THE
POCKET OXFORD
RUSSIAN
DICTIONARY

THE
POCKET OXFORD
RUSSIAN
DICTIONARY

RUSSIAN–ENGLISH
compiled by Jessie Coulson

ENGLISH–RUSSIAN
compiled by Nigel Rankin
and Della Thompson

CLARENDON PRESS · OXFORD

Oxford University Press, Walton Street, Oxford OX2 6DP

Oxford   New York   Toronto
Delhi Bombay Calcutta Madras Karachi
Petaling Jaya Singapore Hong Kong Tokyo
Nairobi Dar es Salaam Cape Town
Melbourne Auckland

and associated companies in
Beirut Berlin Ibadan Nicosia

Oxford is a trade mark of Oxford University Press

Published in the United States
by Oxford University Press, New York

Pocket Oxford Russian–English Dictionary © Oxford University Press 1975
Pocket Oxford English–Russian Dictionary © Oxford University Press 1981

Combined edition first published 1981
Reprinted 1986 (twice)

British Library Cataloguing in Publication Data

Coulson, Jessie
The pocket Oxford Russian dictionary.
1. Russian language—Dictionaries—English
2. English language—Dictionaries—Russian
I. Title II. Rankin, Nigel III. Thompson, Della
IV. The pocket Oxford Russian—English dictionary
491.73'21   PG2640
ISBN 0–19–864122–2

Printed and bound in Great Britain by
William Clowes Limited, Beccles and London

THE
POCKET OXFORD
RUSSIAN – ENGLISH
DICTIONARY

THE
POCKET OXFORD
RUSSIAN – ENGLISH
DICTIONARY

COMPILED BY
JESSIE COULSON

PREFACE

THIS dictionary is based on the *Oxford Russian–English Dictionary* (Oxford, 1972), and like it is designed primarily for English-speaking users. It offers, as far as possible, translations rather than definitions or explanations. Its vocabulary is as large and as wide in range as its size allows, and has been supplemented and brought more nearly up to date by the fullest possible use of the new dictionaries, new editions of existing dictionaries, and other (chiefly Soviet) sources, that have become available in the past three or four years. Unlike most bilingual dictionaries, this is not intended exclusively for students of Russian, but caters also for those whose needs will be served if they can find and translate a limited number of words connected with their own special field, and whose interest in the language as such is minimal.

For such readers, and others whose study of Russian has not advanced very far, there is one respect in which the language presents peculiar difficulties. It has many words of which different parts, such as the oblique cases of pronouns, tenses and aspects of verbs, or alternative forms of prepositions, have different alphabetical positions from the nominative, imperfective infinitive, or simple preposition concerned. For example, the imperfective идти *go* has an alternative infinitive итти, a past tense шёл, шла derived from a different root, and a perfective пойти. Because of this characteristic of Russian we have been particularly careful to supply adequate cross-references to enable those who consult the dictionary to find and identify the word they are looking for from the form in which they have come across it.

Pronunciation. Russian spelling is almost entirely phonetic, and it seems unnecessary for a small dictionary to record the pronunciation of most words. Those abbreviations, however, which consist of groups of capital letters are likely, because the names of the letters of the alphabet are comparatively unfamiliar, to present some difficulties of pronunciation to English-speaking readers. As in English, abbreviations of this kind which do not readily form acceptable syllables must be pronounced by spelling them out, and we give some indication of this pronunciation in italic type within parentheses immediately after the head-word of the entry; as in CCCP (*esesesér*) U.S.S.R., ABM (*avéém*) analogue computer.

Stress. There are some classes of words —prepositions, conjunctions, particles— which are normally unstressed; stress is indicated for all others, except monosyllables, by the placing of a mark like an acute accent over the vowel of the stressed syllable or, if it is a capital letter, immediately after it; thus: го́род, городско́й; ООН. The vowel ё, pronounced *yo* or *o*, is always stressed except in a few compound words, and so has no stress-mark. When two stress-marks are found in the same word or form (as in о́бли́тый), either of the two syllables may be stressed.

Treatment of individual words or entries. An article in this dictionary consists of a word, prefix, abbreviation or other lexical element, or occasionally of two or more synonymous words or forms, or corresponding masculine and feminine forms, with necessary grammatical information, translation(s), and sometimes illustrative examples of usage. In order to save space, related and alphabetically consecutive words may be grouped together in paragraphs, as may consecutive but unrelated entries each consisting only of a cross-reference, and compound words of which the first element is a prefix or other combining form. All head-words, including those grouped together in paragraphs, are printed in bold type to make them easily distinguishable.

Another device to save space is the use of the tilde (~ or ~), which may be substituted in the body of an article for the whole of the head-word or, in a list of compound words, for the prefix or other combining form which is common to all of them. In some adjectives the adjectival ending -ый, -ой or -ий may be separated from the stem by a thin vertical stroke; the tilde will then represent the stem only, and the appropriate form of the ending will be appended to it, as in сáхар|ый sugar; sugary; ~ая головá, sugar-loaf; ~ый завóд, sugar-refinery.

The head-word of an article in this dictionary is usually the nominative case of nouns or pronouns, the nominative singular masculine of adjectives, the infinitive of verbs; the grammatical information that follows the head-word is not intended to enable the grammarian to complete the paradigm but only to identify the specific form he has in mind, or assist him to translate it. The genitive ending of every noun is given, and followed by that of any case showing an irregularity of ending or a change of stress; in the singular any case cited is named, but in the plural the cases can be identified by their endings. The alternative genitive ending in -у is in round brackets immediately after the genitive (see examples below); the term locative (loc.) is used as a distinctive name for the prepositional form ending in -ý after в or на. In those pronouns in which a list of case-endings is given, the accusative is never included and the order of the cases is genitive, dative, instrumental, prepositional. The gender of nouns can usually be deduced from the endings of the nominative and genitive, and it is indicated here only in exceptional instances, as of masculine nouns in -a and neuters in -мя; nouns ending in a soft consonant should be assumed to be feminine unless labelled m. Knowledge of their aspect is essential for the translation of verbs, and all verbs are labelled imp. or perf. or sometimes perf. and imp. The form and stress of the first person singular of the present or future tense are indicated immediately after the infinitive, and other forms of the present (or future) and past tenses are noted if they show a change of stress or an irregularity of ending or contain the vowel ё. When a perfective verb is formed by the addition of a prefix to a simple imperfective, the prefix is divided from the rest of the infinitive by a light vertical stroke. A single bracket, (, before the reflexive ending of an infinitive indicates, especially in cross-references, that the cross-reference, etc., applies to both the active and the reflexive infinitive. When the construction of a verb demands the use of a case other than the accusative or genitive the case required is indicated as in махáть... imp., махнýть... perf. + instr. wave; brandish.

Some adjectives have shifting stress in the short forms; in these the full nominative singular masculine form of the head-word is followed immediately by a semicolon and then by the short forms, as in худóй below.

If a compound word cannot be found in the dictionary its meaning may often be deduced from those of its prefix and its second element. To assist this process full and careful translations and definitions are given of many prefixes, especially verbal prefixes, and other combining forms, all of which are distinguished by a head-word ending with a hyphen.

Examples illustrating many of the points mentioned in this preface follow:

адресовáть, -сýю perf. and imp. address, send; ~ся, address oneself.

налúть, -лью, -льёшь; нáлил, -а, -о perf. (imp. наливáть) pour (out).

плáмя, -мени n. flame; fire, blaze.

по́вод², -а (-у), *loc.* -ý; *pl.* -о́дья, -ьев, rein.
по|проси́ть(ся, -ошу́(сь, -о́сишь(ся *perf.*
прозва́ть, -зову́, -зовёшь; -а́л, -á, -о *perf.* (*imp.* прозыва́ть) nickname, name.
проси́ть, -ошу́, -о́сишь *imp.* (*perf.* по∼) ask; beg; invite; ∼ся, ask; apply.
про|слу́шать, -аю *perf.*, прослу́шивать, -аю *imp.* hear; listen to.
сестра́, -ы́; *pl.* сёстры, сестёр, сёстрам, sister.
сок, -а (-у), *loc.* -ý, juice; sap; в (по́лном) ∼ý, in the prime of life.
худо́й; худ, -á, -о, thin, lean.

ACKNOWLEDGEMENTS

THE compiler wishes to record her gratitude for the patience and kindness of the many scholars and friends in Oxford, Moscow, and elsewhere who have answered her questions and given her generous help and guidance, and in particular her debt to Professor J. G. Nicholson, Chairman of the Department of Russian at McGill University, Montreal, and Professor M. C. C. Wheeler, of the Queen's University of Belfast, author of the *Oxford Russian-English Dictionary*.

CORRIGENDA

THE entry for лзс appears out of sequence on p. 137 instead of on p. 133.
The entry for отс appears out of sequence on p. 198 instead of on p. 207.

ABBREVIATIONS

abbr. abbreviation (of)
acc. accusative
adj. adjective(s)
adv., *advs.* adverb(s)
approx. approximately
collect. collective(ly)
comb. combination
comp. comparative
conj. conjunction
dat. dative
dim. diminutive(s)
etc. etcetera
f. feminine
fut. future
gen. genitive
imp. imperfective
impers. impersonal
indecl. indeclinable
inf. infinitive
instr. instrumental
int. interjection
loc. locative

m. masculine
n. neuter
neg. negative(s)
nom. nominative
part. particle
perf. perfective
pl. plural
predic. predicative adjective
pref. prefix
prep. prepositional, preposition(s)
pron. pronoun(s)
refl. reflexive
sb., *sbs.* substantive(s)
sing. singular
sl. slang
superl. superlative
usu. usually
vb., *vbs.* verb(s)
vbl. verbal
voc. vocative
= equals, the same as
+ plus

A

a *n. indecl.* the letter a.

a *conj.* and, but; a (не) то́, or else, otherwise.

a *part.* eh?

a *int.* oh, ah.

абажу́р, -a, lampshade.

абба́т, -a, abbot; abbé. абба́тиса, -ы, abbess. абба́тство, -a, abbey.

аббревиату́ра, -ы, abbreviation; acronym.

абза́ц, -a, indention; paragraph; сде́лать ~, indent.

абонеме́нт, -a, subscription, season ticket; сверх ~a, extra. абоне́нт, -a, subscriber. абони́ровать, -рую *perf. and imp.* subscribe for, subscribe to, take a (season-)ticket for; ~ся, subscribe, take out a subscription, be a subscriber.

або́рт, -a, abortion; abort, failure, cancellation. абортивный, abortive; causing abortion. абортист, -a, -и́стка, -и, abortionist.

абрико́с, -a, apricot.

а́брис, -a, outline, contour.

абсолю́т, -a, absolute. абсолю́тно *adv.* absolutely, utterly. абсолю́тный, absolute; utter; ~ слух, perfect pitch.

абсу́рд, -a, absurdity; the absurd. абсу́рдный, absurd.

аванга́рд, -a, advanced guard, van; vanguard; avantgarde. аванга́рдистский, avantgarde. аванпо́ст, -a, outpost; forward position.

ава́нс, -a, advance, advance payment; *pl.* advances, overtures. авансировать, -рую *perf. and imp.* advance. ава́нсом, *adv.* in advance, on account.

авансце́на, -ы, proscenium.

авантю́ра, -ы, adventure; venture; escapade; shady, risky, or speculative en-terprise. авантюри́ст, -a, adventurer. авантюри́стка, -и, adventuress. авантю́рный, adventurous; adventure, of adventure.

авари́йка, -и, breakdown vehicle. авари́йный, accident, breakdown, crash; emergency; spare; ~ сигна́л, distress signal. ава́рия, -и, accident, crash, wreck; breakdown; damage; loss; потерпе́ть ава́рию, have an accident.

а́вгуст, -a, August.

а́виа *abbr.* авиапо́чтой, by airmail.

авиа- *abbr. in comb.* of авиацио́нный, air-, aero-; aircraft; aviation. авиали́ния, -и, air-route, airway. ~но́сец, -сца, aircraft carrier. ~по́чта, -ы, airmail. ~разве́дка, -и, air reconnaissance. ~съёмка, -и, aerial survey.

авиацио́нный, aviation; flying; aircraft. авиа́ция, -и, aviation, flying; aircraft; air-force.

ABM (аве́эм) *abbr.* анало́говая вычисли́тельная маши́на, analogue computer.

аво́сь *adv.* perhaps, maybe; на ~, at random, on the off-chance. аво́ська, -и, shopping-bag.

авра́л, -a, work involving all hands; emergency; rush job; *int.* all hands on deck! all hands to the pump! авра́льный, rush, emergency.

австрали́ец, -и́йца, австрали́йка, -и, Australian. австрали́йский, Australian.

австри́ец, -и́йца, австри́йка, -и, Austrian. австри́йский, Austrian.

авто́ *n. indecl.* car.

авто- *in comb.,* self-; auto-; automatic; motor-; bus. автоба́за, -ы, motor--transport depot. ~биогра́фия, -и, autobiography. **автóбус**, -a, bus. **~вокза́л**, -a, bus-station. **автóграф**, -a, autograph. **~запра́вочная ста́нция**, petrol station. **~ка́р**, -a, motor trolley. **~кла́в**, -a, autoclave. **~кра́т**, -a, autocrat. **~крати́ческий**, autocratic. **~магистра́ль**, -и, motor high-way. **~маши́на**, -ы, motor vehicle. **~нóмия**, -и, autonomy. **~нóмный**, autonomous; self-contained. **~павильóн**, -a, (long-distance) bus halt. **~пилóт**, -a, automatic pilot. **~ру́чка**, -и, fountain-pen. **~ста́нция**, -и, bus station. **~стóп**, -a, automatic brakes; hitch-hiking, hitch-hike. **~стра́да**, -ы, motorway.

автома́т, -a, slot-machine; automatic device, weapon, etc.; sub-machine gun; robot; automaton; (телефóн-)**~**, dial telephone, automatic telephone; public call-box. **автоматиза́ция**, -и, automation. **автоматизи́ровать**, -рую *perf. and imp.* automate; make automatic; **~ся**, become automatic. **автомати́ческий**, **автомати́чный**, **автома́тный**, automatic.

а́втор, -a, author; composer, producer, inventor; **~** предложéния, **~** резолю́ции, mover of a resolution. **авториза́ция**, -и, authorization. **авторизóванный**, authorized. **авторизова́ть**, -зу́ю *perf. and imp.* authorize.

авторитéт, -a, authority; prestige. **авторитéтный**, authoritative.

а́вторск|**ий**, author's; **~ий** гонора́р, royalty; **~ое** пра́во, copyright; **~ие** права́ зая́влены, all rights reserved; **~ие** *sb. pl.* royalties. **а́вторство**, -a, authorship.

ага́ *int.* ah; aha.

агéнт, -a, agent; attaché. **агéнтство**, -a, agency. **агенту́ра**, -ы, secret service; agents, network of agents.

агита́тор, -a, agitator, propagandist; canvasser. **агитациóнный**, propaganda. **агита́ция**, -и, propaganda, agitation; campaign. **агити́ровать**, -рую *imp. (perf.* с**~**) agitate, campaign; (try to) persuade, win over. **агитка**, -и, piece of propaganda. **агитпрóп**, -a *abbr.* agitation and propaganda sec-

tion. **агитпу́нкт**, -a *abbr.* agitation centre; committee-rooms.

агонизи́ровать, -рую *perf. and imp.* be in the throes of death. **агóния**, -и, agony of death, death-pangs.

агрега́т, -a, aggregate; assembly, unit, outfit, set.

агронóм, -a, -нóмша, -и, agronomist. **агронóмия**, -и, agriculture.

ад, -a, *loc.* -у́, hell.

адвока́т, -a, lawyer, advocate. **адвокату́ра**, -ы, legal profession; lawyers.

адéпт, -a, adherent, follower, disciple.

администрати́вный, administrative. **администра́тор**, -a, administrator, manager. **администра́ция** -и, administration; management. **администри́рование**, -я, bureaucracy, red tape. **администри́ровать**, -рую *imp.* act as administrator or manager (of); send into exile.

адмира́л, -a, admiral. **адмиралтéйский**, Admiralty. **адмиралтéйство**, -a, (Admiralty; naval dockyard. **адмира́льский**, admiral's; flag. **адмира́льша**, -и, admiral's wife.

а́дов *adj.* infernal, diabolical.

а́дрес, -a; *pl.* -á, -óв, address; не по **~**у, to the wrong address. **адреса́нт**, -a, sender. **адреса́т**, -a, addressee. **а́дресн**|**ый**, address; **~ая** кни́га, directory; **~ый** стол, address bureau. **адресова́ть**, -су́ю *perf. and imp.* address, send; **~ся**, address oneself.

а́дский, infernal, hellish, fiendish, devilish.

адъю́нкт, -a, service student.

адъюта́нт, -a, aide-de-camp; ста́рший **~**, adjutant.

ажу́р, -a, openwork; up-to-date; в **~е**, in order, (all) correct. **ажу́рн**|**ый**, openwork; delicate, lacy; **~ая** рабóта, openwork; tracery.

аза́рт, -a, heat; excitement; fervour, ardour, passion. **аза́ртн**|**ый**, reckless, venturesome; heated; excitable; **~ая** игра́, game of chance.

а́збука, -и, alphabet; ABC; **~** Мóрзе, Morse code. **а́збучный**, alphabetical; elementary.

азóт, -a, nitrogen; **за́кись ~a**, nitrous oxide.

а́ист, -а, stork.

ай *int.* oh; oo; ай да молоде́ц! well done! good lad!

айва́, -ы́, quince, quinces.

айда́, *int.* come on! let's go!

акаде́мик, -а, Academician; member or student of academy. академи́ческий, академи́чный, academic. акаде́мия, -и, academy.

аквала́нг, -а, aqualung.

акварели́ст, -а, water-colour painter. акваре́ль, -и, water-colour, water-colours.

акведу́к, -а, aqueduct.

аккомпанеме́нт, -а, accompaniment; под ~ +*gen.* to the accompaniment of. аккомпаниа́тор, -а, -а́торша, -и, accompanist. аккомпани́ровать, -рую *imp.* +*dat.* accompany.

акко́рд, -а chord; взять ~, strike a chord.

акко́рдн|ый, agreed, by agreement; ~ая рабо́та, piece-work.

аккредити́в, -а, letter of credit; credentials. аккредитова́ть, -ту́ю *perf.* and *imp.* accredit.

аккура́тный, accurate, neat, careful; punctual; exact, thorough.

аксельба́нт, -а, aiguillette.

аксессуа́р, -а, accessory; (stage) property.

аксио́ма, -ы, axiom; truism.

акт, -а, act; deed, document; обвини́тельный ~, indictment.

актёр, -а, actor. актёрский, actor's. актёрство, -а, acting; posing.

акти́в, -а, activists; assets; advantages. активиза́ция, -и, stirring up, making (more) active. активизи́ровать, -рую *perf.* and *imp.* make (more) active, stir up, arouse акти́вный, active; ~ бала́нс, favourable balance.

акти́ровать, -рую *perf.* and *imp.* (*perf.* also с~) register, record, presence or absence of; (*sl.*) write off. актиро́вка, -и (*sl.*) writing off, write-off; cancellation.

а́ктов|ый; ~ая бума́га. official document, stamped paper; ~ый зал, assembly hall.

актри́са, -ы, actress.

актуа́льный, actual; up-to-date, topical; urgent.

аку́ла, -ы, shark.

аку́стика, -и, acoustics. акусти́ческий, acoustic.

акуше́р, -а, obstetrician. акуше́рка, -и, midwife. акуше́рский, obstetric, obstetrical. акуше́рство, -а, obstetrics; midwifery.

акце́нт, -а, accent, stress. акценти́ровать, -рую *perf.* and *imp.* accent; accentuate.

акци́з, -а, duty; Excise. акци́зный, excise.

акционе́р, -а, shareholder. акционе́рн|ый, joint-stock; ~ое о́бщество, joint-stock company. а́кция[1], -и, share; *pl.* stock. а́кция[2], -и, action.

але́ть, -е́ет *imp.* (*perf.* за~) redden, flush, blush; show red.

алле́я, -и, avenue; path, walk.

аллю́р, -а, pace, gait.

алма́з, -а, diamond. алма́зный, diamond; of diamonds.

алта́рь, -я́ *m.* altar; chancel, sanctuary.

а́лчный, greedy, grasping.

а́лый, scarlet.

альбино́с, -а, -а́льбино́ска, -и, albino.

альбо́м, -а, album; sketch-book.

альмана́х, -а, literary miscellany; almanac.

альпи́йск|ий, Alpine; ~ие луга́, alps, mountain meadows, альпини́зм, -а, mountaineering. альпини́ст, -а, -альпини́стка, -и, (mountain-)climber.

альт, -а́; *pl.* -ы́, alto, contralto; viola. альтера́ция, -и, change in pitch; зна́ки альтера́ции, accidentals. альти́ст, -а, -и́стка, -и, viola-player. альто́вый, alto, contralto; viola.

алюми́ниевый, aluminium. алюми́ний, -я, aluminium.

амазо́нка, -и, Amazon; horsewoman; riding-habit.

а́мба, *f. indecl.* (*sl.*) finish, curtains; ki-bosh.

амба́р, -а, barn; storehouse, warehouse. амба́рный, barn.

амби́ция, -и, pride; arrogance. амбицио́зный, vainglorious, conceited; self-loving, egoistic.

а́мбра, -ы, ambergris; scent, perfume,

fragrance. **амбре́** *n. indecl.* scent, perfume.

амбулато́рия, -и, out-patients' department; surgery. **амбулато́рный**; ~ больно́й, out-patient.

амбушю́р, -а, **амбушю́ра**, -ы, mouthpiece.

америка́нец, -нца, American. **америка́нка**, -и, American; racing sulky; snack bar, (*sl.*) vodka stand. **америка́нск|ий**, American; U.S.; ~ие го́ры, switchback; ~ий замо́к, Yale lock; ~ий оре́х Brazil nut.

ами́нь, -я *m.* amen; finis, finish, kibosh.

аммиа́к, -а, ammonia. **аммиа́чный**, ammonia, ammoniac, ammoniacal. **аммо́ний**, -я, ammonium.

амнисти́ровать, -рую *perf. and imp.* amnesty. **амни́стия**, -и, amnesty.

амора́льный, amoral; immoral.

амортиза́тор, -а, shock-absorber. **амортиза́ция**, -и, depreciation, wear and tear; shock-absorption. **амортизи́ровать**, -рую *perf. and imp.* amortize; damp, make shock-proof.

ампи́р, -а, Empire style. **ампи́рный**, Empire.

амплуа́ *n. indecl.* type; role; occupation, job.

АМС *f. indecl. abbr.* автомати́ческая межплане́тная ста́нция, automatic space station.

аму́р, -а, cupid; *pl.* amours, love-affairs. **аму́рный**, love.

амфитеа́тр, -а, amphitheatre; circle.

АН (*аэ́н* or *ан*) *abbr.* Акаде́мия Нау́к, Academy of Sciences.

ана́лиз, -а, analysis; ~ кро́ви, bloodtest. **анализи́ровать**, -рую *perf. and imp.* analyse. **анали́тик**, -а, analyst. **аналити́ческий**, analytic, analytical.

анало́й, -я, lectern.

анана́с, -а, pineapple. **анана́сный**, **анана́совый**, pineapple.

анархи́ст, -а, -и́стка, -и, anarchist. **анархи́ческий**, anarchic, anarchical. **ана́рхия**, -и, anarchy.

анга́р, -а, hangar.

а́нгел, -а, angel; день ~а name-day. **а́нгельский**, angels'; angelic.

анги́на, -ы, quinsy, tonsillitis, ulcerated sore throat.

англизи́ровать, -рую *perf. and imp.* anglicize **англи́йск|ий**, English; ~ая була́вка, safety-pin; ~ая соль, Epsom salts; ~ий рожо́к cor anglais. **англи́зм**, -а, anglicism, English loanword. **англича́нин**, -а; *pl.* -ча́не, -чан, Englishman. **англича́нка**, -и, Englishwoman.

андре́евский, St. Andrew's.

анекдо́т, -а, anecdote, story; funny thing. **анекдоти́ческий**, anecdotal; unlikely; funny, comical. **анекдоти́чный**, improbable; odd; amusing, funny.

анестезио́лог, -а, anaesthetist. **анестези́ровать**, -рую *perf. and imp.* anaesthetize. **анестези́рующ|ий**, anaesthetizing, anaesthetic; ~ее сре́дство, anaesthetic. **анестези́я**, -и, anaesthesia.

ани́с, -а, anise; kind of apple. **ани́совый**; ~ое се́мя aniseed.

анке́та, -ы, questionnaire; form; (opinion) poll, inquiry, survey.

аннули́ровать, -рую *perf. and imp.* annul, nullify; cancel, repeal, revoke, abolish. **аннуля́ция**, -и, annulment, nullification; cancellation, revocation, repeal.

анони́м, -а, anonymous author, work, letter. **анони́мка**, -и, anonymous letter. **анони́мный**, anonymous.

ано́нс, -а, announcement, notice; advertisement. **анонси́ровать**, -рую *perf. and imp.* announce, make an announcement.

анса́мбль, -я, *m.* ensemble; company, troupe.

анте́нна, -ы, antenna; aerial.

антивещество́, -а́, anti-matter.

антидетона́тор, -а, anti-knock (compound). **антидетонацио́нный**, anti-knock.

антиква́р, -а, **антиква́рий**, -я, antiquary, antiquarian; antique-dealer. **антиквариа́т**, -а, antique-dealer's, antique-shop. **антиква́рный**, antiquarian; antique. **анти́чность**, -и, antiquity. **анти́чный** ancient, antique.

антираке́та, -ы, anti-missile missile. **антите́ло**, -а; *pl.* -а, antibody.

антра́кт, -а, interval; entr'acte.

антрепренёр, -а, impresario.

антерсо́ли, -ей *pl.* mezzanine; attic floor; attics; gallery.

антропофа́г, -а, cannibal. **антропофа́гия**, -и, cannibalism.

антура́ж, -а, surroundings, environment; entourage, associates.

анфа́с *adv.* full face.

анфила́да, -ы, suite.

анчо́ус, -а, anchovy.

аншла́г, -а, 'house full' notice; пройти́ с ~ом, play to full houses.

АО (*ао́*) *abbr.* автоно́мная о́бласть, Autonomous Region.

апелли́ровать, -рую *perf.* and *imp.* appeal. **апелляцио́нный**; ~ суд, Court of Appeal. **апелля́ция**, -и, appeal.

апельси́н, -а, orange, orange-tree. **апельси́нный**, **апельси́новый**, orange; апельси́нное варе́нье, (orange) marmalade.

аппликé *indecl. adj.* plated; appliqué.

аплоди́ровать, -рую *imp.* + *dat.* applaud. **аплодисме́нт**, -а, clap; *pl.* applause; под ~ы, to applause.

аполити́зм, -а, political apathy. **аполити́чный**, politically apathetic.

апо́стол, -а, apostle; Acts and Epistles. **апо́стольский**, apostolic.

аппара́т, -а, apparatus, apparat; machinery, organs; staff, establishment; camera. **аппарату́ра**, -ы, apparatus, gear. **аппара́тчик**, -а, operator; apparatchik, functionary.

аппликату́ра, -ы, fingering. **апплика́ция**, -и, appliqué, appliqué-work. **аппликацио́нный**, appliqué.

апре́ль, -я *m.* April. **апре́льский**, April.

апроба́ция, -и, approval. **апроби́ровать**, -рую *perf.* and *imp.* approve.

апси́да, -ы, apse.

апте́ка, -и, (dispensing) chemist's; medicine chest; first-aid kit. **апте́карский**, chemist's; pharmaceutical. **апте́карь**, -я *m.* chemist, pharmacist. **апте́карша**, -и, pharmacist; chemist's wife. **апте́чка**, -и, medicine chest; first-aid kit. **апте́чный**, medicine, drug.

ара́б, -а, ара́бка, -и, Arab. **ара́бский**, Arab, Arabian; Arabic; arabic. **арави́йский**, Arabian.

ара́п, -а, Negro; trickster, swindler.

ара́пник, -а, (huntsman's) whip.

арба́, -ы́; *pl.* -ы, (bullock-)cart.

арби́тр, -а, arbitrator. **арбитра́ж**, -а, arbitration.

арбу́з, -а, water-melon.

аргуме́нт, -а, argument. **аргумента́ция**, -и, reasoning; arguments. **аргументи́ровать**, -рую *perf.* and *imp.* argue, (try to) prove.

аре́на, -ы, arena, ring.

аре́нда, -ы, lease; rent; в аре́нду, on lease. **аренда́тор**, -а, leaseholder, tenant. **арендова́ть**, -ду́ю *perf.* and *imp.* lease, take or hold on lease.

аре́ст, -а, arrest; seizure, sequestration. **аре́стант**, -а, **-а́нтка**, -и prisoner. **аре́стантская** *sb.* lock-up, cells. **арестова́ть**, -ту́ю *perf.*, **аресто́вывать**, -аю *imp.* arrest; seize, sequestrate.

арифме́тика, -и, arithmetic. **арифмети́ческий**, arithmetical. **арифмо́граф**, -а, **арифмо́метр**, -а, a calculating machine.

а́рка, -и, arch. **арка́да**, -ы, arcade.

арка́н, -а, lasso. **арка́нить**, -ню *imp.* (*perf.* за~) lasso.

армату́ра, -ы, fittings, accessories; equipment; reinforcement; armature; trophy (of arms). **армату́рщик**, -а, fitter.

арме́ец, -е́йца, soldier; *pl.* Soviet Army Sports-Club team. **арме́йский**, army. **а́рмия**, -и, army.

армя́к, -а́, peasant's heavy overcoat.

армяни́н, -а; *pl.* -я́не, -я́н, **армя́нка**, -и, Armenian. **армя́нский**, Armenian.

арома́т, -а, scent, odour, aroma. **аромати́ческий**, **арома́тичный**, **арома́тный**, aromatic, fragrant.

а́рочный, arched, vaulted.

арсена́л, -а, arsenal.

арта́читься, -чусь *imp.* jib, be restive; dig one's heels in; be pigheaded, be obstinate.

арте́ль, -и, artel. **арте́льный**, of an artel; common, collective. **арте́льщик**, -а, **арте́льщица**, -ы, member, leader, of an artel.

артериа́льный, arterial. **арте́рия**, -и, artery.

артиллери́йский, artillery, ordnance. **артилле́рия**, -и, artillery.

арти́ст, -а, **-и́стка**, -и, artiste, artist,

performer; expert. **артисти́ческая** *sb.* dressing-room, green-room, artists' room. **артисти́ческий**, artistic.

а́рфа, -ы, harp. **арфи́ст**, -a, -и́стка, -и, harpist.

архи́в, -a, archives. **архива́риус**, -a, archivist. **архи́вный**, archive, archival.

архидья́кон, -a, archdeacon. **архиепи́скоп**, -a, archbishop. **архиере́й**, -я, bishop.

архите́ктор, -a, architect. **архитекту́ра**, -ы, architecture. **архитекту́рный**, architectural.

арши́н, -a; *gen. pl.* -ши́н(ов), arshin (71 cm.); arshin-rule; **как бу́дто ~ проглоти́л**, bolt upright, as stiff as a poker.

асе́ссор, -a; **колле́жский ~**, Collegiate Assessor (8th grade: see чин).

аске́т, -a, ascetic. **аскети́зм**, -a, asceticism. **аскети́ческий**, ascetic.

а́спид[1], -a, asp; viper.

а́спид[2], -a, slate. **а́спиди|ый**; **~ая доска́**, slate.

аспира́нт, -a, -а́нтка, -и, post-graduate student. **аспиранту́ра** -ы, post-graduate course; post-graduate students.

ассигна́ция, -и, banknote.

ассамбле́я, -и, assembly; ball.

ассисте́нт, -a, assistant; junior lecturer, research assistant. **ассисти́ровать**, -рую, *imp.*+*dat.* assist.

ассоциа́ция, -и, association. **ассоции́ровать**, -рую *perf.* and *imp.* associate.

АССР (*a-eseseŕ*) *abbr.* автоно́мная сове́тская социалисти́ческая респу́блика, Autonomous Soviet Socialist Republic.

астрона́вт, -a, astronaut. **астрона́втика**, -и, space-travel. **астроно́м**, -a, astronomer. **астрономи́ческий**, astronomical. **астроно́мия**, -и, astronomy.

ась *int.* eh?

атама́н, -a, ataman; Cossack chieftain, commander; (gang-)leader; robber chieftain.

ателье́ *n. indecl.* studio; atelier.

а́тлас[1], -a, atlas.

атла́с[2], -a, satin. **атла́систый**, **атла́сный**, satin; like satin, satiny.

атле́т, -a, athlete; acrobat; strong man. **атле́тика**, -и, athletics; **лёгкая ~**, track and field sports; **тяжёлая ~**, weight-lifting, boxing, wrestling. **атлети́ческий**, athletic.

атмосфе́ра, -ы, atmosphere. **атмосфери́ческий**, **атмосфе́рный**, atmospheric; **атмосфе́рные оса́дки**, rainfall.

а́том, -a, atom. **атоми́стика**, -и, atomics; atomic theory. **атоми́стический**, atomistic. **а́томник**, -a, atomic scientist. **а́томный**, atomic.

АТС (*ateés*) *abbr.* автомати́ческая телефо́нная ста́нция, automatic telephone exchange.

аттеста́т, -a, testimonial, recommendation; reference; certificate; pedigree. **аттеста́ция**, -и, attestation; testimonial; confidential report. **аттестова́ть**, -ту́ю *perf.* and *imp.* attest; recommend.

ау́ *int.* halloo, cooee.

аудито́рия, -и, auditorium; lecture-room; audience.

ау́кать(ся, -аю(сь *imp.*, **ау́кнуть(ся**, -ну(сь *perf.* halloo, cooee.

аул, -a, aul, Caucasian or Central Asian village.

а́утборт, -a, outboard motor.

афи́нский, Athenian. **афи́нянин**, -a; *pl.* -яне, афи́нянка, -и, Athenian.

афи́ша, -и, placard, poster. **афиши́ровать**, -рую *perf.* and *imp.* parade, advertise; **~ся**, be exhibitionist, seek the limelight.

африка́нец, -нца, **африка́нка**, -и, African. **африка́нский**, African.

аффе́кт, -a, fit of passion, rage, nervous excitement; temporary insanity.

ах *int.* ah, oh. **а́хи**, -ов *pl.* ahs, ohs. **а́ханье**, -я, sighing; exclamations. **а́хать**, -аю *imp.* (*perf.* а́хнуть) sigh; exclaim; gasp.

ахине́я, -и, nonsense, rubbish; **нести́ ахине́ю**, talk nonsense.

а́хнуть, -ну *perf.* (*imp.* а́хать) gasp, exclaim; bang; strike.

аэро- in *comb.* aero-, air-, aerial. **аэровокза́л**, -a, air terminal, airport building. ~дро́м, -а, aerodrome, air-field. ~зо́ль, -я *m.* aerosol. ~на́вт, -а, aeronaut. ~по́рт, -а airport. ~по́чта, -и, air-mail. ~сни́мок, -мка,

aerial photograph. ~ста́т, -а, balloon. ~съёмка, -и, aerial photography. АЭС (*a-és*) *abbr.* а́томная электро-ста́нция, atomic power-station.

Б

б *letter*: see бэ.

б *part.*: see бы.

ба *int.* expressing surprise.

ба́ба, -ы, (married) peasant woman; woman; ка́менная ~, ancient stone image; снежная ~, snowman. ба́б|ий; ~ье ле́то, Indian summer; ~ьи ска́зки, old wives' tales. ба́бка[1], -и, grandmother; (повива́льная) ~, mid-wife.

ба́бка[2], -и, knucklebone; pastern; игра́ть в ба́бки, play at knucklebones.

ба́бочка, -и, butterfly; ночна́я ~, moth.

ба́бушка, -и, grandmother; granny.

бага́ж, -а́, luggage. бага́жник, -а, carrier; luggage-rack; boot. бага́ж-ный, luggage; ~ ваго́н. luggage-van.

багрове́ть, -е́ю *imp.* (*perf.* по~) crim-son, flush, go red. багро́вый, багря́-ный, crimson, purple.

бадья́, -и́; *gen. pl.* -де́й, tub, bucket, pail.

ба́за, -ы, base; centre; stock, stores; basis.

база́р, -а, market, fair; bazaar; row, din. база́рный, market.

бази́ровать, -рую *imp.* base; ~ся, be based, rest (on).

байда́рка, -и, canoe; kayak. байда́роч-ный, canoe.

ба́йка, flannelette flannel. ба́йковый, flannelette, flannel; ~ плато́к, woollen shawl.

бак[1], -а, tank, cistern; can, billy.

бак[2], -а, forecastle.

бакале́йный, grocer's, grocery. бакале́йщик, -а, grocer. бакале́я, -и, groceries.

ба́кан, -а, ба́кен, -а, buoy.

бакенба́рды, -ба́рд *pl.*, ба́кены, -ов *pl.*

whiskers; side-whiskers. ба́ки, бак *pl.* sideburns, (short) side-whiskers.

баклажа́н, -а; *gen. pl.* -ов or -жа́н aubergine.

бактериа́льный, бактери́йный, bac-terial. бактерио́лог, -а, bacteriologist. бакте́рия, -и, bacterium.

бал, -а, *loc.* -у́; *pl.* -ы́, dance, ball.

балага́н, -а, booth; side-show; popular show; farce, buffoonery. балага́нить, -ню *imp.* play the fool. балага́нщик, -а, showman; clown, buffoon.

балала́ечник, -а, balalaika-player. балала́йка, -и, balalaika.

баламу́т, -а, trouble-maker. баламу́-тить, -у́чу *imp.* (*perf.* вз~) stir up, trouble; disturb; upset.

бала́нда, -ы, (*sl.*) watery soup, skilly, swill.

балансёр, -а, rope-walker.

баланси́р, -а, balance, balance-wheel. баланси́ровать, -рую *imp.* (*perf.* с~) balance; keep one's balance.

балахо́н, -а, loose overall; shapeless garment.

балбе́с, -а, booby.

балдахи́н, -а, canopy.

балери́на, -ы, ballerina. бале́т, -а, ballet.

ба́лка[1], -и, beam, girder.

ба́лка[2], -и, ravine, gully.

балл, -а, mark, number, point, degree; force; ве́тер в пять ~ов, wind force 5.

балла́ст, -а, ballast; lumber.

балло́н, -а, container, carboy, cylinder; balloon tyre.

баллоти́ровать, -рую *imp.* ballot, vote; put to the vote; ~ся, stand, be a candi-date (в or на + *acc.* for). баллотиро́в-ка, -и, vote, ballot, poll; polling, voting.

бало́ванный, spoilt. **балова́ть**, -лу́ю *imp.* (*perf.* из~) spoil; indulge, pamper; play about, play up; +*instr.* play with, play at, amuse oneself with; ~ся, play about, get up to tricks; amuse oneself, play; +*instr.* indulge in. **ба́ловень**, -вня *m.* spoilt child; pet, favourite. **баловство́**, -а́, spoiling, over-indulgence; pampering; monkey tricks, mischief.

балти́йский, Baltic.

бальза́м, -а, balsam; balm. **бальзами́ровать**, -рую *imp.* (*perf.* на~) embalm.

ба́льный, ball, dance.

балюстра́да, -ы, balustrade; banister. **баля́сина**, -ы, baluster, banister. **баля́сы**, -яс *pl.* banisters; точи́ть ~, jest, joke.

бамбу́к, -а, bamboo. **бамбу́ко́в|ый**, bamboo; ~ое положе́ние, awkward situation.

бан, -а, *loc.* -у́, (*sl.*) railway station.

ба́нда, -ы, band, gang.

банда́ж, -а́, truss; belt, bandage; tyre.

бандеро́ль, -и, wrapper; printed matter, book-post.

банди́т, -а, bandit, brigand; gangster.

банк, -а, bank.

ба́нка[1], -и, jar; tin.

ба́нка[2], -и, (sand-)bank, shoal.

банки́р, -а, banker. **банкро́т**, -а, bankrupt.

бант, -а, bow. **ба́нтик**, -а, bow; гу́бки ~ом, Cupid's bow. **бантов|о́й**; ~а́я скла́дка, box-pleat.

ба́ня, -и, bath, bath-house.

бар, -а, a bar; snack-bar.

бараба́н, -а, drum. **бараба́нить**, -ню *imp.* drum, thump. **бараба́нн|ый**, drum; ~ая дробь, drum-roll; ~ая перепо́нка, ear-drum. **бараба́нщик**, -а, drummer.

бара́к, -а, barrack; *pl.* hutments.

бара́н, -а, ram; sheep. **бара́ний**, sheep's; sheepskin; mutton. **бара́нина**, -ы, mutton.

бара́нка, -и, baranka, ring-shaped roll; (steering-)wheel.

барахли́ть, -лю́ *imp.* pink, knock; talk rubbish.

барахло́, -а́, old clothes, jumble; odds and ends; trash, junk; rubbish. **барахо́лка**, -и, second-hand market, junk-stall.

бара́хтаться, -аюсь *imp.* flounder, wallow, thrash about.

бара́шек, -шка, young ram; lamb; lambskin; wing nut; catkin; *pl.* white horses; fleecy clouds. **бара́шковый**, lambskin.

баржа́, -и́ or -й; *gen. pl.* барж(е́й), barge.

ба́рин, -а; *pl.* -ре or -ры, бар, barin; land-owner; gentleman; master; sir.

ба́рка, -и, barge.

баро́чный, baroque.

барс, -а, ounce, snow-leopard.

ба́рский, gentleman's; lordly; grand. **ба́рственный**, lordly, grand, arrogant.

барсу́к, -а́, badger. **барсу́чий**, badger; badger-skin.

барха́н, -а, sand-hill, dune.

ба́рхат, -а (-у), velvet. **бархати́стый**, velvety. **ба́рхатка**, -и, velvet ribbon. **ба́рхатный**, velvet; velvety.

барчо́нок, -нка; *pl.* -ча́та -ча́т. **барчу́к**, -а́, barin's son; young master, young gentleman.

бары́га, -и, (*sl.*) fence.

ба́рыня, -и, barin's wife; lady; mistress; madam.

бары́ш, -а́, profit. **бары́шник**, -а, dealer; buyer for re-sale; jobber; (ticket) speculator. **бары́шничать**, -аю *imp.* deal, speculate, job (+*instr.* in).

ба́рышня, -и; *gen. pl.* -шень, barin's daughter; young lady, young mistress; miss.

барье́р, -а, barrier; obstacle; bar; fence, jump, hurdle. **барьери́ст**, -а, -и́стка, -и. hurdler. **барье́рный**, hurdle; ~ бег hurdle-race.

бас, -а; *pl.* -ы́, bass. **баси́стый**, bass.

баскетбо́л, -а, basket-ball. **баскетболи́ст**, -а, -и́стка, -и, basket-ball player. **баскетбо́льный**, basket-ball.

баснопи́сец, -сца, fabulist, writer of fables. **баснословный**, mythical, legendary; fabulous. **ба́сня**, -и; *gen. pl.* -сен, fable; legend; fabrication.

ба́со́вый, bass.

бассе́йн, -а, basin; pool; pond; reser-

voir; swimming-pool; каменноугольный ~, угольный ~, coal-field.
бастова́ть, -тую *imp.* be on strike.
батаре́ец, -е́йца, gunner. **батаре́йка**, -и, батаре́я, -и, battery; radiator.
бати́ст, -а (-у), batiste, cambric, lawn.
бато́н, -а, long loaf; stick, bar. **бато́нчик**, -а, a stick, bar; шокола́дный ~, bar of chocolate.
батра́к, -а́, батра́чка, -и, farm-hand, farm-worker, farm labourer. **батра́цкий**, farm, farm labourer's.
ба́тька, -и *m.*, **ба́тюшка**, -и *m.*, **ба́тя**, -и *m.* father; my dear chap. **ба́тюшки** *int.* expressing amazement or fright.
бах *int.* bang! **ба́хать(ся**, -аю(сь *imp.* of **ба́хнуть(ся**.
бахва́л, -а, boaster, braggart. **бахва́льство**, -а, bragging, boasting.
ба́хнуть, -ну *perf.* (*imp.* ба́хать) bang; thump; ~ся, fall or bump heavily and noisily; let oneself fall, plump down; ~ся голово́й, bang one's head.
бахрома́, -ы́ fringe. **бахро́мчатый**, fringed.
бац *int.* bang! crack! **ба́цать**, -аю *imp.*, **ба́цнуть**, -ну *perf.* crack, bang, bash.
баци́лла, -ы, bacillus. **бациллоноси́тель**, -я *m.* carrier.
ба́шенка, -и, turret. **ба́шенный**, tower, turret.
башка́, -и́, head. **башкови́тый**, brainy.
башлы́к, -а́, hood.
башма́к, -а́, shoe; chock; под ~о́м у + *gen.* under the thumb of.
ба́шня, -и; *gen. pl.* -шен, tower, turret.
ба́ю-бай, **ба́юшки-баю́** *int.* hushabye, lullaby. **баю́кать**, -аю *imp.* (*perf.* y~) lull, rock, sing to sleep.
БГДТ (*begedeté*) *abbr.* Большо́й госуда́рственный драмати́ческий теа́тр, Great State Dramatic Theatre.
бде́ние, -я, vigil, wakefulness. **бди́тельность**, -и, vigilance, watchfulness. **бди́тельный**, vigilant, watchful.
бег, -а, *loc.* -у; *pl.* -а́, run, running; double; race; *pl.* trotting-races. **бе́гать**, -аю *indet.* (*det.* бежа́ть) *imp.* run; move quickly.
бегемо́т, -а, hippopotamus.
бегле́ц, -а́, бегля́нка, -и, fugitive. **бе́глость**, -и, speed, fluency, dexterity.

бе́глый, fugitive; quick, rapid, fluent; fleeting, cursory, passing; ~ гла́сный, fugitive vowel, fill-vowel; *sb.* fugitive, runaway. **бего́вой**, running; race; ~ круг, race-course, ring. **бего́м** *adv.* running, at a run, at the double. **бего́тня**, -и́, running about; bustle. **бе́гство**, -а, flight, hasty retreat; escape. **бегу́н**, -а́, **бегу́нья**, -и; *gen. pl.* -ний, runner.
беда́, -ы́; *pl.* -ы, misfortune; calamity; disaster; trouble; ~ в том, что, the trouble is (that); ~ как, terribly, awfully; на беду́, unfortunately; не ~, it doesn't matter; что за ~! what does it matter? so what? **бедне́ть**, -е́ю *imp.* (*perf.* о~) grow poor. **бе́дность**, -и, poverty, the poor. **бе́дный**; -ден, -дна́, -дно, poor; poverty-stricken. **бедня́га**, -и *m.*, **бедня́жка**, -и *m.* and *f.* poor thing, poor creature. **бедня́к**, -а́, **бедня́чка**, -и, poor peasant; poor man, poor woman. **бедня́чество**, -а, poor peasants.
бе́дренный, femoral, thigh-. **бедро́**, -а́; *pl.* бёдра, -дер, thigh; hip; leg.
бе́дственный, disastrous, calamitous. **бе́дствие**, -я, disaster, calamity; сигна́л бе́дствия, distress signal. **бе́дствовать**, -твую *imp.* be in want, live in poverty.
бежа́ть, бегу́ *det.* (*indet.* бе́гать) *imp.* (*perf.* по~) run; flow; fly; boil over; *perf.* and *imp.* escape. **бе́женец**, -нца, **бе́женка**, -и, refugee.
без, **безо** *prep.* + *gen.* without; in the absence of; minus, less, short of; ~ вас, in your absence; ~ ма́лого, almost, all but; ~ пяти́ (мину́т), five (minutes) to; ~ ума́ (от + *gen.*) mad, crazy (about); ~ че́тверти, a quarter to.
без-, **безъ-**, **бес-** in *comb.* in-, un-; non-; -less. **безава́рийный**, accident-free; without breakdowns. **~ала́берный**, disorderly, unsystematic; slovenly, careless. **~алкого́льный**, non-alcoholic, soft. **~апелляцио́нный**, without appeal; peremptory, categorical. **~биле́тник**, -а, -ница, -ы, passenger without a ticket; stowaway. **~бо́жие**, -я,

atheism, ~бо́жный, atheistic; irreligious, anti-religious; godless; shameless, scandalous, outrageous. ~боле́зненный, painless. ~бра́чность, -и, unmarried state, living in sin. ~бра́чный, celibate. ~бре́жный, boundless. ~ве́рие, -я, unbelief. ~ве́стный, unknown; obscure. ~ве́тренный, calm, windless. ~ви́нный, guiltless, innocent. ~вку́сие, -я. ~вку́сица, -ы, lack of taste bad taste. ~вку́сный, tasteless. ~вла́стие, -я, anarchy. ~во́дный, arid, waterless; anhydrous. ~возвра́тный, irrevocable; irretrievable; irrecoverable. ~возме́здный, free, gratis; unpaid. ~во́лие -я, weakness of will, lack of will-power. ~во́льный, weak-willed, spineless. ~вре́дный, harmless, innocuous. ~вре́менный, untimely; premature. ~вы́ходный, hopeless, desperate; without going out; uninterrupted. ~гла́зый, one-eyed, eyeless. ~гла́сный, silent, dumb; powerless to protest ~голо́сный, voiceless, unvoiced. ~гра́мотный, illiterate; ignorant. ~грани́чный, boundless, limitless, infinite. ~гре́шный, innocent, sinless, without sin. ~да́рный, ungifted, untalented. ~де́йственный, inactive; idle, passive. ~де́йствие, -я, inaction, inactivity, inertia, idleness; negligence. ~де́йствовать, -твую *imp.* to be idle, be inactive; stand idle, not work.

безде́лица, -ы, безде́лка, -и, trifle, bagatelle. **безделу́шка, -и,** trinket, knick-knack; toy. **безде́льник, -а,** idler, loafer; ne'er-do-well. **безде́льничать, -аю** *imp.* idle, loaf. **безде́льный,** idle; trifling.

бе́здна, -ы, abyss, chasm; enormous numbers, a multitude, masses.

без-. бездо́ждье, -я, dry weather, drought. ~доказа́тельный, unsupported, unsubstantiated, unproved. ~до́мный, homeless. ~до́нный, bottomless, fathomless. ~доро́жный, without roads. ~доро́жье, -я, lack of (good) roads; season when roads are impassable. ~ду́шный, heartless, callous; soulless, lifeless. ~жа́лостный, pitiless, ruthless. ~жи́зненный, life-

less. ~забо́тный, carefree, untroubled, careless. ~заве́тный, selfless, wholehearted. ~зако́ние, -я, lawlessness; unlawful act. ~зако́нный, illegal, unlawful; lawless. ~засте́нчивый, shameless, unblushing, barefaced. ~защи́тный, defenceless, unprotected. ~земе́льный, landless. ~зло́бный, good-natured, kindly. ~ли́чный, characterless without personality, without individuality; impersonal. ~лу́нный, moonless. ~лю́дный, uninhabited; sparsely populated; lonely, solitary; empty, unfrequented.

безме́н, -а, steelyard; spring balance.

без-. безме́рный, boundless, limitless. ~мо́зглый, brainless. ~мо́лвие, -я, silence. ~мо́лвный, silent, mute. ~мото́рный, engineless; ~мото́рный самолёт, glider. ~мяте́жный, serene, placid. ~надёжный, hopeless. ~надзо́рный, neglected. ~нака́занно *adv.* with impunity, unpunished. ~нака́занный, unpunished. ~но́гий, legless; one-legged. ~нра́вственный, immoral.

безо *prep.*: see **без.**

безобра́зие, -я, ugliness; outrage; disgrace, scandal. **безобра́зить, -а́жу** *imp.* (*perf.* о~) disfigure, mutilate; create a disturbance, make a nuisance of oneself. **безобра́зничать, -аю** *imp.* behave outrageously; make a nuisance of oneself.

без-. безогово́рочный, unconditional. ~опа́сность, -и, safety, security. ~опа́сный, safe; secure; ~опа́сная бри́тва, safety razor. ~ору́жный, unarmed. ~оско́лочный, unsplinterable; splinter-proof, shatter-proof. ~основа́тельный, groundless. ~остано́вочный, unceasing, continuous; without a break; sustained; non-stop. ~отве́тный, meek, unanswering; unanswered; dumb. ~отве́тственный, irresponsible. ~отка́зно *adv.* without a hitch. ~отка́зный, trouble-free, smooth(-running). ~отлага́тельный, urgent. ~отлу́чный, uninterrupted; continual, continuous; ever-present. ~относи́тельно *adv.* + к dat. irrespective of. ~относи́тельный, absolute, unconditional. ~отра́дный, cheerless, dreary. ~отчётный, uncontrolled; unaccountable; instinctive. ~оши́бочный, unerring mark; correct. ~рабо́тица, -ы, unemployment. ~рабо́тный, unemployed. ~разде́льный, undivided; wholehearted; complete. ~разли́чие, -я, indifference. ~разли́чно adv. indifferently; it is all the same. ~разли́чный, indifferent; neutral. ~разме́рный, one-size, stretch. ~рассу́дный, reckless, foolhardy, imprudent. ~ро́дный, alone in the world; without relatives; of unknown antecedents. ~ро́потный, uncomplaining, unmurmuring; meek, resigned. ~рука́вка, -и, sleeveless jacket, jerkin. ~ру́кий, armless; one-armed; awkward. ~уда́рный, unstressed, unaccented. ~уде́ржный, unrestrained, uncontrolled; uncontrollable. ~укори́зненный, irreproachable, impecable.

безу́мец, -мца, madman. **безу́мие**, -я, madness, insanity; distraction. **безу́мный**, mad, insane; crazy, senseless; terrible. ~у́мство, -а, madness.

без-. ~безупре́чный, irreproachable, faultless. ~уря́дица, -ы, disorder, confusion. ~уса́дочный, non-shrink. ~сло́вно adv. unconditionally, absolutely; of course, undoubtedly, certainly. ~усло́вный, unconditional, absolute; undoubted, indisputable. ~успе́шный, unsuccessful. ~уста́нный, tireless; ceaseless, unremitting. ~уте́шный, inconsolable. ~уча́стие, -я, ~уча́стность, -и, indifference, apathy. ~уча́стный, indifferent, apathetic, unconcerned. ~ыде́йный, without ideas or ideals; unideological; unprincipled. ~изве́стный, unknown, obscure. ~ымённый, ~имя́нный, nameless, anonymous. ~имя́нный па́лец, third finger, ring-finger. ~интере́сный, uninteresting. ~иску́сственный, ~иску́сный, artless, ingenuous, unsophisticated. ~исхо́дный, hopeless, inconsolable; irreparable; interminable.

бейсбо́л, -а, baseball. **бейсболи́ст**, -а, baseball player.

бека́р, -а, бека́р indecl. adj. natural.

бека́с, -а, snipe. **бекаси́нник**, -а, small shot.

беко́н, -а, bacon.

беле́ть, -е́ю imp. (perf. по~) grow white, turn white; show white; ~ся, show white.

белизна́, -ы́, whiteness. бели́ла, -и́л pl. whitewash, whiting; ceruse. бели́льный, bleaching. бели́ть, -лю́, бе́ли́шь imp. (perf. вы́~, на~, по~) whitewash; whiten; bleach; ~ся, put ceruse on.

бе́личий, squirrel, squirrel's. бе́лка, -и, -и.

белко́вый, albuminous.

беллетри́ст, -а, writer of fiction. беллетри́стика, -и, fiction.

бело- in comb., white-, leuco-. белогварде́ец, -е́йца, White Guard. ~кро́вие, -я, leukaemia. ~ку́рый, fair, blonde. ~ру́с, -а, ~ру́ска, -и, ~ру́сский, Belorussian. ~ры́бица, -ы, white salmon. ~сне́жный, snow-white.

белови́к, -лка́, fair copy. белово́й, fair.

бело́к, бел, -а́, бело́, white; clean, blank; ~а́я берёза, silver birch; ~ый день, broad daylight; ~ое кале́ние, white heat; ~ый медве́дь, polar bear; ~ые но́чи, white nights, midnight sun; ~ые стихи́, blank verse.

бельё, -я́, linen; bedclothes, underclothes, underclothing; washing.

бельмо́, -а́; pl. -ма, cataract; wall-eye.

бельэта́ж, -а, first floor; dress circle

бемо́ль, -я m., бемо́ль indecl. adj. flat.

бенефи́с, -а, a benefit (performance).

бензи́н, -а, petrol; benzine. бензи́новый, petrol; ~ая коло́нка, petrol pump. бензиноме́р, -а, petrol-gauge. бензиопрово́д, -а, petrol pipe.

бензо- in comb., petrol. бензоба́к, -а, petrol-tank. ~запра́вка, -и, ~запра́вочная sb., filling-station, petrol-station. ~запра́вщик, -а, petrol bowser,

~коло́нка, -и, petrol pump. ~ме́р, -a, fuel gauge. ~очисти́тель, -я *m.* petrol filter. ~прово́д, -a, petrol pipe, fuel line. ~храни́лище -a, petrol (storage) tank. ~цисте́рна, -ы, petrol tanker.

бензо́л, -a, benzene; benzol.

берёг, etc.: see бере́чь.

бе́рег, -a, *loc.* -ý; *pl.* -á, bank, shore; coast; на ~ý мо́ря, at the seaside. берего|во́й, coast; coastal; ~бе судохо́дство, coastal shipping.

бережёшь, etc.: see бере́чь. бережли́|вый, thrifty, economical; careful. бе́режный, careful; cautious; solicitous.

берёза, -ы, birch. бере́зник, -a, березня́к, -á, birch grove, birch wood. берёзовый, birch.

бере́йтор, -a, horse-breaker; riding-master.

бере́менеть, -ею *imp.* (*perf.* за~) become pregnant; be pregnant. бере́менный, pregnant (+*instr.*, with). бере́менность, -и, pregnancy; gestation.

бере́чь, -регу́, -режёшь; -рёг, -лá *imp.* take care of, look after; keep; cherish; husband; be sparing of; ~ся, be careful, take care; beware; береги́(те)сь! look out!

берли́нск|ий, Berlin; ~ая лазу́рь, Prussian blue.

берло́га, -и, den, lair.

беру́, etc.: see брать.

бес, -a, devil; the devil.

бес-: see без-.

бесе́да, -ы, talk, conversation; discussion. бесе́дка, -и, summer-house. бесе́д|овать, -дую *imp.* talk, converse. бесе́дчик, -a, discussion-leader.

беси́ть, бешу́, бе́сишь *imp.* (*perf.* вз~) enrage, madden, infuriate; ~ся, go mad; rage, be furious.

бес-. бескла́ссовый, classless. ~коне́чный, endless; infinite; interminable; ~коне́чная дробь, recurring decimal. ~коры́стие, -я, disinterestedness. ~коры́стный, disinterested. ~кра́йний, boundless. ~кро́вный, bloodless. беснова́тый, like one possessed; raving,

frenzied. беснова́ться, -ну́юсь *imp.* rage, storm, rave; be possessed. бесо́вский, devilish; devil's.

бес-. беспа́мятный, forgetful. ~па́-мятство, -a, unconsciousness; forgetfulness; delirium. ~пардо́нный, shameless, brazen. ~парти́йный, non-party. ~перспекти́вный, without prospects; hopeless. ~пе́чность, -и, carelessness, unconcern. ~пе́чный, carefree; careless, unconcerned. ~пла́тно *adv.* free. ~пла́тный, free; rent-free; complimentary. ~пло́-дие, -я, sterility, barrenness. ~пло́дность, -и, fruitlessness, futility. ~пло́дный, sterile, barren; fruitless, futile. ~поворо́тный, irrevocable, final. ~подо́бный, incomparable; superb, magnificent. ~позвоно́чный, invertebrate.

беспоко́ить, -ою *imp.* (*perf.* о~, по~) disturb, make anxious, make uneasy; trouble; ~ся, worry, be anxious; trouble, put oneself out. беспоко́йный, restless; anxious; uneasy; troubled; disturbing; fidgety.

бес-. беспо́ле́зный, useless. ~по́лый, sexless, asexual. ~по́мощный, helpless, powerless; feeble. ~поро́дный, mongrel, not thoroughbred. ~поро́ч-ный, blameless, irreproachable; immaculate. ~поря́док, -дка, disorder; untidy state; *pl.* disorders, disturbances, rioting. ~поря́дочный, disorderly; untidy. ~поса́дочный, non-stop. ~по́чвенный, groundless; unsound. ~по́шлинный, duty-free; ~по́шлинная торго́вля, free trade. ~поща́дный, merciless, relentless. ~пра́вный, without rights, deprived of civil rights. ~преде́льный, boundless, infinite. ~предме́тный, aimless, purposeless; abstract. ~прекосло́вный, unquestioning, absolute. ~препя́тственный, unhindered; free, clear, unimpeded. ~преры́вный, continuous, uninterrupted. ~преста́нный, continual, incessant.

беспризо́рник, -a, -ница, -ы, waif, homeless child. беспризо́рный, neglected, stray; homeless; *sb.* waif, homeless child or young person.

бес-. **беспримерный**, unexampled, unparalleled. **~пристрастие, -я, ~пристрастность,** -и, impartiality. **~пристрастный,** impartial, unbiased. **~приютный,** homeless; not affording shelter. **~проволочный,** wireless. **~просветный,** pitch-dark, pitch-black; hopeless, gloomy; unrelieved. **~путный,** debauched, dissipated, dissolute. **~связный,** incoherent. **~семянный,** seedless. **~сердечие, -я, ~сердечность,** -и, heartlessness, callousness. **~сердечный,** heartless; callous, unfeeling, hard-hearted. **~силие, -я,** impotence; debility, feebleness. **~сильный,** weak, feeble; impotent, powerless. **~славие, -я,** infamy. **~славный,** ignominious; infamous; inglorious. **~следно** *adv.* without trace; utterly, completely. **~следный,** without leaving a trace, complete. **~словесный,** dumb, speechless; silent, unmurmuring, meek, humble; walking-on. **~сменный,** permanent, continuous. **~смертие, -я,** immortality. **~смертный,** immortal, undying. **~смысленный,** senseless; foolish; meaningless, nonsensical. **~смыслица, -ы,** nonsense. **~совестный,** unscrupulous; shameless. **~сознательный,** unconscious; involuntary. **~сонница, -ы,** insomnia, sleeplessness. **~сонный,** sleepless. **~спорный,** indisputable, undeniable, unquestionable; incontrovertible. **~срочный,** indefinite; indeterminate; unlimited. **~страстный,** impassive. **~страшный,** intrepid, fearless. **~таланный,** untalented, without talent.

бестолковщина, -ы muddle, confusion, disorder. **бестолковый,** muddle-headed, slow, stupid; confused, incoherent. **бестолочь, -и,** confusion, muddle; stupid creature; blockheads.

бес-. **бестрепетный,** dauntless, undaunted, intrepid. **~форменный,** shapeless, formless. **~характерный,** weak, spineless. **~хитростный,** artless; ingenuous; unsophisticated. **~цветный,** colourless. **~цельный,** aimless; pointless. **~ценный,** priceless. **~ценок; за ~ценок,** very cheap,

for a song. **~церемонный,** unceremonious; free and easy, familiar, off-hand. **~человечный,** inhuman. **~честить, -ещу** *imp.* (*perf.* о~честить) dishonour, disgrace. **~честный,** dishonourable, disgraceful. **~численный,** innumerable, countless.

бесчувственный, insensible, unconscious; insensitive, unfeeling. **бесчувствие, -я,** unconsciousness, insensibility; callousness, heartlessness; пьян до бесчувствия, dead drunk. бес-. **бесшумный.** noiseless.

бетон, -а, concrete. **бетонировать, -рую** *imp.* (*perf.* за-), concrete. **бетонный,** concrete. **бетономешалка, -и,** concrete-mixer. **бетонщик, -а,** concrete-worker, concreter.

бечева, бичева, -ы, tow-rope; rope, cord, twine. **бечёвка, бичёвка, -и,** twine, cord, string. **бечевник, -а,** tow-path, towing-path. **бечев|ой,** tow, towing; **~ая** *sb.* tow-path, towing-path.

бешенство, -а, hydrophobia, rabies; fury, rage. **бешеный,** rabid, mad; furious, violent.

бешу etc.: see **бесить.**

бибабо *n. indecl.* glove puppet.

библейский, biblical. **библиограф, -а,** bibliographer. **библиографический,** bibliographical. **библиотека, -и,** library; **~-читальня,** reading-room. **библиотекарь, -я** *m.,* **-текарша, -и,** librarian. **библиотечный,** library. **библия. -и,** bible.

бивак, -а, bivouac, camp.

бивень, -вня *m.* tusk.

бигуди *pl. indecl.* curlers.

бидон, -а, can; milk-churn.

биение, -я beating; beat.

бижутерия, -и, costume jewellery.

бикса, -ы, (*sl.*) whore.

билет, -а, ticket; card; pass, permit; кредитный ~, bank-note. **билетёр, -а, -тёрша, -и,** ticket-collector; usherette. **билетный,** ticket.

бинокль -я *m.* binoculars; полевой ~, field-glasses; театральный ~, opera-glasses. **бинокулярный,** binocular.

бинт, -а, bandage. **бинтовать, -тую**

imp. (*perf.* за~) bandage. **бинто́вка, -и** bandaging.

би́ржа, -и, exchange.

би́рка, -и, tally; name-plate; label.

бирюза́, -ы́, turquoise.

бис *int.* encore; спеть на ~, repeat as encore. **бисирова́ть, -ру́ю** *perf.* and *imp.* repeat; give an encore.

би́сер, -а, glass beads, bugles. **би́серина, -ы, би́серинка, -и,** (small) glass bead.

бискви́т, -а, sponge cake; biscuit. **бискви́тный,** sponge; biscuit.

би́тва, -ы, battle.

битко́м *adv.;* ~ наби́т, crowded, packed.

бито́к -тка́, rissole, hamburger.

би́т|ый, beaten; broken, cracked; ~ые сли́вки, whipped cream; ~ый час, a full hour; hours, ages. **бить, бью, бьёшь** *imp.* (*perf.* за~, по~, про~, уда́рить) beat; hit; defeat; strike; whip; sound; thump, bang; kill, slaughter; smash, shatter; fight, struggle; wage war (по+*dat.* on, against); spurt, gush; shoot, fire; ~ в бараба́н, beat a drum; ~ в ладо́ши, clap one's hands; ~ (в) наба́т, sound, raise, the alarm; ~ в цель, hit the target; ~ за́дом, kick; ~ ключо́м, gush out, well up; be in full swing; ~ на+*acc.* strive for, after; have a range of; ~ отбо́й, beat a retreat; ~ по+*dat.* damage, injure, wound; ~ трево́гу, sound, raise, the alarm; ~ хвосто́м, lash its tail; ~ся, fight; beat; writhe, struggle; break; +*instr.* knock, hit, strike; +*над*+*instr.* struggle with, rack one's brains over; ~ голово́й об сте́ну, be up against a blank wall; ~ об закла́д, bet, wager. **битьё, -я́.** beating, thrashing; thumping, banging; smashing.

бич, -а́, whip, lash; scourge. **бичева́, -ы́, бичёвка:** see бечева́, бечёвка. **бичева́ть, -чу́ю** *imp.* flog; lash, castigate.

бишь *part.* expressing effort to remember name, etc.: как ~ его́? what was the name again? what's-his-name, thingamy; то ~, that is to say.

бла́го, -а, good; blessing; всех благ! all the best! **бла́го** *conj.* since.

бла́го- in *comb.* well-, good-. **Благове́щение, -я,** Annunciation. **~ве́щен-**

ский, of the Annunciation. ~ви́дный, comely; plausible; specious. ~во́ле́ние, -я, goodwill; favour. ~воспи́танный, well-bred.

благодаре́ние, -я, gratitude, thanks. **благодари́ть, -рю́** *imp.* (*perf.* по~) thank; благодарю́ вас, thank you. **благода́рность, -и,** gratitude; thanks; bribe; не сто́ит благода́рности, don't mention it, not at all. **благода́рный,** grateful; rewarding, promising. **благода́рственный,** of gratitude, of thanks; thanksgiving. **благодаря́** *prep.*+*dat.* thanks to, owing to; because of.

благо-. благоде́тель, -я *m.,* **-ница, -ы,** benefactor. **~де́тельный,** beneficial; beneficent. **~ду́шный,** placid, equable; good-humoured. **~жела́тель, -я** *m.* well-wisher. **~жела́тельный,** well-disposed; benevolent. **~зву́чный,** melodious, harmonious. **~мы́слящий,** right-thinking, right-minded. **~надёжный,** reliable, trustworthy, sure; loyal. **~наме́ренный,** well-intentioned. **~нра́вие, -я,** good behaviour. **~нра́вный,** well-behaved; high-principled. **~получие, -я,** well-being; happiness. **~получно** *adv.* all right, well; happily; safely. **~получный,** happy, successful; safe. **~присто́йный,** decent, seemly, decorous. **~прия́тный,** favourable. **~прия́тствовать** *imp.*+*dat.* favour; наибо́лее ~приятствуемая держа́ва, most-favoured nation. **~разу́мие, -я,** sense; prudence. **~разу́мный,** judicious, sensible, prudent. **~ро́дие, -я;** ва́ше ~ро́дие, your Honour. **~ро́дный,** noble. **~ро́дство, -а,** nobility. **~скло́нность, -и** favour, good graces. **~скло́нный,** favourable; gracious. **~слови́ть, -влю́** *perf.,* **благословля́ть, -я́ю** *imp.* bless. **~состоя́ние, -я,** prosperity. **~твори́тель, -я** *m.,* **-ница, -ы,** philanthropist. **~твори́тельный,** charitable, charity. **~тво́рный,** salutary; beneficial; wholesome. **~устро́енный,** well-equipped, well-arranged, well-planned; with all amenities.

блаже́нный, blessed; blissful; simple-minded. **блаже́нство, -а,** bliss, blessedness.

бланк, -а, form; анкéтный ~, questionnaire. **бла́нков|ый**, form; ~ая на́дпись. endorsement.

блат, -а, (*sl.*) thieves' cant, criminals' slang; pull, protection; racket, fiddle. **блата́рь**, -я́ *m.*, **блатя́к**, -а́, блатя́га, -и *m.* professional criminal; racketeer. **блатн|о́й**, criminal; soft, cushy; ~а́я му́зыка, thieves' cant; ~о́й *sb.* criminal, thief.

бледне́ть, -е́ю *imp.* (*perf.* по~), grow pale; pale. **бледноли́цый**, pale; *sb.* paleface. **бле́дность**, -и, бледнота́, -ы, paleness, pallor. **бле́дный** -ден, -дна́, -о, pale; colourless; ~ как полотно́, as white as a sheet.

бле́клый, faded. **бле́кнуть**, -ну; блёк-(нул) *imp.* (*perf.* по~) fade, wither.

блеск, -а (-у), brightness, brilliance, lustre, shine; splendour, magnificence.

блесну́ть, -ну́, -нёшь *perf.* flash, gleam; shine. **блесте́ть**, -ещу́, -сти́шь or блéщешь *imp.* shine; glitter; sparkle. **блёстка**, -и, sparkle, flash; spangle, sequin. **блестя́щий**, shining, bright; brilliant.

бле́яние, -я, bleat, bleating. **бле́ять**, -éет *imp.* bleat.

ближа́йший, nearest, closest; next; immediate; ~ ро́дственник, next of kin. **бли́же** *comp.* of бли́зкий. **близко**. **бли́жний**, near, close; neighbouring; *sb.* neighbour. **близ** *prep.*+*gen.* near, close to, by. **бли́зиться**, -зится *imp.* approach, draw near. **бли́зкий**, -зок, -изка́, -о, near, close; imminent; intimate; ~кие *sb. pl.* one's nearest and dearest, near relatives. **бли́зко** *adv.* near, close (от+*gen.* to); nearly, closely. **близне́ц**, -á, twin; *pl.* Gemini. **близору́кий**, short-sighted. **бли́зость**, -и, nearness, closeness, proximity; intimacy.

блик, -а. spot or patch of light; light, high-light.

блин, -á, pancake.

блинда́ж, -á, dug-out.

блиста́тельный, brilliant, splendid. **блиста́ть**, -áю *imp.* shine; glitter; sparkle.

блок¹, -а, block, pulley, sheave.

блок², -а, bloc, block; section, unit, slab. **блоки́ровать**, -рую *perf.* and *imp.* blockade; block; ~ся, form a bloc. **блокиро́вка**, -и, block system. **блокно́т**, -а, writing-pad, note-pad, note-book.

блонди́н, -а, **блонди́нка**, -и, blond(e).

блоха́, -и́; *pl.* -и, -áм flea. **блоши́ный**, flea. **бло́шки**, -шек *pl.* tiddlywinks.

блудни́ца, -ы, whore.

блужда́ть, -áю *imp.* roam, wander, rove. **блужда́ющ|ий**, wandering; ~ий огонёк, will-o'-the-wisp; ~ая по́чка, floating kidney.

блу́за, -ы, блу́зка, -и, blouse.

блю́дечко, -а, saucer; small dish; на блю́дечке, on a plate. **блю́до**, -а, dish; course. **блю́дце**, -а, saucer.

блюсти́, -юду́, -дёшь; блюл, -á *imp.* (*perf.* со~), guard, keep; watch over; observe. **блюсти́тель**, -я *m.* keeper, guardian.

БНТИ (be-entei) *abbr.* бюро́ нау́чно-техни́ческой информа́ции, Scientific and Technical Information Bureau.

боб, -á, bean. **бобо́в|ый**, bean; ~ые *sb. pl.* leguminous plants. **бобо́к**, -бка́, bean.

бобр, -á, beaver. **бо́брик**, -а, beaver cloth; во́лосы ~ом, crew cut. **бо́бровый**, beaver.

бобы́ль, -я́ *m.* poor landless peasant; solitary person.

бог, -а, *voc.* Бо́же, god; Бог дай ~, God grant; с его́ зна́ет, who knows? не дай ~, God forbid; Бо́же (мой)! my God! good God! ра́ди ~а, for God's sake; с ~ом! good luck!; сла́ва ~у, thank God. **богаде́льня**, -и, almshouse, workhouse.

богате́й, -я, rich man. **богате́ть**, -е́ю *imp.* (*perf.* раз~), grow rich. **бога́тство**, -а, riches, wealth; richness. **бога́тый**, rich, wealthy; *sb.* rich man. **бога́ч**, -á, rich man.

боги́ня, -и, goddess. **богома́терь**, -и, Mother of God. **богомо́лец**, -льца, -мо́лка, -и, devout person; pilgrim. **богомо́лье**, -я, pilgrimage. **богомо́льный**, religious, devout. **богоро́дица**, -ы, the Virgin Mary. **богосло́в**, -а, theologian. **богосло́вие**, -я, theology.

боготвори́ть, -рю́ *imp.* worship, idolize; deify.

бодáть(ся, -áю(сь *imp.*, боднýть, -нý, -нёшь *perf.* (*perf.* also забодáть) butt. бодли́вый, inclined to butt.

бодри́ть, -рю́ *imp.* stimulate, invigorate, brace up; ∼ся, try to keep up one's spirits. бóдрость, -и, cheerfulness, good spirits, courage. бóдрствовать, -твую *imp.* be awake; stay awake, keep awake; sit up. бóдрый; бодр, -á, -о, cheerful, brisk, bright; hale and hearty. бодря́щий, invigorating, bracing.

боеви́к, -á, active revolutionary, militant; smash hit. боевóй, fighting, battle, war; urgent; militant, determined, unyielding; ∼óй клич, war-cry; ∼óе креще́ние, baptism of fire; ∼óй механи́зм, striking mechanism. боеголóвка, -и, warhead. боеприпáсы, -ов *pl.* ammunition. боéц, бойцá, soldier; fighter, warrior; butcher, slaughterer: *pl.* men.

Бóже: see бог. божéеский, divine; fair, just. божествó, -á, deity; divinity. бóж|ий, God's; ∼ья корóвка, ladybird; кáждый ∼ий день, every blessed day. божи́ться, -жýсь *imp.* (*perf.* по∼). swear. божóк, -жкá idol.

бой, -я (-ю), *loc.* -ю́; *pl.* -и́, -ёв. battle, action, fight; bout; fighting; killing, slaughtering; striking; breakage(s), broken glass, crockery, etc.; барáбанный ∼, drumbeat; ∼ быкóв bullfight; ∼ китóв, whaling; ∼ тюле́ней, sealing; с бóю, by force; часы́ с бóем, striking clock.

бóй|кий; бóек, бойкá, -о, bold, spry, smart, sharp; glib; lively, animated; busy.

бойни́ца, -ы, loophole, embrasure.

бóйня, -и; *gen. pl.* бóен, slaughter-house, abattoir, shambles; massacre, slaughter, butchery.

бóйче, *comp.* of бóйкий.

бок, -а (-у), *loc.* -ý; *pl.* -á, side; flank; ∼ ó ∼, side by side; в ∼, sideways; нá ∼, sideways, to the side; на ∼ý, on one side; пóд ∼ом, near by, close by; с ∼у from the side, from the flank; с ∼у нá бок from side to side.

бокáл, -а, glass; goblet.

боковóй, side, flank; lateral; sidelong. бóком *adv.* sideways.

бокс, -а, boxing. боксёр, -а, boxer. боксёрский, boxing. бокси́ровать, -рую *imp.* box.

болвáн, -а, block; blockhead; dummy; idol. болвáнка, -и, block; pig; желéзо в ∼х, pig-iron.

болевóй, of pain painful.

бóлее *adv.* more; ∼ всегó, most of all; тем ∼, что, especially as.

болéзнен|ный, sickly; unhealthy; abnormal morbid; painful. болéзнь, -и, illness, disease, ailment; abnormality; ∼ рóста, growing pains.

болéльщик, -а, -щица, -ы, fan, supporter. болéть[1], -éю *imp.* be ill, suffer; be worried; +за+*acc.* support, be a fan of. болéть[2], -ли́т *imp.* ache, hurt.

болóнья, -и, (cape of) waterproof nylon.

болóтистый, marshy, boggy, swampy. болóто, -а, marsh, bog, swamp. болóтный, marsh, bog.

болтáнка, -и, air-pocket. болтáть[1], -áю *imp.* stir; shake; dangle; ∼ся, dangle; swing; hang loosely; hang about: fly bumpily. bump.

болтáть[2], -áю *imp.* chatter, jabber, natter. болтли́вый, garrulous, talkative; indiscreet. болтнýть, -нý, -нёшь *perf.* blurt out. болтовня́, -и́, talk; chatter; gossip. болтýн[1], -á, болтýнья, -и, talker, chatterer; chatterbox; gossip. болтýн[2]. -á. addled egg.

болтýшка, -и, scrambled eggs; mixture; swill, mash; whisk.

боль, -и, pain; ache; ∼ в бокý, stitch. больни́ца, -ы, hospital. больни́чный, hospital; ∼ листóк, medical certificate. бóльно[1] *adv.* painfully. badly; *predic.* + *dat.* it hurts. бóльно[2] *adv.* very, extremely, terribly. больнóй; -лен, -льнá, ill. sick; diseased; sore; *sb.* patient, invalid.

большáк, -á, high road. бóльше *comp.* of большóй, вели́кий, мнóго; bigger, larger; greater; more; ∼ не, not any more, no more, no longer; ∼ тогó, and what is more; *adv.* for the most part. бóльш|ий, greater, larger; ∼ей чáстью for the most part; сáмое ∼ее at most, at the utmost, at the outside. **большинство́**, -á, majority; most people. **больш|о́й**, big, large; great; grown-up; ~áя бу́ква, capital letter; ~áя доро́га, high road; ~о́й па́лец, thumb, big toe; ~о́й свет, high society, the world; ~и́е *sb. pl.* grown-ups. **большу́щий**, huge, enormous.

боля́чка, -и, sore, scab; defect, weakness.

бо́мба, -ы, bomb. **бомбардирова́ть**, -ру́ю *imp.* bombard; bomb. **бомбарди́ровка**, -и, bombardment, bombing. **бомбёжка**, -и, *coll.* bombing. **бомби́ть**, -блю́ *imp.* bomb. **бомбово́з**, -а, bomber. **бо́мбовый**, bomb. **бомбоубе́жище**, -а, bomb shelter.

бо́на, -ы, bond, bill; money order; *pl.* paper money.

бор, -а, *loc.* -ý; *pl.* -ы́, pine-wood, coniferous forest.

бордо́ *n. indecl.* claret; red Bordeaux. **бордо́** *indecl. adj.*, **бордо́вый**, wine-red, claret-coloured.

бордю́р, -а, border.

боре́ц, -рца́ fighter; wrestler.

борза́я *sb.* borzoi. **бо́рзый**, swift.

бормота́ние, -я, muttering, mumbling; mutter, mumble. **бормота́ть**, -очу́, -о́чешь *imp.* (*perf.* про~), mutter, mumble.

бо́рный, boric, boracic.

бо́ров, -а, hog.

борови́к, -á, boletus.

борода́, -ы́, *acc.* бо́роду; *pl.* бо́роды, -ро́д, -áм, beard; wattles. **борода́вка**, -и, wart. **борода́тый**, bearded. **борода́ч**, -á, bearded man. **боро́дка**, -и, small beard, tuft; (key-)bit.

борозда́, -ы́; *pl.* бо́розды, -озд, -áм, furrow; fissure. **борозди́ть**, -зжу́ *imp.* (*perf.* вз~) furrow; plough; leave wake or track on; score. **борозди́нка**, -и, furrow, groove. **борозди́тый**, furrowed; grooved, scored.

борона́, -ы́, *acc.* бо́рону; *pl.* бо́роны, -ро́н, -áм, harrow. **борони́ть**, -ню́ *imp.* (*perf.* вз~) harrow.

боро́ться, -рю́сь, -решься *imp.* wrestle, grapple; struggle, fight.

борт, -а, *loc.* -ý; *pl.* -á, -о́в, side, ship's

side; front; cushion; зá ~, overboard; на ~, на ~ý, on board. **борт-** in *comb.* ship's; air, flight, flying. **бортово́й**, ship's; onboard; flight, flying; ~áя ка́чка, rolling. **бортпроводни́к**, -á, air steward. **бортпроводни́ца**, -ы, air hostess.

борщ, -á, borshch.

борьба́, -ы́, wrestling; struggle, fight; conflict.

босико́м *adv.* barefoot. **босо́й**, бос, -á, -о, **босоно́гий**, barefooted; на бо́су но́гу, on one's bare feet. **босоно́жка**, -и, barefooted woman or girl; barefoot dancer; *pl.* sandals. mules. **бося́к**, -á, бося́чка, -и, tramp; down-and-out.

бот[1], -а, **бо́тик**[1], -а, small boat.

бот[2], -а, **бо́тик**[2], -а, high overshoe. **боти́нок**, -нка. boot.

боца́ть, буца́ть, -áю *imp.* (*perf.* за~) clatter, tramp.

бо́цман, -а, boatswain, boatswain's mate.

боча́г, -á, pool; deep puddle.

бочко́м *adv.* sideways.

бо́чка, -и, barrel. cask. **бочо́нок**, -нка, keg. small barrel.

боязли́вый, timid, timorous. **боя́знь**, -и, fear, dread.

боя́рин, -а; *pl.* -я́ре, -я́р, boyar. **боя́рский|ий**, boyar's, boyars'; ~ие де́ти, small landowners.

боя́рышник, -а, hawthorn.

боя́ться, бою́сь *imp.* (+ *gen.* be afraid of, fear; dislike, be intolerant of.

бр. *abbr.* бра́тья, brothers.

бра, *n. indecl.* sconce, bracket.

бра́га, -и, home-brewed beer.

брак[1], -а, marriage.

брак[2], -а, defective goods, defective part; reject, waste. **бракёр**, -а, inspector. **бракова́ть**, -ку́ю *imp.* (*perf.* за~), reject. **бракоде́л**, -а, bad workman.

бракоразво́дный, divorce.

брандахлы́ст, -а, slops, swipes.

брани́ть, -ню́ *imp.* (*perf.* вы~) scold; abuse, curse; ~ся (*perf.* по~ся) swear, curse; quarrel. **бра́нный|ый**[1], abusive, profane; ~ое сло́во, swear-word.

бра́нный[2], martial, battle. **брань**[1], -и, war; battle.

брань[2], -и, swearing, bad language; abuse.

браслет, -а, bracelet; pl. (sl.) handcuffs.

брасс, -а, breast stroke. **брасси́ст**, -а, **-и́стка**, -и, breast-stroke swimmer.

брат, -а; pl. -ться, -тьев, brother; comrade; old man, my lad, mate; lay brother, monk, friar; pl. friends, boys; на ~а, per head; наш ~, we, the likes of us, our sort. **брата́ние**, -я, fraternization. **брата́ться**, -а́юсь imp. (perf. по~) fraternize. **братва́**, -ы́, comrades, friends. **бра́тия**, -и; gen. pl. -тий, **бра́тья**, -и, brotherhood, fraternity. **братоуби́йство**, -а, **братоуби́йца**, -ы, m. and f. fratricide. **бра́тский**, brotherly, fraternal. **бра́тство**, -а, brotherhood, fraternity.

брать, беру́, -рёшь; брал, -а́, -о imp. (perf. взять) take; get, obtain, book; hire; seize, grip; exact, demand, require; surmount, clear; work; be effective; take bribes; +instr. succeed through, succeed by means of; +adv. bear; ~ верх, get the upper hand; ~ в ско́бки, put in brackets; ~ на+acc. have a range of; ~ на букси́р, take in tow; ~ на пору́ки, go bail for; ~ но́ту, sing (play) a note; ~ под аре́ст, put under arrest; ~ своё, get one's (own) way; take its toll, tell; ~ сло́во, take the floor; **~ся**+за+acc. touch; take hold of, seize; take up; get down to; +за+acc. or inf. undertake, take on oneself; appear, come; **~ся** за ум, come to one's senses; **~ся** нарасхва́т, go (sell) like hot cakes.

бра́чный, marriage; mating.

бревенча́тый, log. **бревно́**, -а́; pl. -ёвна, -вен, log, beam.

бред, -а, loc. -у́, delirium; raving(s); gibberish. **бре́дить**, -е́жу imp. be delirious, rave; +instr. rave about, be infatuated with. **бре́дни**, -ей pl. ravings; fantasies. **бредово́й**, **бре́довый**, delirious; fantastic, nonsensical.

бреду́, etc.: see брести́. **бре́жу**, etc.: see бре́дить.

брезга́ть, -аю imp. (perf. по~)+inf. or instr. be squeamish about, be fastidious

about; be nauseated by, be sickened by; shrink from, scruple or hesitate to. **брезгли́вый**, squeamish, fastidious.

брезе́нт, -а, tarpaulin.

бре́зжить(ся, -ит(ся imp. dawn; gleam faintly, glimmer.

брёл, etc.: see брести́.

брело́к, -а, a charm, trinket.

бремени́ть, -ню́ imp. (perf. о~) burden. **бре́мя**, -мени pl. burden; load.

бренча́ть, -чу́ imp. strum; jingle.

брести́, -еду́, -едёшь; брёл, -а́ imp. stroll, amble; struggle along, drag oneself along.

брете́ль, -я, **брете́лька**, -и, shoulder-strap.

бре́ю etc.: see брить.

брига́да, -ы, brigade; squadron; crew, team, gang, squad. **брига́дир**, -а, brigadier; brigade-leader team-leader; foreman. **брига́дник**, -а, **-ница**, -ы, member of brigade, crew, team.

бри́джи, -ей pl. breeches.

бриза́нтный, high-explosive.

бриллиа́нт, -а, **брилья́нт**, -а, brilliant, diamond.

брита́нец, -нца, **брита́нка**, -и, Briton, British subject; Englishman, English-woman. **брита́нский**, British.

бри́тва, -ы, razor. **бри́твенный**, shaving. **бри́тый**, shaved; clean-shaven. **брить**, бре́ю imp. (perf. по~) shave; **~ся**, shave (oneself). **бритьё**, -я, shave; shaving.

бри́чка, -и, britzka, trap.

бро́вка, -и, brow; edge. **бровь**, -и; pl. -и, -е́й, eyebrow; brow.

брод, -а, ford.

броди́ть, -ожу́, -о́дишь imp. wander, roam, stray; amble, stroll; ferment. **бродя́га**, -и m. and f., **бродя́жка**, -и m. and f. tramp, vagrant, down-and-out; wanderer. **бродя́жничать**, -аю imp. be on the road, be a tramp. **бродя́жничество**, -а, vagrancy. **бродя́чий**, vagrant; wandering, roving; strolling; stray; restless. **броже́ние**, -я, ferment, fermentation.

бром, -а, bromine; bromide. **бро́мистый**, bromic, bromidic; ~ ка́лий, potassium bromide. **бро́мный**, **бро́мовый**, bromine.

броне- in *comb.*, armoured, armour. **бронебо́йный**, armour-piercing. **~ви́к**, -á, armoured car. **~во́й**, armoured, armour. **~но́сец**, -сца, battleship, iron-clad; armadillo. **~но́сный**, **~та́нко-вый**, armoured.

бро́нза, -ы, bronze; (collection of) bronzes. **бронзова́ть**, -ру́ю, *perf.* and *imp.* bronze. **бронзиро́вка**, -и, bronzing. **бро́нзовый**, bronze; bronzed.

брони́рованный, armoured, **брониро-ва́ть**[1], -ру́ю *perf.* and *imp.* (*perf.* also за~) armour.

брони́ровать[2], -ру́ю *perf.* and *imp.* (*perf.* also за~), reserve, book. **бро́ня**[2], -и, reservation; commandeering; warrant, permit; exemption. **броня́**[1], -и́ armour.

броса́ть, -а́ю *imp.*, **бро́сить**, -о́шу *perf.* throw, cast, fling; drop; throw down; leave, abandon, desert; give up, leave off; бро́с(те)ть! stop it! drop it!; ~ся, throw oneself, fling oneself, rush; + *inf.* begin, start; + *instr.* throw away, squander; throw at one another, pelt one another with; ~ся в глаза́, be striking, arrest the attention; ~ся на коле́ни, fall on one's knees; ~ся на по́мощь +*dat.* rush to the assistance of. **бро́ский**, arresting, striking; loud, garish, glaring. **бро́совый**, worthless, rubbishy; ~ая цена́, giveaway price; ~ый э́кспорт, dumping. **бросо́к**, -ска́, throw; burst; bound, spurt; thrust.

бро́шка, -и, **брошь**, -и, brooch.

брошю́ра, -ы, pamphlet, booklet, brochure. **брошюрова́ть**, -ру́ю *imp.* (*perf.* с~) stitch. **брошюро́вка**, -и, stitching. **брошюро́вщик**, -а, a stitcher.

брус, -а; *pl.* -сья, -сьев, squared timber; beam, joist; bar; (паралле́льные) ~ья, parallel bars. **бру́сковый**, bar.

брусни́ка, -и, cowberry, red whortle-berry; cowberries, red whortleberries.

брусо́к, -ска́, bar; ingot; slug.

бру́ствер, -а, breastwork, parapet.

бру́тто *indecl. adj.* gross.

бры́згать, -зжу or -гаю *imp.*, **бры́знуть**, -ну *perf.* splash, spatter; sprinkle; spurt, gush; ~ слюно́й sputter, splut-

ter; ~ся, splash; splash oneself, splash one another; spray oneself. **бры́зги**, брызг *pl.* spray, splashes; fragments; sparks.

брыка́ть, -а́ю *imp.*, **брыкну́ть**, -ну́, -нёшь *perf.* kick; ~ся, kick, rebel.

брысь *int.* shoo.

БРЭ *m. indecl.*, *abbr.* биологи́ческий рентге́н-эквивале́нт, man roentgen equivalent.

брюзга́, -и́ *m.* and *f.* grumbler. **брюзгли́вый**, grumbling, peevish. **брюз-жа́ть**, -жу́ *imp.* grumble.

брю́ква, -ы, swede.

брю́ки, брюк *pl.* trousers.

брюне́т, -а, dark man, dark-haired man. **брюне́тка**, -и, brunette.

брюха́стый, **брюха́тый**, big-bellied. **брю́хо** -а; *pl.* -и, belly; paunch, corporation; stomach.

брю́чный, trouser; ~ костю́м, trouser suit.

брюшко́, -á; *pl.* -и́, -о́в, abdomen; paunch. **брюшно́й**, abdominal; ~ тиф, typhoid.

бря́канье, -я, clatter. **бря́кать**, -аю *imp.*, **бря́кнуть**, -ну *perf.* crash down, drop with a crash; blurt out; (+*instr.*) clatter, make a clatter; ~ся, crash, fall heavily. **бряца́ние**, -я, rattling, rattle; clanking; clank; clang. **бряца́ть**, -а́ю *imp.* rattle; clank, clang.

бу́бен, -бна, tambourine. **бубене́ц**, -нца́, **бубе́нчик**, -а, small bell.

бу́бны, -бён, -бна́м *pl.* diamonds. **буб-но́вый**, diamond; ~ вале́т, knave of diamonds.

буго́р, -гра́, mound, hillock, knoll; bump, lump. **буго́рок**, -рка́, small mound or lump; protuberance; tubercle. **бугорча́тка**, -и, tuberculosis, consumption. **бугри́стый**, hilly, bumpy.

бу́дет, that's enough, that will do; + *inf.* it's time to stop; ~ вам писа́ть, don't do any more writing.

буди́льник, -а, alarm-clock. **буди́ть**, бужу́, бу́дишь *imp.* (*perf.* про~) wake, awaken; rouse, arouse.

бу́дка, -и, box, booth; hut; stall; со-ба́чья ~, dog-kennel.

бу́дни, -ней *pl.* weekdays; workdays,

working days; humdrum existence. бу́дний, бу́дничный, weekday; everyday; dull, humdrum.

бу́дто *conj.* as if, as though; ~ (бы) (как) ~, apparently, allegedly, ostensibly; *part.* really?

бу́ду, etc.: see быть. бу́дучи, being. бу́дущ|ий, future; next, coming; to be, to come; ~ee *sb.* future. бу́дущность, -и, future. будь(те): see быть.

бу́ер, -а; *pl.* -а́, -о́в, ice-boat, ice-yacht.

бужу́: see буди́ть.

буза́ -ы́, home brew; (*sl.*) row, shindy; rubbish.

бузина́, -ы́, elder. бузи́нник, -а, thicket of elders. бузи́нный, бузи́новый, elder. бузи́ть, -и́шь *imp.* (*sl.*) kick up a row. бузотёр -а, (*sl.*) rowdy; trouble-maker.

буй, -я; *pl.* -и́, -ёв, buoy.

бу́йвол, -а, buffalo.

бу́йный; бу́ен, буйна́, -о, violent, turbulent; tempestuous; ungovernable; wild; luxuriant, lush. бу́йство, -а, tumult, uproar; unruly conduct, riotous behaviour. бу́йствовать, -твую *imp.* create an uproar, behave violently.

бук, -а, beech.

бука́шка, -и, small insect.

бу́ква, -ы; *gen. pl.* букв, letter; ~ в букву, literally, word for word. буква́льно *adv.* literally. буква́льный, literal. буква́рь, -я́, ABC. буквое́д, -а, pedant. буквое́дство, -а, pedantry.

букети́ровать, -рую *imp.* thin out.

букини́ст, -а, second-hand bookseller.

буклиро́ванн|ый, bouclé; ~ая ткань, bouclé fabric. бу́кля, -и, curl, ringlet.

бу́ковый, beech, beech-wood.

букс, -а, box(-tree).

букси́р, -а, tug, tug-boat; tow-rope, hawser. букси́ровать, -рую *imp.* tow, be towing, have in tow.

буксова́ние, -я, wheel-spin. буксова́ть, -су́ет *imp.* spin, slip.

булава́, -ы́, mace. була́вка, -и, pin; английская ~, safety-pin. була́вочный, pin.

бу́лка, -и, roll; сдо́бная ~, bun. бу́лочная *sb.* bakery; baker's shop. бу́лочник, -а, baker.

булты́х *int.* splash, plump. бултыха́ться, -а́юсь *imp.*, бултыхну́ться, -нёшь

-нёшься *perf.* fall with heavy splash, plunge, plump.

булы́жник, -а, cobble-stone, cobbles. булы́жный, cobbled.

бу́льканье, -я, gurgling, gurgle. бу́лькать, -аю *imp.* gurgle.

бум, -а, beam.

бума́га, -и, cotton; paper; document; *pl.* securities. бумагодержа́тель, -я, security-holder, bond-holder; paper-clip. бума́жка, -и, piece of paper; paper; note. бума́жник, -а, wallet; paper-maker. бума́жн|ый, cotton; paper; ~ая волоки́та, red tape; ~ый змей, kite; ~ая фа́брика, paper-mill. бума́жонка, -и, scrap of paper.

бунт[1], -а, bale; package; bundle.

бунт[2], -а; *pl.* -ы́, rebellion, revolt, rising; riot; mutiny. бунта́рский, seditious, mutinous; rebellious; turbulent. бунта́рь, -я́ *m.* rebel; insurgent; mutineer; rioter; inciter to rebellion or mutiny. бунтова́ть(ся, -ту́ю(сь *imp.* (*perf.* вз~), revolt, rebel; mutiny, riot; incite to rebellion or mutiny. бунтовщи́к, -а́, -щица, -ы, rebel; insurgent; mutineer; rioter.

бур, -а, auger; bore; drill.

бура́, -ы́, borax.

бура́в, -а; *pl.* -а́, auger; gimlet. бура́вить, -влю *imp.* (*perf.* про~) bore, drill. бура́вчик, -а, gimlet.

бура́н, -а, snowstorm.

бурда́, -ы́, (*sl.*) slops, swill, hog-wash.

буреве́стник, -а, stormy petrel. бурево́й, storm; stormy. бурело́м, -а, wind-fallen trees.

буре́ние, -я, boring, drilling.

буржуа́, *m. indecl.* bourgeois. буржуази́я, -и, bourgeoisie. буржуа́зный, bourgeois. буржуй, -я, bourgeois. буржу́йка, -и, bourgeois; small stove. буржу́йский, bourgeois.

бури́льный, boring, drilling. бури́льщик, -а, borer, driller, drill-operator. бури́ть, -рю́ *imp.* bore, drill.

бу́ркать, -аю *imp.*, бу́ркнуть, -ну *perf.* growl, grumble, mutter.

бурли́вый, stormy; seething, turbulent.

бурли́ть, -лю́ *imp.* boil, seethe.

бу́рный, -рен, -рна́, -о, stormy; rough; impetuous; rapid; energetic.

бурово́й, boring, bore, drilling; ~а́я вы́шка, derrick; ~а́я (сква́жина), borehole; ~о́й стано́к, ~а́я устано́вка, drilling rig.

бурт, -а, clamp. **буртова́ние**, -я, storing in clamps.

бурча́ть, -чу́ *imp.* (*perf.* про~) grumble; mumble, mutter; rumble; bubble.

бу́рый; бур, -а́, -о, brown; liver chestnut, (dark) chestnut; ~ая лиси́ца, red fox.

бурья́н, -а, tall weeds.

бу́ря, -и, storm; tempest; gale.

бу́сать, -аю *imp.* (*sl.*) drink, swallow.

бу́сина, -ы, **бу́синка**, -и, bead. **бу́сы**, бус *pl.* beads.

бутафо́р, -а, property-man, props. **бутафо́рия**, -и, properties, props; window-dressing. **бутафо́рский**, property.

бутербро́д, -а, open sandwich.

буто́н, -а, bud. **бутонье́рка**, -и, button-hole, spray of flowers.

бу́тсы, бу́тс, -ов *pl.* football boots.

буты́лка, -и, bottle. **буты́лочный**, bottle; ~ цвет, bottle green. **буты́ль**, -и, large bottle; demijohn; carboy.

буфе́т, -а, sideboard; buffet, refreshment room; bar, counter. **буфе́тная** *sb.* pantry. **буфе́тчик**, -а, barman; steward. **буфе́тчица**, -ы, barmaid.

бу́фы, буф *pl.* gathered fullness, close gathering, puffs.

бух *int.* thump, thud. **бу́хать**, -аю *imp.* (*perf.* **бу́хнуть**) thump, bang; drop noisily, bang down; thunder; thud; blurt out; ~ся, fall heavily; plump oneself down.

бухга́лтер, -а, book-keeper, accountant. **бухгалте́рия**, -и, book-keeping, accountancy; counting-house; accounts office, department. **бухга́лтерский**, book-keeping account.

бу́хнуть[1], -ну; бух *imp.* swell.

бу́хнуть[2](**бу́хнуть**) -ну(сь *perf.* of **бу́хать**(ся).

бу́хта, -ы, bay, bight. **бу́хточка**, -и, cove, creek, inlet.

буца́ть: see **боца́ть**. **бу́цы**: see **бу́тсы**.

бушева́ть, -шу́ю *imp.* rage, storm.

бушла́т, -а, pea-jacket; wadded jacket; (*sl.*) деревя́нный ~, coffin.

буя́н, -а, rowdy, brawler. **буя́нить**, -ню *imp.* make a row, create an uproar, brawl. **буя́нство**, -а, rowdyism, brawling.

бы, б *part.* I. +*pa. t.* or *inf.* indicates the conditional or subjunctive, expresses possibility, a wish, a polite suggestion or exhortation; II. (+ни), forms indefinite pronouns and conjunctions; see е́сли, как, когда́, кто, etc.

быва́ло: see **быва́ть**. **быва́лый**, experienced; worldly-wise; past, former; not new; habitual, familiar. **быва́ть**, -а́ю *imp.* be, be present; happen; take place; be inclined to be, tend to be; как не быва́ло ~ have completely disappeared; как ни в чём не быва́ло, as if nothing had happened, as though everything was all right; **быва́ло** *part.* used to, would; мать быва́ло ча́сто пе́ла э́ту пе́сню, my mother would often sing this song. **бы́вший**, former, one-time, ex-.

бык, -а́, bull, ox; stag; pier.

были́на, -ы, bylina. **были́нный**, of byliny; epic, heroic.

бы́ло *part.* nearly, on the point of; (only) just; чуть ~ не, very nearly, all but. **был**[ой], former, past, bygone; ~о́е *sb.* the past. **быль**, -и, the past, what really happened; true story, true happening.

быстрина́, -ы́; *pl.* -ы, rapids. **быстроно́гий**, swift-footed, fleet-footed; fast. **быстрота́**, -ы́, quickness, swiftness, rapidity; speed. **быстроте́чный**, fleeting, transient. **быстрохо́дный**, fast, high-speed. **бы́стрый**; быстр, -а́, -о, rapid, fast, quick; prompt.

быт, -а, *loc.* -у́, way of life, life; everyday life; слу́жба ~а, consumer services. **бытие́**, -я́ бе́нед, existence; objective reality; кни́га Бытия́, Genesis. **бытова́ть**, -тует *imp.* exist; occur; be current. **бытови́к**, -а́ (*sl.*) criminal, non-political prisoner. **бытово́й** of everyday life; everyday; domestic; social; ~а́я жи́вопись, genre painting

~бое обслу́живание. consumer services. **бытописа́ние**, -я, annals, chronicles. **бытописа́тель**, -я *m.* annalist, chronicler; writer on social themes.

быть, *pres. 3rd sing.* есть, *pl.* суть; *fut.* бу́ду; *past* был, -а́ -о; *imper.* будь(те) *imp.* be; exist; be situated; happen, take place; *impers.+dat.* be sure to happen, be inevitable: будь, что бу́дет, come what may; ~бёде, there's sure to be trouble; должно́ ~, probably, very likely; как ~? what is to be done?; не будь его́, but for him, if it weren't for him; так и ~, so be it; all right, very well, have it your own way. **бытьё**, -я́, way of life.

быча́чий, **бы́чий**, bull, ox. **бычо́к**[1], -чка́, young ox, steer.

бычо́к[2], -чка́, (*sl.*) cigarette end, fag-end. **бью** etc.: see **бить**.

бэ *n. indecl.* the letter б.

БЭР, бэр, -а; *gen. pl.* бэр *abbr.* биологи́ческий эквивале́нт рентге́на, man roentgen equivalent.

бюллете́нь, -я *m.* bulletin; voting-paper; ballot-paper; medical certificate; быть на бюллете́не, be on the sick-list, be on sick-leave.

бюро́ *n. indecl.* bureau; office; writing-desk. **бюрокра́т**, -а, bureaucrat. **бюрократи́зм**, -а, bureaucracy. **бюрократи́ческий** bureaucratic. **бюрокра́тия**, -и, bureaucracy; bureaucrats.

бюст, -а. bust; bosom. **бюстга́льтер**, -а, brassière, bra.

В

в *letter:* see **вэ**.

в, во *prep.* I.+*acc.* into, to; on; at; within; for. as; through; быть в, take after, be like; в два ра́за бо́льше, twice as big, twice the size; в на́ши дни, in our day; войти́ в дом, go into the house; в понеде́льник, on Monday; в тече́ние+*gen.* during, in the course of; в четы́ре часа́, at four o'clock; высото́й в три ме́тра, three metres high; игра́ть в ша́хматы, play chess; моро́з в де́сять гра́дусов, ten degrees of frost; пое́хать в Москву́, go to Moscow; положи́ть в я́щик стола́, put in(to) a drawer; преврати́ть во́ду в лёд, turn water into ice; разби́ть в куски́, smash to pieces; руба́шка в кле́тку check(ed) shirt; сесть в ваго́н, get into the carriage; сказа́ть в шу́тку, say as a joke; смотре́ть в окно́, look out of the window; э́то мо́жно сде́лать в неде́лю, it can be done in a week. II.+*prep.* in; on; at; of; at a distance of; в двадца́том ве́ке, in the twentieth century; в теа́тре, at the theatre; в трёх киломе́трах от го́рода,

three kilometres from the town; в четвёртом часу́, between three (o'clock) and four; в э́том году́, this year; в январе́, in January; лицо́ в весну́шках, freckled face; пье́са в пяти́ а́ктах, a play in five acts, a five-act play; роди́ться в Москве́, be born in Moscow; са́хар в куска́х, lump sugar; служи́ть в куха́рках, be a cook.

в. *abbr.* век, century; восто́к, Е.

в *abbr.* вольт, volt.

в-, во-, въ- *vbl. pref.* expressing direction of action or motion inwards or upwards; occurrence wholly within the agent.

ваго́н, -а, (railway-)carriage; coach; van; car; wagon-load; loads, an awful lot; ~-рестора́н, restaurant car, dining-car. **ваго́нетка**, -и, truck, trolley. **вагоновожа́тый** sb. tram-driver.

ва́жничанье, -я, airs. **ва́жничать**, -аю *imp.* give oneself airs; +*instr.* plume oneself, pride oneself, on. **ва́жность**, -и, importance, consequence; significance; pomposity, pretentiousness. **ва́жный**; -жен, -жна́, -о, important;

weighty, consequential; pompous, pretentious.

ва́за, -ы, vase, bowl.

ва́кса, -ы, (shoe-)polish, blacking; чи́стить ва́ксой, polish. **ва́ксить**, -кшу *imp.* (*perf.* на~) black, polish.

вал[1], -a, *loc.* -ý; *pl.* -ы́, bank, earthen wall; rampart; billow, roller, wave; barrage.

вал[2], -a, *loc.* -ý; *pl.* -ы́, shaft, spindle.

вал[3], -a, gross output.

валанда́ться, -аюсь *imp.* loiter, hang about; mess about.

валёк, -лька́, battledore; swingle-tree; roll; roller; flail; loom.

валёнок -нка; *gen. pl.* -нок, felt boot. **ва́леный**, felt.

валёт, -a, knave, Jack.

ва́лик, -a, bolster; roller; cylinder; spindle, shaft; platen.

вали́ть[1], -лю́ *imp.* flock, throng; pour; ва́лом ~, throng, flock; вали́(те)! go on! have a go!

вали́ть[2], -лю́, -лишь *imp.* (*perf.* по~, c~), throw down, bring down, knock down; overthrow; fell; lay low; heap, pile up; ~ся, fall, collapse; drop; topple; у него́ всё из рук ва́лится, his fingers are all thumbs; he can't give his mind to anything.

ва́лка, -и, felling. **ва́лкий**; -лок, -лка́, -o, unsteady, shaky.

валово́й, gross; wholesale.

валто́рна, -ы, French horn. **валтор-ни́ст**, -a, French-horn (player).

валу́н, -á, boulder.

вальс, -a, waltz. **вальси́ровать**, -и́рую *imp.* waltz.

вальцева́ть, -цу́ю *imp.* roll. **вальцо́вка**, -и, rolling; rolling press. **вальцо́вый**, rolling. **вальцы́**, *pl.* -о́в, rolling press. **вальцо́вщик**, -a, roller.

валю́та, -ы, currency; foreign currency. **валю́тчик**, -a, -чица, -ы, speculator in foreign currency.

ва́ляный, felt. **валя́ть**, -я́ю *imp.* (*perf.* на~, c~), drag; roll; shape; full, felt; botch, bungle; make a mess (of); mess about; ~ дурака́, play the fool; валя́й(те)! go ahead! carry on!; ~ся, lie, lie about, loll; roll, wallow; ~ся в нога́х у+gen. fall at the feet of.

вам, **ва́ми**: see вы.

вани́ль, -и, vanilla, vanilla-pod.

ва́нна, -ы, **ва́нночка**, -и, bath. **ва́нный**, bath; ~ая *sb.* bathroom.

ва́нька, -и *m.* cabby.

ва́рвар, -a, barbarian. **варвари́зм**, -a, loan-word; barbarism. **ва́рварский**, barbarian; barbarous; barbaric. **ва́рварство**, -a, barbarity; vandalism.

ва́режка, -и, mitten.

варёный, boiled; limp. **варе́нье**, -я, jam, marmalade. **вари́ть**, -рю́, -ришь *imp.* (*perf.* c~) boil; cook; brew; make; digest; ~ся, boil; cook. **ва́рка**, -и, boiling; cooking; making; brewing.

вас: see вы.

василёк, -лька́, cornflower. **василько́-вый**, cornflower blue.

ва́та, -ы, cotton wool; wadding.

вата́га, -и, band, gang.

ватерли́ния, -и, water-line. **ватерпа́с**, -a, level, spirit-level.

вати́н, -a, (sheet) wadding, quilting. **ва́тник**, -a, quilted jacket. **ва́тный**, quilted, wadded.

ватру́шка, -и, open tart; curd tart; cheese-cake.

ватт, -a; *gen. pl.* ватт, watt.

ва́фельный, waffle. **ва́фля**, -и, *gen. pl.* -фель, waffle.

вахла́к, -a, lout; sloven; (*sl.*) goner, wreck.

ва́хта, -ы, watch. **ва́хтенн|ый**, watch; ~ журна́л, log, log-book; ~ командир, officer of the watch, duty officer.

ваш, -его *m.*, **ва́ша**, -ей *f.*, **ва́ше**, -его *n.*, **ва́ши**, -их *pl.*, *pron.* your, yours.

вая́ние, -я, sculpture. **вая́тель**, -я *m.* sculptor. **вая́ть**, -я́ю *imp.* (*perf.* из~) sculpture; carve, model.

вбега́ть, -а́ю *imp.*, **вбежа́ть**, вбегу́ *perf.* run in, rush in.

вберу́ etc.: see вобра́ть.

вбива́ть, -а́ю *imp.* of вбить. **вби́вка**, -и, knocking in, driving in, hammering in.

вбира́ть, -а́ю, *imp.* of вобра́ть.

вбить, вобью́, -бьёшь *perf.* (*imp.* вби-ва́ть) drive in, hammer in, knock in.

вблизи́ *adv.* (+от+*gen.*), close (to), near (to), not far (from); closely.

вбок *adv.* sideways, to one side.

вбра́сывание, -я, throw-in. **вбра́сывать**, -аю *imp.* of **вбро́сить**.

вброд *adv.* by fording or wading; переходи́ть ~, ford, wade.

вбро́сить, -о́шу *perf.* (*imp.* вбра́сывать) throw in.

вв. *abbr.* века́, centuries.

вва́ливать, -аю *imp.*, **ввали́ть**, -лю́, -лишь *perf.* throw heavily, heave, fling, bundle, tumble; ~ся, fall heavily; sink, become hollow or sunken; burst in. **вва́лившийся**, sunken, hollow.

введе́ние, -я, leading in; introduction. **введу́**, etc.: see **ввести́**.

ввезти́, -зу́, -зёшь; ввёз, -ла́ *perf.* (*imp.* **ввози́ть**) import; bring in, take in, carry in.

ввек *adv.* ever; for ever.

вве́рить, -рю *perf.* (*imp.* вверя́ть) entrust, confide; ~ся *+dat.* trust in, put one's faith in; put oneself in the hands of.

вверну́ть, -ну́, -нёшь *perf.*, **ввёртывать**, -аю *imp.* screw in; insert; put in.

вверх *adv.* up, upward(s); ~ дном, ~ нога́ми ~ торма́шками, upside down, topsy-turvy; ~ (по ле́стнице), upstairs; ~ (по тече́нию) upstream. **вверху́** *adv.* above, overhead; upstairs; upstream; at the top.

вверя́ть(ся, -я́ю(сь *imp.* of **вве́рить(ся**.

ввести́, -еду́, -едёшь; ввёл, -а́ *perf.* (*imp.* вводи́ть) bring in, lead in; introduce; insert, interpolate, incorporate; administer.

ве́черу *adv.* in the evening.

ввиду́ *prep.+gen.* in view of.

ввинти́ть, -нчу́ *perf.*, **вви́нчивать**, -аю *imp.* screw in.

ввод, -а, bringing in, leading in; lead-in, lead; input, intake. **вводи́ть**, -ожу́ -о́дишь *imp.* of ввести́. **вво́дн|ый**, introductory; parenthetic; ~ое предложе́ние, ~ое сло́во, parenthesis; ~ый тон, leading note.

ввожу́: see вводи́ть, ввози́ть.

ввоз, -а, importation, importing; import, imports. **ввози́ть**, -ожу́, -о́зишь *imp.* of ввезти́. **ввозный**, imported, import.

вво́лю *adv.* to one's heart's content; enough and to spare; ad lib.

вво́сьмеро *adv.* eight times. **ввосьмеро́м** *adv.* eight together; мы ~, eight of us.

BBC (*veve-és*) *abbr.* вое́нно-возду́шные си́лы, air force.

ввысь *adv.* up, upward(s).

ввяза́ть, -яжу́, -я́жешь *perf.*, **ввя́зывать**, -аю *imp.* knit in; involve; ~ся, meddle, get involved, get or be mixed up (in).

вгиб, -а, inward bend; concavity, dent, sag. **вгиба́ть(ся**, -а́ю(сь *imp.* of **вогну́ть(ся**.

вглубь *adv.* deep, deep into, into the depths.

вгляде́ться, -яжу́сь *perf.*, **вгля́дываться**, -а́юсь *imp.* peer, look closely or intently (в *+acc.* at).

вгоня́ть, -я́ю *imp.* of вогна́ть. **вдава́ться**, вдаю́сь, -даёшься *imp* of вда́ться.

вдави́ть, -авлю́, -а́вишь *perf.*, **вда́вливать**, -аю *imp.* press in, crush in; ~ся, give, give way; be crushed or pressed in; press in.

вдалеке́, **вдали́** *adv.* in the distance, far away; ~ от, a long way from. **вдаль** *adv.* into the distance.

вда́ться, -а́мся, -а́шься, -а́стся, -ади́мся; -а́лся, -ла́сь *perf.* (*imp.* вдава́ться) jut out; penetrate, go in; ~ в то́нкости, split hairs.

ВДВ (*vedevé*) *abbr.* возду́шно-деса́нтные войска́, airborne troops.

вдвига́ть(ся, -а́ю(сь *imp.*, **вдви́нуть**(ся, -ну(сь *perf.* push in, move in, thrust in.

вдво́е *adv.* twice; double; ~ бо́льше, twice as big, as much, as many. **вдвоём** *adv.* (the) two together, both. **вдвойне́** *adv.* twice as much, double; doubly.

вде́вать, -а́ю, *imp.* of вдеть.

вдёжка, -и, threading; thread, tape, cord, lace.

вде́лать, -аю *perf.*, **вде́лывать**, -аю *imp.* set in, fit in.

вде́ржка, -и, bodkin; threading. **вдёргивать**, -аю *imp.*, **вдёрнуть**, -ну *perf.* в *+acc.* thread through, pull through.

вде́сятеро *adv.* ten times; ~ бо́льше, ten times as much, as many. **вдесятеро́м** *adv.* ten together; мы ~, ten of us.

вдеть, -éну *perf.* (*imp.* вдевáть) put in, thread.

ВДНХ (*vede-enkhá*) *abbr.* Вы́ставка достижéний нарóдного хозя́йства, Exhibition of National Economic Achievements.

вдобáвок *adv.* in addition; besides, as well, into the bargain.

вдовá, -ы́; *pl.* -ы, widow. вдовéц, -вцá, widower. вдóвий, widow's, widows'. вдови́ца, -ы, widow.

вдóволь *adv.* enough; in abundance; plenty (of).

вдóвствующая *sb.* dowager. вдóвый, widowed.

вдогóнку *adv.* (за+*instr.*) after, in pursuit (of).

вдоль *adv.* lengthways, lengthwise; ~ и попérek, in all directions, far and wide; minutely, in detail; *prep.* + *gen.* or по+*dat.* along.

вдох, -a, breath. вдохновéние, -я, inspiration. вдохновéнный, inspired. вдохнови́тель, -я *m.*, -тельница, -ы inspirer, inspiration. вдохнови́ть, -влю *perf.*, вдохновля́ть, -я́ю *imp.* inspire. вдохну́ть, -ну́, -нёшь *perf.* (*imp.* вдыхáть) breathe in, inhale; +в+*acc.* inspire with, breathe into.

вдребезги *adv.* to pieces, to smithereens; ~ пьян dead drunk.

вдруг *adv.* suddenly; all at once; what if? suppose; все ~, all together.

вдувáть, -áю *imp.* of вдуну́ть, вдуть.

вдуматься, -аюсь *perf.*, вдумываться, -аюсь *imp.* ponder, meditate; +в+ *acc.* think over. вдумчивый, thoughtful.

вдуну́ть, -ну *perf.*, вдуть, -ую *perf.* (*imp.* вдувáть) blow in pump in.

вдыхáние, -я, inhalation, inspiration. вдыхáтельный, respiratory. вдыхáть, -áю *imp.* of вдохну́ть.

ве́дать, -аю *imp.* know; +*instr.* manage, handle; be in charge of. ве́дение[1], -я, authority, jurisdiction; в ве́дении +*gen.* under the jurisdiction of; вне моегó ве́дения, outside my province.

ве́дение[2], -я, conducting, conduct, management; ~ книг, book-keeping.

ведёрный, bucket, pail; holding a bucketful, holding one vedro.

ве́домость, -и; *gen. pl.* -éй, list, register; *pl.* gazette. ве́домственный, departmental. ве́домство, -а, department.

ведрó, -á; *pl.* вёдра, -дер, bucket, pail; vedro (approx. 12 litres).

веду́ *etc.*: see вести́. веду́щ|ий, leading; ~ee колесó, driving-wheel.

ведь *part.* and *conj.* you see, you know; but; why; isn't it? is it?

ве́дьма, -ы witch; old bitch, hag.

вéер, -a; *pl.* -á, fan. веерообрáзный, fan-shaped; ~ свод, fan vault(ing).

вéжливость, -и, politeness, courtesy, civility. вéжливый, polite, courteous, civil.

вездé *adv.* everywhere. вездехóд, -a, cross-country vehicle. вездехóдный, cross-country.

везéние, -я, luck. везу́чий, fortunate, lucky. везти́, -зу́, -зёшь, вёз, -лá *imp.* (*perf.* по~), cart, convey, carry; bring, take; *impers.* + *dat.* be lucky, be in luck have luck; ему́ не везлó, he had no luck.

век, -a (-y), *loc.* -ý; *pl.* -á, century; age; life, lifetime; испокóн ~óв, from time immemorial. век *adv.* for ages, for ever; always, constantly.

вéко, -a; *pl.* -и, век, eyelid.

вековéчный, eternal, everlasting. вековóй, ancient, age-old; secular.

вéксель, -я; *pl.* -я́, -éй *m.* promissory note, bill (of exchange). вéксельный; ~ курс, rate of exchange.

вёл, *etc.*: see вести́.

велéть, -лю́ *perf.* and *imp.* order, tell; не ~, forbid, not allow.

великáн, -a, giant. великáнша, -и, giantess. великáнский, gigantic. велúк|ий; велúк, -а or -á, great; big, large; too big; ~ие держáвы, Great Powers; ~ий князь, grand prince, grand duke; ~ий пост, Lent.

велико- *in comb.* great. великодержáвный, great-power. ~ду́шие, -я, magnanimity, generosity. ~ду́шный, magnanimous; generous. ~лéпие, -я, splendour, magnificence. ~лéпный, splendid, magnificent; excellent. ~пóстный, Lenten. ~ру́с, -а, -ру́ска, -и, Great Russian. ~ру́сский, Great Russian.

велича́вый, stately, majestic. **велича́йший**, greatest, extreme. supreme. **вели́чественный**, majestic, grand. **вели́чество**, -а, Majesty. **вели́чие**, -я, greatness, grandeur, sublimity. **величина́**, -ы́; pl. -ы, size; quantity, magnitude; value; great figure.

велосипе́д, -а, cycle; bicycle, tricycle. **велосипеди́ст**, -а, cyclist.

вельве́т, -а, velveteen, cotton velvet; ~ в рубчи́к, corduroy. **вельве́товый**, velveteen.

вельмо́жа, -и m. grandee, dignitary, magnate.

ве́на, -ы, vein.

венге́рка, -и, Hungarian; dolman; Hungarian ballroom dance. **венге́рский**, Hungarian. **венгр**, -а, Hungarian.

Вене́ра, -ы, Venus. **вене́рин** adj. Venusian, of Venus; ~ волосо́к, maidenhair fern.

ве́нец[1], -нца, Viennese.

вене́ц[2], -нца́, crown; wreath, garland; corona; halo. **вене́чный**, coronal; coronary.

ве́нзель, -я; pl. -я́, -е́й m. monogram.

ве́ник, -а, besom, (birch-)broom, birchwhisk.

ве́нка, -и, Viennese.

вено́к, -нка́, wreath, garland.

ве́нский, Viennese; ~ стул, ballroom chair.

ве́нтиль, -я m. valve.

венча́льный, wedding. **венча́ние**, -я, wedding; coronation. **венча́ть**, -а́ю imp. (perf. об~, по~, у~) crown; marry; ~ся, be married, marry. **ве́нчик**, -а, halo, nimbus; corolla; edge, rim; crown; ring, bolt.

ве́ра, -ы, faith, belief; trust, confidence; на ~у, on trust.

верба́, -ы, willow, osier, pussy-willow; willow branch. **ве́рбн|ый**; ~ое воскресе́нье, Palm Sunday.

верблю́д, -а, -ю́дица, -ы, camel. **верблю́ж|ий**, camel's; camelhair; ~ья шерсть, camel's hair.

ве́рбный: see ве́рба.

вербова́ть, -бу́ю imp. (perf. за~) recruit, enlist. **вербо́вка**, -и, recruitment.

ве́рбовый, willow, osier; wicker.

верёвка, -и, rope; string; cord. **верёвочный**, rope.

вред, -а, boil, abscess.

верени́ца, -ы, row, file, line, string.

ве́реск, -а, heather.

веретено́, -а́; pl. -тёна, spindle, shank, axle.

вереща́ть, -щу́ imp. squeal; chirp.

ве́рить, -рю imp. believe, have faith; + dat. or в + acc. trust (in), believe in; ~ на́ слово, take on trust.

верне́е adv. rather. **верноподда́нный**, loyal, faithful. **ве́рно** part. probably, I suppose; that's right! **ве́рность**, -и, faithfulness, loyalty; truth, correctness.

верну́ть, -ну́, -нёшь perf. (imp. возвраща́ть) give back, return; get back, recover, retrieve; ~ся, return, revert.

ве́рный; -рен, -рна́, -о, faithful, loyal; true; correct; sure; reliable; certain.

ве́рование, -я, belief; creed. **ве́ровать**, -рую imp. believe. **вероиспове́дание**, -я, religion; denomination. **вероло́мный**, treacherous, perfidious. **вероотсту́пник**, -а, apostate. **вероте́рпи́мость**, -и, (religious) toleration. **вероя́тно** adv. probably. **вероя́тность**, -и, probability. **вероя́тный**, probable, likely.

ве́рсия, -и, version.

верста́, -ы́, acc. -у́ от вёрсту; pl. вёрсты, verst (1·06 km.); verst-post; за́ ~у, miles away.

верста́к, -а́, bench.

верстово́й, verst; ~ столб, milestone.

ве́ртел, -а; pl. -а́, spit, skewer. **верте́ть**, -чу́, -тишь imp. turn (round); twirl; spin; ~ся, rotate, turn (round), revolve, spin; move about, hang about, go round; fidget; turn and twist, dodge. **ве́ткий** -ток, -тка, nimble, agile. **вертлю́г**, -а́, swivel. **вертля́вый**, restless, fidgety; flighty, frivolous.

вертодро́м, -а, heliport. **вертолёт**, -а, helicopter.

верту́н, -а́, fidget; tumbler-pigeon. **верту́шка**, -и, revolving door, revolving stand; flirt, coquette.

ве́рующий sb. believer.

верфь, -и, dockyard, shipyard.

верх, -а (-у), *loc.* -ý; *pl.* -ѝ or -á, top, summit; height; upper part, upper side; upper reaches; bonnet, hood; upper hand; outside; right side; *pl.* upper ten, bosses, leadership, management, top brass; high notes. **верхний**, upper; outer; top. **верховный**, supreme. **верховой**¹, riding; *sb.* rider.

верховой², up-stream, up-river; upper.

верховье, -я; *gen. pl.* -вьев, upper reaches, head. **верхолаз**, -а, steeplejack. **верхом**¹ *adv.* on high ground; quite full, brim-full. **верхом**² *adv.* on horseback; astride; ездить ∼, ride. **верхушка**, -и, top, summit; apex; bosses, top brass, management.

верчу, etc.: see вертеть.

вершина, -ы, top, summit; peak; height; apex, vertex. **вершить**, -шý *imp.* top, top out; decide, settle; +*instr.* manage, control, direct; control, sway.

вершковый, a vershok long. **вершок**, -шкá, vershok (4.4 cm.); inch; smattering.

вес, -а (-у), *loc.* -ý; *pl.* -á, weight; authority, influence; на ∼, by weight; на ∼ý, suspended, balanced.

веселеть, -ею *imp.* (*perf.* по∼), cheer up, be cheerful. **веселить**, -лю *imp.* (*perf.* раз∼) cheer up, gladden; amuse; ∼ся, enjoy oneself; amuse oneself. **весело** *adv.* gaily, merrily. **весёлость**, -и, gaiety; cheerfulness. **весёлый**; весел, -á, -о, gay, merry; cheerful, lively. **весéлье**, -я, gaiety, merriment.

весенний, spring; vernal; ∼ее равноденствие, vernal equinox.

весить, вешу *imp.* weigh. **веский**, weighty.

весло, -á; *pl.* вёсла, -сел, oar; scull; paddle.

весна, -ы́; *pl.* вёсны, -сен, spring; spring-time. **весной**, -ою *adv.* in (the) spring. **веснушка**, -и, freckle. **веснушчатый**, freckled. **веснянка**, -и, may-fly.

весовой, weight, of weight; sold by weight. **весомый**, heavy, weighty; ponderable.

вести, веду, -дёшь; вёл, -á *imp.* (*perf.* по∼) lead, take; conduct, carry on; be engaged in, wage; drive; conduct; direct, run; keep; +*instr.* pass, run (по+*dat.* over, across); ∼ корабль, navigate a ship; ∼ (своё) начáло, originate, take rise; ∼ огóнь, fire; ∼ самолёт, pilot an aircraft; ∼ свой род от, be descended from; ∼ себя, behave, conduct oneself; ∼сь, be observed, be the custom.

вестник, -а, messenger, herald; bulletin. **вестовой**, signal; *sb.* orderly. **весть**, -и; *gen. pl.* -ей, news; *pl.* tales, talk, gossip; бéз вести, without trace. **весть**: Бог ∼, God knows; не ∼, goodness knows, there's no knowing.

весы́, -óв *pl.* scales, balance; Libra.

весь, всего *т.*, вся, всей *f.*, всё, всего *n.*, все, всех *pl.*, *pron.* all, the whole of; all gone; бумáга вся, the paper is used up, there's no paper left; во∼ гóлос, at the top of one's voice; во∼всю, like anything; вот и всё, that's all; при всём том, for all that; moreover; всегó хорóшего! goodbye; all the best!; всё, everything; без всегó, without anything, with nothing; все, everybody.

весьма, *adv.* very, highly; very much.

ветвистый, spreading, (many-)branched, branching. **ветвиться**, -влюсь *imp.* branch. **ветвь**, -и; *gen. pl.* -ей, branch; bough.

ветер, -тра (-у), *loc.* -ý; *gen. pl.* вéтрóв, wind; *pl.* по вéтру, before the wind; down wind; подбитый вéтром, empty-headed; light, flimsy; под вéтром, (to) leeward; против вéтра, close to the wind, against the wind. **ветерóк**, -ркá, breeze.

ветка, -и, branch; twig.

ветла, -ы́; *pl.* вётлы, -сел, (white) willow.

веточка, -и, twig, sprig, shoot.

ветошка, -и, rag. **ветошник**, -а, old-clothes dealer, rag-dealer. **ветошь**, -и, old clothes, rags.

ветренеть, -еет *imp.* become windy, get windy. **ветреный**, windy; frivolous, inconstant, unstable. **ветровой**, wind, of wind; ∼ое окнó, ∼ое стеклó, windscreen. **ветромéр**, -а, anemometer. **ветроуказáтель**, -я *m.* drogue, wind cone, wind sock. **ветрáк**, -á, wind motor; windmill. **ветряно́й**, **ве́тряный**, wind; **ве́тряная о́спа**, chicken-pox.

ве́тхий; ветх, -á, -о, old, ancient; dilapidated, ramshackle, tumbledown; decrepit; **В~ заве́т**, Old Testament. **ветхозаве́тный**, Old-Testament; antiquated, out-of-date. **ве́тхость**, -и, decrepitude, dilapidation, decay.

ветчина́, -ы́, ham.

ветша́ть, -а́ю *imp.* (*perf.* об~), decay; become dilapidated.

ве́ха, -и, landmark; marker post, stake; spar-buoy.

ве́чер, -a; *pl.* -á, evening; party; soirée. **вече́рн|ий**, evening; ~яя заря́, sunset; dusk. **вече́рник**, -a, evening student, evening worker. **вече́рня**, -и; *gen. pl.* -рен, vespers. **ве́чером** *adv.* in the evening.

ве́чно *adv.* for ever, eternally; everlastingly. **вечнозелёный**, evergreen. **ве́чность**, -и, eternity; an age, ages. **ве́чн|ый**, eternal, everlasting; endless; perpetual; ~ая мерзлота́, permafrost; ~ое перо́, fountain-pen.

ве́шалка, -и, peg, rack, stand; hanger; cloak-room. **ве́шать**, -аю *imp.* (*perf.* взве́сить, пове́сить, све́шать) hang; weigh, weigh out; ~ся, be hung, be hanged; hang oneself; weigh oneself.

ве́шний, spring, vernal.

ве́шу etc.: see **ве́сить**.

веща́ние, -я, radio; prophecy. **веща́ть**, -а́ю *imp.* broadcast; prophesy; pontificate.

вещево́й, clothing, kit; in kind; ~ мешо́к, knapsack; pack, hold-all, kit-bag; ~ склад, clothing store, stores. **веще́ственный**, substantial, material, real. **вещество́**, -á, substance; matter. **вещмешо́к**, -шка́ rucksack. **вещь**, -и; *gen. pl.* -ей, thing.

ве́ялка, -и, winnowing-fan; winnowing-machine. **ве́яние**, -я, winnowing; breathing, blowing; current, tendency, trend. **ве́ять**, ве́ю *imp.* (*perf.* про~) winnow, fan; blow, breathe; wave, flutter.

вз-, **взо-**, **взъ-**, **вс-** *vbl. pref.* expressing direction of motion or action upwards **or** on to; rapidity or suddenness of occurrence; completion or finality of action.

взад *adv.* backwards; ~ и вперёд, backwards and forwards, to and fro.

взаи́мность, -и, reciprocity; requital, return. **взаи́мный** mutual, reciprocal.

взаимо- in *comb.* inter-. **взаимоде́йствие**, -я interaction; co-operation, co-ordination. **~де́йствовать**, -твую *imp.* interact; co-operate. **~отноше́ние**, -я, interrelation; *pl.* relations. **~по́мощь**, -и, mutual aid. **~связь**, -и, intercommunication; interdependence, correlation.

взаймы́ *adv.* as a loan; взять ~, borrow; дать ~, lend.

взаме́н *prep.*+*gen.* instead of; in return for, in exchange for.

взаперти́ *adv.* under lock and key; in seclusion, in isolation.

взапра́вду *adv.* in truth, really and truly.

вз|баламу́тить, -у́чу *perf.*

взба́лмошный, unbalanced, eccentric.

взба́лтывание, -я, shaking (up). **взба́лтывать**, -аю *imp.* of взболта́ть.

взбега́ть, -а́ю *imp.*, **взбежа́ть**, -егу́ *perf.* run up.

взберу́сь, etc.: see взобра́ться. **вз|беси́ть(ся**, -ешу́(сь, -е́сишь(ся *perf.* **взбива́ть**, -а́ю *imp.* of взбить. **взбира́ться**, -а́юсь *imp.* of взобра́ться.

взби́тый, whipped, beaten. **взбить**, взобью́, -бьёшь *perf.* (*imp.* взбива́ть) beat (up); whip; shake up, fluff up.

взболта́ть, -а́ю *perf.* (*imp.* взба́лтывать) shake (up).

вз|борозди́ть, -зжу́ *perf.* **вз|борони́ть**, -ню́ *perf.* **взбра́сывать**, -аю *imp.* of взбро́сить.

взбреда́ть, -а́ю *imp.*, **взбрести́**, -еду́, -ёшь; -ёл, -ела́ *perf.*+на+*acc.* climb (up), mount, with difficulty; struggle up; ~ в го́лову, на ум, come into one's head.

взбро́сить, -о́шу *perf.* (*imp.* взбра́сывать) throw up, toss up.

вз|будора́жить, -жу *perf.* **вз|бунтова́ться**, -ту́юсь *perf.*

взбуха́ть, -а́ет *imp.*, **взбу́хнуть**, -нет -ух *perf.* swell (out).

взва́ливать, -аю *imp.*, **взвали́ть**, -лю́,

-лишь *perf.* hoist, heave (up); load; +на+*acc.* saddle with.

взве́сить, -е́шу *perf.* (*imp.* ве́шать, взве́шивать) weigh.

взвести́, -еду́, -еде́шь; -ёл, -а́ *perf.* (*imp.* взводи́ть) lead up, take up; lift up, raise; cock, arm; +на+*acc.* impute to, bring against.

взвесь, -и, suspension. **взве́шенный**, weighed; suspended; of suspension. **взве́шивать**, -аю *imp.* of взве́сить.

взви́ть(ся, -а́ю(сь *imp.* of взви́ть(ся.

взвизг, -а, scream, squeal, screech; yelp. **взви́згивать**, -аю *imp.*, **взви́згнуть**, -ну *perf.* let out screams, a scream; scream, screech; yelp.

взвинти́ть, -нчу́ *perf.*, **взви́нчивать**, -аю *imp.* excite, work up; inflate; ~ся, work oneself up; spiral up. **взви́нченный**, excited, worked up; nervy, on edge; highly strung; inflated.

взви́ть, взовью́ -ёшь; -и́л, -ила́, -о *perf.* (*imp.* взвива́ть) raise; ~ся, rise, be hoisted; fly up, soar.

взвод[1], -а, platoon, troop.

взвод[2], -а, cocking; notch; на боево́м ~е, cocked; на пе́рвом ~е, at half-cock. **взводи́ть**, -ожу́, -о́дишь *imp.* of взвести́. **взводно́й**, cocking.

взво́дный, platoon; *sb.* platoon commander.

взд воить, -ою́ *perf.*

взволно́ванный, agitated, disturbed; ruffled; anxious, troubled, worried. **взволнова́ть(ся**, -ну́ю(сь *perf.*

взвыть, взво́ю *perf.* howl, set up a howl.

взгляд, -а, look; glance; gaze, stare; view; opinion; на ~, to judge from appearances; на пе́рвый ~, с пе́рвого ~а, at first sight. **взгля́дывать**, -аю *imp.*, **взгляну́ть**, -яну́ -янешь *perf.* look, glance.

взго́рок, -рка, **взго́рье**, -я, hill, hillock.

взгроможда́ть, -а́ю *imp.*, **взгромозди́ть**, -зжу́ *perf.* pile up; ~ся, clamber up.

вздёргивать, -аю *imp.*, **вздёрнуть**, -ну *perf.* hitch up; jerk up; turn up; hang.

вздор, -а, nonsense. **вздо́рный**, cantankerous, quarrelsome; foolish, stupid.

вздорожа́ние, -я, rise in price. **вз дорожа́ть**, -а́ет *perf.*

вздох, -а, sigh; deep breath. **вздохну́ть**, -ну́, -нёшь *perf.* (*imp.* вздыха́ть) sigh; heave a sigh; take a deep breath; take a breather, pause for breath.

вздра́гивать, -аю *imp.* (*perf.* вздро́гнуть) shudder, quiver.

вздремну́ть, -ну́, нёшь *perf.* have a nap, doze.

вздро́гнуть, -ну *perf.* (*imp.* вздра́гивать) start, jump; wince, flinch.

вздува́ть(ся, -а́ю(сь *imp.* of вздуть[1](ся.

взду́мать, -аю *perf.* take it into one's head; не взду́май(те! mind you don't, don't you dare! **взду́маться**, -ается *impers.*+*dat.* come into one's head; как взду́мается, as the fancy takes one, as one likes.

взду́тие, -я, swelling; inflation. **взду́тый**, swollen. **взду́ть**[1], -ую *perf.* (*imp.* вздува́ть) blow up, swell, inflate; ~ся, swell.

взду́ть[2], -у́ю *perf.* thrash, lick, give a hiding.

вздыха́ние, -я, sighing; sigh. **вздыха́тель**, -я *m.* admirer, suitor. **вздыха́ть**, -а́ю *imp.* (*perf.* вздохну́ть) breathe; sigh.

взима́ть, -а́ю *imp.* levy, collect.

взла́мывать, -аю *imp.* of взлома́ть.

вз лелея́ть, -е́ю *perf.*

взлёт, -а, flight; taking wing; take-off. **взлета́ть**, -а́ю *imp.*, **взлете́ть**, -лечу́ *perf.* fly (up); take off. **взлётный**, flying; take-off; взлётно-поса́дочная полоса́, runway, landing-strip.

взлом, -а, breaking open, breaking in; break-in. **взлома́ть**, -а́ю *perf.* (*imp.* взла́мывать) break open, force; smash; break up, break through. **взло́мщик**, -а, burglar, house-breaker.

взлохма́ченный, dishevelled, tousled.

взмах, -а, stroke, sweep, wave, flap. **взма́хивать**, -аю *imp.*, **взмахну́ть**, -ну́, -нёшь *perf.*+*instr.* wave, flap.

взмо́рье, -я, (sea-)shore, coast; seaside; beach; coastal waters.

вз мути́ть, -учу́ -у́тишь *perf.*

взнос, -а, payment; fee, dues; subscription; instalment.

взнузда́ть, -а́ю *perf.*, **взну́здывать**, -аю *imp.* bridle.

взо-: see вз-.

взобра́ться, взберу́сь, -ёшься; -а́лся, -ла́сь, -а́ло́сь *perf.* (*imp.* взбира́ться) на+*acc.* climb (up), clamber up.

взобью́, etc.: see взбить. **взовью́**, etc.: see взвить.

взойти́, -йду́, -йдёшь; -ошёл, -шла́, *perf.* (*imp.* всходи́ть), rise, go up, come up; на+*acc.* mount, ascend, enter.

взор, -а, look, glance.

взорва́ть, -ву́, -вёшь; -а́л, -а́, -о *perf.* (*imp.* взрыва́ть) blow up; blast; fire, explode, detonate; exasperate madden, make furiously angry; ~ся, blow up, burst, explode.

взро́слый, grown-up, adult.

взрыв, -а, explosion; burst, outburst; plosion. **взрыва́тель**, -я *m.* fuse. **взрыва́ть**, -а́ю *imp.*, **взрыть**, -ро́ю *(perf.* also взорва́ть) blow up; ~ся, blow up, explode. **взрывно́й**, explosive; explosion; blasting; plosive; ~а́я волна́, shock wave, blast. **взры́вчатка**, -и, explosive. **взры́вчатый**, explosive.

взъ-: see вз-.

взъеро́шенный, tousled, dishevelled, ruffled. **взъеро́шивать**, -аю *imp.*, **взъеро́шить**, -шу *perf.* tousle, ruffle, rumple; ~ся, become dishevelled, bristle up, stand on end.

взыва́ть, -а́ю *imp.* of воззва́ть.

взыска́ние, -я, penalty, punishment; recovery, exaction; prosecution. **взыска́тельный**, exacting; demanding. **взыска́ть**, -ышу́, -ы́шешь *perf.*, **взы́скивать**, -аю *imp.* exact, recover; call to account, make answer.

взя́тие, -я, taking, capture, seizure. **взя́тка**, -и, bribe; trick. **взя́точничество**, -а, bribery, corruption. **взя́ть(ся**, возьму́(сь, -мёшь(ся; -ял(ся, -а́(сь, -о(сь *perf.* of брать(ся; ни дать ни ~, exactly, neither more nor less than; отку́да ни возьми́сь, out of the blue, from nowhere.

вибри́ровать, -рует *imp.* vibrate, oscillate.

вид[1], -а (-у), *loc.* -у́, look; appearance; air; shape, form; condition; view; prospect; sight; де́лать ~, pretend; име́ть в ~у, plan, intend; mean; bear in mind, not forget; из ~у, out of sight; на ~у, in the public eye; теря́ть из ~у, lose sight of; под ~ом, under the pretext; при ~е, at the sight.

вид[2], -а, kind, sort; species.

ви́данный, seen; heard of. **вида́ть**, -а́ю *imp.* (*perf.* по~, у~) see; ~ся, see one another. **виде́ние**[1], -я, sight, vision. **виде́ние**[2], -я, vision, apparition. **ви́деть**, ви́жу *imp.* (*perf.* у~) see; ~ во сне, dream (of); ~ся, see one another, meet; appear. **ви́димо** *adv.* visibly; evidently; seemingly. **ви́димо-неви́димо** *adv.* immense numbers of. **ви́димость**, -и, visibility; vision; appearance, semblance; show; appearances. **ви́димый**, visible, in sight; apparent, evident, seeming. **видне́ться**, -е́ется, be visible. **ви́дный**; -ден, -дна́, -о, -ы or -ы́, visible; conspicuous; prominent, stately, portly, dignified. **видово́й**[1], landscape; ~ фильм, travelogue, travel-film.

видово́й[2], specific; aspectual.

видоизмене́ние, -я, modification; alteration; variety. **видоизмени́ть**, -ню́ *perf.*, **видоизменя́ть**, -я́ю *imp.* modify, alter; ~ся, alter; be modified, be altered.

видоиска́тель, -я *m.* view-finder.

ви́жу: see ви́деть.

ви́за, -ы, visa; visa; official stamp.

визг, -а, squeal; scream; yelp. **визгли́вый**, shrill; screaming, squealing, squalling. **визжа́ть**, -жу́ *imp.* squeal, scream, yelp, squeak.

визи́ровать, -рую *perf.* and *imp.* (*perf.* also за~) visa, visé.

визи́т, -а, visit; call. **визита́ция**, -и, call; round; search. **визи́тка**, -и, morning coat.

виктори́на, -ы, quiz.

ви́лка, -и, fork; plug; bracket. **вилообра́зный**, forked. **ви́лочный**, fork-lift. **ви́лы**, вил *pl.* pitchfork.

вильну́ть, -ну́, -нёшь *perf.*, **виля́ть**, -я́ю *imp.* twist and turn; turn sharply; prevaricate, be evasive; +*instr.* wag.

вина́, -ы́; *pl.* ви́ны, fault, guilt; blame.

винегре́т, -а, Russian salad; medley, farrago.

вини́тельный, accusative. **вини́ть**, -ню́ *imp.* accuse, blame; reproach; **~ся** (*perf.* по~) confess.

ви́нкель, -я; *pl.* -я́ *m.* set-square.

виннока́менный, tartaric. **ви́нн|ый**, wine; winy; vinous; ~ый ка́мень, tartar; ~ая я́года, fig. вино́, -а́; *pl.* -а, wine; vodka.

винова́тый, guilty; to blame; винова́т(а)! (I'm) sorry. **вино́вник**, -а, author, initiator; culprit; ~ торжества́, founder of the feast. **вино́вный**, guilty.

виногра́д, -а (-у) vine; grapes. **виногра́дарь**, -я *m.* wine-grower. **виногра́дина**, -ы, grape. **виногра́дник**, -а, vineyard. **виногра́дный**, vine; grape; wine, vintage. **виноку́р**, -а, distiller. **винокуре́ние**, -я, distillation. **виноку́ренный**, distilling; ~ заво́д, distillery.

винт, -а́, screw; propeller; rotor; spiral; vint. **винти́ть**, -нчу́ *imp.* screw in; unscrew; turn. **винто́вка**, -и, rifle. **винтово́й**, screw; spiral; helical. **винто́вочный**, rifle-. **винто́м** *adv.* spirally.

вира́ж, -а, turn; bend; curve.

вис, -а, hang, hanging. **ви́селица**, -ы, gallows. **висе́ть**, вишу́ *imp.* hang; hover. **вислоу́хий**, lop-eared. **ви́снуть**, -ну; вис(ну́л) *imp.* hang; droop.

висо́к, -ска́, temple.

високо́сный; ~ год, leap-year.

висо́чный, temporal.

висю́лька, -и, pendant. **вися́чий**, hanging; ~ замо́к, padlock; ~ мост, suspension bridge.

вито́й, twisted, spiral. **вито́к**, -тка́, turn, coil, loop; orbit.

витра́ж, -а́, stained-glass window, panel, etc. **витри́на**, -ы, shop-window; show-case.

вить, вью, вьёшь; вил, -а́, -о *imp.* (*perf.* с~) twist, wind, weave; ~ гнездо́, build a nest; ~ верёвки из+*gen.* twist round one's little finger; **~ся**, wind, twine; curl, wave; hover, circle; twist, turn; whirl, eddy; writhe.

вихо́р, -хра́, tuft. **вихра́стый**, shaggy, wiry; shock-headed.

вихрево́й, vortical. **вихрь**, -я *m.* whirlwind; whirl, eddy, vortex; снежный ~, blizzard.

ви́це- *perf.* vice-. **вице-коро́ль**, -я́ *m.* viceroy. **~-президе́нт**, -а, vice-president.

вицмунди́р, -а, (dress) uniform.

ви́шенник, -а, вишня́к, -а, cherry-orchard, cherry-grove; wild cherry. **вишнёвый**, cherry; cherry-coloured. **ви́шня**, -и; *gen. pl.* -шен, cherry, cherries; cherry-tree.

вишу́: see висе́ть.

вишь *part.* look, just look; well!

вка́лывать, -аю *imp.* (*perf.* вколо́ть) (*sl.*) work hard, slave; get stuck in.

вка́пывать, -аю *imp.* of вкопа́ть.

вкати́ть, -ачу́, -а́тишь *perf.*, **вка́тывать**, -аю *imp.* roll in, wheel in; roll up; put in, put on; administer; **~ся**, roll in; run in.

вклад, -а, deposit; investment; endowment; contribution. **вкла́дка**, -и, вкла́дыш, -а, a supplementary sheet, inset. **вкладно́й**, deposit; supplementary, inserted; ~ лист, loose leaf, insert. **вкла́дчик**, -а, a depositor; investor. **вкла́дывать**, -аю *imp.* of вложи́ть. **вкла́дыш**: see вкла́дка.

вкле́ивать, -аю *imp.*, **вкле́ить**, -е́ю *perf.* stick in, glue in, paste in; put in. **вкле́йка**, -и, sticking in; inset.

вкли́нивать, -аю *imp.*, **вкли́нить**, -иню́ *perf.* wedge in; put in; **~ся**, edge one's way in; drive a wedge (into).

включа́тель, -я *m.* switch. **включа́ть**, -а́ю *imp.*, **включи́ть**, -чу́ *perf.* include; insert; switch on, turn on, start; plug in, connect; engage, let in; **~ся в** +*acc.* join in, enter into. **включа́я**, including. **включе́ние**, -я, inclusion insertion; switching on, turning on. **включи́тельно** *adv.* inclusive.

вкола́чивать, -аю *imp.*, **вколоти́ть**, -очу́, -о́тишь *perf.* hammer in, knock in.

вколо́ть, -олю́, -о́лешь *perf.* (*imp.* вка́лывать), stick (in), pin (in).

вконе́ц *adv.* completely, absolutely.

вко́панный, dug in; rooted to the ground. **вкопа́ть**, -а́ю *perf.* (*imp.* вка́пывать) dig in.

вкорени́ть, -ню́ *perf.*, **вкореня́ть**, -я́ю *imp.* inculcate; **~ся**, take root.

вкось *adv.* obliquely, slantwise; **~ и вкривь**, вкривь и **~**, at random, all over the place; indiscriminately.

ВКП(б) (*vekapebé*) *abbr.* Всесою́зная Коммунисти́ческая па́ртия (большевико́в), All-Union Communist Party (Bolsheviks).

вкра́дчивый, insinuating, ingratiating. **вкра́дываться**, -аюсь *imp.*, **вкра́сться**, -адусь, -адёшься *perf.* steal in, creep in; worm oneself, insinuate oneself, (into).

вкра́тце *adv.* briefly, succinctly.

вкривь *adv.* aslant; wrongly, perversely; **~ и вкось**: see вкось.

вкруг: see вокруг.

вкруту́ю *adv.* hard(-boiled).

вку́пе *adv.* together.

вкус, -а, taste; manner, style; де́ло **~а**, a matter of taste. **вкуси́ть**, -ушу́, -у́сишь *perf.*, **вкуша́ть**, -а́ю *imp.* taste; partake of; savour, experience. **вку́сный**; -сен, -сна́, -о, tasty, nice, good; appetizing.

вла́га, -и, moisture, damp, liquid.

влага́лище, -а, vagina; sheath.

влага́ть, -а́ю *imp.* of вложи́ть.

владе́лец, -льца, -льца, -ы, owner; proprietor. **владе́ние**, -я, ownership; possession; property; domain, estate. **владе́тель**, -я *m.*, -ница, *pl.* possessor; sovereign. **владе́тельный**, sovereign. **владе́ть**, -е́ю *imp.* + *instr.* own, possess; control; be in possession of; have (a) command of; have the use of.

влады́ка, -и *m.* master, sovereign; Orthodox prelate; my Lord. **влады́чество**, -а, dominion, rule, sway.

влажне́ть, -е́ет *imp.* (*perf.* по**~**) become humid, grow damp. **вла́жный**; -жен, -жна́, -о, damp moist, humid.

вла́мываться, -аюсь *imp.* of вломи́ться.

вла́ствовать, -твую *imp.* + (над +) *instr.* rule, hold sway over. **власти́тель**, -я *m.* sovereign; ruler. **вла́стный**, imperious, commanding; masterful; empowered competent. **власть**, -и; *gen. pl.* -е́й, power; authority; control; *pl.*

authorities; ва́ша **~**, as you like, please yourself, it's up to you.

вле́во *adv.* to the left.

влеза́ть, -а́ю *imp.*, **влезть**, -зу; *perf.* climb in, climb up; get in; fit in, go in, go on; ско́лько вле́зет, as much as will go in, any amount.

влёк, etc.: see влечь.

влепи́ть, -плю́, -пишь *perf.*, **влепля́ть**, -я́ю *imp.* stick in, fasten in; **~ пощёчину** + *dat.* give a slap in the face.

влета́ть, -а́ю *imp.* **влете́ть**, -ечу́ *perf.* fly in; rush in.

влече́ние, -я, attraction; bent, inclination. **влечь**, -еку́, -ечёшь; влёк, -ла́ *imp.* draw, drag; attract; **~ за собо́й**, involve, entail; **~ся к** + *dat.* be drawn to, be attracted by.

влива́ть, -а́ю *imp.*, **влить**, волью́, -ёшь; влил, -а́, -о *perf.* pour in; infuse; instil; bring in; **~ся**, flow in.

влия́ние, -я, influence. **влия́тельный**, influential. **влия́ть**, -я́ю *imp.* (*perf.* по**~**) на + *acc.* influence, have an influence on, affect.

вложе́ние, -я, enclosure; investment. **вложи́ть**, -ожу́, -о́жишь *perf.* (*imp.* вкла́дывать, влага́ть) put in, insert; enclose; invest.

вломи́ться, -млю́сь, -мишься *perf.* (*imp.* вла́мываться) break in.

влюби́ть, -блю́ -бишь *perf.*, **влюбля́ть**, -я́ю *imp.* capture the heart of, make fall in love (в + *acc.* with); **~ся**, fall in love. **влюблённый**; -лён, -а́, in love; loving tender; *sb.* lover. **влю́бчивый**, susceptible.

вма́зать, -а́жу *perf.*, **вма́зывать**, -аю *imp.* cement in, putty in, mortar in.

вм. *abbr.* вме́сто, instead of, in place of

вменя́ть, -ню́ *perf.*, **вменя́ть**, -я́ю *imp.* impute; **~ в вину́**, lay to the charge of; **~ в обя́занность**, impose as a duty **вменя́емый**, responsible, liable; of sound mind.

вме́сте *adv.* together; at the same time **~ с тем**, at the same time, also.

вмести́лище, -а, receptacle. **вмести́мость**, -и, capacity; tonnage. **вмести́тельный**, capacious; spacious, roomy **вмести́ть**, -ещу́ *perf.* (*imp.* вмеща́ть) contain, hold, accommodate; find room for; put, place; ~ся, go in.

вместо *prep.* + *gen.* instead of, in place of.

вмешательство, -a interference; intervention. вмеша́ть, -а́ю *perf.*, вме́шивать, -аю *imp.* mix in; mix up, implicate; ~ся interfere, meddle.

вмеща́ть(ся, -а́ю(сь *imp.* of вмести́ться.

вмиг *adv.* in an instant, in a flash.

вмина́ть, -а́ю *imp.*, вмять, вомну́, -нёшь *perf.* crush in, press in; dent. вмя́тина, -ы, dent.

ВМФ (*ve-emef*) *abbr.* военно-морской флот, navy.

внаём, внаймы́ *adv.* to let; for hire; брать ~, hire rent; отдава́ться ~, let, hire out rent; сдава́ться ~, to be to let.

внаки́дку *adv.* thrown over the shoulders.

внача́ле *adv.* at first, in the beginning.

вне *prep.* + *gen.* outside; out of; without; ~ себя́, beside oneself; ~ сомне́ния, without doubt, undoubtedly.

вне-, *pref.*, extra-: situated outside, lying outside the province or scope of; -less. внебра́чный, extra-marital; illegitimate, born outside wedlock. ~вре́менный, timeless. ~кла́ссный, out-of-school, extracurricular. ~ма́точный, extra-uterine. ~очередно́й, out of turn, out of order; extraordinary; extra. ~парти́йный, non-party. ~служе́бный, leisure-time, leisure. ~студи́йный, outside. ~шко́льный, adult; extra-scholastic; out-of-school. ~шта́тный, not established; not permanent; part-time.

внедре́ние, -я, introduction; inculcation; indoctrination; intrusion. внедри́ть, -рю́ *perf.*, внедря́ть, яю *imp.* inculcate, instil; introduce; ~ся, take root.

внеза́пно *adv.* suddenly, all of a sudden, all at once. внеза́пный, sudden, unexpected; surprise.

внемлю, etc.: see внима́ть.

внесе́ние, -я, bringing in, carrying in; paying in, deposit; entry, insertion; moving, submission. внести́, -су́, -сёшь, внёс, -ла́ *perf.* (*imp.* вноси́ть) bring in, carry in; introduce, put in;

pay in, deposit; move, table; insert, enter; bring about, cause.

внешне *adv.* outwardly. вне́шний, outer, exterior; outward, external; outside; surface, superficial; foreign. вне́шность, -и, exterior; surface; appearance.

вниз *adv.* down, downwards; downstream; ~ по + *dat.* down; ~ по тече́нию, downstream. внизу́ *adv.* below; downstairs; *prep.* + *gen.* at the foot of, in the lower part of.

ВНИИ' *abbr.* всесою́зный нау́чно-иссле́довательский институ́т, All-Union Scientific-research Institute.

вника́ть. -а́ю *imp.*, вни́кнуть, -ну вник *perf.* + в + *acc.* go carefully into, investigate thoroughly, get to the heart or root of.

внима́ние, -я, attention; notice; note; heed; consideration; attentions, kindness; ~! look out!; ~ на старт! get set! внима́тельный, attentive; thoughtful, considerate, kind. внима́ть, -а́ю ог вне́млю *imp.* (*perf.* внять) listen to; hear; heed.

вничью́ *adv.*; око́нчиться ~, end in a draw, be drawn; сыгра́ть ~, draw.

вноси́ть, -ошу́ -о́сишь *imp.* of внести́.

внук, -a, grandson; *pl.* grandchildren; descendants.

вну́тренн|ий, inner, interior; internal; intrinsic; home, inland; -ие дохо́ды, inland revenue. вну́тренность, -и, interior; *pl.* entrails, intestines; internal organs; viscera. внутри́ *adv.* and *prep.* + *gen.* inside, within. внутрь *adv.* and *prep* + *gen.* inside, in; inwards.

внуча́та, -ча́т *pl.* grandchildren. внуча́тный, внуча́тый, second, great-; ~ брат, second cousin; ~ племя́нник, great-nephew. вну́чка, -и, grand-daughter; grandchild.

внуша́емость, -и, suggestibility. внуша́ть, -а́ю *imp.*, внуши́ть, -шу́ *perf.* instil; suggest; + *dat.* inspire with, fill with. внуше́ние, -я, suggestion; reproof reprimand. внуши́тельный, inspiring, impressive; imposing, striking.

вня́тный, distinct; intelligible. внять, no *fut.*~ял, -а́, -о *perf.* of внима́ть.

во: see в².

ВО *abbr.* военный округ, military district.

во-: see **в-**.

вобра́ть вберу́, -рёшь; -а́л, -а́, -о *perf.* (*imp.* вбира́ть) absorb, draw in, soak up, inhale.

вобью́, etc.: see вбить.

вове́к, **вове́ки** *adv.* for ever; ~ не, never.

во́время *adv.* in time; on time; не ~, at the wrong time.

во́все *adv.* quite; ~ не, not at all.

во-вторы́х *adv.* secondly, in the second place.

вогна́ть, вгоню́, -о́нишь; -гна́л, -а́, -о *perf.* (*imp.* вгоня́ть) drive in. **во́гнутый**, concave; dented. **вогну́ть**, -ну́, -нёшь *perf.* (*imp.* вгиба́ть) bend or curve inwards; ~ся, bend inwards, curve inwards.

-вод in *comb.* -breeder, -grower, -raiser.

вода́, *acc.* во́ду; *pl.* -ы, water; *pl.* the waters; watering-place, spa.

водворе́ние, -я, settlement; establishment. **водвори́ть**, -рю́ *perf.*, **водворя́ть**, -я́ю *imp.* settle, install, house; establish.

води́тель, -я *m.* driver; leader. **води́тельница**, -ы, (woman) driver. **води́тельство**, -а, leadership. **води́ть**, вожу́, во́дишь *imp.* lead; conduct; take; drive;+*instr.* (по+*dat.*) pass (over, across); ~ автомоби́ль, маши́ну, drive a car; ~ глаза́ми по+*dat.*, cast one's eyes over; ~ся, be, be found; associate, play (with); be the custom, happen.

во́дка, -и, vodka. **воднолы́жник**, -а, -ница, -ы, water-skier. **во́дный**, water; watery; aquatic; aqueous; ~ые лы́жи, water-skiing; water-skis.

водо- in *comb.* water, water-; hydraulic; hydro-. **водобоя́знь**, -и, hydrophobia. **~вмести́лище**, -а, reservoir. **~воз**, -а, water-carrier. **~воро́т**, -а, whirlpool, eddy; vortex, maelstrom, whirl. **~ём**, -а, reservoir. **~измеще́ние**, -я, displacement. **~ка́чка**, -и, water-tower, pump-house, pumping station. **~лаз**, -а, diver; Newfoundland. **~ла́зный**, diving. **~лей**, -я, Aquarius. **~непроница́емый**, watertight; waterproof. **~но́сный**, water-bearing. **~отво́д**, -а,

drain, overflow. **~отво́дный**, drainage, overflow. **~отта́лкивающий**, water-repellent. **~па́д**, -а, waterfall; falls, cataract. **~по́й**, -я, watering-place; water-supply; watering. **~прово́д**, -а, water-pipe, water-main; water supply. **~прово́дный**, water-main, mains; tap-. **~прово́дчик**, -а, plumber. **~разде́л**, -а, watershed. **~распыли́тель**, -я *m.* sprinkler. **~ро́д**, -а, hydrogen. **во́доросль**, -и, water-plant, water-weed; seaweed; alga. **~снабже́ние**, -я, water-supply. **~сто́к**, -а, drain, gutter.

во́дочный, vodka.

водружа́ть, -а́ю *imp.*, **водрузи́ть**, -ужу́ *perf.* hoist; set up, fix up.

водяни́стый, watery. **водя́нка**, -и, dropsy. **водяно́й**, water; aquatic; ~ знак, watermark; *sb.* water-sprite. **водяни́чный**, dropsical.

воева́ть, вою́ю *imp.* wage war, make war, be at war; quarrel. **воево́да**, -ы *m.* voivode; commander of army; governor of province. **воево́дство**, -а, office of voivode; voivode's province.

воеди́но *adv.* together, into one.

воен- *abbr.* in *comb.* of военный, military, war-. **военко́м**, -а, military commissar. **~ко́р**, -а, war-correspondent.

воениза́ция, -и, militarization. **военизи́рованный**, militarized, armed; paramilitary.

военно- in *comb.* military; war-. **вое́нно-возду́шный**, air-, air-force; ~-возду́шные си́лы, air-force. **вое́нно-морско́й**, naval; ~-морско́й флот, navy. **~пле́нный** *sb.* prisoner of war. **вое́нно-полево́й**; ~-полево́й суд, (drumhead) court-martial. **~слу́жащий** *sb.* serviceman.

вое́нный, military; war; army; ~ое положе́ние, martial law; ~ый суд, court-martial; *sb.* soldier, serviceman; *pl.* the military.

вожа́к, -а́, guide; leader. **вожа́тый** *sb.* guide; leader; tram-driver. **вожде́ние**, -я, leading; driving, steering, piloting. **вождь**, -я *m.* leader, chief.

вожжа́, -и́; *pl.* -и, -е́й, reins.

вожу́ etc.: see води́ть, вози́ть.

воз, -а (-у), *loc.* -у́; *pl.* -ы́ or -á, cart, wagon; cart-load; loads, heaps.

воз-, **возо-**, **вос-** *vbl. pref.* indicates direction or movement upwards; renewed action; action in response; beginning of action; intensity, excitement, solemnity.

возбуди́мый, excitable, irritable. **возбуди́тель**, -я *m.* agent; stimulus; stimulant; exciter; instigator. **возбуди́ть**, -ужу́ *perf.*, **возбужда́ть**, -áю *imp.* excite, rouse, arouse; stimulate, whet; stir up, incite; provoke; institute, bring, raise. **возбужда́ющий**; ~ее сре́дство, stimulant. **возбужде́ние**, -я, excitement, agitation. **возбуждённый**, excited, agitated.

возвести́, -еду́, -дёшь; -вёл, -лá *perf.* (*imp.* возводи́ть) elevate; raise; erect, put up; bring, advance; level; +к+ *dat.* trace to, derive from.

возвести́ть, -ещу́ *perf.*, **возвеща́ть**, -áю *imp.* proclaim, announce.

возводи́ть, -ожу́, -о́дишь *imp.* of возвести́.

возвра́т, -а, return; repayment, reimbursement; restitution; ~ боле́зни, relapse; ~ со́лнца, solstice. **возврати́ть**, -ащу́ *perf.*, **возвраща́ть**, -áю *imp.* (*perf.* also верну́ть) return, give back, restore; pay back; recover, retrieve; send back, bring back; ~ся, return; go back, come back; revert. **возвра́тный**, back, return; relapsing; recurrent; reflexive. **возвраще́ние**, -я, return; recurrence; restoration, restitution.

возвы́сить, -ы́шу *perf.*, **возвыша́ть**, -áю *imp.* raise; ennoble; ~ся, rise, go up; tower. **возвыше́ние**, -я, rise; raising; eminence; raised place. **возвы́шенность**, -и, height; eminence; loftiness, sublimity. **возвы́шенный**, high, elevated; lofty, sublime.

возгла́вить, -влю *perf.*, **возглавля́ть**, -я́ю *imp.* head, be at the head of.

во́зглас, -а, cry, exclamation. **возгласи́ть**, -ашу́ *perf.*, **возглаша́ть**, -áю *imp.* proclaim. **возглаше́ние**, -я, proclamation; exclamation.

возгора́емость, -и, inflammability. **возгора́емый**, inflammable. **возгора́ние**

-я, ignition; то́чка возгора́ния, flash-point. **возгора́ться**, -áюсь *imp.*, **возгоре́ться**, -рю́сь *perf.* flare up; be seized (with); be smitten.

воздава́ть, -даю́, -даёшь *imp.*, **возда́ть**, -áм, -áшь, -áст; -áл, -адм, -áл, -á, -о *perf.* render; ~ до́лжное+*dat.* do justice to.

воздвига́ть, -áю *imp.*, **воздви́гнуть**, -ну; -дви́г *perf.* raise, erect; ~ся, rise, arise.

возде́йствие, -я, influence; физи́ческое ~, coercion. **возде́йствовать**, -твую *perf.* and *imp.* influence, affect; act on, work on.

возде́лать, -аю *perf.*, **возде́лывать**, -аю *imp.* cultivate till.

воздержа́вшийся *sb.* abstainer; abstention. **воздержа́ние**, -я, abstinence; abstention. **возде́ржанный**, **возде́ржный**, abstemious; temperate; abstinent. **воздержа́ться**, -жу́сь, -жи́шься *perf.*, **возде́рживаться**, -аюсь *imp.* refrain; abstain; withhold acceptance, decline.

во́здух, -а, air; в ~е, in the air; на ~, на ~е, out of doors. **воздухо́дувка**, -и, blower. **воздухонепроница́емый**, air-tight. **воздухоохлажда́емый**, air-cooled. **возду́шн**|ый, air, aerial; overhead; air-raid; airy, light; flimsy; ~ые за́мки, castles in the air; ~ый змей, kite; ~ая пе́тля, chain (stitch); ~ый пиро́г, soufflé; ~ый флот, air force; ~ый шар, balloon.

воззва́ние, -я, appeal. **воззва́ть**, -зову́, -вёшь *perf.* (*imp.* взыва́ть) appeal, call (о+*prep.* for).

воззре́ние, -я, view, opinion, outlook.

вози́ть, вожу́, во́зишь *imp.* cart, convey; carry; bring, take; drive; draw; beat, flog; ~ся, romp, run about, play noisily; take trouble, spend time, busy oneself; potter about; tinker, fiddle about, mess about. **во́зка**, -и, carting, carriage.

возлага́ть, -áю *imp.* of возложи́ть.

во́зле *adv.* and *prep.*+*gen.* by, near; near by; past.

возложи́ть, -жу́, -жишь, *perf.* (*imp.* возлага́ть) lay; place.

возлю́бленный, beloved; *sb.* boy-friend, girl-friend; lover, mistress.

возме́здие, -я, retribution; requital; punishment.

возмести́ть, -ещу́ perf., возмеща́ть, -а́ю imp. compensate for, make up for; refund, reimburse. возмеще́ние, -я, compensation, indemnity; damages; replacement; refund, reimbursement.

возмо́жно adv. possibly; +comp. as ... as possible. возмо́жность, -и, possibility; opportunity; pl. means, resources; potentialities; по (ме́ре) возмо́жности, as far as possible; при пе́рвой возмо́жности, as soon as possible, at the first opportunity. возмо́жный, possible; greatest possible.

возмужа́лость, -и, maturity; manhood, womanhood. возмужа́лый, mature; grown up. возмужа́ть, -а́ю perf. grow up, reach maturity; gain strength, become strong.

возмути́тельный, disgraceful, scandalous; seditious, subversive. возмути́ть, -ущу́ perf., возмуща́ть, -а́ю imp. disturb, trouble; stir up, incite; anger, rouse to indignation; ~ся, be indignant, be roused to indignation, be exasperated; rebel, rise in revolt. возмуще́ние, -я, indignation; revolt, rebellion; perturbation; disturbance. возмущённый; -щён, -щена́, indignant, troubled, disturbed.

вознагради́ть, -ажу́ perf., вознагражда́ть, -а́ю imp. reward; recompense; make up for (за +acc. for). вознагражде́ние, -я, reward, recompense; compensation; fee, remuneration.

возненави́деть, -и́жу perf. conceive a hatred for, come to hate.

вознесе́ние, -я, ascent; Ascension. вознести́, -несу́, -несёшь; -нёс, -ла́ perf. (imp. возноси́ть) raise, lift up; ~сь, rise; ascend.

возника́ть, -а́ет imp., возни́кнуть, -нет; -ник perf. arise, spring up. возникнове́ние, -я, rise, beginning, origin.

возни́ца, -ы m. coachman, driver. возни́чий sb. coachman, driver.

возноси́ть(ся, -ошу́(сь, -о́сишь(ся imp. of вознести́(сь. вознопе́ние, -я, raising, elevation.

возня́, -и́, row, noise; horse-play; bother, trouble.

возобнови́ть, -влю́ perf., возобновля́ть, -я́ю imp. renew, resume; restore; begin again. возобновле́ние, -я, renewal, resumption; revival.

возража́ть, -а́ю imp., возрази́ть, -ажу́ perf. object, have or raise an objection; take exception; retort; say. возраже́ние, -я, objection; retort; answer.

во́зраст, -а, age; на ~е, grown up. возраста́ние, -я, growth, increase; increment. возраста́ть, -а́ет imp., возрасти́, -тёт; -ро́с, -ла́ perf. grow, increase.

возроди́ть, -ожу́ perf., возрожда́ть, -а́ю imp. regenerate; revive; ~ся, revive. возрожде́ние, -я, rebirth; revival; Renaissance.

возро́с etc.: see возрасти́. возро́сший, increased.

во́зчик, -а, carter, carrier; drayman.

возьму́ etc.: see взять.

во́ин, -а, warrior; soldier; serviceman. во́инск|ий, military; soldierly; army, troop; ~ая пови́нность, conscription. во́инственный, warlike; bellicose. во́инствующий, militant.

вои́стину adv. indeed; verily.

вой, -я, howl, howling; wail, wailing.

войду́ etc.: see войти́.

во́йлок, -а, felt; strip of felt. во́йлочный, felt.

война́, -ы́; pl. -ы, war.

во́йско, -а; pl. -а́, army; host; multitude; pl. troops, forces. войсково́й, military; of the (Cossack) host.

войти́, -йду́, -йдёшь; вошёл, -шла́ perf. (imp. входи́ть), go in, come in, enter; get in(to); ~ в аза́рт, grow heated; ~ в лета́, get on (in years); ~ в мо́ду, become fashionable; ~ во вкус, acquire a taste; ~ в си́лу, come into force.

вокза́л, -а, (railway) station.

вокру́г adv. and prep.+gen. round, around.

вол, -а́, ox, bullock.

вола́н, -а, flounce; shuttlecock.

волды́рь, -я́ m. blister; lump, bump.

волево́й, volitional; strong-willed. во́лей-нево́лей adv. willy-nilly.

во́лжский, Volga, of the Volga.

волк, -а; -и, -о́в, wolf. волкода́в, -а, wolf-hound.

волна́, -ы́; -и, во́лна́м, wave. волне́ние, -я, roughness, choppiness; agitation, disturbance; emotion, excitement; (usu. *pl.*) unrest. волни́стый, wavy; undulating; corrugated; watered. волнова́ть, -ну́ю *imp.* (*perf.* вз~) disturb, agitate; excite; worry; ~ся, be disturbed or agitated; fret, worry, be nervous, be excited; be in a state of ferment or unrest; be rough or choppy; ripple, wave. волноло́м, -а, breakwater. волнообра́зный, wavelike; undulatory; wavy, undulating. волноре́з, -а, breakwater. волну́ющий, disturbing; worrying; exciting, thrilling, stirring.

воло́к -а; *pl.* -и or -а́, portage.

волоки́та, -ы, red tape.

волокни́стый, fibrous, stringy. волокно́, -а́; *pl.* -а, fibre, filament.

волоку́ etc.: see воло́чь.

во́лос, -а; *pl.* -ы or -а́, -о́с hair; *pl.* hair. волоса́тый, hairy; hirsute; pilose. волоси́стый, fibrous. волосно́й, capillary. волосо́к, -ска́, hair, fine hair; hair-spring; filament.

волостно́й, of a volost. во́лость, -и; *pl.* -и, -е́й, volost.

волосяно́й, hair.

воло́чить, -очу́ -о́чишь *imp.* drag; draw; ~ся drag, trail; +за+*instr.* run after. воло́чь, -очу́, -о́чешь; -о́к, -ла́ *imp.* drag; ~ся, drag, trail; be oneself along; shuffle.

волча́та etc.: see волчо́нок. во́лчий, wolf, wolf's; wolfish. волчи́ха, -и, волчи́ца, -ы, she-wolf.

волчо́к, -чка́, top; gyroscope.

волчо́нок, -нка; *pl.* -ча́та, -ча́т, wolf-cub.

волше́бник, -а, magician; wizard. волше́бница, -ы, enchantress. волше́бный, magic, magical; enchanted; bewitching, enchanting: ~ая па́лочка, magic wand; ~ое ца́рство, fairyland, enchanted kingdom. волшебство́, -а́, magic, enchantment.

во́льно adv. freely; ~! stand at ease! вольнонаёмный, civilian. во́льность, -и, freedom, liberty; license; familiar-ity. во́льный; -лен, -льна́ -о, -ы or -ы́, free; unrestricted; loose; free-style; familiar; private; at liberty; ~ ка́меньщик, Freemason.

вольт[1], -а, volt.

вольт[2], -а, *loc.* -у́. vault; volte. вольтижёр, -а. trick-rider. вольтижи́ровать, -рую *imp.* vault.

во́льтов *adj.* voltaic.

вольфра́м, -а, tungsten; wolfram.

волью́ etc.: see влить.

во́ля, -и, will; volition; wish(es); freedom, liberty; ~ ва́ша, as you please, as you like; дать во́лю+*dat.*, give rein to; дать себе́ во́лю, let oneself go; на во́ле, at liberty; не по свое́й во́ле, against one's will; по до́брой во́ле, freely, of one's own free will.

вомну́ etc.: see вмять.

вон adv. out; off away.

вон *part.* there, over there.

вонза́ть, -а́ю *imp.*, вонзи́ть -нжу́ *perf.* plunge, thrust; ~ся в + *acc.* pierce, penetrate.

вонь, -и, stink. stench. воню́чий, stinking, fetid. воню́чка, -и, stinker; skunk. воня́ть, -я́ю *imp.* stink, reek.

вообража́емый, imaginary; fictitious. вообража́ть, -а́ю *imp.*, вообрази́ть, -ажу́ *perf.* imagine; fancy; ~ся, imagine oneself. воображе́ние -я, imagination; fancy. вообрази́мый, imaginable.

вообще́ adv. in general; generally (speaking); on the whole; always; altogether; at all; ~ говоря́, generally speaking; as a matter of fact.

воодушеви́ть, -влю́ *perf.*, воодушевля́ть, -я́ю *imp* inspire, rouse; in-spirit, hearten. воодушевле́ние, -я, rousing; inspiration; inspiriting; ani-mation; enthusiasm, fervour. воодушевлённый, animated; enthusiastic, fervent.

вооружа́ть, -а́ю *imp.*, вооружи́ть, -жу́ *perf.* arm equip; fit out; set turn; ~ про́тив себя́, antagonize; ~ся, arm oneself take up arms; equip oneself, provide oneself. вооруже́ние, -я, arm-ing; arms, armament; equipment.

вооружённый; -жён, -á, armed; equipped.

воóчию *adv.* with one's own eyes, for oneself; clearly, plainly.

во-пéрвых *adv.* first, first of all, in the first place.

вопить, -плю́ *imp.* yell, howl, wail. вопию́щий, crying, glaring; flagrant, scandalous. вопия́ть, -ию́, -иéшь *imp.* cry out, clamour.

воплотить, -ощу́ *perf.*, воплощáть, -áю *imp.* embody, incarnate; ~ в себé, be the embodiment of. воплощéние, -я, embodiment; incarnation. воплощённый; -щён, -щенá, incarnate; personified.

вопль, -я *m.* cry wail; wailing howling.

вопреки́ *prep.* + *dat.* despite, in spite of; against, contrary to.

вопрóс, -а a question; problem; matter; ~ по существу́, substance of the matter; под ~ом in question, undecided; что за ~! of course! вопроси́тельный, interrogative; questioning; ~ знак, question-mark. вопрошáющий, questioning, inquiring.

вопью́ etc.: see впить.

вор, -а; *pl.* -ы́ -óв. thief; criminal.

ворвáться, -вýсь -вёшься; -áлся, -лáсь, -áлóсь *perf.* (*imp.* врывáться) burst in.

воркова́ть, -кýю *imp.* coo; bill and coo.

воркотня́, -и́, grumbling.

воробéй, -бья́ sparrow. воробьи́ный sparrow's; passerine.

ворóванный, stolen. ворова́тый, thievish; furtive. ворова́ть, -рýю *imp.* (*perf.* с~) steal; be a thief. воровка, -и woman thief. воровскóй *adv.* furtively. воровскóй, thieves'; illegal. воровствó -á, stealing; theft.

вóрон, -а, a raven. ворóна, -ы, crow. воронёный, blued. ворóний, crow's-corvine. ворони́ть, -ню́ *imp.* blue.

ворóнка, -и, funnel; crater.

воронóй, black; *sb.* black horse.

ворóньё, -я́, carrion crows.

вóрот[1], -а neckline; collar; neckband.

вóрот[2], -а winch; windlass.

ворóта, -рóт *pl.* gate, gates; gateway; goal.

вороти́ть[1], -очу́ -óтишь *imp.* + *instr.* be in charge of; ~ нос, turn up one's

nose; меня́ ворóтит от э́того дéла, this business makes me sick.

вороти́ть[2], -очу́, -óтишь *perf.* bring back, get back; turn back, send back; ~ся. return, come back, go back.

ворóтник, -á, воротничóк, -чкá, collar.

ворóт|ый, gate; ~ая вéна, portal vein.

вóрох, -а; *pl.* -á, a heap, pile; masses lots, heaps.

ворочáть, -аю *imp.* turn (over); move, shift; + *instr.* control, have control of; boss; ~ глазáми, roll one's eyes; ~ миллиóнами, deal in millions; ~ся, move turn; toss and turn.

ворочу́(сь etc.: see вороти́ть(ся.

вороши́ть, -шý *imp.* stir stir up; turn (over); ~ся, move about, stir.

ворс, -а, nap. pile. ворси́нка, -и hair, nap, lint; fibre. ворси́стый, fleecy.

ворчáть, -чý *imp.* grumble growl. ворчли́вый, querulous, peevish; grumpy.

вос-: see воз-

восвоя́си *adv.* home; отпрáвиться ~, go back home.

восемнáдцатый eighteenth. восемнáдцать, -и, eighteen. вóсемь, -сьми́, *instr.* -сьмью́ or -семью́, eight. вóсемьдесят -сьми́десяти, eighty. восемьсóт, -сьмисóт -стáми, eight hundred восьмерó *adv.* eight times.

воск, -а (-у) wax. beeswax.

восклúкнуть -ну *perf.*, восклицáть, -áю *imp.* exclaim. восклицáние, -я, exclamation. восклицáтельный, exclamatory; ~ знак, exclamation mark.

восковка, -и, waxed paper; stencil. восковóй, wax, waxen; waxy; waxed; ~ая бумáга, greaseproof paper.

воскресáть, -áю *imp.*, воскрéснуть, -ну; -ec *perf.* rise again, rise from the dead; revive. воскресéние, -я, resurrection. воскресéнье, -я Sunday. воскресить -ешý *perf.*, воскресúть, -áю *imp.* raise from the dead, resurrect; revive. воскрéсник, -а voluntary Sunday work. воскрéсный, Sunday. воскрешéние, -я, raising from the dead, resurrection; revival.

воспалéние, -я, inflammation. воспалённый; -лён, -á, inflamed; sore. воспалúть, -лю́ *perf* воспаля́ть, -я́ю *imp.* inflame; ~ся become inflamed.

воспита́ние, -я, upbringing, education; training; (good) breeding. воспита́нник, -а, -ница, -ы, pupil, schoolboy, schoolgirl; ward. воспи́танность, -и, (good) breeding. воспи́танный, well-brought-up. воспита́тельный, educational; ~ дом, foundling hospital. воспита́ть, -а́ю perf., воспи́тывать, -аю imp. bring up, rear; cultivate, foster; inculcate; educate; train.

воспламени́ть, -ню́ perf., воспламеня́ть, -я́ю imp. kindle, set on fire, ignite; fire, inflame; ~ся, ignite catch fire; blaze up; take fire, flare up. воспламеня́емый, inflammable.

вос|по́льзоваться, -зуюсь perf.

воспомина́ние, -я, recollection, memory; pl. memoirs; reminiscences.

вос|препя́тствовать, -твую perf.

воспрети́ть, -ещу́ perf., воспреща́ть, -а́ю imp. forbid, prohibit. воспреще́ние, -я, prohibition. воспрещённый, -щён, -а, forbidden, prohibited.

восприе́мник, -а, godfather. восприе́мница, -ы, godmother. восприи́мчивый, receptive, impressionable; susceptible. воспринима́емый, perceptible, apprehensible. воспринима́ть, -а́ю imp., восприня́ть, -иму́, -и́мешь; -и́нял, -а́, -о perf. perceive, apprehend; grasp, take in; interpret take (как, for). восприя́тие, -я, perception.

воспроизведе́ние, -я, reproduction. вос|произвести́, -еду́, -еде́шь; -вёл, -а́ perf., воспроизводи́ть, -ожу́, -о́дишь imp. reproduce; renew; recall. воспроизводи́тельный, reproductive. воспроизво́дство, reproduction.

вос|проти́виться, -влюсь perf.

воссоедине́ние, -я, reunion, reunification. воссоедини́ть, -ню́ perf., воссоединя́ть, -я́ю imp. reunite.

восстава́ть, -таю́, -таёшь imp. of восста́ть. восстана́вливать, -аю imp. of восстанови́ть.

восста́ть, -а́ну perf. (imp. восстава́ть) rise (up), arise.

восстанови́тельный, of restoration, of reconstruction. восстанови́ть, -влю́, -вишь perf. (imp. восстана́вливать) restore, renew, re-establish, revive; recall, recollect; reduce; ~ про́тив + gen. set against; ~ про́тив себя́, an-

tagonize. восстановле́ние, -я, restoration, renewal, reinstatement; rehabilitation; reconstruction; reduction.

восста́ть, -а́ну perf. (imp. восстава́ть) rise (up), arise.

восто́к, -а, east. востокове́дение, -я, oriental studies.

восто́рг, -а, delight, rapture; в ~е от + gen. delighted with. восторга́ть, -а́ю imp. delight, enrapture; ~ся + instr. be delighted with, go into raptures over. восто́рженный, enthusiastic. восторжествова́ть, -тву́ю perf. triumph.

восто́чник, -а, orientalist. восто́чный, east, eastern; oriental.

востре́бование, -я, claiming; demand; до востре́бования, to be called for, poste restante. востре́бовать, -бую perf. claim, call for.

восхвали́ть, -лю́, -лишь perf., восхваля́ть, -я́ю imp. praise, extol.

восхити́тельный, entrancing, ravishing; delightful; delicious. восхити́ть, -хищу́ perf., восхища́ть, -а́ю imp. carry away, delight, enrapture. восхище́ние, -я, delight, rapture; admiration. восхищённый; -щён, -а́, rapt, admiring.

восхо́д, -а, rising; east. восходи́ть, -ожу́, -о́дишь imp. of взойти́; ~ к + dat. go back to, date from. восходи́тель, -я m. mountaineer, climber. восхожде́ние, -я, ascent. восходя́щий, rising.

восше́ствие, -я, accession.

восьма́я sb. eighth; octave. восьмёрка, -и, eight; No. 8; figure of eight. во́сьмеро, -ры́х, eight; eight pairs. восьми- in comb. eight; octo-. восьмигра́нник, -а, octahedron. ~деся́тый, eightieth. ~кла́ссник, -а, -ница, -ы, eighth-year pupil. ~кра́тный, eightfold, octuple. ~ле́тний, eight-year; eight-year-old. ~со́тый, eight-hundredth. ~уго́льник, -а, octagon. ~уго́льный, octagonal. ~часово́й, eight-hour.

восьмо́й, eighth.

вот, part. here (is), there (is); this is; here's a . . ! there's a . . !; ~ ещё! well, what next?; ~ и всё, and that's all; ~ как! no! really?; ~ та́к! that's it!; that's right!; ~ тебé! take that!; ~ тебé и .., so much for ..; ~ что! no! not really? **вот-вот** adv. a moment more, and . . : this moment, just; part. that's right!

воткнýть, -нý, -нёшь perf. (imp. втыкáть) stick in, drive in, thrust in.

вотрý etc.: see втерéть.

воцарéние, -я, accession. **воцарúться**, -úтся perf., **воцарáться**, -áется imp. come to the throne; fall, set in; reign; establish oneself.

вошёл etc.: see войтú.

вошь, вши; gen. pl. вшей louse.

вошью etc.: see вшить.

вощáнка, -и, wax paper, wax(ed) cloth; cobbler's wax. **вощанóй**, wax. **вощúть**, -щý imp. (perf. на~) wax, wax-polish.

вою, etc.: see быть.

воюю, etc.: see воевáть. **воюющий**, warring; belligerent.

впадáть, -áю imp., **впасть**, -адý perf. fall, flow; lapse, sink; fall in; + в + acc. verge on, approximate to. **впадéние**, -я, confluence, (river-)mouth. **впадúна**, -ы, cavity, hollow; socket. **впáлый**, hollow, sunken.

впервóй, впервыé adv. for the first time, first.

вперёд, adv. forward(s), ahead; in future; in advance; идтú ~, be fast. **впередú** adv. in front, ahead; in (the) future; prep. + gen. in front of, ahead of, before.

вперемéшку adv. pell-mell, higgledy-piggledy.

вперúть, -рю perf., **вперя́ть**, -я́ю imp. fix, fasten; direct; ~ся, be fixed; gaze fixedly, stare.

впечатлéние, -я, impression; effect. **впечатлúтельный**, impressionable; sensitive.

впивáть(ся, -áю(сь imp. of впить(ся.

вписáть, -ишý, -úшешь perf., **впúсывать**, -аю imp. enter insert; inscribe; ~ся, be enrolled, join. **впúска**, -и, entry; insertion.

впитáть, -áю perf., **впúтывать**, -аю imp. absorb, take in; ~ся soak.

впить, вопью, -ьёшь; -úл, -á, -о perf. (imp. впивáть) imbibe, absorb; ~ся,

dig in, stick in; cling to; ~ся взóром, глазáми, fix one's gaze, one's eyes (on).

впúхивать, -аю imp., **впихнýть**, -нý, -нёшь perf. stuff in, cram in; shove in.

вплавь adv. (by) swimming; перепрáвиться ~, swim across.

вплестú, -етý, -етёшь; -ёл, -á perf., **вплетáть**, -áю imp. plait in, intertwine; involve.

вплотнýю adv. close; closely; in earnest. **вплоть** adv.; ~ до + gen. (right) up to; ~ к + dat. right against, close to, right up to.

вполгóлоса adv. under one's breath, in an undertone.

вползáть, -áю imp., **вползтú**, -зý, -зёшь; -з, -лá perf. creep in, creep up, crawl in.

вполнé adv. fully, entirely; quite.

вполовúну adv. (by) half.

впопáд adv. to the point; opportunely.

впопыхáх adv. in a hurry, hastily; in one's haste.

впóру adv. at the right time, opportune(ly); just right, exactly; быть ~ (+ dat.) fit.

впослéдствии adv. subsequently afterwards.

впотьмáх adv. in the dark.

впрáвду adv. really.

впрáве adv.; быть ~, have a right.

впрáвить, -влю perf., **вправлять**, -я́ю imp. set, reduce; tuck in. **впрáвка**, -и, setting, reduction.

впрáво adv. to the right (от + gen. of).

впредь adv. in (the) future; ~ до + gen. until.

впрóчем conj. however, but; though; or rather.

впрыгивать, -аю imp., **впрыгнуть**, -ну perf. jump in, jump up (on).

впрыскивани:е, -я, injection. **впрыскивать**, -аю imp., **впрыснуть**, -ну perf. inject.

впрягáть, -áю imp., **впрячь**, -ягý, -яжёшь; -яг, -лá perf. harness.

впуск, -a, admission, admittance. **впускáть**, -áю imp., **впустúть**, -ущý -ýстишь perf. admit, let in. **впускнóй**, admittance; inlet.

впусту́ю *adv.* for nothing, to no purpose, in vain.

впута́ть, -аю *perf.*, **впу́тывать**, -аю *imp.* entangle, involve, implicate; **~ся**, get mixed up in.

впущу́, etc.: see впусти́ть.

впя́теро *adv.* five times. **впятеро́м** *adv.* five (together).

враг, -á, enemy; the Devil. **вражда́**, -ы́, enmity, hostility. **вражде́бный**, hostile; enemy. **враждова́ть**, -ду́ю, be at war, be at enmity, be hostile, quarrel. **вра́жеский**, enemy. **вра́жий**, enemy, hos'ile.

вразби́вку *adv.* at random.

вразбро́д *adv.* separately not in concert, disunitedly.

вразре́з *adv.* contrary; идти́ ~ с + *instr.* go against.

вразуми́тельный, intelligible, clear; instructive; persuasive. **вразуми́ть**, -млю́ *perf.*, **вразумля́ть**, -я́ю *imp.* make understand make listen to reason, make see sense.

врасплóх *adv.* unexpectedly, unawares, by surprise.

враста́ть, -а́ет *imp.*, **врасти́**, -тёт; врос-ла́ *perf.* grow in; take root. **враста́ю-щий**, ingrowing.

врата́рь, -я́ *m.* gate-keeper; goalkeeper.

врать, вру, врёшь; -ал, -á, -о *imp.* (*perf.* на~, со~) lie, tell lies; talk nonsense.

врач, -á, doctor; medical officer; зуб-но́й ~, dentist. **враче́бный**, medical.

враща́тельный, rotary. **враща́ть**, -а́ю *imp.* turn rotate, revolve; ~ глаза́ми, roll one's eyes; **~ся**, turn, revolve, rotate; **~ся** в худо́жественных кру-га́х, move in artistic circles. **враще́ние**, -я rotation, revolution, gyration.

вред, -á, harm, hurt, injury; damage. **вреди́тель**, -я *m.* pest; wrecker, sabo-teur; *pl.* vermin. **вреди́тельство**, -а, wrecking, (act of) sabotage. **вреди́ть**, -ежу́ *imp.* (*perf.* по~) + *dat.* injure, harm, hurt; damage. **вре́дный**, -ден, -дна́, -о, harmful, injurious; unhealthy.

врежу́: see вреди́ть. **вре́жу**(сь, etc.: see вре́зать(ся.

вре́зать, -е́жу *perf.*, **вреза́ть**, -а́ю *imp.* cut in, engrave; set in, fit in, insert; (*sl.*) + *dat.* hit, smash; slang; curse; **~ся**,

cut, force one's way, run (into); en-graved; fall in love; **~ся** в зе́млю, plunge to the ground. **врезно́й**, inset; mortise; notch.

времена́ми *adv.* at times, now and then, from time to time. **вре́менник**, -a, chronicle, annals. **вре́менно** *adv.* tem-porarily; ~ исполня́ющий обя́зан-ности, acting; ~ пове́ренный в дела́х, acting chargé d'affaires. **вре-менно́й**, temporal; time; of tense(s). **вре́менный**, temporary; provisional; acting. **вре́менщик**, -á, favourite. **вре́мя**, -мени; *pl.* -мена́, -мён, -áм *n.* time, times; tense; ~ гóда, season; ~ от вре́мени, at times, from time to time, now and then; в своё ~, in one's time; once, at one time; in due course, in one's own time; до того́ вре́мени, till then, till that time; на ~, for a time; са́мое ~, just the time (the right time); ско́лько вре́мени? what is the time?; тем вре́менем, mean-while. **вре́мянка**, -и, portable or makeshift stove; temporary structure.

врид, *n. abbr.* вре́менно исполня́ющий до́лжность, temporary, acting (as).

вро́вень *adv.* level, on a level.

вро́де *prep.* + *gen.* like; не́что ~, a sort of, a kind of; *part.* such as, like; apparently, seemingly.

врождённый, -дён, -á, innate; congeni-tal; inherent.

врознь, **врозь** *adv.* separately, apart.

врос, etc.: see врасти́. **врою́**(сь, etc.: see врыть(ся. **вру**, etc.: see врать.

врун, -á, **вру́нья**, -и, liar.

вруча́ть, -а́ю *imp.*, **вручи́ть**, -чу́ *perf.* hand, deliver; entrust; serve. **вручи́-тель**, -я, *m.* bearer.

вручну́ю *adv.* by hand.

врыва́ть(ся, -а́ю(сь *imp.* of ворва́ться, врыть(ся.

врыть, врóю *perf.* (*imp.* врыва́ть) dig in, bury; **~ся**, dig oneself in.

вряд (ли) *adv.* it's not likely; hardly, scarcely; ~ ли стóит, it's hardly worth while.

вс-: see вз-.

всади́ть, -ажу́, -а́дишь *perf.*, **вса́жи-вать**, -аю *imp.* thrust in, plunge in; set in; put in, sink in. **вса́дник**, -a, rider, horseman; knight. вса́дница, -ы, rider, horsewoman.

вса́сывание, -я, suction; absorption. вса́сывать(ся, -аю(сь *imp.* of всоса́ть(ся.

всё, все *pron.*: see весь. всё *adv.* always, all the time; only, all; ~ (ещё), still; ~ из-за тебя, all because of you; ~ лу́чше и лу́чше, better and better; *conj.* however, nevertheless; ~ же, all the same.

все- in *comb.* all-, omni-. всевозмо́ж-ный, of every kind; all possible. ~волново́й, all-wave. ~ме́рно *adv.* in every way, to the utmost. всеме́рный, of every kind, every possible kind of. ~ми́рный, world, world-wide, universal. ~могу́щий, omnipotent, all-powerful. ~наро́дно *adv.* publicly. ~наро́дный, national; nation-wide. ~ору́жие; во всеору́жии, completely ready; fully armed, equipped. ~побежда́ющий, all-conquering. ~росси́йский, All-Russian. ~си́льный, omnipotent, all-powerful. ~славя́н-ский, pan-Slav. ~сою́зный, All-Union. ~сторо́нний, all-round; thorough, detailed; comprehensive.

всегда́, always, ever. всегда́шний, usual, habitual, customary.

всего́ (-vo) *adv.* in all, all told; only.

вселе́ние, -я, installation, moving in. вселе́нная *sb.* universe. вселе́нский, universal; oecumenical.

всели́ть, -лю́ *perf.*, вселя́ть, -я́ю *imp.* install, settle, lodge; move; inspire, instill; ~ся, move in, install oneself; settle in; be implanted.

все́меро *adv.* seven times. все́мером *adv.* seven (together).

всео́буч, -a *abbr.* всео́бщее обуче́ние, compulsory education. всео́бщий, general, universal.

всерьёз *adv.* seriously, in earnest.

всё-таки *conj.* and *part.* all the same, for all that, still. всеце́ло *adv.* completely; exclusively.

вска́кивать, -аю *imp.* of вскочи́ть.

вс|кара́бкаться, -аюсь *perf.*, вскара́б-киваться, -аюсь *imp.* scramble up, clamber up.

вскачь *adv.* at a gallop.

вски́дывать, -аю *imp.*, вски́нуть, -ну *perf.* throw up, toss; ~ся, leap up; +на+*acc.* turn on, go for.

вскипа́ть, -а́ю *imp.*, вс|кипе́ть, -плю́ *perf.* boil up; flare up.

вс|кипяти́ть(ся, -ячу́(сь *perf.*

всклоко́чивать, -аю *imp.*, всклоко́чить, -чу *perf.* dishevel, tousle.

всколыхну́ть, -ну́, -нёшь *perf.* stir; stir up, rouse.

вско́льзь *adv.* slightly; in passing.

вско́ре *adv.* soon, shortly after.

вскочи́ть, -очу́, о́чишь *perf.* (*imp.* вска́кивать) jump up, spring up, leap up; come up.

вскри́кивать, -аю *imp.*, вскри́кнуть, -ну *perf.* cry out, shriek, scream. вскри-ча́ть, -чу́ *perf.* exclaim.

вскрыва́ть, -а́ю *imp.*, вскрыть, -ро́ю *perf.* open; reveal, disclose; turn up; lance; cut open, dissect; ~ся, come to light, be revealed; become clear of ice, become open; burst. вскры́тие, -я, opening; revelation, disclosure; lancing; dissection, post-mortem.

вслед *adv.* and *prep.*+*dat.* after; ~ за+ *instr.* after, following. всле́дствие *prep.*+*gen.* in consequence of, because of, on account of.

вслепу́ю *adv.* blindly; blindfold.

вслух *adv.* aloud.

вслу́шаться, -аюсь *perf.* вслу́шиваться, -аюсь *imp.* listen attentively, listen hard.

ВСМ (*re-esém*) *abbr.* Всеми́рный Сове́т Ми́ра, World Peace Council.

всма́триваться, -аюсь *imp.*, всмотре́ть-ся, -рю́сь, -ришься *perf.* look closely, peer, look hard.

всмя́тку *adv.* soft(-boiled), lightly (boiled).

всо́вывать, -аю *imp.* of всу́нуть.

всоса́ть, -су́, -сёшь *perf.* (*imp.* вса́сы-вать) suck in; absorb; imbibe; ~ся, be absorbed, soak in; sink in.

вспа́рхивать, -аю *imp.* of вспорхну́ть. вспа́рывать, -аю *imp.* of вспоро́ть.

вс|паха́ть, -ашу́, -а́шешь *perf.*, вспа́хи-вать, -аю *imp.* plough up. вспа́шка, -и, ploughing.

вс|пе́нить, -ню *perf.*

всплеск, -a, splash; blip. всплёскивать,

-аю *imp.*, всплесну́ть, -ну́, -нёшь *perf.* splash; ~ рука́ми, fling up, throw up, one's hands.

всплыва́ть, -а́ю *imp.*, всплыть, -ыву́, -ывёшь; -ыл, -а́, о *perf.* rise to the surface, surface; arise, come up; come to light, be revealed.

вс|полоши́ть(ся), -шу́(сь) *perf.*

вспомина́ть, -а́ю *imp.*, вспо́мнить, -ню *perf.* remember, recall, recollect; ~ся *impers.*+*dat.*: мне вспо́мнилось, I remembered.

вспомога́тельный, auxiliary; subsidiary; branch.

вспоро́ть, -орю́, -о́решь *perf.* (*imp.* вспа́рывать) rip open.

вспорхну́ть, -ну́, -нёшь *perf.* (*imp.* вспа́рхивать) take wing, start up, fly up.

вс|поте́ть, -е́ю *perf.*

вспры́гивать, -аю *imp.*, вспры́гнуть, -ну *perf.* jump up, spring up.

вспры́скивать, -аю *imp.*, вспры́снуть, -ну *perf.* sprinkle.

вспуха́ть, -а́ет *imp.*, вс|пу́хнуть, -нет; -ух *perf.* swell up.

вспыли́ть, -лю́ *perf.* flare up; fly into a rage (на+*acc.* with). вспы́льчивый, hot-tempered, irritable.

вспы́хивать, -аю *imp.*, вспы́хнуть, -ну *perf.* burst into flame blaze up; flare up; break out; blush. вспы́шка, -и, flash; flare, spurt; outburst, burst; outbreak.

встава́ние, -я, rising, standing. встава́ть, -таю́, -таёшь *imp.* of встать.

вста́вить, -влю *perf.*, вставля́ть, -я́ю *imp.* put in, set in, insert. вста́вка, -и, fixing, insertion; framing, mounting; inset; front: interpolation. вставн|о́й, inserted; set in; ~ы́е зу́бы, false teeth; ~ы́е ра́мы, double window-frames.

встать, -а́ну *perf.* (*imp.* встава́ть), get up, rise; stand up; stand; arise, come up; stop; go, fit (в+*acc.* into); ~ на коле́ни, kneel down; ~ с ле́вой ноги́, get out of bed on the wrong side.

встрево́женный *adj.* anxious, worried, alarmed. вс|трево́жить, -жу *perf.*

встрёпанный, dishevelled.

встрепену́ться, -ну́сь, -нёшься *perf.* rouse oneself; shake its wings; start, start up; beat faster, begin to thump.

встре́тить, -е́чу *perf.*, встреча́ть, -а́ю *imp.* meet, meet with, encounter; greet, welcome, receive; ~ся, meet; be found, be met with. встре́ча, -и, meeting; reception; encounter; match. встре́чный, coming to meet; contrary, head; counter; ~ ве́тер, head wind; ~ иск, counter-claim; *sb.* person met with; ка́ждый ~ и попере́чный, anybody and everybody, every Tom, Dick, and Harry; пе́рвый ~, the first person you meet, anybody.

встря́ска, -и, shaking; shock. встря́хивать, -аю *imp.*, встряхну́ть, -ну́, -нёшь *perf.* shake; shake up, rouse; ~ся, shake oneself; rouse oneself, pull oneself together; have a good time.

вступа́ть, -а́ю *imp.*, вступи́ть, -плю́, -пишь *perf.*+в+*acc.* enter, enter into, join, join in; come into; +на+*acc.* go up, mount; ~ в брак, marry; ~ на престо́л, ascend the throne; ~ся, in-tervene; +за+*acc.* stand up for. вступи́тельный, introductory; in-augural, opening; entrance. вступле́-ние, -я, entry, joining; accession; pre-lude, opening, introduction, preamble.

всу́нуть, -ну *perf.* (*imp.* всо́вывать) put in, stick in, push in; slip in.

всхли́пнуть, -ну *perf.*, всхли́пывать, -аю *imp.* sob. всхли́пывание, -я, sobbing; sobs.

всходи́ть, -ожу́, -о́дишь *imp.* of взойти́. всхо́ды, -ов *pl.* new growth, shoots.

всхрапну́ть, -ну́, -нёшь *perf.* всхра́пы-вать, -аю *imp.* snore; snort; have a nap.

всю: see весь.

всю́ду *adv.* everywhere.

вся: see весь.

вся́к|ий, any; every, all kinds of; во ~ом слу́чае, in any case, anyhow, at any rate; на ~ий слу́чай, just in case, to be on the safe side; *pron.* anyone, everyone; anything. вся́чески *adv.* in every possible way, in all ways. вся́ческий, all kinds of.

вт *abbr.* ватт, watt.

вта́йне *adv.* secretly, in secret.

вта́лкивать, -аю *imp.* of втолкну́ть.

вта́птывать, -аю *imp.* of втопта́ть.

вта́скивать, -аю *imp.* of втащи́ть.

втача́ть, -а́ю *perf.*, вта́чивать, -аю *imp.* sew in, sew on; set in. вта́чка, -и, sewing in, sewing on; patch. вта́чанный, вта́чный sewn in, sewn on; set in.

втащи́ть, -щу́, -щишь *perf.* (*imp.* вта́скивать) drag in, drag on, drag up; ~ся, drag oneself.

втека́ть, -а́ет *imp.* of втечь.

втере́ть, вотру́, вотрёшь; втёр *perf.* (*imp.* втира́ть) rub in; ~ся, insinuate oneself, worm oneself.

втечь, -чёт; втёк, -ла́ *perf.* (*imp.* втека́ть) flow in.

втира́ние, -я rubbing in; embrocation, liniment. втира́ть(ся, -а́ю(сь *imp.* of втере́ть(ся.

вти́скивать, -аю *imp.*, вти́снуть, -ну *perf.* squeeze in; ~ся, squeeze (oneself) in.

втихомо́лку, втихую́ *advs.* surreptitiously; on the quiet.

втолкну́ть, -ну́ -нёшь *perf.* (*imp.* вта́лкивать) push in, shove in.

втопта́ть, -пчу́ -пчешь *perf.* (*imp.* вта́птывать) trample (in).

вто́ра, -ы, second voice, violin etc. вто́рить, -рю *imp.* play or sing second; +*dat.* repeat, echo. втори́чный, second, secondary. вто́рник, -а Tuesday. втор|о́й, second; ~о́е as *sb.* second course. второочередно́й, secondary. второстепе́нный, secondary, minor.

в-тре́тьих *adv.* thirdly, in the third place. втро́е *adv.* three times, treble. втроём *adv.* three (together). втро́йне́ *adv.* three times as much, treble.

втуз, -а *abbr.* вы́сшее техни́ческое уче́бное заведе́ние, technical college.

вту́лка, -и, bush; plug bung; liner, sleeve.

втыка́ть, -а́ю *imp.* of воткну́ть. вты́чка -и, thrusting, driving in; plug, bung.

втя́гивать, -аю *imp.*, втяну́ть, -ну́, -нишь *perf.* draw in, up; pull in, up; absorb take in; involve; ~ся, sink, fall in; +*acc.* draw into enter; get used to; get keen on.

вуалетка, -и, veil. вуали́ровать, -рую *imp.* (*perf.* за~), veil, draw a veil over; fog. вуа́ль, *f.* veil; fog.

вуз, -а *abbr.* вы́сшее уче́бное заведе́-

ние, higher educational establishment; university, college, institute. ву́зовец, -вца, -овка, -и, student.

вулка́н, -а, volcano. вулкани́ческий, volcanic.

вундерки́нд, -а, infant prodigy.

ВФП (*ve-efpé*) *abbr.* Всеми́рная федера́ция профсою́зов, World Federation of Trade Unions.

вход, -а, entrance; entry. входи́ть, -ожу́, -о́дишь *imp.* of войти́. входн|о́й, entrance, input; ~о́е отве́рстие, inlet, inlet port. входя́щий, incoming, entering; reentrant; male.

вхолосту́ю *adv.* idle, free; рабо́тать ~, idle.

ВЦ (*vetsé*) *abbr.* вычисли́тельный центр, computer centre.

ВЦСПС (*vetse-espeés*) *abbr.* Всесою́зный Центра́льный Сове́т Профессиона́льных Сою́зов, All-Union Central Trade-Union Council.

вцепи́ться, -плю́сь, -пишься *perf.*, вцепля́ться, -я́юсь *imp.* clutch, cling to; seize, catch hold of.

ВЧ (*veché*) *abbr.* высокочасто́тный, high-frequency, radio-frequency.

вчера́ *adv.* yesterday. вчера́шний, yesterday's.

вчерне́ *adv.* in rough, roughly.

вче́тверо *adv.* four times, by four, in four. вчетверо́м *adv.* four (together). в-четвёртых *adv.* fourthly, in the fourth place.

вши, etc.: see вошь.

вшестеро *adv.* six times, by six. вшестеро́м *adv.* six (together).

вшива́ть, -а́ю *imp.* of вшить. вши́вка, -и, sewing in; patch. вшивно́й, sewn in, set in.

вши́вый, lousy.

вширь *adv.* in breadth; widely.

вшить, вошью́, -ьёшь *perf.* (*imp.* вшива́ть) sew in, set in.

въ-: see в-.

въеда́ться, -а́ется *imp.* of въе́сться. въе́дливый, въе́дчивый *adjs.* corrosive; caustic; acid.

въезд, а, entry; entrance. въезжа́ть, -а́ю *imp.* of въе́хать.

въе́сться, -е́стся, -едя́тся *perf.* (*imp.* въеда́ться) в+*acc.* eat into, corrode.

въе́хать, -е́ду *perf.* (*imp.* въезжа́ть), ride in, up; drive in, up; +в+*acc.* move into; run into.

въя́вь *adv.* in reality; before one's eyes, with one's own eyes.

вы, вас, вам, ва́ми, вас *pron.* you.

вы- *vbl. pref.* expressing direction of motion or action outwards; achievement or attainment by means of action; completion of action or process.

выбега́ть, -а́ю *imp.*, **вы́бежать**, -егу *perf.* run out.

вы́|**белить**, -лю *perf.* **вы́белка** *f.* bleaching; whitening.

вы́беру, etc.: see **выбрать**. **выбива́ть**(**ся**, -а́ю(сь *imp.* of **вы́бить**(ся. **выбира́ть**(ся, -а́ю(сь *imp.* of **вы́брать**(ся.

вы́бить, -бью *perf.* (*imp.* выбива́ть) knock out, kick out; dislodge; beat; beat down; beat out; stamp, strike; hammer out; **~ся**, get out; break loose; come out, show; ~ся из сил, exhaust oneself, be exhausted.

вы́боина, -ы, rut; pot-hole; dent; groove.

вы́бор, -а, choice, option; selection; assortment; *pl.* election, elections. **вы́борка**, -и, selection; excerpt. **вы́**|**борн**|**ый**, elective; electoral; elected; ~ бюллете́нь, ballot-paper; ~ый, ~ая *sb.* delegate. **вы́борочный**, selective.

вы́|**бранить**(ся, -ню(сь *perf.* **выбра́сывать**(ся, -аю(сь *imp.* of **вы́бросить**(ся.

вы́брать, -беру *perf.* (*imp.* выбира́ть), choose, select, pick out; elect; take out; haul in; **~ся**, get out; move, remove; manage to go out.

выбрива́ть, -а́ю *imp.*, **вы́брить**, -рею *perf.* shave; **~ся**, shave (oneself).

вы́брос, -а, blip, pip. **вы́бросить**, -ошу *perf.* (*imp.* выбра́сывать) throw out; reject, discard, throw away; put out; **~ся**, throw oneself out, leap out; ~ся с парашю́том, bale out.

выбыва́ть, -а́ю *imp.*, **вы́быть**, -буду *perf.* из+*gen.* leave, quit; be out of. **вы́бытие**, -я, departure, removal, absence.

выва́ливать, -аю *imp.*, **вы́валить**, -лю *perf.* throw out; pour out; **~ся**, fall out; pour out.

выва́ривать, -аю *imp.*, **вы́варить**, -рю *perf.* boil out; extract by boiling; boil thoroughly. **вы́варка**, -и, decoction, extraction; residue, concentrate.

вы́везти -зу; -ез *perf.* (*imp.* вывози́ть) take out, remove; bring out; export; save, rescue.

вы́верить, -рю *perf.* (*imp.* выверя́ть) verify; regulate.

вы́вернуть, -ну *perf.*, **вывёртывать**, -аю *imp.* turn inside out; unscrew; pull out; twist, wrench; dislocate; **~ся**, come unscrewed; slip out; get out, extricate oneself, wriggle out; be dislocated; emerge. **вы́верт**, -а, caper; mannerism; affectation.

выверя́ть, -я́ю *imp.* of **вы́верить**.

вы́весить, -ешу *perf.* (*imp.* выве́шивать) weigh; hang out; put up, post up. **вы́веска**, -и, sign, signboard; screen, pretext; mug.

вы́вести, -еду -ел *perf.* (*imp.* выводи́ть) lead out, bring out; drive out; turn out, force out; remove; exterminate; deduce, conclude; hatch; grow, breed, raise; put up, erect; depict, portray; write, draw, trace out; **~сь**, go out of use; lapse; disappear; become extinct; come out; hatch out.

выве́тривание, -я, airing; weathering. **выве́тривать**, -аю *imp.*, **вы́ветрить**, -рю *perf.* air; drive out, remove, efface; weather, erode; **~ся**, weather; disappear, be driven out, be effaced.

выве́шивать, -аю *imp.* of **вы́весить**.

вы́вих, -а, dislocation; sprain; kink, oddity, quirk. **вы́вихнуть**, -ну *perf.* dislocate, put out; sprain.

вы́вод, -а, deduction; conclusion; withdrawal, removal. **выводи́ть**(ся, -ожу́(сь, -о́дишь(ся *imp.* of **вы́вести**(сь. **вы́водка**, -и, removal; exercising. **вы́водок**, -дка, brood; hatch, litter.

вы́вожу: see **выводи́ть**, **вывози́ть**.

вы́воз, -а, export; removal. **вывози́ть**, -ожу́, -о́зишь *imp.* of **вы́везти**. **вы́возка**, -и, carting out. **вывозно́й**, export.

вы́гарки, -ов *pl.* slag, dross.

вы́гиб, -а, curve, curvature. **выгиба́ть**(ся, -а́ю(сь *imp.* of **вы́гнуть**(ся.

вы́|гладить, -ажу *perf.*

вы́глядеть, -яжу *imp.* look look like. **выгля́дывать**, -аю *imp.*, **вы́глянуть**, -ну *perf.* look out; peep out, emerge, become visible.

вы́гнать, -гоню *perf.* (*imp.* выгоня́ть) drive out; expel; distil; force.

вы́гнутый, curved, convex. **вы́гнуть**, -ну *perf.* (*imp.* выгиба́ть) bend, arch; ~ся, arch up.

выгова́ривать, -аю *imp.* **вы́говорить**, -рю *perf.* pronounce, utter, speak; reserve; stipulate for; +*dat.* reprimand; ~ся, speak out, have one's say out. **вы́говор**, -а, accent, pronunciation; reprimand, rebuke.

вы́года, -ы advantage, benefit; profit, gain; interest. **вы́годный**, advantageous, beneficial; profitable; ~о, it pays.

вы́гон, -а pasture, common. **вы́гонка**, -и, distillation. **выгоня́ть**, -я́ю *imp.* of вы́гнать.

выгора́живать, -аю *imp.* of вы́городить.

выгора́ть, -а́ет *imp.*, **вы́гореть**, -рит *perf.* burn down; burn out; fade, bleach; turn out well, come off.

вы́городить, -ожу *perf.* (*imp.* выгора́живать) fence off; shield screen.

вы́|гравировать, -рую *perf.*

выгружа́ть, -а́ю *imp.*, **вы́грузить**, -ужу *perf.* unload; discharge; disembark; ~ся, unload; disembark; detrain, debus. **вы́грузка**, -и unloading; disembarkation.

выдава́ть, -даю́, -даёшь *imp.*, **вы́дать**, -ам, -ашь -аст, -адим *perf.* give out, issue, produce; give away, betray; deliver up, extradite; +за +*acc.* pass off as give out to be; ~ за́муж, give in marriage; ~ся, protrude, project; jut out; stand out; present itself, happen to be. **вы́дача**, -и, issuing; issue; payment; extradition. **выдаю́щийся**, prominent, salient; eminent, outstanding.

выдвига́ть, -а́ю *imp.*, **вы́двинуть**, -ну *perf.* move out; pull out, open; put forward, advance; promote; nominate, propose; ~ся, move forward, move out, come out; rise, get on.

выдвиже́нец, -нца -же́нка, -и, worker promoted from rank and file. **выдвиже́ние**, -я, nomination; promotion, advancement.

выделе́ние, -я, secretion; excretion; isolation; apportionment. **вы́делить**, -лю *perf.*, **выделя́ть**, -я́ю *imp.* pick out, single out; detach, detail; assign, earmark; allot; secrete; excrete; isolate; ~ курси́вом italicize; ~ся, take one's share; ooze out exude; stand out, be noted (+*instr.* for).

вы́держанный, consistent; self-possessed; firm; matured, seasoned. **вы́держать** -жу *perf.* **выде́рживать**, -аю *imp.* bear hold; stand, stand up to, endure; contain oneself; pass; keep; lay up; mature season; maintain, sustain. **вы́держка**[1], -и, endurance; self-possession; exposure.

вы́держка[2], -и, extract, excerpt, quotation.

вы́дох, -а, expiration. **вы́дохнуть**, -ну *perf.* (*imp.* выдыха́ть) breathe out; ~ся, have lost fragrance or smell; be played out; be flat; be past one's best.

вы́дра, -ы, otter.

вы́|драть, -деру *perf.* **вы́|дрессировать**, -рую *perf.* **вы́|дубить**, -блю *perf.*

выдува́льщик, -а, glass-blower. **выдува́ть**, -а́ю *imp.* of вы́дуть. **вы́дувка**, -и glass-blowing. **выдувно́й**, blown.

вы́думанный, made-up, invented, fabricated. **вы́думать**, -аю *perf.*, **выду́мывать**, -аю *imp.* invent; make up fabricate. **вы́думка**, -и, invention; idea, gadget, device; inventiveness; fabrication, fiction.

вы́|дуть, -ую *perf.* (*imp.* also выдува́ть) blow; blow out; blow up.

выдыха́ние, -я, expiration. **выдыха́ть(ся**, -а́ю(сь *imp.* of вы́дохнуть(ся.

вы́езд, -а, departure; exit; turn-out, equipage; going out. **выездно́й**, going-out; travelling; visiting; exit; away; ~ой матч, away match; ~ая се́ссия суда́, assizes. **выезжа́ть**, -а́ю *imp.* of вы́ехать.

вы́емка, -и taking out; seizure; collection; excavation; hollow, groove; fluting, flute; cutting, cut.

вы́ехать, -еду *perf.* (*imp.* выезжа́ть) go out depart; drive out, ride out; move, remove, leave; +на+*prep.* make use of, exploit take advantage of.

вы́жать, -жму *perf.* (*imp.* выжима́ть) squeeze out; wring out, press out; lift, press-lift.

вы́ждать, -ду *perf.* (*imp.* выжида́ть) wait for, wait out.

вы́жечь, -жгу *perf.* (*imp.* выжига́ть) burn low, burn out; burn. scorch; cauterize. **вы́жженн|ый**, **~ая земля́**, scorched earth.

выжива́|ние, -я, survival. **выжива́ть**, -а́ю *imp.* of вы́жить.

выжига́|ние, -я, burning out, scorching; cauterization; **~ по де́реву** poker-work. **выжига́ть**, -а́ю *imp.* of вы́жечь.

выжида́|ние, -я, waiting, temporizing. **выжида́тельный**, waiting; expectant; temporizing. **выжида́ть**, -а́ю *imp.* of выжда́ть.

вы́жим, -а, press-up. **выжима́|ние**, -я, squeezing; wringing (out); (weight-)lifting. **выжима́ть**, -а́ю *imp.* of вы́жать. **вы́жимка**, -и, squeezing, pressing, wringing; abstract, brief summary.

вы́жить, -иву *perf.* (*imp.* выжива́ть) survive; live through; stay alive, hold out, stick it out; drive out, hound out; get rid of; **~ из ума́**, become senile.

вы́звать, -зову *perf.* (*imp.* вызыва́ть) call, call out; send for; challenge; call forth, provoke; cause; stimulate; rouse; **~ по телефо́ну**, ring up; **~ся**, volunteer, offer.

выздора́вливать, -аю *imp.*, **вы́здороветь**, -ею *perf.* recover get better. **выздоровле́ние**, -я, recovery; convalescence.

вы́зов, -а, call; summons; challenge.

вы́|золотить, -лочу *perf.* **вы́золоченный**, gilt.

вызу́бривать, -аю *imp.*, **вы́|зубрить**, -рю *perf.* learn by heart, cram.

вызыва́ть(ся, -а́ю(сь *imp.* of вы́звать(-ся. **вызыва́ющий**, defiant; challenging, provocative.

вы́играть, -аю *perf.*, **выи́грывать**, -аю *imp.* win; gain. **вы́игрыш**, -а, win; winning; winnings; gain; prize. **вы́и-**

игрышный, winning; premium; lottery; advantageous; effective.

вы́йти, -йду, -шел, -шла *perf.* (*imp.* выходи́ть) go out; come out; get out; appear; turn out; come of; be used up; have expired; **~ в свет**, appear; **~ в фина́л**, reach the final; **~ за́муж (за+***acc.*) marry; **~ из грани́ц**, **~ из преде́лов**, exceed the bounds; **~ из себя́**, lose one's temper, be beside oneself; **~ на вы́зовы**, take a call; **~ на сце́ну**, come on to the stage.

вы́казать, -ажу *perf.*, **выка́зывать**, -аю *imp.* show; display.

выка́лывать, -аю *imp.* of вы́колоть.

выка́пчивать, -аю *imp.* of вы́коптить.

выка́пывать, -аю *imp.* of вы́копать.

вы́карабкаться, -аюсь *perf.*, **выкара́бкиваться**, -аюсь *imp.* scramble out; get out.

вы́|катать, -аю *perf.*

вы́качать, -аю *perf.*, **выка́чивать**, -аю *imp.* pump out.

выки́дывать, -аю *imp.*, **вы́кинуть**, -ну *perf.* throw out, reject; put out; miscarry, abort; **~ флаг**, hoist a flag. **вы́кидыш**, -а, miscarriage, abortion.

вы́кладка, -и, laying out; lay-out; facing; kit; computation, calculation. **выкла́дывать**, -аю *imp.* of вы́ложить.

выкли́ка́ть, -а́ю *imp.*, **вы́кликнуть**, -ну *perf.* call out.

выключа́тель, -я *m.* switch. **выключа́ть**, -а́ю *imp.*, **вы́ключить**, -чу *perf.* turn off, switch off; remove, exclude; justify.

вы́|клянчить, -чу *perf.*

выкола́чивать, -аю *imp.*, **вы́колотить**, -лочу *perf.* knock out, beat out; beat; extort, wring out.

вы́колоть, -лю *perf.* (*imp.* выка́лывать) put out; gouge out; tattoo.

вы́|копать, -аю *perf.* (*imp.* also выка́пывать) dig out, dig up; exhume; unearth; **~ся**, dig oneself out.

вы́коптить, -пчу *perf.* (*imp.* выка́пчивать) smoke.

выко́рчевать, -чую *perf.*, **выкорчёвывать**, -аю *imp.* uproot, root out; extirpate, eradicate.

выкра́ивать, -аю *imp.* of вы́кроить.

вы́|красить, -ашу *perf.*, выкра́шивать, -аю *imp.* paint; dye.

вы́крик -а, cry, shout; yell. **выкри́кивать**, -аю *imp.*, **вы́крикнуть**, -ну *perf.* cry out; yell.

вы́кроить, -ою *perf.* (*imp.* выкра́ивать) cut out; (manage to) find. **вы́кройка**, -и, pattern.

вы́крутить, -учу *perf.*, выкру́чивать, -аю *imp.* unscrew; twist; ~ся, extricate oneself, get oneself out.

вы́куп, -а, ransom; redemption.

вы́|купать[1](ся), -аю(сь *perf.*

выкупа́ть[2], -а́ю *imp.*, **вы́купить**, -плю *perf.* ransom, redeem. **вы́купить**, ransom; redemption.

выку́ривать, -аю *imp.*, **вы́курить**, -рю *perf.* smoke; smoke out; distil.

вала́вливать, -аю *imp.* of **вы́ловить**.

вы́лазка, -и, sally, sortie; raid; ramble, excursion outing.

вы́|лакать, -аю *perf.* **выла́мывать**, -аю *imp.* of **вы́ломать**. **выла́щивать**, -аю *imp.* of **вы́лощить**.

вылеза́ть, -а́ю *imp.*, **вы́лезти**, **вы́лезть**, -зу; -лез *perf.* crawl out; climb out; fall out, come out.

вы́|лепить, -плю *perf.*

вы́лет, -а, flight; take-off, departure; emission, escape; overhang. **выле-та́ть**, -а́ю *imp.*, **вы́лететь**, -ечу *perf.* fly out, off, away; take off; rush out, dash out; escape.

выле́чивать, -аю *imp.*, **вы́лечить**, -чу *perf.* cure, heal; ~ся, recover, be cured; ~ся от+*gen.* get over.

вылива́ть(ся, -а́ю(сь *imp.* of **вы́лить(ся**. **вы́|линять**, -яет *perf.*

вы́лить, -лью *perf.* (*imp.* вылива́ть) pour out; empty (out); cast, found; mould; ~ся, run out, flow (out); be expressed, express itself.

вы́ловить, -влю *perf.* (*imp.* выла́вливать) fish out, catch.

вы́ложить, -жу *perf.* (*imp.* выкла́дывать) lay out, spread out; cover, lay; face; tell, reveal.

вы́лом, -а, breaking down, in, out, open; breach, break, gap. **вы́ломать**, -аю *perf.*, **вы́ломить**, -млю *perf.* (*imp.* выла́мывать) break down, break out, break open. **вы́ломка**, -и, breaking off.

вы́лощенный, glossy; polished, smooth. **вы́лощить**, -щу *perf.* (*imp.* выла́щивать) polish.

вы́|лудить, -ужу *perf.* **вы́лью**, etc.: see **вы́лить**.

вы́|мазать, -мажу *perf.*, **выма́зывать**, -аю *imp.* smear, daub, dirty; ~ся, get dirty, make oneself dirty.

выма́ливать, -аю *imp.* of **вы́молить**.

выма́нивать, -аю *imp.*, **вы́манить**, -ню *perf.* entice, lure; +у+*gen.* swindle, cheat, out of; wheedle, coax, out of.

вы́|марать, -аю *perf.* **вы́мени**, etc.: see **вы́мя**.

вы́мереть, -мрет; -мер *perf.* (*imp.* выми-ра́ть) die out; become extinct; be, become, deserted. **вы́мерший**, extinct.

вымина́ть, -а́ю *imp.* of **вы́мять**. **выми-ра́ть**, -а́ю *imp.* of **вы́мереть**. **вы́мну**, etc.: see **вы́мять**.

вымога́тель, -я *m.*, -ница, -ы, blackmailer, extortioner. **вымога́тельство**, -а, blackmail, extortion. **вымога́ть**, -а́ю *imp.* extort, wring out.

вымока́ть, -а́ю *imp.*, **вы́мокнуть**, -ну; -ок *perf.* be soaked, drenched, wet through; soak, steep; rot.

вымола́чивать, -аю *imp.* of **вы́моло-тить**.

вы́молвить, -влю *perf.* say, utter.

вы́молить, -лю *perf.* (*imp.* выма́ливать) beg; obtain by prayer(s).

вы́молот, -а, threshing; grain. **вы́моло-тить**, -очу *perf.* (*imp.* вымола́чивать) thresh. **вы́молотки**, -ток or -тков *pl.* chaff.

вы́|мостить, -ощу *perf.* **вы́мою** etc.: see **вы́мыть**.

вы́мпел, -а, pennant.

вы́мрет: see **вы́мереть**. **вымыва́ть(ся** *imp.* of **вы́мыть(ся**.

вы́мысел, -сла, invention, fabrication; fantasy, flight of fancy. **вы́мыслить**, -лю *perf.* (*imp.* вымышля́ть) think up, make up, invent; imagine.

вы́|мыть, -мою *perf.* (*imp.* also вымы-ва́ть) wash; wash out, off; wash away; ~ся, wash, wash oneself.

вы́мышленный, fictitious, imaginary. **вымышля́ть**, -я́ю *imp.* of **вы́мыслить**.

вы́мя -мени *n.* udder.

вы́мять, -мну perf. (imp. вымина́ть) knead, work; trample down.

вы́нести, -су; -нес perf. (imp. выноси́ть) carry out, take out; take away; carry away; bear, stand, endure; pass; ~ вопро́с, submit a question; ~ на бе́рег, wash up; **~сь**, fly out, rush out.

вынима́ть(ся, -а́ю(сь imp. of вы́нуть(-ся.

вы́нос, -а, carrying out; removal; drift; trace. **выноси́ть**, -ошу́, -о́сишь imp. of вы́нести; не ~, be unable to bear, to stand; **~ся** imp. of вы́нестись. **вы́носка**, -и, taking out, carrying out; removal; marginal note, footnote. **выно́сливость**, -и, endurance, staying-power; hardiness.

вы́нудить, -ужу perf., **вынужда́ть**, -а́ю imp. force, compel, oblige; extort. **вы́нужденный**, forced, compulsory.

вы́нуть, -ну perf. (imp. вынима́ть) take out; pull out; extract; draw out; **~ся**, come out, pull out.

вы́пад, -а, attack; lunge, thrust. **выпада́ть**, -а́ю imp. of вы́пасть. **выпаде́ние**, -я, falling out; fall-out; precipitation; prolapsus.

вы́палывать, -аю imp. of вы́полоть.

выпа́ривать, -аю imp., **вы́парить**, -рю, evaporate.

вы́парывать, -аю imp. of вы́пороть².

вы́пасть, -аду; -ал perf. (imp. выпада́ть) fall out; fall; occur, turn out; lunge, thrust.

выпека́ть, -а́ю imp., **вы́печь**, -еку; -ек perf. bake. **вы́печка**, -и, baking, batch.

выпива́ть, -а́ю imp. of вы́пить; enjoy a drink. **вы́пивка**, -и, drinking; drinks.

выпи́ливать, -аю imp., **вы́пилить**, -лю perf. saw, cut out, make with fretsaw.

вы́писать, -ишу perf., **выпи́сывать**, -аю imp. copy out, excerpt; trace out; write out; order; subscribe to; send for, write for; strike off the list; ~ из больни́цы, discharge from hospital; **~ся**, leave, be discharged. **вы́писка**, -и, copying out, making extracts; writing out; extract, excerpt, cutting; ordering, subscription; discharge. **вы́пись**, -и, extract, copy.

вы́пить, -пью perf. (imp. also выпива́ть) drink; drink up, drink off.

вы́плавить, -влю perf., **выплавля́ть**, -я́ю imp. smelt. **вы́плавка**, -и, smelting; smelted metal.

вы́плата, -ы, payment. **вы́платить**, -ачу perf., **выпла́чивать**, -аю imp. pay, pay out; pay off.

выплёвывать, -аю imp. of вы́плюнуть.

вы́плести, -ету perf., **выплета́ть**, -а́ю imp. undo, untie; unplait; weave.

выплыва́ть, -а́ю imp., **вы́плыть**, -ыву perf. swim out, sail out; come to the surface, come up; emerge; appear, crop up.

вы́плюнуть, -ну perf. (imp. выплёвывать) spit out.

выполза́ть, -а́ю imp., **вы́ползти**, -зу; -олз perf. crawl out, creep out.

выполне́ние, -я, execution, carrying out; fulfilment. **выполни́мый**, practicable, feasible. **вы́полнить**, -ню perf., **выполня́ть**, -я́ю imp. execute, carry out; fulfil; discharge.

вы́полоскать, -ощу perf.

вы́полоть, -лю perf. (imp. also выпа́лывать) weed out; weed.

вы́пороть¹, -рю perf.

вы́пороть², -рю perf. (imp. выпа́рывать) rip out, rip up.

вы́потрошить, -шу perf.

вы́править, -влю perf., **выправля́ть**, -я́ю imp. straighten (out); correct; improve; get, obtain; **~ся**, become straight; improve; bearing; correction. **вы́правка**, -и,

выпра́шивать, -аю imp. of вы́просить; solicit.

выпрова́живать, -аю imp., **вы́проводить**, -ожу perf. send packing; show the door.

вы́просить, -ошу perf. (imp. выпра́шивать) (ask for and) get.

выпряга́ть, -а́ю imp. of вы́прячь.

выпрями́тель, -я m. rectifier. **вы́прямить**, -млю perf., **выпрямля́ть**, -я́ю imp. straighten (out); rectify; **~ся**, become straight; straighten up, draw oneself up.

вы́прячь, -ягу; -яг perf. (imp. выпряга́ть) unharness.

выпу́тивать, -аю imp., **вы́пугнуть**, -ну perf. scare off; start.

вы́пукло *adv.* in relief. **вы́пукло-, convexo-. вы́пуклость, -и,** protuberance; prominence, bulge; convexity; relief; clarity, distinctness. **вы́пуклый,** protuberant; prominent; bulging, convex; in relief; clear, distinct.

вы́пуск, -а, output; issue; discharge; part, number, instalment; final-year students, pupils; cut, omission; edging, piping. **выпуска́ть, -а́ю** *imp.,* **вы́пустить, -ущу** *perf.* let out, release; put out, issue; turn out, produce; cut, cut out, omit; let out, let down; issue; see through the press. **выпускни́к, -а́,** final-year student, pupil. **вы́пускно́й,** output; discharge; exhaust; ~**ой экза́мен,** finals, final examination; ~**а́я цена́,** market-price; ~**о́й** *sb.* final-year student.

вы́путать, -аю *perf.,* **выпу́тывать, -аю** *imp.* disentangle; ~**ся,** disentangle oneself, extricate oneself; ~**ся из беды́,** get out of a scrape.

вы́пушка, -и, edging, braid, piping.

вы́пытать, -аю *perf.,* **выпы́тывать, -аю** *imp.* elicit, worm out.

выпь, -и, bittern.

вы́пью, etc.: see **вы́пить.**

вы́пятить(ся, -ячу(сь *perf.,* **выпя́чивать(ся, -аю(сь** *imp.* stick out, protrude.

выраба́тывать, -аю *imp.,* **вы́работать, -аю** *perf.* work out; work up; draw up; elaborate; manufacture; produce, make; earn. **вы́работка, -и,** manufacture; production, making; working; working out, drawing up; output, yield; make.

выра́внивать(ся, -аю(сь *imp.* of **вы́ровнять(ся.**

выража́ть, -а́ю *imp.,* **вы́разить, -ажу** *perf.* express; convey; voice; ~**ся,** express oneself; manifest itself; amount, come (в+*prep.* to). **выраже́ние, -я,** expression. **выраженный,** pronounced, marked. **вырази́тель, -я** *m.* spokesman, exponent; voice. **вырази́тельный,** expressive; significant.

выраста́ть, -а́ю *imp.,* **вы́расти, -ту; -рос** *perf.* grow, grow up; develop; increase; appear, rise up; ~ **из**+*gen.* grow out of. **вы́растить, -ащу** *perf.,*

выра́щивать, -аю *imp.* bring up; rear, breed; grow, cultivate.

вы́рвать[1], -ву *perf.* (*imp.* **вырыва́ть**) pull out, tear out; extort, wring out; ~**ся,** tear oneself away; break out, break loose, break free; get away; come loose, come out; break, burst, shoot up, shoot (out).

вы́|рвать[2], -ву *perf.*

вы́рез, -а, cut; notch; décolletage. **вы́резать, -ежу** *perf.,* **выреза́ть, -а́ю** *imp.,* **вырезывать, -аю** *imp.* cut out; excise; cut, carve; engrave; slaughter, butcher. **вы́резка, -и,** cutting-out, excision; carving; engraving; cutting; fillet. **вырезно́й,** cut; carved; lownecked, décolleté. **вы́резывание, -я,** cutting out; excision; carving; engraving.

вырисова́ть, -су́ю *perf.,* **вырисо́вывать, -аю** *imp.* draw carefully, draw in detail; ~**ся,** appear; stand out.

вы́ровнять, -яю *perf.* (*imp.* **выра́внивать**) smooth level; straighten (out); draw up; ~**ся,** become level, become even; form up; equalize; catch up, draw level; improve.

вырожда́ться, -ится *perf.,* **вырожда́ться, -а́ется** *imp.* degenerate. **вы́родок, -дка** degenerate; black sheep. **вырожде́нец, -нца** degenerate. **вырожде́ние, -я,** degeneration.

вы́ронить, -ню *perf.* drop.

вы́рос, etc.: see **вы́расти. вы́рост, -а,** growth, excrescence; offshoot. **вы́ростковый,** calf. **вы́росток, -тка,** yearling; calf.

вы́рою etc.: see **вы́рыть.**

выруба́ть, -а́ю *imp.,* **вы́рубить, -блю** *perf.* cut down, fell; hew out; cut (out); carve (out); cut one's way out. **вы́рубка, -и** cutting down, felling; hewing out; clearing.

вы́ругать(ся, -аю(сь *perf.*

выру́ливать, -аю *imp.,* **вы́|рулить, -лю** *perf.* taxi.

выруча́ть, -а́ю *imp.,* **вы́ручить, -чу** *perf.* rescue; help out; gain; make. **вы́ручка, -и,** rescue, assistance; gain; proceeds, receipts; earnings.

вырыва́ние[1], -я, pulling out, extraction; uprooting.

вырыва́ние². -я, digging (up). **вырыва́ть**², -а́ю *imp.*, **вы́рыть**, -ро́ю *perf.* dig up, dig out, unearth.

вырыва́ть¹(**ся** *imp. of* **вы́рвать**(**ся**.

выса́дить, -ажу *perf.*, **выса́живать**, -аю *imp.* set down; help down; put off; detrain, debus; put ashore, land; plant out, transplant; smash; break in; ~ся, alight, get off; land; disembark; detrain, debus. **вы́садка**, -и, disembarkation; landing; transplanting, planting out.

выса́сывать, -аю *imp. of* **вы́сосать**.

высве́рливать, -аю *imp.*, **вы́сверлить**, -лю *perf.* drill, bore.

вы́свободить, -божу *perf.*, **высвобожда́ть**, -а́ю *imp.* free; disengage, disentangle; release; help to escape.

вы́секать, -а́ю *imp. of* **вы́сечь**².
вы́секу etc.: see **вы́сечь**.

выселе́нец, -нца, evacuee. **выселе́ние**, -я, eviction. **вы́селить**, -лю *perf.*, **выселя́ть**, -я́ю *imp.* evict; evacuate, move; ~ся, move, remove. **вы́селок**, -лка, settlement.

вы́сечка, -и, carving; hewing. **вы́сечь**¹, -еку *perf.* **вы́сечь**² -еку -сек (*imp.* высека́ть) cut, cut out; carve; hew.

вы́сидеть, -ижу *perf.*, **выси́живать**, -аю *imp.* sit out; stay; hatch, hatch out.

вы́ситься, -ится *imp.* rise, tower.

вы́сказать, -ажу *perf.*, **выска́зывать**, -аю *imp.* express; state; ~ся, speak out; speak one's mind, have one's say; speak. **выска́зывание**, -я, utterance; pronouncement, opinion.

выска́кивать, -аю *imp. of* **вы́скочить**. **выска́льзывать**, -аю *imp. of* **вы́скользнуть**.

вы́скоблить, -лю *perf.* scrape out; erase; remove.

вы́скользнуть, -ну *perf.* (*imp.* выска́льзывать) slip out.

вы́скочить, -чу *perf.* (*imp.* выска́кивать) jump out; leap out, spring out, rush out; come up; drop out, fall out; ~ с + *instr.* come out with. **вы́скочка**, -и, upstart, parvenu.

вы́сланный *sb.* exile, deportee. **вы́слать** вы́шлю *perf.* (*imp.* высыла́ть) send, send out; dispatch; exile; deport.

вы́следить, -ежу *perf.*, **высле́живать**, -аю *imp.* trace, track; stalk; shadow.

вы́слуга, -и; ~ лет, long service. **вы́слу́живать**, -аю *imp.*, **вы́служить**, -жу *perf.* qualify for, earn; serve (out); ~ся, gain promotion, be promoted; curry favour, get in (with).

вы́слушать, -аю *perf.*, **выслу́шивать**, -аю *imp.* hear out; sound; listen to. **выслу́шивание**, -я, auscultation.

вы́|смолить, -лю *perf.* **вы́|сморкать**(-ся, -аю(сь *perf.* of **вы́сунуть**(ся.

высо́кий, -о́к, -á, -о́ко́, high; tall; lofty; elevated, sublime.

высоко- in *comb.* high-, highly. **высокоблагоро́дие**, -я, (your) Honour, Worship. ~во́льтный, high-tension. ~го́рный, Alpine. mountain. ~ка́чественный, high-quality. ~ме́рие, -я, haughtiness, arrogance. ~ме́рный, haughty, arrogant. ~па́рный, high-flown, stilted; bombastic, turgid. ~про́бный, sterling; standard; of high quality. ~со́ртный, high-grade. ~часто́тный, high-frequency.

вы́сосать, -осу *perf.* (*imp.* выса́сывать) suck out.

высота́, -ы́; *pl.* -ы, height, altitude; pitch; eminence; high level; high quality. **высо́тник**, -а, high-building worker; high-altitude flier. **высо́тн|ый**, high; high-rise; tall, multi-storey, high-rise; ~ое зда́ние, tower block. **высотоме́р**, -а, altimeter, height-finder.

вы́|сохнуть, -ну; -ох *perf.* (*imp.* also высыха́ть) dry, dry out; dry up; wither, fade; waste away, fade away. **вы́сохший**, dried up; shrivelled; wizened.

вы́ставить, -влю *perf.*, **выставля́ть**, -я́ю *imp.* bring out, bring forward; display, exhibit; post; put forward; adduce; put down, set down; take out, remove; send out, turn out, throw out; + *instr.* represent as, make out to be; ~ свою́ кандидату́ру, stand for election; ~ся, lean out, thrust oneself forward; show off. **вы́ставка**, -и, exhibition, show; display; showcase, (shop-)window. **выставно́й**, removable.

вы́|стегать, -аю *perf.* **вы́стелю**, etc.: see **вы́слать**. **выстила́ть**, -а́ю *imp.* of **вы́стлать**. **вы́|стирать**, -аю *perf.*

вы́стлать, -телю *perf.* (*imp.* выстила́ть) cover; line; pave.

вы́страдать, -аю *perf.* suffer, go through; gain through suffering.

выстра́ивать(ся, -аю(сь *imp.* of **вы́строить(ся**. **выстра́чивать**, -аю *imp.* of **вы́строчить**.

вы́стрел, -а, shot; report. **вы́стрелить**, -лю *perf.* shoot, fire.

вы́|строгать, -аю *perf.*

вы́строить, -ою *perf.* (*imp.* выстра́ивать) build; draw up, order, arrange; form up; **~ся** form up.

вы́строчить, -чу *perf.* (*imp.* выстра́чивать) hemstitch; stitch.

вы́стукать, -аю *perf.* **выстру́кивать**, -аю *imp.* tap, percuss; tap out. **выстру́кивание**, -я, percussion; tapping.

вы́ступ, -а, protuberance, projection, ledge; bulge, salient; lug. **выступа́ть**, -а́ю *imp.* **вы́ступить**, -плю *perf.* come forward, go forward; come out; appear; perform; speak; **~ из** + *gen.* go beyond exceed; **~ из берего́в**, overflow its banks; **~ с докла́дом**, give a talk; **~ с ре́чью**, make a speech. **выступле́ние**, -я appearance, performance; speech; setting out.

вы́сунуть, -ну *perf.* (*imp.* высо́вывать) put out, thrust out; **~ся**, show oneself, thrust oneself forward; **~ся в окно́**, lean out of the window.

вы́|сушить(ся, -шу(сь *perf.*

вы́сш|ий, highest; supreme; high; higher; **~ая то́чка**, climax.

высыла́ть, -а́ю *imp.* of **вы́слать**. **вы́сылка**, -и, sending, dispatching; expulsion, exile.

высыпа́ть, -плю *perf.*, **высыпа́ть**, -а́ю *imp.* pour out; empty (out); spill; **~ся**, pour out, spill.

высыха́ть, -а́ю *imp.* of **вы́сохнуть**.

высь, -и, height; summit.

выта́лкивать, -аю *imp.* of **вы́толкать**, **вы́толкнуть**. **вы́|тарашить**, -шу *perf.* **выта́скивать**, -аю *imp.* of **вы́тащить**.

вы́|тачать, -аю *perf.* **выта́чивать**, -аю *imp.* of **вы́точить**.

выта́чка, -и, tuck; dart.

вы́|тащить, -щу *perf.* (*imp.* also выта́скивать) drag out; pull out, extract; steal, pinch.

вы́|твердить -ржу *perf.*

вытека́ть, -а́ю *imp.* (*perf.* вы́течь); **~ из** + *gen.* flow from, out of; result from, follow from.

вы́|теребить, -блю *perf.*

вы́тереть, -тру; -тру *perf.* (*imp.* вытира́ть) wipe, wipe up; dry, rub dry; wear out.

вы́терпеть, -плю *perf.* bear, endure.

вы́тертый, threadbare.

вытесне́ние, -я, ousting; supplanting; displacement. **вы́теснить**, -ню *perf.*, **вытесня́ть**, -я́ю *imp.* crowd out; force out; oust; supplant; displace.

вы́течь, -чет; -чет *perf.* (*imp.* вытека́ть) flow out, run out.

вытира́ть, -а́ю *imp.* of **вы́тереть**.

вы́тиснить, -ню, *perf.*, **вытисня́ть**, -я́ю *imp.* stamp, imprint, impress.

вы́толкать, -аю *perf.*, **вы́толкнуть**, -ну *perf.* (*imp.* выта́лкивать) throw out, sling out; push out, force out.

вы́точенный, turned; сло́вно **~**, chiselled; perfectly formed. **вы́|точить**, -чу *perf.* (*imp.*, also выта́чивать) turn; sharpen; gnaw through.

вы́|травить, -влю *perf.*, **вытра́вливать**, -аю, *perf.*, **вытравля́ть**, -я́ю *imp.* exterminate, destroy; poison; remove, get out; etch; trample down, damage.

вы́требовать, -бую *perf.* summon, send for; get on demand.

вытрезви́тель, -я *m.* sobering-up treatment, station. **вы́трезвить(ся**, -влю(сь *perf.*, **вытрезвля́ть(ся**, -я́ю(сь *imp.* sober up.

вы́тру etc.: see **вы́тереть**.

вытряса́ть, -а́ю *imp.*, **вы́|трясти**, -су; -яс *perf.* shake out.

вытря́хивать, -аю *imp.*, **вы́тряхнуть**, -ну *perf.* shake out.

выть, во́ю *imp.* howl; wail. **вытьё**, -я́, howling; wailing.

вытя́гивать, -аю *imp.*, **вы́тянуть**, -ну *perf.* stretch, stretch out; extend; draw out, extract; endure, stand, stick;

weigh; **~ся**, stretch, stretch out, stretch oneself; grow, shoot up; draw oneself up. **вы́тяжка**, -и, drawing out, extraction; extract; stretching extension. **вытяжно́й**, drawing; exhaust; ventilating; **~ шкаф**, fume chamber.

вы́|утюжить, -жу perf.

вы́учивать, -аю imp.; **~ся**, **вы́|учить**, -чу perf. learn; teach; **~ся** + dat. or inf. learn. **вы́учка**, -и, teaching, training.

выха́живать, -аю imp. of выходить.

вы́хватить, -ачу perf., **выхва́тывать**, -аю imp. snatch out, up; snatch away; pull out, draw; take out; take up.

вы́хлоп, -а, exhaust.

выхло́патывать, -аю imp. of вы́хлопотать.

выхлопно́й, exhaust, discharge.

вы́хлопотать, -очу perf. (imp. выхло́па́тывать) obtain with much trouble.

вы́ход, -а, going out; leaving, departure; way out, exit; outlet, vent; appearance; entrance; output, yield; outcrop; все хо́ды и **~ы**, all the ins and outs; **~** в отста́вку, retirement; **~** за́муж, marriage. **выхо́дец**, -дца, emigrant; immigrant. **выходи́ть**[1], -ожу -о́дишь imp. of вы́йти; +на+acc. look out on, give on, face.

выходи́ть[2], -ожу perf. (imp. выха́живать) tend, nurse; rear, bring up; grow.

выходи́ть[3], -ожу perf. (imp. выха́живать) pass through; go all over.

вы́ходка, -и, trick; escapade; prank. **выходн|о́й**, exit, outlet; going-out, outgoing; leaving, departure, discharge; publication, issue; output; **~а́я дверь**, street door; **~о́й день**, day off, free day, rest-day; **~о́й лист**, title-page; **~а́я роль**, walking-on part; **~ые све́дения**, imprint; **~о́й день**, person off duty; day off; **~а́я** sb. person off duty. **вы́ходец**, etc.: see. **выхожу́** etc.: see выходи́ть[1].

выхола́щивать, -аю imp., **выхолости́ть**, -ощу perf. castrate, geld; emasculate.

вы́хухоль, -я m., musk-rat; musquash. **вы́хухолевый**, musquash.

вы́щарапать, -аю perf., **выцара́пывать**,

-аю imp. scratch; scratch out; extract, get out.

вы́вести, -ветет perf., **выцвета́ть**, -а́ет imp. fade. **вы́цветший**, faded.

вы́цедить, -ежу perf., **выце́живать**, -аю imp. filter, rack off; strain; decant; drink off, drain.

вычека́нивать, -аю imp., **вы́|чеканить**, -ню perf. mint; strike.

вычёркивать, -аю imp., **вы́черкнуть**, -ну perf. cross out, strike out; expunge, erase.

вы́черпать, -аю perf., **вычёрпывать**, -аю imp. bale out.

вы́честь, -чту, -чел, -чла perf. (imp. вычита́ть) subtract; deduct; keep back. **вы́чет**, -а, deduction; за **~ом**, except; less, minus, allowing for.

вычисле́ние, -я, calculation. **вычисли́тель**, -я m. calculator; plotter; computer. **вычисли́тельн|ый**, calculating, computing; **~ая маши́на**, computer. **вы́числить**, -лю perf., **вычисля́ть**, -я́ю imp. calculate, compute.

вы́|чистить, -ищу perf. (imp. also вычища́ть) clean, clean up, clean out; purge.

вычита́емое sb. subtrahend. **вычита́ние**, -я, subtraction. **вычита́ть**, -а́ю imp. of вы́честь.

вычища́ть, -а́ю imp. of вы́чистить. **вычту**, etc.: see вы́честь.

вы́швырнуть, -ну perf., **вышвы́ривать**, -аю imp. throw out, hurl out; chuck out.

вы́ше, higher, taller; prep.+gen. above, beyond; over; adv. above.

вы́ше- in comb. above-, afore-. **вышеизло́женный**, foregoing. **~на́званный**, afore-named. **~озна́ченный**, aforesaid, above-mentioned. **~сказа́нный**, **~ука́занный**, aforesaid. **~упомя́нутый**, afore-mentioned.

вы́шел, etc.: see вы́йти.

вышиба́ла, -ы m. chucker-out. **вышиба́ть**, -а́ю imp., **вы́шибить**, -бу; -иб perf. knock out; chuck out.

вышива́льный, embroidery. **вышива́льщица**, -ы, embroideress, needlewoman. **вышива́ние**, -я, embroidery needlework. **вышива́ть**, -а́ю imp. of вы́шить. **вы́шивка**, -и, embroidery.

вышина́, -ы́ height.

вы́шить, -шью perf. (imp. вышива́ть) embroider. вы́шитый, embroidered.

вы́шка, -и, turret; tower; (бурова́я) ~ derrick.

вы́|школить, -лю perf. вы́шлю, etc.: see вы́слать. вы́шью, etc.: see вы́шить.

вы́щипать, -плю perf. вы́щипнуть, -ну perf., вы́щипывать, -аю imp. pluck out, pull out.

вы́явить, -влю perf., выявля́ть, -я́ю imp. reveal; bring out; make known; display; show up, expose; ~ся, appear, come to light, be revealed. выявле́ние, -я, revelation; showing up, exposure.

выясне́ние, -я, elucidation; explanation. вы́яснить, -ню perf. выясня́ть, -я́ю imp. elucidate; clear up, explain; ~ся, become clear; turn out, prove.

вью etc.: see вить.

вью́га, -и, snow-storm, blizzard.

вьюк, -а, pack; load.

вьюно́к, -нка́, bindweed, convolvulus.

вью́чн|ый, pack; ~ое живо́тное, pack animal, beast of burden; ~ая ло́шадь, pack-horse; ~ое седло́, pack-saddle.

вью́шка, -и, damper.

вью́щийся, creeping, climbing; curly frizzy.

вэ n. indecl. the letter в.

вяжу́, etc.: see вяза́ть. вя́жущий, binding, cementing; astringent.

вяз, -a, elm.

вяза́льный, knitting, crochet. вяза́ние, -я, knitting, crocheting; binding, tying. вя́занка¹, -и, knitted garment. вяза́нка², -и, bundle, truss. вя́заный, knitted, crocheted. вяза́нье, -я, knitting; crochet(-work). вяза́ть, вяжу́, вя́жешь imp. (perf. c~) tie, bind; clamp; knit, crochet; be astringent; ~ся, accord, agree; fit in, be in keeping, tally. вя́зка, -и, tying, binding; knitting, crocheting; bunch, string.

вя́зкий; -зок, -зка́, -о, viscous, glutinous, sticky; boggy; ductile, malleable; tough; astringent. вя́знуть, -ну; вяз(нул), -зла imp. (perf. за~, у~) stick, get stuck; sink.

вя́зовый, elm.

вя́зчик, -a, binder. вязь, -и, ligature; arabesque.

вял, etc.: see вя́нуть.

вя́ление, -я, dry-curing; drying. вя́леный, dried; sun-cured. вя́лить, -лю imp. (perf. про~) dry, dry-cure.

вя́лый, flabby, flaccid; limp; sluggish; inert; slack. вя́нуть, -ну; вял imp. (pref. за~, у~) fade, wither; droop, flag.

Г

г letter: see гэ.

г. abbr. год, year; гора́, mountain, mount; го́род, city, town; господи́н, Mr.

г abbr. грамм, gramme.

га abbr. некта́р, hectare.

габари́т, -a, clearance; clearance diagram; size, dimension. габари́тн|ый, clearance; overall; ~ые воро́та, loading gauge; ~ая высота́, headroom.

га́вань, -и, harbour.

га́врик, -a, (sl.) petty crook; man, fellow, mate.

га́га, -и, eider(-duck).

гага́ра, -ы, loon, diver. гага́рка, -и, razorbill.

гага́т, -a, jet.

гага́чий, eider-; ~ пух, eiderdown.

гад, -a, reptile, amphibian; vile creature; pl. vermin.

гада́лка, -и, fortune-teller. гада́ние, -я, fortune-telling, divination; guess-work. гада́тельный, fortune-telling; problematical, conjectural, hypothetical. гада́ть, -а́ю imp. (perf. по~) tell fortunes; guess, conjecture, surmise.

гáдина, -ы, reptile; vile creature; *pl.* vermin. **гáдить**, **гáжу** *imp.* (*perf.* на~) +в+*prep.*, на+*acc.*, *prep.* foul, dirty, defile. **гáдкий**, -док, -дка, -о, nasty, vile, foul, loathsome; ~ утёнок, ugly duckling. **гáдливость**, -и, aversion, disgust. **гáдливый**, of disgust, disgusted. **гáдость**, -и, filth, muck; dirty trick; *pl.* filthy expressions. **гадю́ка**, -и, adder, viper; repulsive person.

ráер, -a, buffoon, clown. **ráерничать**, -аю *imp.*, **ráерствовать**, -твую *imp.* clown, play the fool.

ráечный, nut; ~ ключ, spanner, wrench.

ráже, *comp.* of гáдкий.

газ¹, -a, gauze.

газ², -a (-y), gas; wind; дать ~, step on the gas; сбáвить ~, reduce speed; на пóлном гáзе, at top speed. **газану́ть**, -нý, -нёшь *perf.* (*imp.* газовáть) accelerate; scram. **газáция**, -и, aeration. **газго́льдер**, -a, gasholder.

газéта, -ы, newspaper, paper. **газéтный**, newspaper, news. **газéтчик**, -a, -чица, -ы, journalist; newspaper-seller. **газирóванный**, aerated. **газирóвать**, -рую *imp.* aerate. **газирóвка**, -и, aeration; aerated water. **газовáть**, -зýю *imp.* (*perf.* газану́ть) accelerate; scram. **гáзовый¹**, gas; ~ счётчик, gas-meter.

гáзовый², gauze.

газокали́льный, incandescent. **газоли́н**, -a, gasolene. **газомéр**, -a, gas-meter. **газо́н**, -a, lawn, turf, grass. **газонокоси́лка**, -ы, lawn-mower. **газообрáзный**, gaseous. **газопровóд**, -a, gas pipeline; gas-main. **газопровóдный**, gas.

ГАИ *abbr.* Госудáрственная автомоби́льная инспéкция, State Motor-vehicle Inspectorate.

гайду́к, -á, heyduck.

гáйка, -и, nut; female screw.

галáктика, -и, galaxy.

галантерéйный, haberdasher's, haberdashery. **галантерéя**, -и, haberdashery fancy goods.

галанти́н, -a, a galantine.

галдёж, -á, din, racket, row. **галдéть**, -ди́шь *imp.* make a din, make a row.

галéра, -ы, galley.

галерéя, -и, gallery. **галёрка**, -и, gallery, gods.

гáлечник, -a, shingle, pebbles.

галифé *indecl. pl.* riding-breeches; jodhpurs.

гáлка, -и, jackdaw, daw.

галл, -a, Gaul. **гáлльский**, Gaulish; Gallic.

гало́п, -a, gallop; galop. **галопи́ровать**, -рую *imp.* gallop.

гáлочий, jackdaw's, daw's. **гáлочка**, -и, tick.

галóша, -и. galosh.

галс, -a, tack.

гáлстук, -a, tie; neckerchief.

галу́шка, -и, dumpling.

гáлька, -и, pebble; pebbles, shingle.

гам, -a (-y), din, uproar.

гáмма, -ы, scale; gamut; range.

гантéль, -и, dumb-bell.

гардерóб, -a, wardrobe; cloakroom. **гардерóбная** *sb.* cloakroom. **гардерóбщик**, -a, -щица, -ы, cloakroom attendant.

гарди́на, -ы, curtain.

гаревóй, **гáревый**, cinder; ~ая доро́жка, cinder track, cinder-path.

гáркать, -аю *imp.*, **гáркнуть**, -ну *perf.* shout, bark.

гармóника, -и, accordion, concertina; pleats; гармóникой, (accordion-) pleated, in pleats. **гармони́ческий**, harmonic; harmonious; rhythmic. **гармони́чный**, harmonious. **гармо́ния**, -и, harmony; concord; accordion, concertina. **гармо́нь**, -и, гармо́шка, -и, accordion, concertina.

гарнизо́н, -a, garrison.

гарни́р, -a, garnish; trimmings; vegetables.

гарниту́р, -a, set; suite.

гарт, -a, type-metal.

гарь, -и, burning; cinders, ashes.

гаси́льник, -a, extinguisher, **гаси́тель**, -я *m.* extinguisher; damper; suppressor. **гаси́ть**, гашу́, гáсишь *imp.* (*perf.* за~, по~) put out, extinguish; slake; suppress, stifle; cancel; liquidate. **гáснуть**, -ну; гас *imp.* (*perf.* за~, по~, у~) be extinguished, go out; grow dim; sink.

гастролёр, -а, -ёрша, -и, guest-artist; touring actor, actress; casual worker. гастроли́ровать, -рую *imp.* tour, be on tour. гастро́ль, -и, tour; guest-appearance, performance; temporary engagement.

гастроно́м, -а, gastronome, gourmet; provision shop. гастрономи́ческий, gastronomic; provision. гастроно́мия, -и, gastronomy; provisions; delicatessen.

га́убица, -ы, howitzer.

гауптва́хта, -ы, guardhouse, guard-room.

гаше́ние, -я, extinguishing; slaking; cancellation, suppression. гашёный, slaked.

гаше́тка, -и, trigger; button.

гварде́ец, -е́йца, guardsman. гварде́йский, guards. гва́рдия, -и, Guards.

гво́здик, -а, tack; stiletto heel. гвозди́ка, -и pink(s), carnation(s); cloves. гвоздь, -я́; *pl.* -и, -е́й *m.* nail; tack; peg; crux; highlight, hit.

ГВФ (geveéf) *abbr.* Гражда́нский возду́шный флот СССР, U.S.S.R. Civil Air Fleet.

гг. *abbr.* го́ды, years.

где *adv.* where; somewhere; anywhere; how; ~ бы ни, wherever; ~ мне знать? how should I know? где́-либо *adv.* anywhere. где́-нибудь *adv.* somewhere; anywhere. где́-то *adv.* somewhere.

ГДР (gede-ér) *abbr.* Герма́нская Демократи́ческая Респу́блика, German Democratic Republic.

гекта́р, -а, hectare. гекто- in *comb.* hecto-.

ге́лий, -я, helium.

геморро́й, -я, haemorrhoids, piles. гемофили́я, -и, haemophilia.

ген, -а, gene.

ген- *abbr.* in *comb.* of генера́льный, general.

генера́л, -а, general; ~-губерна́тор, governor-general. генералите́т, -а, general's; high command. генера́льн|ый, general; radical, basic; ~ая репети́ция, dress rehearsal. генера́льский, general's. генера́льша, -и, general's wife.

генера́ция, -и, generation; oscillation.

гениа́льный, of genius, great; brilliant. ге́ний, -я, genius.

гео- in *comb.* geo-. гео́граф, -а, geographer. ~графи́ческий, geographical. ~гра́фия, -и, geography. гео́лог, -а, geologist. ~логи́ческий, geological. ~ло́гия, -и, geology. гео́метр, -а, geometrician. ~метри́ческий, geometric, geometrical. ~ме́трия, -и, geometry.

георги́н, -а, георги́на, -ы, dahlia.

гепа́рд, -а, cheetah.

гера́нь, -и, geranium.

герб, -а́, arms, coat of arms. гербов|ы́й, heraldic; bearing coat of arms; stamped; ~ая печа́ть, official stamp; ~ый сбор, stamp-duty.

геркуле́с, -а, Hercules; rolled oats. геркуле́совский, Herculean.

герма́нец, -нца, Teuton, German. герма́нский, Germanic, Teutonic; German.

P гермети́ческий, гермети́чный, hermetic, secret; hermetically sealed, air-tight, water-tight, pressurized.

геро́изм, -а, heroism. геро́ика, -и, heroics; heroic spirit; heroic style. геро́иня, -и, heroine. геро́ический, heroic. геро́й, -я, hero. геро́йский, heroic. геро́йство, -а, heroism.

герц, -а; *gen. pl.* герц, hertz.

ге́тман, -а, hetman.

г-жа *abbr.* госпожа́, Mrs., Miss.

гиаци́нт, -а, hyacinth; jacinth.

ги́бель, -и, death; destruction; ruin; loss; wreck; downfall. ги́бельный, disastrous, fatal.

ги́бкий; -бок, -бка́, -бко, flexible, pliant; lithe; adaptable, versatile, resourceful; tractable. ги́бкость, -и, flexibility, pliancy; suppleness.

ги́бнуть, -ну; ги́б(нул) *imp.* (*perf.* по~) perish.

гига́нт, -а, giant. гига́нтский, gigantic.

гид, -а, гиде́сса, -ы, guide.

гидро- *perf.* hydro-. гидро́лиз, -а, hydrolysis. ~о́кись, -и, hydroxide. ~ста́нция, -и, hydro-electric power-station. ~те́хник, -а, hydraulic engineer. ~те́хника, -и, hydraulic engineering. ~фо́н, -а, hydrophone.

гиéна, -ы, hyena.

гик, -а, whoop, whooping. гикать, -аю *imp.*, гикнуть, -ну *perf.* whoop.

гиль, -и, nonsense, rubbish.

гильдия, -и, guild.

гильза, -ы, case; cartridge-case; sleeve; liner; (cigarette-)wrapper.

гимн, -а, hymn.

гимназист, -а, -истка, -и, grammar--school or high-school pupil. гимназия, -и, grammar school, high school.

гипноз, -а, hypnosis. гипнотизёр, -а, hypnotist. гипнотизировать, -рую *imp.* (*perf.* за~), hypnotize. гипнотизм, -а, hypnotism. гипнотический, hypnotic.

гипотеза, -ы, hypothesis. гипотетический, гипотетичный, hypothetical.

гипс-, -а, gypsum, plaster of Paris; plaster; plaster cast. гипсовый, plaster.

гиревик, -á, weight-lifter.

гирлянда, -ы, garland.

гиря, -и, weight.

гитара, -ы, guitar.

гл. *abbr.* глава, chapter.

гл *abbr.* гектолитр, hectolitre.

глав- *abbr.* in comb. of главный, head, chief, main; главное управление, central administration, central board. главбух, -а, chief accountant. главк, -а, chief directorate; central committee, central administration. ~реж, -а, head producer, chief director.

глава, -ы; *pl.* -ы, head; chief; chapter; cupola. главарь, -я *m.* leader, ring-leader. главенство, -а, supremacy. главенствовать, -твую *imp.* be in command, lead, dominate. главнокомандующий *sb.* commander-in-chief. главный, chief, main, principal; head, senior; ~ая книга, ledger; ~ый нерв, nerve-centre; ~ым образом, chiefly, mainly, for the most part; ~ое *sb.* the chief thing, the main thing; the essentials; и самое ~ое, and above all.

глагол, -а, verb; word. глагольный, verbal.

гладильный, ironing. гладить, -ажу *imp.* (*perf.* вы~, по~), stroke; iron, press. гладкий, smooth; sleek; plain; fluent, facile. гладко *adv.* smoothly;

swimmingly; ~ выбритый, clean--shaven. гладь, -и, smooth surface; satin-stitch. глаже *comp.* of гладкий, гладко. глаженье, -я, ironing.

глаз, -а (-у), *loc.* -ý; *pl.* -á, глаз, eye; eyesight; в ~á, to one's face; за ~á + *gen.* in the absence of, behind the back of; в ~á, на ~áх, before one's eyes; с ~у на ~, without witnesses; смотреть во все ~á, be all eyes. глазастый, big-eyed; quick-sighted.

глазированный, glazed; glossy; iced, glacé. глазировать, -рую *perf.* and *imp.* glaze; candy; ice. глазировка, -и glazing; icing.

глазник, -á, oculist. глазница, -ы, eye-socket. глазной, eye; optic; ~ врач, oculist, eye-specialist.

глазунья, -и, fried eggs.

глазурь, -и, glaze; syrup; icing.

гланда, -ы, gland; tonsil.

глас, -а, voice. гласить, -сит *imp.* announce; say, run. гласность, -и, publicity. гласный, open, public; vowel vocalic; *sb.* vowel. глашатай, -я, crier; herald.

глетчер, -а, glacier.

глина, -ы, clay. глинистый, clay, clayey, argillaceous. глинозём, -а, alumina. глиняный, clay; earthenware, pottery; clayey; ~ая посуда, earthenware.

глиссер, -а, speed-boat; hydroplane.

гл. обр. *abbr.* главным образом, chiefly, mainly.

глобус, -а, globe.

глодать, -ожу -ожешь *imp.* gnaw.

глотать, -аю *imp.* swallow. глотка, -и, gullet; throat. глоток, -тка, gulp; mouthful.

глохнуть, -ну глох *imp.* (*perf.* за~, о~) become deaf; die away, subside; decay; die; grow wild, become a wilderness, run to seed.

глубже *comp.* of глубокий, глубоко. глубина, -ы; *pl.* -ы. depth; depths, deep places; heart, interior; recesses; profundity; intensity. глубинный, deep; deep-laid; deep-sea; depth; remote, out-of-the-way. глубокий, -ок, -á, -окó, deep; profound; intense; thorough, thorough-going; considerable, serious; late, advanced, extreme; ~ий вира́ж, steep turn; ~ой о́сенью, in the late autumn; ~ая ста́рость, extreme old age; ~ая таре́лка, soup-plate. глубоко́ adv. deep; deeply, profoundly. глубоково́дный, deep-water, deep-sea. глубокомы́слие, -я, profundity; perspicacity. глубоме́р, -а, depth gauge. глубоча́йший superl. of глубо́кий. глубь, -и, depth; (the) depths.

глуми́ться, -млю́сь imp. mock, jeer (над + instr. at). глумле́ние, -я, mockery; gibe, jeer. глумли́вый, mocking; gibing, jeering.

глупе́ть, -е́ю imp. (perf. по~) grow stupid. глупе́ц, -пца́, fool, blockhead. глупи́ть, -плю́ imp. (perf. с~) make a fool of oneself; do something foolish. глупова́тый, silly; rather stupid. глу́пость, -и, foolishness, stupidity; nonsense; глу́пости! (stuff and) nonsense! глу́пый, глуп, -а́, -о, foolish, stupid, silly.

глуха́рь, -я́ m. capercailzie; deaf person; coach screw. глухова́тый, rather deaf, hard of hearing. глухо́й, глух, -а́, -о, deaf; muffled, confused, indistinct; obscure, vague; voiceless; thick, dense; wild; remote, lonely, deserted; god-forsaken; sealed; blank, blind; buttoned up, done up; not open; late; ~а́я крапи́ва, dead-nettle; ~о́й, ~а́я sb. deaf man, deaf woman. глухонемо́й, deaf and dumb; sb. deaf mute. глухота́, -ы́ deafness. глу́ше, comp. of глухо́й. глуши́лка, -и, jamming, jammer. глуши́тель, -я m. silencer; damper; suppressor; jammer. глуши́ть, -шу́ imp. (perf. за~, о~) stun, stupefy; muffle; dull, deaden, damp; drown, jam; switch off; put out, extinguish; choke; stifle; suppress; soak up, swill. глушь, -и, backwoods; solitary place.

глы́ба, -ы, clod; lump; block.

гляде́ть, -яжу́ imp. (perf. по~, гля́-нуть) look, gaze; heed, take notice; look for, seek; show, appear; + за + instr. look after, see to; + на + acc. look on (to), give on (to); face; take example from, imitate; + instr. or adv.

look, look like; ~ в о́ба, be on one's guard; ~ ко́со на, take a poor view of; гляди́(те), mind (out); (того́ и) гляди́, it looks as if; I'm afraid; at any moment; гля́дя по + dat., depending on; не гля́дя на + acc., unmindful of, heedless of; ~ся, look at oneself.

гля́нец, -нца, gloss, lustre; polish.

гля́нуть, -ну perf. (imp. гляде́ть) glance.

глянцеви́тый, glossy, lustrous.

гм, int. hm!

гнать, гоню́, го́нишь; гнал, -а́, -о imp. drive; urge (on); whip up; drive hard; dash, tear; hunt, chase; persecute; turn out; distil; ~ся за + instr. pursue; strive for, strive after; keep up with.

гнев, -а, anger, rage; wrath. гне́ваться, -аюсь imp. (perf. раз~) be angry. гне́вить, -влю́ imp. (perf. про~) anger, enrage. гневли́вый, irascible. гне́вный, angry, irate.

гнедо́й, bay.

гнезди́ться, -зжу́сь imp. nest, build a nest; roost; have its seat; be lodged. гнездо́, -а́; pl. гнёзда, nest; eyrie; den, lair; brood; cluster; socket; seat; housing. гнездова́ние, -я, nesting.

гнести́, -ету́, -ете́шь imp. oppress, weigh down; press. гнёт, -а, press; weight; oppression. гнету́щий, oppressive.

гни́да, -ы nit.

гние́ние, -я, decay, putrefaction, rot. гнило́й; -ил, -а́, -о, rotten; decayed; putrid; corrupt; damp, muggy. гнить, -ию́, -иёшь; -ил, -а́, -о imp. (perf. с~) rot, decay; decompose. гное́ние, -я, suppuration. гнои́ть, -ою́ imp. (perf. с~) let rot, leave to rot; allow to decay; ~ся, suppurate, discharge matter. гной, -я (-ю), loc. -ю́, pus, matter. гно́йник, -а́, abscess; ulcer. гно́йный, purulent.

гнуса́вить, -влю imp. talk, speak, through one's nose. гнуса́вость, -и, nasal twang. гнуса́вый, гнусли́вый, nasal.

гну́сный; -сен, -сна́, -о, vile, foul.

гну́т|ый, bent; ~ая ме́бель, bentwood furniture. гнуть, гну, гнёшь imp. (perf. со~) bend, bow; drive at, aim at; ~ся, bend; be bowed; stoop; be flexible. гнутьё, -я́, bending.

гнуша́ться, -а́юсь *imp.* (*perf.* по~) disdain; +*gen.* or *instr.* shun; abhor, have an aversion to.

гобеле́н, -а, tapestry.

гобои́ст, -а, oboist. гобо́й, -я, oboe.

говѣнье, -я, fasting. говѣть, -ѣю *imp.* fast.

говно́, -á, shit.

го́вор, -а, sound of voices; murmur, babble; talk, rumour; pronunciation, accent; dialect. говори́льня, -и, talking-shop. говори́ть, -рю́ *imp.* say; speak, talk; say; tell; mean, convey, signify; point, testify; говори́т Москва́! this is Moscow; говоря́ в по́льзу +*gen.* tell in favour of; support, back; не говоря́ уже́ о +*prep.*, not to mention; не́чего (и) ~, it goes without saying, needless to say; что и ~, it can't be denied; ~ся; как говори́тся, as they say, as the saying goes. говорли́вый, garrulous, talkative. говору́н, -á, -ру́нья, -и, talker, chatterer, chatterbox.

говя́дина, -ы, beef. говя́жий, beef.

го́гот, -а, cackle; shouts of laughter. гогота́нье, -я, cackling. гогота́ть, -очу́ -о́чешь *imp.* cackle; laugh aloud, shout with laughter.

год, -а (-y), *loc.* -ý; *pl.* -ы or -á, *gen.* -óв or лет, year; *pl.* years, age, time; без ~у неде́ля, only a few days; в ~ы, in the days (of); during; в ~áх, advanced in years; ~ от ~у, every year; из ~а в ~, year in, year out; не по ~áм, beyond one's years, precocious(ly). года́ми *adv.* for years (on end). годи́на, -ы, time, period; year.

годи́ться, -жу́сь *imp.* be fit, suitable, suited; do, serve; +в+*nom.* or *acc.* be cut out for; be old enough to be; не годи́тся, it's no good, it won't do; +*inf.* it does not do to, one should not.

годи́чный, lasting a year, a year's; annual, yearly.

го́дный, -ден, -дна́, -о, -ы or -ы́, fit, suitable, valid.

годова́лый, a year old; yearling. годови́к, -á, yearling. годово́й, annual, yearly. годовщи́на, -ы, anniversary.

гожу́сь etc.: see годи́ться.

гол, -а, goal.

гола́вль, -я́ *m.* chub.

голена́ст|ый, long-legged; ~ые *sb. pl.* wading birds, Grallatores. голени́ще, -а, (boot-)top. го́лень, -и, shin.

голла́ндец, -дца, Dutchman. голла́ндка, -и, Dutchwoman; tiled stove; jumper. голла́ндск|ий, Dutch; ~ая печь, tiled stove; ~ое полотно́, holland.

голова́, -ы́, *acc.* го́лову; *pl.* го́ловы, -óв, -áм, head; brain; mind; wits; life; van; *m.* and *f.* person in charge, head; в пе́рвую го́лову, first of all; городско́й ~, mayor; ~ сы́ру, a cheese; на свою́ го́лову, to one's cost; с головы́, per head. голова́стик, -а, tadpole. голо́вка, -и, head; cap, nose, tip; head-scarf; *pl.* vamp. головн|о́й, head; brain, cerebral; leading, advance; ~áя боль, headache; ~о́й го́лос, head-voice, falsetto; ~о́й мозг, brain, cerebrum; ~о́й убо́р, headgear, head-dress. головокруже́ние, -я, giddiness, dizziness; vertigo. головокружи́тельный, dizzy, giddy. головоло́мка, -и, puzzle, riddle, conundrum. головоло́мный, puzzling. головомо́йка, -и, reprimand, dressing-down, telling-off. головоно́гие *sb. pl.* Cephalopoda. головоре́з, -а, cut-throat; bandit; black-guard, ruffian, rascal. головотя́п, -а, bungler, muddler.

го́лод, -а (-y), hunger; starvation; famine; dearth, acute shortage. голода́ние, -я, starvation; fasting. голода́ть, -а́ю *imp.* go hungry, hunger, starve; fast, go without food. голо́дный; го́лоден, -дна́, -о, -ы or -ы́, hungry; hunger, starvation; meagre, scanty, poor. голодо́вка, -и, starvation; hunger-strike.

голоно́гий, bare-legged; bare-foot.

го́лос, -а; *pl.* -á, -óв, voice; part; word, opinion; say; vote; во весь ~, at the top of one's voice; пода́ть ~ за +*acc.*, vote for; пра́во ~а, vote, suffrage, franchise; с ~а, by ear. голоси́стый, loud-voiced; vociferous; loud. голоси́ть, -ошу́ *imp.* sing loudly; cry; wail, keen.

голосло́вный, unsubstantiated, unfounded; unsupported by evidence.

голосова́ние, -я, voting; poll; hitching lifts, hitch-hiking; всео́бщее ~, universal suffrage. **голосова́ть**, -су́ю *imp.* (*perf.* про~) vote; put to the vote, vote on; hitch lifts, hitch-hike. **голосово́й**, vocal.

голошта́нник, -а, ragamuffin.

голубе́ть, -е́ет *imp.* (*perf.* по~) turn blue, show blue. **голубизна́**, -ы́, blueness. **голу́бка**, -и, pigeon; (my) dear, darling. **голуб|о́й**, blue; light blue, pale blue; ~о́е то́пливо, natural gas; ~о́й экра́н, television screen. **голу́бчик**, -а, my dear, my dear fellow; darling. **го́лубь**, -я; *pl.* -и, -е́й *m.* pigeon, dove. **голубя́тник**, -а, pigeon-fancier; dovecote. **голубя́тня**, -и; *gen. pl.* -тен, dovecote, pigeon-loft.

го́л|ый; гол, -а́, -ло, naked, bare; poor; unmixed, unadorned; pure, neat. **голытьба́**, -ы́, the poor. **голы́ш**, -а́, naked child, naked person; pauper; pebble, smooth round stone. **голышо́м** *adv.* stark naked. **голя́к**, -а́, beggar, tramp.

гомоге́нный, homogeneous.

го́мон, -а (-у) hubbub. **гомони́ть**, -ню́ *imp.* shout, talk noisily.

гондо́ла, -ы, gondola; car; nacelle.

гоне́ние, -я, persecution. **гони́тель**, -я *m.*, ~ница, -ы, persecutor. **го́нка**, -и, race; dashing, rushing; haste, hurry. **го́нкий**, -нок, -нка́, -нко, fast, swift; fast-growing.

гонора́р, -а, fee.

го́ночный, racing.

гонча́р, -а́, potter.

го́нщик, -а, racer; drover. **гоню́**, etc.: see гнать. **гоня́ть**, -я́ю *imp.* drive; send on errands; ~ся, race; +за+ *instr.* chase, pursue, hunt.

гор- *abbr.* in *comb.* of городско́й, го́рный.

гор|а́, -ы́, *acc.* го́ру; *pl.* го́ры, -а́м, mountain; hill; heap, pile, mass; в го́ру, uphill; под го́ру, downhill.

гора́здо *adv.* much, far, by far.

горб, -а́, *loc.* -у́, hump; protuberance, bulge. **горба́тый**, humpbacked, hunchbacked; ~ нос, hooked nose. **го́рбить**,

-блю *imp.* (*perf.* с~) arch, bend. ~ся, stoop, become bent. **горбоно́сый**, hook-nosed. **горбу́н**, -а́ *m.*, **горбу́нья**, -и; *gen. pl.* -ний, humpback, hunchback. **горбу́шка**, -и; *gen. pl.* -шек, crust, heel of loaf.

горделивый, haughty, proud. **горди́ться**, -ржу́сь *imp.* put on airs, be haughty; +instr. be proud of, pride oneself on. **го́рдость**, -и, pride. **го́рдый**; горд, -а́, -о, го́рды, proud. **горды́ня**, -и, pride, arrogance.

го́ре, -я, grief, sorrow; distress; woe; misfortune, trouble. **горева́ть**, -рю́ю *imp.* grieve, mourn.

горе́лка, -и, burner. **горе́лый**, burnt. **горе́ние**, -я, burning, combustion; enthusiasm.

горе́стный, sad, sorrowful; pitiful, mournful. **го́ресть**, -и, sorrow, grief; *pl.* afflictions, misfortunes, troubles. **горе́ть**, -рю́ *imp.* (*perf.* с~) burn; be on fire, be alight; glitter, shine.

го́рец, -рца, mountain-dweller, highlander.

го́речь, -и, bitterness; bitter taste; bitter stuff.

горизо́нт, -а, horizon; skyline. **горизонта́ль**, -и, horizontal; contour line.

гори́стый, mountainous, hilly. **го́рка**, -и, hill; hillock; steep climb.

горла́н, -а, bawler. **горла́нить**, -ню *imp.* bawl, yell. **горла́стый**, noisy, loud-mouthed. **го́рло**, -а, throat; neck. **горлово́й**, throat; of the throat; guttural; raucous. **го́рлышко**, -а, neck.

горн[1], -а, furnace, forge.

горн[2], -а, bugle. **горни́ст**, -а, bugler.

го́рничная *sb.* maid, chambermaid; stewardess.

горново́й, furnace, forge; *sb.* furnaceman. **горнозаво́дский**, mining and metallurgical. **горнопромы́шленный**, -и, mining industry. **горнопромы́шленный**, mining. **горнорабо́чий** *sb.* miner.

горноста́евый, ermine. **горноста́й**, -я, ermine.

го́рный, mountain; mountainous; mineral; mining; ~ лён, asbestos; ~ хруста́ль, rock crystal.

го́род, -а; *pl.* -а́, town; city; base, home. **городи́ть**, -ожу́, -о́дишь *imp.* fence, enclose; ~ глýпости, talk nonsense; огорóд ~, make a fuss. **городовóй** sb. policeman. **городск|óй**, urban; city; municipal; ~áя лáсточка, (house-)martin. **гóрод-спýтник**, -a, satellite town. **горожáнин**, -a; pl. -áне, -áн m., -жáнка, -и, town-dweller; townsman. townswoman.

горóх, -a (-у), pea, peas. **горóховый**, pea. **горóшек**, -шка, spots, spotted pattern; душúстый ~, sweet peas; зелёный ~, green peas. **горóшина**, -ы, pea.

горсовéт, -a abbr. городскóй совéт, city soviet, town soviet.

гóрсточка, -и, **гóрсть**, -и; gen. pl. -éй, handful.

гортáнный, guttural; laryngeal. **гортáнь**, -и, larynx.

гóрче, comp. of гóрький. **горчúть**, -чúт imp. taste bitter. **горчúца**, -ы, mustard. **горчúчник**, -a, mustard plaster. **горчúчница**, -ы, mustard-pot.

горшóк, -шкá, pot; chamber-pot.

гóрький, -рек, -рькá, -o, bitter; rancid; hapless, wretched.

горю́ч|ий, combustible, inflammable; ~ee sb. fuel. **горю́чка**, -и, motor fuel.

горячелóмкий, hot-short. **горя́чий**, -ря́ч, -á, hot; passionate; ardent, fervent; hot-tempered; mettlesome; heated; impassioned; busy; high-temperature.

горячúть, -чý imp. (perf. раз~) excite, irritate; ~ся, get excited, become impassioned. **горя́чка**, -и, fever; feverish activity; feverish haste; m. and fem. hothead; firebrand; поро́ть горя́чку, hurry, bustle; rush headlong. **горя́чность**, -и zeal, fervour, enthusiasm.

гос- sb. in comb. of госудáрственный state. **Госдепартáмент**, -a, State Department. ~издáт, -a, State Publishing House. ~плáн, -a, State Planning Commission. ~стрáх, State Insurance.

гóспиталь, -я m. (military) hospital.

гóсподи (ho-) int. good heavens! good Lord! good gracious! **господúн**, -a; pl. -спóд, -óд, -áм, master; gentleman; Mr.; pl. gentlemen; ladies and gentlemen; Messrs. **госпóдский**, seigniorial,

manorial; ~ дом, manor-house; the big house. **госпóдство**, -a, supremacy, dominion, mastery; predominance. **госпóдствовать**, -твую imp. hold sway, exercise dominion; predominate, prevail; ~ над+instr. command, dominate; tower above. **госпóдствующий**, ruling; predominant, prevailing; commanding. **госпóдь**, гóспода, voc. гóсподи m. God, the Lord. **госпожá**, -й, mistress; lady; Mrs. Miss.

ГОСТ, гост, -a abbr. госудáрственный общесою́зный стандáрт, All-Union State Standard.

гостевóй, guest, guests'. **гостеприúмный**, hospitable. **гостеприúмство**, -a, hospitality. **гостúная** sb. drawing-room, sitting-room; drawing-room suite. **гостúница**, -ы, hotel; inn. **гостúный**; ~ двор, arcade, bazaar. **гостúть**, гощý imp. stay, be on a visit. **гость**, -я; gen. pl. -éй m., **гóстья**, -и gen. pl. -ий, guest, visitor.

госудáрственный, State, public. **госудáрство**, -a, State. **госудáрыня**, -и, **госудáрь**, -я m. sovereign; Your Majesty.

гот, -a, Goth. **готúческий**, Gothic; шрифт, black-letter.

готóвить, -влю imp. (perf. c~) prepare, get ready; train; cook; lay in, store; have in store; ~ся, get ready; prepare oneself, make preparations; be at hand, brewing, impending, imminent; loom ahead. **готóвность**, -и, readiness, preparedness, willingness. **готóв|ый**, ready, prepared; willing; on the point, on the verge; ready-made; finished; tight, plastered; на всём ~ом, all found.

гофрирóванный, corrugated; crimped; waved; pleated; goffered. **гофрировáть**, -рую́ perf. and imp. corrugate; wave, crimp; goffer. **гофрирóвка**, -и, corrugation; goffering; waving; waves.

гр. abbr. граждани́н, гражда́нка, citizen.

граб, -a, hornbeam.

грабёж, -á, robbery; pillage, plunder. **грабúтель**, -я m. robber. **грабúтельский**, extortionate, exorbitant. **грабúтельство**, -a, robbery. **грабúть**, -блю *imp.* (*perf.* о∼) rob, pillage. **гра́бленый**, stolen.

гра́бли, -бель or -блей *pl.* rake.

грабо́вый, hornbeam.

гравёр, -а, **гравиро́вщик**, -а, engraver, etcher. **гравёрный**, engraver's, etcher's; engraving, etching.

гра́вий, -я, gravel. **гра́вийный**, gravel.

гравирова́льный, engraving, etching. **гравирова́ть**, -ру́ю *imp.* (*perf.* вы∼) engrave; etch. **гравиро́вка**, -и, engraving, print; etching. **гравю́ра**, -ы, engraving, print; etching; ∼ на де́реве, woodcut; ∼ на лино́леуме, linocut.

град¹, -а, city, town.

град², -а, hail; shower, torrent; volley; ∼ом, thick and fast. **гра́дина**, -ы, hailstone.

гради́рня, -и, salt-pan; cooling tower. **гради́ровать**, -рую *perf.* and *imp.* evaporate.

градово́й, hail. **гра́дом**: see град.

градострои́тель, -я *m.* town-planner. **градострои́тельный**, **градострои́тельство**, -а, town(-)planning.

гра́дус, -а, degree; pitch; stage. **гра́дусник**, -а, thermometer. **гра́дусн|ый**, degree; grade; ∼ая се́тка, grid.

граждани́н, -а; *pl.* гра́ждане, -дан, **гражда́нка**, -и, citizen. **гражда́нский**, civil; citizens'; civic; secular; civilian. **гражда́нство**, -а, citizenship, nationality.

грамза́пись, -и, gramophone recording.

гра́мота, -ы, ability to read and write, reading and writing; official document; deed. **гра́мотность**, -и, literacy. **гра́мотный**, literate; grammatically correct; competent.

грампласти́нка, -и, disc, (gramophone) record.

гран, -а; *gen. pl.* гран, grain.

грана́т, -а, pomegranate; garnet. **грана́та**, -ы, shell, grenade. **грана́тник**, -а, pomegranate. **грана́товый**, pomegranate; garnet; rich red.

гране́ние, -я, cutting. **гранёный**, cut, faceted; cut-glass. **грани́льный**, lapidary; diamond-cutting. **грани́льня**, -и; *gen. pl.* -лен, diamond-cutter's workshop. **грани́льщик**, -а, lapidary, dia-

mond-cutter. **грани́ть**, -ню́ *imp.* cut, facet.

грани́ца, -ы, frontier, border; boundary; limit, bound; за грани́цей за грани́цу, abroad. **грани́чить**, -чит *imp.* border, verge.

гра́нка, -и, galley proof, galley, slip (proof).

грань, -и, border, verge; brink; side, facet; edge; period.

граф, -а, count; earl.

графа́, -ы́, column. **гра́фик**, -а, a graph, chart; schedule; draughtsman, graphic artist. **гра́фика**, -и, drawing, graphic art; script.

графи́н, -а, carafe; decanter.

графи́ня, -и, countess.

графи́ть, -флю́ *imp.* (*perf.* раз-) rule.

графи́ческий, graphic.

графлёный, ruled.

гра́фство, -а, title of earl or count; county.

грацио́зный, graceful. **гра́ция**, -и, grace.

грач, -а́, rook.

гребёнка, -и, comb; rack; hackle. **гре́бень**, -бня *m.* comb; hackle; crest; ridge. **гребе́ц**, -бца́, rower, oarsman. **гребно́й**, rowing. **гребо́к**, -бка́, stroke; blade. **гребу́**, etc.: see грести́.

грёза, -ы, day-dream, dream. **гре́зить**, -е́жу *imp.* dream.

гре́йдер, -а, a grader; unmetalled road.

грек, -а, Greek.

гре́лка, -и, heater; hot-water bottle, foot-warmer.

греме́ть, -млю́ *imp.* (*perf.* про∼) thunder, roar; rumble; peal; rattle; resound, ring out. **гремуч|ий**, roaring, rattling; fulminating; ∼ий газ, fire-damp; ∼ая змея́, rattlesnake; ∼ая ртуть, fulminate of mercury; ∼ий сту́день, nitro-gelatine. **грему́шка**, -и, rattle; sleigh-bell.

грести́, -ебу́, -ебёшь; грёб, -бла́ *imp.* row; scull, paddle; rake.

греть, -е́ю *imp.* warm, heat; give out heat; ∼ся, warm oneself, bask.

грех, -а́, sin. **грехо́вный**, sinful. **грехопаде́ние**, -я, the Fall; fall.

гре́цкий, Greek, Grecian; ∼ оре́х, walnut. **греча́нка**, -и, Greek. **гре́ческий**, Greek, Grecian.

речи́ха, -и, buckwheat. **гре́чневый**, buckwheat.

реши́ть, -шу́ *imp.* (*perf.* по~, со~) sin.

гре́шник, -а, -ница, -ы, sinner. **гре́шный**, -шен, -шна́, -о, sinful; culpable.

риб, -а́, mushroom, toadstool, fungus. **грибно́й**, mushroom.

ри́ва, -ы, mane; wooded ridge; spit, shelf, sandbank.

ри́венник, -а, a ten-copeck piece.

рим, -а, make-up; grease-paint. **гримёр**, -а, -ёрша, -и, make-up man, woman. **гримирова́ть**, -ру́ю *imp.* (*perf.* за~, на~) make up; +*instr.* make up as; ~**ся**, make up. **гримиро́вка**, -и, making up, make-up.

риф[1], -а, gryphon; vulture.

риф[2], -а, finger-board.

риф[3], -а, seal, stamp.

ри́фель, -я *m.* slate-pencil. **гри́фельный**, slate; ~**ая** доска́, slate.

роб, -а, *loc.* -у́; *pl.* -ы́ or -а́, coffin; grave. **гробану́ть**, -ну́, -нёшь *perf.* ~**ся**, have an accident, be killed in an accident. **гробово́й**, coffin; deathly, sepulchral. **гробовщи́к**, -а́, coffin-maker; undertaker.

роза́, -ы́; *pl.* -ы, (thunder-)storm; calamity, disaster; terror; threats.

роздь, -и; *pl.* -ди or -дья, -де́й or -дьев, cluster, bunch.

рози́ть(ся), -ожу́(сь) *imp.* по~, при~) threaten; make a threatening gesture; ~ кулако́м+*dat.* shake one's fist at. **гро́зный**, -зен, -зна́, -зно́, -о, menacing, threatening; dread, terrible; formidable; stern, severe. **грозово́й**, storm, thunder.

ром, -а; *pl.* -ы, -о́в, thunder.

рома́да, -ы, mass; bulk, pile. heaps. **грома́дина**, -ы, vast object. **грома́дный**, huge, vast, enormous; colossal.

роми́ть, -млю́ *imp.* destroy; smash, rout; thunder, fulminate, against. **гро́мкий**, -мок, -мка́, -о, loud; famous; notorious; fine-sounding, specious. **гро́мко** *adv.* loud(ly); aloud. **громкоговори́тель**, -я *m.* loud-speaker. **громово́й**, thunder, of thunder; thunderous, deafening; crushing, smashing.

громогла́сный, loud; loud-voiced; public, open.

громозди́ть, -зжу́ *imp.* (*perf.* на~), pile up, heap up; ~**ся**, tower; clamber up. **громо́здкий**, cumbersome, unwieldy.

гро́мче, *comp.* of гро́мкий; гро́мко.

громыха́ть, -а́ю *imp.* rumble, clatter.

гроссме́йстер, -а, grand master.

гро́хать, -аю *imp.*, гро́хнуть, -ну *perf.* crash, bang; bang down, drop with a crash, bang down; ~**ся**, fall with a crash. **грохот**[1], -а, crash, din.

грохот[2], -а, screen, sieve, riddle.

грохота́ть, -очу́, -о́чешь *imp.* (*perf.* про~) crash; roll, rumble; thunder, roar; roar (with laughter).

грош, -а́, half-copeck piece; farthing, brass farthing, penny. **грошо́вый**, dirt-cheap; cheap, shoddy; insignificant, trifling.

грубе́ть, -е́ю *imp.* (*perf.* за~, о~, по~) grow coarse, coarsen; become rough. **груби́ть**, -блю́ *imp.* (*perf.* на~) be rude. **грубия́н**, -а, boor. **грубия́нить**, -ню *imp.* (*perf.* на~) be rude; behave boorishly. **гру́бо** *adv.* coarsely, roughly; crudely; rudely. **гру́бость**, -и, rudeness; coarseness; grossness; rude remark. **гру́бый**, груб, -а́, -о, coarse; rough; crude, rude; gross, flagrant.

гру́да, -ы, heap, pile.

груди́на, -ы, breastbone. **гру́динка**, -и, brisket; breast. **грудно́й**, breast, chest; pectoral; ~**а́я** жа́ба, angina pectoris; ~**о́й** ребёнок, infant in arms. **грудобрю́шный**; ~**ая** прегра́да, diaphragm. **грудь**, -й or -и, *instr.* -ю, *loc.* -и́; *pl.* -и, -е́й, breast; bosom, bust; chest; (shirt-)front.

груз, -а, weight; load, cargo, freight; burden; bob. **грузи́ло**, -а, sinker.

грузи́н, -а; *gen. pl.* -и́н, грузи́нка, -и, Georgian. **грузи́нский**, Georgian.

грузи́ть, -ужу́, -у́зи́шь *imp.* (*perf.* за~, на~, по~) load, lade, freight; ~**ся**, load, take on cargo. **гру́зка**, -и, lading. **гру́зный**, -зен, -зна́, -о, weighty, bulky; unwieldy; corpulent. **грузови́к**, -а́, lorry, truck. **грузово́й**, goods, cargo, freight, load. **грузопото́к**, -а, freight traffic, goods traffic.

грузотакси́ n. indecl. taxi-lorry. **гру́з- чик**, -а, stevedore, docker; loader.

грунт, -а, ground, soil, earth; subsoil; bottom; priming, primer. **грунтова́ть**, -ту́ю imp. (perf. за~) prime. **грунто́в- ка**, -и, priming, ground coat, ground. **грунтово́й**, soil, earth, ground; subsoil; bottom; priming; unpaved, un- metalled.

гру́ппа, -ы, group. **группирова́ть**, -ру́ю imp. (perf. с~), group, classify; ~ся, group, form groups. **группиро́вка**, -и, grouping; classification: group. **груп- пово́й**, group; team.

грусти́ть, -ущу́ imp. grieve, mourn; +по+dat. pine for. **гру́стный**, -тен, -тна́, -о, sad; melancholy; grievous, distressing. **грусть**, -и, sadness, melancholy.

гру́ша, -и, pear; pear-shaped thing. **гру́шевый**, pear; ~ компо́т, stewed pears.

гры́жа, -и, hernia, rupture. **гры́жевый**, hernial; ~ банда́ж, truss.

грызня́, -и́, dog-fight, fight; squabble. **грызть**, -зу́, -зёшь; грыз imp. (perf. раз~) gnaw; nibble; nag; devour, consume; ~ся, fight; squabble, bicker. **грызу́н**, -á, rodent.

ГРЭС abbr. Госуда́рственная райо́н- ная электроста́нция, State District power-station.

гряда́, -ы́; pl. -ы, -а́м, ridge; bed; row, series; bank. **гря́дка**, -и, (flower-)bed.

гряду́щий, approaching, coming, future; to come; на сон ~, at bedtime; last thing at night.

грязеви́й, mud. **грязни́ть**, -ню́ imp. (perf. за~, на~) dirty, soil; sully, be- smirch; make a mess, be untidy; ~ся, become dirty. **гря́зный**, -зен, -зна́, -о, muddy, mud-stained; dirty; untidy, slovenly; filthy; refuse, garbage, slop. **грязь**, -и, loc. -и́, mud; dirt, filth; pl. mud-baths, mud-cure.

гря́нуть, -ну perf. burst out, crash out, ring out; strike up. ~ся, crash (down).

грясти́, -яду́, -яде́шь imp. approach.

ГСП (ge-espé) abbr. городска́я слу- же́бная по́чта, urban postal service.

губа́, -ы́; pl. -ы, -а́м, lip; pl. pincers. **губа́стый**, thick-lipped.

губерна́тор, -а, governor. **губе́рния**, -и, province. **губе́рнский**, provincial; ~ секрета́рь, Provincial Secretary (12th grade: see чин).

губи́тельный, destructive, ruinous; baneful, pernicious. **губи́ть**, -блю́, -бишь imp. (perf. по~) destroy; be the undoing of; ruin, spoil; ~ся, be des- troyed; be wasted.

гу́бка, -и, sponge.

губн|о́й, lip; labial; ~áя гармо́ника, harmonica, mouth organ.

гу́бчатый, porous, spongy; ~ каучу́к, foam rubber.

гуверна́нтка, -и, governess. **гуверне́р**, -а, tutor.

гугу́; ни ~! not a sound! mum's the word!

гуде́ние, -я, hum; drone; buzzing; hooting, hoot. **гуде́ть**, гужу́ imp. (perf. про~) hum; drone; buzz; hoot. **гудо́к**, -дка́, hooter, siren, horn, whistle; hoot, hooting.

гудро́н, -а, tar. **гудрони́ровать**, -рую perf. and imp. (perf. also за~), tar. **гудро́нный**, tar, tarred.

гул, -а, rumble; hum; boom. **гу́лкий**; -лок, -лка́, -о, resonant; booming, rumbling.

гуля́нье, -я; gen. pl. -ний, walking, going for a walk, walk; fête; outdoor party. **гуля́ть**, -я́ю imp. (perf. по~) walk, stroll; go for a walk, take a walk; have time off, not be working; make merry, carouse, have a good time; +с+instr. go with.

ГУМ, -а abbr. Госуда́рственный универса́льный магази́н, State depart- ment store.

гумани́зм, -а, humanism. **гумани́ст**, -а, humanist. **гуманита́рный**, of the hu- manities; humane. **гума́нный**, humane.

гумно́, -á; pl. -а, -мен or -мён, -ам, threshing-floor; barn.

гурт, -á, herd, drove; flock. **гуртов- щи́к**, -á, herdsman; drover. **гурто́м** adv. wholesale; in bulk; together; in a body, en masse.

гуса́к, -а́, gander.
гу́сеница, -ы, caterpillar; (caterpillar) track. **гу́сеничный**, track, tracked.
гусёнок, -нка; *pl.* -ся́та, -ся́т, gosling.
гуси́н|ый, goose; ~ая ко́жа, goose-flesh; ~ые ла́пки, crow's-feet.
густе́ть, -е́ет *imp.* (*perf.* за~, по~), thicken, get thicker. **густо́й**; густ, -а́, -о, thick, dense; deep, rich. **густота́**, -ы́, thickness, density; deepness, richness.

гусы́ня, -и, goose. **гусь**, -я; *pl.* -и, -е́й *m.* goose. **гусько́м** *adv.* in single file. **гуся́тина**, -ы, goose.
гутали́н, -а, shoe-polish, boot-polish.
гу́ща, -и, dregs, lees, grounds, sediment; thicket; centre, heart. **гу́ще**, *comp.* of густо́й. **гущина́**, -ы́, thickness; thicket.
гэ *n. indecl.* the letter г.
ГЭС *abbr.* гидроэлектроста́нция, hydro-electric power station.

Д

д *letter*: see дэ.
да *conj.* and; but; да (ещё), and what is more; да (и), and besides; да и то́лько, and that's all.
да *part.* yes; yes? really? indeed; well; +3rd pers. of vb., may, let; да здра́вствует . . ! long live . . !
дава́ть, даю́, -ёшь *imp.* of дать; **дава́й(те)**, let us, let's; come on; ~ся, yield; let oneself be caught; come easy; не ~ся+*dat.* dodge, evade; ру́сский язы́к ему́ даётся легко́, Russian comes easy to him.
да́веча *adv.* lately, recently.
дави́|ло, -а, press. **дави́ть**, -влю́, -вишь *imp.* (*perf.* за~, по~, раз~, у~) press; squeeze; weigh, lie heavy; crush; oppress; trample; strangle; ~ся, choke; hang oneself. **да́вка**, -и, crushing, squeezing; throng, crush. **давле́ние**, -я, pressure.
да́вний, ancient; of long standing. **давно́** *adv.* long ago; for a long time; long since. **давнопроше́дший**, remote; long past; pluperfect. **да́вность**, -и, antiquity; remoteness; long standing; prescription. **давны́м-давно́** *adv.* long ago, ages ago.
дади́м, etc.: see дать. **даю́**, etc.: see дава́ть.
да́же *adv.* even.
да́лее *adv.* further; и так ~, and so on,

etc. **далёкий**; -ёк, -а́, -ёко́, distant, remote; far (away). **далеко́** *adv.* far; far off; by a long way; ~ за, long after; ~ не, far from. **даль**, -и, *loc.* -и́, distance. **да́льн|ий**, distant, remote; long; без ~их слов, without more ado; ~ Восто́к, the Far East. **дальнозо́ркий**, long-sighted. **да́льность**, -и, distance; range. **да́льше** *adv.* farther; further; then, next; longer.
дам, etc.: see дать.
да́ма, -ы lady; partner; queen.
да́мба, -ы, dike, embankment; dam.
да́мка, -и, king. **да́мский**, ladies'.
да́нные *sb. pl.* data; facts, information; qualities, gifts; grounds. **да́нный**, given, present; in question, this. **дань**, -и, tribute; debt.
дар, -а; *pl.* -ы́, gift; donation; grant. **даре́ние**, -я, donation. **дари́тель**, -я *m.* donor. **дари́ть**, -рю́, -ришь *imp.* (*perf.* по~) *dat.* give, make a present.
дармое́д, -а, -е́дка -и, parasite, sponger, scrounger. **дармое́дничать**, -аю *imp.* sponge, scrounge.
ДАРМС *abbr.* дрейфу́ющая автомати́ческая радиометеорологи́ческая ста́нция, drifting radio weather-station.
дарова́ние, -я, gift, talent. **дарова́ть**, -ру́ю *perf.* and *imp.* grant, confer. **дарови́тый**, gifted, talented. **дарово́й**, free, gratuitous. **да́ром** *adv.* free, gratis; in vain, to no purpose.

да́та, -ы, date.

дта́ельный, dative.

дати́ровать, -рую *perf.* and *imp.* date.

да́тский, Danish. датча́нин, -а; *pl.* -а́не, -а́н, датча́нка, -и, Dane.

дать, дам, дашь, даст, дади́м; дал, -а́, да́ло́ (*imp.* дава́ть) give; administer; grant; let; ~ взаймы́; lend; ~ газ, step on the gas; ~ доро́гу, make way; ~ кля́тву, take an oath; ~ нача́ло+*dat.* give rise to; ~ сло́во, give one's word; +*dat.* give the floor; ~ ход+*dat.* set in motion, get going; ~ся *perf.* of дава́ться.

да́ча, -и, dacha; на да́че, in the country; на да́чу, (in)to the country. да́чник, -а, (holiday) visitor.

ДВ (*devé*) *abbr.* дли́нные во́лны, long waves; длинново́лновый, long-wave.

два *m.* and *n.*, две *f.*, двух, -ум, -умя́ -ух, two; ~-три, two or three, a couple; ка́ждые ~ дня, every other day. двадцатиле́тний, twenty-year; twenty-year-old. двадца́т|ый, twentieth; ~ые го́ды, the twenties. два́дцать, -и, *instr.* -ью, twenty. два́дцатью *adv.* twenty times. два́жды *adv.* twice; double. двена́дцатый, twelfth. двена́дцать, -и, twelve.

дверн|о́й, door; ~а́я коро́бка, door-frame. две́рца, -ы; *gen. pl.* -рец, door, hatch. дверь, -и, *loc.* -и́; *pl.* -и, -е́й, *instr.* -я́ми or -ьми́, door; *pl.* doors, door.

две́сти, двухсо́т, -умста́м, -умяста́ми, -ухста́х, two hundred.

дви́гатель, -я *m.* engine, motor; (prime) mover, motive force. дви́гательный, motive; motor. дви́гать, -аю or -и́жу *imp.*, дви́нуть, -ну *perf.* move; set in motion, get going; advance, further; ~ся, move; advance; start, get started.

движе́ние, -я, movement; motion; exercise; flow; traffic; promotion, advancement; impulse; железнодоро́жное ~, train service. дви́жимость, -и, movables, chattels; personal property. дви́жимый, movable; moved, prompted, activated. дви́жущий, motive; moving; driving.

дво́е, -и́х, two; two pairs.

двое- in *comb.*, two; double. двоебо́рец,

-рца, competitor in double event. ~бо́рье, -я, double event. ~ду́шие, -я, duplicity, double-dealing. ~ду́шный, two-faced. ~же́нец, -нца, ~му́жница, -ы, bigamist. ~же́нство, -а, ~му́жие, -я, bigamy. ~то́чие, -я, colon.

дво́ить, -о́ю *imp.* (*perf.* вз~) double; divide into two; ~ся, divide in two; appear double. дво́йчный, binary. дво́йка, -и, two; figure 2; No. 2; pair-oar. двойни́к, -а́, double; twin. двойно́й, double, twofold; binary. дво́йня, -и; *gen. pl.* -о́ен, twins. дво́йственный, double-dealing, two-faced; dual; bipartite.

двор, -а́, yard; courtyard; homestead; court; на ~е́, out of doors, outdoors; при ~е́, at court. дворе́ц, -рца́, palace. дворе́цкий *sb.* butler; major-domo. дво́рник, -а, dvornik, yardman; windscreen-wiper. дво́рников|ий, dvornik's; ~ая *sb.* dvornik's lodge. дво́рня, -и, servants, menials. дворо́вый, yard, courtyard; *sb.* house-serf. дворцо́вый, palace. дворяни́н, -а; *pl.* -я́не, -я́н, дворя́нка, -и, member of the nobility or gentry. дворя́нство, -а, nobility, gentry.

двою́родн|ый; ~ый брат, ~ая сестра́, (first) cousin; ~ый дя́дя, ~ая тётка, first cousin once removed. двоя́кий, double; ambiguous; in two ways, of two kinds. двоя́ко-, double-, bi-, di-.

дву-, двух-, in *comb.* two-; bi-, di-; double; diplo-. двубо́ртный, double-breasted. ~гла́вый, two-headed. ~гла́сный *sb.* diphthong. ~гри́венный *sb.* twenty-copeck piece. ~жи́льный, strong; hardy; tough. ~зна́чный, two-digit. ~ли́кий, two-faced. ~ли́чие, -я, double-dealing, duplicity. ~ли́чный, two-faced; hypocritical. ~пла́нный, two-dimensional. ~по́лый, bisexual. ~ру́чный, two-handed; two-handled. ~ру́шник, -а, double-dealer. ~сло́жный, disyllabic. ~сме́нный in two shifts, two-shift. ~смы́сленный, ambiguous, equivocal. ~(х)спа́льный, double. сторо́нний double-sided; two-way; bilateral. ~хато́мный, diatomic. ~хгоди́чный, two-year. ~хкра́сочный, two-colour;

two-tone. ~хлéтний, two-year; two-year-old; biennial. ~хмéстный, two-seater; two-berth. ~хмоторный, twin-engined, two-engined. ~хпалáтный, bicameral. ~хсотлéтие, -я, bicentenary. ~хсóтый, two-hundredth. ~хтáктный, two-beat; two-stroke. ~хъя́русный, two-layer, two-storey, two-tier, double-deck; two-lever. ~хэтáжный, two-storey; double-deck. ~члéн, -a, binomial. ~язы́чный, bilingual.

дебáты, -ов *pl.* debate.

дéбет, -a, debit. **дебетовáть**, -тую *perf.* and *imp.* debit.

дебúт, -a. discharge, flow, yield, output.

дéбри, -ей *pl.* jungle; thickets; the wilds; maze, labyrinth.

дебю́т, -a, début; opening.

дéва, -ы, maid, maiden; girl; spinster; Virgo; стáрая ~, old maid.

девальвáция, -и, devaluation.

девáть(ся, -áю(сь *imp.* of деть(ся.

девúз, -a, motto; device.

девúца, -ы, spinster; girl. **девúческий**, **девúч|ий**, girlish, maidenly; ~ья фамúлия, maiden name. **дéвка**, -и, girl, wench, lass; tart, whore. **дéвочка**, -и, (little) girl. **дéвственник**, -ица, -ы, virgin. **дéвственый**, virgin; virginal, innocent. **дéвушка**, -и, girl; maid.

девянóсто, -a, ninety. **девянóстый**, ninetieth. **дéвятеро**, -ых, nine; nine pairs. **девятúсóтый**, nine-hundredth. **девя́тка**, -и, nine; figure 9; No. 9; group of nine. **девятнáдцать**, -и, nineteen. **девя́тый**, ninth. **дéвять**, -и, *instr.* -ью, nine. **девятьсóт** -тисóт, -тистáм, -тьюстáми, -тистáх, nine hundred. **дéвятью** *adv.* nine times.

дёготь, -гтя, tar, coal-tar, pitch. **дёгтебетóн**, -a, tarmac, tar concrete. **дегтя́рный**, tar, coal-tar, pitch; tarry.

дед, -a, grandfather; grandad, grandpa. **дéдовский**, grandfather's; old-world; old-fashioned. **дéдушка**, -и, grandfather; grandad.

деепричáстие, -я, gerund, adverbial participle.

дежу́рить, -рю *imp.* be on duty, be in (constant) attendance. **дежу́рный**,

duty; on duty. **дежу́рство**, -a, (being on) duty.

дéйственный, efficacious; effective. **дéйствие**, -я, action; operation; activity; functioning; effect; act; под ~м under the influence. **действúтельно** *adv.* really; indeed. **действúтельность**, -и, reality; conditions; validity; efficacy; в действúтельности, in reality, in fact. **действúтельный**, real, actual; true, authentic; valid, efficacious; effective; active; ~ тáйный совéтник — стáтский совéтник, Actual Privy Councillor (2nd grade), Actual State Councillor (4th grade: see чин). **дéйствовать**, -твую *imp.* (*perf.* по~) affect, have an effect; act; work, function; operate; +*instr.* use; не ~, be out of order, not be working. **дéйствующ|ий**, active; in force; working; ~ее лицó, character; active participant; ~ие лúца, dramatis personae, cast.

дéка, -и, sounding-board.

декабрúст, -a, Decembrist. **декáбрь**, -я́ *m.* December. **декáбрьский**, December.

декáда, -ы, ten days; (ten-day) festival.

декáн, -a, a dean. **деканáт**, -a, office of dean.

декламáтор, -a, reciter, declaimer. **деклáмация**, -и, recitation, declamation. **деклáмировать**, -рую *imp.* (*perf.* про~). recite, declaim.

декоратúвный, decorative, ornamental. **декорáтор**, -a, decorator; scene-painter. **декорáция**, -и, scenery, décor; window-dressing.

дéланый, artificial, forced, affected. **дéлать**, -аю *imp.* (*perf.* с~) make; do; give, produce; ~ вид, pretend, feign; ~ предложéние, propose; ~ честь+ *dat.* honour; do credit to; ~ся, become, get, grow; happen; be going on; break out, appear.

дележ, -á, **дележка**, -и, sharing, division; partition. **делéние**, -я, division; point, degree, unit.

делéц, -льцá, business man, dealer; smart operator.

делúмое *sb.* dividend. **делúмость**, -и, divisibility. **делúтель**, -я *m.* divisor.

дели́ть, -лю́ -лишь *imp.* (*perf.* по~, раз~) divide; share; ~ шесть на́ три, divide six by three; ~ся, divide; be divisible; +*instr.* share; communicate, impart.

де́ло, -а; *pl.* ~á, business; affair, affairs; cause; occupation; matter; point; fact; deed; thing; case, action; file, dossier; battle fighting; в са́мом де́ле, really, indeed; ~ в том the point is; в то́м-то и ~, that's just the point; ~ за ва́ми, it's up to you; как (ва́ши) дела́? how are things going? how are you getting on? на са́мом де́ле, in actual fact, as a matter of fact; по де́лу, по дела́м, on business; то и ~, continually, time and again. делови́тый, business-like, efficient. делово́й, business, work; business-like. де́льный, efficient, business-like; sensible, practical.

дельфи́н, -а, dolphin.

демокра́т, -а, democrat; plebeian. демократизи́ровать, -рую *perf.* and *imp.* democratize. демократи́ческий, democratic; plebeian. демокра́тия, -и, democracy; common people, lower classes.

демонстра́ция, -и, demonstration; (public) showing; display, show.

дендра́рий, -я, arboretum.

де́нежн|ый, monetary; money; moneyed; ~ый перево́д, money order, postal order; ~ая рефо́рма, currency reform; ~ый штраф, fine.

де́ну, etc.: see деть.

день, дня *m.* day; afternoon; днём, in the afternoon; на днях, the other day; one of these days; че́рез ~, every other day.

де́ньги, -нег, -ьга́м *pl.* money.

департа́мент, -а, department.

депута́т, -а deputy; delegate. депута́ция, -и, deputation.

дёргать, -аю *imp.* (*perf.* дёрнуть) pull, tug; pull out; harass pester; +*instr.* move sharply, jerk shrug; ~ся, twitch; jerk; move sharply.

дерга́ч, -á, corncrake, landrail.

деревене́ть, -е́ю *imp.* (*perf.* за-, о~) grow stiff, grow numb. дереве́нский, village; rural, country. дере́вня, -и;

pl. -и, -ве́нь, -вня́м, village; the country. де́рево, -а; *pl.* -е́вья, -ьев, tree; wood. дереву́шка, -и, hamlet. деревя́нный, wood; wooden; expressionless, dead; dull.

держа́ва, -ы, power; orb. держа́вный, holding supreme power, sovereign; powerful. держа́ть, -жу́, -жишь *imp.* hold; hold up, support; keep; ~ корректу́ру read proofs; ~ пари́, bet; ~ себя́, behave; ~ экза́мен, take an examination; ~ся, hold; be held up, be supported; keep, stay; be; hold oneself; behave; last; hold together; hold out, stand firm, hold one's ground; +*gen.* keep to; adhere to, stick to; ~ся на ни́точке, hang by a thread.

дерза́ние, -я, daring. дерза́ть, -а́ю *imp.* дерзну́ть, -ну́, -нёшь *perf.* dare. де́рзкий, impertinent, impudent, cheeky; insolent; daring; audacious. дерзнове́нный, audacious, daring. де́рзость, -и, impertinence; cheek; rudeness; insolence; daring, audacity.

дёрн, -а (-у), turf. дерно́вый, turf. дернова́ть, -ну́ю *imp.* turf, edge with turf.

дёрнуть(ся, -ну(сь *perf. of* дёргать(ся. деру́, etc.: see драть.

деса́нт, -а, landing; landing force. деса́нтный, landing.

десна́, -ы́; *pl.* дёсны, -сен, gum.

десятерно́й, tenfold. десятеро, -ы́х, ten. десятиле́тие, -я, decade; tenth anniversary. десятиле́тка, -и, ten-year (secondary) school. десятиле́тний, ten-year, decennial; ten-year-old. десяти́чный, decimal. деся́тка, -и, ten; No. 10; group of ten; ten-rouble note. деся́ток, -тка, ten; ten years, decade. деся́тник, -а, foreman. деся́тский *sb.* peasant policeman. деся́тый, tenth. де́сять, -и *instr.* -ью́, ten. деся́тью *adv.* ten times.

дет- *abbr.* in *comb.* of де́тский, children's. детдо́м, -а, children's home. ~са́д, -а, kindergarten, nursery school.

дета́ль, -и, detail; part, component. дета́льный, detailed; minute.

детвора́, -ы́, children. детёныш, -а, young animal; cub, whelp, etc.; *pl.*

young. де́ти, -те́й, -тям, -тьми́, -тях *pl.* children.

де́тская *sb.* nursery. де́тский, child's, children's; childish. де́тство, -а, childhood.

деть, де́ну *perf.* (*imp.* дева́ть) put; куда́ ты дел моё перо́? what have you done with my pen?; ~ся, get to; куда́ она́ де́лась? what has become of her?

дефи́с, -а, hyphen; писа́ть че́рез ~, hyphen, hyphenate.

дефици́т. -а, deficit; shortage, deficiency. дефици́тный, showing a loss; in short supply; scarce.

децима́льный, decimal.

дешеве́ть, -е́ет *imp.* (*perf.* по~), fall in price, get cheaper. дешеви́зна, -ы, cheapness; low price. деше́вле, *comp.* of дёшево, дешёвый. дёшево *adv.* cheap, cheaply; lightly. дешёвый, дёшев, -á, -о, cheap; empty, worthless.

дешифри́ровать, -рую *perf.* and *imp.* decipher, decode. дешифро́вка, -и, decipherment, deciphering, decoding.

дея́ние, -я, act, deed. де́ятель, -я *m.*; госуда́рственный ~, statesman; ~ нау́ки, scientific worker, scientist; обще́ственный ~, public figure. де́ятельность, -и, activity; activities; work; operation. де́ятельный, active, energetic.

дже́мпер, -а, jumper, pullover, jersey.

джу́нгли, -ей *pl.* jungle.

диама́т, -а *abbr.* диалекти́ческий материали́зм, dialectical materialism. диапазо́н, -а, diapason; range; compass; band.

диапозити́в, -а, slide, transparency.

дива́н, -а, sofa, divan.

диверса́нт, -а, saboteur. диверсио́нный, diversionary; sabotage, wrecking. диве́рсия, -и, diversion; sabotage.

ди́вный, amazing; marvellous, wonderful. ди́во, -а, wonder, marvel.

дие́з, -а, sharp.

ди́зель, -я *m.* diesel; diesel engine. ди́зельный, diesel.

дика́рь, -я́ *m.*, дика́рка, -и, savage; barbarian; shy person. ди́кий, wild; savage; shy, unsociable; queer absurd; fantastic, preposterous; ridicu-

lous. дикобра́з, -а, porcupine. дико́вина, -ы, marvel, wonder. дикорасту́щий, wild. ди́кость, -и, wildness, savagery; shyness, unsociableness; absurdity, queerness.

дикта́нт, -а, dictation. диктова́ть, -ту́ю *imp.* (*perf.* про~) dictate. дикто́вка, -и, dictation. ди́ктор, -а, announcer.

дилижа́нс, -а, stage-coach.

ди́на, -ы, dyne.

диноза́вр, -а, dinosaur.

дипло́м, -а, diploma; degree; degree work, research; pedigree. дипломи́рованный; graduate; professionally qualified, certificated, diplomaed. дипло́мный, diploma, thesis.

директи́ва, -ы, instructions; directions, directives.

дирижёр, -а, conductor. дирижи́ровать, -рую *imp.* + *instr.* conduct.

диск, -а, disc, disk; plate; dial; discus. ди́скант, -а, treble.

дискре́тность, -и, discreteness, discontinuity. дискре́т|ый, discrete; digital; ~ая маши́на, digital computer.

дискуссио́нный, discussion, debating; debatable, open to question. диску́ссия, -и, discussion, debate. дискути́ровать, -рую *perf.* and *imp.* discuss, debate.

диспансе́р, -а, clinic, (health) centre, dispensary.

диспе́тчер, -а, controller, dispatcher. диспе́тчерская *sb.* controller's office; control tower.

дистанцио́н|ный, distance, distant, remote; remote-control; ~ый взрыва́тель, time fuse; ~ое управле́ние, remote control. диста́нция, -и, distance; range; division, region, sector.

дитя́, -я́ти; *pl.* де́ти. -е́й *n.* child; baby.

дифтери́т, -а, дифтери́я, -и, diphtheria.

дича́ть, -а́ю *imp.* (*perf.* о~) grow wild; become unsociable; run wild. дичи́на, -ы, game. дичи́ться, -чу́сь *imp.* be shy; + *gen.* shun, fight shy of. дичь, -и, *loc.* -и́, game; wildfowl; wilderness, wilds.

ДК (*deká*) *abbr.* Дворе́ц культу́ры, Дом культу́ры, Palace (House) of Culture.

длина́, -ы́, length; длино́й, in length, long. дли́нный; -нен, -нна́, -о, long; lengthy. дли́тельность, -и, duration. дли́тельный, long, protracted, long--drawn-out. дли́ться, -и́тся *imp.* (*perf.* про~), last, be protracted.

для *prep.* +*gen.* for; for the sake of; to; of; ~ ви́ду, for the sake of appearances; вре́дно ~ дете́й, bad for children; высо́к ~ свои́х лет, tall for his age; непроница́емый ~ воды́, waterproof, impervious to water; ~ того́, что́бы . . , in order to . . ; э́то ~ вас, this is for you; э́то типи́чно ~ них, it is typical of them.

дм *abbr.* дециме́тр, decimetre.

днева́льный *sb.* orderly, man on duty. дневни́к, -а́, diary, journal. дневн|о́й, day; daylight; day's, daily; ~а́я сме́на, day shift; ~о́й спекта́кль, matinee. днём *adv.* in the day-time, by day; in the afternoon. дни, etc.: see день.

ДНК (*de-enká*) *abbr.* дезоксирибонуклеи́новая кислота́, DNA.

дно, дна; *pl.* до́нья, -ьев, bottom.

до *n. indecl.* C; doh.

до *prep.* +*gen.* to, up to; as far as; until, till; before; to the point of; under; about, approximately; with regard to, concerning; де́ти до пяти́ лет, children under five; до бо́ли, until it hurt(s); до войны́, before the war; до на́шей э́ры, B.C.; до сих пор, up to now, till now, hitherto; до тех пор, till then, before; до того́, как, before; до того́, что, to such an extent that, to the point where; мне не до, I don't feel like, I'm not in the mood for; от Ленингра́да до Москвы́, from Leningrad to Moscow; что до меня́, as far as I am concerned; ю́бка до коле́н, knee-length skirt.

до- *pref.* up (to); pre-; sub- in *comb.* I. with *vbs.* etc. expresses completion of action, indicates that action is carried to a certain point, expresses supplementary action; with *refl. vbs.* expresses eventual attainment of object, or continuation of action with injurious consequences; II. with *adjs.* indicates priority in time sequence.

доба́вить, -влю *perf.*, добавля́ть, -я́ю *imp.* (+*acc.* or *gen.*) add. доба́вка, -и, addition; second helping. добавле́ние, -я, addition; appendix, addendum, supplement; extra. доба́вочный, additional, supplementary; extra; extension, booster.

добега́ть, -а́ю *imp.*, добежа́ть, -егу́ *perf.* +до+*gen.* run to, run as far as; reach.

добела́ *adv.* to white heat, white-hot; clean, white.

добива́ть, -а́ю *imp.*, доби́ть, -бью́, -бьёшь *perf.* finish (off), kill off, deal the final blow to; ~ся+*gen.* get, obtain, secure; achieve; ~ся своего́, get one's way, gain one's end.

добира́ться, -а́юсь *imp.* of добра́ться.

до́блестный, valiant, valorous, brave. до́блесть, -и, valour, prowess.

добра́ться, -беру́сь; -ешься; -а́лся -ла́сь, -а́ло́сь *perf.* (*imp.* добира́ться) +до+*gen.* get to, reach.

добро́, -а́, good; good deed; goods, property; э́то не к добру́, it is a bad sign, it augurs ill.

добро- in *comb.* good, well-. доброво́лец, -льца volunteer. ~во́льно *adv.* voluntarily, of one's own free will. ~во́льный, voluntary. ~де́тель, -и, virtue. ~де́тельный, virtuous. ~ду́шие, -я, good nature. ~ду́шный, good-natured; genial. ~жела́тельный, benevolent. ~ка́чественный, of good quality; benign. ~со́вестный, conscientious.

доброта́, -ы́, goodness, kindness. добр|ый; -бр, -а́, -о, до́бры, good; kind; бу́дте добры́+*imper.* please; would you be kind enough to; в ~ый час! good luck! по ~ой во́ле of one's own accord, of one's own free will.

добыва́ть, -а́ю *imp.*, добы́ть, -бу́ду до́был, -а́, -о *perf.* get, obtain, procure; extract, mine, quarry. добы́ча, -и, output; extraction, mining, quarrying; booty, spoils, loot; bag, catch; mineral products.

добью́, etc.: see доби́ть. доведу́, etc.: see довести́.

довезти́, -зу́, -зёшь; -вёз, -ла́ *perf.*

(*imp.* довози́ть) take (to), carry (to), drive (to).

дове́ренность, -и, warrant; power of attorney; trust. **дове́ренн|ый**, trusted; confidential; ~ое лицо́, confidential agent; ~ый *sb.* agent, proxy. **дове́рие**, -я, trust, confidence. **дове́рить**, -рю *perf.* (*imp.* доверя́ть) entrust; trust, confide; ~ся +*dat.* trust in; confide in. **дове́рчивый**, trustful, credulous.

доверша́ть, -а́ю *imp.*, **доверши́ть**, -шу́ *perf.* complete. **доверше́ние**, -я, completion, accomplishment; в ~ всего́, to crown all.

доверя́ть(ся, -я́ю(сь *imp.* of дове́рить(-ся.

дове́сок, -ска, makeweight.

довести́, -еду́, -еде́шь; -вёл, -а́ *perf.*, **доводи́ть**, -ожу́, -о́дишь *imp.* lead, take, accompany (to); bring, drive, reduce (to). **до́вод**, -а, argument, reason. **дово́енный**, pre-war.

довози́ть, -ожу́, -о́зишь *imp.* of довезти́.

дово́льно *adv.* enough; quite, fairly; rather; pretty. **дово́льный**, contented, satisfied; content; pleased; considerable. **дово́льство**, -а, content, contentment; ease, prosperity. **дово́льствоваться**, -ствуюсь *imp.* (*perf.* у~) be content, be satisfied.

догада́ться, -а́юсь *perf.*, **дога́дываться**, -аюсь *imp.* guess; suspect. **дога́дка**, -и, surmise, conjecture; shrewdness; imagination. **дога́дливый**, quick-witted, shrewd.

догна́ть, -гоню́, -го́нишь; -гна́л, -а́, -о *perf.* (*imp.* догоня́ть), catch up (with); drive; push up.

догова́риваться, -аюсь *imp.*, **договори́ться**, -рю́сь *perf.* come to an agreement or understanding; arrange; negotiate, treat; догова́ривающиеся сто́роны, contracting parties. **догово́р**, -а; *pl.* -ы or -а́, -о́в, agreement; contract; treaty, pact. **догово́рный**, contractual; agreed; fixed by treaty.

догоня́ть, -я́ю *imp.* of догна́ть.

догора́ть, -а́ет *imp.*, **догоре́ть**, -ри́т *perf.* burn out, burn down.

доеду́, etc.: see дое́хать. **доезжа́ть**, -а́ю *imp.* of дое́хать.

дое́ние, -я, milking.

дое́хать, -е́ду *perf.* (*imp.* доезжа́ть)+ до+*gen.* reach, arrive at.

дожда́ться, -ду́сь, -дёшься; -а́лся, -ла́сь, -а́ло́сь *perf.* + *gen.* wait for, wait until.

дождеви́к, -а́, raincoat; puff-ball. **дождево́й**, rain; rainy; ~ червь, earthworm. **до́ждик**, -а, shower. **дождли́вый**, rainy. **дождь**, -я́ *m.* rain; shower, hail; ~ идёт, it is raining.

дожива́ть, -а́ю *imp.*, **дожи́ть**, -иву́ -ивёшь; до́жи́л, -а́, -о *perf.* live out; spend; + до + *gen.* live until; reach; come to be reduced to.

доза́тор, -а, metering device; hopper, feeder, dispenser.

дозволе́ние, -я, permission. **дозво́ленный**, permitted; legal. **дозво́лить**, -лю *perf.*, **дозволя́ть**, -я́ю *imp.* permit, allow.

дозвони́ться, -ню́сь *perf.* get through, reach by telephone; get bell answered.

дозо́р, -а, patrol; ночно́й ~, night watch. **дозо́рный**, patrol, scout.

дозрева́ть, -а́ет *imp.*, **дозре́ть**, -е́ет *perf.* ripen. **дозре́лый**, fully ripe.

доистори́ческий, prehistoric.

дои́ть, дою́, до́ишь *imp.* (*perf.* по~) milk; ~ся, give milk. **до́йка**, -и, milking. **до́йный**, milch.

дойму́ etc.: see доня́ть.

дойти́, дойду́, -дёшь; дошёл, -шла́ *perf.* (*imp.* доходи́ть)+до+*gen.* reach; make an impression on, get through to, penetrate to, touch; come to, be a matter of.

доказа́тельный, demonstrative, conclusive. **доказа́тельство**, -а, proof, evidence; demonstration. **доказа́ть**, -ажу́ *perf.*, **дока́зывать**, -аю *imp.* demonstrate, prove; argue, try to show. **дока́зуемый** demonstrable.

докати́ться, -ачу́сь, -а́тишься *perf.*, **дока́тываться**, -аюсь *imp.* roll; thunder, boom; +до+*gen.* sink into, come to.

докла́д, -а, report; lecture; paper; talk; address; announcement. **докла́дчик**, -а, speaker, lecturer; rapporteur. **докла́дывать(ся**, -аю(сь *imp.* of доложи́ть(ся.

до́красна́ adv. to red heat, to redness; red-hot red.

до́ктор, -а; pl. -á, doctor. **доктора́льный,** didactic. **доктора́нт,** -а, person working for doctorate. **до́кторский,** doctor's; doctoral. **до́кторша,** -и, woman doctor; doctor's wife.

докуме́нт, -а, document, paper; deed, instrument. **документа́льный,** documentary. **документа́ция,** -и, documentation; documents papers.

долби́ть, -блю́ imp. hollow; chisel, gouge; repeat, say over and over again; swot up; learn by rote.

долг, -а (-у). loc. -ý; pl. -и́, duty; debt; в ~, on credit; в ~ý, indebted; взять в ~, borrow; дать в ~, lend.

до́лгий; до́лог, -лга́, -о, long. **до́лго** adv. long, (for) a long time. **долгове́чный.** lasting; durable.

долголе́тие, -я, longevity. **долголе́тний,** of many years; long-standing.

долгота́, -ы́; pl. -ы, length; longitude.

долево́й, lengthwise. **до́лее** adv. longer.

должа́ть, -а́ю imp. (perf. за~) borrow.

до́лжен, -жна́ predic.+dat. in debt to; + inf. obliged, bound; likely; must, have to, ought to; он ~ мне три рубля́, he owes me three roubles; он ~ идти́, he must go; он ~ был отказа́ться, he had to refuse; он ~ ско́ро прийти́, he should be here soon; должно́ быть, probably. **должни́к,** -а́, -ница́, -а, debtor. **должностно́й,** official; ~о́е лицо́, official, functionary, public servant. **до́лжность,** -и; gen. pl. -е́й, post, appointment, office; duties. **до́лжный,** due, fitting, proper.

доли́на, -ы, valley.

доложи́ть[1], -ожу́, -о́жишь perf. (imp. докла́дывать) add.

доложи́ть[2], -ожу́, -о́жишь perf. (imp. докла́дывать) + acc. or о + prep. report; give a report on; announce; ~ся, announce one's arrival.

доло́й adv. away, off; + acc. down with!; с глаз ~, из се́рдца вон, out of sight, out of mind; с глаз мои́х ~! out of my sight!

долото́, -а́; pl. -а, chisel.

до́лька, -и, segment, section, clove.

до́льше adv. longer.

до́ля, -и; gen. pl. -е́й, part, portion; share; quota, allotment; lobe; lot, fate.

дом, -а (-у). loc. -ý; pl. -а́, building, house; home; household; lineage; family; на ~ý, at home. **до́ма** adv. at home; in. **дома́шн|ий,** house; home; domestic; home-made, homespun, home-brewed; tame; ~яя хозя́йка, housewife; ~не sb. pl. family, people.

до́менн|ый, blast-furnace, ironmaking; ~ая печь, blast-furnace.

домини́ровать, -рует imp. dominate, predominate; + над + instr. dominate, command.

домкра́т, -а, jack.

до́мна, -ы blast-furnace.

домовладе́лец, -льца, -лица, -ы, house-owner; landlord. **домово́дство,** -а, household management; domestic science. **домо́в|ый,** house; household; housing; ~ая кни́га, house-register, register of tenants; ~ая конто́ра, house-manager's office; ~ый трест, housing trust.

домога́тельство, -а, solicitation, importunity; demand, bid. **домога́ться,** -а́юсь imp.+gen. seek, solicit, covet, bid for.

домо́й adv. home, homewards. **домостро́ение,** -я, housebuilding. **домостро́ительный,** housebuilding. **домоуправле́ние,** -я, house management (committee). **домохозя́йка,** -и, housewife. **домрабо́тница,** -ы, domestic servant, (daily) maid. **дому́шник,** -а, (sl.) burglar, housebreaker.

дона́шиваться, -вается imp. of доноси́ться[2].

доне́льзя adv. in the extreme; to the utmost degree; он ~ упря́м, he's as stubborn as a mule, he couldn't be more pigheaded.

донесе́ние, -я, dispatch, report, message. **донести́,** -су́, -сёшь; -нёс, -сла́ perf. (imp. доноси́ть) report, announce; + dat. inform; + на + acc. inform against, denounce; ~сь, be heard; + до + gen. reach, reach the ears of; carry as far as.

до́низу adv. to the bottom; све́рху ~, from top to bottom.

донима́ть, -а́ю imp. of доня́ть.

до́нный, bottom, base; ~ лёд, ground ice.

до́нор, -а, blood-donor.

доно́с, -а, denunciation, information. **доноси́ть(ся**[1], -ношу́(сь), -но́сишь(ся imp. of донести́(сь.

доно́шивать(ся, -носится perf. (imp. дона́шиваться) wear out, be worn out.

доно́счик, -а, informer.

донско́й, Don; ~ каза́к, Don Cossack.

до́нья, etc.: see дно.

до н.э. (do-ené) abbr. до на́шей э́ры, B.C.

доня́ть, дойму́, -мёшь; до́нял, -а́, -о perf. (imp. донима́ть), weary to death, pester.

допла́та, -ы, additional payment, extra charge, excess. **доплати́ть** -ачу́, -а́тишь perf., **допла́чивать**, -аю imp. pay in addition; pay the rest.

доплыва́ть, -а́ю imp., **доплы́ть**, -ыву́ -ывёшь; -ыл, -а́, -о perf. + до + gen. swim to, sail to; reach.

допо́длинно adv. for certain. **допо́длинный**, authentic, genuine.

дополне́ние, -я, supplement, addition; appendix; addendum; object. **дополни́тельно** adv. in addition. **дополни́тельн|ый**, supplementary, additional, extra; complementary; ~ые вы́боры, by-election. **допо́лнить**, -ню perf., **дополня́ть**, -я́ю imp. supplement, add to, amplify; complete; complement.

допото́пный, antediluvian.

допра́шивать, -аю imp., **допроси́ть**, -ошу́ -о́сишь perf. interrogate, question, examine. **допро́с**, -а, interrogation, examination.

до́пуск, -а, right of entry, admittance; tolerance. **допуска́ть**, -а́ю imp., **допусти́ть**, -ущу́ -у́стишь perf. admit, allow, permit; tolerate; grant, assume, suppose. **допусти́мый**, permissible, admissible, allowable, acceptable. **допуще́ние**, -я, assumption.

доро́га, -и, road; highway; way; journey; route; в доро́ге, on the journey, on the way, en route; по доро́ге, on the way; the same way; туда́ ему́ и ~! serves him right!

до́рого adv. dear, dearly. **дороговизна́**,

-ы, expensiveness; high cost, high prices. **дорого́й**; до́рог, -а́, -о, dear; expensive; costly.

доро́дный, portly, corpulent, stout; healthy, strong.

дорожа́ть, -а́ет imp. (perf. вз~, по~) rise in price, go up. **доро́же**, comp. of до́рого, дорого́й. **дорожи́ть**, -жу́ imp. + instr. value; prize; care about.

доро́жка, -и, path, walk; track; lane; runway; strip, runner, stair-carpet. **доро́жный**, road; highway; travelling.

доса́да, -ы, annoyance; disappointment; nuisance, pity. **досади́ть**, -ажу́ perf., **досажда́ть**, -а́ю imp. + dat. annoy. **доса́дливый**, annoyed, irritated, disappointed; of annoyance. **доса́дный**, annoying; disappointing. **доса́довать**, -дую, be annoyed (на + acc. with).

досе́ле adv. up to now.

доска́, -и́, acc. до́ску; pl. -и, -со́к, -ска́м, board; plank; slab; plaque, plate.

досло́вный, literal, verbatim; word-for-word.

досмо́тр, -а, inspection, examination. **досмо́трщик**, -а, inspector, examiner.

доспе́хи, -ов pl. armour.

досро́чный, ahead of time, ahead of schedule, early.

доставать(ся, -таю(сь, -ёшь(ся imp. of доста́ть(ся.

доста́вить, -влю perf., **доставля́ть**, -я́ю imp. deliver, convey; supply, furnish; cause, give. **доста́вка**, -и, delivery; conveyance. **доста́вщик**, -а, roundsman, delivery man.

доста́ну, etc.: see доста́ть.

доста́ток, -тка, sufficiency; prosperity; pl. income. **доста́точно** adv. enough, sufficiently; sufficient; adequate; prosperous, well-off.

доста́ть, -а́ну perf. (imp. достава́ть) fetch; get (out), take (out); obtain; + gen. or до + gen. touch; reach; (impers.) suffice, be sufficient; ~ся + dat. pass to, be inherited by; fall to the lot of; ему́ доста́нется, he'll catch it.

достига́ть, -а́ю imp. **дости́гнуть**, **дости́чь**, -и́гну; -сти́г perf. + gen. attain, achieve; + gen. or до + gen.

reach. **достиже́ние**, -я, achievement, attainment. **достижи́мый**, accessible; attainable.

досто- in *comb.*, worthy (of). **достове́рный**, reliable, trustworthy; authentic. **~па́мятный**, memorable. **~примеча́тельность**, -и, notable place or object; *pl.* sights; ~примеча́тельности Ленингра́да, What to see in Leningrad; осма́тривать ~примеча́тельности, go sightseeing. **~примеча́тельный**, noteworthy, remarkable, notable.

досто́инство, -а, dignity; merit, virtue; value; rank, title. **досто́йно** *adv.* suitably, fittingly, adequately, properly; with dignity. **досто́йный**, deserved; fitting, adequate; suitable, fit; worthy; +*gen.* worthy of, deserving.

достоя́ние, -я, property.

до́ступ, -а, access; entrance; admission, admittance. **досту́пный**, accessible; simple; easily understood; intelligible; approachable; moderate, reasonable; ~ для, open to; available to.

досу́г, -а, leisure, (spare) time. **досу́жий** leisure, spare; idle.

до́суха *adv.* dry.

досяга́емый, attainable accessible.

дота́ция, -и, grant, subsidy.

дотла́ *adv.* utterly, completely, out; to the ground.

дото́шный, meticulous.

дотра́гиваться, -аюсь *imp.*, **дотро́нуться**, -нусь *perf.* +до+*gen.* touch.

дотя́гивать, -аю *imp.*, **дотяну́ть**, -яну́, -я́нешь *perf.* draw out; stretch out; hold out; live, last; put off; +до+*gen.* draw, drag, haul as far as; reach, make; ~ся, stretch, reach; drag on; +до+*gen.* reach, touch.

до́хлый, dead; sickly, puny. **до́хнуть**, -нет; дох (*perf.* из~, по~, с~) die, croak, kick the bucket.

дохну́ть, -ну́, -нёшь *perf.* draw a breath.

дохо́д, -а, income; receipts; revenue. **доходи́ть**, -ожу́, -о́дишь *imp.* of дойти́. **дохо́дность**, -и, profitability; income. **дохо́дный**, profitable, lucrative, paying; income-producing, revenue-producing. **дохо́дчивый**, intelligible, easy to understand.

доц. *abbr.*, **доце́нт**, -а, reader, senior lecturer.

до́чери, etc.: see дочь.

до́чиста *adv.* clean; completely.

до́чка, -и, daughter. **дочь**, -чери, *instr.* -черью; *pl.* -чери, -чере́й, *instr.* -черьми́, daughter.

дошёл, etc.: see дойти́.

дошко́льник, -а, -ница, -ы, child under school age. **дошко́льный**, pre-school; nursery.

доща́тый, plank, board, wooden. **доще́чка**, -и, small plank, small board; door-plate, name-plate.

доя́рка, -и, milkmaid.

др. *abbr.* други́е, others.

драгоце́нность, -и, jewel; gem; precious stone; treasure; *pl.* jewellery; valuables. **драгоце́нный**, precious.

дразни́ть, -ню́, -нишь *imp.* tease.

дра́ка, -и, fight; доходи́ть до дра́ки, come to blows.

драко́н, -а, dragon; wyvern.

дра́ма, -ы, drama; tragedy, calamity. **драмати́зм**, -а, dramatic effect; dramatic character, dramatic quality; tension. **драмати́ческий**, dramatic; drama, theatre, of the theatre; theatrical; tense. **драмату́рг**, -а, playwright, dramatist. **драматурги́я**, -и, dramatic art; dramatic composition, play-writing; drama, plays.

драп, -а, heavy woollen cloth.

драпиро́вка, -и, draping; curtain; hangings. **драпиро́вщик**, -а, upholsterer. **драпри́** *indecl. pl.* curtain(s), hangings. **дра́повый**, cloth.

драть, деру́, -рёшь; драл, -á, -о *imp.* (*perf.* вы~, за~, со~) tear, tear up; sting, irritate; run away, make off; tear off; kill; beat, flog, thrash; tear out; +c+*gen.* fleece; sting; ~ го́рло, bawl; ~ у́ши+*dat.* jar on; чёрт его́ (по)дери́! damn him!; ~ся, fight; use one's fists; struggle.

дре́безги *pl.*; в ~, to smithereens. **дребезжа́ние**, -я, rattle, clink, jingle, tinkle. **дребезжа́ть**, -жи́т *imp.* rattle, jingle, tinkle, clink.

древеси́на, -ы, wood; wood-pulp; timber. **древе́с|ный**, wood; ~ая ма́сса, wood-pulp; ~ый пито́мник, arboretum; ~ый у́голь, charcoal.

дре́вко, -а; pl. -и, -ов, pole, (flag-)staff; shaft.

древнееврейский, Hebrew. древнеру́сский, Old Russian. дре́вний, ancient; very old, aged. дре́вность, -и, antiquity.

дрези́на, -ы, trolley.

дрейф, -а, drift; leeway. дрейфова́ть, -фу́ю imp. drift. дрейфу́ющий, drifting; ~ лёд, drift-ice.

дрема́, -ы́, дрёма, -ы, drowsiness, sleepiness. дрема́ть, -млю́, -млешь imp. doze; slumber; drowse; не ~, be wakeful; be wide awake, on the alert. дремо́та, -ы, drowsiness, somnolence. дрему́чий, thick, dense.

дрессиро́ванный, trained; performing. дрессирова́ть, -ру́ю imp. (perf. вы́~) train, school. дрессиро́вка, -и, training. дрессиро́вщик, -а, trainer.

дроби́льный, crushing, grinding. дроби́на, -ы, pellet. дроби́ть, -блю́ imp. (perf. раз~) break up, smash; crush, grind; divide, split up; ~ся, break to pieces, smash; crumble; divide, split up. дроблёный, splintered, crushed, ground, fragmented. дро́бный, separate; subdivided, split up; minute; staccato, abrupt; fractional; ~ дождь, fine rain. дробови́к, -а́, shot-gun. дробь, -и, (small) shot, pellets; drumming; tapping; trilling; fraction.

дрова́, дров, pl. firewood. дро́вни, дро́вней pl. wood-sledge.

дро́ги, дрог pl. dray; hearse. дро́гнуть, -ну perf., дрожа́ть, -жу́ imp. shake, move; tremble; shiver; quiver, quaver; flicker; waver, falter; +над+instr. be concerned over, worry about; grudge.

дрожжево́й, yeast. дро́жжи, -е́й pl. yeast.

дро́жки, -жек pl. droshky.

дрожь, -и, shivering, trembling; tremor, quaver.

дрозд, -а́, thrush.

дро́ссель, -я m. throttle, choke.

дро́тик, -а, javelin, dart.

друг[1], -а; pl. -узья́, -зе́й, friend.
друг[2]; ~ дру́га (дру́гу), each other,

one another; ~ за ~ом, one after another; in single file. друго́й, other, another; different; second; на ~ день, (the) next day. дру́жба, -ы, friendship.

дружелю́бный, дру́жеский, дру́жественный, friendly. дружи́ть, -жу́, -у́жишь imp. be friends. be on friendly terms; ~ся (perf. по~ся) make friends. дру́жно adv. harmoniously, in concord; simultaneously, in concert; rapidly, smoothly. дру́жный, -жен, -жна́, -о, amicable; harmonious; simultaneous, concerted.

друммо́ндов свет, limelight.

дря́блый, дрябл, -а́, -о, flabby; flaccid; sluggish.

дря́зги, -зг pl. squabbles; petty annoyances.

дрянно́й, worthless, rotten; good-for-nothing. дрянь, -и, trash, rubbish. дряхле́ть, -е́ю imp. (perf. о~) become decrepit. дря́хлый, -хл, -ла́, -о, decrepit, senile.

ДСО (десо́) abbr. доброво́льное спорти́вное о́бщество, Voluntary Sports club.

дуб, -а; pl. -ы́, oak; blockhead. дуби́льный, tanning, tannic. дуби́льня, -и; gen. pl. -лен, tannery. дуби́на, -ы; club, cudgel; blockhead. дуби́нка, -и, truncheon, baton. дуби́ть, -блю́ imp. (perf. вы́~) tan.

дублёр, -а, understudy; actor dubbing a part. дубле́т, -а, дублика́т, -а, duplicate. дубли́ровать, -рую imp. duplicate; understudy; dub.

дубова́тый, coarse; stupid, thick. дубо́вый, oak; coarse; clumsy, thick.

дуга́, -и́; pl. -и, shaft-bow; arc; arch.

ду́дка, -и, pipe, fife.

ду́жка, -и, small arch or bow; handle; (croquet-)hoop; wishbone.

ду́ло, -а, muzzle; barrel. ду́льце, -а; gen. pl. -лец, mouthpiece.

ду́ма, -ы, thought; Duma; council. ду́мать, -аю imp. (perf. по~) think; +inf. think of, intend.

дунове́ние, -я, puff, breath. ду́нуть, -ну perf. of ду́ть.

дупли́стый, hollow. дупло́, -а́; pl. -а, -пел, hollow; hole; cavity.

ду́ра, -ы, дура́к, -а́, fool. дура́чить, -чу

imp. (*perf.* o~) fool, dupe; ~ся, play the fool.

дуре́ть, -е́ю *imp.* (*perf.* o~) grow stupid.

дурма́н, -а, datura; drug, narcotic; intoxicant. дурма́нить, -ню *imp.* (*perf.* o~) stupefy.

дурно́й; -рен, -рна́, -о, bad, evil; nasty; ill, faint; ugly; мне ду́рно, I'm going to faint. дурнота́, -ы́, faintness; nausea.

ду́тый, blown, blown up, hollow; inflated; pneumatic; exaggerated. дуть, ду́ю *imp.* (*perf.* вы́-, по~, ду́нуть) blow; ду́ет, there is a draught. дутьё, -я́, blowing; draught; blast; glass-blowing. ду́ться, ду́юсь *imp.* pout; sulk. be sulky.

дух, -а (-у), spirit; spirits; heart; mind; breath; air; ghost; smell; в ~е, in high spirits in a good mood; во весь ~, at full speed, flat out; не в моём ~е, not to my taste; ни слу́ху ни ~у, no news, not a word, not a whisper; одни́м ~ом, in one breath; at one go, at a stretch; па́дать ~ом, lose heart, grow despondent. духи́, -о́в *pl.* scent, perfume. Ду́хов день, Whit Monday. духове́нство, -а, clergy, priesthood. духови́дец, -дца, clairvoyant; medium. духо́вка, -и, oven. духо́вный, spiritual; inner, inward; ecclesiastical; church, religious. духово́й, wind; air; steam; steamed. духота́, -ы́, stuffiness, closeness; stuffy heat.

душ, -а, shower-bath.

душа́, -и́, *acc.* -у; *pl.* -ши, soul; heart; feeling; spirit; moving spirit; inspiration; в глубине́ души́, in one's heart of hearts; в душе́, inwardly, secretly; at heart; за душо́й, in one's name; на ду́шу, per head; от всей души́, with all one's heart.

душева́я *sb.* shower-baths.

душевнобольно́й, mentally ill, insane;

sb. mental patient; lunatic. душе́вный, mental; of the mind; sincere, cordial, heartfelt.

души́стый, fragrant; sweet-scented; ~ горо́шек, sweet pea(s). души́ть[1], -шу́, -шишь *imp.* (*perf.* на~) scent, perfume; ~ся, use scent, put on scent.

души́ть[2], -шу́, -шишь *imp.* (*perf.* за~) strangle; stifle, smother, suffocate; suppress; choke.

ду́шный; -шен, -шна́, -о, stuffy, close; sultry; stifling, suffocating.

дыбо́м *adv.* on end; у меня́ во́лосы вста́ли ~, my hair stood on end. дыбы́: станови́ться на ~, rear; resist, jib, dig one's heels in.

дым, -а (-у), *loc.* -у́; *pl.* -ы́, smoke. дыми́ть, -млю́ *imp.* (*perf.* на~) smoke; ~ся, smoke, steam; billow. ды́мка, -и, haze, mist. ды́мный, smoky. дымово́й, smoke; ~ая труба́, flue, chimney; ~ая труба́, smoke-stack, funnel. дымо́к, -мка́, puff of smoke. дымохо́д, -а, flue. ды́мчатый, smoky; smoked; smoke-coloured.

ды́ня, -и, melon.

дыра́, -ы́; *pl.* -ы ды́рка, -и; *gen. pl.* -рок, hole; gap. дыря́вый, full of holes; holed, perforated.

дыха́ние, -я, breathing, respiration; breath. дыха́тельный, respiratory; breathing, breather; ~ое го́рло, windpipe. дыша́ть, -шу́, -шишь *imp.* breathe.

дья́вол, -а, devil. дья́вольский, devilish, diabolical; damnable.

дьяк, -а́, clerk, secretary. дья́кон, -а; *pl.* -а́, deacon. дьячо́к, -чка́, sacristan, sexton; reader.

дю́жина, -ы, dozen. дю́жинный, ordinary, commonplace.

дэ *n. indecl.* the letter д.

дя́денька, -и *m.*, дя́дюшка, -и *m.* uncle. дя́дя, -и; *gen. pl.* -ей *m.* uncle.

дя́тел, -тла, woodpecker.

Е

е *n. indecl.* the letter e.

ев- *pref.* eu-. **евге́ника, -и,** eugenics. **е́внух, -а,** eunuch. **евразийский,** Eurasian. **евстáхиев,** Eustachian.

ева́нгелие, -я gospel; the Gospels. **евангели́ческий,** evangelical. **ева́нгельский,** gospel.

евре́й, -я, Jew; Hebrew. **евре́йка, -и** Jewess. **евре́йский,** Jewish.

Еврови́дение, -я, Eurovision. **европе́ец, -éйца,** European. **европе́йский,** European.

еги́петский, Egyptian. **египтя́нин, -а;** *pl.* -**я́не, -я́н, египтя́нка, -и,** Egyptian.

его́ see **он, оно́**; *pron.* his; its, of it.

еда́, -ы́, food; meal; eating.

едва́ *adv.* and *conj.* hardly, barely; only just; scarcely; ~ .., как, no sooner .. than; ~ ли, hardly, scarcely; ~ (ли) не, nearly, almost, all but.

еди́м, etc.: see **есть**[1].

едине́ние, -я, unity. **едини́ца, -ы,** one; figure one; unity; unit; individual. **едини́чность, -и,** singleness; single occurrence. **едини́чный,** single, unitary; solitary, isolated; individual.

едино- in *comb.* mono-, uni-; one; co-. **единобо́жие, -я,** monotheism. ~**бо́рство, -а,** single combat. ~**бра́чие, -я,** monogamy. ~**бра́чный,** monogamous. ~**вла́стие, -я,** autocracy, absolute rule. ~**вла́стный,** autocratic; dictatorial; absolute. ~**вре́менно** *adv.* only once; simultaneously. ~**вре́менный,** extraordinary; unique; + *dat.* or c + *instr.* simultaneous with. ~**гла́сие, -я,** ~**ду́шие, -я,** unanimity. ~**гла́сный,** ~**ду́шный,** unanimous. ~**кро́вный,** consanguineous; ~**кро́вный брат,** half-brother. ~**мы́слие, -я,** like-mindedness; agreement in opinion. ~**мы́шленник, -а,** like-minded person; accomplice; мы с ним ~**мы́шленники,** we are in agreement, we think the same way. ~**нача́лие, -я,** unified management command. ~**образ-я** uniformity. ~**обра́зный,** uniform. ~**рог, -а,** unicorn; narwhal. ~**утро́б-**ный, uterine; ~**утро́бный брат,** half-brother.

еди́нственно *adv.* only, solely. **еди́нственный,** only, sole; singular; unique, unequalled. **еди́нство, -а,** unity. **еди́ный,** one; single; sole; united, unified; common.

е́дкий; е́док, е́дка, -о, caustic, corrosive; acrid, pungent; sarcastic; ~ **натр,** caustic soda.

едо́к, -á, mouth; head; eater.

е́ду, etc.: see **е́хать. е́дче,** *comp.* of **е́дкий.**

её: see **она́;** *pron.* her, hers; its.

ёж, ежá, hedgehog.

еже- in *comb.* every; -ly. **ежего́дник, -а,** annual, year-book. ~**го́дный,** annual, yearly. ~**дне́вный,** daily; everyday; quotidian. ~**ме́сячник, -а,** ~**ме́сячный,** monthly. ~**неде́льник, -а,** ~**неде́льный,** weekly. ~**но́шный,** nightly.

ежеви́ка, -и, blackberries; blackberry bush, bramble. **ежеви́чный,** blackberry.

ёжиться, ёжусь *imp.* (*perf.* съ~) huddle up; shrivel; shrink away; hesitate.

езда́, -ы́, ride, riding; drive, driving; going; journey; traffic. **е́здить, е́зжу** *imp.* go; ride, drive; slip; ~ **верхо́м,** ride. **ездо́к, -á,** rider; horseman.

ей: see **она́.**

ей-бо́гу *int.* really! I swear (to God).

ел, etc.: see **есть**[1].

е́ле *adv.* hardly, barely, scarcely; only just.

ёлка, -и, fir, fir-tree; spruce; Christmas tree, Christmas party; herring-bone pattern. **е́ловый,** fir, spruce; deal, white-wood. **ёлочка, -и,** herring-bone pattern, herring-boning. **ёлочный,** Christmas-tree; herring-bone; dendritic. **ель, -и,** fir-tree; spruce; deal, white wood. **е́льник, -а,** fir (spruce) plantation; fir-wood, fir-twigs.

ем, etc.: see **есть**[1].

ёмкий, capacious. **ёмкость, -и,** capacity, cubic content; capacitance.

ему́: see **он, оно́.**

енóт, -а, енóтовый, raccoon.

епи́скоп, -а, bishop. епи́скопский, episcopal.

е́ресь, -и heresy. ерети́к, -á, heretic. ерети́ческий, heretical.

ёрзать, -аю imp. fidget.

еро́шить, -шу imp. (perf. взъ~) ruffle, rumple, tousle; dishevel; ~ся, bristle, stand on end, stick up.

ерундá, -ы́, nonsense, rubbish; trifle, trifling matter.

е́сли, if; ~ бы, if only; ~ бы не, but for, if it were not for: ~ не, unless; ~ то́лько, provided; if only; что, ~ бы, what about, how about.

ест: see есть¹.

есте́ственно adv. naturally. есте́ственный, natural. естество́, -á, nature; essence. естествове́дение, -я, есте́ствознáние, -я, (natural) science; natural history; nature study.

есть¹, ем, ешь, ест, еди́м; ел imp. (perf. съ~) eat; corrode, eat away; sting, make smart; torment, nag (at).

есть²: see быть; is, are; there is, there are; и ~, yes, indeed; как ~, entirely, completely; int. yes, sir; very good, sir; aye, aye sir.

ефре́йтор, -a, lance-corporal.

е́хать, е́ду imp. (perf. по~) go; ride, drive; travel, journey, voyage; ~ верхо́м, ride.

ехи́дный, malicious, spiteful; venomous.

ешь: see есть¹.

ещё adv. still; yet; (some) more; any more; yet; further; again; +comp. still, yet even; всё ~, still; ~ бы! of course! oh yes! can you ask?; ~ не, нет ~, not yet; ~ раз, once more, again; encore!; покá ~, for the present, for the time being.

ЕЭС (éés) abbr. Европе́йское экономи́ческое соо́бщество, E.E.C.

е́ю: see онá.

Ж

ж letter: see жэ.

ж conj.: see же.

жáба, -ы, toad; quinsy.

жáбра, -ы; gen. pl. -бр, gill, branchia.

жáворонок, -нка, lark.

жáдничать, -аю imp. be greedy; be mean. жáдность, -и, greed; greediness; avidity; avarice, meanness. жáдный, -ден, -днá, -о, greedy; avid; avaricious, mean.

жáжда, -ы, thirst; + gen. thirst for, craving for. жáждать, -ду imp. thirst, long, yearn.

жакéт -а, жакéтка, -и, jacket.

жалéть, -éю imp. (perf. по~) pity, feel sorry for; regret, be sorry; +acc. or gen. spare; grudge.

жáлить, -лю imp. (perf. у~) sting, bite.

жáлкий, -лок, -лкá, -о, pitiful, pitiable, pathetic, wretched. жáлко predic.: see жаль.

жáло, -a, sting.

жáлоба, -ы, complaint. жáлобный, plaintive; doleful mournful.

жáлованный, granted, conferred; ~ая грáмота, charter, letters patent. жáлованье, -я, salary, pay, wage(s); reward; donation. жáловать, -лую imp. (perf. по~)+acc. or dat. of person, instr. or acc. of thing, grant, bestow on, confer on; +к+dat. come to see, visit; ~ся, complain (на+acc. of, about).

жáлостливый, compassionate, sympathetic; pitiful. жáлостный, piteous; compassionate, sympathetic. жáлость, -и, pity, compassion. жаль, жáлко, predic. impers. (it is) a pity, a shame; + dat. it grieves; + dat. and gen. regret; feel sorry for; +gen. grudge; ей ~ бы́ло себя́, she felt sorry for herself; ~, что вас там не́ было, it is a pity you were not there; как ~, what a pity; мне ~ его́, I'm sorry for him.

жанр, -а, genre; genre-painting. жанри́ст, -а, genre-painter.

жар, -а (-у), *loc.* -у́, heat; heat of the day; hot place; embers; fever; (high) temperature; ardour. жара́, -ы́, heat; hot weather.

жарго́н, -а, jargon; slang; cant.

жа́рен|ый, roast; grilled; fried; ~ый карто́фель, chips; ~ое *sb.* roast (meat). жа́рить, -рю *imp.* (*perf.* за~, из~) roast; grill; fry; scorch; burn; ~ся, roast, fry; ~ся на со́лнце, sunbathe. жа́рк|ий, -рок, -рка́, -о, hot; torrid; tropical; heated; ardent; passionate; ~ое *sb.* roast (meat). жаро́вня, -и; *gen. pl.* -вен, brazier. жар-пти́ца, -ы, Firebird. жа́рче, *comp.* of жа́ркий.

жа́тва, -ы, harvest; reaping. жа́твенн|ый, harvest; reaping; ~ая маши́на, harvester, reaper. жа́тка, -и, harvester, reaper. жать¹, жну, жнёшь *imp.* (*perf.* с~), reap, cut.

жать², жму, жмёшь *imp.* press, squeeze; pinch, be tight; oppress.

жва́чка, -и chewing, rumination; cud; chewing-gum. жва́чн|ый, ruminant; ~ое *sb.* ruminant.

жгу, etc.: see жечь.

жгут, á, plait; braid; tourniquet.

жгу́чий, burning, smarting; scalding, baking; hot; caustic, corrosive. жёг, etc.: see жечь.

ж.д. *abbr.* желе́зная доро́га, railway.

ждать, жду, ждёшь; -ал, -á, -о *imp.*+ *gen.* wait for, await; expect.

же, ж *conj.* but; and; however; also; *part.* giving emphasis or expressing identity; мне же ка́жется, it seems to me, however; на пе́рвом же шагу́, at the very first step; оди́н и тот же, one and the same; он же ваш брат, he's your brother, after all; сего́дня же, this very day; так же, in the same way; тако́й же, тот же, the same, idem; там же, in the same place, ibid.; что же ты де́лаешь? what on earth are you doing?

жева́тельн|ый, chewing; ~ая рези́нка, chewing-gum. жева́ть, жую́, жуёшь *imp.* chew, masticate; ruminate.

жезл, -á, rod; staff; baton; crozier.

жела́ние, -я wish, desire. жела́нный, wished-for, longed-for; desired; beloved. жела́тельный, desirable; advisable, preferable; optative. жела́ть, -áю *imp.* (*perf.* по~)+*gen.* wish for, desire; want; + что́бы or *inf.* wish, want. жела́ющие *sb. pl.* those who wish.

желе́ *n. indecl.* jelly.

железа́, -ы́; *pl.* же́лезы, -лёз, -зáм, gland; *pl.* tonsils. желе́зистый¹, glandular.

желе́зистый², iron; ferrous; ferriferous; chalybeate. железнодоро́жник, а, railwayman. железнодоро́жн|ый, railway; ~ая ве́тка, branch line; ~ое полотно́, permanent way; ~ый у́зел, junction. желе́зн|ый, iron; ferric; reliable, dependable; ~ая доро́га, railway; ~ый лом, scrap iron. желе́зо, -а, iron.

железо- in *comb.* iron, ferro-, ferri-, ferric. железобето́н, -а, reinforced concrete, ferro-concrete. ~бето́нный, reinforced-concrete. ~пла́вильный заво́д, iron foundry. ~прока́тный, steel-rolling; ~прока́тный заво́д, rolling mill. ~ру́дный, iron-ore.

жёлоб, -а; *pl.* -á, gutter; trough; chute; channel; groove. желобо́к, -бка́, groove, channel flute; slot; furrow.

желте́ть, -е́ю *imp.* (*perf.* по~) turn yellow; show yellow. желтова́тый, yellowish; sallow. желто́к, -тка́. yolk. желту́ха, -и, jaundice. желту́шный, jaundiced; ~ая мель, brass.

желу́док, -дка, stomach. желу́дочный, stomach; gastric.

жёлудь, -я; *gen. pl.* -е́й *m.* acorn.

жёлчный, bilious; bile, gall; peevish, irritable. жёлчь, -и, bile, gall.

жема́ниться, -нюсь *imp.* be affected, put on airs. жема́нный, mincing, affected.

же́мчуг, -а; *pl.* -á, pearl, pearls. жемчу́жина, -ы, pearl. жемчу́жный, pearl; pearly.

жена́ -ы́; *pl.* жёны, wife. жена́тик, -а, married man; *pl.* married couple. жена́тый, married. жени́ть, -ню́, -нишь *perf.* and *imp.* (*perf.* also по~)

marry. **жени́тьба**, -ы, marriage, wedding. **жени́ться**, -ню́сь, -нишься *perf.* and *imp.* (+на+*prep.*) marry, get married (to). **жени́х**, -а́, fiancé; bridegroom. **же́нский**, woman's; feminine; female. **же́нственный**, womanly, feminine. **же́нщина**, -ы, woman.

жердь, -и; *gen. pl.* -е́й pole; stake.

жеребёнок, -нка; *pl.* -бя́та, -бя́т, foal. **жеребе́ц**, -бца́, stallion.

жеребьёвка, -и, casting of lots.

жерло́, -а́; *pl.* -а, muzzle; vent, pipe, crater.

жёрнов, -а; *pl.* -а́, -о́в. millstone.

же́ртва, -ы, sacrifice; victim: пасть же́ртвой+*gen.* fall victim to; принести́ в же́ртву, sacrifice. **же́ртвенный**, sacrificial. **же́ртвовать**, -твую *imp.* (*perf.* по~) present, donate, make a donation (of); +*instr.* sacrifice, give up.

жест, -а, gesture.

жёсткий, -ток, -тка́, -о hard, tough; rigid, strict.

жесто́кий, -то́к, -а́, -о, cruel; brutal; severe, sharp. **жестокосе́рдный**, -се́рдый, hard-hearted. **жесто́кость**, -и, cruelty, brutality.

жёстче *comp.* of жёсткий.

жесть, -и, tin(-plate). **жестя́нка**, -и, tin, can; piece of tin. **жестяно́й**, tin; ~áя посу́да, tinware.

жето́н, -а, medal; counter.

жечь, жгу, жжёшь; жёг жгла *imp.* (*perf.* с~) burn; ~ся, burn, sting; burn oneself. **жжёный**, burnt; scorched; ~ ко́фе, roasted coffee.

живи́тельный, invigorating, revivifying; bracing. **жи́во** *adv.* vividly; with animation; keenly; strikingly; quickly promptly. **живо́й**, жив, -á, -о, living, live, alive; lively; keen; brisk; animated; vivacious; poignant; bright, sparkling; ~áя и́згородь, (quickset) hedge; ~о́й инвента́рь, livestock; на ~у́ю ни́тку, hastily, anyhow; шить на ~у́ю ни́тку, tack; оста́ться в ~ы́х, survive, escape with one's life. **живопи́сец**, -сца, painter. **живопи́сный**, pictorial; picturesque. **жи́вопись**, -и, painting; paintings, art. **жи́вость**, -и, liveliness, vivacity, animation.

живо́т, -á, abdomen, belly; stomach. **живо́тик**, -а, tummy. **животново́дство**, -а, stock-breeding, animal husbandry. **живо́тное** *sb.* animal; beast; brute. **живо́тный**, animal.

живу́, etc.: see жить. **живу́чий**, tenacious of life; hardy; firm, stable. **живьём** *adv.* alive.

жи́дк|ий, -док, -дка́, -о, liquid; fluid; watery; weak, thin; sparse, scanty; feeble; ~ий криста́лл, liquid crystal; ~ое те́ло, liquid. **жи́дкостный**, liquid, fluid; liquid-fuel. **жи́дкость**, -и, liquid, fluid; liquor; wateriness, weakness, thinness. **жи́жа**, -и, жи́жица, -ы, sludge, slurry; slush; wash, swill; liquid, liquor. **жи́же**, *comp.* of жи́дкий.

жи́зненный, life, of life; vital; living; close to life; lifelike; vitally important; ~ые си́лы, vitality, sap; ~ый у́ровень, standard of living. **жизнеописа́ние**, -я, biography. **жизнера́достный**, full of the joy of living; cheerful, buoyant. **жизнеспосо́бный** capable of living; viable; vigorous, flourishing. **жизнь**, -и, life; existence.

жил- *abbr.* in *comb.* of жили́щный, жило́й; living; housing. **жилотде́л**, -а, housing department. **~пло́щадь**, -и, floor-space; housing, accommodation. **~строи́тельство**, -а, house-building. **~фонд**, -а, housing, accommodation.

жи́ла, -ы, vein; tendon, sinew, lode, seam; core, strand; catgut.

жиле́т, -а, жиле́тка, -и, waistcoat.

жиле́ц, -льца́, жили́ца, -ы, lodger; tenant; inhabitant; он не ~ (на бе́лом све́те), he is not long for this world.

жи́листый, sinewy; stringy; wiry.

жили́ца: see жиле́ц. **жили́ще**, -а, dwelling, abode; lodging; (living) quarters. **жили́щн|ый**, housing; living; ~ые усло́вия, living conditions.

жи́лка, -и, vein; fibre, rib; streak; bent. **жил|о́й**, dwelling; residential; inhabited; habitable, fit to live in; ~о́й дом, dwelling house; block of flats; ~áя пло́щадь, floor-space; housing, accommodation. **жильё**, -я́, habitation, dwelling; lodging; (living) accommodation.

жим, -а, press.

жир, -а (-у), *loc.* -ý; *pl.* -ы́, fat; grease. **жире́ть**, -е́ю *imp.* (*perf.* о~, раз~), grow fat, stout, plump. **жи́рный**; -рен, -рна́, -о, fatty; greasy; rich; plump; lush; bold, heavy. **жирова́ть**, -ру́ю *imp.* lubricate, oil, grease; fatten, grow fat. **жирово́й**, fatty; adipose; fat.

жите́йский, worldly; of life, of the world; everyday. **жи́тель**, -я *m.* inhabitant; dweller. **жи́тельство**, -а, residence; ме́сто жи́тельства, residence, domicile; ме́сто постоя́нного жи́тельства, permanent address. **жи́тница**, -ы, granary. **жи́тный**, cereal. **жи́то**, -а, corn, cereal. **жить**, живу́, -вёшь; жил, -á, -о *imp.* live; +*instr.* live for, live on, live in. **житьё**, -я́, life; existence; habitation, residence.

ЖКО (*zhekaó*) *abbr.* жили́щно-коммуна́льный о́тдел, department of housing and public utilities.

жму, etc.: see жать².

жму́риться, -рюсь *imp.* (*perf.* за~) screw up one's eyes, frown. **жму́рки**, -рок *pl.* blind-man's-buff.

жмых, -á, жмыхи́, -óв *pl.* oil-cake.

жне́йка, -и, reaper. **жнец**, -á, **жни́ца**, -ы, reaper. **жну**, etc.: see жать¹.

жоке́й, -я, jockey. **жоке́йка**, -и, jockey cap.

жре́бий, -я, lot; fate, destiny; ~ бро́шен, the die is cast.

жрец, -á, priest. **жре́ческий**, priestly. **жри́ца**, -ы, priestess.

жужжа́ние, -я, humming, buzzing; hum, buzz, drone. **жужжа́ть**, -жжу́, hum, buzz, drone; whiz(z).

жук, -á, beetle.

жу́лик, -а, petty thief; cheat, swindler; card-sharper. **жу́льничать**, -аю *imp.* (*perf.* с~) cheat, swindle, defraud.

жура́вль, -я́ *m.* crane.

жури́ть, -рю́ *imp.* reprove, take to task.

журна́л, -а, magazine, periodical; journal; diary; register; log; ~ заседа́ний minute-book.

журча́ние, -я, ripple, babble; murmur. **журча́ть**, -чи́т *imp.* babble, ripple, murmur.

жу́ткий; -ток, -тка́, -о, awe-inspiring; uncanny; terrible, terrifying. **жу́тко** *adv.* terrifyingly; terribly, awfully.

жую́, etc.: see жева́ть.

жэ *n. indecl.* the letter ж.

жюри́, *n. indecl.* jury, judges; umpire, referee; член ~, judge.

З

з *letter:* see зэ.

з. *abbr.* за́пад, W.

за *prep.* I.+*acc.* (indicating motion or action) or *instr.* (indicating rest or state) behind; beyond; across, the other side of; at; to; вы́йти за́муж за +*acc.* marry, get married to; за́мужем за+*instr.* married to; за́ борт, за бо́ртом, overboard; за́ городом, out of town; за рубежо́м, abroad; сесть за роя́ль, sit down at the piano; сиде́ть за роя́лем, be at the piano; за угол, за угло́м, round the corner. II.+*acc.* after; over; during, in the space of; by;

for; to; боя́ться за, fear for; за ва́ше здоро́вье! your health!; вести́ за́ руку, lead by the hand; далеко́ за по́лночь, long after midnight; за два дня до+ *gen.* two days before; ему́ уже́ за со́рок, he is over forty already; есть за трои́х, eat enough for three; за три киломе́тра от дере́вни, three kilometres from the village; за́ ночь, during the night, overnight; за биле́т, pay for a ticket; за после́днее вре́мя, recently, lately, of late. III.+ *instr.* after; for; on account of, because of; at, during; год за го́дом, year after year; идти за молокóм, go for milk; за неимéнием+*gen*. for want of; за обéдом, at dinner; óчередь за вáми, it is your turn; послáть за дóктором, send for a doctor; следить за, look after; слéдовать за, follow.

за- *perf*. in *comb*. I. with *vbs*.: forms the perfective aspect; indicates beginning of action, direction of action beyond a given point, continuation of action to excess. II. with *sbs*. and *adjs*., trans-, beyond, on the far side.

забáва, -ы, amusement; game; pastime; fun. забавлять, -яю *imp*. amuse, entertain, divert; ~ся, amuse oneself. забáвный, amusing, funny.

забаллотировать, -рую *perf*. blackball, reject, fail to elect.

забастовáть, -тýю *perf*. strike; go on strike, come out on strike. забастóвка, -и, strike; stoppage. забастóвщик, -а, -шица, -ы, striker.

забвéние, -я, oblivion; unconsciousness; drowsiness. забвéнный, forgotten.

забéг, -а, heat, race; trial. забегáть, -áю *imp*.. забежáть, -егý *perf*. run up; run off; stray; +к+*dat*. drop in on, look in to see; ~ вперёд, run ahead; anticipate.

забелéть(ся, -éет(ся *perf*. (begin to) turn white.

за|берéменеть, -ею *perf*. become pregnant.

заберý, etc.: see забрáть. за|бетони́ровать, -рую *perf*.

забивáние, -я, jamming. забивáть(ся, -áю(сь *imp*. of забить(ся[1]. забивка, -и, driving in; blocking up; stopping up.

за|бинтовáть, -тýю *perf*., забинтóвывать *imp*. bandage; ~ся, bandage oneself.

забирáть(ся, -áю(сь *imp*. of забрáть(ся. забитый, cowed, downtrodden. забить[1], -бью, -бьёшь *perf*. (*imp*. забивáть), drive in, hammer in, ram in; score; seal, stop up, block up; obstruct; choke; jam; cram, stuff; beat up, knock senseless; render defenceless;

beat; outdo, surpass; slaughter; ~ себé в гóлову, get it firmly fixed in one's head; ~ся, hide, take refuge; become cluttered, become clogged; +в +*acc*. get into, penetrate. за|бить(ся[2] *perf*. begin to beat. забияка, -и *m*. and *f*. quarrelsome person; squabbler; trouble-maker; bully.

заблаговрéменно *adv*. in good time; well in advance. заблаговрéменный, done in good time.

заблагорассýдиться, -ится *perf*. *impers*. (+*dat*.) come into one's head; seem good (to); он придёт, когдá емý заблагорассýдится, he will come when he thinks fit, feels like it, feels so disposed.

заблестéть, -ещý, -естишь or -éшешь *perf*. begin to shine, glitter, glow.

заблудиться, -ужýсь, -ýдишься *perf*. lose one's way, get lost. заблýдший, lost, stray. заблуждáться, -áюсь *imp*. be mistaken. заблуждéние, -я, error; delusion.

за|бодáть, -áю *perf*.

забóй, -я, (pit)face. забóйщик, -а, face-worker, cutter.

заболевáемость, -и, sickness rate; number of cases. заболевáние, -я, sickness, illness, disease; falling ill. заболевáть[1], -áю *imp*., заболéть[1], -éю *perf*. fall ill, fall sick; be taken; +*instr*. go down with. заболевáть[2], -áет *imp*., заболéть[2], -лит *perf*. (begin to) ache, (begin to) hurt; у меня заболéл зуб, I have tooth-ache.

забóр[1], -а, fence. забóристый, strong; pungent; risqué, racy. забóрный, fence; coarse, indecent; risqué.

забóр[2], -а, taking away; obtaining on credit.

забóртный, outboard.

забóта, -ы, concern; care, attention(s); cares, trouble(s). забóтить, -óчу *imp*. (*perf*. о~) trouble, worry, cause anxiety to; ~ся *imp*. (*perf*. по~) worry, be troubled; take care (о+*prep*. of); take trouble; care. забóтливый, solicitous, thoughtful.

за|боцáть, -áю *perf*.

забракóванный, rejected; ~ товáр, rejects. за|браковáть, -кýю *perf*.

забра́сывать, -аю *imp.* of заброса́ть, забро́сить.

забра́ть, -беру́, -берёшь; -а́л, -а́, -о *perf.* (*imp.* забира́ть), take; take away; seize; appropriate; take in; turn off, turn aside; come over; catch; stop up, block up; ~ся, climb; get to, get into; hide, go into hiding.

забреда́ть, -а́ю *imp.*, **забрести́**, -еду́, -едёшь; -ёл, -а́ *perf.* stray, wander; drop in.

за|брони́рова́ть[1] -ру́ю *perf.* **за|брони́ровать**[2], -ру́ю *perf.*

заброса́ть, -а́ю *perf.* (*imp.* забра́сывать), fill up; shower, bespatter, deluge. **забро́сить**, -о́шу *perf.* (*imp.* забра́сывать) throw; fling; cast; throw up, give up, abandon; neglect; let go; take, bring; leave behind; mislay. **забро́шенный**, neglected; deserted, desolate.

забры́згать, -аю *perf.*, **забры́згивать**, -аю *imp.* splash, spatter, bespatter.

забыва́ть, -а́ю *imp.*, **забы́ть**, -бу́ду *perf.* forget; ~ся, doze off, drop off; lose consciousness; sink into a reverie; forget oneself. **забы́вчивый**, forgetful; absent-minded. **забытьё**, -я́, unconsciousness; drowsiness.

забью́, etc.: see заби́ть.

зав, *abbr.* заве́дующий, manager; chief, head.

зав- *abbr.* in *comb.* of заве́дующий, manager, director, superintendent; заводско́й, factory, works. **завга́р**, -а garage manager. ~ко́м, -а, factory committee. **за́вуч**, -а, director of studies.

зава́ливать, -аю *imp.*, **завали́ть**, -лю́, -лишь *perf.* block up, obstruct; fill; pile; cram; overload; knock down, demolish; make a mess of; ~ся, fall, tumble; collapse; overturn, tip up; come to grief.

зава́ривать, -аю *imp.*, **завари́ть**, -арю́, -а́ришь *perf.* make; brew; scald; weld. **зава́рка**, -и, brewing; scalding; welding.

заведе́ние, -я, establishment, institution; custom, habit. **заве́довать**, -дую *imp.*+*instr.* manage, superintend; be in charge of.

заве́домо *adv.* wittingly. **заве́домый**, notorious, undoubted; well-known.

заведу́ etc.: see завести́.

заве́дующий *sb.* (+*instr.*) manager; head; director, superintendent; person in charge.

завезти́, -зу́, -зёшь; -ёз, -ла́ *perf.* (*imp.* завози́ть) convey, deliver; supply; leave.

за|вербова́ть, -бу́ю *perf.*

заве́ренн|ый, witnessed; certified; ~ая ко́пия, certified true copy. **завери́тель**, -я *m.* witness. **заве́рить**, -рю *perf.* (*imp.* заверя́ть) assure; certify; witness.

заверну́ть, -ну́, -нёшь *perf.* (*imp.* завёртывать, завора́чивать) wrap, wrap up; tuck up, roll up; screw tight, screw up; turn off; drop in, call in; turn; come on, come down; ~ся, wrap oneself up, wrap up, muffle oneself.

заверте́ться, -рчу́сь, -ртишься *perf.* begin to turn, begin to spin; become flustered, lose one's head.

завёртка, -и, wrapping up; package. **завёртывать(ся**, -аю(сь *imp.* of заверну́ть(ся.

заверша́ть, -а́ю *imp.*, **заверши́ть**, -шу́ *perf.* complete, conclude, crown. **заверше́ние**, -я, completion; end, conclusion.

заверя́ть, -я́ю *imp.* of заве́рить.

заве́са, -ы, curtain; veil, screen. **заве́сить**, -е́шу *perf.* (*imp.* заве́шивать) cover; curtain, curtain off.

завести́, -еду́, -едёшь; -ёл, -а́ *perf.* (*imp.* заводи́ть) take, bring; leave, drop off; set up, start; acquire; institute, introduce; wind (up); crank; ~сь, be; appear; be established, be set up; start.

заве́т, -а, behest, bidding; ordinance; Testament. **заве́тный**, cherished; intimate; secret.

заве́шивать, -аю *imp.* of заве́сить.

завеща́ние, -я, will, testament. **завеща́ть**, -а́ю, leave, bequeath; devise.

завзя́тый, inveterate, out-and-out downright; incorrigible.

завива́ть(ся, -а́ю(сь *imp.* of зави́ть(ся. **зави́вка**, -и, waving; curling; wave.

зави́дно *impers.*+*dat.*; мне ~, I fee

envious. зави́дный, enviable. зави́-
довать, -дую imp. (perf. по~) + dat.
envy.

за|визи́ровать, -рую perf.

завинти́ть, -нчу́ perf., зави́нчивать, -аю
imp. screw up; ~ся, screw up.

зави́сеть, -и́шу imp. + от + gen. depend
on; lie in the power of. зави́симость,
-и, dependence; в зави́симости от, depending on, subject to. зави́симый,
dependent.

зави́стливый, envious. за́висть, -и,
envy.

завито́й; за́вит, -á, -о, curled, waved.
завито́к, -тка́, curl, lock; flourish;
volute, scroll; tendril; helix. зави́ть,
-вью́, -вьёшь; -и́л, -á, -о perf. (imp.
завива́ть) curl, wave; twist, wind; ~ся,
curl, wave, twine; curl, wave, one's
hair; have one's hair waved.

завладева́ть, -áю imp., завладе́ть, -е́ю
perf. + instr. take possession of; seize,
capture.

завлека́тельный, alluring; fascinating,
captivating; attractive. завлека́ть,
-áю imp., завле́чь, -еку́, -ечёшь; -лёк,
-лá perf. lure, entice; fascinate captivate.

заво́д[1], -a, factory; mill; works; plant;
stud, studfarm.

заво́д[2], -a, winding up; winding mechanism. заводи́ть(ся, -ожу́(сь, -о́дишь-
(ся imp. of завести́(сь. заво́дка, -и,
winding up; starting. cranking. заводно́й, clockwork, mechanical; winding,
cranking, starting.

заво́дский, заводско́й, factory, works,
mill; prefabricated; stud; sb. factory
worker. заводча́не, -áн pl. factory
workers. заво́дчик, -a, manufacturer,
mill-owner, factory owner.

завоева́ние, -я, winning; conquest;
achievement, gain. завоева́тель, -я m.
conqueror. завоева́тельный, aggressive; of aggression. завоева́ть, -ою́ю
perf., завоёвывать, -аю imp. conquer;
win, gain; try to get.

завожу́ etc.: see заводи́ть, завози́ть.

заво́з, -a, delivery; carriage. завози́ть,
-ожу́, -о́зишь imp. of завезти́.

завора́чивать(ся, -аю(сь imp. of за-
верну́ть(ся. заворо́т[1], -a, turn, turning; sharp bend. за́воро́т[2], -a; ~
кишо́к, twisted intestines, volvulus.

завою́, etc.: see завы́ть.

завсегда́ adv. always. завсегда́тай, -я,
habitué, frequenter.

за́втра, tomorrow. за́втрак, -a, breakfast; lunch. за́втракать, -аю imp.
(perf. по~) have breakfast; have
lunch. за́втрашний, tomorrow's; ~
день, tomorrow, the morrow; the
(near) future.

за|вуали́ровать, -рую perf.

завыва́ть, -áю imp., завы́ть, -во́ю perf.
(begin to) howl.

завяза́ть, -яжу́, -я́жешь perf. (imp.
завя́зывать), tie, tie up; knot; bind,
bind up; start; ~ся, start; arise; (of
fruit) set. завя́зка, -и, string, lace,
band; beginning, start; opening; plot.

за|вя́знуть, -ну; -я́з perf. завя́зывать-
(ся, -аю(сь imp. of завяза́ть(ся.

завя́лый, withered, faded; dead. за|вя́-
нуть, -ну; -я́л perf.

загада́ть, -áю perf., зага́дывать, -аю
imp. think of; plan ahead, look ahead;
guess at the future; ~ зага́дку, ask a
riddle. зага́дка, -и, riddle; enigma,
mystery. зага́дочный, enigmatic, mysterious.

зага́р, -a, sunburn tan.

за|гаси́ть, -ашу́, -а́сишь perf. за|га́с-
нуть, -ну perf.

загвоздка, -и, snag, obstacle; difficulty.

заги́б, -a, fold; bend; exaggeration;
deviation. загиба́ть(ся, -áю(сь imp. of
загну́ть(ся. заги́бщик, -a, deviation-
ist.

за|гипнотизи́ровать, -рую perf.

загла́вие, -я, title; heading. загла́в-
ный, title; ~ая бу́ква, capital letter;
~ая роль, title-role, name-part.

загла́дить, -а́жу perf., загла́живать,
-аю imp. iron, iron out, press; make up
for, make amends for; expiate; ~ся,
iron out, become smooth; fade.

за|гло́хнуть, -ну́; -гло́х perf.

заглуша́ть, -áю imp., за|глуши́ть, -шу́
perf. drown, deaden, muffle; jam;
choke; suppress, stifle; alleviate,
soothe. заглу́шка, -и, choke, plug,
stopper.

загляде́нье, -я, lovely sight. **загляде́ться**, -я́жусь *perf.*, **загля́дываться**, -аюсь *imp.* на+*acc.* stare at; be lost in admiration of. **загля́дывать**, -аю *imp.*, **загляну́ть**, -ну́, -нешь *perf.* peep; glance; look in, drop in.

за́гнанный, driven, at the end of one's tether; tired out, exhausted, down-trodden, cowed. **загна́ть**, -гоню́, -го́нишь; -а́л, -а́, -о *perf.* (*imp.* **загоня́ть**) drive in, drive home; drive; exhaust; sell, flog.

загнива́ние, -я, rotting, putrescence; decay; suppuration. **загнива́ть**, -а́ю *imp.*, **загни́ть**, -ию́, -иёшь; -и́л, -а́, -о *perf.* rot; decay; fester.

загну́ть, -ну́, -нёшь *perf.* (*imp.* **загиба́ть**) turn up, turn down; bend, fold; crease; utter; **~ся**, turn up, stick up; turn down; turn up one's toes.

загова́ривать, -аю *imp.*, **заговори́ть**, -рю́ *perf.* begin to talk; begin to speak; talk to death, tire out with talk; cast a spell over; protect with a charm (от+*gen.* against); ~ c+*instr.* speak to. **за́говор**, -а, plot, conspiracy; charm, spell. **загово́рщик**, -а, conspirator.

заголо́вок, -вка, title; heading; headline.

заго́н, -а, enclosure, pen; driving in; rounding up. **заго́нщик**, -а, beater. **загоня́ть**[1], -я́ю *imp.* of **загна́ть**. **загоня́ть**[2], -я́ю *perf.* tire out; work to death; grill.

загора́живать, -аю(сь) *imp.* of **загороди́ть**.

загора́ть, -а́ю *imp.*, **загоре́ть**, -рю́ *perf.* become sunburnt, brown, tan; (*sl.*) serve a sentence; **~ся**, catch fire; blaze, burn; break out, start; *impers.*+*dat.* become eager, want very much.

за́город, -а, suburbs; ~ом, in the suburbs.

загороди́ть, -рожу́, -ро́дишь *perf.* (*imp.* **загора́живать**), enclose, fence in; barricade; bar; obstruct, block. **загоро́дка**, -и, fence, enclosure.

за́городный, out-of-town; country; suburban.

загота́вливать, -аю *imp.*, **загота́вля́ть**, -я́ю *imp.*, **загото́вить**, -влю *perf.* lay in; lay in a stock of, stockpile, store;

prepare. **загото́вка**, -и, State procurement, purchase; laying in; stocking up, stockpiling; semi-finished product.

загради́тельный, defensive; barrage; mine-laying. **загради́ть**, -ажу́ *perf.*, **загражда́ть**, -а́ю *imp.* block, obstruct; bar. **загражде́ние**, -я, blocking; obstruction; obstacle, barrier.

заграни́ца, -ы, abroad, foreign parts. **заграни́чный**, foreign.

загреба́ть, -а́ю *imp.*, **загрести́**, -ебу́ -ебёшь; -ёб, -ла́ *perf.* rake up, gather; rake in.

загри́вок, -вка, withers; nape (of the neck).

загримирова́ть(ся), -ру́ю(сь *perf.*

загромозжда́ть, -а́ю *imp.*, **загромозди́ть**, -зжу́ *perf.* block up, encumber; pack, cram; overload.

загрубе́лый, coarsened, callous. **за|грубе́ть**, -е́ю *perf.*

загружа́ть, -а́ю *imp.*, **за|грузи́ть**, -ужу́, -у́зишь *perf.* load; overload; feed; keep fully occupied; ~ c+*instr.* load up with, take on. **загру́зка**, -и, loading, feeding; charge, load, capacity.

за|грунтова́ть, -ту́ю *perf.*

загрусти́ть, -ущу́ *perf.* grow sad.

загрязне́ние, -я, soiling; pollution; contamination. **за|грязни́ть**, -ню́ *perf.*, **загрязня́ть**, -я́ю *imp.* soil, make dirty; contaminate, pollute; **~ся**, make oneself dirty, become dirty; be polluted.

загс, -а *abbr.* (отдѣл) за́писи а́ктов гражда́нского состоя́ния, registry office.

загуби́ть, -блю́, -бишь *perf.* ruin; squander, waste.

за|гудрони́ровать, -рую *perf.*

загуля́ть, -я́ю *perf.*, **загу́ливать**, -аю *imp.* take to drink.

за|густе́ть, -е́ет *perf.* thicken, grow thick.

зад, -а (-у). *loc.* -у́; *pl.* -ы́, back; hindquarters; buttocks; seat; croup; rump; *pl.* back-yard(s); бить ~ом, kick; ~ом наперёд, back to front.

задабривать, -аю *imp.* of **задо́брить**. **задава́ть(ся**, -даю́сь *imp.* of **зада́ть(ся**.

за|дави́ть, -влю́, -вишь *perf.* crush; run over, knock down.

задади́м, etc., **за́дал,** etc., **зада́м,** etc.: see **зада́ть.**

зада́ние, -я, task, job; commission, assignment.

зада́ривать, -аю *imp.,* **задари́ть,** -рю́ -ришь *perf.* load with presents; bribe.

зада́тки, -тков *pl.* instincts, inclinations.

зада́ток, -тка, deposit, advance.

зада́ть, -а́м, -а́шь, -а́ст, -ади́м; за́дал, -á -о *perf.* (*imp.* задава́ть) set; give; put; ~ вопро́с, ask a question; ~ тя́гу, take to one's heels; я ему́ зада́м! I'll give him what-for!; ~ся, begin to set well; work out, succeed; ~ся мы́слью, це́лью, set oneself, make up one's mind. зада́ча, -и, problem, sum; task; mission.

задвига́ть, -а́ю *imp.,* **задви́нуть,** -ну *perf.* bolt; bar; close; push, slide; ~ задви́жку, shoot a bolt; ~ за́навес, draw a curtain; ~ся, shut; slide. **задви́жка,** -и, bolt; catch, fastening; slide-valve. **задвижно́й,** sliding.

задво́рки, -рок *pl.* back-yard; back parts; out-of-the-way place, backwoods.

задева́ть, -а́ю *imp.* of заде́ть.

заде́лать, -аю *perf.,* **заде́лывать,** -аю *imp.* do up; block up, close up; wall up; stop (up). **заде́лка,** -и, doing up; blocking up, stopping up.

заде́ну, etc.: see заде́ть. **задёргивать,** -аю *imp.* of задёрнуть. **за|деревене́ть,** -е́ю *perf.*

задержа́ние, -я, detention, arrest; retention; suspension. **задержа́ть,** -жу́, -жишь *perf.,* **заде́рживать,** -аю *imp.* detain; delay; withhold, keep back; retard; arrest; ~ся, stay too long; linger.

задёрнуть, -ну *perf.* (*imp.* задёргивать), pull; draw; cover; curtain off.

задеру́, etc.: see задра́ть.

заде́ть, -е́ну *perf.* (*imp.* задева́ть), touch, brush (against); graze; offend; wound; catch (against); catch on; ~ за живо́е, touch on the raw.

задира, -ы *m.* and *f.* bully; trouble-maker. **задира́ть(ся,** -а́ю(сь *imp.* of задра́ть(ся. **задири́стый,** provocative, pugnacious; cocky, pert.

за́дн|ий, back, rear; hind; дать ~ий

ход, back, reverse; ~яя мысль, ulterior motive; ~ий план, background; ~ий прохо́д, anus, back passage. **за́дник,** -а, back; back drop.

задо́брить, -рю *perf.* (*imp.* задо́бривать) cajole; coax; win over.

задо́к, -дка́, back.

задо́лго *adv.* long before.

за|должа́ть, -а́ю *perf.*; ~ся, run into debt. **задо́лженность,** -и, debts; liabilities.

задо́р, -а, fervour, ardour; enthusiasm; passion; temper. **задо́рный,** provocative; fervent; ardent; impassioned; quick-tempered.

задохну́ться, -ну́сь, -нёшься; -о́хся or -у́лся *perf.* (*imp.* задыха́ться) suffocate; choke; pant; gasp for breath.

за|дра́ть, -деру́, -дерёшь; -а́л, -á, -о *perf.* (*imp.* also задира́ть) tear to pieces, kill; lift up, stretch up; break, split; provoke, insult; ~ нос, put on airs; ~ся, break; split; ride up.

задрема́ть, -млю́, -млешь *perf.* doze off, begin to nod.

задува́ть, -а́ю *imp.* of заду́ть.

заду́мать, -аю *perf.,* **заду́мывать,** -аю *imp.* plan; intend; think of; conceive the idea (of); ~ся, become thoughtful, pensive; meditate; ponder. **заду́мчивость,** -и, thoughtfulness; reverie. **заду́мчивый,** thoughtful, pensive.

заду́ть, -у́ю *perf.* (*imp.* задува́ть) blow out; blow in; begin to blow.

задуше́вный, sincere; cordial; intimate; ~ разгово́р, heart-to-heart talk.

за|души́ть, -ушу́, -у́шишь *perf.* **за́ды** etc.: see зад.

задыха́ться, -а́юсь *imp.* of задохну́ться

заеда́ние, -я, jamming. **заеда́ть,** -а́ю *imp.* of зае́сть. **заеди́м,** etc.: see зае́сть.

зае́зд, -а, calling in; lap, round, heat. **зае́здить,** -зжу *perf.* override; wear out; work too hard. **заезжа́ть,** -а́ю *imp.* of зае́хать. **зае́зженный,** hackneyed, trite; worn out. **зае́зж|ий,** visiting; ~ий двор, wayside inn; ~ая тру́ппа, touring company.

заём, за́йма, loan. **заёмный,** loan. **заёмщик,** -а, -щица, -ы, borrower, debtor.

заесть, -ем, -ешь, -ест, -едим *perf.* (*imp.* заедать) torment, oppress; jam; foul; +*instr.* take with.

заехать, -еду *perf.* (*imp.* заезжать) call in; enter, ride in, drive in; land oneself; reach; +за+*acc.* go beyond, go past; +за+*instr.* call for, fetch.

за|жарить(ся, -рю(сь *perf.*

зажать, -жму, -жмёшь *perf.* (*imp.* зажимать) squeeze; press; clutch; grip; suppress.

зажечь, -жгу, -жжёшь; -жёг, -жгла *perf.* (*imp.* зажигать) set fire to; kindle; light; strike; inflame; ~ ся, catch fire; light up; flame up.

заживать(ся, -аю(сь *imp.* of зажить(ся. **заживить**, -влю *perf.*, **заживлять**, -яю *imp.* heal. **заживо** *adv.* alive.

заживу, etc.: see зажить.

зажигалка, -и, lighter; incendiary. **зажигательн**|ый, inflammatory; ~ая свеча, sparking-plug. **зажи**|**аться(ся**, -аю(сь *imp.* of зажечь(ся.

зажим, -а, clamp; clutch; clip; (screw) terminal; suppression, clamping down. **зажимать**, -аю *imp.* of зажать. **зажимистый**, strong, powerful; tightfisted, stingy. **зажимной**, tight-fisted. **зажимщик**, -а, suppressor.

зажиточность, -и, prosperity; easy circumstances. **зажиточный**, well-to-do; prosperous. **зажить**, -иву, -ивёшь; -ил, -а, -о *perf.* (*imp.* заживать) heal; close up; begin to live; ~ ся, live to a great age; live too long.

зажму, etc.: see зажать. за|**жмуриться**, -рюсь *perf.*

зазеленеть, -еет *perf.* turn green.

заземление, -я, earthing; earth. **за-землить**, -лю *perf.*, **заземлять**, -яю *imp.* earth.

зазнаваться, -наюсь, -наёшься *imp.*, **зазнаться**, -аюсь *perf.* give oneself airs, become conceited.

зазубренный, notched, jagged, serrated. **зазубрина**, -ы, notch, jag. за|**зубрить**[1], -рю *perf.*

за|**зубрить**[2], -рю, -убришь *perf.*

зайгрывать, -аю *imp.* make advances; flirt.

зайка, -и *m.* and *f.* stammerer, stutterer.

заикание, -я, stammer, stutter; stammering, stuttering. **заикаться**, -аюсь *imp.*, **заикнуться**, -нусь, -нёшься *perf.* stammer, stutter; +о+*prep.* hint at, mention, touch on.

заимообразно *adv.* on credit, on loan. **заимствование**, -я, borrowing, adoption. **заимствованн**|ый, borrowed, taken over; ~ое слово, loan-word. **заимствовать**, -твую *perf.* and *imp.* (*perf.* also по~) borrow, take over, adopt.

заинтересованный, interested, concerned. **заинтересовать**, -сую *perf.*, **заинтересовывать**, -аю *imp.* interest; excite the curiosity of; ~ ся+*instr.* become interested in, take an interest in.

заискивать, -аю *imp.* make up (to), ingratiate oneself.

зайду, etc.: see зайти. **займу**, etc.: see занять.

зайти, -йду, -йдёшь; зашёл, -шла *perf.* (*imp.* заходить) call; look in, drop in; go go on; set; water, +в+*acc.* get to; reach; +за+*acc.* go behind, turn; +за+*instr.* call for, go for, fetch.

зайца, etc.: see заяц. **зайчик**, -а, dear little hare; reflection of sunlight. **зай-чиха**, -и, doe (of hare). **зайчонок**, -нка; *pl.* -чата, -чат leveret.

закабалить, -лю *perf.*, **закабалять**, -яю *imp.* enslave.

закавказский, Trans-Caucasian.

закадычный, intimate, bosom.

заказ, -а, order; prohibition; на ~, to order. **заказать**, -ажу, -ажешь *perf.*, **заказывать**, -аю *imp.* order; reserve, book. **заказник**, -а, reserve; preserve. **заказн**|ой, made to order, made to measure; bespoke; registered; ~ое (письмо), registered letter. **заказчик**, -а, a customer, client.

закал, -а, temper, tempering; stamp; cast; strength of character, backbone. **закалённый**, tempered, hardened, hard; seasoned, tough; fully trained. **закалить**, -лю *perf.*, **закалить**, -лю *perf.* (*imp.* also закалять) temper; harden, case-harden; harden off. **закалка**, -и tempering; hardening; temper, calibre.

закáлывать, -аю *imp.* of заколóть.
закалúть, -яю *imp.* of закалúть. за-
кáнчивать(ся, -аю(сь *imp.* of закóн-
чить(ся.

закáпать, -аю *perf.*, закáпывать[1], -аю
imp. begin to drip; rain, fall in drops;
pour in drops; spot, spatter.

закáпывать[2](ся, -аюсь *imp.* of закó-
пáть(ся.

закáт, -а, a setting; sunset; decline; на
~е, at sunset; на ~е дней, in one's
declining years. закатáть, -áю *perf.*,
закáтывать[1], -аю *imp.* begin to roll;
roll up; roll out; ~ в тюрьмý, throw
into prison. закатúть, -ачý, -áтишь
perf., закáтывать[2], -аю *imp.* roll; ~ ся
roll; set; wane; vanish, disappear; go
off; ~ся смéхом, burst out laughing.
закáтный, sunset.

заквáсить, -áшу *perf.*, заквáшивать,
-аю *imp.* ferment; leaven. заквáска,
-и, ferment; leaven.

закидáть, -áю *perf.*, закúдывать[1], -аю
imp. shower; cover up; fill up; spatter,
bespatter; ~ вопрóсами, ply with
questions; ~ грязью, fling mud at.

закúдывать[2], -аю *imp.*, закúнуть, -ну
perf. throw; throw out, away; fling,
cast, toss.

закипáть, -áет *imp.*, закипéть, -пúт
perf. begin to boil; boil, simmer; be in
full swing.

закисáть, -áю *imp.*, закúснуть, -ну; -úс-
.ла *perf.* turn sour; become apathetic.
зáкись, -и, oxide, protoxide; ~ азóта,
nitrous oxide.

заклáд, -а. pawn; pledge; mortgage; bet,
wager; бúться об ~, bet, wager; в
~е, in pawn. заклáдка, -и, laying
laying down; batch, charge; book-
mark. закладнáя *sb.* mortgage. за-
кладнóй, mortgage; pawn. заклáды-
вать, -аю *imp.* of заложúть.

заклéивать, -аю *imp.*, заклéить, -éю
perf. glue up; stick up; seal; ~ся, stick.

заклепáть, -áю *perf.*, заклёпывать, -аю
imp. rivet. заклёпка, -и, rivet; riveting.

заклинáние, -я, incantation; spell,
charm; exorcism. заклинáтель. -я *m.*
exorcist; ~ змей, snake-charmer

заклинáть, -áю *imp.* conjure; invoke;
exorcize; adjure, entreat.

заключáть, -áю *imp.*, заключúть, -чý
perf. conclude; end; infer; enter into;
contain; enclose; comprise; confine.
заключáться, -áется, consist; lie, be;
be contained. заключéние, -я conclusion; end; inference; resolution, decision; confinement, detention. заключённый *sb.* prisoner convict. заклю-
чúтельный, final concluding.

заклятие, -я, oath, pledge. заклятый,
sworn, inveterate; enchanted, bewitched.

заковáть, -кую, -куёшь *perf.*, закóвы-
вать, -аю *imp.* chain; shackle, put in
irons.

заколáчивать, -аю *imp.* of заколотúть.
заколдóванный, bewitched, enchanted;
spellbound; ~ круг, vicious circle.
заколдовáть, -дую *perf.* bewitch, enchant; lay a spell on.

закóлка, -и, hairpin; hair-grip; hair-
-slide.

заколотúть, -лочý, -лóтишь *perf.* (*imp.*
заколáчивать) board up; nail up;
knock in, drive in; beat the life out of,
knock insensible.

за|колóть, -олю, -óлешь *perf.* (*imp.*
also закáлывать) stab; spear, stick;
kill; pin, pin up; fasten; (*impers.*) у
меня заколóло в бокý, I have a stitch
in my side; ~ся, stab oneself.

закóн, -а, law; ~ бóжий, scripture,
divinity. законнорождённый, legitimate. закóнный, lawful, legal; legitimate, rightful.

законо- in *comb.* law, legal. законовé-
дение, -я, law, jurisprudence. ~дá-
тельный, legislative. ~мéрность, -и,
regularity, normality. ~мéрный, regular, natural. ~положéние, -я, statute.
~проéкт, -а, bill.

за|конопáтить, -áчу *perf.* за|консервú-
ровать, -рую *perf.* за|конспектúро-
вать, -рую *perf.* за|контрактовáть(ся,
-тýю(сь *perf.*

закóнченность, -и, finish; completeness. закóнченный, finished; complete;
consummate. закóнчить, -чу *perf.*
(*imp.* закáнчивать), end, finish; ~ся,
end, finish; come to an end.

закопа́ть, -а́ю *perf.* (*imp.* зака́пывать) begin to dig; bury; ~ся, begin to rummage; bury oneself; dig (oneself) in.

закопте́лый, sooty, smutty; smoke-grimed. за|копте́ть, -ти́т *perf.* за|-копти́ть, -пчу́ *perf.*

закоренѐлый, deep-rooted; ingrained; inveterate.

зако́рки, -рок *pl.* back, shoulders.

закосне́лый, deep-rooted; incorrigible, inveterate. за|косне́ть, -е́ю *perf.*

закостене́лый, ossified; stiff.

закоу́лок, -лка, back street, alley, passage; secluded corner, nook; знать все закоу́лки, know all the ins and outs.

закочене́лый, numb with cold. за|кочене́ть, -е́ю *perf.*

закра́дываться, -аюсь *imp.* of за-кра́сться. закра́ивать, -аю *imp.* of закрои́ть.

закра́сить, -а́шу *perf.* (*imp.* закра́шивать) paint over, paint out.

закра́сться, -аду́сь, -адёшься *perf.* (*imp.* закра́дываться) steal in, creep in.

закра́шивать, -аю *imp.* of закра́сить.

закре́па, -ы, catch; fastener. **закрепи́тель**, -я *m.* fastener; fixative, fixing agent, fixer. **закрепи́ть**, -плю́ *perf.*, закрепля́ть, -я́ю *imp.* fasten, secure; make fast; fix; consolidate; +за|*instr.* allot to, assign to; appoint to, attach to; ~ за собо́й secure; ~ся, на+*acc.* consolidate one's hold on.

закрепости́ть, -ощу́ *perf.* закрепоша́ть, -а́ю *imp.* enslave; make a serf of. **за-крепоще́ние**, -я, enslavement; slavery, serfdom.

закрича́ть, -чу́ *perf.* cry out; begin to shout; give a shout.

закрои́ть, -ою́ *perf.* (*imp.* закра́ивать) cut out; groove. **закро́й**, -я, cutting out; cut, style; groove. **закро́йный**, cutting, cutting-out. **закро́йщик**, -а, cutter.

закро́м, -а; *pl.* -а́, corn-bin.

закро́ю, etc.: see закры́ть. **закрою́**, etc.: see закрои́ть.

закругле́ние, -я, rounding, curving; curve; curvature; well-rounded period.

закруглённый: -ён, -а́, rounded; well-rounded. **закругли́ть**, -лю́ *perf.*, за-кругля́ть, -я́ю *imp.* make round; round off; ~ся, become round.

закружи́ться, -ужу́сь, -у́жи́шься *perf.* begin to whirl, begin to go round; be in a whirl.

за|крути́ть, -учу́, -у́тишь *perf.*, закру́-чивать, -аю *imp.* twist, twirl, whirl round; wind round; roll; turn; screw in; turn the head of; ~ся, twist twirl, whirl; wind round; begin to whirl.

закрыва́ть, -а́ю *imp.* закры́ть, -ро́ю *perf.* close, shut; shut off, turn off; close down, shut down; cover; ~ся, close, shut; end; close down; cover oneself, take cover; find shelter, shelter. **закры́тие**, -я, closing; shutting; closing down; shelter, cover. **закры́т**|**ый**, closed, shut; private; ~ое голосова́ние, secret ballot; ~ое заседа́ние, private meeting; closed session; ~ое мо́ре, inland sea; ~ое пла́тье, high-necked dress; ~ый просмо́тр, private view.

закули́сный, behind the scenes; secret; underhand, under-cover.

закупа́ть, -а́ю *imp.*, закупи́ть, -плю́ -пишь *perf.* buy up; lay in; stock up with; bribe. **заку́пка**, -и, purchase. **закупно́й**, bought, purchased.

заку́поривать, -аю *imp.*, заку́порить, -рю *perf.* cork; stop up; plug, clog; shut up; coop up. **заку́порка**, -и, corking; embolism, thrombosis.

заку́почный, purchase. **заку́пщик**, -а, -щица -ы, purchaser; buyer.

заку́ривать, -аю *imp.*, закури́ть, -рю́, -ришь *perf.* light; light up; begin to smoke.

закуси́ть, -ушу́, -у́сишь *perf.*, заку́сывать, -аю *imp.* have a snack have a bite; +*instr.* have a bit of; ~ удила́, take the bit between one's teeth. **заку́ска**, -и, hors-d'oeuvre; appetizer, snack, titbit. **заку́сочная** *sb.* snack-bar.

за|ку́тать, -аю *perf.*, заку́тывать, -аю *imp.* wrap up muffle; tuck up; ~ся, wrap oneself up.

зал, -а, hall, room; ~ ожида́ния, waiting-room.

зала́вок. -вка, chest, locker.

залёг, etc.: see **залёчь**. **залега́ние** -я, bedding; bed, seam. **залега́ть**, -а́ю *imp*. of **залёчь**.

за|ледене́ть, -е́ю *perf*.

залежа́лый, stale, long unused. **за|лежа́ться**, -жу́сь *perf*., **залёживаться**, -аюсь *imp*. lie too long; lie idle a long time; find no market; become stale. **за́лежь**, -и, deposit, bed, seam; stale goods.

залеза́ть, -а́ю *imp*., **залёзть**, -зу; -ёз, *perf*. climb, climb up; get in; creep in; ~ **в долги́**, run into debt.

за|лепи́ть, -плю́, -пишь *perf*., **за-лепля́ть**, -я́ю *imp*. paste up, paste over; glue up, stick up.

залета́ть, -а́ю *imp*., **залете́ть**, -ечу́ *perf*. fly; +**в**+*acc*. fly into; land at; +**за**+ *acc*. fly over, fly beyond. **залётный**, flown in; ~ **ая пти́ца**, bird of passage.

залёчивать, -аю *imp*., **залечи́ть**, -чу́, -чишь *perf*. heal, cure; ~ **ся**, heal, heal up.

залёчь, -ля́гу, -ля́жешь; залёг, -ла́ *perf*. (*imp*. залега́ть) lie down; lie low; lie in wait; lie, be deposited; take root, become ingrained; become blocked.

зали́в, -а, bay; gulf; creek, cove. **зали-ва́ть**, -а́ю *imp*., **зали́ть**, -лью, -льёшь; за́лил, -а́, -о *perf*. flood, inundate; quench, extinguish, put out; lay, spread; stop holes in; +*instr*. pour over, spill on; ~ **ска́терть черни́лами** spill ink on the tablecloth; ~ **ту́шью**, ink in; ~ **ся**, be flooded; pour, spill; +*instr*. break into, burst into; ~ **ся слеза́ми**, burst into tears, dissolve in tears.

зало́г, -а deposit; pledge; security, mortgage; token; voice. **заложи́ть**, -жу́, -жишь *perf*. (*imp*. закла́дывать) lay; put; mislay; pile up, heap up; block up; pawn, mortgage; harness; lay in, store, put by. **зало́жник**, -а, hostage.

залп, -а, volley, salvo; ~ **ом**, without pausing for breath, at one gulp.

залью́, etc.: see **зали́ть**. **заля́гу**, etc.: see **залёчь**.

зам, -а *abbr*. заме́ститель, assistant. deputy. **зам-** *abbr*. in *comb*. of за-ме́ститель assistant, deputy, vice-.

замдире́ктора, deputy director; vice--principal, assistant head. ~ **мини́стра**, deputy minister. ~ **председа́теля**, vice--chairman.

за|ма́зать, -а́жу *perf*., **зама́зывать**, -аю *imp*. paint over; efface; slur over; putty; daub; smear; soil; ~ **ся**, smear oneself; get dirty. **зама́зка**, -и, putty, paste, cement; puttying.

зама́лчивать, -аю *imp*. of замолча́ть.

зама́нивать, -аю *imp*., **замани́ть**, -ню́, -нишь *perf*. entice, lure; attract; decoy. **зама́нчивость**, -и, allurements. **зама́н-чивый**, tempting, alluring.

за|мара́ть(ся, -а́ю(сь *perf*. **за|маринова́ть**, -ну́ю *perf*.

замаскиро́ванный, masked; disguised; concealed. **за|маскирова́ть**, -ру́ю *perf*., **замаскиро́вывать**, -аю *imp*. mask; disguise; camouflage; conceal; ~ **ся**, disguise oneself.

зама́х, -а, threatening gesture. **зама́хи-ваться**, -аюсь *imp*., **замахну́ться**, -ну́сь, -нёшься *perf*. threaten; +*instr*. raise threateningly; ~ **руко́й на**+*acc*. life one's hand against.

зама́чивать, -аю *imp*. of замочи́ть.

зама́щивать, -аю *imp*. of замости́ть.

замедле́ние, -я, slowing down, decelera-tion; delay. **заме́дленный**, retarded, delayed. **заме́длить**, -лю *perf*., **за-медля́ть**, -я́ю *imp*. slow down, retard; reduce, slacken; delay; hold back; be slow (to), be long (in); ~ **ся**, slow down; slacken, grow slower.

замёл, etc.: see замести́.

заме́на, -ы, substitution; replacement; commutation; substitute, **замени́мый**, replaceable. **замени́тель**, -я *m*. (+*gen*.) substitute (for). **замени́ть**, -ню́, -нишь *perf*., **заменя́ть**, -я́ю *imp*. replace; take the place of; be a substitute for.

замере́ть, -мру́ -мрёшь; за́мер, -ла́, -о *perf*. (*imp*. замира́ть) stand still; freeze, be rooted to the spot; die down, die away; die.

замерза́ние, -я, freezing. **замерза́ть**, -а́ю *imp*., **за|мёрзнуть**, -ну *perf*. freeze, freeze up; freeze to death.

заме́рить, -рю *perf*. (*imp*. замеря́ть) measure, gauge. **заме́рный**, gauge, measuring; ~ая ре́йка, dip-stick, gauge rod.

за́мертво adv. like one dead, in a dead faint.

замери́ть. -я́ю imp. of заме́рить.

замеси́ть, -ешу́, -е́сишь perf. (imp. заме́шивать), knead.

замести́ -ету́, -ете́шь; -мёл, -а́ perf. (imp. замета́ть) sweep up; cover; ~ следы́ cover one's traces.

замести́тель, -я m., ~ница, -ы, substitute; assistant, deputy, vice-. замести́ть, -ещу́ perf. (imp. замеща́ть), replace, be substitute for; deputize for, act for; serve in place of.

замета́ть[1], -а́ю imp. of замести́.

замета́ть[2], -а́ю perf. (imp. замётывать) tack, baste.

заме́тить, -е́чу perf. (imp. замеча́ть) notice; take notice of, make a note of; remark, observe. заме́тка, -и, paragraph; mark; note. заме́тный, noticeable; appreciable; outstanding.

замётывать, -аю imp. of замета́ть[2].

замеча́ние, -я, remark, observation; reprimand, reproof. замеча́тельный, remarkable; splendid, wonderful. замеча́ть, -а́ю imp. of заме́тить. заме́ченный, discovered; noticed; detected.

замеша́тельство, -а, confusion; embarrassment. замеша́ть, -а́ю perf., заме́шивать, -аю imp. mix up, entangle; ~ся, become mixed up, become entangled; mix, mingle. заме́шивать, -аю imp. of замеси́ть, замеша́ть.

заме́шка, -и delay. заме́шкаться, -аюсь perf. linger, loiter.

замеща́ть, -а́ю imp. of замести́ть. замеще́ние, -я, substitution; filling.

замина́ть, -а́ю imp. of замя́ть. зами́нка, -и, hitch; hesitation.

замира́ние, -я, dying out, dying down; sinking. замира́ть, -а́ю imp. of замере́ть.

за́мкнутость, -и, reserve, reticence. за́мкнутый, reserved; closed, exclusive. замкну́ть, -ну́, -нёшь perf. (imp. замыка́ть) lock; close; ~ся, close; shut oneself up; become reserved; ~ся в себя́, shrink into oneself.

замну́, etc.: see замя́ть.

за́мок[1] -мка, castle.

замо́к[2], -мка́, lock; padlock; keystone; bolt; clasp, clip; запере́ть на ~, lock; под замко́м, under lock and key.

замо́лвить, -влю perf.; ~ слове́чко, put in a word.

замолка́ть, -а́ю imp., замо́лкнуть, -ну; -мо́лк perf. fall silent; stop, cease. замолча́ть, -чу́ perf. (imp. зама́лчивать) fall silent; cease corresponding; keep silent about, hush up.

замора́живание, -я, freezing; chilling, refrigeration; congealing; quenching. замора́живать, -аю imp., заморо́зить, -ро́жу perf. freeze; refrigerate; ice, chill. заморо́женный, frozen; iced. за́морозки, -ов pl. (slight) frosts.

замо́рский, overseas.

замо́рыш, -а, weakling, puny creature; runt.

замости́ть, -ощу́ perf. (imp. also зама́щивать) pave.

замочи́ть, -чу́, -чишь perf. (imp. also зама́чивать) wet; soak; ret.

замо́ч|ный, lock; ~ая сква́жина, keyhole.

замру́, etc.: see замере́ть.

за́муж adv.; вы́йти ~ (за + acc.) marry; вы́дать ~ за + acc. marry (off) to. за́мужем adv. married (за + instr. to). заму́жество, -а. marriage.

замурова́ть. -ру́ю perf., заму́ровывать, -аю imp. brick up; wall up; immure.

заму́тить(ся), -учу́(сь), -у́тишь(ся perf.

заму́чить, -аю imp., заму́чить, -чу perf. torment; wear out; plague the life out of, bore to tears. заму́читься, -чусь perf.

за́мша, -и, suede; chamois leather, shammy.

замыка́ние, -я, locking, closing; closure; short circuit, shorting. замыка́ть(ся, -а́ю(сь imp. of замкну́ть(ся. замыка́ющ|ий; идти́ ~им, bring up the rear.

за́мысел, -сла, project, plan; design, scheme; idea. замы́слить, -лю perf., замышля́ть, -я́ю imp. plan; contemplate, intend, think of. замыслова́тый, intricate, complicated.

замя́ть, -мну -мнёшь perf. (imp. замина́ть) hush up, stifle, smother;

suppress; put a stop to; distract attention from; **~ся**, falter; stumble; stop short.

за́навес, -а, **занаве́ска**, -и, curtain. **зана-ве́сить**, -е́шу *perf.*, **занаве́шивать**, -аю *imp.* curtain; hang; cover.

занеме́ть, -е́ю *perf.*

занесённый снегом, snowbound. **занести́**, -су́, -сёшь; -ёс, -ла́ *perf.* (*imp.* **заноси́ть**) bring; leave, drop; raise, lift; note down, put down, enter; cover with snow, sand, etc.; **~ в протоко́л**, place on record, record in the minutes; **~сь**, be carried away.

занима́тельный, entertaining, diverting; absorbing. **занима́ть**, -а́ю *imp.* (*perf.* **заня́ть**) occupy; interest; engage, secure; take, take up; borrow; **~ся** + *instr.* be occupied with, be engaged in; work at, work on; study; busy oneself with; devote oneself to.

зано́за, -ы, splinter. **занози́ть**, -ожу́ *perf.* get a splinter in.

зано́с, -а, drift, accumulation; raising lifting; skid, skidding. **заноси́ть(ся** -ошу́(сь, -о́сишь(ся *imp.* of **занести́(сь. зано́сный**, alien, foreign, imported. **зано́счивый**, arrogant, haughty.

занумерова́ть, -ру́ю *perf.*

заня́тие, -я, occupation; pursuit; *pl.* studies, work. **заня́тный**, entertaining, amusing; interesting. **за́нято** *adv.* engaged, number engaged. **за́нятой**, busy. **за́нятый**, -нят, -а́, -о, occupied taken; engaged; employed; busy. **заня́ть(ся, займу́(сь, -мёшь(ся; за́нял(ся, -а́(сь, -о(сь *perf.* of **занима́ть-(ся**.

заодно́ *adv.* in concert; at one; at the same time.

заострённый, pointed, sharp. **заострить**, -рю́ *perf.*, **заостря́ть**, -я́ю *imp.* sharpen; stress, emphasize; **~ся**, grow sharp; become pointed.

зао́чник, -а, -ница, -ы student taking correspondence course. **зао́чно** *adv.* in one's absence; by correspondence course. **зао́чн**|**ый**; -**ый курс**, correspondence course; **~ое обуче́ние**, postal tuition; -**ый пригово́р**, judgment by default.

за́пад, -а, west; the West, the Occident **за́падный**, west, western; westerly.

западня́, -й; *gen. pl.* -ней, trap; pitfall snare.

запа́здывать, -аю *imp.* of **запозда́ть**.

запа́ивать, -аю *imp.* of **запая́ть**. **запа́йка**, soldering; sealing (off), seal.

запакова́ть, -ку́ю *perf.*, **запако́вывать**, -аю, *imp.* pack; wrap up, do up.

запа́костить, -ощу *perf.*

запа́л, -а, ignition; fuse; detonator **запа́ливать**, -аю *imp.*, **запали́ть**, -лю́ light, ignite, kindle; set fire to. **запа́льн**|**ый**, ignition; detonating; **~ая** свеча́, (sparking)plug. **запа́льчивый** quick-tempered.

запа́с, -а, reserve; stock, supply; hem *pl.* turnings; вы́пустить **~**, let out отложи́ть про **~**, put by; про **~**, fo an emergency; прове́рить **~**, take stock; **~ слов**, vocabulary. **запаса́ть** -а́ю *imp.*, **запасти́**, -су́, -сёшь; -а́с, -ла́ *perf.* stock, store; lay in a stock of **~ся**, + *instr.* provide oneself with stock up with; arm oneself with. **за па́сливый**, thrifty; provident. **за па́сник**, -а, reservist. **запасно́й** *sb.* reservist **запа́сн**ый, **запа́сный**, spare; reserve; **~ вы́ход**, emergency exit; **~ путь** siding.

за́пах[1], -а (-у), smell.

запа́х[2], -а, wrapover. **запа́хивать**, -аю *imp.*, **запахну́ть**[2], -ну́, -нёшь *perf* wrap up; **~ся**, wrap (oneself) up.

запа́хнуть[1], -ну; -а́х *perf.* begin t smell.

запа́чкать, -аю *perf.*

запа́шка, -и, ploughing in, ploughin up; plough-land, arable land.

запая́ть, -я́ю *perf.* (*imp.* **запа́ивать** solder; seal, seal off.

запе́в, -а, solo part. **запева́ла**, -ы *m* singer of solo part; leader of chorus leader, instigator. **запева́ть**, -а́ю (*perf.* **запе́ть**) lead the singing, set th tune.

запека́нка, -и, baked pudding, bake dish; spiced brandy. **запека́ть(ся** -а́ю *imp.* of **запе́чь(ся. запеку́** etc. see **запе́чь**.

запелена́ть, -а́ю *perf.*

запере́ть, -пру́, -прёшь; за́пер, -ла́, -

запеть (*imp.* запира́ть) lock; lock in; shut up; bar; block up; ~ на засо́в bolt; ~ся, lock oneself in; shut (oneself) up; +в+*prep.* refuse to admit, refuse to speak about.

запе́ть, -пою́, -поёшь *perf.* (*imp.* запева́ть) begin to sing; ~ друго́е, change one's tune; ~ пе́сню, strike up a song; plug a song.

запеча́тать, -аю *perf.*, **запеча́тывать**, -аю *imp.* seal. **запечатлева́ть**, -а́ю *imp.* **запечатле́ть**, -е́ю *perf.* imprint, impress, engrave; ~ся, imprint, stamp, impress, itself.

запе́чь, -еку́, -ечёшь; -пёк, -ла́ *perf.* (*imp.* запека́ть) bake; ~ся, bake; become parched; clot, coagulate.

запива́ть, -а́ю *imp.* of запи́ть.

запина́ться, -а́юсь *imp.* of запну́ться. **запи́нка**, -и, hesitation; без запи́нки, smoothly.

запира́тельство, -а, denial, disavowal. **запира́ть(ся)**, -а́ю(сь *imp.* of запере́ть(ся.

записа́ть, -ишу́, -и́шешь *perf.* **запи́сывать**, -аю *imp.* note, make a note of, take notes; take down; record; enter, register, enrol; make over (to); begin to write, begin to correspond; ~ся, register, enter one's name, enrol; ~ся в клуб, join a club; ~ся к врачу́, make an appointment with the doctor. **запи́ска**, -и, note; minute, memorandum; *pl.* notes; memoirs; transactions. **записн|о́й**, note, writing; regular; inveterate; ~а́я кни́жка, notebook. **за́пись**, -и, writing down; recording; registration; entry, record; deed.

запи́ть, -пью́, -пьёшь; за́пи́л, -а́, -о *perf.* (*imp.* запива́ть) begin drinking; take to drink; wash down (with), take (with).

запиха́ть, -а́ю *perf.*, **запи́хивать**, -аю *imp.*, **запихну́ть**, -ну́, -нёшь *perf.* push in, cram in.

запишу́, etc.: see записа́ть.

запла́канный, tear-stained; in tears. **запла́кать**, -а́чу *perf.* begin to cry.

заплани́ровать, -рую *perf.*

запла́та, -ы, patch. **запла́танный**, patched, mended.

заплати́ть, -ачу́, -а́тишь *perf.* pay;

+за+*acc.* pay for; ~ по счёту, settle an account.

заплачу́, etc.: see запла́кать. **заплачу́**: see заплати́ть.

заплесневе́лый, mouldy, mildewed. **за|плесневе́ть**, -ве́ет *perf.*

заплести́, -ету́, -етёшь; -ёл, -а́ *perf.*, **заплета́ть**, -а́ю *imp.* plait, braid; ~ся, stumble; be unsteady in one's gait; falter.

за|пломбирова́ть, -ру́ю *perf.*

заплы́в, -а, heat, round. **заплыва́ть**, -а́ю *imp.*, **заплы́ть**, -ыву́, -ывёшь; -ы́л, -а́, -о *perf.* swim in, sail in; swim out, sail out; be swollen, be bloated.

запну́ться, -ну́сь, -нёшься *perf.* (*imp.* запина́ться) hesitate; stumble, halt; stammer; ~ ного́й, trip (up).

запове́дник, -а, reserve; preserve; госуда́рственный ~, national park. **запове́дный**, prohibited; ~ лес, forest reserve. **за́поведь**, -и, precept; commandment.

заподо́зривать, -аю *imp.*, **заподо́зрить**, -рю *perf.* suspect (в+*prep.* of); be suspicious of.

запо́ем: see запо́й.

запозда́лый, belated; late; delayed. **запозда́ть**, -а́ю *perf.* (*imp.* запа́здывать) be late.

запо́й, -я, heavy drinking; alcoholism; кури́ть запо́ем, smoke like a chimney; пить запо́ем, have bouts of heavy drinking. **запо́йный** *adj.*; ~ пья́ница, chronic drunk; old soak.

заползти́, -зу́, -зёшь; -о́лз, -зла́, creep in, creep under; crawl in, crawl under.

запо́лнить, -ню *perf.*, **заполня́ть**, -я́ю *imp.* fill (in, up).

заполя́рный, polar; trans-polar. **за-поля́рье**, -я, polar regions.

запомина́ть, -а́ю *imp.*, **запо́мнить**, -ню *perf.* remember, keep in mind; memorize; ~ся, be retained in memory, stay in one's mind. **запомина́ющ|ий**; ~ее устро́йство, (computer) memory.

за́понка, -и, cuff-link; (collar-)stud.

запо́р, -а, bolt; lock; closing, locking, bolting; constipation; на ~е, locked, bolted.

запроши́ть, -ши́т *perf*. powder, dust, scatter.

запоте́лый, misted, dim. за|поте́ть, -е́ет *perf*. mist over.

запою́, etc.: see запе́ть.

заправи́ла, -ы, boss. **запра́вить**, -влю *perf*., **заправля́ть**, -я́ю *imp*. insert, tuck in; prepare, set up; fuel, refuel, fill up; season, dress. flavour; mix in; ~ ла́мпу, trim a lamp; заправля́ть дела́ми, boss the show; ~ся, refuel. **запра́вка**, -и, refuelling; filling; servicing, setting up; seasoning, dressing, flavouring.

запра́шивать, -аю *imp*. of запроси́ть.

запрёт, -а, prohibition, ban; под ~ом, banned, prohibited. **запрети́тельный**, prohibitive. **запрети́ть**, -ещу́ *perf*., **запреща́ть**, -а́ю *imp*. prohibit, forbid, ban. **запре́тный**, forbidden, prohibited. **запреще́ние**, -я, prohibition; distraint. **запрещённый**, forbidden, illicit.

за|прихо́довать, -дую *perf*. за|программи́ровать, -рую *perf*.

запроки́дывать, -аю *imp*., **запроки́нуть**, -ну *perf*. throw back; ~ся, throw oneself back; fall back, sink back.

запро́с, -а, inquiry; overcharging; *pl*. requirements, needs. **запроси́ть**, -ошу́, -о́сишь *perf*. (*imp*. запра́шивать), inquire; inquire of, question; ask (a high price).

за́просто *adv*. without ceremony, without formality.

за|протоколи́ровать, -рую *perf*. запрошу́, etc.: see запроси́ть. запру́, etc.: see запере́ть.

запру́да, -ы, dam, weir; mill-pond. за|пруди́ть, -ужу́, -у́ди́шь *perf*., запру́живать, -аю *imp*. block; dam; fill to overflowing, cram, jam.

запряга́ть, -а́ю *imp*. of запря́чь. запря́гу́, etc.: see запря́чь. **запря́жка**, -и, harnessing; harness, team.

запря́тать(ся, -я́чу(сь *perf*.), **запря́тывать(ся**, -аю(сь *imp*. hide.

запря́чь, -ягу́, -яжёшь; -яг, -ла́ *perf*. (*imp*. запряга́ть) harness; yoke.

запу́ганный, cowed, intimidated, broken-spirited. **запуга́ть**, -а́ю *perf*., запу́гивать, -аю *imp*. cow, intimidate.

запуска́ть, -а́ю *imp*., **запусти́ть**, -ущу́, -у́стишь *perf*. thrust (in), push (in), dig (in); start, start up; launch; (+*acc*. or *instr*.) throw, fling; neglect, let go. **запусте́лый**, neglected; desolate. запусте́ние, -я, neglect; desolation.

запу́танный, tangled; intricate, involved, knotty. за|пу́тать, -аю *perf*. запу́тывать, -аю *imp*. tangle; confuse; complicate; muddle; involve; ~ся, get tangled, get entangled; be involved, get involved; become complicated.

запу́щенный, neglected. запущу́, etc.: see запусти́ть.

запча́сть, -и; *gen. pl*. -е́й *abbr*. запасна́я часть, spare part, spare.

за|пыли́ть(ся, -лю́(сь *perf*.)

запыха́ться, -а́юсь *perf*. be out of breath.

запью́, etc.: see запи́ть.

запя́стье, -я, wrist; bracelet.

запята́я *sb*. comma; difficulty, snag. за|пята́ть, -а́ю *perf*.

зараба́тывать, -аю *imp*., **зарабо́тать**, -аю *perf*. earn; start (up), begin to work; ~ся, overwork. **за́работ́н|ый**; ~ая пла́та, wages; pay, salary. **за́работок**, -тка, earnings.

заража́ть, -а́ю *imp*., **зарази́ть**, -ажу́ *perf*. infect; ~ся +*instr*. be infected with, catch. **зара́за**, -ы, infection, contagion; pest, plague. **зарази́тельный** infectious; catching. **зара́зный**, infectious, contagious; *sb*. infectious case.

зара́нее *adv*. beforehand; in good time, in advance.

зараста́ть, -а́ю *imp*., **зарасти́**, -ту́ -тёшь; -ро́с, -ла́ *perf*. be overgrown heal, skin over.

за́рево, -а, glow.

за|регистри́ровать(ся, -и́рую(сь *perf*.) за|регули́ровать, -рую *perf*.

заре́з, -а (-у), disaster; до ~у, desperately, badly, urgently. за|ре́зать, -е́жу *perf*. kill, knife; slaughter; ~ся, cut one's throat.

зарека́ться, -а́юсь *imp*. of заре́чься.

зарекомендова́ть, -ду́ю *perf*. ~ себя́ show oneself, present oneself; +*instr* prove oneself. show oneself, to be.

заре́чься, -еку́сь -ечёшься, -ёкся -екла́сь *perf*. (*imp*. зарека́ться) +*inf* renounce; swear off, promise to give up.

рржаветь, -еет *perf.* заржавленный, rusty.

рисовать, -сую *perf.*, зарисовывать, -аю *imp.* sketch. зарисовка, -и, sketching; sketch.

арница, -ы, summer lightning.

родить, -ожу *perf.*, зарождать, -аю *imp.* generate, engender; ~ся be born; arise. зародыш, -а, foetus; bud; embryo, germ. зародышевый, embryonic. зарождение, -я, conception; origin.

рок, -а, (solemn) promise, vow, pledge, undertaking.

рос, etc.: see зарасти. заросль, -и, thicket; brushwood.

рою, etc.: see зарыть.

рплата, -ы *abbr.* заработная плата, wages; pay; salary.

рубать, -аю *imp.* of зарубить.

рубежный, foreign.

рубить, -блю, -бишь *perf.* (*imp.* зарубать, -аю) kill, cut down; notch, cut in. зарубка, -и notch, incision.

румянить(ся, -ню(сь *perf.*

ручаться, -аюсь *imp.*, заручиться, -учусь *perf.* + *instr.* secure. заручка, -и, pull, protection.

рывать, -аю *imp.*, зарыть -рою *perf.* bury; ~ся, bury oneself; dig in.

ря, -и́; *pl.* зо́ри, зорь, за́рям; daybreak; unset, nightfall; reveille, retreat.

ряд, -а, a charge; cartridge; fund, supply. зарядить, -яжу́, -я́дишь *perf.*, аряжать, -аю *imp.* load; charge; toke; ~ся, be loaded; be charged. арядка, -и, loading; charging; exercises, drill. заряжающий *sb.* loader.

сада, -ы, ambush. засадить, -ажу -ади́шь *perf.*, засаживать, -аю *imp.* plant; plunge, drive; shut in, confine; eep in; set (за + *acc.* to); ~ (в тюрьму), put in prison, lock up. засадка, -и, planting. засаживаться, -аюсь *mp.* of засесть.

саливать[1], -аю *imp.* of засолить.

саливать[2], -аю *imp.*, засалить, -лю erf. soil, make greasy.

сасывать, -аю *imp.* of засосать.

сахаренный, candied, crystallized.

светить, -ечу -е́тишь *perf.* light, ~ся,

light up. засветло *adv.* before nightfall, before dark.

за|свидетельствовать, -твую *perf.*

засев, -а, sowing; seed, seed-corn; sown area. засевать, -аю *imp.* of засеять.

заседание, -я, meeting; session, sitting; conference. заседатель, -я *m.* assessor. заседать, -аю *imp.* sit, meet, be in session.

засеивать, -аю *imp.* of засеять. засек, е.с.: see засечь. засекать, -аю *imp.* of засечь.

засекретить, -речу *perf.*, засекречивать, -аю *imp.* classify; restrict; make secret; clear, give access to secret material. засекреченный, classified; cleared; hush-hush, secret.

засеку, etc.: see засечь. засёл, etc.: see засесть.

заселение, -я, settlement; colonization. заселённый; -ён, -ена́, populated, inhabited. заселить, -лю *perf.*, заселя́ть, -я́ю *imp.* settle; colonize; populate; occupy.

засесть, -ся́ду, -ся́л *perf.* (*imp.* заса́живаться) sit down (за + *acc.* to); sit firm, sit tight; settle; ensconce oneself; lodge in, stick in.

засечка, -и, notch, indentation; mark; intersection; fix; serif. засечь, -еку́, -ечёшь; -ёк, -ла́ *perf.* (*imp.* засекать) flog to death; notch; intersect; locate; fix.

засеять, -е́ю *perf.* (*imp.* засевать, засе́ивать) sow.

засидеться. -ижу́сь *perf.*, заси́живаться, -аюсь *imp.* sit too long, stay too long; sit up late; stay late. заси́женный, fly-specked, flyblown.

за|силосовать, -сую *perf.*

засилье, -я, dominance, sway.

заслать, зашлю́, -шлёшь *perf.* (*imp.* засыла́ть) send.

заслон -а, screen; barrier, road-block; (furnace, oven) door. заслони́ть, -оню́ *perf.*, заслоня́ть, -я́ю *imp.* cover; shield, screen; hide, push into the background. засло́нка, -и, (stove-)lid; damper; slide; baffle-plate; (furnace, oven) door.

заслу́га, -и, merit, desert; service. заслу́женный, заслужённый; deserved, merited; meritorious, of merit, distinguished; Honoured; time-honoured, good old. заслу́живать, -аю *imp.*, заслужи́ть, -ужу́, -у́жишь *perf.* deserve, merit; win, earn; +*gen.* be worthy or deserving of.

заслу́шать, -аю *perf.*, заслу́шивать, -аю *imp.* listen to, hear; ~ся (+*gen.*) listen spellbound (to).

засме́ивать, -аю *imp.*, засме́ять, -е́ю, -е́ешь *perf.* ridicule; ~ся, begin to laugh; burst out laughing.

засмоли́ть, -лю́ *perf.* tar, pitch.

засну́ть, -ну́, -нёшь *perf.* (*imp.* засыпа́ть) go to sleep, fall asleep; die down.

засо́в, -а, bolt, bar.

засо́вывать, -аю *imp.* of засу́нуть.

засо́л, -а, salting, pickling. засоли́ть, -олю́, -о́лишь *perf.* (*imp.* заса́ливать), salt, corn, pickle. засо́лка, -и, salting, pickling; brine, pickle.

засоре́ние, -я, littering; pollution, contamination; obstruction, clogging up. засори́ть, -рю́ *perf.*, засоря́ть, -я́ю *imp.* litter; get dirt into; clog, block up, stop.

засоса́ть, -осу́, -осёшь *perf.* (*imp.* заса́сывать) suck in, engulf, swallow up.

за|со́хнуть, -ну; -со́х *perf.* (*imp.* also засыха́ть), dry, dry up; wither.

за́спанный, sleepy.

заста́ва, -ы, gate, gates; barrier; picket, picquet; outpost; пограни́чная ~, frontier post.

застава́ть, -таю́, -таёшь *imp.* of заста́ть.

заста́вить[1], -влю *perf.*, заставля́ть, -я́ю *imp.* cram, fill; block up, obstruct.

заста́вить[2], -влю *perf.*, заставля́ть, -я́ю *imp.* make; compel, force.

заста́иваться, -ается *imp.* of застоя́ться. заста́ну, etc.: see заста́ть.

застаре́лый, chronic; rooted.

заста́ть, -а́ну *perf.* (*imp.* застава́ть) find; catch.

застёгивать, -аю *imp.*, застегну́ть, -ну́, -нёшь *perf.* fasten, do up; button up; hook up. застёжка, -и, fastening; clasp, buckle; hasp; ~-мо́лния, zip fastener, zip.

застекли́ть, -лю́ *perf.*, застекля́ть, -я́ю *imp.* glaze, fit with glass.

застелю́, etc.: see застла́ть.

засте́нчивый, shy.

застига́ть, -а́ю *imp.*, засти́гнуть, -сти́чь, -и́гну; -сти́г *perf.* catch; take unawares.

застила́ть, -а́ю *imp.* of застла́ть. сти́лка, -и, covering; floor-covering.

засти́чь: see засти́гнуть.

застла́ть, -телю́, -те́лешь *perf.* (*imp.* застла́ть) cover; spread over; cloud. ~ ковро́м, carpet.

засто́й, -я, stagnation; standstill; depression. засто́йный, stagnant; sluggish, immobile.

засто́льн|ый, table-; ~ая речь, after-dinner speech.

за|сто́порить, -рю *perf.*

застоя́ться, -и́тся *perf.* (*imp.* заста́иваться) stagnate, stand too long, get stale.

застра́ивать, -аю *imp.* of застро́ить.

застрахо́ванный, insured. за|страхова́ть, -ху́ю *perf.*, застрахо́вывать, -аю *imp.* insure (от+*gen.* against).

застрева́ть, -а́ю *imp.* of застря́ть.

застрели́ть, -елю́, -е́лишь *perf.* shoot (dead); ~ся, shoot oneself; blow one's brains out. застре́льщик, -а, pioneer, leader.

застро́ить, -о́ю *perf.* (*imp.* застра́ивать) build over, build on, build up. застро́йка, -и. building.

застря́ть, -я́ну *perf.* (*imp.* застрева́ть) stick; get stuck; be held up; be bogged down.

за|студене́ть, -е́ет *perf.*

застуди́ть, -ужу́, -у́дишь *perf.*, заста́живать, -аю *imp.* expose to cold, chill; ~ся, catch cold.

за́ступ, -а, spade.

заступа́ться, -а́юсь *imp.*, заступи́ться -плю́сь, -пишься *perf.*+за+*acc.* stand up for, take the part of; plead for. засту́пник, -а, defender; protector. засту́пничество, -а, protection; intercession, defence.

застыва́ть, -а́ю *imp.*, засты́ть, -ы́ну *perf.* congeal; thicken, harden, set; become stiff; freeze; be petrified; be paralysed. засты́лый, congealed, stiff.

засу́нуть, -ну *perf.* (*imp.* засо́вывать) thrust in, push in, shove in; stuff in; tuck in.

за́суха, -и, drought.

засу́чивать, -аю *imp.*, **засучи́ть**, -чу́, -чишь *perf.* roll up.

засу́шивать, -аю *imp.*, **засуши́ть**, -шу́, -шишь *perf.* dry up, shrivel. **засу́шливый**, arid, dry, drought.

засыла́ть -а́ю *imp.* of засла́ть.

засыпа́ть[1], -плю *perf.*, **засыпа́ть**, -а́ю *imp.* fill up, fill in; cover, strew; put in. add; ~ вопро́сами, bombard with questions.

засыпа́ть[2](ся. -а́ю(сь *imp.* of засну́ть, засыпа́ть(ся.

засыпа́ться, -плюсь *perf.* (*imp.* засыпа́ться) be caught; come to grief, slip up; fail an examination.

засы́пка, -и, filling; backfilling; filling up, charging; covering, strewing; putting in.

засыха́ть, -а́ю *imp.* of засо́хнуть. **заси́ду**, etc.: see засе́сть.

зата́енный, -ён, -ена́, secret; repressed, suppressed. **зата́ивать**, -аю *imp.*, **зата́ить**, -а́ю *perf.* suppress, repress; conceal; harbour, cherish; ~ дыха́ние, hold one's breath; ~ оби́ду, nurse a grievance, bear a grudge.

зата́лкивать, -аю *imp.* of затолка́ть.

зата́пливать, -аю *imp.* of затопи́ть.

зата́птывать, -аю *imp.* of затопта́ть.

зата́сканный, worn; threadbare; hackneyed, trite. **затаска́ть**, -а́ю *perf.*, **зата́скивать**[1], -аю *imp.* wear out; make hackneyed, make trite; drag about; ~ по суда́м, drag through the courts; ~ся, wear (out), get dirty or threadbare with use.

зата́скивать[2], -аю *imp.*, **затащи́ть**, -щу́, -щишь *perf.* drag in; drag off, drag away.

затвердева́ть, -а́ет *imp.*, **за|тверде́ть**, -е́ет *perf.* harden, become hard; set; solidify; freeze. **затверде́вший**, затверде́лый, hardened; solidified, set, congealed. **затверде́ние**, -я, hardening; induration, callosity; callus. **за|тверди́ть**, -ржу́ *perf.*

затво́р, -а, bolt, bar; lock; breech-block; shutter; water-gate, flood-gate.

затвори́ть, -рю́, -ришь *perf.*, **затворя́ть**, -я́ю *imp.* shut, close; ~ся, shut oneself up, lock oneself in. **затво́рник**, -а, hermit, anchorite, recluse.

затева́ть, -а́ю *imp.* of зате́ять. **зате́йливый**, ingenious; intricate, involved; original.

затёк, etc.: see зате́чь. **затека́ть**, -а́ет *imp.* of зате́чь.

зате́м *adv.*, then, after that, next; for that reason; ~ что, because, since, as.

затемне́ние, -я, darkening, obscuring; blacking out; black-out; fade-out. **затемни́ть**, -ню́ *perf.*, **затемня́ть**, -я́ю *imp.* darken, obscure; black out. **за́темно** *adv.* before dawn.

затере́ть, -тру́, -трёшь; -тёр *perf.* (*imp.* затира́ть) rub out; block, jam; су́дно затёрло льда́ми, the ship was ice-bound.

зате́рянный, lost; forgotten, forsaken. **затеря́ть**, -я́ю *perf.* lose, mislay; ~ся, be lost; be mislaid; be forgotten.

зате́чь, -ечёт, -еку́т; -тёк, -кла́ *perf.* (*imp.* затека́ть) pour, flow; leak; swell up; become numb.

зате́я, -и, undertaking, enterprise, venture; escapade; joke. **зате́ять**, -е́ю *perf.* (*imp.* затева́ть) undertake, venture; organize; ~ дра́ку, start a fight.

затира́ть, -а́ю *imp.* of затере́ть.

затиха́ть, -а́ю *imp.*, **зати́хнуть**, -ну; -ти́х *perf.* die down, abate; die away, fade; become quiet. **зати́шье**, -я, calm; lull; sheltered corner; backwater.

заткну́ть, -ну́, -нёшь *perf.* (*imp.* затыка́ть) stop up; plug; stick, thrust; ~ про́бкой, cork.

затмева́ть, -а́ю *imp.*, **затми́ть**, -ми́шь *perf.* darken, obscure; eclipse; overshadow. **затме́ние**, -я, eclipse; darkening; black-out.

зато́, *conj.* but then, but on the other hand.

затова́ренность, -и. **затова́ривание**, -я, overstocking; glut.

затолка́ть, -а́ю *perf.* (*imp.* зата́лкивать) jostle.

зато́н, -а, backwater; boat-yard. **зато|ну́ть**, -о́нет *perf.* sink, be submerged.

затопи́ть[1], -плю́, -пишь *perf.* (*imp.* зата́пливать) light; turn on the heating.

затопи́ть[2], -плю́, -пишь *perf.*, **затопля́ть**, -я́ю *imp.* flood, submerge; sink, scuttle.

затопта́ть, -пчу́, -пчешь *perf.* (*imp.* зата́птывать) trample, trample down; trample underfoot.

зато́р, -а, obstruction, block, jam; congestion.

за|тормози́ть, -ожу́ *perf.*

заточа́ть, -а́ю *imp.*, **заточи́ть**, -чу́ *perf.* confine, shut up; incarcerate. **заточе́ние**, -я, confinement; incarceration, captivity.

за|трави́ть, -влю́, -вишь *perf.*, **затра́вливать**, -аю *imp.* hunt down, bring to bay; persecute, harass, harry; badger.

затра́гивать, -аю *imp.* of затро́нуть.

затра́та, -ы, expense; outlay. **затра́тить**, -а́чу *perf.*, **затра́чивать**, -аю *imp.* expend, spend.

затре́бовать, -бую *perf.* request, require; ask for.

затро́нуть, -ну *perf.* (*imp.* затра́гивать) affect; touch, graze; touch on.

затрудне́ние, -я, difficulty. **затрудни́тельный**, difficult; embarrassing. **затрудни́ть**, -ню́ *perf.*, **затрудня́ть**, -я́ю *imp.* trouble; cause trouble to; embarrass; make difficult; hamper; ~ся, be in difficulties; +*inf.* or *instr.* find difficulty in.

затума́нивать, -ает *imp.*, **за|тума́нить**, -ит *perf.* befog; cloud, dim, obscure.

за|тупи́ть, -плю́, -пишь *perf.*

за|тушева́ть, -шу́ю *perf.*, **затушёвывать**, -аю *imp.* shade; conceal; draw a veil over.

за|туши́ть, -шу́, -шишь *perf.* put out, extinguish; suppress.

за́тхлый, musty, mouldy; stuffy, close; stagnant.

затыка́ть, -а́ю *imp.* of заткну́ть.

заты́лок, -лка, back of the head; occiput; scrag scrag-end. **заты́лочный**, occipital.

зати́гивать, -аю *imp.*, **затяну́ть**, -ну́, -нешь *perf.* tighten; lace up; cover; close, heal; drag out, draw out, spin out; ~ся, lace oneself up; be covered; close, skin over; be delayed; linger; be

drawn out, drag on; inhale. **затя́жка**, -и, inhaling; prolongation; dragging on; drawing out; delaying, putting off; lagging. **затяжно́й**, long-drawn-out; lingering.

зауны́вный, mournful, doleful.

заура́дный, ordinary, commonplace; mediocre.

заусе́нец, -нца, **заусе́ница**, -ы, agnail, hangnail, wire-edge, burr.

за|фарширова́ть, -ру́ю *perf.* **за|фикси́ровать**, -рую *perf.* **за|фрахтова́ть**, -ту́ю *perf.*

захва́т, -а, seizure, capture; usurpation; clamp c1aw. **захвати́ть**, -ачу́, -а́тишь *perf.* **захва́тывать**, -аю *imp.* take; seize, capture; carry away; thrill, excite; catch; у меня захвати́ло дух it took my breath away. **захва́тнический**, predatory; aggressive. **захва́тчик**, -а, invader; aggressor. **захва́тывающий**, gripping; ~ся, breath-taking.

захвора́ть -а́ю *perf.* fall ill, be taken ill.

за|хире́ть -е́ю *perf.*

захлебну́ться -ну́сь, -нёшься *perf.*, **захлёбываться**, -аюсь *imp.* choke (от +*gen.* with).

захлестну́ть, -ну́, -нёшь *perf.* **захлёстывать**, -аю *imp.* flow over, swamp, overwhelm; overflow.

захло́пнуть, -ну *perf.*, **захло́пывать**, -аю *imp.* slam, bang; ~ся, slam (to) bang (to), shut with a bang.

захо́д, -а setting, sunset; stopping, calling, putting in. **заходи́ть**, -ожу́, -о́дишь *imp.* of зайти́. **захо́жий**, newly-arrived.

захолу́стный, remote, out-of-the-way, provincial. **захолу́стье**, -я, backwoods; godforsaken hole.

за|хорони́ть, -ню́ -нишь *perf.* **за|хоте́ть(ся**, -очу́(сь, -о́чешь(ся, -оти́м(ся *perf.*

захуда́лый, impoverished, poor, shabby; emaciated.

зацвести́, -ету́; -вёл -а́ *perf.*, **зацвета́ть**, -а́ю *imp.* burst into flower come into bloom.

зацепи́ть, -плю́, -пишь *perf.*, **зацепля́ть**, -я́ю *imp.* hook; engage, catch (за+*acc.* on); ~ся за+*acc.* catch on; catch hold of. **заце́пка**, -и, catch, hook, peg; hooking; hitch, catch; pull, protection.

зачастую *adv.* often, frequently.

зача́тие, -я, conception. **зача́ток**, -тка, embryo; rudiment; beginning, germ. **зача́точный**, rudimentary. **зача́ть**, -чну́ -чнёшь; -ча́л, -а́, -о *perf.* (*imp.* **зачина́ть**) conceive; begin.

за|ча́хнуть -ну; -ча́х *perf.* **зачёл**, etc.: see **заче́сть**.

зачем *adv.* why; what for. **зачем-то** *adv.* for some reason.

зачёркивать -аю *imp.*, **зачеркну́ть**, -ну, -нёшь *perf.* cross out, strike out; delete.

за|черни́ть -ню́ *perf.*

зачерпну́ть -ну́ -нёшь *perf.*, **зачёрпывать**, -аю *imp.* scoop up; ladle; draw up.

зачерстве́лый, stale; hard-hearted. **за|черстве́ть**, -е́ет *perf.*

заче́сть, -чту́, -чтёшь; -чёл -чла́ *perf.* (*imp.* **зачи́тывать**) take into account, reckon as credit; pass. **~**, a, reckoning; instalment; test; в **~** пла́ты in payment, on account; получи́ть сдать, **~** по+*dat.* pass a test in; поста́вить **~** по+*dat.* pass in. **зачётн|ый**; **~ая** квита́нция, receipt; **~ая кни́жка**, (student's) record book.

за|чехли́ть, -лю́ *perf.*

зачина́тель, -я *m.* founder, author. **зачина́ть**, -а́ю *imp.* of **зача́ть**. **зачи́н-щик**, -а, instigator, ringleader.

зачи́слить -лю *perf.*, **зачисля́ть**, -я́ю *imp.* include; enter; enrol, enlist; **~ся**, join, enter.

зачи́тывать, -аю *imp.* of **заче́сть**. **зачну́**, etc.: see **зача́ть**. **зачту́**, etc.: see **заче́сть**. **зашёл**, etc.: see **зайти́**.

зашива́ть, -а́ю *imp.* **заши́ть** -шью, -шьёшь *perf.* sew up; suture; put stitches in.

зашифро́ванный encoded, in cipher. **за|шифрова́ть** -ру́ю *perf.* **зашифро́вывать**, -аю *imp.* encipher, encode.

зашло́ etc.: see **засла́ть**.

за|шнурова́ть -ру́ю *perf.*, **зашнуро́вывать**, -аю *imp.* lace up.

за|шпаклева́ть -лю́ю *perf.* **за|штемпелева́ть** -лю́ю *perf.* **за|што́пать**,

-аю *perf.* **за|штрихова́ть** -ху́ю *perf.* **зашью́**, etc.: see **заши́ть**.

защипну́ть, -ну́ -нёшь *perf.* **защи́пывать** -аю *imp* pinch, nip, tweak; take; curl; punch.

защи́та, -ы, defence; protection; the defence. **защити́ть**, -ишу́ *perf.*, **защища́ть**, -а́ю *imp.* defend, protect; stand up for.

заяви́ть, -влю́, -вишь *perf.*, **заявля́ть**, -я́ю *imp.* announce; declare; claim; show, attest; **~ся**, appear, turn up. **зая́вка**, -и, claim; demand, request. **заявле́ние**, -я, statement, declaration; application.

зая́длый, inveterate, confirmed.

за́яц, за́йца, hare; stowaway; gate-crasher; е́хать за́йцем, travel without a ticket. **за́ячий**, hare, hare's; **~** щаве́ль, wood-sorrel.

зва́ние, -я, calling, profession; rank; title. **зва́ный**, invited; **~** ве́чер, guest-night; **~** гость, guest; **~** обе́д, banquet, dinner, dinner-party. **зва́-тельный**, vocative. **звать**, зову́, -вёшь; звал, -а́, -о *imp.* (*perf.* по**~**) call; ask, invite; как вас зову́т? what is your name?; be called.

звезда́, -ы́; *pl.* звёзды, star. **звёздный**, star; starry; starlit; stellar. **звездо-обра́зный**, star-shaped; radial; stellate. **звездочёт**, -а, astrologer. **звёздочка**, -и, little star; asterisk.

звене́ть, -ню́ *imp.* ring; +*instr.* jingle, clink.

звено́, -а́; *pl.* зве́нья, -ьев, link; bond; team, group, section, flight; unit; component, element; network. **звенье-во́й** *sb.* team leader; section leader.

звери́нец, -нца, menagerie. **звери́ный**, wild-animal, wild-beast. **зверо́бой**, hunter, sealer. **зверово́дство**, -а, fur farming, fur breeding. **зверо́лов**, -а, trapper. **зве́рский** *adv.* brutally, bestially; terribly; awfully. **зве́рский**, brutal, bestial; terrific, tremendous. **зве́рство**, -а, brutality; atrocity. **зве́рствовать**, -твую *imp.* commit atrocities. **зверь**, -я; *pl.* -и, -е́й *m.* wild animal, wild beast; brute. **зверьё**, -я́, wild animals; wild beasts.

звон, -а, ringing; ringing sound, chime,

peal, chink, clink. звони́ть, -ню́ imp. (perf. по~) ring; ring up; -и́ть в колоко́ла, ring the bells; ~ кому́-нибудь (по телефо́ну), ring somebody up; telephone to somebody; вы не туда́ звони́те, you've got the wrong number; звоня́т, the telephone's ringing; there's somebody at the door; ~ся, ring the (door-)bell, ring. звон|ки́й, -нок, -нка́, -о, ringing, clear; voiced; ~ая моне́та, hard cash, coin. звоно́к, -нка́, bell; ~ по телефо́ну, (telephone) call. зво́нче, зво́нчее, comp. of зво́нкий, зво́нко.

звук, -а, sound; ни ~а, not a sound.

звуко- in comb. sound. звукоза́пись, -и, sound recording. ~изоля́ция, -и, sound-proofing. ~непроница́емый, sound-proof. ~подража́тельный, onomatopoeic. ~проводный, sound-conducting. ~снима́тель, -я m. pick-up. ~ула́вливатель, -я m. sound locator. ~часто́тный, audio, audio-frequency.

звуково́й, sound; audio; acoustical, acoustic. звуча́ние, -я, sound vibration; phonation. звуча́ть, -чи́т imp. be heard; sound; + instr. express, convey; ~ и́скренно, ring true. зву́чный, -чен, -чна́, -о, sonorous.

звя́канье, -я, jingling; tinkling. звя́кать, -аю imp, звя́кнуть, -ну perf. (+ instr.) jingle; tinkle.

зда́ние, -я, building.

здесь adv. here; at this point; in this. зде́шний, local; he ~, a stranger here.

здоро́ваться, -аюсь imp. (perf. по~) exchange greetings; ~ за́ руку, shake hands. здо́рово adv. splendidly, magnificently; well done! fine! здоро́вый, healthy, strong; well; health-giving, wholesome, sound. здоро́вье, -я, health; за ва́ше ~! your health!; как ва́ше ~? how are you? здра́вица, -ы, toast. здра́вница, -ы, sanatorium. здра́во adv. soundly; sensibly.

здраво- in comb. health; sound, sensible. здравомы́слящий, sensible, judicious. ~охране́ние, -я, public health; health service. ~охрани́тельный, public-health.

здравпу́нкт, -а, medical post, medical

centre. здра́вствовать, -твую imp. be healthy; thrive, prosper; здра́вствуй(те), how do you do?; good morning, afternoon, evening; да здра́вствует! long live! здра́вый, sensible; healthy; в ~ом уме́, in one's right mind; ~ый смысл, common sense.

зев, -а, pharynx; jaws. зева́ка, -и m. and f. idler, gaper. зева́ть, -а́ю imp., зевну́ть, -ну́, -нёшь perf. (perf. also про~) yawn; gape; miss, let slip, lose. зево́к, -вка́ зево́та, -ы, yawn.

зелене́ть, -е́ет imp. (perf. по~) turn green, go green; show green. зелен|но́й, ~а́я ла́вка, greengrocer's. зеленова́тый, greenish. зелён|ый, -лён, -а́, -о, green; ~ый лук, spring onions; ~ая у́лица, go, green light. зе́лень, -и, green; greenery, vegetation; greens; vegetables.

земле- in comb. land; earth. землеве́дение, -я, physical geography. ~владе́лец, -льца, landowner. ~де́лец, -льца, farmer. ~де́лие, -я, farming, agriculture. ~де́льческий, agricultural. ~ко́п, -а, navvy. ~ме́р, -а, land-surveyor. ~ме́рный, surveying, surveyor's. ~ро́йный, earth-moving, excavating. ~трясе́ние, -я, earthquake. ~черпа́лка, -и, mechanical dredger, bucket dredger. ~черпа́ние, -я, dredging.

земли́стый, earthy; sallow. земля́, -и́, acc. -ю; pl. -и, земе́ль, -ям, earth; land; soil. земля́к, -а́, fellow-countryman. земляни́ка, -и, strawberries; wild strawberries. земля́нка, -и, dug-out; mud hut. земля́н|ой, -и, earthen; earth; earthy. ~а́я гру́ша, Jerusalem artichoke. земля́чка, -и, country-woman. земно́й, earthly; terrestrial; ground; mundane; ~ шар, the globe.

зени́т, -а, zenith. зени́тный, zenith; anti-aircraft.

зе́ркало, -а; pl. -а́, looking-glass; mirror; reflector. зерка́льн|ый, mirror; looking-glass; reflecting; smooth; plate, plate-glass; ~ое изображе́ние, mirror image.

зерни́ст|ый, granular, granulated; grainy; ~ая икра́, unpressed caviare. зерно́, -а́; pl. зёрна, зёрен, grain; seed;

зерца́ло, -a, looking-glass; *pl.* breast-plate.

зима́, -ы́, *acc.* -у; *pl.* -ы, winter. **зи́мний**, winter, wintry. **зимова́ть**, -му́ю *imp.* (*perf.* пере~, про~) winter, spend the winter; hibernate. **зимо́вка**, -и wintering, winter stay; hibernation; polar station. **зимо́вщик**, -a, winterer. **зимо́вье**, -я, winter quarters. **зимо́й** *adv.* in winter. **зимосто́йкий**, hardy.

зия́ние, -я, gaping, yawning; gap; hiatus. **зия́ть**, -я́ет *imp.* gape, yawn.

злак, -a, grass; cereal. **зла́ковый**, grassy, herbaceous: cereal, grain.

злейший *superl.* of злой; ~ враг, worst enemy. **злить**, злю *imp.* (*perf.* обо~, о~, разо~) anger; irritate; ~ся, be angry, be in a bad temper; rage. зло, -a; *gen. pl.* зол; evil; harm; misfortune, disaster; malice, spite; vexation. зло *adv.* maliciously, spitefully.

зло- in comb., evil, harm, malice; wicked, malicious; bad-tempered. зло**ве́щий**, ominous, ill-omened. зло**во́ние**, -я, stink, stench. зло**во́нный**, fetid, stinking. ~**вре́дный**, pernicious, noxious. ~**ка́чественный**, malignant; pernicious. ~**наме́ренный**, ill-intentioned. ~**па́мятный**, rancorous, unforgiving. ~**полу́чный**, unlucky, ill-starred. ~**ра́дный**, malevolent, gloating. ~**сло́вие**, -я, malicious gossip; backbiting. ~**у́мышленник**, -a, malefactor, criminal; plotter. ~**у́мышленный**, with criminal intent. ~**язы́чие**, -я, slander, backbiting. ~**язы́чный**, slanderous.

зло́ба, -ы, malice; spite; anger; ~ дня, topic of the day, latest news. **зло́бный**, malicious, spiteful; bad-tempered. **злободне́вный**, topical; ~ые вопро́сы, burning issues, topics of the day. **злоде́й**, -я, villain; scoundrel. **злоде́йский**, villainous. **злоде́йство**, -a, villainy; crime, evil deed. **злодея́ние**, -я, crime, evil deed. **злой**; зол, зла, evil; bad; wicked; malicious; malevo-

lent; vicious; bad-tempered; savage; dangerous; severe, cruel; bad, nasty; зла́я соба́ка, beware of the dog. **зло́стный**, malicious; conscious, intentional; persistent, hardened; ~ное банкро́тство, fraudulent bankruptcy. **злость**, -и, malice, spite; fury. **злоупотреби́ть**, -блю́ *perf.*, **злоупотребля́ть**, -я́ю *imp.* + *instr.* abuse. **злоупотребле́ние**, -я, + *instr.* abuse of; ~ дове́рием, breach of confidence.

змеи́ный, snake; snake's; cunning, crafty; wicked. **змеи́стый**, serpentine; sinuous. **змей**, -я, snake; dragon; kite. **змея́**, -и́; *pl.* -и, snake. **змия́**, -я́, serpent, dragon.

знак, -a, sign; mark; token, symbol; omen; signal; ~и препина́ния, punctuation marks; ~и разли́чия, insignia, badges of rank.

знако́мить, -млю *imp.* (*perf.* о~, по~), acquaint; introduce; ~ся, become acquainted, acquaint oneself; get to know; introduce oneself; study, investigate; +c+ *instr.* meet, make the acquaintance of. **знако́мство**, -a, acquaintance; (circle of) acquaintances; knowledge (c+ *instr.* of). **знако́мый**, familiar; быть ~ым с+ *instr.* be acquainted with, know; ~ый, ~ая, *sb.* acquaintance, friend.

знамена́тель, -я *m.* denominator; привести́ к одному́ знамена́телю, reduce to a common denominator. **знамена́тельный**, significant, important; principal. **зна́мение**, -я, sign. **знамени́тость**, -и, celebrity. **знамени́тый**, celebrated, famous, renowned; outstanding, superlative. **знаменова́ть**, -ну́ю *imp.* signify, mark. **знаменосец**, -сца, standard-bearer. **зна́мя**, -мени; *pl.* -мёна *n.* banner; flag; standard.

зна́ние, -я, knowledge; *pl.* learning; accomplishments; со зна́нием де́ла, capably, competently.

зна́тный; -тен, -тна́, -о, distinguished; outstanding, notable; noble, aristocratic; splendid.

знато́к, -а́, expert; connoisseur. **знать**, -а́ю *imp.* know; дать ~, let know; да́йте мне ~ о вас, let me hear from you; дать себе́ ~, make itself felt; ~ в лицо́, know by sight; ~ ме́ру, know where to stop; ~ себе́ це́ну, know one's own value; ~ толк в +prep. be knowledgeable about; ~ся, associate.

значе́ние, -я, meaning; significance; importance; value. зна́чит, so, then; that means. значи́тельный, considerable, sizeable; important; significant; meaningful. зна́чить, -чу imp. mean; signify; have significance, be of importance; ~ся, be; be mentioned, appear. значо́к, -чка́, badge; mark.

зна́ющий, expert; learned, erudite; knowledgeable; well-informed.

зноби́ть, -и́т imp., impers.+acc.; меня́, etc., зноби́т, I feel shivery, feverish.

зной, -я, intense heat. зно́йный, hot, sultry; burning.

зов, -а (-у), call, summons; invitation. зову́, etc.: see звать.

зо́дческий, architecture, architectural. зо́дчество, -а, architecture. зо́дчий sb. architect.

зол: see зло, злой.

зола́ -ы́, ashes, cinders.

золо́вка, -и, sister-in-law, husband's sister.

золоти́стый, golden. золоти́ть, -очу́ imp. (perf. вы́~, по~) gild. зо́лото, -а, gold. золот|о́й, gold; golden; ~о́е дно, gold-mine; ~о́й запа́с, gold reserves; ~о́й песо́к, gold-dust; ~ы́е про́мыслы, gold-fields. золотоно́сный, auriferous; gold-bearing.

золоту́ха, -и, scrofula. золоту́шный, scrofulous.

золоче́ние, -я, gilding. золочёный, gilt, gilded.

зо́на, -ы, zone; region; band, belt. зона́льный, zonal, zone; regional.

зонд, -а, probe; bore; sonde. зонди́ровать, -рую imp. sound, probe.

зонт, -а́, umbrella; awning. зо́нтик, -а, umbrella; sunshade; umbel. зо́нтичный, umbellate, umbelliferous.

зоо́лог, -а, zoologist. зоологи́ческий, zoological. зооло́гия, -и, zoology. зоопа́рк, -а, zoo, zoological gardens.

зо́ри, etc.: see заря́.

зо́ркий, -рок, -рка́, -о, sharp-sighted; perspicacious, penetrating; vigilant.

зрачо́к, -чка́, pupil.

зре́лище -а, sight; spectacle; show; pageant.

зре́лость, -и, ripeness; maturity; аттеста́т зре́лости, school-leaving certificate. зре́лый; зрел, -а́, -о, ripe, mature.

зре́ние, -я, sight, eyesight, vision; обма́н зре́ния, optical illusion; по́ле зре́ния, field of vision, field of view; то́чка зре́ния, point of view; у́гол зре́ния, viewing angle, camera angle.

зреть, -е́ю imp. (perf. со~) ripen; mature.

зри́мый, visible. зри́тель, -я m. spectator, observer; onlooker; pl. audience. зри́тельный, visual; optic; ~ зал, hall, auditorium.

зря adv. to no purpose, for nothing, in vain.

зря́чий, sighted, seeing.

зуб, -а; pl. -ы or -бья, -о́в or -бьев, tooth; cog. зуба́стый, large-toothed; sharp-tongued. зубе́ц, -бца́, tooth, cog, tine; blip. зуби́ло, -а, chisel. зубно́й, dental; tooth; ~ врач, dentist. зубовраче́бный, dentists', dental; ~ кабине́т, dental surgery. зубовраче́ва́ние, -я, dentistry. зубо́к, -бка́; pl. -бки́, tooth; cog; clove. зубоска́л, -а, scoffer. зубочи́стка, -и, toothpick.

зубр, -а, (European) bison, aurochs; die-hard.

зубри́ть[1], -рю́ imp. (perf. за~) notch, serrate.

зубри́ть[2], -рю́, зу́бришь imp. (perf. вы́~, за~) cram, learn by rote.

зубча́тка, -и, sprocket; gear-wheel, gear; rack-wheel. зубча́тый, toothed, cogged; gear; gear-wheel; serrate, serrated; jagged, indented.

зуд, -а, itch. зуда́, -ы́ m. and f. bore. зуде́ть, -и́т, itch.

зы́бкий; -бок, -бка́, -о, unsteady, shaky; unstable, shifting; vacillating. зыбу́ч|ий, unsteady, unstable, shifting; ~ие пески́, quicksands. зыбь, -и; gen. pl. -е́й, ripple rippling.

зы́чный, loud, stentorian.

зэ *n. indecl.* the letter з.

зя́бкий, chilly, sensitive to cold.

зя́блик, -а, chaffinch.

зя́блый, frozen; damaged by frost.

зя́бнуть, -ну; зяб *imp.* suffer from cold, feel the cold.

зять, -я; *pl.* **-тья́, -тьёв,** son-in-law; brother-in-law, sister's husband.

И, Й

и *n. indecl.* the letter и; и с кра́ткой. и кра́ткое, the letter й.

и *conj.* and; and so; even; just; too, as well; (with *neg.*) either; в то́м-то и де́ло, that's just it, that's the whole point; и . . и, both . . and; и он не знал, he didn't know either; и про́чее, и так да́лее, etc., etcetera, and so on and so forth; и тому́ подо́бное, and the like; и тот и друго́й, both.

и́бо *conj.* for; because, since.

и́ва, -ы, willow. **ивня́к, -á,** osier-bed; osiers, osier. **и́вовый,** willow.

и́волга, -и, oriole.

игла́, -ы́; *pl.* **-ы,** needle; thorn; spine; quill.

и́го, -а, yoke.

иго́лка, -и, needle. **иго́лочка, -и** *dim.*; с иго́лочки, brand-new, spick and span. **иго́льник, -а,** needle-case. **иго́льный,** needle, needle's. **иго́льчатый,** needle-shaped; acicular; needle.

игра́ный, gaming, gambling. **игра́, -ы́;** *pl.* **-ы,** play, playing; game; hand; turn, lead; ~ приро́ды, sport, freak (of nature); ~ слов, pun. **игра́[льный],** playing; ~ые ко́сти, dice. **игра́ть, -а́ю** *imp.* (*perf.* сыгра́ть) play; act; ~ в+*acc.* play (game); ~ на+*prep.* play (an instrument), play on; +*instr.* or с+*instr.* play with, toy with, trifle with; ~ в билья́рд, на билья́рде, play billiards; э́то не игра́ет ро́ли, it is of no importance, of no significance. **игри́вый,** playful. **игри́стый,** sparkling. **игро́к, -á,** player; gambler. **игру́шечный,** toy. **игру́шка, -и,** toy; plaything.

иде́йность, -и, principle, integrity; ideo-logical content. **иде́йный,** high-principled; acting on principle; ideological.

идёт, etc.: see идти́.

иде́я, -и, idea; notion, concept; счастли́вая ~, happy thought.

идио́т, -а, idiot, imbecile. **идиоти́зм, -а,** idiocy, imbecility. **идиоти́ческий, идио́тский,** idiotic, imbecile.

идти́, итти́, иду́, идёшь; шёл, шла *imp.* (*perf.* пойти́) go; come; go round; run, work; pass; go on, be in progress; be on, be showing; fall; + в + *nom.-acc.* become; +в+*acc.* be used for, go for; +(к +) *dat.* suit, become; + на + *acc.* enter; go to make, go on; + о + *prep.* be about; + *instr.* or с + *gen.* play, lead, move; ей идёт тридца́тый год, she is in her thirtieth year; ~ в лётчики, become a flyer; ~ в лом, go for scrap; ~ на сме́ну+*dat.* take the place of, succeed; ~ ферзём, move the queen; ~ с черве́й, lead a heart; хорошо́ ~, be selling well, be going well; шли го́ды, years passed; э́та шля́па ей не идёт, that hat doesn't suit her.

иере́й, -я, priest. **иере́йство, -а,** priesthood.

иждиве́нец, -нца, -ве́нка, -и, dependant. **иждиве́ние, -я,** maintenance; means, funds; на иждиве́нии, at the expense of; жить на своём иждиве́нии, keep oneself; жить на иждиве́нии роди́телей, live on one's parents. **иждиве́нчество, -а,** a dependence.

из, изо *prep.* + *gen.* from, out of, of; вы́йти из до́ма, go out, leave the house; изо всех сил, with all one's might; из достове́рных исто́чников, from reliable sources, on good authority; ло́жки из серебра́, silver spoons; обе́д из трёх блюд, a three-course dinner; оди́н из ста, one in a hundred.

из-, изо-, изъ-, ис-, *vbl. pref.* indicating motion outwards; action over entire surface of object, in all directions; expenditure of instrument or object in course of action; continuation or repetition of action to extreme point; exhaustiveness of action.

изба́, -ы́; *pl.* -ы, izba; ~-чита́льня, village reading-room.

изба́витель, -я *m.* deliverer. **изба́вить,** -влю *perf.*, **избавля́ть,** -я́ю *imp.* save, deliver; изба́ви Бог! God forbid! ~ся, be saved; escape; ~ся от, get rid of; get out of. **избавле́ние,** -я, deliverance.

избало́ванный, spoilt. **из|бало́вать,** -лу́ю *perf.*, **избало́вывать,** -аю *imp.* spoil.

изба́ч, -а́, village librarian.

избега́ть, -а́ю *imp.*, **избе́гнуть,** -ну; -бе́г(нул) *perf.*, **избежа́ть,** -егу́ *perf.*+ *gen.* or *inf.* avoid; shun, escape, evade. **избежа́ние,** -я; во ~+*gen.* (in order) to avoid.

изберу́, etc.: see **избра́ть.**

избива́ть, -а́ю *imp.* of **изби́ть. избие́ние,** -я, slaughter, massacre; beating, beating-up.

избира́тель, -я *m.*, ~ница, -ы, elector, voter. **избира́тель|ный,** electoral; selective; ~ый бюллете́нь, voting-paper, ballot-paper; ~ая у́рна, ballot-box; ~ый уча́сток, polling station. **избира́ть,** -а́ю *imp.* of **избра́ть.**

изби́|тый, beaten, beaten up; hackneyed, trite. **изби́ть,** изобью́, -бьёшь *perf.* (*imp.* избива́ть) beat unmercifully, beat up; slaughter, massacre; wear down, ruin.

избра́ние, -я, election. **и́збранн|ый,** selected; select; ~ые *sb. pl.* the élite. **избра́ть,** -беру́, -берёшь; -а́л, -а, -о *perf.* (*imp.* избира́ть) elect; choose.

избу́шка, -и, small hut.

избы́т|ок, -тка, surplus, excess; abundance, plenty. **избы́точный,** surplus, abundant, plentiful.

изва́яние, -я, statue, sculpture. **изва́ять,** -я́ю *perf.*

изве́дать, -аю *perf.*, **изве́дывать,** -аю *imp.* come to know, learn the meaning of.

изведу́, etc., **извёл,** etc.: see **извести́.**

изве́рг, -а, monster. **изверга́ть,** -а́ю *imp.*, **изве́ргнуть,** -ну; -ёрг *perf.* disgorge; eject; throw out; excrete; expel; ~ся, erupt. **изверже́ние,** -я, eruption; ejection, expulsion; excretion.

изверну́ться, -ну́сь, -нёшься *perf.*, **изве́ртываться,** -аюсь *imp.* (*imp.* also изворо́чиваться) dodge, take evasive action; be evasive.

извести́, -еду́, -едёшь; -ёл, -ела́ *perf.* (*imp.* изводи́ть) use (up); waste; destroy, exterminate; exhaust; torment.

изве́стие, -я, news; information; intelligence; *pl.* proceedings, transactions. **извести́ть,** -ещу́ *perf.* (*imp.* извеща́ть) inform, notify.

изве́стка, -и, lime. **известкова́ть,** -ку́ю *per.* and *imp.* lime. **известко́вый,** lime; limestone; calcareous.

изве́стно, it is (well) known; of course, certainly; как ~, as everybody knows; наско́лько мне ~, as far as I know. **изве́стность,** -и, fame, reputation; repute; notoriety. **изве́ст|ный,** known; well-known, famous; notorious; certain; в ~ых слу́чаях, in certain cases. **известня́к,** -а́, limestone. **и́звесть,** -и, lime.

извеща́ть, -а́ю *imp.* of **извести́ть. извеще́ние,** -я, notification, notice; advice.

изви́в, -а, winding, bend. **извива́ть,** -а́ю *imp.* of **изви́ть;** ~ся, coil; wriggle, writhe; twist; wind; meander. **извили́на,** -ы, bend, twist, winding; convolution. **изви́листый,** winding; tortuous; sinuous; meandering.

извине́ние, -я, excuse; apology; pardon. **извини́тельный,** excusable, pardonable; apologetic. **извини́ть,** -ню́ *perf.*, **извиня́ть,** -я́ю *imp.* excuse; извини́те (меня́), I beg your pardon, excuse me, (I'm) sorry; извини́те, что я опозда́л, sorry I'm late; ~ся, apologize; make excuses, excuse oneself; извиня́юсь, I apologize, (I'm) sorry; извини́тесь за меня́, present my apologies, make my excuses.

изви́ть, извью́, -вьёшь; -и́л, -а́, -о *perf.* (*imp.* извива́ть) coil, twist, wind; ~ся, coil; writhe, twist.

извлека́ть, -а́ю *imp.*, **извле́чь**, -еку́, -ечёшь; -ёк, -ла́ *perf.* extract; derive, elicit; extricate; ~ уро́к из, learn a lesson from. **извлече́ние**, -я, extraction; extract, excerpt.

извне́ *adv.* from outside.

изводи́ть, -ожу́, -о́дишь *imp.* of извести́.

изво́зчик, -а, cabman, cabby; carrier, carter, drayman; cab.

изво́лить, -лю *imp.*+*inf.* or *gen.* wish, desire; + *inf.* deign, be pleased; изво́льте, if you wish; all right; with pleasure.

изворачиваться, -аюсь *imp.* of изверну́ться. **изворо́т**, -а, bend, twist; *pl.* tricks, wiles. **изворо́тливый**, resourceful, artful; wily, shrewd.

изврати́ть, -ащу́ *perf.*, **извраща́ть**, -а́ю *imp.* distort; pervert; misinterpret, misconstrue. **извраще́ние**, -я, perversion; misinterpretation, distortion. **извращённый**, perverted, unnatural.

изга́дить, -а́жу *perf.* befoul, soil; spoil, make a mess of.

изги́б, -а, bend, twist; winding; inflexion, nuance. **изгиба́ть(ся**, -а́ю(сь *imp.* of изогну́ть(ся.

изгла́дить, -а́жу *perf.*, **изгла́живать**, -аю *imp.* efface, wipe out, blot out.

изгна́ние, -я, banishment; expulsion; exile. **изгна́нник**, -а, exile. **изгна́ть**, -гоню́, -го́нишь; -а́л, -а́, -о *perf.* (*imp.* изгоня́ть) banish, expel; exile; oust, do away with.

изголо́вье, -я, bed-head; bedside; служи́ть изголо́вьем, serve as a pillow.

изголода́ться, -а́юсь, be famished, starve; +по+*dat.* thirst for, yearn for.

изгоню́, etc.: see изгна́ть, **изгоня́ть**, -я́ю *imp.* of изгна́ть.

и́згородь, -и, fence, hedge.

изготовля́ть, -я́ю *imp.*, **изгото́вить**, -влю *perf.*, **изготовля́ть**, -я́ю *imp.* make, manufacture, produce; prepare; cook; ~ся, get ready, make ready.

изгото́вка, -и, **изготовле́ние**, -я making, manufacture, production; preparation.

издава́ть, -даю́, -даёшь *imp.* of изда́ть.

и́здавна *adv.* from time immemorial; for a very long time.

издади́м etc.: see изда́ть.

издалека́, **издалёка**, **и́здали** *advs.* from afar, from far away, from a distance.

изда́ние, -я, publication; edition; promulgation. **изда́тель**, -я *m.*, ~ница, -ы, publisher. **изда́тельство**, -а, publishing house, press, publisher's. **изда́ть**, -а́м, -а́шь -а́ст -ади́м; -а́л, -а́, -о *perf.* (*imp.* издава́ть) publish; promulgate; issue; produce emit; let out, utter; ~ся, be published.

издева́тельский, mocking. **издева́тельство**, -а, mocking, scoffing; mockery; taunt, insult. **издева́ться**, -а́юсь *imp.* (+над+*instr.*) mock, scoff, (at). **издёвка** -и, taunt, insult.

изде́лие, -я make, work; article; *pl.* wares.

издержа́ть, -жу́, -жишь *perf.* spend; ~ся, spend all one's money; be spent up. **изде́ржки**, -жек *pl.* expenses; costs; cost.

издеру́, etc.: see изодра́ть. **издира́ть**, -а́ю *imp.* of изодра́ть.

издо́хнуть, -ну; -до́х *perf.*, **издыха́ть**, -а́ю *imp.* die; peg out, kick the bucket. **издыха́ние**, -я; после́днее ~, last breath, last gasp.

изжа́рить(ся -рю(сь *perf.*

изжива́ть, -а́ю *imp.*, **изжи́ть**, -иву́, -вёшь; -и́л, -а́, -о *perf.* overcome, get over; eliminate, get rid of.

изжо́га, -и, heartburn.

из-за *prep.*+*gen.* from behind, from beyond; because of, through; жени́ться ~ де́нег, marry for money.

излага́ть, -а́ю *imp.* of изложи́ть. **изла́мывать**, -аю *imp.* of излома́ть.

излече́ние, -я, treatment; recovery cure. **изле́чивать**, -аю *imp.*, **изле́чить**, -чу́, -чишь, cure; ~ся, be cured, make a complete recovery; +от+*gen.* rid oneself of, shake off.

излива́ть, -а́ю *imp.*, **изли́ть**, изолью́ -льёшь; -и́л, -а́, -о *perf.* pour out, give vent to; ~ ду́шу, unbosom oneself; unburden one's heart.

излишек, -шка, surplus; remainder; excess; с изли́шком, enough and to spare. **изли́шество**, -а, excess; over-indulgence. **изли́шний**, -шен, -шня, superfluous; excessive; unnecessary.

излия́ние, -я, outpouring, outflow. effusion, discharge.

изловчи́ться, -чу́сь perf. contrive, manage.

изложе́ние, -я, exposition; account. изложи́ть, -жу́, -жишь perf. (imp. излага́ть) expound, state; set forth; word, draft; ~ на бума́ге. commit to paper.

изло́м, -а, break, fracture; sharp bend; salient point. **изло́манный**, broken, fractured; winding, tortuous; worn out. **изломи́ть**, -а́ю perf. (imp. изла́мывать) break; smash; wear out.

излуча́ть, -а́ю imp. radiate, emit; ~ся, be emitted; be radiated; emanate. **излуче́ние**, -я radiation; emanation.

излучи́на, -ы, bend, curve, meander. **излучи́стый**, winding, meandering.

излю́бленный, favourite.

изма́зать, -а́жу perf., dirty, smear all over; use up; ~ся, get dirty, smear oneself all over.

изма́рать, -а́ю perf., **измельча́ть**, -а́ю perf. **измельчи́ть**, -чу́ perf.

изме́на, -ы, betrayal; treachery, treason; infidelity.

измене́ние, -я, change, alteration; inflexion. **измени́ть¹**, -ню́, -нишь perf. (imp. изменя́ть) change, alter; ~ся, change, alter; vary; ~ся в лице́, change countenance.

измени́ть², -ню́, -нишь perf. (imp. изменя́ть) + dat. betray; be unfaithful to; fail. **изме́нник**, -а, traitor. **изме́ннический**, treacherous, traitorous.

изме́нчивый, changeable; inconstant, fickle. **изменя́емый**, variable. **изменя́ть(ся**, -я́ю(сь imp. of измени́ть(ся.

измере́ние, -я, measurement, measuring; mensuration; sounding, fathoming; metering, gauging; taking; dimension. **измери́мый**, measurable. **измери́тель**, -я m. gauge, meter; index. измери́-

тельный, measuring; standard. из-ме́рить, -рю perf., измеря́ть, -я́ю imp. measure, gauge; sound: survey.

изможде́нный, -ён, -ена́, emaciated; worn out.

и́зморозь, -и, hoar-frost; rime.

изму́чать, -аю perf., **изму́чивать**, -аю imp., **изму́чить**, -чу perf. torment; tire out, exhaust; ~ся, be tired out, be exhausted. **изму́ченный**, worn out, tired out.

измы́слить, -лю perf., **измышля́ть**, -я́ю imp. fabricate, invent; contrive. **измышле́ние**, -я, fabrication, invention.

измя́тый, crumpled, creased; haggard, jaded. из|мя́ть(ся, изомну́(сь, -нёшь(ся perf.

изна́нка, -и, wrong side; under side; reverse; seamy side. **изна́ночн|ый**, -ая петля, purl (stitch).

из|наси́ловать, -лую perf. rape, assault, violate.

изна́шивание, -я, wear (and tear). из-на́шивать(ся, -аю(сь imp. of изно-си́ть(ся.

изне́женный, pampered; delicate; soft, effete; effeminate. **изне́живать**, -аю imp., **изне́жить**, -жу perf. pamper, coddle; make effeminate; ~ся, grow soft, grow effete; become effeminate.

изнемога́ть, -а́ю imp., **изнемо́чь**, -огу́, -о́жешь; -о́г, -ла́ perf. be exhausted, be dead tired. **изнеможе́ние**, -я exhaustion. **изнеможённый**; -ён, -а́, exhausted.

изно́с, -а (-у), wear and tear; deterioration; не знать ~у, wear well, stand hard wear. **износи́ть**, -ошу́, -о́сишь perf. (imp. изна́шивать) wear out; ~ся, wear out; be used up; be played out; age (prematurely). **изно́шенный**, worn out; threadbare; worn; aged.

изно́ю, etc.: see изны́ть.

изнуре́ние, -я, exhaustion; emaciation. **изнурённый**, -ён, -ена́, exhausted, worn out; jaded; ~ го́лодом, faint with hunger. **изнури́тельный**, exhausting. **изнури́ть**, -рю́ perf., **изнуря́ть**, -я́ю imp. exhaust, wear out.

изнутри́ adv. from inside, from within.

изныва́ть, -а́ю *imp.*, **изны́ть**, -но́ю *perf.* languish, be exhausted; ~ от жа́жды, be tormented by thirst; ~ по +*dat.* pine for.

изо: see из. **изо-**[1]: see из-. **изо-**[2], **исо-**.

изоби́лие, -я, abundance, plenty; profusion. **изоби́ловать**, -лует *imp.* + *instr.* abound in. be rich in. **изоби́льный**, abundant; +*instr.* abounding in.

изобличи́ть, -а́ю *imp.*, **изобличи́ть**, -чу́ *perf.* expose; unmask; reveal, show. **изобличе́ние**, -я, exposure; conviction. **изобличи́тельный**; -ые докуме́нты, documentary evidence.

изобрести́, -ету́, -ете́шь; -ёл, -а́ *perf.*, **изобрета́ть**, -а́ю *imp.* invent; devise, contrive. **изобрета́тель**, -я *m.* inventor. **изобрета́тельный**, inventive; resourceful. **изобрете́ние**, -я, invention.

изобража́ть, -а́ю *imp.*, **изобрази́ть**, -ажу́ *perf.* represent, depict, portray (+*instr.* as); imitate. take off; ~ из себя́ +*acc.* make oneself out to be, represent oneself as; ~ся, appear, show itself. **изображе́ние**, -я, image; representation; portrayal; imprint. **изобрази́тельный**, graphic; decorative; ~ые иску́сства, fine arts.

изобью́, etc.: see изби́ть. **изовью́**, etc.: see изви́ть.

изо́гнутый, bent, curved; winding. **изогну́ть(ся**, -ну́(сь, -нёшь(ся *perf.* (*imp.* изгиба́ть(ся) bend, curve.

изо́дранный, tattered. **изодра́ть**, издеру́, -ерёшь; -а́л, -а́, -о *perf.* (*imp.* издира́ть) tear to pieces; scratch all over.

изолга́ться, -лгу́сь, -лжёшься; -а́лся, -а́сь, -ось *perf.* become a hardened liar. **изоли́рованный**, isolated; separate; insulated. **изоли́ровать**, -рую *perf.* and *imp.* isolate; quarantine; insulate. **изоляро́вка**, -и, insulation; insulating tape.

изолью́, etc.: see изли́ть.

изоля́тор, -а insulator; isolation ward; solitary confinement cell. **изоля́ция**, -и, isolation; quarantine; insulation.

изомну́(сь, etc.: see измя́ть.

изо́рванный, tattered, torn. **изорва́ть**, -ву́, -вёшь; -а́л, -а́, -о *perf.* tear, tear to pieces; ~ся, be in tatters.

изотру́, etc.: see истере́ть.

изощрённый; -рён, -а́. refined; keen. **изощри́ть**, -рю́ *perf.*, **изощря́ть**, -я́ю *imp.* sharpen; cultivate, refine, develop; ~ся. acquire refinement; excel.

из-под *prep.* +.*gen.* from under; from near: from; буты́лка ~ молока́, milk-bottle.

изразе́ц, -зца́, tile. **изразцо́вый**, tile, tiled.

из/расхо́довать(ся, -дую(сь *perf.*

и́зредка *adv.* now and then; occasionally; from time to time.

изре́занный, cut up; indented, rugged. **изре́зать**, -е́жу *perf.*, **изре́зывать**, -аю *imp.* cut up; cut to pieces; indent.

изрека́ть, -а́ю *imp.*, **изре́чь**, -еку́ -ечёшь; -ёк, -ла́ *perf.* speak solemnly; utter. **изрече́ние**, -я, apophthegm, dictum, saying.

изро́ю, etc.: see изры́ть.

изруба́ть, -а́ю *imp.*, **изруби́ть**, -блю́, -бишь *perf.* cut (up); chop, chop up, mince; cut down, cut to pieces.

изруга́ть, -а́ю *perf.* abuse, swear at, curse.

изрыва́ть, -а́ю *imp.*, **изры́ть**, -ро́ю *perf.* dig up, tear up, plough up. **изры́тый**, pitted; cratered; torn up.

изря́дно *adv.* fairly, pretty; tolerably. **изря́дный**, fair, handsome; fairly large.

изуве́чивать, -аю *imp.*, **изуве́чить**, -чу *perf* maim, mutilate.

изуми́тельный amazing astounding. **изуми́ть** -млю́ *perf.* **изумля́ть** -я́ю *imp.* amaze astonish; ~ся, be amazed. **изумле́ние**, -я, amazement. **изумлён-ный**; -лён, -а́, amazed, astonished; dumbfounded.

изумру́д, -а, emerald.

изуро́дованный, maimed, mutilated; disfigured. **из/уро́довать**, -дую *perf.*

изуча́ть, -а́ю *imp.*, **изучи́ть**, -чу́, -чишь *perf.* learn, study; master; come to know (very well). **изуче́ние**, -я, study.

изъ-: see из-.

изъе́здить, -зжу *perf.* travel all over; wear out. **изъе́зженный**, much--travelled, well-worn; rutted.

изъяви́тельн|ый; ~ое наклоне́ние, indicative (mood). изъяви́ть, -влю́, -вишь *perf.*, изъявля́ть, -я́ю *imp.* express; ~ согла́сие, give consent. изъявле́ние -я, expression.

изъя́н -а (-у), defect, flaw.

изъя́тие -я withdrawal; removal; exception. изъя́ть, изыму́, -мешь *perf.* изыма́ть, -а́ю *imp.* withdraw; remove; confiscate.

изыска́ние, -я investigation, research; prospecting; survey. изы́сканный, refined; recherché. изыска́тель, -я *m.* project surveyor; prospector. изыска́ть -ыщу́, -ы́щешь *perf.*, изы́скивать, -аю *imp.* search (successfully) for; search out; (try to) find; prospect for.

изю́м, -а (-у). raisins; sultanas. изю́мина, -ы, raisin. изю́минка, -и, zest, go, spirit; sparkle; с изю́минкой, spirited, piquant.

изя́щество, -а, elegance, grace. изя́щный, elegant graceful.

ика́ние, -я, hiccupping. ика́ть, -а́ю *imp.*, икну́ть, -ну́, -нёшь *perf.* hiccup.

ико́на, -ы, icon. иконогра́фия, -и, iconography; portraiture, portraits. иконопи́сец, -сца icon-painter. и́конопись, -и, icon-painting.

ико́та, -ы, hiccup, hiccups.

икра́[1], -ы, (hard) roe; spawn; caviare; pâté, paste.

икра́[2], -ы; *pl* -ы, calf.

икс, -а, (letter) x.

ил, -а, silt, mud, ooze; sludge.

и́ли, иль, *conj.* or; ~ . . ~, either . . or. и́листый, muddy, silty, oozy.

иллюзиони́ст, -а illusionist; conjurer, magician. иллю́зия, -и, illusion. иллюзо́рный, illusory.

иллюмина́тор, -а, porthole.

иллюстри́рованный, illustrated. иллюстри́ровать, -рую *perf.* and *imp.* illustrate.

иль: see и́ли. им: see он, они́, оно́.

им. *abbr.* и́мени, named after.

и́мени, etc.: see и́мя.

име́ние, -я, estate; property, possessions.

имени́ны, -и́н *pl.* name-day (party).

имени́тельный, nominative. и́менно

adv. namely; to wit, viz.; just, exactly, precisely; to be exact; вот ~! exactly! precisely! именно́й, named, nominal; bearing the owner's name; inscribed, autographed; name. именова́ть, -ну́ю *imp.* (*perf.* на~) name; ~ся + *instr.* be called; be termed. имену́емый, called.

име́ть, -е́ю *imp.* have; ~ в виду́, bear in mind, think of, mean; ~ де́ло с + *instr.* have dealings with, have to do with; ~ значе́ние, be of importance, matter; ~ ме́сто, take place; ~ся, be; be present, be available.

ймн: see они́.

импера́тор, -а, emperor. импера́торский, imperial. императри́ца, -ы, empress. импе́рия, -и, empire.

импони́ровать, -рую *imp.* + *dat.* impress.

иму́щественный, property. иму́щество, -а, property, belongings; stock; stores, equipment. иму́щий, propertied; well off, wealthy.

и́мя, и́мени; *pl.* имена́, -ён *n.* name; first name, Christian name; reputation; noun; во ~ + *gen.* in the name of; ~ прилага́тельное, adjective; ~ существи́тельное, substantive, noun; ~ числи́тельное numeral; от и́мени + *gen.* on behalf of; по и́мени, by name; in name, nominally; Теа́тр и́мени Го́рького, the Gorky Theatre.

ин- *abbr.* in *comb.* of иностра́нный, foreign. инвалю́та, -ы, foreign currency. инотде́л, -а, foreign department.

и́на́че *adv.* differently, otherwise; так и́ли ~, in either case, in any event, at all events; *conj.* otherwise, or, or else.

инвали́д, -а, disabled person; invalid. инвали́дность, -и, disablement, disability.

инвента́рн|ый, inventory, stock; ~ая о́пись, inventory. инвента́рь, -я́ *m.* stock; equipment, appliances; inventory.

инде́ец, -е́йца, (American) Indian. инде́йка, -и; *gen. pl.* -е́ек, turkey (-hen). инде́йский, (American) Indian; ~ пету́х, turkey-cock. инди́а́нка, -и, Indian; American Indian. инди́ец, -и́йца, Indian. инди́йский, Indian.

индýс, -а, индýска, -и Hindu. индýс-ский, Hindu.

индю́к, -á, индю́шка -и, turkey.

и́ней, -я, hoar-frost, rime.

инéртность, -и, inertness, inertia; slug-gishness, inaction, passivity. инéрт-ный, inert; passive; sluggish, inactive. инéрция, -и, inertia.

инженéр, -а, engineer; ～-механи́к, mechanical engineer; ～-строи́тель, civil engineer. инженéрн|ый, engineer-ing; ～ые войска́, Engineers; ～ое дéло, engineering.

ин-ква́рто n. indecl. quarto.

инкруста́ция, -и, inlaid work, inlay. инкрусти́ровать, -рую perf. and imp. inlay.

ино- in comb. other, different: hetero-иногоро́дн|ый, of, from, for, another town. ～зéмец, -мца, foreigner. ～зéмный, foreign. ～ро́дец, -дца, non--Russian. ～ро́дный, foreign. ～сказа́-ние, -я, allegory. ～сказа́тельный, allegorical. ～стра́нец, -нца, ～стра́н-ка, -и; gen. pl. -нок, foreigner. ～стра́нный, foreign. ～язы́чный, speaking, belonging to, another lan-guage; non-native, foreign.

иногда́ adv. sometimes.

ино́й, different; other; some; ～ раз, sometimes; ины́ми слова́ми, in other words.

и́нок, -а, monk. и́нокиня, -и, nun.

ин-окта́во n. indecl. octavo.

иноты́дел: see ин-.

и́ноходь, -и, amble.

инспéкция, -и inspection; inspectorate.

институ́т, -а, institution; institute; young ladies' boarding school. инсти-ту́тка -и, boarding-school miss; inno-cent unsophisticated girl.

инструкти́ровать, -рую perf. and imp. (perf. also про～), instruct, give in-structions to; brief. инстру́кция, -и, instructions; directions.

инструмéнт, -а, instrument; tool, imple-ment; tools, implements.

инсцени́ровать, -рую perf. and imp. dramatize, adapt; stage. инсцениро́в-ка, -и, dramatization; adaptation; pretence, act.

интеллигéнт, -а, intellectual, member of

intelligentsia. интеллигéнтный, cul-tured, educated. интеллигéнтский, dilettante. интеллигéнция, -и, intelli-gentsia.

интенда́нт, -а, commissary, quarter-master.

интерéс, -а, interest. интерéсный, interesting; striking, attractive. ин-тересова́ть, -сую imp. interest; ～ся, be interested (+ instr. in).

интерна́т -а, boarding-school.

интри́га -и, intrigue; plot.

инфа́ркт, -а, infarct; coronary (throm-bosis), heart attack.

инфля́ция, -и, inflation.

ин-фо́лио n. indecl. folio.

и.о. abbr. исполня́ющий обя́занности, acting.

йод, etc.: see йод.

и пр. abbr. и про́чее, etc. etcetera; and so on; и про́чие, et al., and Co.

ирла́ндец, -дца, Irishman. ирла́ндка, -и, Irishwoman. ирла́ндский, Irish.

ис-: see из-.

ИСЗ (иеэзé) abbr. иску́сственный спу́тник Земли́, artificial Earth satel-lite, sputnik.

иск. -а, suit action.

искажа́ть -а́ю imp. исказить, -ажу́ perf. distort, pervert, twist; misrepre-sent. искажéние, -я distortion, per-version. искажённый, -ён, -ена́, distorted, perverted.

искалéченный, crippled, maimed. ис-калéчивать, -аю imp. ис|калéчить, -чу perf. cripple, maim; break, damage; ～ся, become a cripple; be crippled.

иска́ние, -я, search, quest; pl. strivings. иска́тель, -я m. seeker; searcher; view--finder; selector; scanner. иска́ть, ищу́, и́щешь imp. (+acc. or gen.) seek, look for, search for.

исключа́ть -а́ю imp. исключи́ть, -чу́ perf. exclude; eliminate; expel; dis-miss; rule out. исключа́я, prep. + gen. except, excepting, with the exception of; ～ прису́тствующих, present company excepted. исключéние, -я, exception; exclusion; expulsion; elimi-nation; за исключéнием + gen. with the exception of. исключи́тельно adv.

exceptionally; exclusively, solely; exclusive. исключи́тельный, exceptional; exclusive, sole; excellent.

исковерканный, corrupt, corrupted; broken; spoilt. ис|коверкать, -аю perf.

исколеси́ть, -ешу́ perf. travel all over.

ис|ко́мкать, -аю perf.

ископа́емое sb. mineral; fossil. ископа́емый, fossilized fossil.

искорене́ние, -я, eradication. искорени́ть, -ню́ perf., искореня́ть -яю imp. eradicate.

и́скоса adv. sideways sidelong; askance.

и́скра -ы spark; flash glimmer.

и́скренний, sincere candid. и́скренно adv. sincerely; candidly. и́скренность, -и, sincerity; candour.

искриви́ть, -влю́ perf., искривля́ть, -яю imp. bend; curve; distort, twist, warp. искривле́ние, -я, bend; distortion, warping.

искри́стый, sparkling. искри́ть, -и́т imp. spark; ~ся sparkle; scintillate. искрово́й spark.

ис|кромса́ть, -а́ю perf. ис|кроши́ть(ся, -шу́(сь, -ши́шь(ся perf.

ис|купа́ть¹(ся, -а́ю(сь perf.

искупа́ть², -а́ю imp., искупи́ть, -плю́ -пишь perf. expiate, atone for; make up for, compensate for. искупи́тель, -я m. redeemer. искупле́ние, -я, redemption, expiation, atonement.

искуси́ть, -ушу́ perf. of искуша́ть.

иску́сный, skilful; expert. иску́сственный, artificial; synthetic; feigned, pretended. иску́сство, -а, art; craftsmanship, skill.

искуша́ть, -а́ю imp. искуси́ть(ся), tempt; seduce. искуше́ние, -я, temptation, seduction. искушённый; -ён, -ена́, experienced; tested.

ИСЛ (iésel) abbr. иску́сственный спу́тник Луны́, artificial Moon satellite, sputnik.

ис|па́костить, -ощу perf.

испа́нец, -нца, испа́нка, -и, Spaniard. испа́нский, Spanish.

испаре́ние, -я, evaporation; pl. fumes. испа́рина, -ы, perspiration. испари́тель, -я m. evaporator; vaporizer. ис|пари́ть, -рю́ perf., испаря́ть, -я́ю imp.

evaporate, volatilize; exhale; ~ся, evaporate, vaporize; be evaporated.

ис|па́чкать, -аю perf. ис|пе́чь, -еку́ -ечёшь perf.

испещрённый; -рён, -рена́, speckled. испещри́ть, -рю́ perf., испещря́ть, -я́ю imp. speckle, spot; mark all over, cover.

исписа́ть, -ишу́, -и́шешь perf., испи́сывать, -аю imp. cover, fill, with writing; use up.

испито́й, haggard, gaunt; hollow-cheeked.

испове́довать, -дую perf. and imp. confess; profess; ~ся, confess; make one's confession; +в+prep. unburden oneself of, acknowledge. и́споведь, -и, confession.

исподло́бья adv. sullenly, distrustfully.

исподтишка́ adv. in an underhand way; on the quiet, on the sly; смея́ться ~, laugh in one's sleeve.

испоко́н веко́в, ве́ку: see век.

исполи́н, -а, giant. исполи́нский, gigantic.

исполко́м, -а abbr. исполни́тельный комите́т, executive committee. исполне́ние, -я, fulfilment, execution, discharge; performance; привести́ в ~, carry out, execute. исполни́мый, feasible, practicable. исполни́тель, -я m., -тельница, -ы, executor; performer. исполни́тельный, executive; assiduous, careful, attentive; ~ лист, writ, court order. испо́лнить, -ню perf., исполня́ть, -я́ю imp. carry out, execute; fulfil; perform; ~ обеща́ние, keep a promise; ~ про́сьбу, grant a request; быть fulfilled; impers. (+dat.); ему́ испо́лнилось семь лет, he is seven years old; исполни́лось пять лет с тех пор, как, it is five years since, five years have passed since. исполня́ющий; ~ обя́занности+gen. acting.

испо́льзование, -я, utilization. испо́льзовать, -зую perf. and imp. make (good) use of, utilize; turn to account.

ис|по́ртить(ся, -рчу(сь perf. испо́рченность, -и, depravity. испо́рченный, depraved; corrupted; spoiled; bad, rotten.

исправи́тельный, correctional; corrective; ~ дом, reformatory. испра́вить, -влю perf. исправля́ть, -я́ю imp. rectify, correct, emendate; repair, mend; reform, improve, amend; ~ся, improve, reform. исправле́ние, -я, correcting; repairing; improvement; correction; emendation. испра́вленный, improved, corrected; revised; reformed. испра́вник, -а, district police superintendent. испра́вность, -и, good repair, good condition; punctuality; preciseness; meticulousness. испра́вный, in good order; punctual; precise; meticulous.

ис|про́бовать, -бую perf.

испу́г, -а (-у), fright; alarm. испу́ганный, frightened, scared, startled. ис|пуга́ть(ся, -а́ю(сь perf.

спуска́ть, -а́ю imp., испусти́ть, -ущу́, -у́стишь perf. emit, let out; utter; ~ вздох, heave a sigh; ~ дух, breathe one's last.

испыта́ние, -я, test, trial; ordeal; examination. испы́танный, tried, well-tried tested. испыта́тельный, test, trial; examining; experimental; probationary. испыта́ть, -а́ю perf., испы́тывать, -аю imp. test; try; feel, experience.

иссера- in comb. grey-, greyish.

иссиня- in comb. blue-, bluish.

сследование, -я, investigation; research; analysis; exploration; paper; study. иссле́дователь, -я m. researcher; investigator; explorer. иссле́довательский, research. иссле́довать, -дую perf. and imp. investigate, examine; research into; explore, analyse.

сстари adv. from of old; так ~ веде́тся, it is an old custom.

сступле́ние, -я, frenzy, transport. исступлённый, frenzied; ecstatic.

ссуша́ть, -а́ю imp., иссуши́ть, -шу́, -шишь perf. dry up; consume, waste.

ссяка́ть, -а́ет imp., исся́кнуть, -нет; -я́к perf. run dry, dry up; run low fail. ста́сканный, worn out; threadbare; worn; haggard. истаска́ть, -а́ю perf., иста́скивать, -аю imp. wear out; ~ся, wear out; be worn out.

стека́ть, -а́ет imp. of исте́чь. исте́кший, past, last; preceding, previous.

истере́ть, изотру́, -трёшь; истёр perf. (imp. истира́ть) grate; wear away, wear down; ~ся, wear out; wear away, be worn away.

исте́рзанный, tattered, lacerated; tormented.

исте́рик, -а, истери́чка, -и, hysterical subject. исте́рика, -и, hysterics. истери́чный, hysterical. исте́ри́я, -и, hysteria.

исте́ц, -тца́, исти́ца, -ы, plaintiff; petitioner.

истече́ние, -я, outflow; expiry, expiration; ~ кро́ви, haemorrhage. исте́чь, -ечёт; -тёк; -ла́ perf. (imp. истека́ть) flow out; elapse; expire.

и́стина, -ы, truth. и́стинный, true.

истира́ние, -я, abrasion. истира́ть(ся, -а́юсь imp. of истере́ть(ся.

исти́ца: see исте́ц.

истлева́ть. -а́ю imp., истле́ть, -е́ю perf. rot, decay; be reduced to ashes, smoulder away.

исто́к, -а, source.

истолкова́ть, -ку́ю perf., истолко́вывать, -аю imp. interpret expound; comment on.

ис|толо́чь, -лку́ -лчёшь; -ло́к, -лкла́ perf.

исто́ма, -ы, lassitude; languor. ис|томи́ть, -млю́ perf., истомля́ть, -я́ю imp. exhaust, weary; ~ся, be exhausted, be worn out; be weary. истомлённый, -ён, -ена́, exhausted, tired out, worn out.

исто́пник, -а́ stoker, boilerman.

исторга́ть, -а́ю imp., исто́ргнуть, -ну; -о́рг perf. throw out, expel; wrest; wrench; force, extort.

исто́рик, -а, historian. истори́ческий, historical; historic. истори́чный, historical. исто́рия, -и, history; story; incident, event; забавная ~, a funny thing.

исто́чник, -а, spring; source.

истоща́ть, -а́ю imp., истощи́ть, -щу́ perf. exhaust; drain, sap; deplete; emaciate. истоще́ние, -я, emaciation; exhaustion; depletion. истощённый, -ён, -ена́, emaciated; exhausted.

ис|тра́тить, -а́чу perf.

истреби́тель, -я m. destroyer; fighter.

истреби́тельный, destructive; fighter.
истреби́ть, -блю́ *perf.,* **истребля́ть,** -я́ю *imp.* destroy; exterminate, extirpate.

истрёпанный, torn, frayed; worn. **ис|трепа́ть,** -плю́, -плешь *perf.*

истука́н, -а, idol, image.

ис|тупи́ть, -плю́, -пишь *perf.*

и́стый, true genuine.

истяза́ние, -я, torture. **истяза́ть,** -а́ю *imp.* torture.

исхо́д, -а, outcome, issue; end; Exodus; на ~е, nearing the end, coming to an end; на ~е дня, towards evening. **исходи́ть,** -ожу́, -о́дишь *imp.* (+из or от +gen.) issue (from); come (from); emanate (from); proceed (from), base oneself (on). **исхо́дный,** initial, original, starting; departure, of departure.

исхуда́лый, emaciated, wasted. **исхуда́ть,** -а́ю *perf.* grow thin, become wasted.

исцеле́ние, -я, healing, cure; recovery. **исцели́мый,** curable. **исцели́ть,** -лю́ *perf.,* **исцеля́ть,** -я́ю *imp.* heal, cure.

исчеза́ть, -а́ю *imp.,* **исче́знуть,** -ну; -ёз *perf.* disappear, vanish. **исчезнове́ние,** -я, disappearance.

и́счерна- in *comb.* blackish, very dark.

исче́рпать, -аю *perf.,* **исче́рпывать,** -аю *imp.* exhaust, drain; settle, conclude. **исче́рпывающий,** exhaustive.

исчисле́ние, -я, calculation; calculus. **исчи́слить,** -лю *perf.,* **исчисля́ть,** -я́ю *imp.* calculate, compute; estimate. **исчи́сляться,** -я́ется *imp.* + *instr.* or в + *acc.* amount to, come to; be calculated at.

ита́к *conj.* thus; so then; and so.

италья́нец, -нца, **италья́нка,** -и, Italian. **италья́нск|ий,** Italian; ~ая забасто́вка, sit-down strike, working to rule go-slow.

и т.д. *abbr.* и так да́лее, etc., and so on.

ито́г, -а, sum; total; result, upshot. **итого́** (-vо) *adv.* in all, altogether. **ито́говый,** total, final.

и т.п. *abbr.* и тому́ подо́бное, etc., and so on.

ИТР (*itee´r*) *abbr.* инжене́рно-техни́ческие рабо́тники, engineering and technical staff.

итти́: see идти́.

иуде́й, -я, **иуде́йка,** -и, Jew. **иуде́йский,** Judaic.

их: see они́. **их, и́хний,** their, theirs.

ихтиоза́вр, -а, ichthyosaurus. **ихтиоло́гия,** -и, ichthyology.

иша́к, -а́, donkey, ass; hinny.

ище́йка, -и, bloodhound; police dog sleuth.

ищу́, etc.: see иска́ть.

ию́ль, -я *m.* July. **ию́льский,** July.

ию́нь, -я *m.* June. **ию́ньский,** June.

й *letter:* see и.

йог (*yo-*), -а, Yogi.

йод (*yo-*), -а, iodine.

йо́та (*yo-*), -ы, iota.

К

к *letter:* see ка.

к, ко *prep.* + *dat.* to, towards; by; for; on; on the occasion of; к лу́чшему, for the better; к (не)сча́стью, (un)fortunately, (un)luckily; к пе́рвому января́, by the first of January; к сро́ку, on time; к тому́ вре́мени, by then, by that time; к тому́ же, besides, moreover; к чему́? what for? лицо́м к лицу́, face to face; ни к чему́, no good, no use.

к. *abbr.* ко́мната, room; копе́йка, copeck.

ка *n. indecl.* the letter к.

-ка *part.* modifying force of imper. or expressing decision or intention да́йте-ка пройти́, let me pass, please скажи́-ка мне, do tell me.

каба́к, -а́, tavern, drinking-shop; pub.

кабала́, -ы́, servitude, bondage. **кабали́ть,** -лю́ *imp.* enslave.

кабан, -á wild boar.

кабачок[1], -чкá *dim.* of кабáк.

кабачок[2], -чкá, vegetable marrow.

кабель, -я *m.* cable. **кабельный** *adj.* **кабельтов**, -а, cable, hawser; cable's length.

кабина, -ы, cabin; booth; cockpit; tip. **кабинет**, -а, a study; consulting-room, surgery; room, classroom, laboratory, office; cabinet. **кабинетский** cabinet.

каблук, -á, heel. **каблучок**, -чкá heel ogee; ~-шпилька stiletto heel.

каботаж, -а, cabotage; coastal shipping. **каботажник**, -а, coaster. **каботажный**, cabotage; coastal, coasting, coastwise.

кавалер, -а, knight; partner, gentleman. **кавалергард**, -а, horse-guardsman. **кавалерийский**, cavalry. **кавалерист**, -а, cavalryman. **кавалерия**, -и, cavalry.

каверза, -ы, chicanery; mean trick, dirty trick. **каверзный**, tricky, ticklish.

кавказец, -зца, **кавказка**, -и, Caucasian. **кавказский**, Caucasian.

кавычки, -чек *pl.* inverted commas, quotation marks; открыть ~, quote; закрыть ~, unquote.

кадет[1], -а, cadet. **кадетский**, cadet; ~ корпус, military school.

кадет[2], -а, *abbr.* конституционный демократ, Cadet, Kadet.

кадка, -и, tub, vat.

кадр, -а, a frame, still; close-up; cadre; *pl.* establishment; staff; personnel; specialists, skilled workers. **кадровик**, -а, member of permanent establishment, professional body, etc. **кадровый**, regular; experienced; skilled; trained.

кадык, -á, Adam's apple.

каёмка, -и, (narrow) border, (narrow) edging. **каёмчатый** with a border.

каждодневный, daily, everyday. **каждый**, each, every; *sb.* everybody, everyone.

кажется, etc.: see казаться.

казак, -á; *pl.* -áки, -áков, казачка, -и, Cossack.

казарма, -ы, barracks; barrack.

казаться, кажусь, кáжешься *imp.* (*perf.* по~), seem, appear; *impers.* кáжется,

казáлось, apparently; казáлось бы, it would seem, one would think; +*dat.* мне кáжется, it seems to me; I think.

казацкий, казáчий, Cossack. **казáчка**: see казак. **казачок**, -чкá, page, boy.

казённый, State; government; fiscal; public; bureaucratic, formal; banal, undistinguished, conventional; ~ язык official jargon; на ~ счёт, at the public expense. **казна**, -ы́, Exchequer, Treasury; public purse; the State; money, property. **казначей**, -я, treasurer, bursar; paymaster; purser.

казнить, -ню *perf.* and *imp.* execute, put to death; punish, chastise; castigate. **казнь**, -и, execution.

кайма, -ы́; *gen. pl.* каём, border, edging; hem, selvage.

как *adv.* how; what; all of a sudden, all at once; вот ~! not really! you don't say!; ~ вы думаете? what do you think?; ~ вы поживаете? how are you?; ~ дела? how are you getting on?; ~ его зовут? what is his name? what is he called?; ~ есть, complete(ly), utter(ly); ~ же, naturally, of course; ~ же так? how is that?; ~ ни, however; ~-никак, nevertheless, for all that; он ~ есть дурáк, he's a complete fool. **как** *conj.* as; like; when; since; + *neg.* but, except, than; будьте ~ дóма, make yourself at home; в то врéмя ~, while, whereas; ~ вдруг, when suddenly; ~ мóжно, нельзя, + *comp.* as . . as possible; ~ мóжно скорéе, as soon as possible; ~ нельзя лучше, as well as possible; ~ нарóчно, as luck would have it; ~ .., так и, both . . and; ~ тóлько, as soon as, when; мéжду тем ~, while, whereas; я видел, ~ онá ушлá, I saw her go. **как будто** *conj.* as if, as though; *part.* apparently, it would seem. **как бы**, how; as if, as though; **как бы . . не**, what if, supposing; боюсь, как бы он не был в дурном настроéнии, I am afraid he may be in a bad temper; как бы не так! not likely, certainly not; как бы . . ни, however. **кáк-либо** *adv.* somehow. **кáк-нибудь** *adv.* somehow; in some way or other; anyhow; some time.

как раз *adv.* just, exactly. **как-то** *adv.* somehow; once, one day.

каков *m.*, **какова** *f.*, **каково** *n.*, **каковы** *pl. pron.* what, what sort (of); ~ он? what is he like? ~ он собой? what does he look like?; погода-то какова! what weather! **каково** *adv.* how. **какой** *pron.* what; (such) as; which; ~ .. ни, whatever, whichever; каким образом? how?; ~ такой? which (exactly)?; какое там, nothing of the kind, quite the contrary. **какой-либо**, **какой-нибудь** *pron.* some; any; only. **какой-то** *pron.* some; a; a kind of; something like.

как раз, **как-то**: see как.

каланча, -й, watch-tower.

калека, -и *m.* and *f.* cripple.

каление, -я, incandescence.

калечить, -чу *imp.* (*perf.* ис~, по~) cripple, maim, mutilate; twist, pervert; ~ся, become a cripple, be crippled.

калибр, -а, calibre; bore; gauge.

калий, -я, potassium.

калитка, -и, wicket, (wicket-)gate.

калоша, -и, galosh.

калька, -и, tracing-paper; tracing; calque.

кальций, -я, calcium.

камбала, -ы, flat-fish; plaice; flounder.

каменистый, stony, rocky. **каменно-угольный**, coal; ~ бассейн, coal-field. **каменный**, stone; rock; stony; hard, immovable; ~ый век, Stone Age; ~ая соль, rock-salt; ~ уголь, coal. **каменоломня**, -и; *gen. pl.* -мен, quarry. **каменщик**, -а, (stone)mason; brick-layer. **камень**, -мня; *pl.* -мни, -мней *m.* stone.

камера, -ы, chamber; compartment; cell, ward; camera; inner tube, (football) bladder; ~ хранения (багажа), cloak-room, left-luggage office. **камерный**, chamber. **камертон**, -а, tuning-fork.

камин, -а, fireplace; fire.

каморка, -и, closet, cell, very small room.

кампания, -и campaign; cruise.

камфара, -ы, camphor.

камыш, -á, reed, rush; cane.

канава, -ы, ditch; gutter; drain; trench; inspection pit.

канадец, -дца, **канадка**, -и, Canadian. **канадский**, Canadian.

канал, -а, canal; channel; duct; bore. **канализация**, -и, sewerage sewerage system; drainage; underground cable system.

канареечный, canary; canary-coloured. **канарейка**, -и, canary.

канат, -а, rope; cable, hawser. **канато-ходец**, -дца, rope-walker.

канва, -ы, canvas; groundwork; outline, design. **канвовый**, canvas.

кандалы, -óв *pl.* shackles, fetters, irons.

каникулы, -ул *pl.* vacation; holidays. **каникулярный**, holiday.

канистра, -ы, can, canister.

канифоль, -и, rosin.

канонерка, -и, gunboat. **канонир**, -а, gunner.

кант, -а, edging, piping; welt; mount. **кантовать**, -тую *imp.* (*perf.* о~) border, pipe; mount.

канун, -а, eve; vigil, watch-night.

кануть, -ну *perf.* drop, sink; ~ в вечность, sink into oblivion; как в воду ~, vanish into thin air, disappear without trace.

канцелярия, -и, office. **канцелярский**, office; clerical; ~ие принадлежности, stationery. **канцелярщина**, office-work; red tape.

канцлер, -а, chancellor.

капать, -аю or -плю *imp.* (*perf.* капнуть на~) drip, drop; trickle, dribble; fall in drops; pour out in drops; +*instr.* spill. **капелька**, -и, small drop, droplet; a little; a bit, a grain, a whit; ~ росы, dew-drop.

капельмейстер, -а, conductor; band-master.

капельный, drip, drop, drip-feed, trickle; tiny.

капитал, -а, capital. **капиталисти-ческий**, capitalist, capitalistic. **капи-тальный**, capital; main, fundamental; most important; ~ ремонт, capital repairs, major overhaul.

капитан, -а, captain; master, skipper.

капитель, -и, capital; small caps.

капка́н, -а, trap. капка́нный, trap; trapping.

ка́пля, -и; *gen. pl.* -пель, drop; bit, scrap; ни ка́пли, not a bit, not a scrap, not a whit; по ка́пле drop by drop. ка́пнуть, -ну *perf.* of ка́пать.

ка́пор, -а, hood, bonnet.

капо́т, -а, hood cowl, cowling; bonnet; (loose) dressing-gown, house-coat.

капу́ста, -ы, cabbage.

капюшо́н, а, hood.

ка́ра, -ы, punishment, retribution.

кара́бкаться, -аюсь *imp.* (*perf.* вс~) clamber, scramble up.

карава́й, -я, round loaf, cob; pudding.

карава́н, -а, caravan; convoy.

кара́куль, -я *m.* karakul, Persian lamb.

кара́куля, -и, scrawl, scribble.

карамбо́ль, -я *m.* cannon.

караме́ль, -и, caramel; caramels. караме́лька, -и, caramel.

каранда́ш, -а́, pencil.

карапу́з, -а, chubby little fellow.

кара́сь, -я́ *m.* crucian carp.

кара́тельный, punitive. кара́ть, -а́ю *imp.* (*perf.* по~) punish, chastise.

карау́л, -а, guard; watch; ~! help!; нести́ ~, be on guard. карау́лить, -лю *imp.* guard; watch for, lie in wait for. карау́льный, guard; *sb.* sentry, sentinel, guard.

карбюра́тор, -а, carburettor.

каре́л, -а, каре́лка, -и, Karelian. каре́льск|ий, Karelian; ~ая берёза, Karelian birch.

каре́та, -ы, carriage, coach; ~ ско́рой по́мощи, ambulance.

ка́рий, brown; hazel.

карикату́ра, -ы, caricature; cartoon.

карка́с, -а, frame; framework.

ка́ркать, -аю *imp.*, ка́ркнуть, -ну *perf.* (*perf.* also на~) caw, croak.

ка́рлик, -а, ка́рлица, -ы, dwarf; pygmy. ка́рликовый, dwarf, dwarfish; pygmy.

карма́н, -а, pocket. карма́нный *adj.* pocket; ~ вор, pickpocket.

карни́з, -а, cornice; ledge.

ка́рта, -ы, map; chart; (playing-)card.

карта́вить, -влю *imp.* burr. карта́вость, -и, burr. карта́вый, burring.

ка́ртер, -а, gear casing, crank-case.

карте́чь, -и, case-shot, grape-shot; buckshot.

карти́на, -ы, picture; scene. карти́нка, -и, picture; illustration. карти́нный, picturesque; picture.

карто́н, -а, cardboard, pasteboard; cartoon. карто́нка, -и, cardboard box; hat-box, bandbox.

картоте́ка, -и, card-index.

карто́фелина, -ы, potato. карто́фель, -я (-ю) *m.* potatoes; potato (-plant). карто́фельн|ый, potato; ~ая запека́нка, shepherd's pie; ~ый крахма́л, potato flour; ~ое пюре́, mashed potatoes.

ка́рточка, -и, card; season ticket; photograph; ~ вин, wine-list; ~ ку́шаний, menu, bill of fare. ка́рточный, card; ~ до́мик, house of cards.

карто́шка, -и, potatoes; potato.

карту́з, -а́, (peaked) cap.

карусе́ль, -и, roundabout, merry-go-round.

каса́ние, -я, contact. каса́тельная *sb.* tangent. каса́ться, -а́юсь *imp.* (*perf.* косну́ться) + *gen.* or до + *gen.* touch; touch on; concern, relate to; что каса́ется, as to, as regards, with regard to.

ка́ска, -и, helmet.

каспи́йский, Caspian.

ка́сса, -ы, till; cash-box; booking-office; box-office; cash-desk; cash; case; ~-автома́т, slot-machine, ticket-machine; ~ взаимопо́мощи, benefit fund, mutual aid fund, friendly society.

кассе́та, -ы, cassette; plate-holder.

касси́р, -а, касси́рша, -и, cashier. ка́ссовый, cash; box-office; ~ аппара́т, cash register; ~ счёт, cash-account; ~ успе́х, box-office success.

кастра́т, -а, eunuch. кастра́ция, -и, castration. кастри́ровать, -рую *perf.* and *imp.* castrate, geld.

кастрю́ля, -и, saucepan.

ката́ние, -я, rolling; driving; ~ верхо́м, riding; ~ на конька́х, skating; ~ с rop, tobogganing.

ката́ть, -а́ю *imp.* (*perf.* вы́~, с~) roll; wheel, trundle; drive, take for a drive, take out; roll out; mangle; ~ся roll, roll about; go for a drive; ~ся вер-хо́м ride, go riding; ~ся на конька́х, skate. go skating; ~ся со́ смеху, split one's sides.

катастро́фа, -ы, catastrophe, disaster; accident, crash.

катафа́лк, -а, catafalque; hearse.

ка́тер, -а; *pl.* -а́, cutter; boat, motor-boat, launch.

кати́ть, -ачу́ -а́тишь *imp.* bowl along, rip, tear; ~ся rush, tear; flow, stream, roll; ~ся под гору, go downhill; ~ся с горы, slide downhill; кати́сь, кати́-тесь, get out! clear off! като́к, -тка́, skating-rink; roller; mangle.

ка́торга, -и, penal servitude, hard labour. **каторжа́нин**, -а, convict, ex-convict. **ка́торжник**, -а, convict. **ка́торжн|ый**, penal, convict; ~ые рабо́ты, hard labour; drudgery.

кату́шка, -и, reel, bobbin; spool; coil.

каучу́к, -а, rubber.

кафе́ *n. indecl.* café.

ка́федра, -ы, pulpit; rostrum, platform; chair; department.

кача́лка, -и, rocking-chair; конь-~, rocking-horse. **кача́ние**, -я, rocking, swinging, swing; pumping. **кача́ть**, -а́ю *imp.* (*perf.* качну́ть) + *acc.* or *instr.* rock, swing; shake; lift up, chair; pump; ~ся rock, swing; roll, pitch; reel, stagger. **каче́ли**, -ей *pl.* swing.

ка́чественный, qualitative; high-quality. **ка́чество**, -а, quality; в ка́честве + *gen.* as, in the capacity or character of; вы́играть ~, потеря́ть ~, gain, lose, by an exchange.

ка́чка, -и, rocking; tossing.

качну́ть(ся, -ну́(сь, -нёшь(ся *perf.* of кача́ть(ся. качу́, etc.: see кати́ть.

ка́ша, -и, kasha; gruel, porridge; зава́рить ка́шу, start something, stir up trouble. **кашева́р**, -а, cook.

ка́шель, -шля *m.* cough. **ка́шлянуть**, -ну *perf.*, **ка́шлять**, -яю *imp.* cough; have a cough.

кашне́ *n. indecl.* scarf, muffler.

кашта́н, -а, chestnut. **кашта́новый**, chestnut.

каю́та, -ы, cabin, stateroom. **каю́т-компа́ния**, -и, wardroom; passengers' lounge.

ка́ющийся, repentant, contrite, penitent. **ка́яться**, ка́юсь *imp.* (*perf.* по~, рас~) repent; confess; ка́юсь, I am sorry to say, I (must) confess.

кв. *abbr.* квадра́тный, square; кварти́ра, flat, apartment.

КВ (*кавэ́*) *abbr.* коро́ткие во́лны, short waves, коротковолно́вый, short-wave.

квадра́т, -а, square; quad; в квадра́те, squared; возвести́ в ~, square. **квадра́тный**, square; quadratic. **квадрату́ра**, -ы, squaring; quadrature.

ква́канье, -я, croaking. **ква́кать**, -аю *imp.*, **ква́кнуть**, -ну *perf.* croak.

квалифици́рованный, qualified; skilled, trained, specialized. **квалифици́ро-вать**, -рую *perf.* and *imp.* qualify; check, test.

квант, -а. **ква́нта**, -ы, quantum.

кварта́л, -а, block; quarter. **кварта́ль-ный**, quarterly; *sb.* police officer.

кварти́ра, -ы. flat; lodging(s); apart-ment(s); quarters; billets. **квартира́нт**, -а, -ра́нтка, -и, lodger; tenant. **квартирн|ый**; ~ая пла́та, **квартирпла́-та**, -ы, rent.

кварц, -а, quartz.

квас, -а (-у); *pl.* ~ы́, kvass. **ква́сить**, -а́шу *imp.* sour; ferment; pickle; leaven. **квасцо́вый**, alum. **квасцы́**, -о́в *pl.* alum. **ква́шен|ый**, sour, fer-mented; ~ая капу́ста, sauerkraut.

кве́рху *adv.* up, upwards.

квит, кви́ты, quits.

квита́нция, -и, receipt. **квито́к**, -тка́, ticket, check.

квт *abbr.* килова́тт, kilowatt; **квт-ч**, kilowatt-hour.

кг *abbr.* килогра́мм, kilogram.

КГБ (*кагебэ́*) *abbr.* Комите́т госуда́р-ственной безопа́сности, State Secur-ity Committee.

КДП (*кадепэ́*) *abbr.* команди́о-дис-пе́тчерский пункт, control tower.

кегль, -я *m.* point size, body size.

ке́гля, -и, skittle.

кедр, -а, cedar. **ке́дровый**, cedar.

ке́ды, -ов *pl.* sports boots, sneakers.

кекс, -а, cake; fruit-cake.

ке́лья, -и; *gen. pl.* -лий, cell.

кем: see **кто**.

ке́мпинг, **кэ́мпинг**, -а, camping site, tourist camp.

кенгуру́ *n. indecl.* kangaroo.

ке́пка, -и, cap, cloth cap.

керога́з, -а, oil pressure stove. **кероси́н**, -а, paraffin, kerosene. **кероси́нка**, -и, oil-stove.

ке́та, -ы, Siberian salmon. **ке́то́вый**; ~ая икра́, red caviare.

киберне́тика, -и, cybernetics. **кибернети́ческий**, cybernetic.

киби́тка, -и, kibitka, covered wagon; nomad tent.

кива́ть, -а́ю *imp.* (*perf.* **ки́внуть**) throw, fling; ~ся, throw oneself, fling oneself; rush; + *instr.* throw, fling, shy. **кив** *imp.* кивну́ть, -ну́, -нёшь *perf.* (голово́й) nod, nod one's head; (+ на + *acc.*) motion (to). **кивок**, -вка́, nod.

кида́ть, -а́ю *imp.* (*perf.* **ки́нуть**) throw, fling, cast; ~ся, throw oneself, fling oneself; rush; + *instr.* throw, fling, shy.

кий, -я́; *pl.* -и́, -ёв, (billiard) cue.

килева́й, keel; ~а́я ка́чка, pitching. **киль**, -я *m.* keel; fin. **кильва́тер**, -а, wake.

ки́лька, -и, sprat.

кинжа́л, -а, dagger.

кино́ *n. indecl.* cinema.

кино- in *comb.* film-, cine-. **киноаппара́т**, -а, cinecamera. ~**арти́ст**, -а, ~**арти́стка**, -и, film actor, actress. ~**ателье́** *n. indecl.* film studio. ~**журна́л**, -а, news-reel. ~**звезда́**, -ы́, film-star. ~**зри́тель**, -я *m.* film-goer. ~**карти́на**, -ы, film, picture. ~**опера́тор**, -а, camera-man. ~**плёнка**, -и, film. ~**режиссёр**, -а, a film director. ~**хро́ника**, -и, news-reel.

ки́нуть(ся, -ну(сь *perf.* of кида́ть(ся.

кио́ск, -а, kiosk, stall, stand.

ки́па, -ы, pile stack; pack, bale.

кипари́с, -а, cypress.

кипе́ние, -я, boiling. **кипе́ть**, -плю́ *imp.* (*perf.* вс~) boil, seethe; рабо́та кипе́ла, work was in full swing. **кипу́чий**, boiling, seething; ebullient, turbulent. **кипяти́льник**, -а, kettle, boiler. **кипяти́льный**, boiling, boiler. **кипяти́ть**, -ячу́ *imp.* (*perf.* вс~) boil; ~ся, boil; get excited, be enraged, be in a

rage. **кипято́к**, -тка́, boiling water. **кипячёный**, boiled.

кирка́, -и́, pickaxe pick.

кирпи́ч, -а́ brick; bricks; 'no-entry' sign. **кирпи́чный**, brick; brick-red; ~ заво́д, brickworks; brick-field brick-yard.

кисе́йный, muslin.

кисе́т, -а tobacco-pouch.

кисея́, -и́, muslin.

ки́ска, -и, pussy.

кислоро́д, -а, oxygen. **кислота́**, -ы́; *pl.* -ы, acid; sourness, acidity. **кисло́тный**, acid. **ки́слый** sour; ~ая капу́ста, sauerkraut. **ки́снуть**, -ну; кис *imp.* (*perf.* про~) turn sour, go sour; mope.

ки́сточка, -и, brush; tassel. **кисть**, -и; *gen. pl.* -е́й, cluster, bunch; brush; tassel; hand.

кит, -а́, whale.

кита́ец -а́йца; *pl.* -ы, -цев, **китая́нка**, -и, Chinese. **кита́йка**, -и, nankeen. **кита́йск**|ий Chinese; ~ая тушь, Indian ink.

китобо́й, -я, whaler, whaling ship. **кито́вый**; whale; ~ ус, whalebone. **китобо́йный**, whaling. **китообра́зный**, cetacean.

кише́ть, -ши́т *imp.* swarm, teem.

кише́чник, -а, bowels, intestines. **кише́чный**, intestinal. **кишка́**, -и́, gut, intestine; hose.

кишми́ *adv.*; ~ кише́ть, swarm.

кл. *abbr.* класс, class form.

к.-л. *abbr.* како́й-либо, some.

клавеси́н, -а harpsichord. **клавиату́ра**, -ы, keyboard. **кла́виш**, -а, **кла́виша**, -ы, key. **кла́вишн**|ый; ~ые инструме́нты keyboard instruments.

клад, -а, treasure.

кла́дбище, -а, cemetery, graveyard, churchyard.

кла́дка, -и, laying; masonry, walling. **кладова́я** *sb.* pantry, larder; store-room. **кладовщи́к**, -а́, storeman; shopman. **кладу́**, etc.: see **класть**.

кла́дчик, -а, bricklayer.

кла́няться, -я́юсь *imp.* (*perf.* поклони́ться)+*dat.* bow to; greet; send, convey greetings; humble oneself; go cap in hand to.

кла́пан, -а, valve; vent; flap.

кларне́т, -а clarinet.

класс, -а, class; form; class-room; *pl.* hopscotch. кла́сс|ый class; class-room; high-class; first-class; ~ый ваго́н, passenger coach; ~ая доска́, blackboard; ~ая каю́та, private cabin. кла́ссовый, class.

класть, -аду́, -адёшь; -ал *imp.* (*perf.* положи́ть, сложи́ть) lay; put; place; construct, build.

клева́ть, клюю́, клюёшь *imp.* (*perf.* клю́нуть) peck; bite; ~ но́сом, nod.

кле́вер, -а; *pl.* -а́ clover.

клевета́, -ы́, slander; calumny, aspersion; libel. клевета́ть, -ещу́, -е́щешь *imp.* (*perf.* на~)+на+*acc.* slander, calumniate; libel. клеветни́к, -а́, -ни́ца, -ы, slanderer. клеветни́ческий, slanderous; libellous, defamatory.

клеево́й, glue; adhesive; size. кле́енка, -и, oilcloth; oilskin. кле́ить, -е́ю *imp.* (*perf.* с~) glue; gum; paste; stick; ~ся, stick; become sticky: get on, go well. клей, -я (-ю), *loc.* -ю́, glue, adhesive; gum; size. кле́йкий, sticky.

клеймёный, branded. клейми́ть, -млю́ *imp.* (*perf.* за~) brand; stamp; stigmatize. клеймо́, -а́; *pl.* -а, brand; stamp; mark.

кле́мма, -ы clamp, clip; terminal.

клён, -а, maple.

клёпаный, riveted. клепа́ть, -а́ю *imp.* rivet.

кле́тка, -и, cage; coop; hutch; square; check; cell. кле́точка, -и, cell. кле́точный, cage; cell, cellular. кле́тчатка, -и, cellulose. кле́тчатый, checked; squared; cellular.

клёш, -а, flare; брю́ки ~, bell-bottoms; ю́бка ~, flared skirt.

клешня́ -й; *gen. pl.* -е́й, claw.

кле́щи, -е́й *pl.* pincers; tongs; pincer-movement.

клие́нт, -а, client; customer. клиенту́ра, -ы, clientèle.

клик -а cry, call. кли́кать, -и́чу *imp.*, кли́кнуть, -ну *perf.* call; hail; honk.

клин, -а; *pl.* -нья, -ньев, wedge; quoin; gore; gusset; field. клино́к, -нка́ blade. кли́нопись, -и, cuneiform.

кли́рос, -а, choir.

клич, -а, call. кли́чка, -и, name; alias; nickname. кли́чу, etc.: see кли́кать.

клок, -а́; *pl.* -о́чья, -ьев or -и́, -о́в, рag, shred; tuft; ~ се́на, wisp of hay.

клоко́т, -а, bubbling; gurgling. клокота́ть, -о́чет *imp.* bubble; gurgle; boil up.

клони́ть, -ню́, -нишь *imp.* bend; incline; +к+*dat.* lead; drive at; ~ся, bow, bend; ~к+*dat.* approach, lead up to, head for; день клони́лся к ве́черу, the day was declining.

клоп, -а, bug.

кло́ун, -а clown.

клочо́к, -чка́ scrap, shred, wisp; plot. кло́чья, etc.: see клок.

клуб, -а; *pl.* -ы́, puff; ~ы́ пы́ли, clouds of dust.

клубе́нь, -бня *m.* tuber.

клуби́ться, -и́тся *imp.* swirl; wreathe, curl.

клубни́ка, -и, strawberry; strawberries. клубни́чный, strawberry.

клубо́к, -бка́, ball; tangle, mass; ~ в го́рле, lump in the throat.

клу́мба, -ы, (flower-)bed.

клык -а́, fang; tusk; canine (tooth).

клюв, -а, beak.

клю́ква, -ы, cranberry; cranberries; развѐсистая ~, traveller's tale, tall story.

клю́нуть, -ну *perf.* of клева́ть.

ключ[1], -а́, key; clue; keystone; clef; wrench, spanner; запере́ть на ~, lock. ключ[2], -а́, spring; source; бить ~о́м, spout, jet; be in full swing.

ключево́й, key; ~ знак, clef; ~ ка́мень, keystone. ключи́ца, -ы, collar-bone, clavicle.

клю́шка, -и, (hockey) stick; (golf-)club.

клюю́, etc.: see клева́ть.

кля́кса, -ы, blot, smudge.

кляну́, etc.: see клясть.

кля́нчить, -чу *imp.* (*perf.* вы́~) beg.

клясть, -яну́, -янёшь; -ял, -а́, -о *imp.* curse; ~ся (*perf.* по~ся) swear, vow. кля́тва, -ы, oath, vow; дать кля́тву, take an oath. **кля́твенный**, sworn, on oath.

км _abbr._ киломе́тр, kilometre.

к.-н. _abbr._ како́й-нибудь, some, any.

кни́га, -и, book.

кни́го- in _comb._ book, biblio-. **кни́гове́дение**[1], -я, bibliography. **~ве́дение**[2], -я, book-keeping. **~держа́тель**, -я _m._ book-end. **~е́д**, -а, bookworm. **~изда́тель**, -я _m._ publisher. **~люб**, -а, bibliophile, book-lover. **~храни́лище**, -а, library; book-stack; book-storage, shelving.

кни́жечка, -и, booklet. **кни́жка**, -и, book; note-book; bank-book. **кни́жный**, book; **~ая по́лка**, bookshelf; **~ый червь**, bookworm; **~ый шкаф**, bookcase.

кни́зу _adv._ downwards.

кно́пка, -и, drawing-pin; press-stud; (push-)button, knob.

КНР (kaené́r) _abbr._ Кита́йская Наро́дная Респу́блика, Chinese People's Republic.

кнут, -а́, whip; knout.

княги́ня, -и, princess. **кня́жество**, -а, principality. **княжна́**, -ы́; _gen. pl._ **-жо́н**, princess. **князь**, -я; _pl._ **-зья́**, **-зе́й** _m._ prince.

ко: see **к** _prep._

кобура́, -ы́, holster.

кобы́ла, -ы, mare; (vaulting-)horse. **кобы́лка**, -и, filly; bridge.

ко́ваный, forged; hammered; wrought; iron-bound, iron-tipped; terse.

кова́рный, insidious, crafty; perfidious, treacherous. **кова́рство**, -а, insidiousness, craftiness; perfidy, treachery.

кова́ть, кую́, -ёшь _imp._ (_perf._ под~) forge; hammer; shoe.

ковёр, -вра́, carpet; rug; **~-самолёт**, magic carpet.

коверка́ть, -аю _imp._ (_perf._ ис~) distort, mangle, mispronounce; spoil, ruin.

ко́вка, -и, forging; shoeing. **ко́вкий**, -вок, -вка́, -вко, malleable, ductile.

коври́га, -и, loaf. **коври́жка**, -и, honey-cake, gingerbread.

ковш, -а́, scoop, ladle, dipper; bucket.

ковы́ль, -я _m._ feather-grass.

ковыля́ть, -я́ю _imp._ hobble; stump; toddle.

ковырну́ть, -ну́, -нёшь _perf._, **ковыря́ть**, -я́ю _imp._ dig into; tinker, potter; **+в+** _prep._ pick; pick at; **~ в зуба́х**, pick one's teeth; **~ся**, rummage; tinker, potter.

когда́ _adv._ when; **~ .. , ~**, sometimes .. , sometimes; **~ (бы) ни**, whenever; **~ как**, it depends; _conj._ when; while, as; if; **~ так**, if so, if that is the case. **когда́-либо**, **когда́-нибудь** _advs._ some time, some day; ever. **когда́-то** _adv._ once, at one time; at some time; formerly; some day, some time.

кого́: see **кто**.

ко́готь, -гтя; _pl._ -гти, -гте́й _m._ claw; talon; **показа́ть свои́ ко́гти**, show one's teeth.

ко́декс, -а, code; codex.

ко́е-где́ _adv._ here and there, in places. **ко́е-ка́к** _adv._ anyhow; somehow (or other), just. **ко́е-како́й** _pron._ some. **ко́е-кто́**, -кого́ _pron._ somebody; some people. **ко́е-что́**, -чего́ _pron._ something; a little.

ко́жа, -и, skin, hide; leather; peel, rind; epidermis. **кожа́н**, -а́, leather coat. **кожа́нка**, -и, leather jacket, leather coat. **ко́жаный**, leather. **кожеве́нный**, leather; tanning, leather-dressing; **~ заво́д**, tannery. **коже́вник**, -а, tanner, leather-dresser, currier. **ко́жица**, -ы, thin skin; film, pellicle; peel, skin. **ко́жный**, skin; cutaneous. **кожура́**, -ы́, rind, peel, skin.

коза́, -ы́; _pl._ -ы, she-goat, nanny-goat. **козёл**, -зла́, goat; he-goat, billy-goat. **козеро́г**, -а, ibex; Capricorn. **ко́зий**, goat; **~ пух**, angora. **козлёнок**, -нка; _pl._ -ля́та, -ля́т, kid. **козло́вый**, goat-skin.

ко́злы, -зел _pl._ (coach-)box; trestle(s); saw-horse.

ко́зни, -ей _pl._ machinations, intrigues.

козырёк, -рька́, peak; eye-shade; **взять под ~+** _dat._ salute.

козырно́й, trump, of trumps. **козырну́ть**, -ну́, -нёшь _perf._, **козыря́ть**, -я́ю _imp._ lead trumps; trump; play one's trump card; salute. **ко́зырь**, -я; _pl._ -и, -е́й _m._ trump; **откры́ть свои́ ко́зыри**, lay one's cards on the table.

ко́йка, -и; *gen. pl.* ко́ек, berth, bunk; hammock; bed.

коклю́ш, -а, whooping-cough.

кокс, -а, coke.

кол, -а́; *pl.* -лья, -ьев, stake, picket; ни ~а́ ни двора́, neither house nor home.

ко́лба, -ы, retort.

колбаса́, -ы́; *pl.* -ы, sausage.

колго́тки, -ток *pl.* tights.

колдовство́, -а́, witchcraft, sorcery, magic. колду́н, -а́, sorcerer, magician, wizard. колду́нья, -и; *gen. pl.* -ний, witch, sorceress.

колеба́ние, -я, oscillation, vibration; fluctuation, variation; hesitation; wavering, vacillation. колеба́тельный, oscillatory, vibratory. колеба́ть, -éблю *imp.* (*perf.* по~) shake; ~ся, oscillate, vibrate, swing; shake; fluctuate, vary; hesitate; waver.

коленко́р, -а, calico. коленко́ровый, calico.

коле́но, -а; *pl.* -и or -а or -нья, -ей or -лен or -ньев, knee; joint, node; bend; elbow, crank; по ~, по коле́ни knee-deep, up to one's knees; стать на коле́ни, kneel (down); стоя́ть на коле́нях, be kneeling, be on one's knees. коле́нчатый, crank, cranked; bent, elbow; ~ вал, crankshaft.

коле́сник, -а, wheelwright. колесни́ца, -ы, chariot. колёсный, wheel; wheeled. колесо́, -а́; *pl.* -ёса, wheel.

коле́чко, -а, ringlet.

колея́, -и́, rut; track, gauge.

коли́чественн|ый, quantitative; ~ое числи́тельное, cardinal number. коли́чество, -а, quantity, amount; number.

ко́лкий; -лок, -лка́, -о, prickly; sharp, biting, caustic.

колле́га, -и, colleague. коллегиа́льный, joint, collective; corporate. колле́гия, -и, board; college. колле́жский, collegiate; ~ асе́ссор, регистра́тор, секрета́рь, councillor (8th, 14th, 10th, 6th grade: see чин).

колли́зия, -и, clash, conflict, collision.

коло́да, -ы, block; log; pack (of cards). коло́дезный, well; well-deck. коло́дец, -дца, well; shaft.

коло́дка, -и, last; block, chock.

ко́локол, -а; *pl.* -а́, -о́в, bell. колоко́льный, bell; ~ звон, peal, chime. колоко́льня, -и, bell-tower. колоко́льчик, -а, small bell; handbell; campanula, harebell.

коло́нка, -и, geyser; (street) fountain; stand-pipe; column; бензи́новая ~, petrol pump. коло́нна, -ы, column. коло́нный, columned. колонти́тул, -а, running title, catchword. колонци́фра, -ы, page number, folio.

колори́т, -а, colouring, colour. колори́тный, colourful, picturesque, graphic.

ко́лос, -а; -о́сья, -ьев, ear, spike. колоси́ться, -и́тся *imp.* form ears.

колосни́ки, -о́в *pl.* fire-bars; grate; flies.

колоти́ть, -очу́, -о́тишь *imp.* (*perf.* по~) beat; batter, pound; thrash, drub; break, smash; shake; ~ся, pound, thump; shake; +o+*acc.* beat, strike, against.

коло́ть[1], -лю́, -лешь *imp.* (*perf.* рас~), break, chop, split; ~ оре́хи, crack nuts.

коло́ть[2], -лю́, -лешь *imp.* (*perf.* за~, кольну́ть) prick; stab; sting; taunt; slaughter; ~ся, prick.

колпа́к, -а́, cap; lamp-shade; hood, cover, cowl.

колу́н, -а́, axe; chopper.

колхо́з, -а *abbr.* коллекти́вное хозя́йство, collective farm.

колыбе́ль, -и, cradle.

колыха́ть, -ы́шу *imp.*, колыхну́ть, -ну́, -нёшь *perf.* sway, rock; ~ся, sway, heave; flutter, flicker.

ко́лышек, -шка, peg.

кольну́ть, -ну́, -нёшь *perf.* of коло́ть.

кольцева́ть, -цу́ю *imp.* (*perf.* о~) ring. кольцево́й, annular; circular. кольцо́, -а́; *pl.* -а, -ле́ц, -льцам ring; hoop.

колю́ч|ий, prickly; thorny; sharp, biting; ~ая про́волока barbed wire. колю́чка, -и, prickle; thorn; quill; burr.

коля́ска, -и, carriage; pram; side-car.

ком, -а; *pl.* -мья, -ьев, lump; ball; clod. ком: see кто.

ком- *abbr.* in *comb.* of коммунисти́ческий, Communist; команди́р, commander; кома́нда, command. комба́т, -а, battalion commander. ~ди́в,

-a, divisional commander. ~интéрн, -a, Comintern. ~пáртия, -и, Communist Party. ~сомóл, -a, Komsomol, Young Communist League. ~сомóлец, -льца, -óлка, -и, member of Komsomol.

комáнда, -ы, command; order; party; detachment, crew; ship's company, team. командúр, -a, commander, commanding officer; captain. командировáть, -рýю perf. and imp. post, send, dispatch on mission, on official business. командирóвка, -и, posting, dispatching; mission, commission, business trip; warrant authority. командирóвочн|ый adj.; ~ые дéньги, travelling allowance; ~ые sb. pl. travelling allowance, expenses. комáндн|ый adj.; commanding; control; ~ая вы́шка, control tower; ~ый пункт, command post; ~ый состáв, officers; executive (body). комáндование, -я, commanding; command; headquarters. комáндовать, -дую imp. (perf. c~) give orders; be in command; +instr. command; +instr. or над+instr. order about; +над+ instr. command. комáндующий sb. commander.

комáр, -á, mosquito.

комбинáт, -a, industrial complex; combine; training centre. комбинáция, -и, combination; merger; scheme, system; manoeuvre; combinations, slip. комбинезóн, -a, overalls, boiler suit. комбинúровать, -рую imp. (perf. c~) combine.

комендáнт, -a, commandant; manager; warden; superintendent. комендатýра, -ы, commandant's office.

комúзм, -a, humour; the funny side, the comic element; the comic. кóмик, -a, comic actor; comedian, funny man. кóмикс, -a, comic, comic strip, comic book; pl. the funnies.

комиссáр, -a, commissar. комиссариáт, -a, ministry department.

комиссионéр, -a, (commission-)agent, factor, broker. комиссиóнн|ый, commission; committee; board; ~ый магазúн, second-hand shop; ~ые sb.

commission. комúссия, -и, commission; committee, board.

комитéт, -a, committee.

комúческий, comic; comical, funny. комúчный, comic, comical, funny.

кóмкать, -аю imp. (perf. ис~, с~) crumple; make a hash of, muff.

коммéнтарий, -я, commentary; pl. comment. комментúровать, -рую perf. and imp. comment (on).

коммерсáнт, -a, merchant; business man. коммéрция, -и, commerce, trade. коммéрческий, commercial, mercantile.

коммýна, -ы, commune. коммунáльн|ый, communal; municipal; ~ые услýги, public utilities. коммунáр, -a, Communard.

коммутáтор, -a, commutator; switchboard.

кóмната, -ы, room. кóмнатный, room; indoor.

комóд, -a, chest of drawers.

комóк, -мкá, lump; ~ нéрвов, bundle of nerves.

компáния, -и, company. компаньóн, -a, -óнка, -и, companion; partner.

компенсáция, -и, compensation. компенсúровать, -рую, perf. and imp. compensate; indemnify; equilibrate.

кóмплексный, complex, compound, composite; combined; over-all, all-in; ~ обéд, table d'hôte dinner. комплéкт, -a, a complete set; complement; specified number; ~ белья́, bedclothes. комплéктный, complete, комплектовáть, -тýю imp. (perf. у~) complete; replenish; bring up to strength, (re)man. комплéкция, -и. build; constitution.

композúтор, -a, composer. композúция, -и, composition.

компóстер, -a, punch. компостúровать, -рую imp. (perf. про~) punch.

компрометúровать, -рую imp. (perf. c~) compromise. компромúсс, -a, compromise.

комý: see кто.

конвéйер, -a, conveyor.

конвéрт, -a, envelope; sleeve.

конвои́р, -a, escort. конвои́ровать,

-рую *imp.* escort, convoy. конво́й, -я, escort, convoy.

конденса́тор, -а, a capacitor; condenser.

конди́терская *sb.* confectioner's, sweet--shop, cake-shop.

кондиционе́р, -а, air-conditioning plant. кондицио́нный, air-conditioning.

конду́ктор, -а; *pl.* -а́, -торша, -и, conductor; guard.

конево́дство, -а, horse-breeding. конево́дческий, horse-breeding. конёк, -нька́ *dim.* of конь; hobby-horse, hobby.

коне́ц, -нца́, end; distance; way; в конце́ концо́в, in the end, after all; в о́ба конца́, there and back; в оди́н ~, one way; и концы́ в во́ду, and nobody any the wiser; оди́н ~, it comes to the same thing in the end; своди́ть концы́ с конца́ми make (both) ends meet; со всех концо́в, from all quarters. коне́чно *adv.* of course, certainly; no doubt. коне́чность, -и, extremity. коне́чн|ый, final, last; ultimate; terminal; finite; ~ая остано́вка, ~ая ста́нция, terminus.

кони́на, -ы, horse-meat.

кони́ческий, conic, conical.

конкуре́нт, -а, a competitor. конкуре́нция, -и, competition; вне конкуре́нции, *hors concours.* конкури́ровать, -рую *imp.* compete. ко́нкурс, -а, competition; вне ~а, *hors concours.* ко́нкурсный, competitive.

ко́нник, -а, cavalryman. ко́нница, -ы, cavalry; horse. конногварде́ец, -е́йца, horse-guardsman; life-guard. конно-заво́дство, -а, horse-breeding; stud, stud-farm. ко́нный, horse; mounted; equestrian; ~ заво́д, stud.

конопа́тить, -а́чу *imp.* (*perf.* за~), caulk.

конопля́, -и́, hemp.

консерва́ция, -и, conservation; temporary closing-down. консерви́ровать, -рую *perf.* and *imp.* (*perf.* also за~), preserve; can, tin, bottle, pot; close down temporarily. консе́рвн|ый, preserving; ~ая ба́нка, tin; can. консе́рвы, -ов *pl.* tinned goods; goggles.

конси́лиум, -а, consultation.

консо́ль, -и, console; cantilever; pedestal.

конспе́кт, -а, synopsis, summary, abstract, précis. конспекти́вный, concise, summary. конспекти́ровать, -рую *imp.* (*perf.* за~, про~) make an abstract of.

конспирати́вный, secret, clandestine.

констата́ция, -и, ascertaining; verification, establishment. констати́ровать, -рую *perf.* and *imp.* ascertain; verify, establish; certify.

конструкти́вный, structural; constructional; constructive. констру́ктор, -а, designer, constructor. констру́кция, -и, construction; structure; design.

консульта́ция, -и, consultation; advice; advice bureau; clinic, surgery; tutorial; supervision. консульти́ровать, -рую *imp.* (*perf.* про~) advise; act as tutor (to); +с+*instr.* consult; ~ся, have a consultation; obtain advice; +с+*instr.* be a pupil of; consult.

конта́кт, -а, contact; touch. конта́ктный, contact; ~ рельс, live rail.

конто́ра, -ы, office. конто́рск|ий, office; -ая кни́га, account-book, ledger. конто́рщик, -а, clerk.

контр- in *comb.* counter-.

контраба́с, -а, double-bass.

контраге́нт, -а, contracting party; subcontractor. контра́кт, -а, contract. контрактова́ть, -ту́ю *imp.* (*perf.* за~) contract for; engage; ~ся, contract, undertake.

контрама́рка, -и, complimentary ticket.

контрапу́нкт, -а, counterpoint. контрапункти́ческий, контрапу́нктный, contrapuntal.

контра́ст, -а, контра́стность, -и, contrast.

контрибу́ция, -и, indemnity; contribution.

контрнаступле́ние, -я, counter-offensive.

контролёр, -а, inspector; ticket-collector. контроли́ровать, -рую *imp.* (*perf.* про~) check; inspect. контро́ль, -я *m.* control; check, checking; inspection; inspectors. контро́льн|ый, control; check; monitoring; reference; ~ая вы́шка, conning-tower.

контрразве́дка, -и, counter-intelligence; security service, secret service.

конту́женный, contused, bruised; shell-shocked. конту́зить, -ужу *perf*. contuse, bruise; shell-shock. конту́зия, -и, contusion; shell-shock.

ко́нтур, -а, contour, outline; circuit.

кону́ра, -ы, kennel.

ко́нус, -а, cone. конусообра́зный, conical.

конфекцио́н, -а, ready-made clothes shop, department.

конфе́та, -ы, sweet, chocolate.

конфу́з, -а, discomfiture, embarrassment. конфу́зить, -ужу *imp*. (*perf*. c~) confuse, embarrass; place in an awkward or embarrassing position; ~ся, feel awkward or embarrassed; be shy. конфу́зливый, bashful; shy. конфу́зный, awkward, embarrassing.

концентра́т, -а, concentrate концентрацио́нный, concentration. концентра́ция -и, concentration. концентри́ровать, -рую *imp*. (*perf*. c~) concentrate; mass.

конце́рт, -а, concert; recital; concerto. концерта́нт, -а, -а́нтка, -и performer. концертме́йстер, -а, first violin; leader; soloist; accompanist. конце́ртный, concert.

концла́герь, -я *m*. *abbr*. концентрацио́нный ла́герь, concentration camp.

концо́вка, -и, tail-piece; colophon; ending.

конча́ть, -а́ю *imp*., ко́нчить, -чу *perf*. finish; end; +*inf*. stop; ~ся, end, finish; come to an end; be over; expire. ко́нченый, finished; decided, settled; всё ~о, it's all over; it's all up. ко́нчик, -а, tip; point. кончи́на, -ы, decease, demise; end.

конь, -я́; *pl*. -и, -е́й. horse; vaulting-horse; knight; ~-кача́лка, rocking-horse. коньки́, -о́в *pl*. skates; на ро́ликах, roller skates. конькобе́жец, -жца, skater. конькобе́жный, skating. ко́нюх, -а, groom, stable-boy. коню́шня, -и; *gen*. *pl*. -шен, stable.

копа́ть -а́ю *imp*. (*perf*. копну́ть, вы́~) dig; dig up dig out; ~ся, rummage; root; dawdle.

копе́ечный, worth, costing, a copeck;

cheap; petty, trifling. копе́йка, -и, copeck.

ко́пи, -ей *pl*. mines.

копи́лка, -и, money-box.

копи́рка, -и, carbon paper copying paper. копирова́льный, copying. копи́ровать, -рую *imp*. (*perf*. c~) copy; imitate, mimic. копиро́вка, -и, copying. копиро́вщик, -а, -щица, -ы, copyist.

копи́ть, -плю́, -пишь *imp*. (*perf*. на~) save (up); accumulate, amass; store up; ~ся, accumulate.

ко́пия, -и, copy; duplicate; replica.

копна́, -ы́; *pl*. -ны, -пён, -пнам, stook, heap, pile; ~ се́на, hay-cock. копни́ть, -ню́ *imp*. (*perf*. c~) shock, stook; cock.

копну́ть, -ну́, -нёшь *perf*. of копа́ть.

ко́поть, -и, soot; lamp-black.

копоши́ться, -шу́сь *imp*. swarm; potter (about).

копте́ть -и́т *imp*. (*perf*. за~) be covered with soot; smoke. копти́лка, -и, oil-lamp. копти́ть, -пчу́ *imp*. (*perf*. за~, на~) smoke, (smoke-)cure; blacken with smoke; cover with soot. копче́ние, -я, smoking, curing; smoked foods. копчёный, smoked, cured.

копы́тный, hoof; hoofed, ungulate. копы́то, -а, hoof.

копьё, -я́; *pl*. -я, -пий, spear, lance. копьеви́дный, lanceolate.

кора́, -ы́, bark, rind; cortex; crust. кора́бельный, ship's, ship; marine, naval. кора́бельщик, -а, shipwright. кораблево́ждение, -я, navigation. кораблекруше́ние, -я, shipwreck. кораблестрое́ние, -я, shipbuilding. кораблестрои́тель, -я *m*. shipbuilder, naval architect. кора́бль, -я́ *m*. ship, vessel; nave.

корево́й, measles.

коре́ец, -е́йца, коре́йка, -и, Korean. коре́йский, Korean.

корена́стый, thickset, stocky. корени́ться, -и́тся *imp*. be rooted. коренно́й, radical, fundamental; ~о́й жи́тель, native; ~о́й зуб, molar; ~а́я ло́шадь, shaft-horse; ~о́е населе́ние, indigenous population. ко́рень, -рня; *pl*. -и, -е́й *m*. root; radical. коре́нья,

-ьев *pl.* root vegetables. корешо́к, -шка́, rootlet; root; back, spine; counterfoil; pal, mate.

коре́йнка: see коре́ец.

корзи́на, -ы, корзи́нка, -и, basket. корзи́нный, basket.

кори́нка, -и, currants.

кори́ца, -ы, cinnamon.

кори́чневый, brown.

ко́рка, -и, crust; rind, peel; scab.

корм, -а (-у), *loc.* -у́; *pl.* -а́, fodder, food, feed; forage.

корма́, -ы́, stern, poop.

корми́лец, -льца, bread-winner; benefactor. корми́лица, -ы, wet-nurse; benefactress. корми́ть, -млю́, -мишь *imp.* (*perf.* на~, по~, про~) feed; keep, maintain; ~ся, eat, feed; +*instr.* live on, make a living by. кормле́ние, -я, feeding. кормово́й¹, fodder, forage; ~а́я свёкла, mangel-wurzel.

кормово́й², stern, poop; after.

корневи́ще, -а, rhizome. корнево́й, root; radical. корнепло́ды, -ов, root-crops.

корнишо́н, -а, gherkin.

коро́бить, -блю *imp.* (*perf.* по~) warp; jar upon, grate upon; ~ся (*perf. also* с~ся) warp, buckle.

коро́бка, -и, box, case; ~ скоросте́й, gear-box.

коро́ва, -ы, cow. коро́в|ий, cow, cow's; ~ье ма́сло, butter. коро́вник, -а, cow-shed.

короле́ва, -ы, queen. короле́вич, -а, king's son. короле́вна, -ы, king's daughter. короле́вский, royal; king's; regal, kingly. короле́вство, -а, kingdom. королёк, -лька́, petty king, kinglet; gold-crest; blood-orange. коро́ль, -я́ *m.* king.

коромы́сло, -а, yoke; beam; rocking shaft, rocker (arm); balance arm.

коро́на, -ы, crown; coronet; corona. коро́нка, -и, crown. коро́нный, crown, of state. коронова́ть, -ну́ю *perf.* and *imp.* crown.

коросте́ль, -я *m.* corncrake.

корота́ть, -а́ю *imp.* (*perf.* с~) while away, pass. коротк|ий; коро́ток, -тка́, коро́тко́, коро́ткий, short; brief;

close, intimate; ~ая распра́ва, short shrift; на ~ой ноге́, on intimate terms. ко́ротко *adv.* briefly; intimately; ~ говоря́, in short. коротковолно́вый, short-wave. коро́че, *comp.* of коро́ткий, коро́тко.

корпе́ть, -плю́ *imp.* sweat, pore (над+ *instr.* over).

ко́рпус, -а́; *pl.* -ы, -ов or -а́, -о́в, corps; services high school; building; hull; housing, frame, case; long primer; body; trunk, torso; length.

корректи́в, -а, amendment, correction. корректи́ровать, -рую *imp.* (*perf.* про~, с~) correct, read, edit. корре́ктный, correct, proper. корре́ктор, -а; *pl.* -а́, proof-reader, corrector. корректу́ра, -ы, proof-reading; proof.

корт, -а, (tennis-)court.

ко́ртик, -а, dirk.

ко́рточки, -чек *pl.*; сесть на ~, сиде́ть на ко́рточках, squat.

корчева́ть, -чу́ю *imp.* grub up, root out. корчёвка, -и, grubbing up, rooting out.

ко́рчить, -чу *imp.* (*perf.* с~) contort; *impers.* convulse; make writhe; ~ грима́сы, ро́жи, make faces, pull faces; ~ дурака́, play the fool; ~ из себя́, pose as; ~ся, writhe.

ко́ршун, -а, kite.

коры́стный, mercenary. корыстолюби́вый, self-interested, mercenary. корыстолю́бие, -я, self-interest, cupidity. коры́сть, -и, cupidity, avarice; profit, gain.

коры́то, -а, trough; wash-tub.

корь, -и, measles.

коря́вый, rough, uneven; gnarled; clumsy, uncouth; pock-marked.

коса́¹, -ы́, *acc.* -у; *pl.* -ы, plait, tress, braid.

коса́², -ы́, *acc.* ко́су; *pl.* -ы, spit.

коса́³, -ы́, *acc.* ко́су; *pl.* -ы, scythe. коса́рь, -я́ *m.* mower, hay-maker.

ко́свенн|ый, indirect; oblique; ~ые ули́ки, circumstantial evidence.

коси́лка, -и, mower, mowing-machine. коси́ть¹, кошу́, ко́сишь *imp.* (*perf.* с~) mow; cut; mow down

коси́ть², кошу́ *imp.* (*perf.* по~, с~)

squint; be crooked; ~ся, slant; look sideways; look askance.

коси́ца, -ы, lock; pigtail.

косма́тый, shaggy.

косми́ческ|ий, cosmic; space; ~ое пространство, (outer) space. космодро́м, -а, spacecraft launching-site. космона́вт, -а, -на́втка, -и, cosmonaut, astronaut. ко́смос, -а, cosmos; (outer) space.

косне́ть, -е́ю imp. (perf. за~) stagnate; stick. косноязы́чный, tongue-tied.

косну́ться, -ну́сь, -нёшься perf. of каса́ться.

ко́сный, inert, sluggish; stagnant.

ко́со adv. slantwise, aslant, askew; sidelong, obliquely. косогла́зие, -я, squint, cast. косогла́зый, cross-eyed, squint-eyed. косого́р, -а, slope, hillside. косо́й, кос, -а́ -о, slanting; oblique; sloping; sidelong; squinting, cross-eyed; скро́ енный по ~ cut on the cross. косола́пый, pigeon-toed; clumsy, awkward.

костёр -тра́, bonfire; camp-fire.

кости́стый, костля́вый, bony; ко́стный, bone, bony, osseous. ко́сточка, -и, dim. of кость; bone; kernel, stone, pip.

косты́ль, -я́ m. crutch; tail skid.

кость, -и, loc. -и́; pl. -и, -е́й, bone; die; игра́ть в ко́сти, dice.

костю́м, -а, dress, clothes; suit; costume, coat and skirt; англи́йский ~, tailor-made (coat and skirt). костюми́рованный, in costume; fancy-dress. костю́ми|ый adj.; ~ая пье́са, period play, costume play.

костя́к, -а́, skeleton; backbone. костяно́й, bone; ivory.

косы́нка, -и, (three-cornered) head-scarf, shawl.

кот, -а́, tom-cat.

котёл, -тла́, boiler; copper, cauldron. котело́к, -лка́, pot; mess-tin; bowler (hat); head. коте́льная sb. boiler-room, boiler-house.

котёнок, -нка́ pl. -тя́та, -тя́т, kitten.

ко́тик, -а, a fur-seal; sealskin. ко́тиковый, sealskin.

котле́та, -ы, rissole croquette; отбивна́я ~, cutlet, chop.

котлова́н, -а, foundation pit, excavation. котлови́на, -ы, basin, hollow; trough.

кото́мка, -и, knapsack.

кото́рый, pron. which, what; who; that; в кото́ром часу́, (at) what time; кото́рые .., кото́рые, some .., some; ~ раз, how many times; ~ час? what time is it? кото́рый-либо, кото́рый-нибудь prons.; some; one or other.

котя́та, etc.: see котёнок.

ко́фе m. indecl. coffee. кофеи́н, -а, caffeine. кофе́йник, -а, coffee-pot. кофе́йный, coffee. кофемо́лка, coffee-mill, coffee-grinder.

ко́фта, -ы, ко́фточка, -и, blouse.

коча́н, -а о́р -чна́ (cabbage-)head.

кочева́ть, -чу́ю imp. lead a nomadic life; rove, wander; migrate. кочёвка, -и, nomad camp; wandering, migration; nomadic existence. коче́вник, -а, nomad. кочево́й, nomadic; migratory. кочевье, -я; gen. pl. -вий, nomad encampment; nomad territory.

кочега́р, -а, stoker, fireman. кочега́рка, -и, stokehold, stokehole.

кочене́ть, -е́ю imp. (perf. за~, о~) grow numb; stiffen.

кочерга́, -и́; gen. pl. -рёг poker.

кочеры́жка, -и. cabbage-stalk.

ко́чка, -и, hummock; tussock. кочкова́тый, hummocky, tussocky.

коша́чий, cat, cat's; catlike; feline; ~ конце́рт, caterwauling; hooting, barracking.

кошелёк, -лька́, purse.

ко́шка, -и, cat; pl. grapnel, drag; pl. climbing-irons; cat(-o'-nine-tails).

кошма́р, -а, nightmare. кошма́рный, nightmarish; horrible. awful.

кошу́, etc.: see коси́ть.

кощу́нственный, blasphemous. кощу́нство, -а, blasphemy.

КП (kapé) abbr. кома́ндный пункт, Command Post; Коммунисти́ческая па́ртия, Communist Party. КПСС, (kapeesés) abbr. Коммунисти́ческая па́ртия Сове́тского Сою́за, Communist Party of the Soviet Union, C.P.S.U.

кра́деный, stolen. краду́, etc.: see красть. кра́дучись adv. stealthily, furtively.

краеве́дение, -я, regional studies. краеуго́льный; ~ ка́мень, corner-stone.

кра́жа, -и, theft; ~ со взло́мом, burglary.

край, -я (-ю), *loc.* -ю́; *pl.* -я́ -ёв, edge; brim; brink; land; country; territory; region; side (of meat); в чужи́х края́х, in foreign parts; на краю́ све́та, at the world's end; че́рез ~, overmuch, beyond measure. кра́йне *adv.* extremely. кра́йний, extreme; last; uttermost; outside, wing. кра́йность, -и, extreme; extremity.

крал, -а: see красть.

кран, -а, tap, cock, faucet; crane.

крапи́ва, -ы, nettle. крапи́вница, -ы, nettle-rash. крапи́вный, nettle.

кра́пина, -ы, кра́пинка, -и, speck, spot. краплёный, marked.

краса́вец, -вца, handsome man; Adonis. краса́вица, -ы, beauty. краси́вость, -и, (mere) prettiness. краси́вый, beautiful; handsome; fine.

краси́льный, dye, dyeing. краси́льня, -и; *gen. pl.* -лен, dye-house, dye-works. краси́льщик, -а, dyer. краси́тель, -я *m.* dye, dye-stuff. кра́сить, -а́шу *imp.* (*perf.* вы́-, о~, по~) paint; colour; dye; stain; ~ ся, (*perf.* на~) make up. кра́ска, -и, paint, dye; colour; painting, colouring, dyeing; (printer's) ink.

красне́ть, -е́ю *imp.* (*perf.* по~) blush; redden, grow red; show red; colour; ~ ся, show red.

красно- *in comb.* red; beautiful. красноарме́ец, -е́йца, Red Army man. ~арме́йский, Red-Army. ~ва́тый, reddish. ~гварде́ец, -е́йца, Red Guard. ~дере́вец, -вца, ~дере́вщик, -а, cabinet-maker. ~знамённый, Red-Banner. ~ко́жий, red-skinned; *sb.* redskin. ~речи́вый, eloquent; expressive. ~ре́чие, -я, eloquence; oratory.

краснота́, -ы, redness; red spot. кра́сн|ый; -сен, -сна́, -о, red; beautiful; fine; of high quality or value; ~ое де́рево, mahogany; ~ый лес, coniferous forest; ~ая строка́, (first line of) new paragraph; ~ый у́гол, place of honour; ~ый уголо́к, Red Corner.

красова́ться, -су́юсь *imp.* (*perf.* по~) stand in beauty; show off; +*instr.* flaunt. красота́, -ы́; *pl.* -ы, beauty. кра́сочный, paint; ink; colourful; (highly) coloured.

красть, -аду́, -аде́шь; крал *imp.* (*perf.* у~), steal; ~ ся, steal, creep, sneak.

кра́тк|ий; -ток, -тка́, -о, short; brief; concise; ~ое содержа́ние, summary. кра́тко *adv.* briefly. кратковре́менный, short, brief; short-lived; transitory. краткосро́чный, short-term; short-dated.

кра́тное *sb.* multiple. кра́тный, divisible without remainder.

кратча́йший *superl.* of кра́ткий. кра́тче *comp.* of кра́ткий, кра́тко.

крах, -а, crash; failure.

крахма́л, -а, starch. крахма́лить, -лю *imp.* (*perf.* на~) starch. крахма́льный, starched.

кра́ше, *comp.* of краси́вый, краси́во.

кра́шеный, painted; coloured; dyed; made up, wearing make-up. кра́шу, etc.: see кра́сить.

краю́ха, -и, hunk, thick slice.

креди́тка, -и, bank-note. креди́тный, credit, on credit; ~ биле́т, bank-note. кредитоспосо́бный, solvent.

кре́йсер, -а; *pl.* -а́, -о́в, cruiser. кре́йсерский, cruiser, cruising. крейси́ровать, -рую *imp.* cruise.

крем, -а, cream.

креме́нь, -мня́ *m.*, кремешо́к, -шка́ flint.

кремлёвский, Kremlin. кремль, -я́ *m.* citadel; Kremlin.

кремнёв|ый, flint; silicon; siliceous; ~ое ружьё, flint-lock. кремнезём, -а, silica. кре́мний, -я, silicon. кремни́стый, siliceous; stony.

кре́мовый, cream; cream-coloured.

крен, -а, list, heel; bank. крени́ть, -ню́ *imp.* (*perf.* на~) heel; bank; ~ ся, heel over, lis ; bank.

кре́па, -ы, *srépe*; crape.

крепи́ть, -плю́ *imp.* strengthen; support, shore up; timber; make fast, hitch, lash; furl; constipate, make costive; ~ ся, hold out. кре́пк|ий; -пок, -пка́, -о, strong; sound; sturdy; robust; firm; ~ий моро́з, hard frost; ~ие напи́тки, spirits; ~ое слóво, словцó, swear-word, curse. **крéпко** *adv.* strongly; firmly; soundly. **креплéние**, -я, strengthening; fastening; timbering, shoring up; lashing, furling.

крéпнуть, -ну; -еп *imp.* (*perf.* о~) get stronger.

крепостни́чество, -а, serfdom. **крепостн|óй**, serf; ~óе прáво serfdom; ~óй *sb.* serf.

крéпость, -и fortress; strength. **крепчáть**, -áет *imp.* (*perf.* по~) strengthen; get stronger, get harder, get up. **крéпче**, *comp.* of крéпкий, крéпко.

крéсло, -а; *gen. pl.* -сел, arm-chair, easy-chair; stall.

крест, -á cross; поставáить ~ на+ *prep.* give up for lost. **крести́ны**, -и́н *pl.* christening. **крести́ть**, крещу́, -éстишь *perf. and imp.* (*perf. also* о~, пере~) baptize, christen; nickname; make sign of the cross over; ~ся, cross oneself; be baptized, be christened. **крест-нáкрест** *adv.* crosswise. **крéстник**, -а, **крéстница**, -ы, godchild. **крéст|ный|**; ~áя (мáть), godmother; ~ый отéц, godfather. **крестóвый**, of the cross; ~ похóд, crusade. **крестонóсец**, -сца, crusader. **крестообрáзный** cruciform.

крестья́н|ин, -а; *pl.* -я́не -я́н, **крестья́нка**, -и, peasant. **крестья́нский**, peasant. **крестья́нство**, -а, peasants, peasantry.

крещéние, -я, baptism, christening; Epiphany. **крещён|ый|**; -ён, -енá, baptized; *sb.* Christian. **крещу́**, etc.: see крести́ть.

кривáя *sb.* curve. **кривизнá**, -ы́, crookedness; curvature. **криви́ть**, -влю́ *imp.* (*perf.* по~, с~) bend distort; ~ душóй, go against one's conscience; ~ся, become crooked or bent; make a wry face. **кривля́ка**, -и, *m. and f.* poseur; affected person. **кривля́нье**, -я affectation. **кривля́ться**, -я́юсь *imp.* be affected give oneself airs.

криво- in *comb.* curved, crooked; one-sided. **кривобóкий**, lopsided. ~**глáзый** blind in one eye, one-eyed. ~**линéйный**, curvilinear. ~**нóгий**,

bandy-legged, bow-legged. ~**тóлки**, -ов *pl.* false rumours. ~**ши́п**, -а, crank; crankshaft.

кривóй| крив, -á, -о, crooked; curved; one-eyed.

крик, -а, a cry, shout; *pl.* clamour, outcry. **крикли́вый**, clamorous, shouting; bawling; loud; penetrating; blatant. **кри́кнуть**, -ну *perf.* of кричáть. **крику́н**, -á, shouter, bawler; babbler.

кри́тик, -а, critic. **кри́тика**, -и, criticism; critique. **критиковáть**, -кую́ *imp.* criticize. **крити́ческий**, critical.

кричáть, -чу́ *imp.* (*perf.* кри́кнуть) cry, shout; yell; scream. **кричáщий**, loud; blatant.

кров, -а roof; shelter; лишённый ~а homeless.

кровáвый, bloody.

кровáть, -и, bed; bedstead.

крóвельный, roof, roofing.

кровенóсный, blood-; circulatory. **крови́нка**, -и, drop of blood.

крóвля, -и; *gen. pl.* -вель, roof.

крóвн|ый|, blood; thoroughbred; vital, deep, intimate; deadly; ~ая месть, blood-feud.

крóво- in *comb.* blood, sangui-, haemo-. **кровожáдный**, bloodthirsty. ~**излия́ние**, -я, haemorrhage. ~**обращéние**, -я, circulation. ~**подтёк**, -а, a bruise. ~**проли́тие**, -я, bloodshed. ~**проли́тный**, bloody; sanguinary. ~**сóс**, -а, vampire bat; blood-sucker. ~**течéние**, -я, bleeding; haemorrhage. ~**точи́вость**, -и, haemophilia. ~**точи́ть**, -чи́т *imp.* bleed. ~**харкание**, -я, spitting of blood; haemoptysis.

кровь, -и, *loc.* -и́, blood. **кровянóй**, blood.

кроúть, крою́ *imp.* (*perf.* с~) cut, cut out. **крóйка**, -и, cutting out.

крóлик, -а, rabbit. **кроликовóдство**, -а, rabbit-breeding. **крóлич|ий**, ~ья, rabbit.

кроль, -я *m.* crawl (-stroke).

крольчáтник, -а, rabbit-hutch; rabbit farm. **крольчи́ха**, -и she-rabbit, doe.

крóме *prep.*+*gen.* except; besides; in addition to; ~ тогó, besides, moreover, furthermore; ~ шу́ток, joking apart.

кро́мка, -и edge; selvage; rim brim.
кромса́ть, -а́ю *imp.* (*perf.* ис~) cut up carelessly; hack to pieces; shred.
кро́на, -ы crown top.
кронште́йн, -а, bracket; corbel.
кропотли́вый painstaking; minute; laborious; precise.
кросс, -а, cross-country race. кроссме́н, -а, competitor in cross-country race(s).
крот, -а́, mole moleskin.
кро́ткий, -ток, -тка́, -тко, meek, gentle; mild. кро́тость, -и, gentleness; mildness. meekness.
кроха́, -и́, *acc.* -у; *pl.* -и, -ох, -а́м, crumb. кро́хотный, кро́шечный, tiny, minute. кро́шево, -а, hash; medley.
кроши́ть, -шу́, -шишь *imp.* (*perf.* ис~, на~, рас~) crumble; chop, hack; hack to pieces; + *instr.* drop crumbs of; ~ся. crumble; break up small. кро́шка, -и, crumb; a bit.
круг, -а (-у). *loc.* -у́; *pl.* -и́, circle; ring; circuit, lap; sphere range compass; на ~, on average, taking it all round.
круглосу́точный. round-the-clock, twenty-four-hour. кру́гл|ый| кругл, -а́ -о, round; complete utter, perfect; ~ый год all the year round; ~ый, ~ая сирота́, (complete) orphan; ~ые су́тки day and night. кругов|о́й circular; all-round; cyclic; ~ая пору́ка, mutual responsibility guarantee; ~ая ча́ша loving-cup. кругозо́р, -а, prospect; outlook horizon, range of interests. круго́м *adv.* round, around; round about; completely entirely; *prep.+gen.* round, around. кругооборо́т, -а, circulation. кругосве́тный, round-the-world.
кружевно́й lace; lacy. кру́жево, -а; *pl.* -а́ -ев -а́м. lace.
кружи́ть, -ужу́, -у́жи́шь *imp.* whirl; spin round; circle; wander; ~ся, whirl round spin round, go round.
кру́жка, -и, mug; tankard; collecting-box.
кру́жный, roundabout, circuitous. кружо́к -жка́ circle, society, group; disc; washer.
круи́з, -а cruise.
крупа́, -ы́; *pl.* -ы groats; sleet. крупи́нка -и, grain. крупи́ца, -ы grain,

fragment, atom. крупно- in *comb.* large, coarse, macro-, megalo-. кру́пный, large, big; large-scale; coarse; important; serious; prominent, outstanding; ~ый план, close-up; ~ый разгово́р, high words; ~ый шаг, coarse pitch; ~ым ша́гом, at a round pace. крупча́тка, -и, finest (white) flour. крупча́тый, granular.
крутизна́, -ы́, steepness; steep slope.
крути́льный, torsion torsional; doubling. крути́ть, -чу́, -у́тишь *imp.* (*perf.* за~, с~) twist, twirl; roll; turn, wind; whirl; ~ся, turn, spin, revolve; whirl; be in a whirl.
кру́то *adv.* steeply; suddenly; abruptly; sharply; sternly, severely; drastically; thoroughly. крут|о́й; крут, -а́, -о, steep; sudden; abrupt, sharp; stern, severe; drastic; thick; well-done; ~о́е яйцо́, hard-boiled egg. кру́ча, -и, steep slope, cliff. кру́че, *comp.* of круто́й круто.
кручу́, etc.: see крути́ть.
круше́ние, -я, wreck; crash; ruin; collapse.
крыжо́венный, gooseberry. крыжо́вник, -а, gooseberries; gooseberry bush.
крыла́тый, winged. крыло́, -а́; *pl.* -лья, -льев, wing; sail, vane; splashboard, mudguard.
крыльцо́, -а́; *pl.* -а, -ле́ц, -ца́м, porch; (front, back) steps.
кры́мский, Crimean.
кры́са, -ы, rat. крысоло́в, -а, rat-catcher. крысоло́вка, -и, rat-trap.
кры́тый, covered. крыть, крою *imp.* cover; roof; coat; trump; ~ся, be. lie; be concealed. кры́ша, -и, roof. кры́шка, -и, lid; cover.
крюк, -а́ (-у); *pl.* -ки́, -ко́в or -ю́чья, -чьев, hook; detour. крючкова́тый, hooked. крючо́к, -чка́, hook; hitch, catch.
кря́ду *adv.* in succession running.
кряж, -а, ridge.
кря́кать, -аю *imp.* кря́кнуть, -ну *perf.* quack; grunt.
кряхте́ть, -хчу́ *imp.* groan.
кста́ти *adv.* to the point, to the purpose; opportunely; at the same time, incidentally; by the way.

кто, кого́, кому́, кем, ком *pron* who; anyone, anybody; кому́ как, tastes differ; ~ (бы) ни whoever. whosoever; ~ идёт? who goes there?; ~ кого́? who will win, who will come out on top?; ~.., ~.., some.. others; ~ куда́, in all directions; ~ что лю́бит, tastes differ. **кто́-либо**, **кто́-нибудь** *pron.* anyone, anybody; someone, somebody. **кто́-то** *pron.* someone, somebody.

куб, -а́; *pl.* -ы́. cube: cubic metre; boiler, water-heater, urn; still; vat; в ~е, cubed.

куб, *abbr.* куби́ческий, cubic.

куба́рем *adv.* head over heels: headlong.

куба́тура, -ы, cubic content. **ку́бик**, -а, brick, block; cubic centimetre.

кубинец, -нца **куби́нка**, -и, Cuban. **куби́нский**, Cuban.

куби́ческий, cubic, cubical; cube.

ку́бовый, indigo

ку́бок, -бка, goblet, bowl, beaker; cup; встре́ча на ~, cup-tie.

кубоме́тр, -а cubic metre.

кувши́н, -а a jug; pitcher. **кувши́нка**, -и, water-lily.

кувырка́ться, -а́юсь *imp.* **кувыркну́ться**, -ну́сь *perf.* turn somersaults, go head over heels **кувырко́м** *adv.* head over heels; topsy-turvy.

куда́ *adv.* where, where to; what for; +*comp.* much far; ~ (бы) ни wherever; ~ бы то ни́ было, anywhere; ~ лу́чше, much better; хоть ~, fine, excellent. **куда́-либо**, **куда́-нибудь** *adv.* anywhere, somewhere. **куда́-то** *adv.* somewhere.

куда́хтанье, -я, cackling, clucking. **куда́хтать**, -хчу *imp.* cackle, cluck.

ку́дри, -е́й *pl* curls. **кудря́вый**, curly; curly-headed; leafy, bushy; flowery, florid, ornate; ~ая капу́ста, curly kale. **кудря́шки**, -шек *pl.* ringlets.

кузне́ц, -а́ smith blacksmith. **кузне́чик**, -а, grasshopper. **кузне́чный**, blacksmith's; ~ мех, bellows; ~ мо́лот, sledge-hammer. **ку́зница**, -ы, forge, smithy.

ку́зов, -а; *pl.* -а́ basket; body.

кукаре́кать, -ает *imp.*, **кукаре́кнуть**,

-нет *perf.* (*perf.* also про~) crow. **кукареку́**, cock-a-doodle-doo.

ку́киш, -а fico. fig.

ку́кла, -ы, doll; puppet; теа́тр ку́кол, puppet theatre.

кукова́ть, -ку́ю *imp.* (*perf.* про~) cuckoo.

ку́колка, -и, dolly; chrysalis, pupa. **ку́кольник**, -а, puppeteer. **ку́кольный**, doll's; doll-like; puppet.

кукуру́за, -ы, maize. Indian corn.

куку́шка, -и, cuckoo.

кула́к, -а́, fist; striking force; kulak: **кула́цкий**, kulak, kulak's. **кула́чный**, fist.

кулёк, -лька́. bag.

кули́к, -а́, sandpiper.

кули́сы, -и́с, wings; за кули́сами. behind the scenes.

кули́ч, -а́, Easter cake.

кулуа́ры, -ов *pl* lobby.

культ- *abbr.* in *comb.* of культу́рно-, культу́рный, cultural, educational, recreational. **культотде́л**, -а, Cultural Section. **~похо́д**, -а, cultural crusade; cultural outing. **~рабо́та**, -ы, cultural and educational work.

культу́ра, -ы, culture; standard, level; cultivation, growing; культу́рно *adv.* in a civilized manner. **культу́рность**, -и, (level of) culture. **культу́рный**, cultivated; cultural.

культя́, -и́, **культя́пка**, -и, stump.

кум, -а; *pl.* -мовья́, -ьёв, кума́, -ы́, god-parent of one's child.

кума́ч, -а́, red cotton.

куми́р, -а, idol.

кумы́с, -а, koumiss.

ку́ний, marten, marten-fur. **куни́ца**, -ы, marten.

купа́льный, bathing, swimming. **купа́льня**, -и, bathing-place. **купа́льщик**, -а, -щица, -ы, bather. **купа́ть**, -а́ю *imp.* (*perf.* вы́~ ис~) bathe; bath; ~ся, bathe; take a bath.

купе́ *n. indecl.* compartment.

купе́ц, -пца́, merchant. **купе́ческий**, merchant, mercantile. **купе́чество**, -а, merchant class. **купи́ть**, -плю́ -пишь *perf.* (*imp.* покупа́ть) buy. **купля**, -и, buying, purchase.

ку́пол, -а; *pl.* -а́, cupola, dome.

купо́н, -а, coupon.

купоро́с, -а, vitriol.

купчи́ха, -и, merchant's wife; woman of merchant class.

кура́нты, -ов *pl.* chiming clock; chimes.

курга́н, -а, barrow; tumulus.

куре́ние, -я, smoking; incense. кури́льница, -ы, censer; incense-burner. кури́льщик, -а, -щица, -ы, smoker.

кури́н|ый, hen's; chicken's.

кури́тельн|ый, smoking; ~ая бума́га, cigarette paper. кури́ть, -рю́, -ришь *imp. (perf.* по~) smoke; distil; +*acc.* or *instr.* burn; ~ся, burn; smoke; +*instr.* produce, emit.

ку́рица, -ы; *pl.* ку́ры, кур, hen, chicken.

курно́сый, snub; snub-nosed.

куро́к, -рка́, cock, cocking-piece; взвести́ ~, cock a gun; спусти́ть ~, pull the trigger.

куропа́тка, -и, partridge; ptarmigan.

куро́рт, -а, health-resort; spa.

курс, -а, course; policy; year; rate (of exchange). курса́нт, -а, student.

курси́в, -а, italics; ~ом in italics. курси́вный, italic.

курси́ровать, -рую *imp.* ply.

курси́стка, -и, woman student.

ку́ртка, -и, jacket.

курча́виться, -ится *imp.* curl. курча́вый, curly; curly-headed.

ку́ры, etc.: see ку́рица.

курьёз, -а, a funny thing; для ~а, ра́ди ~а, for a joke, for amusement. курьёзный, curious, funny.

курье́р, -а, messenger; courier. курье́рский, fast, express.

куря́тина, -ы, chicken. куря́тник, -а, hen-house, hen-coop.

куря́щий, *sb.* smoker; ваго́н для куря́щих smoking-carriage, smoker.

куса́ть, -а́ю *imp.* bite; sting; ~ся, bite; bite one another.

кусково́й, in lumps; lump. кусо́к, -ска́, piece, bit; slice; lump; cake.

куст, -а́, bush, shrub. куста́рник, -а, shrubbery; bush, shrub, bushes, shrubs.

куста́рн|ый, hand-made, home-made; handicrafts; amateurish, primitive; ~ая промы́шленность, cottage industry. куста́рь, -я́ *m.* handicrafts-man.

ку́тать, -аю *imp. (perf.* за~) wrap up, muffle up; ~ся, muffle oneself up.

кутёж, -а́, drinking-bout; drunken revel, binge. кутерьма́, -ы́, commotion, stir, bustle. кути́ть, кучу́, ку́тишь *imp.,* кутну́ть, -ну́, -нёшь *perf.* drink, carouse; go on a binge, the spree.

кухáрка, -и, cook. ку́хня, -и; *gen. pl.* -хонь, kitchen; cook-house; cooking, cuisine. ку́хонн|ый, kitchen; ~ая посу́да, kitchen utensils.

ку́ц|ый, tailless; bob-tailed; short; limited, abbreviated.

ку́ча, -и, heap, pile; heaps, piles, lots. кучево́й, cumulus.

ку́чер, -а; *pl.* -а́, coachman, driver. кучерско́й, coachman's.

ку́чка, -и, small heap; small group. ку́чный, closely-grouped.

кучу́: see кути́ть.

куша́к, -а́ sash; (plaited) girdle; belt.

ку́шанье. -я, food; dish ку́шать. -аю *imp. (perf.* по~, с~) eat, have.

куше́тка, -и, couch, chaise-longue.

кую́, etc.: see кова́ть.

кэ́мпинг: see ке́мпинг.

кюве́т, -а, ditch, drain; tray, dish, bath.

Л

л *letter*: see эль.

л. *abbr.* лист, sheet.

л *abbr.* литр, litre.

лабора́нт, -а, -а́нтка, -и, laboratory assistant. лаборато́рия, -и, laboratory. лаборато́рный, laboratory.

лави́на, -ы, avalanche.

ла́вка, -и, bench; shop. ла́вочка, -и, small shop. ла́вочник, -а, -ница, -ы, shopkeeper, retailer.

лавр, -а, bay-tree, laurel; *pl.* laurels.

ла́вра, -ы, monastery.

ла́вровый, laurel, bay; ~ вено́к, laurel wreath, laurels.

ла́герник, -а, inmate of camp. ла́гер|ный, camp; ~ая жизнь, nomad existence; ~ый сбор, annual camp. ла́герь, -я; *pl.* -я ог -и, -е́й ог -ей *m.* camp.

лад, -а (-у), *loc.* -у́; -ы́, -о́в, harmony, concord; manner, way; stop, fret key, stud; в ~, не в ~, in, out of, tune; идти́ на ~ go well, be successful; на свой ~, in one's own way, after one's own fashion; не в ~а́х, at odds at variance; они́ не в ~а́х, they don't get on.

ла́дан, -а, incense; дыша́ть на ~, have one foot in the grave.

ла́дить, ла́жу *imp.* get on, be on good terms; ~ся, go well, succeed. ла́дно *adv.* harmoniously; well; all right; very well! ла́дный, fine, excellent; harmonious.

ладо́нный, palmar. ладо́нь, -и, palm.

ладья́[1], -ьи́, rook, castle.

ладья́[2], -ьи́, boat, barge.

ла́жу, etc.: see ла́дить, ла́зить.

лазаре́т, -а, field hospital; sick quarters; sick-bay; infirmary.

ла́зать: see ла́зить. лазе́йка, -и, hole, gap; loop-hole.

ла́зер, -а, a laser.

ла́зить, ла́жу, ла́зать, -аю *imp.* climb, clamber; +в+*acc.* climb into, get into.

лазу́рный, sky-blue, azure. лазу́рь, -и, azure.

лазу́тчик, -а, scout; spy.

лай, -я, bark, barking. ла́йка[1], -и, (Siberian) husky, laika.

ла́йка[2], -и, kid. ла́йковый, kid; kidskin.

ла́йнер, -а, liner air-liner.

лак, -а (-у), varnish lacquer.

лака́ть, -а́ю *imp.* (*perf.* вы́~) lap.

лаке́й, -я, footman, man-servant; lackey, flunkey. лаке́йский, man-servant's; servile.

лакиро́ванн|ый, varnished, lacquered; ~ая ко́жа, patent leather. лакирова́ть, -ру́ю *imp.* (*perf.* от~) varnish; lacquer. лакиро́вка, -и, varnishing, lacquering; varnish; gloss, polish.

ла́кмус, -а, litmus. ла́кмусов|ый, litmus; ~ая бума́га, litmus paper.

ла́ков|ый, varnished, lacquered; ~ая ко́жа, patent leather.

ла́комить, -млю *imp.* (*perf.* по~) regale, treat; ~ся+*instr.* treat oneself to. ла́комка, -и *m.* and *f.* gourmand; lover of sweet things. ла́комство, -а, delicacy; *pl.* dainties, sweet things. ла́комый, dainty, tasty; +до, fond of, partial to.

ла́мпа, -ы, lamp; valve, tube. ла́мпочка, -и, lamp; bulb; light.

ландша́фт, -а, landscape.

ла́ндыш, -а, lily of the valley.

лань, -и, fallow deer; doe.

ла́па, -ы, paw; tenon, dovetail; fluke; (*sl.*) bribe; попа́сть в ла́пы к+*dat.*, fall into the clutches of.

ла́поть, -птя́; *pl.* -и, -е́й *m.* bast shoe, bast sandal.

ла́пчатый, palmate; web-footed.

лапша́, -и́, noodles; noodle soup.

ларёк, -рька́ stall. ларёчник, -а, stall-keeper. ларь, -я́ *m.* chest, coffer; bin; stall.

ла́ска, -и, caress, endearment; kindness. ласка́тельн|ый, caressing; affectionate; ~ое и́мя, pet name. ласка́ть, -а́ю, *imp.* caress, fondle, pet; comfort, console; ~ся+к+*dat.* make up to; snuggle up to; coax; fawn upon. ла́сковый, affectionate, tender.

ла́стик, -а, (india-)rubber, eraser.

ла́сточка, -и, swallow.

лату́к, -а, lettuce.

лату́нный, brass. лату́нь, -и, brass.

ла́ты, лат *pl.* armour.

латы́нь, -и Latin.

латы́ш, -а́ латы́шка, -и, Lett, Latvian. латы́шский, Lettish, Latvian.

лауреа́т, -а, prize-winner.

лафе́т, -а, gun-carriage.

ла́цкан, -а, lapel.

лачу́га, -и, hovel, shack.

ла́ять, ла́ю *imp.* bark; bay.

лба, etc.: see лоб.

лганьё, -я́, lying. **лга́ть**, лгу, лжёшь; лгал, -а́, -о *imp.* (*perf.* на~, со~) lie; tell lies; +на+*acc.* slander. **лгун**, -а́, лгу́нья, -и, liar.

ЛГУ (*elgéu*) *abbr.* Ленингра́дский госуда́рственный университе́т, Leningrad State University.

лебедёнок, -нка; *pl.* -дя́та, -дя́т, cygnet. **лебеди́ный**, swan, swan's. **лебёдка**, -и, swan, pen; winch, windlass. **ле́бедь**, -я; *pl.* -и, -е́й *m.* swan, cob.

лебези́ть, -ежу́ *imp.* fawn, cringe.

лев, льва, lion.

левко́й, -я, stock.

лево- in *comb.* left, left-hand; laevo-. **левобере́жный** left-bank. **левша́**, -и́; *gen. pl.* -е́й *m.* and *f.* left-handed person, left-hander, southpaw. **ле́вый** *adj.* left; left-hand; port; left-wing; -ая сторона́, left-hand side, near side, wrong side.

лёг, etc.: see лечь.

лёгк|ий, -гок -гка́, лёгкий. light; easy; slight, mild; ~ая атле́тика, field and track events; лёгок на поми́не, talk of the devil!; у него́ ~ая рука́, he brings luck. **легко́** *adv.* easily, lightly, slightly.

легко- in *comb.* light, light-weight; easy, easily, readily. **легкове́рие**, -я, credulity, gullibility. ~ **ве́рный**, credulous, gullible. ~**ве́с**, -а, ~**ве́сный**, light-weight. ~**ву́шка**, -и, (private) car. ~**мы́сленный**, light-minded; thoughtless, careless, irresponsible; flippant, frivolous, superficial. ~**мы́слие**, -я, flippancy, frivolity, levity.

легков|о́й; ~о́й автомоби́ль, ~а́я маши́на, (private) car. **лёгкое** *sb.* lung; lights. **лёгкость**, -и, lightness; easiness. **лего́нько** *adv.* slightly; gently. **лёгочный**, lung, pulmonary. **ле́гче** *comp.* of лёгкий, легко́.

лёд, льда (-у), *loc.* -у, ice. **ледене́ть**, -е́ю *imp.* (*perf.* за~, о~) freeze; grow numb with cold. **ледене́ц**, -нца́, fruit-drop. **леденцо́вый**, frozen; icy. **ледени́ть**, -йт *imp.* (*perf.* о~) freeze; chill. **ледяни́ный**, chilling, icy.

ле́дник¹, -а, ice-house; ice-box; ваго́н-~, refrigerator van. **ледни́к²**, -а́, glacier. **леднико́вый**, glacial; glacier; ice; refrigerator; ~ пери́од, Ice Age.

ледоко́л, -а, ice-breaker. **ледору́б**, -а, ice-axe. **ледян|о́й**, ice; icy; ice-cold; ~ая гора́, tobogganing run, ice slope; iceberg.

лежа́ть, -жу́ *imp.* lie; be, be situated. **лежа́чий**, lying (down); ~ больно́й, bed-patient.

ле́звие, -я, (cutting) edge; blade.

лезть, -зу; лез *imp.* (*perf.* по~), climb; clamber, crawl; make one's way; come on, keep on; creep, get, go; fall out; come to pieces; ~ в пе́тлю, stick one's neck out; ~ на́ стену, climb up the wall; не ~ за сло́вом в карма́н, not be at a loss for words.

ле́йка, -и, watering-can; pourer; funnel.

лейтена́нт, -а, lieutenant.

лека́рственный, medicinal. **лека́рство**, -а, medicine, drug.

лексико́н, -а, vocabulary. **лекси́ческий**, lexical.

ле́ктор, -а, lecturer. **лекцио́нный**, lecture. **ле́кция**, -и, lecture; чита́ть ле́кцию, lecture, deliver a lecture.

леле́ять, -е́ю *imp.* (*perf.* вз~) cherish, foster; coddle, pamper.

лён, льна, flax.

лени́вый, lazy, idle; sluggish. **лени́ться**, -ню́сь, -нишься *imp.* (*perf.* по~) be lazy, be idle; +*inf.* be too lazy to.

ле́нта, -ы, ribbon; band; tape; film; belt; track.

лент|я́й, -я, -**я́йка**, -и, lazy-bones; sluggard. **лентя́йничать**, -аю *imp.* be lazy, be idle, loaf. **лень**, -и, laziness idleness; indolence; ей ~ встать, she is too lazy to move.

лепесто́к, -тка́, petal.

лепет, -а, babble; prattle. **лепета́ть**, -ечу́, -е́чешь *imp.* (*perf.* про~) babble, prattle.

лепёшка, -и, scone; tablet, lozenge, pastille.

лепи́ть, -плю́, -пишь *imp.* (*perf.* вы́~, за~, на~, с~) model, fashion; mould; stick; ~**ся**, cling; crawl. **ле́пка**, -и, modelling. **лепн|о́й**, modelled, moulded; ~**ое украше́ние**, stucco moulding.

лес, -а (-у), *loc.* -у́; *pl.* -а́, forest, wood,

woods; timber; *pl.* scaffold, scaffolding.

ле́са́, -ы́ or -ы; *pl.* лёсы, fishing-line.

леси́стый, wooded, forest, woodland.

лесни́к, -а́, forester; gamekeeper. **лесни́чество**, -а, forestry area. **лесни́чий** *sb.* forestry officer; forest warden; gamekeeper. **лесно́й**, forest, forestry; timber.

лесо- in *comb.* forest, forestry; timber wood. **лесово́дство**, -а, forestry. **~заготóвка**, -и, logging, lumbering. **~защи́тный**, forest-protection. **~насажде́ние**, -я, afforestation; (forest) plantation. **~пи́лка**, -и, *gen. pl.* -лен, sawmill. **~руб**, -а, woodcutter, logger. **~спла́в**, -а, (timber)-rafting. **~степь**, -и, partially wooded steppe. **~ту́ндра**, -ы, forest-tundra.

ле́стница, -ы, stairs, staircase; ladder; steps. **ле́стничный**; **~ая кле́тка**, (stair)-well.

ле́стный, flattering; complimentary. **лесть**, -и, flattery; adulation.

лёт, -а, *loc.* -у́, flight, flying; на ~у́, in the air, on the wing; hurriedly, in passing.

лета́, лет *pl.* years; age; в ~х, elderly, getting on (in years); на ста́рости лет, in one's old age; прошло́ мно́го лет, many years passed; ско́лько вам лет? how old are you? сре́дних лет, middle-aged.

лета́тельный, flying. **лета́ть**, -а́ю *imp.*, **лете́ть**, лечу́ *imp.* (*perf.* полете́ть) fly; rush, tear; fall, drop.

ле́тний, summer. **ле́тник**, -а, annual.

лётный, flying, flight; **~ состáв**, air-crew.

ле́то, -а; *pl.* -á, summer; *pl.* years. **ле́том** *adv.* in summer.

летопи́сец, -сца, chronicler, annalist. **ле́топись** -и, chronicle, annals. **летосчисле́ние**, -я, (system of) chronology; era.

лету́н, -а́, летýнья, -и, flyer; rolling stone, drifter. **лету́ч|ий**, flying; passing, ephemeral; brief; volatile; **~ий листо́к**, leaflet; **~ий ми́тинг**, emergency meeting, extraordinary meeting, impromptu meeting; **~ая мышь**, bat; hurricane lamp. **лету́чка**, -и, leaflet;

emergency meeting; mobile detachment, road patrol; mobile dressing station. **лётчик**, -а, -чица, -ы, pilot; aviator, flyer; **~-испыта́тель**, test pilot.

лече́бница, -ы, clinic, hospital. **лече́бный**, medical; medicinal. **лече́ние**, -я, (medical) treatment; cure. **лечи́ть**, -чу́, -чишь *imp.* treat (от, for); **~ся**, be given, have, treatment (от, for); +*instr.* take a course of.

лечу́, etc.: see лете́ть, лечи́ть.

лечь, ля́гу, ля́жешь; лёг, -ла́ *perf.* (*imp.* ложи́ться) lie, lie down; go to bed, turn in; +на+*acc.* fall on, rest on, lie on.

лещ, -а́ bream.

лже- in *comb.* false, pseudo-, mock-. **лженау́ка**, -и, pseudo-science. **~сви-де́тель**, -я *m.*, **~ница**, -ы, perjuror, perjured witness. **~свиде́тельство**, -а, false evidence. **~уче́ние**, -я, false doctrine.

лжец, -а́ liar. **лжи́вый**, lying; mendacious; false, deceitful.

ли, ль *interrog.* *part.* and *conj.* whether, if; ли.. ли, whether .. or; ра́но ли, поздно ли, sooner or later.

ли́бо *conj.* or; **~ .. ~**, either, .. or.

ли́вень, -вня *m.* heavy shower, downpour, rainstorm; cloud-burst; hail.

ливре́йный, livery, liveried. **ливре́я**, -и, livery.

ли́га, -и, league.

ли́дер, -а, a leader; flotilla leader. **ли́дер-ство**, -а, leadership; first place, lead. **лиди́ровать**, -рую *perf.* and *imp.* be in the lead.

лиза́ть, лижу́, -ешь *imp.*, **лизну́ть**, -ну́, -нёшь *perf.* lick.

лик, -а, face.

ликёр, -а, liqueur.

ликова́ние, -я, rejoicing, exultation; triumph. **ликова́ть**, -ку́ю *imp.* rejoice, exult, triumph.

лиле́йный, lily-white; liliaceous. **ли́лия**, -и, lily.

лило́вый. mauve, violet.

лима́н, -а, estuary.

лимо́н, -а, lemon. **лимо́нн|ый**, lemon; **~ая кислота́**, citric acid.

лингви́ст, -а, linguist. **лингви́стика**, -и,

linguistics. **лингвисти́ческий**, linguistic.

лине́йка, -и, ruler; rule; line. **лине́йный**, linear, line; of the line; ~ **кора́бль**, battleship.

ли́нза, -ы, lens.

ли́ния, -и, line. **лино́ваный**, lined, ruled. **линова́ть**, -ну́ю *imp. (perf.* на~) rule.

линогравю́ра, -ы, linocut.

лино́чий, liable to fade not fast. **линя́лый**, faded, discoloured; moulted. **линя́ть**, -я́ет *imp. (perf.* вы~ по~, с~) fade, lose colour; run; cast the coat, skin; shed hair; moult; slough.

ли́па, -ы, lime(-tree).

ли́пкий, -пок, -пка́, -о, sticky, adhesive. **ли́пнуть**, -ну; лип *imp.* stick, adhere.

липня́к, -а́, lime-grove. **ли́повый**, lime, linden.

ли́ра, -ы, lyre. **ли́рик**, -а, lyric poet. **ли́рика**, -и, lyric poetry. **лири́ческий**, lyric; lyrical. **лири́чный**, lyrical.

лиса́, -ы́; *pl.* -ы, fox. **лисёнок**, -нка; *pl.* -ся́та, -ся́т, fox-cub. **ли́сий**, fox, fox's. **лиси́ца**, -ы, fox.

лист, -а́; *pl.* -ы́ or -ья, -о́в or -ьев, leaf; sheet; quire; page; form; certificate; в ~, in folio; игра́ть с ~а́, play at sight; корректу́ра в ~а́х, pageproofs. **листа́ть**, -а́ю *imp.* leaf through, turn over the pages of. **листва́**, -ы́, leaves, foliage. **ли́ственный**, deciduous. **листо́вка**, -и, leaflet. **листово́й**, sheet, plate; leaf. **листо́к**, -тка́, *dim.* of лист; leaflet; form, proforma. **листопа́д**, -а, fall of the leaf.

лит- *abbr.* in *comb.* of литерату́ра, -ту́рный literature literary.

лите́йная *sb.* foundry, smelting-house. **лите́йный**, founding, casting. **лите́йщик**, -а, founder.

ли́тера, -ы, type, letter. **литера́тор**, -а, literary man, man of letters. **литерату́ра**, -ы, literature. **литерату́рн|ый**, literary; ~ое воровство́, plagiarism.

ли́тий, -я, lithium.

лито́вец, -вца, **лито́вка**, -и, Lithuanian. **лито́вский**, Lithuanian.

литой, cast. **лить**, лью, льёшь; лил, -а́, -о *imp. (perf.* с~) pour; shed, spill; found, cast, mould. **литьё**, -я́ founding, casting, moulding; castings,

mouldings. **ли́ться**, льётся; ли́лся, -а́сь, ли́ло́сь *imp.* flow; stream, pour.

лиф, -а, bodice. **ли́фчик**, -а, bodice; bra.

лиха́ч, -а́, (driver of) smart cab; reckless driver, road-hog. **лихо́й**[1], лих, -а́, -о, dashing, spirited.

лихо́й[2], лих, -а́, -о, ли́хи́, evil.

лихора́дка, -и, fever. **лихора́дочный**, feverish.

лицева́ть, -цу́ю *imp. (perf.* пере~) turn. **лицев|о́й**, facial; exterior; ~а́я ру́копись, illuminated manuscript; ~а́я пе́тля, plain (stitch); ~а́я сторона́, facade, front; right side; obverse.

лицеме́р, -а, hypocrite, dissembler. **лицеме́рие**, -я, hypocrisy, dissimulation. **лицеме́рный**, hypocritical.

лицо́, -а́; *pl.* -а, face; exterior; right side; person; быть к лицу́+*dat.* suit, become; befit; в лице́+*gen.* in the person of; знать в ~, know by sight; ~м к лицу́, face to face; на нём лица́ нет, he looks awful; невзира́я на ли́ца, without respect of persons; от лица́+*gen.*, in the name of, on behalf of; сказа́ть в ~+*dat.* say to his, etc., face; черты́ лица́, features. **лично́йка**, -ы, mask; guise; escutcheon, key-plate. **личи́нка**, -и, larva, grub; maggot. **ли́чно** *adv.* personally, in person. **личн|о́й**, face; facial. **ли́чность**, -и, personality; person, individual; *pl.* personalities, personal remarks. **ли́чный**, personal; individual; private; ~ секрета́рь, private secretary; ~ соста́в, staff, personnel.

лиша́й, -я, lichen; herpes; опоя́сывающий ~, shingles. **лиша́йник**, -а, lichen.

лиша́ть(ся, -а́ю(сь *imp.* of лиши́ть(ся.

ли́шек, -шка (-у), surplus; с ли́шком, odd, and more, just over.

лише́нец, -нца, disfranchised person. **лише́ние**, -я, deprivation; privation; hardship; ~ гражда́нских прав, disfranchisement. **лишённ|ый**, -ён, -ена́+*gen.* lacking in, devoid of. **лиши́|ть**, -шу́ *perf. (imp.* лиша́ть)+*gen.* deprive of; ~ себя́ жи́зни, take one's own life; ~ся+*gen.* lose, be deprived of. **ли́шн|ий**, superfluous; unnecessary;

left over; spare, odd; ~ раз, once more; с ~им, odd, and more.

лишь *adv.* only; *conj.* as soon as; ~ бы, if only, provided that; ~ (то́лько), as soon as.

лл. *abbr.* листы́, sheets.

лоб, лба, *loc.* лбу, forehead; brow.

лобзик, -а, fret-saw.

лобн|ый, frontal; front; ~ое ме́сто, place of execution. **лобово́й**, frontal, front.

лове́ц, -ца́, fisherman; hunter. **лови́|ть**, -влю́, -вишь *imp.* (*perf.* пойма́ть) catch, try to catch; ~ на сло́ве, take at his, etc. word; ~ ста́нцию, try to pick up a (radio-)station.

ло́вкий, -вок -вка́, -о, adroit, dexterous, deft; cunning, smart; comfortable. **ло́вкость**, -и, adroitness, dexterity, deftness; cunning, smartness.

ло́вля, -и; *gen. pl.* -вель, catching, hunting; fishing-ground. **лову́шка**, -и, snare trap.

ло́вче, *comp.* of ло́вкий.

ло́говище, -а, ло́гово, -а, den, lair.

логопе́д, -а, speech therapist. **логопе́дия**, -и, speech therapy.

ло́дка, -и, ло́дочка, -и, boat. **ло́дочник**, -а boatman. **ло́дочный**, boat, boat-.

лоды́рничать, -аю *imp.* loaf, idle about. **лоды́рь**, -я *m.* loafer, idler.

ло́жа, -и, box; (masonic) lodge.

ложби́на, -ы, hollow.

ло́же, -а, couch; bed; channel; gun-stock.

ложи́ться, -жу́сь *imp.* of лечь.

ло́жка, -и, spoon; spoonful.

ло́жн|ый, false, erroneous; sham, dummy. **ложь**, лжи, lie, falsehood.

лоза́, -ы́; *pl.* -ы, vine. **лозня́к**, -а́, willow withy.

ло́зунг, -а, slogan, catchword; watch-word; pass-word.

ло́кон, -а, lock, curl, ringlet.

локотни́к, -а́, (chair-, sofa-)arm. **ло́коть**, -ктя; *pl.* -и, -ей *m.* elbow.

лом, -а; *pl.* -ы, -о́в, crowbar; scrap, waste. **ло́маный**, broken. **лома́ть**, -а́ю *imp.* (*perf.* по~, с~) break; fracture; rack, cause to ache; ~ ка́мень, quarry stone; ~ ру́ки, wring one's hands; ~ себе́ го́лову, rack one's

brains; меня́ всего́ лома́ло, I was aching all over; ~ся, break; crack; pose, put on airs; make difficulties, be obstinate.

ломба́рд, -а, pawnshop. **ломба́рдн|ый**; ~ная квита́нция pawn-ticket.

ло́мберный; ~ стол, card-table.

лом|и́ть, -ми́т *imp.* break; break through, rush; *impers.* cause to ache; у меня́ ло́мит спи́ну my back aches; ~ся, be (near to) breaking; +в+*acc.* force; + от + *gen.* be bursting, crammed, loaded, with. **ло́мка**, -и, breaking; *pl.* quarry. **ло́мкий**; -мок, -мка́, -о, fragile, brittle.

ломов|о́й, dray, draught; ~о́й изво́з-чик, drayman, carter; ~а́я ло́шадь, cart-horse dray-horse, draught-horse.

ломо́та, -ы, ache (in one's bones).

ломо́ть, -мтя́; *pl.* -мти́ *m.* large slice, round; hunk chunk. **ло́мтик**, -а, slice.

ло́но, -а bosom, lap.

лопа́рь, -я *m.*, лопа́рка, -и, Lapp, Lap-lander. **лопа́рский**, Lapp Lappish.

ло́пасть, -и; *pl.* -и, -е́й, blade; fan, vane; paddle; lamina; ~ о́си axle-tree.

лопа́та, -ы, spade; shovel. **лопа́тка**, -и, shoulder-blade; shovel; trowel; blade.

ло́паться, -аюсь *imp.*, **ло́пнуть**, -ну *perf.* burst; split, crack; break; fail, be a failure; go bankrupt, crash.

лопоу́хий, lop-eared.

лопу́х, -а́, burdock.

лоси́на, -ы elk-skin, chamois leather; elk-meat; (*pl.*) buckskins. **лоси́ный**, elk, elk-.

лоск, -а (-у) lustre. gloss, shine.

лоску́т, -а́; *pl.* -ы́ ог -ья, -о́в ог -ьев rag, shred, scrap. **лоску́тн|ый**, scrappy; made of scraps, patchwork; ~ое одея́ло, patchwork quilt.

лосни́ться, -ню́сь *imp.* be glossy, shine.

лососи́на, -ы, salmon. **ло́сось**, -я *m.* salmon.

лось, -я; *pl.* -и, -е́й *m.* elk.

лосьо́н, -а, lotion.

лот, -а, lead, plummet.

лотере́йный, lottery, raffle. **лотере́я**, -и, lottery, raffle.

лото́к, -тка́, hawker's stand; hawker's tray; chute; gutter; trough. **лото́чник**, -а, **-ница**, -ы, hawker.

лоха́нка, -и, **лоха́нь**, -и, (wash-)tub.

лохма́тить, -а́чу *imp.* (*perf.* раз~) tousle, ruffle; ~ся, become tousled, be dishevelled. **лохма́тый**, shaggy(-haired); dishevelled tousled.

лохмо́тья, -ьев *pl.* rags.

ло́цман a pilot; pilot-fish.

лошади́н|ый, horse; equine; ~ая си́ла, horsepower. **лоша́дка**, -и, (small) horse; hobby-horse; rocking-horse. **ло́шадь**, -и; *pl.* -и, -е́й, *instr.* -дьми́ or -дя́ми, horse.

лощёный, glossy, polished.

лощи́на, -ы, hollow, depression.

лощи́ть, -щу́ *imp.* (*perf.* на~), polish; gloss, glaze.

л.с. *abbr.* лошади́ная си́ла, horsepower.

луб, -а, bast. **лубо́к**, -бка́, splint; wood-block; popular print. **лубо́чн|ый**; ~ карти́нка, popular print.

луг, -а, *loc.* -ý; *pl.* -а́, meadow.

луди́ть, лужу́, лу́дишь *imp.* (*perf.* вы́~), tin.

лу́жа, -и, puddle, pool.

лужа́йка, -и, grass-plot, lawn, (forest) glade.

луже́ние, -я, tinning. **лужёный**, tinned, tin-plate. **лужу́**, etc.: see луди́ть.

лу́за, -ы, pocket.

лук[1], -а (-у), onions; зелёный лук, spring onions.

лук[2], -а, bow.

лука́вить, -влю *imp.* (*perf.* с~), be cunning. **лука́вство**, -а, craftiness slyness. **лука́вый**, crafty, sly, cunning; arch.

лу́ковица, -ы, onion; bulb; onion dome. **лу́ковичный**, onion-shaped; bulbous.

лукомо́рье, -я, cove, bay.

луна́, -ы́; *pl.* -ы, moon. **луна́тик**, -а, sleep-walker, somnambulist.

луко́шко, -а; *pl.* -и, punnet, bast basket.

лу́нка, -и, hole; socket, alveolus.

лу́нник, -а, moon-rocket. **лу́нн|ый**, moon; lunar; ~ый ка́мень, moonstone; ~ая ночь, moonlight night; ~ый свет, moonlight.

лу́па, -ы, magnifying-glass.

лупи́ть, -плю́ -пишь *imp.* (*perf.* об~,

с~) peel (off); bark; fleece; ~ся, peel (off), scale; come off, chip.

луч, -а́, ray; beam. **лучево́й**, ray, beam; radial, radiating; radiation. **лучеза́р-ный**, radiant, resplendent. **лучеис-пуска́ние**, -я, radiation. **лучепрелом-ле́ние**, -я, refraction.

лучи́на, -ы, spill; chip; splinter.

лучи́стый, radiant; radial.

лу́чше, better; ~ всего́, ~ всех, best of all; нам ~ верну́ться, we had better go back; тем ~, so much the better. **лу́чш|ий**, better; best; в ~ем слу́чае, at best; всего́ ~его! all the (very) best! к ~ему, for the better.

лущёный, -ён, -ена́, hulled, shelled, husked. **лущи́ть**, -щу́ *imp.* (*perf.* об~) shell, husk, hull, pod.

лы́жа, -и, ski; snow-shoe. **лы́жник**, -а, skier. **лы́жный**, ski, skiing; ~ спорт, skiing. **лыжня́**, -и́, ski-track.

лы́ко -а, bast, bass.

лысе́ть -е́ю *imp.* (*perf.* об~, по~) grow bald. **лы́сина**, -ы, bald spot, bald patch; blaze, star, patch. **лы́сый**, лыс, -а́, -о, bald.

ль: see ли.

льва, etc.: see лев. **львёнок** -нка; *pl.* львя́та, -я́т, lion-cub. **льви́ный**, lion, lion's; ~ зев, snapdragon. **льви́ца**, -ы, lioness.

льго́та, -ы, privilege; advantage. **льго́тн|ый**, privileged; favourable; ~ый биле́т, complimentary ticket, free ticket; на ~ых усло́виях, on easy terms.

льда, etc.: see лёд. **льди́на**, -ы, block of ice; ice-floe. **льди́нка**, -и, piece of ice. **льди́стый**, icy; ice-covered.

льна, etc.: see лён. **льново́дство**, -а, flax-growing. **льнопряде́ние**, -я, flax-spinning. **льнопряди́льн|я**, -и; *gen. pl.* -лен, flax-mill.

льнуть, -ну, -нёшь *imp.* (*perf.* при~) + к + *dat.* cling to, stick to; have a weakness for; make up to, try to get in with. **льняно́й**, flax, flaxen; linen; linseed.

льстец, -а́, flatterer. **льсти́вый**, flattering; smooth-tongued. **льстить**, льщу *imp.* (*perf.* по~) + *dat.* flatter; gratify;

+ *acc.* delude; ~ся, + на + *acc.* be tempted by.

лью, etc.: see лить.

ЛЗС (*elzeés*) *abbr.* лесозащи́тная ста́нция, Forest-protection Station.

любе́зность, -и, courtesy; politeness; civility; kindness; compliment. любе́зн|ый, courteous, polite; obliging; kind, amiable.

люби́мец, -мца, -мица, -ы, pet, favourite. люби́мый, beloved, loved; favourite. люби́тель, -я *m.*, -ница, -ы, lover; amateur. люби́тельский, amateur; amateurish; choice. люби́ть, -блю́, -бишь *imp.* love; like, be fond of; need, require.

любова́ться, -бу́юсь *imp.* (*perf.* по~) admire; feast one's eyes (на + *acc.* on). любо́вник, -а, lover. любо́вница, -ы, mistress. любо́вный, love-; loving. любо́вь, -бви́, *instr.* -бо́вью, love.

любозна́тельный, of an inquiring turn of mind, desirous of knowledge.

любо́й, any; either; *sb.* anyone, anybody.

любопы́тный, curious; inquisitive; prying; interesting. любопы́тство, -а, curiosity. любопы́тствовать, -твую *imp.* (*perf.* по~) be curious.

лю́бящий, loving, affectionate; ~ вас, yours affectionately.

лю́ди, -е́й, -ям, -дьми́, -ях *pl.* people; men; servants; в ~, away from home; на лю́дях, in the presence of others, in company. лю́дный, populous, crowded. людое́д, -а, cannibal; ogre. людско́й, human; servants'.

люк, -а. hatch, hatchway; trap.

лю́лька, -и, cradle.

лю́стра, -ы, chandelier.

лю́тик, -а, buttercup.

лю́тый, лют, -а́, -о, ferocious, fierce, cruel.

ля *n. indecl.* A; lah.

ляга́ть, -а́ю *imp.*, лягну́ть, -ну́, -нёшь *perf.* kick; ~ся, kick.

ля́гу, etc.: see лечь.

лягуша́тник, -а, paddling-pool. лягу́шка, -и, frog.

ля́жка, -и, thigh, haunch.

ля́згать, -аю *imp.* clank, clang; + *instr.* rattle, clatter; он ля́згал зуба́ми, his teeth were chattering.

ля́мка, -и, strap; тяну́ть ля́мку, toil, sweat, drudge.

ля́пис, -а, silver nitrate, lunar caustic.

ля́псус, -а blunder; slip (of the tongue, of the pen).

M

м *letter*: see эм.

м. *abbr.* мину́та, minute; мыс, cape.

м *abbr.* метр, metre.

мавзоле́й -я, mausoleum.

мавр, -а мавритáнка, -и, Moor. мавритáнский, Moorish; Moresque; Mauretanian.

магази́н, -а, shop; store; depot; magazine. магази́нный *adj.*; ~ вор, shoplifter.

магисте́рский, master's. маги́стр, -а, (holder of) master's degree; head of knightly or monastic order.

магистра́ль, -и, main; main line, main road.

маги́ческий, magic, magical. ма́гия, -и, magic.

ма́гний, -я, magnesium.

магни́т, -а, magnet. магни́тный magnetic. магнитофо́н, -а, tape-recorder. магнитофо́нн|ый; ~ая за́пись, tape-recording.

мада́м *f. indecl.* madam, madame; governess; dressmaker.

мадемуазе́ль, -и, mademoiselle; governess.

мадья́р, -а; *p.* -ы, -я́р, мадья́рка, -и, Magyar, Hungarian. мадья́рский, Magyar, Hungarian.

мажо́р, -а, major (key); cheerful mood,

good spirits. **мажо́рный,** major; cheerful.

ма́заный, dirty, soiled; cob, daub, clay. **ма́зать,** dirty, **ма́жу** *imp.* (*perf.* вы́~, за~, из~, на~, по~, про~) oil, grease, lubricate; smear, grease; soil, dirty; daub; miss; ~**ся,** get dirty; soil; make up. **мазо́к,** -зка́, touch, dab; smear; miss. **мазу́т,** -а, crude oil, fuel oil. **мазь,** -и, ointment; grease.

майс, -а, maize. **ма́йсов|ый;** ~**ая ка́ша,** polenta.

май, -я, May.

ма́йка, -и, (sleeveless) vest.

ма́йский, May; May-day; ~ **жук,** cock-chafer.

мак, -а (-у), poppy; poppy-seeds.

мака́ть, -а́ю *imp.* (*perf.* макну́ть) dip.

маке́т, -а, model; dummy.

макну́ть, -ну́, -нёшь, *perf.* of **мака́ть.**

ма́ковка, -и, poppy-head; crown; cupola. **ма́ковый,** poppy; poppy-seed.

максима́льный, maximum. **ма́ксимум,** -а, maximum; at most.

маку́шка, -и, top, summit; crown.

мал, etc.: see **ма́лый.**

малева́ть, -лю́ю *imp.* (*perf.* на~) paint. **мале́йший,** least, slightest. **ма́ленький,** little; small; slight; young.

мали́на, -ы, raspberries; raspberry-bush, raspberry-cane; raspberry tea. **мали́нник,** -а, raspberry-bushes. **мали́новый,** raspberry; crimson.

ма́ло *adv.* little, few; not enough; ~ кто, few (people); ~ ли что! what does it matter? ~ ли что мо́жет случи́ться, who knows what may happen? anything may happen; ~ того́, moreover; ~ того́ что .., not only .., it is not enough that ..; э́того ма́ло, this is not enough.

мало- in *comb.* (too) little, small-, low-, under-. **малова́жный,** of little importance, insignificant. **~вероя́тный,** unlikely, improbable. **~ве́сный,** light, light-weight. **~во́дье,** -я, shortage of water. **~во́льтный,** low-voltage. **~гра́мотный,** semi-literate; crude, ignorant. **~достове́рный,** improbable; not well-founded. **~ду́шие,** -я, faint-heartedness, cowardice. **~ду́шный,** faint-hearted, cowardly. **~заме́тный,**

barely visible, hardly noticeable; ordinary, undistinguished. **~земе́лье,** -я, shortage of (arable) land. **~земе́льный,** without enough (arable) land; land-hungry. **~иму́щий,** needy, indigent, poor. **~кро́вие,** -я, anaemia. **~кро́вный,** anaemic. **~ле́тний,** young; juvenile; minor, under age. **~ле́тство,** -а infancy; nonage, minority. **~лю́дный,** not crowded, unfrequented; poorly attended; thinly populated. **~ро́слый,** undersized, stunted. **~содержа́тельный,** empty, shallow. **~сро́чный,** short-term. **~употреби́тельный,** infrequent, rarely used. **~це́нный,** of little value. **~чи́сленный,** small (in number), few.

мало-ма́льски *adv.* in the slightest degree; at all. **малома́льский,** slightest, most insignificant. **мало-пома́лу** *adv.* little by little bit by bit.

ма́л|ый; мал, -а́, little, (too) small; без ~ого, almost, all but; са́мое ~ое, at the least; с ~ых лет, from childhood; *sb.* fellow, chap; lad, boy. **малы́ш,** -а́, child, kiddy; little boy. **ма́льчик,** -а, boy, lad; child; apprentice. **мальчико́вый,** boy's, boys'. **мальчи́шеский,** boyish; childish, puerile. **мальчи́шка,** -и, *m.* urchin, boy. **мальчуга́н,** -а, little boy. **малю́тка,** -и *m.* and *f.* baby, little one.

ма́ма, -ы, mother, mummy, mamma. **мама́ша,** -и, **ма́менька,** -и, mummy, mamma. **ма́менькин, ма́мин,** mother's.

ма́монт, -а, mammoth.

мандари́н, -а, mandarin, tangerine.

манда́т, -а, warrant; mandate, credentials. **манда́тн|ый,** mandate, mandated; ~**ая систе́ма голосова́ния,** card-vote system.

манёвр, -а, manoeuvre; shunting. **манёвренный,** manoeuvre, manoeuvring, manoeuvrable; shunting, switching. **маневри́ровать,** -рую *imp.* (*perf.* с~) manoeuvre; shunt; + *instr.* make good use of, use to advantage. **маневро́вый,** shunting.

мане́ж, -а, riding-school; manège. **мане́жик,** -а, play-pen.

манекéн, -а, lay figure; dummy; mannequin. манекéнщик, -а, -щица, -ы,
model, mannequin.

манéр, -а, манéра, -ы, manner, way;
style. манéрный, affected; precious.

манжéта, -ы, cuff.

маникю́рша, -и, manicurist.

манипули́ровать, -рую *imp.* manipulate. манипуля́ция, -и, manipulation;
machination, intrigue.

мани́ть, -ню́, -нишь *imp.* (*perf.* по~)
beckon; attract; lure, allure.

манифéст, -а, manifesto. манифестáнт,
-а, demonstrator. манифестáция, -и,
demonstration.   манифести́ровать,
-рую *imp.* demonstrate.

мани́шка, -и, false shirt-front, dickey.

мáния, -и, mania; passion, craze; ~
вели́чия megalomania.

манки́ровать, -рую *perf.* and *imp.* be
absent; +*instr.* neglect; +*dat.* be impolite to.

мáнный, ~ая кáша, ~ая крупá,
semolina.

манóметр, -а, pressure-gauge mano-
meter.

мáнтия, -и, cloak; mantle; robe, gown.

мануфактýра, -ы, manufacture; textiles; workshop; (textile) mill.

марáтель, -я *m.* dauber; scribbler.
марáть, -áю *imp.* (*perf.* вы́~, за~,
из~, на~) soil, stain; daub; scribble;
cross out, strike out; ~ся, get dirty;
soil one's hands.

марафóнский бег, Marathon.

мáрганец, -нца manganese.

маргари́тка, -и, daisy.

маринóванный, pickled. маринова́ть,
-ную *imp.* (*perf.* за~) pickle, marin-
ate; delay, hold up, shelve.

марионéтка, -и, puppet, marionette.
марионéточный, puppet, marionette.

мáрка, -и, stamp; mark; counter;
brand, make; trade-mark; grade, sort;
name, reputation.

мáркий, easily soiled. маркирова́ть,
-рую *perf.* and *imp.* mark.

мáрлевый, gauze. мáрля, -и, gauze;
butter muslin, cheesecloth.

мармелáд, -а, fruit jellies. мармелáдка,
-и, fruit jelly.

марморировать, -рую *perf.* and *imp.*
marble.

Марс, -а Mars. марсиáнин, -а; *pl.*
-áне, -áн. марсиáнка, -и, Martian.
марсиáнский, Martian.

март, -а, March. мáртовский, March.

мартышка, -и, marmoset; monkey.

маршировáть, -рую *imp.* march; ~ на
мéсте mark time. марширóвка, -и,
marching.

маршрýт, -а, route, itinerary. мар-
шрýтка, -и, маршрýтное такси́, fixed-
route taxi.

мáска, -и, mask. маскарáд, -а masked
ball; masquerade. маскирова́ть, -рую
imp. (*perf.* за~) mask, disguise;
camouflage. маскирóвка, -и, mask-
ing, disguise; camouflage. маскирóв-
щик, -а, camouflage expert.

мáсленица, -ы, Shrovetide; carnival.
маслёнка, -и, butter-dish; oil-can.
мáсленый, buttered; oiled, oily; unctuous; ~ая недéля, Shrove-tide. мас-
ли́на, -ы, olive. мáсло, -лю *pl.*
(*perf.* на~, по~) butter; oil, grease.
мáсло, -а; *pl.* -áсел, -слáм, butter;
oil; oil paints, oils; как по мáслу,
swimmingly. маслобóйка, -и, churn;
oil press. маслобóйный завод, масло-
бóйня, -и; *gen. pl.* -óен, маслозавóд,
-а, creamery; dairy; oil-mill. масло-
мéр, -а, oil gauge; dipstick. масляни́с-
тый, oily. мáсляный, oil; butter.

мáсса, -ы, mass; paste; pulp; a lot, lots.

масси́в, -а, massif; expanse, tract.
масси́вный, massive.

массóвка, -и, mass meeting; outing;
crowd scene. мáссовый, mass; popular; back; ~ая постáвка, bulk delivery; ~ые сцéны, crowd scenes.

мастáк, -á, expert, past master. мáстер,
-а; *pl.* -á, мастери́ца, -ы, foreman,
forewoman; master craftsman, skilled
worker; expert, master; ~ на все
рýки, Jack of all trades. мастери́ть,
-рю́ *imp.* (*perf.* с~) make, build construct. мастерскáя *sb.* workshop;
shop; studio. мастерскóй, masterly.
мастерствó, -á, trade, craft; skill,
craftsmanship.

масти́ка, -и, mastic; putty; floor-polish.

масти́тый, venerable.

масть, -и; *pl.* -и -е́й, colour; suit; ходи́ть в ~, follow suit.

масшта́б, -а, scale. **масшта́бность**, -и, (large) scale, range, dimensions.

мат, -а, checkmate, mate; объяви́ть ~, mate, checkmate.

материа́л, -а, material; stuff. **материа́льный** material; physical; financial; pecuniary, economic.

матери́к, -а́, continent; mainland; subsoil. **материко́вый**, continental.

матери́нский, maternal, motherly. **матери́нство**, -а, maternity, motherhood.

мате́рия, -и, material, cloth, stuff; matter; pus; subject, topic.

ма́тка, -и, uterus, womb; female, queen; (submarine) tender, depot ship.

ма́товый, matt; dull; suffused; ~ое стекло́, frosted glass.

матра́с, -а, matráц, -а, mattress.

ма́трица, -ы, matrix; die, mould.

матро́с, -а, sailor seaman. **матро́ска**, -и, sailor's wife; sailor's blouse, sailor blouse. **матро́сский**, sailor's, sailors', seaman's, seamen's; ~ воротни́к, sailor collar.

ма́тушка, -и, mother; priest's wife.

матч, -а, match.

мать, ма́тери, *instr.* -рью; *pl.* -тери -ре́й, mother.

мах, -а (-у), swing, stroke; дать ~у, let a chance slip, make a blunder; одни́м ~ом, at one stroke, in a trice; с ~у, rashly, without thinking. **маха́ть**, машу́ ма́шешь *imp.*, **махну́ть**, -ну́, -нёшь *perf.*+*instr.* wave; brandish; wag; flap; go travel; rush, leap jump. **махови́к**, -а́, fly-wheel. **махово́й**; ~о́е колесо́, fly-wheel; ~ые пе́рья, wing-feathers.

ма́хонький, very little, tiny.

махро́вый, double; double-dyed, dyed-in-the-wool; terry; ~ая ткань, terry towelling.

ма́чеха, -и, stepmother.

ма́чта, -ы, mast.

маши́на, -ы, machine; mechanism; engine; (motor) vehicle; car; bicycle; train. **машина́льный**, mechanical; automatic, absent-minded; machine-like. **машинизи́ровать**, -рую *perf.* and *imp.* mechanize. **машини́ст**, -а, opera-

tor; engineer; engine-driver; scene-shifter. **машини́стка**, -и, typist. **маши́нка**, -и, machine; typewriter; sewing-machine; clippers. **маши́нно-тра́кторный**; ~ая ста́нция, machine and tractor station. **маши́нный**, machine, engine; mechanical, mechanized; power-driven; ~ое бюро́ typing office, typing agency; ~ый зал, engine-room; machine-room. **маши́нописный**, typewritten; ~ текст, typescript. **маши́нопись**, -и, typewriting; typescript. **машинострое́ние**, -я, mechanical engineering, machine-building.

мая́к, -а́ lighthouse; beacon.

ма́ятник, -а, pendulum. **ма́ять**, ма́ю *imp.* wear out, exhaust, weary; ~ся, suffer, languish; loaf, loiter about.

ма́ячить, -чу *imp.* loom, loom up; appear indistinctly.

МБР (*embeér*) *abbr.* межконтинента́льная баллисти́ческая раке́та, intercontinental ballistic missile.

МБТ (*embeté*) *abbr.* Междунаро́дное бюро́ труда́, I.L.O.

МВТ (*emveté*) *abbr.* министе́рство вне́шней торго́вли, Ministry of Foreign Trade.

мг *abbr.* миллигра́мм, milligram.

мгла, -ы, haze; mist; gloom, darkness. **мгли́стый**, hazy.

мгнове́ние, -я, instant, moment. **мгнове́нный**, instantaneous, momentary.

МГУ (*emgeú*) *abbr.* Моско́вский госуда́рственный университе́т, Moscow State University.

ме́бель, -и, furniture. **ме́бельщик**, -а, upholsterer; furniture-dealer. **меблиро́ванный**, furnished. **меблирова́ть**, -рую *perf.* and *imp.* furnish. **меблиро́вка**, -и, furnishing; furniture.

мег-, мега́-, mega-, meg-. мегава́тт, -а; *gen. pl.* -атт, megawatt. ~**ге́рц**, -а, megacycle. **мего́м**, -а, megohm. ~**то́нна**, -ы, megaton.

мёд, -а (-у), *loc.* -у́; *pl.* -ы́, honey; mead.

мед- *abbr.* in *comb.* of медици́нский, of medicine, medical. **медву́з**, -а, Medical School, School of Medicine. ~**осмо́тр**, -а, medical examination.

~пу́нкт, -a, first aid post, medical station; surgery. ~сестра́, -ы́, (hospital) nurse.

медве́дица, -ы, she-bear; Bear, Ursa.

медве́дь, -я *m.* bear. медве́жий, bear bear's; bearskin; bear-like. медвежо́нок, -нка; *pl.* -жа́та, -жа́т, bear-cub.

медеплави́льный, copper-smelting.

ме́дик, -a, medical student; doctor. медикаме́нт, -a, medicine; *pl.* medical supplies. медици́на, -ы, medicine. медици́нск|ий, medical; ~ое обслу́живание, medical attendance, medical care; ~ий пункт, dressing-station, first-aid post. меди́чка, -и medical student.

ме́дленно *adv.* slowly. ме́дленный, slow. медли́тельный, sluggish; slow, tardy. ме́длить, -лю *imp.* linger; tarry; be slow.

ме́дник, -a, coppersmith; tinker. ме́дный, copper; brass, brazen; cupric, cuprous.

медо́вый honey; honeyed; ~ ме́сяц, honeymoon.

меду́за, -ы. jellyfish, medusa.

медь, -и, copper.

меж *prep.*+*instr.* between.

меж- in *comb.* inter-; between. межгалакти́ческий, intergalactic. ~контине́нта́льный, intercontinental. ~плане́тный interplanetary.

межа́, -и́; *pl.* -и, меж, -а́м, boundary; boundary-strip.

междоме́тие, -я, interjection.

ме́жду *prep.* + *instr.* between; among, amongst; ~ на́ми (говоря́), between ourselves, between you and me; ~ про́чим incidentally, by the way; ~ тем meanwhile; all the same; ~ тем как, while, whereas.

между- in *comb.*, inter-, between. междугоро́дный, inter-urban, inter-city; ~-горо́дный телефо́н, trunk-line. ~наро́дный, international.

мезони́н, -a, attic (storey); mezzanine (floor).

мел -a, *loc.* -у́, chalk; whiting; white-wash.

мёл, etc.: see мести́.

меле́ть, -е́ет *imp.* (*perf.* об~) grow shallow.

мели́ть, -лю́ *imp.* (*perf.* на~) chalk.

ме́лк|ий; -лок, -лка́, -о, small; shallow; shallow-draught; fine; petty, small-minded; ~ая таре́лка, flat plate. ме́лко *adv.* fine, small.

мелко- in *comb.* small; fine, finely; petty; shallow. мелкобуржуа́зный, petty-bourgeois. ~во́дье, -я, shallow water; shallow. ~зерни́стый, fine-grained, small-grained. ~со́бственнический, of small property holders.

мело́к, -лка́, chalk.

ме́лочность, -и, pettiness, small-mindedness, meanness. ме́лочный petty, trifling; paltry; small-minded. ме́лочь, -и; *pl.* -е́й, small items; small fry; small coin; (small) change; *pl.* minutiae; trifles, trivialities.

мель, -и, *loc.* -и́, shoal; bank; на мели́, aground; on the rocks in low water; сесть на ~, run aground.

мелька́ть, -а́ю *imp.*, мелькну́ть, -ну́, -нёшь *perf.* be glimpsed fleetingly; flash, gleam (for a moment). ме́льком *adv.* in passing; for a moment.

ме́льник, -a, miller. ме́льница, -ы, mill. ме́льничный, mill; ~ лото́к, mill-race.

мельча́йший *superl.* of ме́лкий. мельча́ть, -а́ю *imp.* (*perf.* из~) grow shallow; become small(er); become petty. ме́льче *comp.* of ме́лкий, ме́лко. мельчи́ть, -чу́ *imp.* (*perf.* из~, раз~) crush, crumble; pulverize; grind mill; reduce size or significance of. мелюзга́, -и́, small fry.

мелю́ etc.: see моло́ть.

мембра́на, -ы, membrane; diaphragm.

ме́на, -ы, exchange, barter.

менаже́р, -a, ме́неджер, -a, manager. менажи́ровать, -рую *imp.* manage, be manager of.

ме́нее *adv.* less; ~ всего́, least of all; тем не ~, none the less, all the same.

мензу́рка, -и, measuring-glass; graduated measure.

меново́й, exchange barter.

ме́ньше, smaller; less. ме́ньш|ий, lesser, smaller; younger; по ~ей ме́ре, at least; са́мое ~ee, at the least. меньшинство́. -a. minority.

меня́: see я *pron.*

меня́ть, -я́ю *imp.* (*perf.* об~, по~) change; exchange; ~ся, change; +*instr.* exchange.

ме́ра, -ы measure; в ме́ру, fairly, moderately; в ме́ру+*gen.* to the extent of; по ме́ре возмо́жности, as far as possible; по ме́ре того́, как, as (in proportion) as; не в ме́ру, сверх ме́ры, чрез ме́ру, excessively, immoderately.

мере́жка, -и, hem-stitching, open-work.

мере́щиться, -щусь *imp.* (*perf.* по~) seem, appear; appear dimly, glimmer.

мерза́вец, -вца, blackguard, scoundrel. ме́рзкий, -зок, -зка́, -о, disgusting, loathsome; abominable foul.

мерзлота́, -ы́; ве́чная ~, permafrost. мёрзлый, frozen, congealed. мёрзнуть, -ну; мёрз *imp.* (*perf.* за~) freeze.

ме́рзость, -и, vileness, loathsomeness; loathsome thing, nasty thing; abomination.

мери́ло, -а, standard, criterion. мери́льный, measuring.

ме́рить, -рю *imp.* (*perf.* по~, с~) measure; try on; ~ся+*instr.* measure. ме́рка, -и, measure.

ме́ркнуть, -нет; ме́рк(нул) *imp.* (*perf.* по~) grow dark, grow dim; fade.

ме́рный, measured; rhythmical; measuring. мероприя́тие, -я, measure.

мёртвенный, deathly, ghastly. мертве́ть, -е́ю *imp.* (*perf.* о~, по~) grow numb; mortify; be benumbed. мертве́ц, -а́, corpse, dead man. мертве́цкая *sb.* mortuary, morgue. мёртв|ый; мёртв, -а́, мёртво́, dead; ~ая зыбь, swell; ~ая пе́тля, loop; noose; спать ~ым сном, sleep like the dead.

мерца́ть, -а́ет *imp.* twinkle; shimmer, glimmer; flicker.

ме́сиво, -а, mash; medley; jumble. меси́ть, мешу́, ме́сишь *imp.* (*perf.* с~) knead.

места́ми *adv.* here and there, in places. месте́чко, -а; *p².* -и -чек, small town.

мести́, мету́, -тёшь; мёл -а́ *imp.* sweep; whirl; метёт, there is a snow-storm.

местко́м, -а *abbr.* local (trade-union) committee. ме́стность, -и, locality,

district; area; ground, country, terrain. ме́стный, local; localized; locative. -ме́стный in *comb.* -berth, -seater, -place. ме́сто, -а; *pl.* -а́, place; site; seat; berth; space, room; post, situation, job; passage; piece of luggage; *pl.* the provinces, the country; без ме́ста, out of work; име́ть ~, take place; ~ де́йствия, scene (of action); на ме́сте преступле́ния, in the act, red-handed; не к ме́сту, out of place; ни с ме́ста! don't move! stay where you are! местожи́тельство, -а, (place of) residence; без определённого местожи́тельства of no fixed abode. местоиме́ние, -я, pronoun. местоиме́нный, pronominal. местонахожде́ние, -я, location, whereabouts. местопребыва́ние, -я, abode, residence. месторожде́ние, -я birthplace; deposit, bed; layer; ~ угля́, coal-field.

месть, -и, vengeance, revenge.

ме́сяц, -а, month; moon. ме́сячный, monthly.

мета́лл, -а, metal. металли́ст, -а, metal-worker. метали́ческий, metal, metallic. металло́м, -а, scrap (-metal).

мета́ние, -я, throwing, casting, flinging; ~ копья́, throwing the javelin. мета́тель, -я *m.* thrower. мета́ть[1], мечу́, ме́чешь *imp.* (*perf.* метну́ть) throw, cast, fling; ~ банк, keep the bank; ~ икру́, spawn; ~ся, rush about; toss (and turn).

мета́ть[2], -а́ю *imp.* (*perf.* на~, с~) tack, baste.

мете́лка, -и, whisk; panicle.

мете́ль, -и, snow-storm; blizzard.

метео- *abbr.* in *comb.* of метеорологи́ческий, meteorological; weather-. метеосво́дка, -и, weather report. ~слу́жба, -ы, weather service. ~ста́нция, weather-station. ~усло́вия, weather conditions.

метеорологи́ческ|ий, meteorological; ~ая сво́дка, weather report.

ме́тить[1], ме́чу *imp.* (*perf.* на~, по~) mark.

ме́тить[2], ме́чу *imp.* (*perf.* на~, по~) aim; +в+*acc. pl.* aim at, aspire to; + в or на+*acc.* drive at, mean.

ме́тка, -и, marking, mark.

ме́ткий; -ток, -тка́, -о, well-aimed, accurate. **ме́ткость**, -и, marksmanship; accuracy; neatness, pointedness

метла́, -ы́; pl. **мётлы**, -тел, broom.

метну́ть, -ну́, -нёшь perf. of мета́ть[1].

ме́тод, -а. method. **мето́дика**, -и, method(s), system; principles. **мето́дология**. **методи́ческий**, methodical, systematic. **методи́чный**, methodical, orderly.

метр, -а. metre. **метра́ж**, -а, metric area; length in me res.

ме́трика, -и, birth-certificate. **метри́ческий**[1]; ~ая кни́га, register of births deaths and marriages; ~ое свиде́тельство, birth-certificate.

метри́ческий[2], metric; metrical.

метро́ n. indecl. Metro; underground; на ~, by Metro, by underground.

мету́, etc.: see мести́.

ме́тче comp. of ме́ткий.

мех[1], -а, loc. -у́; pl. -а́, fur; на ~у́, fur-lined.

мех[2], -а; pl. -и́, wine-skin, water-skin; pl. bellows.

механиза́ция, -и, mechanization. **механи́зм**, -а, mechanism; gear. gearing; pl. machinery. **меха́ник**, -а, mechanic. **меха́ника**, -и, mechanics; trick; knack. **механи́ческий**, mechanical; power-driven; of mechanics; mechanistic; ~ моме́нт, momentum; ~ цех, machine shop. **механи́чный**, mechanical, automatic.

мехово́й, fur. **меховщи́к**, -а́, furrier.

меч, -а́, sword.

ме́ченый, marked; labelled; tagged; ~ а́том, tracer atom; tracer element.

мече́ть, -и, mosque.

мечта́, -ы́, dream, day-dream. **мечта́тельный**, dreamy. **мечта́ть**, -а́ю imp. dream.

мечу́, etc.: see ме́тить. **мечу́**, etc.: see мета́ть.

меша́лка, -и, mixer, stirrer.

меша́ть[1], -а́ю imp. (perf. по~)+dat. hinder, impede, hamper; prevent; disturb; не меша́ло бы +inf.. it would be advisable to, it would not be a bad thing to.

меша́ть[2], -а́ю imp. (perf. по~, с~),

stir; agitate; mix, blend, confuse, mix up; ~ся (в+acc.) interfere (in), meddle (with).

ме́шкать, -аю imp. linger, delay; loiter.

мешкова́тый, baggy; awkward, clumsy. **мешкови́на**, -ы, sacking, hessian. **мешо́к**, -шка́, bag; sack; clumsy fellow.

меща́нин, -а; pl. -а́не, -а́н, petty bourgeois; Philistine. **меща́нский**, lower--middle-class; bourgeois, vulgar, narrow-minded; Philistine. **меща́нство**, -а, petty bourgeoisie, lower middle class; philistinism, vulgarity, narrow-mindedness.

ми, n. indecl. E; me.

миг. -а. moment, instant.

мига́ть, -а́ю imp., **мигну́ть**, -ну́, -нёшь perf. blink; wink, twinkle; +dat. wink at.

ми́гом adv. in a flash; in a jiffy.

МИД, мид, -а abbr. Министе́рство иностра́нных дел. Ministry for Foreign Affairs, Foreign Office, State Department.

мизе́рный, scanty, wretched.

мизи́нец, -нца, little finger; little toe.

микро- micro-; small. **микроавто́бус**, -а, minibus. ~**ампе́р**, -а, microampere. ~**органи́зм**, -а, micro-organism. ~**ско́п**, -а, microscope. ~**скопи́ческий**, ~**скопи́чный**, microscopic. ~**фо́н**, -а, microphone.

микро́н, -а, micron.

микстура, -ы, medicine, mixture.

ми́ленький, pretty; nice; sweet; dear, darling.

милиционе́р, -а, militiaman, policeman. **мили́ция**, -и, militia, police force.

миллиа́рд, -а, milliard, a thousand millions. **миллиарде́р**, -а, multi-millionaire. **миллио́н**, -а, million. **миллионе́р**, -а, millionaire. **миллио́нный**, millionth; worth, numbered in, millions.

милосе́рдие, -я, mercy, charity; сестра́ милосе́рдия, (hospital) nurse. **милосе́рдный**, merciful, charitable.

ми́лостивый, gracious, kind; ~ый госуда́рь, sir; (Dear) Sir; ~ая госуда́рыня, madam; (Dear) Madam. **ми́лостыня**, -и, alms. **ми́лость**, -и, favour, grace; mercy; charity; ва́ша

~, your worship; ми́лости про́сим! welcome!; you are always welcome; come and see us. ми́лочка, -и, dear, darling. ми́лый; мил, -а́, -о; nice; kind; sweet, lovable; dear, darling.

ми́ля, -и, mile.

ми́мика, -и, (facial) expression; miming. ми́мо adv. and prep.+gen. by, past. мимое́здом adv. in passing. мимолёт-ный, fleeting, transient. мимохо́дом adv. in passing.

мин. abbr. мину́та, minute.

ми́на¹, -ы; mine; bomb; rocket.

ми́на², -ы; expression; face, countenance.

миндалеви́дн|ый, almond-shaped. минда́лина, -ы, almond; tonsil. минда́ль, -я m. almond(-tree); almonds. минда́льн|ый, almond; ~ое пече́нье, macaroon.

минера́л, -а, mineral. минерало́гия, -и, mineralogy. минера́льный, mineral.

минима́льный, minimum. ми́нимум, -а, minimum; at the least.

министе́рский, ministerial. министе́рство, -а, ministry. мини́стр, -а, minister.

минова́ть, -ну́ю perf. and imp. pass, pass by, pass over; be over, be past; impers.+dat escape, avoid; тебе́ э́того не ~, you can't escape it.

миномёт, -а, mortar. миноно́сец, -сца, torpedo-boat.

мино́р, -а, minor (key); blues.

ми́нувш|ий, past; ~ее sb. the past.

ми́нус, -а, minus; defect, shortcoming. ми́нусовый, negative.

мину́та, minute. мину́тный, minute; momentary; transient, ephemeral, brief.

мину́ть, -нешь; ми́ну́л perf. pass; pass by; be over, be past; past; ему́ ми́нуло два́дцать лет, he is turned twenty.

мир¹, -а; pl. -ы́, world; universe; mir, village community.

мир², -а, peace. мири́ть, -рю́ imp. (perf. по~, при~) reconcile; ~ся, be reconciled, make it up; reconcile oneself (с + instr. to). ми́рный, peaceful; peaceable.

мировоззре́ние, -я, (world-)outlook;

philosophy. миров|о́й, world; ~а́я держа́ва, world power.

миролюби́вость, -и, peaceable disposition. миролюби́вый, peace-loving, peaceful.

ми́ска, -и, basin bowl, tureen.

ми́ссия, -и, mission; legation.

мисте́рия, -и, mystery(-play).

ми́стика, -и, mysticism.

мистифика́тор, -а, hoaxer. мистифика́ция, -и, hoax, leg-pull.

мисти́ческий, mystic, mystical.

ми́тинг, -а, mass meeting. митингова́ть, -гу́ю imp. hold a mass meeting; discuss endlessly.

миф, -а, myth. мифи́ческий, mythical. мифологи́ческий, mythological. мифоло́гия, -и, mythology.

мише́нь, -и, target.

ми́шка, -и, bear; Teddy bear.

мишура́, -ы́, tinsel; tawdriness, show. мишу́рный, tinsel; trumpery, tawdry.

МК (emka) abbr. ме́стный комите́т, local committee, mestkom.

мл. abbr. мла́дший, junior.

млд. abbr. миллиа́рд, milliard.

млн. abbr. миллио́н, million.

младе́нец, -нца, baby; infant. младе́нческий, infantile. младе́нчество, -а, infancy, babyhood. мла́дший, younger; youngest; junior; ~ кома́ндный соста́в, non-commissioned officers; ~ офице́рский соста́в, junior officers.

млекопита́ющие sb. pl. mammals. мле́чный, milk; lactic; ~ Путь, Milky Way, Galaxy.

мм abbr. миллиме́тр, millimetre.

мне: see я pron.

мне́ние, -я opinion; по моему́ мне́нию in my opinion.

мни́мый, imaginary; sham, pretended. мни́тельный, hypochondriac; mistrustful, suspicious. мнить, мню imp. think, imagine; мно́го мнить о себе́, think much of oneself.

мно́г|ий; much; many; ~ие sb. many (people); ~ое sb. much, a great deal, many things; во мно́гом, in many respects. мно́го adv. + gen. much; many; a great deal; a lot of; ~ лу́чше, much better; на ~ by far; ни ~ ни ма́ло, neither more nor less (than), no less (than).

мно́го- in *comb.* many-, poly-, multi-, multiple-. **многобо́жие**, -я, polytheism. **~бо́рец**, -рца, competitor in combined event; all-rounder. **~бо́рье**, -я, combined event, combined competition. **~бра́чие**, -я, polygamy. **~веково́й**, centuries-old. **~во́дный**, full, in spate; well-watered, abounding in water. **~гра́нник**, -а, polyhedron. **~гра́нный**, polyhedral; many-sided. **~де́тный**, having many children. **~же́нец**, -нца, polygamist. **~же́нство**, -а, polygamy. **~значи́тельный**, significant. **~зна́чный**, multi-digit; polysemantic. **~каска́дный**, multi-stage. **~кра́тный**, repeated, reiterated; multiple; frequentative, iterative. **~ле́тний**, lasting, living, many years'; of many years' standing; perennial. **~ле́тник**, -а, perennial. **~лю́дный**, populous; crowded. **~му́жие**, -я, polyandry. **~национа́льный**, multi-national. **~обеща́ющий**, promising, hopeful; significant. **~обра́зие**, -я, variety, diversity. **~обра́зный**, varied, diverse. **~семе́йный**, having a large family. **~сло́вный**, verbose, prolix. **~сло́жный**, complex, complicated; polysyllabic. **~сло́йный**, multi-layer; multi-ply; **~сло́йная фане́ра**, plywood. **~сторо́нний**, polygonal; multi-lateral; many-sided, versatile. **~ступе́нчатый**, multistage. **~тира́жка**, -и, factory newspaper; house organ. **~то́мный**, in many volumes. **~то́чие**, -я, dots, omission points. **~уважа́емый**, respected; Dear. **~уго́льник**, -а, polygon. **~уго́льный**, polygonal. **~цве́тный**, many-coloured, multi-coloured; polychromatic; multiflorous, floribunda. **~чи́сленный**, numerous. **~чле́н**, -а, polynomial. **~эта́жный**, multi-storey, many-storeyed. **~язы́чный**, polyglot; multi-lingual.

мно́жественный, plural. **мно́жество**, -а, great number; value; set; aggregate; great quantities; multitude. **мно́жимое** *sb.* multiplicand. **мно́житель**, -я, *m.* multiplier; factor. **мно́жить**, -жу imp. (*perf.* по-, у-) multiply; increase, augment; **~ся**, multiply, increase.

мной, etc.: see я *pron.* мог, etc.: see мочь. мну, etc.: see мять.

моги́ла, -ы, grave. моги́льник, -а, burial ground, cemetery. моги́льный grave; of the grave; sepulchral; **~ая плита́**, tombstone, gravestone, headstone. моги́льщик, -а, grave-digger.

могу́, etc.: see мочь. могу́чий, mighty, powerful. могу́щественный, powerful. могу́щество, -а, power, might.

мо́да, -ы, fashion, vogue.

модели́ровать, -рую *perf.* and *imp.* design. моде́ль, -и, model; pattern. модельер, -а, dress-designer. моде́льный, model; fashionable.

моди́стка, -и, milliner; modiste. мо́дный; -ден, -дна́, -о, fashionable, stylish; fashion.

мо́жет: see мочь.

можжеве́льник, -а, juniper.

мо́жно, one may, one can; it is permissible; it is possible; как **~+comp.** as .. as possible; как **~ лу́чше**, as well as possible, to the best of one's abilities; как **~ скоре́е**, as soon as possible.

мозг, -а (-у), *loc.* -ý; *pl.* -и́, brain; marrow; **шевели́ть ~а́ми**, use one's head. мозгови́тый, brainy. мозгово́й, cerebral; brain.

мозо́листый, calloused; horny. мозо́ль, -и, corn; callus, callosity.

мой, моего́ *m.*, моя́, мое́й *f.*, моё, моего́ *n.*, мои́, -и́х *pl. pron.* my; mine; по-мо́ему, in my opinion, I think; in my way, as I think right.

МОК, -а *abbr.* Междунаро́дный олимпи́йский комите́т, International Olympics Committee.

мо́кнуть, -ну; мок *imp.* get wet, get soaked; soak. мокрова́тый, moist, damp. мокрота́[1], -ы, phlegm. мокрота́[2], -ы́, humidity, damp. мо́крый, wet, damp; soggy.

мол, -а, *loc.* -ý, mole, pier.

молва́, -ы́, rumour, talk. мо́лвить, -влю *perf.* and *imp.* utter; say.

моле́ние, -я, prayer; entreaty, supplication. моли́тва, -ы, prayer. моли́ть, -лю́, -лишь *imp.* pray; entreat, supplicate, beg (o+*prep.* for); **~ся** (*perf.* по~ся) pray, offer prayers; say one's prayers; +на+*acc.* idolize.

мо́лкнуть, -ну; молк imp. fall silent.

молниено́сн|ый, lightning; ~ая война́, blitzkrieg. **молниеотво́д**, -а, lightning-conductor. **мо́лния**, -и, lightning; zip (-fastener); (телегра́мма)~, express telegram.

молодёжь, -и, youth, young people; the younger generation. **молоде́ть**, -е́ю imp. (perf. по~), get younger, look younger. **молоде́ц**, -дца́ fine fellow; brick; ~! well done! good man!; вести́ себя́ молодцо́м, put up a good show. **молоде́цкий**, dashing, spirited. **молодня́к**, -а́, saplings; young animals; youth, young people. **молодо́|й**; мо́лод, -а́, -о, young, youthful; ~о́й карто́фель, new potatoes; ~о́й ме́сяц, new moon; ~о́й sb. bridegroom; ~а́я sb. bride; ~ы́е sb. pl. young couple, newly-weds. **мо́лодость**, -и, youth; youthfulness. **моложа́вый**, young-looking; име́ть ~ вид, look young for one's age. **моло́же** comp. of молодо́й.

молоко́, -а́, milk. **молокосо́с**, -а, greenhorn, raw youth.

мо́лот, -а, hammer. **молоти́лка**, -и, threshing-machine. **молоти́ть**, -очу́, -о́тишь imp. (perf. с~), thresh; hammer. **молото́к**, -тка́, hammer.

мо́лотый, ground. **моло́ть**, мелю́, ме́лешь imp. (perf. с~), grind, mill; ~ вздор, talk nonsense, talk rot.

молотьба́, -ы́, threshing. **моло́ченный**, threshed.

моло́чник, -а, milk-jug, milk-can; milkman. **моло́чница**, -ы, milkwoman, milk-seller. **моло́чн|ый**, milk; dairy; milky; lactic; ~ый брат, foster-brother; ~ое стекло́, frosted glass, opal glass; ~ое хозя́йство, dairy-farm(ing); ~ая sb. dairy; creamery.

мо́лча adv. silently, in silence. **молчали́вый**, silent, taciturn; tacit, unspoken. **молча́ние**, -я, silence. **молча́ть**, -чу́ imp. be silent, keep silence.

моль, -и, (clothes-)moth.

мольба́, -ы́, entreaty, supplication.

мольбе́рт, -а, easel.

моме́нт, -а, moment; instant; feature; element, factor. **момента́льно** adv. in a moment, instantly. **момента́льный**,

instantaneous; ~ сни́мок, snap(shot). **моме́нтами** adv. now and then.

монасты́рь, -я́ m. monastery; convent. **мона́х**, -а, monk; friar. **мона́хиня**, -и, nun. **мона́шеский**, monastic; monkish.

моне́та, -ы, coin; приня́ть за чи́стую моне́ту, take at face value, take in good faith. **моне́тный**, monetary; ~ двор, mint.

моноли́т, -а, monolith. **моноли́тность**, -и, monolithic character; solidity. **моноли́тный**, monolithic; massive, united.

моното́нный, monotonous.

монта́ж, -а́, assembling, mounting, installation; montage; editing, cutting; arrangement. **монта́жник**, -а rigger, erector, fitter. **монтёр**, -а, fitter, maintenance man, mechanic. **монти́ровать**, -рую imp. (perf. с~) mount; install, fit; erect; edit, cut.

мор, -а, pestilence, plague.

мора́ль, -и, moral; morals, ethics. **мора́льн|ый**, moral; ethical; ~ое состоя́ние, morale.

морга́ть, -а́ю imp., **моргну́ть**, -ну́, -нёшь perf. blink; wink.

мо́рда, -ы, snout, muzzle; face, (ugly) mug.

мо́ре, -я; pl. -я́, -е́й, sea; в откры́том мо́ре, on the open sea; за́ морем, oversea(s).

море́на, -ы, moraine.

морепла́вание, -я, navigation; voyaging. **морепла́ватель**, -я m. navigator, seafarer. **морепла́вательный**, nautical, navigational. **морехо́д**, -а, seafarer.

морж, -а́, моржи́ха, -и, walrus; all-the-year-round swimmer. **моржо́вый**, walrus, walrus-hide.

Мо́рзе, Morse; а́збука ~, Morse code. **морзя́нка**, -и, Morse code.

мори́ть, -рю́ imp. (perf. по~, у~), exterminate; exhaust, wear out; ~ го́лодом, starve.

морко́вка, -и, carrot. **морко́вный**, carrot; carroty. **морко́вь**, -и, carrots.

моро́женое sb. ice-cream, ice. **моро́женый**, frozen, chilled. **моро́з**, -а, frost; pl. intensely cold weather. **моро́зить**, -о́жу, freeze. **моро́зный**, frost, frosty. **морозоусто́йчивый**, frost-resistant, hardy.

моросить, -ит *imp.* drizzle.

морс, -а, fruit-juice, fruit syrup; fruit drink.

морск|ой, sea; maritime; marine, nautical; shipping; naval; ~ой волк, old salt; ~ая звезда, starfish; ~ой конёк, sea-horse; ~ая пенка, meerschaum; ~ая пехота, marines; ~ой разбойник, pirate; ~ая свинья, porpoise; ~ой флот navy, fleet.

морфология, -и, morphology; accidence.

морщин|а, -ы, wrinkle; crease. **морщинистый**, wrinkled, lined; creased. **морщить**[1], -щу *imp.* (*perf.* на~, по~, с~) wrinkle; pucker; ~ лоб, knit one's brow; ~ся, make a wry face; knit one's brow; wince; crease, wrinkle. **морщить**[2], -ит *imp.* crease; ruck up.

моряк, -а sailor seaman.

московск|ий, Moscow of Moscow.

мост, моста (-у), *loc.* -у; *pl.* -ы, bridge. **мостик**, -а, bridge. **мостить**, -ощу *imp.* (*perf.* вы~, за~, на~) pave; lay. **мостки**, -ов *pl.* planked footway, board-walk; wooden platform. **мостовая** *sb.* roadway; pavement. **мостовой**, bridge.

мотальный, winding. **мотать**[1], -аю *imp.* (*perf.* мотнуть, на~) wind, reel; shake.

мотать[2], -аю *imp.* (*perf.* про~) squander.

мотаться, -аюсь *imp.* dangle; wander; rush about; ~ по свету, knock about the world.

мотив, -а, a motive; reason; tune; motif. **мотивировать**, -рую *perf. and imp.* give reasons for, justify. **мотивировка**, -и reason(s); motivation; justification.

мотнуть, -ну, -нёшь *perf.* of мотать.

мото- in *comb.*, motor-, engine-; motor-cycle; motorized. **мотогонки**, -нок *pl.* motor-cycle races. **~дрезина**, -ы, (rail) motor-trolley. **~дром**, -а, motor-cycle race-track. **~кросс**, -а, motor-cross. **~пед**, -а, moped. **~пехота**, -ы, motorized infantry. **~роллер**, -а, (motor-)scooter. **~цикл**, -а, **~циклет**, -а, motor-cycle.

мотовской, wasteful, extravagant. **мотовство**, -а, wastefulness, extravagance, prodigality.

моток, -тка, skein, hank.

мотор, -а, motor, engine. **моторист**, -а, motor-mechanic. **моторка**, -и, motor-boat. **моторный**, motor; engine.

мотыга, -и hoe, mattock. **мотыжить**, -жу *imp.* hoe.

мотылёк, -лька, butterfly, moth.

мох, мха or моха, *loc.* мху; *pl.* мхи, мхов, moss. **мохнат|ый**, hairy, shaggy; ~ое полотенце, Turkish towel.

моцион, -а, exercise.

моча, -и, urine; water.

мочалка, -и, wisp of bast. **мочало**, -а, bast bass.

мочевина, -ы, urea. **мочевой**, urinary; uric; ~ пузырь bladder. **моченный**, wetted; steeped; soused. **мочёный**, soaked, steeped. **мочить**, -чу, -чишь *imp.* (*perf.* за~, на~), wet, moisten; soak; steep, macerate; ~ся (*perf.* по~ся) urinate, make water.

мочь, могу, можешь; мог, -ла *imp.* (*perf.* с~), be able; может (быть), perhaps, maybe; не могу знать, I don't know. **мочь**, -и, power, might; во всю ~, изо всей мочи, что есть мочи, with all one's might, with might and main.

мошенник, -а, rogue, scoundrel; swindler. **мошенничать**, -аю *imp.* (*perf.* с~) play the rogue, cheat, swindle. **мошеннический**, rascally, swindling.

мошка, -и, midge. **мошкара**, -ы, (swarm of) midges.

мощёный, paved.

мощность, -и, power; capacity, rating; output. **мощный**; -щен, -щна, -о, powerful; vigorous.

мощу, etc.: see мостить.

мощь, -и, power, might.

мою, etc.: see мыть. **моющий**, washing; detergent.

мрак, -а, darkness, gloom. **мракобес**, -а, obscurantist. **мракобесие**, -я, obscurantism.

мрамор, -а, marble; marbled; marmoreal.

мрачнеть, -ею *imp.* (*perf.* по~), grow

dark; grow gloomy. мра́чный, dark, sombre; gloomy, dismal.

мсти́тель -я m. avenger. мсти́тельный, vindictive. мстить, мщу imp. (perf. ото~) take vengeance on, revenge oneself; +acc. avenge.

МТС (emteés) abbr. машинно-тра́кторная ста́нция, agricultural-machinery pool.

мудрёный, -рён -á, strange queer odd; difficult, abstruse, complicated; не мудрено́ что, no wonder (that). мудре́ц, -á, sage, wise man. мудри́ть -рю́ imp. (perf. на~, с~) subtilize, complicate matters unnecessarily. му́дрость, -и, wisdom. му́дрый; -др, -á, -о, wise, sage.

муж, -á; pl. -жья́ or -и́, husband; man. мужа́ть, -а́ю imp. grow up; mature; ripen; grow strong; ~ся, take heart, take courage. мужеподо́бный, mannish; masculine. му́жеский, male; masculine. му́жественный, manly, steadfast. му́жество, -а, courage, fortitude.

мужи́к, -á, moujik, muzhik; peasant; man, fellow.

мужск|о́й, masculine; male; ~о́й род, masculine gender; ~а́я шко́ла, boys' school. мужчи́на, -ы, man.

музе́й -я, museum.

му́зыка, -и, music; instrumental music; band; business, affair. музыка́льность, -и, melodiousness; musical talent. музыка́льный, musical. музыка́нт, -а, musician.

му́ка¹, -и, torment; torture; suffering; pangs, throes.

мука́², -и́, meal; flour. мукомо́л, -а, miller.

мультиплика́тор, -а, multiplier; multiplying camera; animator, animated-cartoon artist. мультипликацио́нный, cartoon, animated-cartoon. мультиплика́ция, -и, мультфи́льм, -а, cartoon film.

мунди́р, -а (full-dress) uniform; карто́фель в ~е, baked potatoes, jacket-potatoes.

мундшту́к, -á, mouthpiece; cigarette-holder, cigar-holder; curb.

МУР, -а abbr. Моско́вский уголо́вный ро́зыск, Moscow C.I.D.

муравей́, -вья́, ant. муравей́ник, -а, ant-hill; ant-bear. мура́шка, -и, small ant; мура́шки по спине́ бе́гают, it sends a shiver down one's spine.

мурлы́кать, -ы́чу -ы́каю imp. purr; hum.

муска́т, -а, nutmeg; muscat, muscatel. муска́тный; ~ оре́х, nutmeg; ~ цвет, mace.

му́скул. -а, muscle. му́скулистый, muscular, sinewy, brawny. му́скульный, muscular.

му́сор, -а, refuse; sweepings; dust; rubbish; garbage; debris. му́сорн|ый; ~ая пово́зка, dust-cart; ~ая сва́лка rubbish heap; ~ый я́щик, dustbin. мусоропрово́д, -а, refuse chute.

муссо́н, -а, monsoon.

мути́ть, мучу́, му́ти́шь imp. (perf. вз~, за~, по~) trouble, make muddy; stir up, upset; dull, make dull; ~ся, grow turbid, muddy, dull; dim. мутне́ть, -е́ет imp. (perf. по~) grow or become turbid, muddy, dull. му́тность, -и, turbidity; dullness. му́тный; -тен, -тна́, -о, turbid, troubled; dull, dulled, lack-lustre; confused.

му́фта, -ы, muff; sleeve, coupling, clutch; ~ сцепле́ния, clutch.

му́ха, -и, fly. мухомо́р, -а, fly-agaric, toadstool.

муче́ние, -я, torment, torture; mealy. му́ченик, -а, му́ченица, -ы, martyr. му́читель, -я m. torturer; tormentor. му́чить, -чу imp. (perf. за~, из~) torment; worry, harass; ~ся, torment oneself; worry, feel unhappy; suffer agonies; ~ся от бо́ли, be racked with pain.

мучни́стый, farinaceous, starchy; mealy, floury. мучно́й, flour, meal; farinaceous, starchy; ~о́е sb. starchy foods.

мха, etc.: see мох.

МХАТ. -а, МХТ (emkhaté) abbr. Моско́вский худо́жественный (академи́ческий) теа́тр, Moscow Arts Theatre.

мчать, мчу imp. rush along, whirl along: ~ся, rush, race, tear along.

мши́стый, mossy.

мщу, etc.: see мстить.

мы, мы́сли, нас. на́ми, нас pron. we; мы с ва́ми, мы с тобо́й, you and I.

мы́лить, -лю imp. (perf. на~) soap,

lather; **~ся**, soap oneself; lather, make a lather. **мы́лкий**, lathering easily; soapy. **мы́ло**, -а; *pl.* -а́, soap; foam, lather. **мылова́рение**, -я, soap-boiling, soap-making. **мылова́ренный**, soap-making; **~ заво́д**, soap works. **мы́льница**, -ы, soap-dish; soap-box. **мы́льн|ый**, soap, soapy; **~ ка́мень**, soapstone; **~ые хло́пья**, soap-flakes.

мыс, -а cape, promontory.

мы́сленный, mental. **мысли́мый**, conceivable, thinkable. **мысли́тель** -я *m.* thinker. **мысли́тельный**, intellectual; thought, of thought. **мы́слить**, -лю *imp.* think; reason; conceive. **мысль**, -и, thought; idea. **мы́слящий**, thinking.

мыть, мо́ю *imp.* (*perf.* вы́~, по~) wash; **~ся**, wash (oneself); **~ся в ва́нне**, have a bath; **~ся под ду́шем**, take a shower.

мыча́ть, -чу́ *imp.* (*perf.* про~) low, moo; bellow; mumble.

мышело́вка, -и, mousetrap.

мы́шечный, muscular.

мышле́ние, -я, thinking, thought.

мы́шца, -ы, muscle.

мышь, -и; *gen. pl.* -е́й, mouse. **мышья́к**, -á (-у́), arsenic.

мя́гк|ий; -гок, -гка́, -о, soft; mild; gentle; **~ий ваго́н**, 'soft-class' carriage, sleeping-car; sleeper; **~ий знак**, soft sign, the letter ь; **~ое кре́сло**, easy-chair; **~ий хлеб**, new bread. **мя́гко** *adv.* softly; mildly; gently. **мя́гче**, *comp.* of мя́гкий. **мягко́.** **мя́киш**, -а, soft part (of loaf), crumb. **мя́кнуть**, -нет; мяк *imp.* (*perf.* раз~) soften, become soft. **мя́коть**, -и, fleshy part, flesh; pulp.

мя́млить, -лю *imp.* (*perf.* про~), mumble; vacillate; procrastinate.

мяси́стый, fleshy; meaty; pulpy. **мясни́к**, -á, butcher. **мясно́й**, meat; **~ые консе́рвы**, tinned meat; **~а́я** *sb.* butcher's (shop). **мя́со**, -а, flesh; meat; beef. **мясору́бка**, -и, mincer.

мя́та, -ы, mint; peppermint.

мятёж, -á, mutiny, revolt. **мяте́жник**, -а, mutineer, rebel. **мяте́жный**, rebellious, mutinous; restless; stormy.

мя́тный, mint, peppermint.

мя́тый, crushed; rumpled, crumpled; **~ пар**, exhaust steam. **мять**, мну, мнёшь *imp.* (*perf.* из~, раз~, с~) work up; knead; crumple, rumple; **~ся**, become crumpled; get creased; get crushed; crush (easily); hesitate; vacillate, hum and haw.

мяу́кать, -аю *imp.* mew, miaow.

мяч, -á, **мя́чик**, -а, ball.

Н

н *letter:* see эн.

на *prep.* I. +*acc.* on; on to, to, into; at; till, until; for; by; ко́мната на двои́х, a room for two; коро́че на дюйм, shorter by an inch, an inch shorter; на беду́, unfortunately; на вес, by weight; на друго́й день, (the) next day; на́ зиму, for the winter; на Но́вый год, on New Year's Day; на рубль ма́рок, a rouble's worth of stamps; на се́вер от, (to the) north of; на со́лнце, in the sun; на чёрный день, for a rainy day; на что э́то вам ну́жно? what do you want it for? на э́тот раз, this time, for this once; отложи́ть на за́втра, put off till tomorrow; перевести́ на, translate into; сесть на, get on, get in, go on board. II. +*prep.* on, upon; in; at; жа́рить на ма́сле, fry (in butter); игра́ть на рояле, play the piano; на ва́те, padded; на дворе́, на у́лице, out of doors; на его́ па́мяти, within his recollection; на кани́кулах, during the holidays, in the holidays; на конце́рте, at a concert; на лету́, in flight; на лю́дях, in public; на мои́х глаза́х, in my presence; на́ мо́ре, at sea; на рабо́те, at work; на э́тих дня́х, one of these days; на э́той неде́ле, this week; рабо́тать на не́фти, run on oil.

на *part.* here; here you are; here, take it.

на- *pref.* I. of *vbs.*, forms the perfective aspect; indicates direction on to, action applied to a surface, or to a certain quantity or number, or continued to sufficiency, excess, or the point of satisfaction or exhaustion. II. of *sbs.* and *adjs.* on. III. of *advs.* extremely, very.

наб. *abbr.* на́бережная, embankment, quay.

наба́вить, -влю *perf.*, **набавля́ть**, -я́ю *imp.* add; add to, increase, raise. **наба́вка**, -и, adding, addition, increase, rise. **наба́вочный**, extra, additional.

набалда́шник, -а, knob.

на|бальзами́ровать, -рую *perf.*

наба́т, -а, alarm, alarm-bell; бить в ~, sound the alarm, raise an alarm.

набе́г, -а, raid, foray. **набега́ть**, -а́ю *imp.*, **набежа́ть**, -егу́ *perf.* run against, run into; come running, pour in; spring up; *impers.* pucker, wrinkle.

набекре́нь *adv.* on one side, over one ear.

на|бели́ть(ся, -елю́(сь, -е́лишь(ся *perf.* на́бело *adv.*; переписа́ть ~, make a fair copy of.

на́бережная *sb.* embankment, quay.

наберу́, etc.: see набра́ть.

набива́ть(ся, -а́ю(сь *imp.* of наби́ть(ся. **наби́вка**, -и, stuffing, padding, packing; (textile) printing. **набивно́й**, printed.

набира́ть(ся, -а́ю(сь *imp.* of набра́ть(ся.

наби́т|ый, packed, stuffed, filled; crowded; битко́м ~, crammed, packed out; ~ый дура́к, utter fool. **наби́ть**, -бью́, -бьёшь *perf.* (*imp.* набива́ть), stuff, pack, fill; break to pieces, smash; kill, bag; print; beat, hammer, drive, knock; ~ оско́мину, set the teeth on edge; ~ ру́ку, get one's hand in, become skilled; ~ це́ну, put up the price; bid up; ~ся, crowd in; be crowded; +*dat.* impose or force oneself on.

наблюда́тель, -я *m.* observer; spectator.

наблюда́тельность, -и, (power of) observation. **наблюда́тельный**, observant; observation. **наблюда́ть**, -а́ю *imp.* observe, watch; ~за+*instr.* take care of, look after; supervise, superintend, control. **наблюде́ние**, -я, observation; supervision, superintendence, control.

на́божный, devout, pious.

набо́йка, -и, print; printed fabric; printed pattern; (rubber, etc.) heel.

на́бок *adv.* on one side, crooked.

наболе́вший, sore, painful; ~ вопро́с, burning question, pressing problem. **наболе́ть**, -е́ет *perf.* ache, be painful.

набо́р, -а, recruiting, enlisting, engaging; collection, set; setting up, composing; matter set up; metal plaques, (horse-) brasses; ~ слов, mere verbiage. **набо́рная** *sb.* composing-room. **набо́рщик**, -а, compositor.

набра́сывать(ся, -аю(сь *imp.* of набро-са́ть, набро́сить(ся.

набра́ть, -беру́, -берёшь; -а́л, -а́, -о perf. (*imp.* набира́ть), gather, collect, assemble; enlist, engage; compose, set up; ~ высоту́, gain height; ~ но́мер, dial a number; ~ ско́рость, pick up speed, gather speed; ~ся, assemble, collect; +*gen.* find, acquire, pick up; ~ся сме́лости, pluck up courage.

набрести́, -еду́, -дёшь; -ёл, -ела́ *perf.*+ на+*acc.* come across, hit upon.

наброса́ть, -а́ю *perf.* (*imp.* набра́сывать) throw, throw down; sketch, outline; jot down. **набро́сить**, -о́шу *perf.* (*imp.* набра́сывать) throw; ~ся, throw oneself, fling oneself; ~ся на, attack, assail. **набро́сок**, -ска, sketch, outline, (rough) draft.

набуха́ть, -а́ет *imp.*, **набу́хнуть**, -нет; -ух *perf.* swell.

набью́, etc.: see наби́ть.

наважде́ние, -я, delusion, hallucination.

на|ва́ксить, -кшу *perf.*

нава́ливать, -аю *imp.*, **навали́ть**, -лю́, -лишь *perf.* heap, pile up; put on top; load overload; ~ся, lean, throw all one's weight to bear; +на+*acc.* fall (up)on. **нава́лка**, -и, loading; list; listing; в нава́лку, in bulk, loose. **нава́лом** *adv.* in bulk, loose.

на|валя́ть, -я́ю *perf.*

наво́р, -а, fat; goodness. нава́ристый, нава́рный, rich and nourishing. нава́ривать, -аю *imp.*, навари́ть, -рю́, -ришь *perf.* weld (on); boil, cook. наварно́й, welded.

навева́ть, -а́ю *imp.* of наве́ять.

наведа́ться, -аюсь *perf.*, наве́дываться, -аюсь *imp.* call, look in.

наведе́ние, -я, laying, laying on; placing; induction; ~ спра́вок, making inquiries; ~ поря́дка, putting in order.

наведу́, etc.: see навести́.

навезти́, -зу́, -зёшь; -вёз, -ла́ *perf.* (*imp.* навози́ть) cart, bring in; + на + *acc.* drive against, drive into.

наве́ивать, -аю, *imp.* of наве́ять.

наве́к, наве́ки *adv.* for ever, for good.

навёл, etc.: see навести́.

наве́рно, наве́рное *adv.* probably, most likely; certainly, for sure. наверняка́ *adv.* certainly, for sure; safely; держа́ть пари́ ~, bet on a certainty.

наверста́ть, -а́ю *perf.*, навёрстывать, -аю *imp.* make up for, compensate for.

наве́рх *adv.* up, upwards; upstairs; to the top. наверху́ *adv.* above; upstairs.

наве́с, -а, awning, roof, canopy; penthouse; (open) shed; car-port.

навеселе́ *adv.* merry, a bit tight.

наве́систый, overhanging, jutting. наве́сить, -е́шу *perf.* (*imp.* наве́шивать) hang, hang up. наве́ска, -и, hanging; hinge. навесно́й, hanging; ~áя дверь, hinged door.

навести́, -еду́, -едёшь; -вёл, -á *perf.* (*imp.* наводи́ть) direct, lead; aim; cover, coat; cover with, spread; introduce, bring, produce; make; cause; ~ красоту́, make up; ~ спра́вку, make inquiries.

навести́ть, -ещу́ *perf.* (*imp.* навеща́ть) visit, call on.

наве́тренный, windward, exposed to the wind.

наве́чно *adv.* for ever; in perpetuity.

наве́шать, -аю *perf.*, наве́шивать[1], -аю *imp.* hang, hang out; weigh out.

наве́шивать[2], -аю *imp.* of наве́сить.

навеща́ть, -а́ю *imp.* of навести́ть.

наве́ять, -е́ю *perf.* (*imp.* навева́ть, на-

ве́ивать) blow; cast, bring, bring about; winnow.

на́взничь *adv.* backwards, on one's back.

навзры́д *adv.*; пла́кать ~, sob.

нависа́ть, -а́ет *imp.*, нави́снуть, -нет; -ви́с *perf.* hang, overhang, hang over; threaten, impend. нави́слый, нави́с-ший, beetling, overhanging.

навлека́ть, -а́ю *imp.*, навле́чь, -еку́, -ечёшь; -ёк, -ла́ *perf.* bring, draw, call down; incur.

наводи́ть, -ожу́, -о́дишь *imp.* of навести́; наводя́щий вопро́с, leading question. наво́дка, -и, aiming, directing; applying.

наводне́ние, -я, flood. наводни́ть, -ню́ *perf.*, наводня́ть, -я́ю *imp.* flood; inundate.

навожу́: see навози́ть. навожу́: see навози́ть.

наво́з, -а (-у) dung, manure, muck. навози́ть[1], -ожу́ *imp.* (*perf.* у~) manure. наво́зный, dung-, muck-; ~áя ку́ча, dunghill.

навози́ть[2], -ожу́, -о́зишь *imp.* of навезти́.

на́волока, -и, на́волочка, -и, pillowcase.

навостри́ть, -рю́ *perf.* sharpen; prick up; ~ лы́жи, clear off, clear out; ~ся, train oneself, grow skilful, become good.

на|вощи́ть, -щу́ *perf.*

на|вра́ть, -ру́, -рёшь; -а́л, -á, -о *perf.* tell lies, romance; talk nonsense; +в + *prep.* make a mistake (mistakes) in; get wrong.

навреди́ть, -ежу́ *perf.*+ *dat.* harm.

навсегда́ *adv.* for ever, for good; раз ~, once (and) for all.

навстре́чу *adv.* to meet; идти́ ~, go to meet; meet half-way; compromise with; consider sympathetically.

навы́ворот *adv.* inside out; back to front.

на́вык, -а, habit; knack; experience, skill.

навы́кат *adv.* protuberant, bulging.

навы́лет *adv.* right through.

навы́нос *adv.* to take away; for consumption off the premises, off-licence.

навы́пуск *adv.* worn outside.

навы́тяжку *adv.*; стоя́ть ~, stand at attention.

навью́чивать, -аю *imp.*, **на\вью́чить**, -чу *perf.* load.

навяза́ть[1], -а́ет *imp.*, **навя́знуть**, -нет; -я́з *perf.* stick; э́то навя́зло у меня́ в зуба́х, I'm sick and tired of it.

навяза́ть[2], -яжу́, -я́жешь *perf.*, **навя́зывать** -аю *imp.* tie, fasten; knit; force, foist, press; ~ся, thrust oneself, intrude; be importunate. **навя́зчив\вый**, importunate, intrusive; persistent; ~ая иде́я, fixed idea, obsession.

нагада́ть, -а́ю *perf.* predict, foretell.

на\га́дить, -а́жу *perf.*

нага́йка, -и, whip; riding-crop.

нага́н, -а, revolver.

нага́р, -а, snuff, scale.

нагиба́ть(ся, -а́ю(сь *imp.* of нагну́ть(ся.

нагишо́м *adv.* stark naked.

нагла́зник, -а, blinker; eye-shade, patch.

нагле́ц, -а́, impudent fellow. **на́глость**, -и, impudence, insolence, effrontery.

на́глухо *adv.* tightly, hermetically.

нагля́дн\ый, clear, graphic; visual; ~ые посо́бия, visual aids; ~ый уро́к, object-lesson.

нагна́ть, -гоню́, -го́нишь; -а́л, -а́, -о *perf.* (*imp.* нагоня́ть) overtake, catch up (with); drive; inspire, arouse, cause.

нагнести́, -ету́, -ете́шь *perf.*, **нагнета́ть**, -а́ю *imp.* compress; supercharge. **нагнета́тель**, -я *m.* supercharger.

на́глый, -гл, -а, -о, impudent, insolent, impertinent; bold-faced, brazen.

нагное́ние, -я, suppuration. **нагнои́ться**, -и́тся *perf.* fester, suppurate.

нагну́ть, -ну́, -нёшь *perf.* (*imp.* нагиба́ть) bend; ~ся, bend, stoop.

нагова́ривать, -аю *imp.*, **наговори́ть**, -рю́ *perf.* slander, calumniate; talk a lot of, say a lot (of); record; ~ пласти́нку, make a record; ~ся, talk oneself out.

наго́й; наг, -а́, -о, naked; bare.

на́голо *adv.* naked, bare. остри́женный на́голо, close-cropped; с ша́шками на́голо, with drawn swords.

наго́нй, -я, scolding, telling-off. **на\гоня́ть**, -я́ю *imp.* of нагна́ть.

нагора́живать, -аю *imp.* of нагороди́ть.

нагора́ть, -а́ет *imp.*, **нагоре́ть**, -ри́т *perf.* gutter; be consumed; *impers.*+ *dat.*, catch it, be scolded; ему́ за э́то нагоре́ло, he was told off for it.

наго́рн\ый, upland, mountain; mountainous; ~ая про́поведь, Sermon on the Mount.

нагороди́ть, -ожу́, -о́ди\шь *perf.* (*imp.* нагора́живать) pile up; erect, build; ~ вздо́р(a), talk a lot of nonsense.

нагота́, -ы́, nakedness, nudity, bareness.

нагота́вливать, -аю *imp.*, **нагото́вить**, -влю *perf.* get in, lay in; prepare. **нагото́ве**, *adv.* in readiness.

награ́бить, -блю *perf.* amass by dishonest means; acquire as loot.

награ́да, -ы, reward; award; decoration; prize. **награди́ть**, -ажу́ *perf.*, **награжда́ть**, -а́ю *imp.* reward; decorate; award prize to. **наградны́е** *sb.* bonus. **награжде́ние**, -я, rewarding, award, decoration.

нагрева́тельный, heating. **нагрева́ть**, -а́ю *imp.*, **нагре́ть**, -е́ю *perf.* warm, heat; ~ся, get hot, warm up.

нагромажда́ть, -а́ю *imp.*, **на\громозди́ть**, -зжу́ *perf.* heap up, pile up.

нагру́дник, -а, bib; breastplate. **нагру́дный**, breast; pectoral; ~ крест, pectoral cross.

нагружа́ть, -а́ю *imp.*, **на\грузи́ть**, -ужу́, -у́зишь *perf.* load, burden; ~ся, load oneself, burden oneself. **нагру́зка**, -и, loading; load; work; commitments, obligation(s).

на\грязни́ть, -ню́ *perf.*

нагря́нуть, -ну *perf.* appear unexpectedly; + на + *acc.* descend on, take unawares.

над, надо *prep.*+*instr.* over, above; on, at; ~ голово́й, overhead; рабо́тать ~ диссерта́цией, be working on a dissertation; смея́ться над, laugh at.

над-, надо-. I. *vbl. pref.* indicating increase, addition; incomplete or partial action, superficiality, slightness. II. *pref.* of nouns and adjs., over-, super-above-. **надво́дный**, above-water, surface-. **~гро́бие**, -я, epitaph. **~гро́бный**, on or over и grave. **~дув**, -а, supercharge, boost; pressurization. **~зе́мный**, above-ground; surface-. **~по́чечник**, -а, adrenal (gland). **~по́чечный**, adrenal.

надави́ть, -влю́, -вишь *perf.*, **нада́вливать**, -аю *imp.* press; squeeze out; crush.

надба́вить, -влю *perf.*, **надбавля́ть**, -я́ю *imp.* add; add to, increase, raise. **надба́вка**, -и, addition, increase; rise.

надвига́ть, -а́ю *imp.*, **надви́нуть**, -ну *perf.* move, pull, push; **~ся**, approach, advance, draw near.

на́двое *adv.* in two; ambiguously.

надво́рный: **~ сове́тник**, Court Councillor (7th grade: see чин).

надёванный, worn, used. **надева́ть**, -а́ю *imp.* of наде́ть.

наде́жда, -ы, hope; **в наде́жде**+*inf.* or **на**+*acc.* in the hope of. **надёжный**, reliable, trustworthy, safe.

наде́л, -а, allotment.

наде́лать, -аю *perf.* make; cause; do.

надели́ть, -лю́, -лишь *perf.*, **наделя́ть**, -я́ю *imp.* endow, provide; allot to, give to.

наде́ть, -е́ну *perf.* (*imp.* надева́ть) put on.

наде́яться, -е́юсь *imp.* (*perf.* по~) hope, expect; rely.

надзира́тель, -я *m.* overseer, supervisor, superintendent; (police) inspector. **надзира́ть**, -а́ю *imp.*+**за**+*instr.* supervise, superintend, oversee. **надзо́р**, -а, supervision; surveillance; inspectorate.

надла́мывать(ся, -аю(сь *imp.* of надломи́ть(ся.

надлежа́щ|ий, fitting, proper, appropriate; **~им о́бразом**, properly. **~ло-жи́т**; **~жа́ло** *impers.*+*dat.* it is necessary, required; **~ яви́ться в де́сять часо́в**, you are required to present yourself at ten o'clock; **~ э́то сде́лать**, it must be done.

надло́м, -а, break; fracture; crack; breakdown, crack-up. **надломи́ть**, -млю́, -мишь *perf.* (*imp.* надла́мывать) break; fracture; crack; break

down; **~ся**, break, crack break down.
надло́мленный, broken, cracked.

надме́нный, haughty, arrogant, supercilious.

на дня́х *adv.* one of these days; the other day, recently, lately.

на́до[1], **на́добно** (+*dat.*) it is necessary; I (etc.) must, ought to; I (etc.) need; **так ему́ и ~**, serve him right!; **~ быть**, probably. **на́добность**, -и necessity need; **в слу́чае на́добности**, in case of need.

на́до[2]: see над. **надо-**: see над-.

надоеда́ть, -а́ю *imp.*, **надое́сть**, -е́м, -е́шь, -е́ст, -еди́м *perf.* + *dat.* bore, bother, pester, plague; annoy. **надое́дливый**, boring, tiresome.

надо́лго *adv.* for a long time, for long.

надорва́ть, -ву́ -вёшь; -а́л, -а́, -о *perf.* (*imp.* надрыва́ть) tear; strain, overtax; **~ся**, tear; overstrain oneself, rupture oneself.

надоу́мить, -млю *perf.*, **надоу́мливать**, -аю *imp.* advise, suggest an idea to.

надо́шью, etc.: see надши́ть.

надписа́ть, -ишу́ -и́шешь *perf.*, **надпи́сывать**, -аю *imp.* inscribe, write. **на́дпись**, -и, inscription; notice; writing, legend; superscription, address.

надре́з, -а, а cut, incision; notch. **надре́зать**, -е́жу *perf.*, **надреза́ть**, -а́ю *imp.*, **надре́зывать**, -аю *imp.* make an incision in.

надруга́тельство, -а, outrage. **надруга́ться**, -а́юсь *perf.*+**над**+*instr.* outrage, insult, abuse.

надры́в, -а, tear; strain; breakdown; outburst. **надрыва́ть(ся**, -а́ю(сь *imp.* of надорва́ть(ся. **надры́вный**, violent, hysterical; heartrending.

надсмо́тр, -а, supervision; surveillance. **надсмо́трщик**, -а, -щица, -ы, overseer; supervisor.

надста́вить, -влю *perf.*, **надставля́ть**, -я́ю *imp.* lengthen. **надста́вка**, -и, lengthening; piece put on.

надстра́ивать, -аю *imp.*, **надстро́ить**, -о́ю *perf.* build on top; extend upwards. **надстро́йка**, -и, building upwards; superstructure.

надува́ла, -ы *m.* and *f.* swindler, cheat. **надува́тельство**, -а, swindle, cheating, trickery. **надува́ть(ся**, -а́ю(сь *imp.* of наду́ть(ся. **надувно́й**, pneumatic, inflatable.

наду́манный, far-fetched, artificial, invented. **наду́мать**, -аю *perf.*, **наду́мывать**, -аю *imp.* make up one's mind; think up, make up.

наду́тый, swollen, inflated; haughty; sulky. **наду́ть**, -у́ю *perf.* (*imp.* надува́ть) inflate, blow up; puff out; dupe, swindle; ~ гу́бы, pout; **~ся**, fill out, swell out; be puffed up; pout, sulk.

надушённый, scented, perfumed. **на|души́ть(ся**, -ушу́(сь, -у́шишь(ся *perf.*

надшива́ть, -а́ю *imp.*, **надши́ть**, -дошью́, -дошьёшь *perf.* lengthen; sew on.

на|дыми́ть, -млю́ *perf.* **наеда́ться**, -а́юсь *imp.* of нае́сться.

наедине́ *adv.* privately, alone.

нае́зд, -а, a flying visit; raid. **нае́здить**, -зжу *perf.*. **наезжа́ть**, -а́ю *imp.* travel, cover; travel over; make by driving; break in. **нае́здник**, -а, horseman, rider; jockey. **нае́здница**, -ы, horsewoman, rider. **наезжа́ть**, -а́ю *imp.* of нае́здить, наеха́ть; pay occasional visits. **нае́зженный**, well-travelled. **нае́зжий**, newly-arrived.

наём, на́йма, hire, hiring; renting; взять в ~ rent; сдать в ~ let. **наёмник**, -а, hireling; mercenary. **наёмный**, hired, rented. **наёмщик**, -а, a tenant, lessee.

нае́сться, -е́мся, -е́шься, -е́стся, -еди́мся *perf.* (*imp.* наеда́ться) eat one's fill; stuff oneself.

нае́хать, -е́ду *perf.* (*imp.* наезжа́ть) come down arrive unexpectedly; +на +acc. run into, collide with.

нажа́ть[1], -жму́, -жмёшь *perf.* (*imp.* нажима́ть) press; squeeze; press on; put pressure (on).

нажа́ть[2], -жну́, -жнёшь *perf.* (*imp.* нажина́ть) reap harvest.

нажда́к, -а́, emery. **нажда́чн|ый**; ~ая бума́га, emery paper.

нажи́ва, -ы, profit gain.

нажива́ть(ся, -а́ю(сь *imp.* of нажи́ть(ся. **наживно́й**, that may be acquired.

нажи́м, -а, pressure; clamp. **нажима́ть**, -а́ю *imp.* of нажа́ть[1]. **нажи́мистый**,

exacting. **нажимно́й**, **нажи́мный**, pressure.

нажина́ть, -а́ю *imp.* of нажа́ть[2].

нажи́ть, -иву́, -ивёшь; на́жил, -а́, -о *perf.* (*imp.* нажива́ть) acquire, gain; contract, incur; ~ враго́в make enemies; **~ся** -жи́лся, -а́сь, get rich, make a fortune.

нажму́, etc.: see нажа́ть[1]. **нажну́**, etc.: see нажа́ть[2].

наза́втра *adv.* (the) next day.

наза́д *adv.* back, backwards; (тому́) ~, ago. **наза́ди** *adv.* behind.

назва́н|ие, -я, name; title. **на́званый**, adopted; sworn. **назва́ть**, -зову́, -зовёшь; -а́л, -а́, -о *perf.* (*imp.* называ́ть) call, name; invite; **~ся**, be called; call oneself; give one's name.

назём, -а, dung.

назе́мный, ground, surface. **на́земь** *adv.* to the ground.

назида́ние, -я, edification. **назида́тельный**, edifying.

на́зло́ *adv.* out of spite; to spite.

назнача́ть, -а́ю *imp.*, **назна́чить**, -чу *perf.* appoint; nominate; fix, set; prescribe.

назову́, etc.: see назва́ть.

назо́йливый, importunate, persistent; tiresome.

назрева́ть, -а́ет *imp.*, **назре́ть**, -е́ет *perf.* ripen, mature; become urgent, imminent, inevitable.

назубо́к *adv.*; знать ~, know by heart.

называ́емый; так ~, so-called. **называ́ть(ся** -а́ю(сь *imp.* of назва́ть(ся; что называ́ется, as they say.

наи- *pref.* used with comparatives and superlatives to signify the very highest degree. **наибо́лее** *adv.* (the) most. **~бо́льший**, greatest, biggest; **~бо́льший** о́бщий дели́тель, highest common factor. **~вы́сший**, highest. **~лу́чший**, best. **~ме́нее** *adv.* (the) least. **~ме́ньший**, least, smallest; **~ме́ньшее** о́бщее кра́тное, lowest common multiple. **~па́че** *adv.* most of all, especially. **~ху́дший**, worst.

наи́гранный, put on, assumed; forced. **наигра́ть**, -а́ю *perf.*, **наи́грывать**, -аю *imp.* win; play, strum, pick out; ~

пласти́нку, make a recording. **на́игрыш**, -а, folk-tune; artificiality, staginess.

наизна́нку *adv.* inside out.

наизу́сть *adv.* by heart.

наименова́ние, -я, name; title. **на|именова́ние**, -ную *perf.*

наискосо́к, **на́искось** *adv.* obliquely, diagonally, aslant.

наи́тие, -я, inspiration; influence; по наи́тию, instinctively, by intuition.

найдёныш, -а, foundling.

наймит, -а, hireling.

найму, etc.: see наня́ть

найти́, -йду́, -йдёшь; нашёл, -шла́, -шло́ *perf.* (*imp.* находи́ть) find; find out, discover; gather, collect; +на+ *acc.* come across, come over, come upon; ~ся, be found; be, be situated; turn up; rise to the occasion, find the right thing (to do, say, etc.); не ~ся, be at a loss.

нака́з, -а, order, instructions; mandate. **наказа́ние**, -я, punishment. **наказа́ть**, -ажу́, -а́жешь *perf.*, **нака́зывать**, -аю *imp.*; order; tell. **наказу́емый**, punishable.

нака́л, -а, heating; incandescence; (white-)heat. **накалённый**, heated; red-hot, white-hot. **накалённость**, incandescent; strained, tense. **нака́ливать**, -аю *imp.*, **накали́ть**, -лю́ *perf.*, **накаля́ть**, -я́ю *imp.* heat; make red-hot, white-hot strain, make tense; ~ся, glow, become incandescent; heat up; become strained, become tense.

нака́лывать(ся, -аю(сь *imp.* of наколо́ть(ся.

накану́не *adv.* the day before; *prep.* + *gen.* on the eve of the day before.

на|ка́пать, -аю *perf.* (*imp.* нака́пывать) pour out (drop by drop), measure out +*instr.* spill.

нака́пливать(ся, -аю(сь *imp.* of накопи́ть(ся. **на|ка́ркать**, -аю *perf.*

накача́ть, -а́ю *perf.*, **нака́чивать**, -аю *imp.* pump; pump up; ~ся, get tight.

наки́д, -а, a loop; made stitch. **накида́ть**, -а́ю *perf.*, **наки́дывать**, -аю *imp.* throw, throw down. **наки́дка**, -и, cloak, cape; wrap; pillow-cover; increase, extra charge. **наки́нуть**, -ну *perf.*, **наки́дывать**, -аю *imp.* throw; throw on, slip on; ~ся, throw oneself, fling oneself on, attack, assail.

накипа́ть, -а́ет *imp.*, **накипе́ть**, -пи́т *perf.* form a scum, form a scale; boil up. **на́кипь**, -и, scum; scale, fur, deposit.

накла́дка, -и, bracket; hair-piece, wig; appliqué. **накладна́я** *sb.* invoice, way-bill. **накладно́й**, laid on; false; ~о́е зо́лото, rolled gold; ~о́й карма́н, patch pocket; ~о́е серебро́, plated silver, (silver) plate; ~ые расхо́ды, overheads. **накла́дывать**, -аю *imp.* of наложи́ть.

на|клевета́ть, -ещу́, -е́щешь *perf.* **наклёвываться**, -ается *imp.* of наклю́нуться.

накле́ивать, -аю *imp.*, **накле́ить**, -е́ю *perf.* stick on, paste on. **накле́йка**, -и, sticking (on, up); label; patch.

наклепа́ть, -а́ю *perf.*, **наклёпывать**, -аю *imp.* rivet; make roughly, knock together.

накло́н, -а, slope, inclination, incline; bend. **наклоне́ние**, -я, inclination; mood. **наклони́ть**, -ню́, -ни́шь *perf.* **наклоня́ть**, -я́ю *imp.* incline, bend; ~ся, stoop, bend; bow. **накло́нность**, -и, learning, inclination, propensity. **накло́нный**, inclined, sloping.

наклю́нуться, -нется *perf.* (*imp.* наклёвываться) peck its way out of the shell; turn up.

накова́льня, -и anvil.

нако́жный, cutaneous, skin.

нако́лка, -и, pinning, sticking; (pinned-on) ornament for hair; tattooing, tattoo. **наколо́ть**[1], -лю́, -лешь *perf.* (*imp.* нака́лывать) prick; pin; stick; ~ся, prick oneself.

наколо́ть[2], -лю́, -лешь *perf.* (*imp.* нака́лывать) chop. split.

наконе́ц *adv.* at last; in the end; finally. **наконе́чник**, -а, tip, point. **наконе́чный**, final; on the end.

на|копи́ть, -плю́, -пишь *perf.*, **накопля́ть**, -я́ю *imp.* (*imp.* also нака́пливать) accumulate, amass, pile up, store; ~ся, accumulate. **накопле́ние**, -я, accumulation; storage; build-up;

~ да́нных, data storage; (computer) memory.

на|копти́ть, -пчу́ perf. на|корми́ть, -млю́, -мишь perf.

накра́пывать, -ает imp. spit, drizzle.

накра́сить, -а́шу perf. (imp. накра́шивать) paint; make up. на|кра́ситься, -а́шусь perf.

на|крахма́лить, -лю perf. накра́шивать, -аю, imp. of накра́сить.

на|крени́ть, -ню́ perf. накрени́ться, -нится perf., накреня́ться, -я́ется imp. tilt; list, take a list, heel.

на́крепко adv. fast, tight; strictly.

на́крест adv. crosswise.

накрича́ть, -чу́ perf. (+на+acc.) shout (at).

на|кроши́ть, -шу́, -шишь perf. накро́ю, etc.: see накры́ть.

накрути́ть, -учу́, -у́тишь perf., накру́чивать, -аю imp. wind, twist.

накрыва́ть, -а́ю imp., накры́ть, -ро́ю perf. cover; catch; ~ (на) стол, lay the table; ~ на ме́сте, catch red--handed; ~ся, cover oneself.

накупа́ть, -а́ю imp., накупи́ть, -плю́, -пишь perf. buy up.

наку́ренный, smoky, smoke-filled. на|кури́ть, -рю́, -ришь perf. fill with smoke; distil.

налага́ть, -а́ю imp. of наложи́ть.

нала́дить, -а́жу perf. нала́живать, -аю imp. regulate, adjust; tune; repair; organize; ~ся, come right; get going.

на|лга́ть, -лгу́, -лжёшь; -а́л, -а́, -о perf.

нале́во adv. to the left; on the side.

налёг, etc.: see нале́чь. налега́ть, -а́ю imp. of нале́чь.

налегке́ adv. lightly dressed; without luggage.

на|лепи́ть, -плю́, -пишь perf.

налёт, -а, raid, swoop; flight; thin coating, bloom, patina; touch, shade; с ~а, suddenly, without warning or preparation, just like that. налета́ть[1] -а́ю perf. have flown. налета́ть[2], -а́ю imp., налете́ть, -лечу́ perf. swoop down; come flying; spring up; +на+acc. fly or drive into, run into. налётчик, -а, raider, robber.

нале́чь, -ля́гу, -ля́жешь; -лёг, -ла́ perf. (imp. налега́ть) lean, apply one's

weight, lie; apply oneself; +на+acc. put one's weight behind.

налжёшь, etc.: see налга́ть.

нали́в, -а, pouring in; ripening, swelling. налива́ть(ся), -а́ю(сь imp. of нали́ть(ся. нали́вка, -и, (fruit-flavoured) liqueur. наливно́й, ripe, juicy; for carriage of liquids; overshot; ~о́й док, wet dock; ~о́е су́дно, tanker.

на|линова́ть, -ну́ю perf.

налипа́ть, -а́ет imp., нали́пнуть, -нет; -и́п perf. stick.

налито́й, plump, juicy; ~ кро́вью, bloodshot. нали́ть, -лью́, -льёшь; на́ли́л, -а, -о perf. (imp. налива́ть) pour (out); fill; pour on; ~ся, -и́лся, -а́сь, -и́ло́сь, pour in, run in; ripen, swell.

налицо́ adv. present, manifest; available, on hand.

нали́чие, -я, presence. нали́чность, -и, presence; amount on hand; cash, ready money. нали́чный on hand, in hand, available; cash; ~ые (де́ньги), cash, ready money.

наловчи́ться, -чу́сь perf. become skilful.

нало́г, -а, tax. нало́говый, tax. налогоплате́льщик, -а, taxpayer. нало́женный; ~ым платежо́м, C.O.D. наложи́ть, -жу́, -жишь perf. (imp. накла́дывать, налага́ть) lay (in on), put (in, on); apply; impose; ~ отпеча́ток, leave traces; ~ штраф, impose a fine; ~ на себя́ ру́ки, lay hands on oneself, commit suicide.

на|лощи́ть, -щу́ perf. налью́, etc.: see нали́ть.

налюбова́ться, -бу́юсь perf.+instr. or на+acc., gaze one's fill at, admire (sufficiently).

наля́гу, etc.: see нале́чь.

нам, etc.: see мы.

на|ма́зать, -а́жу perf., нама́зывать, -аю imp. oil, grease; smear, spread; daub; ~ся, make up.

намалева́ть, -лю́ю perf. на|мара́ть, -а́ю perf. на|ма́слить, -лю perf. нама́тывать, -аю imp. of намота́ть. нама́чивать, -аю imp. of намочи́ть.

наме́дни adv. the other day, recently.

намёк, -а, hint. намека́ть, -а́ю imp.,

намекну́ть, -ну́, -нёшь *perf.* hint, allude.

на|ме́лить, -лю *perf.*

намерева́ться, -а́юсь *imp.* + *inf.* intend to, mean to, be about to. **наме́рен** *predic.*; я ~ + *inf.* I intend to, I mean to; что она́ ~а сде́лать? what is she going to do? **наме́рение**, -я, intention, purpose. **наме́ренный**, intentional, deliberate.

на|мета́ть, -а́ю *perf.* **на|ме́тить**[1], -е́чу *perf.*

наме́тить[2], -е́чу *perf.* (*imp.* намеча́ть) plan, project; outline; nominate, select; ~ся, be outlined, take shape.

наме́тка[1], -и, draft, preliminary outline.

наме́тка[2], -и, tacking, basting; tacking thread.

намеча́ть(ся), -а́ю(сь *imp. of* наме́тить(ся).

намно́го *adv.* much, far.

намока́ть, -а́ю *imp.*, **намо́кнуть**, -ну *perf.* get wet.

намо́рдник, -а, muzzle.

на|мо́рщить(ся, -щу(сь *perf.* **на|мости́ть**, -ощу́ *perf.*

на|мота́ть(ся, -а́ю *perf.* (*imp. also* нама́тывать) wind, reel.

на|мочи́ть, -очу́, -о́чишь *perf.* (*imp. also* нама́чивать) wet; soak, steep; splash, spill.

намы́в, -а, alluvium. **намывно́й**, alluvial. **намыва́ть**, -а́ю *imp.*, **на|мы́ть**, -мо́ю *perf.* wash; wash down, wash up.

нанести́, -су́, -сёшь, -ёс, -ла́ *perf.* (*imp.* наноси́ть) carry, bring; draw, plot; cause, inflict; ~ оскорбле́ние insult; ~ уда́р + *dat.* deal a blow; hit, punch, strike; ~ уще́рб, damage.

на|низа́ть, -ижу́, -и́жешь *perf.*, **нани́зывать**, -аю *imp.* string, thread.

нанима́тель, -я *m.* tenant; employer. **нанима́ть(ся**, -а́ю(сь *imp. of* наня́ть(ся.

нано́с, -а, alluvial deposit; drift. **наноси́ть**, -ошу́ -о́сишь *imp. of* нанести́. **нано́сный**, alluvial; alien, borrowed.

наня́ть, найму́, -мёшь; на́нял, -а́, -о

perf. (*imp.* нанима́ть) hire, engage; rent; ~ся, get a job, get work.

наоборо́т *adv.* on the contrary; back to front; the other, the wrong, way (round); и ~, and vice versa.

наобу́м *adv.* without thinking, at random.

на́отмашь *adv.* with a wild swing (of the hand), violently, full.

наотре́з *adv.* flatly, point-blank.

напада́ть, -а́ю *imp. of* напа́сть. **напада́ющий** *sb.* forward. **нападе́ние**, -я, attack; forwards. **напа́дки**, -док *pl.* attacks, accusations.

на|па́костить, -ощу *perf.*

напа́рник, -а, co-driver, fellow-worker; team-mate; mate.

напа́сть, -аду́, -адёшь; -а́л *perf.* (*imp.* напада́ть) на + *acc.* attack; descend on; grip, seize, come over; come upon, come across. **напа́сть**, -и, misfortune, disaster.

на|па́чкать, -аю *perf.*

напе́в, -а, melody, tune. **напева́ть**, -а́ю *imp.* the melody. **напе́вный**, melodious.

наперебо́й, **наперерыв** *adv.* interrupting, vying with one another.

наперёд *adv.* in advance, beforehand.

напереко́р *adv.* + *dat.* in defiance of, counter to.

наперерыв: see наперебо́й.

напёрсток, -тка, thimble.

на|пе́рчить, -чу *perf.*

напе́ть, -пою́, -поёшь *perf.* (*imp.* напева́ть) sing; hum, croon; ~ пласти́нку, make a record.

на|печа́тать(ся, -аю(сь *perf.* **напива́ться**, -а́юсь *imp. of* напи́ться.

напи́лок, -лка, **напи́льник**, -а, file.

на|писа́ть, -ишу́, -и́шешь *perf.*

напи́ток, -тка, drink, beverage. **напи́ться**, -пью́сь, -пьёшься; -и́лся, -а́сь, -и́ло́сь *perf.* (*imp.* напива́ться) quench one's thirst, drink; get drunk.

напиха́ть, -а́ю *perf.*, **напи́хивать**, -аю *imp.* cram, stuff.

на|плева́ть, -люю́, -люёшь *perf.*; ~! to hell with it! who cares?

наплечник, -а, shoulder-strap. **наплечный**, shoulder-.

наплы́в, -а, flow, influx; accumulation; dissolve; canker.

наплюю́ etc.: see наплева́ть.

напова́л adv. outright on the spot.

наподо́бие prep.+gen. like, not unlike.

на|по́ить, -ою́, -о́ишь perf.

напока́з adv. for show; выставля́ть ~, display; show off.

наполне́ние, -я, filling; inflation. **наполни́тель,** -я m. filler. **наполни́ть(ся,** -ню(сь perf., **наполня́ть(ся,** -я́ю(сь imp. fill.

наполови́ну adv. half.

напомина́ние, -я, reminder. **напомина́ть,** -а́ю imp., **напо́мнить,** -мню perf. remind.

напо́р, -а, pressure. **напо́ристость,** -и, energy; push, go. **напо́ристый,** energetic, pushing. **напо́рный,** pressure.

напо́ртить, -рчу perf. spoil; damage; +dat. injure, harm.

напосле́док adv. in the end; after all.

напою́, etc.: see напе́ть, напои́ть.

напр. abbr. например, for example.

напра́вить, -влю perf., **направля́ть,** -я́ю imp. direct; aim; send; refer; sharpen, whet; organize; ~ся, make (for), go (towards); get going, get under way. **напра́вка,** -и, setting, whetting. **направле́ние,** -я, direction; trend, tendency, turn; order, warrant, directive; action, effect; sector. **напра́вленный,** purposeful, unswerving; directional. **направля́ющая** sb. guide. **направля́ющий,** guiding, guide; leading.

напра́во adv. to the right, on the right.

напра́сно adv. vainly, in vain, to no purpose, for nothing; wrong, unjustly, mistakenly. **напра́сный,** vain, idle; unfounded, unjust.

напра́шиваться, -аюсь imp. of напроси́ться

наприме́р, for example, for instance.

на|прока́зить, -а́жу perf. **на|прока́зничать,** -аю perf.

напрока́т adv. for hire, on hire; взять ~, hire.

напролёт adv. through, without a break; всю ночь ~, all night long.

напроло́м adv. straight, regardless of obstacles; идти́ ~, push one's way through.

на|проро́чить, -чу perf.

напроси́ться, -ошу́сь, -о́сишься perf. (imp. напра́шиваться) thrust oneself, force oneself; suggest itself; ~ на, ask for, invite; ~ на комплиме́нты, fish for compliments.

напро́тив adv. opposite; on the contrary; + dat. against, to spite. **напро́тив** prep.+gen. opposite.

напру́живать, -аю imp., **напру́жить,** -жу perf. strain; tense; ~ся, become tense, become taut.

напряга́ть(ся, -а́ю(сь imp. of напря́чь(ся. **напряже́ние,** -я, tension; effort, exertion, strain; stress; voltage; смеще́ния, grid bias. **напряжённый,** tense, strained; intense; intensive.

напрями́к adv. straight, straight out.

напря́чь, -ягу́, -яжёшь; -я́г, -ла́ perf. (imp. напряга́ть) tense, strain; ~ся, exert oneself, strain oneself; become tense.

на|пуга́ть(ся, -а́ю(сь perf. **на|пу́дрить(ся,** -рю(сь perf.

напу́ск, -а, letting in; slipping, letting loose; bloused or loosely hanging part. **напуска́ть,** -а́ю imp., **напусти́ть,** -ущу́, -у́стишь perf. let in, admit; let loose, slip; ~ на себя́ affect, put on, assume; ~ся+на+acc. fly at, go for. **напускно́й,** assumed, put on; artificial.

напу́тать, -аю perf. (imp. напу́тывать) + в + prep. make a mess of, make a hash of; confuse; get wrong.

напу́тственный, parting, farewell. **напу́тствие,** -я, parting words, farewell speech.

напу́тывать, -аю imp. of напу́тать.

напуха́ть, -а́ет imp., **напу́хнуть,** -нет perf. swell (up).

на|пыли́ть, -лю́ perf.

напы́шен|ный, pompous, bombastic, high-flown.

напью́сь, etc.: see напи́ться.

наравне́ adv. level, keeping pace; equally; on an equal footing.

нараспа́шку adv. unbuttoned; у него́ душа́ ~, he wears his heart on his sleeve.

нараспе́в adv. in a sing-song (way).

нараста́ние, -я, growth, accumulation; build-up. **нараста́ть,** -а́ет imp., **нараста-**

сти́, -тёт, -рос, -ла́ perf. grow, form; increase, swell; accumulate.

нарасхва́т adv. very quickly, like hot cakes; раскупа́ться ~, be in great demand.

нарва́ть[1], -рву́, -рвёшь; -а́л, -а́, -о perf. (imp. нарыва́ть) pick; tear up.

нарва́ть[2], -вёт; -а́л, -а́, -о perf. (imp. нарыва́ть) gather, come to a head.

нарва́ться, -вусь, -вёшься; -а́лся, -ала́сь, -а́лось perf. (imp. нарыва́ть-ся) +на +acc. run into, run up against.

наре́з, -а, thread, groove; rifling; plot. **наре́зать**, -е́жу perf., **нареза́ть**, -а́ю imp. cut, cut up, slice, carve; thread, rifle; allot, parcel out. **наре́зка**, -и, cutting, slicing; thread, rifling. **наре́зно́й**, rifled.

нарека́ние, -я, censure.

наре́чие[1], -я, dialect.

наре́чие[2], -я, adverb. **наре́чный**, adverbial.

нарисова́ть, -су́ю perf.

нарица́тельный, nominal; и́мя ~ое, common noun; ~ая сто́имость, face value, nominal value.

нарко́з, -а, anaesthesia; narcosis; anaesthetic. **наркома́н**, -а, -ма́нка, -и, drug addict. **наркома́ния**, -и, drug addiction.

наро́д, -а (-у), people.

народи́ться, -ожу́сь perf. (imp. нарожда́ться) be born; come into being, arise.

наро́дник, -а, narodnik, populist. **наро́днический** populist. **наро́дность**, -и, nationality; people; national character. **наро́дный**, national; folk; popular; people's. **народонаселе́ние**, -я, population.

нарожда́ться, -а́юсь imp. of народи́ть-ся. **нарожде́ние**, -я, birth; springing up.

наро́с, etc.: see нарасти́. **наро́ст**, -а, outgrowth, excrescence; burr, tumour; incrustation, scale.

наро́читый, deliberate, intentional. **наро́чно** adv. on purpose, purposely, deliberately; for fun, jokingly. **на́рочный** sb. courier; express messenger, special messenger; с ~м, express delivery.

на́рты, нарт pl., **на́рта**, -ы. sledge.

нару́жно adv. outwardly, on the surface. **нару́жность**, -и, exterior, (outward) appearance. **нару́жный**, external, exterior, outward; for external use only, not to be taken. **нару́жу** adv. outside, out.

на|румя́нить(ся), -ню(сь) perf.

нару́чник, -а, handcuff, manacle. **нару́чный**; ~ые часы́, wrist-watch.

наруше́ние, -я, breach; infringement, violation; offence. **наруши́тель**, -я m. transgressor, infringer, violator; ~ грани́цы illegal entrant. **наруши́ть**, -шу perf., **наруша́ть**, -а́ю imp. break; disturb, infringe, violate, transgress.

на́ры, нар pl. plank-bed.

нары́в, -а, abscess, boil. **нарыва́ть(ся)**, -а́ю(сь) imp. of нарва́ть(ся).

наря́д[1], -а, order warrant; duty; detail.

наря́д[2], -а, attire, apparel, dress. **наряди́ть**, -яжу́ perf. (imp. наряжа́ть), dress array; dress up; ~ся, dress up, array oneself. **наря́дный**, well-dressed, elegant, smart.

наряду́ adv. alike, equally; side by side; ~ с э́тим, at the same time.

наряжа́ть(ся), -а́ю(сь) imp. of наряди́ть(ся). нас: see мы.

насади́ть, -ажу́, -а́дишь perf., **насажа́ть**, -а́ю imp. (imp. also наса́живать) plant; seat; propagate; implant, inculcate; set fix, stick, pin. **наса́дка**, -и, setting, fixing, putting on; hafting; bait; nozzle, mouthpiece. **насажа́ть**, -а́ю perf. (imp. наса́живать) plant, seat. **насажде́ние**, -я, planting; plantation stand, wood; spreading, dissemination, propagation. **наса́живать**, -а́ю imp. of насади́ть, насажа́ть.

наса́ливать, -а́ю imp. of насоли́ть.

наса́сывать, -а́ю imp. of насоса́ть.

насви́стывать, -а́ю imp. whistle.

наседа́ть, -а́ю imp. (perf. насе́сть) press; settle, collect. **насе́дка**, -и, sitting hen.

насека́ть, -а́ю imp. of насе́чь. **насеко́мое** sb. insect. **насеку́**, etc.: see насе́чь.

населе́ние, -я, population, inhabitants; settling, peopling. **населённость**, -и, density of population. **населённый**, populated, settled, inhabited; thickly populated, populous; ~ пункт, settlement; inhabited place; built-up area. населить, -лю *perf.*, населять, -яю *imp.* settle, people, inhabit. насельник, -а, inhabitant.

насест, -а, roost, perch. насесть, -сяду, -сёл *perf.* of наседать.

насечка, -и, incision, cut; notch; inlay. насечь, -еку, -ечёшь; -ек, -ла *perf.* (*imp.* насекать) cut; cut up; incise; damascene.

насидеть, -ижу *perf.*, насиживать, -аю *imp.* hatch; warm. насиженный, long occupied; ~ое место, old haunt, old home.

насилие, -я, violence, force, aggression. насиловать, -лую *imp.* (*perf.* из~) coerce constrain; rape. насилу *adv.* with difficulty, hardly. насильник, -а, aggressor, user of violence, violator. насильно *adv.* by force, forcibly. насильственный, violent, forcible.

наскакивать, -аю *imp.* of наскочить. на|скандалить, -лю *perf.*

насквозь *adv.* through, throughout.

насколько *adv.* how much? how far?; as far as, so far as.

наскоро *adv.* hastily hurriedly.

наскочить, -очу, -очишь *perf.* (*imp.* наскакивать) + на + *acc.* run into, collide with; fly at.

наскребать, -аю *imp.*, наскрести, -ебу, -ебёшь; -ёб, -ла *perf.* scrape up, scrape together.

наскучить, -чу *perf.* bore.

насладить, -ажу *perf.*, наслаждать, -аю *imp.* delight, please; ~ся, enjoy, take pleasure, delight. наслаждение, -я, delight pleasure, enjoyment.

наслаиваться, -ается *imp.* of наслоиться.

наследие, -я, legacy; heritage. на|следить, -ежу *perf.* наследник, -а, heir, legatee; successor. наследница, -ы, heiress. наследный, next in succession; ~ принц, crown prince. наследование, -я, inheritance, succession. наследовать, -дую *perf.* and *imp.* (*perf.* also y~) inherit, succeed to. наследственный, hereditary, inherited.

наследство, -а, inheritance, legacy; heritage.

наслоение, -я, stratification; stratum, layer, deposit. наслоиться, -ойтся *perf.* (*imp.* наслаиваться) form a layer or stratum, be deposited.

наслышаться, -шусь *perf.* have heard a lot. наслышка, -и: по наслышке, by hearsay.

насмерть *adv.* to death; to the death.

насмехаться, -аюсь *imp.* jeer, gibe; + над + *instr.* ridicule. на|смешить, -шу *perf.* насмешка, -и, mockery, ridicule; gibe. насмешливый, mocking, derisive; sarcastic.

насморк, -а, cold in the head.

насмотреться, -рюсь, -ришься *perf.* see a lot; ~ на, see enough of, have looked enough at.

насолить, -олю, -олишь *perf.* (*imp.* насаливать) salt, pickle; oversalt; annoy, spite, injure.

на|сорить, -рю *perf.*

насос, -а, pump. насосать, -осу, -осёшь *perf.* (*imp.* насасывать) pump; suck; ~ся, suck one's fill; drink oneself drunk. насосный, pumping.

наспех *adv.* hastily.

на|сплетничать, -аю *perf.* наставать, -таёт *imp.* of настать.

наставительный, edifying, instructive. наставить[1], -влю *perf.* (*imp.* наставлять) edify; exhort, admonish.

наставить[2], -влю *perf.* (*imp.* наставлять) lengthen; add, add on; aim, point; set up, place. наставка, -и, addition.

наставление, -я, exhortation, admonition; directions, instructions, manual. наставлять, -яю *imp.* of наставить.

наставник, -а, tutor, teacher, mentor; классный ~, form-master. наставничество, а, tutorship, tutelage.

наставной, lengthened; added.

наставать(ся, -аю(сь *imp.* of настоять(ся.

настать, -анет *perf.* (*imp.* наставать) come, begin, set in.

настежь *adv.* wide, wide open.

настелю, etc.: see настлать.

настенный, hanging; ~ые часы, wall-clock.

настига́ть, -а́ю *imp.*, насти́гнуть, насти́чь, -и́гну; -и́г *perf.* catch up with, overtake.

насти́л, -а, flooring, planking. настила́ть, -а́ю *imp.* of настла́ть.

насти́чь: see настига́ть.

настла́ть, -телю́, -те́лешь *perf.* (*imp.* настила́ть) lay, spread.

насто́й, -я, infusion; (fruit-flavoured) liqueur, cordial. насто́йка, -и, (fruit-flavoured) liqueur, cordial.

насто́йчивый, persistent; urgent, insistent.

насто́лько *adv.* so, so much; ~, наско́лько, as much as.

насто́льник, -а, table-lamp, desk-lamp. насто́льный, table, desk; for constant reference, in constant use.

настора́живать, -аю *imp.*, насторожи́ть, -жу́ *perf.* set; prick up, strain; ~ся, prick up one's ears. насторожё́ adv. on the alert, on one's guard. насторожё́нный, -ен, -енна, насторожё́нный, -ён, -ена́ or -ённа, guarded; alert.

настоя́ние, -я, insistence. настоя́тельный, persistent, insistent; urgent, pressing. настоя́ть[1], -ою́ *perf.* (*imp.* наста́ивать) insist.

настоя́ть[2], -ою́ *perf.* (*imp.* наста́ивать) brew, draw, infuse; ~ся, draw, stand; stand a long time.

настоя́щее *sb.* the present. настоя́щий (the) present, this; real, genuine.

настра́ивать(ся, -аю(сь *imp.* of настро́ить(ся.

настри́г, -а, shearing, clipping; clip. настри́чь, -игу́, -ижёшь; -и́г *perf.* shear, clip.

на́строго *adv.* strictly.

настрое́ние, -я, mood, temper, humour; ~ умо́в, public feeling, general mood. настро́ить, -о́ю *perf.* (*imp.* настра́ивать) tune, tune in in; dispose, incline; incite; ~ся, dispose oneself, incline, settle; make up one's mind. настро́йка, -и, tuning; tuning in; tuning signal. настро́йщик, -а, a tuner.

на|строчи́ть, -чу́ *perf.*

настря́пать, -аю *perf.* cook; cook up.

наступа́тельный, offensive; aggressive.

наступа́ть[1], -а́ю *imp.* of наступи́ть[1].

наступа́ть[2], -а́ет *imp.* of наступи́ть[2].

наступа́ющий, coming, beginning.

наступа́ющий *sb.* attacker.

наступи́ть[1], -плю́, -пишь *perf.* (*imp.* наступа́ть) tread, step; attack; advance.

наступи́ть[2], -у́пит *perf.* (*imp.* наступа́ть) come, set in; fall; наступи́ла ночь, night had fallen; наступи́ла тишина́, silence fell. наступле́ние[1], -я, coming, approach; с ~м но́чи, at nightfall.

наступле́ние[2], -я, offensive, attack.

насу́питься, -плюсь *perf.*, насу́пливаться, -аюсь *imp.* frown, knit one's brows.

на́сухо *adv.* dry. насу́шивать, -аю *imp.*, насуши́ть, -шу́, -шишь *perf.* dry.

насу́щность, -и, urgency. насу́щный, urgent, vital, essential; хлеб ~, daily bread.

насчёт *prep.*+*gen.* about, concerning; as regards. насчита́ть, -а́ю *perf.*, насчи́тывать, -аю *imp.* count; hold, contain; ~ся+*gen.* number.

насыпа́ть, -плю *perf.*, насыпа́ть, -а́ю *imp.* pour in, pour on; fill; spread, scatter; raise, heap up. насы́пка, -и, pouring; filling. насыпно́й, bulk; piled up; ~ холм, artificial mound. на́сыпь, -и, embankment.

насы́тить, -ы́щу *perf.*, насыща́ть, -а́ю *imp.* sate, satiate; saturate, impregnate; ~ся, be full, be sated; be saturated. насыще́нный, saturated; rich, concentrated.

нася́ду, etc.: see насе́сть.

ната́лкивать(ся, -аю(сь *imp.* of натолкну́ть(ся. ната́пливать, -аю *imp.* of натопи́ть.

натаска́ть, -а́ю *perf.*, ната́скивать, -аю *imp.* train; coach, cram; bring in, lay in; fish out, drag out, fetch out.

натвори́ть, -рю́ *perf.* do, get up to.

натере́ть, -тру́, -трёшь; -тёр *perf.* (*imp.* натира́ть) rub on, rub in; polish; chafe, rub; grate; ~ся rub oneself.

натерпе́ться, -плю́сь, -пишься *perf.* have suffered much, have gone through a great deal.

натира́ть(ся, -а́ю(сь *imp.* of натере́ть(ся.

на́тиск, -а, onslaught, charge, onset; pressure; impress, impression. **нати́-**
скать, -аю *perf*. impress; cram in; shove, push about.

наткну́ться, -ну́сь, -нёшься *perf*. (*imp*. **натыка́ться**) + **на** + *acc*. run against, run into; strike, stumble on, come across.

натолкну́ть, -ну́, -нёшь *perf*. (*imp*. **ната́лкивать**) push; lead; ~ **на**, suggest; ~**ся**, run against, run across.

натопи́ть, -плю́, -пишь *perf*. (*imp*. **ната́пливать**) heat, heat up; stoke up; melt.

на́точи́ть, -чу́, -чишь *perf*.

натоща́к *adv*. on an empty stomach.

натр, a, natron, soda; е́дкий ~, caustic soda.

натрави́ть, -влю́, -вишь *perf*., **натра́вливать**, -аю *imp*., **натравля́ть**, -я́ю *imp*. set (on); stir up; etch; exterminate (by poison).

натрениро́ванный, trained. **на|трениро-**
ва́ть(ся, -ру́ю(сь *perf*.

на́трий, -я, sodium.

нату́га, -и, effort, strain. **на́туго** *adv*. tight, tightly. **нату́жный**, strained, forced.

нату́ра, -ы, nature; kind; model; на нату́ре, on location; плати́ть нату́-
рой, pay in kind; с нату́ры, from life. **натура́льно** *adv*. naturally, of course. **натура́льный**, natural; real, genuine; in kind; ~ обме́н, barter. **нату́рный**, life, from life; on location. **нату́рщик**, -а, -щица, -ы, artist's model.

натыка́ть(ся, -а́ю(сь *imp*. of **наткну́ть-**
(ся.

натюрмо́рт, -а, still life.

натя́гивать, -аю *imp*., **натяну́ть**, -ну́, -нешь *perf*. stretch; draw; pull tight, tauten; pull on; ~**ся**, stretch. **натя́жка**, -и, stretching, straining; tension; stretch; допусти́ть натя́жку, stretch a point; с натя́жкой, by stretching a point, at a pinch. **натяжно́й**, tension. **натя́нутость**, -и, tension. **натя́нутый**, tight; strained, forced.

науга́д *adv*. at random; by guesswork. **нау́ка**, -и, science; learning, scholarship; study; lesson. **наукообра́зный**, scientific; pseudo-scientific.

наутёк *adv*.: пусти́ться ~, take to one's heels, take to flight.

нау́тро *adv*. (the) next morning.

на|учи́ть, -чу́, -чишь *perf*.

нау́чн|ый, scientific; ~ая фанта́стика, science fiction.

нау́шник, -а, ear-flap, ear-muff; ear-
-phone, head-phone; informer, tale-
-bearer. **нау́шничать**, -аю *imp*. tell tales, inform.

нафтали́н, -а (-у), naphthalene. **нафта-**
ли́новый, naphthalene; ~ ша́рик, moth-ball.

наха́л, -а, -ха́лка, -и, impudent creature brazen creature; lout, hussy. **на-**
ха́льный, impudent, impertinent; cheeky; brazen, bold-faced. **наха́ль-**
ство, -а, impudence, effrontery.

нахвата́ть, -а́ю *perf*., **нахва́тывать**, -аю *imp*. pick up, get hold of, come by; ~**ся** + *gen*. pick up, get a smattering of.

нахле́бник, -а, parasite, hanger-on; boarder, paying guest.

нахлобу́чивать, -аю *imp*., **нахлобу́чить**, -чу *perf*. pull down; + *dat*. tell off, dress down. **нахлобу́чка**, -и, telling-
-off, dressing-down.

нахлы́нуть, -нет *perf*. well up; surge; flow, gush; crowd.

нахму́ренный, frowning, scowling. **на|**
хму́рить(ся, -рю(сь *perf*.

находи́ть(ся, -ожу́(сь, -о́дишь(ся *imp*. of **найти́(сь**. **нахо́дка**, -и, find; godsend. **нахо́дчивый**, resourceful, ready, quick-witted.

на|холоди́ть, -ожу́ *perf*.

нацеди́ть, -ежу́, -е́дишь *perf*., **наце́жи-**
вать, -аю *imp*. strain.

наце́ливать, -аю *imp*., **на|це́лить**, -лю *perf*. aim, level, direct; ~**ся**, aim, take aim.

наце́нка, -и, extra, addition; additional charge.

национализи́ровать, -рую *perf*. and *imp*. nationalize. **националисти́ческий**, nationalist, nationalistic. **национа́ль-**
ность, -и, nationality; ethnic group; national character. **национа́льный**, national. **на́ция**, -и, nation. **нацме́н**, -а, -ме́нка, -и *abbr*. member of national minority. **нацменьшинство́**, -а́; *pl*. -а *abbr*. national minority.

на|чади́ть, -ажу́ perf.

нача́ло, -a, beginning, start; origin, source; principle, basis; command, authority; для нача́ла, to start with; с нача́ла, at, from, the beginning. нача́льник, -a, head, chief; superior boss. нача́льный, initial, first; primary. нача́льственный, overbearing, domineering. нача́льство, -a, the authorities; command, direction; head, boss. нача́льствование, -я, command. нача́льствовать, -твую imp. be in command; + над + instr. command.

нача́тки, -ков pl. rudiments, elements.

нача́ть, -чну́, -чнёшь; на́чал, -а́, -о perf. (imp. начина́ть) begin, start; ~ся, begin, start.

начеку́ adv. on the alert, ready.

на|черни́ть, -ню́ perf. на́черно adv. roughly, in rough.

начерта́ние, -я, tracing; outline. начерта́тельн|ый; ~ая геоме́трия, descriptive geometry. начерта́ть, -а́ю perf. trace, inscribe. на|черти́ть, -рчу́, -ртишь perf.

начина́ние, -я, undertaking; project; initiative. начина́тель, -я m., -тельница, -ы, originator, initiator. начина́тельный, inchoative, inceptive. начина́ть(ся, -а́ю imp. of нача́ть(ся. начина́ющий sb. beginner. начина́я с prep.+gen. as from, starting with.

начина́ть, -а́ю imp., начини́ть¹, -ню́, -нишь perf. mend; sharpen.

начини́ть², -ню́ perf., начиня́ть, -я́ю imp. stuff, fill. начи́нка, -и, stuffing, filling.

начисле́ние, -я, extra charge, supplement, addition. начи́слить, -лю perf., начисля́ть, -я́ю imp. add.

начи́стить, -и́щу perf. (imp. начища́ть) clean; polish, shine; peel. на́чисто adv. flatly, decidedly; openly, frankly; переписа́ть ~, make a clean copy (of). начистоту́, начисту́ю adv. openly, frankly.

начи́танность, -и, learning, erudition; wide reading. начи́танный, well-read. начита́ть, -а́ю perf. have read; ~ся, have read (too) much, have read enough.

начища́ть, -а́ю imp. of начи́стить.

наш, -его m., на́ша, -ей f., на́ше, -его n., на́ши, -их pl., pron. our, ours; ~a взяла́, we've won; ~его (after comp.) than we (have, etc.); ~и, our (own) people; оди́н из ~их, one of us; служи́ть, угожда́ть, и ~им и ва́шим, run with the hare and hunt with the hounds.

нашата́рный; ~ спирт, ammonia. нашаты́рь, -я́ m. sal-ammoniac; ammonia.

нашёл, etc.: see найти́.

нашепта́ть, -пчу́ -пчешь perf., нашёптывать, -аю imp. whisper; cast a spell.

наше́ствие, -я, invasion.

нашива́ть, -а́ю imp. наши́ть, -шью, -шьёшь perf. sew on. наши́вка, -и, stripe, chevron; tab. нашивно́й, sewn on; ~ карма́н, patch pocket.

нашинкова́ть, -ку́ю perf., нашинко́вывать, -аю imp. shred, chop.

нашпи́ливать, -аю imp., нашпи́лить, -лю perf. pin on.

нашлёпать, -аю imp. slap.

нашуме́ть, -млю perf. make a din; cause a sensation.

нашью́, etc.: see наши́ть.

нащу́пать, -аю perf., нащу́пывать, -аю imp. grope for, fumble for, feel (about) for; grope one's way to, find by groping.

на|электризова́ть, -зу́ю perf.

на|я́бедничать, -аю perf.

наяву́ adv. awake; in reality; сон ~, waking dream.

не part. not; не раз, more than once.

не- pref. un-, in-, non-, mis-, dis-; -less; not. неаккура́тный, careless, inaccurate; unpunctual; untidy. небезопа́сный, unsafe. небезразли́чный, not indifferent. небезызве́стный, not unknown; notorious; well-known; ~o, что, it is no secret that; нам ~o, we are not unaware. небезынтере́сный, not without interest.

небеса́, etc.: see не́бо². небе́сный, heavenly, of heaven; celestial.

не-. небесполе́зный, of some use, useful. неблагода́рный, ungrateful, thankless. неблагожела́тельный, malevolent, ill-disposed. **неблагозву́-чие**, -я, disharmony, dissonance. **не-благозву́чный**, inharmonious, discordant. **неблагонадёжный**, unreliable. **неблагополу́чие**, -я, trouble. **неблаго-получный**, unsuccessful, bad, unfavourable. **неблагопристо́йный**, obscene, indecent, improper. **неблаго-разу́мный**, imprudent, ill-advised, unwise. **неблагоро́дный**, ignoble, base.

нёбный, palatal, palatine. **нёбо¹**, -а, palate.

нёбо², -а; *pl.* -беса́, -бёс, sky; heaven.

не-. небога́тый, of modest means, modest. **небольшо́й**, small, not great; **с небольши́м**, a little over.

небосво́д -а, firmament, vault of heaven. **небоскло́н**, -а, horizon. **небоскрёб**, -а, skyscraper.

небо́сь *adv.* I dare say; probably, very likely; I suppose.

не-. небре́жничать, -аю *imp.* be careless. **небре́жный**, careless, negligent; slipshod; offhand. **небыва́лый**, unprecedented; fantastic, imaginary; inexperienced. **небыли́ца**, -ы, fable, cock-and-bull story. **небытие́**, -я́, non-existence. **небью́щийся**, unbreakable. **нева́жно** *adv.* not too well, indifferently. **нева́жный**, unimportant, insignificant; poor, indifferent. **невдалеке́** *adv.* not far away. **неве́дение**, -я, ignorance. **неве́домо** *adv.* God (only) knows. **неве́домый**, unknown; mysterious. **неве́жа**, -и *m.* and *f.* boor, lout. **неве́жда**, -ы, *m.* and *f.* ignoramus. **неве́жественный**, ignorant, unenlightened. **неве́жество**, -а, ignorance; rudeness, bad manners, discourtesy. **неве́жливый**, rude, impolite, ill-mannered. **невели́кий** -и́к, -а́, -и́ко́, small; short; slight, insignificant. **неве́рие**, -я, unbelief, atheism; lack of faith, scepticism. **неве́рный**, -рен, -рна́, -о. incorrect, wrong; inaccurate, uncertain, unsteady; false; faithless, disloyal; unfaithful; Фома́ ~, doubting Thomas. **невероя́тный**, improbable, unlikely; incredible, unbelievable. **неве́рующий**, unbelieving; *sb.* unbeliever, atheist. **невесёлый**, joyless, sad. **невесо́мость**, -и, weightlessness. **не-весо́мый**, weightless; imponderable, insignificant.

неве́ста, -ы, fiancée; bride. **неве́стка**, -и, daughter-in-law; brother's wife, sister-in-law.

не-. невзго́да, -ы, adversity, misfortune. **невзира́я на** *prep.* + *acc.* in spite of; regardless of. **невзнача́й** *adv.* by chance, unexpectedly. **невзра́чный**, unattractive, plain. **невзыска́тель-ный**, unexacting, undemanding. **неви́-даль**, -и, wonder, prodigy. **невида́н-ный**, unprecedented, unheard of; mysterious. **невиди́мый**, invisible. **неви́дящий**, unseeing. **неви́нность**, -и, innocence. **неви́нный**, innocent. **невино́вный**, innocent, not guilty. **невку́с-ный**, tasteless, unappetizing, not nice. **невменя́емый**, irresponsible, not responsible; beside oneself. **невмеша́-тельство**, -а, non-intervention; non-interference. **невмоготу́, невмо́чь** *advs.* unbearable, unendurable, too much (for). **невнима́ние**, -я, inattention; carelessness; lack of consideration. **невнима́тельный**, inattentive, thoughtless. **невня́тный**, indistinct, incomprehensible.

не́вод, -а, seine, seine-net.

не-. невозврати́мый, невозвра́тный, irrevocable, irrecoverable. **невозвра-ще́нец**, -нца, defector. **невозде́лан-ный**, untilled, waste. **невоздержанный, невозде́ржный**, intemperate; incontinent; uncontrolled, unrestrained. **не-возмо́жный**, impossible; insufferable. **невозмути́мый**, imperturbable; calm, unruffled.

нево́лить, -лю *imp.* (*perf.* при~) force, compel. **нево́льник**, -а, -ница, -ы, slave. **нево́льно** *adv.* involuntarily; unintentionally. **нево́льный**, involuntary; unintentional; forced; ~ная поса́дка, forced landing. **нево́ля**, -и, bondage, captivity; necessity.

не-. невообрази́мый, unimaginable, inconceivable. **невооружён**|**ный**, unarmed; ~ным гла́зом, with the naked eye. **невоспи́танность**, -и, ill breeding, bad manners. **невоспи́танный**, ill-bred. **невоспламеня́емый** not inflammable, non-flam. **невосприи́мчивый,** unreceptive; immune. **невпопа́д** *adv.* out of place; irrelevant, inopportune. **невралги́ческий,** neuralgic. **невралги́я, -и,** neuralgia.

невреди́мый, safe, unharmed, uninjured. **неври́т, -а,** neuritis. **невро́з, -а,** neurosis. **невроло́гический,** neurological. **невроло́гия, -и,** neurology. **невроти́ческий,** neurotic.

не-. невруче́ние, -я, non-delivery. **невы́года, -ы,** disadvantage, loss. **невы́годный,** disadvantageous, unfavourable; unprofitable, unremunerative. **невы́держанный,** lacking self-control; unmatured. **невыноси́мый,** unbearable, insufferable, intolerable. **невыполне́ние, -я,** non-fulfilment, non-compliance. **невыполни́мый,** impracticable. **невырази́мый,** inexpressible, unmentionable. **невысо́кий; -со́к, -а́, -о́ко,** not high, low; not tall, short. **невы́ясненный,** obscure, uncertain. **невя́зка, -и,** discrepancy.

не́га, -и, luxury; bliss, delight; voluptuousness.

негашён|ый, unslaked; ~**ая и́звесть,** quicklime.

не́где *adv.* there is nowhere.

не-. неги́бкий; -бок, -бка́, -о. inflexible, stiff. **негла́сный,** secret. **неглубо́кий; -о́к, -а́, -о,** rather shallow; superficial. **неглу́п|ый; -уп, -а́, -о,** sensible, quite intelligent; **он** ~**,** he is no fool. **него́дник, -а,** reprobate, scoundrel good-for-nothing. **него́дный; -ден, -дна́, -о,** unfit, unsuitable; worthless. **негодова́ние, -я,** indignation. **негодова́ть, -ду́ю** *imp.* be indignant. **негоду́ющий,** indignant. **негодя́й, -я.** scoundrel, rascal. **негостеприи́мный,** inhospitable.

негр, -а, Negro.

негра́мотность, -и, illiteracy. **негра́мотный,** illiterate.

негритёнок, -нка; *pl.* -**тя́та, -тя́т,** Negro child. **негритя́нка, -и,** Negress. **негритя́нский, не́грский,** Negro.

не-. неда́вний, recent. **неда́вно** *adv.* recently. **недалёкий; -ёк, -а́, -ёко, -о.** not far away, near; short; not bright, dull-witted. **недалеко́** *adv.* not far, near.

неда́ром *adv.* not for nothing, not without reason, not without purpose. **недви́жимость, -и,** real property, real estate. **недви́жимый,** immovable, motionless. **недвусмы́сленный,** unequivocal. **недействи́тельный,** ineffective, ineffectual; invalid, null and void. **недели́мый,** indivisible.

неде́льный, of a week, week's. **неде́ля, -и,** week.

не-. недёшево *adv.* not cheap(ly), dear(ly). **недоброжела́тель, -я** *m.* ill-wisher. **недоброжела́тельность, -и, недоброжела́тельство, -а,** hostility, ill-will, malevolence. **недоброжела́тельный,** ill-disposed, hostile, malevolent. **недоброка́чественный,** of poor quality, low-grade; bad. **недобросо́вестный,** unscrupulous; not conscientious, careless. **недо́брый; -бр, -бра́, -о,** unkind, unfriendly; bad; evil, wicked. **недове́рие, -я,** distrust; mistrust; lack of confidence. **недове́рчивый,** distrustful, not confident, mistrustful. **недове́с, -а,** short weight. **недово́льный,** dissatisfied, discontented, displeased; *sb.* malcontent. **недово́льство, -а,** dissatisfaction, discontent, displeasure. **недога́дливый,** slow-witted. **недогляде́ть, -яжу́** *perf.* overlook; take insufficient care of. **недоеда́ние, -я,** malnutrition. **недоеда́ть, -а́ю** *imp.* be undernourished, be underfed, not eat enough. **недозво́ленный,** unlawful; illicit.

недои́мка, -и, arrears. **недои́мочность, -и,** non-payment. **недои́мщик, -а,** defaulter, person in arrears.

не-. недо́лг|ий; -лог, -лга́, -о short, brief; **вот и вся** ~**а́,** that's all there is to it. **недо́лго** *adv.* not long. **недолгове́чный,** short-lived, ephemeral. **недоме́р, -а,** short measure. **недоме́рок, -рка,** undersized object; small size. **недомога́ние, -я,** indisposition. **недомога́ть, -а́ю** *imp.* be unwell, be indisposed. **недомо́лвка, -и,** reservation, omission. **недомы́слие, -я,** thoughtlessness. **недоно́сок, -ска,** premature child. **недоно́шенный,** premature. **недооце́нивать, -аю** *imp.,* **недооцени́ть, -ню́, -нишь** *perf.* underestimate, underrate. **недооцéнка**, -и, underestimation. **недопроизвóдство**, -а, underproduction. **недопустúмый**, inadmissible, intolerable. **недоразумéние**, -я, misunderstanding. **недорогóй**, -дóрог, -á, -о, not dear, inexpensive; reasonable, modest. **недорóд**, -а, crop failure, bad harvest. **недосмóтр**, -а, oversight. **недосмотрéть**, -рю́ -ришь perf. overlook, miss; take insufficient care. **недоспáть**, -плю́ -áл, -á, -о perf. (imp. **недосыпáть**) have not enough sleep.

недоставáть, -таёт imp., **недостáть**, -áнет perf. impers. be missing, be lacking, be wanting. **недостáток**, -тка, shortage, lack, deficiency; want; shortcoming, defect. **недостáточно** adv. insufficiently, not enough. **недостáточный**, insufficient, inadequate; ~ глагóл, defective verb. **недостáча**, -и, lack, shortage, deficit.

не-. **недостижúмый**, unattainable. **недостовéрный**, not authentic, doubtful. apocryphal. **недостóйный**, unworthy. **недостýпный**, inaccessible. **недосýг**, а, lack of time, being too busy; ~ом for lack of time. **недосчитáться**, -áюсь perf. **недосчúтываться**, -аюсь imp. miss, find missing, be short (of). **недосыпáть**, -áю imp. of недоспáть. **недосягáемый**, unattainable. **недотрóга**, и m. and f. touch-me-not person; f. mimosa.

недоумевáть, -áю imp. be puzzled, be at a loss, be bewildered. **недоумéние**, -я, perplexity, bewilderment. **недоумéнный**, puzzled, perplexed.

не-. **недóучка**, -и m. and f. half-educated person. **недохвáтка**, -и, shortage, lack. **недочёт**, -а, a deficit, shortage; shortcoming, defect.

нéдра, недр pl. depths, heart, bowels; богáтство недр, mineral wealth.

не-. **недремлющий**, unsleeping, watchful, vigilant. **недрýг**, -а, enemy. **недружелюбный**, unfriendly.

недýг, а, illness, disease.

недурнóй, not bad; not bad-looking.

недюжинный, out of the ordinary, outstanding, exceptional.

не-. **неестéственный**, unnatural. **нежданно** adv. unexpectedly; ~-негá-

данно, quite unexpectedly. **нежданный**, unexpected, unlooked-for. **нежелáние**, -я, unwillingness, disinclination. **нежелáтельный**, undesirable, unwanted. **женáтый**, unmarried. **нéженка**, -и m. and f. mollycoddle. **нежилóй**, uninhabited; not habitable. **нéжить**, -жу imp. pamper; indulge; caress; ~ся, luxuriate, bask. **нéжничать**, -аю imp. bill and coo; be soft, be over-indulgent. **нéжность**, -и, tenderness; delicacy; pl. endearments, compliments, flattery. **нéжный**, tender; delicate; affectionate.

не-. **незабвéнный**, unforgettable. **незабýдка**, -и, forget-me-not. **незабывáемый**, unforgettable. **незавéренный**, uncertified. **незавúсимо** adv. independently; ~ от, irrespective of. **незавúсимый**, independent; sovereign. **незавúсящ|ий**, по ~им от нас обстоятельствам, owing to circumstances beyond our control. **незадáча**, -и, ill luck, bad luck. **незадáчливый**, unlucky; luckless. **незадóлго** adv. not long. **незакóнный**, illegal, illicit, unlawful; illegitimate. **незакóнченный**, unfinished incomplete. **незаменúмый**, irreplaceable, indispensable. **незамерзáющ|ий**, ice-free; anti-freeze; ~ая смесь, anti-freeze. **незамéтно** adv. imperceptibly, insensibly. **незамéтный**, imperceptible; inconspicuous, insignificant. **незамýжняя**, unmarried. **незамысловáтый**, simple, uncomplicated. **незапамятный**, immemorial. **незапятнанный**, unstained, unsullied. **незарáзный**, non-contagious. **незаслýженный**, unmerited, undeserved. **незастрóенный**, not built on, undeveloped; vacant. **незатéйливый**, simple, plain; modest. **незаурядный**, uncommon, outstanding out of the ordinary.

нéзачем adv. there is no need; it is useless, pointless, no use.

не-. **незащищённый**, unprotected. **незвáный**, uninvited. **нездорóвиться**, -ится imp. impers.; мне нездорóвится, I don't feel well, I am not well. **нездорóвый**, unhealthy, sickly; morbid; unwholesome; unwell. **нездорóвье**, -я, indisposition; ill health. **неземнóй**, not of the earth; unearthly. **незло́бивый**, gentle, mild, forgiving. **незнако́мец**, -мца, **незнако́мка**, -и, stranger. **незнако́мый**, unknown, unfamiliar; unacquainted. **незна́ние**, -я, ignorance. **незна́чащий**, **незначи́тельный** insignificant. unimportant, of no consequence. **незре́лый**, unripe, immature. **незри́мый**, invisible. **незы́блемый**, unshakable, stable, firm. **неизбе́жный** inevitable, unavoidable, inescapable. **незве́данный**, unknown, unexplored; not experienced before.

неизве́стное *sb.* unknown quantity. **неизве́стность**, -и, uncertainty; ignorance; obscurity. **неизве́стный**, unknown; *sb.* stranger, unknown.

не-. **неизглади́мый**, indelible, uneffaceable. **неизда́нный**, unpublished. **неизлечи́мый**, incurable. **неизме́нный**, unchanged, unchanging; devoted, true. **неизменя́емый**, invariable, unalterable. **неизмери́мый**, immeasurable, immense. **неизу́ченный**, unstudied; obscure, unknown; unexplored. **неиме́ние**, -я, lack, want; absence; за ~м + *gen.* for want of. **неимове́рный**, incredible, unbelievable. **неиму́щий**, indigent needy, poor. **нейскренний**, insincere; false. **неиску́сный**, unskilful, inexpert. **неискушённый**, inexperienced, innocent, unsophisticated. **неисполне́ние**, -я, non-performance, non-observance, non-execution. **неисполни́мый**, impracticable, unrealizable. **неисправи́мый**, incorrigible; irremediable, irreparable. **неиспра́вность**, -и, disrepair, fault, defect; carelessness. **неиспра́вный**, out of order, faulty, defective; careless. **неиссле́дованный**, unexplored, uninvestigated. **неиссяка́емый**, inexhaustible. **неи́стовство**, -а, fury, frenzy; violence; savagery, atrocity. **неи́стовый**, furious, frenzied, uncontrolled. **неистощи́мый**, **неисчерпа́емый**, inexhaustible. **неисчисли́мый**, innumerable, incalculable.

нейло́н, -а, **нейло́новый**, nylon.

нейро́н, -а, neuron.

нейтрализа́ция, -и, neutralization. **нейтрализова́ть**, -зу́ю *perf.* and *imp.* neutralize. **нейтралите́т**, -а, **нейтра́ль-**ность, -и, neutrality. **нейтра́льный**, neutral. **нейтри́но**, -а, neutrino. **нейтро́н**, -а, neutron.

неквалифици́рованный, unskilled; unqualified.

не́кий *pron.* a certain, some.

не́когда[1] *adv.* once, long ago, in the old days.

не́когда[2] *adv.* there is no time; мне ~, I have no time.

не́кого (*-го*), **не́кому**, **не́кем**, **не́ о ком** *pron.* (with separable *pref.*), there is nobody.

неколеби́мый, unshakeable.

некомпете́нтный, not competent, unqualified.

не́котор|ый *pron.* some; ~ым о́бразом, somehow, in a way; ~ые *sb. pl.* some, some people.

некраси́вый, plain, ugly, unsightly, unpleasant.

некро́з, -а, necrosis. **некроло́г**, -а, obituary (notice). **некрома́нтия**, -и, necromancy; telling fortunes.

некры́тый, roofless.

некста́ти *adv.* malapropos, unseasonably, at the wrong time, out of place.

не́кто *pron.* somebody; one, a certain.

не́куда *adv.* there is nowhere.

не-. **некульту́рный**, uncivilized, uncultured; uncultivated; barbarous, ill-mannered; uncouth, boorish. **некуря́щий** *sb.* non-smoker. **нела́дн|ый**, wrong; здесь что́-то ~о, something is wrong here; будь он ~ен! blast him! **нела́ды**, -ов *pl.* discord, disagreement; trouble, something wrong. **нелега́льный**, illegal. **нелега́льщина**, -ы, illegal literature, illegal activity. **нелёгкая** *sb.* the devil, the deuce. **нелёгкий**, difficult, not easy; heavy, not light. **неле́пость**, -и, absurdity, nonsense. **неле́пый**, absurd, ridiculous. **нело́вк|ий**, awkward, clumsy, gauche; uncomfortable, embarrassing; мне ~о, I'm uncomfortable. **нело́вко** *adv.* awkwardly, uncomfortably. **нело́вкость**, -и, awkwardness, gaucherie, clumsiness; blunder.

нельзя́ *adv.* it is impossible, it is not allowed; one ought not, one should not, one can't; здесь кури́ть ~, smoking is not allowed here; как ~ лу́чше, in the best possible way.

не-. нелюбёзный, ungracious; discourteous. нелюби́мый, unloved. нелюди́м, -а нелюди́мка, -и, unsociable person. нелюди́мый, unsociable; unpeopled lonely. нема́ло adv. not a little, not a few; a considerable amount or number. немалова́жный, of no small importance. нема́лый, no small, considerable. неме́дленно adv. immediately, at once, without delay. неме́дленный, immediate.

неме́ть, -ею imp. (perf. за~, о~) become dumb; grow numb. не́мец, -мца, German. неме́цк|ий, German; ~ая овча́рка, Alsatian.

неми́лость, -и, disgrace, disfavour. неминуемый, inevitable, unavoidable.

не́мка -и, German.

немно́г|ий, a little; not much; (a) few; ~ие sb. pl. few, a few. немно́го adv. a little; some, not much; a few; somewhat, slightly. немногосло́вный, laconic, brief, terse. немно́жко adv. a little, a bit, a trifle.

немну́щийся, uncrushable, crease-resistant.

нем|о́й; нем, -а́, -о, dumb, mute, (utterly) silent; ~а́я а́збука, deaf-and--dumb alphabet; ~о́й согла́сный, voiceless consonant; ~о́й фильм, silent film. ~ота́, -ы, dumbness.

не́мощный, feeble, ill, sick. не́мощь, -и, sickness; feebleness, infirmity.

немудрёный, simple, easy; немудрено́, no wonder.

ненави́деть, -и́жу imp. hate, detest, loathe. ненави́стник, -а, hater. ненави́стный, hated, hateful. не́нависть, -и, hatred.

не-. ненагля́дный, dear, beloved. ненадёжный, insecure; unreliable, untrustworthy. ненадёжность, -и, uselessness ненадо́лго adv. for a short time, not for long. ненападе́ние, -я, non-aggression. ненаруши́мый, inviolable. ненаси́лие, -я, non-violence. нена́стный, bad, foul, rainy. нена́стье, -я, bad weather, wet weather. ненасто́ящий, artificial, imitation, counterfeit. ненасы́тный, insatiable. нену́жный, unnecessary, superfluous.

нео- pref. neo-. нео́зойский, neozoic. ~класси́цизм, -а, neo-classicism. ~колониали́зм, -а, neo-colonialism. ~фаши́стский, neo-fascist. ~фи́т, -а, neophyte.

не-. необду́манный, thoughtless, hasty, precipitate. необеспе́ченный, without means, unprovided for, not provided (with). необита́емый, uninhabited; ~ о́стров, desert island. необозна́ченный, not indicated, not marked. необозри́мый, boundless, immense, необосно́ванный, unfounded, groundless. необрабо́танный, uncultivated, untilled; raw, crude; unpolished, untrained. необразо́ванный, uneducated. необу́зданный, unbridled, ungovernable. необу́ченный, untrained.

необходи́мость, -и, necessity; по необходи́мости, of necessity, perforce. необходи́мый, necessary, essential.

не-. необъясни́мый, inexplicable, unaccountable. необъя́тный, immense, unbounded. необыкнове́нный, unusual, uncommon. необыча́йный, extraordinary, exceptional, unaccustomed. необы́чный, unusual singular. необяза́тельный, optional. неограни́ченный, unlimited, absolute. неоднокра́тно adv. repeatedly, more than once. неоднокра́тный, repeated. неодобре́ние, -я, disapproval. неодобри́тельный, disapproving. неодушевлённый, inanimate.

неожи́данность, -и, unexpectedness, suddenness; surprise. неожи́данный, unexpected, sudden.

не-. неоконча́тельный, inconclusive. неоко́нченный, unfinished. неописуемый, indescribable. неопла́тный, that cannot be repaid; insolvent. неопла́ченный, unpaid. неопра́вданный, unjustified, unwarranted. неопределённый, indefinite, indeterminate; infinitive; vague, uncertain. неопредели́мый, indefinable. неопрове́ржимый, irrefutable; incontestable. неопря́тный, slovenly, untidy, sloppy. неопублико́ванный, unpublished. нео́пытность, -и, inexperience. нео́пытный, inexperienced. **неосведомлённый**, ill-informed. **неосéдлый**, nomadic. **неослáбный**, unremitting, unabated, untiring. **неосмотрѝтельный**, imprudent, incautious; indiscreet. **неослѝовáтельный**, unfounded, unwarranted; frivolous. **неоспорѝмый**, unquestionable, incontestable, indisputable. **неосторóжный**, careless, imprudent, indiscreet, incautious. **неосуществѝмый**, impracticable, unrealizable. **неосязáмый**, intangible. **неотвратѝмый**, inevitable. **неотвя́зный, неотвя́зчивый**, importunate; obsessive. **неотёсанный**, rough, undressed; unpolished, uncouth.

нéоткуда adv. there is nowhere; there is no reason; мне ∼ э́то получѝть, there is nowhere I can get it from.

не-. неотлóжн|ый, urgent, pressing; ∼ая пóмощь, first aid. **неотлу́чно** adv. constantly, continually, unremittingly; permanent. **неотлу́чный**, continual, constant, permanent. **неотрази́мый**, irresistible; incontrovertible, irrefutable. **неотсту́пный**, persistent, importunate. **неотъéмлемый**, inalienable; inseparable, integral. **неохóта**, -ы, reluctance. **неохóтно** adv. reluctantly; unwillingly. **неоценѝмый**, inestimable invaluable. **неощутѝмый**, imperceptible. **непáрный**, odd. **непартѝйный**, non-party; unbefitting a member of the (Communist) Party. **непереводѝмый**, untranslatable. **непередавáемый**, incommunicable, inexpressive. **непереходный**, intransitive. **непечáтный**, unprintable.

неплатёж, -ежá, non-payment. **неплатёжеспосóбный**, insolvent. **неплатéльщик**, -а, defaulter; person in arrears.

не-. неплодорóдный, infertile. **неплóхо** adv. not badly, quite well. **неплохóй**, not bad, quite good. **непобедѝмый**, invincible, unbeatable. **неповиновéние**, -я, insubordination, disobedience. **неповорóтливый**, clumsy, awkward; sluggish, slow. **неповторѝмый**, inimitable, unique. **непогóда**, -ы, bad weather. **непогрешѝмый**, infallible. **неподалёку** adv. not far (away). **не-**

подáтливый, stubborn, intractable, unyielding. **неподвѝжный**, motionless, immobile, immovable; fixed, stationary. **неподдéльный**, genuine, sincere, unfeigned. **неподку́пный**, incorruptible, unbribable. **неподражáемый**, inimitable. **неподходя́щий**, unsuitable, inappropriate. **непокóйный**, troubled, disturbed, restless. **непоколебѝмый**, unshakable, steadfast. **непокóрный**, recalcitrant, unruly, insubordinate. **непокры́тый**, uncovered, bare.

не-. неполáдки **-док** pl. defects. **неполноцéнность**, -и; кóмплекс неполноцéнности, inferiority complex. **неполноцéнный**, defective, imperfect; inadequate. **непóлный**, incomplete; defective; not quite, not (a) full. **непомéрный**, excessive, inordinate. **непонимáние**, -я, incomprehension, lack of understanding. **непоня́тливый**, slow-witted, stupid, dull. **непоня́тный**, unintelligible, incomprehensible. **непоправѝмый**, irreparable, irremediable. **непоря́док**, -дка, disorder. **непоря́дочный**, dishonourable. **непосвящённый**, uninitiated. **непосéда**, -ы, m. and f. fidget, restless person. **непосѝльный**, beyond one's strength, excessive. **непослéдовательный**, inconsistent; inconsequent. **непослушáние**, -я, disobedience. **непослу́шный**, disobedient, naughty. **непосрéдственный**, immediate, direct; spontaneous; ingenuous. **непостижѝмый**, incomprehensible. **непостоя́нный**, inconstant, changeable. **непостоя́нство**, -а, inconstancy. **непотопля́емый**, unsinkable. **непотрéбный**, obscene, indecent; useless; bad. **непочáтый**, untouched, not begun; ∼ край, у́гол, a lot, a wealth, no end. **непочтéние**, -я, disrespect. **непочтѝтельный**, disrespectful.

не-. непрáвда, -ы, untruth, falsehood, lie. **неправдоподóбие**, -я, improbability, unlikelihood. **неправдоподóбный**, improbable, unlikely, implausible. **непрáвильно** adv. wrong; irregularly; incorrectly; erroneously. **непрáвильность**, -и, irregularity; anomaly; incorrectness. **непрáвильн|ый**, irregular; anomalous; incorrect, erroneous, wrong, mistaken; ~ая дробь, improper fraction. неправомо́чный, incompetent; not entitled. неправоспосо́бный, disqualified. неправота́, -ы́, error; injustice. непра́вый, wrong, mistaken; unjust. непракти́чный, unpractical. непревзойдённый, unsurpassed, matchless. непредви́денный, unforeseen. непредубеждённый, unprejudiced. непредусмо́тренный, unforeseen; unprovided for. непредусмотри́тельный, improvident, short-sighted. непрекло́нный, inflexible, unbending; inexorable, adamant. непрело́жный immutable, unalterable; indisputable.

не-. непреме́нно adv. without fail; certainly; absolutely. непреме́нный, indispensable, necessary; ~ секрета́рь, permanent secretary. непреодоли́мый, insuperable, insurmountable; irresistible. непреры́вно adv. uninterruptedly, continuously. непреры́вный, uninterrupted, unbroken; continuous. непреста́нный, incessant, continual. неприве́тливый, unfriendly, ungracious; bleak. непривлека́тельный, unattractive. непривы́чный, unaccustomed, unwonted, unusual. непригля́дный, unattractive, unsightly. неприго́дный, unfit, unserviceable, useless; ineligible. неприе́млемый, unacceptable. неприкоснове́нность, -и, inviolability; immunity. неприкосно́ве́нный, inviolable; to be kept intact; reserve, emergency. неприкра́шенный, plain, unadorned, unvarnished. неприли́чный, indecent, improper; unseemly, unbecoming. неприме́ни́мый, inapplicable. неприми́ри́мый, irreconcilable. непринуждённый, unconstrained; natural, relaxed, easy; spontaneous. неприспосо́бленный, unadapted; maladjusted. непристо́йный, obscene, indecent. непристу́пный, inaccessible, impregnable; unapproachable, haughty. непритво́рный unfeigned. непритяза́тельный. неприхотли́вый, modest, unpretentious, simple, plain. неприя́зненный, hostile, inimical. неприя́знь, -и, hostility, enmity. неприя́тель, -я m.

enemy. неприя́тельский, hostile, enemy. неприя́тный, unpleasant, disagreeable; annoying, troublesome; obnoxious.

не-. непрове́ренный, unverified, unchecked. непроводни́к, -а́, non-conductor. непроводя́щий, non-conducting. непрогля́дный, impenetrable; pitch-dark. непродолжи́тельный, short, short-lived. непроду́манный, rash, unconsidered. непрое́зжий impassable. непрозра́чный, opaque. непроизводи́тельный, unproductive; wasteful. непроизво́льный, involuntary. непрола́зный, impassable, impenetrable. непромока́емый, waterproof. непроница́емый, impenetrable, impervious; inscrutable; +для+gen. proof against. непрости́тельный, unforgivable, unpardonable, inexcusable. непроходи́мый, impassable; complete, utter, hopeless. непро́чный; -чен, -чна́, -о, fragile flimsy; precarious, unstable; not durable.

не прочь predic. not averse; я ~ пойти́ туда́, I wouldn't mind going there.

не-. непро́шеный, uninvited, unasked (-for). нерабо́тоспосо́бный, incapacitated, disabled. нерабо́чий; ~ день, day off, free day. нера́венство, -а, inequality, disparity. неравноме́рный, uneven, irregular. нера́вный, unequal. неради́вый, negligent, indolent, careless, remiss. неразбери́ха, -и muddle, confusion. неразбо́рчивый, not fastidious; unscrupulous; illegible. неразви́то́й; -ра́звит, -á, -о, undeveloped; backward. неразгово́рчивый taciturn, not talkative. неразде́ли́мый, неразде́льный, indivisible, inseparable. неразличи́мый, indistinguishable. неразлу́чный, inseparable. неразрешённый, unsolved; forbidden, prohibited. неразреши́мый, insoluble. неразры́вный, indissoluble, inseparable. неразу́мный, unwise, unreasonable. нерасположе́ние, -я, dislike; disinclination. нерасполо́женный, ill-disposed; unwilling, disinclined. нераствори́мый, insoluble. нерасчётливый, extravagant, wasteful; improvident.

нерв, -а, nerve; гла́вный ~, nerve-centre. **нерви́ческий**, nervous. **нервнобольно́й** sb. neurotic, nervous case. **не́рвный**; -вен, -вна́, -о, nervous; neural; irritable, highly strung; ~ у́зел, ganglion. **нервю́ра**, -ы, rib.

не-. **нереа́льный**, unreal; unrealistic. **нере́дкий**; -док, -дка́, -о, not infrequent, not uncommon. **нере́дко** adv. not infrequently. **нереши́мость**, -и, **нереши́тельность**, -и, indecision; irresolution. **нереши́тельный**, indecisive, irresolute, undecided. **нержаве́ющ|ий**, rustless; ~ая сталь, stainless steel. **неро́вный**; -вен, -вна́, -о, uneven, rough; unequal, irregular. **нерукотво́рный**, not made with hands. **неруши́мый**, inviolable, indestructible, indissoluble.

неря́ха, -и m. and f. sloven; slattern, slut. **неря́шливый**, slovenly, untidy, slatternly; careless, slipshod.

не-. **несбы́точн|ый**, unrealizable; ~ые мечты́, castles in the air; ~ые наде́жды, vain hopes. **несваре́ние** -я; ~ желу́дка, indigestion. **несве́жий**; -е́ж, -а́, not fresh; stale; tainted; weary, washed-out. **несвоевре́менный**, ill-timed, inopportune; overdue, not at the right time. **несво́йственный**, not characteristic, unusual, unlike. **несвя́зный**, disconnected, incoherent. **несгиба́емый**, unbending, inflexible. **несгово́рчивый**, intractable, hard to handle. **несгора́емый**, fireproof; ~ шкаф, safe.

несессе́р, -а, dressing-case.

нескла́дный, incoherent; ungainly, awkward; absurd.

несклоня́емый, indeclinable.

не́сколько, -их pron. some, several; a number a few; adv. somewhat, a little, rather.

не-. **несконча́емый**, interminable, never-ending. **нескро́мный**; -мен, -мна́, -о, immodest; vain; indelicate, tactless, indiscreet. **несло́жный**, simple. **неслы́ханный**, unheard of, unprecedented. **неслы́шный**, inaudible; noiseless. **несме́тный**, countless, incalculable, innumerable. **не-**

смина́емый, uncrushable, crease-resistant. **несмолка́емый**, ceaseless, unremitting.

несмотря́ на prep.+acc. in spite of, despite notwithstanding.

не-. **несно́сный**, intolerable, insupportable, unbearable. **несоблюде́ние**, -я, non-observance. **несовершенноле́тие** -я, minority. **несовершенноле́тний**, under age; sb. minor. **несоверше́нный**, imperfect, incomplete; imperfective. **несовмести́мость**, -и, incompatibility. **несовмести́мый**, incompatible. **несогла́сие**, disagreement, difference; discord, variance; refusal. **несогла́сный**, not agreeing; inconsistent, incompatible; discordant; not consenting. **несогласова́ние**, -я, non-agreement. **несогласо́ванный**, uncoordinated, not concerted. **несозна́тельный**, irresponsible. **несоизмери́мый**, incommensurable. **несокруши́мый**, indestructible; unconquerable. **несоло́но**: уйти́ ~ хлеба́вши, get nothing for one's pains, go away empty-handed. **несомне́нно** adv. undoubtedly, doubtless, beyond question. **несомне́нный**, undoubted, indubitable; unquestionable. **несообра́зный**, incongruous, incompatible; absurd. **несоотве́тствие**, -я, disparity, incongruity. **несоразме́рный**, disproportionate. **несостоя́тельный**, insolvent, bankrupt; not wealthy, of modest means; groundless, unsupported. **неспе́лый**, unripe. **неспоко́йный**, restless; uneasy. **неспосо́бный**, dull, not able; incapable, not competent. **несправедли́вый**, unjust, unfair; incorrect, unfounded. **неспроста́** adv. not without purpose; with an ulterior motive. **несравне́нно** adv. incomparably, matchlessly; far, by far. **несравне́нный**; -е́нен, -е́нна, incomparable, matchless. **несрави́мый**, not comparable; incomparable, unmatched. **нестерпи́мый**, unbearable, unendurable.

нести́, -су́, -сёшь; нёс, -ла́ imp. (perf. по~, с~) carry; bear; bring, take; support; suffer; incur; perform; talk; lay; impers.+instr. stink of, reek of; **~сь**, rush, tear, fly; float, drift, be carried; skim; spread, be diffused; lay, lay eggs.

не-. **нестойкий**, unstable. **нестроевик**, -а, non-combatant. **нестроевой**, non--combatant. **нестройный**; -óен, -ойна, -о, discordant, dissonant; disorderly; clumsily built. **несудоходный**, unnavigable. **несущественный**, immaterial, inessential.

несу́, etc.: see **нести́**. **несу́щий**, supporting, carrying, bearing, lifting.

несхо́дный, unlike, dissimilar; unreasonable.

несчастли́вец, -вца, ~ вица, -ы, unlucky person; unfortunate. **несчастли́вый**, unfortunate, unlucky; unhappy. **несча́стный**, unhappy, unfortunate, unlucky; *sb.* wretch, unfortunate. **несча́стье**, -я, misfortune; accident; к несча́стью, unfortunately.

несчётный, innumerable, countless.

нет *part.* no, not; nothing; ~ да ~, ~ как ~, absolutely not; свести́ на ~, bring to naught; ~-~ да и, from time to time, every now and then. **нет**, **нету**, there is not, there are not.

не-. **нетакти́чный**, tactless. **нетвёрдый**; -ёрд, -á, -о, unsteady, shaky; not firm. **нетерпели́вый**, impatient. **нетерпе́ние**, -я, impatience. **нетерпи́мый**, intolerable, intolerant. **нето́чный**; -чен, -чнá, -о, inaccurate, inexact. **нетре́бовательный**, not exacting, undemanding, unpretentious. **нетре́звый**, drunk, intoxicated. **нетро́нутый**, untouched; chaste, virginal. **нетрудово́й**; ~ дохо́д, unearned income. **нетрудоспосо́бность**, -и, disablement, disability.

не́тто *indecl. adj.* and *adv.*, net, nett.

не́ту: see **нет**.

не-. **неубеди́тельный**, unconvincing. **неуваже́ние**, -я, disrespect. **неуважи́тельный**, inadequate; disrespectful. **неуве́ренный**, uncertain; hesitant; ~ в себе́, diffident. **неувяда́емый**, **неувяда́ющий**, unfading, eternal, immortal. **неувя́зка**, -и, lack of co-ordination; misunderstanding. **неугаси́мый**, inextinguishable, unquenchable; never extinguished. **неугомо́нный**, restless; unsleeping, indefatigable. **неуда́ча**, -и,

failure. **неуда́чливый**, unlucky. **неуда́чник**, -а, -ница, -ы, unlucky person, failure. **неуда́чный**, unsuccessful, unfortunate. **неудержи́мый**, irrepressible. **неудо́бный**, uncomfortable; inconvenient, awkward, embarrassing. **неудо́бство**, -а, discomfort, inconvenience, embarrassment. **неудовлетворе́ние**, -я, dissatisfaction. **неудовлетворённый**, discontented. **неудовлетвори́тельный**, unsatisfactory. **неудово́льствие**, -я, displeasure.

неуже́ли? *part.* indeed? really? surely not?; ~ он так ду́мает? does he really think that?

не-. **неузнава́емый**, unrecognizable. **неуклóнный**, steady, steadfast; undeviating, unswerving, strict. **неуклю́жий**, clumsy, awkward. **неукроти́мый**, ungovernable, untamable. **неукрощённый**; -ён, -á, untamed. **неулови́мый**, elusive, difficult to catch; imperceptible, subtle. **неуме́лый**, unskilful; clumsy. **неуме́ренный**, immoderate; excessive. **неуме́стный**, inappropriate; out of place, misplaced; irrelevant. **неумоли́мый**, implacable, inexorable. **неумы́шленный**, unintentional.

не-. **неупла́та**, -ы, non-payment. **неупотреби́тельный**, not in use, not current. **неуравнове́шенный**, unbalanced. **неурожа́й**, -я, bad harvest, crop failure. **неуро́чный**, untimely, unseasonable, inopportune. **неуря́дица**, -ы, disorder, mess; squabbling, squabble. **неуспева́емость**, -и, poor progress. **неуспева́ющий**, not making satisfactory progress. **неуспе́х**, -а, failure, ill success. **неусто́йка**, -и, forfeit, penalty; failure. **неусто́йчивый**, unstable; unsteady. **неустраши́мый**, fearless, intrepid. **неусту́пчивый**, unyielding, uncompromising. **неусы́пный**, vigilant, unremitting. **неуте́шный**, inconsolable, disconsolate. **неутоли́мый**, unquenchable; unappeasable; insatiable. **неутоми́мый**, tireless, indefatigable. **неу́ч**, -а. ignoramus. **неучти́вый**, discourteous, impolite. **неуязви́мый**, invulnerable; unassailable.

неф, -а, nave.

нефри́т, -а, jade.

нефте- in *comb.* oil, petroleum. **нефтево́з**, -а, tanker. **~но́сный**, oil-bearing. **~перего́нный заво́д**, oil refinery. **~прово́д**, -а, (oil) pipeline. **~проду́кты**, -ов *pl.* petroleum products. **~хими́ческий**, petrochemical.

нефть, -и, oil, petroleum; **~-сыре́ц**, crude oil. **нефтян|о́й**, oil, petroleum; oil-fired; **~о́е покрыва́ло**, **~а́я плёнка**, oil-slick.

не-. **нехва́тка**, -и shortage, deficiency. **нехорошо́** *adv.* badly. **нехоро́ш|ий**, -о́ш, -а́, bad; **~о́**, it is bad, it is wrong; как **~о́!** what a shame!; чу́вствовать себя́ **~о́**, feel unwell. **не́хотя** *adv.* reluctantly, unwillingly; unintentionally. **нецелесообра́зн|ый**, inexpedient; purposeless, pointless; **~ая тра́та**, waste. **нецензу́рный**, unprintable. **неча́янный**, unexpected; accidental; unintentional.

не́чего, не́чему, -чем, не́ о чем *pron.* (with separable *pref.*), (there is) nothing; it's no good, it's no use; there is no need; **~ де́лать**, there is nothing to be done; it can't be helped; **~ сказа́ть!** well, really! well, I must say!; от **~** де́лать, for want of something better to do, idly.

нечелове́ческий, inhuman, superhuman. **нечести́вый**, impious, profane. **нече́стно** *adv.* dishonestly, unfairly. **нече́стный**, dishonest, unfair.

не́чет, -а odd number. **нече́тный** *adj.* odd. **нечистопло́тный**, dirty; slovenly; unscrupulous. **нечистота́**, -ы́; *pl.* -о́ты, -о́т, dirtiness, dirt, filth; *pl.* sewage. **нечи́ст|ый**, -и́ст, -а́, -о, dirty, unclean; impure; adulterated; careless, inaccurate; dishonourable, dishonest; *sb.* the evil one, the devil. **не́чисть**, -и, evil spirits; scum, vermin.

нечленоразде́льный, inarticulate. **не́что** *pron.* something.

не-. **нешу́точн|ый**, grave, serious; **~ое де́ло**, no joke, no laughing matter. **неща́дный**, merciless, pitiless. **неэвкли́дов**, non-Euclidean. **нея́вка**, -и, non-appearance, failure to appear, absence. **неядови́тый**, non-poisonous,

non-toxic. **нея́ркий**, not bright; not vivid, not striking; dull, subdued. **нея́сный**; -сен, -сна́, -о, not clear; vague, obscure.

НЗ (*enzé*) *abbr.* неприкоснове́нный запа́с, emergency ration.

ни *part.* not a; ни оди́н (одна́, одно́), not one, not a single; (with *prons.* and *pronominal advs.*) -ever; как .. ни, however; кто .. ни, whoever; что .. ни, whatever; како́й ни на есть, any whatsoever. **ни**, *conj.*; ни .. ни, neither .. nor; ни за что ни про что, for no reason, without rhyme or reason; ни ры́ба ни мя́со, neither fish, flesh, nor good red herring; ни с того́, ни с сего́, all of a sudden, for no apparent reason; ни то ни сё, neither one thing nor the other.

ни́ва, -ы, cornfield, field.

нивели́р, -а, level. **нивели́ровать**, -рую *perf.* and *imp.* level; survey, contour. **нивелиро́вщик**, -а, surveyor.

нигде́ *adv.* nowhere.

нидерла́ндец, -дца; *gen. pl.* -дцев, Dutchman. **нидерла́ндка**, -и, Dutchwoman. **нидерла́ндский**, Dutch.

нижа́йший, lowest, humblest; very low, very humble. **ни́же** *adj.* lower humbler; *adv.* below; *prep.* + *gen.* below, beneath. **нижеподписа́вшийся**, (the) undersigned. **нижесле́дующий**, following. **нижестоя́щий**, subordinate. **нижеупомя́нутый**, (the) undermentioned. **нижн|ий**, lower, under-; **~ее бельё**, underclothes; **~ий эта́ж**, ground floor. **низ**, -а (-у), *loc.* -ý; *pl.* -ы́, bottom; ground floor; *pl.* lower classes; low notes.

низ-, **нис-**, *vbl. pref.* down, downward(s). **низа́ть**, нижу́, ни́жешь *imp.* (*perf.* на~), string, thread.

низверга́ть, -а́ю *imp.*, **низве́ргнуть**, -ну; -е́рг *perf.* precipitate; throw down, overthrow; **~ся**, crash down; be overthrown. **низверже́ние**, -я, overthrow.

низи́на, -ы, depression, hollow. **ни́зк|ий**; -зок, -зка́, -о, low; humble; base, mean. **ни́зко** *adv.* low; basely, meanly, despicably. **низкопокло́нник**, -а, toady, crawler. **низкопокло́нничать**,

-аю *imp.* crawl, cringe, grovel. **низко-
поклонство**, -а, obsequiousness, cringing, servility. **низкопро́бный**, base;
low-grade; inferior. **низкоро́слый**,
undersized, stunted, dwarfish. **низ-
косо́ртный**, low-grade, of inferior
quality.

ни́зменность, -и, lowland; baseness.
ни́зменный, low-lying; low, base, vile.
низово́й, lower; down-stream, from
lower down the Volga; local. **ни-
зо́вье**, -я; *gen. pl.* -ьев, the lower
reaches; **низо́вья Во́лги**, the lower
Volga. **ни́зость**, -и, lowness; baseness,
meanness. **ни́зш**|**ий**, lower, lowest;
~ее образова́ние, primary education;
~ий сорт, inferior quality.

НИИ (*nii*) *abbr.* нау́чно-иссле́доватеь-
ский институ́т, scientific research institute.

ника́к *adv.* by no means, in no way. **ни-
како́й** *pron.* no; no . . whatever.

ни́кель, -я *m.* nickel.

нике́м: see никто́. **никогда́** *adv.* never.
ник|**о́й**, no; ~о́им о́бразом, by no
means, in no way. **никто́**, -ого́,
-кому́, -ке́м, ни о ко́м *pron.* (with
separable *pref.*) nobody, no one.
никуда́, nowhere; ~ не годи́тся, (it)
is worthless, (it) is no good at all, (it)
won't do. **никудышный**, useless,
worthless, good-for-nothing. **ничем-
ный**, pointless, useless; no good.
нима́ло *adv.* not at all, not in the least.
нимб, -а, halo, nimbus.
ни́мфа, -ы, nymph; pupa. **нимфома́нка**,
-и, nymphomaniac.

ниоткуда *adv.* from nowhere; not from
anywhere.

нипочём *adv.* it is nothing; for nothing,
dirt cheap; never, in no circumstances.

ни́ппель, -я; *pl.* -я *m.* nipple.

НИС *abbr.* нау́чно-иссле́довательская
ста́нция, scientific research station.

нис-: see низ-.

ниско́лько *adv.* not at all, not in the
least.

ниспроверга́ть, -а́ю *imp.*, **ниспрове́рг-
нуть**, -ну -ерг *perf.* overthrow, overturn. **ниспроверже́ние**, -я, overthrow.

нисходя́щий, descending, of descent;
falling.

ни́тка, -и, thread; string; до ни́тки, to
the skin; на живу́ю ни́тку, hastily,
carelessly, anyhow. **ни́точка**, -и,
thread. **ни́точный**, thread; spinning.

нитро- in *comb.* nitro-. **нитробензо́л**, -а,
nitrobenzene. ~**глицери́н**, -а, nitroglycerine. ~**клетча́тка**, -и, nitrocellu-
lose.

ни́тчатый, filiform. **нить**, -и, thread;
filament; suture; (путево́дная) ~
clue. **нитяно́й**, **ни́тяный**, cotton,
thread.

ничего́, etc.: see ничто́. **ничего́** *adv.* all
right; so-so, passably, not too badly;
as *indecl. adj.* not bad, passable. **ниче́й**,
-чья, -чьё *pron.* nobody's, no-one's;
ничья́ земля́, no man's land. **ничья́** *sb.*
draw, drawn game; tie; dead heat.

ничко́м *adv.* face downwards, prone.

ничто́, -чего́, -чему́, -чём, ни о чём
pron. (with separable *pref.*) nothing;
naught; nil; ничего́! that's all right! it
doesn't matter, never mind! **ничто́-
жество**, -а, nonentity, nobody; noth-
ingness. **ничто́жный**, insignificant;
paltry, worthless.

ничу́ть *adv.* not at all, not in the least,
not a bit.

ничье́, etc.: see ниче́й.

ни́ша, -и, niche, recess; bay.

ни́щенка, -и, beggar-woman. **ни́щен-
ский**, beggarly. **ни́щенствовать**,
-твую *imp.* beg, be a beggar; be destitute. **нищета́**, -ы́, destitution, indi-
gence, poverty; beggars, the poor.
ни́щий, нищ, -а́, -е, destitute, indigent,
poverty-stricken, poor; *sb.* beggar,
mendicant, pauper.

НК (*enká*) *abbr.* Наро́дный комисса́р,
Наро́дный комиссариа́т, Peoples'
Commissar(iat); натура́льный каучу́к,
natural rubber; нау́чный комите́т,
scientific committee. **НКВД** (*enkavedé*)
abbr. Наро́дный комиссариа́т вну́т-
ренних дел, People's Commissariat
for Internal Affairs.

но *conj.* but; still, nevertheless; as *sb.*,
snag, difficulty.

но *int.* gee up!

н.о., **НО** *abbr.* Национа́льный о́круг,
National Area.

нова́тор, -а, innovator. **нова́торство**, -а, innovation.

нове́йший, newest, latest.

нове́лла, -ы, short story. **новелли́ст**, -а, short-story writer.

но́веньк|ий, brand-new; ~**ий**, ~**ая** *sb.* new boy, new girl.

новизна́, -ы́, novelty; newness. **нови́нка**, -и, novelty. **новичо́к**, -чка́, novice, beginner, tyro; new recruit; new boy, new girl.

ново- in *comb.* new, newly; recent, recently; modern. **новобра́нец**, -нца, new recruit. **~бра́чный** *sb.* bride-groom; ~**бра́чная** *sb.* bride; ~**бра́чные** *sb. pl.* newly-weds. ~**введе́ние**, -я, innovation. ~**го́дний**, new year's, new-year. ~**зела́ндец**, -дца; *gen. pl.* -дцев, ~**зела́ндка**, -и, New Zealander. ~**зела́ндский**, New Zealand. ~**лу́ние**, -я, new moon. ~**мо́дный**, up-to-date, fashionable; newfangled. ~**прибы́вший**, newly-arrived; *sb.* newcomer. ~**сёл**, -а́, ~**сёлка**, -и, new settler. ~**се́лье**, -я, new home; house-warming.

но́вость, -и, news; novelty. **но́вшество**, -а, innovation, novelty. **но́вый**, нов, -а́, -о, new, novel, fresh; modern, recent; ~ **год** New Year's Day. **новь**, -и, virgin soil.

нога́, -и́, *acc.* но́гу; *pl.* но́ги, ногам, foot, leg; без (за́дних) ног, dead beat; встать с ле́вой ноги́, get out of bed on the wrong side; дать но́гу, get in step; итти́ в но́гу с + *instr.*, keep in step with; на коро́ткой ноге́ с + *instr.* intimate with, on good terms with; на широ́кую (большу́ю, ба́рскую) но́гу, in style, like a lord; протяну́ть но́ги, turn up one's toes; сбить с ног, knock down; сби́ться с ног, get out of step; со всех ног, as fast as one's legs will carry one; стать на́ ноги, стоя́ть на нога́х, stand on one's own feet.

ногото́к, -тка́, nail; *pl.* marigold. **но́готь**, -гтя; *pl.* -и *m.* finger-nail, toe-nail.

нож, -а́, knife; на ~а́х, at daggers drawn. **ножев|о́й**, knife; ~**ые** изде́лия, ~**о́й** това́р, cutlery; ~**о́й** ма́стер, cutler.

но́жка, -и, small foot or leg; leg; stem, stalk.

но́жницы, -иц *pl.* scissors; shears.

ножно́й, foot, pedal, treadle.

но́жны, -жен *pl.* sheath, scabbard.

ножо́вка, -и, saw, hacksaw.

ножо́вщик, -а, cutler.

ноздрева́тый, porous, spongy. **ноздря́**, -и́; *pl.* -и, -е́й, nostril.

нока́ут, -а, knock-out. **нокаути́рованный**, knocked out. **нокаути́ровать**, -рую *perf.* and *imp.* knock out.

нолево́й, **нулево́й**, zero. **ноль**, -я́, **нуль**, -я́ *m.* nought, zero, nil, love; cipher; абсолю́тный ~, absolute zero; в семна́дцать ~-~, at seventeen hundred hours, at five p.m.

но́мер, -а; *pl.* -а́, number; size; (hotel-) room; item, turn; trick. **нумера́тор**, etc.: see **нумера́тор** etc. **номерно́й** *sb.* floor waiter, hotel servant. **номеро́к**, -рка́, tag; label, ticket; small room.

номина́л, -а, face value. **номина́льный**, nominal; rated, indicated.

нора́, -ы́; *pl.* -ы, burrow, hole; lair, form.

норве́жец, -жца, **норве́жка**, -и, Norwegian. **норве́жский**, Norwegian.

норд, -а, north, north wind. **норд-вест**, -а, north-west, north-wester. **норд-о́ст**, -а north-east, north-easter.

но́рка, -и, mink.

но́рма, -ы, standard, norm; rate; ~ вре́мени, time norm. **нормализа́ция**, -и, standardization. **нормализова́ть**, -зу́ю *perf.* and *imp.* standardize. **норма́льный**, normal; standard. **норма́тив**, -а, norm, standard. **нормирова́ние**, -я, **нормиро́вка**, -и, regulation, normalization; rate-fixing. **нормирова́ть**, -ру́ю *perf.* and *imp.* regulate, standardize, normalize. **нормиро́вщик**, -а -щица, -ы, rate-fixer, rate-setter.

нос, -а (-у), *loc.* -у́; *pl.* -ы́, nose; beak; bow, prow; на ~у́, near (at hand), imminent; оста́вить с ~ом, dupe, make a fool of; пове́сить ~, be crest-fallen, be discouraged. **но́сик**, -а, (small) nose; toe; spout.

носи́лки, -лок *pl.* stretcher; litter; hand-barrow. **носи́льщик**, -а, porter. **носи́тель**, -я *m.*, -**тельница**, -ы, bearer;

carrier; vehicle. **носить**, -ошу́, -о́сишь *imp.* carry, bear; wear; ~ на рука́х, make much of, make a fuss of, spoil; ~ся, rush, tear along, fly; float, drift, be carried; wear; + c + *instr.* make much of, make a fuss of. **но́ска**, -и, carrying, bearing, wearing; laying. **но́ский**, hard-wearing, durable; laying, that lays well.

носово́й. of or for the nose; nasal; bow, fore; ~ плато́к, (pocket) handkerchief. **носо́к**, -ска́, little nose; toe; sock. **носоро́г**, -а, rhinoceros.

НОТ, -а *abbr.* нау́чная организа́ция труда́, scientific organization of labour; work study.

но́та, -ы, note; *pl.* music. **нота́ция**, -и, notation; lecture, reprimand.

ночева́ть, -чу́ю *imp.* (*perf.* пере~), spend the night. **ночёвка**, -и, spending the night. **ночле́г**, -а, a shelter for the night, a night's lodging; passing the night. **ночле́жка**, -и, **ночле́жный дом**, -а, doss-house, common lodging-house. **ночни́к**, -а́, night-light. **ночн|о́й**, night, nocturnal; ~а́я ба́бочка, moth; ~а́я руба́шка, nightdress, nightgown, nightshirt; ~о́й сто́лик, bedside table; ~ы́е ту́фли, bedroom slippers. **ночь**, -и, *loc.* -и́; *gen. pl.* -е́й, night; глуха́я ~, dead of night. **но́чью** *adv.* at night, by night.

но́ша, -и, burden. **но́шеный**, in use, worn; part-worn, second-hand.

но́ю, etc.: see **ныть**.

ноя́брь, -я́ *m.* November. **ноя́брьский**, November.

нрав, -а, disposition, temper; *pl.* manners, customs, ways; по ~у, to one's taste, pleasing. **нра́виться**, -влюсь *imp.* (*perf.* по~), + *dat.* please; мне нра́вится, I like. **нравоуче́ние**, -я, moralizing, moral lecture; moral. **нравоучи́тельный**, edifying. **нра́вственность**, -и, morality, morals. **нра́вственный**, moral.

н. ст. *abbr.* но́вый стиль, New Style.

ну, *int.* and *part.* well, well then; what?; really; what a .. !, there's a .. !; да ну

+ *gen.*, to hell with; (да) ну? not really?; ну́ как+*future*, suppose, what if?

ну́дный, tedious, boring.

нужда́, -ы́; *pl.* -ы, want, straits; need; indigence; necessity; call of nature; нужды́ нет, never mind, it doesn't matter. **нужда́ться**, -а́юсь *imp.* be in want, be poor, be hard up; + в + *prep.* need, require, want. **ну́жник**, -а, lavatory, public convenience, latrine. **ну́жн|ый**, -жен, -жна́, -о, -жны́, necessary, requisite; ~о, it is necessary, + *dat.* I, etc., must, ought to, should, need.

нуклеи́новый, nucleic.

нулево́й, **нуль**: see **нолево́й**, **ноль**.

нумера́тор, ном-, -а, numberer, numbering machine; annunciation. **нумера́ция**, ном-, -и, numeration; numbering. **нумерова́ть**, ном-, -ру́ю *imp.* (*perf.* за~, про~) number.

нутро́, -а́, inside, interior; core, kernel; instinct(s), intuition; всем ~м, with one's whole being, completely; по нутру́ + *dat.*, to the liking of. **нутряно́й**, internal.

НЧ (*enché*) *abbr.* ни́зкая частота́, низкочасто́тный, low(-)frequency.

ны́не *adv.* now; today. **ны́нешний**, the present, this; today's. **ны́нче** *adv.* today; now.

нырну́ть, -ну́, -нёшь *perf.*, **ныря́ть**, -я́ю *imp.* dive, plunge; duck. **ныро́к**, -рка́, dive, plunge; duck, ducking; diver. **ныря́ло**, -а, plunger.

ны́тик, -а, whiner, moaner. **ныть**, но́ю *imp.* ache; whine, moan. **нытьё**, -я́, whining, moaning.

н.э. *abbr.* на́шей э́ры, A.D.

нюх, -а, scent; nose, flair. **ню́хательный** таба́к, snuff. **ню́хать**, -аю *imp.* (*perf.* по~) smell, sniff; ~ таба́к, take snuff.

ня́нчить, -чу *imp.* nurse, look after; dandle; ~ся с + *instr.* be nurse to, act as nurse to; fuss over, make a fuss of. **ня́нька**, -и, nanny. **ня́ня**, -и, (children's) nurse, nanny; hospital nurse.

O

o *n. indecl.* the letter o.

о, об, обо *prep.* of, about, concerning; on; with; having; стол о трёх но́жках, a three-legged table. II. +*acc.* against; on, upon; бок о́ бок, side by side; опере́ться о сте́ну, lean against the wall; рука́ о́б руку, hand in hand; споткну́ться о ка́мень, stumble against a stone. II.+*acc.* or *prep.* on, at, about; об э́ту по́ру, about this time; о заре́, about dawn.

o *int.* oh!

о. *abbr.* о́стров, island, isle.

о-, об-, обо-, объ-, *vbl. pref.* indicates transformation, process of becoming, action applied to entire surface of object or to series of objects.

об: see **о** *prep.*

об-, обо- объ- *vbl. pref.* = о-, or indicates action or motion about an object.

о́ба обо́их *m.* and *n.,* **о́бе, обе́их** *f.* both; обе́ими рука́ми, with both hands; very willingly, readily; смотре́ть в о́ба, keep one's eyes open, be on one's guard.

обагри́ть, -рю́ *perf.,* **обагря́ть, -я́ю** *imp.* crimson, incarnadine; ~ кро́вью, stain with blood; ~ ру́ки в крови́, steep one's hands in blood; ~ся, be crimsoned; ~ся (кро́вью), be stained with blood.

обалдева́ть, -а́ю *imp.,* **обалде́ть, -е́ю** *perf.* go crazy; become dulled; be stunned.

обанкро́титься, -о́чусь *perf.* go bankrupt.

обая́ние, -я, fascination, charm. **обая́тельный,** fascinating, charming.

обва́л, -а, fall, falling, crumbling; collapse; caving-in; landslide; (сне́жный) ~, avalanche. **обва́ливать(ся, -аю(сь** *imp.* of обвали́ть(ся, обваля́ть. **обва́листый,** liable to fall, liable to cave in. **обвали́ть, -лю́, -лишь** *perf.* (*imp.* обва́ливать) cause to fall, cause to collapse; crumble; heap round; ~ся, fall, collapse, cave in; crumble.

обваля́ть, -я́ю *perf.* (*imp.* обва́ливать) roll; ~ в сухаря́х, roll in bread--crumbs.

обва́ривать, -аю *imp.,* **обвари́ть, -рю́, -ришь** *perf.* pour boiling water over; scald; ~ся, scald oneself.

обве́ду, etc.: see обвести́. **обвёл, etc.:** see обвести́. **об|венча́ть(ся, -а́ю(сь** *perf.*

обверну́ть, -ну́, -нёшь *perf.,* **обвёртывать, -аю** *imp.* wrap, wrap up.

обве́с, -а, short weight. **обве́сить, -е́шу** *perf.* (*imp.* обве́шивать) give short weight (to); cheat in weighing.

обвести́, -еду́, -еде́шь; -ёл, -ела́ *perf.* (*imp.* обводи́ть) lead round, take round; encircle; surround; outline; dodge, get past; deceive, fool, cheat; ~ взо́ром, глаза́ми, look round (at), take in; ~ вокру́г па́льца, twist round one's little finger.

обве́тренный, weather-beaten; chapped. **обветша́лый,** decrepit, decayed; dilapidated. **об|ветша́ть, -а́ю** *perf.*

обве́шивать, -аю *imp.* of обве́сить. **обвива́ть(ся, -а́ю(сь** *imp.* of обви́ть-(ся.

обвине́ние, -я, charge, accusation; prosecution; вы́нести ~ в +*prep.* find guilty of. **обвини́тель, -я** *m.* accuser; prosecutor. **обвини́тельный,** accusatory; ~ный акт, indictment; ~ный пригово́р, verdict of guilty; ~ая речь, speech for the prosecution. **обвини́ть, -ню́** *perf.,* **обвиня́ть, -я́ю** *imp.* prosecute, indict; + в +*prep.* accuse of, charge with. **обвиня́емый** *sb.* the accused; defendant.

обвиса́ть, -а́ет *imp.,* **обви́снуть, -нет; -вис** *perf.* sag; hang, droop; grow flabby. **обви́слый,** flabby; hanging, drooping.

обви́ть, обовью́, обовьёшь; обви́л, -а́, -о *perf.* (*imp.* обвива́ть) wind round, entwine; ~ся, wind round, twine oneself round.

обво́д, -а, enclosing, surrounding; outlining. **обводи́ть, -ожу́, -о́дишь** *imp.* of обвести́.

обводне́ние, -я, irrigation; filling up. обводни́тельный, irrigation. обводни́ть, -ню́ perf., обводня́ть, -ня́ю imp. irrigate; fill with water.

обво́дный, bypass, leading round.

обвора́живать, -аю imp., обворожи́ть, -жу́ perf. charm, fascinate, enchant. обворожи́тельный, charming, fascinating, enchanting.

обвяза́ть, -яжу́, -я́жешь perf., обвя́зывать, -аю imp. tie round; edge; ~ся instr. tie round oneself.

обгла́дывать, -аю imp., обглода́ть, -ожу́, -о́жешь perf. pick, gnaw (round). обгло́док, -дка, bare bone.

обго́н, -а, passing. обгоня́ть, -я́ю imp. of обогна́ть.

обгора́ть, -а́ю imp., обгоре́ть, -рю́ perf. be burnt, be scorched. обгоре́лый, burnt, charred, scorched.

обдава́ть, -даю́, -даёшь imp., обда́ть, -а́м, -а́шь, -а́ст, -ади́м; о́бдал, -а́, -о perf.+instr. pour over, cover with; overcome overwhelm, with; ~ся + instr. pour over oneself.

обде́лать, -аю imp. of обде́лать. (imp. обде́лывать), finish; cut polish; set; manage, arrange; cheat.

обдели́ть, -лю́, -лишь perf. (imp. обделя́ть)+instr. do out of one's (fair) share of.

обде́лывать, -аю imp. of обде́лать. обделя́ть, -я́ю imp. of обдели́ть.

обдеру́, etc.: see ободра́ть. обдира́ть, -аю imp. of ободра́ть. обди́рка -и, peeling; hulling, shelling; skinning, flaying; groats. обди́рный, peeled, hulled.

обдува́ла, -ы m. and f. cheat, trickster. обдува́ть, -а́ю imp. of обду́ть.

обду́манно adv. after careful consideration, deliberately. обду́манный, deliberate, well-considered, well-weighed, carefully-thought-out. обду́мать, -аю perf., обду́мывать, -аю imp. consider, think over, weigh.

обду́ть, -у́ю perf. (imp. обдува́ть) blow on, blow round; cheat, fool, dupe.

обе́: see о́ба. обега́ть, -а́ю imp. of обежа́ть. обегу́, обегу́, etc.: see обежа́ть.

обе́д, -а, dinner; пе́ред ~ом, in the morning; по́сле ~а, in the afternoon.

обе́дать, -аю imp. (perf. по~) have dinner, dine. обе́денный, dinner; ~ переры́в, dinner hour.

обедне́вший, обедне́лый, impoverished. обедне́ние, -я, impoverishment. о|бедне́ть, -е́ю perf., обедни́ть, -ню́ perf., обедня́ть, -я́ю imp. impoverish.

обе́дня, -и; gen. pl. -ден, mass.

обежа́ть, -егу́ perf. (imp. обега́ть) run round; run past; outrun, pass.

обезбо́ливание, -я, anaesthetization. обезбо́ливать, -аю imp., обезбо́лить, -лю perf. anaesthetize.

обезвре́дить, -е́жу perf., обезвре́живать, -аю imp. render harmless; neutralize.

обездо́ленный, deprived; unfortunate, hapless. обездо́ливать, -аю imp., обездо́лить, -лю perf. deprive of one's share.

обеззара́живать, -аю imp., обеззара́зить, -а́жу perf. disinfect. обеззара́живающий, disinfectant.

обезли́ченный, depersonalized; generalized; reduced to a standard; mechanical. обезли́чивать, -аю imp., обезли́чить, -чу perf. deprive of individuality, depersonalize; do away with personal responsibility for. обезли́чка, -и, lack of personal responsibility.

обезобра́живать, -аю imp., о|безобра́зить, -а́жу perf. disfigure, mutilate.

обезопа́сить, -а́шу perf. secure, make safe; ~ся, secure oneself.

обезору́живание, -я, disarmament. обезору́живать, -аю imp., обезору́жить, -жу perf. disarm.

обезу́меть, -ею perf. lose one's senses, lose one's head; ~ от испуга, become panic-stricken.

обезья́на, -ы, monkey; ape. обезья́ний, monkey; simian; ape-like. обезья́нник, -а, monkey-house. обезья́нничать, -аю imp. (perf. с~) ape.

обели́ть, -лю́ perf., обеля́ть, -я́ю imp. vindicate, prove the innocence; clear of blame; whitewash; ~ся, vindicate oneself, prove one's innocence.

оберега́ть, -а́ю imp., обере́чь, -егу́, -ежёшь; -рёг, -ла́ perf. guard; protect; ~ся, guard oneself, protect oneself.

обернуть, -ну, -нёшь *perf.*, обёртывать, -аю *imp.* (*imp.* also оборачивать) wind, twist; wrap up; turn; turn over; ~ книгу, jacket a book; cover a book; ~ся, turn, turn round; turn out; come back; manage, get by; +*instr.* or в+ *acc.* turn into; ~ся лицом к, turn towards; - envelope; (dust-)jacket, cover. обёрточный, wrapping; ~ая бумага, brown paper, wrapping paper.
оберу, etc.: see обобрать.

обескуражывать, -аю *imp.*, обескуражить, -жу *perf.* discourage; dismay.

обескровить, -влю *perf.*, обескровливать, -аю *imp.* drain of blood, bleed white; render lifeless. обескровленный, bloodless; pallid, anaemic, lifeless.

обеспечение, -я, securing, guaranteeing; ensuring; providing; provision; guarantee; security; safeguard(s); protection. обеспеченность, -и, security; +*instr.* being provided with, provision of. обеспеченный, well-to-do; well provided for. обеспечивать, -аю *imp.*, обеспечить, -чу *perf.* provide for; secure, guarantee; ensure, assure; safeguard, protect; + *instr.* provide with guarantee supply of.

о|беспокоить(ся, -о́ю(сь *perf.*

обессилеть, -ею *perf.* grow weak, lose one's strength; collapse, break down. обессиливать, -аю *imp.*, обессилить, -лю *perf.* weaken.

о|бесславить, -влю *perf.*

обессмертить, -рчу *perf.* immortalize.

обесцветить, -ечу *perf.*, обесцвечивать, -аю *imp.* fade, deprive of colour; make colourless, tone down; ~ся, fade; become colourless.

обесценение, -я, depreciation; loss of value. обесценивать, -аю *imp.*, обесценить, -ню *perf.* depreciate, cheapen; ~ся, depreciate, lose value.

о|бесчестить, -ещу *perf.*

обет, -а, vow, promise. обетованный, promised. обещание, -я, promise; дать ~, give a promise, give one's word; сдержать ~, keep a promise. обещать, -аю *perf.* and *imp.* (*perf.* also по~) promise.

обжалование, -я, appeal. обжаловать, -лую *perf.* appeal against, lodge a complaint against.

обжечь, обожгу обожжёшь; обжёг, обожгла *perf.*, обжигать, -аю *imp.* burn; scorch; bake; fire, calcine; sting; ~ся, burn oneself; scald oneself; burn one's fingers; ~ся крапивой, be stung by a nettle. обжигательный, glazing; baking; roasting; ~ая печь, kiln.

обжора, -ы *m.* and *f.* glutton, gormandizer. обжорливый, gluttonous. обжорство, -а, gluttony.

обзаведение, -я, providing, fitting out; establishment; fittings, appointments; bits and pieces. обзавестись, -едусь, -едёшься; -вёлся, -лась *perf.*, обзаводиться, -ожусь, -одишься *imp.*+ *instr.* provide oneself with; set up.

обзову, etc.: see обозвать.

обзор, -а, survey, review.

обзывать, -аю *imp.* of обозвать.

обивать, -аю *imp.* of обить. обивка, -и, upholstering; upholstery.

обида, -ы, offence, injury, insult; annoying thing, nuisance; не в обиду будь сказано, no offence meant; не дать себя в обиду, stand up for oneself. обидеть, -ижу *perf.*, обижать, -аю *imp.* offend; hurt, wound; мухи не обидит, he would not harm a fly; ~ся, take offence, take umbrage; feel hurt; ~ся на+*acc.* resent; не обижайтесь, don't be offended. обидный, offensive; annoying, tiresome; мне обидно, I feel hurt, it pains me; обидно, it is a pity, it is a nuisance. обидчивый, touchy, sensitive. обиженный, offended, hurt, aggrieved.

обилие, -я, abundance, plenty. обильный, abundant, plentiful; +*instr.* rich in.

обиняк, -а, circumlocution; hint, evasion; без ~ов, plainly, in plain terms; говорить ~ами, beat about the bush.

обирать, -аю *imp.* of обобрать.

обитаемый, inhabited. обитатель, -я *m.* inhabitant; resident; inmate. обитать, -аю *imp.* live, dwell, reside.

обить, обобью, -ьёшь *perf.* (*imp.* обивать) upholster, cover; knock off knock down; ~ гвоздя́ми, stud; ~ желе́зом, bind with iron.

обихо́д, -а, custom, (general) use, practice; в дома́шнем ~е, in domestic use, in the household. обихо́дный, everyday.

обката́ть, -а́ю perf., обка́тывать, -аю imp. roll; roll smooth; run in. обка́тка, -и, running in.

обкла́дка, -и, facing; ~ дёрном, turfing. обкла́дывать(ся, -аю(сь imp. of обложи́ть(ся.

обко́м, -а abbr. областно́й комите́т, regional committee.

обкра́дывать, -аю imp. of обокра́сть.

обл. abbr. о́бласть, oblast, region.

обла́ва, -ы, raid sweep (game); round-up; cordon, cordoning off; battue.

облага́емый, taxable. облага́ть(ся, -а́ю(сь imp. of обложи́ть(ся; ~ся нало́гом, be liable to tax, be taxable.

облагора́живать, -аю imp., облагоро́дить, -о́жу perf. ennoble.

облада́ние, -я, possession. облада́тель, -я m. possessor. облада́ть, -а́ю imp.+ instr. possess, be possessed of; ~ пра́вом, have the right; ~ хоро́шим здоро́вьем, enjoy good health.

о́блако, -а; pl. -а́, -о́в, cloud.

обла́мывать(ся, -аю(сь imp. of обломи́ть(ся, обломи́ться.

обласка́ть, -а́ю perf. treat with affection, show much kindness or consideration to.

областно́й, oblast; provincial; regional; dialectal. о́бласть, -и; gen. pl. -е́й, oblast, province; region; district; belt; tract; field, sphere, realm, domain.

обла́тка, -и, wafer; capsule; paper seal.

обла́чко, -а; pl. -а́, -о́в dim. of о́блако. о́блачность, -и, cloudiness; cloud. о́блачный, cloudy.

облёг, etc.: see обле́чь. облега́ть, -а́ет imp. of обле́чь. облега́ющий, tight-fitting.

облегча́ть, -а́ю imp., облегчи́ть, -чу́ perf. lighten; relieve; alleviate, mitigate; commute; facilitate. облегче́ние, -я, relief.

обледене́лый, ice-covered. обледене́ние, -я, icing over; пери́од обледене́ния, Ice Age. обледене́ть, -е́ет perf. ice over, become covered with ice.

облеза́ть, -а́ет imp., обле́зть, -зет; -ле́з perf. come out, fall out, come off; grow bare, grow mangy; peel off. обле́злый, shabby, bare; mangy.

облека́ть(ся, -а́ю(сь imp. of обле́чь² (ся, облеку́, etc.: see обле́чь².

облени́ваться, -аюсь imp., облени́ться, -ню́сь, -нишься perf. grow lazy, get lazy.

облепи́ть, -плю́, -пишь perf., обле́пля́ть, -я́ю imp. stick to, cling to; surround, throng round; paste all over, plaster.

облета́ть, -а́ю imp., облете́ть, -лечу́, fly (round); spread (round, all over); fall.

обле́чь¹, -ля́жет; -лёг, -ла́ perf. (imp. облега́ть) cover, surround, envelop; fit tightly.

обле́чь², -еку́, -ечёшь; -ёк, -кла́ perf. (imp. облека́ть) clothe, invest; wrap, shroud; ~ся, clothe oneself, dress oneself; +gen. take the form of, assume the shape of.

облива́ние, -я, spilling over, pouring over; shower-bath; sponge-down. облива́ть(ся, -а́ю(сь imp. of обли́ть(ся; се́рдце у меня́ кро́вью облива́ется, my heart bleeds. обли́вка, -и, glazing; glaze. обливно́й, glazed.

облига́ция, -и, bond, debenture.

обли́занный, smooth. облиза́ть, -ижу́, -и́жешь perf., обли́зывать, -аю imp. lick (all over); lick clean; ~ся, smack one's lips; lick itself.

о́блик, -а, look, aspect, appearance; cast of mind, temper.

облисполко́м, -а abbr. областно́й исполни́тельный комите́т, regional executive committee.

обли́тый; о́бли́т, -а́, -о, covered, enveloped; ~ све́том луны́, bathed in moonlight. обли́ть, оболью́, -льёшь; о́бли́л, -ила́, -о perf. (imp. облива́ть) pour, sluice, spill; glaze; ~ся, sponge down, take a shower; pour over oneself, spill over oneself; ~ся по́том, be bathed in sweat; ~ся слеза́ми, melt into tears.

облицева́ть, -цу́ю perf., облицо́вывать, -аю imp. face, revet. облицо́вка, -и, facing, revetment; lining, coating.

обличáть, -áю imp., обличи́ть, -чу́ perf. expose, unmask, denounce; reveal, display, manifest; point to. обличе́ние, -я, exposure, unmasking, denunciation. обличи́тельный, denunciatory; ~ая речь, ~ая статья́, diatribe, tirade.

обложе́ние, -я, taxation; assessment, rating. обложи́ть, -жу́, -жишь perf. (imp. обкла́дывать, облага́ть) put round; edge; surface, face; cover; surround; close round, corner; assess; круго́м обложи́ло (не́бо), the sky is completely overcast; ~ ме́стным нало́гом, rate; ~ нало́гом tax; обло́жило язы́к, the tongue is furred; ~ся + instr. put round oneself, surround oneself with. обло́жка, -и, (dust-)cover; folder.

облока́чиваться, -аюсь imp., облокоти́ться, -очу́сь, -о́тишься perf. на + acc. lean one's elbows on.

обло́м, -а, breaking off; break; profile. обломáть, -áю perf. (imp. обла́мывать) break off; make yield; ~ся break off, snap. обломи́ться, -ло́мится perf. (imp. обла́мываться) break off. обло́мок, -мка, fragment; debris, wreckage.

об|лупи́ть, -плю́, -пишь perf., облу́пливать, -аю imp. peel; shell; fleece; ~ся, peel, peel off; scale; come off, chip. облу́пленный, chipped.

облучáть, -чу́ perf., облучáть, -áю imp. irradiate. облуче́ние, -я, irradiation. об|лущи́ть, -щу́ perf.; see лущи́ть, -аю perf.

облюбова́ть, -бу́ю perf., облюбо́вывать, -аю imp. pick, choose, select.

обля́жет, etc.: see обле́чь[1].

обма́зать, -а́жу perf., обма́зывать, -аю imp. coat; putty; soil, besmear; ~ся + instr. besmear oneself with, get covered with. обма́зка, -и, coating, puttying.

обма́кивать, -аю imp., обмакну́ть, -ну́, -нёшь perf. dip.

обма́н, -а, fraud, deception; illusion; ~ зре́ния, optical illusion. обма́нный, fraudulent, deceitful. обману́ть,

-ну́, -нешь perf., обма́нывать, -аю imp. deceive; cheat, swindle; betray, disappoint; ~ся, be deceived, be disappointed. обма́нчивый, deceptive, delusive. обма́нщик, -а, deceiver; cheat, fraud.

обма́тывать(ся, -аю(сь imp. of обмота́ть(ся.

обма́хивать, -аю imp., обмахну́ть, -ну́, -нёшь perf. brush off, dust (off); fan; ~ся, fan oneself.

обмёл, etc.: see обмести́.

обмеле́ние, -я, shallowing, shoaling. об|меле́ть, -е́ет perf. become shallow, shoal; run aground.

обме́н -а, exchange, interchange; barter; в ~ за + acc. in exchange for; ~ веще́ств, metabolism; ~ мне́ниями, exchange of opinions. обме́нивать, -аю imp., обмени́ть, -ню́, -нишь perf., об|меня́ть, -я́ю perf. exchange; barter; swop; ~ся + instr. exchange; обменя́ться впечатле́ниями, compare notes. обме́нный, exchange; metabolic.

обме́р, -а, measurement; false measure. обмере́ть, обомру́, -рёшь; о́бмер, -лá, -ло perf. (imp. обмира́ть) faint; ~ от у́жаса, be horror-struck; я о́бмер, my heart stood still.

обме́ривать, -аю imp., обме́рить, -рю perf. measure; cheat in measuring, give short measure (to); ~ся, make a mistake in measuring.

обмести́, -ету́, -етёшь; -мёл, -á perf., обметáть[1], -áю imp. sweep off, dust.

обметáть[2], -ечу́ or -áю, -е́чешь or -áешь perf. (imp. обмётывать) oversew, overcast; whip; blanket-stitch.

обмету́, etc.: see обмести́. обмётывать, -аю imp. of обметáть. обмира́ть, -аю imp. of обмере́ть.

обмозгова́ть, -гу́ю perf., обмозго́вывать, -аю imp. think over, turn over (in one's mind).

обмолáчивать, -аю imp. of обмоло́тить.

обмо́лвиться, -влюсь perf. make a slip of the tongue; say, utter. обмо́лвка, -и, slip of the tongue.

обмоло́т, -а, threshing. обмолоти́ть,

-лочу́ -ло́тишь *perf.* (*imp.* обмола́чивать) thresh.

обмора́живать, -аю *imp.*, обморо́зить, -ро́жу *perf.* expose to frost subject to frost-bite, get frost-bitten; я обморо́зил себе́ ру́ки, I have got my hands frost-bitten; **~ся**, suffer frost-bite, be frost-bitten. обморо́женный, frost-bitten.

о́бморок, -а, fainting-fit, swoon; syncope.

обмота́ть, -а́ю *perf.* обма́тывать) wind round; **~ся** + *instr.* wrap oneself in. обмо́тка, -и, winding; lagging; taping; *pl.* puttees, leg-wrappings.

обмо́ю, etc.: see обмы́ть.

обмундирова́ние, -я, обмундиро́вка, -и, fitting out (with uniform), issuing of uniform; uniform. обмундирова́ть, -ру́ю *perf.*, обмундиро́вывать, -аю *imp.* fit out (with uniform), issue with clothing; **~ся**, fit oneself out; draw uniform. обмундиро́вочный; ~ые де́ньги. uniform allowance.

обмыва́ние, -я, bathing, washing. обмыва́ть, -а́ю *imp.*, обмы́ть. -мо́ю *perf.* bathe, wash; sponge down; **~ся**, wash, bathe; sponge down.

обмяка́ть, -а́ю *imp.*, обмя́кнуть, -ну; -мя́к *perf.* become soft; go limp, become flabby.

обнадёживать, -аю *imp.*, обнадёжить, -жу *perf.* give hope to, reassure.

обнажа́ть, -а́ю *imp.*, обнажи́ть, -жу́ *perf.* bare, uncover; unsheathe; lay bare, reveal. обнажённый, -ён, -ена́, naked, bare; nude.

обнаро́дование, -я, publication, promulgation. обнаро́довать, -дую *perf.* and *imp.* publish, promulgate.

обнаруже́ние, -я, disclosure; displaying, revealing; discovery; detection. обнару́живать, -аю *imp.*, обнару́жить, -жу *perf.* disclose; display; reveal, betray; discover, bring to light; detect; **~ся**, be revealed, come to light.

обнести́, -су́, -сёшь; -нёс, -ла́ *perf.* (*imp.* обноси́ть) enclose; + *instr.* serve round, pass round; pass over, leave out; меня́ обнесли́ вино́м, I have not been offered wine; **~** и́згородью,

fence (in); **~** пери́лами, rail in, rail off.

обнима́ть(ся, -а́ю(сь *imp.* of обня́ть(ся. обниму́, etc.: see обня́ть.

обнища́лый, impoverished; beggarly. обнища́ние, -я, impoverishment.

обнови́ть, -влю́ *perf.*, обновля́ть, -я́ю *imp.* renovate; renew; re-form; repair, restore; use or wear for the first time; **~ся**, be restored. обно́вка, -и, new acquisition, new toy; new dress. обновле́ние, -я, renovation, renewal.

обноси́ть, -ошу́ -о́сишь *imp.* of обнести́; **~ся**, have worn out one's clothes; be out at elbow. обно́ски, -ов *pl.* old clothes, cast-offs.

обню́хать, -аю *perf.*, обню́хивать, -аю *imp.* smell, sniff at.

обня́ть, -ниму́, -ни́мешь; о́бнял, -á, -о *perf.* (*imp.* обнима́ть) embrace; clasp in one's arms; take in; **~** взгля́дом, survey; **~** умо́м, comprehend, take in; **~ся**, embrace; hug one another.

обо: see о *prep.* обо-: see о-.

обобра́ть, беру́, -рёшь; обобра́л, -á, -о *perf.* (*imp.* обира́ть) rob; clean out; pick; gather all of.

обобща́ть, -а́ю *imp.*, обобщи́ть, -щу́ *perf.* generalize. обобще́ние, -я, generalization. обобществи́ть, -влю́ *perf.*, обобществля́ть, -я́ю *imp.* socialize; collectivize. обобществле́ние, -я, socialization; collectivization.

обобью́, etc.: see обби́ть. обовью́, etc.: see обви́ть.

обогати́ть, -ащу́ *perf.*, обогаща́ть, -а́ю *imp.* enrich; concentrate; **~ся**, become rich; enrich oneself. обогаще́ние, -я, enrichment; concentration.

обогна́ть, обгоню́, -о́нишь; обогна́л, -á, -о *perf.* (*imp.* обгоня́ть) pass, leave behind; outstrip, outdistance.

обогну́ть, -ну́, -нёшь *perf.* (*imp.* огиба́ть) round, skirt; double; bend round.

обогре́в, -а, heating. обогрева́ние, -я, heating, warming. обогрева́тель, -я *m.* heater. обогрева́ть, -а́ю *imp.*, обогре́ть, -е́ю *perf.* heat, warm; **~ся**, warm oneself; warm up.

о́бод, -а; *pl.* -о́дья, -ьев, rim; felloe.

ободо́к, -дка́, thin rim, narrow border; fillet.

ободра́нец, -нца, ragamuffin, ragged fellow. **обо́дранный**, ragged. **ободра́ть**, обдеру́, -рёшь; -а́л, -а́, -о *perf.* (*imp.* обдира́ть) strip; skin, flay; peel; fleece.

ободре́ние, -я encouragement, reassurance. **ободри́тельный**, encouraging, reassuring. **ободри́ть**, -рю́ *perf.*, **ободря́ть**, -я́ю *imp.* cheer up; encourage, reassure; ~**ся**, cheer up, take heart.

обожа́ние, -я, adoration. **обожа́тель**, -я *m.* adorer; admirer. **обожа́ть**, -а́ю *imp.* worship.

обожгу́, etc.: see **обжёчь**.

обожестви́ть, -влю́ *perf.*, **обожествля́ть**, -я́ю *imp.* deify; worship, idolize. **обожествле́ние**, -я, deification, worship.

обожжённый; -ён, -ена́, burnt, scorched; scalded; stung.

обо́з, -а, string of carts, string of sledges; transport; collection of vehicles.

обозва́ть, обзову́, -вёшь; -а́л, -а́, -о *perf.* (*imp.* обзыва́ть) call; call names; ~ дурако́м, call a fool.

обозлённый; -ён, -а́, angered; embittered. **обо|зли́ть**, -лю́ *perf.*, **о|зли́ть**, -лю́ *perf.* enrage; anger; embitter; ~**ся**, get angry, grow angry.

обознача́ть, -а́ю *imp.*, **обозна́чить**, -чу *perf.* mean; mark; reveal; emphasize; ~**ся**, appear, reveal oneself. **обозначе́ние**, -я, marking; sign, symbol.

обо́зник, -а, driver.

обозрева́тель, -я *m.* reviewer, observer; columnist; полити́ческий ~, political correspondent. **обозрева́ть**, -а́ю *imp.*, **обозре́ть**, -рю́ *perf.* survey; view; look round; (pass in) review. **обозре́ние**, -я, surveying; viewing; looking round; survey; review; revue. **обозри́мый**, visible.

обо́и, -ев *pl* wall-paper.

обо́йма, -ы; *gen. pl.* -о́йм, cartridge-clip.

обойти́, -йду́, -йдёшь; -ошёл, -ошла́ *perf.* (*imp.* обходи́ть) go round, pass; make the round of, go (all) round;

avoid; leave out; pass over; ~ молча́нием, pass over in silence; ~**сь**, cost, come to; manage, make do; turn out, end; +*c*+*instr.* treat.

обо́йщик, -а, upholsterer.

обокра́сть, обкраду́, -дёшь *perf.* (*imp.* обкра́дывать) rob.

оболо́чка, -и, casing; membrane; cover, envelope, jacket; shell; coat.

обо́лтус, -а, blockhead, booby.

обольсти́тель, -я *m.* seducer. **обольсти́тельный**, seductive, captivating. **обольсти́ть**, -льщу́ *perf.*, **обольща́ть**, -а́ю *imp.* captivate; seduce. **обольще́ние**, -я, seduction; delusion.

оболью́, etc.: see **обли́ть**.

обомле́ть, -е́ю *perf.* be stupefied, be stunned.

обомру́, etc.: see **обмере́ть**.

обомше́лый, moss-grown.

обоня́ние, -я, (sense of) smell. **обоня́тельный**, olfactory. **обоня́ть**, -я́ю *imp.* smell.

обопру́, etc.: see **опере́ть**.

обора́чиваемость, -и, turnover. **обора́чивать(ся**, -аюсь *imp.* of обверну́ть(ся, оборо́тить(ся.

оборва́нец, -нца, ragamuffin, ragged fellow. **обо́рванный**, torn, ragged. **оборва́ть**, -ву́, -вёшь; -а́л, -а́, -о *perf.* (*imp.* обрыва́ть) tear off, pluck; strip; break; snap; cut short, interrupt; ~**ся**, break; snap; fall; come away; stop suddenly, stop short.

обо́рка, -и, frill, flounce.

оборо́на, -ы, defence; defences. **оборони́тельный**, defensive. **оборони́ть**, -ню́ *perf.*, **оборони́ть**, -я́ю *imp.* defend; ~**ся**, defend oneself. **оборо́нный**, defence, defensive. **обороноспосо́бность**, -и, defence potential.

оборо́т, -а, turn; revolution, rotation; circulation; turnover; back; ~, (turn of) phrase; locution; смотри́ на ~е, P.T.O., please turn over; see other side. **оборо́тистый**, resourceful. **оборо́ти́ть**, -рочу́, -ро́тишь *perf.* (*imp.* обора́чивать) turn; ~**ся**, turn (round); + *instr.* or в + *acc.* turn into. **оборо́тливый**, resourceful. **оборо́тн|ый**, circulating; working; turn-round; reverse; ~**ый** капита́л, working capital; ~ая сторона́, reverse side; verso; э ~ое, the letter э.

оборудование, -я, equipping; equipment. обору́довать, -дую perf. and imp. equip, fit out; manage, arrange.

обо́рыш, -а, left-over, remnant.

обоснова́ние, -я, basing; basis; ground. обосно́ванный, well-founded, well--grounded. обоснова́ть, -ну́ю, -нуёшь perf., обосно́вывать, -аю imp. ground, base; substantiate; ~ся, settle down.

обосо́бить, -блю perf., обособля́ть, -я́ю imp. isolate; ~ся, stand apart; keep aloof. обособле́ние, -я, isolation. обосо́бленный, isolated, solitary.

обостре́ние, -я, aggravation, exacerbation. обостре́нный, keen; strained; tense; sharp, pointed. обостри́ть, -рю́ perf., обостря́ть, -я́ю imp. sharpen, intensify; strain; aggravate, exacerbate; ~ся, become sharp, become more pointed; become keener, become more sensitive; become strained; be aggravated; become acute.

оботру́, etc.: see обтере́ть.

обо́чина, -ы, verge; shoulder, edge, side.

обошёл, etc.: see обойти́. обошью́, etc.: see обши́ть.

обою́дность, -и, mutuality, reciprocity. обою́дный, mutual, reciprocal. обою́доо́стрый, double-edged, two-edged.

обраба́тывать, -аю imp., обрабо́тать, -аю perf., till, cultivate; work, work up; treat, process; machine; polish, perfect; work upon, win round. обраба́тывающий, ~ая промы́шленность, manufacturing industry. обрабо́тка, -и, working (up); treatment, processing; cultivation.

об|ра́довать(ся, -дую(сь perf.

о́браз, -а, shape, form; appearance; image; type; figure; mode, manner; way; icon; гла́вным ~ом, mainly, chiefly, largely; каки́м ~ом? how? ~ де́йствий, line of action, policy; ~ жи́зни, way of life; ~ мы́слей, way of thinking; ~ правле́ния, form of government; таки́м ~ом, thus. образе́ц, -зца́, model; pattern; example; specimen, sample. о́бразный, picturesque, graphic; figurative; employing images. образова́ние, -я, forma-

tion; education. образо́ванный, educated. образова́тельный, educational. образова́ть, -зу́ю perf. and imp., разо́вывать, -аю imp. form; make (up); organize; educate; ~ся, form; arise; turn out well.

образу́мить, -млю perf. bring to reason; make listen to reason; ~ся, come to one's senses, see reason.

образу́ющая sb. generatrix.

образцо́вый, model; exemplary. обра́зчик, -а, specimen, sample; pattern.

обра́мить, -млю perf., обрамля́ть, -я́ю imp. frame. обрамле́ние, -я, framing; frame; setting.

обраста́ть, -а́ю imp., обрасти́, -ту́, -тёшь; -ро́с, -ла́ perf. be overgrown; be covered, surrounded, cluttered; + instr. acquire, accumulate.

обрати́м|ый, reversible, convertible; ~ая валю́та, convertible currency. обрати́ть, -ащу́ perf., обраща́ть, -а́ю imp. turn; convert; ~ в бе́гство, put to flight; ~ внима́ние на + acc. pay attention to, take notice of, notice; call, draw, attention to; ~ на себя́ внима́ние, attract attention to one-self); ~ в шу́тку, turn into a joke; ~ся, turn; revert; appeal; apply; ac-cost, address; circulate; + в + acc. turn into, become; + с + instr. treat; handle, manage; ~ся в бе́гство, take to flight; ~ся в слух, be all ears; prick up one's ears. обра́тно, adv. back; backwards; conversely; inversely; ~ пропорциона́льный, inversely pro-portional; туда́ и ~, there and back. обра́тный, reverse; return; opposite; inverse; в ~ую сто́рону, in the oppo-site direction; ~ый а́дрес, sender's ad-dress, return address; ~ая вспы́шка, back-firing; ~ой по́чтой, by return (of post); ~ый уда́р, backfire; ~ый ход, reverse motion, back stroke. обраще́-ние, -я, appeal, address; conversion; circulation; manner; (+ с + instr.) treatment (of); handling (of), use (of).

об|ревизова́ть, -зу́ю perf.

обре́з, -а, edge, side; sawn-off gun; в ~ + gen. only just enough; де́нег у меня́ в ~, I haven't a penny to spare. обре́зать, -е́жу perf., обреза́ть, -а́ю imp.

cut; cut off; clip trim; pare; prune; bevel; circumcise; cut short, snub; **~ся,** cut oneself. обре́зок, -зка, scrap; remnant; *pl.* ends; clippings.

обрека́ть, -а́ю *imp.* of обре́чь. обреку́, etc.: see обре́чь. обрёл, etc.: see обрести́.

обремени́тельный, burdensome, onerous. о|бремени́ть, -ню́ *perf.,* обременя́ть, -я́ю *imp.* burden.

обрести́, -ету́, -ете́шь, -рёл, -а́ *perf.,* обрета́ть, -а́ю *imp.* find. обрета́ться, -а́юсь *imp.* be; live.

обрече́ние, -я, doom. обречённый, doomed. обре́чь, -еку́, -ече́шь, -ёк, -ла́ *perf.* (*imp.* обрека́ть) condemn, doom.

обрисова́ть, -су́ю *perf.,* обрисо́вывать, -аю *imp.* outline, delineate; depict; **~ся,** appear (in outline), take shape.

обро́к, -а, quit-rent.

оброни́ть, -ню́, -нишь *perf.* drop; let drop, let fall.

обро́с, etc : see обрасти́. обро́сший, overgrown.

обруба́ть, -а́ю *imp.,* обруби́ть, -блю́ -бишь *perf.* chop off; lop off, cut off; dock; hem seam. обру́бок, -бка, stump.

об|руга́ть, -а́ю *perf.*

о́бруч, -а; *pl.* -и, -е́й, hoop. обруча́льный, engagement, betrothal; **~** кольцо́, betrothal ring, wedding-ring. обруча́ть, -а́ю *imp.,* обручи́ть, -чу́, betroth; **~ся** + с + *instr.* become engaged to. обруче́ние, -я, betrothal.

обру́шивать, -аю *imp.,* об|ру́шить, -шу *perf.* bring down, rain down; **~ся,** come down, collapse, cave in; + на + *acc.* beat down on; come down on, fall on, pounce on.

обры́в -а, precipice; break, rupture. обрыва́ть(ся, -а́ю(сь *imp.* of оборва́ть(ся. обры́вистый, steep, precipitous; abrupt. обры́вок, -вка, scrap; snatch.

обры́згать, -аю *imp.,* обры́згивать, -аю *imp.,* обры́знуть, -ну *perf.* splash, spatter; sprinkle.

обрю́зглый, обрю́згший, fat and flabby.

обря́д, -а, rite, ceremony. обря́дный, обря́довый, ritual, ceremonial.

обслу́живание, -я, service; servicing; maintenance; бытово́е **~,** consumer service(s); медии́нское **~,** medical attendance, medical care. обслу́живать, -аю *imp.,* обслужи́ть, -жу́, -жишь *perf.* serve, attend to; service; mind, operate; обслу́живающий персона́л, staff; assistants, attendants.

обсле́дование, -я, inspection; inquiry; investigation. обсле́дователь, -я *m.* inspector, investigator. обсле́довать, -дую *perf.* and *imp.* inspect; investigate; examine.

обсо́хнуть, -ну; -о́х *perf.* (*imp.* обсыха́ть) dry, dry up.

обста́вить, -влю *perf.,* обставля́ть, -я́ю *imp.* surround, encircle; furnish; arrange; organize; **~ся,** establish oneself, furnish one's home. обстано́вка, -и, furniture; décor; situation, conditions; environment; set-up.

обстоя́тельный, thorough, reliable; detailed, circumstantial. обстоя́тельственный, adverbial. обстоя́тельство, -a, circumstance; adverbial modifier, adverb, adverbial phrase. обстоя́ть, -о́ит *imp.* be; get on go; как обстои́т де́ло? how is it going? how are things going?

обстра́гивать, -аю *imp.* of обстрога́ть. обстра́ивать(ся, -аю(сь *imp.* of об|стро́ить(ся.

обстре́л, -а firing, fire; под **~ом,** under fire. обстре́ливать, -аю *imp.,* обстреля́ть, -я́ю *perf.* fire at, fire on; bombard; **~ся,** become seasoned (in battle), receive one's baptism of fire. обстре́лянный, seasoned, experienced.

обстрога́ть, -а́ю, обструга́ть, -а́ю *perf.* (*imp.* обстра́гивать) plane; whittle.

обстро́ить, -о́ю *perf.* (*imp.* обстра́ивать), build up, build round; **~ся,** be built; spring up; build for oneself.

обструга́ть: see обстрога́ть.

обступа́ть, -а́ет *imp.,* обступи́ть, -у́пит *perf.* surround; cluster round.

обсуди́ть, -ужу́, -у́дишь *perf.,* обсужда́ть, -а́ю *imp.* discuss; consider. обсужде́ние, -я, discussion.

обсчита́ть, -а́ю *perf.,* обсчи́тывать, -аю *imp.* cheat (in reckoning); **~ся,** make a mistake (in counting), miscalculate;

вы обсчита́лись на шесть копе́ек, you were six copecks out.

обсы́пать, -плю *perf.* обсыпа́ть, -а́ю *imp.* strew; sprinkle.

обсыха́ть, -а́ю *imp.* of обсо́хнуть. обта́чивать, -аю *imp.* of обточи́ть.

обтека́емый, streamlined, streamline. обтека́тель, -я *m.* fairing, cowling.

обтере́ть, оботру́, -трёшь; обтёр *perf.* (*imp.* обтира́ть) wipe; wipe dry; rub; ~ся, wipe oneself dry, dry oneself; sponge down.

обтерпе́ться, -плю́сь, -пишься *perf.* become acclimatized, get used.

о(б)теса́ть, -ешу́, -е́шешь *perf.*, о(б)тёсывать, -аю *imp.* square; rough-hew; dress, trim; lick into shape.

обти́рание, -я, sponge-down; lotion. обтира́ть(ся, -а́ю(сь *perf.* of обтере́ть(ся.

обточи́ть, -чу́, -чишь *perf.* (*imp.* обта́чивать) grind; turn, machine, round off. обто́чка, -и, turning, machining, rounding off.

обтрёпанный, frayed; shabby. обтрепа́ть, -плю́, -плешь *perf.* fray; ~ся, fray become frayed; get shabby.

обтя́гивать, -аю *imp.*, обтяну́ть, -ну́, -нешь *perf.* cover; fit close. fit tight. обтя́жка, -и, cover; skin; в обтя́жку, close-fitting.

обува́ть(ся, -а́ю(сь *imp.* of обу́ть(ся. обу́вка, -и, boots, shoes. обувно́й, shoe. о́бувь, -и, footwear; boots, shoes.

обу́гливание, -я, carbonization. обу́гливать, -аю *imp.*, обу́глить, -лю *perf.* char; carbonize; ~ся, char, become charred.

обу́живать, -аю *imp.* of обу́зить.

обу́за, -ы, burden, encumbrance.

обузда́ть, -а́ю *perf.*, обу́здывать, -аю *imp.* bridle, curb; restrain, control.

обу́зить, -у́жу *perf.* (*imp.* обу́живать) make too tight, too narrow.

обурева́емый, possessed; + *instr.* a prey to. обурева́ть, -а́ет *imp.* shake; grip. possess.

обусло́вить, -влю *perf.*, обусло́вливать, -аю *imp.* cause, bring about; + *instr.* make conditional on, limit by; ~ся +

instr. be conditioned by, be conditional on; depend on.

обу́ть, shod. обу́ть, -у́ю *perf.* (*imp.* обува́ть) put boots, shoes, on; provide with boots, shoes; ~ся, put on one's boots shoes.

о́бух, -a or -á, butt, back.

обуча́ть, -а́ю *imp.*, об|учи́ть, -чу́, -чишь *perf.* teach; train, instruct; ~ся + *dat.* or *inf.* learn. обуче́ние, -я, teaching; instruction, training.

обхва́т, -a girth; в ~e, in circumference. обхвати́ть, -ачу́, -а́тишь *perf.*, обхва́тывать, -аю *imp.* embrace; clasp.

обхо́д, -a, round; beat; roundabout way; bypass; evasion, circumvention. обходи́тельный, amiable; courteous; pleasant. обходи́ть(ся, -ожу́(сь, -о́дишь(ся *imp.* of обойти́(сь. обхо́дный, roundabout, circuitous; ~ путь, detour. обхожде́ние, -я, manners; treatment; behaviour.

обша́ривать, -аю *imp.*, обша́рить, -рю *perf.* rummage through, ransack.

обшива́ть, -а́ю *imp.* of обши́ть. обши́вка, -и, edging, bordering; trimming; facing; boarding, panelling; sheathing; plating; ~ фане́рой, veneering.

обши́рный, extensive, spacious; vast.

обши́ть, обошью́, -шьёшь *perf.* (*imp.* обшива́ть) edge, border; sew round; trim, face; fit out make outfit(s) for; plank; panel; sheathe, plate.

обшла́г, -á; *pl.* -á, -о́в, cuff.

обща́ться, -а́юсь *imp.* associate, mix.

обще- in *comb.* common(ly), general(ly). общедосту́пный, moderate in price; popular. ~жи́тие, -я, hostel; community; communal life. ~изве́стный, well-known, generally known; notorious. ~наро́дный, general, national, public; ~наро́дный пра́здник, public holiday. ~образова́тельный, general, of general education. ~при́нятый, generally accepted. ~сою́зный, All-Union. ~употреби́тельный, in general use. ~челове́ческий, common to all mankind; human; universal, general, ordinary.

общение, -я, intercourse; relations; links; личное ~, personal contact.

общественник, -а, -ица, -ы, public-spirited person. общественность, -и, (the) public; public opinion; community; communal organizations; дух общественности, public spirit. общественный, social, public; voluntary, unpaid, amateur; на ~ых началах, voluntary, unpaid; ~ые науки social sciences; ~ое питание, public catering. общество, -а, society; association; company.

общий, general; common; on the whole, in general, in sum; ~ий итог, ~ая сумма, sum total. община, -ы, community; commune. общинный, communal; common.

общипать, -плю, -плешь perf.

общительный, sociable. общность, -и, community.

обо-: see о-, об-.

объедать(ся, -аю(сь imp. of объесть(ся.

объединение, -я, unification; merger; union, association. объединённый, -ён, -а, united. объединительный, unifying, uniting. объединить, -ню perf., объединять, -яю imp. unite; join; pool, combine; ~ся unite.

объедки, -ов pl. leavings, leftovers, scraps.

объездить, -зжу, -здишь perf. (imp. объезжать) travel over; break in. объезжать, -аю imp. of объездить. объехать, -аю imp. of объездить, объехать, объезжий, roundabout, circuitous.

объект, -а, object; objective; establishment, works объективный, -а, objective, lens. объективный, objective; unbiassed.

объём. -а volume; bulk, size, capacity. объёмистый, voluminous, bulky. объёмный, by volume, volumetric.

объесть, -ём -ешь, -ест, -едим perf. (imp. -едать) gnaw (round), nibble; ~ся, overeat.

объехать -еду perf. (imp. объезжать) drive round; go round; go past, skirt; visit, make the round of; travel over.

объявить, -влю, -вишь perf., объявлять, -яю imp. declare, announce; publish, proclaim; advertise; ~ся, turn up,

appear; + instr. announce oneself, declare oneself. объявление, -я, declaration, announcement; notice; advertisement.

объяснение, -я, explanation; ~ в любви, declaration of love. объяснимый, explicable, explainable. объяснительный, explanatory. объяснить, -ню perf., объяснять, -яю imp. explain; ~ся, explain oneself; become clear, be explained; speak, make oneself understood; +c+instr. have a talk with; have it out with; + instr. be explained, accounted for, by.

объятие, -я, embrace.

обыватель, -я m. man in the street; inhabitant, resident. обывательский, commonplace; of the local inhabitants; narrow-minded.

обыграть, -аю perf. обыгрывать, -аю imp. beat; win; use with effect, play up; turn to advantage, turn to account.

обыденный, ordinary, usual; commonplace, everyday.

обыкновение, -я, habit, wont; иметь ~ +inf. be in the habit of; по обыкновению, as usual. обыкновенно adv. usually as a rule. обыкновенный, usual; ordinary; commonplace; everyday.

обыск, -а, search. обыскать, -ыщу, -ышешь perf. обыскивать, -аю imp. search.

обычай, -я, custom; usage. обычно adv. usually, as a rule. обычный, usual, ordinary.

обязанность, -и, duty; responsibility; исполняющий обязанности, acting. обязанный, (+inf.) obliged, bound; +dat. obliged to, indebted to (+instr. for). обязательно adv. without fail; он ~ там будет, he is sure to be there, he is bound to be there. обязательный, obligatory; compulsory; binding; obliging, kind. обязательство, -а, obligation; engagement; pl. liabilities; взять на себя ~, pledge oneself, undertake. обязать, -яжу, -яжешь perf., обязывать, -аю imp. bind; commit, oblige; ~ся, bind oneself, pledge oneself, undertake; не хочу ни перед кем обя́зываться, I do not want to be beholden to anybody.

ОВ (*ové*) *abbr.* отравля́ющее вещество́, poison, poisonous material; war gas.

овдове́вший, widowed. **овдове́ть**, -е́ю *perf.* become a widow, widower.

ове́н, овна́, Aries, the Ram.

ове́с, овса́, oats.

ове́чий, sheep, sheep's. **ове́чка**, -и *dim.* of овца́; lamb, harmless person, gentle creature.

ови́н, -а, barn.

овладева́ть, -а́ю *imp.*, **овладе́ть**, -е́ю *perf.* + *instr.* take possession of; master; seize; ~ собо́й, get control of oneself, regain self-control. **овладе́ние**, -я, mastery; mastering.

о-во *abbr.* о́бщество, society.

о́вод, -а; *pl.* -ы or -á, оводо́в, gadfly.

о́вощ, -а; *pl.* -и, -ей, vegetable, vegetables. **овощно́й**, vegetable; ~ мага́зи́н, greengrocer's; greengrocery.

овра́г, -а, ravine, gully.

овся́нка, -и, oatmeal; porridge. **овся́но́й**, oat, of oats. **овся́н**|**ый**, oat, oatmeal; ~ая крупа́, (coarse) oatmeal.

овца́, -ы́; *pl.* -ы, ове́ц, о́вцам, sheep; ewe. **овцево́дство**, -а, sheep-breeding. **овча́р**, -а, shepherd. **овча́рка**, -и, sheep-dog. **овчи́на**, -ы, sheepskin. **овчи́нный**, sheepskin.

ога́рок, -рка, candle-end.

огиба́ть, -а́ю *imp.* of огну́ть.

ОГИ́З, -а *abbr.* Объедине́ние госуда́рственных изда́тельств, Central State Publishing House.

оглавле́ние, -я, table of contents.

огласи́ть, -ашу́ *perf.*, **оглаша́ть**, -а́ю *imp.* proclaim; announce; divulge; make public; fill (with sound); ~ся, resound, ring. **огла́ска**, -и, publicity; получи́ть огла́ску, be given publicity; оглаше́ние, -я, proclaiming, publication; не подлежи́т оглаше́нию, confidential, not for publication.

огло́бля, -и; *gen. pl.* -бель, shaft.

о|**гло́хнуть**, -ну, -óх *perf.*

оглуша́ть, -а́ю *imp.*, **о**|**глуши́ть**, -шу́ *perf.* deafen; stun. **оглуши́тельный**, deafening.

огляде́ть, -яжу́ *perf.*, **огля́дывать**, -аю

imp., **огляну́ть**, -ну́, -нешь *perf.* look round; look over, examine, inspect; ~ся, look round, look about; look back; turn to look; adapt oneself, become acclimatized. **огля́дка**, -и, looking round, looking back; care, caution; бежа́ть без огля́дки, run for one's life.

огнево́й, fire; fiery; igneous. **огнемёт**, -а, flame-thrower. **о́гненный**, fiery. **огнеопа́сный**, inflammable. **огнеприпа́сы**, -ов *pl.* ammunition. **огнесто́йкий**, fire-proof, fire-resistant. **огнестре́льн**|**ый**; ~ое ору́жие, firearm(s). **огнетуши́тель**, -я *m.* fire-extinguisher. **огнеупо́рн**|**ый**, fire-resistant, fire-proof; refractory; ~ая гли́на, fire-clay; ~ый кирпи́ч, fire-brick.

ого́ (*ohó*) *int.* oho!

огова́ривать, -аю *imp.*, **оговори́ть**, -рю́ *perf.* slander; stipulate (for); fix, agree on; ~ся, make a reservation, make a proviso; make a slip (of the tongue); я оговори́лся, it was a slip of the tongue. **огово́р**, -а, slander. **огово́рка**, -и, reservation, proviso; slip of the tongue; без огово́рок, without reserve.

оголённый, bare, nude; uncovered, exposed. **оголи́ть**, -лю́ *perf.* (*imp.* оголя́ть) bare; strip; uncover; ~ся, strip, strip oneself; become exposed.

оголте́лый, wild, frantic; frenzied; unbridled.

оголя́ть(ся, -я́ю(сь *imp.* of оголи́ть(ся.

огонёк, -нька́, (small) light; zest, spirit. **ого́нь**, огня́ *m.* fire; firing; light.

огора́живать, -аю *imp.*, **огороди́ть**, -рожу́, -ро́ди́шь *perf.* fence in, enclose; ~ся, fence oneself in. **огоро́д**, -а, kitchen-garden; market-garden. **огоро́дник**, -а market-gardener. **огоро́дничество**, -а, market-gardening. **огоро́дный**, kitchen-garden, market-garden.

огоро́шить, -шу *perf.* take aback, dumbfound; startle.

огорча́ть, -а́ю *imp.*, **огорчи́ть**, -чу́ *perf.* grieve, distress, pain; ~ся, grieve; distress oneself, be distressed, be pained. **огорче́ние**, -я, grief, affliction; chagrin. **огорчи́тельный**, distressing.

ОГПУ' *abbr.* Объединённое госудáрственное политическое управлéние, OGPU.

о|грáбить, -блю *perf.* ограблéние, -я, robbery; burglary.

огрáда, -ы, fence. огради́ть, -ажý *perf.*, огражда́ть, -áю *imp.* guard, protect; enclose, fence in; ~ся, defend oneself, protect oneself; guard oneself.

ограничéние, -я, limitation, restriction. ограни́ченный, limited, narrow. ограни́чивать, -аю *imp.*, ограни́чить, -чу *perf.* limit, restrict, cut down; ~ся + *instr.* limit oneself to, confine oneself to; be limited, be confined, to.

огро́мный, huge; vast; enormous.

огрубéлый, coarse, hardened, rough. о|грубéть, -éю *perf.*

огрыза́ться, -áюсь *imp.*, огрызну́ться, -нýсь, -нёшься *perf.* snap (на + *acc.* at).

огры́зок, -зка, bit, end; stub, stump.

огу́зок, -зка, rump.

огу́лом *adv.* all together; wholesale, indiscriminately. огу́льно *adv.* without grounds. огу́льный, wholesale, indiscriminate; unfounded, groundless.

огурéц, -рцá, cucumber.

одарённый, gifted, talented. одáривать, -аю *imp.*, одари́ть, -рю́ *perf.*, одаря́ть, -я́ю *imp.* give presents (to); + *instr.* endow with.

одевáть(ся, -áю(сь *imp.* of одéть(ся.

одéжда, -ы, clothes; garments; clothing; revetment; surfacing.

одеколóн, -а, eau-de-Cologne.

одели́ть, -лю́ *perf.*, оделя́ть, -я́ю *imp.* (+ *instr.*) present (with); endow (with).

одéну, etc.: see одéть. одёргивать, -аю *imp.* of одёрнуть.

одеревенéлый, numb; lifeless. о|деревенéть, -éю *perf.*

одержáть, -жý, -жишь *perf.*, одéрживать, -аю *imp.* gain, win; ~ верх, gain the upper hand, prevail. одержи́мый, possessed.

одёрнуть, -ну *perf.* (*imp.* одёргивать) pull down, straighten; call to order; silence.

одéтый, dressed; clothed. одéть, -éну *perf.* (*imp.* одевáть) dress; clothe; ~ся, dress (oneself); + в + *acc.* put on.

одея́ло, -а, blanket; coverlet. одея́ние, -я, garb, attire.

оди́н, однóго, однá, однóй, однó, однóго; *pl.* одни́, одни́х *num.* one; a, an; a certain; alone; only; by oneself; nothing but; same; в оди́н гóлос, with one voice, with one accord; все до однóго, (all) to a man; мне это всё однó, it is all one to me; одни́ .., други́е, some .., others; оди́н за други́м, one after the other; оди́н и тот же, one and the same; оди́н и то же, the same thing; оди́н на оди́н, in private, tête-à-tête; face to face; одни́ нóжницы, one pair of scissors; оди́н раз, once; одни́м слóвом, in a word; in short; по одному́, one by one, one at a time; in single file.

одинáково *adv.* equally. одинáковый, identical, the same, equal. одинáрный, single.

оди́ннадцатый, eleventh. оди́ннадцать, -и, eleven.

одинóкий, solitary; lonely; single. одинóчество, -а, solitude; loneliness. одинóчка, -и *m.* and *f.* (one) person alone; в одинóчку, alone, on one's own; мать-~, unmarried mother; по одинóчке, one by one. одинóчный *adv.* alone, by oneself, by itself. одинóчный, individual; one-man; single; ~ое заключéние, solitary confinement. одинóчник, -а individual competitor; skiff.

одио́зный, odious.

одичáлый, wild, gone wild. одичáние, -я, running wild. о|дичáть, -áю *perf.*

одна́жды *adv.* once; one day; once upon a time; ~ ýтром, ~ вéчером, ~ нóчью, one morning, evening, night.

одна́ко *conj.* however; but; though; *int.* you don't say so! not really!

одно- in comb. single, one; uni-, mono-, homo-. однобóкий, one-sided. ~бóртный, single-breasted. ~вре́ме́нно *adv.* simultaneously, at the same time. ~гóдок, -дка, ~гóдка, -и, person of the same age (c + *instr.* as). ~дне́вный, one-day. ~зву́чный, monotonous. ~знáчащий, synonymous; monosemantic. ~знáчный, synonymous; mono-semantic; simple; one-digit. ~имён-

ный, of the same name; eponymous. ~-кла́ссник, class mate. ~ кле́точ-
ный, unicellular. ~коле́йный, single-track. ~кра́тный, single; ~ кра́тный
вид, momentary aspect. ~ле́тний, one-year; annual. ~ле́тник, -а, (a annual. ~лёток, -тка, ~лётка, -и, (person) of the same age (c+instr. as).
~ме́стный, for one (person); single-seater. ~мото́рный, single-engined.
~обра́зие, ~обра́зность, -и, monotony. ~обра́зный, monotonous. ~-
по́люсный, unipolar. ~пу́тка, -и, single-track railway. ~пу́тный, one-
way. ~ро́дность, -и, homogeneity, uniformity. ~ро́дный, homogeneous,
uniform; similar. ~сло́жный, mono-syllabic; terse, abrupt. ~сло́йный,
single-layer; one-ply, single-ply. ~сторо́нний, one-sided; unilateral;
one-way; one-track. ~та́ктный, one-stroke; single-cycle. ~ти́пный, of the
same type; of the same kind. ~то́м-ник, one-volume edition. ~то́мный,
one-volume. ~фами́лец, -льца, person of the same surname. ~цве́тный, one-
-colour; monochrome. ~эта́жный, single-stage; one-storeyed. ~я́русный,
single-tier, single-deck; single-layer.

одобре́ние, -я, approval. **одобри́тель-ный**, approving. **одо́брить**, -рю perf.,
одобря́ть, -я́ю imp. approve of, approve.

одолева́ть, -а́ю imp., **одоле́ть**, -е́ю perf. overcome, conquer; master, cope with.

одолжа́ть, -а́ю imp., **одолжи́ть**, -жу́ perf. lend; +y+gen. borrow from;
~ся, be obliged, be beholden; borrow, get into debt. **одолже́ние**, -я, favour,
service.

одома́шненный, domesticated. **одома́ш-нивать**, -аю imp., **одома́шнить**, -ню
perf. domesticate, tame.

о|дряхле́ть, -е́ю perf.

одува́нчик, -а dandelion.

оду́маться, -аюсь perf., **оду́мываться**, -аюсь imp. change one's mind; think
better of it; have time to think.

одура́чивать, -аю imp., **о|дура́чить**, -чу perf. fool, make a fool of.

одуре́лый, stupid. **одуре́ние**, -я, stupe-faction, torpor. **о|дуре́ть**, -е́ю perf.

одура́нивать, -аю imp., **о|дура́нить**, -ню perf. stupefy. **о́дурь**, -и, stupefac-
tion, torpor. **одуря́ть**, -я́ю imp. stupefy; **одуря́ющий за́пах**, over-
powering scent.

одухотворённый, inspired; spiritual. **одухотвори́ть**, -рю́ perf., **одухотво-
ря́ть**, -я́ю imp. inspire.

одушеви́ть, -влю́ perf., **одушевля́ть**, -я́ю imp. animate; ~ся, be animated.
одушевле́ние, -я, animation. **одушев-лённый**, animated; animate.

оды́шка, -и, shortness of breath; **страда́ть одышкой**, be short-winded.

ожере́лье, -я, necklace.

ожесточа́ть, -а́ю imp., **ожесточи́ть**, -чу́ perf. embitter, harden; ~ся, become
embittered, become hard. **ожесточе́-ние**, -я, **ожесточённость**, -и, bitterness;
hardness. **ожесточённый**, bitter, em-bittered.

ожива́ть, -а́ю imp. of ожи́ть.

оживи́ть, -влю́ perf., **оживля́ть**, -я́ю imp. revive; enliven, vivify, animate;
~ся, become animated, liven up. **оживле́ние**, -я, animation, gusto; re-
viving; enlivening. **оживлённый**, animated, lively.

ожида́ние, -я, expectation; waiting; в ожида́нии, expecting; +gen. pending;
про́тив ожида́ния, unexpectedly; сверх ожида́ния, beyond expectation.
ожида́ть, -а́ю imp.+gen. wait for; ex-pect, anticipate.

ожире́ние, -я, obesity. **о|жире́ть**, -е́ю perf.

ожи́ть, -иву́, -ивёшь; о́жил, -а́, -о perf. (imp. ожива́ть) come to life, revive.

ожо́г, -а, burn, scald.

оз. abbr. о́зеро, lake.

о|забо́тить, -о́чу perf., **озабо́чивать**, -аю imp. trouble, worry; cause anxiety
to; ~ся + instr. attend to, see to. **озабо́ченность**, -и, preoccupation;
anxiety. **озабо́ченный**, preoccupied; anxious, worried.

озагла́вить, -лю perf., **озагла́вливать**, -аю imp. entitle, call; head.

озада́ченный, perplexed, puzzled. **озада́чивать**, -аю imp., **озада́чить**, -чу
perf. perplex, puzzle; take aback.

озари́ть, -рю́ perf., **озаря́ть**, -я́ю imp.

light up, illuminate; их озари́ло, it dawned on them; ~ся, light up.

озвере́лый, brutal; brutalized. о|з-вере́ть, -е́ю perf.

озву́ченный фильм, sound film.

оздорови́тельный, sanitary. оздорови́ть, -влю́ perf., оздоровля́ть, -я́ю imp. render (more) healthy; improve sanitary conditions of.

озелени́ть, -ню́ perf., озеленя́ть, -я́ю imp. plant (with trees, grass, etc.).

озёрный, lake; ~ райо́н, lake district. о́зеро, -а; pl. озёра, lake.

ози́мые sb. winter crops. ози́мый, winter. о́зимь, -и, winter crop.

озира́ться, -а́юсь imp. look round; look about.

о|зли́ть(ся: see обозли́ть(ся.

озло́бить, -блю perf., озлобля́ть, -я́ю imp. embitter; ~ся, grow bitter, be embittered. озлобле́ние, -я, bitterness, animosity. озло́бленный, embittered, bitter; angry.

о|знако́мить, -млю perf., ознакомля́ть, -я́ю imp. c+instr. acquaint with; ~ся c+instr. familiarize oneself with.

ознаменова́ние, -я, marking, commemoration; в ~+gen. to mark, to commemorate, in commemoration of. ознаменова́ть, -ну́ю perf., ознаменовывать, -аю imp. mark, commemorate; celebrate.

означа́ть, -а́ет imp. mean, signify, stand for. озна́ченный, aforesaid.

озно́б, -а, shivering, chill.

озорни́к, -а́, naughty child, mischievous child; rowdy person. озорнича́ть, -а́ю imp. (perf. c~) be naughty, get up to mischief. озорно́й, naughty, mischievous; rowdy. озорство́, -а́, naughtiness, mischief.

озя́бнуть, -ну; озя́б perf. be cold, be freezing.

ой int. oh.

ок. abbr. о́коло, about.

оказа́ть, -ажу́, -а́жешь perf. (imp. ока́зывать) render, show; ~ влия́ние на+acc. influence, exert influence on; ~ де́йствие, have an effect, take effect; ~ предпочте́ние, show preference; ~ услу́гу, do a service, do a good

turn; ~ честь, do honour; ~ся, turn out, prove; find oneself, be found.

ока́зия, -и, opportunity; unexpected happening, funny thing.

ока́зывать(ся, -аю(сь imp. of оказа́ть-(ся.

окайми́ть, -млю́ perf., окаймля́ть, -я́ю imp. border, edge.

окамене́лость, -и, fossil. окамене́лый, fossil; fossilized; petrified. о|камене́ть, -е́ю perf.

о|кантова́ть, -ту́ю perf. оканто́вка, -и, mount; edge.

ока́нчивать(ся, -аю(сь imp. of око́нчить(ся. ока́пывать(ся, -аю(сь imp. of окопа́ть(ся.

окая́нный, damned, cursed.

океа́н, -а. ocean. океа́нский, ocean; oceanic; ocean-going; ~ парохо́д, ocean liner.

оки́дывать, -аю imp., оки́нуть, -ну perf. cast round; ~ взгля́дом, take in at a glance, glance over.

о́кисел, -сла, oxide. окисле́ние, -я, oxidation. окисли́ть, -лю́ perf., окисля́ть, -я́ю imp. oxidize; ~ся, oxidize. о́кись, -и, oxide.

оккупа́нт, -а, invader; pl. occupying forces, occupiers. оккупа́ция, -и, occupation. оккупи́ровать, -рую perf and imp. occupy.

окла́д, -а, salary scale; (basic) pay; tax(-rate); metal overlay, setting.

оклевета́ть, -ещу́, -е́щешь perf. slander, calumniate, defame.

окле́ивать, -аю imp., окле́ить, -е́ю perf. cover; glue over, paste over; ~ обо́ями, paper.

окно́, -а́; pl. о́кна, window; port; gap; aperture; interval, free period.

о́ко, -а; pl. о́чи, оче́й, eye; в мгнове́ние о́ка, in the twinkling of an eye.

окова́ть, окую́, -ёшь perf., око́вывать, -аю imp. bind; fetter, shackle. око́вы, -о́в pl. fetters.

окола́чиваться, -аюсь imp. lounge about, kick one's heels.

околдова́ть, -ду́ю perf., околдо́вывать, -аю imp. bewitch, entrance, enchant.

околева́ть, -а́ю imp., околе́ть, -е́ю perf. die. околе́лый, dead.

о́коло *adv. and prep.* + *gen.* by; close (to), near; around; about; где-нибудь ~, hereabouts, somewhere here; ~ э́того, ~ того́, thereabouts.

око́лыш, -а, cap-band.

око́льн|ый, roundabout; ~ым путём, in a roundabout way.

о|кольцева́ть, -цу́ю *perf.*

око́нный, window; ~ переплёт, sash.

оконча́ние, -я, end; conclusion, termination; ending; ~ сле́дует, to be concluded. **оконча́тельно** *adv.* finally, definitively; completely. **оконча́тельный**, final; definitive, decisive. **око́нчить**, -чу *perf.* (*imp.* ока́нчивать) finish, end; ~ся, finish, end, terminate; be over.

око́п, -а, trench; entrenchment. **окопа́ть**, -а́ю *perf.* (*imp.* ока́пывать) dig up, dig round; ~ся, entrench oneself, dig in. **око́пн|ый**, trench; ~ая война́, trench warfare.

о́корок, -а; *pl.* -а́, -о́в, ham, gammon, leg.

окостенева́ть, -а́ю *imp.*, **окостене́ть**, -е́ю *perf.* ossify; stiffen. **окостене́лый**, ossified; stiff.

окочене́лый, stiff with cold. **о|коченеть**, -е́ю *perf.*

око́шечко, -а, *окошко*, -а, (small) window; opening.

окра́ина, -ы, outskirts, outlying districts; borders, marches.

о|кра́снть, -а́шу *perf.*, **окра́шивать**, -аю *imp.* paint, colour; stain. **окра́ска**, -и, painting; colouring; dyeing, staining; coloration; tinge, tint, touch, slant.

о|кре́пнуть, -ну *perf.* **о|крести́ть(ся**, -ещу́(сь, -е́стишь(ся *perf.*

окре́стность, -и, environs; neighbourhood, vicinity. **окре́стный**, neighbouring, surrounding.

о́крик, -а, hail, call; cry, shout. **окри́кивать**, -аю *imp.*, **окри́кнуть**, -ну *perf.* hail, call, shout to.

окрова́вленный, blood-stained, bloody.

окро́шка, -и, okroshka; hotch-potch, jumble.

о́круг, -а, okrug; region, district; circuit. **округа́**, -и, neighbourhood. **округлённый**; -лён, -а́, rounded.

округли́ть, -лю́ *perf.*, **округля́ть**, -я́ю *imp.* round; round off; express in round numbers; ~ся, become rounded; be expressed in round numbers. **окру́глый**, rounded, roundish. **окружа́ть**, -а́ю *imp.*, **окружи́ть**, -жу́ *perf.* surround; encircle. **окружа́ющ|ий**, surrounding; ~ая среда́, environment; ~ее *sb.* environment; ~ие *sb. pl.* associates: entourage. **окруже́ние**, -я, encirclement; surroundings; environment; milieu; в окруже́нии + *gen.* accompanied by; surrounded by, in the midst of. **окружн|о́й**, okrug, district, circuit; circle; ~а́я желе́зная доро́га, circle line. **окру́жность**, -и, circumference; circle; neighbourhood; на три ми́ли в окру́жности, within a radius of three miles, for three miles round. **окру́жный**, neighbouring.

окрыли́ть, -лю́ *perf.*, **окрыля́ть**, -я́ю *imp.* inspire, encourage.

окта́н, -а, octane. **окта́нов|ый**, octane; ~ое число́, octane rating.

октя́брь, -я́ *m.* October. **октя́брьский**, October.

окуна́ть, -а́ю *imp.*, **окуну́ть**, -ну́, -нёшь *perf.* dip; ~ся, dip; plunge; become absorbed, become engrossed.

о́кунь, -я; *pl.* -и, -ей *m.* perch.

окупа́ть, -а́ю *imp.*, **окупи́ть**, -плю́, -пишь *perf.* compensate, repay, make up for; ~ся, be compensated, be repaid, pay for itself; pay; be justified, be required, be rewarded.

оку́ривание, -я, fumigation. **оку́ривать**, -аю *imp.*, **окури́ть**, -рю́, -ришь *perf.* fumigate. **окуро́к**, -рка́, cigarette-end; (cigar-)stub.

оку́тать, -аю *perf.*, **оку́тывать**, -аю *imp.* wrap up; shroud, cloak; ~ся, wrap up; be shrouded be cloaked.

оку́чивать, -аю *imp.*, **оку́чить**, -чу *perf.* earth up.

ола́дья, -и; *gen. pl.* -ий, fritter; girdle scone, drop-scone.

оледене́лый, frozen. **о|ледене́ть**, -е́ю *perf.* **о|ледени́ть**, -и́т *perf.*

оле́н|ий, deer, deer's; reindeer; hart, hart's; ~ий мох, reindeer moss; ~ьи рога́, antlers. **оле́нина**, -ы, venison.

оле́нь, -я *m.* deer; reindeer; (*sl.*) simpleton, greenhorn.

оли́ва, -ы, olive. оли́вковый, olive; olive(-coloured).

олимпиа́да, -ы olympiad; competition. олимпи́йский, олимпи́ец, олимпи́йка, -и, contestant in Olympic games.

оли́фа, -ы, drying oil.

олицетворе́ние, -я, personification; embodiment. олицетворённый, -рён, -á, personified. олицетвори́ть, -рю́ *perf.*, олицетворя́ть, -я́ю *imp.* personify, embody.

о́лово, -a tin. оловя́нн|ый, tin; stannic; ~ая посу́да, tinware; pewter; ~ая фо́льга, tinfoil.

ом, -a, ohm.

омерзе́ние, -я, loathing. омерзе́ть, -е́ю *perf.* become loathsome. омерзи́тельн|ый loathsome, sickening; ~ое настрое́ние, foul mood.

омертве́лость, -и, stiffness; numbness; necrosis, mortification. омертве́л|ый, stiff, numb; necrotic; ~ая ткань dead tissue. омертве́ние, -я, necrosis. о|мертве́ть, -е́ю *perf.*

омоложе́ние, -я, rejuvenation.

омо́ним, -a, homonym.

омо́ю, etc.: see омы́ть.

омрача́ть, -а́ю *imp.*, омрачи́ть, -чу́ *perf.* darken, cloud, overcloud; ~ся, become darkened, become clouded.

о́мут, -a, pool; whirlpool; whirl, maelstrom.

омыва́ть, -а́ю *imp.*, омы́ть, омо́ю *perf.* wash; wash away, wash out; wash down; ~ся, be washed.

он, -á, -ó, им, о нём *pron.* he. она́, её, ей, ей (е́ю), о ней *pron.* she.

онда́тра, -ы musk-rat; musquash. онда́тровый, musquash.

онеме́лый, dumb; numb. о|неме́ть, -е́ю *perf.*

они́, их, им, и́ми, о них *pron.* they. оно́, его́, ему́ им, о нём *pron.* it; this, that.

ОНО́ *abbr.* отде́л наро́дного образова́ния, (local) education department.

ОО́Н *abbr.* Организа́ция объединённых на́ций, U.N.(O.), United Nations

(Organisation). ообно́вский, United Nations.

опада́ть, -áет *imp.* of опа́сть. опада́ющий, deciduous.

опа́здывать, -аю *imp.* of опозда́ть.

опа́ла, -ы, disgrace, disfavour.

о|пали́ть, -лю́ *perf.*

опа́ловый, opal; opaline.

опа́лубка, -и, shuttering, casing.

опаса́ться, -а́юсь *imp.*+*gen.* fear, be afraid of; +*gen.* or *inf.* beware (of); avoid, keep off. опасе́ние, -я, fear; apprehension; misgiving(s). опа́сливый, cautious; wary.

опа́сность, -и, danger; peril. опа́сный, dangerous, perilous.

опа́сть, -адёт *perf.* (*imp.* опада́ть) fall, fall off; subside, go down.

опе́ка, -и, guardianship, tutelage; trusteeship; guardians, trustees; care; surveillance. опека́емый *sb.* ward. опека́ть, -а́ю *imp.* be guardian of; take care of, watch over. опеку́н, -á, -у́нша, -и, guardian; tutor; trustee.

операти́вность, -и, drive, energy. операти́вный, energetic; efficient; executive; operative, surgical; operation(s) operational; strategical. опера́тор, -a, operator; cameraman; (computer) instruction. опера́торная *sb.* management and control centre. операцио́нн|ый, operating; surgical; ~ая *sb.* operating theatre. опера́ция, -и, operation.

опереди́ть, -режу́ *perf.*, опережа́ть, -а́ю *imp.* outstrip, leave behind; forestall.

опере́ние, -я, plumage. опере́нный; -ён, -á, feathered.

опере́тта, -ы, -е́тка, -и, musical comedy, operetta.

опере́ть, обопру́, -прёшь; опёр, -лá *perf.* (*imp.* опира́ть)+o+*acc.* lean against; ~ся, на о *acc.* lean on, lean against.

опери́ровать, -рую *perf.* and *imp.* operate on; operate, act; + *instr.* operate with; use, handle.

опери́ть, -рю́ *perf.* (*imp.* опери́ть) feather; adorn with feathers; ~ся, be fledged; stand on one's own feet.

о́перный, opera; operatic; ~ теа́тр, opera-house.

оперуполномо́ченный, sb. C.I.D. officer; security officer.

опёршись на + acc. leaning on.

опере́ть(ся, -я́ю(сь imp. of опере́ть(ся. о|печа́лить(ся, -лю(сь perf.

опеча́тать, -аю perf. (imp. опеча́тывать) seal up.

опеча́тка, -и, misprint; спи́сок опеча́ток, errata.

опеча́тывать, -аю imp. of опеча́тать.

опеши́ть, -шу perf. be taken aback.

опи́вки, -вок pl. dregs.

опи́лки, -лок pl. sawdust; (metal) filings.

опира́ть(ся, -а́ю(сь imp. of опере́ть(ся.

описа́ние, -я, description; account. опи́санный, circumscribed. описа́тельный, descriptive. описа́ть, -ишу́ -и́шешь perf. описа́ться, -а́ю imp. describe; take inventory; circumscribe; distrain; ~ся, make a slip of the pen. о́пись, -и, list, schedule; inventory.

опла́кать, -а́чу perf., опла́кивать, -аю imp. mourn for; bewail, deplore.

опла́та, -ы, pay, payment; remuneration. оплати́ть, -ачу́ -а́тишь perf., опла́чивать, -аю imp. pay for. pay; ~ расхо́ды, meet the expenses, foot the bill; ~ счёт, settle the account, pay the bill. опла́ченный, paid; с ~ым отве́том, reply-paid.

оплачу́, etc.: see опла́кать. оплачу́, etc.: see оплати́ть.

оплева́ть, -люю́, -люёшь perf., оплёвывать, -аю imp. spit on; humiliate.

оплеу́ха, -и, slap in the face.

о|плеши́веть, -ею perf.

оплодотворе́ние, -я, impregnation, fecundation; fertilization. оплодотвори́тель, -я m. fertilizer. оплодотвори́ть, -рю́ perf., оплодотворя́ть, -я́ю imp. impregnate, fecundate; fertilize.

о|пломбирова́ть, -ру́ю perf.

опло́т, -а, stronghold, bulwark.

опло́шность, -и, blunder, oversight. опло́шный, mistaken, blundering.

оплюю́, etc.: see оплева́ть.

оповести́ть, -ещу́ perf., оповеща́ть, -а́ю imp. notify, inform. оповеще́ние, -я, notification; warning.

о|пога́нить, -ню perf.

опозда́вший sb. late-comer. опозда́ние, -я, being late, lateness; delay; без опозда́ния, on time; с ~м на де́сять мину́т, ten minutes late. опозда́ть, -а́ю perf. (imp. опа́здывать) be late; be overdue; be slow.

опознава́тельный, distinguishing; ~ знак, landmark, beacon; marking. опознава́ть, -наю́, -наёшь imp., опозна́ть, -а́ю perf. identify. опозна́ние, -я, identification.

опозо́рение, -я, defamation. о|позо́рить(ся, -рю(сь perf.

оползти́, -а́ет imp., оползти́, -зёт; -о́лз, -ла́ perf. slip, slide. о́ползень, -зня m. landslide; landslip.

ополча́ться, -а́юсь imp., ополчи́ться, -чу́сь perf. take up arms; be up in arms; + на + acc. fall on, attack. ополче́нец, -нца, militiaman. ополче́ние, -я, militia; irregulars; levies.

опо́мниться, -нюсь perf. come to one's senses, collect oneself.

опо́р, -а; во весь ~, at full speed, at top speed, full tilt.

опо́ра, -ы, support; bearing; pier; buttress; то́чка опо́ры, fulcrum, bearing.

опора́жнивать, -аю imp. of опоро́жнить.

опо́рный, support, supporting, supported; bearing; ~ый прыжо́к, vault; ~ый пункт, strong point; ~ая то́чка, fulcrum.

опоро́жни́ть, -ню́ or -ню perf., опорожня́ть, -я́ю imp. (imp. also опора́жнивать) empty; drain.

о|пороси́ться, -и́тся perf. о|поро́чить, -чу perf.

опохмели́ться, -лю́сь perf., опохмеля́ться, -я́юсь imp. take a hair of the dog that bit you.

опо́шлить, -лю perf., опошля́ть, -я́ю imp. vulgarize, debase.

опоя́сать, -я́шу perf., опоя́сывать, -аю imp. gird on; girdle.

оппозицио́нный, opposition, in opposition; antagonistic, of opposition. оппози́ция, -и, opposition.

опра́ва, -ы, setting, mounting; case; rim.

оправда́ние, -я, justification; excuse;

acquittal, discharge. **оправда́тель-**
ный пригово́р, verdict of not guilty.
оправда́ть, -а́ю *perf.,* **опра́вдывать,**
-аю *imp.* justify, warrant; vindicate;
authorize; excuse; acquit, discharge;
~ся, justify oneself; vindicate oneself;
be justified.

опра́вить, -влю *perf.,* **оправля́ть, -я́ю**
imp. put in order, set right adjust; set,
mount; **~ся,** put one's dress in order;
recover; **+от+**gen. get over.

опра́шивать, -аю *imp.* of **опроси́ть.**

определе́ние, -я, definition; determination; decision; attribute. **определён-**
ный, definite; determinate; fixed; certain. **определи́мый,** definable. **опре-**
дели́ть, -лю́ *perf.,* **определя́ть, -я́ю**
imp. define; determine; fix, appoint;
allot, assign; **~ на слу́жбу,** appoint;
~ся, be formed; take shape; be determined; obtain a fix, find one's position.

опроверга́ть, -а́ю *imp.,* **опрове́ргнуть,**
-ну; -ве́рг *perf.* refute, disprove. **опро-**
верже́ние, -я, refutation; disproof;
denial.

опрокиди|о́й, tipping, tip-up. **опроки́-**
дывать, -аю *imp.,* **опроки́нуть, -ну**
perf. overturn; upset; topple; overthrow; overrun; refute; knock back;
~ся, overturn; topple over, tip over,
tip up; capsize.

опроме́тчивый, precipitate, rash, hasty,
unconsidered. **о́прометью** *adv.* headlong.

опро́с, -а, interrogation; (cross-)examin-
ation; referendum; (opinion) poll.
опроси́ть, -ошу́ -о́сишь *perf.* (*imp.*
опра́шивать) interrogate, question;
(cross-)examine. **опро́сный,** interroga-
tory; **~ лист,** questionnaire.

опроти́веть, -ею *perf.* become loathsome, become repulsive.

опры́скать, -аю *perf.,* **опры́скивать,**
-аю *imp.* sprinkle; spray. **опры́скива-**
тель, -я m sprinkler; spray(er).

опря́тный, neat, tidy.

о́птик, -а, optician. **о́птика, -и,** optics;
optical instruments. **опти́ческий,** optic, optical; **~ обма́н,** optical illusion.

опто́вый. wholesale. **о́птом** *adv.* wholesale; **~ и в ро́зницу,** wholesale and
retail.

опубликова́ние, -я, publication; pro-
mulgation. **о|публикова́ть, -ку́ю** *perf.,*
опублико́вывать, -аю *imp.* publish;
promulgate.

опуска́ть(ся, -а́ю(сь *imp.* of **опусти́ть-**
(ся.

опускн|о́й, movable; **~а́я дверь,** trap-
-door.

опусте́лый, deserted. **о|пусте́ть, -е́ет**
perf.

опусти́ть, -ущу́ -у́стишь *perf.* (*imp.*
опуска́ть) lower; let down; turn down;
omit; **~ глаза́,** look down; **~ го́лову,**
hang one's head; **~ ру́ки,** lose heart;
~ што́ры, draw the blinds; **~ся,**
lower oneself; sink; fall; go down; let
oneself go, go to pieces.

опустоша́ть, -а́ю *imp.,* **опустоши́ть, -шу́**
perf. devastate, lay waste, ravage.
опустоше́ние, -я, devastation, ruin.
опустоши́тельный, devastating.

опу́тать, -аю *perf.,* **опу́тывать, -аю** *imp.*
enmesh, entangle; ensnare.

опуха́ть, -а́ю *imp.,* **о|пу́хнуть, -ну;**
опу́х *perf.* swell, swell up. **опу́хлый,**
swollen; **~ся.** **о́пухоль, -и,** swelling; tumour.

опущу́, etc.: see **опусти́ть.**

опыле́ние, -я, pollination. **опыли́ть,**
-лю́ *perf.,* **опыля́ть, -я́ю** *imp.* pollinate.

о́пыт, -а, experience; experiment; test,
trial; attempt. **о́пытный,** experienced;
experimental.

опьяне́лый, intoxicated. **опьяне́ние, -я,**
intoxication. **о|пьяне́ть, -е́ю** *perf.*
о|пьяни́ть, -и́т *perf.,* **опьяня́ть, -я́ет**
imp. intoxicate, make drunk. **опьяня́ю-**
щий, intoxicating.

опя́ть *adv.* again.

ора́ва, -ы, crowd, horde.

ора́нжевый, orange. **оранжере́йный,**
hothouse, greenhouse. **оранжере́я, -и,**
hothouse, greenhouse, conservatory.

ора́тор, -а, orator, (public) speaker.
ора́торский, orator's, speaker's; oratorical. **ора́торствовать, -твую** *imp.*
orate, harangue, speechify.

ора́ть, ору́, орёшь *imp.* bawl, yell.

орби́та, -ы, orbit; (eye-)socket; **вы́-**
вести на орби́ту, put into orbit; **~**
влия́ния, sphere of influence.

орг- abbr. in comb. organization, organizational.

о́рган[1], -a, organ; organization; unit, element; department, body; исполни́тельный ~, executive; agency. **орга́н**[2], -a, organ. **организа́тор**, -a, organizer. **организацио́нный**, organization, organizational. **организа́ция**, -и, organization; ~ Объединённых На́ций, United Nations Organisation. **организо́ванный**, organized; orderly; disciplined. **организова́ть**, -зу́ю perf. and imp. (perf. also с~) organize; ~ся, be organized; organize. **органи́ческий**, **органи́чный**, organic.

о́ргия, -и, orgy.

орда́, -ы́; pl. -ы, horde.

о́рден, -a; pl. -á, order. **орденоно́сец**, -сца, holder of an order or decoration. **орденоно́сный**, decorated with an order.

о́рдер, -a; pl. -á, order; warrant; writ.

ордина́рец, -рца, orderly; batman.

ордина́тор, -a, house-surgeon. **ордина-ту́ра**, -ы, house-surgeon's appointment; clinical studies.

орды́нский, of the (Tartar) horde(s).

орёл, орла́, eagle; ~ и́ли ре́шка? heads or tails?

орео́л, -a, halo, aureole.

оре́х, -a, nut, nuts; nut-tree; walnut. **оре́ховый**, nut; walnut. **оре́шник**, -a, hazel; hazel-thicket.

оригина́л, -a, original; eccentric, oddity. **оригина́льный**, original.

ориента́ция, -и, orientation (на+acc. towards); understanding, grasp (в+prep. of). **ориенти́р**, -a, landmark; reference point, guiding line. **ориенти́рование**, -я, orienteering. **ориенти́роваться**, -а́юсь perf. and imp. orient oneself; find, get, one's bearings; +на +acc. head for, make for; aim at. **ориентиро́вка**, -и, orientation. **ориенти́ровочный**, serving for orientation, position-finding; tentative; provisional; rough approximate.

орли́ный, eagle's, eagle; aquiline. **орли́ца**, -ы, female eagle.

орна́мент, -a, ornament; ornamental design; plaster cast.

оробе́лый, timid; frightened. **о|робе́ть**, -е́ю perf.

ороси́тельный, irrigation. **ороси́ть**, -ошу́ perf., **ороша́ть**, -а́ю imp. irrigate. **ороше́ние**, -я, irrigation; поля́ ороше́ния, sewage farm.

ору́, etc.: see ора́ть.

ору́дие, -я, instrument; implement; tool; gun. **оруди́йный**, gun. **ору́довать**, -дую imp.+instr. handle; be active in; run; он там всем ору́дует, he bosses the whole show. **оруже́йн|ый**, arms; gun; ~ый заво́д, arms factory; ~ая пала́та, armoury. **ору́жие**, -я, arm, arms; weapons.

орфографи́ческ|ий, orthographic, orthographical; ~ая оши́бка, spelling mistake. **орфогра́фия**, -и, orthography, spelling.

оса́, -ы́; pl. -ы, wasp.

оса́да, -ы, siege. **осади́ть**[1], -ажу́ perf. (imp. осажда́ть) besiege, lay siege to; beleaguer; ~ вопро́сами, ply with questions; ~ про́сьбами, bombard with requests.

осади́ть[2], -ажу́, -а́дишь perf. (imp. осажда́ть) precipitate.

осади́ть[3], -ажу́, -а́дишь perf. (imp. оса́живать) check, halt; force back; rein in; put in his (her) place; take down a peg.

оса́дн|ый, siege; ~ое положе́ние, state of siege.

оса́док, -дка, sediment; precipitate; fall-out; after-taste; pl. precipitation, fall-out. **оса́дочный**, precipitation; sedimentary.

осажда́ть, -а́ю imp. of осади́ть. **осажда́ться**, -а́ется imp. fall; be precipitated, fall out.

оса́живать, -аю imp. of осади́ть. **осажу́**: see осади́ть.

оса́нистый, portly. **оса́нка**, -и, carriage, bearing.

осва́ивать(ся, -аю(сь imp. of осво́ить-(ся.

осведоми́тель, -я m. informer. **осведоми́тельный**, informative; information. **осве́домить**, -млю perf., **осведомля́ть**, -я́ю imp. inform; ~ся о+prep. inquire about, ask after. **осведомле́ние**, -я, informing, notification. **осведомлённость**, -и, knowledge, information. **осведомлённый**, well-informed, knowledgeable; conversant, versed.

освежа́ть, -а́ю *imp.*, **освежи́ть**, -жу́ *perf.* refresh; freshen; air; revive. **освежи́тельный**, refreshing.

освети́тельный, lighting, illuminating. **освети́ть**, -ещу́ *perf.*, **освеща́ть**, -а́ю *perf.* light; light up; illuminate, illumine; throw light on; ~ся, light up, brighten; be lighted. **освеще́ние**, -я, light, lighting illumination. **освещённый**, -ён, -а́, lit; ~ луно́й, moonlit.

о|свиде́тельствовать, -твую *perf.*

освиста́ть, -ищу́, -и́щешь *perf.*, **освистывать**, -аю *imp.* hiss (off); boo, hoot; greet with catcalls.

освободи́тель, -я *m.* liberator. **освободи́тельный**, liberation, emancipation. **освободи́ть**, -ожу́ *perf.*, **освобожда́ть**, -а́ю *imp.* free, liberate; release, set free; emancipate; dismiss; vacate; clear, empty; ~ся, free oneself; become free. **освобожде́ние**, -я, liberation; release; emancipation; discharge; dismissal; vacation. **освобождённый**, -ён, -а́, freed, free; exempt; ~ от нало́га, tax-free.

освое́ние, -я, assimilation, mastery, familiarization; reclamation, opening up. **осво́ить**, -о́ю *perf.* (*imp.* осва́ивать) assimilate, master; cope with; become familiar with; acclimatize; ~ся, familiarize oneself; feel at home.

о|святи́ть, -ящу́ *perf.* **освящённый**; -ён, -ена́, consecrated; sanctified, hallowed; обы́чай, ~ века́ми, time-honoured custom.

осево́й, axle; axis; axial.

оседа́ние, -я, settling, subsidence; settlement. **оседа́ть**, -а́ю *imp.* of осе́сть.

осёдланный, saddled. **о|седла́ть**, -а́ю *perf.*, **осёдлывать**, -аю *imp.* saddle.

осёдлый, settled.

осека́ться, -а́юсь *imp.* of осе́чься.

осёл, -сла́, donkey; ass.

осело́к, -лка́, touchstone; hone, whetstone, oil-stone.

осени́ть, -ню́ *perf.* (*imp.* осеня́ть) cover; overshadow; shield; dawn

upon, strike; ~ся кресто́м, cross oneself.

осе́нний, autumn, autumnal. **о́сень**, -и, autumn. **о́сенью** *adv.* in autumn.

осеня́ть(ся, -я́ю(сь *imp.* of осени́ть(ся.

осерди́ться, -ржу́сь, -рди́шься *perf.* (+на +*acc.*) become angry (with).

осеребри́ть, -рю́т *perf.* silver (over).

осе́сть, ося́ду; осе́л *perf.* (*imp.* оседа́ть) settle; subside; sink; form a sediment.

осётр, -а́, sturgeon. **осетри́на**, -ы, sturgeon. **осетро́вый**, sturgeon, sturgeon's.

осе́чка, -и, misfire. **осе́чься**, -еку́сь, -ечёшься *perf.* (*imp.* осека́ться) misfire; stop short, break (off).

оси́ливать, -аю *imp.*, **оси́лить**, -лю *perf.* overpower; master; manage.

оси́на, -ы, aspen. **оси́новый**, aspen.

оси́ный, wasp, wasp's; hornets'.

оси́плый, hoarse, husky. **о|си́пнуть**, -ну; оси́п *perf.* get hoarse, grow hoarse.

осироте́лый, orphaned. **осироте́ть**, -е́ю *perf.* be orphaned.

оска́ливать, -аю *imp.*, **о|ска́лить**, -лю *perf.*; ~ зу́бы, ~ся, show one's teeth, bare one's teeth.

о|сканда́лить(ся, -лю(сь *perf.*

оскверне́ние, -я, defilement; profanation. **оскверни́ть**, -ню́ *perf.*, **оскверня́ть**, -я́ю *imp.* profane; defile.

оскла́биться, -блюсь *perf.* grin.

оско́лок, -лка, splinter; fragment. **оско́лочный** *adj.* splinter; fragmentation.

оско́мина, -ы, bitter taste (in the mouth); наби́ть оско́мину, set the teeth on edge. **оско́мистый**, sour, bitter.

оскорби́тельный, insulting, abusive. **оскорби́ть**, -блю́ *perf.*, **оскорбля́ть**, -я́ю *imp.* insult; offend; ~ся, take offence; be offended, be hurt. **оскорбле́ние**, -я, insult; ~ де́йствием, assault and battery. **оскорблённый**, -ён, -а́, offended, insulted; ~ая неви́нность, outraged innocence.

ослабева́ть, -а́ю *imp.*, **о|слабе́ть**, -е́ю *perf.* weaken, become weak; slacken; abate. **осла́бнуть**, weakened, enfeebled. **осла́бить**, -блю *perf.*, **ослабля́ть**, -я́ю *imp.* weaken; slacken, relax; loosen. ослабле́ние, -я, weakening; slackening, relaxation.

ослепи́тельный, blinding, dazzling. осле́пить, -плю́ perf., ослепля́ть, -я́ю imp. blind, dazzle. ослепле́ние, -я, blinding, dazzling; blindness. о|сле́пнуть, -ну; -еп perf.

осли́ный, donkey; ass's, asses'; asinine. осли́ца, -ы, she-ass.

осложне́ние, -я, complication. осложни́ть, -ню́ perf., осложня́ть, -я́ю imp. complicate; ~ся, become complicated.

ослуша́ние, -я, disobedience. ослу́шаться, -аюсь perf., ослу́шиваться, -аюсь imp. disobey.

ослы́шаться, -шусь perf. mishear. ослы́шка, -и, mishearing, mistake of hearing.

осма́тривать(ся, -аю(сь imp. of осмотре́ть(ся. осме́ивать, -аю imp. of осмея́ть.

о|сме́лить, -ею perf. осме́ливаться, -аюсь imp., осме́литься, -люсь perf. dare; beg to, take the liberty of.

осмея́ть, -ею, -е́ешь perf. (imp. осме́ивать) mock, ridicule.

о|смоли́ть, -лю́ perf.

осмо́тр, -а, examination, inspection. осмотре́ть, -рю́, -ришь perf. (imp. осма́тривать) examine, inspect; look round, look over; ~ся, look round; take one's bearings, see how the land lies. осмотри́тельный, circumspect. осмо́трщик, -а, inspector.

осмы́сленный, sensible, intelligent. осмы́сливать, -аю imp., осмы́слить, -лю perf., осмысля́ть, -я́ю imp. interpret, give a meaning to; comprehend.

оснасти́ть, -ащу́ perf., оснаща́ть, -а́ю imp. rig; fit out, equip. осна́стка, -и, rigging. оснаще́ние, -я, rigging; fitting out; equipment.

осно́ва, -ы, base, basis, foundation; pl. principles, fundamentals; на осно́ве + gen. on the basis of; положи́ть в осно́ву, take as a principle. основа́ние, -я, founding, foundation; base; basis; ground, reason; на како́м основа́нии? on what grounds?; разру́шить до основа́ния, raze to the ground. основа́тель, -я m. founder. основа́тельный, well-founded; just; solid, sound;

thorough; bulky. основа́ть, -ную́, -нуёшь perf., осно́вывать, -аю imp. found; base; ~ся, settle; base oneself; be founded, be based. основно́й, fundamental, basic; principal main; primary; в основно́м, in the main, on the whole. основополо́жник, -а, founder, initiator.

осо́ба, -ы, person, individual, personage. осо́бенно adv. especially; particularly; unusually; не ~, not very, not particularly; not very much. осо́бенность, -и, peculiarity; в осо́бенности, especially, in particular; (more) particularly. осо́бенный, special particular, peculiar; ничего́ осо́бенного, nothing in particular; nothing (very) much. особня́к, -а́, private residence; detached house. особняко́м adv. by oneself. осо́бо adv. apart, separately; particularly, especially. осо́бый, special; particular; peculiar.

ОТС (оте-э́с) abbr. областна́я трансляцио́нная сеть, regional broadcasting network.

осознава́ть, -наю́, -наёшь imp., осозна́ть, -а́ю perf. realize.

осо́ка, -и sedge.

о́спа, -ы, smallpox; pock-marks; vaccination marks.

оспа́ривать, -аю imp., оспо́рить, -рю perf. dispute, question; challenge, contest; contend for.

о|срами́ть(ся, -млю́(сь perf. оставаться, -таю́сь, -таёшься imp. of оста́ться.

оста́вить, -влю perf., оставля́ть, -я́ю imp. leave; abandon, give up; reserve, keep; ~ в поко́е, leave alone, let alone; ~ за собо́й пра́во, reserve the right; ~ь(те)! stop it! stop that! lay off!

остальн|о́й the rest of; в ~о́м, in other respects; ~о́е sb. the rest; ~ы́е sb. the others.

остана́вливать(ся, -аю(сь imp. of останови́ть(ся.

оста́нки, -ов pl. remains.

остано́в, -а, stop, stopper, ratchet-gear. останови́ть, -влю́, -вишь perf. (imp. остана́вливать) stop; interrupt; pull up, restrain; check; direct, concentrate; ~ся, stop, come to a stop, come to a halt; stay, put up; + на + prep.

dwell on; settle on, rest on. **остано́вка**, stop; stoppage; hold-up; ~ за ва́ми, you are holding us up.

оста́ток, -тка, remainder; rest; residue; remnant; residuum; balance; *pl.* remains; leavings; leftovers. **оста́точный**, residual, remaining. **оста́ться**, -а́нусь *perf.* (*imp.* оставаться) remain; stay; be left, be left over; за ним оста́лось пять рубле́й, he owes five roubles; ~ в живы́х, survive, come through; ~ на́ ночь, stay the night; *impers.* it remains, it is necessary; нам не оста́ётся ничего́ друго́го, как, there is nothing for us to do but, we have no choice but.

о|стекле́ть, -е́ет *perf.* **остекли́ть**, -лю́ *perf.*, **остекля́ть**, -я́ю *imp.* glaze.

остепени́ться, -ню́сь *perf.*, **остепеня́ться**, -я́юсь *imp.* settle down; become staid, become respectable; mellow.

остерега́ть, -а́ю *imp.*, **остере́чь**, -регу́, -режёшь; -рёг, -гла́ *perf.* warn, caution; ~ся (+*gen.*) beware (of); be careful (of), be on one's guard (against).

о́стов, -а, frame, framework; shell; hull; skeleton.

остолбене́лый, dumbfounded. **о|столбене́ть**, -е́ю *perf.*

осторо́жно *adv.* carefully; cautiously; guardedly; ~! with care; look out! **осторо́жность**, -и, care, caution; prudence. **осторо́жный**, careful, cautious; prudent.

острига́ть(ся, -а́ю(сь *imp.* of остри́чь(ся.

острие́, -я́ point; spike; (cutting) edge. **остри́ть**[1], -рю́ *imp.* sharpen; point. **остри́ть**[2], -рю́ *imp.* (*perf.* с~) be witty.

о|стри́чь, -игу́, -ижёшь; -иг *perf.* (*imp.* also острига́ть) clip; cut; ~ся, cut one's hair; have one's hair cut.

остро- in *comb.* sharp, pointed. **о|строгла́зый**, sharp-sighted, keen-eyed. ~коне́чный, pointed. ~лист, -а, holly. ~но́сый, sharp-nosed; pointed, tapered. ~сло́в, -а, wit. ~уго́льный, acute-angled. ~у́мие, -я, wit. ~у́мный, witty.

о́стров, -а; *pl.* -а́, island; isle. **островно́й**, island; insular. **острово́к**, -вка́ islet; ~ безопа́сности, (traffic) island.

острота́[1], -ы́, witticism, joke. **острота́**[2], -ы́, sharpness; keenness; acuteness; pungency, poignancy.

о́стр|ый, остр, -а́, -о, sharp; pointed; acute; keen; ~ое положе́ние, critical situation; ~ый сыр, strong cheese; ~ый у́гол, acute angle. **остря́к**, -а́, wit.

о|студи́ть, -ужу́, -у́дишь *perf.*, **остужа́ть**, -а́ю *imp.* cool.

оступа́ться, -а́юсь *imp.*, **оступи́ться**, -плю́сь, -пишься *perf.* stumble.

остыва́ть, -а́ю *imp.*, **осты́ть**, -ы́ну *perf.* get cold; cool, cool down.

осуди́ть, -ужу́, -у́дишь *perf.*, **осужда́ть**, -а́ю *imp.* condemn, sentence; convict; censure, blame. **осужде́ние**, -я, censure, condemnation; conviction. **осуждённый**; -ён, -а́, condemned, convicted; *sb.* convict, convicted person.

осу́нуться, -нусь *perf.* grow thin, get pinched-looking.

осуша́ть, -а́ю *imp.*, **осуши́ть**, -шу́, -шишь *perf.* drain; dry. **осуше́ние**, -я, drainage. **осуши́тельный**, drainage.

осуществи́мый practicable, realizable, feasible. **осуществи́ть**, -влю́ *perf.*, **осуществля́ть**, -я́ю *imp.* realize, bring about; accomplish, carry out; implement; ~ся, be fulfilled, come true. **осуществле́ние**, -я, realization; accomplishment; implementation.

осчастли́вить, -влю *perf.*, **осчастли́вливать**, -аю *imp.* make happy.

осыпа́ть, -плю *perf.*, **осыпа́ть**, -а́ю *imp.* strew; shower; heap; pull down, knock down; ~ уда́рами, rain blows on; ~ся, crumble; fall. **о́сыпь**, -и, scree.

ось, -и; *gen. pl.* -е́й, axis; axle; spindle; pin.

осяду́, etc.: see осе́сть.

осяза́емый, tangible; palpable. **осяза́ние**, -я, touch. **осяза́тельный**, tactile, tactual; tangible, palpable, sensible. **осяза́ть**, -а́ю *imp.* feel.

от, **ото** *prep.* + *gen.* from; of; for; against; бли́зко от го́рода, near the town; вре́мя от вре́мени, from time to time; день ото дня, from day to day; дрожа́ть от стра́ха, tremble with fear; застрахова́ть от огня́, insure against fire; ключ от две́ри, door-key; на се́вер от Ленингра́да, north of Leningrad; от всей души́, with all one's heart; от и́мени+gen., on behalf of; от нача́ла до конца́, from beginning to end; от ра́дости, for joy; письмо́ от пе́рвого а́вгуста, letter of the first of August; рабо́чий от станка́, machine operative; сре́дство от, a remedy for; сын от пре́жнего бра́ка, a son by a previous marriage; умере́ть от го́лода die of hunger; це́ны от рубля́ и вы́ше, prices from a rouble upwards.

от-, ото-, отъ- vbl. pref. indicating completion of action or task, fulfilment of duty or obligation; action or motion away from a point; action continued through a certain time; (with verbs reflexive in form) action of negative character, cancelling or undoing of a state, omission, etc.

ота́пливать, -аю imp. of отопи́ть.

отба́вить, -влю perf., отбавля́ть, -я́ю imp. take away; pour off; хоть отбавля́й more than enough.

отбега́ть, -а́ю imp., отбежа́ть, -егу́ perf. run off.

отберу́, etc.: see отобра́ть.

отбива́ть(ся, -а́ю(сь imp. of отби́ть(ся. отби́вка, -и, marking out, delineation; whetting, sharpening.

отбивн|о́й, ~а́я котле́та, cutlet, chop.

отбира́ть, -а́ю imp. of отобра́ть.

отби́тие, -я, repulse; repelling. отби́ть, отобью́, -ёшь perf. (imp. отбива́ть) beat off, repulse, repel; parry; take; win over; break off, knock off; knock up; damage by knocks or blows; whet, sharpen; ~ся, break off; drop behind, straggle; + от + gen. defend oneself against; repulse, beat off; ~ся от рук, get out of hand.

от|благове́стить, -ещу perf.

о́тблеск, -а, reflection.

отбо́й, -я (-ю), repulse, repelling; retreat; ringing off; бить ~, beat a retreat; ringing off; дать ~, ring off; ~ возду́шной трево́ги, the all-clear; ~ мяча́, return; отбо́ю нет от, there is no getting rid of.

отбо́р, -а, selection. отбо́рный, choice, select(ed); picked. отбо́рочн|ый, selection; ~ая коми́ссия, selection board; ~ое соревнова́ние, knock-out competition.

отбра́сывать, -аю imp., отбро́сить, -о́шу perf. throw off; cast away; throw back, thrust back, hurl back; give up, reject, discard; ~ тень, cast a shadow. отбро́с, -а, garbage, refuse; offal.

отбыва́ть, -а́ю imp., отбы́ть, -бу́ду; о́тбыл, -а́, -о perf. depart, leave; serve, do; ~ наказа́ние, serve one's sentence, do time.

отва́га, -и, courage, bravery.

отва́дить, -а́жу perf., отва́живать, -аю imp. scare away; +от+gen. break of, cure of.

отва́живаться, -аюсь imp., отва́житься, -жусь perf. dare, venture; have the courage. отва́жный, courageous, brave.

отва́л, -а, mould-board; dump, slag-heap; putting off, pushing off, casting off; до ~а, to satiety; нае́сться до ~а, eat one's fill, stuff oneself. отва́ливать, -аю imp., отвали́ть, -лю́, -лишь perf. heave off; push aside; put off, push off, cast off; fork out, stump up.

отва́р, -а, broth; decoction. отва́ривать, -аю imp., отвари́ть, -рю́, -ришь perf. boil. отварно́й, boiled.

отве́дать, -аю perf. (imp. отве́дывать), taste, try.

отведённый, allotted. отведу́, etc.: see отвести́.

отве́дывать, -аю imp. of отве́дать.

отвезти́, -зу́, -зёшь; -вёз, -ла́ perf. (imp. отвози́ть) take, take away; cart away.

отвёл, etc.: see отвести́.

отверга́ть, -а́ю imp., отве́ргнуть, -ну; -ве́рг perf. reject, turn down; repudiate; spurn.

отвердева́ть, -а́ет imp., отверде́ть, -е́ет perf. harden. отверде́лость, и, hardening; callus. отверде́лый, hardened.

отве́ржен, -нца, outcast. отве́рженный, outcast.

отверну́ть, -ну́, -нёшь perf. (imp. отвёртывать, отвора́чивать) turn away, turn aside; turn down; turn on; unscrew; screw off, twist off; ~ся, turn away, turn aside; come on; come unscrewed.

отверстие, -я, opening, aperture, orifice; hole; slot.

отвертеть, -рчу́, -ртишь *perf.* (*imp.* отвёртывать) unscrew; screw off, twist off; ~ся, come unscrewed; get off; get out, wriggle out. **отвёртка**, -и, screwdriver.

отвёртывать(ся, -аю(сь *imp.* of отверну́ть(ся, отвертеть(ся.

отве́с, -а, plumb plummet; sag. **отве́сить**, -е́шу *perf.* (*imp.* отве́шивать) weigh out. **отве́сно** *adv.* plumb; sheer. **отве́сный** perpendicular, sheer.

отвести́, -еду́, -едёшь; -вёл, -а́ *perf.* (*imp.* отводи́ть) lead, take, conduct; draw aside, take aside; deflect; draw off; reject; challenge; allot, assign; ~ глаза́, look aside, look away; ~ глаза́ от, take one's eyes off; ~ ду́шу, unburden one's heart; ~ обвине́ние, justify oneself.

отве́т, -а, answer, reply, response; responsibility; быть в отве́те (за), be answerable (for).

ответвиться, -и́тся *perf.*, **ответвля́ться**, -я́ется *imp.* branch off. **ответвле́ние**, -я, branch, offshoot; branch pipe; tap, shunt.

отве́тить, -е́чу *perf.*, **отвеча́ть**, -а́ю *imp.* answer, reply; ~ на + *acc.* return; + за +*acc.* answer for, pay for. **отве́тный**, given in answer answering. **отве́тственность**, -и, responsibility; привле́чь к отве́тственности, call to account, bring to book. **отве́тственный**, responsible; crucial; ~ реда́ктор, editor-in-chief. **отве́тчик**, -а, defendant, respondent; bearer of responsibility.

отве́шивать, -аю *imp.* of отве́сить. **отве́шу**, etc.: see отве́сить.

отви́ливать, -аю *imp.*, **отвильну́ть**, -ну́, -нёшь *perf.* dodge.

отвинти́ть, -нчу́ *perf.*, **отви́нчивать**, -аю *imp.* unscrew; ~ся, unscrew come unscrewed.

отвиса́ть, -а́ет *imp.*, **отви́снуть**, -нет; -ис *perf.* hang down, sag. **отви́слый**, hanging, baggy; с ~ыми уша́ми, lop-eared.

отвлека́ть, -а́ю *imp.*, **отвле́чь**, -еку́, -ечёшь; -влёк, -ла́ *perf.* distract, divert; draw away attention of; ~ся, be distracted; become abstracted. **отвлече́ние**, -я, abstraction; distraction. **отвлечённый** abstract.

отво́д, -а, taking aside; deflection; diversion; leading, taking, conducting; withdrawal; rejection; challenge; allotment, allocation; tap, tapping. **отводи́ть**, -ожу́, -о́дишь *imp.* of отвести́. **отво́дка**, -и, branch; diversion; shifting device, shifter. **отво́док**, -дка, cutting, layer.

отвоева́ть, -ою́ю *perf.*, **отвоёвывать**, -аю *imp.* win back, reconquer; fight, spend in fighting; finish fighting, finish the war.

отвози́ть, -ожу́, -о́зишь *imp.* of отвезти́. **отвора́чивать(ся**, -аю(сь *imp.* of отверну́ть(ся.

отвори́ть, -рю́ -ришь *perf.* (*imp.* отворя́ть) open; ~ся, open. **отворо́т**, -а, lapel flap; top. **отворя́ть(ся**, -я́ю(сь *imp.* of отвори́ть(ся. отворю́ю, etc.: see отвоева́ть.

отврати́тельный, отвра́тный, repulsive, disgusting, loathsome; abominable. **отврати́ть**, -ащу́ *perf.*, **отвраща́ть**, -а́ю *imp.* avert, stave off; deter, stay the hand of. **отвраще́ние**, aversion, disgust, repugnance; loathing.

отвяза́ть, -яжу́ -я́жешь *perf.*, **отвя́зывать**, -аю *imp.* untie unfasten; untether; ~ся, come untied, come loose; +от+*gen.* get rid of, shake off, get shut of; leave alone, leave in peace; stop nagging at; отвяжи́сь от меня́! leave me alone!

отвыка́ть, -а́ю *imp.*, **отвы́кнуть**, -ну; -вык *perf.*+от or *inf.* break oneself of, give up; lose the habit of; grow out of.

отгада́ть, -а́ю *perf.*, **отга́дывать**, -аю *imp.* guess. **отга́дка** -и, answer. **отга́дчик**, -а, guesser, solver, diviner.

отгиба́ть(ся, -а́ю(сь *imp.* of отогну́ть(ся.

отглаго́льный, verbal.

отгла́дить, -а́жу *perf.*, **отгла́живать**, -аю *imp.* iron (out).

отгова́ривать, -аю *imp.* **отговори́ть**, -рю́ *perf.* dissuade; talk out of; ~ся +

instr. plead, excuse oneself on the ground of. **отгово́рка, -и,** excuse, pretext.

отголо́сок, -ска echo.

отго́н, -а, driving off; distillation; distillate. **отго́нка, -и,** driving off; distillation. **отго́нн|ый, -ые па́стбища,** distant pastures. **отгоня́ть, -я́ю** *imp.* of отогна́ть.

отгора́живать, -аю *imp.*, **отгороди́ть, -ожу́, -о́дишь** *perf.* fence off; partition off, screen off; **~ся** fence oneself off; shut oneself off, cut oneself off.

отгрыза́ть, -а́ю *imp.*, **отгры́зть, -зу́, -зёшь** *perf.* gnaw off, bite off.

отдава́ть¹(ся, -даю́(сь *imp.* of отда́ть(ся. **отдава́ть², -аёт** *imp. impers.* + *instr.* taste of; smell of; smack of; от него́ отдаёт во́дкой, he reeks of vodka.

отдави́ть, -влю, -вишь *perf.* crush; **~** но́гу + *dat.* tread on the foot of.

отдале́ние, -я, removal; estrangement; distance; держа́ть в отдале́нии, keep at a distance. **отдалённость, -и,** remoteness. **отдалённый,** distant, remote. **отдали́ть, -лю́** *perf.*, **отдаля́ть, -я́ю** *imp.* remove; estrange; alienate; postpone, put off; **~ся,** move away; digress.

отда́ние, -я giving back; returning. **отда́|ть, -а́м, -а́шь, -а́ст, -ади́м;** о́тдал, -а́, -о *perf.* (*imp.* отдава́ть) give back, return; give; give up; devote; give in marriage; give away; put, place; make; sell; let have; recoil, kick; let go; cast off; **~** в шко́лу, send to school; **~** до́лжное + *dat.* render his due to; **~** под суд, prosecute; **~** прика́з, issue an order, give orders; **~** честь + *dat.* salute; **~ся,** give oneself (up); devote oneself; resound; reverberate; ring. **отда́ча, -и,** return; payment; reimbursement; letting go, casting off; efficiency; performance; output; recoil, kick.

отде́л, -а, department; section; part. **отде́лать, -аю** *perf.* (*imp.* отде́лывать) finish, put the finishing touches to; trim; **~ся** + от + *gen.* get rid of, finish with; + *instr.* escape with, get off with. **отделе́ние, -я,** separation; department;

branch; compartment; section; part; **~** шка́фа, pigeon-hole. **отделённый,** section; *sb.* section commander. **отделе́нческий, отделе́нческий, департамент(al), branch. отдели́мый,** separable. **отдели́ть, -елю́, -е́лишь** *perf.* (*imp.* отделя́ть) separate part; detach; separate off; cut off; **~ся,** separate, part; detach oneself, itself; get detached; come apart; come off.

отде́лка, -и, finishing; trimming; finish, decoration. **отде́лывать(ся, -аю(сь** *imp.* of отде́лать(ся.

отде́льно, separately; apart. **отде́льность, -и;** в отде́льности, taken separately, individually. **отде́льный,** separate, individual; independent. **отделя́ть(ся, -я́ю(сь** *imp.* of отдели́ть(ся.

отдёргивать, -аю *imp.*, **отдёрнуть, -ну** *perf.* draw aside, pull aside; draw back, pull back; jerk back.

отдеру́, etc.: see отодра́ть. **отдира́ть, -а́ю** *imp.* of отодра́ть.

отдохну́ть, -ну́, -нёшь *perf.* (*imp.* отдыха́ть) rest; have a rest, take a rest.

отду́шина, -ы, air-hole, vent; safety-valve. **отду́шник, -а,** air-hole, vent.

о́тдых, -а, rest; relaxation; holiday. **отдыха́ть, -а́ю** *imp.* (*perf.* отдохну́ть), be resting; be on holiday. **отдыха́ющий** *sb.* holiday-maker.

отдыша́ться, -шу́сь, -шишься *perf.* recover one's breath.

отека́ть, -а́ю *imp.* of оте́чь. **о|тели́ться, -е́лится** *perf.* отела́ть, etc.: see обтеса́ть.

оте́ц, отца́, father. **оте́ческий,** fatherly, paternal. **оте́чественн|ый,** home, native; **~ая** промы́шленность, home industry; Вели́кая **~ая** война́, Great Patriotic War. **оте́чество, -а,** native land, fatherland, home country.

оте́чь, -еку́, -ечёшь; отёк, -ла́ *perf.* (*imp.* отека́ть) swell, become swollen; gutter.

отжива́ть, -а́ю *imp.*, **отжи́ть, -иву́, -ивёшь; о́тжил, -а́, -о** *perf.* become obsolete; become outmoded; **~** свой век have had one's day; go out of fashion. **отжи́вший,** obsolete; outmoded.

о́тзвук, -а, echo.

о́тзыв[1], -а, opinion, judgement; reference; testimonial; review; reply, response; похва́льный ~, honourable mention. **отзы́в**[2], -а, recall. **отзыва́ть(ся, -а́ю(сь** *imp.* of отозва́ть(ся. **отзывно́й**, -ы́е гра́моты, letters of recall. **отзы́вчивый**, responsive.

отка́з, -а, refusal; denial; repudiation; rejection; renunciation; giving up; failure; natural; де́йствовать без ~а, run smoothly; получи́ть ~, be refused, be turned down; по́лный до ~а, full to capacity, cram-full. **отказа́ть**, -ажу́, -а́жешь *perf.*, **отка́зывать**, -аю *imp.* fail, break down; (+*dat.* в +*prep.*) refuse, deny; + *dat.* от + *gen.* dismiss discharge; ~ от до́ма, forbid the house; ~ся (+ от + *gen.* or + *inf.*) refuse, decline; turn down; retract; renounce, give up; relinquish, abdicate; ~ся от свое́й по́дписи, repudiate one's signature; ~ся служи́ть, be out of order.

отка́лывать(ся, -аю(сь *imp.* of отколо́ть(ся. **отка́пывать**, -аю *imp.* of откопа́ть. **отка́рмливать**, -аю *imp.* of откорми́ть.

откати́ть, -ачу́, -а́тишь *perf.*, **отка́тывать**, -аю *imp.* roll away; ~ся, roll away; roll back, be forced back.

откача́ть, -а́ю *perf.*, **отка́чивать**, -аю *imp.* pump out; resuscitate, give artificial respiration to.

отка́шливаться, -аюсь *imp.*, **отка́шляться**, -яюсь *perf.* clear one's throat.

откидно́й, folding, collapsible. **отки́дывать**, -аю *imp.*, **отки́нуть**, -ну *perf.* turn back, fold back; throw aside; cast away.

откла́дывать, -аю *imp.* of отложи́ть.

откла́няться, -яюсь *perf.* take one's leave.

откле́ивать, -аю *imp.*, **откле́ить**, -е́ю *perf.* unstick; ~ся, come unstuck.

о́тклик, -а, response; comment; echo; repercussion. **откли́каться**, -аюсь *imp.*, **откли́кнуться**, -нусь *perf.* answer, respond.

отклоне́ние, -я deviation; divergence; declining refusal; deflection, declination; error; diffraction; ~ в сто́рону, deviation; ~ от те́мы digression.

отклони́ть, -ню́, -нишь *perf.*, **отклоня́ть**, -я́ю *imp.* deflect; decline; ~ся, deviate; diverge; swerve.

отключа́ть, -а́ю *imp.*, **отключи́ть**, -чу́ *perf.* cut off, disconnect.

отколоти́ть, -очу́, -о́тишь *perf.* knock off; beat up, thrash, give a good hiding.

отколо́ть, -лю́, -лешь *perf.* (*imp.* отка́лывать) break off; chop off; unpin; ~ся, break off; come unpinned, come undone; break away, cut oneself off.

откопа́ть, -а́ю *perf.* (*imp.* отка́пывать) dig out; exhume, disinter; dig up, unearth.

откорми́ть, -млю́, -мишь *perf.* (*imp.* отка́рмливать) fatten, fatten up. **отко́рмленный**, fat, fatted, fattened.

отко́с, -а, slope; пусти́ть под отко́с, derail.

открепи́ть, -плю́ *perf.*, **открепи́ть**, -я́ю *imp.* unfasten, untie; ~ся, become unfastened.

открове́ние, -я, revelation. **открове́нничать**, -аю *imp.* be candid, be frank; open one's heart. **открове́нный**, candid, frank; blunt, outspoken; open, unconcealed; revealing. **откро́ю**, etc.: see открыть.

открути́ть, -учу́, -у́тишь *perf.*, **откру́чивать**, -аю *imp.* untwist, unscrew; ~ся, come untwisted; + от + *gen.* get out of.

открыва́ть, -а́ю *imp.*, **откры́ть**, -ро́ю *perf.* open; uncover, reveal, bare; discover; turn on; ~ па́мятник, unveil a monument; ~ся, open; come to light, be revealed; confide. **откры́тие**, -я, discovery; revelation; opening; inauguration; unveiling. **откры́тка**, -и, postcard. **откры́то**, openly. **откры́т|ый**, open; на ~ом во́здухе, под ~ым не́бом, out of doors, in the open air; ~ое заседа́ние, public sitting; ~ое письмо́ postcard; open letter.

откуда *adv.* whence; where from; from which; ~ вы об э́том зна́ете? how do you come to know about that?; ~ ни возьми́сь, quite unexpectedly, suddenly. **откуда-либо, -нибудь**, from somewhere or other. **откуда-то**, from somewhere.

отку́поривать -аю *imp.*, отку́порить, -рю *perf.* uncork; open. отку́порка, -и, opening, uncorking.

откуси́ть -ушу́, -у́сишь *perf.*, отку́сывать, -аю *imp.* bite off; snap off; nip off.

отлага́тельство, -а, delay; procrastination; де́ло не те́рпит отлага́тельства, the matter is urgent. отлага́ть(ся, -а́юсь *imp.* of отложи́ть(ся.

от|лакирова́ть, -ру́ю *perf.* отла́мывать, -аю *imp.* of отломи́ть, отломи́ть.

отлежа́ть, -жу́ *perf.*, отлёживать, -аю *imp.*; я отлежа́л но́гу, my foot has gone to sleep.

отлепи́ть -плю́, -пишь *perf.*, отлепля́ть, -я́ю *imp.* unstick, take off; ~ся, come unstuck, come off.

отлёт, -а, flying away; departure; на ~е, on the point of departure, about to leave; in one's outstretched hand; (standing) by itself. отлета́ть, -а́ю *imp.* отлете́ть, -лечу́ *perf.*, fly, fly away, fly off; vanish; rebound, bounce back; come off, burst off.

отли́в, -а, ebb, ebb-tide; tint; play of colours; с золоты́м ~ом, shot with gold. отлива́ть, -а́ю *imp.*, отли́ть, отолью́; о́тли́л, -á, -о *perf.* pour off; pump out; cast, found; (no *perf.*) + *instr.* be shot with. отли́вка, -и, casting; founding; cast, ingot, moulding. отливно́й, cast, casting; founded, moulded.

отлича́ть, -а́ю *imp.*, отличи́ть, -чу́ *perf.* distinguish; single out; ~ одно́ от друго́го tell one (thing) from another; ~ся, distinguish oneself, excel; differ; + *instr.* be notable for. отли́чие, -я, difference; distinction; в ~ от, unlike, as dis'inguished from, in contradistinction to; знак отли́чия, order, decoration; с отли́чием, with honours. отли́чник, -а, outstanding student, worker, etc. отличи́тельный, distinctive; distinguishing. отли́чно *adv.* excellently; perfectly; extremely well. отли́чный, different; excellent; perfect; extremely good.

отло́гий, sloping. отло́гость, -и, slope. отло́же, *compr.* of отло́гий.

отложе́ние, -я, sediment; precipitation; deposit. отложи́ть, -ожу́ -о́жишь *perf.* (*imp.* откла́дывать, отлага́ть) put aside, set aside; put away, put by; put off, postpone; adjourn; turn back, turn down; unharness; deposit; ~ся, detach oneself, separate; deposit, be deposited. отложно́й воротни́к, turn-down collar.

отлома́ть, -а́ю, отломи́ть, -млю́ -мишь *perf.* (*imp.* отла́мывать) break off.

отлуча́ть, -а́ю *imp.*, отлучи́ть, -чу́ *perf.* separate, remove; ~ (от це́ркви), excommunicate; ~ся, absent oneself. отлу́чка, -и, absence; быть в отлу́чке, be absent, be away.

отлы́нивать, -аю *imp.* + от + *gen.* shirk.

отма́лчиваться, -аюсь *imp.* of отмолча́ться.

отма́хивать, -аю *imp.*, отмахну́ть, -ну́, -нёшь *perf.*; wave away; ~ся от + *gen.* brush off; brush aside.

отмежева́ться, -жу́юсь *perf.*, отмежёвываться, -аюсь *imp.* от + *gen.* dissociate oneself from; refuse to acknowledge.

о́тмель, -и, bar, (sand-)bank; shallow.

отме́на, -ы, abolition; abrogation, repeal, revocation; cancellation; countermand. отмени́ть, -ню́, -нишь *perf.*, отменя́ть, -я́ю *imp.* abrogate, repeal, revoke, rescind; abolish; cancel, countermand; disaffirm.

отмере́ть, отомрёт; о́тмер, -ла́, -ло *perf.* (*imp.* отмира́ть) die off; die out, die away.

отме́ривать, -аю *imp.*, отме́рить, -рю *perf.*, отмеря́ть, -я́ю *imp.* measure off.

отмести́, -ету́, -етёшь; -ёл, -á *perf.* (*imp.* отмета́ть) sweep aside.

отме́стка, -и, revenge.

отмета́ть, -а́ю *imp.* of отмести́.

отме́тина, -ы, mark, notch; star, blaze. отме́тить, -е́чу *perf.*, отмеча́ть -а́ю *imp.* mark, note; make a note of; point to, mention, record; celebrate, mark by celebration; ~ся, sign one's name; sign out. отме́тка, -и, note; mark; blip. отме́тчик, -а, marker.

отмира́ние, -я, dying off; dying away,

fading away, withering away. **отми-
ра́ть**, -áет *imp.* of отмере́ть.

отмолча́ться, -чу́сь *perf.* (*imp.* от-
мáлчиваться) keep silent, say nothing.

отмора́живать, -аю *imp.*, **отморо́зить**,
-óжу *perf.* injure by frost-bite. **отморо́-
жение**, -я, frost-bite. **отморо́женный**,
frost-bitten.

отмóю, etc.: see отмы́ть.

от|мсти́ть, -мщу́ *perf.* **отмще́ние**, -я,
vengeance.

отмыва́ть, -áю *imp.*, **отмы́ть**, -мóю
perf. wash clean; wash off, wash away;
~ся, wash oneself clean; come out,
come off.

отмы́чка, -и, picklock; master-key.

отнéкиваться, -аюсь *imp.* refuse.

отнести́, -су́, -сёшь; -нёс, -ла́ *perf.* (*imp.*
относи́ть) take; carry away, carry off;
ascribe, attribute, refer; **~ся к** + *dat.*
treat; regard; apply to; concern, have
to do with; date from; э́то к де́лу не
отно́сится, that's beside the point,
that is not relevant.

отнима́ть(ся), -áю(сь *imp.* of отня́ть(ся.

относи́тельно *adv.* relatively; *prep.* +
gen. concerning, about, with regard to.
относи́тельность, -и, relativity. **от-
носи́тельн|ый**, relative. **~ое местои-
мéние**, relative pronoun. **относи́ть**[1]
-ошу́(сь, -о́сишь(ся *imp.* of от-
нести́(сь. **относи́ть**[2], -ошу́ -о́сишь
perf. stop wearing. **отноше́ние**, -я,
attitude; treatment; relation; respect;
ratio; letter, memorandum; *pl.* relations; terms; в нéкоторых отноше́-
ниях, in some respects; в отноше́нии
+ *gen.* по отношéнию к + *dat.*, with
respect to, with regard to; в прямо́м
(обра́тном) отноше́нии, in direct (inverse) ratio; не имéть отноше́ния к +
dat., bear no relation to, have nothing
to do with.

отны́не *adv.* henceforward, henceforward.

отня́тие, -я, taking away; amputation.
отня́ть, -ниму́, -ни́мешь; о́тнял, -á,
-о *perf.* (*imp.* отнима́ть) take (away);
amputate; **~ от груди́**, wean; **~ три
от шести́**, take three away from six;
э́то о́тняло у меня́ три часá, it took
me three hours; **~ся**, be paralysed; у

негó отняла́сь пра́вая рука́, he has
lost the use of his right arm.

ото: see от. **ото-**: see от-.

отобража́ть, -áю *imp.*, **отобрази́ть**,
-ажу́ *perf.* reflect; represent. **отобра-
же́ние**, -я, reflection; representation.

отобра́ть, отберу́, -рёшь; отобра́л, -á,
-о *perf.* (*imp.* отбира́ть) take (away);
seize; select, pick out.

отобью́, etc.: see отби́ть.

отовсю́ду *adv.* from everywhere.

отогна́ть, отгоню́, -о́нишь; отогна́л
-á, -о *perf.* (*imp.* отгоня́ть) drive away,
off; keep off; distil (off).

отогну́ть, -ну́, -нёшь *perf.* (*imp.* отги-
ба́ть) bend back; flange; **~ся**, bend
back.

отогрева́ть, -áю *imp.*, **отогре́ть**, -éю
perf. warm; **~ся**, warm oneself.

отодвига́ть, -áю *imp.*, **отодви́нуть**, -ну
perf. move aside; put off, put back;
~ся, move aside.

отодра́ть, отдеру́, -рёшь; отодра́л, -á,
-о *perf.* (*imp.* отдира́ть) tear off, rip
off; flog.

отож(д)естви́ть, -влю́ *perf.*, **отож-
(д)ествля́ть**, -я́ю *imp.* identify.

отожжённый, -ён -á, annealed.

отозва́ть, отзову́, -вёшь; отозва́л, -á,
-о *perf.* (*imp.* отзыва́ть) take aside; recall; **~ся на** + *acc.* answer; respond
to; о + *acc.* speak of; на + *acc.* or *prep.*
tell on; have an effect on.

отойти́, -йду́, -йдёшь; отошёл, -шла́
perf. (*imp.* отходи́ть) move away;
move off; leave, depart; withdraw;
recede; fall back; digress, diverge;
come out, come away, come off; recover; come to oneself, come round;
pass, go; be lost.

отолью́, etc.: see отли́ть. **отомрёт**,
etc.: see отмере́ть. **ото|мсти́ть**, -мщу́
perf.

отопи́тельный, heating. **отопи́ть**, -плю́,
-пишь *perf.* (*imp.* отáпливать) heat.
отоплéние, -я, heating.

отопру́, etc.: see отпере́ть. **отопью́**,
etc.: see отпи́ть.

отóрванность, -и, detachment, isolation; loneliness. **отóрванный**, cut off,
isolated, out of touch. **оторва́ть**, -ву́,
-вёшь *perf.* (*imp.* отрыва́ть) tear off;

tear away; ~ся, come off, be torn off; be cut off, lose touch, lose contact; break away; tear oneself away; ~ся от земли, take off.

оторопе́лый, dumbfounded. **оторопе́ть**, -е́ю *perf.* be struck dumb.

отосла́ть, -ошлю́, -ошлёшь *perf.* (*imp.* отсыла́ть) send (off), dispatch; send back; + к + *dat.* refer to.

отошёл, etc.: see отойти́. **отошлю́**, etc.: see отосла́ть.

отоща́лый, emaciated. о|тоща́ть, -а́ю *perf.*

отпада́ть, -а́ет *imp.* of отпа́сть. **отпаде́ние**, -я, falling away; defection.

от|пари́ровать, -рую *perf.* отпа́рывать, -аю *imp.* of отпоро́ть.

отпа́сть, -адёт *perf.* (*imp.* отпада́ть) fall off, drop off; fall away; defect, drop away; pass, fade.

отпере́ть, отопру́, -прёшь; о́тпер, -ла́, -ло *perf.* (*imp.* отпира́ть) unlock; open; ~ся, open; + от + *gen.* deny; disown.

отпе́тый, arrant, inveterate.

от|печа́тать, -аю *perf.*, отпеча́тывать, -аю *imp.* print (off); type (out); imprint; unseal, open (up); ~ся, leave an imprint; be printed. **отпеча́ток**, -тка, imprint, print; impress.

отпива́ть, -а́ю *imp.* of отпи́ть.

отпи́ливать, -аю *imp.*, отпили́ть, -лю́, -лишь *perf.* saw off.

отпира́тельство, -а, denial, disavowal. ~пира́ть(ся, -а́ю(сь *imp.* of отпере́ть(ся.

отпи́ть, отопью́, -пьёшь; о́тпи́л, -а́, -о *perf.* (*imp.* отпива́ть) sip, take a sip of.

отпи́хивать, -аю *imp.*, отпихну́ть, -ну́, -нёшь *perf.* push off; shove aside.

отпла́та, -ы, repayment. **отплати́ть**, -ачу́, -а́тишь *perf.*, отпла́чивать, -аю *imp.* + *dat.* pay back, repay, requite; ~ той же моне́той, pay back in his own coin.

отплыва́ть, -а́ю *imp.*, отплы́ть, -ыву́, -ывёшь; -ы́л, -а́, -о *perf.* sail, set sail; swim off. **отплы́тие**, -я, sailing, departure.

о́тповедь, -и, reproof, rebuke.

отполза́ть, -а́ю *imp.*, отползти́, -зу́, -зёшь; -о́лз, -ла́, *perf.* crawl away.

от|полирова́ть, -ру́ю *perf.* от|поло-ска́ть, -ощу́ *perf.*

отпо́р, -а, repulse; rebuff; встре́тить ~, meet with a rebuff; дать ~, repulse.

отпоро́ть[1], -рю́, -решь *perf.* (*imp.* отпа́рывать) rip off, rip out.

отпоро́ть[2], -рю́, -решь *perf.* flog, thrash, give a thrashing.

отправи́тель, -я *m.* sender. **отпра́вить**, -влю *perf.*, отправля́ть, -я́ю *imp.* send, forward, dispatch; ~ся, set out, set off, start; leave, depart. **отпра́вка**, -и, sending off, forwarding, dispatch. **отправле́ние**, -я, sending; departure; exercise, performance; ~ обя́занностей, performance of one's duties. **отправн|о́й**, ~о́й пункт, ~а́я то́чка, starting-point.

от|пра́здновать, -ную *perf.*

отпра́шиваться, -аюсь *imp.*, отпроси́ться, -ошу́сь, -о́сишься *perf.* ask for leave, get leave.

отпры́гивать, -аю *imp.*, отпры́гнуть, -ну *perf.* jump back, spring back; jump aside, spring aside; bounce back.

о́тпрыск, -а, offshoot, scion.

отпряга́ть, -а́ю *imp.* of отпря́чь.

отпря́дывать, -аю *imp.*, отпря́нуть, -ну *perf.* recoil, start back.

отпря́чь, -ягу́, -яжёшь; -я́г, -ла́ *perf.* (*imp.* отпряга́ть) unharness.

отпу́гивать, -аю *imp.*, отпугну́ть, -ну́, -нёшь *perf.* frighten off, scare away.

о́тпуск, -а, *loc.* -у́; *pl.* -а́, leave, holiday(s); furlough; issue, delivery, distribution; tempering, drawing; в ~е, в ~у́, on leave; ~ по боле́зни, sick-leave. **отпуска́ть**, -а́ю *imp.*, отпусти́ть, -ущу́, -у́стишь *perf.* let go, let off; let out; set free; release; give leave (of absence); relax, slacken; (let) grow; issue, give out; serve; assign, allot; remit; forgive; temper, draw; ~ шу́тку, crack a joke. **отпускни́к**, -а́, person on leave, holiday-maker; soldier on leave. **отпускн|о́й**, holiday; leave; on leave; ~ые де́ньги, holiday pay; ~а́я цена́, (wholesale) selling price. **отпуще́ние**, -я, remission; козёл отпуще́ния, scapegoat. **отпу́щенник**, -а, freedman.

отраба́тывать, -аю *imp.*, отрабо́тать, -аю *perf.* work off; work (for); finish work; finish working on; master. **от-рабо́танный**, worked out; waste, spent, exhaust.

отра́ва, -ы, poison; bane. **отрави́тель**, -я *m.* poisoner. **отрави́ть**, -влю́, -вишь *perf.*, **отравля́ть**, -я́ю *imp.* poison; **~ся**, poison oneself.

отра́да, -ы, joy, delight; comfort. **отра́дный**, gratifying, pleasing; comforting.

отража́тель, -я *m.* reflector; scanner; ejector. **отража́тельный**, reflecting, deflecting; reverberatory. **отража́ть**, -а́ю *imp.*, **отрази́ть**, -ажу́ *perf.* reflect; repulse, repel, parry; ward off; **~ся**, be reflected; reverberate; + на + *prep.* affect, tell on.

отраслево́й, branch. **о́трасль**, -и, branch.

отраста́ть, -а́ет *imp.*, **отрасти́**, -тёт; отро́с, -ла́ *perf.* grow. **отрасти́ть**, -ащу́ *perf.*, **отра́щивать**, -аю *imp.* (let) grow.

от|реаги́ровать, -рую *perf.* **от|регули́ровать**, -рую *perf.* **от|редакти́ровать**, -рую *perf.*

отре́з, -а, cut; length; ~ на пла́тье, dress-length. **отре́зать**, -е́жу *perf.*, **отреза́ть**, -а́ю *imp.* cut off; divide, apportion; snap.

о|трезве́ть, -е́ю *perf.* **отрезви́тельный**, sobering. **отрезви́ть**, -влю́, -вишь *perf.*, **отрезвля́ть**, -я́ю *imp.* sober; **~ся**, become sober, sober up. **отрезвле́ние**, -я, sobering (up).

отрезно́й, cutting; tear-off, cut-off. **отре́зок**, -зка, piece, cut; section; portion; segment; ~ вре́мени, period, space of time.

отрека́ться, -а́юсь *imp.* of отре́чься. **от|рекомендова́ть(ся**, -ду́ю(сь *perf.* **отрёкся**, etc.: see отре́чься. **от|ремонти́ровать**, -рую *perf.* **от|репети́ровать**, -рую *perf.*

отре́пье, -я, отре́пья, -ьев *pl.* rags.

от|реставри́ровать, -рую *perf.*

отрече́ние, -я, renunciation; ~ от престо́ла, abdication. **отре́чься**, -еку́сь, -ечёшься *perf.* (*imp.* отрека́ться) renounce, disavow, give up.

отреша́ть -а́ю *imp.*, **отреши́ть**, -шу́ *perf.* release; dismiss, suspend; **~ся**,

renounce, give up; get rid of. **отрешённость**, -и, estrangement, aloofness.

отрица́ние, -я, denial; negation. **отрица́тельный**, negative; bad, unfavourable. **отрица́ть**, -а́ю *imp.* deny; disclaim.

отро́г, -а, spur.

отро́дье, -я, race, breed, spawn.

отро́с, etc.: see отрасти́. **отро́сток**, -тка, shoot, sprout; branch, extension; appendix.

о́троческий, adolescent. **о́трочество**, -а, adolescence.

отруби, -е́й *pl.* of отруби́ть.

о́труби, -е́й *pl.* bran.

отруби́ть, -блю́ -бишь *perf.* (*imp.* отруба́ть) chop off; snap back.

отры́в, -а, tearing off; alienation, isolation; loss of contract, estrangement; без ~а от произво́дства, while remaining at work; в ~е от+*gen.*, out of touch with; ~ (от земли́), take-off. **отрыва́ть(ся**, -а́ю(сь *imp.* of оторва́ть(ся. **отры́вистый**, jerky, abrupt; curt. **отрывно́й**, detachable, tear-off. **отры́вок**, -вка, fragment, except; passage. **отры́вочный**, fragmentary, scrappy.

отры́жка, -и, belch; belching, eructation; survival, throw-back.

от|ры́ть, -ро́ю *perf.*

отря́д, -а, detachment; order. **отряди́ть**, -яжу́ *perf.*, **отряжа́ть**, -а́ю *imp.* detach, detail, tell off.

отря́хивать, -аю *imp.*, **отряхну́ть**, -ну́, -нёшь *perf.* shake down, shake off; **~ся**, shake oneself down.

от|салютова́ть, -ту́ю *perf.*

отса́сывание, -я, suction. **отса́сыватель**, -я *m.* suction pump. **отса́сывать**, -аю *imp.* of отсоса́ть.

отсве́т, -а, reflection; reflected light. **отсве́чивать**, -аю *imp.* be reflected; + *instr.* shine with, reflect.

отсебя́тина, -ы, words of one's own; ad-libbing.

отсе́в, -а, sifting, selection; siftings, residue. **отсева́ть(ся**, -а́ю(сь, **отсе́ивать(ся**, -аю(сь *imp.* of отсе́ять(ся. **отсе́вки**, -ов *pl.* siftings, residue.

отсе́к, -а, compartment. **отсека́ть**, -а́ю

imp., **отсе́чь**, -еку́ -ечёшь; -сёк, -ла́ *perf.* sever, chop off, cut off. **отсече́ние**, -я, cutting off, severance; дать го́лову на ~, stake one's life. **отсе́чка**, -и, cut-off.

отсе́ять, -е́ю *perf.* (*imp.* отсева́ть, отсе́ивать) sift, screen; eliminate; ~ся, fall out, fall off; fall away, drop out.

отска́кивать, -аю *imp.*, **отскочи́ть**, -чу́, -чишь *perf.* jump aside, jump away; rebound, bounce back; come off, break off.

отслу́живать, -аю *imp.*, **отслужи́ть**, -жу́, -жишь *perf.* serve; serve one's time; have served its turn, be worn out.

отсове́товать, -тую *perf.* + *dat.* dissuade.

отсоса́ть, -осу́, -осёшь *perf.* (*imp.* отса́сывать) suck off, draw off; filter by suction.

отсро́чивать, -аю *imp.*, **отсро́чить**, -чу *perf.* postpone, delay, defer; adjourn; extend (date of). **отсро́чка**, -и, postponement, delay, deferment; adjournment; respite; extension.

отстава́ние, -я, lag; lagging behind. **отстава́ть**, -таю́, -аёшь *imp.* of отста́ть.

отста́вить, -влю *perf.*, **отставля́ть** -я́ю *imp.* set aside, put aside; dismiss, discharge; rescind; ~! as you were! **отста́вка**, -и, dismissal, discharge; resignation; retirement; в отста́вке, retired, in retirement; вы́йти в отста́вку, resign, retire. **отставно́й** retired.

отста́ивать(ся, -аю(сь *imp.* of отстоя́ть(ся.

отста́лость, -и, backwardness. **отста́лый**, backward. **отста́ть**, -а́ну *perf.* (*imp.* отстава́ть) fall behind, drop behind; lag behind; be backward, be retarded; be behind(hand); be left behind, become detached; lose touch; break (off); break oneself; be slow; come off, ~ на полчаса́, be half an hour late; ~ от, break oneself of, give up; leave alone.

от|**стега́ть**, -а́ю *perf.*

отстёгивать, -аю *imp.*, **отстегну́ть**, -ну́, -нёшь *perf.* unfasten, undo; unbutton; ~ся, come unfastened, come undone.

отстой, -я, sediment, deposit. **отстой-**

ник, -а, settling tank; sedimentation tank; cesspool.

отстоя́ть[1], -ою́ *perf.* (*imp.* отста́ивать) defend, save; stand up for; ~ свои́ права́, assert one's rights. **отстоя́ть**[2], -ои́т *imp.* be . . away: стои́т от це́нтра го́рода на два киломе́тра, the station is two kilometres from the town centre. **отстоя́ться**, -ои́тся *perf.* (*imp.* отста́иваться) settle; precipitate; become stabilized, become fixed.

отстра́ивать(ся, -аю(сь *imp.* of отстро́ить(ся.

отстране́ние, -я, pushing aside; dismissal, discharge. **отстрани́ть**, -ню́ *perf.*, **отстраня́ть**, -я́ю *imp.* push aside, lay aside; dismiss, discharge, remove; suspend; ~ся, move away; keep out of the way, keep aloof; ~ся от, dodge; relinquish.

отстре́ливаться, -аюсь *imp.*, **отстре-ля́ться**, -я́юсь *perf.* fire back.

отстрига́ть, -а́ю *imp.*, **отстри́чь**, -игу́, -ижёшь; -ри́г *perf.* cut off, clip.

отстро́ить, -о́ю *perf.* (*imp.* отстра́ивать), complete the construction of, finish building; build up; ~ся, finish building; be built up.

отступа́ть, -а́ю *imp.*, **отступи́ть**, -плю́, -пишь *perf.* step back; recede; retreat, fall back; back down; ~ от + *gen.* go back on; give up; swerve from; deviate from; ~ся от + *gen.* give up, renounce; go back on. **отступле́ние**, -я, retreat; deviation; digression. **отсту́пник**, -а, apostate; recreant. **отступни́|к**, -ые де́ньги, ~о́е *sb.* indemnity, compensation. **отступя́** *adv.* (farther) off, away (от + *gen.* from).

отсу́тствие, -я absence; lack; want; за ~м + *gen.*, in the absence of; for lack of, for want of; находи́ться в отсу́т-ствии, be absent. **отсу́тствовать**, -твую *imp.* be absent; default. **отсу́т-ствующий**, absent; *sb.* absentee.

отсчита́ть, -а́ю *perf.*, **отсчи́тывать**, -аю *imp.* count off, count out; read off.

отсыла́ть, -а́ю *imp.* of отосла́ть. **от-сы́лка**, -и, dispatch; reference; ~ де́нег, remittance.

отсыпа́ть, -плю *perf.*, **отсыпа́ть**, -а́ю

imp. pour off; measure off; **~ся,** pour out.

отсыре́лый, damp. **от|сыре́ть,** -е́ет *perf.*

отсю́да *adv.* from here; hence; from this.

отта́ивать, -аю *imp.* of отта́ять.

отта́лкивание, -я, repulsion. **отта́лкивать,** -аю *imp.* of оттолкну́ть. **отта́лкивающий,** repulsive, repellent.

отта́чивать, -аю *imp.* of отточи́ть.

отта́ять, -а́ю *perf.* (*imp.* отта́ивать) thaw out.

оттени́ть, -ню́ *perf.,* **оттеня́ть,** -я́ю *imp.* shade, shade in; set off, make more prominent. **отте́нок,** -нка, shade, nuance; tint, hue.

о́ттепель, -и, thaw.

оттесни́ть, -ню́ *perf.,* **оттесня́ть,** -я́ю *imp.* drive back, press back; push aside, shove aside.

оттого́ (*-vo*) *adv.* that is why; **~, что,** because.

о́ттиск, -а, impression; off-print, reprint.

оттолкну́ть, -ну́, -нёшь *perf.* (*imp.* отта́лкивать) push away, push aside; antagonize, alienate; **~ся,** push off.

оттопы́ренный, protruding, sticking out. **оттопы́ривать,** -аю *imp.,* **оттопы́рить,** -рю *perf.* stick out; **~ гу́бы,** pout; **~ся,** protrude, stick out; bulge.

отточи́ть, -чу́, -чишь *perf.* (*imp.* отта́чивать) sharpen, whet.

отту́да *adv.* from there.

оття́гивать, -аю *imp.,* **оттяну́ть,** -ну́, -нешь *perf.* draw out, pull away; draw off; delay. **оття́жка,** -и, delay, procrastination; guy-rope; strut, brace, stay.

отупе́лый, stupefied, dulled. **отупе́ние,** -я, stupefaction, dullness, torpor. **о|тупе́ть,** -е́ю *perf.* grow dull, sink into torpor.

от|утю́жить, -жу *perf.*

отуча́ть, -а́ю *imp.,* **отучи́ть,** -чу́, -чишь *perf.* break (of); **~ся,** break oneself (of).

от|футбо́лить, -лю *perf.,* **отфутбо́ливать,** -аю *imp.* pass on; send from pillar to post.

отха́ркать, -аю *perf.,* **отха́ркивать,** -аю *imp.* expectorate. **отха́ркивающий** *adj.;* **~ee (сре́дство),** expectorant.

отхлебну́ть, -ну́, -нёшь *perf.,* **отхлёбывать,** -аю *imp.* sip, take a sip of; take a mouthful of.

отхлы́нуть, -нет *perf.* flood back, rush back, rush away.

отхо́д, -а, departure, sailing; withdrawal, retirement, falling back; **~ от,** deviation from; break with. **отходи́ть,** -ожу́, -о́дишь *imp.* of отойти́. **отхо́дчивый,** not bearing grudges. **отхо́ды,** -ов *pl.* waste; siftings, screenings; tailings.

отцвести́, -ету́, -етёшь; -ёл, -а́ *perf.,* **отцвета́ть,** -а́ю *imp.* finish blossoming, fade.

отцепи́ть, -плю́, -пишь *perf.,* **отцепля́ть,** -я́ю *imp.* unhook; uncouple; **~ся,** come unhooked, come uncoupled; **+ от + gen.** leave alone. **отце́пка,** -и uncoupling.

отцо́вский, father's; paternal. **отцо́вство,** -а, paternity.

отча́иваться, -аюсь *imp.* of отча́яться.

отча́ливать, -аю *imp.,* **отча́лить,** -лю *perf.* cast off; push off.

отча́сти *adv.* partly.

отча́яние, -я, despair. **отча́янный,** despairing; desperate; daredevil. **отча́яться,** -аюсь *perf.* (*imp.* отча́иваться) despair.

отчего́ (*-vo*) *adv.* why. **отчего́-либо,** **-нибудь** *adv.* for some reason or other. **отчего́-то** *adv.* for some reason.

от|чека́нить, -ню *perf.*

о́тчество, -а, patronymic; как его́ по о́тчеству? what is his patronymic?

отчёт, -а, account; дать **~ в + prep.,** give an account of; report on; отда́ть себе́ **~ в + prep.** be aware of, realize. **отчётливый,** distinct; precise; intelligible, clear. **отчётность,** -и, book-keeping; accounts. **отчётный** *adj.;* **~ год,** financial year; current year; **~ докла́д,** report.

отчи́зна, -ы, country, native land; fatherland. **о́тчий,** paternal. **о́тчим,** -а, step-father.

отчисле́ние, -я, deduction; assignment;

dismissal. **отчи́слить**, -лю *perf.*, отчисля́ть, -я́ю *imp.* deduct; assign; dismiss.

отчита́ть, -а́ю *perf.*, **отчи́тывать**, -аю *imp.* scold, read a lecture, tell off; ~ся, report back; + в + *prep.* give an account of, report on.

отчуди́ть, -ужу́ *perf.*, **отчужда́ть**, -а́ю *imp.* alienate; estrange. **отчужде́ние**, -я, alienation; estrangement.

отшатну́ться, -ну́сь, -нёшься *perf.*, **отша́тываться**, -аюсь *imp.* start back, recoil; + от + *gen.* give up, forsake, break with.

отшвы́ривать, -аю *imp.*, **отшвырну́ть**, -ну́, -нёшь *perf.* fling away; throw off.

отше́льник, -а, hermit, anchorite; recluse.

от|шлифова́ть, -фу́ю *perf.* **от|штукату́рить**, -рю *perf.*

отшути́ться, -учу́сь, -у́тишься *perf.*, **отшу́чиваться**, -аюсь *imp.* reply with a joke; laugh it off.

отщепе́нец, -нца, renegade.

отъ-: see **от-**.

отъе́зд, -а, departure. **отъезжа́ть**, -а́ю *imp.*, **отъе́хать**, -е́ду *perf.* drive off, go off. **отъе́зжий**, distant.

отъя́вленный, thorough; inveterate.

отыгра́ть, -а́ю *perf.*, **оты́грывать**, -аю *imp.* win back; ~ся, win, get, back what one has lost; get one's own back, get one's revenge.

отыска́ть, -ыщу́, -ы́щешь *perf.*, **оты́скивать**, -аю *imp.* find; track down, run to earth; look for, try to find; ~ся, turn up, appear.

офице́р, -а, officer. **офице́рский**, officer's, officers'. **офице́рство**, -а, officers; commissioned rank.

официа́льный, official.

официа́нт, -а, waiter. **официа́нтка**, -и, waitress.

официо́з, -а, semi-official organ (of the press). **официо́зный**, semi-official.

оформи́тель, -я *m.* decorator, stage-painter. **офо́рмить**, -млю *perf.*, **оформля́ть**, -я́ю *imp.* get up, mount, put into shape; register officially, legalize; ~ пье́су, stage a play; ~ся, take shape; be registered; legalize one's position; be taken on the staff,

join the staff. **оформле́ние**, -я, get-up; mounting, staging; registration, legalization.

ox *int.* oh! ah!

оха́пка, -и, armful; взять в оха́пку, take in one's arms.

о|характеризова́ть, -зу́ю *perf.*

о́хать, -аю *imp.* (*perf.* **о́хнуть**) moan, groan; sigh.

охва́т, -а, scope, range; inclusion; outflanking, envelopment. **охвати́ть**, -ачу́, -а́тишь *perf.*, **охва́тывать**, -аю *imp.* envelop; enclose; grip; seize; comprehend, take in; outflank; + *instr.* draw into, involve in. **охва́ченный**, seized, gripped; ~ у́жасом, terror-stricken.

охладева́ть, -а́ю *imp.*, **охладе́ть**, -е́ю *perf.* grow cold. **охлади́лый**, cold; grown cold. **охлади́тельный**, cooling, cool. **охлади́ть**, -ажу́ *perf.*, **охлажда́ть**, -а́ю *imp.* cool, chill; refrigerate, freeze; ~ся, become cool, cool down. **охлажда́ющ|ий**, cooling, refrigerating; ~ая жи́дкость, coolant. **охлажде́ние**, -я, cooling, chilling; refrigerating; freezing; coolness; с возду́шным ~м, air-cooled.

о|хмеле́ть, -е́ю *perf.* **о́хнуть**, -ну *perf.* of **о́хать**.

охо́та[1], -ы, hunt, hunting; chase.

охо́та[2], -ы, desire, wish; inclination.

охо́титься, -о́чусь *imp.* hunt. **охо́тник**[1], -а, hunter; sportsman.

охо́тник[2], -а, volunteer; + до + *gen.*, or + *inf.* lover of, enthusiast for.

охо́тничий, hunting; sporting, shooting.

охо́тно *adv.* willingly, gladly, readily.

о́хра, -ы, ochre.

охра́на, -ы, guarding; protection; conservation, preservation; guard. **охрани́ть**, -ню́ *perf.*, **охраня́ть**, -я́ю *imp.* guard, protect; preserve. **охра́нка**, -и, secret police. **охра́нн|ый**, guard, protection; ~ая гра́мота, ~ый лист, safe-conduct, pass.

охри́плый, **охри́пший**, hoarse, husky. **о|хри́пнуть**, -ну; охри́п *perf.* become hoarse.

о|хрому́ть, -ну *perf.*

о|цара́пать(ся, -аю(сь *perf.*

оце́нивать, -аю *imp.*, **оцени́ть**, -ню́,

-нишь *perf*. estimate, evaluate; appraise; appreciate. **оце́нка**, -и, estimation, evaluation; appraisal; estimate; appreciation. **оце́нщик**, -а, valuer.

оцепене́лый, torpid, benumbed. о|цепене́ть, -е́ю *perf*.

оцепи́ть, -плю́, -пишь *perf*., **оцепля́ть**, -я́ю *imp*. surround; cordon off. **оцепле́ние**, -я, surrounding; cordoning off; cordon.

оцинко́ванный, galvanized.

оча́г, -а́, hearth; centre, seat; focus; nidus; дома́шний ~, hearth, home; ~ зара́зы, nidus of infection; ~ землетрясе́ния, focus of earthquake; ~ сопротивле́ния, pocket of resistance.

очарова́ние, -я, charm, fascination. **очарова́тельный**, charming, fascinating. **очарова́ть**, -ру́ю *perf*., **очаро́вывать**, -аю, charm, fascinate.

очеви́дец, -дца, eye-witness. **очеви́дно** *adv*. obviously, evidently. **очеви́дный**, obvious, evident, manifest, patent.

о́чень *adv*. very; very much.

очередн|о́й, next; next in turn; periodic, periodical; recurrent; usual, regular; routine; ~а́я зада́ча, immediate task; ~о́й о́тпуск, usual holiday. **о́чередь**, -и; *gen. pl.* -е́й, turn; queue, line; burst, salvo; на о́череди, next (in turn); по о́череди in turn, in order, in rotation; в пе́рвую ~, in the first place, in the first instance; ~ за ва́ми, it is your turn; стоя́ть в о́череди (за + *instr.*), queue (for), stand in line (for).

о́черк, -а, essay, sketch, study; outline. о|черни́ть, -ню́ *perf*.

очерстве́лый, hardened, callous. о|черстве́ть, -е́ю *perf*.

очерта́ние, -я, outline(s), contour(s). **очерти́ть**, -рчу́, -ртишь *perf*., **оче́рчивать**, -аю *imp*. outline, trace.

оче́ски, -ов *pl*. combings; flocks.

оче́чник, -а spectacle case.

о́чи, etc. see **о́ко**.

очи́нивать, -аю *imp*. о|чини́ть, -ню́, -нишь *perf*. sharpen, point.

очисти́тельный, purifying, cleansing. о|чи́стить, -и́щу *perf*., **очища́ть**, -а́ю *imp*. clean; cleanse, purify; refine; rectify; clear; free; peel; ~ся, clear oneself; become clear (от + *gen*. of).

очи́стка, -и. cleaning; cleansing, purification; refinement, rectification; clearance; freeing; mopping up; для очи́стки со́вести, for conscience sake. **очи́стки**, -ов *pl*. peelings. **очище́ние**, -я, cleansing; purification.

очки́, -о́в *pl*. glasses, spectacles. **очко́**, -а́; *gen. pl.* -о́в, pip; point; hole. **очко́в|ый**[1]; ~ая систе́ма, points system. **очко́в|ый**[2]; ~ая змея́, cobra.

очну́ться, -ну́сь, -нёшься *perf*. wake, wake up; come to (oneself), regain consciousness.

о́чн|ый; ~ое обуче́ние, internal courses; ~ая ста́вка, confrontation.

очути́ться, -у́тишься *perf*. find oneself; come to be.

о|швартова́ть, -ту́ю *perf*.

оше́йник, -а, collar.

ошеломи́тельный, stunning. **ошеломи́ть**, -млю́ *perf*., **ошеломля́ть**, -я́ю *imp*. stun. **ошеломле́ние**, -я, stupefaction.

ошиба́ться, -а́юсь *imp*., **ошиби́ться**, -бу́сь, -бёшься; -и́бся *perf*. be mistaken, make a mistake, make mistakes; be wrong; err, be at fault. **оши́бка**, -и, mistake; error; blunder; по оши́бке, by mistake. **оши́бочный**, erroneous, mistaken.

ошпа́ривать, -аю *imp*., о|шпа́рить, -рю *perf*. scald.

о|штрафова́ть, -фу́ю *perf*. о|штукату́рить, -рю *perf*. о|щени́ться, -и́тся *perf*.

ощети́ниваться, -ается *imp*., **ощети́ниться**, -нится *perf*. bristle (up).

о|щипа́ть, -плю́, -плешь *perf*., **ощи́пывать**, -аю *imp*. pluck.

ощу́пать, -аю *perf*., **ощу́пывать**, -аю *imp*. feel, touch; grope about. **о́щупь**, -и; на ~, to the touch; by touch; идти́ на ~ feel one's way, feel one's way. **о́щупью** *adv*. gropingly, fumblingly; by touch; blindly; идти́ ~, grope one's way, feel one's way; иска́ть ~, grope for.

ощути́мый, **ощути́тельный**, perceptible, tangible, palpable; appreciable. **ощути́ть**, -ущу́ *perf*., **ощуща́ть**, -а́ю *imp*. feel, sense, experience. **ощуще́ние**, -я, sensation; feeling; sense.

П

п *letter*: see пэ.

па *n. indecl.* step, *pas*.

па́ва, -ы, peahen.

павильо́н, -а, pavilion; film studio.

павли́н, -а, peacock.

па́водок, -дка, (sudden) flood, freshet.

па́вший, fallen; ~ие в бою́, (those) who fell in action.

па́губа, -ы, ruin, destruction; bane.

па́губный, pernicious, ruinous; baneful; fatal.

па́даль, -и, carrion.

па́дать, -аю *imp.* (*perf.* пасть, упа́сть) fall; sink; drop; decline; fall out, drop out; die; ~ ду́хом, lose heart, lose courage; ~ от уста́лости, be ready to drop. **па́дающий**, falling; incident; ~ие звёзды, shooting stars. **паде́ж**, -а́. case. **паде́ние**, -я, fall; drop, sinking; degradation; slump; incidence; dip. **па́дкий на** + *acc.* или до + *gen.* having a weakness for; susceptible to; greedy for. **паду́чий**, falling; ~ая (боле́знь), falling sickness, epilepsy.

па́дчерица, -ы, step-daughter.

па́дший, fallen; ~ие *sb. pl.* the fallen.

паёк, пайка́, ration.

па́зуха, -и, bosom; sinus; axil; за па́зухой, in one's bosom.

пай, -я; *pl.* -и́, -ёв, share. **па́йщик**, -а, shareholder.

пак, -а, pack-ice.

паке́т, -а, parcel, package; packet; (official) letter; paper bag.

па́кля, -и tow; oakum.

пакова́ть, -ку́ю *imp.* (*perf.* за~, у~) pack.

па́костить, -ощу *imp.* (*perf.* за~, ис~, на~) soil, dirty; spoil, mess up; + *dat.* play dirty tricks on. **па́костный**, dirty, mean, foul; nasty. **па́кость**, -и, filth; dirty trick, nasty trick; obscenity, dirty word.

пакт, -а, pact; ~ догово́ра, covenant; ~ о ненападе́нии, non-aggression pact.

паланти́н -а (fur) stole, cape.

пала́та, -ы, ward; chamber, house; hall; *pl.* palace; Оруже́йная ~, Armoury; ~ мер и весо́в, Board of Weights and Measures; ~ о́бщин, House of Commons; торго́вая ~, Chamber of Commerce. **пала́тка**, -и, tent; marquee; stall, booth; в ~х, under canvas. **пала́тный**, ward; ~ая сестра́, (ward) sister. **пала́точный**, tent; tented, of tents.

пала́ч, -а́, hangman; executioner; butcher.

па́лец, -льца, finger; toe; pin, peg; cam, cog, tooth; знать как свои́ пять па́льцев, have at one's finger-tips; он па́льцем никого́ не тро́нет, he wouldn't lay a finger on anybody; he wouldn't harm a fly; ~ о ~ не уда́рить, not lift a finger; смотре́ть сквозь па́льцы на + *acc.*, wink at, shut one's eyes to.

палиса́д, -а, paling; palisade, stockade.

палиса́дник, -а, (small) front garden.

палиса́ндр, -а, rosewood.

пали́тра, -ы, palette.

пали́ть[1], -лю́ *imp.* (*perf.* о~, с~) burn; scorch.

пали́ть[2], -лю́ *imp.* (*perf.* вы́~, пальну́ть) fire, shoot.

па́лка, -и, stick; walking-stick, cane; staff; из-под па́лки, under the lash, under duress; ~ о двух конца́х, double-edged weapon.

пало́мник, -а, pilgrim. **пало́мничество**, -а, pilgrimage.

па́лочка, -и, stick; bacillus; дирижёрская ~, (conductor's) baton. **па́лочковый**, bacillary. **па́лочный**, stick, cane.

па́луба, -ы, deck. **па́лубный**; ~ груз, deck cargo.

пальба́, -ы́, fire, cannonade.

па́льма, -ы, palm(-tree). **па́льмовый**, palm; ~ая ветвь, olive-branch; ~ое де́рево, box-wood.

пальну́ть, -ну́, -нёшь *perf.* of пали́ть.

пальто́ *n. indecl.* (over)coat; topcoat.

паля́щий, burning; scorching.

па́мятник, -а, monument; memorial;

tombstone. **пáмятн|ый**, memorable; memorial; ~ая кни́жка, notebook, memorandum book. **пáмять**, -и, memory; recollection, remembrance; mind, consciousness; без пáмяти, unconscious; на ~, by heart; from memory; подари́ть на ~, give as a keepsake.

панáма, -ы, **панáмка**, -и, Panama (hat).

панéль, -и, pavement, footpath; panel-(ling), wainscot(ing). **панéльн|ый**, panelling; ~ая обши́вка, panelling, wainscot.

пáника, -и, panic. **паникёр**, -а, panic-monger, scaremonger, alarmist.

панихи́да, -ы, office for the dead; requiem; гражда́нская ~, (civil) funeral. **панихи́дный**, requiem; funereal.

пани́ческий panic; panicky.

панно́ n. indecl. panel.

пансио́н, -а, boarding-school; boarding-house; board and lodging; ко́мната с ~ом, room and board. **пансиона́т**, -а, living in; holiday hotel. **пансионе́р**, -а, boarder; guest.

пантало́ны, -о́н pl. trousers; knickers, panties.

пантéра, -ы, panther.

пантолéты, -лéт pl. open sandals.

пáпа¹, -ы, Pope.

пáпа², -ы m., **папáша**, -и m. daddy; papa.

папиро́са, -ы, (Russian) cigarette. **папиро́сн|ый** adj.; ~ая бума́га, rice-paper.

пáпка, -и, file; document case; folder; cardboard, pasteboard.

пáпоротник, -а, fern.

пáпский, papal. **пáпство**, -а, papacy.

пар¹, -а (-у), loc. -ý; pl. -ы́, steam; exhalation; на всех пара́х, full steam ahead; at full speed.

пар², -а, loc. -ý; pl. -ы́, fallow.

пáра, -ы, pair, couple; (two-piece) suit.

парáграф, -а, paragraph.

парáд, -а, parade; review. **парáдность**, -и, magnificence; ostentation. **парáдн|ый**, parade; gala; main; front; ~ая дверь, front door; ~ые ко́мнаты, state rooms, (suite of) reception rooms; ~ый подъéзд, main entrance; ~ая фóрма, full dress (uniform).

парализо́ванный, paralysed. **парализова́ть**, -зýю perf. and imp. paralyse.

парали́ч, -á, paralysis, palsy. **паралич-ный**, paralytic.

паралле́ль, -и, parallel. **паралле́льн|ый**, parallel; ~ые бру́сья, parallel bars.

парáф, -а, flourish; initials. **парафи́ровать**, -рую perf. and imp. initial.

парéние, -я, soaring.

пáрень, -рня́; gen. pl. -рнéй m. boy, lad; chap, fellow.

пари́ n. indecl. bet; держа́ть ~, bet, lay a bet.

парижа́нин, -а; pl. -áне, -áн, **парижа́нка**, -и, Parisian. **Пари́жский**, Parisian.

пари́к, -á, wig. **парикма́хер**, -а, barber; hairdresser. **парикма́херская** sb. barber's, hairdresser's.

пари́ровать, -и́рую perf. and imp. (perf. also от~) parry, counter.

паритéт, -а, parity. **паритéтн|ый**; на ~ых нача́лах, on a par, on an equal footing.

пари́ть¹, -рю́ imp. soar, swoop, hover.

пáрить², -рю imp. steam, induce sweating in; stew; impers. пáрит it is sultry; ~ся (perf. по~ся), steam, sweat, stew.

парк, -а, park; yard; depot; fleet; stock; pool; ваго́нный ~, rolling-stock.

пáрка, -и, steaming; stewing.

паркéт, -а, parquet.

пáркий, steamy.

парламéнт, -а, parliament. **парламента́рный**, parliamentarian. **парламентёр**, -а, envoy; bearer of flag of truce. **парламентёрский**; ~ флаг, flag of truce. **парламéнтский**, parliamentary; ~ зако́н, Act of Parliament.

парни́к, -á, hot bed, seed-bed; frame. **парнико́в|ый** adj.; ~ые расте́ния, hothouse plants.

парни́шка, -и, boy, lad.

парн|о́й, fresh; steamy; ~о́е молоко́, milk fresh from the cow. **пáрный¹**, steamy.

пáрный², pair; forming a pair; twin; pair-horse.

паро- in comb. steam-. **парово́з**, -а, (steam-)engine, locomotive. **~во́зник**, -а, engine-driver, engineer. **~во́зный**, engine. ~выпускной, exhaust. ~непроницаемый, steam-tight, steam-proof. ~образный, vaporous. ~провод, -а, steam-pipe. ~силовой, steam-power. ~ход, -а, steamer; steamship. ~ходный, steam; steamship; ~ходное общество, steamship company. ~ходство, -а, steam-navigation; steamship-line.

паров|ой, steam; steamed; ~ая машина steam-engine; ~ое отопление, steam heating; central heating.

пароль, -я m. password, countersign.

паром, -а, ferry(-boat). паромщик, -а, ferryman.

паросский, Parian.

парт- abbr. in comb. Party. партактив, -а, Party activists ~билет, -а, Party (membership) card. ~кабинет, -а, Party educational centre. ~ком, -а, Party committee. ~орг, -а, Party organizer. ~организация, -и, Party organization. ~съезд, -а, Party congress.

парта, -ы, (school) desk.

партер, -а, stalls; pit.

партиец, -ийца, Party member.

партизан, -а; gen. pl. -ан, partisan; guerilla. партизанск|ий, partisan, guerilla; unplanned, haphazard; ~ая война, guerilla warfare; ~ое движение, Resistance (movement).

партийка, -и, Party member. партийность, -и, Party membership; Party spirit, Party principles. партийный, party, Party; sb. Party member.

партитура, -ы, score.

парт|ия, -и, party; group; batch; lot; consignment; game, set; part.

партнёр, -а, partner.

парус, -а; pl. -а, -ов, sail; идти под ~ами, sail, be under sail; на всех ~ах, in full sail; поднять ~, set sail. парусина, -ы, canvas, sail-cloth; duck. парусник, -а, sailing vessel. парусный, sail; ~ спорт, sailing.

парча, -и; gen. pl. -ей, brocade. парчевой, парчовый, brocade.

паря́щ|ий, soaring, hovering; ~ая машина, hovercraft.

пасека, -и, apiary, beehive. пасечный adj. beekeeper's, beekeeping.

пасётся: see пастись.

пасмурный, dull, cloudy; overcast; gloomy, sullen.

пасова|ть, -сую imp. (perf. с~) pass; be unable to cope (with), give up, give in.

паспорт, -а; pl. -а, passport; registration certificate.

пассаж, -а, passage; arcade.

пассажир, -а, passenger. пассажирск|ий, passenger; ~ое движение, passenger services.

паста, -ы, paste.

пастбище, -а, pasture.

пастернак, -а, parsnip.

пасти, -су, -сёшь; пас, -ла imp. graze, pasture; shepherd, tend.

пастись, -сётся; пасся, -лась imp. graze; browse. пастух, -а, shepherd, herdsman. пастушеский, shepherd's, herdsman's; pastoral. пастушок, -шка, shepherd. пастушка, -и, shepherdess.

пасть, -и, mouth; jaws.

пасть, паду, -дёшь; пал perf. of падать.

пасха, -и, Easter; Passover.

пасынок, -нка, stepson, stepchild; outcast.

пат, -а, stalemate.

патетический, патетичный, pathetic.

патефон, -а, (portable) gramophone.

патока, -и, treacle; syrup. паточный, treacle; treacly.

патрон, -а, cartridge; chuck, holder; lamp-socket lamp-holder; pattern.

патронаж, -а, patronage; home health service. патронажн|ый; ~ая сестра, health visitor, district nurse.

патронка, -и, pattern.

патронный, cartridge.

патруль, -я m. patrol.

пауза, -ы, pause; interval; rest.

паук, -а, spider. паутина, -ы, cobweb, spider's web; gossamer; web. паучий, spider, spider's.

пафос, -а, (excessive) feeling; zeal, enthusiasm; spirit.

пах, -а, loc. -у, groin.

паханый, ploughed. пахарь, -я m. ploughman. паха́ть, пашу, па́шешь imp. (perf. вс~) plough, till.

па́хнуть[1], -ну; пах *imp.*+*instr.* smell of; reek of; savour of, smack of.

пахну́ть[2], -нёт *perf.* puff, blow.

па́хота, -ы, ploughing, tillage. па́хотный, arable.

паху́чий, odorous, strong-smelling.

па́чка, -и, bundle; batch; packet, pack; tutu.

па́чкать, -аю *imp.* (*perf.* за~, ис~, на~) dirty, soil, stain, sully; daub. пачкотня́, -и́, daub. пачку́н, -а́, sloven; dauber.

пашу́, etc.: see паха́ть. па́шня, -и; *gen. pl.* -шен, ploughed field.

паште́т, -а, pie; pâté.

па́юсн|ый; ~ая икра́, pressed caviare.

пая́льник, -а, soldering iron. пая́льн|ый, soldering; ~ая ла́мпа, blow-lamp. пая́льщик, -а, tinman, tinsmith. па́янный, soldered. пая́ть, -я́ю *imp.* solder.

пая́ц, -а, clown.

певе́ц, -вца́, певи́ца, -ы, singer. певу́чий, melodious. пе́вч|ий, singing; ~ая пти́ца, song-bird; *sb.* chorister.

пе́гий, skewbald, piebald.

пед- *abbr.* in *comb.* of педагоги́ческий, pedagogic(al); teachers'; education, educational. педву́з, -а, ~институ́т, -а, (teachers') training college. ~ку́рсы, -ов *pl.* teachers' training courses. ~сове́т, -а, staff-meeting. ~фа́к, -а, education department.

педаго́г, -а, teacher; pedagogue, educationist. педаго́гика, -и, pedagogy, pedagogics. педагоги́ческий, pedagogical; educational; ~ институ́т, (teachers') training college; ~ факульте́т, education department.

педа́ль, -и, pedal; treadle. педа́льный, pedal.

пейза́ж, -а, landscape; scenery. пейзажи́ст, -а, landscape painter.

пёк: see печь. пека́рный, baking, bakery. пека́рня, -и; *gen. pl.* -рен, bakery, bakehouse. пе́карь, -я; *pl.* -я́, -ей *m.* baker. пекло́, -а, scorching heat; hell-fire. пеку́, etc.: see печь.

пелена́ -ы́; *gen. pl.* -лён, shroud. пелена́ть, -а́ю *imp.* (*perf.* за~, с~) swaddle; put nappy on, change.

пе́ленг, -а, bearing. пеленга́тор, -а,

direction finder. пеленгова́ть, -гу́ю *perf.* and *imp.* take the bearings of.

пелёнка, -и, napkin, nappy; *pl.* swaddling-clothes; с пелёнок, from the cradle.

пе́мза, -ы, pumice(-stone). пе́мзовый, pumice.

пе́на, -ы, foam, spume; scum; froth, head; lather; (мы́льная) ~, soapsuds.

пена́л, -а, pencil-box, pencil-case.

пе́ние, -я, singing; ~ петуха́, crowing.

пе́нист|ый, foamy; frothy; ~ое вино́, sparkling wine. пе́нить, -ню *imp.* (*perf.* вс~) froth; ~ся, foam, froth.

пе́нка, -и, skin; (морска́я) ~, meerschaum. пе́нковый, meerschaum. пенопла́ст, -а, plastic foam, cellular plastic. пенопластма́сса, -ы, expanded plastic. пеностекло́, -а́, fibreglass.

пенсионе́р, -а, pensioner. пенсио́нный, pension. пе́нсия, -и, pension; ~ по инвали́дности, disability pension; ~ по ста́рости, old-age pension.

пенсне́ *n. indecl.* pince-nez.

пень, пня *m.* stump, stub.

пенька́, -и́, hemp. пенько́вый, hempen.

пе́ня, -и, fine. пеня́ть, -я́ю *imp.* (*perf.* по~)+*dat.* reproach; + на+*acc.* blame.

пе́пел, -пла, ash, ashes. пепели́ще, -а, site of fire; (hearth and) home; родно́е ~, old home. пе́пельница, -ы, ashtray. пе́пельный, ashy.

пер. *abbr.* переу́лок, Street, Lane.

перве́йший, the first, the most important; first-class. пе́рвенец, -нца, first-born; first of its kind. пе́рвенство, -а, first place; championship; ~ по футбо́лу, football championship. пе́рвенствовать, -твую *imp.* take first place; take precedence, take priority. перви́чный, primary; initial.

перво- in *comb.* first, primary; prime, top; newly, just; archi-, archaeo-, proto-; prim(o)-. первобы́тный, primitive; primordial; primeval; pristine. ~зда́нный, primordial; primitive, primary. ~-исто́чник, -а, primary source; origin. ~катего́рник, -а, first-rank player. ~кла́ссный, first-class, first--rate. ~ку́рсник, -a, first-year student, freshman. ~ма́йский, May-day. ~нача́льно adv. originally. ~нача́льный, original; primary; initial; prime; elementary. ~о́браз, -a, prototype, original; protoplast. ~очередно́й, ~очередно́й, first and foremost, immediate. ~печа́тный, early printed, incunabular; first printed, first-edition; ~печа́тные кни́ги, incunabula. ~причи́на, -ы, first cause. ~разря́дный, first-class, first-rank. ~ро́дный, first--born; primal original. ~рождённый, first-born. ~со́ртный, best-quality; first-class, first-rate. ~степе́нный, paramount, of the first order.

пе́рвое sb. first course. пе́рво-на́перво adv. first of all. пе́рв|ый, former; earliest; быть ~ым, идти́ ~ым come first, lead; ~ое де́ло, ~ым де́лом, first of all, first thing; с ~ого ра́за, from the first.

перга́мент -a, parchment; greaseproof paper. перга́ментный, parchment; parchment-like; greaseproof.

пере-, vbl. pref. indicating action across or through something; repetition of action; superiority, excess, etc.; extension of action to encompass many or all objects or cases of a given kind; division into two or more parts; reciprocity of action; trans-, re-, over-, out-.

переадресова́ть, ~сую perf., переадресо́вывать, -аю imp. re-address.

перебега́ть, -а́ю imp., перебежа́ть, -бегу́ perf. cross; run across; desert, go over. перебе́жка, -и, bound; rush; re-run. перебе́жчик, -a, deserter; turncoat.

перебели́ть, -а́ю imp., перебели́ть, -елю́, -е́лишь perf. re-whitewash; make a fair copy of.

переберу́, etc.: see перебра́ть.

перебива́ть(ся, -а́ю(сь imp. of переби́ть(ся. переби́вка, -и, re-upholstering.

перебира́ть(ся, -а́ю(сь imp. of перебра́ть(ся.

переби́ть, -бью -бьёшь perf. (imp. перебива́ть) interrupt; intercept; kill, slay, slaughter; beat; beat up again;

break; re-upholster; ~ся, break; make ends meet; get by. перебо́й, interruption, intermission; stoppage, hold-up; irregularity; misfire. перебо́йный, interrupted, intermittent.

перебо́рка, -и, sorting out; re-assembly; partition; bulkhead.

переборо́ть, -рю́, -решь perf. overcome; master.

перебо́рщить, -щу́ perf. go too far; overdo it.

перебра́нка, -и, wrangle squabble.

перебра́сывать(ся, -аю(сь imp. of перебро́сить(ся.

перебра́ть, -беру́, -берёшь; -а́л, -а́, -о perf. (imp. перебира́ть) sort out, pick over; look through, look over; turn over; turn over in one's mind; finger; dismantle and re-assemble; reset; take in excess; score more than enough; ~ся, get over, cross; move.

перебро́сить, -о́шу perf. (imp. перебра́сывать) throw over; transfer; ~ся, fling oneself; spread; + instr. throw to one another; ~ся не́сколькими слова́ми, exchange a few words. перебро́ска, -и, transfer.

перебью́, etc.: see переби́ть.

перева́л, -a, passing, crossing; pass. перева́ливать, -аю imp., перевали́ть, -лю́, -лишь perf. transfer, shift; cross, pass; impers. перевали́ло за по́лночь, it is past midnight; ей перевали́ло за со́рок, she's turned forty, she's over forty; ~ся, waddle.

перева́ривать, -аю imp., перевари́ть, -рю́, -ришь perf. boil again; reheat; overdo, overcook; digest; swallow, bear, stand.

переведу́, etc.: see перевести́.

перевезти́, -зу́, -зёшь; -вёз, -ла́ perf. (imp. перевози́ть) take across, put across; transport, convey; (re)move.

переверну́ть, -ну́, -нёшь perf., переверты́вать, -аю imp. (imp. also перевора́чивать) turn (over); overturn, upset; turn inside out; ~ вверх дном, turn upside-down; ~ся, turn (over).

переве́с, -a, preponderance; predominance; advantage, superiority; с ~ом в пять голосо́в, with a majority of five votes. переве́сить, -е́шу perf. (imp.

переве́шивать) re-weigh, weigh again; outweigh, outbalance; tip the scales; hang somewhere else.

перевести́, -веду́, -ведёшь; -вёл, -а́, *perf.* (*imp.* переводи́ть), take across; transfer move, switch, shift; translate; convert, express; transfer, copy; ~ дух, take breath; ~ часы́ вперёд (наза́д), put a clock forward (back); ~сь, be transferred; come to an end, run out; become extinct; у меня́ перевели́сь де́ньги, my money ran out, I was spent up.

переве́шивать, -аю *imp.* of переве́сить.

перевира́ть, -а́ю *imp.* of перевра́ть.

перево́д, -а (-у), transfer, move, switch, shift; translation; version; conversion; spending, using up, waste; нет ~у + *dat.*, there is no shortage of, there is an inexhaustible supply of. переводи́ть(ся, -ожу́(сь, -о́дишь(ся *imp.* of перевести́(сь. переводно́й, transfer; ~а́я бума́га, carbon paper, transfer paper; ~а́я карти́нка. transfer. перево́дный, transfer; translated. перево́дчик, -а, translator; interpreter.

перево́з, -а, transporting, conveyance; crossing; ferry. перевози́ть, -ожу́, -о́зишь *imp.* of перевезти́. перево́зка, -и conveyance, carriage. перево́зчик, -а, ferryman; boatman; carrier, carter, removal man.

перевооружа́ть, -а́ю *imp.*, перевооружи́ть, -жу́ *perf.* rearm; ~ся, rearm. перевооруже́ние, -я, rearmament.

перевоплоти́ть, -лощу́ *perf.*, перевоплоща́ть, -а́ю *imp.* reincarnate; transform; ~ся, be reincarnated; transform oneself, be transformed. перевоплоще́ние, -я, reincarnation; transformation.

перевора́чивать(ся, -аю(сь *imp.* of переверну́ть(ся. переворо́т, -а, revolution; overturn; cataclysm; госуда́рственный ~, coup d'état.

перевоспита́ние, -я, re-education. перевоспита́ть, -а́ю *perf.*, перевоспи́тывать, -аю *imp.* re-educate.

переврать, -ру́, -рёшь; -а́л, -а́, -о *perf.* (*imp.* перевира́ть) garble, confuse; misinterpret; misquote.

перевыполне́ние, -я, over-fulfilment.

перевы́полнить, -ню *perf.*, перевыполня́ть, -я́ю *imp.* over-fulfil.

перевяза́ть, -яжу́, -я́жешь *perf.*, перевя́зывать, -аю *imp.* dress, bandage; tie up, cord; tie again, re-tie; knit again. перевя́зка, -и, dressing, bandage. перевя́зочный = материа́л, dressing; ~ пункт, dressing station. пе́ревязь, -и, cross-belt, shoulder-belt; sling.

переги́б, -а, bend, twist; fold; exaggeration; допусти́ть ~ в+*prep.*, carry too far. перегиба́ть(ся, -а́ю(сь *imp.* of перегну́ть(ся.

перегля́дываться, -аюсь *imp.*, перегляну́ться, -ну́сь, -нешься *perf.* exchange glances.

перегна́ть, -гоню́, -го́нишь; -а́л, -а́, -о *perf.* (*imp.* перегоня́ть) outdistance, leave behind; overtake, surpass; drive; ferry; distil, sublimate.

перегно́й, -я, humus.

перегну́ть, -ну́, -нёшь *perf.* (*imp.* перегиба́ть) bend; ~ па́лку, go too far; ~ся, bend; lean over.

перегова́ривать, -аю *imp.* переговори́ть, -рю́ *perf.* talk, speak; silence, out-talk; +о+*prep.* talk over, discuss; ~ся (с+ *instr.*) exchange remarks (with). перегово́р, -а, (telephone) call, conversation; *pl.* negotiations, parley; вести́ ~ы, negotiate, conduct negotiations, parley. перегово́рный *adj.*; ~ая бу́дка, call-box, telephone booth; ~ый пункт, public call-boxes; trunk-call office.

перего́н, -а, driving; stage. перего́нка, -и. distillation. перего́нный, distilling, distillation; ~ заво́д, distillery; ~ куб, still. перегоню́, etc.: see перегна́ть. перегоня́ть, -я́ю *imp.* of перегна́ть.

перегора́живать, -аю *imp.* of перегороди́ть.

перегора́ть, -а́ет *imp.*, перегоре́ть, -ри́т *perf.* burn out, fuse; burn through; rot through.

перегороди́ть, -рожу́, -ро́дишь *perf.* (*imp.* перегора́живать) partition off; block. перегоро́дка, -и, partition; baffle (plate). перегоро́женный, partitioned off; blocked.

перегре́в, -а, overheating; superheating.

перегрева́ть, -а́ю *imp.*, перегре́ть, -е́ю *perf.* overheat; burn, burn out, get burned.

перегружа́ть, -а́ю *imp.*, перегрузи́ть, -ужу́, -у́зишь *perf.* overload; transfer, trans-ship; overwork. перегру́зка, -и, overload; overwork; transfer; reloading.

перегрыза́ть, -а́ю *imp.*, перегры́зть, -зу́, -зёшь; -гры́з *perf.* gnaw through, bite through; ~ся, fight; quarrel, wrangle.

пе́ред, пе́редо, пред, пре́до, *prep.* + *instr.* before; in front of; in the face of; to; compared to, in comparison with; извини́ться ~, apologize to. пе́редо, пе́реда; *pl.* -а́, front, forepart.

передава́ть, -даю́, -даёшь *imp.*, переда́ть, -а́м, -а́шь, -а́ст, -ади́м; пе́редал, -а́, -о *perf.* pass, hand, hand over; hand down; make over; tell; communicate; transmit, convey; pay too much; give too much to; вы пе́редали три рубля́, you have paid three roubles too much; ~ де́ло в суд, take a matter to court, sue; ~ приве́т, convey one's greetings, send one's regards; переда́й(те) им приве́т, remember me to them; ~ся, pass; be transmitted; be communicated; be inherited; + *dat.* go over to. переда́точн|ый; ~ый механи́зм, drive, driving mechanism, transmission; ~ое число́, gear ratio. переда́тчик, -а, transmitter, sender; conductor. переда́ча, -и, passing; transmission; communication; broadcast; drive; gear, gearing; transfer.

передвига́ть, -а́ю *imp.*, передви́нуть, -ну *perf.* move, shift; ~ часы́ вперёд (наза́д), put the clock forward (back); ~ сро́ки экза́менов change the date of examinations; ~ся, move, shift; travel. передвиже́ние, -я, movement, moving; conveyance; travel; сре́дства передвиже́ния, means of transport. передви́жка, -и, movement; moving; travel; in *comb.*, travelling, itinerant; библиоте́ка-~, travelling library, mobile library; теа́тр-~, strolling players. передвижно́й, movable, mobile; travelling, itinerant.

переде́л, -а, re-partition; re-division, redistribution; re-allotment.

переде́лать, -аю *perf.*, переде́лывать, -аю *imp.* alter; change; refashion, recast; do. переде́лка, -и, alteration; adaptation; отда́ть в переде́лку, have altered; попа́сть в переде́лку, get into a pretty mess.

передёргивать(ся, -аю(сь *imp.* of передёрнуть(ся.

передержа́ть, -жу́, -жишь *perf.*, переде́рживать, -аю *imp.* keep too long; overdo; overcook; overexpose. переде́ржка, -и, overexposure.

передёрнуть, -ну *perf.* (*imp.* передёргивать) pull aside, pull across; cheat; distort, misrepresent; ~ фа́кты, juggle with facts; ~ся, flinch, wince.

пере́дний, front, fore; anterior; first, leading; ~ план, foreground. пере́дник, -а apron; pinafore. пере́дняя *sb.* ante-room; (entrance) hall, lobby. пе́редо: see пе́ред. передови́к, -а́, peredovik, leader; standard-bearer, pioneer; leader-writer. передови́ца, -ы, leading article, leader; editorial. передово́|й, forward; advanced; foremost; ~ы́е взгля́ды, advanced views; ~о́й отря́д, advanced detachment; vanguard; ~а́я (статья́), leading article, leader; editorial.

передохну́ть, -ну́, -нёшь *perf.* pause for breath, take a breather.

передра́знивать, -аю *imp.*, передразни́ть, -ню́, -нишь *perf.* take off, mimic.

передря́га, -и, scrape, tight corner; unpleasantness.

переду́мать, -аю *perf.*, переду́мывать, -аю *imp.* change one's mind, think better of it; do a lot of thinking.

переды́шка, -и, respite, breathing-space.

перее́зд, -а, crossing; removal. переезжа́ть, -а́ю *imp.*, перее́хать, -е́ду *perf.* cross; run over, knock down; move, remove.

пережа́ренный, overdone; burnt. пережа́ривать, -аю *imp.*, пережа́рить, -рю *perf.* overdo, overcook.

пережда́ть, -жду́, -ждёшь; -а́л, -а́, -о *perf.* (*imp.* пережида́ть) wait; wait through, wait for the end of.

пережёвывать, -аю *imp.* masticate, chew; repeat over and over again.

пережива́ние, -я, experience. **пережи-ва́ть** -а́ю *imp.* of **пережи́ть**.

пережида́ть, -а́ю *imp.* of **пережда́ть**.

пережи́тое *sb.* the past. **пережи́ток**, -тка, survival; vestige. **пережи́ть**, -иву́ -ивёшь; пережи́л, -а́, -о *perf.* (*imp.* пережива́ть) live through; experience; go through; endure, suffer; outlive, outlast, survive.

перезаряди́ть, -яжу́, -я́дишь *perf.*, **перезаряжа́ть**, -а́ю *imp.* re-charge, reload. **перезаря́дка**, -и, re-charging, reloading.

перезво́н, -а ringing, chime.

пере|зимова́ть, -му́ю *perf.*

перезрева́ть, -а́ю *imp.*, **перезре́ть**, -е́ю *perf.* become overripe; be past one's prime. **перезре́лый**, overripe; past one's first youth, past one's prime.

переизбира́ть, -а́ю *imp.*, **переизбра́ть**, -беру́, -берёшь; -бра́л, -а́, -о *perf.* re-elect. **переизбра́ние**, -я, re-election.

переиздава́ть, -даю́, -даёшь *imp.*, **переизда́ть**, -а́м, -а́шь, -а́ст, -ади́м; -а́л, -а́, -о *perf.* republish, reprint. **переизда́ние**, -я, re-publication; new edition, reprint.

переименова́ть, -ну́ю *perf.*, **переименова́вывать**, -а́ю *imp.* rename.

переймý, etc.: see **переня́ть**.

перейти́, -йду́, -йдёшь; перешёл, -шла́ *perf.* (*imp.* переходи́ть) cross; get across, get over, go over; pass; turn (в+*acc.* to, into); ~ в наступле́ние, go over to the offensive; ~ грани́цу, cross the frontier; ~ из рук в ру́ки, change hands; ~ на другу́ю рабо́ту, change one's job; ~ че́рез мост, cross a bridge.

перека́рмливать, -аю *imp.* of **перекорми́ть**.

переквалифика́ция, -и, training for a new profession; re-training. **переквалифици́роваться**, -руюсь *perf.* and *imp.* change one's profession; re-train.

перекидно́й; ~ мо́стик, footbridge, gangway. **переки́дывать**, -аю *imp.*, **переки́нуть**, -ну *perf.* throw over; ~ся, leap; spread; go over, deal; ~ся слова́ми, exchange a few remarks.

переки́сать, -а́ет *imp.*, **переки́снуть**,

-нет *perf.* turn sour, go sour. **пе́рекись**, -и, peroxide.

перекла́дина, -ы, cross-beam cross-piece, transom; joist; horizontal bar. **перекла́дывать**, -аю *imp.* of **переложи́ть**.

перекли́каться, -а́юсь *imp.*, **перекли́кнуться**, -нусь *perf.* call to one another. **перекли́чка**, -и, roll-call, call-over; hook-up.

переключа́тель, -я *m.* switch. **переключа́ть**, -а́ю *imp.*, **переключи́ть**, -чу́ *perf.* switch, switch over; ~ся, switch (over).

перекова́ть, -кую́, -куёшь *perf.*, **переко́вывать**, -аю *imp.* re-shoe; re-forge; hammer out, beat out.

переколоти́ть, -лочу́, -ло́тишь *perf.* break, smash.

перекорми́ть, -млю́, -мишь *perf.* (*imp.* перека́рмливать) overfeed, surfeit; feed.

перекоси́ть, -ошу́, -о́сишь *perf.* warp; distort; ~ся, warp, be warped; become distorted.

перекочева́ть, -чу́ю *perf.*, **перекочёвывать**, -аю *imp.* migrate move on.

перекоше́нный, distorted, twisted.

перекра́ивать, -аю *imp.* of **перекрои́ть**.

перекра́сить, -а́шу *perf.*, **перекра́шивать**, -аю *imp.* (re-)colour, (re-)paint; (re-)dye; ~ся, change colour; turn one's coat.

пере|крести́ть, -ещу́, -е́стишь *perf.*, **перекре́щивать**, -аю *imp.* cross; ~ся, cross, intersect; cross oneself. **перекре́стн|ый**, cross; ~ый допро́с, cross-examination; ~ый ого́нь, cross-fire; ~ая ссы́лка, cross-reference. **перекрёсток**, -тка, cross-roads, crossing.

перекри́кивать, -аю *imp.*, **перекрича́ть**, -чу́ *perf.* out-shout, outroar; shout down.

перекрои́ть, -ою́ *perf.* (*imp.* перекра́ивать) cut out again; rehash; reshape.

перекрыва́ть, -а́ю *imp.*, **перекры́ть**, -ро́ю *perf.* re-cover; exceed; ~ реко́рд, break a record.

перекую́, etc.: see **перекова́ть**.

перекупа́ть, -а́ю *imp.*, **перекупи́ть**, -плю́, -пишь *perf.* buy; buy up; buy secondhand. **перекӳпщик**, -а, second-hand dealer.

перекуси́ть, -ушу́, -у́сишь *perf.*, **перекӳсывать**, -аю *imp.* bite through; have a bite, have a snack.

перелага́ть, -а́ю *imp.* of переложи́ть. **перела́мывать**, -аю *imp.* of переломи́ть.

перелеза́ть, -а́ю *imp.* **переле́зть**, -зу; -ёз *perf.* climb over, get over.

перелёт, -а, migration; flight. **перелета́ть**, -а́ю *imp.*, **перелете́ть**, -лечӳ *perf.* fly over, fly across; overshoot the mark. **перелётн|ый**, migratory; ~ая пти́ца, bird of passage.

перелива́ние, -я, decanting; transfusion; ~ кро́ви, blood transfusion. **перелива́ть**, -а́ю *imp.* of перели́ть. **перелива́ться**, -а́ется *imp.* of перели́ться play; modulate. **переливчатый**, iridescent; shot; modulating.

перелиста́ть, -а́ю *perf.*, **перели́стывать**, -аю *imp.* turn over, leaf through; look through glance at.

перели́ть, -лью́, -льёшь; -и́л, -а́, -о *perf.* (*imp.* перелива́ть) pour; decant; let overflow; transfuse. **перели́ться**, -льётся; -ли́лся, -лила́сь, -ли́ло́сь *perf.* (*imp.* перелива́ться) flow; overflow, run over.

пере|лицева́ть, -цу́ю *perf.*, **перелицо́вывать**, -аю *imp.* turn; have turned.

переложе́ние, -я, arrangement. **переложи́ть**, -жӳ, -жишь *perf.* (*imp.* перекла́дывать, перелага́ть) put somewhere else; shift, move; transfer; interlay; re-set, re-lay; put in too much; put, set arrange; transpose; ~ в стихи́, put into verse; ~ на мӳзыку, set to music.

перело́м, -а, break, breaking; fracture; turning-point, crisis; sudden change; на ~e+*gen.*, on the eve of. **переломи́ть**, -а́ю *perf.* break; ~ся, break. be broken. **переломи́ть**, -млю́, -мишь *perf.* (*imp.* перела́мывать) break in two; break; fracture; master; ~ себя́, master oneself, restrain one's feelings. **перело́мный**; ~ моме́нт, critical moment, crucial moment.

перелью́, etc.: see перели́ть. **перема́лывать**, -аю *imp.* of перемоло́ть.

перема́нивать, -аю *imp.*, **перемани́ть**, -ню́ -нишь *perf.* win over; entice.

перемежа́ться, -а́ется *imp.* alternate; перемежа́ющаяся лихора́дка, intermittent fever.

перемелю́, etc.: see перемоло́ть. **переме́на**, -ы, change, alteration; change (of clothes); interval, break. **перемени́ть**, -ню́, -нишь *perf.*, **переменя́ть**, -я́ю *imp.* change; ~ся, change. **переме́нный**, variable, changeable; ~ ток, alternating current. **переме́нчивый** changeable.

перемести́ть, -мещӳ *perf.* (*imp.* перемеща́ть) move; transfer; ~ся, move.

перемеша́ть, -а́ю *perf.*, **переме́шивать**, -аю *imp.* mix, intermingle; mix up; confuse; ~ся, get mixed; get mixed up.

перемеща́ть(ся), -а́ю(ся) *imp.* of перемести́ть(ся). **перемеще́ние**, -я, transference, shift; displacement; dislocation; travel. **перемещён|ый**, displaced; ~ые ли́ца, displaced persons.

переми́гиваться, -аюсь *imp.*, **перемигнӳться**, -нӳсь, -нёшься *perf.* wink at each other; + с + *instr.* wink at.

переми́рие, -я, armistice, truce.

перемога́ть, -а́ю *imp.* (try to) overcome; ~ся, struggle (against illness, tears, etc.).

перемоло́ть, -мелю́, -ме́лешь *perf.* (*imp.* перема́лывать) grind, mill; pulverize.

перемыва́ть, -а́ю *imp.*, **перемы́ть**, -мо́ю *perf.* wash (up) again.

перенапряга́ть, -а́ю *imp.*, **перенапря́чь**, -ягу́, -яжёшь; -я́г, -ла́ *perf.* overstrain; ~ся, overstrain oneself.

перенаселе́ние, -я, overpopulation. **перенаселённый** -лён, -а́, overpopulated; overcrowded. **перенаселя́ть**, -лю́ *perf.*, **перенаселя́ть**, -я́ю *imp.* overpopulate; overcrowd.

перенести́, -сӳ, -сёшь; -нёс, -ла́ *perf.* (*imp.* переноси́ть) carry, move, take; transport; transfer; carry over; take over; put off, postpone; endure, bear, stand; ~сь, be carried; be borne; be carried away.

перенима́ть, -а́ю *imp.* of переня́ть.

перено́с, -а, transfer; transportation; division of words; знак ~a, hyphen.

переноси́мый, bearable, endurable. **переноси́ть(ся**, -ошу́(сь, -о́сишь(ся *imp.* of перенести́(сь.

перено́сица, -ы, bridge (of the nose).

перено́ска, -и, carrying over; transporting; carriage. **перено́сный**, portable; figurative, metaphorical.

пере|ночева́ть, -чу́ю *perf.* **переношу́**, etc.: see переноси́ть.

переня́ть, -ейму́, -еймёшь, пе́реня́л, -а́, -о *perf.* (*imp.* перенима́ть) imitate, copy; adopt.

переобору́довать, -дую *perf. and imp.* re-equip.

переосвиде́тельствовать, -твую *perf. and imp.* re-examine.

переоце́нивать, -аю *imp.*, **переоцени́ть**, -ню́, -нишь *perf.* overestimate, over-rate; revalue, reappraise. **переоце́нка**, -и, overestimation; revaluation; re-appraisal.

перепа́чкать, -аю *perf.* dirty, make dirty; **~ся**, get dirty.

пе́репел, -а; *pl.* -а́, перепёлка, -и, quail.

перепеча́тать, -аю *perf.*, **перепеча́тывать**, -аю *imp.* reprint; type (out). **перепеча́тка**, -и, reprinting; reprint.

перепи́ливать, -аю *imp.*, **перепили́ть**, -лю́, -лишь *perf.* saw in two.

переписа́ть, -ишу́, -и́шешь *perf.*, **перепи́сывать**, -аю *imp.* copy; type; re-write; list, make a list of. **перепи́ска**, -и, copying; typing; correspondence; letters; быть в перепи́ске с + *instr.* be in correspondence with. **перепи́счик**, -а, -чица, -ы, copyist; typist. **перепи́сываться**, -аюсь *imp.* correspond. **пе́репись**, -и, census; inventory.

переплавля́ть, -влю *perf.*, **переплавля́ть**, -я́ю *imp.* smelt.

перепла́та, -ы, overpayment; surplus. **переплати́ть**, -ачу́, -а́тишь *perf.*, **перепла́чивать**, -аю *imp.* overpay, pay too much.

переплести́, -лету́ -летёшь; -лёл, -а *perf.*, **переплета́ть**, -а́ю *imp.* bind; interlace, interknit; re-plait; **~ся**, interlace, interweave; get mixed up. **переплёт**, -а, binding; cover; transom; caning; mess, scrape. **переплётная** *sb.* bindery; bookbinder's. **переплётчик**, -а, bookbinder.

переплыва́ть, -а́ю *imp.*, **переплы́ть**, -ыву́, -ывёшь; -ы́л, -а́, -о *perf.* swim (across); sail across, row across, cross.

переподгота́вливать, -аю *imp.*, **переподгото́вить**, -влю *perf.* re-train; give further training. **переподгото́вка**, -и, further training; re-training; ку́рсы по переподгото́вке, refresher courses.

переполза́ть, -а́ю *imp.*, **переползти́**, -зу́, -зёшь; -о́лз, -ла́ *perf.* crawl across; creep across.

переполне́ние, -я, overfilling; over-crowding. **перепо́лненный**, over-crowded, too full, overfull. **переполни́ть**, -ню *perf.*, **переполня́ть**, -я́ю *imp.* overfill; overcrowd; **~ся**, be overflowing; be overcrowded.

переполо́х, -а, alarm; commotion; rumpus. **переполоши́ть**, -шу́ *perf.* alarm; arouse, alert; **~ся**, take alarm; became alarmed.

перепо́нка, -и, membrane; web. **перепо́нчатый**, membranous; webbed; web-footed.

переправля́ть, -влю *perf.*, **переправля́ть**, -я́ю *imp.* convey, transport; take across; forward; correct; **~ся**, cross, get across.

перепродава́ть, -даю́, -даёшь *imp.*, **перепрода́ть**, -а́м, -а́шь, -а́ст, -ади́м; -про́дал, -а́, -о *perf.* re-sell. **перепрода́жа**, -и, re-sale.

перепроизво́дство, -а, overproduction.

перепры́гивать, -аю *imp.*, **перепры́гнуть**, -ну *perf.* jump, jump over.

перепу́г, -а (-у), fright. **перепуга́ть**, -а́ю *perf.* frighten, give a fright, give a turn; **~ся**, get a fright.

пере|пу́тать, -аю *perf.*, **перепу́тывать**, -аю *imp.* entangle; confuse, mix up, muddle up.

перепу́тье, -я, cross-roads.

перераба́тывать, -аю *imp.*, **перерабо́тать**, -аю *perf.* work up, make; convert; treat; re-make; recast, re-shape; process; work overtime; overwork; **~ся**, overwork.

перераспределе́ние, -я, redistribution. **перераспредели́ть**, -лю́ *perf.*, **перераспределя́ть**, -я́ю *imp.* redistribute.

перераста́ние, -я, outgrowing; escalation; growing (into), development (into). **перераста́ть**, -а́ю imp., **перасти́**, -ту́, -тёшь; -ро́с, -ла́ perf. outgrow, overtop; outstrip; be too old (for); + в + acc. grow into, develop into, turn into.

перерасхо́д, -a, over-expenditure; overdraft. **перерасхо́довать**, -дую perf. and imp. overspend, expend too much of; overdraw.

перерасчёт, -a, recalculation, recomputation.

перерва́ть, -ву́, -вёшь; -а́л, -а́, -о perf. (imp. перерыва́ть) break, tear asunder; ∼ся, break, come apart.

перерегистра́ция, -и, re-registration. **перерегистри́ровать**, -рую perf. and imp. re-register.

переро́зать, -е́жу perf., **перереза́ть**, -а́ю imp., **перере́зывать**, -аю imp. cut; cut off; cut across; break; kill, slaughter.

перереша́ть, -а́ю imp., **перереши́ть**, -шу́ perf. re-solve; decide differently; change one's mind, reconsider one's decision.

перероди́ть, -ожу́ perf., **перерожда́ть**, -а́ю imp. regenerate; ∼ся, be re-born; be regenerated; degenerate. **перерожде́ние**, -я, regeneration; degeneration.

перерос, etc.: see перерасти́. **перерою́**, etc.: see перерыть.

переруба́ть, -а́ю imp., **переруби́ть**, -блю́, -бишь perf. chop in two; cut up, chop up.

переры́в, -a, interruption; interval, break, intermission; с ∼ами, off and on.

перерыва́ть¹(ся, -а́ю(сь imp. of перерва́ть(ся.

перерыва́ть², -а́ю imp., **переры́ть**, -ро́ю perf. dig up; rummage through, search thoroughly.

пересади́ть, -ажу́, -а́дишь perf., **переса́живать**, -аю imp. transplant; graft; seat somewhere else; make change, help change; ∼ че́рез + acc. help across. **переса́дка**, -и, transplantation; grafting; change, changing.

переса́живаться, -аюсь imp. of пересе́сть. **переса́ливать**, -аю imp. of пересоли́ть; пересека́ть(ся, -а́ю(сь imp. of пересе́чь(ся.

переселе́нец, -нца, settler; migrant,

emigrant; immigrant. **переселе́ние**, -я, migration, emigration; immigration, resettlement; move, removal. **пересели́ть**, -лю́ perf., **переселя́ть**, -я́ю imp. move; transplant; resettle; ∼ся, move; migrate.

пересе́сть, -ся́ду perf. (imp. переса́живаться) change one's seat; change, change trains, etc.

пересече́ние, -я, crossing, intersection. **пересе́чь**, -секу́ -сечёшь; -сёк, -ла́ perf. (imp. пересека́ть) cross; traverse; intersect; cut, cut up; ∼ся, cross, intersect.

пере́силивать, -аю imp., **переси́лить**, -лю perf. overpower; overcome; master.

переска́з, -a, (re)telling; exposition. **пересказа́ть**, -ажу́ -а́жешь perf., **переска́зывать**, -аю imp. tell, retell; expound; retail, relate.

переска́кивать, -аю imp., **перескочи́ть**, -чу́, -чишь perf. jump (over), vault (over); skip (over).

пересла́ть, -ешлю́, -шлёшь perf. (imp. пересыла́ть) send; remit; send on, forward.

пересма́тривать, -аю imp., **пересмотре́ть**, -рю́, -тришь perf. revise; reconsider; review. **пересмо́тр**, -a, revision; reconsideration; review; re-trial.

пересоли́ть, -олю́, -о́лишь perf. (imp. переса́ливать) put too much salt in, over-salt; exaggerate, overdo it.

пересо́хнуть, -нет; -о́х perf. (imp. пересыха́ть) dry up, become parched; dry out.

переспа́ть, -плю́; -а́л, -а́, -о perf. oversleep; spend the night; ∼ с + instr. sleep with.

переспе́лый, overripe.

переспо́рить, -рю perf. out-argue, defeat in argument.

переспра́шивать, -аю imp., **переспроси́ть**, -ошу́ -о́сишь perf. ask again; ask to repeat.

пересо́риться, -рюсь perf. quarrel, fall out.

перестава́ть, -таю́, -таёшь imp. of переста́ть.

переста́вить, -влю *perf.*, **переставля́ть**, -я́ю *imp.* move, shift; re-arrange; transpose; ~ часы́ вперёд (наза́д), put the clock forward (back).

перестара́ться, -а́юсь *perf.* overdo it, try too hard.

переста́ть, -а́ну *perf.* (*imp.* переставать) stop, cease.

перестрада́ть, -а́ю *perf.* have suffered, have gone through.

перестра́ивать(ся, -аю(сь *imp.* of перестро́ить(ся.

перестре́лка, -п, exchange of fire; firing; skirmish. **перестреля́ть**, -я́ю *perf.* shoot (down).

перестро́ить, -о́ю *perf.* (*imp.* перестра́ивать) rebuild, reconstruct; re-design, refashion, reshape; reorganize; retune; ~ся, re-form; reorganize oneself; switch over, retune (на+*acc.* to). **перестро́йка**, -и, rebuilding, reconstruction; reorganization; retuning.

переступа́ть, -а́ю *imp.*, **переступи́ть**, -плю́, -пишь *perf.* step over; cross; overstep; ~ с ноги́ на́ ногу, shuffle one's feet.

пересу́ды, -ов *pl.* gossip.

пересчита́ть, -а́ю *perf.*, **пересчи́тывать**, -аю *imp.* (*perf.* also перече́сть) re-count; count; + на + *acc.* convert to, express in terms of.

пересыла́ть, -а́ет *imp.* of пересла́ть. **пересы́лка**, -и, sending, forwarding; ~ беспла́тно, post free; carriage paid; сто́имость пересы́лки, postage. **пересы́льный**, transit.

пересыха́ть, -а́ет *imp.* of пересо́хнуть. **пересяду**, etc.: see пересе́сть. **перета́пливаю**, -аю *imp.* of перетопи́ть.

перета́скивать, -аю *imp.*, **перетащи́ть**, -щу́, -щишь *perf.* drag (over, through); move, remove.

перетере́ть, -тру́, -трёшь, -тёр *perf.*, **перетира́ть**, -а́ю *imp.* wear out, wear down; grind; wipe, dry; ~ся, wear out, wear through.

перетопи́ть, -плю́, -пишь *perf.* (*imp.* перета́пливать) melt.

перетру́, etc.: see перетере́ть.

перетя́гивать, -аю *imp.*, ~ кана́та, tug-of-war. **перетя́гивать**, -аю *imp.*, **перетяну́ть**, -ну́, -нешь *perf.* pull, draw;

attract, win over; outbalance, outweigh; ~ на свою́ сто́рону, win over.

переу́лок, -лка, narrow street; cross-street; lane, passage.

переустро́йство, -а, reconstruction, re-organization.

переутоми́ть, -млю́ *perf.*, **переутомля́ть**, -я́ю *imp.* overtire, overstrain; overwork; ~ся, overtire oneself, over-strain oneself; overwork; be run down. **переутомле́ние**, -я, overstrain; over-work.

переформирова́ть, -ру́ю *perf.*, **переформиро́вывать**, -аю *imp.* re-form.

перехвати́ть, -ачу́, -а́тишь *perf.*, **перехва́тывать**, -аю *imp.* intercept, catch; snatch a bite (of); borrow; go too far, overdo it. **перехва́тчик**, -а, inter-ceptor.

перехитри́ть, -рю́ *perf.* outwit, over-reach.

перехо́д, -а, passage, transition; cross-ing; day's march; going over, conver-sion. **переходи́ть**, -ожу́, -о́дишь *imp.* of перейти́. **перехо́дный**, transitional; transitive; transient. **перехо́дящий**, transient, transitory; intermittent; brought forward, carried over; ~ ку́бок, challenge cup.

пе́рец, -рца, pepper.

перечёл, etc.: see перече́сть.

пе́речень, -чня *m.* list, enumeration.

перечёркивать, -аю *imp.*, **перечеркну́ть**, -ну́, -нёшь *perf.* cross out, cancel.

перече́сть, -чту́, -чтёшь; -чёл, -чла́ *perf.*: see пересчита́ть, перечта́ть.

перечисле́ние, -я, enumeration; list; transfer, transferring. **перечи́слить**, -лю *perf.*, **перечисля́ть**, -я́ю *imp.* enumerate, list; transfer.

перечи́тывать, -аю *perf.*, **перечи́тывать**, -аю *imp.* (*perf.* also перече́сть) re-read.

перечи́ть, -чу *imp.* contradict; cross, go against.

пе́речница, -ы, pepper-pot. **пере́чн|ый**, pepper; ~ая мя́та, peppermint.

перечту́, etc.: see перече́сть. **перечу́**, etc.: see перечи́ть.

переша́гивать, -аю *imp.*, **перешагну́ть**, -ну́, -нёшь *perf.* step over; ~ поро́г, cross the threshold.

перешеёк, -е́йка, isthmus, neck.

перешёл, etc.: see перейти́.

перешёптываться, -аюсь *imp.* whisper (together), exchange whispers.

перешива́ть, -а́ю *imp.*, переши́ть, -шью́, -шьёшь *perf.* alter; have altered. переши́вка, -и, altering, alteration.

перешлю́, etc.: see пересла́ть.

перещеголя́ть, -я́ю *perf.* outdo, surpass.

переэкзамено́вывать, -аю, re-examine; ~ ся, take an examination again.

пери́ла, -ил *pl.* rail, railing(s); handrail; banisters.

пери́на, -ы, feather-bed.

пери́од, -а, period. перио́дика, -и, periodicals, journals. периоди́ческ|ий, periodic; periodical; recurring, recurrent; ~ая дробь, recurring decimal.

пе́ристо-кучево́й, cirro-cumulus. пе́рист|ый, feathery; plumose; pinnate; ~ые облака́, fleecy clouds; cirrus.

перифери́я, -и, periphery; the provinces; outlying districts.

перл, -а, pearl. перламу́тр, -а, mother-of-pearl; nacre. перламу́тров|ый; ~ая пу́говица, pearl button. перло́в|ый; ~ая крупа́, pearl barley.

перма́нент, -а, permanent wave, perm. перма́нентный, permanent.

перна́тый, feathered. перна́тые *sb. pl.* birds. перо́, -а́; *pl.* пе́рья, -ьев, feather; pen; fin; blade, paddle. перочи́нный нож, но́жик, penknife.

перро́н, -а, platform.

перс, -а, Persian. перси́дский, Persian.

пе́рсик, -а, peach.

персия́нин, -а; *pl.* -я́не, -я́н, перси́янка, -и, Persian.

персо́на, -ы, person; со́бственной персо́ной, in person. персона́ж, -а, character; personage. персона́л, -а, personnel, staff. персона́льный, personal; individual; ~ соста́в, staff, personnel.

перспекти́ва, -ы, perspective; vista; prospect; outlook. перспекти́вный, perspective; prospective, forward-looking; long-term; having prospects, promising.

перст, -а́, finger. пе́рстень, -тня *m.* ring; signet-ring.

перфока́рта, -ы, punched card.

пе́рхоть, -и, dandruff; scurf.

перцо́вый, pepper.

перча́тка, -и, glove; gauntlet.

перчи́нка, -и, peppercorn. пе́рчить, -чу *imp.* (*perf.* на~, по~) pepper.

перши́ть, -и́т *imp. impers.*; у меня́ перши́т в го́рле, I have a tickle in my throat.

пёс, пса, dog.

пе́сенник, -а, song-book; (choral) singer; song-writer. пе́сенный, song; of songs.

песе́ц, -сца́, (polar) fox.

пёс|ий, dog; dog's, dogs'; ~ья звезда́, dog-star, Sirius.

песнь, -и; *gen. pl.* -ей, song; canto, book; ~ пе́сней, Song of Songs. пе́сня, -и; *gen. pl.* -сен, song; air.

песо́к, -ска́ (-у́), sand; *pl.* sands, stretches of sand. песо́чница, -ы, sand-box; sand-pit. песо́чн|ый, sand; sandy; short; ~ое пече́нье, ~ое те́сто, shortbread; ~ые часы́, sand-glass, hourglass.

пест, -а́, pestle. пе́стик, -а, pistil; pestle.

пестрота́, -ы́, variegation, diversity of colours; mixed character. пёстрый, motley, variegated, many-coloured, particoloured; colourful.

песча́ник, -а, sandstone. песча́ный, sand, sandy. песчи́нка, -и, grain of sand.

пета́рда, -ы, petard; squib, cracker.

петли́ца, -ы, buttonhole; tab. пе́тля, -и; *gen. pl.* -тель, loop; noose; button-hole; stitch; hinge.

петру́шка¹, -и, parsley.

петру́шка², -и, *m.* Punch; *f.* Punch-and-Judy show; foolishness, absurdity.

пету́х, -а́, cock; встать с ~а́ми, be up with the lark; ~-бое́ц, fighting-cock. пету́ший, петуши́ный, cock, cock's. петушо́к, -шка́, cockerel.

петь, пою́, поёшь *imp.* (*perf.* про~, с~) sing; chant, intone; crow; ~ вполго́лоса, hum.

пехо́та, -ы, infantry, foot. пехоти́нец, -нца, infantryman. пехо́тный, infantry.

печа́лить, -лю *imp.* (*perf.* о~) grieve,

sadden; ~ся, grieve, be sad. печа́ль, -и, grief, sorrow. печа́льный, sad, mournful, sorrowful; sorry, bad.

печа́тание, -я, printing. печа́тать, -аю imp. (perf. на~, от~), print; type; ~ся, write, be published; ~ся be at the printer's. печа́тка, -и, signet, seal, stamp. печа́тн|ый, printing; printer's; printed; ~ые бу́квы, block letters, block capitals; ~ая кра́ска, printer's ink; ~ый лист, quire, sheet; ~ый стано́к, printing-press. печа́ть, -и, seal, stamp; print; printing; type; press.

пече́ние, -я, baking.

печёнка, -и, liver.

печёный, baked.

пе́чень, -и, liver.

пече́нье, -я, pastry; biscuit; cake. пе́чка, -и, stove. печно́й, stove; oven; furnace; kiln. печь, -и, loc. -и́; gen. pl. -е́й, stove; oven; furnace, kiln. печь, пеку́, -чёшь; пёк, -ла́ imp. (perf. ис~), bake; scorch, parch; ~ся, bake; broil.

пешехо́д, -а, pedestrian. пешехо́дн|ый, pedestrian; foot; ~ая доро́жка, ~ая тропа́, footpath; ~ый мост, foot-bridge. пе́шечный, pawn's. пе́ший, pedestrian; unmounted, foot. пе́шка, -и, pawn. пешко́м adv. on foot.

пеще́ра, -ы, cave, cavern; grotto. пеще́ристый, cavernous. пеще́рник, -а, caver, pot-holer. пеще́рный, cave; ~ челове́к, caveman, cave-dweller.

пиани́но n. indecl. (upright) piano.

пивна́я sb. alehouse; pub. пивн|о́й, beer; ~ы́е дро́жжи, brewer's yeast. пи́во, -а, beer, ale. пивова́р, -а, brewer.

пиджа́к, -а́, jacket, coat. пиджа́чн|ый, ~ый костю́м, ~ая па́ра, (lounge-)suit.

пижа́ма, -ы, pyjamas.

пик, -а, peak; часы́ ~, rush-hour.

пи́ка, -и, pike, lance.

пика́нтный, piquant; spicy; savoury.

пика́п, -а, pick-up (van).

пике́ n. indecl. dive.

пике́т, -а, picket; piquet. пике́тчик, -а, picket.

пи́ки, пик pl. spades.

пики́рование, -я, dive, diving. пики́ровать, -рую perf. and imp. (perf. also с~) dive.

пики́роваться, -руюсь imp. exchange caustic remarks, cross swords. пики́ро́вка, -и, altercation, slanging-match.

пики́ро́вщик, -а, dive-bomber. пики́рующий, diving; ~ бомбарди́ро́вщик, dive-bomber.

пи́кнуть perf. squeak, let out a squeak; make a sound.

пи́ковый, of spades; awkward, unfavourable.

пила́, -ы́; pl. -ы, saw; nagger. пилёный, sawed, sawn; ~ са́хар, lump sugar. пили́ть, -лю́, -лишь imp. saw; nag (at). пи́лка, -и, sawing; fret-saw; nail-file. пилообра́зный, serrated, notched.

пило́тка, -и, forage-cap.

пилоти́ровать, -рую imp. pilot. пилоти́руемый, manned.

пилю́ля, -и, pill.

пина́ть, -а́ю imp. (perf. пнуть) kick. пино́к, -нка́, kick.

пинце́т, -а, pincers, tweezers.

пио́н, -а, peony.

пионе́р, -а, pioneer. пионе́рский, pioneer.

пир, -а, loc. -у́; pl. -ы́, feast, banquet. пирова́ть, -ру́ю imp. feast; celebrate.

пиро́г, -а́, pie; tart. пиро́жное sb. pastries; cake, pastry. пирожо́к, -жка́, patty, pastry, pie.

пиру́шка, -и, party, celebration. пи́ршество, -а, feast, banquet; celebration.

писа́ка, -и m. and f. scribbler, quill-driver, pen-pusher. пи́сан|ый, written, manuscript; ~ая краса́вица, as pretty as a picture. писа́рь, -я; pl. -я́ m. clerk. писа́тель, -я m., писа́тельница, -ы, writer, author. писа́ть, пишу́, пи́шешь imp. (perf. на~) write; paint; ~ ма́слом, paint in oils; ~ся, be written; be spelt. писе́ц, -сца́, clerk; scribe.

писк, -а, squeak, cheep, chirp, peep. пискли́вый, пискля́вый, squeaky. пи́скнуть, -ну perf. squeak.

пистоле́т, -а, pistol; gun; ~-пулемёт, sub-machine gun.

пистóн, -а, (percussion-)cap; piston; hollow rivet.

писчебума́жный, writing-paper; stationery; ~ магази́н, stationer's (shop). **пи́сч|ий**, writing; ~ая бума́га, writing paper. **пи́сьменно** *adv.* in writing. **пи́сьменн|ый**, writing, written; в ~ом ви́де, в ~ой фо́рме, in writing; ~ый знак, letter; ~ый стол, writing-table, desk. **письмо́**, -а́; *pl.* -а, -сем, letter; writing; script; hand(-writing). **письмоно́сец**, -сца, postman.

пита́ние, -я, nourishment, nutrition; feeding, feed. **пита́тельн|ый**, nourishing, nutritious; alimentary; feed, feeding; ~ая среда́, culture medium; breeding-ground. **пита́ть**, -а́ю *imp.* (*perf.* на~) feed; nourish; sustain; supply; ~ся, be fed, eat; + *instr.* feed on, live on.

пи́терский, of St. Petersburg.

пито́мец, -мца, foster-child, nursling; charge; pupil; alumnus. **пито́мник**, -а, nursery.

пить, пью, пьёшь; пил, -а́, -о *imp.* (*perf.* вы́~) drink; have, take; мне хо́чется ~, я хочу́ ~, I am thirsty. **питьё**, -я́, drinking; drink, beverage. **питьево́й**, drinkable; ~ая вода́, drinking-water.

пи́хта, -ы, (silver) fir.

пи́чкать, -аю *imp.* (*perf.* на~) stuff, cram.

пи́шущ|ий, writing; ~ая маши́нка, typewriter.

пи́ща, -и, food.

пища́ть, -щу́ *imp.* (*perf.* пи́скнуть) squeak; cheep, peep; whine; sing.

пищеваре́ние, -я digestion; расстро́йство пищеваре́ния, indigestion. **пищево́д**, -а, oesophagus, gullet. **пищев|о́й**, food; ~ые проду́кты, foodstuffs; foods; eatables.

пия́вка, -и, leech.

ПКиО (*pekeió*) *abbr.* парк культу́ры и о́тдыха, Park of Culture and Rest.

пл. *abbr.* пло́щадь, Square.

пла́вание, -я, swimming; sailing; navigation; voyage; су́дно да́льнего пла́вания, ocean-going ship. **пла́вательный**, swimming, bathing; ~ бассе́йн, swimming-bath, pool. **пла́вать**, -аю *imp.* swim; float; sail. **плавба́за**, -ы,

depot ship, factory ship, factory trawler.

плави́льник, -а, crucible. **плави́льный**, melting, smelting; fusion. **плави́льня**, -и, foundry. **плави́льщик**, -а, founder, smelter. **пла́вить**, -влю *imp.* (*perf.* рас~) melt, smelt; fuse; ~ся, melt; fuse. **пла́вка**, -и, fusing; fusion.

пла́вки, -вок *pl.* bathing trunks.

пла́вк|ий, fusible; fuse; ~ая вста́вка, ~ий предохрани́тель, ~ая про́бка, fuse. **плавле́ние**, -я, melting, fusion. **пла́вленый сыр**, processed cheese.

плавни́к, -а́, fin; flipper. **пла́вный**, smooth, flowing; liquid. **плаву́ч|ий**, floating; buoyant; ~ая льди́на, ice-floe; ~ий мая́к, lightship, floating light; ~ий рыбозаво́д, factory ship.

плагиа́т -а, plagiarism. **плагиа́тор**, -а, plagiarist.

плака́т, -а, poster, bill; placard. **плакати́ст**, -а, poster artist.

пла́кать, -а́чу *imp.* cry, weep; cry for, weep for; mourn; ~ навзры́д, sob; ~ся, complain, lament; + на + *acc.* complain of; lament, bewail, bemoan.

плакирова́ть, -ру́ю *perf. and imp.* plate. **плакиро́вка**, -и, plating.

пла́кса, -ы, cry-baby. **плакси́вый**, whining; piteous, pathetic. **плаку́чий**, weeping.

пла́менность, -и, ardour. **пла́менный**, flaming, fiery; ardent, burning. **пла́мя**, -мени *n.* flame; fire, blaze.

план, -а, plan; scheme; plane.

планёр, -а, glider. **планери́зм**, -а, gliding. **планери́ст**, -а, glider-pilot. **планёрный**, gliding; ~ спорт, gliding.

плане́та, -ы, planet. **плане́тный**, planetary.

плани́рование[1], -я, planning.

плани́рование[2], -я, gliding; glide.

плани́ровать[1], -рую *imp.* (*perf.* за~) plan.

плани́ровать[2], -рую *imp.* (*perf.* с~), glide, glide down.

пла́нка, -и, lath, slat.

пла́новый, planned, systematic; planning. **планоме́рный**, systematic, planned, balanced, regular.

планше́т, -а, plane-table; map-case.

пласт, -á, layer; sheet; course; stratum, bed. **пласти́на**, -ы, plate. **пласти́нка**, -и, plate; (gramophone) record, disc.

пласти́ческий, plastic. **пласти́чность**, -и, plasticity. **пласти́чный**, plastic; supple, pliant; rhythmical; fluent, flowing. **пластма́сса**, -ы, plastic. **пластма́ссовый**, plastic.

пла́та, -ы, pay; salary; payment, charge; fee; fare. **платёж**, -á, payment. **платёжеспосо́бный**, solvent. **платёжный**, payment; pay. **плате́льщик**, -а, payer.

пла́тина, -ы, platinum. **пла́тиновый**, platinum.

плати́ть, -ачу́, -а́тишь *imp.* (*perf.* за~, у~) pay; + *instr.* pay back, return; ~ся (*perf.* по~ся) за + *acc.* pay for. **пла́тный**, paid; requiring payment, chargeable; paying.

плато́к, -тка́, shawl; head-scarf; handkerchief.

платфо́рма, -ы, platform; truck.

пла́тье, -я; *gen. pl.* -ьев, clothes, clothing; dress; gown, frock. **платяно́й**, clothes; ~ шкаф, wardrobe.

плафо́н, -а, ceiling; lamp shade, ceiling light; bowl.

плац, -а, *loc.* -у́, parade-ground. **плацда́рм**, -а, bridgehead, beach-head; base; springboard. **плацка́рта**, -ы, reserved-seat ticket.

плач, -а, weeping, crying; wailing; keening; lament. **плаче́вный**, mournful, sad; sorry; lamentable, deplorable. ~ плачу́, etc.: see пла́кать.

плачу́, etc.: see плати́ть.

плашмя́ *adv.* flat, prone.

плащ, -á, cloak; raincoat; waterproof cape.

плева́тельница, -ы, spittoon. **плева́ть**, плюю́, плюёшь *imp.* (*perf.* на~, плю́нуть) spit; ~ в потоло́к, idle, fritter away the time; *impers.* + *dat.*: мне ~, I don't give a damn, I don't care a rap (на + *acc.* about); ~ся, spit.

плево́к, -вка́, spit, spittle.

плеври́т, -а, pleurisy.

плед, -а, rug; plaid.

плёл, etc.: see плести́.

племенно́й, tribal; pedigree. **пле́мя**, -мени; *pl.* -мена́, -мён *n.* tribe; breed; stock. **племя́нник**, -а, nephew. **племя́нница**, -ы, niece.

плен, -а, *loc.* -у́, captivity.

плена́рный, plenary.

плени́тельный, captivating, fascinating, charming. **плени́ть**, -ню́ *perf.* (*imp.* пленя́ть) take prisoner take captive; captivate, fascinate, charm; ~ся, be captivated, be fascinated.

плёнка, -и, film; pellicle.

пле́нник, -а, prisoner, captive. **пле́нный**, captive.

плёночный, film; filmy.

пленя́ть(ся, -я́ю(сь *imp.* of плени́ть(ся.

плесе́нный, mouldy, musty. **пле́сень**, -и, mould.

плеск, -а, splash, plash, lapping. **плеска́тельный бассе́йн**, paddling pool. **плеска́ть**, -ещу́, -е́щешь *imp.* (*perf.* плесну́ть) splash, plash; lap; ~ся, splash; lap.

пле́сневеть, -еет *imp.* (*perf.* за~), go mouldy, grow musty.

плесну́ть, -ну́, -нёшь *perf.* of плеска́ть.

плести́, -ету́, -етёшь; плёл, -á *imp.* (*perf.* с~) plait, braid; weave; tat; spin; net; ~ вздор, ~ чепуху́, talk rubbish; ~сь, drag oneself along; trudge; ~сь в хвосте́, lag behind. **плете́ние**, -я, plaiting, braiding; wickerwork. **плетёнка**, -и, (wicker) mat, basket; hurdle. **плетён**ый, woven; wattled; wicker. **плете́нь**, -тня́ *m.* hurdle; wattle fencing. **плётка**, -и, lash; *cf. pl.* -ей, lash.

пле́чико, -а; *pl.* -и, -ов, shoulder-strap; *pl.* coat-hanger; padded shoulders. **плечи́стый**, broad-shouldered. **плечо́**, -á; *pl.* -и, -а́м, shoulder; arm.

плешиве́ть, -ею *imp.* (*perf.* о~) grow bald. **плеши́вый**, bald. **плеши́на**, -ы, **плешь**, -и, bald patch; bare patch.

плещу́, etc.: see плеска́ть.

плис, -а, velveteen. **пли́совый**, velveteen.

плиссиро́ванный, pleated. **плиссиро́вать**, -ру́ю *imp.* pleat.

плита́, -ы́; *pl.* -ы plate, slab; flag-(stone); stove, cooker; моги́льная ~, gravestone, tombstone. **пли́тка**, -и, tile; (thin) slab; stove, cooker; ~

шокола́да, bar, block, of chocolate. пли́точный, tile, of tiles; ~ пол, tiled floor.

пловéц, -вца́, пловчи́ха, -и, swimmer. пловучий, floating; buoyant.

плод, -á, fruit; приноси́ть ~ы́, bear fruit. плоди́ть, -ожу́ imp. (perf. рас~) produce, procreate; engender; ~ся, multiply; propagate. пло́дный, fertile; fertilized.

плодо- in comb. fruit-. плодови́тый, fruitful, prolific; fertile. ~во́дство, -а, fruit-growing. ~но́сный, fruit-bearing, fruitful. ~овощно́й, fruit and vegetable. ~ро́дный, fertile. ~сменн|ый; ~сме́нная систе́ма, rotation of crops. ~тво́рный, fruitful.

пло́мба, -ы, stamp, seal; stopping; filling. пломбирова́ть, -рую imp. (perf. за~, о~) seal; stop, fill.

пло́ский; -сок, скá, -о, flat; plane; trivial, tame.

пло́ско- in comb. flat. плоскогóрье, -я, plateau; tableland. ~гру́дый, flat-chested. ~гу́бцы, -ев pl. pliers. ~до́нный, flat-bottomed. ~стóпие, -я, flat feet.

пло́скость, -и; gen. pl. -éй, flatness; plane; platitude, triviality.

плот, -á, raft.

плоти́на, -ы, dam; weir; dike, dyke.

пло́тник, -а, carpenter, joiner.

пло́тно adv. close(ly), tight(ly). пло́тность, -и, thickness; compactness; solidity, strength; density. пло́тный; -тен, -тнá, -о, thick; compact; dense; solid, strong; thickset, solidly built; tightly-filled; square, hearty.

плотоя́дный, carnivorous; lustful. плоть -и flesh

пло́хо adv. badly; ill; bad; ~ ко́нчить, come to a bad end; чу́вствовать себя́ ~, feel unwell, feel bad; sb. bad mark. плохова́тый, rather bad, not too good. плохо́й, bad; poor.

площа́дка, -и, area, (sports) ground, playground; site; landing; platform. пло́щадь, -и; gen. pl. -éй, area; space; square.

пло́ще, comp. of пло́ский.

плуг, -а; pl, -и́, plough.

плут, -á, cheat, swindler, knave; rogue. плутова́тый, cunning. плутова́ть, -тую imp. (perf. с~) cheat, swindle. плутовско́й, knavish; roguish, mischievous; picaresque.

плыть, -ыву́, -ывёшь; плыл, -á, -о imp. swim; float; drift; sail; ~ стóя, tread water.

плю́нуть, -ну perf. of плева́ть.

плюс, -а, plus; advantage.

плюш, -а, plush. плю́шевый, plush; plush-covered.

плющ, -á, ivy.

плюю́, etc.: see плева́ть.

пляж, -а, beach.

пляса́ть, -яшу́, -я́шешь imp. (perf. с~) dance. пля́ска, -и, dance; dancing. пля́сово́й, dancing; ~а́я sb. dance tune, dancing song. пляску́н, -á, пляску́нья, -и; gen. pl. -ий, dancer.

пневма́тик, -а, pneumatic tyre. пневмати́ческий, pneumatic.

пнуть, пну, пнёшь perf. of пина́ть. пня, etc.. see пень.

по prep. I. + dat. on; along; round, about; by; over; according to; in accordance with; for; in: at; by (reason of); on account of; from; жить по сре́дствам, live within one's means; идти́ по следáм + gen. follow in the track(s) of; идти́ по траве́, walk on the grass; лу́чший по ка́честву, better in quality; переда́ть по ра́дио, broadcast; по áдресу + gen.., to the address of; по áдресу, by air; по дéлу, on business; по и́мени, by name; по любви́, for love; по ма́тери, on the mother's side; по оши́бке, by mistake; по положе́нию, by one's position; ex officio; по понеде́льникам, on Mondays; по по́чте, by post; по пра́ву, by right, by rights; по происхожде́нию, by descent, by origin; по профе́ссии, by profession; по ра́дио, over the radio; по рассе́янности, from absent-mindedness; по утра́м, in the mornings; това́рищ по шко́ле, schoolfellow; тоскá по до́му, по ро́дине, homesickness; чемпио́н по ша́хматам, chess champion. II. + dat. or acc. of cardinal number, forms distributive number; по́ два, по́ двое, or twos, two by two; по пять рубле́й шту́ка, at five roubles each; по рублю́ шту́ка, one rouble each; по ча́су в день, an hour a day. III. + *acc.* to, up to; for, to get; идти́ по грибы́, go to get mushrooms; по пе́рвое сентября́, up to (and including) the first of September; по по́яс, up to the waist; по ту сто́рону, on that side. IV. + *prep.* on, (immediately) after; by; носи́ть тра́ур, be in mourning for; по нём, to his liking; по прибы́тии, on arrival.

по-¹ *vbl. pref.* forms the perfective aspect; indicates action of short duration or incomplete or indefinite character, and action repeated at intervals or of indeterminate duration.

по-² *pref.* I. in *comb.* with dative case of adjectives, or with adverbs ending in -и, indicates manner of action, conduct, etc., use of a named language, or accordance with the opinion or wish of; говори́ть по-ру́сски, speak Russian; жить по-ста́рому, live in the old style; по-мо́ему, in my opinion. II. in *comb.* with adjectives and nouns, indicates situation along or near something. пово́лжский, situated on the Volga. пово́лжье, -я, the Volga region. помо́ры, -ов *pl.* native Russian inhabitants of White-Sea coasts. помо́рье, -я, seaboard, coastal region. III. in *comb.* with comparative of adjectives indicates a smaller degree of comparison, slightly more (or less) ...; поме́ньше, a little less; помоло́же, rather younger.

по|багрове́ть, -е́ю *perf.*

поба́иваться, -аюсь *imp.* be rather afraid.

побе́г¹, -а, flight; escape.

побе́г², -а, sprout, shoot; sucker; set; graft.

побегу́шки; быть на побегу́шках у + *gen.* run errands for; be at the beck and call of.

побе́да, -ы, victory. победи́тель, -я *m.* victor, conqueror; winner. победи́ть, -и́шь *perf.* (*imp.* побежда́ть) conquer, vanquish; defeat; master, overcome. побе́дный победоно́сный, victorious, triumphant.

побежда́ть, -а́ю *imp.* of победи́ть.
по|беле́ть, -е́ю *perf.* по|бели́ть, -лю́, -е́ли́шь *perf.*

побере́жный, coastal. побере́жье, -я, (sea-)coast, seaboard, littoral.

по|беспоко́ить(ся, -о́ю(сь *perf.*

побира́ться, -а́юсь *imp.* beg; live by begging.

по|би́ть(ся, -бью́(сь, -бьёшь(ся *perf.*
по|благодари́ть, -рю́ *perf.*

по|бледне́ть, -е́ю *perf.* по|блёкнуть, -ну; -блёк *perf.*

поблизости *adv.* near at hand, hereabouts.

по|божи́ться -жу́сь, -жи́шься *perf.*

побо́и, -ев *pl.* beating, blows. побо́ище, -а, slaughter, carnage; bloody battle. побо́рник, -а, champion, upholder, advocate. поборо́ть, -рю́. -решь *perf.* overcome; fight down; beat.

побо́чн|ый, secondary, accessory; collateral; ~ый проду́кт, by-product; ~ая рабо́та, side-line; ~ый сын, natural son.

по|брани́ться, -ню́сь *perf.*

по|брата́ться, -а́юсь *perf.* по-бра́тски *adv.* like a brother; fraternally. побрати́мы, -ов *pl.* twin cities.

по|брезгать, -аю *perf.* по|бри́ть(ся, -бре́ю(сь *perf.*

побуди́тельный, stimulating. побуди́ть, -ужу́ *perf.*, побужда́ть, -а́ю *imp.* induce, impel, prompt, spur. побужде́ние, -я, motive; inducement; incentive.

побыва́ть, -а́ю *perf.* have been, have visited; look in, visit. побы́вка, -и, leave, furlough; прие́хать на побы́вку, come on leave. побы́ть, -бу́ду, -бу́дешь *perf.* (imp. побыва́ть) stay (for a short time).

побыл(сь, etc.: see побы́ть(ся.

повадиться, -а́жу *perf.*, пова́живать, -аю *imp.* accustom; train; ~ся, get into the habit (of). пова́дка, -и, habit.

по|вали́ть(ся, -лю́(сь, -лишь(ся *perf.*

пова́льно *adv.* without exception. пова́льный, general, mass; epidemic.

по́вар, -а; *pl.* -а́, cook, chef. пова́ренный culinary; cookery, cooking.

по-ва́шему *adv.* in your opinion; as you wish.

поведе́ние, -я, conduct, behaviour.

поведу́, etc.: see **повести́.**

повелева́ть, -а́ю *imp.* + *instr.* command, rule; + *dat.* enjoin. **повеле́ние, -я,** command, injunction. **повели́тельный,** imperious, peremptory; authoritative; imperative.

по|венча́ть(ся), -а́ю(сь *perf.*

поверга́ть, -а́ю *imp.,* **пове́ргнуть, -ну; -вёрг** *perf.* throw down; lay low; plunge.

пове́ренная *sb.* confidante. **пове́ренный** *sb.* attorney; confidant; ~ в дела́х, chargé d'affaires. **пове́рить, -рю** *perf.* (*imp.* **поверя́ть**) believe; check, verify; confide, entrust. **пове́рка, -и,** check-up, check; verification; proof; roll-call; ~ вре́мени, time-signal.

поверну́ть, -ну́, -нёшь *perf.,* **повёртывать, -аю** *imp.* (*imp.* also **повора́чивать**) turn; change; ~ся, turn; ~ся спино́й к + *dat.* turn one's back on.

пове́рх *prep.* + *gen.* over, above. **пове́рхностный,** surface, superficial; shallow; perfunctory; ~ое унавожение, top dressing. **пове́рхность, -и** surface.

пове́рье, -я; *gen. pl.* **-ий,** popular belief, superstition. **поверя́ть, -я́ю** *imp.* of **пове́рить.**

по|весели́ть, -е́ю *perf.* **пове́сить(ся, -е́шу(сь** *perf.* of **ве́шать(ся.**

повествова́ние, -я narrative, narration. **повествова́тельный,** narrative. **повествова́ть, -тву́ю** *imp.* + о + *prep.* narrate, recount, relate, tell about.

по|вести́, -еду́ -едёшь; -вёл, -а́ *perf.* (*imp.* also **поводи́ть**) + *instr.* move; ~ бровя́ми, raise one's eyebrows.

пове́стка, -и, notice, notification; summons; writ; signal; last post; ~ (дня), agenda.

по́весть. -и; *gen. pl.* **-е́й,** story, tale.

повéтрие, -я, epidemic; infection.

повéшу, etc.: see **повéсить.** **по|взодри́ть, -рю́** *perf.*

повива́льный, obstetric; ~ая ба́бка, midwife.

по|вида́ть(ся, -а́ю(сь *perf.* **по|вини́ться, -ню́сь** *perf.*

пови́нность, -и, duty, obligation; во́инская ~, conscription. **пови́нный,** guilty, obliged; bound.

повинова́ться, -ну́юсь *perf.* and *imp.* obey. **повинове́ние, -я,** obedience.

повиса́ть, -а́ю *imp.,* **по|ви́снуть, -ну; -вис** *perf.* hang on; hang down, droop; hang; ~ в во́здухе, hang in mid-air.

по|влажне́ть, -е́ет *perf.*

повле́чь, -еку́ -ечёшь; -ёк, -ла́ *perf.* drag; pull behind one; ~ (за собо́й), entail, bring in its train.

по|влия́ть, -я́ю *perf.*

по́вод[1], -а, occasion, cause, ground; по ~у + *gen.* a propos of, as regards, concerning.

по́вод[2], -а, *loc.* **-ý;** *pl.* **-о́дья, -ьев,** rein; быть на ~ý у + *gen.* be under the thumb of. **поводи́ть, -ожу́, -о́дишь** *imp.* of **повести́. пово́док, -дка́,** rein; lead.

пово́зка, -и, cart; vehicle, conveyance; (unsprung) carriage.

пово́лжский, поволжье: see **по-[2]** II.

повора́чивать(ся, -аю(сь *imp.* of **поверну́ть(ся, повороти́ть(ся;** **повора́чивайся, -айтесь!** get a move on! look sharp! look lively!

по|вороши́ть, -жу́ *perf.*

поворо́т, -а, turn, turning; bend; turning-point. **повороти́ть(ся, -рочу́(сь -ро́тишь(ся** *perf.* (*imp.* **повора́чивать(ся)** turn. **повортли́вый,** nimble, agile, quick; manoeuvrable. **поворо́тный,** turning; rotary, rotating; revolving; ~ круг, turntable; ~ мост, swing bridge; ~ пункт, turning point.

по|вреди́ть, -ежу́ *perf.,* **поврежда́ть, -а́ю** *imp.* damage; injure, hurt; ~ся, be damaged; be injured; be hurt. **повреждéние, -я,** damage, injury.

повремени́ть, -ню́ *perf.* wait a little; + с + *instr.* linger over, delay. **повремéнный,** periodic, periodical; by time.

повседнéвно *adv.* daily, every day. **повседнéвный,** daily; everyday.

повсемéстно *adv.* everywhere, in all parts. **повсемéстный,** universal, general.

повста́н**ец**, -нца, rebel, insurgent, insurrectionist. повста́нческий, rebel; insurgent.

повсю́ду adv. everywhere.

повторе́ние, -я, repetition; reiteration. повтори́тельный, repeated; revision. повтори́ть, -рю́ perf., повторя́ть, -я́ю imp. repeat; ~ся, repeat oneself; be repeated; recur. повто́рный, repeated; recurring.

повы́сить, -ы́шу perf., повыша́ть, -а́ю imp. raise, heighten; promote, prefer, advance; ~ в вдво́е, втро́е, double, treble; ~ го́лос, ~ тон, raise one's voice; ~ся, rise; improve; be promoted, receive advancement. повыше́ние, -я, rise, increase; advancement, promotion. повы́шенн|ый, heightened, increased; ~ое настрое́ние, state of excitement; ~ая температу́ра, high temperature.

повяза́ть, -яжу́, -я́жешь perf., повя́зывать, -аю imp. tie. повя́зка, -и, band, bandeau, fillet; bandage.

по|гада́ть, -а́ю perf.

пога́н|ец, -нца, swine; scoundrel. пога́нить, -ню imp. (perf. о~) pollute, defile. пога́нка, -и, toadstool. пога́н|ый, foul; unclean; filthy, vile; ~ гриб, toadstool, poisonous mushroom.

погаса́ть, -а́ю imp., по|га́снуть, -ну perf. go out, be extinguished. по|гаси́ть, -ашу́, -а́сишь perf. погаша́ть, -а́ю imp. liquidate, cancel. пога́шенный, used, cancelled, cashed.

погиба́ть, -а́ю imp., по|ги́бнуть, -ну; -ги́б perf. perish; be lost. поги́бель, -и, ruin, perdition. поги́бельный, ruinous, fatal. поги́бший, lost; ruined; killed; число́ поги́бших, death-roll.

по|гла́дить, -а́жу perf.

поглоти́ть, -ощу́, -о́тишь perf., по|глоща́ть, -а́ю imp. swallow up; take up; absorb.

по|глупе́ть, -е́ю perf.

по|гляде́ть, -яжу́ (ся perf. погля́дывать, -аю imp. glance; look from time to time; + за + instr. keep an eye on.

погна́ть, -гоню́ -го́нишь; -гна́л, -а́, -о perf. drive; begin to drive; ~ся за + instr. run after; start in pursuit of, give chase to; strive for, strive after.

по|гну́ть(ся), -ну́(сь, -нёшь(ся perf. по|гнуша́ться, -а́юсь perf.

погово́рка, -и, saying, proverb; byword.

пого́да, -ы, weather.

погоди́ть, -ожу́ perf. wait a little, wait a bit; немно́го погодя́, a little later.

поголо́вно adv. one and all; to a man. поголо́вный, general, universal; capitation, poll. поголо́вье, -я, head, number.

по|голубе́ть, -е́ет perf.

пого́н, -а; gen. pl. -о́н, shoulder-strap; (rifle-)sling.

пого́нщик, -а, driver. пого́ню, etc.: see погна́ть. пого́ня, -и, pursuit, chase. погоня́ть, -я́ю imp. urge on, drive.

погора́ть, -а́ю imp., погоре́ть, -рю́ perf. burn down; be burnt out; lose everything in a fire. погоре́лец, -льца, one who has been burnt out.

пограни́чн|ик, -а, frontier guard. пограни́чн|ый, frontier; boundary; ~ая полоса́, border; ~ая стра́жа, frontier guards.

по́греб, -а; pl. -а́, cellar. погреба́льн|ый, funeral; ~ая колесни́ца, hearse. погреба́ть, -а́ю imp. of погрести́. погребе́ние, -я, burial.

погрему́шка, -и, rattle.

погрести́[1], -ебу́, -ебёшь; -рёб, -ла́ perf. (imp. погреба́ть) bury.

погрести́[2], -ебу́, -ебёшь; -рёб, -ла́ perf. row for a while.

погре́ть, -е́ю perf. warm; ~ся, warm oneself.

погреша́ть, -а́ю imp., по|греши́ть, -шу́ perf. sin; err. погре́шность, -и, error, mistake, inaccuracy.

по|грози́ть(ся, -ожу́(сь perf. по|грубе́ть, -е́ю perf.

погружа́ть, -а́ю imp., по|грузи́ть, -ужу́, -у́зишь perf. load; ship; dip, plunge, immerse; submerge; duck; ~ся, sink, plunge; submerge, dive; be plunged, absorbed, buried, lost. погруже́ние, -я, sinking, submergence; immersion; dive, diving. погру́зка, -и, loading; shipment.

погря́зать, -а́ю imp., по|гря́знуть, -ну; -я́з perf. be bogged down, be stuck.

по|губи́ть, -блю́, -бишь perf. по|-гуля́ть, -я́ю perf. по|густе́ть, -е́ет perf.

под; подо prep. I. + acc. or instr. under; near, close to; быть ~ ружьём, be under arms; взять по́д руку + acc. take the arm of; ~ ви́дом + gen. under the guise of; по́д гору, down hill; ~ замко́м, under lock and key; ~ землёй, underground; ~ Москво́й, in the neighbourhood of Moscow; ~ руко́й, (close) at hand, to hand. II. + instr. occupied by, used as; (meant, implied) by; in, with; говя́дина ~ хре́-ном, beef with horse-radish; по́ле ~ карто́фелем potato-field. III. + acc. towards; on the eve of; to (the accompaniment of); in imitation of; on; for, to serve as; ему́ ~ пятьдеся́т (лет), he is getting on for fifty; ~ аплодисме́нты, to applause; ~ ве́чер, towards evening; подде́лка ~ же́мчуг, fake pearls; ~ дикто́вку, from dictation; ~ зву́ки му́зыки, to the sound of music; ~ коне́ц, towards the end; ~ Но́вый год, on New Year's Eve; шу́ба ~ ко́тик, imitation sealskin coat.

под-, подо-, подъ-. I. vbl. pref. indicating action from beneath or affecting lower part of something, motion upwards or towards a point, slight or insufficient action or effect, supplementary action, underhand action. II. pref. of nouns and adjs., under-, sub-.

подава́льщик, -a, waiter; supplier. подава́льщица, -ы, waitress. подава́ть(ся, -даю́(сь, -даёшь(ся imp. of пода́ть(ся.

подави́ть, -влю́, -вишь perf., подавля́ть, -я́ю imp. suppress, put down; repress; depress; crush, overwhelm. по|дави́ться, -влю́сь, -вишься perf. подавле́ние, -я, suppression; repression. пода́вленность, -и, depression; blues. пода́вленный, suppressed; depressed, dispirited. подавля́ющ|ий, overwhelming; overpowering; ~ee большинство́, overwhelming majority.

пода́вно adv. much less, all the more.

пода́льше adv. a little further.

по|дари́ть, -рю́, -ришь perf. пода́рок, -рка, present gift.

пода́тель, -я m. bearer; ~ проше́ния, petitioner. пода́тливый, pliant, pliable; complaisant. пода́ть, -и; gen. pl. -éй, tax duty, assessment. пода́ть, -а́м, -а́шь, -а́ст, -ади́м; по́дал, -á, -o perf. (imp. подава́ть) serve; give; put, move, turn; put forward, present, hand in; display; обе́д по́дан, dinner is served; ~ в отста́вку, send in one's resignation; ~ в суд на + acc., bring an action against; ~ го́лос, vote; ~ жа́лобу, lodge a complaint; ~ заявле́ние, hand in an application; ~ мяч, serve; ~ ру́ку, hold out one's hand; ~ телегра́мму, send a telegram; ~ся, move; give way, yield; cave in, collapse; ~ на + acc. make for, set out for; ~ся в сто́рону, move aside; ~ся наза́д, draw back. пода́ча, -и, giving, presenting; service, serve; feed, supply; introduction; ~ голосо́в, voting. пода́чка, -и, (charitable) gift; pittance. пода́й, etc.: see подава́ть. подая́ние, -я, charity, alms; dole.

подбега́ть, -а́ю imp., подбежа́ть, -eгу́ perf. run up, come running up.

подбива́ть, -а́ю imp. of подби́ть. подби́вка, -и, lining; re-soling.

подберу́, etc.: see подобра́ться. подбира́ть(ся, -а́ю(сь imp. of подобра́ть(ся.

подби́тый, bruised; lined; padded; ~ глаз, black eye. подби́ть, -добью́, -добьёшь perf. (imp. подбива́ть), line; pad, wad; re-sole; injure, bruise; put out of action, knock out, shoot down; incite. instigate.

подбодри́ть, -рю́ perf., подбодря́ть, -я́ю imp., cheer up, encourage; ~ся, cheer up, take heart.

подбо́йка, -и, lining; re-soling.

подбо́р, -a, selection. assortment; в ~ run on; (как) на ~, choice, well--matched.

подборо́док, -дка. chin.

подбоче́ниваться, -аюсь imp. подбоче́-ниться, -нюсь perf. place one's arms akimbo. подбоче́нившись adv. with arms akimbo, with hands on hips.

подбра́сывать, -аю *imp.*, подбро́сить, -ро́шу *perf.* throw up, toss up; throw in, throw on; abandon, leave surreptitiously.

подва́л, -а, cellar; basement; (article appearing at) foot of page. подва́льный, basement, cellar.

подведу́, etc.: see подвести́.

подвезти́, -зу́, -зёшь; -вёз, -ла́ *perf.* (*imp.* подвози́ть) bring, take; give a lift.

подвене́чн|ый, wedding; ~ое пла́тье, wedding-dress.

подверга́ть, -а́ю *imp.*, подве́ргнуть, -ну; -ве́рг *perf.* subject; expose; ~ опа́сности, expose to danger; ~ сомне́нию, call in question. подве́рженный subject, liable; susceptible.

подве́сить, -е́шу *perf.* (*imp.* подве́шивать) hang up, suspend; ~ся, hang, be suspended. подвесно́й, hanging, overhead; suspension; ~ дви́гатель, мото́р, outboard motor, engine.

подвести́, -еду́, -едёшь; -вёл, -а́ *perf.* (*imp.* подводи́ть) lead up, bring up; place (under); bring under, subsume; put together; let down; ~ ито́ги, reckon up; sum up; ~ фунда́мент, underpin.

подве́шивать(ся, -аю(сь *imp.* of подве́сить(ся.

по́двиг, -а, exploit, feat; heroic deed.

подвига́ть(ся, -а́ю(сь *imp.* of подви́нуть(ся.

подвижно́й, mobile; movable; travelling; lively; agile; ~ соста́в, rolling-stock. подви́жный, mobile; lively; agile.

подвиза́ться, -а́юсь *imp.* (в or на + *prep.*) work (in), make a career (in).

подви́нуть, -ну *perf.* (*imp.* подвига́ть) move; push; advance, push forward; ~ся, move; advance, progress.

подвла́стный + *dat.* subject to; under the jurisdiction of.

подво́да, -ы, cart. подводи́ть, -ожу́, -о́дишь *imp.* of подвести́.

подво́дник, -а, submariner. подво́дн|ый, submarine; underwater; ~ая скала́ reef.

подво́з, -а, transport; supply. под-

вози́ть, -ожу́, -о́зишь *imp.* of подвезти́.

подворо́тня, -и; *gen. pl.* -тен, gateway.

подво́х, -а, trick.

подвы́пивший, a bit tight.

подвяза́ть, -яжу́, -я́жешь *perf.*, подвя́зывать, -аю *imp.* tie up; keep up. подвя́зка, -и, garter; suspender.

подгиба́ть(ся, -а́ю(сь *imp.* of подогну́ть(ся.

подгляде́ть, -яжу́ *perf.*, подгля́дывать, -аю *imp.* peep; spy, watch furtively.

подгова́ривать, -аю *imp.*, подговори́ть, -рю́ *perf.* put up, incite, instigate.

подголо́сок, -ска, second part, supporting voice; yes-man.

подгоню́, etc.: see подгна́ть. подгоня́ть, -я́ю *imp.* of подогна́ть.

подгора́ть, -а́ет *imp.*, подгоре́ть, -ри́т *perf.* get a bit burnt. подгоре́лый, slightly burnt.

подготови́тельный, preparatory. подгото́вить, -влю *perf.*, подготовля́ть, -я́ю *imp.* prepare; ~ по́чву, pave the way; ~ся, prepare, get ready. подгото́вка, -и, preparation; training; grounding, schooling. подгото́вленность, -и, preparedness.

поддава́ться, -даю́сь, -даёшься *imp.* of подда́ться.

подда́кивать, -аю *imp.* agree, assent.

по́дданный *sb.* subject; national. по́дданство, -а, citizenship, nationality. подда́ться, -а́мся, -а́шься, -а́стся, -ади́мся; -а́лся, -лась *perf.* (*imp.* поддава́ться) yield, give way, give in; не ~ описа́нию, beggar description.

подде́лать, -аю *perf.*, подде́лывать, -аю *imp.* counterfeit, falsify, fake; forge; fabricate. подде́лка, -и, falsification; forgery; counterfeit; imitation, fake; ~ под жемчуг, artificial pearls. подде́льный, false, counterfeit; forged; sham, spurious.

подде́ржание, -я, maintenance, support. поддержа́ть, -жу́, -жишь *perf.*, подде́рживать, -аю *imp.* support; back up, second; keep up, maintain; bear; ~ поря́док, maintain order. подде́ржка, -и, support; encouragement, backing; seconding; prop, stay; при подде́ржке + *gen.* with the support of.

поддра́знивать, -аю *imp.*, поддразни́ть, -ню́, -нишь *perf.* tease (slightly).

поддува́ло, -а, ash-pit.

по|де́йствовать, -твую *perf.*

поде́лать, -аю *perf.* do; ничего́ не поде́лаешь, it can't be helped, there's nothing to be done about it.

по|дели́ть(ся, -лю́(сь, -лишь(ся *perf.*

поде́лка, -и, *pl.* small (hand-made) articles.

подело́м *adv.*; ~ ему́ (etc.), it serves him (etc.) right.

подённо *adv.*, подённый, by the day; подённая опла́та, payment by the day. подёнщик, -а, day-labourer; workman hired by the day. подёнщица, -ы, daily, char.

подёргивание, -я, twitch, twitching; jerk. подёргиваться, -аюсь *imp.* twitch.

подёржанный, second-hand.

подёрнуть, -нет *perf.* cover, coat; ~ся, be covered.

подеру́, etc.: see подра́ть. по|дешеве́ть, -е́ет *perf.*

поджа́ривать(ся, -аю(сь *imp.*, поджа́рить(ся, -рю(сь *perf.* fry, roast, grill; brown, toast. поджа́ристый, brown, browned; crisp.

поджа́рый, lean, wiry, sinewy.

поджа́ть, -дожму́, -дожмёшь *perf.* (*imp.* поджима́ть) draw in, draw under; ~ гу́бы, purse one's lips; ~ хвост, have one's tail between one's legs.

поджечь, -дожгу́, -ожжёшь; -жёг, -дожгла́ *perf.* (*imp.* поджига́ть, -а́ю *imp.* set fire to, set on fire; burn. поджига́тель, -я *m.* incendiary; instigator; ~ войны́, warmonger. поджига́тельский, inflammatory.

поджида́ть, -а́ю *imp.* (+ *gen.*) wait (for); lie in wait (for).

поджима́ть, -а́ю *imp.* of поджа́ть.

поджо́г, -а, arson.

подзаголо́вок, -вка, subtitle, sub-heading.

подзадо́ривать, -аю *imp.*, подзадо́рить, -рю *perf.* egg on, set on.

подзащи́тный *sb.* client.

подземе́лье, -я; *gen. pl.* -лий, cave, dungeon. подзе́мка, -и, underground,

tube. подзе́мный, underground, subterranean.

подзо́рн|ый; ~ая труба́ telescope.

подзову́, etc.: see подозва́ть. подзыва́ть, -а́ю *imp.* of подозва́ть.

подиви́ть, -влю́ *perf.* astonish, amaze. по|диви́ться, -влю́сь *perf.*

подка́пывать(ся, -аю(сь *imp.* of подкопа́ть(ся.

подкарау́ливать, -аю *imp.*, подкарау́лить, -лю *perf.* be on the watch (for), lie in wait (for); catch.

подка́рмливать, -аю *imp.* of подкорми́ть.

подкати́ть, -ачу́, -а́тишь *perf.*, подка́тывать, -аю *imp.* roll up, drive up; roll.

подка́шивать(ся, -аю(сь *imp.* of подкоси́ть(ся.

подки́дывать, -аю *imp.*, подки́нуть, -ну *perf.* throw up, toss up; throw in, throw on; abandon. подки́дыш, -а, foundling.

подкла́дка, -и, lining; на шёлковой подкла́дке, silk-lined. подкла́дочный, lining. подкла́дывать, -аю *imp.* of подложи́ть.

подкле́ивать, -аю *imp.*, подкле́ить, -е́ю *perf.* glue, paste; glue up, paste up; stick together, mend. подкле́йка, -и, glueing, pasting; sticking.

подко́ва, -ы, (horse-)shoe. под|кова́ть, -кую́, -ёшь *perf.*, подко́вывать, -аю *imp.* shoe.

подко́жный, subcutaneous, hypodermic.

подкоми́ссия, -и, подкомите́т, -а, sub-committee.

подко́п, -а, undermining; underground passage; intrigue, underhand plotting. подкопа́ть, -а́ю *perf.* (*imp.* подка́пывать), undermine, sap; ~ся под + *acc.* undermine, sap; burrow under; intrigue against.

подкорми́ть, -млю́ -мишь *perf.* (*imp.* подка́рмливать) top-dress, give a top-dressing; feed up. подко́рмка, -и, top-dressing.

подкоси́ть, -ошу́, -о́сишь *perf.* (*imp.* подка́шивать) cut down; fell, lay low; ~ся, give way, fail one.

подкра́дываться, -аюсь *imp.* of подкра́сться.

подкра́сить, -а́шу perf. (imp. подкра́шивать), touch up; tint, colour; ~ся, make up lightly.

подкра́сться, -адусь, -адёшься perf. (imp. подкра́дываться) steal up, sneak up.

подкра́шивать(ся, -аю(сь imp. of подкра́сить(ся. подкра́шу, etc.: see подкра́сить.

подкрепи́ть, -плю́ perf., подкрепля́ть, -я́ю imp. reinforce; support; back; confirm, corroborate; fortify recruit the strength of; ~ся, fortify oneself. подкрепле́ние, -я, confirmation, corroboration; sustenance; reinforcement.

подку́п, -а, bribery. подкупа́ть, -а́ю imp., подкупи́ть, -плю́, -пишь perf. bribe; suborn; win over.

подлади́ться, -а́жусь perf., подла́живаться -аюсь imp. + к + dat. adapt oneself to, fit in with; humour; make up to.

подла́мываться, -ается imp. of подломи́ться.

по́дле prep. + gen. by the side of, beside.

подлежа́ть, -жу́ imp. + dat. be liable to, be subject to; не подлежи́т сомне́нию, it is beyond doubt; unquestionably. подлежа́щий sb. subject. подлежа́щий + dat. liable to, subject to; не ~ огла́шению, confidential, private; off the record.

подле́зть, -а́ю imp., подле́зть, -зу, -зз perf. crawl (under), creep (under).

подле́ц, -а́, scoundrel, villain.

подлива́ть, -а́ю imp. of подли́ть. подли́вка, -и, sauce, dressing; gravy. подливн|о́й, -о́е колесо́ undershot wheel.

подлиза́, -ы m. and f. lickspittle, toady. подлиза́ться, -ижусь, -ижешься perf., подли́зываться, -аюсь imp. + к + dat. make up to, suck up to; wheedle.

по́длинник, -а, original. по́длинно adv. really; genuinely. по́длин|ый, genuine; authentic; original; true, real; с ~ым ве́рно, certified true copy.

подли́ть, -долью́, -дольёшь; по́дли́л, -а́, -о perf. (imp. подлива́ть) pour; add; ~ ма́сла в ого́нь, add fuel to the flames.

подло́г, -а, forgery.

подложи́ть, -жу́, -жишь perf. (imp. подкла́дывать) add; + под + acc. lay under; line.

подло́жный, false, spurious; counterfeit, forged.

подломи́ться, -о́мится perf. (imp. подла́мываться) break; give way under one.

по́длость, -и, meanness, baseness; mean trick, low trick.

подлу́нный, sublunar.

по́длый; подл, -а́, -о, mean, base, ignoble.

подма́зать, -а́жу perf., подма́зывать, -аю imp. grease, oil; paint; give bribes, grease palms.

подманда́тный, mandated.

подмасте́рье, -я; gen. pl. -ьев m. apprentice.

подме́н, -а, подме́на, -ы, replacement. подме́нивать, -аю imp., подмени́ть, -ню́, -нишь perf., подменя́ть, -я́ю imp. replace.

подмести́, -ету́, -етёшь; -мёл, -а́ perf., подмета́ть[1], -а́ю imp. sweep.

подмета́ть[2], -а́ю perf. (imp. подмёты-вать) baste, tack.

подме́тить, -е́чу perf. (imp. подмеча́ть) notice.

подме́тка, -и, sole.

подмётывать, -аю imp. of подмета́ть[2]. подмеча́ть, -а́ю imp. of подме́тить.

подме́шивать, -аю imp., подме́сить, -аю imp. mix in, stir in.

подми́гивать, -аю imp., подмигну́ть, -ну́, -нёшь perf. + dat. wink at.

подмо́га, -и, help, assistance; идти́ на подмо́гу, lend a hand.

подмока́ть, -а́ет imp., подмо́кнуть, -нет; -мо́к perf. get damp, get wet.

подмора́живать, -ает imp., подморо́зить, -зит perf. freeze. подморо́жен-ный, frost-bitten, frozen.

подмо́стки, -ов pl. scaffolding, staging; stage.

подмо́ченный, damp; tarnished, tainted, blemished.

подмы́в, -а, washing away, undermining. подмыва́ть, -а́ю imp., подмы́ть, -о́ю perf. wash; wash away, undermine; его́ так и подмыва́ет, he feels an urge (to), he can hardly help (doing).

подмы́шка, -и, armpit. подмы́шник, -а, dress-protector.

поднево́льный, dependent; subordinate; forced.

поднести́, -су́, -сёшь; -ёс, -ла́ perf. (imp. подноси́ть) present; take, bring.

поднима́ть(ся, -а́ю(сь imp. of подня́ть-(ся.

поднови́ть, -влю́ perf., подновля́ть, -я́ю imp. renew, renovate.

подно́жие, -я, foot; pedestal. подно́жка, -и, step; running-board. подно́жный; ~ корм, pasture.

подно́с, -а, tray; salver. подноси́ть, -ошу́, -о́сишь imp. of поднести́. подноше́ние, -я, giving; present, gift.

подня́тие, -я, raising; rise; rising. подня́ть, -ниму́, -ни́мешь; по́днял, -á, -о perf. (imp. поднима́ть, подыма́ть) raise; lift (up); hoist; pick up; rouse, stir up; open up; improve, enhance; ~ на смех, hold up to ridicule; ~ пе́тли, pick up stitches; ~ ору́жие, take up arms; ~ целину́, break fresh ground; open up virgin lands; ~ся, rise; go up; get up; climb, ascend; arise; break out, develop; improve; recover.

подо: see под. подо-: see под-.

подоба́ть, -а́ет imp. be becoming, be fitting. подоба́ющий, proper, fitting.

подо́бие, -я, likeness; similarity. подо́бн|ый, like, similar; и тому́ ~ое, and the like, and so on, and such like; ничего́ ~ого! nothing of the sort!

подобостра́стие, -я, servility. подобостра́стный, servile.

подобра́ть, -дберу́, -дберёшь; -бра́л, -á, -о perf. (imp. подбира́ть) pick up; tuck up, put up; select, pick; ~ся, steal up, approach stealthily; make oneself tidy.

подобью́, etc.: see подби́ть.

подогна́ть, -дгоню́, -дго́нишь; -а́л, -á, -о perf. (imp. подгоня́ть) drive; drive on, urge on, hurry; adjust, fit.

подогну́ть, -ну́, -нёшь perf. (imp. подгиба́ть) tuck in; bend under; ~ся, bend.

подогрева́ть, -а́ю imp., подогре́ть, -е́ю perf. warm up, heat up; arouse.

подвига́ть, -а́ю imp., подви́нуть, -ну perf. move up, push up.

пододея́льник, -а, quilt cover, blanket cover; top sheet.

подожгу́, etc.: see подже́чь.

подожда́ть, -ду́, -дёшь; -а́л, -á, -о perf. wait (+ gen. or acc. for).

подожму́, etc.: see поджа́ть.

подзыва́ть, -зову́, -зовёшь; -а́л, -á, -о perf. (imp. подзыва́ть) call up; beckon.

подозрева́емый, suspected; suspect. подозрева́ть, -а́ю imp. suspect. подозре́ние, -я, suspicion. подозри́тельный, suspicious; suspect; shady, fishy.

по|дои́ть, -ою́, -о́ишь perf. подо́йник, -а milk-pail.

подойти́, -йду́, -йдёшь; -ошёл, -шла́ perf. (imp. подходи́ть) approach; come up, go up; + dat. do for; suit, fit.

подоко́нник, -а, window-sill.

подо́л, -а, hem; lower part, lower slopes, foot.

подо́лгу adv. for a long time; for ages; for hours (etc.) together.

подолью́, etc.: see подли́ть.

подо́нки, -ов pl. dregs; scum.

подоплёка, -и, underlying cause, hidden motive.

подопру́, etc.: see подпере́ть.

подо́пытный, experimental; ~ кро́лик, guinea-pig.

подорва́ть, -рву́, -рвёшь; -а́л, -á, -о perf. (imp. подрыва́ть) undermine, sap; damage severely; blow up; blast.

по|дорожа́ть, -а́ет perf.

подоро́жник, -а, plantain; provisions for a journey. подоро́жный, on the road; along the road; ~ столб, milestone.

подосла́ть, -ошлю́, -ошлёшь perf. (imp. подсыла́ть) send (secretly).

подоспева́ть, -а́ю imp. подоспе́ть, -е́ю perf. arrive, appear (at the right moment).

подостла́ть, -дстелю́, -дсте́лешь perf. (imp. подстила́ть) lay underneath.

подотде́л, -а, section, subdivision.

подотру́, etc.: see подтере́ть.

подотчётный accountable; on account.

по|до́хнуть, -ну perf. (imp. also подыха́ть) die; peg out, kick the bucket.

подохо́дный; ~ нало́г, income-tax.

подо́шва, -ы, sole; foot; base.

подойдёт, etc.: see подойти́. подошлю́, etc.: see подосла́ть. подошью́, etc.: see подши́ть. подпада́ть, -а́ю *imp.* of подпа́сть. подпа́ивать, -аю *imp.* of подпои́ть.

подпа́сть, -аду́, -адёшь; -а́л *perf. (imp.* подпада́ть) под + *acc.* fall under; ~ под влия́ние + *gen.* fall under the influence of.

подпева́ла, -ы *m.* and *f.* yes-man.

подпере́ть, -допру́; -пёр *perf. (imp.* подпира́ть) prop up.

подпи́ливать, -аю *imp.*, подпили́ть, -лю́, -лишь *perf.* saw; saw a little off; file, file down. подпи́лок, -лка, file.

подпира́ть, -а́ю *imp.* of подпере́ть.

подписа́вший *sb.* signatory. подписа́ние, -я, signing, signature. подписа́ть, -ишу́, -и́шешь *perf.*, подпи́сывать, -аю *imp.* sign; write underneath, add; ~ ся, sign; subscribe. подпи́ска, -и, -и, subscription; engagement, written undertaking; signed statement. подписно́й, subscription; ~ лист, subscription list. подпи́счик, -а, a subscriber. по́дпись, -и, signature; caption; inscription; за ~ю + *gen.* signed by; за ~ю и печа́тью, signed and sealed.

подпои́ть, -ою́, -ои́шь *perf. (imp.* подпа́ивать) make tipsy.

подполко́вник, -а, lieutenant-colonel.

подпо́лье, -я, cellar; underground. подпо́льный, under the floor; underground.

подпо́ра, -ы, подпо́рка, -и, prop, support; brace, strut.

подпры́гивать, -аю *imp.*, подпры́гнуть, -ну *perf.* leap up, jump up.

подпуска́ть, -а́ю *imp.*, подпусти́ть, -ущу́, -у́стишь *perf.* allow to approach; add in; get in, put in; ~ шпи́льку, sting.

подража́ние, -я, imitation. подража́ть, -а́ю *imp.* imitate.

подразде́л, -а, a subsection. подразделе́ние, -я, subdivision; sub-unit. подраздели́ть, -лю́ *perf.*, подразделя́ть, -я́ю subdivide.

подразумева́ть, -а́ю *imp.* imply, mean;

~ ся, be implied, be meant, be understood.

подраста́ть, -а́ю *imp.*, подрасти́, -ту́, -тёшь; -ро́с, -ла́ *perf.* grow.

по|дра́ть(ся, -деру́(сь, -дерёшь(ся, -а́л-(ся, -а́(сь, -о́(сь *perf.* or -ось *perf.*

подре́зать, -е́жу *perf.*, подреза́ть, -а́ю *imp.* cut; clip, trim; prune, lop; + *gen.* cut (off) more of.

подро́бно *adv.* minutely, in detail; at (great) length. подро́бность, -и, detail; minuteness. подро́бный, detailed, minute.

подровня́ть, -я́ю *perf.* level, even; trim.

подро́с, etc.: see подрасти́. подросто́к, -тка, adolescent; teenager; youth, young girl.

подро́ю, etc.: see подры́ть.

подруба́ть[1], -а́ю *imp.*, подруби́ть, -блю́, -бишь *perf.* chop down; cut short(er); hew.

подруба́ть[2], -а́ю *imp.*, подруби́ть, -блю́, -бишь *perf.* hem.

подру́га, -и, friend. по-дру́жески *adv.* in a friendly way; as a friend. по|дружи́ться, -жу́сь *perf.*

подру́ливать, -аю *imp.*, подрули́ть, -лю́ *perf.* taxi up.

подру́чный, at hand, to hand; improvised, makeshift; *sb.* assistant, mate.

подры́в, -а, undermining; injury, blow, detriment.

подрыва́ть[1], -а́ю *imp.* of подорва́ть.

подрыва́ть[2], -а́ю *imp.*, подры́ть, -ро́ю *perf.* undermine, sap. подрывно́й, blasting, demolition; undermining; subversive.

подря́д *adv.* in succession; running; on end.

подря́д, -а, contract. подря́дный, (done by) contract. подря́дчик, -а, contractor.

подса́живаться, -аюсь *imp.* of подсе́сть.

подсве́чник, -а, candlestick.

подсе́сть, -ся́ду; -се́л *perf. (imp.* подса́живаться) sit down, take a seat (к + *dat.* by, near, next to).

под|сини́ть, -ню́ *perf.*

подсказа́ть, -ажу́, -а́жешь *perf.*, подска́зывать, -аю *imp.* prompt; suggest. подска́зка, -и, prompting.

подска́кивать, -аю *imp.*, подскочи́ть, -чу́, -чишь *perf.* jump (up), leap up, soar; run up, come running.

подслепова́тый, weak-sighted.

подслу́шать, -аю *perf.*, подслу́шивать, -аю *imp.* overhear; eavesdrop, listen.

подсма́тривать, -аю *imp.* of подсмотре́ть.

подсме́иваться, -аюсь *imp.* над + *instr.* laugh at, make fun of.

подсмотре́ть, -рю́, -ришь *perf.* (*imp.* подсма́тривать) spy (on).

подсне́жник, -а, snowdrop.

подсо́бный, subsidiary, supplementary; secondary; auxiliary; accessory.

подсо́вывать, -аю *imp.* of подсу́нуть.

подсозна́ние, -я, subconscious (mind). подсозна́тельный, subconscious.

подсо́лнечник, -а, sunflower. подсо́лнечн|ый, sunflower; ~ое ма́сло, sunflower(-seed) oil. подсо́лнух, -а, sunflower; sunflower seed.

подсо́хнуть, -ну *perf.* (*imp.* подсыха́ть) get dry, dry out a little.

подспо́рье, -я, help, support.

подста́вить, -влю *perf.*, подставля́ть, -я́ю *imp.* put (under), place (under); bring up, put up; hold up; expose, lay bare; substitute; ~ но́жку + *dat.* trip up. подста́вка, -и, stand; support, rest, prop. подставн|о́й, false; substitute; ~о́е лицо́, dummy, figure-head.

подстака́нник, -а, glass-holder.

подстела́ть, etc.: see подстла́ть.

подстерега́ть, -а́ю *imp.*, подстере́чь, -егу́, -ежёшь; -рёг, -ла́ *perf.* be on the watch for, lie in wait for.

подстила́ть, -а́ю *imp.* of подостла́ть. подсти́лка, -и, bedding; litter.

подстра́ивать, -аю *imp.* of подстро́ить. одстрека́тель, -я *m.* instigator. подпстрека́тельство, -а, instigation, incitement, setting-on. подстрека́ть, -а́ю *imp.*, подстрекну́ть, -ну́, -нёшь *perf.* instigate, incite, set on; excite.

подстре́ливать, -аю *imp.*, подстрели́ть, -лю́, -лишь *perf.* wound; wing.

подстрига́ть, -а́ю *imp.*, подстри́чь, -игу́, -ижёшь; -иг *perf.* cut; clip, trim; prune; ~ся, trim one's hair; have a hair-cut, a trim.

подстро́ить, -о́ю *perf.* (*imp.* подстра́ивать) build on; tune (up); arrange, contrive.

подстро́чн|ый, interlinear; literal; word--for-word; ~ое примеча́ние, footnote.

по́дступ, -а, approach. подступи́ть, -плю́ -пишь *perf.* approach, come up, come near; ~ся к + *dat.* approach.

подсуди́мый *sb.* defendant; the accused. подсу́дн|ый + *dat.* under the jurisdiction of, within the competence of; ~ое де́ло, punishable offence.

подсчёт, -а, calculation; count. подсчита́ть, -а́ю *perf.*, подсчи́тывать, -аю, count (up); calculate.

подсыла́ть, -а́ю *imp.* of подосла́ть. подсыпа́ть, -а́ю *imp.* of подсо́вывать. подся́ду, etc.: see подсе́сть. подта́лкивать, -аю *imp.* of подтолкну́ть.

подтасова́ть, -су́ю *perf.*, подтасо́вывать, -аю *imp.* shuffle unfairly; garble, juggle with.

подта́чивать, -аю *imp.* of подточи́ть.

подтверди́тельный, confirmatory; of acknowledgement. подтверди́ть, -ржу́ *perf.*, подтвержда́ть, -а́ю *imp.* confirm; corroborate. bear out; ~ получе́ние + *gen.* acknowledge receipt of. подтвержде́ние, -я, confirmation, corroboration; acknowledgement.

подтёк, -а, bruise. подтека́ть, -а́ет *imp.* of подте́чь; leak, be leaking.

подтере́ть, -дотру́, -дотрёшь; подтёр *perf.* (*imp.* подтира́ть) wipe, wipe up.

подте́чь, -ечёт; -тёк, -ла́ *perf.* (*imp.* подтека́ть) под + *acc.* flow under, run under.

подтира́ть, -а́ю *imp.* of подтере́ть.

подтолкну́ть, -ну́, -нёшь *perf.* (*imp.* подта́лкивать) push, nudge; urge on.

подточи́ть, -чу́, -чишь *perf.* (*imp.* подта́чивать) sharpen slightly, give an edge (to); eat away, gnaw; undermine.

подтру́нивать, -аю *imp.*, подтруни́ть, -ню́ *perf.* над + *instr.* chaff, tease.

подтя́гивать, -аю *imp.*, подтяну́ть, -нешь *perf.* tighten; pull up, haul up; bring up move up; take in hand, chase up; ~ся, tighten one's belt, etc.; pull oneself up; move up, move in; pull oneself together, take oneself in hand. подтяжки, -жек *pl.* braces, suspenders. подтянутый, smart.

по|думать, -аю *perf.* think; think a little, think for a while. подумывать, -аю *imp.* + *inf.* or o + *prep.* think of, think about.

по|дуть, -ую *perf.*

подучивать, -аю *imp.*, подучить, -чу, -чишь *perf.* + *acc.* study, learn; + *acc.* and *dat.* instruct in; ~ся (+ *dat.*) learn.

подушка, -и, pillow; cushion.

подхалим, -а *m.* toady, lickspittle. подхалимничать, -аю *imp.* toady. подхалимство, -а, toadying, grovelling.

подхватить, -ачу, -атишь *perf.*, подхватывать, -аю *imp.* catch (up), pick up, take up; ~ песню, take up, join in, a song.

подход, -а, approach. подходить, -ожу, -одишь *imp.* of подойти. подходящий, suitable, proper, appropriate.

подцепить, -плю, -пишь *perf.*, подцеплять, -яю *imp.* hook on, couple on; pick up.

подчас *adv.* sometimes, at times.

подчёркивать, -аю *imp.*, подчеркнуть, -ну, -нёшь *perf.* underline; emphasize.

подчинение, -я, subordination; submission, subjection. подчинённый, subordinate; tributary; *sb.* subordinate. подчинить, -ню *perf.*, подчинять, -яю, subordinate; subject; place (under); ~ся + *dat.* submit to, obey.

подшефный, aided, assisted; + *dat.* under the patronage of, sponsored by. подшивать, -аю *imp.* of подшить. подшивка, -и, hemming; lining; soling; hem, facing; filing, file.

подшипник, -а, bearing.

подшить, -дошью, -дошьёшь *perf.* (*imp.* подшивать) hem, line, face; sole; sew underneath; file.

подшутить, -учу, -утишь *perf.*, подшучивать, -аю *imp.* над + *instr.* chaff, mock; play a trick on.

подъ-: see под-. подъеду, etc.: see подъехать.

подъезд, -а, porch, entrance, doorway; approach, approaches. подъездн|ой, approach; ~ая аллея, drive; ~ая дорога, access road; ~ой путь, spur (track). подъездный, entrance. подъезжать, -аю *imp.* of подъехать.

подъём, -а, lifting; raising; hoisting; ascent; climb; rise; upward slope; development; élan; enthusiasm, animation; instep; reveille; тяжёл (лёгок) на ~, slow (quick) off the mark, (not) easily persuaded to go somewhere. подъёмник, -а, lift, elevator, hoist; jack. подъёмн|ый, lifting; ~ые деньги, removal allowance; travelling expenses; ~ кран, crane, jenny, derrick; ~ машина, lift; ~ мост, drawbridge; ~ые *sb. pl.* removal allowance, travelling expenses.

подъехать, -еду *perf.* (*imp.* подъезжать) drive up, draw up; call; get round.

подыматься, -аюсь *imp.* of подняться.

подыскать, -ыщу, -ыщешь *perf.*, подыскивать, -аю *imp.* seek (out), (try to) find.

подытоживать, -аю *imp.*, подытожить, -жу *perf.* sum up.

подыхать, -аю *imp.* of подохнуть.

подышать, -шу, -шишь *perf.* breathe; ~ свежим воздухом, have, get, a breath of fresh air.

поедать, -аю *imp.* of поесть.

поединок, -нка, duel; single combat.

поезд, -а; *pl.* -а, train; convoy, procession; ~ом, by train. поездка, -и, journey; trip, excursion, outing, tour. поездн|ой, train; ~ая бригада, train crew.

поесть, -ем, -ешь, -ест, -едим; -ел *perf.* (*imp.* поедать) eat, eat up; have a bite to eat.

по|ехать, -еду *perf.* go; set off, depart.

по|жалеть, -ею *perf.*

по|жаловать(ся, -лую(сь *perf.* пожалуй *adv.* perhaps; very likely; it may be. пожалуйста *part.* please; certainly! by all means! with pleasure!; not at all, don't mention it.

пожа́р, -а, fire; conflagration. пожа́рка, -и, fire-station. пожа́рник, -а, пожа́рный *sb.* fireman. пожа́рн|ый, fire; ~ая кома́нда, fire-brigade; ~ая ле́стница, fire-escape; ~ая маши́на, fire-engine.

пожа́тие, -я; ~ ру́ки, handshake. пожа́ть[1], -жму́, -жмёшь *perf.* (*imp.* пожима́ть) press, squeeze; ~ ру́ку + *dat.*, shake hands with; ~ плеча́ми, shrug one's shoulders; ~ся, shrink, huddle up, hug oneself.

пожа́ть[2], -жну́, -жнёшь *perf.* (*imp.* пожина́ть) reap.

пожела́ние, -я, wish, desire. по|жела́ть, -а́ю *perf.*

пожелте́лый, yellowed; gone yellow. по|желте́ть, -е́ю *perf.*

по|жени́ть, -ню́, -нишь *perf.* пожени́ться, -же́нимся *perf.* get married

поже́ртвование, -я, donation; sacrifice. по|же́ртвовать, -твую *perf.*

пожива́ть, -а́ю *imp.* live; как (вы) пожива́ете? how are you (getting on)?; ста́ли они́ жить-~ да добра́ нажива́ть, they lived happily ever after. пожи́ться *perf.* (+ *instr.*) profit (by), live (off). пожи́вший, experienced. пожило́й, middle-aged; elderly.

пожима́ть(ся, -а́ю(сь *imp.* of пожа́ть[1]- (ся. пожина́ть, -а́ю *imp.* of пожа́ть[2].

пожира́ть, -а́ю *imp.* of пожра́ть.

пожи́тки, -ов *pl.* belongings; things; goods and chattels; со все́ми пожи́тками, bag and baggage.

пожму́, etc.: see пожа́ть[1]. пожну́, etc.: see пожа́ть[2].

пожра́ть, -ру́, -рёшь; -а́л, -а́, -о *perf.* (*imp.* пожира́ть) devour.

по́за, -ы, pose; attitude, posture.

по|забо́титься, -о́чусь *perf.* по|зави́довать, -дую *perf.* по|за́втракать, -аю *perf.*

позавчера́ *adv.* the day before yesterday.

позади́ *adv.* and *prep.* + *gen.* behind.

по|займствовать, -твую *perf.* по|зва́ть, -зову́, -зовёшь; -а́л, -а́, -о *perf.*

позволе́ние, -я, permission, leave; с ва́шего позволе́ния, with your permission, by your leave; с позволе́ния сказа́ть, if one may say so. позволи́-

тельный, permissible. позво́лить, -лю *perf.*, позволя́ть, -я́ю *imp.* + *dat.* or *acc.* allow, permit; ~ себе́ пое́здку в Пари́ж, be able to afford a trip to Paris; позво́ль(те), allow me; excuse me.

по|звони́ть(ся, -ню́(сь *perf.*

позвоно́к, -нка́, vertebra. позвоно́чник, -а, spine, backbone; spinal column. позвоно́чн|ый, spinal, vertebral; vertebrate; ~ые *sb. pl.* vertebrates.

поздне́е *adv.* later. поздне́йший, latest. по́здний, late; по́здно, it is late. по́здно *adv.* late.

по|здоро́ваться, -аюсь *perf.* по|здра́вить, -влю *perf.*, поздравля́ть, -я́ю *imp.* с + *instr.* congratulate on; ~ с днём рожде́ния, wish many happy returns. поздравле́ние, -я, congratulation.

по|зелене́ть. -е́ет *perf.*

поземе́льный, land; ~ нало́г, land-tax.

по́зже *adv.* later (on).

позицио́нн|ый, positional, position; static; ~ая война́, trench warfare. пози́ция, -и, position; stand; заня́ть пози́цию, take one's stand.

познава́емый, cognizable, knowable. познава́тельный, cognitive. познава́ть, -наю́, -наёшь *imp.* of позна́ть. познава́ться, -наю́сь, -наёшься *imp.* become known, be recognized.

по|знако́мить(ся, -млю(сь *perf.*

позна́ние, -я, cognition; *pl.* knowledge. позна́ть, -а́ю *perf.* (*imp.* познава́ть) get to know, become acquainted with.

позоло́та. -ы, gilding, gilt. по|золоти́ть, -лочу́ *perf.*

позо́р, -а, shame, disgrace; infamy, ignominy. позо́рить, -рю *imp.* (*perf.* о~) disgrace; ~ся, disgrace oneself. позо́рный, shameful, disgraceful; infamous, ignominious.

позы́в, -а, urge, call; inclination. позывн|о́й, call; ~о́й сигна́л, ~ы́е *sb. pl.*, call sign.

поимённо *adv.* by name; вызыва́ть ~, call over, call the roll of. поимённый, nominal; ~ спи́сок, list of names.

по́иски, -ов *pl.* search; в по́исках + *gen.* in search of, in quest of.

пои́стине *adv.* indeed, in truth.

пойть, пою, пойшь *imp.* (*perf.* на~) give something to drink; water.

пойду, etc.: see **пойти**.

пойло, -а, swill, mash.

поймать, -аю *perf.* of **ловить**. **поймý**, etc.: see **понять**.

пойти, -иду, -йдёшь; пошёл, -шлá *perf.* of **идти**, **ходить**; go, walk; begin to walk; + *inf.* begin; + в + *acc.* take after; пошёл! off you go! I'm off; пошёл вон! be off! get out! (так) не пойдёт, that won't work, that won't wash; это ей не пойдёт, it won't suit her.

покá *adv.* for the present, for the time being; ~ что, in the meanwhile. **покá** *conj.* while; ~ не, until, till.

покáз, -а, showing, demonstration. **показáние**, -я, testimony, evidence; deposition; affidavit; reading. **показáтель**, -я *m.* index, exponent; showing. **показáтельный**, significant; instructive; revealing; model; demonstration; exponential; ~ суд, show-trial. **показáть**, -ажý, -áжешь *perf.*, **показывать**, -аю *imp.* show; display, reveal; register, read; testify, give evidence; + на + *acc.* point at, point to; ~ вид, pretend; ~ лýчшее время, clock (make) the best time; ~ на дверь + *dat.* show the door (to). **по**|**казáться**, -ажýсь, -áжешься *perf.*, **показываться**, -аюсь *imp.* show oneself (itself); come in sight; appear; seem. **показнóй**, for show; ostentatious.

по-какóвски *adv.* in what language?

по|**калéчить(ся**, -чу(сь *perf.*

покáмест *adv.* and *conj.* for the present; while; meanwhile.

по|**карáть(ся**, *perf.*

покáтость, -и, slope, incline. **покáтый**, sloping; slanting.

покачáть, -áю *perf.* rock. swing: ~ головóй, shake one's head. **покáчивать**, -аю *imp.* rock; swing; stagger, totter. **покачнýть**, -нý, -нёшь, shake; rock; ~ся, sway, totter, lurch.

покаяние, -я, confession; penitence, repentance. **покáянный**, penitential. **по**|**кáяться**, -áюсь *perf.*

поквитáться, -áюсь *perf.* be quits; get even.

покидáть, -áю *imp.*, **покинуть**, -ну *perf.* leave; desert, abandon, forsake. **покинутый**, deserted; abandoned.

поклáдистый, complaisant, obliging; easy to get on with.

поклáжа, -и, load; baggage, luggage.

поклёп, -а, slander, calumny.

поклóн, -а, bow; greeting; передáть мой ~ + *dat.* remember me to, give my regards to; послáть ~, send one's compliments, one's kind regards. **поклонéние**, -я, worship. **поклониться**, -нюсь -нишься *perf.* of **клáняться**. **поклонник**, -а, admirer; worshipper. **поклоняться**, -яюсь *imp.* + *dat.* worship.

по|**клясться**, -янýсь, -нёшься; -ялся, -лáсь *perf.*

покóиться, -óюсь *imp.* rest. repose, be based; lie. **покóй**, -я, rest, peace; room, chamber. **покóйник**, -а, the deceased. **покóйный**, calm, quiet; comfortable; restful; ~ой нóчи! good night!

по|**колебáть(ся**, -éблю(сь *perf.*

поколéние, -я, generation.

по|**колотить(ся**, -очý(сь, -óтишь(ся *perf.*

покóнчить, -чу *perf.* с + *instr.* finish; finish with, have done with; put an end to, do away with; ~ с собóй, commit suicide; с этим покóнчено, that's done with.

покорéние, -я, subjugation, subdual; conquest. **покорить**, -рю *perf.* (*imp.* покорять) subjugate, subdue; conquer; ~ся, submit, resign oneself.

по|**кормить(ся**, -млю(сь, -мишь(ся *perf.*

покóрно *adv.* humbly; submissively, obediently.

по|**коробить(ся**, -блю(сь *perf.* **покорóбленный**, warped.

покорять(ся, -яю(сь *imp.* of **покорить**(ся.

покóс, -а, mowing, haymaking; meadow (-land); вторóй ~, aftermath.

покосившийся, rickety, crazy, ramshackle; leaning. **по**|**косить(ся**, -ошý-(сь *perf.*

покра́жа, -и, theft; stolen goods.

по|кра́сить, -а́шу perf. покра́ска, -и, painting, colouring.

по|красне́ть, -е́ю perf. по|красова́ться, -су́юсь perf. по|крепча́ть, -а́ет perf.

по|криви́ть, -влю́(сь perf.

покри́кивать, -аю imp. shout (на + acc. at).

покро́в, -а, cover; covering; pall; cloak, shroud; protection. покрови́тель, -я m., покрови́тельница, -ы, patron; sponsor. покрови́тельственный, protective; condescending, patronizing. покрови́тельство, -а, protection, patronage. покрови́тельствовать, -твую imp. + dat. protect, patronize.

покро́й, -я, cut.

покроши́ть, -шу́, -шишь perf. crumble; mince, chop.

покрыва́ло, -а, cover; bedspread, counterpane; shawl; veil. покрыва́ть, -а́ю imp., по|кры́ть, -ро́ю perf. cover; coat; roof; drown; shield, cover up for; hush up; discharge, pay off; ~ся, cover oneself; get covered. покры́тие, -я, covering; surfacing; discharge, payment. покры́шка, -и, cover, covering; outer cover.

покупа́тель, -я m. buyer, purchaser; customer, client. покупа́тельный, purchasing. покупа́ть, -а́ю imp. of купи́ть. поку́пка, -и, buying; purchasing; purchase. покупно́й, bought, purchased; purchase, purchasing; ~а́я цена́, purchase-price.

по|кури́ть, -рю́, -ришь perf., поку́ривать, -аю imp. smoke a little; have a smoke.

по|ку́шать, -аю perf.

пол¹, -а (-у), loc. -у́; pl. -ы́, floor.

пол², -а, sex.

пол-¹ in comb. with noun in gen., in oblique cases usu. полу-, half. полве́ка, half a century. ~го́да, half a year, six months. ~доро́ги, half-way. ~дю́жины, half a dozen. ~миллио́на, half a million. ~мину́ты, half a minute. ~цены́, half price. ~часа́, half an hour.

пол-² abbr. in comb. of полномо́чный, plenipotentiary. полпре́д, -а, (ambas-

sador) plenipotentiary. ~пре́дство, -а, embassy.

пола́, -ы́; pl. -ы, skirt, flap; из-под полы́, on the sly, under cover.

полага́ть, -а́ю imp. suppose, think, believe; lay, place. полага́ться, -а́юсь imp. of положи́ться; полага́ется impers. one is supposed to; + dat. it is due to; нам э́то полага́ется, it is our due, we have a right to it; не полага́ется, it is not done; так полага́ется, it is the custom.

пола́дить, -а́жу perf. come to an understanding; get on good terms.

по|ла́комить(ся, -млю(сь perf.

по́лдень, -дня or -лу́дня m. noon, midday; south. полу́дневный adj.

по́ле, -я; pl. -я́, field; ground; margin; brim; ~ де́ятельности, sphere of action. полев|о́й, field; ~ы́е цветы́, wild flowers; ~о́й шпат, feldspar.

поле́зн|ый, useful; helpful; good, wholesome; effective; ~ая нагру́зка, payload.

по|ле́зть, -зу; -ле́з perf.

поле́мика, -и, controversy, dispute; polemics. полемизи́ровать, -рую imp. argue, debate, engage in controversy. полеми́ческий, controversial; polemical.

по|лени́ться, -ню́сь, -нишься perf.

поле́но, -а; pl. -е́нья, -ьев, log.

поле́сье, -я, woodlands, wooded region.

полёт, -а, flight; flying; вид с пти́чьего ~а, bird's-eye view. по|лете́ть, -лечу́ perf.

по́лзать, -аю indet. imp., ползти́, -зу́, -зёшь; полз, -ла́ det. imp. crawl, creep; ooze; spread; fray, ravel; slip, slide, collapse. ползу́ч|ий, creeping; ~ие расте́ния, creepers.

поли- in comb. poly-.

поли́ва, -ы, glaze. полива́ть(ся, -а́ю(сь imp. of поли́ть(ся. поли́вка, -и, watering.

полиграфи́ст, -а, printing-trades worker. полиграфи́ческ|ий, printing-trades; ~ая промы́шленность, printing industry. полигра́фия, -и, printing.

полиго́н, -а, range.

поликли́ника, -и, polyclinic; outpatients' (department).

полиня́лый, faded, discoloured. **по|линя́ть**, -я́ет *perf.*

полирова́льн|ый, polishing; **~ая бума́га**, sandpaper. **полирова́ть**, **-ру́ю** *imp.* (*perf.* **от~**) polish. **полиро́вка**, **-и**, polishing; polish. **полиро́вщик**, **-а**, polisher.

полит- *abbr.* in *comb.* of **полити́ческий**, political. **политбюро́** *n. indecl.* Politbureau. **~гра́мота**, **-ы**, elementary political education. **~заключённый** *sb.* political prisoner. **~кружо́к**, **-жка́**, political study circle. **~просве́т**, **-а**, political education. **~рабо́тник**, **-а**, political worker.

полите́хник, **-а**, polytechnic student. **политехникум**, **-а**, polytechnic. **политехни́ческий**, polytechnic, polytechnical.

поли́тика, **-и**, policy; politics. **полити́ческий**, political.

поли́ть, **-лью́**, **-льёшь**; **по́ли́л**, **-а́**, **-о** *perf.* (*imp.* **полива́ть**) pour on, pour over; **~** (**водо́й**) water; **~ся** + *instr.* pour over oneself.

полице́йский, police; *sb.* policeman. **полиция**, **-и**, police.

поли́чн|ое *sb.*; **с ~ым**, red-handed.

полк, **-а́**, *loc.* **-у́**, regiment.

по́лка¹, **-и**, shelf; berth.

по́лка², **-и**, weeding.

полко́вник, **-а**, colonel. **полково́дец**, **-дца**, commander; general. **полково́й**, regimental.

полне́ть, **-е́ю** *imp.* (*perf.* **по~**) put on weight, fill out.

по́лно *adv.* that's enough! that will do! stop it! **~ ворча́ть!** stop grumbling.

полно- in *comb.* full; completely. **полновла́стный**, sovereign. **~кро́вный**, full-blooded. **~лу́ние**, **-я**, full moon. **~метра́жный**, full-length. **~пра́вный**, enjoying full rights; competent; **~правный член**, full member. **~сбо́рный**, prefabricated. **~це́нный**, of full value.

полномо́чие, **-я**, authority; power; plenary powers; commission; proxy; *pl.* terms of reference; credentials; **дать полномо́чия** + *dat.* empower, commission; **превы́сить полномо́чия**, exceed one's commission. **полномо́чный**, plenipotentiary.

по́лностью *adv.* fully, in full; completely, utterly. **полнота́**, **-ы́**, fullness, completeness; plenitude; stoutness, corpulence; plumpness.

по́лночь, **-л(у́)ночи**, midnight; north; **за ~**, after midnight.

по́лн|ый; **-лон**, **-лна́**, **по́лно́**, full; complete; entire, total; absolute; stout, portly; plump; **в ~ом соста́ве**, in full force; in a body; **~ым го́лосом**, at the top of one's voice; **~ым-полно́**, chock-full, cram-full; **~ый сбор**, full house; **~ое собра́ние сочине́ний**, complete works; **~ый стенографи́ческий отчёт**, verbatim record.

полови́к, **-а́**, mat, matting; door-mat. **полови́на**, **-ы**, half; middle; два с половиной, two and a half; **~** (**две́ри**), leaf; **~ шесто́го**, half-past five. **полови́нка**, **-и**, half; leaf. **полови́нчатый**, halved; half-and-half; half-hearted; undecided; indeterminate.

полово́й¹, floor.

полово́й², sexual.

по́лог, **-а**, curtains; cover, blanket.

поло́гий, gently sloping.

положе́ние, **-я**, position; whereabouts; posture; attitude; condition, state; situation; status, standing; circumstances; regulations, statute; thesis; tenet; clause, provisions; **быть на высоте́ положе́ния**, rise to the situation; **по положе́нию**, according to the regulations. **поло́женный**, agreed; determined. **поло́жим**, let us assume; suppose; though, even if. **положи́тельный**, positive; affirmative; favourable; complete, absolute; practical. **положи́ть**, **-жу́**, **-жишь** *perf.* (*imp.* **класть**) put, place; lay (down); decide; agree; propose; offer; fix; **~ся** (*imp.* **полага́ться**) rely, count; pin one's hopes.

по́лоз, **-а**; *pl.* **-о́зья**, **-ьев**, runner.

по|лома́ть(ся, **-а́ю(сь** *perf.* **поло́мка**, **-и**, breakage.

полоса́, **-ы́**, *acc.* **по́лосу́**; *pl.* **по́лосы**, **-ло́с**, **-а́м**, stripe, streak; strip; band;

region; zone; belt; period; phase; spell, run. полосáтый, striped, stripy.

полоскáние, -я, rinse, rinsing; gargle, gargling. полоскáтельница, -ы, slop--basin. полоскáть, -ощý -óщешь *imp.* (*perf.* вы~, от~, про~) rinse; ~ гóрло, gargle; ~ся, paddle; flap.

пóлость[1], -и; *gen. pl.* -éй, cavity.

пóлость[2], -и; *gen. pl.* -éй, carriage-rug.

полотéнце, -а; *gen. pl.* -нец, towel.

полотёр, -а, floor-polisher.

полóтнище, -а, width; panel. полотнó, -á; *pl.* -а, -тен, linen; canvas. полотня́ный, linen.

полóть, -лю́, -лишь *imp.* (*perf.* вы~) weed.

полошить, -шý *imp.* (*perf.* вс~) agitate, alarm; ~ся, take alarm, take fright.

полощý, etc.: see полоскáть.

полтинá, -ы, полтинник, -а, fifty copecks; fifty-copeck piece.

полторá, -лýтора *m.* and *n.,* полторы́, -лýтора *f.* one and a half. полторáста, полýт-, a hundred and fifty.

полу-[1]: see пол-[1].

полу-[2] in *comb.* half, semi, demi-. полуботи́нок, -нка; *gen. pl.* -нок, shoe. ~гóдие, -я, six months, half a year. ~годи́чный, six months', lasting six months. ~годовáлый, six-month-old. ~годовóй, half-yearly, six-monthly. ~грáмотный, semi-literate. ~гýсеничный, half-track. ~защи́та, -ы, halfbacks; центр ~защи́ты, centre half. ~защи́тник, -а, half-back. ~круг, -а, semicircle. ~крýглый, semicircular. ~мéра, -ы, half-measure. ~мéсяц, -а, crescent (moon). ~оборóт, -а, halfturn. ~óстров, -а, peninsula. ~открытый, half-open; ajar. ~официáльный, semi-official. ~подвáльный, semi-basement. ~проводни́к, -á, semi-conductor, transistor. ~проводникóвый, transistor, transistorized. ~сóнный, half-asleep; dozing. ~стáнок, -нка, halt. ~тóнка, -и, half-ton lorry. ~тьмá, -ы, semi-darkness; twilight, dusk. ~фабрикáт, -а, semi-finished product, convenience food. ~финáл, -а, semi-final. ~шáрие, -я, hemisphere. ~шýбок, -бка, sheepskin coat.

полýда, -ы, tinning. по|лудить, -ужý, -ýдишь *perf.*

полýденный, midday.

полýторка, -и, thirty-hundredweight lorry.

получáтель, -я *m.* recipient. получáть, -áю *imp.,* получи́ть, -чý, -чишь *perf.* get, receive, obtain; ~ся, come, arrive, turn up; turn out, prove, be; из этого ничегó не получи́лось, nothing came of it; результáты получи́лись невáжные, the results are poor. получéние, -я, receipt. полýчка, -и, receipt; pay(-packet).

полýчше *adv.* rather better, a little better.

пóлчище, -а, horde; mass, flock.

полынный, wormwood; ~ая вóдка, absinthe. полынь, -и, wormwood.

по|лысéть, -éю *perf.*

пóльза, -ы, use; advantage, benefit, profit; в пóльзу + *gen.* in favour of, on behalf of. пóльзование, -я, use. пóльзоваться, -зуюсь *imp.* (*perf.* вос~) + *instr.* make use of, utilize; profit by; enjoy; take advantage of, ~ довéрием + *gen.* enjoy the confidence of; ~ кредитом, be credit-worthy; ~ слýчаем, take the opportunity; ~ уважéнием, be held in respect.

пóлька, -и, Pole; polka. пóльский, Polish; *sb.* polonaise.

по|льсти́ть(ся, -льщý(сь *perf.* полью́, etc.: see поли́ть.

полюби́ть, -блю́, -бишь *perf.* come to like, take to; fall in love with.

по|любовáться, -бýюсь *perf.*

полюбóвный, amicable.

по|любопы́тствовать, -твую *perf.*

пóлюс, -а, pole.

поля́к, -а, Pole.

поля́на, -ы, glade, clearing.

поля́рник, -а, polar explorer, member of polar expedition. поля́рный, polar, arctic; diametrically opposed; ~ая звездá, pole-star; (сéверное) ~ое сия́ние, aurora borealis, Northern Lights.

пом- *abbr.* in *comb.* of помóщник, assistant. помбýх. -а, assistant accountant. ~дирéктор, -а, assistant manager. **~нáч**, -а, assistant chief, assistant head.

помáда, -ы, pomade; lipstick.

по|мáзать(ся, -áжу(сь *perf*. **помазóк**, -зкá small brush.

помалéньку *adv*. gradually, little by little; gently; in a small way, modestly; tolerably, so-so.

помáлкивать, -аю *imp*. hold one's tongue, keep mum.

по|манить, -ню, -нишь *perf*.

помáрка, -и, blot; pencil mark; correction.

по|мáслить, -лю *perf*.

помахáть, -машу, -мáшешь *perf*., **помáхивать**, -аю *imp*. + *instr*. wave; brandish, swing; wag.

помéньше, somewhat smaller, rather smaller, a little smaller; somewhat less, a little less, rather less.

по|менять(ся, -яю(сь *perf*. **по|мерéщиться**, -щусь *perf*. **по|мéрить(ся**, -рю(сь *perf*. **по|мéркнуть**, -нет, -мéрк(нул) *perf*.

помертвéлый, deathly pale. **по|мертвéть**, -éю *perf*.

поместительный, roomy; capacious; spacious. **поместить**, -ещу *perf*. (*imp*. помещáть), lodge, accommodate; put up; place, locate; invest; publish an article; **~ся**, lodge, find room; put up; go in. **помéстье**, -я; *gen. pl*. -тий, -тьям estate.

пóмесь, -и, cross-breed, hybrid; cross; mongrel; mixture, hotch-potch.

помéсячный, monthly.

помёт, -а, dung, excrement; droppings; litter, brood, farrow.

помéта, -ы, mark, note. **по|мéтить**, -éчу *perf*. (*imp*. also помечáть) mark; date; **~ гáлочкой**, tick.

помéха, -и, hindrance; obstacle; encumbrance; *pl*. interference; **быть (служить) помéхой** + *dat*. hinder, impede, stand in the way of. **помехоустóйчивый**, anti-static, anti-interference

помечáть, -áю *imp*. of помéтить.

помéшанный, mad, crazy; insane; *sb*. madman, madwoman. **помешáтельство**, -а, madness, craziness; lunacy, insanity; craze. **по|мешáть**, -áю *perf*.

помешáться, -áюсь *perf*. go mad, go crazy.

помéшивать, -аю *imp*. stir slowly.

помещáть, -áю *imp*. of поместить. **помещáться**, -áюсь *imp*. of поместиться; be; be located, be situated; be housed; be accommodated, find room; **в э́тот стадио́н помеща́ются се́мьдесят ты́сяч челове́к**, this stadium holds seventy thousand people. **помещéние**, -я, premises; apartment, room, lodging; placing, location; investment; **жилóе ~**, housing, living accommodation. **помéщик**, -а, landowner, landlord. **помéщичий**, landowner's; **~ дом**, manor-house, gentleman's residence.

помидóр, -а, tomato.

помилование, -я, forgiveness, pardon. **помиловать**, -лую *perf*. forgive, pardon.

помимо *prep*. + *gen*. apart from; besides; without the knowledge of, unbeknown to

помин, -а (-у), mention; **лёгок на ~е**, talk of the devil. **поминáть**, -áю *imp*. of помяну́ть; **не ~ лихом**, remember kindly; not bear a grudge against; **помина́й как зва́ли**, he (etc.) has vanished into thin air; **~ добро́м**, speak well of. **поми́нки**, -нок *pl*. funeral repast.

по|мирить(ся, -рю́(сь *perf*.

пóмнить, -ню *imp*. remember.

помножáть, -áю *imp*. **по|мнóжить**, -жу *perf*. multiply; **~ два на́ три**, multiply two by three.

помогáть, -áю *imp*. of помóчь.

по-мóему *adv*. I think; in my opinion; to my mind, to my way of thinking; as I (would) think, as I would have it.

помóи, -ев *pl*. slops. **помóйка**, -и; *gen. pl*. -óек dustbin; rubbish heap, rubbish dump; cesspit. **помóйн|ый**, slop; **~ое ведрó**, slop-pail.

помóл, -а, grinding, milling; grist.

помóлвка, -и, betrothal, engagement.

по|молиться, -лю́сь, -лишься *perf*. **по|молодéть**, -éю *perf*.

помолчáть, -чу́ *perf*. be silent for a time, pause.

помóр, **помóрский**, etc.: see по-² II.

по|мори́ть, -рю́ *perf.* по|мо́рщиться, -щусь *perf.*

помо́ст, -а, dais; platform, stage, rostrum; scaffold.

по|мочи́ться, -чу́сь, -чишься *perf.*

помо́чь, -огу́, -о́жешь; -о́г, -ла́ *perf.* (*imp.* помога́ть) help, aid, assist; relieve, bring relief. помо́щник, -а, помо́щница, -ы, assistant, mate; help, helper, helpmeet. по́мощь, -и, help, aid, assistance; relief; без посторо́нней по́мощи, unaided, single-handed; на ~! help!; пода́ть ру́ку по́мощи, lend a hand, give a helping hand; при по́мощи, с по́мощью, + *gen.* with the help of, by means of.

помо́ю, etc.: see помы́ть.

по́мпа, -ы, pump.

по|мрачне́ть, -е́ю *perf.*

по|мути́ть(ся, -учу́(сь, -ути́шь(ся *perf.* помутне́ние, -я, dimness, dullness, clouding. по|мутне́ть, -е́ет *perf.*

помча́ться, -чу́сь *perf.* dash, rush, tear; dart off.

помыка́ть, -а́ю *imp.* + *instr.* order about.

по́мысел, -сла, intention, design; thought.

по|мы́ть(ся, -мо́ю(сь *perf.*

помяну́ть, -ну́ -нешь *perf.* (*imp.* помина́ть) mention; remember in one's prayers; помяни́ моё сло́во, mark my words.

помя́тый, crushed; flabby, baggy. по|мя́ть(ся, -мну́сь, -мнётся *perf.*

по|наде́яться, -е́юсь *perf.* count, rely.

пона́добиться, -блюсь *perf.* become necessary, be needed; е́сли пона́добится, if necessary.

понапра́сну *adv.* in vain.

понаслы́шке *adv.* by hearsay.

по-настоя́щему *adv.* in the right way, properly, truly.

понево́ле *adv.* willynilly; against one's will.

понеде́льник, -а, Monday. понеде́льный, weekly.

понемно́гу, понемно́жку *adv.* little by little; a little.

по|нести́(сь, -су́(сь, -сёшь(ся; -нёс(ся, -ла́сь *perf.*

понижа́ть, -а́ю *imp.*, пони́зить, -ни́жу *perf.* lower; reduce; ~ся, fall, drop, go down, fall off. пониже́ние, -я, fall, drop; lowering; reduction.

поника́ть, -а́ю *imp.*, пони́кнуть, -ну- -ни́к *perf.* droop, flag, wilt; ~ голово́й, hang one's head.

понима́ние, -я, understanding; comprehension; interpretation, conception. понима́ть, -а́ю *imp.* of поня́ть.

по-но́вому *adv.* in a new fashion; нача́ть жить ~, begin a new life, turn over a new leaf.

поно́с, -а diarrhoea.

поноси́ть[1], -ошу́ -о́сишь *perf.* carry; wear.

поноси́ть[2], -ошу́, -о́сишь *imp.* abuse, revile. поно́сный, abusive, defamatory.

поно́шенный, worn; shabby, threadbare. по|нра́виться, -влюсь *perf.*

понто́н, -а, pontoon; pontoon bridge. понто́нный, pontoon.

понуди́тельный, compelling, pressing; coercive. пону́дить, -у́жу *perf.* понужда́ть, -а́ю *imp.* force, compel, coerce; impel.

понука́ть, -а́ю *imp.* urge on.

пону́рить, -рю *perf.*; ~ го́лову, hang one's head. пону́рый, downcast, depressed.

по|ню́хать, -аю *perf.* поню́шка, -и; ~ табаку́, pinch of snuff.

поня́тие, -я, concept, conception; notion, idea. поня́тливость, -и, comprehension, understanding. поня́тливый, bright, quick. поня́тный, understandable; clear, intelligible; perspicuous; ~о, of course, naturally; ~о? (do you) see? is that clear?; ~но! I see! I understand; quite! поня́ть, пойму́, -мёшь; по́нял, -а́, -о *perf.* (*imp.* понима́ть) understand, comprehend; realize.

по|обе́дать, -аю *perf.* по|обеща́ть, -а́ю *perf.*

пода́ль *adv.* at some distance, a little way away.

поодино́чке *adv.* one by one, one at a time.

поочерёдно *adv.* in turn, by turns.

поощре́ние, -я, encouragement; incentive, spur. поощри́ть, -рю́ *perf.*, поощря́ть, -я́ю *imp.* encourage.

поп, -á, priest.

попадáние, -я, hit. попадáться, -áю(сь *imp.* of попáсть(ся.

попадья́, -и́, priest's wife.

попáло: see попáсть. по|пáриться, -рюсь *perf.*

попáрно *adv.* in pairs, two by two.

попáсть, -адý, -адёшь; -áл *perf.* (*imp.* попадáть) + в + *acc.* hit; get to, get into, find oneself in; + на + *acc.* hit upon, come on; не тудá ∼, get the wrong number; ∼ в плен, be taken prisoner; ∼ в цель, hit the target; ∼ на поезд, catch a train; ∼ на рабóту, land a job; ∼ся, be caught; find oneself; turn up; пéрвый попáвшийся, the first person who happens to meet; ∼ся на удóчку, swallow the bait; что попадётся among *prons.* and *advs.*; где ∼, anywhere; как ∼, anyhow; helter-skelter; что ∼, first to hand.

по|пенять, -я́ю *perf.*

поперёк *adv.* and *prep.* + *gen.* across; вдоль и ∼, far and wide; знать вдоль и ∼, know inside out, know the ins and outs of; стать ∼ гóрла + *dat.* stick in the throat of; стоя́ть ∼ дорóги + *dat.* be in the way of.

поперемéнно *adv.* in turn, by turns.

попере́чник, -а, diameter. попере́чн|ый, transverse, diametrical; cross; dihedral; ∼ый разрéз, ∼ое сечéние, cross-section.

по|пе́рчить, -чу *perf.*

попечéние, -я, care; charge; быть на попечéнии + *gen.*, be under the charge of, be left to the care of. попечи́тель, -я *m.* guardian, trustee.

попирáть, -áю *imp.* (*perf.* попрáть) trample on; flout.

поплавкóв|ый, float; ∼ая кáмера, float chamber. поплавóк, -вкá, float; floating research.

поплáкать, -áчу *perf.* cry a little; shed a few tears.

по|плати́ться, -чýсь, -ти́шься *perf.*

попóйка, -и, drinking-bout.

пополáм *adv.* in two, in half; half-and-half; fifty-fifty.

поползновéние, -я, feeble impulse; half-formed intention, half a mind; pretension(s).

пополнéние, -я, replenishment; re-stocking; re-fuelling; reinforcement. по|полнéть, -éю *perf.* попóлнить, -ню *perf.*, пополня́ть, -я́ю *imp.* replenish, supplement, fill up; re-stock; re-fuel; reinforce.

пополýдни *adv.* in the afternoon, p.m. пополýночи *adv.* after midnight, a.m.

попóна, -ы, horse-cloth.

поправи́мый, reparable, remediable. попрáвить, -влю *perf.*, поправля́ть, -я́ю *imp.* mend, repair; correct, set right, put right; adjust, set straight, tidy; improve, better; ∼ся, correct oneself; tidy one's hair; get better, recover; put on weight; look better; improve. попрáвка, -и, correction, amendment; mending, repairing; adjustment; recovery.

попрáть; -áл *perf.* of попирáть.

по-прéжнему *adv.* as before; as usual.

попрёк, -а, reproach. попрекáть, -áю *imp.*, попрекнýть, -нý, -нёшь *perf.* reproach.

пóприще, -а, field; walk of life, profession career.

по|прóбовать, -бую *perf.* по|проси́ть-(ся, -ошý(сь, -óсишь(ся *perf.*

пóпросту *adv.* simply; without ceremony.

попрошáйка, -и *m.* and *f.* cadger; beggar. попрошáйничать, -аю *imp.* beg; cadge.

попугáй, -я, parrot.

популя́рность, -и, popularity. популя́рный, popular.

попусти́тельство, -а, connivance; toleration; tolerance.

по-пустóму, пóпусту *adv.* in vain, to no purpose.

попýтно *adv.* at the same time; in passing; incidentally. попýтный, accompanying; following; passing; incidental; ∼ вéтер, fair wind. попýтчик, -а, fellow-traveller.

попытáть, -áю *perf.* try; ∼ счáстья, try one's luck. по|пытáться, -áюсь *perf.* попы́тка, -и, attempt, endeavour.

по|пя́титься, -я́чусь *perf.* попя́тный,

backward; идти́ на ~, go back on one's word.

порá, -ы́, *acc.* -у; *pl.* -ы, пор, -а́м, time, season; it is time; в (са́мую) по́ру, opportunely, at the right time; давно́ ~, it is high time; до поры́ до вре́мени, for the time being; до каки́х пор? till when? till what time? how long? до сих пор, till now, up to now, so far; hitherto; на пе́рвых ~х, at first; с каки́х пор? с кото́рых пор? since when?

порабо́тить, -ощу́ *perf.*, **порабоща́ть**, -а́ю *imp.* enslave. **порабоще́ние**, -я, enslavement.

по́|ра́довать(ся, -дую(сь *perf.*

поража́ть, -а́ю *imp.*, **порази́ть**, -ажу́ *perf.* rout; hit; strike; defeat; affect; stagger, startle; ~ся, be astounded, be startled; be staggered. **пораже́нец**, -нца defeatist. **пораже́ние**, -я, defeat; hitting, striking; affection; lesion; ~ в права́х, disfranchisement. **пораже́нчество**, -а, defeatism. **порази́тельный**, striking; staggering, startling.

пора́нить, -ню *perf.* wound; injure; hurt.

порва́ть, -ву́, -вёшь; -ва́л, -а́, -о *perf.* (*imp.* порыва́ть) tear (up); break, break off; ~ся, tear; break (off); snap; be broken off.

по|реде́ть, -е́ет *perf.*

поре́з, -а, cut. **поре́зать**, -е́жу *perf.* cut; kill, slaughter; ~ся, cut oneself.

поре́й, -я, leek.

по|рекомендова́ть, -ду́ю *perf.* **по|ржа́веть**, -еет *perf.*

по́ристый, porous.

порица́ние, -я, censure; reproof, reprimand; blame; обще́ственное ~, public censure. **порица́тельный**, disapproving; reproving. **порица́ть**, -а́ю *imp.* blame; censure.

поро́вну *adv.* equally, in equal parts.

поро́г, -а, threshold; rapids.

поро́да, -ы, breed, race, strain, species, stock; kind, sort, type; breeding; rock; layer, bed, stratum; matrix. **поро́дистый**, thoroughbred. pedigree. **по|роди́ть**, -ожу́ *perf.* (*imp.* порожда́ть) give birth to, beget; raise, generate, engender, give rise to.

породнённ|ый; ~ые города́, twin cities.

по|родни́ть(ся, -ню́(сь *perf.* **поро́дность**, -и, race, breed; stock, strain. **поро́дный**, pedigree.

порожда́ть, -а́ю *imp.* of породи́ть.

поро́жний, empty.

по́рознь *adv.* separately, apart.

поро́й, поро́ю *adv.* at times, now and then.

поро́к, -а, vice; defect; flaw, blemish; ~ се́рдца, heart-disease.

поросёнок, -нка; *pl.* -ся́та, -ся́т, piglet; sucking-pig. **пороси́ться**, -и́тся *imp.* (*perf.* о~) farrow.

по́росль, -и, suckers, shoots; young wood.

поро́ть[1], -рю́, -решь *imp.* (*perf.* вы́~) flog, thrash; whip, lash.

поро́ть[2], -рю́, -решь *imp.* (*perf.* рас~), undo, unpick; rip (out); ~ вздор, ерунду́, чушь, talk rot, talk nonsense; ~ горя́чку, be in a frantic hurry; ~ся, come unstitched, come undone.

по́рох, -а (-у); *pl.* ~á, gunpowder, powder; он ~а не вы́думает, he'll never set the Thames on fire. **порохово́й**, powder; ~ по́греб, ~ склад, powder-magazine.

поро́чить, -чу *imp.* (*perf.* о~) discredit; bring into disrepute; defame, denigrate, blacken, smear. **поро́чный**, vicious, depraved; wanton; faulty, defective, fallacious.

порошо́к, -шка́ powder.

порт, -а, *loc.* -у́; *pl.* -ы, -о́в, port; harbour; dockyard.

по́ртить, -чу *imp.* (*perf.* ис~), spoil, mar; damage; corrupt; ~ся, deteriorate; go bad; decay, rot; get out of order; be corrupted, become corrupt.

портни́ха, -и, dressmaker. **портно́й** *sb.* tailor. **портно́вский**, tailor's; tailoring. **портно́й** *sb.* tailor.

портови́к, -á, docker. **порто́вый**, port, harbour; ~ рабо́чий, docker.

портре́т, -а portrait; likeness.

портсига́р, -а, cigarette-case, cigar-case.

портфе́ль, -я *m.* brief-case; portfolio.

портье́ра, -ы, curtain(s), portière.

портя́нка, -и, foot-binding puttee.

поро́ганный, profaned, desecrated; outraged. **поруга́ть**, -а́ю *perf.* scold, swear at; **~ся**, curse, swear; fall out, quarrel.

порýка, -и, bail; guarantee; surety; на порýки, on bail.

по-рýсски *adv.* (in) Russian; говорúть **~**, speak Russian.

поручáть, -áю *imp.* of поручúть. поручéнец, -нца, special messenger. поручéние, -я, commission, errand; message; mission.

пóручень, -чня *m.* handrail.

порýчик, -а, lieutenant.

поручúть, -чý, -чишь *perf.* (*imp.* поручáть) charge, commission; entrust; instruct.

поручúться, -чýсь, -чишься *perf.* of ручáться.

порхáть, -áю *imp.*, **порхнýть**, -нý, -нёшь *perf.* flutter, flit; fly about.

порцион, -а, ration. **порциóнный**, à la carte. **пóрция**, -и, portion; helping.

пóрча, -и, spoiling; damage; wear and tear.

пóршень, -шня *m.* piston; plunger. поршнев|óй, piston, plunger; reciprocating; **~óе кольцó** piston ring.

порýв[1], -а, gust; rush; fit; uprush, upsurge; impulse.

порýв[2], -а, a breaking, snapping. порывáть(ся[1], -áю(сь *imp.* of порвáть(ся.

порывáться[2], -áюсь *imp.* make jerky movements; try, endeavour, strive. **порывисто** *adv.* fitfully, by fits and starts. **порывистый**, fitfully, gusty; jerky; impetuous; violent; fitful.

порядковый, ordinal. **порядком** *adv.* pretty, rather; properly, thoroughly. **порядок**, -дка (-у) order; sequence; manner, way; procedure; *pl.* customs, usages, observances; в обязáтельном порядке, without fail; всё в порядке, everything is all right, it's all in order; в спéшном порядке, quickly, in haste; не в порядке, out of order; по порядку, in order, in succession; **~ дня**, agenda, order of business, order of the day. **порядочно** *adv.* decently; honestly; respectably; fairly, pretty; a fair amount; fairly well, quite decently. **порядочный**, decent; honest; respectable; fair, considerable.

пос. *abbr.* посёлок, settlement, housing estate.

посадúть, -ажý, -áдишь *perf.* of садúть, сажáть. **посáдка**, -и, planting; embarkation; boarding; landing; seat. **посáдочн|ый**, planting; landing; **~ые огнú**, flare-path; **~ фáры**, landing lights.

посажý, etc.: see посадúть. по|сáхарить, -рю *perf.* по|свáтать(ся, -аю(сь *perf.* по|свежéть, -éет *perf.* по|светúть, -ечý, -éтишь *perf.* по|светлéть, -éет *perf.*

пóсвист, -а, whistle; whistling. посвúстывать, -аю *imp.* whistle.

посвятúть, -ящý *perf.*, **посвящáть**, -áю *imp.* devote, give up; dedicate; initiate, let in; ordain, consecrate. **посвящéние**, -я, dedication; initiation; consecration, ordination.

посéв, -а, sowing; crops. посевн|óй, sowing; **~áя плóщадь**, sown area, area under crops.

по|седéть, -éю *perf.* посéкся, etc.: see посéчься.

поселéнец, -нца, settler; deportee, exile. **поселéние**, -я, settling, settlement; deportation, exile. по|селúть, -лю *perf.*, **поселять**, -яю *imp.* settle; lodge; inspire, arouse, engender; **~ся**, settle, take up residence, make one's home. **посёлок**, -лка, settlement; housing estate.

посеребрённый, -рён, -á, silver-plated; silvered. по|серебрúть, -рю *perf.* по|серéть, -éю *perf.*

посетúтель, -я *m.* visitor; caller; guest. **посетúть**, -ещý *perf.* (*imp.* посещáть) visit; call on; attend.

по|сéтовать, -тую *perf.* по|сéчься, -ечётся, -екýтся *perf.* посéкся, -лáсь *perf.*

посещáемость, -и, attendance, (number of) visitors. посещáть, -áю *imp.* of посетúть. **посещéние**, -я, visiting; visit.

по|сéять, -éю *perf.*

посúльн|ый, within one's powers.

посинéлый, gone blue. по|синéть, -éю *perf.*

по|скакáть, -ачý, -áчешь *perf.*

поскользну́ться, -ну́сь, -нёшься *perf.* slip.

поско́льку *conj.* as far as, as much as, (in) so far as; since.

по|скро́мничать, -аю *perf.* по|скупи́ться, -плю́сь *perf.*

посла́нец, -нца, messenger, envoy. посла́ние, -я, message; epistle. посла́нник, -а, envoy, minister. посла́ть, -шлю́, -шлёшь *perf.* (*imp.* посыла́ть), send, dispatch; move, thrust; ~ за до́ктором, send for the doctor; ~ по по́чте, post.

по́сле *adv.* and *prep.* + *gen.* after; afterwards, later (on); since; ~ всего́, after all, when all is said and done; ~ всех, last (of all).

по́сле- in *comb.* post-; after-. послевое́нный, post-war. ~за́втра *adv.* the day after tomorrow. ~обе́денный, after--dinner. ~родово́й, post-natal. ~сло́вие, epilogue; concluding remarks. ~уда́рный, post-tonic.

после́дн|ий, last; final; recent; latest; latter; (в) ~ее вре́мя, за ~ее вре́мя, lately recently; (в) ~ий раз, for the last time; до ~его вре́мени, until very recently; ~яя ка́пля, the last straw; ~яя мо́да, the latest fashion. после́дователь, -я *m.* follower. после́довательный, successive, consecutive; consistent, logical. по|сле́довать, -дую *perf.* после́дствие, -я consequence, sequel; after-effect. после́дующий, subsequent, succeeding, following, ensuing; consequent.

посло́вица, -ы, proverb, saying. посло́вичный, proverbial.

по|служи́ть, -жу́, -жишь *perf.* послужно́й, service; ~ спи́сок, service record.

послуша́ние, -я, obedience. по|слу́шать(ся), -аю(сь) *perf.* послу́шный, obedient, dutiful.

по|слы́шаться, -шится *perf.*

посма́тривать, -аю *imp.* look from time to time (at); glance occasionally.

посме́иваться, -аюсь *imp.* chuckle, laugh softly.

посме́ртный, posthumous.

по|сме́ть, -е́ю *perf.*

посме́шище, -а, laughing-stock, butt. посмея́ние, -я, mockery, ridicule. по-

смея́ться, -ею́сь, -еёшься *perf.* laugh; + над + *instr.* laugh at, ridicule, make fun of.

посо́бие, -я, aid, help, relief, assistance; allowance, benefit; textbook; (educational) aid; *pl.* teaching equipment; уче́бные посо́бия, educational supplies. посо́бник, -а, accomplice; abettor.

по|сове́товать(ся), -тую(сь) *perf.* по|соде́йствовать, -твую *perf.*

посо́л, -сла́ ambassador.

по|соли́ть, -олю́, -о́ли́шь *perf.*

посо́льский, ambassadorial, ambassador's; embassy. посо́льство, -а, embassy.

поспа́ть, -сплю́, -а́л, -а́, -о *perf.* sleep; have a nap.

поспева́ть[1], -а́ет *imp.*, по|спе́ть[1], -е́ет *perf.* ripen; be done, be ready.

поспева́ть[2], -а́ю *imp.*, поспе́ть[2], -е́ю *perf.* have time; be in time (к + *dat.*, на + *acc.* for); + за + *instr.* keep up with, keep pace with; не ~ к по́езду, miss the train; ~ на по́езд, catch the train.

по|спеши́ть, -шу́ *perf.* поспе́шно *adv.* in a hurry, hurriedly, hastily. поспе́шный, hasty, hurried.

по|спо́рить, -рю *perf.* по|спосо́бствовать, -твую *perf.*

посреди́ *adv.* and *prep.* + *gen.* in the middle (of), in the midst (of). посреди́не *adv.* in the middle. посре́дник, -а, mediator, intermediary; go-between; middleman; umpire. посре́дничество, -а, mediation. посре́дственно *adv.* so-so, (only) fairly well; fair; satisfactory. посре́дственность, -и, mediocrity. посре́дственный, mediocre, middling; fair, satisfactory. посре́дством *prep.* + *gen.* by means of; by dint of; with the aid of.

по|ссо́рить(ся), -рю(сь) *perf.*

пост[1], -а́, *loc.* -у́, post; занима́ть ~, occupy a post; на ~у́, at one's post; on one's beat; on point-duty.

пост[2], -а́, *loc.* -у́, fasting; abstinence; fast.

по|ста́вить[1], -влю *perf.*

поста́вить[2], -влю *perf.*, поставля́ть, -я́ю

imp. supply, purvey. **поста́вка**, -и, supply; delivery. **поставщи́к**, -á, supplier, purveyor, provider; caterer; outfitter.

постана́вливать, -аю *imp.*, **постанови́ть**, -влю́ -вишь *perf.* (*imp.* also постановля́ть) decree, enact; ordain; decide resolve.

постано́вка, -и, staging, production; arrangement, organization; putting, placing, setting; erection, raising; ~ го́лоса, voice training; ~ па́льцев, fingering.

постановле́ние, -я, decree, enactment; decision, resolution. **постановля́ть**, -я́ю *imp.* of постанови́ть.

постано́вочный, stage, staging, production. **постано́вщик**, -а, producer, stage-manager; (film) director.

по|стара́ться, -а́юсь *perf.*

по|старе́ть, -е́ю *perf.* **по-ста́рому** *adv.* as before; as of old.

посте́ль, -и, bed; bottom. **посте́льн|ый**, bed; ~ое бельё, bed-clothes; ~ режи́м, confinement to bed. **посте́ю**, etc.: see постла́ть.

постепе́нно *adv.* gradually, little by little. **постепе́нный**, gradual.

по|стеся́ться, -я́юсь *perf.*

постига́ть, -а́ю *imp.* of пости́чь. **по-сти́гнуть**: see пости́чь. **постиже́ние**, -я comprehension, grasp. **постижи́мый**, comprehensible.

постила́ть, -а́ю *imp.* of постла́ть. **пости́лка**, -и, spreading, laying; bedding; litter.

пости́чь, пости́гнуть, -и́гну -и́г(нул) *perf.* (*imp.* постига́ть) comprehend, grasp; befall.

по|стла́ть, -стелю́, -сте́лешь *perf.* (*imp.* also постила́ть) spread, lay; ~ по-сте́ль, make a bed.

по́стн|ый, lenten; lean; glum; ~ое ма́сло, vegetable oil.

посто́й, -я, billeting, quartering.

посто́льку *conj.* to the same extent, to the same degree; (so).

по|стоя́ться, -ню́сь, -ни́шься *perf.* **посторо́нн|ий**, strange; foreign; extraneous, outside; *sb.* stranger, outsider; ~им вход запрещён, no admission; private.

постоя́нно *adv.* constantly, continually, perpetually, always. **постоя́нн|ый**, permanent; constant; continual; invariable; steadfast, unchanging; ~ый а́дрес, permanent address; ~ая (величина́), constant; ~ый ток, direct current. **постоя́нство**, -а, constancy; permanency.

по|стоя́ть -ою́ *perf.* stand, stop; + за + *acc.* stand up for.

пострада́вший *sb.* victim. **по|страда́ть**, -а́ю *perf.*

постро́ение, -я, construction; building; formation. **по|стро́ить(ся**, -ро́ю(сь *perf.* **постро́йка**, -и, building; erection, construction; building-site.

постро́мка, -и, trace; strap.

поступа́тельный, progressive, forward, advancing. **поступа́ть** -а́ю *imp.*, **по-ступи́ть**, -плю́, -пишь *perf.* act; do; come through come in, be received; + в и́ога на + *acc.* enter, join go to, go into; + с + *instr.* treat, deal with; ~ в прода́жу, go on sale, come on the market; ~ в шко́лу, go to school, start school; поступи́ла жа́лоба, a complaint has been received; ~ся + *instr.* waive, forgo; give up. **поступле́ние**, -я, entering, joining; receipt; entry. **посту́пок**, -пка, action; act, deed; *pl.* conduct, behaviour. **по́ступь**, -и, gait; step, tread.

по|стуча́ть(ся, -чу́(сь *perf.*

по|стыди́ться, -ыжу́сь *perf.* **посты́дный**, shameful.

посу́да, -ы, crockery; plates and dishes; service; ware; utensils; vessel, crock. **посу́дн|ый**, china; dish; ~ое полоте́нце, tea-towel; ~ый шкаф, dresser, china-cupboard.

по|сули́ть, -лю́ *perf.*

посу́точный, 24-hour, round-the-clock; by the day.

посчастли́виться, ится *perf. impers.* (+ *dat.*) turn out well, go well (for); ей посчастли́вилось + *inf.* she had the luck to, she was lucky enough to.

по|счита́ть, -а́ю *perf.* count (up). **по|счита́ться**, -а́юсь *perf.*

посыла́ть, -а́ю *imp.* of посла́ть. **посы́лка**, -и, sending; parcel, package;

errand; premise. посы́лочный, parcel. посы́льный sb. messenger.

посыпа́ть, -плю -плешь perf., посыпа́ть, -а́ю imp. strew; sprinkle; powder.

посяга́тельство, -а, encroachment; infringement. посяга́ть, -а́ю imp., посягну́ть, -ну́, -нёшь perf. encroach, infringe; make an attempt (на + acc. on).

пот, -а (-у), loc. -у́; pl. -ы́, sweat, perspiration.

потаённый потайно́й, secret.

по-тво́ему adv. in your opinion; as you wish; as you advise; пусть бу́дет ~, have it your own way; just as you think.

потака́ть, -а́ю imp. + dat. indulge, pander to.

потасо́вка, -и, brawl, fight; hiding, beating.

потво́рствовать, -твую imp. (+ dat.) be indulgent (towards), connive (at), pander (to).

потёмки, -мок pl. darkness. по|темне́ть, -е́ет perf.

потерпе́вший sb. victim; survivor. по|терпе́ть, -плю́ -пишь perf.

поте́ря, -и, loss; waste; pl. losses, casualties. по|теря́ть(ся, -я́ю(сь perf.

потесни́ть, -ню́ perf. потесни́ться, -ню́сь perf.; make room; sit closer, stand closer. squeeze up, move up.

поте́ть, -е́ю imp. (perf. вс~, за~) sweat, perspire; mist over, steam up (+ над + instr.) sweat, toil (over).

поте́ха, -и, fun, amusement. по|те́шить(ся, -шу(сь perf. поте́шный, funny amusing.

потира́ть, -а́ю imp. rub.

потихо́ньку adv. noiselessly, softly; secretly, by stealth. on the sly; slowly.

по́тный, -тен, -тна́, -тно, sweaty, damp with perspiration; misty, steamed up; ~ые ру́ки, clammy hands.

пото́к, -а, stream; flow; torrent; flood; production line; group; пото́к маши́н, traffic flow.

потоло́к, -лка́, ceiling.

по|толсте́ть, -е́ю perf.

пото́м adv. afterwards; later (on); then, after that. пото́мок, -мка, descendant; scion; offspring, progeny. пото́мство, -а, posterity, descendants.

потому́ adv. that is why; ~ что conj. because, as.

по|тону́ть, -ну́, -нешь perf. пото́п, -а, flood, deluge. по|топи́ть, -топлю́, -пишь perf., потопля́ть, -я́ю imp. sink. потопле́ние, -я, sinking.

по|топта́ть, -пчу́, -пчешь perf. по|торопи́ть(ся -плю́(сь, -пишь(ся perf.

пото́чный, continuous; production-line; ~ая ли́ния, production line; ма́ссовое ~ое произво́дство, mass production.

по|тра́тить, -а́чу perf.

потреби́тель, -я m. consumer, user. потреби́тельск|ий, consumer; consumer's, consumers'; ~ие това́ры, consumer goods. потреби́ть, -блю́ perf., потребля́ть, -я́ю imp. consume, use. потребле́ние, -я, consumption, use. потре́бность, -и, need, want, necessity. requirement. потре́бный, necessary, required requisite. по|тре́бовать(ся, -бую(сь perf.

по|трево́жить(ся, -жу(сь perf.

потрёпанный, shabby; ragged, tattered; battered; worn, seedy. по|трепа́ть(ся, -плю́(сь, -плешь(ся perf.

по|тре́скаться, -ается perf. потре́скивать, -ает imp. crackle.

потроха́, -о́в pl. giblets; pluck. по|троши́ть, -шу́ imp. (perf. вы́~) disembowel, clean; draw.

потруди́ться, -ужу́сь, -у́дишься perf. take some pains do some work; take the trouble.

потряса́ть, -а́ю imp., потрясти́, -су́, -сёшь; -я́с, -лá perf. shake; rock; stagger, stun; + acc. or instr. brandish, shake; ~ кулако́м, shake one's fist. потряса́ющий, staggering, stupendous, tremendous.

поту́га, -и, muscular contraction; pl. labours; vain attempts; родовы́е поту́ги, labour.

поту́пить -плю perf., потупля́ть, -я́ю imp. lower cast down; ~ся, look down, cast down one's eyes.

потускне́лый, tarnished; lack-lustre. по|тускне́ть, -е́ет perf.

потуха́ть, -а́ет imp., по|ту́хнуть, -нет, -ух perf. go out; die out. потуха́ть, -а́ет imp., по|ту́хнуть, -нет, -ух perf. go out; die out. потухший, extinct; lifeless, lack-lustre.

по|туши́ть, -шу́, -шишь perf. по|тя́-га́ться, -а́юсь perf.

потя́гиваться, -аюсь imp., по|тяну́ться, -ну́сь, -нешься perf. stretch oneself. по|тяну́ть, -ну́, -нешь perf.

по|у́жинать, -аю perf. по|умне́ть, -е́ю perf.

поучи́тельный, instructive.

похвала́, -ы́, praise. по|хвали́ть(ся, -лю́(сь, -лишь(ся perf. похвальба́, -ы́, bragging, boasting. похва́льный, praiseworthy, laudable, commendable; laudatory.

по|хва́статься, -аюсь perf.

похити́тель, -я m. kidnapper; abductor; thief. похи́тить, -и́щу perf., похи-ща́ть, -а́ю imp. kidnap; abduct, carry off; steal. похище́ние, -я, theft; kid-napping; abduction.

похлёбка, -и, broth, soup.

по|хлопота́ть, -очу́, -о́чешь perf.

похме́лье, -я, hangover.

похо́д, -а, campaign; march; cruise; (long) walk, hike; outing, excursion. вы́ступить в ~, take the field; set out; на ~е, on the march.

по|хода́тайствовать, -твую perf.

походи́ть, -ожу́, -о́дишь imp. на + acc. be like, look like, resemble.

похо́дка, -и, gait, walk, step. похо́д-н|ый, mobile, field; marching, cruis-ing; ~ая крова́ть, camp-bed; ~ая ку́хня, mobile kitchen, field kitchen; ~ый мешо́к, kit-bag; ~ый поря́док, marching order; ~ая ра́ция, walkie-talkie. похожде́ние, -я, adventure, escapade.

похо́жий, similar, alike; ~ на, like.

по|хорони́ть, -ню́, -нишь perf. по-хоро́нный, funeral. по́хороны, -ро́н pl. funeral; burial.

по|хороше́ть, -е́ю perf.

по́хоть, -и, lust.

по|худе́ть, -е́ю perf.

по|целова́ть(ся, -лу́ю(сь perf. по-целу́й, -я, kiss.

по|церемо́ниться, -нюсь perf.

по́чва, -ы, soil, earth; ground; basis, footing. по́чвенный, soil, ground; ~ покро́в, top-soil.

почём adv. how much? how; ~ знать? who can tell? how is one to know?; ~ сего́дня я́блоки? how much are apples today?; ~ я зна́ю? how should I know?

почему́ adv. why; (and) so, that's why. почему́-либо, -нибудь advs. for some reason or other. почему́-то adv. for some reason.

о́черк, -а, hand(writing).

почерне́лый, blackened, darkened. по|-пчерне́ть, -е́ю perf.

почерпа́ть, -а́ю imp., почерпну́ть, -ну́, -нёшь perf. get, draw, scoop up; pick up.

по|черстве́ть, -е́ю perf. по|чеса́ть(ся, -ешу́(сь, -е́шешь(ся perf.

по́честь, -и, honour. почёт, -а, honour; respect, esteem. почётный, honoured, respected, esteemed; of honour; honourable; honorary; ~ карау́л, guard of honour.

по́чечный, renal; kidney.

почива́ть, -а́ю imp. of почи́ть.

почи́н, -а, initiative; beginning, start.

по|чини́ть, -ню́, -нишь perf., починя́ть, -я́ю imp. repair, mend. почи́нка, -и, repairing, mending.

по|чи́стить(ся, -и́щу(сь perf.

почита́ние, -я, honouring; respect, esteem. почита́ть[1], -а́ю imp. honour, respect, esteem; revere; worship.

почита́ть[2], -а́ю perf. read for a while, look at.

почи́ть, -и́ю perf. (imp. почива́ть) rest, take one's rest; pass away; ~ на ла́-врах, rest on one's laurels.

по́чка[1], -и, bud.

по́чка[2], -и, kidney.

по́чта, -ы, post, mail; post-office. по-чтальо́н, -а, postman. почтальо́нша, -и, postwoman. почта́мт, -а, (head) post-office.

почте́ние, -я, respect; esteem; deference. почте́нный, honourable; respectable, estimable; venerable; considerable.

почти́ adv. almost, nearly.

почти́тельный, respectful, deferential; considerable. почти́ть, -чту́ perf. honour.

почтóв|ый, post, mail; postal; ~ая карéта, stage coach, mail; ~ая кáрточка, postcard; ~ый перевóд, postal order; ~ый пóезд, mail (train); ~ый я́щик, letter-box.

по|чýдиться, -ишься perf. по|шабáшить, -шу perf.

пошатнýть, -нý -нёшь perf. shake; ~ся, shake; totter, reel, stagger; be shaken.

по|шевели́ть(ся, -елю́(сь, -éли́шь(ся perf. пошёл, etc.: see пойти́.

пошивка, -и, sewing. **поши́вочный**, sewing.

пóшлина, -ы, duty; customs.

пóшлость, -и, vulgarity, commonness; triviality; triteness, banality. **пóшлый**, vulgar, common; commonplace, trivial; trite, banal. **пошля́к**, -á, vulgarian, Philistine.

поштýчно adv. by the piece. **поштýчный**, by the piece; piece-work.

по|шути́ть, -учý, -ýтишь perf.

пощáда, -ы, mercy. **по|щади́ть**, -ажý perf.

по|щекотáть, -очý -óчешь perf.

пощёчина, -ы box on the ear; slap in the face.

по|щýпать, -аю perf.

поэ́зия, -и, poetry. **поэ́ма**, -ы, poem. **поэ́т**, -а, poet. **поэти́ческий**, poetic, poetical.

поэ́тому adv. therefore, and so.

пою́, etc.: see петь, пойти́.

появи́ться, -влю́сь -вишься perf, **появля́ться**, -я́юсь imp. appear; show up; emerge. **появле́ние**, -я, appearance.

пóяс, -а; pl. -á, belt; girdle; waist-band; waist; zone; по ~, up to the waist, waist-deep, waist-high.

поясне́ние, -я, explanation, elucidation. **поясни́тельный**, explanatory. **поясни́ть**, -ню́ perf. (imp поясня́ть) explain, elucidate.

поясни́ца, -ы, small of the back. **поясн|óй**, waist; to the waist, waist-high; zone, zonal; ~áя вáнна, hip-bath.

поясня́ть, -я́ю imp. of поясни́ть.

пр. abbr. прое́зд, passage, thoroughfare; проспе́кт, Prospect, avenue; прóчие, (the) others.

пра- pref. original, first, oldest; great-. **прабáбушка**, -и, great-grandmother. **прáвнук**, -а, great-grandson. **прáвнучка**, -и, great-granddaughter. **прáдед**, -а, great-grandfather; pl. ancestors, forefathers; ~дéдовский, great-grandfather's; ancestral; ancient. ~дéдушка, -и m. great-grandfather. **прáотец**, -тца, forefather. ~прáдед, -а, great-great-grandfather. ~роди́тель, -я m. primogenitor; forefather. ~язы́к, -á, parent language.

прáвда, -ы, (the) truth; true; justice; всéми ~ми и непрáвдами, by fair means or foul, by hook or by crook; э́то ~, that's true. **правди́вый**, true; truthful; honest, upright. **правдоподóбный**, probable, likely; plausible.

прáвило, -а, rule; regulation; principle; взять за ~, положи́ть за ~, make it a rule; взять себé за ~, make a point of; как ~, as a rule; прáвила ýличного движе́ния, traffic regulations.

прáвильно adv. rightly; correctly; regularly. **прáвильн|ый**, right, correct; regular; rectilinear, rectilineal; ~о! that's right! exactly!

прави́тельственный, government, governmental. **прави́тельство**, -а, government. **прáвить**[1], -влю + instr. rule, govern; drive.

прáвить[2], -влю imp. correct; ~ корректýру, read proofs, correct proofs. **прáвка**, -и, correcting; (proof-)reading.

правле́ние, -я, board, governing body; administration, management; governing, government.

прáвленый, corrected.

прáвнук, ~внýчка: see пра-.

прáво, -а; pl. -á, law; right; (води́тельские) правá, driving licence; на правáх + gen. in the capacity, character, or position of; на правáх рýкописи, all rights reserved; ~ гóлоса, the vote, suffrage.

прáво adv. really, truly, indeed.

прáво-[1] in comb. law; right. **правовéд**, -а, jurist; law-student. ~ве́дение, -я, jurisprudence. ~ве́рный, orthodox; sb. true believer, Moslem. ~ме́рный, lawful, rightful. **~мо́чие**, **-я**, competence. **~мо́чный**, competent, authorized. **~наруше́ние**, **-я**, infringement of the law, offence. **~наруши́тель**, **-я** *m*. offender, delinquent. **~писа́ние**, **-я**, spelling, orthography. **~сла́вный**, orthodox; *sb*. member of Orthodox Church. **~су́дие**, **-я**, justice.

право-[2] in *comb*. right, right-hand. **правобере́жный**, on the right bank right-bank. **~сторо́нний**, right; right-hand. **~фла́нговый**, right-flank, right-wing.

правово́й, legal, of the law; lawful, rightful.

правота́, **-ы́**, rightness; innocence.

пра́вый[1], right; right-hand; right-wing **пра́в**|**ый**[2]; прав, **-а́**, **-о**, right, correct; righteous, just; innocent not guilty; **~ое де́ло**, a just cause.

пра́вящий, ruling.

пра́дед, etc.: see пра-.

пра́здник, **-а**, (public) holiday; feast; festival; festive occasion. **пра́зднование**, **-я**, celebration. **пра́здновать**, **-ную** *imp*. (*perf*. от**~**) celebrate. **пра́здность**, **-и**, idleness, inactivity; emptiness. **пра́здный**; **-ден**, inactive; empty; vain, useless.

пра́ктика, **-и**, practice; practical work; **на пра́ктике**, in practice. **практикова́ть**, **-ку́ю** *imp*. practise; apply in practice; **~ся** (*perf*. на**~ся**) practise; be used, be practised; **+ в** *prep*. have practice in. **практику́м**, **-а**, practical work. **практи́ческий**, **практи́чный**, practical.

пра́отец: see пра-.

пра́порщик, **-а**, ensign.

прапра́дед, etc.: see пра-.

прах, **-а**, dust; ashes, remains; **пойти́ ~ом**, go to rack and ruin.

пра́чечная *sb*. laundry; wash-house. **пра́чка**, **-и**, laundress.

пра́язык: see пра-.

пре- *pref*. I. of verbs, indicating action in extreme degree or superior measure; sur-, over-, out-. II. of adjs. and advs., indicating superlative degree; very, most, exceedingly.

пребыва́ние, **-я**, stay; residence; tenure, period; **~ в до́лжности**, tenure of office, period in office. **пребыва́ть**, **-а́ю** *imp*. be; reside; **~ в неве́дении**, be in the dark; **~ в отсу́тствии**, be absent; **~ у вла́сти**, be in power.

превзойти́, **-йду́**, **-йдёшь**; **-ошёл**, **-шла́** *perf*. (*imp*. **превосходи́ть**) surpass; excel; **~ самого́ себя́**, surpass oneself; **~ чи́сленностью**, outnumber.

превозмога́ть, **-а́ю** *imp*., **превозмо́чь**, **-огу́**, **-о́жешь**; **-о́г**, **-ла́** *perf*. overcome; surmount.

превознести́, **-су́**, **-сёшь**; **-ёс**, **-ла́** *perf*., **превозноси́ть**, **-ошу́**, **-о́сишь** *imp*. extol, praise.

превосходи́тельство, **-а**, Excellency. **превосходи́ть**, **-ожу́**, **-о́дишь** *imp*. of превзойти́. **превосхо́дн**|**ый** superlative; superb, outstanding, excellent; superior; **~ая сте́пень**, superlative (degree). **превосходя́щий**, superior.

преврати́ть, **-ащу́** *perf*., **превраща́ть**, **-а́ю** *imp*. convert, turn, reduce; transmute; **~ся**, turn, change. **превра́тно** *adv*. wrongly; **~ истолкова́ть**, misinterpret; **~ поня́ть**, misunderstand. **превра́тный**, wrong, false; changeful, inconstant, perverse. **превраще́ние** **-я**, transformation, conversion; transmutation; metamorphosis.

превы́сить, **-ы́шу** *perf*., **превыша́ть**, **-а́ю** *imp*. exceed. **превыше́ние**, **-я**, exceeding, excess.

прегра́да, **-ы**, obstacle; bar, barrier. **прегради́ть**, **-ажу́** *perf*., **прегражда́ть**, **-а́ю** *imp*. bar, obstruct, block.

пред *prep*. + *instr*.: see пе́ред.

пред-[1], **предъ-** *pref*. pre-, fore-, ante-.

пред-[2] *abbr*. in *comb*. of председа́тель, chairman.

-пред, **-а**, *abbr*. in *comb* of представи́тель, representative, spokesman.

предава́ть(ся, **-даю́(сь**, **-даёшь(ся** *imp*. of преда́ть(ся.

преда́ние, **-я**, legend; tradition; handing over, committal. **пре́данность**, **-и**, devotion; faithfulness; loyalty. **пре́данный**, devoted, faithful. **преда́тель**, **-я** *m*. traitor; betrayer. **преда́тельский**, traitorous; perfidious; treacherous. **преда́тельство**, **-а**, treachery, betrayal, perfidy. **преда́ть**, **-а́м**, **-а́шь**,

-áст, -ади́м; пре́дал, -á, -о perf. (imp. предава́ть) hand over, commit; betray; ~ забве́нию, bury in oblivion; ~ земле́, commit to the earth; ~ суду́, bring to trial; ~ся give oneself up, abandon oneself; give way, indulge; + dat. go over to, put oneself in the hands of.

предаю́, etc.: see предава́ть.

предвари́тель|ый, preliminary; prior; по ~ому соглаше́нию by prior arrangement; ~ое заключе́ние, detention before trial; ~ая прода́жа биле́тов, advance sale of tickets, advance booking. предвари́ть, -рю́ perf., предваря́ть, -я́ю imp. forestall, anticipate; forewarn inform beforehand.

предве́стник, -а, forerunner, precursor; herald, harbinger; presage, portent.

предвеща́ть, -а́ю imp. foretell; herald, presage, portend; э́то предвеща́ет хорошее, this augurs well.

предвзя́тый, preconceived; prejudiced; biased.

предви́деть. -и́жу imp. foresee; ~ся be foreseen; be expected.

предвкуси́ть, -ушу́, -у́сишь perf., предвкуша́ть, -а́ю imp. look forward to, anticipate (with pleasure).

предводи́тель, -я m. leader. предводи́тельствовать, -твую imp. + instr. lead.

предвое́нный pre-war.

предвосхи́тить -и́щу perf., предвосхища́ть. -а́ю imp. anticipate.

предвы́борный, (pre-)election.

предго́рье, -я, foothills.

преде́л, -а, limit; bound. boundary; end; pl. range; положи́ть ~ + dat. put an end to terminate. преде́льн|ый, boundary; limiting; maximum; utmost; critical; saturated; ~ый во́зраст, age-limit; ~ое напряже́ние, breaking load, maximum stress; ~ая ско́рость, maximum speed; ~ый срок time-limit deadline.

предзнаменова́ние, -я, omen, augury. предзнаменова́ть, -ну́ю imp. bode, augur, portend.

предисло́вие, -я, preface, foreword.

предлага́ть, -а́ю imp. of предложи́ть.

предло́г[1], -а, pretext; под ~ом + gen. on the pretext of.

предло́г[2], -а, preposition.

предложе́ние[1], -я, sentence; clause; proposition.

предложе́ние[2], -я, offer; proposition; proposal; motion; suggestion; supply; внести́ ~, move, introduce, put down, a motion; сде́лать ~ + dat. make an offer to; propose to; спрос и ~, supply and demand. предложи́ть, -жу́, -жишь perf. (imp. предлага́ть) offer; propose; suggest; put, set, propound; order, require; ~ резолю́цию, move a resolution.

предло́жный, prepositional.

предме́т, -а, object; article, item; subject; topic, theme; (pl.) goods; на сей ~, to this end, with this object; ~ спо́ра, point at issue; ~ы пе́рвой необходи́мости, necessities. предме́тн|ый, object; ~ катало́г, subject catalogue; ~ сто́лик stage; ~ уро́к, object-lesson.

предназнача́ть, -а́ю imp., предназна́чить, -чу perf. destine, intend, mean; earmark, set aside. предназначе́ние, -я earmarking; destiny.

преднаме́ренный, premeditated; aforethought; deliberate.

пре́до: see пе́ред.

пре́док, -дка, forefather, ancestor; pl. forebears.

предоста́вить, -влю perf., предоставля́ть, -я́ю imp. grant; leave; give; ~ в его́ распоряже́ние, put at his disposal; ~ пра́во, concede a right; ~ сло́во + dat. give the floor to, call on to speak.

предостерега́ть, -а́ю imp., предостере́чь, -егу́, -ежёшь; -ёг, -ла́ perf. warn, caution. предостереже́ние, -я, warning, caution. предосторо́жность, -и, caution; precaution; ме́ры предосторо́жности, precautionary measures.

предосуди́тельный, wrong, reprehensible, blameworthy.

предотврати́ть, -ащу́ perf., предотвраща́ть. -а́ю imp. avert, prevent; ward off, stave off.

предохране́ние, -я, protection; preservation. предохрани́тель, -я m. guard;

safety device, safety-catch; fuse. **предохрани́тельн|ый**, preservative; preventive; safety; protective; ~ый кла́пан, safety-valve; ~ая коро́бка, fuse-box. **предохрани́ть**, -ню́ *perf.*, **предохраня́ть**, -я́ю *imp.* preserve, protect.

предписа́ние, -я, order, injunction; *pl.* directions, instructions; prescription; согла́сно предписа́нию, by order. **предписа́ть**, -ишу́, -и́шешь *perf.*, **предпи́сывать**, -аю *imp.* order, direct, instruct; prescribe.

предполага́емый, supposed, conjectural. **предполага́ть**, -а́ю *imp.*, **предположи́ть**, -ожу́, -о́жишь *perf.* suppose, assume; conjecture, surmise; intend, propose; contemplate; presuppose; предполага́ется *impers.* it is proposed, it is intended. **предположе́ние**, -я, supposition; assumption; intention. **предположи́тельно** *adv.* supposedly, presumably; probably. **предположи́тельный**, conjectural; hypothetical.

предпосле́дний, penultimate, last but one, next to the last.

предпосы́лка, -и, prerequisite, pre-condition; premise.

предпоче́сть, -чту́, -чтёшь; -чёл, -чла́ *perf.*, **предпочита́ть**, -а́ю *imp.* prefer; я предпочёл бы, I would rather. **предпочте́ние**, -я, preference. **предпочти́тельный**, preferable.

предприи́мчивость, -и, enterprise. **предприи́мчивый**, enterprising.

предпринима́тель, -я *m.* owner; employer; entrepreneur; contractor. **предпринима́тельство**, -а, business undertakings; свобо́дное ~, free enterprise. **предпринима́ть**, -а́ю *imp.*, **предприня́ть**, -иму́, -и́мешь; -и́нял, -а́, -о *perf.* undertake; ~ ата́ку, launch an attack; ~ шаги́, take steps. **предприя́тие**, -я, undertaking, enterprise; business; concern; works; риско́ванное ~, venture risky undertaking

предрасположе́ние, -я, predisposition. **предрасполо́женный**, predisposition.

предрассу́док, -дка, prejudice.

предреша́ть, -а́ю *imp.* **предреши́ть**, -шу́ *perf.* decide beforehand; predetermine.

председа́тель, -я *m.*, **председа́тельница**, -ы, chairman. **председа́тельск|ий**, chairman's; ~ое кре́сло, the chair. **председа́тельствовать**, -твую *imp.* preside, be in the chair.

предсказа́ние, -я, prediction, forecast, prophecy; prognostication. **предсказа́тель**, -я *m.* foreteller, forecaster; soothsayer. **предсказа́ть**, -ажу́ -а́жешь *perf.*, **предска́зывать**, -аю *imp.* foretell, predict; forecast prophesy.

предсме́ртный, dying; ~ час, one's last hour.

представи́тель, -я *m.* representative; spokesman; specimen. **представи́тельный**, representative; imposing. **представи́тельство**, -а, representation; re-presentatives; delegation.

представа́ть, -таю́, -таёшь *imp.* of предста́ть.

предста́вить, -влю *perf.*, **представля́ть**, -я́ю *imp.* present; produce, submit; introduce; recommend, put forward; display; perform; play; represent; ~ себе́, imagine, fancy, picture, conceive; представля́ть собо́й, represent, be; constitute; ~ся, present itself, occur, arise; seem; introduce oneself; + *instr.* pretend to be, pass oneself off as. **представле́ние**, -я, presentation, introduction; declaration statement; representation; performance; idea, notion, conception.

предста́ть, -а́ну *perf.* (*imp.* представа́ть), appear; ~ пе́ред судо́м, appear in court.

предстоя́ть, -ои́т *imp.* be in prospect, lie ahead, be at hand; мне предстои́т пойти́ туда́, I shall have to go there. **предстоя́щий**, coming, forthcoming; impending, imminent.

предте́ча, -и *m.* and *f.* forerunner, precursor; Иоа́нн ~, John the Baptist.

предубежде́ние, -я, prejudice, bias.

предуга́дать, -а́ю *perf.*, **предуга́дывать**, -аю *imp.* guess; foresee.

предупреди́тельность, -и, courtesy; attentiveness. **предупреди́тельный**, preventive; precautionary; courteous, attentive; obliging. **предупреди́ть**, -ежу́ *perf.*, **предупрежда́ть**, -а́ю *imp.*

notify in advance, let know beforehand; warn; give notice; prevent, avert; anticipate, forestall. **предупрежде́ние**, -я *notice*; notification; warning, caution; prevention; anticipation; forestalling.

предусма́тривать, -аю *imp.*, **предусмотре́ть**, -рю́, -ришь *perf.* envisage, foresee; provide for, make provision for. **предусмотри́тельный**, prudent; provident; far-sighted.

предчу́вствие, -я, presentiment; foreboding, misgiving. premonition. **предчу́вствовать** -твую *imp.* have a presentiment (about) have a premonition of.

предше́ственник, -а, predecessor; forerunner, precursor. **предше́ствовать**, -твую *imp.* + *dat.* go in front of; precede.

предъ-: see **пред-**¹.

предъяви́тель -я *m.* bearer; а́кция на предъяви́теля, ordinary share. **предъяви́ть**, -влю́ -вишь *perf.*, **предъявля́ть**, -я́ю *imp* show, produce, present; bring, bring forward; ~ иск к + *dat.* bring suit against: ~ обвине́ние + *dat.* charge; ~ пра́во на + *acc.* lay claim to.

предыду́щ|ий previous, preceding; ~ее *sb.* the foregoing.

прее́мник -а, successor. **прее́мственность**, -и succession; continuity.

пре́жде *adv.* before; first; formerly, in former times; ~ чем, before; *prep.* + *gen.* before; ~ всего́, first of all, to begin with; first and foremost. **преждевре́менный**, premature; untimely. **пре́жний**, previous, former.

президе́нт, -а, president; **президе́нтский**, presidential. **прези́диум**, -а, presidium.

презира́ть, -а́ю *imp* despise hold in contempt; disdain scorn. **презре́ние**, -я, contempt; scorn. **презре́нный**, contemptible, despicable **презри́тельный**, contemptuous scornful.

преиму́щественно *adv.* mainly, chiefly, principally. **преиму́щественный**, main. principal primary prime; preferential; priority **преиму́щество**, -а, advantage;

preference; по преиму́ществу for the most part, chiefly.

преклоне́ние, -я. admiration. worship. **преклони́ть**, -ню́ *perf.*, **преклоня́ть**, -я́ю *imp.* bow bend; ~ го́лову, bow; ~ коле́на genuflect kneel; ~ся bow down; + *dat.* or перед + *instr.* admire, worship. **прекло́нный**; ~ во́зраст. old age; declining years.

прекра́сно *adv.* excellently; perfectly well. **прекра́сный**, beautiful; fine; excellent, capital first-rate; в оди́н ~ день, one fine day; ~ пол, the fair sex.

прекрати́ть, -ащу́ *perf.*, **прекраща́ть**, -а́ю *imp.* stop, cease discontinue; put a stop to, end; break off sever, cut off; ~ войну́ end the war; ~ подпи́ску, discontinue a subscription, stop subscribing; ~ся, cease, end.

преле́стный charming. delightful lovely. **пре́лесть**, -и, charm fascination.

преломи́ть, -млю́, -мишь *perf.*, **преломля́ть**, -я́ю *imp.* refract; ~ся, be refracted. **преломле́ние** -я, refraction.

пре́лый fusty, musty; rotten. **прель**, -и, mouldiness, mould, rot.

прельсти́ть, -льщу́ *perf.*, **прельща́ть**, -а́ю *imp.* attract; lure, entice; ~ся, be attracted; be tempted; fall (+ *instr.* for)

премиа́льн|ый, bonus; prize; ~ые *sb. pl.* bonus.

премину́ть, -ну *perf.* with *neg.* (not) fail.

премирова́ть, -ру́ю *perf. and imp.* award a prize to; give a bonus. **пре́мия**, -и, prize; bonus; bounty, gratuity; premium.

премье́р, -а, prime minister; leading actor, lead. **премье́ра**, -ы, premiére; first performance. **премье́рша**, -и, leading lady, lead.

пренебрега́ть, -а́ю *imp.*, **пренебре́чь**, -егу́, -ежёшь; -ёг, -ла́ *perf.* + *instr.* scorn despise; neglect, disregard. **пренебреже́ние**, -я, scorn, contempt; disdain; neglect, disregard. **пренебрежи́тельный**, scornful; slighting; disdainful.

пре́ния -ий *pl.* debate; discussion; pleadings; вы́ступить в ~х, take part in a discussion.

преоблада́ние, -я, predominance. пре-облада́ть, -а́ет *imp.* predominate; pre-vail.

преображать, -а́ю *imp.* преобрази́ть, -ажу́, transform. преображе́ние, -я, transformation; Transfiguration. пре-образова́ние, -я, transformation; re-form; reorganization. преобразова́ть, -зу́ю *perf.*, преобразо́вывать, -аю *imp.* transform; reform, reorganize.

преодолева́ть, -а́ю *imp.*, преодоле́ть, -е́ю *perf.* overcome, get over, sur-mount.

препара́т, -а, preparation.

препина́ние, -я; зна́ки препина́ния, punctuation marks.

препира́тельство, -а, altercation, wrang-ling squabbling. препира́ться, -а́юсь *imp.* wrangle, squabble.

преподава́ние, -я, teaching, tuition, in-struction. преподава́тель, -я *m.*, -ница, -ы, teacher; lecturer, instructor. преподава́тельский, teaching; teach-er's, teachers'; ~ соста́в, teaching staff. преподава́ть, -даю́, -даёшь *imp.* teach.

преподнести́, -су́, -сёшь ёс, -ла́ *perf.*, преподноси́ть, -ошу́, -о́сишь, present with, make a present of.

препроводи́тельный, accompanying. препроводи́ть, -вожу́, -во́дишь *perf.*, препровожда́ть, -а́ю *imp.* send, for-ward, dispatch.

препя́тствие, -я, obstacle, impediment, hindrance; hurdle; ска́чки (бег) с препя́тствиями, steeplechase; hurdle--race, obstacle-race. препя́тствовать, -твую *imp.* (*perf.* вос~) + *dat.* hinder, impede hamper; stand in the way of.

прерва́ть, -ву́, -вёшь; -а́л, -а́, -о *perf.* (*imp.* прерыва́ть) interrupt; break off; cut off, sever; cut short; нас прерва́ли we've been cut off; ~ся, be interrupted; be broken off; break down; break.

пререка́ние, -я, altercation, argument, wrangle. пререка́ться, -а́юсь *imp.* argue, wrangle, dispute.

прерыва́ть(ся, -а́ю(сь *imp.* of пре-рва́ть(ся.

пресека́ть, -а́ю *imp.*, пресе́чь, -еку́ -ечёшь; -ёк, -екла́ *perf.* stop, cut short;

put an end to; ~ в ко́рне, nip in the bud; ~ся, stop; break.

пресле́дование, -я, pursuit, chase; per-secution, victimization; prosecution. пресле́довать, -дую *imp.* pursue, chase, be after; haunt; persecute, tor-ment; victimize; prosecute.

пресловутый, notorious.

пресмыка́ться, -а́юсь *imp.* grovel, cringe; creep, crawl. пресмыка́ющее-ся *sb.* reptile.

пре́сный, fresh; unsalted; unleavened; flavourless, tasteless; insipid, vapid, flat.

престаре́лый, aged; advanced in years.

престо́л, -а, throne; altar.

преступле́ние, -я crime, offence; felony; transgression. престу́пник, -а, criminal, offender delinquent; felon; вое́нный ~, war criminal. престу́п-ность, -и, criminality; crime, delin-quency. престу́пный, criminal; feloni-ous.

пресыти́ться, -ы́щусь *perf.*, пресы-ща́ться, -а́юсь *imp.* be satiated, be sur-feited. пресыще́ние, -я, surfeit, satiety.

претвори́ть, -рю́ *perf.*, претворя́ть, -я́ю *imp* (в + *acc.*) turn, change, convert; ~ в жизнь, put into practice, realize, carry out; ~ся в + *acc.* turn into be-come; ~ в жизнь, be realized, come true.

претенде́нт, -а, claimant; aspirant; candidate; pretender. претендова́ть, -ду́ю *imp.* на + *acc.* claim, lay claim to; have pretensions to; aspire to. прете́нзия, -и, claim; pretension; быть в прете́нзии на + *acc.* have a grudge, a grievance, against; bear a grudge.

претерпева́ть, -а́ю *imp.*, претерпе́ть, -плю́, -пишь *perf.* undergo; suffer, en-dure.

преувеличе́ние, -я, exaggeration; over-statement. преувели́чивать, -аю *imp.*, преувели́чить, -чу *perf.* exaggerate; overstate.

преуменьша́ть, -а́ю *imp.*, преуме́нь-шить, -е́ньшу *perf.* underestimate; minimize; belittle; understate.

преуспева́ть, -а́ю *imp.*, преуспе́ть, -е́ю *perf.* succeed be successful; thrive, prosper, flourish.

преходя́щий, transient.

при *prep.* + *prep.* by, at; in the presence of; attached to, affiliated to, under the auspices of; with; about; on; for, notwithstanding; in the time of, in the days of; under; during; when, in case of; би́тва ~ Бородине́, the battle of Borodino; ~ всём том, with it all, moreover; for all that; ~ де́тях, in front of the children; ~ дневно́м све́те, by daylight; ~ доро́ге, by the road(-side); ~ Ива́не Гро́зном, in the reign of Ivan the Terrible; under Ivan the Terrible; при мне, in my presence; ~ перехо́де че́рез у́лицу, when crossing the street; ~ Пу́шкине, in Pushkin's day; ~ слу́чае, when the occasion arises; ~ све́те ла́мпы, by lamplight; у него́ не́ было ~ себе́ де́нег, he had no money on him.

при-. I. *vbl. pref.* indicating action or motion continued to a given terminal point; action of attaching or adding; direction of action towards speaker or from above downward; incomplete or tentative action; exhaustive action; action to an accompaniment. II. *pref.* of nouns and adjs., indicating juxtaposition or proximity.

приба́вить, -влю *perf.*, **прибавля́ть**, -я́ю, add, put on, increase, augment; exaggerate, lay it on (thick); ~ в ве́се), put on weight; ~ хо́ду, put on speed; ~ ша́гу, mend one's pace; ~ся, increase; rise; wax; день приба́вился, the days are getting longer, are drawing out. **приба́вка**, -и, addition, augmentation; increase, supplement, rise. **прибавле́ние**, -я, addition, augmentation; supplement, appendix. **приба́вочный**, additional; surplus.

прибега́ть[1], -а́ю *imp.* of прибежа́ть.
прибега́ть[2], -а́ю *imp.*, **прибе́гнуть**, -ну; -бе́г *perf.* + к + *dat.* resort to, fall back on.

прибежа́ть, -егу́ *perf.* (*imp.* прибега́ть) come running, run up.

прибе́жище, -а, refuge; verst ~, last resort.

приберега́ть, -а́ю *imp.*, **прибере́чь**, -егу́, -ежёшь; -ёг, -ла́ *perf.* save (up), reserve.

приберу́, etc.: see прибра́ть. **прибива́ть**, -а́ю *imp.* of прибить. **прибира́ть**, -а́ю *imp.* of прибра́ть.

прибить, -бью́, -бьёшь *perf.* (*imp.* прибива́ть), nail, fix with nails; lay, flatten; drive, carry; beat up.

приближа́ть, -а́ю *imp.*, **прибли́зить**, -и́жу *perf.* bring nearer, move nearer; hasten, advance; ~ся, approach, draw near; draw (come) nearer.

прибо́й, -я, surf, breakers.

прибо́р, -а, instrument, device, apparatus, appliance, gadget; set, service, things; fittings; бри́твенный ~, shaving things; ча́йный ~, tea-service, tea-things. **прибо́рн|ый**, instrument; ~ая доска́, dash-board, instrument panel.

прибра́ть, -беру́, -берёшь; -а́л, -а́, -о *perf.* (*imp.* прибира́ть) tidy (up), clear up, clean up; put away; ~ ко́мнату, do (out) a room; ~ посте́ль, make a bed.

прибре́жн|ый, coastal; littoral, riverside; riparian; ~ые острова́, off-shore islands.

прибыва́ть, -а́ю *imp.*, **прибы́ть**, -бу́ду; прибыл, -а́, -о *perf.* arrive; get in; increase, grow; rise, swell; wax. **при́быль**, -и, profit, gain; return; increase, rise. **при́быльный**, profitable, lucrative. **прибы́тие**, -я, arrival.

прибью́, etc.: see прибить.

прива́л -а, halt, stop; stopping-place.

приведу́, etc.: see привести́.

привезти́, -зу́, -зёшь; -ёз, -ла́ (*imp.* привози́ть), bring.

приве́редливый, fastidious, squeamish, hard to please. **привере́дничать**, -аю *imp.* be hard to please, be fastidious, be squeamish.

приве́сить, -е́шу *perf.* (*imp.* приве́шивать) hang up, suspend.

привести́, -еду́, -едёшь; -ёл, -а́ *perf.* (*imp.* приводи́ть) bring; lead; take; reduce; adduce, cite; + к + *dat.* lead to, bring to, conduce to, result in; + в + *acc.* put in(to), set; ~ в движе́ние, в де́йствие, set in motion, set going; ~ в изумле́ние, astonish, astound; ~ в исполне́ние, execute, carry out; ~ в отча́яние, drive to despair; ~ в поря́док, put in order, tidy (up); arrange, fix; ~ в у́жас, horrify.

приве́т, -а, greeting(s); regards; переда́йте ~ from me to my regards to; с серде́чным ~ом, yours sincerely. приве́тливость, -и, affability; cordiality. приве́тливый, cordial, friendly; affable. приве́тствие, -я, greeting, salutation; speech of welcome. приве́тствовать, -твую perf. and imp. greet, salute, hail; welcome; ~ стоя́, give a standing ovation (to).

приве́шивать, -аю imp. of приве́сить.

привива́ть(ся, -а́ю(сь, -а́ешь(ся imp. of приви́ть(ся. приви́вка, -и, inoculation; vaccination; grafting, graft.

привиде́ние, -я, ghost, spectre; apparition. при|ви́деться, -дится perf.

привилегиро́ванн|ый, privileged; ~ая а́кция, preference share. привиле́гия, -и, privilege.

привинти́ть, -нчу́ perf., приви́нчивать, -аю imp. screw on.

приви́ть, -вью, -вьёшь; -и́л, -а́, -о perf. (imp. привива́ть) inoculate, vaccinate; graft; implant; inculcate; cultivate, foster; ~ о́спу + dat. vaccinate; ~ся, take; become established, find acceptance, catch on.

приву́кус, а, after-taste; smack.

привлека́тельный, attractive. привлека́ть, -а́ю imp., привле́чь, -еку́, -ечёшь; -ёк, -ла́ perf. attract; draw; draw in, win over; have up; ~ внима́ние, attract attention; ~ к суду́, sue, take to court; prosecute; put on trial.

приво́д, -а, drive, driving-gear. приводи́ть, -ожу́ -о́дишь imp. of привести́. приводно́й, driving.

привожу́, etc.: see приводи́ть, привози́ть.

приво́з, -а, bringing, supply; importation; import. привози́ть, -ожу́ -о́зишь imp. of привезти́. привозно́й, привозный, imported.

приво́льный, free.

привстава́ть, -таю́, -таёшь imp., привста́ть, -а́ну perf. half-rise; rise, stand up.

привыка́ть, -а́ю imp., привы́кнуть, -ну; -ы́к perf. get used, get accustomed; get into the habit, get into the way. привы́чка, -и, habit. привы́чный, habitual, usual, customary; accustomed, used; of habit.

привью́, etc.: see приви́ть.

привя́занность, -и, attachment; affection. привя́занный, attached. привяза́ть, -яжу́, -я́жешь perf., привя́зывать, -аю imp. attach; tie, bind, fasten, secure, tether; ~ся, become attached; attach oneself; + к + dat. pester, bother. привязно́й, fastened, secured, tethered. привя́зчивый, importunate, insistent, annoying; affectionate; susceptible. при́вязь, -и, tie; lead, leash; tether.

пригласи́ть, -ашу́ perf., приглаша́ть, -а́ю imp. invite, ask; call (in); ~ на обе́д, ask to dinner. приглаше́ние, -я, invitation; offer.

пригляде́ться, -яжу́сь perf., пригля́дываться, -аюсь imp. look closely; + к + dat. scrutinize, examine; get used to. get accustomed.

пригна́ть, -гоню́, -го́нишь; -а́л, -а́, -о perf. (imp. пригоня́ть) drive in, bring in; fit, adjust.

пригова́ривать[1], -аю imp. keep saying, keep (on) repeating.

пригова́ривать[2], -аю imp., приговори́ть, -рю́ perf. sentence; condemn.

пригоди́ться, -ожу́сь perf. prove useful; be of use; come in useful come in handy. приго́дный, fit, suitable, good; useful. приго́жий, fine.

пригоня́ть, -я́ю imp. of пригна́ть.

пригора́ть, -а́ет imp., пригоре́ть, -ри́т perf. be burnt. пригоре́лый, burnt.

при́город, -а, suburb. при́городный, suburban.

приго́рок, -рка, hillock, knoll.

при́горшня, -и, gen. pl. -ей, handful.

пригото́вительный, preparatory. пригото́вить, -влю perf., приготовля́ть, -я́ю imp. prepare, cook, ~ роль, learn a part; ~ся, prepare; prepare oneself. приготовле́ние, -я, preparation.

пригрева́ть, -а́ю imp. of пригре́ть.

при|гре́зиться, -е́жусь perf.

пригре́ть, -е́ю *perf.* (*imp.* пригрева́ть) warm; cherish.

при|грози́ть, -ожу́ *perf.*

придава́ть, -даю́, -даёшь *imp.*, **прида́ть**, -а́м, -а́шь, -а́ст, -ади́м; при́дал, -а́, -о *perf.* add; increase, strengthen; give, impart; attach; ~ значе́ние + *dat.* attach importance to. **прида́ча**, -и, adding; addition; supplement; в прида́чу, into the bargain, in addition.

придвига́ть, -а́ю *imp.* придви́нуть, -ну *perf.* move up, draw up; ~ся, move up, draw near.

придво́рный, court; *sb.* courtier.

приде́лать, -аю *perf.*, **приде́лывать**, -аю *imp.* fix, attach.

приде́рживаться, -аюсь *imp.* hold on, hold; + *gen.* hold to, keep to; stick to, adhere to; ~ пра́вой стороны́, keep to the right; ~ мне́ния, be of the opinion.

придеру́сь, etc.: see придра́ться. **приди́раться**, -а́юсь *imp.* of придра́ться. **приди́рка**, -и, cavil, captious objection; fault-finding; carping. **приди́рчивый**, niggling; captious.

придоро́жный, roadside wayside.

придра́ться, -деру́сь, -дерёшься; -а́лся, -а́сь, -а́лось *perf.* (*imp.* придира́ться) find fault, cavil carp; seize; ~ к слу́чаю, seize an opportunity.

приду́, etc.: see прийти́.

приду́мать, -аю *perf.*, **приду́мывать**, -аю *imp.* think up, devise, invent; think of.

придыха́тельное *sb.* aspirate.

прие́ду, etc.: see прие́хать. **прие́зд**, -а, arrival, coming. **приезжа́ть**, -а́ю *imp.* of прие́хать. **прие́зжий**, newly arrived; *sb.* newcomer; visitor.

прие́м, -а, receiving; reception; surgery; welcome; admittance; dose; go; motion, movement; method, way, mode; device, trick; hold, grip; в оди́н ~, at one go. **прие́млемый**, acceptable; admissible. **прие́мная** *sb.* waiting-room; reception room. **прие́мник**, -а, radio, wireless, receiver. **прие́мн|ый**, receiving; reception; entrance; foster, adoptive, adopted; ~ый день, visiting day; ~ая коми́ссия, selection board; ~ая мать, foster-mother; ~ые часы́, (business) hours; surgery (hours);

~ый экза́мен, entrance examination. **прие́мо-переда́ющий**, two-way. **прие́мщик**, -а, inspector, examiner. **прие́мочный**, inspection, examining.

прие́хать, -е́ду *perf.* (*imp.* приезжа́ть) arrive, come.

прижа́ть, -жму́, -жмёшь *perf.* (*imp.* прижима́ть) press; clasp; ~ся, press oneself; cuddle up, snuggle up, nestle up.

приже́чь, -жгу́, -жжёшь; -жёг, -жгла́ *perf.* (*imp.* прижига́ть) cauterize, sear.

прижива́лка, -и, **прижива́льщик**, -а, dependant; hanger-on, sponger, parasite.

прижига́ние, -я, cauterization. **прижига́ть**, -а́ю *imp.* of приже́чь.

прижима́ть(ся), -а́ю(сь) *imp.* of прижа́ть(ся). **прижи́мистый**, tight-fisted, stingy. **прижму́**, etc.: see прижа́ть.

приз, -а; *pl.* -ы́, prize.

призаду́маться, -аюсь *perf.*, **призаду́мываться**, -аюсь *imp.* become thoughtful, become pensive.

призва́ние, -я, vocation, calling; по призва́нию, by vocation. **призва́ть**, -зову́, -зовёшь; -а́л, -а́, -о *perf.* (*imp.* призыва́ть) call, summon; call upon, appeal to; call up; ~ся, be called up.

призе́мистый, stocky, squat; thickset. **приземле́ние**, -я, landing, touch-down. **приземля́ться**, -лю́сь *perf.*, **приземля́ться**, -я́юсь *imp.* land, touch down.

призёр, -а, призёрша, и, prizewinner.

признава́ть, -наю́, -наёшь *imp.*, **призна́ть**, -а́ю *perf.* recognize; spot, identify; admit, own, acknowledge; deem vote; (не) ~ себя́ вино́вным, plead (not) guilty; ~ся, confess, own; ~ся (сказа́ть), to tell the truth. **при́знак**, -а, sign, symptom; indication. **призна́ние**, -я, confession, declaration; admission, acknowledgement; recognition. **при́знанный**, acknowledged, recognized. **призна́тельный**, grateful.

призову́, etc.: see призва́ть.

при́зрак, -а, spectre, ghost, phantom, apparition. **при́зрачный**, spectral, ghostly, phantasmal; illusory, imagined.

призы́в, -а, call, appeal; slogan; call-up, conscription. **призыва́ть(ся**, -а́ю(сь *imp.* of призва́ть(ся. призывно́й, conscription; ~ во́зраст, military age; *sb.* conscript.

при́иск, -a, mine; золоты́е ~и, gold-field(s).

прийти́, приду́, -дёшь; пришёл, -шла́ *perf.* (*imp.* приходи́ть) come; arrive; ~ в себя́, come round, regain consciousness; ~ в у́жас, be horrified; ~ к концу́, come to an end; ~ к заключе́нию, come to the conclusion, arrive at a conclusion; ~сь + по + *dat.* fit; suit; ~ на + *acc.* fall on; *impers.* + *dat.* have to; happen (to), fall to the lot (of); ~ на + *acc.* or c + *gen.* be owing to from; нам пришло́сь верну́ться в Москву́, we had to return to Moscow; как придётся, anyhow, at haphazard.

прика́з, -a, order, command; order of the day; office, department. **приказа́ние**, -я, order, command, injunction. **приказа́ть**, -ажу́, -а́жешь *perf.*, **прика́зывать**, -аю *imp.* order, command; give orders, direct.

прика́лывать, -аю *imp.* of приколо́ть. **прика́лываться**, -аюсь *imp.* of приколо́ться.

прики́дывать, -аю *imp.*, **прики́нуть**, -ну *perf.* throw in, add; weigh; estimate; calculate, reckon; ~ся + *instr.* pretend (to be); feign; ~ся больны́м, pretend to be ill, feign illness.

прикла́д¹, -a, butt.

прикла́д², -a, trimmings, findings. **прикладно́й**, applied. **прикла́дывать(ся**, -аю(сь *imp.* of приложи́ть(ся.

прикле́ивать, -аю *imp.*, **прикле́ить**, -е́ю *perf.* stick; glue; paste; affix; ~ся, stick, adhere.

приключа́ться, -а́ется *imp.*, **приключи́ться**, -и́тся *perf.* happen, occur. **приключе́ние**, -я, adventure. **приключе́нческий**, adventure.

прико́вывать, -аю *imp.*, **прикова́ть**, -кую́, -куёшь *perf.* chain; rivet.

прико́л, -a, stake; на ~е, laid up, idle.

прика́лачивать, -аю *imp.*, **приколоти́ть**, -очу́, -о́тишь *perf.* nail, fasten with nails; beat up.

приколо́ть, -лю́, -лешь *perf.* (*imp.* прика́лывать) pin, fasten with a pin; stab, transfix.

прикомандирова́ть, -ру́ю *perf.*, **прикомандиро́вывать**, -аю *imp.* attach, second.

прикоснове́ние, -я, touch, contact; concern. **прикоснове́нный**, concerned, involved, implicated (к + *dat.* in). **прикосну́ться**, -ну́сь, -нёшься *perf.* (*imp.* прикаса́ться) к + *dat.* touch.

прикра́сить, -а́шу *perf.*, **прикра́шивать**, -аю *imp.* embellish, embroider.

прикрепи́ть, -плю́ *perf.*, **прикрепля́ть**, -я́ю *imp.* fasten, attach. **прикрепле́ние**, -я, fastening; attachment; registration.

прикрыва́ть, -а́ю *imp.*, **прикры́ть**, -ро́ю *perf.* cover; screen; protect, shelter, shield; cover up, conceal; close down, wind up; ~ся, cover oneself; close down, go out of business; + *instr.* use as cover, take refuge in, shelter behind.

прику́ривать, -аю *imp.*, **прикури́ть**, -рю́, -ришь *perf.* get a light; light a cigarette from another.

прику́с, -a, bite. **прикуси́ть**, -ушу́ -у́сишь *perf.*, **прику́сывать**, -аю *imp.* bite; ~ язы́к, hold one's tongue, keep one's mouth shut.

прила́вок, -вка, counter; рабо́тник прила́вка, counter-hand; (shop) assistant.

прилага́тельн|ый, adjective; ~oe *sb.* adjective. **прилага́ть**, -а́ю *imp.* of приложи́ть.

прила́дить, -а́жу *perf.*, **прила́живать**, -аю *imp.* fit, adjust.

приласка́ть, -а́ю *perf.* caress, fondle, pet; ~ся, snuggle up, nestle up.

прилега́ть, -а́ет *imp.* (*perf.* приле́чь) к + *dat.* fit; adjoin, be adjacent to, border (on). **прилега́ющий**, close-fitting, tight-fitting; adjoining, adjacent, contiguous.

прилежа́ние, -я, diligence, industry; application. **приле́жный**, diligent, industrious, assiduous.

прилепи́ть(ся, -плю́(сь, -пишь(ся *perf.*, **прилепля́ть(ся**, -я́ю(сь *imp.* stick.

прилёт, -a, arrival. **прилета́ть**, -а́ю *imp.*, **прилете́ть**, -ечу́ *perf.* arrive, fly in; fly, come flying.

прилечь, -ля́гу, -ля́жешь; -ёг, -гла́ perf. (imp. прилега́ть) lie down; be laid flat; + к + dat. fit.

прили́в, a, flow, flood; rising tide; surge, influx; congestion; ~ кро́ви, rush of blood; ~ эне́ргии, burst of energy. прилива́ть, -а́ет imp. of прили́ть. прили́вный, tidal.

прилипа́ть, -а́ет imp., прили́пнуть, -нет -ли́п perf. stick, adhere. прили́пчивый, sticking, adhesive; clinging; not to be shaken off; tiresome; catching

прили́ть, -лье́т; -и́л, -а́, -о perf. (imp. прилива́ть) flow; rush.

прили́чие, -я, decency, propriety; decorum. прили́чный, decent, proper, decorous, seemly; tolerable, fair.

приложе́ние, -я, application; affixing; enclosure; supplement; appendix; schedule, exhibit; apposition. приложи́ть, -жу́ -жишь perf. (imp. прикла́дывать, прилага́ть) put; apply; affix; add, join; enclose; ~ все стара́ния, do one's best, try one's hardest; ~ся, take aim; + instr. put, apply; + к + dat. kiss.

прилуни́ться, -ню́сь perf. land on the moon.

прилёт, etc.: see прили́ть. при|лью́ну́ть, -ну́, -нёшь perf. приля́гу, etc.: see прилечь.

прима́нивать, -аю imp., примани́ть, -ню́, -нишь perf. lure; entice, allure. прима́нка, -и, bait, lure; enticement, allurement.

примене́ние, -я, application; employment, use. примени́ть, -ню́, -нишь perf., применя́ть, -я́ю imp. apply; employ, use; ~ на пра́ктике, put into practice; ~ся, adapt oneself, conform.

приме́р, a, example; instance; model; не в ~ + dat. unlike; + comp. far more, by far; подава́ть в ~, set an example; привести́ в ~, cite as an example.

при|ме́рить, -рю perf. (imp. also примеря́ть) try on; fit. приме́рка, -и, trying on; fitting.

приме́рно adv. in exemplary fashion; approximately, roughly. приме́рный, exemplary, model; approximate, rough.

примеря́ть, -я́ю imp. of приме́рить.

при́месь, -и, admixture; dash; без при́меси, unadulterated.

приме́та, -ы, sign, token; mark, приме́тный, perceptible, visible, noticeable; conspicuous, prominent.

примеча́ние, -я, note, footnote; pl. comments.

примеша́ть, -а́ю perf., приме́шивать, -аю imp. add, mix in.

примина́ть, -а́ю imp. of примя́ть.

примире́ние, -я, reconciliation. примире́нчество, -а, appeasement; compromise. примири́мый, reconcilable. примири́тель, -я m. reconciler, conciliator, peace-maker. примири́тельный, conciliatory. при|мири́ть, -рю́ perf., примиря́ть, -я́ю imp. reconcile; conciliate; ~ся, be reconciled, make it up; + с + instr. reconcile oneself to, put up with.

примкну́ть, -ну́, -нёшь perf. (imp. примыка́ть) join; fix, attach.

примну́, etc.: see примя́ть.

примо́рский, seaside; maritime. примо́рье, -я, seaside; littoral.

примо́чка, -и, wash, lotion.

приму́, etc.: see приня́ть.

примча́ться, -чу́сь perf. come tearing along.

примыка́ние, -я, contiguity; agglutination. примыка́ть, -а́ю imp. of примкну́ть; + к + dat. adjoin, abut on, border on. примыка́ющий, affiliated.

примя́ть, -мну́, -мнёшь perf. (imp. примина́ть) crush, flatten; trample down.

принадлежа́ть, -жу́ imp. belong. принадле́жность, -и, belonging; membership; pl. accessories, appurtenances; equipment; outfit, tackle.

при|нево́лить, -лю perf.

принести́, -су́, -сёшь perf. (imp. приноси́ть) bring; fetch; bear, yield; bring in; ~ в же́ртву, sacrifice; ~ по́льзу, be of use, be of benefit.

принима́ть(ся, -а́ю(сь imp. of приня́ть(ся; принима́ющая сторона́, host country.

принора́вливать, -аю imp., приноро́вить, -влю́ perf. fit, adapt, adjust;

~ся, adapt oneself, accommodate oneself.

приноси́ть, -ошу́ -о́сишь *imp.* of принести́. приноше́ние, -я, gift, offering.

прину́ди́тельн|ый, compulsory; forced, coercive; ~ые рабо́ты, forced labour, hard labour. прину́дить, -у́жу *perf.* принужда́ть, -а́ю *imp.* force, compel, coerce, constrain. принужде́ние, -я, compulsion, coercion, constraint; duress. принуждённый, constrained, forced.

при́нцип, -а, principle. принципиа́льно *adv.* on principle; in principle. принципиа́льный, of principle; in principle; general.

приня́тие, -я, taking; taking up, assumption; acceptance, adoption; admission, admittance; ~ при́нято, it is accepted, it is usual; не ~, it is not done. приня́ть, -иму́, -и́мешь; при́нял, -á, -о *perf.* (*imp.* принима́ть) take; accept; take up; take over; pass, approve; admit; receive; + за + *acc.* take for; ~ ва́нну, take (have) a bath; ~ в шко́лу, admit to, accept for, a school; ~ зако́н, pass a law; ~ лека́рство, take medicine; ~ ме́ры, take measures; ~ резолю́цию, pass, adopt, carry a resolution; ~ уча́стье, take part; ~ся, begin; start; take; take root, strike root; + за + *acc.* take in hand; set to, get down to; ~ за рабо́ту, to set to work.

приобрести́ть, -рбу́ *perf.*, приобрета́ть, -я́ю *imp.* cheer up, encourage, hearten; ~ся, cheer up.

приобрести́, -ету́, -етёшь; -рёл, -á *perf.*, приобрета́ть, -а́ю *imp.* acquire, gain. приобрете́ние, -я, acquisition; gain; bargain, find.

приобща́ть, -а́ю *imp.*, приобщи́ть, -щу́ *perf.* join, attach, unite; ~ к де́лу, file, ~ся к + *dat.* join in.

приозёрный, lakeside, lakeland.

приостана́вливать, -аю *imp.* приостанови́ть, -влю́, -вишь *perf.* stop, suspend, check; ~ся, halt, stop, pause. приостано́вка, -и, halt, check, stoppage, suspension.

приотвори́ть, -рю́, -ришь *perf.*, приотворя́ть, -я́ю *imp.* open slightly, half-open, set ajar.

припа́док, -дка, fit; attack; paroxysm. припаса́ть, -а́ю *imp.*, припасти́, -су́ -сёшь; -áс, -лá *perf.* store, lay in, lay up. припа́сы, -ов *pl.* stores, supplies; provisions; munitions.

припёв, -а, refrain, burden.

приписа́ть, -ишу́ -и́шешь *perf.*, припи́сывать, -аю *imp.* add; attribute, ascribe; put down, impute. припи́ска, -и, addition; postscript; codicil.

припла́та, -ы, extra pay; additional payment. приплати́ть, -ачу́, -а́тишь *perf.* припла́чивать, -аю *imp.* pay in addition.

припло́д, -а. issue, increase.

приплыва́ть, -а́ю *imp.*, приплы́ть, -ыву́, -ывёшь; -ы́л, -á, -о *perf.* swim up, sail up.

приплю́снуть, -ну *perf.*, приплю́щивать, -аю *imp.* flatten.

приподнима́ть, -а́ю *imp.*, приподня́ть, -ниму́, -ни́мешь; -о́дня́л, -á, -о *perf.* raise (a little); ~ся, raise oneself (a little), rise.

припо́й, -я, solder.

припомина́ть, -а́ю *imp.*, припо́мнить, -ню *perf.* remember, recollect, recall; + *dat.* remind.

припра́ва, -ы, seasoning, flavouring; relish, condiment, dressing. припра́вить, -влю *perf.*, приправля́ть, -я́ю *imp.* season, flavour, dress.

припря́тать, -я́чу *perf.*, припря́тывать, -аю *imp.* secrete, put by.

припу́гивать, -аю *imp.*, припугну́ть, -ну́, -нёшь *perf.* intimidate, scare.

при́пуск, -а, allowance, margin.

прираба́тывать, -аю *imp.*, прирабо́тать, -аю *perf.* earn . . . extra, earn in addition. при́работок, -тка, supplementary earnings, additional earnings.

прира́внивать, -аю *imp.*, приравня́ть, -я́ю *perf.* equate, place on the same footing; compare (к + *dat.* to).

прираста́ть, -а́ю *imp.*, прирасти́, -тёт; -рбс, -лá *perf.* adhere; take; increase; accrue; ~ к ме́сту, be rooted to the spot.

прире́чный, riverside.

приро́да, -ы, nature; character. приро́дный, natural; native; born, by birth;

inborn, innate. прирождённый, in-born, innate; born.

приро́с, etc.: see прирасти́. приро́ст, -а, increase, growth.

прируча́ть, -а́ю *imp.*, приручи́ть, -чу́ *perf.* tame; domesticate. прируче́ние, -я, taming, domestication.

приса́живаться, -аюсь *imp.* of присе́сть.

присва́ивать, -аю *imp.*, присво́ить, -о́ю *perf.* appropriate; give, award, confer; ~ и́мя + *dat.* and *gen.* name after.

приседа́ть, -а́ю *imp.*, присе́сть, -ся́ду *perf.* (*imp.* also приса́живаться) sit down, take a seat; squat; cower; bend the knees (in walking).

прискака́ть, -ачу́, -а́чешь *perf.* come galloping, arrive at a gallop; rush, tear.

приско́рбный, sorrowful, regrettable, lamentable.

присла́ть, -ишлю́, -ишлёшь *perf.* (*imp.* присыла́ть) send, dispatch.

прислони́ть(ся, -оню́(сь, -о́ни́шь(ся *perf.*, прислоня́ть(ся, -я́ю(сь *imp.* lean, rest (к + *dat.* against).

прислу́га, -и, maid, servant; servants, domestics; crew. прислу́живать, -аю *imp.* (к + *dat.*) wait (upon) ~ ся к + *dat.* fawn upon, cringe to.

прислу́шаться, -аюсь *perf.*, прислу́шиваться, -аюсь *imp.* listen; + к + *dat.* listen to; heed, pay attention to; get used to (the sound of), cease to notice.

присма́тривать, -аю *imp.*, присмотре́ть, -рю́, -ришь *perf.* look for, find; + за + *instr.* look after, keep an eye on; supervise, superintend; ~ за ребён-ком, mind the baby; ~ ся (к + *dat.*) look closely (at); get accustomed, get used (to).

присни́ться, -ню́сь *perf.*

присовокупи́ть, -плю́ *perf.*, присовокупля́ть, -я́ю *imp.* add; attach.

присоедине́ние -я, joining; addition; annexation; connection. присоедини́ть, -ню́ *perf.*, присоединя́ть, -я́ю *imp.* join; add; annex; connect; ~ ся к + *dat.* join; associate oneself with; ~ к мне́нию, subscribe to an opinion.

приспосо́бить, -блю *perf.*, приспособля́ть, -я́ю *imp.* fit, adjust, adapt, accommodate; ~ ся, adapt oneself,

accommodate oneself. приспособле́-ние, -я, adaptation, accommodation; device, contrivance; appliance; gadget. приспосо́бленность, -и, fitness, suitability. приспособля́емость, -и, adaptability.

при́став, -а; *pl.* -а́ or -ы, police officer police sergeant.

пристава́ть, -таю́, -таёшь *imp.* of приста́ть.

приста́вить, -влю *perf.* (*imp.* приставля́ть) к + *dat.* put, place, set to, against; lean against; add to; appoint to look after.

приста́вка, -и, prefix.

приставля́ть, -я́ю *imp.* of приста́вить. пристав|о́й, added, attached; ~а́я ле́стница, step-ladder.

при́стальный, fixed, intent.

при́стань, -и; *gen. pl.* -е́й, landing-stage, jetty; pier; wharf; refuge; haven.

приста́ть, -а́ну *perf.* (*imp.* пристава́ть) stick, adhere; attach oneself; pester, bother, badger; put in, come along-side.

пристёгивать, -аю *imp.*, пристегну́ть, -ну́, -нёшь *perf.* fasten. пристежно́й; ~ воротничо́к, separate collar.

пристра́ивать(ся, -аю(сь *imp.* of при-стро́ить(ся.

пристра́стие, -я, weakness, predilection, passion; partiality, bias. пристра́ст-ный partial, biased.

пристро́ить, -о́ю *perf.* (*imp.* пристра́и-вать), add, build on; place, settle, fix up; ~ ся, be placed, be settled, be fixed up, get a place; join up form up. пристро́йка, -и, annexe, extension; outhouse; lean-to.

при́ступ, -а, assault, storm; fit, attack; bout, touch; access approach. приступа́ть, -а́ю *imp.* приступи́ть, -плю́, -пишь *perf.* к + *dat.* set about, start; get down to; approach; importune, pester. при́ступок, -пка, step.

присты́ди́ть, -ы́жу *perf.* пристыжён-ный; -жён, -а́ ashamed.

пристыко́ва́ться, -ку́ется *perf.*

пристя́жка, -и, пристяжна́я *sb.* trace-horse, outrunner.

присуди́ть, -ужу́, -у́дишь *perf.*, присужда́ть, -а́ю *imp.* sentence, condemn; award; confer; ~ к штра́фу, fine, impose a fine on. присужде́ние, -я, awarding, adjudication; conferment.

прису́тственн|ый, -ое ме́сто government office. прису́тствие -я, presence; attendance; government office; ~ ду́ха, presence of mind. прису́тствовать, -твую, be present, attend. прису́тствующ|ий, present; ~ие *sb.* those present, present company.

прису́щий, inherent; characteristic, distinctive.

присыла́ть, -а́ю *imp.* of присла́ть.

прися́га, -и, oath; привести́ к прися́ге, swear in, administer the oath to. присяга́ть, -а́ю *imp.*, присягну́ть, -ну́, -нёшь *perf.* take one's oath, swear; ~ в ве́рности, swear allegiance.

прися́ду, etc.: see присе́сть.

прися́жн|ый, sworn; born, inveterate; ~ заседа́тель, juror, juryman; ~ пове́ренный, barrister.

притаи́ться, -аю́сь *perf.* hide, conceal oneself.

прита́скивать, -аю *imp*, притащи́ть, -ащу́, -а́щишь *perf.* bring, drag, haul; ~ся drag oneself.

притвори́ться, -рю́сь *perf*, притворя́ться, -я́юсь *imp.* + *instr.* pretend to be; feign; sham; ~ больны́м, pretend to be ill, feign illness. притво́рный, pretended, feigned, sham. притво́рство, -а, pretence, sham. притво́рщик, -а, sham; dissembler, hypocrite.

притека́ть, -а́ю *imp.* of прите́чь.

притесне́ние, -я, oppression. притесни́ть, -ню́ *perf.*, притесня́ть, -я́ю *imp.* oppress.

прите́чь, -ечёт, -еку́т; -ёк, -ла́ *perf.* (*imp.* притека́ть) flow in, pour in.

притиха́ть, -а́ю *imp.*, прити́хнуть, -ну; -и́х *perf.* quiet down, grow quiet, hush.

прито́к, -а, tributary; flow, influx; intake.

прито́м *conj.* (and) besides.

прито́н, -а, den, haunt.

прито́рный, sickly-sweet, luscious, cloying.

притра́гиваться, -аюсь *imp.*, притро́нуться, -нусь *perf.* touch.

притупи́ть, -плю́ -пишь *perf.*, притупля́ть, -я́ю *imp.* blunt, dull; deaden; ~ся, become blunt, lose its edge; become dull.

при́тча, -и, parable.

притяга́тельный, attractive, magnetic. притя́гивать, -аю *imp.* of притяну́ть.

притяжа́тельный, possessive.

притяже́ние, -я, attraction; земно́е ~, gravity.

притяза́ние, -я, claim, pretension. притяза́ть, -а́ю *imp.* на + *acc.* lay claim to, have pretensions to.

притя́нутый: ~ за́ уши, за́ волосы, far-fetched. притяну́ть, -ну́ -нешь *perf.* (*imp.* притя́гивать) draw, attract; drag (up), pull (up).

приуро́чивать, -аю *imp.*, приуро́чить, -чу *perf.* к + *dat.* time for, time to coincide with.

приуса́дебный; ~ уча́сток, individual holding (in kolkhoz), personal plot.

приуча́ть, -а́ю *imp.*, приучи́ть, -чу́, -чишь *perf.* accustom; train, school.

прихва́рывать, -аю *imp.*, прихворну́ть, -ну́, -нёшь *perf.* be unwell, be indisposed.

при́хвостень, -тня *m.* hanger-on.

прихлеба́тель, -я *m.* sponger, parasite.

прихо́д, -а, coming, arrival; advent; receipts; parish; ~ и расхо́д, credit and debit. приходи́ть(ся, -ожу́(сь, -о́дишь(ся *imp.* of прийти́(сь. прихо́дный, receipt. прихо́довать, -дую *imp.* (*perf.* за~) credit. приходя́щ|ий, non-resident; ~ий больно́й, outpatient; ~ая домрабо́тница, daily (maid), char(woman).

прихотли́вый, capricious, whimsical; fanciful; intricate. при́хоть, -и, whim, caprice, fancy.

прихра́мывать, -аю *imp.* limp (slightly).

прице́л, -а, sight; aiming. прице́ливаться, -аюсь *imp.*, прице́литься, -люсь *perf.* aim, take aim.

прице́ниваться, -аюсь *imp.*, прицени́ться, -ню́сь, -нишься (к + *dat.*) ask the price (of).

прице́п, -а, trailer. прицепи́ть, -плю́ -пишь *perf.*, прицепля́ть, -я́ю *imp.* hitch, hook on; couple; ~ся к + *dat.*

stick to, cling to; pester; nag at. **при**|**цéпка**, -и, hitching, hooking on; coupling; trailer; pestering; nagging. **прицепнóй**; ~ вагóн, trailer.

причáл, -а, mooring, making fast; mooring line; berth, moorings. **при**|**чáливать**, -аю *imp.*, **причáлить**, -лю *perf.* moor.

причáстие[1], -я, participle. **причáстие**[2], -я, communion.

причáстный[1], participial. **причáстный**[2], participating, concerned; involved; accessary, privy.

причём *conj.* moreover, and; while. **причём** *adv.* why? what for?; а ~ же я тут? what has it to do with me?

причёс|**ать**, -ешý, -éшешь *perf.*, **причёсывать**, -аю *imp.* brush, comb; do the hair (of); ~ся, do one's hair, have one's hair done. **причёска**, -и, hair-do, hair-style; haircut.

причи́на, -ы, cause; reason. **причини́ть**, -ню́ *perf.*, **причиня́ть**, -я́ю *imp.* cause; occasion.

причи́слить, -лю *perf.*, **причисля́ть**, -я́ю *imp.* reckon, number, rank (к + *dat.* among); add on; attach.

причита́ние, -я, lamentation.

причита́ться, -а́ется *imp.* be due; вам причита́ется два рубля́, there is two roubles due to you, you have two roubles to come; с вас причита́ется два рубля́, you have two roubles to pay.

причу́да, -ы, caprice, whim, fancy; oddity, vagary.

при|**чу́диться**, -ится *perf.*

причу́дливый, odd, queer; fantastic; capricious, whimsical.

пришвартова́ть, -ту́ю *perf.* пришёл, etc.: see прийти́.

пришиблённый, crest-fallen, dejected.

пришива́ть, -а́ю *imp.*, **приши́ть**, -шью́, -шьёшь *perf.* sew on, attach; nail (on).

пришлю́, etc.: see присла́ть.

пришпо́ривать, -аю *imp.*, **пришпо́рить**, -рю *perf.* spur (on).

прищеми́ть, -млю́ *perf.* **прищемля́ть**, -я́ю *imp.* pinch, squeeze.

прищё|**пка**, -и, **прищёпок**, -пка, clothes-peg.

прищу́риваться, -аюсь *imp.*, **прищу́рить**|**ся**, -рюсь *perf.* screw up one's eyes.

прию́т, -а, asylum, orphanage; shelter, refuge. **приюти́ть**, -ючу́ *perf.* shelter, give refuge; ~ся, take shelter.

прия́тель, -я *m.*, **прия́тельница**, -ы, friend. **прия́тельский**, friendly, amicable. **прия́тный**, nice, pleasant, agreeable, pleasing; ~ на вкус, nice, palatable, tasty.

про *prep.* + *acc.* about; for; ~ себя́, to oneself.

про-[1] *vbl. pref.* indicating action through, across, or past object; action continued throughout given period of time; overall or exhaustive action or effect; loss or failure.

про-[2] *pref.* of nouns and adjs., pro-.

про́ба, -ы, trial, test; try-out; assay, hallmark; sample; standard, measure of fineness of gold; зо́лото 96-о́й про́бы, 24-carat gold, pure gold.

пробе́г, -а, run; race; mileage, distance. **пробе́га́ть**, -а́ю *imp.*, **пробежа́ть**, -егу́ *perf.* run; cover; pass, run past, run by; run through; run along, run over.

пробе́л, -а, blank, gap; hiatus; lacuna; deficiency, flaw.

проберу́, etc.: see пробра́ть. **пробива́ть**(**ся**, -а́ю(сь *imp.* of проби́ть(ся. **пробира́ть**(**ся**, -а́ю(сь *imp.* of пробра́ть(ся.

проби́рка, -и, test-tube. **проби́рный**, test, assay; ~ое клеймо́, hallmark. **проби́ровать**, -рую *imp.* test, assay.

про|**би́ть**, -бью́ -бьёшь *perf.* (*imp.* also пробива́ть) make a hole in; hole; pierce; punch; strike; ~ся, fight, force, make, one's way through; break through, strike through.

про́бка, -и, cork; stopper; plug; fuse; (traffic) jam, blockage, congestion. **про́бковый**, cork; ~ по́яс, life-belt, life-jacket.

про́блеск, -а. flash; gleam, ray.

про́бный, trial, test, experimental; hall-marked; ~ ка́мень, touchstone. **про́бовать**, -бую *imp.* (*perf.* ис~, по~), try; attempt, endeavour; test; taste, feel.

пробо́ина, -ы, hole.

проболта́ться, -а́юсь *perf.* blab, let out a secret; hang about.

пробо́р, -а, parting; де́лать (себе́) ~, part one's hair.

про|бормота́ть, -очу́, -о́чешь *perf.*

пробра́ть, -беру́, -берёшь; -а́л, -а́, -о *perf.* (*imp.* пробира́ть) go through; scold, rate; clear, weed; ~ся, make one's way; force one's way; steal (through); ~ озно́б, feel one's way.

пробу́ду, etc.: see пробы́ть.

про|буди́ть, -ужу́, -у́дишь *perf.*, пробужда́ть, -а́ю *imp.* wake (up); awaken, rouse, arouse; ~ся, wake, wake up. **пробужде́ние**, -я, waking (up), awakening.

про|бура́вить, -влю *perf.*, пробура́вливать, -аю *imp.* bore (through), drill.

про|бурча́ть, -чу́ *perf.*

пробы́ть, -бу́ду; про́бы́л, -а́, -о *perf.* remain, stay; be.

пробью́, etc.: see проби́ть.

прова́л, -а, failure; flop; downfall; gap; funnel. **прова́ливать**, -аю *imp.*, провали́ть, -лю́, -лишь *perf.* cause to fall in, bring down; ruin, make a mess of; reject, fail; ~ся, collapse; fall in, come down; fall through; fail; disappear, vanish.

прова́нск|ий, Provençal; ~ое ма́сло, olive oil.

прове́дать, -аю *perf.*, прове́дывать, -аю *imp.* come to see, call on; find out, learn.

провезти́, -зу́, -зёшь; -ёз, -ла́ *perf.* (*imp.* провози́ть) convey, transport; smuggle (through, in, out); bring.

прове́рить, -рю *perf.* проверя́ть, -я́ю *imp.* check, check up on; verify; audit; control; test; ~ биле́ты, examine tickets; ~ тетра́ди, correct exercise-books. **прове́рка**, -и, checking, check; examination; verification; control; testing.

про|вести́, -еду́, -едёшь; -ёл, -а́ *perf.* (*imp.* also проводи́ть) lead, take; pilot; build; install; carry out, carry on; conduct, hold; carry through; carry; pass; advance, put forward; draw; spend; + *instr.* pass over, run over; ~ в жизнь, put into effect, put into practice; ~ водопрово́д, lay on

water; ~ вре́мя, pass the time; ~ черту́, draw a line; хорошо́ ~ вре́мя, have a good time.

прове́тривать, -аю *imp.*, прове́трить, -рю *perf.* air; ventilate.

про|ве́ять, -е́ю *perf.*

провиде́ние, -я, Providence. **прови́деть**, -и́жу *imp.* foresee.

прови́зия, -и, provisions.

провизо́рный, preliminary, provisional; temporary.

провини́ться, -ню́сь *perf.* be guilty; do wrong; ~ пе́ред + *instr.* wrong.

провинциа́льный, provincial. **прови́нция**, -и, province; the provinces.

про́вод, -а; *pl.* -а́, wire, lead, conductor. **проводи́мость**, -и, conductivity; conductance. **проводи́ть¹**, -ожу́, -о́дишь *imp.* of провести́; conduct, be a conductor.

проводи́ть², -ожу́, -о́дишь *perf.* (*imp.* провожа́ть) accompany; see off; ~ глаза́ми, follow with one's eyes; ~ домо́й, see home.

прово́дка, -и, leading, taking; building; installation; wiring, wires.

проводни́к¹, -а́, guide; conductor; guard.

проводни́к², -а́, conductor; bearer; transmitter. **проводни́к**, wire, line.

про́воды, -ов *pl.* seeing off, send-off. **провожа́тый** *sb.* guide, escort. **провожа́ть**, -а́ю *imp.* of проводи́ть.

прово́з, -а, carriage, conveyance, transport.

провозгласи́ть, -ашу́ *perf.*, провозгла-ша́ть, -а́ю *imp.* proclaim, declare; announce; + *instr.* proclaim, hail as; ~ тост, propose a toast. **провозгла-ше́ние**, -я, proclamation; declaration.

провози́ть, -ожу́, -о́зишь *imp.* of про-везти́.

провока́тор, -а, agent provocateur; in-stigator, provoker. **провокацио́нный**, provocative. **провока́ция**, -и, provoca-tion.

про́волока, -и, wire. **про́волочн|ый**, wire; ~ая сеть, wire netting.

прово́рный, quick, swift, prompt; agile, nimble, adroit, dexterous. **прово́рство**, -а, quickness, swiftness; agility, nimble-ness, adroitness, dexterity.

провоци́ровать, -рую *perf.* and *imp.* (*perf.* also c~) provoke.

про|вя́лить, -лю *perf.*

прогада́ть, -а́ю *perf.*, прога́дывать, -аю *imp.* miscalculate.

прога́лина, -ы, glade; (clear) space.

прогла́тывать, -аю *imp.*, проглоти́ть, -очу́, -о́тишь *perf.* swallow.

прогляде́ть, -яжу́ *perf.*, прогля́дывать[1], -аю *imp.* overlook, miss; look through, glance through. прогляну́ть, -я́нет *perf.*, прогля́дывать[2], -ает *imp.* show, show through, peep out, peep through, appear.

прогна́ть, -гоню́ -го́нишь; -а́л, -а́, -о *perf.* (*imp.* прогоня́ть) drive away; banish; drive; sack, fire.

про|гне́вить, -влю́ *perf.*

прогнива́ть, -а́ет *imp.*, прогни́ть, -ниёт -и́л, -а́, -о *perf.* rot through, be rotten.

прогно́з, -а, prognosis; (weather) forecast. прогнози́рование, -я, forecasting. прогнози́ст, -а, forecaster.

проголода́ться, -а́юсь *perf.* get hungry, grow hungry.

про|голосова́ть, -су́ю *perf.* прогоня́ть, -я́ю *imp.* of прогна́ть.

прогора́ть, -а́ю *imp.*, прогоре́ть, -рю́ *perf.* burn; burn out; get burnt; go bankrupt, go bust.

прого́рклый, rancid, rank.

програ́мма, -ы, programme; schedule; syllabus, curriculum. программи́ровать, -рую *imp.* (*perf.* за~), programme.

прогре́в, -а, warming up. прогрева́ть, -а́ю *imp.*, прогре́ть, -е́ю *perf.* heat, warm thoroughly; warm up; ~ся, get warmed through, get thoroughly warmed; warm up.

про|греме́ть, -млю́ *perf.* про|грохота́ть, -очу́ -о́чешь *perf.*

прогрыза́ть, -а́ю *imp.*, прогры́зть, -зу́, -зёшь; -ы́з *perf.* gnaw through.

про|гуде́ть, -гужу́ *perf.*

прогу́л, -а, absence (from work); absenteeism. прогу́ливать, -аю *imp.*, прогуля́ть, -я́ю *perf.* be absent from work; miss; take for a walk, walk; ~ уро́ки, play truant; ~ся, stroll, saunter; take a walk. прогу́лка, -и, walk,

stroll; ramble; outing. прогу́льщик, -а, absentee, truant.

прод- *abbr.* in *comb.* of продово́льственный, food-, provision-. продма́г, -а, grocery; provision-shop. ~пу́нкт, -а, food centre. ~това́ры, -ов *pl.* food products.

продава́ть, -даю́, -даёшь *imp.*, прода́ть, -а́м, -а́шь, -а́ст, -ади́м; про́дал, -а́, -о *perf.* sell. продава́ться, -даётся *imp.* be for sale; sell. продаве́ц, -вца́, seller, vendor; salesman; shop-assistant. продавщи́ца, -ы, seller, vendor; saleswoman; shop-assistant. прода́жа, -и, sale, selling. прода́жный, for sale, to be sold; mercenary, venal.

продвига́ть, -а́ю *imp.*, продви́нуть, -ну *perf.* move forward, push forward; promote, further, advance; ~ся, advance; move on, move forward; push on, push forward, forge ahead; be promoted.

про|деклами́ровать, -рую *perf.*

проде́лать, -аю *perf.*, проде́лывать, -аю *imp.* do, perform, accomplish. проде́лка, -и, trick; prank, escapade.

продёргивать, -аю *imp.* of продёрнуть.

продержа́ть, -жу́, -жишь *perf.* hold; keep; ~ся, hold out.

продёрнуть, -ну, -нешь *perf.* (*imp.* продёргивать) pass, run; put through; criticize, pull to pieces; ~ ни́тку в иго́лку, thread a needle).

продешеви́ть, -влю́ *perf.* sell too cheap.

про|диктова́ть, -ту́ю *perf.*

продлева́ть, -а́ю *imp.*, продли́ть, -лю́ *perf.* extend, prolong. продле́ние, -я, extension, prolongation. про|дли́ться, -и́тся *perf.*

продово́льственн|ый, food, provision; ~ая ка́рточка, ration book, ration card; ~ый магази́н, grocery, provision shop. продово́льствие, -я, food, food-stuffs; provisions.

продолгова́тый, oblong.

продолжа́тель, -я *m.* continuer, successor. продолжа́ть, -а́ю *imp.*, продо́лжить, -жу *perf.* continue, go on (with), proceed (with); extend, prolong; ~ся, continue, last, go on, be in progress. продолже́ние, -я, continuation; sequel;

extension prolongation; в ~ + *gen.* in the course of, during, for, throughout; ~ сле́дует, to be continued. **продолжи́тельность**, -и, duration, length. **продолжи́тельный**, long; prolonged, protracted. **продо́льный**, longitudinal, lengthwise, linear.

продро́гнуть, -ну, -о́г *perf.* be chilled to the marrow, be half frozen.

проду́кт, -а, product; produce; provisions, food-stuffs. **продукти́вно** *adv.* productively; to good effect, with a good result. **продукти́вность**, -и, productivity. **продукти́вный**, productive; fruitful. **проду́ктовый**, food, provision; ~ магази́н, grocery, food-shop. **проду́кция**, -и, production, output.

проду́мать, -аю *perf.*, **проду́мывать**, -аю *imp.* think over; think out.

продыря́вить, -влю *perf.* make a hole in, pierce.

продю́с(с)ер, -а, (film) producer.

прое́дать, -а́ю *imp.* of прое́сть. **прое́ду**, etc.: see прое́хать.

прое́зд, -а, passage, thoroughfare; journey; ~а нет, no thoroughfare. **прое́здить**, -зжу *perf.* (*imp.* проезжа́ть) spend on a journey, spend in travelling; spend travelling (driving, riding). **проездн**|**о́й**, travelling; ~о́й биле́т, ticket; ~а́я пла́та, fare; ~ые *sb.* travelling expenses. **прое́здом** *adv.* en route, in transit, while passing through. **проезжа́ть**, -а́ю *imp.* of прое́здить, прое́хать. **проезж**|**и́й**, passing (by); ~ая доро́га, highway, thoroughfare; ~ий *sb.* passer-by.

прое́кт, -а, project, scheme, design; draft; ~ догово́ра, draft treaty; ~ резолю́ции, draft resolution. **проекти́ровать**, -рую *imp.* (*perf.* за~, с~) project; plan, design. **прое́ктный**, planning, designing; planned. **прое́ктор**, -а, projector.

проекцио́нный, ~ фона́рь, projector. **прое́кция**, -и, projection.

прое́сть, -е́м, -е́шь, -е́ст, -еди́м; -е́л *perf.* (*imp.* проеда́ть) eat through, corrode; spend on food.

прое́хать, -е́ду *perf.* (*imp.* проезжа́ть) pass by, through; drive by, through;

ride by, through; go past, pass; go, do, make, cover.

прожа́ренный, well-done.

проже́ктор, -а; *pl.* -ы or -а́, searchlight; floodlight.

проже́чь, -жгу́, -жжёшь; -жёг, -жгла́ *perf.* (*imp.* прожига́ть) burn; burn through.

прожива́ть, -а́ю *imp.* of прожи́ть. **прожига́ть**, -а́ю *imp.* of проже́чь.

прожи́точный, enough to live on; ~ ми́нимум, living wage. **прожи́ть**, -иву́, -ивёшь; -о́жил, -а, -о *perf.* (*imp.* прожива́ть) live; spend; run through.

прожо́рливый, voracious, gluttonous.

про́за, -ы, prose. **проза́ический**, prose; prosaic; prosy.

прозва́ние, -я, **про́звище**, -а, nickname. **прозва́ть**, -зову́, -зовёшь; -а́л, -а́, -о *perf.* (*imp.* прозыва́ть) nickname, name.

про|**зева́ть**, -а́ю *perf.* **про**|**зимова́ть**, -мую *perf.* **прозову́**, etc.: see прозва́ть.

прозоде́жда, -ы *abbr.* working clothes; overalls.

прозорли́вый, sagacious; perspicacious.

прозра́чный, transparent; limpid, pellucid.

прозыва́ть, -а́ю *imp.* of прозва́ть.

прозяба́ние, -я, vegetation. **прозяба́ть**, -а́ю *imp.* vegetate.

проигра́ть, -а́ю *perf.*, **прои́грывать**, -аю *imp.* lose; play; ~ся, lose everything, gamble away all one's money. **прои́грыватель**, -я *m.* record-player. **про́игрыш**, -а, loss.

произведе́ние, -я, work; production; product. **произвести́**, -еду́, -едёшь; -ёл, -а́ *perf.*, **производи́ть**, -ожу́, -о́дишь *imp.* make; carry out; execute; produce; cause; effect; give birth to; + в + *acc./nom. pl.* promote to (the rank of); ~ впечатле́ние, make an impression, create an impression; ~ на свет, bring into the world. **производи́тельность**, -и, productivity, output; productiveness. **производи́тельный**, productive; efficient. **производ**|**ный**, derivative, derived; ~ое сло́во, derivative. **произво́дственный**, industrial;

production; commercial; ~ стаж, industrial experience, industrial work
record. **произво́дство**, -а, production,
manufacture; factory, works; carrying
out, execution.

произво́л, -а, arbitrariness; arbitrary
rule; оста́вить на ~ судьбы́, leave to
the mercy of fate; чини́ть ~, impose
arbitrary rule. **произво́льный**, arbitrary.

произнести́, -су́, -сёшь; -ёс, -ла́ *perf.*,
произноси́ть, -ошу́, -о́сишь *imp.* pronounce; articulate; say, utter; ~ речь,
deliver a speech. **произноше́ние**, -я,
pronunciation; articulation.

произойти́, -ойдёт; -ошёл, -шла́ *perf.*
(*imp.* происходи́ть) happen, occur,
take place; spring, arise, result; come,
descend, be descended.

про|инструкти́ровать, -рую *perf.*

про́иски, -ов *pl.* intrigues; machinations, schemes, underhand plotting.

происте́кать, -а́ет *imp.*, **происте́чь**,
-ечёт; -ёк, -ла́ *perf.* spring, result;
stem.

происходи́ть, -ожу́, -о́дишь *imp.* of
произойти́; go on, be going on. **про-
исхожде́ние**, -я, origin; provenance;
parentage, descent, extraction, birth;
по происхожде́нию, by birth.

происше́ствие, -я, event, incident, happening, occurrence; accident.

пройти́, -йду́, -йдёшь; -ошёл, -шла́
perf. (*imp.* проходи́ть) pass; go; go
past, go by, elapse; do, cover; be over;
pass off, abate, let up; go off; take,
study, learn; go through, get through;
fall; ~ в + *acc.* or *acc./nom. pl.*, become, be made; be taken on; ему́ э́то
да́ром не пройдёт, he will have to pay
for it; ~ ми́мо, pass by, go by, go
past; overlook, disregard; ~ че́рез,
pass, get through; э́то не пройдёт, it
won't work; **~сь**, walk up and down;
take a stroll, a walk; dance.

прок. -а (-у), use, benefit.

прокажённый *sb.* leper. **прока́за**[1], -ы,
leprosy.

прока́за[2], -ы, mischief, prank, trick.
прока́зить, -а́жу *imp.*, **прока́зничать**,
-аю *imp.* (*perf.* на~) be up to mischief,

play pranks. **прока́зник**, -а, mischievous child.

прока́лывать, -аю *imp.* of проколо́ть.

прока́т, -а, hire.

прокати́ться, -ачу́сь, -а́тишься *perf.*
roll; go for a drive, go for a run.

прока́тный, rolling; rolled; ~ стан,
rolling-mill.

прокипяти́ть, -ячу́ *perf.* boil; boil
thoroughly.

прокиса́ть, -а́ет *imp.*, **про|ки́снуть**, -нет
perf. turn (sour).

прокла́дка, -и, laying; building, construction; washer, gasket; packing.
прокла́дывать, -аю *imp.* of про-
ложи́ть.

проклама́ция, -и, proclamation, leaflet.

проклина́ть, -а́ю *imp.*, **прокля́сть**, -яну́,
-янёшь; -о́клял, -а́, -о *perf.* curse;
damn; swear at. **прокля́тие**, -я, curse;
damnation, perdition; imprecation.
прокля́тый, -ят, -а́, -о, accursed,
damned; damnable, confounded.

проколо́ть, -лю́, -лешь *perf.* (*imp.* про-
ка́лывать) prick, pierce; perforate;
run through.

про|компости́ровать, -рую *perf.* **про|
конопа́тить**, -а́чу *perf.* **про|конспекти́-
ровать**, -рую *perf.* **про|консульти́ро-
вать(ся**, -рую(сь *perf.* **про|контроли́-
ровать**, -рую *perf.*

прокорм, -а, nourishment, sustenance.
про|корми́ть(ся, -млю́(сь, -мишь(ся
perf.

про|корректи́ровать, -рую *perf.*

прокра́дываться, -аюсь *imp.*, **про-
кра́сться**, -аду́сь, -адёшься *perf.* steal
in.

про|кукаре́кать, -ает *perf.* **про|куко-
ва́ть**, -ку́ю *perf.*

прокуро́р, -а, public prosecutor; pro-
curator; investigating magistrate.

прокути́ть, -учу́, -у́тишь *perf.* **проку́чи-
вать**, -аю *imp.* squander, dissipate; go
on the spree, go on the binge.

пролага́ть, -а́ю *imp.* of проложи́ть.

пролега́ть, -а́ет *imp.* lie, run.

проле́жень, -жня *m.* bedsore.

пролеза́ть, -а́ю *imp.*, **проле́зть**, -зу;
-ле́з *perf.* get through, climb through;
get in, worm oneself in.

про|лепета́ть, -ечу́, -е́чешь *perf.*

проле́т, -а span; stair-well; bay.

пролета́рий, -я, proletarian; пролета́рии всех стран, соединя́йтесь! workers of the world, unite! пролета́рский, proletarian.

пролета́ть, -а́ю *imp.*, пролете́ть, -ечу́ *perf.* fly; cover; fly by, fly past, fly through; flash, flit.

проли́в, -а, strait sound. пролива́ть, -а́ю *imp.*, проли́ть, -лью́, -льёшь; -о́ли́л, -а́, -о *perf.* spill, shed; ~ свет на + *acc.* throw light on; shed light on.

проложи́ть, -жу́ -жишь *perf.* (*imp.* прокла́дывать, пролага́ть) lay; build, construct; interlay; insert; interleave; ~ доро́гу, build a road; pave the way, blaze a trail; ~ себе́ доро́гу, carve one's way.

проло́м, -а, breach, break; gap; fracture. проломи́ть, -а́ю *perf.* break, break through.

пролью́, etc.: see проли́ть.

пром- *abbr.* in *comb.* of промы́шленный; industrial. промтова́ры, -ов *pl.* manufactured goods. ~финпла́н -а, industrial and financial plan.

про|мота́ть, -а́ю *perf.* (*imp.* also прома́тывать) squander; ~ся, run through one's money.

прома́хиваться(ся, -аюсь(ся *imp.* of промота́ть(ся.

прома́х, -а, miss; slip, blunder. прома́хиваться, -аюсь *imp.*, промахну́ться, -ну́сь, -нёшься *perf.* miss; miss the mark; miscue; be wide of the mark, make a mistake, miss an opportunity.

прома́чивать, -аю *imp.* of промочи́ть.

промедле́ние, -я, delay; procrastination. проме́длить, -лю *perf.* delay, dally; procrastinate.

промежу́ток, -тка, interval; space. промежу́точный, intermediate; intervening; interim.

промелькну́ть, -ну́, -нёшь *perf.* flash; flash past, fly by; be perceptible, be discernible.

проме́нивать, -аю *imp.*, променя́ть, -я́ю *perf.* exchange, trade, barter; change.

промерза́ть, -а́ю *imp.*, промёрзнуть, -ну; -ёрз *perf.* freeze through. промёрзлый, frozen.

промока́тельн|ый: ~ая бума́га, blotting-paper. промока́ть, -а́ю *imp.*,

промо́кнуть, -ну; -мо́к *perf.* get soaked, get drenched.

промо́лвить, -влю *perf.* say, utter.

промочи́ть, -чу́ -чишь *perf.* (*imp.* прома́чивать) get wet (through); soak, drench; ~ но́ги, get one's feet wet.

промою́, etc.: see промы́ть.

промча́ться, -чу́сь *perf.* tear, dart, rush (by, past, through); fly.

промыва́ние, -я, washing (out, down); bathing; irrigation. промыва́ть, -а́ю *imp.* of промы́ть.

про́мысел, -сла, trade business; *pl.* works; го́рный ~, mining; охо́тничий ~, hunting, trapping; ры́бный ~, fishing, fishery. промысло́в|ый, producers'; business; hunters', trappers'; game; ~ая коопера́ция, producers' cooperative.

промы́ть, -мо́ю *perf.* (*imp.* промыва́ть) wash well, wash thoroughly; wash, irrigate; wash; scrub; ~ мозги́ + *dat.* brain-wash.

про|мыча́ть, -чу́ *perf.*

промы́шленник, -а, manufacturer, industrialist. промы́шленность, -и, industry. промы́шленный, industrial.

про|мя́млить, -лю *perf.*

пронести́, -су́, -сёшь; -ёс, -ла́ *perf.* (*imp.* проноси́ть) carry; carry by, past, through; pass (over), be over, be past; ~сь, rush by, past, through; scud (past); fly; be carried, spread; пронёсся слух, there was a rumour.

пронза́ть, -а́ю *imp.*, пронзи́ть, -нжу́ *perf.* pierce, run through, transfix. пронзи́тельный, penetrating; piercing; shrill, strident.

прониза́ть, -а́жу -и́жешь *perf.*, прони́зывать, -аю *imp.* pierce; permeate, penetrate; run through. пронизываю́щий, piercing, penetrating.

проника́ть, -а́ю *imp.*, прони́кнуть, -ну́; -и́к *perf.* penetrate; percolate; run through; ~ся, be imbued, be filled. проникнове́ние, -я, penetration; feeling; heartfelt conviction. проникнове́нный, full of feeling; heartfelt.

прони́кнутый + *instr*. imbued with, instinct with, full of.

проница́емый, permeable, pervious. **проница́тельный**, penetrating; perspicacious; acute, shrewd.

проноси́ть(ся, -ошу́(сь, -о́сишь(ся *imp*. of пронести́(сь. **про|нумерова́ть**, -ру́ю *perf*.

проны́рливый, pushful, pushing.

проню́хать, -аю *perf*., **проню́хивать**, -аю *imp*. smell out, nose out, get wind of.

прообра́з, -а, prototype.

пропада́ть, -а́ю *imp*. of пропа́сть. **пропа́жа**, -и, loss; lost object; missing thing.

пропа́лывать, -аю *imp*. of прополо́ть.

про́пасть, -и, precipice; abyss; a mass, masses.

пропа́сть, -аду́, -адёшь *perf*. (*imp*. пропада́ть) be missing; be lost; disappear, vanish; be done for, die; be wasted; мы пропа́ли, we're lost, we're done for; ~ без ве́сти, be missing.

пропека́ть(ся, -а́ю(сь *imp*. of пропе́чь(ся. **про|пе́ть**, -пою́, -поёшь *perf*.

пропе́чь, -еку́, -ечёшь; ~ёк, -ла́ *perf*. (*imp*. пропека́ть) bake well, bake thoroughly; **~ся**, bake well; get baked through.

пропива́ть, -а́ю *imp*. of пропи́ть.

прописа́ть, -ишу́, -и́шешь *perf*., **пропи́сывать**, -аю *imp*. prescribe; register; **~ся**, register. **пропи́ска**, -и, registration; residence permit. **прописн|о́й**, capital; commonplace, trivial; ~а́я бу́ква, capital letter; ~а́я и́стина, truism. **про́пись**, -и, copy; copy-book maxim. **про́писью** *adv*. in words, in full; писа́ть ци́фры ~, write out figures in words.

пропита́ние, -я, subsistence, sustenance, food; зарабо́тать себе́ на ~, earn one's living. **пропита́ть**, -а́ю *perf*., **пропи́тывать**, -аю *imp*. impregnate, saturate; soak, steep; keep; provide for; **~ся**, be saturated, be steeped; keep oneself.

пропи́ть, -пью, -пьёшь, *perf*. -о́пи́л, -а́, -о *perf*. (*imp*. пропива́ть) spend on drink, squander on drink.

проплы́в, -а, (swimming) race, heat. **проплыва́ть**, -а́ю *imp*., **проплы́ть**, -ыву́, -ывёшь; -ы́л, -а́, -о *perf*. swim, swim by, past; through; sail by, past, through; float; drift by, past, through; ~ стометро́вку, swim the hundred metres.

пропове́довать, -дую *imp*. preach; advocate. **про́поведь**, -и, sermon; homily; preaching, advocacy; наго́рная ~, Sermon on the Mount.

пропо́лка, -и, weeding. **прополо́ть**, -лю́, -лешь *perf*. (*imp*. пропа́лывать) weed.

про|полоска́ть, -ощу́, -о́щешь *perf*.

пропорциона́льный, proportional, proportionate. **пропо́рция**, -и, proportion; ratio.

про́пуск, -а; *pl*. -а́ or -и, -о́в or -ов, pass, permit; password; admission; omission, lapse; absence, non-attendance; blank, gap. **пропуска́ть**, -а́ю *imp*., **пропусти́ть**, -ущу́, -у́стишь *perf*. let pass, let through; let in, admit; absorb; pass; omit, leave out; skip; miss; let slip; ~ ми́мо уше́й, pay no heed to, turn a deaf ear to; не пропуска́ть воды́, be waterproof; пропуска́ть во́ду, leak. **пропускн|о́й**; ~а́я бума́га, blotting-paper; ~о́й свет, transmitted light; ~а́я спосо́бность, capacity.

пропью́, etc.: see пропи́ть.

прораба́тывать, -аю *imp*., **прорабо́тать**, -аю *perf*. work, work through; work at, study; get up; slate, pick holes in. **прорабо́тка**, -и, study, studying, getting up; slating.

прораста́ть, -а́ет *imp*., **прорасти́**, -тёт; -ро́с, -ла́ *perf*. germinate, sprout, shoot. **прорва́ть**, -ву́, -вёшь; -а́л, -а́, -о *perf*. (*imp*. прорыва́ть) break through; tear, make a hole in; ~ блока́ду, run the blockade; **~ся**, burst open, break; tear; break out break through.

про|реаги́ровать, -рую *perf*.

проре́з, -а, cut; slit, notch, nick. **про|ре́зать**, -е́жу *perf*., **проре́зывать**, -аю *imp*. (*imp*. also проре́зывать) cut through; **~ся**, be cut, come through.

прорези́нивать, -аю *imp*., **прорези́нить** -ню *perf*. rubberize.

прорёзывать(ся, -аю(сь *imp.* of прорéзать(ся. про|репети́ровать, -рую *perf.*

прорéха, -и, rent, tear, slit; fly, flies; gap deficiency.

про|рецензи́ровать, -рую *perf.*

проро́к, -а, prophet.

проро́с, etc.: see прорасти́.

пророни́ть, -ню́ -нишь *perf.* utter, breathe, drop.

проро́ческий, prophetic, oracular. проро́чество -а prophecy. проро́чить, -чу *imp.* (*perf.* на~) prophesy; predict.

проро́ю, etc.: see прорыть.

проруба́ть, -аю *imp.*, проруби́ть, -блю́ -бишь *perf.* cut through, hack through; break. про́рубь, -и, ice-hole.

проры́в, -а, break; break-through, breach; hitch, hold-up ликвиди́ровать ~, put things right; по́лный ~, breakdown. прорыва́ть¹(ся, -а́ю(сь *imp.* of прорва́ть(ся.

прорыва́ть², -а́ю *imp.*, проры́ть, -ро́ю *perf.* dig through; ~ся, dig one's way through, tunnel through.

проса́чиваться, -а́ется *imp.* of просочи́ться.

просвéрливать, -аю *imp.*, про|сверли́ть, -лю́ *perf.* drill, bore; perforate, pierce.

просвéт, -а, (clear) space; shaft of light; ray of hope; aperture, opening. просвети́тельный, educational; cultural. просвети́тельство, -а, educational activities, cultural activities. просвети́ть¹, -ещу́ *perf.* (*imp.* просвеща́ть) educate; enlighten.

просвети́ть², -ечу́ -éтишь *perf.* (*imp.* просвéчивать) X-ray.

просветлéние, -я, clearing up; brightening (up); clarity lucidity. просветлённый, clear, lucid. про|светлéть, -éет *perf.*

просвéчивание -я, fluoroscopy; radioscopy. просвéчивать, -аю *imp.* of просвети́ть; be translucent; be visible; show, appear, shine.

просвеща́ть, -аю *imp.* of просвети́ть. просвещéние, -я, enlightenment; education, instruction; наро́дное ~, public education. просвещённый, enlightened; educated, cultured.

про́седь, -и, streak(s) of grey; во́лосы с ~ю, greying hair, hair touched with grey.

просéивать, -аю *imp.* of просéять.

просéка, -и, cutting, ride.

просёлок, -лка, country road, cart-track.

просéять, -éю *perf.* (*imp.* просéивать) sift, riddle, screen.

про|сигнализи́ровать, -рую *perf.*

просидéть, -ижу́ *perf.*, проси́живать, -аю *imp.* sit; ~ всю ночь, sit up all night.

проси́тель, -я *m.* applicant; suppliant; petitioner. проси́тельный, pleading. проси́ть, -ошу́ -óсишь *imp.* (*perf.* по~) ask; beg; plead, intercede; invite; про́сят не кури́ть, no smoking, please; ~ся, ask; apply.

проси́ять, -я́ю *perf.* brighten; begin to shine; beam, light up.

проска́кивать, -аю *imp.* of проскочи́ть.

проска́льзывать -аю *imp.*, проскользну́ть, -ну́, -нёшь *perf.* slip in, creep in; ~ ми́мо, slip past.

проскочи́ть, -чу́, -чишь *perf.* (*imp.* проска́кивать) rush, tear; slip through; slip in, creep in.

про|слáбить, -бит *perf.*

прослáвить, -влю *perf.*, прославля́ть, -я́ю *imp.* glorify; bring fame to; make famous; ~ся, become famous, be renowned. прослáвленный, famous, renowned, celebrated, illustrious.

проследи́ть, -ежу́ *perf.* track (down); trace.

прослези́ться, -ежу́сь *perf.* shed a tear, a few tears.

прослои́ть, -ою́ *perf.* layer; sandwich. просло́йка, -и, layer, stratum; seam, streak.

про|слу́шать, -аю *perf.*, прослу́шивать, -аю *imp.* hear; listen to; miss, not catch.

про|слы́ть, -ыву́ -ывёшь; -ы́л, -á, -о *perf.*

просмáтривать, -аю *imp.*, просмотрéть, -рю́, -ришь *perf.* look over, look through; glance over, glance through; survey; view; run over; overlook miss.

просмо́тр, -а, survey; view, viewing;

examination; закрытый ∼, private view; предварительный ∼, preview.

проснуться, -нусь, -нёшься *perf.* (*imp.* просыпаться) wake up, awake.

просо, -a millet.

просовывать(ся, -аю(сь *imp.* of просунуть(ся.

про|сохнуть, -ну; -óx *perf.* (*imp.* also просыхáть) get dry, dry out. **просохший**, dried.

просочиться, -ится *perf.* (*imp.* просáчиваться) percolate; filter; leak, ooze; seep out; filter through, leak out.

проспáть, -плю; -áл, -á, -о *perf.* (*imp.* просыпáть) sleep (for, through); oversleep; miss.

проспéкт, -a, avenue.

проспóрить, -рю *perf.* lose, lose a bet; argue.

про|спрягáть, -áю *perf.*

просрóчен|ный, overdue; out of date, expired; пáспорт ∼ the passport is out of date. **просрóчивать**, -аю *imp.*, **просрóчить**, -чу *perf.* allow to run out; be behind with; overstay; ∼ óтпуск, overstay one's leave. **просрóчка**, -и, delay; expiration of time limit.

простáк, -á, simpleton. **простéйший** *superl.* of простóй.

простéн|ок, -нка; *pl.* ∼ки; partition.

простерéться, -трётся; -тёрся *perf.*, **простирáться**, -áется *imp.* stretch, extend.

простительный, pardonable, excusable, justifiable. **простить**, -ощу *perf.* (*imp.* прощáть) forgive, pardon; excuse; ∼ся (с + *instr.*) say goodbye (to), take (one's) leave (of), bid farewell.

прóсто *adv.* simply; ∼ так, for no particular reason.

прóсто- in *comb.* simple; open; mere. **простоволóсый**, bare-headed, with head uncovered. ∼ **дýшный**, open-hearted; simple-hearted, simple-minded; ingenuous, artless. ∼ **квáша**, -и, (thick) sour milk, yoghurt. ∼ **людин**, -a, man of the common people. ∼ **нарóдный**, of the common people. ∼ **рéчие**, -я, popular speech; в ∼речии, colloquially. ∼ **рéчный**, popular, of popular speech. ∼ **сердéчный**, simple-hearted; frank; open.

standing idle, enforced idleness; stoppage.

прост|óй, simple; easy; ordinary; plain; unaffected, unpretentious; mere; ∼ым глáзом, with the naked eye; ∼ые люди, ordinary people; homely people; ∼óй нарóд, the common people; ∼óе предложéние, simple sentence; ∼óе числó, prime number.

прóсто-напрóсто *adv.* simply.

простóр, -a, spaciousness; space, expanse; freedom, scope; elbow-room; дать ∼, give scope free range, full play. **простóр|ный**, spacious, roomy; ample; здесь ∼o, there is plenty of room here.

простотá, -ы, simplicity.

прострáнный, extensive, vast; diffuse; verbose. **прострáнственный**, spatial. **прострáнство**, -a, space; expanse; area.

прострéл, -a, lumbago. **прострéливать**, -аю *imp.*, **прострелить**, -лю, -лишь *perf.* shoot through.

прострётся, etc.: see простерéться.

про|строчить, -очу -óчишь *perf.*

простýда, -ы, cold; chill. **простудить**, -ужý, -ýдишь *perf.*, **простужáть**, -áю *imp.* let catch cold; ∼ся, catch (a) cold, a chill.

простýп|ок, -пка, fault; misdemeanour.

простын|ный, sheet; ∼óе полотнó, sheeting. **простыня** -и́; *pl.* прóстыни, -ынь, -ня́м, sheet.

простýть, -ýну *perf.* get cold; cool; catch cold.

просýнуть, -ну *perf.* (*imp.* просóвывать) push, shove, thrust; ∼ся, push through force one's way through.

просýшивать, -аю *imp.*, **просушить**, -шý, -шишь *perf.* dry (thoroughly, properly); ∼ся, dry, get dry. **просýшка**, -и, drying.

просуществовáть, -твýю *perf.* exist; last, endure.

просчитáться, -áюсь *perf.*, **просчитываться**, -аюсь *imp.* miscalculate.

прóсып -a (-у); без ∼у, without waking. without stirring.

просыпáть, -плю *perf.* **просыпáть**[1], -áю *imp.* spill; ∼ся, spill, get spilt; fail, be ploughed.

просыпа́ть, -а́ю *imp.* of проспа́ть.
просыпа́ться, -а́юсь *imp.* of просну́ть-
ся. просыха́ть, -а́ю *imp.* of просо́х-
нуть.

про́сьба, -ы, request; application,
petition; ~ не кури́ть, no smoking,
please; у меня́ к вам ~, I have a
favour to ask you.

прота́лкивать, -аю *imp.* of протолк-
ну́ть. прота́пливать, -аю *imp.* of
протопи́ть.

прога́скивать, -аю *imp.* of протащи́ть,
-щу́, -щишь *perf.* pull, drag, trail.

проте́з, -а, artificial limb; (artificial)
aid; prosthesis, prosthetic appliance;
зубно́й ~, false teeth, denture; слу-
хово́й ~, hearing aid. проте́зный,
prosthetic.

протека́ть, -а́ет *imp.* of проте́чь. про-
тёкший, past, last.

проте́кция, -и, patronage, influence.

протере́ть, -тру́, -трёшь, -тёр *perf.*
(*imp.* протира́ть) wipe (over); wipe
dry; rub (through).

проте́чь, -ечёт, -тёк, -ла́ *perf.* (*imp.*
протека́ть) flow; run; leak; ooze,
seep; elapse, pass; take its course.

про́тив *prep.* + *gen.* against; opposite;
facing; contrary to, as against; in proportion to, according to; име́ть что́-
-нибудь ~, have something against,
mind, object; ничего́ не име́ть ~, not
mind, not object.

про́тивень, -вня *m.* dripping-pan; meat-
-tin; girdle, griddle.

проти́виться, -влюсь *imp.* (*perf.* вос~)
+ *dat.* oppose; resist, stand up against.
проти́вник, -а, opponent, adversary,
antagonist; the enemy. проти́вно
prep. + *dat.* against; contrary to.
проти́вн|ый[1], opposite; contrary; op-
posing, opposed; в ~ом слу́чае,
otherwise; ~ый ве́тер, contrary wind,
head wind. проти́вный[2], nasty, offensive, disgusting; unpleasant, disagreeable; мне проти́вно, I am disgusted.

противо- in *comb.* anti-, contra- coun-
ter- противове́с, -а, counterbalance,
counterpoise. ~возду́шный, anti-aircraft. ~га́з, -а, gas-mask, respirator.
~га́зовый, anti-gas. ~де́йствие, -я,
opposition, counteraction. ~де́йство-

вать, -твую *imp.* + *dat.* oppose,
counteract. ~есте́ственный, unnatural. ~зако́нный, unlawful; illegal.
~зача́точный, contraceptive. ~лежа́-
щий, opposite. ~обще́ственный, anti-
-social. ~пожа́рный, fire-fighting, fire-
-prevention. ~поло́жность, -и, opposition; contrast; opposite, antithesis;
пряма́я ~поло́жность, exact opposite. ~поло́жный, opposite; opposed,
contrary. ~поста́вить, -влю *perf.*,
~поставля́ть, -я́ю *imp.* oppose; contrast, set off. ~раке́та, -ы, anti-missile
missile. ~раке́тный, anti-missile.
~речи́вый, contradictory; discrepant,
conflicting. ~ре́чие, -я, contradiction;
inconsistency; conflict, clash. ~ре́-
чить, -чу *imp.* + *dat.* contradict; be at
variance with, conflict with be contrary to, run counter to. ~стоя́ть, -ою́
imp. + *dat.* resist, withstand. ~та́нко-
вый, anti-tank. ~хими́ческий, anti-
-gas. ~я́дие, -я, antidote.

протира́ть, -а́ю *imp.* of протере́ть.
проти́рка, -и, cleaning rag.

проткну́ть, -ну́, -нёшь *perf.* (*imp.* про-
тыка́ть) pierce; transfix; spit, skewer.

протоко́л, -а, minutes, record of proceedings; report; statement; charge-
-sheet; protocol; вести́ ~, take,
record, the minutes; занести́ в ~,
enter in the minutes. протоколи́ро-
вать, -рую *perf.* and *imp.* (*perf.* also
за~) minute, record. протоко́льный,
of protocol; exact, factual.

протолкну́ть, -ну́, -нёшь *perf.* (*imp.*
прота́лкивать) push through.

протопи́ть, -плю́, -пишь *perf.* (*imp.*
прота́пливать) heat (thoroughly).

проторённ|ый, beaten, well-trodden;
~ая доро́жка, beaten track.

прото́чный, flowing, running.

про|тра́лить, -лю *perf.*, etc.:
see протере́ть. про|тру́|тить, -блю́
perf.

протуха́ть, -а́ет *imp.*, проту́хнуть, -нет,
-ух *perf.* become foul, become rotten;
go bad. проту́хший, foul, rotten; bad,
tainted.

протыка́ть, -а́ю *imp.* of проткну́ть.

протя́гивать, -аю *imp.*, протяну́ть, -ну́,
-нешь *perf.* stretch; extend; stretch

out, hold out; reach out; protract; drawl out; last; **~ся**, stretch out; reach out; extend, stretch, reach; last, go on. **протяже́ние**, **-я**, extent, stretch; distance, expanse, area; space; **на всём протяже́нии** + gen. along the whole length of, all along; **на протяже́нии**, during, for the space of. **протя́женность**, **-и**, extent, length. **протя́жность**, **-и**, slowness; **~ ре́чи**, drawl. **протя́жный**, long-drawn-out; drawling.

проу́чивать, **-аю** imp., **проучи́ть**, **-чу́**, **-чишь** perf. study, learn (up); teach a lesson. punish.

проф. abbr. профе́ссор, professor.

проф- abbr. in comb. of профессиона́льный, professional, occupational; профсою́зный, trade-union. **профбиле́т**, **-а**, trade-union card. **~боле́знь**, **-и** occupational disease. **~ко́м**, **-а**, trade-union commitee. **~о́рг**, **-а**, trade-union organizer. **~ориента́ция**, **-и**, vocational guidance. **~рабо́тник**, **-а** trade-union official. **~сою́з**, **-а**, trade-union. **~сою́зный**, trade-union. **~техучи́лище**, **-а**, a technical college. **~техшко́ла**, **-ы**, trade school. **~шко́ла**, **-ы**, trade-union school.

профа́н, **-а**, a layman; ignoramus.

профессиона́льный, professional; occupational; **~ сою́з**, trade union. **профе́ссия**, **-и**, profession, occupation, trade.

про́филь, **-я** m. profile; side-view; outline; section; type.

прохла́да, **-ы**, coolness, cool. прохлади́тельный, refreshing, cooling. прохла́дный, cool, fresh.

прохо́д, **-а** (**-у**) passage; passageway; gangway, aisle; duct; пра́во **~а**, right of way; **~а нет**, no thoroughfare. проходи́мец, **-мца**, rogue, rascal. проходи́мый, passable. проходи́ть, **-ожу́**, **-о́дишь** imp. of пройти́. **прохо́дка**, **-и**, going through, getting through; tunnelling, driving. **проходно́й**, of passage; through, communicating. прохо́жий, passing, in transit; sb. passer-by.

процвета́ние, **-я**, prosperity, well-being;

flourishing, thriving. процвета́ть, **-а́ю** imp. prosper, flourish, thrive.

процеди́ть, **-ежу́**, **-е́дишь** perf. (imp. проце́живать) filter, strain; **~ сквозь зу́бы**, mutter, mumble.

процеду́ра, **-ы**, procedure; treatment; лече́бные процеду́ры, medical treatment.

проце́живать, **-аю** perf. of процеди́ть.

проце́нт, **-а**, percentage; per cent; interest; сто **~ов**, a hundred per cent.

проце́сс, **-а**, process; trial; legal action, legal proceedings; lawsuit; cause, case. **проце́ссия**, **-и**, procession. **процессуа́льный**, trial; legal.

про|цити́ровать, **-рую** perf.

прочёска, **-и**, screening; combing.

проче́сть, **-чту́**, **-чтёшь**; **-чёл**, **-чла́** perf. of прочита́ть.

про́ч|ий, other; и **~ее**, etc., etcetera, and so on; ме́жду **~им**, incidentally, by the way; **~ее** sb. (the) others.

прочи́стить, **-и́щу** perf. (imp. прочища́ть) clean; cleanse thoroughly.

про|чита́ть, **-а́ю** perf., прочи́тывать, **-аю** imp. read (through).

прочища́ть, **-а́ю** imp. of прочи́стить.

про́чно adv. firmly, soundly, solidly, well. про́чн|ый; **-чен**, **-чна́**, **-о**, firm, sound, stable, solid; durable, lasting; enduring; **~ая кра́ска**, fast colour.

прочте́ние, **-я**, reading; reciting; giving, delivering. прочту́, etc.; see проче́сть.

прочу́вствовать, **-твую** perf. feel; feel deeply, acutely, keenly; experience, go through; get the feel of.

прочь adv. away, off; averse to; (поди́) **~!** go away! be off!; (пошёл) **~** отсю́да! get out of here!; **~ с доро́ги!** get out of the way!; ру́ки **~!** hands off!; я не прочь, I have no objection, I am not averse to, I am quite willing.

проше́дш|ий, past; last; **~ее** sb. the past. прошёл, etc.; see пройти́.

проше́ние, **-я**, application, petition.

прошепта́ть, **-пчу́**, **-пчешь** perf. whisper.

проше́ствие, **-я**; по проше́ствии + gen. after the lapse of, after the expiration of.

прошива́ть, **-а́ю** imp., проши́ть, **-шью́**, **-шьёшь** perf. sew, stitch. **проши́вка**, **-и**, insertion.

прошлого́дний, last year's. прошл|ый, past; of the past; bygone, former; last; в ~ом году́, last year; ~ое sb. the past.

прошма́нивать, -аю *imp.*, про|шмона́ть, -а́ю *perf.*, про|шмони́ть, -ню́, -ни́шь *perf.* (*sl.*) search, frisk.

прошурова́ть, -ру́ю *perf.*, про|штуди́ровать, -рую *perf.* прошью́, etc.: see проши́ть.

проща́й(те), goodbye; farewell. проща́льный, parting; farewell. проща́ние, -я, farewell; parting, leave-taking. проща́ть(ся, -а́ю(сь *imp.* of прости́ть(ся.

про́ще, simpler, plainer, easier.

проще́ние, -я, forgiveness, pardon; прошу́ проще́ния, I beg your pardon; (I'm) sorry.

прощу́пать, -аю *perf.*, прощу́пывать, -аю *imp.* feel; detect; sound (out).

про|экзамену́ю, -ну́ю *perf.*

проявн́тель, -я *m.* developer. прояви́ть, -влю́, -вишь *perf.*, проявля́ть -я́ю *imp.* show, display, manifest, reveal; develop.

проясне́ть[1], -еет *perf.* clear; проя́снело, it cleared up. проясне́ть[2], -е́ет *perf.* brighten (up). проясни́ться, -и́тся *perf.*, проясня́ться, -я́ется *imp.* clear, clear up.

пруд, -а́, *loc.* -у́, pond. пруди́ть, -ужу́, -у́ди́шь *imp.* (*perf.* за~) dam. прудово́й, pond.

пружи́на, -ы, spring. пружи́нистый, springy, elastic. пружи́нка, -и, mainspring; hairspring. пружи́нный, spring.

пруса́к, -а́, cockroach.

прусса́к, -а́ прусса́чка, -и, Prussian. пру́сский, Prussian.

прут, -а or -а́, *pl.* -тья twig; switch; rod.

прыга́лка, -и, skipping-rope. пры́гать, -аю *imp.*, пры́гнуть, -ну *perf.* jump, leap, spring; bound; hop; bounce; ~ со скака́лкой, skip; ~ с упо́ром, vault; ~ с шесто́м, pole-vault. прыгу́н, -а́, пры́гунья, -и; *gen. pl.* -ний, jumper. прыжо́к, -жка́, jump; leap, spring; caper; прыжки́, jumping; прыжки́ в во́ду, diving; ~ в высоту́, high jump; ~ в длину́, long jump; ~ с ме́ста, standing jump; ~ с разбе́га,

running jump; ~ с упо́ром, vault, vaulting; ~ с шесто́м, pole-vault.

пры́скать, -аю *imp.*, пры́снуть, -ну *perf.* spurt, gush; ~ на or в + *acc.* spray, sprinkle; ~ (со́ смеху) burst out laughing.

пры́ткий, quick, lively, sharp. прыть, -и, speed; quickness, liveliness, go.

прыщ, -а́, пры́щик, -а, pimple; pustule, pimply, pimpled.

пряде́ние, -я, spinning. пря́деный, spun. пряди́льный, spinning. пряди́льня, -и; *gen. pl.* -лен, (spinning-)mill. пряди́льщик, -а, spinner. пряду́, etc.: see прясть. прядь, -и, lock; strand. пря́жа, -и, yarn, thread.

пря́жка, -и, buckle, clasp.

пря́лка, -и, distaff; spinning-wheel.

пряма́я *sb.* straight line; по прямо́й, on the straight. пря́мо *adv.* straight; straight on; directly; frankly, openly, bluntly; really.

прямо- in *comb.* straight-; direct; ortho-, rect(i)-, right. прямоду́шие, -я, directness, frankness, straightforwardness. ~ду́шный, direct, frank, straightforward. ~кры́лый, orthopterous. ~лине́йный, rectilinear; straightforward, forthright. ~сло́йный, straight-grained. ~уго́льник, -а, rectangle. ~уго́льный, right-angled, rectangular.

прямо́й, -я́м, -а́, -о, straight; upright, erect; through; direct; straightforward; real.

пря́ник, -а, spice cake; gingerbread; honey-cake. пря́ничный, gingerbread. пря́ность, -и, spice; spiciness. пря́ный, spicy, heady.

прясть, -яду́, -ядёшь; -ял, -яла́, -о *imp.* (*perf.* с~) spin.

пря́тать, -ячу *imp.* (*perf.* с~) hide, conceal; ~ся, hide, conceal oneself. пря́тки, -ток *pl.* hide-and-seek.

пря́ха, -и, spinner.

пса, etc.: see пёс.

псало́м, -лма́, psalm. псало́мщик, -а, (psalm-)reader; sexton.

псевдони́м, -а, pseudonym; pen-name.

псих, -а, madman, lunatic, crank. пси́хика, -и, state of mind; psyche; psychology. психи́ческий, mental,

psychical. психо́з, -а, psychosis. пси-
хопа́т, -а, psychopath; lunatic.
птене́ц, -нца́, nestling; fledgeling.
пти́ца, -ы, bird; ва́жная ~, big noise;
дома́шняя ~, poultry. птицево́д, -а,
poultry-farmer poultry-breeder. пти́-
ч|ий, bird, bird's; poultry; вид с
~ьего полёта, bird's-eye view; ~ий
двор, poultry-yard. пти́чка, -и, bird.
ПТО (пете́о) abbr. профессиона́льно-
-техни́ческое обуче́ние, technical education.
ПТУ (пете́у) abbr. профтехучи́лище,
профессиона́льно-техни́ческое учи́-
лище, technical college.
публика, -и, public; audience. публи-
ка́ция, -и, publication; notice, advertisement. публикова́ть, -ку́ю imp.
(perf. o~) publish. публици́стика, -и,
social and political journalism; writing
on current affairs. публи́чно adv.
publicly; in public; openly. публи́ч-
ность, -и publicity. публи́чный,
public.
пу́гало, -а, scarecrow. пу́ганый, scared,
frightened. пуга́ть, -а́ю imp. (perf.
ис~, на~) frighten; scare; intimidate;
+ instr. threaten with; ~ся (+ gen.)
be frightened (of), be scared (of); take
fright (at); shy (at). пуга́ч, -а́, toy
pistol; screech owl. пугли́вый, fearful,
timorous; timid. пугну́ть, -ну́, -нёшь
perf. scare, frighten; give a fright.
пу́говица, -ы, пу́говка, -и, button.
пуд, -а́; pl. -ы́, pood (= 16·3 kg).
пудово́й, пудо́вый, one pood in weight.
пу́дра, -ы powder. пу́дреный, powdered.
пу́дрить, -рю imp. (perf. на~) powder; ~ся, powder one's face, use powder.
пуза́тый, big-bellied, pot-bellied.
пузырёк, -рька́, phial, vial; bubble;
bleb. пузы́рь, -я́ m. bubble; blister;
bladder.
пук, -а; pl. -и́, bunch, bundle; tuft;
wisp.
пулево́й, bullet. пулемёт, -а, machine-
-gun. пулемётный, machine-gun. пу-
лемётчик, -а, machine-gunner. пу-
лесто́йкий, bullet-proof.
пульс, -а, pulse. пу́льсар, -а, pulsar.

пульси́ровать, -рует imp. pulse, pulsate; beat, throb.
пульт, -а, desk, stand; control panel.
пу́ля, -и, bullet.
пункт, -а, point; spot; post; centre;
item; plank; по всем ~ам, at all
points. пункти́р, -а, dotted line.
пункти́рный, dotted, broken.
пунцо́вый, crimson.
пуп, -а́, navel; umbilicus; ~ земли́,
hub of the universe. пупови́на, -ы, umbilical cord. пупо́к, -пка́, navel; gizzard. пупо́чный, umbilical.
пурга́ -и́, snow-storm, blizzard.
пу́рпур, -а, purple, crimson. пурпу́р-
ный, пурпу́ровый, purple, crimson.
пуск, -а, starting (up); setting in motion. пуска́й: see пусть. пуска́ть(ся,
-а́ю(сь imp. of пусти́ть(ся. пуско-
в|о́й, starting; initial; ~а́я площа́дка,
(rocket-)launching platform.
пусте́ть, -е́ет imp. (perf. o~) empty;
become deserted.
пусти́ть, пущу́, пу́стишь perf. (imp.
пуска́ть) let go; set free; let in, allow
to enter; let, allow, permit; start; set,
put; send; set in motion, set going, set
working; throw, shy; put forth, put
out; не ~, keep out; ~ во́ду, turn on
the water; ~ в ход, start, launch, set
going, set in train; ~ ко́рни, take
root; ~ ростки́, shoot, sprout; ~
слух, start, spread, a rumour; ~
фейерве́рк, let off fireworks; ~ в
сбыт; start; begin; ~ся в путь, set out,
get on one's way.
пустобрёх, -а, chatterbox, windbag.
пустова́ть, -ту́ет imp. be empty, stand
empty; lie fallow. пуст|о́й; see -а́, -о,
empty; void; tenantless, vacant, uninhabited; deserted; idle; shallow;
futile, frivolous; vain, ungrounded;
~о́е ме́сто, blank space; ~а́я от-
гово́рка, lame excuse; hollow pretence; ~ые слова́, mere words; ~о́й
чай, just tea. пустота́, -ы́; pl. -ы,
emptiness; void; vacuum; shallow-
ness; futility, frivolousness. пусто-
те́лый, hollow.
пусты́нник, -а, hermit, anchorite. пуст-
ы́нный, uninhabited; deserted; ~
о́стров, desert island. пу́стынь, -и,

hermitage, monastery. пусты́ня, -и, desert, wilderness. пусты́рь, -я́ *m.* waste land; vacant plot; desolate area.

пусты́шка, -и, dummy; hollow object; (baby's) dummy; empty-headed person.

пусть, пуска́й *part.* let; all right, very well; though, even if; ~ бу́дет так, so be it; ~ *x* ра́вен 3, let *x* = 3.

пустя́к, -а́, trifle; bagatelle. пустяко́вый, trifling, trivial.

пу́таница, -ы, muddle, confusion; mess, tangle. пу́таный, muddled, confused; tangled; confusing; muddle-headed. пу́тать, -аю *imp.* (*perf.* за~, пере~, с~) tangle; confuse; muddle; mix up; ~ся, get tangled; get confused; get muddled; get mixed up.

путёвка, -и, pass, authorization; permit; проси́ть путёвку в санато́рий, apply for a place in a sanatorium. путеводи́тель, -я *m.* guide, guide-book. путево́дный, guiding; ~ая звезда́, guiding star; lodestar. путёвой, travelling, itinerary; ~ая ка́рта, road-map; ~ая ско́рость, ground-speed. путём *prep.* + *gen.* by means of, by dint of. путепрово́д, -а, overpass; underpass; bridge. путеше́ственник, -а, traveller. путеше́ствие, -я, journey; trip; voyage; cruise; *pl.* travels. путеше́ствовать, -твую *imp.* travel; voyage. путь, -и́, *instr.* -ём, *prep.* -и́, way; track; path; road; course; journey; voyage; passage; duct; means; use, benefit; во́дный ~, water-way; в пути́, en route, on one's way; в четырёх днях пути́ от, four days' journey from; ми́рным путём, amicably, peaceably; морски́е пути́, shipping-routes, sea-lanes; нам с ва́ми по пути́, we are going the same way; на обра́тном пути́, on the way back; пойти́ по пути́ + *gen.* take, follow, the path of; по пути́, on the way; путём сообще́ния, communications; стоя́ть на пути́, be in the way.

пух, -а (-у), *loc.* -у́, down; fluff; разби́ть в ~ и прах, put to complete rout. пухл|ый, -хл, -а́, -о, chubby, plump. пу́хнуть, -ну; пух *imp.* (*perf.* вс~) swell.

пухови́к, -а́, feather-bed; down quilt; eiderdown. пухо́вка, -и, powder-puff. пухо́вый, downy.

пучегла́зый, goggle-eyed.

пучи́на, -ы, gulf, abyss; the deep.

пучо́к, -чка́, bunch, bundle; tuft, fascicle; wisp.

пу́шечн|ый, gun, cannon; ~ое мя́со, cannon-fodder.

пуши́нка, -и, bit of fluff; ~ сне́га, snow-flake. пуши́стый, fluffy, downy.

пу́шка, -и, gun, cannon.

пушни́на, -ы, furs, fur-skins, pelts. пушно́й, fur; fur-bearing; ~ зверь, fur-bearing animals.

пу́ще *adv.* more; ~ всего́, most of all.

пущу́, etc.: see пусти́ть.

пчела́, -ы́; *pl.* -ёлы, bee. пчели́ный, bee, bees', of bees; ~ воск, beeswax. пчелово́д, -а, bee-keeper, bee-master, apiarist. пче́льник, -а, apiary.

пшени́ца, -ы, wheat. пшени́чный, wheaten, wheat.

пшённый, millet. пшено́, -а́, millet.

пыл, -а (-у), *loc.* -у́, heat, ardour, passion. пыла́ть, -а́ю *imp.* blaze, flame; burn; glow.

пылеви́дный, powdered, pulverized. пылесо́с, -а, vacuum cleaner. пылесо́сить, -сю *imp.* vacuum(-clean). пыли́нка, -и, speck of dust. пыли́ть, -лю́ *imp.* (*perf.* за~, на~) raise a dust, raise the dust; cover with dust, make dusty; ~ся, get dusty, get covered with dust.

пы́лкий, ardent, passionate; fervent; fervid. пы́лкость, -и, ardour, passion; fervency.

пыль, -и, *loc.* -и́, dust. пы́льн|ый; -лен, -льна́, -о, dusty; ~ый котёл, dust-bowl; ~ая тря́пка, duster. пыльца́, -ы́, pollen.

пыта́ть, -а́ю *imp.* torture, torment. пыта́ться, -а́юсь *imp.* (*perf.* по~) try. пы́тка, -и, torture, torment. пытли́вый, inquisitive searching.

пыха́ть, пы́шет *imp.* blaze.

пыхте́ть, -хчу́ *imp.* puff, pant.

пы́шет: see пыха́ть.

пы́шка, -и, bun; doughnut; chubby child; plump woman.

пы́шность, -и, splendour, magnificence. пы́шный; -шен, -шна́, шно, splendid, magnificent; fluffy, light; luxuriant.

пье́ксы, -с *pl.* ski boots.

пье́са, -ы, play; piece.

пью, etc.: see пить.

пьяне́ть, -е́ю *imp.* (*perf.* о~) get drunk. пьяни́ть, -ни́т *imp.* (*perf.* о~) intoxicate, make drunk; go to one's head. пья́ница, -ы *m.* and *f.* drunkard; tippler, toper. пья́нство, -a, drunkenness; hard drinking. пья́нствовать, -твую *imp.* drink hard, drink heavily. пья́ный, drunk; drunken; tipsy, tight; intoxicated; heady, intoxicating.

пэ *n. indecl.* the letter п.

пюпи́тр, -a, desk; reading-desk; music-stand.

пюре́ *n. indecl.* purée.

пядь, -и; *gen. pl.* -е́й, span; ни пя́ди, not an inch.

пя́льцы, -лец *pl.* tambour; embroidery frame.

пята́, -ы́; *pl.* -ы, -а́м, heel.

пята́к, -а́, пятачо́к, -чка́, five-copeck piece. пятёрка, -и, five; figure 5; No. 5; group of five; five-rouble note. пя́теро, -ы́х, five.

пяти- in *comb.* five; penta-. пятибо́рье, -я, pentathlon. ~гла́вый, five-headed; five-domed. ~десятиле́тие, -я, fifty years; fiftieth anniversary; fiftieth birthday. ~деся́тница, -ы, Pentecost. ~деся́тый, fiftieth; the fifties, the fifties. ~кла́ссник, -a, -ница, -ы, ~кла́шка, -и *m.* and *f.* class-five pupil. ~кни́жие, -я, Pentateuch. ~коне́чный, five-pointed. ~кра́тный, fivefold, quintuple. ~ле́тие, -я, five years; fifth anniversary. ~ле́тка, -и, five years; five-year plan; five-year-old. ~со́тенный, five-hundred-rouble. ~~сотле́тие, -я, five centuries; quincentenary. ~со́тый, five-hundredth. ~сто́пный, pentameter. ~то́нка, -и, five-ton lorry. ~ты́сячный, five-thousandth. ~уго́льник, -a, pentagon. ~уго́льный, pentagonal.

пя́тка, -и, heel.

пятна́дцатый, fifteenth. пятна́дцать, -и, fifteen.

пятна́ть, -а́ю *imp.* (*perf.* за~) spot, stain, smirch; tig, catch. пятна́шки, -шек *pl.* tag, tig. пятни́стый, spotted, dappled.

пя́тница, -ы, Friday.

пятно́, -а́; *pl.* -а, -тен, stain; spot; patch; blot; stigma, blemish; роди́мое ~, birth-mark.

пято́к, -тка́, five. пя́тый, fifth. пять, -и́, *instr.* -ью́, five. пятьдеся́т, -и́десяти, *instr.* -ью́десятью, fifty. пятьсо́т, -тисо́т, -тиста́м, five hundred. пя́тью *adv.* five times.

Р

p *letter*: see эр.

р. *abbr.* река́, river; рубль, rouble.

р *abbr.* рентге́н, roentgen.

раб, -а́, slave, bondsman.

раб- *abbr.* in *comb.* of рабо́чий, worker. рабко́р, -a, Workers' Correspondent. ~селько́р, -a, Workers' and Rural Correspondent. ~си́ла, -ы, man-power, labour force.

раба́, -ы́, slave; bondswoman. рабовладе́лец, -льца, slave-owner. рабовладе́льческий, slave-owning. раболе́пие, -я, servility. раболе́пный, servile. раболе́пствовать, -твую, cringe, fawn. рабо́та, -ы, work; labour; job, employment; working; functioning, running; workmanship. рабо́тать, -аю *imp.* work; run, function; be open; + *instr.* work, operate; не ~, not work, be out of order; ~ над + *instr.* work at, work on. рабо́тник, -a, рабо́тница, -ы, worker; workman; hand, labourer. рабо́тный, working; ~ дом, work-house. работоспосо́бность, -и, capacity for work, efficiency. **работоспосо́бный**, able-bodied, efficient. **работя́щий**, hardworking, industrious. **рабо́чий** sb. worker; working man; workman; hand, labourer. **рабо́ч|ий**, worker's; work; working; working-class; driving; ~ее движе́ние, working-class movement, labour movement; ~ий день, working day; ~ее колесо́, driving wheel; ~ая ло́шадь, draught-horse; ~ие ру́ки, hands; ~ая си́ла, manpower, labour force; slave.

ра́бский, slave; servile. **ра́бство**, -а, slavery, servitude.

равви́н, -а, rabbi.

ра́венство, -а, equality; знак ра́венства, equals sign. **равне́ние**, -я, dressing, alignment; ~ напра́во! eyes right! **равни́на**, -ы, plain. **равни́нный**, plain; level, flat.

равно́ adv. alike; equally; ~ как, as well as; and also, as also. **равно́** predic.: see **ра́вный**.

равно- in comb. equi-, iso-. **равнобе́дренный**, isosceles. ~ве́сие, -я, equilibrium; balance, equipoise; привести́ в ~ве́сие, balance. ~де́йствующая sb. resultant force. ~де́йствие, -я, equinox. ~ду́шие, -я, indifference. ~ду́шный, indifferent. ~зна́чащий, ~зна́чный, equivalent, equipollent. ~ме́рный, even; uniform. ~отстоя́щий, equidistant. ~пра́вие, -я, equality of rights. ~пра́вный, equal in rights, having equal rights. ~си́льный, of equal strength; equal, equivalent, tantamount. ~сторо́нний, equilateral. ~уго́льный, equiangular. ~це́нный, of equal value, of equal worth; equivalent.

ра́вн|ый, -вен, -вна́, equal as, equals, on an equal footing; на ~ых, as equals; при про́чих ~ых усло́виях, other things being equal; ~ым о́бразом, equally, likewise; **равно́** predic. make(s), equals; всё ~о́, it is all the same, it makes no difference; all the same; мне всё ~о́, I don't mind, it's all the same to me; не всё ли ~о́? what difference does it make? what does it matter? **равня́ть**, -я́ю imp. (perf. c~) make even; treat equally; + c + instr. compare with,

treat as equal to; ~ счёт, equalize; ~ся, compete, compare; be equal; be equivalent, be tantamount; dress; + dat. equal, amount to; + c + instr. compete with, match.

рад, -а, -о predic. glad.

ра́ди prep. + gen. for the sake of; чего́ ~? what for?

ра́диевый, radium. **ра́дий**, -я, radium. **ра́дио** n. indecl. radio, wireless; radio set; переда́ть по~, broadcast; слу́шать ~, listen in.

радио- in comb., radio-; radioactive. ~акти́вность, -и, radioactivity. ~акти́вный, radioactive. ~аппара́т, -а, radio set. ~веща́ние, -я, broadcasting. ~веща́тельный, broadcasting. ~гра́мма, -ы, radiogram; wireless message. ~зо́нд, -а, radiosonde. **радио́лог**, -а, radiologist. ~логи́ческий, radiological. ~ло́гия, -и, radiology. ~лока́тор, -а, radar (set). ~люби́тель -я m. radio amateur, ham. ~мая́к, -а, radio beacon. ~переда́тчик, -а, transmitter. ~переда́ча, -и, transmission, broadcast. ~перекли́чка, -и, radio hook-up. ~приёмник, -а, receiver radio (set). ~связь, -и, radio communication, radio link. ~слу́шатель, -я m. listener. ~ста́нция, -и, radio station, set. ~те́хника, -и, radio-engineering. ~фици́ровать, -рую perf. and imp. instal radio in, equip with radio. ~хими́ческий, radiochemical. ~хи́мия, -и, radiochemistry. ~электро́ника, -и, radio-electronics.

радио́ла, -ы, radiogram.

ради́ровать, -рую perf. and imp. radio.

ра́довать, -дую imp. (perf. об~, по~) gladden, make glad, make happy; ~ся, be glad, be happy, rejoice. **ра́достный**, glad, joyous, joyful. **ра́дость**, -и, gladness, joy; от ра́дости, for joy, with joy; с ~ю, with pleasure, gladly.

ра́дуга, -и, rainbow. **ра́дужн|ый**, iridescent, opalescent, rainbow-coloured; cheerful; optimistic; ~ая оболо́чка, iris.

раду́шие, -я, cordiality. **раду́шный**, cordial; ~ приём, hearty welcome.

раёк, райка́, gallery; gods.

раз, -а, *pl.* -ы́, раз, time, occasion; one; в друго́й ~, another time, some other time; в са́мый ~, at the right moment, just right; ещё ~, (once) again, once more; как ~, just, exactly; как ~ то, the very thing; на э́тот ~, this time, on this occasion, (for) this once; не ~, more than once; time and again; ни ~у, not once, never; оди́н ~, once; ~ навсегда́, once (and) for all. **раз** *adv.* once, one day. **раз** *conj.* if; since; ~ так, in that case.

раз-, **разо-**, **разъ-**, **рас-** *vbl. pref.* indicating division into parts; distribution; action in different directions; action in reverse; termination of action or state; intensification of action or state; dis-, un-.

разба́вить, -влю *perf.*, **разбавля́ть**, -я́ю *imp.* dilute.

разбаза́ривание, -я, squandering; sell-out. **разбаза́ривать**, -аю *imp.*, **разбаза́рить**, -рю *perf.* squander, waste; (*sl.*) sell (government property).

разба́лтывать(ся, -аюсь *imp.* of разболта́ть(ся.

разбе́г, -а (-у), run, running start; прыжо́к с разбе́га (-éгу), running jump. **разбега́ться**, -а́юсь *imp.*, **разбежа́ться**, -егу́сь *perf.* take a run, run up; scatter, disperse; be scattered; у меня́ разбежа́лись глаза́, I was dazzled.

разберу́, etc.: see разобра́ть.

разбива́ть(ся, -а́ю(сь *imp.* of разби́ть(ся. **разби́вка**, и, laying out; spacing (out).

разбинтова́ть, -ту́ю *perf.*, **разбинто́вывать**, -аю *imp.* unbandage remove a bandage from; ~ся, remove one's bandage(s); come off, come undone; come unbandaged, lose its bandage.

разбира́тельство, -а, examination, investigation. **разбира́ть**, -а́ю *imp.* of разобра́ть; be particular; не разбира́я, indiscriminately; ~ся *imp.* of разобра́ться.

разби́ть, -зобью́, -зобьёшь *perf.* (*imp.* разбива́ть) break; smash; break up, break down; divide (up), split; damage; fracture; beat, defeat; lay out, mark out; space (out); ~ся, break, get broken, get smashed; hurt oneself

badly; smash oneself up. **разби́тый**, broken; jaded.

раз|благовести́ть, -ещу́ *perf.* **раз|богате́ть**, -е́ю *perf.*

разбо́й, -я, robbery, brigandage. **разбо́йник**, -а, robber, brigand, bandit. **разбо́йничий**, robber; thieves'; ~ья ша́йка, gang of robbers.

разболе́ться[1], -ли́тся *perf.* ache; у меня́ разболе́лась голова́, I've got a (bad) headache.

разболе́ться[2], -е́юсь *perf.* become ill, lose one's health.

разболта́ть[1], -а́ю *perf.* (*imp.* разба́лтывать) divulge, let out, give away.

разболта́ть[2], -а́ю *perf.* (*imp.* разба́лтывать) shake up, stir up; loosen; ~ся, mix; come loose, work loose; get slack, get out of hand.

разбомби́ть, -блю́ *perf.* bomb, destroy by bombing.

разбо́р, -а (-у), analysis; parsing; criticism, critique; selectiveness, discrimination; investigation; stripping, dismantling; buying up; sorting out; sort, quality; без ~у (-а) indiscriminately. **разбо́рный**, collapsible. **разбо́рчивость**, -и, legibility; scrupulousness; fastidiousness. **разбо́рчивый**, legible; scrupulous; fastidious exacting; discriminating.

разбра́сывать -аю *imp.* of разброса́ть.

разбреда́ться -а́ется *imp.*, **разбрести́сь**, -едётся; -ёлся, -ла́сь *perf.* disperse; straggle. **разбро́д**, -а, disorder.

разбро́санный, sparse, scattered; straggling; disconnected, incoherent. **разброса́ть**, -а́ю *perf.* (*imp.* разбра́сывать) throw about; scatter, spread, strew.

раз|буди́ть, -ужу́, -у́дишь *perf.*

разбуха́ние, -я, swelling; ~ шта́та, over-staffing. **разбуха́ть**, -а́ет *imp.*, **разбу́хнуть**, -нет; -ух *perf.* swell.

разбушева́ться, -шу́юсь *perf.* fly into a rage; blow up; turn high.

разва́л, -а, breakdown, disintegration, disruption; disorganization. **разва́ливать**, -аю *imp.*, **развали́ть**, -лю́, -лишь *perf.* pull down; break up; mess up; ~ся, collapse; go to pieces, fall to pieces; fall down, tumble down; break down; sprawl, lounge. **разва́лина** -ы, ruin; wreck; гру́да разва́лин, a heap of ruins.

разварно́й boiled soft.

ра́зве *part.* really?; ~ вы не зна́ете? don't you know?; ~ (то́лько), ~ (что) only; perhaps; except that, only. **ра́зве** *conj.* unless.

развева́ться, -ается *imp.* fly, flutter.

разве́д- *abbr.* in *comb.* of разве́дывательный, reconnaissance; intelligence. **разведгру́ппа**, -ы, reconnaissance party. ~**о́рган**, -а, intelligence agency; reconnaissance unit. ~**сво́дка**, -и, intelligence summary. ~**слу́жба**, -ы, intelligence service.

разве́дать, -аю *perf.* (*imp.* разве́дывать) find out; investigate; reconnoitre; prospect.

разведе́ние, -я, breeding, rearing; cultivation.

разведённ|**ый**, divorced; ~**ый**, ~**ая** *sb.* divorcee.

разве́дка, -и, intelligence; secret service, intelligence service; reconnaissance; prospecting; идти́ в разве́дку, reconnoitre. **разве́дочный**, prospecting, exploratory.

разведу́, etc.: see развести́.

разве́дчик, -а, intelligence officer; scout; prospector. **разве́дывать**, -аю *imp.* of разве́дать.

развезти́, -зу, -зёшь, -зёт, -ла́ *perf.* (*imp.* развози́ть), convey, transport; deliver; exhaust, wear out; make impassable, make unfit for traffic.

развёивать(ся, -аю(сь *imp.* of развеять(ся. развёл, etc.: see развести́.

развенча́ть. -аю *perf.*, **развёнчивать**, -аю *imp.* dethrone; debunk.

развёрнутый, extensive, large-scale, all-out; detailed; deployed, extended. **разверну́ть**, -ну́, -нёшь *perf.* (*imp.* развёртывать, развора́чивать) unfold, unwrap, open; unroll; unfurl; deploy; expand; develop; turn, swing; scan; show, display; ~**ся**, unfold, unroll, come unwrapped; deploy; develop; spread; expand; turn, swing.

разверста́ть. -аю *perf.*, **развёрстывать**, -аю *imp.* distribute, allot, apportion.

развёрстка, allotment, apportionment; distribution.

развёртывать(ся, -аю(сь *imp.* of развернуть(ся.

разве́с, -а, weighing out.

разве́селить, -лю *perf.* cheer up, amuse; ~**ся**, cheer up.

разве́систый, branchy, spreading. **разве́сить**[1], -е́шу *perf.* (*imp.* разве́шивать) spread; hang (out).

разве́сить[2], -е́шу *perf.* (*imp.* разве́шивать) weigh out. **развесно́й**, sold by weight.

развести́, -еду́, -еде́шь; -ёл, -а́ *perf.* (*imp.* разводи́ть), take, conduct; part, separate; divorce; dilute; dissolve; start; breed, rear; cultivate; ~ мост, raise a bridge, swing a bridge open; ~ ого́нь, light a fire; ~**сь**, be divorced; breed, multiply.

разветви́ться, -ви́тся *perf.* **разветвля́ться**, -яется *imp.* branch; fork; ramify. **разветвле́ние**, -я, branching, ramification, forking; branch; fork.

разве́шать, -аю *perf.*, **разве́шивать**, -аю *imp.* hang.

разве́шивать, -аю *imp.* of разве́сить, разве́шать. **разве́шу**, etc.: see разве́сить.

разве́ять, -е́ю *perf.* (*imp.* разве́ивать) scatter, disperse; dispel; destroy; ~**ся**, disperse; be dispelled.

развива́ть(ся, -а́ю(сь *imp.* of развить(ся.

развинти́ть, -нчу́ *perf.*, **разви́нчивать**, -аю *imp.* unscrew. **разви́нченный**, unstrung; unsteady, lurching.

разви́тие, -я, development; evolution; progress; maturity. **развито́й**; ра́звит, -а́, -о, developed; mature, adult. **разви́ть**, -зовью́; зовьёшь; -и́л, -а́, -о *perf.* (*imp.* развива́ть) develop; unwind, untwist; ~**ся**, develop.

развлека́ть, -а́ю *imp.*, **развле́чь**, -еку́ -ече́шь; -ёк, -ла́ *perf.* entertain, amuse; divert; ~**ся**, have a good time; amuse oneself; be diverted, be distracted.

разво́д, -а, divorce. **разводи́ть**(ся, -ожу́(сь, -о́дишь(ся *imp.* of разве-сти́(сь. **разво́дка**, -и, separation.

разводно́й; ~ **ключ**, adjustable spanner, monkey-wrench; ~ **мост**, drawbridge, swing bridge.

развози́ть, -ожу́, -о́зишь *imp.* of развезти́.

разволнова́ться, -ну́ю(сь *perf.* get excited, be agitated.

развора́чивать(ся, -аю(сь *imp.* of развернуть(ся.

раз|вороши́ть, -шу́ *perf.*

развра́т, -а, debauchery, depravity, dissipation. **разврати́ть**, -ащу́ *perf.* **развраща́ть**, -а́ю *imp.* debauch, corrupt; deprave. **развра́тничать**, -аю *imp.* indulge in debauchery, lead a depraved life. **развра́тный**, debauched, depraved, profligate; corrupt. **развращённый**; -ён, -а́, corrupt.

развяза́ть, -яжу́, -я́жешь *perf.*, **развя́зывать**, -аю *imp.* untie, unbind, undo; unleash; ~ся, come untied, come undone; ~ся с + *instr.* rid oneself of, have done with. **развя́зка**, -и, dénouement; outcome, issue, upshot; (motorway) junction; де́ло идёт к развя́зке, things are coming to a head. **развя́зный**, familiar; free-and-easy.

разгада́ть, -а́ю *perf.*, **разга́дывать**, -аю *imp.* solve, guess, puzzle out, make out; ~ сны, interpret dreams; ~ шифр, break a cipher. **разга́дка**, -и, solution.

разга́р, -а, height, peak, climax; в по́лном ~е, in full swing; в ~е ле́та, in the height of summer.

разгиба́ть(ся, -а́ю(сь *imp.* of разогну́ться.

разглаго́льствовать, -твую *imp.* hold forth, expatiate.

разгла́дить, -а́жу *perf.*, **разгла́живать**, -аю *imp.* smooth out; iron out, press.

разгласи́ть, -ашу́ *perf.*, **разглаша́ть**, -а́ю *imp.* divulge, give away, let out; + о *prep.* spread, broadcast; herald, trumpet. **разглаше́ние**, -я, divulging, disclosure.

разгляде́ть, -яжу́ *perf.*, **разгля́дывать**, -аю *imp.* make out, discern, descry; examine closely, scrutinize.

разгне́ванный, angry. **разгне́вать**, -аю, *perf.* anger, incense. **раз|гне́ваться**, -аюсь *perf.*

разгова́ривать, -аю *imp.* talk, speak,

converse. **разгово́р**, -а (-у), talk, conversation. **разгово́рник**, -а, phrasebook. **разгово́рный**, colloquial; conversational. **разгово́рчивый**, talkative, loquacious.

разго́н, -а, dispersal; breaking up; run, running start; distance; space. **разго́нистый**, widely-spaced. **разгоня́ть(ся**, -я́ю(сь *imp.* of разогна́ть(ся.

разгора́живать, -аю *imp.* of разгороди́ть.

разгоря́ться, -а́юсь *imp.*, **разгоре́ться**, -рю́сь *perf.* flame up, flare up; flush; стра́сти разгоре́лись, feeling ran high, passions rose.

разгороди́ть, -ожу́, -о́дишь *perf.* (*imp.* разгора́живать) partition off.

раз|горячи́ть(ся, -чу́(сь *perf.*); ~ся от вина́, be flushed with wine.

разгра́бить, -блю *perf.* plunder, pillage, loot. **разграбле́ние**, -я, plunder, pillage; looting.

разграниче́ние, -я, demarcation, delimitation; differentiation. **разграни́чивать**, -аю *imp.*, **разграни́чить**, -чу *perf.* delimit, demarcate; differentiate, distinguish.

раз|графи́ть, -флю́ *perf.*, **разграфля́ть**, -я́ю *imp.* rule, square. **разграфле́ние**, -я, ruling.

разгреба́ть, -а́ю *imp.*, **разгрести́**, -ебу́, -ебёшь; -ёб, -ла́ *perf.* rake (away), shovel (away).

разгро́м, -а, rout, crushing defeat; knock-out blow; havoc, devastation. **разгроми́ть**, -млю́ *perf.* rout, defeat.

разгружа́ть, -а́ю *imp.*, **разгрузи́ть**, -ужу́, -у́зишь *perf.* unload; relieve; ~ся, unload; be relieved. **разгру́зка**, -и, unloading; relief, relieving.

разгрыза́ть, -а́ю *imp.*, **раз|грызть**, -зу́ -зёшь; -ы́з *perf.* crack; bite through.

разгу́л, -а, revelry, debauch; raging; (wild) outburst. **разгу́ливать**, -аю *imp.* stroll about, walk about. **разгу́ливаться**, -аюсь *imp.*, **разгуля́ться**, -а́юсь *perf.* spread oneself; have free scope; wake up, be wide awake; clear up; improve. **разгу́льный**, loose, wild, rakish.

раздава́ть(ся, -даю́(сь, -даёшь(ся *imp.* of разда́ть(ся.

раз|дави́ть, -влю́, -вишь *perf.* **разда́вливать**, -аю *imp.* crush; squash; run down, run over; overwhelm.

разда́ть, -а́м, -а́шь, -а́ст, -адим; ро́зог разда́л, -а́, -о *perf.* (*imp.* раздава́ть) distribute, give out, serve out, dispense; **~ся**, be heard; resound; ring out; make way; stretch, expand; put on weight.

разда́ча, -и, distribution. **раздаю́**, etc.: see **разда́ть**.

раздава́ть(ся, -аю(сь *imp.* of **раздво́ить**ся.

раздвига́ть, -а́ю *imp.*, **раздви́нуть**, -ну *perf.* move apart, slide apart; draw back; **~** стол, extend a table; **~ся**, move apart, slide apart; be drawn back; за́навес раздви́нулся, the curtain rose. **раздвижно́й**, expanding; sliding; extensible.

раздвое́ние, -я, division into two; bifurcation; **~** ли́чности, split personality. **раздво́енный, раздвоённый**, forked; bifurcated; cloven; split. **раз|дво́ить**, -ою́ *perf.* (*imp.* раздва́ивать), divide into two; bisect; **~ся**, bifurcate, fork; become double.

раздева́лка, -и, **раздева́льня**, -и; *gen. pl.* -лен, cloakroom. **раздева́ть(ся**, -а́ю(сь *imp.* of разде́ть(ся.

разде́л, -а, division; partition; allotment; section, part.

разде́латься, -аюсь *perf.* + с + *instr.* finish with; be through with; settle accounts with; pay off; get even with.

разделе́ние, -я, division; **~** труда́, division of labour. **раздели́мый**, divisible. **раз|дели́ть**, -лю́, -лишь *perf.*, **разделя́ть**, -я́ю *imp.* divide; separate, part; share; **~ся**, divide; be divided; be divisible; separate, part. **разде́льный**, separate; clear, distinct.

разде́ну, etc.: see разде́ть. **раздеру́**, etc.: see раздира́ть.

разде́ть, -де́ну *perf.* (*imp.* раздева́ть) undress; **~ся**, undress (oneself); strip; take off one's coat, one's things.

раздира́ть, -а́ю *imp.* of разодра́ть. **раздира́ющий** (ду́шу), heart-rending, harrowing.

раздобыва́ть, -а́ю *imp.*, **раздобы́ть**, -бу́ду *perf.* get, procure, come by, get hold of.

раздо́лье, -я, expanse; freedom, liberty. **раздо́льный**, free.

раздо́р, -а, discord, dissension; се́ять **~**, breed strife, sow discord.

раздоса́довать, -дую *perf.* vex.

раздража́ть, -а́ю *imp.*, **раздражи́ть**, -жу́ *perf.* irritate; annoy, exasperate, put out; **~ся**, lose one's temper, get annoyed; get irritated; become inflamed. **раздраже́ние**, -я, irritation; в раздраже́нии, in a temper. **раздражи́тельный**, irritable; short-tempered.

раздразни́ть, -ню́, -нишь *perf.* tease; arouse, stimulate.

раз|дроби́ть, -блю́ *perf.*, **раздробля́ть**, -я́ю *imp.* break; smash to pieces, splinter; turn, convert, reduce. **раздро́бленный, раздроблённый**, shattered; small-scale; fragmented.

раздува́ть(ся, -а́ю(сь *imp.* of раздуть-(ся.

разду́мать, -аю *perf.*, **разду́мывать**, -аю *imp.* change one's mind; + *inf.* decide not to; ponder, consider; hesitate; не разду́мывая, without a moment's thought. **разду́мье**, -я, meditation; thought, thoughtful mood; hesitation; в глубо́ком **~**, deep in thought.

разду́ть, -у́ю *perf.* (*imp.* раздува́ть), blow; fan; blow out; exaggerate; whip up; inflate, swell; blow about; **~ся**, swell.

разева́ть, -а́ю *imp.* of рази́нуть.

разжа́лобить, -блю *perf.* move (to pity).

разжа́ловать, -лую *perf.* degrade, demote.

разжа́ть, -зожму́, -мёшь *perf.* (*imp.* разжима́ть) unclasp, open; release, unfasten, undo.

разжёвывать, -жую́ -жуёшь *perf.*, **разжёвывать**, -аю *imp.* chew, masticate; chew over.

разже́чь, -зожгу́, -зожжёшь; -жёг, -зожгла́ *perf.*, **разжига́ть**, -а́ю *imp.* kindle; rouse, stir up.

разжима́ть, -а́ю *imp.* of разжа́ть. **раз|жи́ть**, -ве́ю *perf.*

рази́нуть, -ну *perf.* (*imp.* разева́ть) open; **~** рот, gape; рази́нув рот, open-mouthed. рази́ня, -и *m.* and *f.* scatter-brained person.

рази́тельный, striking. рази́ть, ражу́ *imp.* (*perf.* по~) strike.

разлага́ть(ся, -а́ю(сь *imp.* of разложи́ть(ся.

разла́д, -а, discord, dissension; disorder.

разла́мывать(ся, -аю(сь *imp.* of разлома́ть(ся, разломи́ть(ся. разлёгся, разлёгся, etc.: see разле́чься.

разлеза́ться, -а́ется *imp.*, разле́зться, -зется; -ле́зся *perf.* come to pieces; come apart, fall apart.

разлени́ться, -ню́сь, -нишься *perf.* get very lazy, sink into sloth.

разлета́ться, -а́юсь *imp.*, разлете́ться, -лечу́сь *perf.* fly away; fly about; scatter; shatter; vanish, be shattered; fly, rush; rush up.

разле́чься, -ля́гусь; -лёгся, -гла́сь *perf.* stretch out; sprawl.

разли́в, -а, bottling; flood; overflow. разлива́ть(ся, -а́ю *imp.*, разли́ть, -золью́, -золье́шь; -и́л, -а́, -о *perf.* pour out; spill; flood (with), drench (with); ~ся, spill; overflow, flood; spread. разли́вка, -и, bottling. разливно́й, on tap, on draught; ~о́е вино́, wine from the wood. разли́тие, -я, flooding.

различа́ть, -а́ю *imp.*, различи́ть, -чу́ *perf.* distinguish; tell the difference; discern, make out; ~ся, differ. разли́чие, -я, distinction; difference; зна́ки разли́чия, badges of rank. различи́тельный, distinctive, distinguishing. разли́чный, different; various, diverse.

разложе́ние, -я, breaking down; decomposition; decay; putrefaction; demoralization, corruption; disintegration; expansion; resolution. разложи́ть, -жу́, -жишь *perf.* (*imp.* разлага́ть, раскла́дывать) put away; lay out; spread (out); distribute, apportion; break down; decompose; expand; resolve; demoralize, corrupt; ~ костёр, make a fire; ~ся, decompose; rot, decay; become demoralized; be corrupted; disintegrate, crack up, go to pieces.

разло́м, -а, breaking; break. разло-

мать, -а́ю, разломи́ть, -млю́, -мишь *perf.* (*imp.* разла́мывать) break, break to pieces; pull down; ~ся, break to pieces.

раз|лохма́тить, -а́чу *perf.*

разлу́ка, -и, separation; parting. разлуча́ть, -а́ю *imp.*, разлучи́ть, -чу́ *perf.* separate, part, sever; ~ся, separate, part.

разлюби́ть, -блю́, -бишь *perf.* cease to love, stop loving; stop liking, no longer like.

разля́гусь, etc.: see разле́чься.

разма́зать, -а́жу *perf.*, разма́зывать, -аю *imp.* spread, smear.

разма́лывать, -аю *imp.* of размоло́ть.

разма́тывать, -аю *imp.* of размота́ть.

разма́х, -а (-у), sweep; swing; span; amplitude; scope, range, scale. разма́хивать, -аю *imp.* + *instr.* swing; brandish; ~ рука́ми, gesticulate. разма́хиваться, -аюсь *imp.*, размахну́ться, -ну́сь, -нёшься *perf.* swing one's arm. разма́шистый, sweeping.

размежева́ние, -я, demarcation, delimitation. размежева́ть, -жу́ю *perf.*, размежёвывать, -аю *imp.* divide out, delimit; ~ся, fix one's boundaries; delimit functions or spheres of action.

размёл, etc.: see разме́сти.

размельча́ть, -а́ю *imp.*, раз|мельчи́ть, -чу́ *perf.* crumble, crush, pulverize.

размелю́, etc.: see размоло́ть.

разме́н, -а, exchange; changing. разме́нивать, -аю *imp.*, разменя́ть, -я́ю *perf.* change; ~ся + *instr.* exchange; dissipate. разме́нный, exchange; ~ая моне́та, (small) change.

разме́р, -а, dimension(s); size; measurement; rate, amount; scale, extent; metre; measure; (*pl.*) proportions. разме́ренный, measured. разме́рить, -рю *perf.*, размеря́ть, -я́ю *imp.* measure off; measure.

размести́, -ету́, -ете́шь; -мёл, -а́ *perf.* (*imp.* размета́ть) sweep clear; clear; sweep away.

размести́ть, -ещу́ *perf.* (*imp.* размеща́ть) place, accommodate; quarter; stow; distribute; ~ся, take one's seat.

размета́ть, -а́ю *imp.* of размести́.

разме́тить, -е́чу perf., размеча́ть, -а́ю imp. mark.

размеша́ть, -а́ю perf., разме́шивать, -аю imp. stir (in).

размести́ть(ся, -а́ю(сь imp. of разме-сти́ть(ся. **размеще́ние**, -я, placing; accommodation; distribution; disposal, allocation; investment. **размещу́**, etc.: see размести́ть.

размина́ть(ся, -а́ю(сь imp. of размя́ть-(ся.

размину́ться, -ну́сь, -нёшься perf. pass (one another); cross; + с + instr. pass; miss.

размножа́ть, -а́ю imp., размно́жить, -жу perf. multiply, manifold, duplicate; breed; rear; ~ся, propagate itself; breed; spawn.

размозжи́ть, -жу́ perf. smash.

размо́лвка, -и, tiff, disagreement.

размоло́ть, -мелю́, -ме́лишь perf. (imp. разма́лывать) grind.

размора́живать, -а́ю imp., размо-ро́зить, -о́жу perf. unfreeze, defreeze; defrost; ~ся, unfreeze; become defrosted.

размота́ть, -а́ю perf. (imp. разма́ты-вать) unwind, unreel; squander.

размыва́ть, -а́ет imp., размы́ть, -о́ет perf. wash away; erode.

размышле́ние, -я, reflection; meditation, thought. **размышля́ть**, -я́ю imp. reflect, ponder; think (things) over.

размягча́ть, -а́ю imp., размягчи́ть, -чу́ perf. soften; ~ся, soften, grow soft. **размягче́ние**, -я, softening.

размяка́ть, -а́ю imp., раз|мя́кнуть, -ну; -мя́к perf. soften, become soft.

раз|мя́ть, -зомну́, -зомнёшь perf. (imp. also размина́ть) knead; mash; ~ся, soften, grow soft; stretch one's legs; limber up, loosen up.

разна́шивать, -аю imp. of разноси́ть.

разнести́, -су́, -сёшь; ёс, -ла́ perf. (imp. разноси́ть) carry, convey; take round, deliver; spread; enter, note down; smash, break up, destroy; blow up; scatter, disperse; impers. make puffy, swell, blow out; меня́ разнесло́, I've got fat.

разнима́ть, -а́ю imp. of разня́ть.

ра́зниться, -нюсь imp. differ. **ра́зница**, -ы, difference; disparity; кака́я ~? what difference does it make?

ра́зно- in comb. different, vari-, hetero-. **разнобо́й**, -я, lack of co-ordination; difference, disagreement. ~**вес**, -а, (set of) weights. ~**ви́дность**, -и variety. ~**гла́сие**, -я, difference, disagreement; discrepancy. ~**голо́сый**, discordant. ~**кали́берный**, of different calibres; mixed, heterogeneous. ~**мы́слие**, -я, diff'rence of opinions. ~**обра́зие**, -я, variety, diversity; для ~образия, for a change. ~**обра́зить**, -а́жу imp. vary, diversify. ~**обра́зный**, various, varied, diverse. ~**рабо́чий** sb. unskilled labourer. ~**речи́вый**, contradictory, conflicting. ~**ро́дный**, heterogeneous. ~**скло́няемый**, irregularly declined. ~**сторо́нний**, many-sided; versatile; all-round; scalene. ~**хара́ктерный**, diverse, varied. ~**цве́тный**, of different colours; many-coloured; variegated, motley. ~**чте́ние**, -я, variant reading. ~**шёрст-ный**, -шёрстый, with coats of different colours; mixed, ill-assorted. ~**язы́чный**, polyglot.

ра́зность[1], -ощу, -о́сишь perf. (imp. разна́шивать) break in, wear in; ~ся, become comfortable with wear.

разноси́ть[2], -ощу́, -о́сишь imp. of раз-нести́. **разно́ска**, -и, delivery. **разно́сный**, delivery; abusive; ~ые слова́, swear-words.

ра́зность, -и, difference; diversity.

разно́счик, -а, pedlar, hawker.

разношу́, etc.: see разноси́ть.

разну́зданный, unbridled, unruly.

ра́зный, different, differing; various, diverse; ~**ое** sb. different things; various matters, any other business.

разня́ть, -ниму́, -ни́мешь; ро́з- or раз-ня́л -а́, -о perf. (imp. разнима́ть) take to pieces, dismantle; disjoint; part, separate.

разо-: see раз-.

разоблача́ть, -а́ю imp., разоблачи́ть, -чу́ perf. expose, unmask. **разобла-че́ние**, -я, exposure, unmasking.

разобра́ть, -зберу́, -рёшь; -а́л, -а́, -о perf. (imp. разбира́ть) take; take to pieces, strip, dismantle; buy up; sort out; investigate, look into; analyse; parse; make out, understand; ничего́ нельзя́ ~, one can't make head or tail of it; ~ся, sort things out; + в + *prep.* investigate, look into; understand.

разобща́ть, -а́ю *imp.*, **разобщи́ть**, -щу́ *perf.* separate; estrange, alienate; disconnect, uncouple, disengage. **разобще́ние**, -я, disconnection, uncoupling. **разобщённо** *adv.* apart, separately.

разобью́, etc.: see разби́ть. **разовью́**, etc.: see разви́ть.

разгоня́ть, -зго́ню, -о́нишь; -гна́л, -á, -о *perf.* (*imp.* разгоня́ть) scatter, drive away; disperse; dispel; drive fast, race; space; ~ся, gather speed, gather momentum.

разгну́ть, -ну́, -нёшь *perf.* (*imp.* разгиба́ть), unbend, straighten; ~ся, straighten (oneself) up.

разгрева́ть, -а́ю *imp.*, **разгре́ть**, -е́ю *perf.* warm up; ~ся, warm up, grow warm.

разоде́ть(ся, -е́ну(сь *perf.* dress up.

раздра́ть, -здеру́, -рёшь; -а́л, -á, -о *perf.* (*imp.* раздира́ть) tear (up); lacerate, harrow.

разожгу́, etc.: see разже́чь. **разожму́**, etc.: see разжа́ть.

разо|зли́ть, -лю́ *perf.* anger, enrage; ~ся, get angry, fly into a rage.

разойти́сь, -йду́сь, -йдёшься; -ошёлся, -ошла́сь *perf.* (*imp.* расходи́ться) go away; break up, disperse; branch off, diverge; radiate; differ, be at variance, conflict; part, separate, be divorced; dissolve, melt; be spent; be sold out; be out of print; gather speed; be carried away.

разолью́, etc.: see разли́ть.

ра́зом *adv.* at once, at one go. **разомну́**, etc.: see размя́ть.

разорва́ть, -ву́, -вёшь; -а́л, -á, -о *perf.* (*imp.* разрыва́ть) tear (off), sever; blow up, burst; ~ся, tear, become torn; break, snap; blow up, burst; explode, go off.

разоре́ние, -я, ruin; destruction, havoc. **разори́тельный**, ruinous; wasteful. **разори́ть**, -рю́ *perf.* (*imp.* разоря́ть)

ruin, bring to ruin; destroy, ravage; ~ся, ruin oneself, be ruined.

разоружа́ть, -а́ю *imp.*, **разоружи́ть**, -жу́ *perf.* disarm; ~ся, disarm. **разоруже́ние**, -я, disarmament.

разоря́ть(ся, -я́ю(сь *imp.* of разори́ть(ся.

разосла́ть, -ошлю́, -ошлёшь *perf.* (*imp.* рассыла́ть) send round, distribute, circulate; send out, dispatch.

разостла́ть, **рассте́лить**, -сстелю́, -те́лешь *perf.* (*imp.* расстила́ть) spread (out); lay; ~ся, spread.

разотру́, etc.: see растере́ть.

разочарова́ние, -я, disappointment. **разочаро́ванный**, disappointed, disillusioned. **разочарова́ть**, -ру́ю *perf.*, **разочаро́вывать**, -аю *imp.* disappoint, disillusion, disenchant; ~ся, be disappointed, be disillusioned.

разочту́, etc.: see расче́сть. **разошёлся**, etc.: see разойти́сь. **разошлю́**, etc.: see разосла́ть. **разошью́**, etc.: see расши́ть.

разраба́тывать, -аю *imp.*, **разрабо́тать**, -аю *perf.* cultivate; work, exploit; work out, work up; develop; elaborate. **разрабо́тка**, -и, cultivation; working out, working up; elaboration; field; pit, working, quarry.

разража́ться, -а́юсь *imp.*, **разрази́ться**, -ажу́сь *perf.* break out; burst out; ~ сме́хом, burst out laughing.

разраста́ться, -а́ется *imp.*, **разрасти́сь**, -тётся; -ро́сся, -ла́сь *perf.* grow, grow up; grow thickly; spread.

разрежённ|ый, -ён, -а́, rarefied; rare; ~ое простра́нство, vacuum.

разре́з, -а, cut; slit, slash; section; point of view; в ~е + *gen.* from the point of view of, in the context of; в э́том ~е, in this connection. **разре́зать**, -е́жу *perf.*, **разреза́ть**, -а́ю *imp.* cut; slit. **разрезно́й**, cutting; slit, with slits; ~ нож, paper-knife.

разреша́ть, -а́ю *imp.*, **разреши́ть**, -шу́ *perf.* (+ *dat.*) allow, permit; authorize; (+ *acc.*) release, absolve; solve; settle; разреши́те пройти́, let me pass; do you mind letting me pass?; ~ся, be allowed; be solved; be settled

~ся от бре́мени, be delivered of; кури́ть не разреша́ется, no smoking. **разреше́ние**, -я, permission; authorization, permit; solution; settlement. **разреши́мый**, solvable.

разро́зненный, uncoordinated; odd; incomplete, broken.

разро́сся, etc.: see разрасти́сь. **разро́ю**, etc.: see разры́ть.

разруба́ть, -а́ю *imp.*, **разруби́ть**, -блю́, -бишь *perf.* cut, cleave; hack; chop.

разру́ха, -и, ruin, collapse. **разруша́ть**, -а́ю *imp.*, **разру́шить**, -шу *perf.* destroy; demolish, wreck; ruin; frustrate, blast, blight; ~ся, go to ruin, collapse. **разруше́ние**, -я, destruction. **разруши́тельный**, destructive.

разры́в, -а, breach; break; gap; rupture, severance; burst, explosion. **разрыва́ть¹(ся**, -а́ю(сь *imp.* of разорва́ть(ся.

разрыва́ть², -а́ю *imp.* of разры́ть.

разрывно́й, explosive, bursting.

разры́ть, -ро́ю *perf.* (*imp.* разрыва́ть) dig (up); turn upside down, rummage through.

раз|рыхли́ть, -лю́ *perf.*, **разрыхля́ть**, -я́ю *imp.* loosen; hoe.

разря́д¹, -а, category, rank; sort; class, rating.

разря́д², -а, discharge. **разряди́ть**, -яжу́, -я́дишь *perf.* (*imp.* разряжа́ть) unload; discharge; space out; ~ся, run down; clear, ease. **разря́дка**, -и, spacing (out); discharging; unloading; ~ напряжённости, lessening of tension, détente.

разря́дник, -а, -ница, -ы, ranking player or competitor.

разряжа́ть(ся, -а́ю(сь *imp.* of разряди́ть(ся.

разубеди́ть, -ежу́ *perf.*, **разубежда́ть**, -а́ю *imp.* dissuade; ~ся, change one's mind, change one's opinion.

разува́ться, -а́юсь *imp.* of разу́ться.

разуве́рить, -рю *perf.*, **разуверя́ть**, -я́ю *imp.* dissuade, undeceive; + в + *prep.* argue out of; ~ся (в + *prep.*) lose faith (in), cease to believe.

разузнава́ть, -наю́, -наёшь *imp.*, **разузна́ть**, -а́ю *imp.* (try to) find out; make inquiries.

разукра́сить, -а́шу *perf.*, **разукра́шивать**, -аю *imp.* adorn, decorate, embellish.

разукрупни́ть(ся, -ню́(сь *perf.*, **разукрупня́ть(ся**, -я́ю(сь *imp.* break up into smaller units.

ра́зум, -а, reason; mind, intellect; у него́ ум за ~ зашёл, he is (was) at his wit's end. **разуме́ться**, -е́ется *imp.* be understood, be meant; (само́ собо́й) разуме́ется, of course; it stands to reason, it goes without saying. **разу́мный**, possessing reason; judicious, intelligent; sensible; reasonable; wise.

разу́ться, -у́юсь *perf.* (*imp.* разува́ться), take off one's shoes.

разучи́ть, -аю *imp.*, **разучи́ть**, -чу́ -чишь *perf.* study; learn (up). **разу́чиваться**, -аюсь *imp.*, **разучи́ться**, -чу́сь, -чишься *perf.* forget (how to).

разъ-: see раз-.

разъеда́ть, -а́ет *imp.* of разъе́сть.

разъедини́ть, -ню́ *perf.*, **разъединя́ть**, -я́ю *imp.* separate, disunite; disconnect; нас разъедини́ли, we were cut off.

разъе́здить, etc.: see разъе́зжать(ся.

разъе́зд, -а, departure; dispersal; passing loop, siding (track); mounted patrol; travelling (about); journeys. **разъездно́й**, travelling. **разъезжа́ть**, -а́ю *imp.* drive about, ride about; travel, wander; ~ся *imp.* of разъе́хаться.

разъе́сть, -е́ст, -едя́т; -е́л *perf.* (*imp.* разъеда́ть) eat away; corrode.

разъе́хаться, -е́дусь *perf.* (*imp.* разъезжа́ться) depart; disperse; separate; (be able to) pass; pass one another, miss one another; slide apart.

разъярённый, -ён, -а́, furious, in a furious temper, frantic with rage. **разъяри́ть**, -рю́ *perf.*, **разъяря́ть**, -я́ю *imp.* infuriate, rouse to fury; ~ся, get furious, become frantic with rage.

разъясне́ние, -я, explanation, elucidation; interpretation. **разъясни́тельный**, explanatory, elucidatory.

разъясня́ться, -я́ется *imp.*, **разъ**яс**ни́ться**, -и́тся *perf.* clear (up).

разъясни́ть, -ню́ *perf.*, **разъясни́ть**, -я́ю, *imp.* explain, elucidate; interpret; ~ся, become clear, be cleared up.

разыгра́ть, -а́ю *perf.*, **разы́грывать**, -аю *imp.* play (through); perform; draw; raffle; play a trick on; ~ **ся**, rise, get up; run high.

разыска́ть, -ыщу́, -ы́щешь *perf.* find. **разы́скивать**, -аю *imp.* look for, search for; ~ **ся**, be wanted.

рай, -я, *loc.* -ю́, paradise; garden of Eden.

рай- *abbr.* in *comb.* of ра́йонный, district. **райко́м**, -а, district committee. ~ **сове́т**, -а, district soviet.

райо́н, -а, region; area; zone; (administrative) district. **райо́нный**, district.

ра́йский, heavenly.

рак, -а, crawfish, crayfish; cancer, canker; Crab; Cancer.

раке́та[1], -ы, **раке́тка**, -и, racket.

раке́та[2], -ы, rocket; ballistic missile; flare; ~ **-носи́тель**, carrier rocket. **раке́тный**, rocket; jet.

ра́ковина, -ы, shell; sink.

ра́ковый, cancer; cancerous.

ра́ма, -ы, frame; chassis, carriage; вста́вить в ра́му, frame. **ра́мка**, -и, frame; *pl.* framework, limits; в ра́мке, framed.

ра́мпа, -ы, footlights.

ра́на, -ы, wound. **ране́ние**, -я, wounding; wound, injury. **ра́неный**, wounded; injured.

ра́нец, -нца, knapsack, haversack; satchel.

ра́нить, -ню *perf.* and *imp.* wound; injure.

ра́нний, early. **ра́но** *predic.* it is (too) early. **ра́но** *adv.* early; ~ и́ли по́здно, sooner or later. **ра́ньше** *adv.* earlier; before; formerly; first (of all).

рапи́ра, -ы, foil. **рапири́ст**, -а, **рапири́стка**, -и, fencer.

ра́порт, -а, a report. **рапортова́ть**, -ту́ю *perf.* and *imp.* report.

рас-: see раз-. **раска́иваться**, -аюсь *imp.* of раска́яться.

раскалённый; -ён, -а́, scorching, burning hot; incandescent. **раскали́ть**, -лю́ *perf.* (*imp.* раскаля́ть) make very hot, make red-hot, white-hot; ~ **ся**, heat up, glow, become red-hot, white-hot.

раска́лывать(ся, -аю(сь *imp.* of расколо́ть(ся. **раскаля́ть(ся**, -я́ю(сь *imp.* of раскали́ть(ся. **раска́пывать**, -аю *imp.* of раскопа́ть.

раска́т, -а, roll, peal. **раската́ть**, -а́ю *perf.*, **раска́тывать**, -аю *imp.* roll, roll out, smooth out, level; drive, ride, (about). **раска́тистый**, rolling, booming. **раската́ться**, -а́юсь, -а́тишься *perf.*, **раска́тываться**, -аюсь *imp.* gather speed; roll away; peal, boom.

раскача́ть, -а́ю *perf.*, **раска́чивать**, -аю *imp.* swing; rock; loosen, shake loose; shake up, stir up; ~ **ся**, swing, rock; shake loose; bestir oneself.

раска́яние, -я, repentance, remorse. **рас|ка́яться**, -а́юсь *perf.* (*imp.* also раска́иваться) repent.

расквита́ться, -а́юсь *perf.* settle accounts; get even, be quits.

раски́дывать, -аю *imp.*, **раски́нуть**, -ну *perf.* stretch (out); spread; scatter; set up, pitch; ~ умо́м, ponder, think things over, consider; ~ **ся**, spread out, lie; sprawl.

раскла́дка, -и, laying; putting up; allotment. **раскладн|о́й**, folding; ~ а́я крова́ть, camp-bed. **раскладу́шка**, -и, camp-bed. **раскла́дывать**, -аю *imp.* of разложи́ть.

раскла́няться, -яюсь *perf.* bow; exchange bows; take leave.

расклеивать, -аю *imp.*, **раскле́ить**, -е́ю *perf.* unstick; stick (up), paste (up); ~ **ся**, come unstuck; fall through, fail to come off; feel seedy, be off colour.

раскле́шенный, flared.

раско́л, -а, split, division; schism; dissent. **рас|коло́ть**, -лю́, -лешь *perf.* (*imp.* also раска́лывать) split; chop; break; disrupt, break up; ~ **ся**, split; crack, break. **раско́льник**, -а, dissenter, schismatic. **раско́льнический**, dissenting, schismatic.

раскопа́ть, -а́ю *perf.* (*imp.* раска́пывать) dig up, unearth, excavate. **раско́пка**, -и, digging up; *pl.* excavation, excavations.

раско́сый, slanting, slant.

раскра́сть, etc.: see раскра́сть. **раскра́дывать**, -аю *imp.* of раскра́сть. **раскра́ивать**, -аю *imp.* of раскрои́ть.

раскра́сить, -а́шу *perf.* (*imp.* раскра́шивать) paint, colour. раскра́ска, -и, painting, colouring; colours, colour scheme.

раскрасне́ться, -е́юсь *perf.* flush, go red.

раскра́сть, -аду́, -адёшь *perf.* (*imp.* раскра́дывать) loot, clean out.

раскра́шивать, -аю *imp.* of раскра́сить.

раскрепости́ть, -ощу́ *perf.*, раскрепоща́ть, -а́ю *imp.* set free, liberate, emancipate. раскрепоще́ние, -я, liberation, emancipation.

раскритикова́ть, -ку́ю *perf.* criticize harshly, slate.

раскрои́ть, -ою́ *perf.* (*imp.* раскра́ивать) cut out; cut open.

рас|кроши́ть(ся, -шу́(сь, -шишь(ся *perf.* раскро́ю, etc.: see раскры́ть.

раскрути́ть, -учу́ -у́тишь *perf.*, раскру́чивать, -аю *imp.* untwist, undo; ～ся, come untwisted, come undone.

раскрыва́ть, -а́ю *imp.*, раскры́ть, -о́ю *perf.* open; expose, bare; reveal, disclose, lay bare; discover; ～ся, open; uncover oneself; come out, come to light, be discovered.

раскупа́ть, -а́ет *imp.*, раскупи́ть, -у́пит *perf.* buy up.

раску́поривать, -аю *imp.*, раску́порить, -рю *perf.* uncork, open.

раскуси́ть, -ушу́, -у́сишь *perf.*, раску́сывать, -аю *imp.* bite through; get to the core of; see through.

раску́тать, -аю *imp.* unwrap.

ра́совый, racial.

распа́д, -а, disintegration, break-up; collapse; decomposition. распада́ться, -а́ется *imp.* of распа́сться.

распакова́ть, -ку́ю *perf.*, распако́вывать, -аю *imp.* unpack; ～ся, unpack; come undone.

распа́ривать(ся, -аю(сь *imp.* of распоро́ть(ся.

распа́сться, -адётся *perf.* (*imp.* распада́ться) disintegrate, fall to pieces; break up; collapse; decompose, dissociate.

распаха́ть, -ашу́, -а́шешь *perf.*, распа́хивать, -аю *imp.* plough up.

распа́хивать², -аю *imp.*, распахну́ть, -ну́, -нёшь *perf.* open (wide); fling open, throw open; ～ся, open; fly open, swing open; throw open one's coat.

распая́ть, -я́ю *perf.* unsolder; ～ся, come unsoldered.

распева́ть, -а́ю *imp.* sing.

распеча́тать, -аю *perf.*, распеча́тывать, -аю *imp.* open; unseal.

распи́вочный, for consumption on the premises; ～ая *sb.* tavern, bar.

распи́ливать, -аю *imp.*, распили́ть, -лю́, -лишь *perf.* saw up.

расписа́ние, -я, time-table, schedule. расписа́ть, -ишу́, -и́шешь *perf.*, распи́сывать, -аю *imp.* enter; assign allot; paint; decorate; ～ся, sign; register one's marriage; + в + *prep.* sign for; acknowledge; testify to. распи́ска, -и, receipt. расписно́й, painted, decorated.

рас|пла́вить, -влю *perf.*, расплавля́ть, -я́ю *imp.* melt, fuse. расплавле́ние, -я, melting, fusion.

распла́каться, -а́чусь *perf.* burst into tears.

распласта́ть, -а́ю *perf.* spread; flatten; split, divide into layers; ～ся, sprawl.

распла́та, -ы, payment; retribution; час распла́ты, day of reckoning. расплати́ться, -ачу́сь, -а́тишься *perf.*, распла́чиваться, -аюсь *imp.* (+ с + *instr.*) pay off; settle accounts, get even; + за + *acc.* pay for.

расплеска́ть(ся, -ещу́(сь, -е́шешь(ся *perf.*, расплёскивать(ся, -аю(сь *imp.* spill.

расплести́, -ету́, -етёшь; -ёл, -а́ *perf.*, расплета́ть, -а́ю *imp.* unplait; untwine, untwist, undo; ～сь, come unplaited, come undone; untwine, untwist.

рас|плоди́ть(ся, -ожу́(сь *perf.*

расплыва́ться, -а́ется *imp.*, расплы́ться, -ывётся; -ы́лся, -а́сь *perf.* run; spread. расплы́вчатый, dim, indistinct; diffuse, vague.

расплющивать, -аю *imp.*, расплю́щить, -щу *perf.* flatten out, hammer out.

распну́, etc.: see распя́ть.

распознава́емый, recognizable, identifiable. распознава́ть, -наю́, -наёшь *imp.*, распозна́ть, -а́ю *perf.* recognize, identify; distinguish; diagnose.

располага́ть, -а́ю *imp.* (*perf.* расположи́ть) + *instr.* dispose of, have at one's disposal, have available; не ~ вре́менем, have no time to spare. **располага́ться**, -а́юсь *imp.* of расположи́ться. **располага́ющий**, prepossessing.

располза́ться, -а́ется *imp.*, **расползти́сь**, -зётся / -о́лзся, -зла́сь *perf.* crawl, crawl away; ravel out; give (at the seams).

расположе́ние, -я, disposition; arrangement; situation, location; inclination; tendency, propensity; bias, penchant; favour, liking; sympathies; mood, humour. **расположенный**, well-disposed; disposed, inclined, in the mood; я не о́чень расположён сего́дня рабо́тать, I don't feel much like working today. **расположи́ть**, -жу́, -жишь *perf.* (*imp.* располага́ть) dispose; arrange, set out; win over, gain; ~ся, settle down; compose oneself, make oneself comfortable.

рас|поро́ть, -рю́, -решь *perf.* (*imp.* also **распа́рывать**) unpick, undo, rip; ~ся, rip, come undone.

распоряди́тель, -я *m.* manager. **распоряди́тельность**, -и, good management; efficiency; отсу́тствие распоряди́тельности, mismanagement. **распоряди́тельный**, capable; efficient; active. **распоряди́ться**, -яжу́сь *perf.*, **распоряжа́ться**, -я́юсь *imp.* order, give orders; see; + *instr.* manage, deal with, dispose of. **распоря́док**, -дка, order; routine; пра́вила вну́треннего распоря́дка на фа́брике, factory regulations. **распоряже́ние**, -я, order; instruction, direction; disposal, command; быть в распоряже́нии + *gen.* be at the disposal of; до особо́го распоряже́ния, until further notice.

распра́ва, -ы, punishment, execution; violence; reprisal; крова́вая ~, massacre, butchery.

распра́вить, -влю *perf.*, **расправля́ть**, -я́ю *imp.* straighten; smooth out; spread, stretch; ~ кры́лья, spread one's wings.

распра́виться, -влюсь *perf.*, **расправля́ться**, -я́юсь *imp.* с + *instr.* deal with, make short work of; give short shrift to.

распределе́ние, -я, distribution; allocation, assignment. **распредели́тель** *m.* distributor; retailer. **распредели́тельный**, distributive, distributing; ~ щит, switchboard. **распредели́ть**, -лю́ *perf.*, **распределя́ть**, -я́ю *imp.* distribute; allocate, allot, assign; ~ своё вре́мя, allocate one's time.

распродава́ть, -даю́, -даёшь *imp.*, **распрода́ть**, -а́м, -а́шь, -а́ст, -ади́м; -о́дал, -а́, -о *perf.* sell off; sell out. **распрода́жа**, -и, sale; clearance sale.

распростёрт|ый, outstretched; prostrate, prone; с ~ыми объя́тиями, with open arms.

распрости́ться, -ощу́сь *perf.*, **распроща́ться**, -а́юсь *perf.* take leave, bid farewell.

распростране́ние, -я, spreading, diffusion; dissemination; circulation. **распространённый**, -ён, -а́, widespread, prevalent. **распространи́ть**, -ню́ *perf.*, **распространя́ть**, -я́ю *imp.* spread; give currency to; diffuse; disseminate, propagate; popularize; extend; give off, give out; ~ся, spread; extend; apply; enlarge, expatiate, dilate (о + *prep.* on).

распроща́ться, etc.: see распрости́ться.

ра́спря, -и; *gen. pl.* -ей, quarrel, feud.

распряга́ть, -а́ю *imp.*, **распря́чь**, -ягу́, -яжёшь; -яг, -ла́ *perf.* unharness.

распуска́ть, -а́ю *imp.*, **распусти́ть**, -ущу́, -у́стишь *perf.* dismiss; dissolve; disband; let out; relax; let get out of hand; spoil; dissolve; melt; spread; ~ во́лосы, loosen one's hair; ~ на кани́кулы, dismiss for the holidays; ~ся, open, come out; come loose; dissolve; melt; get out of hand; let oneself go.

распу́тать, -аю *perf.* (*imp.* распу́тывать) disentangle, untangle; unravel; untie, loose; puzzle out.

распу́тица, -ы, season of bad roads; slush.

распу́тный, dissolute, dissipated, debauched.

распу́тывать, -аю *imp.* of распу́тать.

распу́тье, -я, crossroads; parting of the ways.

распуха́ть, -а́ю *imp.*, распу́хнуть, -ну; -у́х *perf.* swell (up).

распу́щенный, undisciplined; spoilt; dissolute, dissipated.

распыле́ние, -я, dispersion, scattering; spraying; atomization. распыли́тель, -я *m.* spray, atomizer. распыли́ть, -лю́ *perf.*, распыля́ть, -я́ю *imp.* spray; atomize; pulverize; disperse, scatter; ~ся, disperse, get scattered.

распя́тие, -я, crucifixion; crucifix, cross. распя́ть, -пну́, -пнёшь *perf.* crucify.

расса́да, -ы, seedlings. рассади́ть, -ажу́, -а́дишь *perf.*, расса́живать, -аю *imp.* plant out, transplant; seat, offer seats; separate, seat separately.

расса́живаться, -ается *imp.* of рассе́сться. рассасываться, -ается *imp.* of рассоса́ться.

рассвести́, -етёт; -ело́ *perf.*, рассвета́ть, -а́ет *imp.* dawn; рассвета́ет, day is breaking; совершенно рассвело́, it is (was) broad daylight. рассве́т, -а, dawn, daybreak.

рас|свирепе́ть, -е́ю *perf.* unsaddle.

расседла́ть, -а́ю *perf.* unsaddle.

рассе́ивание, -я, dispersion; dispersal, scattering, dissipation. рассе́иваться(ся, -аю(сь *imp.* of рассе́ять(ся.

рассека́ть, -а́ю *imp.* of рассе́чь.

расселе́ние, -я, settling, resettlement; separation.

рассе́лина, -ы, cleft, fissure; crevasse.

рассели́ть, -лю́ *perf.*, расселя́ть, -я́ю *imp.* settle, resettle; separate, settle apart.

рас|серди́ть(ся, -жу́(сь, -рдишь(ся *perf.* рассе́рженный, angry.

рассе́сться, -ся́дусь *perf.* (*imp.* расса́живаться) take seats; sprawl.

рассе́чь, -еку́, -ечёшь; -ёк, -ла́ *perf.* (*imp.* рассека́ть) cut, cut through; cleave.

рассе́янность, -и, absent-mindedness, distraction; diffusion; dispersion; dissipation. рассе́янный, absent-minded; diffused; scattered, dispersed; dissipated; ~ свет, diffused light. рассе́ять, -е́ю *perf.* (*imp.* рассе́ивать) sow, broadcast; place at intervals, dot

about; disperse, scatter; dispel; ~ся, disperse, scatter; clear, lift; divert oneself, have some distraction.

расска́з, -а, story, tale; account, narrative. рассказа́ть, -ажу́, -а́жешь *perf.*, расска́зывать, -аю *imp.* tell, narrate, recount. расска́зчик, -а, story-teller, narrator.

рассла́бить, -блю *perf.*, расслабля́ть, -я́ю *imp.* weaken, enfeeble; enervate. расслабле́ние, -я, weakening, enfeeblement; relaxation.

рассла́ивать(ся, -аю(сь *imp.* of расслои́ть(ся.

рассле́дование, -я, investigation, examination; inquiry; произвести́ ~ + *gen.* hold an inquiry into. рассле́довать, -дую *perf.* and *imp.* investigate, look into, hold an inquiry into.

расслое́ние, -я, stratification; exfoliation. расслои́ть, -ою́ *perf.* (*imp.* рассла́ивать) divide into layers, stratify; ~ся, become stratified; exfoliate, flake off.

рассл́ушать, -шу *perf.* catch.

рассма́тривать, -аю *imp.* of рассмотре́ть; examine, scrutinize; regard as, consider.

рас|смеши́ть, -шу́ *perf.*

рассмея́ться, -е́юсь, -еёшься *perf.* burst out laughing.

рассмотре́ние, -я, examination, scrutiny; consideration; предста́вить на ~, submit for consideration. рассмотре́ть, -рю́, -ришь *perf.* (*imp.* рассма́тривать) examine, consider; descry, discern, make out.

рассова́ть, -сую́, -суёшь *perf.*, рассо́вывать, -аю *imp.* по + *dat.* shove into, stuff into.

рассо́л, -а (-у), brine; pickle.

рассо́риться, -рюсь *perf.* с + *instr.* fall out with, quarrel with.

рас|сортирова́ть, -ру́ю *perf.*, рассортиро́вывать, -аю *imp.* sort out.

рассоса́ться, -сётся *perf.* (*imp.* расса́сываться) resolve.

рассо́хнуться, -нется *perf.* (*imp.* рассыха́ться) warp, crack, shrink.

расспра́шивать, -аю *imp.*, расспроси́ть, -ошу́, -о́сишь *perf.* question; make inquiries of.

рассро́чить, -чу perf. spread (over), divide into instalments. рассро́чка, -и, instalment; в рассро́чку, in instalments, by instalments.

расстава́ние, -я, parting. расстава́ться, -таю́сь, -таёшься imp. of расста́ться.

расста́вить, -влю perf., расставля́ть, -я́ю imp., расстана́вливать, -аю imp. place, arrange, post; move apart, set apart; let out; ~ часовы́х, post sentries. расстано́вка, -и, placing; arrangement; pause; spacing; говори́ть с расстано́вкой, speak slowly and deliberately.

расста́ться, -а́нусь perf. (imp. расстава́ться) part; separate; + с + instr. leave; give up.

расстёгивать, -аю imp., расстегну́ть, -ну́, -нёшь perf. undo, unfasten; unbutton; unhook, unclasp, unbuckle; ~ся, come undone; undo one's coat.

расстели́ть(ся, etc.: see разостла́ть(ся. расстила́ть(ся, -а́ю(сь imp. of разостла́ть(ся.

расстоя́ние, -я, distance, space, interval; на далёком расстоя́нии, a long way off, in the far distance.

расстра́ивать(ся, -аю(сь imp. of расстро́ить(ся.

расстре́л, -а, execution, shooting. расстре́ливать, -аю imp., расстреля́ть, -я́ю perf. shoot.

расстро́енный, disordered, deranged; upset; out of tune. расстро́ить, -о́ю perf. (imp. расстра́ивать) upset; thwart, frustrate; put out; disorder, derange; disturb; throw into confusion; unsettle; put out of tune; ~ ряды́ проти́вника, break the enemy's ranks; ~ся, be frustrated; be shattered; be upset, be put out; get out of tune; fall into confusion; fall apart; fall through. расстро́йство, -а, disorder, disarray; derangement; confusion; frustration; discomposure; ~ желу́дка, indigestion; diarrhoea.

расступа́ться, -а́ется imp., расступи́ться, -у́пится perf. part, make way.

рассту́коваться, -ку́ется perf. disengage, cast off. рассты́ко́вка, -и, disengagement, casting off.

рассуди́тельность, -и, reasonableness;

good sense. рассуди́тельный, reasonable; sober-minded; sensible. рассуди́ть, -ужу́, -у́дишь perf. judge, arbitrate; think, consider; decide. рассу́док, -дка, reason; intellect, mind; good sense. рассужда́ть, -а́ю imp. reason; deliberate; debate; argue; + о + prep. discuss. рассужде́ние, -я, reasoning; discussion, debate; argument; без рассужде́ний, without arguing.

рассую́, etc.: see рассова́ть.

рассчи́танный, calculated, deliberate; meant, intended, designed. рассчита́ть, -а́ю perf., рассчи́тывать, -аю imp. + расче́сть, разочту́, -тёшь; расчёл, разочла́ perf. calculate; compute; rate; count, reckon; expect, hope; rely, depend; ~ся, settle accounts, reckon.

рассыла́ть, -а́ю imp. of разосла́ть. рассы́лка, -и, delivery, distribution. рассы́льный sb. messenger; delivery man.

рассы́пать, -плю perf., рассыпа́ть, -а́ю imp. spill; strew, scatter; ~ся, spill, scatter; spread out, deploy; crumble; go to pieces, disintegrate; be profuse; ~ся в похвала́х + dat. shower praises on. рассыпно́й, (sold) loose. рассы́пчатый, friable, short, crumbly; floury.

рассыха́ться, -а́ется imp. of рассо́хнуться. рассяду́сь, etc.: see рассе́сться. раста́лкивать, -аю imp. of растолка́ть. раста́пливать(ся, -аю(сь imp. of растопи́ть(ся. раста́птывать, -аю imp. of растопта́ть.

растаска́ть, -а́ю perf., раста́скивать, -аю imp., растащи́ть, -щу́, -щишь perf. pilfer, filch.

растачи́вать, -аю imp. of расточи́ть. растащи́ть: see растаска́ть. расста́ять, -а́ю perf.

раство́р², -а, (extent of) opening, span. раство́р¹, -а, solution; mortar. раствори́мый, soluble. раствори́тель, -я m. solvent. раствори́ть¹, -рю́ perf. (imp. растворя́ть) dissolve; mix; ~ся, dissolve.

раствори́ть², -рю́, -ришь perf. (imp. растворя́ть) open; ~ся, open.

раствори́ть(ся, -я́ю(сь *imp.* of раствори́ть(ся. **растека́ться**, -а́ется *imp.* of растечься.

расте́ние, -я, plant.

растере́ть, разотру́, -трёшь; растёр *perf.* (*imp.* растира́ть) grind; pound; triturate; spread; rub; massage; ~ся, rub oneself briskly.

растерза́ть, -а́ю *perf.*, **расте́рзывать**, -аю *imp.* tear to pieces; lacerate, harrow.

растерянность, -и, confusion, perplexity, dismay. **расте́рянный**, confused, perplexed, dismayed. **растеря́ть**, -я́ю *perf.* lose; ~ся, get lost; lose one's head, get confused.

расте́чься, -ечётся, -еку́тся; -тёкся -ла́сь *perf.* (*imp.* растека́ться) spill; run; spread.

расти́, -ту́, -тёшь; рос, -ла́ *imp.* grow; increase; grow up; advance, develop.

растира́ние, -я, grinding; rubbing, massage. **растира́ть(ся**, -а́ю(сь *imp.* of растере́ть(ся.

расти́тельность, -и, vegetation; hair. **расти́тельный**, vegetable. **расти́ть**, ращу́ *imp.* raise, bring up; train; grow, cultivate.

растолка́ть, -а́ю *perf.* (*imp.* раста́лкивать) push apart; shake. **растолкну́ть**, -ну́, -нёшь *perf.* part forcibly, push apart.

растолкова́ть, -ку́ю *perf.*, **растолко́вывать**, -аю *imp.* explain, make clear.

рас|**толо́чь**, -лку́ -лчёшь; -ло́к, -лкла́ *perf.*

растолсте́ть, -е́ю *perf.* put on weight, grow stout.

расто́пить, -плю́ -пишь *perf.* (*imp.* раста́пливать) melt; thaw; ~ся, melt.

растопи́ть[2], -плю́, -пишь *perf.* (*imp.* раста́пливать) light, kindle; ~ся, begin to burn. **расто́пка**, -и, lighting; kindling; firewood.

растопта́ть, -пчу́ -пчешь *perf.* (*imp.* раста́птывать) trample, stamp on; crush.

расто́ргать, -а́ю *imp.*, **расто́ргнуть**, -ну, -о́рг *perf.* cancel dissolve annul, abrogate. **расторже́ние**, -я, cancellation, dissolution, annulment; abrogation.

расторо́пный, quick, prompt, smart; efficient.

расточа́ть, -а́ю *imp.*, **расточи́ть**[1], -чу́ *perf.* waste, squander dissipate; lavish, shower. **расточи́тельный**, extravagant, wasteful.

расточи́ть[2], -чу́, -чишь *perf.* (*imp.* раста́чивать) bore, bore out.

растра́вить, -влю́, -вишь *perf.*, **раста́вливать** -а́ю *imp.* irritate.

растра́та, -ы, spending; waste, squandering; embezzlement. **растра́тить**, -а́чу *perf.*, **растра́чивать**, -аю *imp.* spend; waste, squander, dissipate; fritter away; embezzle. **растра́тчик**, -а, embezzler.

растрёпанный, tousled, dishevelled; tattered. **рас**|**трепа́ть**, -плю́ -плешь *perf.* disarrange; tousle, dishevel; tatter, tear; ~ся, get tousled, be dishevelled; get tattered.

растре́скаться, -ается *perf.*, **растре́скиваться**, -ается *imp.* crack, chap.

растро́гать, -аю *perf.* move, touch; ~ся, be moved.

раст́ягивать, -аю *imp.*, **растяну́ть**, -ну́, -нешь *perf.* stretch (out); strain, sprain; prolong, drag out; ~ себе мы́шцу, pull a muscle; ~ся, stretch; lengthen; be prolonged, drag out; stretch oneself out, sprawl; measure one's length, fall flat. **растяже́ние**, -я, tension; stretch, stretching; strain, sprain. **растяжи́мость**, -и, stretchability; tensility; extensibility. **растяжи́мый**, tensile; extensible; stretchable. **растя́нутый**, stretched; long-winded, prolix.

рас|**цвести́**, -сцвету́ *perf.*

расформирова́ние, -я, breaking up; disbandment. **расформирова́ть**, -ру́ю *perf.*, **расформиро́вывать**, -аю *imp.* break up; disband.

расха́живать, -аю *imp.* walk about; pace up and down; ~ по ко́мнате, pace the floor.

расхва́ливать, -аю *imp.*, **расхвали́ть**, -лю́, -лишь *perf.* lavish, shower, praises on.

расхва́рываться, -аюсь *imp.* of расхвора́ться.

расхвата́ть, -а́ю *perf.*, **расхва́тывать**, -аю *imp.* seize on, buy up.

расхвора́ться, -а́юсь *perf.* (*imp.* **расхва́рываться**) fall (seriously) ill.

расхити́тель, -я *m.* plunderer. **расхи́тить**, -и́щу *perf.*, **расхища́ть**, -а́ю *imp.* plunder, misappropriate. **расхище́ние**, -я, plundering, misappropriation.

расхля́банный, loose; unstable; lax, undisciplined.

расхо́д, -а, expenditure; consumption; outlay; expense; *pl.* expenses, outlay, cost; списа́ть в ~, write off. **расхо́диться**, -ожу́сь, -о́дишься *imp.* of разойти́сь. **расхо́дование**, -я, expense, expenditure. **расхо́довать**, -дую *imp.* (*perf.* из~) spend, expend; use up, consume; ~ся, spend money; be spent, be consumed. **расхожде́ние**, -я, divergence; ~ во мне́ниях, difference of opinion.

расхола́живать, -аю *imp.*, **расхолоди́ть**, -ожу́ *perf.* damp the ardour of.

расхоте́ть, -очу́, -о́чешь, -о́тим *perf.* cease to want, no longer want.

расхохота́ться, -очу́сь, -о́чешься *perf.* burst out laughing.

расцара́пать, -аю *perf.* scratch (all over).

расцвести́, -ету́, -ете́шь; -ёл, -а́ *perf.*, **расцвета́ть**, -а́ю *imp.* blossom, come into bloom; flourish. **расцве́т**, -а, bloom, blossoming (out); flourishing; flowering, heyday; в ~e сил, in the prime of life, in one's prime.

расцве́тка, -и, colours; colouring.

расце́нивать, -аю *imp.*, **расцени́ть**, -ню́, -нишь *perf.* estimate, assess value; rate; consider, think. **расце́нка**, -и, valuation; price; (wage-)rate.

расцепи́ть, -плю́ -пишь *perf.*, **расцепля́ть**, -я́ю *imp.* uncouple, unhook; disengage, release. **расцепле́ние**, -я, uncoupling, unhooking; disengaging; release.

расчеса́ть, -ешу́, -е́шешь *perf.* (*imp.* **расчёсывать**) comb; scratch. **расчёска**, -и, comb.

расче́сть, etc.: see рассчита́ть. **расчёсывать**, -аю *imp.* of расчеса́ть.

расчёт[1], -а, calculation; computation; estimate, reckoning; gain, advantage;

settling, settlement; dismissal, discharge; быть в ~e, be quits, be even; дать ~ + *dat.* dismiss, sack; не принима́ть в ~, leave out of account; приня́ть в ~, take into consideration. **расчётливый**, economical, thrifty; careful. **расчётный**, calculation, computation; reckoning; pay; accounts; rated, calculated designed; ~ день, pay-day; ~ отде́л, accounts department.

расчи́стить, -и́щу *perf.*, **расчища́ть**, -а́ю *imp.* clear; ~ся, clear. **расчи́стка**, -и, clearing.

расчлене́ние, -я, dismemberment; partition. **расч|лени́ть**, -ню́ *perf.*, **-члени́ть**, -я́ю *imp.* dismember; partition; break up, divide.

расшата́ть, -а́ю *perf.*, **расша́тывать**, -аю *imp.* shake loose, make rickety; shatter, impair; ~ся, get loose, get rickety; go to pieces, crack up.

расшевели́ть, -лю́ -е́лишь *perf.* stir, shake; rouse.

расшиба́ть, -а́ю *imp.*, **расшиби́ть**, -бу́, -бёшь; -и́б *perf.* break up, smash to pieces; hurt; knock, stub; ~ся, hurt oneself, knock oneself; ~ся в лепёшку, go flat out.

расши́ть, разошью́ -шьёшь *perf.* (*imp.* **расшива́ть**) embroider; undo, unpick.

расшивно́й, embroidered.

расшире́ние, -я, broadening, widening; expansion; extension; dilation, dilatation; distension. **расши́рить**, -рю *perf.*, **расширя́ть**, -я́ю *imp.* broaden, widen; enlarge; expand; extend; ~ся, broaden, widen, gain in breadth; extend; expand, dilate.

расшифрова́ть, -ру́ю *perf.*, **расшифро́вывать**, -аю *imp.* decipher, decode; interpret.

расшнурова́ть, -ру́ю *perf.*, **расшнуро́вывать**, -аю *imp.* unlace, undo.

расщедри́ться, -рю́сь *perf.* be generous, turn generous.

расще́лина, -ы, cleft, crevice, crack.

расще́п, -а, split. **расщепи́ть**, -плю́ *perf.*, **расщепля́ть**, -я́ю *imp.* split; splinter; break up; ~ся, split, splinter. **расщепле́ние**, -я, splitting; splintering;

fission; break-up, disintegration; ~ ядра́, nuclear fission. расщепля́емый, расщепля́ющийся, fissile, fissionable. ратифици́ровать, -рую perf. and imp. ratify.

рационализа́тор, -a, efficiency expert. рационализа́торский, rationalization. рационализа́ция, -и, rationalization, improvement. рационализи́ровать, -рую perf. and imp. rationalize, improve. рациона́льный, rational; efficient.

ра́ция, -и, portable radio transmitter; walkie-talkie.

РВ (ervé) abbr. радиоакти́вные веще́ства, radioactive substances.

рвану́ться, -ну́сь, -нёшься perf. dart, rush, dash.

рва́ный, torn; lacerated. рвать[1], рву, рвёшь; рва́л, -а́, -о imp. tear; rend; rip; pull out, tear out; pick, pluck; blow up; break off, sever; ~ и мета́ть, rant and rave; ~ся, break; tear; burst, explode; strive; be eager, be bursting; ~ с привя́зи, strain at the leash.

рвать[2], рвёт; рва́ло imp. (perf. вы́ ~) impers. vomit, be sick, throw up.

рве́ние, -я, zeal, fervour, ardour.

рво́та, -ы, vomiting; retching; vomit. рво́тн|ый, emetic; ~ое sb. emetic.

ре n. indecl. D; ray.

реаги́ровать, -рую imp. (perf. от~, про~) react; respond.

реакти́вный, reactive; jet; jet-propelled; rocket; ~ самолёт, jet (plane). реа́ктор, -a, reactor, pile.

реакционе́р, -a, reactionary. реакцио́нный, reactionary. реа́кция, -и, reaction.

реа́льность, -и, reality; practicability. реа́льный, real; realizable, practicable, workable; realistic; practical.

ребёнок, -нка; pl. ребя́та, -я́т and де́ти, -е́й, child; infant.

ребро́, -а́; pl. рёбра, -бер, rib; fin; edge, verge; поста́вить вопро́с ~м, put a question point-blank.

ребя́та, -я́т pl. children; boys, lads. ребя́ческий, child's; childish; infantile; puerile. ребя́чество, -a, childishness, puerility. ребя́чий, childish. ребя́читься, -чусь imp. behave like a child.

рёв, -a, roar; bellow, howl.

рев- abbr in comb. of революцио́нный, revolutionary; ревизио́нный, inspection. ревко́м, -a, revolutionary committee. ~коми́ссия, -и, Inspection Board.

рева́нш, -a, revenge; return match.

реве́ть, -ву́, -вёшь imp. roar; bellow; howl.

ревизио́нный, inspection; auditing. реви́зия, -и, inspection; audit; revision. ревизова́ть, -зу́ю perf. and imp. (perf. also об~) inspect; revise. ревизо́р, -a, inspector.

ревни́вый, jealous. ревнова́ть, -ну́ю imp. (perf. при~) be jealous. ре́вностный, zealous, earnest, fervent. ре́вность, -и, jealousy; zeal, earnestness, fervour.

революционе́р, -a, revolutionary. революцио́нный, revolutionary. револю́ция, -и, revolution.

регистра́тор, -a, registrar. регистрату́ра, -ы, registry. регистра́ция, registration. регистри́ровать, -рую perf. and imp. (perf. also за~), register, record; ~ся, register; register one's marriage.

регла́мент, -a, regulations; standing orders; time-limit; установи́ть ~, agree on procedure. регламента́ция, -и, regulation. регламенти́ровать, -рую perf. and imp. regulate.

регули́рование, -я, regulation, control; adjustment. регули́ровать, -рую imp. (perf. за~, от~, у~) regulate; control; adjust, tune. регули́ровщик, -a, traffic controller; man on point duty.

ред- abbr. in comb. of редакцио́нный, editorial. редколле́гия, -и, editorial board. ~отде́л, -a, editorial department. ~сове́т, -a, editorial committee.

-ред abbrev. in comb. of реда́ктор, editor.

редакти́рование, -я, editing. редакти́ровать, -рую imp. (perf. от~) edit, be editor of; word. реда́ктор, -a, editor; гла́вный ~, editor-in-chief; ~ отде́ла, sub-editor. реда́кторский, editorial. редакцио́нн|ый, editorial, editing; ~ая коми́ссия, drafting committee. реда́кция, -и, editorial staff;

editorial office; editing; wording; под
реда́кцией + *gen.* edited by.

редѣ́ть, -еет *imp.* (*perf.* по~) thin, thin
out.

реди́с, -а, radishes. **реди́ска**, -и, radish.

ре́дкий, -док, -дка́, -о, thin; sparse;
rare; uncommon. **ре́дко** *adv.* sparsely;
far apart; rarely, seldom. **ре́дкость**,
-и, rarity; curiosity; curio.

ре́дька, -и, black radish.

рее́стр, -а, list, roll, register.

режи́м, -а, régime; routine; procedure;
regimen; mode of operation; conditions; rate; ~ пита́ния, diet.

режиссёр, -а, producer; director.
режисси́ровать, -рую *imp.* produce;
direct.

ре́жущий, cutting, sharp. **ре́зать**,
ре́жу *imp.* (*perf.* за~, про~, с~) cut;
slice; carve; engrave; pass close to,
shave; cut into; kill, slaughter, knife;
speak bluntly; ~ся, be cut, come
through; gamble.

резви́ться, -влю́сь *imp.* sport, gambol,
play. **ре́звый**, frisky, playful, sportive.

резерву́ар, -а, reservoir, vessel, tank.

резе́ц, -зца́, cutter; cutting tool; chisel;
incisor.

рези́на, -ы, rubber. **рези́нка**, -и, rubber
(piece of) elastic. **рези́новый**, rubber;
elastic; ~ые сапоги́, gum-boots.

ре́зкий, sharp; harsh; abrupt; shrill.
резно́й, carved, fretted. **резня́**, -й,
slaughter, butchery, carnage.

результа́т, -а, result, outcome. **резуль-
та́тивный**, resulting.

резьба́, -ы, carving, fretwork.

рейд[1], -а, roads, roadstead.

рейд[2], -а, a raid.

рейнве́йн, -а (-у), hock. **ре́йнский**,
Rhine, Rhenish.

рейс, -а, trip, run; voyage, passage;
flight.

река́, -й *асс.* ре́ку́; *pl.* -и, ре́ка́м, river.

реквизи́т, -а, properties, props.

рекла́ма, -ы, advertising, advertisement; publicity. **реклами́ровать**, -рую
perf. and *imp.* advertise, publicize,
push. **рекла́мный**, publicity.

рекоменда́тель|ный, of recommenda-
tion; ~ое письмо́, letter of introduction. **рекоменда́ция**, -и, recommenda-

tion; reference. **рекомендова́ть**, -ду́ю
perf. and *imp.* (*perf.* also от~, по~)
recommend; speak well for; advise;
~ся, introduce oneself; be advisable.

реконструи́ровать, -рую *perf.* and *imp.*
reconstruct.

реко́рд, -а, record; поби́ть ~, break,
beat, a record. **реко́рдный**, record,
record-breaking. **рекордсме́н**, -а,
-éнка, -и, record-holder.

религио́зный, religious; of religion;
pious. **рели́гия**, -и, religion.

релье́ф, -а, relief. **релье́фно** *adv.*
boldly. **релье́фный**, relief; raised, embossed, bold.

рельс, -а, rail; сойти́ с ~ов, be derailed, go off the rails. **ре́льсовый**,
rail, railway.

рема́рка, -и, stage direction.

реме́нь, -мня́ *m.* strap; belt; thong.

реме́сленник, -а, artisan, craftsman;
hack. **реме́сленничество**, -а, workmanship, craftsmanship; hack-work.
реме́слен|ный, handicraft; trade;
mechanical; stereotyped; ~ое учи́-
лище, trade school. **ремесло́**, -á; *pl.*
-ёсла, -ёсел, handicraft; trade; profession.

ремо́нт, -а, repair, repairs; maintenance.
ремонти́ровать, -рую *perf.* and *imp.*
(*perf.* also от~), repair; refit, recondition, overhaul. **ремо́нтный**, repair,
repairing.

ре́нта, -ы, rent; income. **рента́бель-
ный**, paying, profitable.

рентге́н, -а, X-rays; roentgen. **рент-
генизи́ровать**, -рую *perf.* and *imp.*
X-ray. **рентге́новский**, X-ray. **рент-
гено́лог**, -а, radiologist. **рентгено-
ло́гия**, -и, radiology.

реомю́р, -а, Réaumur.

ре́па, -ы, turnip.

репети́ровать, -рую *imp.* (*perf.* от~,
про~, с~) rehearse; coach. **репети́-
тор**, -а, coach. **репети́ция**, -и, rehearsal; repeater mechanism; часы́ с
репети́цией, repeater.

ре́плика, -и, rejoinder, retort; cue.

репортёр, -а, reporter.

репроду́ктор, -а, a loud-speaker.

респу́блика, -и, republic.

рессо́ра, -ы, spring. рессо́рный, spring; sprung.

реставра́ция, -и, restoration. реставри́ровать, -рую perf. and imp. (perf. also от~) restore.

рестора́н, -а, restaurant.

рети́вый, zealous, ardent.

ретирова́ться, -ру́юсь perf. and imp. retire, withdraw; make off.

ретрансля́тор, -а, (radio-)relay. ретрансля́ция, -и, relaying, retransmission.

ретроракета, -ы, retro-rocket.

рефера́т, -а, synopsis, abstract; paper, essay.

реценз́ент, -а, reviewer. рецензи́ровать, -рую imp. (perf. про~) review, criticize. реце́нзия, -и, review; notice.

реце́пт, -а, prescription; recipe; method, way, practice.

рециди́в, -а, recurrence; relapse; repetition. рецидиви́ст, -а, a recidivist.

речево́й, speech; vocal.

ре́чка, -и, river. речно́й, river; riverine; fluvial; ~ вокза́л, river-steamer and water-bus station; ~ трамва́й, water-bus.

речь, -и; gen. pl. -е́й, speech; enunciation, way of speaking; language; discourse; oration; address; вы́ступить с ~ю, make a speech; не об э́том ~, that's not the point; об э́том не мо́жет бы́ть и ре́чи, it is out of the question; о чём ~? what are you talking about? what is it all about?; ~ идёт о том . ., the question is . . .

реша́ть, -а́ю(сь imp. of реши́ть(ся. реша́ющий, decisive, deciding; key, conclusive. реше́ние, -я, decision; decree; judgement; verdict; solution, answer; вы́нести ~, pass a resolution.

решётка, -и, grating; grille, railing; lattice; trellis; fender, (fire)guard; (fire)grate; tail; орёл или ~ (ре́шка)? heads or tails? решето́, -а́; pl. -ёта, sieve. решётчатый, lattice, latticed; trellised.

реши́мость, -и, resolution, resoluteness; resolve. реши́тельно adv. resolutely; decidedly, definitely; absolutely; всё равно́, it makes no difference whatever. реши́тельность, -и, resolution, determination, firmness. реши́тель-

ный, resolute, determined; decided; firm; definite; decisive; crucial; absolute. реши́ть, -шу́ perf. (imp. реша́ть) decide, determine; make up one's mind; solve, settle; ~ся, make up one's mind, resolve; bring oneself; + gen. lose, be deprived of.

ре́шка: see реше́тка.

ржа́веть, -еет imp. (perf. за~, по~), rust. ржа́вчина, -ы, rust; mildew. ржа́вый, rusty.

ржано́й, гуе.

ржать, ржу, ржёшь imp. neigh.

ри́га, -и, (threshing-)barn.

ри́млянин, -а; pl. -яне, -ян, ри́млянка, -и, Roman. ри́мск|ий, Roman; па́па ~ий, роре; ~ие ци́фры, Roman numerals.

ри́нуться, -нусь perf. rush, dash, dart.

рис, -а (-у), rice.

риск, -а, risk; hazard; пойти́ на ~, run risks, take chances. риско́ванный, risky; risqué. рискова́ть, -ку́ю imp. run risks, take chances; + instr. or inf. risk, take the risk of.

рисова́ние, -я, drawing. рисова́ть, -су́ю imp. (perf. на~) draw; paint, depict, portray; ~ся, be silhouetted; appear, present oneself; pose, act.

ри́с|ый, rice; ~ая ка́ша, rice pudding; boiled rice.

рису́нок, -нка, drawing; illustration; figure; pattern, design; outline; draughtsmanship.

риф, -а, reef.

ри́фма, -ы, rhyme. рифмова́ть, -му́ю imp. (perf. с~) rhyme; ~ся, rhyme. рифмо́вка, -и, rhyming (system).

р-н abbr. райо́н, district.

РНК (эрэнка́) abbr. рибонуклеи́новая кислота́, RNA, ribonucleic acid.

робе́ть, -е́ю imp. (perf. о~) be timid; be afraid, quail. ро́бкий, -бок, -бка́, -о, timid, shy. ро́бость, -и, timidity, shyness. робче, comp. of ро́бкий.

ров, рва, loc. -у, ditch.

рове́сник, -а, coeval. ро́вно adv. regularly, evenly; exactly; sharp; absolutely; just as, exactly like; ~ в час, at one sharp, on the stroke of one; ~ ничего́, absolutely nothing, nothing at all. ро́вный, flat; even; level; regular;

equable; exact; equal. **ро́вня**, **ро́вни** *m*. and *f*. equal; match. **ровня́ть**, **-я́ю** *imp*. (*perf*. с∼) even, level; ∼ с землёй, raze to the ground.

рог, -а; *pl*. -а́, -о́в, horn; antler; bugle. **порга́тый**, horned. **роговица**, -ы. cornea. **роговой**, horny; horny; horn-rimmed.

рого́жа, -и, bast mat(ting).

род, -а (-у), *loc*. -у́; *pl*. -ы́, birth; family, kin, clan; birth, origin, stock; generation; genus; sort, kind; без ∼у, без пле́мени, without kith or kin; ∼ э́того, of this sort, of the kind; ей де́сять лет от ∼у, she is ten years old; он своего́ ∼а ге́ний, he is a genius in his (own) way; ∼ом, by birth; своего́ ∼а, a kind of, a sort of; челове́ческий ∼, mankind, the human race. **роди́льный**, maternity; puerperal. **ро́дина**, -ы, native land, mother country; home, homeland. **роди́нка**, -и, birth-mark. **роди́тель**, -я *m*. father; ∼ница, -ы, mother; **роди́тели**, -ей *pl*. parents. **роди́тельный**, genitive. **роди́тельский**, parental, parents'; paternal. **роди́ть**, рожу́, -и́л, -ила́, -о *perf*. and *imp*. (*imp*. also рожа́ть, рожда́ть), bear; give birth to; give rise to; ∼ся, be born; arise; come into being; spring up, thrive.

родни́к, -а́, spring. **роднико́вый**, spring.

родни́ть, -ни́т (*perf*. по∼) make related, link; make similar, make alike; ∼ся, become related, be linked. **роди́н|ой**, own; native; home; ∼о́й брат, brother; ∼о́й язы́к, mother tongue; ∼ые *sb*. relations, relatives, family. **родня́**, -и́, relation(s), relative(s); kinsfolk. **родово́й**, clan, tribal; ancestral; generic; gender. **родонача́льник**, -а, ancestor, forefather; father. **родосло́в|ный|**, genealogical; ∼ая *sb*. genealogy, pedigree. **ро́дственник**, -а, relation, relative. **ро́дственный**, kindred, related; allied; cognate; familiar, intimate. **родство́**, -а́, relationship, kinship; relations, relatives. **ро́ды**, -ов *pl*. birth; childbirth, delivery; labour.

ро́жа[1], -и, erysipelas.

ро́жа[2], -и, mug; стро́ить ро́жи, pull faces.

рожа́ть, -а́ю, рожда́ть(ся, -а́ю(сь *imp*. of роди́ть(ся. **рожда́емость**, -и, birth-rate. **рожде́ние**, -я, birth; birthday. **рождённый**, -ён, -а́, born. **рождество́**, -а́, Christmas.

рожь, ржи, rye.

ро́за, -ы, rose; rose-bush, rose-tree; rose window.

ро́зга, -и; *gen*. *pl*. -зог, birch.

ро́здал, etc.: see разда́ть.

ро́зница, -ы, retail; в ∼у, retail. **ро́зничный**, retail. **ро́зно** *adv*. apart, separately, in difference; dissension. **ро́знял**, etc.: see разня́ть.

ро́зовый, pink; rose-coloured; rosy; rose.

ро́зыгрыш, -а, draw; drawing; drawn game; playing off; tournament, competition, championship.

ро́зыск, -а, search; inquiry; investigation.

ро́иться, -и́тся, swarm. **рой**, -я, *loc*. -ю́; *pl*. -и́, -ёв, swarm.

рок, -а, fate.

рокирова́ть(ся, -ру́ю(сь *perf*. and *imp*. castle. **рокиро́вка**, -и, castling.

РОКК, -а *abbr*. Росси́йское О́бщество Кра́сного Креста́, Russian Red Cross.

роково́й, fateful; fated; fatal.

ро́кот, -а, roar, rumble. **рокота́ть**, -о́чет *imp*. roar, rumble.

ро́лик, -а, roller; castor; *pl*. roller skates. **ро́ллер**, -а, scooter.

роль, -и; *gen*. *pl*. -ей, role, part.

ром, -а (-у), rum.

рома́н, -а, novel; romance; love affair. **романи́ст**, -а, novelist.

рома́нс, -а, song; romance.

рома́шка, -и, **рома́шковый**, camomile.

рони́ть, -я́ю *imp*. (*perf*. урони́ть) drop, let fall; shed; lower, injure, discredit.

ро́пот, -а, murmur, grumble. **ропта́ть**, -пщу́, -пщешь *imp*. murmur, grumble.

рос, etc.: see расти́.

роса́, -ы́; *pl*. -ы, dew. **роси́стый**, dewy.

роско́шный, luxurious; sumptuous; luxuriant; splendid. **ро́скошь**, -и, luxury; luxuriance; splendour.

ро́слый, tall, strapping.

ро́спись, -и, list, inventory; painting(s); mural(s).

ро́спуск, -a, dismissal; disbandment; breaking up.

росси́йский, Russian.

ро́ссказни, -ей *pl.* old wives' tales, cock-and-bull stories.

ро́ссыпь, -и, scattering, *pl.* deposit; ~ю, in bulk, loose.

рост, -a (-у), growth; increase; rise; height, stature; во весь ~, upright, straight; ~ом, in height.

ростовщи́к, -á, usurer, money-lender.

росто́к, -тка́, sprout, shoot; пусти́ть ростки́, sprout, put out shoots.

ро́счерк, -a, flourish, одни́м ~ом пера́, with a stroke of the pen.

рот, рта (рту), *loc.* рту, mouth.

ро́та, -ы, company.

рота́тор, -a, duplicator. **ротацио́нн|ый**, rotary; ~ая маши́на, rotary press. **рота́ция**, -и, rotary press.

ро́тный, company; *sb.* company commander.

ротозе́й, -я, -зе́йка, -и, gaper, rubberneck; scatter-brain. **ротозе́йство**, -a, carelessness, absent-mindedness.

ро́ща, -и, **ро́щица**, -ы, grove.

ро́ю, etc.: see рыть.

роя́ль, -я *m.* (grand) piano; игра́ть на роя́ле, play the piano.

РСФСР (*eresefesér*) *abbr.* Росси́йская Сове́тская Федерати́вная Социалисти́ческая Респу́блика, Russian Soviet Federative Socialist Republic.

ртýтный, mercury, mercurial. **ртуть**, -и, mercury; quicksilver.

руба́нок, -нка, plane.

руба́шка, -нка, shirt; ночна́я ~, night-shirt, nightgown, nightdress.

рубе́ж, -á, boundary, border(line), frontier; line; за ~о́м, abroad.

рубе́ц, -бца́, scar, cicatrice; weal; hem; seam; tripe.

руби́н, -a, ruby. **руби́новый**, ruby; ruby-coloured.

руби́ть, -блю́, -бишь *imp.* (*perf.* с~) fell; hew, chop, hack; mince, chop up; build (of logs), put up, erect.

ру́бище, -a, rags, tatters.

ру́бка¹, -и, felling; hewing, hacking; chopping; mincing.

ру́бка², -и, deck house, deck cabin; боева́я ~, conning-tower; рулева́я ~, wheelhouse.

рублёвка, -и, one-rouble note. **рублё́вый**, (one-)rouble.

ру́блен|ый, minced, chopped; log, of logs; ~ые котле́ты, rissoles; ~ое мя́со, mince, minced meat, hash.

рубль, -я́ *m.* rouble.

ру́брика, -и, rubric, heading; column.

рубча́тый, ribbed. **ру́бчик**, -a, scar, seam, rib.

ру́гань, -и, abuse, bad language, swearing. **руга́тельн|ый**, abusive; ~ые слова́, bad language, swear-words. **руга́тельство**, -a, oath, swear-word. **руга́ть**, -а́ю *imp.* (*perf.* вы́~, об~, от~) curse, swear at; abuse; tear to pieces; criticize severely; ~ся, curse, swear, use bad language; swear at, abuse, one another.

руда́, -ы́; *pl.* ру́ды, ore. **рудни́к**, -á, mine, pit. **рудни́чный**, mine, pit; mining; ~ газ, fire-damp. **рудоко́п**, -a, miner.

руже́йный, rifle, gun; ~ вы́стрел, rifle-shot. **ружьё**, -ья́; *pl.* ~ья, -жей, -жьям, gun, rifle.

рука́, -и́, *acc.* -у; *pl.* ру́к, -а́м, hand; arm; в со́бственные ру́ки, personal; игра́ть в четы́ре руки́, play duets; идти́ по́д руку с + *instr.*, walk arm in arm with; маха́ть руко́й, wave one's hand; махну́ть руко́й на + *acc.* give up as lost; на ско́рую ру́ку, hastily; extempore; не поднима́ется ~ + *inf.* one cannot bring oneself to; под руко́й, at hand; по рука́м! done! it's a bargain!; приложи́ть ру́ку, append one's signature; рука́ми не тро́гать! (please) don't touch!; ру́ки вверх! hands up; ру́ки прочь! hands off!; руко́й пода́ть, a stone's throw away; у вас на ~х, on you; чёткая ~, a clear hand; э́то мне на́ руку, that suits me.

рука́в, -а́; *pl.* -а́, -о́в sleeve; branch, arm; hose; пожа́рный ~, fire-hose.

рукави́ца, -ы, mitten; gauntlet.

руководи́тель, -я *m.* leader; manager; instructor; guide. **руководи́ть**, -ожу́ *imp.* + *instr.* lead; guide; direct, manage. **руково́дство**, -a, leadership; guidance; direction; guide; handbook, manual; instructions; leaders; governing body. **руково́дствоваться**, -твуюсь + *instr.* follow; be guided by, be influenced by. **руководя́щий**, leading; guiding; **~ая статья́**, leader; **~ий комите́т**, steering committee.

рукоде́лие, -я, needlework; *pl.* hand-made goods.

рукомо́йник, -а, wash-stand.

рукопа́шн|ый, hand-to-hand; **~ая** *sb.* hand-to-hand fighting.

рукопи́сный, manuscript. **ру́копись**, -и, manuscript.

рукоплеска́ние, -я, applause. **рукоплеска́ть**, -ещу́, -е́щешь *imp.* + *dat.* applaud, clap.

рукопожа́тие, -я, handshake; **обменя́ться рукопожа́тиями**, shake hands.

рукоя́тка, -и, handle; hilt; haft, helve; shaft; grip.

рулев|о́й, steering; **~о́е колесо́**, steering wheel; *sb.* helmsman, man at the wheel.

руле́тка, -и, tape-measure; roulette.

рули́ть, -лю́ *imp.* (*perf.* вы́~) taxi.

руль, -я́ *m.* rudder; helm; (steering-)wheel; handlebar.

румы́н, -а; *gen. pl.* -ы́н, **румы́нка**, -и, Rumanian. **румы́нский**, Rumanian.

румя́на, -я́н *pl.* rouge. **румя́нец**, -нца, (high) colour; flush; blush. **румя́нить**, -ню *imp.* (*perf.* за~, на~) redden, bring colour to; rouge; brown; **~ся**, redden; glow; flush; use rouge, put on rouge. **румя́ный**, rosy, ruddy; brown.

ру́пор, -а, megaphone, speaking-trumpet; loud-hailer; mouthpiece.

руса́лка, -и, mermaid. **руса́лочий**, mermaid, mermaid's.

ру́сский, Russian; *sb.* Russian.

ру́сый, light brown.

ру́хлядь, -и, junk, lumber.

ру́хнуть, -ну *perf.* crash down; fall heavily; crash (to the ground).

руча́тельство, -а, guarantee; **с ~м**, warranted, guaranteed. **руча́ться**, -а́юсь *imp.* (*perf.* поручи́ться) answer, vouch; + за + *acc.* warrant, guarantee, certify.

руче́й, -чья́, stream, brook.

ру́чка, -и, handle; (door-)knob; (chair-)

-arm; penholder. **ручн|о́й**, hand; arm; manual; hand-made; tame; **~ые часы́**, wrist-watch.

ру́шить, -у *imp.* (*perf.* об~) pull down; **~ся**, fall, fall in; collapse.

ры́ба, -ы, fish; *pl.* Pisces. **рыба́к**, -а́, fisherman. **рыба́лка**, -и, fishing. **рыба́цкий**, **рыба́чий**, fishing. **ры́бий**, fish; fishlike, fishy; **~ жир**, cod-liver oil. **ры́бн|ый**, fish; **~ые консе́рвы**, tinned fish. **рыболо́в**, -а, fisherman; angler. **рыболо́вный**, fishing.

рыво́к, -вка́, jerk; dash, burst, spurt.

рыда́ние, -я, sobbing, sobs. **рыда́ть**, -а́ю *imp.* sob.

ры́жий, рыж, -а́, -е, red, red-haired; ginger; chestnut; reddish-brown, brown with age; gold. **ры́жики**, -ов *pl.* (*sl.*) gold watch.

ры́ло, -а, snout; mug.

ры́нок, -нка, market; market-place. **ры́ночный**, market.

рыса́к, -а́, trotter.

ры́сий, lynx.

рыси́стый, trotting. **рыси́ть**, -и́шь *imp.* trot. **рысь**[1], -и, *loc.* -и́, trot; **~ю**, на **рыся́х**, at a trot.

рысь[2], -и, lynx.

ры́твина, -ы, rut, groove. **рыть**, ро́ю *imp.* (*perf.* вы́~, от~) dig; rummage about (in), ransack, burrow into; **~ся**, dig; rummage.

рыхли́ть, -лю́ *imp.* (*perf.* вз~, раз~) loosen, make friable. **ры́хлый**, -л, -а́, -о, friable; loose; porous; podgy, podgy.

ры́царский, knightly; chivalrous. **ры́царь**, -я *m.* knight.

рыча́г, -а́ lever.

рыча́ть, -чу́ *imp.* growl, snarl.

рья́ный, zealous, ardent.

РЭС *abbr.* райо́нная электроста́нция, Regional power station.

рю́мка, -и, wineglass.

ряби́на[1], -ы, rowan. mountain ash; service(-tree); rowan-berry.

ряби́на[2], -ы, pit, pock. **ряби́ть**, -и́т *imp.*; *impers.* у меня́ ряби́т в глаза́х, I am dazzled. **рябо́й**, pitted, pock-marked; speckled. **ря́бчик**, -а, hazel-hen, hazel grouse. **рябь**, -и, ripple; ripples; dazzle.

ря́вкать, -аю *imp.*, **ря́вкнуть**, -ну *perf.* bellow, roar.

ряд, -а (-у), *loc.* -ý; *pl.* -ы́, row; line; file, rank; series; number; из ~а вон выходя́щий, outstanding, exceptional, out of the common run; пе́рвый ~ front row; после́дний ~, back row; стоя́ть в одно́м ~ý с + *instr.* rank with. **рядово́й**, ordinary common; ~ соста́в, rank and file; men other ranks; *sb.* private. **ря́дом** *adv.* alongside; near, close by, next door; + с + *instr.* next to.

ря́са, -ы cassock.

С

с *letter*: see эс.

с, со *prep.* I. + *gen.* from; since; off; for, with; on; by; дово́льно с тебя́! that's enough from you!; перево́д с ру́сского, translation from Russian; с большо́й бу́квы, with a capital letter; сда́ча с рубля́ change for a rouble; с ле́вой стороны́ on the left-hand side; с одно́й стороны́ с друго́й стороны́, on the one hand, on the other hand; со сна, just up, half awake; со стыда́, for shame, with shame; с пе́рвого взгля́да, at first sight; с ра́дости, for joy; с утра́, since morning. II. + *acc.* about; the size of; ма́льчик с па́льчик, Tom Thumb; на́ша до́чка ро́стом с ва́шу, our daughter is about the same height as yours; с неде́лю for about a week. III. + *instr.* with; and; мы с ва́ми, you and I; получи́ть с пе́рвой по́чтой, receive by the first post; что с ва́ми? what is the matter with you? what's up?

с. *abbr.* се́вер, N.; село́, village; страни́ца, page.

с-, со-, съ- *vbl. pref.* indicating perfective aspect: unification, joining, fastening; accompaniment, participation; comparison: copying: removal; movement away (from), to one side, downwards, down (from), off, there and back, directed to a point or centre; action in concert.

СА (*esá*) *abbr.* Сове́тская А́рмия, Soviet Army.

са́бельный, sabre. **са́бля**, -и; *gen. pl.* -бель, sabre; (cavalry) sword.

саботи́ровать, -рую *perf.* and *imp.* sabotage.

са́ван, -а, shroud; blanket.

с|агити́ровать, -рую *perf.*

сад, -а, *loc.* -ý; *pl.* -ы́, garden, gardens. **сади́ть**, сажу́, са́дишь *imp.* (*perf.* по~) plant. **сади́ться**, сажу́сь, *imp.* of сесть. **садо́вник**, -а, -ница, -ы, gardener. **садово́дство**, -а, gardening; horticulture; nursery; garden(s). **садо́вый**, garden; cultivated.

са́жа, -и, soot.

сажа́ть, -а́ю *imp.* (*perf.* посади́ть) plant; seat; set put; ~ в тюрьму́, put in prison, imprison, jail; ~ под аре́ст, put under arrest. **са́женец**, -нца, seedling; sapling.

са́жень, -и; *pl.* -и, -жен or -же́ней, sazhen (2·13 metres).

сажу́, etc.: see сади́ть.

са́йка, -и, roll.

с|акти́ровать, -рую *perf.*

сала́зки, -зок *pl.* sled, toboggan.

сала́т, -а (-у), lettuce; salad. **сала́тник**, -а, **сала́тница**, -ы, salad-dish, salad-bowl.

са́ло, -а, fat, lard; suet; tallow.

салфе́тка, -и, napkin, serviette.

са́льный, greasy; fat; tallow; obscene, bawdy.

салю́т, -а, salute. **салютова́ть**, -ту́ю *perf.* and *imp.* (*perf.* also от~) + *dat.* salute.

сам, -ого́ *m.*, **сама́**, -о́й, *acc.* -о́ё *f.*, **само́**, -ого́ *n.*, **са́ми**, -их *pl.*, *pron.* -self, -selves; myself, etc., ourselves, etc.; она́ — ~á доброта́ she is kindness itself; ~ по себе́, in itself; by oneself, unassisted; ~ собо́й, of itself, of its own accord; ~ó собо́й (разуме́ется), of course; it goes without saying.

са́мбо *n. indecl. abbr.* самозащи́та без ору́жия, unarmed combat.

саме́ц -мца́, male. **са́мка**, -и, female.

само- *perf.* self-, auto-. **самобы́тный**, original, distinctive. **~внуше́ние**, -я, auto-suggestion. **~возгора́ние**, -я, spontaneous combustion. **~во́льный**, wilful, self-willed; unauthorized; unwarranted. **~дви́жущийся**, self-propelled. **~де́лка**, -и, home-made. **~де́льный**, home-made; self-made. **~держа́вие**, -я. autocracy. **~держа́вный**, autocratic. **~де́ятельность**, -и, amateur work, amateur performance; initiative. **~дово́льный**, self-satisfied, smug, complacent. **~ду́р**, a, petty tyrant; self-willed person. **~ду́рство**, -а, petty tyranny, obstinate wilfulness. **~забве́ние**, -я, selflessness. **~забве́нный**, selfless. **~защи́та**, -ы, self-defence. **~зва́нец** -нца, impostor, pretender. **~зва́нство**, -а, imposture. **~ка́т**, -а, scooter; bicycle. **~кри́тика**, -и, self-criticism. **~люби́вый**, proud; touchy. **~люби́е** -я, pride self-esteem. **~мне́ние**, -я conceit, self-importance. **~наде́янный**, presumptuous. **~облада́ние**, -я, self-control, self-possession; composure. **~обма́н**, -а, self-deception. **~оборо́на**, -ы, self-defence. **~образова́ние**, -я, self-education. **~обслу́живание**, -я, self-service. **~определе́ние**, -я, self-determination. **~опроки́дывающийся**, self-tipping; **~опроки́дывающийся грузови́к**, tip-up lorry. **~отверже́ние**, -я, **~отве́рженность**, -и, selflessness. **~отве́рженный**, selfless, self-sacrificing. **~пи́шущий**, recording, registering; **~пи́шущее перо́** fountain-pen. **~поже́ртвование**, -я, self-sacrifice. **~пу́ск**, -а, self-starter. **~рекла́ма**, -ы, self-advertisement. **~ро́дный**, native. **~ро́док**, -дка, nugget; rough diamond. **~сва́л**, -а, a tip-up lorry. **~-созна́ние**, -я, self-consciousness.

~сохране́ние, -я, self-preservation. **~стоя́тельно** *adv.* independently; on one's own. **~стоя́тельность**, -и, independence. **~стоя́тельный**, independent. **~су́д**, -а, lynch law, mob law. **~тёк**, -а, drift. **~тёком** *adv.* by gravity; haphazard of its own accord; идти́ ~тёком, drift. **~уби́йственный**, suicidal. **~уби́йство**, -а, suicide. **~уби́йца**, -ы *m.* and *f.* suicide. **~уве́ренность**, -и, self-confidence, self-assurance. **~уве́ренный**, self-confident, self-assured; cocksure. **~униже́ние**, -я, self-abasement, self-disparagement. **~управле́ние**, -я, self-government; local authority. **~управля́ющийся**, self-governing. **~упра́вный**, arbitrary. **~упра́вство**, -а, arbitrariness. **~учи́тель**, -я, self-instructor, manual. **~у́чка**, -и *m.* and *f.* self-taught person. **~хо́дный**, self-propelled. **~чу́вствие**, -я, general state; как ва́ше ~чу́вствие? how do you feel?

самова́р, -а, samovar.

самолёт, -а, aeroplane, aircraft, plane.

самоцве́т, -а, semi-precious stone.

са́м|**ый** *pron.* (the) very (the) right; (the) same; (the) most; в ~ое вре́мя, at the right time; в ~ом де́ле, indeed; в ~ом де́ле? indeed? really?; в ~ый раз, just right; на ~ом де́ле, actually, in fact; ~ый глу́пый, the stupidest, the most stupid; ~ые пустяки́, the merest trifles; с ~ого нача́ла, from the very beginning, right from the start; с ~ого утра́, ever since the morning, since first thing.

can, -а, dignity, office.

сан- *abbr.* in *comb.* of санита́рный, medical, hospital; sanitary. **санвра́ч**, -á, medical officer of health; sanitary inspector. **~по́езд**, -а, hospital train, ambulance train. **~пу́нкт**, -а, medical centre; dressing-station aid-post. **~у́зел**, -зла, sanitary arrangements. **~ча́сть**, -и, medical unit.

са́ни, -ей *pl.* sledge, sleigh.

санита́р, -а, medical orderly, hospital orderly, male nurse; stretcher-bearer. **санита́рия**, -и, hygiene, public health. **санита́рка**, -и, nurse. **санита́рн**|**ый**, medical; hospital; (public) health; sanitary; ~ый автомоби́ль, ~ая каре́та, ~ая маши́на, ambulance; ~ый у́зел, sanitary arrangements.

са́нки, -нок *pl.* sledge; toboggan. са́нный, sledge, sleigh; ~ путь, sleigh-road. са́ночник, -а, tobogganist.

сантиме́тр, -а, centimetre; tape-measure, ruler.

сапёр, -а, sapper; pioneer. сапёрный, sapper, pioneer; engineer.

сапо́г, -а́; *gen. pl* -о́г boot; top-boot, jackboot. сапо́жник, -а, a shoemaker; bootmaker; cobbler. сапо́жный, boot, shoe.

сапфи́р, -а sapphire.

сара́й, -я, shed; barn, barrack.

саранча́, -и́ locust; locusts.

сарафа́н, -а, sarafan; pinafore dress, pinafore skirt.

сарде́лька, -и, small fat sausage; sardine.

сатана́, -ы́ *m.* Satan. сатани́нский, satanic.

сати́н, -а, sateen. сати́новый, sateen.

сафья́н, -а, morocco. сафья́новый, morocco.

са́хар, -а (-у), sugar. сахари́н, -а, saccharine. са́харистый, sugary; saccharine. са́харить, -рю *imp.* (*perf.* по~) sugar, sweeten. са́харница, -ы, sugar-basin. са́харн|ый, sugar; sugary; ~ая голова́, sugar-loaf; ~ый заво́д, sugar-refinery; ~ый песо́к granulated sugar; ~ая пу́дра, castor sugar; ~ая свёкла, sugar-beet.

сачо́к, -чка́, net; landing net; butterfly-net.

сб. *abbr.* сбо́рник, collection.

сба́вить, -влю *perf.* сбавля́ть, -я́ю *imp.* take off, deduct; reduce; ~ в ве́се, lose weight; ~ газ, throttle down; ~ с цены́ reduce the price.

сбаланси́ровать, -рую *perf.*

сбе́гать[1], -аю *perf.* run; + за + *instr.* run for. сбега́ть[2], -а́ю *imp.*, сбежа́ть, -erу́ *perf.* run down (from); run away; disappear, vanish; ~ся, come running; gather, collect

сберега́тельн|ый, ~ая ка́сса savings bank. сберега́ть, -а́ю *imp.*, сбере́чь,

-егу́ -ежёшь; -ёг -ла́ *perf.* save; save up, put aside; preserve, protect. сбереже́ние, -я, economy; saving, preservation; savings. сберка́сса, -ы *abbr* savings bank.

сбива́ть, -а́ю *imp.*, с|бить, собью, -бьёшь *perf.* bring down, knock down, throw down; knock off, dislodge; put out; distract; deflect; wear down, tread down; knock together; churn; beat up, whip, whisk; ~ с доро́ги, misdirect; ~ с ног, knock down; ~ це́ну, beat down the price; ~ся, be dislodged; slip; be deflected; go wrong; be confused; be inconsistent; ~ся в ку́чу, ~ся толпо́й, bunch, huddle; ~ся с доро́ги, ~ся с пути́, lose one's way, go astray; ~ся с ног, be run off one's feet; ~ся со счёта, lose count. сби́вчивый, confused, indistinct; inconsistent, contradictory. сби́т|ый; ~ые сли́вки, whipped cream.

сближа́ть, -а́ю *imp.*, сбли́зить, -и́жу *perf.* bring (closer) together, draw together; ~ся, draw together, converge; become good friends. сближе́ние, -я, rapprochement; intimacy; approach, closing in.

сбо́ку *adv.* from one side; on one side; at the side.

сбор, -а, collection; dues; duty; charge(s), fee, toll; takings; returns; salvage; assemblage, gathering; course of instruction; быть в ~е, be assembled, be in session; ~ урожа́я, harvest. сбо́рище, -а, crowd, mob. сбо́рка, -и, assembling, assembly, erection; gather. сбо́рник, -а, collection; ~ пра́вил, code of rules. сбо́рн|ый, assembly; mixed, combined; that can be taken to pieces; prefabricated; sectional; detachable; ~ая кома́нда, combined team, representative team; picked team; scratch team; ~ый пункт, assembly point, rallying point. сбо́рочный, assembly; ~ цех, assembly shop. сбо́рчатый, gathered. сбо́рщик, -а, collector; assembler, fitter, mounter.

сбра́сывать(ся, -аю(сь *imp.* of сбро́сить(ся.

сбрива́ть, -а́ю *imp.*, **сбрить**, **сбре́ю** *perf.* shave off.

сброд, -а, riff-raff, rabble.

сброс, -а, fault, break. **сбро́сить**, -о́шу *perf.* (*imp.* **сбра́сывать**) throw down, drop; throw off; cast off, shed; throw away, discard; ~**ся**, throw oneself down, leap (+ *gen.* from).

с|**брошюрова́ть**, -рю́ю *perf.*

сбру́я, -и, harness.

сбыва́ть, -а́ю *imp.*, **сбыть**, **сбу́ду**; **сбыл**, -а́, -о *perf.* sell, market; get rid of; dump; ~ с рук, get off one's hands; ~**ся**, come true, be realized; happen; что сбу́дется с ней? what will become of her? **сбыт**, -а, sale; market. **сбытово́й**, selling, marketing.

CB (*esvé*) *abbr.* сре́дние во́лны, medium waves; medium-wave.

св. *abbr.* свы́ше, over; свято́й, saint.

сва́дебный, wedding; nuptial. **сва́дьба**, -ы; *gen. pl.* -деб, wedding.

сва́ливать, -аю *imp.*, **с**|**вали́ть**, -лю́, -лишь *perf.* throw down, bring down; overthrow; lay low; heap up, pile up; abate; ~**ся**, fall, fall down, collapse. **сва́лка**, -и, dump; scrap-heap, rubbish-heap; scuffle; вы́бросить на сва́лку, dump.

с|**валя́ть**, -я́ю **сваля́ться**, -я́ется *perf.* get tangled, get matted.

сва́ривать, -аю *imp.*, **с**|**вари́ть**, -рю́, -ришь *perf.* boil; cook; weld; ~**ся**, boil, cook; weld (together), unite. **сва́рка**, -и, welding.

сварли́вый, peevish; shrewish.

сварно́й, welded. **сва́рочный**, welding. **сва́рщик**, -а, welder.

сва́тать, -аю *imp* (*perf.* по~, со~) propose as a husband or wife; ask in marriage; ~**ся** к + *dat.* or за + *acc.* ask, seek in marriage.

свая́. -и, pile.

све́дение, -я piece of information; knowledge; attention, notice; report, minute; *pl.* information, intelligence; knowledge. **све́дущий**, knowledgeable; versed experienced; ~**ие ли́ца,** experts, informed persons.

сведу́, etc.: see **свести́.**

свежезаморо́женный, fresh-frozen; chilled. **све́жесть**, -и, freshness; cool-

ness. **свеже́ть**, -е́ет *imp.* (*perf.* по~) become cooler; freshen. **свеж**|**ий**; -еж, -а́, fresh; ~ее бельё clean underclothes; ~ие проду́кты, fresh food; ~ий хлеб, new bread.

свезти́, -зу́, -зёшь; свёз, -ла́ *perf.* (*imp.* свози́ть) take, convey; bring down, take down; take away, clear away.

свёкла, -ы, beet, beetroot.

свёкор, -кра, father-in-law. **свекро́вь**, -и, mother-in-law.

свёл, etc.: see **свести́.**

сверга́ть, -а́ю *imp.*, **све́ргнуть**, -ну; сверг *perf.* throw down, overthrow. **сверже́ние**, -я, overthrow; ~ с престо́ла, dethronement.

све́рить, -рю *perf.* (*imp.* сверя́ть) collate; check.

сверка́ние, -я, sparkling, sparkle; twinkling, twinkle; glitter; glare. **сверка́ть**, -а́ю *imp.* sparkle, twinkle; glitter; gleam. **сверкну́ть**, -ну́, -нёшь *perf.* flash.

сверли́льный, drill, drilling; boring. **сверли́ть**, -лю́ *imp.* (*perf.* про~) drill; bore, bore through; nag, gnaw. **сверло́**, -а́, drill. **сверля́щий**, nagging, gnawing, piercing.

сверну́ть, -ну́, -нёшь *perf.* (*imp.* свёртывать, свора́чивать) roll, roll up; turn; reduce, contract, curtail, cut down; wind up; ~ ла́герь, break camp; ~ ше́ю + *dat.* wring the neck of; ~**ся**, roll up, curl up; coil up; fold; curdle, coagulate; turn; contract.

све́рстник, -а, coeval, contemporary; мы с ним ~и, he and I are the same age.

свёрток, -тка, package, parcel, bundle. **свёртывание**, -я, rolling, rolling up; curdling, turning; coagulation; reduction, curtailment; cutting down, cuts. **свёртывать**(**ся**, -аю(сь *imp.* of сверну́ть(ся.

сверх *prep.* + *gen.* over, above on top of; beyond; over and above; in addition to; in excess of; ~ того́, moreover, besides.

сверх- in *comb.* super-, supra-, extra-, over-, preter-, hyper-. **сверхзвезда́**, -ы́, quasar. ~**звуково́й**, supersonic. ~**пла́новый**, over and above the plan.

~при́быль, -и, excess profit, excessive profit. ~проводни́к, -á, superconductor. ~секре́тный, top secret. ~совреме́нный, ultra-modern. ~уро́чный, overtime; уро́чный *sb. pl.* overtime. ~челове́к, -a, superman. ~челове́ческий, superhuman. ~шпио́н, -a, super-spy. ~шта́тный, supernumerary. ~есте́ственный, supernatural, preternatural.

све́рху *adv.* from above; from the top; on the surface; ~ до́низу, from top to bottom.

сверчо́к, -чка́ cricket.

све́рить, -яю *imp.* of све́рить.

свес, -a, overhang. све́сить, -е́шу *perf.* (*imp.* све́шивать) let down, lower; dangle; weigh; ~ся, hang over, overhang; lean over.

свести́, -еду́, -еде́шь; -ёл, -á *perf.* (*imp.* своди́ть) take; take down; take away, lead off; remove, take out; bring together; unite; reduce, bring; cramp, convulse; ~ дру́жбу, ~ знако́мство, make friends; ~ концы́ с конца́ми, make (both) ends meet; ~ на нет, bring to naught; ~ с ума́, drive mad; ~ счёты, settle accounts, get even; у меня́ свело́ но́гу, I've got cramp in the leg.

свет¹, -a (-y), light; daybreak; при ~е + *gen.* by the light of.

свет², -a (-y), world; society, beau monde.

света́ть, -а́ет *imp. impers.* dawn; ~а́ет, day is breaking, it is getting light. свети́лка, -и, attic. свети́ло, -a, luminary. свети́льный, illuminating; ~ газ, coal-gas. свети́ть, -ечу́, -е́тишь *imp.* (*perf.* по~) shine; + *dat.* light; hold a light for, light the way for; ~ся, shine, gleam. светле́ть, -е́ет *imp.* (*perf.* по~, про~) brighten; grow lighter; clear up, brighten up. све́тлый, light; bright; light-coloured; radiant, joyous; pure, unclouded; lucid, clear. светля́к, -á, светлячо́к, -чка́, glow-worm; fire-fly.

свето- in *comb.* light, photo-. свето-боя́знь, -и, photophobia. ~ко́пия, -и, photostat; blueprint; photocopy. ~маскиро́вка, -и, black-out. ~не-проница́емый, light-proof, light-tight, opaque. ~си́ла, -ы, candlepower; rapidity; speed, focal ratio. ~фи́льтр, -a, light filter; (colour) filter. ~фо́р, -a, traffic light(s). ~чувстви́тельный, photosensitive, light-sensitive, photographic, sensitized.

свето́во́й, lighting; luminous; ~ой год, light-year; ~áя рекла́ма, illuminated light sign(s).

све́тский, society, fashionable; genteel, refined; temporal, lay, secular; ~ челове́к, man of the world, man of fashion.

светя́щийся, luminous, luminescent, fluorescent, phosphorescent. свеча́, -и́; *pl.* -и, -е́й, candle; taper; (sparking)-plug. свече́ние, -я, luminescence, fluorescence; phosphorescence. све́чка, -и, candle. свечно́й, candle; ~ ога́рок, candle-end. свечу́, etc.: see свети́ть.

с|ве́шать, -аю *perf.* све́шивать(ся, -аю(сь *imp.* of све́сить(ся. свива́ть, -а́ю *imp.* of свить.

свида́ние, -я, meeting; appointment; rendezvous; date; до свида́ния! goodbye!; назна́чить ~, make an appointment; make a date.

свиде́тель, -я *m.*, -ница, -ы, witness. свиде́тельство, -a, evidence; testimony; certificate; ~ о бра́ке, marriage certificate; ~ о прода́же, bill of sale. свиде́тельствовать, -твую *imp.* (*perf.* за~, о~) give evidence, testify; be evidence (of), show; witness; attest, certify; examine, inspect.

свина́рник -a, свина́рня, -и, pigsty.

свине́ц, -нца́, lead.

свини́на, -ы, pork. свин|о́й, pig; pork; ~áя ко́жа, pigskin; ~о́е са́ло, lard.

свинцо́в|ый, lead; leaden; lead-coloured; ~ые бели́ла, white lead.

свинья́, -и́; *pl.* -и́н, -е́й, -я́м, pig, swine; hog; sow.

свире́ль, -и, (reed-)pipe.

свирепе́ть, -е́ю *imp.* (*perf.* рас~), grow fierce, grow savage. свире́пствовать, -твую *imp.* rage; be rife. свире́пый, fierce, ferocious, savage; violent.

свиса́ть, -а́ю *imp.*, сви́снуть, -ну; -ис *perf.* hang down, droop, dangle; trail.

свист, -а, whistle; whistling; singing, piping, warbling. **свиста́ть**, -ищу́, -и́щешь *imp.* whistle; sing, pipe, warble. **свисте́ть**, -ищу́ *imp.*, **свисту́ть**, -ну *perf.* whistle; hiss. **свисто́к**, -тка́, whistle.

сви́та, -ы, suite; retinue; series, formation.

сви́тер, -а, sweater.

сви́ток, -тка roll, scroll. **с|вить**, совью́ совьёшь; -ил, -а, -о *perf.* (*imp.* also **свива́ть**) twist, wind; **~ся**, roll up, curl up, coil.

свищ, -а́, flaw; (knot-)hole; fistula.

свищу́, etc.: see **свиста́ть**, **свисте́ть**.

свобо́да, -ы, freedom, liberty; **на свобо́де**, at leisure; at large, at liberty; **~ рук**, a free hand; **~ сло́ва**, freedom of speech. **свобо́дно** *adv.* freely; easily, with ease; fluently; loose, loosely. **свобо́дн|ый**, free; easy; vacant; spare; free-and-easy; loose, loose-fitting; flowing; **~ое вре́мя**, free time time off; spare time; **~ый до́ступ**, easy access; **~ый уда́р**, free kick. **свободолюби́вый**, freedom-loving. **свободомы́слие**, -я, free-thinking. **свободомы́слящий**, free-thinking; *sb.* free-thinker.

свод, -а code; collection; arch, vault; **~ зако́нов**, code of laws.

своди́ть, -ожу́, -о́дишь *imp.* of **свести́**.

сво́дка, -и, summary, résumé; report; communiqué; revise. **сво́дный**, composite combined; collated; step-; **~ брат**, step-brother.

сво́дчатый, arched, vaulted.

своево́лие, -я, self-will, wilfulness. **своево́льный**, self-willed, wilful.

своевре́менно *adv.* in good time; opportunely. **своевре́менный**, timely, opportune; well-timed.

своенра́вие, -я, wilfulness, waywardness, capriciousness. **своенра́вный**, wilful, wayward, capricious.

своеобра́зие, -я originality; peculiarity. **своеобра́зный**, original, peculiar, distinctive.

свожу́ etc.: see **своди́ть**, **свози́ть**.

свози́ть, -ожу́ -о́зишь *imp.* of **свезти́**.

свой, своего́ *m.*, **своя́**, свое́й *f.*, **своё**, своего́ *n.*, **свои́** *pl.*, *pron.* one's (own); my his, her, its; our, your, their; **доби́ться своего́**, to get one's own way; **она́ сама́ не своя́**, she is not herself; **он не в своём уме́**, he is not in his right mind. **сво́йственный**, peculiar, characteristic. **сво́йство**, -а, property, quality, attribute, characteristic.

сво́ра, -ы, leash, pair; pack; gang.

свора́чивать, -аю *imp.* of **сверну́ть**, **свороти́ть**. **с|вороба́ть**, -рую *perf.*

свороти́ть, -очу́, -о́тишь *perf.* (*imp.* **свора́чивать**) dislodge, displace, shift; turn, swing; twist, dislocate.

свыка́ться, -а́юсь *imp.*, **свы́кнуться**, -нусь, -ыкся *perf.* get used, accustom oneself.

высока́ *adv.* haughtily; condescendingly. **свы́ше** *adv.* from above; from on high. **свы́ше** *prep.* + *gen.* over, more than; beyond.

свя́занный, constrained; combined, fixed; bound; coupled. **с|вяза́ть**, -яжу́, -я́жешь *perf.*, **свя́зывать**, -аю *imp.* tie together; tie, bind; connect, link; associate; **~ся**, get in touch, communicate; get involved, get mixed up. **связи́ст**, -а, -и́стка, -и, signaller; worker in communication services. **свя́зка**, -и, sheaf, bunch bundle; chord; ligament; copula. **связно́й**, liaison, communication. **свя́зный**, connected, coherent. **связу́ющий**, connecting, linking; liaison. **связь**, -и, *loc.* -и́, connection; causation; link, tie, bond; liaison, association; communication(s); signals; tie, stay, brace, strut; coupling; *pl.* connections, contacts.

святи́лище, -а, sanctuary. **святи́тель**, -я *m.* prelate. **святи́ть**, -ячу́ *imp.* (*perf.* о**~**) consecrate; bless, sanctify. **свя́тки**, -ток *pl.* Christmas-tide. **свя́то** *adv.* piously; religiously; **~ бере́чь**, treasure; **~ чтить**, hold sacred. **свят|о́й**; -ят, -а́, -о holy; sacred; saintly; pious; **~о́й**, **~а́я** *sb.* saint. **свяще́нник**, -а, priest. **свяще́нный**, holy; sacred. **свяще́нство**, -а, priesthood; priests.

с.г. *abbr.* сего́ го́да, of this year.

сгиб, -а, bend. **сгиба́емый**, flexible, pliable. **сгиба́ть**, -а́ю *imp.* of **согну́ть**.

сгла́дить, -а́жу perf., сгла́живать, -аю imp. smooth out; smooth over, soften; ~ся, smooth out, become smooth; be smoothed over, be softened; diminish, abate.

сглупи́ть, -плю́ perf.

сгнива́ть, -а́ю imp., сгнить, -ию́, -иёшь; -ил, -а́, -о perf. rot, decay.

сгнои́ть, -ою́ perf.

сгова́риваться, -аюсь imp., сговори́ться, -рю́сь perf. come to an arrangement, reach an understanding; arrange; make an appointment. сго́вор, -а, agreement, compact, deal; betrothal. сгово́рчивый, compliant, complaisant, tractable.

сгон, -а, driving; herding, rounding-up. сго́нка, -и, rafting, floating. сго́нщик, -а, herdsman, drover; rafter. сгоня́ть, -я́ю imp. of согна́ть.

сгора́ние, -я, combustion; дви́гатель вну́треннего сгора́ния, internal-combustion engine. сгора́ть, -а́ю imp. of сгоре́ть.

с|го́рбить(ся), -блю(сь) perf. сго́рбленный, crooked, bent; hunchbacked.

с|горе́ть, -рю́ perf. (imp. also сгора́ть) burn down; be burnt out, be burnt down; be burned be used up; burn; burn oneself out; ~ от стыда́, burn with shame. сгоряча́ adv. in the heat of the moment; in a fit of temper.

с|гото́вить, -влю perf.

сгреба́ть, -а́ю imp., сгрести́, -ебу́, -ебёшь; -ёб, -ла́ perf. rake up, rake together; shovel away, off.

сгружа́ть, -а́ю imp., сгрузи́ть, -ужу́, -у́зишь perf. unload.

с|группирова́ть(ся), -ру́ю(сь) perf.

сгусти́ть, -ущу́ perf., сгуща́ть, -а́ю imp. thicken; condense; ~ся, thicken; condense; clot. сгу́сток, -тка, clot. сгуще́ние, -я, thickening, condensation; clotting. сгущённый; -ён, -а́, condensed; ~ое молоко́, condensed milk; evaporated milk.

сда́бривать, -аю imp. of сдо́брить.

сдава́ть, слаю́, сдаёшь imp. of сдать; ~ экза́мен, take sit for, an examination; ~ся imp. of сда́ться. сдави́ть, -влю́, -вишь perf., сдавли-

вать, -аю imp. squeeze. сда́вленный, squeezed; constrained.

сда́точн|ый, delivery; ~ая квита́нция, receipt. сда́ть, -ам, -ашь, -аст, -ади́м; -ал, -а́, -о perf. (imp. сдава́ть), hand over; pass; let, let out, hire out; give in change; surrender, yield, give up; deal; ~ бага́ж на хране́ние, deposit, leave, one's luggage; ~ экза́мен, pass an examination; ~ся, surrender, yield. сда́ча, -и, handing over; letting out, hiring out; surrender; change; deal; дать сда́чи, give change; give as good as one gets.

сдвиг, -а, displacement; fault, dislocation; change, improvement. сдвига́ть, -а́ю imp., сдви́нуть, -ну perf. shift, move, displace; move together, bring together; ~ся, move, budge; come together. сдвижно́й, movable.

с|де́лать(ся), -аю(сь) perf. сде́лка, -и, transaction; deal, bargain; agreement. сде́льн|ый, piece-work; ~ая рабо́та, piece-work. сде́льщик, -а, piece-worker. сде́льщина, -ы, piece-work.

сдёргивать, -аю imp. of сдёрнуть.

сде́ржанно adv. with restraint, with reserve. сде́ржанный, restrained, reserved. сдержа́ть, -жу́, -жишь perf., сде́рживать, -аю imp. hold, hold back; hold in check, contain; keep back, restrain; keep; ~ сло́во, keep one's word.

сдёрнуть, -ну perf. (imp. сдёргивать) pull off.

сдеру́, etc.: see содра́ть. сдира́ть, -а́ю imp. of содра́ть.

сдо́ба, -ы, shortening; fancy bread, bun(s). сдо́бн|ый; -бен, -бна́, -о, rich, short; ~ая бу́лка, bun. сдо́брить, -рю perf. (imp. сда́бривать) flavour; spice; enrich.

с|до́хнуть, -нет; сдох perf. (imp. also сдыха́ть) die; croak, kick the bucket.

сдружи́ться, -жу́сь perf. become friends.

сдубли́рованный, bonded.

сдува́ть, -а́ю imp., сду́нуть, -ну perf., сдуть, -у́ю perf. blow away, blow off; crib.

сду́ру adv.: see сдо́хнуть.

сеа́нс, -а, performance; showing, house; sitting.

себестóимость, -и, prime cost; cost (price).

себя́, *dat.*, *prep.* oneself; myself, yourself, himself, etc.; ничего́ себе́, not bad; собóй, in appearance; так себе́, so-so; хорóш собóй, good-looking, nice-looking.

сев, -а sowing.

сéвер, -а, north. сéвернее *adv.* + *gen.* northwards of, to the north of. сéверн|ый, north, northern; northerly; ~ый олéнь, reindeer; ~ое сия́ние, northern lights, aurora borealis. сéверо-востóк, -а, north-east. сéверо-востóчный, north-east, north-eastern. сéверо-зáпад, -а, north-west. сéверо-зáпадный, north-west, north-western. северя́нин, -а; *pl.* -я́не, -я́н, northerner.

севооборóт, -а, rotation of crops.

сегó: see сей. сегóдня (-*vo*-) *adv.* today; ~ вéчером, this evening, tonight. сегóдняшний, of today, today's.

седéльник, -а, saddler. седéльный, saddle.

седéть, -éю *imp.* (*perf.* по~) go grey, turn grey. седéющий, grizzled, greying. седина́, -ы́; *pl.* -ы, grey hairs; grey streak.

седла́ть, -а́ю *imp.* (*perf.* о~) saddle. седлó, -а́; *pl.* сёдла, -дел, saddle. седловина, -ы, arch; saddle; col.

седоборóдый, grey-bearded. седовла́сый, седоволóсый, grey-haired. седóй; сед, -а́, -о, grey; hoary; grey-haired; flecked with white.

седóк, -а́, fare, passenger; rider, horseman.

седьмóй, seventh.

сезóн, -а, season. сезóнник, -а, seasonal worker. сезóнный, seasonal.

сей, сегó *m.*, сия́ *f.*, сиé, сегó *n.*, сий, сих *pl.*, *pron.* this; these; на сей раз, this time, for this once; сегó мéсяца, this month's; сию́ минýту, this (very) minute; at once, instantly.

сейча́с *adv.* now, at present, at the (present) moment; just, just now; presently, soon; straight away, immediately.

сек. etc.: see сечь.

сек. *abbr.* секýнда, second.

секрéт, -а, secret; hidden mechanism; listening post; по ~у, secretly; confidentially, in confidence.

секретáрский, secretarial; secretary's. секретáрша, -и, секретáрь, -я́ *m.* secretary.

секрéтно *adv.* secretly, in secret; secret, confidential; совершéнно ~, top secret. секрéтный, secret; confidential; ~ сотрýдник, secret agent, under-cover agent. сексóт, -а *abbr.* (*sl.*) prison informer, collaborator.

сéкта, -ы, sect. сектáнт, -а, sectarian, sectary. сектáнтство, -а, sectarianism.

секý, etc.: see сечь.

секýнда, -ы, second; сию́ секýнду! (in) just a moment! секундáнт, -а, second; second string. секýнд|ый, second; ~ая стрéлка, second hand. секундомéр, -а, stop-watch.

секциóнный, sectional. сéкция, -и, section.

селёдка, -и, herring. селёдочный, herring, of herring(s).

селéзень, -зня *m.* drake.

селéние, -я, settlement, village.

селитра, -ы, saltpetre, nitre. селитрян|ый, saltpetre; ~ая кислота́, nitric acid.

сели́ть, -лю́ *imp.* (*perf.* по~) settle; ~ся, settle. сели́тебный, built-up; building, development. сели́тьба, -ы; *gen. pl.* -итьб, developed land; built-up area; settlement. селó, -а́; *pl.* сёла, village.

сель- *abbr.* in *comb.* of сéльский, village; country, rural. селькóр, -а, rural correspondent. ~мáг, -а, ~пó *n. indecl.* village shop. ~совéт, -а, village soviet.

сельдь, -и; *pl.* -и, -éй, herring. сельдяно́й, herring.

сéльск|ий, country, rural; village; ~ое хозя́йство, agriculture, farming. сельскохозя́йственный, agricultural, farming.

семафóр, -а, semaphore; signal.

сёмга, -и, salmon; smoked salmon.

семéйный, family; domestic; ~ человéк, married man, family man. семéйство, -а family.

сéмени, etc.: see сéмя.

семени́ть, -ню́ *imp.* mince.

семени́ться, -и́тся *imp.* seed. семенни́к, -а́, testicle; pericarp, seed-vessel; seed-plant. семенно́й, seed; seminal, spermatic.

семери́чный, septenary. семёрка, -и, seven; figure 7; No. 7; group of seven. семерно́й, sevenfold, septuple. се́меро, -ых, seven.

семе́стр, -а, term, semester. семестро́вый, terminal.

се́мечко, -а; *pl.* -и, seed; *pl.* sunflower seeds.

семидесятиле́тие, -я, seventy years; seventieth anniversary, birthday. семидесятиле́тний, seventy-year, seventy years; seventy-year-old. семидеся́тый, seventieth; ~ые го́ды, the seventies. семикра́тный, sevenfold, septuple. семиле́тка, -и, seven-year school; seven-year plan; seven-year-old. семиле́тний, seven-year; septennial; seven-year-old; ~ ребёнок, child of seven, seven-year-old.

семина́рист, -а, seminarist. семина́рия, -и, seminary; training college.

семисо́тый, seven-hundredth. семиты́сячный, seven-thousandth. семиуго́льник, -а, heptagon. семиуго́льный, heptagonal. семина́дцатый, seventeenth. семина́дцать, -и, seventeen. семь, -ми́, -мью́, seven. се́мьдесят, -ми́десяти, -мью́десятью, seventy. семьсо́т, -мисо́т, *instr.* -мьюста́ми, seven hundred. се́мью *adv.* seven times.

семья́, -и́; *pl.* -и, -ей, -ям, family. семьяни́н, -а, family man.

се́мя, -мени; *pl.* -мена́, -мя́н, -мена́м, seed; semen, sperm.

се́ни, -е́й *pl.* (entrance-)hall; (enclosed) porch

сенно́й, hay. се́но, -а, hay. сенова́л, -а, hayloft, hay-mow. сеноко́с, -а mowing, haymaking; hayfield. сенокоси́лка, -и, mowing-machine. сеноко́сный, haymaking.

сенсацио́нный, sensational. сенса́ция, -и, sensation.

сентя́брь, -я́ *m.*, сентя́брьский, September.

се́ра, -ы, sulphur; brimstone; ear-wax.

серва́нт, -а, sideboard.

серви́з, -а, service, set. сервирова́ть, -ру́ю *perf.* and *imp.* serve; ~ стол, lay a table. сервиро́вка, -и, laying; serving, service.

серде́чник, -а, core. серде́чность, -и, cordiality; warmth. серде́чный, heart; of the heart; cardiac; cordial, hearty; heartfelt, sincere; warm, warm-hearted. серди́тый, angry, cross; strong. серди́ть, -ржу́, -рдишь *imp.* (*perf.* рас~) anger, make angry; ~ся, be angry, be cross. се́рдце, -а; *pl.* -а́, -де́ц, heart; в сердца́х, in anger, in a fit of temper; от всего́ се́рдца, from the bottom of one's heart, whole-heartedly. сердцебие́ние, -я, palpitation. сердцеви́дный, heart-shaped; cordate. сердцеви́на, -ы, core, pith, heart.

серебрёный, silver-plated. серебри́стый, silvery. серебри́ть, -рю́ *imp.* (*perf.* по~) silver, silver-plate; ~ся, silver, become silvery. серебро́, -а́, silver. сере́бряник, -а, silversmith. сере́бряный, silver; ~ая сва́дьба, silver wedding.

середи́на, -ы, middle, midst; золота́я ~, golden mean. середи́нный, middle, mean, intermediate. середка, -и, middle, centre.

серёжка, -и, earring; catkin.

се́ренький, grey; dull, drab. сере́ть, -е́ю *imp.* (*perf.* по~), turn grey, go grey; show grey.

сержа́нт, -а, sergeant.

сери́йный, serial; ~ое произво́дство, mass production. се́рия, -и, series; range; part.

се́рный, sulphur; sulphuric; ~ая кислота́ sulphuric acid.

серова́тый, greyish. серогла́зый, grey-eyed.

серп, -а́, sickle, reaping-hook; ~ луны́, crescent moon.

серпанти́н, -а, paper streamer; serpentine road.

серпови́дный, crescent(-shaped).

серсо́ *n. indecl.* hoop.

се́рый, сер, -а́, -о, grey; dull; drab; dim; ignorant, uncouth, uneducated.

серьга́, -и́; *pl.* -и, -рёг, earring.

серьёзно *adv.* seriously; earnestly; in earnest. серьёзный, serious; earnest; grave.

céссия, -и, session, sitting; conference; congress; term.

сестрá, -ы́; *pl.* сёстры, сестёр, сёстрам, sister.

сесть, ся́ду *perf.* (*imp.* сади́ться) sit down; alight, settle, perch; land; set; shrink; + на + *acc.* board, take, get on; ~ за рабóту, set to work; ~ на корáбль, go on board, go aboard; ~ на лóшадь, mount a horse; ~ на пóезд, board a train.

сетевóй, net, netting, mesh. сéтка, -и, net, netting; (luggage-)rack; string bag; grid; co-ordinates; scale.

céтовать, -тую *imp.* (*perf.* по~) complain; lament, mourn.

céточный, net; grid. сетчáтка, -и, retina. сетчáтый, netted, network; reticular. сеть, -и, *loc.* -и́; *pl.* -и, -ей, net; network; circuit, system.

сечéние, -я, cutting; section. сечь, секу́, сечёшь; сек *imp.* (*perf.* вы́~) cut to pieces; beat, flog; ~ся (*perf.* по~ся) split; cut.

сéялка, -и, sowing-machine, seed drill. сéяльщик, -а, сéятель, -я *m.* sower. сéять, -éю *imp.* (*perf.* по~) sow; throw about.

сжáлиться, -люсь *perf.* take pity (над + *instr.*) on.

сжáтие, -я, pressing, pressure; grasp, grip; compression; condensation. сжáтость, -и, compression; conciseness, concision. сжáтый, compressed; condensed compact; concise, brief.

с|жать[1], сожну́, -нёшь *perf.*

сжать[2], сожму́, -мёшь *perf.* (*imp.* сжимáть) squeeze; compress; grip; clench; ~ зу́бы, grit one's teeth; ~ся, tighten, clench; shrink, contract.

с|жечь, сожгу́, сожжёшь; сжёг, сожглá *perf.* (*imp.* also сжигáть), burn; burn up, burn down; cremate.

сживáться, -áюсь *imp.* of сжи́ться. сжигáть, -áю *imp.* of сжечь.

сжим, -а, clip, grip, clamp. сжимáемость, -и, compressibility. сжимáть(ся *imp.* of сжать[2](ся.

сжи́ться, -иву́сь, -ивёшься, -и́лся, -ась

perf. (*imp.* сживáться) с + *instr.* get used to, get accustomed to.

с|жульничать, -аю *perf.*

сзáди *adv.* from behind; behind; from the end; from the rear. сзáди *prep.* + *gen.* behind.

сзывáть, -áю *imp.* of созвáть.

си *n. indecl.* В; te.

сиби́рский, Siberian; ~ кедр, Siberian pine. сибиря́к, -á, сибиря́чка, -и, Siberian.

сигáра, -ы, cigar. сигарéта, -ы, cigarette; small cigar. сигáрка, -и (home-made) cigarette. сигáрный, cigar.

сигнáл, -а, signal. сигнализáция, -и, signalling. сигнализи́ровать, -рую *perf.* and *imp.* (*perf.* also про~) signal; give warning. сигнáльный, signal. сигнáльщик, -а, signaller, signal-man.

сидéлка, -и (untrained) nurse, sick-nurse. сидéние, -я, sitting. сидéнье, -я, seat. сидéть, -ижу́ *imp.* sit; be; fit; плáтье хорошо́ сиди́т на ней, the dress fits her; ~ без дéла, have nothing to do; ~ верхóм, be on horseback; ~ (в тюрьмé), be in prison; ~ на насéсте, roost, perch. си́дка, -и (*sl.*) imprisonment. сидя́чий, sitting; sedentary; sessile.

сиé, etc.: see сей.

си́зый, сиз, -á, -о, dove-coloured, (blue-)grey; bluish, blue.

сий: see сей.

си́ла, -ы, strength; force; power; energy; quantity, multitude; point, essence; *pl.* force(s); в си́ле, in force, valid; в си́лу + *gen.*, on the strength of, by virtue of, because of; имéющий си́лу, valid; не по ~ам, beyond one's powers, beyond one's strength; свои́ми ~ами, unaided; си́лой, by force. силáч, -á, strong man. си́литься, -люсь *imp.* try, make efforts. силов|óй, power; of force. ~óе пóле, field of force. ~ая стáнция, power-station, power-house; ~ая устанóвка power-plant.

силóк, -лкá, noose, snare.

си́лос, -а, silo, silage. силосовáть, -су́ю *perf.* and *imp.* (*perf.* also за~), silo, ensile.

сильно *adv.* strongly, violently; very much, greatly; badly. **сильный**; -лен or -лён, -льна, -о, strong; powerful; intense, keen, hard; он не силён в языках, he is not good at languages; ~ мороз, hard frost.

символ, -а, symbol; emblem; ~ веры, creed. **символизировать**, -рую *imp.* symbolize. **символизм**, -а, symbolism. **символический**, symbolic.

симпатизировать, -рую *imp.* + *dat.* be in sympathy with, sympathize with. **симпатический**, sympathetic. **симпатичный**, likeable, attractive, nice. **симпатия**, -и, liking; sympathy.

симулировать, -рую *perf.* and *imp.* simulate, feign, sham. **симулянт**, -а, malingerer, sham. **симуляция**, -и, simulation, pretence.

симфония, -и, symphony; concordance.

синева, -ы, blue; ~ под глазами, dark rings under the eyes. **синеватый**, bluish. **синеглазый**, blue-eyed. **синеть**, -ею *imp.* (*perf.* по~), turn blue, become blue; show blue. **синий**; синь, -ня, -не, (dark) blue. **синильная кислота**, prussic acid. **синить**, -ню *imp.* (*perf.* под~) paint blue; blue.

синоним, -а, synonym. **синонимика**, -и, synonymy; synonyms.

синоптик, -а, **синоптичка**, -и, weather-forecaster. **синоптика**, -и, weather-forecasting.

синтез, -а, synthesis. **синтезировать**, -рую *perf.* and *imp.* synthesize. **синтетический**, synthetic.

синус, -а, sine; sinus.

синхронист, -а, simultaneous interpreter.

синь[1], -и, blue. **синь**[2]: see **синий**. **синька**, -и, blue, blueing; blue-print. **синяк**, -а, bruise; ~ (под глазом) black eye.

сиплый, hoarse, husky. **сипнуть**, -ну; сип *imp.* (*perf.* о~) become hoarse, become husky.

сирена, -ы, siren; hooter.

сиреневый, lilac(-coloured). **сирень**, -и, lilac.

сироп, -а, syrup.

сирота, -ы; *pl.* -ы *m.* and *f.* orphan.

сиротливый, lonely. **сиротский**, orphan's, orphans'; ~ дом, orphanage.

система, -ы, system; type. **систематизировать**, -рую *perf.* and *imp.* systematize. **систематика**, -и, systematics; classification; taxonomy. **систематический**, **систематичный**, systematic; methodical.

ситец -тца (-тцу), (cotton) print, (printed) cotton; chintz.

сито, -а, sieve; screen; riddle.

ситцевый, print, chintz; chintz-covered.

сия: see **сей**.

сияние -я, radiance; halo. **сиять**, -яю *imp.* shine, beam; be radiant.

СКА (*ska, eská*) *m. indecl. abbr.* спортивный клуб армии, Soviet Army Sports Club.

сказ, -а, tale. lay. **сказание** -я, story, tale, legend lay. **сказать**, -ажу, -ажешь *perf.* (*imp.* говорить) say; speak; tell; как ~, how shall I put it?; сказано — сделано, no sooner said than done; так сказать, so to say. **сказаться**, -ажусь -ажешься *perf.*, **сказываться**, -аюсь *imp.* give notice, give warning; tell (on); declare oneself; ~ больным, report sick. **сказитель**, -я *m.* narrator, story-teller. **сказка**, -и, tale; story; fairy-tale; fib. **сказочник**, -а, story-teller. **сказочный**, fairy-tale; fabulous, fantastic; ~ая страна, fairyland. **сказуемое**, *sb.* predicate.

скакалка, -и, skipping-rope. **скакать**, -ачу -ачешь *imp.* (*perf.* по~) skip, jump; hop; gallop. **скаковой**, race, racing. **скакун**, -а, fast horse, race-horse.

скала, -ы; *pl.* -ы, rock face, crag; cliff; подводная ~, reef. **скалистый**, rocky; precipitous.

скалить, -лю *imp.* (*perf.* о~); ~ зубы, bare one's teeth; grin.

скалка, -и, rolling-pin.

скалолаз, -а, rock-climber. **скалолазание**, -я, rock-climbing.

скалывать, -аю *imp.* of **сколоть**.

скамеечка, -и, footstool; small bench. **скамейка**, -и, bench. **скамья**, -и; *pl.* скамьи, -ей, bench; ~ подсудимых, dock; со шкóльной скамьи́, straight from school.

скандáл, -а, scandal; disgrace; brawl; rowdy scene. **скандали́ст**, -а, brawler; trouble-maker; rowdy. **скандáлить**, -лю *imp.* (*perf.* на~, о~) brawl; kick up a row; shame; ~**ся**, disgrace oneself; cut a poor figure. **скандáльный**, scandalous; rowdy; scandal.

сканди́рование, -я scansion.

скáпливать(ся, -аю(сь *imp.* of скопи́ть-(ся.

скарб, -а, goods and chattels, bits and pieces.

скáред, -а, **скáреда**, -ы *m.* and *f.* miser. **скáредничать**, -аю *imp.* be stingy. **скáредный**, stingy, miserly, niggardly.

скат -а slope, incline; pitch.

с|кáтать, -áю *perf.* (*imp.* скáтывать) roll (up); furl.

скáтерть, -и; *pl.* -и, -éй. table-cloth; ~ю дорóга! good riddance!

скати́ть, -ачý, -áтишь *perf.*, **скáтывать**[1], -аю *imp.* roll down; ~**ся**, roll down; slip, slide. **скáтывать**[2], -аю *imp.* of скатáть.

скафáндр, -а, diving-suit; space-suit.

скáчка, -и, gallop, galloping. **скáчки**, -чек *pl.* horse-race; races, race-meeting; ~ с препя́тствиями, steeple-chase, obstacle-race. **скачкообрáзный**, spasmodic; uneven. **скачóк**, -чкá, jump, leap, bound.

скáшивать, -аю *imp.* of скоси́ть.

сквáжина, -ы, slit, chink; bore-hole; well. **сквáжистый, сквáжный**, porous.

сквер, -а a public garden; square.

скве́рно, badly; bad, poorly. **скверносло́вить**, -влю *imp.* use foul language. **скве́рный**, nasty, foul; bad.

сквози́ть, -и́т *imp.* be transparent; show light through; show through; сквози́т *impers.* there is a draught. **сквозно́й**, through; all-round; transparent; ~ ве́тер, draught. **сквозня́к**, -á, draught. **сквозь** *prep.* + *gen.* through.

скворе́ц, -рцá, starling.

скеле́т, -а, skeleton.

ски́дка, -и, rebate, reduction, discount; allowance(s); со ски́дкой в + *acc.*, with a reduction of, at a discount of. **ски́дывать**, -аю *imp.*, **ски́нуть**, -ну

perf. throw off, throw down; knock off.

ски́петр, -а, sceptre.

скипидáр, -а (-у), turpentine.

скирд, -á; *pl.* -ы́, **скирдá**, -ы́; *pl.* -ы, -áм, stack, rick.

скисáть, -áю *imp.*, **ски́снуть**, -ну; скис *perf.* go sour, turn (sour).

скитáлец -льца, wanderer. **скитáльческий** wandering. **скитáться**, -áюсь *imp.* wander.

скиф, -а, Scythian. **ски́фский**, Scythian.

склад[1], -а, storehouse; depot; store.

склад[2], -а (-у), stamp, mould; turn; logical connection; ~ умá, turn of mind, mentality.

склáдка, -и, fold; pleat, tuck; crease; wrinkle.

склáдно *adv.* smoothly, coherently.

склáдн|ой, folding, collapsible; ~áя кровáть, camp-bed; ~áя ле́стница, steps, step-ladder.

склáдный; -ден, -днá, -о, well-knit, well-built; well-made; rounded, smooth, coherent.

склáдочный, складско́й, storage, ware-housing; складско́е ме́сто, store-room, lumber-room. box-room.

склáдчатый, plicated, folded.

склáдчина, -ы, clubbing; pooling; в склáдчину, by clubbing together. **склáдывать(ся**, -аю(сь *imp.* of сло-жи́ть(ся.

скле́ивать, -аю *imp.*, **с|кле́ить**, -е́ю *perf.* stick together; glue together; paste together; ~**ся**, stick together. **скле́йка**, -и, glueing, pasting, together.

склеп, -а, (burial) vault, crypt.

склепáть, -áю *perf.*, **склёпывать**, -аю *imp.* rivet. **склёпка**, -и riveting.

скло́ка, -и, squabble; row.

склон, -а, slope; на ~е лет, in one's declining years. **склоне́ние** -я, inclination; declination; declension. **склони́ть**, -ню́, -нишь *perf.*, **склоня́ть**, -я́ю *imp.* incline; bend, bow; win over, gain over; decline; ~**ся**, bend, bow; give in, yield; decline, be declined. **скло́нность**, -и, inclination; disposition; susceptibility; bent, penchant. **скло́нный**; -нен, -ннá, -нно, inclined,

склóчник, -а, squabbler, trouble-maker. **склóчный**, troublesome, trouble-making.

склянка, -и, phial; bottle; hour-glass; bell; шесть склянок six bells.

скобá, ы́; pl. -ы, -áм, cramp, clamp; staple; catch, fastening; shackle.

скóбель, -я m. spoke-shave, draw(ing)--knife.

скóбка, -и, dim. of скобá; bracket, (pl.) parenthesis, parentheses; в ~х, in brackets; in parenthesis, by the way, incidentally

скоблить, -облю́, -óблишь imp. scrape, plane.

скóбочный, cramp, clamp staple; shackle; bracket; ~ая машина, stapler, stapling machine.

скóванность, -и, constraint. **скóванный**, constrained; locked; bound; ~ льдáми, ice-bound. **сковáть**, скую́, скуёшь perf. (imp. скóвывать) forge; hammer out; chain; fetter, bind; pin down, hold, contain; лёд сковáл рéку, the river is ice-bound.

сковородá, -ы́; pl. сковороды, -рóд, -áм, **сковорóдка**, -и frying-pan.

скóвывать, -аю imp of сковáть.

сколáчивать, -аю imp., **сколотить**, -очу́, -óтишь perf. knock together; knock up; put together.

сколóть, -лю́, -лешь perf. (imp. скáлывать) split off chop off: pin together.

скольжéние, -я, sliding, slipping; glide; ~ на крылó, side-slip. **скользить**, -льжу́ imp., **скользнуть**, -ну́, -нёшь perf. slide; slip; glide. **скóльзкий**, -зок, -зка́, -о, slippery. **скользя́щий**, sliding; ~ у́зел, slip-knot.

скóлько adv. how much; how many; as far as, so far as; ~ вам лет? how old are you?; ~ врéмени? what time is it? how long?; ~ раз? how many times? **скóлько-нибудь** adv. any.

с|**командовать**, -дую perf. **с**|**комбинировать**, -рую perf. **с**|**комкать**, -аю perf. **с**|**комплектовáть**, -тую perf. **с**|**компрометировать**, -рую perf.

сконфуженный, embarrassed, confused,

abashed, disconcerted. **с**|**конфузить-**(ся, -ужу(сь perf.

с|**концентрировать**, -рую perf.

скончáние, -я, end; passing, death. **скончáться**, -áюсь perf. pass away, die.

с|**копировать**, -рую perf.

скопить, -плю́, -пишь perf. (imp. скáпливать) save, save up; amass pile up; ~ся, accumulate, pile up; gather, collect. **скоплéние**, -я, accumulation; crowd; concentration, conglomeration.

с|**копить**, -ню́ perf. скóпом adv. in a crowd, in a bunch, en masse.

скорбéть, -блю́ imp. grieve, mourn, lament. **скóрбный**, sorrowful, mournful, doleful. **скорбь**, -и; pl. -и, -éй, sorrow, grief.

скорée, **скорéй** comp. of скóро, скóрый; adv. rather, sooner; как мóжно ~, as soon as possible; ~ всегó, most likely, most probably.

скорлупá, -ы́; pl. -ы, shell.

скорня́жный, fur, fur-dressing; ~ое дéло, fur-trade, furrier's art; ~ый товáр, furs. **скорня́к**, -á, furrier, fur--dresser.

скóро adv. quickly, fast; soon.

скоро- in comb. quick-, fast-. **скороварка**, -и, pressure-cooker. **~говóрка**, -и, patter; tongue-twister. **~дум**, -а, quick-witted person. **~писный**, cursive. **скóропись**, -и, cursive; shorthand. **~подъёмность**, -и, rate of climb. **~пóртящийся**, perishable. **~постижный**, sudden. **~спéлый**, early; fast--ripening; premature; hasty. **~стрéльный**, rapid-firing, quick-firing. **~сшивáтель**, -я m. loose-leaf binder; folder, file. **~течный**, transient, short-lived; ~течная чахотка, galloping consumption. **~хóд**, -а, runner, messenger; fast runner; high-speed skater.

с|**коробиться**, -ится perf.

скоростник, -á, high-speed worker, performer. **скоростнóй**, high-speed; ~ автóбус, express bus. **скóрость**, -и; gen. pl. -éй, speed; velocity; rate; в скóрости, soon, in the near future; коробка скоростéй, gear-box.

с|**коротáть**, -áю perf.

скорпион, -а, scorpion; Scorpio.

с|корректировать, -рую *perf.* **с|корчить(ся**, -чу(сь *perf.*

скор|ый; скор, -á, -о, quick, fast; rapid; near; short; forthcoming; ~ом будущем, in the near future; ~ом времени, shortly, before long; на ~ую руку, off-hand, in a rough-and-ready way; ~ый поезд, fast train, express; ~ая помощь, first aid; ambulance service.

скос, -а, mowing. **с|косить**[1], -ошý, -осишь *perf.* (*imp.* also **скáшивать**) mow.

с|косить[2], -ошý *perf.* (*imp.* also скáшивать) squint; be drawn to one side; cut on the cross.

скот, -á, **скотина**, -ы, cattle; livestock; beast, swine. **скотник**, -а, herdsman; cowman. **скотный**, cattle, livestock; ~ двор, cattle-yard, farmyard.

ското- in *comb.* cattle. **скотобойня**, -и; *gen. pl.* -óен, slaughter-house. ~вóд, -а, cattle-breeder, stock-breeder. ~вóдство, -а, cattle-raising, stock-breeding. ~крáдство, -а, cattle-stealing. ~пригóнный двор, stock-yard. ~промышленник, -а, cattle-dealer. ~сбрáсыватель, -я *m.* cow-catcher.

скотский, cattle; brutal, brutish, bestial. **скотство**, -а, brutish condition; brutality, bestiality.

скрасить, -áшу *perf.*, **скрáшивать**, -аю *imp.* smooth over; relieve, take the edge off; improve.

скребóк, -бкá, scraper. **скребý**, etc.: see скрести.

скрéжет, -а, grating; gnashing, grinding. **скрежетáть**, -ещý, -éшешь *imp.* grate, grit; + *instr.* scrape, grind, gnash.

скрéпа, -ы, tie, clamp, brace; counter-signature, authentication.

скрéпер, -а, scraper.

скрепить, -плю *perf.*, **скреплять**, -яю *imp.* fasten (together), make fast; pin (together); clamp, brace; countersign, authenticate, ratify; скрепя сéрдце, reluctantly, grudgingly. **скрéпка**, -и, paper-clip. **скреплéние**, -я, fastening; clamping; tie, clamp.

скрести, -ебý, -ебёшь; -ёб, -лá *imp.* scrape; scratch, claw; ~сь, scratch.

скрестить, -ещý *perf.*, **скрéщивать**, -аю *imp.* cross; interbreed; ~ся, cross, clash; interbreed. **скрещéние**, -я, crossing; intersection. **скрéщивание**, -я, crossing; interbreeding.

с|кривить(ся, -влю(сь *perf.*

скрип, -а, squeak, creak. **скрипáч**, -á, violinist; fiddler. **скрипéть**, -плю *imp.* squeak, creak; **скрипнуть**, -ну *perf.* squeak, creak; scratch. **скрипичный**, violin; ~ ключ, treble clef. **скрипка**, -и, violin, fiddle. **скрипучий**, squeaking, creaking; rasping, scratching.

с|кроить, -ою *perf.*

скрóмник, -а, modest man. **скрóмничать**, -аю *imp.* (*perf.* по~) be (too) modest. **скрóмность**, -и, modesty. **скрóмный**; -мен, -мнá, -о, modest.

скрóю etc.: see скрыть. **скрою́**, etc.: see скроить.

скрýпул, -а, scruple. **скрупулёзный**, scrupulous.

с|крутить, -учý, -ýтишь *perf.*, **скрýчивать**, -аю *imp.* twist; roll; bind, tie up.

скрывáть, -áю *imp.*, **скрыть**, -óю *perf.* hide, conceal; ~ся, hide, go into hiding, be hidden; steal away, escape; disappear, vanish. **скрытничать**, -аю *imp.* be secretive, be reticent. **скрытный**, reticent, secretive. **скрытый**, secret, concealed, hidden; latent.

скряга, -и *m.* and *f.* miser. **скряжничать**, -аю *imp.* pinch, scrape; be miserly.

скýдный; -ден, -днá, -о, scanty, poor; slender, meagre; scant; + *instr.* poor in, short of. **скýдость**, -и, scarcity, poverty.

скýка, -и, boredom, tedium.

скулá, -ы́; *pl.* -ы, cheek-bone. **скулáстый**, with high cheek-bones.

скулить, -лю *imp.* whine, whimper.

скупáть, -áю *imp.* of скупить.

скупéц, -пцá, miser.

скупить, -плю -пишь *perf.* (*imp.* скупáть) buy (up); corner.

скупиться, -плюсь *imp.* (*perf.* по~), pinch, scrape, be stingy, be miserly; be sparing; + на + *acc.* stint, grudge; ~ на дéньги, be close-fisted.

скýпка, -и, buying (up); cornering.

скýпо *adv.* sparingly. скупóй; -п, -á, -о, stingy, miserly, niggardly; inadequate. скýпость, -и, stinginess, miserliness, niggardliness.

скýпщик, -а, buyer(-up); ~ крáденого, fence.

скýрвиться, -влюсь *perf.* (*sl.*) turn informer.

скýтер, -а; *pl.* -á, outboard speed-boat.

скучáть, -áю *imp.* be bored; + по + *dat.* or *prep.* miss, yearn for.

скýченность, -и, density, congestion; ~ населéния, overcrowding. скýченный, dense, congested. скýчивать, -аю *imp.*, скýчить, -чу *perf.* crowd (together); ~ся, flock, cluster; crowd together, huddle together.

скýчный; -чен, -чнá, -о, boring, tedious, dull; bored; мне скýчно, I'm bored.

с|кýшать, -аю *perf.* скушý, etc.: see сковáть.

слабéть, -éю *imp.* (*perf.* о~) weaken, grow weak; slacken, drop. слабинá, -ы́, slack; weak spot, weak point. слабúтель|ый; -ьно, laxative, purgative; ~ое *sb.* purge. слабúть, -ит *imp.* (*perf.* про~) purge, act as a laxative; *impers.* егó слабúт, he has diarrhoea.

слабо- in *comb.* weak, feeble, slight. слабовóлие, -я, weakness of will. ~вóльный, weak-willed. ~дýшный, faint-hearted. ~нéрвный, nervy, nervous; neurasthenic. ~рáзвитый, under-developed. ~сúльный, weak, feeble; low-powered. ~тóчный, low-current; weak-current, low-power. ~ýмие, -я, feeble-mindedness, imbecility; dementia. ~ýмный, feeble-minded, imbecile. ~харáктерный, characterless, of weak character.

слáбый; -б, -á, -о, weak; feeble; slack, loose; poor.

слáва, -ы, glory; fame; name, repute, reputation; rumour; на слáву, wonderfully well, excellently, famously. слáвить, -влю *imp.* celebrate, hymn, sing the praises of; ~ся (+ *instr.*) be famous, famed, renowned, (for) have a reputation (for). слáвный, glorious, famous, renowned; nice, splendid.

славянúн, -а; *pl.* -я́не, -я́н, славя́нка, и,

Slav. славянофúл, -а, Slavophil(e). славя́нский, Slav, Slavonic.

слагáемое *sb.* component, term, member. слагáть, -áю *imp.* of сложúть.

слáдить, -áжу *perf.* с + *instr.* cope with, manage, handle; make, construct.

слáдк|ий; -док, -дкá, -о, sweet; sugary, sugared, honeyed; ~кое мя́со, sweetbread; ~ое *sb.* sweet course. сладострáстник, -а, voluptuary. сладострáстный, voluptuous. слáдость, -и, joy; sweetness; sweetening; *pl.* sweets.

слáженность, -и, co-ordination, harmony, order. слáженный, co-ordinated, harmonious, orderly.

слáнец, -нца shale, slate; schist. сланцевáтый, слáнцевый, shale; shaly, slaty, schistose.

сластёна *m.* and *f.* person with a sweet tooth. слáсть, -и; *pl.* -и, -éй, delight, pleasure; *pl.* sweets, sweet things.

слать шлю, шлёшь *imp.* send.

слащáвый, sugary, sickly-sweet. слáще *comp.* of слáдкий.

слéва *adv.* from (the) left; on, to, the left; ~ напрáво, from left to right.

слёг, etc.: see слечь.

слегкá *adv.* slightly; lightly, gently; somewhat.

след, следá (-y), *dat.* -y; *loc.* -ý; *pl.* -ы́, track; trail, footprint, footstep; trace, sign, vestige. следúть[1], -ежý *imp.* + за + *instr.* watch; track; shadow; follow; keep up with; look after; keep an eye on. следúть[2], -ежý *imp.* (*perf.* на~) leave traces, marks, footmarks, footprints. слéдование, -я, movement, proceeding. слéдователь, -я *m.* investigator. слéдовательно *adv.* consequently, therefore, hence. слéдовать, -дую *imp.* (*perf.* по~), I. + *dat.* or за + *instr.* follow; go after; comply with; result; go, be bound; пóезд слéдует до Москвы́, the train goes to Moscow; II. *impers.* + *dat.* ought, should; be owing, be owed; вам слéдует + *inf.* you should, you ought to; как и слéдовало ожидáть, as was to be expected; как слéдует, properly, well; as it should be; кудá слéдует, to the proper quarter; скóлько с меня́ сле́дует? how much do I owe (you)? сле́дом *adv.* (за + *instr.*) immediately after, behind, close behind. следопы́т, -а, pathfinder, tracker. сле́дственн|ый, investigation, inquiry; ~ая коми́ссия commission (committee) of inquiry. сле́дствие[1], -я, consequence, result. сле́дствие[2], -я, investigation. сле́дующ|ий, following, next; в ~ий раз, next time; на ~ей неде́ле, next week; ~им о́бразом, in the following way. слёжка, -и, shadowing.

слеза́, -ы́; *pl.* -ёзы, -а́м, tear.

слеза́ть, -а́ю *imp.* of слезть.

слези́ться, -и́тся *imp.* water. слезли́вый, tearful, lachrymose. слёзный, tear; lachrymal. слезоточи́вый, watering, running; lachrymatory; ~ газ, tear-gas.

слезть, -зу; слез *perf.* (*imp.* слеза́ть) climb down, get down; dismount, alight, get off; come off, peel.

слепе́нь, -пня́ *m.* gadfly horse-fly.

слепе́ц, -пца́ blind man. слепи́ть[1], -пи́т *imp.* blind; dazzle.

с|лепи́ть[2], -плю́, -пишь *perf.*, слепля́ть, -я́ю *imp.* stick together; mould, model.

сле́пнуть, -ну; слеп *imp.* (*perf.* о~) go blind, become blind. сле́по *adv.* blindly; indistinctly. слеп|о́й; -п, -а́, -о, blind; indistinct; ~ы́е *sb. pl.* the blind.

слепо́к, -пка, cast.

слепота́, -ы́, blindness.

сле́сарь, -я; *pl.* -я́ or -и *m.* metal worker; locksmith.

слёт, -а, gathering, meeting; rally. слета́ть, -а́ю *imp.*, слете́ть, -ечу́ *perf.* fly down; fall down, fall off; fly away; ~ся, fly together; congregate.

слечь, сля́гу, -я́жешь; слёг, -ла́ *perf.* take to one's bed.

сли́ва, -ы, plum; plum-tree.

слива́ть(ся, -а́ю(сь *imp.* of слить(ся. сли́вки, -вок *pl.* cream. сли́вочник, -а, cream-jug. сли́вочн|ый, cream; creamy; ~ое ма́сло, butter; ~ое моро́женое, ice-cream.

сли́зистый, mucous; slimy. слизня́к, -а́, slug. слизь, -и, mucus; slime.

с|линя́ть, -я́ет *perf.*

слипа́ться, -а́ется *imp.*, сли́пнуться, -нется; -и́пся *perf.* stick together.

сли́тно, together, as one word. сли́ток, -тка, ingot, bar. с|лить, со́лью, -льёшь; -ил, -а́, -о *perf.* (*imp.* also слива́ть) pour, pour out, pour off; fuse, merge, amalgamate; ~ся, flow together; blend, mingle; merge, amalgamate.

слича́ть, -а́ю *imp.*, сличи́ть, -чу́ *perf.* collate; check. сличе́ние, -я, collation, checking. сличи́тельный, checking, check.

слия́ние, -я, confluence; blending, merging, amalgamation; merger.

сли́шком *adv.* too; too much.

слова́рный, lexical; lexicographic(al); dictionary. слова́рь, -я́ *m.* dictionary; glossary; vocabulary. слове́сник, -а, -ница, -ы, philologist; student of philology; (Russian) language and literature teacher. слове́сность, -и, literature; philology. слове́сный, verbal, oral; literary; philological. сло́вник, -а, glossary, word-list, vocabulary. сло́вно *conj.* as if; like, as. сло́во, -а; *pl.* -á; word; speech; speaking; address; lay, tale; by the way, by the by; одни́м ~м, in a word. сло́вом *adv.* in a word, in short. словообразова́ние, -я, word-formation. словоохо́тли́вый, talkative, loquacious. словосочета́ние, -я, word combination, word-group, phrase. словоупотребле́ние, -я, use of words, usage. словцо́, -а́; word; apt word, the right word; для кра́сного словца́, for effect, to display one's wit.

слог[1], -а, style.

слог[2], -а; *pl.* -и, -о́в, syllable. слогово́й, syllabic.

слое́ние, -я, stratification. слоё|ный, flaky; ~ое те́сто, puff pastry, flaky pastry.

сложе́ние, -я, adding; composition; addition; build, constitution. сложи́ть, -жу́, -жишь *perf.* (*imp.* класть, скла́дывать, слага́ть) put (together) lay (together); pile, heap, stack; add, add up; fold (up); make up, compose; take off, put down, set down; lay down; сложа́ ру́ки, with arms folded; idle; ~ ве́щи, pack pack up; ~ наказа́ние, remit a punishment; ~ся, form, turn out; take shape; arise; club together, pool one's resources. **слож-носокращённ**|**ый**, acronymic; ~ое сло́во, acronym. **сло́жность**, -и, complication; complexity; в о́бщей сло́жности, all in all, in sum. **сло́жный**, -жен, -жна́, -о, compound; complex; multiple; complicated, intricate; ~ое сло́во, compound (word).

сло́йстый, stratified; lamellar; flaky, foliated; schistose. **сло́ить**, -о́ю imp. stratify; layer; make flaky. **слой**, -я, pl. -и́, -ёв, layer; stratum; coat, coating, film.

слом, -а, demolition, pulling down, breaking up; пойти́ на ~, be scrapped. **с**|**лома́ть(ся**, -а́ю(сь perf. **сломи́ть**, -млю́ -мишь perf. break, smash; overcome; сломя́ го́лову, like mad, at breakneck speed; ~**ся**, break.

слон, -а́, elephant; bishop. **слони́ха** -и, she-elephant. **слоно́в**|**ый**, elephant; elephantine; ~ая кость, ivory.

слою́, etc.: see **сло́ить**.

слоня́ться, -я́юсь imp. loiter (about), mooch about.

слуга́, -и́; pl. -и m. man, (man)servant. **служа́нка**, -и, servant, maid. **служа́щий** sb. e·mployee; pl. staff. **слу́жба**, -ы, serv.ce; work; employment. **служе́бн**|**ый**, service; office; official; work; auxiliary; secondary; ~ый вход, staff entrance; ~ое вре́мя, office hours; ~ое де́ло, official business. **служе́ние**, -я, service, serving. **служи́ть** -жу́. -жишь imp. (perf. по~) serve; work, be employed; be used, do; be in use, do duty; + dat. devote oneself to; ~ доказа́тельством + gen. serve as evidence of; ~ при́знаком, indicate, be a sign of.

с|**лука́вить**, -влю perf. **с**|**лупи́ть**, -плю́ -пишь perf.

слух, -а, hearing; ear; rumour, hearsay; по ~у по ear. **слуха́ч** -а́, monitor. **слухов**|**о́й**, acoustic, auditory, aural; ~о́й аппара́т, hearing aid; ~о́е окно́, dormer (window).

слу́чай, -я, incident, occurrence, event; case; accident; opportunity, chance; ни в ко́ем слу́чае, in no circumstances; по слу́чаю, secondhand;

+ gen. by reason of, on account of; on the occasion of. **случа́йно** adv. by chance, by accident, accidentally; by any chance. **случа́йность**, -и, chance; по счастли́вой случа́йности, by a lucky chance, by sheer luck. **случа́й-н**|**ый**, accidental, fortuitous; chance; casual, incidental; ~ая встре́ча, chance meeting. **случа́ться**, -а́ется imp. **случи́ться**, -и́тся perf. happen; come about, come to pass; befall; turn up, show up; что случи́лось? what has happened? what's up?

слу́шатель, -я m. hearer, listener; student; pl. audience. **слу́шать**, -аю imp. (perf. по~, про~), listen to; hear; attend lectures on; (я) слу́шаю! hello!; very well, very good; yes, sir; ~ся + gen. obey, listen to.

слыть, -ыву́, -ывёшь; -ыл, -а́, -о imp. (perf. про~) have the reputation, be known, be said; pass (+ instr. or за + acc., for).

слыха́ть imp., **слы́шать**, -шу imp. (perf. y~) hear; notice; feel, sense. **слы́шаться**, -шится imp. (perf. по~) be heard, be audible. **слы́шимость**, -и, audibility. **слы́шимый**, audible. **слы́шно** adv. audibly. **слы́шн**|**ый**, audible; ~но predic. impers. (+ dat.) one can hear; it is said they say; нам никого́ не́ было ~но, we could not hear anyone; что ~? what news? any news?

слюда́, -ы́, mica. **слюдяно́й**, mica.

слюна́, -ы́; pl. -и -ей, saliva; spit; pl. slobber, spittle. **слюня́вый**, dribbling, drivelling, slavering.

сля́гу, etc.: see **слечь**.

сля́котный, slushy. **сля́коть**, -и, slush.

см. abbr. смотри́, see, vide.

с.м. abbr. сего́ ме́сяца, this month's, of this month; inst

сма́зать, -а́жу perf., **сма́зывать**, -аю imp. oil, lubricate; grease; smudge; rub over; slur over. **сма́зка**, -и, oiling, lubrication; oil, lubricant; greasing; grease. **сма́зочн**|**ый**, oil; lubricating; ~ое ма́сло, lubricating oil. **сма́зчик**, -а, greaser. **сма́зывание**, -я, oiling, lubrication; greasing; slurring over.

смак, -а (-у), relish, savour. **смакова́ть**, -ку́ю imp. relish, enjoy; savour.

с|маневри́ровать, -рую *perf.*

сма́нивать, -аю *imp.,* смани́ть, -ню́, -нишь *perf.* entice, lure.

с|мастери́ть, -рю́ *perf.* сма́тывать, -аю *imp.* of смота́ть.

сма́хивать, -аю *imp.,* смахну́ть, -ну́, -нёшь *perf.* brush away, off; flick away, off.

сма́чивать, -аю *imp.* of смочи́ть.

сме́жный, adjacent, contiguous, adjoining, neighbouring.

смека́лка, -и, native wit, mother wit; sharpness.

смёл, etc.: see смести́

смеле́ть, -е́ю *imp.* (*perf.* о~), grow bold, grow bolder. сме́ло *adv.* boldly; easily, with ease. сме́лость, -и, boldness, audacity, courage. сме́лый, bold, audacious, courageous, daring. смельча́к, -á, bold spirit; daredevil.

смелю́, etc.: see смоло́ть.

сме́на, -ы, changing, change; replacement(s); relief; shift; change; идти́ на сме́ну + *dat.* take the place of, relieve; ~ карау́ла, changing of the guard. смени́ть, -ню́, -нишь *perf.,* сменя́ть[1], -я́ю *imp.* change; replace; relieve; succeed; ~ся, hand over; be relieved; take turns; + *instr.* give place to. сме́нность, -и, shift system; shiftwork. сме́нный, shift; changeable; ~ое колесо́, spare wheel. сме́нщик, -а, relief; *pl.* new shift. сменя́емый, removable, interchangeable. сменя́ть[2], -я́ю *perf.* exchange.

с|ме́рить, -рю *perf.*

смерка́ться, -а́ется *imp.,* сме́ркнуться, -нется *perf.* get dark.

смерте́льно *adv.* mortally; extremely; terribly; ~ уста́ть, be dead tired. смерте́льный, mortal, fatal, death; extreme, terrible. сме́ртность, -и, mortality, death-rate. сме́ртный, mortal; death; deadly, extreme; ~ая казнь, death penalty; capital punishment; ~ый пригово́р, death sentence. смерть, -и; *gen. pl.* -éй; death; decease; до сме́рти, to death; умере́ть свое́й сме́ртью, die a natural death; ~ как *adv.* awfully, terribly.

смерч, -а, whirlwind, tornado; waterspout; sandstorm.

смеси́тельный, mixing. с|меси́ть, -ешу́, -éсишь *perf.*

смести́, -ету́, -етёшь -ёл, -á *perf.* (*imp.* смета́ть) sweep off, sweep (away).

смести́ть, -ещу́ *perf.* (*imp.* смеша́ть) displace; remove; move; dismiss; ~ся, change position, become displaced.

смесь, -и, mixture; blend, miscellany, medley.

смета́, -ы, estimate.

смета́на, -ы, smetana sour cream.

с|мета́ть[1], -а́ю *perf.* (*imp.* also смёты-вать), tack (together).

смета́ть[2], -а́ю *imp.* of смести́.

сметли́вый, quick, sharp; resourceful.

сме́тный, estimated, budget, planned.

смету́, etc.: see смести́. смётывать, -аю *imp.* of смета́ть.

сметь, -е́ю *imp.* (*perf.* по~) dare; have the right.

смех, -а (-у), laughter; laugh; ~а ра́ди, for a joke, for fun. смехотво́рный, laughable, ludicrous, ridiculous.

сме́шанн|ый, mixed; combined; ~ое акционе́рное о́бщество, joint-stock company. с|меша́ть, -а́ю *perf.,* сме́шивать, -аю *imp.* mix, blend; lump together; confuse, mix up; ~ся, mix, (inter)blend, blend in; mingle; become confused, get mixed up. смеше́ние, -я, mixture, blending, merging; confusion, mixing up.

смеши́ть, -шу́ *imp.* (*perf.* на~, рас~) amuse, make laugh. смешли́вость, -и, risibility. смешли́вый, inclined to laugh, easily amused, given to laughing. смешн|о́й, funny; amusing; absurd, ridiculous, ludicrous; здесь нет ничего́ ~о́го, there's nothing to laugh at, it is no laughing matter; ~о́ *predic.* it is funny; it makes one laugh.

смешу́, etc.: see смеси́ть, смеши́ть.

смеша́ть(ся, -а́ю(сь *imp.* of смести́ть-(ся. смеще́ние, -я, displacement, removal; shifting; shift; drift; bias. смещу́, etc.: see смести́ть.

смея́ться, -éюсь, -е́ешься *imp.* laugh; + над + *instr.* laugh at, make fun of.

смире́ние, -я, humility, meekness. смире́нный, humble, meek. смири́-тельн|ый; ~ая руба́шка, straitjacket. смири́ть, -рю́ *perf.,* смиря́ть, -я́ю *imp.*

restrain subdue; humble; ~ся, submit; resign oneself. **смирно** adv. quietly; ~! attention! **смирный**, quiet; submissive.

смогу́, etc.: see **смочь**.

смола́, -ы́; pl. -ы, resin; pitch, tar; rosin. **смолёный**, resined; tarred; pitched. **смоли́стый**, resinous. **смоли́ть**, -лю́ imp. (perf. вы́~, о~) resin; tar, pitch.

смолка́ть, -а́ю imp., **смо́лкнуть**, -ну; -олк perf. fall silent be silent; cease.

смо́лоду adv. from one's youth.

c|**молоти́ть**, -очу́, -о́тишь perf. c|**молоть**, смелю, смелешь perf.

смоляно́й, pitch, tar. resin.

c|**монти́ровать**, -рую perf.

сморка́ть, -а́ю imp. (perf. вы́~) blow; ~ся, blow one's nose.

сморо́дина, -ы, currants; currant (-bush). **сморо́динный**, currant.

смо́рщенный, wrinkled. c|**мо́рщить(ся**, -щу(сь perf.

смота́ть, -а́ю perf. (imp. сма́тывать) wind, reel; ~ся, hurry (away); go, drop in.

смотр, -а loc. -у́; pl. -о́тры, review, inspection; public showing; произвести́ ~ + dat.. inspect. review; ~ худо́жественной самоде́ятельности, amateur arts festival. **смотре́ть**, -рю́, -ришь imp. (perf. по~) look; see; watch; look through; examine; review, inspect; + за + instr. look after; be in charge of; supervise: + в + acc., на + acc. look on to. look over; + instr. look (like); смотри́(те)! mind! take care!; ~ за поря́дком, keep order; **смотря́** it depends; смотря́ по, depending on, in accordance with; ~ся, look at oneself. **смотри́тель**, -я m. supervisor; custodian keeper. **смотрово́й**, review; observation, inspection, sight.

смочи́ть, -чу́, -чишь perf. (imp. сма́чивать) damp, wet, moisten.

c|**мочь**, -огу́, -о́жешь; смог, -ла́ perf.

c|**моше́нничать**, -аю perf. **смою́**, etc.: see **смыть**.

смрад, -а, stink, stench. **сма́дный**, stinking.

смуглоли́цый, **сму́глый**; -гл, -а́, -о, dark-complexioned; swarthy.

c|**мудри́ть**, -рю́ perf.

сму́та, -ы, disturbance, sedition. **смути́ть**, -ущу́ perf., **смуща́ть**, -а́ю imp. embarrass, confuse; disturb, trouble; ~ся, be embarrassed. be confused. **сму́тный**, vague; indistinct; dim; disturbed, troubled; ~ое вре́мя, Time of Troubles. **смутья́н**, -а, trouble-maker. **смуще́ние**, -я, embarrassment, confusion. **смущённый**; -ён, -а́ embarrassed, confused.

смыва́ть(ся, -а́ю(сь imp. of **смыть(ся**. **смыка́ть(ся**, -а́ю(сь imp. of **сомкну́ть(ся**.

смысл, -а, sense; meaning; purport; point; в по́лном ~е сло́ва. in the full sense of the word; нет ~а, there is no sense, there is no point. **смы́слить**, -лю imp. understand. **смыслово́й**, sense, semantic; of meaning.

смыть, смо́ю perf. (imp. смыва́ть) wash off; wash away; ~ся, wash off, come off; slip away, run away, disappear.

смы́чка, -и. union; linking.

смычо́к, -чка́ bow.

смышлёный, clever. bright.

смягча́ть, -а́ю imp., **смягчи́ть**, -чу́ perf. soften; mollify; ease, alleviate; assuage; palatalize; ~ся, soften, become soft, grow softer; be mollified; relent, relax; grow mild; ease (off).

смяте́ние, -я, confusion, disarray; commotion; приводи́ть в ~, confuse, perturb. c|**мять(ся**, сомну́(сь, -нёшь(ся perf.

снабди́ть, -бжу́ perf., **снабжа́ть**, -а́ю imp. + instr. supply with, furnish with, provide with. **снабже́ние**, -я, supply, supplying, provision.

сна́добье, -я; gen. pl. -ий, drug, concoction.

снару́жи adv. on the outside; from (the) outside.

снаря́д, -а, projectile, missile; shell; contrivance, machine, gadget; tackle, gear. **снаряди́ть**, -яжу́ perf., **снаряжа́ть**, -а́ю imp. equip, fit out; ~ся, equip oneself, get ready. **снаря́дный**, shell, projectile; ammunition; apparatus. **снаряже́ние**, -я, equipment, outfit.

снасть, -и; *gen. pl.* -е́й, tackle, gear; (*pl.*) rigging.

снача́ла *adv.* at first, at the beginning; all over again.

сна́шивать, -аю *imp.* of сноси́ть.

снег, -а (-у); *pl.* -а́, snow.

снеги́рь, -я, bullfinch.

снегово́й, snow. **снегоочисти́тель**, -я *m.* snow-plough. **снегопа́д**, -а, snowfall, fall of snow. **снегосту́пы**, -ов *pl.* snow-shoes. **снегохо́д**, -а, snow-tractor. **снегу́рочка**, -и, Snow-maiden. **снежи́нка**, -и, snow-flake. **сне́жн|ый**, snow; snowy; ~ая ба́ба, snowman. **снежо́к**, -жка́, light snow; snowball.

снести́¹(-сь, -сёшь; ёс, -ла́ *perf.* (*imp.* сноси́ть) take; bring together, pile up; bring down, fetch down; carry away; blow off; take off; demolish, take down, pull down; bear endure, stand, put up with; **~сь**, communicate (с *instr.* with).

с|нести́²(сь, -су́(сь, -сёшь(ся; снёс(ся, -сла́(сь *perf.*

снижа́ть, -а́ю *imp.*, **сни́зить**, -и́жу *perf.* lower; bring down; reduce; **~ся**, descend; come down; lose height; fall, sink. **сниже́ние**, -я, lowering; reduction; loss of height.

снизойти́, -йду́, -йдёшь; -ошёл, -шла́ *perf.* (*imp.* снисходи́ть) condescend, deign.

сни́зу *adv.* from below; from the bottom; ~ доверху, from top to bottom.

снима́ть(ся, -а́ю(сь *imp.* of снять(ся. **сни́мок**, -мка, photograph; print. **сниму́**, etc.: see снять.

сниска́ть, -ищу́ -и́щешь *perf.*, **сни́скивать**, -аю *imp.* gain, get, win.

снисходи́тельность, -и, condescension; indulgence, tolerance, leniency. **снисходи́тельный**, condescending; indulgent, tolerant, lenient. **снисходи́ть**, -ожу́, -о́дишь *imp.* of снизойти́. **снисхожде́ние**, -я, indulgence; leniency.

сни́ться, снюсь *imp.* (*perf.* при~) *impers.* + *dat.* dream: ей сни́лось, she dreamed; мне сни́лся сон, I had a dream.

сно́ва *adv.* again, anew, afresh.

сновиде́ние, -я, dream.

сноп, -а́, sheaf; ~ луче́й, shaft of light.

сноповяза́лка, -и, binder.

снорови́стый, quick, smart, nimble, clever. **сноро́вка**, -и, knack, skill.

снос, -а, demolition, pulling down; drift; wear. **сноси́ть**¹, -ошу́ -о́сишь *perf.* (*imp.* сна́шивать) wear out. **сноси́ть**²(сь -ошу́(сь, -о́сишь(ся *imp.* of снести́(сь. **сно́ска**, -и, footnote. **сно́сно** *adv.* tolerably, so-so. **сно́сный**, tolerable; fair, reasonable.

снотво́рн|ый, soporific; ~ые *sb. pl.* sleeping-pills.

сноха́, -и́ *pl.* -и, daughter-in-law.

сноше́ние, -я, intercourse; relations, dealings.

сношу́, etc.: see сноси́ть.

сня́тие, -я, taking down; removal, lifting; raising; taking; making; ~ ко́пии, copying. **снят|о́й**, ~о́е молоко́, skim milk. **снять**, сниму́, -и́мешь; -я́л, -а́, -о *perf.* (*imp.* снима́ть) take off; take down; gather in; remove; withdraw, cancel; take; make; photograph; ~ запре́т, lift a ban; ~ с рабо́ты, discharge, sack; ~ с учёта, strike off the register; ~ фильм, shoot, make, a film; **~ся**, come off; move off; have one's photograph taken; ~ с я́коря, weigh anchor; get under way.

со: see с *prep.*

со- *pref.* I. of verbs, used instead of с- before и, й, о, before two or more consonants, and before single consonants followed by ь. II. forming *sbs.* and *adjs.*, co-, joint. **соа́втор**, -а, co-author, joint author. **соа́вторство**, -а, coauthorship, joint authorship. **~брат**, -а; *pl.* -ья, -ьев, colleague. **~владе́лец**, -льца, joint owner, joint proprietor. **~владе́ние**, -я, joint ownership. **~вме́стно** *adv.* in common, jointly. **~вме́стный**, joint, combined; ~вме́стное обуче́ние, co-education; ~вме́стная рабо́та, team-work. **~вою́ющий**, co-belligerent. **согражда́н|ин**, -а; *pl.* -а́ждане, -ан, fellow-citizen. **~докла́д**, -а, supplementary report, paper. **~жи́тель**, -я *m.* room-mate, flat-mate; lover. **~жи́тельница**, -ы, room-mate, flat-mate; mistress. **~жи́тельство**, -а, living together, lodging together; cohabitation. **~квартирáнт**, -а, co-tenant, sharer of flat or lodgings. **~насле́дник**, -а, co-heir. **~о́бщник**, -а, accomplice, confederate. **~оте́чественник**, -а, compatriot, fellow-countryman. **~племе́нник**, -а, fellow-tribesman. **~подчине́ние**, -я, co-ordination. **~преде́льный**, contiguous. **~прича́стность** -и, complicity, participation. **~ра́тник**, -а, comrade-in-arms. **~слу́живец**, -вца, colleague, fellow-employee. **~существовáние**, -я, co-existence. **~умы́шленник**, -а, accomplice. **~учени́к**, -á, schoolfellow. **~член**, -а, fellow-member.

собáка, -и, dog; hound. **собáчий**, dog, dog's; canine. **собáчка**, -и little dog, doggie; trigger. **собáчник**, -а, dog-lover.

с|обезья́нничать, -аю perf.

соберу́, etc.: see собрáть.

собе́с, -а abbr. социáльное обеспече́ние, social security (department).

собесе́дник, -а, interlocutor; party to conversation, companion; он ~ забáвный ~, he is amusing to talk to, amusing company.

собирáние, -я, collecting, collection. **собирáтель**, -я m. collector. **собирáтельный**, collective. **собирáть(ся**, -áю(сь imp. of собрáться.

собла́зн, -а, temptation. **соблазни́тель**, -я m. tempter; seducer. **соблазни́тельница**, -ы, temptress. **соблазни́тельный**, tempting; alluring; seductive; suggestive, corrupting. **соблазни́ть**, -ню́ perf., **соблазня́ть**, -я́ю imp. tempt; seduce, entice.

соблюдáть, -áю imp., **со|блюсти́**, -юду́, -дёшь, -юл, -á perf. observe; keep (to), stick to. **соблюде́ние**, -я, observance; maintenance.

собо́й, **собо́ю**: see себя́.

соболе́знование, -я, sympathy, condolence(s). **соболе́зновать**, -ную imp. + dat. sympathize with, condole with.

собо́лий, sable, sableskin(s), sable. **со́боль**, -я; pl. -и or -я́ m. sable.

собо́р, -а, cathedral; council, synod, assembly. **собо́рный**, cathedral; synod, council.

собрáние, -я, meeting; gathering; assembly; collection; ~ сочине́ний, collected works. **со́бранный**, collected; concentrated. **собрáть**, -беру́, -берёшь, -áл, -á, -о perf. (imp. собирáть), gather; collect; pick; assemble, muster; convoke, convene; mount; obtain; poll; prepare, make ready, equip; **~ся**, gather, assemble, muster; be amassed; prepare, make ready, get ready; intend, be about, be going; + с + instr. collect; ~ся с ду́хом, take a deep breath; pluck up one's courage; pull oneself together; ~ся с мы́слями, collect one's thoughts.

со́бственник, -а, owner, proprietor. **со́бственнический**, proprietary; proprietorial, possessive. **со́бственно** adv. strictly; ~ (говоря́), strictly speaking, properly speaking, as a matter of fact. **со́бственнору́чно** adv. personally, with one's own hand. **со́бственнору́чн|ый**, done, made, written, with one's own hand(s); ~ая по́дпись, autograph. **со́бственность**, -и, property; possession, ownership. **со́бственн|ый**, (one's) own; proper; true; natural; internal; в ~ые ру́ки, personal; и́мя ~ое, proper name; ~ой персо́ной, in person. **собы́тие**, -я, event; теку́щие собы́тия, current affairs.

собью́, etc.: see сбить.

сов- abbr. in comb. of сове́т, soviet, Soviet, council; сове́тский, Soviet. **совми́н**, -а, Council of Ministers. **~нарко́м**, -а, Council of People's Commissars. **~нархо́з**, -а (Regional) Economic Council. **~хо́з**, -а, Sovkhoz, State farm.

совá, -ы́; pl. -ы, owl.

совáть, сую́, суёшь imp. (perf. су́нуть) thrust, shove, poke; **~ся**, push, push in; poke one's nose in, butt in.

совершáть, -áю imp. **соверши́ть**, -шу́ perf. accomplish; carry out; perform; commit, perpetuate; complete, conclude; **~ся**, happen; be accomplished, be completed. **соверше́ние**, -я, accomplishment, fulfilment; perpetration, commission. **соверше́нно** *adv.* perfectly; absolutely, utterly, completely, totally. **совершенноле́тие**, -я, majority. **совершенноле́тний**, of age. **соверше́нный**[1], perfect; absolute, utter, complete, total. **соверше́нный**[2], perfective. **соверше́нство**, -а, perfection. **соверше́нствовать**, -твую *imp.* (*perf.* y~) perfect; improve; ~ся в + *instr.* perfect oneself in; pursue advanced studies in.

со́вестливый, conscientious. **со́вестно** *impers.* + *dat.* be ashamed; ему́ бы́ло ~, he was ashamed. **со́весть**, -и, conscience; по со́вести (говоря́), to be honest.

сове́т, -а, advice, counsel; opinion; council; conference; soviet, Soviet; ~ Безопа́сности, Security Council. **сове́тник**, -а, adviser; counsellor. **сове́товать**, -тую *imp.* (*perf.* по~) advise; ~ся с + *instr.* consult, ask advice of, seek advice from. **советове́д**, -а, Sovietologist. **сове́толог**, -а, a Kremlinologist. **сове́тск**|**ий**, Soviet; of soviets; of the Soviet Union; ~ая власть, the Soviet regime; ~кий Сою́з, the Soviet Union. **сове́тчик**, -а, adviser, counsellor.

совеща́ние, -я, conference, meeting. **совеща́тельный**, consultative, deliberative. **совеща́ться**, -а́юсь *imp.* deliberate; consult; confer.

совлада́ть, -а́ю *perf.* с + *instr.* control, cope with.

совмести́мый, compatible. **совмести́тель**, -я *m.* person holding more than one office, combining jobs; pluralist. **совмести́ть**, -ещу́ *perf.*, **совмеща́ть**, -а́ю *imp.* combine; ~ся, coincide; be combined, combine.

сово́к, -вка́, shovel; scoop; dust-pan; садо́вый ~, trowel.

совокупи́ть, -плю́ *perf.*, **совокупля́ть**, -я́ю *imp.* combine, unite; ~ся, copulate. **совокупле́ние**, -я, copulation. **совоку́пно** *adv.* in common, jointly. **совоку́пность**, -и, aggregate, sum total; totality. **совоку́пный**, joint, combined, aggregate.

совпада́ть, -а́ет *imp.*, **совпа́сть**, -аде́т *perf.* coincide; agree, concur, tally.

соврати́ть, -ащу́ *perf.* (*imp.* совраща́ть) pervert, seduce; ~ся, go astray.

со|**вра́ть**, -вру́, -врёшь; -а́л, -а́, -о *perf.* **совраща́ть**(**ся**, -а́ю(сь *imp.* of со|врати́ть(ся. **совраще́ние**, -я, perverting, seducing, seduction.

совреме́нник, -а, contemporary. **совреме́нность**, -и, the present (time); contemporaneity. **совреме́нный**, contemporary, present-day; modern; up-to-date; + *dat.* contemporaneous with, of the time of.

совру́, etc.: see **свить**.

совсе́м *adv.* quite; entirely, completely, altogether; ~ не, not at all, not in the least.

совью́, etc.: see **свить**.

согла́сие, -я, consent; assent; agreement; accordance; accord; concord, harmony. **согласи́ть**, -ашу́ *perf.* (*imp.* соглаша́ть) reconcile; ~ся, consent; agree; concur. **согла́сно** *adv.* in accord, in harmony, in concord; *prep.* + *dat.* in accordance with; according to. **согла́сность**, -и, harmony harmoniousness. **согла́сн**|**ый**[1], agreeable (to); in agreement; concordant; harmonious; быть ~ым, agree (with). **согла́сн**|**ый**[2], consonant, consonantal; ~ое *sb.* consonant.

согласова́ние, -я, co-ordination; concordance; agreement; concord. **согласо́ванность**, -и, co-ordination; ~ во вре́мени, synchronization. **согласова́ть**, -су́ю *perf.*, **согла́совывать**, -аю *imp.* co-ordinate; agree; make agree; ~ся, accord; conform; agree.

соглаша́тель, -я *m.* appeaser; compromiser. **соглаша́тельский**, conciliatory. **соглаша́тельство**, -а, appeasement; compromise. **соглаша́ть**(**ся**, -а́ю(сь *imp.* of согласи́ть(ся. **соглаше́ние**, -я, agreement; understanding; covenant. **соглашу́**, etc.: see **согласи́ть**.

согна́ть, сгоню́, сго́нишь; -а́л, -а́, -о *perf.* (*imp.* сгоня́ть), drive away; drive together, round up.

со|**гну́ть**, -ну́, -нёшь *perf.* (*imp.* also сгиба́ть) bend, curve, crook; ~ся, bend (down), bow (down); stoop.

согрева́ть, -а́ю *imp.*, **согре́ть**, -е́ю *perf.*

warm heat; **~ся**, get warm; warm oneself.

согрешéние, -я, sin, trespass. **со|грешить**, -шу́ *perf.*

содéйствие, -я, assistance, help; good offices. **содéйствовать**, -твую *perf.* and *imp.* (*perf.* also по~) + *dat.* assist, help; further, promote; make for, contribute to.

содержáние, -я, maintenance, upkeep; keeping; allowance; pay; content; matter, substance; contents; plot; table of contents; быть на содержáнии у + *gen.* be kept, supported, by. **содержáнка**, -и, kept woman. **содержáтельный**, rich in content; pithy, sapid. **содержáть**, -жу́, -жишь *imp.* keep; maintain; support; have, contain; **~ся**, be kept; be maintained; be contained. **содержи́мое** *sb.* contents.

со|дра́ть, сдеру́, -рёшь; -áл -á, -о *perf.* (*imp.* also сдира́ть) tear off, strip off; fleece.

содрогáние, -я, shudder. **содрогáться**, -áюсь *imp.*, **содрогну́ться**, -ну́сь, -нёшься *perf.* shudder, shake, quake.

содру́жество, -а, concord, community, commonwealth.

со́евый, soya.

соединéние, -я, joining, conjunction, combination; joint, join, junction; compound; formation. **соединённый**, -ён, -á, united, joint. **соедини́тельный**, connective, connecting; copulative. **соедини́ть**, -ню́ *perf.*, **соединя́ть**, -я́ю *imp.* join, unite; connect, link; combine; ~ (по телефо́ну), put through; **~ся**, join, unite; combine.

сожалéние, -я, regret; pity; к сожалéнию, unfortunately. **сожалéть**, -éю *imp.* regret deplore.

сожгу́ etc.: see **сжечь**. **сожжéние**, -я, burning; cremation.

сожму́ etc.: see **сжать**[2]. **сожну́** etc.: see **сжать**[1]. **сова́ниваться**, -аюсь *imp.* of **созвони́ться**.

созвáть, -зову́, -зовёшь; -áл, -á, -о *perf.* (*imp.* сзыва́ть, созыва́ть) call together; call; invite; summon; convoke, convene.

созвéздие, -я, constellation.

созвони́ться, -ню́сь *perf.* (*imp.* созва́ниваться) ring up; speak on the telephone.

созвýчие, -я, accord, consonance; assonance. **созвýчный**, harmonious; + *dat.* consonant with, in keeping with.

создава́ть, -даю́, -даёшь *imp.*, **создáть**, -áм, -áшь, -áст, -ади́м; со́здал, -á, -о *perf.* create; found, originate; set up, establish; **~ся**, be created; arise; spring up. **создáние**, -я, creation; making; work; creature. **создáтель**, -я *m.* creator; founder, originator.

созерцáние, -я, contemplation. **созерцáтельный**, contemplative, meditative. **созерцáть**, -áю *imp.* contemplate.

сознавáть, -наю́, -наёшь *imp.*, **сознáть**, -áю *perf.* be conscious of, realize; recognize, acknowledge; **~ся**, confess; plead guilty. **сознáние**, -я consciousness; recognition, acknowledgement; admission, confession; прийти́ в ~, recover consciousness; ~ до́лга, sense of duty. **сознáтельность**, -и, awareness, consciousness; intelligence, acumen; deliberation, deliberateness. **сознáтельный**, conscious; politically conscious; intelligent; deliberate.

созову́, etc.: see **созва́ть**. **с|озорнича́ть**, -áю *perf.*

созревáть, -áю *imp.*, **со|зрéть**, -éю *perf.* ripen, mature; come to a head.

созы́в, -а, convocation; summoning; calling. **созыва́ть**, -áю *imp.* of **созва́ть**.

соизво́лить, -лю *perf.*, **соизволя́ть**, -я́ю *imp.* deign, condescend, be pleased.

соизмери́мый, commensurable.

соискáние, -я, competition, candidacy **соискáтель**, -я *m.*, -ница, -ы, competitor, candidate.

сойти́, -йду́, -йдёшь; сошёл, -шла́ *perf.* (*imp.* сходи́ть), go down, come down; descend, get off, alight; leave; come off; pass, go off; + за + *acc.* pass for, be taken for; снег сошёл, the snow has melted; сойдёт и так, it will do (as it is); ~ с доро́ги, get out of the way, step aside; ~ с умá, go mad, go out of one's mind; сошло́ благополу́чно, it went off all right; ~сь, meet; come together, gather; become friends; become intimate; agree; tally; ~сь хара́ктером, get on, hit it off.

сок, -а (-у), *loc.* -у́, juice; sap; в (по́лном) ~у́, in the prime of life. **соковыжима́лка**, -и, juicer, juice-extractor.

со́кол, -а (-у), falcon.

сократи́ть, -ащу́ *perf.*, **сокраща́ть**, -а́ю *imp.* shorten; curtail; abbreviate; abridge; reduce; cut down; dismiss, discharge; lay off; cancel; ~ся, grow shorter; get shorter; decrease, decline; cut down; be cancelled; contract. **сокраще́ние**, -я, shortening; abridgement; abbreviation; reduction, cutting down; curtailment; cancellation; contraction; ~ шта́тов, staff reduction; уво́лить по сокраще́нию шта́тов, dismiss as redundant. **сокращённ|ый**, brief; abbreviated; ~ое сло́во, abbreviation.

сокрове́нный, secret, concealed; innermost. **сокро́вище**, -а, a treasure. **сокро́вищница**, -ы, treasure-house, treasury.

сокруша́ть, -а́ю *imp.*, **сокруши́ть**, -шу́ *perf.* shatter; smash; crush; distress, grieve; ~ся, grieve; be distressed. **сокруше́ние**, -я, smashing, shattering; grief, distress. **сокрушённый**, -ён, -á, grief-stricken. **сокруши́тельный**, shattering; crippling, withering, destructive.

сокры́тие, -я, concealment. **сокры́ть**, -ро́ю *perf.* conceal, hide, cover up; ~ся, hide, conceal oneself.

со|лга́ть, -лгу́, -лжёшь; ~а́л, -á, -о *perf.*

солда́т, -а; *gen. pl.* -а́т, soldier. **солда́тский** soldier's; army.

соле́ние, -я, salting; pickling. **солён|ый**; со́лон, -á, -о, salt; salty; salted; pickled; corned; spicy; hot. **соле́нье**, -я, salted food(s); pickles.

солида́рность, -и, solidarity; collective (joint) responsibility. **солида́рный**, at one, in sympathy; collective, joint, solidary. **соли́дность**, -и, solidity; reliability. **соли́дн|ый**, solid; strong, sound; reliable; respectable; sizeable;

~ый во́зраст, middle age; челове́к ~ых лет, a middle-aged man.

соли́ст, -а, **соли́стка**, -и, soloist.

соли́ть, -лю́, со́ли́шь *imp.* (*perf.* по~) salt; pickle, corn.

со́лнечн|ый, sun; solar; sunny; ~ый свет, sunlight, sunshine; ~ый уда́р, sunstroke; ~ые часы́, sundial. со́лнце (-он-), -а, sun. **солнцепёк**, -а; на ~e, right in the sun, in the full blaze of the sun. **солнцестоя́ние**, -я, solstice.

солове́й, -вья́, nightingale. **соловьи́ный**, nightingale's.

со́лод, -а (-у), malt.

соло́дка, -и, liquorice. **соло́дковый**, liquorice.

соло́ма, -ы, straw; thatch. **соло́менн|ый**, straw; straw-coloured; ~ая вдова́, grass widow; ~ая кры́ша, thatch, thatched roof. **соло́минка**, -и, straw.

со́лон, etc.: see **солёный**. **солони́на**, -ы, salted beef, corned beef. **соло́нка**, -и, salt-cellar. **солонча́к**, -á, saline soil; *pl.* salt marshes. **соль¹**, -и; *pl.* -и, -е́й, salt.

соль², *n. indecl.* G; sol, soh.

со́льный, solo.

со́лью, etc.: see **слить**.

соляно́й, соля́ный, salt, saline; соля́ная кислота́, hydrochloric acid.

со́мкнутый, close; ~ строй, close order. **сомкну́ть**, -ну́, -нёшь *perf.* (*imp.* смыка́ть) close; ~ся, close, close up.

сомнева́ться, -а́юсь *imp.* doubt; have doubts; question; worry; не ~ в + *prep.* have no doubts of. **сомне́ние**, -я, doubt; uncertainty; без сомне́ния, without doubt, undoubtedly. **сомни́тельн|ый**, doubtful, questionable; dubious; equivocal; ~o, it is doubtful, it is open to question.

сомну́, etc.: see **смять**.

сон, сна, sleep; dream; ви́деть во сне, dream, dream about. **сонли́вость**, -и, sleepiness, drowsiness; somnolence. **сонли́вый**, sleepy, drowsy; somnolent. **со́нный**, sleepy, drowsy; somnolent; slumberous; sleeping, soporific.

соображ́ать, -а́ю *imp.*, **сообрази́ть**, -ажу́ *perf.* consider, ponder, think out;

weigh; understand, grasp; think up, arrange; have a quick one, have a round of drinks. **сообрази́тельный,** quick-witted, quick, sharp, bright.

сообра́зный с + *instr.* conformable to, in conformity with, consistent with. **сообразова́ть,** -зу́ю *perf.* and *imp.* conform, make conformable; adapt; ~ся, conform, adapt oneself.

сообща́ *adv.* together, jointly. **сообща́ть,** -а́ю *imp.,* **сообщи́ть,** -щу́ *perf.* communicate, report, announce; impart; + *dat.* inform of, tell that. **сообще́ние,** -я, communication report; information; announcement; connection.

сооруди́ть, -ужу́ *perf.,* **сооружа́ть,** -а́ю *imp.* build erect. **сооруже́ние,** -я, building; erection; construction; structure.

соотве́тственно *adv.* accordingly, correspondingly; *prep.* + *dat.* according to, in accordance with, in conformity with, in compliance with. **соотве́тственный,** corresponding. **соотве́тствие,** -я, accordance, conformity, correspondence. **соотве́тствовать,** -твую *imp.* correspond, conform, be in keeping. **соотве́тствующий,** corresponding; proper, appropriate, suitable.

сопе́рник, -а, rival. **сопе́рничать,** -аю *imp.* be rivals; compete, vie. **сопе́рничество,** -а, rivalry.

сопе́ть, -плю́ *imp.* breathe heavily; sniff; snuffle; huff and puff.

со́пка, -и, knoll, hill, mound.

сопли́вый, snotty.

сопостави́мый, comparable. **сопоста́вить,** -влю *perf.,* **сопоставля́ть,** -я́ю *imp.* compare. **сопоставле́ние,** -я, comparison.

соприкаса́ться, -а́юсь *imp.,* **соприкосну́ться,** -ну́сь, -нёшься *perf.* adjoin, be contiguous (to); come into contact. **соприкоснове́ние,** -я, contiguity; contact.

сопроводи́тель, -я *m.* escort. **сопроводи́тельный** accompanying. **сопроводи́ть,** -ожу́ *perf.,* **сопровожда́ть,** -а́ю *imp.* accompany; escort. **сопровожде́ние,** -я, accompaniment; escort.

сопротивле́ние, -я, resistance; opposition. **сопротивля́ться,** -я́юсь *imp.* + *dat.* resist, oppose.

сопу́тствовать, -твую *imp.* + *dat.* accompany.

сопью́сь, etc.: see спи́ться.

сор, -а (-у), litter, dust, rubbish.

соразме́рить, -рю *perf.,* **соразмеря́ть,** -я́ю *imp.* proportion, balance, match. **соразме́рный,** proportionate, commensurate.

сорва́ть, -ву́, -вёшь; -а́л, -а́, -о *perf.* (*imp.* срыва́ть) tear off, away, down; break off; pick, pluck; get, extract; break; smash, wreck, ruin, spoil; vent; ~ся, break away, break loose; fall, come down; fall through, fall to the ground, miscarry; ~ с ме́ста, dart off; ~ с пе́тель, come off its hinges.

с|организова́ть, -зу́ю *perf.*

соревнова́ние, -я, competition; contest; tournament; event; emulation. **соревнова́ться,** -ну́юсь *imp.* compete, contend. **соревну́ющийся** *sb.* competitor, contestant, contender.

сори́ть, -рю́ *imp.* (*perf.* на~) + *acc.* or *instr.* litter; throw about. **со́р|ный,** dust, rubbish, refuse; ~ая трава́, weed, weeds. **сорня́к,** -а́, weed.

со́рок, -а́, forty.

соро́ка, -и, magpie.

сороков|о́й, fortieth; ~ы́е го́ды, the forties.

соро́чка, -и, shirt; blouse; shift.

сорт, -а; *pl.* -а́, grade, quality; brand; sort, kind, variety. **сортирова́ть,** -ру́ю *imp.* (*perf.* рас~) sort, assort, grade, size. **сортиро́вка,** -и, sorting, grading, sizing. **сортиро́вочный,** sorting; ~ая *sb.* marshalling-yard. **сортиро́вщик,** -а, sorter. **со́ртность,** -и, grade, quality. **со́ртный,** of high quality. **сортово́й,** high-grade, of high quality.

соса́ть, -су́, -сёшь *imp.* suck.

со|сва́тать, -аю *perf.*

сосе́д, -а; *pl.* -и, neighbour. **сосе́дний,** neighbouring; adjacent, next; ~ дом, the house next door. **сосе́дский,** neighbours', neighbouring, next-door. **сосе́дство,** -а, neighbourhood, vicinity.

соси́ска, -и, sausage; frankfurter.

со́ска, -и, (baby's) dummy.

соска́кивать, -аю *imp.* of соскочи́ть.

соска́льзывать, -аю *imp.*, соскользну́ть, -ну, -нёшь *perf.* slide down, glide down; slip off, slide off.

соскочи́ть, -чу́, -чишь *perf.* (*imp.* соска́кивать) jump off, leap off; jump down, leap down; come off; vanish suddenly.

соску́читься, -чусь *perf.* get bored, be bored; ~ по, miss.

сослага́тельный, subjunctive.

сосла́ть, сошлю́, -лёшь *perf.* (*imp.* ссыла́ть) exile, banish, deport; ~ся на + *acc.* refer to, allude to; cite, quote; plead, allege.

сосло́вие, -я, estate; corporation, professional association.

сосна́, -ы́; *pl.* -ы, -сен, pine(-tree). сосно́вый, -ая, pine; deal.

сосну́ть, -ну́, -нёшь *perf.* have a nap.

сосо́к, -ска́ nipple, teat.

сосредото́ченность, -и, concentration. сосредото́ченный, concentrated. сосредото́чивать, -аю *imp.*, сосредото́чить, -чу *perf.* concentrate; focus; ~ся, concentrate.

соста́в, -а, composition, make-up; structure; compound; staff; personnel; membership; strength; train; в ~е + *gen.* numbering, consisting of, amounting to; в по́лном ~е, with its full complement; in, at, full strength; in a body. состави́тель, -я *m.* compiler, author. соста́вить, -влю *perf.*, составля́ть, -я́ю *imp.* put together; make (up); compose; draw up; compile; work out; form; construct; be, constitute; amount to, total; ~ в сре́днем, average; ~ся, form, be formed, come into being. составно́й, compound, composite; sectional; component, constituent.

со|ста́рить(ся, -рю(сь *perf.*

состоя́ние, -я, state, condition; position; status; fortune; в состоя́нии + *inf.* able to, in a position to. состоя́тельный, solvent; well-off, well-to-do; well-grounded. состоя́ть, -ою *imp.* be; + из + *gen.* consist of, comprise, be made up of; + в + *prep.* consist in, lie in, be; ~ в до́лжности + *gen.* occupy the post of. состоя́ться, -ои́тся *perf.* take place.

сострада́ние, -я, compassion, sympathy. сострада́тельный, compassionate, sympathetic.

с|остри́ть, -рю́ *perf.* со|стря́пать, -аю *perf.*

со|стыкова́ть, -у́ю *perf.*, состыко́вывать, -аю *imp.* dock; ~ся, dock.

состяза́ние, -я, competition, contest; match; уча́стник состяза́ния, competitor. состяза́ться, -а́юсь *imp.* compete, contend.

сосу́д, -а, vessel.

сосу́лька, -и, icicle.

со|счита́ть, -а́ю *perf.* сот; see сто. со|твори́ть, -рю́ *perf.*

со́тенная *sb.* hundred-rouble note.

со|тка́ть, -ку́, -кёшь; -а́л, -ала́, -о *perf.*

со́тня, -и; *gen. pl.* -тен, a hundred.

сото́видный, honeycomb. со́товый, honeycomb; ~ мёд, honey in the comb.

сотру́, etc.: see стере́ть.

сотру́дник, -а, collaborator; employee, assistant, official; contributor. сотру́дничать, -аю *imp.* collaborate; + в + *prep.* contribute to. сотру́дничество, -а, collaboration; co-operation.

сотряса́ть, -а́ю *imp.*, сотрясти́, -су́, -сёшь; -я́с, -ла́ *perf.* shake; ~ся, shake, tremble. сотрясе́ние, -я, shaking; concussion.

со́ты, -ов *pl.* honeycomb; мёд в со́тах, honey in the comb.

со́тый, hundredth.

со́ус, -а (-у), sauce; gravy; dressing.

соуча́стие, -я, participation, taking part; complicity. соуча́стник, -а, partner; participant; accessory, accomplice.

соха́, -и́; *pl.* -и, (wooden) plough.

со́хнуть, -ну; сох *imp.* (*perf.* вы~, за~, про~) dry, get dry; become parched; wither.

сохране́ние, -я, preservation; conservation; care, custody, charge, keeping; retention. сохрани́ть, -ню́ *perf.*, сохраня́ть, -я́ю *imp.* preserve, keep; keep safe; retain, reserve; ~ся, remain (intact); last out, hold out; be preserved. сохра́нность, -и, safety, undamaged state; safe-keeping. сохра́нный, safe.

соц- *abbr.* in *comb.* of социа́льный, social; социалисти́ческий, socialist. **соцреали́зм**, -а, socialist realism. **~соревнова́ние**, -я, socialist emulation. **~стра́х**, -а, social insurance.

социа́л-демокра́т, -а, Social Democrat. **социа́л-демократи́ческий**, Social-Democratic. **социализа́ция**, -и, socialization. **социализи́ровать**, -рую *perf.* and *imp.* socialize. **социали́ст**, -а, socialist. **социалисти́ческий**, socialist. **социа́льн|ый**, social; ~ое обеспече́ние, social security; ~ое положе́ние, social status; ~ое страхова́ние, social insurance. **социо́лог**, -а, sociologist.

соч- *abbr.* сочине́ния, works.

сочета́ние, -я, combination. **сочета́ть**, -а́ю *perf.* and *imp.* combine; + с + *instr.* go with, harmonize with; match; ~ бра́ком, marry; **~ся**, combine; harmonize; match; ~ся бра́ком, be married.

сочине́ние, -я, composition; work; essay; co-ordination. **сочини́ть**, -ню́ *perf.*, **сочиня́ть**, -я́ю *imp.* compose; write; make up, fabricate.

сочи́ться, -и́тся *imp.* ooze (out), trickle; ~ кро́вью, bleed.

сочлени́ть, -ню́ *perf.*, **сочленя́ть**, -я́ю *imp.* join, couple.

со́чн|ый, -чен, -чна́, -о, juicy; succulent; rich; lush.

сочту́, etc.: see счесть.

сочу́вственный, sympathetic. **сочу́вствие**, -я, sympathy. **сочу́вствовать**, -твую *imp.* + *dat.* sympathize with, feel for.

сошёл, etc.: see сойти́. **сошлю́**, etc.: see сосла́ть. **сошью́**, etc.: see сшить.

сощу́ривать, -аю *imp.*, **сощу́рить**, -рю *perf.* screw up, narrow; **~ся**, screw up one's eyes; narrow.

сою́з[1], -а, union; alliance; agreement; league. **сою́з**[2], -а, conjunction. **сою́зник**, -а, ally. **сою́зный**, allied; of the (Soviet) Union.

СП (*espé*) *m.* indecl. *abbr.* Се́верный по́люс, North Pole.

спад, -а, slump, recession; abatement. **спада́ть**, -а́ет *imp.* of спасть.

спа́ивать, -аю *imp.* of спая́ть, спои́ть.

спа́йка, -и, soldered joint; solidarity, unity.

с|пали́ть, -лю́ *perf.*

спа́льник, -а, sleeping-bag. **спа́льн|ый**, sleeping; ~ый ваго́н, sleeper, sleeping-car; ~ое ме́сто, berth, bunk. **спа́льня**, -и; *gen. pl.* -лен, bedroom; bedroom suite.

спа́ржа, -и, asparagus.

спартакиа́да, -ы, sports, sports meeting.

спа́рывать, -аю *imp.* of споро́ть.

спасе́ние, -я, rescue, life-saving. **спаса́тельн|ый**, rescue, life-saving; ~ый круг, lifebuoy; ~ый по́яс, life-belt; ~ая экспеди́ция, rescue party. **спаса́ть(ся**, -а́ю(сь *imp.* of спасти́(сь. **спасе́ние**, -я, rescuing, saving; rescue; escape; salvation. **спаси́бо**, thanks; thank you. **спаси́тель**, -я *m.* rescuer, saver; saviour. **спаси́тельный**, saving; of rescue, of escape; salutary.

с|пасова́ть, -су́ю *perf.*

спасти́, -су́, -сёшь; спас, -ла́ *perf.* (*imp.* спаса́ть) save; rescue; **~сь**, save oneself, escape; be saved.

спасть, -адёт *perf.* (*imp.* спада́ть) fall (down); abate.

спать, сплю; -ал, -а́, -о *imp.* sleep, be asleep; лечь ~, go to bed; пора́ ~, it is bedtime.

спа́янность, -и, cohesion, unity; solidarity. **спа́янный**, united. **спая́ть**, -я́ю *perf.* (*imp.* спа́ивать) solder together, weld; unite, knit together.

спекта́кль, -я *m.* performance.

спектр, -а, spectrum.

спекули́ровать, -рую *imp.* speculate; profiteer; gamble; + на + *prep.* gamble on, reckon on; profit by. **спекуля́нт**, -а, speculator; profiteer. **спекуля́ция**, -и, speculation; profiteering; gamble.

с|пелена́ть, -а́ю *perf.*

спелео́лог, -а, caver, pot-holer.

спе́лый, ripe.

спе́рва *adv.* at first; first.

спе́реди *adv.* in front at the front, from the front; *prep.* + *gen.* (from) in front of.

спёртый, close, stuffy.

спеси́вый, arrogant, haughty, lofty. спесь, -и, arrogance, haughtiness, loftiness.

спеть¹, -е́ет *imp.* (*perf.* по~) ripen.

с|петь², спою́, споёшь *perf.*

спец, -еца́; *pl.* -ецы́, -ев or -о́в, *abbr.* specialist, expert, authority.

спец- *abbr.* in *comb.* of специа́льный, special. спецко́р, -a, special correspondent. ~ ку́рс, -a, special course of lectures. ~ оде́жда, -ы, working clothes, protective clothing; overalls.

специализи́роваться, -руюсь *perf.* and *imp.* specialize. специали́ст, -a, specialist, expert, authority. специа́льность, -и, speciality, special interest; profession; trade. специа́льный, special; specialist; ~ те́рмин, technical term.

специ́фика, -и, specific character. специфи́ческий, specific.

спецо́вка, -и, protective clothing, working clothes; overall(s).

спеши́ть, -шу́ *imp.* (*perf.* по~), hurry, be in a hurry; make haste, hasten; hurry up; be fast.

спе́шка, -и, hurry, haste, rush. спе́шн|ый, urgent, pressing; ~ый зака́з, rush order; ~ая по́чта, express delivery.

спива́ться, -а́юсь *imp.* of спи́ться.

с|пи́ки́ровать, -рую *perf.*

спи́ливать, -аю *imp.*, спили́ть, -лю́, -лишь *perf.* saw down; saw off.

спина́, -ы́; *acc.* -у; *pl.* -ы, back. спи́нка, -и, back. спинно́й, spinal; ~ мозг, spinal cord; ~ хребе́т, spinal column.

спирт, -a (-у), alcohol, spirit(s). спиртн|о́й, spirituous; ~ые напи́тки, spirits; ~ое *sb.* spirits. спирто́вка, -и, spirit-stove. спиртово́й, spirit, spirituous.

списа́ть, -ишу́, -и́шешь *perf.*, спи́сывать, -аю *imp.* copy; crib; write off; ~ся, exchange letters. спи́сок, -ска, list; roll; record; manuscript copy; ~ избира́телей, voters' list, electoral roll; ~ уби́тых и ра́неных, casualty list.

спи́ться, спою́сь, -ьёшься *perf.*, спива́ться *perf.* (*imp.* спива́ться) take to drink, become a drunkard.

спи́хивать, -аю *imp.*, спихну́ть, -ну́, -нёшь *perf.* push aside; push down.

спи́ца, -ы, knitting-needle; spoke.

спи́чечн|ый, match; ~ая коро́бка, match-box. спи́чка, -и, match.

спишу́ etc.: see списа́ть.

сплав¹, -a, floating, rafting. сплав², -a, alloy. сплавля́ть¹, -влю *perf.* сплавля́ть¹, -я́ю *imp.* float; raft; get rid of. сплавля́ть², -влю *perf.*, сплавля́ть², -я́ю *imp.* alloy; ~ся, fuse, coalesce.

с|плани́ровать, -рую *perf.* спла́чивать-(ся, -аю(сь *imp.* of сплоти́ть(ся.

сплёвывать, -аю *imp.* of сплю́нуть.

с|плести́, -ету́, -етёшь; -ёл, -а́ *perf.*, сплета́ть, -а́ю *imp.* weave; plait; interlace. сплете́ние, -я, interlacing; plexus.

спле́тник, -a, -ница, -ы, gossip, scandal-monger. спле́тничать, -аю *imp.* (*perf.* на~) gossip, tittle-tattle; talk scandal. спле́тня, -и; *gen. pl.* -тен, gossip, scandal.

сплоти́ть, -очу́ *perf.* (*imp.* спла́чивать) join; unite, rally; ~ ряды́, close the ranks; ~ся, unite, rally; close the ranks. сплочённость, -и, cohesion, unity. сплочённый, -ён, -а́, united, firm; unbroken.

сплошн|о́й, solid; all-round, complete; unbroken, continuous; sheer, utter, unreserved. сплошь *adv.* all over; throughout; without a break; completely, utterly; without exception; ~ да ря́дом, nearly always; pretty often.

с|плутова́ть, -ту́ю *perf.*

сплыва́ть, -а́ет *imp.*, сплыть, -ывёт; -ыл, -á, -о *perf.* sail down, float down; be carried away; overflow, run over; бы́ло да сплы́ло those were the days; it's all over; ~ся, run (together), merge, blend.

сплю́: see спать.

сплю́нуть, -ну *perf.* (*imp.* сплёвывать) spit; spit out.

сплю́щенный, flattened out. сплю́щивать, -аю *imp.*, сплю́щить, -щу *perf.* flatten; ~ся, become flat.

с|пляса́ть, -яшу́, -я́шешь *perf.*

сподви́жник, -a, comrade-in-arms.

спои́ть, -ою́, -о́ишь *perf.* (*imp.* спа́ивать) accustom to drinking, make a drunkard of.

спокойн|ый, quiet; calm, tranquil; placid; serene; composed; comfortable; ~ой ночи! good night! спокойствие, -я, quiet; tranquillity; calm, calmness; order; composure, serenity.

сползаскивать, -аю *imp.* of сползнуть.

сползать. -аю *imp.*, сползти, -зу, -зёшь, -олз, -ла *perf.* climb down; slip (down); fall away.

сполна́ *adv.* completely, in full.

сполоснуть, -ну, -нёшь *perf.* (*imp.* споласкивать) rinse.

спор, -а (-у), argument; controversy; debate; dispute. спо́рить, -рю *imp.* (*perf.* по~) argue; dispute; debate; bet, have a bet. спо́рный, disputable, debatable, questionable; disputed, at issue; ~ вопрос, moot point, vexed question; ~ мяч, jump ball; held ball.

спороть, -рю́, -решь *perf.* (*imp.* спарывать) rip off.

спорт, -а, sport sports; лы́жный ~, skiing; парашю́тный ~, parachute-jumping. спорти́вный, sports; ~ый зал, gymnasium; ~ая площа́дка, sports ground, playing-field; ~ые состяза́ния, sports. спортсме́н, -а, спортсме́нка, -и, athlete player.

спо́рый, -ор, -а́, -о, successful, profitable; skilful, efficient.

спо́соб, -а, way, manner, method; mode; means; ~ употребле́ния directions for use; таки́м ~ом, in this way. спосо́бность, -и, ability, talent, aptitude, flair; capacity. спосо́бный, able; talented, gifted, clever; capable. спосо́бствовать, -твую *imp.* (*perf.* по~) + *dat.* assist; be conducive to, further, promote, make for.

споткну́ться, -ну́сь, -нёшься *perf.*, спотыка́ться, -а́юсь *imp.* stumble; get stuck, come to a stop.

спохвати́ться, -ачу́сь, -а́тишься *perf.*, спохва́тываться, -аюсь *imp.* remember suddenly.

спою́, etc.: see спеть, спойть.

спра́ва *adv.* to the right.

справедли́вость, -и, justice; equity; fairness; truth, correctness. справедли́вый, just; equitable, fair; justified.

спра́вить, -влю *perf.*, справля́ть, -я́ю *imp.* celebrate. спра́виться¹, -влюсь

perf. справля́ться, -я́юсь *imp.* с + *instr.* cope with, manage; deal with.

спра́виться², -влюсь *perf.*, справля́ться, -я́юсь *imp.* ask, inquire; inform oneself; ~ в словаре́, consult a dictionary. спра́вка, -и, information; reference; certificate; навести́ спра́вку, inquire; наводи́ть спра́вку, make inquiries. справочник, -а, reference-book, handbook, guide, directory. спра́вочный, inquiry; information; ~ая кни́га, reference-book, handbook.

спра́шивать(ся, -аю(сь *imp.* of спроси́ть(ся. с|провоци́ровать, -рую *perf.* с|проекти́ровать, -рую *perf.*

спрос, -а (-у), demand; asking; без ~у, without asking leave, without permission; по́льзоваться (больши́м) ~ом, be in (great) demand; ~ на + *acc.* demand for, run on. спроси́ть, -ошу́, -о́сишь *perf.* (*imp.* спра́шивать) ask (for); inquire; ask to see; + с + *gen.* make answer for, make responsible for; ~ся, ask permission.

спросо́нок *adv.* (being) only half-awake.

спры́гивать, -аю *imp.*, спры́гнуть, -ну *perf.* jump off, jump down.

спры́скивать, -аю *imp.*, спры́снуть, -ну *perf.* sprinkle.

спряга́ть, -а́ю *imp.* (*perf.* про~) conjugate; ~ся, be conjugated. спряже́ние, -я, conjugation.

с|прясть, -яду́, -ядёшь; -ял, -яла́, -о *perf.* с|пря́тать(ся, -ячу(сь *perf.*

спу́гивать, -аю *imp.*, спугну́ть, -ну́, -нёшь *perf.* frighten off, scare off.

спуртова́ть, -ту́ю *perf.* and *imp.* spurt.

спуск, -а, lowering, hauling down; descent; descending; landing; release; draining; slope. спуска́ть, -а́ю *imp.*, спусти́ть, -ущу́, -у́стишь *perf.* let down, lower; haul down; let go, let loose release; let out, drain; send out; go down; forgive, let off, let go, let pass; lose; throw away, squander; ~ кора́бль, launch a ship; ~ куро́к, pull the trigger; ~ пе́тлю, drop a stitch; ~ с це́пи, unchain; спусти́ рукава́, carelessly. спуски́ой, drain; ~ая труба́, drain-pipe. спусково́й, trigger. спустя́ *prep.* + *acc.* after; later; немно́го ~ not long after.

с|пу́тать(ся, -аю(сь *perf.*

спу́тник, -а, satellite, sputnik; (travelling) companion; fellow-traveller; concomitant.

спущу́, etc.: see спусти́ть.

спя́чка, -и, hibernation; sleepiness, lethargy.

ср. *abbr.* сравни́, compare, cf.; сре́дний, mean.

сравне́ние, -я, comparison; simile; по сравне́нию с + *instr.*, as compared with, as against.

сра́внивать, of сравни́ть, сравня́ть.

сравни́тельно *adv.* comparatively; ~ с + *instr.* compared with. сравни́тельный, comparative. сравни́ть (*imp.* сра́внивать) compare; ~ся с + *instr.* compare with, come up to, touch.

с|равня́ть, -я́ю *perf.* (*imp.* also сра́внивать) make even, make equal; level.

сража́ть, -а́ю *imp.*, срази́ть, -ажу́ *perf.* slay, strike down, fell; overwhelm, crush; ~ся, fight, join battle. сраже́ние, -я, battle, engagement.

сра́зу *adv.* at once; straight away, right away.

срам, -а (-у), shame. срами́ть, -млю́ *imp.* (*perf.* о~) shame, put to shame; ~ся, cover oneself with shame. срамни́к, -а́, shameless person. срамно́й, shameless. срамота́, -ы́, shame.

срастание, -я, growing together; knitting. сраста́ться, -а́ется *imp.*, срасти́сь, -тётся; сро́сся, -ла́сь *perf.* grow together; knit.

сребролюби́вый, money-grubbing. сребро́носный, argentiferous.

среда́[1], -ы́; *pl.* -ы, environment, surroundings; milieu; habitat; medium; в на́шей среде́, in our midst, among us. среда́[2], -ы́, *acc.* -у; *pl.* -ы, -а́м or -ам, Wednesday. среди́ *prep.* + *gen.* among, amongst; amidst; in the middle of; ~ бе́ла дня, in broad daylight. средиземномо́рский, Mediterranean. среди́на, -ы middle. сре́дне *adv.* middling, so-so. средневеко́вый, medieval. средневеко́вье, -я, the Middle Ages. средневи́к, -а́, middle-distance runner. сре́дн|ий, middle;

medium; mean; average; middling; secondary; neuter; ~ие века́, the Middle Ages; ~яя величина́, mean value; ~ий па́лец, middle finger, second finger; ~ee *sb.* mean, average; вы́ше ~его, above (the) average. сре́дство, -а, means; remedy; *pl.* means; resources; credits; жить не по сре́дствам, live beyond one's means.

срез, -а, cut; section; shear, shearing, slice, slicing. с|ре́зать, -е́жу *perf.* срезать, -а́ю *imp.* cut off; slice, cut, chop; fail, plough; ~ся, fail, be ploughed.

с|репети́ровать, -рую *perf.*

срисова́ть, -су́ю *perf.*, срисо́вывать, -аю *imp.* copy.

с|рифмова́ть(ся, -му́ю(сь *perf.* с|ровни́ть, -я́ю *perf.*

сродство́, -а́, affinity.

срок, -а (-у), date; term; time, period; в ~, к ~y, in time to time.

сро́сся, etc.: see срасти́сь.

сро́чно *adv.* urgently; quickly. сро́чность, -и, urgency; hurry; что за ~? what's the hurry? сро́чный, urgent, pressing; at a fixed date; for a fixed period; periodic, routine; ~ зака́з, rush order.

сро́ю, etc.: see срыть.

сруб, -а, felling; framework. сруба́ть, -а́ю *imp.*, с|руби́ть, -блю́, -бишь *perf.* fell, cut down; build (of logs).

срыв, -а, disruption; derangement, frustration; foiling, spoiling, ruining, wrecking; ~ перегово́ров, breaking-off of talks, breakdown in negotiations. срыва́ть[1](ся, -а́ю(сь *imp.* of сорва́ть(ся.

срыва́ть[2], -а́ю *imp.*, срыть, сро́ю *perf.* raze, level, to the ground.

сря́ду *adv.* running.

сса́дина, -ы, scratch, abrasion. ссади́ть, -ажу́, -а́дишь *perf.*, сса́живать, -аю *imp.* set down; help down, help to alight; put off, turn off.

ссо́ра, -ы, quarrel; falling-out; slanging-match; быть в ссо́ре, be on bad terms, have fallen out. ссо́рить, -рю *imp.* (*perf.* по~) cause to quarrel, embroil; ~ся, quarrel, fall out.

CCCP (*esesesér*) *abbr*. Сою́з Сове́тских Социалисти́ческих Респу́блик, U.S.S.R.

ссу́да, -ы, loan. **ссуди́ть**, -ужу́, -у́дишь *perf.*, **ссужа́ть**, -а́ю *imp.* lend, loan.

с|**сучи́ть**, -чу́, -чишь perf.

ссыла́ть(**ся**), -а́ю(сь *imp.* of сосла́ть(ся. **ссы́лка**[1], -и, exile. banishment; deportation. **ссы́лка**[2], -и, reference. **ссы́льный**, **ссы́льная** *sb*. exile.

ссыпа́ть. -плю *perf.*, **ссыпа́ть**, -а́ю *imp.* pour. **ссыпно́й пункт**, grain-collecting station.

ст. *abbr*. статья́, article; столе́тие, century.

стабилиза́тор, -а, stabilizer; tail-plane. **стабилизи́ровать**, -рую *perf.* and *imp.*, **стабилизова́ть**, -зу́ю *perf.* and *imp.* stabilize; **~ся**, become stable. **стаби́льный**, stable, firm; **~** уче́бник, standard textbook.

ста́вень, -вня; *gen. pl.* -вней *m.*, **ста́вня**, -и; *gen. pl.* -вен. shutter.

ста́вить, -влю *imp.* (*perf.* по**~**) put, place, set; stand; station; put up, erect; install; put in; put on apply; present, stage; stake. **ста́вка**[1], -и, rate; stake; **~** зарпла́ты, rate of pay. **ста́вка**[2], -и, headquarters.

ста́вня: see ста́вень.

стадио́н -а, stadium. **ста́дия**, -и, stage.

ста́дность. -и, herd instinct. **ста́дный**, gregarious. **ста́до**, -а; *pl.* -а́, herd, flock.

стаж, -а length of service; record; probation. **стажёр**, -а, probationer, houseman; trainee. **стажи́ровать**(**ся**), -рую(сь *imp.* go through period of training.

ста́ивать, -ает *imp.* of ста́ять.

ста́йер, -а, long-distance runner, stayer.

стака́н, -а, a glass, tumbler beaker.

сталелите́йный, steel-founding, steel-casting; **~** заво́д, steel foundry. **сталепла́вильный**, steel-making; **~** заво́д, steel works. **сталепрока́тный**, (steel-)rolling; **~** стан, rolling-mill.

ста́лкивать(**ся**, -аю(сь *imp.* of столкну́ть(ся.

ста́ло быть *conj.* consequently, therefore, so.

сталь, -и, steel. **стально́й**, steel.

стаме́ска, -и, chisel.

стан[1] -а, figure, torso.

стан[2], -а, camp.

стан[3], -а, mill.

станио́ль, -я *m.* foil, tinfoil.

станко́вый, machine; mounted; (free-)standing. **станкострое́ние**, -я, machine-tool engineering.

станови́ться, -влю́сь, -вишься *imp.* of стать.

стано́к, -нка́, machine tool, machine; bench; mount, mounting.

ста́ну, etc.: see стать.

станцио́нный, station. **ста́нция**, -и, station.

ста́пель, -я; *pl.* -я́ *m.* stocks.

ста́птывать(**ся**), -аю(сь *imp.* of стопта́ть(ся.

стара́ние, -я, effort, endeavour, pains, diligence. **стара́тель**, -я *m.* prospector (for gold), (gold-)digger. **стара́тельность**, -и, application, diligence. **стара́тельный**, diligent, painstaking, assiduous. **стара́ться**, -а́юсь *imp.* (*perf.* по**~**) try, endeavour; take pains; make an effort.

старе́ть, -е́ю *imp.* (*perf.* по**~** у**~**) grow old, age. **ста́рец**, -рца, elder, (venerable) old man; hermit **стари́к**, -а́, old man. **старина́**, -ы́, antiquity, olden times; antique(s); old man, old fellow. **стари́нный**, ancient; old; antique. **ста́рить**, -рю *imp.* (*perf.* со**~**) age, make old; **~ся**, age, grow old.

старо- in *comb.* old. **старове́р**, -а, Old Believer. **~да́вний**, ancient. **~жи́л**, -а, old inhabitant; old resident. **~заве́тный**, old-fashioned, conservative; antiquated. **~мо́дный**, old-fashioned, out-moded; out-of-date. **~печа́тный**; **~печа́тные кни́ги**, early printed books. **~све́тский**, old-world; old-fashioned. **~славя́нский**, Old Slavonic.

ста́роста, -ы, head; senior; monitor; churchwarden. **ста́рость**, -и, old age.

старт, -а, start; на **~**! on your marks! **ста́ртер**, -а, a starter. **стартова́ть**, -ту́ю *perf.* and *imp.* start. **ста́ртовый**, starting.

стару́ха, -и, old woman. **ста́рческ|ий**,

old man's; senile; ~ое слабоу́мие, senility, senile decay. ста́рше, *comp.* of ста́рый. ста́рш|ий, oldest, eldest; senior; superior; chief, head; upper, higher; ~ий адъюта́нт, adjutant; ~e *sb.* (one's) elders; ~ий *sb.* chief; man in charge; кто здесь ~ий? who is in charge here? старшина́, -ы́ *m.* sergeant-major; petty officer; leader, senior representative, foreman. старшинство́, -а́, seniority; по старшинству́, by right of, in order of, seniority. ста́р|ый; -ар, -а́, -о, old. старьё, -я́, old things, old clothes, old junk.

ста́скивать, -аю *imp.* of стащи́ть.

с|тасова́ть -су́ю *perf.*

стати́ст, -а, super, extra.

стати́стика, -и, statistics. статисти́ческий, statistical.

ста́тный, stately.

ста́тский, civil, civilian; State; ~ сове́тник, State Councillor (5th grade: see чин).

ста́туя, -и, statue.

стать, -а́ну *perf.* (*imp.* станови́ться) stand; take up position; stop, come to a halt; cost; suffice, do; begin, start; + *instr.* become, get, grow; + c + *instr.* become of happen to; не ~ *impers.* + *gen.* cease to be; disappear, be gone; его́ не ста́ло, he is no more; её отца́ давно́ не ста́ло, her father has been dead a long time; ~ в о́чередь, queue up; в по́зу, strike an attitude; ~ на коле́ни, kneel; ~ на рабо́ту, begin work; часы́ ста́ли, the clock (has) stopped.

стать, -и; *gen. pl.* -е́й, need, necessity; physique, build; points; быть под ~, be well-matched; + *dat.* be like; с како́й ста́ти? why? what for?

ста́ться, -а́нется *perf.* happen; become; вполне́ мо́жет ~, it is quite possible.

статья́, -и́; *gen. pl.* -е́й, article; clause; item; matter, job; class, rating; э́то осо́бая ~, that is another matter.

стациона́р, -а, permanent establishment; hospital. стациона́рный, stationary; permanent, fixed; ~ больно́й, in-patient.

с|тача́ть, -а́ю *perf.*

ста́чечник, -а, striker. ста́чка, -и, strike.

с|тащи́ть, -щу́ -щишь *perf.* (*imp.* also ста́скивать) drag off, pull off; drag down; pinch, swipe, whip.

ста́я, -и, flock, flight; school, shoal; pack.

ста́ять, -а́ет *perf.* (*imp.* ста́ивать) melt.

ствол, -а́, trunk; stem; bole, barrel; tube, pipe; shaft.

ство́рка, -и, leaf, fold; door, gate, shutter. ство́рчатый, folding; valved.

сте́бель, -бля; *gen. pl.* -бле́й *m.* stem, stalk. стебе́льчатый, stalky, stalk-like; ~ шов, feather-stitch.

стёганка, -и, quilted jacket. стёган|ый, quilted; ~ое одея́ло, quilt. стега́ть[1], -а́ю *imp.* (*perf.* вы́~) quilt.

стега́ть[2], -а́ю *imp.*, стегну́ть, -ну́ *perf.* (*perf.* also от~) whip, lash.

стежо́к, -жка́, stitch.

стёк, etc.: see стечь. стека́ть(ся, -а́ет(ся *imp.* of стечь(ся.

стекле́не́ть, -е́ет *imp.* (*perf.* о~), become glassy. стекло́, -а́; *pl.* -ёкла, -кол, glass; lens; (window-)pane.

стекло- in *comb.* glass. стекловолокно́, -а́, glass fibre. ~ду́в, -а, glass-blower. ~ма́сса, -ы, molten glass. ~очисти́тель, -я *m.* windscreen-wiper. ~пла́ст, -а, fibreglass laminate. ~ре́з, -а, glass-cutter. ~тка́нь, -и, fibreglass.

стекля́нн|ый; glass; glassy; ~ый колпа́к, bell-glass, glass case; ~ая посу́да, glassware. стекольный, glass; vitreous. стеко́льщик, -а glazier.

стели́ть: see стлать.

стелла́ж, -а́, shelves, shelving; rack, stand.

сте́лька, -и, insole, sock.

сте́льная коро́ва, cow in calf.

стёр, etc.: see стере́ть.

с|темне́ть, -е́ет *perf.*

стена́, -ы́, *acc.* -у; *pl.* -ы, -а́м, wall. стенгазе́та, -ы, wall newspaper. стенно́й, wall; mural.

стеногра́мма, -ы, shorthand record. стено́граф, -а, стенографи́ст, -а, стенографи́стка, -и, stenographer, shorthand-writer. стенографи́ровать, -рую *perf.* and *imp.* take down in shorthand. **стенографи́ческий**, shorthand. **стеногра́фия**, -и, shorthand, stenography.

сте́нопись, -и, mural.

степе́нный, staid, steady; middle-aged. **сте́пень**, -и; *gen. pl.* -е́й, degree; extent; power.

степно́й, steppe. **степня́к**, -а́, steppe-dweller; steppe horse. **степь**, -и, *loc.* -и́; *gen. pl.* -е́й, steppe.

стерегу́, etc.: see **стере́чь**.

стере́ть, сотру́, сотрёшь; стёр *perf.* (*imp.* стира́ть) wipe off; rub out, erase; rub sore; rind; grind down; ~ся, rub off; fade; wear down; be effaced; be obliterated.

стере́чь, -регу́, -режёшь; -ёг, -ла́ *imp.* guard; watch (over); watch for.

сте́ржень, -жня *m.* pivot; shank, rod; core. **стержнево́й**, pivoted; ~ вопро́с, key question.

сте́рлядь, -и; *gen. pl.* -е́й, sterlet.

стерпе́ть, -плю́, -пишь *perf.* bear, suffer, endure.

стёртый, worn, effaced.

стесне́ние, -я, constraint. **стесни́тельный**, shy; inhibited; difficult, inconvenient. **с|тесни́ть**, -ню́ *perf.*, **стесня́ть**, -я́ю *imp.* constrain; hamper; inhibit. **стесня́ться**, -я́юсь *imp.* (*perf. also* по~) + *inf.* feel too shy to, be ashamed to; (+ *gen.*) feel shy (of).

стече́ние, -я, confluence; ~ наро́да, concourse; ~ обстоя́тельств, coincidence. **стечь**, -чёт; -ёк, -ла́ *perf.* (*imp.* стека́ть) flow down; ~ся, flow together; gather, throng.

стиль, -я *m.* style. **сти́льный**, stylish; period.

сти́мул, -а, stimulus, incentive. **стимули́ровать**, -рую *perf. and imp.* stimulate.

стипенди́ат, -а, grant-aided student. **стипе́ндия**, -и, grant.

стира́льный, washing.

стира́ть[1], -а́ю(сь) *imp.* of стере́ть(ся).

стира́ть[2], -а́ю *imp.* (*perf.* вы́~) wash, launder; ~ся, wash. **сти́рка**, -и, washing, wash, laundering, laundry.

сти́скивать, -аю *imp.*, **сти́снуть**, -ну *perf.* squeeze; clench; hug.

стих, -а́, verse; line; *pl.* verses, poetry.

стиха́ть, -а́ю *imp.* of стихнуть.

стихи́йный, elemental; spontaneous, uncontrolled; ~ое бе́дствие, disaster. **стихи́я**, -и, element.

сти́хнуть, -ну; стих *perf.* (*imp.* стиха́ть) abate, subside; die down; calm down.

стихове́дение, -я, prosody. **стихосложе́ние**, -я, versification; prosody. **стихотворе́ние**, -я, poem. **стихотво́рный**, in verse form; of verse; poetic; ~ разме́р, metre.

стлать (*sl*-), стели́ть, стелю́, сте́лешь *imp.* (*perf.* по~) spread; ~ посте́ль, make a bed; ~ ска́терть, lay the cloth; ~ся, spread; drift, creep.

сто, ста; *gen. pl.* сот, a hundred.

стог, -а, *loc.* -е & -ý; *pl.* -á, stack, rick.

стогра́дусный, centigrade.

сто́имость, -и, cost; value. **сто́ить**, -о́ю *imp.* cost; be worth; be worthy of, deserve; не сто́ит, don't mention it; сто́ит, it is worth while; ~ то́лько + *inf.* one has only to.

стой: see стоять.

сто́йка, -и, counter, bar; support, prop; stanchion, upright; strut; set; stand, stance. **сто́йкий**, firm; stable; persistent; steadfast, staunch, steady. **сто́йкость**, -и, firmness, stability; steadfastness, staunchness; determination. **сто́йло**, -а, stall. **стоймя́** *adv.* upright.

сток, -а, flow; drainage, outflow; drain, gutter; sewer.

стол, -а́, table; desk; board; cooking, cuisine; department, section; office, bureau.

столб, -а́, post, pole, pillar, column. **столбене́ть**, -е́ю *imp.* (*perf.* o~) be rooted to the ground, be transfixed. **столбе́ц**, -бца́, column. **сто́лбик**, -а, column; style; double crochet; treble. **столбня́к**, -а́, stupor; tetanus. **столбово́й**, main, chief.

столе́тие, -я, century; centenary. **столе́тний**, of a hundred years; a hundred years old; ~ стари́к, centenarian.

столи́ца, -ы, capital; metropolis. **столи́чный**, capital; of the capital.

столкнове́ние, -я, collision; clash.
столкну́ть, -ну́ -нёшь *perf.* (*imp.* **ста́лкивать**) push off, push away; cause to collide, bring into collision; bring together; ~ся, collide, come into collision; clash, conflict; + с + *instr.* run into, bump into.

столова́ться, -лу́юсь *imp.* have meals, board, mess. **столо́вая** *sb.* dining-room; mess; canteen; dining-room suite. **столо́вый**, table; dinner; feeding, catering, messing.

столп, -á, pillar, column.

столпи́ться, -и́тся *perf.* crowd.

столь *adv.* so. **сто́лько** *adv.* so much, so many.

столя́р, -á, joiner, carpenter. **столя́рный**, joiner's, carpenter's.

стометро́вка, -и, (the) hundred metres; hundred-metre event.

стон, -a, groan, moan. **стона́ть**, -ну́, -нешь *imp.* groan, moan.

стоп! *int.* stop! **indecl. adj.** stop.

стопа́¹, -ы́; *pl.* -ы, foot.

стопа́², -ы́; *pl.* -ы, goblet.

стопа́³, -ы́; *pl.* -ы, ream; pile, heap. **сто́пка¹**, -и, pile, heap.

сто́пка², -и, small glass.

сто́пор, -a, stop, catch, pawl. **сто́порить**, -рю *imp.* (*perf.* за~) stop, lock; slow down, bring to a stop; ~ся, slow down, come to a stop.

стопроце́нтный, hundred-per-cent.

стоп-сигна́л, a brake-light.

стопта́ть, -пчу́ -пчешь *perf.* (*imp.* **ста́птывать**) wear down; trample; ~ся, wear down, be worn down.

с|торгова́ть(ся, -гу́ю(сь *perf.*

сто́рож, -a; *pl.* -á, watchman, guard. **сторожево́й**, watch; ~а́я бу́дка, sentry-box; ~о́й кора́бль, escort vessel; ~о́е су́дно, patrol-boat. **сторожи́ть**, -жу́ *imp.* guard, watch, keep watch over.

сторона́, -ы́, *асс.* сто́рону; *pl.* сто́роны, -ро́н, -áм, side; quarter; hand; feature, aspect; part; party; land, place; parts; в стороне́, aside, aloof; на чужо́й стороне́, in foreign parts; по ту сто́рону + *gen.* across;

on the other, the far, side of; с мое́й стороны́, for my part; с одно́й стороны́, on the one hand; шу́тки в сто́рону, joking apart. **сторони́ться**, -ню́сь, -нишься *imp.* (*perf.* по~) stand aside, make way; + *gen.* shun, avoid. **сторо́нний**, strange, foreign; detached; indirect. **сторо́нник**, -a, supporter, adherent, advocate.

сто́чн|ый, sewage, drainage; ~ые во́ды, sewage; ~ая труба́, drainpipe; sewer.

стоя́к, -á, post, stanchion, upright; stand-pipe; chimney. **стоя́нка**, -и, stop; parking; stopping place, parking space; stand; rank; moorage; site; ~ запрещена́! no parking; ~ такси́, taxi-rank. **стоя́ть**, -ою́ *imp.* (*perf.* по~) stand; be; be situated, lie; continue; stay; be stationed; stop; have stopped, have come to a stop; + *acc.* stand up for; мои́ часы́ стоя́т, my watch has stopped; рабо́та стои́т, work has come to a standstill; стой(те)! stop! halt!; ~ во главе́ + *gen.* head, be at the head of; ~ ла́герем, be encamped, be under canvas; ~ на коле́нях kneel, be kneeling; ~ у вла́сти, be in power, be in office; стоя́ла хоро́шая пого́да, the weather kept fine. **сто́йчий**, standing, upright, vertical; stagnant.

сто́ящий deserving; worth-while.

стр. *abbr.* страни́ца page.

страда́лец, -льца, sufferer. **страда́ние**, -я, suffering. **страда́тельный**, passive. **страда́ть**, -áю or -ра́жду *imp.* (*perf.* по~) suffer; be subject; be in pain; be weak, be poor; ~ за + *gen.* feel for; ~ по + *dat.* or *prep.* miss, long for, pine for; ~ от зубно́й бо́ли, have toothache.

стра́жа, -и, guard, watch; взять под стра́жу, take into custody; под стра́жей, under arrest, in custody; стоя́ть на стра́же + *gen.* guard.

страна́, -ы́; *pl.* -ы, country; land; ~ све́та, cardinal point.

страни́ца, -ы, page.

стра́нник, -a, **стра́нница**, -ы, wanderer; pilgrim.

стра́нно adv. strangely. oddly. **стра́нность**, -и, strangeness; oddity, eccentricity, singularity. **стра́нн|ый** -а́нен, -анна́, -о, strange; funny, odd, queer.

стра́нствие, -я, wandering, journeying, travelling. **стра́нствовать**, -твую imp. wander, journey, travel.

страстн|о́й, of Holy Week; ~а́я пя́тница, Good Friday. **стра́стный**; -тен, -тна́, -о passionate; impassioned; ardent. **страсть**, -и; gen. pl. -е́й, passion; + к + dat. passion for; до стра́сти, passionately. **страсть** adv. awfully, frightfully; an awful lot, a terrific number.

стратоста́т, -а, stratosphere balloon.

стра́ус, -а, ostrich. **стра́усовый**, ostrich.

страх, -а (-у), fear; terror; risk, responsibility; на свой ~, at one's own risk; под ~ом сме́рти, on pain of death. **страх** adv. terribly.

страхка́сса, -ы, insurance office. **страхова́ние**, -я, insurance; ~ жи́зни, life insurance; ~ от огня́, fire insurance. **страхова́ть**, -ху́ю imp. (perf. за~) insure (от + gen. against); ~ся, insure oneself. **страхо́вка**, -и, insurance; guarantee.

стра́шно adv. terribly, awfully. **стра́шн|ый**; -шен, -шна́, -о, terrible, awful, dreadful, frightful, fearful; terrifying, frightening; ~ый сон, bad dream.

стрекоза́, -ы́; pl. -ы, dragonfly.

стре́кот, -а, **стрекота́ние**, -й, chirr; rattle, chatter, clatter. **стрекота́ть**, -очу́, -о́чешь imp. chirr; rattle, chatter, clatter.

стрела́, -ы́; pl. -ы, arrow; shaft; dart; arm, boom, jib; derrick. **стреле́ц**, -льца́, Sagittarius. **стре́лка**, -и, pointer, indicator; needle; arrow; spit; points. **стрелко́вый**, rifle; shooting, fire; small-arms; infantry. **стрелови́дность**, -и, angle, sweep. **стрелови́дн|ый**, arrow-shaped; ~ое крыло́, swept-back wing. **стрело́к**, -лка́, shot; rifleman, gunner. **стре́лочник**, -а, pointsman. **стрельба́**, -ы́; pl. -ы, shooting, firing; shoot, fire. **стрельну́ть**, -ну́, -нёшь perf. fire, fire a shot; rush away. **стре́льчатый**, lancet; arched, pointed. **стреля́ный**, shot;

used, fired, spent; that has been under fire. **стреля́ть**, -я́ю imp. shoot; fire; ~ глаза́ми, dart glances; make eyes; ~ кнуто́м, crack a whip.

стремгла́в adv. headlong.

стременно́й, stirrup.

стреми́тельный, swift, headlong; impetuous. **стреми́ться**, -млю́сь imp. strive; seek, aspire; try; rush, speed, charge. **стремле́ние**, -я, striving, aspiration. **стремни́на**, -ы, rapid, rapids; precipice.

стре́мя, -мени; pl. -мена́, -мя́н, -а́м n. stirrup. **стремя́нка**, -и, step-ladder, steps. **стремя́нный**, stirrup.

стреха́, -и́; pl. -и, eaves.

стрига́льщик, -а, shearer. **стри́женый**, short; short-haired, cropped; shorn, sheared; clipped. **стри́жка**, -и. hair-cut; cut; shearing; clipping. **стричь**, -игу́, -ижёшь; -иг imp. (perf. о~) cut, clip; cut the hair of; shear; cut into pieces; ~ся, cut one's hair, have one's hair cut; wear one's hair short.

строга́ль, -я m., **строга́льщик**, -а, plane operator, planer. **строга́льный**, planing; ~ резе́ц, planer cutter. **строга́ть**, -а́ю imp. (perf. вы́~) plane, shave.

стро́гий, strict; severe; stern. **стро́гость**, -и, strictness; severity; pl. strong measures.

строев|о́й, combatant; line; drill; -а́я слу́жба, combatant service. **строе́ние**, -я, building; structure; composition; texture.

строжа́йший, **стро́же**, superl. and comp. of **стро́гий**.

строи́тель, -я m. builder. **строи́тельн|ый**, building, construction; ~ое иску́сство, civil engineering; ~ая пло́щадка, building site. **строи́тельство**, -а, a building, construction; building site, construction site. **стро́ить**, -о́ю imp. (perf. по~) build; construct; make; formulate, express; base; draw up, form up; ~ся, be built, be under construction; draw up, form up; **стро́йся!** fall in! **строй**, -я, loc. -ю́; pl. -и or -и́, -ев or -ёв, system; order; régime; structure; pitch; formation; service, commission. **стро́йка**, -и, building, construction; building-site. **стро́йность**, -и, proportion; harmony; balance, order. **стро́йный**; -о́ен, -о́йна, -о. harmonious, well-balanced, orderly, well put together, well-proportioned, shapely.

строка́, -и́, *acc.* -о́ку́, *pl.* -и, -а́м, line; кра́сная ~, break-line, new paragraph.

строп, -а, **стро́па**, -ы, sling; shroud line.

стропи́ло, -а, rafter, truss, beam.

стропти́в|ый, obstinate, refractory; ~**ая** *sb.* shrew.

строфа́, -ы́; *pl.* -ы, -а́м, stanza, strophe.

строчёный, stitched; hem-stitched. **строчи́ть**, -чу́, -о́чишь *imp.* (*perf.* на~, про~) sew, stitch; back-stitch; scribble, dash off. **стро́чка**, -и, stitch; back-stitching; hem-stitching; line.

строчно́й, lower-case, small.

стро́ю, etc.: see **стро́ить**.

струг, -а, plane. **струга́ть**, -а́ю *imp.* (*perf.* вы́~) plane, shave. **стру́жка**, -и, shaving, filing.

струи́ться, -и́тся, *imp.* stream, flow.

струна́, -ы́; *pl.* -ы, string. **стру́нный**, stringed.

с|тру́сить, -у́шу *perf.*

стручко́вый, leguminous, podded; ~ пе́рец, capsicum; ~ горо́шек, peas in the pod. **стручо́к**, -чка́, pod.

струя́, -и́; *pl.* -и, -уй, jet, spurt, stream; current; spirit; impetus.

стря́пать, -аю *imp.* (*perf.* со~) cook; cook up; concoct. **стряпня́**, -и́, cooking. **стряпу́ха**, -и, cook.

стря́хивать, -аю *imp.*, **стряхну́ть**, -ну́, -нёшь *perf.* shake off.

ст. ст. *abbr.* ста́рый стиль, Old Style.

студене́ть, -е́ет *imp.* (*perf.* за~) thicken, set. **студени́стый**, jelly-like.

студе́нт, -а, **студе́нтка**, -и, student. **студе́нческий**, student.

сту́день, -дня *m.* jelly; galantine; aspic.

студи́ец, -и́йца, **студи́йка**, -и, student. **студи́йный**, studio.

студи́ть, -ужу́, -у́дишь *imp.* (*perf.* о~) cool.

сту́дия, -и, studio, workshop; school.

стук, -а, knock; tap; thump; rumble; clatter. **сту́кать**, -аю *imp.*, **сту́кнуть**, -ну *perf.* knock; bang; tap; rap; hit,

strike; ~**ся**, knock (oneself), bang, bump.

стул, -а; *pl.* -лья, -льев, chair. **стульча́к**, -а́, (lavatory) seat. **сту́льчик**, -а, stool.

ступа́, -ы, mortar.

ступа́ть, -а́ю *imp.*, **ступи́ть**, -плю́, -пишь *perf.* step; tread; ступа́й(те)! be off! clear out! **ступе́нчатый**, stepped, graduated, graded; multi-stage. **ступе́нь**, -и; *gen.* -е́ней, step, rung; stage, grade, level, phase. **ступня́**, -и́, foot; sole.

стуча́ть, -чу́ *imp.* (*perf.* по~) knock; bang; tap; rap; chatter; hammer, pulse, thump, pound; ~**ся** в + *acc.* knock at.

стушева́ться, -шу́юсь *perf.*, **стушёвываться**, -аюсь *imp.* efface oneself, retire to the background; be covered with confusion; shade off, fade out.

с|туши́ть, -шу́, -шишь *perf.*

стыд, -а́, shame. **стыди́ть**, -ыжу́ *imp.* (*perf.* при~) shame, put to shame; ~**ся** (*perf.* по~ся) be ashamed. **стыдли́вый**, bashful. **сты́дный**, shameful; ~о! shame! for shame!; ~о *impers.* + *dat.* ему́ ~о, he is ashamed; как тебе́ не ~о! you ought to be ashamed of yourself!

стык, -а, joint; junction; meeting-point. **стыкова́ть**, -ку́ю *imp.* (*perf.* со~) join end to end; dock; ~**ся** (*perf.* при~ся) dock. **стыко́вка**, -и, docking. **стыко́вочный**, docking.

сты́нуть, **стыть**, -ы́ну; стыл *imp.* cool; get cold; run cold; freeze.

сты́чка, -и, skirmish, clash; squabble.

стюарде́сса, -ы, stewardess; air hostess.

стя́гивать, -аю *imp.*, **стяну́ть**, -ну́, -нешь *perf.* tighten; pull together; gather, assemble; pull off; pinch, steal; ~**ся**, tighten; gird oneself tightly; gather, assemble.

суббо́та, -ы, Saturday.

субсиди́ровать, -рую *perf. and imp.* subsidize. **субси́дия**, -и, subsidy, grant.

субъе́кт, -а, subject; self, ego; person, individual; character, type. **субъекти́вный**, subjective.

сувере́нный, sovereign.

сугли́нок, -нка, loam.

сугро́б, -а snowdrift.

сугу́бо *adv.* especially, particularly; exclusively.

суд, -а́, court; law-court; trial, legal proceedings; the judges; the bench; judgement, verdict; пода́ть ~ на + *acc.*, bring an action against; ~ че́сти, court of honour.

суда́, etc.: see суд, су́дно¹.

суда́к, -а́ pike-perch.

суде́бный, judicial; legal; forensic. **суде́йский**, judge's; referee's, umpire's. **суде́йство**, -а, refereeing, umpiring; judging. **суди́мость**, -и, previous convictions, record. **суди́ть**, сужу́, су́дишь *imp.* judge; form an opinion; try; pass judgement; referee, umpire; foreordain; ~ся, go to law.

су́дно¹, -а; *pl.* -да́, -о́в, vessel, craft.

су́дно², -а; *gen. pl.* -ден, bed-pan.

судово́дитель, -я *m.* navigator. **судово́ждение**, -я, navigation. **судово́й**, ship's; marine.

судомо́йка, -и, kitchen-maid, scullery maid, washer-up; scullery.

судопроизво́дство, -а, legal proceedings.

су́дорога, -и, cramp, convulsion, spasm. **су́дорожный**, convulsive, spasmodic.

судостро́ение, -я, shipbuilding. **судостро́ительный**, shipbuilding. **судохо́дный**, navigable; shipping; ~ кана́л, ship canal.

судьба́, -ы́; *pl.* -ы, -деб, fate, fortune, destiny, lot; каки́ми судьба́ми? how do you come to be here?

судья́, -и́; *pl.* -и, -е́й, -ям *m.* judge; referee; umpire.

суеве́р, -а, superstitious person. **суеве́рие**, -я, superstition. **суеве́рный**, superstitious.

суета́, -ы́, bustle, fuss. **суети́ться**, -ечу́сь *imp.* bustle, fuss. **суетли́вый**, fussy, bustling.

сужде́ние, -я, opinion; judgement.

су́женая *sb.* fiancée; intended (wife). **су́женый** *sb.* fiancé; intended (husband).

суже́ние, -я, narrowing; constriction. **су́живать**, -аю *imp.*, **су́зить**, -у́жу *perf.* narrow, contract; make too narrow; ~ся, taper.

сук, -а́, *loc.* -у́; *pl.* су́чья, -ьев or -и́, -о́в, bough; knot.

су́ка, -и, bitch. **су́кин** *adj.*; ~ сын, son of a bitch.

сукно́, -а́; *pl.* -а, -кон, cloth; положи́ть под ~, shelve. **суко́нный**, cloth; rough, clumsy, crude.

сули́ть, -лю́ *imp.* (*perf.* по~), promise.

султа́н, -а, plume.

сума́, -ы́ bag; pouch.

сумасбро́д, -а, **сумасбро́дка**, -и, madcap. **сумасбро́дный**, wild, extravagant. **сумасбро́дство**, -а, extravagance, wild behaviour. **сумасше́дш|ий**, mad; lunatic; ~ий *sb.* madman, lunatic; ~ая *sb.* madwoman, lunatic. **сумасше́ствие**, -я, madness, lunacy.

сумато́ха, -и, hurly-burly, turmoil; bustle; confusion, chaos.

сумбу́р, -а, confusion, chaos. **сумбу́рный**, confused, chaotic.

су́меречный, twilight; crepuscular. **су́мерки**, -рек *pl.* twilight, dusk; half-light.

суме́ть, -е́ю *perf.* + *inf.* be able to, manage to.

су́мка, -и, bag; handbag; shopping-bag; case; satchel; pouch.

су́мма, -ы, sum. **сумма́рный**, summary; total. **сумми́ровать**, -рую *perf.* and *imp.* sum up, total up; summarize.

су́мрак, -а, dusk, twilight; murk. **су́мрачный**, gloomy; murky; dusky.

су́мчатый, marsupial.

сундук, -а́, trunk, box, chest.

су́нуть(ся, -ну(сь *perf.* of сова́ть(ся.

суп, -а (-у); *pl.* -ы́, soup.

суперобло́жка, -и, (book-)jacket, dust-cover.

супово́й, soup; ~ая ло́жка, soup-spoon; ~ая ми́ска, soup-tureen.

супру́г, -а, husband, spouse; *pl.* husband and wife (married) couple. **супру́га**, -и, wife, spouse. **супру́жеск|ий**, conjugal, matrimonial; ~ая изме́на, infidelity. **супру́жество**, -а, matrimony, wedlock.

сургу́ч, -а́, sealing-wax.

сурди́нка, -и mute; под сурди́нку, on the quiet, on the sly. **сурдока́мера**, -ы, sound-proof room.

суро́вость, -и, severity, sternness. **суро́в|ый**, severe, stern; rigorous; bleak; unbleached; brown; ∼ое полотно́, crash; brown holland.

суро́к, -рка́, marmot.

суррога́т -а, substitute.

су́слик, -а, ground-squirrel.

су́сло, -а, must; wort; grape-juice.

суста́в, -а, joint, articulation.

су́тки, -ток *pl.* twenty-four hours; a day (and a night); дво́е с полови́ной су́ток, sixty hours.

сутоло́ка, -и, commotion, hubbub, hurly-burly.

су́точн|ый twenty-four-hour; daily; per diem; round-the-clock; ∼ые де́ньги, ∼ые *sb.* per diem allowance.

суту́литься, -люсь *imp.* stoop. **суту́лый**, round-shouldered, stooping.

суть, -и, essence, main point; по су́ти де́ла, as a matter of fact, in point of fact; ∼ де́ла, the heart of the matter.

суфлёр, -а, prompter. **суфлёрск|ий**, prompt; ∼ая бу́дка, prompt-box. **суфли́ровать**, -рую *imp.* + *dat.* prompt.

суха́рь, -я́ *m.* rusk; *pl.* bread-crumbs. **су́хо** *adv* drily; coldly.

сухожи́лие, -я tendon, sinew.

сухо́й; сух, -а́, -о, dry; dried-up; arid; dried; withered; chilly, cold. **сухопу́тный**, land. **су́хость**, -и dryness. aridity; chilliness, coldness. **сухоща́вый**, lean, skinny.

сучи́ть, -чу́, су́чи́шь *imp.* (*perf.* с∼) twist, spin; throw; roll out.

сучкова́тый, knotty; gnarled. **сучо́к**, -чка́, twig; knot.

су́ша, -и, (dry) land. **су́ше** *comp.* of сухо́й. **сушёный**, dried. **суши́лка**, -и, drýer; drying-room. **суши́льня**, -и; *gen. pl.* -лен, drying-room. **суши́ть**, -шу́, -шишь *imp.* (*perf.* вы́∼) dry, dry out, dry up; ∼ся, dry, get dry.

суще́ственный, essential, vital; material; important. **существи́тельное** *sb.* noun, substantive. **существо́**, -а́, being, creature; essence. **существова́ние**, existence **существова́ть**, -тву́ю *imp.* exist. **су́щий**, existing; real; absolute, utter; downright. **су́щность**, -и, essence; ∼ де́ла, the point; в су́щ-

ности, in essence, at bottom; as a matter of fact.

сую́, etc.: see сова́ть. **с|фабрикова́ть**, -ку́ю *perf.* **с|фальши́вить**, -влю *perf.* **с|фантази́ровать**, -рую *perf.*

сфе́ра, -ы; realm; zone, area; ∼ влия́ния, sphere of influence. **сфери́ческий**, spherical.

с|формирова́ть(ся, -ру́ю(сь *perf.* **с|формова́ть**, -му́ю *perf.* **с|формули́ровать**, -рую *perf.* **с|фотографи́ровать(ся**, -рую(сь *perf.*

с.-х. *abbr.* се́льское хозя́йство, agriculture.

схвати́ть, -ачу́, -а́тишь *perf.*, **схва́тывать**, -аю *imp.* (*imp.* also хвата́ть) seize; catch; grasp, comprehend; clamp together; ∼ся, snatch, catch; grapple, come to grips. **схва́тка**, -и, skirmish, fight, encounter; squabble; *pl.* contractions; fit, spasm; родовы́е схва́тки, labour.

схе́ма, -ы, diagram, chart; sketch, outline, plan; circuit. **схемати́ческий**, diagrammatic, schematic; sketchy, over-simplified. **схемати́чный**, sketchy, over-simplified.

с|хитри́ть, -рю́ *perf.*

схлы́нуть, -нет *perf.* (break and) flow back; break up, rush away; subside, vanish.

сход, -а, coming off, alighting; descent; gathering, assembly. **сходи́ть[1](ся**, -ожу́(сь, -о́дишь(ся *imp.* of сойти́(сь. **с|ходи́ть[2]**, -ожу́, -о́дишь *perf.* go; + за + *instr.* go for, go to fetch. **сходка**, -и, gathering, assembly, meeting. **схо́дный**; -ден, -дна́ -о, similar; reasonable, fair. **схо́дня**, -и; *gen. pl.* -ей, (*usu. pl.*) gangway, gang-plank. **схо́дство**, -а, likeness, similarity, resemblance.

схола́стика, -и, scholasticism. **схола́сти́ческий**, scholastic.

с|хорони́ть(ся, -ню́(сь, -нишь(ся *perf.*

сцеди́ть, -ежу́, -е́дишь *perf.*, **сце́живать**, -аю *imp.* strain off, pour off, decant.

сце́на, -ы, stage; scene. **сцена́рий**, -я, scenario; script; stage directions. **сценари́ст**, -а, script-writer. **сцени́ческ|ий**, stage; ∼ая рема́рка, stage direction. **сцени́чный**, good theatre.

сцеп, -а, coupling; drawbar. **сцепи́ть**, -плю́, -пишь *perf.*, **сцепля́ть**, -я́ю *imp.* couple; ~ся, be coupled; grapple, come to grips. **сце́пка**, -и, coupling. **сцепле́ние**, -я, coupling; adhesion; cohesion; accumulation, chain; clutch.

счастли́вец, -вца, **счастли́вчик**, -а, lucky man. **счастли́вица**, -ы, lucky woman. **счастли́в|ый**; **счастли́в**, ~а, happy; lucky, fortunate; successful; ~ая иде́я, happy thought; ~ого пути́, ~ого пла́вания, bon voyage, pleasant journey. **сча́стье**, -я, happiness; luck, good fortune.

счесть(ся, сочту́(сь, -тёшь(ся; счёл(ся, сочла́(сь *perf.* of счита́ть(ся. **счёт**, -а (-у), *loc.* -ý; *pl.* -á, bill; account; counting, calculation, reckoning; score; expense; быть на хоро́шем ~ý, be in good repute, stand well; в два ~а, in two ticks, in two shakes; за ~ + *gen.*, at the expense of; на ~, on account; + *gen.* on the account, to the account, of; потеря́ть ~ + *dat.* lose count of. **счёт|ный**, counting, calculating, computing; accounts, accounting; ~ая лине́йка, slide-rule; ~ая маши́на, calculating machine. **счетово́д**, -а, accountant, book-keeper. **счетово́дство**, -а, accounting, book-keeping. **счётчик**, -а, **счётчица**, -ы, teller; counter; meter. **счёты**, -ов *pl.* abacus.

счи́стить, -и́щу *perf.* (*imp.* счища́ть) clean off; clear away; ~ся, come off, clean off.

счита́ть, -а́ю *imp.* (*perf.* со~, счесть) count; compute, reckon; consider, think; regard (as); ~ся (*perf.* also по~ся) settle accounts; be considered, be thought, be reputed; be regarded (as); + с + *instr.* take into consideration; take into account, reckon with.

счища́ть(ся, -а́ю(сь *imp.* of счи́стить(ся.

сшиба́ть, -а́ю *imp.*, **сшиби́ть**, -бу́, -бёшь; сшиб *perf.* strike, hit, knock (off); ~ с ног knock down; ~ся, collide; come to blows.

сшива́ть, -а́ю *imp.*, **с|шить**, сошью́, -бёшь *perf.* sew; sew together, sew up. **сши́вка**, -и, sewing together.

сыр- *vbl. pref.*: see с-.

съеда́ть, -а́ю *imp.* of съесть. **съедо́бный**, edible; eatable, nice.

съе́ду, etc.: see съе́хать.

съёживаться, -аюсь *imp.*, **съ|ёжиться**, -жусь *perf.* huddle up; shrivel, shrink.

съезд, -а, congress; conference, convention; arrival, gathering. **съе́здить**, -зжу *perf.* go, drive, travel.

съезжа́ть(ся, -а́ю(сь *imp.* of съе́хать(ся. съел. etc.: see съесть.

съём, -а, removal. **съёмка**, -и, removal; survey, surveying; plotting; exposure; shooting. **съёмный**, detachable, removable. **съёмщик**, -а, **съёмщица**, -ы, tenant, lessee; surveyor.

съестн|о́й, food; ~ы́е припа́сы, ~о́е *sb.* food supplies, provisions, eatables, food-stuffs. **с|есть**, -ем, -ешь, -ест, -еди́м; съел *perf.* (*imp.* also съеда́ть).

съе́хать, -е́ду *perf.* (*imp.* съезжа́ть) go down; come down; move, remove; slip; ~ся, meet; arrive, gather, assemble.

съ|язви́ть, -влю́ *perf.*

сы́воротка, -и, whey; serum. **сы́вороточный**, serum; serous.

сы́гранность, -и, team-work. **сыгра́ть**, -а́ю *perf.* of игра́ть; ~ на рояле, (*sl.*) be finger-printed; ~ся, play (well) together, play as a team.

сын, -а; *pl.* сыновья́, -е́й or -ы́, -о́в, son. **сыно́вий**, **сыно́вний**, filial. **сыно́к**, -нка́, little son, little boy; sonny.

сы́пать, -плю *imp.* pour; strew; pour forth; ~ся, fall; pour out, run out; scatter; fly; rain down; fray. **сыпно́й тиф**, typhus. **сыпу́ч|ий**, friable; free-flowing; shifting; ме́ры ~их тел, dry measures; ~ий песо́к, quicksand; shifting sand. **сыпь**, -и, rash; eruption.

сыр, -а (-у), *loc.* -ý; *pl.* -ы́, cheese.

сыре́ть, -е́ю *imp.* (*perf.* от~) become damp.

сыре́ц, -рца́, unfinished product, raw product; шёлк-~, raw silk.

сы́рный, cheese; cheesy. **сырова́р**, -а, cheese-maker. **сырова́рение**, -я, сыроде́лие, -я, cheese-making.

сыр|о́й, сыр, -á, -о, damp; raw; uncooked; unfinished; green, unripe;

~áя водá, unboiled water; ~ые материáлы, raw materials. **сы́рость,** -и, dampness, humidity. **сырьё,** -я́, raw material(s).

сыск, -а, investigation, detection. **сыскáть,** сыщу́, сы́щешь *perf.* find; ~ся, be found, come to light. **сыскнóй,** investigation.

сы́тный; -тен, -тнá, -о, satisfying, substantial, copious. **сы́тость,** -и, satiety, repletion. **сы́тый;** сыт, -á, -о, satis-

fied, replete, full; fat; ~ по гóрло, full up; ~ скот, fat stock.

сыч, -á, little owl.

сы́щик, -а, **сы́щица,** -ы, detective.

с|экономить, -млю *perf.*

сюдá *adv.* here, hither.

сюжéт, -а, subject; plot; topic. **сюжéтный,** subject; based on having, a theme.

сюртýк, -á, frock-coat.

сюсю́кать, -аю *imp.* lisp.

сяк *adv.*: see так. **сям** *adv.*: see там.

Т

т *letter*: see тэ.

т. *abbr.* товáрищ, Comrade; том, volume.

та: see тот.

табáк, -á (-ý), tobacco; snuff. **табакéрка,** -и, snuff-box. **табáчн|ый,** tobacco; ~oгo цвéта, snuff-coloured.

тáбель, -я; *pl.* -и, -ей or -я́, -éй *m.* table, list, scale. **тáбельн|ый,** table; time; ~ые часы́, time-clock. **тáбельщик,** -а, -щица, -ы, timekeeper.

таблéтка, -и, tablet.

таблúца, -ы, табурéтка, -и, plate; ~ вы́игрышей, prize-list; таблúцы логарúфмов, logarithm tables; ~ Менделéева, periodic table; ~ умножéния, multiplication table. **таблúчный,** tabular; standard.

тáбор, -а, camp; gipsy encampment. **тáборный,** camp; gipsy.

табулягрáмма, -ы, tabulation, printout. **табуля́тор,** -а, tabulator.

табýн, -á, herd.

табурéт, -а, **табурéтка,** -и, stool.

таврёный, branded. **таврó,** -á; *pl.* -а, -áм, brand.

таёжник, -а, -ница, -ы, taiga dweller. **таёжный,** taiga.

таз, -а *loc.* -ý; *pl.* -ы́, basin; wash-basin; pelvis. **тазобéдренный,** hip; ~ сустáв, hip-joint. **тáзовый,** pelvic.

таúнственный, mysterious; enigmatic; secret; secretive. **таúть,** таю́ *imp.* hide,

conceal; harbour; ~ся, hide, be in hiding; lurk.

тайгá, -и́, taiga.

тайкóм *adv.* in secret, surreptitiously, by stealth; ~ от + *gen.* behind the back of.

тайм, -а, half; period of play.

тáйна, -ы, mystery; secret. **тайнúк,** -á, hiding-place; *pl.* secret places, recesses. **тайнопúсный,** cryptographic. **тáйнопись,** -и, cryptography, cryptogram. **тáйный,** secret; clandestine; privy; ~ совéтник, Privy Councillor (3rd grade: see чин).

так *adv.* so; thus, in this way, like this; in such a way; as it should be; just like that; ~, even so; as it is, as it stands; и ~ дáлее, and so on, and so forth; ~ и сяк, this way and that; мы сдéлали ~, this is what we did, we did it this way; не ~, amiss, wrong; прóсто ~, ~ (тóлько), for no special reason, just for fun; ~ же, in the same way; ~ же . . как, as . . as; ~ и, simply, just; ~ и бы́ть, all right, right you are; ~ и есть, I thought so!; ~ ему́ и нáдо, serves him right; ~ и́ли инáче, in any event, whatever happens; one way or another; ~ себé, so-so, middling, not too good; чтó-то бы́ло не совсéм ~, something was amiss, something was not quite right; я ~ и забы́л, I clean forgot, I've gone and forgotten. **так** *conj.* then; so;

не сего́дня, ~ за́втра, if not today, then tomorrow; ~ как, as, since. так part. yes.

такела́ж, -а, rigging; tackle, gear. такела́жник, -а, rigger, scaffolder. такела́жный, rigging; scaffolding.

та́кже adv. also, too, as well.

таки -таки part. after all; всё-~ nevertheless; опя́ть-~, again; та́к-~, after all, really.

тако́в m., -á f., -ó n., -ы́ pl., pron. such; все они́ ~ы́, they are all the same.

так|о́й pron. such; so; a kind of; в ~о́м слу́чае, in that case; кто он ~о́й? who is he? ~о́й же, the same; ~и́м о́бразом, thus, in this way; что ~о́е? what's that? what did you say? что э́то ~о́е? what is this? тако́й-то pron. so-and-so; such-and-such.

та́кса, -ы, fixed price, statutory price; tariff. такса́тор, -а, price-fixer; valuer. такса́ция, -и, price-fixing; valuation.

таксёр, -а, taxi-driver. такси́, n. indecl. taxi.

такси́ровать, -рую perf. and imp. fix the price of, value.

такси́ст, -а, taxi-driver. таксомото́рный, taxi. таксомото́рщик, -а, taxi-driver. таксопа́рк, -а, taxi depot, fleet of taxis.

такт, -а, time; measure; bar; stroke; tact.

та́к-таки: see таки.

такти́чность, -и, tact. такти́чный, tactful.

та́ктов|ый, time, timing; ~ая черта́, bar.

тала́нт, -а, talent, gift; talented man. тала́нтливый, talented, gifted.

та́лия, -и, waist.

тало́н, -а, тало́нчик, -а coupon; stub.

та́л|ый, thawed, melted; ~ая вода́, melted snow; ~ый снег, slush.

там adv. there; и ~ и сям, here, there, and everywhere; ~ же, in the same place; ibid, ibidem.

тамада́, -ы́ m. master of ceremonies; toast-master.

та́мбур¹, -а, tambour; lobby; platform. та́мбур², -а, tambour-stitch, chain-stitch. та́мбурный, tambour; ~ шов, tambour-stitch; chain-stitch.

тамо́женный, customs. тамо́жня, -и, custom-house.

та́нгенс, -а, tangent. тангенциа́льный, tangential.

та́нец, -нца, dance; dancing.

та́нковый, tank, armoured.

танцева́льный, dancing; ~ ве́чер, dance. танцева́ть, -цу́ю imp. dance. танцо́вщик, -а, танцо́вщица, -ы (ballet) dancer. танцо́р, -а, танцо́рка, -и, dancer.

та́пка, -и, та́почка, -и, (heelless) slipper; sports shoe, gym shoe.

та́ра, -ы, packing, packaging; tare.

тарака́н, -а, cockroach, black-beetle.

тара́щить, -щу imp. (perf. вы́~); ~ глаза́, goggle.

таре́лка, -и, plate; disc; быть не в свое́й таре́лке, feel uneasy, feel unsettled, be not quite oneself. таре́льчатый, plate; disc.

таска́ть, -а́ю imp. drag, lug; carry; pull; take; drag off; pull out; pinch, swipe; wear; ~ся, drag, trail; roam about, hang about.

тасова́ть, -су́ю imp. (perf. с~) shuffle. тасо́вка, -и, shuffle, shuffling.

ТАСС abbr. Телегра́фное аге́нтство Сове́тского Сою́за, Telegraph Agency of the Soviet Union.

тафта́, -ы́, taffeta.

тахта́, -ы́, divan, ottoman.

тача́ть, -а́ю imp. (perf. вы́~, с~) stitch.

та́чка, -и, wheelbarrow.

тащи́ть, -щу́, -щишь imp. (perf. вы́~ с~) pull; drag, lug; carry; take; drag off; pull out; pinch, swipe; ~ся, drag oneself along; drag, trail.

та́яние, -я, thaw, thawing. та́ять, та́ю imp. (perf. рас~) melt; thaw; melt away, dwindle, wane; waste away.

тварь, -и, creature; creatures; wretch.

тверде́ть, -е́ет imp. (perf. за~) harden, become hard. тверди́ть, -ржу́ imp. (perf. вы́~, за~) repeat, say again and again; memorize, learn by heart.

твёрдо adv. hard; firmly, firm. твердоло́бый, thick-skulled; diehard.

твёрд|ый, hard; firm; solid; stable; steadfast; ~ый знак, hard sign, ъ;

~ое те́ло, solid; ~ые це́ны, fixed prices. тверды́ня, -и, stronghold.

твой, -его́ *m.* твоя́, -ей *f.*, твоё, -его́ *n.*, твои́, -и́х *pl.* your, yours; твои́ *sb. pl.* your people.

творе́ние, -я, creation, work; creature; being. творе́ц, -рца́, creator. твори́тельный, instrumental. твори́ть, -рю́ *imp.* (*perf.* со~) create; do; make; ~ чудеса́, work wonders; ~ся, happen, go on; что тут твори́тся? what is going on here?

творо́г, -а́ (-у́) or -а (-у) curds; cottage cheese. творо́жный, curd.

тво́рческий, creative. тво́рчество, -а, creation; creative work; works.

те: see тот.

т.е. *abbr.* то есть, that is, i.e.

теа́тр, -а, theatre; stage; plays, dramatic works. театра́л, -а, theatre-goer, playgoer. театра́льн|ый, theatre; theatrical; stage; ~ая ка́сса, box-office. театрове́дение, -я, the theatre, theatre studies.

тебя́, etc.: see ты.

те́зис, -а, thesis; proposition, point.

тёзка, -и, namesake.

тёк: see течь.

текст, -а, text; words, libretto, lyrics.

тексти́ль, -я *m.* textiles. тексти́льный, textile. тексти́льщик, -а, ~щица, -ы, textile worker.

текстуа́льный, verbatim, word-for-word; textual.

теку́честь, -и, fluidity; fluctuation; instability. теку́чий, fluid; fluctuating, unstable. теку́щ|ий, current, of the present moment; instant; routine, ordinary; ~ий ремо́нт, running repair(s), routine maintenance; ~ие собы́тия current affairs; ~ий счёт, current account; 6-го числа́ ~его ме́сяца, the 6th inst.

теле- in *comb.* tele-; television. телеателье́ *n. indecl.* television maintenance workshop. ~ви́дение, -я, television. ~визио́нный, television, TV. ~ви́зор -а, television (set). ~ви́к, -а́, telephoto lens. ~гра́мма, -ы, telegram, wire. ~гра́ф, -а, telegraph (office). ~графи́ровать, -рую *perf.* and *imp.* telegraph, wire. ~гра́фный, telegraph;

telegraphic; ~гра́фный столб, telegraph-pole. ~зри́тель, -я *m.* (television) viewer. ~мо́ст, -а, TV link or transmission by satellite. ~объекти́в, -а, telephoto lens. ~пати́ческий, telepathic. ~па́тия, -и, telepathy. ~скоп, -а, telescope. ~скопи́ческий, telescopic. ~ста́нция, -и, television station. ~сту́дия, -и, television studio. ~управле́ние, -я, remote control. ~фо́н, -а, telephone; (telephone) number; (по)звони́ть по ~фо́ну + *dat.* telephone, ring up; ~фон-автома́т, automatic telephone; public telephone, call-box. ~фони́ровать, -рую *perf.* and *imp.* telephone. ~фони́ст, -а, ~и́стка, -и, telephone operator. ~фони́я, -и, telephony. ~фо́нный, telephone; ~фо́нная кни́га, telephone directory; ~фо́нная ста́нция, telephone exchange; ~фо́нная тру́бка, receiver. ~фотогра́фия, -и, telephotography. ~це́нтр, -а, television centre.

теле́га, -и, cart, waggon. теле́жка, -и, small cart; handcart; bogie, trolley. теле́жный, cart.

телёнок, -нка; *pl.* -я́та, -я́т, calf.

теле́сн|ый, bodily; corporal; somatic; physical; corporeal; ~ое наказа́ние, corporal punishment; ~ого цве́та, flesh-coloured.

тели́ться, -и́тся *imp.* (*perf.* о~) calve. тёлка, -и. heifer.

те́ло, -а; *pl.* -а́, body; держа́ть в чёрном те́ле, ill-treat, maltreat. телогре́йка, -и, quilted jacket, padded jacket. телодвиже́ние, -я, movement, motion; gesture. телосложе́ние, -я, build, frame. телохрани́тель, -я *m.* bodyguard. тельня́шка, -и, vest.

теля́та, etc.: see телёнок. теля́тина, -ы, veal. теля́чий, calf; veal.

тем *conj.* (so much) the; ~ лу́чше, so much the better; ~ не ме́нее, none the less, nevertheless.

тем: see тот, тьма.

те́ма, -ы, subject; topic; theme. тема́тика, -и, subject-matter; themes, subjects. темати́ческий, subject; thematic.

тембр, -а, timbre.

темне́ть, -е́ет *imp.* (*perf.* по~, с~) grow dark, become dark; darken; show dark; темне́ет, it gets dark, it is getting dark. темни́ца, -ы, dungeon. темно́ *predic.* it is dark. темноко́жий, dark-skinned, swarthy. темноси́ний, dark blue. темнота́, -ы́, dark, darkness; ignorance; backwardness. тёмный, dark; obscure; vague; sombre; shady, fishy, suspicious; ignorant, benighted.

темп, -а, tempo; rate, speed, pace.

те́мпера, -ы distemper; tempera.

температу́ра, -ы, temperature; ~ кипе́ния, boiling-point; ~ замерза́ния, freezing-point.

те́мя, -мени *n.* crown, top of the head.

тенде́нция, -и, tendency; bias.

теневой тени́стый, shady.

те́ннис, -а, tennis. тенниси́ст, -а, -и́стка, -и, tennis-player. те́ннис|ый, tennis; ~ая площа́дка, tennis-court.

тент, -а, awning, canopy.

тень, -и, *loc.* -и́; *pl.* -и, -е́й, shade; shadow; phantom, ghost; particle, vestige, atom; suspicion.

тепе́решн|ий, present; в ~ее вре́мя, at the present time, nowadays. тепе́рь *adv.* now; nowadays, today.

тепле́ть, -е́ет *imp.* (*perf.* по~) get warm. тепли́ться, -ится *imp.* flicker; glimmer. тепли́ца, -ы, greenhouse, hothouse, conservatory. тепли́чный, hothouse. тепло́, -а́, heat; warmth. тепло́ *adv.* warmly; *predic.* it is warm.

тепло- in *comb.* heat; thermal; thermo-. теплово́з, -а, diesel locomotive. ~во́зный, diesel. ~ёмкость, -и, heat capacity, thermal capacity; heat. ~кро́вный, warm-blooded. ~обме́н, -а, heat exchange. ~прово́д, -а, hot-water system. ~прово́дный, heat-conducting. ~сто́йкий, heat-proof, heat-resistant. ~те́хник, -а, heating engineer. ~те́хника, -и, heat engineering. ~хо́д, -а, motor ship. ~центра́ль, -и, heat and power station.

теплово́й, heat; thermal; ~ дви́гатель, heat-engine; ~ уда́р, heat-stroke; thermal shock. теплота́, -ы́, heat; warmth. теплу́шка, -и, heated railway van. тёплый; -пел, -пла́, -пло́, -пло́, warm; warmed, heated; cordial; kindly, affectionate; heartfelt.

терапе́вт, -а, therapeutist. терапи́я, -и, therapy.

тереби́ть, -блю́ *imp.* (*perf.* вы́~), pull, pick; pull at, pull about; pester, bother.

тере́ть, тру, трёшь; тёр *imp.* rub; grate, grind; chafe; ~ся, rub oneself; ~ся о + *acc.* rub against; ~ся о́коло + *gen.* hang about, hang around; ~ся среди́ + *gen.* mix with, hobnob with.

терза́ть, -а́ю *imp.* tear to pieces; pull about; torment, torture; ~ся + *instr.* suffer; be a prey to.

тёрка, -и, grater.

те́рмин, -а, term. терминоло́гия, -и, terminology.

терми́ческий, thermic, thermal. те́рмос, -а, thermos (flask). термоя́дерный, thermonuclear.

тёрн, -а, терно́вник, -а, sloe, blackthorn. терни́стый, терно́вый, thorny, prickly.

терпели́вый, patient. терпе́ние, -я, patience; endurance, perseverance; запасти́сь ~м, be patient. терпе́ть, -плю́, -пишь *imp.* (*perf.* по~) suffer; undergo; bear, endure, stand; have patience; tolerate, put up with; вре́мя не те́рпит, there is no time to be lost, time is getting short; вре́мя те́рпит, there is plenty of time; ~ не могу́, I can't stand, I hate. терпе́ться, -пится *imp. impers.* + *dat.*; ему́ не те́рпится + *inf.* he is impatient to. терпи́мость, -и, tolerance; indulgence. терпи́мый, tolerant; indulgent, forbearing; tolerable, bearable, supportable.

те́рпкий; -пок, -пка́, -о, astringent; tart, sharp. те́рпкость, -и, astringency; tartness, sharpness, acerbity.

терра́са, -ы, terrace.

террито́рия, -и, territory, confines, grounds; area.

тёртый, ground; grated; hardened, experienced.

теря́ть, -я́ю *imp.* (*perf.* по~, у~) lose; shed; ~ в ве́се, lose weight; ~ из виду, lose sight of; ~ си́лу, become invalid; ~ся, get lost; disappear, vanish; fail, decline. decrease, weaken; become flustered; be at a loss; ~ся в дога́дках, be at a loss.

тёс, -а (-у) boards, planks. теса́ть, тешу́, те́шешь *imp.* cut, hew; trim, square.

тесёмка, -и, tape, ribbon, lace, braid. тесёмчатый, ribbon, braid; ~ глист, tapeworm.

тесни́ть, -ню́ *imp.* (*perf.* по~, с~) press; crowd; squeeze, constrict; be too tight; ~ся, press through, push a way through; move up, make room; crowd, cluster, jostle. те́сно *adv.* closely; tightly; narrowly. теснота́, -ы́, crowded state; narrowness; crush, squash. те́сн|ый, crowded; cramped; narrow; (too) tight; close; compact; hard, difficult; ~о, it is crowded, there is not enough room.

тесо́вый, board, plank.

те́сто, -а, dough; pastry; paste.

тесть, -я *m.* father-in-law.

тесьма́, -ы́ tape, ribbon, lace, braid.

те́терев, -а; *pl.* ~а́, black grouse, blackcock. те́тёрка, -и, grey hen.

тётка, -и, aunt.

тетра́дка, -и, тетра́дь, -и, exercise book; copy-book; part, fascicule.

тётя, -и; *gen. pl.* -ей, aunt.

тех- *abbr.* in *comb.* of техни́ческий, technical. техми́нимум, -а, minimum (technical) qualifications. ~персона́л, -а, technical personnel. ~ре́д, -а, technical editor.

те́хник, -а, technician. те́хника, -и, machinery, technical equipment; technical devices; engineering; technology; technique, art. те́хникум, -а, technical college, technical school. техни́ческий, technical; engineering; maintenance; industrial; commercial -(grade); assistant, subordinate; ~ие усло́вия, specifications.

тече́ние, -я, flow; course; current, stream; trend, tendency; вверх по тече́нию, upstream.

течь, -чёт; тёк, -ла́ *imp.* flow; stream; pass; leak, be leaky.

те́шить, -шу *imp.* (*perf.* по~), amuse, entertain; gratify, please; ~ся

(+ *instr.*) amuse oneself (with), play (with).

тешу́, etc.: see теса́ть.

тёша, -и, mother-in-law.

тигр, -а, tiger. тигри́ца, -ы, tigress тигро́вый, tiger.

ти́на, -ы, slime, mud; mire. ти́нистый slimy, muddy.

тип, -а, type. типи́чный, typical. типово́й, standard; model; type. типогра́фия, -и, printing-house, press типогра́фск|ий, typographical; printing, printer's; ~ая кра́ска, printer's ink.

тир, -а, shooting-range; shooting-gallery. тира́ж, -а́, draw; circulation; edition; вы́йти в тира́ж, be drawn have served one's turn, become redundant, be superannuated.

тире́ *n. indecl.* dash.

ти́скать, -аю *imp.*, ти́снуть, -ну *perf* press, squeeze; pull. тиски́, -о́в *pl* vice; в тиска́х + *gen.* in the grip of, in the clutches of. тисне́ние, -я, stamping, printing; imprint; design. тисне́ный, stamped; printed.

ти́тул, -а, title; title-page. ти́тульный title; ~ лист, title-page; ~ спи́сок itemized list. титуля́рный, titular; ~ сове́тник, Titular Councillor (9th grade: see чин).

тиф, -а, *loc.* -у́, typhus; typhoid.

ти́хий; тих, -а́, -о, quiet; low, soft, faint; silent, noiseless; still; calm; gentle; slow, slow-moving; ~ ход, slow speed slow pace. ти́хо *adv.* quietly; softly; gently; silently, noiselessly; calmly; still; silently. тихоокеа́нский, Pacific ти́ше *comp.* of ти́хий, ти́хо; ти́ше! quiet! silence! hush! gently! careful! тишина́, -ы́, quiet, silence; stillness; нару́шить тишину́, break the silence; соблюда́ть тишину́, keep quiet.

тка́невый, tissue. тка́ный, woven ткань, -и, fabric, cloth; tissue; substance, essence. ткать, тку, ткёшь; -ал, -а́ла, -о *imp.* (*perf.* со~), weave. тка́цкий, weaver's; weaving; ~ стано́к loom. ткач, -а, ткачи́ха, -и, weaver.

ткну́ть(ся, -у(сь, -ёшь(ся *perf.* of ты́-кать(ся.

тле́ние, -я, decay, decomposition, putrefaction; smouldering. **тлеть**, -е́ет *imp.* rot, decay, decompose, putrefy; moulder; smoulder; **~ся**, smoulder.

тмин, -а (-у), caraway-seeds.

то pron. that; а не то́, or else, otherwise; (да) и то́, and even then and that; то́ есть, that is (to say); то и де́ло, every now and then; то . . то, either . . or; не то . ., не то, either . . or; whether . . or; half . ., half; не то, что́бы . ., no, it is (was) not that . ., (but); то . ., то, now . ., now; то ли . ., то ли, whether . . or; то тут, то там, now here, now there.

-то *part.* just, precisely, exactly; в то́м-то и де́ло, that's just it.

тобо́й: see ты.

тов. *abbr.* това́рищ, Comrade.

това́р, -а, goods; wares; article; commodity.

това́рищ, -а, comrade; friend; companion; colleague; person; assistant, deputy, vice-; ~ по рабо́те, colleague; mate; ~ по шко́ле, school-friend; ~ председа́теля, vice-president. **това́рищеск|ий**, comradely; friendly; communal; unofficial; с ~им приве́том, with fraternal greetings. **това́рищество**, -а, comradeship, fellowship; company; association, society.

това́рность, -и, marketability. **това́рный**, goods; freight; commodity; marketable; ~ ваго́н, goods truck; ~ склад, warehouse; ~ соста́в, goods train.

товаро- in *comb.* commodity; goods. **товарообме́н**, -а, barter, commodity exchange. **~оборо́т**, -а, (sales) turnover; commodity circulation. **~отправи́тель**, -я *m.* consignor, forwarder (of goods). **~получа́тель**, -я *m.* consignee.

тогда́ *adv.* then; ~ как, whereas, while. **тогда́шний**, of that time, of those days; the then.

того́: see тот.

тожде́ственный, identical, one and the same. **тожде́ство**, -а, identity.

то́же *adv.* also, as well, too.

ток, -а (-у); *pl.* -и, current.

тока́рный, turning; ~ стано́к, lathe. **тока́рь**, -я; *pl.* -я́, -е́й or -и, -е́й *m.* turner, lathe operator.

толк, -а (-у), sense; understanding; use, profit; бе́з ~у, senselessly, wildly; to no purpose; знать ~ в + *prep.* know what's what in; be a good judge of; сбить с ~у, confuse, muddle; с ~ом, sensibly, intelligently.

толка́ть, -а́ю *imp.* (*perf.* толкну́ть) push, shove; jog; ~ ло́ктем, nudge; ~ ядро́, put the shot; **~ся**, jostle.

то́лки, -ов *pl.* talk; rumours, gossip.

толкну́ть(ся, -ну́(сь, -нёшь(ся *perf.* of толка́ть(ся.

толкова́ние, -я, interpretation; *pl.* commentary. **толкова́ть**, -ку́ю *imp.* interpret; explain; talk; say; ло́жно ~ misinterpret, misconstrue. **толко́вый**, intelligent, sensible; intelligible, clear; ~ слова́рь, defining dictionary. **то́лком** *adv.* plainly, clearly.

толкотня́, -и́, crush, scrum, squash; crowding.

толку́, etc.: see толо́чь.

толку́чий ры́нок second-hand market, junk-market. **толку́чка**, -и, crush, scrum, squash; crowded place; second-hand market.

толокно́, -а́, oatmeal.

толо́чь, -лку́, -лчёшь; -ло́к, -лкла́ *imp.* (*perf.* ис~, рас~) pound, crush.

толпа́, -ы́; *pl.* -ы, crowd; throng; multitude. **толпи́ться**, -и́тся *imp.* crowd; throng; cluster.

толсте́ть, -е́ю *imp.* (*perf.* по~) grow fat, get stout; put on weight. **толсти́ть**, -и́т *imp.* fatten; make look fat. **толстоко́жий**, thick-skinned; pachydermatous. **толстомо́рдый**, fat-faced. **то́лстый**, -а́, -о, fat; stout; thick; heavy. **толстя́к**, -а́, fat man; fat boy.

толчёный, pounded, crushed; ground. **толчёт**, etc.: see толо́чь.

толче́я́, -и́, crush, scrum, squash.

толчо́к, -чка́, push, shove; put; jolt; bump; shock, tremor; incitement, stimulus.

то́лща, -и, thickness; thick. **то́лще** *comp.* of то́лстый. **толщина́**, -ы́ thickness; fatness; stoutness.

то́лько *adv.* only, merely; solely; just; ~ что, just, only just; ~-~, barely; *conj.* only, but; (как) ~, (лишь) ~, as soon as; ~ бы, if only.

том, -а; *pl.* ~а́. volume. **то́мик**, -а small volume, slim volume.

томи́тельный, wearisome, tedious, wearing; tiresome, trying; agonizing. **томи́ть**, -млю́ *imp.* (*perf.* ис~), tire, wear, weary; torment; wear down; stew, steam, braise; ~ся, pine; languish; be tormented. **томле́ние**, -я, languor. **томлёный**, stewed, steamed, braised. **то́мность**, -и, languor. **то́мный**; -мен, -мна́, -о, languid, languorous.

тон, -а; *pl.* -а́ or -ы, -о́в, tone; note; shade; tint; дурно́й ~, bad form; хоро́ший ~, good form. **тона́льность**, -и, key; tonality.

то́ненький, thin; slender, slim. **то́нкий**; -нок, -нка́, -о, thin; slender, slim; fine; delicate; refined; dainty; subtle; nice; keen; crafty, sly; ~ вкус, refined taste; ~ за́пах, delicate perfume; ~ знато́к, connoisseur; ~ слух, good ear; ~ сон, light sleep. **то́нкость**, -и, thinness; slenderness, slimness; fineness; subtlety; nice point; nicety.

тонне́ль: see **тунне́ль**.

тону́ть, -ну́, -нешь *imp.* (*perf.* по~) sink; drown; go down; be lost, be hidden, be covered.

тонфи́льм, -а, sound film; (sound) recording.

то́ньше, *comp.* of то́нкий.

то́пать, -аю *imp.* (*perf.* то́пнуть) stamp; ~ ного́й, stamp one's foot.

топи́ть¹, -плю́, -пишь *imp.* (*perf.* по~, у~), sink; drown; wreck, ruin; ~ся, drown oneself.

топи́ть², -плю́, -пишь *imp.* stoke; heat; melt (down); render; ~ся, burn, be alight; melt. **то́пка**, -и, stoking; heating; melting (down); furnace. fire-box.

то́пкий, boggy, marshy, swampy. **то́пливный**, fuel; ~ая нефть, fuel oil. **то́пливо**, -а, fuel.

то́пнуть, -ну *perf.* of то́пать.

то́полевый, poplar. **то́поль**, -я; *pl.* -я́ or -и *m.* poplar.

топо́р, -а́, axe. **топо́рик**, -а, hatchet. **топори́ще**, -а, axe-handle. **топо́рный**, axe; clumsy, crude; uncouth.

то́пот, -а, tread; tramp; ко́нский ~, clatter of hooves. **топта́ть**, -пчу́ -пчешь *imp.* (*perf.* по~) trample (down); ~ся, stamp; ~ся на ме́сте, mark time.

торг¹, -а, *loc.* -у́; *pl.* -и́, trading; bargaining, haggling; market; *pl.* auction. **торг²**, -а *abbr.* торго́вое учрежде́ние, trading organization. **торгова́ть**, -гу́ю *imp.* (*perf.* с~), trade, deal; bargain for; be open; + *instr.* sell; ~ся bargain, chaffer, haggle. **торго́вец**, -вца, merchant; trader; dealer; tradesman. **торго́вка**, -и, market-woman; stall-holder; street-trader. **торго́вля**, -и, trade, commerce. **торго́в**\|ый, trade, commercial; mercantile; ~ое су́дно, merchant ship; ~ый флот, merchant navy. **торгпре́д**, -а *abbr.* trade representative. **торгпре́дство**, -а *abbr.* trade delegation.

торже́ственный, solemn; ceremonial, festive; gala. **торжество́**, -а́, celebration; triumph; exultation; *pl.* festivities, rejoicings. **торжествова́ть**, -тву́ю *imp.* celebrate; triumph, exult. **торжеству́ющий**, triumphant, exultant.

торможе́ние, -я, braking; deceleration; inhibition. **то́рмоз**, -а; *pl.* -а́ or -ы, brake; drag, hindrance, obstacle. **тормози́ть**, -ожу́ *imp.* (*perf.* за~) brake; apply the brake(s); hamper, impede, be a drag on; retard, damp; inhibit. **тормозно́й**, brake, braking.

тормоши́ть, -шу́ *imp.* pester, plague, worry, torment; bother.

торопи́ть, -плю́, -пишь *imp.* (*perf.* по~) hurry; hasten; press; ~ся, hurry, be in a hurry; make haste. **торопли́вый**, hurried, hasty.

торт, -а, cake.

торф, -а, peat. **торфобо́лотный**, peat-moss. **торфяни́стый**, peaty. **торфян**\|о́й, peat; ~о́е боло́то, peat-moss peat-bog.

торча́ть, -чу́ *imp.* stick up, stick out; protrude, jut out; hang about. **торчко́м** *adv.* on end, sticking up.

торшéр, -а, standard lamp.

тоскá, -и, melancholy; anguish; pangs; depression; boredom; nostalgia; ~ по, longing for, yearning for; ~ по рóдине, homesickness. тоскли́вый, melancholy; depressed, miserable; dull, dreary, depressing. тосковáть, -ку́ю *imp.* be melancholy, depressed, miserable; long, yearn, pine; ~ по, miss.

тост, -а, toast; toasted sandwich.

тот *m.*, та *f.*, то *n.*, те *pl. pron.* that; the former; he, she, it; the other; the opposite; the one; the same; the right; *pl.* those; в том слу́чае, in that case; и тому́ подóбное, and so on, and so forth; и ~ и другóй, both; к тому́ же, moreover; на той сторонé, on the other side; не ~, the wrong; не ~, так другóй, if not one, then the other; ни с тогó ни с сегó, for no reason at all; without rhyme or reason; ни ~ ни другóй, neither; однó и то же, one and the same thing, the same thing over again; по ту стóрону + *gen.*, beyond, on the other side of; с тем, чтóбы, in order to, with a view to; on condition that, provided that; с тогó бéрега, from the other shore; тем врéменем, in the meantime; тогó и гляди́, any minute now; before you know where you are; тот, кто, the one who, the person who; э́то не та дверь, that's the wrong door. тóтчас *adv.* at once; immediately.

точи́лка, -и, steel, knife-sharpener; pencil-sharpener. точи́ло, -а, whetstone, grindstone. точи́льный, grinding, sharpening; ~ кáмень, whetstone, grindstone. точи́льщик, -а, (knife-) grinder. точи́ть, -чу́ -чишь *imp.* (*perf.* вы́~, на~) sharpen; grind; whet, hone; turn; eat away, gnaw away; corrode; gnaw at, prey upon.

тóчка, -и, spot; dot; full stop; point; попáсть в тóчку, hit the nail on the head; ~ в тóчку, exactly; to the letter, word for word; ~ зрéния, point of view; ~ с запятóй, semicolon. тóчно[1] *adv.* exactly, precisely; punctually; ~ в час, at one o'clock sharp. тóчно[2] *conj.* as though, as if; like.

тóчность, -и, punctuality; exactness; precision; accuracy; в тóчности, exactly, precisely; accurately; to the letter. тóчный; -чен, -чнá, -о, exact, precise; accurate; punctual; ~ые науки, exact sciences; ~ый прибóр precision instrument. тóчь-в-тóчь *adv.* exactly; to the letter; word for word.

тошни́ть, -и́т *imp. impers.*: меня́ тошни́т, I feel sick; меня́ от э́того тошни́т, it makes me sick, it sickens me. тошнотá, -ы́, sickness, nausea. тошнотвóрный, sickening, nauseating.

тощáть, -áю *imp.* (*perf.* о~), become thin, get thin. тóщ|ий; тощ, -á, -е gaunt, emaciated; scraggy skinny, scrawny; lean; empty; poor; ~ая пóчва, poor soil.

тпру *int.* whoa.

травá, -ы́; *pl.* -ы, grass; herb. трави́нка, -и, blade of grass.

трави́ть, -влю́, -вишь *imp.* (*perf.* вы́~, за~) poison; exterminate, destroy; etch; hunt; persecute, torment; badger; bait; worry the life out of. травлéние, -я, extermination, destruction; etching. трáвленый, etched. трáвля, -и, hunting; persecution tormenting; badgering.

трáвма, -ы, trauma, injury; shock. травмати́зм, -а, traumatism; injuries. травоя́дный, herbivorous. травяни́стый, grass; herbaceous; grassy; tasteless, insipid. травянóй, grass; herbaceous; herb; grassy.

трагéдия, -и, tragedy. трáгик, -а, tragic actor; tragedian. траги́ческий, траги́чный, tragic.

традициóнный, traditional. тради́ция, -и, tradition.

тракт, -а, high road, highway; route; channel.

трактáт, -а, treatise; treaty.

тракти́р, -а, inn, tavern. тракти́рный, inn. тракти́рщик, -а тракти́рщица, -ы, innkeeper.

трактовáть, -ту́ю *imp.* interpret; treat, discuss. трактóвка, -и, treatment; interpretation.

трал, -а, trawl. трáлить, -лю *imp.* (*perf.* про~) trawl; sweep. трáльщик, -а, trawler; mine-sweeper.

трамбова́ть, -бу́ю *imp.* (*perf.* у~) ram, tamp. **трамбо́вка**, -и, ramming; rammer, beetle.

трамва́й, -я, tram-line; tram. **трамва́йный**, tram.

трампли́н, -а, spring-board; ski-jump; trampoline; jumping-off place.

транзи́стор, -а, transistor; transistor radio, transistor set. **транзи́сторный**, transistor; transistorized.

трансли́ровать, -рую *perf.* and *imp.* broadcast, transmit; relay. **трансля́тор**, -а, repeater. **трансляцио́нный**, transmission; broadcasting; relaying. **трансля́ция**, -и, broadcast, transmission; relay.

тра́нспорт, -а, transport; transportation, conveyance; consignment; train; supply ship; troopship. **транспорта́бельный**, transportable, mobile. **транспортёр**, -а conveyer; carrier. **транспорти́р**, -а, protractor. **транспорти́ровать**, -рую *perf.* and *imp.* transport. **тра́нспортник**, -а, transport worker; transport plane.

трансформа́тор, -а, transformer; quick-change artist; conjurer, illusionist.

транше́йный, trench. **транше́я**, -и, trench.

трап, -а, ladder; steps.

тра́пеза, -ы, (monastery) dining-table; meal; refectory. **тра́пезная** *sb.* refectory.

трапе́ция, -и trapezium; trapeze.

тра́сса, -ы, line, course, direction; route, road. **трасси́ровать**, -рую *perf.* and *imp.* mark out, trace. **трасси́рующий**, tracer.

тра́та, -ы, expenditure; expense; waste. **тра́тить**, -а́чу *imp.* (*perf.* ис~, по~) spend, expend; waste.

тра́улер, -а, trawler.

тра́ур, -а, mourning. **тра́урный**, mourning; funeral; mournful, sorrowful.

трафаре́т, -а, stencil; conventional pattern; cliché. **трафаре́тный**, stencilled; conventional, stereotyped; trite, hackneyed.

тра́чу, etc.: see **тра́тить**.

ТРД (*te-erdé*) *abbr.* турбореакти́вный дви́гатель, turbo-jet engine.

тре́бование, -я demand; request; claim; requirement, condition; requisition; order; *pl.* aspirations; needs. **тре́бовательный**, demanding, exacting; particular; requisition, order. **тре́бовать** -бую *imp.* (*perf.* по~) send for, call; summon; + *gen.* demand, request; require; expect, ask; need, call for; ~ся, be needed, be required; на э́то тре́буется мно́го вре́мени, it takes a lot of time; что и тре́бовалось доказа́ть, Q.E.D.

трево́га, -и, alarm; anxiety; uneasiness; disquiet; alert. **трево́жить**, -жу *imp.* (*perf.* вс~, по~) alarm; disturb, worry, trouble; interrupt; ~ся, worry, be anxious, be alarmed, be uneasy, worry oneself, trouble oneself, put oneself out. **трево́жный**, worried, anxious, uneasy, troubled; alarming, disturbing, disquieting; alarm.

тре́звенник, -а, teetotaller, abstainer. **трезве́ть**, -е́ю *imp.* (*perf.* о~), sober up, become sober.

трезво́н, -а, peal (of bells); rumours, gossip; row, shindy.

тре́звый; -зв, -а́, -о, sober; teetotal, abstinent.

тре́йлер, -а, trailer.

трель, -и, trill, shake; warble.

тре́нер -а, trainer, coach. **тре́нерский**, trainer's, training.

тре́ние, -я friction; rubbing; *pl.* friction.

тренирова́ть, -ру́ю *imp.* (*perf.* на~) train coach; ~ся, train oneself; be in training. **трениро́вка**, -и, training; coaching. **трениро́вочный**, training; practice.

трепа́ть -плю́, -плешь *imp.* (*perf.* ис~, по~ рас~) scutch, swingle; pull about; blow about; dishevel, tousle; tear; wear out; pat; его́ трёплет лихора́дка, he is feverish; ~ся, tear; fray; wear out; flutter, blow about; go round; hang out; blather, talk rubbish; play the fool. **тре́пет**, -а, trembling, quivering; trepidation. **трепета́ть** -пещу́, -пе́шешь *imp.* tremble; quiver flicker; palpitate. **тре́петный**, trembling; flickering; palpitating; anxious; timid.

треск, -а, crack, crash; crackle, crackling; noise, fuss.

треска́, -и́, cod.

тре́скаться[1], -ается *imp.* (*perf.* по~) crack; chap.

тре́скаться[2], -аюсь *imp.* of тре́снуться.

треско́вый, cod.

треско́тня, -и́, crackle, crackling; chirring; chatter, blather. **трескучий**, crackling; highfaluting, high-flown; ~ моро́з, hard frost. **тре́снуть**, -нет *perf.* snap, crackle; crack; chap; ~ся (*imp.* тре́скаться) + *instr.* bang.

трест, -а trust.

трете́йский, arbitration; ~ суд, arbitration tribunal.

тре́т|ий, -ья, -ье, third; в ~ьем часу́, between two and three; полови́на ~ьего, half past two; ~ьего дня, the day before yesterday; ~ье *sb.* sweet (course).

трети́ровать, -рую *imp.* slight.

трети́чный, tertiary, ternary. **треть**, -и; *gen. pl.* -е́й, third. **тре́тье**, etc.: see тре́тий. **треуго́льник**, -а, triangle. **треуго́льный**, three-cornered, triangular.

трефо́вый, of clubs. **тре́фы**, треф *pl.* clubs.

трёх- in *comb.* three-, три-. **трёхгоди́чный**, three-year. **~годова́лый**, three--year-old. **~голо́сный**, three-part. **~гра́нный**, three-edged; trihedral. **~дне́вный**, three-day; tertian. **~зна́чный**, three-digit, three-figure. **~колёсный**, three-wheeled. **~ле́тний**, three-year: three-year-old. **~ме́рный**, three-dimensional. **~ме́стный**, three--seater. **~ме́сячный**, three-month; quarterly; three-month-old. **~сло́жный**, trisyllabic. **~сло́йный**, three--layered; three-ply. **~со́тый**, three--hundredth. **~сторо́нний**, three-sided; trilateral; tripartite. **~то́нка**, -и, three-ton lorry. **~ходово́й**, three-way, three-pass; three-move. **~цветно́й**, three-coloured; tricolour; trichromatic. **~эта́жный**, three-storeyed.

треща́ть, -щу́ *imp.* crack; crackle; creak; chirr; crack up; jabber, chatter. тре́щина, -ы, crack, split; cleft, fissure. chap.

три, трёх -ём -емя́, -ёх, three.

трибу́на, -ы, platform, rostrum; tribune; stand.

тридцатиле́тний, thirty-year; thirty--year old. тридца́тый, thirtieth. три́дцать, -и, *instr.* -ью́, thirty. три́дцатью *adv.* thirty times. три́жды *adv.* three times; thrice.

трико́ *n. indecl.* jersey, tricot stockinet; knitted fabric; tights; pants, knickers. трико́вый, jersey, tricot. трикота́ж, -а, jersey, tricot, stockinet; knitted fabric; knitted wear, knitted garments. трикота́жный, jersey, tricot; knitted.

тринадцатый, thirteenth. тринадцать, -и, thirteen. трино́м, -а, trinomial. трио́ль, -и, triplet.

три́ппер, -а, gonorrhoea.

три́ста, трёхсо́т, -ёмста́м, -емяста́ми, -ёхста́х, three hundred.

тро́гательный, touching, moving, affecting. тро́гать(ся, -аю(сь *imp.* of тро́нуть(ся.

тро́е, -и́х *pl.* three. троебо́рье, -я, triathlon. троекра́тный, thrice-repeated. тро́ить, -ою́ *imp.* treble; divide into three; ~ся, be trebled; appear treble. Тро́ица, -ы, Trinity; trio. Тро́ицын день, Whit Sunday. тро́йка, -и, (figure) three; troika; No. 3; three--piece suit; three-man commission. тройно́й, triple, threefold; treble; three-ply. тро́йственный, triple; tripartite.

тролле́й, -я, trolley. тролле́йбус, -а, trolley-bus. тролле́йбусный, trolley-bus.

трон, -а, throne. тро́нный, throne.

тро́нуть, -ну *perf.* (*imp.* тро́гать) touch; disturb, trouble; move, affect; start; ~ся, start, set out; go bad; be touched; be moved, be affected; be cracked.

тропа́, -ы́, path.

тро́пик, -а, tropic.

тропи́нка, -и, path.

тропи́ческий, tropical; ~ по́яс, torrid zone.

трос, -а. rope, cable, hawser.

тростни́к, -á, reed, rush. **тростнико́-вый**, reed.

тро́сточка, -и, **трость**, -и; *gen. pl.* -éй, cane, walking-stick.

тротуа́р, -a, pavement.

трофе́й, -я, trophy; spoils (of war); booty; captured material. **трофе́йный**, captured.

трою́родн|**ый**; ~ый брат, ~ая сестра́, second cousin.

тру *etc.*: see тере́ть.

труба́, -ы́; *pl.* -ы, pipe; conduit; chimney, flue; funnel, smoke-stack; trumpet; tube; duct. **труба́ч**, -á, a trumpeter; trumpet-player. **труби́ть**, -блю́ *imp.* (*perf.* про~) blow, sound; blare; ~ в + *acc.* blow. **тру́бка**, -и, tube; pipe; fuse; (telephone) receiver. **тру́бный**, trumpet. **трубопрово́д**, -a, pipe-line; piping, tubing; manifold. **трубочи́ст**, -a, chimney-sweep. **тру́бочный**, pipe; ~ таба́к, pipe tobacco. **тру́бчатый**, tubular.

труд, -á, labour; work; effort; *pl.* works; transactions; не сто́ит ~á, it is not worth the trouble; с ~о́м, with difficulty, hardly. **труди́ться**, -ужу́сь, -у́дишься *imp.* toil, labour, work; trouble. **тру́дно** *predic.* it is hard, it is difficult. **тру́дность**, -и, difficulty; obstacle. **тру́дный**; -ден, -дна́, -о, difficult; hard; arduous; awkward; serious grave.

трудо- in *comb.* labour, work. **трудо-де́нь**, -дня́ *m.* work-day (unit), labour-day (unit). ~**люби́вый**, hard-working, industrious. ~**лю́бие**, -я, industry, diligence. ~**спосо́бность**, -и, ability to work, capacity for work. ~**спосо́б-ный**, able-bodied; capable of working.

трудово́й, labour, work; working; earned; hard-earned; ~ стаж, working life. **трудя́щ**|**ийся**, working; ~**неся** *sb. pl.* the workers. **тру́женик**, -а **тру́женица** -ы, toiler. **тру́жениче-ский**, toiling; of toil.

труп, -a, dead body, corpse; carcass. **тру́пный**, corpse; post-mortem; pto-maine.

тру́ппа, -ы, troupe company.

трус, -a, coward.

тру́сики, -ов *pl.* shorts; (swimming) trunks.

труси́ть[1], -ушу́ *imp.* trot along, jog along.

тру́сить[2], -ýшу *imp.* (*perf.* с~) be a coward; lose one's nerve; quail; be afraid, be frightened. **труси́ха**, -и, coward. **трусли́вый**, cowardly; faint-hearted; timorous; apprehensive. **тру́сость**, -и, cowardice.

трусы́, -óв *pl.* shorts; trunks; pants.

тру́шу́, *etc.*: see труси́ть, тру́сить.

трущо́ба, -ы, godforsaken hole; slum.

трюк, -a, feat, stunt; trick. **трю́ковый**, trick.

трюм, -a, hold.

трюмо́ *n. indecl.* pier-glass.

тряпи́чный, rag; soft, spineless. **тря́пка**, -и, rag; duster; spineless creature; *pl.* finery, clothes. **тряпьё**, -я, rags; clothes, things.

тряси́на, -ы, bog, swampy ground; quagmire. **тря́ска**, -и, shaking, jolting. **тря́ский**, shaky, jolty; bumpy. **трясти́**, -су́, -сёшь; -яс, -ла́ *imp.*, **тряхну́ть**, -ну́, -нёшь *perf.* (*perf.* also вы~) shake; shake out; jolt; + *instr.* shake, swing, toss; ~**сь**, shake; tremble, shiver; quake; bump along, jolt.

тсс *int.* sh! hush!

тт. *abbr.* това́рищи, Comrades; тома́, volumes.

туале́т, -a, dress; toilet; dressing; dressing-table; lavatory, cloak-room. **туале́тный** toilet; ~ сто́лик, dres-sing-table. **туале́тчик**, -а, **туале́тчица** -ы, lavatory attendant, cloak-room attendant.

туберкулёз, -a, tuberculosis, consump-tion. **туберкулёзник**, -a, -**ница**, -ы, consumptive. **туберкулёзный**, tuber-cular, consumptive; tuberculosis.

тýго *adv.* tight(ly), taut; with difficulty; ~ наби́ть, pack tight, cram; *predic. impers.* с деньга́ми у нас ~, we are in a tight spot financially, money is tight with us; емý ~ приходи́ться, he is in straits, he is in a spot. **тугóй**; туг, -á, -о, tight; taut; tightly filled, tightly stuffed; blown up hard; close-fisted; difficult; ~ на́ ухо, hard of hearing. **тугопла́вкий**, refractory.

туда́ *adv.* there, thither; that way; to the right place; не ~! not that way!; ни ~ ни сюда́, neither one way nor the other; ~ и обра́тно, there and back.

ту́же, *comp.* of ту́го, туго́й.

тужу́рка, -и, (double-breasted) jacket.

туз, -а́, *acc.* -а́, ace; dignitary; big name

тузе́мец, -мца, тузе́мка, -и, native. тузе́мный, native, indigenous.

ту́ловище, -а, trunk; torso.

тулу́п, -а, sheepskin coat.

тума́н, -а (-у) fog; mist; haze. тума́нить, -ит *imp.* (*perf.* за~) dim, cloud, obscure; ~ся, grow misty, grow hazy; be enveloped in mist; be befogged; grow gloomy, be depressed. тума́нность, -и, fog, mist; nebula; haziness, obscurity. тума́нный, foggy; misty; hazy; dull lacklustre; obscure, vague.

ту́мба, -ы, post; bollard; pedestal. ту́мбочка, -и, bedside table.

туне́ядец, -дца, parasite, sponger. туне́ядствовать, -твую *imp.* be a parasite, sponge.

туни́ка, -и, tunic.

тунне́ль, -я *m.*, тонне́ль, -я *m.* tunnel; subway. тунне́льный, тонне́льный, tunnel; subway.

тупе́ть, -е́ю *imp.* (*perf.* о~), become blunt; grow dull. тупи́к, -а́, blind alley, cul-de-sac, dead end; siding; impasse, deadlock; зайти́ в ~, reach a deadlock; поста́вить в ~, stump, nonplus. тупи́ть, -плю́, -пишь *imp.* (*perf.* за~, ис~) blunt; ~ся, become blunt. тупи́ца, -ы *m.* and *f.* dolt, blockhead, dimwit. тупо́й, туп, -а́, -о, -о blunt; obtuse; dull; vacant, stupid, meaningless; slow; dim; blind, unquestioning. ту́пость, -и, bluntness; vacancy; dullness, slowness. тупоу́мный, dull, obtuse.

тур, -а, turn; round.

туре́цкий, Turkish; ~ бараба́н, big drum, bass drum.

тури́ст, -а, -и́стка, -и, tourist, hiker. тури́стский, tourist; ~ похо́д: see турпохо́д.

турне́ *n. indecl.* tour.

турни́к, -а, horizontal bar.

турнике́т, -а, turnstile; tourniquet.

турни́р, -а, tournament.

туро́к, -рка, Turk. турча́нка, -и, Turkish woman.

турпохо́д, -а *abbr.* тури́стский похо́д, walking-tour; tourist excursion; outing.

ту́склый, dim, dull; matt; tarnished; wan; lacklustre; colourless, tame. тускне́ть, -е́ет *imp.* (*perf.* по~), dim; grow dim, grow dull; tarnish; pale.

тут *adv.* here; now; ~ же, there and then. ту́т-то *adv.* just here; there and then.

ту́фля, -и, shoe; slipper.

ту́хлый; -хл, -а́, -о, rotten, bad. ту́хнуть[1], -нет; тух, go bad.

ту́хнуть[2], -нет; тух *imp.* (*perf.* по~) go out.

ту́ча, -и, cloud; storm-cloud; swarm, host. тучево́й, cloud.

ту́чный; -чен, -чна́, -чно, fat obese; rich, fertile; succulent.

туш, -а, flourish.

ту́ша, -и, carcass.

тушева́ть, -шу́ю *imp.* (*perf.* за~) shade. тушёвка, -и shading.

тушёный, braised, stewed. туши́ть[1], -шу́, -шишь *imp.* (*perf.* с~) braise, stew.

туши́ть[2], -шу́, -шишь *imp.* (*perf.* за~, по~) extinguish, put out; suppress, stifle, quell.

тушу́ю, etc.: see тушева́ть. тушь, -и, Indian ink.

тща́тельность, -и, thoroughness, carefulness; care. тща́тельный, thorough, careful; painstaking.

тщеду́шный, feeble, frail, weak; puny.

тщесла́вие, -я, vanity, vainglory. тщесла́вный, vain, vainglorious. тщета́, -ы́, vanity. тще́тно *adv.* vainly, in vain. тще́тный, vain, futile; unavailing.

ты, тебя́, -бе́, тобо́й, тебе́, you; thou; быть на ты с ~ + *instr.*, be on intimate terms with.

ты́кать, ты́чу *imp.* (*perf.* ткнуть) poke; prod; jab; stick; ~ па́льцем, point; ~ся, knock (в ~ + *acc.* against, into); rush about, fuss about.

ты́ква, -ы, pumpkin; gourd.

тыл, -а (-у), *loc.* -ý; *pl.* -ы́, back; rear; the interior. тылово́й, rear; ~ го́спиталь, base hospital. ты́льный, back; rear.

тын, -а, paling; palisade, stockade.

ты́сяча, -и *instr.* -ей or -ью, thousand. тысячеле́тие, -я, a thousand years; millennium; thousandth anniversary. тысячеле́тний, thousand-year; millennial. ты́сячный, thousandth; of (many) thousands.

тычи́нка, -и stamen.

тьма¹, -ы, dark, darkness.

тьма², -ы; *gen. pl.* тем, ten thousand; host, swarm, multitude.

тэ *n. indecl.* the letter т.

ТЭЦ *f. indecl., abbr.* теплоэлектроцентра́ль, district-heating and power station.

тю́бик, -а, tube.

ТЮЗ *m. indecl., abbr.* теа́тр ю́ного зри́теля, young people's theatre.

тюк, -а́, bale, package.

тюле́невый, sealskin. тюле́ний, seal. тюле́нь, -я *m.* seal.

тюль, -я *m.* tulle.

тюльпа́н, -а, tulip.

тюни́ка, -и, over-skirt; 'romantic' tutu, long ballet dress.

тюре́мн|ый, prison; ~ое заключе́ние, imprisonment. тюре́мщик, -а, gaoler, warder; enslaver. тюре́мщица, -ы, wardress. тюрьма́, -ы́; *pl.* -ы, -рем, prison; jail gaol; imprisonment.

тю́ря, -и, (*sl.*) 'bread soup', sop(s), slops.

тюфя́к, -а́, mattress. тюфя́чный, mattress.

тя́га, -и, traction; locomotion; locomotives; thrust; draught; pull, attraction; thirst, craving; taste; да́ть тя́гу, take to one's heels. тяга́ться, -а́юсь *imp.* (*perf.* по~) measure one's

strength (against): vie, contend; have a tug-of-war. тяга́ч, -а́, tractor.

тя́гостный, burdensome, onerous; painful, distressing. тя́гость, -и, weight, burden; fatigue. тяготе́ние, -я, gravity, gravitation; attraction, taste; bent, inclination. тяготе́ть, -е́ю *imp.* gravitate; be drawn, be attracted; ~ над, hang over, threaten. тяготи́ть, -ощу́ *imp.* burden, be a burden on; lie heavy on, oppress.

тягу́чий, malleable, ductile; viscous; slow leisurely, unhurried.

тя́жба, -ы, lawsuit; litigation; competition, rivalry.

тяжело́ *adv.* heavily; seriously, gravely; with difficulty. тяжело́ *predic.* it is hard; it is painful; it is distressing; ему́ ~, he feels miserable, he feels wretched. тяжелоатле́т, -а, weight-lifter. тяжелове́с, -а, heavy-weight. тяжелове́сный, heavy; ponderous, clumsy. тяжелово́з, -а, heavy draught-horse; heavy lorry. тяжёлый; -ёл, -а́, heavy; hard; difficult; slow; severe; serious, grave, bad; seriously ill; painful; ponderous, unwieldy. тя́жесть, -и, gravity; weight; heavy object; heaviness; difficulty; severity. тя́жкий, heavy, hard; severe; serious, grave.

тяну́ть, -ну́, -нешь *imp.* (*perf.* по~) pull; draw; haul; drag; tug; drawl; drag out, protract; delay; weigh, weigh down; draw up; take in; extract; extort; *impers.* draw, attract; be tight; его́ тя́нет домо́й, he wants to go home; тя́нет в плеча́х, it feels tight across the shoulders; ~ жре́бий, draw lots; ~ на букси́ре, tow; ~ся, stretch; extend; stretch out; stretch oneself; drag on; crawl; drift; move along one after another; last out, hold out; reach (out), strive (к + *dat.* after); + за + *instr.* try to keep up with, try to equal.

тяну́чка, -и, toffee, caramel.

У

у *n. indecl.* the letter y.

у *int.* oh.

у *prep.* + *gen.* by; at; with; from, of; belonging to; спроси́те у него́ о́ттиск, ask him to let you have an offprint; у вла́сти, in power; у воро́т, at the gate; у меня́ (есть), I have; у меня́ к вам ма́ленькая про́сьба, I have a small favour to ask of you; у нас, at our place, with us; in our country; у неё нет вре́мени, she has no time; у окна́, by the window; я за́нял де́сять рубле́й у сосе́да, I borrowed ten roubles from a neighbour.

у- *vbl. pref.* indicating movement away from a place, insertion in something, covering all over, reduction or curtailment, achievement of aim; and, with adjectival roots, forming verbs expressing comparative degree.

уба́вить, -влю *perf.,* **убавля́ть,** -я́ю *imp.* reduce, lessen, diminish; ~ в ве́се, lose weight.

у|ба́юкать, -аю *perf.,* **убаю́кивать,** -аю *imp.* lull (to sleep); rock to sleep, sing to sleep.

убега́ть, -а́ю *imp.* of убежа́ть.

убеди́тельн|ый, convincing, persuasive, cogent; pressing; earnest; быть ~ым, carry conviction. **убеди́ть,** -и́шь *perf.* (*imp.* убежда́ть) convince; persuade; prevail on; ~ся, be convinced; make certain, satisfy oneself.

убежа́ть, -егу́ *perf* (*imp.* убега́ть) run away, run off, make off; escape; boil over.

убежда́ть(ся, -а́ю(сь *imp.* of убеди́ть(ся. **убежде́ние,** -я, persuasion; conviction, belief. **убеждённость,** -и, conviction. **убеждённый;** -ён, -а́, convinced; persuaded; confirmed; staunch, stalwart.

убе́жище, -а, refuge, asylum; sanctuary; shelter; dug-out; иска́ть убе́жища, seek refuge seek sanctuary; пра́во убе́жища, right of asylum.

убелённый; -ён, -а́, whitened, white; ~ седина́ми, white-haired; ~ седино́й, white. **убели́ть,** -и́т *perf.* whiten.

уберега́ть, -а́ю *imp.,* **убере́чь,** -регу́, -режёшь; -рёг, -гла́ *perf.* protect, guard, keep safe, preserve; ~ся от + *gen.* protect oneself against, guard against.

уберу́, etc.: see убра́ть.

убива́ть(ся, -а́ю(сь *imp.* of уби́ть(ся. **уби́йственный,** deadly; murderous; killing. **уби́йство,** -а, murder, assassination. **уби́йца,** -ы *m.* and *f.* murderer; killer; assassin.

убира́ть(ся, -а́ю(сь *imp.* of убра́ть(ся; убира́йся! clear off! hop it! **убира́ющийся,** retractable.

уби́тый, killed; crushed, broken; *sb.* dead man. **уби́ть,** убью́, -ьёшь *perf.* (*imp.* убива́ть) kill; murder; assassinate; finish; break, smash; expend; waste; ~ся, hurt oneself, bruise oneself; grieve.

убо́гий, wretched; poverty-stricken, beggarly; squalid; *sb.* pauper, beggar. **убо́жество,** -а, poverty; squalor; mediocrity; physical disability; infirmity.

убо́й, -я, slaughter; корми́ть на ~, fatten; feed up, stuff. **убо́йность,** -и, effectiveness. destructive power. **убо́йный,** killing, destructive, lethal; for slaughter.

убо́р, -а, dress, attire; головно́й ~, headgear, head-dress.

убо́ристый, close, small.

убо́рка, -и, harvesting, reaping, gathering in; picking; collection, removal; clearing up, tidying up. **убо́рная** *sb.* lavatory; public convenience; dressing-room. **убо́рочный,** harvest, harvesting; ~ая маши́на, harvester. **убо́рщик,** -а, **убо́рщица,** -ы, cleaner. **убра́нство,** -а furniture appointments; decoration; attire. **убра́ть,** уберу́, -рёшь; -а́л, -а́, -о *perf.* (*imp.* убира́ть) remove; take away; kick out; sack; put away, store; harvest, reap, gather in; clear up, tidy up; decorate, adorn; ~ ко́мнату, do a room; ~ посте́ль, make a bed; ~ с доро́ги, put out of the way; ~ со стола́, clear the table; **~ся**, clear up, tidy up, clean up; clear off, clear out; attire oneself.

убыва́ть, -а́ю *imp.*, **убы́ть**, убу́лу; у́был, -а́, -о *perf.* decrease, diminish; subside, fall, go down; wane; go away, leave. **убы́ль**, -и, diminution, decrease; subsidence; losses, casualties. **убы́ток**, -тка (-тку), loss; *pl.* damages. **убы́точно** *adv.* at a loss. **убы́точн|ый**, unprofitable; ~ая прода́жа, sale at a loss.

убу́ю, etc.: see уби́ть.

уважа́емый, respected, esteemed, honoured; dear. **уважа́ть**, -а́ю *imp.* respect, esteem; **уваже́ние**, -я, respect, esteem; с ~м, yours sincerely. **уважи́тельный**, valid, good; respectful, deferential.

ува́риваться, -ается *imp.*, **ува́ри́ться**, -а́рится *perf.* be thoroughly cooked; boil down, boil away.

уведомля́тельн|ый, notifying, informing; ~ое письмо́, letter of advice; notice. **уве́домить**, -млю *perf.*, **уведомля́ть**, -я́ю *imp.* inform, notify. **уведомле́ние**, -я, information, notification.

уведу́, etc.: see увести́.

увезти́, -зу́, -зёшь; увёз, -ла́ *perf.* (*imp.* **увози́ть**) take (away); take with one; steal; abduct, kidnap.

увекове́чивать, -аю *imp.*, **увекове́чить**, -чу *perf.* immortalize; perpetuate.

увёл, etc.: see увести́.

увеличе́ние, -я, increase; augmentation; extension; magnification; enlargement. **увели́чивать**, -аю *imp.*, **увели́чить**, -чу *perf.* increase; augment; extend; enhance; magnify; enlarge; **~ся**, increase, grow, rise. **увеличи́тель**, -я *m.* enlarger. **увеличи́тельн|ый**, magnifying; enlarging; augmentative; ~ое стекло́, magnifying glass.

у|венча́ть, -а́ю *perf.*, **~ве́нчивать**, -аю *imp.* crown; **~ся** be crowned.

увере́ние, -я, assurance; protestation. **уве́ренность**, -и, confidence; certitude, certainty; в по́лной уве́ренности, in the firm belief, quite certain. **уве́ренн|ый**, confident; sure; certain; бу́дь(те) уве́рен(ы)! you may be sure, you may rely on it. **уве́рить**, -рю *perf.* (*imp.*

уверя́ть) assure; convince, persuade; **~ся**, assure oneself, satisfy oneself; be convinced.

уве́рнуться, -нусь, -нёшься *perf.*, **уве́ртываться**, -аюсь *imp.* от + *gen.* dodge; evade. **уве́ртка**, -и, dodge, evasion; subterfuge; *pl.* wiles. **уве́ртли́вый**, evasive, shifty.

увертю́ра, -ы, overture.

уверя́ть(ся, -я́ю(сь *imp.* of уве́рить(ся.

увеселе́ние, -я, amusement, entertainment. **увесели́тельн|ый**, amusement, entertainment; pleasure; ~ая пое́здка, pleasure trip. **увесели́ть**, -я́ю *imp.* amuse, entertain.

уве́систый, weighty; heavy.

увести́, -еду́ -еде́шь; -ёл, -а́ *perf.* (*imp.* **уводи́ть**) take (away); take with one; carry off, walk off with.

уве́чить, -чу *imp.* maim, mutilate, cripple. **уве́чный**, maimed, mutilated, crippled; *sb.* cripple. **уве́чье**, -я, maiming; mutilation; injury.

уве́шать, -аю *perf.*, **уве́шивать**, -аю *imp.* hang, cover (+ *instr.* with).

увеща́ние, -я, exhortation, admonition. **увеща́ть**, -а́ю *imp.*, **увещева́ть**, -а́ю *imp.* exhort, admonish.

у|ви́да́ть(ся, -а́ю(сь *perf.* **у|ви́деть(ся**, -и́жу(сь *perf.*

увили́вать, -аю *imp.*, **увильну́ть**, -ну́, -нёшь *perf.* от + *gen.* dodge; evade, shirk; (try to) wriggle out of.

увлажни́ть, -ню́ *perf.*, **увлажня́ть**, -я́ю *imp.* moisten, damp, wet.

увлека́тельный, fascinating; absorbing. **увлека́ть**, -а́ю *imp.*, **увле́чь**, -еку́, -ече́шь; -ёк, -ла́ *perf.* carry along; carry away, distract; captivate, fascinate; entice, allure; **~ся**, be carried away; become keen; become mad (+ *instr.* about); become enamoured, fall (+ *instr.* for).

уво́д, -а, taking away, withdrawal; carrying off; stealing. **уводи́ть**, -ожу́, -о́дишь *imp.* of увести́.

увожу́, etc.: see уводи́ть, увози́ть.

уво́з, -а, abduction; carrying off; сва́дьба ~ом, elopement. **увози́ть**, -ожу́, -о́зишь *imp.* of увезти́.

уво́лить, -лю *perf.*, **увольня́ть**, -я́ю *imp.* discharge, dismiss; retire; sack;

fire; **~ся**, retire; resign, leave the service. **увольне́ние**, -я, discharge, dismissal; retiring, pensioning off. **уво́льни́тельный**, discharge, dismissal; leave.

УВЧ (*uveché*) *abbr.* ультравысо́кая частота́, ультравысокочасто́тный, ultrahigh frequency, UHF.

увы́ *int.* alas!

увяда́ние, -я, fading. withering. **увяда́ть**, -а́ю *imp.* of увя́нуть. **увя́дший**, withered.

увяза́ть¹, -а́ю *imp.* of увя́знуть.

увяза́ть², -яжу́ -я́жешь *perf.* (*imp.* увя́зывать) tie up; pack up; co-ordinate; **~ся**, pack; tag along. **увя́зка**, -и, tying up, roping, strapping; co-ordination.

у|вя́знуть, -ну; -я́з *perf.* (*imp.* also увяза́ть) get bogged down, get stuck.

увя́зывать(ся, -аю(сь *imp.* of увяза́ть(ся.

у|вя́нуть, -ну *perf.* (*imp.* also увяда́ть) fade, wither, wilt, droop.

угада́ть, -а́ю *perf.*, **уга́дывать**, -аю *imp.* guess (right).

уга́р, -а, charcoal fumes; carbon monoxide (poisoning); ecstasy, intoxication. **уга́рный**, full of fumes; **~ газ**, carbon monoxide.

угаса́ть, -а́ет *imp.*, **у|га́снуть**, -нет; -а́с *perf.* go out; die down.

угле- in *comb.* coal; charcoal; carbon. **углево́д**, -а, carbohydrate. **~водоро́д**, -а, hydrocarbon. **~добы́ча**, -и. coal extraction. **~жже́ние**, -я, charcoal burning. **~жо́г**, -а, charcoal-burner. **~кислота́**, -ы́, carbonic acid; carbon dioxide. **~ки́слый**, carbonate (of); **~ки́слый аммо́ний**, ammonium carbonate. **~ро́д**, -а, carbon.

углова́тый, angular; awkward. **углово́й**, corner; angular.

углубля́ть, -блю́ *perf.*, **углубля́ть**, -я́ю *imp.* deepen; make deeper; sink deeper; extend; **~ся**, deepen; become deeper; become intensified; go deep; delve deeply; become absorbed. **углубле́ние**, -я, hollow, depression; dip; draught; deepening; extending; intensification. **углублённый**, deepened; deep; profound; absorbed.

угна́ть, угоню́, -о́нишь; -а́л, -а́, -о perf. (*imp.* угоня́ть) drive away; send off, despatch; steal; **~ся за** + *instr.* keep pace with, keep up with.

угнета́тель, -я *m.* oppressor. **угнета́тельский**, oppressive. **угнета́ть**, -а́ю *imp.* oppress; depress, dispirit. **угнете́ние**, -я, oppression; depression. **угнетённый**, oppressed; depressed; **~ое состоя́ние**, low spirits, depression.

угова́ривать, -аю *imp.*, **уговори́ть**, -рю́ *perf.* persuade, induce; urge; talk into; **~ся**, arrange, agree. **угово́р**, -а (-у), persuasion; agreement compact.

уго́да, -ы; в уго́ду + *dat.* to please. **угоди́ть**, -ожу́ -оди́шь *perf.*, **угожда́ть**, -а́ю *imp.* fall, get; bang; (+ *dat.*) hit; + *dat.* or на + *acc.* please, oblige. **уго́дливый**, obsequious. **уго́дно** *predic.* + *dat.*; как вам **~**, as you wish, as you please; please yourself; что вам **~**? what would you like? what can I do for you?; *part.* кто **~**, anyone (you like), whoever you like; что **~**, anything (you like), whatever you like. **уго́дный**, pleasing; welcome.

у́гол, угла́, *loc.* -у́, corner; angle; part of a room; place; из-за угла́, (from) round the corner; on the sly; име́ть свой **~**, have a place of one's own; **~** зре́ния, visual angle; point of view.

уголо́вник, -а, -ница, -ы, criminal. **уголо́вный**, criminal.

уголо́к, -лка́, *loc.* -у́, corner.

у́голь, угля́; *pl.* у́гли, -ей or -ей *m.* coal; charcoal.

уго́льник, -а, set square; angle iron, angle bracket. **уго́льный¹**, corner.

уго́льный², coal; carbon; carbonic. **у́гольщик**, -а, collier; coal-miner; coal-man; charcoal-burner.

угомони́ть, -ню́ *perf.* calm down, pacify; **~ся**, calm down.

уго́н, -а, driving away; stealing. **угоня́ть**, -я́ю *imp.* of угна́ть.

угора́ть, -а́ю *imp.*, **угоре́ть**, -рю́ *perf.* get carbon monoxide poisoning; be mad, be crazy. **угоре́лый**; как **~**, like a madman, like one possessed.

у́горь¹, угря́ *m.* eel.

у́горь², угря́ *m.* blackhead.

угости́ть, -ощу́ *perf.*, **угоща́ть**, -а́ю *imp.* entertain; treat. **угоще́ние**, -я, entertaining; treating; refreshments; fare.

угро́бить, -блю *perf.* (*sl.*) do in; ruin, wreck.

угрожа́ть, -а́ю *imp.* threaten. **угрожа́ю-щий**, threatening, menacing. **угро́за**, -ы, threat, menace.

угро́зыск, -а *abbr.* criminal investigation department.

угрызе́ние, -я, pangs; угрызе́ния со́вести, remorse.

угрю́мый, sullen, morose, gloomy.

уда́в, -а, boa, boa-constrictor.

удава́ться, удаётся *imp.* of уда́ться.

у|дави́ть(ся, -влю́(сь, -вишь(ся *perf.* **уда́вка**, -и, running knot, half hitch. **удавле́ние**, -я, strangling, strangulation.

удале́ние, -я, removal; extraction; sending away, sending off; moving off. **удали́ть**, -лю́ *perf.* (*imp.* удаля́ть) re-move; extract; send away; move away; ~ся, move off, move away; leave, withdraw, retire.

удало́й, **уда́лый**, -а́л, -а́, -о, daring, bold. **уда́ль**, -и, **удальство́**, -а́, daring, boldness.

удаля́ть(ся, -я́ю(сь *imp.* of удали́ть(ся.

уда́р, -а, blow; stroke; shock; attack; thrust; seizure; быть в ~е, be in good form; нанести́ ~, strike a blow; ~ гро́ма, thunder-clap. **ударе́ние**, -я, accent; stress; stress-mark; emphasis. **уда́ренный** stressed, accented. **уда́р-ить**, -рю *perf.*, **ударя́ть**, -я́ю *imp.* (*imp.* also бить) strike; hit; sound; beat; attack; set in; ~ся, strike, hit; ~ся в бе́гство, break into a run; ~ся в слёзы, burst into tears. **уда́рник**, -а, **-ница**, -ы, shock-worker. **уда́рный**, percussive; percussion; shock; of shock-workers; urgent, rush. **ударо-про́чный** ударосто́йкий, shockproof, shock-resistant.

уда́ться, -а́стся, -аду́тся -а́лся, -ла́сь *perf.* (*imp.* удава́ться) succeed, be a success, turn out well, work. **уда́ча**, -и, good luck, good fortune; success. **уда́чный**, successful; felicitous, apt, good.

удва́ивать, -аю *imp.*, **удво́ить**, -о́ю *perf.* double, redouble; reduplicate. **удвое́ние**, -я, doubling; reduplication. **удво́енный**, doubled, redoubled; re-duplicated.

уде́л, -а, lot, destiny; apanage; crown lands.

уделя́ть, -лю́ *perf.* (*imp.* уделя́ть) spare, devote, give.

уде́льный[1], specific; ~ вес, specific gravity.

уде́льный[2], apanage, crown.

уделя́ть, -я́ю *imp.* of удели́ть.

у́держ, -у; без ~у, unrestrainedly, without restraint, uncontrollably. **удержа́ние**, -я, deduction; retention; keeping, holding. **удержа́ть**, -жу́, -жишь *perf.*, **уде́рживать**, -аю *imp.* hold, hold on to, not let go; keep, re-tain; hold back, keep back; restrain; keep down, suppress; deduct; ~ в па́мяти, bear in mind, retain in one's memory; ~ся, hold one's ground, hold on, hold out; stand firm; keep one's feet; keep (from); refrain (from); мы не могли́ ~ся от сме́ха, we couldn't help laughing; ~ся от собла́зна, resist a temptation.

удеру́, etc.: see удра́ть.

удешеви́ть, -влю́ *perf.*, **удешевля́ть**, -я́ю *imp.* reduce the price of; ~ся, be-come cheaper. **удешевле́ние**, -я, price-reduction.

удиви́тельный, astonishing, surprising, amazing; wonderful, marvellous; не удиви́тельно, что, no wonder (that). **удиви́ть**, -влю́ *perf.*, **удивля́ть**, -я́ю *imp.* astonish, surprise, amaze; ~ся, be astonished, be surprised, be amazed; marvel. **удивле́ние**, -я, astonishment, surprise, amazement; к моему́ удив-ле́нию, to my surprise; на ~, excel-lently, splendidly, marvellously.

удила́, -и́л *pl.* bit.

уди́лище, -а, fishing-rod. **уди́льщик**, -а, -щица, -ы, angler.

удира́ть, -а́ю *imp.* of удра́ть.

уди́ть, ужу́, у́дишь *imp.* fish for; ~ ры́бу, fish; ~ся, bite.

удлине́ние, -я, lengthening; extension. **удлини́ть**, -ню́ *perf.*, **удлиня́ть**, -я́ю *imp.* lengthen; extend, prolong; ~ся, become longer, lengthen; be extended, be prolonged.

удо́бно adv. comfortably; conveniently.
удо́бн|ый, comfortable; cosy; convenient, suitable, opportune; proper, in order; ~ый слу́чай, opportunity; ~o + dat. it is convenient for, it suits.

удобо- in comb. conveniently, easily, well. удобовари́мый, digestible. ~исполни́мый, easy to carry out. ~обтека́емый, streamlined. ~переноси́мый, portable, easily carried. ~поня́тный, comprehensible, intelligible. ~произноси́мый, easy to pronounce. ~управля́емый, easily controlled. ~усвоя́емый, easily assimilated. ~чита́емый, legible, easy to read.

удобре́ние, -я, fertilization, manuring; fertilizer. удо́брить, -рю perf., удобря́ть, -я́ю imp. fertilize.

удо́бство, -а, comfort; convenience; amenity; кварти́ра со все́ми удо́бствами, flat with all conveniences.

удовлетворе́ние, -я, satisfaction; gratification. удовлетворённый, -рён, -а́, satisfied, contented. удовлетвори́тельно adv. satisfactorily; fair, satisfactory. удовлетвори́тельный, satisfactory. удовлетвори́ть, -рю perf., удовлетворя́ть, -я́ю imp. satisfy; gratify; give satisfaction to; comply with; + dat. answer, meet; + instr. supply with, furnish with; ~ жела́ние, gratify a wish; ~ потре́бности, satisfy the requirements; ~ про́сьбу, comply with a request; ~ся, content oneself; be satisfied.

удово́льствие, -я, pleasure; amusement. у|дово́льствоваться, -твуюсь perf.

удо́й, -я, milk-yield; milking. удо́йлив|ый, yielding much milk; ~ая коро́ва, good milker.

удоста́ивать(ся, -аю(сь imp. of удосто́ить(ся.

удостовере́ние, -я, certification, attestation; certificate; ~ ли́чности, identity card. удостове́рить, -рю perf., удостоверя́ть, -я́ю imp. certify, attest, witness; ~ ли́чность + gen. prove the identity of, identify; ~ся, make sure (в + prep. of), assure oneself.

удосто́ить, -о́ю perf. (imp. удоста́ивать) make an award to; + gen. award to, confer on; + instr. favour with, vouchsafe to; ~ся + gen. receive, be awarded; be favoured with, be vouchsafed; be found worthy.

удосу́живаться, -аюсь imp., удосу́житься, -жусь perf. find time.

у́дочка, -и, (fishing-)rod.

удра́ть, удеру́, -ёшь; удра́л, -а́, -о perf. (imp. удира́ть) make off, clear out, run away.

удружи́ть, -жу́ perf. + dat. do a good turn.

удруча́ть, -а́ю imp., удручи́ть, -чу́ perf. depress, dispirit. удручённый; -чён, -а́, depressed, despondent.

удуша́ть, -а́ю imp., удуши́ть, -шу́, -шишь perf. smother, stifle, suffocate; asphyxiate. удуше́ние, -я, suffocation; asphyxiation. удушли́вый, stifling, suffocating; asphyxiating. уду́шье, -я, asthma; suffocation, asphyxia.

уедине́ние, -я, solitude; seclusion. уединённый, solitary, secluded; lonely. уедини́ться, -ню́сь perf., уединя́ться, -я́юсь imp. retire, withdraw; seclude oneself.

уе́зд, -а, uezd, District.

уезжа́ть, -а́ю imp., уе́хать, уе́ду perf. go away, leave, depart.

уж, -а́, grass-snake.

уж adv. see уже́. уж, уже́ part. to be sure, indeed, certainly.

у|жа́лить, -лю perf.

у́жас, -а, horror, terror; predic. it is awful, it is terrible; ~ (как), awfully, terribly; ~ ско́лько, an awful lot of. ужаса́ть, -а́ю imp., ужасну́ть, -ну́, -нёшь perf. horrify, terrify; ~ся, be horrified, be terrified. ужа́сно adv. horribly, terribly; awfully; frightfully. ужа́сный, awful, terrible, ghastly, frightful.

у́же, comp. of у́зкий.

уже́, уж adv. already; now; by now; ~ давно́, it's a long time ago; ~ не, no longer. уже́ part.: see уж part.

уже́ние, -я, fishing, angling.

ужесточа́ться, -а́ется imp. become, be made, stricter, tighter, more rigorous.

ужесточéние, -я, tightening up intensi-fication; making stricter, more rigorous. ужесточи́ть, -чý *perf.* make stricter, make more rigorous; intensify, tighten (up).

ужива́ться, -а́юсь, *imp. of* ужи́ться. ужи́вчивый, easy to get on with.

у́жимка, -и, grimace.

у́жин, -а, supper. у́жинать, -аю *imp.* (*perf.* по~) have supper.

ужи́ться, -иву́сь, -ивёшься; -и́лся, -ла́сь *perf.* (*imp.* ужива́ться) get on.

ужу́: *see* уди́ть.

узаконéние, -я, legalization, legitimiza-tion; statute. узакóнивать, -аю *imp.*, узакóнить, -ню *perf.*, узаконя́ть, -я́ю *imp.* legalize, legitimize.

уздá, -ы́; *pl.* -ы, bridle.

у́зел, узлá, knot; bend, hitch; junction; centre; node; bundle, pack; нéрвный ~, nerve-centre, ganglion.

у́зкий; у́зок, узкá, -о, narrow; tight; limited; narrow-minded; ~ое мéсто, bottleneck. узкоколéйка, -и, narrow--gauge railway. узкоколéйный, narrow-gauge. узкоплёночный, 16-mm, sixteen-millimetre.

узловáтый, knotty; nodose; gnarled. узлов|óй, junction; main, principal, central, key; ~áя стáнция, junction.

узнавáть, -наю́, -наёшь *imp.*, узнáть, -áю *perf.* recognize; get to know, be-come familiar with; learn, find out.

у́зник, -а, у́зница, -ы, prisoner.

узóр, -а, pattern, design. узóрный, pattern; patterned. узóрчатый, pat-terned.

у́зость, -и, narrowness; tightness.

у́зы, уз *pl.* bonds, ties.

уйду́, etc.: *see* уйти́. уйму́, etc.: *see* уня́ть.

уйти́, уйду́, -дёшь; ушёл, ушлá *perf.* (*imp.* уходи́ть) go away, leave, depart; escape, get away; evade; retire; sink; bury oneself; be used up, be spent; pass away, slip away; boil over; spill; ~ (вперёд), gain, be fast; на э́то уйдёт мнóго врéмени, it will take a lot of time; так вы далекó не уйдёте, you won't get very far like that; ~ на пéнсию, retire on a pension; ~ co

сцéны, quit the stage; ~ c рабóты, leave work, give up work.

укáз, -а, decree; edict, ukase. указáние, -я, indication, pointing out; instruc-tion, direction. укáзанный, fixed, ap-pointed, stated. указáтель, -я *m.* indicator; marker; gauge; index; guide, directory; ~ направлéния, road-sign. указáтельный, indicating; demonstrative; ~ый пáлец, index finger, forefinger; ~ая стрéлка, pointer. указáть, -ажý, -áжешь *perf.*, укáзывать, -аю *imp.* show; indicate; point; point out; explain; give direc-tions; give orders. укáзка, -и, pointer; orders; по чужóй укáзке, at someone else's bidding.

укáлывать, -аю *imp. of* уколóть.

укатáть, -áю *perf.*, укáтывать[1], -аю *imp.* roll, roll out; flatten; wear out, tire out; ~ся, become smooth. укати́ть, -ачý, -áтишь *perf.*, укáты-вать[2], -аю *imp.* roll away; drive off; ~ся, roll away.

укачáть, -áю *perf.*, укáчивать, -аю *imp.* rock to sleep; make sick.

УКВ (*ukavé*) *abbr.* ультракорóткие вóлны, ультракоротковóлновый, ul-tra-short waves, ultrashort-wave.

уклáд, -а, structure; form; organiza-tion, set-up; ~ жи́зни, style of life, mode of life; общéственно-экономи́-ческий ~, social and economic struc-ture. уклáдка, -и, packing; stacking, piling; stowing; laying; setting, set. уклáдчик, -а, packer; layer. уклáды-вать(ся[1], -аю(сь *imp. of* уложи́ть(ся.

уклáдываться[2], -аюсь *imp. of* улéчься.

уклóн, -а, slope, declivity; inclination; incline; gradient; bias, tendency; de-viation. уклонéние, -я, deviation; evasion; digression. уклони́ст, -а, de-viationist. уклони́ться, -ню́сь, -ни́шь-ся *perf.*, уклоня́ться, -я́юсь *imp.* deviate; + *от* + *gen.* turn, turn off, turn aside; avoid; evade. уклóнчивый, evasive.

уключи́на, -ы, rowlock.

укóл, -а, prick; jab; injection; thrust. уколóть, -лю́, -лешь *perf.* (*imp.* укá-лывать) prick; sting, wound.

укомплектова́ние, -я, bringing up to strength. укомплекто́ванный, complete, at full strength. у|комплекто-ва́ть, -тую *perf.*, укомплекто́вывать, -аю *imp.* complete; bring up to (full) strength; man; + *instr.* equip with, furnish with.

уко́р, -а, reproach.

укора́чивать, -аю *imp.* of укороти́ть.

укорени́ть, -ню́ *perf.*, укореня́ть, -я́ю *imp.* implant, inculcate; ~ ся, take root, strike root.

укори́зна, -ы, reproach. укори́зненный, reproachful. укори́ть, -рю́ *perf.* (*imp.* укоря́ть) reproach (в + *prep.* with).

укороти́ть, -очу́ *perf.* (*imp.* укора́чивать) shorten.

укоря́ть, -я́ю *imp.* of укори́ть.

уко́с, -а, (hay-)crop.

укра́дкой *adv.* stealthily, by stealth, furtively. укра́дкy, etc.: see укра́сть.

украи́нец, -нца, украи́нка, -и, Ukrainian. украи́нский, Ukrainian.

укра́сить, -а́шу *perf.* (*imp.* украша́ть) adorn, decorate, ornament; ~ ся, be decorated; adorn oneself.

у|кра́сть, -аду́, -дёшь *perf.*

украша́ть(ся, -а́ю(сь *imp.* of укра́сить(ся. украше́ние, -я, adorning; decoration; adornment, ornament.

укрепи́ть, -плю́ *perf.*, укрепля́ть, -я́ю *imp.* strengthen; reinforce; fix, make fast; fortify; consolidate; brace; enhance; ~ ся, become stronger; fortify one's position. укрепле́ние, -я, strengthening; reinforcement; consolidation; fortification; work. укрепля́ющее *sb.* tonic, restorative.

укро́мный, secluded, sheltered, cosy.

укро́п, -а (-y), dill.

укроти́тель, -я *m.* (animal-)tamer. укроти́ть, -ощу́ *perf.*, укроща́ть, -а́ю *imp.* tame; curb, subdue, check; ~ ся, become tame, be tamed; calm down, die down. укроще́ние, -я, taming.

укро́ю, etc.: see укры́ть.

укрупне́ние, -я, enlargement, extension; amalgamation. укрупни́ть, -ню́ *perf.*, укрупня́ть, -я́ю *imp.* enlarge; extend; amalgamate.

укрыва́тель, -я *m.* concealer, harbourer; ~ кра́деного, receiver (of stolen goods). укрыва́тельство, -а, concealment, harbouring; receiving. укрыва́ть, -а́ю *imp.*, укры́ть, -ро́ю *perf.* cover, cover up; conceal, harbour; give shelter (to); receive, act as receiver of; ~ ся, cover oneself; take cover; find shelter; escape notice. укры́тие, -я, cover; concealment; shelter.

у́ксус, -а (-y), vinegar.

уку́с, -а, bite; sting. укуси́ть, -ушу́ -у́сишь *perf.* bite; sting.

уку́тать, -аю *perf.*, уку́тывать, -аю *imp.* wrap up; ~ ся wrap oneself up.

укушу́, etc.: see укуси́ть.

ул. *abbr.* у́лица, street, road.

ула́вливать, -аю *imp.* of улови́ть.

ула́дить, -а́жу *perf.*, ула́живать, -аю *imp.* settle, arrange; reconcile.

ула́мывать, -аю *imp.* of уломáть.

у́лей, у́лья, (bee)hive.

улета́ть, -а́ю *imp.*, улете́ть, -ечу́ *perf.* fly, fly away; vanish. улету́чиваться, -аюсь *imp.*, улету́читься, -чусь *perf.* evaporate, volatilize; vanish, disappear.

уле́чься, уля́гусь, -я́жешься; улёгся, -гла́сь *perf.* (*imp.* укла́дываться) lie down; find room; settle; subside; calm down.

улизну́ть, -ну́, -нёшь *perf.* slip away, steal away.

ули́ка, -и, clue; evidence.

ули́тка, -и, snail.

у́лица, -ы, street; на у́лице, in the street; out of doors, outside.

улича́ть, -а́ю *imp.*, уличи́ть, -чу́ *perf.* establish the guilt of; ~ в + *prep.* catch out in.

у́личный, street.

уло́в, -а, catch, take, haul. улови́мый, perceptible; audible. улови́ть, -влю́, -вишь *perf.* (*imp.* ула́вливать) catch, pick up, locate; detect, perceive; seize. уло́вка, -и, trick, ruse, subterfuge.

уложе́ние, -я, code. уложи́ть, -жу́, -жишь *perf.* (*imp.* укла́дывать) lay; pack; stow; pile, stack; cover; set; ~ спать, put to bed; ~ ся, pack, pack up; go in; fit in; sink in; + в + *acc.* keep within, confine oneself to.

уломáть, -а́ю (*imp.* ула́мывать) talk round, prevail on.

улуча́ть, -а́ю imp., улучи́ть, -чу́ perf. find, seize, catch.

улучша́ть, -а́ю imp., улу́чшить, -шу perf. improve; ameliorate; better; ~ся, improve; get better. улучше́ние, -я, improvement; amelioration.

улыба́ться, -а́юсь imp., улыбну́ться, -ну́сь, -нёшься perf. smile; + dat. appeal to. улы́бка, -и, smile.

ультра- in comb. ultra-. ультравысо́кий, ultra-high. ~звуково́й, super-sonic, ultrasonic. ~коро́ткий, ultra-short. ~фиоле́товый, ultra-violet.

уля́гусь, etc.: see уле́чься.

ум, -а́, mind, intellect; wits; head; свести́ с ~а́, drive mad; склад ~а́, mentality turn of mind; сойти́ с ~а́, go mad; go crazy.

умале́ние, -я, belittling, disparagement. умали́ть, -лю́ perf. (imp. умаля́ть) be-little, disparage; decrease, lessen.

умалишённый, mad, lunatic; sb. luna-tic, madman, madwoman.

ума́лчивать, -аю imp. of умолча́ть. умаля́ть, -я́ю imp. of умали́ть.

уме́лец, -льца, skilled workman, crafts-man. уме́лый, able, skilful; capable; skilled. уме́ние, -я, ability, skill; know--how.

уменьша́ть, -а́ю imp., уме́ньшить, -шу or -шу́ perf. reduce, diminish, decrease, lessen; ~ расхо́ды, cut down ex-penditure; ~ ско́рость, slow down; ~ся, diminish, decrease, drop, dwindle; abate. уменьше́ние, -я, de-crease, reduction, diminution, lessen-ing, abatement. уменьши́тельный, diminutive.

уме́ренность, -и, moderation. уме́рен-ный, moderate; temperate.

умере́ть, -мру́, -рёшь; у́мер, -ла́, -о perf. (imp. умира́ть) die.

уме́рить, -рю perf. (imp. умеря́ть) moderate; restrain.

умертви́ть, -рщвлю́ perf., умерщвля́ть, -я́ю imp. kill, destroy; mortify. уме́рший, dead; sb. the deceased. умерщвле́ние, -я, killing, destruction; mortification.

умеря́ть, -я́ю imp. of уме́рить.

умести́ть, -ещу́ perf. (imp. умеща́ть) get in, fit in, find room for; ~ся, go in,

fit in, find room. уме́стно adv. appro-priately; opportunely; to the point. уме́стный, appropriate; pertinent, to the point; opportune, timely.

уме́ть, -е́ю imp. be able, know how.

умеща́ть(ся, -а́ю(сь imp. of умести́ть-(ся.

умиле́ние, -я, tenderness; emotion. умили́тельный, moving, touching, affecting. умили́ть, -лю́ perf., умил-я́ть, -я́ю imp. move, touch; ~ся, be moved, be touched.

умира́ние, -я, dying. умира́ть, -а́ю imp. of умере́ть. умира́ющий, dying; sb. dying person.

умне́ть, -е́ю imp. (perf. по~) grow wiser. у́мник, -а, good boy; clever person. у́мница, -ы, good girl; m. and f. clever person. у́мно adv. cleverly, wisely; sensibly.

умножа́ть, -а́ю imp., у|мно́жить, -жу perf. multiply; increase; augment; ~ся, increase, multiply. умноже́ние, -я, multiplication; increase, rise. умно́житель, -я m. multiplier.

у́мный; умён, умна́, у́мно, clever, wise, intelligent; sensible. умозаключа́ть, -а́ю imp., умозаключи́ть, -чу́ perf. deduce; infer, conclude. умозаключ-е́ние, -я, deduction; conclusion, in-ference.

умоли́ть, -лю́ perf. (imp. умоля́ть) move by entreaties.

у́молк, -у; без ~у, without stopping, incessantly. умолка́ть, -а́ю imp., умо́лкнуть, -ну; -о́лк perf. fall silent; stop; cease. умолча́ть, -чу́ perf. (imp. ума́лчивать) pass over in silence, fail to mention, suppress.

умоля́ть, -я́ю imp. of умоли́ть; beg, entreat, implore, beseech. умоля́ю-щий, imploring, pleading.

умопомеша́тельство, -а, derangement, madness, insanity.

умори́тельный, incredibly funny, kil-ling. у|мори́ть, -рю́ perf. kill; tire out, exhaust.

умру́, etc.: see умы́ть. умру́, etc.: see умере́ть.

у́мственный, mental, intellectual; ~ труд, brainwork.

~

умудри́ть, -рю́ *perf.*, **умудря́ть**, -я́ю *imp.* make wise, make wiser; ∼ся, contrive, manage.

умча́ть, -чу́ *perf.* whirl away, dash away; ∼ся, whirl away, dash away.

умыва́льная *sb.* lavatory, cloak-room. **умыва́льник**, -а, wash-stand, wash-basin. **умыва́льный**, wash, washing. **умыва́ть**, -а́ю(сь) *imp.* of умы́ть(ся).

у́мысел, -сла, design, intention; злой ∼ evil intent; с у́мыслом, of set purpose.

умы́ть, умо́ю *perf.* (*imp.* умыва́ть) wash; ∼ся, wash (oneself).

умы́шленный, intentional, deliberate.

унаво́живать, -аю *imp.*, **у|наво́зить**, -о́жу *perf.* manure.

у|насле́довать, -дую *perf.*

унести́, -су́, -сёшь; -ёс, -ла́ *perf.* (*imp.* уноси́ть) take away; carry off, make off with; carry away, remove; ∼сь, whirl away; fly away, fly by; be carried (away).

универма́г, -а, *abbr.* department store. **универса́ль|ный**, universal; all-round; many-sided; versatile; multi-purpose, all-purpose; ∼ магази́н, department store; ∼ое сре́дство, panacea. **универса́м**, -а *abbr.* supermarket.

университе́т, -а, university. **университе́тский**, university.

унижа́ть, -а́ю *imp.*, **уни́зить**, -и́жу *perf.* humble humiliate, lower, degrade; ∼ся, debase oneself, lower oneself, stoop. **униже́ние**, -я, humiliation, degradation, abasement. **уни́женный**, humble, humiliated, oppressed, degraded. **унизи́тельный**, humiliating, degrading.

унима́ть(ся, -а́ю(сь *imp.* of уня́ть(ся.

унита́з, -а, lavatory pan.

уничтожа́ть, -а́ю *imp.*, **уничто́жить**, -жу *perf.* destroy, annihilate; wipe out; exterminate, obliterate; abolish; do away with, eliminate; put an end to; crush. **уничтожа́ющий**, destructive, annihilating. **уничтоже́ние**, -я, destruction, annihilation; extermination, obliteration; abolition; elimination.

уноси́ть(ся, -ошу́(сь, -о́сишь(ся *imp.* of унести́(сь.

у́нтер, -а, **у́нтер-офице́р**, -а, non-commissioned officer.

уныва́ть, -а́ю *imp.* be depressed, be dejected. **уны́лый**, depressed, dejected, despondent, downcast; melancholy, doleful, cheerless. **уны́ние**, -я, depression, dejection, despondency.

уня́ть, уйму́, -мёшь; -я́л, -а́, -о *perf.* (*imp.* унима́ть) calm, soothe, pacify; stop, check; suppress; ∼ся, calm down; stop, abate, die down.

упа́док, -дка, decline, decay, collapse; decadence; depression; ∼ ду́ха, depression. **упа́дочнический**, decadent. **упа́дочный**, depressive; decadent.

упа́сть etc.: see упа́сть.

у|пакова́ть, -ку́ю *perf.*, **упако́вывать**, -аю *imp.* pack (up); wrap (up), bale. **упако́вка**, -и, packing, wrapping, baling; package. **упако́вочный**, packing. **упако́вщик**, -а, packer.

упа́сть, -аду́, -адёшь *perf.* of па́дать.

упере́ть, упру́, -рёшь; -ёр *perf.*, **упира́ть**, -а́ю *imp.* rest, prop, lean (heavily): (*sl.*) pinch, steal; ∼ глаза́ в + *acc.* fix one's eyes on; ∼ на + *acc.* stress, insist on; ∼ся, rest, lean, prop oneself; resist; jib; dig one's heels in; + в + *acc.* come up against; run into.

упи́танный, well-fed; fattened; plump.

упла́та, -ы, payment, paying. **у|плати́ть**, -ачу́, -а́тишь *perf.*, **упла́чивать**, -аю *imp.* pay.

уплотне́ние, -я, compression; condensation; consolidation; sealing. **уплотни́ть**, -ню́ *perf.*, **уплотня́ть**, -я́ю *imp.* condense; consolidate, concentrate, compress; pack (in).

уплыва́ть, -а́ю *imp.*, **уплы́ть**, -ыву́, -ывёшь; -ы́л, -а́, -о *perf.* swim away; sail away, steam away; pass, elapse; be lost to sight; vanish, ebb.

уподо́биться, -блюсь *perf.*, **уподобля́ться**, -я́юсь *imp.* + *dat.* become like; be assimilated to. **уподобле́ние**, -я, likening, comparison; assimilation.

упое́ние, -я, ecstasy, rapture, thrill. **упоённый**, intoxicated, thrilled, in raptures. **упои́тельный**, intoxicating, ravishing.

уползать, -áю *imp.*, **уползти**, -зý, -зёшь; -óлз, -злá *perf.* creep away, crawl away.

уполномо́ченный *sb.* (authorized) agent, delegate, representative; proxy; commissioner. **уполномо́чивать**, -аю *imp.*, **уполномо́чить**, -чу *perf.* authorize, empower. **уполномо́чие**, -я, authorization; authority; credentials.

упомина́ние, -я, mention; reference; reminder. **упомина́ть**, -áю *imp.*, **упомяну́ть**, -нý, -нешь *perf.* mention, refer to.

упо́р, -а, rest, prop, support; stay, brace; в ~, point-blank; сде́лать ~ на + *acc.* or *prep.* lay stress on; смотре́ть в ~ на + *acc.* stare straight at. **упо́рный**, stubborn, unyielding, obstinate; dogged, persistent; sustained. -упо́рный in *comb.* -resistant. **упо́рство**, -а, stubbornness, obstinacy; doggedness, persistence. **упо́рствовать**, -твую *imp.* be stubborn; persist (в + *prep.* in).

упоря́дочивать, -аю *imp.*, **упоря́дочить**, -чу *perf.* regulate, put in (good) order, set to rights.

употреби́тельный, (widely-)used; common, generally accepted, usual. **употреби́ть**, -блю́ *perf.*, **употребля́ть**, -я́ю *imp.* use; make use of; take. **употребле́ние**, -я, use; usage; application; вы́йти из употребле́ния, go out of use, fall into disuse; спо́соб употребле́ния, directions for use.

управде́л, -а *abbr.* office manager, business manager. **управдо́м**, -а *abbr.* manager (of block of flats), house manager. **управи́тель**, -я *m.* manager; bailiff, steward. **упра́виться**, -влюсь *perf.*, **управля́ться**, -яюсь *imp.* cope, manage; + с + *instr.* deal with. **управле́ние**, -я management; administration; direction; control; driving, piloting, steering; government; authority, directorate, board; controls; под управле́нием + *gen.* conducted by; ~ автомоби́лем, driving; ~ на расстоя́нии, remote control; ~ по ра́дио, radio control. **управля́емый снаря́д**, guided missile. **управля́ть**, -я́ю *imp.* + *instr.*

manage, administer, direct, run; govern; be in charge of; control, operate; drive, pilot, steer, navigate; ~ ве́слом, paddle. **управля́ющий**, control, controlling; *sb.* manager; bailiff, steward; ~ по́ртом, harbour-master.

упражне́ние, -я, exercise. **упражня́ть**, -я́ю *imp.* exercise, train; ~ся, practise, train.

упраздне́ние, -я, abolition; cancellation, annulment. **упраздни́ть**, -ню́ *perf.*, **упраздня́ть**, -я́ю *imp.* abolish; cancel, annul.

упра́шивать, -аю *imp.* of упроси́ть. **упре́ть**, -е́ет *perf.* of упре́ть.

упрёк, -а, reproach, reproof. **упрека́ть**, -а́ю *imp.*, **упрекну́ть**, -нý, -нёшь *perf.* reproach, reprove; accuse, charge.

у|пре́ть, -е́ет *perf.* (*imp.* also упрева́ть) stew.

упроси́ть, -ошу́ -о́сишь *perf.* (*imp.* упра́шивать) beg, entreat; prevail upon.

упрости́ть, -ощу́ *perf.* (*imp.* упроща́ть) simplify; over-simplify; ~ся, be simplified, get simpler.

упро́чивать, -аю *imp.*, **упро́чить** -чу *perf.* strengthen, consolidate; fix; secure; establish firmly; + за + *instr.* leave to; establish for, ensure for; ~ся, be strengthened be consolidated; become firmer; be firmly established; establish oneself settle oneself; + за + *instr.* become attached to, stick to.

упрошу́, etc.: see упроси́ть.

упроща́ть(ся, -а́ю(сь *imp.* of упрости́ть(ся. **упроще́ние**, -я, simplification. **упрощённый**, -щён, -á, simplified; over-simplified.

упру́, etc.: see упере́ть.

упру́гий, elastic; resilient, flexible; springy. **упру́гость**, -и, elasticity; pressure, tension; spring, bound. **упру́же** *comp.* of упру́гий.

упря́жка, -и, harness, gear; team, relay. **упряжно́й**; ~áя ло́шадь, draught-horse, carriage-horse. **у́пряжь**, -и, harness, gear.

упря́миться, -млюсь *imp.* be obstinate; persist. **упря́мство**, -а, obstinacy, stubbornness. **упря́мый**, obstinate, stubborn; persistent.

упря́тать, -я́чу *perf.*, упря́тывать, -аю *imp.* hide, conceal; put away, banish; ~ ся, hide.

упуска́ть, -а́ю *imp.*, упусти́ть, -ущу́, -у́стишь *perf.* let go, let slip, let fall; miss; lose; neglect; ~ из виду, lose sight of, overlook, fail to take account of. упуще́ние, -я, omission; slip; negligence.

ура́ *int.* hurrah.

уравне́ние, -я, equalization; equation. ура́внивать, -аю *imp.*, уравня́ть, -я́ю *perf.* equalize, make equal, make level; equate. уравни́тельный, equalizing, levelling. уравнове́сить, -е́шу *perf.*, уравнове́шивать, -аю *imp.* balance; equilibrate; counterbalance; neutralize. уравнове́шенность, -и, balance, steadiness, composure. уравнове́шенный, -balanced, steady, composed.

урага́н, -а, hurricane; storm.

ура́н, -а, uranium; Uranus. ура́новый, uranium; uranic.

урва́ть, -ву́, -вёшь, -а́л, -а́, -о *perf.* (*imp.* урыва́ть) snatch, grab.

урегули́рование, -я, regulation; settlement, adjustment. у|регули́ровать, -рую *perf.*

уре́з, -а, reduction, cut. уре́зать, -е́жу *perf.*, уреза́ть, -а́ю, уре́зывать, -аю *imp.* cut off; shorten; cut down, reduce; axe.

у́рка, -и *m.* and *f.* (*sl.*) lag, convict, (non-political) prisoner.

у́рна, -ы, urn; ballot-box; refuse-bin, litter-bin.

у́ровень, -вня *m.* level; plane; standard; grade; gauge.

уро́д, -а, freak, monster; deformed person; ugly person; depraved person. уроди́ться, -ожу́сь *perf.* ripen; grow; be born; + в + *acc.* take after.

уро́дливость, -и, deformity; ugliness. уро́дливый, deformed, misshapen; ugly; bad; abnormal; faulty; distorting, distorted. уро́довать, -дую *imp.* (*perf.* из~) deform, disfigure, mutilate; make ugly; distort. уро́дство, -а, deformity; disfigurement; ugliness; abnormality.

урожа́й, -я, harvest; crop, yield; abundance. урожа́йность, -и, yield;

productivity. урожа́йный, harvest; productive, high-yield; ~ год, good year.

урождённый, née; inborn, born. уро-же́нец, -нца, уроже́нка, -и, native. урожу́сь: see уроди́ться.

уро́к, -а, lesson; homework; task.

уро́н, -а, losses, casualties; damage. уроня́ть, -ню́, -нишь *perf.* of роня́ть.

уро́чный, fixed, agreed; usual, established.

УРС, -а *abbr.* управля́емый реакти́вный снаря́д, guided missile.

урыва́ть, -а́ю *imp.* of урва́ть. уры́вками *adv.* in snatches, by fits and starts; at odd moments. уры́вочный, fitful; occasional.

ус, -а; *pl.* -ы́, whisker; antenna; tendril; awn; *pl.* moustache.

усади́ть, -ажу́ -а́лишь *perf.*, уса́живать, -аю *imp.* seat, offer a seat; make sit down; set; plant; cover; ~ в тюрьму́, clap in prison. уса́дьба, -ы; *gen. pl.* -деб or -дьб, country estate, country seat; farmstead; farm centre. уса́живаться, -аюсь *imp.* of усе́сться.

уса́тый, moustached; whiskery; whiskered.

усва́ивать, -аю *imp.*, усво́ить, -о́ю *perf.* master; assimilate; adopt; acquire; imitate; pick up. усвое́ние, -я, mastering; assimilation; adoption.

усе́ивать, -аю *imp.* of усе́ять.

усе́рдие, -я *neut.* diligence. усе́рдный, zealous; diligent, painstaking.

усе́сться, усяду́сь, -е́лся *perf.* (*imp.* уса́живаться) take a seat; settle; set (to), settle down (to).

усе́ять, -е́ю *perf.* (*imp.* усе́ивать) sow; cover, dot, stud; litter, strew.

усиде́ть, -ижу́ *perf.* keep one's place, remain seated, sit still; hold down a job. уси́дчивый, -и, assiduity. уси́дчивый, assiduous; painstaking.

у́сик, -а, tendril; awn; runner; antenna; *pl.* small moustache.

усиле́ние, -я, strengthening; reinforcement; intensification; aggravation; amplification. уси́ленный, reinforced; intensified; increased; earnest, urgent, importunate; copious. уси́ливать, -аю imp., уси́лить, -лю perf. intensify, increase, heighten; aggravate; amplify; strengthen, reinforce; ~ся, increase, intensify; become stronger; become aggravated; swell, grow louder; make efforts, try. уси́лие, -я, effort; exertion. уси́литель, -я m. amplifier; booster. уси́лительный, amplifying; booster.

ускака́ть, -ачу́, -а́чешь perf. bound away; skip off; gallop off.

ускольза́ть, -а́ю imp., ускользну́ть, -ну́, -нёшь perf. slip off; steal away; get away; disappear; escape; + от + gen. evade, avoid.

ускоре́ние, -я, acceleration; speeding-up. ускори́тель, -я, accelerator. ускори́ть, -рю perf., ускоря́ть, -я́ю imp. quicken; speed up, accelerate; hasten; precipitate; ~ся, accelerate, be accelerated; quicken.

усла́вливаться: see усло́виться.

услади́ть, -ажу́, усложжа́ть, -а́ю imp. delight, charm; soften, mitigate.

уследи́ть, -ежу́ perf. + за + instr. keep an eye on, mind; follow.

усло́вие, -я, condition; clause, term; stipulation, proviso; agreement; pl. conditions; усло́вия приёма, reception. усло́виться, -влюсь perf., усла́вливаться, усло́вливаться, -аюсь imp. agree, settle; arrange, make arrangements. усло́вленный, agreed, fixed, stipulated. усло́вность, -и, convention, conventionality; conditional character. усло́вный, conditional; conditioned; conventional; agreed, prearranged; relative; theoretical; ~ знак, conventional sign.

усложне́ние, -я, complication. усложни́ть, -ню́ perf. усложня́ть, -я́ю imp. complicate; ~ся, become complicated.

услу́га, -и, service; good turn; pl. service(s), public utilities; оказа́ть услу́гу, do a service. услу́живать, -аю imp. услужи́ть, -жу́, -жишь perf. serve, act as a servant; + dat. do a service, do a good turn. услу́жливый, obliging.

услыха́ть, -ышу perf., услы́шать, -ышу perf. hear; sense; scent.

усма́тривать, -аю imp. of усмотре́ть.

усмеха́ться, -а́юсь imp., усмехну́ться, -ну́сь, -нёшься perf. smile; grin; sneer; smirk. усме́шка, -и, smile; grin; sneer.

усмире́ние, -я, pacification; suppression, putting down. усмири́ть, -рю́ perf., усмиря́ть, -я́ю imp. pacify; calm, quieten; tame; suppress, put down.

усмотре́ние, -я, discretion, judgement; по усмотре́нию, at one's discretion, as one thinks best. усмотре́ть, -рю́, -ришь perf. (imp. усма́тривать) perceive, observe; see; regard, interpret.

усну́ть, -ну́, -нёшь perf. go to sleep, fall asleep.

усоверше́нствование, -я, perfecting; finishing, qualifying; advanced studies; improvement, refinement. усоверше́нствованный, improved; finished, complete. у|соверше́нствовать(ся, -твую(сь perf.

усомни́ться, -ню́сь perf. doubt.

усо́пший, (the) deceased.

успева́емость, -и, progress. успева́ть, -а́ю imp., успе́ть, -е́ю perf. have time; manage; succeed, be successful. успе́ется impers. there is still time, there is no hurry. успе́х, -а, success; progress. успе́шный, successful.

успока́ивать, -аю imp., успоко́ить, -о́ю perf. calm, quiet, soothe, tranquillize; reassure, set one's mind at rest; assuage, deaden; reduce to order, control; ~ся, calm down; compose oneself; rest content; abate; become still; drop. успока́ивающий, calming, soothing, sedative; ~ее сре́дство, sedative tranquillizer. успокое́ние, -я, calming, quieting, soothing; calm; peace, tranquillity. успокои́тельный, calming, soothing; reassuring; ~ое sb. sedative, tranquillizer.

УССР (u-eseсér) abbr. Украи́нская Сове́тская Социалисти́ческая Респу́блика, Ukrainian Soviet Socialist Republic.

уста́в, -а, regulations, rules, statutes; service regulations; rule; charter.

уставáть, -таю́, -ёшь imp. of уста́ть; не уставая, incessantly, uninterruptedly.

уста́вить, -влю *perf.*, уставля́ть, -я́ю *imp.* set, arrange, dispose; cover, fill, pile; direct, fix; ~ся, find room, go in; fix one's gaze, stare; become fixed, become steady. **уста́вный**, regulation, statutory, prescribed.

уста́лость, -и, fatigue, tiredness, weariness. **уста́лый** tired, weary, fatigued.

устана́вливать, -аю *imp.*, установи́ть, -влю́, -вишь *perf.* place, put, set up; install, mount, rig up; adjust, regulate; set; establish; institute; fix; prescribe; secure obtain; determine; ascertain; ~ся, take position, dispose oneself; be settled, be established; set in; be formed be fixed. **устано́вка**, -и, placing, putting, setting up, arrangement; installation; mounting, rigging; adjustment, regulation, setting; plant, unit; directions, directive. **установле́ние**, -я, establishment; statute; institution. **устано́вленный**, established, fixed, secured, regulation.

уста́ну, etc.: see уста́ть.

устарева́ть, -а́ю *imp.*, у|старе́ть, -е́ю *perf.* grow old; become obsolete; become antiquated, go out of date. **устаре́лый**, obsolete; antiquated, out of date.

уста́ть, -а́ну *perf.* become tired, tire; я уста́ла, I am tired.

у́стно *adv.* orally, by word of mouth. **у́стный**, oral, verbal; ~ая речь, spoken language.

усто́й, -я, abutment, buttress, pier; foundation, support; *pl.* foundations, bases. **усто́йчивость**, -и, stability, steadiness, firmness; resistance. **усто́йчивый**, stable, steady, firm; settled; resistant (к + *dat.* to). **устоя́ть**, -ою́ *perf.* keep one's balance, keep one's feet; stand firm, stand one's ground; resist, hold out.

устра́ивать(ся, -аю(сь *imp.* of устро́ить(ся.

устране́ние, -я, removal, elimination, clearing. **устрани́ть**, -ню́ *perf.*, устраня́ть, -я́ю *imp.* remove; eliminate, clear; dismiss; ~ся, resign, retire, withdraw.

устраша́ть, -а́ю *imp.*, устраши́ть, -шу́ *perf.* frighten; scare; ~ся, be afraid; be

frightened, be terrified. **устраша́ющий**, frightening; deterrent. **устраше́ние**, -я, frightening; fright, fear; сре́дство устраше́ния, deterrent.

устреми́ть, -млю́ *perf.*, устремля́ть, -я́ю *imp.* direct, fix; ~ся, rush; head; be directed, be fixed, be concentrated; concentrate. **устремле́ние**, -я, rush; striving, aspiration. **устремлённость**, -и tendency.

у́стрица, -ы, oyster. **у́стричный**, oyster.

устрое́ние, -я, arranging, organization. **устро́итель**, -я *m.*, -ница, -ы, organizer. **устро́ить**, -о́ю *perf.* (*imp.* устра́ивать) arrange, organize; establish; make; construct; cause, create; settle, order, put in order; place, fix up; get, secure; suit, be convenient; ~ на рабо́ту, fix up with, a job; ~ сканда́л, make a scene; ~ся, work out; come right; manage, make arrangements; settle down, get settled; be found, get fixed up. **устро́йство**, -а, arrangement, organization; (mode of) construction; layout; apparatus, mechanism, device; structure, system.

усту́п, -а, shelf, ledge; terrace; bench. **уступа́ть**, -а́ю *imp.*, уступи́ть, -плю́, -пишь *perf.* yield; give in; cede; concede; let have, give up; be inferior; take off, knock off; ~ доро́гу, make way; ~ ме́сто, give up one's place, seat. **усту́пка**, -и, concession, compromise; reduction. **усту́пчатый**, ledged, stepped, terraced. **усту́пчивый**, pliant pliable; compliant; tractable.

устыди́ться, -ыжу́сь *perf.* (+ *gen.*) be ashamed (of).

у́стье, -я; *gen. pl.* -ьев, mouth; estuary.

усугуби́ть, -у́блю *perf.* усугубля́ть, -я́ю *imp.* increase; intensify; aggravate, make worse.

усы́: see ус.

усынови́ть, -влю́ *perf.*, усыновля́ть, -я́ю *imp.* adopt. **усыновле́ние**, -я, adoption.

усы́пать, -плю *perf.*, усыпа́ть, -а́ю *imp.* strew, scatter; cover.

усыпи́тельный, soporific. **усыпи́ть**, -плю́ *perf.*, усыпля́ть, -я́ю *imp.* put to sleep; lull; weaken, undermine, neutralize; ~ боль, deaden pain.

усядусь, etc.: see усесться.

утаивать, -аю *imp.*, **утаить**, -аю *perf.* conceal; keep to oneself, keep secret; appropriate.

утаптывать, -аю *imp.* of утоптать.

утаскивать, -аю *imp.*, **утащить**, -щу -щишь *perf.* drag away, drag off; make off with.

утварь, -и, utensils, equipment.

утвердительный, affirmative. **утвердить**, -ржу *perf.*, **утверждать**, -аю *imp.* confirm; approve; sanction, ratify; establish; assert, maintain, hold, claim, allege. **утверждение**, -я, approval; confirmation; ratification; assertion, affirmation, claim, allegation; establishment.

утекать, -аю *imp.* of утечь.

утёнок, -нка; *p'.* утята, -ят, duckling.

утереть, утру, -рёшь, утёр *perf.* (*imp.* утирать) wipe; wipe off; wipe dry; ~ нос + *dat.* score off.

утерпеть, -плю, -пишь *perf.* restrain oneself.

утеря, -и, loss. **у|терять**, -яю *perf.*

утёс, -а, cliff, crag. **утёсистый**, steep, precipitous.

утечка, -и, leak, leakage; escape; loss, wastage, dissipation; ~ газа, escape of gas. **утечь**, -еку -ечёшь, -ёк, -ла *perf.* (*imp.* утекать) flow away; leak, escape; run away; pass, elapse, go by.

утешать, -аю *imp.*, **утешить**, -шу *perf.* comfort, console; ~ся, console oneself. **утешение**, -я, comfort, consolation. **утешительный**, comforting, consoling.

утиль, -я *m.*, **утильсырьё**, -я, salvage; scrap; rubbish, refuse. **утильный**, scrap.

утиный, duck, duck's.

утирать(ся), -аю(сь *imp.* of утереть(ся).

утихать, -аю *imp.*, **утихнуть**, -ну, -их *perf.* abate, subside; cease, die away; slacken; drop; become calm, calm down.

утка, -и, duck; canard.

уткнуть, -ну, -нёшь *perf.* bury; fix; ~ся, bury oneself; ~ся головой в подушку, bury one's head in the pillow.

утолить, -лю *perf.* (*imp.* утолять)

quench, slake; satisfy; relieve, alleviate, soothe.

утолстить, -лщу *perf.*, **утолщать**, -аю *imp.* thicken, make thicker; ~ся, thicken, become thicker. **утолщение**, -я, thickening; thickened part, bulge; reinforcement, rib, boss.

утолять, -яю *imp.* of утолить.

утомительный, tiresome; tedious; wearisome, tiring, fatiguing. **утомить**, -млю *perf.*, **утомлять**, -яю *imp.* tire, weary, fatigue; ~ся, get tired. **утомление**, -я, tiredness, weariness, fatigue. **утомлённый**, tired, weary, fatigued.

у|тонуть, -ну, -нешь *perf.* (*imp.* also утопать) drown, be drowned; sink, go down.

утончённость, -и, refinement. **утончённый**, refined; exquisite, subtle.

утопать, -аю *imp.* of утонуть; roll, wallow. **у|топить(ся**, -плю(сь -пишь(ся *perf.* **утопленник**, -а, drowned man.

утоптать, -пчу, -пчешь *perf.* (*imp.* утаптывать) trample down, pound.

уточнение, -я, more precise definition; amplification, elaboration. **уточнить**, -ню *perf.*, **уточнять**, -яю *imp.* define more precisely; amplify, elaborate.

утраивать, -аю *imp.* of утроить.

у|трамбовать, -бую *perf.*, **утрамбовывать**, -аю *imp.* ram, tamp; ~ся, become flat, become level.

утрата, -ы, loss. **утратить**, -ачу *perf.*, **утрачивать**, -аю *imp.* lose.

утренний, morning, early. **утренник**, -а, morning performance, matinée; early-morning frost.

утрировать, -рую *perf.* and *imp.* exaggerate; overplay. **утрировка**, -и, exaggeration.

утро, -а or -á, -у or -ý; *pl.* -а, -ам or -ám, morning.

утроба, -ы, womb; belly.

утроить, -ою *perf.* (*imp.* утраивать) triple, treble.

утром *adv.* in the morning; сегодня ~, this morning.

утру, etc.: see утереть, утро.

утрудить, -ужу *perf.*, **утруждать**, -аю *imp.* trouble, tire.

утю́г, -á, iron. **утю́жить**, -жу *imp.* (*perf.* вы́~, от~) iron, press; smooth.

утю́жка, -и, ironing, pressing.

ух *int.* oh, ooh, ah.

уха́, -и́, fish soup.

уха́б, -а, pot-hole. **уха́бистый**, full of pot-holes; bumpy.

уха́живать, -аю *imp.* за + *instr.* nurse, tend; look after; court; pay court to, make advances to.

у́хать, -аю *imp.* of у́хнуть.

ухвати́ть, -ачу́ -а́тишь *perf.*, **ухва́ты-вать**, -аю *imp.* catch, lay hold of; seize; grasp; ~ся за + *acc.* grasp, lay hold of; set to, set about; seize; jump at; take up. **ухва́тка**, -и, grip; grasp; skill; trick; manner.

ухитри́ться, -рю́сь *perf.*, **ухитря́ться**, -я́юсь *imp.* manage, contrive.

ухло́пать, -аю *perf.*, **ухло́пывать**, -аю *imp.* squander, waste; (*sl.*) kill.

ухмы́лка, -и, smirk, grin. **ухмыльну́ть-ся**, -ну́сь, -нёшься *perf.*, **ухмыля́ться**, -я́юсь *imp.* smirk, grin.

у́хнуть, -ну *perf.* (*imp.* у́хать) cry out; hoot; crash; bang; rumble; slip, fall; come a cropper; come to grief; drop; lose, squander, spend away.

у́хо, -а; *pl.* у́ши, уше́й, ear; ear-flap, ear-piece; lug, hanger; заткну́ть у́ши, stop one's ears; кра́ем у́ха, with half an ear; по́ уши, up to one's ears; слу́-шать во все у́ши, be all ears; туго́й на́ ~, hard of hearing.

ухо́д[1], -а, + за + *instr.* care of; main-tenance of; nursing, tending, looking after.

ухо́д[2], -а, going away, leaving, depart-ure; withdrawal. **уходи́ть**, -ожу́, -о́дишь *imp.* of уйти́; stretch, extend.

уху́дшать, -áю *imp.*, **уху́дшить**, -шу *perf.* make worse, aggravate; ~ся, get worse.

уцеле́ть, -е́ю *perf.* remain intact, escape destruction; survive; escape.

уцепи́ть, -плю́ -пишь *perf.*, **уцепля́ть**, -я́ю *imp.* catch hold of, grasp, seize; ~ся за + *acc.* catch hold of, grasp, seize; jump at.

уча́ствовать, -твую *imp.* take part, participate; have a share, hold shares.

уча́ствующий *sb.* participant. **уча́стие**,

-я, participation, taking part; share, sharing; sympathy, concern.

участи́ть, -ащу́ *perf.* (*imp.* учаща́ть) make more frequent, quicken; ~ся, become more frequent, become more rapid.

уча́стливый, sympathetic. **уча́стник**, -а, participant, member; ~ состяза́ния, competitor. **уча́сток**, -тка, plot, strip; allotment; lot, parcel; part, section, portion; length; division; sector, area, zone, district; police district, police-station; field, sphere. **у́часть**, -и, lot, fate, portion.

учаща́ть(ся, -áю(сь *imp.* of участи́ть (ся. **учащённый**; -ён, -ена́), quickened; faster.

уча́щийся *sb.* student; pupil. **учёба**, -ы, studies; course; studying, learning; drill, training. **уче́бник**, -а, text-book; manual, primer. **уче́бн|ый**, education-al; school; training, practice; ~ый год, academic year, school year; ~ые посо́бия, teaching equipment, teach-ing aids; ~ое су́дно, training-ship. **уче́ние**, -я, learning; studies; appren-ticeship; teaching, instruction; doc-trine; exercise; *pl.* training. **учени́к**, -á, **учени́ца**, -ы, pupil; student; learner; apprentice; disciple, follower. **учени́-ческий**, pupil('s); apprentice('s); un-skilled; raw, crude, immature. **учени́-чество**, -а, time spent as pupil or stu-dent; apprenticeship; rawness, im-maturity. **учёность**, -и, learning, erudi-tion. **учён|ый**, learned, erudite; edu-cated; scholarly; academic; scientific; trained, performing; ~ая сте́пень, (university) degree; ~ый *sb.* scholar; scientist.

уче́сть, учту́, -тёшь; учёл, учла́ *perf.* (*imp.* учи́тывать) take stock of, make an inventory of; take into account, take into consideration; allow for; bear in mind; discount. **учёт**, -а, stock-taking; reckoning, calculation; taking into account; registration; dis-count, discounting; без ~а + *gen.*, disregarding; взять на ~ register. **учётн|ый**, registration; discount; ~ое отделе́ние, records section.

учи́лище, -а, school; (training) college.

у|чини́ть, -ню́ *perf.*, учиня́ть, -я́ю *imp.* make; carry out, execute; commit.

учи́тель, -я; *pl.* -я́ *m.*, учи́тельница, -ы, teacher. учи́тельск|ий, teacher's, teachers'; ~ая *sb.* staff-room.

учи́тывать, -аю *imp.* of уче́сть.

учи́ть, учу́, у́чишь *imp.* (*perf.* вы́~, на~, об~) teach; be a teacher; learn, memorize; ~ся, be a student; + *dat.* or *inf.* learn, study.

учреди́тель, -я *m.* founder. учреди́тельница, -ы, foundress. учреди́тельн|ый, constituent; ~ый акт, constituent act; ~ое собра́ние, constituent assembly. учреди́ть, -ежу́ *perf.*, учрежда́ть, -а́ю *imp.* found, establish, set up; introduce, institute учрежде́ние, -я, founding, setting up; establishment; institution.

учти́вый, civil, courteous, polite.

учту́. etc.: see уче́сть.

учхо́з, -а *abbr.* (school) experimental farm

ушёл, etc.: see уйти́. у́ши, etc.: see у́хо.

уши́б, -а, injury; knock; bruise, contusion. ушиба́ть, -а́ю *imp.*, ушиби́ть, -бу́, -бёшь; уши́б *perf.* injure; bruise; hurt, shock; ~ся, hurt oneself, give oneself a knock; bruise oneself.

ушко́. -а́; *pl.* -и, -о́в, eye; lug; tab, tag; *pl.* pasta shells.

ушно́й, ear, aural.

уще́лье, -я, ravine gorge. canyon.

ущеми́ть, -млю́ *perf.*, ущемля́ть, -я́ю *imp.* pinch jam. nip; limit; encroach on; wound, hurt. ущемле́ние, -я, pinching, jamming, nipping; limitation; wounding hurting.

уще́рб, -а, detriment; loss; damage, injury; prejudice; на ~e, waning. уще́рбный, waning.

ущипну́ть, -ну́, -нёшь *perf* of щипа́ть.

ую́т, -а, cosiness, comfort. ую́тный, cosy comfortable.

уязви́мый, vulnerable. уязви́ть, -влю́ *perf.*, уязвля́ть, -я́ю *imp.* wound, hurt.

уясне́ние, -я, explanation, elucidation. уясни́ть, -ню́ *perf.* уясня́ть, -я́ю *imp.* understand, make out; explain.

Ф

ф *letter:* see эф.

фа *n. indecl.* F; fah.

фаб- *abbr.* in *comb.* of фабри́чный, factory, works. фабзавко́м, -а, factory and works committee. ~завместко́м, -а, factory, plant, and local committee. ~за́вуч, -а, factory industrial-training school. ~ко́м, -а, works committee. ~мас, -а, mass-production factory.

фа́брика, -и, factory, mill, works. фабрика́нт, -а, manufacturer. фабрика́т, -а, finished product, manufactured product. фабрикова́ть, -ку́ю *imp.* (*perf.* с~) manufacture, make, fabricate, forge. фабри́чн|ый, factory; industrial, manufacturing; factory-made; ~ая ма́рка ~ое клеймо́ trade-mark.

фа́була, -ы, plot, story.

фаго́т, -а, bassoon. фаготи́ст, -а, bassoon-player.

фа́за, -ы, phase; stage.

фаза́н, -а, фаза́ниха, -и, pheasant. фаза́ний, pheasant, pheasants'.

фа́зис, -а, phase. фа́зный, фа́зовый, phase.

фа́кел, -а, torch, flare. flame. фа́кельный, torch(-light). фа́кельщик, -а, torch-bearer; incendiary.

факт, -а. fact; соверши́вшийся ~, fait accompli. факти́чески *adv.* in fact, actually; practically, virtually, to all intents and purposes. факти́ческий, actual; real; virtual.

факту́ра, -ы, invoice, bill; style, execution, texture; structure.

факультати́вный, optional. **факульте́т**, -а, faculty, department. **факульте́тский**, faculty.

фа́лда, -ы, tail, skirt.

фальсифика́тор, -а, falsifier, forger. **фальсифика́ция**, -и, falsification; forging; adulteration; forgery, fake, counterfeit. **фальсифици́ровать**, -рую *perf. and imp.* falsify; forge; adulterate. **фальши́вить**, -влю *imp.* (*perf.* с~) be a hypocrite, act insincerely; sing or play out of tune. **фальши́вка**, -и, forged document. **фальши́вый**, false; spurious; forged, fake; artificial, imitation; out of tune; hypocritical, insincere. **фальшь**, -и, deception, trickery; falsity; falseness; hypocrisy, insincerity.

фами́лия, -и, surname; family, kin. **фами́льный**, family. **фамилья́рничать**, -аю, be over-familiar, take liberties. **фамилья́рность**, -и, familiarity; liberty, liberties. **фамилья́рный**, (over-)familiar; unceremonious; off-hand, casual.

фане́ра, -ы, veneer; plywood. **фане́рный**, veneer, of veneer; plywood.

фантазёр, -а, dreamer, visionary. **фантази́ровать**, -рую *imp.* (*perf.* с~) dream, indulge in fantasies; make up, dream up; improvise. **фанта́зия**, -и, fantasy; fancy; imagination; whim; fabrication. **фанта́стика**, -и, fiction, fantasy; the fantastic; works of fantasy; нау́чная ~, science fiction. **фантасти́ческий**, **фантасти́чный**, fantastic; fabulous; imaginary.

фа́ра, -ы, headlight; посáдочные фа́ры, landing lights.

фарао́н, -а, pharaoh; faro. **фарао́нов**, pharaoh's.

фарва́тер, -а, fairway, channel.

фармазо́н, -а, freemason.

фарт, -а, (*sl.*) luck, success.

фа́ртук, -а, apron; carriage-rug.

фарфо́р, -а, china; porcelain. **фарфо́ровый**, china; ~ая посу́да, china. **фарцева́ть**, -цу́ю *imp.* speculate in currency. **фарцо́вщик**, -а, currency speculator.

фарш, -а, stuffing, force-meat; minced meat, sausage-meat. **фарширо́ванный**, stuffed. **фарширова́ть**, -ру́ю *imp.* (*perf.* за~) stuff.

фасова́ть, -су́ю *imp.* (*perf.* рас~) package, pre-pack. **фасо́вка**, -и, packaging, pre-packing.

фасо́ль, -и, kidney bean(s), French bean(s); haricot beans.

фасо́н, -а, cut; fashion; style; manner, way; держа́ть ~, show off, put on airs. **фасо́нистый**, fashionable, stylish. **фасо́нный**, fashioned, shaped; form, forming, shaping.

фая́нс, -а, faience, pottery. **фая́нсовый**, pottery.

ФБР (*febeér*) *abbr.* Федера́льное бюро́ рассле́дований, F.B.I.

февра́ль, -я́ *m.* February. **февра́льский**, February.

фееpи́ческий, fairy-tale, magical.

фейерве́рк, -а, firework, fireworks.

фельдшер, -а; *pl.* -á, -шери́ца, -ы, doctor's assistant; (partly-qualified) medical attendant; hospital attendant; trained nurse.

фельето́н, -а, feuilleton, feature.

фен, -а, (hair-)dryer.

фе́рзевый, queen's. **ферзь**, -я́ *m.* queen.

фе́рма[1], -ы, farm.

фе́рма[2], -ы, girder, truss. **фе́рменный**, lattice.

фетр, -а, felt. **фе́тровый**, felt.

фехтова́льный, fencing, of fencing. **фехтова́льщик**, -а, -щица, -ы, fencer. **фехтова́ние**, -я, fencing. **фехтова́ть**, -ту́ю *imp.* fence.

фе́я, -и, fairy.

фиа́лка, -и, violet.

фибролит, -а, chipboard.

фигаро́ *n. indecl.* bolero.

фигля́р, -а, (circus) acrobat; clown; mountebank; buffoon. **фигля́рить**, -рю, **фигля́рничать**, -аю **фигля́рствовать**, -твую *imp.* put on an act.

фигу́ра, -ы, figure; court-card; (chess-)piece. **фигура́льный**, figurative, metaphorical; ornate, involved. **фигура́нт**, -а, figurant; super, extra. **фигури́ровать**, -рую *imp.* figure, appear. **фигури́ст**, -а, -и́стка, -и, figure-skater. **фигу́рка**, -и, figurine, statuette; figure. **фигу́рн|ый**, figured;

ornamented, patterned; figure; ~ое ката́ние, figure skating.

фи́зик, -а, physicist. **фи́зика**, -и, physics. **физио́лог**, -а, physiologist. **физиотерапе́вт**, -а, physiotherapist. **физи́ческ|ий**, physical; physics; ~ая культу́ра, physical culture; gymnastics. **физкульту́ра**, -ы abbr. P.T., gymnastics. **физкульту́рник**, -а, -у́рница, -ы abbr. gymnast, athlete. **физкульту́рный** abbr. gymnastic; athletic; sports; ~ зал, gymnasium.

фикс, -а, fixed price, fixed sum. **фикса́ж**, -а, fixing, fixer, fixing solution. **фикси́ровать**, -рую perf. and imp. (perf. also за~) fix; record, register.

фикти́вный, fictitious. **фи́кция**, -и, fiction.

филе́ n. indecl. sirloin; fillet; drawn-thread work, filet (lace). **филе́й**, -я, sirloin. **филе́йн|ый**, sirloin; filet-lace, drawn-thread; ~ая рабо́та, drawn-thread work, filet.

филиа́л, -а, branch. **филиа́льный**, branch.

фи́лин, -а, eagle-owl.

фили́стер, -а, philistine. **фили́стерский**, philistine. **фили́стерство**, -а, philistinism.

фило́лог, -а, philologist; student of language and literature. **филологи́ческий**, philological. **филоло́гия**, -и, philology, study of language and literature.

фило́н, -а, (sl.) shirker, lazy-bones. **фило́нить**, -ню imp. (sl.), loaf about, slack, shirk work.

фильм, -а, **фи́льма**, -ы, film.

фин- abbr. of фина́нсовый, financial, finance. **фининспе́ктор**, -а, financial officer. ~**отде́л**, finance department.

фина́л, -а, finale; final. **фина́льный**, final.

фина́нсовый, financial. **фина́нсы**, -ов pl. finance, finances; money.

фи́ник, -а, date. **фи́никовый**, date.

фи́ниш, -а, finish; finishing post. **фи́нишный**, finishing.

фи́нка, -и, Finn; Finnish knife; Finnish cap; Finnish pony. **финля́ндский**, Finnish. **финн**, -а, Finn. **фи́нно-уго́рский**, Finno-Ugrian. **фи́нский**, Finnish.

финт, -а, feint.

фиоле́товый, violet.

фи́рма, -ы, firm; company; combine; large enterprise; trade name; appearance, guise.

фисгармо́ния, -и, harmonium.

фити́ль, -я́ m. wick; fuse.

флаг, -а, flag; под ~ом + gen. flying the flag of; under the guise of; приспу́щенные ~и, flags at half-mast; спусти́ть ~, lower a flag.

флако́н, -а, (scent-)bottle, flask.

флама́ндец, -дца, **флама́ндка**, -и, Fleming. **флама́ндский**, Flemish.

фле́йта, -ы, flute. **флейти́ст**, -а, -и́стка, -и, flautist. **фле́йтовый**, flute.

фле́ксия, -и, inflexion. **флекти́вный**, inflexional; inflected.

фли́гель, -я; pl. -я́ m. wing; pavilion, extension, annexe.

флот, -а, fleet; возду́шный ~, air force; aviation. **фло́тский**, naval; sb. sailor.

флю́гер, -а; pl. -á, weather-vane, weathercock; pennant.

флюс[1], -а, gumboil, abscess.

флюс[2], -а; pl. -ы́, flux.

фля́га, -и, flask; water-bottle; (milk-) churn, milk-can. **фля́жка**, -и, flask.

фо́кус[1], -а, trick; conjuring trick.

фо́кус[2], -а, focus. **фокуси́ровать**, -рую imp. focus. **фокусиро́вка**, -и, focusing.

фо́кусник, -а, conjurer, juggler.

фо́кусный, focal.

фо́льга, -и, foil.

фо́мка, -и, (sl.) jemmy.

фон, -а, background.

фона́рик, -а, small lamp; torch, flashlight. **фона́рный**, lamp; ~ столб, lamp-post. **фона́рщик**, -а, lamplighter. **фона́рь**, -я́ m. lantern; lamp; light; skylight; black eye, bruise.

фонд, -а, fund; stock; reserves, resources; stocks; foundation.

фонта́н, -а, a fountain; stream; gusher.

форе́ль, -и, trout.

фо́рзац, -а, fly-leaf.

фóрма, -ы, form; shape; mould, cast; uniform; *pl.* contours; в пи́сьменной фóрме, in writing; в фóрме, in form; отли́ть в фóрму, mould, cast. **формáльный**, formal. **формáция**, -и, structure; stage; formation; stamp, mentality. **фóрменный**, uniform; regulation; formal; proper, regular, positive. **формировáние**, -я, forming; organization; unit, formation. **формировáть**, -рýю *imp.* (*perf.* c~) form; organize; shape; ~ся, form, shape, develop. **формовáть**, -мýю *imp.* (*perf.* c~) form shape; model; mould, cast. **формóвщик**, -а, moulder.

фóрмула, -ы, formula; formulation. **формули́ровать**, -рую *perf.* and *imp.* (*perf.* also c~) formulate. **формулирóвка**, -и, formulation; wording; formula. **формуля́р**, -а, record of service; log-book; library card; (*sl.*) dossier.

форси́рованный, forced; accelerated. **форси́ровать**, -рую *perf.* and *imp.* force; speed up.

фóрточка, -и, fortochka; small hinged (window-)pane; air vent.

фóто *n. indecl.* photo(graph).

фото- *in comb.*, photo-, photo-electric. **фотоаппарáт**, -а, camera. ~ **бумáга**, -и, photographic paper. ~**гени́чный**, photogenic. **фотóграф**, -а, photographer. ~**графи́ровать**, -рую *imp.* (*perf.* c~) photograph ~**графи́роваться**, be photographed; have one's photograph taken. ~**графи́ческий**, photographic. ~**грáфия**, -и, photography; photograph; photographer's studio. ~**кóпия**, photocopy. ~ **лáмпа**, -ы, dark-room lamp; photoelectric cell. ~**люби́тель**, -я *m.* amateur photographer. ~**нáбор**, -а, film-setting; photo-setting. ~**объекти́в**, -а, (camera) lens. ~**паннó** *n. indecl.* photo-mural; blow-up. ~**репортёр**, -а, press photographer. ~**хрóника**, -и, news in pictures. ~**элемéнт**, -а, photoelectric cell.

фрáза, -ы, sentence; phrase. **фразёр**, -а, phrase-monger.

фрак, -а, tail-coat, dress coat; tails; evening dress.

фракциóнный, fractional; factional. **фрáкция**, -и, fraction; faction.

франкоязы́чный, Francophone.

франкмасóн, -а, freemason.

франт, -а, dandy. **франтовскóй**, dandyish, dandyfied. **франтовствó**, -á, dandyism.

францýженка, -и, Frenchwoman. **францýз**, -а, Frenchman. **францýзский**, French; ~ ключ, monkeywrench.

фрахт, -а, freight. **фрахтовáть**, -тýю *imp.* (*perf.* за~) charter.

ФРГ (*fe-ergé*) *abbr.* Федерати́вная Респу́блика Герма́нии, German Federal Republic.

фрéйлина, -ы, maid of honour.

френч, -а, service jacket.

фронт, -а; *pl.* -ы, -óв, front; стать во ~, stand to attention. **фронтови́к**, -á, front-line soldier. **фронтовóй**, front- (-line).

фронтóн, -а, pediment.

фрукт, -а, fruit. **фрукто́вый**, fruit; ~ сад, orchard.

фтор, -а, fluorine. **фтóристый**, fluorine, fluoride; ~ кáльций, calcium fluoride.

фу *int.* ugh! uh!

фугáс, -а, landmine. **фугáсный**, high-explosive.

фундáмент, -а, foundation, base; substructure; seating. **фундаментáльный**, fundamental; solid, sound; thorough(-going); main; basic.

фунди́рованный, funded, consolidated.

функциони́ровать, -рую *imp.* function. **фýнкция**, -и, function.

фунт, -а, pound. **фýнтик**, -а, paper bag, paper cone, screw of paper.

фурáж, -á, forage, fodder. **фурáжка**, -и, peaked cap, service cap, forage-cap.

фургóн, -а, van; estate car, station wagon; caravan; pantechnicon.

фурниту́ра, -ы, accessories; parts, components; fittings.

фут, -а, foot; foot-rule. **футбóл**, -а, football, soccer. **футболи́ст**, -а, footballer. **футбóлить**, -лю *perf.* and *imp.* (*perf.* also от~) give, be given, the run-around. **футбо́лка**, -и, football jersey, sports shirt. **футбо́льный**, football: ~ мяч, football.

футля́р, -a case, container; sheath; cabinet; casing, housing.

фу́товый. one-foot.

футуроло́гия -и, futurology.

фуфа́йка, -и, jersey; sweater.

фы́ркать, -аю *imp.*, **фы́ркнуть**. -ну *perf.* snort; chuckle; grouse, grumble.

X

ха *n. indecl.* the letter x.

хаба́р, -a, **хабара́**, -ы́, bribe.

хавро́нья, -и, sow.

хала́т, -a, robe; dressing-gown; overall. **хала́тность**, -и carelessnesss, negligence. **хала́тный**. careless, negligent.

халту́ра, -ы, pot-boiler; hackwork; money made on the side, extra earnings. **халту́рить**, -рю *imp.* do hackwork; earn a little extra. **халту́рщик**, -a, hack.

хам, -a, boor, lout. **ха́мский**, boorish, loutish. **ха́мство**, -a, boorishness, loutishness.

хан, -a, khan.

хандра́, -ы́, depression, dejection. **хандри́ть**, -рю́ *imp.* suffer from melancholy; be dejected, be depressed.

ханжа́, -и́, canting hypocrite, sanctimonious person. **ха́нжеский**, **ханжеской**, sanctimonious, hypocritical.

ха́нство, -a, khanate.

хара́ктер, -a, character; personality; nature; disposition; type. **характеризова́ть**, -зу́ю *perf.* and *imp.* (*perf.* also о~) describe; characterize, be characteristic of; ~ся, be characterized. **характери́стика**, -и, reference; description. **характе́рный**[1], characteristic; typical; distinctive; character. **хара́ктерный**[2], of strong character, strong-willed; temperamental; quick-tempered.

ха́ркать, -аю *imp.*, **ха́ркнуть**, -ну *perf.* spit, hawk; ~ кро́вью, spit blood.

ха́ртия, -и, charter.

ха́ря, -и, mug, face.

ха́та, -ы, peasant hut.

ха́ять, ха́ю *imp.* run down; abuse; slate, slang, swear at, curse.

хвала́, -ы́, praise. **хвале́бный**, laudatory, eulogistic, complimentary. **хвалёный**, highly-praised much-vaunted. **хвали́ть**, -лю́ -лишь *imp.* (*perf.* по~) praise, compliment; ~ся, boast.

хва́стать(ся, -аю(сь *imp.* (*perf.* по~) boast, brag. **хвастли́вый**, boastful. **хвастовство́**, -а́, boasting, bragging. **хвасту́н**, -а́, boaster, braggart.

хвата́ть[1], -а́ю *imp.*, **хвати́ть**, -ачу́, -а́тишь *perf.* (*perf.* also **схвати́ть**) snatch, seize, catch hold of; grab, grasp; bite; hit, strike, knock; ~ся, wake up (to), remember; + *gen.* realize the absence of; + за + *acc.* snatch at, clutch at, catch at; take up, try out; по́здно хвати́лись, you thought of it too late; ~ся за ум, come to one's senses.

хвата́ть[2], -а́ет *imp.*, **хвати́ть**, *perf.*, *impers.* (+ *gen.*) suffice, be sufficient, be enough; last out; вре́мени не хвата́ло, there was not enough time; мне его́ не хвата́ет, I miss him; на сего́дня хва́тит, that will do for today, let's call it a day; у нас не хвата́ет де́нег, we haven't enough money; хва́тит! that will do! that's enough!; э́того ещё не хвата́ло! that's all we needed! that's the last straw!; э́того мне хва́тит на ме́сяц, this will last me a month. **хва́тка**, -и, grasp, grip, clutch; method, technique; skill. **хва́ткий**, strong; tenacious; skilful, crafty.

хвойн|ый, coniferous; **~ые** sb. pl. conifers.

хворать, -áю imp. be ill.

хворост, -а (-у), brushwood; straws. **хворостúна, -ы,** stick, switch. **хворостнóй,** brushwood.

хвост, -á, tail; end, tail-end; train; queue. **хвóстик, -a,** tail; c **~ом,** and a bit; сто с **~ом,** a hundred odd. **хвостовóй,** tail.

хвоя, -и, needle, needles; (coniferous) branch(es).

хижина, -ы, shack, hut, cabin.

хим- abbr. in comb. Of химúческий, chemical. **химкомбинáт, -а,** chemical plant. **~продýкты,** chemical products. **~чúстка, -и,** dry-cleaning; dry-cleaner's.

химéра, -ы, chimera. **химерúческий,** chimerical.

химик, -a, chemist. **химúческ|ий,** chemical; **~ая войнá** chemical warfare. **химия, и,** chemistry.

хина, -ы, хинúн, quinine. **хúнный,** cinchona.

хирéть, -éю imp. (perf. за**~**), grow sickly; wither; decay.

хирург, -a, surgeon. **хирургúческ|ий,** surgical; **~ая сестрá,** theatre nurse, theatre sister. **хирургúя, -и,** surgery.

хитрéц, -á, sly, cunning person. **хитрúть, -рю** imp. (perf. с**~**) use cunning, be cunning; be crafty; dissemble. **хúтрость, -и,** cunning, craftiness; ruse, stratagem; skill, resource; intricacy, subtlety. **хúтрый,** cunning, sly, crafty, wily; skilful, resourceful; intricate, subtle; complicated.

хихúкать, -аю imp., **хихúкнуть, -ну** perf. giggle, titter, snigger.

хищéние, -я, theft; embezzlement, misappropriation. **хúшник, -a,** predator, bird of prey, beast of prey; plunderer, despoiler. **хúшнический,** predatory, rapacious; destructive; injurious. **хúшн|ый,** predatory; rapacious; grasping, greedy; **~ые птúцы,** birds of prey.

хладагéнт, -a, a refrigerant; coolant. **хладнокрóвие, -я,** coolness, composure, presence of mind, sang-froid; **сохранять ~,** keep one's head. **хладнокрóвный** cool, composed self-possessed. **хладостóйкий,** cold-resistant; anti-freeze.

хлам, -a, rubbish, trash, lumber.

хлеб, -a; pl. **-ы, -ов** or **-á, - óв,** bread; loaf; grain, corn, cereal; **~-сóль,** bread and salt, hospitality. **хлебáть, -áю** imp., **хлебнуть, -нý, -нёшь** perf. gulp down, drink down; eat; go through, experience. **хлéбный,** bread; baker's; grain, corn, cereal; rich, abundant; grain-producing.

хлебо- in comb., bread; baking; grain. **хлебобýлочный,** bread. **~заготóвка, -и,** grain-procurement. **~завóд, -а,** (mechanized) bakery. **~пекáрня, -и,** gen. pl. **-рен,** bakery; bake-house. **~постáвка,** grain delivery. **~рéз, -a,** **~рéзка, -и,** bread-cutter. **~рóдный,** grain-growing; rich; **~рóдный год,** good year (for cereals).

хлев, -а, loc. **-ý;** pl. **-á,** cow-house, cattle-shed, byre.

хлестáть, -ещý, -éшешь imp., **хлестнýть, -нý, -нёшь** perf. !ash; whip; beat (down), teem, pour; gush, spout.

хлоп int. bang! **хлоп. -a,** bang, clatter. **хлóпать -аю** imp. (perf. хлóпнуть) bang; slap; **~ (в ладóши),** clap, applaud.

хлопковóдство, -a, cotton-growing. **хлóпковый,** cotton.

хлóпнуть, -ну perf. of хлóпать.

хлопóк[1], -пкá, clap.

хлопóк[2], -пка, cotton.

хлопотáть, -очý, -óчешь imp. (perf. по**~**), busy oneself; bustle about; take trouble, make efforts; **+ о + prep.** or **за + acc.** petition for, plead for, solicit for. **хлопотлúвый,** troublesome, bothersome; exacting; busy, bustling, restless. **хлóпоты, -óт** pl. trouble; efforts; pains.

хлопчáтка, -и, cotton. **хлопчато-бумáжный,** cotton.

хлóпья, -ьев pl. flakes.

хлор, -a, chlorine. **хлорвинúловый,** vinyl chloride. **хлóристый, хлóрный,** chlorine; **хлóрная извéсть,** chloride of lime. **хлóрка, -и,** bleaching powder, bleach liquor.

хлынуть, -нет perf. gush, pour; rush, surge.

хлыст, -á, whip, switch.

хмелевóд, -a, hop-grower. **хмелевóй**, hop. **хмелéть**, -éю *imp.* (*perf.* за~, о~) get tipsy, get tight. **хмель**, -я, *loc.* -ю́ *m.* hop, hops; drunkenness, tipsiness; во хмелю́ tipsy, tight. **хмельнóй**, -лён, -льнá, drunken, drunk; tipsy; intoxicating.

хму́рить, -рю *imp.* (*perf.* на~); ~ брóви, knit one's brows; ~ся, frown; become gloomy; be overcast, be cloudy. **хму́рый**, gloomy, sullen; overcast, dull, cloudy; lowering.

хны́кать, -ы́чу *or* -аю *imp.* whimper, snivel; whine.

хóбот, -a, trunk, proboscis. **хоботóк**, -ткá, proboscis.

ход, -a (-y), *loc.* -ý; *pl.* -ы, -ов *or* -ы́ *or* -á, -óв, motion, movement; travel, going; speed, pace; procession; course, progress; work, operation, running; stroke; move; lead; gambit, manœuvre; entrance; passage; thoroughfare, covered way; wheel-base; runners; быть в ~ý, be in demand, be in vogue; дать зáдний ~, back, reverse; дать ~, set in motion, set going; знать все ~ы и вы́ходы, know all the ins and outs; на ~ý, in transit, on the move, without halting; in motion; in operation; пóлным ~ом, at full speed, in full swing; пусти́ть в ~, start, set in motion, set going; put into operation, put into service; три часá ~y, three hours' journey.

ходáтай, -я, intercessor, mediator. **ходáтайство** -a, petitioning; entreaty, pleading; petition, application. **ходáтайствовать**, -твую *imp.* (*perf.* по~) petition, apply.

хóдики, -ов *pl.* wall-clock.

ходи́ть, хожу́, хóдишь *imp.* walk; go; run; pass, go round; lead, play; move; sway, shake; + в + *prep.* be; wear; + за + *instr.* look after, take care of tend; ~ с пик, lead a spade; ~ ферзём, move one's queen. **хóдкий** -док, -дкá, -о, fast; saleable, marketable; popular, in demand, sought after; current. **ходу́ли**, -ей *pl.* stilts. **ходу́льный**, stilted. **ходьбá**, -ы́,

walking; walk; полчасá хольбы́, half an hour's walk. **ходя́чий**, walking; able to walk; popular; current; ~ ая добродéтель, virtue personified; ~ая монéта, currency.

хозрасчёт, -a *abbr.* хозя́йственный расчёт, self-financing system. **хозя́ин**, -a; *pl.* -яева, -яев, owner, proprietor; master; boss; landlord; host; хозяéва пóля, home team. **хозя́йка**, -и, owner; mistress; hostess; landlady; wife, missus. **хозя́йничать**, -аю *imp.* keep house; be in charge; play the master, take charge. **хозя́йственник**, -a, financial manager, economic manager. **хозя́йственный**, economic, of the economy; management; household; economical, thrifty. **хозя́йство**, -a, economy; management; housekeeping; equipment; farm, holding; домáшнее ~, housekeeping; сéльское ~, agriculture.

хоккеи́ст, -a, (ice-)hockey-player. **хоккéй**, -я, hockey, ice-hockey. **хоккéйный**, (ice-)hockey.

холестери́н, -a, cholesterol. **холестери́новый**, cholesteric.

холм, -á, hill. **холми́стый**, hilly.

хóлод, -a (-y); *pl.* -á, -óв, cold; coldness; cold spell, cold weather. **холоди́льник**, -a, refrigerator; cooler, condenser. **холоди́льный**, cooling; refrigerating, freezing. **холоди́ть**, -ожу́ *imp.* (*perf.* на~) cool, chill; produce feeling of cold. **хóлодно** *adv.* coldly. **хóлодность**, -и, coldness. **холóдн**|**ый**; хóлоден, -днá, -о, cold; inadequate, thin; ~ое ору́жие, side-arms, cold steel; ~ая *sb.* cooler, lock-up.

холóп, -a, serf. **холóпий**, serf's, of serfdom, servile.

холостóй; хóлост, -á, unmarried, single; bachelor; idle, free; blank, dummy. **холостя́к**, -á, bachelor. **холостя́цкий**, bachelor.

холст -á, (canvas); coarse linen. **холщóвый**, canvas, (coarse) linen.

хому́т, -á, (horse-)collar; burden; clamp, clip.

хор, -a; *pl.* хóры, choir; chorus.

хорва́т, -а, **хорва́тка**, -и, Croat. **хорва́тский**, Croatian.

хорёк, -рька́, polecat.

хори́ст, -а, member of choir or chorus. **хорово́д**, -а, round dance.

хорони́ть, -ню́, -нишь *imp.* (*perf.* за~, по~, с~) bury; hide, conceal; ~ся, hide, conceal oneself.

хоро́шенький, pretty; nice. **хоро́шенько** *adv.* properly, thoroughly, well and truly. **хорошо́ть**, -е́ю *imp.* (*perf.* по~) grow prettier. **хоро́ший**; -о́ш, -а́, -о́, good; nice; pretty, nice-looking. **хорошо́** *predic.* it is good; it is nice, it is pleasant. **хорошо́** *adv.* well; nicely; all right! very well!; good.

хо́ры, хор or -ов *pl.* gallery.

хоте́ние, -я, desire, wish. **хоте́ть**, хочу́, хо́чешь, хоти́м *imp.* (*perf.* за~) wish; + *gen.* want; *е́сли хоти́те*, perhaps; ~ пить, be thirsty; ~ сказа́ть, mean; ~ся *impers.* + *dat.* want; *мне хо́те́лось бы*, I should like; *мне хо́чется*, I want; *мне хо́чется спать*, I am sleepy.

хоть *conj.* although; even if; *part.* at least, if only; for example, even; ~ бы, if only. **хотя́** *conj.* although, though; ~ бы, even if; if only.

хохла́тый, crested, tufted.

хо́хот, -а, guffaw, loud laugh. **хохота́ть**, -очу́, -о́чешь *imp.* guffaw, laugh loudly.

хочу́, etc.: see хоте́ть.

храбре́ц, -а́, brave man. **храбри́ться**, -рю́сь, make a show of bravery; pluck up one's courage. **хра́брость**, -и, bravery, courage. **хра́брый**, brave, courageous, valiant.

храм, -а, temple, church.

хране́ние, -я, keeping, custody; storage; conservation; ка́мера хране́ния, cloak-room, left-luggage office; сдать на ~, store, deposit, leave in a cloakroom. **храни́лище**, -а, storehouse, depository. **храни́тель**, -я *m.* keeper, custodian; repository; curator. **храни́ть**, -ню́ *imp.* keep; preserve, maintain; store; ~ся, be, be kept; be preserved.

храпе́ть, -плю́ *imp.* snore; snort.

хребе́т, -бта́, spine; back; (mountain) range; ridge; crest, peak. **хребто́вый**, spinal; range, ridge, crest.

хрен, -а (-у), horseradish. **хрено́вый**, horseradish.

хрестома́тия, -и, reader.

хрип, -а, wheeze; hoarse sound. **хрипе́ть**, -плю́ *imp.* wheeze. **хри́плый**; -пл, -а́, -о, hoarse, wheezing. **хри́пнуть**, -ну; хрип *imp.* (*perf.* о~) become hoarse, lose one's voice. **хрипота́**, -ы́, hoarseness.

христиани́н, -а; *pl.* -а́не, -а́н **христиа́нка**, -и, Christian. **христиа́нский**, Christian. **христиа́нство**, -а, Christianity; Christendom. **Христо́с**, -иста́, Christ.

хром, -а, box-calf.

хрома́ть, -а́ю *imp.* limp, be lame; be poor, be shaky. **хроме́ть**, -е́ю *imp.* (*perf.* о~) go lame. **хромо́й**; хром, -а́, -о, lame, limping; game, gammy; shaky, rickety; *sb.* lame man, woman. **хромота́**, -ы́, lameness.

хро́ник, -а, chronic invalid. **хро́ника**, -и, chronicle; news items; newsreel; historical film. **хроника́льный**, news; documentary. **хрони́ческий**, chronic.

хронологи́ческий, chronological. **хроноло́гия**, -и, chronology. **хроно́метр**, -а, chronometer. **хронометра́ж**, -а, time-study.

хру́пкий; -пок, -пка́, -о, fragile; brittle; frail; delicate. **хру́пкость**, -и, fragility; brittleness; frailness.

хруст, -а, crunch; crackle.

хруста́лик, -а, crystalline lens. **хруста́ль**, -я́ *m.* cut glass; crystal. **хруста́льный**, cut-glass; crystal; crystal-clear.

хрусте́ть, -ущу́ *imp.*, **хру́стнуть**, -ну *perf.* crunch; crackle. **хрустя́щий**, crackling; crisp, crunchy; ~ карто́фель, potato crisps.

хрю́кать, -аю *imp.*, **хрю́кнуть**, -ну *perf.* grunt.

хрящ[1], -а́, cartilage, gristle.

хрящ[2], -а́, gravel, shingle. **хрящева́тый**[2], **хрящево́й**[2], gravelly, shingly.

хрящева́тый[1], **хрящево́й**[1], cartilaginous, gristly.

худа́пать, -е́ю *imp.* (*perf.* по~) grow thin.

ху́до, -а, harm, ill; evil. **ху́до** *adv.* ill, badly.

худо́жественный, art, arts; artistic; aesthetic; ~ фильм, feature film. **худо́жество**, -а, art; artistry; *pl.* the arts. **худо́жник**, -а, artist.

худо́й[1], худ, -а́, -о, thin, lean.

худо́й[2]; худ, -а́, -о, bad; full of holes; worn; tumbledown; ему́ ~ до, he feels bad; на ~ коне́ц, if the worst comes to the worst, at (the) worst.

худоща́вый, thin, lean.

ху́дший, *superl.* of худо́й, плохо́й (the) worst. **ху́же**, *comp.* of худо́й, ху́до, плохо́й, пло́хо, worse.

хула́, -ы́, abuse, criticism.

хулига́н, -а, hooligan. **хулига́нить**, -ню *imp.* behave like a hooligan. **хулига́нство**, -а, hooliganism.

ху́тор, -а; *pl.* -а́, farm; farmstead; small village.

ХФ (*khaef*) *abbr.* холо́дный фронт, cold front.

Ц

ц *letter*: see цэ.

ца́пля, -и; *gen. pl.* -пель, heron.

цара́пать, -аю *imp.*, **цара́пнуть**, -ну *perf.* (*perf.* also на~, о~) scratch; scribble; ~ся, scratch; scratch one another; scramble, scrabble. **цара́пина**, -ы, scratch; abrasion.

цари́зм, -а, tsarism. **цари́стский**, tsarist. **цари́ть**, -рю́ *imp.* be tsar; hold sway; reign, prevail. **цари́ца**, -ы, tsarina; queen. **ца́рский**, of the tsar, tsar's; royal; tsarist; regal, kingly. **ца́рство**, -а, kingdom, realm; reign; domain. **ца́рствование**, -я, reign. **ца́рствовать**, -твую *imp.* reign. **царь**, -я́ *m.* tsar; king, ruler.

цвести́, -ету́, -ете́шь; -ёл, -а́ *imp.* flower, bloom, blossom; prosper, flourish; grow mouldy.

цвет[1], -а; *pl.* -а́, colour; ~ лица́, complexion.

цвет[2], -а (-у), *loc.* -у́; *pl.* -ы́, flower; cream, pick; blossom-time; prime; blossom; во ~е лет, in the prime of life; во ~е сил, at the height of one's powers; в цвету́, in blossom. **цветни́к**, -а́, flower-bed, flower-garden.

цветн|о́й, coloured; colour; non-ferrous; ~а́я капу́ста, cauliflower; ~ые мета́ллы, non-ferrous metals; ~ое

стекло́, stained glass; ~о́й фильм, colour-film.

цветово́дство, -а, flower-growing, floriculture.

цветов|о́й, colour; ~а́я слепота́, colour-blindness.

цвето́к, -тка́; *pl.* цветы́ от цветки́, -о́в, flower. **цвето́чный**, flower; ~ магази́н, flower-shop. **цвету́щий**, flowering, blossoming, blooming; prosperous, flourishing.

ЦВМ (*tseveem*) *abbr.* цифрова́я вычисли́тельная маши́на, digital computer.

цеди́лка, -и, strainer, filter. **цеди́ть**, цежу́, це́дишь *imp.* strain, filter; percolate; mutter (through clenched teeth).

целе́бный, curative, healing.

целево́й, special; earmarked for a specific purpose. **целенапра́вленный**, purposeful. **целесообра́зный**, expedient. **целеустремлённый**, -ён, -ённа от -ена́, purposeful.

целико́м *adv.* whole; wholly, entirely.

целина́, -ы́, virgin lands, virgin soil. **цели́нн**|ый, virgin; ~ые зе́мли, virgin lands.

цели́тельный, curative, healing, medicinal.

це́лить(ся, -лю(сь *imp.* (*perf.* на~), aim, take aim.

целко́вый *sb.* one rouble.

целова́ть, -лу́ю *imp.* (*perf.* по~) kiss; ~ся, kiss.

це́лое *sb.* whole; integer. целому́дренный, chaste. целому́дрие, -я, chastity. це́лостность, -и, integrity. це́лостный, integral; entire, complete. це́лый; цел, -á, -о, whole, entire; safe, intact.

цель, -и, target; aim, object, goal, end, purpose; с це́лью, with the object (of), in order to.

цельнометалли́ческий, all-metal. це́льный; -лен, -льна́, -о; of one piece, solid; entire; whole; integral; single; undiluted. це́льность, -и, wholeness, entirety, integrity.

цеме́нт, -а, cement. цементи́ровать, -рую *perf.* and *imp.* cement; case-harden.

цена́, -ы́, *acc.* -у; *pl.* -ы, price, cost; worth, value; цено́й + *gen.* at the price of, at the cost of; любо́й цено́й, at any price.

ценз, -а, qualification. це́нзовый, qualifying. це́нзор, -а, censor. цензу́ра, -ы, censorship.

цени́тель, -я *m.* judge, connoisseur, expert. цени́ть, -ню́, -нишь *imp.* value; assess; estimate; appreciate. це́нник, -а, price-list. це́нность, -и, value; price; importance; *pl.* valuables; values. це́нный, valuable; costly; precious; important.

центр, -а, centre. центра́ль, -и, main. центра́льный, central. центробе́жный, centrifugal.

цеп, -á, flail.

цепене́ть, -е́ю *imp.* (*perf.* о~) freeze; be numbed; be rooted to the spot. це́пкий, tenacious, strong; prehensile; sticky, tacky, loamy; obstinate, persistent, strong-willed. це́пкость, -и, tenacity, strength; obstinacy, persistence. цепля́ться, -я́юсь *imp.* за + *acc.* clutch at, try to grasp; cling to; stick to. цепн|о́й, chain; ~а́я реа́кция, chain reaction. цепо́чка, -и, chain; file, series. цепь, -и, *loc.* -и́; *gen. pl.* -е́й, chain; row; series; range; line, file; succession; circuit; *pl.* chains, bonds.

церемо́ниться, -нюсь *imp.* (*perf.* по~) stand on ceremony; be (over-)con-siderate. церемо́ния, -и, ceremony; без церемо́ний, informally.

церковнославя́нский, Church Slavonic. церко́вный, church; ecclesiastical. це́рковь, -кви; *gen. pl.* -е́й, church.

цех, -а, *loc.* -у́; *pl.* -и or -á, shop; section; guild, corporation.

цивилиза́ция, -и, civilization. цивилизо́ванный, civilized. цивилизова́ть, -зу́ю *perf.* and *imp.* civilize.

циге́йка, -и, beaver lamb. циге́йковый, beaver-lamb.

цикл, -а, cycle.

цико́рий, -я, chicory. цико́рный, chicory.

цили́ндр, -а, cylinder; drum; top hat. цилиндри́ческий, cylindrical.

цимба́лы, -а́л *pl.* cymbals.

цинга́, -и́, scurvy. цинго́тный, scorbutic.

цинк, -а, zinc. ци́нковый, zinc.

цино́вка, -и, mat. цино́вочный, mat, of mats.

цирк, -а, circus. цирково́й, circus.

циркули́ровать, -рует *imp.* circulate. ци́ркуль, -я *m.* (pair of) compasses; dividers. циркуля́р, -а, circular.

цирю́льник, -а, barber.

цисте́рна, -ы, cistern, tank.

цитаде́ль, -и, citadel; bulwark, stronghold.

цита́та, -ы, quotation. цити́ровать, -рую *imp.* (*perf.* про~) quote.

ци́тра, -ы, zither.

ци́трус, -а, citrus. ци́трусов|ый, citrous; ~ые *pl.* citrus plants.

цифербла́т, -а, dial, face.

ци́фра, -ы, figure; number, numeral. цифров|о́й, numerical, in figures; ~ые да́нные, figures.

ЦК (*tseká*) *abbr.* Центра́льный Комите́т, Central Committee.

цо́кать, -аю *imp.*, цо́кнуть, -ну *perf.* clatter, clang; click.

цо́коль, -я *m.* socle, plinth, pedestal. цо́кольный, plinth; ~ эта́ж, ground floor.

ЦРУ (*tse-erú*) *abbr.* Центра́льное разве́дывательное управле́ние, C.I.A.

ЦС (*tse-és*) *abbr.* Центра́льный сове́т, Central Soviet, Central Council.

ЦСУ (*tse-esú* or -*séй*) *abbr.* Центра́льное статисти́ческое управле́ние, Central Statistical Board.

цука́т, -а, a candied fruit, candied peel.

цыга́н, -а; *pl.* -е, -а́н ог -ы, -ов, **цыга́нка**, -и, gipsy. **цыга́нский**, gipsy.

цыплёнок, -нка; *pl.* -ля́та, -ля́т, chicken; chick.

цы́почки; на ~, на цы́почках, on tiptoe.

цэ *n. indecl.* the letter ц.

Ч

ч *letter*: see чэ.

ч. *abbr.* час, hour, (after numerals) o'clock; часть, part.

чад, -а (-у), *loc.* -ý, fumes, smoke. **чади́ть**, чажу́ *imp.* (*perf.* на~) smoke. **ча́дный**, smoky, smoke-laden; stupefied, stupefying.

чай, -я (-ю); *pl.* -и́, -ёв, tea.

чай *part.* perhaps; no doubt; I suppose; after all.

ча́йка, -и; *gen. pl.* ча́ек, gull, sea-gull.

ча́йник, -а, teapot; kettle. **ча́йн|ый**, tea; ~ая посу́да, tea-service; ~ая ро́за, tea-rose. **чайхана́**, -ы́, tea-house.

чалма́, -ы́, turban.

ча́лый, roan.

чан, -а, *loc.* -ý; *pl.* -ы́, vat, tub, tank.

ча́рка, -и, cup, goblet, small glass.

чарова́ть, -ру́ю *imp.* bewitch; charm, captivate, enchant.

ча́ртерный, chartered.

час, -а (-у), with numerals -а́, *loc.* -ý; *pl.* -ы́, hour; hours, time, period; *pl.* guard-duty; ~, one o'clock; в два ~а́, at two o'clock; стоя́ть на ~а́х, stand guard; ~ы́ пик, rush-hour. **часовня**, -и; *gen. pl.* -вен, chapel. **часово́й** *sb.* sentry, sentinel, guard. **часов|о́й**, clock, watch; time; of one hour, an hour's; by the hour; one o'clock; ~о́й переры́в, an hour's interval; ~а́я пла́та, payment by the hour; ~о́й по́яс, time zone; ~а́я стре́лка, (hour-)hand. **часовщи́к**, -а́, watchmaker. **ча́сом** *adv.* sometimes, at times; by the way.

части́ца, -ы, small part, element; particle. **части́чно** *adv.* partly, partially. **части́чный**, partial.

ча́стность, -и, detail; в ча́стности, in particular. **ча́стн|ый**, private; personal; particular, individual; local; district; ~ая со́бственность, private property.

ча́сто *adv.* often, frequently; close, thickly. **частоко́л**, -а, paling, palisade. **частота́**, -ы́; *pl.* -ы, frequency. **часто́тный**, frequency. **часту́шка**, -и, ditty, folk-song. **ча́ст|ый**; част, -а́, -о, frequent; close, close together; dense, thick; close-woven; quick, rapid; ~ый гре́бень, fine-tooth comb.

часть, -и; *gen. pl.* -е́й, part; portion; section, department, side; sphere, field; share; unit; ча́сти ре́чи, parts of speech.

часы́, -о́в *pl.* clock, watch; нару́чные ~, ручны́е ~, wrist-watch.

ча́хлый, stunted; poor, sorry; weakly, sickly, puny. **ча́хнуть**, -ну; чах *imp.* (*perf.* за~) wither away; become weak, go into a decline. **чахо́тка**, -и, consumption. **чахо́точный**, consumptive; poor, sorry, feeble.

ча́ша, -и, cup, bowl; chalice; ~ весо́в, scale, pan. **ча́шка**, -и, cup; bowl; scale, pan.

ча́ща, -и, thicket.

ча́ще *comp.* of ча́сто, ча́стый; ~ всего́, most often, mostly.

ча́яние, -я, expectation; hope. **ча́ять**, ча́ю *imp.* hope, expect; think, suppose.

чва́ниться, -нюсь *imp.* (+ *instr.*) boast (of). **чва́нство**, -а, conceit, arrogance, pride.

чв-д (*chevedé*) *abbr.* челове́ко-де́нь, man-day. **чв-ч(ас)** *abbr.* челове́ко-ча́с, man-hour.

чего́: see что.

чей *m.*, **чья** *f.*, **чьё** *n.*, **чьи** *pl.*, *pron.* whose. **чей-либо**, **чей-нибудь**, anyone's. **чей-то**, someone's.

чек, -а, cheque; check, bill; receipt.

Чека́ *f. indecl.*, or -и́, **ЧК** (cheká) *abbr.* Чрезвыча́йная Коми́ссия (по борьбе́ с контрреволю́цией, сабота́жем и спекуля́цией), Cheka.

чека́н, -а stamp, die. **чека́нить**, -ню *imp.* (*perf.* вы~, от~) mint, coin; stamp, engrave, emboss, chase; ~ слова́, enunciate words clearly; rap out; ~ шаг, step out. **чека́нный**, stamping, engraving, embossing; stamped, engraved, embossed, chased; precise, expressive, chiselled; ~ шаг, measured tread.

чёлка, -и, fringe; forelock.

челн, -а́; *pl.* чёлны, dug-out canoe; boat. **челно́к**, -а́, dug-out canoe; shuttle.

челове́к, -а; *pl.* лю́ди; with numerals, *gen.* -ве́к, -ам, man, person, human being; (man-)servant, waiter.

челове́ко- in *comb.* man-, anthropo-. **челове́ко-де́нь**, -дня *m.* man-day. **~люби́вый**, philanthropic. **~люби́е**, -я, philanthropy; humanity, humaneness. **~ненави́стнический**, misanthropic. **~обра́зный**, anthropomorphous; anthropoid. **челове́ко-ча́с**, -а; *pl.* -ы, man-hour.

челове́чек, -чка, little man. **челове́ческий**, human; humane. **челове́чество**, -а, humanity, mankind. **челове́чий**, human. **челове́чный**, humane.

че́люсть, -и, jaw, jaw-bone; denture, dental plate, false teeth.

чем, чём: see что. **чем** *conj.* than; + *inf.* rather than, instead of; ~.., тем .. + *comp.* the more .., the more.

чемода́н, -а, suitcase.

чемпио́н, -а, **чемпио́нка**, -и, champion(s), title-holder(s). **чемпиона́т**, -а, championship.

чему́: see что.

чепуха́, -и́, nonsense, rubbish; trifle, triviality.

че́пчик, -а, cap; bonnet.

че́рви, -е́й, **че́рвы**, черв *pl.* hearts. **черво́нн|ый**, of hearts; red; ~ое зо́лото, pure gold; ~ый туз, ace of hearts.

червь, -я́; *pl.* -и, -е́й *m.* worm; maggot; bug, virus, germ. **червя́к**, -а́, worm; screw.

черда́к, -а́, attic, loft.

черёд, -а́, *loc.* -у́, turn; queue; идти́ свои́м ~о́м, take its course. **чередова́ние**, -я, alternation, interchange, rotation; (vowel) gradation, ablaut. **чередова́ть**, -ду́ю *imp.* alternate; **~ся**, alternate, take turns.

че́рез, чрез *prep.* + *acc.* across; over; through; via; in; after; (further) on; every (other); ~ день, every other day, on alternate days; ~ полчаса́, in half an hour; ~ три киломе́тра, three kilometres further on; ~ ка́ждые три страни́цы, every four pages.

черёмуха, -и, bird cherry.

че́реп, -а; *pl.* -а́, skull, cranium. **черепа́ха**, -и, tortoise; turtle; tortoiseshell. **черепа́ховый**, tortoise; turtle; tortoiseshell. **черепа́ший**, tortoise, turtle; very slow.

черепи́ца, -ы, tile. **черепи́чный**, tile; tiled.

черепо́к, -пка́, crock, potsherd, broken piece of pottery.

чересчу́р *adv.* too; too much.

чере́шневый, cherry; cherry-wood. **чере́шня**, -и; *gen. pl.* -шен, cherry; cherry-tree.

черке́с, -а, **черке́шенка**, -и, Circassian. **черке́сский**, Circassian.

черкну́ть, -ну́, -нёшь *perf.* scrape; leave a mark on; scribble, dash off.

черне́ть, -е́ю *imp.* (*perf.* по~) turn black, go black; show black. **черни́ка**, -и, bilberry, whortleberry. **черни́ла**, -и́л *pl.* ink. **черни́льница**, -ы, ink-pot ink-well. **черни́льный**, ink; ~ каранда́ш, indelible pencil. **черни́ть**, -ню́ *imp.* (*perf.* за~, на~, о~) blacken; paint black; slander. **черни́чный**, bilberry.

черно- in *comb.* black; unskilled; rough. **чёрно-бе́лый**, black-and-white. **черно-бу́рка**, -и, silver fox (fur). **~бу́рый**, dark-brown; ~бу́рая лиса́, silver fox,

~волóсый, black-haired. ~глáзый, black-eyed. ~зём, -а, chernozem, black earth. ~зёмный, black-earth. ~кóжий, black, coloured; sb. Negro, black. ~мóрский, Black-Sea. ~рабóчий sb. unskilled worker, labourer. ~слив, -а (-у), prunes. ~смородинный, blackcurrant.

черновик, -á, rough copy, draft. черновóй, rough; draft, preparatory; heavy, dirty; crude. чернотá, -ы, blackness; darkness. чёрн|ый, -рен, -рнá, black; back; heavy, unskilled; ferrous; gloomy, melancholy; на ~ый день, for a rainy day; ~ый вóрон, (sl.) Black Maria; ~ые метáллы, ferrous metals; ~ый хлеб black bread, rye-bread; ~ый ход, back way, back door; ~ый sb. Negro, black.

черпáк, -á, scoop; bucket; grab. черпáлка, -и, scoop; ladle. чéрпать, -аю imp. ~нуть, -ну, -нёшь perf. draw; scoop ladle; extract, derive.

черстветь, -éю imp. (perf. за~, о~, по~) grow stale. get stale; become hardened, grow callous. чёрствый; чёрств, -á, -о, stale; hard callous.

чёрт, -а; pl. чéрти, -éй, devil; the devil. чертá, -ы, line; boundary; trait, characteristic; в óбщих ~x, in general outline; в чертé гóрода, within the town boundary. чертёж, -á, drawing; blueprint, plan, scheme. чертёжная sb. drawing-office. чертёжник, -а, draughtsman. чертёжный, drawing. чертить, -рчý, -ртишь imp. (perf. на~) draw; draw up.

чёртов adj. devil's: devilish. hellish. чертóвский devilish, damnable.

чёрточка, -и line; hyphen. черчéние, -я. drawing. черчý, etc.: see чертить.

чесáть, чешý, чéшешь imp. (perf. по~) scratch; comb; card; ~ся, scratch oneself; comb one's hair; у негó рýки чéшутся + inf. he is itching to.

чеснóк, -á (-ý), garlic. чеснóчный, garlic.

чесóтка, -и, scab; rash; mange; itch.

чéствование, -я, celebration. чéствовать, -твую imp. celebrate; honour. чéстность, -и, honesty, integrity. чéстный; -тен, -тнá, -о, honest, upright. честолюбивый, ambitious. честолюбие, -я, ambition. честь, -и, loc. -и, honour; regard, respect; отдáть ~ + dat. salute.

четвéрг, -á, Thursday. четверéньки; на ~, на четверéньках, on all fours, on hands and knees. четвёрка, -и, figure 4; No. 4; four; good. чéтверо, -ых four. четверонóг|ий, four-legged; ~ое sb. quadruped. четверостишие, -я, quatrain. четвёртый, fourth. чéтверть, -и; gen. pl. -éй, quarter; quarter of an hour; term; без четверти час, a quarter to one. четвертьфинáл, -а, quarter-final.

чёткий; -ток, -ткá, -о, precise; clear-cut; clear well-defined; legible; plain, distinct; articulate. чёткость, -и, precision; clarity, clearness, definition; legibility; distinctness.

чётный, even.

чéтыре, -рёх, -рьмя, -рёх, four. четыреста, -рёхсóт, -ьмястáми, -ёхстáх, four hundred.

четырёх- in comb. four-, tetra-. четырёхголóсый, four-part. ~грáнник, -а, tetrahedron. ~крáтный, fourfold. ~лéтие, -я, four-year period; fourth anniversary. ~мéстный, four-seater. ~мотóрный, four-engined. ~сóтый, four-hundredth. ~стóпный, tetrameter. ~тáктный, four-stroke. ~угóльник, -а, square, quadrangle. ~угóльный, square, quadrangular. ~часовóй, four hours', four-hour; four-o'clock.

четырнадцатый, fourteenth. четырнадцать, -и, fourteen.

чех, -а, Czech.

чехардá, -ы, leap-frog.

чехлить, -лю imp. (perf. за~) cover. чехóл, -хлá, cover, case; loose cover.

чечевица, -ы, lentil; lens. чечевичн|ый, lentil; ~ая похлёбка, mess of pottage.

чéшка, -и, Czech. чéшский, Czech.

чешý, etc.: see чесáть.

чешýйка, -и, scale. чешуя, -и, scales.

чиж, -á, чижик, -а, siskin.

чин, -а; pl. -ы, rank; any of fourteen grades (numbered from the top) of Tsarist Civil Service; official; rite, ceremony, order; быть в ~áх, hold high rank, be of high rank.

чина́рик, -a, (sl.) cigarette end.

чини́ть[1], -ню́, -нишь imp. (perf. по~) repair, mend.

чини́ть[2], -ню́, -нишь imp. (perf. o~) sharpen.

чини́ть[3], -ню́ imp. (perf. y~) carry out, execute; cause; ~ препя́тствия + dat. put obstacles in the way of.

чино́вник, -a, civil servant; official, functionary; bureaucrat. чино́вни-ческий, чино́вничий, civil-service; bureaucratic.

чи́псы, -ов pl. chips.

чири́кать, -аю imp., чири́кнуть, -ну perf. chirp.

чи́ркать, -аю imp., чи́ркнуть, -ну perf. + instr. strike; ~ спи́чкой, strike a match.

чи́сленность, -и, numbers; strength. чи́сленный, numerical. числи́тель, -я m. numerator. числи́тельное sb. numeral. чи́слить, -лю imp. count, reckon; ~ся, be; + instr. be reckoned, be on paper; be attributed; за ним чи́слится мно́го недоста́тков, he has many failings; ~ся больны́м, be on the sick-list; ~ся в спи́ске, be on the list. число́, -á; pl. -a, -сел, number; date, day; в числе́ + gen. among; в том числе́, including; еди́нственное ~, singular; мно́жественное ~, plural; сего́дня восемна́дцатое ~, today is the eighteenth. числово́й, numerical.

чи́стильщик, -a, cleaner; ~ сапо́г, bootblack, shoeblack. чи́стить, чи́щу imp. (perf. вы́~, о~, по~) clean; brush, scour, sweep; peel, shell; purge; clear; dredge. чи́стка, -и, cleaning; purge; отда́ть в чи́стку, have cleaned, send to the cleaner's. чи́сто adv. cleanly, clean; purely, merely; completely, clean. чисто́вой, fair, clean; ~áя ко́пия, fair copy, чисто́вой экземпля́р, clean copy. чистокро́вный, thorough-bred, pure-blooded. чистописа́ние, -я, calligraphy, (hand)writing. чистопло́тный, clean; neat, tidy; decent. чистосерде́чный, frank, sincere, candid.

чистота́, -ы́, cleanness, cleanliness; neatness, tidiness; purity, innocence. чи́стый, clean; neat; tidy; pure; unsullied; undiluted; clear; net; utter; mere, sheer; complete, absolute; на ~ом во́здухе, in the open air; ~ый вес, net weight; ~ые де́ньги, cash; ~ый лист, blank sheet; ~ая при́быль, clear profit; ~ая случа́йность, pure chance.

чита́емый, widely-read, popular. чита́льный, reading. чита́льня, -и; gen. pl. -лен, reading-room. чита́тель, -я m. reader. чита́ть, -áю imp. (perf. про~, проче́сть) read; recite, say; ~ ле́кции, lecture, give lectures; ~ся, be legible; be visible, be discernible. чи́тка, -и, reading; reading through.

чих, -a, sneeze. чиха́ть, -áю imp., чихну́ть, -ну́, -нёшь perf. sneeze, cough, splutter.

чи́ще, comp. of чи́сто, чи́стый.

чи́щу, etc.: see чи́стить.

ЧК: see Чека́.

член, -a, member; limb; term; part; article. члене́ние, -я, articulation. члени́ть, -ню́ imp. (perf. рас~) divide; articulate. член(-)ко́р(р), -a abbr., член-корреспонде́нт, -a, чл.-ко́р. abbr. corresponding member, associate. членоразде́льный, articulate. чле́н-ск|ий, membership; ~ие взно́сы, membership fee, dues. чле́нство, -a, membership. чл.-ко́р.: see членко́рр.

чмо́кать, -аю imp., чмо́кнуть, -ну perf. make smacking or sucking sound; kiss noisily; ~ губа́ми, smack one's lips.

чо́канье, -я, clinking of glasses. чо́кать-ся, -аюсь imp., чо́кнуться, -нусь perf. clink glasses.

чо́порный, prim, stiff; stuck-up, stand-offish.

чрева́тый + instr. fraught with, pregnant with. чре́во, -a, belly, womb. чревовеща́ние, -я, ventriloquism. чревовеща́тель, -я m. ventriloquist.

чрез: see че́рез. чрезвыча́йн|ый, extraordinary; special; extreme; ~ое положе́ние, state of emergency. чрезме́рный, excessive, inordinate, extreme.

чтéние, -я, reading; reading-matter.

чтец, -á, чтицá, -ы, reader; reciter.

чтúво, -a, reading-matter, trash.

чтить verb *imp.* honour.

чтúца: see чтец.

что, чегó, чемý, чем, о чём *pron.* what?; how?; why?; how much?; which, what, who; anything; в чём дéло? what is the matter?; для чегó? what .. for? why?; éсли ~ случúтся, if anything happens; к чемý? why?; ~ емý до этого? what does it matter to him?; ~ касáется меня, as for me, as far as I am concerned; ~ с тобóй? what's the matter (with you)?; я знáю, ~ вы имéете в видý, I know what you mean; ~ ж, yes; all right, right you are; ~ за, what? what sort of?; что (а) .. !; ~ за ерундá! what (utter) nonsense! **что** *conj.* that. **что (бы) ни** *pron.* whatever, no matter what; во что бы то ни стáло, at whatever cost.

чтоб, чтóбы *conj.* in order (to), so as; that; to; он сказáл, чтóбы вы к немý зашлú, he said you were to go and see him; он хóчет, чтóбы я сдéлал это сейчáс же, he wants me to do it at once. **чтó-либо, чтó-нибудь** *pron.* anything. **чтó-то,** *pron.* something. **чтó-то** *adv.* somewhat, slightly; somehow, for some reason.

чýвственность, -и, sensuality. **чýвственный**, sensual; perceptible, sensible. **чувствúтельность**, -и, sensitivity, sensitiveness, sensibility; perceptibility; sentimentality; tenderness, feeling; (film) speed. **чувствúтельный**, sensitive, susceptible; sensible, perceptible; sentimental; tender. **чýвство**, -a, feeling; sense; senses; прийтú в ~, come round, regain consciousness. **чýвствовать**, -твую *imp.* realize; appreciate, have a feeling for; ~**ся**, be perceptible; make itself felt.

чугýн, -á, cast iron. **чугýнка, -и,** (cast-iron) pot; (cast-iron) stove; railway. **чугýнный**, cast-iron.

чудáк, -á, чудáчка, -и, eccentric, crank. **чудáческий**, eccentric, extravagant. **чудáчество**, -a, eccentricity, extravagance.

чудесá, etc.: see чýдо. **чудéсный**, miraculous; marvellous, wonderful.

чýдиться, -ишься *imp.* (*perf.* по~, при~), seem.

чýдно *adv.* wonderfully, beautifully. **чуднóй**; -дён, -днá, odd, strange. **чýдный**, wonderful, marvellous; beautiful, lovely; magical. **чýдо, -a;** *pl.* -десá, miracle; wonder, marvel. **чудóвище, -a,** monster. **чудóвищный**, monstrous; enormous. **чудóдей, -я, -дéйка, -и,** miracle-worker. **чудодéйственный**, miracle-working; miraculous. **чýдом** *adv.* miraculously. **чудотвóрный**, miraculous, miracle-working.

чужбúна, -ы, foreign land, foreign country. **чуждáться** -áюсь *imp.* + *gen.* shun, avoid; stand aloof from, be untouched by. **чýждый**; -ждт, -á, -о, alien (to); + *gen.* free from, devoid of, a stranger to. **чужезéмец, -мца, -зéмка, -и,** foreigner stranger. **чужезéмный**, foreign. **чуж|óй**, someone else's, another's, others'; strange, alien; foreign; на ~óй счёт, at somebody else's expense; ~ие края, foreign lands; *sb.* stranger.

чулáн, -a, store-room, lumber-room; larder; built-in cupboard.

чулóк, -лкá; *gen. pl.* -лóк, stocking. **чулóчн|ый**, stocking; ~ая вязка, stocking-stitch.

чум, -a, tent.

чумá, -ы, plague.

чурбáн, -a, block, chock; blockhead. **чýрка**, -и, block, lump.

чýткий; -ток, -ткá, -о, keen, sharp, quick; sensitive; sympathetic; tactful, delicate, considerate; ~ сон, light sleep. **чýткость, -и,** keeness, sharpness, quickness; delicacy, tact, consideration.

чýточка, -и; ни чýточки, not in the least; чýточку, a little (bit), a wee bit.

чýтче *comp.* of чýткий.

чуть *adv.* hardly, scarcely; just; a little, very slightly; ~ не, almost, nearly, all but; ~ свет, at daybreak, at first light; ~-чуть, a tiny bit.

ухо́нец, -нца, **чухо́нка**, -и, Finn. **чухо́нск|ий**, Finnish; ~ое ма́сло, butter.

ýчело, -а, stuffed animal, stuffed bird; scarecrow.

чушь, -и, nonsense, rubbish.

чу́ять, чу́ю *imp.* scent, smell; sense feel.

чье́, etc.: see чей.

чэ *n. indecl.* the letter ч.

Ш

ша *n. indecl.* the letter ш.

шаба́ш[1], -а, sabbath. **шаба́ш**[2], -á, end of work, break; finish; ~! that's all! that's enough! that'll do! **шаба́шить**, -шу *imp.* (*perf.* по~) (*sl.*) knock off, stop work; take a break.

шабло́н, -а, template, pattern; mould, form; stencil; cliché; routine. **шабло́н-ный**, stencil, pattern; trite, banal; stereotyped; routine.

шаг, -а (-у), with numerals -á, *loc.* -ý; *pl.* -й, step; footstep; pace; stride. **шага́ть**, -áю *imp.*, **шагну́ть**, -ну́, -нёшь *perf.* step; walk, stride; pace; go, come; make progress. **ша́гом** *adv.* at walking pace, at a walk; slowly.

ша́йба, -ы, washer; puck.

ша́йка[1], -и, tub.

ша́йка[2], -и, gang, band.

шака́л, -а, jackal.

шала́нда, -ы, barge, lighter.

шала́ш, -á, cabin, hut.

шали́ть, -лю́ *imp.* be naughty; play up, play tricks. **шаловли́вый**, naughty, mischievous, playful. **ша́лость**, -и, prank, game; *pl.* mischief, naughtiness. **шалу́н**, -á, **шалу́нья**, -и; *gen. pl.* -ний, naughty child.

шаль, -и, shawl.

пальн|о́й, mad, crazy; wild; ~áя пу́ля, stray bullet.

ша́мать, -аю *imp.* (*sl.*) scoff, eat.

ша́мкать, -аю *imp.* mumble, lisp.

шамо́вка, -и (*sl.*) grub, food.

шампа́нское *sb.* champagne.

шанда́л, -а, candlestick.

шанта́ж, -á, blackmail. **шантажи́ро-вать**, -рую *imp.* blackmail.

ша́пка, -и, cap; banner headline. **ша́почка**, -и, cap.

шар, -а, with numerals -á; *pl.* -ы́, sphere; ball; balloon; ballot; *pl.* (*sl.*) eyes; ~-зо́нд, sonde.

шара́хать, -аю *imp.*, **шара́хнуть**, -ну, hit; ~ся, rush, dash; shy.

шарж, -а, caricature, cartoon. **шаржи́-ровать**, -рую *imp.* caricature.

ша́рик, -а, ball; corpuscle. **ша́рико-в|ый**; ~ая (а́вто)ру́чка, ball-point pen; ~ый подши́пник, ball-bearing. **шарикоподши́пник**, -а, ball-bearing.

ша́рить, -рю *imp.* grope, feel, fumble; sweep.

ша́ркать, -аю *imp.*, **ша́ркнуть**, -ну *perf.* shuffle; scrape; ~ ного́й, click one's heels.

шарма́нка, -и, barrel-organ, street organ. **шарма́нщик**, -а, organ-grinder.

шарни́р, -а, hinge, joint.

шарова́ры, -áр *pl.* (wide) trousers; bloomers.

шарови́дный, spherical, globular. **шаро-во́й**, ball; globular. **шарообра́зный**, spherical, globular.

шарф, -а, scarf.

шасси́ *n. indecl.* chassis; undercarriage.

шата́ть, -áю *imp.*, rock, shake; *impers.* его́ шата́ет, he is reeling, staggering; ~ся, rock, sway; reel, stagger, totter; come loose, be loose; be unsteady; wander; loaf, lounge about. **шата́ю-щийся**, loose.

шатёр, -трá, tent; marquee; tent--shaped roof or steeple.

ша́тия, -и (*sl.*) gang, band, crowd, mob.

ша́ткий, unsteady; shaky; loose; unstable, insecure; unreliable; vacillating.

шатро́вый, tent-shaped.

шату́н, -á, connecting-rod.

ша́фер, -а; pl. -á, best man.

шафра́н, -а, saffron. шафра́нный, шафра́новый, saffron.

шах¹, -а, Shah.

шах², -а, check; ~ и мат, checkmate. шахмати́ст, -а, chess-player. ша́хматн|ый, chess; chess-board, chequered, check; ~ая па́ртия, game of chess; в ~ом поря́дке, quincunx fashion. ша́хматы, -ат pl. chess; chessmen.

ша́хта, -ы, mine, pit; shaft. шахтёр, -а, miner. шахтёрский, miner's, miners'; mining. ша́хтный, pit, mine.

ша́шечница, -ы, draught-board, chess-board. ша́шка¹, -и, draught; pl. draughts.

ша́шка², -и, sabre, cavalry sword.

шашлы́к, -á, shashlik, kebab.

шва, etc.: see шов.

шва́бра, -ы, mop, swab.

шваль, -и, rubbish; trash; riff-raff.

швартóв, -а, hawser; mooring-line; pl. moorings. швартова́ть, -ту́ю imp. (perf. о~, при~) moor; ~ся, moor, make fast.

швах, indecl. weak, poor; bad; in a bad way.

швед, -а, шве́дка, -и, Swede. шве́дский, Swedish.

швей́н|ый, sewing; ~ая маши́на, sewing-machine; ~ая мастерска́я, dressmaker's.

швейца́р, -а, (hall-)porter, door-keeper, commissionaire.

швейца́рец, -рца, -ца́рка, -и, Swiss. швейца́рский, Swiss.

швея́, -и́, seamstress, machinist.

швырну́ть, -ну́, -нёшь perf. швыря́ть, -я́ю imp. throw, fling, chuck, hurl; ~ся + instr. throw; throw about; treat carelessly, muck about.

шевели́ть, -елю́, -éли́шь imp.; шевельну́ть, -ну́, -нёшь perf. (perf. also по~), turn (over); (+ instr.) move, stir, budge; ~ся, move, stir, budge.

шевро́ n. indecl. kid.

шеде́вр, -а, masterpiece, chef d'œuvre.

шёл: see идти́.

ше́лест, -а rustle, rustling. шелесте́ть, -сти́шь imp. rustle.

шёлк, -а (-у), loc. -у́; pl. -á, silk. шелкови́стый, silk, silky. шелкови́ца, -ы, mulberry(-tree). шелкови́чный, mulberry; ~ червь, silkworm. шёлко́вый, silk.

шелохну́ть, -ну́, -нёшь perf. stir, agitate; ~ся, stir, move.

шелуха́, -и́, skin; peel, peelings; pod; scale. шелуши́ть, -шу́, peel; shell; ~ся, peel; peel off, flake off.

шепеля́вить, -влю imp. lisp. шепеля́вый, lisping; hissing.

шепну́ть, -ну́, -нёшь perf., шепта́ть, -пчу́, -пчешь imp. whisper; ~ся, whisper (together). шёпот, -а, whisper. шёпотом adv. in a whisper.

шере́нга, -и, rank; file, column.

шерохова́тый, rough; uneven; rugged.

шерсть, -и, wool, woollen; fleece; hair, coat. шерстяно́й, wool, woollen.

шерша́веть, -еет imp. become rough, get rough. шерша́вый, rough.

шест, -á, pole; staff.

ше́ствие, -я, procession. ше́ствовать, -твую, walk in procession, process; march, pace, proceed.

шестёрка, -и, six; figure 6; No. 6; group of six.

шестерня́, -и́; gen. pl. -рён, gear-wheel, cogwheel, pinion.

ше́стеро, -ы́х, six.

шести- in comb. six-, hexa-, sex(i)-. шестигра́нник, -а, hexahedron. ~дне́вка, -и, six-day (working) week. ~деся́тый, sixtieth. ~кла́ссник -а, ~кла́ссница, -ы, sixth-class pupil. ~ле́тний, six-year; six-year-old. ~ме́сячный, six-month; six-month-old. ~ сотле́тие, -я, six hundred years; sexcentenary. ~со́тый, six-hundredth anniversary. ~со́тый, six-hundredth. ~уго́льник, -а, hexagon. ~уго́льный, hexagonal. ~часово́й, six-hour; six-o'clock.

шестнадцатиле́тний, sixteen-year; sixteen-year-old. шестна́дцатый, sixteenth. шестна́дцать, -и, sixteen. шест|о́й, sixth; одна́ ~а́я, one-sixth. шесть, -и́, instr. -ью́ six. шестьдеся́т

-и́десяти, *instr.* -ью́десятью, sixty. шестьсо́т, -исо́т, -иста́м, -ьюста́ми, -иста́х, six hundred. ше́стью *adv.* six times.

шеф, -а, boss, chief; patron, sponsor. ше́фский, patronage, sponsorship, adoption; sponsored. ше́фство, -а, patronage, adoption. ше́фствовать, -твую *imp.* + над + *instr.* adopt; sponsor.

ше́я, -и neck; сиде́ть на ше́е y, be a burden to.

ши́ворот, -а, collar.

шика́рный, chic, smart, stylish; splendid, magnificent; done for effect.

ши́кать, -аю *imp.*, ши́кнуть, -ну *perf.* + *dat.* hiss, boo; + на + *acc.* hush, call 'sh' to.

ши́ло, -а; *pl.* -ья, -ьев, awl.

ши́на, -ы, tyre; splint.

шине́ль, -и, greatcoat, overcoat.

шинко́ванный, shredded, chopped. шинкова́ть, -ку́ю *imp.* shred, chop.

ши́нный tyre. шиноремо́нтный, tyre-repairing, tyre-maintenance.

шип, -а́, thorn, spine; spike, crampon, nail; pin; tenon.

шипе́ние, -я, hissing; sizzling; sputtering. шипе́ть, -плю́ *imp.* hiss; sizzle; fizz; sputter.

шипо́вник, -а, wild rose, dog-rose.

шипу́чий, sparkling; fizzy. шипу́чка, -и, fizzy drink. шипя́щий, sibilant.

ши́ре *comp.* of широ́кий, широко́. ширина́, -ы́, width, breadth; gauge. ши́рить, -рю *imp.* extend, expand; ~ся, spread, extend.

ши́рма, -ы, screen.

широ́к|ий, -о́к, -а́, -о́ко́. wide, broad; това́ры ~ого потребле́ния, consumer goods; ~ие ма́ссы, the broad masses; ~ое пла́тье, loose dress; ~ая пу́блика, the general public; ~ий экра́н, wide screen. широко́ *adv.* wide, widely, broadly; extensively, on a large scale; ~ смотре́ть на ве́щи, be broad-minded.

широко- in *comb.* wide-, broad-. широковеща́ние, -я, broadcasting. ~веща́тельный, broadcasting. ~коле́йный, broad-gauge. ~ко́стный, big-boned. ~пле́чий, broad-shouldered.

~по́лый, wide-brimmed; full-skirted. ~форма́тный, ~экра́нный, wide-screen.

широта́, -ы́; *pl.* -ы, width, breadth; latitude. широ́тный, of latitude; latitudinal. широча́йший *superl.* of широ́кий. широтре́б, -а *abbr.* consumption; consumer goods. ширь, -и, (wide) expanse; во всю ~, to full width; to the full extent.

ши́тый, embroidered. шить, шью, шьёшь *imp.* (*perf.* c~) sew; make; embroider. шитьё, -я́, sewing, needlework; embroidery.

шифр, -а, cipher, code; press-mark; monogram. шифро́ванный, in cipher, coded. шифрова́ть, -ру́ю *imp.* (*perf.* за~) encipher, code. шифро́вка, -и, enciphering, coding; coded communication, communication in cipher.

шиш, -а́, fico, fig; nothing; ruffian, brigand; ни ~а́, damn all. ши́шка, -и, cone; bump; lump, knob; core; (*sl.*) big shot, big noise. шишкова́тый, knobby, knobbly; bumpy. шишко-ви́дный, cone-shaped. шишконо́сный, coniferous.

шкала́, -ы́; *pl.* -ы, scale; dial.

шкап: see шкаф.

шкату́лка, -и, box, casket, case.

шкаф, шкап, -а, *loc.* -у́; *pl.* -ы́, cupboard; wardrobe; dresser; кни́жный ~, bookcase; несгора́емый ~, safe. шка́фчик, -а, cupboard, locker.

шквал, -а, squall. шква́листый, squally.

шкет, -а, (*sl.*) boy; apprentice criminal.

шкив, -а; *pl.* -ы, pulley; sheave.

шко́ла, -ы, school; ~-интерна́т, boarding-school. шко́лить, -лю *imp.* (*perf.* вы́~) train, discipline. шко́льник, -а, schoolboy. шко́льница, -ы, schoolgirl. шко́льный, school; ~ учи́тель, school-teacher, school-master.

шку́ра, -ы, skin, hide, pelt. шку́рка, -и, skin; rind; emery paper, sandpaper. шку́рник, -а, -ница, -ы, person who looks after number one. шку́рный, self-centred, selfish.

шла: see идти́.

шлагба́ум, -а, barrier; arm.

шлак, -а, slag; dross; cinder; clinker. шлакоблóк, -а, breeze-block. шлáковый, slag.

шланг, -а, hose.

шлейф, -а, train.

шлем, -а, helmet.

шлёпать, -аю *imp.*, шлёпнуть, -ну *perf.* smack, spank; shuffle; tramp; (*sl.*) shoot, execute by shooting; ~ся, fall flat, plop down, plump down.

шли: see идти.

шлифовáльный, polishing; grinding; abrasive. шлифовáть, -фýю *imp.* (*perf.* от~) polish; grind; abrade. шлифóвка, -и, polishing; grinding; polish.

шлю: see идти. шлю́, etc.: see слать.

шлюз, -а, lock, sluice, floodgate. шлюзовóй, lock, sluice.

шлю́пка, -и, launch, boat.

шля́па, -ы, hat; hélpless feeble creature. дéло в шля́пе, it's in the bag. шля́пка, -и, hat, bonnet; head; cap. шля́пник, -а, шля́пница, -ы, milliner, hatter. шля́пный, hat.

шмель, -я́, bumble-bee.

шмон, -а, (*sl.*) search, frisking. шмонáть, -áю *imp.*, шмони́ть, -ню́, -ни́шь *perf.*, шмоня́ть, -я́ю *imp.* (*perf.* also про~), (*sl.*) search, frisk.

шмы́гать, -аю *imp.*, шмыгнýть, -ыгнý, -ыгнёшь *perf.* dart, rush, slip, sneak; + *instr.* rub, brush; ~ нóсом, sniff.

шнур, -á, cord; lace; flex, cable. шнуровáть, -рýю *imp.* (*perf.* за~, про~) lace up; tie. шнурóк, -ркá, lace.

шныря́ть, -я́ю *imp.* dart about, run in and out.

шов, шва, seam; stitch; suture; joint; weld.

шоколáд, -а, chocolate. шоколáдка, -и, chocolate, bar of chocolate. шоколáдный, chocolate; chocolate-coloured.

шóрох, -а, rustle.

шóры, шор *pl.* blinkers.

шоссé *n. indecl.* highway, main road; (made) road. шоссéйник, -а, road-racer.

шотлáндец, -дца, Scotsman, Scot. шотлáндка[1], -и, Scotswoman. шот-

лáндка[2], -и, tartan, plaid. шотлáндский, Scottish, Scots.

шофёр, -а, driver; chauffeur. шофёрша, -и, driver. шофёрский, driver's; driving.

шпáга, -и, sword.

шпагáт, -а, cord; twine; string; splits.

шпаклевáть, -лю́ю *imp.* (*perf.* за~) caulk; fill, stop, putty. шпаклёвка, -и, filling, puttying, stopping; putty.

шпáла, -ы, sleeper.

шпанá, -ы́ (*sl.*) hooligan(s), rowdy, rowdies; riff-raff, rabble; petty criminals.

шпаргáлка, -и, crib.

шпáрить, -рю *imp.* (*perf.* о~) scald.

шпат, -а, spar.

шпиль, -я *m.* spire, steeple; capstan, windlass. шпи́лька, -и, hairpin; hat-pin; tack, brad; stiletto heel.

шпинáт, -а, spinach.

шпингалéт, -а, espagnolette, (vertical) bolt; catch, latch.

шпиóн, -а, spy. шпионáж, -а, espionage. шпиóнить, -ню *imp.* be a spy; spy (за + *instr.* on). шпиóнский, spy's; espionage.

шпóра, -ы, spur.

шприц, -а, syringe.

шпрóта, -ы, sprat; *pl.* smoked sprats in oil.

шпýлька, -и, spool, bobbin.

шрам, -а, scar.

шрифт, -а; *pl.* -ы́, type, print; script; курси́вный ~, italic(s). шрифтовóй, type.

шт. *abbr.* штýка, item, piece.

штаб, -а; *pl.* -ы́, staff; headquarters.

штáбель, -я; *pl.* -я́ *m.* stack, pile.

штаби́ст, -а, штáбник, -а, staff-officer.

штабнóй, staff, headquarters.

штамп, -а, die, punch; stamp, impress; letter-head; cliché, stock phrase. штампóванный, punched, stamped, pressed; trite, hackneyed, stock, standard.

штáнга, -и, bar, rod, beam; weight; crossbar. штанги́ст, -а, weight-lifter.

штани́шки, -шек *pl.* (child's) shorts. штаны́, -óв, trousers.

штат[1], -а, State.

штат[2], -а, штáты, -ов *pl.* staff, establishment.

штати́в, -а, tripod, base, support, stand.

шта́тный, staff; established, permanent.

шта́тск|ий, civilian; ~ое (пла́тье), civilian clothes, mufti, civvies; ~ий sb. civilian.

штемпелева́ть, -лю́ю imp. (perf. за~) stamp; frank, postmark. ште́мпель, -я; pl. -я́ m. stamp; почто́вый ~, postmark.

ште́псель, -я, pl. -я́ m. plug, socket. ште́псельный, plug, socket.

штиль, -я m. calm.

што́льня, -и; gen. pl. -лен, gallery.

што́пальный, darning. што́паный, darned. што́пать, -аю imp. (perf. за~) darn. што́пка, -и, darning; darn; darning wool, darning thread.

што́пор, -а, corkscrew; spin.

што́ра, -ы, blind.

шторм, -а, gale, storm.

штраф, -а, fine. штрафба́т, -а abbr. (sl.) penal battalion. штрафно́й, penal, penalty; ~ батальо́н, penal battalion; ~ уда́р, penalty kick. штрафова́ть, -фу́ю imp. (perf. о~) fine.

штрих, -а́, stroke; hatching; feature, trait. штрихова́ть, -ху́ю imp. (perf. за~) shade, hatch.

штуди́ровать, -рую imp. (perf. про~) study.

шту́ка, -и, item, one; piece; trick; thing; вот так ~! well, I'll be damned! в то́м-то и ~! that's just the point; пять штук яи́ц, five eggs.

штукату́р, -а, plasterer. штукату́рить, -рю imp. (perf. от~, о~) plaster, parget. штукату́рка, -и, plastering; plaster; facing, rendering; stucco. штукату́рный, plaster, stucco.

штурва́л, -а, (steering-)wheel, helm; controls. штурва́льный, steering, control; sb. helmsman, pilot.

штурм, -а, storm, assault.

штурма́н, -а; pl. -ы or -а́, navigator.

штурмова́ть, -му́ю imp. storm, assault. штурмов|о́й, assault; storming; ~а́я авиа́ция, ground-attack aircraft; ~а́я ле́стница, scaling-ladder; ~а́я поло-

cá, assault course. штурмовщи́на, -ы, rushed work, production spurt, sporadic effort.

шту́чн|ый, piece, by the piece; ~ый пол, parquet floor; ~ая рабо́та, piece-work; ~ый това́р, piece-goods.

штык, -а́, bayonet. штыково́й, bayonet.

штырь, -я́ m. pintle, pin.

шу́ба, -ы, winter coat, fur coat.

шу́лер, -а; pl. -а́, card-sharper, cheat. шу́лерство, -а, card-sharping, sharp practice.

шум, -а (-у), noise; din, uproar, racket; sensation, stir; мно́го ~у из-за ниче́го, much ado about nothing; наде́лать ~у, cause a sensation. шуме́ть, -млю́ imp. make a noise; row, wrangle; make a stir; make a fuss; cause a sensation. шу́мный, -мен, -мна́, -о, noisy; loud; sensational. шумови́к, -а́, sound-effects man.

шумо́вка, -и, perforated spoon; skimmer.

шумов|о́й, sound, noise; ~ы́е эффе́кты, sound effects. шумо́к, -мка́, noise; под ~, under cover, on the quiet.

шу́рин, -а, brother-in-law.

шурша́ть, -шу́ imp. rustle, crackle.

шу́стрый, -тёр, -тра́, -о, smart, bright, sharp.

шут, -а́, fool; jester; buffoon, clown. шути́ть, -чу́, -ти́шь imp. (perf. по~) joke, jest; play, trifle; + над + instr. laugh at, make fun of. шу́тка, -и, joke, jest; trick; farce; без шу́ток, кро́ме шу́ток, joking apart; в шу́тку, as a joke, in jest; не на шу́тку, in earnest; сыгра́ть шу́тку с + instr. play a trick on. шутли́вый, humorous; joking, light-hearted. шу́точн|ый, comic; joking; де́ло не ~ое, it's no joke, no laughing matter. шутя́ adv. for fun, in jest; easily, lightly.

шушу́каться, -аюсь imp. whisper together.

шху́на, -ы, schooner.

шью, etc.: see шить.

Щ

ща *n. indecl.* the letter щ.

щаве́ль, -я́ *m.* sorrel.

щади́ть, щажу́ *imp.* (*perf.* по~) spare; have mercy on.

щебёнка, -и, ще́бень, -бня *m.* gravel, crushed stone, ballast; road-metal.

щебе́т, -а, twitter, chirp. щебета́ть, -ечу́, -е́чешь *imp.* twitter, chirp.

щего́л, -гла́, goldfinch.

щёголь, -я *m.* dandy, fop. щегольну́ть, -ну́, -нёшь *perf.*, щеголя́ть, -я́ю *imp.* dress fashionably; strut about; + *instr.* show off, parade, flaunt. щегольско́й, foppish, dandified.

ще́дрость, -и, generosity. ще́дрый; -др, -а́, -о, generous; lavish, liberal.

щека́, -и́, *acc.* щёку; *pl.* щёки, -а́м, cheek.

щеко́лда, -ы, latch, catch.

щекота́ть, -очу́, -о́чешь *imp.* (*perf.* по~) tickle. щеко́тка, -и, tickling, tickle. щекотли́вый, ticklish, delicate.

щёлкать, -аю *imp.*, щёлкнуть, -ну *perf.* crack; flick, fillip; trill; + *instr.* click, snap, pop; он щёлкает зубами, his teeth are chattering; ~ па́льцами, snap one's fingers.

щёлок, -а, lye, liquor. щелочно́й, alkaline. щёлочь, -и; *gen. pl.* -ей, alkali.

щелчо́к, -чка́, flick, flip, fillip; slight; blow.

щель, -и; *gen. pl.* -ей, crack; chink; slit; fissure, crevice; slit trench; голосова́я ~, glottis.

щени́ться, -и́тся *imp.* (*perf.* о~) pup, whelp, cub. щено́к, -нка́; *pl.* -нки́, -о́в *or* -ня́та, -я́т, puppy, pup; whelp, cub.

щепа́, -ы́; *pl.* -ы, -а́м, ще́пка, -и; splinter, chip; kindling; худо́й как

ще́пка, as thin as a rake. щепа́ть, -плю́, -плешь *imp.* chip, chop.

щепети́льный, punctilious, correct; pernickety, fussy, finicky.

ще́пка: see щепа́.

щепо́тка, -и, щепо́ть, -и, pinch.

щети́на, -ы, bristle; stubble. щети́нистый, bristly, bristling. щети́ниться, -ится *imp.* (*perf.* о~) bristle. щётка, -и, brush; fetlock. щёточный, brush.

щёчный, cheek.

щи, щей *or* щец, шам, ща́ми *pl.* shchi, cabbage soup.

щи́колотка, -и, ankle.

щипа́ть, -плю́, -плешь *imp.*, щипну́ть, -ну́, -нёшь *perf.* (*perf. also* об~, о~, ущипну́ть) pinch, nip, tweak; sting, bite; burn; pluck; nibble; ~ся, pinch. щипко́м *adv.* pizzicato. щипо́к, -пка́, pinch, nip, tweak. щипцы́, -о́в *pl.* tongs, pincers, pliers; forceps. щи́пчики, -ов *pl.* tweezers.

щит, -а́, shield; screen; sluice-gate; (tortoise-)shell; hoarding; board; panel; распредели́тельный ~, switchboard; ~ управле́ния, control panel. щитови́дный, thyroid. щито́к, -тка́, dashboard.

щу́ка, -и, pike.

щуп, -а, probe. щу́пальце, -а; *gen. pl.* -лец, tentacle; antenna. щу́пать, -аю (*perf.* по~) feel, touch; feel for; probe.

щу́плый; -пл, -а́, -о, weak, puny, frail.

щу́рить, -рю *imp.* (*perf.* со~) screw up, narrow; ~ся, screw up one's eyes; narrow.

щу́чий, pike's; (как) по ~ьему веле́нью, of its own accord, as if by magic.

Э

э *n. indecl.*, э обор**о**тное, the letter э.

эв *abbr.* электр**о**н-в**о**льт, electron volt, eV.

эвакуацио**нный**, evacuation. **эваку**а**ция**, -и, evacuation. **эваку**и**рованный** *sb.* evacuee. **эваку**и**ровать**, -рую *perf.* and *imp.* evacuate.

ЭВМ (*eveém*) *abbrev.* of электр**о**нная вычисл**и**тельная маш**и**на, (electronic) computer.

эволюцио**нировать**, -рую *perf.* and *imp.* evolve. **эволюци**о**нный**, evolutionary. **эвол**ю**ция**, -и, evolution; manœuvre.

эй *int.* hi! hey!

эква**тор**, -а, equator. **экватори**а**льный**, equatorial.

экз. *abbr.* экземпл**я**р, copy, specimen.

экза**мен**, -а, examination, exam; в**ы**держать, сдать, ∼, pass an examination. **экзаменов**а**ть**, -н**у**ю *imp.* (*perf.* про∼) examine; ∼ся, take an examination.

экземпля**р**, -а, specimen, example; copy.

экипа**ж**[1], -а, carriage.

экипа**ж**[2], -а, crew; ship's company. **экипиров**а**ть**, -р**у**ю *perf.* and *imp.* equip. **экипир**о**вка**, -и, equipping; equipment.

эконо**м**, -а, steward, housekeeper; economist. **экон**о**мика**, -и, economics; economy. **эконо**м**ить**, -млю *imp.* (*perf.* с∼) use sparingly, husband; save; economize. **эконом**и**ческий**, economic; economical. **эконом**и**чный**, economical. **экон**о**мия**, -и, economy; saving. **эконо**м**ка**, -и, housekeeper. **экон**о**мный**, economical; careful, thrifty.

экра**н**, -а, screen; голуб**о**й ∼, television (screen). **экраниз**а**ция**, -и, filming, screening; film version.

экскурса**нт**, -а, tourist. **экскурси**о**нный**, excursion. **экск**у**рсия**, -и, (conducted) tour; excursion, trip; outing; group, party (of tourists). **экскурсов**о**д**, -а, guide.

экспанси**вный**, effusive, expansive, talkative.

экспеди**ровать**, -рую *perf.* and *imp.* dispatch. **экспед**и**ция**, -и, expedition; dispatch, forwarding; forwarding office.

экспе**рт**, -а, expert. **эксперт**и**за**, -ы, (expert) examination, expert opinion; commission of experts.

эксплуата**тор**, -а, exploiter. **эксплуатаци**о**нн**|**ый**, exploitational, operating; ∼ые расх**о**ды, running costs; ∼ые усл**о**вия, working conditions. **эксплуат**а**ция**, -и, exploitation; utilization; operation, running. **эксплуат**и**ровать**, -рую *imp.* exploit; operate, run, work.

экспо́ *f. indecl.* Expo. **экспоз**и**ция**, -и, lay-out; exposition; exposure. **экспон**а**т**, -а, exhibit. **экспон**и**ровать**, -рую *perf.* and *imp.* exhibit; expose. **экспон**о**метр**, -а, exposure meter.

экспро**мт**, -а, impromptu. **экспр**о**мтом** *adv.* impromptu; suddenly, without warning; игр**а**ть ∼, improvise.

эксте**рн**, -а, external student. **экстерн**а**т**, -а, extramural course(s).

э́**кстра** *indecl. adj.* highest, best; jolly good, splendid, smashing.

экстравага**нтный**, extravagant, eccentric, bizarre, preposterous.

э́**кстра(-)кл**а**сс**, -а, first class; highest rating, qualification, standing, etc.

э́**кстренн**|**ый**, urgent; emergency; extra, special; ∼ое засед**а**ние, extraordinary session; ∼ое изд**а**ние, special edition; ∼ый в**ы**пуск, special edition; ∼ые расх**о**ды, unforeseen expenses.

эксцентри**чный**, eccentric.

электризова**ть**, -з**у**ю *imp.* (*perf.* на∼) electrify. **эл**е**ктрик**, -а, electrician. **электрифиц**и**ровать**, -рую *perf.* and *imp.* electrify. **электр**и**ческий**, electric; ∼ фон**а**рик, torch, flashlight. **электр**и**чество**, -а, electricity; electric light. **электр**и**чка**, -и, electric train.

электро- in *comb.* electro-, electric, electrical. **электробытов**о**й**, electrical.

~во́з, -а, electric locomotive. ~дви́гатель, -я *m.* electric motor. ~дина́мика, -и, electrodynamics. ~дугово́й, electric-arc. ~изгородь, -и, electric fence. электро́лиз, -а, electrolysis. ~маши́нка, -и, electric typewriter. ~монтёр, -а, electrician. ~одея́ло, -а, electric blanket. ~подогрева́тель, -я *m.* electric heater. ~по́езд, -а, electric train. ~полотёр, -а, electric floor-polisher. ~прибо́р, -а, electrical appliance. ~про́вод, -а; *pl.* -а́, electric cable. ~прово́дка, -и, electric wiring. ~прои́грыватель, -я *m.* record-player. ~сва́рка, -и, electric welding. ~ста́нция, -и, power-station. ~те́хник, -а, electrical engineer. ~те́хника, -и, electrical engineering. ~тя́га, -и, electric traction. ~шо́к, -а, electric-shock treatment. ~энцефалогра́мма, -ы, (electro-)encephalogram. ~энцефало́граф, -а, (electro-)encephalograph.

электро́н, -а, electron. электро́н-во́льт, -а, электроново́льт, -а, electron volt, eV. электро́ник, see электро́нщик. электро́ника, -и, electronics.

электро́нно- in *comb.* electron, electronic. электро́нно-вычисли́тельный, electronic-computer. ~ лучево́й, electron-beam, cathode-ray. ~микроскопи́ческий, electron-microscope.

электро́нный, electron; electronic.

электроново́льт: see электро́н-во́льт.

электро́нщик, -а, электро́ник, -а, specialist in electronics.

элеме́нт, -а, element; cell; type, character. элемента́рный, elementary; simple.

эль *n. indecl.* the letter л.

эм *n. indecl.* the letter м.

эма́левый, enamel. эмали́рованный, enamelled. эмали́ровать, -рую *imp.* enamel. эма́ль, -и, enamel.

эмбле́ма, -ы, emblem; insignia.

эмбрио́н, -а, embryo.

эмигра́нт, -а, emigrant, émigré. эмигра́ция, -и, emigration.

эмпири́зм, -а, empiricism. эмпи́рик, -а, empiricist. эмпири́ческий, empiricist; empirical.

эн *n. indecl.* the letter н.

э́ндшпиль, -я *m.* end-game.

энерге́тика, -и, power engineering. энерги́чный, energetic, vigorous, forceful. эне́ргия, -и, energy; vigour, effort.

энерго- in *comb.* power, energy. энерговооружённость, -и, power capacity, power supply. ~ёмкий, power-consuming. ~затра́та, energy expenditure. ~систе́ма, -ы, electric power system.

эпиде́мия, -и, epidemic.

эпизо́д, -а, episode. эпизоди́ческий, episodic; occasional, sporadic.

эпопе́я, -и, epic.

эпо́ха, -и, epoch, age, era. эпоха́льный, epoch-making.

эр *n. indecl.* the letter р.

э́ра, -ы, era; до на́шей э́ры, B.C.; на́шей э́ры, A.D.

эрс́, -а *abbr.* реакти́вный снаря́д, missile.

эро́тика, -и, sensuality. эроти́ческий, эроти́чный, erotic, sensual.

эс *n. indecl.* the letter с.

эсе́р, -а *abbr.* S.R., Socialist Revolutionary. эсе́ровский, Socialist-Revolutionary.

эска́дра, -ы; squadron. эска́дренный, squadron; ~ миноно́сец, destroyer. эскадри́льный, squadron. эскадри́лья, -и; *gen. pl.* -лий, squadron. эска́дрон, -а, squadron, troop. эскадро́нный, squadron, troop.

эски́з, -а, sketch, study; draft, outline. эски́зный, sketch; sketchy; draft.

эскимо́ *n. indecl.* choc-ice.

эскимо́с, -а, эскимо́ска, -и, Eskimo. эскимо́сский, Eskimo.

эсми́нец, -нца *abbr.* эска́дренный миноно́сец, destroyer.

эстака́да, -ы, trestle, platform; trestle bridge; gantry; overpass; pier, boom.

эста́мп, -а, print, engraving, plate.

эстафе́та, -ы, relay race; baton.

эсте́тика, -и, aesthetics; design. эстети́ческий, aesthetic.

эстра́да, -ы, stage, platform; variety, music hall; арти́ст эстра́ды, music-hall artiste. эстра́дный, stage; variety; ~ конце́рт, variety show.

эта́ж, -á, storey, floor. этажёрка, -и, shelves; whatnot; stand. эта́жность, -и, number of floors.

э́так adv. so, thus; about, approximately. э́такий, such (a), what (a).

этало́н, -a, standard.

эта́п, -a, stage, phase; lap; halting-place; transport, shipment, of prisoners. этапи́ровать, -рую imp. ship, transport.

этике́тка, -и, label.

этиче́ский, эти́чный, ethical.

эти́ческий, ethnic.

э́то part. this (is), that (is), it (is). э́тот m., э́та f., э́то n., э́ти pl. pron. this, these.

этю́д, -a, study, sketch; étude; exercise; problem.

эф n. indecl. the letter ф.

эфе́с, -a, hilt, handle.

эфио́п, -a, эфио́пка, -и, Ethiopian. эфио́пский, Ethiopian.

эфи́р, -a, ether; air. эфи́рн|ый, ethereal; ether, ester; ~ое ма́сло, essential oil; volatile oil.

эффе́кт, -a, effect, impact; result, consequences; pl. effects. эффекти́вный, effective; efficient. эффе́ктный, effective; striking; done for effect.

эх int. eh! oh!

э́хо, -a, echo. эхоло́т, -a, echo-sounder. эхолока́ция, -и, echo location.

ЭЦВМ (etseveém) abbr. электро́нная цифрова́я вычисли́тельная маши́на, electronic digital computer.

эшафо́т, -a, scaffold.

эшело́н, -a, echelon; special train, troop-train.

Ю

ю n. indecl. the letter ю.

ю. abbr. юг, S., south.

ЮА́Р (yuár) abbr. Ю́жно-Африка́нская Респу́блика, Republic of South Africa.

юбиле́й, -я, anniversary; jubilee. юбиле́йный, jubilee.

ю́бка, -и, skirt. ю́бочка, -и, short skirt.

ювели́р, -a, jeweller. ювели́рный, jeweller's, jewellery; fine, intricate; ~ магази́н, jeweller's.

юг, -a, south; на ~е, in the south. ю́го-восто́к, -a, south-east. ю́го-за́пад, -a, south-west. югосла́в, -a, югосла́вка, -и, Yugoslav. югосла́вский, Yugoslav. южа́нин, -a; pl. -а́не, -а́н, southerner. ю́жный, south, southern.

ю́мор, -a, humour. юмореска, -и, humoresque. юмори́ст, -a, humourist. юмори́стика, -и, humour. юмористи́ческий, humorous, comic, funny.

юнио́р, -a, юнио́рка, -и, junior; junior competitor, player, etc. юнко́р, -a abbr. young contributor, youth correspondent.

ю́ность, -и, youth. ю́ноша, -и m. youth. ю́ношеский, youthful. ю́ношество, -a, youth; young people. ю́ный; юн, -á, -о, young; youthful.

юпи́тер, -a, floodlight.

юриди́ческ|ий, legal, juridical; ~ие нау́ки, jurisprudence; law; ~ий факульте́т, faculty of law. юриско́нсульт, -a, legal adviser. юри́ст, -a, legal expert, lawyer.

ю́ркий; -рок, -рка́, -рко, quick-moving, brisk; sharp, smart.

ю́рта, -ы, yurt, nomad's tent.

юсти́ция, -и, justice.

юти́ться, ючу́сь imp. huddle (together); take shelter.

ю́шка, -и (sl.) watery gruel; blood.

Я

я, *n. indecl.* the letter я.

я, меня́, мне, мной (-о́ю), (обо) мне *pron.* I.

я́беда, -ы *m.* and *f.*, **я́бедник**, -а, sneak, tell-tale; informer. **я́бедничать**, -аю *imp.* (*perf.* на~) inform, tell tales, sneak.

я́блоко, -а; *pl.* -и, -ок, apple; в я́блоках, dappled, dapple; глазно́е ~, eyeball. **я́блоневый**, **я́блонный**, **я́блочный**, apple. **я́блоня**, -и, apple-tree.

яви́ться, явлю́сь, я́вишься *perf.*, **явля́ться**, -я́юсь *imp.* appear; present oneself, report; turn up, arrive, show up; arise, occur; + *instr.* be, serve as. **я́вка**, -и, appearance, attendance, presence; secret rendez-vous; ~ обяза́тельна, attendance obligatory. **явле́ние**, -я, phenomenon; appearance; occurrence, happening; scene. **я́вный**, obvious, manifest, patent; overt, explicit. **я́вственный**, clear, distinct. **я́вствовать**, -твует, appear; be clear, be obvious: follow.

ягнёнок, -нка; *pl.* -ня́та, -я́т, lamb.

я́года, -ы, berry; berries.

ягоди́ца, -ы, buttock, buttocks.

яд, -а (-у), poison; venom.

я́дерник, -а, **я́дерщик**, -а, a nuclear physicist. **я́дерный**, nuclear.

ядови́тый, venomous; toxic.

ядрёный, vigorous, healthy; bracing; sound, crisp, juicy. **ядро́**, -á; *pl.* -а, я́дер, kernel, core; nucleus; main body; (cannon-)ball; shot. **ядро-толка́тель**, -я *m.* shot-putter.

я́зва, -ы, ulcer, sore. **я́звенный**, ulcerous; ~ая боле́знь, ulcers. **язви́на**, -ы, large ulcer; indentation, pit. **язви́тельный**, caustic, biting, sarcastic. **язви́ть**, -влю́ *imp.* (*perf.* съ~), wound, sting; be sarcastic.

язы́к, -á, tongue; clapper; language; англи́йский ~, English. **языка́стый**, sharp-tongued. **языкове́д**, -а, linguist, language specialist. **языкове́дение**, -я, **языкозна́ние**, -я, linguistics. **языково́й**, linguistic. **языко́вый**, tongue;

lingual. **язычко́вый**, uvular; reed. **язы́чник**, -а, heathen, pagan. **язы́чный**, lingual. **язычо́к**, -чка́, tongue; uvula; reed; catch.

яи́чко, -а; *pl.* -и, -чек, egg; testicle. **яи́чник**, -а, ovary. **яи́чница**, -ы, fried eggs. **яйцеви́дный**, oval; oviform, ovoid, egg-shaped. **яйцо́**, -á; *pl.* я́йца, яи́ц, egg; ovum.

я́кобы *conj.* as if, as though; *part.* supposedly, ostensibly; allegedly.

я́корный, anchor; mooring; ~ая стоя́нка, anchorage. **я́корь**, -я; *pl.* -я *m.* anchor; armature.

ял, -а, whaleboat, whaler; yawl. **я́лик**, -а, skiff, dinghy; yawl. **я́личник**, -а, ferryman.

я́ма, -ы, pit, hole; depression, hollow; (*sl.*) fence.

ямщи́к, -á, coachman.

янва́рский, January. **янва́рь**, -я́ *m.* January.

янта́рный, amber. **янта́рь**, -я́ *m.* amber.

япо́нец, -нца, **япо́нка**, -и, Japanese. **япо́нский**, Japanese; ~ лак, japan.

я́ркий; я́рок, ярка́, -о, bright; colourful, striking; vivid, graphic; ~ приме́р, striking example, glaring example.

ярлы́к, -á, label; tag.

я́рмарка, -и, fair. **я́рмарочный**, fair, market.

ярмо́, -á; *pl.* -а, yoke.

ярово́й, spring, spring-sown.

я́ростный, furious, fierce, savage, frenzied. **я́рость**, -и, fury, rage, frenzy.

я́рус, -а, circle; tier; layer.

я́рче *comp.* of я́ркий.

я́рый, vehement, fervent; furious, raging; violent.

я́сельный, creche, day-nursery.

я́сеневый, ash. **я́сень**, -я *m.* ash(-tree).

я́сли, -ей *pl.* manger, crib; creche, day nursery.

ясне́ть, -е́ет *imp.* become clear, clear. **я́сно** *adv.* clearly. **яснови́дение**, -я, clairvoyance. **яснови́дец**, -дца, **яснови́дица**, -ы, clairvoyant. **я́сный**; -я́сен, ясна́, -о, clear; bright; fine;

distinct; serene; plain; lucid; precise, logical.

я́ства, яств *pl.* viands, victuals.

я́стреб, -а; *pl.* ·á, hawk. **ястреби́н|ый,** hawk; с ~ым взгля́дом, hawk-eyed. **ястребо́к,** -бка́, hawk; fighter (plane).

я́хта. -ы, yacht.

яче́истый, cellular, porous. **яче́йка,** -и, **ячея́,** -и́, cell.

ячме́нный, barley. **ячме́нь**[1], -я́ *m.* barley.

ячме́нь[2], -я́ *m.* stye.

я́щерица -ы, lizard.

я́щик, -а, box, chest, case; cabinet; drawer; му́сорный ~, dustbin; откла́дывать в до́лгий ~, shelve, put off.

я́щур, -а, foot-and-mouth disease.

THE
POCKET OXFORD
ENGLISH–RUSSIAN
DICTIONARY

THE
POCKET OXFORD
ENGLISH–RUSSIAN
DICTIONARY

COMPILED BY
NIGEL RANKIN
AND
DELLA THOMPSON

PREFACE

This dictionary forms a companion volume to the *Pocket Oxford Russian–English Dictionary* (1975), and is likewise designed primarily for English-speaking users who do not have an advanced knowledge of Russian.

For this reason, particular attention has been given to the provision of the inflected forms of nouns, pronouns, adjectives, and verbs wherever they occur as translations and are not within the group of regular forms defined in the Introduction (pp. vii–xi). The stressed syllable of every Russian word is shown, and changes of stress are also marked. Perfective and imperfective aspects are distinguished, and both are given wherever appropriate.

The English vocabulary is drawn from that of the smaller Oxford English dictionaries, and the Russian translations are based on the best bilingual and monolingual dictionaries and grammars published in the Soviet Union and elsewhere. The aim has been to meet the needs of as wide a range of users as possible, by providing a single alphabetical list of almost 30,000 words in the general, technical, colloquial, and idiomatic areas of the language.

PUBLISHER'S NOTE

The major part of this dictionary was compiled by Mr Nigel Rankin. After his death on 4 October 1979, the remaining work was undertaken by Miss Della Thompson, under the supervision of Dr John Sykes, Editor of the *Concise Oxford Dictionary* and of the *Pocket Oxford Dictionary*.

ACKNOWLEDGEMENTS

The Publisher takes this opportunity to thank Dr Jane Grayson, Mrs Vera Konnova-Stone, and Miss Helen Szamuely for valuable comments on the galley proofs; the late Professor R. Auty, Professor J. L. I. Fennell, Mr P. S. Falla, Mr I. P. Foote, Mrs Konnova-Stone, Professor A. E. Pennington, Miss Szamuely, and Professor M. C. C. Wheeler for useful remarks on a preliminary specimen of the dictionary; Mrs Jessie Coulson for a considerable amount of preliminary drafting done before her retirement; and Mr and Mrs A. Levtov for their valuable advice on contemporary Russian usage.

INTRODUCTION

NOTES ON THE USE OF THE DICTIONARY

General

In order to save space, several English words are sometimes included in one entry. They are printed in **bold type** and separated by full stops. Compounds and phrases within an entry are printed in *italics* and separated by semicolons. When a bold-type word is used in a compound or phrase, it is abbreviated to its first letter, e.g. **crash** . . . *c. landing.* A swung dash ∼ stands for the preceding Russian word, e.g. **Georgian** . . . грузи́н, ∼ка indicates грузи́нка; **sing** . . . петь *imp.*, про ∼, с ∼ *perf.* indicates пропе́ть, спеть. In giving grammatical forms a hyphen is often used to stand for the whole or a part of the preceding or following Russian word, e.g. **grey** . . . седо́й (сед, -á, -о)=седо́й (сед, седá, сéдо); **come** . . . приходи́ть (-ожу́, -о́дишь)=приходи́ть (прихожу́, прихо́дишь); **prepare** . . . при-, под-, гото́вливаться =пригото́вливаться, подгото́вливаться. Superscript numbers are used to distinguish unrelated headwords spelt alike, and glosses may follow in brackets, e.g. **bank**[1] *n.* (*of river*), **bank**[2] *n.* (*econ.*).

The comma is used to show alternatives, e.g.

(i) **want** . . . хоте́ть+*gen.*, *acc.* means that the Russian verb may govern either the genitive or (less often) the accusative;

(ii) **classify** . . . классифици́ровать *imp.*, *perf.* means that the Russian verb is both imperfective and perfective.

The ampersand (&) also shows alternatives, e.g.

(i) **dilate** *v.t.* & *i.* . . . . расширя́ть(ся) means that the Russian verb forms given cover both the transitive and the intransitive English verb;

(ii) **orphan** . . . сирота́ *m.* & *f.* means that the Russian noun can be treated as either masculine or feminine according to the sex of the person it denotes;

(iii) **move** . . . дви́гаться (-аюсь, -аешься & дви́жусь,

-жешься) shows alternative forms for the first and second persons singular present.

The double hyphen is used when a hyphenated word is split between two lines, to show that the hyphen is not simply the result of printing convention. Where the first part is abbreviated, the hyphen is not repeated, e.g. **red** ... *r.-/handed.*

Stress

The stress of each Russian word is indicated by an acute accent over the vowel of the stressed syllable. It is not given for monosyllabic words, except those which bear the main stress in a phrase, e.g. **be** ... нé было; **year** ... год óт году; here, the stressed monosyllable and the next word are pronounced as one. The vowel ё has no stress-mark, since it is almost always stressed; when the stress falls elsewhere, this is shown, e.g. **three-ply** ... трёхслóйный. The presence of two stress-marks indicates that either of the marked syllables may be stressed, e.g. **decrease** ... умéньши́ть = умéньшить or уменьши́ть. Changes of stress which take place in conjugation, or declension, or in the short forms of adjectives, are shown, e.g.

(i) **suggest** ... предложи́ть (-жý, -жишь). Here, the absence of a stress-mark on the second person singular indicates that the stress is on the preceding syllable: предлóжишь.

(ii) **begin** ... нача́ть (-чнý, -чнёшь; нáчал, -á, -о). When the stress of the two preceding forms is not identical as it is in (i), the final form takes the stress of the first of these: нáчало. Forms not shown at all, e.g. the rest of the conjugation of начáть, and the rest of the future and the past plural of начáть, are stressed like the last form given: предлóжит etc., начнёт etc., нáчали.

(iii) **boring**[2] ... скýчный (-чен, -чнá, -чно) = (скýчен, скучнá, скýчно, скýчны); where the ending (e.g. -чны here) is not given, the stress is the same as for the previous form.

(iv) **rain** ... дождь (-дя́). The single form in brackets is the genitive (see *Declension* below), and all other forms have the same stressed syllable. If only one case-labelled form is given in the singular, it is an exception to the regular paradigm. For example, **leg**... ногá (*acc.* -гу; *pl.* -ги, -г, -гáм); the other singular forms have end-stress, while the unmentioned plural forms follow the stress of the last form given: ногáми, ногáх.

Nouns

Gender This can usually be deduced from the ending of the nominative singular: a final consonant or -й indicates a masculine noun, -а or -я or -ь a feminine, -e or -о a neuter. Gender is shown explicitly for masculine nouns in -а, -я, or -ь, neuter nouns in -мя, and indeclinable nouns. If a noun is given only as a plural form, the gender is shown where possible; otherwise, the genitive plural is shown. Nouns denoting persons are often given a masculine and a feminine translation, e.g. **teacher** ... учи́тель, ~ница; **Cossack** ... каза́к, -а́чка; these correspond to the sex of the person concerned.

Declension The declensions treated as regular here are exemplified on pp. 38–41, 44–5, 58–60, and 64–5 of B. O. Unbegaun's *Russian Grammar* (Clarendon Press, 1957). (Some of the points mentioned there have been regarded in this dictionary as irregularities.) When a single inflected form is added in brackets with no label of case or number, it is the genitive singular, e.g. **Indian** ... инде́ец (-е́йца), and all other inflected cases have the genitive stem. Apart from changes in stress (see *Stress* above), the following irregularities are among those indicated:

(i) The 'mobile vowel' in masculine nouns, e.g. **stub** ... оку́рок (-рка).

(ii) The alternative genitive singular in -y or -ю of masculine nouns, e.g. **cheese** ... сыр (-а(у)), i.e. сы́ра or сы́ру. For nouns denoting a substance, a number of objects, or a collective unit, the -y/-ю form has partitive value; with other nouns, it is used only in some set phrases.

(iii) The prepositional singular of masculine nouns, when ending in -у́ (or -ю́) after в or на. Here the term *locative* is used, e.g. **shore** ... бе́рег (*loc.* -у́).

(iv) Substantivized adjectives are followed by *sb.* to show that they retain the adjectival declension.

Adjectives

The declensions treated as regular here are exemplified on pp. 96–8 and 131–5 of B. O. Unbegaun's *Russian Grammar* (Clarendon Press, 1957). The short forms of adjectives are shown when they are irregular, when the stress moves (see *Stress* above), and for all adjectives in -нный or -нний, e.g. **sickly** ... болéзне-нный (-ен, -енна); **sincere** ... и́скренний (-нен, -нна, -нно & -нне).

Verbs

The conjugations treated as regular here are exemplified in B. O. Unbegaun's *Russian Grammar* (Clarendon Press, 1957): verbs in -ать, -еть, and -ять on p. 195, those in -ить on p. 198, those in -нуть on p. 192, and those in -овать on p. 197. Persons and tenses treated as irregular, and changes of stress in conjugation, are shown in brackets, e.g. **come** ... приходи́ть (-ожу́, -о́дишь) *imp.*, прийти́ (приду́, -дёшь; пришёл, -шла́) *perf.* The first two forms in brackets are the first and second persons singular of the present or future tense; other persons and the past tense follow where necessary. Each verb is labelled with its aspect. The case construction is shown for transitive verbs *not* followed by the accusative.

The conjugation of быть is given only under *be*. Irregularities of imperative, participial, and gerundial forms are not usually shown.

The following changes in the first person singular of the present or future tense of verbs in -ить are treated as regular:

(i) insertion of л after a stem in -б, -в, -м, -п, or -ф, e.g. **add** ... доба́вить: доба́влю, доба́вишь.

(ii) change of д or з to ж, к or т to ч, с or х to ш, ск or ст to щ, e.g. **annoy** ... досади́ть: досажу́, досади́шь; **answer** ... отве́тить: отве́чу, отве́тишь; **paint** ... кра́сить: кра́шу, кра́сишь; **clean** ... чи́стить: чи́щу, чи́стишь.

The reflexive suffix -ся or -сь is placed in brackets when the verb may be used with or without it, usually as an intransitive or a transitive verb respectively, e.g. **open** *v.t.* & *i.* открыва́ть(ся) *imp.*, откры́ть(ся) (-ро́ю(сь), -ро́ешь(ся)).

ABBREVIATIONS
USED IN THE DICTIONARY

abbr. abbreviation	*dim.* diminutive
abs. absolute	*dipl.* diplomacy
acc. accusative	*eccl.* ecclesiastical
adj. adjective	*econ.* economics
adv. adverb	*electr.* electrical
aeron. aeronautics	*electron.* electronics
agr(ic). agriculture	*emph.* emphatic
anat. anatomy	*ent.* entomology
approx. approximately	*esp.* especially
archaeol. archaeology	*euphem.* euphemism
arch(it). architecture	*f.* feminine
astron. astronomy	*fig.* figurative
attrib. attributive	*fut.* future
aux. auxiliary	*gen.* genitive
Bibl. Biblical	*geog.* geography
biol. biology	*geol.* geology
bot. botany	*geom.* geometry
chem. chemistry	*gram.* grammar
cin. cinema	*hist.* history
coll. colloquial	*hort.* horticulture
collect. collective(ly)	*i.* intransitive
comb. combination	*imp.* imperfective
comm. commerce	*imper.* imperative
comp. comparative, complement	*impers.* impersonal
	inc. including
conj. conjunction	*indecl.* indeclinable
cul. culinary	*indet.* indeterminate
dat. dative	*inf.* infinitive
demonstr. demonstrative	*instr.* instrumental
derog. derogatory	*interj.* interjection
det. determinate	*interrog.* interrogative

journ. journalism
leg. legal
ling. linguistics
lit. literary
loc. locative
m. masculine
math. mathematics
med. medicine
meteorol. meteorology
mil. military
min. mineralogy
mus. music
myth. mythology
n. noun
naut. nautical
neg. negative
neut. neuter
nom. nominative
obl. oblique
opp. opposed
orn. ornithology
parl. parliamentary
perf. perfective
pers. person
phon. phonetics
phot. photography
phys. physics
pl. plural
poet. poetical
polit. politics
poss. possessive
predic. predicative
pref. prefix
prep. preposition(al)

pres. present
print. printing
pron. pronoun
psych. psychology
refl. reflexive
relig. religion
rly. railway
sb. substantive
s.b. somebody
sing. singular
sl. slang
s.o. someone
s.th. something
superl. superlative
surg. surgery
t. transitive
tech. technical
tel. telephone
theat. theatre
theol. theology
trigon. trigonometry
univ. university
usu. usually
v. verb
v.abs. verb absolute
var. various
v.aux. verb auxiliary
vet. veterinary
v.i. verb intransitive
voc. vocative
v.t. verb transitive
zool. zoology
~ see Introduction, p.vii

A

A *n.* (*mus.*) ля *neut.indecl.*; *from A to Z*, с нача́ла до конца́.

a, an *indef. article, not translated; adj.* оди́н, не́кий, како́й-то; *fifty miles an hour*, пятьдеся́т миль в час; *twice a week*, два ра́за в неде́лю.

aback *adv.*: *take a.*, поража́ть *imp.*, порази́ть *perf.*; засти́гнуть *perf.* враспло́х.

abacus *n.* счёты *m.pl.*

abandon *v.t.* (*leave*) оставля́ть *imp.*, оста́вить *perf.*; (*desert*) покида́ть *imp.*, поки́нуть *perf.*; (*give up*) броса́ть *imp.*, бро́сить *perf.*; *a. oneself to*, предава́ться (-даю́сь, -даёшься) *imp.*, преда́ться (-а́мся, -а́шься, -а́стся, -ади́мся, -а́лся, -ала́сь) *perf.* + *dat.* **abandoned** *adj.* забро́шенный, поки́нутый; (*profligate*) распу́тный. **abandonment** *n.* (*action*) оставле́ние; (*state*) забро́шенность.

abase *v.t.* унижа́ть *imp.*, уни́зить *perf.* **abasement** *n.* униже́ние.

abate *v.i.* (*lessen*) уменьша́ться *imp.*, уме́ньшиться *perf.*; (*weaken*) слабе́ть *imp.*, о~ *perf.*; (*calm*) успока́иваться *imp.*, успоко́иться *perf.*; (*die down*) затиха́ть *imp.*, зати́хнуть (-х) *perf.* **abatement** *n.* уменьше́ние.

abattoir *n.* скотобо́йня (*gen.pl.* -о́ен).

abbess *n.* абба́тиса. **abbey** *n.* абба́тство. **abbot** *n.* абба́т.

abbreviate *v.t.* сокраща́ть *imp.*, сократи́ть (-ащу́, -ати́шь) *perf.* **abbreviation** *n.* сокраще́ние.

ABC *abbr.* а́збука, алфави́т.

abdicate *v.i.* отрека́ться *imp.*, отре́чься (-еку́сь, -ечёшься; -ёкся, -екла́сь) *perf.* от престо́ла. **abdication** *n.* отрече́ние (от престо́ла).

abdomen *n.* брюшна́я по́лость (*pl.* -ти, -те́й); (*entom.*) брюшко́ (*pl.* -ки́, -ко́в). **abdominal** *adj.* брюшно́й.

abduct *v.t.* наси́льно увози́ть (-ожу́, -о́зишь) *imp.*, увезти́ (увезу́, -зёшь; увёз, -ла́) *perf.* **abduction** *n.* наси́льственный уво́з.

aberration *n.* аберра́ция; (*mental*) помраче́ние ума́.

abet *v.t.* подстрека́ть *imp.*, подстрекну́ть *perf.* (к соверше́нию преступле́ния *etc.*); соде́йствовать *imp., perf.* соверше́нию (преступле́ния *etc.*).

abhor *v.t.* пита́ть *imp.* отвраще́ние к + *dat.*; (*hate*) ненави́деть (-и́жу, -и́дишь) *imp.* **abhorrence** *n.* отвраще́ние. **abhorrent** *adj.* отврати́тельный.

abide *v.t.* (*tolerate*) выноси́ть (-ошу́, -о́сишь) *imp.*, вы́нести (-су, -сешь; -с) *perf.*; *v.i.* (*remain*) остава́ться (-таю́сь, -таёшься) *imp.*, оста́ться (-а́нусь, -а́нешься) *perf.*; *a. by*, (*promise etc.*) выполня́ть *imp.*, вы́полнить *perf.*

ability *n.* спосо́бность, уме́ние.

abject *adj.* (*miserable*) жа́лкий (-лок, -лка́, -лко) (*low*) ни́зкий (-зок, -зка́, -зко); (*craven*) малоду́шный.

abjure *v.t.* отрека́ться *imp.*, отре́чься (-еку́сь, -ечёшься; -ёкся, -екла́сь) *perf.* от + *gen.*

ablative *n.* абляти́в.

ablaze *predic.*: *be a.*, горе́ть (-ри́т) *imp.*, сверка́ть *imp.*

able *adj.* спосо́бный, уме́лый; (*talented*) тала́нтливый; *be a. to*, мочь (могу́, мо́жешь; мог, -ла́) *imp.*, с~ *perf.*; быть в состоя́нии; (*know how to*) уме́ть *imp.*, с~ *perf.*

abnormal *adj.* ненорма́льный. **abnormality** *n.* ненорма́льность.

aboard *adv.* на борт(у́); (*train*) на по́езд(е).

abolish *v.t.* отменя́ть *imp.*, отмени́ть (-ню́, -нишь) *perf.*; уничтожа́ть *imp.*, уничто́жить *perf.* **abolition** *n.* отме́на, уничтоже́ние.

abominable *adj.* отврати́тельный; (*bad*) ужа́сный. **abomination** *n.* отвраще́ние; (*also object of a.*) ме́рзость.

aboriginal *adj.* исконный, коренно́й; *n.* абориге́н, коренно́й жи́тель *m.*

aborigines *n.* абориге́ны *m.pl.*, коренны́е жи́тели *m.pl.*

abort *v.i.* (*med.*) выки́дывать *imp.*, вы́кинуть *perf.*; *v.t.* (*terminate*) прекраща́ть *imp.*, прекрати́ть (-ащу́, -ати́шь) *perf.*; обрыва́ть *imp.*, оборва́ть (-ву́, -вёшь; оборва́л, -á, -о) *perf.* **abortion** *n.* або́рт, вы́кидыш. **abortive** *adj.* неуда́вшийся, безуспе́шный.

abound *v.i.* быть в большо́м коли́честве; *a. in*, изоби́ловать *imp.* + *instr.*; *a. with*, кише́ть (-ши́т) *imp.* + *instr.*

about *adv.*, *prep.* о́коло + *gen.*; (*concerning*) о + *prep.*, насчёт + *gen.*; (*up and down*) по + *dat.*; *be a. to*, собира́ться *imp.*, собра́ться (соберу́сь, -рёшься; собра́лся, -ала́сь, -а́ло́сь) *perf.* + *inf.*

above *adv.* наверху́; (*higher up*) вы́ше; *from a.*, све́рху; свы́ше; *prep.* над + *instr.*; (*more than*) свы́ше + *gen.*; *a.-board* че́стный (-тен, -тна́, -тно), прямо́й (прям, -á, -о); *a.-mentioned*, вышеупомяну́тый.

abrasion *n.* стира́ние, истира́ние; (*wound*) сса́дина. **abrasive** *adj.* абрази́вный; *n.* абрази́в, шлифова́льный материа́л.

abreast *adv.* (*in line*) в ряд, ря́дом; (*on a level*) в у́ровень.

abridge *v.t.* сокраща́ть *imp.*, сократи́ть (-ащу́, -ати́шь) *perf.* **abridgement** *n.* сокраще́ние.

abroad *adv.* за грани́цей, за грани́цу; *from a.*, из-за грани́цы.

abrupt *adj.* (*steep*) обры́вистый, круто́й (крут, -á, -о, кру́ты́); (*sudden*) внеза́пный; (*manner*) ре́зкий (-зок, -зка́, -зко).

abscess *n.* абсце́сс, нары́в, гнойни́к (-á).

abscond *v.i.* скрыва́ться *imp.*, скры́ться (-ро́юсь, -ро́ешься) *perf.*; бежа́ть (бегу́, бежи́шь) *imp.*, *perf.*

absence *n.* отсу́тствие; (*temporary*) отлу́чка; (*from work*) нея́вка, невы́ход, на рабо́ту; *a. of mind*, рассе́янность. **absent** *adj.* отсу́тствующий; в

отлу́чке; *be a.*, отсу́тствовать *imp.*; *a.-minded*, рассе́янный (-ян, -янна); *v.t.: a. oneself*, отлуча́ться *imp.*, отлучи́ться *perf.* **absentee** *n.* отсу́тствующий *sb.*; (*habitual*) прогу́льщик, -ица. **absenteeism** *n.* прогу́л, абсентеи́зм.

absolute *adj.* абсолю́тный; (*complete*) по́лный (-лон, -лна́, по́лно́), соверше́нный (-нен, -нна); (*unrestricted*) безусло́вный, неограни́ченный (-ен, -ена); (*pure*) чи́стый (чист, -á, -о, чи́сты); *a. alcohol*, чи́стый спирт (-a(y), *loc.* -е & -у́); *a. pitch*, (*of sound*) абсолю́тная высота́; (*in person*) абсолю́тный слух; *a. proof*, несомне́нное доказа́тельство; *a. zero*, абсолю́тный нуль (-ля́) *m.*

absolution *n.* отпуще́ние грехо́в. **absolve** *v.t.* проща́ть *imp.*, прости́ть *perf.*

absorb *v.t.* (*take in*) впи́тывать *imp.*, впита́ть *perf.*; (*swallow, also fig.*) поглоща́ть *imp.*, поглоти́ть (-ощу́, -о́тишь) *perf.*; (*suck in*) вса́сывать *imp.*, всоса́ть (-су́, -сёшь) *perf.*; (*tech.*) абсорби́ровать *imp.*, *perf.*; (*engross*) захва́тывать *imp.*, захвати́ть (-ачу́, -а́тишь) *perf.* **absorbed** *adj.* поглощённый (-ён, -ена́), захва́ченный (-ен). **absorbent** *adj.* вса́сывающий; поглоща́ющий. **absorption** *n.* впи́тывание; вса́сывание; поглоще́ние; абсо́рбция; (*mental*) погружённость.

abstain *v.i.* возде́рживаться *imp.*, воздержа́ться (-жу́сь, -жишься) *perf.* (*from*, от + *gen.*). **abstemious** *adj.* возде́ржанный (-ан, -анна). **abstention** *n.* воздержа́ние; (*from vote*) уклоне́ние, отка́з, от голосова́ния; (*person*) воздержа́вшийся *sb.* **abstinence** *n.* воздержа́ние; (*total a.*) тре́звость. **abstinent** *adj.* возде́ржанный (-ан, -анна).

abstract *adj.* абстра́ктный, отвлечённый (-ён, -ённа) *n.* конспе́кт, рефера́т; *in the a.*, абстра́ктно отвлечённо; (*journal of abstract(s*) рефера́тивный журна́л; *v.t.* (*steal*) похища́ть *imp.*, похи́тить (-и́щу -и́тишь) *perf.*; красть (-аду́, -адёшь; -ал) *imp.*, y ~ *perf.*; (*make a. of*) рефери́ровать *imp.*, *perf.*, конспекти́ровать *imp.*, за ~, про ~ *perf.* **abstracted** *adj.* погружённый (-ён, -ена́) в мы́сли, рассе́янный (-ян,

-янна). **abstraction** *n.* абстра́кция, отвлечённость; (*abstractedness*) погружённость в мы́сли, рассе́янность; (*theft*) похище́ние, кра́жа.

absurd *adj.* неле́пый, абсу́рдный. **absurdity** *n.* неле́пость, абсу́рд(ность).

abundance *n.* (из)оби́лие. **abundant** *adj.* (из)оби́льный.

abuse *v.t.* (*revile*) руга́ть *imp.*, вы́~, об~, от~ *perf.*; брани́ть *imp.*, вы́~ *perf.*; (*misuse*) злоупотребля́ть *imp.*, злоупотреби́ть *perf.* **abuse** *n.* (*curses*) брань, ру́гань, руга́тельства *neut.pl.*; (*misuse*) злоупотребле́ние. **abusive** *adj.* оскорби́тельный, бра́нный.

abut *v.i.* примыка́ть *imp.* (on, к + *dat.*) **abutment** *n.* (берегово́й) усто́й.

abysmal *adj.* бездо́нный (-нен, -нна); (*bad*) ужа́сный. **abyss** *n.* бе́здна, про́пасть. **abyssal** *adj.* абисса́льный.

acacia *n.* ака́ция.

academic *adj.* академи́ческий, университе́тский; (*abstract*) академи́чный. **academician** *n.* акаде́мик. **academy** *n.* акаде́мия; уче́бное заведе́ние.

accede *v.i.* вступа́ть *imp.*, вступи́ть (-плю́, -пишь) *perf.* (to, в, на, + *acc.*); (*assent*) соглаша́ться *imp.*, согласи́ться *perf.*

accelerate *v.t.* & *i.* ускоря́ть(ся) *imp.*, уско́рить(ся) *perf.*; *v.i.* ускоря́ть *imp.*, уско́рить *perf.* ход. **acceleration** *n.* ускоре́ние. **accelerator** *n.* ускори́тель *m.*; (*pedal*) акселера́тор.

accent *n.* акце́нт; (*stress*) ударе́ние, знак ударе́ния; *v.t.* де́лать *imp.*, с~ *perf.* ударе́ние на + *acc.*; ста́вить *imp.*, по~ *perf.* зна́ки ударе́ния над + *instr.* **accentuate** *v.t.* подчёркивать *imp.*, подчеркну́ть *perf.* **accentuation** *n.* подчёркивание.

accept *v.t.* принима́ть *imp.*, приня́ть (приму́, -мешь; при́нял, -а, -о); (*agree*) соглаша́ться *imp.*, согласи́ться *perf.* **acceptable** *adj.* прие́млемый; (*pleasing*) уго́дный. **acceptance** *n.* приня́тие. **acceptation** *n.* при́нятое значе́ние. **accepted** *adj.* (обще)при́нятый.

access *n.* до́ступ; (*attack*) при́ступ. **accessary** *n.* (*after the fact*) соуча́стник, -ица (преступле́ния по́сле собы-

тия). **accessible** *adj.* досту́пный. **accession** *n.* вступле́ние, восше́ствие (на престо́л); (*acquisition*) приобрете́ние.

accessories *n.* принадле́жности *f.pl.* **accessory** *adj.* доба́вочный, вспомога́тельный.

accidence *n.* морфоло́гия.

accident *n.* (*chance*) слу́чай, случа́йность; (*mishap*) несча́стный слу́чай; (*crash*) ава́рия, катастро́фа; by a., случа́йно. **accidental** *adj.* случа́йный; *n.* (*mus.*) знак альтера́ции.

acclaim *v.t.* приве́тствовать *imp.* (in past also *perf.*); *n.* приве́тствие.

acclimatization *n.* акклиматиза́ция. **acclimatize** *v.t.* акклиматизи́ровать *imp.*, *perf.*

accommodate *v.t.* помеща́ть *imp.*, помести́ть *perf.*; размеща́ть *imp.*, размести́ть *perf.* **accommodating** *adj.* услу́жливый. **accommodation** *n.* помеще́ние; (*lodging*) жильё; *a. ladder*, нару́жный трап.

accompaniment *n.* сопровожде́ние; (*mus.*) аккомпанеме́нт. **accompanist** *n.* аккомпаниа́тор. **accompany** *v.t.* сопровожда́ть *imp.*, сопроводи́ть *perf.*; (*mus.*) аккомпани́ровать *imp.* + *dat.*

accomplice *n.* соо́бщник, -ица, соуча́стник, -ица.

accomplish *v.t.* соверша́ть *imp.*, соверши́ть *perf.* **accomplished** *adj.* заверше́нный (-ён, -ена́); (*skilled*) превосхо́дный. **accomplishment** *n.* выполне́ние, заверше́ние; *pl.* достои́нства *neut.pl.*, соверше́нства *neut.pl.*

accord *n.* согла́сие; of one's own a., доброво́льно; of its own a., сам собо́й, сам по себе́; with one a., единогла́сно, единоду́шно. **accordance** *n.*: in a. with, в соотве́тствии с + *instr.*, согла́сно + *dat.*, c + *instr.* **according** *adv.*: a. to, по + *dat.*, соотве́тственно + *dat.*, c + *instr.*; a. to him, по его́ слова́м. **accordingly** *adv.* соотве́тственно.

accordion *n.* гармо́ника, аккордео́н.

account *n.* счёт (-а(у); *pl.* -а́); расчёт; отчёт; (*description, narrative*) описа́ние, расска́з; call to a., призыва́ть *imp.* (*description* -зову́, -зовёшь; призва́л, -а́, -о) *perf.* к отве́ту; keep a. of, вести́ (веду́, -дёшь; вёл, -а́) *imp.*

счёт + *dat.*; *not on any a.*, on no a., ни в ко́ем слу́чае; *on a.*, в счёт причита́ющейся су́ммы; *on a. of*, из-за + *gen.*, по причи́не + *gen.*; *settle accounts with*, своди́ть (-ожу́, -о́дишь) *imp.*, свести́ (сведу́, -дёшь; свёл, -а́) *perf.* счёты с + *instr.*; *take into a.*, принима́ть *imp.*, приня́ть (приму́, -мешь; при́нял, -а́, -о) *perf.* во внима́ние, в расчёт; *turn to* (*good*) *a.*, обраща́ть *imp.*, обрати́ть (-ащу́, -ати́шь) *perf.* в свою́ по́льзу; *v.i.*: *a. for*, объясня́ть *imp.*, объясни́ть *perf.* **accountable** *adj.* отве́тственный (-ен, -енна), подотчётный. **accountancy** *n.* бухгалте́рия. **accountant** *n.* бухга́лтер.

accredited *adj.* аккредито́ванный (-ан).

accretion *n.* прираще́ние, приро́ст.

accrue *v.i.* нараста́ть *imp.*, нарасти́ (-тёт; наро́с, -ла́) *perf.*; *accrued interest*, наро́сшие проце́нты *m.pl.*

accumulate *v.t.* & *i.* нака́пливать(ся) *imp.*, копи́ть(ся) (-плю́, -пит(ся)) *imp.*, на ~ *perf.*; *v.i.* ска́пливаться *imp.*, скопи́ться (-ится) *perf.* **accumulation** *n.* накопле́ние, скопле́ние. **accumulator** *n.* аккумуля́тор.

accuracy *n.* то́чность, ме́ткость. **accurate** *adj.* то́чный (-чен, -чна́, -чно), ме́ткий (-ток, -тка́, -тко).

accursed *adj.* прокля́тый.

accusation *n.* обвине́ние. **accusative** *adj.* (*n.*) вини́тельный (паде́ж (-а́)). **accuse** *v.t.* обвиня́ть *imp.*, обвини́ть *perf.* (*of*, в + *prep.*); *the accused*, обвиня́емый *sb.*, подсуди́мый *sb.*

accustom *v.t.* приуча́ть *imp.*, приучи́ть (-чу́, -чишь) *perf.* (*to*, к + *dat.*). **accustomed** *adj.* привы́чный, обы́чный; *be, get, a.*, привыка́ть *imp.*, привы́кнуть (-к) *perf.* (*to*, к + *dat.*).

ace *n.* туз (-а́); (*airman*) ас.

acetic *adj.* у́ксусный. **acetylene** *n.* ацетиле́н; *adj.* ацетиле́новый.

ache *n.* боль; *v.i.* боле́ть (-ли́т) *imp.*

achieve *v.t.* достига́ть *imp.*, дости́чь & дости́гнуть (-и́гну, -и́гнешь; -и́г) *perf.* + *gen.*; добива́ться *imp.*, доби́ться (-бью́сь, -бьёшься) *perf.* + *gen.* **achievement** *n.* достиже́ние.

acid *n.* кислота́; *adj.* ки́слый (-сел, -сла́, -сло). **acidity** *n.* кислота́, кисло́тность.

acknowledge *v.t.* (*admit*) признава́ть (-наю́, -наёшь) *imp.*, призна́ть *perf.*; сознава́ть (-наю́, -наёшь) *imp.*, созна́ть *perf.*; (*express gratitude*) благодари́ть *imp.*, по ~ *perf.* за + *acc.*; (*a. receipt of*) подтвержда́ть *imp.*, подтверди́ть *perf.* получе́ние + *gen.* **acknowledgement** *n.* призна́ние, благода́рность; подтвержде́ние; *in a. of*, в знак благода́рности за + *acc.*

acme *n.* верши́на, верх (*pl.* -и́), вы́сшая то́чка.

acne *n.* прыщи́ *m.pl.*

acorn *n.* жёлудь (*pl.* -ди, -де́й) *m.*

acoustic *adj.* (*of sound*) акусти́ческий, звуково́й; (*of hearing*) слухово́й; (*sound-absorbing*) звукопоглоща́ющий. **acoustics** *n.* аку́стика.

acquaint *v.t.* знако́мить *imp.*, по ~ *perf.*; ознакомля́ть *imp.*, ознако́мить *perf.* **acquaintance** *n.* знако́мство; (*person*) знако́мый *sb.* **acquainted** *adj.* знако́мый.

acquiesce *v.i.* (мо́лча) соглаша́ться *imp.*, согласи́ться *perf.* **acquiescence** *n.* (молчали́вое, неохо́тное) согла́сие. **acquiescent** *adj.* (молчали́во) соглаша́ющийся.

acquire (*v.t.* приобрета́ть *imp.*, приобрести́ (-ету́, -етёшь; -ёл, -ела́) *perf.*; (*habit etc.*) усва́ивать *imp.*, усво́ить *perf.* **acquired** *adj.* приобретённый (-ён, -ена́); *a. taste*, благоприобретённый вкус. **acquisition** *n.* приобрете́ние. **acquisitive** *adj.* жа́дный (-ден, -дна́, -дно).

acquit *v.t.* опра́вдывать *imp.*, оправда́ть *perf.*; *a. oneself*, вести́ (веду́, -дёшь; вёл, -а́) *imp.* себя́. **acquittal** *n.* оправда́ние.

acre *n.* акр; *pl.* зе́мли (-ме́ль, -мля́м) *f.pl.*, поме́стье. **acreage** *n.* пло́щадь в а́крах.

acrid *adj.* о́стрый (остр & о́стёр, остра́, о́стро), е́дкий (е́док, едка́, е́дко). **acridity** *n.* острота́, е́дкость.

acrimonious *adj.* язви́тельный, жёлчный.

acrobat *n.* акроба́т. **acrobatic** *adj.* акробати́ческий. **acrobatics** *n.* акроба́тика.

acronym *n.* акро́ним, аббревиату́ра.

across *adv.*, *prep.* че́рез + *acc.*; поперёк (+ *gen.*); (*to, on, other side*) на, по, ту сто́рону (+ *gen.*), на той стороне́ (+ *gen.*); (*crosswise*) крест-на́крест.

acrylic *adj.* акри́ловый.

act *n.* (*deed*) акт, посту́пок (-пка); (*law*) зако́н; (*of play*) де́йствие, Acts, Дея́ния *neut.pl.* апо́столов; *v.i.* поступа́ть *imp.*, поступи́ть (-плю́, -пишь) *perf.*; де́йствовать *imp.*, по~ *perf.*; *v.t.* игра́ть *imp.*, сыгра́ть *perf.* **acting** *n.* игра́ на сце́не; *adj.* исполня́ющий обя́занности + *gen.* **action** *n.* де́йствие, посту́пок (-пка); (*leg.*) иск, (судебный процесс; (*battle*) бой (*loc.* бою́). **active** *adj.* акти́вный, де́ятельный, энерги́чный; *a. service*, действи́тельная слу́жба; *a. voice*, действи́тельный зало́г. **activity** *n.* де́ятельность; акти́вность; *pl.* де́ятельность. **actor** *n.* актёр. **actress** *n.* актри́са.

actual *adj.* действи́тельный, факти́ческий. **actuality** *n.* действи́тельность. **actually** *adv.* на са́мом де́ле, факти́чески.

actuate *v.t.* приводи́ть (-ожу́, -о́дишь) *imp.*, привести́ (приведу́, -дёшь; привёл, -а́) *perf.* в движе́ние.

acuity *n.* острота́.

acute *adj.* о́стрый (остр & остёр, остра́, о́стро́); (*penetrating*) проница́тельный; *a. accent*, аку́т.

A.D. *abbr.* н. э. (на́шей э́ры).

adamant *adj.* непрекло́нный (-нен, -нна).

adapt *v.t.* приспособля́ть *imp.*, приспосо́бить *perf.*; (*for stage etc.*) инсцени́ровать *imp.*, *perf.*; *a. oneself*, приспособля́ться *imp.*, приспосо́биться *perf.*; применя́ться *imp.*, примени́ться (-ню́сь, -нишься) *perf.* **adaptable** *adj.* приспособля́ющийся. **adaptation** *n.* приспособле́ние, адапта́ция, переде́лка; инсцениро́вка.

add *v.t.* прибавля́ть *imp.*, приба́вить *perf.*; добавля́ть *imp.*, доба́вить *perf.*; (*math.*) скла́дывать *imp.*, сложи́ть (-жу́, -жишь) *perf.*; *a. up to*, своди́ться (-ится) *imp.*, свести́сь (сведётся; свёлся, -ла́сь) *perf.* к + *dat.* **addenda** *n.* дополне́ния *neut.pl.*; приложе́ния *neut.pl.*

adder *n.* гадю́ка.

addict *n.* (*drug a.*) наркома́н, ~ ка. **addicted** *adj.*: *be a. to*, быть рабо́м + *gen.*; *a. to drink*, предаю́щийся пья́нству. **addiction** *n.* па́губная привы́чка; (*to drugs*) наркома́ния.

addition *n.* прибавле́ние, добавле́ние; дополне́ние; (*math.*) сложе́ние; *in a.*, вдоба́вок, кро́ме того́, к тому́ же. **additional** *adj.* доба́вочный, дополни́тельный. **additive** *n.* доба́вка.

address *n.* а́дрес (*pl.* -а́); (*speech*) обраще́ние, речь; *v.t.* адресова́ть *imp.*, *perf.*; (*apply*) обраща́ться *imp.*, обрати́ться (-ащу́сь, -ати́шься) *perf.* к + *dat.*; *a. a meeting*, выступа́ть *imp.*, вы́ступить *perf.* с ре́чью на собра́нии. **addressee** *n.* адреса́т.

adept *n.* знато́к (-а́), экспе́рт; *adj.* све́дущий.

adequacy *n.* адеква́тность, доста́точность. **adequate** *adj.* адеква́тный, доста́точный.

adhere *v.i.* прилипа́ть *imp.*, прили́пнуть (-нет; прили́п) *perf.* (*to*, к + *dat.*); (*fig.*) приде́рживаться *imp.* + *gen.* **adherence** *n.* приве́рженность, ве́рность. **adherent** *n.* приве́рженец (-нца); после́дователь *m.*, ~ ница. **adhesion** *n.* прилипа́ние, скле́ивание. **adhesive** *adj.* ли́пкий (-пок, -пка́, -пко), кле́йкий; *n.* клей (-е́я(ю), *loc.* -е́ю́; *pl.* -е́и).

adjacent *adj.* сме́жный, сосе́дний.

adjectival *adj.* адъекти́вный. **adjective** *n.* (и́мя *neut.*) прилага́тельное *sb.*

adjoin *v.t.* прилега́ть *imp.* к + *dat.*

adjourn *v.t.* откла́дывать *imp.*, отложи́ть (-жу́, -жишь) *perf.*; *v.i.* объявля́ть *imp.*, объяви́ть (-влю́, -вишь) *perf.* переры́в; (*to another place*) переходи́ть (-ожу́, -о́дишь) *imp.*, перейти́ (перейду́, -дёшь; перешёл, -шла́) *perf.*

adjudicate *v.i.* выноси́ть (-ошу́, -о́сишь) *imp.*, вы́нести (-су, -сешь; -с) *perf.* (суде́бное, арбитра́жное) реше́ние; разреша́ть *imp.*, разреши́ть *perf.* спор; рассма́тривать *imp.*, рассмотре́ть (-рю́, -ришь) *perf.* де́ло.

adjust *v.t.* & *i.* приспособля́ть(ся) *imp.*, приспосо́бить(ся) *perf.*; *v.t.* пригоня́ть *imp.*, пригна́ть (-гоню́, -го́нишь;

пригна́л, -á, -о) perf.; (regulate) регули́ровать imp., от~ perf. **adjustable** adj. регули́руемый; a. spanner, разводно́й ключ (-á). **adjustment** n. регули́рование, регулиро́вка, подго́нка.

adjutant n. адъюта́нт.

administer v.t. (manage) управля́ть imp. + instr.; (dispense) отправля́ть imp. + instr.; (give) дава́ть (даю́, даёшь) imp., дать (дам, дашь, даст, дади́м; дал, -á, да́ло, -и) perf. **administration** n. администра́ция, управле́ние; (government) прави́тельство. **administrative** adj. администрати́вный, управле́нческий. **administrator** n. администра́тор.

admirable adj. похва́льный; (excellent) замеча́тельный.

admiral n. адмира́л. **Admiralty** n. адмиралте́йство.

admiration n. любова́ние, восхище́ние. **admire** v.t. любова́ться imp., по~ perf. + instr., на + acc.; восхища́ться imp., восхити́ться (-ищу́сь, -ити́шься) perf. + instr. **admirer** n. покло́нник.

admissible adj. допусти́мый, приёмлемый. **admission** n. до́ступ, впуск, вход; (confession) призна́ние. **admit** v.t. впуска́ть imp., впусти́ть (-ущу́, -у́стишь) perf.; (allow) допуска́ть imp., допусти́ть (-ущу́, -у́стишь) perf.; (accept) принима́ть imp., приня́ть (приму́, -мешь; при́нял, -á, -о) perf.; (confess) признава́ть (-наю́, -наёшь) imp., призна́ть perf. **admittance** n. до́ступ. **admittedly** adv. призна́ться.

admixture n. при́месь.

adolescence n. ю́ность. **adolescent** adj. подро́стковый; n. подро́сток (-тка).

adopt v.t. (child) усыновля́ть imp., усынови́ть perf.; (thing) усва́ивать imp., усво́ить perf.; (approve) принима́ть imp., приня́ть (приму́, -мешь; при́нял, -á, -о) perf. **adopted**, **adoptive** adj. приёмный. **adoption** n. усыновле́ние; приня́тие.

adorable adj. восхити́тельный, преле́стный. **adoration** n. обожа́ние. **adore** v.t. обожа́ть imp. **adorer** n. обожа́тель m.

adorn v.t. украша́ть imp., укра́сить perf. **adornment** n. украше́ние.

adroit adj. ло́вкий (-вок, -вка́, -вко, ло́вки).

adult adj., n. взро́слый (sb.).

adulterate v.t. фальсифици́ровать imp., perf. **adulteration** n. фальсифика́ция.

adultery n. адюльте́р, небра́чная связь.

advance n. (going forward) продвиже́ние (вперёд); (progress) прогре́сс; (mil.) наступле́ние; (rise) повыше́ние; (of pay etc.) ава́нс; (loan) ссу́да; in a., зара́нее, вперёд; ава́нсом; make advances to, уха́живать imp. за + instr.; a. information, предвари́тельные све́дения neut.pl.; a. copy, сигна́льный экземпля́р; v.i. (go forward) продвига́ться imp., продви́нуться perf. вперёд; идти́ (иду́, идёшь; шёл, шла) imp. вперёд; (mil.) наступа́ть imp.; v.t. продвига́ть imp., продви́нуть perf.; (put forward) выдвига́ть imp., вы́двинуть perf.; (promote) повыша́ть imp., повы́сить perf.; (pay in advance) выпла́чивать imp., вы́платить perf. ава́нсом. **advanced** adj. передово́й, продви́нутый; a. in years, престаре́лый; a. studies, вы́сший курс. **advancement** n. продвиже́ние, повыше́ние.

advantage n. преиму́щество; (profit) вы́года, по́льза; take a. of, по́льзоваться imp., вос~ perf. + instr.; to a., вы́годно, хорошо́; in a. вы́годном све́те; to the best a., в са́мом вы́годном све́те. **advantageous** adj. вы́годный.

adventure n. приключе́ние; a. story, приключе́нческий рома́н. **adventurer** n. авантюри́ст. **adventuress** n. авантюри́стка. **adventurous** adj. (rash) риско́ванный (-ан, -анна); (enterprising) предприи́мчивый.

adverb n. наре́чие. **adverbial** adj. наре́чный, обстоя́тельственный. **adverse** adj. неблагоприя́тный; a. winds, проти́вные ве́тры m.pl. **adversity** n. несча́стье.

advert abbr. объявле́ние, рекла́ма.

advertise v.t. реклами́ровать imp., perf.; афиши́ровать imp., perf.; v.i. помеща́ть imp., помести́ть perf. дава́ть (даю́, даёшь) imp., дать (дам, дашь, даст, дади́м; дал, -á, да́ло, -и) perf. объявле́ние (for, o + prep.). **advertisement** n. объявле́ние, рекла́ма.

advice *n.* совет; (*specialist*) консультация; (*notice*) авизо; *a piece, word of a.,* совет. **advisability** *n.* желательность. **advisable** *adj.* рекомендуемый, желательный. **advise** *v.t.* советовать *imp.,* по ~ *perf.+dat.* & *inf.*; рекомендовать *imp., perf.,* по ~ *perf.+acc.* & *inf.*; (*notify*) уведомлять *imp.,* уведомить *perf.* **advisedly** *adv.* обдуманно, намеренно. **adviser** *n.* советник, -ица; консультант; (*legal*) юрисконсульт; *medical a.,* врач (-á). **advisory** *adj.* совещательный, консультативный.

advocacy *n.* (*profession*) адвокатура; (*support*) пропаганда. **advocate** *n.* адвокат; сторонник; *v.t.* пропагандировать *imp.*; выступать *imp.,* выступить *perf.* в защиту + *gen.*

aerial *n.* антенна; *adj.* воздушный.

aero- *in comb.* авиа-, аэро-, воздухо-. **aerodrome** *n.* аэродром. **aerodynamics** *n.* аэродинамика. **aero-engine** *n.* авиационный двигатель *m.* **aeronautical** *adj.* авиационный. **aeroplane** *n.* самолёт. **aerosol** *n.* аэрозоль *m.*

aesthetic *adj.* эстетический.

affable *adj.* приветливый. **affability** *n.* приветливость.

affair *n.* (*business*) дело (*pl.* -ла); (*love*) роман.

affect *v.t.* действовать *imp.,* по ~ *perf.* на + *acc.*; влиять *imp.,* по ~ *perf.* на + *acc.*; (*touch*) трогать *imp.,* тронуть *perf.*; затрагивать *imp.,* затронуть *perf.*; (*concern*) касаться *imp.+gen.*; *it doesn't a. me,* это меня не касается. **affectation** *n.* притворство, жеманство. **affected** *adj.* притворный, жеманный (-нен, -нна). **affecting** *adj.* трогательный. **affection** *n.* привязанность, любовь (-бви, *instr.* -бовью); (*malady*) болезнь. **affectionate** *adj.* любящий, нежный (-жен, -жна, -жно, нежны), ласковый.

affiliate *v.t.* & *i.* присоединять(ся) *imp.,* присоединить(ся) *perf.* как филиал, отделение. **affiliated** *adj.* филиальный. **affiliation** *n.* присоединение как филиал; (*of child*) установление отцовства + *gen.*

affinity *n.* (*relationship*) родство; (*resem-*

blance) сходство, близость; (*attraction*) увлечение.

affirm *v.t.* утверждать *imp.*; *v.i.* торжественно заявлять *imp.,* заявить (-влю, -вишь) *perf.* **affirmation** *n.* заявление. **affirmative** *adj.* утвердительный.

affix *v.t.* прикреплять *imp.,* прикрепить *perf.*; *n.* аффикс.

afflict *v.t.* огорчать *imp.,* огорчить *perf.*; причинять *imp.,* причинить *perf.* страдания + *dat.* **affliction** *n.* огорчение.

affluence *n.* богатство. **affluent** *adj.* богатый; *a. society,* богатеющее общество.

afford *v.t.* позволять *imp.,* позволить *perf.* себе; быть в состоянии + *inf.*; (*supply*) предоставлять *imp.,* предоставить *perf.*; доставлять *imp.,* доставить *perf.*; *I can't afford it,* мне это не по средствам, не по карману.

afforest *v.t.* засаживать *imp.,* засадить (-ажу, -адишь) *perf.* лесом; облесить *perf.* **afforestation** *n.* лесонасаждение, облесение.

affront *n.* (публичное) оскорбление, обида; *v.t.* оскорблять *imp.,* оскорбить *perf.*

afoot *adv.*: *set a.,* пускать *imp.,* пустить (пущу, пустишь) *perf.* в ход.

aforesaid *adj.* вышеупомянутый. **aforethought** *adj.* преднамеренный (-ен, -енна).

afraid *predic.*: *be a.,* бояться (боюсь, боишься) *imp.*

afresh *adv.* снова.

after *adv.* впоследствии; после, потом; *prep.* после + *gen.,* спустя + *acc.*; за + *acc., instr.*; *a. all,* в конце концов; *day a. day,* день за днём; *long a. midnight,* далеко за полночь.

after- *in comb.* после-. **afterbirth** *n.* послед. **after-dinner** *adj.* послеобеденный. **aftermath** *n.* последствия *neut. pl.* **afternoon** *n.* вторая половина дня; *in the a.,* днём, пополудни. **afterthought** *n.* запоздалая мысль.

afterwards *adv.* впоследствии; потом, позже.

again *adv.* опять; (*once more*) ещё раз; (*anew*) снова.

against prep. (opposed to) про́тив + gen.; (a. background of) на фо́не + gen.

agate n. ага́т.

age n. во́зраст; (period) век (на веку́; pl. -а́), эпо́ха; v.t. ста́рить imp., со ~ perf.; v.i. старе́ть imp., по ~ perf.; ста́риться imp., со ~ perf. **aged** adj. ста́рый (стар, -а́, ста́ро́), престаре́лый.

agency n. аге́нтство; (mediation) посре́дничество; by, through, the a. of, посре́дством, при по́мощи, при соде́йствии, + gen. **agenda** n. пове́стка дня. **agent** n. аге́нт.

agglomerate n. агломера́т. **agglomeration** n. скопле́ние, агломера́ция.

agglutination n. агглютина́ция. **agglutinative** adj. агглютинати́вный.

aggravate v.t. ухудша́ть imp., уху́дшить perf.; (annoy) раздража́ть imp., раздражи́ть perf. **aggravation** n. ухудше́ние; раздраже́ние.

aggregate adj. совоку́пный; n. совоку́пность, агрега́т; in the a., в совоку́пности, в це́лом.

aggression n. агре́ссия; агресси́вность. **aggressive** adj. агресси́вный. **aggressor** n. агре́ссор.

aggrieved adj. оби́женный (-ен).

aghast predic. поражён (-á) у́жасом; в у́жасе (at, от + gen.).

agile adj. прово́рный. **agility** n. прово́рство.

agitate v.t. волнова́ть imp., вз ~ perf.; v.i. агити́ровать imp. **agitation** n. волне́ние; агита́ция.

agnostic n. агно́стик; adj. агности́ческий. **agnosticism** n. агностици́зм.

ago adv. (тому́) наза́д; long a., давно́.

agonizing adj. мучи́тельный. **agony** n. мучи́тельная боль; (of death) аго́ния.

agrarian adj. агра́рный, земе́льный.

agree v.i. соглаша́ться imp., согласи́ться perf.; усла́вливаться imp., усло́виться perf. (on, о + prep.); (reach agreement) догова́риваться imp., договори́ться perf.; (gram.) согласова́ться imp., perf. **agreeable** adj. согла́сный; (pleasing) прия́тный. **agreed** adj. согласо́ванный (-ан), усло́вленный (-ен). **agreement** n. согла́сие,

соглаше́ние, догово́р; (gram.) согласова́ние; in a., согла́сен (-сна).

agricultural adj. сельскохозя́йственный, земледе́льческий. **agriculture** n. се́льское хозя́йство, земледе́лие; (science) агроно́мия.

aground predic. на мели́; adv.: run a., сади́ться imp., сесть (ся́ду, -дешь; сел) perf. на мель.

ague n. маляри́я.

ahead adv. (forward) вперёд; (in front) впереди́; a. of time, досро́чно.

aid v.t. помога́ть imp., помо́чь (-огу́, -о́жешь; -о́г, -огла́) perf. + dat.; n. по́мощь; (teaching) посо́бие; in a. of, в по́льзу + gen.; come to the a. of, прийти́ (приду́, -дёшь; пришёл, -шла́) perf. на по́мощь к + dat. **aide-de-camp** n. адъюта́нт (генера́ла).

aileron n. элеро́н.

ailing adj. (ill) больно́й (-лен, -льна́); (sickly) хи́лый (хил, -á, -о). **ailment** n. неду́г.

aim n. (aiming) прице́л; (purpose) цель, наме́рение; v.i. це́лить(ся) imp., на ~ perf. (at, в + acc.); прице́ливаться imp., прице́литься perf. (at, в + acc.); (also fig.) ме́тить imp., на ~ perf. (at, в + acc.); v.t. наце́ливать imp., наце́лить perf. (also fig.) наводи́ть (-ожу́, -о́дишь) imp., навести́ (наведу́, -дёшь; навёл, -á) perf. **aimless** adj. бесце́льный.

air n. во́здух; (look) вид; (mus.) пе́сня (gen.pl. -сен), мело́дия; by a., самолётом; change of a., переме́на обстано́вки; on the a., по ра́дио; attrib. возду́шный; v.t. (ventilate) прове́тривать imp., прове́трить perf.; (make known) выставля́ть imp., вы́ставить perf. напока́з; заявля́ть imp., заяви́ть (-влю́, -вишь) perf. во всеуслы́шание.

air- in comb. **airborne** adj. (mil.) возду́шно-деса́нтный; predic. в во́здухе. **air-conditioning** n. кондициони́рование во́здуха. **air-cooled** adj. с возду́шным охлажде́нием. **aircraft** n. самолёт; (collect.) самолёты m.pl., авиа́ция. **aircraft-carrier** n. авиано́сец (-сца). **air force** n. ВВС (вое́нно-возду́шные си́лы) f.pl. **air hostess** n. стюарде́сса. **airless** adj. (stuffy) ду́шный (-шен, -шна́, -шно); безвозду́шный. **air-lift** n. возду́шные перево́зки f.pl.; v.t. перевози́ть (-ожу́, -о́зишь) imp., перевезти́ (перевезу́, -зёшь; перевёз, -ла́) perf. по во́здуху. **airline** n. авиали́ния. **airlock** n. возду́шная про́бка. **air mail** n. авиа(по́чта). **airman** n. лётчик. **airport** n. аэропо́рт (loc. -ý). **airship** n. дирижа́бль m. **airspeed** n. возду́шная ско́рость. **airstrip** n. лётная полоса́ (acc. полосу́; pl. -осы, -о́с, -оса́м). **airtight** adj. непроница́емый для во́здуха. **airworthy** adj. приго́дный к полёту.

aisle n. боково́й неф; (passage) прохо́д.
alabaster n. алеба́стр.
alacrity n. жи́вость; (readiness) гото́вность.
alarm n. трево́га; v.t. трево́жить imp., вс~ perf.; a. clock, буди́льник. **alarming** adj. трево́жный. **alarmist** n. паникёр; adj. паникёрский.
alas interj. увы́!
albatross n. альба́трос.
albino n. альби́нос.
album n. альбо́м.
alchemist n. алхи́мик. **alchemy** n. алхи́мия.
alcohol n. алкого́ль m., спирт (-а(у), loc. -е & -ý); спиртны́е напи́тки m.pl. **alcoholic** adj. алкого́льный, спиртно́й; n. алкого́лик, -и́чка.
alcove n. алько́в, ни́ша.
alder n. ольха́.
alderman n. о́лдермен.
ale n. пи́во, эль m.
alert adj. бди́тельный, живо́й (жив, -á, -о); predic. на стороже́; n. трево́га; v.t. предупрежда́ть imp., предупреди́ть perf.
algebra n. а́лгебра. **algebraic** adj. алгебраи́ческий. **algorithm** n. алгори́тм.
alias adv. ина́че (называ́емый); n. кли́чка, вы́мышленное и́мя neut.
alibi n. а́либи neut.indecl.
alien n. иностра́нец (-нца), -нка; adj. иностра́нный, чужо́й, чу́ждый (чужд, -á, -о). **alienate** v.t. отчужда́ть imp., отдаля́ть imp., отдали́ть perf. **alienation** n. отчужде́ние, охлажде́ние;

(insanity) умопомеша́тельство. **alienist** n. психиа́тр.
alight [1] v.i. сходи́ть (-ожу́, -о́дишь) imp., сойти́ (сойду́, -дёшь; сошёл, -шла́) perf.; (come down) сади́ться imp., сесть (ся́ду, -дешь; сел) perf.; (dismount) спе́шиваться imp., спе́шиться perf.
alight [2] predic. зажжён (-á); be a., горе́ть (-ри́т) imp.; (shine) сия́ть imp.
align v.t. располага́ть imp., расположи́ть (-жу́, -жишь) perf. по одно́й ли́нии; ста́вить imp., по ~ perf. в ряд. **alignment** n. выра́внивание, равне́ние.
alike predic. похо́ж, одина́ков; adv. одина́ково, то́чно так же.
alimentary adj. пищево́й; a. canal, пищевари́тельный кана́л.
alimony n. алиме́нты m.pl.
alive predic. жив (-á, -о), в живы́х; (brisk) бодр (-á, -о); a. with, киша́щий + instr.
alkali n. щёлочь (pl. -чи, -че́й). **alkaline** adj. щелочно́й.
all adj. весь (вся, всё; все); вся́кий; n. всё, всё pl.; adv. всеце́ло, целико́м, по́лностью; совсе́м, соверше́нно; a. along, всё вре́мя; a. but, почти́, едва́ не; a. in, кра́йне утомлён (-á), совсе́м без сил; a.-in wrestling, борьба́, допуска́ющая любы́е приёмы; a. over, повсю́ду; a. right, хорошо́, ла́дно; (satisfactory) так себе́; непло́х (-á, -о); a.-round, разносторо́нний (-нен, -ння); a. the same, всё равно́; in a., всего́; love a., по нулю́; two, etc., a., по два и т.д.; not at a., ниско́лько; on a. fours, на четвере́ньках.
allay v.t. облегча́ть imp., облегчи́ть perf.; успока́ивать imp., успоко́ить perf.; утоля́ть imp., утоли́ть perf.
allegation n. заявле́ние, утвержде́ние. **allege** v.t. заявля́ть imp., заяви́ть (-влю́, -вишь) perf.; утвержда́ть imp. **allegedly** adv. я́кобы.
allegiance n. ве́рность.
allegorical adj. аллегори́ческий, иноска́зательный. **allegory** n. аллего́рия, иноска́зание.
allegretto adv. (n.) аллегре́тто (neut. indecl.). **allegro** adv. (n.) алле́гро (neut.indecl.).

allergic adj. аллерги́ческий. **allergy** n. аллерги́я.

alleviate v.t. облегча́ть imp., облегчи́ть perf.; смягча́ть imp., смягчи́ть perf. **alleviation** n. облегче́ние, смягче́ние.

alley n. переу́лок (-лка), прохо́д.

alliance n. сою́з. **allied** adj. сою́зный.

alligator n. аллига́тор.

alliterate v.i. аллитери́ровать imp. **alliteration** n. аллитера́ция.

allocate v.t. распределя́ть imp., распредели́ть perf.; ассигнова́ть imp., perf. **allocation** n. распределе́ние; ассигнова́ние.

allot v.t. предназнача́ть imp., предназна́чить perf.; распределя́ть imp., распредели́ть perf.; отводи́ть (-ожу́, -о́дишь) imp., отвести́ (отведу́, -дёшь; отвёл, -а́) perf.; выделя́ть imp., вы́делить perf. **allotment** n. выделе́ние; (plot of land) уча́сток (-тка).

allow v.t. позволя́ть imp., позво́лить perf.; разреша́ть imp., разреши́ть perf.; допуска́ть imp., допусти́ть (-ущу́, -у́стишь) perf.; a. for, принима́ть imp., приня́ть (приму́, -мешь; при́нял, -а́, -о) perf. во внима́ние, в расчёт; учи́тывать imp., уче́сть (учту́, -тёшь; учёл, учла́) perf. **allowance** n. (financial) содержа́ние, посо́бие; (expenses) де́ньги (-нег, -ньга́м) pl. на расхо́ды; (deduction, also fig.) ски́дка; make allowance(s) for, принима́ть imp., приня́ть (приму́, -мешь; при́нял, -а́, -о) perf. во внима́ние, в расчёт; де́лать imp., с ∼ perf. ски́дку на + acc.

alloy n. сплав; v.t. сплавля́ть imp., спла́вить perf.

allude v.i. ссыла́ться imp., сосла́ться (сошлю́сь, -лёшься) perf. (to, на + acc.); намека́ть imp., намекну́ть perf. (to, на + acc.).

allure v.t. зама́нивать imp., замани́ть (-ню́, -нишь) perf.; завлека́ть imp., завле́чь (-еку́, -ечёшь; -ёк, -екла́) perf. **allurement** n. прима́нка. **alluring** adj. зама́нчивый, завлека́тельный, собла́знительный.

allusion n. ссы́лка, намёк.

alluvial adj. аллювиа́льный, нано́сный.

ally n. сою́зник; v.t. соединя́ть imp., соедини́ть perf.

almanac n. календа́рь (-ря́) m.

almighty adj. всемогу́щий (-щ).

almond n. (tree; pl. collect.) минда́ль (-ля́) m.; (nut) минда́льный оре́х; attrib. минда́льный.

almost adv. почти́, едва́ (ли) не, чуть (бы́ло) не.

alms n. ми́лостыня; a.-house, бога-де́льня (gen.pl. -лен).

aloe(s) n. ало́э neut.indecl.

aloft adv. наве́рх(у́).

alone predic. оди́н (одна́, одно́; одни́); одино́к; adv. то́лько; сам по себе́; a. with, наедине́ с + instr.; leave a. оставля́ть imp., оста́вить perf. в поко́е; let a., не говоря́ уже́ о + prep.

along prep. по + dat., вдоль + gen., вдоль по + dat.; adv. (onward) да́льше, вперёд; (with oneself) с собо́й; all a., всё вре́мя; a. with, вме́сте с + instr.

alongside adv., prep. ря́дом (с + instr.), бок о́ бок (с + instr.).

aloof predic., adv. (apart) в стороне́, вдали́; (distant) холо́ден (-дна́, -дно, хо́лодны), равноду́шен (-шна).

aloud adv. вслух, гро́мко.

alphabet n. алфави́т, а́збука. **alphabetical** adj. алфави́тный.

alpine adj. альпи́йский.

already adv. уже́.

also adv. та́кже, то́же.

altar n. алта́рь (-ря́) m.; a.-piece, запресто́льный о́браз (pl. -а́).

alter v.t. переде́лывать imp., переде́лать perf.; v.t. & i. изменя́ть(ся) imp., измени́ть(ся) (-ню́(сь), -нишь(ся)) perf. **alteration** n. переде́лка; переме́на; измене́ние.

altercation n. препира́тельство.

alternate adj. чередую́щийся, перемежа́ющийся; v.t. & i. чередова́ть(ся) imp.; alternating current, переме́нный ток; on a. days, че́рез день. **alternation** n. чередова́ние. **alternative** n. альтернати́ва; adj. альтернати́вный.

although conj. хотя́.

altimeter n. альтиме́тр, высотоме́р. **altitude** n. высота́ (pl. -о́ты). **alto** n. альт (-а́); контра́льто f. & neut. indecl.; attrib. альто́вый; контра́льтовый.

altogether adv. (fully) совсе́м; (in total) всего́; (wholly) всеце́ло.

alum n. квасцы́ m.pl. **aluminium** n. алюми́ний; attrib. алюми́ниевый.

always adv. всегда́; (constantly) постоя́нно.

a.m. abbr. до полу́дня.

amalgamate v.t. & i. амальгами́ровать(ся) imp., perf.; объединя́ть(ся) imp., объедини́ть(ся) perf. **amalgamation** n. амальгами́рование; объедине́ние.

amanuensis n. перепи́счик, -ица.

amass v.t. копи́ть (-плю́, -пишь) imp., на ~ perf.

amateur n. люби́тель m., ~ница f.; adj. самоде́ятельный, люби́тельский. **amateurish** adj. люби́тельский.

amatory adj. любо́вный.

amaze v.t. удивля́ть imp., удиви́ть perf.; изумля́ть imp., изуми́ть perf. **amazement** n. удивле́ние, изумле́ние. **amazing** adj. удиви́тельный, изуми́тельный.

ambassador n. посо́л (-сла́) m.; adj. посо́льский. **ambassadorial** adj. посо́льский.

amber n. янта́рь (-ря́) m.; adj. янта́рный; (coloured) жёлтый (жёлт, -а́, жёлто). **ambergris** n. а́мбра.

ambidextrous adj. одина́ково свобо́дно владе́ющий обе́ими рука́ми.

ambiguity n. двусмы́сленность. **ambiguous** adj. двусмы́сленный (-ен, -енна).

ambition n. честолю́бие. **ambitious** adj. честолюби́вый.

amble v.i. (horse) бе́гать indet., бежа́ть (-жи́т) det. и́ноходью; (ride) е́здить indet., е́хать (е́ду, е́дешь) det. верхо́м на инохо́дце; (on foot) ходи́ть (хожу́, хо́дишь) indet., идти́ (иду́, идёшь; шёл, шла) det. неторопли́вым ша́гом; n. и́ноходь.

ambrosia n. амбро́зия.

ambulance n. каре́та ско́рой по́мощи; ско́рая по́мощь; air a., санита́рный самолёт.

ambush n. заса́да; v.t. напада́ть imp., напа́сть (-аду́, -адёшь; -а́л) perf. из заса́ды на + acc.; устра́ивать imp., устро́ить perf. заса́ду на + acc.

ameliorate v.t. & i. улучша́ть(ся) imp.,

улу́чшить(ся) perf. **amelioration** n. улучше́ние.

amen interj. ами́нь!

amenable adj. усту́пчивый, сгово́рчивый (то, + dat.).

amend v.t. исправля́ть imp., испра́вить perf.; вноси́ть (-ошу́, -о́сишь) imp., внести́ (внесу́, -сёшь; внёс, -ла́) perf. измене́ния, попра́вки, в + acc. **amendment** n. попра́вка, исправле́ние, поправле́ние. **amends** n.: make a. for, загла́живать imp., загла́дить perf.

amenities n. пре́лести f.pl., удо́бства neut.pl.

American adj. америка́нский; n. америка́нец (-нца), -нка. **Americanism** n. американи́зм. **Americanization** n. американиза́ция. **Americanize** v.t. американизи́ровать imp., perf.

amethyst n. амети́ст.

amiability n. любе́зность. **amiable** adj. любе́зный. **amicability** n. дружелю́бие. **amicable** adj. дружелю́бный.

amid(st) prep. среди́ + gen.

amiss adv. ду́рно, пло́хо; take it a., обижа́ться imp., оби́деться (-и́жусь, -и́дишься) perf.

amity n. дру́жественные отноше́ния neut.pl.

ammonia n. аммиа́к; (liquid a.) наша́тырный спирт imp., loc. -е & -у́). **ammonia(cal)** adj. аммиа́чный.

ammunition n. боеприпа́сы m.pl., снаря́ды m.pl., патро́ны m.pl., дробь.

amnesty n. амни́стия; v.t. амнисти́ровать imp., perf.

among(st) prep. среди́ + gen., ме́жду + instr.

amoral adj. амора́льный.

amorous adj. влюбчи́вый; (in love) влюблённый (-ён, -ена́).

amorphous adj. амо́рфный, безфо́рменный (-ен, -енна).

amortization n. амортиза́ция. **amortize** v.t. амортизи́ровать imp., perf.

amount n. коли́чество; v.i.: a. to, составля́ть imp., соста́вить perf.; равня́ться imp. + dat.; быть равноси́льным + dat.

ampere n. ампе́р (gen.pl. -р).

amphibian n. амфи́бия. **amphibious** adj. земново́дный.

amphitheatre *n.* амфитеа́тр.

ample *adj.* (*enough*) (вполне́) доста́точный; (*abundant*) оби́льный; (*spacious*) обши́рный. **amplification** *n.* усиле́ние. **amplifier** *n.* усили́тель *m.* **amplify** *v.t.* (*strengthen*) уси́ливать *imp.*, уси́лить *perf.*; (*enlarge*) расширя́ть *imp.*, расши́рить *perf.* **amplitude** *n.* обши́рность, просто́р. **amply** *adv.* доста́точно.

ampoule *n.* а́мпула.

amputate *v.t.* ампути́ровать *imp.*, *perf.* **amputation** *n.* ампута́ция.

amuse *v.t.* забавля́ть *imp.*; развлека́ть *imp.*, развле́чь (-еку́, -ечёшь; -ёк, -екла́) *perf.*; увеселя́ть *imp.* **amusement** *n.* заба́ва, развлече́ние, увеселе́ние; *pl.* аттракцио́ны *m.pl.* **amusing** *adj.* заба́вный; (*funny*) смешно́й (-шо́н, -шна́).

anachronism *n.* анахрони́зм. **anachronistic** *adj.* анахрони́чный, -ческий.

anaemia *n.* малокро́вие, анеми́я. **anaemic** *adj.* малокро́вный, анеми́чный, -ческий.

anaesthesia *n.* анестези́я, обезбо́ливание. **anaesthetic** *n.* анестези́рующее, обезбо́ливающее; сре́дство; *adj.* анестези́рующий, обезбо́ливающий. **anaesthetist** *n.* наркотиза́тор. **anaesthetize** *v.t.* анестези́ровать *imp.*, *perf.*; обезбо́ливать *imp.*, обезбо́лить *perf.*

anagram *n.* анагра́мма.

anal *adj.* ана́льный.

analogical *adj.* аналоги́ческий. **analogous** *adj.* аналоги́чный. **analogue** *n.* анало́г; *a. computer*, анало́говая вычисли́тельная маши́на, АВМ. **analogy** *n.* анало́гия.

analyse *v.t.* анализи́ровать *imp.*, *perf.*; (*gram.*) разбира́ть *imp.*, разобра́ть (разберу́, -рёшь; разобра́л, -á, -о) *perf.* **analysis** *n.* ана́лиз; разбо́р. **analyst** *n.* анали́тик; психоанали́тик. **analytical** *adj.* аналити́ческий.

anarchism *n.* анархи́зм. **anarchist** *n.* анархи́ст, ~ка; *adj.* анархи́стский. **anarchy** *n.* ана́рхия.

anastigmatic *adj.* анастигмати́ческий.

anatomical *adj.* анатоми́ческий. **anatomist** *n.* ана́том. **anatomy** *n.* анато́мия.

ancestor *n.* пре́док (-дка), прароди́тель *m.* **ancestral** *adj.* родово́й, насле́дственный. **ancestress** *n.* прароди́тельница. **ancestry** *n.* происхожде́ние; пре́дки *m.pl.*, прароди́тели *m.pl.*

anchor *n.* я́корь (*pl.* -ря́) *m.*; *v.t.* ста́вить *imp.*, по~ *perf.* на я́корь; *v.i.* станови́ться (-влю́сь, -вишься) *imp.*, стать (ста́ну, -нешь) *perf.* на я́корь. **anchorage** *n.* я́корная стоя́нка.

anchovy *n.* анчо́ус.

ancient *adj.* анти́чный, дре́вний (-вен, -вня), стари́нный.

and *conj.* и, а; с + *instr.*; *you and I*, мы с ва́ми; *my wife and I*, мы с жено́й.

andante *adv.* (*n.*) анда́нте (*neut.indecl.*).

anecdotal *adj.* анекдоти́ческий. **anecdote** *n.* анекдо́т.

anemometer *n.* анемо́метр, ветроме́р. **anemone** *n.* анемо́н, ве́треница.

aneroid (barometer) *n.* анеро́ид, баро́метр-анеро́ид.

anew *adv.* сно́ва.

angel *n.* а́нгел. **angelic** *adj.* а́нгельский.

anger *n.* гнев; *v.t.* серди́ть (-ржу́, -рдишь) *imp.*, рас~ *perf.*

angle[1] *n.* у́гол (угла́); (*fig.*) то́чка зре́ния.

angle[2] *v.i.* уди́ть (ужу́, у́дишь) *imp.* ры́бу. **angler** *n.* рыболо́в. **angling** *n.* уже́ние.

angrily *adv.* серди́то, гне́вно. **angry** *adj.* серди́тый, гне́вный (-вен, -вна, -вно); (*inflamed*) воспалённый (-ён, -ена́).

anguish *n.* страда́ние, боль. **anguished** *adj.* страда́ющий.

angular *adj.* углово́й; (*sharp*) углова́тый.

aniline *adj.* анили́новый.

animal *n.* живо́тное *sb.*; зверь (*pl.* -ри, -ре́й) *m.*; *adj.* живо́тный. **animate** *adj.* живо́й (жив, -á, -о). **animated** *adj.* оживлённый (-ён, -ена́), живо́й (жив, -á, -о); воодушевлённый (-ён, -ена́); (*film*) мультипликацио́нный; *a. cartoon*, мультфи́льм. **animation** *n.* оживле́ние, жи́вость, воодушевле́ние.

animosity, animus *n.* вражде́бность, неприя́знь.

aniseed *n.* ани́совое се́мя *neut.*

ankle *n.* лоды́жка, щи́колотка; *a. socks*,

коро́ткие носки́ *m.pl.* **anklet** *n.* ножно́й брасле́т.

annals *n.* ле́топись, анна́лы *m.pl.*

annalist *n.* летопи́сец (-сца).

annex *v.t.* аннекси́ровать *imp.*, *perf.*; присоединя́ть *imp.*, присоедини́ть *perf.*; прилага́ть *imp.*, приложи́ть (-жу́, -жишь) *perf.* **annexation** *n.* анне́ксия; присоедине́ние. **annexe** *n.* (*building*) пристро́йка; дополне́ние.

annihilate *v.t.* уничтожа́ть *imp.*, уничто́жить *perf.* **annihilation** *n.* уничтоже́ние.

anniversary *n.* годовщи́на.

annotate *v.t.* анноти́ровать *imp.*, *perf.* **annotated** *adj.* снабжённый (-ён, -ена́) примеча́ниями, коммента́риями. **annotation** *n.* примеча́ние, коммента́рий, анноти́ция.

announce *v.t.* объявля́ть *imp.*, объяви́ть (-влю́, -вишь) *perf.*; (*declare*) заявля́ть *imp.*, заяви́ть (-влю́, -вишь) *perf.*; (*radio*) сообща́ть *imp.*, сообщи́ть *perf.*; (*guest*) докла́дывать *imp.*, доложи́ть (-жу́, -жишь) *perf.* о + *prep.* **announcement** *n.* объявле́ние; сообще́ние. **announcer** *n.* ди́ктор.

annoy *v.t.* досажда́ть *imp.*, досади́ть *perf.*; раздража́ть *imp.*, раздражи́ть *perf.*; *I was annoyed*, мне бы́ло доса́дно. **annoyance** *n.* доса́да, раздраже́ние; (*nuisance*) неприя́тность. **annoying** *adj.* доса́дный.

annual *adj.* ежего́дный, годово́й, годи́чный; (*bot.*) одноле́тний; *n.* ежего́дник; одноле́тник. **annually** *adv.* ежего́дно. **annuity** *n.* (ежего́дная) ре́нта.

annul *v.t.* аннули́ровать *imp.*, *perf.* **annulment** *n.* аннули́рование.

Annunciation *n.* Благове́щение.

anode *n.* ано́д.

anodyne *n.* болеутоля́ющее сре́дство.

anoint *v.t.* пома́зывать *imp.*, пома́зать (-а́жу, -а́жешь) *perf.*

anomalous *adj.* анома́льный. **anomaly** *n.* анома́лия.

anon. *abbr.*, **anonymous** *adj.* анони́мный. **anonymity** *n.* анони́мность.

another *adj.*, *pron.* друго́й; *a.* (*one*) ещё (оди́н); *ask me a.*, почём я зна́ю? *in*

a. ten years, ещё че́рез де́сять лет; *many a.*, мно́гие други́е.

answer *n.* отве́т; *v.t.* отвеча́ть *imp.*, отве́тить *perf.* на + *dat.*; на + *acc.*; *a. back*, дерзи́ть *imp.*, на ~ *perf.* + *dat.*; *a. for*, руча́ться *imp.*, поручи́ться (-чу́сь, -чишься) *perf.* за + *acc.*; *a. the door*, отворя́ть *imp.*, отвори́ть (-рю́, -ришь) *perf.* дверь на звоно́к, на стук. **answerable** *adj.* отве́тственный (-ен, -енна).

ant *n.* мураве́й (-вья́); *a.-eater*, муравье́д; *a.-hill*, мураве́йник.

antagonism *n.* антагони́зм, вражда́. **antagonist** *n.* антагони́ст, проти́вник. **antagonistic** *adj.* антагонисти́ческий, вражде́бный. **antagonize** *v.t.* порожда́ть *imp.*, породи́ть *perf.* антагони́зм, вражду́, у + *gen.*

antarctic *adj.* антаркти́ческий; *n.* Анта́рктика.

antecedent *n.* антецеде́нт; *pl.* про́шлое *sb.*; *adj.* антецеде́нтный; предше́ствующий, предыду́щий.

antechamber *n.* пере́дняя *sb.*, прихо́жая *sb.*

antedate *v.t.* дати́ровать *imp.*, *perf.* за́дним число́м; (*precede*) предше́ствовать *imp.* + *dat.*

antediluvian *adj.* допото́пный.

antelope *n.* антило́па.

antenatal *adj.* до рожде́ния.

antenna *n.* (*ent.*) у́сик, щу́пальце (*gen. pl.* -лец & -льцев); (*also radio*) анте́нна.

anterior *adj.* пере́дний; *a. to*, предше́ствующий + *acc.*

anteroom *n.* пере́дняя *sb.*

anthem *n.* гимн.

anthology *n.* антоло́гия.

anthracite *n.* антраци́т; *adj.* антраци́товый.

anthropoid *adj.* человекообра́зный; *n.* антропо́ид. **anthropological** *adj.* антрополо́гический. **anthropologist** *n.* антропо́лог. **anthropology** *n.* антрополо́гия.

anti- *in comb.* анти-, противо-. **anti-aircraft** *adj.* противовозду́шный, зени́тный. **antibiotic** *n.* антибио́тик. **antibody** *n.* антите́ло (*pl.* -ла́). **Antichrist** *n.* анти́христ. **anticlimax** *n.* неосуществлённые ожида́ния *neut.pl.*, антикли́макс. **anticyclone** *n.* антицикло́н. **antidote** *n.* противоя́дие. **anti-Fascist** *n.* антифаши́ст, ~ ка; *adj.* антифаши́стский. **antifreeze** *n.* антифри́з, хладносто́йкий соста́в. **antihero** *n.* антигеро́й. **antimatter** *n.* антивещество́. **anti-missile missile** *n.* антираке́та. **antipathetic** *adj.* антипати́чный. **antipathy** *n.* антипа́тия. **antipodes** *n.* антипо́д; диаметра́льно противополо́жная то́чка. **anti-Semite** *n.* антисеми́т, ~ ка. **anti-Semitic** *adj.* антисеми́тский. **anti-Semitism** *n.* антисемити́зм. **antiseptic** *adj.* антисепти́ческий; *n.* антисе́птик. **anti-submarine** *adj.* противоло́дочный. **anti-tank** *adj.* противота́нковый. **anti-thesis** *n.* антите́за; (*opposition*) противополо́жность. **antithetical** *adj.* антитети́ческий; противополо́жный. **anticipate** *v.t.* ожида́ть *imp.* + *gen.*; (*with pleasure*) предвкуша́ть *imp.*, предвкуси́ть (-ушу, -у́сишь) *perf.*; (*forestall*) предупрежда́ть *imp.*, предупреди́ть *perf.* **anticipation** *n.* ожида́ние; предвкуше́ние; предупрежде́ние. **antics** *n.* вы́ходки *f.pl.*, ша́лости *f.pl.* **antimony** *n.* сурьма́. **antiquarian** *adj.* антиква́рный; *n.*, **antiquary** *n.* антиква́р. **antiquated** *adj.* устаре́лый. **antique** *adj.* стари́нный; *n.* анти́к; *pl.* старина́. **antiquity** *n.* дре́вность, старина́ *f.*; *pl.* дре́вности *f.pl.* **antler** *n.* оле́ний рог (*pl.* -а́). **anus** *n.* за́дний прохо́д. **anvil** *n.* накова́льня (*gen.pl.* -лен). **anxiety** *n.* беспоко́йство, трево́га, озабо́ченность. **anxious** *adj.* беспоко́йный, трево́жный, озабо́ченный (-ен, -енна); *be a.*, беспоко́иться *imp.*; трево́житься *imp.* **any** *adj.*, *pron.* како́й-нибудь; ско́лько-нибудь; вся́кий, любо́й; кто́-нибудь, что́-нибудь; (*with neg.*) никако́й, ни оди́н; ниско́лько; никто́, ничто́; *adv.* ско́лько-нибудь; (*with neg.*) ниско́лько, ничу́ть. **anybody**, **anyone** *pron.* кто́-нибудь; вся́кий, любо́й; (*with neg.*) никто́. **anyhow** *adv.* ка́к-нибудь; ко́е-как; (*with neg.*) ника́к; *conj.* во вся́ком слу́чае; всё же, всё равно́. **anyone** *see* anybody. **anything** *pron.* что́-нибудь;

всё (что уго́дно); (*with neg.*) ничего́. **anyway** *adv.* во вся́ком слу́чае; как бы то ни́ было. **anywhere** *adv.* где, куда́, отку́да, уго́дно; (*with neg.*, *interrog.*) где-, куда́-, отку́да-нибудь.

aorta *n.* ао́рта.

apart *adv.* (*aside*) в стороне́, в сто́рону; (*separately*) разде́льно, врозь; (*into pieces*) на ча́сти; *a. from*, кро́ме + *gen.*, не счита́я + *gen.*; *take a.*, разбира́ть *imp.*, разобра́ть (разберу́, -рёшь; разобра́л, -а́, -о) *perf.* (на ча́сти); *tell a.*, различа́ть *imp.*, различи́ть *perf.*; отлича́ть *imp.*, отличи́ть *perf.* друг от дру́га.

apartheid *n.* апарте́йд.

apartments *n.pl.* меблиро́ванные ко́мнаты *f.pl.*

apathetic *adj.* апати́чный. **apathy** *n.* апа́тия, безразли́чие.

ape *n.* обезья́на; *v.t.* обезья́нничать *imp.*, с~ *perf.* с + *gen.*

aperient *adj.* слаби́тельный; *n.* слаби́тельное *sb.*

aperture *n.* отве́рстие.

apex *n.* верши́на.

aphorism *n.* афори́зм. **aphoristic** *adj.* афористи́чный, -ческий.

apiarist *n.* пчелово́д. **apiary** *n.* па́сека, пче́льник.

apiece *adv.* (*persons*) на ка́ждого; (*things*) за шту́ку; (*amount*) по + *dat.* or *acc.* with 2, 3, 4, 90, 100, etc.

Apocalypse *n.* Апока́липсис. **apocalyptic** *adj.* апокалипти́ческий.

Apocrypha *n.* апо́крифы *m.pl.* **apocryphal** *adj.* апокрифи́чный, -ческий.

apogee *n.* апоге́й.

apologetic *adj.* извиня́ющийся; *be a.*, извиня́ться *imp.*; *feel a.*, чу́вствовать *imp.* свою́ вину́. **apologetics** *n.* апологе́тика. **apologia** *n.* аполо́гия. **apologize** *v.i.* извиня́ться *imp.*, извини́ться *perf.* (to, пе́ред + *instr.*; for, за + *acc.*). **apology** *n.* извине́ние; *a. for*, жа́лкое подо́бие + *gen.*

apoplectic *adj.* апоплекси́ческий. **apoplexy** *n.* апопле́ксия.

apostasy *n.* (веро)отсту́пничество. **apostate** *n.* (веро)отсту́пник, -ица; *adj.* (веро)отсту́пнический.

apostle *n.* апо́стол. **apostolic** *adj.* апо́стольский.

apostrophe *n.* апостро́ф.

apotheosis *n.* апофео́з, прославле́ние.

appal *v.t.* ужаса́ть *imp.*, ужасну́ть *perf.* **appalling** *adj.* ужаса́ющий, ужа́сный.

apparatus *n.* аппара́т; прибо́р; (*gymnastic*) гимнасти́ческие снаря́ды *m.pl.*

apparel *n.* одея́ние.

apparent *adj.* (*seeing*) ви́димый; (*manifest*) очеви́дный, я́вный; *heir a.*, прямо́й насле́дник. **apparently** *adv.* ка́жется, по-ви́димому; очеви́дно.

apparition *n.* виде́ние, при́зрак.

appeal *n.* (*request*) призы́в, воззва́ние, обраще́ние; (*leg.*) апелля́ция, обжа́лование; (*attraction*) привлека́тельность; *a. court*, апелляцио́нный суд (-а́); *v.i.* (*request*) взыва́ть *imp.*, воззва́ть (-зову́, -зовёшь) *perf.* (to, к+*dat.*; for, о+*prep.*); обраща́ться *imp.*, обрати́ться (-ащу́сь, -ати́шься) *perf.* (с призы́вом); (*leg.*) апелли́ровать *imp.*, *perf.*; *a. against*, обжа́ловать *perf.*; *a. to*, (*attract*) привлека́ть *imp.*, привле́чь (-еку́ -ечёшь; -ёк, -екла́) *perf.*

appear *v.i.* появля́ться *imp.*, появи́ться (-влю́сь, -вишься) *perf.*; выступа́ть *imp.*, вы́ступить *perf.*; (*seem*) каза́ться (кажу́сь, -жешься) *imp.*, по~ *perf.* **appearance** *n.* появле́ние, выступле́ние; (*aspect*) вид, нару́жность; (*pl.*) ви́димость.

appease *v.t.* умиротворя́ть *imp.*, умиротвори́ть *perf.* **appeasement** *n.* умиротворе́ние.

appellant *n.* апелля́нт. **appellate** *adj.* апелляцио́нный.

append *v.t.* прилага́ть *imp.*, приложи́ть (-жу́, -жишь) *perf.*; прибавля́ть *imp.*, приба́вить *perf.* **appendicitis** *n.* аппендици́т. **appendix** *n.* приложе́ние, прибавле́ние; (*anat.*) аппе́ндикс.

appertain *v.i.*: *a.* to, принадлежа́ть (-жи́т) *imp.*+*dat.*; относи́ться (-ится) *imp.*+*dat.*

appetite *n.* аппети́т. **appetizing** *adj.* аппети́тный.

applaud *v.t.* аплоди́ровать *imp.*+*dat.*; рукоплеска́ть (-ещу́, -е́щешь) *imp.*+

dat. **applause** *n.* аплодисме́нты *m.pl.*, рукоплеска́ние.

apple *n.* я́блоко (*pl.* -ки); *adj.* я́блочный; *a. charlotte*, шарло́тка; *a.-tree*, я́блоня.

appliance *n.* приспособле́ние, прибо́р.

applicable *adj.* примени́мый. **applicant** *n.* подате́ль *m.*, ~ница, заявле́ние, проси́тель *m.*, ~ница; кандида́т. **application** *n.* (*use*) примене́ние, приложе́ние; (*putting on*) накла́дывание; (*request*) заявле́ние. **applied** *adj.* прикладно́й. **appliqué** *n.* аппликация. **apply** *v.t.* (*use*) применя́ть *imp.*, примени́ть (-ню́, -нишь) *perf.*; прилага́ть *imp.*, приложи́ть (-жу́, -жишь) *perf.*; (*put on*) накла́дывать *imp.*, наложи́ть (-жу́, -жишь) *perf.*; *v.i.* (*request*) обраща́ться *imp.*, обрати́ться (-ащу́сь, -ати́шься) *perf.* с про́сьбой (for, о+*prep.*); подава́ть (-даю́, -даёшь) *imp.*, пода́ть (-а́м, -а́шь, -а́ст, -ади́м; по́дал, -а́, -о) *perf.* заявле́ние.

appoint *v.t.* назнача́ть *imp.*, назна́чить *perf.* **appointment** *n.* назначе́ние; (*office*) до́лжность, пост (-а́, *loc.* -ý); (*meeting*) свида́ние.

apposite *adj.* уме́стный. **apposition** *n.* приложе́ние; *in a.*, приложённый (-ен).

appraisal *n.* оце́нка. **appraise** *v.t.* оце́нивать *imp.*, оцени́ть (-ню́, -нишь) *perf.* **appreciable** *adj.* ощути́мый, ощути́тельный. **appreciate** *v.t.* цени́ть (-ню́, -нишь) *imp.*; (*правильно*) оце́нивать *imp.*, оцени́ть (-ню́, -нишь) *perf.*; *v.i.* повыша́ться *imp.*, повы́ситься *perf.* **appreciation** *n.* (*estimation*) оце́нка; (*recognition*) призна́тельность; (*rise in value*) повыше́ние це́нности, це́ны. **appreciative** *adj.* призна́тельный (of, за+*acc.*).

apprehend *v.t.* (*arrest*) аресто́вывать *imp.*, арестова́ть *perf.*; (*understand*) понима́ть *imp.*, поня́ть (пойму́, -мёшь; по́нял, -а́, -о) *perf.*; (*anticipate*) опаса́ться *imp.*+*gen.*, *inf.* **apprehension** *n.* аре́ст; опасе́ние. **apprehensive** *adj.* опаса́ющийся.

apprentice *n.* учени́к (-а́), подмасте́рье (*gen.pl.* -в) *m.*; *v.t.* отдава́ть (-даю́, -даёшь) *imp.*, отда́ть (-а́м, -а́шь, -а́ст, -ади́м; о́тдал, -а́, -о) *perf.* в уче́ние.

apprenticeship n. учени́чество; обуче́ние.

appro. abbr.: on a., на про́бу.

approach v.t. подходи́ть (-ожу́, -о́дишь) imp., подойти́ (подойду́, -дёшь) подошёл, -шла́) perf. к + dat.; приближа́ться imp., прибли́зиться perf. к + dat.; (apply to) обраща́ться imp., обрати́ться (-ащу́сь, -ати́шься) perf. к + dat.; n. приближе́ние; подхо́д, подъе́зд, по́дступ.

approbation n. одобре́ние.

appropriate adj. подходя́щий, соотве́тствующий; v.t. присва́ивать imp., присво́ить perf.; (assign money) ассигнова́ть imp., perf. **appropriation** n. присвое́ние, присво́енное sb.; ассигнова́ние.

approval n. одобре́ние; утвержде́ние. **approve** v.t. утвержда́ть imp., утверди́ть perf.; v.t. & i. (a. of) одобря́ть imp., одо́брить perf.

approximate adj. приблизи́тельный; v.i. приближа́ться imp. (to, к + dat.). **approximation** n. приближе́ние.

apricot n. абрико́с.

April n. апре́ль m.; attrib. апре́льский.

apron n. пере́дник; (theatre) авансце́на; (airfield) площа́дка.

apropos adv. кста́ти; a. of, по по́воду + gen.; относи́тельно + gen.; что каса́ется + gen.

apse n. апси́да.

apt adj. (suitable) уда́чный; (quick) спосо́бный; (inclined) скло́нный (-о́нен, -о́нна, -о́нно). **aptitude** n. спосо́бность.

aqualung n. аквала́нг. **aquamarine** n. аквамари́н. **aquarium** n. аква́риум. **Aquarius** n. Водоле́й. **aquatic** adj. водяно́й, во́дный. **aqueduct** n. акведу́к. **aqueous** adj. во́дный; (watery) водяни́стый.

aquiline adj. орли́ный.

Arab n. (person) ара́б, ~ ка; (horse) ара́бская ло́шадь (pl. -ди, -де́й, instr. -дьми́); adj. ара́бский. **arabesque** n. арабе́ска. **Arabic** adj. ара́бский.

arable adj. па́хотный.

arbitrary adj. произво́льный. **arbitrate** v.i. де́йствовать imp. в ка́честве трете́йского судьи́. **arbitration** n. арбитра́ж, трете́йское реше́ние. **arbitrator**

n. арби́тр, трете́йский судья́ (pl. -дьи, -де́й, -дья́м, -дья́м) m.

arbor n. вал (loc. -у́; pl. -ы́), шпи́ндель m.

arboreal adj. древе́сный; (living in trees) обита́ющий на дере́вьях. **arbour** n. бесе́дка.

arc n. дуга́ (pl. -ги); a. lamp, дугова́я ла́мпа. **arcade** n. арка́да, пасса́ж.

arch[1] n. а́рка, свод, дуга́ (pl. -ги); v.t. & i. выгиба́ть(ся) imp., вы́гнуть(ся) perf.; изгиба́ть(ся) imp., изогну́ть(ся) perf.

arch[2] adj. игри́вый.

archaeological adj. археологи́ческий. **archaeologist** n. архео́лог. **archaeology** n. археоло́гия.

archaic adj. архаи́чный. **archaism** n. архаи́зм.

archangel n. арха́нгел.

archbishop n. архиепи́скоп. **archdeacon** n. архидиа́кон.

archducal adj. эрцге́рцогский. **archduchess** n. эрцге́рцоги́ня. **archduchy** n. эрцге́рцогство. **archduke** n. эрцге́рцог.

archer n. стрело́к (-лка́) из лу́ка. **archery** n. стрельба́ из лу́ка.

archipelago n. архипела́г.

architect n. архите́ктор, зо́дчий sb. **architectural** adj. архитекту́рный. **architecture** n. архитекту́ра.

archives n. архи́в. **archivist** n. архива́риус, архиви́ст.

archway n. прохо́д под а́ркой, сво́дчатый прохо́д.

arctic adj. аркти́ческий; n. А́рктика.

ardent adj. горя́чий (-ч, -ча́), пы́лкий (-лок, -лка́, -лко). **ardour** n. пыл (-а(у), loc. -у́), пы́лкость, рве́ние.

arduous adj. тру́дный (-ден, -дна́, -дно).

area n. (extent) пло́щадь (pl. -ди, -де́й); (region) райо́н, зо́на.

arena n. аре́на.

argon n. арго́н.

arguable adj. утвержда́емый, доказу́емый; (disputed) спо́рный. **argue** v.t. (try to prove) аргументи́ровать imp., perf.; (maintain) утвержда́ть imp.; (prove) дока́зывать imp.; v.i. (dispute) спо́рить imp., по ~ perf. **argument** n.

аргуме́нт, до́вод; (*dispute*) спор. **argumentative** *adj.* любя́щий спо́рить.

arid *adj.* сухо́й (сух, -á, -о), безво́дный. **aridity** *n.* су́хость.

Aries *n.* Ове́н (Овна́).

arise *v.i.* возника́ть *imp.*, возни́кнуть (-к) *perf.*; происходи́ть (-ит) *imp.*, произойти́ (-ойдёт) -ошёл, -ошла́) *perf.*

aristocracy *n.* аристокра́тия. **aristocrat** *n.* аристокра́т, ~ ка. **aristocratic** *adj.* аристократи́ческий, -чный.

arithmetic *n.* арифме́тика. **arithmetical** *adj.* арифмети́ческий. **arithmetician** *n.* арифме́тик.

ark *n.* (Но́ев) ковче́г.

arm[1] *n.* (*of body*) рука́ (*acc.* -ку; *pl.* -ки, -к, -ка́м); (*of sea*) морско́й зали́в; (*of chair*) ру́чка; (*of river*) рука́в (-á; *pl.* -á); (*of tree*) больша́я ветвь (*pl.* -ви, -ве́й); *a. in a.*, под руку; *at a.'s length*, (*fig.*) на почти́тельном расстоя́нии; *with open arms*, с распростёртыми объя́тиями.

arm[2] *n.* (*mil.*) род войск; *pl.* (*weapons*) ору́жие; *pl.* (*coat of a.*) герб (-á); *v.t.* вооружа́ть *imp.*, вооружи́ть *perf.* **armaments** *n.* вооруже́ния *neut.pl.*

armchair *n.* кре́сло (*gen.pl.* -сел). **armful** *n.* оха́пка. **armhole** *n.* про́йма.

armistice *n.* переми́рие.

armorial *adj.* ге́рбовый, геральди́ческий. **armour** *n.* (*hist.*) доспе́хи *m.pl.*; броня́; (*vehicles, collect.*) бронеси́лы *f.pl.* **armoured** *adj.* бронир́ованный (-ан), бронево́й; (*vehicles etc.*) бронета́нковый, броне-; *a. car*, броневи́к (-á), бронеавтомоби́ль *m.*; *a. forces*, бронета́нковые войска́ *neut.*, -броне-си́лы *f.pl.* **armourer** *n.* оруже́йник. **armoury** *n.* арсена́л, склад ору́жия.

armpit *n.* подмы́шка.

army *n.* а́рмия; *adj.* арме́йский.

aroma *n.* арома́т. **aromatic** *adj.* аромати́чный.

around *adv.* круго́м, вокру́г; *prep.* вокру́г + *gen.*; *all a.*, повсю́ду.

arouse *v.t.* пробужда́ть *imp.*, буди́ть (бужу́, бу́дишь) *imp.*, про ~ *perf.*; возбужда́ть *imp.*, возбуди́ть *perf.*

arraign *v.t.* привлека́ть *imp.*, привле́чь (-еку́, -ечёшь; -ёк, -екла́) *perf.* к суду́. **arraignment** *n.* привлече́ние к суду́.

arrange *v.t.* (*put in order*) приводи́ть (-ожу́, -о́дишь) *imp.*, привести́ (приведу́, -дёшь; привёл, -á) *perf.* в поря́док; расставля́ть *imp.*, расста́вить *perf.*; (*plan*) устра́ивать *imp.*, устро́ить *perf.*; аранжи́ровать *imp.*, *perf.*; *v.i.*: *a. for*, усла́вливаться *imp.*, усло́виться *perf.* о + *prep.*; угова́риваться *imp.*, уговори́ться *perf.* + *inf.* **arrangement** *n.* расположе́ние; устро́йство; (*agreement*) соглаше́ние; (*mus.*) аранжиро́вка; *pl.* приготовле́ния *neut.pl.*

array *v.t.* наряжа́ть *imp.*, наряди́ть (-яжу́, -я́дишь) *perf.*; (*marshal*) стро́ить *imp.*, вы ~ *perf.*; *n.* наря́д; (*series*) совоку́пность.

arrears *n.* задо́лженность, недои́мка.

arrest *v.t.* аресто́вывать *imp.*, арестова́ть *perf.*; заде́рживать *imp.*, задержа́ть (-жу́, -жишь) *perf.*; (*attention*) прико́вывать *imp.*, прикова́ть (-кую́, -куёшь) *perf.*; *n.* аре́ст, задержа́ние.

arrival *n.* прибы́тие, прие́зд; (*new a.*) вновь прибы́вший *sb.*; (*child*) новорождённый *sb.* **arrive** *v.i.* прибыва́ть *imp.*, прибы́ть (прибу́ду, -дешь; при́был, -á, -о) *perf.*; приезжа́ть *imp.*, прие́хать (-е́ду, -е́дешь) *perf.*; (*succeed*) доби́ться (-бью́сь, -бьёшься) *perf.* успе́ха.

arrogance *n.* высокоме́рие, кичли́вость. **arrogant** *adj.* высокоме́рный, кичли́вый.

arrow *n.* стрела́ (*pl.* -лы); (*pointer etc.*) стре́лка. **arrowhead** *n.* наконе́чник стрелы́.

arsenal *n.* арсена́л.

arsenic *n.* мышья́к (-á); *adj.* мышьяко́вый.

arson *n.* поджо́г.

art *n.* иску́сство; *pl.* гуманита́рные нау́ки *f.pl.*; *adj.* худо́жественный.

arterial *adj.* (*anat.*) артериа́льный; магистра́льный; *a. road*, магистра́ль. **artery** *n.* (*anat.*) арте́рия; магистра́ль.

artesian *adj.* артезиа́нский.

artful *adj.* хи́трый (-тёр, -трá, хи́тро́), ло́вкий (-вок, -вкá, -вко, ло́вки́).

arthritic *adj.* артрити́ческий. **arthritis** *n.* артри́т.

artichoke *n.* артишо́к; (*Jerusalem a.*) земляна́я гру́ша.

article *n.* (*literary*) статья́ (*gen.pl.* -те́й); (*clause*) пункт *m.*; (*thing*) предме́т *m.*; (*gram.*) арти́кль *m.*, член; *v.t.* отдава́ть (-даю́, -даёшь) *imp.*, отда́ть (-а́м, -а́шь, -а́ст, -ади́м; о́тдал, -а́, -о) *perf.* в уче́ние.

articulate *adj.* членоразде́льный, я́сный (я́сен, ясна́, я́сно, я́сны); *v.t.* произноси́ть (-ошу́, -о́сишь) *imp.*, произнести́ (-есу́, -есёшь; -ёс, -есла́) *perf.*; артикули́ровать *imp.* **articulated** *adj.* сочленённый (-ён, -ена́). **articulation** *n.* артикуля́ция; сочлене́ние.

artifice *n.* хи́трость, (иску́сная) вы́думка. **artificer** *n.* (вое́нный) те́хник. **artificial** *adj.* иску́сственный (-ен(ен), -енна).

artillery *n.* артилле́рия; *adj.* артилле́ри́йский. **artilleryman** *n.* артиллери́ст.

artisan *n.* реме́сленник.

artist *n.* худо́жник; арти́ст. **artiste** *n.* арти́ст, ~ ка. **artistic** *adj.* худо́жественный (-ен, -енна); артисти́ческий.

artless *adj.* бесхи́тростный, простоду́шный.

Aryan *n.* арие́ц (-и́йца), ари́йка; *adj.* ари́йский.

as *adv.* как; *conj.* (*time*) когда́; в то вре́мя как; (*cause*) так как; (*manner*) как; (*concession*) как ни; *rel.pron.* како́й; кото́рый; *as ... as*, так (же)... как; *as for*, то, относи́тельно + *gen.*; что каса́ется + *gen.*; *as if*, как бу́дто; *as it were*, ка́к бы; так сказа́ть; *as soon as*, как то́лько; *as well*, та́кже; то́же.

asbestos *n.* асбе́ст; *adj.* асбе́стовый.

ascend *v.t.* поднима́ться *imp.*, подня́ться (-ниму́сь, -ни́мешься; -я́лся, -яла́сь) *perf.* на + *acc.*; всходи́ть (-ожу́, -о́дишь) *imp.*, взойти́ (взойду́, -дёшь; взошёл, -шла́) *perf.* на + *acc.*; *v.i.* возноси́ться (-ошу́сь, -о́сишься) *imp.*, вознести́сь (-есу́сь, -есёшься; -ёсся, -есла́сь) *perf.* **ascendancy** *n.* домини́рующее влия́ние (over, на + *acc.*).

ascendant *adj.* восходя́щий. **Ascension** *n.* (*eccl.*) Вознесе́ние. **ascent** *n.* восхожде́ние (of, на + *acc.*).

ascertain *v.t.* устана́вливать *imp.*, установи́ть (-влю́, -вишь) *perf.*

ascetic *adj.* аскети́ческий; *n.* аске́т. **asceticism** *n.* аскети́зм.

ascribe *v.t.* припи́сывать *imp.*, приписа́ть (-ишу́, -и́шешь) *perf.* (to, + *dat.*). **ascription** *n.* припи́сывание.

asepsis *n.* асе́птика. **aseptic** *adj.* асепти́ческий.

asexual *adj.* беспо́лый.

ash[1] *n.* (*tree*) я́сень *m.*

ash[2], **ashes** *n.* зола́, пе́пел (-пла); (*human remains*) прах. **ashtray** *n.* пе́пельница.

ashamed *predic.*: *he is a.*, ему́ сты́дно; *be, feel, a. of*, стыди́ться *imp.*, по ~ *perf.* + *gen.*

ashen[1] *adj.* (*of tree*) я́сеневый.

ashen[2] *adj.* (*of ash*[2]) пе́пельный; (*pale*) мёртвенно-бле́дный.

ashore *adv.* на берег(у́).

Asian, Asiatic *adj.* азиа́тский; *n.* азиа́т, ~ ка.

aside *adv.* в сто́рону, в стороне́; *n.* слова́ *neut.pl.*, произноси́мые в сто́рону.

asinine *adj.* осли́ный; (*stupid*) глу́пый (глуп, -а́, -о).

ask *v.t.* (*inquire of*) спра́шивать *imp.*, спроси́ть (-ошу́, -о́сишь) *perf.*; (*request*) проси́ть (-ошу́, -о́сишь) *imp.*, по ~ *perf.* (for, *acc.*, gen., o + *prep.*); (*invite*) приглаша́ть *imp.*, пригласи́ть *perf.*; (*demand*) тре́бовать *imp.* + *gen.* (of, от + *gen.*); *a. after*, осведомля́ться *imp.*, осве́домиться *perf.* o + *prep.*; *a. a question*, задава́ть (-даю́, -даёшь) *imp.*, зада́ть (-а́м, -а́шь, -а́ст, -ади́м; за́дал, -а́, -о) *perf.* вопро́с; *you can have it for the asking*, сто́ит то́лько попроси́ть.

askance *adv.* ко́со, с подозре́нием.

askew *adv.* кри́во.

asleep *predic.*, *adv.*: *be a.*, спать (сплю, спишь; спал, -а́, -о) *imp.*; *fall a.*, засыпа́ть *imp.*, засну́ть *perf.*; *my foot's a.*, нога́ затекла́.

asp *n.* а́спид.

asparagus *n.* спа́ржа.

aspect *n.* аспе́кт, вид (-а(у), на виду́), сторона́ (*acc.* -ону; *pl.* -оны, -о́н, -она́м).

aspen *n.* оси́на.

asperity *n.* ре́зкость.

aspersion *n.* клевета́.

asphalt *n.* асфа́льт; *adj.* асфа́льтовый; *v.t.* асфальти́ровать *imp.*, *perf.*

asphyxia *n.* асфи́ксия, уду́шье. **asphyxiate** *v.t.* удуша́ть *imp.*, удуши́ть (-шу́, -ши́шь) *perf.*

aspic *n.* заливно́е *sb.*; *in a.*, заливно́й.

aspirant *n.* претенде́нт. **aspirate** *n.* при-дыха́тельный *sb.* **aspiration** *n.* (*ling.*) придыха́ние; (*desire*) стремле́ние. **aspire** *v.i.* стреми́ться *imp.* (*to*, к + *dat.*).

aspirin *n.* аспири́н; (*tablet*) табле́тка аспири́на.

ass *n.* осёл (осла́).

assail *v.t.* напада́ть *imp.*, напа́сть (-аду́, -адёшь; -а́л) *perf.* на + *acc.*; (*with questions*) забра́сывать *imp.*, заброса́ть *perf.* вопро́сами. **assailant** *n.* напада́ющий *sb.*

assassin *n.* (наёмный, -ная) уби́йца *m.*, *f.* **assassinate** *v.t.* (веро́мно) убива́ть *imp.*, уби́ть (убью́, убьёшь) *perf.* **assassination** *n.* (преда́тельское) уби́й-ство.

assault *n.* нападе́ние; (*mil.*) штурм; (*rape*) изнаси́лование; *a. and battery*, оскорбле́ние де́йствием; *v.t.* напа-да́ть *imp.*, напа́сть (-аду́, -адёшь; -а́л) *perf.* на + *acc.*; штурмова́ть *imp.*; наси́ловать *imp.*, из ~ *perf.*

assay *n.* про́ба; *v.t.* производи́ть (-ожу́, -о́дишь) *imp.*, произвести́ (-еду́, -едёшь; -ёл, -ела́) *perf.* ана́лиз + *gen.*; про́бовать *imp.*, по ~ *perf.*

assemblage *n.* сбор, собира́ние. **assemble** *v.t.* собира́ть *imp.*, собра́ть (собе́ру, -рёшь; собра́л, -а, -о) *perf.*; (*machine*) монти́ровать *imp.*, с ~ *perf.*; *v.i.* со-бира́ться *imp.*, собра́ться (-берётся; собра́лся, -ала́сь, -а́ло́сь) *perf.* **assembly** *n.* собра́ние, ассамбле́я; (*of machine*) сбо́рка.

assent *v.i.* соглаша́ться *imp.*, согла-си́ться *perf.* (*to*, на + *acc.*, *inf.*). *n.* согла́сие; (*royal*) са́нкция.

assert *v.t.* утвержда́ть *imp.*; *a. oneself*, отста́ивать *imp.*, отстоя́ть (-ою́, -ои́шь) *perf.* свои́ права́. **assertion** *n.* утвержде́ние. **assertive** *adj.* насто́й-чивый, самонаде́янный (-ян, -янна).

assess *v.t.* (*amount*) определя́ть *imp.*, определи́ть *perf.*; (*tax*) облага́ть *imp.*, обложи́ть (-жу́, -жишь) *perf.* нало́гом; (*value*) оце́нивать *imp.*, оцени́ть (-ню́, -нишь) *perf.* **assessment** *n.* определе́-ние; обложе́ние; оце́нка.

asset *n.* це́нное ка́чество; бла́го; *pl.* иму́щество; *assets and liabilities*, акти́в и пасси́в.

assiduity *n.* прилежа́ние, усе́рдие. **assiduous** *adj.* приле́жный, усе́рдный.

assign *v.t.* назнача́ть *imp.*, назна́чить *perf.*; ассигнова́ть *imp.*, *perf.*; *n.*: *heirs and assigns*, насле́дники и право-прее́мники *m.pl.* **assignation** *n.* (*meeting*) усло́вленная встре́ча, свида́ние. **assignment** *n.* (*task*) зада́ние; (*mission*) командиро́вка.

assimilate *v.t.* ассимили́ровать *imp.*, *perf.*; усва́ивать *imp.*, усво́ить *perf.* **assimilation** *n.* ассимиля́ция; усво-е́ние.

assist *v.t.* помога́ть *imp.*, помо́чь (-огу́, -о́жешь; -о́г, -огла́) *perf.* + *dat.*; со-де́йствовать *imp.*, *perf.* + *dat.* **assist-ance** *n.* по́мощь, соде́йствие. **assistant** *n.* помо́щник, ассисте́нт.

assizes *n.* выездна́я се́ссия суда́.

associate *v.t.* ассоции́ровать *imp.*, *perf.*; *v.i.* присоединя́ться *imp.*, присоеди-ни́ться *perf.* (*with*, к + *dat.*); обща́ть-ся *imp.* (*with*, с + *instr.*); *n.* (*colleague*) колле́га *m.*; (*subordinate member*) мла́дший член, член-корреспонде́нт. **association** *n.* о́бщество, ассоциа́ция; присоедине́ние; *A. football*, футбо́л.

assonance *n.* ассона́нс.

assorted *adj.* подо́бранный (-ан). **assort-ment** *n.* ассортиме́нт.

assuage *v.t.* успока́ивать *imp.*, успо-ко́ить *perf.*; смягча́ть *imp.*, смягчи́ть *perf.*

assume *v.t.* (*accept*) принима́ть *imp.*, приня́ть (приму́, -мешь; при́нял, -а, -о) *perf.*; (*pretend*) напуска́ть *imp.*, напусти́ть (-ущу́, -у́стишь) *perf.* на себя́; (*suppose*) предполага́ть *imp.*, предположи́ть (-ожу́, -о́жишь) *perf.*; *assumed name*, вы́мышленное и́мя *neut.* assumption *n.* приня́тие на себе́; (*pretence*) притво́рство; (*supposition*) предположе́ние, допуще́ние; (*eccl.*, *the A.*) Успе́ние.

assurance *n.* увере́ние; (*self-a.*) самоуве́ренность; (*insurance*) страхова́ние. assure *v.t.* уверя́ть *imp.*, уве́рить *perf.*; гаранти́ровать *imp.*, *perf.*; (*insure*) страхова́ть *imp.*, за~ *perf.* (*against*, от + *gen.*). assuredly *adv.* несомне́нно.

aster *n.* а́стра.

asterisk *n.* звёздочка.

astern *adv.* позади́, наза́д.

asteroid *n.* астеро́ид.

asthma *n.* а́стма. asthmatic *adj.* астмати́ческий.

astigmatic *adj.* астигмати́ческий. astigmatism *n.* астигмати́зм.

astir *predic.*, *adv.* (*in motion*) в движе́нии; (*out of bed*) на нога́х; (*excited*) в возбужде́нии.

astonish *v.t.* удивля́ть *imp.*, удиви́ть *perf.* astonishing *adj.* удиви́тельный. astonishment *n.* удивле́ние.

astound *v.t.* изумля́ть *imp.*, изуми́ть *perf.* astounding *adj.* изуми́тельный.

astrakhan *n.* кара́куль *m.*

astral *adj.* астра́льный, звёздный.

astray *adv.*: *go a.*, сбива́ться *imp.*, сби́ться (собью́сь, собьёшься) *perf.* с пути́; *lead a.*, сбива́ть *imp.*, сбить (собью́, собьёшь) *perf.* с пути́.

astride *adv.* расста́вив но́ги; верхо́м (*of*, на + *prep.*); *prep.* верхо́м на + *prep.*

astringent *adj.* вя́жущий; *n.* вя́жущее сре́дство.

astro- *in comb.* астро-, звездо-. astrologer *n.* астро́лог. astrological *adj.* астрологи́ческий. astrology *n.* астроло́гия. astronaut *n.* астрона́вт. astronomer *n.* астроно́м. astronomical *adj.* астрономи́ческий. astronomy *n.* астроно́мия. astrophysical *adj.* астрофизи́ческий. astrophysics *n.* астрофи́зика.

astute *adj.* проница́тельный; (*crafty*) хи́трый (-тёр, -тра́, хи́тро).

asunder *adv.* (*apart*) врозь; (*in pieces*) на ча́сти.

asylum *n.* психиатри́ческая больни́ца; (*refuge*) убе́жище.

asymmetrical *adj.* асимметри́чный. asymmetry *n.* асимметри́я.

at *prep.* (*position, condition*) на + *prep.*, в + *prep.*, у + *gen.*; (*time, direction*) на + *acc.*, в + *acc.*; with verbs etc.: see verbs etc., e.g. *look* смотре́ть (at, на + *acc.*); *at all*, вообще́; *not at all*, совсе́м не; *at first*, снача́ла, сперва́; *at home*, до́ма; *at last*, наконе́ц; *at least*, по кра́йней ме́ре; *at most*, са́мое бо́льшее; *at night*, но́чью; *at once*, (*immediately*) сра́зу; (*at the same time*) одновреме́нно; *at present*, в настоя́щее вре́мя; *at that*, на том; (*moreover*) к тому́ же; *at work*, (*working*) за рабо́той; (*at place of work*) на рабо́те.

atheism *n.* атеи́зм. atheist *n.* атеи́ст, ~ ка. atheistic *adj.* атеисти́ческий.

athlete *n.* атле́т; легкоатле́т, ~ ка; спортсме́н, ~ ка. athletic *adj.* атлети́ческий. athletics *n.* (лёгкая) атле́тика.

atlas *n.* а́тлас.

atmosphere *n.* атмосфе́ра. atmospheric *adj.* атмосфе́рный. atmospherics *n.* атмосфе́рные поме́хи *f.pl.*

atom *n.* а́том; *a. bomb*, а́томная бо́мба. atomic *adj.* а́томный.

atone *v.i.* искупа́ть *imp.*, искупи́ть (-плю́, -пишь) *perf.* (*for*, + *acc.*). atonement *n.* искупле́ние.

atrocious *adj.* отврати́тельный, ужа́сный. atrocity *n.* зве́рство, ужа́с.

atrophy *n.* атрофи́я, притупле́ние; *v.i.* атрофи́роваться *imp.*, *perf.*

attach *v.t.* (*fasten*) прикрепля́ть *imp.*, прикрепи́ть *perf.*; (*fig.*) привя́зывать *imp.*, привяза́ть (-яжу́, -я́жешь) *perf.*; (*second*) прикомандиро́вывать *imp.*, прикомандирова́ть *perf.*; (*attribute*) придава́ть (-даю́, -даёшь) *imp.*, прида́ть (-а́м, -а́шь, -а́ст, -ади́м) *perf.*, при́дал, -а́, -о) *perf.* attaché *n.* атташе́ *m.indecl.* attachment *n.* прикрепле́ние; привя́занность; (*mil.*) принадле́жности *f.pl.*

attack *v.t.* напада́ть *imp.*, напа́сть (-аду́, -адёшь; -а́л) *perf.* на + *acc.*; *n.* нападе́ние; (*mil. also*) ата́ка; (*of illness*) при́ступ (-дка).

attain *v.t.* достига́ть *imp.*, дости́чь & дости́гнуть (-и́гну, -и́гнешь; -и́г) *perf.*

+ *gen.*, до + *gen.*; *a. the age of*, доживáть *imp.*, дожи́ть (-иву́, -ивёшь; до́жил, -á, -о) *perf.* до + *gen.* **attainment** *n.* достижéние.

attar (of roses) *n.* ро́зовое мáсло.

attempt *v.t.* пытáться *imp.*, по ~ *perf.* + *inf.*; про́бовать *imp.*, по ~ *perf.* + *inf.*; *n.* попы́тка; (*on the life of*) покушéние (на жизнь + *gen.*); *make an a. on the life of*, покушáться *imp.*, покуси́ться *perf.* на жизнь + *gen.*

attend *v.i.* занимáться *imp.*, заня́ться (займу́сь, -мёшься; -я́лся, -ялáсь) *perf.* (to, + *instr.*); (*be present*) присýтствовать *imp.* (at, на + *prep.*); *v.t.* (*accompany*) сопровождáть *imp.*, сопроводи́ть *perf.*; (*serve*) обслýживать *imp.*, обслужи́ть (-жу́, -жишь) *perf.*; (*visit*) посещáть *imp.*, посети́ть (-ещу́, -ети́шь) *perf.* **attendance** *n.* (*presence*) присýтствие; посещáемость; обслýживание. **attendant** *adj.* сопровождáющий; *n.* (*escort*) провожáтый *sb.*

attention *n.* внимáние; *pay a. to*, обращáть *imp.*, обрати́ть (-ащу́, -ати́шь) *perf.* внимáние на + *acc.*; *interj.* (*mil.*) сми́рно! **attentive** *adj.* внимáтельный; (*polite*) вéжливый.

attenuated *adj.* утончённый (-ён, -енá). **attenuation** *n.* утончéние.

attest *v.t.* заверя́ть *imp.*, завéрить *perf.*; свидéтельствовать *imp.*, за ~ *perf.*

attic *n.* мансáрда, чердáк (-á); (*storey*) мезони́н.

attire *v.t.* наряжáть *imp.*, наряди́ть (-яжý, -я́дишь) *perf.*; *n.* наря́д.

attitude *n.* (*posture*) пóза; (*opinion*) отношéние (towards, к + *dat.*); (*of a. of mind*) склад умá.

attorney *n.* повéренный *sb.*; *by a.*, чéрез повéренного; *power of a.*, довéренность; *A.-General*, генерáльный атторнéй.

attract *v.t.* притя́гивать *imp.*, притяну́ть (-ну́, -нешь) *perf.*; прельщáть *imp.*, прельсти́ть *perf.*; привлекáть *imp.*, привлéчь (-екý, -ечёшь; -ёк, -еклá) *perf.* **attraction** *n.* притяжéние; привлекáтельность; (*entertainment*) аттракцио́н. **attractive** *adj.* привлекáтельный, притягáтельный.

attribute *v.t.* припи́сывать *imp.*, припи-

cáte (-ишý, -и́шешь) *perf.*; *n.* (*object*) атрибýт; (*quality*) свóйство; (*gram.*) определéние. **attribution** *n.* припи́сывание. **attributive** *adj.* атрибути́вный, определи́тельный.

attrition *n.* истирáние; *war of a.*, войнá на истощéние.

aubergine *n.* баклажáн.

auburn *adj.* каштáнового цвéта, рыжевáтый.

auction *n.* аукцио́н; *v.t.* продавáть (-даю́, -даёшь) *imp.*, продáть (-áм, -áшь, -áст, -ади́м; про́дал, -á, -о) *perf.* с аукцио́на. **auctioneer** *n.* аукциони́ст.

audacious *adj.* (*bold*) смéлый (смел, -á, -о); (*impudent*) дéрзкий (-зок, -зкá, -зко). **audacity** *n.* смéлость; дéрзость.

audibility *n.* слы́шимость. **audible** *adj.* слы́шный (-шен, -шнá, -шно). **audience** *n.* публика, аудито́рия; (*radio*) слýшатели *m.pl.*, (*теле*)зри́тели *m.pl.*; (*interview*) аудиéнция. **audit** *n.* провéрка счето́в, реви́зия; *v.t.* проверя́ть *imp.*, провéрить *perf.* (счетá + *gen.*). **audition** *n.* про́ба; *v.t.* & *i.* устрáивать *imp.*, устро́ить *perf.* про́бу + *gen.* **auditor** *n.* ревизо́р. **auditorium** *n.* зри́тельный зал, аудито́рия. **auditory** *adj.* слуховóй.

auger *n.* бурáв (-á), сверло́ (*pl.* свёрла).

augment *n.* увеличивать *imp.*, увеличить *perf.*; прибавля́ть *imp.*, прибáвить *perf.* + *gen.* **augmentation** *n.* увеличéние, прибáвка. **augmentative** *adj.* увеличи́тельный.

augur *v.t.* & *i.* предвещáть *imp.*

August *n.* áвгуст; *attrib.* áвгустовский; **august** *adj.* величéственный (-ен, -енна).

aunt *n.* тётя (*gen.pl.* -тей), тётка. **auntie** *n.* тётушка.

aureole *n.* орео́л.

auriferous *adj.* золотоно́сный.

aurochs *n.* тур.

aurora *n.* авро́ра; *a. borealis*, сéверное сия́ние.

auspices *n.* покрови́тельство. **auspicious** *adj.* благоприя́тный.

austere *adj.* стро́гий (строг, -á, -о), сурóвый. **austerity** *n.* стро́гость, суро́вость.

austral *adj.* ю́жный.

Australian *n.* австрали́ец (-и́йца), -и́йка; *adj.* австрали́йский.

Austrian *n.* австри́ец (-и́йца), -и́йка; *adj.* австри́йский.

authentic *adj.* (*genuine*) по́длинный (-нен, -нна), аутенти́чный; (*reliable*) достове́рный. **authenticate** *v.t.* удостоверя́ть *imp.*, удостове́рить *perf.*; устана́вливать *imp.*, установи́ть (-влю́, -вишь) *perf.* по́длинность + *gen.* **authenticity** *n.* по́длинность, аутенти́чность; достове́рность.

author, authoress *n.* а́втор, писа́тель *m.*, ~ ница.

authoritarian *adj.* авторита́рный; *n.* сторо́нник авторита́рной вла́сти. **authoritative** *adj.* авторите́тный. **authority** *n.* (*power*) власть (*pl.* -ти, -те́й), полномо́чие; (*evidence*) авторите́т; (*source*) авторите́тный исто́чник. **authorize** *v.t.* (*action*) разреша́ть *imp.*, разреши́ть *perf.*; (*person*) уполномо́чивать *imp.*, уполномо́чить *perf.*

authorship *n.* а́вторство.

auto- *in comb.* а́вто-. **autobiographer** *n.* автобио́граф. **autobiographical** *adj.* автобиографи́ческий. **autobiography** *n.* автобиогра́фия. **autoclave** *n.* автокла́в. **autocracy** *n.* автокра́тия. **autocrat** *n.* автокра́т. **autocratic** *adj.* автократи́ческий. **autograph** *n.* авто́граф; *adj.* напи́санный руко́й а́втора; *v.t.* писа́ть (пишу́, -шешь) *imp.*, на ~ *perf.* авто́граф в + *prep.*, на + *prep.* **automatic** *adj.* автомати́ческий; *n.* автомати́ческий пистоле́т. **automation** *n.* автоматиза́ция. **automaton** *n.* автома́т. **autonomous** *adj.* автоно́мный. **autonomy** *n.* автоно́мия. **autopilot** *n.* автопило́т. **autopsy** *n.* вскры́тие трупа; ауто́псия. **autosuggestion** *n.* самовнуше́ние.

autumn *n.* о́сень. **autumn(al)** *adj.* осе́нний.

auxiliary *adj.* вспомога́тельный; *n.* помо́щник, -ица; (*gram.*) вспомога́тельный глаго́л; *pl.* вспомога́тельные войска́ *neut.pl.*

avail *n.*: of no *a.*, беспо́лезен (-зна); to no *a.*, напра́сно; *v.t.*: *a.* oneself of, по́льзоваться *imp.*, вос~ *perf.* + *instr.*

available *adj.* досту́пный, нали́чный; *predic.* налицо́, в нали́чии.

avalanche *n.* лави́на.

avarice *n.* жа́дность. **avaricious** *adj.* жа́дный (-ден, -дна́, -дно).

avenge *v.t.* мстить *imp.*, ото~ *perf.* за + *acc.* **avenger** *n.* мсти́тель *m.*

avenue *n.* (*of trees*) алле́я; (*wide street*) проспе́кт; (*approach*) путь (-ти́, -тём) *m.*

aver *v.t.* утвержда́ть *imp.*; заявля́ть *imp.*, заяви́ть (-влю́, -вишь) *perf.*

average *n.* сре́днее число́ (*pl.* -ла, -сел, -слам), сре́днее *sb.*; on an, the, *a.*, в сре́днем; *adj.* сре́дний; *v.t.* составля́ть *imp.* в сре́днем; де́лать *imp.* в сре́днем.

averse *adj.* нерасполо́женный (-ен), нескло́нный (-нен, -нна́, -нно); not *a.* to, не прочь + *inf.*, не проти́в + *gen.* **aversion** *n.* отвраще́ние. **avert** *v.t.* (*ward off*) предотвраща́ть *imp.*, предотврати́ть (-ащу́, -ати́шь) *perf.*; (*turn away*) отводи́ть (-ожу́, -о́дишь) *imp.*, отвести́ (отведу́, -дёшь; отвёл, -á) *perf.*

aviary *n.* пти́чник.

aviation *n.* авиа́ция. **aviator** *n.* лётчик.

avid *adj.* а́лчный, жа́дный (-ден, -дна́, -дно). **avidity** *n.* а́лчность, жа́дность.

avoid *v.t.* избега́ть *imp.*, избежа́ть (-егу́, -ежи́шь) *perf.* + *gen.*; уклоня́ться *imp.*, уклони́ться (-ню́сь, -ни́шься) *perf.* от + *gen.* **avoidance** *n.* избежа́ние, уклоне́ние.

avoirdupois *n.* эвердьюпо́йс.

avowal *n.* призна́ние.

await *v.t.* ждать (жду, ждёшь; ждал, -á, -о) *imp.* + *gen.*; to *a.* arrival, до востре́бования

awake *predic.*: be *a.*, не спать (сплю, спишь) *imp.*; be *a.* to, понима́ть *imp.*; stay *a.*, бо́дрствовать *imp.* **awake(n)** *v.t.* пробужда́ть *imp.*, пробуди́ть (-ужу́, -у́дишь) *perf.*; *v.i.* просыпа́ться *imp.*, просну́ться *perf.*

award *v.t.* присужда́ть *imp.*, присуди́ть (-ужу́, -у́дишь) *perf.*; награжда́ть *imp.*, награди́ть *perf.*; *n.* (*prize*) награ́да, пре́мия; (*decision*) присужде́ние.

aware *predic.*: be *a.* of, сознава́ть (-аю́, -аёшь) *imp.* + *acc.*; знать *imp.* + *acc.*

away *adv.* прочь; *far a. (from)*, далеко́ (от + *gen.*); *a. game*, игра́ (*pl.* -ры) на чужо́м по́ле; *a. team*, кома́нда госте́й.

awe *n.* благогове́йный страх; *stand in a. of*, испы́тывать *imp.* благогове́йный тре́пет пе́ред + *instr.*; *v.t.* внуша́ть *imp.*, внуши́ть *perf.* (благогове́йный) страх + *dat.*; *a.-struck*, преиспо́лненный (-ен) благогове́йного стра́ха, благогове́ния. **awful** *adj.* ужа́сный, стра́шный (-шен, -шна́, -шно, стра́шны). **awfully** *adv.* ужа́сно, о́чень, стра́шно.

awkward *adj.* нело́вкий (-вок, -вка́, -вко). **awkwardness** *n.* нело́вкость.

awl *n.* ши́ло (*pl.* -лья, -льев).

awning *n.* наве́с, тент.

awry *adv.* кри́во, на́бок; *go a.*, прова́литься (-ится) *perf.*

axe *n.* топо́р (-á); *v.t.* урéзывать, урезáть *imp.*, урéзать (-éжу, -éжешь) *perf.*

axial *adj.* осево́й.

axiom *n.* аксио́ма. **axiomatic** *adj.* аксиоматический.

axis, axle *n.* ось (*pl.* о́си, осе́й).

ay *interj.* да!; *n.* положи́тельный отве́т; *(in vote)* го́лос (*pl.* -á) „за"; *the ayes have it*, большинство́ „за".

azure *n.* лазу́рь; *adj.* лазу́рный.

B

B *n.* (*mus.*) си *neut.indecl.* **B.A.** *abbr.* бакала́вр.

babble *n.* (*voices*) болтовня́; (*water*) журча́ние; *v.i.* болта́ть *imp*; журча́ть (-чи́т) *imp.*

babel *n.* галдёж (-á); *tower of B.*, столпотворе́ние вавило́нское.

baboon *n.* павиа́н.

baby *n.* младе́нец (-нца); *b.-sitter*, приходя́щая ня́ня; *adj.* ма́лый (мал, -á, ма́ло, -ы), де́тский. **babyish** *adj.* ребя́ческий.

Bacchanalia *n.* вакхана́лия. **Bacchanalian** *adj.* вакхи́ческий. **Bacchante** *n.* вакха́нка.

bachelor *n.* холостя́к (-á); (*degree-holder*) бакала́вр; *adj.* холосто́й (-ост).

bacillus *n.* баци́лла.

back *n.* (*of body*) спина́ (*acc.* -ну; *pl.* -ны); (*rear*) за́дняя часть (*pl.* -ти, -те́й); (*reverse*) оборо́т; (*of book*) коре́шок (-шка́); (*of seat*) спи́нка; (*sport*) защи́тник; *adj.* за́дний; (*overdue*) просро́ченный (-ен); *v.t.* подде́рживать *imp.*, поддержа́ть (-жу́, -жишь) *perf.*; *v.i.* пя́титься *imp.* по~ *perf.*;

отступа́ть *imp.*, отступи́ть (-плю́, -пишь) *perf.*; *b. down*, уступа́ть *imp.*, уступи́ть (-плю́, -пишь) *perf.*; *b. out*, уклоня́ться *imp.*, уклони́ться (-ню́сь, -ни́шься) *perf.* (*of*, от + *gen.*). **back-biter** *n.* клеветни́к (-á). **backbiting** *n.* клевета́. **backbone** *n.* позвоно́чник; (*support*) гла́вная опо́ра; (*firmness*) твёрдость хара́ктера. **backer** *n.* лицо́ (*pl.* -ца), субсиди́рующее и́ли подде́рживающее предприя́тие; сторо́нник. **background** *n.* фон, за́дний план; (*person's*) воспита́ние, происхожде́ние, окруже́ние. **backside** *n.* зад (*loc.* -ý; *pl.* -ы́). **backslider** *n.* ренега́т, рецидиви́ст. **backward** *adj.* отста́лый; *adv.* наза́д. **backwash** *n.* отка́т (воды́). **backwater** *n.* за́водь, зато́н.

bacon *n.* бе́кон, груди́нка.

bacterium *n.* бакте́рия.

bad *adj.* плохо́й (плох, -á, -о, плохи́); (*food etc.*) испо́рченный (-ен); (*language*) гру́бый (груб, -á, -о); *b. taste*, безвку́сица.

badge *n.* значо́к (-чка́), эмбле́ма.

badger *n.* барсу́к (-á); *v.t.* пристава́ть (-таю́, -таёшь) *imp.*, приста́ть (-а́ну,

-а́нешь) *perf.* к+*dat.*; трави́ть (-влю́, -вишь) *imp.*, за~ *perf.*

badly *adv.* пло́хо; (*very much*) о́чень, си́льно.

baffle *v.t.* ста́вить *imp.*, по~ *perf.* в тупи́к; приводи́ть (-ожу́, -о́дишь) *imp.*, привести́ (-еду́, -едёшь; привёл, -а́) *perf.* в недоуме́ние; *n.* экра́н.

bag *n.* мешо́к (-шка́), су́мка; *v.t.* (*game*) убива́ть *imp.*, уби́ть (убью́, убьёшь) *perf.*; *v.i.* (*clothes*) сиде́ть (сиди́т) *imp.*, сесть (ся́дет; сел) *perf.* мешко́м.

baggage *n.* бага́ж (-á(ý)); *adj.* бага́жный.

baggy *adj.* мешкова́тый.

bagpipe *n.* волы́нка. **bagpiper** *n.* волы́нщик.

bail[1] *n.* (*security*) поручи́тельство, зало́г; (*surety*) поручи́тель, ~ница; *v.t.* (*b. out*) брать (беру́, -рёшь; брал, -á, -о) *imp.*, взять (возьму́, -мёшь; взял, -á, -о) *perf.* на пору́ки.

bail[2] *n.* (*cricket*) перекла́дина воро́т.

bail[3], **bale**[2] *v.t.* выче́рпывать *imp.*, вы́черпнуть *perf.* (во́ду из+*gen.*); *b. out*, *v.i.* выбра́сываться *imp.*, вы́броситься *perf.* с парашю́том. **bailer** *n.* черпа́к (-á).

bait *n.* нажи́вка; прима́нка (*also fig.*); (*fig.*) собла́зн; *v.t.* (*torment*) трави́ть (-влю́, -вишь) *imp.*, за~ *perf.*

baize *n.* ба́йка.

bake *v.t.* печь (пеку́, печёшь; пёк, -ла́) *imp.*, ис~ *perf.*; (*bricks*) обжига́ть *imp.*, обже́чь (обожгу́, -жжёшь; обжёг, обожгла́) *perf.* **baker** *n.* пе́карь *m.*, бу́лочник. **bakery** *n.* пека́рня (*gen.pl.* -рен), бу́лочная *sb.* **baking** *n.* пече́ние, вы́печка.

balance *n.* (*scales*) весы́ *m.pl.*; (*equilibrium*) равнове́сие; (*econ.*) бала́нс; (*remainder*) оста́ток (-тка); *b. sheet*, бала́нс; *v.t.* уравнове́шивать *imp.*, уравнове́сить *perf.*; (*econ.*) баланси́ровать *imp.*, с~ *perf.*

balcony *n.* балко́н.

bald *adj.* лы́сый (лыс, -á, -о), плеши́вый; *b. patch*, лы́сина.

baldness *n.* плеши́вость.

bale[1] *n.* (*bundle*) тюк (-á), ки́па; *v.t.* укла́дывать *imp.*, уложи́ть (-жу́, -жишь) *perf.* в тюки́, ки́пы.

bale[2] *see* **bail**[3].

baleful *adj.* па́губный, мра́чный (-чен, -чна́, -чно).

balk *n.* ба́лка; (*hindrance*) препя́тствие; *v.t.* препя́тствовать *imp.*, вос~ *perf.*+*dat.*

ball[1] *n.* (*sphere*) мяч (-á), шар (-á with 2, 3, 4; *pl.* -ы́), клубо́к (-бка́); *b. and socket*, шарово́й шарни́р; *b.-bearing*, шарикоподши́пник; *b.-point* (*pen*), ша́риковая ру́чка.

ball[2] *n.* (*dancing*) бал (*loc.* -ý; *pl.* -ы́).

ballad, ballade (*mus.*) *n.* балла́да.

ballast *n.* балла́ст (-а); *v.t.* грузи́ть (-ужу́, -у́зи́шь) *imp.*, за~, на~ *perf.* балла́стом.

ballerina *n.* балери́на.

ballet *n.* бале́т; *b.-dancer*, арти́ст, ~ ка, бале́та, танцо́вщик, -ица.

balloon *n.* возду́шный шар (-á with 2, 3, 4; *pl.* -ы́); *v.i.* раздува́ться *imp.*, разду́ться (-у́ется) *perf.*

ballot *n.* голосова́ние, баллотиро́вка; *b.-paper*, избира́тельный бюллете́нь *m.*; *v.i.* голосова́ть *imp.*, про~ *perf.*

ballyhoo *n.* шуми́ха.

balm *n.* бальза́м. **balmy** *adj.* (*fragrant*) души́стый; (*crazy*) тро́нутый.

baluster *n.* баля́сина. **balustrade** *n.* балюстра́да.

bamboo *n.* бамбу́к.

bamboozle *v.t.* одура́чивать *imp.*, одура́чить *perf.*

ban *n.* запре́т, запреще́ние; *v.t.* запреща́ть *imp.*, запрети́ть (-ещу́, -ети́шь) *perf.*

banal *adj.* бана́льный.

banana *n.* бана́н.

band *n.* (*strip*) о́бод (*pl.* обо́дья, -ьев), тесьма́, поло́ска, кайма́ (*gen.pl.* каём); (*of people*) гру́ппа; (*mus.*) орке́стр; (*radio*) полоса́ (*acc.* по́лосу; *pl.* -осы, -о́с, -оса́м) часто́т; *v.t.*: *b. together*, объединя́ть *imp.*, объедини́ться *perf.*

bandage *n.* бинт (-á), повя́зка; *v.t.* бинтова́ть *imp.*, за~ *perf.*

bandeau *n.* повя́зка, ободо́к (-дка́).

bandit *n.* банди́т.

bandoleer *n.* патронта́ш.

bandy *v.t.* (*throw about*) переб́расывать *imp.*, переб́роситься *perf.*+*instr.*

bandy-legged *adj.* кривоно́гий.

bane *n.* (*ruin*) ги́бель; (*poison*; *fig.*) отра́ва. **baneful** *adj.* ги́бельный, ядови́тый.

bang *n.* (*blow*) (си́льный) уда́р; (*noise*) (гро́мкий) стук; (*of gun*) вы́стрел; *v.t.* ударя́ть *imp.*, уда́рить *perf.*; хло́пать *imp.*, хло́пнуть *perf.*; стуча́ть (-чу́, -чи́шь) *imp.*, сту́кнуть *perf.*

bangle *n.* брасле́т.

banish *v.t.* изгоня́ть *imp.*, изгна́ть (-гоню́, -го́нишь) изгна́л, -á, -о) *perf.*; высыла́ть *imp.*, вы́слать (вы́шлю, -шлешь) *perf.* **banishment** *n.* изгна́ние, вы́сылка, ссы́лка.

banister *n.* пери́ла *neut.pl.*

banjo *n.* ба́нджо *neut.indecl.*

bank [1] *n.* (*of river*) бе́рег (*loc.* -ý; *pl.* -á); (*in sea*) о́тмель; (*of earth*) вал (*loc.* -ý; *pl.* -ы́); (*aeron.*) крен; *v.t.* сгреба́ть *imp.*, сгрести́ (-ебу́, -ебёшь; сгрёб, -лá) *perf.* в ку́чу.

bank [2] *n.* (*econ.*) банк, фонд; **b. holiday**, устано́вленный пра́здник; *v.i.* (*keep money*) держа́ть (-жу́, -жишь) *imp.* де́ньги (в ба́нке); *v.t.* (*put in bank*) класть (кладу́, -дёшь; клал) *imp.*, положи́ть (-жу́, -жишь) *perf.* в банк; **b. on**, полага́ться *imp.*, положи́ться (-жу́сь, -жишься) *perf.* на + *acc.*

bankrupt *n.* банкро́т; *adj.* обанкро́тившийся; *v.t.* доводи́ть (-ожу́, -о́дишь) *imp.*, довести́ (-еду́, -едёшь; -ёл, -елá) *perf.* до банкро́тства. **bankruptcy** *n.* банкро́тство.

banner *n.* зна́мя (*pl.* -ёна) *neut.*, флаг; **b. headline**, ша́пка.

bannister see **banister**.

banquet *n.* банке́т, пир (*loc.* -ý; *pl.* -ы́).

bantam *n.* банта́мка. **bantamweight** *n.* легча́йший вес.

banter *n.* подшу́чивание; *v.i.* шути́ть (шучу́, шу́тишь) *imp.*

baptism *n.* креще́ние. **baptize** *v.t.* крести́ть (-ещу́, -е́стишь) *imp.*, o ~ *perf.*

bar *n.* (*beam*) брус (*pl.* -ья, -ьев), полоса́ (*acc.* по́лосу; *pl.* -осы, -о́с -осáм); (*of chocolate*) пли́тка; (*of soap*) кусо́к (-скá); (*barrier*) прегра́да, барье́р; (*leg.*) колле́гия юри́стов; (*counter*) сто́йка, (*room*) бар; (*mus.*) такт; *v.t.* (*obstruct*) прегражда́ть *imp.*, прегра-

ди́ть *perf.*; (*prohibit*) запреща́ть *imp.*, запрети́ть (-ещу́, -ети́шь) *perf.*

barb *n.* зубе́ц (-бцá); **barbed wire**, колю́чая про́волока.

barbarian *n.* ва́рвар; *adj.* ва́рварский. **barbaric, barbarous** *adj.* ва́рварский, гру́бый (груб, -á, -о).

barber *n.* парикма́хер; **b.'s shop**, парикма́херская *sb.*

bard *n.* бард, певе́ц (-вцá).

bare *adj.* (*naked*) го́лый (гол, -á, -о); (*barefoot*) босо́й (бос, -á, -о); (*exposed*) обнажённый (-ён, -енá); (*unadorned*) неприкра́шенный (-ен); (*scanty*) минима́льный; *v.t.* обнажа́ть *imp.*, обнажи́ть *perf.*; **b. one's head**, снима́ть *imp.*, снять (сниму́, -мешь; снял, -á, -о) *perf.* шля́пу, ша́пку. **barefaced** *adj.* на́глый (нагл, -á, -о). **barely** *adv.* едва́, чуть не, е́ле-е́ле, лишь (с трудо́м).

bargain *n.* вы́годная сде́лка, дешёвая поку́пка; *v.i.* торгова́ться *imp.*, с ~ *perf.*

barge *n.* ба́ржа, ба́рка; *v.i.*: **b. into**, ната́лкиваться *imp.*, натолкну́ться *perf.* на + *acc.* **bargee** *n.* ло́дочник.

baritone *n.* барито́н.

barium *n.* ба́рий.

bark [1] *n.* (*sound*) лай; *v.i.* ла́ять (ла́ю, ла́ешь) *imp.*

bark [2] *n.* (*of tree*) кора́; *v.t.* сдира́ть *imp.*, содра́ть (сдеру́, -рёшь; содра́л, -á, -о) *perf.* ко́жу с + *gen.*

barley *n.* ячме́нь (-ня́) *m.*

barmaid *n.* буфе́тчица. **barman** *n.* ба́рмен, буфе́тчик.

barn *n.* амба́р.

barometer *n.* баро́метр. **barometric(al)** *adj.* барометри́ческий.

baron *n.* баро́н. **baroness** *n.* бароне́сса. **baronet** *n.* бароне́т. **baronial** *adj.* баро́нский.

baroque *n.* баро́кко *neut.indecl.*

barrack [1] *n.* каза́рма.

barrack [2] *v.t.* осви́стывать *imp.*, освиста́ть (-ищу́, -и́щешь) *perf.*

barrage *n.* загражде́ние, барра́ж.

barrel *n.* (*vessel*) бо́чка; (*of gun*) ду́ло; **b.-organ**, шарма́нка.

barren *adj.* беспло́дный.

barricade n. баррика́да, прегра́да; v.t. баррикади́ровать imp., за~ perf.

barrier n. барье́р, прегра́да, шлагба́ум.

barring prep. за исключе́нием + gen.

barrister n. адвока́т.

barrow[1] n. (tumulus) курга́н.

barrow[2] n. (cart) та́чка.

barter n. менова́я торго́вля; v.i. обме́ниваться imp., обменя́ться perf. това́рами.

base[1] adj. (low) ни́зкий (-зок, -зка́, -зко), по́длый (подл, -а́, -о); (metal, also fig.) низкопро́бный.

base[2] n. осно́ва, основа́ние, (also mil.) ба́за; v.t. осно́вывать imp., основа́ть (-ну́ю, -ну́ёшь) perf. **baseless** adj. необосно́ванный. **baseline** n. (sport) за́дняя ли́ния площа́дки. **basement** n. цо́кольный эта́ж (-а́), подва́л.

bash v.t. колоти́ть (-очу́, -о́тишь) imp., по~ perf.

bashful adj. засте́нчивый. **bashfulness** n. засте́нчивость.

basic adj. основно́й.

basil n. базили́к.

basin n. (vessel) ми́ска, таз (loc. -у́; pl. -ы́); (geog., geol.) бассе́йн; (pool) водоём.

basis n. ба́зис, осно́ва.

bask v.i. гре́ться imp.; (fig.) наслажда́ться imp., наслади́ться perf. (in, + instr.).

basket n. корзи́на, корзи́нка. **basketball** n. баскетбо́л; adj. баскетбо́льный.

bas-relief n. барелье́ф.

bass[1] n. (mus.) бас (pl. -ы́); adj. басо́вый; b. drum, большо́й бараба́н.

bass[2] n. (fish) о́кунь (pl. -ни, -не́й) m.

bassoon n. фаго́т.

bastard n. внебра́чный, побо́чный, ребёнок (-нка; pl. де́ти, дете́й); adj. незаконнорождённый.

baste[1] v.t. (tack) мета́ть imp., на~, с~ perf.

baste[2] v.t. (cul.) полива́ть imp., поли́ть (-лью, -льёшь) perf. жи́ром.

baste[3] v.t. (thrash) дуба́сить imp., от~ perf.

bastion n. бастио́н.

bat[1] n. (zool.) лету́чая мышь (pl. -ши, -ше́й).

bat[2] n. (sport) бита́; v.i. бить (бью, бьёшь) imp., по~ perf. по мячу́.

bat[3] v.t. (wink) морга́ть imp., моргну́ть perf. + instr., abs.

batch n. па́чка; (of loaves) вы́печка.

bated adj. уме́ренный (-ен); with b. breath, затаи́в дыха́ние.

bath n. (vessel) ва́нна; pl. пла́вательный бассе́йн; b. house, ба́ня; b. robe, купа́льный хала́т; v.t. купа́ть imp., вы́~, ис~ perf. **bathe** v.i. купа́ться imp., вы́~, ис~ perf.; v.t. омыва́ть imp., омы́ть (омо́ю, омо́ешь) perf. **bather** n. купа́льщик, -и́ца. **bathing** n. купа́ние; b. costume, купа́льный костю́м. **bathroom** n. ва́нная sb.

batiste n. бати́ст.

batman n. (mil.) денщи́к (-а́).

baton n. (mil.) жезл (-а́); (police) дуби́нка; (sport) эстафе́та; (mus.) дирижёрская па́лочка.

battalion n. батальо́н.

batten n. ре́йка; v.t. закола́чивать imp., заколоти́ть (-очу́, -о́тишь) perf. до́сками.

batter n. жи́дкое те́сто; v.t. разбива́ть imp., разби́ть (разобью́, -ьёшь) perf.; размозжи́ть perf.; battering-ram, тара́н.

battery n. (mil., tech.) батаре́я; (leg.) оскорбле́ние де́йствием.

battle n. би́тва, сраже́ние, бой (loc. бою́; pl. бой); adj. боево́й. **battlefield** n. по́ле (pl. -ля́) бо́я. **battlement** n. зубча́тая стена́ (acc. -ну; pl. -ны, -н, -на́м) **battleship** n. лине́йный кора́бль (-ля́) m., линко́р.

bauble n. безделу́шка.

bawdy adj. непристо́йный; b.-house, публи́чный дом (pl. -а́).

bawl v.i. ора́ть (ору́, орёшь) imp.

bay[1] n. (bot.) лавр(о́вое де́рево); pl. лавро́вый вено́к (-нка́), ла́вры m.pl.; adj. лавро́вый.

bay[2] n. (geog.) зали́в, бу́хта.

bay[3] n. (recess) ни́ша; b. window, фона́рь (-ря́) m.; sick b., лазаре́т.

bay[4] v.i. (bark) ла́ять (ла́ю, ла́ешь) imp.; (howl) выть (во́ю, во́ешь) imp.; n. лай; вой.

bay[5] adj. (colour) гнедо́й.

bayonet *n.* штык (-á); *v.t.* коло́ть (-лю́, -лешь) *imp.*, за~ *perf.* штыко́м.

bazaar *n.* база́р.

be[1] *v.* **1.** быть (*fut.* бу́ду, -дешь; был, -á, -о; не́ был, -á, -о): *usually omitted in pres.: he is a teacher,* он учи́тель; + *instr. or nom. in past and fut.: he was, will be, a teacher,* он был, бу́дет, учи́телем. **2.** (*exist*) существова́ть *imp.* **3.** (*frequentative*) быва́ть *imp.* **4.** (*be situated*) находи́ться (-ожу́сь, -о́дишься) *imp.: where is the information office?* где нахо́дится спра́вочное бюро́?; (*upright*) стоя́ть (-ою́, -ои́шь) *imp.: the piano is against the wall,* роя́ль стои́т у стены́; (*laid flat*) лежа́ть (-жу́, -жи́шь) *imp.: the letter is on the table,* письмо́ лежи́т на столе́. **5.** (*in general definitions*) явля́ться *imp.* + *instr.: Moscow is the capital of the USSR,* столи́цей СССР явля́ется го́род Москва́. **6.** *there is, are,* име́ется, име́ются; (*emph.*) есть.

be[2] *v.aux.* **1.** be + inf., *expressing duty, plan:* до́лжен (-жна́) + inf.: *he is to leave on Monday,* он до́лжен отпра́вится в понеде́льник. **2.** be + *past part. pass., expressing passive:* быть + *past part. pass. in short form: this was made by my son,* э́то бы́ло сде́лано мои́м сы́ном; *impersonal construction of 3 pl. + acc.: I was beaten,* меня́ би́ли; *reflexive construction: music was heard,* слы́шалась му́зыка. **3.** be + *pres. part. act., expressing continuous tenses: I am reading,* я чита́ю.

beach *n.* пляж, бе́рег (*loc.* -ý; *pl.* -á); *b.-head,* плацда́рм; *v.t.* выта́скивать *imp.*, вы́тащить *perf.* на бе́рег.

beacon *n.* мая́к (-á), сигна́льный ого́нь (огня́) *m.*

bead *n.* бу́сина; (*of liquid*) ка́пля (*gen. pl.* -пель); *pl.* бу́сы *f.pl.*

beadle *n.* церко́вный сто́рож (*pl.* -á).

beagle *n.* (коротконо́гая) го́нчая *sb.*

beak *n.* клюв.

beaker *n.* стака́н.

beam *n.* (*timber etc.*) ба́лка; (*ray*) луч (-á); (*naut.*) бимс; (*breadth*) ширина́; *v.t.* испуска́ть *imp.*, испусти́ть (-ущу́, -у́стишь) *perf.*; *v.i.* (*shine*) сия́ть *imp.*

bean *n.* фасо́ль, боб (-á).

bear[1] *n.* медве́дь *m.*, -дица; *Great, Little, B.,* Больша́я, Ма́лая, Медве́дица; *b.-cub,* медвежо́нок (-жо́нка; *pl.* -жа́та, -жа́т).

bear[2] *n.* (*carry*) носи́ть (ношу́, но́сишь) *indet.,* нести́ (несу́, -сёшь) нёс, -ла́) *det.,* по~ *perf.*; (*support*) подде́рживать *imp.,* поддержа́ть (-жу́, -жишь) *perf.*; (*endure*) терпе́ть (-плю́, -пишь) *imp.*; выноси́ть (-ошу́, -о́сишь) *imp.,* вы́нести (-су, -сешь; -с) *perf.*; (*give birth to*) рожда́ть *imp.,* роди́ть *imp.,* (роди́л, -á, -о) *perf.* **bearable** *adj.* сно́сный, терпи́мый.

beard *n.* борода́ (*acc.* -оду; *pl.* -оды, -о́д, -ода́м). **bearded** *adj.* борода́тый.

bearer *n.* носи́тель *m.*; (*of cheque*) предъяви́тель *m.*; (*of letter*) пода́тель *m.*

bearing *n.* ноше́ние; (*behaviour*) поведе́ние; (*relation*) отноше́ние; (*position*) пе́ленг; (*tech.*) подши́пник, опо́ра.

beast *n.* живо́тное *sb.*, зверь (*pl.* -ри, -ре́й) *m.*; (*fig.*) скоти́на *m.* & *f.* **beastly** *adj.* (*coll.*) проти́вный, отврати́тельный.

beat *n.* бой; (*round*) обхо́д; (*mus.*) такт; *v.t.* бить (бью, бьёшь) *imp.,* по~ *perf.*; (*cul.*) взбива́ть *imp.,* взбить (взобью́, -ьёшь) *perf.*; *b.* a *carpet,* выбива́ть *imp.,* вы́бить (-бью, -бьешь) *perf.* ковёр; *b. off,* отбива́ть *imp.,* отби́ть (отобью́, -ьёшь) *perf.*; *b. time,* отбива́ть *imp.,* отби́ть (отобью́, -ьёшь) *perf.* такт; *b. up,* избива́ть *imp.,* изби́ть (изобью́, -ьёшь) *perf.* **beating** *n.* битьё; (*defeat*) пораже́ние; бие́ние.

beatific *adj.* блаже́нный (-ён -е́нна).

beatify *v.t.* канонизи́ровать *imp., perf.* **beatitude** *n.* блаже́нство.

beau *n.* (*fop*) франт; (*ladies' man*) уха́жёр.

beautiful *adj.* краси́вый, прекра́сный. **beautify** *v.t.* украша́ть *imp.* укра́сить *perf.* **beauty** *n.* (*quality*) красота́; (*person*) краса́вица.

beaver *n.* (*animal*) бобр (-á); (*fur*) бобёр (-бра́), бобро́вый мех (-a(у), *loc.* -е & -ý; *pl.* -á).

becalmed adj.: be b. штилева́ть (-лю́ю, -лю́ешь) imp.

because conj. потому́ что, так как; adv.: b. of, из-за + gen.

beckon v.t. мани́ть (-ню́, -нишь) imp., по ~ perf. к себе́.

become v.i. станови́ться (-влю́сь, -вишься) imp., стать (-а́ну, -а́нешь) perf. + instr.; b. of, ста́ться (-а́нется) perf. с + instr. **becoming** adj. подоба́ющий, иду́щий к лицу́ + dat.

bed n. крова́ть, посте́ль; (garden) гря́дка; (sea) дно pl. до́нья, -ьев; (river) ру́сло; (geol.) пласт (-а́, loc. -у́). **bedclothes, bedding** n. посте́льное бельё. **bedridden** adj. прико́ванный (-на) к посте́ли боле́знью. **bedrock** n. материко́вая поро́да. **bedroom** n. спа́льня (gen.pl. -лен). **bedtime** n. вре́мя neut. ложи́ться спать.

bedeck v.t. украша́ть imp., укра́сить perf.

bedevil v.t. терза́ть imp.; му́чить imp., за ~ perf.

bedlam n. бедла́м, сумасше́дший дом.

bedraggled adj. заво́женный (-ен).

bee n. пчела́ (pl. -ёлы). **beehive** n. у́лей (у́лья).

beech n. бук.

beef n. говя́дина.

beer n. пи́во. **beer(y)** adj. пивно́й.

beet n. свёкла.

beetle[1] n. (tool) трамбо́вка, кува́лда.

beetle[2] n. (insect) жук (-а́).

beetle[3] adj. нависа́ющий.

beetroot n. свёкла.

befall v.t. & i. случа́ться imp., случи́ться perf. (+ dat.).

befit v.t. подходи́ть (-ит) imp., подойти́ (-ойдёт, -ошёл, -ошла́) perf. + dat.

before adv. пре́жде, ра́ньше; prep. пе́ред + instr., до + gen.; conj. до того́ как, пре́жде чем; (rather than) скоре́е чем; the day b. yesterday, позавчера́. **beforehand** adv. зара́нее, вперёд.

befriend v.t. ока́зывать imp., оказа́ть (-ажу́, -а́жешь) perf. дру́жескую по́мощь + dat.

beg v.t. ни́щенствовать imp.; v.t. (ask) проси́ть (-ошу́, -о́сишь) imp., по ~ perf.; (of dog) служи́ть (-и́т) imp.; b.

pardon, проси́ть (-ошу́, -о́сишь) imp. проще́ние.

beget v.t. порожда́ть imp., породи́ть perf.

beggar n. ни́щий sb.; v.t. разоря́ть imp., разори́ть perf. **beggarly** adj. ни́щенский.

beggarly adj. (poor) бе́дный (-ден, -дна́, -дно); (mean) жа́лкий (-лок, -лка́, -лко).

begin v.t. начина́ть imp., нача́ть (-чну́, -чнёшь; на́чал, -а́, -о) perf.; v.i. начина́ться imp., нача́ться (-чну́сь, -чнёшься; -ался́, -ала́сь) perf. **beginner** n. начина́ющий sb., новичо́к (-чка́). **beginning** n. нача́ло.

begonia n. бего́ния.

begrudge v.t. (spare) скупи́ться imp., по ~ perf. на + acc., + inf.

beguile v.t. (amuse) развлека́ть imp., развле́чь (-еку́, -ечёшь; -ёк, -екла́) perf.

behalf n.: on b. of, от и́мени + gen.; (in interest of) в по́льзу + gen.

behave v.i. вести́ (веду́, -дёшь; вёл, -а́) imp. себя́. **behaviour** n. поведе́ние.

behead v.t. обезгла́вливать imp., обезгла́вить perf.

behest n. заве́т.

behind adv., prep. сза́ди (+ gen.), позади́ (+ gen.), за (+ acc., instr.); n. зад (loc. -у́; pl. -ы́).

behold interj. се! **beholden** predic.: b. to, обя́зан + dat.

beige adj. беж indecl., бе́жевый.

being n. (existence) бытие́ (instr. -ие́м, prep. -ии́); (creature) существо́; for the time being, на не́которое вре́мя; вре́менно.

belabour v.t. бить (бью, бьёшь) imp., по ~ perf.

belated adj. запозда́лый.

belch n. отры́жка; v.i. рыга́ть imp., рыгну́ть perf.; v.t. изверга́ть imp., изве́ргнуть (-г(нул), -гла) perf.

beleaguer v.t. осажда́ть imp., осади́ть perf.

belfry n. колоко́льня (gen.pl. -лен).

belie v.t. противоре́чить imp. + dat.

belief n. (faith) ве́ра; (confidence) убежде́ние. **believable** adj. вероя́тный, правдоподо́бный. **believe** v.t. ве́рить *imp.*, по ~ *perf.* + *dat.*; *I b. so*, ка́жется так; *I b. not*, ду́маю, что нет; едва́ ли.

belittle *v.t.* умаля́ть *imp.*, умали́ть *perf.*

bell *n.* ко́локол (*pl.* -а́); (*small*) колоко́льчик, бубе́нчик; *b.-bottomed trousers*, брю́ки (-к) *pl.* с раструбами; *b.-ringer*, звона́рь (-ря́) *m.*; *b. tower*, колоко́льня (*gen.pl.* -лен).

belle *n.* краса́вица.

belles-lettres *n.* худо́жественная литерату́ра.

bellicose *adj.* войнственный (-ен, -енна), агресси́вный. **belligerency** *n.* войнственность. **belligerent** *n.* вою́ющая сторона́ (*acc.* -ону; *pl.* -оны, -о́н, -она́м); *adj.* вою́ющий.

bellow *n.* мыча́ние, рёв; *v.t.* & *i.* мыча́ть (-чу́, -чи́шь) *imp.*; реве́ть (-ву́, -вёшь) *imp.*

bellows *n.* мехи́ *m.pl.*

belly *n.* живо́т (-а́); (*bowels*) брю́хо (*pl.* -хи).

belong *v.i.* принадлежа́ть (-жу́, -жи́шь) *imp.* (*to*, (к) + *dat.*). **belongings** *n.* пожи́тки (-ков) *pl.*, ве́щи (-ще́й) *f.pl.*

beloved *adj.* люби́мый, возлю́бленный (-ен, -енна).

below *adv.* вниз, внизу́, ни́же; *prep.* ни́же + *gen.*

belt *n.* (*strap*) по́яс (*pl.* -а́), реме́нь (-мня́); (*zone*) зо́на, полоса́ (*acc.* -осу́; *pl.* -осы, -о́с, -оса́м); *v.t.* подпоя́сывать *imp.*, подпоя́сать (-я́шу -я́шешь) *perf.*; (*thrash*) поро́ть (-рю́, -решь) *imp.*, вы ~ *perf.* ремнём.

bench *n.* (*seat*) скамья́ (*pl.* ска́мьи́, -ме́й), скаме́йка; (*for work*) стано́к (-нка́); (*court*) полице́йские судьи (*gen.* -де́й) *pl.*; (*parl.*) ме́сто (*pl.* -та́); *back benches*, скамьи́ рядовы́х чле́нов парла́мента.

bend *n.* сгиб, изги́б, накло́н; *v.t.* сгиба́ть *imp.*, согну́ть *perf.*

beneath *prep.* под + *instr.*

benediction *n.* благослове́ние.

benefaction *n.* ми́лость, дар (*pl.* -ы́). **benefactor** *n.* благоде́тель *m.* **benefactress** *n.* благоде́тельница.

benefice *n.* бенефи́ция. **beneficence** *n.* благодея́ние, милосе́рдие. **beneficent** *adj.* благотво́рный, поле́зный.

beneficial *adj.* поле́зный, вы́годный. **beneficiary** *n.* лицо́ (*pl.* -ца), получаю-

щее дохо́ды; (*in will*) насле́дник.

benefit *n.* по́льза, вы́года; (*allowance*) посо́бие; (*theat.*) бенефи́с; *v.t.* приноси́ть (-ошу́, -о́сишь) *imp.*, принести́ (-есу́, -есёшь; -ёс, -есла́) *perf.* по́льзу + *dat.*; *v.i.* извлека́ть *imp.*, извле́чь (-еку́, -ечёшь; -ёк, -екла́) *perf.* вы́году.

benevolence *n.* благожела́тельность, благодея́ние. **benevolent** *adj.* благоскло́нный (-нен, -нна), благотвори́тельный.

benign *adj.* до́брый (добр, -а́, -о, -ы́), мя́гкий (мя́гок, мягка́, мя́гко, мя́гки); (*of tumour*) доброка́чественный (-нен, -нна).

bent *n.* скло́нность, накло́нность.

benumbed *adj.* окочене́вший, оцепене́лый.

benzene *n.* бензо́л.

bequeath *v.t.* завеща́ть *imp.*, *perf.* (+ *acc.* & *dat.*). **bequest** *n.* насле́дство, посме́ртный дар (*pl.* -ы́).

berate *v.t.* руга́ть *imp.*, вы ~ *perf.*

bereave *v.t.* лиша́ть *imp.*, лиши́ть *perf.* (*of*, + *gen.*). **bereavement** *n.* поте́ря (бли́зкого).

berry *n.* я́года.

berserk *adj.* нейстовый; *go b.*, нействовать *imp.*

berth *n.* (*bunk*) ко́йка; (*naut.*) стоя́нка; *give a wide b. to*, обходи́ть (-ожу́, -о́дишь) *imp.*; избега́ть *imp.*, избе́гнуть (избе́г(нул), -гла) *perf.* + *gen.*; *v.t.* ста́вить *imp.*, по ~ *perf.* на я́корь, на прича́л.

beryl *n.* бери́лл.

beseech *v.t.* умоля́ть *imp.*, умоли́ть *perf.* **beseeching** *adj.* умоля́ющий.

beset *v.t.* осажда́ть *imp.*, осади́ть *perf.*

beside *prep.* о́коло + *gen.*, во́зле + *gen.*, ря́дом с + *instr.*; *b. the point*, некста́ти; *b. oneself*, вне себя́. **besides** *adv.* кро́ме того́, помимо; *prep.* кро́ме + *gen.*

besiege *v.t.* осажда́ть *imp.*, осади́ть *perf.*

besom *n.* садо́вая метла́ (*pl.* мётлы, -тел, -тлам), ве́ник.

besotted *adj.* одуре́лый.

bespoke *adj.* зака́занный (-ан); *b. tailor*, портно́й *sb.*, рабо́тающий на зака́з.

best *adj.* лу́чший, са́мый лу́чший; *adv.* лу́чше всего́, бо́льше всего́; *do one's b.*, де́лать *imp.*, с ~ *perf.* всё возможное; *b. man*, шáфер (*pl.* -á); *b. seller*, ходкая книга.

bestial *adj.* скóтский, звéрский. **bestiality** *n.* скóтство, звéрство.

bestow *v.t.* даровáть *imp.*, *perf.*

bestride *v.t.* (*sit*) сидéть (сижу, сидишь) *imp.* верхóм на + *prep.*; (*stand*) стоять (-óю, -óишь) *imp.*, расстáвив нóги над + *instr.*

bet *n.* пари́ *neut.indecl.*; (*stake*) стáвка; *v.t.* держáть (-жу, -жишь) *imp.* пари́ (on, на + *acc.*). **betting** *n.* заключéние пари́.

betide *v.t. & i.* случáться *imp.*, случи́ться *perf.* (+ *dat.*); *whate'er b.*, что бы ни случи́лось; *woe b. you*, гóре тебé.

betray *v.t.* изменять (-ню, -нишь) *perf.* + *dat.*; предавáть (-даю, -даёшь) *imp.*, предáть (-áм, -áшь, -áст, -ади́м; прéдал, -á, -о) *perf.* **betrayal** *n.* измéна, предáтельство.

betroth *v.t.* обручáть *imp.*, обручи́ть *perf.* **betrothal** *n.* обручéние.

better *adj.* лу́чший; *adv.* лу́чше; (*more*) бóльше; *v.t.* улучшáть *imp.*, улу́чшить *perf.*; *get the b. of*, брать (беру́, -рёшь; брал, -á, -о) *imp.*, взять (возьму́, -мёшь; взял, -á, -о) *perf.* верх над + *instr.*; *had b.: you had b. go*, вам (*dat.*) лу́чше бы пойти́; *think b. of*, передумывать *imp.*, передумать *perf.* **betterment** *n.* улучшéние.

between, betwixt *prep.* между + *instr.*

bevel *n.* (*tool*) мáска.

beverage *n.* напи́ток (-тка).

bevy *n.* собрáние, компáния.

bewail *v.t.* сокрушáться *imp.*, сокруши́ться *perf.* о + *prep.*

beware *v.i.* остерегáться *imp.*, остерéчься (-егу́сь, -ежёшься; -ёгся, -еглáсь) *perf.* (of, + *gen.*).

bewilder *v.t.* сбивáть *imp.*, сбить (собью́, -ьёшь) *perf.* с тóлку. **bewildered** *adj.* смущённый (-ён, -енá), озадáченный (-ен). **bewilderment** *n.* смущéние, замешáтельство.

bewitch *v.t.* заколдóвывать *imp.*, заколдовáть *perf.*; очарóвывать *imp.*, очаровáть *perf.* **bewitching** *adj.* очаровáтельный.

beyond *prep.* за + *acc.*, *instr.*, по ту стóрону + *gen.*; (*above*) сверх + *gen.*;

(*outside*) вне + *gen.*; *the back of b.*, глушь (-ши́), край (*loc.* -аю́) свéта.

bias *n.* (*inclination*) уклóн; (*prejudice*) предубеждéние; *to cut on the b.*, кроить *imp.*, с ~ *perf.* по косóй. **biased** *adj.* предубеждённый (-ён, -енá).

bib *n.* нагру́дник.

Bible *n.* Би́блия. **biblical** *adj.* библéйский.

bibliography *n.* библиогрáфия.

bibliophile *n.* библиофи́л.

bibulous *adj.* пьянствующий.

bicarbonate (*of soda*) *n.* сóда.

bicentenary *n.* двухсотлéтие; *adj.* двухсотлéтний.

biceps *n.* би́цепс, двуглáвая мышца.

bicker *v.i.* пререкáться *imp.*; препирáться *imp.* **bickering** *n.* пререкáния *neut. pl.*, ссóры *f. pl.* из-за мелочéй.

bicycle *n.* велосипéд.

bid *n.* предложéние цены, зая́вка; *v.t. & i.* предлагáть *imp.*, предложи́ть (-жу́, -жишь) *perf.* (цéну) (for, за + *acc.*); *v.t.* (*command*) прикáзывать *imp.*, приказáть (-ажу́, -áжешь) *perf.* + *dat.* **bidding** *n.* предложéние цены, торги́ *m. pl.*; (*command*) приказáние.

bide *v.t.: b. one's time*, ожидáть *imp.* подходя́щего момéнта.

biennial *adj.* двухлéтний; *n.* двухлéтник.

bier *n.* (*похорóнные*) дрóги (-г) *pl.*

bifocal *adj.* двухфóкусный.

big *adj.* большóй, кру́пный (-пен, -пнá, -пно, кру́пны); (*important*) вáжный (-жен, -жнá, -жно, вáжны); *b. business*, дéло большóго масштáба; *b. end*, бóльшая, ни́жняя, кривоши́пная головка; *b. name*, знамени́тость; *b. noise*, ши́шка; *b. top*, цирк; *talk b.*, хвáстаться *imp.*

bigamist *n.* (*man*) двоежéнец (-нца), (*woman*) двуму́жница. **bigamous** *adj.* двубрáчный. **bigamy** *n.* двубрáчие.

bike *n.* велосипéд.

bikini *n.* бики́ни *neut.indecl.*

bilateral *adj.* двусторóнний.

bilberry *n.* черни́ка.

bile *n.* жёлчь. **bilious** *adj.* жёлчный.

bilge *n.* (*sl.*) ерунда́.

bilingual *adj.* двуязы́чный. **bilingualism** *n.* двуязы́чие.

bill n. (account) счёт (pl. -á); (draft of law) законопроéкт; (b. of exchange) вéксель (pl. -ля); (theat.) програ́мма; (poster) афи́ша; v.t. (announce) объявля́ть imp., объяви́ть (-влю́, -вишь) perf. в афи́шах; раскле́ивать imp., раскле́ить perf. афи́ши + gen.; b. of fare, меню́ neut.indecl.; b. of health, санита́рное удостовере́ние; b. of lading, накладна́я sb.; B. of Rights, билль m. о права́х.

billet n. помеще́ние для посто́я, кварти́ры f.pl.; v.t. расквартиро́вывать imp., расквартирова́ть perf.; billeting officer, кварти́рьер.

billhead n. бланк.

billiard-ball n. билья́рдный шар (-á with 2, 3, 4; pl. -ы). **billiard-cue** n. кий (ки́я; pl. кии́). **billiard-room** n. билья́рдная sb. **billiard-table, billiards** n. билья́рд.

billion n. биллио́н.

billow n. больша́я волна́ (pl. -ны, -н, -на́м), вал (loc. -у́; pl. -ы́); v.i. вздыма́ться imp. **billowy** adj. вздыма́ющийся, волни́стый.

billposter n. раскле́йщик афи́ш.

bimonthly adj. (twice a month) выходя́щий два ра́за в ме́сяц; (every two months) выходя́щий раз в два ме́сяца.

bin n. (refuse) му́сорное ведро́ (pl. вёдра, -дер, -драм); (corn) за́кром (pl. -á), ларь (-ря́) m.

bind v.t. (tie) свя́зывать imp., связа́ть (-яжу́, -яжешь) perf.; (oblige) обя́зывать imp., обяза́ть (-яжу́, -яжешь) perf.; (book) переплета́ть imp., переплести́ (-ету́, -етёшь; -ёл, -ела́) perf. **binder** n. (person) переплётчик, -ица; (agr.) вяза́льщик; (for papers) па́пка. **binding** n. (book) переплёт; (braid) опто́рочка. **bindweed** n. вьюно́к (-нка́).

binge n. кутёж (-á).

bingo n. би́нго neut.indecl.

binoculars n. бино́кль m.

binomial adj. двучле́нный.

biochemical adj. биохими́ческий. **biochemist** n. биохи́мик. **biochemistry** n. биохи́мия. **biographer** n. био́граф. **biographical** adj. биографи́ческий. **biography** n. биогра́фия, жизнеописа́ние. **biological** adj. биологи́ческий.

biologist n. био́лог. **biology** n. биоло́гия.

bipartisan adj. двухпарти́йный. **bipartite** adj. двусторо́нний. **biped** n. двуно́гое живо́тное sb. **biplane** n. бипла́н.

birch n. (tree) берёза; (rod) ро́зга (gen.pl. -зог); v.t. сечь (секу́, сечёшь; сек, -ла́) imp., вы~ perf. ро́згой.

bird n. пти́ца; b. of passage, перелётная пти́ца; b. of prey, хи́щная пти́ца; b.'s-eye view, вид с пти́чьего полёта.

birth n. рожде́ние; (origin) происхожде́ние; b. certificate, метри́ка; b. control, противозача́точные ме́ры f.pl. **birthday** n. день (дня) m. рожде́ния. **birthplace** n. ме́сто (pl. -тá) рожде́ния. **birthright** n. пра́во по рожде́нию.

biscuit n. сухо́е пече́нье.

bisect v.t. разреза́ть imp., разре́зать (-éжу, -éжешь) perf. попола́м.

bishop n. епи́скоп; (chess) слон (-á). **bishopric** n. епа́рхия.

bismuth n. ви́смут.

bison n. бизо́н.

bit[1] n. (tech.) сверло́ (pl. -ёрла), бура́в (-á); (bridle) удила́ (-л) pl.

bit[2] n. (piece) кусо́чек (-чка); до́ля (pl. -ли, -лéй); a b., немно́го; not a b., ничу́ть.

bitch n. су́ка.

bite n. уку́с; (fishing) клёв; v.t. куса́ть imp., укуси́ть (-ушу́, -у́сишь) perf.; (fish) клева́ть (клюёт) imp., клю́нуть perf. **biting** adj. е́дкий (е́док, едка́, е́дко), ре́зкий (-зок, -зка́, -зко).

bitter adj. го́рький (-рек, -рька́, -рько). **bitterness** n. го́речь.

bittern n. выпь.

bitumen n. биту́м. **bituminous** adj. биту́м(ин)озный.

bivouac n. бива́к.

bi-weekly adj. (twice a week) выходя́щий два ра́за в неде́лю; (fortnightly) выходя́щий раз в две неде́ли, двухнеде́льный.

bizarre adj. стра́нный (-нен, -нна́ -нно), причу́дливый.

blab v.t. выба́лтывать imp., вы́болтать perf.

black adj. чёрный (-рен, -рна́); (dark-skinned) черноко́жий; b. currant, чёрная сморо́дина; *b. eye*, подби́тый глаз (*pl.* -á, глаз, -áм), фонáрь (-ря́) *m. n.* (*Negro*) чёрный *sb.*; (*mourning*) тра́ур. **blackberry** *n.* ежеви́ка (*collect.*). **blackbird** *n.* чёрный дрозд (-á). **blackboard** *n.* кла́ссная доска́ (*acc.* -ску́; *pl.* -ски, -сóк, -скáм). **blacken** *v.t.* черни́ть *imp.*, за~, на~, (*fig.*) о~ *perf.* **blackguard** *n.* поллéц (-á), мерзáвец (-вца). **blackleg** *n.* штрейкбрéхер. **blackmail** *n.* шантáж (-á); *v.t.* шантажи́ровать *imp.*

bladder *n.* пузы́рь (-ря́) *m.*

blade *n.* (*knife etc.*) лéзвие, клинóк (-нкá); (*oar etc.*) лóпасть (*pl.* -ти, -тéй); (*grass*) были́нка.

blame *n.* винá, порицáние; *v.t.* вини́ть *imp.* (*for*, в + *prep.*); *be to b.*, быть винова́тым. **blameless** *adj.* безупрéчный, неви́нный (-нен, -нна).

blanch *v.t.* бели́ть *imp.*, вы~ *perf.*; (*food*) обва́ривать *imp.*, обвари́ть (-рю́, -ришь) *perf.*; *v.i.* бледнéть *imp.*, по~ *perf.*

bland *adj.* мя́гкий (-гок, -гкá, -гко, мя́гки); (*in manner*) вéжливый.

blandishment *n.*: *pl.* льсти́вые рéчи (-чéй) *pl.*

blank *n.* (*space*) пробéл; (*form*) бланк; (*ticket*) пустóй билéт; *adj.* пустóй (пуст, -á, -о, -ы́); незапóлненный (-ен); чи́стый (чист, -á, -о, чи́сты́); *b. cartridge*, холостóй патрóн; *b. wall*, глухáя стенá (*acc.* -ну; *pl.* -ны, -нáм); *b. verse*, бéлый стих (-á).

blanket *n.* одея́ло.

blare *n.* звук трубы́; *v.i.* труби́ть *imp.*, про~ *perf.*; (*shout*) орáть (орý, орёшь) *imp.*

blasphemous *adj.* богохýльный. **blasphemy** *n.* богохýльство.

blast *n.* (*wind*) порýв вéтра; (*air*) струя́ (*pl.* -ýи); (*sound*) гудóк (-дкá); (*of explosion*) взрывнáя волнá (*pl.* -ны, -н, -нáм); *v.t.* взрывáть *imp.*, взорвáть (-вý, -вёшь; взорвáл, -á, -о) *perf.*; *b. off*, стартовáть *imp.*, *perf.*; взлетáть *imp.*, взлетéть (-ечý, -ети́шь) *perf.*; *b.-furnace*, дóменная печь (*pl.* -чи, -чéй). **blatant** *adj.* (*clear*) я́вный; (*flagrant*) вопию́щий.

blaze[1] *n.* (*flame*) я́ркое плáмя *neut.*; (*light*) я́ркий свет; *v.i.* (*flame*) пылáть *imp.*; (*with light*) сверкáть *imp.*

blaze[2] *v.t.* (*mark*) мéтить *imp.*, на~ *perf.*; *b. the trail*, прокла́дывать *imp.* путь.

blazer *n.* спорти́вная кýртка.

bleach *n.* хлóрная и́звесть; *v.t.* бели́ть *imp.*, вы́~ *perf.* **bleaching** *n.* отбéливание, белéние.

bleak *adj.* (*bare*) оголённый (-ён, -енá); (*dreary*) уны́лый.

bleary *adj.* мýтный (-тен, -тнá, -тно, мýтны), затумáненный (-ен); *b.-eyed*, с затумáненными глазáми.

bleat *v.i.* блéять (-éю, -éешь) *imp.*; *n.* блéяние.

bleed *v.i.* кровоточи́ть *imp.*; *v.t.* пускáть *imp.*, пусти́ть (пущý, пýстишь) *perf.* кровь + *dat.*; *n.* кровотечéние; кровопускáние; *my heart bleeds*, сéрдце обливáется крóвью.

bleep *n.* бип.

blemish *n.* недостáток (-тка), пятнó (*pl.* -тна, -тен, -тнам), порóк; *without b.*, непорóчный, незапя́танный (-ан).

blench *v.i.* вздрóгнуть *perf.*

blend *n.* смесь; *v.t.* смéшивать *imp.*, смешáть *perf.*; *v.i.* гармони́ровать *imp.* **blender** *n.* смеси́тель *m.*

bless *v.t.* благословля́ть *imp.*, благослови́ть *perf.* **blessed** *adj.* благословéнный (-ён, -éнна), счастли́вый (счáстлив). **blessing** *n.* (*action*) благословéние; (*object*) благо.

blind *adj.* слепóй (слеп, -á, -о); *b. alley*, тупи́к (-á); *b. flying*, слепóй полёт; *n.* штóра; *v.t.* ослепля́ть *imp.*, ослепи́ть *perf.*

blink *v.i.* мигáть *imp.*, мигнýть *perf.*; моргáть *imp.*, моргнýть *perf.*; *n.* мигáние. **blinkers** *n.* шóры (-р) *pl.*

blip *n.* сигнáл на экрáне.

bliss *n.* блажéнство. **blissful** *adj.* блажéнный (-ён, -éнна).

blister *n.* пузы́рь (-ря́) *m.*, волды́рь (-ря́) *m.*; *v.i.* покрывáться *imp.*, покры́ться (-рóюсь, -рóешься) *perf.* пузыря́ми, волдыря́ми; *v.t.* вызывáть *imp.*, вы́звать (-зовет) *perf.* пузы́рь, волды́рь на + *prep.*, на кóже + *gen.*

blithe *adj.* весёлый (весел, -а, -от весёлы); (*carefree*) беспечный.
blitz *n.* стремительное нападение; (*aerial*) стремительный налёт. **blitzkrieg** *n.* молниеносная война.
blizzard *n.* метель, вьюга.
bloated *adj.* надутый, раздутый.
bloater *n.* копчёная селёдка.
blob *n.* (*liquid*) капля (*gen.pl.* -пель); (*spot*) пятнышко (*pl.* -шки, -шек, -шкам).
bloc *n.* блок.
block *n.* (*of wood*) чурбан, колода; (*of stone*) глыба; (*obstruction*) затор; (*traffic*) пробка; (*tech.*) блок; (*b. of flats*) жилой дом (*pl.* -á); *b.* and tackle, тали (-лей) *pl.*; *b.* letters, печатные буквы *f.pl.*; *v.t.* преграждать *imp.*, преградить *perf.*; *b.* out, набрасывать *imp.*, набросать *perf.* вчерне.
blockade *n.* блокада; *v.t.* блокировать *imp.*, *perf.*
blockage *n.* затор.
blond *n.* блондин, ~ка; *adj.* белокурый.
blood *n.* кровь (*loc.* -ви; *pl.* -ви, -вей); (*descent*) происхождение; *b.* bank, хранилище крови и плазмы; *b.*-donor, донор; *b.* orange, королёк (-лька́); *b.*-poisoning, заражение крови; *b.* pressure, кровяное давление; *b.*-relation, близкий родственник, -ица; *b.* transfusion, переливание крови; *b.*-vessel, кровеносный сосуд. **bloodhound** *n.* ищейка. **bloodless** *adj.* бескровный. **bloody** *adj.* кровавый, окровавленный (-ен).
bloom *n.* расцвет; *v.i.* расцветать *imp.*, расцвести (-ету, -етёшь; -ёл, -ела) *perf.*
blossom *n.* цветок (-тка; *pl.* цветы); *collect.* цвет; *in b.*, в цвету.
blot *n.* клякса; пятно (*pl.* -тна, -тен, -тнам); *v.t.* промокать *imp.*, промокнуть *perf.*; пачкать *imp.*, за~ *perf.*
blotch *n.* пятно (*pl.* -тна, -тен, -тнам). **blotchy** *adj.* запятнанный (-ан).
blotter, blotting-paper *n.* промокательная бумага.
blouse *n.* кофточка, блузка.
blow[1] *n.* удар.
blow[2] *v.i.* & *t.* дуть (дую, дуешь) *imp.*;

веять (веет) *imp.*; выдувать *imp.*, выдуть (-ую, -уешь) *perf.*; *b. away*, сносить (-ошу, -осишь) *imp.*, снести (-есу, -есёшь; снёс, -ла) *perf.*; *b. down*, сваливать *imp.*, свалить (-лю, -лишь) *perf.*; *b. up*, взрывать *imp.*, взорвать (-ву, -вёшь; взорвал, -а, -о) *perf.*; *b.-up*, фотоснимок *neut.indecl.* **blow-lamp** *n.* паяльная лампа.
blubber[1] *n.* ворвань.
blubber[2] *v.i.* реветь (-ву, -вёшь) *imp.*
bludgeon *n.* дубинка.
blue *adj.* (*dark*) синий (-нь, -ня, -не); (*light*) голубой; *n.* синий, голубой, цвет; (*sky*) небо. **bluebell** *n.* колокольчик. **bluebottle** *n.* синяя муха. **blueprint** *n.* синька, светокопия.
bluff[1] *n.* (*cliff*) отвесный берег (*loc.* -у́; *pl.* -á); *adj.* (*person*) грубовато-добродушный.
bluff[2] *n.* (*deceit*) обман, блеф; *v.i.* притворяться *imp.*, притвориться *perf.*
blunder *n.* грубая ошибка; *v.i.* ошибаться *imp.*, ошибиться (-бусь, -бёшься; -бся) *perf.*; (*stumble*) спотыкаться *imp.*, споткнуться *perf.*
blunt *adj.* (*knife*) тупой (туп, -á, -о, тупы); (*person*) прямой (прям, -á, -о, прямы); (*words*) резкий (-зок, -зка, -зко); *v.t.* тупить (-плю, -пишь) *imp.*, за~, ис~ *perf.*; притуплять *imp.*, притупить (-плю, -пишь) *perf.*
blur *n.* расплывчатая форма; *v.t.* туманить *imp.*, за~ *perf.*; изглаживать *imp.*, изгладить *perf.*
blurb *n.* рекламная надпись (на суперобложке).
blurred *adj.* расплывчатый, неясный (-сен, -сна, -сно, неясны).
blurt *v.t.*: *b. out*, выбалтывать *imp.*, выболтать *perf.*
blush *v.i.* краснеть *imp.*, по~ *perf.*; зардеться *perf.*; *n.* румянец (-нца).
bluster *v.i.* бушевать (-шую, -шуешь) *imp.*; *n.* пустые угрозы *f.pl.*
boa *n.* боа *m.indecl.* (*snake*), *neut.indecl.* (*wrap*); *b. constrictor*, удав.
boar *n.* боров (*pl.* -ы, -ов); (*wild*) вепрь *m.*
board *n.* доска (*acc.* -ску; *pl.* -ски, -сок, -скам); (*table*) стол (-á); (*food*) питание; (*committee*) правление, со-

вёт; *pl.* сцéна, подмóстки (-ков) *pl.*; (*naut.*) борт (*loc.* -ý; *pl.* -á); on b., на борт(ý); *v.i.* столовáться *imp.*; *v.t.* сади́ться *imp.*, сесть (сяду, -дешь; сел) *perf.* (на корáбль, в пóезд и т.д.); (*naut.*) брать (берý, -рёшь; брал, -á, -о) *imp.*, взять (возьмý, -мёшь; взял, -á, -о) *perf.* на абордáж. **boarder** *n.* пансионéр. **boarding-house** *n.* пансиóн. **boarding-school** *n.* интернáт.

boast *v.i.* хвастáться *imp.*, по~ *perf.*; *v.t.* горди́ться *imp.*+*instr.*; *n.* хвастовствó. **boaster** *n.* хвастýн (-á). **boastful** *adj.* хвастли́вый.

boat *n.* лóдка, сýдно (*pl.* -дá, -дóв), корáбль (-ля́) *m.*; b. building, судострóение; b.-hook, багóр (-грá). **boatswain** *n.* бóцман.

bob[1] *n.* (*weight*) баланси́р; (*hair*) стри́жка волóс, покрывáющая ýши.

bob[2] *v.i.* подпры́гивать *imp.*, подпры́гнуть *perf.*

bobbin *n.* катýшка, шпýлька.

bobby *n.* полисмéн, бóбби *m.indecl.*

bobsleigh *n.* бóбслéй.

bobtail *n.* обрéзанный хвост (-á).

bode *v.t.* предвещáть *imp.*

bodice *n.* лиф, корсáж.

bodily *adv.* целикóм; *adj.* телéсный, физи́ческий.

bodkin *n.* тупáя иглá (*pl.* -лы).

body *n.* тéло (*pl.* -лá), тýловище; (*corpse*) труп; (*frame*) óстов; (*troops etc.*) кóрпус (*pl.* -á); (*carriage*) кýзов (*pl.* -á); (*main part*) основнáя часть. **bodyguard** *n.* телохрани́тель *m.*; *collect.* кóрпус телохрани́телей.

bog *n.* болóто, трясина; get bogged down, увязáть *imp.*, увязнуть (-з) *perf.* **boggy** *adj.* болóтистый.

bogus *adj.* поддéльный, фальши́вый.

bogy *n.* пýгало.

boil[1] *n.* (*med.*) фурýнкул, нары́в.

boil[2] *v.i.* кипéть (-пи́т) *imp.*, вс~ *perf.*; *v.t.* кипяти́ть *imp.*, с~ *perf.*; (*cook*) вари́ть (-рю́, -ришь) *imp.*, с~ *perf.*; *n.* кипéние; bring to the b., доводи́ть (-ожý, -óдишь) *imp.*, довести́ (-едý, -едёшь; -ёл, -елá) *perf.* до кипéния. **boiled** *adj.* варёный, кипячёный. **boiler** *n.* (*vessel*) котёл (-тлá); (*fowl*) кýрица гóдная для вáрки; b. house, котéльная

sb.; b. suit, комбинезóн. **boiling** *n.* кипéние; *adj.* кипя́щий; b. water, кипятóк (-ткá).

boisterous *adj.* бýрный (-рен, бýрнá, -рно), шумли́вый.

bold *adj.* смéлый (смел, -á, -о), хрáбрый (храбр, -á, -о, хрáбры́), дéрзкий (-зок, -зкá, -зко); (*clear*) чёткий (-ток, -ткá, -тко); (*type*) жи́рный.

bole *n.* ствол (-á).

bolster *n.* вáлик; *v.t.*: b. up, подпирáть *imp.*, подпéреть (подопрý, -рёшь; подпёр) *perf.*

bolt *n.* засóв, задви́жка; (*tech.*) болт (-á); (*flight*) бéгство; *v.t.* запирáть *imp.*, запереть (-прý, -прёшь; зáпер, -лá, -ло) *perf.* на засóв; скрепля́ть *imp.*, скрепи́ть *perf.* болтáми; *v.i.* (*flee*) удирáть *imp.*, удрáть (удерý, -рёшь; удрáл, -á, -о) *perf.*; (*horse*) понести́ (-сёт; ёс, -еслá) *perf.*

bomb *n.* бóмба; *v.t.* бомби́ть *imp.*; бомбардировáть *imp.* **bombard** *v.t.* бомбардировáть *imp.* **bombardment** *n.* бомбардирóвка. **bomber** *n.* бомбардирóвщик.

bombastic *adj.* напы́щенный (-ен, -енна).

bonanza *n.* золотóе дно.

bond *n.* (*econ.*) облигáция; связь; *pl.* окóвы (-в) *pl.*, (*fig.*) ýзы (уз) *pl.*

bone *n.* кость (*pl.* -ти, -тéй); *pl.* прах; b. of contention, я́блоко раздóра.

bonfire *n.* костёр (-трá).

bonnet *n.* кáпор, чéпчик; (*car*) капóт.

bonny *adj.* здорóвый, хорóшенький.

bony *adj.* костля́вый.

booby *n.* болвáн, óлух; b. trap, ловýшка.

book *n.* кни́га; *v.t.* (*order*) закáзывать *imp.*, заказáть (-ажý, -áжешь) *perf.*; (*reserve*) брони́ровать *imp.*, за~ *perf.* **bookbinder** *n.* переплётчик. **bookkeeper** *n.* бухгáлтер. **bookmaker**, **bookie** *n.* букмéкер. **booking** *n.* (*order*) закáз; (*sale*) продáжа билéтов. b. clerk, касси́р; b. office, кáсса.

boom[1] *n.* (*barrier*) бон.

boom[2] *n.* (*sound*) гул; (*econ.*) бум, экономи́ческий подъём; *v.i.* гудéть (гужý, гуди́шь) *imp.*; (*flourish*) процветáть *imp.*

boon[1] *n.* бла́го.

boon[2] *adj.*: b. **companion**, весёлый друг (*pl.* друзья́, -зе́й).

boor *n.* гру́бый, мужикова́тый челове́к. **boorish** *adj.* мужикова́тый.

boost *v.t.* (*raise*) поднима́ть *imp.*, подня́ть (-ниму́, -ни́мешь; по́днял, -а́, -о) *perf.*; (*increase*) увели́чивать *imp.*, увели́чить *perf.*

boot *n.* боти́нок (-нка) *gen.pl.* -нок), сапо́г (-а́; *gen.pl.* -г); (*football*) бу́тса; *v.t.*: b. **out**, выгоня́ть *imp.*, вы́гнать (вы́гоню, -нишь) *perf.* **bootee** *n.* де́тский вя́заный башмачо́к (-чка́). **boots** *n.* коридо́рный *sb.*

booth *n.* кио́ск, бу́дка; (*polling*) каби́на (для голосова́ния).

bootlegger *n.* торго́вец (-вца) контраба́ндными спиртны́ми напи́тками.

booty *n.* добы́ча; (*mil.*) трофе́и *m.pl.*

booze *n.* вы́пивка; *v.i.* выпива́ть *imp.*

boracic *adj.* бо́рный. **borax** *n.* бура́.

border *n.* (*boundary*) грани́ца; (*edge*) край (*loc.* -аю́; *pl.* -ая́); (*edging*) кайма́, бордю́р; *v.i.* грани́чить *imp.* (on, c + *instr.*); *v.t.* окаймля́ть *imp.*, окайми́ть *perf.* **borderline** *n.* грани́ца.

bore[1] *n.* (*calibre*) кана́л (ствола́), кали́бр (ору́жия); (*borehole*) бурова́я сква́жина; *v.t.* сверли́ть *imp.*, про~ *perf.* **boring**[1] *adj.* сверля́щий, бурово́й.

bore[2] *n.* (*tedium*) ску́ка; (*person*) ну́дный челове́к; *v.t.* надоеда́ть *imp.*, надое́сть (-е́м, -е́шь, -е́ст, -еди́м; -е́л) *perf.* **boredom** *n.* ску́ка. **boring**[2] *adj.* ску́чный.

born *adj.* прирождённый; be b., роди́ться *imp.*, (-и́лся, -и́ла́сь) *perf.*

borough *n.* го́род (*pl.* -а́).

borrow *v.t.* занима́ть *imp.*, заня́ть (займу́, -мёшь; за́нял, -а́, -о) *perf.* (from person), у + *gen.*); займствовать *imp.*, *perf.*

bosh *n.* чепуха́.

bosom *n.* (*breast*) грудь (-ди́, *instr.* -дью; *pl.* -ди, -де́й); (*heart*) се́рдце; (*depths*) не́дра (-р) *pl.*; b. **friend**, закады́чный друг (*pl.* друзья́, -зе́й).

boss *n.* хозя́ин (*pl.* -я́ева, -я́ев), шеф; *v.t.* кома́ндовать *imp.*, с ~ *perf.* + *instr.* **bossy** *adj.* вла́стный.

botanical *adj.* ботани́ческий. **botanist** *n.* бота́ник. **botany** *n.* бота́ника.

botch *v.t.* по́ртить *imp.*, ис~ *perf.*

both *adj.*, *pron.* о́ба (обо́их, -им, -ими) *m.* & *neut.*, о́бе (обе́их, -им, -ими) *f.*; *adv.* то́же; both... and, и... и то́лько... но и; как... так и.

bother *n.* беспоко́йство, хло́поты (gen. -о́т) *pl.*; *v.t.* беспоко́ить *imp.*; надоеда́ть *imp.*, надое́сть (-е́м, -е́шь, -е́ст, -еди́м; -е́л) *perf.*

bottle *n.* буты́лка; b.-neck, у́зкое ме́сто (*pl.* -та́), зато́р; *v.t.* разлива́ть *imp.* разли́ть (разолью́, -ьёшь; разли́л, -а́, -о) *perf.* по буты́лкам; b. up, (*conceal*) зата́ивать *imp.*, затаи́ть *perf.*; (*restrain*) подавля́ть *imp.*, подави́ть (-влю́, -вишь) *perf.*

bottom *n.* ни́жняя часть (*pl.* -ти, -те́й); (*of river etc.*) дно (*pl.* до́нья, -ьев); (*buttocks*) зад (*loc.* -ду́; *pl.* -ы́); *adj.* са́мый ни́жний. **bottomless** *adj.* безло́нный (-нен, -нна); b. pit, ад (*loc.* -у́).

bough *n.* сук (-а́, *loc.* -у́; *pl.* -и, -о́в & су́чья, -ьев), ветвь (*pl.* -ви, -ве́й).

boulder *n.* валу́н (-а́), глы́ба.

bounce *n.* прыжо́к (-жка́), скачо́к (-чка́); *v.i.* подпры́гивать *imp.*, подпры́гнуть *perf.* **bouncing** *adj.* ро́слый, здоро́вый.

bound[1] *n.* (*limit*) преде́л; *v.t.* ограни́чивать *imp.*, ограни́чить *perf.*

bound[2] *n.* (*spring*) прыжо́к (-жка́), скачо́к (-чка́); *v.i.* пры́гать *imp.*, пры́гнуть *perf.*; скака́ть (-ачу́, -а́чешь) *imp.*

bound[3] *adj.* (*tied*) свя́занный (-ан); he is b. to be there, он обяза́тельно там бу́дет.

bound[4] *adj.*: to be b. for, направля́ться *imp.*, напра́виться *perf.* на + *acc.*

boundary *n.* грани́ца, межа́ (*pl.* -жи, -ж, -жа́м).

bounder *n.* хам.

boundless *adj.* беспреде́льный, безграни́чный.

bounteous, bountiful *adj.* (*generous*) ще́дрый (щедр, -а́, -о); (*ample*) оби́льный. **bounty** *n.* ще́дрость; (*gratuity*) пре́мия.

bouquet *n.* буке́т.

bourgeois *n.* буржуа́ *m.indecl.*; *adj.* буржуа́зный. **bourgeoisie** *n.* буржуази́я.

bout n. (of illness) при́ступ; (sport) схва́тка, встре́ча.

bovine adj. быча́чий (-чья, -чье); (fig.) тупо́й (туп, -а́, -о, ту́пы́).

bow¹ n. (weapon) лук; (knot) бант; (mus.) смычо́к (-чка́).

bow² n. (obeisance) покло́н; v.i. кла́няться imp., поклони́ться (-ню́сь, -ни́шься). perf.

bow³ n. (naut.) нос (loc. -у́; pl. -ы́); (rowing) пе́рвый но́мер (pl. -а́).

bowdlerize v.t. очища́ть imp., очи́стить perf.

bowels n. кише́чник; (depths) не́дра (-р) pl.

bower n. бесе́дка.

bowl¹ n. (vessel) ми́ска, таз (loc. -у́; pl. -ы́), ча́ша.

bowl² n. (ball) шар (-á with 2, 3, 4; pl. -ы́); v.i. мета́ть (мечу́, -чешь) imp., метну́ть perf. мяч; подава́ть (-даю́, -даёшь) imp., пода́ть (-а́м, -а́шь, -а́ст, -ади́м; по́дал, -а́, -о) perf. мяч. **bowler** (hat) n. котело́к (-лка́). **bowling** n. кегельба́н. **bowls** n. игра́ в шары́; play b., игра́ть imp., сыгра́ть perf. в шары́.

box¹ n. (container) коро́бка, я́щик, сунду́к (-а́); (theat.) ло́жа; (coach) ко́злы (-зел) pl.; (horse) сто́йло; b.-office, ка́сса; b.-pleat, ба́нтовая скла́дка.

box², **boxwood** n. (bot.) самши́т.

box³ n. (blow) уда́р; v.i. боксирова́ть imp. **boxer** n. боксёр. **boxing** n. бокс.

boy n. ма́льчик, ю́ноша m.; b. friend, друг (pl. друзья́, -зе́й); b. scout, бойска́ут. **boyhood** n. о́трочество. **boyish** adj. мальчи́шеский.

boycott n. бойко́т; v.t. бойкоти́ровать imp., perf.

bra n. бюстга́лтер.

brace n. (clamp) скре́па; pl. подтя́жки f.pl.; (pair) па́ра; v.t. скрепля́ть imp., скрепи́ть perf.; b. oneself, напряга́ть imp., напря́чь (-ягу́, -яжёшь; -я́г, -ягла́) perf. си́лы.

bracelet n. брасле́т.

bracing adj. бодря́щий.

bracket n. (support) кронште́йн (pl. ско́бки f.pl.); (category) катего́рия, ру́брика.

brad n. шти́фтик. **bradawl** n. ши́ло (pl. ши́лья, -ьев).

brag v.i. хва́статься imp., по~ perf. **braggart** n. хвасту́н (-á).

braid n. тесьма́.

Braille n. шрифт Бра́йля.

brain n. мозг (-a(y), loc. -е & -ý; pl. -и́); (intellect) ум (-á); b. drain, уте́чка умо́в; v.t. размозжи́ть perf. го́лову + dat. **brainstorm** n. припа́док (-дка) безу́мия. **brainwashing** n. идеологи́ческая обрабо́тка. **brainwave** n. блестя́щая иде́я.

braise v.t. туши́ть (-шу́, -шишь) imp., с~ perf.

brake n. то́рмоз (pl. -á, fig. -ы); v.t. тормози́ть imp., за~ perf.

bramble n. ежеви́ка.

brambling n. вьюро́к (-рка́).

bran n. о́труби (-бей) pl.

branch n. ве́тка; (subject) о́трасль; (department) отделе́ние, филиа́л; v.i. разветвля́ться imp., разветви́ться perf.

brand n. (mark) клеймо́ (pl. -ма); (make) ма́рка; (sort) сорт (pl. -á); v.t. клейми́ть imp., за~ perf.

brandish v.t. разма́хивать imp. + instr.

brandy n. конья́к (-á(у)).

brass n. лату́нь, жёлтая медь; (mus.) ме́дные инструме́нты m.pl.; adj. лату́нный, ме́дный; b. band, ме́дный духово́й орке́стр; bold as b., на́глый (нагл, -á, -о); b. hats, нача́льство, ста́ршие офице́ры m.pl.; top b., вы́сшее нача́льство.

brassière n. бюстга́лтер.

brat n. ребёнок (-нка; pl. де́ти, -те́й); (derog.) постре́л.

bravado n. брава́да.

brave adj. хра́брый (храбр, -á, -о, хра́бры́), сме́лый (смел, -á, -о); v.t. хра́бро встреча́ть imp., встре́тить perf. **bravery** n. хра́брость, сме́лость.

brawl n. у́личная дра́ка, сканда́л; v.i. дра́ться (деру́сь, -рёшься; дра́лся, -ала́сь, -а́лось) imp., по~ perf.; сканда́лить imp., на~ perf.

brawn n. му́скульная си́ла; (cul.) свино́й сту́день (-дня) m. **brawny** adj. дю́жий (дюж, -á, -е), си́льный (силён, -льна́, -льно, си́льны́).

bray n. крик осла́; v.i. крича́ть (-чи́т) imp.; издава́ть (-даю́, -даёшь) imp.

изда́л (-а́м, -а́шь, -а́ст, -ади́м; изда́л, -а́, -о) perf. ре́зкий звук.

brazen adj. ме́дный, бро́нзовый; (b.-faced) бессты́дный.

brazier n. жаро́вня (gen.pl. -вен).

breach n. наруше́ние; (break) проло́м; (mil.) брешь; v.t. прола́мывать imp., проломи́ть (-млю́, -мишь) perf.

bread n. хлеб; (white) бу́лка; b.-winner, корми́лец (-льца).

breadth n. ширина́, широта́.

break n. проло́м, разры́в; (pause) переры́в, па́уза; b. of day, рассве́т; v.t. лома́ть imp., с~ perf.; разбива́ть imp., разби́ть (разобью́, -ёшь) perf.; (violate) наруша́ть imp., нару́шить perf.; b. in(to), вла́мываться imp., вломи́ться (-млю́сь, -мишься) perf. в + acc.; b. off, отла́мывать imp., отломи́ть (-млю́, -мишь) perf.; (interrupt) прерыва́ть imp., прерва́ть (-ву́, -вёшь; -вал, -вала́, -ва́ло) perf.; b. out, вырыва́ться imp., вы́рваться (-вусь, -вешься) perf.; b. through, проби-ва́ться imp., проби́ться (-бью́сь, -бьёшься) perf.; b. up, разбива́ть(ся) imp., разби́ть(ся) (разобью́, -бьёт(ся)) perf.; b. with, порыва́ть imp., порва́ть (-ву́, -вёшь; порва́л, -а́, -о) perf. + instr. **breakage** n. поло́мка. **breakdown** n. ава́рия; nervous b., не́рвное расстро́йство. **breaker** n. буру́н (-а́). **breakfast** n. у́тренний за́втрак; v.i. за́втракать imp., по~ perf. **breakneck** adj.: at b. speed, сломя́ го́лову. **breakwater** n. мол (loc. -у́).

breast n. грудь (-ди, instr. -дью; pl. -ди, -де́й); b.-feeding, кормле́ние гру́дью; b. stroke, брасс.

breath n. дыха́ние, дунове́ние. **breathe** v.i. дыша́ть (-шу́, -шишь) imp.; b. in, вдыха́ть imp., вдохну́ть perf.; b. out, выдыха́ть imp., вы́дохнуть perf. **breather**, **breathing-space** n. переды́шка. **breathless** adj. запыха́вшийся.

breeches n. бри́джи (-жей) pl., брю́ки (-к) pl.

breed n. поро́да; v.i. размножа́ться imp., размно́житься perf.; v.t. разводи́ть (-ожу́, -о́дишь) imp., развести́ (-еду́, -едёшь; -ёл, -ела́) perf. **breeder**

n. -во́д: cattle b., скотово́д; poultry b., птицево́д. **breeding** n. разведе́ние; (upbringing) воспи́танность.

breeze n. ве́тер (-рка); (naut.) бриз. **breezy** adj. све́жий (свеж, -а́, -о, све́жи); (lively) живо́й (жив, -а́, -о).

breviary n. тре́бник.

brevity n. кра́ткость.

brew v.t. (beer) вари́ть (-рю́, -ришь) imp., с~ perf.; (tea) зава́ривать imp., завари́ть (-рю́, -ришь) perf. **brewer** n. пивова́р. **brewery** n. пивова́ренный заво́д.

bribe n. взя́тка; v.t. дава́ть (даю́, даёшь) imp., дать (дам, дашь, даст, дади́м; дал, -а́, да́ло, -и) perf. взя́тку + dat.; подкупа́ть imp., подкупи́ть (-плю́, -пишь) perf. **bribery** n. по́дкуп.

brick n. кирпи́ч (-а́) (also collect.); (toy) (де́тский) ку́бик; adj. кирпи́чный. **brickbat** n. обло́мок (-мка) кирпича́. **brick-field**, **-yard** n. кирпи́чный заво́д. **bricklayer** n. ка́менщик.

bridal adj. сва́дебный. **bride** n. неве́ста; (after wedding) новобра́чная sb. **bridegroom** n. жени́х (-а́); (after wedding) новобра́чный sb. **bridesmaid** n. подру́жка неве́сты.

bridge[1] n. мост (моста́, loc. -у́; pl. -ы́); мо́стик; (of nose) перено́сица; v.t. наводи́ть (-ожу́, -о́дишь) imp., навести́ (-еду́, -едёшь; -ёл, -ела́) perf. мост че́рез + acc.; стро́ить imp., по~ perf. мост че́рез + acc. **bridgehead** n. плацда́рм.

bridge[2] n. (cards) бридж.

bridle n. узда́ (pl. -ды), узде́чка; v.t. обу́здывать imp., обузда́ть perf.; v.i. возмуща́ться imp., возмути́ться (-ущу́сь, -ути́шься) perf.

brief adj. недо́лгий (-лог, -лга́, -лго), кра́ткий (-ток, -тка́, -тко); n. инстру́кция; v.t. инструкти́ровать imp., perf. **brief-case** n. портфе́ль m. **briefing** n. инструкти́рование, **briefly** adv. кра́тко, сжа́то. **briefs** n. шо́рты (-т & -тов) pl.

brier n. шипо́вник.

brig n. бриг.

brigade n. брига́да. **brigadier** n. бригади́р.

bright adj. я́ркий (я́рок, ярка́, я́рко), блестя́щий; (clever) смышлёный (-ён). **brighten** v.i. проясня́ться imp., про-

ясни́ться *perf.*; *v.t.* придава́ть (-даю́,
-даёшь) *imp.*, прида́ть (-а́м, -а́шь,
-а́ст, -ади́м; -при́дал, -а́, -о) *perf.*
блеск, красоту́. **brightness** *n.* я́ркость.

brilliant *adj.* блестя́щий.

brim *n.* край (*pl.* -ая́); (*hat*) поля́ (-ле́й)
pl. **brimful** *adj.* по́лный (-лон, -лна́,
по́лно) до краёв.

brimstone *n.* саморо́дная се́ра.

brine *n.* рассо́л.

bring *v.t.* (*carry*) приноси́ть (-ошу́,
-о́сишь) *imp.*, принести́ (-есу́, -есёшь,
-ёс, -есла́) *perf.*; (*lead*) приводи́ть
(-ожу́, -о́дишь) *imp.*, привести́ (-еду́,
-едёшь, -ёл, -ела́) *perf.*; (*transport*)
привози́ть (-ожу́, -о́зишь) *imp.*, при-
везти́ (-езу́, -езёшь, -ёз, -езла́) *perf.*;
b. about, быть причи́ной + *gen.*; *b.
back*, возвраща́ть *imp.*, возврати́ть
(-ащу́, -ати́шь) *perf.*; *b. down*, сва́ли-
вать *imp.*, свали́ть (-лю́, -лишь) *perf.*;
b. forward, переноси́ть (-ошу́, -о́сишь)
imp., перенести́ (-есу́, -есёшь, -ёс,
-есла́) *perf.* на сле́дующую страни́цу;
b. up, (*educate*) воспи́тывать *imp.*,
воспита́ть *perf.*; (*question*) подни-
ма́ть *imp.*, подня́ть (-ниму́, -ни́мешь,
подня́л, -а́, -о) *perf.*

brink *n.* край (*pl.* -ая́), грань.

brisk *adj.* (*lively*) живо́й (жив, -а́, -о),
оживлённый (-ён, -ённа); (*air etc.*)
све́жий (свеж, -а́, -о, све́жи́), бодря́-
щий.

brisket *n.* груди́нка.

brisling *n.* бри́слинг, шпро́та.

bristle *n.* щети́на; *v.i.* ощети́ниваться
imp., ощети́ниться *perf.*; *b. with*,
изоби́ловать *imp.* + *instr.*

British *adj.* брита́нский, англи́йский.
Britisher, Briton *n.* брита́нец (-нца),
-нка; англича́нин (*pl.* -а́не, -а́н),
-а́нка.

brittle *adj.* хру́пкий (-пок, -пка́, -пко).
brittleness *n.* хру́пкость.

broach *v.t.* начина́ть *imp.*, нача́ть (-чну́,
-чнёшь; на́чал, -а́, -о) *perf.* обсужда́ть;
затра́гивать *imp.*, затро́нуть. *perf.*

broad *adj.* (*wide*) широ́кий (-о́к, -ока́,
-о́ко); (*general*) о́бщий (общ, -а́);
(*clear*) я́сный (я́сен, ясна́, я́сно,
я́сны); *in b. daylight*, средь бе́ла дня;
in b. outline, в о́бщих черта́х; *b.-*

minded, с широ́кими взгля́дами.
broadly *adv.*: *b. speaking*, вообще́
говоря́.

broadcast *n.* ра́дио-, теле-, переда́ча,
ра́дио-, теле-, програ́мма; *adj.* ра́дио-,
теле-; *v.t.* передава́ть (-даю́, -даёшь)
imp., переда́ть *perf.* (-а́м, -а́шь, -а́ст,
-ади́м; пе́редал, -а́, -о) по ра́дио,
по телеви́дению; (*seed*) се́ять (се́ю,
се́ешь) *imp.*, по ~ *perf.* вразбро́с.
broadcaster *n.* ди́ктор. **broadcasting** *n.*
ра́дио-, теле-, веща́ние.

brocade *n.* парча́; *adj.* парчо́вый.

broccoli *n.* спа́ржевая капу́ста.

brochure *n.* брошю́ра.

brogue *n.* (*shoe*) спорти́вный боти́нок
(-нка; *gen.pl.* -нок); (*accent*) ирла́нд-
ский акце́нт.

broiler *n.* бро́йлер.

broke *predic.* разорён (-а́); *be b. to the
world*, не име́ть *imp.* ни гроша́. **broken**
adj. сло́манный (-ан), разби́тый,
нару́шенный (-ен); *b.-hearted*, уби́тый
го́рем.

broker *n.* бро́кер, ма́клер. **brokerage** *n.*
комиссио́нное вознагражде́ние.

bromide *n.* броми́д. **bromine** *n.* бром
(-а(у)).

bronchitis *n.* бронхи́т.

bronze *n.* бро́нза; *adj.* бро́нзовый; *v.t.*
бронзирова́ть *imp.*, *perf.*

brooch *n.* брошь, брошка.

brood *n.* вы́водок (-дка); *v.i.* мра́чно
размышля́ть *imp.* **broody** *adj.* сидя́-
щий на я́йцах; *b. hen*, насе́дка.

brook[1] *n.* руче́й (-чья́).

brook[2] *v.t.* терпе́ть (-плю́, -пишь) *imp.*

broom *n.* метла́ (*pl.* мётлы, -тел,
-тлам); (*plant*) раки́тник, дрок.
broomstick *n.* (*witches'*) помело́ (*pl.*
-лья, -льев).

broth *n.* суп, похлёбка.

brothel *n.* публи́чный дом (*pl.* -а́).

brother *n.* брат (*pl.* -ья, -ьев); *b. in arms*,
собра́т (*pl.* -ья, -ьев) по ору́жию; *b.-
in-law*, (*sister's husband*) зять (*pl.* -я,
-ёв); (*husband's brother*) де́верь (*pl.*
-рья, -ре́й); (*wife's brother*) шу́рин
pl. (шурья́, -ьёв); (*wife's sister's
husband*) своя́к (-а́). **brotherhood** *n.*
бра́тство. **brotherly** *adj.* бра́тский.

brow *n.* (*eyebrow*) бровь (*pl.* -ви, -ве́й)

(*forehead*) лоб (лба, *loc.* лбу); (*of cliff*) выступ. **browbeaten** *adj.* запуганный (-ан).

brown *adj.* коричневый; (*eyes*) карий; *b.* paper, обёрточная бумага; *v.t.* (*cul.*) подрумянивать *imp.*, подрумянить *perf.*

browse *v.i.* (*feed*) пастись (пасётся; пасся, паслась) *imp.*; (*read*) читать *imp.* бессистемно.

bruise *n.* синяк (-а), ушиб; *v.t.* ушибать *imp.*, ушибить (-бу, -бёшь; -б) *perf.* **bruised** *adj.* (*fruit*) повреждённый (-ён, -ена).

brunette *n.* брюнетка.

brush *n.* щётка; (*paint*) кисть (*pl.* -ти, -тей); *v.t.* (*clean*) чистить *imp.*, вы~, по~ *perf.* щёткой; (*touch*) легко касаться *imp.*, коснуться *perf.* + *gen.*; *b.* one's hair, причёсываться *imp.*, причесаться (-ешусь, -ешешься) *perf.* щёткой; *b.* aside, отстранять *imp.*, отстранить *perf.*; *b.*-off *n.*: give the *b.*-off, отмахиваться *imp.*, отмахнуться *perf.* + *gen.*; *b.* up, собирать *imp.*, собрать (соберу, -рёшь; собрал, -а, -о) *perf.* щёткой; (*renew*) возобновлять *imp.*, возобновить *perf.* знакомство с + *instr.*

brushwood *n.* хворост (-а(у)).

Brussels sprouts *n.* брюссельская капуста.

brutal *adj.* жестокий (-ок, -ока, -око), зверский, грубый (груб, -а, -о). **brutality** *n.* жестокость, зверство. **brutalize** *v.t.* (*treat brutally*) грубо обращаться *imp.*, с + *instr.*; (*make brutal*) доводить (-ожу, -одишь) *imp.*, довести (-еду, -едёшь; -ёл, -ела) *perf.* до озверения. **brute** *n.* животное *sb.*, скотина, жестокий человек. **brutish** *adj.* грубый (груб, -а, -о), жестокий (-ок, -ока, -око).

bubble *n.* пузырь (-ря) *m.*, пузырёк (-рька); *v.i.* пузыриться *imp.*; кипеть (-пит) *imp.*, вс~ *perf.* **bubbly** *n.* шампанское *sb.*

buccaneer *n.* пират.

buck *n.* самец (-мца) оленя, кролика *etc.*; *v.i.* брыкаться *imp.*

bucket *n.* ведро (*pl.* вёдра, -дер, -драм), ведёрко (*pl.* -рки, -рок, -ркам).

buckle *n.* пряжка; *v.t.* застёгивать *imp.*,

застегнуть *perf.* пряжкой; *v.i.* (*crumple*) коробиться *imp.*, по~, с~ *perf.*

buckshot *n.* картечь.

buckskins *n.* лосины (-н) *pl.*

buckthorn *n.* крушина.

buckwheat *n.* гречиха.

bucolic *adj.* буколический, деревенский.

bud *n.* почка, бутон; *v.i.* развиваться *imp.* **budding** *n.* окулировка, почкование.

Buddha *n.* Будда. **Buddhism** *n.* буддизм. **Buddhist** *n.* буддист; *adj.* буддийский.

budge *v.t.* & *i.* шевелить(ся) (-елю(сь), -елишь(ся)) *imp.*, по~ *perf.*

budgerigar *n.* попугайчик.

budget *n.* бюджет; *v.i.*: *b.* for, предусматривать *imp.*, предусмотреть (-рю, -ришь) *perf.* в бюджете.

buff *n.* (*leather*) кожа; *in*, *to the b.*, нагишом; *adj.* желтовато-бежевый.

buffalo *n.* буйвол.

buffoon *n.* шут (-а); *act the b.*, паясничать *imp.*

bug *n.* (*bedbug*) клоп (-а); (*virus*) вирус; (*microphone*) потайной микрофон; *v.t.* (*install b.*) устанавливать *imp.*, установить (-влю, -вишь) *perf.* аппаратуру для подслушивания в + *prep.*; (*listen*) подслушивать *imp.*

bugle *n.* рог (*pl.* -а), горн. **bugler** *n.* горнист.

build *n.* (*person*) телосложение; *v.t.* строить *imp.*, вы~, по~ *perf.* **builder** *n.* строитель *m.* **building** *n.* (*edifice*) здание; (*action*) строительство; *b.* society, общество, предоставляющее средства для покупки жилых помещений.

bulb *n.* луковица; (*electric*) лампочка. **bulbous** *adj.* луковичный.

bulge *n.* выпуклость, выступ; *v.i.* выпячиваться *imp.*; выпирать *imp.* **bulging** *adj.* разбухший, оттопыривающийся; *b.* eyes, глаза (-з) *pl.* на выкате.

bulk *n.* (*size*) объём; (*greater part*) бо́льшая часть; (*mass*) основная масса; (*large object*) громада; *b.* buying, закупки *f.pl.* гуртом; *b.* cargo, груз навалом.

bull *n.* (*ox*) бык (-á); (*male animal*) самéц (-мцá); *adj.* бычáчий (-чья, -чье); **bulldog** *n.* бульдóг. **bulldoze** *v.t.* расчищáть *imp.*, расчистить *perf.* бульдóзером. **bulldozer** *n.* бульдóзер. **bullfinch** *n.* снегирь (-ря) *m.* **bullock** *n.* вол (-á). **bull's-eye** *n.* (*target*) яблоко.

bullet *n.* пуля; **b.-proof,** пулестóйкий.

bulletin *n.* бюллетéнь *m.*

bullion *n.* слиток (-тка).

bully *n.* задира *m. & f.*, забияка *m. & f.*; *v.t.* запугивать *imp.*, запугáть *perf.*; задирáть *imp.*

bulrush *n.* камыш (-á).

bulwark *n.* бастиóн, оплóт.

bum *n.* зад (*loc.* -ý; *pl.* -ы).

bumble-bee *n.* шмель (-ля) *m.*

bump *n.* (*blow*) удáр, толчóк (-чкá); (*swelling*) шишка; *v.i.* удáряться *imp.*, удáриться *perf.*; **b. against,** налетáть *imp.*, налетéть (-ечу -етишь) *perf.* на+*acc.*; нáталкиваться *imp.*, натолкнýться *perf.* на+*acc.* **bumper** *n.* бáмпер; *adj.* óчень крýпный, обильный.

bumpkin *n.* неотёсанный пáрень (-рня; *pl.* -рни, -рнéй) *m.*; *country* b., деревéнщина *m. & f.*

bumptious *adj.* нахáльный, самоувéренный (-ен, -енна).

bun *n.* сдóбная бýлка.

bunch *n.* пучóк (-чкá), связка, гроздь (*pl.* -ди, -дéй & -дья, -дьев); *v.t.* собирáть *imp.*, собрáть (соберý, -рёшь; собрáл, -á, -о) *perf.* в пучки.

bundle *n.* ýзел (узлá), узелóк (-лкá) *v.t.* связывать *imp.*, связáть (-яжý, -яжешь) *perf.* в ýзел; **b. away,** off, спровáживать *imp.*, спровáдить *perf.*

bung *n.* втýлка.

bungalow *n.* бýнгало *neut.indecl.*

bungle *v.t.* пóртить *imp.*, ис~ *perf.*; *n.* пýтаница. **bungler** *n.* пýтаник.

bunk *n.* (*berth*) кóйка.

bunker *n.* бýнкер (*pl.* -á & -ы).

bunkum *n.* чепухá.

buoy *n.* буй (*pl.* буи), бáкен. **buoyancy** *n.* плавýчесть; (*fig.*) бóдрость, оживлéние. **buoyant** *adj.* плавýчий; бóдрый (бодр, -á, -о), жизнерáдостный.

bur(r) *n.* колючка.

burden *n.* брéмя *neut.*; *v.t.* обременять *imp.*, обременить *perf.*

bureau *n.* бюрó *neut.indecl.* **bureaucracy** *n.* бюрокрáтия (*also collect.*), бюрократизм. **bureaucrat** *n.* бюрокрáт. **bureaucratic** *adj.* бюрократический.

burglar *n.* взлóмщик. **burglary** *n.* крáжа со взлóмом. **burgle** *v.t.* совершáть *imp.*, совершить *perf.* крáжу со взлóмом; *v.t.* грáбить *imp.*, о~ *perf.*

burial *n.* погребéние; **b.-service,** заупокóйная слýжба.

burlesque *n.* парóдия; *v.t.* пародировать *imp.*, *perf.*; *adj.* пародийный, паро-дийный.

burly *adj.* здоровéнный.

burn *v.t.* жечь (жгу, жжёшь, жгут; жёг, жглá) *imp.*; с~ (сожгý, сожжёшь, сожгýт; сжёг, сожглá) *perf.*; сжечь & *i.* (*injure*) обжигáть(ся) *imp.*, обжéчь(ся) (обожгý(сь), обожжёшь(ся), обожгýт(ся); обжёг(ся), обожглá(сь)) *perf.*; *v.i.* горéть (-рю, -ришь) *imp.*, с~ *perf.*; (*by sun*) загорáть *imp.*, загорéть (-рю, -ришь) *perf.*; *n.* ожóг. **burner** *n.* горéлка. **burning** *adj.* горячий (-ч, -чá).

burnish *v.t.* полировáть *imp.*, на~, от~ *perf.* **burnishing** *n.* полирóвка; *adj.* полировáльный.

burr *n. see* bur(r).

burrow *n.* норá (*pl.* -ры), нóрка; *v.i.* рыть (рóю, рóешь) *imp.*, вы~ *perf.* норý; (*fig.*) рыться (рóюсь, рóешься) *imp.*

bursar *n.* казначéй, завхóз. **bursary** *n.* стипéндия.

burst *n.* разрыв, вспышка; *v.i.* разрывáться *imp.*, разорвáться (-вётся; -вáлся, -вáлась, -вáлось) *perf.*; лóпаться *imp.*, лóпнуть *perf.*; *v.t.* разрывáть *imp.*, разорвáть (-вý, -вёшь; разорвáл, -á, -о) *perf.*

bury *v.t.* (*dead*) хоронить (-ню, -нишь) *imp.*, по~ *perf.*; (*hide*) закáпывать *imp.*, закопáть *imp.*; зарывáть *imp.*, зарыть (-рóю, -рóешь) *perf.*

bus *n.* автóбус; **b.-conductor,** кондýктор (*pl.* -á).

bush *n.* куст (-á); (*collect.*) кустáрник. **bushy** *adj.* густóй (густ, -á, -о, гýсты).

business *n.* (*matter*) дéло; (*occupation*) занятие; (*firm*) коммéрческое предприятие; *big b.*, крупный капитал; *mind your own b.*, не ваше дело; *no monkey b.*, без фокусов; *on b.*, по делу.

busker *n.* уличный музыкант.

bust *n.* (*sculpture*) бюст; (*bosom*) грудь (-ди, *instr.* -дью; *pl.* -ди, -дей).

bustle¹ *n.* (*fuss*) суматоха, суета; *v.i.* суетиться *imp.*

bustle² *n.* (*garment*) турнюр.

busy *adj.* занятой (занят, -а, -о); *v.t.*: *b. oneself*, заниматься *imp.*, заняться (займусь, -мёшься; занялся, -лась) *perf.* (*with*, + *instr.*). **busybody** *n.* человек, сующий нос в чужие дела.

but *conj.* но, а, кроме; *b. then*, но зато; *prep.* кроме + *gen.*

butcher *n.* мясник (-а); *v.t.* резать (режу, -жешь) *imp.*, за~ *perf.*; *b.'s shop*, мясная *sb.* **butchery** *n.* резня.

butt¹ *n.* (*cask*) бочка.

butt² *n.* (*of gun*) приклад; (*end*) толстый конец (-нца).

butt³ *n.* (*target*) мишень.

butt⁴ *v.t.* бодать *imp.*, за~ *perf.*; *v.i.* бодаться *imp.*

butter *n.* (*slivочное*) масло; *v.t.* намазывать *imp.*, намазать (-ажу, -ажешь) *perf.* маслом. **buttercup** *n.* лютик. **butterfly** *n.* бабочка.

buttock *n.* ягодица.

button *n.* пуговица; (*knob*) кнопка; *v.t.* застёгивать *imp.*, застегнуть *perf.*

buttress *n.* контрфорс; *v.t.* подпирать *imp.*, подпереть (подопру, -рёшь; подпёр) *perf.*

buy *v.t.* покупать *imp.*, купить (-плю, -пишь) *perf.* **buyer** *n.* покупатель *m.*

buzz *n.* жужжание; *v.i.* жужжать (-жит) *imp.*; гудеть (гужу, гудишь) *imp.*

buzzard *n.* канюк (-а).

buzzer *n.* зуммер.

by *adv.* мимо; *by and by*, вскоре; *prep.* (*near*) около + *gen.*, у + *gen.*; (*beside*) рядом с + *instr.*; (*via*) через + *acc.*; (*past*) мимо + *gen.*; (*time*) к + *dat.*; (*means*) *instr.* without *prep.*; *by means of*, посредством + *gen.*

bye-bye *interj.* пока! всего!

by-election *n.* дополнительные выборы *m.pl.* **bygone** *adj.* пережитый, прошлый; *n.*: *pl.* прошлое *sb.*; (*objects*) предметы, *m.pl.* вышедшие из употребления; *let b. be b.*, что пропало, то бульём поросло. **by-law** *n.* постановление местной власти. **bypass** *n.* (*road*) обход, обходный путь (-ти, -тём) *m.*; (*pipe*) обводный канал; *v.t.* обходить (-ожу, -одишь) *imp.*, обойти (обойду, -дёшь; обошёл, -шла) *perf.*; объезжать *imp.*, объехать (-еду, -едешь) *perf.* **by-product** *n.* побочный продукт. **bystander** *n.* наблюдатель *m.* **byway** *n.* просёлочная дорога. **by-word** *n.* (*proverb*) поговорка; (*example*) пример.

Byzantine *adj.* византийский.

C

C *n.* (*mus.*) до *neut.indecl.*

cab *n.* (*taxi*) такси *neut.indecl.*; (*of lorry*) кабина; *c.-rank*, стоянка такси.

cabaret *n.* эстрадное представление.

cabbage *n.* капуста; *c. white*, капустница.

cabin *n.* (*hut*) хижина; (*bathing etc.*) кабина; (*ship's*) каюта; *c.-boy*, юнга *m.*

cabinet *n.* (*polit.*) кабинет; (*cupboard*) (застеклённый) шкаф (*loc.* -у; *pl.* -ы); *c.-maker*, краснодеревец (-вца); *C. Minister*, министр-член кабинета.

cable *n.* (*rope*) канат, трос; (*electric*)

cabotage *n.* каботáж.

cacao *n.* какáо *neut.indecl.*

cache *n.* укрытый, тáйный, запáс.

cackle *n.* (*geese*) гóгот, гоготáнье; (*hens*) кудáхтанье; *v.i.* гоготáть (-очу, -очешь) *imp.*; кудáхтать (-хчу, -хчешь) *imp.*

cactus *n.* кáктус; *adj.* кáктусовый.

cad *n.* хам.

cadaverous *adj.* мёртвенно-блéдный (-ден, -днá, -дно, -блéдны).

caddie *n.* человéк, прислýживающий при игрé в гольф.

caddish *adj.* хáмский.

caddy *n.* (*box*) чáйница.

cadence *n.* (*rhythm*) ритм, такт; (*mus.*) кадéнция. **cadenced** *adj.* мéрный, ритмúчный. **cadenza** *n.* кадéнция.

cadet *n.* кадéт (*gen.pl.* -т & -тов); *adj.* кадéтский.

cadge *v.t.* выпрáшивать *imp.*, выпросить *perf.*

cadre *n.* кáдры *m.pl.*

Caesarean (section) *n.* кéсарево сечéние.

caesura *n.* цезýра.

cafe *n.* кафé *neut.indecl.* **cafeteria** *n.* кафетéрий.

caffeine *n.* кофеúн.

cage *n.* клéтка; (*in mine*) клеть (*loc.* -éтú; *pl.* -ти, -тéй); *v.t.* сажáть *imp.*, посадúть (-ажý, -áдишь) *perf.* в клéтку; *caged*, в клéтке.

cairn *n.* грýда камнéй.

caisson *n.* кессóн.

cajole *v.t.* умáсливать *imp.*, умáслить *perf.* **cajolery** *n.* лесть, умáсливание.

cake *n.* торт, пирóжное *sb.*; (*fruit-c.*) кекс; (*soap*) кусóк (-скá) *fruit-c.*; *v.i.* твердéть *imp.*, за~ *perf.*; отвердевáть *imp.*, отвердéть *perf.*

calamitous *adj.* пáгубный, бéдственный (-ен, -енна). **calamity** *n.* бéдствие.

calcareous *adj.* известкóвый. **calcium** *n.* кáльций; *adj.* кáльциевый.

calculate *v.t.* вычислять *imp.*, вычислить *perf.*; *v.i.* рассчúтывать *imp.*, рассчитáть *perf.* (на, на+*acc.*); *calculated*, преднамéренный (-ен,

-енна); *calculating-machine*, вычислúтельная машúна. **calculation** *n.* вычислéние, расчёт. **calculus** *n.* (*math.*) исчислéние; (*stone*) кáмень (-мня; *pl.* -мни, -мнéй) *m.*

calendar *n.* календáрь (-ря) *m.*; (*register*) спúсок (-ска).

calf[1] *n.* (*cow*) телёнок (-нка; *pl.* телятá, -т); (*other animal*) детёныш; (*leather*) телячья кóжа; *c.-love*, ребячеcкая любóвь (-бви, -бóвю).

calf[2] *n.* (*leg*) икрá (*pl.* -ры).

calibrate *v.t.* калибрúровать *imp. perf.*; калибровáть *imp.* **calibration** *n.* калибрóвка. **calibre** *n.* калúбр.

calico *n.* коленкóр (-а(у)), миткáль (-ля) *m.*

call *v.* звать (зовý, -вёшь; звал, -á, -о) *imp.*, по~ *perf.*; (*name*) называть *imp.*, назвáть (назовý, -вёшь; назвáл, -á, -о) *perf.*; (*cry*) кричáть (-чý, -чúшь) *imp.*, крúкнуть *perf.*; (*wake*) будúть (бужý, бýдишь) *imp.*, раз~ *perf.*; (*visit*) заходúть (-ожý, -óдишь) *imp.*, зайтú (зайдý, -дёшь; зашёл, -шлá) *perf.* (оп, к+*dat.*; at, в+*acc.*); (*stop at*) останáвливаться *imp.*, остановúться (-влюсь, -вишься) *perf.* (at, в, на, +*prep.*); (*summon*) вызывáть *imp.*, вызвать (вызову, -вешь) *perf.*; (*ring up*) звонúть *imp.*, по~ *perf.*+*dat.*; *c. for*, (*require*) трéбовать *imp.*, по~ *perf.*+*gen.*; (*fetch*) заходúть (-ожý, -óдишь) *imp.* зайтú (зайдý, -дёшь; зашёл, -шлá) *perf.* за+*instr.*; *c. off*, отменять *imp.*, отменúть (-ню, -нишь) *perf.*; *c. out*, вскрúкивать *imp.*, вскрúкнуть *perf.*; *c. up*, призывáть *imp.*, призвáть (призовý, -вёшь; призвáл, -á, -о) *perf.*; *n.* (*cry*) крик; (*summons*) зов, призыв; (*telephone*) (телефóнный) вызов, разговóр; (*visit*) визúт; (*signal*) сигнáл; *c.-box*, телефóн-автомáт; *c.-boy*, мáльчик, вызывáющий актёров на сцéну; *c.-over*, переклúчка; *c.-sign*, позывнóй сигнáл, позывные *sb.*; *c.-up*, призыв. **caller** *n.* посетúтель *m.*, ~ница; гость (*pl.* -ти, -тéй) *m.*, гóстья (*gen.pl.* -тий). **calling** *n.* (*summons*) призвáние; (*profession*) профéссия; (*occupation*) занятие; (*trade*) ремеслó.

callous adj. (person) бессерде́чный, бесчу́вственный (-ен(ен), -енна).

callow adj. (unfledged) неопери́вшийся; (raw) нео́пытный.

callus n. мозо́ль.

calm adj. (tranquil) споко́йный, хладно-кро́вный; (quiet) ти́хий (тих, -а́, -о); (windless) безве́тренный (-ен, -енна); n. споко́йствие; безве́трие; v.t. & i. (c. down) успока́ивать(ся) imp., успоко́ить(ся) perf.

calorie n. кало́рия.

calumniate v.t. клевета́ть (-ещу́, -е́щешь) imp., на~ perf. на+acc. **calumniation, calumny** n. клевета́.

calve v.i. тели́ться (-и́тся) imp., о~ perf.

calypso n. кали́псо neut.indecl.

calyx n. ча́шечка.

cam n. кулачо́к (-чка́), кула́к (-а́). **cam-shaft** n. распредели́тельный, кулачко́вый, вал (loc. -у́; pl. -ы́).

camber n. вы́пуклость. **cambered** adj. вы́пуклый.

camel n. верблю́д; camel('s)-hair, вер-блю́жья шерсть.

cameo n. каме́я.

camera n. фотоаппара́т; кино-, теле-, ка́мера. **cameraman** n. кинооперато́р.

camomile n. рома́шка.

camouflage n. маскиро́вка; камуфля́ж; adj. маскиро́вочный; v.t. маскирова́ть imp., за~ perf.

camp n. ла́герь (pl. -я, -е́й) m.; v.i. располага́ться imp., расположи́ться (-жу́сь, -жи́шься) perf. ла́герем; c.-bed, раскладна́я крова́ть, раскла-ду́шка; c.-chair, складно́й стул (pl. -ья, -ьев); c.-fire, бива́чный костёр (-тра́).

campaign n. кампа́ния; похо́д; v.i. (conduct c.) проводи́ть (-ожу́, -о́дишь) imp., провести́ (-еду́, -еде́шь; -ёл, -ела́) perf. кампа́нию; (serve in c.) уча́ствовать imp. в похо́де, в кам-па́нии.

campanula n. колоко́льчик.

camphor n. камфара́. **camphorated oil** n. камфо́рное ма́сло.

campus n. академи́ческий городо́к (-дка́), академгородо́к (-дка́).

camshaft see **cam**.

can[1] n. жестя́нка, (консе́рвная) коро́б-ка, ба́нка; v.t. консерви́ровать imp., за~ perf.

can[2] v. aux. (be able) мочь (могу́, мо́жешь; мог, -ла́) imp., с~ perf.+inf.; (know how) уме́ть imp., с~ perf.+inf.

Canadian n. кана́дец (-дца), -дка n.; adj. кана́дский.

canal n. кана́л.

canary n. канаре́йка.

cancel v.t. аннули́ровать imp., perf.; отменя́ть imp., отмени́ть (-ню́, -нишь) perf.; (math.) сокраща́ть imp., сократи́ть (-ащу́, -ати́шь) perf.; (print.) вычёркивать imp., вы́черкнуть perf.; (stamp) гаси́ть (гашу́, га́сишь) imp., по~ perf.; n. (print.) перепеча́танный лист (-а́). **cancellation** n. аннули́ро-вание, отме́на; (math.) сокраще́ние; (print.) перепеча́тка.

cancer n. рак; (C.) Рак; adj. ра́ковый; c. patient, больно́й ра́ком. **cancerous** adj. ра́ковый.

candelabrum n. канделя́бр.

candid adj. открове́нный (-нен, -нна), и́скренний (-нен, -нна, -нне & -нно); c. camera, скры́тый фотоаппара́т.

candidacy n. кандидату́ра. **candidate** n. кандида́т. **candidature** n. кандидату́ра.

candied adj. заса́харенный; c. peel, цука́т(ы).

candle n. свеча́ (pl. -чи, -че́й); c.-end, ога́рок (-рка). **candlestick** n. подсве́ч-ник. **candlewick** n. фити́ль (-ля́) m., вы́шивка фитилька́ми.

candour n. открове́нность, и́скрен-ность.

candy n. сла́дости f.pl.; v.t. заса́хари-вать imp., заса́харить perf.

cane n. (plant) тростни́к (-а́); (stick) трость (pl. -ти, -те́й), па́лка; c. sugar, тростнико́вый са́хар (-а(у)); v.t. бить (бью, бьёшь) imp., по~ perf. тро́стью, па́лкой.

canine adj. соба́чий (-чья, -чье); n. (tooth) клык (-а́).

canister n. жестяна́я коро́бка.

canker n. рак.

cannibal n. каннниба́л, людое́д; adj. каннниба́льский, людое́дский. **canni-balism** n. каннибали́зм, людое́дство.

cannibalistic *adj.* канниба́льский, людое́дский. **cannibalize** *v.t.* снима́ть *imp.*, снять (сниму́, -мешь; снял, -á, -о) *perf.* ча́сти с + *gen.*

cannon *n.* (*gun*) пу́шка; (*billiards*) карамбо́ль *m.*; *adj.* пу́шечный; *c.-ball*, пу́шечное ядро́ (*pl.* я́дра, я́дер, я́драм); *c.-ball service*, пу́шечная пода́ча; *c.-fodder*, пу́шечное мя́со; *v.i.*: *c. into*, налета́ть *imp.*, налете́ть (-лечу́, -лети́шь) *perf.* на + *acc.*; *c. off*, отска́кивать *imp.*, отскочи́ть (-очу́, -о́чишь) *perf.* от + *gen.* **cannonade** *n.* канона́да

canoe *n.* кано́э *neut.indecl.*; челно́к (-á); *v.i.* пла́вать *indet.*, плыть (плыву́, -вёшь; плыл, -á, -о) *det.* в челноке́, на кано́э.

canon *n.* кано́н; (*person*) кано́ник; *c. law*, канони́ческое пра́во. **canonical** *adj.* канони́ческий; *c. hours*, уста́вные часы́ *m.pl.* моли́тв. **canonicals** *n.* церко́вное облаче́ние. **canonization** *n.* канониза́ция. **canonize** *v.t.* канонизова́ть *imp.*, *perf.*

canopy *n.* балдахи́н.

cant[1] *n.* (*slant*) накло́н, накло́нное положе́ние; *v.t.* наклоня́ть *imp.*, наклони́ть (-ню́, -нишь) *perf.*; придава́ть (-даю́, -даёшь) *imp.*, прида́ть (-áм, -áшь, -áст, -ади́м; при́дал, -á, -о) *perf.* + *dat.* накло́нное положе́ние.

cant[2] *n.* (*hypocrisy*) ха́нжество; (*jargon*) жарго́н, арго́ *neut.indecl.*

cantaloup *n.* канталу́па.

cantankerous *adj.* ворчли́вый.

cantata *n.* канта́та.

canteen *n.* столо́вая *sb.*, буфе́т; (*case*) я́щик; (*flask*) фля́га.

canter *n.* кёнтер, лёгкий гало́п; *v.i.* (*rider*) е́здить *indet.*, е́хать (е́ду, е́дешь) *det.* лёгким гало́пом; (*horse*) ходи́ть (-ди́т) *indet.*, идти́ (идёт; шёл, шла) *det.* лёгким гало́пом; *v.t.* пуска́ть *imp.*, пусти́ть (пущу́, пу́стишь) *perf.* лёгким гало́пом.

cantilever *n.* консо́ль, уко́сина; *c. bridge*, консо́льный мост (мо́ста́, *loc.* -ý; *pl.* -ы́).

canto *n.* песнь.

canton *n.* канто́н.

canvas *n.* холст (-á), канва́, паруси́на; (*painting*) карти́на; (*sails*) паруса́ *m.pl.*; *under c.*, (*on ship*) под паруса́ми; (*in tent*) в пала́тках.

canvass *v.i.* собира́ть *imp.*, собра́ть (соберу́, -рёшь; собра́л, -á, -о) *perf.* голоса́; *c. for*, агити́ровать *imp.*, с ~ *perf.* за + *acc.*; *n.* собира́ние голосо́в, агита́ция. **canvasser** *n.* собира́тель *m.* голосо́в.

canyon *n.* каньо́н.

cap *n.* ша́пка, фура́жка; (*cloth*) ке́пка; (*woman's*) чепе́ц (-пца́); (*percussion*) ка́псюль *m.*, писто́н; (*lid*) кры́шка; *v.t.* (*surpass*) перещеголя́ть *perf.*; превосходи́ть (-ожу́, -о́дишь) *imp.*, превзойти́ (-ойду́, -ойдёшь; -ошёл, -ошла́) *perf.*

capability *n.* спосо́бность. **capable** *adj.* спосо́бный; (*skilful*) уме́лый; *c. of*, (*admitting*) поддаю́щийся + *dat.*; (*able*) спосо́бный на + *acc.*

capacious *adj.* просто́рный, вмести́тельный, ёмкий (ёмок, ёмка́). **capacitance** *n.* ёмкость. **capacity** *n.* ёмкость, вмести́мость; (*ability*) спосо́бность; (*power*) мо́щность; *in the c. of*, в ка́честве + *gen.*

cape[1] *n.* (*geog.*) мыс (*loc.* -е & -ý; *pl.* -ы́).

cape[2] *n.* (*cloak*) пелери́на, плащ (-á). **caped** *adj.* с пелери́ной.

caper[1] *n.* (*plant*) ка́перс; *pl.* ка́персы *pl.*

caper[2] *n.* (*leap*) прыжо́к (-жка́); *cut capers*, выде́лывать *imp.* антраша́; *v.i.* де́лать *imp.* прыжки́.

capillary *n.* капилля́р; *adj.* капилля́рный.

capital *adj.* (*city*) столи́чный; (*letter*) прописно́й; (*main*) капита́льный; (*excellent*) отли́чный; *c. goods*, сре́дства *neut.pl.* произво́дства; *c. punishment*, сме́ртная казнь; *c. ship*, кру́пный боево́й кора́бль (-ля́ *m.*); *n.* (*town*) столи́ца; (*letter*) прописна́я бу́ква; (*econ.*) капита́л; (*arch.*) капите́ль. **capitalism** *n.* капитали́зм. **capitalist** *n.* капитали́ст; *adj.* капиталисти́ческий. **capitalistic** *adj.* капиталисти́ческий. **capitalization** *n.* капитализа́ция. **capitalize** *v.t.* капитализи́ровать *imp.*, *perf.*

capitation *attrib.* поголо́вный.

capitulate *v.i.* капитули́ровать *imp.*, *perf.* **capitulation** *n.* капитуля́ция.
capon *n.* каплу́н (-á).
caprice *n.* капри́з. **capricious** *adj.* капри́зный.
Capricorn *n.* Козеро́г.
capsize *v.t. & i.* опроки́дывать(ся) *imp.*, опроки́нуть(ся) *perf.*
capstan *n.* кабеста́н.
capsule *n.* ка́псула, обла́тка.
captain *n.* капита́н; *v.t.* быть капита́ном + *gen.* **captaincy** *n.* зва́ние, чин, до́лжность, капита́на.
caption *n.* на́дпись, по́дпись; (*cin.*) титр.
captious *adj.* приди́рчивый.
captivate *v.t.* пленя́ть *imp.*, плени́ть *perf.* **captivating** *adj.* плени́тельный.
captive *adj.*, *n.* пле́нный. **captivity** *n.* нево́ля, (*esp. mil.*) плен (*loc.* -ý).
capture *n.* взя́тие, захва́т, пле́н(ение); *v.t.* брать (беру́, -рёшь; брал, -á, -о) *imp.*, взять (возьму́, -мёшь; взял, -á, -о) *perf.* в плен; захва́тывать *imp.*, захвати́ть (-ачу́, -а́тишь) *perf.*
car *n.* маши́на, автомоби́ль *m.*; *attrib.* автомоби́льный.
caracul *n.* каракул *m.*
carafe *n.* графи́н.
caramel(s) *n.* караме́ль.
carat *n.* кара́т (*gen.pl.* -т & -тов).
caravan *n.* (*convoy*) карава́н; (*cart*) фурго́н; (*house*) дом-фурго́н.
caraway (*seeds*) *n.* тмин (-а(у)).
carbide *n.* карби́д.
carbine *n.* карби́н.
carbohydrate *n.* углево́д. **carbolic** (**acid**) *n.* карбо́ловая кислота́. **carbon** *n.* углеро́д; (*copy*) ко́пия (че́рез копи́рку); *c.* **dioxide**, углекислота́; *c.* **paper**, копирова́льная бума́га. **carbonaceous** *adj.* (*carbon*) углеро́дистый; (*coal*) у́глистый. **carbonate** *n.* углеки́слая соль. **carboniferous** *adj.* углено́сный. С., карбо́новый (пери́од). **carborundum** *n.* карбору́нд.
carboy *n.* буты́ль.
carbuncle *n.* карбу́нкул.
carburettor *n.* карбюра́тор.
carcase, carcass *n.* ту́ша, труп.
card *n.* ка́рта, ка́рточка; (*ticket*) биле́т;

a house of cards, ка́рточный до́мик; *c.* **index**, картоте́ка; *c.-sharp(er)*, шу́лер (*pl.* -á); *c.-table*, ло́мберный, ка́рточный, стол (-á). **cardboard** *n.* карто́н; *adj.* карто́нный.
cardiac *adj.* серде́чный.
cardigan *n.* вя́заная ко́фта, кардига́н.
cardinal *adj.* (*important*) кардина́льный; (*scarlet*) а́лый; *c.* **number**, коли́чественное числи́тельное *sb.*; *n.* кардина́л.
care *n.* (*trouble*) забо́та, попече́ние; (*attention*) внима́тельность; (*tending*) ухо́д; *take c.*, осторо́жно! береги́(те)сь!; смотри́(те)!; *take c. of*, забо́титься *imp.*, по~ *perf.* o + *prep.*; *I don't c.*, мне всё равно́! *what do I c.?* *who cares?* а мне всё равно́! а мне-то что?
career *n.* (*movement*) карье́р; (*profession*) карье́ра.
carefree *adj.* беззабо́тный. **careful** *adj.* (*cautious*) осторо́жный; (*thorough*) тща́тельный; (*attentive*) внима́тельный. **careless** *adj.* (*negligent*) небре́жный; (*incautious*) неосторо́жный; (*carefree*) беззабо́тный.
caress *n.* ла́ска (*gen.pl.* -ск); *v.t.* ласка́ть *imp.*
caretaker *n.* смотри́тель *m.*, ~ница; сто́рож (*pl.* -á); *attrib.* вре́менный.
care-worn *adj.* изму́ченный (-ен) забо́тами.
cargo *n.* груз.
caricature *n.* карикату́ра; *v.t.* изобража́ть *imp.*, изобрази́ть *perf.* в карикату́рном ви́де.
caries *n.* карио́з.
carmine *n.* карми́н, карми́нный цвет; *adj.* карми́нный.
carnage *n.* резня́.
carnal *adj.* пло́тский.
carnation *n.* (садо́вая) гвозди́ка.
carnival *n.* карнава́л; (*Shrove-tide*) ма́сленица.
carnivore *n.* плотоя́дное живо́тное *sb.* **carnivorous** *adj.* плотоя́дный.
carol *n.* (рожде́ственский) гимн.
carotid artery *n.* со́нная арте́рия.
carousal *n.* попо́йка.
carp[1] *n.* (*wild*) саза́н; (*domesticated*) карп.

carp² *v.i.* придира́ться *imp.*, придра́ться (-деру́сь, -дерёшся; -дра́лся, -драла́сь, -драло́сь) *perf.* (at, k + *dat.*).

carpenter *n.* пло́тник. **carpentry** *n.* пло́тничество.

carpet *n.* ковёр (-вра́) *v.t.* устила́ть *imp.*, устла́ть (-телю́, -те́лешь) *perf.* ковра́ми; *c.-bag*, саквоя́ж.

carping *adj.* приди́рчивый; *n.* приди́рки (-рок) *pl.*

carriage *n.* (*vehicle*) каре́та, экипа́ж; (*rly.*) ваго́н; (*of machine*) каре́тка; (*conveyance*) прово́з, перево́зка; (*bearing*) оса́нка; *c. forward*, с опла́той доста́вки получа́телем; *c. free*, беспла́тная пересы́лка; *c. paid*, за пересы́лку упла́чено. **carriageway** *n.* прое́зжая часть доро́ги, у́лицы. **carrier** *n.* (*person*) во́зчик; (*object*) бага́жник; *c. pigeon*, почто́вый го́лубь (*pl.* -би, -бе́й) *m.*; *c. wave*, несу́щая волна́ (*pl.* -ны, -н, -на́м).

carrion *n.* па́даль; *c. crow*, чёрная воро́на.

carrot *n.* морко́вка; *pl.* морко́вь (*collect.*).

carry *v.t.* (*by hand*) носи́ть (ношу́, но́сишь) *indet.*, нести́ (несу́, -сёшь; нёс, -ла́) *det.*; переноси́ть (-ошу́, -о́сишь) *imp.*, перенести́ (-есу́, -есёшь; -ёс, -есла́) *perf.*; (*in vehicle*) вози́ть (вожу́, во́зишь) *indet.*, везти́ (везу́, -зёшь; вёз, -ла́) *det.*; *v.i.* нести́сь (несётся; нёсся, несла́сь) (*sound*) быть слы́шен (-шна́, -шно); *c. forward*, переноси́ть (-ошу́, -о́сишь) *imp.*, перенести́ (-есу́, -есёшь; -ёс, -есла́) *perf.*; *c. on*, (*continue*) продолжа́ть *imp.*; (*behaviour*) вести́ (веду́, ведёшь; вёл, -а́) *imp.* себя́ несде́ржанно; *c. out*, выполня́ть *imp.*, вы́полнить *perf.*; доводи́ть (-ожу́, -о́дишь) *imp.*, довести́ (-еду́, -едёшь; -ёл, -ела́) *perf.* до конца́; *c. over*, переноси́ть (-ошу́, -о́сишь) *imp.*, перенести́ (-есу́, -есёшь; -ёс, -есла́) *perf.*

cart *n.* теле́га, пово́зка; *v.t.* вози́ть (вожу́, во́зишь) *indet.*, везти́ (везу́, -зёшь; вёз, -ла́) *det.* в теле́ге; *c.-horse*, ломова́я ло́шадь (*pl.* -ди, -де́й, *instr.* -дьми́); *c.-load*, воз; *c.-track*, гужева́я доро́га, просёлок (-лка); *c.-wheel*

колесо́ (*pl.* -ёса) теле́ги; (*somersault*) переворо́т бо́ком в сто́рону. **cartage** *n.* сто́имость перево́зки.

cartel *n.* карте́ль *m.*

cartilage *n.* хрящ (-а́). **cartilaginous** *adj.* хрящево́й.

cartographer *n.* карто́граф. **cartographic** *adj.* картографи́ческий. **cartography** *n.* картогра́фия.

carton *n.* коро́бка из карто́на, пластма́ссы и т.д.

cartoon *n.* карикату́ра; (*design*) карто́н; (*cin.*) мультфи́льм. **cartoonist** *n.* карикатури́ст, ~ ка.

cartridge *n.* патро́н; *c. belt*, патронта́ш.

carve *v.t.* ре́зать (ре́жу, -жешь) *imp.* по + *dat.*; (*wood*) выреза́ть *imp.*, вы́резать (-ежу, -ежешь) *perf.*; (*stone*) высека́ть *imp.*, вы́сечь (-еку, -ечешь, -ек) *perf.*; (*meat etc.*) нареза́ть *imp.* наре́зать (-е́жу, -е́жешь) *perf.* **carver** *n.* (*person*) ре́зчик; *pl.* (*cutlery*) большо́й нож (-а́) и ви́лка. **carving** *n.* резьба́; резно́й орна́мент; *c.-knife*, нож (-а́) для нареза́ния мя́са.

cascade *n.* каска́д.

case¹ *n.* (*instance*) слу́чай; (*leg.*) де́ло (*pl.* -ла́); (*med.*) больно́й *sb.*; (*gram.*) паде́ж (-а́); *as the c. may be*, в зави́симости от обстоя́тельств; *in c.*, в слу́чае е́сли; *in any c.*, во вся́ком слу́чае; *in no c.*, ни в ко́ем слу́чае; *just in c.*, на вся́кий слу́чай, на аво́сь.

case² *n.* (*box*) я́щик, коро́бка; (*suitcase*) чемода́н; (*casing*) футля́р, чехо́л (-хла́); (*print.*) ка́сса; *v.t.* покрыва́ть *imp.*, покры́ть (-ро́ю, -ро́ешь) *perf.*; *c.-harden*, цементи́ровать *imp.*, *perf.*

casement window *n.* ство́рное окно́ (*pl.* о́кна, о́кон, о́кнам).

cash *n.* нали́чные *sb.*; де́ньги (-нег, -ньга́м) *pl.*; ка́сса; *c. and carry*, прода́жа за нали́чный расчёт без доста́вки на́ дом; *c. down*, де́ньги на бо́чку; *c. on delivery*, нало́жен платежо́м; *c. register*, ка́сса; *v.t.* превраща́ть *imp.*, преврати́ть (-а́щу, -ати́шь) *perf.* в нали́чные *sb.*; *c. a cheque*, получа́ть *imp.*, получи́ть (-чу́, -чишь) *perf.* де́ньги по че́ку. **cashier¹** *n.* касси́р. **cashier²** *v.t.* увольня́ть *imp.*, уво́лить *perf.* со слу́жбы.

cashmere *n.* кашеми́р.

casing *n.* (*tech.*) кожу́х (-а́).

casino *n.* казино́ *neut.indecl.*

cask *n.* бо́чка.

casket *n.* шкату́лка, ларе́ц (-рца́).

casserole *n.* тяжёлая кастрю́ля; блю́до, приготовля́емое в ней.

cassock *n.* ря́са.

cast *v.t.* (*throw*) броса́ть *imp.*, бро́сить *perf.*; (*shed*) сбра́сывать *imp.*, сбро́сить *perf.*; (*theat.*) распределя́ть *imp.*, распредели́ть *perf.* ро́ли + *dat.*; (*found*) лить (лью, льёшь; лил, -а́, -о) *imp.*, с~ (со́лью, -ьёшь; слил, -а́, -о) *perf.*; (*horoscope*) составля́ть *imp.*, соста́вить *perf.*; c. ashore, выбра́сывать *imp.*, вы́бросить *perf.* на бе́рег; c. off, (*knitting*) спуска́ть *imp.*, спусти́ть (-ущу́, -у́стишь) *perf.* пе́тли; (*naut.*) отплыва́ть *imp.*, отплы́ть (-ыву́, -ывёшь; отплы́л, -а́, -о) *perf.*; c. on, (*knitting*) набира́ть *imp.*, набра́ть (наберу́, -рёшь; набра́л, -а́, -о) *perf.* пе́тли; *n.* (*throw*) бросо́к (-ска́), броса́ние; (*of mind etc.*) склад, тип; (*mould*) фо́рма; (*med.*) ги́псовая повя́зка; (*theat.*) де́йствующие ли́ца (-ц) *pl.*; (*in eye*) лёгкое косогла́зие. **castaway** *n.* потерпе́вший *sb.* кораблекруше́ние.

cast iron *n.* чугу́н (-а́). **cast-iron** *adj.* чугу́нный. **cast-offs** *n.* (*clothes*) но́шеное пла́тье.

castanet *n.* кастанье́та.

caste *n.* ка́ста; ка́стовая систе́ма.

castigate *v.t.* бичева́ть *imp.*

castle *n.* за́мок (-мка); (*chess*) ладья́.

castor *n.* (*wheel*) ро́лик, колёсико (*pl.* -ки, -ков); c. sugar, са́харная пу́дра.

castor oil *n.* касто́ровое ма́сло.

castrate *v.t.* кастри́ровать *imp.*, *perf.* **castration** *n.* кастра́ция.

casual *adj.* случа́йный; (*careless*) несерьёзный. **casualty** *n.* (*wounded*) ра́неный *sb.*; (*killed*) уби́тый *sb.*; *pl.* поте́ри (-рь) *pl.*; c. ward, пала́та ско́рой по́мощи.

casuist *n.* казуи́ст. **casuistic(al)** *adj.* казуисти́ческий. **casuistry** *n.* казуи́стика.

cat *n.* ко́шка; (*tom*) кот (-а́); catcall, свист, осви́стывание; *v.t. & i.* осви́стывать *imp.*, освиста́ть (-ищу́, -и́щешь) *perf.*; c.-o'-nine-tails, ко́шки *f.pl.*; c.'s-eye, (*min.*) коша́чий глаз (*loc.* -у́; *pl.* -за́, -з); (*on road*) (доро́жный) рефле́ктор; c.'s-meat, кони́на (для ко́шек); catwalk, у́зкий мо́стик; рабо́чий помо́ст.

cataclysm *n.* катакли́зм.

catalogue *n.* катало́г; (*price list*) прейскура́нт; *v.t.* каталогизи́ровать *imp.*, *perf.*

catalysis *n.* ката́лиз. **catalyst** *n.* катализа́тор. **catalytic** *adj.* каталити́ческий.

catamaran *n.* катамара́н.

catapult *n.* (*child's*) рога́тка; (*hist.*, *aeron.*) катапу́льта; *v.t.* катапульти́ровать *imp.*, *perf.*

cataract *n.* (*waterfall*) водопа́д; (*med.*) катара́кта.

catarrh *n.* ката́р.

catastrophe *n.* катастро́фа. **catastrophic** *adj.* катастрофи́ческий.

catch *v.t.* (*captive*) лови́ть (-влю́, -вишь, *imp.*, пойма́ть *perf.*; (*seize*) захва́тывать *imp.*, захвати́ть (-ачу́, -а́тишь) *perf.*; (*surprise*) застава́ть (-таю́, -таёшь) *imp.*, заста́ть (-а́ну, -а́нешь) *perf.*; (*disease*) заража́ться *imp.*, зарази́ться *perf.* + *instr.*; (*be in time for*) успева́ть *imp.*, успе́ть *perf.* на + *acc.*; c. on, зацепля́ть(ся) *imp.*, зацепи́ть(ся) (-плю́(сь), -пишь(ся)) *perf.* за + *acc.*; (*v.i.*) (*become popular*) привива́ться *imp.*, приви́ться (-вьётся; -ви́лся, -вила́сь) *perf.*; c. up with, догоня́ть *imp.*, догна́ть (догоню́, -нишь; догна́л, -а́, -о) *perf.*; *n.* (*action*) пойма; (*of fish*) уло́в; (*trick*) уло́вка; (*on door etc.*) защёлка, задви́жка; c. crops, междупосевные культу́ры *f.pl.* **catching** *adj.* зара́зный; зарази́тельный; привлека́тельный. **catchment area** *n.* водосбо́рная пло́щадь (*pl.* -ди, -де́й). **catchword** *n.* (*slogan*) ло́зунг; (*running title*) колонти́тул; (*headword*) загла́вное сло́во (*pl.* -ва́). **catchy** *adj.* привлека́тельный, легко́ запомина́ющийся.

catechism *n.* (*eccl.*) катехи́зис; допро́с. **catechize** *v.t.* допра́шивать *imp.*, допроси́ть (-ошу́, -о́сишь) *perf.*

categorical *adj.* категори́ческий. **category** *n.* катего́рия.

catenary *n.* цепна́я ли́ния; *adj.* цепно́й.

cater v.i. поставля́ть imp. прови́зию; c. for, снабжа́ть imp., снабди́ть perf.; обслу́живать imp., обслужи́ть (-жу́, -жишь) perf. caterer n. поставщи́к (-á) (прови́зии).

caterpillar n. гу́сеница; adj. гу́сеничный; c. track, гу́сеничная ле́нта.

caterwaul v.i. крича́ть (-чу́, -чи́шь) кото́м; задава́ть (-даю́) imp., зада́ть (-áст; зáдал, -á, -o) perf. коша́чий конце́рт. caterwauling n. коша́чий конце́рт.

catgut n. кетгу́т.

catharsis n. ка́тарсис.

cathedral n. (кафедра́льный) собо́р.

catheter n. катéтер.

cathode n. като́д; c. rays, като́дные лучи́ m.pl.

Catholic adj. католи́ческий; n. като́лик, -и́чка. **Catholicism** n. католи́чество, католици́зм.

catkin n. серёжка.

cattle n. скот (-á).

cauldron n. котёл (-тлá).

cauliflower n. цветна́я капу́ста.

caulk v.t. конопа́тить imp., за~ perf.

causal adj. причи́нный (-нен, -нна). **causality** n. причи́нность. **causation** n. причинéние; причи́нность. **cause** n. причи́на, по́вод; (leg. etc.) дéло (pl. -лá); v.t. причиня́ть imp., причини́ть perf.; вызыва́ть imp., вы́звать (-зову, -зовешь) perf.; (induce) заставля́ть imp., заста́вить perf. **causeless** adj. беспричи́нный.

caustic adj. каусти́ческий, éдкий (éдок, едкá, éдко); c. soda, éдкий натр; c. éдкое вещество́.

cauterization n. прижига́ние. **cauterize** v.t. прижига́ть imp., прижéчь (-жгу, -жжёшь; -жёг, -жглá) perf. **cautery** n. термокáутер.

caution n. осторо́жность; (warning) предупреждéние; v.t. предостерега́ть imp., предостерéчь (-егу́, -ежёшь; -ёг, -еглá) perf. **cautious** adj. осторо́жный. **cautionary** adj. предостерега́ющий.

cavalcade n. кавалькáда. **cavalier** adj. бесцеремóнный (-нен, -нна), C., (hist.) роялистский; роялист. **cavalry**

n. кавалéрия. **cavalryman** n. кавалерист.

cave n. пещéра; v.i.: c. in, обва́ливаться imp., обвали́ться (-ится) perf.; (yield) уступáть imp., уступи́ть (-плю, -пишь) perf. **caveman** n. пещéрный человéк. **cavern** n. пещéра. **cavernous** adj. пещéристый.

caviare n. икрá.

cavil v.i. придира́ться imp., придра́ться (-дерýсь, -дерёшься; -áлся, -алáсь, -áлось) perf. (at, k + dat.).

cavity n. впáдина, по́лость (pl. -ти, -тéй).

caw n. кáрканье; v.i. кáркать imp., кáркнуть perf.; n. кáрканье.

cayman n. каймáн.

cease v.t. & i. прекращáть(ся) imp., прекрати́ть(ся) (-ащý, -ати́т(ся)) perf.; v.i. переставáть (-таю́, -таёшь) imp., перестáть (-áну, -áнешь) perf. (+ inf.); c.-fire, прекращéние огня́. **ceaseless** adj. непрестáнный (-áнен, -áнна).

cedar n. кедр.

ceiling n. потоло́к (-лкá); (prices etc.) максимáльная ценá (acc. -ну), максимáльный у́ровень (-вня) m.

celandine n. чистотéл.

celebrate v.t. прáздновать imp., от~ perf.; be celebrated, слáвиться imp. (for, + instr.). **celebrated** adj. знамени́тый. **celebration** n. прáзднование. **celebrity** n. знамени́тость.

celery n. сельдерéй.

celestial adj. небéсный.

celibacy n. безбрáчие. **celibate** adj. безбрáчный; (person) холостóй (-ост), незамýжняя.

cell n. (room) кéлья; (prison) (тюрéмная) кáмера; (biol.) клéтка, клéточка; (polit.) ячéйка.

cellar n. подвáл, по́греб (pl. -á); adj. подвáльный.

cellist n. виолончели́ст. **cello** n. виолончéль.

cellophane n. целлофáн; adj. целлофáновый. **cellular** adj. клéточный. **cellule** n. клéточка. **celluloid** n. целлуло́ид; (кино)фи́льм. **cellulose** n. целлюло́за, клетчáтка.

Celsius: C. scale, шкалá термóметра

Цельсия; *C. thermometer*, термометр Цельсия; *10° C.*, 10° по Цельсию.
Celt *n.* кельт. **Celtic** *adj.* кельтский.
cement *n.* цемент; *v.t.* цементировать *imp.*, за~ *perf.*
cemetery *n.* кладбище.
cenotaph *n.* кенотаф.
censer *n.* кадило.
censor *n.* цензор; *v.t.* подвергать *imp.*, подвергнуть (-г) *perf.* цензуре. **censorious** *adj.* строгий (строг, -á, -о); склонный (-онен, -онна, -онно) осуждать. **censorship** *n.* цензура. **censure** *n.* осуждение; порицание; *v.t.* осуждать *imp.*, осудить (-ужу, -удишь) *perf.*; порицать *imp.*
census *n.* перепись (населения).
cent *n.* цент; *per c.*, процент.
centaur *n.* кентавр.
centenarian *n.* столетний; *n.* столетний человек, человек в возрасте ста лет. **centenary** *n.* столетие. **centennial** *adj.* столетний; *n.* столетняя годовщина. **centigrade** *adj.* стоградусный; *10° C.*, 10° по Цельсию. **centigram** *n.* сантиграмм. **centilitre** *n.* сантилитр. **centimetre** *n.* сантиметр. **centipede** *n.* сороконожка.
central *adj.* центральный; *c. heating*, центральное отопление. **centralism** *n.* централизм. **centralization** *n.* централизация. **centralize** *v.t.* централизовать *imp.*, *perf.* **centre** *n.* центр; середина; *c. back*, центр защиты; *c. board*, опускной киль *m.*; *c. forward*, центр нападения; *c. half*, центр полузащиты; *v.i.* сосредоточиваться *imp.*, сосредоточиться *perf.* **centrifugal** *adj.* центробежный. **centrifuge** *n.* центрифуга. **centripetal** *adj.* центростремительный.
centurion *n.* центурион. **century** *n.* столетие, век (*loc.* в -е, на -у́; *pl.* -á); (*sport*) сто очков.
ceramic *adj.* керамический. **ceramics** *n.* керамика.
cereal *adj.* хлебный; *n.*: *pl.* хлеба *m.pl.*, хлебные, зерновые, злаки *m.pl.*; *breakfast cereals*, зерновые хлопья (-ьев) *pl.*
cerebral *adj.* мозговой.

ceremonial *adj.* формальный; торжественный (-ен, -енна), парадный; *n.* церемониал. **ceremonious** *adj.* церемонный (-нен, -нна). **ceremony** *n.* церемония.
cerise *adj.* (*n.*) светло-вишнёвый (цвет).
cert *n.* (*sl.*) верное дело. **certain** *adj.* (*definite*) определённый (-ёнен, -ённа); (*reliable*) верный (-рен, -рна, -рно, верны́); (*doubtless*) несомненный (-нен, -нна); *predic.* уверен (-на); *for c.*, наверняка. **certainly** *adv.* (*of course*) конечно, безусловно; (*without fail*) непременно; (*beyond question*) несомненно. **certainty** *n.* (*conviction*) уверенность; (*undoubted fact*) несомненный факт; безусловность; *bet on a c.*, держать (-жу, -жишь) *imp.* пари наверняка.
certificate *n.* удостоверение, свидетельство; сертификат; аттестат; *birth c.*, метрика. **certify** *v.t.* удостоверять *imp.*, удостоверить *perf.*; свидетельствовать *imp.*, за~ *perf.*; (*as insane*) признавать (-наю, -наёшь) *imp.*, признать *perf.* сумасшедшим.
certitude *n.* уверенность.
cessation *n.* прекращение.
cesspit *n.* помойная яма. **cesspool** *n.* выгребная яма; (*fig.*) клоака.
chafe *v.t.* (*rub*) тереть (тру, трёшь; тёр) *imp.*; (*rub sore*) натирать *imp.*, натереть (-тру, -трёшь; -тёр) *perf.*; *v.i.* (*fret*) раздражаться *imp.*, раздражиться *perf.*
chaff *n.* (*husks*) мякина; (*chopped straw*) сечка; (*banter*) подшучивание; *v.t.* поддразнивать *imp.*, поддразнить (-ню, -нишь) *perf.*; подшучивать *imp.*, подшутить (-учу, -утишь) *perf.* над + *instr.*
chaffinch *n.* зяблик.
chagrin *n.* огорчение.
chain *n.* цепь (*loc.* -пи; *pl.* -пи, -пей); (*crochet*) косичка; *c. reaction*, цепная реакция; *c. stitch*, тамбурный шов (шва), тамбурная строчка.
chair *n.* стул (*pl.* -ья, -ьев), кресло (*gen.pl.* -сел); (*chairmanship*) председательство; (*chairman*) председатель *m.*, ~ ница; (*univ.*) кафедра; *v.t.* (*preside*) председательствовать *imp.* на +

prep.; (*carry aloft*) поднима́ть *imp.*, подня́ть (-ниму́, -ни́мешь; по́днял, -á, -о) *perf.* и нести́ (несу́, -сёшь; нёс, -лá) *imp.* **chairman, -woman** *n.* председа́тель *m.*, -ница.

chalice *n.* ча́ша.

chalk *n.* мел (-a(y), *loc.* -ý & -e); (*piece of c.*) мело́к (-лкá); *not by a long c.*, отню́дь не, далеко́ не; *v.t.* писа́ть (пишу́, пи́шешь) *imp.*, на~ *perf.* ме́лом; черти́ть (-рчу́, -ртишь) *imp.*, на~ *perf.* ме́лом. **chalky** *adj.* мелово́й, известко́вый.

challenge *n.* (*summons*) вы́зов; (*sentry's call*) о́клик (часово́го); (*leg.*) отво́д; *v.t.* вызыва́ть *imp.*, вы́звать (вы́зову, -вешь) *perf.*; оклика́ть *imp.*, окли́кнуть *perf.*; отводи́ть (-ожу́, -о́дишь) *imp.*, отвести́ (-еду́, -едёшь; -ёл, -елá) *perf.*

chalybeate *adj.* желе́зистый.

chamber *n.* ко́мната; (*polit.*) пала́та; *pl.* меблиро́ванные ко́мнаты *f.pl.*; *pl.* (*judge's*) кабине́т (судьи́); *c. music*, ка́мерная му́зыка; *c.-pot*, ночно́й горшо́к (-шка́). **chamberlain** *n.* камерге́р; *c.*, гофме́йстер. **chambermaid** *n.* го́рничная *sb.*

chameleon *n.* хамелео́н.

chamois *n.* (*animal*) се́рна; (*c.-leather*) за́мша; *adj.* за́мшевый.

champ *v.i.* ча́вкать *imp.*, ча́вкнуть *perf.*; *c. the bit*, грызть (-зёт; -з) *imp.* удила́ (*pl.*).

champagne *n.* шампа́нское *sb.*

champion *n.* (*athletic etc.*) чемпио́н, ~ ка; (*animal, plant etc.*) пе́рвый приз; (*upholder*) побо́рник, -ица; *adj.* получи́вший пе́рвый приз; *v.t.* защища́ть *imp.*, защити́ть (-ищу́, -ити́шь) *perf.* **championship** *n.* пе́рвенство, чемпиона́т; побо́рничество.

chance *n.* случа́йность; (*opportunity*) слу́чай; (*possibility*) шанс; *adj.* случа́йный; *v.i.* (*happen*) случа́ться *imp.*, случи́ться *perf.*; *c. it*, рискну́ть *perf.*

chancel *n.* алта́рь (-ря́) *m.*

chancellery *n.* канцеля́рия. **chancellor** *n.* ка́нцлер; (*univ.*) ре́ктор университе́та; *Lord C.*, лорд-ка́нцлер; *C. of the Exchequer*, ка́нцлер казначе́йства.

Chancery *n.* суд (-á) ло́рда-ка́нцлера; *c.*, канцеля́рия.

chancy *adj.* риско́ванный (-ан, -анна).

chandelier *n.* лю́стра.

change *n.* переме́на, измене́ние; (*of clothes etc.*) сме́на; (*money*) сда́ча; (*of trains etc.*) переса́дка; *c. for the better*, переме́на к лу́чшему; *c. of air*, переме́на обстано́вки; *c. of life*, клима́ктерий; *c. of scene*, переме́на обстано́вки; *for a c.*, для разнообра́зия; *v.t. & i.* меня́ть(ся) *imp.*; изменя́ть(ся) *imp.*, измени́ть(ся) (-ню́(сь), -ни́шь(ся)) *perf.*; *v.i.* (*one's clothes*) переодева́ться *imp.*, переоде́ться (-е́нусь, -е́нешься) *perf.*; (*trains etc.*) переса́живаться *imp.*, пересе́сть (-ся́ду, -ся́дешь; -сёл) *perf.*; (*a baby*) перепелёнывать *imp.*, перепелена́ть *perf.*; (*give c. for*) разме́нивать *imp.*, разменя́ть *perf.*; *c. into* превраща́ться *imp.*, преврати́ться (-ащу́сь, -ати́шься) *perf.* в+*acc.* **changeable** *adj.* непостоя́нный (-нен, -нна), неусто́йчивый, изме́нчивый. **changeless** *adj.* неизме́нный (-нен, -нна), постоя́нный (-нен, -нна).

channel *n.* кана́л, проли́в, прото́к; (*fig.*) ру́сло (*gen.pl.* -сл & -сел), путь (-ти́, -тём) *m.*; *the* (*English*) *C.*, Ла-Ма́нш; *v.t.* пуска́ть *imp.*, пусти́ть (пущу́, пу́стишь) *perf.* по кана́лу; (*fig.*, *direct*) направля́ть *imp.*

chaos *n.* ха́ос. **chaotic** *adj.* хаоти́чный.

chap[1] *n.* (*person*) ма́лый *sb.*, па́рень (-рня, *pl.* -рни, -рне́й) *m.*

chap[2] *n.* (*crack*) трещи́на; *v.i.* тре́скаться *imp.*, по~ *perf.*

chapel *n.* часо́вня (*gen.pl.* -вен), капе́лла; моле́льня (*gen.pl.* -лен).

chap-fallen *adj.* удручённый (-ён, -ена́).

chaplain *n.* капелла́н.

chapter *n.* глава́ (*pl.* -вы); (*eccl.*) капи́тул; *c. house*, зда́ние капи́тула.

char[1] *n.* приходя́щая домрабо́тница.

char[2] *v.t. & i.* обу́гливать(ся) *imp.*, обу́глить(ся) *perf.*

character *n.* хара́ктер; (*testimonial*) рекоменда́ция; (*personage*) персона́ж; (*theat.*) де́йствующее лицо́ (*pl.* -ца); (*letter*) бу́ква; (*numeral*) ци́фра;

(*mark*) знак. **characteristic** *adj.* характе́рный; *n.* характе́рная черта́.
characterize *v.t.* характеризова́ть *imp.*, *perf.*

charade *n.* шара́да.

charcoal *n.* древе́сный у́голь (угля́) *m.*

charge *n.* (*load*) нагру́зка; (*for gun*; *electr.*) заря́д; (*fee*) пла́та; (*care*) попече́ние; (*person*) пито́мец (-мца), -мица; (*accusation*) обвине́ние; (*mil.*) ата́ка; *be in c. of,* заве́довать *imp.*+ *instr.*; име́ть *imp.* на попече́нии; *in the c. of,* на попече́нии+*gen.*; *v.t.* (*gun*; *electr.*) заряжа́ть *imp.*, заряди́ть (-яжу́, -я́ди́шь) *perf.*; (*accuse*) обвиня́ть *imp.*, обвини́ть *perf.* (*with,* в+*prep.*); (*mil.*) атакова́ть *imp.*, *perf.*; броса́ться *imp.*, бро́ситься *perf.* в ата́ку; *c.* (*for*), брать (беру́, -рёшь; брал, -а́, -о) *imp.*, взять (возьму́, -мёшь; взял, -а́, -о) *perf.* (за+*acc.*); назнача́ть *imp.*, назна́чить *perf.* пла́ту (за+*acc.*); *c. to* (*the account of*), запи́сывать *imp.*, записа́ть (-ишу́, -и́шешь) *perf.* на счёт +*gen.*

chargé d'affaires *n.* пове́ренный *sb.* в дела́х.

chariot *n.* колесни́ца.

charisma *n.* (*divine gift*) бо́жий дар; (*charm*) обая́ние. **charismatic** *adj.* богодухнове́нный; вдохнове́нный; с бо́жьей и́скрой; обая́тельный.

charitable *adj.* благотвори́тельный; (*merciful*) милосе́рдный; (*lenient*) снисходи́тельный. **charity** *n.* (*kindness*) милосе́рдие; (*leniency*) снисходи́тельность; благотвори́тельность; (*organization*) благотвори́тельное о́бщество; *pl.* благотвори́тельная де́ятельность.

charlatan *n.* шарлата́н.

charlotte *n.:* *apple c.,* шарло́тка.

charm *n.* очарова́ние; пре́лесть; (*spell*) заговор; *pl.* ча́ры (чар) *pl.*; (*amulet*) талисма́н; (*trinket*) брело́к; *act, work, like a c.,* твори́ть *imp.*, со~ *perf.* чудеса́; *v.t.* очаро́вывать *imp.*, очарова́ть *perf.*; *c. away,* отгоня́ть *imp.*, отогна́ть (отгоню́, -нишь; отогна́л, -а́, -о) *perf.* (как бы) колдовство́м; *bear a charmed life,* быть неуязви́мым.

charming *adj.* очарова́тельный, преле́стный.

charring *n.* рабо́та по до́му; *do, go out, c.,* служи́ть (-жу́, -жишь) *imp.* приходя́щей домрабо́тницей.

chart *n.* (*naut.*) морска́я ка́рта; (*table*) гра́фик; *v.t.* наноси́ть (-ошу́, -о́сишь) *imp.*, нанести́ (-су́, -сёшь; нанёс, -ла́) *perf.* на ка́рту; составля́ть *imp.*, соста́вить *perf.* гра́фик+*gen.* **charter** *n.* (*document*) ха́ртия; (*statutes*) уста́в; (*c.-party*) ча́ртер; *v.t.* (*ship*) фрахтова́ть *imp.*, за~ *perf.*; (*vehicle etc.*) нанима́ть *imp.*, наня́ть (найму́, -мёшь; на́нял, -а́, -о) *perf.*

charwoman *n.* приходя́щая домрабо́тница.

chase *v.t.* гоня́ться *indet.*, гна́ться (гоню́сь, го́нишься; гна́лся, -ла́сь, гна́ло́сь) *det.* за+*instr.*; *n.* (*pursuit*) пого́ня, пресле́дование; (*hunting*) охо́та.

chased *adj.* укра́шенный (-н) гравиро́ванием, рельефо́м.

chasm *n.* (*abyss*) бе́здна; (*fissure*) глубо́кая рассе́лина.

chassis *n.* шасси́ *neut.indecl.*

chaste *adj.* целому́дренный (-ен, -енна).

chastise *v.t.* подверга́ть *imp.*, подве́ргнуть (-г) *perf.* наказа́нию.

chastity *n.* целому́дрие.

chat *n.* бесе́да, разгово́р; *v.i.* бесе́довать *imp.*; разгова́ривать *imp.*

chattels *n.* дви́жимость.

chatter *n.* болтовня́; трескотня́; *v.i.* болта́ть *imp.*; треща́ть (-щу́, -щи́шь) *imp.*; (*of teeth*) стуча́ть (-ча́т) *imp.* **chatterbox** *n.* болту́н (-а́), ~ья. **chatty** *adj.* разгово́рчивый.

chauffeur *n.* шофёр.

chauvinism *n.* шовини́зм. **chauvinist** *n.* шовини́ст, ~ ка; *adj.* шовинисти́ческий.

cheap *adj.* дешёвый (дёшев, -а́, -о). **cheapen** *v.t. & i.* обесце́нивать(ся) *imp.*, обесце́нить(ся) *perf.*; удешевля́ть(ся) *imp.*, удешеви́ть(ся) *perf.* **cheaply** *adv.* дёшево. **cheapness** *n.* дешеви́зна.

cheat *v.t.* обма́нывать *imp.*, обману́ть (-ну́, -нешь) *perf.*; *v.i.* плутова́ть *imp.*, на~, с~ *perf.*; моше́нничать *imp.*,

c ~ perf.; n. (person) обма́нщик, -ица;
(act) обма́н. **cheating** n. моше́нни-
чество, плутовство́.

check¹ n. контро́ль m., прове́рка;
(stoppage) заде́ржка; (chess) шах; adj.
контро́льный; v.t. (examine) прове-
ря́ть imp., прове́рить perf.; контроли́-
ровать imp., про~, perf.; (restrain)
сде́рживать imp., сдержа́ть (-жу́,
-жишь) perf.; c.-list, контро́льный
спи́сок (-ска); checkmate, шах и мат;
v.t. наноси́ть (-ошу́, -о́сишь) imp.,
нанести́ (-су́, -сёшь; нанёс, -ла́) perf.
+ dat. пораже́ние; c.-point, контро́ль-
но-пропускно́й пункт.

check² n. (pattern) кле́тка. **check(ed)**
adj. кле́тчатый.

cheek n. щека́ (acc. щёку; pl. щёки,
щёк, -а́м); (impertinence) наха́льство,
де́рзость; v.t. дерзи́ть (-ишь) imp.,
на~ perf. + dat.; c.-bone, скула́ (pl.
-лы). **cheeky** adj. де́рзкий (-зок, -зка́,
-зко), наха́льный.

cheep n. писк; v.i. пища́ть (-щу́, -щи́шь)
imp., пи́скнуть perf.

cheer n. одобри́тельное восклица́ние;
pl. (applause) аплодисме́нты (-тов)
pl.; cheers! за (ва́ше) здоро́вье!; three
cheers for . . ., да здра́вствует (-уют)
+ nom.; v.t. (applaud) аплоди́ровать
imp. + dat.; c. up, ободря́ть(ся) imp.,
ободри́ть(ся) perf. **cheerful** adj. весёлый (ве́сел, -а́, -о, ве́селы), бо́дрый
(бодр, -а́, -о). **cheerless** adj. уны́лый.
cheery adj. бо́дрый (бодр, -а́, -о).

cheese n. сыр (-а(у); pl. -ы́); c.-cake,
ватру́шка; **cheesecloth**, ма́рля; c.-
paring, ску́пость, грошо́вая эконо́мия;
скупо́й (скуп, -а́, -о); c. straw, сы́рная
па́лочка.

cheetah n. гепа́рд.

chef n. (шеф-)по́вар (pl. -а́).

chef-d'oeuvre n. шеде́вр.

chemical adj. хими́ческий; c. warfare,
хими́ческая война́; n. химика́т; pl.
химика́лии (-ий) **chemically** adv.
хими́чески. **chemist** n. хи́мик; (drug-
gist) апте́карь m.; c.'s (shop), апте́ка.
chemistry n. хи́мия.

chenille n. сине́ль; adj. сине́льный.

cheque n. чек; c.-book, че́ковая кни́жка.

chequered adj. (varied) разнообра́зный;
(changing) изме́нчивый.

cherish v.t. (foster) леле́ять (-е́ю,
-е́ешь) imp.; (hold dear) дорожи́ть
imp. + instr.; (preserve in memory) хра-
ни́ть imp. (в па́мяти); (love) не́жно
люби́ть (-блю́, -бишь) imp. **cherished**
adj. заве́тный.

cheroot n. мани́льская сига́ра.

cherry n. ви́шня (gen.pl. -шен); черешня
(gen.pl. -шен); (tree) вишнёвое
де́рево (pl. -е́вья, -е́вьев); (colour)
вишнёвый цвет; adj. вишнёвый, вишнёвого цве́та; c.-wood, древеси́на
вишнёвого де́рева.

cherub n. херуви́м, херуви́мчик.
cherubic adj. пу́хлый и розове́нький.

chervil n. ке́рвель f.

chess n. ша́хматы (-т) pl.; adj. ша́хмат-
ный; c.-board, ша́хматная доска́ (acc.
-ску; pl. -ски, -со́к, -ска́м); c.-cham-
pion, чемпио́н по ша́хматам; c.-
player, шахмати́ст, ~ ка; c.-men, ша́х-
маты (-т) pl.

chest n. я́щик, сунду́к (-а́); (anat.)
грудь (-ди, instr. -дью; pl. -ди, -де́й);
c. of drawers, комо́д.

chestnut n. (tree, fruit) кашта́н; (colour)
кашта́новый цвет; (horse) гнеда́я sb.;
adj. кашта́новый; (horse) гнедо́й.

chevron n. наши́вка.

chew v.t. жева́ть (жую́, жуёшь) imp.;
c. over, пережёвывать imp., пережё-
ва́ть (-жую́, -жуёшь) perf.; c. the cud,
жева́ть (жую́, жуёшь) imp. жва́чку.
chewing n. жева́ние; c.-gum, жева́тель-
ная рези́нка, жва́чка.

chicane n. вре́менное или передвижно́е
препя́тствие на доро́ге, го́ночном
тре́ке. **chicanery** n. крючкотво́рство,
махина́ция.

chick n. цыплёнок (-нка; pl. цепля́та,
-т). **chicken** n. ку́рица (pl. ку́ры, кур);
цыплёнок (-нка; pl. цепля́та, -т);
(meat) куря́тина; adj. трусли́вый; c.-
hearted, -livered, трусли́вый. **chicken-
pox** n. ветряна́я о́спа, ветря́нка.

chicory n. цико́рий.

chief n. глава́ (pl. -вы) m., f.; (mil. etc.)
нача́льник; (of tribe) вождь (-дя́) m.;
(robber) атама́н; adj. гла́вный; ста́р-
ший. **chiefly** adv. гла́вным о́бразом.

chieftain *n.* вождь (-дя́) *m.*; (*robber*) атама́н.

chiffon *n.* шифо́н; *adj.* шифо́новый.

child *n.* ребёнок (-нка; *pl.* де́ти, -те́й); c.-*birth*, ро́ды (-дов) *pl.*; c. *prodigy*, вунде́ркинд; c.'s *play*, де́тские игру́шки *f.pl.*; *childrens' adj.* де́тский. **childhood** *n.* де́тство. **childish** *adj.* де́тский, ребя́ческий. **childless** *adj.* безде́тный. **childlike** *adj.* де́тский.

chili *n.* стручко́вый пе́рец (-рца(у)).

chill *n.* хо́лод (-а(у); *pl.* -á); охлажде́ние; (*ailment*) просту́да, озно́б; (*fig.*) холодно́сть (-дка́) *adj.*; *v.t.* охлажда́ть *imp.*, охлади́ть *perf.*; студи́ть (-ужу́, -у́дишь) *imp.*, о~ *perf.* **chilled** *adj.* охлаждённый (-ён, ена́), моро́женый. **chilly** *adj.* холо́дный (хо́лоден, -дна́, -дно, холо́дны), прохла́дный.

chime *n.* (*set of bells*) набо́р колоколо́в, *pl.* колоко́льный перезво́н, (*of clock*) бой; *v.t.* звони́ть *imp.*, по~ *perf.* в + *acc.*; *v.i.* звене́ть (-ни́т) *imp.*, про~ *perf.*; (*correspond*) соотве́тствовать *imp.* (to, + *dat.*); c. in, вме́шиваться *imp.*, вмеша́ться *perf.*

chimera *n.* химе́ра. **chimerical** *adj.* химери́ческий.

chimney *n.* (*for smoke*) (дымова́я) труба́ (*pl.* -бы); (*lamp c.*) ла́мповое стекло́ (*pl.* стёкла, -кол, -клам); (*cleft*) рассе́лина, камни́н; c.-*pot*, дефле́ктор; c.-*sweep*, трубочи́ст.

chimpanzee *n.* шимпанзе́ *m.indecl.*

chin *n.* подборо́док (-дка); *v.t.*: c. the *bar*, *oneself*, подтя́гиваться *imp.*, подтяну́ться (-ну́сь, -нешься) *perf.* до у́ровня подборо́дка.

China *adj.* кита́йский. **china** *n.* (*material*) фарфо́р; (*objects*) посу́да; *adj.* фарфо́ровый.

chinchilla *n.* (*animal, fur*) шинши́лла.

Chinese *n.* (*person*) кита́ец (-а́йца), -а́нка; *adj.* кита́йский; C. *lantern*, кита́йский фона́рик; C. *white*, кита́йские бели́ла (-л) *pl.*

chink[1] *n.* (*sound*) звон; *v.i.* звене́ть (-ни́т) *imp.*, про~ *perf.*

chink[2] *n.* (*opening, crack*) щель (*pl.* -ли, -ле́й), сква́жина.

chintz *n.* глазиро́ванный си́тец (-тца(у)).

chip *v.t.* отбива́ть *imp.*, отби́ть (отобью́, -ьёшь) *perf.*; щепа́ (*pl.* -пы, -п, -па́м), ще́пка, лучи́на; щерби́на, щерби́нка; (*in games*) фи́шка; *pl.* жа́реная карто́шка (*collect.*); c.-*basket*, корзи́на из стру́жек.

chiropody *n.* педикю́р.

chirp *v.i.* чири́кать *imp.*

chisel *n.* долото́ (*pl.* -та); стаме́ска; зуби́ло; резе́ц (-зца́); *v.t.* высека́ть *imp.*, вы́сечь (-еку, -ечешь; -ек) *perf.*; выреза́ть *imp.*, вы́резать (-ежу, -ежешь) *perf.* **chiseller** *n.* моше́нник.

chit *n.* (*note*) запи́ска.

chit-chat *n.* болтовня́.

chivalrous *adj.* ры́царский. **chivalry** *n.* ры́царство.

chive *n.* лук(-а)-ре́занец (-нца).

chloral *n.* хлоралгидра́т. **chloride** *n.* хлори́д. **chlorinate** *v.t.* хлори́ровать *imp.*, *perf.* **chlorine** *n.* хлор. **chloroform** *n.* хлорофо́рм; *v.t.* хлороформи́ровать *imp.*, *perf.* **chlorophyll** *n.* хлорофи́лл.

chock *n.* клин (*pl.* -ья, -ьев); (*tormozná́я*) коло́дка; c.-*a-block*, c.-*full*, битко́м наби́тый, перепо́лненный (-ен, -енна).

chocolate *n.* шокола́д (-а(у)); (*sweet*) шокола́дка; (*colour*) шокола́дный цвет; *adj.* шокола́дный; шокола́дного цве́та.

choice *n.* вы́бор; *adj.* отбо́рный.

choir *n.* хор (*pl.* хоры́); хорово́й анса́мбль *m.*; c.-*boy*, (ма́льчик) пе́вчий *sb.*

choke *n.* (*valve*) дро́ссель *m.*; (*artichoke*) сердцеви́на артишо́ка; *v.i.* дави́ться (-влю́сь, -вишься) *imp.*, по~ *perf.*; задыха́ться *imp.*, задохну́ться (-ну́лся, -о́х(ну́)лась) *perf.*; *v.t.* (*suffocate*) души́ть (-шу́, -шишь) *imp.*, за~ *perf.*; (*of plants*) заглуша́ть *imp.*, глуши́ть *imp.*, за~ *perf.* **choker** *n.* (*collar*) высо́кий крахма́льный воротничо́к (-чка́); (*necklace*) коро́ткое ожере́лье.

cholera *n.* холе́ра.

choleric *adj.* вспы́льчивый.

cholesterol *n.* холестери́н.

choose *v.t.* (*select*) выбира́ть *imp.*, вы́брать (-беру, -берешь) *perf.*;

chop (*decide*) реша́ть *imp.*, реши́ть *perf.* **choosy** *adj.* разбо́рчивый.

chop[1] *v.t.* руби́ть (-блю́, -бишь) *imp.*, рубну́ть, (*fell*) сруба́ть *imp.*, (*chop up*) кроши́ть (-шу́, -шишь) *imp.*, ис~, на~, рас~ *perf.*; коло́ть (-лю́, -лешь) *imp.*, рас~ *perf.*; ~ **off**, отруба́ть *imp.*, отруби́ть (-блю́, -бишь) *perf.*; *n.* (*blow*) руба́щий уда́р (*cul.*) отбивна́я котле́та.

chop[2] *v.i.*: ~ **and change**, постоя́нно меня́ться *imp.*; колеба́ться (-блюсь, -блешься) *imp.*

chopper *n.* (*knife*) се́чка, коса́рь (-ря́) *m.*; (*axe*) колу́н (-а́). **choppy** *adj.* неспоко́йный; ~ **sea**, зыбь на́ море.

chops *n.* (*jaws*) че́люсти (-тей) *pl.*; ~ **of the Channel**, вход в Ла-Ма́нш; **lick one's** ~, обли́зываться *imp.*, облиза́ться (-жу́сь, -жешься) *perf.*

chop-sticks *n.* па́лочки *f.pl.* для еды́. **chop-suey** *n.* кита́йское рагу́ *neut. indecl.*

choral *adj.* хорово́й. **chorale** *n.* хора́л.

chord[1] *n.* (*math.*) хо́рда; (*anat.*) свя́зка.

chord[2] *n.* (*mus.*) акко́рд.

choreographer *n.* хорео́граф. **choreographic** *adj.* хореографи́ческий. **choreography** *n.* хореогра́фия.

chorister *n.* пе́вчий *sb.*, хори́ст, -ка.

chortle *v.i.* фы́ркать *imp.*, фы́ркнуть *perf.* от сме́ха.

chorus *n.* хор *pl.* хо́ры́); (*refrain*) припе́в; *attr.* ~-**girl**, хори́стка; *v.i.* (*sing*) петь (пою́) *imp.*, про~ *perf.* хо́ром; (*speak*) говори́ть *imp.*, сказа́ть (-ажет) *perf.* хо́ром.

christen *v.t.* (*baptise*) крести́ть (-ещу́, -е́стишь) *imp.*, *perf.*; (*give name*) дава́ть (даю́, даёшь) *imp.*, дать (дам, дашь, даст, дади́м; дал, -а́, да́ло́, -и) *perf.*+*dat.* и́мя при креще́нии. **Christian** *n.* христиани́н (*pl.* -а́не, -а́н), -а́нка; *adj.* христиа́нский; ~ **name**, и́мя *neut.* **Christianity** *n.* христиа́нство.

Christmas *n.* рождество́; *C. Eve*, сочельник; *C.*-*tide*, свя́тки (-ток) *pl.*; *C. tree*, ёлка.

chromatic *adj.* хромати́ческий. **chrome** *n.* крон; (*c. leather*) хроми́рованная ко́жа; *c. steel*, хро́мистая сталь; *c. yellow*, (жёлтый) крон. **chromium** *n.*; *c.*-*plated*, хроми́рованный. **chromolithograph(у)** *n.* хромолитогра́фия. **chromosome** *n.* хромосо́ма.

chronic *adj.* хрони́ческий.

chronicle *n.* хро́ника, ле́топись; (*Book of*) *Chronicles*, Паралипоме́нон; *v.t.* заноси́ть (-ошу́, -о́сишь) *imp.*, занести́ (-есу́, -есёшь; -ёс, -есла́) *perf.* (в дневни́к, в ле́топись); отмеча́ть *imp.*, отме́тить *perf.* **chronicler** *n.* летопи́сец (-сца).

chronological *adj.* хронологи́ческий. **chronology** *n.* хроноло́гия. **chronometer** *n.* хроно́метр.

chrysalis *n.* ку́колка.

chrysanthemum *n.* хризанте́ма.

chub *n.* гола́вль (-ля́) *m.* **chubby** *adj.* пу́хлый (пухл, -а́, -о).

chuck *v.t.* броса́ть *imp.*, бро́сить *perf.*; *c. it!* брось!; *c. out*, выши́бить *imp.*, вы́шибить (-бу, -бешь; -б) *perf.*; *c. under the chin*, трепа́ть (-плю́, -плешь) *imp.*, по~ *perf.* по подборо́дку; *c. up*, броса́ть *imp.*, бро́сить *perf.* **chucker-out** *n.* вышиба́ла *m.*

chuckle *v.i.* посме́иваться *imp.*

chug *v.i.* итти́ (идёт) *imp.* с пыхте́нием; *c. along*, пропы́хать (-тит) *perf.*

chum *n.* това́рищ.

chump *n.* чурба́н; то́лстый коне́ц (-нца́); *c. chop*, то́лстая бара́нья отбивна́я *sb.*; *off one's c.*, спя́тивший с ума́.

chunk *n.* ломо́ть (-мтя́) *m.*, кусо́к (-ска́). **chunky** *adj.* коро́ткий (ко́роток, -тка́, -тко, коро́ткий) и то́лстый (толст, -а́, -о, то́лсты́); корена́стый.

church *n.* це́рковь (-кви, -ко́вью; *pl.* -кви, -кве́й, -ква́м); *C. of England*, англика́нская це́рковь. **churchyard** *n.* (церко́вное) кла́дбище.

churlish *adj.* гру́бый (груб, -а́, -о), нелюбе́зный.

churn *n.* маслобо́йка; *v.t.* сбива́ть *imp.*, сбить (собью́, -ёшь) *perf.*; *v.i.* (*foam*) пе́ниться *imp.*, вс~ *perf.*; (*seethe*) кипе́ть (-пи́т) *imp.*, вс~ *perf.*

chute *n.* скат, жёлоб (*pl.* -а́); (*parachute*) параш(ю́т).

cicada *n.* цика́да.

cider *n.* сидр.

cigar *n.* сига́ра. **cigarette** *n.* сигаре́та, папиро́са; *c. lighter*, зажига́лка.

cinder *n.* шлак; *pl.* зола́; *c.-path*, *c.-track*, гарева́я доро́жка.

cine-camera *n.* киноаппара́т. **cinema** *n.* кино́ *neut.indecl.*, кинематогра́фия. **cinematic** *adj.* кинематографи́ческий.

cinnamon *n.* кори́ца; *(colour)* светло-кори́чневый цвет.

cipher *n.* *(math.)* ноль (-ля́) *m.*, нуль (-ля́) *m.*; шифр.

circle *n.* круг *(loc. -е & -у́; pl. -и́)*; *(theatre)* я́рус; *v.t. & i.* кружи́ть(ся) (-ужу́(сь), -у́жи́шь(ся)) *imp.*; *v.i.* дви́гаться (-аюсь, -аешься & дви́жусь, -жешься) *imp.*, дви́нуться *perf.* по кру́гу. **circlet** *n.* кружо́к (-жка́); вено́к (-нка́). **circuit** *n.* кругооборо́т; объе́зд, обхо́д; *(tour)* турне́ *neut.indecl.*; *(leg.)* выездна́я се́ссия суда́; *(electr.)* цепь, ко́нтур; *short c.*, коро́ткое замыка́ние. **circuitous** *adj.* кружны́й, око́льный. **circular** *adj.* кру́глый (кругл, -а́, -о; кру́глы), круговой; *(circulating)* циркуля́рный; *n.* циркуля́р. **circularize** *v.t.* рассыла́ть *imp.*, разосла́ть (-ошлю́, -ошлёшь) *perf.* + *dat.* циркуля́ры. **circulate** *v.i.* циркули́ровать *imp.*; *v.t.* рассыла́ть *imp.*, разосла́ть (-ошлю́, -ошлёшь) *perf.*; *(spread)* распространя́ть *imp.*, распространи́ть *perf.* **circulation** *n.* *(movement)* циркуля́ция; *(distribution)* распростране́ние; *(of newspaper)* тира́ж (-а́); *(econ.)* обраще́ние; *(med.)* кровообраще́ние.

circumcise *v.t.* обреза́ть *imp.*, обре́зать (-е́жу, -е́жешь) *perf.* **circumcision** *n.* обре́за́ние.

circumference *n.* окру́жность.

circumscribe *v.t.* оче́рчивать *imp.*, очерти́ть (-рчу́, -ртишь) *perf.*; *(restrict)* ограни́чивать *imp.*, ограни́чить *perf.*

circumspect *adj.* осмотри́тельный. **circumspection** *n.* осмотри́тельность.

circumstance *n.* обстоя́тельство; *pl.* *(material situation)* материа́льное положе́ние; *in, under, the circumstances*, при да́нных обстоя́тельствах, в тако́м слу́чае; *in, under, no circumstances*, ни при каки́х обстоя́тельствах, ни в ко́ем слу́чае. **circumstan-**

-tial *adj.* *(detailed)* подро́бный; *c. evidence*, ко́свенные доказа́тельства *neut.pl.*

circumvent *v.t.* *(outwit)* перехитри́ть *perf.*; *(evade)* обходи́ть (-ожу́, -о́дишь) *imp.*, обойти́ (обойду́, -дёшь; обошёл, -шла́) *perf.*

circus *n.* *(show)* цирк; *(arena)* кру́глая пло́щадь *(pl. -ди, -де́й)*.

cirrhosis *n.* цирро́з.

cistern *n.* бак; резервуа́р.

citadel *n.* цита́дель.

citation *n.* *(quotation)* ссы́лка, цита́та. **cite** *v.t.* цити́ровать *imp.*, про ~ *perf.*; ссыла́ться *imp.*, сосла́ться (сошлю́сь, -лёшься) *perf.* на + *acc.*

citizen *n.* граждани́н *(pl. -ане, -ан)*, -а́нка. **citizenship** *n.* гражда́нство.

citric *adj.* лимо́нный. **citron** *n.* цитро́н. **citronella** *n.* цитроне́лла. **citrous** *adj.* ци́трусовый. **citrus** *n.* ци́трус; *adj.* ци́трусовый.

city *n.* го́род *(pl. -а́)*.

civet *n.* *(perfume)* цибети́н; *(c. cat)* виве́рра.

civic *adj.* гражда́нский. **civil** *adj.* гражда́нский; *(polite)* ве́жливый; *c. engineer*, гражда́нский инжене́р; *c. engineering*, гражда́нское строи́тельство; *C. Servant*, госуда́рственный гражда́нский слу́жащий *sb.*; *C. Service*, госуда́рственная слу́жба; *c. war*, гражда́нская война́. **civilian** *n.* шта́тский *sb.*; *adj.* шта́тский; гражда́нский. **civility** *n.* ве́жливость. **civilization** *n.* цивилиза́ция, культу́ра. **civilize** *v.t.* цивилизова́ть *imp.*, *perf.*; де́лать *imp.*, с ~ *perf.* культу́рным. **civilized** *adj.* цивилизо́ванный; культу́рный.

claim *n.* *(demand)* тре́бование, притяза́ние, прете́нзия; *(piece of land)* отведённый уча́сток (-тка) *v.t.* заявля́ть *imp.*, заяви́ть (-влю́, -вишь) *perf.* права́ *pl.* на + *acc.*; претендова́ть *imp.* на + *acc.*

clairvoyance *n.* яснови́дение. **clairvoyant** *n.* яснови́дец (-дца), -дица; *adj.* яснови́дящий.

clam *n.* венерка, рази́нька.

clamber *v.i.* кара́бкаться *imp.*, вс ~ *perf.*

clammy adj. холо́дный и вла́жный на о́щупь.

clamorous adj. крикли́вый. **clamour** n. кри́ки m.pl., шум (-а(у)); v.i. крича́ть (-чу́, -чи́шь) imp.; c. for, шу́мно тре́бовать imp., по ~ perf. + gen.

clamp[1] n. (clasp) зажи́м, скоба́ (pl. -бы, -б, -ба́м), скобка́; v.t. скрепля́ть imp., скрепи́ть perf.

clamp[2] n. (of potatoes) бурт (бурта́; pl. -ы́).

clan n. клан.

clandestine adj. та́йный.

clang, clank n. лязг, бряца́ние; v.t. & i. ля́згать imp., ля́згнуть perf. (+ instr.); бряца́ть imp., про ~ perf. (+ instr., на + prep.).

clap v.t. хло́пать imp., хло́пнуть perf. + dat.; аплоди́ровать imp. + dat.; n. хлопо́к (-пка́); рукоплеска́ние neut. pl.; (thunder) уда́р. **clapper** n. язы́к (-а́). **claptrap** n. треску́чая фра́за; (nonsense) вздор.

claret n. бордо́ neut.indecl.

clarification n. (explanation) разъясне́ние; (of liquid, chem.) осветле́ние; (purification) очище́ние. **clarify** v.t. разъясня́ть imp., разъясни́ть perf.; осветля́ть imp., осветли́ть perf.; очища́ть imp., очи́стить perf.

clarinet n. кларне́т.

clarity n. я́сность.

clash n. (conflict) столкнове́ние; (disharmony) дисгармо́ния; (sound) гро́хот, лязг; v.i. ста́лкиваться imp., столкну́ться perf.; (coincide) совпада́ть imp., совпа́сть (-адёт; -а́л) perf.; не гармони́ровать imp.; (sound) ля́згать imp., ля́згнуть perf.

clasp n. (buckle etc.) пря́жка, застёжка; (handshake) пожа́тие руки́; (embrace) объя́тие; v.t. обнима́ть imp., обня́ть (обниму́, -мешь; о́бнял, -а́, -о) perf.; сжима́ть imp., сжать (сожму́, -мёшь) perf. в объя́тиях; c.-knife, складно́й нож (-а́).

class n. класс; (category) разря́д; c.-conscious, (кла́ссово) созна́тельный; c.-consciousness, кла́ссовое созна́ние; c.-room, класс; c. war, кла́ссовая борьба́; v.t. причисля́ть imp., при-

чи́слить perf. (as, к + dat.); классифици́ровать imp., perf.

classic adj. класси́ческий; (renowned) знамени́тый; n. кла́ссик; класси́ческое произведе́ние; pl. кла́ссика; класси́ческие языки́ m.pl. **classical** adj. класси́ческий.

classification n. классифика́ция. **classify** v.t. классифици́ровать imp., perf.; (c. as secret) засекре́чивать imp., засекре́тить perf.

classy adj. кла́ссный, первокла́ссный, пе́рвый сорт predic.

clatter n. стук, лязг; v.i. стуча́ть (-чу́, -чи́шь) imp., по ~ perf.; ля́згать imp., ля́згнуть perf.

clause n. статья́; (leg.) кла́узула; (gram.) предложе́ние.

claw n. ко́готь (-гтя; pl. -гти, -гте́й); (of crustacean) клешня́; v.t. скрести́ (-ебу́, -ебёшь; -ёб, -ебла́) imp.

clay n. гли́на; (pipe) гли́няная тру́бка; adj. гли́няный. **clayey** adj. гли́нистый.

clean adj. чи́стый (чист, -а́, -о, чи́сты); adv. (fully) соверше́нно, по́лностью; v.t. чи́стить imp., вы́ ~, по ~ perf.; очища́ть imp., очи́стить perf. **cleaner** n. чи́стильщик, -ица; убо́рщик, -ица. **cleaner's** n. хими́стка. **cleaning** n. чи́стка, убо́рка; очи́стка. **clean(li)ness** n. чистота́. **cleanse** v.t. очища́ть imp., очи́стить perf.

clear adj. я́сный (я́сен, ясна́, я́сно, я́сны); (transparent) прозра́чный; (distinct) отчётливый; (free) свобо́дный (of, от + gen.); v.t. & i. очища́ть(ся) imp., очи́стить(ся) perf.; v.t. (jump over) перепры́гивать imp., перепры́гнуть perf.; (acquit) опра́вдывать imp., оправда́ть perf.; c. away, убира́ть imp., убра́ть (уберу́, -рёшь; убра́л, -а́, -о) perf. со стола́; c. off, (go away) убира́ться imp., убра́ться (уберу́сь; -рёшься; убра́лся, -ала́сь, -а́ло́сь) perf.; c. out, (v.t.) вычища́ть imp., вы́чистить perf.; (v.i.) (make off) удира́ть imp., удра́ть (удеру́, -рёшь; удра́л, -а́, -о) perf.; c. up, (make tidy) приводи́ть (-ожу́, -о́дишь) imp., привести́ (-еду́, -едёшь; -ёл, -ела́) perf. в поря́док; (explain) выяснять *imp.*, выяснить *perf.* **clearance** *n.* расчистка; (*permission*) разрешение. **clearing** *n.* расчистка; (*in forest*) поляна. **clearly** *adv.* ясно; отчётливо.

cleavage *n.* разделение. **cleaver** *n.* нож (-а) мясника.

clef *n.* (*mus.*) ключ (-а).

cleft *n.* трещина, расщелина; *adj.*: in a cleft stick, в тупике.

clematis *n.* ломонос.

clemency *n.* милосердие.

clench *v.t.* (*fist*) сжимать *imp.*, сжать (сожму, -мёшь) *perf.*; (*teeth*) стискивать *imp.*, стиснуть *perf.*

clergy *n.* духовенство. **clergyman** *n.* священник. **clerical** *adj.* (*of clergy*) духовный; (*of clerk*) канцелярский.

clerk *n.* конторский служащий *sb.*

clever *adj.* умный (умён, умна, умно), способный. **cleverness** *n.* умение.

cliché *n.* клише *neut.indecl.*, избитая фраза.

click *v.t.* щёлкать *imp.*, щёлкнуть *perf.* + *instr.*; *n.* щёлк.

client *n.* клиент. **clientele** *n.* клиентура.

cliff *n.* утёс, отвесная скала (*pl.* -лы).

climacteric *n.* климактерий; *adj.* климактерический.

climate *n.* климат. **climatic** *adj.* климатический.

climax *n.* кульминационный пункт.

climb *v.t. & i.* лазить *indet.*, лезть (лезу, -зешь) *det.* на + *acc.*; влезать *imp.*, влезть (влезу, -зешь, влез) *perf.* на + *acc.*; подниматься *imp.*, подняться (-нимусь, -нимешься; -нялся, -нялась) *perf.* на + *acc.* (*aeron.*) набирать *imp.*, набрать (наберу, -рёшь; набрал, -а, -о) *perf.* высоту; c. down, спускаться *imp.*, спуститься (-ущусь, -устишься) *perf.* с + *gen.*; (*give in*) уступать *imp.*, уступить (-плю, -пишь) *perf.* **climber** *n.* (*mountain-c.*) альпинист, ~ка; (*social c.*) карьерист, ~ка; (*plant*) вьющееся растение.

climbing *n.* (*sport*) альпинизм; (*ascent*) восхождение; (*plant*) вьющийся.

clinch *n.* (*boxing*) клинч, захват.

cling *v.i.* прилипать *imp.*, прилипнуть (-п) *perf.* (to, к + *dat.*); c. to, (*clothes*) облегать (-ает) *imp.*

clinic *n.* (*consultation*) консультация; (*place*) клиника. **clinical** *adj.* клинический.

clink *v.t. & i.* звенеть (-ню, -нишь) *imp.*, про~ *perf.* (+ *instr.*); c. glasses, чокаться *imp.*, чокнуться *perf.*; *n.* звон.

clinker *n.* (*brick*) клинкер; (*slag*) шлак.

clip¹ *n.* зажим; (*mil.*) обойма; *v.t.* прикреплять *imp.*, прикрепить *perf.*

clip² *v.t.* стричь (-игу, -ижёшь; -иг) *imp.*, об~, о~ *perf.*; подрезать *imp.*, подрезать (-ежу, -ежешь) *perf.* **clipped** *adj.* подрезанный, подстриженный; c. tones, отрывочная речь. **clipper** *n.* (*naut.*) клипер; *pl.* ножницы *f.pl.*

clipping *n.* стрижка; (*newspaper c.*) газетная вырезка; *pl.* настриг, обрезки *f.pl.*

clique *n.* клика. **cliquish** *adj.* замкнутый.

cloak *n.* плащ (-а); *v.t.* покрывать *imp.*, покрыть (-рою, -роешь) *perf.* **cloakroom** *n.* (*for clothing*) гардероб; (*for luggage*) камера хранения; (*lavatory*) уборная *sb.*, туалет.

clock *n.* часы *m.pl.*; c. face, циферблат; clockmaker, часовщик (-а); clockwise, по часовой стрелке; c-work, часовой механизм; *v.i.*: c. in, регистрировать *imp.*, за~ *perf.* приход на работу.

clod *n.* ком (*pl.* -ья, -ьев), глыба; c-hopper, увалень (-льня) *m.*, деревенщина *m. & f.*

clog *n.* башмак (-а) на деревянной подошве; *v.i.*: c. up, засорять *imp.*, засорить *perf.*

cloister *n.* (*monastery*) монастырь (-ря) *m.*; (*arcade*) крытая аркада.

close *adj.* (*near*) близкий (-зок, -зка, -зко, близки); (*stuffy*) душный (-шен, -шна, -шно); (*secret*) скрытый; *v.t.* (*shut*) закрывать *imp.*, закрыть (-рою, -роешь) *perf.*; (*conclude*) заканчивать *imp.*, закончить *perf.*; *adv.* близко (to, от + *gen.*). **closed** *adj.* закрытый. **closeted** *adj.*: be c. together, совещаться *imp.* наедине. **close-up** *n.* съёмка, снятая на крупном плане; in c., крупным планом. **closing** *n.* закрытие; *adj.* заключительный. **closure** *n.* закрытие.

clot n. сгу́сток (-тка); v.i. сгуща́ться imp., сгусти́ться perf. **clotted** adj. сгущённый; c. cream, густы́е топлёные сли́вки (pl.).

cloth n. ткань, сукно́ (pl. -кна, -кон, -кнам); (duster) тря́пка; (table-c.) ска́терть (pl. -ти, -те́й).

clothe v.t. одева́ть imp., оде́ть (-е́ну, -е́нешь) (in, + instr., в + acc.) perf. **clothes** n. оде́жда, пла́тье.

cloud n. о́блако (pl. -ка́, -ко́в); (rain, storm, c.) ту́ча; v.t. затемня́ть imp., затемни́ть perf.; омрача́ть imp., омрачи́ть perf.; c. over, покрыва́ться imp., покры́ться (-ро́ется) perf. облака́ми, ту́чами.

clout n. ударя́ть imp., уда́рить perf.; n. затре́щина.

clove n. гвозди́ка; (garlic) зубо́к (-бка́).

cloven adj. раздвоённый (-ён, -е́нна).

clover n. кле́вер (pl. -а́).

clown n. кло́ун.

club n. (stick) дуби́нка; pl. (cards) тре́фы f.pl.; (association) клуб; v.t. (beat) бить (бью, бьёшь) imp., по ~ perf. дуби́нкой; v.i.: c. together, устра́ивать imp., устро́ить perf. скла́дчину.

cluck v.i. куда́хтать (-а́хчет) imp.

clue n. (evidence) ули́ка; (to puzzle) ключ (-а́ к разга́дке).

clump n. гру́ппа дере́вьев; v.i. тяжело́ ступа́ть imp., ступи́ть (-плю́, -пишь) perf.

clumsiness n. неуклю́жесть, беста́ктность. **clumsy** adj. неуклю́жий.

cluster n. (bunch) пучо́к (-чка́); (group) гру́ппа; v.i. собира́ться imp., собра́ться (-берётся; собра́лся, -ала́сь, -ало́сь) perf. гру́ппами.

clutch[1] n. (grasp) хва́тка; ко́гти (-те́й) m.pl.; (tech.) сцепле́ние, му́фта; v.t. зажима́ть imp., зажа́ть (зажму́, -мёшь) perf.; v.i.: c. at, хвата́ться imp., хвати́ться (-ачу́сь, -а́тишься) imp. за + acc.

clutch[2] n. (of eggs) я́йца (pl. яи́ц, я́йцам).

clutter n. беспоря́док (-дка); v.t. приводи́ть (-ожу́, -о́дишь) imp., привести́ (-еду́, -едёшь; -ёл, -ела́) perf. в беспоря́док.

c/o abbr. по а́дресу + gen.; че́рез + acc.

coach n. (carriage) каре́та; (rly.) ваго́н; (bus) авто́бус; (tutor) репети́тор; (sport) тре́нер; v.t. репети́ровать imp.; тренирова́ть imp., на ~ perf.

coagulate v.i. сгуща́ться imp., сгусти́ться perf.

coal n. у́голь (угля́; pl. у́гли, угле́й) m.; c.-bearing, углено́сный; c.-face, у́гольный забо́й; coalfield, каменноу́гольный бассе́йн; c.-mine, у́гольная ша́хта; c.-miner, шахтёр; c.-owner, шахтовладе́лец (-льца); c.-scuttle, ведёрко (pl. -рки, -рок, -ркам) для угля́; c.-seam, у́гольный пласт (-а́).

coalesce v.i. соединя́ться imp., соедини́ться perf.

coalition n. коали́ция.

coarse adj. гру́бый (груб, -а́, -о); (vulgar) вульга́рный.

coast n. побере́жье, бе́рег (loc. -у́; pl. -а́); c. guard, берегова́я охра́на; v.i. (trade) каботажничать imp.; (move without power) дви́гаться (-и́гается & -и́жется) imp., дви́нуться perf. по ине́рции. **coastal** adj. берегово́й, прибре́жный. **coaster** n. каботажное су́дно (pl. -да́, -до́в).

coat n. (overcoat) пальто́ neut.indecl.; (jacket) пиджа́к (-а́), ку́ртка; (layer) слой (pl. слои́); (animal) шерсть (pl. -ти, -те́й), мех (loc. -у́; pl. -а́); c. of arms, герб (-а́); v.t. покрыва́ть imp., покры́ть (-ро́ю, -ро́ешь) perf. (with, сло́ем + gen.).

coax v.t. зада́бривать imp., задо́брить perf.

cob n. (corn-c.) поча́ток (-тка кукуру́зы; (swan) ле́бедь-дя; pl. -ди, -де́й-саме́ц (-мца́); (horse) ни́зкая верхова́я ло́шадь (pl. -ди, -де́й, instr. -дьми́).

cobalt n. ко́бальт.

cobble n. булы́жник (also collect.); v.t. мости́ть imp., вы ~, за ~ perf. булы́жником.

cobbler n. сапо́жник.

cobra n. очко́вая змея́ (pl. зме́и).

cobweb n. паути́на.

cocaine n. кокаи́н.

cochineal n. кошени́ль.

cock n. (bird) петух (-á); (tap) кран; (of gun) курóк (-кá); v.t. (gun) взводить (-ожý, -óдишь) imp., взвести (-едý, -едёшь; -ёл, -елá) perf. курóк+ gen.; c. a snook, показывать imp., показáть (-ажý, -áжешь) perf. длинный нос. **cocked hat** n. треугóлка.

cockade n. кокáрда.

cockatoo n. какадý m.indecl.

cockchafer n. мáйский жук (-á).

cockerel n. петушóк (-шкá).

cockle n. съедóбная сердцевúдка.

cockney n. уроженéц (-нца), -нка, Лóндона.

cockpit n. (arena) арéна; (aeron.) кабúна.

cockroach n. таракáн.

cocktail n. коктéйль m.

cocky adj. (cheeky) дéрзкий (-зок, -зкá, -зко); (conceited) чвáнный.

cocoa n. какáо neut.indecl.

coco(a)nut n. кокóс; adj. кокóсовый.

cocoon n. кóкон.

cod n. трескá; c.-liver oil, рыбий жир (-а(у)).

coda n. (mus.) кóда.

coddle v.t. изнéживать imp., изнéжить perf.

code n. (collection of laws) кóдекс, закóн m.pl.; (cipher) код, шифр; civil c., граждáнский кóдекс; c. of honour, закóны m.pl. чéсти; penal c., уголóвный кóдекс; Morse c., áзбука Мóрзе; v.t. шифровáть imp., за~ perf. **codicil** n. припúска. **codify** v.t. кодифицúровать imp., perf.

co-education n. совмéстное обучéние.

coefficient n. коэффициéнт.

coerce v.t. принуждáть imp., принýдить perf. **coercion** n. принуждéние; under c., по принуждéнию.

coexist v.i. сосуществовáть imp. **co-existence** n. сосуществовáние.

coffee n. кóфе m. (neut. (coll.)) indecl.; c.-mill, кофéйница; c.-pot, кофéйник.

coffer n. сундýк (-á). **coffin** n. казнá.

coffin n. гроб (loc. -ý; pl. -ы).

cog n. зубéц (-бцá); c. in the machine, вúнтик машúны. **cogwheel** n. зубчáтое колесó (pl. -ёса), шестерня (gen.pl. -рён).

cogent adj. убедúтельный.

cogitate v.i. размышлять imp., размыслить perf. **cogitation** n.: pl. мысли (-лей) f.pl., размышлéния neut.pl.

cognate adj. рóдственный (-ен, -енна); n. рóдственное слóво.

cohabit v.i. сожительствовать imp. **cohabitation** n. сожительство.

coherence n. свясность. **coherent** adj. свясный. **cohesion** n. сплочённость; сцеплéние. **cohesive** adj. спосóбный к сцеплéнию.

cohort n. когóрта.

coil v.t. свёртывать imp., свернýть perf. кольцóм, спирáлью; уклáдывать imp., уложúть (-жý, -жишь) perf. в бýхту; n. кольцó (pl. -льца, -лец, -льцам), бýхта; (electr.) катýшка.

coin n. монéта; v.t. чекáнить imp., от~ perf. **coinage** n. (coining) чекáнка; (system) монéта; монéтная систéма.

coincide v.i. совпадáть imp., совпáсть (-адý, -адёшь; -áл) perf. **coincidence** n. совпадéние. **coincidental** adj. случáйный.

coke[1] n. кокс; adj. кóксовый; v.t. коксовáть imp.; c. oven, коксовáльная печь (pl. -чи, -чéй).

Coke[2] n. кóка-кóла.

colander n. дуршлáг.

cold n. хóлод (-а у); pl. -á); (illness) простýда, нáсморк; adj. холóдный (хóлоден, -дná, -дно, холóдны); c.-blooded, жестóкий (-óк, -óкá, -óко); (zool.) холоднокрóвный; c. steel, холóдное орýжие; c. war, холóдная войнá.

colic n. кóлики f.pl.

collaborate v.i. сотрýдничать imp. **collaboration** n. сотрýдничество. **collaborator** n. сотрýдник, -ица.

collapse v.i. рýшиться imp., об~ perf.; валúться (-люсь, -лишься) imp., по~, с~ perf.; n. падéние; крах; провáл. **collapsible** adj. разбóрный, склáдной, откиднóй.

collar n. воротнúк (-á), воротничóк (-чкá); (dog-c.) ошéйник; (horse-c.) хомýт (-á); c.-bone, ключúца; v.t. (seize) хватáть imp., схватúть (-ачý, -áтишь) perf.

collate v.t. сличáть imp., сличúть perf.

collateral *adj.* побо́чный, дополни́тельный; *n.* (*c. security*) дополни́тельное обеспе́чение.

collation *n.* лёгкая заку́ска.

colleague *n.* колле́га *m. & f.*

collect *v.t.* собира́ть *imp.*, собра́ть (соберу́, -рёшь; собра́л, -а́, -о) *perf.*; (*as hobby*) коллекциони́ровать *imp.*

collected *adj.* со́бранный; *c. works*, собра́ние сочине́ний. collection *n.* сбор, собира́ние; колле́кция. collective *n.* коллекти́в; *adj.* коллекти́вный; *c. farm*, колхо́з; *c. farmer*, колхо́зник, -ица; *c. noun*, собира́тельное существи́тельное *sb.* collectivization *n.* коллективиза́ция. collector *n.* сбо́рщик; коллекционе́р.

college *n.* колле́дж. collegiate *adj.* университе́тский.

collide *v.i.* ста́лкиваться *imp.*, столкну́ться *perf.* collision *n.* столкнове́ние.

collie *n.* шотла́ндская овча́рка.

collier *n.* (*miner*) шахтёр; (*ship*) у́гольщик. colliery *n.* каменноуго́льная ша́хта.

colloquial *adj.* разгово́рный. colloquialism *n.* разгово́рное выраже́ние.

collusion *n.* та́йный сго́вор.

colon[1] *n.* (*anat.*) то́лстая кишка́ (*gen.pl.* -шо́к).

colon[2] *n.* (*punctuation mark*) двоето́чие.

colonel *n.* полко́вник.

colonial *adj.* колониа́льный. colonialism *n.* колониали́зм. colonist *n.* колони́ст, ~ка. colonization *n.* колониза́ция. colonize *v.t.* колонизова́ть *imp.*, *perf.* colony *n.* коло́ния.

colonnade *n.* колонна́да.

coloration *n.* окра́ска, расцве́тка.

coloratura *n.* (*mus.*) колорату́ра.

colossal *adj.* колосса́льный, грома́дный.

colour *n.* цвет (*pl.* -а́), кра́ска; (*pl.*) (*flag*) зна́мя (*pl.* -мёна) *neut.*; *c.-blind* страда́ющий дальтони́змом, цветна́я плёнка; *c. prejudice*, ра́совая дискримина́ция; *v.t.* кра́сить *imp.*, цы́~, о~, по~ *perf.*; раскра́шивать *imp.*, раскра́сить *perf.*; *v.i.* красне́ть *imp.*, по~ *perf.* colouration *see* coloration. coloured *adj.* цветно́й,

раскра́шенный, окра́шенный. colouring. *n.* кра́сящее вещество́; окра́ска.

colt *n.* жеребёнок (-бёнка; *pl.* -бя́та, -бя́т).

column *n.* (*archit., mil.*) коло́нна; столб (-а́); (*of print*) столбе́ц (-бца́). columnist *n.* журнали́ст.

coma *n.* ко́ма. comatose *adj.* комато́зный.

comb *n.* гребёнка; гре́бень (-бня) *m.*; *v.t.* чеса́ть (чешу́, -шешь) *imp.*; причёсывать *imp.*, причеса́ть (-ешу́, -е́шешь) *perf.*

combat *n.* бой (*loc.* бою́), сраже́ние; *v.t.* боро́ться (-рю́сь, -решься) *imp.* *c + instr.*, про́тив + *gen.* combatant *n.* комбата́нт; *adj.* строево́й.

combination *n.* сочета́ние; соедине́ние; комбина́ция. combine *n.* комбина́т; (*c.-harvester*) комба́йн; *v.t. & i.* совмеща́ть(ся) *imp.*, совмести́ть(ся) *perf.* combined *adj.* совме́стный.

combustible *adj.* горю́чий. combustion *n.* горе́ние; *internal c. engine*, дви́гатель *m.* вну́треннего сгора́ния.

come *v.i.* (*on foot*) приходи́ть (-ожу́, -о́дишь) *imp.*, прийти́ (приду́, -дёшь; пришёл, -шла́) *perf.*; (*by transport*) приезжа́ть *imp.*, прие́хать (-е́ду, -е́дешь) *perf.*; *c. about*, случа́ться *imp.*, случи́ться *perf.*; *c. across*, случа́йно ната́лкиваться *imp.*, натолкну́ться *perf.* на + *acc.*; *c. back*, возвраща́ться *imp.*, возврати́ться (-ащу́сь, -ати́шься) *perf.*; *c. from*, происходи́ть (-ожу́, -о́дишь) *imp.*, произойти́ (-ойду́, -ойдёшь) -ошёл, -ошла́) *perf.* из, от + *gen.*; *c. in*, входи́ть (-ожу́, -о́дишь) *imp.*, войти́ (войду́, -дёшь; вошёл, -шла́) *perf.*; *c. in handy*, пригоди́ться *perf.*; *c. through*, проника́ть *imp.*, прони́кнуть (-к) *perf.*; *c. up to*, доходи́ть (-ожу́, -о́дишь) *imp.*, дойти́ (дойду́, -дёшь; дошёл, -шла́) *perf.* до + *gen.* come-back *n.* возвра́т. come-down *n.* паде́ние, ухудше́ние.

comedian *n.* коме́дийный актёр, ко́мик. comedienne *n.* коме́дийная актри́са. comedy *n.* коме́дия.

comet *n.* коме́та.

comfort *n.* комфо́рт, удо́бство; (*consolation*) утеше́ние; *v.t.* утеша́ть *imp.*, уте́шить *perf.* comfortable *adj.* удо́бный. comforter *n.* (*person*) утеши́тель *m.*; (*dummy*) со́ска.

comic *adj.* коми́ческий, юмористи́ческий; c. opera, опере́тта; *n.* ко́микс (*magazine*) ко́микс. comical *adj.* смешно́й, коми́чный.

coming *adj.* наступа́ющий.

comma *n.* запята́я *sb.*; *inverted* c., кавы́чка.

command *n.* (*order*) прика́з; (*order, authority*) кома́нда; *v.t.* прика́зывать *imp.*, приказа́ть (-ажу́, -а́жешь) *perf.* + *dat.*; кома́ндовать *imp.*, c~ *perf.* + *instr.*, над (*terrain*) + *instr.*; (*have c. of, master*) владе́ть *imp.* + *instr.* commandant *n.* коменда́нт. commandeer *v.t.* (*men*) набира́ть *imp.*, набра́ть (наберу́, -рёшь) *perf.*; набра́ть, -а́, -о) *perf.* в а́рмию; (*goods*) реквизи́ровать *imp.*, *perf.* commander *n.* команди́р; кома́ндующий *sb.* (of, + *instr.*); c.-in-chief, главнокома́ндующий *sb.* commanding *adj.* кома́ндующий. commandment *n.* за́поведь *n.* commandos *n.* деса́нтно-диверсио́нные войска́ (*gen.* -к) *pl.*

commemorate *v.t.* ознамено́вывать *imp.*, ознаменова́ть *perf.* commemoration *n.* ознаменова́ние. commemorative *adj.* па́мятный, мемориа́льный.

commence *v.t.* начина́ть *imp.*, нача́ть (-чну́, -чнёшь; на́чал, -а́, -о) *perf.* commencement *n.* нача́ло.

commend *v.t.* (*praise*) хвали́ть (-лю́, -лишь) *imp.*, по~ *perf.* commendable *adj.* похва́льный. commendation *n.* похвала́.

commensurable *adj.* соизмери́мый. commensurate *adj.* соразме́рный.

comment *n.* замеча́ние; *v.i.* де́лать *imp.*, c~ *perf.* замеча́ния; *on* c., комменти́ровать *imp.*, *perf.*, про~ *perf.* commentary *n.* коммента́рий. commentator *n.* коммента́тор.

commerce *n.* торго́вля, комме́рция. commercial *adj.* торго́вый, комме́рческий; *n.* рекла́мная переда́ча. commercialize *v.t.* превраща́ть *imp.*, преврати́ть (-ащу́, -ати́шь) *perf.* в исто́чник дохо́дов.

commiserate *v.i.*: c. *with*, соболе́зновать *imp.* + *dat.* commiseration *n.* соболе́знование.

commissar *n.* комисса́р. commissariat *n.* (*polit.*) комиссариа́т; (*mil. etc.*) интенда́нтство.

commission *n.* (*command*) поруче́ние; (*agent's fee*) комиссио́нные *sb.*; (c. *of inquiry etc.*) коми́ссия; (*mil.*) офице́рское зва́ние; *put into* c., вводи́ть (-ожу́, -о́дишь) *imp.*, ввести́ (введу́, -дёшь; ввёл, -а́) *perf.* в строй; *v.t.* поруча́ть *imp.*, поручи́ть (-чу́, -чишь) *perf.* + *dat.* commissionaire *n.* швейца́р. commissioner *n.* уполномо́ченный представи́тель *m.*; коммисса́р.

commit *v.t.* соверша́ть *imp.*, соверши́ть *perf.*; c. *oneself*, обя́зываться (-я́жусь, -я́жешься) *perf.*; c. *to*, предава́ть (-даю́, -даёшь) *imp.*, преда́ть (-а́м, -а́шь, -а́ст, -ади́м; пре́дал, -а́, -о) *perf.* + *dat.*; c. *to prison*, помеща́ть *imp.*, помести́ть *perf.* в тюрьму́. commitment *n.* обяза́тельство.

committee *n.* комите́т, коми́ссия.

commodity *n.* това́р; *scarce* c., дефици́тный това́р.

commodore *n.* (*officer*) коммодо́р.

common *adj.* о́бщий, просто́й, обыкнове́нный; *n.* о́бщинная земля́ (*acc.* -млю; *pl.* -мли, -ме́ль, -мля́м) c.-*room*, о́бщая ко́мната, учи́тельская *sb.*; c. *sense*, здра́вый смысл. commonly *adv.* обы́чно, обыкнове́нно. commonplace *adj.* избито́й, бана́льный. commonwealth *n.* содру́жество, федера́ция.

commotion *n.* сумато́ха, волне́ние.

communal *adj.* о́бщий, коммуна́льный. commune *n.* комму́на; *v.i.* обща́ться *imp.*

communicate *v.t.* передава́ть (-даю́, -даёшь) *imp.*, переда́ть (-а́м, -а́шь, -а́ст, -ади́м; пе́редал, -а́, -о) *perf.*; сообща́ть *imp.*, сообщи́ть *perf.* communication *n.* сообще́ние; связь; коммуника́ция. communicative *adj.* разгово́рчивый.

communion *n.* (*eccl.*) прича́стие.

communiqué *n.* коммюнике́ *neut.indecl.*

Communism n. коммуни́зм. **Communist** n. коммуни́ст. ~ ка; adj. коммунисти́ческий.

community n. общи́на; содру́жество; о́бщность.

commute v.t. заменя́ть imp., замени́ть (-ню́, -нишь) perf. **commuter** n. пассажи́р, име́ющий сезо́нный биле́т.

compact[1] n. (agreement) соглаше́ние.

compact[2] adj. компа́ктный; пло́тный (-тен, -тна́, -тно, -тны); n. пу́дреница.

companion n. това́рищ; компаньо́н, ~ ка; (fellow traveller) спу́тник; (lady's c.) компаньо́нка; (handbook) спра́вочник. **companionable** adj. общи́тельный, компане́йский. **companionship** n. дру́жеское обще́ние.

company n. о́бщество, компа́ния; (theat.) тру́ппа; (mil.) ро́та; ship's c., экипа́ж.

comparable adj. сравни́мый. **comparative** adj. сравни́тельный; n. сравни́тельная сте́пень (pl. -ни, -ней). **compare** v.t. & i. сра́внивать(ся) imp., сравни́ть(ся) perf. (to, with, c + instr.). **comparison** n. сравне́ние.

compartment n. отделе́ние; (rly.) купе́ neut.indecl.

compass n. ко́мпас; pl. ци́ркуль m.; (extent) преде́лы m.pl.

compassion n. сострада́ние, жа́лость. **compassionate** adj. сострада́тельный.

compatibility n. совмести́мость. **compatible** adj. совмести́мый.

compatriot n. соотечественник, -ица.

compel v.t. заставля́ть imp., заста́вить perf.; принужда́ть imp., прину́дить perf. **compelling** adj. неотрази́мый.

compendium n. кра́ткое руково́дство; конспе́кт.

compensate v.t.: c. for, вознагражда́ть imp., вознагради́ть perf. за + acc.; возмеща́ть imp., возмести́ть perf. + dat.; компенси́ровать imp. & perf. **compensation** n. возмеще́ние, вознагражде́ние, компенса́ция.

compete v.i. конкури́ровать imp.; соревнова́ться imp.; состяза́ться imp. **competence** n. компете́нция; компете́нтность; правомо́чие. **competent** adj. компете́нтный; правомо́чный.

competition n. соревнова́ние, состяза́ние; конку́ренция; ко́нкурс. **competitive** adj. соревну́ющийся, конкури́рующий; c. examination, ко́нкурсный экза́мен. **competitor** n. соревну́ющийся sb.; конкуре́нт, ~ ка.

compilation n. компиля́ция; составле́ние. **compile** v.t. составля́ть imp., соста́вить perf.; компили́ровать imp., с ~ perf. **compiler** n. состави́тель m., ~ ница; компиля́тор.

complacency n. самодово́льство. **complacent** adj. самодово́льный.

complain v.i. жа́ловаться imp., по ~ perf. **complaint** n. жа́лоба; (ailment) боле́знь, неду́г.

complement n. дополне́ние; (full number) (ли́чный) соста́в. **complementary** adj. дополни́тельный.

complete v.t. заверша́ть imp., заверши́ть perf.; adj. по́лный (-лон, -лна́, по́лно); зако́нченный (-ен). **completion** n. заверше́ние, оконча́ние.

complex adj. сло́жный (-жен, -жна́, -жно); n. ко́мплекс. **complexity** n. сло́жность.

complexion n. цвет лица́.

compliance n. усту́пчивость. **compliant** adj. усту́пчивый.

complicate v.t. осложня́ть imp., осложни́ть perf. **complicated** adj. сло́жный (-жен, -жна́, -жно). **complication** n. осложне́ние.

complicity n. соуча́стие.

compliment n. комплиме́нт; pl. приве́т; v.t. говори́ть imp. комплиме́нт(ы) + dat.; хвали́ть (-лю́, -лишь) imp., по ~ perf. **complimentary** adj. ле́стный, хвале́бный; (ticket) беспла́тный.

comply v.i.: c. with, (fulfil) исполня́ть imp., испо́лнить perf.; (submit to) подчиня́ться imp., подчини́ться perf. + dat.

component n. компоне́нт, составна́я часть (pl. -ти, -те́й); adj. составно́й.

comport v.t.: c. oneself, вести́ (веду́, -дёшь; вёл, -а́) perf. себя́. **comportment** n. поведе́ние.

compose v.t. (lit., mus.) сочиня́ть imp., сочини́ть perf.; (institute) составля́ть imp., соста́вить perf.; (print.) набира́ть imp., набра́ть (наберу́, -рёшь;

набра́л, -á, -о) perf. composed adj. споко́йный; be c. of, состоя́ть (-ои́т) imp. из + gen. composer n. компози́тор. composite adj. составно́й. composition n. построе́ние; сочине́ние; соста́в. compositor n. набо́рщик.

compost n. компо́ст.

composure n. самооблада́ние.

compound¹ n. (mixture) соедине́ние, соста́в; (gram.) составно́й; сло́жный.

compound² n. (enclosure) огоро́женное ме́сто (pl. -та́).

comprehend v.t. понима́ть imp., поня́ть (пойму́, -мёшь; по́нял, -á, -о) perf. comprehensible adj. поня́тный. comprehensive adj. всесторо́нний (-нен, -ння); всеобъе́млющий; c. school, общеобразова́тельная шко́ла.

compress v.t. сжима́ть imp., сжать (сожму́, -мёшь) perf.; сда́вливать imp., сдави́ть (-влю, -вишь) perf.; n. компре́сс. compressed adj. сжа́тый. compression n. сжа́тие. compressor n. компре́ссор.

comprise v.t. заключа́ть imp. в себе́; состоя́ть (-ою, -ои́шь) imp. из + gen.

compromise n. компроми́сс; v.t. компромети́ровать imp., с ~ perf.; v.i. идти́ (иду́, идёшь; шёл, шла) imp., пойти́ (пойду́, -дёшь; пошёл, -шла́) perf. на компроми́сс.

compulsion n. принужде́ние. compulsory adj. обяза́тельный.

compunction n. угрызе́ние со́вести.

computation n. вычисле́ние. compute v.t. вычисля́ть imp., вы́числить perf. computer n. вычисли́тельная маши́на; (electronic) ЭВМ; компью́тер.

comrade n. това́рищ; c.-in-arms, сора́тник comradeship n. това́рищество.

concave adj. во́гнутый. concavity n. во́гнутая пове́рхность.

conceal v.t. скрыва́ть imp., скрыть (-ро́ю, -ро́ешь) perf. concealment n. сокры́тие, ута́ивание.

concede v.t. уступа́ть imp., уступи́ть (-плю́, -пишь) perf.

conceit n. самомне́ние; чва́нство. conceited adj. чва́нный (-нен, -нна).

conceivable adj. постижи́мый; мы́слимый. conceive v.t. (plan, contemplate) замышля́ть imp., замы́слить perf.;

(become pregnant) зачина́ть imp. зача́ть (-чну́, -чнёшь; зача́л, -á, -о) perf.

concentrate n. концентра́т; v.t. & i. сосредото́чивать(ся) imp., сосредото́чить(ся) (on, на + prep.); v.t. концентри́ровать imp., с ~ perf. concentrated adj. концентри́рованный, сосредото́ченный (-ен, -енна). concentration n. сосредото́ченность, концентра́ция.

concentric adj. концентри́ческий.

concept n. поня́тие; конце́пция. conception n. понима́ние; представле́ние; (physiol.) зача́тие.

concern n. (worry) забо́та; (business) предприя́тие; v.t. каса́ться imp. + gen.; c. oneself with, занима́ться imp., заня́ться (займу́сь, -мёшься; заня́лся́, -яла́сь) perf. + instr. concerned adj. озабо́ченный (-ен, -енна); с. with, свя́занный (-ан) с + instr.; за́нятый (-т, -та́, -то) + instr. concerning prep. относи́тельно + gen.

concert n. конце́рт; v.t. согласо́вывать imp., согласова́ть perf. concerted adj. согласо́ванный.

concertina n. гармо́ника.

concession n. усту́пка; (econ.) конце́ссия. concessionaire n. концессионе́р.

conch n. ра́ковина.

conciliate v.t. умиротворя́ть imp., умиротвори́ть perf. conciliation n. умиротворе́ние. conciliatory adj. примири́тельный.

concise adj. сжа́тый, кра́ткий (-ток, -тка́, -тко) conciseness n. сжа́тость, кра́ткость.

conclave n. конкла́в.

conclude v.t. (complete) зака́нчивать imp., зако́нчить perf.; (infer, arrange, complete) заключа́ть imp., заключи́ть perf. concluding adj. заключи́тельный; заверша́ющий. conclusion n. заключе́ние, оконча́ние; (deduction) вы́вод. conclusive adj. заключи́тельный; (decisive) реша́ющий.

concoct v.t. стря́пать imp., со ~ perf. concoction n. стряпня́.

concomitant adj. сопу́тствующий.

concord n. согла́сие; согласова́ние. concordance n. согла́сие; соотве́т-

ствие; (*To Bible etc.*) слова́рь (-ря́) *m.*
concordat *n.* конкорда́т.

concourse *n.* скопле́ние; (*area*) откры́-
тое ме́сто.

concrete *n.* бето́н; *c.-mixer*, бетономе-
ша́лка; *adj.* (*made of c.*) бето́нный;
(*not abstract*) конкре́тный.

concubine *n.* любо́вница.

concur *v.i.* соглаша́ться *imp.*, согла-
си́ться *perf.*

concussion *n.* сотрясе́ние.

condemn *v.t.* осужда́ть *imp.*, осуди́ть
(-ужу́, -у́дишь) *perf.*; (*as unfit for use*)
бракова́ть *imp.*, за~ *perf.* **condemnation** *n.* осужде́ние.

condensation *n.* конденса́ция. **condense**
v.t (*liquid etc.*) конденси́ровать *imp.*,
perf.; (*text etc.*) сжа́то излага́ть *imp.*,
изложи́ть (-жу́, -жишь) *perf.* **condensed** *adj.* сжа́тый, кра́ткий (-ток,
-тка́, -тко); сгущённый (-ён, -ена́);
конденси́рованный. **condenser** *n.* кон-
денса́тор.

condescend *v.i.* снисходи́ть (-ожу́,
-о́дишь) *imp.*, снизойти́ (-ойду́,
-ойдёшь) -ошёл, -ошла́) *perf.* **condescending** *adj.* снисходи́тельный.
condescension *n.* снисхожде́ние.

condiment *n.* припра́ва.

condition *n.* усло́вие; (*state of being*)
состоя́ние; положе́ние; *v.t.* обусло́в-
ливать *imp.*, обусло́вить *perf.* **conditional** *adj.* усло́вный. **conditioned**
adj. обусло́вленный (-ен); *c. reflex*,
усло́вный рефле́кс.

condole *v.i.*: *c. with*, соболе́зновать
imp.+dat. **condolence** *n.*: *pl.* соболе́з-
нование.

condone *v.t.* закрыва́ть *imp.*, закры́ть
(-ро́ю, -ро́ешь) *perf.* глаза́ на + *acc.*

conduce *v.i.*: *c. to*, спосо́бствовать *imp.*
+dat. **conducive** *adj.* спосо́бствующий
(to, + *dat.*).

conduct *n.* веде́ние; (*behaviour*) поведе́-
ние; *v.t.* вести́ (веду́, -дёшь; вёл, -á)
imp., по~, про~ *perf.*; (*mus.*) дири-
жи́ровать *imp.+instr.*; (*phys.*) про-
води́ть (-ит) *imp.* **conduction** *n.* прово-
ди́мость. **conductor** *n.* (*bus, tram*)
конду́ктор (*pl.* -á); (*phys.*) провод-
ни́к (-á); (*mus.*) дирижёр.

conduit *n.* трубопрово́д; (*for wires*)
кабелепрово́д.

cone *n.* ко́нус; (*of pine, fir*) ши́шка.

confection *n.* изготовле́ние; конди́тер-
ское изде́лие. **confectioner** *n.* кон-
ди́тер; *c.'s*, конди́терская *sb.* **con-
fectionery** *n.* конди́терские изде́лия
neut.pl.

confederacy *n.* конфедера́ция. **confeder-
ate** *adj.* конфедерати́вный; *n.* сообщ-
ник. **confederation** *n.* конфедера́ция.

confer *v.t.* жа́ловать *imp.*, по~ *perf.*
(+ *acc.* & *instr.*, + *dat.* & *acc.*);
присужда́ть *imp.*, присуди́ть (-ужу́,
-у́дишь) (on, + *dat.*) *perf.*; *v.i.* сове-
ща́ться *imp.* **conference** *n.* совеща́ние,
конфере́нция; *c. hall*, конфере́нц-зал.
conferment *n.* присвое́ние; присужде́-
ние.

confess *v.t.* (*acknowledge*) признава́ть
(-наю́ ,-наёшь) *imp.*, призна́ть *perf.*;
(*eccl.*, *of sinner & priest*) испове́до-
вать *imp.*, perf. **confession** *n.* призна́-
ние; и́споведь. **confessor** *n.* духовни́к
(-á).

confidant(e) *n.* дове́ренное лицо́ (*pl.*
-ца). **confide** *v.t.* поверя́ть *imp.*, пове́-
рить *perf.* **confidence** *n.* (*trust*) дове́-
рие; (*certainty*) уве́ренность; *c. trick*,
моше́нничество. **confident** *adj.* уве́рен-
ный (-ен, -енна). **confidential** *adj.*
секре́тный; конфиденциа́льный.

configuration *n.* конфигура́ция.

confine *v.t.* ограни́чивать *imp.*, огра-
ни́чить *perf.*; (*in prison*) заключа́ть
imp., заключи́ть *perf.* **confinement** *n.*
(*for birth*) ро́ды (-до́в) *pl.*; заключе́-
ние. **confines** *n.* преде́лы *m.pl.*

confirm *v.t.* подтвержда́ть *imp.*, под-
тверди́ть *perf.* **confirmation** *n.* под-
твержде́ние; (*eccl.*) конфирма́ция.
confirmed *adj.* закорене́лый.

confiscate *v.t.* конфискова́ть *imp.*, perf.
confiscation *n.* конфиска́ция.

conflagration *n.* пожа́рище.

conflict *n.* конфли́кт; противоре́чие;
v.i.: *c. with*, (*contradict*) противоре́-
чить *imp.+dat.* **conflicting** *adj.* про-
тиворечи́вый.

confluence *n.* слия́ние.

conform *v.i.*: *c. to*, подчиня́ться *imp.*,
подчини́ться *perf.+dat.* **conformity** *n.*

соотвéтствие; (*compliance*) подчинéние.

confound *v.t.* сбивáть *imp.*, сбить (собью, -ьёшь) *perf.* с тóлку; с. *it!* к чёрту! **confounded** *adj.* проклятый.

confront *v.t.* стоять (-ою, -оишь) *imp.* лицóм к лицу c + *instr.*; *be confronted with*, быть постáвленным пéред + *instr.*

confuse *v.t.* приводить (-ожу, -óдишь) *imp.*, привести (-еду, -едёшь; -ёл, -елá) *perf.* в замешáтельство; путать *imp.*, за~, c ~ *perf.* **confusion** *n.* замешáтельство, путáница.

congeal *v.t.*застывáть *imp.*,застыть (-ыну, -ынешь) *perf.* засты́(ну)ть (-ыну, -ынешь), -ы́(ну)л, -ы́ла) *perf.*

congenial *adj.* близкий (-зок, -зкá, -зко, близки) по духу.

congenital *adj.* врождённый (-ён, -енá).

conger (eel) *n.* морскóй угорь (угря) *m.*

congested *adj.* переполненный (-ен); (*med.*) застóйный. **congestion** *n.* (*population*) перенаселённость; (*traffic*) затóр; (*med.*) застóй крóви.

congratulate *v.t.*поздравлять *imp.*, поздрáвить *perf.* (on, c + *instr.*). **congratulation** *n.* поздравлéние. **congratulatory** *adj.* поздравительный.

congregate *v.i.* собирáться *imp.*, собрáться (-берётся; -брáлся, -бралáсь, -брáлось) *perf.* **congregation** *n.* собрáние; (*eccl.*) прихожáне (-н) *pl.*

congress *n.* конгрéсс, съезд. **congressional** *adj.* относящийся к конгрéссу. **Congressman** *n.* конгрессмéн.

congruent *adj.* конгруэнтный.

conic(al) *adj.* конический.

conifer *n.* хвóйное *sb.* **coniferous** *adj.* хвóйный, шишконóсный.

conjectural *adj.* предположительный. **conjecture** *n.* предположéние; *v.t.* предполагáть *imp.*, предположить (-жу, -жишь) *perf.*

conjugal *adj.* супружеский.

conjugate *v.t.* (*gram.*) спрягáть *imp.*, про~ *perf.* **conjugation** *n.* (*gram.*) спряжéние.

conjunction *n.* (*gram.*) сою́з.

conjure *v.i.*: c. *up*, (*in mind*) вызывáть *imp.*, вызвать (-зову, -зовешь) *perf.* в воображéнии. **conjurer** *n.* фóкусник.

conjuring *n.* покáзывание фóкусов; c. *trick*, фóкус.

conker *n.* кóнский каштáн; *pl.* дéтская игрá в каштáны.

connect *v.t.* связывать *imp.*, связáть (-яжу, -я́жешь) *perf.*; соединять *imp.*, соединить *perf.* **connected** *adj.* связанный (-ан). **connecting** *adj.* соединительный, связующий; c.-*rod*, шатун (-á). **connection, -exion** *n.* связь (*loc.* связи).

conning-tower *n.* боевáя рубка.

connivance *n.* попустительство. **connive** *v.i.*: c. *at*, попустительствовать *imp.* + *dat.*

connoisseur *n.* знатóк (-á).

conquer *v.t.* (*country*) завоёвывать *imp.*, завоевáть (-оюю, -оюешь) *perf.*; (*enemy*) побеждáть *imp.*, победить (-едишь, -едит) *perf.*; (*habit*) преодолевáть *imp.*, преодолеть *perf.* **conqueror** *n.* завоевáтель *m.*; победитель *m.* **conquest** *n.* завоевáние; покорéние.

consanguinity *n.* крóвное родствó.

conscience *n.* сóвесть; *pangs of c.*, угрызéние сóвести. **conscientious** *adj.* добросóвестный. **conscious** *adj.* сознáтельный; *predic.* в сознáнии; *be c. of*, сознавáть (-аю, -аёшь) *imp.* + *acc.* **consciousness** *n.* сознáние.

conscript *v.t.* призывáть *imp.*, призвáть (призову, -вёшь; призвáл, -á, -о) *perf.* на воéнную службу; *n.* новобрáнец (-нца), призывник (-á). **conscription** *n.* вóинская повинность.

consecrate *v.t.* (*church etc.*) освящáть *imp.*, освятить (-ящу, -ятишь) *perf.*; (*bishop etc.*) посвящáть *imp.*, посвятить (-ящу, -ятишь) *perf.* в епископы и т.д.). **consecration** *n.* освящéние; посвящéние.

consecutive *adj.* послéдовательный.

consensus *n.* соглáсие.

consent *v.i.* давáть (даю, даёшь) *imp.*, дать (дам, дашь, даст, дадим; дал, -á, дáло, -и) *perf.* соглáсие; соглашáться *imp.*, согласиться *perf.* (to, + *inf.*, на + *acc.*); *n.* соглáсие.

consequence *n.* послéдствие; *of great c.*, большóго значéния; *of some c.*, довóльно вáжный. **consequent** *adj.*

последовательный; с. on, вытека́ющий из + gen. consequently adv. сле́довательно. consequential adj. ва́жный (-жен, -жна́, -жно, -жны).

conservancy n. охра́на (рек и лесо́в). conservation n. сохране́ние; охра́на приро́ды. conservative adj. консервати́вный; n. консерва́тор. conservatory n. оранжере́я. conserve v.t. сохраня́ть imp., сохрани́ть perf.

consider v.t. обду́мывать imp., обду́мать perf.; рассма́тривать imp., рассмотре́ть (-рю́, -ришь) perf.; (regard as, be of opinion that) счита́ть imp., счесть (сочту́, -тёшь; счёл, сочла́) perf. + instr., за + acc., что. considerable adj. значи́тельный. considerate adj. внима́тельный. consideration n. рассмотре́ние; внима́ние; take into c., принима́ть imp., приня́ть (приму́, -мешь; при́нял, -а́, -о) perf. во внима́ние. considered adj. проду́манный (-ан). considering prep. принима́я + acc. во внима́ние.

consign v.t. отправля́ть imp., отпра́вить perf. consignee n. грузополуча́тель m. consignment n. (goods consigned) па́ртия; (consigning) отпра́вка това́ров; c. note, накладна́я sb. consignor n. грузоотправи́тель m.

consist v.i.: c. of, состоя́ть imp. из + gen. consistency n. после́довательность; консисте́нция. consistent adj. после́довательный; c. with, совмести́мый с + instr. consistently adv. после́довательно; согла́сно с + instr.

consolation n. утеше́ние. consolatory adj. утеши́тельный. console[1] v.t. утеша́ть imp., уте́шить perf. consoling adj. утеши́тельный.

console[2] n. (arch.) консо́ль; (control panel) пульт управле́ния.

consolidate v.t. укрепля́ть imp., укрепи́ть perf. consolidated adj. (econ.) консолиди́рованный (-ан, -анна). consolidation n. укрепле́ние; (econ.) консолида́ция.

consonance n. созву́чие. consonant n. согла́сный (-ая); adj. созву́чный; согла́сный; совмести́мый.

consort v.i. обща́ться imp.; n. супру́г,

~ a; Prince C., супру́г ца́рствующей короле́вы.

consortium n. консо́рциум.

conspicuous adj. заме́тный; ви́дный (-ден, -дна́, -дно, ви́дны). conspicuously adv. я́сно, заме́тно.

conspiracy n. за́говор. conspirator n. заговорщик, -ица. conspiratorial adj. заговорщицкий. conspire v.i. устра́ивать imp., устро́ить perf. за́говор.

constable n. полице́йский sb. constabulary n. поли́ция.

constancy n. постоя́нство. constant adj. постоя́нный (-нен, -нна); (faithful) ве́рный (-рен, -рна́, -рно, ве́рны). constantly adv. постоя́нно.

constellation n. созве́здие.

consternation n. трево́га.

constipation n. запо́р.

constituency n. (area) избира́тельный о́круг (pl. -а́); (voters) избира́тели m.pl. constituent n. (component) составна́я часть (pl. -ти, -те́й); (voter) избира́тель m.; adj. составно́й; c. assembly, учреди́тельное собра́ние. constitute v.t. составля́ть imp., соста́вить perf. constitution n. (polit., med.) конститу́ция; (composition) сложе́ние. constitutional adj. (med.) конституциона́льный; (polit.) конституцио́нный (-нен, -нна). constitutionally adv. зако́нно; в соотве́тствии с конститу́цией.

constrain v.t. принужда́ть imp., прину́дить perf. constrained adj. принуждённый (-ён, -ена́). constraint n. принужде́ние; without c., свобо́дно, непринуждённо.

constrict v.t. (compress) сжима́ть imp., сжать (сожму́, -мёшь) perf.; (narrow) сужива́ть imp., су́зить perf. constriction n. сжа́тие, суже́ние.

construct v.t. стро́ить imp., по ~ perf. construction n. строи́тельство; (also gram.) констру́кция; (interpretation) истолкова́ние; c. site, стро́йка. constructional adj. строи́тельный; (structural) структу́рный. constructive adj. конструкти́вный. constructor n. строи́тель m., констру́ктор.

construe v.t. истолко́вывать imp., истолкова́ть perf.

consul n. ко́нсул; *honorary* c., почётный ко́нсул; C.-*general*, генера́льный ко́нсул. **consular** *adj.* ко́нсульский. **consulate** n. ко́нсульство.

consult v.t. консульти́ровать *imp.*, про~ *perf.* c + *instr.*; сове́товаться *imp.*, по~ *perf.* c + *instr.* **consultation** n. консульта́ция, совеща́ние. **consultative** *adj.* консультати́вный, совеща́тельный. **consulting** *adj.* консульти́рующий; c. *room*, враче́бный кабине́т.

consume v.t. потребля́ть *imp.*, потреби́ть *perf.*; расхо́довать *imp.*, из~ *perf.* **consumer** n. потреби́тель m.; c. *goods*, това́ры m.pl. широ́кого потребле́ния, ширпотре́б; c. *society*, о́бщество потребле́ния.

consummate *adj.* зако́нченный (-ен, -енна); соверше́нный (-нен, -нна); v.t. заверша́ть *imp.*, заверши́ть *perf.*; доводи́ть (-ожу́, -о́дишь) *imp.*, довести́ (-еду́, -едёшь; довёл, -á) *perf.* до конца́. **consummation** n. заверше́ние.

consumption n. потребле́ние, расхо́д; (*disease*) чахо́тка. **consumptive** *adj.* чахо́точный, туберкулёзный; n. больно́й *sb.* чахо́ткой, туберкулёзом.

contact n. конта́кт, соприкоснове́ние; v.t. соприкаса́ться *imp.*, соприкосну́ться *perf.* c + *instr.*; входи́ть (-ожу́, -о́дишь) *imp.*, войти́ (войду́, -дёшь; вошёл, -шла́) *perf.* в конта́кт c + *instr.*

contagion n. зара́за, инфе́кция. **contagious** *adj.* зара́зный, инфекцио́нный; c. *laughter*, зарази́тельный смех.

contain v.t. содержа́ть (-жу́, -жишь) *imp.*; вмеща́ть *imp.*, вмести́ть *perf.*; (*restrain*) сде́рживать *imp.*, сдержа́ть (-жу́, -жишь) *perf.* **container** n. (*vessel*) сосу́д; (*transport*) конте́йнер. **containment** n. сде́рживание.

contaminate v.t. заража́ть *imp.*, зарази́ть *perf.*; загрязня́ть *imp.*, загрязни́ть *perf.* **contamination** n. зараже́ние, загрязне́ние.

contemplate v.t. созерца́ть *imp.*; размышля́ть *imp.*; (*intend*) предполага́ть *imp.*, предположи́ть (-жу́, -жишь) *perf.* **contemplation** n. созерца́ние;

размышле́ние. **contemplative** *adj.* созерца́тельный.

contemporary n. совреме́нник; *adj.* совреме́нный (-нен, -нна).

contempt n. презре́ние; c. *of court*, неуваже́ние к суду́; *hold in* c., презира́ть *imp.* **contemptible** *adj.* презре́нный (-ен, -енна). **contemptuous** *adj.* презри́тельный.

contend v.i. (*compete*) состяза́ться *imp.*; c. *for*, оспа́ривать *imp.*; v.t. утвержда́ть *imp.* **contender** n. соревну́ющийся *sb.*

content[1] n. содержа́ние; *pl.* содержи́мое *sb.*; (*table of*) *contents*, содержа́ние.

content[2] n. дово́льство; *predic.* дово́лен (-льна); v.t.: c. *oneself with*, дово́льствоваться *imp.*, у~ *perf.* + *instr.* **contented** *adj.* дово́льный; удовлетворённый (-ён, -ена́).

contention n. (*dispute*) спор, разногла́сие; (*claim*) утвержде́ние. **contentious** *adj.* (*disputed*) спо́рный; (*quarrelsome*) вздо́рный.

contest n. соревнова́ние, состяза́ние; v.t. оспа́ривать *imp.*, оспо́рить *perf.* **contestant** n. уча́стник, -ица, соревнова́ния; конкуре́нт, ~ ка.

context n. конте́кст.

contiguity n. соприкоснове́ние; бли́зость. **contiguous** *adj.* (*adjoining*) прилега́ющий (to, к + *dat.*); (*touching*) соприкаса́ющийся (to, c + *instr.*); (*near*) бли́зкий (-зок, -зка́, -зко, бли́зки) (to, от + *gen.*).

continence n. воздержа́ние. **continent**[1] *adj.* возде́ржанный (-ан, -анна).

continent[2] n. матери́к (-á), контине́нт. **continental** *adj.* материко́вый, контине́нтальный.

contingency n. случа́йность. **contingent** *adj.* случа́йный, непредви́денный (-ен, -енна); c. *on*, в зави́симости от + *gen.*; n. континге́нт.

continual *adj.* непреста́нный (-нен, -нна). **continuance, continuation** n. продолже́ние. **continue** v.t. & i. продолжа́ть(ся) *imp.*, продо́лжить(ся) *perf.* **continuous** *adj.* непреры́вный.

contort v.t. искажа́ть *imp.*, искази́ть

perf. **contortion** *n.* искажение; искривление. **contortionist** *n.* акробат.

contour *n.* контур, очертание; *c.* line, горизонталь.

contraband *n.* контрабанда; *adj.* контрабандный.

contraception *n.* предупреждение беременности. **contraceptive** *n.* противозачаточное средство; *adj.* противозачаточный.

contract *n.* контракт, договор; *v.i.* (make a c.) заключать *imp.*, заключить *perf.* контракт, договор; *v.t.* & *i.* сокращать(ся) *imp.*, сократить(ся) (-ащу(сь), -атишь(ся)) *perf.* **contracting** *n.* договаривающийся; *c.* parties, договаривающиеся стороны (-он, -онам) *f.pl.* **contraction** *n.* сокращение, сжатие. **contractor** *n.* подрядчик.

contradict *v.t.* противоречить *imp.*+ *dat.* **contradiction** *n.* противоречие. **contradictory** *adj.* противоречивый.

contralto *n.* контральто (voice) *neut.* & (person) *f.indecl.*

contraption *n.* штуковина; устройство.

contrariness *n.* своенравие, упрямство. **contrary** *adj.* (opposite) противоположный; (perverse) упрямый; *c.* to, вопреки + *dat.*; *n.*: on the *c.*, наоборот.

contrast *n.* контраст, противоположность; *v.t.* противопоставлять *imp.*, противопоставить *perf.* (with, + *dat.*).

contravene *v.t.* нарушать *imp.*, нарушить *perf.* **contravention** *n.* нарушение.

contribute *v.t.* (to fund etc.) жертвовать *imp.*, по ~ *perf.* (to, в + *acc.*); *c.* to, (further) содействовать *imp.*, perf. по ~ *perf.*+ *dat.*; (to publication etc.) сотрудничать *imp.* в + *prep.* **contribution** *n.* пожертвование; вклад. **contributor** *n.* жертвователь; сотрудник; соучастник.

contrite *adj.* сокрушающийся, кающийся. **contrition** *n.* раскаяние.

contrivance *n.* приспособление; выдумка. **contrive** *v.t.* умудряться *imp.*, умудриться *perf.*+ *inf.*

control *n.* (check) контроль, проверка; (direction) управление; (restraint) сдержанность; (remote c.) телеуправление; c.-gear, механизм управления;

c. point, контрольный пункт; *c.* tower, диспетчерская вышка; *v.t.* (check) контролировать *imp.*, про ~ *perf.*; управлять *imp.*+ *instr.*; *c.* oneself, сдерживаться *imp.*, сдержаться (-жусь, -жишься) *perf.* **controllable** *adj.* управляемый, регулируемый. **controller** *n.* контролёр; (electr.) контроллер.

controversial *adj.* спорный. **controversy** *n.* спор, дискуссия.

contuse *v.t.* контузить *perf.* **contusion** *n.* контузия.

conundrum *n.* головоломка.

convalesce *v.i.* поправляться *imp.* **convalescence** *n.* поправка, выздоравливание. **convalescent** *n.*, *adj.* выздоравливающий.

convection *n.* конвекция.

convene *v.t.* созывать *imp.*, созвать (созову, -вёшь; созвал, -á, -о) *perf.*

convenience *n.* удобство; (public c.), уборная *sb.*; *c.* foods, полуфабрикаты *m.pl.* **convenient** *adj.* удобный.

convent *n.* женский монастырь (-ря) *m.*

convention *n.* (assembly) съезд, собрание; (agreement) конвенция; (practice, use, custom) обычай; (conventionality) условность. **conventional** *adj.* общепринятый, обычный; условный; *c.* weapons, обычные виды *m.pl.* оружия.

converge *v.i.* сходиться (-дятся) *imp.*, сойтись (-йдутся; сошлись) *perf.* в одну точку. **convergence** *n.* сходимость, конвергенция. **converging** *adj.* сходящийся в одной точке.

conversant *predic.*: *c.* with, осведомлён (-á) в + *prep.*; знаком с + *instr.*

conversation *n.* разговор, беседа. **conversational** *adj.* разговорный. **converse**[1] *v.i.* разговаривать *imp.*; беседовать *imp.*

converse[2] *adj.* обратный, противоположный. **conversely** *adv.* наоборот. **conversion** *n.* (change) превращение; (of faith) обращение; (of building) перестройка. **convert** *n.* (change) превращать *imp.*, превратить (-ащу, -атишь) *perf.* (into, в + *acc.*); (to faith) обращать *imp.*, обратить (-ащу, -атишь) *perf.* (to, в + *acc.*); (a building) перестраивать *imp.*, перестроить *perf.* **convertible** *adj.* обрати́мый; *n.* кабриоле́т, фаэто́н.

convex *adj.* вы́пуклый.

convey *v.t.* (*transport*) перевози́ть (-ожу́, -о́зишь) *imp.*, перевезти́ (-езу́, -езёшь; -ёз, -езла́) *perf.*; (*communicate*) сообща́ть *imp.*, сообщи́ть *perf.*; (*transmit*) передава́ть (-даю́, -даёшь) *imp.*, переда́ть (-а́м, -а́шь, -а́ст, -ади́м; пе́редал, -а́, -о) *perf.* **conveyance** *n.* перево́зка, переда́ча. **conveyancing** *n.* оформле́ние перехо́да пра́ва на недви́жимость. **conveyer** *n.* конве́йер, транспортёр.

convict *n.* осуждённый *sb.*, ка́торжник; *v.t.* осужда́ть *imp.*, осуди́ть (-ужу́, -у́дишь) *perf.* **conviction** *n.* (*leg.*) осужде́ние; (*belief*) убежде́ние. **convince** *v.t.* убежда́ть *imp.*, убеди́ть (-и́шь, -и́т) *perf.* **convincing** *adj.* убеди́тельный.

convivial *adj.* пра́здничный.

convocation *n.* созы́в; собра́ние; (*eccl.*) собо́р, сино́д. **convoke** *v.t.* созыва́ть *imp.*, созва́ть (созову́, -вёшь; созва́л, -а́, -о) *perf.*

convoluted *adj.* свёрнутый спира́лью, изви́листый.

convolvulus *n.* вьюно́к (-нка́)

convoy *n.* конво́й; коло́нна под конво́ем; *v.t.* конвои́ровать *imp.*

convulse *v.t.*: be convulsed with, содрога́ться *imp.*, содрогну́ться *perf.* от + *gen.* **convulsion** *n.* (*med.*) конву́льсия; су́дороги *f.pl.*

coo *n.* воркова́ние; *v.i.* воркова́ть *imp.*

cooee *interj.* ау́!

cook *n.* куха́рка, по́вар (*pl.* -а́), ~и́ха; *v.t.* стря́пать *imp.*; (*roast*) жа́рить *imp.*, за~, из~ *perf.*; (*boil*) вари́ть (-рю́, -ришь) *imp.*, с~ *perf.* **cooker** *n.* плита́ (*pl.* -ты), печь (*loc.* -чи́; *pl.* -чи, -че́й). **cookery** *n.* кулина́рия, стряпня́. **cooking** *adj.* ку́хонный; *c.* salt, пова́ренная соль.

cool *n.* прохла́дный; (*of persons*) хладнокро́вный; *v.t.* студи́ть (-ужу́, -у́дишь) *imp.*, о~ *perf.*; охлажда́ть *imp.*, охлади́ть *perf.*; *c.* down, off, остыва́ть *imp.*, осты́(ну)ть (-ы́ну, -ы́нешь; -ы́(ну)л, -ы́ла) *perf.* **coolant** *n.* сма́зочно-охлажда́ющая жи́дкость.

cooler *n.* охлади́тель *m.* **cooling** *adj.* охлажда́ющий.

coop *n.* куря́тник; *v.t.*: *c.* up, держа́ть (-жу́, -жишь) *imp.* взаперти́.

cooper *n.* бо́ндарь (бондаря́) *m.*, бо́чар (-а́).

co-operate *v.i.* сотру́дничать *imp.*; коопери́роваться *imp.*, *perf.* **co-operation** *n.* сотру́дничество; коопера́ция. **co-operative**, **co-op.** *n.* кооперати́в; *adj.* совме́стный, коопера́тивный. **co-operator** *n.* коопера́тор.

co-opt *v.t.* коопти́ровать *imp.*, *perf.*

co-ordinate *v.t.* координи́ровать *imp.*, *perf.*; согласо́вывать *imp.*, согласова́ть *perf.*; *n.* координа́та; *adj.* согласо́ванный (-ан), координи́рованный (-ан, -анна). **co-ordination** *n.* координа́ция.

coot *n.* лысу́ха.

co-owner *n.* совладе́лец (-льца)

cop *n.* полице́йский *sb.*; *v.t.* пойма́ть *perf.*

cope[1] *n.* ри́за.

cope[2] *v.i.*: *c.* with, справля́ться *imp.*, спра́виться *perf.* с + *instr.*

copious *adj.* оби́льный. **copiousness** *n.* изоби́лие.

copper *n.* (*metal*) медь; (*vessel*) ме́дный котёл (-тла́); (*coin*) медя́к (-а́); (*policeman*) полице́йский *sb.* **copperplate** *n.* (*handwriting*) каллиграфи́ческий по́черк.

coppice, **copse** *n.* ро́щица.

Copt *n.* копт. **Coptic** *adj.* ко́птский.

copulate *v.i.* спа́риваться *imp.*, спа́риться *perf.* **copulation** *n.* копуля́ция.

copy *n.* ко́пия; (*specimen of book etc.*) экземпля́р; *c.-book*, тетра́дь; *copyright*, а́вторское пра́во; *fair c.*, чистови́к (-а́); *rough c.*, чернови́к (-а́); *v.t.* копи́ровать *imp.*, с~ *perf.*; (*transcribe*) перепи́сывать *imp.*, переписа́ть (-ишу́, -и́шешь) *perf.*

coquetry *n.* коке́тство. **coquette** *n.* коке́тка. **coquettish** *adj.* коке́тливый, игри́вый.

coracle *n.* ло́дка из ивняка́, обтя́нутая ко́жей или паруси́ной.

coral *n.* кора́лл; *adj.* кора́лловый.

corbel *n.* вы́ступ; консо́ль; кронште́йн.

cord *n.* шнур (-á), верёвка; umbilical c., пуповина; vocal cords, голосовые связки *f.pl.*; *v.t.* связывать *imp.*, связать (-яжу, -яжешь) *perf.* верёвкой.

cordage *n.* снасти (-тей) *pl.*, такелаж.

cordial *adj.* сердечный, радушный; *n.* (drink) фруктовый напиток (-тка).

cordiality *n.* сердечность, радушие.

corduroy *n.* вельвет (-a(y)) *m.* в рубчик; плис; *pl.* вельветовые штаны (-нóв) *pl.*

core *n.* сердцевина; (fig.) суть; *v.t.* удалять *imp.*, удалить *perf.* сердцевину из + *gen.*

cork *n.* (stopper) пробка; (float) поплавок (-вкá); *attrib.* пробковый; *v.t.* закупоривать *imp.*, закупорить *perf.*

corkscrew *n.* штопор; *v.i.* двигаться (-игается & -ижется) *imp.*, двинуться *perf.* по спирáли.

corm *n.* клубнелуковица.

cormorant *n.* баклан.

corn[1] *n.* зерно, зерновые хлеба *m.pl.*; (wheat) пшеница, (oats) овёс (овсá), (maize) кукуруза; c.-cob, початок (-тка). **cornflakes** *n.* кукурузные хлопья (-ьев) *pl.* **cornflour** *n.* кукурузная мука. **cornflower** *n.* василёк (-лькá). **corny** *adj.* зерновой; (coll.) банальный.

corn[2] *v.t.* засаливать *imp.*, засолить (-олю, -олишь) *perf.*; corned beef, солонина.

corn[3] *n.* (on foot) мозоль.

cornea *n.* роговая оболочка.

cornelian *n.* сердолик.

corner *n.* угол (угла, loc. углу); c.-stone, краеугольный камень (-мня; *pl.* -мни, -мнéй) *m.*; *v.t.* загонять *imp.*, загнать (-гоню, -гонишь; загнал, -á, -о) *perf.* в угол.

cornet *n.* (mus., mil.) корнет; (paper) фунтик; (ice-cream) рожок (-жкá).

cornice *n.* карниз.

cornucopia *n.* рог изобилия.

corolla *n.* венчик.

corollary *n.* следствие; вывод.

corona *n.* корона, венец (-нцá). **coronary** (thrombosis) *n.* венечный тромбоз. **coronation** *n.* коронация. **coroner** *n.* следователь *m.* **coronet** *n.* небольшая корона; (garland) венок (-нкá).

corporal[1] *n.* капрал.

corporal[2] *adj.* телесный; c. punishment, телесное наказание.

corporate *adj.* корпоративный. **corporation** *n.* корпорация.

corps *n.* корпус (*pl.* -á).

corpse *n.* труп.

corpulence *n.* тучность. **corpulent** *adj.* тучный (-чен, -чнá, -чно).

corpuscle *n.* частица, тельце (*pl.* -льцá, -лéц, -льцáм); red, white, c., красные, белые, шарики *m.pl.* **corpuscular** *adj.* корпускулярный.

corral *n.* загон; *v.t.* загонять *imp.*, загнать (-гоню, -гонишь; загнал, -á, -о) *perf.* в загон.

correct *adj.* правильный, верный (-рен, -рнá, -рно, верны); (conduct) корректный; *v.t.* исправлять *imp.*, исправить *perf.* **correction** *n.* исправление; поправка. **corrective** *adj.* исправительный. **corrector** *n.* корректор (*pl.* -ы & -á).

correlate *v.i.* соотноситься (-ошу, -осишь) *imp.*, соотнестись (-есу, -есёшь; -ёс, -еслá) *perf.* **correlation** *n.* соотношение, корреляция.

correspond *v.i.* соответствовать *imp.* (to, with, + *dat.*); (by letter) переписываться *imp.* **correspondence** *n.* соответствие; корреспонденция. **correspondent** *n.* корреспондент. **corresponding** *adj.* соответствующий (to, + *dat.*).

corridor *n.* коридор.

corroborate *v.t.* подтверждать *imp.*, подтвердить *perf.* **corroboration** *n.* подтверждение.

corrode *v.t.* разъедать *imp.*, разъесть (-ест, -едят; -ел) *perf.* **corrosion** *n.* разъедание, коррозия. **corrosive** *adj.* едкий (ёдок, едкá, ёдко); *n.* едкое, разъедающее, вещество.

corrugate *v.t.* гофрировать *imp.*, *perf.*; corrugated iron, рифлёное железо.

corrupt *adj.* испорченный (-ен, -енна); развратный; *v.t.* развращать *imp.*, развратить (-ащу, -атишь) *perf.*; портить *imp.*, ис~ *perf.* **corruption** *n.* порча; развращённость; коррупция.

corsage *n.* корсаж.

corsair *n.* корсар; пират.

corset n. корсе́т.

cortège n. торже́ственное ше́ствие, корте́ж.

cortex n. кора́.

corundum n. кору́нд.

corvette n. корве́т.

cos n. ромэ́н-сала́т.

cosh n. дуби́нка; v.t. ударя́ть imp., уда́рить perf. дуби́нкой.

cosine n. ко́синус.

cosmetic adj. космети́ческий; n. космет́и́ческое сре́дство; pl. косме́тика.

cosmic adj. косми́ческий. **cosmonaut** n. космона́вт.

cosmopolitan adj. космополити́ческий; n. космополи́т.

Cossack n. каза́к (-á; pl. -áки), -áчка; adj. каза́чий (-чья, -чье), каза́цкий.

cosset v.t. не́жить imp.

cost n. сто́имость, цена́ (acc. -ну; pl. -ны); pl. (leg.) суде́бные изде́ржки f.pl.; c. price, себесто́имость; v.t. сто́ить imp.

costermonger n. у́личный торго́вец (-вца).

costly adj. дорого́й (до́рог, -á, -о), це́нный (-нен, -нна).

costume n. костю́м, оде́жда; c. jewellery, ювели́рное украше́ние без драгоце́нных ка́мней; c. play, истори́ческая пье́са.

cosy adj. ую́тный; n. тёплая покры́шка.

cot n. (child's) де́тская крова́тка; (hospital bed) ко́йка.

cottage n. котте́дж.

cotton n. хло́пок (-пка); (cloth) хлопчатобума́жная ткань; (thread) бума́жная ни́тка; c.-plant, хлопча́тник; c. wool, ва́та; adj. хло́пковый, хлопчатобума́жный.

couch n. куше́тка, ло́же.

couch-grass n. пыре́й.

cough n. ка́шель (-шля) m.; v.i. ка́шлять imp.

council n. сове́т; (eccl.) собо́р. **councillor** n. сове́тник; член сове́та.

counsel n. (consultation) обсужде́ние; (advice) сове́т; (lawyer) адвока́т; c. for the defence, защи́тник; c. for the prosecution, обвини́тель m.; v.t. сове́товать imp., по~ perf. + dat.

count[1] v.t. счита́ть imp., со~, сосчи́тать; (sum up) счесть (сочту́, -тёшь; счёл, сочла́) perf.; n. счёт (-а(у)), подсчёт. **countdown** n. отсчёт вре́мени.

count[2] n. (title) граф.

countenance n. лицо́ (pl. -ца); v.t одобря́ть imp., одо́брить perf.

counter n. прила́вок (-вка), сто́йка; (token) фи́шка, жето́н; adj. обра́тный; adv.: run c. to, де́йствовать imp. про́тив + gen.; v.t. пари́ровать imp., от~ perf. **counteract** v.t. противоде́йствовать imp. **counteraction** n. противоде́йствие. **counterbalance** n. противове́с; v.t. уравнове́шивать imp., уравнове́сить perf. **counterfeit** adj. подло́жный, фальши́вый. **counterintelligence** n. контрразве́дка. **countermand** v.t. отменя́ть imp., отмени́ть (-ню́, -нишь) perf. **counterpane** n. покрыва́ло. **counterpart** n. соотве́тственная часть (pl. -ти, -те́й). **counterpoint** n. контрапу́нкт. **counter-revolutionary** n. контрреволюционе́р; adj. контрреволюцио́нный. **countersign** n. паро́ль m.

countess n. графи́ня.

counting-house n. бухгалте́рия.

countless adj. несчётный, бесчи́сленный (-ен, -енна).

countrified adj. дереве́нский. **country** n. (nation) страна́; (land of birth) ро́дина; (rural areas) дере́вня; adj. дереве́нский, се́льский. **countryman**, **-woman** n. земля́к, -я́чка; се́льский жи́тель m., -ница.

county n. гра́фство.

couple n. па́ра; два m. & neut., две f, (двух, двум, двумя́); married c., супру́ги m.pl.; v.t. сцепля́ть imp.. сцепи́ть (-плю́, -пишь) perf. **couplet** n. двусти́шье. **coupling** n. соедине́ние, сцепле́ние.

coupon n. купо́н; тало́н.

courage n. му́жество, хра́брость; **courageous** adj. хра́брый (храбр, -á, -о, хра́бры).

courier n. (messenger) курье́р; (guide) гид.

course n. курс, ход, путь (-ти́, -тём) m.; (of meal) блю́до; of c., коне́чно; v.t. гна́ться (гоню́сь, го́нишься; гна́лся, гнала́сь, гнало́сь) *imp.* за + *instr.* coursing *n.* охо́та с го́нчими.

court *n.* двор (-а́); (*sport*) корт, пло́щадка; (*law*) суд (-а́); (*c. martial*) вое́нный трибуна́л; *v.t.* уха́живать *imp.* за + *instr.* **courteous** *adj.* ве́жливый, любе́зный. **courtesy** *n.* ве́жливость. **courtier** *n.* придво́рный *sb.*

cousin *n.* двою́родный брат (*pl.* -ья, -ьев), -ная сестра́ (*pl.* сёстры, -тёр, -трам); *second c.*, трою́родный брат (*pl.* -ья, -ьев), -ная сестра́ (*pl.* сёстры, -тёр, -трам).

cove *n.* небольша́я бу́хта.

covenant *n.* догово́р; *v.i.* заключа́ть *imp.*, заключи́ть *perf.* догово́р.

cover *n.* покры́шка, покро́в; укры́тие; чехо́л (-хла́); (*bed*) покрыва́ло; (*book*) переплёт, обло́жка; *under separate c.*, в отде́льном конве́рте; *v.t.* покрыва́ть *imp.*, покры́ть (-ро́ю, -ро́ешь) *perf.*; скрыва́ть *imp.*, скрыть (-ро́ю, -ро́ешь) *perf.* **coverage** *n.* репорта́ж, информа́ция. **covering** *n.* покры́шка, оболо́чка; *adj.* покрыва́ющий; *c. letter*, сопроводи́тельное письмо́ (*pl.* -сьма, -сем, -сьмам). **covert** *adj.* скры́тый, та́йный.

covet *v.t.* домога́ться *imp.* + *gen.*; пожела́ть *perf.* + *gen.* **covetous** *adj.* зави́стливый, а́лчный.

covey *n.* вы́водок (-дка).

cow[1] *n.* коро́ва. **cowboy** *n.* ковбо́й. **cowshed** *n.* хлев (*loc.* -е & -у́; *pl.* -а́).

cow[2] *v.t.* запу́гивать *imp.*, запуга́ть *perf.*

coward *n.* трус. **cowardice** *n.* тру́сость. **cowardly** *adj.* трусли́вый.

cower *v.i.* съёживаться *imp.*, съёжиться *perf.*

cowl *n.* (*hood*) капюшо́н; (*of chimney*) колпа́к (-а́) дымово́й трубы́.

cowslip *n.* первоцве́т.

cox(swain) *n.* рулево́й *m.*

coxcomb *n.* фат.

coy *adj.* скро́мный (-мен, -мна́, -мно).

crab *n.* краб; *catch a c.*, пойма́ть *perf.* леща́.

crab-apple *n.* (*fruit*) ди́кое я́блоко (*pl.* -ки, -к); (*tree*) ди́кая я́блоня.

crack *n.* тре́щина; треск; уда́р; *adj.* первокла́ссный, великоле́пный; *v.t.*

(*break*) коло́ть (-лю́, -лешь) *imp.*, рас ~ *perf.*; *v.i.* (*sound*) тре́снуть *perf.* **cracker** *n.* (*Christmas c.*) хлопу́шка; (*firework*) фейерве́рк. **crackle** *v.i.* потре́скивать *imp.*; хрусте́ть (-щу́, -сти́шь) *imp.* п. потре́скивание, хруст (-а(у)). **crackpot** *n.* поме́шанный *sb.*

cradle *n.* колыбе́ль, лю́лька; *v.t.* убаю́кивать *imp.*

craft *n.* (*trade*) ремесло́ (*pl.* -ёсла, -ёсел, -ёслам); (*boat*) су́дно (*pl.* суда́, -до́в). **craftiness** *n.* хи́трость, лука́вство. **craftsman** *n.* реме́сленник. **crafty** *adj.* хи́трый (-тёр, -тра́, хи́тро́), кова́рный.

crag *n.* утёс. **craggy** *adj.* скали́стый.

cram *v.t.* набива́ть *imp.*, наби́ть (набью́, -ьёшь) *perf.*; впи́хивать *imp.*, впихну́ть *perf.*; пи́чкать *imp.*, на ~ *perf.*; (*coach*) ната́скивать *imp.*, натаска́ть *perf.* **crammed** *adj.* битко́м наби́тый.

cramp[1] *n.* (*med.*) су́дорога.

cramp[2] *n.* зажи́м, скоба́ (*pl.* -бы, -б, -ба́м); *v.t.* стесня́ть *imp.*, стесни́ть *perf.*; ограни́чивать *imp.*, ограни́чить *perf.* **cramped** *adj.* сти́снутый; ограни́ченный (-ен, -енна).

cranberry *n.* клю́ква.

crane *n.* (*bird*) жура́вль (-ля́) *m.*; (*machine*) кран; *v.t.* (& *i.*) вытя́гивать *imp.*, вы́тянуть *perf.* (ше́ю).

cranium *n.* че́реп (*pl.* -а́).

crank[1] *n.* кривоши́п, заводна́я ру́чка; *c.-shaft*, коле́нчатый вал (*loc.* -у́; *pl.* -ы́); *v.t.* заводи́ть (-ожу́, -о́дишь) *imp.*, завести́ (-еду́, -еде́шь; -ёл, -ела́) *perf.* **crank**[2] *n.* (*eccentric*) чуда́к (-а́). **cranky** *adj.* чуда́ческий; эксцентри́чный.

cranny *n.* щель (*loc.* ще́ли; *pl.* ще́ли, щеле́й).

crape *n.* креп; (*mourning*) тра́ур.

crash[1] *n.* (*noise*) гро́хот, треск; (*accident*) круше́ние, ава́рия; (*financial*) крах, банкро́тство; (*helmet*) защи́тный шлем; *c. landing*, вы́нужденная поса́дка; *v.i.* ру́шиться *imp.* с тре́ском; разбива́ться *imp.*, разби́ться (разобью́сь, -ьёшься) *perf.*

crash[2] *n.* (*linen*) холст (-а́), гру́бое полотно́.

crass adj. пóлный (-лон, -лнá, пóлно), совершённый (-нен, -нна).

crate n. упакóвочный ящик.

crater n. крáтер, жерлó (pl. -ла).

crave v.t. стрáстно желáть imp. + gen.; c. for, жáждать (-ду, -дешь) imp. + gen. **craving** n. стрáстное желáние.

craven adj. труслúвый, малодýшный.

crawl v.i. пóлзать indet., ползтú (-зý, -зёшь; -з, -злá) det.; тащúться (-щýсь, -щишься) imp.; n. ползáние; мéдленный ход (-a(y)); (sport) кроль.

crayfish n. речнóй рак.

crayon n. цветнóй мелóк (-лкá), цветнóй карандáш (-á); (drawing) пастéль; v.t. рисовáть imp., на ~ perf. цветным мелкóм, карандашóм.

craze n. мáния. **crazy** adj. помéшанный (-ан).

creak n. скрип; v.i. скрипéть (-плю, -пúшь) imp. **creaking, creaky** adj. скрипýчий.

cream n. слúвки (-вок) pl., крем; (cheese, слúвочный сыр (-a(y))); soured c., сметáна; v.t. сбивáть imp., сбить (собью, -ьёшь) perf. **creamed** adj. взбúтый, стёртый. **creamy** adj. слúвочный, крéмовый, густóй.

crease n. мятая склáдка; v.t. мять (мну, мнёшь) imp., из ~ (изомнý, -нёшь), c ~ (comнý, -нёшь) perf. **creased** adj. мятый.

create v.t. создавáть (-даю, -даёшь) imp., создáть (-áм, -áшь, -áст, -адúм; сóздал, -á, -о) perf.; творúть imp., co ~ perf. **creation** n. творéние; создáние. **creative** adj. твóрческий, создáтельный. **creator** n. творéц (-рцá), создáтель m. **creature** n. существó; создáние; тварь.

crèche n. (дéтские) ясли (-лей) pl.

credence n. довéрие; letter of c., рекомендáтельное письмó (pl. -сьма, -сем, -сьмам); give c., вéрить imp. (to, + dat.). **credentials** n. мандáт; удостоверéние лúчности; вверúтельные грáмоты f.pl. **credibility** n. правдоподóбие. **credible** adj. заслýживающий довéрия. **credibly** adv. достовéрно.

credit n. довéрие; кредúт; прихóд; v.t.: credit with, припúсывать imp., приписáть (-ишý, -úшешь) perf. + dat.; give

c., кредитовáть imp., perf. + acc.; отдавáть (-даю, -даёшь) imp., отдáть (-áм, -áшь, -áст, -адúм; óтдал, -á, -о) perf. дóлжное + dat.; it is to your c., это вам дéлает честь. **creditable** adj. дéлающий честь. **creditor** n. кредитóр. **credit-worthy** adj. кредитоспосóбный.

credulity n. легковéрие. **credulous** adj. легковéрный.

creed n. убеждéние; (eccl.) вероисповéдание.

creep v.i. пóлзать indet., ползтú (-зý, -зёшь; -з, -злá) det.; крáсться (-адусь, -адёшься; -áлся) imp. **creeper** n. (plant) ползýчее растéние. **creeping** adj. ползýчий; c. paralysis, прогрессúвный паралúч (-á).

cremate v.t. кремúровать imp., perf. **cremation** n. кремáция. **crematorium** n. кремáторий.

Creole n. креóл, ~ ка.

crêpe n. креп; c. de Chine, крепдешúн.

crescendo adv., adj., n. крещéндо indecl.

crescent n. полумéсяц; adj. серповúдный.

cress n. кресс-салáт.

crest n. грéбень (-бня) m.; вершúна. c.-fallen, удручённый (-ён, -ённа).

cretin n. кретúн.

cretonne n. кретóн.

crevasse, crevice n. расщéлина, рассéлина.

crew n. бригáда; (of ship) экипáж, комáнда.

crib n. (bed) дéтская кровáтка; (in school) шпаргáлка; v.i. спúсывать imp., списáть (-ишý, -úшешь) perf. (from, c + gen.).

crick n. растяжéние мышц.

cricket¹ n. (insect) сверчóк (-чкá).

cricket² n. (sport) крúкет; c.-bat, битá.

crier n. глашáтай.

crime n. преступлéние. **criminal** n. престýпник; adj. престýпный, уголóвный.

crimp v.t. мéлко завивáть imp., завúть (-вью, -вьёшь; завúл, -á, -о) perf.

crimson adj. малúновый, кармазúнный.

cringe v.i. (cower) съёживаться imp., съёжиться perf.; (of behaviour) раболепствовать *imp.* **cringing** *adj.* подобострастный.

crinkle *n.* морщина.

crinoline *n.* кринолин.

cripple *n.* калека *m. & f.; v.t.* калечить *imp.,* ис~ *perf.; (fig.)* наносить (-ошу, -осишь) *imp.,* нанести (нанесу, -сёшь; нанёс, -ла) вред, повреждение, + *dat.*

crisis *n.* кризис.

crisp *adj.* свежий (-á); *(brittle)* хрустящий; *(fresh)* свежий (свеж, -á, -ó, свежи); *(abrupt)* резкий (-зок, -зка, -зко); *n.: pl.* чипсы (-сов) *pl.*

criss-cross *adv.* крест-накрест.

criterion *n.* критерий.

critic *n.* критик. **critical** *adj.* критический; *(dangerous)* опасный. **criticism** *n.* критика. **criticize** *v.t.* критиковать *imp.* **critique** *n.* критика.

croak *n.* кваканье; *v.i.* квакать *imp.,* квакнуть *perf.;* хрипеть (-плю, -пишь) *imp.*

Croat, Croatian *n.* хорват, ~ ка; *adj.* хорватский.

crochet *n.* вязание крючком; *v.t.* вязать (вяжу, вяжешь) *imp.,* с ~ *perf.* (крючком).

crock *n. (broken pottery)* глиняный черепок (-пка). **crockery** *n.* глиняная, фаянсовая, посуда.

crocodile *n. (animal)* крокодил; *(of children)* хождение парами.

crocus *n.* крокус.

croft *n.* мелкое хозяйство. **crofter** *n.* мелкий арендатор.

crone *n.* старая карга.

crony *n.* закадычный друг *(pl.* друзья, -зей, -зьям).

crook *n. (staff)* посох; *(bend)* изгиб; *(swindler)* жулик, мошенник; *v.t.* сгибать *imp.,* согнуть *perf.* **crooked** *adj.* кривой (крив, -á, -о); *(dishonest)* нечестный. **crookedness** *n.* кривизна; *(dishonesty)* жульничество.

croon *v.t. & i.* напевать *imp.;* мурлыкать (-ычу, -ычешь) *imp.* **crooner** *n.* эстрадный певец (-вца).

crop *n. (yield)* урожай; *pl.* культуры *f.pl.; (bird's)* зоб *(pl.* -ы); *(haircut)* короткая стрижка; *v.t. (cut)* подстригать *imp.,* подстричь (-игу, -ижёшь;

-иг) *perf.; c. up,* неожиданно возникать *imp.,* возникнуть (-к) *perf.*

croquet *n.* крокет.

cross *n.* крест (-á); *(biol.) (action)* скрещивание, *(result)* помесь; *adj. (transverse)* поперечный; *(angry)* сердитый; *v.t.* пересекать *imp.,* пересечь (-еку, -ечёшь; -ёк, -екла) *perf.; (biol.)* скрещивать *imp.,* скрестить *perf.; c. off, out,* вычёркивать *imp.,* вычеркнуть *perf.; c. oneself,* креститься (-ещусь, -éстишься) *imp.,* пере~ *perf.; c. over,* переходить (-ожу, -одишь) *imp.,* перейти (-ейду, -ейдёшь; -ешёл, -ешла) *perf.* *(через) + acc.* **crossbar,** поперечина; **crossbow,** самострел; *c.-breed,* помесь; *v.t.* скрещивать *imp.,* скрестить *perf.; c.-country race,* кросс; *c.-examination,* перекрёстный допрос; *c.-examine, c.-question,* подвергать *imp.,* подвергнуть (-г) *perf.* перекрёстному допросу; *c.-eyed,* косоглазый; *c.-legged: sit c.,* сидеть (сижу, сидишь) *imp.* по-турецки; *c.-reference,* перекрёстная ссылка; **crossroad(s),** перекрёсток (-тка); *(fig.)* распутье; *c.-section,* перекрёстное сечение; **crossways, -wise,** крест-накрест; **crossword (puzzle),** кроссворд. **crossing** *n. (intersection)* перекрёсток (-тка); *(foot)* переход; *(transport; rly.)* переезд.

crotch *n. (anat.)* промежность.

crotchet *n. (mus.)* четвертная нота.

crotchety *adj.* сварливый, придирчивый.

crouch *v.i.* пригибаться *imp.,* пригнуться *perf.; n. (sport)* полуприсед, низкая стойка.

croup *n.* круп.

crow *n.* ворона; *as the c. flies,* по прямой линии; *v.i.* кукарекать *imp.; (exult)* ликовать *imp.* **crowbar** *n.* лом *(pl.* ломы, ломов).

crowd *n.* толпа *(pl.* -пы); *v.i.* тесниться *imp.,* с~ *perf.; c. into,* втискиваться *imp.,* втиснуться *perf.; c. out,* вытеснять *imp.,* вытеснить *perf.* **crowded** *adj.* переполненный (-ен).

crown *n.* корона, венец (-нца); *(tooth)* коронка; *(head)* макушка; *(hat)* тулья; *(coin)* крона; *v.t.* короновать *imp.*, *perf.*; (*fig.*) венча́ть *imp.*, у ~ *perf.*; C. prince, кронпри́нц.

crucial *adj.* (*decisive*) реша́ющий; (*critical*) крити́ческий.

crucible *n.* плави́льный ти́гель (-гля) *m.*

crucifix, crucifixion *n.* распя́тие. **crucify** *v.t.* распина́ть *imp.*, распя́ть (-пну́, -пнёшь) *perf.*

crude *adj.* (*rude*) гру́бый (груб, -а́, -о); (*raw*) сыро́й (сыр, -а́, -о). **crudeness, crudity** *n.* гру́бость.

cruel *adj.* жесто́кий (-о́к, -о́ка́, -о́ко). **cruelty** *n.* жесто́кость.

cruet *n.* судо́к (-дка́).

cruise *n.* круи́з; морско́е путеше́ствие; *v.i.* крейси́ровать *imp.*; cruising speed, сре́дняя, экономи́ческая, ско́рость; cruising taxi, свобо́дное такси́ *neut. indecl.* **cruiser** *n.* кре́йсер (*pl.* -а́ & -ы).

crumb *n.* кро́шка; *v.t.* обсыпа́ть *imp.*, обсы́пать (-плю, -плешь) *perf.* кро́шками.

crumble *v.t.* кроши́ть (-ошу́, -о́шишь) *imp.*, ис ~, на ~, рас ~ *perf.*; *v.i.* обва́ливаться *imp.*, обвали́ться (-ится) *perf.* **crumbling** *adj.* осыпа́ющийся. **crumbly** *adj.* рассы́пчатый, кроша́щийся.

crumpet *n.* сдо́бная лепёшка.

crumple *v.t.* мять (мну, мнёшь) *imp.*, с ~ (сомну́, -нёшь) *perf.*; ко́мкать *imp.*, с ~ *perf.*

crunch *n.* хруст; треск; *v.t.* грызть (-зу́, -зёшь, -з) *imp.*, раз ~ *perf.*; *v.i.* хрусте́ть (-ущу́, -усти́шь) *imp.*, хрустну́ть *perf.*

crusade *n.* кресто́вый похо́д; (*fig.*) кампа́ния (в защи́ту + *gen.*); *v.i.* боро́ться (-рю́сь, -решься) *imp.* (for, за + *acc.*). **crusader** *n.* крестоно́сец (-сца); (*fig.*) боре́ц (-рца́) (for, за + *acc.*).

crush *n.* да́вка, толкотня́; (*infatuation*) си́льное увлече́ние; *v.t.* дави́ть (-влю́, -вишь) *imp.*, за ~, раз ~ *perf.*; мять (мну, мнёшь) *imp.*, с ~ (сомну́, -нёшь) *perf.*; (*fig.*) подави́ть *imp.*, подави́ть (-влю́, -вишь) *perf.* **crusher** *n.* дроби́лка. **crushing** *adj.* сокруши́тельный, уничтожа́ющий.

crust *n.* (*of earth*) кора́; (*bread etc.*) ко́рка.

crustacean *n.* ракообра́зное *sb.*

crusty *adj.* с твёрдой ко́ркой; (*irritable*) сварли́вый, раздражи́тельный.

crutch *n.* костыль (-ля́) *m.*

crux *n.* затрудни́тельный вопро́с; c. of the matter, суть де́ла.

cry *n.* плач; крик; a far cry to, далеко́ от + *gen.*; *v.i.* (*weep*) пла́кать (-а́чу, -а́чешь) *imp.*; (*shout*) крича́ть (-чу́, -чи́шь) *imp.*; c. off, отка́зываться *imp.*, отказа́ться (-ажу́сь, -а́жешься) *perf.* (от + *gen.*). **crying** *adj.* пла́чущий, вопию́щий; it's a c. shame, позо́рно! жа́лко.

crypt *n.* склеп. **cryptic** *adj.* зага́дочный. **cryptogram** *n.* та́йнопись.

crystal *n.* криста́лл; (*mineral*) хруста́ль (-ля́) *m.* **crystallize** *v.t. & i.* кристаллизова́ть(ся) *imp.*, *perf.*; *v.t.* (*fruit*) заса́харивать *imp.*, заса́харить *perf.*

cub *n.* детёныш ди́кого зве́ря; bear c., медвежо́нок (-жо́нка; *pl.* -жа́та, -жа́т); fox c., лисёнок (-нка; *pl.* лися́та, -т); lion c., львёнок (-нка; *pl.* льва́та, -т); wolf c., волчо́нок (-нка; *pl.* волча́та, -т).

cubby-hole *n.* чула́н.

cube *n.* куб. **cubic** *adj.* куби́ческий.

cubicle *n.* отгоро́женная спа́льня (*gen. pl.* -лен).

cuckoo *n.* (*bird*) куку́шка; (*fool*) глупе́ц (-пца́); (*fig.*) кукова́ть *imp.*, про ~ *perf.*

cucumber *n.* огуре́ц (-рца́).

cud *n.* жва́чка.

cuddle *v.t.* обнима́ть *imp.*, обня́ть (обниму́, -мешь) обня́л, -а́, -о) *perf.*; *v.i.* обнима́ться *imp.*, обня́ться (обниму́сь, -мешься) обня́лся, -ла́сь) *perf.*

cudgel *n.* дуби́на, дуби́нка.

cue [1] *n.* (*theat.*) ре́плика.

cue [2] *n.* (*billiards*) кий (кия́; *pl.* кии́).

cuff [1] *n.* манже́та, обшла́г (-а́; *pl.* -а́); off the c., экспро́мтом; c.-link, за́понка.

cuff [2] *v.t.* (*hit*) дава́ть (даю́, даёшь) *imp.*, дать (дам, дашь, даст, дади́м; дал, -а́, да́ло, -и) *perf.* пощёчину + *dat.*

cul-de-sac *n.* тупи́к (-а́).

culinary *adj.* кулина́рный.

cull *v.t.* отбира́ть *imp.*, отобра́ть (отберу́, -рёшь; отобра́л, -á, -o) *perf.*

culminate *v.i.* достига́ть *imp.*, дости́чь & дости́гнуть (-и́гну, -и́гнешь; -и́г) *perf.* вы́сшей то́чки. **culmination** *n.* кульминацио́нный пункт.

culpability *n.* вино́вность. **culpable** *adj.* вино́вный. **culprit** *n.* вино́вный *sb.*

cult *n.* культ; *c. of personality*, культ ли́чности.

cultivate *v.t.* (*land*) обраба́тывать *imp.*, обрабо́тать *perf.*; (*crops*; *fig.*) культиви́ровать *imp.*; (*develop*) развива́ть *imp.*, разви́ть (разовью́, -ьёшь; разви́л, -á, -o) *perf.* cultivated *adj.* (*land*) обрабо́танный (-ан); (*plants*) вы́ращенный (-ен); (*person*) культу́рный; *c. crop*, пропашна́я культу́ра. **cultivation** *n.* обрабо́тка, возде́лывание; культива́ция; выра́щивание; *area under c.*, посевна́я пло́щадь. **cultivator** *n.* культива́тор.

cultural *adj.* культу́рный. **culture** *n.* культу́ра; (*of land*) возде́лывание; (*of animals*) разведе́ние; (*of bacteria*) выра́щивание. **cultured** *adj.* культу́рный; развито́й (ра́звит, -á, -o); *c. pearls*, культиви́рованный жéмчуг (-a(y); *pl.* -á).

culvert *n.* водопропускна́я труба́ (*pl.* -бы).

cumbersome *adj.* обремени́тельный; громо́здкий.

cumulative *adj.* постепе́нно увеличи́вающийся. **cumulus** *n.* кучевы́е облака́ (-ко́в) *pl.*

cuneiform *adj.* клинообра́зный; *n.* кли́нопись.

cunning *n.* хи́трость, лука́вство; *adj.* хи́трый (-тёр, -трá, -тро́), лука́вый.

cup *n.* ча́шка, ча́ша; (*prize*) ку́бок (-бка).

cupboard *n.* шкаф (*loc.* -ý; *pl.* -ы́).

cupid *n.* купидо́н.

cupidity *n.* а́лчность.

cupola *n.* ку́пол (*pl.* -á).

cur *n.* (*dog*) дворня́жка; (*person*) гру́бый, ни́зкий, челове́к.

curable *adj.* излечи́мый.

curate *n.* свяще́нник (мла́дшего са́на.)

curative *adj.* целе́бный.

curator *n.* храни́тель *m.* музе́я.

curb *v.t.* обу́здывать *imp.*, обузда́ть *perf.*; *n.* (*check*) обузда́ние, узда́ (*pl.* -ды); (*kerb*) край (*loc.* краю́; *pl.* края́) тротуа́ра.

curd (*cheese*) *n.* творо́г (творога́(ý)). **curdle** *v.t.* & *i.* свёртывать(ся) *imp.*, сверну́ть(ся) *perf.*; *v.t.* (*blood*) ледени́ть *imp.*, о ~ *perf.*

cure *n.* (*treatment*) лече́ние; (*means*) сре́дство (for, про́тив + *gen.*); *v.t.* (*person*) выле́чивать *imp.*, вы́лечить *perf.*; (*smoke*) копти́ть *imp.*, за ~ *perf.*; (*salt*) соли́ть (солю́, со́лишь) *imp.*, по ~ *perf.*

curfew *n.* коменда́нтский час.

curing *n.* лече́ние; (*cul.*) копче́ние, соле́ние.

curio *n.* ре́дкая антиква́рная вещь (*pl.* -щи, -ще́й).

curiosity *n.* любопы́тство. **curious** *adj.* любопы́тный.

curl *n.* (*hair*) ло́кон; (*spiral*; *hair*) завито́к (-тка́); *v.t.* завива́ть *imp.*, зави́ть (-вью, -вьёшь; зави́л, -á, -o) *perf.*; *v.i.* крути́ть (-учу́, -у́тишь) *imp.*, за ~ *perf.*

curlew *n.* кро́ншнеп.

curling *n.* кэ́рлинг.

curly *adj.* вью́щийся; кудря́вый; *c.-haired*, кудря́вый; *c.-headed*, курча́вый.

curmudgeon *n.* скря́га *m.* & *f.*

currants *n.* (*collect.*) кори́нка; *black c.*, чёрная сморо́дина; *red c.*, кра́сная сморо́дина.

currency *n.* валю́та; (*prevalence*) распространённость. **current** *adj.* теку́щий; *n.* тече́ние; (*air*) струя́ (*pl.* -ýи); (*water*; *electr.*) ток (-a(y)).

curriculum *n.* курс обуче́ния; *c. vitae*, жизнеописа́ние.

curry[1] *n.* кэ́рри *neut.indecl.*

curry[2] *v.t.*: *c. favour with*, заи́скивать *imp.* пе́ред + *instr.*, у + *gen.*

curse *n.* прокля́тие, руга́тельство; *v.t.* проклина́ть *imp.*, прокля́сть (-яну́, -янёшь; про́клял, -á, -o) *perf.*; *v.i.* руга́ться *imp.*, по ~ *perf.* **cursed** *adj.* прокля́тый, окая́нный.

cursive *n.* ско́ропись; *adj.* скоропи́сный.

cursory *adj.* бе́глый; пове́рхностный.

curt adj. кра́ткий (-ток, -тка́, -тко); ре́зкий (-зок, -зка́, -зко).

curtail v.t. сокраща́ть imp., сократи́ть (-ащу́, -ати́шь) perf. **curtailment** n. сокраще́ние.

curtain n. за́навес; занаве́ска; c. call, вы́зов актёра; v.t. занаве́шивать imp., занаве́сить perf.

curts(e)y n. реверанс.

curvature n. кривизна́; искривле́ние. **curve** n. изги́б; (math. etc.) крива́я sb.; v.t. гнуть imp., со~ perf.; v.i. изгиба́ться imp., изогну́ться perf. **curvilinear** adj. криволине́йный.

cushion n. поду́шка; v.t. смягча́ть imp., смягчи́ть perf.

cusp n. о́стрый вы́ступ; (geom.) то́чка пересече́ния двух кривы́х.

custard n. сла́дкий зава́рной крем, со́ус; c. powder, концентра́т.

custodian n. храни́тель m.; сто́рож (pl. -а́) **custody** n. опе́ка; хране́ние; (of police) аре́ст; to be in c., находи́ться (-ожу́сь, -о́дишься) imp. под стра́жей, аре́стом; to take into c., арестова́ть perf.

custom n. обы́чай; привы́чка; (customers) клиенту́ра; pl. (duty) тамо́женные по́шлины f.pl.; to go through the c., проходи́ть (-ожу́, -о́дишь) imp., пройти́ (пройду́, -дёшь; прошёл, -шла́) perf. тамо́женный осмо́тр; c.-house, тамо́жня. **customary** adj. обы́чный, привы́чный. **customer** n. клие́нт; покупа́тель m.; зака́зчик.

cut v.t. ре́зать (ре́жу, -жешь) imp., по~ perf.; (hair) стричь (-игу́, -ижёшь; -иг) imp., о~ perf.; (hay) коси́ть (кошу́, ко́сишь) imp., с~ perf.; (price) снижа́ть imp., сни́зить perf.; (cards) снима́ть imp., снять (сниму́, -мешь; снял, -а́, -о) perf. коло́ду; c. down, сруба́ть (-блю́, -бишь) perf.; c. off, отреза́ть imp., отре́зать (-е́жу, -е́жешь) perf.; (interrupt) прерыва́ть imp., прерва́ть (-ву́, -вёшь; -ва́л, -вала́, -ва́ло) perf.; c. out, выреза́ть imp., вы́резать (-е́жу, -е́жешь) perf.; кро́ить imp., вы́~, с~ perf.; c.-out, (switch) предохрани́тель m., выключа́тель m.; (figure) вы́резанная фигу́ра; c. up, разреза́ть imp.

разреза́ть (-е́жу, -е́жешь) perf.; n. поре́з, разре́з; покро́й; сниже́ние; adj. разре́занный (-ан); сре́занный (-ан); поре́занный (-ан); (glass etc.) гранёный; c. out, скро́енный (-ен); c. rate, сни́женная цена́ (acc. -ну); c. up, огорчённый (-ён, -ена́).

cute adj. привлека́тельный, преле́стный, заба́вный.

cuticle n. ко́жица.

cutlass n. аборда́жная са́бля (gen.pl. -бель).

cutler n. ножо́вщик. **cutlery** n. ножевы́е изде́лия neut.pl.; ножи́, ви́лки и ло́жки pl.

cutlet n. отбивна́я котле́та.

cutter n. (tailor) закро́йщик, -ица (naut.) ка́тер (pl. -а́).

cutthroat n. головоре́з; adj. ожесточённый (-ён, -ённа).

cutting n. ре́зание; разреза́ние; (press) вы́резка; (from plant) черено́к (-нка́); (rly.) вы́емка; adj. ре́жущий; прони́зывающий; ре́зкий (-зок, -зка́, -зко).

cuttlefish n. карака́тица.

cyanide n. циани́д.

cybernetics n. киберне́тика.

cyclamen n. цикламе́н.

cycle n. цикл; (electr.) герц (gen.pl. -ц); (bicycle) велосипе́д; v.i. е́здить imp. на велосипе́де. **cyclic(al)** adj. цикли́ческий. **cycling** n. езда́ на велосипе́де; велоспо́рт. **cyclist** n. велосипеди́ст.

cyclone n. цикло́н.

cyclotron n. циклотро́н.

cygnet n. лебедёнок (-нка; pl. лебедя́та, -т).

cylinder n. цили́ндр. **cylindrical** adj. цилиндри́ческий.

cymbals n. таре́лки f.pl.

cynic n. ци́ник. **cynical** adj. цини́чный. **cynicism** n. цини́зм.

cynosure n. центр внима́ния.

cypress n. кипари́с.

Cypriot n. киприо́т, ~ка; Greek (Turkish) C., киприо́т, ~ка, гре́ческого (туре́цкого) происхожде́ния.

Cyrillic n. кири́ллица.

cyst n. киста́.

czar, czarina see tsar, tsarina

Czech n. чех, че́шка; adj. че́шский.

D

D n. (mus.) pe neut.indecl.

dab¹ n. лёгкое каса́ние; мазо́к (-зка́); v.t. легко́ прикаса́ться imp., прикосну́ться perf. k + dat.; d. on, накла́дывать imp., наложи́ть (-жу́, -жишь) perf. мазка́ми.

dab² n. (fish) ка́мбала-лима́нда.

dab³ n. (barrier): be a d. hand at, собаку съесть (-ем, -ешь, -ест, -еди́м; -ел) perf. на + prep.

dabble v.i. плеска́ться (-ещу́сь, -е́щешься) imp.; d. in, пове́рхностно, по-лю́бительски, занима́ться imp., заня́ться (займу́сь, -мёшься; -я́лся, -яла́сь) perf. + instr. **dabbler** n. дилета́нт.

dace n. еле́ц (ельца́).

dachshund n. та́кса.

dad, daddy n. па́па; d.-long-legs, долгоно́жка.

dado n. вну́тренняя пане́ль.

daffodil n. жёлтый нарци́сс.

daft adj. глу́пый (глуп, -а́,-о); бессмы́сленный (-ен, -енна).

dagger n. кинжа́л; (print.) кре́стик.

dahlia n. георги́н.

daily adv. ежедне́вно; adj. ежедне́вный, повседне́вный; d. bread, хлеб насу́щный; d. dozen, заря́дка; n. (char-woman) приходя́щая домрабо́тница; (newspaper) ежедне́вная газе́та.

daintiness n. изя́щество; изы́сканность.

dainty adj. изя́щный; изы́сканный (-ан, -анна).

dairy n. маслобо́йня; (shop) моло́чная sb.; d. farm, моло́чное хозя́йство. **dairymaid** n. доя́рка.

dais n. помо́ст.

daisy n. маргари́тка.

dale n. доли́на.

dalliance n. пра́здное времяпрепровожде́ние. **dally** v.i. развлека́ться imp., развле́чься (-еку́сь, -ечёшься; -ёкся, -екла́сь) perf.

Dalmatian n. далма́тский дог.

dam¹ n. (barrier) плоти́на; перемы́чка; v.t. прегражда́ть imp., прегради́ть perf. плоти́ной; пруди́ть (-ужу́, -у́ди́шь) imp., за ~ perf.

dam² n. (animal) ма́тка.

damage n. повреждé́ние; уще́рб; pl. убы́тки m.pl.; v.t. поврежда́ть imp., повреди́ть perf.; по́ртить imp., ис ~ perf.

damascene v.t. насека́ть imp., насе́чь (-еку́, -ечёшь; -ёк, -екла́) perf. зо́лотом, серебро́м.

damask n. камча́тная ткань; adj. дама́сский; камча́тный.

damn v.t. проклина́ть imp., прокля́сть (-яну́, -янёшь; про́клял, -а́, -о) perf.; (censure) осужда́ть imp., осуди́ть (-ужу́, -у́дишь) perf. **damnable** adj. отврати́тельный, прокля́тый. **damnation** n. прокля́тие. **damned** adj. прокля́тый.

damp n. сы́рость, вла́жность; adj. сыро́й (сыр, -а́, -о); вла́жный (-жен, -жна́, -жно, -жны́); v.t. сма́чивать imp., смочи́ть (-чу́, -чишь) perf.; увлажня́ть imp., увлажни́ть perf.; d.-course, гидроизоля́ция; d.-proof, влагонепроница́емый.

damson n. терносли́ва.

dance v.i. танцева́ть imp.; пляса́ть (-яшу́, -я́шешь) imp., с ~ perf.; n. та́нец (-нца), пля́ска; (party) танцева́льный ве́чер (pl. -а́). **dancer** n. танцо́р, ~ ка; (ballet) танцо́вщик, -ица, балери́на.

dandelion n. одува́нчик.

dandruff n. пе́рхоть.

dandy n. дэ́нди m.indecl., франт.

Dane n. датча́нин (pl. -а́не, -а́н), -а́нка; Great D., дог. **Danish** adj. да́тский.

danger n. опа́сность. **dangerous** adj. опа́сный.

dangle v.t. болта́ть imp. + instr.; v.i. болта́ться imp.; свиса́ть imp.

dank adj. промо́зглый.

dapper adj. аккура́тный; франтова́тый.

dappled adj. пятни́стый. **dapple-grey** adj. се́рый (сер, -а́, -о) в я́блоках.

dare v.i. сметь imp., по ~ perf.; отва́живаться imp., отва́житься perf.; I d. say, полага́ю; n. вы́зов. **daredevil** n. сорвиголова́ m. & f. (pl. -овы, -о́в, -ова́м). **daring** n. сме́лость; adj. сме́лый (смел, -а́, -о); де́рзкий (-зок, -зка́, -зко).

dark adj. тёмный (-мен, -мна́); D. Ages, ра́ннее средневеко́вье; d.-room, тёмная ко́мната; d. secret, вели́кая та́йна; n. темнота́, тьма, мрак. **darken** v.t. затемня́ть imp., затемни́ть perf. **darkly** adv. мра́чно. **darkness** n. темнота́, тьма, мрак.

darling n. дорого́й sb., ми́лый sb.; люби́мец (-мца); adj. дорого́й (до́рог, -а́, -о), люби́мый.

darn v.t. што́пать imp., за~ perf.; n. зашто́панное ме́сто (pl. -та́). **darning** n. што́пка; adj. што́пальный; d. thread, wool, што́пка.

darnel n. плевел.

dart n. стрела́ (pl. -лы); стре́лка; (tuck) вы́тачка; v.t. мета́ть (мечу́, ме́чешь) imp.; броса́ть imp., бро́сить perf.; v.i. носи́ться (ношу́сь, но́сишься) indet., нести́сь (несу́сь, -сёшься) нёсся, несла́сь) det., по~ perf.

dash n. (hyphen) тире́ neut.indecl.; (admixture) при́месь; (rush) рыво́к (-вка́); v.t. швыря́ть imp., швырну́ть perf.; v.i. броса́ться imp., бро́ситься perf.; носи́ться (ношу́сь, но́сишься) indet., нести́сь (несу́сь, -сёшься) нёсся, несла́сь) det., по~ perf.; мча́ться (мчусь, мчи́шься) imp. **dashboard** n. прибо́рная доска́ (acc. -ску; pl. -ски, -со́к, -ска́м). **dashing** adj. лихо́й (лих, -á, -o), удало́й (удал, -á, -o).

data n. да́нные sb.; фа́кты m.pl.

date[1] n. (fruit) фи́ник; d. palm, фи́никовая па́льма.

date[2] n. (number) число́ (pl. -сла, -сел, -слам), да́та; (engagement) свида́ние; out of d., устаре́лый; (overdue) просро́ченный (-ен); up-to-date, совреме́нный (-нен, -нна); в ку́рсе де́ла; v.t. & i. дати́ровать(ся) imp., perf.; (make engagement) назнача́ть imp., назна́чить perf. свида́ние с + instr.

dative adj. (n.) да́тельный (паде́ж (-á)).

daub v.t. ма́зать (ма́жу, -жешь) imp., на~ perf.; малева́ть (-лю́ю, -лю́ешь) imp., на~ perf.; n. плоха́я карти́на.

daughter n. дочь (до́чери, instr. -рью; pl. -ри, -ре́й, instr. -рьми́) d.-in-law, неве́стка (in rel. to mother), сноха́ (pl. -хи) (in rel. to father).

dauntless adj. неустраши́мый.

davit n. шлю́пбалка.

dawdle v.i. безде́льничать imp.

dawn n. рассве́т; заря́ (pl. зо́ри, зорь, зо́рям); v.i. (day) рассвета́ть imp., рассвести́ (-етёт; -ело́) perf.impers.; d. (up)on, осеня́ть imp., осени́ть perf.; it dawned on me, меня́ осени́ло.

day n. день (дня) m.; (working d.) рабо́чий день (дня) m.; (24 hours) су́тки (-ток) pl.; pl. (period) пери́од, вре́мя neut.; d. after d., изо дня в день; the d. after tomorrow, послеза́втра; all d. long, день-деньско́й; the d. before, накану́не; the d. before yesterday, позавчера́; by d., днём; every other day, че́рез день; d. off, выходно́й день (дня) m.; one d., одна́жды; this d. week, че́рез неде́лю; carry, win, the d., одержа́ть imp., одержа́ть (-жу́, -жишь) perf. побе́ду, lose the d., потерпе́ть (-плю, -пишь) perf. пораже́ние. **daybreak** n. рассве́т. **day-dreams** n. мечты́ (gen. мечта́ний) f.pl., грёзы f.pl. **day-labourer** n. поде́нщик, -ица. **daylight** n. дневно́й свет; in broad d., средь бе́ла дня.

daze v.t. ошеломля́ть imp., ошеломи́ть perf.; n. изумле́ние **dazed** adj. изумлённый (-ён, -ена́), потрясённый (-ён, -ена́).

dazzle v.t. ослепля́ть imp., ослепи́ть perf. **dazzling** adj. блестя́щий, ослепи́тельный.

deacon n. дья́кон (pl. -á).

dead adj. мёртвый (мёртв, -а, -o & (fig.) -ó), уме́рший (animals) до́хлый; (plants) увя́дший; (numb) онеме́вший; (lifeless) безжи́зненный (-ен, -енна) (sound) глухо́й (глух, -á, -o); (complete) соверше́нный (-нен, -нна); d. to, глухо́й (глух, -á, -o) к + dat.; n.: the d., мёртвые sb., уме́ршие sb.; d. of night, глуба́я ночь (loc. -чи́); adv. соверше́нно; d.-beat, смерте́льно уста́лый; d. calm, (naut.) мёртвый штиль m.; d. drunk, мертве́цки пья́ный (пьян, -á, -o); d. end, тупи́к (-á) d.-end, безвы́ходный; d. heat, одновреме́нный фи́ниш; (time) преде́льный срок (-a(y)); **deadlock**, тупи́к (-á); reach d., зайти́ (зайду́, -дёшь; зашёл, -шла́) perf. в тупи́к; d. march, похоро́нный марш *d. nettle*, глуха́я крапи́ва; *d. reckoning*, счисле́ние пути́; *d. set*, мёртвая сто́йка; *d. weight*, мёртвый груз.

deaden *v.t. & i.* притупля́ть(ся) *imp.*, притупи́ть(ся) (-плю́(сь), -пи́шь(ся)) *perf.*

deadly *adj.* смерте́льный, смертоно́сный; *d. nightshade*, белладо́нна; *d. sin*, сме́ртный грех (-а́).

deaf *adj.* глухо́й (глух, -а́, -о); *d. and dumb*, глухонемо́й; *d. mute*, глухонемо́й (*sb.*). **deafen** *v.t.* оглуша́ть *imp.*, оглуши́ть *perf.* **deafness** *n.* глухота́.

deal[1] *n.: a great, good, d.*, мно́го (+ *gen.*); (*with compar.*) гора́здо.

deal[2] *n.* (*bargain*) сде́лка; (*cards*) сда́ча; *v.t.* (*cards*) сдава́ть (сдаю́, -аёшь) *imp.*, сдать (-ам, -ашь, -аст, -ади́м; сдал, -а́, -о) *perf.*; (*blow*) наноси́ть (-ошу́, -о́сишь) *imp.*, нанести́ (-есу́, -есёшь; -ёс, -есла́) *perf.*; *d. in*, торгова́ть *imp.* + *instr.*; *d. out*, распределя́ть *imp.*, распредели́ть *perf.*; *d. with*, (*engage in*) занима́ться *imp.*, заня́ться (займу́сь, -мёшься; заня́лся, -ла́сь) *perf.* + *instr.*; (*behave towards*) обходи́ться (-ожу́сь, -о́дишься) *imp.*, обойти́сь (обойду́сь, -дёшься; обошёлся, -шла́сь) *perf.* с + *instr.* **dealer** *n.* (*trader*) торго́вец (-вца) (in, + *instr.*).

deal[3] *n.* (*wood*) ело́вая, сосно́вая древеси́на; *adj.* ело́вый, (*pine*) сосно́вый.

dean *n.* (*univ.*) дека́н; (*church*) насто́ятель *m.* собо́ра. **deanery** *n.* декана́т.

dear *adj.* дорого́й (до́рог, -а́, -о); (*also n.*) ми́лый (мил, -а́, -о, ми́лы) (*sb.*).

dearth *n.* недоста́ток (-тка); нехва́тка.

death *n.* смерть (*pl.* -ти, -те́й) (-а́); сме́ртный, смерте́льный; *at d.'s door*, при сме́рти; *put to d.*, казни́ть *imp.*, *perf.*; **deathbed**, сме́ртное ло́же (-а); *d.-blow*, сме́ртельный уда́р; *d. certificate*, свиде́тельство о сме́рти; *d. duty*, нало́г на насле́дство; *d. penalty*, сме́ртная казнь; *d. rate*, сме́ртность; *d.-roll*, спи́сок (-ска) уби́тых; *d.-warrant*, сме́ртный пригово́р (*also fig.*). **deathless** *adj.* бессме́ртный. **deathly** *adj.* смерте́льный.

debar *v.t.: d. from*, не допуска́ть *imp.* до + *gen.*

debase *v.t.* понижа́ть *imp.*, пони́зить *perf.* ка́чество + *gen.*

debatable *adj.* спо́рный. **debate** *n.* пре́ния (-ий) *pl.*, деба́ты (-тов) *pl.*; *v.t.* обсужда́ть *imp.*, обсуди́ть (-ужу́, -у́дишь) *perf.*; *v.i.* дебати́ровать *imp.*

debauch *v.t.* развраща́ть *imp.*, разврати́ть (-ащу́, -ати́шь) *perf.*; *n.* о́ргия. **debauched** *adj.* развращённый (-ён, -ённа), развра́тный. **debauchery** *n.* разврат.

debenture *n.* долгово́е обяза́тельство.

debilitate *v.t.* рас-, о-, слабля́ть *imp.*, рас-, о-, сла́бить *perf.* **debility** *n.* бесси́лие, тщеду́шие.

debit *n.* де́бет; *debits and credits*, прихо́д и расхо́д; *v.t.* дебетова́ть *imp.*, *perf.*; запи́сывать *imp.*, записа́ть (-ишу́, -и́шешь) *perf.* в де́бет + *dat.*

debouch *v.i.* (*mil.*) дебуши́ровать *imp.*, *perf.*; (*river*) впада́ть *imp.*, впасть (впаду́; впал) *perf.*

debris *n.* оско́лки *m.pl.*, обло́мки *m.pl.*

debt *n.* долг (-а(у), *loc.* -у́; *pl.* -и́). **debtor** *n.* должни́к (-а́).

debunk *v.t.* развенчивать *imp.*, развенча́ть *perf.*

début *n.* дебю́т; *make one's d.*, дебюти́ровать *imp.*, *perf.* **debutante** *n.* дебюта́нтка.

deca- *in comb.* дека-, десяти-.

decade *n.* десятиле́тие.

decadence *n.* декаде́нтство; упа́дочничество. **decadent** *adj.* декаде́нтский; упа́дочный.

decamp *v.i.* удира́ть *imp.*, удра́ть (удеру́, -рёшь; удра́л, -а́, -о) *perf.*

decant *v.t.* сце́живать *imp.*, сцеди́ть (-ежу́, -е́дишь) *perf.*; (*wine*) перелива́ть *imp.*, перели́ть (-лью́, -льёшь; перели́л, -а́, -о) *perf.* (в графи́н). **decanter** *n.* графи́н.

decapitate *v.t.* обезгла́вливать *imp.*, обезгла́вить *perf.*

decarbonize *v.t.* очища́ть *imp.*, очи́стить *perf.* от нага́ра.

decathlon *n.* десятибо́рье.

decay *v.i.* гнить (-ию́, -иёшь; гнил, -а́, -о) *imp.*, с ~ *perf.*; *n.* гние́ние; распа́д (*also phys.*). **decayed** *adj.* прогни́вший, гнило́й (гнил, -а́, -о) *perf.* **decaying** *adj.* гнию́щий.

decease *n.* кончи́на. **deceased** *adj.* поко́йный; *n.* поко́йный *sb.*, поко́йник, -ица.

deceit *n.* обма́н. **deceitful** *adj.* лжи́вый. **deceive** *v.t.* обма́нывать *imp.*, обману́ть (-ну́, -нешь) *perf.*

deceleration *n.* замедле́ние.

December *n.* дека́брь (-ря́) *m.*; *attrib.* декабрьский.

decency *n.* прили́чие, поря́дочность. **decent** *adj.* прили́чный, поря́дочный.

decentralization *n.* децентрализа́ция. **decentralize** *v.t.* децентрализова́ть *imp.*, *perf.*

deception *n.* обма́н. **deceptive** *adj.* обма́нчивый.

deci- *in comb.* деци-.

decibel *n.* деци́бел.

decide *v.t.* реша́ть *imp.*, реши́ть *perf.* **decided** *adj.* (*resolute*) реши́тельный; (*definite*) несомне́нный (-нен, -нна). **decidedly** *adv.* реши́тельно, бесспо́рно, я́вно.

deciduous *adj.* листопа́дный.

decimal *n.* десяти́чная дробь (*pl.* -би, -бей); *adj.* десяти́чный; **d. point**, запята́я *sb.*

decimate *v.t.* (*fig.*) коси́ть (-и́т) *imp.*, с~ *perf.*

decipher *v.t.* расшифро́вывать *imp.*, расшифрова́ть *perf.*

decision *n.* реше́ние. **decisive** *adj.* реша́ющий, реши́тельный.

deck *n.* па́луба; (*bus etc.*) эта́ж (-а́); **d.-chair**, шезло́нг; **d.-hand**, па́лубный матро́с; **d.-house**, ру́бка; *v.t.*: **d. out**, украша́ть *imp.*, укра́сить *perf.*

declaim *v.t.* деклами́ровать *imp.*, про~ *perf.*

declaration *n.* объявле́ние; (*document*) деклара́ция. **declare** *v.t.* за-, объ-, явля́ть *imp.*, за-, объ-, яви́ть (-влю́, -вишь) *perf.*

declassify *v.t.* рассекре́чивать *imp.*, рассекре́чить *perf.*

declension *n.* склоне́ние. **decline** *n.* упа́док (-дка); (*price*) пониже́ние; *v.i.* приходи́ть (-и́т) *imp.*, прийти́ (придёт; пришёл, -шла́) *perf.* в упа́док; *v.t.* (*refuse*) отклоня́ть *imp.*, отклони́ть (-ню́, -нишь) *perf.*; (*gram.*)

склоня́ть *imp.*, про~ *perf.* **declining** *adj.*: **d. years**, прекло́нный во́зраст.

declivity *n.* укло́н.

decoction *n.* отва́р (-а(у)).

decode *v.t.* расшифро́вывать *imp.*, расшифрова́ть *perf.*

decompose *v.t.* разлага́ть *imp.*, разложи́ть (-жу́, -жишь) *perf.*; *v.i.* распада́ться *imp.*, распа́сться (-адётся; -а́лся) *perf.*; (*rot*) гнить (-ию́, -иёшь; гнил, -а́, -о) *imp.*, с~ *perf.*

decompress *v.t.* снижа́ть *imp.*, сни́зить *perf.* давле́ние на + *acc.* **decompression** *n.* декомпре́ссия.

decontaminate *v.t.* (*gas*) дегази́ровать *imp.*, *perf.*; (*radioactivity*) дезактиви́ровать *imp.*, *perf.*

decontrol *v.t.* снима́ть *imp.*, снять (сниму́, -мешь; снял, -а́, -о) *perf.* контро́ль *m.* с + *gen.*

decorate *v.t.* украша́ть *imp.*, укра́сить *perf.*; (*with medal etc.*) награжда́ть *imp.*, награди́ть *perf.* о́рденом (-на́ми). **decoration** *n.* украше́ние, отде́лка; о́рден (*pl.* -а́). **decorative** *adj.* декорати́вный. **decorator** *n.* маля́р (-а́).

decorous *adj.* прили́чный; чи́нный (-нен, -нна́, -нно). **decorum** *n.* прили́чие, деко́рум; (*etiquette*) этике́т.

decoy *n.* (*trap*) западня́; (*bait*) прима́нка; *v.t.* за-, при-, ма́нивать *imp.*, за-, при-, мани́ть (-ню́, -нишь) *perf.*

decrease *v.t.* & *i.* уменьша́ть(ся) *imp.*, уме́ньшить(ся) *perf.*; *n.* уменьше́ние, пониже́ние.

decree *n.* ука́з, декре́т, постановле́ние; *v.t.* постановля́ть *imp.*, постанови́ть (-влю́, -вишь) *perf.*

decrepit *adj.* дря́хлый (дряхл, -а́, -о); (*dilapidated*) ве́тхий (ветх, -а́, -о). **decrepitude** *n.* дря́хлость; ве́тхость.

dedicate *v.t.* посвяща́ть *imp.*, посвяти́ть (-ящу́, -яти́шь) *perf.* **dedication** *n.* посвяще́ние.

deduce *v.t.* заключа́ть *imp.*, заключи́ть *perf.*; де́лать *imp.*, с~ *perf.* вы́вод.

deduct *v.t.* вычита́ть *imp.*, вы́честь (-чту, -чтешь; -чел, -чла) *perf.* **deduction** *n.* (*amount*) вы́чет; (*deducting*) вычита́ние; (*inference*) вы́вод.

deed *n.* посту́пок (-пка); (*heroic*) по́двиг; (*leg.*) акт.

deem *v.t.* счита́ть *imp.*, счесть (сочту́, -тёшь; счёл, сочла́) *perf.* + *acc.* & *instr.*

deep *adj.* глубо́кий (-о́к, -ока́, -о́ко́); (*colour*) тёмный (-мен, -мна́); (*sound*) ни́зкий (-зок, -зка́, -зко, ни́зки); *n.* мо́ре; **d.-rooted**, закоренёлый; **d.-seated**, укорени́вшийся. **deepen** *v.t.* углубля́ть *imp.*, углуби́ть *perf.*, сгуща́ть *imp.*, сгусти́ть *perf.*

deer *n.* оле́нь *m.* **deerskin** *n.* лоси́на. **deer-stalker** *n.* охо́тничья ша́пка.

deface *v.t.* по́ртить *imp.*, ис~ *perf.*; (*erase*) стира́ть *imp.*, стере́ть (сотру́, -рёшь; стёр) *perf.* **defacement** *n.* по́рча; стира́ние.

defamation *n.* диффама́ция, клевета́. **defamatory** *adj.* дискредити́рующий, позо́рящий. **defame** *v.t.* поро́чить *imp.*, о~ *perf.*; позо́рить *imp.*, о~ *perf.*

default *n.* невыполне́ние обяза́тельств; (*leg.*) нея́вка в суд; *v.i.* не выполня́ть *imp.* обяза́тельств.

defeat *n.* пораже́ние; *v.t.* побежда́ть *imp.*, победи́ть (-и́шь) *perf.* **defeatism** *n.* пораже́нчество. **defeatist** *n.* пораже́нец (-нца).

defecate *v.i.* испражня́ться *imp.*, испражни́ться *perf.* **defecation** *n.* испражне́ние.

defect *n.* дефе́кт, недоста́ток (-тка), изъя́н; *v.i.* дезерти́ровать *imp.*, *perf.* **defection** *n.* дезерти́рство. **defective** *adj.* неиспра́вный, повреждённый (-ён, -ена́); дефе́ктный, с изъя́ном.

defector *n.* дезерти́р, невозвраще́нец (-нца).

defence *n.* защи́та (*also leg.*, *sport*), оборо́на (*also mil.*); *pl.* (*mil.*) закрепле́ния *neut.pl.* **defenceless** *adj.* беззащи́тный. **defend** *v.t.* защища́ть *imp.*, защити́ть (-ищу́, -ити́шь) *perf.*; обороня́ть *imp.*, оборони́ть *perf.*; (*uphold*) подде́рживать *imp.*, подержа́ть (-жу́, -жишь) *perf.* **defendant** *n.* подсуди́мый *sb.* **defender** *n.* защи́тник. **defensive** *adj.* оборони́тельный.

defer[1] *v.t.* (*postpone*) отсро́чивать *imp.*, отсро́чить *perf.*

defer[2] *v.i.*: **d. to**, подчиня́ться *imp.* + *dat.* **deference** *n.* уваже́ние, почте́ние. **deferential** *adj.* почти́тельный.

defiance *n.* откры́тое неповинове́ние; **in d. of**, вопреки́ + *dat.*, напереко́р + *dat.* **defiant** *adj.* вызыва́ющий, непоко́рный.

deficiency *n.* нехва́тка, дефици́т. **deficient** *adj.* недоста́точный; (*mentally d.*) слабоу́мный. **deficit** *n.* дефици́т, недочёт.

defile *v.t.* оскверня́ть *imp.*, оскверни́ть *perf.* **defilement** *n.* оскверне́ние, профана́ция.

define *v.t.* определя́ть *imp.*, определи́ть *perf.* **definite** *adj.* определённый (-нен, -нна). **definitely** *adv.* несомне́нно. **definition** *n.* определе́ние. **definitive** *adj.* оконча́тельный.

deflate *v.t.* & *i.* спуска́ть *imp.*, спусти́ть (-ущу́, -у́стишь) *perf.*; *v.t.* (*person*) сбива́ть *imp.*, сбить (собью́, -ьёшь) *perf.* спесь с + *gen.*; *v.i.* (*econ.*) проводи́ть (-ожу́, -о́дишь) *imp.*, провести́ (-еду́, -едёшь; -ёл, -ела́) *perf.* поли́тику дефля́ции. **deflation** *n.* дефля́ция.

deflect *v.t.* отклоня́ть *imp.*, отклони́ть (-ню́, -нишь) *perf.* **deflection** *n.* отклоне́ние.

defoliate *v.t.* уничтожа́ть *imp.*, уничто́жить *perf.* расти́тельность + *gen.* **defoliation** *n.* дефолиа́ция.

deforest *v.t.* обезле́сивать *imp.*, обезле́сить *perf.*

deform *v.t.* уро́довать *imp.*, из~ *perf.*; деформи́ровать *imp.*, *perf.* **deformity** *n.* уро́дство.

defraud *v.t.* обма́нывать *imp.*, обману́ть (-ну́, -нешь) *perf.*; **d. of**, выма́нивать *imp.*, вы́манить *perf.* + *acc.* & у + *gen.* (*of person*).

defray *v.t.* опла́чивать *imp.*, оплати́ть (-ачу́, -а́тишь) *perf.*

defrost *v.t.* размора́живать *imp.*, разморо́зить *perf.*

deft *adj.* ло́вкий (-вок, -вка́, -вко, ло́вки).

defunct *adj.* усо́пший.

defy *v.t.* (*challenge*) вызыва́ть *imp.*, вы́звать (вы́зову, -вешь) *perf.*; (*resist*) откры́то не повинова́ться *imp.* + *dat.*

degeneracy *n.* вырожде́ние, дегенера-ти́вность. **degenerate** *n.* дегенера́т, вы́родок (-дка); *adj.* дегенерати́вный; *v.i.* вырожда́ться *imp.*, вы́родиться *perf.* **degenerative** *adj.* дегенерати́вный.

degradation *n.* деграда́ция; униже́ние. **degrade** *v.t.* унижа́ть *imp.*, уни́зить *perf.* **degrading** *adj.* унизи́тельный.

degree *n.* сте́пень (*pl.* -ни, -не́й); (*math. etc.*) гра́дус; (*univ.*) учёная сте́пень (*pl.* -ни, -не́й).

dehydrate *v.t.* обезво́живать *imp.*, обезво́дить *perf.* **dehydration** *n.* дегидра-та́ция.

deify *v.t.* обожествля́ть *imp.*, обо-жестви́ть *perf.*

deity *n.* божество́.

dejected *adj.* удручённый (-ён, -ённа & -ена́), уны́лый. **dejection** *n.* уны́ние.

delay *n.* заде́ржка; замедле́ние; *without d.*, неме́дленно; *v.t.* заде́рживать *imp.*, задержа́ть (-жу́, -жишь) *perf.*; замед-ля́ть *imp.*, заме́длить *perf.*

delegate *n.* делега́т; *v.t.* делеги́ровать *imp.*, *perf.* **delegation** *n.* делега́ция.

delete *v.t.* вычёркивать *imp.*, вы́черк-нуть *perf.*

deliberate *adj.* (*intentional*) преднаме́-ренный (-ен, -енна), (*unhurried*) нето-ропли́вый; *v.t. & i.* размышля́ть *imp.*, размы́слить *perf.* (*o* + *prep.*). **delibera-tion** *n.* размышле́ние; (*discussion*) об-сужде́ние, совеща́ние.

delicacy *n.* (*tact*) делика́тность; (*dainty*) ла́комство. **delicate** *adj.* то́нкий (-нок, -нка́, -нко, то́нки́); лёгкий (-гок, -гка́, -гко́, лёгки́); (*health*) боле́знен-ный (-ен, -енна).

delicious *adj.* восхити́тельный; (*tasty*) о́чень вку́сный (-сен, -сна́, -сно).

delight *n.* наслажде́ние, пре́лесть. **delightful** *adj.* преле́стный.

delimit *v.t.* размежёвывать *imp.*, раз-межева́ть (-жу́ю, -жу́ешь) *perf.* **de-limitation** *n.* размежева́ние.

delinquency *n.* правонаруше́ние, пре-сту́пность. **delinquent** *n.* правона-руши́тель *m.*, ~ ница.

delirious *adj.* бредово́й; *be d.*, бре́дить *imp.* **delirium** *n.* бред (-а(у), *loc.*, -у́); *d. tremens*, бе́лая горя́чка.

deliver *v.t.* доставля́ть *imp.*, доста́-вить *perf.*; (*rescue*) избавля́ть *imp.*, изба́вить *perf.* (from, от + *gen.*); (*lecture*) прочита́ть *imp.*, проче́сть (-чту́, -чтёшь; -чёл, -чла́) *perf.*; (*letters*) разноси́ть (-ошу́, -о́сишь) *imp.*, разнести́ (-есу́, -есёшь; -ёс, -есла́) *perf.*; (*speech*) произноси́ть (-ошу́, -о́сишь) *imp.*, произнести́ (-есу́, -есёшь; -ёс, -есла́) *perf.* **deliverance** *n.* избавле́ние, освобож-де́ние. **delivery** *n.* доста́вка.

dell *n.* лощи́на.

delphinium *n.* дельфи́ниум.

delta *n.* де́льта.

delude *v.t.* обма́нывать (-ожу́, -о́дишь) *imp.*, ввести́ (-еду́, -едёшь; ввёл, -а́) *perf.* в заблужде́ние.

deluge *n.* (*flood*) пото́п; (*rain*) ли́вень (-вня) *m.*

delusion *n.* заблужде́ние; *delusions of grandeur*, ма́ния вели́чия.

demagogue *n.* демаго́г. **demagogic** *adj.* демагоги́ческий. **demagogy** *n.* дема-го́гия.

demand *n.* тре́бование; (*econ.*) спрос (for, на + *acc.*); *v.t.* тре́бовать *imp.*, по ~ *perf.* + *gen.*

demarcate *v.t.* разграни́чивать *imp.*, разграни́чить *perf.* **demarcation** *n.* де-марка́ция; *line of d.*, демаркацио́нная ли́ния.

demented *adj.* умалишённый (-ён, -ённа). **dementia** *n.* слабоу́мие.

demi- *in comb.* полу-.

demigod *n.* полубо́г (*pl.* -и, -о́в).

demilitarization *n.* демилитариза́ция. **demilitarize** *v.t.* демилитаризова́ть *imp.*, *perf.*

demise *n.* кончи́на.

demobbed *adj.* демобилизо́ванный (-ан). **demobilization** *n.* демобилиза́-ция. **demobilize** *v.t.* демобилизова́ть *imp.*, *perf.*

democracy *n.* демокра́тия. **democrat** *n.* демокра́т. **democratic** *adj.* демократи́-ческий, демократи́чный.

demolish *v.t.* разруша́ть *imp.*, раз-ру́шить *perf.*; (*building*) сноси́ть

(-ошу́, -о́сишь) *imp.*, снести́ (-су́, -сёшь), снёс, -ла́) *perf.*; (*refute*) опроверга́ть *imp.*, опрове́ргнуть (-ве́рг(нул), -ве́ргла) *perf.* demolition *n.* разруше́ние, снос.

demon *n.* де́мон. demonic *adj.* дья́вольский, демони́ческий.

demonstrable *adj.* доказу́емый. demonstrably *adv.* очеви́дно, нагля́дно. demonstrate *v.t.* демонстри́ровать *imp.*, *perf.*; *v.i.* уча́ствовать *imp.* в демонстра́ции. demonstration *n.* демонстра́ция, пока́з. demonstrative *adj.* (*behaviour etc.*) экспанси́вный, несде́ржанный (-ан, -анна); (*gram.*) указа́тельный. demonstrator *n.* (*laboratory*) демонстра́тор; (*polit.*) демонстра́нт.

demoralization *n.* деморализа́ция. demoralize *v.t.* демо́рализова́ть *imp.*, *perf.*

demote *v.t.* понижа́ть *imp.*, пони́зить *perf.* в до́лжности; (*mil.*) разжа́ловать *perf.* demotion *n.* пониже́ние.

demur *v.i.* возража́ть *imp.*, возрази́ть *perf.* (at, to, про́тив + *gen.*); *n.*: without d., без возраже́ний.

demure *adj.* (притво́рно) скро́мный (-мен, -мна́, -мно).

den *n.* (*animal's*) ло́гово, берло́га; (*thieves' etc.*) прито́н.

denial *n.* отрица́ние, опроверже́ние; (*refusal*) отка́з.

denigrate *v.t.* черни́ть *imp.*, о ~ *perf.*

denomination *n.* (*name*) назва́ние; (*category*) катего́рия; (*relig.*) вероисповеда́ние. denominator *n.* знамена́тель *m.*

denote *v.t.* означа́ть *imp.*, озна́чить *perf.*

dénouement *n.* развя́зка.

denounce *v.t.* (*accuse*) облича́ть *imp.*, обличи́ть *perf.*; (*inform on*) доноси́ть (-ошу́, -о́сишь) *imp.*, донести́ (-есу́, -есёшь; -ёс, -есла́) *perf.* на + *acc.*; (*treaty*) денонси́ровать *imp.*, *perf.*

dense *adj.* (*thick*) густо́й (густ, -а́, -о, гу́сты); (*stupid*) тупо́й (туп, -а́, -о, ту́пы). density *n.* (*phys. etc.*) пло́тность.

dent *n.* вы́боина, вмя́тина; *v.t.* вмина́ть *imp.*, вмять (вомну́, -нёшь) *perf.*

dental *adj.* зубно́й. dentifrice *n.* (*paste*) зубна́я па́ста; (*powder*) зубно́й порошо́к (-шка́). dentist *n.* зубно́й врач (-а́). dentistry *n.* зубоврачева́ние. denture *n.* зубно́й проте́з.

denunciation *n.* (*accusation*) обличе́ние; (*informing*) доно́с; (*treaty*) деноса́ция.

deny *v.t.* отрица́ть *imp.*; d. oneself, отка́зывать *imp.*, отказа́ть (-ажу́, -а́жешь) *perf.* себе́ в + *prep.*

deodorant *n.* дезодора́нт; *adj.* уничтожа́ющий за́пах.

depart *v.i.* отбыва́ть *imp.*, отбы́ть (отбу́ду, -дешь; о́тбыл, -а́, -о) *perf.*; d. from, отклоня́ться *imp.*, отклони́ться (-ню́сь, -ни́шься) *perf.* от + *gen.*

department *n.* отде́л; (*government*) департа́мент, ве́домство; (*univ.*) факульте́т, ка́федра; d. store, универма́г. departmental *adj.* ве́домственный.

departure *n.* отбы́тие; отклоне́ние.

depend *v.i.* зави́сеть (-и́шу, -и́сишь) *imp.* (on, от + *gen.*); (*rely*) полага́ться *imp.*, положи́ться (-жу́сь, -жи́шься) *perf.* (on, на + *acc.*) dependable *adj.* надёжный. dependant *n.* иждиве́нец (-нца); *pl.* семья́ и дома́шние *sb.* dependence *n.* зави́симость. dependent *adj.* зави́симый, зави́сящий.

depict *v.t.* изобража́ть *imp.*, изобрази́ть *perf.*; (*in words*) опи́сывать *imp.*, описа́ть (-ишу́, -и́шешь) *perf.*

deplete *v.t.* истоща́ть *imp.*, истощи́ть *perf.* depleted *adj.* истощённый, (-ён, -ённа) depletion *n.* истоще́ние.

deplorable *adj.* приско́рбный, плаче́вный. deplore *v.t.* сожале́ть *imp.* о + *prep.*

deploy *v.t.* & *i.* развёртывать(ся) *imp.*, разверну́ть(ся) *perf.* deployment *n.* развёртывание.

depopulate *v.t.* истребля́ть *imp.*, истреби́ть *perf.* населе́ние + *gen.*

deport *v.t.* высыла́ть *imp.*, вы́слать (вы́шлю, -лешь) *perf.*; (*internal exile*) ссыла́ть *imp.*, сосла́ть (сошлю́, -лёшь) *perf.* deportation *n.* вы́сылка; ссы́лка. deportee *n.* высыла́емый *sb.*; ссы́льный *sb.*

deportment *n.* поведе́ние, оса́нка.

depose v.t. сверга́ть imp., све́ргнуть (-г(нул), -гла) perf. (с престо́ла); v.i. (leg.) пока́зывать imp., показа́ть (-ажу́, -а́жешь) perf. **deposit** n. (econ.) вклад; (pledge) взнос; (sediment) оса́док (-дка); (coal etc.) месторожде́ние; v.t. (econ.) вноси́ть (-ошу́, -о́сишь) imp., внести́ (-есу́, -есёшь; -ёс, -есла́) perf.; (pledge) отлага́ть imp., отложи́ть (-жу́, -жишь) perf. **deposition** n. сверже́ние (с престо́ла); (leg.) показа́ние; (geol.) отложе́ние. **depositor** n. вкла́дчик. **depository** n. храни́лище.

depot n. склад; депо́ neut.indecl.; d. ship, су́дно-ба́за (pl. суда́-ба́зы, судо́в-ба́з).

deprave v.t. развраща́ть imp., разврати́ть (-ащу́, -ати́шь) perf. **depraved** adj. развращённый (-ён, -ённа). **depravity** n. развра́т.

deprecate v.t. возража́ть imp., возрази́ть perf. про́тив + gen. **deprecation** n. неодобре́ние.

depreciate v.t. & i. обесце́нивать(ся) imp., обесце́нить(ся) perf. **depreciation** n. обесце́нение. **depreciatory** adj. обесце́нивающий.

depress v.t. (lower) понижа́ть imp., пони́зить perf.; (dispirit) удруча́ть imp., удручи́ть perf. **depressed** adj. удручённый (-ён, -ённа & -ена́). **depressing** adj. нагоня́ющий тоску́. **depression** n. (hollow) впа́дина; (econ., med., meteor., etc.) депре́ссия.

deprivation n. лише́ние. **deprive** v.t. лиша́ть imp., лиши́ть perf. (of, + gen.)

depth n. глубина́ (pl. -ны); d. of feeling, си́ла пережива́ния; depths of the country, глушь (-ши́); in the d. of winter, в разга́р зимы́; d.-bomb, -charge, глуби́нная бо́мба.

deputation n. делега́ция, депута́ция. **depute** v.t. делеги́ровать imp. & perf. **deputize** v.i. замеща́ть imp., замести́ть perf. (for, + acc.). **deputy** n. замести́тель m.; помо́щник, -ица; (parl.) депута́т.

derail v.t. спуска́ть imp., спусти́ть (-ущу́, -у́стишь) perf. под отко́с; be derailed, сходи́ть (-ожу́, -о́дишь) imp., сойти́ (сойду́, -дёшь; сошёл, -шла́)

perf. с ре́льсов. **derailment** n. круше́ние, сход с ре́льсов.

derange v.t. расстра́ивать imp., расстро́ить perf. **deranged** adj. (mentally) душевнобольно́й, ненорма́льный. **derangement** n. (психи́ческое) расстро́йство.

derelict adj. бро́шенный (-шен). **dereliction** n. упуще́ние; (of duty) наруше́ние до́лга.

deride v.t. высме́ивать imp., вы́смеять (-ею, -еешь) perf. **derision** n. высме́ивание; object of d., посме́шище. **derisive** adj. (mocking) насме́шливый. **derisory** adj. (ridiculous) смехотво́рный.

derivation n. происхожде́ние. **derivative** n. производное sb.; adj. произво́дный. **derive** v.t. извлека́ть imp., извле́чь (-еку́, -ечёшь; -ёк, -екла́) perf.; v.i.: d. from, происходи́ть (-ожу́, -о́дишь) imp., произойти́ (-ойду́, -ойдёшь; -ошёл, -ошла́) perf. от + gen.

dermatitis n. дермати́т.

derogatory adj. умаля́ющий, унижа́ющий.

derrick n. де́ррик; (oil-well etc.) бурова́я вы́шка.

dervish n. де́рвиш.

descend v.t. спуска́ться imp., спусти́ться (-ущу́сь, -у́стишься) perf. с + gen.; сходи́ть (-ожу́, -о́дишь) imp., сойти́ (сойду́, -дёшь; сошёл, -шла́) perf. с + gen.; v.i. (go down) спуска́ться imp., спусти́ться (-ущу́сь, -у́стишься) perf.; (sink) понижа́ться imp., пони́зиться perf.; d. on, (attack) обру́шиваться imp., обру́шиться perf. на + acc.; d. to, (property; to details etc.) переходи́ть (-ожу́, -о́дишь) imp., перейти́ (-йду́, -йдёшь; перешёл, -шла́) perf. к + dat. be descended from, происходи́ть (-ожу́, -о́дишь) imp., произойти́ (-ойду́, -ойдёшь; -ошёл, -ошла́) perf. из, от, + gen. **descendant** n. пото́мок (-мка). **descent** n. спуск; (sinking) пониже́ние; (lineage) происхожде́ние; (property) насле́дование.

describe v.t. опи́сывать imp., описа́ть (-ишу́, -и́шешь) perf. **description** n. описа́ние. **descriptive** adj. описа́тельный.

descry *v.t.* различа́ть *imp.*, различи́ть *perf.*

desecrate *v.t.* оскверня́ть *imp.*, оскверни́ть *perf.* **desecration** *n.* оскверне́ние, профана́ция.

desert[1] *n.* (*wilderness*) пусты́ня; *adj.* пусты́нный (-нен, -нна).

desert[2] *v.t.* покида́ть *imp.*, поки́нуть *perf.*; (*mil.*) дезерти́ровать *imp. & perf.* **deserter** *n.* дезерти́р. **desertion** *n.* дезерти́рство.

desert[3] *n.*: *pl.* заслу́ги *f.pl.* **deserve** *v.t.* заслу́живать *imp.*, заслужи́ть (-жу́, -жишь) *perf.* **deserving** *adj.* заслу́живающий (of, + *gen.*), досто́йный (-о́ин, -о́йна) (of, + *gen.*).

desiccated *adj.* сушёный.

design *n.* (*scheme*) за́мысел (-сла); (*sketch*) рису́нок (-нка); (*model*) констру́кция, прое́кт; *school of d.*, шко́ла изобрази́тельных иску́сств; *v.t.* констру́ировать *imp.*; с ~ *perf.*; создава́ть (-даю́, -даёшь) *imp.*, созда́ть (-а́м, -а́шь, -а́ст, -ади́м; со́здал, -а́, -о) *perf.*

designate *adj.* назна́ченный (-чен); *v.t.* обознача́ть *imp.*, обозна́чить *perf.*; (*appoint*) назнача́ть *imp.*, назна́чить *perf.* **designation** *n.* обозначе́ние, назва́ние.

designer *n.* констру́ктор, проектиро́вщик, диза́йнер; (*of clothes*) модельер.

desirable *adj.* жела́тельный. **desire** *n.* жела́ние; *v.t.* жела́ть *imp.*, по ~ *perf.* + *gen.* **desirous** *adj.* жела́ющий.

desist *v.i.* перестава́ть (-таю́, -таёшь) *imp.*, переста́ть (-а́ну, -а́нешь) *perf.*

desk *n.* пи́сьменный стол (-а́); конто́рка; (*school*) па́рта.

desolate *adj.* (*deserted*) поки́нутый; (*dreary*) уны́лый. **desolation** *n.* запусте́ние.

despair *n.* отча́яние; *v.i.* отча́иваться *imp.*, отча́яться (-а́юсь, -а́ешься) *perf.* **despairing** *adj.* отча́янный (-ян, -янна).

desperado *n.* сорвиголова́ (*pl.* -овы, -о́в, -ова́м). **desperate** *adj.* отча́янный (-ян, -янна). **desperation** *n.* отча́яние.

despatch *see* dispatch.

despicable *adj.* презре́нный (-ён, -е́нна), жа́лкий (-лок, -лка́, -лко). **despise** *v.t.*

презира́ть *imp.*, презре́ть (-рю́, -ри́шь) *perf.*

despite *prep.* вопреки́ + *dat.*, несмотря́ на + *acc.*

despondency *n.* уны́ние, пода́вленность. **despondent** *adj.* уны́лый.

despot *n.* де́спот. **despotic** *adj.* деспоти́ческий, деспоти́чный. **despotism** *n.* деспоти́зм, деспоти́чность.

dessert *n.* десе́рт; сла́дкое *sb.*

destination *n.* ме́сто (*pl.* -та́) назначе́ния, цель. **destiny** *n.* судьба́, у́часть.

destitute *adj.* си́льно нужда́ющийся; без вся́ких средств. **destitution** *n.* нищета́, нужда́.

destroy *v.t.* уничтожа́ть *imp.*, уничто́жить *perf.*; губи́ть (-блю́, -бишь) *imp.*, по ~ *perf.* **destroyer** *n.* (*naut.*) эсми́нец (-нца). **destruction** *n.* разруше́ние, уничтоже́ние. **destructive** *adj.* разруши́тельный, уничтожа́ющий.

desultory *adj.* беспоря́дочный.

detach *v.t.* отделя́ть *imp.*, отдели́ть *perf.* **detachable** *adj.* съёмный, отделя́емый. **detached** *adj.* отде́льный; *d. house*, особня́к (-а́). **detachment** *n.* отделе́ние, разъедине́ние; (*mil.*) отря́д.

detail *n.* дета́ль, подро́бность; (*mil.*) наря́д; *in d.*, подро́бно; *v.t.* подро́бно расска́зывать *imp.*, рассказа́ть (-ажу́, -а́жешь) *perf.*; выделя́ть *imp.*, вы́делить *perf.*; назнача́ть *imp.*, назна́чить *perf.* в наря́д; *d. for guard duty*, назнача́ть *imp.* в карау́л. **detailed** *adj.* дета́льный, подро́бный.

detain *v.t.* заде́рживать *imp.*, задержа́ть (-жу́, -жишь) *perf.*; аресто́вывать *imp.*, арестова́ть *perf.* **detainee** *n.* аресто́ванный *sb.*, (челове́к) под стра́жей.

detect *v.t.* обнару́живать *imp.*, обнару́жить *perf.* **detection** *n.* обнару́жение; рассле́дование. **detective** *n.* сы́щик, детекти́в; *adj.* сыскно́й, детекти́вный; *d. film, story, etc.*, детекти́в. **detector** *n.* дете́ктор, обнаружи́тель *m.*

détente *n.* разря́дка.

detention *n.* задержа́ние, аре́ст.

deter *v.t.* уде́рживать *imp.*, удержа́ть (-жу́, -жишь) *perf.* (from, от + *gen.*).

detergent n. мо́ющее сре́дство; adj. мо́ющий, очища́ющий.

deteriorate v.i. ухудша́ться imp., уху́дшиться perf. **deterioration** n. ухудше́ние.

determination n. (resoluteness) реши́тельность, реши́мость. **determine** v.t. устана́вливать imp., установи́ть (-влю́, -вишь) perf.; определя́ть imp., определи́ть perf. (resolute) реши́тельный.

deterrent n. уде́рживающее сре́дство, сре́дство устраше́ния; adj. сде́рживающий, уде́рживающий.

detest v.t. ненави́деть (-и́жу, -и́дишь) imp. **detestable** adj. отврати́тельный. **detestation** n. отвраще́ние, не́нависть.

dethrone v.t. сверга́ть imp., све́ргнуть (-г(нул), -гла) perf. с престо́ла; разве́нчивать imp., развенча́ть perf. **dethronement** n. сверже́ние с престо́ла; развенча́ние.

detonate v.t. & i. взрыва́ть(ся) imp., взорва́ть(ся) (-ву́, -вёт(ся)) perf.; взрыва́ться (-а́(сь) -о/-а́лось) perf. **detonation** n. детона́ция, взрыв. **detonator** n. детона́тор.

detour n. обхо́д, объе́зд.

detract v.i.: d. from, умаля́ть imp., умали́ть perf. + acc.

detriment n. уще́рб, вред (-а́). **detrimental** adj. вре́дный (-ден, -дна́, -дно), па́губный.

detritus n. детри́т.

deuce n. (tennis) ра́вный счёт; (what) the d., чёрт возьми́!

devaluation n. девальва́ция. **devalue** v.t. проводи́ть (-ожу́, -о́дишь) imp., провести́ (-еду́, -едёшь; -ёл, -ела́) perf. девальва́цию + gen.

devastate v.t. опустоша́ть imp., опустоши́ть perf. **devastation** n. опустоше́ние.

develop v.t. & i. развива́ть(ся), разви́ть(ся) (разовью́(сь), -вёшь(ся)) разви́л(ся), -а́(сь), -о/-и́ло́сь) perf.; v.t. (phot.) проявля́ть imp., прояви́ть (-влю́, -вишь) perf.; (nat. resources) разраба́тывать imp., разрабо́тать perf. **developer** n. (of land etc.) застро́йщик но́вого райо́на; (phot.) проявля́тель m. **development** n. разви́тие; (phot.) проявле́ние.

deviate v.i. отклоня́ться imp., отклони́ться (-ню́сь, -ни́шься) perf. (from, от + gen.). **deviation** n. отклоне́ние; (polit.) уклон.

device n. устро́йство, прибо́р.

devil n. дья́вол, чёрт (pl. че́рти, -те́й) бес; d.-may-care, бесшаба́шный. **devilish** adj. дья́вольский, черто́вск ий.

devious adj. (indirect) непрям ́й (-м, -ма́, -мо); (person) хи́трый (-тёр, -тра́, хи́тро)

devise v.t. приду́мывать imp., приду́мать perf.

devoid adj. лишённый (-ён, -ена́) (of, + gen.).

devolution n. переда́ча; перехо́д. **devolve** v.t. передава́ть (-даю́, -даёшь) imp., переда́ть (-а́м, -а́шь, -а́ст, -ади́м; пе́редал, -а́, -о) perf.; v.i. переходи́ть (-ожу́, -о́дишь) imp., перейти́ (-йду́, -йдёшь; перешёл, -шла́) perf.

devote v.t. посвяща́ть imp., посвяти́ть (-ящу́, -яти́шь) perf. **devoted** adj. пре́данный (-ан). **devotion** n. пре́данность, приве́рженность; pl. религио́зные обя́занности f.pl. **devotional** adj. религио́зный.

devour v.t. пожира́ть imp., пожра́ть (-ру́, -рёшь) пожра́л, -а́, -о) perf.

devout adj. набо́жный, благочести́вый. **devoutness** n. на́божность, благоче́стие.

dew n. роса́. **dewdrop** n. роси́нка. **dewy** adj. вла́жный (-жен, -жна́, -жно), роси́стый.

dexterity n. прово́рство, ло́вкость; сноро́вка. **dext(e)rous** adj. прово́рный ло́вкий (-вок, -вка́, -вко, ло́вки́).

diabetes n. са́харная боле́знь, диабе́т. **diabetic** n. диабе́тик; adj. диабети́ческий.

diabolic(al) adj. дья́вольский; зве́рский.

diagnose v.t. ста́вить imp., по~ perf. диа́гноз + gen. **diagnosis** n. диа́гноз.

diagonal n. диагона́ль; adj. диагона́льный. **diagonally** adv. по диагона́ли.

diagram n. диагра́мма; чертёж (-а́); схе́ма.

dial n. цифербла́т; шкала́ (pl. -лы); (tel.) диск набо́ра; v.t. набира́ть imp., набра́ть (наберу́, -рёшь; набра́л, -а́, -о) perf.

dialect *n.* диале́кт, наре́чие; *adj.* диале́ктный. **dialectical** *adj.* диалекти́ческий.

dialogue *n.* диало́г.

diameter *n.* диа́метр. **diametrical** *adj.* диаметра́льный; *diametrically opposed,* диаметра́льно противополо́жный.

diamond *n.* алма́з, бриллиа́нт; (*rhomb*) ромб; (*cards*) бубна́ (*pl.* бу́бны, бубён, бубна́м); *play a d.,* ходи́ть (хожу́, хо́дишь) *imp.,* пойти́ (пойду́, -дёшь; пошёл, -шла́ *perf.* с бубён; *adj.* алма́зный, бриллиа́нтовый; бубно́вый.

diaper *n.* пелёнка.

diaphanous *adj.* прозра́чный.

diaphragm *n.* диафра́гма; мембра́на.

diarrhoeia *n.* поно́с.

diary *n.* дневни́к (-а́).

diatribe *n.* обличи́тельная речь (*pl.* -чи, -че́й).

dice *n.* see **die**[1].

dicey *adj.* риско́ванный (-ан, -анна).

dictaphone *n.* дикта́фон. **dictate** *n.* веле́ние; *v.t.* диктова́ть *imp.,* про~ *perf.* **dictation** *n.* дикто́вка, дикта́нт. **dictator** *n.* дикта́тор. **dictatorial** *adj.* дикта́торский, повели́тельный. **dictatorship** *n.* диктату́ра.

diction *n.* ди́кция.

dictionary *n.* слова́рь (-ря́) *m.*

dictum *n.* авторите́тное заявле́ние; (*maxim*) изрече́ние.

didactic *adj.* дидакти́ческий.

diddle *v.t.* надува́ть *imp.,* наду́ть (-у́ю, -у́ешь) *perf.*

die[1] *n.* (*pl.* **dice**) игра́льная кость (*pl.* -ти, -те́й); (*pl.* **dies**) (*stamp*) штамп, штёмпель (*pl.* -ля́) *m.*; (*mould*) ма́трица.

die[2] *v.i.* (*person*) умира́ть *imp.,* умере́ть (умру́, умрёшь; у́мер, -ла́, -ло) *perf.*; (*animal*) до́хнуть (дох(нул), до́хла) *imp.,* из~, по~ *perf.*; (*plant*) вя́нуть (вя́(ну)л, вя́ла) *imp.,* за~ *perf.*; сконча́ться *perf.*; *d.-hard,* неисправи́мый *sb.*

diesel *n.* (*engine*) ди́зель *m.*; *attrib.* ди́зельный.

diet *n.* дие́та; (*habitual food*) пита́ние, стол (-а́); *v.i.* соблюда́ть *imp.,* соблюсти́ (-юду́, -юдёшь; -юл, -юла́) *perf.* дие́ту. **dietary** *adj.* диети́ческий.

differ *v.i.* отлича́ться *imp.*; различа́ться *imp.*; (*disagree*) не соглаша́ться *imp.* **difference** *n.* ра́зница; (*disagreement*) разногла́сие. **different** *adj.* разли́чный, ра́зный. **differential** *n.* (*math.*) дифференциа́л; ра́зница; *adj.* дифференциа́льный. **differentiate** *v.t.* различа́ть *imp.,* различи́ть (вб *perf.* **differentiation** *n.* различе́ние, дифференциа́ция.

difficult *adj.* тру́дный (-ден, -дна́, -дно, тру́дны), затрудни́тельный. **difficulty** *n.* тру́дность; затрудне́ние; *without d.,* без труда́.

diffidence *n.* неуве́ренность в себе́. **diffident** *adj.* ро́бкий (-бок, -бка́, -бко), неуве́ренный (-ен) в себе́.

diffused *adj.* рассе́янный (-ян, -янна).

dig *n.* (*archaeol.*) раско́пки *f.pl.*; (*poke*) тычо́к (-чка́) *f.*; (*lodgings*) кварти́ра; *give a d. in the ribs,* ткнуть *perf.* ло́ктем под ребро́; *v.t.* копа́ть *imp.,* вы~ *perf.*; рыть (ро́ю, ро́ешь) *imp.,* вы~ *perf.*; (*prod*) ты́кать (ты́чу, -чешь) *imp.,* ткнуть *perf.*

digest *n.* (*synopsis*) кра́ткое изложе́ние, резюме́ *neut.indecl.*; (*collection*) сбо́рник резюме́; *v.t.* перева́ривать *imp.,* перевари́ть (-рю́, -ришь) *perf.* **digestible** *adj.* удобовари́мый. **digestion** *n.* пищеваре́ние. **digestive** *adj.* пищевари́тельный.

digger *n.* копа́тель *m.*, землеко́п. **digging** *n.* копа́ние, рытьё; *pl.* земляны́е рабо́ты *f.pl.*

digit *n.* (*math.*) ци́фра, однозна́чное число́ (*pl.* -сла, -сел, -слам); (*anat.*) па́лец (-льца).

dignified *adj.* с чу́вством со́бственного досто́инства. **dignify** *v.t.* облагора́живать *imp.,* облагоро́дить *perf.* **dignitary** *n.* сано́вник. **dignity** *n.* досто́инство.

digress *v.i.* отклоня́ться *imp.,* отклони́ться (-ню́сь, -ни́шься) *perf.* (*from, from* + *gen.*). **digression** *n.* отступле́ние, отклоне́ние.

dike *n.* на́сыпь; (*ditch*) ров (рва, *loc.* во рву́).

dilapidated *adj.* обветша́лый. **dilapidation** *n.* (*eccl.*) поврежде́ние.

dilate *v.t. & i.* расширя́ть(ся) *imp.,* расши́рить(ся) *perf.*

dilatory *adj.* оття́гивающий.

dilemma *n.* диле́мма.

dilettante *n.* дилета́нт; *adj.* дилета́нтский, люби́тельский.

diligence *n.* прилежа́ние, усе́рдие. **diligent** *adj.* приле́жный, усе́рдный.

dill *n.* укро́п (-а(у)).

dilly-dally *v.i.* ме́шкать *imp.*

dilute *v.t.* разбавля́ть *imp.*, разба́вить *perf.*; *adj.* разба́вленный (-ен). **dilution** *n.* разбавле́ние.

dim *adj.* ту́склый (тускл, -á, -о), сму́тный (-тен, -тна́, -тно); *d.-sighted*, недальнови́дный; *d.-witted*, тупо́й (туп, -á, -о, ту́пы).

dimension *n.* величина́; *pl.* разме́ры *m.pl.*; (*math.*) измере́ние. **-dimensional** *in comb.* -ме́рный; *three-d.*, трёхме́рный; *two-d.*, двухме́рный.

diminish *v.t. & i.* уменьша́ть(ся) *imp.*, уме́ньшить(ся) *perf.* **diminished** *adj.* уме́ньшенный (-ен). **diminution** *n.* уменьше́ние. **diminutive** *adj.* ма́ленький; (*gram.*) уменьши́тельный; *n.* уменьши́тельное *sb.*

dimity *n.* канифа́с.

dimness *n.* ту́склость; полусве́т.

dimple *n.* я́мочка.

din *n.* шум и гам; *v.t.: d. into one's ears*, прожужжа́ть (-жу́, -жи́шь) у́ши + *dat.*

dine *v.i.* обе́дать *imp.*, по~ *perf.*; *v.t.* угоща́ть *imp.*, угости́ть *perf.* обе́дом. **diner** *n.* обе́дающий *sb.*; (*rly.*) ваго́н(-а)-рестора́н (-а).

ding-dong *n.* череду́ющийся.

dinghy *n.* шлю́пка, я́лик.

dingy *adj.* (*drab*) ту́склый (тускл, -á, -о); (*dirty*) гря́зный (-зен, -зна́, -зно).

dining-car *n.* ваго́н(-а)-рестора́н (-а). **dining-room** *n.* столо́вая *sb.* **dinner** *n.* обе́д; *d.-hour*, обе́денный переры́в; *d.-jacket*, смо́кинг; *d.-time*, обе́денное вре́мя *neut.*

dinosaur *n.* диноза́вр.

dint *n.: by d. of*, посре́дством + *gen.*; с по́мощью + *gen.*

diocesan *adj.* епархиа́льный. **diocese** *n.* епа́рхия.

diode *n.* дио́д.

dioxide *n.* двуо́кись.

dip *v.t. & i.* окуна́ть(ся) *imp.*, окуну́ть(ся) *perf.*; *v.t.* (*flag*) припуска́ть *imp.*,
припусти́ть (-ущу́, -у́стишь) *perf.*; *d. into*, (*book*) перели́стывать *imp.*, перелиста́ть *perf.*; *n.* окуна́ние; (*depression*) впа́дина; (*slope*) укло́н; (*phys.; astr.*) наклоне́ние; *have a d.*, (*bathe*) купа́ться *imp.*, вы~ *perf.*

diphtheria *n.* дифтери́я.

diphthong *n.* дифто́нг.

diploma *n.* дипло́м. **diplomacy** *n.* диплома́тия. **diplomat(ist)** *n.* диплома́т. **diplomatic** *adj.* дипломати́ческий, дипломати́чный; *d. bag*, дипломати́ческая по́чта.

dipper *n.* (*ladle*) ковш (-á); (*bird*) оля́пка.

dipsomania *n.* алкоголи́зм.

dire *adj.* стра́шный (-шен, -шна́, -шно, стра́шны); (*ominous*) злове́щий.

direct *adj.* прямо́й (прям, -á, -о, пря́мы); непосре́дственный (-ен, -енна); *d. current*, постоя́нный ток (-а(у)); *v.t.* направля́ть *imp.*, напра́вить *perf.*; (*guide, manage*) руководи́ть *imp.* + *instr.*; (*film*) режисси́ровать *imp.* **direction** *n.* направле́ние; (*guidance*) руково́дство; (*instruction*) указа́ние; (*film*) режиссу́ра; *stage d.*, рема́рка. **directive** *n.* директи́ва, указа́ние. **directly** *adv.* пря́мо; (*at once*) сра́зу. **director** *n.* дире́ктор (pl. -á), член правле́ния; (*film*) режиссёр; *board of directors*, правле́ние. **directory** *n.* спра́вочник, указа́тель *m.*; *telephone d.*, телефо́нная кни́га.

dirge *n.* погреба́льная песнь.

dirt *n.* грязь (loc. -зи́); *d. cheap*, дешёвле па́реной ре́пы; *d. floor*, земляно́й пол (loc. -ý; pl. -ы́). **dirty** *adj.* гря́зный (-зен, -зна́, -зно); (*mean*) по́длый (подл, -á, -о); (*obscene*) непристо́йный; *v.t. & i.* па́чкать(ся) *imp.*, за~ *perf.*

disability *n.* (*physical*) нетрудоспосо́бность. **disable** *v.t.* де́лать *imp.*, с~ *perf.* неспосо́бным; (*cripple*) кале́чить *imp.*, ис~ *perf.* **disabled** (*adj.*) искале́ченный (-ен); *d. serviceman*, инвали́д войны́. **disablement** *n.* инвали́дность.

disabuse *v.t.* выводи́ть (-ожу́, -о́дишь) *imp.*, вы́вести (-еду, -едешь; -ел) *perf.* из заблужде́ния; *d. of*, освобожда́ть *imp.*, освободи́ть *perf.* от + *gen.*

disadvantage n. невы́годное положе́ние; (defect) недоста́ток (-тка). **disadvantageous** adj. невы́годный.

disaffected adj. недово́льный, нелоя́льный. **disaffection** n. недово́льство, нелоя́льность.

disagree v.i. не соглаша́ться imp., согласи́ться perf.; расходи́ться (-ожу́сь, -о́дишься) imp., разойти́сь (-ойду́сь, -ойдёшься; -ошёлся, -ошла́сь) perf. **disagreeable** adj. неприя́тный. **disagreement** n. расхожде́ние, несогла́сие; (quarrel) ссо́ра.

disallow v.t. отка́зывать imp., отказа́ть (-ажу́, -а́жешь) perf. в + prep.

disappear v.i. исчеза́ть imp., исче́знуть (-ез) perf.; пропада́ть imp., пропа́сть (-аду́, -адёшь; -а́л) perf.; скрыва́ться imp., скры́ться (-ро́юсь, -ро́ешься) perf. **disappearance** n. исчезнове́ние, пропа́жа.

disappoint v.t. разочаро́вывать imp., разочарова́ть perf. **disappointed** adj. разочаро́ванный (-ан, -ан(н)а). **disappointing** adj. вызыва́ющий разочарова́ние. **disappointment** n. разочарова́ние; доса́да.

disapproval n. неодобре́ние. **disapprove** v.t. не одобря́ть imp.

disarm v.t. разоружа́ть imp., разоружи́ть perf.; обезору́живать imp., обезору́жить perf. **disarmament** n. разоруже́ние.

disarray n. беспоря́док (-дка), смяте́ние.

disaster n. бе́дствие, несча́стье. **disastrous** adj. бе́дственный (-ен, -енна); ги́бельный, губи́тельный.

disavow v.t. отрека́ться imp., отре́чься (-еку́сь, -ечёшься; -ёкся, -екла́сь) perf. от + gen.; отрица́ть imp.

disband v.t. распуска́ть imp., распусти́ть (-ущу́, -у́стишь) perf.; (mil.) расформиро́вывать imp., расформирова́ть perf.; v.i. расходи́ться (-ожу́сь, -о́дишься) imp., разойти́сь (-ойду́сь, -ойдёшься; -ошёлся, -ошла́сь) perf.

disbelief n. неве́рие. **disbelieve** v.t. не ве́рить imp. + dat.

disburse v.t. выпла́чивать imp., вы́платить perf. **disbursement** n. вы́плата.

disc, disk n. диск, круг (pl. -и́); (gramophone record) граммпласти́нка; d. **brake**, ди́сковый то́рмоз (pl. -а́); d. **jockey**, веду́щий sb. переда́чу.

discard v.t. отбра́сывать imp., отбро́сить perf.; (cards) сбра́сывать imp., сбро́сить perf.; n. (card) сбро́шенная ка́рта.

discern v.t. различа́ть imp., различи́ть perf.; разгляде́ть (-яжу́, -яди́шь) perf. **discernible** adj. различи́мый. **discerning** adj. проница́тельный. **discernment** n. распознава́ние; уме́ние различа́ть.

discharge v.t. (ship etc.) разгружа́ть imp., разгрузи́ть (-ужу́, -у́зи́шь) perf. (gun; electr.) разряжа́ть imp., разряди́ть (-яжу́, -яди́шь) perf.; (dismiss) увольня́ть imp., уво́лить perf.; (prisoner) освобожда́ть imp., освободи́ть perf.; (debt, duty) выполня́ть imp., вы́полнить perf.; (med.) выделя́ть imp., вы́делить perf.; n. разгру́зка; (gun) вы́стрел; (electr.) разря́д; увольне́ние; освобожде́ние; выполне́ние; (med.) (action) выделе́ние, (matter) выделе́ния neut.pl.

disciple n. учени́к (-а́).

disciplinarian n. сторо́нник стро́гой дисципли́ны. **disciplinary** adj. дисциплина́рный. **discipline** n. дисципли́на; v.t. дисциплини́ровать imp., perf.

disclaim v.t. отрека́ться imp., отре́чься (-еку́сь, -ечёшься; -ёкся, -екла́сь) perf. от + gen. **disclaimer** n. отрече́ние.

disclose v.t. обнару́живать imp., обнару́жить perf. **disclosure** n. обнаруже́ние.

discoloured adj. измени́вший цвет, обесцве́ченный (-ен, -енна), вы́цветший.

discomfit v.t. приводи́ть (-ожу́, -о́дишь) imp., привести́ (-еду́, -едёшь; -ёл, -ела́) perf. в замеша́тельство. **discomfiture** n. замеша́тельство.

discomfort n. неудо́бство, нело́вкость.

disconcert v.t. (plans) расстра́ивать imp., расстро́ить perf.; (person) смуща́ть imp., смути́ть (-ущу́, -ути́шь) perf.

disconnect v.t. разъединя́ть imp., разъедини́ть perf.; (electr.) выключа́ть imp., вы́ключить perf. **disconnected** adj. (incoherent) бессвя́зный.

disconsolate *adj.* неутешный.

discontent *n.* недовольство. **discontented** *adj.* недовольный.

discontinue *v.t.* & *i.* прекращать(ся) *imp.*, прекратить(ся) (-ащу, -атит(ся)) *perf.*

discord *n.* (*disagreement*) разногласие, разлад; (*mus.*) диссонанс. **discordant** *adj.* несогласующийся; диссонирующий.

discount *n.* скидка; *v.t.* (*econ.*) учитывать *imp.*, учесть (учту, -тёшь; учёл, учла) *perf.*; (*disregard*) не принимать *imp.*, принять (-иму, -имешь; принял, -á, -о) *perf.* в расчёт, во внимание.

discountenance *v.t.* не одобрять *imp.*, одобрить *perf.*

discourage *v.t.* обескураживать *imp.*, обескуражить *perf.* **discouragement** *n.* обескураживание.

discourteous *adj.* нелюбезный, невоспитанный (-ан, -анна), **discourtesy** *n.* нелюбезность, невоспитанность.

discover *v.t.* открывать *imp.*, открыть (-рою, -роешь) *perf.*; обнаруживать *imp.*, обнаружить *perf.* **discoverer** *n.* исследователь *m.* **discovery** *n.* открытие.

discredit *n.* позор; *v.t.* дискредитировать *imp.*, *perf.*

discreet *adj.* осмотрительный, благоразумный. **discretion** *n.* усмотрение; (*prudence*) благоразумие; *at one's d.*, по своему усмотрению.

discrepancy *n.* разница, несоответствие.

discriminate *v.t.* различать *imp.*, различить *perf.*; *d. against*, дискриминировать *imp.*, *perf.* **discrimination** *n.* установление различия; дискриминация.

discursive *adj.* непоследовательный, сбивчивый.

discus *n.* диск; *d. throwing*, метание диска.

discuss *v.t.* обсуждать *imp.*, обсудить (-ужу, -удишь) *perf.* **discussion** *n.* обсуждение, дискуссия.

disdain *n.* презрение. **disdainful** *adj.* презрительный, надменный (-енен, -енна).

disease *n.* болезнь. **diseased** *adj.* больной (-лен, -льна).

disembark *v.t.* & *i.* высаживать(ся) *imp.*, высадить(ся) *perf.* **disembarkation** *n.* высадка.

disembodied *adj.* бесплотный.

disembowel *v.t.* потрошить *imp.*, вы~ *perf.*

disenchantment *n.* разочарование.

disengage *v.t.* высвобождать *imp.*, высвободить *perf.*; (*tech.*) разобщать *imp.*, разобщить *perf.*; выключать *imp.*, выключить *perf.* **disengaged** *adj.* свободный. **disengagement** *n.* освобождение; разобщение, выключение.

disentangle *v.t.* распутывать *imp.*, распутать *perf.*

disestablishment *n.* отделение церкви от государства.

disfavour *n.* немилость, неприязнь.

disfigure *v.t.* уродовать *imp.*, из~ *perf.*

disfranchise *v.t.* лишать *imp.*, лишить *perf.* (гражданских, избирательных) прав, привилегий. **disfranchisement** *n.* лишение гражданских, избирательных, прав.

disgorge *v.t.* извергать *imp.*, извергнуть (-г(нул), -гла) *perf.*

disgrace *n.* позор; (*disfavour*) немилость, опала; *v.t.* позорить *imp.*, о~ *perf.* **disgraceful** *adj.* позорный.

disgruntled *adj.* недовольный.

disguise *n.* маскировка; изменение внешности; *v.t.* маскировать *imp.*, за~ *perf.*; изменять *imp.*, изменить (-ню, -нишь) *perf.* внешность + *gen.*; (*conceal*) скрывать *imp.*, скрыть (-рою, -роешь) *perf.* **disguised** *adj.* замаскированный (-ан, -анна); *d. as*, переодетый в + *acc.*

disgust *n.* отвращение; *v.t.* внушать *imp.*, внушить *perf.* отвращение + *dat.* **disgusting** *adj.* отвратительный, противный.

dish *n.* блюдо; *pl.* посуда collect.; *d.-towel*, кухонное полотенце (*gen.pl.* -нец); *d.-washer*, (посудо)моечная машина; *d.-water*, помои (-оев) *pl.*; *v.t.*: *d. up*, класть (-аду, -адёшь; -ал) *imp.*, положить (-ожу, -ожишь) *perf.* на блюдо.

disharmony *n.* дисгармония; (*disagreement*) разногласие.

dishearten v.t. обескура́живать imp., обескура́жить perf.

dishevelled adj. растрёпанный (-ан, -анна).

dishonest adj. нечестный, недобросо́вестный. **dishonesty** n. нечестность.

dishonour n. бесчестье; v.t. бесчестить imp., o ~ perf. **dishonourable** adj. бесчестный, подлый (подл, -á, -о).

disillusion v.t. разочаро́вывать imp., разочарова́ть perf. **disillusionment** n. разочаро́ванность.

disinclination n. несклонность, неохо́та. **disinclined** adj.: be ~, не хоте́ться (хо́чется) impers. + dat.

disinfect v.t. дезинфици́ровать imp., perf. **disinfectant** n. дезинфици́рующее сре́дство; adj. дезинфици́рующий. **disinfection** n. дезинфе́кция, обеззара́живание.

disingenuous adj. нейскренный (-нен, -нна, -нне & -нно).

disinherit v.t. лиша́ть imp., лиши́ть perf. насле́дства.

disintegrate v.t. дезинтегри́ровать imp., perf.; v.i. разлага́ться imp., разложи́ться (-жу́сь, -жи́шься) perf. **disintegration** n. разложе́ние, дезинтегра́ция, распа́д.

disinterested adj. бескоры́стный.

disjointed adj. бессвя́зный.

disk see disc.

dislike n. нелюбо́вь (-бви́, instr. -бо́вью) (for, к + dat.); нерасположе́ние (for, к + dat.); v.t. не люби́ть (-блю́, -бишь) imp.

dislocate v.t. (med.) вывихивать imp., вывихнуть perf.; расстра́ивать imp., расстро́ить perf. **dislocation** n. вы́вих; беспоря́док (-дка).

dislodge v.t. смеща́ть imp., смести́ть perf.

disloyal adj. нелоя́льный, неве́рный (-рен, -рна́, -рно, неве́рность. **disloyalty** n. нелоя́льность, неве́рность.

dismal adj. мра́чный (-чен, -чна́, -чно), уны́лый.

dismantle v.t. разбира́ть imp., разобра́ть (разберу́, -рёшь; разобра́л, -á, -о) perf.; демонти́ровать imp., perf.

dismay v.t. приводи́ть (-ожу́, -о́дишь) imp., привести́ (-еду́, -едёшь; -ёл,

-ела́) perf. в у́жас, уны́ние; n. (alarm) испу́г (-a(y)); уны́ние.

dismember v.t. расчленя́ть imp., расчлени́ть perf. **dismemberment** n. расчлене́ние.

dismiss v.t. (discharge) увольня́ть imp., уво́лить perf.; (disband) распуска́ть imp., распусти́ть (-ущу́, -у́стишь) perf.; d.! interj. (mil.) разойди́сь! **dismissal** n. увольне́ние; ро́спуск.

dismount v.i. (from horse) спе́шиваться imp., спе́шиться perf.

disobedience n. непослуша́ние. **disobedient** adj. непослу́шный. **disobey** v.t. не слу́шаться imp. + gen.

disobliging adj. нелюбе́зный, не услу́жливый.

disorder n. беспоря́док (-дка). **disordered** adj. расстро́енный (-ен). **disorderly** adj. (untidy) беспоря́дочный; (unruly) бу́йный (бу́ен, бу́йна́, -но).

disorganization n. дезорганиза́ция. **disorganize** v.t. дезорганизова́ть imp., perf.

disorientation n. дезориента́ция.

disown v.t. не признава́ть (-наю́, -наёшь) imp., призна́ть perf.; отрица́ть imp.

disparage v.t. умаля́ть imp., умали́ть perf. **disparagement** n. умале́ние.

disparity n. нера́венство.

dispassionate adj. беспристра́стный.

dispatch, des- v.t. (send) отправля́ть imp., отпра́вить perf.; (deal with) распра́виться imp., распра́виться perf. с + instr.; n. отпра́вка; (message) донесе́ние; (rapidity) быстрота́; d.-box, ва́лиза; d.-rider, мотоцикли́ст свя́зи.

dispel v.t. рассе́ивать imp., рассе́ять (-е́ю, -е́ешь) perf.

dispensary n. апте́ка.

dispensation n. (exemption) освобожде́ние (от обяза́тельства, обе́та). **dispense** v.t. (distribute) раздава́ть (-даю́, -даёшь) imp., разда́ть (-а́м, -а́шь, -а́ст, -ади́м; ро́здал & разда́л, раздала́, ро́здало & разда́ло) perf.; (justice, medicine) отпуска́ть imp., отпусти́ть (-ущу́, -у́стишь) perf.; d. with, (do without) обходи́ться (-ожу́сь, -о́дишься) imp., обойти́сь (обойду́сь, -дёшься; обошёлся, -шла́сь) perf.

без + gen. **dispenser** n. (*person*) фармацéвт; (*device*) торгóвый автомáт.
dispersal n. распространéние. **disperse** v.t. разгонять *imp.*, разогнáть (разгоню, -нишь; разогнáл, -á, -о) *perf.*; рассéивать *imp.*, рассéять (-éю, -éешь) *perf.*; v.i. расходиться (-дится) *imp.*, разойтись (-ойдётся; -ошёлся, -ошлáсь) *perf.*
dispirited adj. удручённый (-ён, -енá).
displaced adj.: d. persons, перемещённые лицá neut. pl. **displacement** n. (*of fluid*) водоизмещéние.
display n. покáз; проявлéние; демонстрáция; v.t. покáзывать *imp.*, показáть (-ажý -áжешь) *perf.*; проявлять *imp.*, проявить (-влю, -вишь) *perf.*; демонстрировать *imp.*, *perf.*
displease v.t. раздражáть *imp.*, раздражить *perf.* **displeased** predic. недовóлен (-льна).
disposable adj. могýщий быть выброшенным. **disposal** n. удалéние, избавлéние (of, от + gen.); at your d., (*service*) к вáшим услýгам; (*use*) в вáшем распоряжéнии. **dispose** v.i.: d. of, избавляться *imp.*, избáвиться (of + gen. **disposed** predic.: d. to, склóнен, (-óнна, -óнно) к + dat., располóжен + inf. or к + dat. **disposition** n. расположéние, склóнность; (*temperament*) нрав.
disproof n. опровержéние.
disproportionate adj. непропорционáльный.
disprove v.t. опровергáть *imp.*, опровéргнуть (-г(нул), -гла) *perf.*
disputation n. диспýт. **dispute** n. (*debate*) спор; (*quarrel*) ссóра; v.t. оспáривать *imp.*, оспóрить *perf.*
disqualification n. дисквалификáция. **disqualify** v.t. лишáть *imp.*, лишить *perf.* прáва + inf.; дисквалифицировать *imp.*, *perf.*
disquiet n. беспокóйство, тревóга. **disquieting** adj. тревóжный.
disregard n. невнимáние к + dat.; пренебрежéние + instr.; v.t. игнорировать *imp.*, *perf.*; пренебрегáть *imp.*, пренебрéчь (-егý, -ежёшь; -ёг, -еглá) *perf.* + instr.
disrepair n. неисправность.

disreputable adj. пóльзующийся дурнóй слáвой, дурнóй репутáцией. **disrepute** n. дурнáя слáва.
disrespect n. неуважéние, непочтéние. **disrespectful** adj. непочтительный.
disrupt v.t. срывáть *imp.*, сорвáть (-вý, -вёшь; сорвáл, -á, -о) *perf.* **disruptive** adj. подрывнóй, разрушительный.
dissatisfaction n. неудовлетворённость; недовóльство. **dissatisfied** adj. неудовлетворённый (-ён, -енá & -éнна), недовóльный.
dissect v.t. разрезáть *imp.*, разрéзать (-éжу, -éжешь) *perf.*; (*med. etc.*) вскрывáть *imp.*, вскрыть (-рóю, -рóешь) *perf.*
dissemble v.t. скрывáть *imp.*, скрыть (-рóю, -рóешь) *perf.*; v.i. притворяться *imp.*, притвориться *perf.*
dissemination n. рассéивание; распространéние.
dissension n. разноглáсие, раздóр. **dissent** n. расхождéние, несоглáсие; (*eccl.*) раскóл. **dissenter** n. (*eccl.*) раскóльник, сектáнт.
dissertation n. диссертáция.
disservice n. плохáя услýга.
dissident n. диссидéнт, инакомыслящий sb.
dissimilar adj. несхóдный, непохóжий, различный. **dissimilation** n. диссимиляция.
dissipate v.t. (*dispel*) рассéивать *imp.*, рассéять (-éю, -éешь) *perf.*; (*squander*) промáтывать *imp.*, промотáть *perf.* **dissipated** adj. распýтный, беспýтный.
dissociate v.t.: d. oneself, отмежёвываться *imp.*, отмежевáться (-жýюсь, -жýешься) *perf.* (from, от + gen.). **dissociation** n. разобщéние, отмежевáние.
dissolute adj. распýщенный (-ен, -енна), развратный. **dissolution** n. (*treaty etc.*) расторжéние; (*parl.*) рóспуск; (*solution*) растворéние. **dissolve** v.t. & i. (*in liquid*) растворять(ся) *imp.*, растворить(ся) *perf.*; v.t. (*annul*) расторгáть *imp.*, расторгнуть (-г(нул), -гла) *perf.*; (*parl.*) распускáть *imp.*, распустить (-ущý, -ýстишь) *perf.*
dissonance n. диссонáнс. **dissonant** adj. диссонирующий.

dissuade v.t. отговáривать imp., отговорúть perf. **dissuasion** n. отговáривание.

distaff n. прялка; on the d. side, по жéнской лúнии.

distance n. расстоя́ние; (distant point) даль (loc. -лú); (sport) дистáнция; at a great d., вдалú. **distant** adj. дáльний, далёкий (-ёк, -екá, -ёко); (reserved) сдéржанный (-ан, -анна).

distaste n. неприя́знь. **distasteful** adj. протúвный, неприя́тный.

distemper[1] n. (vet.) чумá.

distemper[2] n. (paint) тéмпера; v.t. крáсить imp., по ~ perf. тéмперой.

distend v.t. расшиýрять imp., расшúрить perf.; надувáть imp., надýть (-ýю, -ýешь) perf. **distension** n. расшире́ние, надувáние.

distil v.t. перегоня́ть imp., перегнáть (-гоню́, -гóнишь; перегнáл, -á, -о) perf.; дистиллúровать imp., perf. **distillation** n. перегóнка, дистилля́ция. **distillery** n. виноку́ренный, перегóнный, завóд.

distinct adj. (separate) отдéльный; (clear) отчётливый; (definite) определённый (-ёнен, -ённа), d. from, отличáющийся от + gen. **distinction** n. отлúчие, разлúчие. **distinctive** adj. особенный, отличúтельный. **distinctly** adj. я́сно, определённо.

distinguish v.t. различáть imp., различúть perf.; d. oneself, отличáться imp., отличúться perf. **distinguished** adj. выдаю́щийся.

distort v.t. искажáть imp., исказúть perf.; (misrepresent) извращáть imp., извратúть (-ащý, -атúшь) perf. **distortion** n. искажéние, искривлéние.

distract v.t. отвлекáть imp., отвлéчь (-екý, -ечёшь; -ёк, -еклá) perf. **distracted** adj. (maddened) обезу́мевший. **distraction** n. (amusement) развлечéние; (madness) безу́мие.

distrain v.i.: d. upon, накла́дывать imp., наложúть (-жý, -жишь) perf. арéст на + acc. **distraint** n. наложéние арéста.

distraught adj. обезу́мевший.

distress n. (calamity) бедá; (ship etc.) бéдствие; (poverty) нужда́; (physical) недомогáние; v.t. огорчáть imp.,

огорчúть perf.; мýчить imp., из~ perf.

distribute v.t. распределя́ть imp., распределúть perf. **distribution** n. распределéние, раздáча. **distributive** adj. распределúтельный. **distributor** n. распределúтель m.; (cin.) кинопрокáтчик.

district n. óкруг (pl. -á), райóн.

distrust n. недовéрие; v.t. не доверя́ть imp. **distrustful** adj. недовéрчивый.

disturb v.t. беспокóить imp., о ~ perf. **disturbance** n. нарушéние покóя; pl. (polit. etc.) беспоря́дки m.pl.

disuse n. неупотреблéние; fall into d., выходúть (-ит) imp., вы́йти (-йдет) perf.; вы́шел, -шла) perf. из употреблéния. **disused** adj. вы́шедший из употреблéния.

ditch n. канáва, ров (рва, loc. во рву).

dither v.i. колебáться (-блю́сь, -блешься) imp.; n.: all of a d., в сúльном возбуждéнии.

ditto n. то же сáмое; adv. так же.

ditty n. пéсенка.

diuretic n. мочегóнное срéдство; adj. мочегóнный.

diurnal adj. дневнóй.

divan n. тахтá.

dive v.i. ныря́ть imp., нырнýть perf. в вóду; прыгáть imp., прыгнуть perf. в вóду; (aeron.) пикúровать imp., perf.; (submarine) погружáться imp., погрузúться perf.; n. нырóк (-ркá), прыжóк (-жкá) в вóду; d-bomber, пикúрующий бомбардирóвщик. **diver** n. водолáз; (bird) гагáра.

diverge v.i. расходúться (-ится) imp., разойтúсь (-ойдётся) -ошёлся, -ошлáсь) perf.; (deviate) отклоня́ться imp., отклонúться (-ню́сь, -нишься) perf. (from, от + gen.). **divergence** n. расхождéние; отклонéние. **divergent** adj. расходя́щийся.

diverse adj. разлúчный, разнообрáзный. **diversification** n. расшире́ние ассортимéнта. **diversified** adj. многообрáзный. **diversify** v.t. разнообрáзить imp. **diversion** n. (deviation) отклонéние; (detour) объéзд; (amusement) развлечéние; (mil.) дивéрсия. **diversionist** n. диверсáнт.

diversity n. разнообра́зие; разли́чие.

divert v.t. отклоня́ть imp., отклони́ть (-ню́, -нишь) perf.; отводи́ть (-ожу́, -о́дишь) imp., отвести́ (-еду́, -едёшь; -ёл, -ела́) perf.; (amuse) развлека́ть imp., развле́чь (-еку́, -ечёшь; -ёк, -екла́) perf. **diverting** adj. заба́вный.

divest v.t. (unclothe) разобла́чать imp., разоблачи́ть perf., (deprive) лиша́ть imp., лиши́ть (of, + gen.).

divide v.t. дели́ть (-лю́, -лишь) imp., по ~ perf.; разделя́ть imp., раздели́ть (-лю́, -лишь) perf. **dividend** n. дивиде́нд. **dividers** n. ци́ркуль m.

divination n. гада́ние; предсказа́ние. **divine** adj. боже́ственный (-ен, -енна); n. богосло́в; v.t. предска́зывать imp., предсказа́ть (-ажу́, -а́жешь) perf. **diviner** n. предсказа́тель m.

diving n. ныря́ние; (profession) водола́зное де́ло; (aeron.) пики́рование; (naut.) погруже́ние; **d.-board**, трампли́н.

divining-rod n. волше́бная лоза́ (pl. -зы).

divinity n. божество́; (theology) богосло́вие, теоло́гия.

divisible adj. дели́мый. **division** n. (dividing) деле́ние, разделе́ние; (section) отде́л, подразделе́ние; (mil.) диви́зия. **divisional** adj. дивизио́нный. **divisive** adj. разделя́ющий, вызыва́ющий разногла́сия. **divisor** n. дели́тель m.

divorce n. разво́д; v.i. разводи́ться (-ожу́сь, -о́дишься) imp., развести́сь (-еду́сь, -едёшься; -ёлся, -ела́сь) perf. **divorced** adj. разведённый (-ён, -ена́). **divorcee** n. разведённая жена́ (pl. жёны).

divulge v.t. разглаша́ть imp., разгласи́ть perf.

dizziness n. головокруже́ние. **dizzy** adj. головокружи́тельный; I am d., у меня́ кру́жится голова́.

do v.t. де́лать imp., с ~ perf.; выполня́ть imp., вы́полнить perf.; (coll.) надува́ть imp., наду́ть (-у́ю, -у́ешь) perf.; v.i. (be suitable) годи́ться imp.; (suffice) быть доста́точным; that will do, хва́тит! how do you do, здра́вствуйте! как вы пожива́ете? do away

with, (abolish) уничтожа́ть imp., уничто́жить perf.; do in, (kill) убива́ть imp., уби́ть (убью́, -ьёшь) perf.; do up, (restore) ремонти́ровать imp., от ~ perf.; (wrap up) завёртывать imp., заверну́ть perf.; (fasten) застёгивать imp., застегну́ть perf.; do without, обходи́ться (-ожу́сь, -о́дишься) imp., обойти́сь (обойду́сь, -дёшься; обошёлся, -шла́сь) perf. без + gen.

docile adj. поко́рный. **docility** n. поко́рность.

dock[1] n. (bot.) щаве́ль (-ля́) m.

dock[2] v.t. (tail) отруба́ть imp., отруби́ть (-блю́, -бишь) perf.; (money) урезывать imp., уреза́ть imp., уре́зать (-е́жу, -е́жешь) perf.

dock[3] n. (naut.) док; v.t. ста́вить imp., по ~ perf. в док; v.i. входи́ть (-ожу́, -о́дишь) imp., войти́ (войду́, -дёшь; вошёл, -шла́) perf. в док; v.t. & i. (spacecraft) стыкова́ться imp., со ~ perf. **docker** n. до́кер, порто́вый рабо́чий sb. **docking** n. (ship) постано́вка в док; (spacecraft) стыко́вка. **dockyard** n. верфь.

dock[4] n. (leg.) скамья́ (pl. ска́мьи, -ме́й) подсуди́мых.

docket n. квита́нция; (label) ярлы́к (-а́), этике́тка.

doctor n. врач (-а́); (also univ. etc.) до́ктор (pl. -а́); v.t. (med.) лечи́ть (-чу́, -чишь) imp.; (falsify) фальсифици́ровать imp., perf. **doctor(i)al** adj. до́кторский. **doctorate** n. сте́пень (pl. -ни, -не́й) до́ктора.

doctrinaire n. доктринёр; adj. доктринёрский. **doctrine** n. доктри́на.

document n. докуме́нт; v.t. документи́ровать imp., perf. **documentary** adj. документа́льный; n. документа́льный фильм. **documentation** n. документа́ция.

dodder n. дрожа́ть (-жу́, -жи́шь) imp. **dodderer** n. ста́рый копу́н (-а́), ~ья.

dodge n. (trick) ло́вкий приём, уве́ртка; v.t. уклоня́ться imp., уклони́ться (-ню́сь, -ни́шься) perf. от + gen.; увили́вать imp., увильну́ть perf. от + gen.

doe n. са́мка. **doeskin** n. за́мша.

dog *n.* соба́ка, пёс (пса); (*male dog*) кобе́ль (-ля́) *m.*; (*male animal*) саме́ц (-мца́); d.-collar, оше́йник; d.-fight, возду́шный бой (*loc.* бою́); *pl.* бой; *v.t.* сле́довать *imp.*, по~ *perf.* по пята́м за+*instr.*; (*fig.*) пресле́довать *imp.*

doggerel *n.* ви́рши (-шей) *pl.*

dogma *n.* до́гма. **dogmatic** *adj.* догмати́ческий.

doing *n.*: *pl.* дела́ *neut.pl.*; (*events*) собы́тия *neut.pl.*

doldrums *n.*: be in the d., хандри́ть *imp.*

dole *n.* посо́бие по безрабо́тице.

doleful *adj.* ско́рбный.

doll *n.* ку́кла (*gen.pl.* -кол).

dollar *n.* до́ллар.

dollop *n.* здоро́вый кусо́к (-ска́).

dolly *n.* ку́колка; (*stick*) валёк (-лька́); (*cin.*) опера́торская теле́жка.

dolphin *n.* дельфи́н, белобо́чка.

dolt *n.* болва́н. **doltish** *adj.* тупо́й (туп, -а́, -о, ту́пы́).

domain *n.* (*estate*) владе́ние; (*field*) о́бласть, сфе́ра.

dome *n.* ку́пол (*pl.* -а́). **domed** *adj.* с ку́полом.

domestic *adj.* (*of household; animals*) дома́шний; (*of family*) семе́йный; (*polit.*) вну́тренний; *n.* прислу́га. **domesticate** *v.t.* прируча́ть *imp.*, приручи́ть *perf.* **domesticity** *n.* дома́шняя, семе́йная, жизнь.

domicile *n.* постоя́нное местожи́тельство; *v.t.* сели́ть *imp.*, по~ *perf.* на постоя́нное жи́тельство. **domiciliary** *adj.* дома́шний.

dominance *n.* госпо́дство. **dominant** *adj.* преоблада́ющий; госпо́дствующий; *n.* домина́нта. **dominate** *v.t.* госпо́дствовать *imp.* над+*instr.* **domineering** *adj.* высокоме́рный.

dominion *n.* домини́он; влады́чество.

domino *n.* кость (*pl.* -ти, -те́й) домино́; *pl.* (*game*) домино́ *neut.indecl.*

don[1] *n.* (D., *title*) дон; (*univ.*) преподава́тель *m.*

don[2] *v.t.* надева́ть *imp.*, наде́ть (-е́ну, -е́нешь) *perf.*

donate *v.t.* же́ртвовать *imp.*, по~ *perf.* **donation** *n.* дар (*pl.* -ы́), поже́ртвование.

donkey *n.* осёл (-сла́); d. engine, вспомога́тельный дви́гатель *m.*

donnish *adj.* педанти́чный.

donor *n.* же́ртвователь *m.*; (*med.*) до́нор.

doom *n.* рок, судьба́; (*ruin*) ги́бель; *v.t.* обрека́ть *imp.*, обре́чь (-еку́, -ечёшь; -ёк, -екла́) *perf.* **doomsday** *n.* стра́шный суд (-а́); коне́ц (-нца́) све́та.

door *n.* (*house*) дверь (*loc.* -ри́; *pl.* -ри, -ре́й, *instr.* -рьми́ & -ря́ми); (*smaller*) две́рца (*gen.pl.* -рец). **doorbell** *n.* (дверно́й) звоно́к (-нка́). **doorknob** *n.* (дверна́я) ру́чка. **doorman** *n.* швейца́р. **doormat** *n.* полови́к (-а́). **doorpost** *n.* (дверно́й) кося́к (-а́). **doorstep** *n.* поро́г. **doorway** *n.* дверно́й проём.

dope *n.* (*drug*) нарко́тик; информа́ция; d.-fiend, наркома́н, ~ка; *v.t.* дава́ть (даю́, даёшь) *imp.*, дать (дам, дашь, даст, дади́м; дал, -а́, да́ло́, -и) *perf.* нарко́тик+*dat.*

dormant *adj.* (*sleeping*) спя́щий; (*inactive*) безде́йствующий.

dormer window *n.* манса́рдное окно́ (*pl.* о́кна, о́кон, о́кнам).

dormitory *n.* дортуа́р.

dormouse *n.* со́ня.

dorsal *adj.* спинно́й.

dose *n.* до́за; *v.t.* дава́ть (даю́, даёшь) *imp.*, дать (дам, дашь, даст, дади́м; дал, -а́, да́ло́, -и) *perf.* лека́рство+*dat.*

doss-house *n.* ночле́жный дом (*pl.* -а́).

dossier *n.* досье́ *neut.indecl.*

dot *n.* то́чка; *v.t.* ста́вить *imp.*, по~ *perf.* то́чки на+*acc.*; (*scatter*) усе́ивать *imp.*, усе́ять (-е́ю, -е́ешь) *perf.* (with, +*instr.*); dotted line, пункти́р.

dotage *n.* (*старческое*) слабоу́мие.

dotard *n.* выжи́вший из ума́ стари́к (-а́). **dote** *v.i.*: d. on, обожа́ть *imp.*

dotty *adj.* рехну́вшийся.

double *adj.* двойно́й, па́рный; (*doubled*) удво́енный (-ен); d.-barrelled, двуство́льный; d.-bass, контраба́с; d. bed, двуспа́льная крова́ть; d.-breasted, двубо́ртный; d.-cross, обма́нывать *imp.*, обману́ть (-ну́, -нешь) *perf.*; d.-dealer, двуру́шник; d.-dealing, двуру́шничество; d.-decker, двухэта́жный авто́бус; d.-edged, обоюдоо́стрый; d.-faced, двули́чный; *adv.* вдвое́; (*two together*) вдвоём; *n.* двойно́е коли́чество; (*person's*) двойни́к (-а́); (*understudy*) дублёр; *pl.* (*sport*) па́рная игра́; *at the* d., бе́глым ша́гом; *v.t.* удва́ивать *imp.*, удвои́ть *perf.*; (*fold*) скла́дывать *imp.*, сложи́ть (-жу́, -жишь) *perf.* вдвое; *pl. the parts of,* (*theat.*) игра́ть *imp.*, сыгра́ть *perf.* ро́ли + *gen.*

doubt *n.* сомне́ние; *v.t.* сомнева́ться *imp.* в + *prep.* **doubtful** *adj.* сомни́тельный. **doubting** *adj.* сомнева́ющийся. **doubtless** *adv.* несомне́нно.

douche *n.* душ; *v.t.* облива́ть *imp.*, обли́ть (оболью́, -ьёшь; о́бли́л, -а́, -о) *perf.* водо́й.

dough *n.* те́сто. **doughnut** *n.* по́нчик, пы́шка.

dour *adj.* угрю́мый, мра́чный (-чен, -чна́, -чно).

douse *v.t.* (*light*) туши́ть (-шу́, -шишь) *imp.*, за ~ по ~ *perf.*

dove *n.* го́лубь (*pl.* -би, -бе́й) *m.*, го́рлица; d.-coloured, си́зый (сиз, -а́, -о).

dovecot(e) *n.* голубя́тня (*gen.pl.* -тен).

dovetail *n.* ла́сточкин хвост (-а́); *v.i.*: d. (*into one another*), соотве́тствовать *imp.* друг дру́гу.

dowager *n.* вдова́ (*pl.* -вы); *in comb.* вдо́вствующая.

dowdy *adj.* безвку́сный, неэлега́нтный.

down[1] *n.* (*geog.*) безле́сная возвы́шенность; *pl.* Да́унс.

down[2] *n.* (*fluff*) пух (-а(у), *loc.* -ý), пушо́к (-шка́).

down[3] *adv.* (*motion*) вниз; (*position*) внизу́; *be d. with,* (*ill*) боле́ть *imp.* + *instr.*; d. with, (*interj.*) доло́й + *acc.*; *prep.* вниз с + *gen.*, по + *dat.*; (*along*) по + *dat.*; *v.t.: d. tools,* (*strike*) бастова́ть *imp.*, за ~ *perf.*; d.-and-out, бедня́к (-а́), оборва́нец (-нца); *down-cast, d.-hearted,* уны́лый. **downfall** *n.* (*ruin*) ги́бель. **downpour** *n.* ли́вень (-вня) *m.* **downright** *adj.* прямо́й (прям, -а́, -о, пря́мы); (*out-and-out*) я́вный; *adv.* соверше́нно. **downstream** *adv.* вниз по тече́нию.

dowry *n.* прида́ное *sb.*

doyen *n.* старшина́ (*pl.* -ны) *m.*

doze *v.i.* дрема́ть (-млю́, -млешь) *imp.*

dozen *n.* дю́жина; baker's d., чёртова дю́жина.

drab *adj.* бесцве́тный; (*boring*) ску́чный (-чен, -чна́, -чно).

draft *n.* (*sketch*) чернови́к (-а́); (*of document*) прое́кт; (*econ.*) тра́тта; *see also* draught; *v.t.* составля́ть *imp.*, соста́вить *perf.* план, прое́кт (-а́).

drag *v.t.* & *i.* тащи́ть(ся) (-щу́(сь), -щишь(ся)) *imp.*; волочи́ть(ся) (-чу́(сь), -чишь(ся)) *imp.*; *v.t.* (*river etc.*) драги́ровать *imp.*, *perf.*; *n.* (*grapnel*) ко́шка; (*puff*) зати́жка; (*burden*) обу́за; (*brake*) тормозно́й башма́к (-а́); (*aeron.*) лобово́е сопротивле́ние; d.-net, бре́день (-дня) *m.*

dragon *n.* драко́н; d.-fly, стрекоза́ (*pl.* -зы).

dragoon *n.* драгу́н (*gen.pl.* -н (collect.) & -нов).

drain *n.* водосто́к; (*leakage, also fig.*) уте́чка; d.-pipe, водосто́чная труба́ (*pl.* -бы); *v.t.* осуша́ть *imp.*, осуши́ть (-шу́, -шишь) *perf.* **drainage** *n.* сток, канализа́ция; дрена́ж.

drake *n.* се́лезень (-зня) *m.*

dram *n.* глото́к (-тка́).

drama *n.* дра́ма. **dramatic** *adj.* драмати́ческий. **dramatis personae** *n. neut.pl.* де́йствующие ли́ца. **dramatist** *n.* драмату́рг. **dramatize** *v.t.* инсцени́ровать *imp.*, *perf.*; (*fig.*) преувели́чивать *imp.*, преувели́чить *perf.*

drape *v.t.* драпирова́ть *imp.*, за ~ *perf.*; *n.* драпиро́вка. **draper** *n.* торго́вец (-вца) тка́нями. **drapery** *n.* драпиро́вка; (*cloth; collect.*) тка́ни *f.pl.*

drastic *adj.* круто́й (крут, -а́, -о), радика́льный.

drat *interj.* чёрт возьми́! **dratted** *adj.* прокля́тый.

draught *n.* (*drink*) глото́к (-тка́); (*air*) тя́га, сквозня́к (-а́); (*naut.*) оса́дка; *pl.* (*game*) ша́шки *f.pl.*; *see also* draft; *be in a d.*, быть на сквозняке́; d. animals, тя́гло collect.; d. beer, пи́во из бо́чки; d. horse, ломова́я ло́шадь (*pl.* -ди, -де́й, *instr.* -дьми́). **draughtsman** *n.* (*person*) чертёжник; (*counter*) ша́шка. **draughty** *adj.*: it's d. here, здесь ду́ет.

draw n. (action) вытя́гивание; (lottery) лотере́я; (attraction) прима́нка; (drawn game) ничья́; v.t. (pull) тяну́ть (-ну́, -нешь) imp., по~ perf.; таска́ть indet., тащи́ть (-щу́, -щишь) det.; (curtains) задёргивать imp., задёрнуть perf. (занаве́ски); (attract) привлека́ть imp., привле́чь (-еку́, -ечёшь; -ёк, -екла́) perf.; (pull out) выта́скивать imp., вы́тащить perf.; (sword) обнажа́ть imp., обнажи́ть perf.; (lots) броса́ть imp., бро́сить perf. (жре́бий); (water; inspiration) че́рпать imp., черпну́ть perf.; (game) конча́ть imp., ко́нчить perf. (игру́) вничью́; (evoke) вызыва́ть imp., вы́звать (вы́зову, -вешь) perf.; (conclusion) выводи́ть (-ожу́, -о́дишь) imp., вы́вести (-еду, -едешь; -ел) perf. (заключе́ние); (fowl) потроши́ть imp., вы́~ perf.; (diagram) черти́ть (-рчу́, -ртишь) imp., на~ perf.; (picture) рисова́ть imp., на~ perf.; d. aside, отводи́ть (-ожу́, -о́дишь) imp., отвести́ (-еду́, -едёшь; -ёл, -ела́) perf. в сто́рону; d. back, (withdraw) отступа́ть imp., отступи́ть (-плю́, -пишь) perf.; d. in, (involve) вовлека́ть imp., вовле́чь (-еку́, -ечёшь; -ёк, -екла́) perf.; d. up, (document) составля́ть imp., соста́вить perf. **drawback** n. недоста́ток (-тка), поме́ха. **drawbridge** n. подъёмный мост (мо́ста́, loc. -у́; pl. -ы́). **drawer** n. (person) чертёжник, рисова́льщик; (of table etc.) выдвижно́й я́щик; pl. кальсо́ны (-н) pl. **drawing** n. (action) рисова́ние, черче́ние; (object) рису́нок (-нка), чертёж (-а́); d.-board, чертёжная доска́ (acc. -ску; pl. -ски, -со́к, -ска́м); d.-pen, рейсфе́дер; d.-pin, кно́пка; d.-room, гости́ная sb.

drawl n. протя́жное, медли́тельное, произноше́ние; v.i. растя́гивать imp., растяну́ть (-ну́, -нешь) perf. слова́.

dray n. подво́да; d.-horse, ломова́я ло́шадь (pl. -ди, -дей, instr. -дьми́). **drayman** n. ломово́й изво́зчик.

dread n. страх; v.t. боя́ться (бою́сь, бои́шься) imp.+gen. **dreadful** adj. стра́шный (-шен, -шна́, -шно, стра́шны).

dreadnought n. дредно́ут.

dream n. сон (сна); мечта́ (gen.pl. -а́ний); v.i. ви́деть (ви́жу, -дишь) imp., у~ perf. сон; d. of, ви́деть (ви́жу, ви́дишь) imp., у~ perf. во сне́; (fig.) мечта́ть imp. o + prep. **dreamer** n. мечта́тель m., фантазёр.

dreariness n. тоскли́вость. **dreary** adj. тоскли́вый, ску́чный (-чен, -чна́, -чно).

dredge[1] v.t. (river etc.) драги́ровать imp., perf. **dredger**[1] n. землечерпа́лка, дра́га.

dredge[2] v.t. (sprinkle) посыпа́ть imp., посы́пать (-плю, -плешь) perf. **dredger**[2] n. си́течко (pl. -чки, -чек, -чкам).

dreg n.: pl. оса́дки (-ков) pl., отбро́сы (-сов) pl.; d. of society, подо́нки (-ков) pl. о́бщества.

drench v.t. (wet) прома́чивать imp., промочи́ть (-чу́, -чишь) perf.; get drenched, промока́ть imp., промо́кнуть (-к) perf.

dress n. пла́тье (gen.pl. -в), оде́жда; d. circle, бельэта́ж; d. coat, фрак; dressmaker, портни́ха; d. rehearsal, генера́льная репети́ция; v.t. & i. одева́ть(ся) imp., оде́ть(ся) (-е́ну(сь), -е́нешь(ся)) perf.; v.t. (cul.) приправля́ть imp., припра́вить perf.; (med.) перевя́зывать imp., перевяза́ть (-яжу́, -я́жешь) perf.; v.i. (mil.) равня́ться imp. **dresser**[1] n. (theat.) костюме́р, ~ ша.

dresser[2] n. ку́хонный шкаф (loc. -у́; pl. -ы́).

dressing n. (cul.) припра́ва; (med.) перевя́зка; d.-case, несессе́р; d. down, вы́говор; d.-gown, хала́т; d.-room, убо́рная sb.; d.-station, перевя́зочный пункт; d.-table, туале́тный стол (-а́).

dribble v.i. (water) ка́пать imp.; (child) пуска́ть imp., пусти́ть (пущу́, пу́стишь) perf. слю́ни; (sport) вести́ (веду́, -дёшь; -вёл, -а́) imp. мяч. **driblet** n. ка́пелька.

dried adj. сушёный. **drier** n. суши́лка.

drift n. тече́ние; (naut.) дрейф; (aeron.) снос; (inaction) безде́йствие; (purpose) тенде́нция; (meaning) смысл; (snow) сугро́б; (sand) нано́с; v.i. плыть (плыву́, -вёшь; плыл, -а́, -о) imp. по тече́нию; (*naut.*) дрейфова́ть *imp.*; (*snow etc.*) скопля́ться *imp.*, скопи́ться (-ится) *perf.*; *v.t.* (*snow*) наноси́ть (-и́т) *imp.*, нанести́ (-есёт; ёс. -есла́) *perf.*; заноси́ть (-и́т) *imp.*, занести́ (-сёт; -сло́) *perf.* (сне́гом, песко́м) *impers.* + *acc.*

drill[1] *n.* сверло́ (*pl.* -ёрла, дрель, бур; *v.t.* сверли́ть *imp.*, про~ *perf.*

drill[2] *n.* (*agr. machine*) се́ялка.

drill[3] *v.t.* обуча́ть *imp.*, обучи́ть (-чу́, -чишь) *perf.* стро́ю; муштрова́ть *imp.*, вы́~ *perf.*; *v.i.* проходи́ть (-ожу́, -о́дишь) *imp.*, пройти́ (-ойду́, -ойдёшь; -ошёл, -ошла́) *perf.* стро-ову́ю подгото́вку; *n.* строева́я подгото́вка.

drink *n.* питьё, напи́ток (-тка); (*mouthful*) глото́к (-тка́); (*strong*) d., спиртно́й напи́ток (-тка); *soft* d., безалкого́льный напи́ток (-тка); *v.t.* пить (пью, пьёшь; пил, -а́, -о) *imp.*, вы́~ *perf.* (*to excess,* си́льно); (*plants; fig.*) впи́тывать *imp.*, впита́ть *perf.* **drinking** *in comb.*: d.-bout, запо́й; d.-song, засто́льная пе́сня (*gen.pl.* -сен); d.-water, питьева́я вода́ (*acc.* -ду).

drip *n.* (*action*) ка́панье; (*object*) ка́пля (*gen.pl.* -пель); *v.i.* ка́пать *imp.*, ка́пнуть *perf.*; d.-dry, быстросо́хну-щий. **dripping** *n.* (*fat*) жир (-а(у), *loc.* -е & -у́); d. wet, промо́кший наскво́зь.

drive *n.* (*journey*) езда́; (*excursion*) ката́нье, прогу́лка; (*campaign*) похо́д, кампа́ния; (*energy*) эне́ргия; (*tech.*) приво́д; (*driveway*) подъездна́я доро́га; *v.t.* (*urge; chase*) гоня́ть *indet.*, гнать (гоню́, -нишь; гнал, -а́, -о) *det.*; (*vehicle*) води́ть (вожу́, во́дишь) *indet.*, вести́ (веду́, -дёшь; вёл, -а́) *det.*; управля́ть *imp.* + *instr.*; (*convey*) вози́ть (вожу́, во́зишь) *indet.*, везти́ (везу́, -зёшь; вёз, -ла́) *det.*, по~ *perf.*; *v.i.* (*travel*) е́здить *indet.*, е́хать (е́ду, е́дешь) *det.*, по~ *perf.*; *v.t.* (*compel*) заставля́ть *imp.*, заста́вить *perf.*; (*nail etc.*) вбива́ть *imp.*, вбить (вобью́, -ьёшь) *perf.* (into, в + *acc.*); (*machine*) приводи́ть (-ожу́, -о́дишь) *imp.*, привести́ (-еду́, -едёшь; -ёл, -ела́) *perf.* в движе́ние (*by steam etc.*, + *instr.*); d. away, *v.t.* прогоня́ть *imp.*,

прогна́ть (прогоню́, -нишь; прогна́л, -а́, -о) *perf.*; *v.i.* уезжа́ть *imp.*, уе́хать (-е́ду, -е́дешь) *perf.*; d. out, *v.t.* (*knock out*) выбива́ть *imp.*, вы́бить (вы́бью, -ьешь) *perf.*; (*expel*) выгоня́ть *imp.*, вы́гнать (вы́гоню, -нишь) *perf.*; d. up, подъезжа́ть *imp.*, подъе́хать (-е́ду, -е́дешь) *perf.* (to, к + *dat.*).

drivel *n.* чепуха́; *v.i.* поро́ть (-рю́, -решь) *imp.* чепуху́.

driver *n.* (*of vehicle*) води́тель *m.*, шофёр. **driving** *n.* вожде́ние; ката́ние; *adj.* дви́жущий; d.-belt, приводно́й ре-ме́нь (-мня́) *m.*; d. force, дви́жущая си́ла; d. licence, води́тельские права́ *neut.pl.*; d.-wheel, веду́щее колесо́ (*pl.* -ёса).

drizzle *n.* ме́лкий дождь (-дя́) *m.*; *v.i.* мороси́ть *imp.*

droll *adj.* смешно́й (-шо́н, -шна́), заба́вный. **drollery** *n.* шу́тка.

dromedary *n.* дромаде́р.

drone *n.* (*bee*) тру́тень (-тня) *m.*; (*buzz*) жужжа́ние; *v.i.* (*buzz*) жужжа́ть (-жжу́, -жжи́шь) *imp.*; (*mutter*) бубни́ть *imp.*

drool *v.i.* пуска́ть *imp.*, пусти́ть (пущу́, пу́стишь) *perf.* слю́ни.

droop *v.i.* ни́кнуть (ник) *imp.*, по~, с~ *perf.*

drop *n.* (*of liquid*) ка́пля (*gen.pl.* -пель); (*pendant*) висю́лька; (*sweet*) ледене́ц (-нца́); (*fall*) паде́ние, пониже́ние; *v.t.* & *i.* ка́пать *imp.*, ка́пнуть *perf.*; (*price*) снижа́ть(ся) *imp.*, сни́зить(ся) *perf.*; *v.i.* (*fall*) па́дать *imp.*, упа́сть (-аду́, -адёшь; -а́л) *perf.*; *v.t.* роня́ть *imp.*, урони́ть (-ню́, -нишь) *perf.*; (*abandon*) броса́ть *imp.*, бро́сить *perf.*; (*eyes*) опуска́ть *imp.*, опусти́ть (-ущу́, -у́стишь) *perf.*; d. behind, отстава́ть (-таю́, -таёшь) *imp.*, отста́ть (-а́ну, -а́нешь) *perf.*; d. in, заходи́ть (-ожу́, -о́дишь) *imp.*, зайти́ (зайду́, -дёшь; зашёл, -шла́) *perf.* (on, к + *dat.*); d. off, (*fall asleep*) засыпа́ть *imp.*, засну́ть *perf.*; d. out, выбыва́ть *imp.*, вы́быть (-буду, -будешь) *perf.* (of, из + *gen.*); d.-out, вы́бывший *sb.* **droplet** *n.* ка́пелька. **dropper** *n.* пипе́тка. **droppings** *n.* помёт, наво́з (-а(у)).

dropsy *n.* водя́нка.

dross n. шлак; (*refuse*) отбро́сы (-сов) pl.

drought n. за́суха; **d.-resistant,** засухоусто́йчивый.

drove n. ста́до (pl. -да́), гурт (-а́). **drover** n. гуртовщи́к (-а́).

drown v.t. топи́ть (-плю́, -пишь) imp., y~ perf.; (*sound*) заглуша́ть imp., заглуши́ть perf.; v.i. тону́ть (-ну́, -нешь) imp., y~ perf.

drowse v.i. дрема́ть (-млю́, -млешь) imp. **drowsiness** n. сонли́вость, дремо́та. **drowsy** adj. сонли́вый, дре́млющий.

drub v.t. поро́ть (-рю́, -решь) imp. вы́~ perf.

drudge n. работя́га. **drudgery** n. тяжёлая, ну́дная, рабо́та.

drug n. медикаме́нт; нарко́тик; **d. addict,** наркома́н, ~ка; v.t. дава́ть (даю́, даёшь) imp., дать (дам, дашь, даст, дади́м; дал, -а́, да́ло, -и) perf. нарко́тик + dat.

druid n. дру́ид.

drum n. бараба́н; v.i. бить (бью, бьёшь) imp. в бараба́н; бараба́нить imp. **drummer** n. бараба́нщик.

drunk adj. пья́ный (пьян, -а́, -о). **drunkard** n. пья́ница m. & f. **drunken** adj. пья́ный. **drunkenness** n. пья́нство.

dry adj. сухо́й (сух, -а́, -о); **d.-cleaning,** химчи́стка; **d. land,** су́ша; v.t. суши́ть (-шу́, -шишь) imp., вы́~ perf.; (*wipe dry*) вытира́ть imp., вы́тереть (-тру, -трешь; -тер) perf.; v.i. со́хнуть (сох) imp., вы́~, про~ perf. **drying** n. су́шка; adj. суши́льный. **dryness** n. су́хость.

dual adj. двойно́й, дво́йственный (-ен, -енна); **d.-purpose,** двойно́го назначе́ния. **duality** n. дво́йственность, раздво́енность.

dub[1] v.t. (*nickname*) дава́ть (даю́, даёшь) imp., дать (дам, дашь, дади́м; дал, -а́, да́ло, -и) про́звище + dat.

dub[2] v.t. (*cin.*) дубли́ровать imp., perf. **dubbing** n. дубля́ж.

dubious adj. сомни́тельный.

ducal adj. ге́рцогский. **duchess** n. герцоги́ня. **duchy** n. ге́рцогство.

duck[1] n. (*bird*) у́тка.

duck[2] v.t. окуна́ть imp., окуну́ть perf.; v.i. увёртываться imp., уверну́ться perf. от уда́ра.

duck[3] n. (*cloth*) паруси́на.

duckling n. утёнок (-нка; pl. утя́та, -т).

duct n. прохо́д, трубопрово́д; (*anat.*) прото́к.

ductile adj. (*metal*) ко́вкий (-вок, -вка́, -вко); (*clay*) пласти́чный. **ductility** n. ко́вкость, пласти́чность.

dud n. (*forgery*) подде́лка; (*shell*) неразорва́вшийся снаря́д; adj. подде́льный; (*worthless*) него́дный (-ден, -дна́, -дно).

dudgeon n. оби́да, возмуще́ние; **in high d.,** в глубо́ком возмуще́нии.

due n. до́лжное sb.; pl. сбо́ры m.pl.; взно́сы m.pl.; adj. до́лжный, надлежа́щий; predic. до́лжен (-жна́); in d. course, со вре́менем; adv. то́чно, пря́мо; **d. to,** благодаря́ + dat., всле́дствие + gen.

duel n. дуэ́ль, поеди́нок (-нка).

duet n. дуэ́т.

duffer n. дура́к (-а́), недотёпа m. & f.

dug-out n. (*boat*) челно́к (-а́); (*mil.*) блинда́ж.

duke n. ге́рцог; **Grand D.,** вели́кий князь (pl. -зья́, -зе́й) m. **dukedom** n. ге́рцогство.

dulcet adj. сла́дкий (-док, -дка́, -дко), не́жный (-жен, -жна́, -жно, не́жны).

dulcimer n. цимба́лы (-л) pl.

dull adj. тупо́й (туп, -а́, -о, ту́пы́); (*tedious*) ску́чный (-чен, -чна́, -чно); (*colour*) тусќлый (-л, -ла́, -ло), ма́товый; (*weather*) па́смурный; v.t. притупля́ть imp., притупи́ть (-плю́, -пишь) perf. **dullard** n. тупи́ца m. & f. **dullness** n. ту́пость; ску́чность.

duly adv. надлежа́щим о́бразом, (*punctually*) в до́лжное вре́мя, своевре́менно.

dumb adj. немо́й (нем, -а́, -о); (*taciturn*) молчали́вый; **deaf and d.,** глухонемо́й; **d.-bell,** ганте́ль. **dumbfound** v.t. ошеломля́ть imp., ошеломи́ть perf.

dummy n. маке́т; (*tailor's*) манеке́н; (*cards*) болва́н; (*baby's*) со́ска(-пус-

ты́шка); *adj.* ненастоя́щий, фальши́-
вый.

dump *n.* сва́лка; *v.t.* сва́ливать *imp.*,
свали́ть (-лю́, -лишь) *perf.* **dumping** *n.*
(*econ.*) де́мпинг, бро́совый э́кспорт.

dumpling *n.* клёцка.

dumpy *adj.* то́лстый (толст, -а́, -о,
то́лсты́), корена́стый.

dun *adj.* серова́то-кори́чневый.

dunce *n.* болва́н, тупи́ца *m. & f.*

dune *n.* дю́на.

dung *n.* помёт, наво́з (-а(у)).

dungarees *n.* рабо́чие брю́ки (-к) *pl.*
на почма́ках.

dungeon *n.* темни́ца.

dunk *v.t.* мака́ть *imp.*, макну́ть *perf.*

dupe *v.t.* обма́нывать *imp.*, обману́ть
(-ну́, -нешь) *perf.*; *n.* же́ртва обма́на,
простофи́ля *m. & f.*

duplicate *n.* дублика́т, ко́пия; *in. d.*, в
двух экземпля́рах; *adj.* двойно́й
(*identical*) иденти́чный; *v.t.*
дубли́ровать *imp.*; снима́ть *imp.*,
снять (сниму́, -мешь; снял, -а́, -о)
perf. ко́пию с + *gen.* **duplicator** *n.*
копирова́льный аппара́т. **duplicity** *n.*
двули́чность.

durability *n.* про́чность. **durable** *adj.*
про́чный (-чен, -чна́, -чно, про́чны).
duration *n.* продолжи́тельность; срок
(-а(у)).

duress *n.* принужде́ние; *under d.*, под
давле́нием.

during *prep.* в тече́ние + *gen.*, во вре́мя
+ *gen.*

dusk *n.* су́мерки (-рек) *pl.*, су́мрак.
dusky *adj.* су́меречный; тёмный
(-мен, -мна́); (*complexion*) сму́глый
(смугл, -а́, -о).

dust *n.* пыль (*loc.* -ли́); *dustbin,* му́сор-
ный я́щик; *d.-jacket,* суперобло́жка;
dustman, му́сорщик; *d.-pan,* сово́к
(-вка́), *v.t.* (*clean*) стира́ть *imp.*,
стере́ть (сотру́, -рёшь; стёр) *perf.*
пыль с + *gen.*; (*sprinkle*) посыпа́ть
imp., посыпа́ть (-плю -плешь) *perf.* +
instr. **duster** *n.* пы́льная тря́пка.

dusting *n.* вытира́ние, сма́хивание,
пы́ли. **dusty** *adj.* пы́льный (-лен
-льна́, -льно), запылённый (-ён, -ена́)

Dutch *adj.* голла́ндский; *D. courage,*
хра́брость во хмелю́; *D. treat,* скла́д-
чина; *n.: the D.,* голла́ндцы *m.pl.*
Dutchman *n.* голла́ндец (-дца)

dutiable *adj.* подлежа́щий обложе́нию
по́шлиной. **dutiful** *adj.* послу́шный.
duty *n.* (*obligation*) долг (-а(у), *loc.* -ý;
pl. -и́), обя́занность; (*office*) дежу́р-
ство; (*tax*) по́шлина; *on d.,* дежу́рный,
be on d., дежу́рить *imp.*; *do one's d.,*
исполня́ть *imp.*, испо́лнить *perf.* свой
долг; *d.-free,* беспо́шлинный; *d.-paid,*
опла́ченный по́шлиной.

dwarf *n.* ка́рлик, -ица; *adj.* ка́рликовый;
v.t. (*stunt*) остана́вливать *imp.*, остано-
ви́ть (-влю́, -вишь) *perf.* рост, разви-
тие, + *gen.*; (*tower above*) возвы-
ша́ться *imp.*, возвы́ситься *perf.* над +
instr.

dwell *v.i.* обита́ть *imp.*; *d. upon,* остa-
на́вливаться *imp.* на + *prep.* **dweller** *n.*
жи́тель *m.*; ~ница. **dwelling** *n.* (*d.
place*) местожи́тельство; *d.-house,*
жило́й дом (*pl.* -а́); *perf.*

dwindle *v.i.* убыва́ть *imp.*, убы́ть (убу́ду,
-дешь; убыл, -а́, -о) *perf.*

dye *n.* краси́тель *m.*, кра́ска; *d.-works,*
краси́льня (*gen.pl.* -лен) *v.t.* окра́ши-
вать *imp.*, окра́сить *perf.*; *dyed-in-the-
wool,* (*fig.*) закоренéлый. **dyeing** *n.*
кра́шение. **dyer** *n.* краси́льщик.

dying *adj.* умира́ющий; (*at time of
death*) предсме́ртный; *n.* умира́ние,
угаса́ние; *d.-out,* вымира́ние.

dynamic *adj.* динами́ческий. **dynamics**
n. дина́мика.

dynamite *n.* динами́т; *v.t.* взрыва́ть,
imp., взорва́ть (-ву́, -вёшь; взорва́л,
-а́, -о) *perf.* динами́том.

dynamo *n.* дина́мо-маши́на.

dynastic *adj.* династи́ческий; *n.* дина́-
стия.

dysentery *n.* дизентери́я.

dyspepsia *n.* диспепси́я. **dyspeptic** *n., adj.*
страда́ющий (*sb.*) диспепси́ей.

E

E *n.* (*mus.*) ми *neut.indecl.*

each *adj., pron.* ка́ждый; e. other, друг дру́га (dat. -гу, etc.).

eager *adj.* стремя́щийся (for, к + dat.); (*impatient*) нетерпели́вый. **eagerness** *n.* пыл -a(-у), loc. -у́), рве́ние.

eagle *n.* орёл (орла́), орли́ца; e.-eyed, зо́ркий (-рок, -рка́, -рко); e.-owl, фи́лин. **eaglet** *n.* орлёнок (-нка; pl. орля́та, -т).

ear¹ *n.* (*corn*) ко́лос (pl. -о́сья, -о́сьев); v.i. колоси́ться *imp.*, вы́~ *perf.*

ear² *n.* (*organ*) у́хо (pl. у́ши, уше́й); (*sense*) слух; by e., по слу́ху; to be all ears, слу́шать *imp.* во все у́ши; *ear-ache*, боль в у́хе; e.-drum, бараба́нная перепо́нка; *earless*, безу́хий; e.-lobe, мо́чка; *earmark*, клеймо́ (pl. -ма); клейми́ть *imp.*, за~ *perf.*; (*assign*) предназнача́ть *imp.*, предназна́чить *perf.*; *earphone*, нау́шник; e.-ring, серьга́ (pl. -рьги, -рёг, -рьга́м); *ear-shot*: within e., в преде́лах слы́шимости; out of e., вне преде́лов слы́шимости; e.-splitting, оглуши́тельный.

earl *n.* граф. **earldom** *n.* гра́фство, ти́тул гра́фа.

early *adj.* ра́нний; (*initial*) нача́льный; *adv.* ра́но.

earn *v.t.* зараба́тывать *imp.*, зарабо́тать *perf.*; (*deserve*) заслу́живать *imp.*, заслужи́ть (-жу́, -жишь) *perf* **earnings** *n.* за́работок (-тка).

earnest *adj.* серьёзный; *n.*: in e., всерьёз.

earth *n.* земля́ (acc. -лю); (*soil*) по́чва; (*fox's*) нора́ (pl. -ры); (*electr.*) заземле́ние; v.t. заземля́ть *imp.*, заземли́ть *perf.*; e. up, окучивать *imp.*, окучить *perf.* **earthen** *adj.* земляно́й. **earthenware** *n.* гли́няная посу́да (*collect.*); *adj.* гли́няный. **earthly** *adj.* земно́й, жите́йский. **earth-moving** *adj.* землеро́йный. **earthquake** *n.* землетрясе́ние. **earthwork** *n.* земляно́е укрепле́ние. **earthworm** *n.* земляно́й червь (-вя́; pl. -ви, -ве́й) *m.* **earthy** *adj.* земляно́й, земли́стый; (*coarse*) гру́бый (груб, -а́, -о).

earwig *n.* уховёртка.

ease *n.* (*facility*) лёгкость; (*unconstraint*) непринуждённость; at e., *interj.* во́льно! with e., легко́, без труда́; v.t. облегча́ть *imp.*, облегчи́ть *perf.*

easel *n.* мольбе́рт.

east *n.* восто́к; (*naut.*) ост; *adj.* восто́чный; о́стовый. **eastern** *adj.* восто́чный. **eastwards** *adv.* на восто́к, к восто́ку.

Easter *n.* па́сха.

easy *adj.* лёгкий (-гок, -гка́, -гко, лёг-ки́); (*unconstrained*) непринуждённый (-ён, -ённа); e.-going, доброду́шный.

eat *v.t.* есть (ем, ешь, ест, еди́м; ел) *imp.*, съ~ *perf.*; ку́шать *imp.*, по~, с~ *perf.*; e. away, разъеда́ть *imp.*, разъе́сть (-е́ст, -е́л) *perf.*; e. into, въеда́ться *imp.*, въе́сться (-е́стся, -е́лся) *perf.* в+acc.; e. up, доеда́ть *imp.*, дое́сть (-е́м, -е́шь, -е́ст, -еди́м; -е́л) *perf.* **eatable** *adj.* съедо́бный.

eau-de-Cologne *n.* одеколо́н.

eaves *n.* стреха́ (pl. -и). **eavesdrop** *v.t.* подслу́шивать *imp.*, подслу́шать *perf.*

ebb *n.* (*tide*) отли́в; (*fig.*) упа́док (-дка).

ebony *n.* чёрное де́рево.

ebullience *n.* кипу́честь. **ebullient** *adj.* кипу́чий.

eccentric *n.* чуда́к (-а́), -а́чка; (*tech.*) эксце́нтрик; *adj.* эксцентри́чный. **eccentricity** *n.* эксцентри́чность, чуда́чество.

ecclesiastic *n.* духо́вное лицо́ (pl. -ца). **ecclesiastical** *adj.* духо́вный, церко́вный.

echelon *n.* эшело́н; v.t. эшелони́ровать *imp.*, *perf.*

echo *n.* э́хо; (*imitation*) о́тклик; e.-sounder, эхоло́т; v.i. (*resound*) оглаша́ться *imp.*, огласи́ться *perf* э́хом; v.t. & i. (*repeat*) повторя́ть(ся) *imp.*, повтори́ть(ся) *perf.*

eclipse *n.* затме́ние; (*fig.*) упа́док (-дка); v.t. затмева́ть *imp.*, затми́ть *perf.*

economic *adj.* экономи́ческий, хозя́йственный; (*profitable*) рента́бельный.

economical *adj.* эконо́мный, бережли́вый. **economist** *n.* экономи́ст. **economize** *v.t. & i.* эконо́мить *imp.*, с ~ *perf.*

economy *n.* хозя́йство, эконо́мика; (*saving*) эконо́мия, сбереже́ние.

ecstasy *n.* экста́з, восхище́ние. **ecstatic** *adj.* исступлённый (-ён, -ённа).

eddy *n.* (*water*) водоворо́т; (*wind*) вихрь *m.*; *v.i.* (*water*) крути́ться (-ится) *imp.*; (*wind*) клуби́ться *imp.*

edelweiss *n.* эдельве́йс.

edge *n.* край (*loc.* -а́е & -аю́; *pl.* -ая́), кро́мка; (*blade*) ле́звие; *on e.*, (*excited*) взволно́ванный (-ан); (*irritable*) раздражённый (-ён, -ена́); *v.t.* (*sharpen*) точи́ть (-чу́, -чишь) *imp.*, на ~ *perf.*; (*border*) окаймля́ть *imp.*, окайми́ть *perf.*; *v.i.* пробира́ться *imp.*, пробра́ться (-беру́сь, -берёшься; -а́лся, -ала́сь, -а́ло́сь) *perf.* **edging** *n.* кайма́. **edgy** *adj.* раздражи́тельный.

edible *adj.* съедо́бный.

edict *n.* ука́з.

edification *n.* назида́ние. **edifice** *n.* зда́ние, сооруже́ние. **edify** *v.t.* наставля́ть *imp.*, наста́вить *perf.* **edifying** *adj.* назида́тельный.

edit *v.t.* редакти́ровать *imp.*, от ~ *perf.*; (*cin.*) монти́ровать *imp.*, с ~ *perf.* **edition** *n.* изда́ние; (*number of copies*) тира́ж (-а́). **editor** *n.* реда́ктор. **editorial** *n.* передова́я статья́; *adj.* реда́кторский, редакцио́нный.

educate *v.t.* воспи́тывать *imp.*, воспита́ть *perf.* **educated** *adj.* образо́ванный (-ан, -анна). **education** *n.* образова́ние, воспита́ние; (*instruction*) обуче́ние. **educational** *adj.* образова́тельный, воспита́тельный; уче́бный.

eel *n.* у́горь (угря́) *m.*

eerie *adj.* (*gloomy*) мра́чный (-чен, -чна́, -чно); (*strange*) стра́нный (-нен, -нна́, -нно).

efface *v.t.* изгла́живать *imp.*, изгла́дить *perf.*; *e. oneself*, стушёвываться *imp.*, стушева́ться (-шу́юсь, -шу́ешься) *perf.*

effect *n.* (*result*) сле́дствие; (*efficacy*) де́йствие; (*impression*; *theat.*, *cin.*) эффе́кт; *pl.* иму́щество, (*personal*)

ли́чные ве́щи (-ще́й) *f.pl.*; *in e.*, факти́чески; *bring into e.*, осуществля́ть *imp.*, осуществи́ть *perf.*; *take e.*, вступа́ть *imp.*, вступи́ть (-ит) *perf.* в си́лу; *v.t.* производи́ть (-ожу́, -о́дишь) *imp.*, произвести́ (-еду́, -едёшь; -ёл, -ела́) *perf.* **effective** *adj.* де́йственный (-ен, -енна), эффекти́вный; (*striking*) эффе́ктный; (*actual*) факти́ческий. **effectiveness** *n.* де́йственность, эффекти́вность. **effectual** *adj.* де́йственный (-ен, -енна).

effeminate *adj.* изне́женный (-ен, -енна).

effervesce *v.i.* пе́ниться *imp.* **effervescent** *adj.* шипу́чий.

efficacious *adj.* де́йственный (-ен, -енна), эффекти́вный. **efficacy** *n.* де́йственность, эффекти́вность. **efficiency** *n.* де́йственность, эффекти́вность; (*of person*) уме́ние; (*mech.*) коэффицие́нт поле́зного де́йствия. **efficient** *adj.* де́йственный (-ен, -енна), эффекти́вный; (*person*) уме́лый.

effigy *n.* изображе́ние.

effort *n.* (*exertion*) уси́лие; (*attempt*) попы́тка.

effrontery *n.* на́глость.

egg[1] *n.* яйцо́ (*pl.* я́йца, яи́ц, я́йцам); *attrib.* яи́чный; *e.-beater*, взбива́лка; *e.-cup*, рю́мка для яйца́; *e.-plant*, баклажа́н; *eggshell*, яи́чная скорлупа́ (*pl.* -пы).

egg[2] *v.t.*: *e. on*, подстрека́ть *imp.*, подстрекну́ть *perf.*

egret *n.* бе́лая ца́пля (*gen. pl.* -пель).

Egyptian *n.* египтя́нин (*pl.* -я́не, -я́н), -я́нка (*gen. pl.* -я́нок); *adj.* еги́петский.

eider *n.* (*duck*) га́га; (*e.-down*) гага́чий пух (*loc.* -у́). **eiderdown** *n.* (*quilt*) пухо́вое одея́ло.

eight *adj., n.* во́семь; (*collect.*; *8 pairs*) во́сьмеро (-ры́х); (*cards*; *boat*; *number 8*) восьмёрка; (*time*) во́семь (часо́в); (*age*) во́семь лет. **eighteen** *adj., n.* восемна́дцать (-ти, -тью); (*age*) восемна́дцать лет. **eighteenth** *adj., n.* восемна́дцатый; (*date*) восемна́дцатое (число́). **eighth** *adj., n.* восьмо́й; (*fraction*) восьма́я (часть (*pl.* -ти, -те́й)); (*date*) восьмо́е (число́). **eightieth** *adj., n.* восьмидеся́тый. **eighty** *adj., n.* во́семьдесят

(-сьми́десяти, -сьмью́десятью); (*age*) во́семьдесят лет; *pl.* (*decade*) восьмидеся́тые го́ды (-до́в) *m.pl.*

either *adj.*, *pron.* (*one of two*) оди́н из двух, тот и́ли друго́й; (*each of two*) и тот, и друго́й; о́ба; любо́й; *adv.*, *conj.*: е. . . . . or, и́ли...и́ли, ли́бо...ли́бо.

eject *v.t.* изверга́ть *imp.*, изве́ргнуть (-г(ну)л, -гла) *perf.* **ejection** *n.* изверже́ние; *e. seat*, катапульти́руемое кре́сло (*gen.pl.* -сел).

eke *v.t.*: *e. out a living*, перебива́ться *imp.*, переби́ться (-бью́сь, -бьёшься) *perf.* ко́е-ка́к.

elaborate *adj.* (*complicated*) сло́жный (-жен, -жна́, -жно); (*detailed*) подро́бный; *v.t.* разраба́тывать *imp.*, разрабо́тать *perf.*; уточня́ть *imp.*, уточни́ть *perf.* **elaboration** *n.* разрабо́тка, уточне́ние.

elapse *v.i.* проходи́ть (-о́дит) *imp.*, пройти́ (пройдёт; прошёл, -шла́) *perf.*; истека́ть *imp.*, исте́чь (-ечёт; -ёк, -екла́) *perf.*

elastic *n.* рези́нка; *adj.* эласти́чный, упру́гий. **elasticity** *n.* эласти́чность, упру́гость.

elate *v.t.* возбужда́ть *imp.*, возбуди́ть *perf.* **elation** *n.* восто́рг.

elbow *n.* ло́коть (-ктя; *pl.* -кти, -ктёй) *m.*; *v.t.* толка́ть *imp.*, толкну́ть *perf.* ло́ктем, -тя́ми; *e.* (*one's way*) *through*, прота́лкиваться *imp.*, протолкну́ться *perf.* че́рез + *acc.*

elder[1] *n.* (*tree*) бузина́; *e.-berry*, я́года бузины́.

elder[2] *n.* (*person*) ста́рец (-рца); *pl.* ста́ршие *sb.*; *adj.* ста́рший. **elderly** *adj.* пожило́й. **eldest** *adj.* ста́рший.

elect *adj.* и́збранный; *v.t.* выбира́ть *imp.*, вы́брать (вы́беру, -решь) *perf.*; избира́ть *imp.*, избра́ть (изберу́, -рёшь; избра́л, -а́, -о) *perf.* **election** *n.* вы́боры *m.pl.*, избра́ние; *adj.* избира́тельный. **elective** *adj.* вы́борный. **elector** *n.* избира́тель *m.* **electoral** *adj.* избира́тельный, вы́борный. **electorate** *n.* избира́тели *m.pl.*

electric(al) *adj.* электри́ческий; *e. light*, электри́чество; *e. shock*, уда́р электри́ческим то́ком. **electrician** *n.*

эле́ктрик, электромонтёр. **electricity** *n.* электри́чество. **electrify** *v.t.* (*convert to electricity*) электрифици́ровать *imp.*, *perf.*; (*charge with electricity*; *fig.*) электризова́ть *imp.*, на~ *perf.* **electrode** *n.* электро́д. **electron** *n.* электро́н. **electronic** *adj.* электро́нный. **electronics** *n.* электро́ника.

electro- *in comb.* электро-. **electrocute** *v.t.* убива́ть *imp.*, уби́ть (убью́, -ьёшь) *perf.* электри́ческим то́ком; (*execute*) казни́ть *imp.*, *perf.* на электри́ческом сту́ле. **electrolysis** *n.* электро́лиз. **electrolyte** *n.* электроли́т. **electromagnetic** *adj.* электромагни́тный. **electrotype** *n.* (*print.*) гальва́но *neut.indecl.*

elegance *n.* элега́нтность, изя́щество. **elegant** *adj.* элега́нтный, изя́щный. **elegiac** *adj.* элеги́ческий. **elegy** *n.* эле́гия.

element *n.* элеме́нт; (*4 e.s*) стихи́я; *pl.* (*rudiments*) нача́тки (-ков) *pl.*; *be in one's e.*, быть в свое́й стихи́и. **elemental** *adj.* стихи́йный. **elementary** *adj.* (*rudimentary*) элемента́рный; (*school etc.*) нача́льный.

elephant *n.* слон (-а́), ~ и́ха. **elephantine** *adj.* слоно́вый; (*clumsy*) тяжелове́сный, неуклю́жий.

elevate *v.t.* поднима́ть *imp.*, подня́ть (подниму́, -мешь; по́днял, -а́, -о) *perf.*; (*in rank*) возводи́ть (-ожу́, -о́дишь) *imp.*, возвести́ (-еду́, -едёшь; -ёл, -ела́) *perf.* **elevation** *n.* подня́тие, возведе́ние; (*height*) высота́; (*angle*) у́гол (угла́) возвыше́ния; (*drawing*) вертика́льная прое́кция. **elevator** *n.* подъёмник; (*for grain*) элева́тор.

eleven *adj.*, *n.* оди́ннадцать (-ти, -тью); (*time*) оди́ннадцать (часо́в); (*age*) оди́ннадцать лет; (*team*) кома́нда (из оди́ннадцати челове́к). **eleventh** *adj.*, *n.* оди́ннадцатый; (*date*) оди́ннадцатое (число́); *at the e. hour*, в после́днюю мину́ту.

elf *n.* эльф.

elicit *v.t.* извлека́ть *imp.*, извле́чь (-еку́, -ечёшь; -ёк, -екла́) *perf.* (*from*, из + *gen.*); (*evoke*) вызыва́ть *imp.*, вы́звать (вы́зову, -вешь) *perf.*

eligibility n. пра́во на избра́ние. **eligible** adj. могу́щий, име́ющий пра́во, быть и́збранным.

eliminate v.t. (exclude) устраня́ть imp., устрани́ть perf.; (remove) уничтожа́ть imp., уничто́жить perf. **elimination** n. устране́ние; уничтоже́ние.

élite n. эли́та; adj. эли́тный.

elk n. лось (pl. -си, -се́й) m.

ellipse n. э́ллипс. **ellipsis** n. э́ллипсис. **elliptic(al)** adj. эллипти́ческий.

elm n. вяз.

elocution n. ора́торское иску́сство.

elongate v.t. удлиня́ть imp., удлини́ть perf.

elope v.i. сбега́ть imp., сбежа́ть (-егу́, -ежи́шь) perf. **elopement** n. (та́йный) побе́г.

eloquence n. красноре́чие. **eloquent** adj. красноречи́вый, вырази́тельный.

else adv. (besides) ещё; (instead) друго́й; (with neg.) бо́льше; nobody e., никто́ бо́льше; or e., ина́че; a (не) то; и́ли же; somebody e., кто́-нибудь друго́й; something e.? ещё что́-нибудь? **elsewhere** adv. (place) в друго́м ме́сте; (direction) в друго́е ме́сто.

elucidate v.t. по-, разъ-, ясня́ть imp., по-, разъ-, ясни́ть perf. **elucidation** n. по-, разъ-, ясне́ние.

elude v.t. избега́ть imp. + gen., уклоня́ться imp., уклони́ться (-ню́сь, -ни́шься) perf. от + gen. **elusive** adj. неулови́мый.

emaciate v.t. истоща́ть imp., истощи́ть perf. **emaciation** n. истоще́ние.

emanate v.i. исходи́ть (-ит) imp. (from, из, от, + gen.); (light) излуча́ться imp., излучи́ться perf. **emanation** n. излуче́ние, эмана́ция.

emancipate v.t. освобожда́ть imp., освободи́ть perf.; эмансипи́ровать imp., perf. **emancipation** n. освобожде́ние, эмансипа́ция.

emasculate v.t. кастри́ровать imp., perf.; (fig.) выхола́щивать imp., вы́холостить perf. **emasculation** n. выхола́щивание.

embalm v.t. бальзами́ровать imp., на- perf. **embalmer** n. бальзами́ровщик. **embalmment** n. бальзами́ро́вка.

embankment n. (river) да́мба, на́бережная sb.; (rly.) на́сыпь.

embargo n. эмба́рго neut.indecl.; v.t. накла́дывать imp., наложи́ть (-жу́, -жишь) perf. эмба́рго на + acc.

embark v.t. грузи́ть (-ужу́, -узи́шь) imp., по ~ perf. на корабль; v.i. сади́ться imp., сесть (ся́ду, -дешь; сел) perf. на корабль; e. upon, предпринима́ть imp., предприня́ть (-иму́, -и́мешь; предпри́нял, -а́, -о) perf. **embarkation** n. поса́дка (на корабль).

embarrass v.t. смуща́ть imp., смути́ть (-ущу́, -ути́шь) perf.; (impede) затрудня́ть imp., затрудни́ть perf.; стесня́ть imp., стесни́ть perf. **embarrassing** adj. неудо́бный. **embarrassment** n. смуще́ние, замеша́тельство.

embassy n. посо́льство.

embed v.t. вставля́ть imp., вста́вить perf.; вде́лывать imp., вде́лать perf.

embellish v.t. (adorn) украша́ть imp., укра́сить perf.; (story) прикраши́вать imp., прикраси́ть perf. **embellishment** n. украше́ние; преувеличе́ние.

embers n. горя́чая зола́, тле́ющие угольки́ m.pl.

embezzle v.t. растра́чивать imp., растра́тить perf. **embezzlement** n. растра́та. **embezzler** n. растра́тчик.

embitter v.t. ожесточа́ть imp., ожесточи́ть perf.

emblem n. эмбле́ма, си́мвол.

embodiment n. воплоще́ние, олицетворе́ние. **embody** v.t. воплоща́ть imp., воплоти́ть (-ощу́, -оти́шь) perf.; олицетворя́ть imp., олицетвори́ть perf.

emboss v.t. чека́нить imp., вы́-, от ~ perf. **embossed** adj. чека́нный (-нен, -нна).

embrace n. объя́тие; v.i. обнима́ться imp., обня́ться (обни́мемся, -етесь; -ня́лся, -няла́сь) perf.; v.t. обнима́ть imp., обня́ть (обниму́, -мешь; о́бнял, -а́, -о) perf.; (accept) принима́ть imp., приня́ть (приму́, -мешь; при́нял, -а́, -о) perf.; (comprise) охва́тывать imp., охвати́ть (-ачу́, -а́тишь) perf.

embrasure n. амбразу́ра.

embrocation n. жи́дкая мазь.

embroider *v.t.* (*cloth*) вышива́ть *imp.*, вы́шить (вы́шью, -ешь) *perf.*; (*story*) прикра́шивать *imp.*, прикра́сить *perf.* **embroidery** *n.* вышива́ние, вы́шивка; преувеличе́ние; e. *frame*, пя́льцы (-лец) *pl.*

embryo *n.* заро́дыш, эмбрио́н. **embryonic** *adj.* заро́дышевый, эмбриона́льный; (*fig.*) элемента́рный.

emend *v.t.* исправля́ть *imp.*, испра́вить *perf.* **emendation** *n.* исправле́ние.

emerald *n.* изумру́д; *adj.* изумру́дный.

emerge *v.i.* появля́ться *imp.*, появи́ться (-влю́сь, -вишься) *perf.* **emergence** *n.* появле́ние. **emergency** *n.* непредви́денный слу́чай; *in case of* e., в слу́чае кра́йней необходи́мости; *state of* e., чрезвыча́йное положе́ние; e. *brake*, экстренный то́рмоз (*pl.* -а́); e. *exit*, запасный вы́ход; e. *landing*, вы́нужденная поса́дка; e. *powers*, чрезвыча́йные полномо́чия *neut.pl.* **emergent** *adj.* появля́ющийся; (*nation*) неда́вно получи́вший незави́симость.

emeritus *adj.*: e. *professor*, заслу́женный профе́ссор (*pl.* -а́) в отста́вке.

emery *n.* нажда́к (-а́); e. *paper*, нажда́чная бума́га.

emetic *adj.* рво́тный; *n.* рво́тное *sb.*

emigrant *n.* эмигра́нт, ~ ка. **emigrate** *v.i.* эмигри́ровать *imp.* & *perf.* **emigration** *n.* эмигра́ция. **émigré** *n.* эмигра́нт; *adj.* эмигра́нтский.

eminence *n.* высота́, возвы́шенность; (*title*) высокопреосвяще́нство. **eminent** *adj.* выдаю́щийся. **eminently** *adv.* чрезвыча́йно.

emission *n.* испуска́ние, излуче́ние. **emit** *v.t.* испуска́ть *imp.*, испусти́ть (-ущу́, -у́стишь) *perf.*; (*light*) излуча́ть *imp.*, излучи́ть *perf.*; (*sound*) издава́ть (-даю́, -даёшь) *imp.*, изда́ть (-а́м, -а́шь, -а́ст, -ади́м; изда́л, -а́, -о) *perf.*

emotion *n.* (*state*) эмо́ция, чу́вство. **emotional** *adj.* эмоциона́льный, волну́ющий.

emperor *n.* импера́тор.

emphasis *n.* ударе́ние; (*expressiveness*) вырази́тельность. **emphasize** *v.t.* подчёркивать *imp.*, подчеркну́ть *perf.*; выделя́ть *imp.*, вы́делить *perf.* **emphatic** *adj.* вырази́тельный, подчёркнутый; (*person*) насто́йчивый.

empire *n.* импе́рия.

empirical *adj.* эмпири́ческий, -чный. **empiricism** *n.* эмпири́зм. **empiricist** *n.* эмпи́рик.

employ *v.t.* (*thing*) по́льзоваться *imp.* + *instr.*; (*person*) нанима́ть *imp.*, наня́ть (найму́, -мёшь; на́нял, -а́, -о) *perf.*; (*busy*) занима́ть *imp.*, заня́ть (займу́, -мёшь; за́нял, -а́, -о) *perf.*; e. *oneself*, занима́ться *imp.*, заня́ться (займу́сь, -мёшься; заня́лся, -ла́сь) *perf.* **employee** *n.* рабо́чий *sb.*, служа́щий *sb.* **employer** *n.* работода́тель *m.* **employment** *n.* рабо́та, слу́жба; испо́льзование; e. *exchange*, би́ржа труда́; *full* e., по́лная за́нятость.

empower *v.t.* уполномо́чивать *imp.*, уполномо́чить *perf.* (to, на + *acc.*).

empress *n.* императри́ца.

emptiness *n.* пустота́. **empty** *adj.* пусто́й (пуст, -а́, -о, пусты́); e.-*headed*, пустоголо́вый; *v.t.* опорожня́ть *imp.*, опорожни́ть *perf.*; (*solid*) высыпа́ть *imp.*, вы́сыпать (-плю, -плешь) *perf.*; (*liquid*) вылива́ть *imp.*, вы́лить (-лью, -льешь) *perf.*; *v.i.* пусте́ть *imp.*, о ~ *perf.*; (*river*) впада́ть *imp.*, впасть (-адёт; -ал) *perf.*

emu *n.* э́му *m.indecl.*

emulate *v.t.* соревнова́ться *imp.* с + *instr.*; подража́ть *imp.* + *dat.* **emulation** *n.* соревнова́ние, подража́ние.

emulsion *n.* эму́льсия.

enable *v.t.* дава́ть (даю́, даёшь) *imp.*, дать (дам, дашь, даст, дади́м; дал, -а́, да́ло, -о) *perf.* возмо́жность + *dat.* & *inf.*

enact *v.t.* (*ordain*) постановля́ть *imp.*, постанови́ть (-влю́, -вишь) *perf.*; (*law etc.*) вводи́ть (-ожу́, -о́дишь) *imp.*, ввести́ (введу́, -дёшь; ввёл, -а́) *perf.* в де́йствие; (*part, scene*) игра́ть *imp.*, сыгра́ть *perf.*

enamel *n.* эма́ль; *adj.* эма́левый; *v.t.* эмалирова́ть *imp.*, *perf.*

enamoured *predic.*: *be* e. *of*, быть влюблённым (-ён, -ена́) в + *acc.*; увлека́ться *imp.*, увле́чься (-еку́сь, -ечёшься; -ёкся, -екла́сь) *perf.* + *instr.*

encamp v.i. располага́ться imp., расположи́ться (-жу́сь, -жи́шься) perf. ла́герем. **encampment** n. ла́герь (pl. -ря́) m.

enchant v.t. (bewitch) заколдо́вывать imp., заколдова́ть perf.; (charm) очаро́вывать imp., очарова́ть perf. **enchanting** adj. очарова́тельный, волше́бный. **enchantment** n. очарова́ние, волшебство́. **enchantress** n. волше́бница.

encircle v.t. окружа́ть imp., окружи́ть perf. **encirclement** n. окруже́ние.

enclave n. анкла́в.

enclose v.t. огора́живать imp., огороди́ть (-ожу́, -о́дишь) perf.; обноси́ть (-ошу́, -о́сишь) imp., обнести́ (-су́, -сёшь; -ёс, -есла́) perf.; (in letter) вкла́дывать imp., вложи́ть (-жу́, -жишь) perf.; please find enclosed, прилага́ется (-а́ются) + nom. **enclosure** n. огоро́женное ме́сто (pl. -та́); в-, при-, ложе́ние.

encode v.t. шифрова́ть imp., за~ perf.

encompass v.t. (encircle) окружа́ть imp., окружи́ть perf.; (contain) заключа́ть imp., заключи́ть perf.

encore interj. бис! n. вы́зов на бис; give an e., бис―рова́ть imp., perf.; v.t. вызыва́ть imp., вы́звать (вы́зову, -вешь) perf. на бис.

encounter n. встре́ча; (in combat) столкнове́ние; v.t. встреча́ть imp., встре́тить perf.; ста́лкиваться imp., столкну́ться perf. с + instr.

encourage v.t. ободря́ть imp., ободри́ть perf.; поощря́ть imp., поощри́ть perf. **encouragement** n. ободре́ние, поощре́ние, подде́ржка. **encouraging** adj. ободри́тельный.

encroach v.i. вторга́ться imp., вто́ргнуться (-г(нул)ся, -глась) perf. (on, в + acc.); (fig.) посяга́ть imp., посягну́ть perf. (on, на + acc.). **encroachment** n. вторже́ние; посяга́тельство.

encumber v.t. загроможда́ть imp., загромозди́ть perf.; обременя́ть imp., обремени́ть perf. **encumbrance** n. обуза, бре́мя.

encyclopaedia n. энциклопе́дия. **encyclopaedic** adj. энциклопеди́ческий.

end n. коне́ц (-нца́), край (loc. -аю́; pl. -ая́); (conclusion) оконча́ние; (death) смерть; (purpose) цель; e.-game, (chess) э́ндшпиль; e.-product, гото́вое изде́лие; an e. in itself, самоце́ль; in the e., в конце́ концо́в; no e., без конца́; no e. of, ма́сса + gen.; on e., (upright) стоймя́; (continuously) подря́д; at a loose e., не у дел; to the bitter e., до после́дней ка́пли кро́ви; come to the e. of one's tether дойти́ (дойду́, -дёшь; дошёл, -шла́) perf. до то́чки, make ends meet, своди́ть (-ожу́, -о́дишь) imp., свести́ (сведу́, -дёшь; свёл, -а́) perf. концы́ с конца́ми; v.t. конча́ть imp., ко́нчить perf.; зака́нчивать imp., зако́нчить perf.; прекраща́ть imp., прекрати́ть (-ащу́, -ати́шь) perf.; v.i. конча́ться imp., ко́нчиться perf.

endanger v.t. подверга́ть imp., подве́ргнуть (-г) perf. опа́сности.

endear v.t. внуша́ть imp., внуши́ть perf. любо́вь к + dat. (to, + dat.). **endearing** adj. привлека́тельный. **endearment** n. ла́ска (gen. pl. -ск).

endeavour n. попы́тка, стара́ние; v.i. стара́ться imp., по~ perf.

endemic adj. эндеми́ческий.

ending n. оконча́ние (also gram.), заключе́ние. **endless** adj. бесконе́чный, беспреде́льный.

endorse v.t. (document) подпи́сывать imp., подписа́ть (-ишу́, -и́шешь) perf.; (bill) индосси́ровать imp., perf. (to, в по́льзу + gen.); (approve) одобря́ть imp., одо́брить perf. **endorsement** n. по́дпись (на оборо́те + gen.); индосса́мент; одобре́ние.

endow v.t. обеспе́чивать imp., обеспе́чить perf. постоя́нным дохо́дом; (fig.) одаря́ть imp., одари́ть perf. **endowment** n. вклад, поже́ртвование; (talent) дарова́ние.

endurance n. (of person) выно́сливость, терпе́ние; (of object) про́чность. **endure** v.t. выноси́ть (-ошу́, -о́сишь) imp., вы́нести (-су, -есешь; -ес) perf.; терпе́ть (-плю́, -пишь) imp., по~ perf.; v.i. продолжа́ться imp., продо́лжиться perf.

enema n. кли́зма.

enemy *n.* враг (-á), проти́вник, неприя́тель *m.*; *adj.* враже́ский.

energetic *adj.* энерги́чный, си́льный (си́лён, -льна́, -льно, си́льны). **energy** *n.* эне́ргия, си́ла; *pl.* уси́лия *neut.pl.*

enervate *v.t.* расслабля́ть *imp.*, рассла́бить *perf.*

enfeeble *v.t.* ослабля́ть *imp.*, осла́бить *perf.*

enfilade *n.* продо́льный ого́нь (огня́) *m.*; *v.t.* обстре́ливать *imp.*, обстреля́ть *perf.* продо́льным огнём.

enforce *v.t.* принужда́ть *imp.*, прину́дить *perf.* к + *dat.* (upon, + *acc.*); (*law*) проводи́ть *imp.*, -óдишь) *imp.*, провести́ (-еду́, -еде́шь; -ёл, -ела́) *perf.* в жизнь. **enforcement** *n.* принужде́ние; (*law etc.*) осуществле́ние, наблюде́ние за + *instr.*, за соблюде́нием + *gen.*

enfranchise *v.t.* предоставля́ть *imp.*, предоста́вить *perf.* избира́тельные права́ (*neut.pl.*) + *dat.*; (set free) освобожда́ть *imp.*, освободи́ть *perf.*

engage *v.t.* (hire) нанима́ть *imp.*, наня́ть (найму́, -мёшь; на́нял, -á, -о) *perf.*; (tech.) зацепля́ть *imp.*, зацепи́ть (-ит *perf.*; *e. the enemy in battle*, завя́зывать *imp.*, завяза́ть (-яжу́, -я́жешь) *perf.* бой с проти́вником. **engaged** *adj.* (occupied) за́нятый (-т, -тá, -то); *be e. in*, занима́ться *imp.*, заня́ться (займу́сь, -мёшься; заня́лся́, -ла́сь) *perf.* + *instr.*; *become e.*, обруча́ться *imp.*, обручи́ться *perf.* (to, c + *instr.*). **engagement** *n.* (appointment) свида́ние; (obligation) обяза́тельство; (betrothal) обруче́ние; (battle) бой (loc. бою́; *pl.* бои́); *e. ring*, обруча́льное кольцо́ (*pl.* -льца, -ле́ц, -льцам). **engaging** *adj.* привлека́тельный.

engender *v.t.* порожда́ть *imp.*, породи́ть *perf.*

engine *n.* мото́р, маши́на, дви́гатель *m.*; (rly.) парово́з; *e.-driver*, (rly.) машини́ст; *e.-room*, маши́нное отделе́ние. **engineer** *n.* инжене́р; *pl.* (mil.) инжене́рные войска́ (-к) *pl.*; *v.t.* (construct) сооружа́ть *imp.*, сооруди́ть *perf.*; (arrange) устра́ивать *imp.*, устро́ить *perf.* **engineering** *n.* инжене́рное де́ло, те́хника, машинострое́ние; *adj.* инжене́рный, техни́ческий.

English *adj.* англи́йский; *n.: the E.*, *pl.* англича́не *pl.* **Englishman**, **-woman** *n.* англича́нин (*pl.* -а́не, -а́н), -а́нка.

engrave *v.t.* гравирова́ть *imp.*, вы́- *perf.*; (fig.) запечатлева́ть *imp.*, запечатле́ть *perf.* **engraver** *n.* гравёр. **engraving** *n.* (picture) гравю́ра; (action) гравиро́вка; *adj.* гравирова́льный, гравёрный.

engross *v.t.* завладева́ть *imp.*, завладе́ть *perf.* + *instr.*; поглоща́ть *imp.*, поглоти́ть (-ощу́, -о́тишь) *perf.*; *be engrossed in*, быть поглощённым + *instr.* **engrossing** *adj.* увлека́тельный.

engulf *v.t.* заса́сывать *imp.*, засоса́ть (-су́, -сёшь) *perf.*

enhance *v.t.* увели́чивать *imp.*, увели́чить *perf.*

enigma *n.* зага́дка. **enigmatic** *adj.* зага́дочный.

enjoin *v.t.* предпи́сывать *imp.*, предписа́ть (-ишу́, -и́шешь) *perf.* + *dat.*; прика́зывать *imp.*, приказа́ть (-ажу́, -а́жешь) *perf.* + *dat.*; (leg.) запреща́ть *imp.*, запрети́ть (-ещу́, -ети́шь) *perf.* + *dat.* (from, + *inf.*).

enjoy *v.t.* получа́ть *imp.*, получи́ть (-чу́, -чишь) *perf.* удово́льствие от + *gen.*; наслажда́ться *imp.*, наслади́ться *perf.* + *instr.*; (have use of) по́льзоваться *imp.* + *instr.*; облада́ть *imp.* + *instr.* **enjoyable** *adj.* прия́тный. **enjoyment** *n.* удово́льствие, наслажде́ние; облада́ние (of, + *instr.*).

enlarge *v.t. & i.* увели́чивать(ся) *imp.*, увели́чить(ся) *perf.*; (widen) расширя́ть(ся) *imp.*, расши́рить(ся) *perf.*; *e. upon*, распространя́ться *imp.*, распространи́ться *perf.* о + *prep.* **enlargement** *n.* увеличе́ние; расшире́ние. **enlarger** *n.* (phot.) увеличи́тель *m.*

enlighten *v.t.* просвеща́ть *imp.*, просвети́ть (-ещу́ -ети́шь) *perf.*; (inform) осведомля́ть *imp.*, осве́домить *perf.* **enlightenment** *n.* просвеще́ние.

enlist *v.i.* поступа́ть *imp.*, поступи́ть (-плю́, -пишь) *perf.* на вое́нную слу́жбу; *v.t.* (mil.) вербова́ть *imp.*, за ~ *perf.*; (support etc.) заруча́ться *imp.*, заручи́ться *perf.* + *instr.*

enliven *v.t.* оживля́ть *imp.*, оживи́ть *perf.*

enmesh *v.t.* опу́тывать *imp.*, опу́тать *perf.*

enmity *n.* вражда́, неприя́знь.

ennoble *v.t.* облагора́живать *imp.*, облагоро́дить *perf.*

ennui *n.* тоска́.

enormity *n.* чудо́вищность. **enormous** *adj.* грома́дный, огро́мный. **enormously** *adv.* кра́йне, чрезвыча́йно.

enough *adj.* доста́точный; *adv.* доста́точно, дово́льно; *e. money*, доста́точно де́нег (*gen.*); *be e.*, хвата́ть *imp.*, хвати́ть (-ит) *perf.impers.* + *gen.*; *I've had e. of him*, он мне надое́л.

enquire, enquiry *see* inquire, inquiry.

enrage *v.t.* беси́ть (бешу́, бе́сишь) *imp.*, вз ~ *perf.*

enrapture *v.t.* восхища́ть *imp.*, восхити́ть (-ищу́, -ити́шь) *perf.*

enrich *v.t.* обогаща́ть *imp.*, обогати́ть (-ащу́, -ати́шь) *perf.*

enrol *v.t. & i.* запи́сывать(ся) *imp.*, записа́ть(ся) (-ишу́(сь), -и́шешь(ся)) *perf.*; *v.t.* (*mil.*) вербова́ть *imp.*, за ~ *perf.*; *v.i.* (*mil.*) поступа́ть *imp.*, поступи́ть (-плю́, -пишь) *perf.* на вое́нную слу́жбу. **enrolment** *n.* регистра́ция, за́пись.

en route *adv.* по пути́ (to, for, в + *acc.*).

ensconce *v.t.*: *e. oneself*, заса́живаться *imp.*, засе́сть (-ся́ду, -ся́дешь; засе́л) *perf.* (with, за + *acc.*).

ensemble *n.* (*mus.*) анса́мбль *m.*

enshrine *v.t.* (*relic*) класть (кладу́, -дёшь; клал) *imp.*, положи́ть (-жу́, -жишь) *perf.* в ра́ку; (*fig.*) храни́ть *imp.*

ensign *n.* (*flag*) флаг; (*rank*) пра́порщик.

enslave *v.t.* порабоща́ть *imp.*, порабо́тить (-ощу́, -о́тишь) *perf.* **enslavement** *n.* порабоще́ние.

ensnare *v.t.* опу́тывать *imp.*, опу́тать *perf.*

ensue *v.i.* сле́довать *imp.*; вытека́ть *imp.* **ensuing** *adj.* после́дующий.

ensure *v.t.* обеспе́чивать *imp.*, обеспе́чить *perf.*

entail *n.* майора́т(ное насле́дование); *v.t.* (*leg.*) определя́ть *imp.*, определи́ть *perf.* насле́дование + *gen.*; (*necessitate*) влечь (влечёт; влёк, -ла́) *imp.* за собо́й.

entangle *v.t.* запу́тывать *imp.*, запу́тать *perf.*

enter *v.t. & i.* входи́ть (-ожу́, -о́дишь) *imp.*, войти́ (войду́, -дёшь; вошёл, -шла́) *perf.* в + *acc.*; (*by transport*) въезжа́ть *imp.*, въе́хать (-е́ду, -е́дешь) *perf.* в + *acc.*; *v.t.* (*join*) поступа́ть *imp.*, поступи́ть (-плю́, -пишь) *perf.* в, на, + *acc.*; (*competition*) вступа́ть *imp.*, вступи́ть (-плю́, -пишь) *perf.* в + *acc.*; (*in list*) вноси́ть (-ошу́, -о́сишь) *imp.*, внести́ (внесу́, -сёшь; внёс, -сла́) *perf.*

enteric *adj.* кише́чный. **enteritis** *n.* энтери́т.

enterprise *n.* (*undertaking*) предприя́тие; (*initiative*) предприи́мчивость; *free, private, e.*, ча́стное предпринима́тельство. **enterprising** *adj.* предприи́мчивый.

entertain *v.t.* (*amuse*) развлека́ть *imp.*, развле́чь (-еку́, -ечёшь; -ёк, -екла́) *perf.*; (*guests*) принима́ть *imp.*, приня́ть (приму́, -мешь; при́нял, -á, -о) *perf.*; угоща́ть *imp.*, угости́ть *perf.* (to, + *instr.*); (*hopes*) пита́ть *imp.* **entertaining** *adj.* занима́тельный, развлека́тельный. **entertainment** *n.* развлече́ние; приём; угоще́ние; (*show*) дивертисме́нт.

enthral *v.t.* порабоща́ть *imp.*, порабо́тить (-ощу́, -о́тишь) *perf.*

enthrone *v.t.* возводи́ть (-ожу́, -о́дишь) *imp.*, возвести́ (-еду́, -еде́шь;-ёл, -ела́) *perf.* на престо́л. **enthronement** *n.* возведе́ние на престо́л.

enthusiasm *n.* энтузиа́зм, воодушевле́ние. **enthusiast** *n.* энтузиа́ст, ~ ка. **enthusiastic** *adj.* восто́рженный (-ен, -енна), воодушевлённый (-ён, -ённа).

entice *v.t.* зама́нивать *imp.*, замани́ть (-ню́, -нишь) *perf.*; соблазня́ть *imp.*, соблазни́ть *perf.* **enticement** *n.* собла́зн, прима́нка, зама́нивание. **enticing** *adj.* соблазни́тельный, зама́нчивый.

entire *adj.* по́лный, це́лый, весь (вся, всё; все). **entirely** *adv.* вполне́, соверше́нно; (*solely*) исключи́тельно. **en-**

tirety *n.* цельность, полнота; *in its e.*, полностью, в целом.

entitle *v.t.* (*book*) озаглавливать *imp.*, озаглавить *perf.*; (*give right to*) давать (даю, даёшь) *imp.*, дать (дам, дашь, даст, дадим; дал, -á, дáлó, -и) *perf.* право + *dat.* (то, на + *acc.*); *be entitled to*, иметь *imp.* право на + *acc.*

entity *n.* существо; (*existence*) бытие (*prep.* -ии, *instr.* -ием).

entomb *v.t.* погребáть *imp.*, погрести (-ебý, -ебёшь; -ёб, -еблá) *perf.* entombment *n.* погребение.

entomological *adj.* энтомологический. entomologist *n.* энтомóлог. entomology *n.* энтомология.

entrails *n.* внутренности (-тей) *pl.*, кишки (-шók) *pl.*; (*fig.*) недра (-др) *pl.*

entrance[1] *v.t.* приводить (-ожý, -óдишь) *imp.*, привести (-едý, -едёшь; -ёл, -елá) *perf.* в состояние трáнса; (*charm*) очаровывать *imp.*, очаровáть *perf.* entrancing *adj.* очаровáтельный.

entrance[2] *n.* вход, въезд; (*theat.*) выход; (*into office etc.*) вступление, поступление; *e. examinations* вступительные экзáмены *m.pl.*; *e. hall*, вестибюль *m.*; *back e.*, чёрный вход; *front e.*, парáдный вход. entrant *n.* (*sport*) учáстник (for, + *gen.*).

entrap *v.t.* поймáть *imp.* в ловýшку; (*fig.*) запýтывать *imp.*, запýтать *perf.*

entreat *v.t.* умолять *imp.*, умолить *perf.* entreaty *n.* мольбá, прóсьба.

entrench *v.t.* окáпывать *imp.*, окопáть *perf.*; *be, become, entrenched*, (*fig.*) укореняться *imp.*, укорениться *perf.*

entropy *n.* энтропия.

entrust *v.t.* (*secret*) вверять *imp.*, вверить (то, + *dat.*); (*object*; *person*) поручáть *imp.*, поручить (-чý, -чишь) *perf.* (то, + *dat.*).

entry *n.* вход, въезд; вступление (*theat.*) выход; (*in book etc.*) запись, статья; (*sport*) записáвшийся.

entwine *v.t.* (*interweave*) сплетáть *imp.*, сплести (-етý, -етёшь; -ёл, -елá) *perf.*; (*wreathe*) обвивáть *imp.*, обвить (обовью, -ьёшь; обвил, -á, -о) *perf.*

enumerate *v.t.* перечислять *imp.*, перечислить *perf.* enumeration *n.* перечисление, перечень (-чня) *m.*

enunciate *v.t.* (*proclaim*) объявлять *imp.*, объявить (-влю, -вишь) *perf.*; (*express*) излагáть *imp.*, изложить (-жý, -жишь) *perf.*; (*pronounce*) произносить (-ошý, -óсишь) *imp.*, произнести (-есý, -есёшь; -ёс, -еслá) *perf.* enunciation *n.* объявление; изложение; произношение.

envelop *v.t.* окýтывать *imp.*, окýтать *perf.*; завёртывать *imp.*, завернýть *perf.* envelope *n.* (*letter*) конверт; (*other senses*) обёртка, оболóчка.

envenom *v.t.* отравлять *imp.*, отравить (-влю, -вишь) *perf.*; (*embitter*) озлоблять *imp.*, озлобить *perf.*

enviable *adj.* завидный. envious *adj.* завистливый.

environment *n.* окружáющая обстановка, средá (*pl.* -ды). environs *n.* окрéстности *f.pl.*

envisage *v.t.* предусмáтривать *imp.*, предусмотреть (-рю, -ришь) *perf.*

envoy *n.* послáнник, агéнт.

envy *n.* зáвисть; *v.t.* завидовать *imp.*, по ~ *perf.* + *dat.*

enzyme *n.* энзим.

epaulette *n.* эполéт(а).

ephemeral *adj.* эфемéрный, недолговéчный.

epic *n.* эпическая поэма, эпопéя; *adj.* эпический.

epicentre *n.* эпицéнтр.

epicure *n.* эпикурéец (-éйца). epicurean *adj.* эпикурéйский.

epidemic *n.* эпидéмия; *adj.* эпидемический.

epigram *n.* эпигрáмма. epigrammatic(al) *adj.* эпиграмматический.

epigraph *n.* эпигрáф.

epilepsy *n.* эпилéпсия. epileptic *n.* эпилéптик; *adj.* эпилептический.

epilogue *n.* эпилóг.

Epiphany *n.* (*eccl.*) Богоявлéние.

episcopal *adj.* епископский. episcopate *n.* епископство.

episode *n.* эпизóд. episodic *adj.* эпизодический.

epistle *n.* послáние. epistolary *adj.* эпистолярный.

epitaph *n.* эпитáфия, надгрóбная надпись.

epithet *n.* эпитет.

epitome n. (summary) конспе́кт; (embodiment) воплоще́ние. **epitomize** v.t. конспекти́ровать imp., за∼, про∼ perf.; воплоща́ть imp., воплоти́ть (-ощу́, -оти́шь) perf.

epoch n. эпо́ха, век (pl. -а́), пери́од.

equable adj. равноме́рный, ро́вный (-вен, -вна́, -вно).

equal adj. ра́вный (-вен, -вна́), одина́ковый; (capable of) спосо́бный (to, на + acc., + inf.); n. ра́вный sb., ро́вня m. & f.; v.t. равня́ться imp. + dat. **equality** n. ра́венство, равнопра́вие. **equalization** n. уравне́ние. **equalize** v.t. ура́внивать imp., уравня́ть perf.; v.i. (sport) равня́ть imp., с∼ perf. счёт. **equally** adv. равно́, ра́вным о́бразом.

equanimity n. хладнокро́вие, невозмути́мость.

equate v.t. прира́внивать imp., приравня́ть perf. (with, к + dat.). **equation** n. (math.) уравне́ние. **equator** n. эква́тор. **equatorial** adj. экваториа́льный.

equestrian n. вса́дник; adj. ко́нный. **equestrienne** n. вса́дница.

equidistant adj. равносто́ящий. **equilateral** adj. равносторо́нний (-нен, -ння). **equilibrium** n. равнове́сие.

equine adj. лошади́ный.

equinox n. равноде́нствие.

equip v.t. обору́довать imp., perf.; снаряжа́ть imp., снаряди́ть perf. **equipment** n. обору́дование, снаряже́ние.

equitable adj. справедли́вый, беспристра́стный. **equity** n. справедли́вость, беспристра́стность; (econ.) ма́ржа; pl. (econ.) обыкнове́нные а́кции f.pl. **equivalence** n. эквивале́нтность, равноце́нность. **equivalent** adj. эквивале́нтный, равноце́нный (-нен, -нна), равноси́льный; n. эквивале́нт.

equivocal adj. (ambiguous) двусмы́сленный (-ен, -енна); (suspicious) сомни́тельный. **equivocate** v.i. говори́ть imp. двусмы́сленно.

era n. э́ра, эпо́ха.

eradicate v.t. искореня́ть imp., искорени́ть perf. **eradication** n. искорене́ние.

erase v.t. стира́ть imp., стере́ть (сотру́, -рёшь; стёр) perf.; подчища́ть imp.,

подчи́стить perf. **eraser** n. ла́стик. **erasure** n. стира́ние, подчи́стка.

erect adj. прямо́й (прям, -а́, -о, пря́мы); v.t. (building) сооружа́ть imp., сооруди́ть perf.; воздвига́ть imp., воздви́гнуть (-г) perf.; (straighten) выпрямля́ть imp., вы́прямить perf. **erection** n. постро́йка, сооруже́ние; выпрямле́ние.

erg n. эрг (gen.pl. эрг & -ов).

ergot n. спорынья́.

ermine n. горноста́й.

erode v.t. разъеда́ть imp., разъе́сть (-е́ст, -едя́т; -е́л) perf.; (geol.) эроди́ровать imp., perf. **erosion** n. разъеда́ние; эро́зия.

erotic adj. эроти́ческий, любо́вный.

err v.i. ошиба́ться imp., ошиби́ться (-бу́сь, -бёшься; -бся) perf.; заблужда́ться imp.; (sin) греши́ть imp., со∼ perf.

errand n. поруче́ние; run errands, быть на посы́лках (for, y + gen.).

errant adj. (knight) стра́нствующий; (thoughts) блужда́ющий.

erratic adj. непостоя́нный (-нен, -нна), изме́нчивый.

erratum n. (print.) опеча́тка; (in writing) опи́ска. **erroneous** adj. оши́бочный, ло́жный. **error** n. оши́бка, заблужде́ние.

erudite adj. учёный. **erudition** n. эруди́ция, учёность.

erupt v.i. прорыва́ться imp., прорва́ться (-вусь, -вёшься; -ва́лся, -вала́сь, -ва́лось) perf.; (volcano) изверга́ться imp., изве́ргнуться (-гся) perf. **eruption** n. (volcano) изверже́ние; (mirth) взрыв; (med.) сыпь.

erysipelas n. ро́жа.

escalator n. эскала́тор.

escapade n. вы́ходка, проде́лка. **escape** n. (from prison) бе́гство, побе́г; (from danger) спасе́ние; (from reality) ухо́д; (of gas) уте́чка; have a narrow e., быть на волоско́м (from, от + gen.); v.i. (flee) бежа́ть (бегу́, бежи́шь) imp., perf.; убега́ть imp., убежа́ть (-eгý, -ежи́шь) perf.; (save oneself) спаса́ться imp., спасти́сь (-су́сь, -сёшься; -сся, -сла́сь) perf.; (leak) утека́ть imp., уте́чь (-ечёт; -ёк, -екла́) perf.; v.t.

избега́ть *imp.*, избежа́ть (-егу́, -ежи́шь) *perf.*+*gen.*; (*groan*) выра́ва́ться *imp.*, вы́рваться (-вется) *perf.* из, у, +*gen.* escapee *n.* бегле́ц (-а́).

escort *n.* конво́й, эско́рт; *v.t.* сопровожда́ть *imp.*, сопроводи́ть *perf.*; (*mil.*) конво́и́ровать *imp.*, от~ *perf.*; эскорти́ровать *imp.*, *perf.*

escutcheon *n.* щит (-а́) герба́.

Eskimo *n.* эскимо́с, ~ка; *adj.* эскимо́сский.

especial *adj.* осо́бенный, осо́бый; (*particular*) ча́стный. **especially** *adv.* осо́бенно, в ча́стности.

espionage *n.* шпиона́ж.

espousal *n.* (*fig.*) подде́ржка. **espouse** *v.t.* (*fig.*) подде́рживать *imp.*, подде́ржа́ть (-жу́, -жишь) *perf.*

espy *v.t.* уви́деть (-и́жу, -и́дишь) *perf.*; (*detect*) замеча́ть *imp.*, заме́тить *perf.*

essay *n.* о́черк, эссе́ *neut.indecl.*; (*attempt*) попы́тка, про́ба; *v.t.* пыта́ться *imp.*, по~ *perf.*+*inf.* **essayist** *n.* очерки́ст, ~ка; эссеи́ст.

essence *n.* су́щность, существо́; (*extract*) эссе́нция. **essential** *adj.* суще́ственный, необходи́мый, неотъе́млемый; *n.* основно́е *sb.*; *pl.* предме́ты *m.pl.* пе́рвой необходи́мости. **essentially** *adv.* по существу́, в основно́м.

establish *v.t.* (*set up*) учрежда́ть *imp.*, учреди́ть *perf.*; (*fact etc.*) устана́вливать *imp.*, установи́ть (-влю́, -вишь) *perf.*; (*appoint*) устра́ивать *imp.*, устро́ить *perf.*; (*secure*) упро́чивать *imp.*, упро́чить *perf.* **establishment** *n.* (*action*) учрежде́ние, установле́ние; (*institution*) учрежде́ние, заведе́ние; (*staff*) штат.

estate *n.* (*property*) поме́стье (*gen.pl.* -тий), име́ние; (*class*) сосло́вие; *real* *e.*, недви́жимость; *e. agent*, аге́нт по прода́же недви́жимости; *e. duty*, нало́г на насле́дство.

esteem *n.* уваже́ние, почте́ние; *v.t.* уважа́ть *imp.*; почита́ть *imp.* **estimable** *adj.* досто́йный (-о́ин, -о́йна) уваже́ния. **estimate** *n.* (*of quality*) оце́нка; (*of cost*) сме́та; *v.t.* оце́нивать *imp.*, оцени́ть (-ню́, -нишь) *perf.* **estimated** *adj.* предполага́емый, приме́рный. **estimation** *n.* оце́нка, мне́ние.

estrange *v.t.* отдаля́ть *imp.*, отдали́ть *perf.* **estrangement** *n.* отчужде́ние, отчуждённость.

estuary *n.* у́стье (*gen.pl.* -в).

etc. *abbr.* и т.д., и т.п. **etcetera** и так да́лее, и тому́ подо́бное.

etch *v.t.* трави́ть (-влю́, -вишь) *imp.*, вы~ *perf.* **etching** *n.* (*action*) травле́ние; (*object*) офо́рт.

eternal *adj.* ве́чный. **eternity** *n.* ве́чность.

ether *n.* эфи́р. **ethereal** *adj.* эфи́рный.

ethical *adj.* эти́ческий, эти́чный. **ethics** *n.* э́тика.

ethnic *adj.* этни́ческий. **ethnography** *n.* этногра́фия.

etiquette *n.* этике́т.

étude *n.* этю́д.

etymological *adj.* этимологи́ческий. **etymologist** *n.* этимо́лог. **etymology** *n.* этимоло́гия.

eucalyptus *n.* эвкали́пт.

Eucharist *n.* евхари́стия, прича́стие.

eulogize *v.t.* превозноси́ть (-ошу́, -о́сишь) *imp.*, превознести́ (-есу́, -есёшь; -ёс, -есла́) *perf.* **eulogy** *n.* похвала́.

eunuch *n.* е́внух.

euphemism *n.* эвфеми́зм. **euphemistic** *adj.* эвфемисти́ческий.

euphonious *adj.* благозву́чный. **euphony** *n.* благозву́чие.

Eurasian *adj.* евразийский.

European *n.* европе́ец (-е́йца) *adj.* европе́йский.

evacuate *v.t.* (*person*) эвакуи́ровать *imp.*, *perf.*; (*med.*) опорожня́ть *imp.*, опорожни́ть *perf.* **evacuation** *n.* эвакуа́ция; опорожне́ние. **evacuee** *n.* эвакуи́рованный *sb.*

evade *v.t.* уклоня́ться *imp.*, уклони́ться (-ню́сь, -ни́шься) *perf.* от+*gen.*; (*law*) обходи́ть (-ожу́, -о́дишь) *imp.*, обойти́ (обойду́, -дёшь; обошёл, -шла́) *perf.*

evaluate *v.t.* оце́нивать *imp.*, оцени́ть (-ню́, -нишь) *perf.* **evaluation** *n.* оце́нка.

evangelical *adj.* ева́нгельский. **evangelist** *n.* евангели́ст.

evaporate *v.t. & i.* испаря́ть(ся) *imp.*, испари́ть(ся) *perf.*; *v.i.* (*lose moisture*) улету́чиваться *imp.*, улету́читься *perf.* **evaporation** *n.* испаре́ние.

evasion *n.* уклоне́ние (of, от + gen.); (of law) обхо́д; (subterfuge) уве́ртка. **evasive** *adj.* укло́нчивый.

eve *n.* кану́н; on the e., накану́не.

even *adj.* ро́вный (-вен, -вна́, -вно); (uniform) равноме́рный; (balanced) уравнове́шенный; (number) чётный; get e., расквита́ться *perf.* (with, c + instr.); *adv.* да́же; (just) как раз; (with comp.) ещё; e. if, да́же е́сли, хотя́ бы и; e. though, хотя́ бы и; e. so, всё-таки; not e., да́же не; *v.t.* выра́внивать *imp.*, вы́ровнять *perf.*

evening *n.* ве́чер (pl. -á); *adj.* вече́рний.

evenly *adv.* ро́вно, одина́ково. **evenness** *n.* ро́вность; равноме́рность.

evensong *n.* вече́рня.

event *n.* собы́тие, происше́ствие, слу́чай; in the e., в слу́чае + gen.; at all events, во вся́ком слу́чае. **eventual** *adj.* (possible) возмо́жный; (final) коне́чный. **eventuality** *n.* возмо́жность. **eventually** *adv.* в конце́ концо́в.

ever *adv.* (at any time) когда́-либо, когда́-нибудь; (always) всегда́; (emph.) же; e. since, с тех пор (как); e. so, о́чень; for e., навсегда́; hardly e., почти́ никогда́. **evergreen** *adj.* вечнозелёный; *n.* вечнозелёное расте́ние. **everlasting** *adj.* ве́чный, постоя́нный. **evermore** *adv.*: for e., навсегда́, наве́ки. **every** *adj.* ка́ждый, вся́кий, все (pl.); e. now and then, вре́мя от вре́мени; e. other, ка́ждый второ́й; e. other day, че́рез день. **everybody, everyone** *pron.* ка́ждый, все (pl.). **everyday** *adj.* (daily) ежедне́вный; (commonplace) повседне́вный. **everything** *pron.* всё. **everywhere** *adv.* всю́ду, везде́.

evict *v.t.* выселя́ть *imp.*, вы́селить *perf.* **eviction** *n.* выселе́ние.

evidence *n.* свиде́тельство, доказа́тельство, ули́ка; in e., (predic.) заме́тен (-тна, -тно); give e., свиде́тельствовать *imp.* (o + prep.; + acc.; + что). **evident** *adj.* очеви́дный, я́сный (я́сен, ясна́, я́сно, я́сны́).

evil *n.* зло (gen. pl. зол), поро́к; *adj.* злой (зол, зла), дурно́й (дурён, -рна́, -рно, ду́рны); *e.-doer*, злоде́й.

evince *v.t.* проявля́ть *imp.*, прояви́ть (-влю́, -вишь) *perf.*

evoke *v.t.* вызыва́ть *imp.*, вы́звать (вы́зову, -вешь) *perf.*

evolution *n.* разви́тие, эволю́ция. **evolutionary** *adj.* эволюцио́нный. **evolve** *v.t. & i.* развива́ть(ся) *imp.*, разви́ть (разовью́(сь), -вьёшь(ся); разви́л(ся), -ила́(сь), -и́ло́(сь)) *perf.*; *v.i.* эволюциони́ровать *imp.*, *perf.*

ewe *n.* овца́ (pl. о́вцы, ове́ц, о́вцам).

ewer *n.* кувши́н.

ex- in comb. бы́вший.

exacerbate *v.t.* обостря́ть *imp.*, обостри́ть *perf.* **exacerbation** *n.* обостре́ние.

exact *adj.* то́чный (-чен, -чна́, -чно), аккура́тный; *v.t.* взы́скивать *imp.*, взыска́ть (взыщу́, -щешь) *perf.* (from, of, c + gen.). **exacting** *adj.* (person) взыска́тельный, тре́бовательный; (circumstance) суро́вый. **exactitude, exactness** *n.* то́чность. **exactly** *adv.* то́чно, как раз, и́менно.

exaggerate *v.t.* преувели́чивать *imp.*, преувели́чить *perf.* **exaggeration** *n.* преувеличе́ние.

exalt *v.t.* возвыша́ть *imp.*, возвы́сить *perf.*; (extol) превозноси́ть (-ошу́, -о́сишь) *imp.*, превознести́ (-есу́, -есёшь; -ёс, -есла́) *perf.* **exaltation** *n.* возвыше́ние; (elation) восто́рг.

examination *n.* осмо́тр, иссле́дование; (of knowledge) экза́мен; (leg.) допро́с. **examine** *v.t.* осма́тривать *imp.*, осмотре́ть (-рю́, -ришь) *perf.*; иссле́довать *imp.*, *perf.*; экзаменова́ть *imp.*, про ~ *perf.*; допра́шивать *imp.*, допроси́ть (-ошу́, -о́сишь) *perf.* **examiner** *n.* экзамена́тор.

example *n.* приме́р, образе́ц (-зца́); for e., наприме́р.

exasperate *v.t.* раздража́ть *imp.*, раздражи́ть *perf.* **exasperation** *n.* раздраже́ние.

excavate *v.t.* выка́пывать *imp.*, вы́копать *perf.*; (archaeol.) раска́пывать *imp.*, раскопа́ть *perf.* **excavation** *n.* выка́пывание; раско́пки *f.pl.* **excavator** *n.* экскава́тор.

exceed *v.t.* превыша́ть *imp.*, превы́сить *perf.* **exceedingly** *adv.* чрезвыча́йно.

excel v.t. превосходи́ть (-ожу́, -о́дишь) imp., превзойти́ (-о йду́, -о́йдёшь, -ошёл, -ошла́) perf. (in, в+prep., + instr.); v.i. отлича́ться imp. отли́чи́ться perf. (at, in, в+prep.). **excellence** n. превосхо́дство. **excellency** n. превосходи́тельство. **excellent** adj. превосхо́дный, отли́чный.

except v.t. исключа́ть imp., исключи́ть perf.; prep. исключа́я+acc., за исключе́нием+gen., кро́ме e. for. **exception** n. исключе́ние; take e. to, возража́ть imp., возрази́ть perf. про́тив+gen. **exceptional** adj. исключи́тельный.

excerpt n. отры́вок (-вка), вы́держка.

excess n. изли́шек (-тка), изли́шек (-шка), изли́шество; e. fare допла́та. **excessive** adj. чрезме́рный, изли́шний (-шен, -шня).

exchange n. обме́н (of, +instr.); (of currency) разме́н; (rate of e.) курс; (building) би́ржа; (telephone) центра́льная телефо́нная ста́нция; v.t. обме́нивать imp., обменя́ть perf. (for, на+acc.); обме́ниваться imp., обменя́ться perf.+instr.

Exchequer n. казначе́йство, казна́.

excise[1] n. (duty) акци́з(ный сбор); v.t. облага́ть imp., обложи́ть (-жу́, -жишь) perf. акци́зным сбо́ром.

excise[2] v.t. (cut out) выреза́ть imp., вы́резать (-ежу, -ежешь) perf. **excision** n. вы́резка.

excitable adj. возбуди́мый. **excite** v.t. возбужда́ть imp., возбуди́ть perf.; волнова́ть imp., вз~ perf. **excitement** n. возбужде́ние, волне́ние.

exclaim v.i. восклица́ть imp., воскли́кнуть perf. **exclamation** n. восклица́ние; e. mark, восклица́тельный знак.

exclude v.t. исключа́ть imp., исключи́ть perf. **exclusion** n. исключе́ние. **exclusive** adj. исключи́тельный; e. of, за исключе́нием+gen., не счита́я+gen.

excommunicate v.t. отлуча́ть imp., отлучи́ть perf. (от це́ркви). **excommunication** n. отлуче́ние.

excrement n. экскреме́нты (-тов) pl.

excrescence n. наро́ст.

excrete v.t. выделя́ть imp., вы́делить perf. **excretion** n. выделе́ние.

excruciating adj. мучи́тельный.

exculpate v.t. опра́вдывать imp., оправда́ть perf. **exculpation** n. оправда́ние.

excursion n. экску́рсия. **excursus** n. э́кскурс.

excusable adj. извини́тельный, прости́тельный. **excuse** n. извине́ние, оправда́ние, отгово́рка; v.t. извиня́ть imp., извини́ть perf.; (release) освобожда́ть imp., освободи́ть perf. (from, от+gen.); e. me! прости́те (меня́)! прошу́ проще́ния!

execrable adj. отврати́тельный, ме́рзкий (-зок, -зка́, -зко).

execute v.t. исполня́ть imp., испо́лнить perf.; выполня́ть imp., вы́полнить perf.; (criminal) казни́ть imp., perf. **execution** n. выполне́ние, исполне́ние; казнь. **executioner** n. пала́ч (-а́). **executive** n. исполни́тельный о́рган; (person) руководи́тель m.; adj. исполни́тельный; e. committee, исполни́тельный комите́т, исполко́м.

exegesis n. толкова́ние.

exemplary adj. приме́рный, образцо́вый. **exemplify** v.t. (illustrate by example) поясня́ть imp., поясни́ть perf. приме́ром, на приме́ре; (serve as example) служи́ть (-жу́, -жишь) imp., по~ perf. приме́ром+gen.

exempt adj. освобождённый (-ён, -ена́) (from, от+gen.), свобо́дный (from, от+gen.); v.t. освобожда́ть imp., освободи́ть perf. (from, от+gen.). **exemption** n. освобожде́ние (from, от+gen.).

exercise n. (application) примене́ние, осуществле́ние; (physical e.; task) упражне́ние; take e., упражня́ться imp.; e.-book, тетра́дь f.; v.t. (apply) применя́ть imp., примени́ть (-ню́, -нишь) perf.; (employ) испо́льзовать imp., perf.; (train) упражня́ть imp.

exert v.t. ока́зывать imp., оказа́ть (-ажу́, -а́жешь) perf.; e. oneself, стара́ться imp., по~ perf. **exertion** n. напряже́ние, уси́лие.

exhalation n. выдыха́ние, вы́дох; (vapour) испаре́ние. **exhale** v.t. (breathe out) выдыха́ть imp., вы́дохнуть perf.; (as vapour) испаря́ть imp., испари́ть perf.

exhaust *n.* вы́хлоп; *e. pipe*, выхлопна́я труба́ (*pl.* -бы); *v.t.* (*use up*) истоща́ть *imp.*, истощи́ть *perf.*; (*person*) изнуря́ть *imp.*, изнури́ть *perf.*; (*subject*) исче́рпывать *imp.*, исче́рпать *perf.* exhausted *adj.*: *be e.*, (*person*) изнемога́ть *imp.*, изнемо́чь (-огу́, -о́жешь; -о́г, -огла́) *perf.* exhausting *adj.* изнури́тельный. exhaustion *n.* изнуре́ние, истоще́ние, изнеможе́ние. exhaustive *adj.* исче́рпывающий.

exhibit *n.* экспона́т; (*leg.*) веще́ственное доказа́тельство; *v.t.* (*show*) пока́зывать *imp.*, показа́ть (-ажу́, -а́жешь) *perf.*; (*manifest quality*) проявля́ть *imp.*, прояви́ть (-влю́, -вишь) *perf.*; (*publicly*) выставля́ть *imp.*, вы́ставить *perf.* exhibition *n.* пока́з, проявле́ние; (*public e.*) вы́ставка. exhibitor *n.* экспоне́нт.

exhilarate *v.t.* (*gladden*) весели́ть, раз ~ *perf.*; (*enliven*) оживля́ть *imp.*, ожив́ить *perf.* exhilaration *n.* весе́лье, оживле́ние.

exhort *v.t.* увещева́ть *imp.* exhortation *n.* увещева́ние.

exhume *v.t.* выка́пывать *imp.*, вы́копать *perf.*

exile *n.* изгна́ние, ссы́лка; (*person*) изгна́нник, ссы́льный *sb.*; *v.t.* изгоня́ть *imp.*, изгна́ть (изгоню́, -нишь; изгна́л, -а́, -о) *perf.*; ссыла́ть *imp.*, сосла́ть (сошлю́, -лёшь) *perf.*

exist *v.i.* существова́ть *imp.*; (*live*) жить (живу́, -вёшь; жил, -а́, -о) *imp.* existence *n.* существова́ние, нали́чие. existent, existing *adj.* существу́ющий, нали́чный.

exit *n.* вы́ход; (*theat.*) ухо́д (со сце́ны); (*death*) смерть; *e. visa*, выездна́я ви́за; *v.i.* уходи́ть (-ожу́, -о́дишь) *imp.*, уйти́ (уйду́, -дёшь; ушёл, ушла́) *perf.*

exonerate *v.t.* освобожда́ть *imp.*, освободи́ть *perf.* (*from*, от + *gen.*); (*from blame*) снима́ть *imp.*, снять (сниму́, -мешь; снял, -а́, -о) *perf.* обвине́ние с + *gen.*

exorbitant *adj.* непоме́рный, чрезме́рный.

exorcism *n.* изгна́ние ду́хов. exorcize

v.t. (*spirits*) изгоня́ть *imp.*, изгна́ть (изгоню́, -нишь; изгна́л, -а́, -о) *perf.*

exotic *adj.* экзоти́ческий.

expand *v.t. & i.* (*broaden*) расширя́ть(ся) *imp.*, расши́рить(ся) *perf.*; (*develop*) развива́ть(ся) *imp.*, разви́ть(ся) (разовью́(сь), -вьёшь(ся) разви́л(ся), -ила́(сь), -и́ло́-и́ло́сь) *perf.*; (*increase*) увели́чивать(ся) *imp.*, увели́чить(ся) *perf.* expanse *n.* простра́нство. expansion *n.* расшире́ние; разви́тие; увеличе́ние; (*of territory*) экспа́нсия. expansive *adj.* (*extensive*) обши́рный; (*effusive*) экспанси́вный.

expatiate *v.i.* распространя́ться *imp.*, распространи́ться *perf.* (on, o + *prep.*).

expatriate *n.* экспатриа́нт.

expect *v.t.* (*await*) ожида́ть *imp.* + *gen.*; ждать (жду, ждёшь; ждал, -а́, -о) *imp.* + *gen.*, что; (*anticipate*) наде́яться (-е́юсь, -е́ешься) *imp.*, по ~ *perf.*; (*require*) тре́бовать *imp.* + *gen.*, чтобы. expectant *adj.* ожида́ющий (of, + *gen.*); *e. mother*, бере́менная же́нщина. expectation *n.* ожида́ние, наде́жда.

expectorant *n.* отха́ркивающее (сре́дство) *sb.* expectorate *v.t.* отха́ркивать *imp.*, отха́ркать *perf.*

expediency *n.* целесообра́зность. expedient *n.* сре́дство, приём; *adj.* целесообра́зный. expedite *v.t.* ускоря́ть *imp.*, уско́рить *perf.*; бы́стро выполня́ть *imp.*, вы́полнить *perf.* expedition *n.* экспеди́ция; (*promptness*) сро́чность. expeditionary *adj.* экспедицио́нный. expeditious *adj.* бы́стрый (быстр, -а́, -о, бы́стры).

expel *v.t.* выгоня́ть *imp.*, вы́гнать (вы́гоню, -нишь) *perf.* (*from school etc.*) исключа́ть *imp.*, исключи́ть *perf.*

expend *v.t.* тра́тить *imp.*, ис ~, по ~ *perf.*; расхо́довать *imp.*, из ~ *perf.* expenditure *n.* расхо́дование, расхо́д, тра́та. expense *n.* расхо́д; *pl.* расхо́ды *m.pl.*, изде́ржки *f.pl.*; *at the e. of*, цено́ю + *gen.*, за счёт + *gen.* expensive *adj.* дорого́й (до́рог, -а́, -о).

experience *n.* о́пыт, о́пытность; (*incident*) пережива́ние; *v.t.* испы́тывать *imp.*, испыта́ть *perf.*; (*undergo*) пережива́ть *imp.*, пережи́ть (-иву́, -ивёшь;

péреж́ил, -á, -о) *perf.* experienced *adj.* óпытный.

experiment *n.* óпыт, эксперимéнт; *v.i.* производи́ть (-ожу́, -óдишь) *imp.*, произвести́ (-еду́, -едёшь; -ёл, -елá) *perf.* óпыты (ол, на + *acc.*); эксперименти́ровать *imp.* (on, with, над, с, + *instr.*). experimental эксперимéнтáльный, óпытный. experimentation *n.* эксперименти́рование.

expert *n.* специали́ст (at, in, в + *prep.*, по + *dat.*), знатóк (-á) (+ *gen.*); *adj.* óпытный. expertise *n.* (*opinion*) эксперти́за; (*knowledge*) специáльные знáния *neut.pl.*

expiate *v.t.* искупáть *imp.*, искупи́ть (-плю́, -пишь) *perf.* expiation *n.* искуплéние.

expiration *n.* (*breathing out*) выдыхáние; (*termination*) истечéние. expire *v.t.* (*exhale*) выдыхáть *imp.*, вы́дохнуть *perf.*; *v.i.* (*period*) истекáть *imp.*, истéчь (-éчёт; -ёк, -еклá) *perf.*; (*die*) умирáть *imp.*, умерéть (умру́, -рёшь; у́мер, -лá, -ло) *perf.* expiry *n.* истечéние.

explain *v.t.* объясня́ть *imp.*, объясни́ть *perf.*; (*justify*) опрáвдывать *imp.*, оправдáть *perf.* explanation *n.* объяснéние. explanatory *adj.* объясни́тельный.

expletive *adj.* вставнóй; *n.* вставнóе слóво (*pl.* -вá); (*oath*) брáнное слóво (*pl.* -вá).

explicit *adj.* я́вный, определённый (-ёнен, -ённа).

explode *v.t. & i.* взрывáть(ся) *imp.*, взорвáть(ся)(-ву́,-вётся; взорвáл (-ся), -áло/-áлось) *perf.*; *v.t.* (*discredit*) разоблачáть *imp.*, разоблачи́ть *perf.*; *v.i.* (*with anger etc.*) разражáться *imp.*, разрази́ться *perf.*

exploit *n.* пóдвиг; *v.t.* эксплуати́ровать *imp.*; (*mine etc.*) разрабáтывать *imp.*, разрабóтать *perf.* exploitation *n.* эксплуатáция; разрабóтка. exploiter *n.* эксплуатáтор.

exploration *n.* исслéдование. exploratory *adj.* исслéдовательский. explore *v.t.* исслéдовать *imp.*, *perf.* explorer *n.* исслéдователь *m.*

explosion *n.* взрыв; (*anger etc.*) вспы́шка. explosive *n.* взры́вчатое вещество́; *adj.* взры́вчатый, взрывнóй.

exponent *n.* (*interpreter*) истолковáтель *m.*; (*representative*) представи́тель *m.*; (*math.*) показáтель *m.* стéпени. exponential *adj.* (*math.*) показáтельный.

export *n.* вы́воз, э́кспорт; *v.t.* вывози́ть (-ожу́, -óзишь) *imp.*, вы́везти (-езу, -езешь; -ез) *perf.*; экспорти́ровать *imp.*, *perf.* exporter *n.* экспортёр.

expose *v.t.* (*to risk etc.*) подвергáть *imp.*, подвéргнуть (-г) *perf.* (to, + *dat.*); (*phot.*) экспони́ровать *imp.*, *perf.*; (*display*) выставля́ть *imp.*, вы́ставить *perf.*; (*discredit*) разоблачáть *imp.*, разоблачи́ть *perf.*

exposition *n.* изложéние, толковáние.

exposure *n.* подвергáние (to, + *dat.*); (*phot.*) вы́держка; выставлéние; разоблачéние.

expound *v.t.* толковáть *imp.*; излагáть *imp.*, изложи́ть (-жу́, -жишь) *perf.*

express *n.* (*train*) экспрéсс; (*messenger*) нáрочный *sb.*, курьéр; *adj.* (*definite*) определённый (-ёнен, -ённа), тóчный (-чен, -чнá, -чно); *v.t.* выражáть *imp.*, вы́разить *perf.* expression *n.* выражéние; (*expressiveness*) вырази́тельность. expressive *adj.* вырази́тельный. expressly *adv.* нарóчно, намéренно.

expropriate *v.t.* экспроприи́ровать *imp.*, *perf.* expropriation *n.* экспроприáция.

expulsion *n.* изгнáние; (*from school etc.*) исключéние.

expunge *v.t.* вычёркивать *imp.*, вы́черкнуть *perf.*

exquisite *adj.* утончённый (-ён, -ённа).

extant *adj.* сохрани́вшийся, существу́ющий.

extemporaneous *adj.* неподготóвленный (-ен), импровизи́рованный (-ан). extempore *adv.* без подготóвки, экспрóмтом. extemporize *v.t. & i.* импровизи́ровать *imp.*, сымпровизи́ровать *perf.*

extend *v.t.* простирáть *imp.*, простерéть (-тру́, -трёшь; -тёр) *perf.*; протя́гивать *imp.*, протяну́ть (-ну́, -нешь) *perf.*; (*enlarge*) расширя́ть *imp.*, расши́рить *perf.*; (*prolong*) продлевáть *imp.*, продли́ть *perf.*; *v.i.* простира́ться *imp.*, простере́ться (-трётся; -тёрся) *perf.*; тяну́ться (-нется) *imp.*, по~ *perf.* **extension** *n.* расшире́ние; продле́ние. **extensive** *adj.* обши́рный, простра́нный (-нен, -нна), протяжённый (-ён, -ённа). **extent** *n.* протяже́ние; (*degree*) сте́пень (*pl.* -ни, -не́й); (*large space*) простра́нство.

extenuate *v.t.* уменьша́ть *imp.*, уме́ньшить *perf.*; *extenuating circumstances*, смягча́ющие вину́ обстоя́тельства *neut.pl.*

exterior *n.* вне́шность, нару́жность; *adj.* вне́шний, нару́жный.

exterminate *v.t.* уничтожа́ть *imp.*, уничто́жить *perf.*; истребля́ть *imp.*, истреби́ть *perf.* **extermination** *n.* уничтоже́ние, истребле́ние.

external *adj.* вне́шний, нару́жный.

extinct *adj.* (*volcano*) поту́хший; (*species*) вы́мерший; *become e.*, ту́хнуть (-х) *imp.*, по~ *perf.*; вымира́ть *imp.*, вы́мереть (-мрет; -мер) *perf.* **extinction** *n.* потуха́ние, вымира́ние.

extinguish *v.t.* гаси́ть (гашу́, га́сишь) *imp.*, по~ *perf.*; туши́ть (-шу́, -шишь) *imp.*, по~ *perf.*; (*debt*) погаша́ть *imp.*, погаси́ть (-ашу́, -а́сишь) *perf.* **extinguisher** *n.* гаси́тель *m.*; (*fire e.*) огнетуши́тель *m.*

extirpate *v.t.* истребля́ть *imp.*, истреби́ть *perf.*; искореня́ть *imp.*, искорени́ть *perf.* **extirpation** *n.* истребле́ние, искорене́ние.

extol *v.t.* превозноси́ть *imp.*, превознести́ (-есу́, -есёшь; -ёс, -есла́) *perf.*

extort *v.t.* вымога́ть *imp.* (from, y + *gen.*); (*information etc.*) выпы́тывать *imp.*, вы́пытать *perf.* (from, y + *gen.*). **extortion** *n.* вымога́тельство. **extortionate** *adj.* вымога́тельский, граби́тельский.

extra *n.* (*theat.*) стати́ст, ~ ка; (*payment*) припла́та, доба́вле́ние; *adj.* доба́вочный, дополни́тельный, э́кстренный; *adj.* осо́бый; *adv.* осо́бо, осо́бенно, дополни́тельно.

extra- *in comb.* вне-.

extract *n.* экстра́кт; (*from book etc.*) вы́держка; *v.t.* извлека́ть *imp.*, извле́чь (-еку́, -ечёшь; -ёк, -екла́) *perf.*; (*pull out*) выта́скивать *imp.*, вы́тащить *perf.*; (*tooth*) удаля́ть *imp.*, удали́ть *perf.* **extraction** *n.* извлече́ние; выта́скивание; удале́ние; (*descent*) происхожде́ние.

extradite *v.t.* выдава́ть (-даю́, -даёшь) *imp.*, вы́дать (-ам, -ашь, -аст, -адим) *perf.* **extradition** *n.* вы́дача.

extraneous *adj.* чу́ждый (чужд, -а́, -о) (to, + *dat.*), посторо́нний.

extraordinary *adj.* необыча́йный, чрезвыча́йный; (*surprising*) удиви́тельный.

extravagance *adj.* (*wild spending*) расточи́тельность; (*wildness*) сумасбро́дство. **extravagant** *adj.* расточи́тельный; сумасбро́дный.

extreme *n.* кра́йность; *adj.* кра́йний, чрезвыча́йный. **extremity** *n.* (*end*) край (*loc.* -а́е & -аю́; *pl.* -а́я), коне́ц (-нца́); (*adversity*) кра́йность; *pl.* (*hands & feet*) коне́чности *f.pl.*

extricate *v.t.* (*disentangle*) распу́тывать *imp.*, распу́тать *perf.*; *e. oneself*, выпу́тываться *imp.*, вы́путаться *perf.*

exuberance *n.* изоби́лие, ро́скошь; (*of person*) жизнера́достность. **exuberant** *adj.* оби́льный, роско́шный; жизнера́достный.

exude *v.t. & i.* выделя́ть(ся) *imp.*, вы́делить(ся) *perf.*

exult *v.i.* икова́ть *imp.* **exultant** *adj.* лику́ющий. **exultation** *n.* икова́ние.

eye *n.* глаз (*loc.* -зу́; *pl.* -за́, -з, -за́м); (*poet.*) о́ко (*pl.* о́чи, оче́й); (*needle etc.*) ушко́ (*pl.* -ки́, -ко́в); *an eye for an eye*, о́ко за о́ко; *up to the eyes in*, по́ уши, по го́рло, в + *prep.*; *v.t.* всма́триваться *imp.*, всмотре́ться (-рю́сь, -ришься) *perf.* в + *acc.* **eyeball** *n.* глазно́е я́блоко (*pl.* -ки, -к). **eyebrow** *n.* бровь (*pl.* -ви, -ве́й). **eyelash** *n.* ресни́ца. **eyelid** *n.* ве́ко (*pl.* -ки, -к). **eyepiece** *n.* окуля́р. **eyesight** *n.* зре́ние. **eyewitness** *n.* очеви́дец (-дца).

eyrie *n.* (орли́ное) гнездо́ (*pl.* -ёзда).

F

F n. (*mus.*) фа *neut.indecl.*
fable n. ба́сня (*gen.pl.* -сен), небыли́ца.
fabric n. (*structure*) структу́ра, устро́й-ство; (*cloth*) ткань. **fabricate** v.t. (*invent*) выду́мывать *imp.*, вы́думать *perf.*; (*forge*) подде́лывать *imp.*, подде́лать *perf.* **fabrication** n. вы́думка; подде́лка.
fabulous adj. ска́зочный.
façade n. фаса́д.
face n. лицо́ (*pl.* -ца); (*expression*) выраже́ние; (*grimace*) грима́са; (*out-ward aspect*) вне́шний вид; (*surface*) пове́рхность; (*clock etc.*) цифербла́т; **have the f.**, име́ть *imp.* наха́льство; **make faces**, ко́рчить *imp.* ро́жи; **f. down**, (*cards*) руба́шкой вверх; **f. to f.**, лицо́м к лицу́; **in the f. of**, пе́ред лицо́м + *gen.*, вопреки́ + *dat.*; **on the f. of it**, на пе́рвый взгляд; **f. card**, фигу́ра; **f. value**, номина́льная сто́и-мость; **take at f. value**, принима́ть *imp.*, приня́ть (приму́, -мешь; при́-нял, -а́, -о) *perf.* за чи́стую моне́ту; v.t. (*be turned towards*) быть обра-щённым к + *dat.*; (*meet firmly*) смо-тре́ть (-рю́, -ришь) *imp.* в лицо́ + *dat.*; (*cover*) облицо́вывать *imp.*, облице-ва́ть (-цу́ю, -цу́ешь) *perf.*; **f. the music**, расхлёбывать *imp.*, расхлеба́ть *perf.* ка́шу. **faceless** adj. безли́кий.
facet n. грань; (*aspect*) аспе́кт.
facetious adj. шутли́вый.
facial adj. лицево́й.
facile adj. лёгкий (-гок, -гка́, -гко́, лёгки), свобо́дный; (*derog.*) пове́рх-ностный. **facilitate** v.t. облегча́ть *imp.*, облегчи́ть *perf.* **facility** n. (*ease*) лёг-кость; (*ability*) спосо́бность; (*oppor-tunity*) возмо́жность.
facing n. облицо́вка; (*of garment*) от-де́лка, обши́вка.
facsimile n. факси́миле *neut.indecl.*
fact n. факт; (*reality*) действи́тель-ность; *pl.* (*information*) да́нные *sb.*; **the f. is that . . .**, де́ло в том, что...; **as a matter of f.**, со́бственно говоря́; **in f.**, действи́тельно, на са́мом де́ле.

faction n. фра́кция. **factional** adj. фрак-цио́нный.
factitious adj. иску́сственный (-вен(ен), -венна).
factor n. (*circumstance*) фа́ктор; (*mer-chant*) комиссионе́р; (*math.*) мно́жи-тель m.; (*of safety etc.*) коэффицие́нт.
factory n. фа́брика, заво́д; **f.-ship**, пла-ву́чий рыбозаво́д.
factual adj. факти́ческий, действи́тель-ный.
faculty n. спосо́бность, дар (*pl.* -ы́); (*univ.*) факульте́т.
fade v.i. вя́нуть (вял) *imp.*, за~ *perf.*; увяда́ть *imp.*, увя́нуть (-я́л) *perf.*; (*colour*) выцвета́ть *imp.*, вы́цвести (-стет, -ел) *perf.*; (*sound*) замира́ть *imp.*, замере́ть (-мрёт; за́мер, -ла́, -ло) *perf.*
faeces n. кал.
fag n.i. корпе́ть (-плю́, -пи́шь) (over, над + *instr.*); v.t. утомля́ть *imp.*, утоми́ть *perf.*; n. (*drudgery*) тяжёлая рабо́та; (*cigarette*) сигаре́тка; **f.-end**, оку́рок (-рка).
faggot n. (*wood*) вяза́нка хво́роста, -ту.
faience n. фая́нс.
fail n.: **without f.**, обяза́тельно, непре-ме́нно; v.t. & i. (*be insufficient*) не хвата́ть *imp.*, не хвати́ть (-тит) *perf.* impers. + *gen.* (*subject*) & y + *gen.* (*object*); v.i. (*weaken*) ослабева́ть *imp.*, ослабе́ть *perf.*; v.i. (*not succeed*) тер-пе́ть (-плю́, -пи́шь) *imp.*, по~ *perf.* неуда́чу; не удава́ться (удаётся) *imp.*, уда́ться (-а́стся; -а́лось) *perf.*impers. + *dat.* (in, + *inf.*); v.t. & i. (*examination*) прова́ливать(ся) *imp.*, провали́ть(ся) (-лю́(сь), -лишь(ся)) *perf.* **failing** n. недоста́ток (-тка), сла́бость; *prep.* за неиме́нием + *gen.*, в слу́чае отсу́т-ствия + *gen.* **failure** n. неуда́ча, прова́л; (*person*) неуда́чник, -ица.
faint n. о́бморок; adj. (*weak*) сла́бый (слаб, -а́, -о); (*pale*) бле́дный (-ден, -дна́, -дно, бле́дны); **f.-hearted**, мало-ду́шный; v.i. па́дать *imp.*, упа́сть (упаду́, -дёшь) *perf.* в о́бморок.
fair[1] n. я́рмарка.

fair² *adj.* (*beautiful*) краси́вый; (*just*) че́стный (-тен, -тна́, -тно), справедли́вый; (*considerable*) поря́дочный; (*blond*) белоку́рый; *f. copy*, чистови́к (-á). **fairly** *adv.* (*tolerably*) дово́льно; (*completely*) соверше́нно. **fairway** *n.* фарва́тер.

fairy *n.* фе́я; *f.-tale*, ска́зка.

faith *n.* (*belief*) ве́ра; (*trust*) дове́рие; (*loyalty*) ве́рность. **faithful** *adj.* ве́рный (-рен, -рна́, -рно, ве́рны́). **faithless** *adj.* вероло́мный, неве́рный (-рен, -рна́, -рно, -рны́).

fake *n.* подде́лка; *v.t.* подде́лывать *imp.*, подде́лать *perf.*

falcon *n.* со́кол. **falconry** *n.* соко́линая охо́та.

fall *n.* паде́ние; *pl.* водопа́д; *v.i.* па́дать *imp.*, (у)па́сть ((у)паду́, -дёшь; (у)па́л) *perf.*; понижа́ться *imp.*, пони́зиться *perf.*; *f. apart*, распада́ться *imp.*, распа́сться (-адётся -а́лся) *perf.*; *f. asleep*, засыпа́ть *imp.*, засну́ть *perf.*; *f. back on*, прибега́ть *imp.*, -гнуть (-г(нул), -гла) *perf.* к + *dat.*; *f. off*, отпада́ть *imp.*, -па́сть (-аду́, -адёшь; -а́л) *perf.*; *f. over*, опроки́дываться *imp.*, опроки́нуться *perf.*; *f. through*, прова́ливаться *imp.*, -ли́ться (-и́тся) *perf.*; *f.-out*, радиоакти́вные оса́дки (-ков) *pl.*

fallacious *adj.* оши́бочный, ло́жный. **fallacy** *n.* оши́бка, заблужде́ние. **fallibility** *n.* оши́бочность. **fallible** *adj.* подве́рженный (-ен) оши́бкам.

fallow *n.* пар (*pl.* -ы́), земля́ (*acc.* -лю) под па́ром; *adj.* под па́ром; *lie f.*, лежа́ть (-жи́т) *imp.* под па́ром.

fallow deer *n.* лань.

false *adj.* ло́жный, фальши́вый. **falsehood** *n.* ложь (лжи, *instr.* ло́жью). **falsetto** *n.* фальце́т. **falsification** *n.* фальсифика́ция, подде́лка. **falsify** *v.t.* фальсифици́ровать *imp.*, *perf.*; подде́лывать *imp.*, подде́лать *perf.* **falsity** *n.* ло́жность.

falter *v.i.* (*stumble*) спотыка́ться *imp.*, споткну́ться *perf.*; (*stammer*) запина́ться *imp.*, запну́ться *perf.*; (*waver*) колеба́ться (-блюсь, -блешься) *imp.*

fame *n.* сла́ва, репута́ция. **famed** *adj.* изве́стный.

familiar *adj.* (*close*) бли́зкий (-зок, -зка́, -зко, бли́зки); (*well known*) знако́мый; (*usual*) обы́чный; (*informal*) фамилья́рный. **familiarity** *n.* бли́зость; знако́мство; фамилья́рность. **familiarize** *v.t.* знакоми́ть *imp.*, ознако́мить *perf.* (*with*, с + *instr.*).

family *n.* семья́ (*pl.* -мьи, -ме́й, -мьям); (*lineage etc.*) род (-а(у)), *loc.* -у́; *pl.* -ы́); (*generic group*) семе́йство; *attrib.* семе́йный, фами́льный; *f. tree*, родосло́вная *sb.*

famine *n.* (*scarcity of food*) го́лод (-а(у)); (*dearth*) недоста́ток (-тка). **famish** *v.t.* мори́ть *imp.*, у~ *perf.* го́лодом; *v.i., be famished*, голода́ть *imp.*

famous *adj.* знамени́тый, изве́стный, просла́вленный.

fan¹ *n.* (*device etc.*) ве́ер (*pl.* -á); (*ventilator*) вентиля́тор; *v.t.* обма́хивать *imp.*, обмахну́ть *perf.*; (*flame*) раздува́ть *imp.*, разду́ть (-у́ю, -у́ешь) *perf.*

fan² *n.* (*devotee*) боле́льщик, -ица. **fanatic** *n.* фана́тик, -и́чка. **fanatical** *adj.* фанати́ческий.

fanciful *adj.* (*capricious*) прихотли́вый; (*imaginary*) вообража́емый. **fancy** *n.* фанта́зия, воображе́ние; (*whim*) причу́да; *adj.* орнамента́льный; *v.t.* (*imagine*) представля́ть *imp.*, предста́вить *perf.* себе́; (*suppose*) каза́ться (ка́жется; каза́лось) *imp.*, по~ *perf.impers.*; (*like*) нра́виться *imp.*, по~ *perf.impers.* + *dat.*; *f. dress*, маскара́дный костю́м; *f.-dress*, костюми́рованный.

fanfare *n.* фанфа́ра.

fang *n.* клык (-á); (*serpent's*) ядови́тый зуб (*pl.* -ы, - о́в).

fantastic *adj.* фантасти́ческий, причу́дливый. **fantasy** *n.* фанта́зия, воображе́ние.

far *adj.* да́льний, далёкий (-ёк, -ека́ -ёко); (*remote*) отдалённый; *adv.* далеко́; (*fig.*) намно́го; *as f. as*, (*prep.*) до + *gen.*; (*conj.*) поско́льку; *by f.*, намно́го; *in so f. as*, поско́льку; *so f.*, до сих пор; *f.-fetched*, натя́нутый; притя́нутый за́ волосы; *f.-reaching*, далеко́ иду́щий;

f.-seeing, дальнови́дный; f.-sighted, дальнови́дный; (physically) дально-зо́ркий.

farce n. фарс. farcical adj. фа́рсовый, смехотво́рный.

fare n. (price) проездна́я пла́та; (passenger) пассажи́р; (food) пи́ща; v.i. пожива́ть imp. farewell interj. проща́й(те)! n. проща́ние; attrib. проща́льный; bid f., проща́ться imp., прости́ться perf. (to, с + instr.).

farinaceous adj. мучни́стый, мучно́й.

farm n. фе́рма, хозя́йство. farmer n. фе́рмер. farming n. се́льское хозя́й-ство.

farrier n. (smith) кузне́ц (-а́); (horse-doctor) кона́вал.

farther comp.adj. бо́лее отдалённый (-ён, -ённа); дальне́йший; (additional) дополни́тельный; adv. да́льше. far-thermost adj. са́мый да́льний. farthest superl.adj. са́мый да́льний, са́мый отдалённый; adv. да́льше всего́.

fascicle n. (bot.) пучо́к (-чка́); (book) вы́пуск.

fascinate v.t. очаро́вывать imp., очаро-ва́ть perf. fascinating adj. очарова́тель-ный. fascination n. очарова́ние.

Fascism n. фаши́зм. Fascist n. фаши́ст, ~ ка; adj. фаши́стский.

fashion n. (manner) мане́ра; (pattern) фасо́н; (style) стиль m.; (style of dress etc.) мо́да; after a f., не́которым о́бразом; after the f. of, по образцу́ + gen.; v.t. придава́ть (-даю́, -даёшь) imp., прида́ть (-а́м, -а́шь, -а́ст, -ади́м; при́дал, -а́, -о) perf. фо́рму + dat.; формирова́ть imp., с ~ perf. fashionable adj. мо́дный (-ден, -дна́, -дно), фешене́бельный.

fast[1] n. пост (-а́, loc. -у́); v.i. пости́ться imp., break (one's) f., разгове́ться imp., разгове́ться perf.

fast[2] adj. (firm) про́чный (-чен, -чна́, -чно), про́чный; кре́пкий (-пок, -пка́, -пко), твёрдый (-д, -да́, -до), сто́йкий (-о́ек, -о́йка, -о́йко); (rapid) ско́рый (скор, -а́, -о), бы́стрый (быстр, -а́, -о, бы́стры); (immoral) беспу́тный; be f., (timepiece) спеши́ть imp. fasten v.t. (attach) прикрепля́ть imp., при-

крепи́ть perf. (to, к + dat.); (tie) при-вя́зывать imp., привяза́ть (-яжу́, -я́жешь) perf. (to, к + dat.); (garment) застёгивать imp., застегну́ть perf. (on garment) застёжка.

fastidious adj. брезгли́вый.

fat n. жир (-а(у), loc. -у́; pl. -ы́), са́ло; adj. (greasy) жи́рный (-рен, -рна́, -рно); (plump) то́лстый (-т, -та́, -то, то́лсты), ту́чный (-чен, -чна́, -чно); get, grow, f., толсте́ть imp., по ~ perf.

fatal adj. фата́льный, роково́й; (deadly) па́губный, сме́ртельный. fatality n. па́губность, фата́льность; (calamity) несча́стье; (death) смерть f.ate n. судьба́ (pl. -дьбы, -деб, -дьбам), рок, жре́бий. fated predic. обречён (-а́).

fateful adj. роково́й.

father n. оте́ц (-тца́); f.-in-law, (husband's f.) свёкор (-кра), (wife's f.) тесть m. fatherland n. оте́чество. fatherly adj. оте́ческий.

fathom n. ше́сть (-ти́, -тью) фу́тов (глубины́ воды́); v.t. измеря́ть imp., изме́рить perf. глубину́ (воды́); (understand) понима́ть imp., поня́ть (пойму́, -мёшь; по́нял, -а́, -о) perf.

fatigue n. уста́лость, утомле́ние; v.t. утомля́ть imp., утоми́ть perf.

fatness n. ту́чность. fatten v.t. отка́рм-ливать imp., откорми́ть (-млю́, -мишь) perf.; v.i. толсте́ть imp., по ~ perf. fatty adj. жи́рный (-рен, -рна́, -рно), жирово́й.

fatuous adj. тупо́й (туп, -а́, -о, ту́пы́).

fault n. недоста́ток (-тка), дефе́кт; (blame) вина́ (pl. -ны); (geol.) сброс. faultless adj. безупре́чный, безоши́бочный. faulty adj. дефе́ктный.

fauna n. фа́уна.

favour n. (goodwill) благоскло́нность; (aid) одолже́ние; in (somebody's) favour, в по́льзу + gen.; be in f. of, стоя́ть (-ою́, -ои́шь) imp. за + acc.; v.t. благоволи́ть imp. + dat.; благо-прия́тствовать imp. + dat. favourable adj. (propitious) благоприя́тный; (ap-proving) благоприя́тный (-нен, -нна). favourite n. люби́мец (-мца), -мица фаво-ри́т, ~ ка; adj. люби́мый.

fawn¹ *n.* оленёнок (-нка; *pl.* оленя́та, -т); *adj.* (*f.-coloured*) желтова́то-кори́чневый.

fawn² *v.i.* (*animal*) ласка́ться *imp.* (upon, к + *dat.*); (*person*) подли́зываться *imp.*, подлиза́ться (-ижу́сь, -и́жешься) *perf.* (upon, к + *dat.*).

fealty *n.* (прися́га на) ве́рность.

fear *n.* страх, боя́знь, опасе́ние; *v.t. & i.* боя́ться (бою́сь, бои́шься) *imp.* + *gen.*; опаса́ться *imp.* + *gen.* **fearful** *adj.* (*terrible*) стра́шный (-шен, -шна́, -шно, стра́шны); (*timid*) пугли́вый. **fearless** *adj.* бесстра́шный. **fearsome** *adj.* гро́зный (-зен, -зна́, -зно). **feasibility** *n.* осуществи́мость, возмо́жность. **feasible** *adj.* осуществи́мый, возмо́жный.

feast *n.* (*meal*) пир (*loc.* -е & -ý; *pl.* -ы́); (*festival*) пра́здник; *v.i.* пирова́ть *imp.*; *v.t.* угоща́ть *imp.*, угости́ть *perf.*; *f. one's eyes on*, любова́ться *imp.*, по~ *perf.* + *instr.*, на + *acc.*

feat *n.* по́двиг.

feather *n.* перо́ (*pl.* пе́рья, -ьев); *pl.* (*plumage*) опере́ние; *v.t.* оперя́ть *imp.*, опери́ть *perf.*; *f. bed*, пери́на; *f.-brained*, ве́треный. **feathery** *adj.* перна́тый.

feature *n.* осо́бенность, черта́; (*newspaper*) статья́; *pl.* (*of face*) черты́ *f.pl.* лица́; *f. film*, худо́жественный фильм; *v.t.* (*in film*) пока́зывать *imp.*, показа́ть (-ажу́, -а́жешь) *perf.* (на экра́не); *v.i.* (*take part*) уча́ствовать *imp.* (in, в + *prep.*).

febrile *adj.* лихора́дочный.

February *n.* февра́ль (-ля́) *m.*; *attrib.* февра́льский.

fecund *adj.* плодоро́дный. **fecundity** *n.* плодоро́дие.

federal *adj.* федерати́вный. **federation** *n.* федера́ция.

fee *n.* гонора́р; (*entrance f. etc.*) взнос; *pl.* (*regular payment, school, etc.*) пла́та.

feeble *adj.* сла́бый (слаб, -á, -о), не́мощный; *f.-minded*, слабоу́мный. **feebleness** *n.* сла́бость.

feed *n.* корм (-а(у), *loc.* -е & -ý; *pl.* -á); *v.t.* корми́ть (-млю́, -мишь) *imp.*, на~, по~ *perf.*; пита́ть *imp.*, на~ *perf.*; *v.i.* корми́ться (-млю́сь, -мишь-ся) *imp.*, по~ *perf.*; пита́ться *imp.* (on, + *instr.*); *f. up*, (*fatten*) отка́рмливать *imp.*, откорми́ть (-млю́, -мишь) *perf.*; *I am fed up with*, мне надое́л (-а, -о, -и) + *nom.* **feedback** *n.* обра́тная связь.

feel *v.t.* осяза́ть *imp.*; ощуща́ть *imp.*, ощути́ть (-ущу́, -ути́шь) *perf.*; чу́вствовать *imp.*, по~ *perf.*; (*undergo*) испы́тывать *imp.*, испыта́ть *perf.*; *v.i.* (*feel bad etc.*) чу́вствовать *imp.*, по~ *perf.* себя́ + *adv.*, + *instr.*; *f. like*, хоте́ться (хо́чется) *imp.impers.* + *dat.* **feeling** *n.* (*sense*) ощуще́ние; (*emotion*) чу́вство, эмо́ция; (*impression*) впечатле́ние; (*mood*) настрое́ние.

feign *v.t.* притворя́ться *imp.*, притвори́ться *perf.* + *instr.* **feigned** *adj.* притво́рный.

feint *n.* ло́жный уда́р; (*pretence*) притво́рство.

felicitate *v.t.* поздравля́ть *imp.*, поздра́вить *perf.* (on, с + *instr.*). **felicitation** *n.* поздравле́ние.

felicitous *adj.* уда́чный, счастли́вый (сча́стлив). **felicity** *n.* сча́стье, блаже́нство.

feline *adj.* коша́чий (-чья, -чье).

fell¹ *n.* (*animal's skin*) шку́ра.

fell² *v.t.* (*tree*) сруба́ть *imp.*, сруби́ть (-блю́, -бишь) *perf.*; (*person*) сбива́ть *imp.*, сбить (собью́, -бёшь) *perf.* с ног.

fellow *n.* челове́к, па́рень (-рня; *pl.* -рни, -рне́й) *m.*, това́рищ; член (колле́гия, нау́чного о́бщества и т.п.). **fellowship** *n.* това́рищество, соо́бщество.

felon *n.* уголо́вный престу́пник, -ица. **felonious** *adj.* престу́пный. **felony** *n.* уголо́вное преступле́ние.

fel(d)spar *n.* полево́й шпат.

felt *n.* фетр, во́йлок; *adj.* фе́тровый, во́йлочный; *f. boots*, ва́ленки (-нок) *pl.*

female *n.* (*animal*) са́мка; (*person*) же́нщина; *adj.* же́нский. **feminine** *adj.* же́нский, же́нственный (-ен, -енна); (*gram.*) же́нского ро́да.

femoral *adj.* бе́дренный. **femur** *n.* бедро́ (*pl.* бёдра, -дер, -драм).

fen *n.* боло́то, боло́тистая ме́стность.

fence *n.* огра́да, забо́р, и́згородь; (*receiver of stolen goods*) бары́га, скупщик кра́деного; *v.t.*: f. in, огора́живать *imp.*, огороди́ть (-ожу́, -оди́шь) *perf.*; f. off, отгора́живать *imp.*, отгороди́ть (-ожу́, -оди́шь) *perf.*; *v.i.* (*sport*) фехтова́ть *imp.* **fencer** *n.* фехтова́льщик, -ица. **fencing** *n.* огора́живание; (*enclosure*) забо́р, и́згородь; (*sport*) фехтова́ние; *adj.* фехтова́льный.

fend *v.t.*: f. off, отража́ть *imp.*, отрази́ть (-ажу́, -ази́шь) *perf.*; (*blow*) пари́ровать *imp.*, от ~ *perf.*; f. for oneself, забо́титься *imp.*, по ~ *perf.* о себе́. **fender** *n.* (*guard*) решётка; (*naut.*) кра́нец (-нца).

fennel *n.* фе́нхель *m.*

ferment *n.* (*substance*) заква́ска; (*action, also fig.*) броже́ние; *v.i.* броди́ть (-дит) *imp.*; *v.t.* ква́сить (-а́шу, -а́сишь) *imp.*, за ~ *perf.*; (*excite*) возбужда́ть *imp.*, возбуди́ть *perf.* **fermentation** *n.* броже́ние; (*excitement*) возбужде́ние.

fern *n.* па́поротник.

ferocious *adj.* свире́пый, лю́тый (лют, -а́, -о). **ferocity** *n.* свире́пость, лю́тость.

ferret *n.* хорёк (-рька́); *v.t.*: f. out, выгоня́ть *imp.*, вы́гнать (вы́гоню, -нишь) *perf.*; (*search out*) разнюхивать *imp.*, разню́хать *perf.*; *v.i.*: f. about, (*rummage*) ры́ться (ро́юсь, ро́ешься) *imp.*

ferro- *in comb.* ферро-, желе́зо-; f.-concrete, железобето́н. **ferrous** *adj.* желе́зный; f. metals, чёрные металлы *m.pl.*

ferry *n.* паро́м, перево́з; *v.t.* перевози́ть (-ожу́, -о́зишь) *imp.*, перевезти́ (-езу́, -езёшь; -ёз, -езла́) *perf.* **ferryman** *n.* паро́мщик, перево́зчик.

fertile *adj.* плодоро́дный, плодови́тый. **fertility** *n.* плодоро́дие, плодови́тость. **fertilize** *v.t.* (*soil*) удобря́ть *imp.*, удобри́ть *perf.*; (*egg*) оплодотворя́ть *imp.*, оплодотвори́ть *perf.* **fertilizer** *n.* удобре́ние.

fervent, fervid *adj.* горя́чий, пы́лкий (-лок, -лка́, -лко). **fervour** *n.* пыл (-а(у), *loc.* -у́), горя́чность, рве́ние.

festal *adj.* (*of feast*) пра́здничный; (*gay*) весёлый (ве́сел, -а́, -о, ве́селы).

fester *v.i.* гнои́ться *imp.*

festival *n.* пра́здник, фестива́ль *m.* **festive** *adj.* пра́здничный; (*jovial*) весёлый (ве́сел, -а́, -о, ве́селы). **festivity** *n.* весе́лье; *pl.* торжества́ *neut.pl.*

festoon *n.* гирля́нда; (*archit.*) фесто́н; *v.t.* украша́ть *imp.*, укра́сить *perf.* гирля́ндами, фесто́нами.

fetch *v.t.* (*carrying*) приноси́ть (-ошу́, -о́сишь) *imp.*, принести́ (-есу́, -есёшь; -ёс, -есла́) *perf.*; (*leading*) приводи́ть (-ожу́, -о́дишь) *imp.*, привести́ (-еду́, -едёшь; -ёл, -ела́) *perf.*; (*go and come back with*) (*on foot*) сходи́ть (-ожу́, -о́дишь) *perf.* за + *instr.*; заходи́ть (-ожу́, -о́дишь) *imp.*, зайти́ (зайду́, -дёшь; зашёл, -шла́) *perf.* за + *instr.*; (*by vehicle*) заезжа́ть *imp.*, зае́хать (-е́ду, -е́дешь) *perf.* за + *instr.*; (*cause*) вызыва́ть *imp.*, вы́звать (вы́зову, -вешь) *perf.*; (*price*) выруча́ть *imp.*, вы́ручить *perf.* **fetching** *adj.* привлека́тельный.

fetid *adj.* злово́нный (-нен, -нна).

fetish *n.* фети́ш.

fetlock *n.* щётка.

fetter *v.t.* ско́вывать *imp.*, скова́ть (скую́, скуёшь) *perf.*; *n.*: *pl.* кандалы́ (-ло́в) *pl.*, око́вы (-в) *pl.*

fettle *n.* состоя́ние.

feud *n.* кро́вная месть.

feudal *adj.* феода́льный. **feudalism** *n.* феодали́зм.

fever *n.* (*med.*) жар (-а(у), *loc.* -у́), лихора́дка; (*agitation*) возбужде́ние. **feverish** *adj.* лихора́дочный; возбуждённый (-ён, -ена́).

few *a.* *adj.*, *pron.* немно́гие (-их) *pl.*; немно́го + *gen.*, ма́ло + *gen.*, не́сколько + *gen.*; quite a f., немало + *gen.*

fez *n.* фе́ска.

fiancé *n.* жени́х (-а́). **fiancée** *n.* неве́ста.

fiasco *n.* прова́л.

fiat *n.* (*sanction*) са́нкция; (*decree*) декре́т.

fib *n.* враньё; *v.i.* привира́ть *imp.*, привра́ть (-ру́, -рёшь; привра́л, -о) *perf.* **fibber** *n.* враль (-ля́) *m.*

fibre n. фи́бра, волокно́ (pl. -о́кна, -о́кон, -о́кнам); (character) хара́ктер. **fibreglass** n. стекловолокно́. **fibrous** adj. фибро́зный, волокни́стый.

fickle adj. непостоя́нный (-нен, -нна), изме́нчивый. **fickleness** n. непостоя́нство, изме́нчивость.

fiction n. (literature) беллетри́стика, худо́жественная литерату́ра; (invention) вы́думка. **fictional** adj. беллетристи́ческий; вы́мышленный. **fictitious** adj. вы́мышленный, фикти́вный.

fiddle n. (violin) скри́пка; (swindle) обма́н; v.i. игра́ть imp. (with, c + instr.); f. about, безде́льничать imp.; v.t. (cheat) надува́ть imp., наду́ть (-у́ю, -у́ешь) perf.

fidelity n. ве́рность.

fidget n. непосе́да m. & f.; v.i. ёрзать imp.; не́рвничать imp. **fidgety** adj. непоседли́вый.

field n. по́ле (pl. -ля́, -ле́й); (sport) площа́дка; (sphere) о́бласть, сфе́ра; attrib. полево́й; (glasses) полево́й бино́кль m.; F. Marshal, фельдма́ршал; f.-mouse, полева́я мышь (pl. -ши, -ше́й).

fiend n. (demon) дья́вол, де́мон; (cruel person) и́зверг. **fiendish** adj. дья́вольский.

fierce adj. свире́пый, лю́тый (лют, -á, -о); (strong) си́льный (си́лён, -льна́, -льно, си́льны). **fiery** adj. о́гненный.

fife n. ду́дка.

fifteen adj., n. пятна́дцать (-ти, -тью); (age) пятна́дцать лет. **fifteenth** adj., n. пятна́дцатый; (date) пятна́дцатое (число́). **fifth** adj., n. пя́тый; (fraction) пя́тая (часть (pl.-ти, -те́й)); (date) пя́тое (число́); (mus.) кви́нта. **fiftieth** adj., n. пятидеся́тый. **fifty** adj., n. пятьдеся́т (-ти́десяти, -тью́десятью); (age) пятьдеся́т лет; pl. (decade) пятидеся́тые го́ды (-до́в) m.pl.; f.-f., adj. ра́вный (-вен, -вна́); adv. по́ровну.

fig n. фи́га, ви́нная я́года, инжи́р.

fight n. дра́ка; (battle) бой (loc. бою́; pl. бой); (fig.) борьба́; v.t. боро́ться (-рю́сь, -решься) imp. c + instr.; сража́ться imp., срази́ться perf. c + instr.; v.i. дра́ться (деру́сь, -рёшься

дра́лся, -ла́сь, дра́ло́сь) imp. **fighter** n. бое́ц (бойца́); (aeron.) истреби́тель m. **fighting** n. бой m.pl., сраже́ние, дра́ка; adj. боево́й.

figment n. вы́мысел (-сла), плод (-á) воображе́ния.

figuration n. оформле́ние; (ornamentation) орнамента́ция. **figurative** adj. о́бразный, перено́сный. **figure** n. (form, body, person) фигу́ра; (number) ци́фра; (diagram) рису́нок (-нка); (image) изображе́ние; (person) ли́чность; (of speech) оборо́т ре́чи; f.-head, (naut.) носово́е украше́ние; (person) подставно́е лицо́ (pl. -ца); v.t. (represent) изобража́ть imp., изобрази́ть perf.; (imagine) представля́ть imp., предста́вить себе́ perf.; f. out, вычисля́ть imp., вы́числить perf. **figurine** n. статуэ́тка.

filament n. волокно́ (pl. -о́кна, -о́кон, -о́кнам), нить.

filch v.t. стяну́ть (-ну́, -нешь) perf.

file [1] n. (tool) напи́льник; v.t. подпи́ливать imp., подпили́ть (-лю́, -лишь) perf.

file [2] n. (folder) подши́вка, па́пка; (set of papers) де́ло (pl. -лá); v.t. подшива́ть imp., подши́ть (подошью́, -ьёшь) perf.; влага́ть imp., вложи́ть (-жу́, -жишь) perf. в па́пку.

file [3] n. (row) ряд (-á with 2, 3, 4, loc. -ý; pl. -ы́), шере́нга; in (single) f., гусько́м.

filial adj. (of son) сыно́вный; (of daughter) доче́рний.

filigree n. филигра́нь; adj. филигра́нный.

fill v.t. & i. наполня́ть(ся) imp., напо́лнить(ся) perf.; v.t. заполня́ть imp., запо́лнить perf.; (tooth) пломбирова́ть imp., за~ perf.; (occupy) занима́ть imp., заня́ть (займу́, -мёшь; за́нял, -á, -о) perf.; (satiate) насыща́ть imp., насы́тить (-ы́щу, -ы́тишь) perf.; f. in, (v.t.) заполня́ть imp., запо́лнить perf.; (words) впи́сывать imp., вписа́ть (-ишу́, -и́шешь) perf.; (v.i.) замеща́ть imp., замести́ть perf.

fillet n. (ribbon) повя́зка; (cul.) филе́ neut.indecl.

filling *n.* наполне́ние; (*tooth*) пло́мба; (*cul.*) начи́нка.

filip *n.* щелчо́к (-чка́); толчо́к (-чка́).

filly *n.* кобы́лка.

film *n.* (*haze*) ды́мка; (*layer*; *phot.*) плёнка; (*cin.*) фильм; *f. star*, кинозвезда́ (*pl.* -ёзды); *v.t.* экранизи́ровать *imp.*, *perf.*; *v.i.* производи́ть (-ожу́, -о́дишь) *imp.*, произвести́ (-еду́, -едёшь; -ёл, -ела́) *perf.* кинносъёмку; снима́ть *imp.*, снять (сниму́, -мешь; снял, -а́, -о) *perf.* фильм. **filmy** *adj.* тума́нный (-нен, -нна).

filter *n.* фильтр; *v.t.* фильтрова́ть *imp.*, про~ *perf.*; проце́живать *imp.*, процеди́ть *perf.*; *f. through, out*, проса́чиваться *imp.*, просочи́ться *perf.*

filth *n.* грязь (*loc.* -зи́); (*obscenity*) непристо́йность. **filthy** *adj.* гря́зный (-зен, -зна́, -зно); непристо́йный.

fin *n.* плавни́к (-а́); (*aeron.*) киль *m.*

final *n.* фина́л; *pl.* выпускны́е экза́мены *m.pl.*; *adj.* после́дний, оконча́тельный. **finale** *n.* фина́л, развя́зка. **finality** *n.* зако́нченность. **finally** *adv.* в конце́ концо́в, оконча́тельно.

finance *n.* фина́нсы (-сов) *pl.*; *pl.* дохо́ды *m.pl.*; *v.t.* финанси́ровать *imp.* & *perf.* **financial** *adj.* фина́нсовый. **financier** *n.* финанси́ст.

finch *n.* see comb., e.g. bullfinch.

find *n.* нахо́дка; *v.t.* находи́ть (-ожу́, -о́дишь) *imp.*, найти́ (найду́, -дёшь; нашёл, -шла́) *perf.*; (*person*) застава́ть (-таю́, -таёшь) *imp.*, заста́ть (-а́ну, -а́нешь) *perf.*; *f. out*, узнава́ть (-наю́, -наёшь) *imp.*, узна́ть *perf.*; *f. fault with*, придира́ться *imp.*, придра́ться (придеру́сь, -рёшься; придра́лся, -ала́сь, -а́лось) *perf.* к + *dat.* **finding** *n.* (*leg.*) пригово́р; *pl.* (*of inquiry*) вы́воды *m.pl.*

fine¹ *n.* (*penalty*) штраф; *v.t.* штрафова́ть *imp.*, о~ *perf.*

fine² *adj.* (*excellent*) прекра́сный, превосхо́дный; (*delicate*) то́нкий (-нок, -нка́, -нко, то́нки́); (*of sand etc.*) ме́лкий (-лок, -лка́, -лко); *f. arts*, изобрази́тельные иску́сства *neut.pl.* **fineness** *n.* то́нкость, изя́щество, острота́. **finery** *n.* наря́д, украше́ние. **finesse** *n.* хи́трость.

finger *n.* па́лец (-льца) (*index*, указа́тельный; *middle*, сре́дний; *ring*, безымя́нный; *little*, мизи́нец (-нца)); *f.-print*, отпеча́ток (-тка) па́льца; *f. tip*, ко́нчик па́льца; *have at* (*one's*) *f.-tips*, знать imp. как свои́ пять па́льцев; *v.t.* тро́гать *imp.*, тро́нуть *perf.*

finish *n.* коне́ц (-нца́), оконча́ние; (*of furniture etc.*) отде́лка; (*sport*) фи́ниш; *v.t.* & *i.* конча́ть(ся) *imp.*, ко́нчить(ся) *perf.*; *v.t.* ока́нчивать *imp.*, око́нчить *perf.*; *finishing touches*, после́дние штрихи́ *m.pl.*

finite *adj.* определённый (-нен, -нна); (*gram.*) ли́чный.

Finn *n.* финн, фи́нка. **Finnish** *adj.* фи́нский.

fir *n.* ель, пи́хта; *f.-cone*, ело́вая ши́шка.

fire *n.* ого́нь (огня́) *m.*; (*grate*) ками́н; (*conflagration*) пожа́р; (*bonfire*) костёр (-тра́); (*fervour*) пыл (-а(у), *loc.* -ý); *be on f.*, горе́ть (-рю́, -ри́шь) *imp.*; *catch f.*, загора́ться *imp.*, загоре́ться (-рю́сь, -ри́шься) *perf.*; *set f. to, set on f.*, поджига́ть *imp.*, подже́чь (подожгу́, -жжёшь; поджёг, подожгла́) *perf.*; *v.t.* зажига́ть *imp.*, заже́чь (-жгу́, -жжёшь; -жёг, -жгла́) *perf.*; воспламеня́ть *imp.*, воспламени́ть *perf.*; (*gun*) стреля́ть *imp.* из + *gen.* (*at*, в + *acc.*, по + *dat.*); (*dismiss*) увольня́ть *imp.*, уво́лить *perf.*; *f.-alarm*, пожа́рная трево́га; *firearm*(s), огнестре́льное ору́жие; *f. brigade*, пожа́рная кома́нда; *f.-engine*, пожа́рная маши́на; *f.-escape*, пожа́рная ле́стница; *f. extinguisher*, огнетуши́тель *m.*; *firefly*, светля́к (-а́); *f.-guard*, ками́нная решётка; *fireman*, пожа́рный *sb.*; (*tending furnace*) кочега́р; *f. place*, ками́н; *fireproof*, *f.-resistant*, огнеупо́рный; *fireside*, ме́сто у ками́на; *f. station*, пожа́рное депо́ *neut.indecl.*; *firewood*, дрова́ (-в) *pl.*; *firework*, фейерве́рк. **firing** *n.* (*of gun*) стрельба́.

firm¹ *n.* (*business*) фи́рма.

firm² *adj.* твёрдый (твёрд, -а́, -о), кре́пкий (-пок, -пка́, -пко), сто́йкий (-о́ек, -о́йка́, -о́йко). **firmament** *n.* небе́сный свод. **firmness** *n.* твёрдость.

first adj. пе́рвый; (foremost) выдаю́щийся; n. (date) пе́рвое (число́); пе́рвый sb.; adv. сперва́, снача́ла, в пе́рвый раз; in the f. place, во-пе́рвых; f. of all, пре́жде всего́; at f. sight, на пе́рвый взгляд, с пе́рвого взгля́да; f. aid, пе́рвая по́мощь; give f. aid, ока́зывать imp. (-а́жу, -а́жешь) perf. пе́рвую по́мощь (to, + dat.); f.-class, первокла́ссный, превосхо́дный; f. cousin, двою́родный брат (pl. -ья, -ьев), двою́родная сестра́ (pl. сёстры, сестёр, сёстрам); f.-hand, из пе́рвых рук; f.-rate, первокла́ссный, превосхо́дный.

fiscal adj. фина́нсовый, фиска́льный.

fish n. ры́ба; adj. ры́бный, ры́бий (-бья, -бье); v.i. лови́ть (-влю́, -вишь imp. ры́бу; удить (ужу́, у́дишь imp. ры́бу; f. for, (compliments etc.) напра́шиваться imp., напроси́ться (-ошу́сь, -о́сишься) perf. на+acc.; f. out, выта́скивать imp., вы́тащить perf. **fisherman** n. рыба́к (-а́), рыболо́в. **fishery** n. ры́бный про́мысел (-сла). **fishing** n. ры́бная ло́вля; f. boat, рыболо́вное су́дно (pl. суда́, -до́в); f. line, ле́са́ (pl. лёсы); f. rod, уди́лище, у́дочка. **fishmonger** n. торго́вец (-вца) ры́бой. **fishy** adj. ры́бный, ры́бий (-бья, -бье); (dubious) подозри́тельный.

fission n. расщепле́ние; nuclear f. деле́ние ядра́; cell f., деле́ние кле́ток. **fissure** n. тре́щина.

fist n. кула́к (-а́). **fisticuffs** n. кула́чный бой (loc. бою́; pl. бои́).

fit¹ n.: be a good f., (clothes) хорошо́ сиде́ть (-дя́т, -дя́т) imp.; adj. подходя́щий, го́дный (-ден, -дна́, -дно); (healthy) здоро́вый; v.t. (be suitable) годи́ться imp.+dat., на+acc., для+gen.; подходи́ть (-ожу́, -о́дишь) imp., подойти́ (подойду́, -дёшь; подошёл, -шла́) perf.+dat.; (adjust) прила́живать imp., прила́дить perf. (to, к+dat.); v.t. & i. приспосо́бливать(ся) imp.; приспосо́бить(ся) perf.; f. out, снабжа́ть imp., снабди́ть perf.

fit² n. (attack) припа́док (-дка), при-

ступ; (fig.) поры́в. **fitful** adj. поры́вистый.

fitter n. монтёр, устано́вщик. **fitting** n. (of clothes) приме́рка; прила́живание, монта́ж; pl. армату́ра; adj. подходя́щий, го́дный (-ден, -дна́, -дно); f.-room, приме́рочная sb.

five adj., n. пять (-ти́, -тью́); (collect.; 5 pairs) пя́теро (-ры́х); (cards; number 5) пятёрка; (time) пять (часо́в); (age) пять лет; f.-year plan, пятиле́тка.

fix n. (dilemma) диле́мма; (radio etc.) засе́чка; v.t. устана́вливать imp., установи́ть (-влю́, -вишь) perf.; (arrange) устра́ивать imp., устро́ить perf.; (repair) поправля́ть imp., попра́вить perf.; v.t. & i. остана́вливать(ся) imp., останови́ть(ся) (-влю́(сь), -вишь(ся) perf. (on, на+acc.). **fixation** n. фикса́ция. **fixed** adj. неподви́жный, постоя́нный (-нен, -нна).

fizz v.i. шипе́ть (-плю́, -пи́шь) imp.; (coll.) шипу́чка. **fizzy** adj. шипу́чий.

flabbergast v.t. ошеломля́ть imp., ошеломи́ть perf.

flabby, flaccid adj. дря́блый (-л, -ла́, -ло), вя́лый.

flag¹ n. (standard) флаг, зна́мя (pl. -мёна) neut.; v.t. (signal) сигнализи́ровать imp., perf., про~ perf. фла́гами.

flag² n. (stone) плита́ (pl. -ты); v.t. мости́ть imp., вы́-, за~ perf. плита́ми.

flag³ v.i. (droop) поника́ть imp., пони́кнуть (-к) perf.

flagellate v.t. бичева́ть (-чу́ю, -чу́ешь) imp.

flagon n. кувши́н.

flagrant adj. вопию́щий, очеви́дный, сканда́льный.

flagship n. флагма́н. **flagstaff** n. флагшто́к.

flail n. цеп (-а́).

flair n. чутьё.

flake n. слой (pl. -ои́); pl. хло́пья (-ьев) pl.; v.i. слои́ться imp.; лупи́ться (-пится) imp., об~ perf. **flaky** adj. слои́стый.

flamboyant adj. цвети́стый.

flame n. пла́мя neut., ого́нь (огня́) m.; (passion) пыл (-а(у), loc. -ý); f.-thrower огнемёт; v.i. пыла́ть imp.; f. up, разгора́ться imp., разгоре́ться (-ри́ться) perf.

flamingo n. флами́нго m. indecl.

flange n. фла́нец (-нца).

flank n. бок (loc. -ý; pl. -á); v.t. быть располо́женным сбо́ку, на фла́нге, +gen.; (mil.) фланки́ровать imp., perf.

flannel n. флане́ль; attrib. флане́левый.

flap n. мах; (wings) взмах; (board) откидна́я доска́ (acc. -ски́; pl. -ски, -со́к, -ска́м); v.t. маха́ть (машу́, -шешь) imp., махну́ть perf.+instr.; взма́хивать imp., взмахну́ть perf.+ instr.; v.i. развева́ться imp.

flare n. вспы́шка; (signal) светово́й сигна́л; v.i. вспы́хивать imp., вспы́хнуть perf.; f. up, вспыли́ть perf.

flash n. вспы́шка, проблеск; in a f., ми́гом; v.i. сверка́ть imp., сверкну́ть perf. **flashy** adj. показно́й.

flask n. фля́жка.

flat[1] n. (dwelling) кварти́ра.

flat[2] n. (f. region) равни́на; (mus.) бемо́ль m.; (tyre) спу́щенная ши́на; adj. пло́ский (-сок, -ска́, -ско), ро́вный (-вен, -вна́, -вно); (dull) ску́чный (-чен, -чна́, -чно); f.-fish, ка́мбала; f. foot, плоскосто́пие; f.-iron, утю́г (-á). **flatten** v.t. де́лать imp., с~ perf. пло́ским; v.i. станови́ться (-ится) imp., стать (ста́нет) perf. пло́ским; v.t. & i. выра́внивать(ся) imp., вы́ровнять(ся) perf.

flatter v.t. льстить imp., по~ perf.+ dat. **flatterer** n. льстец (-á). **flattering** adj. льсти́вый, ле́стный. **flattery** n. лесть.

flaunt v.t. щеголя́ть imp., щегольну́ть perf.+instr.; f. oneself, выставля́ться imp., вы́ставиться perf.

flautist n. флейти́ст.

flavour n. арома́т, вкус; (fig.) при́вкус, отте́нок (-нка); v.t. приправля́ть imp., припра́вить perf. **flavourless** adj. безвку́сный.

flaw n. (crack) тре́щина; (defect) изъя́н.

flax n. лён (льна). **flaxen** adj. льняно́й; (colour) соло́менный.

flay v.t. сдира́ть imp., содра́ть (сдеру́, -рёшь; содра́л, -á, -о) perf. ко́жу с+ gen.

flea n. блоха́ (pl. -хи, -х, -ха́м); f.-bite, блоши́ный уку́с.

fleck n. пятно́ (pl. -тна, -тен, -тнам), кра́пина.

fledge v.t. оперя́ть imp., опери́ть perf.; be(come) fledged, оперя́ться imp., опери́ться perf. **fledg(e)ling** n. птене́ц (-нца́).

flee v.i. бежа́ть (бегу́, бежи́шь) imp., perf. (from, от+gen.); (vanish) исчеза́ть imp., исче́знуть (-з) perf.

fleece n. ове́чья шерсть, руно́ (pl. -на); v.t. обдира́ть imp., ободра́ть (обдеру́, -рёшь; ободра́л, -á, -о) perf. **fleecy** adj. шерсти́стый.

fleet[1] n. флот (pl. -о́ты, -о́то́в); (vehicles) парк.

fleet[2] adj. бы́стрый (быстр, -á, -о, бы́стры); f. of foot, быстроно́гий. **fleeting** adj. мимолётный.

flesh n. (as opp. to mind) плоть; (meat) мя́со; (of fruit) мя́коть; in the f., во пло́ти. **fleshly** adj. пло́тский. **fleshy** adj. мяси́стый.

flex n. электрошну́р (-á); v.t. сгиба́ть imp., согну́ть perf. **flexibility** adj. ги́бкость, податли́вость. **flexible** adj. ги́бкий (-бок, -бка́, -бко), податли́вый. **flexion** n. сгиб(а́ние); (gram.) фле́ксия.

flick n. щелчо́к (-чка́); f.-knife, фи́нка; v.t. & i. щёлкать imp., щёлкнуть perf. (+instr.); f. off, сма́хивать imp., смахну́ть perf.

flicker n. мерца́ние; v.i. мерца́ть imp.

flier see flyer.

flight[1] n. (fleeing) бе́гство; put to f., обраща́ть imp., обрати́ть (-ащу́, -ати́шь) perf. в бе́гство.

flight[2] n. (flying) полёт, перелёт; (trip) рейс; (flock) ста́я; (aeron. unit) звено́ (pl. -нья, -ньев); f. of stairs, ле́стничный марш. **flighty** adj. ве́треный.

flimsy adj. непро́чный (-чен, -чна́, -чно).

flinch v.i. уклоня́ться imp., уклони́ться (-ню́сь, -ни́шься) perf. (from, от+

gen.); (*wince*) вздра́гивать *imp.*, вздро́гнуть *perf.*

fling *v.t.* швыря́ть *imp.*, швырну́ть *perf.*; *v.i.* (*also f. oneself*) броса́ться *imp.*, бро́ситься *perf.*

flint *n.* креме́нь (-мня́) *m.*; *attrib.* кремнёвый.

flip *n.* щелчо́к (-чка́) *v.t.* щёлкать *imp.*, щёлкнуть *perf.*+ *instr.*

flippancy *n.* легкомы́слие. **flippant** *adj.* легкомы́сленный (-ен, -енна).

flipper *n.* плавни́к (-а́), ласт.

flirt *n.* коке́тка; *v.i.* флиртова́ть *imp.* (with, c+*instr.*), (*fig.*) заи́грывать *imp.* (with, c+*instr.*). **flirtation** *n.* флирт.

flit *v.i.* (*migrate*) переезжа́ть *imp.*, перее́хать (-е́ду, -е́дешь) *perf.*; (*fly*) порха́ть *imp.*, порхну́ть *perf.*

float *v.i.* поплаво́к (-вка́), плот (-а́); *v.i.* пла́вать *indet.*, плыть (плыву́, -вёшь; плыл, -а́, -о) *det.*; *v.t.* (*loan*) выпуска́ть *imp.*, вы́пустить *perf.*; (*company*) пуска́ть *imp.*, пусти́ть (пущу́, пу́стишь) *perf.* в ход.

flock *n.* (*animals*) ста́до (*pl.* -да́); (*birds*) ста́я; (*people*) толпа́ (*pl.* -пы); *v.i.* стека́ться *imp.*, сте́чься (стечётся, стёкся, -кла́сь) *perf.*; толпи́ться *imp.*

floe *n.* плаву́чая льди́на.

flog *v.t.* сечь (секу́, сечёшь; сек, -ла́) *imp.*, вы́ ~ *perf.*

flood *n.* наводне́ние, разли́в, пото́п; *f.-tide*, прили́в; *v.i.* (*river etc.*) выступа́ть *imp.*, вы́ступить *perf.* из берего́в; *v.t.* наводня́ть *imp.*, наводни́ть *perf.*; затопля́ть *imp.*, затопи́ть (-плю́, -пишь) *perf.* **floodgate** *n.* шлюз. **floodlight** *n.* прожёктор (*pl.* -ы & -а́).

floor *n.* пол (*loc.* -ý; *pl.* -ы́); (*of sea*) дно (*no pl.*); (*storey*) эта́ж (-а́); *ground, first,* (*etc.*) *f.*, пе́рвый, второ́й, (и т.д.) эта́ж (-а́); *take the f.*, брать (беру́, -рёшь; брал, -а́, -о) *imp.*, взять (возьму́, -мёшь; взял, -а́, -о) *perf.* сло́во; *f.-board*, полови́ца; *f.-cloth*, полова́я тря́пка; *v.t.* настила́ть *imp.*, настла́ть (-телю́, -те́лешь) *perf.* пол+ *gen.*; (*knock down*) вали́ть (-лю́, -лишь) *imp.*, по ~ *perf.* на́ пол; (*con-*

found) ста́вить *imp.*, по~ *perf.* в тупи́к. **flooring** *n.* насти́л(ка).

flop *v.i.* шлёпаться *imp.*, шлёпнуться *perf.*; (*fail*) прова́ливаться *imp.*, провали́ться (-ится) *perf.*

flora *n.* фло́ра. **floral** *adj.* цвето́чный. **florescence** *n.* цвете́ние. **florid** *adj.* цвети́стый; (*ruddy*) румя́ный. **florist** *n.* торго́вец (-вца) цвета́ми.

flotilla *n.* флоти́лия.

flotsam *n.* пла́вающие обло́мки *m.pl.*

flounce[1] *v.i.* броса́ться *imp.*, бро́ситься *perf.*

flounce[2] *n.* (*of skirt*) обо́рка.

flounder[1] *n.* (*fish*) ка́мбала.

flounder[2] *v.i.* бара́хтаться *imp.*; пу́таться *imp.*, с~ *perf.*

flour *n.* мука́; *f.-mill*, ме́льница.

flourish *n.* (*movement*) разма́хивание (+*instr.*); (*of pen*) ро́счерк; (*mus.*) туш; *v.i.* (*thrive*) процвета́ть *imp.*; *v.t.* (*wave*) разма́хивать *imp.*, размахну́ть *perf.*+ *instr.*

floury *adj.* мучни́стый.

flout *v.t.* пренебрега́ть *imp.*, пренебре́чь (-егу́, -ежёшь; -ёг, -егла́) *perf.*+ *instr.*

flow *v.i.* течь (течёт, тёк, -ла́) *imp.*; ли́ться (льётся; лила́сь, лило́сь) *imp.*; *n.* тече́ние, пото́к; (*tide*) прили́в.

flower *n.* цвето́к (-тка́; *pl.* -ты́); (*pick; prime*) цвет; *f.-bed*, клу́мба; *flowerpot*, цвето́чный горшо́к (-шка́); *v.i.* цвести́ (цветёт; цвёл, -а́) *imp.* **flowery** *adj.* покры́тый цвета́ми; (*florid*) цвети́стый.

fluctuate *v.i.* колеба́ться (-блюсь, -блешься) *imp.*, по~ *perf.* **fluctuation** *n.* колеба́ние.

flue *n.* дымохо́д.

fluency *n.* пла́вность, бе́глость. **fluent** *adj.* пла́вный, бе́глый. **fluently** *adv.* бе́гло, свобо́дно.

fluff *n.* пух (-а(у), *loc.* -ý), пушо́к (-шка́). **fluffy** *adj.* пуши́стый.

fluid *n.* жи́дкость; *adj.* жи́дкий (-док, -дка́, -дко), теку́чий.

flunkey *n.* лаке́й.

fluorescence *n.* флуоресце́нция. **fluorescent** *adj.* флуоресци́рующий.

fluoride *n.* фтори́д. **fluorine** *n.* фтор.

flurry n. (squall) порыв ветра; (commotion) суматоха; v.t. (agitate) волновать imp., вз ~ perf.

flush n. прилив; (redness) румянец (-нца); (reddden) краснеть imp., по ~ perf.; v.t. спускать imp., спустить (-ущу, -устишь) perf. воду в + acc.

fluster n. волнение; v.t. волновать imp., вз ~ perf.

flute n. (mus.) флейта; (groove) желобок (-бка); (archit.) каннелюра.

flutter v.i. порхать imp., порхнуть perf.; развеваться imp.; (with excitement) трепетать (-ещу, -ещешь) imp.; n. порхание; трепет.

fluvial adj. речной.

flux n. течение; in a state of f., в состоянии изменения.

fly[1] n. (insect) муха.

fly[2] v.i. летать indet., лететь (лечу, летишь) det., по ~ perf.; (flag) развеваться imp.; (hasten) нестись (несусь, -сёшься); нёсся, неслась) imp., по ~ perf.; (flee) бежать (бегу, бежишь) imp., perf.; v.t. (aircraft) управлять imp. + instr.; (transport) перевозить (-ожу, -озишь) imp., перевезти (-езу, -езёшь; -ёз, -езла) perf. (самолётом); (flag) поднимать imp., поднять (-ниму, -нимешь; поднял, -а, -о) perf. flyer, flier n. лётчик. flying n. полёт(ы).

flywheel n. маховик (-á).

foal n. (horse) жеребёнок (-нка; pl. жеребята, -т); (ass) ослёнок (-нка; pl. ослята, -т); in f., жерёбая; v.i. жеребиться imp., o ~ perf.

foam n. пена; f. plastic, пенопласт; f. rubber, пенорезина; v.i. пениться imp., вс ~ perf. **foamy** adj. пенистый.

focal adj. фокусный.

fo'c's'le see forecastle.

focus n. фокус, центр; v.t. фокусировать imp., с ~ perf.; (concentrate) сосредоточивать imp., сосредоточить perf.

fodder n. корм (loc. -e & -ý; pl. -á), фураж (-á).

foe n. враг (-á).

fog n. туман, мгла. **foggy** adj. туманный (-нен, -нна), неясный (-сен, -сна, -сно).

foible n. слабость.

foil[1] n. (metal) фольга; (contrast) контраст.

foil[2] v.t. (frustrate) расстраивать imp., расстроить perf. (планы + gen.); n. (track) след (pl. -ы) зверя.

foil[3] n. (sword) рапира.

foist v.t. навязывать imp., навязать (-яжу, -яжешь) perf. (on, + dat.).

fold[1] n. (sheep-f.) овчарня (gen.pl. -рен).

fold[2] n. складка, сгиб; v.t. складывать imp., сложить (-жу, -жишь) perf.; сгибать imp., согнуть perf. **folder** n. папка. **folding** adj. складной, откидной, створчатый.

foliage n. листва.

folk n. народ (-a(y)), люди (-дей, -дям, -дьми) pl.; pl. (relatives) родня collect.; attrib. народный. **folklore** n. фольклор.

follow v.t. следовать imp., по ~ perf. + dat., за + instr.; идти (иду, идёшь; шёл, шла) det. за + instr.; следить imp. за + instr. **follower** n. последователь m., ~ница. **following** adj. следующий.

folly n. глупость, безумие.

fond adj. любящий, нежный; be f. of, любить (-блю, -бишь) imp. + acc.

fondle v.t. ласкать imp.

fondness n. нежность, любовь (-бви, instr. -бовью).

font n. (eccl.) купель.

food n. пища, еда; f. value, питательность. **foodstuff** n. пищевой продукт.

fool n. дурак (-á), глупец (-пца); v.t. дурачить imp., o ~ perf.; v.i.: f. about, play the f., дурачиться imp. **foolery** n. дурачество. **foolhardy** adj. безрассудно храбрый (храбр, -á, -о). **foolish** adj. глупый (глуп, -á, -о). **foolishness** n. глупость.

foot n. нога (acc. -гу; pl. -ги, -г, -гам), ступня; (measure) фут; (of hill etc.) подножие; (mil.) пехота; on f., пешком; put one's foot in it, сесть (сяду, -дешь; сел) perf. в лужу. **football** n. футбол; attrib. футбольный. **footballer** n. футболист. **footfall** n. поступь. **footlights** n. pl. рампа. **footman** n. лакей. **footnote** n. сноска, примечание. **footpath** n. тропинка; (pavement) тротуа́р. **footprint** n. след (pl. -ы́) (ноги́). **footstep** n. (tread) шаг (-a(y) & (with 2, 3, 4) -á, loc. -ý; pl. -и́); (footprint) след (pl. -ы́) (ноги́). **footwear** n. óбувь.

fop n. щёголь m., фат. **foppish** adj. щегольско́й, фатова́тый.

for prep. (of time) в тече́ние + gen., на + acc.; (of purpose) для + gen., за + acc., + instr.; (of destination) в + acc.; (on account of) из-за + gen.; (in place of) вме́сто + gen.; for the sake of, ра́ди + gen.; за, то́, что каса́ется + gen.; conj. так как, и́бо.

forage n. фура́ж (-á), корм (loc. -е & -ý; pl. -á); v.i. фуражи́ровать imp.

foray n. набе́г.

forbear¹ n. (ancestor) пре́док (-дка).

forbear² v.i. (refrain) возде́рживаться imp., воздержа́ться (-жу́сь, -жи́шься) perf. (from, от + gen.). **forbearance** n. возде́ржанность.

forbid v.t. запреща́ть imp., запрети́ть (-ещу́, -ети́шь) perf. + dat. (person) & acc. (thing); воспреща́ть imp., воспрети́ть (-ещу́, -ети́шь) perf. + acc., + inf.

force n. (strength) си́ла; (violence) наси́лие; (meaning) смысл; pl. (armed f.) вооружённые си́лы f.pl.; by f., си́лой; by f. of, в си́лу + gen.; in f., в си́ле (in large numbers) толпа́ми; v.t. (compel) заставля́ть imp., заста́вить perf.; принужда́ть imp., прину́дить perf.; (lock etc.) взла́мывать imp., взлома́ть perf.; (hasten) форси́ровать imp., perf. **forceful** adj. си́льный (си́лен, -льна́, -льно, си́льны); (speech) убеди́тельный. **forcible** adj. наси́льственный.

forceps n. щипцы́ (-цо́в) pl.

ford n. брод; v.t. переходи́ть (-ожу́, -о́дишь) imp., перейти́ (-ейду́, -ейдёшь; -ешёл, -ешла́) perf. вброд + acc., че́рез + acc.

fore n.: to the f., на пере́днем пла́не.

forearm n. предпле́чье (gen.pl. -чий).

forebode v.t. (betoken) предвеща́ть imp.; (have presentiment) предчу́вствовать imp. **foreboding** n. предчу́вствие.

forecast n. предсказа́ние; (of weather) прогно́з; v.t. предска́зывать imp., предсказа́ть (-ажу́, -а́жешь) perf.

forecastle, fo'c's'le n. (naut.) бак. **forefather** n. пре́док (-дка). **forefinger** n. указа́тельный па́лец (-льца). **foreground** n. пере́дний план. **forehead** n. лоб (loc. -бу́; pl. -бы́).

foreign adj. (from abroad) иностра́нный (-нен, -нна); (alien) чужо́й; (external) вне́шний; f. body, иноро́дное те́ло (pl. -ла́). **foreigner** n. иностра́нец (-нца).

forelock n. чёлка. **foreman** n. (jury) старшина́ (pl. -ны) m. прися́жных; (factory) ма́стер (pl. -á).

foremost adj. передово́й, пере́дний; (notable) выдаю́щийся.

forensic adj. суде́бный.

forerunner n. предве́стник. **foresee** v.t. предви́деть (-и́жу, -и́дишь) imp. **foreshadow** v.t. предвеща́ть imp. **foresight** n. предви́дение; (caution) предусмотри́тельность.

forest n. лес (-a(y), loc. -ý; pl. -á). **forestall** v.t. предупрежда́ть imp., предупреди́ть perf. **forester** n. лесни́к (-á), лесни́чий sb. **forestry** n. лесово́дство.

foretaste n. предвкуше́ние; v.t. предвкуша́ть imp., предвкуси́ть (-ушу́, -у́сишь) perf. **foretell** v.t. предска́зывать imp., предсказа́ть (-ажу́, -а́жешь) perf. **forethought** n. (intention) преднаме́ренность; (caution) предусмотри́тельность. **forewarn** v.t. предостерега́ть imp., предостере́чь (-егу́, -ежёшь; -ёг, -егла́) perf. **foreword** n. предисло́вие.

forfeit n. (fine) штраф; (deprivation) лише́ние, конфиска́ция; (in game) фант; pl. (game) игра́ в фа́нты; v.t. лиша́ться imp., лиши́ться perf. + gen.; (pay with) плати́ться (-ачу́сь, -а́тишься) imp., по ~ perf. + instr. **forfeiture** n. лише́ние, конфиска́ция, поте́ря.

forge¹ n. (smithy) ку́зница; (furnace) горн; v.t. кова́ть (кую́, куёшь) imp., вы́ ~ perf.; (fabricate) подде́лывать imp., подде́лать perf.

forge² v.i.: f. ahead продвига́ться imp., продви́нуться perf. вперёд.

forger n. подде́лыватель m.; (of money) фальшивомоне́тчик. **forgery** n. подде́лка, подло́г.

forget v.t. забыва́ть imp., забы́ть (забу́ду, -дешь) perf.; f.-me-not. незабу́дка. **forgetful** adj. забы́вчивый.

forgive v.t. проща́ть imp., прости́ть perf. **forgiveness** n. проще́ние.

forgo v.t. возде́рживаться imp., воздержа́ться (-жу́сь, -жишься) perf. от + gen.

fork n. (eating) ви́лка; (digging) ви́лы (-л) pl.; (of tree) разветвле́ние; v.i. рабо́тать imp. ви́лами; (form fork) разветвля́ться imp., разветви́ться perf.

forlorn adj. уны́лый.

form n. фо́рма, вид, фигу́ра; (formality) форма́льность; (class) класс; (document) бланк, анке́та; (bench) скаме́йка; v.t. (shape) придава́ть (-даю́, -даёшь) imp., прида́ть (-а́м, -а́шь, -а́ст, -ади́м) imp.; при́дал, -а́, -о) perf. фо́рму + dat.; (make up) составля́ть imp., соста́вить perf.; образо́вывать imp., образова́ть perf.; формирова́ть imp.; v.i. принима́ть imp., приня́ть (-и́мет; при́нял, -а́, -о) perf. фо́рму; образо́вываться imp., образова́ться perf. **formal** adj. официа́льный, форма́льный. **formality** n. форма́льность. **formation** n. образова́ние, формирова́ние, форма́ция.

former adj. бы́вший, пре́жний; the f. (of two) пе́рвый. **formerly** adv. пре́жде.

formidable adj. (dread) гро́зный (-зен, -зна́, -зно) (arduous) тру́дный (-ден, -дна́, -дно, тру́дны).

formless adj. бесфо́рменный (-ен, -енна).

formula n. фо́рмула. **formulate** v.t. формули́ровать imp., c~ perf. **formulation** n. формулиро́вка.

forsake v.t. (desert) покида́ть imp., поки́нуть perf.; (renounce) отка́зываться imp., отказа́ться (-ажу́сь, -а́жешься) perf. от + gen.

forswear v.t. отрека́ться imp., отре́чься (-еку́сь, -ечёшься, -еку́тся; -ёкся, -екла́сь) perf. от + gen.

fort n. форт (loc. -ý; pl. -ы́).

forth adv. вперёд, да́льше; back and f., взад и вперёд; and so f., и так да́лее. **forthcoming** adj. предстоя́щий. **forthwith** adv. неме́дленно.

fortieth adj., n. сороково́й.

fortification n. фортифика́ция, укрепле́ние. **fortify** v.t. укрепля́ть imp., укрепи́ть perf.; подкрепля́ть imp., подкрепи́ть perf. **fortitude** n. му́жество.

fortnight n. две неде́ли. **fortnightly** adj. двухнеде́льный; adv. раз в две неде́ли.

fortress n. кре́пость.

fortuitous adj. случа́йный.

fortunate adj. счастли́вый (сча́стли́в). **fortunately** adv. к сча́стью. **fortune** n. (destiny) судьба́ (pl. -дьбы, -деб, -дьбам); (good f.) сча́стье; (wealth) состоя́ние; f.-teller, гада́льщик, -ица, гада́лка; f.-telling, гада́ние.

forty adj., n. со́рок (oblique cases -á); (age) со́рок лет; pl. (decade) сороковы́е го́ды (-до́в) m.pl.

forward adj. пере́дний, передово́й; (early) ра́нний; n. (sport) напада́ющий sb.; adv. вперёд, да́льше; v.t. (promote) спосо́бствовать imp., по~ perf. + dat.; (letter etc.) пересыла́ть imp., пересла́ть (перешлю́, -лёшь) perf.

fossil n. окамене́лость, ископа́емое sb.; adj. окамене́лый, ископа́емый. **fossilize** v.t. & i. превраща́ть(ся) imp., преврати́ть(ся) (-ащу́(сь), -ати́шь(ся)) perf. в окамене́лость.

foster v.t. воспи́тывать imp., воспита́ть perf.; (feeling) леле́ять (-е́ю, -е́ешь) imp.; adj. приёмный; f.-child, приёмыш.

foul adj. (dirty) гря́зный (-зен, -зна́, -зно); (repulsive) отврати́тельный; (obscene) непристо́йный; n. (collision) столкнове́ние; (sport) наруше́ние пра́вил; v.t. (dirty) па́чкать(ся) imp., за~, ис~ perf.; (entangle) запу́тывать(ся) imp., запу́тать(ся) perf.

found[1] v.t. (establish) осно́вывать imp., основа́ть (-ную́, -нуёшь) perf.; (building) закла́дывать imp., заложи́ть (-жу́, -жишь) perf.

found[2] v.t. (metal) отлива́ть imp., отли́ть (отолью́, -ьёшь; о́тли́л, -á, -о) perf.

foundation n. (of building) фунда́мент; (basis) осно́ва, основа́ние; (institution) учрежде́ние; (*funds*) фонд. **founder** [1] *n.* основа́тель *m.*, ~ница.

founder [2] *n.* (*of metal*) лите́йщик, пла́вильщик.

founder [3] *v.i.* (*naut.*) идти́ (идёт; шёл, шла) *imp.*, пойти́ (пойдёт; пошёл, -шла́) *perf.* ко дну.

foundling *n.* подки́дыш.

foundry *n.* лите́йная *sb.*

fount [1] *n.* (*print.*) компле́кт шри́фта.

fount [2] *n.* исто́чник. **fountain** *n.* фонта́н, исто́чник; *f.-pen*, авторучка.

four *adj.*, *n.* четы́ре (-рёх, -рём, -рьмя́); (*collect.*; *4 pairs*) четверо (-ры́х); (*cards*; *boat*; *number 4*) четвёрка; (*time*) четы́ре (часа́); (*age*) четы́ре го́да; *on all fours*, на четвере́ньках. **fourteen** *adj.*, *n.* четы́рнадцать (-ти, -тью); (*age*) четы́рнадцать лет. **fourteenth** *adj.*, *n.* четы́рнадцатый; (*date*) четы́рнадцатое (число́). **fourth** *adj.*, *n.* четвёртый; (*quarter*) че́тверть (*pl.* -ти, -те́й); (*mus.*) ква́рта. четвёртое (число́)

fowl *n.* (*bird*) пти́ца (*domestic*) дома́шняя пти́ца; (*wild*) дичь *collect.*

fox *n.* лиса́ (*pl.* -сы), лиси́ца; *attrib.* ли́сий (-сья, -сье); *v.t.* обма́нывать *imp.*, обману́ть (-ну́, -нешь) *perf.* **foxglove** *n.* наперстя́нка. **foxhole** *n.* (*mil.*) яче́йка. **foxy** *adj.* ли́сий (-сья, -сье); (*crafty*) хи́трый (-тёр, -тра́, хи́тро).

fraction *n.* (*math.*) дробь (*pl.* -би, -бе́й); (*portion*) части́ца. **fractional** *adj.* дро́бный.

fractious *adj.* раздражи́тельный.

fracture *n.* перело́м; *v.t. & i.* лома́ть(ся) *imp.*, с~ *perf.*

fragile *adj.* ло́мкий (-мок, -мка́, -мко), хру́пкий (-пок, -пка́, -пко). **fragility** *n.* ло́мкость, хру́пкость.

fragment *n.* обло́мок (-мка), оско́лок (-лка) (*of writing etc.*) отры́вок (-вка), фрагме́нт. **fragmentary** *adj.* отры́вочный.

fragrance *n.* арома́т. **fragrant** *adj.* арома́тный, души́стый.

frail *adj.* хру́пкий (-пок, -пка́, -пко).

frame *n.* о́стов; (*body*) те́ло (*pl.* -ла́); (*build*) телосложе́ние; (*picture*) ра́мка,

ра́мка; (*cin.*) кадр; *f. of mind*, настрое́ние; *v.t.* (*devise*) создава́ть (-даю́, -даёшь) *imp.*, созда́ть (-а́м, -а́шь, -а́ст, -ади́м; со́зда́л, -а́, -о) *perf.*; (*adapt*) приспоса́бливать *imp.*, приспосо́бить *perf.*; (*picture*) вставля́ть *imp.*, вста́вить *perf.* в ра́мку; (*surround*) обрамля́ть *imp.*, обрами́ть *perf.* **framework** *n.* о́стов, структу́ра; (*fig.*) ра́мки *f.pl.*

franc *n.* франк.

franchise *n.* (*privilege*) привиле́гия; (*right to vote*) пра́во го́лоса.

frank [1] *adj.* (*open*) открове́нный (-нен, -нна).

frank [2] *v.t.* (*letter*) франки́ровать *imp.*, *perf.*

frantic *adj.* нейстовый, бе́шеный.

fraternal *adj.* бра́тский. **fraternity** *n.* бра́тство, общи́на. **fraternize** *v.i.* брата́ться *imp.*, по~ *perf.* (with, с+*instr.*).

fraud *n.* (*deception*) обма́н; (*person*) обма́нщик. **fraudulent** *adj.* обма́нный (-нен, -нна).

fraught *adj.*: *f. with*, чрева́тый+*instr.*, по́лный (-лон, -лна́, по́лно)+*gen.*, *instr.*

fray [1] *v.t. & i.* обтрёпывать(ся) *imp.*, обтрепа́ть(ся) (-плю́(сь), -плешь(ся)) *perf.*

fray [2] *n.* (*brawl*) дра́ка.

freak *n.* (*caprice*) причу́да; (*monstrosity*) уро́д.

freckle *n.* весну́шка. **freckled** *adj.* весну́шчатый.

free *adj.* свобо́дный, во́льный; (*gratis*) беспла́тный; *of one's own f. will*, по до́брой во́ле; *f.-lance*, внешта́тный; *f. speech*, свобо́да сло́ва; *f. thinker*, вольноду́мец (-мца); *v.t.* освобожда́ть *imp.*, освободи́ть *perf.* **freedom** *n.* свобо́да. **Freemason** *n.* франкмасо́н.

freeze *v.i.* замерза́ть *imp.*, мёрзнуть (-з) *imp.*, за~ *perf.*; *v.t.* замора́живать *imp.*, заморо́зить *perf.*

freight *n.* фрахт, груз. **freighter** *n.* (*ship*) грузово́е су́дно (*pl.* -да́, -до́в).

French *adj.* францу́зский; *F. bean*, фасо́ль; *F. leave*, уйти́ без проща́ния, без разреше́ния. **Frenchman** *n.* францу́з. **Frenchwoman** *n.* францу́женка.

frenetic *adj.* неи́стовый.

frenzied *adj.* неи́стовый. **frenzy** *n.* неи́стовство.

frequency *n.* частота́ (*pl.* -ты). **frequent** *adj.* ча́стый (част, -á, -о); *v.t.* ча́сто посеща́ть *imp.*

fresco *n.* фре́ска.

fresh *adj.* све́жий (свеж, -á, -ó, све́жи); (*new*) но́вый (нов, -á, -о); (*vigorous*) бо́дрый (бодр, -á, -о, бо́дры); *f. water*, пре́сная вода́ (*acc.* -ду). **freshen** *v.t.* освежа́ть *imp.*, освежи́ть *perf.*; *v.i.* свеже́ть *imp.*, по~ *perf.* **freshly** *adv.* свежо́; (*recently*) неда́вно. **freshness** *n.* све́жесть; бо́дрость. **freshwater** *adj.* пресново́дный.

fret[1] *n.* (*irritation*) раздраже́ние; *v.t.* (*eat away*) разъеда́ть *imp.*, разъе́сть (-е́м, -е́шь, -е́ст, -еди́м; -е́л) *perf.*; *v.t. & i.* (*distress*) беспоко́ить(ся) *imp.*, о~ *perf.* **fretful** *adj.* беспоко́йный.

fret[2] *n.* (*mus.*) лад (*loc.* -ý; *pl.* -ы́).

fretsaw *n.* лобзи́к.

friar *n.* мона́х. **friary** *n.* мужско́й монасты́рь (-ря́) *m.*

friction *n.* тре́ние; (*fig.*) тре́ния *neut.pl.*

Friday *n.* пя́тница; *Good F.*, страстна́я пя́тница.

friend *n.* друг (*pl.* друзья́, -зе́й), подру́га; прия́тель *m.*, ~ница; (*acquaintance*) знако́мый *sb.* **friendly** *adj.* дру́жеский, дру́жественный. **friendship** *n.* дру́жба.

frigate *n.* фрега́т.

fright *n.* испу́г (-а(у)). **frighten** *v.t.* пуга́ть *imp.*, ис~, на~ *perf.* **frightful** *adj.* стра́шный (-шен, -шна́, -шно, стра́шны); ужа́сный.

frigid *adj.* холо́дный (хо́лоден, -дна́, -дно, хо́лодны). **frigidity** *n.* хо́лодность.

frill *n.* обо́рка.

fringe *n.* бахрома́.

frisk *n.* (*leap*) прыжо́к (-жка́); *v.i.* (*frolic*) резви́ться *imp.*; *v.t.* (*search*) шмона́ть *imp.* **frisky** *adj.* игри́вый, резвый (резв, -á, -о).

fritter[1] *n.* ола́дья (*gen.pl.* -дий).

fritter[2] *v.t.: f. away*, растра́чивать *imp.*, растра́тить *perf.* (по мелоча́м и т.п.).

frivolity *n.* легкомы́сленность. **frivolous** *adj.* легкомы́сленный (-ен, -енна).

fro *adv.*: *to and f.*, взад и вперёд.

frock *n.* пла́тье (*gen.pl.* -в); *f.-coat*, сюрту́к (-á).

frog *n.* лягу́шка.

frolic *v.i.* резви́ться *imp.*; (*play pranks*) прока́зничать *imp.*, на~ *perf.*; *n.* весе́лье; (*prank*) прока́за.

from *prep. expressing*: **1.** *starting-point*: (*away f.*; *f. person*) от+*gen.*; (*f. off, down f.*; *in time*) с+*gen.*; (*out of*) из+*gen.* **2.** *change of state*; *distinction*: от +*gen.*, из+*gen.* **3.** *escape, avoidance*: от+*gen.* **4.** *source*: из+*gen.* **5.** *giving, sending*: от+*gen.*; (*stressing sense of possession*) у+*gen.* **6.** *model*: по+*dat.* **7.** *reason, cause*: от+*gen.* **8.** *motive*: из-за+*gen.* **9.** *in phrasal verbs: see verbs*; **10.**: *from . . . to*, (*time*) с+*gen.* . . . до+*gen.*; (*with strictly defined starting-point*) от+*gen.* . . . до+ *gen.*; (*up to and including*) с+*gen.* . . . по+*acc.*; (*space*) от+*gen.* . . . до+*gen.*; (*emphasizing distance*) от+*gen.* . . . до+*gen.*; (*emphasizing journey*) из+*gen.* . . . в+*acc.* **11.** *f. above*, све́рху; *f. abroad*, из-за грани́цы; *f. afar*, и́здали; *f. among*, из числа́+*gen.*; *f. behind*, из-за+*gen.*; *f. day to day*, изо дня в день; *f. everywhere*, отовсю́ду; *f. here*, отсю́да; *f. long ago*, и́здавна; *f. memory*, по па́мяти; *f. nature*, с нату́ры; *f. now on*, отны́не; *f. off*, с+*gen.*; *f. there*, отту́да; *f. time to time*, вре́мя от вре́мени; *f. under*, из-под+*gen.*

front *n.* фаса́д, пере́дняя сторона́ (*acc.* -ону; *pl.* -о́ны, -о́н, -она́м); (*mil.*) фронт (*pl.* -ы́, -о́в); *in f. of*, впереди́ +*gen.*, пе́ред+*instr.* *adj.* пере́дний, пара́дный. **frontal** *adj.* (*anat.*) ло́бный; (*mil.*) лобово́й, фронта́льный.

frontier *n.* грани́ца. **frontier** *adj.* пограни́чный.

frost *n.* моро́з; *f.-bite*, отмороже́ние; *f.-bitten*, отморо́женный (-ен). **frosted** *adj.*: *f. glass*, ма́товое стекло́. **frosty** *adj.* моро́зный; (*fig.*) ледяно́й.

froth *n.* пе́на; *v.t. & i.* пе́ниться *imp.*, вс~ *perf.* **frothy** *adj.* пе́нистый.

frown *n.* хму́рый взгляд; *v.i.* хму́риться *imp.*, на~ *perf.*

frugal *adj.* (*careful*) бережли́вый; (*scanty*) ску́дный (-ден, -дна́, -дно).

fruit *n.* плод (-á); *collect.* фрýкты *m.pl.* **fruitful** *adj.* плодовúтый, плодотвóрный. **fruition** *n.* осуществлéние; *come to f.*, осуществúться *perf.* **fruitless** *adj.* беспло́дный, бесполéзный.

fry[1] *n.* (*collect., fishes*) малькú *m.pl.*

fry[2] *v.t. & i.* жáрить(ся) *imp.*, за ~, из ~ *perf.* **frying-pan** *n.* сковородá (*pl.* сковорóды, -óд, -óдам).

fuel *n.* тóпливо, горю́чее *sb.*

fugitive *n.* беглéц (-á); *adj.* (*transient*) мимолётный.

fugue *n.* фýга.

fulcrum *n.* тóчка опóры, вращéния.

fulfil *v.t.* (*perform*) выы-, ис-, полня́ть *imp.*, вы-, ис-, пóлнить *perf.*; (*bring about*) осуществля́ть *imp.*, осуществúть *perf.* **fulfilment** *n.* вы-, ис-, полнéние; осуществлéние.

full *adj.* пóлный (-лон, -лнá, пóлно) (*of*, +*gen.*, *instr.*); (*complete*) цéлый; (*abundant*) изобúлующий, богáтый; (*replete*) сы́тый (сыт, -á, -о); *f. back*, защúтник; *f.-blooded*, полнокрóвный; *f. stop*, тóчка; *n.*: *in f.*, пóлностью; *to the f.*, в пóлной мéре; *adv.* (*very*) óчень; (*exactly*) прямо, как раз. **fullness** *n.* полнотá. **fully** *adv.* пóлностью, вполнé.

fulsome *adj.* чрезмéрный.

fumble *v.i.*: *f. for*, нащý́пывать *imp.* + *acc.*; *f. with*, нелóвко обращáться *imp.* с + *instr.*

fume *n.* испарéние; *v.i.* испаря́ться *imp.*, испарúться *perf.*; (*with anger*) кипéть (-плю́, -пúшь) *imp.*, вс ~ *perf.* от злóсти. **fumigate** *v.t.* окýривать *imp.*, окурúть (-рю́, -ришь) *perf.* **fumigation** *n.* окýривание.

fun *n.* забáва, весéлье; *make f. of*, смея́ться (-ею́сь, -еёшься) *imp.*, по ~ *perf.* над + *instr.*

function *n.* фýнкция, назначéние; *pl.* (*duties*) обя́занности *f.pl.*; *v.i.* функционúровать *imp.*; дéйствовать *imp.* **functional** *adj.* функционáльный. **functionary** *n.* должностнóе лицó (*pl.* -цá).

fund *n.* запáс; (*of money*) фонд, капитáл.

fundamental *n.* оснóва; *adj.* основнóй.

funeral *n.* пóхороны (-óн, -онáм) *pl.*; *adj.* похорóнный, трáурный. **funereal** *adj.* (*gloomy*) мрáчный (-чен, -чнá, -чно).

fungoid *adj.* грибнóй. **fungus** *n.* гриб (-á).

funnel *n.* ворóнка; (*chimney*) дымовáя трубá (*pl.* -бы).

funny *adj.* смешнóй (-шóн, -шнá), забáвный; (*odd*) стрáнный (-нен, -ннá, -нно).

fur *n.* мех (*loc.* -ý; *pl.* -á); *pl.* (*collect.*) пушнúна, мехá *m.pl.*; *attrib.* мехово́й; *f. coat*, шýба.

furbish *v.t.* полировáть *imp.*, от ~ *perf.*; (*renovate*) подновля́ть *imp.*, подновúть *perf.*

furious *adj.* бéшеный, я́ростный.

furl *v.t.* свёртывать *imp.*, сверну́ть *perf.*

furnace *n.* тóпка, горн; *blast-f.*, дóменная печь (*pl.* -чи, -чéй).

furnish *v.t.* (*provide*) снабжáть *imp.*, снабдúть *perf.* (*with*, с + *instr.*); доставля́ть *imp.*, достáвить *perf.*; (*house*) меблировáть *imp.*, об ~; обставля́ть *imp.*, обстáвить *perf.* **furniture** *n.* мéбель, обстанóвка.

furrier *n.* меховщúк (-á), скорня́к (-á).

furrow *n.* борозда́ (*acc.* бóрозду; *pl.* бóрозды, -óзд, -оздáм); (*wrinkle*) морщúна; *v.t.* бороздúть *imp.*, вз ~, из ~ *perf.*

furry *adj.* мехово́й, пушú́стый.

further *compar.adj.* дальнéйший; (*additional*) добáвочный; *adv.* дáльше, далéе; *v.t.* продвигáть *imp.*, продвúнуть *perf.*; содéйствовать *imp.*, *perf.* + *dat.*; спосóбствовать *imp.*, по ~ *perf.* + *dat.* **furthermore** *adv.* к тому́ же. **furthest** *superl.adj.* сáмый дáльний.

furtive *adj.* скры́тый, тáйный. **furtively** *adv.* украдкой, краду́чись.

fury *n.* я́рость, неúстовство, бéшенство.

furze *n.* утёсник.

fuse[1] *v.t. & i.* (*of metal*) сплавля́ть(ся) *imp.*, сплáвить(ся) *perf.*

fuse[2] *n.* (*in bomb*) запа́л, фити́ль (-ля́) *m.*, взрыва́тель *m.*; *v.t.* вставля́ть *imp.*, вста́вить *perf.* взрыва́тель в + *acc.*

fuse[3] *n.* (*electr.*) пла́вкая про́бка, пла́вкий предохрани́тель *m.*; f. wire, пла́вкая про́волока.

fuselage *n.* фюзеля́ж.

fusible *adj.* пла́вкий (-вок, -вка).

fusillade *n.* расстре́л.

fusion *n.* пла́вка, слия́ние; (*nuclear f.*) си́нтез (я́дер).

fuss *n.* суета́; *v.i.* суети́ться *imp.* **fussy** *adj.* суетли́вый.

fusty *adj.* за́тхлый.

futile *adj.* бесполе́зный, тще́тный. **futility** *n.* бесполе́зность, тще́тность.

future *adj.* бу́дущее *sb.*, бу́дущность; (*gram.*) бу́дущее вре́мя *neut.*; *adj.* бу́дущий.

G

G *n.* (*mus.*) соль *neut.indecl.*

gab *n.* болтовня́.

gabble *v.i.* тарато́рить *imp.*

gable *n.* щипе́ц (-пца́).

gad *n.*: g. *about*, шата́ться *imp.*

gadfly *n.* о́вод (*pl.* -ы & -а́), слепе́нь (-пня́) *m.*

gadget *n.* приспособле́ние.

gag *n.* кляп; *v.t.* засо́вывать *imp.*, засу́нуть *perf.* кляп в рот + *dat.*

gaggle *n.* (*flock*) ста́я; (*cackle*) гогота́нье; *v.i.* гогота́ть (-очу́, -о́чешь) *imp.*

gaiety *n.* весе́лье, весёлость. **gaily** *adv.* ве́село.

gain *n.* при́быль; *pl.* дохо́ды *m.pl.*; (*increase*) прирост; *v.t.* получа́ть *imp.*, получи́ть (-чу́, -чишь) *perf.*; приобрета́ть *imp.*, приобрести́ (-ету́, -етёшь; -ёл, -ела́) *perf.*; g. on, нагоня́ть *imp.*, нагна́ть (нагоню́, -нишь; нагна́л, -а́, -о) *perf.*

gainsay *v.t.* (*deny*) отрица́ть *imp.*; (*contradict*) противоре́чить *imp.* + *dat.*

gait *n.* похо́дка.

gala *n.* пра́зднество.

galaxy *n.* гала́ктика; (G., Milky Way) Мле́чный Путь (-ти́, -тём) *m.*; (*fig.*) плея́да.

gale *n.* си́льный ве́тер (-тра; *loc.* на -тру́); (*naut.*) шторм.

gall[1] *n.* (*bile*) жёлчь; (*bitterness*) жёлчность; g.-bladder, жёлчный пузы́рь (-ря́) *m.*

gall[2] *n.* (*sore*) сса́дина; (*irritation*) раздраже́ние; *v.t.* раздража́ть *imp.*, раздражи́ть *perf.*

gallant *adj.* (*brave*) хра́брый (храбр, -а́, -о); (*courtly*) гала́нтный. **gallantry** *n.* хра́брость; гала́нтность.

gallery *n.* галере́я; (*theat.*) галёрка.

galley *n.* (*ship*) гале́ра; (*kitchen*) ка́мбуз; g. *proof*, гра́нка.

gallon *n.* галло́н.

gallop *n.* гало́п; *v.i.* скака́ть (-ачу́, -а́чешь) *imp.* (гало́пом).

gallows *n.* ви́селица.

gallstone *n.* жёлчный ка́мень (-мня; *pl.* -мни, -мне́й) *m.*

galore *adv.* в изоби́лии.

galosh *n.* гало́ша.

galvanic *adj.* гальвани́ческий. **galvanize** *v.t.* гальванизи́ровать *imp.*, *perf.*; (*coat with zinc*) оцинко́вывать *imp.*, оцинкова́ть *perf.*

gambit *n.* гамби́т.

gamble *n.* аза́ртная игра́ (*pl.* -ры); (*undertaking*) риско́ванное предприя́тие; *v.i.* игра́ть *imp.* в аза́ртные и́гры; рискова́ть *imp.* (with, + *instr.*); g. *away*, проигрывать *imp.*, проигра́ть *perf.* **gambler** *n.* игро́к (-а́). **gambling** *n.* аза́ртные и́гры *f.pl.*

gambol *v.i.* резви́ться *imp.*

game *n.* игра́ (*pl.* -ры); (*single g.*) па́ртия; (*collect.*, *animals*) дичь; *adj.* (*ready*) гото́вый. **gamekeeper** *n.* лесни́к (-а́). **gaming-house** *n.* иго́рный дом (*pl.* -а́). **gaming-table** *n.* иго́рный стол (-а́).

gammon *n.* о́корок.

gamut *n.* га́мма, диапазо́н.

gander *n.* гуса́к (-а́).

gang *n.* брига́да, ба́нда, ша́йка.

gangrene *n.* гангре́на.

gangster *n.* га́нгстер, банди́т.

gangway *n.* (*passage*) прохо́д; (*naut.*) схо́дни (-ней) *pl.*

gaol *n.* тюрьма́ (*pl.* -рьмы, -рем, -рьмам); *v.t.* заключа́ть *imp.*, заключи́ть *perf.* в тюрьму́. **gaoler** *n.* тюре́мщик.

gap *n.* (*breach*) брешь, проло́м; (*crack*) щель (*pl.* -ли, -ле́й); (*blank space*) пробе́л.

gape *v.i.* (*person*) разева́ть *imp.*, рази́нуть *perf.* рот; (*chasm*) зия́ть *imp.*; *g. at*, глазе́ть *imp.*, по ~ *perf.* на + *acc.*

garage *n.* гара́ж (-а́).

garb *n.* одея́ние.

garbage *n.* му́сор.

garble *v.t.* подтасо́вывать *imp.*, подтасова́ть *perf.*

garden *n.* сад (*loc.* -у́; *pl.* -ы́); (*kitchen g.*) огоро́д; *n.* парк; *attrib.* садо́вый. **gardener** *n.* садо́вник, садово́д. **gardening** *n.* садово́дство.

gargle *n.* полоска́ние; *v.i.* полоска́ть (-ощу́, -о́щешь) *imp.*, про ~ *perf.* го́рло.

gargoyle *n.* горгу́лья.

garish *adj.* я́ркий (я́рок, ярка́, я́рко), крича́щий.

garland *n.* гирля́нда, вено́к (-нка́); *v.t.* украша́ть *imp.*, укра́сить *perf.* гирля́ндой, венко́м.

garlic *n.* чесно́к (-а́(у́)).

garment *n.* предме́т оде́жды; *pl.* оде́жда collect.

garnet *n.* манса́рда.

garnish *n.* (*dish*) гарни́р; (*embellishment*) украше́ние; *v.t.* гарни́ровать *imp.*, *perf.*; украша́ть *imp.*, укра́сить *perf.*

garret *n.* манса́рда.

garrison *n.* гарнизо́н.

garrulous *adj.* болтли́вый.

garter *n.* подвя́зка.

gas *n.* газ (-а(у)); (*talk*) болтовня́; *attrib.* га́зовый; *g. cooker*, га́зовая плита́ (*pl.* -ты); *g. main*, газопрово́д; *g. mask*, противога́з; **gasworks**, га́зовый заво́д; *v.t.* отравля́ть *imp.*, отрави́ть (-влю́, -вишь) *perf.* га́зом. **gaseous** *adj.* газообра́зный.

gash *n.* глубо́кая ра́на, разре́з.

gasket *n.* прокла́дка.

gasp *v.i.* задыха́ться *imp.*, задохну́ться (-х(ну́)лся, -х(ну́)лась) *perf.*; (*exclaim*) а́хнуть (-ну) *perf.*

gastric *adj.* желу́дочный.

gate *n.* (*large*) воро́та (-т) *pl.*; (*small*) кали́тка. **gatekeeper** *n.* привра́тник. **gateway** *n.* (*gate*) воро́та (-т) *pl.*; (*entrance*) вход.

gather *v.t.* на-, со-, бира́ть *imp.*, на-, со-, бра́ть (-беру́, -берёшь; -брал, -брала́, -бра́ло) *perf.*; (*infer*) заключа́ть *imp.*, заключи́ть *perf.*; *v.i.* собира́ться *imp.*, собра́ться (-берётся; -бра́лся, -брала́сь, -бра́ло́сь) *perf.* **gathering** *n.* (*action*) собира́ние; (*assembly*) собра́ние.

gaudy *adj.* я́ркий (я́рок, ярка́, я́рко), крича́щий.

gauge *n.* (*measure*) ме́ра; (*instrument*) кали́бр, измери́тельный прибо́р; (*rly.*) коле́я; (*criterion*) крите́рий; *v.t.* измеря́ть *imp.*, изме́рить *perf.*; (*estimate*) оце́нивать *imp.*, оцени́ть (-ню́, -нишь) *perf.*

gaunt *adj.* то́щий (тощ, -а́, -е).

gauntlet *n.* рука́вица.

gauze *n.* ма́рля, газ.

gay *adj.* весёлый (ве́сел, -а́, -о, ве́селы́); (*bright*) пёстрый (пёстр, -а́, пёстро).

gaze *n.* при́стальный взгляд; *v.i.* при́стально гляде́ть (-яжу́, -яди́шь) *imp.* (*at*, на + *acc.*).

gazelle *n.* газе́ль.

gazette *n.* официа́льная газе́та; *v.t.* опублико́вывать *imp.*, опубликова́ть *perf.* в официа́льной газе́те. **gazetteer** *n.* географи́ческий спра́вочник.

gear *n.* (*appliance*) приспособле́ние, механи́зм, устро́йство; (*in motor*) переда́ча; (*high, low, g. etc.*) ско́рость (*pl.* -ти, -те́й); *in g.*, включённый (-ён, -ена́). **gearbox** *n.* коро́бка скоро-

gearwheel *n.* зубчáтое колесó (*pl.* -ёса), шестерня (*gen.pl.* -рён).

geld *v.t.* кастрировать *imp.*, *perf.* **gelding** *n.* мéрин.

gelignite *n.* гелигнит.

gem *n.* драгоцéнный кáмень (-мня; *pl.* -мни, -мнéй) *m.*; (*fig.*) драгоцéнность.

Gemini *n.* Близнецы *m.pl.*

gender *n.* род (*pl.* -ы́).

gene *n.* ген.

genealogical *adj.* генеалогический. **genealogy** *n.* генеалóгия, родослóвная *sb.*

general *n.* генерáл; *adj.* óбщий (общ, -á, -е), всеóбщий; (*chief*) генерáльный, глáвный; *in g.*, вообщé. **generality** *n.* всеóбщность; (*majority*) большинствó. **generalization** *n.* обобщéние. **generalize** *v.t.* обобщáть *imp.*, обобщить *perf.*; *v.i.* говорить *imp.* неопределённо. **generally** *adv.* обычно, вообщé.

generate *v.t.* порождáть *imp.*, породить *perf.*; производить (-ожý, -óдишь) *imp.*, произвести (-едý, -едёшь; -ёл, -елá) *perf.* **generation** *n.* порождéние, производство; (*in descent*) поколéние. **generator** *n.* генерáтор.

generic *adj.* родовóй; (*general*) óбщий (общ, -á, -е).

generosity *n.* (*magnanimity*) великодýшие; (*munificence*) щéдрость. **generous** *adj.* великодýшный; щéдрый (щедр, -á, -о); (*abundant*) обильный.

genesis *n.* происхождéние; (*G.*) Книга Бытия́.

genetic *adj.* генетический. **genetics** *n.* генéтика.

genial *adj.* (*of person*) добродýшный. **geniality** *n.* добродýшие.

genital *adj.* половóй. **genitals** *n.* половые óрганы *m.pl.*

genitive *adj.* (*n.*) родительный (падéж -á)).

genius *n.* (*person*) гéний; (*ability*) гениáльность; (*spirit*) дух.

genocide *n.* геноцид.

genre *n.* жанр.

genteel *adj.* благовоспитанный (-ан, -анна).

gentian *n.* горечáвка.

gentile *adj.* невеврéйский; *n.* нееврéй.

gentility *n.* благовоспитанность.

gentle *adj.* (*mild*) мягкий (-гок, -гкá, -гко); (*meek*) крóткий (-ток, -ткá, -тко); (*quiet*) тихий (тих, -á, -о); (*light*) лёгкий (-гок, -гкá, -гкó, лёгки). **gentleman** *n.* джентльмéн; господин (*pl.* -одá, -óд). **gentleness** *n.* мя́гкость.

genuine *adj.* (*authentic*) пóдлинный (-нен, -нна), настоя́щий; (*sincere*) искренний (-нен, -нна, -нно & -нне). **genuineness** *n.* пóдлинность; искренность.

genus *n.* род (*pl.* -ы́).

geo- *in comb.* гео-. **geographer** *n.* геóграф. **geographical** *adj.* географический. **geography** *n.* геогрáфия. **geological** *adj.* геологический. **geologist** *n.* геóлог. **geology** *n.* геолóгия. **geometric(al)** *adj.* геометрический. **geometrician** *n.* геóметр. **geometry** *n.* геомéтрия.

Georgian *n.* (*USSR*) грузин (*gen.pl.* -н), ~а; *adj.* грузинский.

geranium *n.* герáнь.

germ *n.* микрóб; (*fig.*) зародыш.

German *n.* нéмец (-мца), нéмка; *adj.* немéцкий; *G. measles*, краснýха. **Germanic** *adj.* гермáнский.

germane *adj.* умéстный.

germinate *v.i.* прорастáть *imp.*, прорасти (-тёт; пророс, -лá) *perf.*

gesticulate *v.i.* жестикулировать *imp.* **gesticulation** *n.* жестикуля́ция. **gesture** *n.* жест.

get *v.t.* (*obtain*) доставáть (-таю́, -таёшь) *imp.*, достáть (-áну, -áнешь) *perf.*; добивáться *imp.*, добиться (добью́сь, -бьёшься) *perf.* + *gen.*; (*receive*) получáть *imp.*, получить (-чý, -чишь) *perf.*; (*understand*) понимáть *imp.*, поня́ть (поймý, -мёшь; пóнял, -á, -о) *perf.*; (*disease*) схвáтывать *imp.*, схватить (-ачý, -áтишь) *perf.*; (*induce*) уговáривать *imp.*, уговорить *perf.* (*to do*, + *inf.*); *v.i.* (*become*) становиться (-влю́сь, -вишься) *imp.*, стать (стáну, -нешь) *perf.* + *inf.*; *have got*, (*have*) имéть *imp.*; *have got to*, быть дóлжен (-жнá) + *inf.*; *g. about*, (*spread*) распространя́ться *imp.*, распространиться *perf.*; *g. away*, ускользáть *imp.*, ускользну́ть *perf.*; g. back, (*recover*) получа́ть *imp.*, получи́ть (-чу́, -чишь) *perf.* обра́тно; (*return*) возвраща́ться *imp.*, верну́ться *perf.*; g. down to, принима́ться *imp.*, приня́ться (приму́сь, -мешься; приня́лся, -ла́сь) *perf.* за + *acc.*; g. off, слеза́ть (-за́ю, -за́ешь; -з) *perf.* c + *gen.*; g. on, сади́ться *imp.*, сесть (ся́ду, -дешь; сел) *perf.* в, на, + *acc.*; (*prosper*) преуспева́ть *imp.*, преуспе́ть *perf.*; g. on with, (*person*) ужива́ться *imp.*, ужи́ться (уживу́сь, -вёшься; ужи́лся, -ла́сь) *perf.* c + *instr.*; g. out of, (*avoid*) избавля́ться *imp.*, изба́виться *perf.* от + *gen.*; g. to, (*reach*) достига́ть *imp.*, дости́гнуть & дости́чь (-и́гну, -и́гнешь; -и́г) *perf.* + *gen.*; g. up, (*from bed*) встава́ть (-таю́, -таёшь) *imp.*, встать (-а́ну, -а́нешь) *perf.*

geyser *n.* (*spring*) ге́йзер; (*water-heater*) (га́зовая) коло́нка.

ghastly *adj.* стра́шный (-шен, -шна́, -шно, стра́шны), ужа́сный.

gherkin *n.* огуре́ц (-рца́).

ghetto *n.* ге́тто *neut.indecl.*

ghost *n.* привиде́ние, при́зрак, дух, тень (*pl.* -ни, -не́й). **ghostly** *adj.* при́зрачный.

giant *n.* велика́н, гига́нт; *adj.* грома́дный.

gibber *v.i.* тарато́рить *imp.* **gibberish** *n.* тараба́рщина.

gibbet *n.* ви́селица.

gibe *n.* насме́шка; *v.i.* насмеха́ться *imp.* (at, над + *instr.*).

giblets *n.* потроха́ (-хо́в) *pl.*

giddiness *n.* головокруже́ние; (*frivolity*) легкомы́слие. **giddy** *adj.* (*frivolous*) легкомы́сленный (-ен, -енна); *predic.*: I am, feel, giddy, у меня́ кружи́тся голова́.

gift *n.* (*present*) пода́рок (-рка); (*donation*) дар (*pl.* -ы́); (*talent*) тала́нт (к + *dat.*); (*ability*) спосо́бность (к + *dat.*). **gifted** *adj.* одарённый (-ён, -ённа), тала́нтливый.

gig *n.* (*carriage*) кабриоле́т; (*boat*) ги́чка.

gigantic *adj.* гига́нтский, грома́дный.

giggle *n.* хихи́канье; *v.i.* хихи́кать *imp.* хихи́кнуть *perf.*

gild *v.t.* золоти́ть *imp.*, вы́ ~, по ~ *perf.*

gill *n.* (*of fish*) жа́бра.

gilt *n.* позоло́та; *adj.* золочёный, позоло́ченный.

gimlet *n.* бура́вчик.

gin[1] *n.* (*snare*) западня́; (*winch*) лебёдка; (*cotton-g.*) джин.

gin[2] *n.* (*spirit*) джин.

ginger *n.* имби́рь (-ря́) *m.*; *attrib.* имби́рный; (*in colour*) ры́жий (рыж, -á, -е). **gingerbread** *n.* имби́рный пря́ник.

gingerly *adv.* осторо́жно.

gipsy *n.* цыга́н (*pl.* -не, -н), ~ ка; *attrib.* цыга́нский.

giraffe *n.* жира́ф.

gird *v.t.* опоя́сывать *imp.*, опоя́сать (-я́шу, -я́шешь) *perf.*; (*encircle*) окружа́ть *imp.*, окружи́ть *perf.* **girder** *n.* ба́лка. **girdle** *n.* по́яс (*pl.* -á); *v.t.* подпоя́сывать *imp.*, подпоя́сать (-я́шу, -я́шешь) *perf.*

girl *n.* де́вочка, де́вушка; g.-friend, подру́га. **girlish** *adj.* де́вичий (-чья, -чье).

girth *n.* (*band*) подпру́га; (*measurement*) обхва́т.

gist *n.* суть, су́щность.

give *v.t.* дава́ть (даю́, даёшь) *imp.*, дать (дам, дашь, даст, дади́м; дал, -á, да́ло, -и) *perf.*; дари́ть (-рю́, -ришь) *imp.*, по ~ *perf.*; g. away, выдава́ть (-даю́, -даёшь) *imp.*, вы́дать (-ам, -ашь, -аст, -адим) *perf.*; g. back, возвраща́ть *imp.*, возврати́ть (-ащу́, -ати́шь) *perf.*; g. in, (*yield*, *v.i.*) уступа́ть *imp.*, уступи́ть (-плю́, -пишь) *perf.* (to, + *dat.*); (*hand in*, *v.t.*) вруча́ть *imp.*, вручи́ть *perf.*; g. out, (*emit*) издава́ть (-даю́, -даёшь) *imp.*, изда́ть (-а́м, -а́шь, -а́ст, -ади́м; и́здал, -á, -о) *perf.*; (*distribute*) раздава́ть (-даю́, -даёшь) *imp.*, разда́ть (-а́м, -а́шь, -а́ст, -ади́м; ро́здал, -á, ро́здало & разда́ло) *perf.*; (*cease*) конча́ться *imp.*, ко́нчиться *perf.*; g. up, отка́зываться *imp.*, отказа́ться (-ажу́сь, -а́жешься) *perf.* от + *gen.*; (*habit etc.*) броса́ть *imp.*, бро́сить *perf.*; g. oneself up, сдава́ться (сдаю́сь, сдаёшься) *imp.*, сда́ться (-а́мся, -а́шься, -а́стся, -ади́мся сдался, -лась, сдалось, *perf.* **given** *predic.* (*inclined*) склонён (-о́нна, -о́нно) (to, к + *dat.*); (*devoted*) пре́дан (-а) (to, + *dat.*).

gizzard *n.* (*of bird*) му́скульный желу́док (-дка).

glacial *adj.* леднико́вый; (*fig.*) ледяно́й.

glacier *n.* ледни́к (-а́), глётчер.

glad *adj.* ра́достный, весёлый; *predic.* рад. **gladden** *v.t.* ра́довать *imp.*, об ~ *perf.* **gladness** *n.* ра́дость.

glade *n.* прога́лина, поля́на.

gladiolus *n.* шпа́жник.

glamorous *adj.* (*charming*) обая́тельный; (*attractive*) привлека́тельный. **glamour** *n.* обая́ние; привлека́тельность.

glance *n.* (*look*) бе́глый взгляд; *v.i.*: g. **at**, взгля́дывать *imp.*, взгляну́ть (-ну́, -нешь) *perf.* на + *acc.*; g. **off**, скользи́ть *imp.*, скользну́ть *perf.* по пове́рхности + *gen.*

gland *n.* железа́ (*pl.* же́лезы, -ёз, -еза́м). **glandular** *adj.* желе́зистый.

glare *n.* (*light*) ослепи́тельный блеск; (*look*) при́стальный, свире́пый, взгляд; *v.i.* ослепи́тельно сверка́ть *imp.*; при́стально, свире́по, смотре́ть (-рю́, -ришь) *imp.* (at, на + *acc.*). **glaring** *adj.* (*bright*) я́ркий; (*dazzling*) ослепи́тельный; (*mistake*) гру́бый.

glass *n.* (*substance*) стекло́; (*drinking vessel*) стака́н, рю́мка; (*glassware*) стекля́нная посу́да; (*mirror*) зе́ркало (*pl.* -ла́); *pl.* (*spectacles*) очки́ (-ко́в) *pl.*; *attrib.* стекля́нный; g.-*blower*, стеклоду́в; g. *fibre*, стекловолокно́; *glasshouse*, тепли́ца. **glassy** *adj.* (*of glass*) стекля́нный; (*water*) зерка́льный, гла́дкий (-док, -дка́, -дко); (*look*) ту́склый (тускл, -а́, -о).

glaze *n.* глазу́рь; *v.t.* (*picture*) застекля́ть *imp.*, застекли́ть *perf.*; (*cover with g.*) покрыва́ть *imp.*, покры́ть (-ро́ю, -ро́ешь) *perf.* глазу́рью. **glazier** *n.* стеко́льщик.

gleam *n.* сла́бый свет; (*also of hope etc.*) про́блеск; *v.i.* свети́ться (-ится) *imp.*

glean *v.t.* тща́тельно собира́ть *imp.*, собра́ть (соберу́, -рёшь; собра́л, -со́) *perf.*; *v.i.* подбира́ть *imp.*, подо-

бра́ть (подберу́, -рёшь; подобра́л, -а́, -о) *perf.* колосья.

glee *n.* весе́лье. **gleeful** *adj.* весёлый (ве́сел, -а́, -о, ве́селы).

glib *adj.* бо́йкий (бо́ек, бойка́, бо́йко).

glide *v.i.* скользи́ть *imp.*; (*aeron.*) плани́ровать *imp.*, с ~ *perf.* **glider** *n.* (*aircraft*) планёр; (*person*) планери́ст.

glimmer *n.* мерца́ние; *v.i.* мерца́ть *imp.*

glimpse *n.* (*appearance*) про́блеск; (*view*) мимолётный взгляд; *v.t.* ме́льком ви́деть (ви́жу, ви́дишь) *imp.*, у ~ *perf.*

glint, glitter *n.* блеск; *v.i.* блесте́ть (-ещу́, -ести́шь & -е́щешь) *imp.*; сверка́ть *imp.*

gloat *v.i.* пожира́ть *imp.*, пожра́ть (-ру́, -рёшь; пожра́л, -а́, -о) глаза́ми (over, + *acc.*); (*maliciously*) злора́дствовать *imp.*

global *adj.* (*world-wide*) мирово́й; (*total*) всео́бщий. **globe** *n.* (*sphere*) шар (-а́ with 2, 3, 4; *pl.* -ы́); (*the earth*) земно́й шар; (*chart*) гло́бус. **globular** *adj.* шарови́дный, сфери́ческий. **globule** *n.* ша́рик.

gloom *n.* мрак. **gloomy** *adj.* мра́чный (-чен, -чна́, -чно).

glorification *n.* прославле́ние. **glorify** *v.t.* прославля́ть *imp.*, просла́вить *perf.* **glorious** *adj.* сла́вный (-вен, -вна́, -вно); (*splendid*) великоле́пный. **glory** *n.* сла́ва; *v.i.* торжествова́ть *imp.*

gloss[1] *n.* (*word*) гло́сса; (*explanation*) толкова́ние.

gloss[2] *n.* (*lustre*) лоск, гля́нец (-нца); (*appearance*) ви́димость; *v.t.* наводи́ть (-ожу́, -о́дишь) *imp.*, навести́ (-еду́, -едёшь; навёл, -а́) *perf.* лоск, гля́нец, на + *acc.*; g. *over*, зама́зывать *imp.*, зама́зать (-а́жу, -а́жешь) *perf.*

glossary *n.* глосса́рий, слова́рь (-ря́) *m.*

glove *n.* перча́тка. **glover** *n.* перча́точник, -ица.

glow *n.* нака́л, за́рево; (*of cheeks*) румя́нец (-нца); (*ardour*) пыл (-а(у), *loc.* -у́); *v.i.* (*incandescence*) накаля́ться *imp.*, накали́ться *perf.*; (*shine*) сия́ть *imp.*; g.-*worm*, светля́к (-а́).

glucose *n.* глюко́за.

glue *n.* клей (-е́я (-е́ю), *loc.* -е́е & -ею́; *pl.* -еи́) *v.t.* кле́ить *imp.*, с ~ *perf.*;

(*attach*) приклеивать *imp.*, приклеить *perf.* (to, к + *dat.*).

glum *adj.* угрюмый.

glut *n.* (*surfeit*) пресыщение; (*excess*) избыток (-тка); (*in market*) затоваривание (рынка); *v.t.* пресыщать *imp.*, пресытить (-ыщу, -ытишь) *perf.*; (*overstock*) затоваривать *imp.*, затоварить *perf.*

glutton *n.* обжора *m. & f.* **gluttonous** *adj.* обжорливый. **gluttony** *n.* обжорство.

gnarled *adj.* (*hands*) шишковатый; (*tree*) сучковатый.

gnash *v.t.* скрежетать (-ещу, -ещешь) *imp.* + *instr.* **gnashing** *n.* скрежет.

gnat *n.* комар (-а).

gnaw *v.t.* глодать (-ожу, -ожешь) *imp.*; грызть (-зу, -зёшь; -з) *imp.*

gnome *n.* гном.

go *n.* (*movement*) движение; (*energy*) энергия; (*attempt*) попытка; be on the go, быть в движении; have a go, пытаться *imp.*, по~ *perf.*; *v.i.* (*on foot*) ходить (хожу, ходишь) *indet.*, идти (иду, идёшь; шёл, шла) *det.*, пойти (пойду, -дёшь; пошёл, -шла) *perf.*; (*by transport*) ездить *indet.*, ехать (еду, едешь) *det.*, по~ *perf.*; (*work*) работать *imp.*; (*become*) становиться (-влюсь, -вишься) *imp.*, стать (стану, -нешь) *perf.* + *instr.*; be going (to do), собираться *imp.*, собраться (соберусь, -рёшься; собрался, -алась, -алось) *perf.* (+ *inf.*); go about, (*set to work at*) браться (берусь, -рёшься; брался, -лась) *imp.*, взяться (возьмусь, -мёшься; взялся, -лась) *perf.* за+*acc.*; (*wander*) бродить (-ожу, -одишь) *indet.*; go at, (*attack*) набрасываться *imp.*, наброситься *perf.* на+*acc.*; go away, (*on foot*) уходить (-ожу, -одишь) *imp.*, уйти (уйду, -дёшь; ушёл, ушла) *perf.*; (*by transport*) уезжать *imp.*, уехать (уеду, -дешь) *perf.*; go down, спускаться *imp.*, спуститься (-ущусь, -устишься) *perf.*; go into, (*enter*) входить (-ожу, -одишь) *imp.*, войти (войду, -дёшь; вошёл, -шла) *perf.* в+*acc.*; (*investigate*) расследовать *imp.*, *perf.*; go off, (*go away*) уходить (-ожу, -одишь) *imp.*, уйти (уйду,

-дёшь; ушёл, ушла) *perf.*; (*deteriorate*) портиться *imp.*, ис~ *perf.*; go on, (*continue*) продолжать(ся) *imp.*, продолжить(ся) *perf.*; go out, выходить (-ожу, -одишь) *imp.*, выйти (выйду, -дешь; вышел, -шла) *perf.*; (*flame etc.*) гаснуть (-с) *imp.*, по~ *perf.*; go over, (*inspect*) пересматривать *imp.*, пересмотреть (-рю, -ришь) *perf.*; (*rehearse*) повторять *imp.*, повторить *perf.*; (*change allegiance etc.*) переходить (-ожу, -одишь) *imp.*, перейти (перейду, -дёшь; перешёл, -шла) *perf.* (to, в, на, + *acc.*, к+*dat.*); go through, (*scrutinize*) разбирать *imp.*, разобрать (разберу, -рёшь; разобрал, -а, -о) *perf.*; go through with, доводить (-ожу, -одишь) *imp.*, довести (-еду, -едёшь; -ёл, -ела) *perf.* до конца; go without, обходиться (-ожусь, -одишься) *imp.*, обойтись (обойдусь, -дёшься; обошёлся, -шлась) *perf.* без+*gen.*; go-ahead, предприимчивый; go-between, *n.* посредник.

goad *v.t.* подгонять *imp.*, подогнать (подгоню, -нишь; подогнал, -а, -о) *perf.*; *g. on*, (*instigate*) подстрекать *imp.*, подстрекнуть *perf.* (to, к + *dat.*).

goal *n.* (*aim*) цель; (*sport*) ворота (-т) *pl.*, (*also point(s) won*) гол (*pl.* -ы); score a g., забивать *imp.*, забить (-бью, -бьёшь) *perf.* гол. **goalkeeper** *n.* вратарь (-ря) *m.*

goat *n.* коза (*pl.* -зы), козёл (-зла); *attrib.* козий (-зья, -зье). **goatherd** *n.* козий пастух (-а).

gobble[1] *v.t.* (*eat*) жрать (жру, жрёшь; жрал, -а, -о) *imp.*; *g. up*, пожирать *imp.*, пожрать (-ру, -рёшь; пожрал, -а, -о) *perf.*

gobble[2] *v.i.* (*of turkeys*) кулдыкать *imp.*

goblet *n.* бокал, кубок (-бка).

god *n.* бог (*pl.* -и, -ов); (*idol*) кумир; (*G.*) Бог (*voc.* Боже); *pl.* (*theat.*) галёрка. **godchild** *n.* крестник, -ица. **god-daughter** *n.* крестница. **goddess** *n.* богиня. **godfather** *n.* крёстный *sb.* **God-fearing** *adj.* богобоязненный (-ен, -енна). **godless** *adj.* безбожный. **godlike** *adj.* богоподобный. **godly** *adj.* набожный. **godmother** *n.* крёстная *sb.* **godparent** *n.* крёстный *sb.* **godson** *n.* крёстник.

goggle *v.i.* тара́щить *imp.* глаза́ (at, на~ + *acc.*). **g.-eyed**, пучегла́зый; *n.*: *pl.* защи́тные очки́ (-ко́в) *pl.*

going *adj.* де́йствующий. **goings-on** *n.* поведе́ние; дела́ *neut.pl.*

goitre *n.* зоб (*loc.* -e & -ý; *pl.* -ы́).

gold *n.* зо́лото; *adj.* золото́й; **g.-bearing**, золотоно́сный; **g.-beater**, золотобо́й; **g.-digger**, золотоиска́тель *m.*; (*sl.*) авантюри́стка; **g.-dust**, золотоно́сный песо́к (-ска́ -ску́); **g.-field**, золото́й прии́ск; **g. leaf**, золота́я фо́льга; **g.-mine**, золото́й рудни́к (-á); (*fig.*) золото́е дно; **g. plate**, золота́я посу́да *collect.*; **g.-plate**, золоти́ть *imp.*, по~ *perf.*; **g.-smith**, золоты́х дел ма́стер (*pl.* -á). **golden** *adj.* золото́й, золоти́стый; **g. eagle**, бе́ркут (-á). **goldfinch** *n.* щего́л (-гла́). **goldfish** *n.* золота́я ры́бка.

golf *n.* гольф. **golfer** *n.* игро́к (-á) в гольф.

gondola *n.* гондо́ла. **gondolier** *n.* гондолье́р.

gong *n.* гонг.

good *n.* добро́, бла́го; *pl.* (*wares*) това́р(ы); *do* g., (*benefit*) идти́ (идёт; шёл, шла) *imp.*, пойти́ (пойдёт; пошёл, -шла́) *perf.* на по́льзу + *dat.*; *adj.* хоро́ший (-ш, -ша́), до́брый (добр, -á, -о, до́бры); **g.-humoured**, доброду́шный; **g.-looking**, краси́вый; **g. morning**, до́брое у́тро! **g. night**, споко́йной но́чи! **goodbye** *interj.* проща́й(те)! до свида́ния! **goodness** *n.* доброта́.

goose *n.* гусь (*pl.* -си, -се́й) *m.*, гусы́ня (*cul.*) гуся́тина; (*fool*) простофи́ля *m.* & *f.*; (*iron*) портно́вский утю́г (-á); **g.-flesh**, гуси́ная ко́жа.

gooseberry *n.* крыжо́вник (*plant or collect.*) *berries*).

gore[1] *n.* (*blood*) запёкшаяся кровь (*loc.* -ви́).

gore[2] *n.* (*cloth*) клин (*pl.* -ья, -ьев).

gore[3] *v.t.* бода́ть *imp.*, за~ *perf.*

gorge *n.* гло́тка; (*narrow opening*) уще́лье (*gen.pl.* -лий); *v.t.* жра́ть (жру, жрёшь; жрал, -á, -о) *imp.*, со~

perf.; *v.i.* объеда́ться *imp.*, объе́сться (-е́мся, -е́шься, -е́стся, -еди́мся; -е́лся) *perf.* (on, *+ instr.*).

gorgeous *adj.* пы́шный (-шен, -шна́, -шно), великоле́пный.

gorilla *n.* гори́лла.

gormandize *v.i.* объеда́ться *imp.*, объе́сться (-е́мся, ~~-е́шься, -е́стся, -еди́мся; -е́лся~~) *perf.*

gorse *n.* утёсник.

gory *adj.* окрова́вленный.

gosh *int.* бо́же мой!

goshawk *n.* большо́й я́стреб (*pl.* -ы & -á).

gosling *n.* гусёнок (-нка; *pl.* гуся́та, -т).

Gospel *n.* Ева́нгелие.

gossamer *n.* (*web*) паути́на; (*gauze*) то́нкая ткань.

gossip *n.* (*talk*) болтовня́, сплётня (*gen. pl.* -тен); (*person*) болту́н (-á), ~ья (*gen.pl.* -ний), сплётник, -ица; *v.i.* болта́ть *imp.*; сплётничать *imp.*, на~ *perf.*

Goth *n.* гот. **Gothic** *adj.* го́тский; (*archit.*; *print.*) готи́ческий.

gouache *n.* гуа́шь.

gouge *n.* полукру́глое долото́ (*pl.* -та); *v.t.*: **g. out**, выда́лбливать *imp.*, вы́долбить *perf.*; (*eyes*) выка́лывать *imp.*, вы́колоть (-лю, -лешь) *perf.*

goulash *n.* гуля́ш (-я́ша).

gourd *n.* ты́ква.

gourmand *n.* лако́мка *m.* & *f.*

gourmet *n.* гурма́н.

gout *n.* пода́гра. **gouty** *adj.* подагри́ческий.

govern *v.t.* пра́вить *imp.* + *instr.*; управля́ть *imp.* + *instr.* **governess** *n.* губерна́нтка. **government** *n.* (*of state*) прави́тельство; управле́ние (of, *+ instr.*). **governmental** *adj.* прави́тельственный. **governor** *n.* прави́тель *m.*, губерна́тор; (*head of institution*) заве́дующий *sb.* (of, *+ instr.*).

gown *n.* (*woman's*) пла́тье (*gen.pl.* -ьев); (*official's*) ма́нтия.

grab *n.* (*grasp*) захва́т; (*device*) черпа́к (-á); *v.t.* хвата́ть (-áю, -а́ешь) *perf.* захва́тывать *imp.*, захвати́ть (-ачу́, -а́тишь) *perf.*

grace *n.* (*gracefulness*) гра́ция; (*refinement*) изя́щество; (*kindness*) любе́з-

ность; (favour) ми́лость; (theol.) благода́ть; v.t. (adorn) украша́ть imp., укра́сить perf.; (confer) удоста́ивать imp., удосто́ить perf. (with, + gen.).
graceful adj. грацио́зный, изя́щный.
graceless adj. (improper) неприли́чный; (inelegant) неуклю́жий.
gracious adj. ми́лостивый, снисходи́тельный.

gradation n. града́ция.
grade n. (level) сте́пень (pl. -ни, -не́й) (quality) ка́чество; (sort) сорт (pl. -á); (slope) укло́н; v.t. распределя́ть imp., распредели́ть perf. по степеня́м, гру́ппам и т.п.; сортирова́ть imp., рас~ perf.; (road etc.) нивели́ровать imp., perf.
gradient n. укло́н.
gradual adj. постепе́нный (-нен, -нна).
graduate n. око́нчивший sb. университе́т, вуз; v.i. конча́ть imp., око́нчить perf. (университе́т, вуз); v.t. градуи́ровать imp., perf.
graffito n. сте́нна на́дпись, стенно́й рису́нок (-нка).
graft[1] n. (agric.) приво́й, приви́вка; (med.) переса́дка (живо́й тка́ни); v.t. (agric.) привива́ть imp., приви́ть (-вью, -вьёшь; приви́л, -á, -о) perf. (to, + dat.); (med.) переса́живать imp., пересади́ть (-ажу́, -а́дишь) perf.
graft[2] n. (bribe) взя́тка, по́дкуп; v.i. (give) дава́ть (даю́, даёшь; дал, дам, дашь, даст, дади́м; дал, -á, да́ло́, -и) perf. взя́тку; (take) брать (беру́, -рёшь; брал, -á, -о) imp., взять (возьму́, -мёшь; взял, -á, -о perf. взя́тки.
grain n. (seed; collect.) зерно́ (pl. зёрна, -рен, -рнам); (particle) крупи́нка; (of sand) песчи́нка; (measure) гран (gen. pl. -н); (smallest amount) крупи́ца; (of wood) (древе́сное) волокно́; against the g., не по нутру́; not a g. of, ни гра́на + gen.
gram(me) n. грамм (gen.pl. -м & -мов).
grammar n. грамма́тика; g. school, гимна́зия. **grammarian** n. грамма́тик.
grammatical adj. граммати́ческий.
gramophone n. граммофо́н, прои́грыватель m.; g. record, грампласти́нка.
grampus n. се́рый дельфи́н.

granary n. амба́р.
grand adj. (in titles) вели́кий; (main) гла́вный; (majestic) вели́чественный (-ен, -енна); (splendid) великоле́пный; g. duke, вели́кий ге́рцог; (in Russia) вели́кий князь (pl. -зья́, -зе́й); g. master, гроссме́йстер; g. piano, роя́ль m. **grandchild** n. внук, вну́чка; pl. вну́чата (-т) pl. **granddaughter** n. вну́чка. **grandfather** n. де́душка m. **grandmother** n. ба́бушка. **grandparents** n. ба́бушка и де́душка. **grandson** n. внук. **grandstand** n. трибу́на.
grandee n. (Span., Portug.) гранд; вельмо́жа m.
grandeur n. вели́чие.
grandiloquence n. напы́щенность. **grandiloquent** adj. напы́щенный (-ен, -енна).
grandiose adj. грандио́зный.
grange n. фе́рма.
granite n. грани́т; attrib. грани́тный.
grannie, granny n. ба́бушка.
grant n. дар (pl. -ы); (financial) дота́ция, субси́дия; v.t. дарова́ть imp., perf.; предоставля́ть imp., предоста́вить perf.; (concede) допуска́ть imp., допусти́ть (-ущу́, -у́стишь) perf.; take for granted, счита́ть imp., счесть (сочту́, -тёшь; счёл, сочла́) perf. само́ собо́й разуме́ющимся.
granular adj. зерни́стый.
granulate v.t. гранули́ровать imp., perf.; granulated sugar, са́харный песо́к (-ска́(у́)).
granule n. зёрнышко (pl. -шки, -шек, -шкам).
grape n. виногра́д (-a(y)) (collect.); g.-shot, карте́чь; g.-vine, виногра́дная лоза́ (pl. -зы). **grapefruit** n. гре́йпфрут.
graph n. гра́фик.
graphic adj. графи́ческий; (vivid) я́ркий (я́рок, ярка́, я́рко).
graphite n. графи́т.
grapnel n. дрек, ко́шка.
grapple n. (grapnel) дрек, ко́шка; (grip) захва́т; v.i. сцепля́ться imp., сцепи́ться (-плю́сь, -пишься) perf. (with, c + instr.); (fig.) боро́ться (-рю́сь, -решься) imp. (with, c + instr.); grappling-hook, -iron, дрек, ко́шка.

grasp n. (grip) хва́тка; (control) власть; (mental hold) схва́тывание; v.t. (clutch) хвата́ть imp., схвати́ть (-ачу́, -а́тишь) perf.; (comprehend) понима́ть imp., поня́ть (пойму́, -мёшь; по́нял, -а́, -о) perf. **grasping** adj. жа́дный (-ден, -дна́, -дно).

grass n. трава́ (pl. -вы), злак; (pasture) па́стбище; g. snake, уж (-а́); g. widow, соло́менная вдова́ (pl. -вы). **grasshopper** n. кузне́чик. **grassy** adj. травяни́стый, травяно́й.

grate[1] n. (in fireplace) (ками́нная) решётка.

grate[2] v.t. (rub) тере́ть (тру, трёшь; тёр) imp., на~ perf.; v.i. (sound) скрипе́ть (-пи́т) imp.; g. (up)on, (irritate) раздража́ть imp., раздражи́ть perf.

grateful n. благода́рный.

grater n. тёрка.

gratify v.t. удовлетворя́ть imp., удовлетвори́ть perf.

grating n. решётка.

gratis adv. беспла́тно, да́ром.

gratitude n. благода́рность.

gratuitous adj. (free) дарово́й; (motiveless) беспричи́нный (-нен, -нна).

gratuity n. де́нежный пода́рок (-рка); (tip) чаевы́е sb.; (mil.) награ́дные sb.

grave[1] n. моги́ла; g.-digger, моги́льщик. **gravestone** n. надгро́бный ка́мень (-мня; pl. -мни, -мне́й) m. **graveyard** n. кла́дбище.

grave[2] adj. (serious) серьёзный, ва́жный (-жен, -жна́, -жно, -жны́).

gravel n. гра́вий; g. pit, гра́вийный карье́р.

gravitate v.i. тяготе́ть imp. (towards, к + dat.). **gravitation** n. тяготе́ние.

gravity n. (seriousness) серьёзность; (force) тя́жесть; specific g., уде́льный вес.

gravy n. (мясна́я) подли́вка; g.-boat, со́усник.

grayling n. ха́риус.

graze[1] v.t. & i. (feed) пасти́ (пасу́(сь), пасёшь(ся)) imp.

graze[2] n. (abrasion) цара́пина; v.t. (touch lightly) задева́ть imp., заде́ть (-е́ну, -е́нешь) perf.; (abrade) цара́пать imp., о~ perf.

grease n. жир (-а(у)), loc. -е & -у́), то́пленое са́ло; (lubricant) сма́зка; g.-gun, тавóтный шприц; g.-paint, грим; v.t. сма́зывать imp., сма́зать (-а́жу, -а́жешь) perf. **greasy** adj. жи́рный (-рен, -рна́, -рно), са́льный.

great adj. (large) большо́й; (eminent) вели́кий; (long) до́лгий (-лог, -лга́, -лго); (strong) си́льный (силён, -льна́, -льно, си́льны); to a g. extent, в большо́й сте́пени; a g. deal, мно́го (+ gen.); a g. many, мно́гие; мно́жество (+ gen.); g.-aunt, двоюро́дная ба́бушка; g.-granddaughter, пра́внучка; g.-grandfather, пра́дед; g.-grandmother, праба́бка; g.-grandson, пра́внук; g.-uncle, двоюро́дный де́душка m. **greatly** adv. о́чень.

grebe n. пога́нка.

Grecian adj. гре́ческий.

greed n. жа́дность (for, к + dat.), а́лчность. **greedy** adj. жа́дный (-ден, -дна́, -дно) (for, к + dat.), а́лчный; (for food) прожо́рливый.

Greek n. грек, греча́нка; adj. гре́ческий.

green n. (colour) зелёный цвет; (piece of land) лужо́к (-жка́); pl. зе́лень collect.; adj. зелёный (зе́лен, -а́, -о) (inexperienced) нео́пытный. **greenery** n. зе́лень. **greenfinch** n. зеленýшка. **greenfly** n. тля (gen. pl. тлей). **greengage** n. ренкло́д. **greengrocer** n. зеленщи́к (-а́). **greenhorn** n. новичо́к (-чка́). **greenhouse** n. тепли́ца, оранжере́я.

greet v.t. кла́няться imp., поклони́ться (-ню́сь, -нишься) perf. + dat.; приве́тствовать imp. (& perf. in past tense). **greeting** n. приве́т(ствие).

gregarious adj. ста́дный; (person) общи́тельный.

grenade n. грана́та.

grey adj. се́рый (сер, -а́, -о); (hair) седо́й (сед, -а́, -о); g. hair, седина́ (pl. -ы).

greyhound n. борза́я sb.

grid n. (grating) решётка; (network) сеть (pl. -ти, -те́й); (map) координа́тная се́тка.

grief n. го́ре, печа́ль; come to g., попа́сть imp., попа́сть (попаду́, -дёшь; попа́л) perf. в беду́.

grievance *n.* жалоба, обида.

grieve *v.t.* огорчать *imp.*, огорчить *perf.*; *v.i.* горевать (-рюю, -рюешь) *imp.* (for, о + *prep.*).

grievous *adj.* тяжкий (-жек, -жка, -жко); (*flagrant*) вопиющий.

grill [1] *n.* рашпер; *v.t.* (*cook*) жарить *imp.*, за~, из~ *perf.* (на рашпере, решётке); (*question*) допрашивать, *imp.*, допросить (-ошу, -осишь) *perf.*

grille, grill [2] *n.* (*grating*) решётка.

grim *adj.* (*stern*) суровый (-в, -ва, -во); (*sinister*) мрачный (-чен, -чна, -чно); (*unpleasant*) неприятный.

grimace *n.* гримаса; *v.i.* гримасничать *imp.*

grime *n.* (*soot*) сажа; (*dirt*) грязь (*loc.* -зи). **grimy** *adj.* грязный (-зен, -зна, -зно).

grin *n.* усмешка; *v.i.* усмехаться *imp.*, усмехнуться *perf.*

grind *v.t.* (*flour etc.*) молоть (мелю, -лешь) *imp.*, с~ *perf.*; (*axe*) точить (-чу, -чишь) *imp.*, на~ *perf.*; (*oppress*) мучить *imp.*, за~, из~ *perf.*; g. one's teeth, скрежетать (-ещу, -ещешь) *imp.* зубами.

grip *n.* схватывание; (*control*) власть; *v.t.* схватывать *imp.*, схватить (-ачу, -атишь) *perf.*

grisly *adj.* ужасный.

gristle *n.* хрящ (-á). **gristly** *adj.* хрящеватый.

grit *n.* крупный песок (-ска(у)); (*firmness*) стойкость. **gritty** *adj.* песчаный.

grizzly *adj.* серый (сер, -á, -о); g. bear, гризли *m. indecl.*

groan *n.* стон; *v.i.* стонать (-ну, -нешь) *imp.*

grocer *n.* бакалейщик; g.'s shop, бакалейная лавка, гастрономический магазин. **groceries** *n.* бакалея *collect.*

groin *n.* (*anat.*) пах (*loc.* -ý); (*arch.*) ребро (*pl.* рёбра, -бер, -брам) крестового свода.

groom *n.* грум, конюх; (*bridegroom*) жених (-á); *v.t.* (*horse*) чистить *imp.*, по~ *perf.*; (*person*) холить *imp.*, вы~ *perf.*; (*prepare*) готовить *imp.*, под~ *perf.* (for, к + *dat.*); well-groomed, выхоленный (-ен).

groove *n.* желобок (-бка), паз (*loc.* -ý; *pl.* -ы); (*routine*) колея.

grope *v.i.* нащупывать *imp.* (for, after, + *acc.*); g. one's way, идти (иду, идёшь; шёл, шла) *imp.*, пойти (пойду, -дёшь; пошёл, -шла) *perf.* ощупью.

gross [1] *n.* (*12 dozen*) гросс; by the g., оптом.

gross [2] *adj.* (*luxuriant*) пышный (-шен, -шна, -шно); (*fat*) тучный (-чен, -чна, -чно); (*coarse*) грубый (груб, -á, -о); (*total*) валовой; g. weight, вес брутто.

grotesque *adj.* гротескный; (*absurd*) нелепый.

grotto *n.* грот, пещера.

ground *n.* земля (*acc.* -лю), почва, грунт; *pl.* (*dregs*) гуща; (*sport*) площадка; *pl.* (*of house*) парк; (*background*) фон; (*reason*) основание, причина; break fresh g., прокладывать *imp.*, проложить (-жу, -жишь) *perf.* новые пути; gain g., делать *imp.*, с~ *perf.* успехи; give, lose, g., уступать *imp.*, уступить (-плю, -пишь) *perf.* (to, + *dat.*); stand one's g., стоять (-ою, -оишь) *imp.* на своём; g. floor, цокольный, первый, этаж (-á); g.-nut, земляной орех; *v.t.* (*base*) обосновывать *imp.*, обосновать (-ную, -нуёшь) *perf.*; (*instruct*) обучать *imp.*, обучить (-чу, -чишь) *perf.* основам (in, + *gen.*); *v.i.* (*naut.*) садиться *imp.*, сесть (сядет, сел) *perf.* на мель. **groundless** *adj.* беспричинный (-нен, -нна), необоснованный (-ан, -анна). **groundsheet** *n.* полотнище палатки. **groundwork** *n.* фундамент, основа, основание.

groundsel *n.* крестовник.

group *n.* группа; g. captain, полковник авиации; *v.t.* & *i.* группировать(ся) *imp.*, с~ *perf.*

grouse [1] *n.* (*bird*) тетерев (*pl.* -á); (*red*) g., шотландская куропатка.

grouse [2] *v.i.* (*grumble*) ворчать (-чу, -чишь) *imp.*

grove *n.* роща.

grovel *v.i.* пресмыкаться *imp.* (before, перед + *instr.*).

grow *v.i.* расти́ (-ту́, -тёшь; рос, -ла́) *imp.*; (*become*) станови́ться (-влю́сь, -вишься) *imp.*, стать (ста́ну, -нешь) *perf.* + *instr.*; *v.t.* (*cultivate*) выра́щивать *imp.*, вы́растить *perf.*; *g. up*, (*person*) вырастать *imp.*, вы́расти (-ту, -тешь; вы́рос, -ла) *perf.*; (*custom*) возника́ть *imp.*, возни́кнуть (-к) *perf.*

growl *n.* ворча́ние; *v.i.* ворча́ть (-чу́, -чи́шь) *imp.* (at, на + *acc.*).

grown-up *adj.*, *n.* взро́слый *sb.*

growth *n.* рост (-а(у)); (*tumour*) о́пухоль.

groyne *n.* волноре́з.

grub *n.* (*larva*) личи́нка; (*sl.*) (*food*) жратва́; *v.i.*: *g. about*, рыться (ро́юсь, ро́ешься) *imp.* **grubby** *adj.* чума́зый.

grudge *n.* недово́льство, за́висть; *have a g. against*, име́ть *imp.* зуб про́тив + *gen.*; *v.t.* жале́ть *imp.*, по ~ *perf.* + *acc.* + *gen.*; неохо́тно дава́ть (даю́, даёшь) *imp.*, дать (дам, дашь, даст, дади́м; дал, -а́, да́ло́, -и) *perf.*; неохо́тно де́лать *imp.*, с ~ *perf.* **grudgingly** *adv.* неохо́тно.

gruel *n.* жи́дкая ка́ша; *v.t.* утомля́ть *imp.*, утоми́ть *perf.* **gruelling** *adj.* изнури́тельный, суро́вый.

gruesome *adj.* отврати́тельный.

gruff *adj.* (*surly*) грубова́тый; (*voice*) хри́плый (-л, -ла́, -ло).

grumble *n.* ворча́ние, ро́пот; *v.i.* ворча́ть (-чу́, -чи́шь) *imp.* (at, на + *acc.*).

grumpy *adj.* брюзгли́вый.

grunt *n.* хрю́канье; *v.i.* хрю́кать *imp.*, хрю́кнуть *perf.*

guarantee *n.* (*person*) поручи́тель *m.*, ~ ница; (*security*) гара́нтия, зало́г; *v.t.* гаранти́ровать *imp.*, *perf.* (against, от + *gen.*); руча́ться *imp.*, поручи́ться (-чу́сь, -чишься) *perf.* за + *acc.* **guarantor** *n.* поручи́тель *m.*, ~ ница. **guaranty** *n.* гара́нтия.

guard *n.* (*protection*) охра́на; (*watch*; *body of soldiers*) карау́л; (*sentry*) часово́й *sb.*; (*watchman*) сто́рож (*pl.* -а́); (*rly.*) конду́ктор (*pl.* -а́); *pl.* (*G.*) гва́рдия; *g. of honour*, почётный карау́л; *v.t.* охраня́ть *imp.*, охрани́ть *perf.*; *v.i.*: *g. against*, остерега́ться *imp.*, остере́чься (-егу́сь, -ежёшься, -ёгся, -егла́сь) *perf.* + *gen.*, *inf.* **guard-**

house, -room *n.* гауптва́хта. **guardsman** *n.* гварде́ец (-е́йца).

guardian *n.* храни́тель *m.*, ~ ница; (*leg.*) опеку́н (-а́).

guer(r)illa *n.* партиза́н; *g. warfare*, партиза́нская война́.

guess *n.* дога́дка; *v.t.* & *i.* дога́дываться *imp.*, догада́ться *perf.* (о + *prep.*); *v.t.* (*g. correctly*) уга́дывать *imp.*, угада́ть *perf.*

guest *n.* гость (*pl.* -ти, -те́й) *m.*, ~ я (*gen.pl.* -тий).

guffaw *n.* хо́хот; *v.i.* хохота́ть (-очу́, -о́чешь) *imp.*

guidance *n.* руково́дство. **guide** *n.* проводни́к (-а́), -и́ца; гид; (*adviser*) сове́тчик; (*manual*) руково́дство; (*guidebook*) путеводи́тель *m.*; *g.-post*, указа́тельный столб (-а́) *v.t.* води́ть (вожу́, во́дишь) *indet.*, вести́ (веду́, -дёшь; вёл, -а́) *det.*; (*direct*) руководи́ть *imp.* + *instr.*; (*control*) управля́ть *imp.* + *instr.*; *guided missile*, управля́емая раке́та.

guild *n.* ги́льдия, цех.

guile *n.* кова́рство, хи́трость. **guileful** *adj.* кова́рный. **guileless** *adj.* простоду́шный.

guillemot *n.* ка́йра, чи́стик.

guillotine *n.* гильоти́на; *v.t.* гильотини́ровать *imp.*, *perf.*

guilt *n.* вина́, вино́вность. **guiltless** *adj.* неви́нный (-нен, -нна), невино́вный. **guilty** *adj.* вино́вный (of, в + *prep.*), винова́тый.

guinea *n.* гине́я; *g.-fowl, -hen,* цеса́рка; *g.-pig,* морска́я сви́нка; (*fig.*) подо́пытный кро́лик.

guise *n.* вид, о́блик; *under the g. of*, под ви́дом + *gen.*

guitar *n.* гита́ра.

gulf *n.* зали́в; (*chasm*) про́пасть; *G. Stream,* гольфстри́м.

gull *n.* ча́йка.

gullet *n.* пищево́д; (*throat*) го́рло.

gullible *adj.* легкове́рный.

gully *n.* (*ravine*) овра́г; (*channel*) кана́ва.

gulp *n.* глото́к (-тка́); *v.t.* жа́дно глота́ть *imp.*

gum[1] *n.* (*anat.*) десна́ (*pl.* дёсны, -сен, -снам).

gum² *n.* (*glue*) камедь, клей (-ея(ю), *loc.* -ée & -ею; *pl.* -еи); *v.t.* склеивать *imp.*, склеить *perf.* **gumboot** *n.* резиновый сапог (-á; *gen.pl.* -г). **gum-tree** *n.* эвкалипт.

gumption *n.* находчивость.

gun *n.* (*piece of ordnance*) орудие, пушка; (*rifle etc.*) ружьё (*pl.* -жья, -жей); (*pistol*) пистолет; *starting g.*, стартовый пистолет; *v.t.*: *g. down*, расстреливать *imp.*, расстрелять *perf.* **gunboat** *n.* канонерская лодка. **gun-carriage** *n.* лафет (-á). **gunner** *n.* артиллерист; (*aeron.*) стрелок (-лкá). **gunpowder** *n.* порох (-a(у)). **gunsmith** *n.* оружейный мастер (*pl.* -á).

gunwale *n.* планшир *m.*

gurgle *v.i.* булькать *imp.*, булькнуть *perf.*

gush *n.* сильный поток; излияние; *v.i.* хлынуть *perf.*; изливаться *imp.*, излиться (изольюсь, -ьёшься; излился, -илась, -илось) *perf.*

gusset *n.* клин (*pl.* -ья, -ьев), ластовица.

gust *n.* порыв. **gusty** *adj.* порывистый.

gusto *n.* удовольствие, смак.

gut *n.* кишка (*gen.pl.* -шок); *pl.* (*entrails*) внутренности *f.pl.*; *pl.* (*coll.*,

bravery) мужество; *v.t.* потрошить *imp.*, вы~ *perf.*; (*devastate*) опустошать *imp.*, опустошить *perf.*

gutta-percha *n.* гуттаперча.

gutter *n.* (*watercourse*) жёлоб (*pl.* -á), сточная канава; *g. press*, бульварная пресса.

guttural *adj.* гортанный, горловой.

guy¹ *n.* (*rope*) оттяжка.

guy² *n.* (*fellow*) парень (-рня; *pl.* -рни, -рней) *m.*

guzzle *v.t.* (*food*) пожирать *imp.*, пожрать (-ру, -рёшь; пожрал, -á, -о) *perf.*; (*liquid*) хлебать *imp.*, хлебнуть *perf.*

gym *n.* (*gymnasium*) гимнастический зал; (*gymnastics*) гимнастика. **gymnasium** *n.* гимнастический зал; (*school*) гимназия. **gymnast** *n.* гимнаст, ~ ка. **gymnastic** *adj.* гимнастический. **gymnastics** *n.* гимнастика.

gynaecology *n.* гинекология.

gypsum *n.* гипс.

gyrate *v.i.* вращаться *imp.* по кругу; двигаться (двигается & движется) *imp.* по спирали.

gyro(scope) *n.* гироскоп. **gyro-compass** *n.* гирокомпас.

H

haberdasher *n.* торговец (-вца) галантереей. **haberdashery** *n.* (*articles*) галантерея; (*shop*) галантерейный магазин.

habit *n.* привычка; (*constitution*) сложение; (*dress*) одеяние.

habitable *adj.* годный (-ден, -дна, -дно) для жилья. **habitation** *n.* жилище.

habitual *adj.* обычный, привычный. **habitué** *n.* завсегдатай.

hack¹ *n.* (*mattock*) мотыга; (*miner's pick*) кайла (*pl.* -лы), кайло (*pl.* -ла); *v.t.* рубить (-блю, -бишь) *imp.*; дробить *imp.*, раз~ *perf.*; *h.-saw*, ножовка.

hack² *n.* (*hired horse*) наёмная лошадь (*pl.* -ди, -дей, *instr.* -дьми); (*jade*) кляча; (*person*) подёнщик, писака *m.* & *f.* **hackneyed** *adj.* избитый, банальный.

haddock *n.* пикша.

haematology *n.* гематология. **haemophilia** *n.* гемофилия. **haemorrhage** *n.* кровоизлияние, кровотечение. **haemorrhoids** *n.* геморрой *collect.*

haft *n.* рукоятка.

hag *n.* ведьма, карга.

haggard *adj.* изможденный (-ён, -ена).

haggle *v.i.* торговаться *imp.*, с~ *perf.*

hail¹ *n.* град; *v.i.: it is hailing,* идёт (*past* пошёл) град; *v.t.* осыпáть *imp.*, осы́пать (-плю, -плешь) *perf.* + *case. & instr.*; *v.i.* сы́паться (-плется) *imp.* грáдом. **hailstone** *n.* грáдина.

hail² *v.t.* (*greet*) приве́тствовать *imp.* (& *perf. in past*); (*call*) оклика́ть *imp.*, окли́кнуть *perf.*; *v.i.: h. from,* (*of persons only*) быть рóдом из + *gen.*; происходи́ть (-ожý, -óдишь) *imp.*, произойти́ (произойдý, -дёшь; произошёл, -шлá) *perf.* из + *gen.*

hair *n.* (*single h.*) вóлос (*pl.* -осы, -óс, -осáм) *pl.*; *collect.* (*human*) вóлосы (-óс, -осáм) *pl.*; (*animal*) шерсть *n.*; *do one's hair,* причёсываться *imp.*, причесáться (-ешýсь, -ёшешься) *perf.* **haircut** *n.* стри́жка. **hair-do** *n.* причёска. **hairdresser** *n.* парикмáхер. **hairy** *adj.* волосáтый.

hake *n.* хек.

halberd *n.* алебáрда.

hale *adj.* здорóвый.

half *n.* половина; (*sport*) тайм; *in comb.* пол(у)-; *adj.* половинный; *in h.,* пополáм; *one and a h.,* полторá *m. & neut.,* -ры́ *f.* + *gen. sing.* (*obl. cases:* полýтора + *pl.*); *h. past* (*one etc.*), половина (вторóго и т.д.); *h.-back,* полузащи́тник; *h.-hearted,* равнодýшный; *h.-hour,* полчасá (*obl. cases* получасá); *h.-mast: flag at h.-mast,* приспущённый флаг; *h. moon,* полумéсяц; *h.-time,* переры́в мéжду тáймами; *h.-way,* на полпути́; *h.-witted,* слабоýмный.

halibut *n.* пáлтус.

hall *n.* (*large room*) зал; (*entrance h.*) холл, вестибю́ль *m.*; (*dining h.*) столóвая (коллéджа); (*h. of residence*) общежи́тие. **hallmark** *n.* пробирное клеймó (*pl.* -ма); (*fig.*) при́знак.

halliard *see* halyard.

hallow *v.t.* освящáть *imp.*, освяти́ть (-ящý, -яти́шь) *perf.*

hallucination *n.* галлюцинáция.

halo *n.* галó *neut. indecl.*; (*around Saint*) вéнчик, нимб; (*fig.*) орео́л.

halogen *n.* галогéн.

halt¹ *n.* (*stoppage*) останóвка *n.* (*rly.*) полустанóк (-нкá) *v.t. & i.* останáв-

ливать(ся) *imp.*, останови́ть(ся) (-влю́(сь), -вишь(ся)) *perf.*; *interj.* (*mil.*) стóй(те)!

halt² *v.i.* (*hesitate*) колебáться (-блю́сь, блешься) *imp.*

halter *n.* недоýздок (-дка).

halve *v.t.* дели́ть (-лю́, -лишь) *imp.*, раз ~ *perf.* пополáм.

halyard, halliard *n.* фал.

ham *n.* (*cul.*) ветчинá, óкорок; (*theat.*) плохóй актёр; (*radio h.*) радиолюби́тель *m.*; *v.i.* (*theat.*) переи́грывать *imp.*, переигрáть *perf.*

hamlet *n.* деревýшка.

hammer *n.* мóлот, молотóк (-ткá); *come under the h.,* продавáться (-даётся) *imp.*, продáться (-дáстся; -дáлся, -далáсь) *perf.* с молоткá.; *vt.* бить (бью, бьёшь) *imp.* мóлотом, молоткóм.

hammock *n.* гамáк (-á); (*naut.*) кóйка.

hamper¹ *n.* (*basket*) корзи́на с кры́шкой.

hamper² *v.t.* (*hinder*) мешáть *imp.*, по ~ *perf.* + *dat.*

hamster *n.* хомя́к (-á).

hand *n.* рукá (*acc.* -ку; *pl.* -ки, -к, -кáм); (*worker*) рабóчий *sb.*; (*handwriting*) пóчерк; (*clock h.*) стрéлка; *at h.,* под рукóй; *on hands and knees,* на четверéньках; *v.t.* передавáть (-даю́, -даёшь) *imp.*, передáть (-áм, -áшь, -áст, -ади́м; пéредал, -á, -о) *perf.*; вручáть *imp.*, вручи́ть *perf.* **handbag** *n.* сýмка, сýмочка. **handbook** *n.* спрáвочник, руковóдство. **handcuffs** *n.* нарýчники *m.pl.* **handful** *n.* горсть (*pl.* -ти, -тéй)

handicap *n.* (*sport*) гандикáп; (*hindrance*) помéха. **handicapped** *adj.: h. person,* инвали́д.

handicraft *n.* ремеслó (*pl.* -ёсла, -ёсел, -ёслам)

handiwork *n.* ручнáя рабóта.

handkerchief *n.* носовóй платóк (-ткá).

handle *n.* рýчка, рукоя́тка; *v.t.* (*treat*) обращáться *imp.* с + *instr.*; (*manage*) управля́ть *imp.* + *instr.*; (*touch*) трóгать *imp.*, трóнуть *perf.* рукóй, рукáми. **handlebar(s)** *n.* руль (-ля́) *m.*

handsome *adj.* краси́вый; (*generous*) щéдрый (щедр, -á, -о).

handwriting *n.* пóчерк.

handy adj. (convenient) удо́бный; (skilful) ло́вкий (-вок, -вка́, -вко, ло́вки); come in h., пригоди́ться perf.

hang v.t. ве́шать imp., пове́сить perf.; подве́шивать imp., подве́сить perf.; v.i. висе́ть (вишу́, виси́шь) imp.; h. about, слоня́ться imp.; h. back, колеба́ться (-блю́сь, -блешься) imp.; h. on, (remain) держа́ться (-жу́сь, -жишься) imp. **hanger-on** n. прижива́льщик. **hangman** n. пала́ч (-а́).

hangar n. анга́р.

hangover n. похме́лье.

hanker v.i.: h. after, стра́стно жела́ть imp., по ~ perf. + gen.

hansom n. двухколёсный экипа́ж.

haphazard adj. случа́йный; adv. случа́йно, наудачу.

hapless adj. злополу́чный.

happen v.i. (occur) случа́ться imp., случи́ться perf.; происходи́ть (-ит) imp., произойти́ (-ойдёт; -ошёл, -ошла́) perf.; (h. to be somewhere) ока́зываться imp., оказа́ться (-ажу́сь, -а́жешься) perf.; h. upon, ната́лкиваться imp., натолкну́ться perf. на + acc.

happiness n. сча́стье. **happy** adj. счастли́вый (сча́стли́в); (apt) уда́чный.

harass v.t. беспоко́ить imp., о ~ perf.

harbinger n. предве́стник.

harbour n. га́вань, порт (loc. -ý; pl. -ы, -ов); (shelter) убе́жище; (person) укрыва́ть imp., укры́ть (-ро́ю, -ро́ешь) perf.; (thoughts) зата́ивать imp., зата́ить perf.

hard adj. твёрдый (твёрд, -á, -о), жёсткий (-ток, -тка́, -тко); (difficult) тру́дный (-ден, -дна́, -дно, тру́дны); (difficult to bear) тяжёлый (-л, -ла́); (severe) суро́вый; h.-boiled egg, яйцо́ (pl. я́йца, я́иц, я́йцам) вкруту́ю; h.-headed, практи́чный; h.-hearted, жестокосе́рдный; h.-working, приле́жный.

harden v.t. де́лать imp., с ~ perf. твёрдым; закаля́ть imp., закали́ть perf.; v.i. затвердева́ть imp., затверде́ть perf.; (become callous) ожесточа́ться imp., ожесточи́ться perf.

hardly adv. (scarcely) едва́ (ли); (with difficulty) с трудо́м.

hardship n. (privation) нужда́.

hardware n. скобяны́е изде́лия neut.pl.

hardy adj. (bold) сме́лый (смел, -á, -о); (robust) выно́сливый.

hare n. за́яц (за́йца). **h.-brained**, опроме́тчивый. **harelip** n. за́ячья губа́.

harem n. гаре́м.

haricot (bean) n. фасо́ль.

hark v.i.: h. at, слу́шать imp., по ~ perf. + acc.; h. back to, возвраща́ться imp., верну́ться perf. к + dat.; interj. чу!

harlot n. проститу́тка.

harm n. вред (-á), зло; v.t. вреди́ть imp., по ~ perf. + dat. **harmful** adj. вре́дный (-ден, -дна́, -дно). **harmless** adj. безвре́дный.

harmonic adj. гармони́ческий. **harmonica** n. губна́я гармо́ника. **harmonious** adj. гармони́чный; (amicable) дру́жный (-жен, -жна́, -жно). **harmonium** n. фисгармо́ния. **harmonize** v.t. гармонизи́ровать imp., perf.; v.i. гармони́ровать imp. (with, c + instr.).

harmony n. гармо́ния, созвучие, согла́сие.

harness n. у́пряжь, сбру́я; v.t. за-, в-, пряга́ть imp., за-, в-, пря́чь (-ягу́, -яжёшь; -яг, -ягла́) perf.; (fig.) испо́льзовать imp., perf. как исто́чник эне́ргии.

harp n. а́рфа; v.i. игра́ть imp. на а́рфе; harp on, распространя́ться imp., распространи́ться perf. o + prep. **harpist** n. арфи́ст, ~ ка.

harpoon n. гарпу́н (-á), острога́.

harpsichord n. клавеси́н.

harpy n. га́рпия; (fig.) хи́щник.

harridan n. ве́дьма, карга́.

harrier¹ n. (hound) го́нчая sb.

harrier² n. (falcon) лунь (-ня́) m.

harrow n. борона́ (acc. -ону -у; pl. -оны, -о́н, -она́м); v.t. борони́ть imp., вз ~ perf.; (torment) терза́ть imp.

harry v.t. (ravage) опустоша́ть imp., опустоши́ть perf.; (worry) трево́жить imp., вс ~ perf.

harsh adj. гру́бый (груб, -á, -о); (sound) ре́зкий (-зок, -зка́, -зко); (cruel) суро́вый.

hart n. оле́нь m.

harvest *n.* жа́тва, сбор (плодо́в); (*yield*) урожа́й; (*fig.*) плоды́ *m.pl.*; *v.t.* & *abs.* собира́ть *imp.*, собра́ть (соберу́, -рёшь; собра́л, -á, -о) *perf.* (урожа́й).

hash *n.* ру́бленое мя́со; (*medley*) меша́нина; *make a h. of*, напу́тать *perf.* + *acc.*, в + *prep.*; *v.t.* руби́ть (-блю́, -бишь) *imp.*

hasp *n.* застёжка.

hassock *n.* (*cushion*) поду́шечка; (*tuft of grass*) ко́чка.

haste *n.* поспе́шность, торопли́вость, спе́шка. **hasten** *v.i.* спеши́ть *imp.*, по ~ *perf.*; *v.t.* & *i.* торопи́ть(ся) (-плю́(сь), -пишь(ся)) *imp.*, по ~ *perf.*; *v.t.* ускоря́ть *imp.*, уско́рить *perf.* **hasty** *adj.* (*hurried*) поспе́шный; (*rash*) опроме́тчивый; (*quick-tempered*) вспы́льчивый.

hat *n.* шля́па; *top h.*, цили́ндр.

hatch[1], **-way** *n.* (*naut.*) люк.

hatch[2] *n.* (*brood*) вы́водок (-дка); *v.t.* выси́живать *imp.*, вы́сидеть (-ижу, -идишь) *perf.*; *v.i.* вылупля́ться, вы́лупиться *perf.*

hatch[3] *v.t.* (*line*) штрихова́ть *imp.*, за ~ *perf.*

hatchet *n.* топо́рик.

hate *n.* не́нависть; *v.t.* ненави́деть (-ижу, -идишь) *imp.* **hateful** *adj.* ненави́стный. **hatred** *n.* не́нависть.

haughty *adj.* надме́нный (-нен, -нна), высокоме́рный.

haul *n.* добы́ча; (*distance*) езда́; *v.t.* тяну́ть (-ну́, -нешь) *imp.*; таска́ть *indet.*, тащи́ть (-щу́, -щишь) *det.*; (*transport*) перевози́ть (-ожу́, -о́зишь) *imp.*, перевезти́ (-езу́, -езёшь; -ёз, -езла́) *perf.*

haunch *n.* бедро́ (*pl.* бёдра, -дер, -драм), ля́жка.

haunt *n.* ча́сто посеща́емое ме́сто; (*of criminals*) прито́н; *v.t.* (*frequent*) ча́сто посеща́ть *imp.*

have *v.t.* име́ть *imp.*; (*cheat*) надува́ть *imp.*, наду́ть (-у́ю, -у́ешь) *perf.*; *I have*, (*possess*) у меня́ (есть; был, -á, -о) + *nom.*; *I have not*, у меня́ нет (*past* не́ было) + *gen.*; *I have (got) to*, я до́лжен (-жна́) + *inf.*; *you had better*, вам лу́чше бы + *inf.*; *h. on* (*wear*) быть

оде́тым в + *prep.*; (*be engaged in*) быть за́нятым (-т, -та́, -то) + *instr.*

haven *n.* га́вань; (*refuge*) убе́жище.

haversack *n.* ра́нец (-нца).

havoc *n.* (*devastation*) опустоше́ние; (*disorder*) беспоря́док (-дка).

hawk[1] *n.* (*bird*) я́стреб (*pl.* -ы́ & -á).

hawk[2] *v.t.* (*trade*) торгова́ть вразно́с + *instr.* **hawker** *n.* разно́счик.

hawk[3] (*cough*) *v.t.* отка́шливать *imp.*, отка́шлянуть *perf.*; *v.i.* отка́шливаться *imp.*, отка́шляться *perf.*

hawse(-hole) *n.* (*naut.*) клюз.

hawser *n.* трос.

hawthorn *n.* боя́рышник.

hay *n.* се́но; *make h.*, коси́ть (кошу́, ко́сишь) се́но; *h ~ fever*, се́нная лихора́дка. **haycock** *n.* копна́ (*pl.* -пны, -пён, -пна́м). **hayloft** *n.* сенова́л. **haystack** *n.* стог (*loc.* -е & -ý; *pl.* -á).

hazard *n.* риск; *v.t.* рискова́ть *imp.* + *instr.* **hazardous** *adj.* риско́ванный (-ан, -анна).

haze *n.* тума́н, ды́мка.

hazel *n.* лещи́на. **hazelnut** *n.* лесно́й оре́х.

hazy *adj.* (*misty*) тума́нный (-нен, -нна); (*vague*) сму́тный (-тен, -тна́, -тно).

H-bomb *n.* водоро́дная бо́мба.

he *pron.* он (его́, ему́, им, о нём).

head *n.* голова́ (*acc.* -ову; *pl.* -овы, -о́в, -ова́м); (*mind*) ум (-á); (*h. of cattle*) голова́ скота́; (*h. of coin*) лицева́я сторона́ (*acc.* -ону) моне́ты; *heads or tails?* орёл и́ли ре́шка? (*chief*) глава́ (*pl.* -вы) *m.*, нача́льник; *attrib.* гла́вный; *v.t.* (*lead*) возглавля́ть *imp.*, возгла́вить *perf.*; (*h. chapter*) озагла́вливать *imp.*, озагла́вить *perf.*; *v.i.*: *h. for*, направля́ться *imp.*, напра́виться *perf.* в, на, к + *dat.* **headache** *n.* головна́я боль. **head-dress** *n.* головно́й убо́р. **heading** *n.* (*title*) заголо́вок (-вка). **headland** *n.* мыс (*loc.* -е & -ý; *pl.* мы́сы). **headlight** *n.* фа́ра. **headline** *n.* заголо́вок (-вка). **headlong** *adj.* (*precipitate*) опроме́тчивый; *adv.* стремгла́в. **headmaster**, **-mistress** *n.* дире́ктор (*pl.* -á) шко́лы. **headphone** *n.* нау́шник. **headquarters** *n.* штабкварти́ра. **headstone** *n.* надгро́бный

ка́мень (-мня; *pl.* -мни, -мне́й) *m.*
headstrong *adj.* своево́льный. **headway**
n. движе́ние вперёд. **heady** *adj.* стре-
ми́тельный; (*liquor*) хмельно́й (-лён,
-льна́).

heal *v.t.* изле́чивать *imp.*, излечи́ть
(-чу́, -чишь) *perf.*; исцеля́ть *imp.*,
исцели́ть *perf.*; *v.i.* зажива́ть *imp.*,
зажи́ть (-ивёт; за́жил, -а́, -о) *perf.*
healing *n.* целе́бный.

health *n.* здоро́вье. **healthy** *adj.* здоро́-
вый; (*beneficial*) поле́зный.

heap *n.* ку́ча, гру́да; *v.t.* нагроможда́ть
imp., нагромозди́ть *perf.*; (*load*) на-
гружа́ть *imp.*, нагрузи́ть (-ужу́,
-у́зишь) *perf.* (with, + *instr.*).

hear *v.t.* слы́шать (-шу, -шишь) *imp.*,
у~ *perf.*; (*listen to*) слу́шать *imp.*,
по~ *perf.*; (*learn*) узнава́ть (-наю́,
-наёшь) *imp.*, узна́ть *perf.*; h. out,
выслу́шивать *imp.*, вы́слушать *perf.*
hearing *n.* слух; (*limit*) преде́л слы́-
шимости; (*leg.*) слу́шание, разбо́р,
де́ла. **hearsay** *n.* слух.

hearken *v.i.* внима́ть *imp.*, внять (*past
only*: внял, -а́, -о) *perf.* (to, + *dat.*).

hearse *n.* катафа́лк.

heart *n.* (*organ*, *fig.*) се́рдце (*pl.* -дца́,
-де́ц, -дца́м) (*fig.*) душа́ (*acc.* -шу;
pl. -ши); (*courage*) му́жество; (*of tree
etc.*) сердцеви́на; (*essence*) суть; *pl.*
(*cards*) че́рви (-ве́й) *pl.*; at h., в глу-
бине́ души́; by h., наизу́сть; h. attack,
серде́чный при́ступ. **heartburn** *n.*
изжо́га. **hearten** *v.t.* ободря́ть *imp.*,
ободри́ть *perf.* **heartfelt** *adj.* и́скрен-
ний (-нен, -нна, -нно & -нне), серде́ч-
ный. **heartless** *adj.* бессерде́чный.
heart-rending *adj.* душераздира́ющий.
hearty *adj.* (*cordial*) серде́чный;
(*vigorous*) здоро́вый.

hearth *n.* оча́г (-а́).

heat *n.* жар (*loc.* -е & -у́), жа́ра; (*phys.*)
теплота́; (*of feeling*) пыл (*loc.* -у́);
(*sport*) забе́г, зае́зд; *v.t.* & *i.* нагре-
ва́ть(ся) *imp.*, нагре́ть(ся) *perf.*; *v.t.*
топи́ть (-плю́, -пишь) *imp.* **heater** *n.*
нагрева́тель *m.* **heating** *n.* отопле́ние.

heath *n.* пу́стошь; (*shrub*) вереск.

heathen *n.* язы́чник; *adj.* язы́ческий.

heather *n.* ве́реск.

heave *v.t.* (*lift*) поднима́ть *imp.*, под-
ня́ть (подниму́, -мешь; по́днял, -а́, -о)
perf.; (*pull*) тяну́ть (-ну́, -нешь)
imp., по~ *perf.*

heaven *n.* не́бо, рай (*loc.* раю́); *pl.*
небеса́ *neut.pl.* **heavenly** *adj.* небе́сный,
боже́ственный.

heaviness *n.* тя́жесть. **heavy** *adj.* тяжёлый (-л, -ла́); (*strong*) си́льный
(силён, -льна́, -льно, си́льны); (*abundant*) оби́льный; (*gloomy*) мра́чный
(-чен, -чна́, -чно); (*sea*) бу́рный (-рен,
бу́рна́, -рно). **heavyweight** *n.* тяжело-
ве́с.

Hebrew *n.* евре́й; *adj.* (дре́вне)евре́й-
ский.

heckle *v.t.* пререка́ться *imp.* с + *instr.*

hectare *n.* гекта́р.

hectic *adj.* лихора́дочный.

hedge *n.* (*fence*) жива́я и́згородь;
(*barrier*) прегра́да; *v.t.* огора́живать
imp., огороди́ть (-ожу́, -о́дишь) *perf.*;
v.i. верте́ться (-рчу́сь, -ртишься) *imp.*
hedgerow *n.* шпале́ра. **hedge-sparrow** *n.*
лесна́я завиру́шка.

hedgehog *n.* ёж (-а́).

heed *n.* внима́ние; *v.t.* обраща́ть *imp.*,
обрати́ть (-ащу́, -ати́шь) *perf.* внима́-
ние на + *acc.* **heedful** *adj.* внима́тель-
ный. **heedless** *adj.* небре́жный.

heel[1] *n.* (*of foot*) пята́ (*pl.* -ты, -т,
-та́м); (*of foot, sock*) пя́тка; (*of shoe*)
каблу́к (-а́).

heel[2] *n.* (*of ship*) крен; *v.t.* & *i.* крени́ть-
(ся) *imp.*, на~ *perf.*

hefty *adj.* дю́жий (дюж, -а́, -е).

hegemony *n.* гегемо́ния.

heifer *n.* тёлка.

height *n.* высота́ (*pl.* -ты), вышина́
(*no pl.*); (*elevation*) возвы́шенность.
heighten *v.t.* повыша́ть *imp.*, повы́сить
perf.; (*strengthen*) уси́ливать *imp.*,
уси́лить *perf.*

heinous *adj.* гну́сный (-сен, -сна́, -сно).

heir *n.* насле́дник. **heiress** *n.* насле́д-
ница. **heirloom** *n.* фами́льная вещь
(*pl.* -щи, -ще́й).

helicopter *n.* вертолёт.

heliograph *n.* гелио́граф. **heliotrope** *n.*
гелиотро́п.

helium *n.* ге́лий.

helix *n.* спира́ль.

hell n. ад (loc. -у́). **hellish** adj. а́дский.
Hellene n. э́ллин. **Hellenic** adj. э́ллинский. **Hellenistic** adj. эллинисти́ческий.
helm n. руль (-ля́) m., корми́ло (правле́ния). **helmsman** n. рулево́й sb.; (fig.) ко́рмчий sb.
helmet n. шлем.
help n. по́мощь; (person) помо́щник, -ица; v.t. помога́ть imp., помо́чь (-огу́, -о́жешь; -о́г, -огла́) perf. + dat.; (with negative) не мочь (могу́, мо́жешь; мог, -ла́) imp. не + inf.; h. oneself, брать (беру́, -рёшь; брал, -а́, -о) imp., взять (возьму́, -мёшь; взял, -а́, -о) perf. себе́. **helpful** adj. поле́зный. **helping** n. (of food) по́рция. **helpless** adj. беспо́мощный.
helter-skelter adv. как попа́ло.
helve n. рукоя́тка, черено́к (-нка́).
hem n. рубе́ц (-бца́), кайма́ (gen.pl. каём); v.t. подруба́ть imp., подруби́ть (-блю́, -бишь) perf.; h. about, in, окружа́ть imp., окружи́ть perf.
hemisphere n. полуша́рие.
hemlock n. болиголо́в.
hemp n. (plant) конопля́; (fibre) пенька́. **hempen** adj. конопля́ный, пенько́вый.
hen n. (female bird) са́мка; (domestic fowl) ку́рица (pl. ку́ры, кур). **henbane** n. белена́. **hen-coop** n. куря́тник. **henpecked** adj.: be h., быть у жены́ под башмако́м, под каблуко́м.
hence adv. (from here) отсю́да; (from this time) с э́тих пор; (as a result) сле́довательно. **henceforth, henceforward** adv. отны́не.
henchman n. приве́рженец (-нца).
henna n. хна.
hepatic adj. печёночный.
her poss.pron. её; свой (-оя́, -оё; -ои́).
herald n. геро́льд, предве́стник; v.t. возвеща́ть imp., возвести́ть perf.
herb n. трава́ (pl. -вы). **herbaceous** adj. травяни́стый. **herbal** adj. травяно́й. **herbivorous** adj. травоя́дный.
herd n. ста́до (pl. -да́); (of people) толпа́ (pl. -пы); v.i. ходи́ть (-ит) imp. ста́дом; (people) толпи́ться imp., с~ perf.; v.t. собира́ть imp., собра́ть (собе́ру, -рёшь; собра́л, -а́, -о) perf. в ста́до. **herdsman** n. пасту́х (-а́).

here adv. (position) здесь, тут; (direction) сюда́; h. is..., вот (+nom.); h. and there, там и сям. **hereabout(s)** adv. побли́зости. **hereafter** adv. в бу́дущем. **hereby** adv. э́тим; таки́м о́бразом. **hereupon** adv. (in consequence) всле́дствие э́того; (after) по́сле э́того. **herewith** adv. при сём, при э́том, че́рез э́то.
hereditary adj. насле́дственный. **heredity** n. насле́дственность.
heresy n. е́ресь. **heretic** n. ерети́к (-а́). **heretical** adj. ерети́ческий.
heritable adj. насле́дуемый.
heritage n. насле́дство, насле́дие.
hermaphrodite n. гермафроди́т.
hermetic adj. гермети́ческий.
hermit n. отше́льник, пусты́нник. **hermitage** n. пу́стынь; хили́ще (отше́льника, пусты́нника).
hernia n. гры́жа.
hero n. геро́й. **heroic** adj. герои́ческий. **heroine** n. герои́ня. **heroism** n. геро́изм.
heron n. ца́пля (gen.pl. -пель).
herpes n. лиша́й (-ая́).
herring n. сельдь (pl. -ди, -де́й), селёдка; h.-bone, ёлочка; (attrib.) ёлочкой, в ёлочку.
hers poss.pron. её; свой (-оя́, -оё; -ои́).
herself pron. (emph.) (она́) сама́ (-мо́й, acc. -му́); (refl.) себя́ (себе́, собо́й); -ся (suffixed to v.t.).
hertz n. герц (gen.pl. -ц).
hesitant adj. нереши́тельный. **hesitate** v.i. колеба́ться (-блюсь, -блешься) imp., по~ perf.; (in speech) запина́ться imp., запну́ться perf. колеба́ние, нереши́тельность.
hessian n. мешкови́на.
heterogeneous adj. разноро́дный.
hew v.t. руби́ть (-блю́, -бишь) imp.
hexa- in comb. шести-, гекса-. **hexagon** n. шестиуго́льник. **hexameter** n. гекза́метр.
hey interj. эй!
heyday n. расцве́т.
hi interj. эй! приве́т!
hiatus n. пробе́л; (ling.) зия́ние.
hibernate v.i. находи́ться (-ожу́сь, -о́дишься) imp. в зи́мней спя́чке; зимова́ть imp., пере~, про~ perf.

hibernation n. зи́мняя спя́чка, зимо́вка.

hiccough, hiccup v.i. ика́ть imp., икну́ть perf.; n.: pl. ико́та.

hide¹ n. (animal's skin) шку́ра, ко́жа.

hide² v.t. & i. (conceal) пря́тать(ся) (-я́чу(сь), -я́чешь(ся)) imp., с~ perf.; скрыва́ть(ся) imp., скры́ть(ся) (скро́ю(сь), -о́ешь(ся)) perf.

hideous adj. отврати́тельный, безобра́зный.

hiding n. (flogging) по́рка.

hierarchy n. иера́рхия.

hieroglyph n. иеро́глиф. hieroglyphic adj. иероглифи́ческий.

higgledy-piggledy adv. как придётся.

high n. высо́кий (-о́к, -ока́, -о́ко); (elevated) возвы́шенный; (higher) вы́сший; (intense) си́льный (силён, -льна́, -льно, си́льны); h.-class, высокока́чественный; higher education, вы́сшее образова́ние; h. fidelity, высо́кая то́чность воспроизведе́ния; h.-handed, повели́тельный; h. jump, прыжо́к (-жка́) в высоту́; h.-minded, благоро́дный; h.-pitched, высо́кий (-о́к, -ока́, -о́ко); h.-strung, чувстви́тельный, не́рвный (-вен, -вна́, -вно). highland(s) n. го́рная страна́. highly adv. в вы́сшей сте́пени. highness n. возвы́шенность; (title) высо́чество. highway n. больша́я доро́га, шоссе́ neut.indecl. highwayman n. разбо́йник (с большо́й доро́ги).

hijack v.t. похища́ть imp., похи́тить (-и́щу, -и́тишь) perf. hijacker n. похити́тель m.

hike n. похо́д.

hilarious adj. весёлый (ве́сел, -а́, -о, ве́селы). hilarity n. весе́лье.

hill n. холм (-а́). hillock n. хо́лмик. hilly adj. холми́стый.

hilt n. рукоя́тка.

himself pron. (emph.) (он) сам (-ого́, -ому́, -и́м, -ом); (refl.) себя́ (себе́, собо́й); ся (suffixed to v.t.).

hind¹ n. (deer) са́мка (благоро́дного) оле́ня.

hind² adj. (rear) за́дний. hindmost adj. са́мый за́дний.

hinder v.t. меша́ть imp., по~ perf. + dat. hindrance n. поме́ха, препя́тствие.

Hindu n. инду́с; adj. инду́сский.

hinge n. шарни́р, пе́тля (gen.pl.-тель); v.t. прикрепля́ть imp., прикрепи́ть perf. на пе́тлях; v.i. враща́ться imp. на пе́тлях; h. on, (fig.) зави́сеть (-сит) imp. от + gen.

hint n. намёк; v.i. намека́ть imp., намекну́ть perf. (at, на + acc.).

hinterland n. глубина́ страны́.

hip¹ n. (anat.) бедро́ (pl. бёдра, -дер, -драм).

hip² n. (fruit) я́года шипо́вника.

hippopotamus n. гиппопота́м.

hire n. наём (на́йма), прока́т; h.-purchase, поку́пка в рассро́чку; v.t. нанима́ть imp., наня́ть (найму́, -мёшь; на́нял, -а́, -о) perf.; брать (беру́, -рёшь; брал, -а́, -о) imp., взять, (возьму́, -мёшь; взял, -а́, -о) perf. напрока́т; h. out, отдава́ть (-даю́, -даёшь) imp., отда́ть (-а́м, -а́шь, -а́ст, -ади́м; о́тдал, -а́, -о) perf. внаймы́, напрока́т.

hireling n. наёмник.

hirsute adj. волоса́тый.

his poss.pron. его́; свой (-оя́, -оё; -ои́).

hiss n. шипе́ние, свист; v.i. шипе́ть (-плю́, -пи́шь) imp.; свисте́ть (-ищу́, -исти́шь) imp.; v.t. освисты́вать imp., освиста́ть (-ищу́, -и́щешь) perf.

historian n. исто́рик. historic(al) adj. истори́ческий. history n. исто́рия.

histrionic adj. театра́льный.

hit n. (blow) уда́р; (on target) попада́ние (в цель); (success) успе́х; v.t. (strike) ударя́ть imp., уда́рить perf.; (target) попада́ть imp., попа́сть (-аду́, -адёшь; -а́л) perf. (в цель); h. (up)on, находи́ть (-ожу́, -о́дишь) imp., найти́ (найду́, -дёшь; нашёл, -шла́) perf.

hitch n. (jerk) толчо́к (-чка́); (knot) у́зел (узла́); (stoppage) заде́ржка; v.t. (move) подта́лкивать imp., подтолкну́ть perf.; (fasten) зацепля́ть imp., зацепи́ть (-плю́, -пишь) perf.; привя́зывать imp., привяза́ть (-яжу́, -я́жешь) perf.; h. up, подтя́гивать imp., подтяну́ть (-ну́, -нешь) perf.; h.-hike, голосова́ть imp.

hither adv. сюда́. hitherto adv. до сих пор.

hive n. у́лей (у́лья).

hoard *n.* запа́с; *v.t.* накопля́ть *imp.*, накопи́ть (-плю́, -пишь) *perf.*

hoarding *n.* рекла́мный щит (-а́).

hoar-frost *n.* и́ней.

hoarse *adj.* хри́плый (-л, -ла́, -ло).

hoary *adj.* седо́й (сед, -а́, -о).

hoax *n.* мистифика́ция; *v.t.* мистифици́ровать *imp.*, *perf.*

hobble *n.* (*for horse*) (ко́нские) пу́ты (-т) *pl.*; *v.i.* прихра́мывать *imp.*; *v.t.* (*horse*) тренóжить *imp.*, с~ *perf.*

hobby *n.* конёк (-нька́), хо́бби *neut. indecl.*

hobnail *n.* сапо́жный гвоздь (-дя́; *pl.* -ди, -дéй) *m.*

hob-nob *v.i.* пить (пью, пьёшь) *imp.* вме́сте; *h. with*, якша́ться *imp.* с + *instr.*

hock *n.* (*wine*) рейнвéйн (-а(у)).

hockey *n.* хоккéй; *ice h.*, хоккéй с ша́йбой; *h. stick*, клю́шка.

hod *n.* (*for bricks*) лото́к (-ткá); (*for coal*) ведёрко (*pl.* -рки, -рок, -ркам).

hoe *n.* моты́га; *v.t.* мотыжить *imp.*

hog *n.* бо́ров (*pl.* -ы, -óв), свинья́ (*pl.* -ньи, -нéй, -ньям).

hoist *n.* подъёмник; *v.t.* поднима́ть *imp.*, подня́ть (-ниму́, -ни́мешь; по́днял, -а, -о) *perf.*

hold[1] (*naut.*) трюм.

hold[2] *n.* (*grasp*) хва́тка; (*influence*) влия́ние (on, на + *acc.*); *v.t.* (*grasp*) держа́ть (-жу́, -жишь) *imp.*; (*contain*) вмеща́ть *imp.*, вмести́ть *perf.*; (*possess*) владе́ть *imp.* + *instr.*; (*conduct*) проводи́ть (-ожу́, -о́дишь) *imp.*, провести́ (-еду́, -едёшь; -ёл, -ела́) *perf.*; (*consider*) счита́ть *imp.*, счесть (сочту́, -тёшь; счёл, сочла́) *perf.* (+ *acc.* & *instr.*, за + *acc.*); *v.i.* держа́ться (-жу́сь, -жишься) *imp.*; (*continue*) продолжа́ться *imp.*, продолжи́ться *perf.*; *h. back*, сдéрживать(ся) *imp.*, сдержа́ть(ся) (-жу́(сь), -жишь(ся)) *perf.*; *h. forth*, разглаго́льствовать *imp.*; *h. out*, (*stretch out*) протя́гивать *imp.*, протяну́ть (-ну́, -нешь) *perf.*; (*resist*) не сдава́ться (сдаю́сь, сдаёшься) *imp.*; *h. over*, (*postpone*) откла́дывать *imp.*, отложи́ть (-жу́, -жишь) *perf.*; *h. up*, (*support*) подде́рживать *imp.*, поддержа́ть (-жу́, -жишь) *perf.*;

(*display*) выставля́ть *imp.*, вы́ставить *perf.*; (*impede*) заде́рживать *imp.*, задержа́ть (-жу́, -жишь) *perf.* **holdall** *n.* портплéд. **hold-up** *n.* (*robbery*) налёт; (*delay*) заде́ржка.

hole *n.* дыра́ (*pl.* -ры), я́ма, отвéрстие; (*animal's*) нора́ (*pl.* -ры); *full of holes*, дыря́вый; *pick holes in*, придира́ться *imp.*, придра́ться (придеру́сь, -рёшься; придра́лся, -ала́сь, -ало́сь) *perf.* к + *dat.*; *v.t.* (*make h. in*) продыря́вливать *imp.*, продыря́вить *perf.*

holiday *n.* (*festival*) пра́здник; (*from work*) о́тпуск, *pl.* кани́кулы (-л) *pl.*; *on h.*, в о́тпуске, *adj.*

holiness *n.* свя́тость; (*H.*, *title*) святéйшество.

hollow *n.* впа́дина; (*valley*) лощи́на; (*in tree*) дуплó (*pl.* -пла, -пел, -плам) *adj.* пустóй (пуст, -а́, -о, пу́сты), пóлый; (*sunken*) впа́лый; (*sound*) глухóй (глух, -а́, -о); *v.t.* (*h. out*) выда́лбливать *imp.*, вы́долбить *perf.*

holly *n.* остроли́ст.

hollyhock *n.* штокро́за.

holm[1] *n.* (*islet*) острово́к (-вка́).

holm[2], **-oak** *n.* ка́менный дуб (*loc.* -е & -у́; *pl.* -ы́).

holocaust *n.* (*sacrifice*) всесожжéние; (*destruction*) уничтожéние (в огнé).

holograph *adj.* собственнору́чный.

holster *n.* кобура́.

holy *adj.* свято́й (свят, -а́, -о), свящéнный (-éн, -éнна); *H. Week*, страстна́я недéля.

homage *n.* почтéние, уважéние; *do, pay, h. to*, отдава́ть (-даю́, -даёшь) *imp.*, отда́ть (-а́м, -а́шь, -а́ст, -ади́м; о́тдал, -а́, -о) *perf.* + *dat.* до́лжное + *dat.*

home *n.* дом (-а(у); *pl.* -а́); (*native land*) ро́дина; *at h.*, до́ма; *feel at h.*, чу́вствовать *imp.* себя́ как дóма; *adj.* дома́шний, роднóй; *H. Affairs*, вну́тренние дела́ *neut. pl.*; *adv.* (*direction*) домо́й; (*position*) до́ма; (*as aimed*) в цель. **homeland** *n.* ро́дина. **homeless** *adj.* бездо́мный **home-made** *adj.* дома́шний, самоде́льный. **homesick** *adj.*: *to be h.*, тоскова́ть *imp.* по ро́дине. **homewards** *adv.* домо́й, восвоя́си.

homely *adj.* простóй (прост, -а́, -о, про́сты).

homicide n. (*person*) уби́йца m. & f.; (*action*) уби́йство.

homily n. про́поведь, поуче́ние.

homogeneous adj. одноро́дный.

homonym n. омо́ним.

hone n. точи́льный ка́мень (-мня; pl. -мни, -мне́й) m.; v.t. точи́ть (-чу́, -чишь) imp., на~ perf.

honest n. (*fair*) че́стный (-тен, -тна́, -тно); (*righteous*) пра́ведный; (*sincere*) и́скренний (-нен, -нна, -нне & -нно). **honesty** n. че́стность; пра́ведность; и́скренность.

honey n. мёд (-a(y), loc. -ý & -е; pl. -ы́).

honeycomb n. медо́вые со́ты (-тов) pl.; attrib. со́товый, сото́вый. **honeymoon** n. медо́вый ме́сяц; v.i. проводи́ть (-ожу́, -о́дишь) imp., провести́ (-еду́, -едёшь; -ёл, -ела́) perf. медо́вый ме́сяц. **honeysuckle** n. жи́молость.

honk v.i. гогота́ть (-очу́, -о́чешь) imp.; (*siren etc.*) гуде́ть (-дит) imp.

honorarium n. гонора́р.

honorary adj. почётный.

honour n. честь, почёт; pl. по́чести f.pl.; (*up*)on my h., че́стное сло́во; v.t. (*respect*) почита́ть imp.; (*confer*) удоста́ивать imp., удосто́ить perf. (with, + gen.). **honourable** adj. че́стный (-тен, -тна́, -тно); (*respected*) почте́нный (-нен, -нна).

hood[1] n. капюшо́н; (*tech.*) капо́т.

hood[2], **hoodlum** n. громи́ла m.

hoodwink v.t. втира́ть imp., втере́ть (вотру́, -рёшь; втёр) perf. очки́+dat.

hoof n. копы́то.

hook n. крюк (-á, loc. -é & -ý), крючо́к (-чка́); (*trap*) лову́шка; (*cutting instrument*) серп (-á); v.t. зацепля́ть imp., зацепи́ть (-плю́, -пишь) perf.; (*catch*) лови́ть (-влю́, -вишь) imp., пойма́ть perf.

hookah n. кальян.

hooligan n. хулига́н.

hoop n. о́бруч (pl. -и, -е́й).

hoot v.i. крича́ть (-чу́, -чишь) imp., кри́кнуть perf.; (*owl*) у́хать imp., у́хнуть perf.; (*horn*) гуде́ть (-ди́т) imp.

hop[1] n. (*plant*; *collect.* hops) хмель (-ля́ (-лю)) m.

hop[2] n. (*jump*) прыжо́к (-жка́); v.i. пры́гать imp., пры́гнуть perf. (на одно́й ноге́).

hope n. наде́жда; v.i. наде́яться (-е́юсь, -е́ешься) imp., по~ perf. (for, на + acc.). **hopeful** adj. (*hoping*) наде́ющийся; (*promising*) многообеща́ющий. **hopeless** adj. безнадёжный.

hopper n. бу́нкер (pl. -á & -ы); (*rly.*) хо́ппер.

horde n. (*hist.*, *fig.*) орда́ (pl. -ды).

horizon n. горизо́нт; (*fig.*) кругозо́р. **horizontal** n. горизонта́ль; adj. горизонта́льный.

hormone n. гормо́н.

horn n. рог (pl. -á); (*mus.*) рожо́к (-жка́); (*motor h.*) гудо́к (-дка́); attrib. рогово́й. **hornbeam** n. граб. **horned** adj. рога́тый.

hornet n. ше́ршень (-шня) m.

horny adj. рогово́й; (*calloused*) мозо́листый.

horoscope n. гороско́п; cast a h., составля́ть imp., соста́вить perf. гороско́п.

horrible adj. ужа́сный, стра́шный (-шен, -шна́, -шно, стра́шны). **horrid** adj. ужа́сный, проти́вный. **horrify** v.t. ужаса́ть imp., ужасну́ть perf. **horror** n. у́жас, отвраще́ние.

hors-d'oeuvre n. заку́ска (*usu. in pl.*).

horse n. ло́шадь (pl. -ди, -де́й, instr. -дьми́), конь (-ня́; pl. -ни, -не́й) m.; (*collect.*; *cavalry*) ко́нница; attrib. лошади́ный, ко́нский. **horse-chestnut** n. ко́нский кашта́н. **horseflesh** n. кони́на. **horse-fly** n. слепе́нь (-пня́) m. **horsehair** n. ко́нский во́лос. **horseman**, **-woman** n. вса́дник, -ица. **horseplay** n. возня́. **horsepower** n. лошади́ная си́ла. **horse-radish** n. хрен (-a(y)). **horseshoe** n. подко́ва. **horsewhip** n. хлыст (-á); v.t. хлеста́ть (-ещу́, -е́щешь) imp., хлестну́ть perf.

horticulture n. садово́дство.

hose n. (*stockings*) чулки́ (*gen.* -ло́к) pl.; (*h.-pipe*) шланг, рука́в (-á; pl. -á).

hosier n. торго́вец (-вца) трикота́жными изде́лиями. **hosiery** n. чуло́чные изде́лия neut.pl., трикота́ж.

hospitable adj. гостеприи́мный.

hospital n. больни́ца; (*military h.*) го́спиталь (pl. -ли, -ле́й) m.

hospitality n. гостеприи́мство.

host¹ n. (multitude) мно́жество; (army) во́йско (pl. -ка́).

host² n. (landlord etc.) хозя́ин (pl. -я́ева, -я́ев).

host³ n. (eccl.) обла́тка.

hostage n. зало́жник, -ица.

hostel n. (students') общежи́тие; (tourists') турба́за.

hostelry n. посто́ялый двор (-á).

hostess n. хозя́йка; (air h.) бортпрово́дница.

hostile adj. вражде́бный. **hostility** n. вражде́бность; pl. вое́нные де́йствия neut.pl.

hot adj. горя́чий (-ч, -чá), жа́ркий (-рок, -ркá, -рко); (pungent) о́стрый (остр & о́стёр, остра́, о́стро); (fresh) све́жий (свеж, -á, -ó, све́жи), h. air, бахва́льство; h.-blooded, пы́лкий (-лок, -лкá, -лко); h.-headed, вспы́льчивый; h.-water bottle, гре́лка. **hotbed** n. парни́к (-á); (fig.) расса́дник. **hotfoot** adv. поспе́шно. **hothouse** n. тепли́ца. **hotplate** n. пли́тка.

hotel n. гости́ница, оте́ль m.

hound n. (dog) го́нчая sb.; (person) подле́ц (-á); v.t. трави́ть (-влю́, -вишь) imp., за~ perf.; h. on, подстрека́ть imp., подстрекну́ть perf.

hour n. (period, specific time) час (-á with 2, 3, 4, loc. -ý; pl. -ы́); (time in general) вре́мя neut. **hourly** adj. ежеча́сный.

house n. дом (-a(y); pl. -á); (parl.) пала́та; (theatre) теа́тр; (audience) пу́блика; (performance) сеа́нс; (dynasty) дом (pl. -á), дина́стия; attrib. дома́шний; v.t. помеща́ть imp., помести́ть perf.; (provide houses for) обеспе́чивать imp., обеспе́чить perf. жильём. **housebreaker** n. взло́мщик. **household** n. (people) дома́шние sb.; (establishment) дома́шнее хозя́йство. **house-keeper** n. эконо́мка. **housemaid** n. го́рничная sb. **house-warming** n. новосе́лье. **housewife** n. хозя́йка. **housework** n. дома́шняя рабо́та. **housing** n. (accommodation) жильё; (provision of h.) жили́щное строи́тельство; (casing) кожу́х (-á); h. estate, жило́й масси́в.

hovel n. лачу́га.

hover v.i. (bird) пари́ть imp.; (helicopter) висе́ть (-си́т) imp.; (hesitate) колеба́ться (-блюсь, -блешься) imp. **hovercraft** n. су́дно (pl. -дá, -до́в) на возду́шной поду́шке, СВП.

how adv. как, каки́м о́бразом; h. do you do? здра́вствуйте! h. many, h. much, ско́лько (+ gen.). **however** adv. как бы ни (+ past); conj. одна́ко, тем не ме́нее; however much, ско́лько бы ни (+ gen. & past).

howitzer n. га́убица.

howl n. вой, рёв; v.i. выть (во́ю, во́ешь) imp.; реве́ть (-ву́, -вёшь) imp. **howler** n. (mistake) грубе́йшая оши́бка.

hub n. (of wheel) ступи́ца; (fig.) центр (внима́ния); h. of the universe, пуп (-á) земли́.

hubbub n. шум (-a(y)), гам (-a(y)).

huddle n. (heap) ку́ча; (confusion) сумато́ха; v.t. (heap together) сва́ливать imp., свали́ть (-лю́, -лишь) perf. в ку́чу; v.i.: h. together, съёживаться imp., съёжиться perf.

hue n. (tint) отте́нок (-нка).

huff n. припа́док (-дка) раздраже́ния; v.t. & i. обижа́ть(ся) imp., оби́деть(ся) (-и́жу(сь), -и́дишь(ся)) perf.

hug n. объя́тие; (wrestling) хва́тка; v.t. (embrace) обнима́ть imp., обня́ть (обниму́, -мешь; о́бнял, -á, -о) perf.; (keep close to) держа́ться (-жу́сь, -жишься) imp. + gen.

huge adj. огро́мный.

hulk n. ко́рпус (pl. -á) (корабля́). **hulking** adj. (bulky) грома́дный; (clumsy) неуклю́жий.

hull¹ n. (of pea etc.) стручо́к (-чка́); (of grain) шелуха́; v.t. лущи́ть imp., об~ perf.

hull² n. (of ship) ко́рпус (pl. -á); (of aeroplane) фюзеля́ж.

hum n. жужжа́ние, гуде́ние; v.i. жужжа́ть (-жу́, -жи́шь) imp.; гуде́ть (гужу́, гуди́шь) imp.; v.t. напева́ть imp.; interj. гм!

human adj. челове́ческий, людско́й; n. челове́к. **humane** adj. челове́чный, гума́нный (-нен, -нна). **humanism** n. гумани́зм. **humanist** n. гумани́ст. **humanity** n. (human race) челове́-

чество; (*humaneness*) гума́нность; *the Humanities*, гуманита́рные нау́ки *f.pl.*

humble *adj.* смире́нный (-ён, -е́нна), скро́мный (-мен, -мна́, -мно); *v.t.* унижа́ть *imp.*, уни́зить *perf.*

humdrum *adj.* (*banal*) бана́льный; (*dull*) скучный (-чен, -чна́, -чно).

humid *adj.* вла́жный (-жен, -жна́, -жно).

humidity *n.* вла́жность.

humiliate *v.t.* унижа́ть *imp.*, уни́зить *perf.* **humiliation** *n.* униже́ние.

humility *n.* смире́ние.

humming-bird *n.* коли́бри *m. & f. indecl.*

hummock *n.* (*hillock*) буго́р (-гра́); (*in ice*) (ледяно́й) то́рос.

humorist *n.* юмори́ст. **humorous** *adj.* юмористи́ческий. **humour** *n.* ю́мор; (*mood*) настрое́ние; *out of h.*, не в ду́хе; *v.t.* потака́ть *imp.* + *dat.*

hump *n.* горб (-á, *loc.* -ý); (*of earth*) буго́р (-гра́); *v.t.* го́рбить *imp.*, с ~ *perf.* **humpback** *n.* горб (-á, *loc.* -ý); (*person*) горбу́н (-á), ~ья. **humpbacked** *adj.* горба́тый.

humus *n.* перегно́й.

hunch *n.* (*hump*) горб (-á, *loc.* -ý); (*thick piece*) ломо́ть (-мтя́) *m.*; (*suspicion*) подозре́ние; *v.t.* го́рбить *imp.*, с ~ *perf.* **hunchback** *n.* горб (-á, *loc.* -ý); (*person*) горбу́н (-á), ~ья. **hunchbacked** *adj.* горба́тый.

hundred *n.* сто (*in oblique cases* ста); (*collect.*) со́тня (*gen.pl.* -тен); (*age*) сто лет; *two h.*, две́сти (двухсо́т, двумста́м, двумяста́ми, двухста́х); *three h.*, три́ста (трёхсо́т трёмста́м, тремяста́ми, трёхста́х); *four h.*, четы́реста (-рёхсо́т, -рёмста́м, -рьмяста́ми, -рёхста́х); *five h.*, пятьсо́т (пятисо́т, пятиста́м, пятьюста́ми, пятиста́х). **hundredfold** *adj.* стокра́тный; *adv.* в сто раз. **hundredth** *adj., n.* со́тый.

Hungarian *n.* венгр, венге́рка; *adj.* венге́рский.

hunger *n.* го́лод; (*fig.*) жа́жда (for, + *gen.*); *h.-strike*, голодо́вка; *v.i.* голода́ть *imp.*; *h. for*, жа́ждать (-ду, -дешь) *imp.* + *gen.* **hungry** *adj.* голо́дный (го́лоден, -дна́, -дно, го́лодны).

hunk *n.* ломо́ть (-мтя́) *m.*

hunt *n.* охо́та; (*fig.*) по́иски *m.pl.* (for, + *gen.*); *v.t.* охо́титься *imp.* на + *acc.*, за + *instr.*; трави́ть (-влю́ -вишь) *imp.*, за ~ *perf.*; *h. down*, вы́следить *perf.*; *h. out*, оты́скивать (-щу, -щешь) *perf.* **hunter** *n.* охо́тник.

hunting *n.* охо́та; *attrib.* охо́тничий (-чья, -чье). **huntsman** *n.* охо́тник, е́герь (*pl.* -ря́) *m.*

hurdle *n.* (*fence*) плете́нь (-тня́) *m.*; (*sport*) барье́р; (*fig.*) препя́тствие; **hurdler** *n.* барьери́ст. **hurdles, hurdling** *n.* (*sport*) барье́рный бег.

hurl *v.t.* швыря́ть *imp.*, швырну́ть *perf.*

hurly-burly *n.* сумато́ха.

hurrah, hurray *interj.* ура́!

hurricane *n.* урага́н.

hurried *adj.* торопли́вый. **hurry** *n.* спе́шка, торопли́вость; *in a h.*, второпя́х; *v.t. & i.* торопи́ть(ся) (-плю́(сь), -пишь(ся)) *imp.*, по ~ *perf.*; *v.i.* спеши́ть *imp.*, по ~ *perf.*

hurt *n.* вред (-á), уще́рб, поврежде́ние; *v.i.* боле́ть (-ли́т) *imp.*; *v.t.* повреж-да́ть *imp.*, повреди́ть *perf.*; *h. the feelings of*, задева́ть *imp.*, заде́ть (-е́ну, -е́нешь) *perf.* + *acc.*

hurtle *v.i.* (*move swiftly*) нести́сь (несу́сь, -сёшься) *imp.*, нёсся, -слась) *imp.*, по ~ *perf.*

husband *n.* муж (*pl.* -ья́, -е́й, -ья́м); *v.t.* эконо́мить *imp.*, с ~ *perf.*

hush *n.* тишина́, молча́ние; *v.t.* успо-ка́ивать *imp.*, успоко́ить *perf.*; *interj.* ти́ше! тсс!

husk *n.* шелуха́; *v.t.* шелуши́ть *imp.*

husky[1] *adj.* (*voice*) хри́плый (хрипл, -á, -о).

husky[2] *n.* (*dog*) эскимо́сская ла́йка.

hussar *n.* гуса́р (*gen.pl.* -р (*as collect.*) & -ров).

hustle *n.* толкотня́; *v.t. & i.* (*push*) толка́ть(ся) *imp.*, толкну́ть(ся) *perf.*; (*hurry*) торопи́ть(ся) (-плю́(сь), -пишь(ся)) *imp.*, по ~ *perf.*

hut *n.* хи́жина, бара́к.

hutch *n.* кле́тка.

hyacinth *n.* гиаци́нт.

hybrid *n.* гибри́д; *adj.* гибри́дный.

hydra *n.* ги́дра.

hydrangea *n.* горте́нзия.

hydrant n. гидра́нт.

hydrate n. гидра́т.

hydraulic adj. гидравли́ческий; h. engineering, гидротехника. **hydraulics** n. гидра́влика.

hydro- in comb. гидро-. **hydrocarbon** n. углеводоро́д. **hydrochloric acid** n. соляна́я кислота́. **hydrodynamics** n. гидродина́мика. **hydroelectric** adj. гидроэлектри́ческий; h. plant, гидроэлектроста́нция, ГЭС f.indecl. **hydrofoil** n. подво́дное крыло́ (pl. -лья, -льев); (vessel) су́дно (pl. -да́, -до́в), кора́бль (-ля́) m., на подво́дных кры́льях, СПК, КПК. **hydrogen** n. водоро́д; h. bomb, водоро́дная бо́мба. **hydrolysis** n. гидро́лиз. **hydrophobia** n. водобоя́знь. **hydroplane** n. (fin) горизонта́льный руль (-ля́) m.; (motor boat) гли́ссер; (seaplane) гидросамолёт. **hydroxide** n. гидроо́кись.

hyena n. гие́на.

hygiene n. гигие́на. **hygienic** adj. гигиени́ческий.

hymn n. гимн; v.t. славосло́вить imp.

hyperbola n. гипербо́ла. **hyperbolic** adj. гиперболи́ческий.

hyperbole n. гипербо́ла. **hyperbolical** adj. гиперболи́ческий.

hypercritical adj. приди́рчивый.

hypersensitive adj. сверхчувстви́тельный.

hyphen n. дефи́с. **hyphen(ate)** v.t. писа́ть (пишу́, -шешь) imp., на~ perf. че́рез дефи́с.

hypnosis n. гипно́з. **hypnotic** adj. гипноти́ческий; (soporific) снотво́рный. **hypnotism** n. гипноти́зм. **hypnotist** n. гипнотизёр. **hypnotize** v.t. гипнотизи́ровать imp., за~ perf.

hypocrisy n. лицеме́рие. **hypocrite** n. лицеме́р. **hypocritical** adj. лицеме́рный.

hypodermic adj. подко́жный.

hypotenuse n. гипотену́за.

hypothesis n. гипоте́за, предположе́ние. **hypothesize** v.i. стро́ить imp., по~ perf. гипоте́зу; де́лать imp., с~ perf. предположе́ние. **hypothetical** adj. гипоте́тический, предположи́тельный.

hysteria n. истери́я. **hysterical** adj. истери́чный, истери́ческий. **hysterics** n. исте́рика, истери́ческий припа́док (-дка).

I

I pron. я (меня́, мне, мной & мно́ю, обо мне).

iambic adj. ямби́ческий. **iambus** n. ямб.

ib. abbr., **ibidem** adv. там же.

ice n. лёд (льда(у), loc. льду); (i. cream) моро́женое sb.; i.-age, леднико́вый пери́од; i.-axe, ледору́б; i.-boat, буер (pl. -á); i.-breaker, ледоко́л, i. cream, моро́женое sb.; i.-floe, плаву́чая льди́на; i. hockey, хокке́й с ша́йбой; v.t. замора́живать imp., заморо́зить perf.; (cul.) глазирова́ть imp., perf.; v.i.: i. over, up, обледенева́ть imp., обледене́ть perf. **iceberg** n. а́йсберг. **icicle** n. сосу́лька. **icing** n. (cul.) глазу́рь. **icy** adj. ледяно́й; (also fig.)

холо́дный (хо́лоден, -дна́, -дно, хо́лодны) (как лёд).

icon n. ико́на.

idea n. иде́я, мысль; (conception) поня́тие; (intention) наме́рение.

ideal n. идеа́л; adj. идеа́льный. **idealism** n. идеали́зм. **idealist** n. идеали́ст. **idealize** v.t. идеализи́ровать imp., perf.

identical adj. (one thing) тот же са́мый; (of different things) тожде́ственный (-ен, -енна), одина́ковый. **identification** n. отождествле́ние; (recognition) опозна́ние; (of person) установле́ние ли́чности. **identify** v.t. отождествля́ть imp., отождестви́ть perf.; (recognize) опознава́ть (-наю́,

-наёшь) *imp.*, опознать *perf.* identity *n.* (*sameness*) тождественность; (*of person*) личность; (*math.*) тождество; *i.* card, удостоверение личности.

ideogram, ideograph *n.* идеограмма.

ideological *adj.* идеологический. **ideologist, ideologue** *n.* идеолог. **ideology** *n.* идеология.

idiocy *n.* идиотизм.

idiom *n.* (*expression*) идиома; (*language*) язык (-á), говор. **idiomatic** *adj.* идиоматический.

idiosyncrasy *n.* склад умá, идиосинкразия.

idiot *n.* идиот. **idiotic** *adj.* идиотский.

idle *adj.* (*vain*) тщетный; (*useless*) бесполезный; (*unoccupied*) незанятый; (*lazy*) ленивый; (*machine*) холостой (холост, -á, -о); *v.i.* бездельничать *imp.*; (*engine*) работать *imp.* вхолостую; *v.t.: i. away*, праздно проводить (-ожу, -одишь) *imp.*, провести (-еду, -едёшь; -ёл, -елá) *perf.* **idleness** *n.* тщетность; бесполезность; праздность, безделье. **idler** *n.* бездельник, -ица.

idol *n.* идол, кумир. **idolater, -tress** *n.* идолопоклонник, -ица. **idolatrous** *adj.* идолопоклоннический. **idolatry** *n.* идолопоклонство; (*fig.*) обожание. **idolize** *v.t.* боготворить *imp.*

idyll *n.* идиллия. **idyllic** *adj.* идиллический.

i.e. *abbr.* т.е., то есть.

if *conj.* (*conditions*) если, если бы; (*whether*) ли; *as if*, как будто; *even if*, даже если; *if only*, если бы только.

igloo *n.* иглу *neut.indecl.*

igneous *adj.* огненный, огневой; (*rock*) вулканический. **ignite** *v.t.* зажигать *imp.*, зажечь (-жгу, жжёшь; -жёг, -жглá) *perf.*; *v.i.* загораться *imp.*, загореться (-рюсь, -ришься) *perf.* **ignition** *n.* зажигание.

ignoble *adj.* низкий (-зок, -зкá, -зко) позор.

ignominious *adj.* позорный. **ignominy** *n.* позор.

ignoramus *n.* невежда *m.* **ignorance** *n.* невежество, неведение. **ignorant** *adj.* невежественный (-ен, -енна); (*uninformed*) несведущий (of, в + *prep.*).

ignore *v.t.* не обращать *imp.* внимания на + *acc.*; игнорировать *imp.*, *perf.*

ilex *n.* падуб.

ill *n.* (*evil*) зло; (*harm*) вред (-á); *pl.* (*misfortunes*) несчастья (-тий) *pl.*; *adj.* (*sick*) больной (-лен, -льнá); (*evil*) дурной (дурён, -рнá, -рно, дурны), злой (зол, зла); *adv.* плохо, дурно; (*scarcely*) едва ли; *fall i.*, заболевать *imp.*, заболеть (-éю) *perf.* **i.-advised** *adj.* неблагоразумный; **i.-bred**, невоспитанный (-ан, -анна); *i.-disposed*, недоброжелательный (towards, к + *dat.*); *i.-mannered*, невежливый; **i.-natured**, злобный; *i.-tempered*, раздражительный; *i.-treat*, плохо обращаться *imp.* с + *instr.*

illegal *adj.* незаконный (-нен, -нна), нелегальный. **illegality** *n.* незаконность, нелегальность.

illegible *adj.* неразборчивый.

illegitimacy *n.* незаконность; (*of child*) незаконнорождённость. **illegitimate** *adj.* незаконный (-нен, -нна), незаконнорождённый (-ён, -ённа).

illiberal *adj.* непросвещённый (*bigoted*) нетерпимый; (*stingy*) скупой (скуп, -á, -о).

illicit *adj.* незаконный (-нен, -нна), недозволенный (-ен, -енна).

illimitable *adj.* безграничный.

illiteracy *n.* неграмотность. **illiterate** *adj.* неграмотный.

illness *n.* болезнь.

illogical *adj.* нелогичный.

illuminate *v.t.* освещать *imp.*, осветить (-ещу, -етишь) *perf.*; (*building*) иллюминировать *imp.*, *perf.*; (*manuscript*) украшать *imp.*, украсить *perf.* **illumination** *n.* освещение; (*also pl.*) иллюминация; украшение (рукописи).

illusion *n.* иллюзия. **illusory** *adj.* обманчивый, иллюзорный.

illustrate *v.t.* иллюстрировать *imp.*, *perf.*, про~ *perf.* **illustration** *n.* иллюстрация. **illustrative** *adj.* иллюстративный.

illustrious *adj.* знаменитый.

image *n.* (*statue etc.*) изображение; (*optical i.*) отражение; (*semblance*) подобие; (*literary i. etc.*) образ. **imagery** *n.* образность.

imaginable *adj.* вообрази́мый. **imaginary** *adj.* вообража́емый, мни́мый. **imagination** *n.* воображе́ние, фанта́зия. **imagine** *v.t.* вообража́ть *imp.*, вообрази́ть *perf.*; (*conceive*) представля́ть *imp.*, предста́вить *perf.* себе́.

imbecile *n.* слабоу́мный *sb.*; (*fool*) глупе́ц (-пца́); *adj.* слабоу́мный.

imbed *see* embed.

imbibe *v.t.* (*absorb*) впи́тывать *imp.*, впита́ть *perf.*

imbroglio *n.* пу́таница.

imbue *v.t.* пропи́тывать *imp.*, пропита́ть *perf.* (with, + *instr.*); внуша́ть *imp.*, внуши́ть *perf.* + *dat.* (with, + *acc.*).

imitate *v.t.* подража́ть *imp.* + *dat.* **imitation** *n.* подража́ние (of, + *dat.*), имита́ция; *attrib.* (*counterfeit*) подде́льный; (*artificial*) иску́сственный (-ен(ен), -енна). **imitative** *adj.* подража́тельный.

immaculate *adj.* незапя́тнанный (-ан, -анна); (*irreproachable*) безупре́чный.

immanent *adj.* прису́щий (in, + *dat.*), имма́нентный.

immaterial *adj.* невеще́ственный (-ен(ен), -енна); (*unimportant*) несуще́ственный (-ен(ен), -енна.

immature *adj.* незре́лый.

immeasurable *adj.* неизмери́мый.

immediate *adj.* (*direct*) непосре́дственный (-ен, -енна); (*swift*) неме́дленный (-ен, -енна). **immediately** *adv.* то́тчас, неме́дленно; непосре́дственно.

immemorial *adj.* незапа́мятный.

immense *adj.* необъя́тный, огро́мный.

immerse *v.t.* погружа́ть *imp.*, погрузи́ть *perf.* **immersion** *n.* погруже́ние.

immigrant *n.* иммигра́нт, ~ ка. **immigrate** *v.i.* иммигри́ровать *imp.*, *perf.* **immigration** *n.* иммигра́ция.

imminent *adj.* бли́зкий (-зок, -зка́, -зко, бли́зки); (*danger*) грозя́щий.

immobile *adj.* неподви́жный. **immobility** *n.* неподви́жность.

immoderate *adj.* неуме́ренный (-ен, -енна).

immodest *adj.* нескро́мный (-мен, -мна́, -мно).

immolate *v.t.* приноси́ть (-ошу́, -о́сишь) *imp.*, принести́ (-есу́, -есёшь; -ёс, -есла́) *perf.* в же́ртву; же́ртвовать *imp.*, по ~ *perf.* + *instr.*

immoral *adj.* безнра́вственный (-ен(ен), -енна). **immorality** *n.* безнра́вственность.

immortal *adj.* бессме́ртный. **immortality** *n.* бессме́ртие. **immortalize** *v.t.* обессме́ртить *perf.*

immovable *adj.* неподви́жный, недви́жимый; (*steadfast*) непоколеби́мый.

immune *adj.* (*to illness*) невоспри́мчивый (to, к + *dat.*); (*free from*) свобо́дный (from, от + *gen.*). **immunity** *n.* невоспри́мчивость (to, к + *dat.*), иммуните́т; освобожде́ние (from, от + *gen.*); (*diplomatic etc.*) неприкоснове́нность.

immure *v.t.* заточа́ть *imp.*, заточи́ть *perf.*

immutable *adj.* неизме́нный (-нен, -нна).

imp *n.* бесёнок (-нка; *pl.* -ня́та, -ня́т).

impact *n.* (*striking*) уда́р; (*collision*) столкнове́ние; (*influence*) влия́ние.

impair *v.t.* (*damage*) поврежда́ть *imp.*, повреди́ть *perf.*; (*weaken*) ослабля́ть *imp.*, осла́бить *perf.*

impale *v.t.* прока́лывать *imp.*, проколо́ть (-лю́, -лешь) *perf.*; (*as torture etc.*) сажа́ть *imp.*, посади́ть (-ажу́, -а́дишь) *perf.* на кол.

impalpable *adj.* неосяза́емый.

impart *v.t.* дели́ться (-лю́сь, -лишься) *imp.*, по ~ *perf.* + *instr.* (to, c + *instr.*).

impartial *adj.* беспристра́стный.

impassable *adj.* непроходи́мый, непрое́зжий.

impasse *n.* тупи́к (-а́).

impassioned *adj.* стра́стный (-тен, -тна́, -тно).

impassive *adj.* бесстра́стный.

impatience *n.* нетерпе́ние. **impatient** *adj.* нетерпели́вый.

impeach *v.t.* обвиня́ть *imp.*, обвини́ть *perf.* (of, with, в + *prep.*).

impeccable *adj.* безупре́чный.

impecunious *adj.* безде́нежный.

impedance *n.* по́лное сопротивле́ние.

impede *v.t.* препя́тствовать *imp.*, вос ~ *perf.* + *dat.*; заде́рживать *imp.*, задержа́ть (-жу́, -жишь) *perf.* **impediment** *n.* препя́тствие, заде́ржка; (*in speech*) заика́ние.

impel *v.t.* побужда́ть *imp.*, побуди́ть *perf.* (to + *inf.*, к + *dat.*).

impend *v.i.* нависа́ть *imp.*, нави́снуть (-с) *perf.*

impenetrable *adj.* непроница́емый.

imperative *adj.* (*imperious*) повели́тельный; (*obligatory*) необходи́мый; *n.* (*gram.*) повели́тельное наклоне́ние.

imperceptible *adj.* незаме́тный.

imperfect *n.* имперфе́кт; *adj.* (*incomplete*) несоверше́нный (-нен, -нна), непо́лный (-лон, -лна́, -лно); (*faulty*) дефе́ктный. **imperfection** *n.* несоверше́нство; (*fault*) недоста́ток (-тка). **imperfective** *adj.* (*n.*) несоверше́нный (вид).

imperial *adj.* (*of empire*) импе́рский; (*of emperor*) импера́торский. **imperialism** *n.* империали́зм. **imperialist** *n.* империали́ст; *attrib.* империалисти́ческий.

imperil *v.t.* подверга́ть *imp.*, подве́ргнуть (-г) *perf.* опа́сности.

imperious *adj.* вла́стный; (*urgent*) настоя́тельный.

imperishable *adj.* ве́чный; (*food*) непо́ртящийся.

impersonal *adj.* безли́чный.

impersonate *v.t.* (*personify*) олицетворя́ть *imp.*, олицетвори́ть *perf.*; (*play part*) исполня́ть *imp.*, испо́лнить *perf.* роль + *gen.*; (*pretend to be*) выдава́ть (-даю́, -даёшь) *imp.*, вы́дать (-ам, -ашь, -аст, -адим) *perf.* себя́ за + *acc.*

impertinence *n.* де́рзость. **impertinent** *adj.* (*insolent*) де́рзкий (-зок, -зка́, -зко); (*out of place*) неуме́стный.

imperturbable *adj.* невозмути́мый.

impervious *adj.* непроница́емый (to, для + *gen.*); (*not responsive*) глухо́й (глух, -а́, -о) (to, к + *dat.*).

impetuous *adj.* стреми́тельный.

impetus *n.* дви́жущая си́ла; (*fig.*) и́мпульс.

impiety *n.* нечести́вость.

impinge *v.i.*: i. (*up*)*on*, (*strike*) ударя́ться *imp.*, уда́риться *perf.* o + *acc.*; (*encroach*) покуша́ться *imp.*, покуси́ться *perf.* на + *acc.*

impious *adj.* нечести́вый.

impish *adj.* прока́зливый.

implacable *adj.* неумоли́мый.

implant *v.t.* насажда́ть *imp.*, насади́ть *perf.*

implement[1] *n.* (*tool*) ору́дие, инструме́нт; *pl.* принадле́жности *f.pl.*

implement[2] *v.t.* (*fulfil*) выполня́ть *imp.*, вы́полнить *perf.*

implicate *v.t.* впу́тывать *imp.*, впу́тать *perf.* **implication** *n.* вовлече́ние; (*meaning*) смысл.

implicit *adj.* подразумева́емый; (*absolute*) безогово́рочный.

implore *v.t.* умоля́ть *imp.*

imply *v.t.* подразумева́ть *imp.*

impolite *adj.* неве́жливый.

imponderable *adj.* невесо́мый.

import *n.* (*meaning*) значе́ние; (*of goods*) и́мпорт, ввоз; *v.t.* импорти́ровать *imp.*, *perf.*; ввози́ть (-ожу́, -о́зишь) *imp.*, ввезти́ (ввезу́, -зёшь; ввёз, -ла́) *perf.*

importance *n.* ва́жность. **important** *adj.* ва́жный (-жен, -жна́, -жно, -жны), значи́тельный.

importunate *adj.* назо́йливый.

impose *v.t.* (*tax*) облага́ть *imp.*, обложи́ть (-жу́, -жишь) *perf.* + *instr.* (on, + *acc.*); (*obligation*) налага́ть *imp.*, наложи́ть (-жу́, -жишь) *perf.* (on, на + *acc.*); (*force* (*oneself*) *on*) навя́зывать(ся) *imp.*, навяза́ть(ся) (-яжу́(сь), -я́жешь(ся)) *perf.* (on, + *dat.*). **imposing** *adj.* внуши́тельный. **imposition** *n.* обложе́ние, наложе́ние.

impossibility *n.* невозмо́жность. **impossible** *adj.* невозмо́жный.

imposter *n.* самозва́нец (-нца). **imposture** *n.* самозва́нство, обма́н.

impotence *n.* бесси́лие; (*med.*) импоте́нция. **impotent** *adj.* бесси́льный; (*med.*) импоте́нтный.

impound *v.t.* (*cattle*) загоня́ть *imp.*, загна́ть (загоню́, -нишь; загна́л, -а́ -о) *perf.*; (*confiscate*) конфискова́ть *imp.*, *perf.*

impoverish *v.t.* обедня́ть *imp.*, обедни́ть *perf.*

impracticable *adj.* невыполни́мый; (*impassable*) непроходи́мый.

imprecation *n.* прокля́тие.

impregnable *adj.* непристу́пный.

impregnate *v.t.* (*fertilize*) оплодотворя́ть *imp.*, оплодотвори́ть *perf.*;

(*saturate*) пропи́тывать *imp.*, пропита́ть *perf.*

impresario *n.* импреса́рио *m.indecl.*, антрепренёр.

impress[1] *n.* отпеча́ток (-тка), печа́ть; *v.t.* (*imprint*) отпеча́тывать *imp.*, отпеча́тать *perf.*; (*affect person*) производи́ть (-ожу́, -о́дишь) *imp.*, произвести́ (-еду́, -едёшь; -ёл, -ела́) *perf.* (како́е-либо) впечатле́ние на+*acc.*

impression *n.* (*notion etc.*) впечатле́ние; (*printing*) о́ттиск; (*reprint*) (стереоти́пное) изда́ние, перепеча́тка.

impressionism *n.* импрессиони́зм.

impressive *adj.* вырази́тельный; (*producing great effect*) порази́тельный.

imprint *n.* отпеча́ток (-тка); *v.t.* отпеча́тывать *imp.*, отпеча́тать *perf.*; (*on memory etc.*) запечатлева́ть *imp.*, запечатле́ть *perf.*

imprison *v.t.* заключа́ть *imp.*, заключи́ть *perf.* (в тюрьму́). **imprisonment** *n.* тюре́мное заключе́ние.

improbable *adj.* невероя́тный, неправдоподо́бный.

impromptu *n.* экспро́мт; *adj.* импровизи́рованный (-ан, -ан(н)а); *adv.* без подгото́вки, экспро́мтом.

improper *adj.* (*inaccurate*) непра́вильный; (*indecent*) неприли́чный.

improve *v.t. & i.* улучша́ть(ся) *imp.*, улу́чшить(ся) *perf.* **improvement** *n.* улучше́ние, усоверше́нствование.

improvidence *n.* непредусмотри́тельность. **improvident** *adj.* непредусмотри́тельный.

improvisation *n.* импровиза́ция. **improvise** *v.t.* импровизи́ровать *imp.*, сымпровизи́ровать *perf.*

imprudence *n.* неосторо́жность. **imprudent** *adj.* неосторо́жный.

impudence *n.* на́глость. **impudent** *adj.* на́глый (нагл, -а́, -о).

impugn *v.t.* оспа́ривать *imp.*, оспо́рить *perf.*

impulse *n.* (*push*) толчо́к (-чка́); (*impetus*) и́мпульс; (*sudden tendency*) поры́в. **impulsive** *adj.* импульси́вный.

impunity *n.* безнака́занность; with i., безнака́занно.

impure *adj.* нечи́стый (-т, -та́, -то).

impute *v.t.* припи́сывать *imp.*, приписа́ть (-ишу́, -и́шешь) *perf.* (to, +*dat.*); (*fault*) вменя́ть *imp.*, вмени́ть *perf.* в+*acc.* (to, +*dat.*).

in *prep.* (*place*) в+*prep.*, на+*prep.*; (*into*) в+*acc.*, на+*acc.*; (*point in time*) в+*prep.*, на+*prep.*; *in the morning* (*etc.*) у́тром (*instr.*); *in spring* (*etc.*), весно́й (*instr.*); (*at some stage etc.*; *throughout*) во вре́мя+*gen.*; (*duration*) за+*acc.*; (*after interval of*) че́рез+*acc.*; (*during course of*) в тече́ние+*gen.*; (*circumstance*) в+*prep.*, при+*prep.*; *adv.* (*place*) внутри́; (*motion*) внутрь; (*at home*) у себя́, до́ма; (*in fashion*) в мо́де; *in here, there*, (*place*) здесь, там; (*motion*) сюда́, туда́; *adj.* вну́тренний; (*fashionable*) мо́дный (-ден, -дна́, -дно); *in(-)patient*, стациона́рный больно́й *sb.*; *n.*: *the ins and outs*, все заку́лки *m.pl.*; дета́ли *f.pl.*

inability *n.* неспосо́бность, невозмо́жность.

inaccessible *adj.* недосту́пный.

inaccurate *adj.* нето́чный (-чен, -чна́, -чно).

inaction *n.* безде́йствие. **inactive** *adj.* безде́ятельный. **inactivity** *n.* безде́ятельность.

inadequate *adj.* недоста́точный, неадеква́тный.

inadmissible *adj.* недопусти́мый.

inadvertent *adj.* (*inattentive*) невнима́тельный; (*unintentional*) ненаме́ренный (-ен, -енна).

inalienable *adj.* неотъе́млемый, неотчужда́емый.

inane *adj.* (*empty*) пусто́й (пуст, -а́, -о, пу́сты); (*silly*) глу́пый (глуп, -а́, -о).

inanimate *adj.* (*lifeless*) неодушевлённый (-ён, -ённа); (*dull*) безжи́зненный (-ен, -енна).

inapplicable *adj.* неприми́мый.

inapposite *adj.* неуме́стный.

inappreciable *adj.* незаме́тный.

inappropriate *adj.* неуме́стный.

inapt *adj.* (*unsuitable*) неподходя́щий; (*unskilful*) неиску́сный. **inaptitude** *n.* неуме́стность; неспосо́бность.

inarticulate *adj.* (*not jointed*) нечленоразде́льный; (*indistinct*) невня́тный.

inasmuch adv.: i. as, так как; ввиду того, что.

inattention n. невнима́ние. **inattentive** adj. невнима́тельный.

inaudible adj. неслы́шный.

inaugural adj. (lecture etc.) вступи́тельный. **inaugurate** v.t. (admit to office) торже́ственно вводи́ть (-ожу́, -о́дишь) imp., ввести́ (введу́, -дёшь; ввёл, -á) perf. в до́лжность; (open) открыва́ть imp., откры́ть (-ро́ю, -ро́ешь) perf.; (begin) начина́ть imp., нача́ть (начну́, -нёшь; на́чал, -á, -о) perf. **inauguration** n. торже́ственное введе́ние, вступле́ние, в до́лжность; открытие.

inauspicious adj. неблагоприя́тный.

inborn, inbred adj. врождённый (-ён, -ена́), приро́дный.

incalculable adj. неисчисли́мый.

incandesce v.t. & i. накаля́ть(ся) imp., накали́ть(ся) perf. добела́. **incandescence** n. бе́лое кале́ние. **incandescent** adj. накалённый (-ён, -ена́) добела́.

incantation n. заклина́ние.

incapability n. неспосо́бность. **incapable** adj. неспосо́бный (of, к + dat., на + acc.).

incapacitate v.t. де́лать imp., с ~ perf. неспосо́бным.

incapacity n. неспосо́бность.

incarcerate v.t. заключа́ть imp., заключи́ть perf. (в тюрьму́). **incarceration** n. заключе́ние (в тюрьму́).

incarnate adj. воплощённый (-ён, -ена́); v.t. воплоща́ть imp., воплоти́ть (-ощу́, -оти́шь) perf. **incarnation** n. воплоще́ние.

incautious adj. неосторо́жный.

incendiary adj. зажига́тельный; n. поджига́тель m.; (fig.) подстрека́тель m.; (bomb) зажига́тельная бо́мба.

incense[1] n. фимиа́м, ла́дан.

incense[2] v.t. (enrage) разъяря́ть imp., разъяри́ть perf.

incentive n. побужде́ние.

inception n. нача́ло.

incessant adj. непреста́нный (-нен, -нна).

incest n. кровосмеше́ние.

inch n. дюйм; i. by i., ма́ло-пома́лу.

incidence n. (falling) паде́ние; (range of action) сфе́ра де́йствия. **incident** n. слу́чай, инциде́нт. **incidental** adj. (casual) случа́йный; i. to, прису́щий + dat. **incidentally** adv. случа́йно; (by the way) ме́жду про́чим.

incinerate v.t. испепеля́ть imp., испепели́ть perf. **incineration** n. испепеле́ние. **incinerator** n. мусоросжига́тельная печь (pl. -чи, -че́й).

incipient adj. начина́ющийся.

incise v.t. надре́зывать, надреза́ть imp., надре́зать (-е́жу, -е́жешь) perf. **incision** n. надре́з (in, на + acc.). **incisive** adj. ре́жущий; (fig.) о́стрый (остр & остёр, остра́, о́стро). **incisor** n. резе́ц (-зца́).

incite v.t. побужда́ть imp., побуди́ть perf. (to, к + dat., + inf.); подстрека́ть imp., подстрекну́ть perf. (to, к + dat.). **incitement** n. подстрека́тельство.

incivility n. неве́жливость.

inclement adj. суро́вый.

inclination n. (slope) накло́н; (propensity) скло́нность (for, to, к + dat.). **incline** n. накло́н; v.t. & i. склоня́ть(ся) imp., склони́ть(ся) (-ню́(сь), -ни́шь(ся)) perf. **inclined** adj. (disposed) скло́нный (-о́нен, -о́нна́, -о́нно) (to, к + dat.).

include v.t. включа́ть imp., включи́ть perf. (in, в + acc.); заключа́ть imp., заключи́ть perf. в себе́. **including** prep. включа́я + acc. **inclusion** n. включе́ние. **inclusive** adj. включа́ющий (в себе́); adv. включи́тельно.

incognito adv., n. инко́гнито adv., m. & neut.indecl.

incoherence n. бессвя́зность. **incoherent** adj. бессвя́зный.

incombustible adj. несгора́емый.

income n. дохо́д; i. tax, подохо́дный нало́г.

incommensurable adj. несоизмери́мый. **incommensurate** adj. несоразме́рный.

incommode v.t. беспоко́ить imp., о ~ perf.

incommodious adj. неудо́бный.

incomparable adj. несравни́мый (to, with, с + instr.); (matchless) несравне́нный (-нен, -нна).

incompatible adj. несовмести́мый.

incompetence n. неспосо́бность; (leg.)

неправомо́чность. **incompetent** *adj.* неспосо́бный; (*leg.*) непра́вомо́чный.
incomplete *adj.* непо́лный (-лон, -лна́, -лно), незако́нченный (-ен, -енна).
incomprehensible *adj.* непоня́тный.
inconceivable *adj.* невообрази́мый.
inconclusive *adj.* неубеди́тельный.
incongruity *n.* несоотве́тствие. **incongruous** *adj.* несоотве́тственный (-ен, -енна) (with, + *dat.*); (*out of place*) неуме́стный.
inconsequent *adj.* непосле́довательный. **inconsequential** *adj.* незначи́тельный.
inconsiderable *adj.* незначи́тельный.
inconsiderate *adj.*(*person*) невнима́тельный; (*action*) необду́манный (-ан, -анна).
inconsistency *n.* непосле́довательность; (*incompatibility*) несовмести́мость. **inconsistent** *adj.* непосле́довательный; (*incompatible*) несовмести́мый.
inconsolable *adj.* безуте́шный.
inconsonant *adj.* несозву́чный (with, + *dat.*).
inconspicuous *adj.* незаме́тный.
inconstant *adj.* непостоя́нный (-нен, -нна).
incontestable *adj.* неоспори́мый.
incontinence *n.* невозде́ржанность; (*med.*) недержа́ние. **incontinent** *adj.* невозде́ржанный (-ан, -анна).
incontrovertible *adj.* неопровержи́мый.
inconvenience *n.* неудо́бство; *v.t.* причиня́ть *imp.*, причини́ть *perf.* неудо́бство + *dat.* **inconvenient** *adj.* неудо́бный.
incorporate *v.t.* (*include*) включа́ть *imp.*, включи́ть *perf.*; *v.t. & i.* (*unite*) объединя́ть(ся) *imp.*, объедини́ть(ся) *perf.*; соединя́ть(ся) *imp.*, соедини́ть(ся) *perf.*
incorporeal *adj.* бестеле́сный.
incorrect *adj.* непра́вильный.
incorrigible *adj.* неисправи́мый.
incorruptible *adj.* неподку́пный; (*not decaying*) непортя́щийся.
increase *n.* рост, увеличе́ние; (*in pay etc.*) приба́вка; *v.t. & i.* увели́чивать(ся) *imp.*, увели́чить(ся) *perf.*; (*intensify*) уси́ливать(ся) *imp.*, уси́лить(ся) *perf.*
incredible *adj.* невероя́тный.

incredulous *adj.* недове́рчивый.
increment *n.* приба́вка; (*profit*) при́быль.
incriminate *v.t.* обвиня́ть *imp.*, обвини́ть *perf.* (в преступле́нии).
incubate *v.t.* (*eggs*) выводи́ть (-ожу́, -о́дишь) *imp.*, вы́вести (-еду, -едешь; -ел) *perf.* (в инкуба́торе); (*bacteria*) выра́щивать *imp.*, вы́растить *perf.* **incubator** *n.* инкуба́тор.
inculcate *v.t.* внедря́ть *imp.*, внедри́ть *perf.*
incumbent *adj.*: it is i. (*up*)on you, на вас лежи́т обя́занность.
incur *v.t.* навлека́ть *imp.*, навле́чь (-еку́, -ечёшь; -ёк, -екла́) *perf.* на себя́.
incurable *adj.* неизлечи́мый.
incurious *adj.* нелюбопы́тный.
incursion *n.* (*invasion*) вторже́ние; (*attack, raid*) набе́г.
indebted *predic.* (*owing money*) в долгу́ (to, у + *gen.*); (*owing gratitude*) обя́зан (-а, -о) (to, + *dat.*).
indecency *n.* неприли́чие, непристо́йность. **indecent** *adj.* неприли́чный, непристо́йный.
indecision *n.* нереши́тельность. **indecisive** *adj.* нереши́тельный.
indeclinable *adj.* несклоня́емый.
indecorous *adj.* неприли́чный.
indecorum *n.* неприли́чие.
indeed *adv.* в са́мом де́ле, действи́тельно; (*interrog.*) неуже́ли?
indefatigable *adj.* неутоми́мый.
indefeasible *adj.* неотъе́млемый.
indefensible *adj.* (*by arms*) непригодный для оборо́ны; (*by argument*) не могу́щий быть опра́вданным.
indefinable *adj.* неопредели́мый. **indefinite** *adj.* неопределённый (-нен, -нна).
indelible *adj.* неизглади́мый, несмыва́емый; i. pencil, хими́ческий каранда́ш (-а́).
indelicacy *n.* недели́ка́тность, беста́ктность. **indelicate** *adj.* недели́ка́тный, беста́ктный.
indemnify *v.t.*: i. against, страхова́ть *imp.*, за~ *perf.* от + *gen.*; обезопа́сить *perf.* от + *gen.*; i. for, (*compensate*) компенси́ровать *imp.*, *perf.* **indemnity**

n. (*against loss*) гара́нтия от убы́тков; (*compensation*) компенса́ция; (*war i.*) контрибу́ция.

indent *v.t.* (*notch*) зазу́бривать *imp.*, зазубри́ть *perf.*; (*print.*) де́лать о́тступ, с ~ *perf.* о́тступ; (*order goods*) зака́зывать *imp.*, заказа́ть (-ажу́, -а́жешь) *perf.* (for, + *acc.*). **indentation** *n.* (*notch*) зубе́ц (-бца́); (*print.*) о́тступ. **indenture** *n.* контра́кт.

independence *n.* незави́симость, самостоя́тельность. **independent** *adj.* незави́симый, самостоя́тельный.

indescribable *adj.* неопису́емый.

indestructible *adj.* неразруши́мый.

indeterminate *adj.* неопределённый (-нен, -нна).

index *n.* и́ндекс, указа́тель *m.*, показа́тель *m.*; (*pointer*) стре́лка; (*finger*) указа́тельный па́лец (-льца); *v.t.* (*provide i.*) снабжа́ть *imp.*, снабди́ть *perf.* указа́телем; (*enter in i.*) заноси́ть (-ошу́, -о́сишь) *imp.*, занести́ (-есу́, -есёшь; -ёс, -есла́) *perf.* в указа́тель.

Indian *n.* (*from India*) инди́ец (-и́йца), индиа́нка; (*from America*) индее́ц (-е́йца), индиа́нка; *adj.* инди́йский; инде́йский; I. club, була́ва; I. corn, кукуру́за; I. ink, тушь; I. summer, ба́бье ле́то.

indiarubber *n.* каучу́к; (*eraser*) рези́нка.

indicate *v.t.* ука́зывать *imp.*, указа́ть (-ажу́, -а́жешь) *perf.*; пока́зывать *imp.*, показа́ть (-ажу́, -а́жешь) *perf.* **indication** *n.* указа́ние; (*sign*) при́знак. **indicative** *adj.* ука́зывающий; (*gram.*) изъяви́тельный; *n.* изъяви́тельное наклоне́ние. **indicator** *n.* указа́тель *m.*

indict *v.t.* обвиня́ть *imp.*, обвини́ть *perf.* (for, в + *prep.*).

indifference *n.* равноду́шие, безразли́чие; (*unimportance*) незначи́тельность. **indifferent** *adj.* равноду́шный, безразли́чный; (*mediocre*) посре́дственный (-ен, -енна).

indigenous *adj.* тузе́мный, ме́стный.

indigent *adj.* нужда́ющийся, бе́дный (-ден, -дна́, -дно, бе́дны).

indigestible *adj.* неудобовари́мый. **indigestion** *n.* несваре́ние желу́дка.

indignant *adj.* негоду́ющий; be i., негодова́ть *imp.* (with, на + *acc.*,

про́тив + *gen.*). **indignation** *n.* негодова́ние.

indignity *n.* оскорбле́ние.

indirect *adj.* непрямо́й (-м, -ма́, -мо); (*lighting*) отражённый; (*econ.*; *gram.*) ко́свенный.

indiscernible *adj.* неразличи́мый.

indiscreet *adj.* нескро́мный (-мен, -мна́, -мно), неосторо́жный. **indiscretion** *n.* нескро́мность, неосторо́жность, неосмотри́тельность.

indiscriminate *adj.* неразбо́рчивый, огу́льный; (*confused*) беспоря́дочный. **indiscriminately** *adv.* беспоря́дочно; без разбо́ру.

indispensible *adj.* необходи́мый, незамени́мый.

indisposed *predic.* (*unwell*) нездоро́в (-а, -о); (*averse*) не скло́нен (скло́нна, -но). **indisposition** *n.* (*ill health*) нездоро́вье; (*ailment*) неду́г; (*disinclination*) нерасположе́ние.

indisputable *adj.* бесспо́рный.

indissoluble *adj.* неразры́вный; (*in liquid*) нераствори́мый.

indistinct *adj.* нея́сный (-сен, -сна́, -сно); (*sound only*) невня́тный.

indistinguishable *adj.* неразличи́мый.

indite *v.t.* сочиня́ть *imp.*, сочини́ть *perf.*

individual *n.* индиви́дуум, ли́чность; *adj.* индивидуа́льный, ли́чный. **individualism** *n.* индивидуали́зм. **individualist** *n.* индивидуали́ст. **individualistic** *adj.* индивидуалисти́ческий. **individuality** *n.* индивидуа́льность.

indivisible *adj.* недели́мый.

indoctrinate *v.t.* внуша́ть *imp.*, внуши́ть *perf.* + *dat.* (with, + *acc.*).

indolence *n.* ле́ность. **indolent** *adj.* лени́вый.

indomitable *adj.* неукроти́мый.

indoor *adj.* ко́мнатный, (находя́щийся) внутри́ до́ма. **indoors** *adv.* внутри́ до́ма.

indubitable *adj.* несомне́нный (-е́нен, -е́нна).

induce *v.t.* (*prevail on*) заставля́ть *imp.*, заста́вить *perf.*; (*bring about*) вызыва́ть *imp.*, вы́звать (вы́зову, -вешь) *perf.* **inducement** *n.* побужде́ние.

induct *v.t.* вводи́ть (-ожу́, -о́дишь) *imp.*, ввести́ (введу́, -дёшь; ввёл, -а́) *perf.* (в до́лжность). **induction** *n.* инду́кция; (*inducting*) введе́ние в до́лжность.

indulge *v.t.* потво́рствовать *imp.* + *dat.*; *v.i.* предава́ться (-даю́сь, -даёшься) *imp.*, преда́ться (-а́мся, -а́шься, -а́стся, -ади́мся; -а́лся, -ала́сь) *perf.* (in, + *dat.*). **indulgence** *n.* снисхожде́ние, потво́рство. **indulgent** *adj.* снисходи́тельный.

industrial *adj.* промы́шленный. **industrialist** *n.* промы́шленник. **industrious** *adj.* трудолюби́вый, приле́жный. **industry** *n.* промы́шленность, инду́стрия; (*diligence*) прилежа́ние.

inebriate *n.* пья́ница *m.* & *f.*; *adj.* пья́ный (пьян, -á, -о); *v.t.* опьяня́ть *imp.*, опьяни́ть *perf.*

inedible *adj.* несъедо́бный.

ineffable *adj.* несказа́нный.

ineffective *adj.* безрезульта́тный; (*person*) неспосо́бный.

ineffectual *adj.* безрезульта́тный.

inefficiency *n.* неэффекти́вность; (*of person*) неспосо́бность. **inefficient** *adj.* неэффекти́вный; неспосо́бный.

inelegant *adj.* неэлега́нтный.

ineligible *adj.* не могу́щий быть и́збранным.

inept *adj.* (*out of place*) неуме́стный; (*silly*) глу́пый (глуп, -á, -о); (*unskilful*) неуме́лый.

inequality *n.* нера́венство, неро́вность.

inequitable *adj.* несправедли́вый.

ineradicable *adj.* неискорени́мый.

inert *adj.* ине́ртный; (*sluggish*) ко́сный. **inertia** *n.* (*phys.*) ине́рция; (*sluggishness*) ине́ртность.

inescapable *adj.* неизбе́жный.

inessential *adj.* несуще́ственный (-ен(ен), -енна).

inestimable *adj.* неоцени́мый.

inevitable *adj.* неизбе́жный.

inexact *adj.* нето́чный (-чен, -чна́, -чно).

inexcusable *adj.* непрости́тельный.

inexhaustible *adj.* неистощи́мый.

inexorable *adj.* неумоли́мый.

inexpedient *adj.* нецелесообра́зный.

inexpensive *adj.* недорого́й (недо́рог, -á, -о).

inexperience *n.* нео́пытность. **inexperienced** *adj.* нео́пытный.

inexpert *adj.* неиску́сный.

inexplicable *adj.* необъясни́мый.

inexpressible *adj.* невырази́мый. **inexpressive** *adj.* невырази́тельный.

inextinguishable *adj.* неугаси́мый.

inextricable *adj.* (*of state*) безвы́ходный; (*of problem*) запу́танный (-ан, -анна).

infallible *adj.* непогреши́мый.

infamous *adj.* (*person*) бессла́вный, гну́сный (-сен, -сна́, -сно); (*action*) позо́рный. **infamy** *n.* позо́р, дурна́я сла́ва.

infancy *n.* младе́нчество. **infant** *n.* младе́нец (-нца). **infanticide** *n.* (*action*) детоуби́йство; (*person*) детоуби́йца *m.* & *f.* **infantile** *adj.* младе́нческий, инфанти́льный.

infantry *n.* пехо́та; *adj.* пехо́тный. **infantryman** *n.* пехоти́нец (-нца).

infatuate *v.t.* вскружи́ть (-ужу́, -у́жи́шь) *perf.* го́лову + *dat.* **infatuation** *n.* си́льное увлече́ние.

infect *v.t.* заража́ть *imp.*, зарази́ть *perf.* (with, + *instr.*). **infection** *n.* зара́за, инфе́кция. **infectious** *adj.* зара́зный; (*fig.*) зарази́тельный.

infelicitous *adj.* несча́стный, неуда́чный. **infelicity** *n.* несча́стье.

infer *v.t.* заключа́ть *imp.*, заключи́ть *perf.*; подразумева́ть *imp.* **inference** *n.* заключе́ние.

inferior *adj.* ни́зший; (*in quality*) ху́дший, плохо́й (плох, -á, -о, пло́хи); *n.* подчинённый *sb.* **inferiority** *n.* бо́лее ни́зкое положе́ние, бо́лее ни́зкое ка́чество; *i. complex*, ко́мплекс неполноце́нности.

infernal *adj.* а́дский. **inferno** *n.* (*hell*) ад (*loc.* -у́); (*conflagration*) пожа́рище.

infertile *adj.* неплодоро́дный.

infested *adj.*: be i. with, кише́ть (-шу́, -ши́шь) *imp.* + *instr.*

infidel *n.* неве́рный *sb.*, неве́рующий *sb.*; *adj.* неве́рующий. **infidelity** *n.* (*disloyalty*) неве́рность; (*disbelief*) неве́рие.

infiltrate *v.t.* (*fluid*) фильтрова́ть *imp.*, про ~ *perf.*; (*of persons*) постепе́нно проника́ть *imp.*, прони́кнуть (-к) *perf.* в + *acc.*

infinite *adj.* бесконе́чный, безграни́чный. **infinitesimal** *adj.* бесконе́чно ма́лый. **infinitive** *n.* инфинити́в. **infinity** *n.* бесконе́чность, безграни́чность.

infirm *adj.* не́мощный, сла́бый (слаб, -á, -о). **infirmary** *n.* больни́ца. **infirmity** *n.* не́мощь, сла́бость.

inflame *v.t. & i.* воспламеня́ть(ся) *imp.*, воспламени́ть(ся) *perf.*; (*excite*) возбужда́ть(ся) *imp.*, возбуди́ть(ся) *perf.*; (*med.*) воспаля́ть(ся) *imp.*, воспали́ть(ся) *perf.* **inflammable** *adj.* огнеопа́сный. **inflammation** *n.* воспламене́ние; (*med.*) воспале́ние. **inflammatory** *adj.* подстрека́тельский; (*med.*) воспали́тельный.

inflate *v.t.* надува́ть *imp.*, наду́ть (-у́ю, -у́ешь) *perf.*; (*econ.*) проводи́ть (-ожу́, -о́дишь) *imp.*, провести́ (-еду́, -еде́шь; -ёл, -ела́) *perf.* инфля́цию + *gen.* **inflated** *adj.* (*bombastic*) напы́щенный (-ен, -енна). **inflation** *n.* надува́ние; (*econ.*) инфля́ция.

inflect *v.t.* вгиба́ть *imp.*, вогну́ть *perf.*; (*gram.*) изменя́ть *imp.*, измени́ть (-ню́, -нишь) *perf.* (оконча́ние + *gen.*). **inflection, -xion** *n.* вгиба́ние; (*gram.*) фле́ксия.

inflexible *adj.* неги́бкий (-бок, -бка́, -бко) (*fig.*) непрекло́нный (-нен, -нна).

inflict *v.t.* (*blow*) наноси́ть (-ошу́, -о́сишь) *imp.*, нанести́ (-есу́, -есёшь; -ёс, -есла́) *perf.* (*up*)on, + *dat.*); (*suffering*) причиня́ть *imp.*, причини́ть *perf.* (*up*)on, + *dat.*); (*penalty*) налага́ть *imp.*, наложи́ть (-жу́, -жишь) *perf.* (*up*)on, на + *acc.*); *i. oneself* навя́зываться *imp.*, навяза́ться (-яжу́сь, -я́жешься) *perf.* + *dat.*

inflow *n.* втека́ние, прито́к.

influence *n.* влия́ние; *v.t.* влия́ть *imp.*, по~ *perf.* на + *acc.* **influential** *adj.* влия́тельный.

influenza *n.* грипп.

influx *n.* (*of stream*) впаде́ние; (*of persons*) наплы́в.

inform *v.t.* сообща́ть *imp.*, сообщи́ть *perf.* + *dat.* (of, about, + *acc.*, o + *prep.*); *v.i.* доноси́ть (-ошу́, -о́сишь)

imp., донести́ (-есу́, -есёшь; -ёс, -есла́) *perf.* (against, на + *acc.*).

informal *adj.* неофициа́льный, нефор-ма́льный.

informant *n.* осведоми́тель *m.* **information** *n.* информа́ция, сведе́ния *neut.pl.* **informer** *n.* доно́счик.

infraction *n.* наруше́ние.

infra-red *adj.* инфракра́сный.

infrequent *adj.* ре́дкий (-док, -дка́, -дко).

infringe *v.t.* (*violate*) наруша́ть *imp.*, нару́шить *perf.*; *v.i.*: *i.* (*up*)on, посяга́ть *imp.*, посягну́ть *perf.* на + *acc.* **infringement** *n.* наруше́ние; посяга́тельство.

infuriate *v.t.* разъяря́ть *imp.*, разъяри́ть *perf.*

infuse *v.t.* влива́ть *imp.*, влить (волью́, -ьёшь; влил, -á, -о) *perf.*; (*fig.*) внуша́ть *imp.*, внуши́ть *perf.* (into, + *dat.*); (*steep*) наста́ивать *imp.*, настоя́ть (-ою́, -ои́шь) *perf.* **infusion** *n.* влива́ние; внуше́ние; насто́й.

ingenious *adj.* изобрета́тельный. **ingenuity** *n.* изобрета́тельность.

ingenuous *adj.* открове́нный (-нен, -нна), бесхи́тростный.

inglorious *adj.* бессла́вный.

ingot *n.* сли́ток (-тка).

ingrained *adj.* закорене́лый.

ingratiate *v.t.*: *i. oneself*, вкра́дываться *imp.*, вкра́сться (-аду́сь, -аде́шься; -а́лся) *perf.* в ми́лость (with, + *dat.*).

ingratitude *n.* неблагода́рность.

ingredient *n.* составна́я часть (*pl.* -ти, -те́й).

ingress *n.* вход; (*right*) пра́во вхо́да.

inhabit *v.t.* жить (живу́, -вёшь; жил, -á, -о) *imp.* в, на, + *prep.*; обита́ть *imp.* в, на, + *prep.* **inhabitant** *n.* жи́тель *m.*, ~ ница, обита́тель *m.*, ~ ница.

inhalation *n.* вдыха́ние. **inhale** *v.t.* вдыха́ть *imp.*, вдохну́ть *perf.*

inherent *adj.* прису́щий (in, + *dat.*).

inherit *v.t.* насле́довать *imp.*, *perf.*, у ~ *perf.* **inheritance** *n.* насле́дство. **inheritor** *n.* насле́дник. **inheritress, -trix** *n.* насле́дница.

inhibit *v.t.* (*forbid*) запреща́ть *imp.*, запрети́ть (-ещу́, -ети́шь) *perf.* (+ *dat.* & *inf.*); (*hinder*) препя́тствовать *imp.*, вос~ *perf.* + *dat.* **inhibition** *n.* запреще́ние; сде́рживание; (*psych.*) торможе́ние.

inhospitable *adj.* негостеприи́мный.

inhuman *adj.* (*brutal*) бесчелове́чный; (*not human*) нечелове́ческий.

inimical *adj.* вражде́бный; (*harmful*) вре́дный (-ден, -дна́, -дно).

inimitable *adj.* неподража́емый.

iniquitous *adj.* несправедли́вый. **iniquity** *n.* несправедли́вость.

initial *adj.* (перво)нача́льный; *n.* нача́льная бу́ква; *pl.* инициа́лы *m.pl.*; *v.t.* ста́вить *imp.*, по ~ *perf.* инициа́лы на + *acc.* **initially** *adv.* в нача́ле.

initiate *v.t.* (*begin*) начина́ть *imp.*, нача́ть (начну́, -нёшь; на́чал, -а́, -о) *perf.*; (*admit*) посвяща́ть *imp.*, посвяти́ть (-ящу́, -яти́шь) *perf.* (into, в + *acc.*).

initiative *n.* почи́н, инициати́ва.

inject *v.t.* впры́скивать *imp.*, впры́снуть *perf.* **injection** *n.* впры́скивание, инъе́кция.

injudicious *adj.* неблагоразу́мный.

injunction *n.* предписа́ние; (*leg.*) суде́бное постановле́ние, суде́бный запре́т.

injure *v.t.* вреди́ть *imp.*, по ~ *perf.* + *dat.*; поврежда́ть *imp.*, повреди́ть *perf.*; (*physically*) ра́нить *imp.*, *perf.* **injurious** *adj.* вре́дный (-ден, -дна́, -дно); (*insulting*) оскорби́тельный. **injury** *n.* вред (-а́), поврежде́ние; (*physical*) ра́на.

injustice *n.* несправедли́вость.

ink *n.* черни́ла (-л) *pl.*; (*printer's i.*) типогра́фская кра́ска; *i.*-well, черни́льница.

inkling *n.* (*hint*) намёк (of, на + *acc.*); (*suspicion*) подозре́ние.

inland *adj.* вну́тренний; *adv.* (*motion*) внутрь страны́; (*place*) внутри́ страны́.

inlay *n.* инкруста́ция; *v.t.* инкрусти́ровать *imp.*, *perf.*

inlet *n.* (*of sea*) у́зкий зали́в; впуск.

inmate *n.* жиле́ц (-льца́), жили́ца; (*of prison*) заключённый *sb.*; (*of hospital*) больно́й *sb.*

inmost *adj.* са́мый вну́тренний; (*fig.*) глубоча́йший, сокрове́нный (-ён, -ённа)

inn *n.* гости́ница.

innate *adj.* врождённый (-ён, -ена́).

inner *adj.* вну́тренний.

innkeeper *n.* хозя́ин (*pl.* -я́ева, -я́ев) гости́ницы.

innocence *n.* неви́нность, невино́вность. **innocent** *adj.* неви́нный (-нен, -нна), невино́вный (of, в + *prep.*).

innocuous *adj.* безвре́дный.

innovate *v.i.* вводи́ть (-ожу́, -о́дишь) *imp.*, ввести́ (введу́, -дёшь; ввёл, -а́) *perf.* но́вшества. **innovation** *n.* нововведе́ние, но́вшество. **innovator** *n.* нова́тор.

innuendo *n.* намёк, инсинуа́ция.

innumerable *adj.* бесчи́сленный (-ен, -енна).

inoculate *v.t.* привива́ть *imp.*, приви́ть (-вью́, -вьёшь; приви́л, -а́, -о) *perf.* + *dat.* (against, + *acc.*). **inoculation** *n.* приви́вка (against, от, про́тив, + *gen.*).

inoffensive *adj.* безоби́дный.

inoperative *adj.* недействующий.

inopportune *adj.* несвоевре́менный (-нен, -нна).

inordinate *adj.* чрезме́рный.

inorganic *adj.* неоргани́ческий.

input *n.* (*action*) ввод, вход; (*power supplied*) вводи́мая мо́щность; (*electr. signal*) входно́й сигна́л; (*econ.*) затра́ты *f.pl.*; (*data*) входны́е да́нные *sb.*; (*device*) устро́йство вво́да.

inquest *n.* суде́бное сле́дствие, дозна́ние.

inquietude *n.* беспоко́йство.

inquire *v.t.* спра́шивать *imp.*, спроси́ть (-ошу́, -о́сишь) *perf.*; *v.i.* справля́ться *imp.*, спра́виться *perf.* (about, о + *prep.*); рассле́довать *imp.*, *perf.* (into, + *acc.*). **inquiry** *n.* вопро́с, спра́вка; (*investigation*) рассле́дование; *i. office*, спра́вочное бюро́ *neut.indecl.*

inquisition *n.* рассле́дование; *the I.*, инквизи́ция. **inquisitive** *adj.* пытли́вый, любозна́тельный. **inquisitor** *n.* сле́дователь *m.*; (*hist.*) инквизи́тор.

inroad *n.* набе́г; (*fig.*) посяга́тельство (on, into, на + *acc.*).

insane *adj.* душевнобольно́й, безу́мный. **insanity** *n.* безу́мие.

insatiable *adj.* ненасы́тный.

inscribe v.t. надпи́сывать imp., надписа́ть (-ишу́, -и́шешь) perf.; впи́сывать imp., вписа́ть (-ишу́, -и́шешь) perf.; (dedicate) посвяща́ть imp., посвяти́ть (-ящу́, -яти́шь) perf. **inscription** n. на́дпись; посвяще́ние.

inscrutable adj. непостижи́мый, непроница́емый.

insect n. насеко́мое sb. **insecticide** n. инсектици́д. **insectivorous** adj. насекомоя́дный.

insecure adj. (unsafe) небезопа́сный; (not firm) непро́чный (-чен, -чна́, -чно).

insensate adj. бесчу́вственный (-ен, -енна); (stupid) глу́пый (глуп, -а́, -о).

insensibility n. бесчу́вствие. **insensible** adj. (inappreciable) незаме́тный; (unconscious) потеря́вший созна́ние; (insensitive) нечувстви́тельный.

insensitive adj. нечувстви́тельный.

inseparable adj. неотдели́мый, неразлу́чный.

insert v.t. вставля́ть imp., вста́вить perf.; вкла́дывать imp., вложи́ть (-жу́, -жишь) perf.; (into newspaper etc.) помеща́ть imp., помести́ть perf. (in, в + prep.). **insertion** n. (inserting) вставле́ние, вкла́дывание; (thing inserted) вста́вка; (in newspaper) объявле́ние.

inset n. (in book) вкла́дка, вкле́йка; (in dress) вста́вка.

inshore adj. прибре́жный; adv. бли́зко к бе́регу.

inside n. вну́тренняя сторона́ (acc. -ону; pl. -оны, -он, -она́м), вну́тренность; turn i. out, вы́вернуть imp., вы́вернуть perf. наизна́нку; adj. вну́тренний; i. left, right, (sport) ле́вый, пра́вый, полусре́дний sb.; adv. (place) внутри́; (motion) внутрь; prep. (place) внутри́ + gen., в + prep.; (motion) внутрь + gen., в + acc.

insidious adj. кова́рный.

insight n. проница́тельность.

insignia n. знаки m.pl. отли́чия, разли́чия.

insignificant adj. незначи́тельный.

insincere adj. нейскренний (-нен, -нна).

insinuate v.t. постепе́нно вводи́ть (-ожу́, -о́дишь) imp., ввести́ (введу́, -дёшь; ввёл, -а́) perf. (into, в + acc.);

(hint) намека́ть imp., намекну́ть perf. на + acc.; i. oneself, вкра́дываться imp., вкра́сться (-аду́сь, -адёшься; -а́лся) perf. (into, в + acc.). **insinuation** n. инсинуа́ция.

insipid adj. (tasteless) безвку́сный; (dull) ску́чный (-чен, -чна́, -чно).

insist v.t. & i. утвержда́ть imp.; наста́ивать imp., настоя́ть (-ою́, -ои́шь) perf. (on, на + prep.). **insistent** adj. настойчивый.

insolence n. на́глость. **insolent** adj. на́глый (нагл, -а́, -о).

insoluble adj. (problem) неразреши́мый; (in liquid) нераствори́мый.

insolvent adj. несостоя́тельный.

insomnia n. бессо́нница.

insomuch adv.: i. that, насто́лько..., что; i. as, ввиду́ того́, что; так как.

inspect v.t. осма́тривать imp., осмотре́ть (-рю́, -ришь) perf.; инспекти́ровать imp., про~ perf. **inspection** n. осмо́тр, инспе́кция. **inspector** n. инспе́ктор (pl. -а́), контролёр, ревизо́р.

inspiration n. вдохнове́ние; (breathing in) вдыха́ние. **inspire** v.t. вдохновля́ть imp., вдохнови́ть perf.; внуша́ть imp., внуши́ть perf. + dat. (with, + acc.); (breathe in) вдыха́ть imp., вдохну́ть perf.

instability n. неусто́йчивость.

install v.t. (person in office) вводи́ть (-ожу́, -о́дишь) imp., ввести́ (введу́, -дёшь; ввёл, -а́) perf. в до́лжность; (apparatus) устана́вливать imp., установи́ть (-влю́, -вишь) perf. **installation** n. введе́ние в до́лжность; устано́вка; pl. сооруже́ния neut.pl.

instalment n. (payment) очередно́й взнос; (serial publication) отде́льный вы́пуск; часть (pl. -ти, -те́й); by instalments, в рассро́чку, по частя́м.

instance n. приме́р, слу́чай; (leg.) инста́нция; at the i. of, по тре́бованию + gen.; for i., наприме́р.

instant n. мгнове́ние, моме́нт; adj. (immediate) неме́дленный (-ен, -енна); (urgent) настоя́тельный; (of current month) теку́щего ме́сяца; (of coffee etc.) раствори́мый. **instantaneous** adj.

мгнове́нный (-нен, -нна). **instantly** *adv.* немéдленно, тóтчас.

instead *adv.* вмéсто (of, + *gen.*), взамéн (of, + *gen.*); *i. of going*, вмéсто тогó, чтóбы пойти́.

instep *n.* подъём.

instigate *v.t.* подстрека́ть *imp.*, подстрекну́ть *perf.* (to, к + *dat.*). **instigation** *n.* подстрека́тельство. **instigator** *n.* подстрека́тель *m.*, ~ ница.

instil *v.t.* (*liquid*) влива́ть *imp.*, влить (волью́, -ьёшь; влил, -á, -о) *perf.* по ка́пле; (*ideas etc.*) внуша́ть *imp.*, внуши́ть *perf.* (into, + *dat.*).

instinct *n.* инсти́нкт. **instinctive** *adj.* инстинкти́вный.

institute *n.* институ́т; (*teach*) уче́ждение; *v.t.* устана́вливать *imp.*, установи́ть (-влю́, -вишь) *perf.*; учрежда́ть *imp.*, учреди́ть *perf.*; (*initiate*) начина́ть *imp.*, нача́ть (начну́, -нёшь; на́чал, -á, -о) *perf.* **institution** *n.* установле́ние, учрежде́ние.

instruct *v.t.* (*teach*) обуча́ть *imp.*, обучи́ть (-чу́, -чишь) *perf.* (in, + *dat.*); (*inform*) сообща́ть *imp.*, сообщи́ть *perf.* + *dat.*; (*command*) прика́зывать *imp.*, приказа́ть (-ажу́, -áжешь) *perf.* + *dat.* **instruction** *n.* инстру́кция; (*teaching*) обуче́ние. **instructive** *adj.* поучи́тельный. **instructor** *n.* инстру́ктор.

instrument *n.* ору́дие, инструме́нт; (*leg.*) докуме́нт, акт. **instrumental** *adj.* служа́щий ору́дием; (*mus.*) инструмента́льный; (*gram.*) твори́тельный; *be i. in*, спосо́бствовать *imp.*, по ~ *perf.* + *dat.*; (*gram.*) твори́тельный паде́ж (-á). **instrumentation** *n.* (*mus.*) инструменто́вка.

insubordinate *adj.* неподчиня́ющийся.

insufferable *adj.* невыноси́мый.

insular *adj.* (*of island*) островно́й; (*narrow-minded*) ограни́ченный (-ен, -енна).

insulate *v.t.* изоли́ровать *imp.*, *perf.*; *insulating tape*, изоляцио́нная ле́нта. **insulation** *n.* изоля́ция. **insulator** *n.* изоля́тор.

insulin *n.* инсули́н.

insult *n.* оскорбле́ние; *v.t.* оскорбля́ть *imp.*, оскорби́ть *perf.* **insulting** *adj.* оскорби́тельный.

insurance *n.* страхова́ние; *attrib.* страхово́й. **insure** *v.t.* страхова́ть *imp.*, за ~ *perf.* (against, от + *gen.*).

insurgent *n.* повста́нец (-нца); *adj.* восста́вший.

insurmountable *adj.* непреодоли́мый.

insurrection *n.* восста́ние, мяте́ж (-á).

intact *adj.* (*untouched*) нетро́нутый; (*entire*) це́лый (цел, -á, -о).

intake *n.* (*action*) впуск, вход; (*mechanism*) впускно́е, приёмное, устро́йство; (*of water*) водозабо́р; (*airway in mine*) вентиляцио́нная вы́работка; (*of persons*) набо́р, о́бщее число́; (*quantity*) потребле́ние.

intangible *adj.* неосяза́емый.

integral *adj.* неотъе́млемый; (*whole*) це́льный (-лен, -льна́, -льно); (*math.*) интегра́льный; *n.* интегра́л. **integrate** *v.t.* (*combine*) объединя́ть *imp.*, объедини́ть *perf.*; (*math.*) интегри́ровать *imp.*, *perf.* **integration** *n.* объедине́ние, интегра́ция.

integrity *n.* (*wholeness*) це́лостность; (*honesty*) че́стность.

intellect *n.* интелле́кт, ум (-á). **intellectual** *n.* интеллиге́нт; *adj.* у́мственный; интеллектуа́льный.

intelligence *n.* (*intellect*) ум (-á); (*cleverness*) смышлёность; (*information*) све́дения *neut.pl.*; (*i. service*) разве́дка, разве́дывательная слу́жба. **intelligent** *adj.* у́мный (умён, умна́, умно́).

intelligentsia *n.* интеллиге́нция.

intelligible *adj.* поня́тный.

intemperate *adj.* невозде́ржанный.

intend *v.t.* намерева́ться *imp.* + *inf.*; быть наме́ренным (-ен) + *inf.*; собира́ться *imp.*, собра́ться (соберу́сь, -рёшься; собра́лся, -ала́сь, -áлóсь) *perf.*; (*design*) предназнача́ть *imp.*, предназна́чить *perf.* (for, для + *gen.*, на + *acc.*); (*mean*) име́ть *imp.* в виду́.

intense *adj.* си́льный (си́лён, -льна́, -льно, си́льны); напряжённый (-ён, -ённа). **intensify** *v.t. & i.* уси́ливать(ся) *imp.*, уси́лить(ся) *perf.* **intensity** *n.* интенси́вность, напряжённость, си́ла. **intensive** *adj.* интенси́вный.

intent *n.* наме́рение, цель; *adj.* (*resolved*) стремя́щийся (on, к + *dat.*); (*occupied*) погружённый (-ён, -ена́) (on, в + *acc.*);

(*earnest*) внима́тельный. **intention** *n.* наме́рение, цель. **intentional** *adj.* наме́ренный (-ен, -енна), умы́шленный (-ен, -енна).

inter[1] *v.t.* (*bury*) хорони́ть (-ню́, -нишь) *imp.*, по~ *perf.*

inter-[2] *pref.* (*mutually*) взаимо-; (*between*) меж-, между-; (*in verbs*) пере-.

interact *v.i.* взаимоде́йствовать *imp.* **interaction** *n.* взаимоде́йствие.

inter alia *adv.* ме́жду про́чим.

interbreed *v.t. & i.* скре́щивать(ся) *imp.*, скрести́ть(ся) *perf.*

intercede *v.i.* хода́тайствовать *imp.*, по~ *perf.* (for, за + *acc.*; with, пе́ред + *instr.*).

intercept *v.t.* перехва́тывать *imp.*, перехвати́ть (-ачу́, -а́тишь) *perf.*; (*cut off*) прерыва́ть *imp.*, прерва́ть (-ву́, -вёшь; прерва́л, -а́, -о) *perf.* **interception** *n.* перехва́т.

intercession *n.* хода́тайство. **intercessor** *n.* хода́тай.

interchange *n.* (*exchange*) обме́н (of, + *instr.*); (*alternation*) чередова́ние; (*road junction*) тра́нспортная развя́зка; *v.t.* обме́нивать *imp.*, обменя́ться *perf.* + *instr.*; чередова́ть *imp.* **interchangeable** *adj.* взаимозаменя́емый.

inter-city *adj.* междугоро́дный.

intercom *n.* вну́тренняя телефо́нная связь.

interconnection *n.* взаимосвя́зь.

inter-continental *adj.* межконтинента́льный.

intercourse *n.* (*social*) обще́ние; (*trade etc.*) сноше́ния *neut.pl.*; (*sexual*) половы́е сноше́ния *neut.pl.*

inter-departmental *adj.* меж(ду)ве́домственный.

interdependent *adj.* взаимозави́симый.

interdict *n.* запреще́ние; *v.t.* запреща́ть *imp.*, запрети́ть (-ещу́, -ети́шь) *perf.* (person, + *dat.*).

interdisciplinary *adj.* межотраслево́й.

interest *n.* интере́с (in, к + *dat.*); (*profit*) вы́года; (*econ.*) проце́нты *m.pl.*; *v.t.* интересова́ть *imp.*; (*i. person in*) заинтересо́вывать *imp.*, заинтересова́ть *perf.* (in, + *instr.*); be interested in,

интересова́ться *imp.* + *instr.* **interesting** *adj.* интере́сный.

interfere *v.i.* меша́ть *imp.*, по~ *perf.* (with, + *dat.*); вме́шиваться *imp.*, вмеша́ться *perf.* (in, в + *acc.*). **interference** *n.* вмеша́тельство; (*radio*) поме́хи *f.pl.*

inter-governmental *adj.* межправи́тельственный.

interim *n.* промежу́ток (-тка) (вре́мени); *in the i.*, тем вре́менем; *adj.* промежу́точный; (*temporary*) вре́менный.

interior *n.* вну́тренность; (*polit.*) вну́тренние дела́ *neut.pl.*; *adj.* вну́тренний.

interjection *n.* восклица́ние; (*gram.*) междоме́тие.

interlace *v.t. & i.* переплета́ть(ся) *imp.*, переплести́(сь) (-ету́(сь), -етёшь(ся); -ёл(ся), -ела́(сь)) *perf.*

interlinear *adj.* междустро́чный.

interlock *v.t. & i.* сцепля́ть(ся) *imp.*, сцепи́ть(ся) (-плю́(сь), -пишь(ся)) *perf.*

interlocutor *n.* собесе́дник, -ица.

interlope *v.i.* вме́шиваться *imp.*, вмеша́ться *perf.* в чужи́е дела́.

interlude *n.* промежу́точный эпизо́д; (*theat.*) антра́кт.

intermediary *n.* посре́дник; *adj.* посре́днический; (*intermediate*) промежу́точный.

intermediate *adj.* промежу́точный.

interment *n.* погребе́ние.

interminable *adj.* бесконе́чный.

intermission *n.* переры́в, па́уза.

intermittent *adj.* преры́вистый.

intermix *v.t. & i.* переме́шивать(ся) *imp.*, перемеша́ть(ся) *perf.*

intern *v.t.* интерни́ровать *imp.*, *perf.*

internal *adj.* вну́тренний; *i. combustion engine*, дви́гатель *m.* вну́треннего сгора́ния.

international *n.* (*contest*) междунаро́дное состяза́ние; *adj.* междунаро́дный, интернациона́льный. **internationalism** *n.* интернационали́зм.

internecine *adj.* междоусо́бный.

internee *n.* интерни́рованный *sb.* **internment** *n.* интерни́рование.

interplanetary *adj.* межпланéтный.

interplay *n.* взаимоде́йствие.

interpolate v.t. (insert) вставля́ть imp., вста́вить perf.; (math.) интерполи́ровать imp., perf. interpolation n. вста́вка f.; (math.) интерполя́ция.

interpose v.t. (insert) вставля́ть imp., вста́вить perf.; v.i. (intervene) вме́шиваться imp., вмеша́ться perf.

interpret v.t. толкова́ть imp.; (speech etc.) у́стно переводи́ть (-ожу́, -о́дишь) imp., перевести́ (-еду́, -еде́шь; -ёл, -ела́) perf. interpretation n. толкова́ние. interpreter n. толкова́тель m.; перево́дчик, -ица.

interregnum n. междуца́рствие; (interval) переры́в.

interrogate v.t. допра́шивать imp., допроси́ть (-ошу́ -о́сишь) perf. interrogation n. допро́с; (question) вопро́с. interrogative adj. вопроси́тельный.

interrupt v.t. прерыва́ть imp., прерва́ть (-ву́, -вёшь; -вал, -вала́, -ва́ло) perf. interruption n. переры́в.

intersect v.t. & i. пересека́ть(ся) imp., пересе́чь(ся) (-еку́(сь), -ече́шь(ся); -е́к(ся), -екла́(сь)) perf. intersection n. пересече́ние.

intersperse v.t. (scatter) рассыпа́ть imp., рассы́пать (-плю, -плешь) perf. (between, among, ме́жду + instr., среди́ + gen.); (diversify) разнообра́зить imp.

intertwine v.t. & i. переплета́ть(ся) imp., переплести́(сь) (-ету́(сь), -ете́шь(ся); -ёл(ся), -ела́(сь)) perf.

interval n. промежу́ток (-тка); (also mus.) интерва́л; (school) переме́на.

intervene v.i. (occur) происходи́ть (-ит) imp., произойти́ (-ойдёт; -ошёл, -ошла́) perf.; i. in, вме́шиваться imp., вмеша́ться perf. в + acc. intervention n. вмеша́тельство; (polit.) интерве́нция.

interview n. делово́е свида́ние, встре́ча; (press i.) интервью́ neut.indecl.; v.t. интервьюи́ровать imp., perf., про ~ perf. interviewer n. интервьюе́р.

interweave v.t. вотка́ть (-ку́, -кёшь; -ка́л, -кала́, -ка́ло) perf.

intestate adj. уме́рший без завеща́ния.

intestinal adj. кише́чный. intestine[1] n. кишка́ (gen.pl. -шо́к); pl. кише́чник. intestine[2] adj. вну́тренний, междоусо́бный.

intimacy n. инти́мность, бли́зость. intimate[1] adj. инти́мный, бли́зкий (-зок, -зка́, -зко, бли́зки). intimate[2] v.t. (state) сообща́ть imp., сообщи́ть perf.; (hint) намека́ть imp., намекну́ть на + acc. intimation n. сообще́ние; намёк.

intimidate v.t. запу́гивать imp., запуга́ть perf.

into prep. в, во + acc., на + acc.

intolerable adj. невыноси́мый. intolerance n. нетерпи́мость. intolerant adj. нетерпи́мый.

intonation n. интона́ция. intone v.t. интони́ровать imp.

intoxicant adj. (n.) опьяня́ющий (напи́ток (-тка)). intoxicate v.t. опьяня́ть imp., опьяни́ть perf. intoxication n. опьяне́ние; in a state of i., в нетре́звом состоя́нии.

intra- pref. внутри-.

intractable adj. неподатли́вый.

intransigent adj. непримири́мый.

intransitive adj. неперехо́дный.

intrepid adj. неустраши́мый.

intricacy n. запу́танность, сло́жность. intricate adj. запу́танный (-ан, -анна), сло́жный (-жен, -жна́, -жно).

intrigue n. интри́га; v.i. интригова́ть imp.; v.t. интригова́ть imp., за ~ perf. intriguer n. интрига́н, ~ ка.

intrinsic adj. прису́щий, суще́ственный (-ен, -енна).

introduce v.t. вводи́ть (-ожу́, -о́дишь) imp., ввести́ (введу́, -дёшь; ввёл, -а́) perf.; вноси́ть (-ошу́, -о́сишь) imp., внести́ (внесу́, -дёшь; внёс, -ла́) perf.; (person) представля́ть imp., предста́вить perf. introduction n. введе́ние, внесе́ние; представле́ние; (to book) предисло́вие. introductory adj. вво́дный, вступи́тельный.

introspection n. самонаблюде́ние.

intrude v.t. вторга́ться imp., вто́ргнуться (-г(нул)ся, -гла́сь) perf. (into, в + acc.); v.t. & i. навя́зывать(ся) imp., навяза́ть(ся) (-яжу́(сь), -я́жешь(ся)) perf. (upon, + dat.). intrusion n. вторже́ние.

intuition n. интуи́ция. intuitive adj. интуити́вный.

inundate v.t. наводня́ть *imp.*, наводни́ть *perf.* **inundation** n. наводне́ние.

inure v.t. приуча́ть *imp.*, приучи́ть (-чу́, -чишь) *perf.* (to, k + *dat.*, + *inf.*).

invade v.t. вторга́ться *imp.*, вто́ргнуться (-гнул)ся, -гласъ) *perf.* в + *acc.* **invader** n. захва́тчик.

invalid[1] n. (*disabled person*) инвали́д, больно́й sb.; adj. (*disabled*) нетрудоспосо́бный.

invalid[2] adj. (*not valid*) недействи́тельный. **invalidate** v.t. де́лать *imp.*, с ~ *perf.* недействи́тельным.

invaluable adj. неоцени́мый.

invariable adj. неизме́нный (-нен, -нна); (*math.*) постоя́нный (-нен, -нна).

invasion n. вторже́ние (в + *acc.*); (*encroachment*) посяга́тельство (на + *acc.*).

invective n. (*verbal attack*) обличи́тельная речь; (*abuse*) руга́тельства *neut.pl.*

inveigh v.i. поноси́ть (-ошу́, -о́сишь) *imp.* (against, + *acc.*).

inveigle v.t. завлека́ть *imp.*, завле́чь (-еку́, -ече́шь; -ёк, -екла́) *perf.*

invent v.t. изобрета́ть *imp.*, изобрести́ (-ету́, -ете́шь; -ёл, -ела́) *perf.*; выду́мывать *imp.*, вы́думать *perf.* **invention** n. изобрете́ние; вы́думка. **inventive** adj. изобрета́тельный. **inventor** n. изобрета́тель m.

inventory n. инвента́рь (-ря́) m., о́пись (иму́щества); v.t. инвентаризова́ть *imp.*, *perf.*

inverse adj. обра́тный. **inversion** n. перестано́вка.

invertebrate adj. беспозвоно́чный; n. беспозвоно́чное sb.

invest v.t. (*clothe*, *endue*) облека́ть *imp.*, обле́чь (-еку́, -ече́шь; -ёк, -екла́) *perf.* (in, в + *acc.*; with, + *instr.*); (*lay siege to*) осажда́ть *imp.*, осади́ть *perf.*; v.t. & i. (*econ.*) вкла́дывать *imp.*, вложи́ть (-жу́, -жишь) *perf.* (де́ньги) (in, в + *acc.*); инвести́ровать *imp.*, *perf.*

investigate v.t. иссле́довать *imp.*, *perf.*; (*leg.*) рассле́довать *imp.*, *perf.* **investigation** n. иссле́дование; рассле́дова-

ние. **investigator** n. иссле́дователь m.; (*leg.*) сле́дователь m.

investiture n. введе́ние в до́лжность.

investment n. (*econ.*) вложе́ние, вклад, инвести́ция; (*mil.*) оса́да. **investor** n. вкла́дчик.

inveterate adj. закоренéлый, застаре́лый.

invigorate v.t. укрепля́ть *imp.*, укрепи́ть *perf.*; (*animate*) оживля́ть *imp.*, оживи́ть *perf.*

invincible adj. непобеди́мый.

inviolable adj. неприкосновéнный (-нен, -нна), неруши́мый. **inviolate** adj. ненару́шенный.

invisible adj. неви́димый; i. ink, симпати́ческие черни́ла (-л) pl.

invitation n. приглаше́ние. **invite** v.t. приглаша́ть *imp.*, пригласи́ть *perf.*; (*request*) проси́ть (-ошу́, -о́сишь) *imp.*, по ~ *perf.*; (*attract*) привлека́ть *imp.*, привле́чь (-еку́, -ече́шь; -ёк, -екла́) *perf.* **inviting** adj. привлека́тельный.

invocation n. призы́в.

invoice n. факту́ра, накладна́я sb.

invoke v.t. призыва́ть *imp.*, призва́ть (-зову́, -зовёшь; призва́л, -а́, -о); взыва́ть *imp.*, воззва́ть (-зову́, -зовёшь) *perf.*

involuntary adj. нево́льный; непроизво́льный.

involve v.t. (*entail*) вовлека́ть *imp.*, вовле́чь (-еку́, -ече́шь; -ёк, -екла́) *perf.*; (*include*) включа́ть *imp.*, включи́ть *perf.* в себе́. **involved** adj. (*complex*) сло́жный (-жен, -жна́, -жно).

invulnerable adj. неуязви́мый.

inward adj. вну́тренний. **inwardly** adv. внутри́, вну́тренне. **inwards** adv. внутрь.

iodine n. йод; *attrib.* йо́дный.

ion n. ио́н. **ionic** adj. ио́нный.

iota n. йо́та; not an i., ни на йо́ту.

IOU n. долгова́я распи́ска.

irascible adj. раздражи́тельный.

irate adj. гне́вный (-вен, -вна́, -вно). **ire** n. гнев.

iridescent adj. ра́дужный.

iris n. (*anat.*) ра́дужная оболо́чка; (*bot.*) каса́тик.

Irish adj. ирла́ндский. **Irishman** n. ирла́ндец (-дца). **Irishwoman** n. ирла́ндка.

irk v.t. надоеда́ть imp., надое́сть (-е́м, -е́шь, -е́ст, -еди́м; -е́л) perf. + dat. **irksome** adj. ску́чный (-чен, -чна́, -чно).

iron n. желе́зо; (for clothes) утю́г (-á); pl. (fetters) кандалы́ (-ло́в) pl.; adj. желе́зный; (clothes) утю́жить imp., вы́~, от~ perf.; гла́дить imp., вы́~ perf.

ironic(al) adj. ирони́ческий. **irony** n. иро́ния.

irradiate v.t. (light up) освеща́ть imp., освети́ть (-ещу́, -ети́шь) perf.; (subject to radiation) облуча́ть imp., облучи́ть perf. **irradiation** n. освеще́ние; облуче́ние.

irrational adj. неразу́мный; (math.) иррациона́льный.

irreconcilable adj. (persons) непримири́мый; (ideas) несовмести́мый.

irrecoverable adj. невозвра́тный.

irredeemable adj. (econ.) не подлежа́щий вы́купу; (hopeless) безнадёжный.

irrefutable adj. неопровержи́мый.

irregular adj. нерегуля́рный; (gram.) непра́вильный; (not even) неро́вный (-вен, -вна́, -вно); (disorderly) беспоря́дочный.

irrelevant adj. неуме́стный.

irreligious adj. неве́рующий.

irremediable adj. непоправи́мый, неизлечи́мый.

irremovable adj. неустрани́мый; (from office) несменя́емый.

irreparable adj. непоправи́мый.

irreplaceable adj. незамени́мый.

irrepressible adj. неудержи́мый.

irreproachable adj. безупре́чный.

irresistible adj. неотрази́мый.

irresolute adj. нереши́тельный.

irrespective adj.: i. of, безотноси́тельно к + dat., незави́симо от + gen.

irresponsible adj. (of conduct etc.) безотве́тственный (-ен, -енна); (not responsible) неотве́тственный (-ен, -енна); (leg.) невменя́емый.

irretrievable adj. непоправи́мый, невозвра́тный.

irreverent adj. непочти́тельный.

irreversible adj. необрати́мый.

irrevocable adj. неотменя́емый.

irrigate v.t. ороша́ть imp., ороси́ть perf. **irrigation** n. ороше́ние, иррига́ция.

irritable adj. раздражи́тельный. **irritate** v.t. раздража́ть imp., раздражи́ть perf. **irritation** n. раздраже́ние.

irrupt v.i. вторга́ться imp., вто́ргнуться (-г(нул)ся, -глась) perf. (into, в + acc.). **irruption** n. вторже́ние.

Islam n. исла́м. **Islamic** adj. мусульма́нский, исла́мистский.

island, isle n. о́стров (pl. -á); adj. островно́й. **islander** n. острови́тянин (pl. -яне, -ян), -янка. **islet** n. острово́к (-вка́).

iso- in comb. изо-, равно-. **isobar** n. изоба́ра. **isomer** n. изоме́р. **isosceles** adj. равнобе́дренный. **isotherm** n. изоте́рма. **isotope** n. изото́п.

isolate v.t. изоли́ровать imp., perf.; обособля́ть imp., обосо́бить perf.; (chem.) выделя́ть imp., вы́делить perf. **isolation** n. изоля́ция; i. hospital, инфекцио́нная больни́ца; i. ward, изоля́тор.

Israeli n. израильтя́нин (pl. -я́не, -я́н), -я́нка; adj. изра́ильский.

issue n. (outlet) вы́ход, (outflow) вытека́ние; (progeny) пото́мство; (outcome) исхо́д, результа́т; (question) (спо́рный) вопро́с; (of book etc.) вы́пуск, изда́ние; v.i. выходи́ть (-ожу́, -о́дишь) imp., вы́йти (вы́йду, -дешь; вы́шел, -шла) perf.; (flow) вытека́ть imp., вы́течь (-еку, -ечешь; -ек) perf.; v.t. выпуска́ть imp., вы́пустить perf.; выдава́ть (-даю́, -даёшь) imp., вы́дать (-ам, -ашь, -аст, -адим) perf.

isthmus n. переше́ек (-е́йка).

it pron. он, оно́ (его́, ему́, им, о нём), она́ (её, ей, ей & е́ю, о ней); demonstr. э́то.

Italian n. италья́нец (-нца), -нка; adj. италья́нский.

italic adj. (I.) италийский; (print.) курси́вный; n. курси́в. **italicize** v.t. выделя́ть imp., вы́делить perf. курси́вом.

itch n. зуд, чесо́тка; v.i. зуде́ть (-ди́т) imp.; чеса́ться чешета́ imp.

item *n.* (*on list*) предме́т; (*in account*) пункт; (*on agenda*) вопро́с; (*in programme*) но́мер (*pl.* -á); *adv.* та́кже, то́же.

iterate *v.t.* повторя́ть *imp.*, повтори́ть *perf.*

itinerant *adj.* стра́нствующий. **itinerary** *n.* (*route*) маршру́т; (*guidebook*) путеводи́тель *m.*

its *poss.pron.* его́, её; свой (-оя́, -оё; -ой).

itself *pron.* (*emph.*) (он(о́)) сам(о́) (-ого́, -ому́, -им, -о́м), (она́) сама́ (-мо́й, -му́); (*refl.*) себя́ (себе́, собо́й); -ся (*suffixed to v.t.*).

ivory *n.* слоно́вая кость.

ivy *n.* плющ (-á).

J

jab *n.* уко́л, толчо́к (-чка́); *v.t.* ты́кать (ты́чу, -чешь) *imp.*, ткнуть *perf.* (+ *instr.* в+*acc.*; +*acc.* в+*acc.*).

jabber *n.* болтовня́; *v.t. & i.* болта́ть *imp.*

jack¹ *n.* (*fellow*) па́рень (-рня; *pl.* -рни, -рне́й) *m.*; (*cards*) вале́т; (*lifting machine*) домкра́т; *v.t.* (*j. up*) поднима́ть *imp.*, подня́ть (-ниму́, -ни́мешь; по́дня́л, -á, -о) *perf.* домкра́том.

jack² *n.* (*naut.*) гюйс.

jackal *n.* шака́л.

jackass *n.* осёл (осла́).

jackdaw *n.* га́лка.

jacket *n.* ку́ртка; (*woman's*) жаке́тка; (*animal's*) шку́ра; (*tech.*) кожу́х (-á); (*on boiler*) руба́шка; (*on book*) (супер)обло́жка.

jack-knife *n.* большо́й складно́й нож (-á).

jade¹ *n.* (*horse*) кля́ча. **jaded** *adj.* изнурённый (-ён, -е́нна).

jade² *n.* (*mineral*) нефри́т.

jagged *adj.* зубча́тый, зазу́бренный (-ен, -ена).

jaguar *n.* ягуа́р.

jail *see* **gaol**.

jam¹ *n.* (*crush*) да́вка; (*of machine*) заеда́ние, перебо́й; (*in traffic*) про́бка; *v.t.* (*squeeze*) сжима́ть *imp.*, сжать (сожму́, -мёшь) *perf.*; (*thrust*) впи́хивать *imp.*, впихну́ть *perf.* (into, в+*acc.*); (*block*) загроможда́ть *imp.*, загромозди́ть *perf.*; (*radio*) заглу-

ша́ть *imp.*, заглуши́ть *perf.*; *v.i.* (*machine*) заеда́ть *imp.*, зае́сть (-е́ст; -е́ло) *perf. impers.*+*acc.*

jam² *n.* (*conserve*) варе́нье, джем.

jamb *n.* кося́к (-á).

jangle *n.* ре́зкий звук; *v.i.* издава́ть (-даю́, -даёшь) *imp.*, изда́ть (-а́м, -а́шь, -а́ст, -ади́м; изда́л, -á, -о) *perf.* ре́зкие зву́ки.

janissary, -izary *n.* янычáр (*gen.pl.* -ров & (*collect.*) -р).

janitor *n.* (*door-keeper*) привра́тник, -ица; (*caretaker*) дво́рник.

January *n.* янва́рь (-pя́) *m.*; *attrib.* янва́рский.

Japanese *n.* япо́нец (-нца), -нка; *adj.* япо́нский.

jape *n.* шу́тка; *v.i.* шути́ть (шучу́, шу́тишь) *imp.*, по~ *perf.*

jar¹ *n.* (*container*) ба́нка.

jar² *v.i.* (*sound*) скрипе́ть (-пи́т) *imp.*; (*irritate*) раздража́ть *imp.*, раздражи́ть *perf.* (upon, +*acc.*).

jargon *n.* жарго́н.

jasmin(e), jessamin(e) *n.* жасми́н.

jasper *n.* я́шма; *attrib.* я́шмовый.

jaundice *n.* желту́ха; (*fig.*) за́висть. **jaundiced** *adj.* желту́шный, больно́й (-лен, -льна́) желту́хой; (*fig.*) зави́стливый.

jaunt *n.* прогу́лка, пое́здка.

jaunty *adj.* бо́дрый (бодр, -á, -о, бо́дры).

javelin *n.* копьё (*pl.* -пья, -пий, -пьям).

jaw *n.* чéлюсть; *pl.* пасть, рот (рта, *loc.* во рту); *pl.* (*of valley etc.*) ýзкий вход; *pl.* (*of vice*) гýбка.

jay *n.* (*bird*) сóйка; (*fig.*) болтýн (-á); ~ья.

jazz *n.* джаз; *adj.* джáзовый.

jealous *adj.* ревнúвый, завúстливый; *be j. of*, (*person*) ревновáть *imp.*; (*thing*) завúдовать *imp.*, по~ *perf.* + *dat.*; (*rights*) ревнúво оберегáть *imp.*, оберéчь (-егý, -ежёшь; -ёг, -еглá) *perf.* **jealousy** *n.* рéвность, зáвисть.

jeans *n.* джúнсы (-сов) *pl.*

jeer *n.* насмéшка; *v.t. & i.* насмехáться *imp.* (над + *instr.*).

jejune *adj.* (*scanty*) скýдный (-ден, -днá, -дно); (*to mind*) неинтерéсный.

jelly *n.* (*sweet*) желé *neut.indecl.*; (*meat, fish*) стýдень (-дня) *m.* **jellyfish** *n.* медýза.

jemmy *n.* фóмка, лом (*pl.* -ы, -óв).

jeopardize *v.t.* подвергáть *imp.*, подвéргнуть (-г) *perf.* опáсности. **jeopardy** *n.* опáсность.

jerk *n.* толчóк (-чкá); (*of muscle*) вздрáгивание; *v.t.* дёргать *imp.* + *instr.*; *v.i.* (*twitch*) дёргаться *imp.*, дёрнуться *perf.* **jerky** *adj.* тряскúй (-сок, -скá), отрывúстый.

jersey *n.* (*garment*) фуфáйка; (*fabric*) джéрси *neut.indecl.*

jest *n.* шýтка, насмéшка; *v.i.* шутúть (шучý, шýтишь) *imp.*, по~ *perf.* **jester** *n.* шутнúк (-á), -úца; (*hist.*) шут (-á).

Jesuit *n.* иезуúт. **Jesuitical** *adj.* иезуúтский.

jet[1] *n.* (*stream*) струя́ (*pl.* -ýи); (*nozzle*) форсýнка, соплó (*pl.* сóпла, сóп(е)л); j. engine, реактúвный двúгатель *m.*; j. plane, реактúвный самолёт. **jet**[2] *n.* (*min.*) гагáт; *adj.* гагáтовый; j.-black, чёрный (-рен, -рнá) как смоль.

jetsam *n.* товáры *m.pl.*, сбрóшенные с корабля́.

jettison *v.t.* выбрáсывать *imp.*, выбросить *perf.* зá борт.

jetty *n.* (*mole*) мол (*loc.* -ý); (*landing-pier*) прúстань (*pl.* -ни, -нéй).

Jew *n.* еврéй. **Jewess** *n.* еврéйка. **Jewish** *adj.* еврéйский. **Jewry** *n.* еврéйство.

jewel *n.* драгоцéнность, драгоцéнный кáмень (-мня; *pl.* -мни, -мнéй) *m.* **jeweller** *n.* ювелúр. **jewellery, jewelry** *n.* драгоцéнности *f.pl.*, ювелúрные издéлия *neut.pl.*

jib *n.* (*naut.*) клúвер (*pl.* -á & -ы); (*of crane*) стрелá (*pl.* -лы) (крáна).

jingle *n.* звякáнье; *v.t.* & *i.* звякать *imp.*, звякнуть *perf.* (+ *instr.*).

jingo *n.* урá-патриóт. **jingoism** *n.* урá-патриотúзм. **jingoistic** *adj.* урá-патриотúческий.

job *n.* (*work*) рабóта; (*task*) задáние; (*position*) мéсто (*pl.* -á). **jobless** *adj.* безрабóтный.

jockey *n.* жокéй; *v.t.* (*cheat*) надувáть *imp.*, надýть (-ýю, -ýешь) *perf.*

jocose *adj.* игрúвый.

jocular *adj.* шутлúвый.

jocund *adj.* весёлый (вéсел, -á, -о, вéселы).

jog *n.* (*push*) толчóк (-чкá); (*movement*) мéдленная ходьбá, еэдá; *v.t.* толкáть *imp.*, толкнýть *perf.*; (*nudge*) подтáлкивать *imp.*, подтолкнýть *perf.* **jog-trot** *n.* рысцá.

join *v.t. & i.* соединя́ть(ся) *imp.*, соединúть(ся) *perf.*; *v.t.* присоединя́ть *imp.*, присоединúть *perf.* к + *dat.*; (*become member of*) вступáть *imp.*, вступúть (-плю́, -пишь) *perf.* в + *acc.*; *v.i.*: j. up, вступáть *imp.*, вступúть (-плю́, -пишь) *perf.* в áрмию.

joiner *n.* столя́р (-á). **joinery** *n.* (*goods*) столя́рные издéлия *neut.pl.*; (*work*) столя́рная рабóта.

joint *n.* соединéние, мéсто (*pl.* -тá) соединéния; (*anat.*) сустáв; (*tech.*) стык, шов (шва), шарнúр; *adj.* соединённый, óбщий; j. stock, акционéрный капитáл; (*attrib.*) акционéрный; *v.t.* (*join*) сочленя́ть *imp.*, сочленúть *perf.*; (*divide*) расчленя́ть *imp.*, расчленúть *perf.*

joist *n.* переклáдина.

joke *n.* шýтка, острóта, анекдóт; *v.i.* шутúть (шучý, шýтишь) *imp.*, по~ *perf.* **joker** *n.* шутнúк (-á), -úца.

jollity *n.* весéлье. **jolly** *adj.* весёлый (вéсел, -á, -о, вéселы); *adv.* óчень.

jolt *n.* тряскá; *v.t.* трястú (-сý, -сёшь; -с, -слá) *imp.*

jostle n. толкотня; v.t. & i. толкать(ся) imp., толкнуть(ся) perf.

jot n. йота; not a j., ни на йоту; v.t. (j. down) быстро, кратко, записывать imp., записать (-ишу, -ишешь) perf.

joule n. джоуль m.

journal n. журнал, дневник (-á); (tech.) цапфа, шейка. **journalese** n. газетный язык (-á). **journalism** n. журналистика. **journalist** n. журналист.

journey n. путешествие, поездка; (specific j. of vehicle) рейс; v.i. путешествовать imp.

jovial adj. (merry) весёлый (весел, -á, -о, веселы); (sociable) общительный.

jowl n. (jaw) чёлюсть; (cheek) щека (acc. щёку; pl. щёки, щёк, -áм).

joy n. радость. **joyful**, **joyous** adj. радостный. **joyless** adj. безрадостный.

jubilant adj. ликующий. **jubilate** v.i. ликовать imp.

jubilee n. юбилей.

Judaic adj. иудейский.

judge n. судья (pl. -дьи, -дей, -дьям) m.; (connoisseur) ценитель m.; v.t. & i. судить (сужу, судишь) imp.; v.t. (appraise) оценивать imp., оценить (-ню, -нишь) perf. **judgement** n. (sentence) приговор; (decision) решение; (opinion) мнение; (estimate) оценка.

judicature n. отправление правосудия; (judiciary) судейская корпорация.

judicial adj. (of law) судебный; (of judge) судейский; (impartial) беспристрастный. **judicious** adj. здравомыслящий.

judo n. дзюдо neut.indecl.

jug n. кувшин; v.t. тушить (-шу, -шишь) imp., с~ perf.

juggle v.i. жонглировать imp. **juggler** n. жонглёр.

jugular adj. шейный; j. vein, яремная вена.

juice n. сок (-a(y), loc. -е & -ý); (fig.) сущность. **juicy** adj. сочный (-чен, -чнá, -чно).

July n. июль m.; attrib. июльский.

jumble n. (disorder) беспорядок (-дка); (articles) барахло́; v.t. перепутывать imp., перепутать perf.

jump n. прыжок (-жка), скачок (-чка); (in price etc.) резкое повышение; v.i. прыгать imp., прыгнуть perf.; скакать (-ачу, -ачешь) imp.; (from shock) вздрагивать imp., вздрогнуть perf.; (of price etc.) подскакивать imp., подскочить (-ит) perf.; v.t. (j. over) перепрыгивать imp., перепрыгнуть perf.; j. at, (accept eagerly) хватáться imp., ухватиться (-ачусь, -áтишься) perf. за + acc.; j. the rails, сходить (-ит) imp., сойти (сойдёт; сошёл, -шлá) perf. с рельсов.

jumper n. (garment) джемпер.

jumpy adj. нервный (-вен, нервнá, -вно).

junction n. (joining) соединение; (rly.) железнодорожный узел (узлá) (roads) перекрёсток (-тка).

juncture n. (joining) соединение; (state of affairs) положение дел; at this j., в этот момент.

June n. июнь m.; attrib. июньский.

jungle n. джунгли (-лей) pl.

junior adj. младший.

juniper n. можжевельник.

junk[1] n. (rubbish) барахло́.

junk[2] n. (ship) джонка.

junta n. хунта.

Jupiter n. Юпитер.

jurisdiction n. (administration of law) отправление правосудия; (legal authority) юрисдикция.

jurisprudence n. юриспруденция.

jurist n. юрист.

juror n. присяжный sb.; (in competition) член жюри. **jury** n. присяжные sb.; жюри neut.indecl.

just adj. (fair) справедливый; (deserved) заслуженный, должный; adv. (exactly) точно, именно; (barely) едвá; (at this, that, moment) только что; j. in case, на всякий случай.

justice n. правосудие; (fairness) справедливость; (judge) судья (pl. -дьи, -дей, -дьям); (proceedings) суд (-á); bring to j., отдавать (-даю, -даёшь) imp., отдать (-áм, -áшь, -áст, -адим; отдал, -á, -о) perf. под суд; do j. to, отдавать (-даю, -аёшь) imp., отдать (-áм, -áшь, -áст, -адим; отдал, -á, -о) perf. должное + dat.

justify *v.t.* опра́вдывать *imp.*, оправда́ть *perf.* **justification** *n.* оправда́ние.

jut *v.i.* (*j. out, forth*) выдава́ться (-даётся) *imp.*, вы́даться (-астся, -адутся) *perf.*; выступа́ть *imp.*

jute *n.* джут.

juvenile *n.* ю́ноша *m.*, подро́сток (-тка); *adj.* ю́ный (юн, -а́, -о), ю́ношеский.

juxtapose *v.t.* помеща́ть *imp.*, помести́ть *perf.* ря́дом; сопоставля́ть *imp.*, сопоста́вить *perf.* (with, c + *instr.*).

K

kale, kail *n.* кормова́я капу́ста.

kaleidoscope *n.* калейдоско́п.

kangaroo *n.* кенгуру́ *m.indecl.*

keel *n.* киль *m.*; *v.t. & i.*: *k. over*, опроки́дывать(ся) *imp.*, опроки́нуть(ся) *perf.*

keen *adj.* (*sharp*) о́стрый (остр & остёр, остра́, о́стро); (*strong*) си́льный (-лён, -льна́, -льно, си́льны); (*penetrating*) проница́тельный; (*ardent*) стра́стный (-тен, -тна́, -тно).

keep[1] *n.* (*of castle*) гла́вная ба́шня (*gen.pl.* -шен); (*maintenance*) содержа́ние; (*food*) пи́ща.

keep[2] *v.t.* (*observe*) соблюда́ть *imp.*, соблюсти́ (-юду́, -юдёшь; -ю́л, -юла́) *perf.* (*the law*); сде́рживать *imp.*, сдержа́ть (-жу́, -жишь) *perf.* (*one's word*); (*celebrate*) пра́здновать *imp.*, от ~ *perf.*; (*possess, maintain*) держа́ть (-жу́, -жишь) *imp.*; храни́ть *imp.*; (*family*) содержа́ть (-жу́, -жишь) *imp.*; (*diary*) вести́ (веду́, -дёшь; вёл, -а́) *imp.*; (*detain*) заде́рживать *imp.*, задержа́ть (-жу́, -жишь) *perf.*; (*retain, reserve*) сохраня́ть *imp.*, сохрани́ть *perf.*; *v.i.* (*remain*) остава́ться (-таю́сь, -таёшься) *imp.*, оста́ться (-а́нусь, -а́нешься) *perf.*; (*of food*) не по́ртиться *imp.*; *k. away*, держа́ть(ся) (-жу́(сь), -жишь(ся)) *imp.* в отдале́нии; *k. back*, (*hold back*) уде́рживать *imp.*, удержа́ть (-жу́, -жишь) *perf.*; (*conceal*) скрыва́ть *imp.*, скрыть (-ро́ю, -ро́ешь) *perf.*; *k. down*, подавля́ть *imp.*, подави́ть (-влю́, -вишь) *perf.*; *k. from*, уде́рживаться *imp.*, удержа́ться (-жу́сь, -жишься) *perf.* от + *gen.*; *k. on*, продолжа́ть *imp.*, продо́лжить *perf.* (+ *inf.*).

keepsake *n.* пода́рок (-рка) на па́мять.

keg *n.* бочо́нок (-нка).

ken *n.* (*knowledge*) преде́л позна́ний; (*sight*) кругозо́р.

kennel *n.* конура́.

kerb *n.* край (*loc.* -аю́; *pl.* -ая́, -аёв) тротуа́ра. **kerbstone** *n.* бордю́рный ка́мень (-мня; *pl.* -мни, -мне́й) *m.*

kerchief *n.* (головно́й) плато́к (-тка́).

kernel *n.* (*nut*) ядро́ (*pl.* я́дра, я́дер, я́драм); (*grain*) зерно́ (*pl.* зёрна, -рен, -рнам); (*fig.*) суть.

kerosene *n.* кероси́н (-а(у)).

kestrel *n.* пустельга́.

kettle *n.* ча́йник. **kettledrum** *n.* лита́вра.

key *n.* ключ (-а́); (*piano, typewriter*) кла́виш(а); (*mus.*) тона́льность; *attrib.* веду́щий, ключево́й. **keyboard** *n.* клавиату́ра. **keyhole** *n.* замо́чная сква́жина. **keynote** *n.* (*mus.*) то́ника; (*fig.*) тон. **keystone** *n.* (*archit.*) замко́вый ка́мень (-мня; *pl.* -мни, -мне́й) *m.*; (*fig.*) основно́й при́нцип.

khaki *n.*, *adj.* ха́ки *neut.*, *adj.indecl.*

khan *n.* хан. **khanate** *n.* ха́нство.

kick *n.* уда́р ного́й, пино́к (-нка́); (*recoil of gun*) отда́ча; *v.t.* удари́ть *imp.*, уда́рить *perf.* ного́й; пина́ть *imp.*, пнуть *perf.*; (*score goal*) забива́ть *imp.*, заби́ть (-бью, -бьёшь) *perf.* (гол, мяч); *v.i.* (*of horse etc.*) ляга́ться *imp.*; *k. out*, вышвы́ривать *imp.*, вы́швырнуть *perf.*

kid[1] *n.* (*goat*) козлёнок (-лёнка; *pl.* -лята, -лят); (*leather*) лайка; (*child*) малыш (-á).

kid[2] *v.t.* (*deceive*) обма́нывать *imp.*, обману́ть (-ну́, -нешь) *perf.*; (*tease*) поддра́знивать *imp.*, поддразни́ть (-ню́, -нишь) *perf.*

kidnap *v.t.* похища́ть *imp.*, похи́тить (-и́щу, -и́тишь) *perf.*

kidney *n.* по́чка; *attrib.* по́чечный; *k. bean*, фасо́ль.

kill *v.t.* убива́ть *imp.*, уби́ть (убью́, -бьёшь) *perf.*; (*cattle*) ре́зать (ре́жу, -жешь) *imp.*, за~ *perf.*; *k. off*, ликвиди́ровать *imp.* & *perf.* **killer** *n.* уби́йца *m. & f.* **killing** *n.* уби́йство; *adj.* (*murderous, fig.*) уби́йственный (-ен, -енна); (*amusing, coll.*) умори́тельный.

kiln *n.* о́бжиговая печь (*pl.* -чи, -че́й).

kilo- *in comb.* кило-. **kilocycle, kilogerz** *n.* килоге́рц (*gen.pl.* -ц). **kilogram(me)** *n.* килогра́мм. **kilometre** *n.* киломе́тр. **kiloton(ne)** *n.* килото́нна. **kilowatt** *n.* килова́тт (*gen.pl.* -т).

kimono *n.* кимоно́ *neut.indecl.*

kin *n.* (*family*) семья́ (*pl.* -мьи, -мéй, -мьям); (*collect., relatives*) родня́.

kind[1] *n.* сорт (*pl.* -á), род (*pl.* -ы, -о́в); *a k. of*, что-то вро́де+*gen.*; *this k. of*, тако́й; *what k. of*, что (э́то, он, *etc.*) за+*nom.*; *k. of*, (*adv.*) как бу́дто, ка́к-то; *pay in k.*, плати́ть (-ачу́, -áтишь) *imp.*, за~ *perf.* натýрой; *return in k.*, отпла́чивать *imp.*, отплати́ть (-ачу́, -áтишь) *perf.* той же моне́той+*dat.*

kind[2] *adj.* до́брый (добр, -á, -о, до́бры), любе́зный.

kindergarten *n.* де́тский сад (*loc.* -ý; *pl.* -ы́).

kindle *v.t.* зажига́ть *imp.*, заже́чь (-жгý, -жжёшь; -жёг, -жгла́) *perf.*; *v.i.* загора́ться *imp.*, загоре́ться (-рю́сь, -ри́шься) *perf.* **kindling** *n.* расто́пка.

kindly *adj.* до́брый (добр, -á, -о, до́бры); *adv.* любе́зно; (*with imper.*), (*request*) бýдьте добры́, +*imper.* **kindness** *n.* доброта́, любе́зность.

kindred *n.* (*relationship*) кро́вное родство́; (*relatives*) ро́дственники *m.pl.*; *adj.* ро́дственный (-ен, -енна); (*similar*) схо́дный (-ден, -дна́, -дно).

kinetic *adj.* кинети́ческий.

king *n.* коро́ль (-ля́) *m.* (*also chess, cards, fig.*); (*fig.*) царь (-ря́) *m.*; (*draughts*) да́мка. **kingdom** *n.* короле́вство; (*fig.*) ца́рство. **kingfisher** *n.* зиморо́док (-дка). **kingpin** *n.* шкво́рень (-рня) *m.*

kink *n.* пе́тля (-тель, -тель). **kinky** *adj.* кудря́вый.

kinsfolk *n.* кро́вные ро́дственники *m.pl.* **kinship** *n.* родство́; (*similarity*) схо́дство. **kinsman, -woman** *n.* ро́дственник, -ица.

kiosk *n.* кио́ск; (*telephone*) бýдка.

kip *v.i.* дры́хнуть (дрых(ну)л, -хла) *imp.*

kipper *n.* копчёная селёдка.

kiss *n.* поцелу́й; *v.t.* целова́ть(ся) *imp.*, по~ *perf.*

kit *n.* (*soldier's*) ли́чное обмундирова́ние; (*clothing*) снаряже́ние; (*tools*) компле́кт. **kitbag** *n.* вещево́й мешо́к (-шка́).

kitchen *n.* ку́хня (*gen.pl.* -хонь); *attrib.* ку́хонный; *k. garden*, огоро́д; *k.-maid*, судомо́йка.

kite *n.* (*bird*) ко́ршун; (*person*) хи́щник; (*toy*) бума́жный змей.

kith *n.*: *k. and kin*, знако́мые *sb.* и родня́.

kitten *n.* котёнок (-тёнка; *pl.* -тя́та, -тя́т); *v.i.* коти́ться *imp.*, о~ *perf.*

kleptomania *n.* клептома́ния. **kleptomaniac** *n.* клептома́н.

knack *n.* сноро́вка, трюк.

knacker *n.* живодёр.

knapsack *n.* рюкза́к (-á), ра́нец (-нца).

knave *n.* (*rogue*) плут (-á); (*cards*) вале́т. **knavery** *n.* плутовство́. **knavish** *adj.* плутовско́й.

knead *v.t.* меси́ть (мешу́, ме́сишь) *imp.*, с~ *perf.*

knee *n.* коле́но (*pl.* (*anat.*) -ни, -не́й; (*tech.*) -нья, -ньев); *k.-joint*, коле́нный суста́в. **kneecap** *n.* (*bone*) коле́нная ча́шка; (*protective covering*) наколе́нник.

kneel *v.i.* стоя́ть (-ою́, -ои́шь) *imp.* на коле́нях; (*k. down*) станови́ться (-влю́сь, -вишься) *imp.*, стать (-á́ну, -а́нешь) *perf.* на коле́ни.

knell *n.* похоро́нный звон.

knickers *n.* панталóны (-н) *pl.*

knick-knack *n.* безделýшка.

knife *n.* нож (-á); *v.t.* колóть (-лю́, -лешь) *imp.*, за~ *perf.* ножóм.

knight *n.* ры́царь *m.*; (*holder of order*) кавалéр (óрдена); (*chess*) конь (-ня́; *pl.* -ни, -нéй) *m.* **knighthood** *n.* ры́царство. **knightly** *adj.* ры́царский.

knit *v.t.* (*garment*) вязáть (вяжý, -жешь) *imp.*, с~ *perf.*; (*unite*) свя́зывать *imp.*, связáть (-яжý, -я́жешь) *perf.*; *v.t. & i.* (*unite*) соединя́ть(ся) *imp.*, соедини́ть(ся) *perf.*; *v.i.* (*bones*) сраста́ться *imp.*, срасти́сь (-тётся; срóсся, срослáсь) *perf.*; *k. one's brows*, хмýрить *imp.*, на~ *perf.* брóви. **knitting** *n.* (*action*) вязáние; (*object*) вязáнье; *k.-needle*, спи́ца. **knitwear** *n.* трикотáж.

knob *n.* ши́шка, кнóпка; (*door handle*) (крýглая) рýчка (двéри). **knob(b)(l)y** *adj.* шишковáтый.

knock *n.* (*noise*) стук; (*blow*) удáр; *v.t. & i.* (*strike*) ударя́ть *imp.*, удáрить *perf.*; (*strike door etc.*) стучáть (-чý, -чи́шь) *imp.*, по~ *perf.* (at, в + *acc.*); *k. about*, (*treat roughly*) колоти́ть (-очý, -óтишь) *imp.*, по~ *perf.*; (*wander*) шатáться *imp.*; *k. down*, (*person*) сбивáть *imp.*, сбить (собью́, -ьёшь) *perf.* с ног; (*building*) сноси́ть (-ошý, -óсишь) *imp.*, снести́ (снесý, -сёшь; снёс, -лá) *perf.*; (*at auction*) продавáть (-даю́, -даёшь) *imp.*, продáть (-áм, -áшь, -áст, -ади́м; прóдал, -á, -о) *perf.* с молоткá; *k. in*, вбивáть *imp.*, вбить (вобью́, -ьёшь) *perf.* (в + *acc.*); *k. off*, сбивáть *imp.*, сбить (собью́, -ьёшь) *perf.*; (*leave work*) прекращáть *imp.*, прекрати́ть (-ащý, -ати́шь) *perf.*

(рабóту), *k. out*, выбивáть *imp.*, вы́бить (-бью, -бьешь) *perf.*; (*sport*) нокаути́ровать *imp.*, *perf.*; *k.-out*, нокáут. **knocker** *n.* (*door-k.*) двернóй молотóк (-ткá).

knoll *n.* бугóр (-грá).

knot *n.* ýзел (узлá) (*also fig.*, *naut.*); (*hard lump*) нарóст; (*in wood*) сучóк (-чкá); (*group*) кýчка; *v.t.* завя́зывать *imp.*, завязáть (-яжý, -я́жешь) *perf.* узлóм. **knotty** *adj.* узловáтый; (*fig.*) запýтанный (-ан, -анна).

knout *n.* кнут (-á).

know *v.t.* знать *imp.*; (*k. how to*) умéть *imp.*, с~ *perf.*; (*be acquainted*) быть знакóмым с + *instr.*; (*recognize*) узнавáть (-наю́, -наёшь) *imp.*, узнáть *perf.*; *k.-all*, всезнáйка *m. & f.*; *k.-how*, умéние. **knowing** *adj.* (*cunning*) хи́трый (-тёр, -трá, хи́трó). **knowingly** *adv.* сознáтельно. **knowledge** *n.* знáние, познáния (-ний) *pl.*; (*familiarity*) знакóмство (of, с + *instr.*); (*sum of what is known*) наýка; *to my k.*, наскóлько мне извéстно.

knuckle *n.* сустáв пáльца; (*cul.*) нóжка; *v.i.*: *k. down to*, реши́тельно брáться (берýсь, -рёшься; брáлся, -лáсь) *imp.*, взя́ться (возьмýсь, -мёшься; взя́лся, -лáсь) *perf.* за + *acc.*; *k. under*, подчиня́ться *imp.*, подчини́ться *perf.* (to, + *dat.*).

ko(w)tow *n.* ни́зкий поклóн; *v.i.* ни́зко кла́няться *imp.*, поклони́ться (-ню́сь, -ни́шься) *perf.*; (*fig.*) раболéпствовать *imp.* (to, пéред + *instr.*).

Kremlin *n.* Кремль (-ля́) *m.*

kudos *n.* слáва.

L

label *n.* этикéтка; (*also fig.*) ярлы́к (-á); *v.t.* прикле́ивать *imp.*, прикле́ить *perf.* ярлы́к к + *dat.*

labial *adj.* (*n.*) губнóй (звук).

laboratory *n.* лаборатóрия; *l. assistant, technician*, лаборáнт, ~ ка.

laborious *adj.* (*arduous*) трýдный (-ден, -днá, -дно, трýдны); (*industrious*) трудолюби́вый; (*of style*) вы́мученный (-ен).

labour *n.* труд (-á), рабóта; (*workers*) рабóчие *sb.*; (*task*) задáча; (*childbirth*) ро́ды (-дов) *pl.*; *attrib.* трудово́й, рабо́чий; *l. exchange*, би́ржа труда́; *l. force*, рабо́чая си́ла; *l.-intensive*, трудоёмкий; *l. pains*, родовы́е схва́тки *f.pl.*; *L. Party*, лейбори́стская па́ртия; *v.i.* труди́ться *imp.*; работа́ть *imp.*; *v.t.* (*elaborate*) подро́бно разраба́тывать *imp.*, разрабо́тать *perf.* **laboured** *adj.* затруднённый (-ён, -ённа); (*style*) вы́мученный (-ен, -енна). **labourer** *n.* чернорабо́чий *sb.* **labourite** *n.* лейбори́ст.

laburnum *n.* раки́тник-золото́й дождь (-дя́) *m.*

labyrinth *n.* лабири́нт.

lace *n.* (*fabric*) кру́жево; (*cord*) шнур (-а́), шнуро́к (-рка́); *v.t.* (*l. up*) шнурова́ть *imp.*, за~ *perf.*

lacerate *v.t.* рвать (рву, рвёшь; рвал, -а́, -о) *imp.*; (*fig.*) раздира́ть *imp.* **laceration** *n.* (*wound*) рва́ная ра́на.

lachrymose *adj.* слезли́вый.

lack *n.* недоста́ток (-тка) (*of* + *gen.*, в + *prep.*), отсу́тствие; *v.t.* испы́тывать *imp.*, испыта́ть *perf.* недоста́ток в + *prep.*; недостава́ть (-таёт) *imp.*, недоста́ть (-а́нет) *perf.impers.* + *dat.* (*person*), + *gen.* (*object*).

lackadaisical *adj.* (*languid*) то́мный (-мен, -мна́, -мно); (*affected*) жема́нный (-нен, -нна).

lackey *n.* лаке́й.

lack-lustre *adj.* ту́склый (-л, -ла́, -ло).

laconic *adj.* лакони́чный, чески́й.

lacquer *n.* лак; *v.t.* лакирова́ть *imp.*, от~ *perf.*

lactic *adj.* моло́чный.

lacuna *n.* пробе́л.

lad *n.* па́рень (-рня; *pl.* -рни, -рне́й) *m.*

ladder *n.* ле́стница; (*naut.*) трап.

laden *adj.* нагру́женный (-ён, -ена́) (*fig.*) обременённый (-ён, -ена́).

ladle *n.* (*spoon*) поло́вник; (*for metal*) ковш (-а́); *v.t.* че́рпать *imp.*, черпну́ть *perf.*

lady *n.* да́ма, ле́ди *f.indecl.* **ladybird** *n.* бо́жья коро́вка.

lag[1] *v.i.*: *l. behind*, отстава́ть (-таю́, -таёшь) *imp.*, отста́ть (-а́ну, -а́нешь) *perf.* (от + *gen.*).

lag[2] *n.* (*convict*) ка́торжник.

lag[3] *v.t.* (*insulate*) покрыва́ть *imp.*, покры́ть (-ро́ю, -ро́ешь) *perf.* изоля́цией. **lagging** *n.* теплова́я изоля́ция.

lagoon *n.* лагу́на.

lair *n.* ло́говище, берло́га.

laity *n.* (*in religion*) миря́не (-н) *pl.*; (*in profession*) профа́ны (-нов) *pl.*

lake *n.* о́зеро (*pl.* озёра); *attrib.* озёрный.

lamb *n.* ягнёнок (-нка; *pl.* ягня́та, -я́т); (*eccl.*) а́гнец (-нца); *v.i.* ягни́ться *imp.*, о~ *perf.*

lame *adj.* хромо́й (хром, -а́, -о); (*fig.*) неубеди́тельный; *be l.*, хрома́ть *imp.*; *go l.*, хроме́ть *imp.*, о~ *perf.*; *v.t.* кале́чить *imp.*, о~ *perf.* **lameness** *n.* хромота́.

lament *n.* плач; *v.t.* опла́кивать *imp.*, опла́кать (-а́чу, -а́чешь) *perf.* **lamentable** *adj.* приско́рбный.

lamina *n.* то́нкая пласти́нка, то́нкий слой (*pl.* -о́и). **laminated** *adj.* листово́й, пласти́нчатый.

lamp *n.* ла́мпа, фона́рь (-ря́) *m.* **lamp-post** *n.* фона́рный столб (-а́). **lamp-shade** *n.* абажу́р.

lampoon *n.* па́сквиль *m.*

lamprey *n.* мино́га.

lance *n.* пи́ка, копьё (*pl.* -пья, -пий, -пьям); (*fish-spear*) острога́; *l.-corporal*, ефре́йтор; *v.t.* пронза́ть *imp.*, пронзи́ть *perf.* пи́кой, копьём; (*med.*) вскрыва́ть *imp.*, вскрыть (-ро́ю, -ро́ешь) *perf.* (ланце́том). **lancer** *n.* ула́н (*pl.* -нов & -н (*collect.*)). **lancet** *n.* ланце́т.

land *n.* земля́ (*acc.* -млю; *pl.* -мли, -ме́ль, -млям); (*dry l.*) су́ша; (*country*) страна́ (*pl.* -ны); (*soil*) по́чва; (*estates*) поме́стья (-тий) *pl.*; *v.t.* (*unload*) выгружа́ть *imp.*, вы́грузить *perf.*; *v.t. & i.* (*persons*) выса́живать(ся) *imp.*, вы́садить(ся) *perf.*; (*aeron.*) приземля́ть(ся) *imp.*, приземли́ть(ся) *perf.* **landfall** *n.* подхо́д к бе́регу. **landing** *n.* вы́садка; (*aeron.*) поса́дка; (*mil.*) деса́нт; (*on stairs*) ле́стничная площа́дка; *l.-stage*, при́стань (*pl.* -ни, -не́й). **landlady** *n.* домовладе́лица, хозя́йка. **landlord** *n.* землевладе́лец (-льца); (*of house*) домовладе́лец (-льца); (*of inn*) хозя́ин (*pl.* -я́ева,

-я́ев). **landmark** n. (boundary stone; fig.) ве́ха; (conspicuous object) ориенти́р. **landowner** n. землевладе́лец (-льца). **landscape** n. ландша́фт; (also picture) пейза́ж; l.-painter, пейзажи́ст. **landslide, landslip** n. о́ползень (-зня) m.

landau n. ландо́ neut.indecl.

lane n. у́зкая доро́га; (street) переу́лок (-лка); (passage) прохо́д; (on road) ряд (-á with 2, 3, 4, loc. -ý; pl. -ы́); (in race) доро́жка; (for ships) морско́й путь (-ти́, -тём) m.; (for aircraft) тра́сса полёта.

language n. язы́к (-á); (style, form of speech) речь.

languid adj. то́мный (-мен, -мна́, -мно).

languish v.i. (pine) томи́ться imp.

languor n. томле́ние, то́мность; (fatigue) уста́лость. **languorous** adj. то́мный (-мен, -мна́, -мно), уста́лый.

lank adj. (person) худоща́вый; (hair) гла́дкий (-док, -дка́, -дко). **lanky** adj. долговя́зый.

lantern n. фона́рь (-ря́) m.

lanyard n. (naut.) тро́совый та́лреп; (cord) шнур (-á).

lap[1] n. (flap; of skirt) пола́ (pl. -лы); (ear-lobe) мо́чка; (of person) коле́ни (-ней) pl.; (racing) круг (pl. -и́).

lap[2] v.t. (drink) лака́ть imp., вы~ perf.; v.i. (water) плеска́ться (-е́щется) imp.

lapel n. отворо́т, ла́цкан.

lapidary n. грани́льщик; adj. грани́льный; (fig.) сжа́тый.

lapis lazuli n. ля́пис-лазу́рь.

lapse n. (mistake) оши́бка; (of pen) опи́ска; (of memory) прова́л па́мяти; (decline) паде́ние; (expiry) истече́ние; (of time) тече́ние, ход вре́мени; v.i. впада́ть imp., впасть (-аду́, -адёшь; -ал) perf. (into, в + acc.); (expire) истека́ть imp., исте́чь (-ечёт; -ёк, -екла́) perf.

lapwing n. чи́бис.

larceny n. воровство́.

larch n. ли́ственница.

lard n. свино́е са́ло; v.t. (cul.) шпигова́ть imp., на~ perf.; (fig.) уснаща́ть imp., уснасти́ть perf. (with, + instr.).

larder n. кладова́я sb.

large adj. большо́й, кру́пный (-пен, -пна́, -пно, кру́пны́); (wide, broad) широ́кий (-о́к, -ока́, -о́ко́); n.: at l. (free) на свобо́де; (in detail) подро́бно; (as a whole) целико́м. **largely** adv. (to a great extent) в значи́тельной сте́пени.

largess(e) n. ще́дрость.

lark[1] n. (bird) жа́воронок (-нка).

lark[2] n. шу́тка, прока́за; v.i. (about) резви́ться imp.

larva n. личи́нка. **larval** adj. личи́ночный.

laryngeal adj. горта́нный. **laryngitis** n. лангри́т. **larynx** n. горта́нь.

lascivious adj. похотли́вый.

laser n. ла́зер.

lash n. плеть (pl. -ти, -те́й), бич (-á); (blow) уда́р плётью, бичо́м; (eyelash) ресни́ца; v.t. (beat) хлеста́ть (хлещу́, -щешь), хлестну́ть perf.; (with words) бичева́ть (-чу́ю, -чу́ешь) imp.; (fasten) привя́зывать imp., привяза́ть (-яжу́, -я́жешь) perf. (to, к + dat.); l. together, свя́зывать imp., связа́ть (-яжу́, -я́жешь) perf.

lass n. де́вушка, де́вочка.

lassitude n. уста́лость.

lasso n. лассо́ neut.indecl.; v.t. лови́ть (-влю́, -вишь) imp., пойма́ть perf. лассо́.

last[1] n. (cobbler's) коло́дка.

last[2] adj. (final) после́дний; (most recent) про́шлый; (extreme) кра́йний; the year (etc.) before l., позапро́шлый год (и т.д.); l. but one, предпосле́дний; l. but two, тре́тий (-тья, -тье) с конца́; l. night, вчера́ ве́чером, но́чью; n. (l.-mentioned) после́дний sb.; (end) коне́ц (-нца́); at l., наконе́ц, в конце́ концо́в; adv. (after all others) по́сле всех; (on last occasion) в после́дний раз; (in last place) в конце́.

last[3] v.i. (go on) продолжа́ться imp., продо́лжиться perf.; дли́ться imp., про~ perf.; (food, health) сохраня́ться imp., сохрани́ться perf.; (suffice) хвата́ть imp., хвати́ть (-ит) perf.

lasting adj. (enduring) дли́тельный; (permanent) постоя́нный (-нен, -нна); (durable) про́чный (-чен, -чна́, -чно, про́чны).

lastly adj. в конце́, в заключе́ние, наконе́ц.

latch n. щеко́лда.

late adj. по́здний; (recent) неда́вний; (dead) поко́йный; (former) бы́вший; be l. for, опа́здывать imp., опозда́ть perf. на + acc.; adv. по́здно; n.: of l., неда́вно, за после́днее вре́мя.

latent adj. скры́тый.

lateral adj. боково́й. **laterally** adv. (from side) сбо́ку; (towards side) вбок.

latex n. мле́чный сок (-а(у)), loc. -е & -у́); (synthetic) ла́текс.

lath n. ре́йка, дра́нка (also collect.).

lathe n. тока́рный стано́к (-нка́).

lather n. (мыльная пе́на; (of horse) мы́ло; v.t. & i. мы́лить(ся) imp., на ~ perf.; (of horse) взмы́ливаться imp., взмы́литься perf.

Latin adj. лати́нский; (Romance) рома́нский; n. лати́нский язы́к (-а́); (when qualified) латы́нь; L.-American, латиноамерика́нский.

latitude n. свобо́да; (geog.) широта́.

latrine n. убо́рная sb.; (esp. in camp) отхо́жее ме́сто (pl. -та́).

latter adj. после́дний; l.-day, совреме́нный. **latterly** adv. (towards end) к концу́; (of late) неда́вно.

lattice n. решётка. **latticed** adj. решётчатый.

laud n. хвала́; v.t. хвали́ть (-лю́, -лишь) imp., по ~ perf. **laudable** adj. похва́льный. **laudatory** adj. хвале́бный.

laugh n. смех (-а(у)), хо́хот; v.i. смея́ться (-ею́сь, -еёшься) imp. (at, над + instr.); l. it off, отшу́чиваться imp., отшути́ться (-учу́сь, -у́тишься) perf.; laughing-stock, посме́шище. **laughable** adj. смешно́й (-шо́н, -шна́). **laughter** n. смех (-а(у)), хо́хот.

launch[1] v.t. броса́ть imp., бро́сить perf.; (ship) спуска́ть imp., спусти́ть (-ущу́, -у́стишь) perf. на́ воду; (rocket) запуска́ть imp., запусти́ть (-ущу́, -у́стишь) perf.; (undertake) предпринима́ть imp., предприня́ть (-ниму́, -ни́мешь; предпри́нял, -а́, -о) perf.; n. спуск на́ воду; за́пуск. **launcher** n. (for rocket) пусково́е установка. **launching pad** n. пускова́я площа́дка.

launch[2] n. (naut.) барка́с; (motor-l.) мото́рный ка́тер (pl. -а́).

launder v.t. стира́ть imp., вы́ ~ perf. **laund(e)rette** n. пра́чечная sb. самообслу́живания. **laundress** n. пра́чка. **laundry** n. (place) пра́чечная sb.; (articles) бельё.

laurel n. ла́вр(овое де́рево); (ornamental plant, Japanese l.) золото́е де́рево (pl. -е́вья, -е́вьев); pl. ла́вры m.pl., по́чести f.pl.

lava n. ла́ва.

lavatory n. убо́рная sb.

lavender n. лава́нда.

lavish adj. ще́дрый (щедр, -а́, -о); (abundant) оби́льный; v.t. расточа́ть imp. (upon, + dat.).

law n. зако́н, пра́во; (jurisprudence) юриспруде́нция; (rule) пра́вило; l. and order, правопоря́док (-дка). **law-court** n. суд (-а́). **lawful** adj. зако́нный (-нен, -нна). **lawgiver** n. законода́тель m. **lawless** adj. беззако́нный (-нен, -нна).

lawn[1] n. (fabric) бати́ст.

lawn[2] n. (grass) газо́н; l.-mower, газонокоси́лка.

lawsuit n. проце́сс.

lawyer n. адвока́т, юри́ст.

lax adj. (loose) сла́бый (слаб, -а́, -о); (careless) небре́жный; (not strict) нестро́гий. **laxity** n. сла́бость; небре́жность; (moral l.) распу́щенность. **laxative** adj. слаби́тельный; n. слаби́тельное sb.

lay[1] n. пе́сенка, балла́да.

lay[2] adj. (non-clerical) све́тский; (non-professional) непрофессиона́льный.

lay[3] n. (position) положе́ние; v.t. (place) класть (кладу́, -дёшь; клал) imp., положи́ть (-жу́, -жишь) perf.; (impose) налага́ть imp., наложи́ть (-жу́, -жишь) perf.; (present) излага́ть imp., изложи́ть (-жу́, -жишь) perf.; (trap etc.) устра́ивать imp., устро́ить perf.; (crops, dust) прибива́ть imp., приби́ть (-бью́, -бьёшь) perf.; (calm) успока́ивать imp., успоко́ить perf.; (ghost) изгоня́ть imp., изгна́ть (изгоню́, -нишь; изгна́л, -а́ -о) perf.; (meal) накрыва́ть imp., накры́ть (-ро́ю, -ро́ешь) perf. стол к + dat.; (eggs) класть (-аде́т; -ал) imp., положи́ть (-и́т) perf.; v.abs. (lay eggs) нести́сь (несётся; нёсся, несла́сь) *imp.*, с ~ *perf.*; *l. bare, open,* раскрыва́ть *imp.*, раскры́ть (-ро́ю, -ро́ешь) *perf.*; *l. a bet, wager.* держа́ть (-жу, -жишь) *imp.* пари́ (on, на + *acc.*); *l. claim to,* име́ть *imp.* прете́нзию на + *acc.*; *l. hands on, (seize)* завладева́ть *imp.*, завладе́ть *perf.* + *instr.*; *l. siege to,* осажда́ть *imp.*, осади́ть *perf.*; *l. table,* накрыва́ть *imp.*, накры́ть (-ро́ю, -ро́ешь) *perf.* стол (for *meal*), к + *dat.*); *l. waste,* опустоша́ть *imp.*, опустоши́ть *perf.*; *l. aside, (put a)* откла́дывать *imp.*, отложи́ть (-жу, -жишь) *perf.*; *(save)* прибере́чь (-егу́, -ежёшь; -ёг, -егла́) *perf.*; *l. down, (relinquish)* отка́зываться *imp.*, отказа́ться (-ажу́сь, -а́жешься) *perf.* от + *gen.*; *(formulate)* составля́ть *imp.*, соста́вить *perf.* *(rule etc.)* устана́вливать *imp.*, установи́ть (-влю́, -вишь) *perf.*; *(ship etc.)* закла́дывать *imp.*, заложи́ть (-жу, -жишь) *perf.*; *l. down one's arms,* скла́дывать *imp.*, слага́ть *imp.*, сложи́ть (-жу, -жишь) *perf.* ору́жие; *l. down one's life,* положи́ть (-жу, -жишь) *perf.* жизнь (for, за + *acc.*); *l. in (stock of),* запаса́ть *imp.*, запасти́ (-су́, -сёшь; с ~, -сла́) *perf.* + *acc.*, + *gen.*; *l. off, (workmen)* временно увольня́ть *imp.*, уво́лить *perf.*; *l. out, (spread)* выкла́дывать *imp.*, вы́ложить *perf.*; *(arrange)* разбива́ть *imp.*, разби́ть (разобью́, -ьёшь) *perf.*; *(expend)* тра́тить *imp.*, ис ~, по ~ *perf.*; *l. up,* запаса́ть *imp.*, запасти́ (-су́, -сёшь; -с, -сла́) *perf.* + *acc.*, + *gen.*; *be laid up,* быть прико́ванным к посте́ли, к до́му. **layabout** *n.* безде́льник.

layer *n.* слой (*pl.* -ои), пласт (-á, *loc.* -ý); *(hort.)* отво́док (-дка) (*hen*) несу́шка.

layman *n.* миря́нин (*pl.* -я́не, -я́н) *(non-expert)* неспециали́ст.

laze *v.i.* безде́льничать *imp.* **laziness** *n.* лень. **lazy** *adj.* лени́вый; *l.-bones,* лентя́й, ~ка.

lea *n.* луг (*loc.* -ý; *pl.* -á).

lead[1] *n.* *(example)* приме́р; *(leadership)* руково́дство; *(position)* пе́рвое ме́сто; *(theat.)* гла́вная роль (*pl.* -ли, -ле́й)

(cards) пе́рвый ход; *(electr.)* про́вод (*pl.* -á); *(dog's)* поводо́к (-дка́); *v.t.* води́ть (вожу́, во́дишь) *indet.*, вести́ (веду́, -дёшь; вёл, -á) *det.*; *(guide)* руководи́ть *imp.* + *instr.*; *(army)* кома́ндовать *imp.*, с ~ *perf.* + *instr.*; *(induce)* заставля́ть *imp.*, заста́вить *perf.*; *v.t. & i. (cards)* ходи́ть (хожу́, хо́дишь) *imp.* (с + *gen.*); *v.i. (sport)* занима́ть *imp.*, заня́ть (займу́, -мёшь; за́нял, -á, -о) *perf.* пе́рвое ме́сто; *l. astray,* сбива́ть *imp.*, сбить (собью́, -ьёшь) *perf.* с пути́; *l. away,* уводи́ть (-ожу́, -о́дишь) *imp.*, увести́ (-еду́, -едёшь; увёл, -á) *perf.*; *l. on,* увлека́ть *imp.*, увле́чь (-еку́, -ечёшь; -ёк, -екла́) *perf.*; *l. to, (result in)* приводи́ть (-ит) *imp.*, привести́ (-едёт; -ёл, -ела́) *perf.* к + *dat.*

lead[2] *n.* *(metal)* свине́ц (-нца́) *(naut.)* лот; *(print.)* шпон(a). **leaden** *adj.* свинцо́вый.

leader *n.* руководи́тель *m.*, ~ница, ли́дер, вождь (-дя́) *m.*; *(mus.)* конце́ртмейстер; *(editorial)* передова́я статья́. **leadership** *n.* руково́дство; *under the l. of,* во главе́ с + *instr.*

leading *adj.* веду́щий, выдаю́щийся; *l. article,* передова́я статья́.

leaf *n.* лист (*pl.* (*plant*) -ья, -ьев & (*paper*) -ы, -о́в); *(of door)* ство́рка; *(of table)* опускна́я доска́ (*acc.* -ску; *pl.* -ски, -со́к, -ска́м); *l.-mould,* листово́й перегно́й; *v.i.: l. through,* перели́стывать *imp.*, перелиста́ть *perf.* **leaflet** *n.* листо́вка. **leafy** *adj.* покры́тый ли́стьями.

league *n.* ли́га, сою́з; *(sport)* класс.

leak *n.* течь, уте́чка; *spring a l.,* (даёт) *imp.*, дать (даст; дал, -á, да́ло́, -и) *perf.* течь; *v.i. (escape)* течь (чёт; тёк, -ла́) *imp.*; *(allow water to l.)* пропуска́ть *imp.* во́ду; *l. out,* проса́чиваться *imp.*, просочи́ться *perf.*

lean[1] *adj.* *(thin)* худо́й (худ, -á, -о); *(meat)* по́стный (-тен, -тна́, -тно) *(meagre)* ску́дный (-ден, -дна́, -дно).

lean[2] *v.t. & i.* прислоня́ть(ся) *imp.*, прислони́ть(ся) (-оню́(сь), -о́ни́шь(ся)) *perf. (against,* к + *dat.*); *l. on, rely on)* опира́ться *imp.*, опере́ться (обопру́сь, -рёшься; опёрся, опёрла́сь) *perf.* (оп, на + *acc.*); (*be inclined*) быть скло́нным (-о́нен, -о́нна, -о́нно) (to(wards)), к + *dat.*); l. back, откидываться *imp.*, откинуться *perf.*; l. out of, высовываться *imp.*, высунуться *perf.* в + *acc.* leaning *n.* скло́нность.

leap *n.* прыжо́к (-жка́), скачо́к (-чка́); *v.i.* пры́гать *imp.*, пры́гнуть *perf.*; скака́ть (-ачу́, -а́чешь) *imp.* (*l. over*) перепры́гивать *imp.*, перепры́гнуть *perf.*; l.-frog, чехарда́; l. year, високо́сный год (*loc.* -у́; *pl.* -ы & -а́, -о́в).

learn *v.t.* учи́ться (учу́сь, у́чишься) *imp.*, об ~ *perf.*; (*find out*) узнава́ть (-наю́, -наёшь) *imp.*, узна́ть *perf.* learned *adj.* учёный. learner *n.* уча́щийся *sb.*, учени́к (-а́), -и́ца. learning *n.* (*studies*) уче́ние; (*erudition*) учёность.

lease *n.* аре́нда; *v.t.* (*of owner*) сдава́ть (сдаю́, сдаёшь) *imp.*, сдать (-ам, -ашь -аст, -адим; сдал, -а́, -о) *perf.* в аре́нду; (*of tenant*) брать (беру́, -рёшь; брал, -а́, -о) *imp.*, взять (возьму́, -мёшь; взял, -а́, -о) *perf.* в аре́нду. leaseholder *n.* аренда́тор.

leash *n.* сво́ра, при́вязь.

least *adj.* наиме́ньший, мале́йший; *adv.* ме́нее всего́; at l., по кра́йней ме́ре; not in the l., ничу́ть.

leather *n.* ко́жа; *attrib.* ко́жаный.

leave[1] *n.* (*permission*) разреше́ние; (l. of absence) о́тпуск (*loc.* -е & -у́); on l., в о́тпуске, -ку́; take (one's) l., проща́ться *imp.*, прости́ться *perf.* (of, с + *instr.*).

leave[2] *v.t.* & *i.* оставля́ть *imp.*, оста́вить *perf.*; (*abandon*) покида́ть *imp.*, поки́нуть *perf.*; (*go away*) уходи́ть (-ожу́, -о́дишь) *imp.*, уйти́ (уйду́, -дёшь; ушёл, ушла́) *perf.* (from, от + *gen.*); уезжа́ть *imp.*, уе́хать (уе́ду, -дешь) *perf.* from, от + *gen.*); (*entrust*) предоставля́ть *imp.*, предоста́вить *perf.* (to, + *dat.*); l. out, пропуска́ть *imp.*, пропусти́ть (-ущу́, -у́стишь) *perf.*

leaven *n.* (*yeast*) дро́жжи (-же́й) *pl.*; заква́ска; *v.t.* ста́вить *imp.*, по ~ *perf.* на дрожжа́х; заква́шивать *imp.*, заква́сить *perf.*

leavings *n.* оста́тки *m.pl.*; (*food*) объе́дки (-ков) *pl.*

lecherous *adj.* распу́тный.

lectern *n.* анало́й.

lecture *n.* (*discourse*) ле́кция; (*reproof*) нота́ция; *v.i.* (*deliver l.(s*)) чита́ть *imp.*, про ~ *perf.* ле́кцию (-ии) (on, по + *dat.*); *v.t.* (*admonish*) чита́ть *imp.*, про ~ *perf.* нота́цию + *dat.*; l. room, аудито́рия. lecturer *n.* ле́ктор; (*univ.*) преподава́тель *m.*, -ница.

ledge *n.* вы́ступ; (*under water*) риф.

ledger *n.* гла́вная кни́га, гроссбу́х.

lee *n.* защи́та; l. side, подве́тренная сторона́ (*acc.* -ону) l. shore, подве́тренный бе́рег (*loc.* -у́).

leech[1] *n.* (*doctor*) ле́карь (*pl.* -ри, -ре́й) *m.*

leech[2] *n.* (*worm*) пия́вка; (*person*) вымога́тель *m.*

leek *n.* лук-поре́й.

leer *v.i.* смотре́ть (-рю́, -ришь) *imp.*, по ~ *perf.* и́скоса (at, на + *acc.*).

lees *n.* оса́док (-дка), подо́нки (-ков) *pl.*

leeward *n.* подве́тренная сторона́ (*acc.* -ону); *adj.* подве́тренный.

leeway *n.* (*naut.*) дрейф.

left *n.* ле́вая сторона́ (*acc.* -ону); (L.; *polit.*) ле́вые *sb.*; *adj.* ле́вый; *adv.* нале́во, сле́ва (of, от + *gen.*); l.-hander, левша́ *m.* & *f.*

left-luggage office *n.* ка́мера хране́ния.

left-overs *n.* оста́тки *m.pl.*; (*food*) объе́дки (-ков) *pl.*

leg *n.* нога́ (*acc.* -гу; *pl.* -ги, -г, -га́м); (*furniture etc.*) но́жка; (*support*) подста́вка; (*stage of journey etc.*) эта́п; pull someone's l., моро́чить *imp.* го́лову + *dat.*

legacy *n.* насле́дство.

legal *adj.* (*of the law*) правово́й; (*lawful*) зако́нный; l. adviser юриско́нсульт. legality *n.* зако́нность. legalize *v.t.* узако́нивать *imp.*, узако́нить *perf.*

legate *n.* лега́т.

legatee *n.* насле́дник.

legation *n.* (*diplomatic*) ми́ссия.

legend *n.* леге́нда. legendary *adj.* легенда́рный.

leggings *n.* гама́ши *f.pl.*

legible *adj.* разбо́рчивый.

legion *n.* легио́н; (*great number*) мно́жество. legionary *n.* легионе́р.

legislate v.i. издава́ть (-даю́, -даёшь) imp., изда́ть (-а́м, -а́шь, -а́ст, -ади́м; изда́л, -а́, -о) perf. зако́ны. **legislation** n. законода́тельство. **legislative** adj. законода́тельный. **legislator** n. законода́тель m.

legitimacy n. зако́нность; (of child) законнорождённость. **legitimate** adj. зако́нный (-нен, -нна); (child) законнорождённый (-ён, -ённа). **legitimize** v.t. узако́нивать imp., узако́нить perf.

leguminous adj. бобо́вый, стручко́вый.

leisure n. досу́г; at l., на досу́ге. **leisurely** adj. неторопли́вый; adv. не спеша́.

leitmotiv n. лейтмоти́в.

lemon n. лимо́н; attrib. лимо́нный. **lemonade** n. лимона́д.

lend v.t. дава́ть (даю́, даёшь) imp., дать (дам, дашь, даст, дади́м; дал, -а́, да́ло́, -и) perf. взаймы́ (то, + dat.); ода́лживать imp., одолжи́ть (то, + dat.).

length n. длина́, расстоя́ние; (duration) продолжи́тельность; (of cloth) отре́з; at l., (at last) наконе́ц; (in detail) подро́бно. **lengthen** v.t. & i. удлиня́ть(ся) imp., удлини́ть(ся) perf. **lengthways, -wise** adv. в длину́, вдоль. **lengthy** adj. дли́нный (-нен, -нна́, дли́нно́).

lenience, -cy n. снисходи́тельность. **lenient** adj. снисходи́тельный.

lens n. ли́нза; (anat.) хруста́лик гла́за.

Lent n. вели́кий пост (-а́, loc. -у́). **Lenten** adj. великопо́стный; (food) по́стный (-тен, -тна́, -тно).

lentil n. чечеви́ца.

Leo n. Лев (Льва).

leonine adj. льви́ный.

leopard n. леопа́рд.

leper n. прокажённый sb. **leprosy** n. прока́за.

lesion n. поврежде́ние; (med.) пораже́ние.

less adj. ме́ньший; adv. ме́ньше, ме́нее; prep. без + gen., за вы́четом + gen.

lessee n. аренда́тор.

lessen v.t. & i. уменьша́ть(ся) imp., уме́ньшить(ся) perf.

lesser adj. ме́ньший.

lesson n. уро́к.

lest conj. (in order that not) что́бы не; (that) как бы не.

let[1] n. (hindrance) поме́ха.

let[2] n. (lease) сда́ча в наём; v.t. (allow) позволя́ть imp., позво́лить perf. + dat.; разреша́ть imp., разреши́ть perf. + dat.; (allow to escape) пуска́ть imp., пусти́ть (пущу́, пу́стишь) perf.; (rent out) слава́ть (сдаю́, -аёшь) imp., сдать (-ам, -ашь, -аст, -ади́м; сдал, -а́, -о) perf. внаём (то, + dat.); v.aux. (imperative) (1st person) дава́й(те); (3rd person) пусть; (assumption) допу́стим; l. alone, оставля́ть imp., оста́вить perf. в поко́е; (in imperative) не говоря́ уже́ о + prep.; l. down, (lower) опуска́ть imp., опусти́ть (-ущу́, -у́стишь) perf.; (fail) подводи́ть (-ожу́, -о́дишь) imp., подвести́ (-еду́, -едёшь; -ёл, -ела́) perf.; (disappoint) разоча́ровывать imp., разочарова́ть perf.; l. go, выпуска́ть imp., вы́пустить perf.; let's go, пойдёмте! пошли́! поёхали! l. in(to), (admit) впуска́ть imp., впусти́ть (-ущу́, -у́стишь) perf. в + acc.; (into secret) посвяща́ть imp., посвяти́ть (-ящу́, -яти́шь) perf. в + acc.; l. know, дава́ть (даю́, даёшь) imp., дать (дам, дашь, даст, дади́м; дал, -а́, да́ло́, -и) perf. знать + dat.; l. off, (gun) выстрелить perf. из + gen.; (not punish) отпуска́ть imp., отпусти́ть (-ущу́, -у́стишь) perf. без наказа́ния; l. out, (release, loosen) выпуска́ть imp., вы́пустить perf.

lethal adj. смертоно́сный.

lethargic adj. летарги́ческий; (inert) вя́лый. **lethargy** n. летарги́я; вя́лость.

letter n. (symbol) бу́ква; (print) ли́тера (missive) письмо́ (pl. -сьма, -сем, -сьмам); pl. (literature) литерату́ра; pl. (erudition) учёность; to the l., буква́льно; l.-box, почто́вый я́щик.

lettuce n. сала́т.

leukaemia n. лейкеми́я.

level n. у́ровень (-вня) m.; (spirit-l.) ватерпа́с; (surveyor's) нивели́р; (flat country) равни́на; adj. горизонта́льный, ро́вный (-вен, -вна́, -вно); l. crossing, (железнодоро́жный) перее́зд; l.-headed, уравнове́шенный (-ен, -енна); v.t. (make l.) выра́внивать *imp.*, вы́ровнять *perf.*; (*make equal*) ура́внивать *imp.*, уравня́ть *perf.*; (*raze*) ровня́ть *imp.*, с~ *perf.* с землёй; (*gun*) наводи́ть (-ожу́, -о́дишь) *imp.*, навести́ (-еду́, -едёшь; -ёл, -ела́) *perf.* (at, в, на, + *acc.*); (*criticism*) направля́ть *imp.*, напра́вить *perf.* (at, про́тив + *gen.*); (*surveying*) нивели́ровать *imp.*, *perf.*

lever *n.* рыча́г (-а́). **leverage** *n.* де́йствие рычага́; (*influence*) влия́ние.

leveret *n.* зайчо́нок (-чонка; *pl.* -ча́та, -ча́т).

levity *n.* легкомы́слие.

levy *n.* (*tax*) сбор; (*mil.*) набо́р; *v.t.* (*tax*) взима́ть *imp.* (from, с + *gen.*); (*mil.*) набира́ть *imp.*, набра́ть (наберу́, -рёшь; набра́л, -а́, -о) *perf.*

lewd *adj.* (*lascivious*) похотли́вый; (*indecent*) непристо́йный.

lexicographer *n.* лексико́граф. **lexicography** *n.* лексикогра́фия.

lexicon *n.* слова́рь (-ря́) *m.*

liability *n.* (*responsibility*) отве́тственность (for, за + *acc.*); (*obligation*) обяза́тельство; *pl.* (*debts*) долги́ *m.pl.*; (*susceptibility*) подве́рженность (to, + *dat.*). **liable** *adj.* отве́тственный (-ен, -енна) (for, за + *acc.*); обя́занный (-ан); подве́рженный (-ен) (to, + *dat.*).

liaison *n.* любо́вная связь; (*mil.*) связь (взаимоде́йствия); *l. officer*, офице́р свя́зи.

liar *n.* лгун (-а́), ~ья.

libation *n.* возлия́ние.

libel *n.* клевета́; *v.t.* клевета́ть (-ещу́, -е́щешь) на~ *perf.* на + *acc.* **libellous** *adj.* клеветни́ческий.

liberal *n.* либера́л; *adj.* либера́льный; (*generous*) ще́дрый (щедр, -а́, -о); (*abundant*) оби́льный.

liberate *v.t.* освобожда́ть *imp.*, освободи́ть *perf.* **liberation** *n.* освобожде́ние; *attrib.* освободи́тельный. **liberator** *n.* освободи́тель *m.*

libertine *n.* (*profligate*) распу́тник; (*free-thinker*) вольноду́мец (-мца).

liberty *n.* свобо́да, во́льность; *at l.*, на свобо́де.

libidinous *adj.* похотли́вый.

Libra *n.* Весы́ (-со́в) *pl.*

librarian *n.* библиоте́карь *m.* **library** *n.* библиоте́ка.

libretto *n.* либре́тто *neut.indecl.*

licence[1] *n.* (*permission, permit*) разреше́ние, пра́во (*pl.* -ва́), лице́нзия; (*liberty*) (изли́шняя) во́льность. **license**[2] *v.t.* (*allow*) разреша́ть *imp.*, разреши́ть *perf.* + *dat.*; дава́ть (даю́, даёшь) *imp.*, дать (дам, дашь, даст, дади́м; дал, -а́, да́ло́, -и) *perf.* пра́во + *dat.*

licentious *adj.* похотли́вый, распу́щенный.

lichen *n.* (*bot.*) лиша́йник; (*med.*) лиша́й (-а́я).

lick *n.* лиза́ние; *go at full l.*, нести́сь (несу́сь, -сёшься; нёсся, несла́сь) *det.*, по~ *perf.*; *v.t.* лиза́ть (лижу́, -жешь) *imp.*, лизну́ть *perf.*; (*l. all over*) обли́зывать *imp.*, облиза́ть (-ижу́, -и́жешь) *perf.*; (*thrash*) колоти́ть (-очу́, -о́тишь) *imp.*, по~ *perf.*; (*defeat*) побежда́ть *imp.*, победи́ть (-и́шь) *perf.* **lickspittle** *n.* подхали́м.

lid *n.* (*cover*) кры́шка; (*eyelid*) ве́ко (*pl.* -ки, -к).

lie[1] *n.* (*untruth*) ложь (лжи, *instr.* ло́жью); (*deceit*) обма́н; *v.i.* лгать (лгу, лжёшь; лгал, -а́, -о) *imp.*, со~ *perf.*

lie[2] *n.* (*position*) положе́ние; *l. of the land*, (*fig.*) положе́ние веще́й; *v.i.* лежа́ть (-жу́, -жи́шь) *imp.*; (*be situated*) находи́ться (-ожу́сь, -о́дишься) *imp.*; *l. down*, ложи́ться *imp.*, лечь (ля́гу, ля́жешь; лёг, -ла́) *perf.*; *l. in wait for*, подстерега́ть *imp.*, подстере́чь (-егу́, -ежёшь; -ёг, -егла́) *perf.* + *acc.*

lieu *n.*: *in l. of*, вме́сто + *gen.*

lieutenant *n.* лейтена́нт; *l.-colonel*, подполко́вник; *l.-general*, генера́л-лейтена́нт.

life *n.* жизнь; (*way of l.*) о́браз жи́зни; (*energy*) живо́сть; (*biography*) жизнеописа́ние; (*of inanimate object*) срок рабо́ты, слу́жбы; *for l.*, на всю жизнь; *from l.*, с нату́ры. **lifebelt** *n.* спаса́тельный по́яс (*pl.* -а́). **lifeboat** *n.* спаса́тельная шлю́пка. **lifebuoy** *n.* спаса́тельный буй (*pl.* буи́). **life-guard** *n.* (*bodyguard*) ли́чная охра́на. **Life-Guards** *n.* лейб-гва́рдия. **life-jacket** *n.*

спаса́тельный жиле́т. **lifeless** *adj.* безжи́зненный (-ен, -енна). **lifelike** *adj.* сло́вно живо́й (жив, -а́, -о). **lifelong** *adj.* пожи́зненный (-ен, -енна). **life-size(d)** *adj.* в натура́льную величину́. **lifetime** *n.* продолжи́тельность жи́зни.

lift *n.* подня́тие; (*machine*) лифт, подъёмная маши́на, подъёмник; (*force*) подъёмная си́ла; *give a l.*, подвезти́ (-озу́, -озёшь) *imp.*, подвезти́ (-езу́, -езёшь, -ёз, -езла́) *perf.*; *v.t. & i.* поднима́ть(ся) *imp.*, подня́ть(ся) (-ниму́(сь), -ни́мешь(ся); по́дня́л/подня́лся, -ла́(сь), -ло/-ло́сь) *perf.*; *v.t.* (*steal*) красть (краду́, -дёшь; крал) *imp.*, с~ *perf.*

ligament *n.* свя́зка.

ligature *n.* лигату́ра; (*mus.*) ли́га.

light *n.* свет, освеще́ние; (*source of l.*) ого́нь (огня́) *m.*, ла́мпа, фона́рь (-ря́) *m.*; *pl.* (*traffic l.*) светофо́р; *bring to l.*, выводи́ть (-ожу́, -о́дишь) *imp.*, вы́вести (-еду, -едешь; -ел) *perf.* на чи́стую во́ду; *come to l.*, обнару́живаться *imp.*, обнару́житься *perf.*; *shed l. on*, пролива́ть *imp.*, проли́ть (-лью, -льёшь; про́ли́л, -а́, -о) *perf.* свет на + *acc.*; *l. meter*, (*phot.*) экспоно́метр; *l.-year*, светово́й год (*pl.* го́ды, лет, года́м); *adj.* (*bright*) све́тлый (-тел, -тла́, -тло); (*pale*) бле́дный (-ден, -дна́, -дно, бле́дны́); *it is l. in the room*, в ко́мнате светло́; *v.t. & i.* (*ignite*) зажига́ть(ся) *imp.*, заже́чь(ся) (-жгу́(сь), -жжёшь(ся), -жёг(ся), -жгла́(сь)) *perf.*; (*give l. to*) освеща́ть *imp.*, освети́ть (-ещу́, -ети́шь) *perf.*; *l. up*, (*begin to smoke*) закури́ть (-рю́, -ришь) *perf.*

light *adj.* (*not heavy*) лёгкий (-гок, -гка́, -гко, лёгки́); (*unimportant*) незначи́тельный; (*nimble*) бы́стрый (быстр, -а́, -о, бы́стры); (*cheerful*) весёлый (ве́сел, -а́, -о, ве́селы); *l.-fingered*, на́ руку нечи́стый (-т, -та́, -то); *l.-headed*, (*frivolous*) легкомы́сленный (-ен, -енна); (*delirious*) *predic.* в бреду́; *l.-hearted*, беззабо́тный (-тен, -тна); *l. industry*, лёгкая промы́шленность; *l. infantry*, лёгкая пехо́та; *l.-minded*, легкомы́сленный (-ен, -енна).

light *v.i.*: *l. upon*, неожи́данно ната́лкиваться *imp.*, натолкну́ться *perf.* на + *acc.*

lighten *v.t. & i.* (*make lighter*) облегча́ть(ся) *imp.*, облегчи́ть(ся) *perf.*; *v.t.* (*mitigate*) смягча́ть *imp.*, смягчи́ть *perf.*

lighten *v.t.* (*illuminate*) освеща́ть *imp.*, освети́ть (-ещу́, -ети́шь) *perf.*; *v.i.* (*grow bright*) светле́ть *imp.*, по~ *perf.*; (*flash*) сверка́ть *imp.*, сверкну́ть *perf.*; *it lightens*, сверка́ет мо́лния.

lighter *n.* (*cigarette l. etc.*) зажига́лка.

lighter *n.* (*boat*) ли́хтер.

lighthouse *n.* мая́к (-а́).

lighting *n.* освеще́ние; (*lights*) освети́тельные устано́вки *f.pl.*

lightning *n.* мо́лния; *ball l.*, шарова́я мо́лния; *summer l.*, зарни́ца; *l.-conductor*, молниеотво́д.

lights *n.* (*cul.*) лёгкое *sb.*

lightship *n.* плаву́чий мая́к (-а́).

lightweight *n.* (*sport*) легкове́с; *adj.* легкове́сный.

ligneous *adj.* деревя́нный.

lignite *n.* лигни́т.

like *adj.* (*similar*) похо́жий (на + *acc.*), подо́бный; *what is he l.?* что он за челове́к? *n.*: *and the l.*, и тому́ подо́бное, и т.п.

like *v.t.* нра́виться *imp.*, по~ *perf.* *impers.* + *dat.*; люби́ть (-блю́, -бишь) *imp.*; (*wish for*) хоте́ть (хочу́, -чешь, хоти́м) *imp.*; *I should l.*, я хоте́л бы; *I would l.*, мне хо́чется; *as you l.*, как вам уго́дно. **likeable** *adj.* симпати́чный.

likelihood *n.* вероя́тность. **likely** *adj.* (*probable*) вероя́тный; (*suitable*) подходя́щий.

liken *v.t.* уподобля́ть *imp.*, уподо́бить *perf.* (to, + *dat.*).

likeness *n.* (*resemblance*) схо́дство; (*semblance*) вид; (*portrait*) портре́т.

likewise *adv.* (*similarly*) подо́бно; (*also*) то́же, та́кже.

liking *n.* вкус (for, к + *dat.*).

lilac *n.* сире́нь; *adj.* сире́невый.

lily *n.* ли́лия; *l. of the valley*, ла́ндыш.

limb *n.* член те́ла; (*of tree*) сук (-а́, *loc.* -ý; *pl.* -и́, -о́в & су́чья, -ьев).

limber[1] *n.* (*mil.*) передо́к (-дка́); *v.t. & abs.* (*l. up*) прицепля́ть *imp.*, прицепи́ть (-плю́, -пишь) *perf.* (ору́дие, -ия) к передка́м.

limber[2] *adj.* (*flexible*) ги́бкий (-бок, -бка́, -бко); (*nimble*) прово́рный; *v.i.*: *l. up*, размина́ться *imp.*, размя́ться (разомну́сь, -нёшься) *perf.*

limbo *n.* преддве́рие а́да; (*fig.*) забро́шенность, забве́ние.

lime[1] *n.* (*min.*) и́звесть. **limekiln** *n.* печь (*loc.* печи́; *pl.* -чи, -че́й) для о́бжига известняка́. **limelight** *n.* друммо́ндов свет; *in the l.*, (*fig.*) в це́нтре внима́ния. **limestone** *n.* известня́к (-а́).

lime[2] *n.* (*fruit*) лайм.

lime[3] *n.* (*l.-tree*) ли́па.

limit *n.* грани́ца, преде́л; *v.t.* ограни́чивать *imp.*, ограни́чить *perf.* **limitation** *n.* ограниче́ние; (*leg.*) иско́вая да́вность. **limitless** *adj.* безграни́чный.

limousine *n.* лимузи́н.

limp[1] *n.* (*lameness*) хромота́; *v.i.* хрома́ть *imp.*

limp[2] *adj.* (*not stiff*) мя́гкий (-гок, -гка́, -гко); (*fig.*) вя́лый.

limpet *n.* морско́е блю́дечко (*pl.* -чки, -чек, -чкам).

limpid *adj.* прозра́чный.

linchpin *n.* чека́.

linden *n.* ли́па.

line[1] *n.* ли́ния, черта́; (*cord*) верёвка; (*fishing l.*) лёса (*pl.* лёсы); (*wrinkle*) морщи́на; (*limit*) грани́ца; (*row*) ряд (-á *with* 2, 3, 4, *loc.* -ý; *pl.* -ы́); (*of words*) строка́ (*pl.* -ки, -к, -ка́м); (*of verse*) стих (-á); *v.t.* (*paper*) линова́ть *imp.*, раз~ *perf.*; *v.t. & i.* (*l. up*) выстра́ивать(ся) *imp.*, вы́строить(ся) *perf.* в ряд.

line[2] *v.t.* (*clothes*) класть (кладу́, -дёшь; клал) *imp.*, положи́ть (-жу́, -жишь) *perf.* на подкла́дку.

lineage *n.* происхожде́ние (по прямо́й ли́нии).

lineal *adj.* (происходя́щий) по прямо́й ли́нии.

linear *adj.* лине́йный.

lined[1] *adj.* лино́ванный; (*face*) морщи́нистый.

lined[2] *adj.* (*garment*) на подкла́дке, с подкла́дкой.

linen *n.* полотно́ (*pl.* -тна, -тен, -тнам); *collect.* бельё; *adj.* льняно́й, полотня́ный.

liner *n.* ла́йнер.

linesman *n.* (*sport*) судья́ (*pl.* -дьи, -дей, -дьям) *m.* на ли́нии.

ling[1] *n.* (*fish*) морска́я щу́ка.

ling[2] *n.* (*heather*) ве́реск.

linger *v.i.* ме́длить *imp.*; заде́рживаться *imp.*, задержа́ться (-жу́сь, -жишься) *perf.*

lingerie *n.* да́мское бельё.

lingering *adj.* (*illness*) затяжно́й.

lingo *n.* (*special language*) жарго́н.

linguist *n.* лингви́ст, языкове́д. **linguistic** *adj.* лингвисти́ческий. **linguistics** *n.* лингви́стика, языкозна́ние.

liniment *n.* жи́дкая мазь.

lining *n.* (*clothing etc.*) подкла́дка; (*tech.*) облицо́вка.

link *n.* звено́ (*pl.* -нья, -ньев), связь; *v.t.* соединя́ть *imp.*, соедини́ть *perf.*; свя́зывать *imp.*, связа́ть (свяжу́, -жешь) *perf.*

linnet *n.* конопля́нка.

linoleum *n.* лино́леум.

linotype *n.* линоти́п.

linseed *n.* льняно́е се́мя (*gen.pl.* -мя́н) *neut.*; *l. cake*, льняны́е жмыхи́ (-хо́в) *pl.*; *l. oil*, льняно́е ма́сло.

lint *n.* ко́рпия.

lintel *n.* перемы́чка.

lion *n.* лев (льва); *l.-cub*, львёнок (-нка; *pl.* льва́та, -т). **lioness** *n.* льви́ца.

lip *n.* губа́ (*pl.* -бы, -б, -ба́м); (*of vessel*) край (*loc.* -аю́; *pl.* -ая́); (*fig.*) де́рзость. **lipstick** *n.* губна́я пома́да.

liquefaction *n.* сжиже́ние. **liquefy** *v.t. & i.* превраща́ть(ся) *imp.*, преврати́ть(ся) (-ащу́, -ати́т(ся)) *perf.* в жи́дкое состоя́ние.

liqueur *n.* ликёр (-a(y)).

liquid *n.* жи́дкость; *adj.* жи́дкий (-док, -дка́, -дко); (*transparent*) прозра́чный; (*ling.*) пла́вный; (*econ.*) ликви́дный.

liquidate *v.t.* ликвиди́ровать *imp.*, *perf.* **liquidation** *n.* ликвида́ция; *go into l.*, ликвиди́роваться *imp.*, *perf.*

liquidity *n.* жи́дкое состоя́ние.

liquor *n.* (спиртно́й) напи́ток (-тка).

liquorice n. (plant) лакри́чник, соло́дка; (root) лакри́ца, солодко́вый ко́рень (-рня) m.

lissom adj. (lithe) ги́бкий (-бок, -бка́, -бко); (agile) прово́рный.

list[1] n. (roll) спи́сок (-ска), пе́речень (-чня) m.; v.t. вноси́ть (-ошу́, -о́сишь) imp., внести́ (внесу́, -сёшь; внёс, -ла́) perf. в спи́сок.

list[2] n. (naut.) крен (-а); v.i. накреня́ться imp., крени́ться imp.; на ~ perf.

listen v.i. слу́шать imp., по ~ perf. (to, + acc.); (heed) прислу́шиваться imp., прислу́шаться perf. (to, к + dat.); l. in, (telephone) подслу́шивать imp., подслу́шать perf. (to, + acc.); (radio) слу́шать imp. ра́дио.

listless adj. (languid) то́мный (-мен, -мна́, -мно); (indifferent) безразли́чный.

litany n. литани́я.

literacy n. гра́мотность.

literal adj. (in letters) бу́квенный; (sense etc.) буква́льный.

literary adj. литерату́рный.

literate adj. гра́мотный.

literature n. литерату́ра.

lithe adj. ги́бкий (-бок, -бка́, -бко).

lithograph n. литогра́фия; v.t. литографи́ровать imp., perf. **lithographer** n. литогра́ф. **lithographic** adj. литографи́ческий. **lithography** n. литогра́фия.

litigant n. сторона́ (acc. -ону; pl. -оны, -о́н, -она́м) adj. тя́жущийся. **litigate** v.i. суди́ться (сужу́сь, су́дишься) imp. **litigation** n. тя́жба. **litigious** adj. сутя́жнический.

litmus n. ла́кмус; l. paper, ла́кмусовая бума́га.

litre n. литр.

litter n. (vehicle, stretcher) носи́лки (-лок) pl.; (bedding) подсти́лка; (disorder) беспоря́док (-дка); (rubbish) сор (-а(у)); (brood) помёт; v.t. (make untidy) сори́ть imp., на ~ perf. (with, + instr.); (scatter) разбра́сывать imp., разброса́ть perf.

little n. немно́гое; l. by l., ма́ло-пома́лу; a l., немно́го + gen.; not a l., нема́ло + gen.; adj. ма́ленький, небольшо́й; (in height) небольшо́го ро́ста; (in distance, time) коро́ткий (ко́роток, коротка́, ко́ротко); (unimportant) незначи́тельный; adv. ма́ло, немно́го; (not at all) совсе́м не.

littoral n. побере́жье; adj. прибре́жный.

liturgical adj. литурги́ческий. **liturgy** n. литурги́я.

live[1] adj. живо́й (жив, -а́, -о); (coals) горя́щий; (mil.) боево́й; (electr.) под напряже́нием; (active) де́ятельный; (real) жи́зненный (-ен, -енна).

live[2] v.i. жить (живу́, -вёшь; жил, -а́, -о) imp.; существова́ть imp.; l. down, загла́живать imp., загла́дить perf.; l. on, (feed on) пита́ться imp.+ instr.; l. through, пережива́ть imp., пережи́ть (-иву́, -ивёшь; пережи́л, -а́, -о) perf.; l. until, to see, дожива́ть imp., дожи́ть (-иву́, -ивёшь; до́жил, -а́, -о) perf. до + gen.; l. up to, жить (живу́, -вёшь; жил, -а́, -о) imp. согла́сно + dat.

livelihood n. сре́дства neut.pl. к существова́нию.

lively adj. живо́й (жив, -а́, -о), весёлый (ве́сел, -а́, -о, ве́селы).

liven (up) v.t. & i. оживля́ть(ся) imp., оживи́ть(ся) perf.

liver n. пе́чень; (cul.) печёнка.

livery n. ливре́я.

livestock n. скот (-а́), живо́й инвента́рь (-ря́) m.

livid adj. (colour) синева́то-се́рый; predic. (angry) зол (зла).

living n. сре́дства neut.pl. к существова́нию; (eccl.) бенефи́ций; earn a l., зараба́тывать imp., зарабо́тать perf. на жизнь; adj. живо́й (жив, -а́, -о), живу́щий; (of likeness) то́чный; l. image, ко́пия; l.-room, гости́ная sb.

lizard n. я́щерица.

lo interj. вот! се!

loach n. голе́ц (-льца́).

load n. груз; (also fig.) бре́мя neut.; (tech.) нагру́зка; pl. (lots) ку́ча; v.t. нагружа́ть imp., грузи́ть (-ужу́, -у́зишь) imp., на ~ perf.; (fig.) обременя́ть imp., обремени́ть perf.; (gun, camera) заряжа́ть imp., заряди́ть (-яжу́, -я́дишь) perf.

loadstar see lodestar.

loadstone, lode- n. магни́тный желе́зняк (-á); (magnet) магни́т.

loaf[1] n. хлеб, бу́лка.

loaf[2] *v.i.* безде́льничать *imp.*; шата́ться *imp.* **loafer** *n.* безде́льник.

loam *n.* сугли́нок (-нка).

loan *n.* заём (за́йма); *v.t.* дава́ть (даю́, даёшь) *imp.*, дать (дам, дашь, даст, дади́м; дал, -á, да́ло́, -и) *perf.* взаймы́.

loath, loth *predic.*: *be l. to,* не хоте́ть (хочу́, -чешь; хоти́м) *imp.*+*inf.*

loathe *v.t.* пита́ть *imp.* отвраще́ние к + *dat.* **loathing** *n.* отвраще́ние. **loathsome** *adj.* отврати́тельный.

lob *n.* (*sport*) свеча́ (*pl.* -чи, -че́й).

lobar *adj.* долево́й.

lobby *n.* прихо́жая *sb.*, вестибю́ль *m.*; (*parl.*) кулуа́ры (-ров) *pl.*

lobe *n.* до́ля (*pl.* -ли, -ле́й); (*of ear*) мо́чка.

lobster *n.* ома́р; *l.-pot,* ве́рша для ома́ров.

local *adj.* ме́стный; (*train*) при́городный.

locality *n.* (*site*) местоположе́ние; (*district*) ме́стность.

localize *v.t.* (*restrict*) локализова́ть *imp.*, *perf.*

locate *v.t.* (*place*) помеща́ть *imp.*, помести́ть *perf.*; (*discover*) обнару́живать *imp.*, обнару́жить *perf.*; *be located,* находи́ться (-и́тся) *imp.*

location *n.* (*position*) местонахожде́ние; определе́ние ме́ста; *on l.,* (*cin.*) на нату́ре.

locative *adj.* (*n.*) ме́стный (паде́ж (-á).

loch, lough *n.* (*lake*) о́зеро (*pl.* -ёра); (*sea l.*) (у́зкий) зали́в.

lock[1] *n.* (*of hair*) ло́кон (*pl.* воло́сы (-ло́с, -ám) *pl.*

lock[2] *n.* замо́к (-мка́), запо́р; (*tech.*) сто́пор; (*canal*) шлюз; *l.-keeper,* нача́льник шлю́за; *v.t.* запира́ть *imp.*, запере́ть (-пру́, -прёшь; за́пер, -ла́, -ло) *perf.*; *v.i.* запира́ться *imp.*, запере́ться (-прётся; за́перся, -рла́сь, заперло́сь) *perf.*; *l.-out,* лока́ут; *l.-up,* (*cell*) аресtáнтский *sb.*

locker *n.* шка́фчик.

locket *n.* медальо́н.

lockjaw *n.* столбня́к (-á).

locksmith *n.* сле́сарь (*pl.* -ри & -ря́) *m.*

locomotion *n.* передвиже́ние. **locomotive** *adj.* дви́жущий(ся); *n.* (*rly.*) локомоти́в.

locum (tenens) *n.* вре́менный замести́тель *m.*

locust *n.* саранча́ (*also collect.*; *fig.*).

locution *n.* оборо́т ре́чи.

lode *n.* ру́дная жи́ла. **lodestar, load-** *n.* Поля́рная звезда́; (*fig.*) путево́дная звезда́ (*pl.* звёзды). **lodestone** *see* **loadstone.**

lodge *n.* (*hunting*) (охо́тничий) до́мик; (*porter's*) швейца́рская *sb.*, сторо́жка; (*Masonic*) ло́жа; *v.t.* (*accommodate*) помеща́ть *imp.*, помести́ть *perf.*; (*deposit*) дава́ть (даю́, даёшь) *imp.*, дать (дам, дашь, даст, дади́м; дал, -á, да́ло́, -и) *perf.* на хране́ние (with, + *dat.*); (*complaint*) подава́ть (-даю́, -даёшь) *imp.*, пода́ть (-áм, -áшь, -áст, -ади́м; по́дал, -á, -о) *perf.*; *v.i.* (*reside*) жить (живу́, -вёшь; жил, -á, -о) *imp.* (with, + *gen.*); (*stick*) заса́живать *imp.*, засе́сть (-ся́дет; -сёл) *perf.* **lodger** *n.* жиле́ц (-льца́), жили́ца. **lodging** *n.* (*also pl.*) кварти́ра, (снима́емая) ко́мната.

loft *n.* (*attic*) черда́к (-á); (*for hay*) сенова́л; (*for pigeons*) голубя́тня (*gen.pl.* -тен); (*gallery*) галере́я.

lofty *adj.* о́чень высо́кий (-о́к, -ока́, -о́ко); (*elevated*) возвы́шенный.

log *n.* бревно́ (*pl.* брёвна, -вен, -внам); (*for fire*) поле́но (*pl.* -нья, -ньев); (*naut.*) лаг; *l.-book,* (*naut.*) ва́хтенный журна́л; (*aeron.*) бортово́й журна́л; (*registration book*) формуля́р.

logarithm *n.* логари́фм. **logarithmic** *adj.* логарифми́ческий.

loggerhead *n.*: *be at l.s,* ссо́риться *imp.*, по~ *perf.* (with, с + *instr.*).

logic *n.* ло́гика. **logical** *adj.* (*of logic*) логи́ческий; (*consistent*) логи́чный. **logician** *n.* ло́гик.

logistics *n.* материа́льно-техни́ческое обеспе́чение.

loin *n.* (*pl.*) поясни́ца; (*cul.*) филе́йная часть.

loiter *v.i.* слоня́ться *imp.*

lone, lonely *adj.* одино́кий, уединённый (-ён, -ённа). **loneliness** *n.* одино́чество, уединённость.

long[1] *v.i.* страстно желать *imp.*, по~ *perf.* (for, + *gen.*); тосковать *imp.* (for, по + *dat.*).

long[2] *adj.* (*space*) длинный (-нен, -нна, длинно); (*time*) долгий (-лог, -лга, -лго); (*protracted*) длительный; (*in measurements*) длиной в + *acc.*; *in the l. run*, в конечном счёте; *l.-boat*, баркас; *l.-lived*, долговечный; *l.-sighted*, дальнозоркий (-рок, -рка); (*fig.*) дальновидный; *l.-suffering*, долготерпение; долготерпеливый; *l.-term*, долгосрочный; *l.-winded*, многоречивый; *adv.* долго; *l. after*, спустя много времени; *l. ago*, (уже) давно; *as l. as*, пока; *l. before*, задолго до.

longevity *n.* долговечность.

longing *n.* страстное желание (for, + *gen.*); тоска (for, по + *dat.*).

longitude *n.* долгота (*pl.* -ты).

longways *adv.* в длину.

look *n.* (*glance*) взгляд; (*appearance*) вид; (*expression*) выражение; *v.i.* смотреть (-рю, -ришь) *imp.*, по~ *perf.* (at, на + *acc.*); глядеть (-яжу, -ядишь) *imp.*, по~ *perf.* (at, на + *acc.*); (*appear*) выглядеть (-яжу, -ядишь) *imp.* + *instr.*; (*face*) выходить (-ит) *imp.* (towards, onto, на + *acc.*); *l. about*, осматриваться *imp.*, осмотреться (-рюсь, -ришься) *perf.*; *l. after*, (*attend to*) присматривать *imp.*, присмотреть (-рю, -ришь) *perf.* за + *instr.*; *l. down on*, презирать *imp.*; *l. for*, искать (ищу, ищешь) *imp.* + *acc.*, + *gen.*; *l. forward to*, предвкушать *imp.*, предвкусить (-ушу, -усишь) *perf.*; *l. in on*, заглядывать *imp.*, заглянуть (-ну, -нешь) *perf.* к + *dat.*; *l. into*, (*investigate*) разбираться *imp.*, разобраться (разберусь, -рёшься -ался, -алась, -алось) *perf.* в + *prep.*; *l. like*, быть похожим на + *acc.*; *it looks like rain*, похоже на то, что будет дождь; *l. on*, (*regard*) считать *imp.*, счесть (сочту, -тёшь; счёл, сочла) *perf.* (as, + *instr.*, за + *instr.*); *l. out*, выглядывать *imp.*, выглянуть *perf.* (в окно); быть настороже; *imper.* осторожно! береги(те)сь!; *l. over, through*, просматривать *imp.*,

просмотреть (-рю, -ришь) *perf.*; *l. up*, (*raise eyes*) поднимать *imp.*, поднять (подниму, -нимешь; поднял, -а, -о) *perf.* глаза; (*in dictionary etc.*) искать (ищу, ищешь) *imp.*; (*improve*) улучшаться *imp.*, улучшиться *perf.*; *l. up to*, уважать *imp.* **looker-on** *n.* зритель *m.*, ~ница. **looking-glass** *n.* зеркало (*pl.* -ла).

loom[1] *n.* ткацкий станок (-нка).

loom[2] *v.i.* неясно вырисовываться *imp.*, вырисоваться *perf.*; (*fig.*) готовиться *imp.*

loop *n.* петля (*gen.pl.* -тель); *v.i.* образовывать *imp.*, образовать *perf.* петлю; *l. the l.*, (*aeron.*) делать *imp.*, с~ *perf.* мёртвую петлю.

loophole *n.* бойница; (*fig.*) лазейка.

loose *adj.* (*free*) свободный; (*not fixed*) неприкреплённый; (*inexact*) неточный (-чен, -чна, -чно); (*not compact*) рыхлый (рыхл, -а, -о); (*lax*) распущенный (-ен, -енна); *be at a l. end*, бездельничать *imp.*; *v.t.* (*free*) освобождать *imp.*, освободить *perf.*; (*untie*) отвязывать *imp.*, отвязать (-яжу, -яжешь) *perf.* **loosen** *v.t. & i.* ослаблять(ся) *imp.*, ослабить(ся) *perf.*

loot *n.* добыча; *v.t.* грабить *imp.*, о~ *perf.*

lop[1] *v.t.* (*tree*) подрезать *imp.*, подрезать (-ежу, -ежешь) *perf.*; (*l. off*) отрубать *imp.*, отрубить (-блю, -бишь) *perf.*

lop[2] *v.i.* (*hang*) свисать *imp.*, свиснуть (-с) *perf.*

lope *v.i.* бегать *indet.*, бежать (бегу, бежишь) *det.* вприпрыжку.

lopsided *adj.* кривобокий.

loquacious *adj.* болтливый. **loquacity** *n.* болтливость.

lord *n.* (*master*) господин (*pl.* -да, -д, -дам), владыка *m.*; (*the L.*); *eccl.*) Господь (-ода, *voc.* -оди); (*peer*; *title*) лорд; *v.t.*: *l. it over*, помыкать *imp.* + *instr.* **lordly** *adj.* (*haughty*) высокомерный. **lordship** *n.* власть (over, над + *instr.*); (*title*) светлость.

lore *n.* знания *neut.pl.*

lorgnette *n.* лорнет.

lorry *n.* грузовик (-а).

lose *v.t.* терять *imp.*, по~ *perf.*; (*forfeit*) лишаться *imp.*, лишиться *perf.* + *gen.*; (*game etc.*) проигрывать *imp.*, проиграть *perf.*; *v.i.* (*suffer loss*) терпеть (-плю, -пишь) *imp.*, по~ *perf.* ущерб (by, от+*gen.*); (*clock*) отставать (-таёт) *imp.*, отстать (-анет) *perf.*

loss *n.* потеря, ущерб; (*in game*) проигрыш; at a l., (*puzzled*) в затруднении.

lot *n.* жребий; (*destiny*) участь; (*of goods*) партия; a l., lots, много, масса; the l., все (всего), все (всех) *pl.*

loth see **loath**.

lotion *n.* примочка.

lottery *n.* лотерея.

lotto *n.* лото *neut.indecl.*

lotus *n.* лотос.

loud *adj.* (*sound*) громкий (-мок, -мка, -мко); (*noisy*) шумный (-мен, -мна, -мно); (*colour*) кричащий; out l., вслух. **loudspeaker** *n.* громкоговоритель *m.*

lough see **loch**.

lounge *n.* фойе *neut.indecl.*; (*sitting-room*) гостиная *sb.*; *v.i.* сидеть (сижу, сидишь) *imp.* развалясь; (*idle*) бездельничать *imp.*

lour, lower² *v.i.* (*person, sky*) хмуриться *imp.*, на~ *perf.*

louse *n.* вошь (вши, *instr.* вошью).

lousy *adj.* вшивый; (*coll.*) паршивый.

lout *n.* увалень (-льня) *m.*, грубиян. **loutish** *adj.* неотёсанный (-ан, -анна).

lovable *adj.* милый (мил, -а, -о, милы).

love *n.* любовь (-бви, *instr.* -бовью) (of, for, к+*dat.*); (*sweetheart*) возлюбленный *sb.*; in l. with, влюблённый (-ён, -ена) в+*acc.*; *v.t.* любить (-блю, -бишь) *imp.* **lovely** *adj.* красивый; (*delightful*) прелестный. **lover** *n.* любовник, -ица.

low¹ *n.* (*of cow*) мычание; *v.i.* мычать (-чу, -чишь) *imp.*

low² *adj.* низкий (-зок, -зка, -зко), невысокий (-ок, -ока, -око); (*quiet*) тихий (тих, -а, -о); (*coarse*) грубый (груб, -а, -о); (*weak*) слабый (слаб, -а, -о).

lower¹ *v.t.* опускать *imp.*, опустить (-ущу, -устишь) *perf.*; снижать *imp.*, снизить *perf.*

lower² see **lour**.

lower³ *adj.* низший, нижний.

lowland *n.* низменность.

lowly *adj.* скромный (-мен, -мна, -мно).

loyal *adj.* верный (-рен, -рна, -рно, верны), лояльный. **loyalty** *n.* верность, лояльность.

lozenge *n.* (*shape*) ромб; (*tablet*) лепёшка.

lubber *n.* увалень (-льня) *m.*

lubricant *n.* смазка, смазочный материал. **lubricate** *v.t.* смазывать *imp.*, смазать (-ажу, -ажешь) *perf.* **lubrication** *n.* смазка.

lubricity *n.* скользкость; (*lewdness*) похотливость.

lucerne *n.* люцерна.

lucid *adj.* ясный (ясен, ясна, ясно, ясны).

luck *n.* (*chance*) случай; (*good l.*) счастье, удача; (*bad l.*) неудача. **luckily** *adv.* к счастью. **luckless** *adj.* несчастный. **lucky** *adj.* счастливый (счастлив); (*successful*) удачный.

lucrative *adj.* прибыльный.

lucre *n.* прибыль.

ludicrous *adj.* смехотворный.

lug¹ *v.t.* (*drag*) таскать *indet.*, тащить (-щу, -щишь) *det.*

lug² *n.* (*ear*) ухо (*pl.* уши, ушей); (*tech.*) ушко (*pl.* -ки, -ков), выступ, прилив.

luggage *n.* багаж (-а).

lugubrious *adj.* печальный.

lukewarm *adj.* тепловатый; (*fig.*) равнодушный.

lull *n.* (*in storm*) затишье; (*interval*) перерыв; *v.t.* (*to sleep*) убаюкивать *imp.*, убаюкать *perf.*; (*suspicions*) усыплять *imp.*, усыпить *perf.*; *v.i.* затихать *imp.*, затихнуть (-х) *perf.* **lullaby** *n.* колыбельная песня (*gen.pl.* -сен).

lumbago *n.* люмбаго *neut.indecl.*

lumbar *adj.* поясничный.

lumber¹ *v.i.* (*move*) двигаться (-аюсь, -аешься & движусь, -жешься) *imp.*, двинуться *perf.* тяжело, шумно, неуклюже.

lumber² *n.* (*domestic*) рухлядь; (*timber*) лесоматериалы *m.pl.*; l.-room, чулан;

v.t. загромождáть *imp.*, загромоздить *perf.* **lumberjack** *n.* лесорýб.

luminary *n.* светило.

luminous *adj.* светящийся.

lump *n.* ком (*pl.* -ья, -ьев), кусóк (-скá); (*swelling*) óпухоль (*f.*); (*lot*) кýча; *v.t.* *l. together*, смéшивать *imp.*, смешáть *perf.* (в кýчу).

lunacy *n.* безýмие.

lunar *adj.* лýнный.

lunatic *adj.* (*n.*) сумасшéдший (*sb.*); безýмный (*sb.*).

lunch *n.* обéд, вторóй зáвтрак; *l.-hour, -time*, обéденный перерыв; *v.i.* обéдать *imp.*, по ~ *perf.*

lung *n.* лёгкое *sb.*

lunge *n.* (*sport*) выпад; толчóк (-чкá); *v.i.* (*fencing*) дéлать *imp.*, с ~ *perf.* выпад; наносить (-ошý, -óсишь) *imp.*, нанести (-есý, -есёшь; -ёс, -еслá) *perf.* удáр (с плечá) (at + *dat.*).

lupin(e) *n.* люпин.

lupine *adj.* вóлчий (-чья, -чье).

lupus *n.* волчáнка.

lurch[1] *n.: leave in the l.*, покидáть *imp.*, покинуть *perf.* в бедé.

lurch[2] *v.i.* (*stagger*) ходить (хожý, хóдишь) *indet.*, идти (идý, идёшь; шёл, шла) *det.* шатáясь.

lure *n.* примáнка; *v.t.* примáнивать *imp.*, приманить (-ню, -нишь) *perf.*

lurid *adj.* мрáчный (-чен, -чнá, -чно); (*sensational*) сенсациóнный.

lurk *v.i.* прятаться (-ячусь, -ячешься) *imp.*, с ~ *perf.*; (*fig.*) тáиться *imp.*

luscious *adj.* притóрный.

lush *adj.* сóчный (-чен, -чнá, -чно).

lust *n.* пóхоть, вожделéние (of, for, к + *dat.*); *v.i.* стрáстно желáть *imp.*, по ~ *perf.* (for, + *gen.*). **lustful** *adj.* похотливый.

lustre *n.* (*gloss*) глянец (-нца); (*splendour*) блеск; (*chandelier*) люстра. **lustrous** *adj.* глянцевитый, блестящий.

lusty *adj.* (*healthy*) здорóвый; (*lively*) живóй (жив, -á, -о).

lute[1] *n.* (*mus.*) лютня (*gen.pl.* -тен).

lute[2] *n.* (*clay etc.*) замáзка.

luxuriant *adj.* пышный (-шен, -шнá, -шно).

luxuriate *v.i.* наслаждáться *imp.*, насладиться (in, + *instr.*).

luxurious *adj.* роскóшный. **luxury** *n.* рóскошь.

lye *n.* щёлок (-а(у)).

lymph *n.* лимфа. **lymphatic** *adj.* лимфатический.

lynch *v.t.* линчевáть (-чýю, -чýешь) *imp.*, *perf.*; *l. law*, суд (-á) Линча.

lynx *n.* рысь.

lyre *n.* лира.

lyric *n.* лирика; *pl.* словá *neut.pl.* песни. **lyrical** *adj.* лирический. **lyricism** *n.* лиризм.

M

macabre *adj.* жýткий (-ток, -ткá, -тко).

macadam *n.* щéбень (-бня) *m.* **macadamize** *v.t.* мостить *imp.*, вы ~, за ~ *perf.* щéбнем.

macaroni *n.* макарóны (-н) *pl.*

macaroon *n.* миндáльное печéнье.

macaw *n.* макáо *m.indecl.*

mace *n.* (*weapon*) булавá; (*staff of office*) жезл; *m.-bearer*, жезлонóсец (-сца).

Mach (number) *n.* числó М(áха).

machete *n.* мачéте *neut.indecl.*

machination *n.* махинáция, интрига, кóзни (-ней) *pl.*

machine *n.* машина, станóк (-нкá); (*state m.*) аппарáт; *attrib.* машинный; *m.-gun*, пулемёт; *m.-made*, машинного производства, машинной выработки; *m. tool*, станóк (-нкá); *v.t.* обрáбатывать *imp.*, обрабóтать *perf.*

на станке́; (*sew*) шить (шью, шьёшь) *imp.*, с~ *perf.* (на маши́не). **machinery** *n.* (*machines*) маши́ны *f.pl.*; (*mechanism*) механи́зм; (*of state*) аппара́т.

machinist *n.* машини́ст; (*sewing*) швейни́к, -ица́, швея́.

mackerel *n.* ску́мбрия, макре́ль; *m. sky*, не́бо бара́шками.

mackintosh *n.* (*material*) прорези́ненная мате́рия; (*coat*) непромока́емое пальто́ *neut.indecl.*

macrocephalic *adj.* макроцефали́ческий. **macrocosm** *n.* макроко́см, вселе́нная *sb.*

mad *adj.*, сумасше́дший, поме́шанный (-ан, -анна); (*animal*) бе́шеный; (*fig.*) безу́мный. **madcap** *n.* сорване́ц (-нца́). **madden** *v.t.* своди́ть (-ожу́, -о́дишь) *imp.*, свести́ (-дёшь, -дёшь, свёл, -а́) *perf.* с ума́; (*irritate*) выводи́ть (-ожу́, -о́дишь) *imp.*, вы́вести (-еду, -едешь; -ел) *perf.* из себя́. **madhouse** *n.* сумасше́дший дом (-а(у); *pl.* -а́). **madly** *adv.* безу́мно. **madman** *n.* сумасше́дший *sb.*, безу́мец (-мца). **madness** *n.* сумасше́ствие, безу́мие. **madwoman** *n.* сумасше́дшая *sb.*, безу́мная *sb.*

made *see* **make**.

madder *n.* (*plant*) маре́на; (*dye*) крапп.

madrigal *n.* мадрига́л.

maestro *n.* маэ́стро *m.indecl.*

mafia *n.* ма́фия.

magazine *n.* журна́л; (*mil.*) скла́д боеприпа́сов, веще́вой склад; (*of gun*) магази́н.

maggot *n.* личи́нка. **maggoty** *adj.* черви́вый.

magic *n.* ма́гия, волшебство́, колдовство́; *adj.* волше́бный, маги́ческий. **magician** *n.* волше́бник, колду́н (-а́); (*conjurer*) фо́кусник.

magisterial *adj.* авторите́тный.

magistracy *n.* магистрату́ра. **magistrate** *n.* полице́йский судья́ (*pl.* -дьи, -де́й, -дьям) *m.*

magma *n.* ма́гма.

magnanimous *adj.* великоду́шный.

magnate *n.* магна́т.

magnesia *n.* о́кись ма́гния. **magnesium** *n.* ма́гний.

magnet *n.* магни́т. **magnetic** *adj.* магни́тный; (*attractive*) притяга́тельный.

magnetism *n.* магнети́зм; притяга́тельность. **magnetize** *v.t.* намагни́чивать *imp.*, намагни́тить *perf.* **magneto** *n.* магне́то *neut.indecl.*

magnification *n.* увеличе́ние.

magnificence *n.* великоле́пие, пы́шность. **magnificent** *adj.* великоле́пный, пы́шный (-шен, -шна́, -шно).

magnify *v.t.* увели́чивать *imp.*, увели́чить *perf.*; (*exaggerate*) преувели́чивать *imp.*, преувели́чить *perf.*

magnitude *n.* величина́.

magnolia *n.* магно́лия.

magpie *n.* соро́ка.

maharajah *n.* магара́джа *m.* **maharanee** *n.* магара́ни *f.indecl.*

mahogany *n.* кра́сное де́рево.

maid *n.* служа́нка, го́рничная *sb.*; *m. of honour*, фре́йлина. **maiden** *adj.* незаму́жняя; де́вичий; (*first*) пе́рвый; *m. name*, де́вичья фами́лия.

mail[1] *n.* (*letters etc.*) по́чта; (*train*) почто́вый по́езд (*pl.* -а́); *m. order*, почто́вый зака́з, зака́з по по́чте; *v.t.* посыла́ть *imp.*, посла́ть (пошлю́, -лёшь) *perf.* по по́чте.

mail[2] *n.* (*armour*) кольчу́га; броня́; *mailed fist*, вое́нная, физи́ческая, си́ла.

maim *v.t.* кале́чить *imp.*, ис~ *perf.*; уве́чить *imp.*

main *n.* (*sea*) откры́тое мо́ре; (*gas m.*; *pl.*) магистра́ль; *in the m.*, в основно́м; гла́вным о́бразом; *with might and m.*, не щадя́ сил; *adj.* основно́й, гла́вный; (*road*) магистра́льный; *by m. force*, изо всех си́л; *the m. chance*, путь (-ти́, -тём) *m.* к нажи́ве; *m. line* (*rly.*) магистра́ль. **mainland** *n.* матери́к (-а́); *attrib.* материко́вый. **mainly** *adv.* в основно́м; гла́вным о́бразом; (*for most part*) бо́льшей ча́стью. **mainmast** *n.* грот-ма́чта. **mainsail** *n.* грот. **mainspring** *n.* ходова́я пружи́на. **mainstay** *n.* гро́та-штаг; (*fig.*) гла́вная опо́ра.

maintain *v.t.* (*continue*) продолжа́ть *imp.*, продо́лжить *perf.*; (*support*) подде́рживать *imp.*, поддержа́ть (-жу́, -жишь) *perf.*; (*family*) содержа́ть (-жу́, -жишь) *imp.*; (*machine*) обслу́живать *imp.*, обслужи́ть (-жу́,

-жишь) *perf.*; (*assert*) утверждáть *imp.* maintenance *n.* поддéржка; содержáние; обслýживание, ухóд.

maize *n.* кукурýза.

majestic *adj.* велúчественный (-ен, -енна). **majesty** *n.* велúчественность; (*title*) велúчество.

majolica *n.* майóлика.

major[1] *n.* (*mil.*) майóр; m.-general, генерáл-майóр.

major[2] *adj.* (*greater*) бóльший; (*more important*) бóлее вáжный; (*main*) глáвный; (*mus.*) мажóрный; (*senior*) стáрший; *n.* совершеннолéтний *sb.* (*mus.*) мажóр. **majority** *n.* (*greater number*) большинствó; (*rank*) чин майóра; (*full age*) совершеннолéтие.

make *v.t.* дéлать *imp.*, с~ *perf.*; (*create*) создавáть (-даю, -даёшь) *imp.*, создáть (-áм, -áшь, -áст, -адúм; сóздал, -á, -о) *perf.*; (*produce*) производúть (-ожý, -óдишь) *imp.*, произвестú (-едý, -едёшь; -ёл, -елá) *perf.*; (*compose*) составлять *imp.*, состáвить *perf.*; (*prepare*) готóвить *imp.*, при~ *perf.*; (*amount to*) равняться *imp.*+ *dat.*; (*become*) становúться (-влюсь, -вишься) *imp.*, стать (стáну, -нешь) *perf.*+ *instr.*; (*earn*) зарабáтывать *imp.*, зарабóтать *perf.*; (*compel*) заставлять *imp.*, застáвить *perf.*; *made in the USSR*, изготóвлено в СССР; *be made of*, состоять (-ою, -оúшь) *imp.* из+ *gen.*; *m. as if*, *though*, дéлать вид, с~ *perf.* вид, бýдто; *m. a bed*, стелúть (стелю, -лешь) *imp.*, по~ *perf.* постéль; *m. believe*, притворяться *imp.*, притворúться *perf.*; *m.-believe*, притвóрство; притвóрный; *m. do with*, довóльствоваться *imp.*, у~ *perf.*+ *instr.*; *m. fun of*, высмéивать *imp.*, вýсмеять (-ею, -еешь) *perf.*; *m. oneself at home*, быть как дóма; *m. oneself scarce*, исчезáть *imp.*, исчéзнуть (-з) *perf.*; *m. sure of*, удостоверяться *imp.*, удостовéриться *perf.* в+ *prep.*; *m. way for*, уступáть *imp.*, уступúть (-плю, -пишь) *perf.* дорóгу+ *dat.*; *m. away with*, покончúть *perf.* с+ *instr.*; *m. off*, удирáть *imp.*, удрáть (удерý, -рёшь; удрáл, -á, -о) *perf.*; *m. out*, (*document*) состав-

лять *imp.*, состáвить *perf.*; (*cheque*) выпúсывать *imp.*, вýписать (-ишу, -ишешь) *perf.*; (*understand*) разбирáть *imp.*, разобрáть (разберý, -рёшь; разобрáл, -á, -о) *perf.*; *m. over*, передавáть (-даю, -даёшь) *imp.*, передáть (-áм, -áшь, -áст, -адúм; пéредал, -á, -о) *perf.*; *m. up*, (*compound*) составлять *imp.*, состáвить *perf.* (*theat.*) гримировáть(ся) *imp.*, на~ *perf.*; *m.-up*, (*theat.*) грим; (*cosmetics*) космéтика; (*composition*) состáв; *m. it up*, мирúться *imp.*, по~ *perf.* (with, с+ *instr.*); *m. up for*, возмещáть *imp.*, возместúть *perf.*; *m. up one's mind*, решáться *imp.*, решúться *perf.*; *m. up to*, заúскивать *imp.* пéред+ *instr.* **make** *n.* мáрка, тип, сорт (*pl.* -á). **makeshift** *adj.* врéменный *n.* **makeweight** *n.* довéсок (-ска).

malachite *n.* малахúт.

maladjusted *adj.* плóхо приспосóбленный (-ен).

maladministration *n.* плохóе управлéние.

maladroit *adj.* нелóвкий (-óвок, -óвкá, -óвко); (*tactless*) бестáктный.

malady *n.* болéзнь.

malaria *n.* малярúя.

malcontent *n.* недовóльный *sb.*

male *n.* (*animal*) самéц (-мцá); (*person*) мужчúна *m.*; *adj.* мужскóй.

malevolence *n.* недоброжелáтельность.

malevolent *adj.* недоброжелáтельный.

malformation *n.* непрáвильное образовáние.

malice *n.* злóба; (*leg.*) злой ýмысел (-сла); *with m. aforethought*, со злым ýмыслом. **malicious** *adj.* злóбный.

malign *adj.* пáгубный; *v.t.* клеветáть (-ещý, -éщешь) *imp.*, на~ *perf.* на+ *acc.* **malignant** *adj.* (*harmful*) зловéщный; (*malicious*) злóбный; (*med.*) злокáчественный.

malinger *v.i.* притворяться *imp.*, притворúться *perf.* больным. **malingerer** *n.* симулянт.

mallard *n.* кряква.

malleable *adj.* кóвкий (-вок, -вкá, -вко); (*fig.*) податливый.

mallet *n.* (дервянный) молотóк (-ткá).

mallow *n.* мáльва, просвúрник.

malnutrition *n.* недоеда́ние.

malpractice *n.* (*wrongdoing*) противозако́нное де́йствие; (*negligence*) престу́пная небре́жность.

malt *n.* со́лод; *v.t.* солоди́ть *imp.*, на ~ *perf.*

maltreat *v.t.* пло́хо обраща́ться *imp.* с + *instr.*

mamba *n.* ма́мба.

mambo *n.* ма́мбо *neut.indecl.*

mamma *n.* ма́ма.

mammal *n.* млекопита́ющее *sb.* **mammalian** *adj.* млекопита́ющий.

mammary *adj.* грудно́й.

mammon *n.* мамо́на, бога́тство.

mammoth *n.* ма́монт; *adj.* грома́дный.

man *n.* (*human*) челове́к (*pl.* лю́ди, -де́й, -дям, -дьми́); (*human race*) челове́чество; (*male*) мужчи́на *m.*; (*husband*) муж (*pl.* -ья́, -е́й, -ья́м); (*servant*) слуга́ *m.*; (*labourer*) рабо́чий *sb.*; *pl.* (*soldiers*) солда́ты *m.pl.*, рядовы́е *sb.*; *pl.* (*sailors*) матро́сы *m.pl.*; (*draughts*) ша́шка *f.*; m. in the street, заура́дный челове́к; *m.*-hour, челове́ко-час (*pl.* -ы́); *m.*-of-war, вое́нный кора́бль (-ля́) *m.*; *v.t.* (*furnish with men*) укомплекто́вывать *imp.*, укомплектова́ть *perf.* ли́чным соста́вом; ста́вить *imp.*, по ~ *perf.* людьми́ к + *dat.*; (*act thus*) станови́ться (-влю́сь, -вишься) *imp.*, стать (ста́ну, -нешь) *perf.* к + *dat.*

manacle *n.* нару́чник; *v.t.* надева́ть *imp.*, наде́ть (-е́ну, -е́нешь) *perf.* нару́чники на + *acc.*

manage *v.t.* (*control*) управля́ть *imp.* + *instr.*; заве́довать *imp.* + *instr.*; (*cope*) справля́ться *imp.*, спра́виться *perf.* с + *instr.* **management** *n.* управле́ние (*of*, + *instr.*), заве́дование (*of*, + *instr.*); (*the m.*) администра́ция, дире́кция. **manager** *n.* управля́ющий *sb.* (*of*, + *instr.*), заве́дующий *sb.* (*of*, + *instr.*), администра́тор, дире́ктор (*pl.* -а́); (*good, bad, m.*) хозя́ин; (*in entertainment*) импреса́рио *m.indecl.*; (*sport*) ме́неджер. **managerial** *adj.* администрати́вный, дире́кторский.

mandarin *n.* мандари́н.

mandatary *n.* мандата́рий. **mandate** *n.*

манда́т. **mandated** *adj.* подманда́тный. **mandatory** *adj.* обяза́тельный.

mandible *n.* ни́жняя че́люсть; (*of insect*) жва́ло.

mandolin(e) *n.* мандоли́на.

mane *n.* гри́ва.

manful *adj.* му́жественный (-ен, -енна).

manganese *n.* ма́рганец (-нца).

manger *n.* я́сли (-лей) *pl.*; dog in the m., соба́ка на се́не.

mangle[1] *n.* (*for clothes*) като́к (-тка́); *v.t.* ката́ть *imp.*, вы ~ *perf.*

mangle[2] *v.t.* (*mutilate*) кале́чить *imp.*, ис ~ *perf.*; (*words*) кове́ркать *imp.*, ис ~ *perf.*

mango *n.* ма́нго *neut.indecl.*

mangrove *n.* ма́нгровое де́рево (*pl.* -е́вья, -е́вьев).

manhandle *v.t.* передвига́ть *imp.*, передви́нуть *perf.* вручну́ю; (*treat roughly*) гру́бо обраща́ться *imp.* с + *instr.*

manhole *n.* смотрово́й коло́дец (-дца).

manhood *n.* возму́жалость; (*courage*) му́жественность.

mania *n.* ма́ния. **maniac** *n.* манья́к, -я́чка. **maniacal** *adj.* маниака́льный.

manicure *n.* маникю́р; *v.t.* де́лать *imp.*, с ~ *perf.* маникю́р + *dat.* **manicurist** *n.* маникю́рша.

manifest *adj.* очеви́дный; *v.t.* де́лать *imp.*, с ~ *perf.* очеви́дным; (*display*) проявля́ть *imp.*, прояви́ть (-влю́, -вишь) *perf.*; *n.* манифе́ст. **manifestation** *n.* проявле́ние. **manifesto** *n.* манифе́ст.

manifold *adj.* разнообра́зный; *n.* (*tech.*) колле́ктор, трубопрово́д.

manikin *n.* (*little man*) челове́чек (-чка); (*lay figure*) манеке́н.

Manil(l)a *n.* (*hemp*), мани́льская пенька́; (*paper*), мани́льская бума́га.

manipulate *v.t.* манипули́ровать *imp.* + *instr.* **manipulation** *n.* манипуля́ция.

manly *adj.* му́жественный (-ен, -енна).

mankind *n.* челове́чество.

manna *n.* ма́нна (небе́сная).

mannequin *n.* манеке́нщица.

manner *n.* спо́соб, о́браз, мане́ра; *pl.* нра́вы *m.pl.*; *pl.* (*good m.*) (хоро́шие) мане́ры *f.pl.* **mannered** *adj.* вы́чурный, мане́рный. **mannerism** *n.* мане́ра, мане́рность.

mannish adj. (masculine) мужеподо́бный; (characteristic of man) сво́йственный (-ен, -енна) мужчи́не.

manoeuvrable adj. легко́ управля́емый.

manoeuvre n. манёвр; v.i. меневри́ровать imp., с ~ perf.; проводи́ть (-ожу́, -о́дишь) imp., провести́ (-еду́, -едёшь; -ёл, -ела́) perf. манёвры.

manor n. (estate) поме́стье (gen.pl. -тий); (house) поме́щичий дом (-а(у); pl. -а́). **manorial** adj. манориа́льный.

manpower n. людски́е ресу́рсы m.pl.

mansard (roof) n. манса́рдная кры́ша.

manservant n. слуга́ m.

mansion n. большо́й дом (pl. -а́); pl. многокварти́рный дом.

manslaughter n. человекоуби́йство; (leg.) непредумы́шленное уби́йство.

mantelpiece n. ками́нная доска́ (acc. -ску; pl. -ски, -со́к, -ска́м) **mantelshelf** n. ками́нная по́лка.

mantis n. богомо́л.

mantle n. (cloak) наки́дка; (gas m.) газокали́льная се́тка; (earth's) ма́нтия.

manual adj. ручно́й; m. labour, физи́ческий, ручно́й, труд (-а́); n. спра́вочник, руково́дство, уче́бник; (of organ) мануа́л. **manually** adv. вручну́ю.

manufacture n. произво́дство, изготовле́ние; v.t. производи́ть (-ожу́, -о́дишь) imp., произвести́ (-еду́, -едёшь; -ёл, -ела́) perf.; изготовля́ть imp., изгото́вить perf.; (fabricate) фабрикова́ть imp., с ~ perf. **manufacturer** n. фабрика́нт, промы́шленник, производи́тель m.

manure n. наво́з; v.t. унаво́живать imp., унаво́зить perf.

manuscript n. ру́копись f.; adj. рукопи́сный.

many adj., n. мно́го + gen., мно́гие pl.; how m., ско́лько + gen.

Maoism n. маои́зм. **Maoist** n. маои́ст; adj. маои́стский.

map n. ка́рта; v.t. черти́ть (-рчу́, -ртишь) imp., на ~ perf. план + gen.; m. out, составля́ть imp., соста́вить perf. план + gen.

maple n. клён; attrib. клёновый.

mar v.t. по́ртить imp., ис ~ perf.

marathon n. марафо́н.

marauder n. мароде́р. **marauding** adj. мароде́рский.

marble n. мра́мор; (toy) ша́рик; pl. (game) игра́ в ша́рики; attrib. мра́морный. **marbled** adj. мра́морный.

March[1] n. март; attrib. ма́ртовский.

march[2] v.i. марширова́ть imp., про ~ perf.; m. marш; ход; m. past, прохожде́ние торже́ственным ма́ршем.

mare n. кобы́ла; m.'s nest, иллю́зия; find a m.'s nest, попа́сть (-аду́, -адёшь; -а́л) perf. па́льцем в не́бо.

margarine n. маргари́н (-а(у)).

margin n. край (loc. -аю́; pl. -ая́), кайма́ (gen.pl. каём); (on page) по́ле (pl. -ля́); m. of error, преде́лы m.pl. погре́шности; profit m., при́быль; safety m., запа́с про́чности.

marigold n. (Tagetes) ба́рхатцы (-цев) pl.; (Calendula) ноготки́ (-ко́в) pl.

marijuana n. марихуа́на.

marinade n. марина́д; v.t. maринова́ть imp., за ~ perf.

marine adj. (maritime) морско́й; (naval) вое́нно-морско́й; (fleet) морско́й n.; (soldier) солда́т морско́й пехо́ты; pl. морска́я пехо́та. **mariner** n. моря́к (-а́), матро́с.

marionette n. марионе́тка.

marital adj. супру́жеский, бра́чный.

maritime adj. морско́й; (near sea) примо́рский.

marjoram n. (Majorana) майора́н; (Origanum) души́ца.

mark[1] n. (coin) ма́рка.

mark[2] n. (target, aim) цель; (sign) знак; (school) отме́тка, (numerical) балл; (trace) след (pl. -ы́); (level) у́ровень (-вня m.); high-, low-, water m., отме́тка у́ровня по́лной, ма́лой, воды́; hit the m., попада́ть imp., попа́сть (-аду́, -адёшь; -а́л) perf. в то́чку; make one's m., отлича́ться imp., отличи́ться perf.; on your marks, на старт! v.t. отмеча́ть imp., отме́тить perf.; ста́вить imp., по ~ perf. знак, (goods) расце́нку, на + acc., (school) отме́тку, балл, за + acc.; (leave trace(s)) оставля́ть imp., оста́вить perf. след(ы́) на + prep.; (football) закрыва́ть imp., закры́ть (-ро́ю, -ро́ешь) perf.; m. my words, попо́мни(те) мой слова́! m.

time, топта́ться (-пчу́сь, -пчешься) *imp.* на ме́сте; *m. off*, отделя́ть *imp.*, отдели́ть (-лю́, -лишь) *perf.*; *m. out*, размеча́ть *imp.*, разме́тить *perf.*
marker *n.* знак, указа́тель *m.*; (*in book*) закла́дка.
market *n.* ры́нок (-нка), база́р; (*demand*) спрос; (*trade*) торго́вля; (*conditions*) конъюнкту́ра; *black m.*, чёрный ры́нок (-нка), конъюнкту́ра ры́нка, вы́годная для покупа́теля, для продавца́; (*European*) *Common M.*, (европе́йский) о́бщий ры́нок (-нка); *find a m.*, находи́ть (-ожу́, -о́дишь) *imp.*, найти́ (найду́, -дёшь; нашёл, -шла) *perf.* сбыт; *m.-day*, база́рный день (дня) *m.*; *m. garden*, огоро́д; *m.place*, база́рная пло́щадь (*pl.* -ди, -де́й); *m. price*, ры́ночная цена́ (*acc.* -ну; *pl.* -ны); *v.t.* продава́ть (-даю́, -даёшь) *imp.*, прода́ть (-а́м, -а́шь, -а́ст, -ади́м; про́дал, -а́, -о) *perf.* **marketable** *adj.* хо́дкий (-док, -дка́, -дко) (*econ.*) това́рный.
marksman *n.* ме́ткий стрело́к (-лка́).
marksmanship *n.* ме́ткая стрельба́.
marl *n.* ме́ргель *m.*
marmalade *n.* апельси́новый джем.
marmoset *n.* игру́нка.
marmot *n.* суро́к (-рка́).
maroon[1] *adj.* (*n.*) (*colour*) тёмно-бордо́вый (цвет).
maroon[2] *v.t.* (*put ashore*) выса́живать *imp.*, вы́садить *perf.* (на необита́емом о́строве); (*cut off*) отреза́ть *imp.*, отре́зать (-е́жет) *perf.*
marquee *n.* шатёр (-тра́).
marquis *n.* марки́з.
marriage *n.* брак; (*wedding*) сва́дьба; *attrib.* бра́чный. **marriageable** *adj.* взро́слый; *m. age*, бра́чный во́зраст.
married *adj.* (*man*) жена́тый; (*woman*) заму́жняя, за́мужем; (*of m. persons*) супру́жеский.
marrow *n.* ко́стный мозг (*loc.* -у́); (*essence*) су́щность; (*vegetable*) кабачо́к (-чка́). **marrowbone** *n.* мозгова́я кость (*pl.* -ти, -те́й).
marry *v.t.* (*of man*) жени́ться (-ню́сь, -нишься) *imp.*, *perf.* на+*prep.*; (*of woman*) выходи́ть (-ожу́, -о́дишь)

imp., вы́йти (вы́йду, -дешь; вы́шла) *perf.* за́муж за+*acc.*; (*give in marriage*) (*man*) жени́ть (-ню́, -нишь) *imp.*, *perf.*, по~ *perf.* (то, на+*prep.*); (*woman*) выдава́ть (-даю́, -даёшь) *imp.*, вы́дать (-ам, -ашь, -аст, -адим) *perf.* за́муж (то, за+*acc.*).
Mars *n.* Марс.
marsh *n.* боло́то; *m.-gas*, боло́тный газ; *m.* ле́карственное *m. marigold*, калу́жница боло́тная. **marshy** *adj.* боло́тистый.
marshal *n.* ма́ршал; *v.t.* выстра́ивать *imp.*, вы́строить *perf.*; приводи́ть (-ожу́, -о́дишь) *imp.*, привести́ (-еду́, -едёшь; -ёл, -ела́) *perf.* в поря́док; *marshalling yard*, сортиро́вочная ста́нция.
marsupial *adj.* су́мчатый; *n.* су́мчатое живо́тное *sb.*
marten *n.* куни́ца.
martial *adj.* вое́нный; (*warlike*) во́инский; *m. law*, вое́нное положе́ние.
Martian *n.* марсиа́нин (*pl.* -а́не, -а́н); *adj.* марсиа́нский.
martin *n.* стриж (-а́); (*house-m.*) городска́я ла́сточка.
martinet *n.* сторо́нник стро́гой дисципли́ны.
martyr *n.* му́ченик, -ица; *v.t.* му́чить *imp.*, за~ *perf.* **martyrdom** *n.* му́чени-чество.
marvel *n.* чу́до (*pl.* -деса́), ди́во; *v.i.* изумля́ться *imp.*, изуми́ться *perf.*; удивля́ться *imp.*, удиви́ться *perf.* **marvellous** *adj.* чуде́сный, изуми́тельный, удиви́тельный.
Marxian, Marxist *n.* маркси́ст; *adj.* маркси́стский. **Marxism** *n.* маркси́зм.
marzipan *n.* марципа́н; *adj.* марципа́нный.
mascot *n.* талисма́н.
masculine *adj.* мужско́й; (*gram.*) мужско́го ро́да; (*of woman*) мужеподо́бный; *n.* (*gram.*) мужско́й род.
maser *n.* ма́зер.
mash *n.* (*of malt*) су́сло; (*of bran*) по́йло; (*mashed potatoes*) карто́фельное пюре́ *neut.indecl.*; *v.t.* размина́ть *imp.*, размя́ть (разомну́, -нёшь) *perf.*
mask *n.* ма́ска; (*gas-m.*) противога́з;

v.t. маскирова́ть *imp.*, за~ *perf.*; *masked ball*, бал-маскара́д.

masochism *m.* мазохи́зм. **masochist** *n.* мазохи́ст. **masochistic** *adj.* мазохи́стский.

mason *n.* ка́менщик; (*M.*) масо́н. **Masonic** *adj.* масо́нский. **masonry** *n.* ка́менная кла́дка; (*M.*) масо́нство.

masque *n.* ма́ска. **masquer** *n.* уча́стник, -ица, бала-маскара́да. **masquerade** *n.* маскара́д; *v.i.*: *m. as*, притворя́ться *imp.*, притвори́ться *perf.* + *instr.*; выдава́ть (-даю́, -даёшь) *imp.*, вы́дать (-ам, -ашь, -аст, -адим) *perf.* себя́ за + *acc.*

mass¹ *n.* (*eccl.*) обе́дня (*gen.pl.* -ден), ме́сса.

mass² *n.* ма́сса; (*majority*) большинство́; *pl.* (*the m.*) наро́дные ма́ссы *f.pl.*; *attrib.* ма́ссовый; *m. media*, сре́дства *neut.pl.* ма́ссовой информа́ции; *m. meeting*, ми́тинг; *m.-produced*, ма́ссового произво́дства; *m. production*, ма́ссовое произво́дство; *m.* масси́ровать *imp.*, *perf.*

massacre *n.* резня́; *v.t.* ре́зать (ре́жу, -жешь) *imp.*, за~ *perf.*

massage *n.* масса́ж; *v.t.* масси́ровать *imp.*, *perf.* **masseur, -euse** *n.* массажи́ст, ~ ка.

massif *n.* го́рный масси́в.

massive *adj.* масси́вный.

mast *n.* ма́чта; *m.-head*, топ ма́чты.

master *n.* (*owner*) хозя́ин (*pl.* -я́ева, -я́ев), владе́лец (-льца); (*of household, college*) глава́ (*pl.* -вы) *m.* (семьи́, ко́лледжа); (*of ship*) капита́н; (*teacher*) учи́тель (*pl.* -ля́) *m.* (*M.*, *univ.*) маги́стр; (*workman*; *artist*) ма́стер (*pl.* -á); (*of film*) контро́льная ко́пия; (*of record*) пе́рвый оригина́л; *be m. of*, владе́ть *imp.* + *instr.*; *M. of Arts*, маги́стр гуманита́рных нау́к; *m.-key*, отмы́чка; *m.-switch*, гла́вный выключа́тель *m.*; *v.t.* (*overcome*) преодолева́ть *imp.*, преодоле́ть *perf.*; справля́ться *imp.*, спра́виться *perf.* c + *instr.*; (*subjugate*) подчиня́ть *imp.*, подчини́ть *perf.* себе́; (*acquire knowledge of*) овладева́ть *imp.*, овладе́ть *perf.* + *instr.* **masterful** *adj.* вла́стный. **masterly** *adj.* мастерско́й. **masterpiece** *n.* ше-

де́вр. **mastery** *n.* (*dominion*) госпо́дство; (*skill*) мастерство́; (*knowledge*) соверше́нное владе́ние (*of*, + *instr.*).

masticate *v.t.* жева́ть (жую́, жуёшь) *imp.*

mastodon *n.* мастодо́нт.

mastiff *n.* масти́фф.

mat¹ *n.* ко́врик, полови́к (-á); (*of rushes, straw*) цино́вка; (*under dish etc.*) подста́вка.

mat² *adj. see* matt.

match¹ *n.* спи́чка. **matchbox** *n.* спи́чечная коро́бка.

match² *n.* (*equal*) ро́вня *m. & f.*; (*contest*) матч, состяза́ние; (*marriage*) брак; *a m. for*, па́ра + *dat.*; *meet one's m.*, встреча́ть *imp.*, встре́тить *perf.* ра́вного себе́, досто́йного проти́вника; *v.t.* (*correspond*) соотве́тствовать *imp.* + *dat.*; (*of colour*) гармони́ровать *imp.* c + *instr.*; (*select*) подбира́ть *imp.*, подобра́ть (подберу́, -рёшь; подобра́л, -á, -о) *perf.* **matchboard** *n.* шпунто́вая доска́ (*acc.* -ску; *pl.* -ски, -со́к, -ска́м). **matchless** *adj.* несравне́нный (-нен, -нна). **matchmaker** *n.* сват, сва́ха.

mate¹ *n.* (*chess*) мат; *v.t.* объявля́ть *imp.*, объяви́ть (-влю́, -вишь) *perf.* мат + *dat.*

mate² *n.* (*one of a pair*) саме́ц (-мца́), са́мка; (*fellow worker*) напа́рник, това́рищ; (*assistant*) помо́щник; (*naut.*) помо́щник капита́на; *v.i.* (*of animals*) спа́риваться *imp.*, спа́риться *perf.*

material *adj.* материа́льный; (*essential*) суще́ственный (-ен, -енна); *n.* материа́л; (*cloth*) мате́рия; *pl.* (*necessary articles*) принадле́жности *f.pl.* **materialism** *n.* материали́зм; материалисти́чность. **materialist** *n.* материали́ст. **materialistic** *adj.* материалисти́чный, -ческий. **materialization** *n.* материализа́ция. **materialize** *v.t. & i.* материализова́ть(ся) *imp.*, *perf.*; осуществля́ть *imp.*, осуществи́ть(ся) *perf.*

maternal *adj.* матери́нский; (*kinship*) по ма́тери; *m. grandfather*, де́душка с матери́нской стороны́. **maternity** *n.* матери́нство; *m. benefit*, посо́бие роже́нице; *m. dress*, пла́тье (*gen.pl.* -в) для бере́менных; m. home, hospital, роди́льный дом (-а(у); pl. -á); m. ward, роди́льная пала́та.

mathematical adj. математи́ческий. **mathematician** n. матема́тик. **mathematics** n. матема́тика.

matinée n. дневно́й спекта́кль m.; m. coat, распашо́нка.

matins n. у́треня.

matriarchal adj. матриарха́льный. **matriarchy** n. матриарха́т. **matricidal** adj. матереуби́йственный. **matricide** n. (action) матереуби́йство; (person) матереуби́йца m. & f.

matriculate v.t. принима́ть imp., приня́ть (приму́, -мешь; при́нял, -á, -о) perf. в вуз; v.i. быть при́нятым в вуз. **matriculation** n. зачисле́ние в вуз; (examination) вступи́тельный экза́мен в вуз.

matrimonial adj. супру́жеский. **matrimony** n. брак, супру́жество.

matrix n. (womb) ма́тка; (rock) ма́точная поро́да; (mould) ма́трица.

matron n. замужняя же́нщина; (hospital) сестра́-хозя́йка; (school) заве́дующая sb. хозя́йством.

matt adj. ма́товый.

matted adj. спу́танный (-ан).

matter n. (substance) вещество́; (philos., med.) мате́рия; (content) содержа́ние; (affair) де́ло (pl. -лá); (question) вопро́с; a m. of form, форма́льность; a m. of life and death, вопро́с жи́зни и сме́рти; a m. of opinion, спо́рное де́ло; a m. of taste, де́ло вку́са; an easy m., просто́е де́ло; as a m. of fact, факти́чески; собственно говоря́; for that m., что каса́ется э́того; в э́том отноше́нии; money matters, де́нежные дела́ neut.pl.; no laughing m., не шу́точное де́ло; what's the m.? в чём де́ло? что случи́лось? what's the m. with him? что с ним? m.-of-fact, проза́йчный; v.i. име́ть imp. значе́ние; (med.) гнои́ться imp.; it doesn't m., э́то не име́ет значе́ния; it matters a lot to me, э́то для меня́ о́чень ва́жно; what does it m.? како́е э́то име́ет значе́ние?

matting n. (rushes) цино́вка; (bast) рого́жа.

mattock n. моты́га.

mattress n. матра́с, тюфя́к (-á).

mature adj. зре́лый (зрел, -á, -о); (well-considered) хорошо́ обду́манный (-ан, -анна); v.i. зреть imp., со ~ perf.; v.t. доводи́ть (-ожу́, -о́дишь) imp., довести́ (-еду́, -едёшь; -ёл, -ела́) perf. до зре́лости; (plan) обду́мывать imp., обду́мать perf. **maturity** n. зре́лость.

maul v.t. терза́ть imp.; кале́чить imp., ис ~ perf.; (criticize) раскритикова́ть perf.

mausoleum n. мавзоле́й.

mauve adj. (n.) розова́то-лило́вый (цвет).

maxim n. сенте́нция.

maximum n. ма́ксимум; adj. максима́льный.

may[1] v.aux. (possibility; permission) мочь (могу́, мо́жешь; мог, -ла́) imp.; с ~ perf.; (possibility) возмо́жно, что + indicative; (wish) пусть + indicative.

May[2] n. (month) май; (m., hawthorn) боя́рышник; m.-bug, ма́йский жук (-á); M. Day, Пе́рвое sb. ма́я; attrib. ма́йский; mayfly n. подёнка.

maybe adv. мо́жет быть.

mayonnaise n. майоне́з.

mayor n. мэр. **mayoress** n. жена́ (pl. жёны) мэ́ра; же́нщина-мэр.

maze n. лабири́нт; (fig.) пу́таница.

mazurka n. мазу́рка.

mead n. мёд (-у, loc. -у́; pl. -ы́).

meadow n. луг (loc. -у́; pl. -á). **meadowsweet** n. та́волга.

meagre adj. (thin) худо́й (худ, -á, -о); (scanty) ску́дный (-ден, -дна́, -дно).

meal[1] n. еда́; at mealtimes, во вре́мя еды́.

meal[2] n. (ground grain) мука́ кру́пного помо́ла. **mealy** adj. рассы́пчатый; m.-mouthed, сладкоречи́вый.

mean[1] adj. (average) сре́дний; n. (middle point) середи́на, сре́днее sb.; pl. (method) сре́дство, спо́соб; pl. (resources) сре́дства neut.pl., состоя́ние; by all means, коне́чно, пожа́луйста; by means of, при по́мощи + gen., посре́дством + gen.; by no means, совсе́м не; means test, прове́рка нужда́емости.

mean[2] adj. (ignoble) по́длый (подл, -á,

-о), ни́зкий (-зок, -зка́, -зко); (*miserly*) скупо́й (скуп, -а́, -о); (*poor*) убо́гий.

mean³ *v.t.* (*have in mind*) име́ть *imp.* в виду́; (*intend*) намерева́ться *imp.*+ *inf.*; (*signify*) зна́чить *imp.*

meander *v.i.* (*stream*) извива́ться *imp.*; (*person*) броди́ть (-ожу́, -о́дишь) *imp.* без це́ли. **meandering** *adj.* изви́листый.

meaning *n.* значе́ние, смысл; *adj.* значи́тельный. **meaningful** *adj.* (мно́го)знача́щий. **meaningless** *adj.* бессмы́сленный (-ен, -енна).

meantime, meanwhile *adv.* тем вре́менем, ме́жду тем.

measles *n.* корь. **measly** *adj.* ничто́жный.

measurable *adj.* измери́мый. **measure** *n.* ме́ра; (*size*) ме́рка; (*degree*) сте́пень (*pl.* -ни, -не́й); (*limit*) преде́л; *made to* ~, сши́тый по ме́рке; сде́ланный (-ан) на зака́з; *v.t.* измеря́ть *imp.*, изме́рить *perf.*; ме́рить *imp.*, с~ *perf.*; (*for clothes*) снима́ть *imp.*, снять (сниму́, -мешь; снял, -а́, -о) *perf.* ме́рку с+*gen.*; (*estimate*) оце́нивать *imp.*, оцени́ть (-ню́, -нишь) *perf.*; *v.i.* (*be of specified size*) име́ть *imp.*+ *acc.*; *the room measures 30 feet in length*, ко́мната име́ет три́дцать фу́тов в длину́; *m. off*, отмеря́ть *imp.*, отме́рить *perf.*; *m. out*, (*deal out*) отмеря́ть *imp.*, распределя́ть *imp.*, распредели́ть *perf.*; *m. up to*, соотве́тствовать *imp.*+*dat.* **measured** *adj.* (*rhythmical*) ме́рный. **measurement** *n.* (*action*) измере́ние; *pl.* (*dimensions*) разме́ры *m.pl.*

meat *n.* мя́со. **meaty** *adj.* мясно́й, мяси́стый.

mechanic *n.* меха́ник. **mechanical** *adj.* механи́ческий; (*automatic*) машина́льный; *m. engineer*, инжене́р-меха́ник; *m. engineering*, машинострое́ние. **mechanics** *n.* меха́ника. **mechanism** *n.* механи́зм. **mechanistic** *adj.* механи́стический. **mechanization** *n.* механиза́ция. **mechanize** *v.t.* механизи́ровать *imp., perf.*

medal *n.* меда́ль. **medallion** *n.* медальо́н. **medallist** *n.* (*recipient*) медали́ст.

meddle *v.i.* вме́шиваться *imp.*, вмеша́ться *perf.* (in, with, в+*acc.*).

media *pl. of* **medium.**

mediaeval *adj.* средневеко́вый.

mediate *v.i.* посре́дничать *imp.* **mediation** *n.* посре́дничество. **mediator** *n.* посре́дник.

medical *adj.* медици́нский; *m. jurisprudence*, суде́бная медици́на; *m. man*, врач (-а́); *m. student*, ме́дик, -и́чка. **medicated** *adj.* (*impregnated*) пропи́танный (-ан) лека́рством. **medicinal** *adj.* (*of medicine*) лека́рственный; (*healing*) целе́бный. **medicine** *n.* медици́на; (*substance*) лека́рство; *m. man*, зна́харь *m.*, шама́н.

mediocre *adj.* посре́дственный (-ен, -енна), зауря́дный. **mediocrity** *n.* посре́дственность.

meditate *v.i.* размышля́ть *imp.* **meditation** *n.* размышле́ние. **meditative** *adj.* заду́мчивый.

Mediterranean *adj.* средиземномо́рский; *n.* Средизе́мное мо́ре.

medium *n.* (*middle*) середи́на; (*means*) сре́дство; (*environment*; *phys.*) среда́ (*pl.* -ды); (*person*) ме́диум; *pl.* (*mass media*) сре́дства *neut.pl.* ма́ссовой информа́ции; *adj.* сре́дний.

medley *n.* смесь, вся́кая вся́чина.

meek *adj.* кро́ткий (-ток, -тка́, -тко), смире́нный (-ён, -е́нна). **meekness** *n.* кро́тость, смире́нность.

meet *v.t. & i.* встреча́ть(ся) *imp.*, встре́тить(ся) *perf.*; *v.t.* (*make acquaintance*) знако́миться *imp.*, по~ *perf.* с+ *instr.*; *v.i.* (*assemble*) собира́ться *imp.*, собра́ться (соберётся; собра́лся, -ала́сь, -ало́сь) *perf.* **meeting** *n.* встре́ча; собра́ние, заседа́ние, ми́тинг.

mega- *in comb.* ме́га-. **megacycle** *n.* мегаци́кл.

megahertz *n.* мегаге́рц (*gen.pl.* -ц). **megalith** *n.* мегали́т. **megalithic** *adj.* мегалити́ческий. **megaphone** *n.* мегафо́н; **megaton(ne)** *n.* мегато́нна.

megavolt *n.* мегаво́льт (*gen.pl.* -т). **megawatt** *n.* мегава́тт (*gen.pl.* -т). **megohm** *n.* мего́м (*gen.pl.* -м).

megalomania *n.* мегалома́ния.

melancholia *n.* меланхо́лия. **melancholic** *adj.* меланхоли́ческий. **melancholy** *n.* грусть, тоска́; *adj.* уны́лый, гру́стный (-тен, -тна́, -тно).

mêlée *n.* сва́лка.

mellow *adj.* (*ripe*) спе́лый (спел, -а́, -о); (*juicy*) со́чный (-чен, -чна́, -чно);

(*soft*) мя́гкий (-гок, -гка́, -гко); (*intoxicated*) подвыпи́вший; *v.i.* спеть *imp.*; смягча́ться *imp.*, смягчи́ться *perf.*

melodic *adj.* мелоди́ческий. **melodious** *adj.* мелоди́чный. **melody** *n.* мело́дия, напе́в.

melodrama *n.* мелодра́ма. **melodramatic** *adj.* мелодрамати́ческий.

melon *n.* ды́ня; (*water-m.*) арбу́з.

melt *v.t.* & *i.* раста́пливать(ся) *imp.*, растопи́ть(ся) (-плю́, -пи́т(ся)) *perf.*; (*smelt*) пла́вить(ся) *imp.*, рас~ *perf.*; (*dissolve*) растворя́ть(ся) *imp.*, раствори́ть(ся) *perf.*; *v.i.* (*thaw*) та́ять (та́ет) *imp.*, рас~ *perf.*; **melting-point**, то́чка плавле́ния.

member *n.* член. **membership** *n.* чле́нство; (*number of members*) коли́чество чле́нов; *attrib.* чле́нский.

membrane *n.* перепо́нка. **membran(e)ous** *adj.* перепо́нчатый.

memento *n.* напомина́ние. **memoir** *n.* кра́ткая биогра́фия; *pl.* мемуа́ры (-ров) *pl.*; воспомина́ния *neut.pl.* **memorable** *adj.* достопа́мятный. **memorandum** *n.* па́мятная запи́ска; (*diplomatic m.*) мемора́ндум. **memorial** *adj.* па́мятный, мемориа́льный; *n.* па́мятник. **memorize** *v.t.* зау́чивать *imp.*, заучи́ть (-чу́, -чишь) *perf.* наизу́сть. **memory** *n.* па́мять; (*recollection*) воспомина́ние; (*computer*) запомина́ющее устро́йство.

menace *n.* угро́за; *v.t.* угрожа́ть *imp.*+ *dat.* **menacing** *adj.* угрожа́ющий.

menagerie *n.* звери́нец (-нца).

mend *v.t.* чини́ть (-ню́, -нишь) *imp.*, по~ *perf.*; (*clothes*) што́пать *imp.*, за~ *perf.*; (*road*) ремонти́ровать *imp.*, от~ *perf.*; *n.* one's ways, исправля́ться *imp.*, испра́виться *perf.*

mendacious *adj.* лжи́вый. **mendacity** *n.* лжи́вость.

mendicancy *n.* ни́щенство. **mendicant** *adj.* ни́щий, ни́щенствующий; *n.* ни́щий *sb.*

menial *adj.* лаке́йский, ни́зкий (-зок, -зка́, -зко).

meningitis *n.* менинги́т.

menopause *n.* кли́макс.

menstrual *adj.* менструа́льный. **menstruation** *n.* менструа́ция.

mental *adj.* у́мственный, психи́ческий, душе́вный; *m. arithmetic*, счёт в уме́; *m. deficiency*, у́мственная отста́лость; *m. home, hospital, institution*, психиатри́ческая больни́ца. **mentality** *n.* ум (-а́); (*character*) склад ума́. **mentally** *adv.* у́мственно, мы́сленно.

menthol *n.* менто́л.

mention *v.t.* упомина́ть *imp.*, упомяну́ть (-ну́, -нешь) *perf.*; *not to m.*, не говоря́ уже́ о + *prep.*; *n.* упомина́ние.

mentor *n.* ме́нтор.

menu *n.* меню́ *neut.indecl.*

mercantile *adj.* торго́вый; *m. marine*, торго́вый флот.

mercenary *adj.* коры́стный; (*hired*) наёмный; *n.* наёмник.

mercerize *v.t.* мерсеризова́ть *imp.*, *perf.*

merchandise *n.* това́ры *m.pl.* **merchant** *n.* купе́ц (-пца́); торго́вец (-вца) *attrib.* торго́вый; *m. navy*, торго́вый флот; *m. ship*, торго́вое су́дно (*pl.* -да́, -до́в).

merciful *adj.* милосе́рдный. **mercifully** *adv.* к сча́стью. **merciless** *adj.* беспоща́дный.

mercurial *adj.* (*person*) живо́й (жив, -а́, -о); (*of mercury*) рту́тный. **mercury** *n.* (*metal*) ртуть; (*M., planet*) Мерку́рий.

mercy *n.* милосе́рдие; поща́да; *at the m. of*, во вла́сти+*gen.*

mere *adj.* просто́й, чи́стый, су́щий; *a m. child*, су́щий ребёнок, всего́ лишь ребёнок. **merely** *adv.* то́лько, про́сто.

meretricious *adj.* показно́й, мишу́рный.

merge *v.t.* & *i.* слива́ть(ся) *imp.*, сли́ть-(ся) (солью́(сь), -ьёшь(ся); слил(ся), -ила́(сь), -и́ло/ило́(сь) *perf.* **merger** *n.* объедине́ние.

meridian *n.* меридиа́н.

meringue *n.* мере́нга.

merit *n.* заслу́га, досто́инство; *v.t.* заслу́живать *imp.*, заслужи́ть (-жу́, -жишь) *perf.*+ *gen.* **meritorious** *adj.* похва́льный.

mermaid *n.* руса́лка. **merman** *n.* водяно́й *sb.*

merrily *adv.* ве́село. **merriment** *n.* весе́лье. **merry** *adj.* весёлый (ве́сел, -а́, -о, ве́селы); *m.-go-round*, карусе́ль; *m.-making*, весе́лье.

mesh *n.* пётля (*gen.pl.* -тель); *pl.* (*network*) сёти (-тёй) *pl.*; *pl.* (*fig.*) западня; *v.i.* сцепляться *imp.*, сцепиться (-ится) *perf.*

mesmeric *adj.* гипнотический. **mesmerize** *v.t.* гипнотизировать *imp.*, за~ *perf.*

meson *n.* мезон.

mess *n.* (*disorder*) беспорядок (-дка); (*trouble*) беда; (*eating-place*) столовая *sb.*; *v.i.* столоваться *imp.* (with, вместе с + *instr.*); *m. about*, лодырничать *imp.*; *m. up*, портить *imp.*, ис~ *perf.*

message *n.* сообщение; (*errand*) поручение. **messenger** *n.* посыльный *sb.*, курьер.

Messiah *n.* мессия *m.* **Messianic** *adj.* мессианский.

Messrs. *abbr.* господа (*gen.* -д) *m.pl.*

messy *adj.* (*untidy*) беспорядочный; (*dirty*) грязный (-зен, -зна, -зно).

metabolism *n.* метаболизм, обмён веществ.

metal *n.* металл; (*road-m.*) щёбень (-бня) *m.*; (*rly.*) балласт; *pl.* (*rails*) рёльсы *m.pl.*; *adj.* металлический; *v.t.* (*road*) шоссировать *imp.*, *perf.*; *metalled road*, шоссё *neut.indecl.* **metallic** *adj.* металлический. **metallurgical** *adj.* металлургический. **metallurgy** *n.* металлургия.

metamorphose *v.t.* подвергать *imp.*, подвергнуть (-г) *perf.* метаморфозе. **metamorphosis** *n.* метаморфоза; (*biol.*) метаморфоз.

metaphor *n.* метафора. **metaphorical** *adj.* метафорический.

metaphysical *adj.* метафизический. **metaphysician** *n.* метафизик. **metaphysics** *n.* метафизика.

meteor *n.* метеор. **meteoric** *adj.* метеорический, метеорный. **meteorite** *n.* метеорит. **meteorological** *adj.* метеорологический. **meteorologist** *n.* метеоролог. **meteorology** *n.* метеорология.

meter *n.* счётчик; *v.t.* измерять *imp.*, измёрить *perf.* при помощи счётчика.

methane *n.* метан.

method *n.* метод, способ; (*system*) система. **methodical** *adj.* систематический, методичный.

Methodism *n.* методизм. **Methodist** *n.* методист; *adj.* методистский.

methyl *n.* метил; *m. alcohol*, метиловый спирт. **methylated** *adj.*: *m. spirit(s)* денатурат.

meticulous *adj.* тщательный.

metre *n.* метр. **metric(al)** *adj.* метрический.

metronome *n.* метроном.

metropolis *n.* (*capital*) столица. **metropolitan** *adj.* столичный; *n.* (*eccl.*) митрополит.

mettle *n.* темперамент; (*ardour*) пыл (-а(у)). **mettlesome** *adj.* горячий (-ч, -ча).

mew *see* **miaow**.

mezzanine *n.* антресоли *f.pl.*

mezzo-soprano *n.* мёццо-сопрано (*voice*) *neut.* & (*person*) *pl.indecl.*

miaow *interj.* мяу; *n.* мяуканье; *v.i.* мяукать *imp.*, мяукнуть *perf.*

mica *n.* слюда.

Michaelmas *n.* Михайлов день (дня) *m.*

micro- *in comb.* микро-. **microbe** *n.* микроб. **microcosm** *n.* микрокосм. **microfilm** *n.* микрофильм. **micron** *n.* микрон (*gen.pl.* -н). **micro-organism** *n.* микроорганизм. **microphone** *n.* микрофон. **microscope** *n.* микроскоп. **microscopic** *adj.* микроскопический. **microsecond** *n.* микросекунда. **microwave** *adj.* микроволновый; *n.* микроволна (*pl.* -олны, *dat.* -олнам).

mid *adj.* срёдний, середийный; **midday** *n.* полдень (полудня & полдня) *m.*; *attrib.* полуденный. **middle** *n.* середина; *adj.* срёдний; *m.-aged*, срёдних лет; *M. Ages*, срёдние века *m.pl.*; *m. man*, посрёдник; *m.-sized*, срёднего размёра. **middleweight** *n.* срёдний вес.

midge *n.* мошка.

midget *n.* карлик, -ица; *adj.* очень маленький, миниатюрный.

Midlands *n.* центральные графства *neut.pl.* Англии. **midnight** *n.* полночь (полуночи & полночи); *attrib.* полуночный. **midriff** *n.* диафрагма. **midshipman** *n.* корабельный гардемарин. **midst** *n.* середина. **midsummer** *n.* середина лёта. **midway** *adv.* на полпути, на полдороге. **mid-week** *n.*

середи́на неде́ли. **midwinter** *n.* середи́на зимы́.

midwife *n.* акуше́рка. **midwifery** *n.* акуше́рство.

might *n.* мощь, могу́щество; си́ла; *with all one's m.*, with m. and main, не щадя́ сил. **mighty** *adj.* могу́щественный (-ен, -енна), мо́щный (-щен, -щна́, -щно).

mignonette *n.* резеда́.

migraine *n.* мигре́нь.

migrant *adj.* кочу́ющий; (*bird*) перелётный; *n.* (*person*) пересе́ленец (-нца); (*bird*) перелётная пти́ца. **migrate** *v.i.* мигри́ровать *imp.*, *perf.*; пересе́ля́ться *imp.*, пересели́ться *perf.* **migration** *n.* мигра́ция; (*birds*) кочу́ющий; (*bird*) перелётный. **migratory** *adj.* кочу́ющий; (*bird*) перелётный.

mike *n.* микрофо́н.

milch *adj.* моло́чный; *m.-cow*, до́йная коро́ва.

mild *adj.* (*soft*) мя́гкий (-гок, -гка́, -гко); (*light*) лёгкий (-гок, -гка́, -гко, лёгки); (*not sharp*) нео́стрый (не остр & остёр, остра́, о́стро); (*not strong*) некре́пкий (-пок, -пка́, -пко), мя́гкая сталь. *m. steel*,

mildew *n.* (*fungi*) мильдью́ *neut.indecl.*; (*on paper etc.*) плесень.

mile *n.* ми́ля. **mileage** *n.* расстоя́ние в ми́лях; (*distance travelled*) коли́чество про́йденных миль; (*expenses*) де́ньги (-нег, -ньга́м) *pl.* на прое́зд. **milestone** *n.* ми́льный ка́мень (-мня; *pl.* -мни, -мне́й) *m.*; (*fig.*) ве́ха.

militancy *n.* войнственность. **militant** *adj.* войнствующий; (*combative*) боево́й; *n.* бое́ц (бойца́); активи́ст. **military** *adj.* вое́нный; *m. band*, духово́й орке́стр; *n.* вое́нные *pl.* (*USSR*) **militate** *v.i.: m. against*, говори́ть *imp.* про́тив + gen. **militia** *n.* ополче́ние; (*USSR*) мили́ция. **militiaman** *n.* ополче́нец (-нца); (*USSR*) милиционе́р.

milk *n.* молоко́; (*of plants*) млечный сок; *attrib.* моло́чный; *v.t.* дои́ть *imp.*, по~ *perf.* **milkmaid** *n.* доя́рка. **milkman** *n.* продаве́ц (-вца́) молока́. **milksop** *n.* тря́пка. **milk-tooth** *n.* моло́чный зуб (*pl.* -ы, -о́в). **milky** *adj.* моло́чный; *M. Way*, Мле́чный Путь (-ти́, -тём) *m.*

mill *n.* ме́льница; (*factory*) фа́брика, заво́д; (*rolling-m.*) прока́тный стан; *m.-hand*, фабри́чный рабо́чий *sb.*; *m.-pond*, ме́льничный пруд (-á, *loc.* -ý); *m.-race*, ме́льничный лото́к (-тка́); *m.-wheel*, ме́льничное колесо́ (*pl.* -ёса); *v.t.* (*grain etc.*) моло́ть (мелю́, -лешь) *imp.*, с~ *perf.*; (*cloth*) валя́ть *imp.*, с~ *perf.*; (*metal*) фрезерова́ть *imp.*, от~ *perf.*; (*coin*) гурти́ть *imp.*; *milled edge*, (*of coin*) гурт; *v.i.* кружи́ть (-ужу́, -ужишь) *imp.* **miller** *n.* ме́льник.

millenium *n.* тысячеле́тие.

millepede, **milli-** *n.* многоно́жка.

millet *n.* (*plant*) про́со; (*grain*) пшено́.

milli- *in comb.* милли-. **milliard** *n.* миллиа́рд. **millibar** *n.* миллиба́р. **milligram(me)** *n.* миллигра́мм. **millimetre** *n.* миллиме́тр.

milliner *n.* моди́стка; шля́пница. **millinery** *n.* да́мские шля́пы *f.pl.*

million *n.* миллио́н. **millionaire** *n.* миллионе́р. **millionth** *adj.* миллио́нный.

millipede *see* mille-.

millstone *n.* жёрнов (*pl.* -á); (*fig.*) бре́мя *neut.*

milt *n.* моло́ки (-к) *pl.*

mime *n.* мим; *v.t.* изобража́ть *imp.*, изобрази́ть *perf.* мими́чески; *v.i.* исполня́ть *imp.*, испо́лнить *perf.* роль в пантоми́ме. **mimic** *adj.* мими́ческий, подража́тельный; *n.* мими́ст; *v.t.* имити́ровать *imp.*, сымити́ровать *perf.*; (*ape*) обезья́нничать *imp.*, с~ *perf.* c + gen. **mimicry** *n.* имита́ция; (*biol.*) мимикри́я.

mimosa *n.* мимо́за; (*acacia*) ака́ция.

minaret *n.* минаре́т.

mince *n.* (*meat*) ру́бленое мя́со; *v.t.* руби́ть (-блю́, -бишь) *imp.*; (*in machine*) пропуска́ть *imp.*, пропусти́ть (-ущу́, -у́стишь) *perf.* че́рез мясору́бку; *v.i.* (*speak*) говори́ть *imp.* жема́нно; (*walk*) семени́ть *imp.*; *not to m. matters*, говори́ть *imp.* пря́мо, без обиняко́в. **mincemeat** *n.* начи́нка из изю́ма, минда́ля и т.п. **mincer** *n.* мясору́бка.

mind *n.* ум (-á), ра́зум; (*memory*) па́мять; (*opinion*) мне́ние; *absence of m.*, забы́вчивость, рассе́янность;

bear in m., иметь *imp.* в виду; по́мнить *imp.*; be in one's right m., быть в здра́вом уме́; be out of one's m., быть не в своём уме́; change one's m., переду́мывать *imp.*, переду́мать *perf.*; make up one's m., реша́ться *imp.*, реши́ться *perf.*; presence of m., прису́тствие ду́ха; v.t. (give heed to) обраща́ть *imp.*, обрати́ть (-ащу́, -ати́шь) *perf.* внима́ние на + *acc.*; (look after) присма́тривать *imp.*, присмотре́ть (-рю́, -ришь) *perf.* за + *instr.*; I don't m., я не возража́ю; я ничего́ не име́ю про́тив; don't m. me, не обраща́й(те) внима́ния на меня́! m. you don't forget, смотри́ не забу́дь! m. your own business, не вме́шивайтесь в чужи́е дела́! never m., ничего́, не беспоко́йтесь! ничего́! **minded** *adj.* (disposed) располо́женный (-ен). **mindful** *adj.* по́мнящий, внима́тельный (of, к + *dat.*).

mine[1] poss.pron. мой (моя́, моё; мой); свой (своя́, своё; свой).

mine[2] n. ша́хта, рудни́к (-а́); (fig.) исто́чник; (mil.) ми́на; v.t. (obtain from m.) добыва́ть *imp.*, добы́ть (добу́ду, -дешь; добы́л, -а́, -о) *perf.*; (mil.) мини́ровать *imp.*, perf. **minefield** n. ми́нное по́ле (pl. -ля́). **minelayer** n. ми́нный загради́тель m. **miner** n. шахтёр, горня́к (-а́). **minesweeper** n. ми́нный тра́льщик.

mineral n. минера́л; adj. минера́льный; m.-water, минера́льная вода́ (acc. -ду). **mineralogist** n. минерало́г. **mineralogy** n. минерало́гия.

mingle v.t. & i. сме́шивать(ся) *imp.*, смеша́ть(ся) perf.

miniature n. миниатю́ра; adj. миниатю́рный. **miniaturist** n. миниатюри́ст.

minibus n. микроавто́бус.

minim n. (mus.) полови́нная но́та. **minimal** adj. минима́льный. **minimize** v.t. (reduce) доводи́ть (-ожу́, -о́дишь) *imp.*, довести́ (-еду́, -едёшь; -ёл, -ела́) perf. до ми́нимума; (underestimate) преуменьша́ть *imp.*, преуме́ньшить perf. **minimum** n. ми́нимум; adj. минима́льный.

mining n. го́рное де́ло.

miniskirt n. ми́ни-ю́бка.

minister n. (polit.) мини́стр; (diplomat) посла́нник; (eccl.) свяще́нник. **ministerial** adj. министе́рский; (eccl.) па́стырский. **ministration** n. по́мощь. **ministry** n. (polit.) министе́рство; (eccl.) духове́нство.

mink n. но́рка; attrib. но́рковый.

minnow n. гольян.

minor adj. (lesser) ме́ньший; (less important) второстепе́нный (-нен, -нна); (mus.) мино́рный; (person under age) несовершенноле́тний n.; (mus.) мино́р. **minority** n. (small number) меньшинство́ (pl. -ва); (age) несовершенноле́тие; national m., нацменьшинство́ (pl. -ва).

minstrel n. менестре́ль m.

mint[1] n. (plant) мя́та; (peppermint) пе́речная мя́та; attrib. мя́тный.

mint[2] n. (econ.) моне́тный двор (-á); in m. condition, блестя́щий, но́вый (нов, -á, -о); (book etc.) непотрёпанный (-ан); v.t. чека́нить *imp.*, от ~, вы ~ perf.

minuet n. менуэ́т.

minus prep. ми́нус + acc.; без + gen.; n. ми́нус; adj. (math., electr.) отрица́тельный.

minuscule adj. минускульный; (о́чень) ма́ленький; n. минускул.

minute[1] n. мину́та; pl. протоко́л; v.t. заноси́ть (-ошу́, -о́сишь) *imp.*, занести́ (-есу́, -есёшь; -ёс, -есла́) perf. в протоко́л.

minute[2] adj. ме́лкий (-лок, -лка́, -лко), мельча́йший. **minutiae** n. ме́лочи (-че́й) f.pl.

minx n. коке́тка.

miracle n. чу́до (pl. -деса́). **miraculous** adj. чуде́сный.

mirage n. мира́ж.

mire n. (mud) грязь (loc. -зи́); (swamp) боло́то. **miry** adj. гря́зный (зен, зна́, зно).

mirror n. зе́ркало (pl. -ла́); (fig.) отображе́ние; m. image, зерка́льное изображе́ние; v.t. отража́ть *imp.*, отрази́ть perf.

mirth n. весе́лье.

misadventure n. несча́стный слу́чай.

misanthrope n. мизантро́п. **misanthropic** adj. мизантропи́ческий. **misanthropy** n. мизантро́пия.
misapplication n. непра́вильное испо́льзование. **misapply** v.t. непра́вильно испо́льзовать imp., perf. **misapprehend** v.t. непра́вильно понима́ть imp., поня́ть (пойму́, -мёшь; -поня́л, -а́, -о) perf. **misapprehension** n. непра́вильное понима́ние. **misappropriate** v.t. незако́нно присва́ивать imp., присво́ить perf. **misappropriation** n. незако́нное присвое́ние. **misbehave** v.i. ду́рно вести́ (веду́, -дёшь; вёл, -а́) imp. себя́. **miscalculate** v.t. непра́вильно рассчи́тывать imp., рассчита́ть perf.; (fig., abs.) просчи́тываться imp., просчита́ться perf. **miscalculation** n. (mistake) оши́бка; (med.) вы́кидыш, або́рт; m. of justice, суде́бная оши́бка. **miscarry** v.i. терпе́ть (-плю́, -пишь) imp., по~ perf. неуда́чу; (med.) име́ть imp. вы́кидыш. **miscast** v.t. непра́вильно распределя́ть imp., распредели́ть perf. роль + dat.
miscellaneous adj. ра́зный, разнообра́зный. **miscellany** n. (mixture) смесь; (book) сбо́рник.
mischance n. несча́стный слу́чай. **mischief** n. (harm) вред (-á); (naughtiness) озорство́; (pranks) прока́зы pl.f.pl. **mischievous** adj. озорно́й. **misconception** n. непра́вильное представле́ние. **misconduct** n. дурно́е поведе́ние; (adultery) супру́жеская неве́рность; v.t.: m. oneself, ду́рно вести́ (веду́, -дёшь; вёл, -а́) imp. себя́. **misconstruction** n. непра́вильное истолкова́ние. **misconstrue** v.t. непра́вильно истолко́вывать imp., истолкова́ть perf. **miscount** n. оши́бка при подсчёте; непра́вильный подсчёт; v.t. ошиба́ться imp., ошиби́ться (-бу́сь, -бёшься; -бся) perf. при подсчёте + gen.
misdeal v.i. ошиба́ться imp., ошиби́ться (-бу́сь, -бёшься; -бся) perf. при сда́че карт. **misdeed** n. злодея́ние. **misdirect** v.t. непра́вильно направля́ть imp., напра́вить perf.; (letter) непра́вильно адресова́ть imp., perf. **misdirection** n.

непра́вильное указа́ние, руково́дство.
miser n. скупе́ц (-пца́), скря́га m. & f. **miserable** adj. (unhappy) несча́стный; (wretched) жа́лкий (-лок, -лка́, -лко), убо́гий. **miserly** adj. скупо́й (скуп, -á, -о). **misery** n. страда́ние, несча́стье.
misfire v.i. дава́ть (даёт) imp., дать (даст, даду́т, да́ло, -и) perf. осе́чку; n. осе́чка. **misfit** n. (garment) пло́хо сидя́щее пла́тье (gen.pl. -ев); (person) неуда́чник. **misfortune** n. несча́стье, беда́. **misgiving** n. опасе́ние. **misgovern** v.t. пло́хо управля́ть imp. + instr. **misgovernment** n. пло́хое управле́ние. **misguided** adj. введённый (-ён, -ена́) в заблужде́ние.
mishap n. неуда́ча, несча́стье. **misinform** v.t. дезинформи́ровать imp., perf. **misinformation** n. дезинформа́ция. **misinterpret** v.t. неве́рно понима́ть imp., поня́ть (пойму́, -мёшь; по́нял, -á, -о) perf. **misjudge** v.t. неве́рно оце́нивать imp., оцени́ть (-ню́, -нишь) perf. **misjudgement** n. неве́рная оце́нка. **mislay** v.t. класть (-аду́, -адёшь; -ал) imp., положи́ть (-жу́, -жишь) perf. не на ме́сто; затеря́ть perf. **mislead** v.t. вводи́ть (-ожу́, -одишь) imp., ввести́ (введу́, -дёшь; ввёл, -á) perf. в заблужде́ние. **mismanage** v.t. пло́хо управля́ть imp. + instr. **mismanagement** n. плохо́е управле́ние. **misnomer** n. непра́вильное назва́ние.
misogynist n. женоненави́стник, мисоги́ну n. женоненави́стничество.
misplace v.t. класть (-аду́, -адёшь; -ал) imp., положи́ть (-жу́, -жишь) perf. не на ме́сто; misplaced confidence, незаслу́женное дове́рие. **misprint** n. опеча́тка; v.t. непра́вильно печа́тать imp., на~ perf. **mispronounce** v.t. непра́вильно произноси́ть (-ошу́, -о́сишь) imp., произнести́ (-есу́, -есёшь; -ёс, -есла́) perf. **mispronunciation** n. непра́вильное произноше́ние. **misquotation** n. непра́вильная цита́та; непра́вильное цити́рование. **misquote** v.t. непра́вильно цити́ровать imp., про~ perf. **misread** v.t. непра́вильно чита́ть imp., про~ perf. **misrepresent**

v.t. искажа́ть *imp.*, искази́ть *perf.* **misrepresentation** *n.* искаже́ние.

Miss[1] *n.* (*title*) мисс.

miss[2] *n.* про́мах, неуда́ча; *v.i.* прома́хиваться *imp.*, промахну́ться *perf.*; *v.t.* (*let slip*) упуска́ть *imp.*, упусти́ть (-ущу́, -у́стишь) *perf.*; (*train*) опа́здывать *imp.*, опозда́ть *perf.* на + *acc.*; *m. out*, пропуска́ть *imp.*, пропусти́ть (-ущу́, -у́стишь) *perf.*; *m. the point*, не понима́ть *imp.*, поня́ть (пойму́, -мёшь; по́нял, -а́, -о) *perf.* су́ти.

missel-thrush *n.* дрозд-деря́ба.

misshapen *adj.* уро́дливый.

missile *n.* снаря́д, раке́та.

missing *adj.* отсу́тствующий, недоста́ющий; (*person*) пропа́вший без вести.

mission *n.* ми́ссия; командиро́вка. **missionary** *n.* миссионе́р; *adj.* миссионе́рский. **missive** *n.* письмо́ (*pl.* -сьма, -сем, -сьмам) посла́ние.

misspell *v.t.* непра́вильно писа́ть (пишу́ -шешь) *imp.*, на ~ *perf.* **misspelling** *n.* непра́вильное написа́ние. **misspent** *adj.* растра́ченный (-ен) (впусту́ю).

misstatement *n.* непра́вильное заявле́ние.

mist *n.* тума́н, мгла.

mistake *v.t.* непра́вильно понима́ть *imp.*, поня́ть (пойму́, -мёшь; по́нял, -а́, -о) *perf.*; *m. for*, принима́ть *imp.*, приня́ть (приму́, -мешь; при́нял, -а́, -о) *perf.* за + *acc.*; *n.* оши́бка; *make a m.*, ошиба́ться *imp.*, ошиби́ться (-бу́сь, -бёшься; -бся) *perf.* **mistaken** *adj.* оши́бочный; *be m.*, ошиба́ться *imp.*, ошиби́ться (-бу́сь, -бёшься; -бся) *perf.*

mister *n.* ми́стер, господи́н.

mistletoe *n.* оме́ла.

mistranslate *v.t.* непра́вильно переводи́ть (-ожу́, -о́дишь) *imp.*, перевести́ (-еду́, -едёшь; -ёл, -ела́) *perf.* **mistranslation** *n.* непра́вильный перево́д.

mistress *n.* хозя́йка; (*teacher*) учи́тельница; (*lover*) любо́вница.

mistrust *v.t.* не доверя́ть *imp.* + *dat.*; *n.* недове́рие. **mistrustful** *adj.* недове́рчивый.

misty *adj.* тума́нный.

misunderstand *v.t.* непра́вильно понима́ть *imp.*, поня́ть (пойму́, -мёшь; по́нял, -а́, -о) *perf.* **misunderstanding** *n.* непра́вильное понима́ние, недоразуме́ние; (*disagreement*) размо́лвка.

misuse *v.t.* непра́вильно употребля́ть *imp.*, употреби́ть *perf.*; (*ill-treat*) ду́рно обраща́ться *imp.* с + *instr.*; *n.* непра́вильное употребле́ние.

mite *n.* (*cheese-m.*) (сы́рный) клещ (-á); (*child*) ма́ленький ребёнок (-нка; *pl.* де́ти, -те́й, -тям, -тьми́), кро́шка; *widow's m.*, ле́пта вдови́цы; *not a m.*, ничу́ть.

mitigate *v.t.* смягча́ть *imp.*, смягчи́ть *perf.* **mitigation** *n.* смягче́ние.

mitre *n.* ми́тра.

mitten *n.* рукави́ца, мите́нка; *pl.* (*boxing-gloves*) боксёрские перча́тки *f.pl.*

mix *v.t.* меша́ть *imp.*, с ~ *perf.*; *v.i.* сме́шиваться *imp.*, смеша́ться *perf.*; (*person*) обща́ться *imp.*; *m. up*, (*confuse*) пу́тать *imp.*, с ~ *perf.*; *get mixed up in*, впу́тываться *imp.*, впу́таться *perf.* в + *acc.*; *n.* смесь; (*food m.*) (пищево́й) полуфабрика́т. **mixer** *n.* смеси́тель. **n. mixture** *n.* смесь; (*medicine*) миксту́ра.

mnemonic *adj.* мнемони́ческий; *n.* мнемони́ческий приём; *pl.* мнемо́ника.

mo *n.* мину́тка; *half a mo*, (одну́) мину́тку!

moan *n.* стон; *v.i.* стона́ть (-ну́, -нешь) *imp.*, про ~ *perf.*

moat *n.* (крепостно́й) ров (рва, *loc.* во рву). **moated** *adj.* обнесённый (-ён, -ена́) рвом.

mob *n.* (*populace*) чернь; (*crowd*) толпа́ (*pl.* -пы); (*gang*) ша́йка; *v.t.* (*attack*) напада́ть *imp.*, напа́сть (-аду́т; -а́л) *perf.* толпо́й на + *acc.*; (*crowd around*) толпи́ться *imp.* вокру́г + *gen.* **mobster** *n.* га́нгстер.

mobile *adj.* подвижно́й, передвижно́й. **mobility** *n.* подви́жность. **mobilization** *n.* мобилиза́ция. **mobilize** *v.t. & i.* мобилизова́ть(ся) *imp.*, *perf.*

moccasin *n.* мокаси́н (*gen.pl.* -н).

mocha *n.* мо́кко *n. & neut.indecl.*

mock *v.t. & i.* издева́ться *imp.* над + *instr.*; осме́ивать *imp.*, осмея́ть (-ею́

-ёшь) *perf.*; *adj.* (*sham*) поддёльный; (*pretended*) мнимый; *mocking-bird*, пересмёшник; *m.* turtle soup, суп из телячьей головы; *m.-up*, макёт, модёль. **mockery** *n.* (*derision*) издевательство, насмёшка; (*travesty*) пародия (of, на+*acc.*; +*gen.*).

mode *n.* (*manner*) о́браз; (*method*) спо́соб.

model *n.* (*representation*) модёль, макёт; (*pattern*) образёц (-зца́); (*artist's*) нату́рщик, -ица; (*mannequin*) манекёнщик, -ица; *adj.* образцо́вый, примёрный; *v.t.* лепи́ть (-плю́, -пишь) *imp.*, вы́~, с~ *perf.*; (*document*) оформля́ть *imp.*, офо́рмить *perf.*; *v.i.* (*act as m.*) быть нату́рщиком, -ицей; быть манекёнщиком, -ицей; *m. after, on*, создава́ть (-да́ю, -даёшь) *imp.*, созда́ть (-а́м, -а́шь, -а́ст, -ади́м) со́здал, -а́, -о) *perf.* по образцу́+*gen.*; *m. oneself on*, брать (беру́, -рёшь; брал, -а́, -о) *imp.*, взять (возьму́, -мёшь; взял, -а́, -о) *perf.*+*acc.* за образёц, примёр.

moderate *adj.* (*var. senses*; *polit.*) умёренный (-ен, -енна); (*person, conduct*) сдёржанный (-ан, -анна); (*quantity*) небольшо́й; *v.t.* умеря́ть *imp.*, умёрить *perf.*; *v.i.* стиха́ть *imp.*, сти́хнуть (-x) *perf.* **moderation** *n.* умёренность; *in m.*, умёренно.

modern *adj.* совремённый (-нен, -нна), но́вый (нов, -а́, -о). **modernism** *n.* модерни́зм. **modernistic** *adj.* модерни́стский. **modernity** *n.* совремённость. **modernization** *n.* модерниза́ция. **modernize** *v.t.* модернизи́ровать *imp.*, *perf.*

modest *adj.* скро́мный (-мен, -мна́, -мно). **modesty** *n.* скро́мность.

modification *n.* видоизменёние, модифика́ция. **modify** *v.t.* (*soften*) смягча́ть *imp.*, смягчи́ть *perf.*; (*partially change*) модифици́ровать *imp.*, *perf.*

modish *adj.* мо́дный (-ден, -дна́, -дно).

modular *adj.* мо́дульный. **modulate** *v.t.* модули́ровать *imp.* **modulation** *n.* модуля́ция. **module** *n.* (*measure*) едини́ца измерёния; (*unit*) мо́дульный, автоно́мный, отсёк; *lunar excursion* *m.*, лу́нная ка́псула. **modulus** *n.* мо́дуль *n.*

mohair *n.* мохёр.

Mohammedan *adj.* мусульма́нский; *n.* мусульма́нин (*pl.* -а́не, -а́н), -а́нка. **Mohammedanism** *n.* исла́м.

moiré *adj.* муа́ровый.

moist *adj.* сыро́й (сыр, -а́, -о), вла́жный (-жен, -жна́, -о). **moisten** *v.t.* & *i.* увлажня́ть(ся) *imp.*, увлажни́ть(ся) *perf.* **moisture** *n.* вла́га.

mol see **mole**[4].

molar[1] *n.* (*tooth*) коренно́й зуб (*pl.* -ы, -о́в); *adj.* коренно́й.

molar[2] *adj.* (*chem.*) мо́льный, моля́рный.

molasses *n.* чёрная па́тока.

mole[1] *n.* (*on skin*) ро́динка.

mole[2] *n.* (*animal*) крот (-а́). **molehill** *n.* крото́вина. **moleskin** *n.* крото́вый мех; (*fabric*) молески́н; *pl.* моле-ски́новые брю́ки (-к) *pl.*

mole[3] *n.* (*pier*) мол (*loc.* -у́).

mole[4] *n.* (*chem.*) моль *n.*

molecular *adj.* молекуля́рный. **molecule** *n.* моле́кула.

molest *v.t.* пристава́ть (-таю́, -таёшь) *imp.*, приста́ть (-а́ну, -а́нешь) *perf.* к+ *dat.* **molestation** *n.* пристава́ние.

mollify *v.t.* смягча́ть *imp.*, смягчи́ть *perf.*

mollusc *n.* моллю́ск.

mollycoddle *n.* нёженка *m.* & *f.*; *v.t.* нёжить *imp.*

molten *adj.* распла́вленный (-ен).

moment *n.* момёнт, миг, мгновёние; (*phys.*) момёнт; (*importance*) значё-ние; *a m. ago*, то́лько что; *at a m.'s notice*, по пёрвому трёбованию; *at the last m.*, в послёднюю мину́ту; *just a m.*, сейча́с! погоди́! **momentarily** *adv.* на мгновёние. **momentary** *adj.* преходя́щий, кратковрёменный (-нен, -нна). **momentous** *adj.* ва́жный (-жен, -жна́, -жно, ва́жны). **momentum** *n.* коли́чество движёния; (*impetus*) дви́жущая си́ла; *gather m.*, набира́ть *imp.*, набра́ть (наберу́, -рёшь; набра́л, -а́, -о) *perf.* ско́рость.

monarch *n.* мона́рх, ~ иня. **monarchical** *adj.* монархи́ческий. **monarchism** *n.*

монархи́зм. **monarchist** n. монархи́ст. **monarchy** n. мона́рхия.

monastery n. (мужско́й) монасты́рь (-ря́) m. **monastic** adj. (of monastery) монасты́рский. (of monks) мона́шеский. **monasticism** n. мона́шество.

Monday n. понеде́льник.

monetary adj. де́нежный; **money** n. де́ньги (-нег, -ньга́м) pl.; m.-box, копи́лка; m.-changer, меня́ла m.; m.-grubbing, стяжа́тельский; m.-lender, ростовщи́к (-а́), -и́ца; m.-market, де́нежный ры́нок (-нка); m. order, (де́нежный) почто́вый перево́д. **moneyed** adj. бога́тый.

Mongol n. монго́л, ~ ка; adj. монго́льский.

mongoose n. мангу́ста.

mongrel adj. нечистокро́вный, сме́шанный; n. дворня́жка, (also fig.) ублю́док (-дка).

monitor n. (school) ста́роста m. (кла́сса); (lizard) вара́н; (naut.; TV) монито́р; (of broadcasts etc.) слуха́ч (-а́); (of radioactivity) дози́метр; v.t. проверя́ть imp., прове́рить perf.; контроли́ровать imp., про~ perf.; v.i. вести́ (веду́, -дёшь; вёл, -а́) imp. радиопереха́т.

monk n. мона́х.

monkey n. обезья́на; v.i.: m. (about) with, неуме́ло обраща́ться imp. с + instr.; m. business, прока́за; m.-jacket, коро́ткая (матро́сская) ку́ртка; m.-nut, земляно́й оре́х; m.-puzzle, араука́рия; m. tricks, ша́лости f.pl.; m.-wrench, разводно́й га́ечный ключ (-а́).

mono- in comb. одно- моно-, едино-. **monochrome** adj. одноцве́тный; n. однокра́сочное изображе́ние. **monocle** n. моно́кль n. **monogamous** adj. единобра́чный. **monogamy** n. единобра́чие. **monogram** n. моногра́мма. **monograph** n. моногра́фия. **monolith** n. моноли́т. **monolithic** adj. моноли́тный. **monologue** n. моноло́г. **monomania** n. монома́ния. **monomaniac** n. манья́к. **monoplane** n. монопла́н. **monopolist** n. монополи́ст. **monopolize** v.t. монополизи́ровать imp., perf. **monopoly** n. монопо́лия. **monorail** n. монорельсо́вая доро́га. **monosyllabic** adj. односло́жный. **monosyllable** n. односло́жное сло́во (pl. -ва́). **monotheism** n. единобо́жие, монотеи́зм. **monotheistic** adj. монотеисти́ческий. **monotone** n. моното́нность; in a m., моното́нно. **monotonous** adj. моното́нный, однообра́зный. **monotony** n. моното́нность, однообра́зие. **monoxide** n. одноо́кись.

monsoon n. (wind) муссо́н; (rainy season) дождли́вый сезо́н.

monster n. чудо́вище, уро́д; adj. грома́дный. **monstrosity** n. уро́дство, чудо́вищность; чудо́вище. **monstrous** adj. чудо́вищный; (huge) грома́дный; (atrocious) безобра́зный.

montage n. (cin.) монта́ж; (of photographs) фотомонта́ж.

month n. ме́сяц. **monthly** adj. ежеме́сячный, ме́сячный; n. ежеме́сячник; adv. ежеме́сячно.

monument n. па́мятник. **monumental** adj. монумента́льный; (stupendous) изуми́тельный, колосса́льный.

moo v.i. мыча́ть (-чу́, -чи́шь); n. мыча́ние.

mood[1] n. (gram.) наклоне́ние.

mood[2] n. настрое́ние. **moody** adj. уны́лый, в дурно́м настрое́нии.

moon n. (of earth) луна́; (of other planets) спу́тник; v.i. бесце́льно слоня́ться imp. **moonlight** n. лу́нный свет; v.i. халту́рить imp. **moonshine** n. фанта́зия; (liquor) самого́н. **moonstone** n. лу́нный ка́мень (-мня) m. **moonstruck** adj. поме́шанный (-ан).

moor[1] n. ме́стность, поро́сшая ве́реском. **moorcock** n. саме́ц (-мца́) шотла́ндской куропа́тки. **moorhen** n. (water-hen) водяна́я ку́рочка. **moorland** n. ве́ресковая пу́стошь.

Moor[2] n. мавр. **Moorish** adj. маврита́нский.

moor[3] v.t. & i. швартова́ть(ся) imp., при~ perf. **mooring** n.: pl. шварто́вы m.pl.; (place) прича́л; m.-mast, прича́льная ма́чта.

moose n. америка́нский лось (pl. -си, -се́й) m.

moot adj. спо́рный.

mop n. швабра; (of hair) копна волос; v.t. протирать imp., протереть (-тру, -трёшь; -тёр) perf. (шваброй); m. one's brow, вытирать (-тру, -трешь; -тер) perf. лоб; m. up, вытирать imp., вытереть (-тру, -трешь; -тер) perf.; (mil.) очищать imp., очистить perf. (от противника).

mope v.i. хандрить imp.

moped n. мопед.

moraine n. морена.

moral adj. моральный, нравственный (-ен, -енна); n. мораль; pl. нравы m.pl., нравственность. morale n. моральное состояние; (of troops) боевой дух. moralist n. моралист, ~ка. moralistic adj. моралистический. morality n. нравственность, мораль. moralize v.i. морализировать imp.

morass n. болото, трясина.

moratorium n. мораторий.

morbid adj. болезненный (-ен, -енна), нездоровый; (med.) патологический.

mordant adj. едкий (едок, едка, едко).

more (larger) больший; (greater quantity) больше + gen.; (additional) ещё; adv. больше; (in addition) ещё; (forming comparative) более; and what is m., и вдобавок; и больше того; m. fool you, тем хуже для тебя; m. or less, более или менее; once m., ещё раз; what m. do you want? что ещё ты хочешь? without m. ado, без дальнейших церемоний. moreover adv. сверх того; кроме того.

mores n. нравы m.pl.

morganatic adj. морганатический.

morgue n. морг; (journ.) справочный отдел.

moribund adj. умирающий.

morning n. утро; in the mornings, по утрам; since m., с утра; towards m., к утру; until m., до утра; at seven o'clock in the m., в семь часов утра; attrib. утренний; m. coat, визитка.

morocco n. сафьян; attrib. сафьяновый.

moron n. умственно отсталый sb. moronic adj. отсталый.

morose adj. угрюмый.

morpheme n. морфема.

morphine n. морфий.

morphology n. морфология.

Morse (code) n. азбука Морзе.

morsel n. кусочек (-чка).

mortal adj. смертный, смертельный; n. смертный sb. mortality n. смертельность; (death-rate) смертность.

mortar n. (vessel) ступа, ступка; (cannon) миномёт, мортира; (cement) (известковый) раствор; m.-board, (cap) академическая шапочка с плоским квадратным верхом.

mortgage n. ипотека, (deed) закладная sb.; v.t. закладывать imp., заложить (-жу, -жишь) perf.

mortification n. (humiliation) унижение; (of the flesh) умерщвление. mortify v.t. унижать imp., унизить perf.; умерщвлять imp., умертвить (-рцвлю, -ртвишь) perf.

mortise n. гнездо (pl. -ёзда), паз (loc. -у; pl. -ы); m. lock, врезной замок (-мка).

mortuary adj. похоронный; n. морг, покойницкая sb.

mosaic n. мозаика; adj. мозаичный.

Mosaic² adj. Моисеев.

Moslem n. мусульманин (pl. -áне, -áн); -áнка; adj. мусульманский.

mosque n. мечеть.

mosquito n. москит; m.-net, москитная сетка.

moss n. мох (м(о)ха, loc. м(о)хе & мху; pl. мхи); m.-grown, поросший мхом. mossy adj. мшистый.

most adj. наибольший; n. наибольшее количество; adj. & n. (majority) большинство + gen.; большая часть + gen.; adv. больше всего, наиболее; (forming superlative) самый; mostly adv. главным образом.

mote n. пылинка.

motel n. мотель m.

moth n. моль, ночная бабочка; m.-ball, нафталиновый шарик; m.-eaten, изъеденный молью.

mother n. мать (-тери, instr. -терью; pl. -тери, -терей); v.t. относиться (-ошусь, -осишься) imp. по-матерински к + dat.; m. country, метрополия; m.-in-law, (wife's m.) тёща; (husband's m.) свекровь; m. of pearl, перламутр; перламутровый; m. tongue, родной язык (-á). motherhood n. материнство.

motherland *n.* ро́дина. **motherless** *adj.* лишённый (-ён, -ена́) ма́тери. **motherly** *adj.* матери́нский.

motif *n.* основна́я те́ма.

motion *n.* движе́ние, ход; (*gesture*) жест; (*proposal*) предложе́ние; (*of bowels*) испражне́ние; *in m.*, в движе́нии, на ходу́; *v.t.* пока́зывать *imp.*, показа́ть (-ажу́, -а́жешь) *perf.* + *dat.* же́стом, что́бы... **motionless** *adj.* неподви́жный. **motivate** *v.t.* побужда́ть *imp.*, побуди́ть *perf.* **motivation** *n.* побужде́ние. **motive** *n.* по́вод, моти́в; *adj.* дви́жущий, дви́гательный.

motley *adj.* (*in colour*) разноцве́тный; (*varied*) пёстрый (-р, -ра́, пёстро́); *n.* вся́кая вся́чина; (*costume*) шутовско́й костю́м.

motor *n.* дви́гатель *m.*, мото́р; *adj.* дви́гательный, мото́рный; (*of m. vehicles*) автомоби́льный; *m. boat*, мото́рная ло́дка; *m. bus*, автобу́с; *m. car*, (легково́й) автомоби́ль *m.*; *m. cycle* мотоци́кл; *m. racing*, автомоби́льные го́нки *f.pl.*; *m. scooter*, моторо́ллер; *m. vehicle*, автомоби́ль *m. motoring n.* автомобили́зм. **motorist** *n.* автомобили́ст, ~ ка. **motorize** *v.t.* моторизова́ть *imp., perf.* **motorway** *n.* автостра́да.

mottled *adj.* испещрённый (-ён, -ена́), кра́пчатый.

motto *n.* деви́з.

mould[1] *n.* (*earth*) взрыхлённая земля́ (*acc.* -лю).

mould[2] *n.* (*shape*) фо́рма, фо́рмочка; *v.t.* формова́ть *imp.*, с~ *perf.*; лепи́ть (-плю́, -пишь) *imp.*, вы~, с~ *perf.* **moulding** *n.* (*action*) формо́вка; (*decoration*) ле́пное украше́ние; (*in wood*) баге́т.

mould[3] *n.* (*fungi*) пле́сень. **mouldy** *adj.* заплесневе́лый; (*coll.*) дрянно́й (-не́н, -нна́, -нно).

moulder *v.i.* разлага́ться *imp.*, разложи́ться (-жи́тся) *perf.*

moult *v.i.* линя́ть *imp.*, вы~ *perf.*; *n.* ли́нька.

mound *n.* холм (-а́); (*heap*) на́сыпь.

Mount[1] *n.* (*in names*) гора́ (*acc.* -ру).

Mount[2] *v.t.* (*ascend*) поднима́ться *imp.*, подня́ться (-ниму́сь, -ни́мешься,

-ня́лся, -няла́сь) *perf.* на + *acc.*; (*m. a horse etc.*) сади́ться (сяду, -дешь; сел) *perf.* на + *acc.*; (*picture*) накле́ивать *imp.*, накле́ить *perf.* на карто́н; (*gem*) вставля́ть *imp.*, вста́вить *perf.* в опра́ву; (*gun*) устана́вливать *imp.*, установи́ть (-влю́, -вишь) *perf.* на лафе́т; *m. up*, (*accumulate*) нака́пливаться *imp.*, накопи́ться (-ится) *perf.*; *m. guard*, стоя́ть (-ою, -ойшь) *imp.* на часа́х; *n.* (*for picture*) карто́н, подло́жка; (*for gem*) опра́ва; (*horse*) верхова́я ло́шадь (*pl.* -ди, -дей, *instr.* дьми́).

mountain *n.* гора́ (*acc.* -ру; *pl.* -ры, -р, -ра́м); *attrib.* го́рный; *m. ash*, ряби́на. **mountaineer** *n.* альпини́ст, ~ ка. **mountaineering** *n.* альпини́зм. **mountainous** *adj.* гори́стый; (*huge*) грома́дный.

mountebank *n.* (*clown*) шут (-а́); (*charlatan*) шарлата́н.

mourn *v.t.* опла́кивать *imp.*, опла́кать (-а́чу, -а́чешь) *perf.*; *v.i.* скорбе́ть (-блю́, -би́шь) *imp.* (over, о + *prep.*). **mournful** *adj.* печа́льный, ско́рбный. **mourning** *n.* (*sorrow*) печа́ль; (*dress*) тра́ур.

mouse *n.* мышь (*pl.* -ши, -ше́й); *v.i.* лови́ть (-влю́, -вишь) *imp.*, пойма́ть *perf.* мыше́й. **mouser** *n.* мышело́в. **mousetrap** *n.* мышело́вка.

mousse *n.* мусс.

moustache *n.* усы́ (усо́в) *pl.*

mousy *adj.* мыши́ный; (*timid*) ро́бкий (-бок, -бка́, -бко).

mouth *n.* рот (рта, *loc.* во рту); (*poet.*) уста́ (-т) *pl.*; (*entrance*) вход; (*of river*) у́стье (*gen.pl.* -ьев); (*of gun, volcano*) жерло́ (*pl.* -ла); *m.* to feed, едо́к (-а́); by word of *m.*, у́стно; *v.t.* говори́ть *imp.*, сказа́ть (-ажу́, -а́жешь) *perf.* напы́щенно. **mouthful** *n.* по́лный рот (рта); (*small amount*) кусо́к (-ска́), глото́к (-тка́). **mouth-organ** *n.* губна́я гармо́ника. **mouthpiece** *n.* мундшту́к (-а́); (*person*) ру́пор.

movable *adj.* подвижно́й; (*property*) дви́жимый.

move *n.* (*in game*) ход (-а(у); *pl.* хо́ды); (*change of location*) переме́на ме́ста; (*step*) шаг (*loc.* -у́; *pl.* -и́); *v.t. & i.* дви-

гать(ся) (-аю(сь), -аешь(ся) & дви-
жу(сь), -жешь(ся)) *imp.*, двинуть(ся)
perf.; *v.t.* (*affect*) трогать *imp.*, тронуть *perf.*; (*propose*) вносить (-ошу,
-осишь) *imp.*, внести (внесу, -сёшь,
внёс, -ла) *perf.*; *v.i.* (*events*) развиваться *imp.*, развиться (разовьётся,
развился, -илась, -илось) *perf.*; (*m.
house*) переезжать *imp.*, переехать
(-еду, -едешь) *perf.*; *m. away*, (*v.i.*)
уезжать *imp.*, уехать (уеду, -едешь
perf.; *m. in*, въезжать *imp.*, въехать
(-еду, -едешь) *perf.*; *m. on*, идти (иду,
идёшь; шёл, шла) *imp.*, пойти (пойду,
-дёшь; пошёл, -шла) *perf.* дальше; *m.
on!* проходите (дальше)! *m. out*,
съезжать *imp.*, съехать (-еду, -едешь)
perf. (*of*, c + *gen.*). **movement** *n.* движение; (*mus.*) часть (*pl.* -ти, -тей).
moving *n.* движущийся; (*touching*)
трогательный; *m. staircase*, эскала-
тор.

mow *v.t.* (*also m. down*) косить (кошу,
косишь) *imp.*, c~ *perf.* **mower** *n.* (*person*) косец (-сца); (*machine*) косилка.

Mr. *abbr.* мистер, господин. **Mrs.** *abbr.*
миссис *f.indecl.*, госпожа.

MS. *abbr.* рукопись.

Mt. *abbr.* гора.

much *adj., n.* много + *gen.*; многое *sb.*;
adv. очень; (*with comp. adj.*) гораздо.

muck *n.* (*dung*) навоз; (*dirt*) грязь (*loc.*
-зи); *v.t.* (*dirty*) пачкать *imp.*, за~,
ис~ *perf.*; *m. out*, чистить *imp.*, вы~
perf.; *m. up*, изгаживать *imp.*, изга-
дить *perf.*

mucous *adj.* слизистый. **mucus** *n.* слизь.

mud *n.* грязь (*loc.* -зи). **mudguard** *n.*
крыло (*pl.* -лья, -льев). **mudslinger** *n.*
клеветник (-а).

muddle *v.t.* путать *imp.*, c~ *perf.*; *v.i.*:
m. along, действовать *imp.* наобум;
m. through, кое-как доводить (-ожу,
-одишь) *imp.*, довести (-еду, -едёшь,
-ёл, -ела) *perf.* дело до конца *n.* не-
разбериха, путаница; *m.-headed*, бестолковый.

muddy *adj.* грязный (-зен, -зна, -зно);
(*of liquid*) мутный (-тен, -тна, -тно);
(*of light*) тусклый (-л, -ла, -ло); *v.t.*
обрызгивать *imp.*, обрызгать *perf.*

грязью; (*water*) мутить (мучу, му-
тишь) *imp.*, вз~, за~ *perf.*

muezzin *n.* муэдзин.

muff *n.* муфта.

muffle *v.t.* закутывать *imp.*, закутать
perf.; (*sound*) глушить *imp.*, за~ *perf.*;
muffled oars, обмотанные вёсла (*gen.*
-сел) *perf.* **muffler** *n.* кашне *neut.
indecl.*, шарф.

mufti *n.*: *in m.*, в штатском.

mug *n.* (*vessel*) кружка; (*face*) морда.

muggy *adj.* сырой (сыр, -а, -о) и тёплый
(-пел, -пла).

mulatto *n.* мулат; ~ ка.

mulberry *n.* (*tree*) шелковица, тутовое
дерево (*pl.* -евья, -евьев); (*fruit*)
тутовая ягода.

mulch *n.* мульча; *v.t.* мульчировать
imp., *perf.* **mulching** *n.* мульчирование.

mule *n.* мул; (*machine*) мюль-машина.
muleteer *n.* погонщик мулов. **mulish**
adj. упрямый как осёл.

mull *v.t.* подогревать *imp.*, подогреть
perf. c пряностями; *mulled wine*,
глинтвейн.

mullah *n.* мулла *m.*

mullet *n.* (*grey m.*) кефаль; (*red m.*)
барабулька.

mullion *n.* средник.

multi- *in comb.* много-. **multicoloured**
adj. многокрасочный. **multifarious**
adj. разнообразный. **multilateral** *adj.*
многосторонний. **multimillionaire** *n.*
мультимиллионер.

multiple *adj.* составной, сложный (-жен,
-жна, -жно); (*varied*) разнообразный;
(*numerous*) многочисленный; (*math.*)
кратный; *m. sclerosis*, рассеянный
склероз; *m. shop*, магазин с филиа-
лами; *n.* кратное число (*pl.* -сла,
-сел, -слам); *least common m.*, общее
наименьшее кратное *sb.* **multiplication**
n. размножение; (*math.*) умножение.
multiplicity *n.* многочисленность,
многообразие. **multiply** *v.t. & i.* раз-
множать(ся) *imp.*, размножить(ся)
perf.; *v.t.* (*math.*) умножать *imp.*,
умножить *perf.*

multitude *n.* множество; (*crowd*) толпа
(*pl.* -пы).

mum[1] *interj.* тише! *mum's the word!*

(об э́том) ни гугу́! *keep m.*, молча́ть (-чу́, -чи́шь) *imp.*

mum² *n.* (*mother*) ма́ма.

mumble *v.t. & i.* мя́млить *imp.*, про~ *perf.*

mummify *v.t.* мумифици́ровать *imp.*, *perf.* **mummy**¹ *n.* му́мия.

mummy² *n.* (*mother*) ма́ма, ма́мочка.

mumps *n.* сви́нка.

munch *v.t.* жева́ть (жую́, жуёшь) *imp.*

mundane *adj.* земно́й.

municipal *adj.* муниципа́льный, городско́й. **municipality** *n.* муниципалите́т.

munificence *n.* ще́дрость. **munificent** *adj.* ще́дрый (щедр, -á, -о).

munitions *n.* вое́нное иму́щество.

mural *adj.* стенно́й; *n.* стенна́я ро́спись.

murder *n.* уби́йство; *v.t.* убива́ть *imp.*, уби́ть (убью́, -ьёшь) *perf.*; (*language*) кове́ркать *imp.*, ис~ *perf.* **murderer**, **murderess** *n.* уби́йца *m. & f.* **murderous** *adj.* уби́йственный (-ен, -енна), смерто́носный.

murky *adj.* тёмный (-мен, -мна́), мра́чный (-чен, -чна́, -чно).

murmur *n.* (*of water*) журча́ние; (*of voices*) шёпот; (*of discontent*) ро́пот; *without a m.*, безро́потно; *v.i.* журча́ть (-чи́т) *imp.*; ропта́ть (ропщу́, -щешь) *imp.* (at, на+*acc.*); *v.t.* шепта́ть (шепчу́, -чешь) *imp.*, шепну́ть *perf.*

muscle *n.* мы́шца, му́скул. **muscular** *adj.* мы́шечный, му́скульный; (*person*) му́скулистый.

Muscovite *n.* москви́ч (-á), ~ка.

muse¹ *v.i.* размышля́ть *imp.*

muse² *n.* му́за.

museum *n.* музе́й.

mushroom *n.* гриб (-á); *m. cloud*, грибови́дное облако (*pl.* -кá, -ко́в).

music *n.* му́зыка; (*sheet m.*) но́ты *f.pl.*; *play without m.*, игра́ть *imp.*, сыгра́ть *perf.* без нот; *m.-hall*, мюзик-холл; *m.-paper*, но́тная бума́га; *m.-stand*, пюпи́тр. **musical** *adj.* музыка́льный; *m. comedy*, музыка́льная коме́дия; *n.* музыка́льная (кино)коме́дия. **musician** *n.* музыка́нт; (*composer*) компози́тор. **musicologist** *n.* музыко́вед. **musicology** *n.* музыкове́дение.

musk *n.* му́скус; *m.-deer*, кабарга́ (*gen. pl.* -ро́г); *m.-melon*, ды́ня; *m.-rat*, онда́тра. **musky** *adj.* му́скусный.

musket *n.* мушке́т. **musketeer** *n.* мушкетёр.

muslin *n.* мусли́н, кисея́; *adj.* мусли́новый, кисе́йный.

mussel *n.* съедо́бная ми́дия.

must¹ *n.* муст; (*new wine*) молодо́е вино́.

must² *v.aux.* (*obligation*) до́лжен (-жнá) *predic.+inf.*; на́до *impers.+dat. & inf.*; (*necessity*) ну́жно *impers.+dat. & inf.*; *m. not*, (*prohibition*) нельзя́ *impers.+ dat. & inf.*; *n.* необходи́мость.

mustard *n.* горчи́ца; *m. gas*, горчи́чный газ; *m. plaster*, горчи́чник; *m.-pot*, горчи́чница.

musty *adj.* за́тхлый.

mutant *adj.* мута́нтный; *n.* мута́нт. **mutation** *n.* мута́ция.

mute *adj.* (*dumb*) немо́й (нем, -á, -о); (*silent*) безмо́лвный; *n.* немо́й *sb.* (*mus.*) сурди́нка. **muted** *adj.* приглушённый (-ён, -ена́); *with m. strings*, под сурди́нку.

mutilate *v.t.* уве́чить *imp.*, из~ *perf.* кале́чить *imp.*, ис~ *perf.* нанести́ уве́чье. **mutilation** *n.* уве́чье.

mutineer *n.* мяте́жник. **mutinous** *adj.* мяте́жный. **mutiny** *n.* мяте́ж (-á); *v.i.* бунтова́ть *imp.*, взбунтова́ться *perf.*

mutism *n.* немота́.

mutter *v.i.* бормота́ть (-очу́, -о́чешь) *imp.*, ворча́ть (-чу́, -чи́шь) *imp.*; *n.* бормота́ние, ворча́ние.

mutton *n.* бара́нина.

mutual *adj.* взаи́мный, взаи́мо-; (*common*) о́бщий; *m. benefit*, ка́сса взаимопо́мощи; *m. friend*, о́бщий друг (*pl.* друзья́, -зе́й).

muzzle *n.* (*animal's*) мо́рда; (*on animal*) намо́рдник; (*of gun*) ду́ло; *v.t.* надева́ть *imp.*, наде́ть (-е́ну, -е́нешь) *perf.* намо́рдник на+*acc.*; (*impose silence*) заставля́ть *imp.*, заста́вить *perf.* молча́ть.

muzzy *adj.* тума́нный (-нен, -нна).

my *poss.pron.* мой (моя́, моё; мои́); свой (-оя́, -оё; -ои́).

myopia *n.* близору́кость. **myopic** *adj.* близору́кий.

myriad *n.* мириа́ды (-д) *pl.*; *adj.* бесчи́сленный (-ен, -енна).

myrrh *n.* ми́рра.

myrtle *n.* мирт; *attrib.* ми́ртовый.

myself *pron.* (*emph.*) (я) сам (-ого́, -ому́, -им, -ом), сама́ (-мо́й, *acc.* -му́); (*refl.*) себя́ (себе́, собо́й); -ся (*suffixed to v.t.*).

mysterious *adj.* тайнственный (-ен,

-енна). **mystery** *n.* та́йна; (*relig. rite; play*) мисте́рия.

mystic(al) *adj.* мисти́ческий; *n.* ми́стик. **mysticism** *n.* мистици́зм. **mystification** *n.* мистифика́ция. **mystify** *v.t.* озада́чивать *imp.*, озада́чить *perf.*

myth *n.* миф. **mythical** *adj.* мифи́ческий. **mythological** *adj.* мифологи́ческий. **mythologist** *n.* мифо́лог. **mythology** *n.* мифоло́гия.

N

nacre *n.* перламу́тр. **nacr(e)ous** *adj.* перламу́тровый.

nadir *n.* нади́р; (*lowest point*) са́мый ни́зкий у́ровень (-вня) *m.*

nag[1] *n.* (*horse*) ло́шадь (*pl.* -ди, -де́й, *instr.* -дьми́).

nag[2] *v.i. & t.: n. at*, пили́ть (-лю́, -лишь) *imp.* + *acc.*; (*of pain*) ныть (но́ет) *imp.*

naiad *n.* найда.

nail *n.* (*finger-, toe-n.*) но́готь (-гтя; *pl.* -гти, -гте́й) *m.*; (*claw*) ко́готь (-гтя; *pl.* -гти, -гте́й) *m.*; (*metal spike*) гвоздь (-дя́; *pl.* -ди, -де́й) *m.*; *n.-brush*, щёточка для ногте́й; *n.-file*, пи́лка для ногте́й; *n.-scissors*, но́жницы (-ц) *pl.* для ногте́й; *n.-varnish*, лак для ногте́й; *v.t.* прибива́ть *imp.*, приби́ть (-бью́, -бьёшь) *perf.* (гвоздя́ми).

naive *adj.* найвный. **naivety** *n.* найвность.

naked *adj.* го́лый (гол, -а́, -о), нагой (наг, -а́, -о); обнажённый (-ён, -ена́); *n. eye*, невооружённый глаз; *n. light*, незащищённый свет; *n. sword*, обнажённый меч (-а́); *n. truth*, чи́стая пра́вда. **nakedness** *n.* нагота́.

name *n.* назва́ние; (*forename*) и́мя *neut.*; (*surname*) фами́лия; (*reputation*) репута́ция; *what is his n.?* как его́ зову́т? *in the n. of*, во и́мя + *gen.*; *v.t.* называ́ть *imp.*, назва́ть (назову́,

-вёшь; назва́л, -а́, -о) *perf.*; (*appoint*) назнача́ть *imp.*, назна́чить *perf.* **nameless** *adj.* безымя́нный. **namely** *adv.* (*a*) и́менно; то есть.

nanny *n.* ня́ня; *n.-goat*, коза́ (*pl.* -зы).

nano-second *n.* на́но-секу́нда.

nap[1] *n.* (*sleep*) коро́ткий сон (сна) *m.*; *v.i.* вздремну́ть *perf.*

nap[2] *n.* (*on cloth*) ворс.

napalm *n.* напа́лм.

nape *n.* загри́вок (-вка).

napkin *n.* (*table-n.*) салфе́тка; (*nappy*) пелёнка.

narcissus *n.* нарци́сс.

narcosis *n.* нарко́з. **narcotic** *adj.* наркоти́ческий; *n.* нарко́тик.

nark *n.* (*spy*) лега́вый *sb.*, стука́ч (-а́); *v.t.* (*irritate*) раздража́ть *imp.*, раздражи́ть *perf.*

narrate *v.t.* расска́зывать *imp.*, рассказа́ть (-ажу́, -а́жешь) *perf.*; *повествова́ть imp.* о + *prep.* **narration** *n.* повествова́ние. **narrative** *n.* расска́з, по́весть (*pl.* -ти, -те́й); *adj.* повествова́тельный. **narrator** *n.* расска́зчик, повествова́тель *m.*

narrow *adj.* у́зкий (у́зок, узка́, у́зко у́зки), те́сный (-сен, -сна́ -сно); (*restricted*) ограни́ченный (-ен, -енна), *n.-gauge*, узкоколе́йный. *n.-minded*, ограни́ченный (-ен, -енна); *n.: pl.* у́зкая часть, (*strait*) у́зкий проли́в; *v.t. & i.* су́живать(ся) *imp.*, су́зить(ся) *perf.* **narrowly** *adv.* (*hardly*) чуть, е́ле-

-éле; *he n. escaped drowning*, он чуть не утонýл. **narrowness** *n.* ýзость, ограниченность.

narwhal *n.* нарвáл.

nasal *adj.* носовóй; (*voice*) гнусáвый.

nascent *adj.* рождáющийся.

nasturtium *n.* настýрция.

nasty *adj.* гáдкий (-док, -дкá, -дко), протúвный; (*dirty*) грязный (-зен, -знá, -зно); (*person*) злóбный.

nation *n.* нáция; (*people*) нарóд; (*country*) странá (*pl.* -ны). **national** *adj.* национáльный, нарóдный; (*of the state*) госудáрственный; *n.* пóдданный *sb.* **nationalism** *n.* националúзм. **nationalist** *n.* националúст, ~ ка. **nationalistic** *adj.* националистúческий. **nationality** *n.* национáльность; (*citizenship*) граждáнство, пóдданство. **nationalization** *n.* национализáция. **nationalize** *v.t.* национализúровать *imp.*, *perf.*

native *n.* (*n. of*) уроженец (-нца), -нка (+*gen.*); туземец (-мца), -мка; *adj.* (*natural*) природный; (*of one's birth*) роднóй; (*indigenous*) тузéмный; (*local*) мéстный; *n. land*, рóдина; *n. language*, роднóй язык (-á); *n. speaker*, носúтель *m.* языкá.

nativity *n.* рождествó (Христóво).

natter *v.i.* болтáть *imp.*; *n.* болтовня.

natural *adj.* естéственный (-ен, -енна), природный; *n. death*, естéственная смерть; *n. resources*, природные богáтства *neut.pl.*; *n. selection*, естéственный отбóр; *n.* (*person*) саморóдок (-дка); (*mus.*) бекáр. **naturalism** *n.* натуралúзм. **naturalist** *n.* натуралúст. **naturalistic** *adj.* натуралистúческий. **naturalization** *n.* (*of alien*) натурализáция; (*of plant, animal*) акклиматизáция. **naturalize** *v.t.* натурализúровать *imp.*, *perf.*; акклиматизúровать *imp.*, *perf.* **naturally** *adv.* естéственно, по прирóде; (*of course*) конéчно, как и слéдовало ожидáть. *n.* прирóда; (*character*) харáктер; *by n.*, по прирóде; *in the n. of*, врóде+*gen.*; *second n.*, вторáя натýра; *state of n.*, первобытное состояние.

naughtiness *n.* (*disobedience*) непослушáние; (*mischief*) шáлости *f.pl.*

naughty *adj.* непослýшный; шаловлúвый.

nausea *n.* тошнотá; (*loathing*) отвращéние. **nauseate** *v.t.* тошнúть *imp. impers.* от+*gen.*; быть протúвным+*dat.*; *the idea nauseates me*, меня тошнúт от этой мысли; эта мысль мне протúвна. **nauseous** *adj.* тошнотвóрный; (*loathsome*) отвратúтельный.

nautical *adj.* морскóй.

naval *adj.* (воéнно-)морскóй, флóтский.

nave *n.* неф.

navel *n.* пупóк (-пкá); *n.-string*, пуповúна.

navigable *adj.* судохóдный. **navigate** *v.t.* (*ship*) вестú (ведý, -дёшь; вёл, -á) *imp.*; (*sea*) плáвать *imp.* **navigation** *n.* навигáция. **navigator** *n.* штýрман.

navvy *n.* землекóп.

navy *n.* воéнно-морскóй флот (*pl.* -óты, -óтов); *n. blue*, тёмно-сúний.

Nazi *n.* нацúст, ~ ка; *adj.* нацúстский. **Nazism** *n.* нацúзм.

near *adv.* блúзко, недалекó; *far and n.*, повсюду; *n. at hand*, под рукóй; *n. by*, рядом; *prep.* вóзле+*gen.*, óколо+*gen.*, у+*gen.*; *adj.* блúзкий (-зок, -зкá, -зко, блúзки), недалёкий (-ёк, -екá, -ёко); *n. miss*, блúзкий прóмах; *n.-sighted*, близорýкий; *v.t. & i.*, приближáться *imp.*, приблúзиться *perf.* к+*dat.*; подходúть (-ожý, -óдишь) *imp.*, подойтú (-ойдý, -ойдёшь; -ошёл, -ошлá) *perf.* к+*dat.*

nearly *adv.* почтú, приблизúтельно.

neat *adj.* (*tidy*) опрятный, аккурáтный; (*clear*) чёткий (-ток, -ткá, -тко); (*undiluted*) неразбáвленный (-ен).

nebula *n.* тумáнность. **nebular** *adj.* небулярный. **nebulous** *adj.* неясный (-сен, -снá, -сно), тумáнный (-нен, -нна).

necessarily *adv.* неизбéжно. **necessary** *adj.* нýжный (-жен, -жнá, -жно, нýжны), необходúмый; (*inevitable*) неизбéжный; *n. необходúмое sb.* **necessitate** *v.t.* дéлать *imp.*, с~ *perf.* необходúмым; (*involve*) влéчь (-чёт, -екýт; влёк, -лá) *imp.* за собóй. **necessity** *n.* необходúмость; неизбéжность; (*object*) предмéт пéрвой необходúмости; (*poverty*) нуждá.

neck n. шея; (of garment) вырез; (of bottle) горлышко (pl. -шки, -шек, -шкам); (isthmus) перешеек (-ейка); get it in the n., получить perf. по шее; risk one's n., рисковать imp. головой; up to one's n., по горло, по уши; n. and n., голова в голову. n. or nothing, либо пан, либо пропал. **neckband** n. ворот. **neckerchief** n. шейный платок (-тка). **necklace** n. ожерелье (gen.pl. -лий). **necklet** n. ожерелье (gen.pl. -лий); (fur) горжетка. **neckline** n. вырез. **necktie** n. галстук.

necromancer n. колдун (-а). **necromancy** n. чёрная магия, колдовство.

nectar n. нектар.

née adj. урождённая.

need n. нужда, надобность, потребность; v.t. нуждаться imp. в + prep.; I (etc.) n., мне (dat.) нужен (-жна, -жно, -жны) + nom.; I n. five roubles, мне нужно пять рублей.

needle n. игла (pl. -лы), иголка; (knitting) спица; (pointer) стрелка; pl. (pine-n.) хвоя; v.t. раздражать imp., раздражить perf.

needless adj. ненужный, излишний; n. to say, не приходится и говорить. **needy** adj. нуждающийся, бедствующий.

negation n. отрицание. **negative** adj. отрицательный; негативный; n. quantity, отрицательная величина; n. result, негативный результат; n. отрицание; (gram.) отрицательное слово (pl. -ва); (phot.) негатив; in the n., отрицательно; отрицательный.

neglect v.t. пренебрегать imp., пренебречь (-егу, -ежёшь; -ёг, -егла) perf. + instr.; не заботиться imp. о + prep.; (abandon) забрасывать imp., забросить perf.; (not fulfil) не выполнять imp. + gen.; n. пренебрежение; (condition) заброшенность. **neglectful** adj. небрежный, невнимательный (of, к + dat.). **negligence** n. небрежность, нерадивость. **negligent** adj. небрежный, нерадивый. **negligible** adj. незначительный.

negotiate v.i. вести (веду, -дёшь; вёл, -а) imp. переговоры; v.t. (arrange)

заключать imp., заключить perf.; (overcome) преодолевать imp., преодолеть perf. **negotiation** n. (discussion) переговоры m.pl.

Negress n. негритянка. **Negro** n. негр; adj. негритянский.

neigh n. ржание; v.i. ржать (ржу, ржёшь) imp.

neighbour n. сосед (pl. -и, -ей), ~ка. **neighbourhood** n. (vicinity) соседство; (area) местность; in the n. of, около + gen. **neighbouring** adj. соседний. **neighbourly** adj. соседский.

neither adv. также не, тоже не; pron. ни тот, ни другой; n. . . . nor, ни . . . ни.

nemesis n. возмездие.

neocolonialism n. неоколониализм.

neolithic adj. неолитический.

neologism n. неологизм.

neon n. неон; attrib. неоновый.

nephew n. племянник.

nepotism n. кумовство.

Neptune n. Нептун. **neptunium** n. нептуний.

nerve n. нерв; (assurance) самообладание; (impudence) наглость; pl. (nervousness) нервозность; get on the nerves of, действовать imp., по~ perf. + dat. на нервы. **nerveless** adj. бессильный. **nervous** adj. нервный (нервен, нервна, нервно); n. breakdown, нервное расстройство. **nervy** adj. нервозный.

nest n. гнездо (pl. -ёзда); n.-egg, сбережения neut.pl.; v.i. гнездиться imp.; вить (вью, вьёшь; вил, -а, -о) imp., свить (совью, -ьёшь, свил, -а, -о) perf. (себе) гнездо. **nestle** v.i. льнуть imp., при~ perf. **nestling** n. птенец (-нца).

net[1] n. сеть (loc. сети; pl. -ти, -тей), сетка; v.t. (catch) ловить (-влю, -вишь) imp., поймать perf. сетями; (cover) закрывать imp., закрыть (-рою, -роешь) perf. сеткой.

net[2], **nett** adj. нетто indecl., чистый (чист, -а, -о, чисты); n. price, цена нетто; n. profit, чистая прибыль; n. weight, чистый вес, вес нетто; v.t. получать imp., получить (-чу, -чишь) perf. . . . чистого дохода.

nettle *n.* крапи́ва; *n.-rash*, крапи́вница; *v.t.* (*fig.*) раздража́ть *imp.*, раздражи́ть *perf.*

network *n.* сеть (*loc.* сети́; *pl.* -ти, -те́й).

neuralgia *n.* невралги́я. **neurasthenia** *n.* неврастени́я. **neuritis** *n.* неври́т. **neurologist** *n.* невро́лог. **neurology** *n.* невроло́гия. **neurosis** *n.* невро́з. **neurotic** *adj.* невроти́ческий; *n.* невро́тик, нервнобольно́й *sb.*

neuter *adj.* сре́дний, сре́днего ро́да; *n.* (*gender*) сре́дний род; (*word*) сло́во (*pl.* -ва́) сре́днего ро́да; (*animal*) кастри́рованное живо́тное *sb.*; *v.t.* кастри́ровать *imp.*, *perf.* **neutral** *adj.* нейтра́льный; (*indifferent*) безуча́стный; *n.* (*state*) нейтра́льное госуда́рство; (*person*) граждани́н (*pl.* -а́не, -а́н), -а́нка, нейтра́льного госуда́рства; (*gear*) нейтра́льное положе́ние рычага́ коро́бки переда́ч; *in n.*, не включённый (-ён, -ена́). **neutrality** *n.* нейтралите́т; безуча́стность. **neutralization** *n.* нейтрализа́ция. **neutralize** *v.t.* нейтрализова́ть *imp.*, *perf.* **neutrino** *n.* нейтри́но *neut.indecl.* **neutron** *n.* нейтро́н.

never *adv.* никогда́; *n.* не мо́жет быть! *n. again*, никогда́ бо́льше, бо́льше не; *n. fear!* бу́дь(те) уве́рен(ы)! *n. mind*, ничего́! всё равно́! *n. once*, ни ра́зу; *on the n.-n.*, в рассро́чку. **nevertheless** *conj.*, *adv.* тем не ме́нее.

new *adj.* но́вый (нов, -а́, -о); (*fresh*) све́жий (свеж, -а́, -о́, све́жи); (*young*) молодо́й (мо́лод, -а́, -о). **new-born** *adj.* новорождённый. **newcomer** *n.* прише́лец (-льца). **newfangled** *adj.* новомо́дный. **newly** *adv.* (*recently*) неда́вно; (*in new manner*) за́ново, вновь.

newel *n.* коло́нка винтово́й ле́стницы.

Newfoundland *n.* ньюфаундле́нд, водола́з.

news *n.* но́вость, -ти *pl.*, изве́стие, -ия *pl.* **newsagent** *n.* газе́тчик. **news-letter** *n.* ·информацио́нный бюллете́нь *m.* **newspaper** *n.* газе́та. **newsprint** *n.* газе́тная бума́га. **newsreel** *n.* кинохро́ника. **news-vendor** *n.* газе́тчик, продаве́ц (-вца́) газе́т.

newt *n.* трито́н.

next *adj.* сле́дующий, бу́дущий; *adv.* в сле́дующий раз; пото́м, зате́м; *n. door*, по сосе́дству; (*house*) в сосе́днем до́ме; (*flat*) в сосе́дней кварти́ре; *n.-door*, сосе́дний; *n. door to*, (*fig.*) почти́; *n. of kin*, ближа́йший ро́дственник, *n. to*, ря́дом с + *instr.*, о́коло + *gen.*; (*fig.*) почти́.

nexus *n.* связь.

nib *n.* перо́ *n.* (*pl.* пе́рья, -ьев).

nibble *v.t.* & *i.* грызть (-зу́, -зёшь; -з) *imp.*; обгрыза́ть *imp.*, обгры́зть (-зу́, -зёшь; -з) *perf.*; (*grass*) щипа́ть (-плю́ -плет) *imp.*; (*fish*) клева́ть (клюёт) *imp.*

nice *adj.* (*precise*) то́чный (-чен, -чна́, -чно); (*subtle*) то́нкий (-нок, -нка́, -нко, то́нки); (*pleasant*) прия́тный (*also iron.*); хоро́ший (-ш, -ша́); (*person*) ми́лый (мил, -а́, -о, ми́лы), любе́зный. **nicety** *n.* то́чность; то́нкость; *to a n.*, то́чно, вполне́.

niche *n.* ни́ша; (*fig.*) своё, надлежа́щее ме́сто.

nick *n.* зару́бка, засе́чка; *in the n. of time*, в са́мый после́дний моме́нт; как раз во́время; *v.t.* де́лать *imp.*, с ~ *perf.* зару́бку, засе́чку, на + *acc.*

nickel *n.* ни́кель *m.*; *attrib.* ни́келевый; *n.-plate*, никелирова́ть *imp.*, *perf.*

nickname *n.* про́звище, прозва́ние; *v.t.* прозыва́ть *imp.*, прозва́ть (прозову́, -вёшь; прозва́л, -а́, -о) *perf.*

nicotine *n.* никоти́н. **nicotinic acid** *n.* никоти́новая кислота́.

niece *n.* племя́нница.

niggardly *adj.* (*miserly*) скупо́й (скуп, -а́, -о); (*scanty*) ску́дный (-ден, -дна́, -дно).

niggling *adj.* ме́лочный.

night *n.* ночь (*loc.* -чи́; *pl.* -чи, -че́й); (*evening*) ве́чер (*pl.* -а́); *at n.*, но́чью; *first n.*, премье́ра; *last n.*, вчера́ ве́чером; *n. and day*, непреста́нно; *attrib.* ночно́й; *n.-club*, ночно́й клуб; *n.-dress*, *-gown*, ночна́я руба́шка; *n.-light*, ночни́к (-а́). **nightcap** *n.* ночно́й колпа́к; (*drink*) стака́нчик спиртно́го на́ ночь. **nightfall** *n.* наступле́ние но́чи. **nightingale** *n.* солове́й (-вья́). **nightjar** *n.* козодо́й. **nightly** *adj.* ночно́й; (*every night*) ежено́щный; *adv.*

ежено́щно. **nightmare** *n.* кошма́р.
nightmarish *adj.* кошма́рный.
nihilism *n.* нигили́зм. **nihilist** *n.* нигили́ст. **nihilistic** *adj.* нигилисти́ческий.
nil *n.* ноль (-ля́) *m.*
nimble *adj.* прово́рный; (*mind*) ги́бкий (-бок, -бка́, -бко).
nimbus *n.* нимб; (*cloud*) дождево́е облако (*pl.* -ка́, -ко́в).
nine *adj.*, *n.* де́вять (-ти́, -тью́); (*collect.*; *9 pairs*) де́ватеро (-рых); (*cards*; *number* 9) девя́тка; (*time*) де́вять (часо́в); (*age*) де́вять лет. **ninepins** *n.* ке́гли (-лей) *pl.* **nineteen** *n.*, *adj.* девятна́дцать (-ти, -тью); (*age*) девятна́дцать лет. **nineteenth** *adj.*, *n.* девятна́дцатый; (*date*) девятна́дцатое (число́). **ninetieth** *adj.*, *n.* девяно́стый. **ninety** *adj.*, *n.* девяно́сто (-та); (*age*) девяно́сто лет; *pl.* (*decade*) девяно́стые го́ды (-до́в) *m.pl.* **ninth** *adj.*, *n.* девя́тый (часть (*pl.* -ти, -те́й)); (*fraction*) девя́тая (часть (*pl.* -ти, -те́й)); (*date*) девя́тое (число́); (*mus.*) но́на.
nip[1] *v.t.* (*pinch*) щипа́ть *imp.*, (-плю́, -плешь) *imp.*, щипну́ть *perf.*; (*bite*) куса́ть *imp.*, укуси́ть (-ушу́, -у́сишь) *perf.*; *n.* along, слета́ть *perf.*; *n. in the bud*, пресека́ть *imp.*, пресе́чь (-еку́, -ече́шь; -е́к, -екла́) *perf.* в ко́рне; *n.* щипо́к (-пка́); уку́с; *there's a n. in the air*, во́здух па́хнет моро́зцем. **nipper** *n.* (*boy*) мальчуга́н.
nip[2] *n.* (*drink*) глото́к (-тка́), рю́мочка.
nipple *n.* сосо́к (-ска́); (*tech.*) ни́ппель (*pl.* -ли & -ля́) *m.*
nirvana *n.* нирва́на.
nit *n.* гни́да.
nitrate *n.* нитра́т. **nitre** *n.* сели́тра. **nitric** *adj.* азо́тный. **nitrogen** *n.* азо́т. **nitrogenous** *adj.* азо́тный. **nitroglycerine** *n.* нитроглицери́н. **nitrous** *adj.* азо́тистый; *n. oxide*, за́кись азо́та.
nitwit *n.* простофи́ля *m.* & *f.*
no *adj.* (*not any*) никако́й, не оди́н; (*not a*) (совсе́м) не; *adv.* нет; (*nisколько*) не + *compar.*; *n.* отрица́ние, отка́з; (*in vote*) го́лос (*pl.* -а́) „про́тив"; *no doubt*, коне́чно, несомне́нно; *no fear*, коне́чно, нет! *no longer*, уже́ не, бо́льше не; *no one*, никто́, *no wonder*, не удиви́тельно.
Noah's ark *n.* Но́ев ковче́г.

nobelium *n.* нобе́лий.
nobility *n.* (*class*) дворя́нство; (*quality*) благоро́дство. **noble** *adj.* дворя́нский, зна́тный; благоро́дный. **nobleman** *n.* дворяни́н (*pl.* -я́не, -я́н).
nobody *pron.* никто́; *n.* ничто́жество.
nocturnal *adj.* ночно́й. **nocturne** *n.* ноктю́рн.
nod *v.i.* кива́ть *imp.*, кивну́ть *perf.* голово́й; (*drowsily*) клева́ть (клюю́, клюёшь) *imp.* но́сом; *nodding acquaintance*, пове́рхностное знако́мство; *n.* киво́к (-вка́).
nodule *n.* узело́к (-лка́).
noggin *n.* кру́жечка.
noise *n.* шум (-а(у)); (*radio*) поме́хи *f.pl.* **noiseless** *adj.* бесшу́мный. **noisy** *adj.* шу́мный (-мен, -мна́, -мно).
nomad *n.* коче́вник. **nomadic** *adj.* кочево́й, кочу́ющий.
nomenclature *n.* номенклату́ра. **nominal** *adj.* номина́льный; (*gram.*) именно́й. **nominate** *v.t.* (*propose*) выдвига́ть *imp.*, вы́двинуть *perf.*; (*appoint*) назнача́ть *imp.*, назна́чить *perf.* **nomination** *n.* выдвиже́ние; назначе́ние. **nominative** *adj.* (*n.*) имени́тельный (паде́ж (-а́)). **nominee** *n.* кандида́т.
non- *pref.* не-, без-. **non-acceptance** *n.* неприня́тие.
nonage *n.* несовершенноле́тие.
nonagenarian *n.* девяностоле́тний стари́к (-а́), -няя стару́ха.
non-aggression *n.* ненападе́ние; *n. pact*, пакт о ненападе́нии. **non-alcoholic** *adj.* безалкого́льный. **non-alignment** *n.* неприсоедине́ние. **non-appearance** *n.* (*leg.*) нея́вка (в суд). **non-arrival** *n.* неприбы́тие.
nonchalance *n.* (*indifference*) безразли́чие; (*carelessness*) беспе́чность. **nonchalant** *n.* безразли́чный; беспе́чный.
non-combatant *n.* нестроево́й. **non-commissioned** *adj.*; *n. officer*, у́нтерофице́р. **non-committal** *adj.* укло́нчивый. **non-conductor** *n.* непроводни́к (-а́).
nonconformist *n.* диссиде́нт; *adj.* диссиде́нтский.
nondescript *adj.* неопределённый (-нен, -нна), неопределённого ви́да.
none *pron.* (*no one*) никто́; (*nothing*) ничто́; (*not one*) не оди́н; *adv.* совсе́м

не; ничуть не; *n.* the less, тем не менее.

nonentity *n.* ничтожество.

non-essential *adj.* несущественный (-ен(ен), -енна). **non-existence** *n.* небытие (*instr.* -ием, *prep.* -ии). **non-existent** *adj.* несуществующий. **non-ferrous** *adj.* цветной. **non-interference, -intervention** *n.* невмешательство. **non-party** *adj.* беспартийный. **non-payment** *n.* неплатёж (-á).

nonplus *v.t.* ставить *imp.*, по~ *perf.* в тупик.

non-proliferation *n.* нераспространение (ядерного оружия). **non-productive** *adj.* непроизводительный. **non-resident** *adj.* не проживающий по месту службы. **non-resistance** *n.* непротивление.

nonsense *n.* вздор, ерунда, чепуха. **nonsensical** *adj.* бессмысленный (-ен, -енна).

non sequitur n. нелогичное заключение.

non-skid, -slip *adj.* нескользящий. **non-smoker** *n.* (*person*) некурящий *sb.*; (*compartment*) вагон, купе *neut.indecl.*, для некурящих. **non-stop** *adj.* безостановочный; (*flight*) беспосадочный; *adv.* без остановок; без посадок.

noodles *n.* лапша.

nook *n.* укромный уголок (-лка); *every n. and cranny*, все углы и закоулки *m.pl.*

noon *n.* полдень (-лудня & -лдня) *m.*; *attrib.* полуденный.

no one see **no.**

noose *n.* петля (*gen.pl.* -тель); *v.t.* поймать *perf.* арканом.

nor *conj.* и не; также не, тоже не; *neither . . . n.*, ни . . . ни.

norm *n.* норма. **normal** *adj.* нормальный. **normality** *n.* нормальность. **normalize** *v.t.* нормализовать *imp.*, *perf.*

north *n.* север; (*naut.*) норд; *adj.* северный; (*naut.*) нордовый; *adv.* к северу, на север; *n.-east*, северо-восток; (*naut.*) норд-ост; *n.-easterly, -eastern*, северо-восточный (*naut.*). норд-остовый; *N. Star*, Полярная звезда; *n.-west*, северо-запад; (*naut.*)

норд-вест; *n.-westerly, -western*, северо-западный; (*naut.*) норд-вестовый; *n. wind*, норд. **northeaster** *n.* норд-ост. **northerly** *adj.* северный; (*naut.*) нордовый. **northern** *adj.* северный; *n. lights*, северное сияние. **northerner** *n.* северянин (*pl.* -яне, -ян); житель *m.*, ~ница *f.* севера. **northernmost** *adj.* самый северный. **northward(s)** *adv.* к северу, на север. **northwester** *n.* норд-вест.

Norwegian *adj.* норвежский; *n.* норвежец (-жца), -жка.

nose *n.* нос (*loc.* -ý; *pl.* -ы); (*sense*) чутьё; (*of ship etc.*) носовая часть (*pl.* -ти, -тей); (*of rocket*) головка; *v.t.* нюхать *imp.*, по~ *perf.*; *n. out*, разнюхивать *imp.*, разнюхать *perf.*; *v.i.* (*of ship etc.*) осторожно продвигаться *imp.*, продвинуться *perf.* вперёд. **nosebag** *n.* торба. **nosebleed** *n.* кровотечение из носу. **nosedive** *n.* пике *neut.indecl.*; *v.i.* пикировать *imp.*, *perf.*

nostalgia *n.* тоска (по родине, по прежнему). **nostalgic** *adj.* вызывающий тоску.

nostril *n.* ноздря (*pl.* -ри, -рей).

not *adv.* не; нет; ни; *n. at all*, нисколько, ничуть; (*reply to thanks*) не стоит (благодарности); *n. half*, (*not at all*) совсем не; (*very much*) ужасно; *n. once*, ни разу; *n. that*, не то, чтобы; *n. too*, довольно + *neg.*; *n. to say*, чтобы не сказать; *n. to speak of*, не говоря уже о + *prep.*

notable *adj.* заметный, замечательный. **notably** *adv.* особенно, заметно.

notary (**public**) *n.* нотариус.

notation *n.* нотация; (*mus.*) нотное письмо.

notch *n.* зарубка; *v.t.* зарубать *imp.*, зарубить (-блю, -бишь) *perf.*

note *n.* (*record*) заметка, записка; (*annotation*) примечание; (*letter*) записка; (*banknote*) банкнот; (*mus.*; *dipl.*) нота; (*tone*) тон; (*attention*) внимание; *n. of hand*, вексель (*pl.* -ля) *m.*; *man of n.*, выдающийся человек; *strike the right (a false) n.*, брать (беру, -рёшь; брал, -á, -о) *imp.*, взять (возьму, -мёшь; взял, -á, -о) *perf.* (не)ве́рный тон; take n. of, обраща́ть *imp.*, обрати́ть (-ащу́, -ати́шь) *perf.* внима́ние на + *acc.*; *v.t.* отмеча́ть *imp.*, отме́тить *perf.*; *n. down*, запи́сывать *imp.*, записа́ть (-ишу́, -и́шешь) *perf.* **notebook** *n.* записна́я кни́жка, блокно́т. **notecase** *n.* бума́жник; (*for*, + *instr.*). **notepaper** *n.* почто́вая бума́га. **noteworthy** *adj.* досто́йный (-о́ин, -о́йна) внима́ния.

nothing *n.* ничто́, ничего́; *n. but*, ничего́ кро́ме + *gen.*, то́лько; *n. of the kind*, ничего́ подо́бного; come to n., конча́ться *imp.*, ко́нчиться *perf.* ниче́м; for n., (free) да́ром; (in vain) зря, напра́сно; have n. to do with, не име́ть *imp.* никако́го отноше́ния к + *dat.*; there is (was) n. for it (but to), ничего́ друго́го не остаётся (остава́лось) (как); придётся (пришло́сь) + *inf.*; to say n. of, не говоря́ уже́ о + *prep.*

notice *n.* (sign) объявле́ние; (intimation) извеще́ние; (warning) предупрежде́ние; (attention) внима́ние; (review) (печа́тный) о́тзыв; at a moment's n., неме́дленно; give (in) one's n., подава́ть (-даю́, -даёшь) *imp.*, пода́ть (-а́м, -а́шь, -а́ст, -ади́м; по́дал, -а́, -о) *perf.* заявле́ние об ухо́де с рабо́ты; give someone n., предупрежда́ть *imp.*, предупреди́ть *perf.* об увольне́нии; take no n. of, не обраща́ть *imp.* внима́ния на + *acc.*; *n.-board*, доска́ (*acc.* -ску; *pl.* -ски, -со́к, -ска́м) для объявле́ний; *v.t.* замеча́ть *imp.*, заме́тить *perf.*; (take n. of) обраща́ть *imp.*, обрати́ть (-ащу́, -ати́шь) *perf.* внима́ние на + *acc.* **noticeable** *adj.* заме́тный. **notifiable** *adj.* подлежа́щий регистра́ции. **notification** *n.* извеще́ние, уведомле́ние; (of death etc.) регистра́ция. **notify** *v.t.* извеща́ть *imp.*, извести́ть *perf.* (of, o + *prep.*); уведомля́ть *imp.*, уве́домить *perf.* (of, o + *prep.*).

notion *n.* поня́тие, представле́ние.

notoriety *n.* дурна́я сла́ва. **notorious** *adj.* пресловут́ый.

notwithstanding *prep.* несмотря́ на + *acc.*; *adv.* тем не ме́нее.

nougat *n.* нуга́.

nought *n.* (nothing) ничто́; (figure 0) нуль (-ля́) *m.*, ноль (-ля́) *m.*; noughts and crosses, кре́стики и но́лики *m.pl.*

noun *n.* (*имя neut.*) существи́тельное *sb.*

nourish *v.t.* пита́ть *imp.* на~ *perf.* **nourishing** *adj.* пита́тельный. **nourishment** *n.* пита́ние.

nova *n.* но́вая звезда́ (*pl.* -ёзды).

novel *adj.* но́вый (нов, -а́, -о); (unusual) необыкнове́нный (-нен, -нна); *n.* рома́н. **novelist** *n.* романи́ст, а́втор рома́нов. **novelty** *n.* (newness) новизна́; (new thing) нови́нка.

November *n.* ноя́брь (-ря́) *m.*; attrib. ноя́брьский.

novice *n.* (eccl.) по́слушник, -ица; (beginner) новичо́к (-чка́).

now *adv.* тепе́рь, сейча́с; (immediately) то́тчас же; (next) тогда́; *conj.*: *n.* (that) раз, когда́; (every) and again, then, вре́мя от вре́мени; *n. . . . . n. . . . ,* то. . .то. . .; by n., уже́; from n. on, в дальне́йшем, впредь. **nowadays** *adv.* в на́ше вре́мя.

nowhere *adv.* (place) нигде́; (direction) никуда́; *pron.*: *I have n. to go,* мне не́куда пойти́.

noxious *adj.* вре́дный (-ден, -дна́, -дно).

nozzle *n.* сопло́ (*pl.* -пла, -п(е)л), форсу́нка, па́трубок (-бка).

nuance *n.* нюа́нс.

nuclear *adj.* я́дерный. **nucleic** *adj.*: *n. acid,* нуклеи́новая кислота́. **nucleus** *n.* ядро́ (*pl.* я́дра, я́дер, я́драм).

nude *adj.* обнажённый (-ён, -ена́), наго́й (наг, -а́, -о); *n.* обнажённая фигу́ра.

nudge *v.t.* подта́лкивать *imp.*, подтолкну́ть *perf.* ло́ктем; *n.* лёгкий толчо́к (-чка́).

nudity *n.* нагота́.

nugget *n.* (gold) саморо́док (-дка).

nuisance *n.* (person) доса́да, неприя́тность; (person) раздража́ющий, надоедли́вый, челове́к.

null *adj.*: *n. and void,* недействи́тельный. **nullify** *v.t.* аннули́ровать *imp.*, *perf.* **nullity** *n.* недействи́тельность.

numb *adj.* онеме́лый, онеме́ний (-ме́ний); *v.t.* вызыва́ть *imp.*, вы́звать (-зовет) *perf.* онеме́ние в + *prep.*, у + *gen.*

number *n.* (total) коли́чество; (total; symbol; math.; gram.) число́ (*pl.* -сла,

-сел, -слам); (*item*) но́мер (*pl.* -á); *n. plate*, номерна́я доще́чка; *v.t.* (*count*) счита́ть *imp.*, со~, счесть (сочту́, -тёшь; счёл, сочла́) *perf.*; (*assign n. to*) нумерова́ть *imp.*, за~, про~ *perf.*; (*contain*) начи́тывать *imp.*; *n. among*, причисля́ть *imp.*, причи́слить *perf.* к+*dat.*; *his days are numbered*, его́ дни сочтены́. **numberless** *adj.* бесчи́сленный (-ен, -енна).

numeral *adj.* числово́й, цифрово́й; *n.* ци́фра; (*gram.*) (и́мя *neut.*) числи́тельное *sb.* **numerator** *n.* числи́тель *m.* **numerical** *adj.* числово́й, цифрово́й. **numerous** *adj.* многочи́сленный (-ен, -енна); (*many*) мно́го+*gen.pl.*

numismatic *adj.* нумизмати́ческий. **numismatics** *n.* нумизма́тика. **numismatist** *n.* нумизма́т.

numskull *n.* тупи́ца *m.* & *f.*, о́лух.

nun *n.* мона́хиня. **nunnery** *n.* (же́нский) монасты́рь (-ря́) *m.*

nuptial *adj.* бра́чный, сва́дебный; *n.: pl.* сва́дьба (*gen.pl.* -деб).

nurse *n.* (*child's*) ня́ня; (*medical*) медсестра́ (*pl.* -ёстры, -ёстёр, -ёстрам), сиде́лка; (*country*) колыбе́ль; *v.t.* (*suckle*) корми́ть (-млю́, -мишь) *imp.*,

на~, по~ *perf.*; (*tend sick*) уха́живать *imp.* за+*instr.*; (*treat illness*) лечи́ть (-чу́, -чишь) *imp.*; **nursing home**, ча́стная лече́бница, ча́стный санато́рий. **nursery** *n.* (*room*) де́тская *sb.*; (*day n.*) я́сли (-лей) *pl.*; (*for plants*) пито́мник; *n. rhyme*, де́тские стишки́ *m.pl.*; *n. school*, де́тский сад (*loc.* -ý; *pl.* -ы́). **nurs(e)ling** *n.* пито́мец (-мца) -мица.

nut *n.* оре́х; (*for bolt etc.*) га́йка; (*sl., head*) башка́; (*sl., person*) псих. **nut-crackers** *n.* щипцы́ (-цо́в) *pl.* для оре́хов. **nuthatch** *n.* по́ползень (-зня) *m.* **nutshell** *n.* оре́ховая скорлупа́ (*pl.* -пы); *in a n.*, в двух слова́х. **nut-tree** *n.* оре́шник.

nutmeg *n.* муска́тный оре́х.

nutria *n.* ну́трия.

nutriment *n.* пита́тельная еда́. **nutrition** *n.* пита́ние. **nutritious** *adj.* пита́тельный.

nylon *n.* нейло́н; *pl.* нейло́новые чулки́ (-ло́к) *pl.*; *attrib.* нейло́новый.

nymph *n.* ни́мфа. **nymphomaniac** *n.* нимфома́нка.

nystagmus *n.* ниста́гм.

O

O *interj.* о! ах! ох!

oaf *n.* неуклю́жий, неотёсанный, челове́к. **oafish** *adj.* неуклю́жий.

oak *n.* (*tree*) дуб (*loc.* -е & -ý; *pl.* -ы́); (*wood*) древеси́на ду́ба; *attrib.* дубо́вый.

oakum *n.* па́кля.

oar *n.* весло́ (*pl.* вёсла, -сел, -слам). **oarsman** *n.* гребе́ц (-бца́).

oasis *n.* оа́зис.

oast-house *n.* хмелесуши́лка.

oat *n.: pl.* ове́с (овса́) *collect.* **oatcake** *n.* овся́ная лепёшка. **oatmeal** *n.* овся́нка.

oath *n.* кля́тва, прися́га; (*expletive*)

руга́тельство; *on, under, o.,* под прися́гой.

obduracy *n.* упря́мство. **obdurate** *adj.* упря́мый.

obedience *n.* послуша́ние. **obedient** *adj.* послу́шный.

obelisk *n.* обели́ск; (*print.; obelus*) кре́стик.

obese *n.* ту́чный (-чен, -чна́, -чно). **obesity** *n.* ту́чность.

obey *v.t.* слу́шаться *imp.*, по~ *perf.*+ *gen.*; повинова́ться *imp.* (*also perf. in past*)+*dat.*

obituary *n.* некроло́г; *adj.* некрологи́ческий.

object n. (thing) предмéт; (aim) цель; (gram.) дополнéние; o.-glass, объектúв; o.-lesson, (fig.) нагля́дный примéр; v.i. возражáть imp., возразúть perf. (to, прóтив + gen.); протестовáть imp. (to, прóтив + gen.); я не прóтив, я не возражáю. **objection** n. возражéние, протéст; I have no o., я не возражáю. **objectionable** adj. неприя́тный. **objective** adj. объектúвный; (gram.) объектúвный; n. (mil.) объéкт; (aim) цель; (lens) объектúв; (gram.) объектúвный падéж (-á). **objectivity** n. объектúвность. **objector** n. возражáющий sb.

obligation n. обязáтельство; I am under an o., я обя́зан (-а). **obligatory** adj. обязáтельный. **oblige** v.t. обя́зывать imp., обязáть (-я́жу, -я́жешь) perf.; заставля́ть imp., застáвить perf.; be obliged to, (grateful) быть благодáрным + dat. **obliging** adj. услýжливый, любéзный.

oblique adj. косóй (кос, -á, -о); (indirect) непрямóй (-м, -мá, -мо); (gram.) кóсвенный.

obliterate v.t. (efface) стирáть imp., стерéть (сотрý, -рёшь; стёр) perf.; (destroy) уничтожáть imp., уничтóжить perf. **obliteration** n. стирáние; уничтожéние.

oblivion n. забвéние. **oblivious** adj. (forgetful) забы́вчивый; to be o. of, не замечáть imp. + gen.

oblong adj. продолговáтый.

obnoxious adj. протúвный.

oboe n. гобóй.

obscene adj. непристóйный. **obscenity** n. непристóйность.

obscure adj. (dark) тёмный (-мен, -мнá); (unclear) нея́сный (-сен, -снá, -сно); (little known) мáло извéстный; v.t. затемня́ть imp., затемнúть perf.; дéлать imp., с~ perf. нея́сным. **obscurity** n. нея́сность, неизвéстность.

obsequious adj. подобострáстный.

observance n. соблюдéние; (rite) обря́д. **observant** adj. наблюдáтельный. **observation** n. наблюдéние; (remark) замечáние. **observatory** n. обсервáтория. **observe** v.t. (law etc.) соблюдáть imp., соблюстú (-юдý, -юдёшь, -юдáл, -юдлá) perf.; (watch) наблюдáть

imp.; (remark) замечáть imp., замéтить perf. **observer** n. наблюдáтель m.

obsess v.t. преслéдовать imp.; мýчить imp. **obsession** n. одержúмость; (idea) навя́зчивая идéя. **obsessive** adj. навя́зчивый.

obsidian n. обсидиáн.

obsolescence n. устаревáние. **obsolescent** adj. устаревáющий. **obsolete** adj. устарéлый, вы́шедший из употреблéния.

obstacle n. препя́тствие, помéха; o.-race, бег с препя́тствиями.

obstetric(al) adj. акушéрский. **obstetrician** n. акушéр. **obstetrics** n. акушéрство.

obstinacy n. упря́мство. **obstinate** adj. упря́мый.

obstreperous adj. бýйный (бýен, буйнá, -но).

obstruct v.t. пре-, за-, граждáть imp., пре-, за-, градúть perf.; (prevent, impede) препя́тствовать imp., вос~ perf.+ dat.; мешáть imp., по~ perf.+ dat. **obstruction** n. пре-, за-, граждéние; (obstacle) препя́тствие. **obstructive** adj. пре-, за-, граждáющий; препя́тствующий, мешáющий.

obtain v.t. получáть imp., получúть (-чý, -чишь) perf.; доставáть (-таю́, -таёшь) imp., достáть (-áну, -áнешь) perf.

obtrude v.t. навя́зывать imp., навязáть (-яжý, -я́жешь) perf. ((up)on, + dat.). **obtrusive** adj. навя́зчивый.

obtuse adj. тупóй (туп, -á, -о, тýпы́).

obverse n. (of coin etc.) лицевáя сторонá (acc. -ону; pl. -оны, -óн, -онáм).

obviate v.t. (remove) устраня́ть imp., устранúть perf.; (get round) обходúть (-ожý, -óдишь) imp., обойтú (обойдý, -дёшь; обошёл, -шлá) perf.

obvious adj. очевúдный, я́вный.

ocarina n. окарúна.

occasion n. (juncture) слýчай; (cause) пóвод; (occurrence) собы́тие; v.t. причиня́ть imp., причинúть perf. **occasional** adj. случáйный, рéдкий (-док, -дкá, -дко). **occasionally** adv. иногдá, врéмя от врéмени.

Occident n. Зáпад. **Occidental** adj. зáпадный.

occlude v.t. прегражда́ть imp., прегради́ть perf. **occlusion** n. прегражде́ние.

occult adj. та́йный, оккульти́ный.

occupancy n. заня́тие; (possession) владе́ние (of, + instr.). **occupant** n. (of land) владе́лец (-льца), -лица; (of house etc.) жи́тель m., ~ ница. **occupation** n. заня́тие; (military o.) оккупа́ция; (profession) профе́ссия. **occupational** adj. профессиона́льный; o. disease, профессиона́льное заболева́ние; o. therapy, трудотерапи́я. **occupy** v.t. занима́ть imp., заня́ть (займу́, -мёшь; за́нял, -а́, -о) perf.; (mil.) оккупи́ровать imp., perf.

occur v.i. (happen) случа́ться imp., случи́ться perf.; (be met with) встреча́ться imp.; o. to, приходи́ть (-ит) imp., прийти́ (придёт; пришёл, -шла́) perf. в го́лову + dat. **occurrence** n. слу́чай, происше́ствие.

ocean n. океа́н; (fig.) ма́сса, мо́ре; attrib. океа́нский; o.-going, океа́нский. **oceanic** adj. океа́нский, океани́ческий.

ochre n. о́хра.

o'clock adv.: at six o., в шесть часо́в.

octagon n. восьмиуго́льник. **octagonal** adj. восьмиуго́льный.

octane n. окта́н; o. number, окта́новое число́.

octave n. (mus.) окта́ва.

octet n. окте́т.

October n. октя́брь (-ря́) m.; attrib. октя́брьский.

octogenarian n. восьмидесятиле́тний стари́к (-а́) /-няя стару́ха.

octopus n. осьмино́г, спрут.

ocular adj. глазно́й, окуля́рный. **oculist** n. окули́ст.

odd adj. (number) нечётный; (not paired) непа́рный; (casual) случа́йный; (strange) стра́нный (-нен, -нна́, -нно); five hundred o., пятьсо́т с ли́шним; o. job, случа́йная рабо́та; o. man out, (тре́тий) ли́шний sb. **oddity** n. стра́нность; (person) чуда́к (-а́), -а́чка. **oddly** adv. стра́нно; o. enough, как э́то ни стра́нно. **oddment** n. оста́ток (-тка); pl. разро́зненные предме́ты m.pl. **odds** n. (advantage) переве́с; (variance) разногла́сие;

(chance) ша́нсы m.pl.; be at o. with, (person) не ла́дить с + instr.; (things) не соотве́тствовать imp. + dat.; long (short) o., нера́вные (почти́ ра́вные) ша́нсы m.pl.; the o. are that, вероя́тно всего́, что; o. and ends, обры́вки m.pl.

ode n. о́да.

odious adj. ненави́стный, отврати́тельный. **odium** n. не́нависть, отвраще́ние.

odour n. за́пах; be in good (bad) o. with, быть в (не)ми́лости у + gen. **odourless** adj. без за́паха.

odyssey n. одиссе́я.

oedema n. отёк.

oesophagus n. пищево́д.

of prep. expressing 1. origin: из + gen.: he comes of a working-class family, он из рабо́чей семьи́; 2. cause: от + gen.: he died of hunger, он у́мер от го́лода; 3. authorship: genitive: the works of Pushkin, сочине́ния Пу́шкина; 4. material: из + gen.: made of wood, сде́ланный из де́рева; adjective: a heart of stone, ка́менное се́рдце; 5. identity: apposition: the city of Moscow, го́род Москва́; adjective: the University of Moscow, Моско́вский университе́т; 6. concern, reference: о + prep.: he talked of Lenin, он говори́л о Ле́нине; 7. quality: genitive: a man of strong character, челове́к си́льного хара́ктера; adjective: a man of importance, ва́жный челове́к; 8. partition: genitive (often in -у(-ю)): see Introduction): a glass of milk, tea, стака́н молока́, ча́ю; из + gen.: one of them, оди́н из них; 9. belonging: genitive: the capital of England, столи́ца А́нглии; poss. adj.: the house of his father, отцо́вский дом; 10. following other parts of speech: see individual entries, e.g. be afraid, боя́ться (+ gen.); dispose of, избавля́ться от + gen.

off adv.: in phrasal verbs, see verb, e.g. clear o., убира́ться; prep. (from surface of) с + gen.; (away from) от + gen.; adj. (far) да́льний; (right hand) пра́вый; (free) свобо́дный; o. and on, вре́мя от вре́мени; on the o. chance, на вся́кий слу́чай; o. colour, нездоро́вый *o. the cuff*, без подготовки; *o. the point*, не относящийся к делу; *o. white*, не совсем белый (бел, -а, бело́).

offal *n.* (*food*) требуха́, потроха́ (-хо́в) *pl.*; (*carrion*) па́даль.

offence *n.* (*attack*) нападе́ние; (*insult*) оби́да; (*against law*) просту́пок (-пка), преступле́ние; *take o.*, обижа́ться *imp.*, оби́деться (-ижусь, -идишься) *perf.* (*at*, на + *acc.*). **offend** *v.t.* оскорбля́ть *imp.*, оскорби́ть *perf.*; обижа́ть *imp.*, оби́деть (-и́жу, -и́дишь) *perf.*; *o. against*, наруша́ть *imp.*, нару́шить *perf.* (*at*, на + *acc.*). **offender** *n.* правонаруши́тель *m.*, ~ница; престу́пник, ~ица. **offensive** *adj.* (*attacking*) наступа́тельный; (*insulting*) оскорби́тельный, оби́дный; (*repulsive*) проти́вный; *n.* нападе́ние.

offer *v.t.* предлага́ть *imp.*, предложи́ть (-жу́, -жишь) *perf.*; *n.* предложе́ние; *on o.*, в прода́же.

offhand *adj.* бесцеремо́нный (-нен,-нна), небре́жный; *adv.* (*without preparation*) без подготовки, экспро́мтом.

office *n.* (*position*) до́лжность; (*place, room, etc.*) бюро́ *neut.indecl.*, конто́ра, канцеля́рия; (*eccl.*) (церко́вная) слу́жба. **officer** *n.* должностно́е лицо́ (*pl.* -ца); (*mil.*) офице́р. **official** *adj.* служе́бный, должностно́й; (*authorized*) официа́льный; *n.* должностно́е лицо́ (*pl.* -ца). **officiate** *v.i.* (*eccl.*) соверша́ть *imp.*, соверши́ть *perf.* богослуже́ние. **officious** *adj.* (*intrusive*) навя́зчивый.

offing *n.*: *in the o.*, в недалёком бу́дущем.

offprint *n.* отде́льный о́ттиск. **offscourings** *n.* отбро́сы (-сов) *pl.*, подо́нки (-ков) *pl.* **offset** *n.* (*compensation*) возмеще́ние; (*offshoot*) о́тпрыск; (*in pipe*) отво́д; *o. process*, (*print.*) офсе́тный спо́соб; *v.t.* возмеща́ть *imp.*, возмести́ть *perf.* **offshoot** *n.* о́тпрыск. **offside** *adv.* вне игры́. **offspring** *n.* пото́мок (-мка); (*collect.*) пото́мки *m.pl.*

often *adv.* ча́сто.

ogle *v.t. & i.* стро́ить *imp.* гла́зки + *dat.*

ogre *n.* велика́н-людое́д. **ogress** *n.* велика́нша-людое́дка.

oh *interj.* о! ах! ох!

ohm *n.* ом (*gen./pl.* ом).

oho *interj.* ого́!

oil *n.* ма́сло (*pl.* -сла́, -сел, -сла́м); (*petroleum*) нефть; (*lubricant*) жи́дкая сма́зка *f.pl.*; (*paint*) ма́сло, ма́сляные кра́ски *f.pl.*; *v.t.* сма́зывать *imp.*, сма́зать (сма́жу, -жешь) *perf.*; *o.-colour, -paint*, ма́сляная кра́ска; *o.-painting*, карти́на, напи́санная ма́сляными кра́сками; *o.-rig*, бурова́я устано́вка; *o.-tanker*, та́нкер; *o.-well*, нефтяна́я сква́жина. **oilcake** *n.* жмых *m.* **oilcan** *n.* маслёнка. **oilcloth** *n.* клеёнка. **oilfield** *n.* месторожде́ние не́фти. **oilskin** *n.* то́нкая клеёнка; *pl.* дождево́е пла́тье. **oily** *adj.* масляни́стый; (*unctuous*) елейный.

ointment *n.* мазь.

O.K. *adv.* хорошо́; *interj.* ла́дно!; *v.t.* одобря́ть *imp.*, одобрить *perf.*

okapi *n.* ока́пи *m. & f.indecl.*

old *adj.* ста́рый (стар, -а́, ста́ро); (*ancient*) стари́нный; (*of long standing*) стари́нный; (*former*) бы́вший; *how o. are you?* ско́лько тебе́, вам, (*dat.*) лет? *she is three years o.*, ей (*dat.*) три го́да; *the o.*, старики́ *m.pl.*; *o. age*, ста́рость; *o.-age pension*, пе́нсия по ста́рости; *O. Believer*, старообря́дец (-дца); *o. chap, fellow, etc.*, старина́; *the o. country*, ро́дина, оте́чество; *o.-fashioned*, старомо́дный; *o. maid*, ста́рая де́ва; *o. man*, (*also father, husband*) стари́к (-а́); (*boss*) шеф; *o. man's beard*, ломоно́с; *o.-time*, стари́нный, пре́жних времён; *o. woman*, стару́ха; (*coll.*) стару́шка; *o.-world*, стари́нный.

oleaginous *adj.* масляни́стый, жи́рный (-рен, -рна́, -рно).

oleander *n.* олеа́ндр.

olfactory *adj.* обоня́тельный.

oligarch *n.* олига́рх. **oligarchic(al)** *adj.* олигархи́ческий. **oligarchy** *n.* олига́рхия.

olive *n.* (*fruit*) масли́на, оли́вка; (*colour*) оли́вковый цвет; *adj.* оли́вковый; *o.-branch*, оли́вковая ветвь (*pl.* -ви, -вёй); *o. oil*, оли́вковое ма́сло, *o.-tree*, масли́на, оли́вковое де́рево (*pl.* дере́вья, -ьев).

Olympic *adj.* олимпи́йский; *O. games*, Олимпи́йские и́гры *f.pl.*

omelet(te) *n.* омле́т.

omen n. предзнаменова́ние. **ominous** adj. злове́щий.

omission n. про́пуск; (*neglect*) упущё́ние. **omit** v.t. (*leave out*) пропуска́ть *imp.*, пропусти́ть (-ущу́, -у́стишь) *perf.*; (*neglect*) упуска́ть *imp.*, упусти́ть (-ущу́, -у́стишь) *perf.*

omnibus n. (*bus*) авто́бус; (*book*) одното́мник.

omnipotence n. всемогу́щество. **omnipotent** adj. всемогу́щий. **omnipresent** adj. вездесу́щий. **omniscient** adj. всеве́дущий. **omnivorous** adj. всея́дный; (*fig.*) всепоглоща́ющий.

on prep. (*position*) на + prep.; *on the right of*, (*relative position*) с пра́вой стороны́ от + gen.; (*direction*) на + acc.; (*time*) в + acc.; *on the next day*, на сле́дующий день; *on Mondays*, (*repeated action*) по понеде́льникам (dat.pl.); *on (the morning of) the first of June*, (у́тром) пе́рвого ию́ня (gen.); *on arrival*, по прибы́тии (prep.); (*concerning*) по + prep., o + prep., на + acc.; adv. да́льше, вперёд; in phrasal verbs, see verbs, e.g. *move on*, идти́ да́льше; *and so on*, и так да́лее, и т.д.; *further on*, да́льше; *later on*, по́зже.

once adv. (оди́н) раз; (*on past occasion*) одна́жды; (*at a*), неожи́данно; *at o.*, сра́зу, неме́дленно; (*if, when*) o., как то́лько; *o. again*, *more*, ещё раз; *o. and for all*, раз и навсегда́; *o. or twice*, не́сколько раз; *o. upon a time there lived*, жил-был...

oncoming n. приближе́ние; adj. приближа́ющийся; *o. traffic*, встре́чное движе́ние.

one adj. оди́н (одна́, -но́); (*only, single*) еди́нственный; (*unified*) еди́ный; n. оди́н; (*unit*) едини́ца; pron.: not usu. translated; verb translated in 2nd pers. sing. or by impers. construction: *one never knows*, никогда́ не зна́ешь; *where can one buy this book?* где мо́жно купи́ть э́ту кни́гу? *chapter o.*, пе́рвая глава́; *I for o.*, что каса́ется меня́; я со свое́й стороны́; *o. after another*, оди́н за други́м; *o. and all*, все до одного́; все как оди́н; *o. and only*, еди́нственный; *o. and the same*, оди́н и тот же; *o. another*, друг дру́га

(dat. -гу, etc.); *o. fine day*, в оди́н прекра́сный день; *o. o'clock*, час; *o.-armed*, *-handed*, одно́ру́кий; *o.-eyed*, одногла́зый; *o.-legged*, одноно́гий; *o.-sided*, *-track*, *-way*, односторо́нний; *o.-time*, бы́вший; *o.-way street*, у́лица односторо́ннего движе́ния.

onerous adj. тя́гостный.

oneself pron. себя́ (себе́, собо́й); -ся (suffixed to v.refl.).

onion n. (*plant*; pl. collect.) лук; (*single o.*) лу́ковица.

onlooker n. наблюда́тель m., ~ ница.

only adj. еди́нственный; adv. то́лько; *if o.*, е́сли бы то́лько; *o. just*, то́лько что; conj. но.

onomatopoeia n. звукоподража́ние. **onomatopoeic** adj. звукоподража́тельный.

onset, onslaught n. на́тиск, ата́ка.

onus n. (*burden*) бре́мя neut.; (*responsibility*) отве́тственность.

onward adj. дви́жущийся вперёд. **onwards** adv. вперёд.

onyx n. о́никс; attrib. о́никсовый.

ooze n. ил, ти́на; v.t. & i. сочи́ться imp.

oozy adj. и́листый, ти́нистый.

opacity n. непрозра́чность.

opal n. опа́л; *o. glass*, моло́чное стекло́. **opalescence** n. опалесце́нция. **opalescent** adj. опалесци́рующий. **opaline** adj. опа́ловый.

opaque adj. непрозра́чный.

open adj. откры́тый; (*frank*) открове́нный (-нен, -нна); (*accessible*) досту́пный; (*boat*) беспалу́бный; *in the o. air*, на откры́том во́здухе; *opencast mining*, откры́тые го́рные рабо́ты f.pl.; *o.-handed*, ще́дрый (щедр, -á, -o); *o.-minded*, непредубеждённый (-ён, -ённа); *o.-mouthed*, с раз́инутым ртом; *o.-work*, ажу́рный; ажу́рная рабо́та; v.t. & i. открыва́ть(ся) imp., откры́ть(ся) (-ро́ю(сь), -ро́ешь(ся)) perf.; (*o. wide*) раскрыва́ть(ся) imp., раскры́ть(ся) (-ро́ю(сь), -ро́ешь(ся)) perf.; v.i. (*begin*) начина́ться imp., нача́ться (-чнётся; начался́, -ла́сь) perf. **opening** n. откры́тие; (*aperture*) отве́рстие; (*beginning*) нача́ло; adj. вступи́тельный, нача́льный, пе́рвый.

opera n. о́пера; attrib. о́перный; o.-glasses, бино́кль m.; o.-hat, складно́й цили́ндр; o.-house, о́пера, о́перный теа́тр.

operate v.i. де́йствовать imp. (upon, на+acc.); де́лать imp., c~ perf. опера́цию; (med.) опери́ровать imp., perf. (on, +acc.); v.t. управля́ть imp. +instr.

operatic adj. о́перный.

operating-theatre n. операцио́нная sb.

operation n. де́йствие; (med.; mil.) опера́ция. **operational** adj. операти́вный. **operative** adj. де́йствующий, операти́вный; n. рабо́чий sb. **operator** n. опера́тор; (telephone o.) телефони́ст, ~ка.

operetta n. опере́тта.

ophthalmia n. офтальми́я. **ophthalmic** adj. глазно́й.

opiate n. опиа́т.

opine v.t. полага́ть imp. **opinion** n. мне́ние; (expert's o.) заключе́ние (специали́ста); o. poll, опро́с обще́ственного мне́ния. **opinionated** adj. упо́рствующий в свои́х взгля́дах.

opium n. о́пий, о́пиум; o. poppy, снотво́рный мак.

opossum n. опо́ссум.

opponent n. проти́вник.

opportune adj. своевре́менный (-нен, -нна). **opportunism** n. оппортуни́зм. **opportunist** n. оппортуни́ст. **opportunity** n. слу́чай, возмо́жность.

oppose v.t. (contrast) противопоставля́ть imp., противопоста́вить perf. (to, +dat.); (resist) проти́виться imp., вос~ perf.+dat.; (speak etc. against) выступа́ть imp., вы́ступить perf. про́тив+gen. **opposed** adj. (contrasted) противопоста́вленный (-ен); (of person) про́тив (to, +gen.); as o. to, в противополо́жность+dat. **opposite** adj. противополо́жный, обра́тный; n. противополо́жность; just the o., как раз наоборо́т; adv. напро́тив, prep. (на)про́тив+gen. **opposition** n. (contrast) противопоставле́ние; (resistance) сопротивле́ние; (polit.) оппози́ция.

oppress v.t. притесня́ть imp., притесни́ть perf.; угнета́ть imp. **oppression** n.

притесне́ние, угнете́ние. **oppressive** adj. гнету́щий, угнета́тельский; (weather) ду́шный (-шен, -шна́, -шно). **oppressor** n. угнета́тель m., ~ница.

opprobrious adj. оскорби́тельный. **opprobrium** n. позо́р.

opt v.i. выбира́ть imp., вы́брать (вы́беру, -решь) perf. (for, +acc.); o. out, не принима́ть уча́стия (of, в+prep.). **optative** (mood) n. оптати́в.

optic adj. глазно́й, зри́тельный. **optical** adj. опти́ческий. **optician** n. о́птик. **optics** n. о́птика.

optimism n. оптими́зм. **optimist** n. оптими́ст. **optimistic** adj. оптимисти́чный, -ческий. **optimum** adj. оптима́льный.

option n. вы́бор; without the o. (of a fine), без пра́ва заме́ны штра́фом. **optional** adj. необяза́тельный, факультати́вный.

opulence n. бога́тство. **opulent** adj. бога́тый.

opus n. о́пус.

or conj. и́ли; or else, ина́че; or so, приблизи́тельно.

oracle n. ора́кул. **oracular** adj. ора́кульский; (mysterious) зага́дочный.

oral adj. у́стный; n. у́стный экза́мен.

orange n. (fruit) апельси́н; (colour) ора́нжевый цвет; attrib. апельси́нный, апельси́новый; adj. ора́нжевый; o.-blossom, помера́нцевый цвет; (decoration) флёрдора́нж; o.-peel, апельси́новая ко́рка. **orangery** n. оранжере́я.

orang-(o)utan(g) n. орангута́нг.

oration n. речь. **orator** n. ора́тор. **oratorical** adj. ора́торский. **oratorio** n. орато́рия. **oratory**[1] n. (chapel) часо́вня (gen.pl. -вен). **oratory**[2] n. (speech) ора́торское иску́сство, красноре́чие.

orb n. шар (-á with 2, 3, 4; pl. -ы́); (part of regalia) держа́ва.

orbit n. орби́та; (eye-socket) глазна́я впа́дина; in o., на орби́те; v.t. враща́ться imp. по орби́те вокру́г+gen. **orbital** adj. орбита́льный.

orchard n. фрукто́вый сад (loc. -ý; pl. -ы́).

orchestra n. оркéстр. **orchestral** adj. оркестрóвый. **orchestrate** v.t. оркестровáть imp., perf. **orchestration** n. оркестрóвка.

orchid n. орхидéя. **orchis** n. ятрышник.

ordain v.t. предписывать imp., предписáть (-ишý, -ишешь) perf.; (eccl.) посвящáть imp., посвятить (-ящý, -ятишь) perf. (в духóвный сан (v. abs.); в + nom.-acc.pl. (of rank)).

ordeal n. испытáние.

order n. порядок (-дка); (system) строй; (command) прикáз; (for goods) закáз; (document) óрдер (pl. -á); (archit.) óрдер; (biol.) отряд; (of monks, knights) óрден; (insignia) óрден (pl. -á); pl. (holy o.) духóвный сан; by o., по приказу; in o. to, для тогó чтóбы; made to o., сдéланный (на) закáз; v.t. (command) прикáзывать imp., приказáть (-ажý, -áжешь) perf.+ dat.; велéть (-лю, -лишь) imp., perf.+ dat.; (goods etc.) закáзывать imp., заказáть (-ажý, -áжешь) perf. **orderly** adj. аккурáтный, опрятный; n. officer, дежýрный офицéр; n. (med.) санитáр; (mil.) ординáрец (-рца).

ordinal adj. порядковый; n. порядковое числительное sb.

ordinance n. декрéт.

ordinary adj. обыкновéнный (-нен, -нна), обычный; (mediocre) заурядный.

ordination n. посвящéние.

ordnance n. артиллéрия; attrib. артиллерийский.

ore n. рудá (pl. -ды).

organ n. óрган; (mus.) оргáн; o.-grinder, шармáнщик; o.-stop, регистр оргáна. **organic** adj. органический; o. whole, единое цéлое sb. **organism** n. организм. **organist** n. органист. **organization** n. организáция. **organize** v.t. организóвывать imp. (pres. not used), организовáть imp. (in pres.), perf.; устрáивать imp., устрóить perf.

orgy n. óргия.

oriel n. эркер; (o. window) окнó (pl. óкна, óкон, óкнам) эркера.

Orient[1] n. Востóк. **oriental** adj. востóчный.

orient[2], **orientate** v.t. ориентировать imp., perf. (oneself, -ся). **orientation** n. ориентáция, ориентирóвка.

orifice n. отвéрстие.

origin n. происхождéние, начáло. **original** adj. оригинáльный; (initial) первоначáльный; (genuine) пóдлинный (-нен, -нна); n. оригинáл, пóдлинник. **originality** n. оригинáльность; пóдлинность. **originate** v.t. порождáть imp., породить perf.; v.i. происходить (-ожý, -óдишь) imp., произойти (-ойдý, -ойдёшь) -ошёл, -ошлá) perf. (from, in, от + gen.); брать (берý, -рёшь; брал, -á, -о) imp., взять (возьмý, -мёшь; взял, -á, -о) perf. начáло (from, in, в + prep., от + gen.). **originator** n. áвтор, инициáтор.

oriole n. иволга.

ormolu n. золочёная брóнза.

ornament n. украшéние, орнáмент; v.t. украшáть imp., укрáсить perf. **ornamental** adj. орнаментáльный, декоративный.

ornate adj. разукрáшенный (-ен); (lit. style) витиевáтый.

ornithological adj. орнитологический. **ornithologist** n. орнитóлог. **ornithology** n. орнитолóгия.

orphan n. сиротá (pl. -ты) m. & f.; v.t. дéлать imp., с~ perf. сиротóй; be orphaned, сиротéть imp., о~ perf. **orphanage** n. приют, сирóтский дом (pl. -á). **orphaned** adj. осиротéлый.

orris-root n. фиáлковый кóрень (-рня) (pl. -á).

orthodox adj. ортодоксáльный; (eccl., O.) православный. **orthodoxy** n. ортодóксия; (O.) православие.

orthographic(al) adj. орфографический. **orthography** n. орфогрáфия, правописáние.

orthopaedic adj. ортопедический. **orthopaedics** n. ортопéдия.

oscillate v.i. вибрировать imp.; (also of person) колебáться (-блюсь, -блешься) imp., по~ perf. **oscillation** n. вибрáция, осцилляция; колебáние. **oscilloscope** n. осциллоскóп.

osier n. (tree) ива; (shoot) лозá (pl. -зы); pl. ивняк (-á) (collect.).

osmosis n. óсмос.

osprey n. (*bird*) скопа́; (*plume*) эгре́т.

osseous adj. ко́стный; (*bony*) кости́стый. **ossified** adj. окостене́лый.

ostensible adj. мни́мый. **ostensibly** adv. я́кобы.

ostentation n. показно́е проявле́ние, выставле́ние напока́з. **ostentatious** adj. показно́й.

osteopath n. остеопа́т. **osteopathy** n. остеопа́тия.

ostler n. ко́нюх.

ostracism n. остраки́зм. **ostracize** v.t. подверга́ть imp., подве́ргнуть (-г) perf. остраки́зму.

ostrich n. стра́ус.

other adj. друго́й, ино́й; тот; pl. други́е sb.; any o. business, теку́щие дела́ neut.pl.; ра́зное sb.; every o., ка́ждый второ́й; every o. day, че́рез день; in o. words, ины́ми слова́ми; on the o. hand, с друго́й стороны́; on the o. side, на той стороне́, по ту сто́рону; one after the o., оди́н за други́м; one or the o., тот или ино́й; the o. day, на дня́х, неда́вно; the o. way round, наоборо́т; the others, остальны́е. **otherwise** adv., conj. ина́че, а то.

otiose adj. нену́жный.

otter n. вы́дра.

ouch interj. ай!

ought v.aux. до́лжен (-жна́) (бы) + inf.; сле́довало (бы) impers. + dat. & inf.; (probability) вероя́тно, по всей вероя́тности + finite verb; o. not, не сле́довало (бы) impers. + dat. & inf.; нельзя́ + dat. & inf.

ounce n. у́нция.

our, **ours** poss.pron. наш (-а, -е; -и); свой (-оя́, -оё; -ои́). **ourselves** pron. (emph.) (мы) са́ми (-и́х, -и́м, -и́ми); (refl.) себя́ (себе́, собо́й); -ся (suffixed to v.t.).

oust v.t. вытесня́ть imp., вы́теснить perf.

out adv. 1. нару́жу, вон; (to the end) до конца́; in phrasal verbs often rendered by prefix вы- (вы́- in perf.), e.g. pull o., выта́скивать imp., вы́тащить perf.; 2. to be o., in various senses: he is o., (not at home) его́ нет до́ма; (not in office etc.) он вы́шел; they are o., (on strike) они́ басту́ют; the secret is o.,

та́йна раскры́та; the truth will o., пра́вды не скрыть; to be o. rendered by perf. verb in past (English pres., past) or fut. (English fut.): (be at an end) ко́нчиться perf.; (be o. of fashion) вы́йти (вы́йду, -дешь; вы́шел, -шла) perf. из мо́ды; (of book, be published) вы́йти (вы́йдет; вы́шел, -шла) perf. из печа́ти; (of candle etc.) поту́хнуть (-x) perf.; (of chicken etc.) вы́лупиться perf.; (of flower) распусти́ться (-и́тся) perf.; (of person, be unconscious) потеря́ть perf. созна́ние; (of rash) вы́ступить perf.; 3.: o. and o., отъя́вленный, соверше́нный; o. with you! вон отсю́да! 4.: o. of, из + gen., вне + gen.; o. of date, устаре́лый, старомо́дный; o. of doors, на откры́том во́здухе; o. of gear, вы́ключенный (-ен); o. of order, неиспра́вный; o. of the way, отдалённый (-ён, -ённа), тру́дно находи́мый; o. of work, безрабо́тный.

outbalance v.t. переве́шивать imp., переве́сить perf. **outbid** v.t. предлага́ть imp., предложи́ть (-жу́, -жишь) perf. бо́лее высо́кую це́ну, чем + nom.

outboard adj.: o. motor, подвесно́й дви́гатель m. **outbreak** n. (of anger, disease) вспы́шка; (of war) нача́ло.

outbuilding n. надво́рная постро́йка.

outburst n. взрыв, вспы́шка. **outcast** n. отве́рженец (-нца); adj. отве́рженный. **outclass** v.t. оставля́ть imp., оста́вить perf. далеко́ позади́. **outcome** n. результа́т, исхо́д. **outcrop** n. обнажённая поро́да. **outcry** n. (шу́мные) проте́сты m.pl. **outdistance** v.t. обгоня́ть imp., обогна́ть (обгоню́, -нишь; обогна́л, -а́, -о) perf. **outdo** v.t. превосходи́ть (-ожу́, -о́дишь) imp., превзойти́ (-ойду́, -ойдёшь; -ошёл, -ошла́) perf.

outdoor adj., **outdoors** adv. на откры́том во́здухе, на у́лице.

outer adj. (external) вне́шний, нару́жный; (far from centre) отдалённый (от це́нтра). **outermost** adj. са́мый да́льний, кра́йний.

outfit n. снаряже́ние; (set of things) набо́р; (clothes) оде́жда. **outfitter** n. торго́вец (-вца) оде́ждой. **outgoings** n. издéржки *f.pl.* **outgrow** *v.t.* перераста́ть *imp.*, перерасти́ (-расту́, -растёшь; -ро́с, -росла́) *perf.*; (*clothes*) выраста́ть *imp.*, вы́расти (-ту, -тешь; вы́рос) *perf.* из + *gen.*; (*habit*) избавля́ться *imp.*, изба́виться *perf.* с во́зрастом от + *gen.* **outhouse** *n.* надво́рная постро́йка.

outing *n.* прогу́лка, экску́рсия.

outlandish *adj.* стра́нный (-нен, -нна́, -нно). **outlast** *v.t.* продолжа́ться *imp.*, продо́лжиться *perf.* до́льше, чем + *nom.* **outlaw** *n.* лицо́ (*pl.* -ца) вне зако́на; банди́т; *v.t.* объявля́ть *imp.*, объяви́ть (-влю́, -вишь) *perf.* вне зако́на. **outlay** *n.* изде́ржки *f.pl.*, расхо́ды *m.pl.* **outlet** *n.* вы́пуск; (*fig.*) вы́ход; (*for goods*) торго́вая то́чка. **outline** *n.* очерта́ние, ко́нтур; (*sketch, draft*) о́черк; *v.t.* оче́рчивать *imp.*, очерти́ть (-рчу́, -ртишь) *perf.* **outlive** *v.t.* пережи́ть (-иву́, -ивёшь; пе́режи́л, -а́, -о) *perf.* **outlook** *n.* вид, перспекти́вы *f.pl.* **outlying** *adj.* отдалённый (-ён, -ённа). **outmoded** *adj.* старомо́дный. **outnumber** *v.t.* чи́сленно превосходи́ть (-ожу́, -о́дишь) *imp.*, превзойти́ (-ойду́, -ойдёшь; -ошёл, -ошла́) *perf.* **out-patient** *n.* амбулато́рный больно́й *sb.* **outpost** *n.* аванпо́ст. **output** *n.* вы́пуск, проду́кция.

outrage *n.* (*violation of rights*) наси́льственное наруше́ние чужи́х прав; (*gross offence*) надруга́тельство (upon, над + *instr.*); *v.t.* оскорбля́ть *imp.*, оскорби́ть *perf.*; надруга́ться *perf.* над + *instr.*; (*infringe*) наруша́ть *imp.*, нару́шить *perf.* **outrageous** *adj.* (*immoderate*) возмути́тельный; (*offensive*) оскорби́тельный.

outrigger *n.* (*boat*) аутри́гер. **outright** *adv.* (*entirely*) вполне́; (*once for all*) раз на всегда́; (*openly*) откры́то; *adj.* прямо́й (прям, -а́, -о, пря́мы). **outset** *n.* нача́ло; at the о., внача́ле; from the о., с са́мого нача́ла. **outshine** *v.t.* затмева́ть *imp.*, затми́ть *perf.*

outside *n.* (*external side*) нару́жная сторона́ (*acc.* -ону; *pl.* -оны, -о́н, -она́м); (*exterior, appearance*) нару́жность, вне́шность; at the о., са́мое бо́льшее, в кра́йнем слу́чае; from the

о., извне́; on the о., снару́жи; *adj.* нару́жный, вне́шний; (*sport*) кра́йний; *adv.* (on the o.) снару́жи; (to the o.) нару́жу; (*out of doors*) на откры́том во́здухе, на у́лице; *prep.* вне + *gen.*; за + *instr.*, за преде́лами + *gen.*; (*other than*) кро́ме + *gen.* **outsider** *n.* посторо́нний *sb.*; (*sport*) аутса́йдер.

outsize *adj.* бо́льше станда́ртного разме́ра. **outskirts** *n.* окра́ина. **outspoken** *adj.* открове́нный (-нен, -нна), прямо́й (прям, -а́, -о, пря́мы). **outspread** *adj.* распростёртый. **outstanding** *adj.* (*person*) выдаю́щийся; (*debt*) неупла́ченный. **outstay** *v.t.* переси́живать *imp.*, пересиде́ть (-ижу́, -иди́шь) *perf.*; о. one's welcome, заси́живаться *imp.*, засиде́ться (-ижу́сь, -иди́шься) *perf.* **outstretched** *adj.*: with o. arms, с распростёртыми объя́тиями. **outstrip** *v.t.* обгоня́ть *imp.*, обогна́ть (обгоню́, -нишь; обогна́л, -а́, -о) *perf.* **outvote** *v.t.* побежда́ть *imp.*, победи́ть (-ди́шь) *perf.* большинство́м голосо́в. **outward** *adj.* (*external*) вне́шний, нару́жный; o. bound, уходя́щий в пла́вание. **outwardly** *adv.* вне́шне, на вид. **outwards** *adv.* нару́жу.

outweigh *v.t.* переве́шивать *imp.*, переве́сить *perf.* **outwit** *v.t.* перехитри́ть *perf.*

oval *adj.* ова́льный *n.* ова́л.
ovary *n.* (*anat.*) яи́чник; (*bot.*) за́вязь.
ovation *n.* ова́ция.
oven *n.* печь (*loc.* -чи́; *pl.* -чи, -чéй) духо́вка.

over *adv.*, *prep.* with verbs: see verbs, e.g. *jump o.*, перепры́гивать *imp.*; *think o.*, обду́мывать *imp.*; *adv.* (*in excess*) сли́шком; (*in addition*) вдоба́вок; (*again*) сно́ва; *prep.* (*above*) над + *instr.*; (*through; covering*) по + *dat.*; (*concerning*) о + *prep.*; (*across*) че́рез + *acc.*; (on the other side of) по ту сто́рону + *gen.*; (*more than*) свы́ше + *gen.*; бо́лее + *gen.*; (*with age*) за + *acc.*; all o. (*finished*) всё ко́нчено; (*everywhere*) повсю́ду; all o. the country, по всей стране́; o. again, ещё раз; o. against, напро́тив + *gen.*; (*in contrast to*) по сравне́нию с + *instr.*; o. and above, сверх + *gen.*; не говоря́ уже́ о + *prep.*;

o. the radio, по ра́дио; *o. there*, вон там; *o. the way*, че́рез доро́гу.

overact *v.t. & i.* переи́грывать *imp.*, переигра́ть *perf.* **overall** *n.* хала́т; *pl.* комбинезо́н, спецоде́жда; *adj.* о́бщий. **overawe** *v.t.* внуша́ть *imp.*, внуши́ть *perf.* благогове́йный страх + *dat.* **overbalance** *v.i.* теря́ть *imp.*, по ~ *perf.* равнове́сие. **overbearing** *adj.* вла́стный, повели́тельный. **overboard** *adv.* (*motion*) за́ борт; (*position*) за бо́ртом. **overcast** *adj.* (*sky*) покры́тый облака́ми. **overcoat** *n.* пальто́ *neut. indecl.* **overcome** *v.t.* преодолева́ть *imp.*, преодоле́ть *perf.*; *adj.* охва́ченный (-ен). **overcrowded** *adj.* переполненный (-ен), перенаселённый (-ён, -ена́). **overcrowding** *n.* перенаселённость. **overdo** *v.t.* (*cook*) пережа́ривать *imp.*, пережа́рить *perf.*; *o. it, things*, (*work too hard*) переутомля́ться *imp.*, переутоми́ться *perf.*; (*go too far*) перебра́щивать *imp.*, переборщи́ть *perf.*

overdose *n.* чрезме́рная до́за. **overdraft** *n.* превыше́ние креди́та; (*amount*) долг ба́нку. **overdraw** *v.i.* превыша́ть *imp.*, превы́сить *perf.* креди́т (в ба́нке). **overdrive** *n.* ускоря́ющая переда́ча. **overdue** *adj.* просро́ченный (-ен); *be o.*, (*late*) запа́здывать *imp.*, запозда́ть *perf.* **overestimate** *v.t.* переоце́нивать *imp.*, переоцени́ть (-ню, -нишь) *perf.*; *n.* переоце́нка. **overflow** *v.i.* перелива́ться *imp.*, перели́ться (-льётся; -лился, -лила́сь, -ли́лось) *perf.*; (*river etc.*) разлива́ться *imp.*, разли́ться (разольётся; разли́лся, -ила́сь, -и́лось) *perf.*; *n.* разли́в; (*outlet*) перелива́я труба́ (*pl.* -бы). **overgrown** *adj.* заро́сший. **overhang** *v.t. & i.* выступа́ть *imp.* над + *instr.*; (*also fig.*) нависа́ть *imp.*, нави́снуть (-с) *perf.* над + *instr.*; *n.* свес, вы́ступ.

overhaul *v.t.* разбира́ть *imp.* (разберу́, -рёшь; разобра́л, -а́, -о) *perf.*; (*repair*) капита́льно ремонти́ровать *imp., perf.*; (*overtake*) догоня́ть *imp.*, догна́ть (догоню́, -нишь; догна́л, -а́, -о) *perf.* **overhead** *adv.* наверху́, над голово́й; *adj.* возду́шный, подвесно́й; (*expenses*) накладно́й; *n.: pl.*

накладны́е расхо́ды *m.pl.* *v.t.* нечая́нно слы́шать (-шу, -шишь) *imp.*, у ~ *perf.*; (*eavesdrop*) подслу́шивать *imp.*, подслу́шать *perf.* **overjoyed** *adj.* в восто́рге (at, от + *gen.*), о́чень дово́льный (at, + *instr.*). **overland** *adj.* сухопу́тный; *adv.* по су́ше. **overlap** *v.t. & i.* (*completely*) перекрыва́ть *imp.*, перекры́ть (-ро́ю, -ро́ешь) *perf.* (друг дру́га); *v.t.* (in part) части́чно покрыва́ть *imp.*, покры́ть (-ро́ю, -ро́ешь) *perf.*; *v.i.* части́чно совпада́ть *imp.*, совпа́сть (-аду́, -адёшь; -а́л) *perf.*

overleaf *adv.* на обра́тной стороне́ (листа́, страни́цы). **overlook** *v.t.* (*look down on*) смотре́ть (-рю́, -ришь) *imp.* све́рху на + *acc.*; (*of window*) выходи́ть (-ит) *imp.* на, в, + *acc.*; (*not notice*) не замеча́ть *imp.*, заме́тить *perf.* + *gen.*; (*o. offence etc.*) проща́ть *imp.*, прости́ть *perf.* **overlord** *n.* сюзере́н, влады́ка *m.* **overmaster** *v.t.* подчиня́ть *imp.*, подчини́ть себе́; (*fig.*) всеце́ло овладева́ть *imp.*, овладе́ть *perf.* + *instr.* **overnight** *adv.* накану́не ве́чером; (*all night*) с ве́чера, всю ночь; (*suddenly*) неожи́данно, ско́ро; *stay o.*, ночева́ть (-чу́ю, -чу́ешь) *imp.*, пере ~ *perf.*; *adj.* ночно́й. **overpass** *n.* путепрово́д. **overpay** *v.t.* перепла́чивать *imp.*, переплати́ть (-ачу́, -а́тишь) *perf.*

over-populated *adj.* перенаселённый (-ён, -ена́). **over-population** *n.* перенаселённость. **overpower** *v.t.* переси́ливать *imp.*, переси́лить *perf.*; (*heat etc.*) одолева́ть *imp.*, одоле́ть *perf.* **over-production** *n.* перепроизво́дство. **overrate** *v.t.* переоце́нивать *imp.*, переоцени́ть (-ню, -нишь) *perf.* **overreach** *v.t.* перехитри́ть *perf.*; *o. oneself*, зарыва́ться *imp.*, зарва́ться (-ву́сь, -вёшься; -ва́лся, -вала́сь, -ва́ло́сь) *perf.* **override** *v.t.* (*fig.*) отверга́ть *imp.*, отве́ргнуть (-г(нул), -гла) *perf.* **overrule** *v.t.* аннули́ровать *imp.*, *perf.* **overrun** *v.t.* (*flood*) наводня́ть *imp.*, наводни́ть *perf.*; (*ravage*) опусто́шать *imp.*, опустоши́ть *perf.*

oversea(s) *adv.* за мо́рем, че́рез мо́ре; *adj.* замо́рский. **oversee** *v.t.* надзира́ть *imp.* за + *instr.* **overseer** *n.* надзира́тель *m.*, ~ница. **overshadow** *v.t.* затмева́ть *imp.*, затми́ть *perf.* **oversight** *n.* (*supervision*) надзо́р; (*mistake*) недосмо́тр, опло́шность. **oversleep** *v.i.* просыпа́ть *imp.*, проспа́ть (-плю́, -пи́шь; -па́л, -пала́, -па́ло) *perf.* **overstate** *v.t.* преувели́чивать *imp.*, преувели́чить *perf.* **overstatement** *n.* преувеличе́ние. **overstep** *v.t.* переступа́ть *imp.*, переступи́ть (-плю́, -пишь) *perf.* + *acc.*, через + *acc.*

overt *adj.* я́вный, откры́тый.
overtake *v.t.* догоня́ть *imp.*, догна́ть (догоню́, -нишь; догна́л, -а́, -о) *perf.*; (*of misfortune etc.*) постига́ть *imp.*, пости́чь & постигну́ть (-и́гну, -и́гнешь; -и́г) *perf.* **overthrow** *v.t.* (*upset*) опроки́дывать *imp.*, опроки́нуть *perf.*; (*from power*) сверга́ть *imp.*, све́ргнуть (-г(нул), -гла) *perf.*; *n.* сверже́ние. **overtime** *n.* (*time*) сверхуро́чные часы́ *m.pl.*; (*payment*) сверхуро́чное *sb.*; *adv.* сверхуро́чно.
overtone *n.* (*mus.*) оберто́н; (*fig.*) скры́тый намёк.
overture *n.* предложе́ние, инициати́ва; (*mus.*) увертю́ра.
overturn *v.t.* & *i.* опроки́дывать(ся) *imp.*, опроки́нуть(ся) *perf.*; *v.t.* сверга́ть *imp.*, све́ргнуть (-г) *perf.* **overweening** *adj.* высокоме́рный, самонаде́янный (-ян, -янна). **overwhelm** *v.t.* подавля́ть *imp.*, подави́ть (-влю́, -вишь) *perf.*; (*of emotions*) овладева́ть *imp.*, овладе́ть *perf.* + *instr.* **overwhelm-**ing *adj.* подавля́ющий. **overwork** *v.t.* & *i.* переутомля́ть(ся) *imp.*, переутоми́ть(ся) *perf.*

owe *v.t.* (*money*) быть до́лжен (-жен, -жна́) + *acc.* & *dat.*; (*be indebted*) быть обя́занным (-ан) + *instr.* & *dat.*; he, she, owes him three roubles, он до́лжен, она́ должна́, мне три рубля́; she owes him her life, она́ обя́зана ему́ жи́знью. **owing** *adj.*: be o., причита́ться *imp.* (to, + *dat.*); o., из-за + *gen.*, по причи́не + *gen.*, всле́дствие + *gen.*
owl *n.* сова́ (*pl.* -вы). **owlet** *n.* совёнок (-нка; *pl.* совя́та, -т).
own *adj.* свой (-оя́, -оё; -ой); (*свой*) со́бственный; (*relative*) родно́й; on one's o., самостоя́тельно; *v.t.* (*possess*) владе́ть *imp.* + *instr.*; (*admit*) признава́ть (-наю́, -наёшь) *imp.*, призна́ть *perf.*; o. up, признава́ться (-наю́сь, -наёшься) *imp.*, призна́ться *perf.* **owner** *n.* владе́лец (-льца), со́бственник. **ownership** *n.* владе́ние (of, + *instr.*), со́бственность.
ox *n.* вол (-а́).
oxalic *adj.*: o. acid, щаве́льная кислота́.
oxidation *n.* окисле́ние. **oxide** *n.* о́кись, о́кисел (-сла). **oxidize** *v.t.* & *i.* окисля́ть(ся) *imp.*, окисли́ть(ся) *perf.* **oxyacetylene** *adj.* кислоро́дно-ацетиле́новый. **oxygen** *n.* кислоро́д; *attrib.* кислоро́дный.
oyster *n.* у́стрица; o.-catcher, кули́к-соро́ка.
ozone *n.* озо́н.

P

pace *n.* шаг (-а́ with 2, 3, 4, loc. -у́; *pl.* -и́); (*fig.*) темп; keep p. with, идти́ (иду́, идёшь; шёл, шла) *imp.* в но́гу с + *instr.*; set the p., задава́ть (-даю́, -даёшь) *imp.*, зада́ть (-а́м, -а́шь, -а́ст, -ади́м; за́дал, -а́, -о) *perf.* темп. *v.i.* шага́ть *imp.*, шагну́ть *perf.*; *v.t.*: p.

out, измеря́ть *imp.*, изме́рить *perf.* шага́ми.
pachyderm *n.* толстоко́жее (живо́тное) *sb.*
pacific *adj.* ми́рный; P., тихоокеа́нский; *n.* Ти́хий океа́н. **pacification** *n.* усмире́ние, умиротворе́ние. **pacifism**

n. пацифи́зм. **pacifist** *n.* пацифи́ст.
pacify *v.t.* усмиря́ть *imp.*, усмири́ть
perf.; умиротворя́ть *imp.*, умиротвори́ть *perf.*

pack *n.* у́зел (узла́), вьюк (*pl.* -ю́ки)
(*soldier's*) ра́нец (-нца); (*hounds*)
сво́ра; (*wolves, birds*) ста́я; (*cards*)
коло́да (*pl.* -ди, -де́й, *instr.* -дьми́); *p.-ice*, пак,
па́ковый лёд (льда, *loc.* льду); *p. of
lies*, сплошна́я ложь (лжи, *instr.*
ло́жью); *v.t.* пакова́ть *imp.*, y ~ *perf.*;
укла́дывать *imp.*, уложи́ть (-жу́,
-жишь) *perf.*; (*cram*) набива́ть *imp.*,
наби́ть (-бью, -бьёшь) *perf.* **package**
n. паке́т, свёрток (-тка); (*packaging*)
упако́вка. **packaging** *n.* упако́вка.
packet *n.* паке́т; па́чка; (*money*) куш.
packing-case *n.* я́щик. **packing-needle** *n.*
упако́вочная игла́ (*pl.* -лы).

pact *n.* догово́р, пакт.

pad[1] *v.i.* (*walk*) идти́ (иду́, идёшь; шёл,
шла) *imp.*, пойти́ (пойду́, -дёшь;
пошёл, -шла́) *perf.* неслы́шным
ша́гом.

pad[2] *n.* (*cushion*) поду́шка, поду́шечка;
(*guard*) щито́к (-тка́); (*of paper*) блокно́т; (*paw*) ла́па; *v.t.* набива́ть *imp.*,
наби́ть (-бью, -бьёшь) *perf.*; подбива́ть *imp.*, подби́ть (подобью, -ьёшь)
perf. **padding** *n.* наби́вка.

paddle[1] *n.* (*oar*) (байда́рочное) весло́
(*pl.* вёсла, -сел, -слам); (*of p.-wheel*)
ло́пасть (*pl.* -ти, -те́й); *p.-boat*, колёсный парохо́д; *p.-wheel*, гребно́е
колесо́ (*pl.* -ёса); *v.i.* (*row*) грести́
(гребу́, -бёшь; грёб, -ла́) *imp.* байда́рочным весло́м.

paddle[2] *v.i.* (*wade*) ходи́ть (хожу́,
хо́дишь) *indet.*, идти́ (иду́, идёшь;
шёл, шла) *det.*, пойти́ (пойду́, -дёшь;
пошёл, -шла́) *perf.* босико́м по воде́.

paddock *n.* небольшо́й луг (*loc.* -у́; *pl.*
-а́).

padlock *n.* вися́чий замо́к (-мка́); *v.t.*
запира́ть *imp.*, запере́ть (запру́,
-рёшь; за́пер, -ла́, -ло) *perf.* на вися́чий замо́к.

padre *n.* полково́й свяще́нник.

paediatric *adj.* педиатри́ческий. **paediatrician** *n.* педиа́тр. **paediatrics** *n.*
педиатри́я.

---

pagan *n.* язы́чник, -ица; *adj.* язы́ческий.
paganism *n.* язы́чество.

page[1] *n.* (*p.-boy*) паж (-а́), ма́льчик-слуга́ *m.*; (*summon*) вызыва́ть
imp., вы́звать (вы́зову, -вешь) *perf.*

page[2] *n.* (*of book*) страни́ца.

pageant *n.* пы́шная проце́ссия; великоле́пное зре́лище. **pageantry** *n.* великоле́пие.

paginate *v.t.* нумерова́ть *imp.*, про ~
perf. страни́цы + *gen.*

pagoda *n.* па́года.

paid, paid-up *adj.* опла́ченный (-ен); *see*
pay.

pail *n.* ведро́ (*pl.* вёдра, -дер, -драм).

pain *n.* боль; *f.* (*of childbirth*) родовы́е
схва́тки *f.pl.*; (*efforts*) уси́лия *neut.
pl.*; *on p. of death*, под стра́хом
сме́рти; *take pains over*, прилага́ть
imp., приложи́ть (-жу́, -жишь) *perf.*
уси́лия к + *dat.*; *p.-killer*, болеутоля́ющее сре́дство; *v.t.* причиня́ть *imp.*,
причини́ть *perf.* боль + *dat.*; (*fig.*)
огорча́ть *imp.*, огорчи́ть *perf.* **painful**
adj. боле́зненный (-ен, -енна); *be p.*,
(*part of body*) боле́ть (-ли́т) *imp.* **painless** *adj.* безболе́зненный (-ен, -енна).
painstaking *adj.* стара́тельный, усе́рдный.

paint *n.* кра́ска; *v.t.* кра́сить *imp.*, по ~
perf.; (*portray*) писа́ть (пишу́, -шешь)
imp., на ~ *perf.* кра́сками. **paintbrush**
n. кисть (*pl.* -ти, -те́й). **painter**[1] *n.*
(*artist*) худо́жник, -ица; (*decorator*)
маля́р (-а́).

painter[2] *n.* (*rope*) фа́линь *m.*

painting *n.* (*art*) жи́вопись; (*picture*)
карти́на.

pair *n.* па́ра; not translated with nouns
denoting a single object, eg *a p. of
scissors*, но́жницы (-ц) *pl.*; *one p. of
scissors*, одни́ но́жницы; *v.t. & i.* располага́ть(ся) *imp.*, расположи́ть(ся)
(-жу́, -жит(ся)) *perf.* па́рами; *p. off*,
уходи́ть (-жу́, -дишь) *imp.*, уйти́
(уйду́, -дёшь; ушёл, ушла́) *perf.*
па́рами.

pal *n.* това́рищ, прия́тель *m.*; *p. up with*,
дружи́ть (-жу́, -у́жишь) *imp.*, подружи́ться (-ужу́сь, -у́жишься) *perf.* с +
instr.

palace n. дворе́ц (-рца́); attrib. дворцо́вый.

palaeographer n. палео́граф. **palaeography** n. палеогра́фия. **palaeolithic** adj. палеолити́ческий. **palaeontologist** n. палеонто́лог. **palaeontology** n. палеонтоло́гия. **palaeozoic** adj. палеозо́йский.

palatable adj. вку́сный (-сен, -сна́, -сно); (fig.) прия́тный. **palatal** adj. нёбный; (ling. also) палата́льный; sb. палата́льный (звук). **palatalize** v.t. палатализова́ть imp., perf. **palate** n. нёбо; (taste) вкус.

palatial adj. дворцо́вый; (splendid) великоле́пный.

palaver n. (idle talk) пуста́я болтовня́; (affair) де́ло.

pale [1] n. (stake) кол (-а́, loc. -у́; pl. -ья); (boundary) грани́ца; (fig.) преде́лы m.pl.

pale [2] adj. бле́дный (-ден, -дна́, -дно, бле́дны); p.-face, бледноли́цый sb.; v.i. бледне́ть imp., по~ perf.

palette n. пали́тра; p.-knife, мастихи́н, шпа́тель m.

paling(s) n. частоко́л.

palisade n. частоко́л, палиса́д.

palish adj. бледнова́тый.

pall [1] n. покро́в. **pallbearer** n. несу́щий sb. гроб.

pall [2] v.i.: p. on., надоеда́ть imp., надое́сть (-е́м, -е́шь, -е́ст, -еди́м; -е́л) perf. + dat.

palliasse n. соло́менный тюфя́к (-а́).

palliative adj. смягча́ющий, паллиати́вный; n. смягча́ющее сре́дство, паллиати́в.

pallid adj. бле́дный (-ден, -дна́, -дно, бле́дны). **pallor** n. бле́дность.

palm [1] n. (tree) па́льма; (branch) па́льмовая ветвь; (p. -ви, -вёй); (willow-branch as substitute) ве́точка ве́рбы; p.-oil, па́льмовое ма́сло; P. Sunday, ве́рбное воскресе́нье.

palm [2] n. (of hand) ладо́нь; v.t. (conceal) пря́тать (-я́чу, -я́чешь) imp., с~ perf. в руке́; p. off, всучива́ть imp., всучи́ть (-учу́, -у́чишь) perf. (on, + dat.).

palmist n. хирома́нт, ~ ка. **palmistry** n. хирома́нтия.

palmy adj. (flourishing) цвету́щий.

palpable adj. осяза́емый.

palpitate v.i. (throb) (си́льно) би́ться (бьётся) imp.; (tremble) трепета́ть (-ещу́, -е́щешь) imp. **palpitations** n. (си́льное) сердцебие́ние, пульса́ция.

palsy n. парали́ч (-а́).

paltry adj. ничто́жный.

pampas n. па́мпасы (-сов) pl.; p.-grass, па́мпасная трава́.

pamper v.t. балова́ть imp., из ~ perf.

pamphlet n. брошю́ра.

pan [1] n. (saucepan) кастрю́ля; (frying-p.) сковорода́ (pl. ско́вороды, -о́д, -ода́м); (bowl of scales) ча́шка; v.t.: p. off, out, промыва́ть imp., промы́ть (-мо́ю, -мо́ешь) perf.

pan [2] v.i. (cin.) панорами́ровать imp., perf.

panama (hat) n. пана́ма.

panacea n. панаце́я.

pan-American adj. панамерика́нский.

pancake n. блин (-а́); v.i. (aeron.) парашюти́ровать imp., с~ perf.

panchromatic adj. панхромати́ческий.

pancreas n. поджелу́дочная железа́ (pl. -е́зы, -ёз, -еза́м).

panda n. па́нда; giant p., бамбу́ковый медве́дь m.

pandemonium n. гвалт.

pander n. сво́дник; v.i.: p. to, потво́рствовать imp.+ dat.

pane n. око́нное стекло́ (pl. стёкла, -кол, -клам).

panel n. пане́ль, филёнка; (control-p.) щит (-а́) управле́ния; (list of jurors) спи́сок (-ска) прися́жных; (jury) прися́жные sb.; (team in discussion, quiz) уча́стники m.pl. (диску́ссии, викторины); (team of experts) гру́ппа специали́стов; v.t. обшива́ть imp., обши́ть (обошью́, -ьёшь) perf. пане́лями, филёнками. **panelling** n. пане́льная обши́вка.

pang n. о́страя боль; p. му́ки (-к) pl.

panic n. па́ника; p.-monger, паникёр; p.-stricken, охва́ченный (-ен) па́никой; adj. пани́ческий; v.i. впада́ть imp., впасть (-аду́, -адёшь; -ал) perf. в па́нику. **panicky** adj. пани́ческий.

panicle n. метёлка.

pannier n. корзи́нка.

panorama n. панора́ма. **panoramic** adj. панора́мный.

pansy *n.* анютины глазки (-зок) *pl.*

pant *v.i.* задыхаться *imp.*, задохнуться (-óх(ну́)ся, -óх(ну́)лась) *perf.*; пыхтеть (-хчу́, -хти́шь) *imp.*

pantheism *n.* пантеизм. **pantheist** *n.* пантеист. **pantheistic** *adj.* пантеистический.

panther *n.* пантера, барс.

panties *n.* трусики (-ков) *pl.*

pantomime *n.* рождественское представление для детей; (*dumb show*) пантомима.

pantry *n.* кладовая *sb.*; (*butler's*) буфетная *sb.*

pants *n.* (*trousers*) брюки (-к) *pl.*; (*underpants*) кальсоны (-н) *pl.*, трусы (-сов) *pl.*

papacy *n.* папство. **papal** *adj.* папский.

paper *n.* бумага; (*p. document*) *m.pl.*; (*newspaper*) газета; (*wallpaper*) обои (-óев) *pl.*; (*dissertation*) доклад; *adj.* бумажный; *v.t.* оклеивать *imp.*, оклеить *perf.* обоями. **paperback** *n.* книга в бумажной обложке. **paper-clip** *n.* скрепка. **paper-hanger** *n.* обойщик. **paper-knife** *n.* разрезной нож (-á). **paper-mill** *n.* бумажная фабрика. **paperweight** *n.* пресс-папье *neut.indecl.* **papery** *adj.* бумажный.

papier mâché *n.* папье-маше *neut.indecl.*

paprika *n.* красный перец (-рца(у)).

papyrus *n.* папирус.

par *n.* (*equality*) равенство; (*normal condition*) нормальное состояние; *p. of exchange*, паритет; *above, below, p. of*, выше, ниже, номинальной цены; *on a p. with*, наравне с + *instr.*

parable *n.* притча.

parabola *n.* парабола. **parabolic** *adj.* параболический.

parachute *n.* парашют; *v.t.* сбрасывать *imp.*, сбросить *perf.* с парашютом; *v.i.* спускаться *imp.*, спуститься (-ущусь, -устишься) *perf.* с парашютом. **parachutist** *n.* парашютист; *n.* парашютно-десантные войска *neut.indecl.*

parade *n.* парад; (*display*) выставление напоказ; *p.-ground*, плац; *v.t. & i.* строить(ся) *imp.*, по ~ *perf.*; *v.t.* (*show off*) выставлять *imp.*, выставить *perf.* напоказ.

paradigm *n.* парадигма.

paradise *n.* рай (*loc.* раю).

paradox *n.* парадокс. **paradoxical** *adj.* парадоксальный.

paraffin *n.* парафин; (*p. oil*) керосин; *liquid p.*, парафиновое масло; *attrib.* парафиновый; *p. wax*, твёрдый парафин.

paragon *n.* образец (-зца́).

paragraph *n.* абзац; (*news item*) (газетная) заметка.

parakeet *n.* длиннохвостый попугай.

parallax *n.* параллакс.

parallel *adj.* параллельный; *p. bars*, параллельные брусья *m.pl.*; *in parallel*, параллельно. **parallelogram** *n.* параллелограмм.

paralyse *v.t.* парализовать *imp.*, *perf.* **paralysis** *n.* паралич (-á). **paralytic** *n.* паралитик; *adj.* параличный.

parameter *n.* параметр.

paramilitary *adj.* полувоенный.

paramount *adj.* (*supreme*) верховный; (*pre-eminent*) верховный; (*pre-eminent*) высочайший (-нен, -нна).

paramour *n.* любовник, -ица.

paranoia *n.* паранойя.

parapet *n.* парапет; (*mil.*) бруствер.

paraphernalia *n.* (*personal belongings*) личное имущество; (*accessories*) принадлежности *f.pl.*

paraphrase *n.* пересказ, парафраза; *v.t.* пересказывать *imp.*, пересказать (-ажу, -ажешь) *perf.*; парафразировать *imp.*, *perf.*

paraplegia *n.* параплегия.

parapsychology *n.* парапсихология.

parasite *n.* паразит; (*person*) тунеядец (-дца). **parasitic(al)** *adj.* паразитический, паразитный.

parasol *n.* зонтик.

paratrooper *n.* парашютист. **paratroops** *n.* парашютно-десантные войска *neut. pl.*

paratyphoid *n.* паратиф.

parboil *v.t.* слегка отваривать *imp.*, отварить (-рю, -ришь) *perf.*

parcel *n.* пакет, посылка; (*of land*) участок (-тка); *p. post*, почтово-посылочная служба; *v.t.*: *p. out*, делить (-лю, -лишь) *imp.*, раз ~ *perf.*;

p. up, завёртывать *imp.*, заверну́ть *perf.* в паке́т.

parch *v.t.* иссуша́ть *imp.*, иссуши́ть (-и́т) *perf.*; *become parched*, пересыха́ть *imp.*, пересо́хнуть (-х) *perf.*

parchment *n.* перга́мент; *attrib.* перга́мен(т)ный.

pardon *n.* проще́ние; извине́ние; (*leg.*) поми́лование; *v.t.* проща́ть *imp.*, прости́ть *perf.*; (*leg.*) поми́ловать *perf.* **pardonable** *adj.* прости́тельный.

pare *v.t.* обреза́ть *imp.*, обре́зать (-е́жу, -е́жешь) *perf.*; (*fruit*) чи́стить *imp.*, о~ *perf.*; *p. away, down*, (*fig.*) сокраща́ть *imp.*, сократи́ть (-ащу́, -ати́шь) *perf.*

parent *n.* роди́тель *m.*, ~ница; (*forefather*) пре́док (-дка); (*origin*) причи́на. **parentage** *n.* происхожде́ние. **parental** *adj.* роди́тельский.

parenthesis *n.* (*word, clause*) вво́дное сло́во (*pl.* -ва́), предложе́ние; *pl.* (*brackets*) ско́бки *f.pl.*; *in p.*, в ско́бках.

pariah *n.* па́рия *m. & f.*

parings *n.* обре́зки *f.pl.*

parish *n.* (*area*) прихо́д; (*inhabitants*) прихожа́не (-н) *pl.*; *attrib.* прихо́дский. **parishioner** *n.* прихожа́нин (*pl.* -а́не, -а́н), -а́нка.

parity *n.* ра́венство; (*econ.*) парите́т.

park *n.* парк; (*national p.*) запове́дник; (*for cars etc.*) стоя́нка; *v.t. & abs.* ста́вить *imp.*, по~ *perf.* (маши́ну). **parking** *n.* стоя́нка.

parley *n.* перегово́ры (-ров) *pl.*; *v.i.* вести́ (веду́, -дёшь; вёл, -а́) *imp.* перегово́ры.

parliament *n.* парла́мент. **parliamentarian** *n.* знато́к (-а́) парла́ментской пра́ктики. **parliamentary** *adj.* парла́ментский.

parlour *n.* гости́ная *sb.*; приёмная *sb.* **parlourmaid** *n.* го́рничная *sb.*

parochial *adj.* прихо́дский; (*fig.*) ограни́ченный (-ен, -енна). **parochialism** *n.* ограни́ченность интере́сов.

parody *n.* паро́дия; *v.t.* пароди́ровать *imp.*, *perf.*

parole *n.* че́стное сло́во; освобожде́ние под че́стное сло́во; (*password*) паро́ль

m.; *on p.*, освобождённый (-ён, -ена́) под че́стное сло́во.

paroxysm *n.* парокси́зм, припа́док (-дка).

parquet *n.* парке́т; *attrib.* парке́тный; *v.t.* устила́ть *imp.*, устла́ть (устелю́, -лешь) *perf.* парке́том.

parricidal *adj.* отцеуби́йственный (-ен, -енна). **parricide** *n.* (*action*) отцеуби́йство; (*person*) отцеуби́йца *m. & f.*

parrot *n.* попуга́й; *v.t.* повторя́ть *imp.*, повтори́ть *perf.* как попуга́й.

parry *v.t.* пари́ровать *imp.*, *perf.*, от~ *perf.*

parse *v.t.* де́лать *imp.*, с~ *perf.* разбо́р + *gen.*

parsec *n.* парсе́к.

parsimonious *adj.* бережли́вый; (*mean*) скупо́й (скуп, -а́, -о). **parsimony** *n.* бережли́вость; ску́пость.

parsley *n.* петру́шка.

parsnip *n.* пастерна́к.

parson *n.* прихо́дский свяще́нник. **parsonage** *n.* дом (*pl.* -а́) прихо́дского свяще́нника.

part *n.* часть (*pl.* -ти, -те́й), до́ля (*pl.* -ли, -ле́й); (*taking p.*) уча́стие; (*in play*) роль (*pl.* -ли, -ле́й); (*mus.*) па́ртия; (*in dispute*) сторона́ (*acc.* -ону; *pl.* -оны, -о́н, -она́м); *for the most p.*, бо́льшей ча́стью; *in p.*, ча́стью; *for my p.*, что каса́ется меня́; *take p. in*, уча́ствовать *imp.* в + *prep.*; *p. and parcel*, неотъе́млемая часть; *p.-owner*, совладе́лец (-льца); *p.-time*, (за́нятый (-т, -та́, -то)) непо́лный рабо́чий день; *v.t. & i.* (*divide*) разделя́ть(ся) *imp.*, раздели́ть(ся) (-лю́(сь), -лишь(ся)) *perf.*; *v.i.* (*leave*) расстава́ться (-таю́сь, -таёшься) *imp.*, расста́ться (-а́нусь, -а́нешься) *perf.* (*from, with*, c + *instr.*); *p. one's hair*, де́лать *imp.*, с~ *perf.* себе́ пробо́р.

partake *v.i.* принима́ть *imp.*, приня́ть (приму́, -мешь; при́нял, -а́, -о) *perf.* уча́стие (*in, of*, в + *prep.*); (*eat*) есть (ем, ешь, ест, еди́м; ел) *imp.*, съ~ *perf.* (*of*, + *acc.*).

partial *adj.* (*incomplete*) части́чный, непо́лный (-лон, -лна́, -лно); (*biased*) пристра́стный; *p. to*, неравноду́шный

participant к+*dat.* **partiality** *n.* пристра́стие (for, к+*dat.*). **partially** *adv.* части́чно.

participant *n.* уча́стник, -ица (in, +*gen.*).

participate *v.i.* уча́ствовать (in, в+*prep.*). **participation** *n.* уча́стие (in, в+*prep.*).

participial *adj.* прича́стный. **participle** *n.* прича́стие.

particle *n.* части́ца.

particoloured *adj.* разноцве́тный.

particular *adj.* осо́бый, осо́бенный; (*careful*) тща́тельный; *n.* подро́бность; *pl.* подро́бный отчёт; in p., в ча́стности.

parting *n.* (*leave-taking*) проща́ние; (*of hair*) пробо́р.

partisan *n.* (*adherent*) сторо́нник; (*mil.*) партиза́н (*gen.pl.* -н); *attrib.* узкопарти́йный; партиза́нский.

partition *n.* разделе́ние, расчлене́ние; (*wall*) перегоро́дка, перебо́рка; *v.t.* разделя́ть *imp.*, раздели́ть (-лю́, -лишь) *perf.*; p. off, отделя́ть *imp.*, отдели́ть (-лю́, -лишь) *perf.* перегоро́дкой.

partitive *adj.* раздели́тельный. p. genitive, роди́тельный раздели́тельный *sb.*

partly *adv.* ча́стью, отча́сти.

partner *n.* (со)уча́стник; (in business) компаньо́н; (in dance, game) партнёр, ~ша. **partnership** *n.* (со)уча́стие, сотру́дничество; (business) това́рищество.

partridge *n.* куропа́тка.

party *n.* (*polit.*) па́ртия; (*group*) гру́ппа; (*social gathering*) вечери́нка; (*leg.*) сторона́ (*acc.* -ону; *pl.* -оны, -о́н, -она́м); (*accomplice*) (со)уча́стник; be a p. to, принима́ть *imp.*, приня́ть (приму́, -мешь; при́нял, -а́, -о) *perf.* уча́стие в+*prep.*; *attrib.* парти́йный; p. line, (*polit.*) ли́ния па́ртии; (*telephone*) о́бщий телефо́нный про́вод (*pl.* -а́); p. wall, о́бщая стена́ (*acc.* -ну; *pl.* -ны, -н, -на́м).

paschal *adj.* пасха́льный.

pasha *n.* паша́ *m.*

pass *v.t. & i.* (*go past*; p. test; *of time*) проходи́ть (-ожу́, -о́дишь) *imp.*, пройти́ (пройду́, -дёшь; прошёл, -шла́) *perf.* (by, ми́мо+*gen.*); (*travel*

past) проезжа́ть *imp.*, прое́хать (-е́ду, -е́дешь) *perf.* (by, ми́мо+*gen.*); (*go across; change*) переходи́ть (-ожу́, -о́дишь) *imp.*, перейти́ (-йду́, -йдёшь; -ешёл, -ешла́) *perf.* (+*acc.*, че́рез+*acc.*; to, в+*acc.*, к+*dat.*); (*p. examination*) сдава́ть (сдаю́, -аёшь) *imp.*, сдать (-ам, -ашь, -аст, -ади́м; сдал, -а́, -о) *perf.* (экза́мен); *v.i.* (*happen*) происходи́ть (-ит) *imp.*, произойти́ (-ойдёт; -ошёл, -ошла́) *perf.*; (*cards*) пасова́ть *imp.*, с~ *perf.*; *v.t.* (*sport*) пасова́ть *imp.*, пасну́ть *perf.*; (*overtake*) обгоня́ть *imp.*, обогна́ть (обгоню́, -нишь; обогна́л, -а́, -о) *perf.*; (*time*) проводи́ть (-ожу́, -о́дишь) *imp.*, провести́ (-еду́, -едёшь; -ёл, -ела́) *perf.*; (*hand on*) передава́ть (-даю́, -даёшь) *imp.*, переда́ть (-а́м, -а́шь, -а́ст, -ади́м; пе́редал, -а́, -о) *perf.*; (*law, resolution*) принима́ть *imp.*, приня́ть (приму́, -мешь; при́нял, -а́, -о) *perf.*; (*sentence*) выноси́ть (-ошу́, -о́сишь) *imp.*, вы́нести (-су, -сешь; -ес) *perf.* (upon, +*dat.*); p. as, for, слыть (слыву́, -вёшь; слыл, -а́, -о) *imp.*, про~ *perf.*+*instr.*, за+*acc.*; p. away, (*die*) сконча́ться *perf.*; p. by, (*omit*) пропуска́ть *imp.*, пропусти́ть (-ущу́, -у́стишь) *perf.*; p. off, (*postpone*) хорошо́) проходи́ть (-ит) *imp.*, пройти́ (-йдёт; прошёл, -шла́) *perf.*; p. out, (*coll.*) отключа́ться *imp.*, отключи́ться *perf.*; p. over, (in silence) обходи́ть (-ожу́, -о́дишь) *imp.*, обойти́ (обойду́, -дёшь; обошёл, -шла́) *perf.* молча́нием; p. through, (*experience*) пережива́ть *imp.*, пережи́ть (-иву́, -ивёшь; пережи́л, -а́, -о) *perf.*; *n.* (*permit*) про́пуск (*pl.* -а́); (*free p.*) беспла́тный биле́т; (*cards*; *sport*) пас; (*fencing*) вы́пад; (*juggling*) фо́кус; (*hypnotism*) пасс; (*mountain p.*) перева́л; bring to p., соверша́ть *imp.*, соверши́ть *perf.*; come to p., случа́ться *imp.*, случи́ться *perf.*; make a p. at, пристава́ть (-таю́, -таёшь) *imp.*, приста́ть (-а́ну, -а́нешь) *perf.* к+*dat.*; p. degree, дипло́м без отли́чия; p.-mark, посре́дственная оце́нка.

passable *adj.* проходи́мый, прое́зжий; (*fairly good*) неплохо́й (-х, -ха́, -хо).

passage *n.* прохо́д, прое́зд; (*of time*) ход; (*sea trip*) рейс; (*in house*) коридо́р; (*in book*) отры́вок (-вка); (*musical*) пасса́ж.

passenger *n.* пассажи́р.

passer-by *n.* прохо́жий *sb.*

passing *adj.* (*transient*) мимолётный, преходя́щий; (*cursory*) бе́глый; *n.*: *in p.*, мимохо́дом.

passion *n.* страсть (*pl.* -ти, -те́й) (for, к + *dat.*); (*attraction*) увлече́ние; (*anger*) вспы́шка гне́ва; *P.* (*of Christ*; *mus.*) стра́сти (-те́й) *f.pl.* (Христо́вы); *p.-flower*, страстноцве́т. **passionate** *adj.* стра́стный (-тен, -тна́, -тно), пы́лкий (-лок, -лка́, -лко).

passive *adj.* пасси́вный; (*gram.*) страда́тельный; *n.* страда́тельный зало́г. **passivity** *n.* пасси́вность.

passkey *n.* отмы́чка.

Passover *n.* евре́йская па́сха.

passport *n.* па́спорт (*pl.* -а́).

password *n.* паро́ль *m.*

past *adj.* про́шлый; (*gram.*) проше́дший; *n.* про́шлое *sb.*; (*gram.*) проше́дшее вре́мя *neut.*; *prep.* ми́мо + *gen.*; (*beyond*) за + *instr.*; *adv.* ми́мо.

paste *n.* (*of flour*) те́сто; (*similar mixture*) па́ста; (*adhesive*) клейстер; (*of imitation gem*) страз; *v.t.* накле́ивать *imp.*, накле́ить *perf.*; *p. up*, раскле́ивать *imp.*, раскле́ить *perf.* **pasteboard** *n.* карто́н.

pastel *n.* (*crayon*) пасте́ль*f.*; (*drawing*) рису́нок (-нка) пасте́лью; *attrib.* пасте́льный.

pastern *n.* ба́бка.

pasteurization *n.* пастериза́ция. **pasteurize** *v.t.* пастеризова́ть *imp.*, *perf.*

pastille *n.* лепёшка.

pastime *n.* развлече́ние; (*game*) игра́ (*pl.* -ры).

pastor *n.* па́стор. **pastoral** *adj.* (*bucolic*) пастора́льный; (*of pastor*) па́сторский; *n.* пастора́ль.

pastry *n.* пече́нье, пиро́жное *sb.*

pasturage *n.* пастьба́. **pasture** *n.* (*land*) па́стбище; (*herbage*) подно́жный корм (*loc.* -е & -у́); *v.t.* пасти́ (-су́, -сёшь; -с, -сла́) *imp.*

pasty[1] *n.* пиро́г (-а́).

pasty[2] *adj.* тестообра́зный; (*p.-faced*) бле́дный (-ден, -дна́, -дно, бле́дны).

pat *n.* шлепо́к (-пка́); (*of butter etc.*) кусо́к (-ска́); *v.t.* хло́пать *imp.*, по ~ *perf.*; *adj.* уме́стный; *adv.* кста́ти, своевре́менно.

patch *n.* запла́та; (*over eye*) повя́зка (на глазу́); (*on face*) му́шка; (*spot*) пятно́ (*pl.* -тна, -тен, -тнам); (*piece of land*) уча́сток (-тка) земли́; *p.-pocket*, накладно́й карма́н; *v.t.* ста́вить *imp.*, по ~ *perf.* запла́ту, -ты, на + *acc.*; *p. up*, (*fig.*) ула́живать *imp.*, ула́дить *perf.* **patchwork** *n.* лоску́тная рабо́та; *attrib.* лоску́тный. **patchy** *adj.* пёстрый (пёстр, -а́, пёстро); (*uneven*) неро́вный (-вен, -вна́, -вно).

pâté *n.* паште́т.

patella *n.* коле́нная ча́шка.

patent *adj.* патенто́ванный (-ан); (*obvious*) я́вный; *p. leather*, лакиро́ванная ко́жа; *n.* пате́нт; *v.t.* патентова́ть *imp.*, за ~ *perf.* **patentee** *n.* владе́лец (-льца) пате́нта.

paternal *adj.* отцо́вский; (*fatherly*) оте́ческий; *p. uncle*, дя́дя *m.* со стороны́ отца́. **paternity** *n.* отцо́вство.

path *n.* тропи́нка, тропа́ (*pl.* -пы, -п, тро́пам); (*way*) путь (-ти́, -тём) *m.*

pathetic *adj.* жа́лостный, тро́гательный.

pathless *adj.* бездоро́жный.

pathological *adj.* патологи́ческий. **pathologist** *n.* пато́лог. **pathology** *n.* патоло́гия.

pathos *n.* па́фос.

pathway *n.* тропи́нка, тропа́ (*pl.* -пы, -п, тро́пам).

patience *n.* терпе́ние; (*persistence*) упо́рство; (*cards*) пасья́нс. **patient** *adj.* терпели́вый; (*persistent*) упо́рный; *n.* больно́й *sb.*, пацие́нт, ~ ка.

patina *n.* пати́на.

patio *n.* (*court*) вну́тренний дво́рик; (*terrace*) терра́са.

patriarch *n.* патриа́рх. **patriarchal** *adj.* патриарха́льный; (*relig.*) патриа́рший.

patrician *n.* аристокра́т, ~ ка; (*hist.*) патри́ций; *adj.* аристократи́ческий; (*hist.*) патрициа́нский.

patricidal *etc. see* **parricide**.

patrimonial adj. насле́дственный. **patri-mony** n. насле́дство.

patriot n. патрио́т, ~ ка. **patriotic** adj. патриоти́ческий. **patriotism** n. патрио-ти́зм.

patrol n. патру́ль (-ля́) m.; (action) патрули́рование; v.t. & i. патрули́ро-вать imp.

patron n. покрови́тель m.; (of shop) клие́нт, ~ ка; p. saint, засту́пник, -ица. **patronage** n. покрови́тельство. **patroness** n. покрови́тельница. **patron-ize** v.t. покрови́тельствовать imp.+dat.; (shop) быть клие́нтом, клие́нт-кой, +gen.; (treat condescendingly) снисходи́тельно относи́ться (-ошу́сь, -о́сишься) imp. к+dat.

patronymic n. родово́е и́мя neut. (Russian name) о́тчество.

patter[1] v.i. (sound) постуки́вать imp.; n. посту́кивание, лёгкий то́пот.

patter[2] n. (speech) скорогово́рка.

pattern n. (paragon) образе́ц (-зца́); (model) моде́ль; (sewing) вы́кройка; (design) узо́р.

patty n. пирожо́к (-жка́).

paunch n. брюшко́ (pl. -ки́, -ко́в), пу́зо.

pauper n. бедня́к (-а́), ни́щий sb.

pause n. па́уза, переры́в; v.i. де́лать imp., c~ perf. па́узу; остана́вливаться imp., останови́ться (-влю́сь, -вишься) perf.

pave v.t. мости́ть imp., вы́~, за~ perf.; p. the way, подготовля́ть imp., подгото́вить perf. по́чву (for, для+gen.). **pavement** n. тротуа́р, пане́ль.

pavilion n. (building) павильо́н; (tent) пала́тка, шатёр (-тра́).

paw n. ла́па; v.t. тро́гать imp. ла́пой; (horse) бить (бьёт) imp. копы́том.

pawl n. защёлка; (naut.) пал.

pawn[1] n. (chess) пе́шка.

pawn[2] n. : in p., в закла́де; v.t. закла́ды-вать imp., заложи́ть (-жу́, -жишь) perf.; отдава́ть (-даю́, -даёшь) imp., отда́ть (-а́м, -а́шь, -а́ст, -ади́м; о́тдал, -а́, -о) perf. в зало́г. **pawn-broker** n. ростовщи́к (-а́), -и́ца. **pawn-shop** n. ломба́рд.

pay v.t. плати́ть (-ачу́, -а́тишь) imp., за~, у~ perf. (for, за+acc.); (bill etc.) опла́чивать imp., оплати́ть

(-ачу́, -а́тишь) perf.; v.i. (be profitable) окупа́ться imp., окупи́ться (-ится) perf.; n. (payment) упла́та; (wages) жа́лованье, зарпла́та; p. packet, полу́чка; p.-roll, платёжная ве́до-мость. **payable** adj. подлежа́щий упла́те. **payee** n. получа́тель m., ~ ница; (of cheque etc.) предъяви́тель m., ~ ница. **payload** n. поле́зная на-гру́зка. **payment** n. упла́та, платёж (-а́); p. by instalments, платёж (-а́) в рассро́чку; p. in kind, пла́та нату́рой.

pea n. (also pl., collect.) горо́х (-a(y)).

peace n. мир; (treaty) ми́рный догово́р; (public order; tranquillity) споко́йст-вие; (quiet) поко́й; attrib. ми́рный; at p. with, в ми́ре c+instr.; in p., в поко́е; make p., заключа́ть imp., за-ключи́ть perf. мир; make one's p., мири́ться imp., по~ perf. (with, c+instr.); p. and quiet, мир и тишина́; p.-loving, миролюби́вый; p.-offering, искупи́тельная же́ртва; p.-time, ми́р-ное вре́мя neut. **peaceable, peaceful** adj. ми́рный.

peach n. пе́рсик; (p.-tree) пе́рсиковое де́рево (pl. дере́вья, -вьев); p.-coloured, пе́рсикового цве́та.

peacock n. павли́н; p. butterfly, дневно́й павли́ний глаз. **peafowl** n. павли́н. **peahen** n. па́ва.

pea-jacket n. бушла́т.

peak n. (of cap) козырёк (-рька́); (sum-mit; highest point) верши́на; p. hour, часы́ m.pl. пик; p.-load, максима́ль-ная, пи́ковая, нагру́зка.

peaky adj. (worn out) изможлённый (-ён, -ена́).

peal n. (sound) звон колоколо́в, тре-зво́н; (set of bells) набо́р колоколо́в; (of thunder) раска́т; (of laughter) взрыв; v.i. (bells) трезво́нить imp.; (thunder) греме́ть (-ми́т) imp., по~perf.; p. the bells, звони́ть imp., по~perf. в колокола́.

peanut n. земляно́й оре́х, ара́хис.

pear n. гру́ша; (p.-tree) гру́шевое де́рево (pl. дере́вья, -вьев); p.-shaped, грушеви́дный.

pearl n. же́мчуг (-a(y); pl. -а́); (single p., also fig.) жемчу́жина; p. barley, перло́-вая крупа́; p. button, перламу́тровая пу́говица; *p.-oyster*, жемчу́жница. **pearly** *adj.* жемчу́жный.

peasant *n.* крестья́нин (*pl.* -я́не, -я́н), -я́нка; *attrib.* крестья́нский; *p. woman*, крестья́нка. **peasantry** *n.* крестья́нство.

peat *n.* торф (-a(y)). **peatbog** *n.* торфяни́к (-á). **peaty** *adj.* торфяно́й.

pebble *n.* га́лька. **pebbly** *adj.* покры́тый га́лькой.

peccadillo *n.* грешо́к (-шка́).

peck *v.t. & i.* клева́ть (клюю́, клюёшь) *imp.*, клю́нуть *perf.*; *n.* клево́к (-вка́).

pectoral *adj.* грудно́й; (*worn on chest*) нагру́дный.

peculiar *adj.* (*distinctive*) своеобра́зный; (*special*) осо́бенный; (*strange*) стра́нный (-нен, -нна́, -нно); *p. to*, сво́йственный (-ен(ен), -енна) + *dat.* **peculiarity** *n.* осо́бенность; стра́нность.

pecuniary *adj.* де́нежный.

pedagogical *adj.* педагоги́ческий. **pedagogics** *n.* педаго́гика. **pedagogue** *n.* учи́тель (*pl.* -ля́) *m.*, педаго́г.

pedal *n.* педа́ль; *v.i.* нажима́ть *imp.*, нажа́ть (-жму́, -жмёшь) *perf.* педа́ль; (*ride bicycle*) е́хать (е́ду, е́дешь) *imp.*, по~ *perf.* на велосипе́де.

pedant *n.* педа́нт, ~ ка. **pedantic** *adj.* педанти́чный. **pedantry** *n.* педанти́чность.

peddle *v.t.* торгова́ть *imp.* вразно́с + *instr.*

pedestal *n.* пьедеста́л, подно́жие; (*of table*) ту́мба.

pedestrian *adj.* пе́ший, пешехо́дный; (*prosaic*) прозаи́ческий; *n.* пешехо́д; *p. crossing*, перехо́д.

pedicure *n.* педикю́р.

pedigree *n.* (*genealogy*) родосло́вная *sb.*; (*descent*) происхожде́ние; *adj.* поро́дистый, племенно́й.

pediment *n.* фронто́н.

pedlar *n.* разно́счик.

pedometer *n.* шагоме́р.

peek *v.i.* (*p. in*) загля́дывать *imp.*, загляну́ть (-ну́, -нешь) *perf.*; (*p. out*) выгля́дывать *imp.*, вы́глянуть *perf.*

peel *n.* ко́рка, ко́жица; *v.t.* очища́ть *imp.*, очи́стить *perf.*; *v.i.*: *p. off*, (*detach oneself*) сходи́ть (-ит) *imp.*,

сойти́ (сойдёт; сошёл, -шла́) *perf.* **peelings** *n.* очи́стки (-ков) *pl.*, шелуха́.

peep *v.i.* (*p. in*) загля́дывать *imp.*, загляну́ть (-ну́, -нешь) *perf.*; (*p. out*) выгля́дывать *imp.*, вы́глянуть *perf.*; *n.* (*glance*) бы́стрый взгляд; *p. of day*, рассве́т; *p.-hole*, глазо́к (-зка́).

peer [1] *v.i.* всма́триваться *imp.*, всмотре́ться (-рю́сь, -ришься) *perf.* (at, в + *acc.*).

peer [2] *n.* (*noble*) пэр, лорд; (*equal*) ра́вный *sb.*, ро́вня *m.* & *f.* **peerage** *n.* (*class*) сосло́вие пэ́ров; (*rank*) зва́ние пэ́ра. **peeress** *n.* (*peer's wife*) супру́га пэ́ра; ле́ди, *f.indecl.* **peerless** *adj.* несравне́нный (-е́нен, -е́нна), бесподо́бный.

peeved *adj.* раздражённый (-ён, -ена́). **peevish** *adj.* раздражи́тельный, брюзгли́вый.

peewit *see* pewit.

peg *n.* ко́лышек (-шка), деревя́нный гвоздь (-дя́; *pl.* -ди, -де́й) *m.*; (*for hat etc.*) ве́шалка; (*on violin etc.*) коло́к (-лка́); *off the p.*, гото́вый; *take down a p.*, осажива́ть *imp.*, осади́ть (-ажу́, -а́дишь) *perf.*; *v.t.* прикрепля́ть *imp.*, прикрепи́ть *perf.* ко́лышком, -ками; (*price etc.*) иску́сственно подде́рживать *imp.*, поддержа́ть (-жу́, -жишь) *perf.*; *v.i.*: *p. away*, приле́жно рабо́тать *imp.* (at, над + *instr.*); *p. out*, (*die*) помира́ть *imp.*, помере́ть (-мру́, -мрёшь; по́мер, -ла́, -ло) *perf.*

pejorative *adj.* уничижи́тельный.

peke, Pekin(g)ese *n.* кита́йский мопс.

pelican *n.* пелика́н.

pellagra *n.* пелла́гра.

pellet *n.* ка́тышек (-шка); (*shot*) дроби́на.

pellicle *n.* ко́жица, плёнка.

pell-mell *adv.* (*in disorder*) беспоря́дочно; (*headlong*) очертя́, сломя́, го́лову.

pellucid *adj.* (*transparent*) прозра́чный; (*clear*) я́сный (я́сен, ясна́, я́сно, я́сны).

pelmet *n.* ламбреке́н.

pelt [1] *n.* (*animal skin*) шку́ра, ко́жа. **pelt** [2] *v.t.* забра́сывать *imp.*, заброса́ть *perf.*; *v.i.* (*rain*) бараба́нить (-ит) *imp.*; *n.*: (*at*) *full p.*, со всех ног.

pelvic adj. тáзовый. **pelvis** n. таз (loc. -é & -ý; pl. -ы).

pen[1] n. (for writing) перó (pl. -рья, -рьев); p. and ink, пи́сьменные принадлéжности f.pl.; slip of the p., опи́ска; p.-friend, знакóмый sb. по пи́сьмам; p.-name, псевдони́м.

pen[2] n. (enclosure) загóн; v.t. загоня́ть imp., загна́ть (загоню́, -нишь; загна́л, -á, -о) perf.

pen[3] n. (female swan) сáмка лéбедя.

penal adj. уголóвный; (punishable) накáзуемый; p. battalion, штрафнóй батальóн; p. code, уголóвный кóдекс; p. servitude, кáторжные рабóты f.pl. **penalize** v.t. накáзывать imp., наказáть (-ажу́, -áжешь) perf.; (sport) штрафовáть imp., о ~ perf. **penalty** n. наказáние, взыскáние; (sport) штраф; p. area, штрафнáя площáдка; p. kick, штрафнóй удáр. **penance** n. епитимья́ (gen.pl. -ми́й).

penchant n. склóнность (for, к + dat.).

pencil n. карандáш (-á); p.-case, пенáл; p.-sharpener, точи́лка; v.t. (write) писáть (пишу́, -шешь) imp., на ~ perf. карандашóм; (draw) рисовáть imp., на ~ perf. карандашóм.

pendant n. подвéска, кулóн; adj. вися́чий.

pending adj. (awaiting decision) ожидáющий решéния; patent p., патéнт зая́влен; prep. (during) во врéмя + gen.; (until) в ожидáнии + gen., до + gen.

pendulous adj. вися́чий, отви́слый.

pendulum n. мáятник.

penetrate v.t. прони́зывать imp., пронизáть (-ижу́, -и́жешь) perf.; v.i. проникáть imp., прони́кнуть (-к) perf. (into, в + acc.); through, чéрез + acc.). **penetrating** adj. проницáтельный; (sound) пронзи́тельный. **penetration** n. проникновéние; (insight) проницáтельность.

penguin n. пингви́н.

penicillin n. пеницилли́н.

peninsula n. полуóстров (pl. -á). **peninsular** adj. полуостровнóй.

penis n. мужскóй половóй член.

penitence n. раскáяние, покая́ние. **penitent** adj. раскáивающийся; n. кáю-

щийся грéшник. **penitential** adj. покая́нный.

penknife n. перочи́нный нож (-á).

pennant n. вы́мпел.

penniless adj. бездéнежный; (predic.) без грошá; (poor) бéдный (-ден, -днá, -дно, бéдны).

pennon n. вы́мпел.

penny n. пéнни neut.indecl., пенс.

pension n. пéнсия; v.t.: p. off, увольня́ть imp., уво́лить perf. на пéнсию. **pensionable** adj. даю́щий, имéющий, прáво на пéнсию; (age) пенсиóнный. **pensioner** n. пенсионéр, ~ ка.

pensive adj. задýмчивый.

penta- in comb. пяти-, пента-. **pentacle** n. маги́ческая фигýра. **pentagon** n. пятиугóльник; the P., Пентагóн. **pentagonal** adj. пятиугóльный. **pentagram** n. пентагра́мма. **pentahedron** n. пятигрáнник. **pentameter** n. пентáметр. **pentathlon** n. пятибóрье. **pentatonic** adj. пентатóнный.

Pentecost n. пятидесятни́ца.

penthouse n. особня́к (-á) на кры́ше многоэтáжного дóма.

pent-up adj. (anger etc.) сдéрживаемый.

penultimate adj. (n.) предпослéдний (слог).

penumbra n. полутéнь (loc. -éни; pl. -éни, -енéй).

penurious adj. бéдный (-ден, -днá, -дно, бéдны); (stingy) скупóй (скуп, -á, -о).

penury n. нуждá.

peony n. пиóн.

people n. нарóд; (as pl., persons) лю́ди (-дéй, -дям, -дьми́) pl.; (relatives) родны́е sb.; (occupy) населя́ть imp., насели́ть perf.; (populate) заселя́ть imp., засели́ть perf.

pepper n. пéрец (-рца(у)); v.t. пéрчить imp., на ~ perf.; (pelt) забрáсывать imp., забросáть perf. **peppercorn** n. пéрчинка. **pepper-pot** n. пéречница.

peppermint n. пéречная мя́та; (sweet) мя́тная конфéта.

peppery adj. напéрченный; (fig.) вспы́льчивый.

per prep. (by means of) expressed by instrumental case, по + dat.; (person) чéрез + acc.; (for each) (person) на + acc.; (time) в + acc.; (quantity) за +

acc.; *as* p., согла́сно + *dat.*; p. *annum*, ежего́дно, в год; p. *capita*, p. *head*, на челове́ка; p. *diem*, в день; p. *hour*, в час; p. *se*, сам (-á, -ó) по себе́, по существу́.

perambulator n. де́тская коля́ска.

perceive *v.t.* воспринима́ть *imp.*, воспри́нять (-иму́, -и́мешь; восприня́л, -á, -о) *perf.*

per cent *adv.*, n. проце́нт, на со́тню. **percentage** n. проце́нтное содержа́ние, проце́нт.

perceptible *adj.* воспринима́емый, заме́тный. **perception** n. восприя́тие, понима́ние. **perceptive** *adj.* воспринима́ющий, восприи́мчивый.

perch[1] n. (*fish*) о́кунь (*pl.* -ни, -ней) m.

perch[2] n. (*roost*) насе́ст, жёрдочка; (*fig.*) высо́кое, про́чное, положе́ние; *v.i.* сади́ться *imp.*, сесть (ся́ду, -дешь; сел) *perf.*; *v.t.* сажа́ть *imp.*, посади́ть (-ажу́, -а́дишь) *perf.* (на насе́ст); высоко́ помеща́ть *imp.*, помести́ть *perf.* **perched** *adj.* высоко́ сидя́щий, располо́женный (-ен).

perchance *adv.* быть мо́жет.

percussion n. уда́р, столкнове́ние; (*mus. instruments*) уда́рные инструме́нты m.pl.; p. *cap*, уда́рный ка́псюль m. **percussive** *adj.* уда́рный.

perdition n. ги́бель.

peregrine (*falcon*) n. со́кол, сапса́н.

peremptory *adj.* повели́тельный.

perennial *adj.* ве́чный; (*plant*) многоле́тний; n. многоле́тнее расте́ние.

perfect *adj.* соверше́нный (-нен, -нна); (*exact*) то́чный (-чен, -чна́, -чно); (*gram.*) перфе́ктный; (*mus.*) чи́стый; n. перфе́кт; *v.t.* соверше́нствовать *imp.*, у~ *perf.* **perfection** n. соверше́нство. **perfective** *adj.* (n.) соверше́нный (вид).

perfidious *adj.* веро́мный, преда́тельский. **perfidy** n. веро́мство, преда́тельство.

perforate *v.t.* перфори́ровать *imp.*, *perf.* **perforation** n. перфора́ция; (*hole*) отве́рстие.

perforce *adv.* по необходи́мости, во́лей-нево́лей.

perform *v.t.* (*carry out*) исполня́ть *imp.*, испо́лнить *perf.*; соверша́ть *imp.*, со-

верши́ть *perf.*; (*play*; *music*) игра́ть *imp.*, сыгра́ть *perf.*; *v.i.* выступа́ть *imp.*, вы́ступить *perf.* **performance** n. исполне́ние; (*of play etc.*) представле́ние, спекта́кль m.; (*of engine etc.*) эксплуатацио́нные ка́чества *neut.pl.* **performer** n. исполни́тель m. **performing** *adj.* (*animal*) дрессиро́ванный.

perfume n. (*sweet smell*) арома́т; (*smell*) за́пах; (*scent*) духи́ (-хо́в) *pl.*; *v.t.* души́ть (-шу́, -шишь) *imp.*, на~ *perf.* **perfumery** n. парфюме́рия.

perfunctory *adj.* пове́рхностный.

pergola n. пе́ргола.

perhaps *adv.* мо́жет быть.

peri n. пе́ри *f.indecl.*

pericarp n. перика́рпий. **perigee** n. периге́й. **perihelion** n. периге́лий.

peril n. опа́сность, риск. **perilous** *adj.* опа́сный, риско́ванный (-ан, -анна).

perimeter n. (*geom.*) пери́метр; (*boundary*) вне́шняя грани́ца.

period n. пери́од; (*term*) срок (-a(y)); (*epoch*) эпо́ха; (*full stop*) то́чка; *adj.* относя́щийся к определённому пери́оду. **periodic** *adj.* периоди́ческий; p. *table*, периоди́ческая систе́ма элеме́нтов Менделе́ева. **periodical** *adj.* периоди́ческий; n. периоди́ческое изда́ние, журна́л. **periodicity** n. периоди́чность.

peripheral *adj.* перифери́йный. **periphery** n. (*outline*) ко́нтур; перифери́я.

periscope n. периско́п.

perish *v.i.* погиба́ть *imp.*, поги́бнуть (-б) *perf.*; (*die*) умира́ть *imp.*, умере́ть (умру́, -рёшь; у́мер, -ла́, -ло) *perf.*; (*spoil*) по́ртиться *imp.*, ис~ *perf.* **perishable** *adj.* скоропо́ртящийся; n.; *pl.* скоропо́ртящиеся това́ры *m.pl.*

peristyle n. перисти́ль m.

peritoneum n. брюши́на. **peritonitis** n. воспале́ние брюши́ны.

periwig n. пари́к (-á).

periwinkle[1] n. (*plant*) барви́нок (-нка).

periwinkle[2] n. (*winkle*) литори́на.

perjure *v.t.*: p. *oneself*, наруша́ть *imp.*, нару́шить *perf.* кля́тву. **perjurer** n. лжесвиде́тель m., ~ ница *f.* **perjury** n. ло́жное показа́ние под прися́гой, лжесвиде́тельство.

perk[1] *see* perquisite.

perk [2] *v.i.*: *p. up*, оживля́ться *imp.*, оживи́ться *perf.*; приободря́ться *imp.*, приободри́ться *perf.* **perky** *adj.* бо́йкий (бо́ек, бойка́, -ко); (*pert*) де́рзкий (-зок, -зка́, -зко).

permafrost *n.* ве́чная мерзлота́.

permanence *n.* постоя́нство. **permanency** *n.* постоя́нство; (*permanent employment*) постоя́нная рабо́та. **permanent** *adj.* постоя́нный; *p. wave*, перма́нент.

permeable *adj.* проница́емый. **permeate** *v.t.* (*penetrate*) проника́ть *imp.*, прони́кнуть (-к) *perf.* в+*acc.*; (*saturate*) пропи́тывать *imp.*, пропита́ть *perf.*; *v.i.* распространя́ться *imp.*, распространи́ться *perf.* **permeation** *n.* проника́ние.

permissible *adj.* допусти́мый, позволи́тельный. **permission** *n.* разреше́ние, позволе́ние. **permissive** *adj.* разреша́ющий, позволя́ющий; (*liberal*) либера́льный. **permissiveness** *n.* (сексуа́льная) вседозво́ленность. **permit** *v.t.* разреша́ть *imp.*, разреши́ть *perf.*+*dat.*; позволя́ть *imp.*, позво́лить *perf.*+*dat.*; *v.i.*: *p. of*, допуска́ть *imp.*, допусти́ть (-ущу́, -у́стишь) *perf.*+*acc.*; *n.* про́пуск (*pl.* -á); (*permission*) разреше́ние.

permutation *n.* перестано́вка.

pernicious *adj.* па́губный.

peroration *n.* заключи́тельная часть (*pl.* -ти, -те́й) (ре́чи).

peroxide *n.* пе́рекись; (*hydrogen p.*) пе́рекись водоро́да; *p. blonde*, хими́ческая блонди́нка.

perpendicular *adj.* перпендикуля́рный; (*cliff etc.*) отве́сный; *n.* перпендикуля́р.

perpetrate *v.t.* соверша́ть *imp.*, соверши́ть *perf.* **perpetration** *n.* соверше́ние.

perpetual *adj.* ве́чный, бесконе́чный; (*for life*) пожи́зненный; (*without limit*) бессро́чный. **perpetuate** *v.t.* увекове́чивать *imp.*, увекове́чить *perf.* **perpetuation** *n.* увекове́чение. **perpetuity** *n.* ве́чность, бесконе́чность; *in p.*, навсегда́, наве́чно.

perplex *v.t.* приводи́ть (-ожу́, -о́дишь) *imp.*, привести́ (-еду́, -едёшь; -ёл, -ела́) в недоуме́ние; озада́чивать *imp.*, озада́чить *perf.* **perplexity** *n.* недоуме́ние, озада́ченность.

perquisite, perk [1] *n.* случа́йный, дополни́тельный дохо́д.

perry *n.* гру́шевый сидр.

persecute *v.t.* пресле́довать *imp.*; (*pester*) надоеда́ть *imp.* надое́сть (-е́м, -е́шь, -е́ст, -еди́м; -е́л) *perf.*+*dat.* (*with*, +*instr.*). **persecution** *n.* пресле́дование.

perseverance *n.* насто́йчивость, сто́йкость. **persevere** *v.i.* сто́йко, насто́йчиво, продолжа́ть *imp.* (*in, at, etc.*, +*acc.*, *inf.*).

Persian *n.* перс, ~ ия́нка; (*cat*) перси́дская ко́шка; *adj.* перси́дский; *P. lamb*, кара́куль *m.*

persist *v.i.* упо́рствовать *imp.* (*in, in* +*prep.*); насто́йчиво продолжа́ть *imp.* (*in*, +*acc.*, *inf.*); (*continue to exist*) продолжа́ть *imp.* существова́ть. **persistence** *n.* упо́рство, насто́йчивость. **persistent** *adj.* упо́рный, насто́йчивый.

person *n.* челове́к (*pl.* лю́ди, -де́й, -дя́м, -дьми́), осо́ба; (*appearance*) вне́шность; (*in play*; *gram.*) лицо́ (*pl.* -ца); *in p.*, ли́чно. **personable** *adj.* привлека́тельный. **personage** *n.* осо́ба (ва́жная) персо́на, выдаю́щаяся ли́чность. **personal** *adj.* ли́чный, персона́льный; *p. property*, дви́жимое иму́щество; *p. remarks*, ли́чности *f.pl.* **personality** *n.* ли́чность. **personally** *adv.* ли́чно; *I p.*, что каса́ется меня́. **personalty** *n.* дви́жимое иму́щество. **personate** *v.t.* игра́ть *imp.*, сыгра́ть *perf.* роль+*gen.*; (*pretend to be*) выдава́ть (-даю́, -даёшь) *imp.*, вы́дать (-ам, -ашь, -аст, -адим) *perf.* себя́ за+*acc.* **personification** *n.* олицетворе́ние. **personify** *v.t.* олицетворя́ть *imp.*, олицетвори́ть *perf.*

personnel *n.* ка́дры (-ров) *pl.*, персона́л; (*mil.*) ли́чный соста́в; *p. carrier*, транспортёр; *p. department*, отде́л ка́дров; *p. manager*, нача́льник отде́ла ка́дров.

perspective *n.* перспекти́ва; *adj.* перспекти́вный.

perspicacious *adj.* проница́тельный. **perspicacity** *n.* проница́тельность.

perspiration n. пот (loc. -ý; pl. -ы́), испáрина; (action) потéние. **perspire** v.i. потéть imp., вс~ perf.

persuade v.t. убеждáть imp., убедить (-ишь) perf. (of, в + prep.); уговáривать imp., уговорить perf. **persuasion** n. убеждéние; (religious belief) религиóзные убеждéния neut.pl.; (joc.) род, сорт. **persuasive** adj. убеди́тельный.

pert adj. дéрзкий (-зок, -зкá, -зко).

pertain v.i.: p. to, (belong) принадлежáть imp. + dat.; (relate) имéть imp. отношéние к + dat.

pertinacious adj. упря́мый, неустýпчивый. **pertinacity** n. упрямство, неустýпчивость.

pertinence n. умéстность. **pertinent** adj. умéстный.

perturb v.t. (disturb) трево́жить imp., вс~ perf.; (agitate) волновáть imp., вз~ perf. **perturbation** n. трево́га, волнéние.

perusal n. внимáтельное чтéние. **peruse** v.t. (read) внимáтельно читáть imp., про~ perf.; (fig.) рассмáтривать imp., рассмотрéть (-рю, -ришь) perf.

pervade v.t. (permeate) проникáть imp., прони́кнуть (-к) perf. в + acc.; (spread) распространя́ться imp., распространи́ться perf. по + dat.

perverse adj. (persistent) упря́мый; (wayward) капри́зный; (perverted) извращéнный (-ён, -ённа). **perversion** n. извращéние. **perversity** n. упря́мство. **pervert** v.t. извращáть imp., изврати́ть (-ащý, -ати́шь) perf.; n. извращéнный человéк.

pessimism n. пессими́зм. **pessimist** n. пессими́ст. **pessimistic** adj. пессимисти́ческий.

pest n. вреди́тель m.; (fig.) я́зва. **pester** v.t. надоедáть imp., надоéсть (-éм, -éшь, -éст, -еди́м) perf.+dat.; (importune) приставáть (-таю́, -таёшь) imp., пристáть (-áну, -áнешь) perf. к + dat. **pesticide** n. пестици́д. **pestilence** n. чумá. **pestilent(ial)** adj. (deadly) смертонóсный; (injurious) врéдный (-ден, -днá, -дно); (of pestilence) чумнóй; (coll.) неснóсный, надоéдливый.

pestle n. пест (-á), пéстик.

pet n. (animal) люби́мое, домáшнее, живóтное sb.; (favourite) люби́мец (-мца), -мица, бáловень (-вня) m.; adj. (favourite) комнáтный, домáшний; (favourite) люби́мый; p. name, ласкáтельное и́мя neut.; v.t. ласкáть imp.; p. shop, зоомагази́н; v.t. ласкáть imp., баловáть imp., из~ perf.

petal n. лепестóк (-ткá).

peter v.i.: p. out, истощáться imp., истощи́ться perf.; (stream) иссякáть imp., иссяќнуть (-к) perf.

petition n. ходáтайство, прошéние; (formal written p.) пети́ция; (leg.) заявлéние; v.t. подавáть (-даю́, -даёшь) imp., подáть (-áм, -áшь, -áст, -ади́м) perf. прошéние, ходáтайство, + dat.; обращáться imp., обрати́ться (-ащýсь, -ати́шься) perf. с пети́цией в + acc. **petitioner** n. проси́тель m.

petrel n. буревéстник, качýрка.

petrifaction n. окаменéние. **petrified** adj. окаменéлый; be p., (fig.) оцепенéть perf. (with, of + gen.). **petrify** v.t. превращáть imp., преврати́ть (-ащý, -ати́шь) perf. в кáмень; v.i. каменéть imp., о~ perf.

petrochemical adj. нефтехими́ческий. **petrochemistry** n. нефтехи́мия. **petrodollar** n. нефтедóллар. **petrol** n. бензи́н; attrib. бензи́новый; p. gauge, бензомéр; p. pipe, бензопровóд; p. pump, (in engine) бензонасóс; (at p. station) бензоколóнка; p. station, бензозапрáвочная стáнция; p. tank, бензобáк. **petroleum** n. нефть.

petticoat n. ни́жняя юбка.

pettifogger n. крючкотвóр. **pettifoggery** n. крючкотвóрство. **pettifogging** adj. кля́узный.

petty adj. мéлкий (-лок, -лкá, -лко); p. bourgeois, мелкобуржуáзный; p. cash, мéлкие сýммы mp.pl.; p. officer, старшинá (pl. -ны) m.

petulance n. нетерпели́вость, раздражи́тельность. **petulant** adj. нетерпели́вый, приди́рчивый.

pew n. церкóвная скамья́ (pl. скáмьи, -мéй).

pewit n. чи́бис.

pewter n. сплав о́лова со свинцо́м; (*dishes*) оловя́нная посу́да.

phalanx n. фала́нга.

phallic adj. фалли́ческий. **phallus** n. фа́ллос.

phantom n. фанто́м, при́зрак.

Pharaoh n. фарао́н.

Pharisaic(al) adj. фарисе́йский. **Pharisee** n. фарисе́й.

pharmaceutical adj. фармацевти́ческий. **pharmacist** n. фармаце́вт. **pharmacology** n. фармаколо́гия. **pharmacopeia** n. фармакопе́я. **pharmacy** n. фарма́ция; (*dispensary*) апте́ка.

pharynx n. гло́тка.

phase n. фа́за, ста́дия.

pheasant n. фаза́н.

phenomenal adj. феномена́льный. **phenomenon** n. явле́ние; (*also person, event*) феноме́н.

phial n. скля́нка, пузырёк (-рька́).

philander v.i. волочи́ться (-чу́сь, -чи́шься) imp. (with, за + instr.). **philanderer** n. волоки́та m.

philanthrope, -pist n. филантро́п. **philanthropic** adj. филантропи́ческий. **philanthropy** n. филантро́пия.

philatelic adj. филателисти́ческий. **philatelist** n. филатели́ст. **philately** n. филате́лия.

philharmonic adj. (*in titles*) филармони́ческий.

philippic n. филиппика.

Philistine n. (*fig.*) фили́стер, меща́нин (*pl.* -а́не, -а́н) -а́нка; adj. фили́стерский, меща́нский. **philistinism** n. фили́стерство, меща́нство.

philological adj. филологи́ческий. **philologist** n. фило́лог. **philology** n. филоло́гия.

philosopher n. фило́соф. **philosophic(al)** adj. филосо́фский. **philosophize** v.i. филосо́фствовать imp. **philosophy** n. филосо́фия.

philtre n. приворо́тное зе́лье (*gen.pl.* -лий).

phlegm n. мокро́та; (*quality*) флегма. **phlegmatic** adj. флегмати́ческий.

phlox n. флокс.

phobia n. фо́бия, страх.

phoenix n. фе́никс.

phone n. телефо́н; v.t. & i. звони́ть imp., по ~ perf. + dat. (по телефо́ну).

phoneme n. фоне́ма. **phonemic** adj. фонемати́ческий. **phonetic** adj. фонети́ческий. **phonetician** n. фонети́ст. **phonetics** n. фоне́тика. **phonograph** n. фоно́граф. **phonological** adj. фонологи́ческий. **phonology** n. фоноло́гия.

phosphate n. фосфа́т. **phosphorescence** n. фосфоресце́нция. **phosphorescent** adj. светя́щийся, фосфоресци́рующий. **phosphorous** adj. фо́сфористый. **phosphorus** n. фо́сфор.

photo n. сни́мок (-мка); v.t. снима́ть imp., снять (сниму́, -мешь; снял, -á, -о) perf.; *p. finish*, фотофи́ниш.

photocopy n. фотоко́пия. **photoelectric** adj. фотоэлектри́ческий; *p. cell*, фотоэлеме́нт. **photogenic** adj. фотогени́чный. **photograph** n. фотогра́фия, сни́мок (-мка); v.t. фотографи́ровать imp., с ~ perf.; снима́ть imp., снять (сниму́, -мешь; снял, -á, -о) perf. **photographer** n. фото́граф. **photographic** adj. фотографи́ческий. **photography** n. фотогра́фия. **photogravure** n. фотогравю́ра. **photolithography** n. фотолитогра́фия. **photometer** n. фото́метр. **photosynthesis** n. фотоси́нтез.

phrase n. фра́за; (*diction*) стиль m.; (*expression*) оборо́т (ре́чи); v.t. выража́ть imp., вы́разить perf. слова́ми. **phraseological** adj. фразеологи́ческий. **phraseology** n. фразеоло́гия.

phrenology n. френоло́гия.

physical adj. физи́ческий; *p. culture*, физкульту́ра; *p. examination*, медици́нский осмо́тр; *p. exercises*, заря́дка. **physician** n. врач (-á). **physicist** n. фи́зик. **physics** n. фи́зика.

physiognomy n. физионо́мия.

physiological adj. физиологи́ческий. **physiologist** n. физио́лог. **physiology** n. физиоло́гия. **physiotherapist** n. физиотерапе́вт. **physiotherapy** n. физиотерапи́я.

physique n. телосложе́ние.

pianist n. пиани́ст, ~ка. **piano** n. фортепья́но neut.indecl.; (*grand*) роя́ль m.; (*upright*) пиани́но neut.indecl. **pianoforte** n. фортепья́но neut.indecl.

piccolo n. пи́кколо neut.indecl.

pick[1] *v.t.* (*ground*) разрыхля́ть *imp.*, разрыхли́ть *perf.*; (*bone*) обгла́дывать *imp.*, обглода́ть (-ожу́, -о́жешь) *perf.*; (*flower*) срыва́ть *imp.*, сорва́ть (-ву́, -вёшь) сорва́л, -а́, -о) *perf.*; (*gather*) собира́ть *imp.*, собра́ть (собе́ру, -рёшь) собра́л, -а́, -о) *perf.*; (*select*) выбира́ть *imp.*, вы́брать (вы́беру, -решь) *perf.*; *p. someone's brains*, присва́ивать *imp.*, присво́ить *perf.* (*чужи́е*) мы́сли; *p. a lock*, открыва́ть *imp.*, откры́ть (-ро́ю, -ро́ешь) *perf.* замо́к отмы́чкой; *p. one's nose, teeth*, ковыря́ть *imp.*, ковырну́ть *perf.* в носу́, в зуба́х; *p. a quarrel*, иска́ть (ищу́, и́щешь) *imp.* ссо́ры (*with*, с + *instr.*); *p. to pieces*, (*fig.*) раскритикова́ть *perf.*; *p. someone's pocket*, залеза́ть *imp.*, зале́зть (-зу, -зешь; -з) *perf.* в карма́н + *dat.*; *p. one's way*, выбира́ть *imp.*, вы́брать (вы́беру, -решь) *perf.* доро́гу; *p. off*, (*pluck off*) обрыва́ть *imp.*, оборва́ть (-ву́, -вёшь) оборва́л, -а́, -о) *perf.*; (*shoot*) перестре́ливать *imp.*, перестреля́ть *perf.* (одного́ за други́м); *p. on*, (*nag*) пили́ть (-лю́, -лишь) *imp.*; *p. out*, отбира́ть *imp.*, отобра́ть (отберу́, -рёшь) отобра́л, -а́, -о) *perf.*; *p. up*, (*lift*) поднима́ть *imp.*, подня́ть (подниму́, -мешь; по́днял, -а́, -о) *perf.*; (*gain*) добыва́ть *imp.*, добы́ть (добу́ду, -дешь; до́был, -а́, -о) *perf.*; (*fetch*) заезжа́ть *imp.*, зае́хать (зае́ду, -дешь) *perf.* за + *instr.*; (*recover*) поправля́ться *imp.*, попра́виться *perf.*; *p. oneself up*, поднима́ться *imp.*, подня́ться (подниму́сь, -мешься; подня́лся, -ла́сь) *perf.*; *p.-up*, (*truck*) пика́п; (*electron.*) звукоснима́тель *m.*

pick[2] *n.* вы́бор; (*best part*) лу́чшая часть, са́мое лу́чшее; *take your p.*, выбира́й(те)!

pick[3], **pickaxe** *n.* кирка́ (*pl.* ки́рки, -ро́к, ки́рка́м).

picket *n.* (*stake*) кол (-а́, *loc.* -у́; *pl.* -ья, -ьев); (*person*) пике́тчик, -и́ца (*collect.*) пике́т; *v.t.* пикети́ровать *imp.*

pickle *n.* (*brine*) рассо́л; (*vinegar*) марина́д; *pl.* соле́нья, марина́ды *m.pl.*, пи́кули (-лей) *pl.*; (*plight*) напа́сть; *v.t.* соли́ть (солю́, со́ли́шь) *imp.*, по~

perf.; маринова́ть *imp.*, за~ *perf.*
pickled *adj.* солёный (со́лон, -а́, -о) марино́ванный; (*drunk*) пья́ный (пьян, -а́, -о).

pickpocket *n.* карма́нник.

picnic *n.* пикни́к (-а́); *v.i.* уча́ствовать *imp.* в пикнике́.

pictorial *adj.* изобрази́тельный; (*illustrated*) иллюстри́рованный. **picture** *n.* карти́на; (*p. of health etc.*) воплоще́ние; (*film*) фильм; *the pictures*, кино́ *neut.indecl.*; *p.-book*, кни́га с карти́нками; *p.-gallery*, карти́нная галере́я; *p. postcard*, худо́жественная откры́тка; *p. window*, цельнометное окно́ (*pl.* о́кна, о́кон, о́кнам); *v.t.* изобража́ть *imp.*, изобрази́ть *perf.*; (*to oneself*) представля́ть *imp.*, предста́вить *perf.* себе́. **picturesque** *adj.* живопи́сный; (*language etc.*) о́бразный.

pie *n.* пиро́г (-а́), пирожо́к (-жка́).

piebald *adj.* пе́гий; *n.* (*horse*) пе́гая ло́шадь (*pl.* -ди, -де́й, *instr.* -дьми́).

piece *n.* кусо́к (-ска́), часть (*pl.* -ти, -те́й); (*one of set*) шту́ка; (*of land*) уча́сток (-тка); (*of paper*) листо́к (-тка́); (*mus., lit.*) произведе́ние; (*picture*) карти́на; (*drama*) пье́са; (*chess*) фигу́ра; (*coin*) моне́та; *take to pieces*, разбира́ть *imp.*, разобра́ть (разберу́, -рёшь) разобра́л, -а́, -о) *perf.* (на ча́сти); *p. of advice*, сове́т; *p. of information*, све́дение; *p. of news*, но́вость; *p.-work*, сде́льщина; *p.-worker*, сде́льщик; *v.t.*: *p. together*, собира́ть *imp.*, собра́ть (собе́ру, -рёшь) собра́л, -а́, -о) *perf.* из кусо́чков; своди́ть (-ожу́, -о́дишь) *imp.*, свести́ (сведу́, -дёшь; свёл, -а́) *perf.* воеди́но. **piecemeal** *adv.* по частя́м.

pied *adj.* разноцве́тный.

pier *n.* (*mole*) мол (*loc.* -у́); (*in harbour*) пирс; (*of bridge*) бык (-а́); (*between windows etc.*) просте́нок (-нка); *p.-glass*, трюмо́ *neut.indecl.*

pierce *v.t.* пронза́ть *imp.*, пронзи́ть *perf.*; прока́лывать *imp.*, проколо́ть (-лю́, -лешь) *perf.*; (*of cold, look, etc.*) прони́зывать *imp.*, пронза́ть (-ижу́, -и́жешь) *perf.* **piercing** *adj.* о́стрый (остр & остёр, остра́, о́стро́), пронзи́тельный.

piety n. на́божность.

piffle n. чепуха́, вздор. **piffling** adj. ничто́жный.

pig n. свинья́ (pl. -ньи, -не́й, -нья́м) (also of person); (of metal) болва́нка, чу́шка; v.t.: p. it, жить (живу́, -вёшь, жил, -а́, -о) imp., по-сви́нски; v. abs. пороси́ться imp., о ~ perf. **pigheaded** adj. упря́мый. **pig-iron** n. чугу́н (-а́) в чу́шках. **piglet** n. поросёнок (-сёнка; pl. -ся́та, -ся́т). **pigskin** n. свина́я ко́жа. **pigsty** n. свина́рник. **pigswill** n. помо́и (-о́ев) pl. **pigtail** n. коси́ца.

pigeon n. го́лубь (pl. -би, -бе́й) m.; p.-hole, (n.) отделе́ние для бума́г; (v.t.) раскла́дывать imp., разложи́ть (-ожу́, -о́жишь) perf. по отделе́ниям, по я́щикам; (put aside) откла́дывать imp., отложи́ть (-ожу́, -о́жишь) perf. в до́лгий я́щик.

pigment n. пигме́нт. **pigmentation** n. пигмента́ция.

pigmy see **pygmy**.

pike[1] n. (weapon) пи́ка.

pike[2] n. (fish) щу́ка;. p-perch, суда́к (-а́).

pilaster n. пиля́стр.

pilchard n. сарди́н(к)а.

pile[1] n. (heap) ку́ча, ки́па; (funeral p.) погреба́льный костёр (-тра́); (building) огро́мное зда́ние; (electr.) батаре́я; (atomic p.) я́дерный реа́ктор; v.t.: p. up, скла́дывать imp., сложи́ть (-жу́, -жишь) perf. в ку́чу; сва́ливать imp., свали́ть (-лю́, -лишь) perf. в ку́чу; (load) нагружа́ть imp., нагрузи́ть (-ужу́, -у́зи́шь) perf. (with, +instr.); p. in(to), on, забира́ться imp., забра́ться (заберу́сь, -рёшься, забра́лся, -ала́сь, -ало́сь) perf. в+acc.; p. up, накопля́ться, нака́пливаться imp., накопи́ться (-ится) perf.

pile[2] n. (support) сва́я; p.-driver, копёр (-пра́).

pile[3] n. (on cloth etc.) ворс.

piles n. геморро́й.

pilfer v.t. ворова́ть imp. **pilfering** n. ме́лкая кра́жа.

pilgrim n. пилигри́м, пало́мник, -ица. **pilgrimage** n. пало́мничество.

pill n. пилю́ля; the p., противозача́точная пилю́ля.

pillage n. мародёрство; v.t. гра́бить

imp., о ~ perf.; v. abs. мародёрствовать imp.

pillar n. столб (-а́); (fig.) столп (-а́); p.-box, стоя́чий почто́вый я́щик.

pillion n. за́днее сиде́нье (мотоци́кла).

pillory n. позо́рный столб (-а́); v.t. (fig.) пригвожда́ть imp., пригвозди́ть perf. к позо́рному столбу́.

pillow n. поду́шка; v.t. подпира́ть imp., подпере́ть (подопру́, -рёшь; подпёр) perf. **pillowcase** n. на́волочка.

pilot n. (naut.) ло́цман; (aeron.) пило́т, лётчик; adj. о́пытный, про́бный; v.t. управля́ть imp.+instr.; (aeron.) пилоти́ровать imp.

pimento n. пе́рец (-рца(у)).

pimp n. сво́дник, -ица; v.i. сво́дничать imp.

pimpernel n. о́чный цвет.

pimple n. прыщ (-а́). **pimpled, pimply** adj. прыща́вый, прыщева́тый.

pin n. була́вка; (peg) па́лец (-льца); p.-head, (fig.) ме́лочь (pl. -чи, -че́й); (person) тупи́ца m. & f.; p-hole, була́вочное отве́рстие; p.-point, то́чно определя́ть imp., определи́ть perf.; p-prick, (fig.) ме́лкая неприя́тность; p.-stripe, то́нкая поло́ска; p.-tuck, ме́лкая скла́дочка; v.t. прика́лывать imp., приколо́ть (-лю́, -лешь) perf. (press) прижима́ть imp., прижа́ть (-жму́, -жмёшь) perf. (against, к+dat.); p.-up, карти́нка краса́вици, прикреплённая на сте́ну.

pinafore n. пере́дник.

pince-nez n. пенсне́ neut.indecl.

pincers n. клещи́ (-ще́й) pl., пинце́т; (crab's) клешни́ f.pl.; pincer movement, захва́т в клещи́.

pinch v.t. щипа́ть (-плю́, -плешь) imp., (у)щипну́ть perf.; прищи́пывать imp., прищипну́ть perf.; (of shoe) жать (жмёт) imp.; (steal) стяну́ть (-ну́, -нешь) perf.; (arrest) сца́пать perf.; v.i. скупи́ться imp.; where the shoe pinches, в чём загво́здка; n. щипо́к (-пка́); (of salt) щепо́тка; (of snuff) поню́шка (табаку́); at a p., в кра́йнем слу́чае.

pinchbeck n. томпа́к (-а́); adj. томпа́ковый.

pincushion *n.* поду́шечка для була́-
вок.

pine[1] *v.i.* томи́ться *imp.*; *p. for*, тоско-
ва́ть *imp.* по + *dat.*, *prep.*

pine[2] *n.* (*tree*) сосна́ (*pl.* -сны, -сен,
-снам); *attrib.* сосно́вый; *p.-cone*,
сосно́вая ши́шка; *p.-needles*, сосно́вая
хво́я *collect.*

pineal *adj.* шишкови́дный.

pineapple *n.* анана́с.

ping-pong *n.* насто́льный те́ннис, пинг-
-по́нг.

pinion[1] *n.* (*of wing*) оконе́чность пти́-
чьего крыла́; (*flight-feather*) махово́е
перо́ (*pl.* -рья, -рьев); *v.t.* подреза́ть
imp., подре́зать (-е́жу, -е́жешь) *perf.*
кры́лья + *dat.*; (*person*) свя́зывать
imp., связа́ть (-яжу́, -я́жешь) *perf.*
ру́ки + *dat.*

pinion[2] *n.* (*cog-wheel*) шестерня́ (*gen.pl.*
-рён).

pink[1] *n.* (*flower*) гвозди́ка; (*colour*)
ро́зовый цвет; *the p.*, вы́сшая сте́-
пень, верх; *in the p.*, в прекра́сном
состоя́нии; *adj.* ро́зовый.

pink[2] *v.t.* (*pierce*) протыка́ть *imp.*,
проткну́ть *perf.*; *p. out*, украша́ть
imp., укра́сить *perf.* зубца́ми.

pink[3] *v.i.* (*of engine*) рабо́тать *imp.* с
детона́цией.

pinnace *n.* пина́с.

pinnacle *n.* (*peak; fig.*) верши́на; (*turret*)
остроконе́чная ба́шенка.

pint *n.* пи́нта.

pintail *n.* (*duck*) шилохво́сть.

piny *adj.* сосно́вый.

pioneer *n.* пионе́р, ~ ка; (*mil.*) сапёр;
adj. пионе́рский; сапёрный.

pious *adj.* набо́жный.

pip[1] *n.* (*on dice etc.*) очко́ (*pl.* -ки́, -ко́в);
(*star*) звёздочка.

pip[2] *n.* (*seed*) зёрнышко (*pl.* -шки,
-шек, -шкам).

pip[3] *n.* (*sound*) бип.

pipe *n.* труба́ (*pl.* -бы); (*mus.*) ду́дка,
свире́ль; (*for smoking*)
тру́бка; *p.-dream*, пуста́я мечта́ (*gen.*
pl. -ний); *v.t.* (*play on p.*) игра́ть *imp.*,
сыгра́ть *perf.* на ду́дке, на свире́ли;
(*convey by p.*) пуска́ть *imp.*, пусти́ть
(пущу́, пу́стишь) *perf.* по труба́м,
по трубопрово́ду; *v.i.*: *p. down*,

замолка́ть *imp.*, замо́лкнуть (-к) *perf.*

pipeclay *n.* бе́лая тру́бочная гли́на.

pipeline *n.* трубопрово́д; (*oil p.*)
нефтепрово́д. **piper** *n.* волы́нщик.

pipette *n.* пипе́тка. **piping** *n.* (*on dress
etc.*) кант; *adj.* (*voice*) пискли́вый; *p.
hot*, с пы́лу, с жа́ру.

pipit *n.* щеври́ца, конёк (-нька́).

piquancy *n.* пика́нтность. **piquant** *adj.*
пика́нтный.

piqué *n.* пике́ *neut.indecl.*

piracy *n.* пира́тство. **pirate** *n.* пира́т;
v.t. (*book*) самово́льно переиздава́ть
(-даю́, -даёшь) *imp.*, переизда́ть (-а́м,
-а́шь, -а́ст, -ади́м; -а́л, -ала́, -а́ло)
perf. piratical *adj.* пира́тский.

pirouette *n.* пируэ́т; *v.i.* де́лать *imp.*,
с ~ *perf.* пируэ́т(ы)

piscatorial *adj.* рыболо́вный.

Pisces *n.* Ры́бы *f.pl.*

pistachio *n.* фиста́шка; *attrib.* фиста́ш-
ковый.

pistil *n.* пе́стик.

pistol *n.* пистоле́т.

piston *n.* по́ршень (-шня) *m.*; (*in cornet
etc.*) писто́н; *adj.* поршнево́й; *p.-ring*,
поршнево́е кольцо́ (*pl.* -льца, -ле́ц,
-льцам); *p.-rod*, шток по́ршня.

pit[1] *n.* я́ма; (*mine*) ша́хта; (*quarry*)
карье́р; (*theat.*) партёр; (*in workshop*)
ремо́нтная я́ма; (*car-racing*) запра-
вочно-ремо́нтный пункт; *the bottomless p.*, преиспо́дняя *sb.*; *in the p. of the
stomach*, под ло́жечкой; *p.-head*, над-
ша́хтный копёр (-пра́); *v.t.*: *p. against*,
выставля́ть *imp.*, вы́ставить *perf.*
про́тив + *gen.*

pit-a-pat *adv.* с ча́стым бие́нием; *go p.*,
(*heart*) затрепета́ть (-е́щет) *perf.*

pitch[1] *n.* (*resin*) смола́; *p.-black*, чёрный
(-рен, -рна́) как смоль; *p.-dark*, о́чень
тёмный (-мен, -мна́); *p.-darkness*,
тьма кроме́шная; *v.t.* смоли́ть *imp.*,
вы́-, о ~ *perf.*

pitch[2] *v.t.* (*camp, tent*) разбива́ть *imp.*,
разби́ть (разобью́, -ьёшь) *perf.*;
(*ball*) подава́ть (-даю́, -даёшь) *imp.*,
пода́ть (-а́м, -а́шь, -а́ст, -ади́м;
по́дал, -ала́, -о) *perf.*; (*fling*) кида́ть
imp., ки́нуть *perf.*; *v.i.* (*fall*) па́дать
imp., (у)па́сть (-аду́, -адёшь; -а́л) *perf.*
(*ship*) испы́тывать *imp.*, испыта́ть

perf. килеву́ю ка́чку; *p. into,* набра́сываться *imp.,* набро́ситься *perf.* на + *acc.; pitched battle,* генера́льное сраже́ние; *n. (of ship)* килева́я ка́чка; *(of ball)* пода́ча; *(football p. etc.)* площа́дка; *(degree)* у́ровень (-вня) *m.; (mus.)* высота́ *(pl.* -ты); *(slope)* укло́н; *p.-pipe,* камерто́н-ду́дка.

pitchblende *n.* уранини́т.

pitcher[1] *n. (sport)* подаю́щий *sb.* (мяч).

pitcher[2] *n. (vessel)* кувши́н.

pitchfork *n.* ви́лы (-л) *pl.*

pitchy *adj.* смоли́стый.

piteous *adj.* жа́лостный, жа́лкий (-лок, -лка́, -лко).

pitfall *n.* западня́.

pith *n.* сердцеви́на; *(essence)* суть; *(vigour)* си́ла, эне́ргия. **pithy** *adj. (fig.)* сжа́тый, содержа́тельный.

pitiable *adj.* жа́лкий (-лок, -лка́, -лко), несча́стный. **pitiful** *adj.* жа́лостный, жа́лкий (-лок, -лка́, -лко). **pitiless** *adj.* безжа́лостный.

pittance *n.* ску́дное жа́лованье, жа́лкие гроши́ (-ше́й) *pl.*

pitted *adj. (of face)* изры́тый, рябо́й (ряб, -а́, -о).

pituitary *adj.* сли́зистый; *n. (gland)* гипо́физ.

pity *n.* сожале́ние; *it's a p.,* жа́лко, жаль; *take p. on,* сжа́литься *perf.* над + *instr.; what a p.,* как жа́лко! *v.t.* жале́ть *imp.,* по~ *perf.; I p. you* мне жаль тебя́.

pivot *n.* сте́ржень (-жня) *m.; (fig.)* центр; *v.i.* враща́ться *imp.* **pivotal** *adj. (fig.)* центра́льный.

placard *n.* афи́ша, плака́т; *v.t. (wall)* раскле́ивать *imp.,* раскле́ить *perf.* афи́ши, плака́ты, на + *prep.,* по + *dat.*

placate *v.t.* умиротворя́ть *imp.,* умиротвори́ть *perf.*

place *n.* ме́сто *(pl.* -та́); *change places with,* обме́ниваться *imp.,* обменя́ться *perf.* места́ми с + *instr.; give p. to,* уступа́ть *imp.,* уступи́ть (-плю́, -пишь) *perf.* ме́сто + *dat.; in p.,* на ме́сте; *(suitable)* уме́стный; *in p. of,* вме́сто + *gen.; in the first, second, p.,* во-пе́рвых, во-вторы́х; *out of p.,* не на ме́сте; *(unsuitable)* неуме́стный; *take p.,* случа́ться *imp.,* случи́ться

perf.; (pre-arranged event) состоя́ться (-ои́тся) *perf.; take the p. of,* заменя́ть *imp.,* замени́ть (-ню́, -нишь) *perf.; p.-name,* географи́ческое назва́ние; *p.-setting,* столо́вый прибо́р; *v.t.* помеща́ть *imp.,* помести́ть *perf.; (stand)* ста́вить *imp.,* по~ *perf.; (lay)* класть (кладу́, -дёшь; -ал) *imp.,* положи́ть (-жу́, -жишь) *perf.; (determine)* определя́ть *imp.,* определи́ть *perf.*

placenta *n.* плаце́нта.

placid *adj.* споко́йный. **placidity** *n.* споко́йствие.

plagiarism *n.* плагиа́т. **plagiarist** *n.* плагиа́тор. **plagiarize** *v.t.* заи́мствовать *imp., perf.*

plague *n.* чума́, морова́я я́зва; *v.t.* му́чить *imp.,* за~, из~ *perf.*

plaice *n.* ка́мбала.

plaid *n. (cloth)* плед; *(adj.)* в шотла́ндскую кле́тку.

plain *n.* равни́на; *adj. (clear)* я́сный (я́сен, ясна́, я́сно, я́сны); *(simple)* просто́й (прост, -а́, -о, про́сты́); *(direct)* прямо́й (прям, -а́, -о, пря́мы́); *(ugly)* некраси́вый; *p.-clothes policeman,* шпик (-а́); *p.-spoken,* открове́нный (-нен, -нна); *p. stitch,* пряма́я петля́.

plaintiff *n.* исте́ц (-тца́), исти́ца.

plaintive *adj.* жа́лобный.

plait *n.* коса́ *(acc.* ко́су; *pl.* -сы); *v.t.* плести́ (плету́, -тёшь, плёл, -а́) *imp.,* с~ *perf.*

plan *n.* план; *v.t.* плани́ровать *imp.,* за~, с~ *perf.; (intend)* намерева́ться *imp.* + *inf.*

plane[1] *n. (tree)* плата́н.

plane[2] *n. (tool)* руба́нок (-нка); *v.t.* строга́ть *imp.,* вы~ *perf.*

plane[3] *n. (surface)* пло́скость; *(level)* у́ровень (-вня) *m.; (aeroplane)* самолёт; *v.i.* плани́ровать *imp.,* с~ *perf.*

plane[4] *adj. (level)* пло́ский (-сок, -ска́, -ско), плоскостно́й.

planet *n.* плане́та. **planetarium** *n.* планета́рий. **planetary** *adj.* плане́тный, плане́тарный.

plank *n.* доска́ *(acc.* -ску; *pl.* -ски, -со́к, -ска́м); *(polit.)* пункт парти́йной програ́ммы; *p. bed,* на́ры (-р) *pl.; v.t.* выстила́ть *imp.,* вы́стлать (-телю,

-телешь) *perf.* доска́ми. **planking** *n.* насти́л; (*collect.*) до́ски (-со́к, -ска́м) *f.pl.*

plankton *n.* планкто́н.

plant *n.* расте́ние; (*fixtures*) устано́вка; (*factory*) заво́д; *v.t.* сажа́ть *imp.*, посади́ть (-ажу́, -а́дишь) *perf.*; насажда́ть *imp.*, насади́ть (-ажу́, -а́дишь) *perf.*; (*fix firmly*) про́чно ста́вить *imp.*, по ~ *perf.*; (*garden etc.*) заса́живать *imp.*, засади́ть (-ажу́, -а́дишь) *perf.* (with, + *instr.*); (*palm off*) всучива́ть *imp.*, всучи́ть (-учу́, -у́чишь) *perf.* (on, + *dat.*); p. out, выса́живать *imp.*, вы́садить *perf.* в грунт.

plantain *n.* подоро́жник.

plantation *n.* (*of trees*) (лесо)насажде́ние; (*of cotton etc.*) планта́ция. **planter** *n.* планта́тор.

plaque *n.* доще́чка, мемориа́льная доска́ (*acc.* -ску; *pl.* -ски, -со́к, -ска́м); (*plate*) декорати́вная таре́лка.

plasma *n.* пла́зма; протопла́зма.

plaster *n.* пла́стырь *m.*; (*for walls etc.*) штукату́рка; p. of Paris, (*n.*) гипс; (*attrib.*) ги́псовый; p. cast, (*mould*) ги́псовый сле́пок (-пка); (*for leg etc.*) ги́псовая повя́зка; *v.t.* (*wall*) штукату́рить *imp.*, от ~, о ~ *perf.*; (*daub*) зама́зывать *imp.*, зама́зать (-а́жу, -а́жешь) *perf.*; (*apply a p. to*) накла́дывать *imp.*, наложи́ть (-жу́, -жишь) *perf.* пла́стырь на + *acc.* **plasterboard** *n.* суха́я штукату́рка. **plastered** *adj.* (*drunk*) пья́ный (пьян, -а́. -о). **plasterer** *n.* штукату́р.

plastic *n.* пластма́сса; *adj.* пласти́чный, пласти́ческий; (*made of p.*) пластма́ссовый; p. arts, пла́стика; p. surgery, пласти́ческая хирурги́я.

plate *n.* пласти́нка; (*for food*) таре́лка; (*collect.; silver, gold p.*) столо́вое серебро́, зо́лото; (*metal sheet*) лист (-а́); (*print.*) печа́тная фо́рма; (*illustration*) (вкладна́я) иллюстра́ция; (*name-p. etc.*) фотопласти́нка; (*phot.*) фотопласти́нка; p.-armour, бронево́е плиты́ *f.pl.*; p. glass, зерка́льное стекло́; p.-rack, суши́лка для посу́ды; *v.t.* плакирова́ть *imp.*, *perf.* **plateful** *n.* по́лная таре́лка. **platelayer** *n.* путево́й рабо́чий *sb.*

plateau *n.* плато́ *neut.indecl.*, плоского́рье.

platform *n.* платфо́рма; (*rly.*) перро́н; p. ticket перро́нный биле́т.

platinum *n.* пла́тина; *attrib.* пла́тиновый.

platitude *n.* бана́льность, пло́скость. **platitudinous** *adj.* бана́льный, пло́ский (-сок, -ска́, -ско).

platoon *n.* взвод.

platypus *n.* утконо́с.

plaudits *n.* аплодисме́нты (-тов) *pl.*

plausibility *n.* (*probability*) правдоподо́бие; (*speciosity*) благови́дие. **plausible** *adj.* правдоподо́бный; благови́дный.

play *v.t. & i.* игра́ть *imp.*, сыгра́ть *perf.* (*game*) в + *acc.*, (*instrument*) на + *prep.*, (*in p.*) в + *prep.*, (*for prize*) на + *acc.*, (*opponent*) с + *instr.*; *v.t.* (*p. part of; also fig.*) игра́ть *imp.*, сыгра́ть *perf.* роль + *gen.*; (*mus. composition*) исполня́ть *imp.*, испо́лнить *perf.*; (*chessman, card*) ходи́ть (хожу́, хо́дишь) *imp.* + *instr.*; (*record*) ста́вить *imp.*, по ~ *perf.*; (*searchlight*) направля́ть *imp.*, напра́вить *perf.* (on, на + *acc.*); *v.i.* (*frolic*) резви́ться *imp.*; (*fountain*) бить (бьёт) *imp.*; (*light*) перелива́ться *imp.*; p. down, преуменьша́ть *imp.*, преуме́ньшить *perf.*; p. fair, че́стно поступа́ть *imp.*, поступи́ть (-плю́, -пишь) *perf.*; p. false, изменя́ть *imp.*, измени́ть (-ню́, -нишь) *perf.* (+ *dat.*); p. the fool, валя́ть *imp.* дурака́; p. into the hands of, игра́ть *imp.*, сыгра́ть *perf.* на́ руку + *dat.*; p. a joke, trick, on подшу́чивать *imp.*, подшути́ть (-учу́, -у́тишь) *perf.* над + *instr.*; p. off, игра́ть *imp.*, сыгра́ть *perf.* реша́ющую па́ртию; p.-off, реша́ющая встре́ча; p. off against, стра́вливать *imp.*, страви́ть (-влю́, -вишь) *perf.* с + *instr.*; p. safe, де́йствовать *imp.* наверняка́; played out, изму́танный (-ан) *n.* игра́; (*theat.*) пье́са. **playbill** *n.* театра́льная афи́ша. **playboy** *n.* прожига́тель *m.* жи́зни. **player** *n.* игро́к (-а́); (*actor*) актёр, актри́са; (*musician*) музыка́нт. **playfellow**, **playmate** *n.* друг (*pl.* друзья́, -зе́й) де́тства. **playful** *adj.* игри́вый. **playgoer** *n.* театра́л. **play-**

ground *n.* площа́дка для игр. **playhouse** *n.* теа́тр. **playing** *n.:* p.-card, игра́льная ка́рта. p.-field, спорти́вная площа́дка. **plaything** *n.* игру́шка. **playwright** *n.* драмату́рг.

plea *n.* (*appeal*) обраще́ние; (*entreaty*) мольба́; (*statement*) заявле́ние; on a p. of, под предло́гом + *gen.* **plead** *v.i.* умоля́ть *imp.*, (with, + *dat.*); *v.t.* ссыла́ться *imp.*, сосла́ться (сошлю́сь, -лёшься) *perf.* на + *acc.*; p. (not) guilty, (не) признава́ть (-на́ю, -наёшь) *imp.*, призна́ть *perf.* себя́ вино́вным.

pleasant *adj.* прия́тный. **pleasantry** *n.* шу́тка. **please** *v.t.* нра́виться *imp.*, по~ *perf.* + *dat.*; угожда́ть *imp.*, угоди́ть *perf.* + *dat.*, на + *acc.*; *v.i.:* as you p., как вам уго́дно; if you p., пожа́луйста, бу́дьте добры́; (*iron.*) предста́вьте себе́! *imper.* пожа́луйста; бу́дьте добры́. **pleased** *adj.* дово́льный; *predic.* рад. **pleasing, pleasurable** *adj.* прия́тный. **pleasure** *n.* (*enjoyment*) удово́льствие; (*will, desire*) во́ля, жела́ние.

pleat *n.* скла́дка; *pl.* плиссе́ *neut.indecl.*; *v.t.* де́лать скла́дки, с~ *perf.* скла́дки на + *prep.*; плиссирова́ть *imp.* **pleated** *adj.* плиссе́ *indecl.* (*follows noun*)

plebeian *adj.* плебе́йский; *n.* плебе́й.

plebiscite *n.* плебисци́т.

plectrum *n.* плектр.

pledge *n.* (*security*) зало́г; (*promise*) заро́к, обеща́ние; sign, take, the p., дать (дам, дашь, даст, дади́м; дал, -а́, да́ло, -и) *perf.* заро́к не пить; *v.t.* отдава́ть (-даю́, -даёшь) *imp.*, отда́ть (-а́м, -а́шь, -а́ст, -ади́м; о́тдал, -а́, -о) *perf.* в зало́г; p. oneself, брать (беру́, -рёшь; брал, -а́, -о) *imp.*, взять (возьму́, -мёшь; взял, -а́, -о) *perf.* на себя́ обяза́тельство; p. one's word, дава́ть (даю́, даёшь) *imp.*, дать (дам, дашь, даст, дади́м; дал, -а́, да́ло, -и) *perf.* сло́во.

plenary *adj.* по́лный (-лон, -лна́, по́лно́); (*assembly*) плена́рный. **plenipotentiary** *adj.* полномо́чный (представи́тель *m.*). **plenteous, plentiful** *adj.* оби́льный. **plenty** *n.* изоби́лие, избы́ток (-тка).

plethora *n.* (*med.*) полнокро́вие; (*fig.*) изоби́лие.

pleurisy *n.* плеври́т.

plexus *n.* сплете́ние.

pliability, pliancy *n.* ги́бкость; (*fig.*) пода́тливость. **pliable, pliant** *adj.* ги́бкий (-бок, -бка́, -бко); (*fig.*) пода́тливый.

pliers *n.* плоскогу́бцы (-цев) *pl.*; кле́щи (-ще́й) *pl.*

plight *n.* (бе́дственное, тру́дное) положе́ние.

Plimsoll line *n.* грузова́я ма́рка. **plimsolls** *n.* спорти́вные та́почки *f.pl.*, ке́ды (-д(ов)) *m.pl.*

plinth *n.* плинтус; (*of wall*) цо́коль *m.*

plod *v.i.* плести́сь (плету́сь, -тёшься; плёлся, -ла́сь) *imp.*; тащи́ться (-щу́сь, -щишься) *imp.*; (*work*) упо́рно рабо́тать *imp.* на + *instr.* **plodder** *n.* работя́га *m. & f.*

plot *n.* (*of land*) уча́сток (-тка (земли́); (*of book etc.*) фа́була; (*conspiracy*) за́говор; *v.t.* (*on graph, map, etc.*) наноси́ть (-ошу́, -о́сишь) *imp.*, нанести́ (-су́, -сёшь; нанёс, -ла́) на гра́фик, на ка́рту; (*a course*) прокла́дывать *imp.*, проложи́ть (-ожу́, -о́жишь) *perf.*; *v. abs.* (*conspire*) составля́ть *imp.*, соста́вить *perf.* за́говор. **plotter** *n.* загово́рщик, -ица.

plough *n.* плуг (*pl.* -и́); the P., (*astron.*) Больша́я Медве́дица; (*land*) па́шня; *v.t.* паха́ть (пашу́, -шешь) *imp.*, вс~ *perf.*; *v.t. & i.* (*fail in examination*) прова́ливать(ся) *imp.*, провали́ть(ся) (-лю́(сь), -лишь(ся)) *perf.*; *v.i.:* p. through, пробива́ться *imp.*, проби́ться (-бью́сь, -бьёшься) *perf.* сквозь + *acc.*

plover *n.* ржа́нка.

ploy *n.* уло́вка.

pluck *n.* (*cul.*) потроха́ (-хо́в) *pl.*, ли́вер (*courage*) му́жество; *v.t.* (*chicken*) щипа́ть (-плю́, -плешь) *imp.*, об~ *perf.*; p. up (one's) courage, собира́ться *imp.*, собра́ться (соберу́сь, -рёшься; собра́лся, -ала́сь, -а́ло́сь) *perf.* с ду́хом; *v.i.:* p. at, дёргать *imp.*, дёрнуть *perf.* за + *acc.* **plucky** *adj.* сме́лый (смел, -а́, -о).

plug *n.* про́бка; (*electr.*) штепсельная ви́лка; (*electr. socket*) ште́псель (*pl.*

-ля́) *m.*; (*sparking-p.*) запа́льная свеча́ (*pl.* -чи, -че́й); (*tobacco*) прессо́ванный таба́к (-á(ý)); (*advertisement*) рекла́ма; *v.t.* (*p. up*) затыка́ть *imp.*, заткну́ть *perf.*; (*sl., shoot*) ба́хать *imp.*, ба́хнуть *perf.*; (*advertise*) реклами́ровать *imp.*, *perf.*; *p. in*, включа́ть *imp.*, включи́ть *perf.*; *v.i.*: *p. away at*, корпе́ть (-плю́, -пи́шь) *imp.* над + *instr.*

plum *n.* (*fruit*) сли́ва; (*colour*) тёмно-фиоле́товый цвет; *p.-cake*, кекс.

plumage *n.* опере́ние, пе́рья (-ьев) *neut. pl.*

plumb *n.* отве́с; (*naut.*) лот; *adj.* верти-ка́льный; (*fig.*) я́вный; *adv.* верти-ка́льно; (*fig.*) то́чно; *v.t.* измеря́ть *imp.*, изме́рить *perf.* глубину́ + *gen.*; (*fig.*) проника́ть *imp.*, прони́кнуть (-к) *perf.* в + *acc.*

plumbago *n.* графи́т.

plumber *n.* водопрово́дчик. **plumbing** *n.* (*work*) водопрово́дное де́ло; (*system of pipes*) водопрово́дная систе́ма.

plume *n.* (*feather*) перо́ (*pl.* -ья, -рьев); (*on hat etc.*) султа́н, плюма́ж; *p. of smoke*, дымо́к (-мка́); *v.t.*: *p. oneself on*, кичи́ться *imp.* + *instr.*

plummet *n.* (*plumb*) отве́с; (*sounding-lead*) лот; (*on fishing-line*) грузи́ло; *v.i.* слета́ть *imp.*, слете́ть (-ечу́, -ети́шь) *perf.*

plump[1] *adj.* по́лный (-лон, -лна́, по́лно), пу́хлый (пухл, -а́, -о).

plump[2] *v.t. & i.* бу́хать(ся) *imp.*, бу́хнуть(ся) *perf.*; *v.i.*: *p. for*, (*vote for*) голосова́ть *imp.*, про ~ *perf.* то́лько за + *acc.*; (*fig.*) выбира́ть *imp.*, вы́брать (вы́беру, -решь) *perf.*

plunder *v.t.* гра́бить *imp.*, о ~ *perf.*; *n.* добы́ча.

plunge *v.t. & i.* (*immerse*) погружа́ть(ся) *imp.*, погрузи́ть(ся) *perf.* (*into*, в + *acc.*); *v.i.* (*dive*) ныря́ть *imp.*, нырну́ть *perf.*; (*rush*) броса́ться *imp.*, бро́ситься *perf.* **plunger** *n.* плу́нжер.

pluperfect *adj.* предпроше́дший; *n.* предпроше́дшее вре́мя *neut.*

plural *n.* мно́жественное число́; *adj.* мно́жественный. **pluralism** *n.* плюрали́зм. **pluralistic** *adj.* плюралисти́ческий.

plus *prep.* плюс + *acc.*; *adj.* (*additional*) доба́вочный; (*positive*) положи́тельный; *n.* (знак) плюс.

plush *n.* плюш; *adj.* плю́шевый. **plushy** *adj.* шика́рный.

Pluto *n.* Плуто́н.

plutocracy *n.* плутокра́тия. **plutocrat** *n.* плутокра́т. **plutocratic** *adj.* плуто-крати́ческий.

plutonium *n.* плуто́ний.

ply[1] *v.i.* курси́ровать *imp.*; *v.t.* (*tool*) рабо́тать *imp.* + *instr.*; (*task*) занима́ться *imp.* + *instr.*; *p. with questions*, засыпа́ть *imp.*, засы́пать (-плю, -плешь) *perf.* вопро́сами.

ply[2] *n.* (*layer*) слой (*pl.* слои́); (*strand*) прядь. **plywood** *n.* фане́ра.

p.m. *adv.* по́сле полу́дня.

pneumatic *adj.* пневмати́ческий.

pneumonia *n.* пневмони́я, воспале́ние лёгких.

poach[1] *v.t.* (*cook*) вари́ть (-рю́, -ришь) *imp.*, опуска́я в кипято́к; кипяти́ть *imp.* на ме́дленном огне́; *poached egg*, яйцо́-пашо́т.

poach[2] *v.i.* (*hunt*) незако́нно охо́титься *imp.*; (*trespass*) вторга́ться *imp.*, вто́ргнуться (-г(нул)ся, -гла́сь) *perf.* в чужи́е владе́ния; *v.t.* охо́титься *imp.* на + *acc.* на чужо́й земле́. **poacher** *n.* браконье́р.

pochard *n.* ныро́к (-рка́).

pocket *n.* карма́н; (*billiards*) лу́за; (*air-p.*) возду́шная я́ма; *in p.*, в вы́игрыше; *in person's p.* в рука́х у + *gen.*; *out of p.*, в убы́тке; *adj.* карма́нный; *v.t.* класть (-аду́, -адёшь; -ал) *imp.*, положи́ть (-жу́, -жишь) *perf.* в карма́н; (*appropriate*) прика́рмнивать *imp.*, прикарма́нить *perf.*; (*billiards*) загоня́ть *imp.*, загна́ть (загоню́, -нишь; загна́л, -а́, -о) *perf.* в лу́зу. **pocketful** *n.* по́лный карма́н.

pock-marked *adj.* рябо́й (ряб, -á, -о).

pod *n.* стручо́к (-чка́), шелуха́; *v.t.* лущи́ть *imp.*, об ~ *perf.*

podgy *adj.* то́лстенький, пу́хлый (пухл, -á, -о).

podium *n.* (*conductor's*) пульт.

poem *n.* стихотворе́ние; (*longer p.*) поэ́ма. **poet** *n.* поэ́т; *P. Laureate*, поэ́т-лауреа́т. **poetaster** *n.* стихопле́т.

poetess *n.* поэтéсса. **poetic(al)** *adj.* поэти́ческий, поэти́чный; (*in verse*) стихотвóрный. **poetry** *n.* поэ́зия, стихи́ *m.pl.*; (*quality*) поэти́чность.

pogrom *n.* погрóм.

poignancy *n.* острота́. **poignant** *adj.* óстрый (остр & остёр, остра́, óстро).

point[1] *n.* тóчка; (*place; in list; print.*) пункт; (*in score*) очкó (*pl.* -ки́, -кóв); (*in time*) момéнт; (*in space*) мéсто (*pl.* -та́); (*essence*) суть; (*sense*) смысл; (*sharp p.*) остриё; (*tip*) кóнчик; (*promontory*) мыс (*loc.* -é & -у́; *pl.* мы́сы); (*decimal p.*) запята́я *sb.*; (*power p.*) штéпсель (*pl.* -ля́) *m.*; *pl.* (*rly.*) стрéлка; *be on the p. of* (*doing*), собира́ться *imp.*, собра́ться (соберу́сь, -рёшься; собра́лся, -ала́сь, -áлось) *perf.* + *inf.*; *beside, off, the p.*, некста́ти; *in p. of fact*, факти́чески; *that is the p.*, в э́том и дéло; *the p. is that*, дéло в том, что; *there is no point* (*in doing*), не имéет смы́сла (+ *inf.*); *to the p.*, кста́ти; *p.-blank*, прямóй (прям, -á, -о, пря́мы); *p.-duty*, регули́рование движéния; *p. of view*, тóчка зрéния.

point[2] *v.t.* (*wall*) расши́вать *imp.*, расши́ть (разошью́, -ьёшь) *perf.* швы + *gen.*; (*gun etc.*) наводи́ть (-ожу́, -óдишь) *imp.*, навести́ (-еду́, -едёшь, -ёл, -ела́) *perf.* (at, на + *acc.*); *v. abs.* (*dog*) дéлать *imp.*, с~ *perf.* стóйку; *v.i.* (*with finger*) по-, у-, ка́зывать *imp.*, по-, у-, каза́ть (-ажу́, -áжешь) *perf.* пáльцем (at, to, на + *acc.*); (*draw attention*; *p. out*) обраща́ть *imp.*, обрати́ть (-ащу́, -ати́шь) *perf.* внима́ние (to, на + *acc.*). **pointed** *adj.* (*sharp*) óстрый (остр & остёр, остра́, óстро); (*of arch etc.*) стрéльчатый; (*of remark*) кóлкий (-лок, -лка́, -лко). **pointer** *n.* указа́тель *m.*; (*of clock etc.*) стрéлка; (*dog*) пóйнтер (*pl.* -ы & -á). **pointless** *adj.* (*meaningless*) бессмы́сленный (-ен, -енна); (*without score*) с неоткры́тым счётом.

poise *v.t.* уравновéшивать *imp.*, уравновéсить *perf.*; *be poised*, (*hover*) висéть (-си́т) *imp.* в вóздухе; *n.* уравновéшенность.

poison *n.* яд (-а(у)), отра́ва; *p. gas*, ядови́тый газ; *p. ivy*, ядонóсный сума́х; *p. pen*, а́втор анони́мных пи́сем; *v.t.* отравля́ть *imp.*, отрави́ть (-влю́, -вишь) *perf.* **poisoner** *n.* отрави́тель *m.* **poisonous** *adj.* ядови́тый.

poke *v.t.* ты́кать (ты́чу, -чешь) *imp.*, ткнуть *perf.*; *p. fun at*, подшу́чивать *imp.*, подшути́ть (-учу́, -у́тишь) *perf.* над + *instr.*; *p. one's nose into*, сова́ть (сую́, суёшь) *imp.*, су́нуть *perf.* нос в + *acc.*; *p. the fire*, меша́ть *imp.*, по~ *perf.* (кочергóй) у́гли в ками́не; *n.* тычóк (-чка́) *perf.* **poker**[1] *n.* (*metal rod*) кочерга́ (*gen.pl.* -рёг).

poker[2] *n.* (*cards*) пóкер; *p.-face*, бесстра́стное лицó.

poky *adj.* тéсный (-сен, -сна́, -сно).

polar *adj.* поля́рный; (*phys.*) полюсны́й; *p. bear*, бéлый медвéдь *m.* **polarity** *n.* поля́рность. **polarize** *v.t.* поляризова́ть *imp.*, *perf.* **pole**[1] *n.* (*geog.*) пóлюс; *p.-star*, Поля́рная звезда́.

pole[2] *n.* (*rod*) столб (-á), шест (-á); *p.-vaulting*, прыжóк (-жка́) с шестóм.

Pole[3] *n.* поля́к, пóлька.

pole-axe *n.* секи́ра, берды́ш (-á).

polecat *n.* хорёк (-рька́).

polemic *adj.* полеми́ческий *n.* полéмика.

police *n.* поли́ция; (*as pl.*) полицéйские *sb.*; *p. constable*, полицéйский *sb.*; *p. court*, полицéйский суд (-á) *perf.*; *p. station*, полицéйский учáсток (-тка). **policeman** *n.* полицéйский *sb.*, полисмéн.

policy[1] *n.* (*course of action*) поли́тика.

policy[2] *n.* (*document*) пóлис.

polio(myelitis) *n.* полиомиели́т.

Polish[1] *adj.* пóльский.

polish[2] *n.* (*gloss*) гля́нец (-нца); (*process*) полирóвка; (*substance*) политу́ра; (*fig.*) изы́сканность; *v.t.* полирова́ть *imp.*, на~ от~ *perf.*; *p. off*, распра́вливаться *imp.*, распра́виться *perf.* с + *instr.* **polished** *adj.* (*refined*) изы́сканный (-ан, -анна).

polite *adj.* вéжливый. **politeness** *n.* вéжливость.

politic *adj.* полити́чный. **political** *adj.* полити́ческий; (*of the state*) госудáрственный; *p. economy*, политэконóмика; *p. prisoner*, политзаключённый *sb.* **politician** *n.* поли́тик. **politics** *n.* поли́тика.

polka *n.* по́лька.

poll *n.* (*voting*) голосова́ние; (*number of votes*) число́ голосо́в; (*opinion*) опро́с; *v.t.* (*receive votes*) получа́ть *imp.*, получи́ть (-чу́, -чишь) *perf.*; *v.i.* голосова́ть *imp.*, про~ *perf.*

pollard *v.t.* подстрига́ть *imp.*, подстри́чь (-игу́, -ижёшь; -и́г) *perf.*

pollen *n.* пыльца́. **pollinate** *v.t.* опыля́ть *imp.*, опыли́ть *perf.*

polling *attrib.*: *p. booth*, каби́на для голосова́ния; *p. station*, избира́тельный уча́сток (-тка).

pollute *v.t.* загрязня́ть *imp.*, загрязни́ть *perf.* **pollution** *n.* загрязне́ние.

polo *n.* по́ло *neut.indecl.*; *p.-necked*, с высо́ким воротнико́м.

polonaise *n.* полоне́з.

polyandry *n.* полиа́ндрия, многому́жие. **polychromatic** *adj.* многокра́сочный. **polychrome** *adj.* (*statue*) раскра́шенная ста́туя. **polyester** *n.* полиэфи́р. **polyethylene** *n.* полиэтиле́н. **polygamous** *adj.* многобра́чный. **polygamy** *n.* многобра́чие. **polyglot** *n.* полигло́т; *adj.* многоязы́чный; (*person*) говоря́щий на мно́гих языка́х. **polygon** *n.* многоуго́льник. **polygonal** *adj.* многоуго́льный. **polyhedral** *adj.* многогра́нный. **polyhedron** *n.* многогра́нник. **polymer** *n.* полиме́р. **polymeric** *adj.* полиме́рный. **polymerize** *v.t. & i.* полимеризова́ть(ся) *imp.*

polyp *n.* поли́п.

polyphonic *adj.* полифони́ческий. **polyphony** *n.* полифо́ния. **polystyrene** *n.* полистиро́л. **polysyllabic** *adj.* многосло́жный. **polysyllable** *n.* многосло́жное сло́во (*pl.* -ва́). **polytechnic** *adj.* политехни́ческий; *n.* политехникум. **polytheism** *n.* многобо́жие. **polythene** *n.* полиэтиле́н. **polyurethane** *n.* полиурета́н. **polyvalent** *adj.* многовале́нтный.

pom *n.* шпиц.

pomade *n.* пома́да; *v.t.* пома́дить *imp.*, на~ *perf.*

pomegranate *n.* грана́т.

Pomeranian *n.* шпиц.

pommel *n.* (*hilt*) голо́вка; (*of saddle*) лука́ (*pl.* -ки).

pomp *n.* пы́шность, великоле́пие. **pomposity** *n.* напы́щенность. **pompous** *adj.* напы́щенный (-ен, -енна).

pom-pom, pompon *n.* помпо́н.

poncho *n.* по́нчо *neut.indecl.*

pond *n.* пруд (-á, *loc.* -ý). **pondweed** *n.* рдест.

ponder *v.t.* обду́мывать *imp.*, обду́мать *perf.*; *v.i.* размышля́ть *imp.*, размы́слить *perf.* (over, о + *prep.*).

ponderous *adj.* тяжелове́сный.

poniard *n.* кинжа́л.

pontiff *n.* (*pope*) ри́мский па́па *m.*; (*bishop*) епи́скоп; (*chief priest*) первосвяще́нник.

pontoon[1] *n.* понто́н; *p. bridge*, понто́нный мост (мо́ста, *loc.* -ý; *pl.* -ы́).

pontoon[2] *n.* (*cards*) два́дцать одно́.

pony *n.* по́ни *m.indecl.*

poodle *n.* пу́дель (*pl.* -ли & -ля́) *m.*

pooh *interj.* фу! **pooh-pooh** *v.t.* пренебрега́ть *imp.*, пренебре́чь (-егу́, -ежёшь; -ёг, -егла́) *perf. + instr.*

pool[1] *n.* (*of water*) прудо́к (-дка́), лу́жа; (*swimming*) бассе́йн.

pool[2] *n.* (*collective stakes*) совоку́пность ста́вок; (*common fund*) о́бщий фонд; (*common resources*) объединённые запа́сы *m.pl.*; *car p.*, автоба́за; *typing p.*, машинопи́сное бюро́ *neut. indecl.*; *v.t.* объединя́ть *imp.*, объедини́ть *perf.*

poop *n.* полуют; (*stern*) корма́.

poor *adj.* бе́дный (-ден, -дна́, -дно, бе́дны); (*bad*) плохо́й (плох, -á, -о, пло́хи); (*scanty*) ску́дный (-ден, -дна́, -дно); (*weak*) сла́бый (слаб, -á, -о); *n.*: *the p.*, беднота́, бедняки́ *m.pl.*; *p.-house*, рабо́тный дом (*pl.* -á); *p.-spirited*, малоду́шный. **poorly** *predic.* нездоро́в (-а, -о).

pop[1] *v.i.* хло́пать *imp.*, хло́пнуть *perf.*; щёлкать *imp.*, щёлкнуть *perf.*; *v.t.* бы́стро всу́нуть *perf.* (into, в + *acc.*); *p. in on*, забега́ть *imp.*, забежа́ть (-егу́, -ежи́шь) *perf.* к + *dat.*; *n.* хлопо́к (-пка́), щёлк; (*drink*) шипу́чий напи́ток (-тка). **popgun** *n.* (*toy*) пуга́ч (-á).

pop[2] *adj.* популя́рный, поп-; *p. art*,

pop-árt; *p. concert*, концéрт поп-мýзыки; *p. music*, поп-мýзыка.

pope *n.* пáпа рúмский *m.* popery *n.* папúзм. popish *adj.* папúстский.

poplar *n.* тóполь (*pl.* -ля) *m.*

poppet *n.* крóшка.

poppy *n.* мак; *p.-seed*, (*collect.*) мак (-а(у)).

poppycock *n.* чепухá.

populace *n.* простóй нарóд. popular *adj.* нарóдный; (*liked*) популáрный. popularity *n.* популáрность. popularize *v.t.* популяризúровать *imp.*, *perf.* populate *v.t.* населя́ть *imp.*, насели́ть *perf.* population *n.* населéние. populous *adj.* (мно́го)лю́дный.

porcelain *n.* фарфóр; *attrib.* фарфóровый.

porch *n.* подъéзд, крыльцó (*pl.* -льца, -лéц, -льцáм).

porcupine *n.* дикобрáз.

pore[1] *n.* пóра.

pore[2] *v.i.*: *p. over*, погружáться *imp.*, погрузи́ться (-ужу́сь, -у́зи́шься) *perf.* в + *acc.*

pork *n.* свини́на; *p.-butcher*, колбáсник; *p. pie*, пиро́г (-á) со свини́ной.

pornographic *adj.* порнографи́ческий. pornography *n.* порногрáфия.

porous *adj.* пóристый.

porphyry *n.* порфи́р.

porpoise *n.* морскáя свинья́ (*pl.* -ньи, -ней, -ньям).

porridge *n.* кáша.

port[1] *n.* (*harbour*) порт (*loc.* -ý; *pl.* -ы, -óв); (*town*) портóвый гóрод (*pl.* -á).

port[2] *n.* (*naut.*, *aeron.*) лéвый борт (*loc.* -ý).

port[3] *n.* (*wine*) портвéйн (-а(у)).

portable *adj.* портати́вный.

portal *n.* портáл.

portcullis *n.* опускнáя решётка.

portend *v.t.* предвещáть *imp.* portent *n.* предзнаменовáние. portentous *adj.* злове́щий.

porter[1] *n.* (*gate-*, *door-*, *keeper*) швейцáр, привратник; *p.'s lodge*, швейцáрская *sb.*, дóмик привратника.

porter[2] *n.* (*carrier*) носи́льщик.

porter[3] *n.* (*beer*) пóртер.

portfolio *n.* портфéль *m.*

porthole *n.* иллюминáтор.

portico *n.* пóртик.

portion *n.* часть (*pl.* -ти, -тéй), дóля (*pl.* -ли, -лéй); (*of food*) пóрция; *v.t.*: *p. out*, разделя́ть *imp.*, раздели́ть (-лю́, -лишь) *perf.*

portly *adj.* дорóдный.

portmanteau *n.* чемодáн; *p. word*, сло́во-гибри́д.

portrait *n.* портрéт. portraiture *n.* портрéтная жи́вопись. portray *v.t.* рисовáть *imp.*, на~ *perf.*; изображáть *imp.*, изобрази́ть *perf.* portrayal *n.* рисовáние, изображéние.

Portuguese *n.* португáлец (-льца), -лка *adj.* португáльский.

pose *n.* пóза; *v.t.* (*question*) стáвить *imp.*, по~ *perf.*; *v.i.* пози́ровать *imp.*; *p. as*, принимáть *imp.*, приня́ть (прими́-, -мешь; при́нял, -á, -о) *perf.* пóзу + *gen.*

poser *n.* трýдный вопрóс, трýдная задáча.

poseur *n.* позёр. poseuse *n.* позёрка.

posh *adj.* шикáрный.

posit *v.t.* (*assume*) постули́ровать *imp.*, *perf.*

position *n.* положéние, пози́ция; *in a p. to*, в состоя́нии + *inf.*; *v.t.* стáвить *imp.*, по~ *perf.* positional *adj.* позицио́нный.

positive *adj.* положи́тельный; (*person*) увéренный (-ен, -енна); (*proof*) несомнéнный (-нен, -нна); (*phot.*) позити́вный; *n.* (*phot.*) позити́в.

positivism *n.* позитиви́зм. positron *n.* позитро́н.

posse *n.* отря́д (шери́фа).

possess *v.t.* облада́ть *imp.* + *instr.*; владéть *imp.* + *instr.*; (*of feeling etc.*) овладевáть *imp.*, овладéть *perf.* + *instr.* possessed *adj.* одержи́мый. possession *n.* владéние (of, + *instr.*); *pl.* собствéнность. possessive *adj.* собствени́ческий; (*gram.*) притяжáтельный. possessor *n.* облада́тель *m.*, ~ница.

possibility *n.* возмóжность. possible *adj.* возмóжный; *as much as p.*, скóлько возмóжно; *as soon as p.*, как мóжно скорéе; *n.* возмóжное *sb.* possibly *adv.* возмóжно, мóжет (быть).

post[1] *n.* (*pole*) столб (-á); *v.t.* (*p. up*) вывéшивать *imp.*, вы́весить *perf.*

post[2] *n.* (*station*) пост (-á, *loc.* на -ý); (*trading-p.*) факто́рия; *v.t.* (*station*) расставля́ть *imp.*, расста́вить *perf.*; (*appoint*) назнача́ть *imp.*, назна́чить *perf.*

post[3] *n.* (*letters, p. office, etc.*) по́чта; *by return of p.*, с обра́тной по́чтой; *attrib.* почто́вый; *p.-box*, почто́вый я́щик; *p.-code*, почто́вый и́ндекс; *p.-free*, без почто́вой опла́ты; *P. Office*, (*ministry*) Министе́рство свя́зи; *p. office*, по́чта, почто́вое отделе́ние; *General P. Office*, (гла́вный) почта́мт; *p.-paid*, с опла́ченными почто́выми расхо́дами; *v.t.* (*send by p.*) отправля́ть *imp.*, отпра́вить *perf.* по по́чте; (*put in p.-box*) опуска́ть *imp.*, опусти́ть (-ущу́, -ýстишь) в почто́вый я́щик. **postage** *n.* почто́вая опла́та, почто́вые расхо́ды *m.pl.*; *p. stamp*, почто́вая ма́рка. **postal** *adj.* почто́вый; *p.-order*, почто́вый перево́д. **postcard** *n.* откры́тка.

post-date *v.t.* дати́ровать *imp.*, *perf.* бо́лее по́здним число́м.

poster *n.* афи́ша, плака́т.

poste restante *n.* (*in address*) до востре́бования.

posterior *adj.* (*later*) после́дующий; (*hinder*) за́дний; *n.* зад (-у; *pl.* -ы́).

posterity *n.* (*descendants*) пото́мство; (*later generations*) после́дующие поколе́ния *neut.pl.*

postern *n.* за́дняя дверь (*loc.* -ри́; *pl.* -ри, -ре́й, *instr.* -ря́ми & -рьми́).

postface *n.* послесло́вие.

post-graduate *n.* аспира́нт; *adj.* аспира́нтский; *p. course*, аспиранту́ра.

posthumous *adj.* посме́ртный.

postlude *n.* постлю́дия.

postman *n.* почтальо́н. **postmark** *n.* почто́вый ште́мпель (*pl.* -ля́) *m.*; *v.t.* штемпелева́ть (-лю́ю, -лю́ешь) *imp.*, за~ *perf.* **postmaster, -mistress** *n.* нача́льник почто́вого отделе́ния.

post-mortem *adj.* посме́ртный; *n.* вскры́тие тру́па.

postpone *v.t.* отсро́чивать *imp.*, отсро́чить *perf.* **postponement** *n.* отсро́чка.

postprandial *adj.* послеобе́денный.

postscript *n.* постскри́птум.

postulate *n.* постула́т; *v.t.* постули́ровать *imp.*, *perf.*

posture *n.* по́за, положе́ние; *v.i.* рисова́ться *imp.*

post-war *adj.* послевое́нный.

posy *n.* буке́тик.

pot *n.* горшо́к (-шка́), котело́к (-лка́); (*as prize*) ку́бок (-бка); *pots of money*, ку́ча де́нег; *p.-bellied*, пуза́тый; *p.-belly*, пу́зо; *p.-boiler*, халту́ра; (*person*) халту́рщик; *p.-roast*, тушёное мя́со; туши́ть (-шу́, -шишь) *imp.*; *p.-shot*, вы́стрел наугáд; (*food*) консерви́ровать *imp.*, за~ *perf.* (*plant*) сажа́ть *imp.*, посади́ть (-ажу́, -а́дишь) *perf.* в горшо́к; (*billiards*) загоня́ть *imp.*, загна́ть (загоню́, -нишь; загна́л, -а, -о) *perf.* в лу́зу.

potash *n.* пота́ш (-á). **potassium** *n.* ка́лий.

potato *n.* (*plant; pl. collect.*) карто́фель *m.* (*no pl.*); карто́фелина, карто́шка (*also collect.; coll.*); *two potatoes*, две карто́фелины, карто́шки.

potence, -cy *n.* си́ла, могу́щество; (*of drug etc.*) де́йственность. **potent** *adj.* (*reason etc.*) убеди́тельный; (*drug etc.*) сильноде́йствующий; (*mighty*) могу́щественный (-ен, -енна). **potentate** *n.* власте́лин.

potential *adj.* потенциа́льный, возмо́жный; *n.* потенциа́л, возмо́жность. **potentially** *n.* потенциа́льность.

pot-hole *n.* пеще́ра; (*in road*) вы́боина. **pot-holer** *n.* пеще́рник.

potion *n.* до́за лека́рства, зе́лье.

pot-pourri *n.* попурри́ *neut.indecl.*

potsherd *n.* черепо́к (-пка́).

potter[1] *v.i.*: *p. at, in*, рабо́тать *imp.* ко́е-как над + *instr.*; *p. about*, лоды́рничать *imp.*

potter[2] *n.* гонча́р (-á). **pottery** *n.* (*goods*) гонча́рные изде́лия *neut.pl.*; (*place*) гонча́рная *sb.*

potty[1] *adj.* (*trivial*) пустяко́вый; (*crazy*) поме́шанный (-ан) (*about*, на + *prep.*).

potty[2] *n.* ночно́й горшо́к (-шка́).

pouch *n.* су́мка, мешо́к (-шка́).

pouffe *n.* пуф.

poulterer *n.* торго́вец (-вца) дома́шней пти́цей.

poultice n. припа́рка; v.t. ста́вить imp., по~ perf. припа́рку+dat.

poultry n. дома́шняя пти́ца; p.-farm, птицефе́рма.

pounce v.i.: p. (up)on, налета́ть imp., налете́ть (-ечу́, -ети́шь) perf. на + acc.; набра́сываться imp., набро́ситься perf. на+acc.; (fig.) ухвати́ться (-ачу́сь, -а́тишься) perf. за+ acc.

pound[1] n. (measure) фунт; p. sterling, фунт сте́рлингов.

pound[2] n. (enclosure) заго́н.

pound[3] v.t. (crush) толо́чь (-лку́, -лчёшь; -ло́к, -лкла́) imp., ис~, рас~ perf.; (strike) колоти́ть (-очу́, -о́тишь) imp., по~ perf. по+dat., в+acc.; v.i. (heart) колоти́ться (-ится) imp.; p. along, тяжело́ ходи́ть (хожу́, хо́дишь) imp.; (run) тяжело́ бе́гать imp.; p. away at, (with guns) обстре́ливать imp., обстреля́ть perf.

pour v.t. лить (лью, льёшь; лил, -á, -о) imp.; p. out, налива́ть imp., нали́ть (налью́, -ьёшь; на́лил, -á, -о) perf.; v.i. ли́ться (льётся; ли́лся, лила́сь, лило́сь) imp.; it is pouring, (with rain) дождь льёт как из ведра́. **pouring** adj. (rain) проливно́й.

pout v.t. & i. надува́ть(ся) imp., наду́ть(ся) (-у́ю(сь), -у́ешь(ся)) perf.

poverty n. бе́дность, убо́гость; p.-stricken, убо́гий.

P.O.W. abbr. военнопле́нный sb.

powder n. порошо́к (-шка́); (cosmetic) пу́дра; (gun-p.) по́рох (-а(у)); p.-blue, се́ро-голубо́й; p. compact, пу́дреница; p.-flask, порохо́вница; p.-magazine, порохово́й по́греб (pl. -á); p.-puff, пухо́вка; v.t. (sprinkle with p.) посыпа́ть imp., посы́пать (-плю, -плешь) perf. порошко́м; (nose etc.) пу́дрить imp., на~ perf.; powdered milk, моло́чный порошо́к (-шка́). **powdery** adj. порошкообра́зный.

power n. (vigour) си́ла; (might) могу́щество; (ability) спосо́бность; (control) власть; (authorization) полномо́чие; (State) держа́ва; (math.) сте́пень (pl. -ни, -не́й); attrib. силово́й, механи́ческий; party in p., па́ртия у вла́сти; p. of attorney, дове́ренность;

p. cut, прекраще́ние пода́чи эне́ргии; p. point, штéпсель (pl. -ля́) m.; p.-station, электроста́нция. **powerful** adj. си́льный (си́лён, -льна́, -льно, си́льны); могу́щественный (-ен, -енна). **powerless** adj. бесси́льный.

practicable adj. осуществи́мый; (theat.) настоя́щий. **practical** adj. (of practice) практи́ческий; (useful in practice; person) практи́чный; p. joke, гру́бая шу́тка. **practically** adv. (in effect) факти́чески; (almost) почти́. **practice** n. пра́ктика; (custom) обы́чай; (exercise) упражне́ние; in p., на де́ле; put into p., осуществля́ть imp., осуществи́ть perf.; attrib. уче́бный. **practise** v.t. (carry out) применя́ть imp., примени́ть (-ню́, -нишь) perf. на пра́ктике; (also abs. of doctor etc.) практикова́ть imp.; (engage in) занима́ться imp., заня́ться (займу́сь, -мёшься; заня́лся, -яла́сь) perf.+instr.; упражня́ться imp. в+prep.; (mus. instrument, в игре́ на+prep.). **practised** adj. о́пытный. **practitioner** n. (doctor) практику́ющий врач (-á); (lawyer) практику́ющий юри́ст; general p., врач (-á) о́бщей пра́ктики.

pragmatic adj. прагмати́ческий. **pragmatism** n. прагмати́зм. **pragmatist** n. прагма́тик.

prairie n. степь (loc. -пи́; pl. -пи, -пе́й); (in N. America) пре́рия.

praise v.t. хвали́ть (-лю́, -лишь) imp., по~ perf.; n. похвала́. **praiseworthy** adj. похва́льный.

pram n. де́тская коля́ска.

prance v.i. (horse) станови́ться (-ится) imp., стать (ста́нет) perf. на дыбы́; (fig.) зада́ваться (-даю́сь, -даёшься) imp.

prank n. вы́ходка, ша́лость.

prate v.i. болта́ть imp.

prattle v.i. лепета́ть (-ечу́, -е́чешь); n. ле́пет.

prawn n. креве́тка.

pray v.t. моли́ть (-лю́, -лишь) imp. (for, o+prep.); v.i. моли́ться (-лю́сь, -лишься) imp., по~ perf. (to, +dat.; for, o+prep.). **prayer** n. моли́тва; p.-book, моли́твенник.

preach v.t. пропове́довать imp.; v.i. произноси́ть (-ошу́, -о́сишь) imp., произнести́ (-есу́, -есёшь; -ёс, -есла́) perf. про́поведь. **preacher** n. пропове́дник.

preamble n. преа́мбула.

pre-arrange v.t. зара́нее плани́ровать imp., за~ perf. **pre-arrangement** n. предвари́тельная договорённость.

precarious adj. ненадёжный; (insecure) непро́чный (-чен, -чна́, -чно).

pre-cast adj. сбо́рный.

precaution n. предосторо́жность; (action) ме́ра предосторо́жности.

precede v.t. предше́ствовать imp. + dat. **precedence** n. предше́ствование; (seniority) старшинство́. **precedent** n. прецеде́нт.

precept n. наставле́ние.

precinct n. огоро́женное ме́сто; pl. окре́стности f.pl.; (boundary) преде́л.

precious adj. драгоце́нный (-нен, -нна); (beloved) дорого́й (до́рог, -á, -о); (refined) изы́сканный (-ан, -анна) adv. о́чень, весьма́.

precipice n. обры́в; (also fig.) про́пасть. **precipitate** n. оса́док (-дка) adj. стреми́тельный; (person) опроме́тчивый; v.t. (throw down) низверга́ть imp., низве́ргнуть (-г) perf.; (hurry) уско́ря́ть imp., уско́рить perf.; (chem.) осажда́ть imp., осади́ть (-ажу́, -а́дишь) perf. **precipitation** n. низверже́ние; ускоре́ние; осажде́ние; (hastiness) стреми́тельность; (meteorol.) оса́дки m.pl. **precipitous** adj. обры́вистый.

précis n. конспе́кт.

precise adj. то́чный (-чен, -чна́, -чно). **precisely** adv. то́чно; (in answer) и́менно, то́чно так; precision n. то́чность; adj. то́чный.

pre-classical adj. доклассический.

preclude v.t. предотвраща́ть imp., предотврати́ть (-ащу́, -ати́шь) perf.

precocious adj. не по года́м развито́й (ра́звит, -á, -о); ра́но разви́вшийся. **precocity** n. ра́ннее разви́тие.

preconceived adj. предвзя́тый. **preconception** n. предвзя́тое мне́ние.

pre-condition n. предпосы́лка.

precursor n. предте́ча m. & f., предше́ственник.

predator n. хи́щник. **predatory** adj. хи́щнический; (animal) хи́щный.

predecease v.t. умира́ть imp., умере́ть (умру́, -рёшь; у́мер, -ла́, -ло) perf. ра́ньше + gen.

predecessor n. предше́ственник, -ица.

predestination n. предопределе́ние. **predestine** v.t. предопределя́ть imp., предопредели́ть perf.

predetermine v.t. предреша́ть imp., предреши́ть perf.; предопределя́ть imp., предопредели́ть perf.

predicament n. затрудни́тельное положе́ние.

predicate n. (gram.) сказу́емое sb.; предика́т. **predicate** v.t. утвержда́ть imp. **predicative** adj. предикати́вный.

predict v.t. предска́зывать imp., предсказа́ть (-ажу́, -а́жешь) perf. **prediction** n. предсказа́ние.

predilection n. пристра́стие (for, к + dat.).

predispose v.t. предрасполага́ть imp., предрасположи́ть (-ожу́, -о́жишь) perf. (to, к + dat.). **predisposition** n. предрасположе́ние (to, к + dat.).

predominance n. преоблада́ние. **predominant** adj. преоблада́ющий. **predominate** v.i. преоблада́ть imp.

pre-eminence n. превосхо́дство. **pre-eminent** adj. выдаю́щийся.

pre-empt v.t. покупа́ть imp., купи́ть (-плю́, -пишь) perf. пре́жде други́х; (fig.) завладева́ть imp., завладе́ть perf.+instr. пре́жде други́х. **pre-emption** n. поку́пка пре́жде други́х; (right) преиму́щественное пра́во на поку́пку. **pre-emptive** adj. преиму́щественный; (mil.) упрежда́ющий.

preen v.t. (of bird) чи́стить imp., по~ perf. клю́вом; p. oneself, (smarten) прихора́шиваться imp.; (be proud) горди́ться imp. собо́й.

pre-fab n. сбо́рный дом (pl. -á). **pre-fabricated** adj. заводско́го изготовле́ния; сбо́рный.

preface n. предисло́вие; v.t. де́лать imp., с~ perf. предвари́тельные замеча́ния к + dat. **prefatory** adj. вступи́тельный.

prefect n. префе́кт; (school) ста́роста m. **prefecture** n. префекту́ра.

prefer v.t. (*promote*) продвига́ть *imp.*, продви́нуть *perf.* (по слу́жбе); (*like better*) предпочита́ть *imp.*, предпоче́сть (-чту́, -чтёшь; -чёл, -чла́) *perf.*; p. *a charge against*, выдвига́ть *imp.*, вы́двинуть *perf.* обвине́ние про́тив+*gen.* **preferable** *adj.* предпочти́тельный. **preference** n. предпочте́ние; p. *share*, привилегиро́ванная а́кция. **preferential** *adj.* предпочти́тельный; (*econ.*) преференциа́льный. **preferment** n. продвиже́ние по слу́жбе.

prefiguration n. прообраз. **prefigure** v.t. служи́ть (-жу́, -жишь) *imp.* прообразом+*gen.*

prefix n. приста́вка, префикс.

pregnancy n. бере́менность. **pregnant** *adj.* (*woman*) бере́менная (with, +*instr.*), по́лный (-лон, -лна́, по́лно) (with, +*gen.*).

prehensile *adj.* хвата́тельный.

prehistoric *adj.* доистори́ческий. **prehistory** n. (*of situation etc.*) предысто́рия.

pre-ignition n. преждевре́менное зажига́ние.

prejudge v.t. предреша́ть *imp.*, предреши́ть *perf.*

prejudice n. предрассу́док (-дка) (*bias*) предубежде́ние; (*injury*) уще́рб; *without p. to*, без уще́рба для+*gen.*; v.t. наноси́ть (-ошу́, -о́сишь) *imp.*, нанести́ (-есу́, -есёшь; -ёс, -есла́) *perf.* уще́рб+*dat.*; p. *against*, восстана́вливать *imp.*, восстанови́ть (-влю́, -вишь) *perf.* про́тив+*gen.*; p. *in favour of*, располага́ть *imp.*, расположи́ть (-жу́, -жишь) *perf.* в по́льзу+*gen.*

prelate n. прела́т.

prelim n.: pl. (*print.*) сбо́рный лист (-а́). **preliminary** *adj.* предвари́тельный; n.: pl. (*discussion*) предвари́тельные перегово́ры m.pl.

prelude n. вступле́ние; (*mus.*; *fig.*) прелю́дия.

pre-marital *adj.* добра́чный.

premature *adj.* преждевре́менный (-нен, -нна).

premeditated *adj.* преднаме́ренный (-ен, -енна). **premeditation** n. преднаме́ренность.

premier *adj.* пе́рвый; n. премье́р-мини́стр. *première* n. премье́ра.

premise, premiss n. (*logic*) (пред)посы́лка. **premises** n. помеще́ние.

premium n. пре́мия.

premonition n. предчу́вствие. **premonitory** *adj.* предупрежда́ющий.

pre-natal *adj.* предродово́й.

preoccupation n. озабо́ченность. **preoccupied** *adj.* озабо́ченный (-ен, -енна). **preoccupy** v.t. поглоща́ть *imp.*, поглоти́ть (-ощу́, -о́тишь) *perf.* внима́ние+*gen.*

pre-ordain v.t. предопределя́ть *imp.*, предопредели́ть *perf.*

prep n. приготовле́ние уро́ков; *adj.*: p. *school*, приготови́тельная шко́ла.

pre-pack(age) v.t. расфасо́вывать *imp.*, расфасова́ть *perf.*

prepaid *adj.* опла́ченный (-ен) вперёд.

preparation n. приготовле́ние; pl. подгото́вка (for, к+*dat.*); (*medicine etc.*) препара́т. **preparatory** *adj.* под-, при-, готови́тельный; p. *to*, пре́жде чем. **prepare** v.t. & i. при-, под-, готовля́ть(ся) *imp.*, при-, под-, гото́вить(ся) *perf.* (for, к+*dat.*). **prepared** *adj.* гото́вый.

preponderance n. переве́с. **preponderant** *adj.* преоблада́ющий. **preponderate** v.i. име́ть *imp.* переве́с.

preposition n. предло́г. **prepositional** *adj.* предло́жный.

prepossess v.t. предрасполага́ть *imp.*, предрасположи́ть (-жу́, -жишь) *perf.* (in favour of, к+*dat.*). **prepossessing** *adj.* привлека́тельный.

preposterous *adj.* (*absurd*) неле́пый, абсу́рдный.

prepuce n. кра́йняя плоть.

pre-record v.t. предвари́тельно запи́сывать *imp.*, записа́ть (-ишу́, -и́шешь) *perf.*

prerequisite n. предпосы́лка.

prerogative n. прерогати́ва.

presage n. предве́стник, предзнаменова́ние; (*foreboding*) предчу́вствие; v.t. предвеща́ть *imp.*

presbyter n. пресви́тер. **Presbyterian** n. пресвитериа́нин (pl. -а́не, -а́н), -а́нка; *adj.* пресвитериа́нский. **presbytery** n. пресвите́рия.

prescience *n.* предви́дение. **prescient** *adj.* предви́дящий.

prescribe *v.t.* устана́вливать *imp.*, установи́ть (-влю́, -вишь) *perf.*; (*med.*) пропи́сывать *imp.*, прописа́ть (-ишу́, -и́шешь) *perf.* (to, for, (*person*) + *dat.*; for, (*complaint*) про́тив + *gen.*). **prescription** *n.* устано́вка; (*med.*) реце́пт.

presence *n.* прису́тствие; (*appearance*) (вне́шний) вид; *p. of mind*, прису́тствие ду́ха. **present** *adj.* прису́тствующий; (*being dealt with*) да́нный; (*existing now*) ны́нешний; (*also gram.*) настоя́щий; *predic.* налицо́; *be p.*, прису́тствовать *imp.* (at, на + *prep.*). *p.-day*, ны́нешний, совреме́нный (-нен, -нна); *n.: the p.*, настоя́щее *sb.*; (*gram.*) настоя́щее вре́мя *neut.*; (*gift*) пода́рок (-рка); *at p.*, в настоя́щее, да́нное, вре́мя *neut.*; *for the p.*, пока́; *v.t.* (*introduce*) представля́ть *imp.*, предста́вить *perf.* (to, + *dat.*); (*hand in*) подава́ть (-даю́, -даёшь) *imp.*, пода́ть (-а́м, -а́шь, -а́ст, -ади́м; по́дал, -а́, -о) *imp.*, по~ *perf.*; (*a gift*) подноси́ть (-ошу́, -о́сишь) *imp.*, поднести́ (-есу́, -есёшь; -ёс, -есла́) *perf.* + *dat.* (with, + *acc.*); *p. arms*, брать (беру́, -рёшь; брал, -а́, -о) *imp.*, взять (возьму́, -мёшь; взял, -а́, -о) *perf.* ору́жие на карау́л; (*command*) на карау́л!; *p. oneself*, явля́ться *imp.*, яви́ться (явлю́сь, я́вишься) *perf.* **presentable** *adj.* прили́чный. **presentation** *n.* представле́ние, поднесе́ние.

presentiment *n.* предчу́вствие.

presently *adv.* вско́ре, сейча́с.

preservation *n.* сохране́ние, предохране́ние; (*state of p.*) сохра́нность; (*of game etc.*) охра́на. **preservative** *adj.* предохрани́тельный; *n.* предохраня́ющее сре́дство. **preserve** *v.t.* (*keep safe*) сохраня́ть *imp.*, сохрани́ть *perf.*; (*maintain*) храни́ть *imp.*; *p. fruit etc.*) храни́ть *imp.*; (*food*) консерви́ровать *imp.*, за~ *perf.*; (*game*) охраня́ть *imp.*, охрани́ть *perf.*; *n.* (for game, fish) охо́тничий, рыболо́вный, запове́дник; *pl.* консе́рвы (-вов) *pl.*; (*jam*) джем, варе́нье. **preside** *v.i.* председа́тельствовать *imp.* (at, на + *prep.*). **presidency** *n.* пред-

седа́тельство, президе́нтство. **president** *n.* председа́тель *m.*, президе́нт. **presidential** *adj.* президе́нтский. **presidium** *n.* прези́диум.

press[1] *n.* (of people) толпа́; (of affairs) спе́шка; (*machine*) пресс; (*printing-p.*) печа́тный стано́к (-нка́); (*printing firm*) типогра́фия; (*publishing house*) изда́тельство; (the p.) пре́сса, печа́ть; (*cupboard*) шкаф (loc. -у́; pl. -ы́); *p. attaché*, пресс-атташе́ *m.indecl.*; *p. conference*, пресс-конфере́нция; *p.-cutting*, газе́тная вы́резка; *p.-mark*, шифр; *p. photographer* фотокорреспонде́нт; *v.t.* жать (жму, жмёшь) *imp.*; (*p. down on*) нажима́ть *imp.*, нажа́ть (-жму́, -жмёшь) *perf.* + *acc.*, на + *acc.*; (*clasp*) прижима́ть *imp.*, прижа́ть (-жму́, -жмёшь) *perf.* (to, к + *dat.*); (*with iron*) гла́дить *imp.*, вы́~ *perf.*; (*oppress, p. on*) тяготи́ть (-ощу́, -оти́шь) *imp.*; (*insist on*) наста́ивать *imp.*, настоя́ть (-ою́, -ои́шь) *perf.* на + *prep.*; *p. forward*, продвига́ться *imp.*, продви́нуться *perf.* вперёд; *p.-stud*, кно́пка.

press[2] *v.t.* (*hist.*) наси́льственно вербова́ть *imp.*, за~ *perf.* во флот; *p. into service*, по́льзоваться *imp.* + *instr.*; *p.-gang*, отря́д вербо́вщиков.

pressing *adj.* (*urgent*) неотло́жный; (*persistent*) насто́йчивый. **pressure** *n.* давле́ние, нажи́м; *p.-cooker*, скорова́рка; *p.-gauge*, мано́метр. **pressurized** *adj.* (*aircraft cabin etc.*) гермети́ческий.

prestige *n.* прести́ж.

pre-stressed *adj.* предвари́тельно напряжённый (-ён, -ённа).

presumably *adv.* вероя́тно, предположи́тельно. **presume** *v.t.* счита́ть *imp.* дока́занным; полага́ть *imp.*; (*venture*) позволя́ть *imp.* себе́. **presumption** *n.* предположе́ние; (*arrogance*) самонаде́янность. **presumptive** *adj.* предполага́емый. **presumptuous** *adj.* самонаде́янный (-ян, -янна), наха́льный.

presuppose *v.t.* предполага́ть *imp.*

pretence *n.* притво́рство. **pretend** *v.t.* притворя́ться *imp.*, притвори́ться *perf.* (to be, +*instr.*); де́лать *imp.* с~ *perf.* вид (что); *v.i.*: *p. to,* претендова́ть *imp.* на+*acc.* **pretender** *n.* претенде́нт. **pretension** *n.* прете́нзия. **pretentious** *adj.* претенцио́зный.

preternatural *adj.* сверхъесте́ственный (-ен, -енна).

pretext *n.* предло́г.

pretonic *adj.* предуда́рный.

prettiness *n.* милови́дность. **pretty** *adj.* милови́дный; (*also iron.*) хоро́шенький; *a p. penny,* кру́гленькая су́мма; *adv.* дово́льно.

prevail *v.i.* (*predominate*) преоблада́ть *imp.*; *p.* (*up*)*on,* угова́ривать *imp.*, уговори́ть *perf.* **prevailing** *adj.* преоблада́ющий. **prevalent** *adj.* распространённый (-ён, -ена́).

prevaricate *v.i.* говори́ть *imp.* укло́нчиво.

prevent *v.t.* предупрежда́ть *imp.*, предупреди́ть *perf.*; меша́ть *imp.*, по~ *perf.* +*dat.* **prevention** *n.* предупрежде́ние. **preventive** *adj.* предупреди́тельный; (*med.*) профилакти́ческий.

preview *n.* предвари́тельный просмо́тр.

previous *adj.* предыду́щий; *adv.: p. to,* пре́жде чем. **previously** *adv.* зара́нее, пре́жде.

pre-war *adj.* довое́нный.

prey *n.* (*animal*) добы́ча; (*victim*) же́ртва (to, +gen.); *bird of p.,* хи́щная пти́ца; *v.i.: p.* (*up*)*on,* (*emotion etc.*) му́чить *imp.*

price *n.* цена́ (*acc.* -ну; *pl.* -ны); *at any p.,* любо́й цено́й, во что бы то ни ста́ло; *at a p.,* по дорого́й цене́; *not at any p.,* ни за что; *what p. . . . ,* каки́е ша́нсы на+*acc.*; *p.-list,* прейскура́нт; *v.t.* назнача́ть *imp.*, назна́чить *perf.* це́ну+*gen.*; (*fig.*) оце́нивать *imp.*, оцени́ть (-ню́, -нишь) *perf.* **priceless** *adj.* бесце́нный.

prick *v.t.* коло́ть (-лю́, -лешь) *imp.*, укола́ывать *imp.*, уколо́ть (-лю́, -лешь) *perf.*; (*conscience*) му́чить *imp.*; *p. out,* (*plants*) пики́ровать *imp.*, *perf.*; *p. up one's ears,* навостри́ть *perf.* у́ши; *n.* уко́л. **pricker** *n.* ши́ло (*pl.* -лья, -льев). **prickle** *n.* (*thorn*) колю́чка; (*spine*) игла́ (*pl.* -лы). **prickly** *adj.*

колю́чий; *p. heat,* потни́ца; *p. pear,* опу́нция.

pride *n.* го́рдость; (*of lions*) прайд; *take a p. in, p. oneself on,* горди́ться *imp.*+*instr.*

priest *n.* свяще́нник; (*non-Christian*) жрец (-а́). **priestess** *n.* жри́ца. **priesthood** *n.* свяще́нство. **priestly** *adj.* свяще́ннический.

prig *n.* самодово́льный педа́нт. **priggish** *adj.* педанти́чный.

prim *adj.* чо́порный.

primacy *n.* пе́рвенство. **primarily** *adv.* первонача́льно; (*above all*) пре́жде всего́. **primary** *adj.* перви́чный; (*chief*) основно́й; *p. colour,* основно́й цвет (*pl.* -а́); *p. feather,* махово́е перо́ (*pl.* -рья, -рьев); *p. school,* нача́льная шко́ла. **primate** *n.* прима́с; (*zool.*) прима́т. **prime** *n.* расцве́т; *in one's p., in the p. of life,* в расцве́те сил; *adj.* (*chief*) гла́вный; (*excellent*) превосхо́дный; (*primary*) перви́чный; *p. cost,* себесто́имость; *p. minister,* премье́р-мини́стр; *p. number,* просто́е число́ (*pl.* -сла, -сел, -слам); *v.t.* (*engine*) заправля́ть *imp.*, запра́вить *perf.*; (*with information etc.*) зара́нее снабжа́ть *imp.*, снабди́ть *perf.* (with, +*instr.*); (*with paint etc.*) грунтова́ть *imp.*, за~ *perf.* **primer** *n.* буква́рь (-ря́) *m.*; (*textbook*) уче́бник (*paint etc.*) грунт. **prim(a)eval** *adj.* первобы́тный. **priming** *n.* (*with paint etc.*) грунто́вка. **primitive** *adj.* первобы́тный, примити́вный. **primogeniture** *n.* перворо́дство. **primordial** *adj.* первобы́тный; (*original*) первозда́нный.

primrose *n.* первоцве́т; (*colour*) бле́дно-жёлтый цвет.

primula *n.* первоцве́т.

primus (stove) *n.* при́мус (*pl.* -ы & -а́).

prince *n.* (*in W. Europe*) принц; (*in Russia*) князь (*pl.* -зья, -зе́й). **princely** *adj.* кня́жеский; (*splendid*) великоле́пный. **princess** *n.* принце́сса; (*wife*) княги́ня; (*daughter*) княжна́ (*gen.pl.* -жо́н). **principality** *n.* кня́жество.

principal *adj.* гла́вный, основно́й; *n.* нача́льник, -ица; (*of school*) дире́ктор (*pl.* -а́); (*econ.*) капита́л. **principally**

adv. гла́вным о́бразом, преиму́щественно.

principle *n.* при́нцип; *in p.*, в при́нципе; *on p.*, принципиа́льно. **principled** *adj.* принципиа́льный.

print *n.* (*mark*) след (*pl.* -ы́); (*also phot.*) отпеча́ток (-тка); (*fabric*) си́тец (-тца(у)); (*print.*) печа́ть; (*picture*) гравю́ра, эста́мп; *in p.*, в прода́же; *out of p.*, распро́данный (-ан); *v.t.* (*impress*) запеча́тлева́ть *imp.*, запеча́тле́ть *perf.*; (*book etc.*) печа́тать *imp.*, на~ *perf.*; (*write*) писа́ть (пишу́, -шешь) *imp.*, на~ *perf.* печа́тными бу́квами; (*fabric*) набива́ть *imp.*, наби́ть (-бью, -бьёшь) *perf.*; (*phot.*; *p. out*, *off*) отпеча́тывать *imp.*, отпеча́тать *perf.*; *p. out*, (*of computer etc.*) распеча́тывать *imp.*, распеча́тать *perf.*; *p-out*, распеча́тка, табуля́грамма. **printed** *adj.* печа́тный; (*fabric*) набивно́й; *p. circuit*, печа́тная схе́ма; *p. matter*, бандеро́ль. **printer** *n.* печа́тник, типо́граф; (*of fabric*) набо́йщик; *p's ink*, типогра́фская кра́ска. **printing** *n.* печа́тание, печа́ть; *p-press*, печа́тный стано́к (-нка́).

prior *n.* настоя́тель *m.*; *adj.* (*earlier*) пре́жний, предше́ствующий; (*more important*) бо́лее ва́жный; *adv.*: *p. to*, до +*gen.* **prioress** *n.* настоя́тельница. **priority** *n.* приорите́т; *in order of p.*, в поря́дке очерёдности. **priory** *n.* монасты́рь (-ря́) *m.*

prise *see* **prize**³.

prism *n.* при́зма. **prismatic** *adj.* призмати́ческий.

prison *n.* тюрьма́ (*pl.* -рьмы, -рем, -рьмам); *attrib.* тюре́мный; *p.-breaking*, побе́г из тюрьмы́; *p. camp*, ла́герь (*pl.* -ря́) *m.* **prisoner** *n.* заключённый *sb.*; (*p. of war*) (военно-)пле́нный *sb.*; *p. of State*, политзаключённый *sb.*

pristine *adj.* (*ancient*) первонача́льный; (*untouched*) нетро́нутый.

privacy *n.* (*seclusion*) уедине́ние; (*private life*) ча́стная жизнь. **private** *adj.* (*personal*) ча́стный, ли́чный; (*unofficial*) неофициа́льный; (*confidential*) конфиденциа́льный; *in p.*,

наедине́; в ча́стной жи́зни; *p. view*, закры́тый просмо́тр; *n.* рядово́й *sb.* **privateer** *n.* ка́пер.

privation *n.* лише́ние. **privative** *adj.* (*gram.*) привати́вный.

privet *n.* бирючи́на.

privilege *n.* привиле́гия. **privileged** *adj.* привилегиро́ванный.

privy *adj.* та́йный; *p. to*, прича́стный к +*dat.*, посвящённый (-ён, -ена́) в +*acc.*; *P. Council*, та́йный сове́т.

prize¹ *n.* (*reward*) пре́мия, приз, награ́да; *adj.* удосто́енный пре́мии, награ́ды; *p.-fight*, состяза́ние на приз; *p.-fighter*, боксёр-профессиона́л; *p.-winner*, призёр, лауреа́т; *v.t.* высоко́ цени́ть (-ню́, -нишь) *imp.*

prize² *n.* (*ship*) приз.

prize³ *v.t.*: *p. open*, взла́мывать *imp.*, взлома́ть *perf.* с по́мощью рычага́.

pro¹ *n.*: *pros and cons*, до́воды *m.pl.* за и про́тив.

pro² *n.* (*professional*) профессиона́л; (спортсме́н-)профессиона́л.

probability *n.* вероя́тность, правдоподо́бие; *in all p.*, по всей вероя́тности. **probable** *adj.* вероя́тный, правдоподо́бный. **probably** *adv.* вероя́тно.

probate *n.* утвержде́ние завеща́ния.

probation *n.* испыта́ние, стажиро́вка; (*leg.*) усло́вный пригово́р. **probationary** *adj.* испыта́тельный. **probationer** *n.* стажёр.

probe *n.* (*med.*) зонд; (*spacecraft*) иссле́довательская раке́та; (*fig.*) рассле́дование; *v.t.* зонди́ровать *imp.*; (*fig.*) рассле́довать *imp.*, *perf.*

probity *n.* че́стность.

problem *n.* пробле́ма, вопро́с; (*math., chess, etc.*) зада́ча; *p. child*, тру́дный ребёнок (-нка; *pl.* де́ти, -те́й, -тям, -тьми́). **problematic(al)** *adj.* проблемати́чный, проблемати́ческий.

proboscis *n.* хо́бот; (*of insects*) хобото́к (-тка́).

procedural *adj.* процеду́рный. **procedure** *n.* процеду́ра. **proceed** *v.i.* (*go further*) идти́ (иду́, идёшь; шёл, шла) *imp.*, пойти́ (пойду́, -дёшь; пошёл, -шла́) *perf.* да́льше; (*act*) поступа́ть *imp.*, поступи́ть (-плю́, -пишь) *perf.*; (*abs.*, *p. to say*) продолжа́ть *imp.*

продóлжить *perf.*; (*of action*) продолжáться *imp.*, продóлжиться *perf.*; *p. against*, возбуждáть *imp.*, возбудить *perf.* дéло, процéсс, прóтив + *gen.*; *p. from*, исходить (-ожý, -óдишь) *imp.* из, от, + *gen.*; *p. in, with*, возобновлять *imp.*, возобновить *perf.*; продолжáть *imp.*, продóлжить *perf.*; *p. to*, приступáть *imp.*, приступить (-плю, -пишь) *perf.* к + *dat.* **proceeding** *n.* (*action*) постýпок (-пка) *perf.*; *pl.* (*legal p.*) судопроизвóдство; *pl.* (*published report*) трудý *m.pl.*, записки *f.pl.* **proceeds** *n.* вырýчка. **process** *n.* (*course*), ход; процéсс; *v.t.* обрабáтывать *imp.*, обрабóтать *perf.*; *processed cheese*, плáвленный сыр (-a(y); *pl.* -ы́). **processing** *n.* обрабóтка. **procession** *n.* процéссия, шéствие.

proclaim *v.t.* провозглашáть *imp.*, провозгласить *perf.*; объявлять *imp.*, объявить (-влю, -вишь) *perf.* **proclamation** *n.* провозглашéние; объявлéние.

proclivity *n.* наклóнность (to(wards), к + *dat.*).

procrastinate *v.i.* мéдлить *imp.* **procrastination** *n.* оття́жка.

procreation *n.* деторождéние.

proctor *n.* прóктор. **proctorial** *adj.* прóкторский.

procuration *n.* (*obtaining*) получéние, (*pimping*) свóдничество. **procure** *v.t.* добывáть *imp.*, добыть (добýду, -дешь; дóбыл, -á, дóбыло) *perf.*; доставáть (-таю, -таёшь) *imp.*, достáть (-áну, -áнешь) *perf.*; *v.i.* (*pimp*) свóдничать *imp.* **procurer** *n.* свóдник. **procuress** *n.* свóдница.

prod *v.t.* ты́кать (ты́чу, -чешь) *imp.*, ткнýть *perf.*; *n.* тычóк (-чкá).

prodigal *adj.* (*wasteful*) расточи́тельный, (*lavish*) щéдрый (щедр, -á, -o) (*of*, на + *acc.*); *p. son*, блýдный сын; *n.* мот. **prodigality** *n.* мотóвство; изоби́лие.

prodigious *adj.* (*amazing*) удиви́тельный; (*enormous*) огрóмный. **prodigy** *n.* чýдо (*pl.* -десá); *infant p.*, вундеркинд.

produce *v.t.* (*evidence etc.*) представлять *imp.*, представить *perf.*; (*ticket etc.*) предъявлять *imp.*, предъявить (-влю,

-вишь) *perf.*; (*play etc.*) стáвить *imp.*, по~ *perf.*; (*manufacture; cause*) производить (-ожý, -óдишь) *imp.*, произвести (-едý, -едёшь; -ёл, -елá) *perf.*; *n.* продýкция (*collect.*) продýкты *m.pl.* **producer** *n.* (*econ.*) производи́тель *m.*; (*of play etc.*) постанóвщик, режиссёр; *p. gas*, генерáторный газ. **product** *n.* продýкт, фабрикáт; (*result*) результáт; (*math.*) произведéние. **production** *n.* производство; (*yield*) продýкция; (*artistic p.*) произведéние; (*of play etc.*) постанóвка. **productive** *adj.* производи́тельный, продукти́вный; (*fruitful*) плодорóдный. **productivity** *n.* производи́тельность.

profanation *n.* профанáция, осквернéние. **profane** *adj.* свéтский; (*blasphemous*) богохýльный; *v.t.* осквернять *imp.*, осквернить *perf.* **profanity** *n.* богохýльство.

profess *v.t.* (*pretend*) притворяться *imp.*, притвори́ться *perf.* (*to be*, + *instr.*); (*declare*) заявлять *imp.*, заяви́ть (-влю, -вишь) *perf.*; (*affirm faith*) испове́довать *imp.*; (*engage in*) занимáться *imp.*, заня́ться (займýсь, -мёшься; заня́лся, -лáсь) *perf.* + *instr.* **professed** *adj.* откры́тый; (*alleged*) мни́мый. **profession** *n.* (*declaration*) заявлéние; (*of faith*) испове́дание; (*vocation*) профéссия. **professional** *n.* профессионáл; (*спортсмéн*) профессионáл. **professor** *n.* профéссор (*pl.* -á). **professorial** *adj.* профéссорский.

proffer *v.t.* предлагáть *imp.*, предложи́ть (-ожý, -óжишь) *perf.*; *n.* предложéние.

proficiency *n.* умéние. **proficient** *adj.* умéлый.

profile *n.* прóфиль *m.*; (*biographical sketch*) крáткий биографи́ческий óчерк.

profit *n.* (*advantage*) пóльза, вы́года; (*gain*) при́быль; *at a p.*, с при́былью; *v.t.* приноси́ть (-ит) *imp.*, принести́ (-есёт; -ёс, -еслá) *perf.* пóльзу + *dat.*; *v.i.* получáть *imp.*, получи́ть (-чý, -чишь) *perf.* при́быль; *p. by*, пóльзоваться *imp.*, вос~ *perf.* + *instr.* **profitable** *adj.* вы́годный, при́быльный.

profiteer v.i. спекули́ровать imp.; n. спекуля́нт, ~ ка. **profiteering** n. спекуля́ция. **profitless** adj. беспо́лезный.

profligacy n. распу́тство. **profligate** n. распу́тник; adj. распу́тный.

pro forma adv. для профо́рмы.

profound adj. глубо́кий (-о́к, -ока́, -о́ко). **profundity** n. глубина́.

profuse adj. (lavish) ще́дрый (щедр, -а́, -о) (in, на + acc.); (abundant) изоби́льный. **profusion** n. изоби́лие.

progenitor n. прароди́тель m. **progeny** n. пото́мок (-мка); (collect.) пото́мство.

prognathous adj. (jaw) выдаю́щийся.

prognosis n. прогно́з. **prognosticate** v.t. предска́зывать imp., предсказа́ть (-ажу́, -а́жешь) perf. **prognostication** n. предсказа́ние.

programme n. програ́мма; adj. программный; v.t. программи́ровать imp., за ~ perf. **programmer** n. программи́ст.

progress n. прогре́сс; (success) успе́хи m.pl.; make p., де́лать imp., с ~ perf. успе́хи; v.i. продвига́ться imp., продви́нуться perf. вперёд. **progression** n. продвиже́ние; (math.) прогре́ссия. **progressive** adj. прогресси́вный.

prohibit v.t. запреща́ть imp., запрети́ть (-ещу́, -ети́шь) perf. **prohibition** n. запреще́ние; (on alcohol) сухо́й зако́н. **prohibitive** adj. запрети́тельный; (price) недосту́пный.

project v.t. (plan) проекти́ровать imp. с ~ perf.; (cast) броса́ть imp., бро́сить perf.; (a film) демонстри́ровать imp., про ~ perf.; v.i. (jut out) выступа́ть imp.; n. прое́кт. **projectile** n. снаря́д. **projection** n. прое́кция; (protrusion) вы́ступ. **projectionist** n. киномеха́ник. **projector** n. (apparatus) проекцио́нный аппара́т.

proletarian adj. пролета́рский; n. пролета́рий, -рка. **proletariat** n. пролетариа́т.

proliferate v.i. размножа́ться imp., размно́житься perf.; (spread) распространя́ться imp., распространи́ться perf.

prolific adj. плодови́тый; (abounding) изоби́лующий (in, + instr.).

prolix adj. многосло́вный. **prolixity** n. многосло́вие.

prologue n. проло́г.

prolong v.t. продлева́ть imp., продли́ть perf. **prolongation** n. продле́ние.

promenade n. ме́сто (pl. -та́) для гуля́нья; (at seaside) набережная sb.; p. deck, ве́рхняя па́луба; v.i. прогу́ливаться imp., прогуля́ться perf.

prominence n. возвыше́ние, вы́пуклость; (distinction) изве́стность; solar p., протубера́нец (-нца). **prominent** adj. вы́пуклый; (conspicuous) ви́дный; (distinguished) выдаю́щийся.

promiscuity n. разноро́дность; (sexual p.) промискуите́т. **promiscuous** adj. (varied) разноро́дный; (indiscriminate) беспоря́дочный; (casual) случа́йный.

promise n. обеща́ние; v.t. обеща́ть imp., perf.; promised land, земля́ (acc. -лю) обетова́нная. **promising** adj. многообеща́ющий, перспекти́вный. **promissory** adj.: p. note, долгово́е обяза́тельство.

promontory n. мыс (loc. -е & -у́; pl. мы́сы).

promote v.t. (advance) продвига́ть imp. продви́нуть perf.; (assist) спосо́бствовать imp., perf. + dat.; (product) соде́йствовать imp., perf. прода́же + gen.; p. to, (mil.) производи́ть (-ожу́, -о́дишь) imp., произвести́ (-еду́, -едёшь; -ёл, -ела́) perf. в + nom.-acc.-pl. **promoter** n. (company p.) учреди́тель m.; (of sporting event etc.) антрепренёр. **promotion** n. продвиже́ние, повыше́ние; соде́йствие.

prompt adj. бы́стрый (быстр, -а́, -о, бы́стры), неме́дленный (-ен, -енна); adv. ро́вно; v.t. (incite) побуди́ть perf. (то, к + dat.; + inf.); (speaker; also fig.) подска́зывать imp., подсказа́ть (-ажу́, -а́жешь) perf. + dat.; (theat.) суфли́ровать imp. + dat.; n. подска́зка; p.-box, суфлёрская бу́дка. **prompter** n. суфлёр.

promulgate v.t. обнаро́довать perf.; публикова́ть imp., о ~ perf.; (disseminate) распространя́ть imp., распространи́ть perf. **promulgation** n. обнаро́дование, опубликова́ние; распростране́ние.

prone adj. (лежа́щий) ничко́м; predic.: p. to, скло́нен (-о́нна, -о́нно) к + dat.

prong n. зубе́ц (-бца́).

pronominal adj. местоиме́нный. **pronoun** n. местоиме́ние.

pronounce v.t. (declare) объявля́ть imp., объяви́ть (-влю́, -вишь) perf.; (articulate) произноси́ть (-ошу́, -о́сишь) imp., произнести́ (-есу́, -есёшь; -ёс, -есла́) perf.; v.i. (give opinion) выска́зываться imp., вы́сказаться (-ажусь, -ажешься) perf. **pronounced** adj. ре́зко вы́раженный (-ен). **pronouncement** n. выска́зывание. **pronunciation** n. произноше́ние.

proof n. доказа́тельство; (test) испыта́ние; (strength of alcohol) устано́вленный гра́дус; (print.) корректу́ра; (phot.) про́бный отпеча́ток (-тка); (of engraving) про́бный о́ттиск; p.-reader, корре́ктор (pl. -ы & -а́); adj. (impenetrable) непроница́емый (against, для + gen.); (not yielding) неподда́ющийся (against, + dat.).

prop[1] n. (support) подпо́рка, сто́йка; (fig.) опо́ра; v.t. (p. up) подпира́ть imp., подпере́ть (-допру́, -допрёшь; -дпёр) perf.; (fig.) подде́рживать imp., поддержа́ть (-жу́, -жишь) perf.

prop[2] n. (theat.): pl. (collect.) реквизи́т, бутафо́рия.

prop[3] n. (aeron.) пропе́ллер.

propaganda n. пропага́нда. **propagandist** n. пропаганди́ст.

propagate v.t. & i. размножа́ть(ся) imp., размно́жить(ся) perf.; (disseminate) распространя́ть(ся) imp., распространи́ть(ся) perf. **propagation** n. размноже́ние; распростране́ние.

propane n. пропа́н.

propel v.t. приводи́ть (-ожу́, -о́дишь) imp., привести́ (-еду́, -едёшь; -ёл, -ела́) perf. в движе́ние; (fig.) дви́гать (-аю, -аешь & -жу, -жешь) imp., дви́нуть perf.; propelling pencil, винтово́й каранда́ш (-а́). **propellant** n. (in firearm) по́рох; (in rocket engine) то́пливо. **propeller** n. (aeron.) пропе́ллер; (aeron.; naut.) винт (-а́).

propensity n. накло́нность (to, к + dat. & + inf.).

proper adj. (characteristic) сво́йственный (-ен(ен), -енна) (to, + dat.); (gram.) со́бственный; (correct) пра́вильный; (strictly so called; after n.) в у́зком смы́сле сло́ва; (suitable) надлежа́щий, до́лжный; (decent) присто́йный; p. fraction, пра́вильная дробь (pl. -би, -бе́й). **properly** adv. (fittingly, duly) до́лжным о́бразом, как сле́дует; (correctly) со́бственно; (decently) прили́чно.

property n. (possessions) со́бственность, иму́щество; (attribute) сво́йство; pl. (theat.) реквизи́т, бутафо́рия; p.-man, реквизи́тор, бутафо́р.

prophecy n. проро́чество. **prophesy** v.t. проро́чить imp., на~ perf. **prophet** n. проро́к. **prophetess** n. проро́чица. **prophetic** adj. проро́ческий.

prophylactic adj. профилакти́ческий; n. профилакти́ческое сре́дство. **prophylaxis** n. профила́ктика.

propinquity n. (nearness) бли́зость; (kinship) родство́.

propitiate v.t. умиротворя́ть imp., умиротвори́ть perf. **propitiation** n. умиротворе́ние.

propitious adj. благоприя́тный.

proponent n. сторо́нник, -ица.

proportion n. пропо́рция; (correct relation) пропорциона́льность; pl. разме́ры m.pl. **proportional** adj. пропорциона́льный; p. representation, пропорциона́льное представи́тельство. **proportionate** adj. соразме́рный (to, + dat.; c + instr.).

proposal n. предложе́ние. **propose** v.t. предлага́ть imp., предложи́ть (-жу́, -жишь) perf.; (intend) предполага́ть imp.; v.i. (p. marriage) де́лать imp., с~ perf. предложе́ние (to, + dat.). **proposition** n. (assertion) утвержде́ние; (math.) теоре́ма; (proposal) предложе́ние; (undertaking) (coll.) де́ло.

propound v.t. предлага́ть imp., предложи́ть (-жу́, -жишь) perf. на обсужде́ние.

proprietary adj. (of owner) со́бственнический; (medicine) патенто́ванный. **proprietor** n. со́бственник, хозя́ин (pl. -я́ева, -я́ев). **proprietress** n. со́бственница, хозя́йка.

propriety n. присто́йность, прили́чие.

propulsion *n.* движе́ние вперёд; (*fig.*) дви́жущая си́ла.

prorogue *v.t.* назнача́ть *imp.*, назна́чить *perf.* переры́в в рабо́те + *gen.*

prosaic *adj.* прозаи́ческий, прозаи́чный.

proscenium *n.* авансце́на.

proscribe *v.t.* (*put outside the law*) объявля́ть *imp.*, объяви́ть (-влю́, -вишь) *perf.* вне зако́на; (*banish*) изгоня́ть *imp.*, изгна́ть (изгоню́, -нишь; изгна́л, -а́, -о) *perf.*; (*forbid*) запреща́ть *imp.*, запрети́ть (-ещу́, -ети́шь) *perf.*

prose *n.* про́за.

prosecute *v.t.* (*pursue*) вести́ (веду́, -дёшь; вёл, -а́) *imp.*; (*leg.*) пресле́довать *imp.* prosecution *n.* веде́ние; (*leg.*) суде́бное пресле́дование; (*prosecuting party*) обвине́ние. prosecutor *n.* обвини́тель *m.*

proselyte *n.* прозели́т. proselytize *v.t.* обраща́ть *imp.*, обрати́ть (-ащу́, -ати́шь) *perf.* в другу́ю ве́ру.

prosody *n.* прос́одия.

prospect *n.* вид, перспекти́ва; *v.t. & i.* разве́дывать *imp.*, разве́дать *perf.* (*for*, на + *acc.*). prospective *adj.* бу́дущий, предполага́емый. prospector *n.* разве́дчик. prospectus *n.* проспе́кт.

prosper *v.i.* процвета́ть *imp.*, преуспева́ть *imp.* prosperity *n.* процвета́ние, преуспева́ние. prosperous *adj.* процвета́ющий, преуспева́ющий; (*wealthy*) зажи́точный.

prostate (gland) *n.* предста́тельная железа́ (*pl.* же́лезы, -лёз, -леза́м).

prostitute *n.* проститу́тка; *v.t.* проститу́ировать *imp.*, *perf.* prostitution *n.* проститу́ция.

prostrate *adj.* распростёртый, (лежа́щий) ничко́м; (*exhausted*) обесси́ленный (-ен); (*with grief*) уби́тый (with, + *instr.*); *v.t.* (*exhaust*) истоща́ть *imp.*, истощи́ть *perf.*; p. oneself, па́дать *imp.*, пасть (паду́, -дёшь; пал) *perf.* ниц. prostration *n.* простра́ция.

prosy *adj.* прозаи́ческий, прозаи́чный.

protagonist *n.* гла́вный геро́й; (*advocate*) сторо́нник.

protean *adj.* (*having many forms*) многообра́зный; (*versatile*) многосторо́нний (-нен, -ння).

protect *v.t.* защища́ть *imp.*, защити́ть (-ищу́, -ити́шь) *perf.* (from, от + *gen.*; against, про́тив + *gen.*). protection *n.* защи́та, охра́на; (*patronage*) покрови́тельство. protectionism *n.* протекциони́зм. protective *adj.* защи́тный, покрови́тельственный. protector *n.* защи́тник, покрови́тель *m.*; (*regent*) прот́ектор. protectorate *n.* протектора́т.

protégé(e) *n.* протеже́ *m.* & *f. indecl.*

protein *n.* протеи́н, бело́к (-лка́).

protest *n.* проте́ст; *v.i.* протестова́ть *imp.*, *perf.*; *v.t.* (*affirm*) заявля́ть *imp.*, заяви́ть (-влю́, -вишь) *perf.* + *acc.*, о + *prep.*, что.

Protestant *n.* протеста́нт, ~ ка; *adj.* протеста́нтский. **Protestantism** *n.* протеста́нтство.

protestation *n.* (торже́ственное) заявле́ние (о + *prep.*; что); (*protest*) проте́ст.

protocol *n.* протоко́л.

proton *n.* прото́н.

protoplasm *n.* протопла́зма.

prototype *n.* прототи́п.

protozoon *n.* просте́йшее (живо́тное) *sb.*

protract *v.t.* тяну́ть (-ну́, -нешь) *imp.*; (*plan*) черти́ть (-рчу́, -ртишь) *imp.*, на ~ *perf.* protracted *adj.* дли́тельный. protraction *n.* промедле́ние; начерта́ние. protractor *n.* (*instrument*) транспорти́р; (*muscle*) разгиба́тельная мы́шца.

protrude *v.t.* высо́вывать *imp.*, вы́сунуть *perf.*; *v.i.* выдава́ться (-даёшься) *imp.*, вы́даться (-астся) *perf.* protrusion *n.* вы́ступ.

protuberance *n.* вы́пуклость, вы́ступ, бугоро́к (-рка́). protuberant *adj.* вы́пуклый; p. eyes, глаза́ (-з, -за́м) *m.pl.* навы́кате.

proud *adj.* го́рдый (горд, -а́, -о, го́рды); be p. of, горди́ться *imp.* + *instr.*

provable *adj.* доказу́емый. **prove** *v.t.* дока́зывать *imp.*, доказа́ть (-ажу́, -а́жешь) *perf.*; удостоверя́ть *imp.*, удостове́рить *perf.*; (a will) утвержда́ть *imp.*, утверди́ть *perf.*; *v.i.* ока́зываться *imp.*, оказа́ться (-ажу́сь, -а́жешься) *perf.* (to be, + *instr.*).

proven *adj.* дока́занный (-ан).

provenance *n.* происхожде́ние.

provender *n.* корм (*loc.* -е & -ý; *pl.* -á).

proverb *n.* посло́вица. **proverbial** *adj.* воше́дший в погово́рку (*that*); (*well-known*) общеизве́стный; *p. saying*, погово́рка.

provide *v.t.* (*stipulate*) ста́вить *imp.*, по~ *perf.* усло́вием (that, что); (*supply person*) снабжа́ть *imp.*, снабди́ть *perf.* (with, + *instr.*); обеспе́чивать *imp.*, обеспе́чить *perf.* (with, + *instr.*); (*supply thing*) предоставля́ть *imp.*, предоста́вить *perf.* (to, for, + *dat.*); дава́ть (даю́, даёшь) *imp.*, дать (дам, дашь, даст, дади́м; дал, -á, да́ло, -и) *perf.* (to, for, + *dat.*): *v.i.*: *p. against*, принима́ть *imp.*, приня́ть (приму́, -мешь; при́нял, -á, -о) *perf.* ме́ры про́тив + *gen.*; *p. for*, предусма́тривать *imp.*, предусмотре́ть (-рю́, -ришь) *perf.* + *acc.*; (*p. for family etc.*) содержа́ть (-жу́, -жишь) *imp. i acc.* **provided (that)** *conj.* при усло́вии, е́сли то́лько. **providence** *n.* провиде́ние; (*foresight*) предусмотри́тельность. **provident** *adj.* предусмотри́тельный; (*thrifty*) бережли́вый. **providential** *adj.* (*lucky*) счастли́вый (-лив). **providing** *see* **provided (that)**.

province *n.* о́бласть (*pl.* -ти, -те́й) (*also fig.*) прови́нция; *pl.* (*the p.*) прови́нция. **provincial** *adj.* провинциа́льный; *n.* провинциа́л, ~ ка. **provincialism** *n.* провинциа́льность; (*expression*) обла́стно́е выраже́ние.

provision *n.* снабже́ние, обеспе́чение; *pl.* прови́зия; (*in agreement etc.*) положе́ние; *make p. against*, принима́ть *imp.*, приня́ть (приму́, -мешь; при́нял, -á, -о) *perf.* ме́ры про́тив + *gen.*; *make p. for*, предусма́тривать *imp.*, предусмотре́ть (-рю́, -ришь) *perf.* + *acc.*; *v.t.* снабжа́ть *imp.*, снабди́ть *perf.* прови́зией. **provisional** *adj.* вре́менный. **proviso** *n.* усло́вие, огово́рка. **provisory** *adj.* усло́вный.

provocation *n.* провока́ция. **provocative** *adj.* провокацио́нный; *p. of*, вызыва́ющий + *acc.* **provoke** *v.t.* провоци́ровать *imp.*, с~ *perf.*; (*call forth, cause*) вызыва́ть *imp.* вы́звать (вы́зову,

-вешь) *perf.*; (*irritate*) раздража́ть *imp.*, раздражи́ть *perf.*

provost *n.* (*univ.*) ре́ктор; (*mayor*) мэр; *p. marshal*, нача́льник вое́нной поли́ции.

prow *n.* нос (*loc.* -ý; *pl.* -ы́).

prowess *n.* (*valour*) до́блесть; (*skill*) уме́ние.

prowl *v.i.* ры́скать (ры́щу, -щешь) *imp.*; *v.t.* броди́ть (-ожу́, -о́дишь) *imp.* по + *dat.*

proximity *n.* бли́зость.

proxy *n.* полномо́чие, дове́ренность; (*person*) уполномо́ченный *sb.*, замести́тель *m.*; *by p.*, по дове́ренности; *stand p. for*, быть *imp.* замести́телем + *gen.*

prude *n.* скро́мник, -ица.

prudence *n.* благоразу́мие. **prudent** *adj.* благоразу́мный.

prudery *n.* притво́рная стыдли́вость. **prudish** *adj.* не в ме́ру стыдли́вый.

prune[1] *n.* (*plum*) черносли́вина; *pl.* черносли́в (-а(у)) (*collect.*).

prune[2] *v.t.* (*trim*) об-, под-, реза́ть *imp.*, об-, под-, ре́зать (-е́жу, -е́жешь) *perf.*; (*fig.*) сокраща́ть *imp.*, сократи́ть (-ащу́, -ати́шь) *perf.* **pruning-hook** *n.* приви́вочный нож (-á).

prurience *n.* похотли́вость. **prurient** *adj.* похотли́вый.

Prussian *n.* прусса́к (-á), -а́чка (*adj.*) пру́сский; *P. blue*, берли́нская лазу́рь. **prussic** *adj.*: *p. acid*, сини́льная кислота́.

pry *v.i.* сова́ть (сую́, суёшь) *imp.* нос (into, в + *acc.*). **prying** *adj.* пытли́вый, любопы́тный.

psalm *n.* псало́м (-лма́). **psalter** *n.* псалты́рь (-ри & -ря́) *f.* & *m.*

pseudo- *in comb.* псевдо-. **pseudonym** *n.* псевдони́м.

psyche *n.* пси́хика. **psychiatric** *adj.* психиатри́ческий. **psychiatrist** *n.* психиа́тр. **psychiatry** *n.* психиатри́я. **psychic(al)** *adj.* психи́ческий, душе́вный. **psycho** *n.* псих. **psycho-** *in comb.* психо-. **psycho-analyse** *v.t.* подверга́ть *imp.*, подве́ргнуть (-г) *perf.* психоана́лизу. **psycho-analysis** *n.* психоана́лиз. **psycho-analyst** *n.* специали́ст по психоана́лизу. **psycho-analytic(al)** *adj.*

психоаналити́ческий. **psychological** *adj.* психологи́ческий. **psychologist** *n.* психо́лог. **psychology** *n.* психоло́гия (*coll.*) пси́хика. **psychomotor** *adj.* психомото́рный. **psychoneurosis** *n.* психоневро́з. **psychopath** *n.* психопа́т. **psychopathic** *adj.* психопати́ческий. **psychopathology** *n.* психопатоло́гия. **psychosis** *n.* психо́з. **psychotherapy** *n.* психотерапи́я.

ptarmigan *n.* тундря́нка.

pterodactyl *n.* птерода́ктиль *m.*

pub *n.* пивна́я *sb.*, каба́к (-а́).

puberty *n.* полова́я зре́лость.

public *adj.* (*n.*) обще́ственный (*open*) публи́чный, откры́тый; *p. health,* здравоохране́ние; *p. house,* пивна́я *sb.*; *p. relations officer,* слу́жащий *sb.* отде́ла информа́ции; *p. school,* ча́стная сре́дняя шко́ла; *p. servant,* госуда́рственный слу́жащий *sb.*; *p. spirit,* обще́ственный дух; *p. utility,* предприя́тие обще́ственного по́льзования; *in p.,* пу́блика, обще́ственность; *in p.,* откры́то, публи́чно. **publication** *n.* (*action*) опубликова́ние; (*also book etc.*) изда́ние. **publicist** *n.* публици́ст. **publicity** *n.* рекла́ма; *p. agent,* аге́нт по рекла́ме. **publicize** *v.t.* реклами́ровать *imp.*, *perf.* **publicly** *adv.* публи́чно, откры́то; *o~ perf.*; **publish** *v.t.* публикова́ть *imp.*, (*book*) издава́ть (-даю́, -даёшь) *imp.*, изда́ть (-да́м, -да́шь, -да́ст, -ади́м; изда́л, -а́, -о) *perf.* **publisher** *n.* изда́тель *m.* **publishing** *n.* (*business*) изда́тельское де́ло; *p. house,* изда́тельство.

puce *adj.* (*n.*) краснова́то-кори́чневый (цвет).

puck *n.* (*in ice hockey*) ша́йба.

pucker *v.t. & i.* мо́рщить(ся) *imp.*, с~ *perf.*; *n.* морщи́на.

pudding *n.* пу́динг, запека́нка; *p.-head,* болва́н; *p.-stone,* конгломера́т.

puddle *n.* лу́жа.

pudgy *adj.* пу́хлый (пухл, -а́, -о).

puerile *adj.* ребя́ческий. **puerility** *n.* ребя́чество.

puff *n.* (*of wind*) поры́в; (*of smoke*) дымо́к (-мка́); (*on dress*) буфы́ (-ф) *pl. only*; *p.-ball,* (*fungus*) дождеви́к (-а́); *p. pastry,* сло́ёное те́сто; *p. sleeves,*

рукава́ *m.pl.* с бу́фами; *v.i.* пыхте́ть (-хчу́, -хти́шь) *imp.*; *p. at,* (*pipe etc.*) попы́хивать *imp.+instr.*; *v.t.*: *p. up, out,* (*inflate*) надува́ть *imp.*, наду́ть (-у́ю, -у́ешь) *perf.*

puffin *n.* ту́пик.

pug[1] *n.* (*dog*) мопс; *p.-nosed,* курно́сый.

pug[2] *n.* (*clay*) мя́тая гли́на.

pugilism *n.* бокс. **pugilist** *n.* боксёр.

pugnacious *adj.* драчли́вый. **pugnacity** *n.* драчли́вость.

puissant *adj.* могу́щественный (-ен, -енна).

puke *v.i.* рвать (рвёт; рва́ло) *imp.*, вы́~ *perf. impers.+acc.*; *n.* рво́та.

pull *v.t.* тяну́ть (-ну́, -нешь) *imp.*, по~ *perf.*; таска́ть *indet.*, тащи́ть (-щу́ -щишь) *det.*, по~ *perf.*; (*a muscle*) растя́гивать *imp.*, растяну́ть (-ну́, -нешь) *perf.*; (*a cork*) выта́скивать *imp.*, вы́тащить *perf.*; (*a tooth*) удаля́ть *imp.*, удали́ть *perf.*; *v.t. & i.* дёргать *imp.*, дёрнуть *perf.* (*at,* (*за*)+*acc.*); *p. faces,* грима́сничать *imp.*; *p. someone's leg,* моро́чить *imp.* го́лову+*dat.*; *p.* (*the*) *strings, wires,* нажима́ть *imp.*, нажа́ть (нажму́, -мёшь) *perf.* на та́йные пружи́ны; *p. the trigger,* спуска́ть *imp.*, спусти́ть (-ущу́, -у́стишь) *perf.* куро́к; *p. apart, to pieces,* разрыва́ть *imp.*, разорва́ть (-ву́, -вёшь) *perf.*; (*fig.*) раскри́тико́вывать *perf.*; *p. at,* (*pipe etc.*) затя́гиваться *imp.*, затяну́ться (-ну́сь, -нешься) *perf.+instr.*; *p. down,* (*demolish*) сноси́ть (-ошу́, -о́сишь) *imp.*, снести́ (снесу́, -сёшь; снёс, -ла́) *perf.*; *p. in,* (*earn*) зараба́тывать *imp.*, зарабо́тать *perf.*; (*of train*) прибыва́ть *imp.*, прибы́ть (-бу́дет; при́был, -а́, -о) *perf.*; (*of vehicle*) подъезжа́ть *imp.*, подъе́хать (-е́дет) *perf.* к обо́чине доро́ги; *p. off,* (*garment*) стя́гивать *imp.*, стяну́ть (-ну́, -нешь) *perf.*; (*achieve*) успе́шно заверша́ть *imp.*, заверши́ть *perf.*; (*win*) выи́грывать *imp.*, вы́играть *perf.*; *p. on,* (*garment*) натя́гивать *imp.*, натяну́ть (-ну́, -нешь) *perf.*; *p. out,* (*v.t.*) (*remove*) выта́скивать *imp.*, вы́тащить *imp.*; (*v.i.*) (*withdraw*) отка́зываться *imp.*

отказа́ться (-ажу́сь, -а́жешься) *perf.* от уча́стия (of, в + *prep.*); (*of vehicle*) отъезжа́ть *imp.*, отъе́хать (-е́дет) *perf.* от обо́чины (доро́ги); (*of train*) отходи́ть (-ит) *imp.*, отойти́ (-йдёт; отошёл, -шла́) *perf.* (от ста́нции); *p. through*, выжива́ть *imp.*, вы́жить (вы́живу, -вешь) *perf.*; *p. oneself together*, брать (беру́, -рёшь; брал, -а́, -о) *imp.*, взять (возьму́, -мёшь; взял, -а́, -о) *perf.* себя́ в ру́ки; *p. up*, (*v.t.*) подтя́гивать *imp.*, подтяну́ть (-ну́, -нешь) *perf.*; (*v.t. & i.*) (*stop*) остана́вливать(ся) *imp.*, останови́ть(ся) (-влю́(сь), -вишь(ся)) *perf.*; *p. in*, *p.-up*, заку́сочная *sb.* на доро́ге; *p. through*, проти́рка; *n.* тя́га; (*fig.*) зару́чка.

pullet *n.* моло́дка.

pulley *n.* блок, шкив (*pl.* -ы́).

Pullman *n.* пу́льман(овский ваго́н).

pullover *n.* пуло́вер.

pulmonary *adj.* лёгочный.

pulp *n.* (*of fruit*) мя́коть; (*anat.*) пу́льпа; (*of paper*) бума́жная ма́сса; *v.t.* превраща́ть *imp.*, преврати́ть (-ащу́, -ати́шь) *perf.* в мя́гкую ма́ссу.

pulpit *n.* ка́федра.

pulsar *n.* пульса́р. **pulsate** *v.i.* пульси́ровать *imp.* **pulsation** *n.* пульса́ция. **pulse**[1] *n.* (*throbbing*) пульс; *v.i.* пульси́ровать *imp.*

pulse[2] *n.* (*food*) бобо́вые *sb.*

pulverize *v.t.* размельча́ть *imp.*, размельчи́ть *perf.*; (*fig.*) сокруша́ть *imp.*, сокруши́ть *perf.*

puma *n.* пу́ма.

pumice(-stone) *n.* пе́мза.

pummel *v.t.* колоти́ть (-очу́, -о́тишь) *imp.*, по~ *perf.*; тузи́ть *imp.*, от~ *perf.*

pump[1] *n.* (*machine*) насо́с; *v.t.* (*use p.*) кача́ть *imp.*; (*person*) выпра́шивать *imp.*, вы́просить *perf.* у + *gen.*; *p. in(to)*, вка́чивать *imp.*, вкача́ть *perf.*; *p. out*, выка́чивать *imp.*, вы́качать *perf.*; *p. up*, нака́чивать *imp.*, накача́ть *perf.*

pump[2] *n.* (*shoe*) ту́фля (*gen.pl.* -фель).

pumpkin *n.* ты́ква.

pun *n.* каламбу́р; *v.i.* каламбу́рить *imp.*, с~ *perf.*

punch[1] *v.t.* (*with fist*) ударя́ть *imp.*,

ударить *perf.* кулако́м; (*pierce*) пробива́ть *imp.*, проби́ть (-бью́, -бьёшь) *perf.*; (*a ticket*) компости́ровать *imp.*, про~ *perf.*; *p.-ball*, пенчингбо́л, гру́ша; *p.-up*, дра́ка; *n.* (*blow*) уда́р кулако́м; (*for tickets*) компо́стер; (*for piercing*) проби́вник; (*for stamping*) пуансо́н.

punch[2] *n.* (*drink*) пунш.

punctilio *n.* форма́льность. **punctilious** *adj.* соблюда́ющий форма́льности, щепети́льный.

punctual *adj.* пунктуа́льный. **punctuality** *n.* пунктуа́льность.

punctuate *v.t.* ста́вить *imp.*, по~ *perf.* зна́ки препина́ния в + *acc.*; прерыва́ть *imp.*, прерва́ть (-ву́, -вёшь; прерва́л, -а́, -о) *perf.* **punctuation** *n.* пунктуа́ция; *p. marks*, зна́ки *m.pl.* препина́ния.

puncture *n.* проко́л; *v.t.* прока́лывать *imp.*, проколо́ть (-лю́, -лешь) *perf.*; *v.i.* получа́ть *imp.*, получи́ть (-чу́, -чишь) *perf.* проко́л.

pundit *n.* (*fig.*) знато́к (-а́).

pungency *n.* е́дкость. **pungent** *adj.* е́дкий (е́док, едка́, е́дко).

punish *v.t.* нака́зывать *imp.*, наказа́ть (-ажу́, -а́жешь) *perf.* **punishable** *adj.* наказу́емый. **punishment** *n.* наказа́ние. **punitive** *adj.* кара́тельный.

punnet *n.* корзи́нка.

punster *n.* каламбури́ст.

punt *n.* (*boat*) плоскодо́нка.

punter *n.* (*gambler*) игро́к (-а́).

puny *adj.* хи́лый (хил, -а́, -о), тщеду́шный.

pup *n.* щено́к (-нка́; *pl.* щенки́, -ко́в & щеня́та, -т); *v.i.* щени́ться *imp.*, о~ *perf.*

pupa *n.* ку́колка.

pupil *n.* учени́к (-а́), -и́ца; (*of eye*) зрачо́к (-чка́).

puppet *n.* марионе́тка, ку́кла (*gen.pl.* -кол); *p. regime*, марионе́точный режи́м; *p.-theatre*, ку́кольный теа́тр.

puppy *n.* щено́к (-нка́; *pl.* щенки́, -ко́в & щеня́та, -т).

purblind *adj.* близору́кий.

purchase *n.* поку́пка; (*leverage*) то́чка опо́ры; *v.t.* покупа́ть *imp.*, купи́ть

(-плю́, -пи́шь) *perf.* **purchaser** *n.* покупа́тель *m.*, ~ница.

pure *adj.* чи́стый (чист, -а́, -о, чи́сты); (*of science*) теорети́ческий; p.-blooded, чистокро́вный; p.-bred, поро́дистый; p.-minded, чи́стый (чист, -а́, -о, чи́сты) душо́й.

purée *n.* пюре́ *neut.indecl.*

purely *adv.* чи́сто; (*entirely*) соверше́нно.

purgative *adj.* слаби́тельный; (*purifying*) очисти́тельный; *n.* слаби́тельное *sb.* **purgatory** *n.* чисти́лище. **purge** *v.t.* (*cleanse*) очища́ть *imp.*, очи́стить *perf.*; (*of medicine*; *abs.*) слаби́ть *imp.*; (*atone for*) искупа́ть *imp.*, искупи́ть (-плю́, -пишь) *perf.*; (*p. party, army, etc.*) проводи́ть (-ожу́, -о́дишь) *imp.*, провести́ (-еду́, -едёшь; -ёл, -ела́) *perf.* чи́стку в + *acc.*; *n.* очище́ние; (*of party, army, etc.*) чи́стка.

purification *n.* очище́ние, очи́стка. **purify** *v.t.* очища́ть *imp.*, очи́стить *perf.*

purism *n.* пури́зм. **purist** *n.* пури́ст.

puritan, P., *n.* пурита́нин (*pl.* -а́не, -а́н), -а́нка. **puritanical** *adj.* пурита́нский.

purity *n.* чистота́.

purlieu *n.* : *pl.* окре́стности *f.pl.*

purloin *v.t.* похища́ть *imp.*, похи́тить (-и́щу, -и́тишь) *perf.*

purple *adj.* (*n.*) пу́рпурный, фиолéтовый (цвет).

purport *n.* смысл.

purpose *n.* цель, намéрение; on p., наро́чно; to no p., напра́сно; to the p., кста́ти. **purposeful** *adj.* целеустремлённый (-ён, -ённа). **purposeless** *adj.* бесце́льный. **purposely** *adv.* наро́чно.

purr *n.* мурлы́канье; *v.i.* мурлы́кать (-ы́чу, -ы́чешь) *imp.*

purse *n.* кошелёк (-лька́); *v.t.* поджима́ть *imp.*, поджа́ть (подожму́, -мёшь) *perf.* **purser** *n.* казначе́й.

pursuance *n.* выполне́ние. **pursuant** *adv.*: p. to, в соотвéтствии с + *instr.*; согла́сно + *dat.* **pursue** *v.t.* пресле́довать *imp.* **pursuit** *n.* пресле́дование; (*occupation*) заня́тие.

purulent *adj.* гно́йный.

purvey *v.t.* поставля́ть *imp.*, поста́вить *perf.* **purveyor** *n.* поставщи́к (-а́).

purview *n.* кругозо́р.

pus *n.* гной (-о́я(ю)), *loc.* -óе & -о́ю).

push *v.t.* толка́ть *imp.*, толкну́ть *perf.*; (*goods*) реклами́ровать *imp.*, *perf.*; *v.i.* толка́ться *imp.*; be pushed for, имéть *imp.* ма́ло + *gen.*; he is pushing fifty, ему́ ско́ро сту́кнет пятьдеся́т; p. one's way, проти́скиваться *imp.*, проти́снуться *perf.*; p. ahead, on, продвига́ться *imp.*, продви́нуться *perf.*; p. around, (*person*) помыка́ть *imp.* + *instr.*; p. aside, (*also fig.*) отстраня́ть *imp.*, отстрани́ть *perf.*; p. away, отта́лкивать *imp.*, оттолкну́ть *perf.*; p. into, (*v.t.*) вта́лкивать *imp.*, втолкну́ть *perf.* в + *acc.*; (*urge*) толка́ть *imp.*, толкну́ть *perf.* на + *acc.*; p. off, (*v.i.*) in boat) отта́лкиваться *imp.*, оттолкну́ться *perf.* (от бе́рега); (*go away*) убира́ться *imp.*, убра́ться (уберу́сь, -рёшься; убра́лся - ала́сь, -ало́сь) *perf.*; p. through, (*v.t.*) прота́лкивать *imp.*, протолкну́ть *perf.*; (*conclude*) доводи́ть (-ожу́, -о́дишь) *imp.*, довести́ (-еду́, -едёшь; -ёл, -ела́) до конца́; *n.* толчо́к (-чка́); (*energy*) эне́ргия; p.-ball, пушбо́л; p.-bike, велосипе́д. **pushing** *adj.* (*of person*) напо́ристый.

puss, pussy(-cat) *n.* ко́шечка, ки́ска; p. willow, вéрба.

pustular *adj.* пустулёзный, прыща́вый. **pustule** *n.* пу́стула, прыщ (-а́).

put *v.t.* класть (кладу́, -дёшь; клал) *imp.*, положи́ть (-жу́, -жишь) *perf.*; (*upright*) ста́вить *imp.*, по~ *perf.*; помеща́ть *imp.*, помести́ть *perf.*; (*into specified state*) приводи́ть (-ожу́, -о́дишь) *imp.*, привести́ (-еду́, -едёшь; -ёл, -ела́) *perf.*; (*estimate*) определя́ть *imp.*, определи́ть *perf.* (at, в + *acc.*); (*express*) выража́ть *imp.*, вы́разить *perf.*; (*translate*) переводи́ть (-ожу́, -о́дишь) *imp.*, перевести́ (-еду́, -едёшь; -ёл, -ела́) *perf.* (into, на + *acc.*); (*a question*) задава́ть (-даю́, -даёшь) *imp.*, зада́ть (-а́м, -а́шь, -а́ст, -ади́м; за́дал, -а́, -о) *perf.*; p. an end, a stop, to, класть (кладу́, -дёшь; клал) *imp.*, положи́ть (-жу́, -жишь) *perf.* коне́ц + *dat.*; p. oneself in another's place, ста́вить *imp.*, по~ *perf.* себя́ на ме́сто

+*gen.*; *p. the shot*, толка́ть *imp.*, толкну́ть *perf.* ядро́; *p. to death*, казни́ть *imp.*, *perf.*; *p. to flight*, обраща́ть *imp.*, обрати́ть (-ащу́, -ати́шь) *perf.* в бе́гство; *p. to shame*, стыди́ть *imp.*, при∼ *perf.*; *p. about*, (*of ship*) лечь (ля́жет, ля́гут; лёг, -ла́) *perf.* на друго́й галс; (*rumour etc.*) распространя́ть *imp.*, распространи́ть *perf.*; *p. away*, (*for future*) откла́дывать *imp.*, отложи́ть (-жу́, -жишь) *perf.*; (*in prison*) сажа́ть *imp.*, посади́ть (-ажу́, -а́дишь) *perf.*; *p. back*, (*in place*) ста́вить *imp.*, по∼ *perf.* на ме́сто; *p. the clock back*, передвига́ть *imp.*, передви́нуть *perf.* стре́лки часо́в наза́д; *p. by*, (*money*) откла́дывать *imp.*, отложи́ть (-жу́, -жишь) *perf.*; *p. down*, (*suppress*) подавля́ть *imp.*, подави́ть (-влю́, -вишь) *perf.*; (*write down*) запи́сывать *imp.*, записа́ть (-ишу́, -и́шешь) *perf.*; (*passengers*) выса́живать *imp.*, вы́садить *perf.*; (*attribute*) припи́сывать *imp.*, приписа́ть (-ишу́, -и́шешь) *perf.* (to, +*dat.*); *p. forth*, (*of plant*) пуска́ть *imp.*, пусти́ть (-ит) *perf.* (побе́ги); *p. forward*, (*proposal*) предлага́ть *imp.*, предложи́ть (-жу́, -жишь) *perf.*; *p. the clock forward*, передвига́ть *imp.*, передви́нуть *perf.* стре́лки часо́в вперёд; *p. in*, (*install*) устана́вливать *imp.*, установи́ть (-влю́, -вишь) *perf.*; (*a claim*) предъявля́ть *imp.*, предъяви́ть (-влю́, -вишь) *perf.*; (*interpose*) вставля́ть *imp.*, вста́вить *perf.*; (*spend time*) проводи́ть (-ожу́, -о́дишь) *imp.*, провести́ (-еду́, -едёшь; -ёл, -ела́) *perf.*; *p. in an appearance*, появля́ться *imp.*, появи́ться (-влю́сь, -вишься) *perf.*; *p. off*, (*postpone*) откла́дывать *imp.*, отложи́ть (-жу́, -жишь) *perf.*; (*evade*) отде́лываться *imp.*, отде́латься *perf.* от+*gen.*; (*dissuade*) отгова́ривать *imp.*, отговори́ть *perf.* от+*gen.*, +*inf.*; *p. on*, (*clothes*) надева́ть *imp.*, наде́ть (-е́ну, -е́нешь) *perf.*; (*appearance*) принима́ть *imp.*, приня́ть (приму́, -мешь; при́нял, -а́, -о) *perf.*; (*a play*) ста́вить *imp.*, по∼ *perf.*; (*turn on*) включа́ть *imp.*, включи́ть *perf.*; (*add to*) при-

бавля́ть *imp.*, приба́вить *perf.*; *p. on airs*, ва́жничать *imp.*; *p. on weight*, толсте́ть *imp.*, по∼ *perf.*; *p. out*, (*dislocate*) вы́вихнуть *perf.*; (*a fire etc.*) туши́ть (-шу́, -шишь) *imp.*, по∼ *perf.*; (*annoy*) раздража́ть *imp.*, раздражи́ть *perf.*; *p. out to sea*, (*of ship*) выходи́ть (-ит) *imp.*, вы́йти (вы́йдет; вы́шел, -шла) *perf.* в мо́ре; *p. through*, (*carry out*) выполня́ть *imp.*, вы́полнить *perf.*; (*on telephone*) соединя́ть *imp.*, соедини́ть *perf.* по телефо́ну; *p. up*, (*building*) стро́ить *imp.*, по∼ *perf.*; (*price*) повыша́ть *imp.*, повы́сить *perf.*; (*a guest*) дава́ть (даю́, даёшь) *imp.*, дать (дам, дашь, даст, дади́м; дал, -а́, да́ло́, -и) *perf.* прию́т +*gen.*; (*as guest*) остана́вливаться *imp.*, останови́ться (-влю́сь, -вишься) *perf.*; *p. up to*, (*instigate*) подстрека́ть *imp.*, подстрекну́ть *perf.* к+*dat.*; *p. up with*, терпе́ть (-плю́, -пишь) *imp.*

putative *adj.* предполага́емый.

putrefaction *n.* гние́ние. **putrefy** *v.i.* гнить (-ию́, -иёшь; гнил, -а́, -о) *imp.*, с∼ *perf.* **putrid** *adj.* гнило́й (гнил, -а́, -о), гни́лостный.

putsch *n.* путч.

puttee *n.* обмо́тка.

putty *n.* зама́зка, шпаклёвка; *v.t.* шпаклева́ть (-лю́ю, -лю́ешь) *imp.*, за∼ *perf.*

puzzle *n.* (*perplexity*) недоуме́ние; (*enigma*) зага́дка; (*toy etc.*) головоло́мка; *v.t.* озада́чивать *imp.*, озада́чить *perf.*; *p. out*, разгада́ть *perf.*; *p. over*, лома́ть *imp.* себе́ го́лову над +*instr.*

pygmy *n.* пигме́й; *adj.* ка́рликовый.

pyjamas *n.* пижа́ма.

pylon *n.* пило́н, опо́ра.

pyorrhoea *n.* пиоре́я.

pyramid *n.* пирами́да. **pyramidal** *adj.* пирамида́льный.

pyre *n.* погреба́льный костёр (-тра́).

pyrites *n.*: (*iron*) p., пири́т; *copper* p., халькопири́т.

pyromania *n.* пирома́ния.

pyrotechnic(al) *adj.* пиротехни́ческий. **pyrotechnics** *n.* пироте́хника.

Pyrrhic *adj.*: P. *victory*, пи́ррова побе́да.

python *n.* пито́н.

Q

qua *conj.* в ка́честве + *gen.*

quack[1] *n.* (*sound*) кря́канье; *v.i.* кря́кать *imp.*, кря́кнуть *perf.*

quack[2] *n.* зна́харь *m.*, шарлата́н. **quackery** *n.* зна́харство, шарлата́нство.

quad *n.* (*quadrangle*) четырёхуго́льный двор (-а́); (*quadrat*) шпа́ция; *pl.* (*quadruplets*) че́тверо (-ры́х) близнецо́в. **quadrangle** *n.* (*figure*) четырёхуго́льник; (*court*) четырёхуго́льный двор (-а́). **quadrangular** *adj.* четырёхуго́льный. **quadrant** *n.* квадра́нт. **quadrat** *n.* шпа́ция. **quadratic** *adj.* квадра́тный; *q. equation,* квадра́тное уравне́ние. **quadrilateral** *adj.* четырёхсторо́нний.

quadrille *n.* кадри́ль.

quadroon *n.* кварте́рон.

quadruped *n.* четвероно́гое живо́тное *sb.* **quadruple** *adj.* четверно́й, учетверённый (-ён, -ена́); *v.t. & i.* учетверя́ть(ся) *imp.*, учетвери́ть(ся) *perf.* **quadruplets** *n.* че́тверо (-ры́х) близнецо́в.

quaff *v.t.* пить (пью, пьёшь; пил, -а́, -о) *imp.*, вы́ ~ *perf.* больши́ми глотка́ми.

quag, quagmire *n.* тряси́на; (*also fig.*) боло́то.

quail[1] *n.* (*bird*) пе́репел (*pl.* -а́), -ёлка.

quail[2] *v.i.* (*flinch*) дро́гнуть *perf.*; тру́сить *imp.*, с ~ *perf.* (*before,* + *acc.*, пе́ред + *instr.*).

quaint *adj.* причу́дливый, оригина́льный.

quake *v.i.* трясти́сь (трясу́сь, -сёшься; тря́сся, -сла́сь) *imp.*; дрожа́ть (-жу́, -жи́шь) *imp.* (*for,* with, от + *gen.*); *n.* землетрясе́ние.

Quaker *n.* ква́кер, ~ ка.

qualification *n.* (*restriction*) ограниче́ние, огово́рка; (*for post etc.*) квалифика́ция; (*for citizenship etc.*) ценз; (*description*) характери́стика. **qualify** *v.t.* (*describe*) квалифици́ровать *imp.*, *perf.*; (*restrict*) ограни́чивать *imp.*, ограни́чить *perf.*; *v.t. & i.* (*prepare for*) гото́вить(ся) *imp.* (*for,* к + *dat.*; + *inf.*).

qualitative *adj.* ка́чественный. **quality** *n.* ка́чество; сорт; (*excellence*) высо́кое ка́чество; (*ability*) спосо́бность.

qualm *n.* (*queasiness*) при́ступ тошноты́; (*doubt, scruple*) колеба́ние, угрызе́ние со́вести.

quandary *n.* затрудни́тельное положе́ние, диле́мма.

quantify *v.t.* определя́ть *imp.*, определи́ть *perf.* коли́чество + *gen.* **quantitative** *adj.* коли́чественный. **quantity** *n.* коли́чество; (*math.*) величина́ (*pl.* -ны).

quantum *n.* (*amount*) коли́чество; (*share*) до́ля (*pl.* -ли, -ле́й); (*phys.*) квант; *attrib.* ква́нтовый.

quarantine *n.* каранти́н; *v.t.* подверга́ть *imp.*, подве́ргнуть (-г) *perf.* каранти́ну.

quark *n.* кварк.

quarrel *n.* ссо́ра; *v.i.* ссо́риться *imp.*, по ~ *perf.* (*with,* с + *instr.*; *about, for,* из-за + *gen.*). **quarrelsome** *adj.* вздо́рный.

quarry[1] *n.* (*for stone etc.*) каменоло́мня (*gen.pl.* -мен), карье́р; *v.t.* добыва́ть *imp.*, добы́ть (добу́ду, -дешь; до́был, -а́, -о) *perf.*

quarry[2] *n.* (*object of pursuit*) пресле́дуемый зверь (*pl.* -ри, -ре́й) *m.*

quart *n.* ква́рта. **quarter** *n.* че́тверть (*pl.* -ти, -те́й); (*of year; of town*) кварта́л; (*direction*) сторона́ (*acc.* -ону; *pl.* -оны, -о́н, -она́м); (*mercy*) поща́да; *pl.* кварти́ры *f.pl.*; *a q. to one,* без че́тверти час; *q.-day,* пе́рвый день (дня) *m.* кварта́ла; *q.-final,* четвертьфина́л(ьная игра́); *v.t. (divide)* дели́ть (-лю́, -лишь) *imp.*, раз~ *perf.* на четы́ре (ра́вные) ча́сти, *(traitor's body)* четвертова́ть *imp., perf.*; *(lodge)* расквартиро́вывать *imp.*, расквартирова́ть *perf.* **quarterdeck** *n.* шка́нцы (-цев) *pl.* **quarterly** *adj.* трёхме́сячный, кварта́льный; *n.* журна́л, выходя́щий раз в три ме́сяца, раз в кварта́л, раз в три ме́сяца; *adv.* раз в три ме́сяца. **quartermaster** *n.* квартирме́йстер. **quartet(te)** *n.* кварте́т. **quarto** *n.* (ин-)ква́рто *neut.indecl.*

quartz *n.* кварц.

quasar *n.* кваза́р.

quash *v.t. (annul)* аннули́ровать *imp., perf.*; *(crush)* подавля́ть *imp.*, подави́ть (-влю́, -вишь) *perf.*

quasi *adv.* как бу́дто.

quasi- *in comb.* квази-.

quater-centenary *n.* четырёхсотле́тие.

quatrain *n.* четверости́шие.

quaver *v.i.* дрожа́ть (-жу́, -жи́шь) *imp.*; *n.* дрожа́ние; *(mus.)* восьма́я *sb.* но́ты.

quay *n.* на́бережная *sb.*

queasy *adj. (stomach)* сла́бый (слаб, -á, -о); *(person)* испы́тывающий тошноту́.

queen *n.* короле́ва *(cards)* да́ма; *(chess)* ферзь (-зя́) *m.*; *q. bee,* ма́тка; *q. mother,* вдо́вствующая короле́ва; *(chess)* проводи́ть (-ожу́, -о́дишь) *imp.*, провести́ (-еду́, -едёшь; -ёл, -ела́) *perf.* в ферзи́; *в* ферзи́ *(chess)*. **queenly** *adj.* ца́рственный (-ен(ен), -енна).

queer *adj.* стра́нный (-нен, -нна́, -нно); *feel q.,* чу́вствовать *imp.* недомога́ние.

quell *v.t.* подавля́ть *imp.*, подави́ть (-влю́, -вишь) *perf.*

quench *v.t. (thirst)* утоля́ть *imp.*, утоли́ть (-лю́, -ли́шь) *perf.*; *(fire, desire)* туши́ть (-шу́, -шишь) *imp.*, по~ *perf.*

querulous *adj.* ворчли́вый.

query *n.* вопро́с, сомне́ние; *v.t. (express doubt)* выража́ть *imp.*, вы́разить *perf.* сомне́ние в + *prep.* **quest** *n.* по́иски *m.pl.*; *in q. of,* в по́исках + *gen.* **question** *n.* вопро́с; *(doubt)* сомне́ние; *beyond all q.,* вне сомне́ния; *it is (merely) a q. of,* э́то вопро́с + *gen.*; де́ло то́лько в том, что́бы + *inf.*; *it is*

out of the q., об э́том не мо́жет быть и ре́чи; *the person in q.,* челове́к, о кото́ром идёт речь; *the q. is this,* де́ло в э́том; *q. mark,* вопроси́тельный знак; *v.t. (ask)* спра́шивать *imp.*, спроси́ть (-ошу́, -о́сишь) *perf.*; *(doubt)* сомнева́ться *imp.* в + *prep.* **questionable** *adj.* сомни́тельный. **questionnaire** *n.* анке́та, вопро́сник.

queue *n.* о́чередь *(pl.* -ди, -де́й); *v.i.* стоя́ть (-ою́, -ои́шь) *imp.* в о́череди.

quibble *n.* софи́зм, увёртка; *v.i.* уклоня́ться *imp.*, уклони́ться (-ню́сь, -ни́шься) *perf.* от су́ти вопро́са, от прямо́го отве́та.

quick *adj.* ско́рый (скор, -á, -о), бы́стрый (быстр, -á, -о, бы́стры); *(nimble)* прово́рный; *(clever)* смышлёный; *q.-tempered,* вспы́льчивый; *q.-witted,* нахо́дчивый; *n.: to the q.,* за живо́е, до мя́са; *the q. and the dead,* живы́е и мёртвые *sb.*; *adv.* ско́ро, бы́стро; *as imper.* скоре́е! **quicken** *v.t. & i. (accelerate)* ускоря́ть(ся) *imp.*, ускори́ть(ся) *perf.*; *v.t. (animate)* оживля́ть *imp.*, оживи́ть *perf.* **quicklime** *n.* негашёная и́звесть. **quickness** *n.* быстрота́; прово́рство. **quicksand** *n.* плыву́н (-á), зыбу́чий песо́к (-ска́). **quickset** *n. (hedge)* жива́я и́згородь. **quicksilver** *n.* ртуть.

quid *n.* фунт.

quiescence *n.* неподви́жность, поко́й. **quiescent** *adj.* неподви́жный, в состоя́нии поко́я. **quiet** *n. (silence)* тишина́; *the person in q.,* челове́к; *(calm)* споко́йствие; *adj.* ти́хий (тих, -á, -о); споко́йный; *interj.* ти́ше!; *v.t. & i.* успока́ивать(ся) *imp.*, успоко́ить(ся) *perf.*

quill *n. (feather)* перо́ *(pl.* -рья, -рьев); *(spine)* игла́ *(pl.* -лы).

quilt *n. (stéganoe)* одея́ло; *v.t.* стега́ть *imp.*, вы́~ *perf.* **quilting** *n.* стёжка.

quince *n.* айва́.

quincentenary *n.* пятисотле́тие.

quinine *n.* хини́н.

quinquennial *adj.* пятиле́тний.

quintessence *n.* квинтэссе́нция.

quintet(te) *n.* квинте́т. **quintuple** *adj.* пятикра́тный. **quins, quintuplets** *n.* пять (-ти́, -тью) близнецо́в.

quip n. остро́та.

quire n. (*in manuscript*) тетра́дь; (*24 sheets*) ру́сская де́сть (*pl.* -ти, -те́й).

quirk n. причу́да.

quisling n. квислинг.

quit v.t. покида́ть *imp.*, поки́нуть *perf.*; (*dwelling*) выезжа́ть *imp.*, вы́ехать (-еду, -едешь) *perf.* из + *gen.*

quite adv. (*wholly*) совсе́м, вполне́; (*somewhat*) дово́льно; q. a few, дово́льно мно́го.

quits predic.: we are q., мы с тобо́й кви́ты; I am q. with him, я расквита́лся (*past*) с ним.

quiver[1] (*for arrows*) колча́н.

quiver[2] v.i. (*tremble*) трепета́ть (-ещу́, -е́щешь) *imp.*, дрожа́ть (-жу́, -жи́шь) *imp.* (ме́лкой дро́жью); n. тре́пет, ме́лкая дрожь.

quixotic adj. донкихо́тский.

quiz n. викторина. **quizzical** adj. насме́шливый.

quod n. тюрьма́.

quoit n. мета́тельное кольцо́ (*pl.* -льца, -ле́ц, -льцам); *pl.* (*game*) мета́ние коле́ц в цель.

quondam adj. бы́вший.

quorum n. кво́рум.

quota n. кво́та.

quotation n. (*quoting*) цити́рование; (*passage quoted*) цита́та; (*estimate*) сме́та; (*of stocks etc.*) котиро́вка; q.-marks, кавы́чки (-чек) *pl.* **quote** v.t. цити́ровать *imp.*, про~ *perf.*; ссыла́ться *imp.*, сосла́ться (сошлю́сь, -лёшься) *perf.* на + *acc.*; (*price*) назнача́ть *imp.*, назна́чить *perf.*

quotidian adj. (*daily*) ежедне́вный; (*commonplace*) обыде́нный.

quotient n. ча́стное sb.

R

rabbet n. шпунт (-á).

rabbi n. равви́н. **rabbinical** adj. равви́нский.

rabbit n. кро́лик; r. punch, уда́р в заты́лок.

rabble n. сброд, чернь.

rabid adj. бе́шеный. **rabies** n. водобоя́знь, бе́шенство.

raccoon see racoon.

race[1] n. (*ethnic r.*) ра́са; род.

race[2] n. (*contest*) (*on foot*) бег; (*of cars etc.*, *fig.*) го́нка, го́нки *f.pl.*; (*of horses*) ска́чки *f.pl.*; r.-meeting, ска́чки *f.pl.*; r.-track, трек; (*for horse r.*) скакова́я доро́жка; v.i. (*compete*) состяза́ться *imp.* в ско́рости; (*rush*) мча́ться (мчусь, мчи́шься) *imp.*; v.t. гнать (гоню́, -нишь; гнал, гнала́, гна́ло) *imp.* **racecard** n. програ́мма ска́чек. **racecourse** n. ипподро́м. **racehorse** n. скакова́я ло́шадь (*pl.* -ди, -де́й, *instr.*

-дьми́). **racer** n. (*person*) го́нщик; (*car*) го́ночный автомоби́ль m.

racial adj. ра́совый. **rac(ial)ism** n. раси́зм. **rac(ial)ist** n. раси́ст, ~ ка; adj. раси́стский.

rack[1] n. (*for fodder*) корму́шка; (*for hats etc.*) ве́шалка; (*for plates etc.*) стелла́ж (-á); (*in train etc.*) се́тка для веще́й; (*for torture*) дыба; (*cogged bar*) зубча́тая ре́йка; v.t. му́чить *imp.*, пыта́ть *imp.*; r. one's brains, лома́ть *imp.* себе́ го́лову.

rack[2] n.: go to r. and ruin, разоря́ться *imp.*, разори́ться *perf.*

racket[1] n. (*bat*) раке́тка.

racket[2] n. (*uproar*) шум (-а(у)); (*illegal activity*) рэ́кет. **racketeer** n. рэкети́р.

rac(c)oon n. ено́т.

racy adj. колори́тный.

rad n. рад.

radar n. (*system*) радиолока́ция;

(*apparatus*) радиолока́тор, рада́р; *attrib.* радиолокацио́нный, рада́рный. **radial** *adj.* радиа́льный, лучево́й.

radiance *n.* сия́ние. **radiant** *adj.* сия́ющий; лучи́стый; *n.* исто́чник (лучи́стого) тепла́, све́та. **radiate** (*v.t.* излуча́ть *imp.*; лучи́ться *imp.* + *instr.*; *v.i.* исходи́ть (-и́т) *imp.* из одно́й то́чки; (*diverge*) расходи́ться (-дя́тся) *imp.* луча́ми. **radiation** *n.* излуче́ние, радиа́ция; *r. sickness*, лучева́я боле́знь. **radiator** *n.* радиа́тор; *(in central heating)* батаре́я.

radical *adj.* коренно́й; (*polit.*) радика́льный; (*ling.*) корнево́й; *n.* (*polit., chem.*) радика́л; (*math., ling.*) ко́рень (-рня; *pl.* -рни, -рне́й) *m.* **radically** *adv.* коренны́м о́бразом, соверше́нно.

radicle *n.* корешо́к (-шка́).

radio *n.* ра́дио *neut.indecl.*; *adj.* радио-; *v.t.* ради́ровать *imp., perf.*

radio- *in comb.* радио-; *r. astronomy*, радиоастроно́мия; *r.-carbon*, радиоакти́вный изото́п углеро́да; *r.-carbon dating*, дати́рование радиоуглеро́дным ме́тодом; *r.-chemistry*, радиохи́мия; *r.-element*, радиоакти́вный элеме́нт; *r.-frequency*, (*n.*) радиочасто́та (*pl.* -ты); (*adj.*) радиочасто́тный; *r. star*, радиозвезда́ (*pl.* -ёзды); *r.-telegraphy*, радиотелегра́фия; *r.-telephone*, радиотелефо́н; *r. telescope*, радиотелеско́п; *r. wave*, радиоволна́ (*pl.* -о́лны, *dat.* -о́лнам). **radioactive** *adj.* радиоакти́вный. **radioactivity** *n.* радиоакти́вность. **radiogram** *n.* (*X-ray picture*) рентгеногра́мма; (*radiotelegram*) радиогра́мма; (*radio and gramophone*) радиогра́мма. **radiographer** *n.* рентгено́лог. **radiography** *n.* рентгеногра́фия. **radioisotope** *n.* радиоизото́п. **radiolocation** *n.* радиолока́ция. **radiologist** *n.* радио́лог; (*spec. X-ray*) рентгено́лог. **radiology** *n.* радиоло́гия. **radiometer** *n.* радио́метр. **radioscopy** *n.* рентгеноско́пия. **radiosonde** *n.* радиозо́нд. **radiotherapy** *n.* радиотерапи́я; (*spec. X-ray*) рентгенотерапи́я.

radish *n.* реди́ска; реди́с (*no pl.: plant, collect.*).

radium *n.* ра́дий.

radius *n.* (*math.*) ра́диус; (*bone*) лучева́я кость.

radon *n.* радо́н.

raffia *n.* ра́фия.

raffish *adj.* беспу́тный.

raffle *n.* лотере́я; *v.t.* разы́грывать *imp.*, разыгра́ть *perf.* в лотере́е.

raft *n.* плот (-а́, *loc.* -у́).

rafter *n.* (*beam*) стропи́ло.

raftsman *n.* плотовщи́к (-а́).

rag¹ *n.* тря́пка, лоску́т (-а́; *pl.* -а́, -о́в & -ья, -ьев); *pl.* (*clothes*) лохмо́тья (-ьев) *pl.*; *r.-and-bone man*, тряпи́чник; *r. doll*, тряпи́чная ку́кла (*gen.pl.* -кои). **rag²** *v.t.* (*tease*) дразни́ть (-ню́, -нишь) *imp.*

ragamuffin *n.* оборва́нец (-нца).

rage *n.* (*anger*) я́рость, гнев; (*desire*) страсть (for, к + *dat.*); *all the r.*, после́дний крик мо́ды; *v.i.* беси́ться (бешу́сь, бе́сишься) *imp.*; (*storm etc.*) свире́пствовать *imp.*

ragged *adj.* (*jagged*) зазу́бренный (-ен); (*of clothes*) изо́дранный (-ан, -анна); (*of person*) в лохмо́тьях.

raglan *n.* регла́н *m.*; *r. sleeve*, рука́в (-а́; *pl.* -а́) регла́н (*indecl.*).

ragout *n.* рагу́ *neut.indecl.*

ragtime *n.* рэгта́йм.

ragwort *n.* крестовник.

raid *n.* набе́г, налёт; (*by police*) обла́ва; *v.t.* де́лать *imp.*, с~ *perf.* налёт на + *acc.*

rail *n.* пери́ла (-л) *pl.*; (*rly.*) рельс; (*railway*) желе́зная доро́га; *by r.*, по́ездом, по желе́зной доро́ге; *v.t.*: *r. in, off*, обнести́ (-есу́, -есёшь) *imp.*, обноси́ть (-ошу́, -о́сишь) *imp.*, обнести́ (-есу́, -есёшь; -ёс, -есла́) *perf.* пери́лами. **railhead** *n.* коне́чный пункт (желе́зной доро́ги). **railing** *n.* пери́ла (-л) *pl.*, огра́да.

raillery *n.* доброду́шное подшу́чивание.

railway *n.* желе́зная доро́га; *attrib.* железнодоро́жный. **railwayman** *n.* железнодоро́жник.

raiment *n.* одея́ние.

rain *n.* дождь (-дя́) *m.*; *pl.* (*the r.*) пери́од (тропи́ческих) дожде́й; *r.-gauge*, дождеме́р; *r.-water*, дождева́я вода́ (*acc.* -ду); *v.impers. it is* (*was*) raining, идёт (шёл) дождь; v.t. осыпа́ть imp., осы́пать (-плю, -плешь) perf. + instr. (upon, + acc.); v.i. осыпа́ться imp., осы́паться (-плется) perf. **rainbow** n. ра́дуга; r. trout, ра́дужная форе́ль. **raincoat** n. непромока́емое пальто́ neut.indecl., плащ (-а́). **raindrop** n. дождева́я ка́пля (gen.pl. -пель). **rainfall** n. (shower) ли́вень (-вня) m.; (amount of rain) коли́чество оса́дков. **rainproof** adj. непромока́емый. **rainy** adj. дождли́вый; r. day, чёрный день (дня) m.

raise v.t. (lift) поднима́ть imp., подня́ть (подниму́, -мешь; по́дня́л, -а́, -о) perf.; (heighten) повыша́ть imp., повы́сить perf.; (erect) воздвига́ть imp., воздви́гнуть (-г) perf.; (provoke) вызыва́ть imp., вы́звать (вы́зову, -вешь) perf.; (procure) добыва́ть imp., добы́ть (добу́ду, -дешь; до́бы́л, -а́, -о) perf.; (children) расти́ть imp.

raisin n. изю́минка; pl. (collect.) изю́м (-а(у)).

raja(h) n. ра́джа (gen.pl. -жей) m.

rake[1] n. (tool) гра́бли (-блей & -бель) pl.; v.t. (r. together, up) сгреба́ть imp., сгрести́ (сгребу́, -бёшь; сгрёб, -бла́) perf.; (with shot) обстре́ливать imp., обстреля́ть perf. продо́льным огнём.

rake[2] n. (person) пове́са m. **rakish** adj. распу́тный.

rally[1] v.t. & i. спла́чивать(ся) imp., сплоти́ть(ся) perf.; v.i. (after illness etc.) оправля́ться imp., опра́виться perf.; n. (meeting) слёт (-а); ма́ссовый ми́тинг; (motoring r.) (авто)ра́лли neut.indecl.; (tennis) обме́н уда́рами.

rally[2] v.t. (ridicule) подшу́чивать imp., подшути́ть (-учу́, -у́тишь) perf. над + instr.

ram n. (sheep) бара́н; (the R., Aries) Ове́н (Овна́); (machine) тара́н; v.t. (beat down) трамбова́ть imp., у~ perf.; (drive in) вбива́ть imp., вбить (вобью́, -ьёшь) perf.; (strike with r.) тара́нить imp., про~ perf.

ramble v.i. (walk) броди́ть (-ожу́, -о́дишь) imp.; (speak) говори́ть несвя́зно; n. прогу́лка. **rambler** (rose) n. вью́щаяся ро́за. **rambling** adj.

(scattered) разбро́санный; (incoherent) бессвя́зный.

ramification n. разветвле́ние. **ramify** v.i. разветвля́ться imp., разветви́ться perf.

ramp n. скат, укло́н.

rampage v.i. нейстовствовать imp.; n. нейстовство.

rampant adj. (of lion etc.) стоя́щий на за́дних ла́пах; (raging) свире́пствующий.

rampart n. вал (loc. -у́; pl. -ы́).

ramrod n. шо́мпол (pl. -а́).

ramshackle adj. ве́тхий (ветх, -а́, -о).

ranch n. ра́нчо neut.indecl.

rancid adj. прого́рклый.

rancour n. зло́ба. **rancorous** adj. зло́бный.

random n.: at r., науда́чу, науга́д, наобу́м; adj. сде́ланный (-ан), вы́бранный (-ан), науга́д; случа́йный.

range n. (of mountains) цепь (pl. -пи, -пе́й); (grazing ground) неогоро́женное па́стбище; (artillery r.) полиго́н; (of voice) диапазо́н; (scope) круг (loc. -у́; pl. -и́), преде́лы m.pl.; (distance) да́льность; r.-finder, дальноме́р; v.t. (arrange in row) выстра́ивать imp., вы́строить perf. в ряд; v.i. (extend) тяну́ться (-нется) imp.; (occur) встреча́ться imp., встре́титься perf.; (vary) колеба́ться (-блется) imp., по~ perf.; (wander) броди́ть (-ожу́, -о́дишь) imp.

rank[1] n. (row) ряд (-а́ with 2, 3, 4; loc. -у́; pl. -ы́); (taxi r.) стоя́нка такси́; (grade) зва́ние, чин, ранг; v.t. (classify) классифици́ровать imp., perf.; (consider) счита́ть imp. (as, + instr.); v.i.: r. with, быть (fut. бу́ду, -дешь; был, -а́, не́ был, -о) perf. в числе́ + gen., на у́ровне + gen.

rank[2] adj. (luxuriant) бу́йный (бу́ен, буйна́, -но); (in smell) злово́нный (-нен, -нна); (repulsive) отврати́тельный; (clear) я́вный.

rankle v.i. причиня́ть imp., причини́ть perf. боль.

ransack v.t. (search) обша́ривать imp., обша́рить perf.; (plunder) гра́бить imp., о~ perf.

ransom n. вы́куп; v.t. выкупа́ть imp., вы́купить perf.

rant *v.t. & i.* напы́щенно декламировать *imp.*

rap[1] *n.* (*blow*) стук, ре́зкий уда́р; *v.t.* (*резко*) ударя́ть *imp.*, уда́рить *perf.*; *v.i.* стуча́ть (-чу́, -чи́шь) *imp.*, сту́кнуть *perf.*; r. *out*, (*words*) отчека́нивать *imp.*, отчека́нить *perf.*

rap[2] *n.*: not a r., ниско́лько; I don't care a r., мне наплева́ть.

rapacious *adj.* неуме́ренно жа́дный (-ден, -дна́, -дно), хи́щнический.

rape[1] *v.t.* наси́ловать *imp.*, из~ *perf.*; *n.* изнаси́лование; (*abduction*) похище́ние.

rape[2] *n.* (*plant*) рапс; r.-oil, ра́псовое ма́сло.

rapid *adj.* бы́стрый (быстр, -а́, -о бы́стры); *pl.* поро́г, быстрина́ (*pl.* -ны); **rapidity** *n.* быстрота́.

rapier *n.* рапи́ра.

rapt *adj.* восхищённый (-ён, -ённа); (*absorbed*) поглощённый (-ён, -ена́). **rapture** *n.* восто́рг. **rapturous** *adj.* восто́рженный (-ен, -енна).

rare[1] *adj.* (*of meat*) недожа́ренный (-ен).

rare[2] *adj.* ре́дкий (-док, -дка́, -дко), ре́дкостный. **rarefy** *v.t.* разрежа́ть *imp.*, разреди́ть *perf.* **rarity** *n.* ре́дкость.

rascal *n.* плут (-а́).

rase see **raze**.

rash[1] *n.* сыпь.

rash[2] *adj.* опроме́тчивый.

rasher *n.* ло́мтик (беко́на, ветчины́).

rasp *n.* (*file*) ра́шпиль *m.*; (*sound*) ре́жущий звук; a r. in the voice, скрипу́чий го́лос; *v.t.*: r. the nerves, де́йствовать *imp.*, по~ *perf.* на не́рвы.

raspberry *n.* (*plant*) мали́на (also collect., *fruit*); *attrib.* мали́новый.

rasping *adj.* (*sound*) ре́жущий, скрипу́чий.

rat *n.* кры́са; (*turncoat*) перебе́жчик; r.-catcher *n.* крысоло́в; r.-race, бе́шеная пого́ня за успе́хом; r.-trap, крысоло́вка; *v.i.*: r. on, предава́ть (-даю́, -даёшь) *imp.*, преда́ть (-а́м, -а́шь, -а́ст, -ади́м; пре́дал, -а́, -о) *perf.* + *acc.*

ratchet *n.* храпови́к (-а́); *attrib.* храпово́й.

rate *n.* но́рма, ста́вка; (*speed*) ско́рость; *pl.* ме́стные нало́ги *m.pl.*; at any r., во вся́ком слу́чае, по ме́ньшей ме́ре; at the r. of, по + *dat.*, со ско́ростью + *gen.*; *v.t.* оце́нивать *imp.*, оцени́ть (-ню́, -нишь) *perf.*; (*consider*) счита́ть *imp.* **rateable** *adj.* подлежа́щий обложе́нию ме́стным нало́гом; r. value, облага́емая сто́имость. **rate-payer** *n.* налогоплате́льщик, -ица.

rather *adv.* лу́чше, скоре́е; (*somewhat*) не́сколько, дово́льно; (*as answer*) ещё бы!; he (she) had (would) r., он (она́) предпочёл (-чла́) бы + *inf.*; or r., (и́ли) верне́е (сказа́ть), точне́е (сказа́ть); r. . . . than, скоре́е . . . чем.

ratification *n.* ратифика́ция. **ratify** *v.t.* ратифици́ровать *imp.*, *perf.*

rating *n.* оце́нка; (*naut.*) рядово́й *sb.*

ratio *n.* пропо́рция.

ration *n.* паёк (пайка́), рацио́н; *v.t.* нормирова́ть *imp.*, *perf.*; be rationed, выдава́ться (-даётся) *imp.*, вы́даться (-астся, -адутся) *perf.* по ка́рточкам.

rational *adj.* разу́мный; (also math.) рациона́льный. **rationalism** *n.* рационали́зм. **rationalist** *n.* рационали́ст. **rationalize** *v.t.* дава́ть (даю́, даёшь) *imp.*, дать (дам, дашь, даст, дади́м; дал, -а́, да́ло, -и) *perf.* рационалисти́ческое объясне́ние + *gen.*; (*industry etc.*) рационализи́ровать *imp.*, *perf.*

rattan *n.* рота́нг.

rattle *v.i. & t.* (*sound*) греме́ть (-млю́, -ми́шь) *imp.* (+ *instr.*); бряца́ть *imp.* (+ *instr.*); (*speak*) болта́ть *imp.*; *v.t.* (*fluster*) смуща́ть *imp.*, смути́ть (-ущу́, -ути́шь) *perf.*; r. along, (*move*) мча́ться (мчусь, мчи́шься) *imp.* с гро́хотом; r. off, (*utter*) отбараба́нить *perf.*; *n.* (*sound*) треск, гро́хот; (*instrument*) погрему́шка. **rattlesnake** *n.* грему́чая змея́ (*pl.* -е́и, -е́й). **rattling** *adj.* (*brisk*) бы́стрый; r. good, великоле́пный.

raucous *adj.* ре́зкий (-зок, -зка́, -зко).

ravage *v.t.* опустоша́ть *imp.*, опусто́шить *perf.*; *n.*: *pl.* разруши́тельное де́йствие.

rave *v.i.* бре́дить *imp.*; (*wind, sea*) реве́ть (-вёт) *imp.*; r. about, бре́дить *imp.* + *instr.*; восторга́ться *imp.* + *instr.*

raven n. во́рон.

ravenous adj. прожо́рливый; (*famished*) голо́дный (го́лоден, -дна́, -дно, го́лодны) как волк; r. *appetite*, во́лчий аппети́т.

ravine n. уще́лье (*gen.pl.* -лий).

ravish v.t. наси́ловать *imp.*, из~ *perf.*; (*charm*) восхища́ть *imp.*, восхити́ть (-ищу́, -ити́шь) *perf.* **ravishing** adj. восхити́тельный.

raw adj. сыро́й (сыр, -а́, -о); (*brick*) необожжённый; (*alcohol*) неразба́вленный; (*style*) неотде́ланный; (*inexperienced*) нео́пытный; (*edge of skin*) обо́дранный; (*sensitive*) чувстви́тельный; (*edge of cloth*) неподру́бленный; r.-*boned*, костля́вый; r. *material(s)*, сырьё (*no pl.*); r. *place*, (*abrasion*) цара́пина; r. *silk*, шёлк-сыре́ц (-рца́); r. *wound*, жива́я ра́на; r. *больно́е ме́сто; touch on the* r., задева́ть *imp.*, заде́ть (-е́ну, -е́нешь) *perf.* за живо́е.

rawhide n. недублёная ко́жа.

ray[1] n. (*beam*) луч (-а́); (*fig.*) про́блеск.

ray[2] n. (*fish*) скат.

rayon n. виско́за.

raze v.t.: r. *to the ground*, ровня́ть *imp.*, с~ *perf.* с землёй.

razor n. бри́тва; r.-*back*, (*ridge*) о́стрый хребе́т (-бта́); (*whale*) полоса́тик; r.-*bill*, гага́рка.

reach v.t. (*extend*) протя́гивать *imp.*, протяну́ть (-ну́, -нешь) *perf.*; (*attain, arrive at*) достига́ть *imp.*, дости́чь & дости́гнуть (-и́гну, -и́гнешь, -и́г) *perf.*+*gen.*, до+*gen.*; доходи́ть (-ожу́, -о́дишь) *imp.*, дойти́ (дойду́, -дёшь; дошёл, -шла́) *perf.* до+*gen.*; v.i. (*extend*) простира́ться *imp.*; r. до-ся-га́емость; (*of river*) плёс.

react v.i. реаги́ровать *imp.*, от~, про~ *perf.* (*to*, на+*acc.*). **reaction** n. реа́кция. **reactionary** adj. реакцио́нный; n. реакционе́р, ~ка. **reactive** adj. реаги́рующий; (*tech.*) реакти́вный. **reactor** n. реа́ктор.

read v.t. чита́ть *imp.*, про~, проче́сть (-чту́, -чтёшь; -чёл, -чла́) *perf.*; (*piece of music*) разбира́ть *imp.*, разобра́ть (разберу́, -рёшь; разобра́л, -а́, -о) *perf.*; (*of meter etc.*) пока́зывать *imp.*, показа́ть (-а́жет) *perf.*; (r. *a meter etc.*)

снима́ть *imp.*, снять (сниму́, -мешь; снял, -а́, -о) *perf.* показа́ния+*gen.*; (*univ.*) изуча́ть *imp.*; (*interpret*) толкова́ть *imp.*; v.i. чита́ться *imp.* **readable** adj. интере́сный, хорошо́ напи́санный (-ан); (*legible*) разбо́рчивый. **reader** n. чита́тель m., ~ница; (*publisher's* r.) рецензе́нт; (*printer's* r.) корре́ктор (*pl.* -а́ & -á); (*univ.*) ста́рший преподава́тель m.; (*book*) хрестома́тия.

readily adv. (*willingly*) охо́тно; (*easily*) легко́. **readiness** n. гото́вность.

reading n. чте́ние; (*erudition*) начи́танность; (*variant*) вариа́нт; (*interpretation*) толкова́ние; r.-*desk*, пюпи́тр; r.-*lamp*, насто́льная ла́мпа; r. *matter*, литерату́ра; r.-*room*, чита́льня (*gen. pl.* -лен), чита́льный зал.

ready adj. гото́вый (гот, к+*dat.*, на+*acc.*); r.-*made*, гото́вый; r. *money*, нали́чные де́ньги (-нег, -ньга́м) *pl.*; r. *reckoner*, арифмети́ческие табли́цы *f.pl.*

reagent n. реакти́в.

real adj. настоя́щий, действи́тельный, реа́льный; r. *estate*, недви́жимость. **realism** n. реали́зм. **realist** n. реали́ст. **realistic** adj. реалисти́чный, -и́ческий. **reality** n. действи́тельность; *in* r., действи́тельно. **realization** n. (*of plan etc.*) осуществле́ние; (*of assets*) реализа́ция; (*understanding*) осозна́ние. **realize** v.t. (*plan etc.*) осуществля́ть *imp.*, осуществи́ть *perf.*; (*assets*) реализова́ть *imp.*, *perf.*; (*apprehend*) осознава́ть (-наю́, -наёшь) *imp.*, осозна́ть *perf.* **really** adv. действи́тельно, в са́мом де́ле.

realm n. (*kingdom*) короле́вство; (*sphere*) о́бласть (*pl.* -ти, -те́й).

ream[1] n. сто́па (*pl.* -пы).

ream[2] v.t. развёртывать *imp.*, разверну́ть *perf.*

reap v.t. жать (жну, жнёшь) *imp.*, сжать (сожну́, -нёшь) *perf.*; (*fig.*) пожина́ть *imp.*, пожа́ть (-жну́, -жнёшь) *perf.* **reaper** n. (*person*) жнец (-а́), жни́ца; (*machine*) жа́тка; r. *and binder*, жа́тка-сноповяза́лка. **reaping-hook** n. серп (-а́).

rear[1] v.t. (*lift*) поднима́ть *imp.*, подня́ть (-ниму́, -ни́мешь; по́дня́л, -а́, -о) *perf.*; (*children*) воспи́тывать *imp.*, воспита́ть *perf.*; *v.i.* (*of horse*) станови́ться (-и́тся) *imp.*, стать (-а́нет) *perf.* на дыбы́.

rear[2] *n.* тыл (*loc.* -ý; *pl.* -ы́); bring up the r., замыка́ть *imp.*, замкну́ть *perf.* ше́ствие; *adj.* за́дний; (*also mil.*) ты́льный; (*mil.*) тылово́й; r.-admiral, контр-адмира́л; r.-light, (*of car*) за́дний фона́рь (-ря́) *m.*; r.-view mirror, зе́ркало (*pl.* -ла́) за́дней обзо́рности.

rearguard *n.* арьерга́рд; r. action, арьерга́рдный бой (*pl.* бои́). **rearwards** *adv.* наза́д.

rearm *v.t. & i.* перевооружа́ть(ся) *imp.*, перевооружи́ть(ся) *perf.* **rearmament** *n.* перевооруже́ние.

reason *n.* (*cause*) причи́на, основа́ние; (*intellect*) ра́зум, рассу́док (-дка); it stands to r., разуме́ется; not without r., не без основа́ния; *v.t.* (*discuss*) обсужда́ть *imp.*, обсуди́ть (-ужу́, -у́дишь) *perf.*; *v.i.* рассужда́ть *imp.*; r. with, (*person*) угова́ривать *imp.*+ *acc.* **reasonable** *adj.* (*sensible*) разу́мный; (*well-founded*) основа́тельный; (*inexpensive*) недорого́й (недо́рог, -а́, -о).

reassurance *n.* успока́ивание. **reassure** *v.t.* успока́ивать *imp.*, успоко́ить *perf.*

rebate *n.* ски́дка.

rebel *n.* повста́нец (-нца), бунтовщи́к (-а́); *adj.* повста́нческий; *v.i.* бунтова́ть *imp.*, взбунтова́ться *perf.* **rebellion** *n.* восста́ние, бунт. **rebellious** *adj.* мяте́жный, повста́нческий.

rebirth *n.* возрожде́ние.

rebound *v.i.* отска́кивать *imp.*, отскочи́ть (-чу́, -чишь) *perf.*; *n.* рикоше́т, отско́к.

rebuff *n.* отпо́р; *v.t.* дава́ть (даю́, даёшь) *imp.*, дать (дам, дашь, даст, дади́м; дал, -а́, да́ло́, -и) *perf.*+ *dat.* отпо́р.

rebuke *v.t.* упрека́ть *imp.*, упрекну́ть *perf.*; *n.* упрёк.

rebut *v.t.* (*refute*) опроверга́ть *imp.*, опрове́ргнуть (-г(нул), -гла) *perf.* **rebuttal** *n.* опроверже́ние.

recalcitrant *adj.* непоко́рный.

recall *v.t.* (*summon*) призыва́ть *imp.*, призва́ть (призову́, -вёшь; призва́л,

-á, -о) *perf.* обра́тно; (*an official*) отзыва́ть *imp.*, отозва́ть (отзову́, -вёшь, отозва́л, -á, -о) *perf.*; (*remember*) вспомина́ть *imp.*, вспо́мнить *perf.*; (*remind*) напомина́ть *imp.*, напо́мнить *perf.*; (r. to life) возвраща́ть *imp.*, верну́ть *perf.* к жи́зни; *n.* призы́в верну́ться; о́тзыв.

recant *v.t. & i.* отрека́ться *imp.*, отре́чься (-еку́сь, -ечёшься; -ёкся, -екла́сь) *perf.* (от+ *gen.*). **recantation** *n.* отрече́ние.

recapitulate *v.t.* резюми́ровать *imp.*, *perf.* **recapitulation** *n.* резюме́ *neut. indecl.*

recast *v.t.* перераба́тывать *imp.*, перерабо́тать *perf.*; переде́лывать *imp.*, переде́лать *perf.*

recede *v.i.* отходи́ть (-ожу́, -о́дишь) *imp.*,отойти́ (отойду́, -дёшь; отошёл, -шла́) *perf.*; отступа́ть *imp.*, отступи́ть (-плю́, -пишь) *perf.*

receipt *n.* (*receiving*) получе́ние; *pl.* (*amount*) прихо́д; (*written r.*) распи́ска, квита́нция; *v.t.* распи́сываться *imp.*, расписа́ться (-ишу́сь, -и́шешься) *perf.* на+ *prep.* **receive** *v.t.* (*accept, admit, entertain*) принима́ть *imp.*, приня́ть (приму́, -мешь; при́нял, -á, -о) *perf.*; (*acquire, be given, be sent*) получа́ть *imp.*, получи́ть (-чу́, -чишь) *perf.*; (*stolen goods*) укрыва́ть *imp.*, укры́ть (-ро́ю, -ро́ешь) *perf.* **receiver** *n.* (*official r.*) управля́ющий *sb.* иму́ществом (банкро́та); (*of stolen goods*) укрыва́тель *m.* кра́деного; (*radio, television*) приёмник; (*telephone*) тру́бка.

recension *n.* изво́д.

recent *adj.* неда́вний; (*new*) но́вый (нов, -á, -о). **recently** *adv.* неда́вно.

receptacle *n.* вмести́лище. **reception** *n.* приём; r.-room, приёмная *sb.* **receptionist** *n.* секрета́рь (-ря́) *m.*, -рша, в приёмной. **receptive** *adj.* восприи́мчивый.

recess *n.* переры́в в рабо́те; (*parl.*) кани́кулы (-л) *pl.*; (*niche*) ни́ша; *pl.* (*of the heart*) тайники́ *m.pl.* **recession** *n.* спад.

recidivist *n.* рецидиви́ст.

recipe *n.* реце́пт.

recipient *n.* получа́тель *m.*, ~ница.

reciprocal *adj.* взаи́мный; (*corresponding*) соотве́тственный; *n.* (*math.*) обра́тная величина́ (*pl.* -ны). **reciprocate** *v.t.* отвеча́ть *imp.* (взаи́мностью) на + *acc.* **reciprocating** *adj.* (*motion*) возвра́тно-поступа́тельный; (*engine*) поршнево́й. **reciprocity** *n.* взаи́мность.

recital *n.* (*account*) изложе́ние, подро́бное перечисле́ние; (*concert*) (со́льный) конце́рт. **recitation** *n.* публи́чное чте́ние. **recitative** *n.* речитати́в. **recite** *v.t.* деклами́ровать *imp.*, про ~ perf.; чита́ть *imp.*, про ~ perf. вслух; (*enumerate*) перечисля́ть *imp.*, перечи́слить perf.

reckless *adj.* (*rash*) опроме́тчивый; (*careless*) неосторо́жный.

reckon *v.t.* подсчи́тывать *imp.*, подсчита́ть perf.; (*also regard as*) счита́ть *imp.*, счесть (сочту́, -тёшь; счёл, сочла́) perf. (+ *instr.*, за + *acc.*); *v.i.*: r. with, счита́ться *imp.* c + *instr.* **reckoning** *n.* счёт, расчёт; *day of* r., час распла́ты.

reclaim *v.t.* (*reform*) исправля́ть *imp.*, испра́вить perf.; (*land*) осва́ивать *imp.*, осво́ить perf.

recline *v.i.* откидываться *imp.*, откинуться perf.; полулежа́ть (-жу́, -жишь) *imp.*

recluse *n.* затво́рник, -ица.

recognition *n.* узнава́ние; (*acknowledgement*) призна́ние. **recognize** *v.t.* (*know again*) узнава́ть (-наю́, -наёшь) *imp.*, узна́ть perf.; (*acknowledge*) признава́ть (-наю́, -наёшь) *imp.*, призна́ть perf.

recoil *v.i.* отпря́дывать *imp.*, отпря́нуть perf.; отша́тываться *imp.*, отшатну́ться perf. (from, от + *gen.*); (*of gun*) отдава́ть (-даёт) *imp.*, отда́ть (-а́ст, -аду́т; о́тдал, -а́, -о) perf.; *n.* отско́к; отда́ча.

recollect *v.t.* вспомина́ть *imp.*, вспо́мнить perf. **recollection** *n.* воспомина́ние.

recommend *v.t.* рекомендова́ть *imp.*, perf.; (*for prize etc.*) представля́ть *imp.*, предста́вить perf. (for, к + *dat.*). **recommendation** *n.* рекоменда́ция; представле́ние.

recompense *n.* вознагражде́ние; *v.t.* вознагражда́ть *imp.*, вознагради́ть perf.

reconcile *v.t.* примиря́ть *imp.*, примири́ть perf.; r. *oneself*, примиря́ться *imp.*, примири́ться perf. (to, c + *instr.*). **reconciliation** *n.* примире́ние.

recondition *v.t.* приводи́ть (-ожу́, -о́дишь) *imp.*, привести́ (-еду́, -едёшь; -ёл, -ела́) perf. в испра́вное состоя́ние.

reconnaissance *n.* разве́дка. **reconnoitre** *v.t.* разве́дывать *imp.*, разве́дать perf.

reconstruct *v.t.* перестра́ивать *imp.*, перестро́ить perf.; реконструи́ровать *imp.*, perf.; воссоздава́ть (-даю́, -даёшь) *imp.*, воссозда́ть (-а́м, -а́шь, -а́ст, -ади́м; -а́л, -ала́, -а́ло) perf. **reconstruction** *n.* перестро́йка; реконстру́кция; воссозда́ние.

record *v.t.* запи́сывать *imp.*, записа́ть (-ишу́, -и́шешь) perf.; *n.* за́пись; (*minutes*) протоко́л; (*gramophone* r.) грампласти́нка; (*sport etc.*) реко́рд; *pl.* архи́в; *off the r.*, неофициа́льно; *adj.* реко́рдный; r.-breaker, -holder, рекордсме́н, ~ ка; r.-player, пройгрыватель *m.* **recorder** *n.* (*person who records*) регистра́тор; (*judge*) рико́рдер; (*tech.*) регистри́рующий, самопи́шущий, прибо́р; (*flute*) блок-фле́йта. **recording** *n.* за́пись; (*sound* r.) звукоза́пись.

recount[1] *v.t.* (*narrate*) переска́зывать *imp.*, пересказа́ть (-ажу́, -а́жешь) perf.

re-count[2] *v.t.* (*count again*) пересчи́тывать *imp.*, пересчита́ть perf.; *n.* пересчёт.

recoup *v.t.* возмеша́ть *imp.*, возмести́ть perf. (*person, + dat.*; *loss etc., + acc.*). **recoupment** *n.* возмеще́ние.

recourse *n.*: *have* r. *to*, прибега́ть *imp.*, прибе́гнуть (-г(нул), -гла) perf. к по́мощи + *gen.*

recover *v.t.* (*regain possession*) получа́ть *imp.*, получи́ть (-чу́, -чишь) perf. обра́тно; (*debt etc.*) взы́скивать *imp.*, взыска́ть (-ыщу́, -ы́щешь) perf. (from, c + *gen.*); *v.i.* (*in health*) поправля́ться *imp.*, попра́виться perf. (from, по́сле + *gen.*). **recovery** *n.* получе́ние обра́тно; выздоровле́ние.

re-create *v.t.* вновь создава́ть (-даю́, -даёшь) *imp.*, созда́ть (-а́м, -а́шь, -аст, -ади́м) созда́л, -а́, -о) *perf.*

recreation *n.* развлече́ние, о́тдых.

recrimination *n.* взаи́мное обвине́ние.

recruit *n.* новобра́нец (-нца); *v.t.* вербова́ть (-бу́ю), за~ *perf.* **recruitment** *n.* вербо́вка.

rectangle *n.* прямоуго́льник. **rectangular** *adj.* прямоуго́льный.

rectification *n.* исправле́ние; (*chem.*) ректифика́ция; (*electr.*) выпрямле́ние. **rectify** *v.t.* исправля́ть *imp.*, испра́вить *perf.*; ректифици́ровать *imp.*, *perf.*; выпрямля́ть *imp.*, вы́прямить *perf.*

rectilinear *adj.* прямолине́йный.

rectitude *n.* че́стность.

recto *n.* нечётная пра́вая страни́ца; (*of folio*) лицева́я сторона́ (*acc.* -ону; *pl.* -о́ны, -о́н, -о́нам).

rector *n.* (*priest*) прихо́дский свяще́нник; (*univ. etc.*) ре́ктор. **rectorship** *n.* ре́кторство; *n.* дом (*pl.* -а́) прихо́дского свяще́нника.

rectum *n.* пряма́я кишка́ (*gen.pl.* -шо́к).

recumbent *adj.* лежа́чий.

recuperate *v.i.* восстана́вливать *imp.*, восстанови́ть (-влю́, -вишь) *perf.* своё здоро́вье. **recuperation** *n.* восстановле́ние здоро́вья.

recur *v.i.* повторя́ться *imp.*, повтори́ться *perf.*; *recurring decimal*, периоди́ческая дробь (*pl.* -би, -бе́й). **recurrence** *n.* повторе́ние. **recurrent** *adj.* повторя́ющийся.

red *adj.* (*in colour*, *fig.*, *polit.*) кра́сный (-сен, -сна́, -сно); (*of hair*) рыжий (рыж, -а́, -е); *n.* (*colour*) кра́сный цвет; (*fig.*, *polit.*) кра́сный *sb.*; *in the r.*, в долгу́; *r. admiral*, адмира́л; *r. blooded*, энерги́чный; *r. cabbage*, краснокоча́нная капу́ста; *r. currant*, кра́сная сморо́дина (*also collect.*); *r. deer*, благоро́дный оле́нь *m.*; *r. handed*, с поли́чным; *r. herring*, ло́жный след (*pl.* -ы́); *draw a r. herring across the track*, сбива́ть *imp.*, сбить (собью́, -ьёшь) *perf.* с то́лку; *r.-hot*, раскалённый (-ён, -ена́) докрасна́; *R. Indian*, индеец (-ейца), индиа́нка; *r. lead*, свинцо́вый су́рик (-а); *r. light*, кра́сный фона́рь (-ря́) *m.*; *see the r.*

light, предчу́вствовать *imp.* приближе́ние опа́сности; *r. pepper*, стручко́вый пе́рец (-рца); *r. tape*, волоки́та.

redbreast *n.* малиновка. **redden** *v.t.* окра́шивать *imp.*, окра́сить *perf.* в кра́сный цвет; *v.i.* красне́ть *imp.*, по~ *perf.* **reddish** *adj.* краснова́тый; (*hair*) рыжева́тый.

redeem *v.t.* (*buy back*) выкупа́ть *imp.*, вы́купить *perf.*; (*from sin*) искупа́ть *imp.*, искупи́ть (-плю́, -пишь) *perf.* **redeemer** *n.* искупи́тель *m.* **redemption** *n.* вы́куп; искупле́ние.

redolent *adj.*: *r. of*, па́хнущий + *instr.*; *be r. of*, па́хнуть (-х(нул), -хла) *imp.* + *instr.*

redouble *v.t.* удва́ивать *imp.*, удво́ить *perf.*

redoubt *n.* реду́т.

redoubtable *adj.* гро́зный (-зен, -зна́, -зно).

redound *v.i.* спосо́бствовать *imp.*, по~ *perf.* (to, + *dat.*); *r. to someone's credit*, де́лать (с~ *perf.* честь + *dat.*

redox *n.* окисле́ние-восстановле́ние.

redpoll *n.* чечётка.

redress *v.t.* исправля́ть *imp.*, испра́вить *perf.*; *r. the balance*, восстана́вливать *imp.*, восстанови́ть (-влю́, -вишь) *perf.* равнове́сие; *n.* возмеще́ние.

redshank *n.* тра́вник. **redskin** *n.* красноко́жий *sb.* **redstart** *n.* горихво́стка (-лысу́шка).

reduce *v.t.* (*decrease*) уменьша́ть *imp.*, уме́ньшить *perf.*; (*lower*) снижа́ть *imp.*, сни́зить *perf.*; (*shorten*) сокраща́ть *imp.*, сократи́ть (-ащу́, -ати́шь) *perf.*; (*bring to*) приводи́ть (-ожу́, -о́дишь) *imp.*, привести́ (-еду́, -едёшь; -ёл, -ела́) *perf.* (to, в + *acc.*); *v.i.* худе́ть *imp.*, по~ *perf.* **reduction** *n.* уменьше́ние, сниже́ние, сокраще́ние; (*amount of r.*) ски́дка.

redundancy *n.* (*excess of workers*) изли́шек (-шка) рабо́чей си́лы; (*dismissal*) увольне́ние (рабо́чих, слу́жащих). **redundant** *adj.* (*excessive*) изли́шний; (*dismissed*) уво́ленный (-ен) (по сокраще́нии шта́тов).

reduplicate *v.t.* удва́ивать *imp.*, удво́ить *perf.* **reduplication** *n.* удвое́ние.

redwing n. белобро́вик. **redwood** n. секво́йя.

reed n. (plant) тростни́к (-á), камы́ш (-á); (in mus. instrument) язычо́к (-чка́); (mus.) язычко́вый инструме́нт; a broken r., ненаде́жная опо́ра; attrib. тростнико́вый, камышо́вый; (mus.) язычко́вый; r.-pipe, свире́ль. **reedy** adj. (slender) то́нкий (-нок, -нка́, -нко, то́нки); (voice) пронзи́тельный.

reef n. (of sail; ridge) риф; r.-knot, ри́фовый у́зел (узла́) n.abs. брать (беру́, -рёшь; брал, -á, -о) impf., взять (возьму́, -мёшь, взял, -á, -о) pf. ри́фы. **reefer** n. (jacket) бушла́т; (cigarette) сигаре́та с марихуа́ной.

reek n. вонь, дурно́й за́пах; v.i.: r. (of), воня́ть impf. (+ instr.).

reel¹ n. кату́шка; (of film) руло́н; (straight) off the r., (fig.) сра́зу, без переры́ва; v.t. (on to r.) нама́тывать impf., намота́ть pf. на кату́шку; r. off, разма́тывать impf., размота́ть pf.; (story etc.) отбараба́нить pf.

reel² v.i. (be dizzy) кружи́ться (-и́тся) impf., за~ pf.; (stagger) поша́тываться impf., пошатну́ться pf.

reel³ n. (dance) рил.

refectory n. (in monastery) тра́пезная sb.; (in college) столо́вая sb.; r. table, дли́нный у́зкий обе́денный стол (-á).

refer v.t. (direct) отсыла́ть impf., ото-сла́ть (отошлю́, -лёшь) pf. (to, к + dat.); v.i.: r. to, (cite) ссыла́ться impf., сосла́ться (сошлю́сь, -лёшься) pf. на + acc.; (mention) упомина́ть impf., упомяну́ть (-ну́, -нешь) pf. + acc.; r. to drawer, обрати́тесь к чекода́телю. **referee** n. судья́ (pl. -дьи, -де́й, -дьям) m.; v.t. суди́ть (сужу́, су́дишь) impf. **reference** n. (in book etc.) ссы́лка; (mention) упомина́ние; (testimonial) рекоменда́ция; r. book, спра́вочник, r. library, спра́вочная библиоте́ка (без вы́дачи книг нá дом). **referendum** n. рефере́ндум.

refine v.t. очища́ть impf., очи́стить pf.; рафини́ровать impf., perf. **refined** adj. (in style etc.) утончённый (-ён, -ённа); (in manners) культу́рный; r. sugar, рафина́д. **refinery** n. (oil-r.) нефте-

очисти́тельный заво́д; (sugar-r.) рафина́дный заво́д.

refit n. переобору́дование; v.t. переобору́довать impf., perf.

reflect v.t. отража́ть impf., отрази́ть pf.; v.i. (meditate) размышля́ть impf., размы́слить pf. (on, о + prep.). **reflection** n. отраже́ние; размышле́ние; on r., поду́мав. **reflector** n. рефле́ктор. **reflex** n. рефле́кс; adj. рефлекто́рный; r. camera, зерка́льный фотоаппара́т. **reflexive** adj. (gram.) возвра́тный.

reform v.t. реформи́ровать impf., perf.; v.t. & i. (of people) исправля́ть(ся) impf., испра́вить(ся) pf.; n. рефо́рма, исправле́ние. **reformation** n. рефо́рма; the R., Реформа́ция. **reformatory** adj. исправи́тельный; n. исправи́тельное заведе́ние.

refract v.t. преломля́ть impf., преломи́ть (-и́т) pf. **refraction** n. рефра́кция, преломле́ние. **refractive** adj. преломля́ющий. **refractory** adj. (person) упря́мый, непоко́рный; (substance) тугопла́вкий.

refrain¹ n. припе́в.

refrain² v.i. уде́рживаться impf., удержа́ться (-жу́сь, -жишься) pf. (from, от + gen.).

refresh v.t. освежа́ть impf., освежи́ть pf.; r. oneself, подкрепля́ться impf., подкрепи́ться pf. **refreshment** n. (drink) освежа́ющий напи́ток (-тка); pl. заку́ска; r. room, буфе́т.

refrigerate v.t. охлажда́ть impf., охлади́ть pf. **refrigeration** n. охлажде́ние. **refrigerator** n. холоди́льник.

refuge n. убе́жище, прибе́жище; take r., находи́ть (-ожу́, -о́дишь) impf., найти́ (найду́, -дёшь; нашёл, -шла́) pf. убе́жище. **refugee** n. бе́женец (-нца), -нка.

refund n. возвраще́ние impf., возврати́ть (-ащу́, -ати́шь) pf.; (expenses) возмеща́ть impf., возмести́ть pf.; n. возвраще́ние (де́нег); возмеще́ние.

refusal n. отка́з; first r., пра́во пе́рвого вы́бора. **refuse**¹ v.t. отка́зывать(ся) impf., отказа́ть (-ажу́, -а́жешь) pf.

refuse² n. отбро́сы (-сов) pl., му́сор.

refutation *n.* опроверже́ние. **refute** *v.t.* опроверга́ть *imp.*, опрове́ргнуть (-г(ну)л, -гла) *perf.*

regain *v.t.* (*recover*) сно́ва приобрета́ть *imp.*, приобрести́ (-ету́, -ете́шь, -ёл, -ела́) *perf.*; (*reach*) сно́ва достига́ть *imp.*, дости́гнуть & дости́чь (-и́гну, -и́гнешь; -и́г) *perf.*

regal *adj.* короле́вский.

regale *v.t.* угоща́ть *imp.*, угости́ть *perf.* (with, + *instr.*).

regalia *n.* рега́лии *f.pl.*

regard *v.t.* смотре́ть (-рю́, -ришь) *imp.*, по ~ *perf.* на + *acc.*; (*take into account*) счита́ться *imp.* с + *instr.*; *r. as,* счита́ть *imp.* + *instr.*, за + *instr.*; *as regards,* что каса́ется + *gen.*; *n.* (*esteem*) уваже́ние; (*attention*) внима́ние; *pl.* покло́н, приве́т; *with r. to,* относи́тельно + *gen.*, что каса́ется + *gen.* **regarding** *prep.* относи́тельно + *gen.*, что каса́ется + *gen.* **regardless** *adv.* не обраща́я внима́ния; *r. of,* не счита́ясь с + *instr.*

regatta *n.* рега́та.

regency *n.* реге́нтство.

regenerate *v.t.* перерожда́ть *imp.*, переродить *perf.*; *adj.* перерождённый (-ён, -ена́). **regeneration** *n.* перерожде́ние.

regent *n.* ре́гент.

regicide *n.* (*action*) цареуби́йство; (*person*) цареуби́йца *m. & f.*

régime *n.* режи́м. **regimen** *n.* (*med.*) режи́м; (*gram.*) управле́ние.

regiment *n.* полк (-а́, *loc.* -у́). **regimental** *adj.* полково́й. **regimentation** *n.* регламента́ция.

region *n.* о́бласть (*pl.* -ти, -те́й). **regional** *adj.* областно́й, региона́льный, ме́стный.

register *n.* рее́стр, кни́га за́писей (*also mus.*); *v.t.* регистри́ровать *imp.*, за ~ *perf.*; (*express*) выража́ть *imp.*, вы́разить *perf.*; (*a letter*) отправля́ть *imp.*, отпра́вить *perf.* заказны́м. **registered** *adj.* (*letter*) заказно́й. **registrar** *n.* регистра́тор. **registration** *n.* регистра́ция, за́пись; *r. mark,* номерно́й знак. **registry** *n.* регистрату́ра; (*r. office*) отде́л за́писей а́ктов гражда́нского состоя́ния, загс.

regression *n.* регре́сс. **regressive** *adj.* регресси́вный.

regret *v.t.* сожале́ть *imp.* о + *prep.*; *I r. to say,* с сожале́нию, до́лжен сказа́ть; *n.* сожале́ние. **regretful** *adj.* по́лный (-лон, -лна́, по́лно́) сожале́ния. **regrettable** *adj.* приско́рбный.

regular *adj.* регуля́рный; (*also gram.*) пра́вильный; (*recurring*) очередно́й; (*of officer*) ка́дровый; *n.* (*coll.*) завсегда́тай. **regularity** *n.* регуля́рность. **regularize** *v.t.* упоря́дочивать *imp.*, упоря́дочить *perf.* **regulate** *v.t.* регули́ровать *imp.*, у ~ *perf.* **regulation** *n.* регули́рование; *pl.* пра́вила *neut.pl.*, уста́в; *adj.* устано́вленный.

rehabilitate *v.t.* реабилити́ровать *imp.*, *perf.* **rehabilitation** *n.* реабилита́ция.

rehash *v.t.* переде́лывать *imp.*, переде́лать *perf.*; *n.* переде́лка.

rehearsal *n.* репети́ция. **rehearse** *v.t.* репети́ровать *imp.*, от ~ *perf.*

reign *n.* ца́рствование; *v.i.* ца́рствовать *imp.*; (*prevail*) цари́ть *imp.*

reimburse *v.t.* возмеща́ть *imp.*, возмести́ть *perf.* (+ *dat. of person*). **reimbursement** *n.* возмеще́ние.

rein *n.* по́вод (*loc.* -у́; *pl.* пово́дья, -ьев); *pl.* во́жжи (-же́й) *pl.*

reincarnation *n.* перевоплоще́ние.

reindeer *n.* се́верный оле́нь *m.*; *r. moss,* оле́ний мох (м(о́)ха, *loc.* мху & м(о́)хе).

reinforce *v.t.* подкрепля́ть *imp.*, подкрепи́ть (-плю́, -пишь) *perf.*; усили́вать *imp.*, уси́лить *perf.*; *reinforced concrete,* железобето́н. **reinforcement** *n.* (*also pl.*) подкрепле́ние, усиле́ние.

reinstate *v.t.* восстана́вливать *imp.*, восстанови́ть (-влю́, -вишь) *perf.* **reinstatement** *n.* восстановле́ние.

reinsurance *n.* перестрахо́вка. **reinsure** *v.t.* перестрахо́вывать *imp.*, перестрахова́ть *perf.*

reiterate *v.t.* повторя́ть *imp.*, повторя́ть *perf.* **reiteration** *n.* повторе́ние.

reject *v.t.* отверга́ть *imp.*, отве́ргнуть (-г(ну)л, -гла) *perf.*; (*as defective*) брако́вать *imp.*, за ~ *perf.*; *n.* брако́ванное изде́лие. **rejection** *n.* отка́з (*of,* от + *gen.*); брако́вка.

rejoice v.t. ра́довать imp., об~ perf.; v.i. ра́доваться imp., об~ perf. (in, at, +dat.). **rejoicing** n. ликова́ние.

rejoin v.t. (вновь) присоединя́ться imp., присоедини́ться perf. к+dat.

rejoinder n. отве́т.

rejuvenate v.t. & i. омола́живать(ся) imp., омолоди́ть(ся) perf. **rejuvenation** n. омоложе́ние.

relapse n. рециди́в; v.i. сно́ва впада́ть imp., впасть (-аду́, -адёшь, -ал) perf. (into, в+acc.); (into illness) сно́ва заболева́ть imp., заболе́ть perf.

relate v.t. (narrate) расска́зывать imp., рассказа́ть (-ажу́, -а́жешь) perf.; (establish relation) устана́вливать imp., установи́ть (-влю́, -вишь) perf. связь между+instr.; v.i. относи́ться (-ится) imp. (to, к+dat.). **related** adj. ро́дственный (-ен, -енна). **relation** n. (narration) повествова́ние; (connection etc.) связь, отноше́ние; (person) ро́дственник, -ица; in r. to, относи́тельно+gen. **relationship** n. родство́. **relative** adj. относи́тельный; n. ро́дственник, -ица. **relativity** n. относи́тельность; (phys.) тео́рия относи́тельности.

relax v.t. & i. ослабля́ть(ся) imp., осла́бить(ся) perf.; смягча́ть(ся) imp., смягчи́ть(ся) perf. **relaxation** n. ослабле́ние, смягче́ние; (rest) о́тдых.

relay n. сме́на; (sport) эстафе́та; (electr.) реле́ neut.indecl.; (broadcast etc.) трансля́ция; v.t. сменя́ть imp., смени́ть (-ню́, -нишь) perf.; (radio) трансли́ровать imp. & perf.

release v.t. (set free) освобожда́ть imp., освободи́ть perf.; отпуска́ть imp., отпусти́ть (-ущу́, -у́стишь) perf.; (film etc.) выпуска́ть imp., вы́пустить perf.; n. освобожде́ние; вы́пуск.

relegate v.t. переводи́ть (-ожу́, -о́дишь) imp., перевести́ (-еду́, -едёшь; -ёл, -ела́) perf. (в бо́лее ни́зкий класс, (sport) в ни́зшую ли́гу). **relegation** n. перево́д (в бо́лее ни́зкий класс, в ни́зшую ли́гу).

relent v.i. смягча́ться imp., смягчи́ться perf. **relentless** adj. неумоли́мый, непрекло́нный (-нен, -нна).

relevance n. уме́стность. **relevant** adj. относя́щийся к де́лу; уме́стный.

reliable adj. надёжный. **reliance** n. дове́рие. **reliant** adj. уве́ренный (-ен, -енна).

relic n. оста́ток (-тка), рели́квия; pl. (of saint) мо́щи (-ще́й) pl.

relief[1] n. (art, geol.) релье́ф.

relief[2] n. (alleviation) облегче́ние; (assistance) по́мощь; (in duty) сме́на; (raising of siege) сня́тие оса́ды. **relieve** v.t. (alleviate) облегча́ть imp., облегчи́ть perf.; (help) ока́зывать imp., оказа́ть (-ажу́, -а́жешь) perf. по́мощь +dat.; (replace) сменя́ть imp., смени́ть (-ню́, -нишь) perf.; (raise siege) снима́ть imp., снять (сниму́, -мешь; снял, -á, -о) perf. оса́ду с+gen.

religion n. рели́гия. **religious** adj. религио́зный.

relinquish v.t. оставля́ть imp., оста́вить perf.; (right etc.) отка́зываться imp., отказа́ться (-ажу́сь, -а́жешься) perf. от+gen.

reliquary n. ра́ка.

relish n. (enjoyment) смак, наслажде́ние; (condiment) припра́ва; v.t. смакова́ть imp.

reluctance n. неохо́та. **reluctant** adj. неохо́тный; be r. to, не жела́ть imp.+ inf.

rely v.i. полага́ться imp., положи́ться (-жу́сь, -жишься) perf. (on, на+acc.).

remain v.i. остава́ться (-аю́сь, -аёшься) imp., оста́ться (-а́нусь, -а́нешься) perf. **remainder** n. оста́ток (-тка); (books) кни́жные оста́тки m.pl.; v.t. распродава́ть (-даю́, -даёшь) imp., распрода́ть (-а́м, -а́шь, -а́ст, -ади́м; распро́дал, -á, -о) perf. по дешёвой цене́. **remains** n. оста́тки m.pl.; (human r.) оста́нки (-ков) pl.

remand v.t. отсыла́ть imp., отосла́ть (отошлю́, -лёшь) perf. под стра́жу; n. отсы́лка под стра́жу; prisoner on r., подсле́дственный sb.

remark v.t. замеча́ть imp., заме́тить perf.; n. замеча́ние. **remarkable** adj. замеча́тельный.

remedial adj. лече́бный. **remedy** n. сре́дство (for, от, про́тив, +gen.); v.t. исправля́ть imp., испра́вить perf.

remember *v.t.* вспомина́ть *imp.*, вспо́мнить *perf.* o+*prep.*; по́мниться *imp. impers.*+*dat.*; (*greet*) передава́ть (-даю́, -даёшь) *imp.*, переда́ть (-а́м, -а́шь, -а́ст, -ади́м) *perf.* приве́т от+*gen.* (*to*, +*dat.*). **remembrance** *n.* па́мять; *pl.* приве́т.

remind *v.t.* напомина́ть *imp.*, напо́мнить *perf.*+*dat.* (*of*, +*acc.*, o+*prep.*). **reminder** *n.* напомина́ние.

reminiscence *n.* воспомина́ние. **reminiscent** *adj.* напомина́ющий.

remiss *predic.* небре́жен (-жна). **remission** *n.* отпуще́ние. **remit** *v.t.* пересыла́ть *imp.*, пересла́ть (-ешлю́, -ешлёшь) *perf.* **remittance** *n.* пересы́лка; (*money*) де́нежный перево́д.

remnant *n.* оста́ток (-тка).

remonstrance *n.* проте́ст. **remonstrate** *v.i.* *r. with*, увещева́ть *imp.*+*acc.*

remorse *n.* угрызе́ния *neut.pl.* со́вести. **remorseful** *adj.* по́лный (-лон, -лна́, по́лно́) раска́яния. **remorseless** *adj.* беспоща́дный.

remote *adj.* да́льний, отдалённый (-ён, -ённа), *r. control*, дистанцио́нное управле́ние, телеуправле́ние.

removal *n.* смеще́ние, устране́ние; (*change of house*) перее́зд. **remove** *v.t.* смеща́ть *imp.*, смести́ть *perf.*; устраня́ть *imp.*, устрани́ть *perf.*; *v.i.* переезжа́ть *imp.*, перее́хать (-е́ду, -е́дешь) *perf.*; *n.* шаг, сте́пень (*pl.* -ни, -не́й) (отдаления). **removed** *adj.* далёкий (-ёк, -ека́, -ёко́); *once r.*, двою́родный; *twice r.*, трою́родный.

remuneration *n.* вознагражде́ние. **remunerative** *adj.* вы́годный.

renaissance *n.* возрожде́ние; *the R.*, Ренесса́нс.

renal *adj.* по́чечный.

renascence *n.* возрожде́ние.

render *v.t.* воздава́ть (-даю́, -даёшь) *imp.*, возда́ть (-а́м, -а́шь, -а́ст, -ади́м; во́зда́л, -а́, -о) *perf.*; (*help etc.*) ока́зывать *imp.*, оказа́ть (-ажу́, -а́жешь) *perf.*; (*role etc.*) исполня́ть *imp.*, испо́лнить *perf.*; (*transmit*) передава́ть (-даю́, -даёшь) *imp.*, переда́ть (-а́м, -а́шь, -а́ст, -ади́м; пе́реда́л, -а́, -о) *perf.*; (*fat*) топи́ть (-плю́, -пишь) *imp.*; (*stone*) штука-

ту́рить *imp.*, o~, от~ *perf.* **rendering** *n.* исполне́ние; переда́ча; выта́пливание.

rendezvous *n.* (*meeting*) свида́ние, встре́ча; (*meeting-place*) ме́сто (*pl.* -та́) свида́ния, встре́чи; *v.i.* встреча́ться *imp.*, встре́титься *perf.*; собира́ться *imp.*, собра́ться (-берётся, собра́лся, -ало́сь) *perf.*

renegade *n.* ренега́т, ~ка.

renew *v.t.* (*возобновля́ть *imp.*, (воз)обнови́ть *perf.*; (*of agreement etc.*) продлева́ть *imp.*, продли́ть *perf.* срок де́йствия+*gen.* **renewal** *n.* (воз)обновле́ние; продле́ние (сро́ка де́йствия).

rennet *n.* сычу́жина.

renounce *v.t.* отка́зываться *imp.*, отка́за́ться (-ажу́сь, -а́жешься) *perf.* от+*gen.*; отрека́ться *imp.*, отре́чься (-еку́сь, -ечёшься; -ёкся, -екла́сь) *perf.* от+*gen.*

renovate *v.t.* ремонти́ровать *imp.*, от~ *perf.* **renovation** *n.* ремо́нт.

renown *n.* изве́стность, сла́ва. **renowned** *adj.* изве́стный; *be r. for*, сла́виться *imp.*+*instr.*

rent[1] *n.* (*tear*) проре́ха, дыра́ (*pl.* -ры).

rent[2] *n.* (*for premises*) аре́нда; аре́ндная, кварти́рная, пла́та; (*for land*) ре́нта; *v.t.* (*of tenant*) арендова́ть *imp.*, *perf.*; брать (беру́, -рёшь; брал, -а́, -о) *imp.*, взять (возьму́, -мёшь; взял, -а́, -о) *perf.* в аре́нду; (*of owner*) сдава́ть (сдаю́, сдаёшь) *imp.*, сдать (-а́м, -а́шь, -а́ст, -ади́м; сдал, -а́, -о) *perf.* в аре́нду.

renunciation *n.* отка́з, отрече́ние (*of*, от+*gen.*).

rep(p)[1] *n.* (*fabric*) репс.

rep[2] *n.* (*commercial traveller*) комми-вояжёр.

repair[1] *v.t.* (*resort*) направля́ться *imp.*, напра́виться *perf.*

repair[2] *v.t.* (*restore*) ремонти́ровать *imp.*, от~ *perf.*; (*clothing etc.*) чини́ть (-ню́, -нишь) *imp.*, по~ *perf.*; (*error etc.*) исправля́ть *imp.*, испра́вить *perf.*; *n.* (*also pl.*) ремо́нт (*only sing.*); почи́нка; (*good condition*) испра́вность; *out of r.*, в неиспра́вном состоя́нии; *attrib.* ремо́нтный; почи́ночный.

reparation *n.* возмещение; *pl.* репарации *f.pl.*

repartee *n.* остроумный, находчивый, ответ.

repatriate *v.t.* репатриировать *imp.*, *perf.* **repatriation** *n.* репатриация.

repay *v.t.* отплачивать *imp.*, отплатить (-ачу, -атишь) *perf.* (person, + *dat.*); вознаграждать *imp.*, вознаградить *perf.* (action, за + *instr.*). **repayment** *n.* отплата; вознаграждение.

repeal *v.t.* отменять *imp.*, отменить (-ню, -нишь) *perf.*; *n.* отмена.

repeat *v.t.* & *i.* повторять(ся) *imp.*, повторить(ся) *perf.*; *n.* повторение. **repeatedly** *adv.* неоднократно.

repel *v.t.* отталкивать *imp.*, оттолкнуть *perf.*; отражать *imp.*, отразить *perf.*

repent *v.i.* раскаиваться *imp.*, раскаяться (-аюсь, -аешься) *perf.* (of, в + *prep.*). **repentance** *n.* раскаяние. **repentant** *adj.* раскаивающийся.

repercussion *n.* (of event) последствие.

repertoire *n.* репертуар. **repertory** *n.* (store) запас; (repertoire) репертуар; *r. company*, постоянная труппа.

repetition *n.* повторение. **repetitious, repetitive** *adj.* (беспрестанно) повторяющийся.

replace *v.t.* (put back) класть (-аду, -адёшь; -ал) *imp.*, положить (-жу, -жишь) *perf.* обратно (на место); (substitute) заменять *imp.*, заменить (-ню, -нишь) *perf.* (by, + *instr.*); замещать *imp.*, заместить *perf.* **replacement** *n.* замена, замещение.

replenish *v.t.* пополнять *imp.*, пополнить *perf.* **replenishment** *n.* пополнение.

replete *adj.* пресыщенный (-ен), наполненный (-ен); (sated) сытый (сыт, -а, -о).

replica *n.* точная копия.

reply *v.t.* & *i.* отвечать *imp.*, ответить *perf.* (to, на + *acc.*); *n.* ответ; *r. paid*, с оплаченным ответом.

report *v.t.* (relate) сообщать *imp.*, сообщить *perf.*; (formally) докладывать *imp.*, доложить (-жу, -жишь) *perf.*; *v.i.* (present oneself) являться *imp.*, явиться (явлюсь, явишься) *perf.*; *n.* сообщение; доклад; (school)

табель *m.* успеваемости; (sound) звук взрыва, выстрела. **reporter** *n.* репортёр, корреспондент.

repose *v.i.* (lie) лежать (-жу, -жишь) *imp.*; (rest) отдыхать *imp.*, отдохнуть *perf.*; *n.* (rest) отдых; (peace) покой.

repository *n.* хранилище.

repp *see* **rep**[1].

reprehensible *adj.* предосудительный.

represent *v.t.* представлять *imp.*; (portray) изображать *imp.*, изобразить *perf.* **representation** *n.* представительство, представление; изображение. **representative** *adj.* изображающий (of, + *acc.*); (typical) типичный; (polit.) представительный; *n.* представитель *m.*

repress *v.t.* подавлять *imp.*, подавить (-влю, -вишь) *perf.* репрессировать *imp.*, *perf.* **repression** *n.* подавление, репрессия. **repressive** *adj.* репрессивный.

reprieve *v.t.* отсрочивать *imp.*, отсрочить *perf.* + *dat.* приведение в исполнение (смертного) приговора; *n.* отсрочка приведения в исполнение (смертного) приговора.

reprimand *n.* выговор; *v.t.* делать *imp.*, с~ *perf.* выговор + *dat.*

reprint *v.t.* переиздавать (-даю, -даёшь) *imp.*, переиздать (-ам, -ашь, -аст, -адим; -ал, -ала, -ало) *perf.*; перепечатывать *imp.*, перепечатать *perf.*; *n.* переиздание; перепечатка.

reprisal *n.* репрессалия.

reproach *v.t.* упрекать *imp.*, упрекнуть *perf.* (with, в + *prep.*); укорять *imp.*, укорить *perf.* (with, в + *prep.*); *n.* упрёк, укор. **reproachful** *adj.* укоризненный.

reproduce *v.t.* воспроизводить (-ожу, -одишь) *imp.*, воспроизвести (-еду, -едёшь; -ёл, -ела) *perf.* **reproduction** *n.* (action) воспроизведение; (object) копия, репродукция. **reproductive** *adj.* воспроизводительный.

reproof *n.* порицание. **reprove** *v.t.* порицать *imp.*

reptile *n.* пресмыкающееся *sb.*

republic *n.* республика. **republican** *adj.* республиканский; *n.* республиканец (-нца), -нка.

repudiate *v.t.* отказываться *imp.*, отказаться (-ажусь, -ажешься) *perf.* от + *gen.*; (*reject*) отвергать *imp.*, отвергнуть (-г(нул), -гла) *perf.* **repudiation** *n.* отказ (of, от + *gen.*).

repugnance *n.* отвращение. **repugnant** *adj.* противный.

repulse *v.t.* отражать *imp.*, отразить *perf.* **repulsion** *n.* отвращение. **repulsive** *adj.* отвратительный, противный.

reputable *adj.* пользующийся хорошей репутацией. **reputation**, **repute** *n.* репутация, слава. **reputed** *adj.* предполагаемый.

request *n.* просьба; *by*, *on*, *r.*, по просьбе; *in* (*great*) *r.*, в (большом) спросе; *r. stop*, остановка по требованию; *v.t.* просить (-ошу, -осишь) *imp.*, по ~ *perf.* + *acc.*, + *gen.*, о + *prep.* (*person*, + *acc.*).

requiem *n.* реквием.

require *v.t.* (*demand*, *need*) требовать *imp.*, по ~ *perf.* + *gen.*; (*need*) нуждаться *imp.* в + *prep.* **requirement** *n.* (*necessity*) потребность. **requisite** *adj.* необходимый; *n.* необходимое *sb.*, необходимая вещь (*pl.* -щи, -щей). **requisition** *n.* реквизиция; *v.t.* реквизировать *imp.*, *perf.*

requite *v.t.* отплачивать *imp.*, отплатить (-ачу, -атишь) *perf.* (for, за + *acc.*; with, + *instr.*)

rescind *v.t.* отменять *imp.*, отменить (-ню, -нишь) *perf.*

rescue *v.t.* спасать *imp.*, спасти (-су, -сёшь; -с, -сла) *perf.*; *n.* спасение; *attrib.* спасательный. **rescuer** *n.* спаситель *m.*

research *n.* исследование (+ *gen.*); (*occupation*) научно-исследовательская работа; *v.i.* заниматься *imp.*, заняться (займусь, -мёшься; занялся, -лась) *perf.* исследованиями, научно-исследовательской работой; *r. into*, исследовать *imp.*, *perf.* + *acc.* **researcher** *n.* исследователь *m.*

resemblance *n.* сходство. **resemble** *v.t.* походить (-ожу, -одишь) *imp.* на + *acc.*

resent *v.t.* (*be indignant*) негодовать *imp.* на + *acc.*, против + *gen.*; (*take offence*) обижаться *imp.*, обидеться

(-ижусь, -идишься) *perf.* на + *acc.* **resentful** *adj.* обидчивый. **resentment** *n.* негодование; обида.

reservation *n.* (*proviso etc.*) оговорка; (*booking*) предварительный заказ; (*tract of land*) резервация. **reserve** *v.t.* (*postpone*) откладывать *imp.*, отложить (-жу, -жишь); (*keep in stock*) резервировать *imp.*, *perf.*; (*book*) заранее заказывать *imp.*, заказать (-ажу, -ажешь) *perf.*; бронировать *imp.*, за ~ *perf.*; *n.* (*stock*; *mil.*) запас, резерв; (*sport*) запасной игрок (-а); (*nature r. etc.*) заповедник; (*proviso*) оговорка; (*r. price*) низшая отплатная цена (*acc.* -ну); (*self-restraint*) сдержанность; *attrib.* запасной, запасный, резервный. **reserved** *adj.* (*person*) сдержанный (-ан, -анна). **reservist** *n.* резервист. **reservoir** *n.* резервуар, водохранилище; (*of knowledge etc.*) запас.

reside *v.i.* проживать *imp.*; (*of right etc.*) принадлежать (-жит) *imp.* (in, + *dat.*). **residence** *n.* (*residing*) проживание; (*abode*) местожительство; (*official r. etc.*) резиденция. **resident** *n.* (*permanent*) житель *m.*, ~ ница; (*adj.* проживающий; (*population*) постоянный; *r. physician*, врач, живущий при больнице. **residential** *adj.* жилой; *r. qualification*, ценз оседлости.

residual *adj.* остаточный. **residuary** *adj.* (*of estate*) оставшийся. **residue** *n.* остаток (-тка); (*of estate*) оставшееся наследство.

resign *v.t.* отказываться *imp.*, отказаться (-ажусь, -ажешься) *perf.* от + *gen.*; *v.i.* уходить (-ожу, -одишь) *imp.*, уйти (уйду, -дёшь; ушёл, ушла) *perf.* в отставку; (*chess*) сдавать (слаю, слаёшь) *imp.*, сдать (-ам, -ашь, -аст, -адим; сдал, -а, -о) *perf.* партию; *r. oneself to*, покоряться *imp.*, покориться *perf.* + *dat.* **resignation** *n.* отставка, заявление об отставке; (*being resigned*) покорность; (*chess*) сдача. **resigned** *adj.* покорный.

resilient *adj.* упругий; (*person*) неунывающий.

resin *n.* смола (*pl.* -лы). **resinous** *adj.* смолистый.

resist *v.t.* сопротивля́ться *imp.* + *dat.*; не поддава́ться (-даю́сь, -даёшься) *imp.* + *dat.* **resistance** *n.* сопротивле́ние; (*r. movement*) движе́ние сопротивле́ния. **resistant** *adj.* про́чный (-чен, -чна́, -чно, про́чны). **resistor** *n.* резисто́р.

resolute *adj.* реши́тельный. **resolution** *n.* (*character*) реши́тельность, реши́мость; (*at meeting etc.*) резолю́ция; (*of problem; mus.*) разреше́ние. **resolve** *v.t.* реша́ть *imp.*, реши́ть *perf.*; разреша́ть *imp.*, разреши́ть *perf.*; *v.t.* & *i.* (*decide*) реша́ться *imp.*, реши́ться *perf.* + *inf.*, на + *acc.*; (*of meeting etc.*) выноси́ть (-ит) *imp.*, вы́нести (-сет; -с) *perf.* резолю́цию; *n.* реше́ние.

resonance *n.* резона́нс. **resonant** *adj.* раздаю́щийся; зву́чный (-чен, -чна́, -чно). **resonate** *v.i.* резони́ровать *imp.*

resort *v.i.* *r. to*, прибега́ть *imp.*, прибе́гнуть (-г(нул), -гла) *perf.* к + *dat.*; (*visit*) (ча́сто) посеща́ть *imp.* + *acc.*; *n.* (*expedient*) сре́дство; (*health r. etc.*) куро́рт; *in the last r.*, в кра́йнем слу́чае; *without r. to*, не прибега́я к + *dat.*

resound *v.i.* (*of sound etc.*) раздава́ться (-даётся) *imp.*, разда́ться (-а́стся, -аду́тся; -а́лся, -ала́сь) *perf.*; (*of place etc.*) оглаша́ться *imp.*, огласи́ться *perf.* (with, + *instr.*).

resource *n.* (*usu. pl.*) ресу́рс, сре́дство; (*expedient*) сре́дство, возмо́жность; (*ingenuity*) нахо́дчивость. **resourceful** *adj.* нахо́дчивый.

respect *n.* (*relation*) отноше́ние; (*esteem*) уваже́ние; *in r. of*, *with r. to*, что каса́ется + *gen.*, в отноше́нии + *gen.*; *v.t.* уважа́ть *imp.*, почита́ть *imp.* **respectability** *n.* почте́нность, респекта́бельность. **respectable** *adj.* почте́нный (-нен, -нна), респекта́бельный. **respectful** *adj.* почти́тельный. **respective** *adj.* соотве́тственный (-ен, -енна). **respectively** *adv.* соотве́тственно.

respiration *n.* дыха́ние; *artificial r.*, иску́сственное дыха́ние. **respirator** *n.* респира́тор.

respite *n.* переды́шка.

resplendent *adj.* блестя́щий; сверка́ющий.

respond *v.i.* *r. to*, отзыва́ться *imp.*, отозва́ться (отзову́сь, -вёшься; отозва́лся, -ала́сь, -а́ло́сь) *perf.* на + *acc.*; реаги́ровать *imp.*, про —, от — *perf.* на + *acc.* **respondent** *n.* отве́тчик, -ица.

response *n.* отве́т; о́тклик. **responsibility** *n.* отве́тственность, обя́занность. **responsible** *adj.* отве́тственный (-ен, -енна) (to, пе́ред + *instr.*; for, за + *acc.*). **responsive** *adj.* отзы́вчивый.

rest[1] *v.i.* отдыха́ть *imp.*, отдохну́ть *perf.*; поко́иться *imp.* (upon, на + *prep.*); *v.t.* (*place*) класть (-аду́, -адёшь; -ал) *imp.*, положи́ть (-жу́, -жишь) *perf.*; (*allow to r.*) дава́ть (даю́, даёшь) *imp.*, дать (дам, дашь, даст, дади́м; дал, -а́, да́ло́, -и) *perf.* о́тдых + *dat.*; (*in repose*) о́тдых; (*peace*) поко́й; (*mus.*) па́уза; (*support*) опо́ра, подста́вка.

rest[2] *n.* (*the remainder*) оста́ток (-тка), остально́е (-о́го); (*the others*) остальны́е *sb.*, други́е *sb.*; *for the r.*, что каса́ется остально́го, что до остально́го.

restaurant *n.* рестора́н.

restful *adj.* споко́йный, ти́хий (тих, -а́, -о); (*soothing*) успока́ивающий.

restitution *n.* (*restoring*) возвраще́ние; (*reparation*) возмеще́ние убы́тков.

restive *adj.* (*horse*) норови́стый; (*person; restless*) беспоко́йный; (*wilful*) своенра́вный.

restless *adj.* беспоко́йный; (*uneasy*) неспоко́йный, трево́жный.

restoration *n.* реставра́ция, восстановле́ние. **restore** *v.t.* реставри́ровать *imp.*, *perf.*; восстана́вливать *imp.*, восстанови́ть (-влю́, -вишь) *perf.*

restrain *v.t.* сде́рживать *imp.*, сдержа́ть (-жу́, -жишь) *perf.*; уде́рживать *imp.*, удержа́ть (-жу́, -жишь) *perf.* (from, от + *gen.*). **restraint** *n.* (*reserve*) сде́ржанность; (*restriction*) ограниче́ние; (*confinement*) заключе́ние; *without r.*, свобо́дно, без у́держу.

restrict *v.t.* ограни́чивать *imp.*, ограни́чить *perf.* **restriction** *n.* ограниче́ние. **restrictive** *adj.* ограничи́тельный.

result *v.i.* сле́довать (-дует) *imp.*, произойти́ (-ойдёт; -ошёл, -ошла́) *perf.* в результа́те; *r. in*, конча́ться *imp.*, ко́нчиться *perf.* + *instr.*

n. результа́т.

resume *v.t.* возобновля́ть *imp.*, возобнови́ть *perf.* **résumé** *n.* резюме́ *neut.indecl.* **resumption** *n.* возобновле́ние.

resurrect *v.t.* воскреша́ть *imp.*, воскреси́ть *perf.* **resurrection** *n.* (*of the dead*) воскресе́ние; (*to memory etc.*) воскреше́ние.

resuscitate *v.t.* приводи́ть (-ожу́, -о́дишь) *imp.*, привести́ (-еду́, -едёшь, -ёл, -ела́) *perf.* в созна́ние.

retail *n.* ро́зничная прода́жа; *attrib.* ро́зничный; *adv.* в ро́зницу; *v.t.* продава́ть (-даю́, -даёшь) *imp.*, прода́ть (-а́м, -а́шь, -а́ст, -ади́м; про́дал, -а́, -о) *perf.* в ро́зницу; *v.i.* продава́ться (-даётся) *imp.* в ро́зницу. **retailer** *n.* ро́зничный торго́вец (-вца).

retain *v.t.* уде́рживать *imp.*, удержа́ть (-жу́, -жишь) *perf.*; (*preserve*) сохраня́ть *imp.*, сохрани́ть *perf.*

retaliate *v.i.* отпла́чивать *imp.*, отплати́ть (-ачу́, -а́тишь) *perf.* тем же (са́мым); (*make reprisals*) применя́ть *imp.*, примени́ть (-ню́, -нишь) *perf.* репресса́лии. **retaliation** *n.* отпла́та, возме́здие.

retard *v.t.* замедля́ть *imp.*, заме́длить *perf.* **retarded** *adj.* отста́лый.

retch *v.i.* рвать (рвёт; рва́ло) *imp. impers.* + *acc.*

retention *n.* удержа́ние; (*preservation*) сохране́ние. **retentive** *adj.* уде́рживающий; (*memory*) хоро́ший.

reticence *n.* (*restraint*) сде́ржанность; (*secretiveness*) скры́тность. **reticent** *adj.* сде́ржанный (-ан, -анна); скры́тный.

reticulated *adj.* се́тчатый. **reticulation** *n.* се́тчатый узо́р, се́тчатое строе́ние.

retina *n.* сетча́тка.

retinue *n.* сви́та.

retire *v.i.* (*withdraw*) уединя́ться *imp.*, уедини́ться *perf.*; (*from office etc.*) уходи́ть (-ожу́, -о́дишь) *imp.*, уйти́ (уйду́, -дёшь; ушёл, ушла́) *perf.* в отста́вку. **retired** *adj.* отставно́й, в отста́вке. **retirement** *n.* отста́вка. **retiring** *adj.* скро́мный (-мен, -мна́, -мно).

retort[1] *v.t.* отвеча́ть *imp.*, отве́тить *perf.* тем же (on, на + *acc.*); *v.i.* возража́ть *imp.*, возрази́ть *perf.*; *n.* возраже́ние; (*reply*) нахо́дчивый отве́т, остроу́мная ре́плика.

retort[2] *n.* (*vessel*) рето́рта.

retouch *v.t.* ретуши́ровать *imp.*, *perf.*, or ~ *perf.*

retrace *v.t.*: *r. one's steps*, возвраща́ться *imp.*, возврати́ться (-ащу́сь, -ати́шься) *perf.*

retract *v.t.* (*draw in*) втя́гивать *imp.*, втяну́ть (-яну́, -я́нешь) *perf.*; (*take back*) брать (беру́, -рёшь; брал, -а́, -о) *imp.*, взять (возьму́, -мёшь; взял, -а́, -о) *perf.* наза́д.

retread *v.t.* (*tyre*) возобновля́ть *imp.*, возобнови́ть *perf.* проте́ктор + *gen.*; *n.* ши́на с возобновлённым проте́ктором.

retreat *v.i.* отступа́ть *imp.*, отступи́ть (-плю́, -пишь) *perf.*; *n.* отступле́ние; (*signal*) отбо́й; (*withdrawal*) уедине́ние; (*refuge*) убе́жище.

retrench *v.t. & i.* сокраща́ть *imp.*, сократи́ть (-ащу́, -ати́шь) *perf.* (рас-хо́ды). **retrenchment** *n.* сокраще́ние расхо́дов.

retribution *n.* возме́здие, ка́ра.

retrieval *n.* (*recovery*) восстановле́ние; (*computing*) по́иск (информа́ции); (*repair*) исправле́ние; *v.t.* восстана́вливать *imp.*, восстанови́ть (-влю́, -вишь) *perf.*; (*repair*) исправля́ть *imp.*, испра́вить *perf.*

retroactive *adj.* (*leg.*) име́ющий обра́тную си́лу. **retrograde** *adj.* ретрогра́дный. **retrogress** *v.i.* дви́гаться (-аюсь, -аешься & дви́жусь, -жешься) *imp.* наза́д; регресси́ровать *imp.* **retro-rocket** *n.* ретрораке́та. **retrospect** *n.* ретроспекти́вный взгляд; *in r.*, ретроспекти́вно. **retrospective** *adj.* обращённый (-ён, -ена́) в про́шлое, ретроспекти́вный; (*leg.*) име́ющий обра́тную си́лу.

return *v.t. & i.* (*give back; come back*) возвраща́ть(ся), возврати́ть(ся) (-ащу́(сь), -ати́шь(ся)) *imp.*, верну́ть(ся) *perf.*; *v.t.* (*reply to*) отвеча́ть *imp.*, отве́тить *perf.* на + *acc.*; (*elect*) избира́ть *imp.*, избра́ть (избери́, -рёшь; избра́л, -á, -о) *perf.*; *n.* возвраще́ние; возвра́т; (*proceeds*) при́быль; by r., обра́тной по́чтой; in r., взаме́н (for, + *gen.*); r. match, отве́тный матч; r. ticket, обра́тный биле́т.

reunion *n.* встре́ча (друзе́й и т.п.); family r., сбор всей семьи́. **reunite** *v.t.* воссоединя́ть *imp.*, воссоедини́ть *perf.*

rev *n.* оборо́т; *v.t. & i.:* r. up, ускоря́ть *imp.*, ускори́ть *perf.* (дви́гатель *m.*).

revanchism *n.* реванши́зм. **revanchist** *n.* реванши́ст.

reveal *v.t.* обнару́живать *imp.*, обнару́жить *perf.*; раскрыва́ть *imp.*, раскры́ть (-ро́ю, -ро́ешь) *perf.*

reveille *n.* подъём.

revel *v.i.* пирова́ть *imp.*; r. in, наслажда́ться *imp.* + *instr.*

revelation *n.* открове́ние; откры́тие; R. (*eccl.*) апока́липсис.

revenge *v.t.:* r. oneself, мстить *imp.*, ото~ *perf.* (for, за + *acc.*; on, + *dat.*); *n.* месть, отомще́ние. **revengeful** *adj.* мсти́тельный.

revenue *n.* дохо́д; *adj.* тамо́женный.

reverberate *v.t. & i.* отража́ть(ся) *imp.* **reverberation** *n.* отраже́ние; (*fig.*) о́тзвук.

revere *v.t.* почита́ть *imp.*, уважа́ть *imp.* **reverence** *n.* благогове́ние; почте́ние. **reverend** *adj.* (in title) (его́) преподо́бие. **reverential** *adj.* благогове́йный.

reverie *n.* мечты́ (*gen.* -та́ний) *f.pl.*

reversal *n.* по́лное измене́ние; (of decision) отме́на. **reverse** *adj.* обра́тный; r. gear, за́дний ход; *v.t.* изменя́ть *imp.*, измени́ть (-ню́, -нишь) *perf.* на обра́тный; (*revoke*) отменя́ть *imp.*, отмени́ть (-ню́, -нишь) *perf.*; *v.i.* дава́ть (даю́, даёшь) *imp.*, дать (дам, дашь, даст, дади́м; дал, -á, да́ло, -и) *perf.* за́дний ход; *n.* (the r.) обра́тное *sb.*, противополо́жное *sb.*; (r. gear) за́дний ход; (r. side) за́дняя сторона́ (*acc.* -ону, *pl.* -оны, -óн, -она́м); (*misfortune*) неуда́ча; (*defeat*) пораже́ние. **reversible** *adj.* обра́тимый; (*cloth*) двусторо́нний. **reversion** *n.* возвраще́ние. **reversion** *n.* реве́рсия. **revert** *v.i.*

возвраща́ться (-аю́сь, -ати́шься) *imp.* (to, в + *acc.*, к + *dat.*); (*leg.*) переходи́ть (-и́т) *imp.*, перейти́ (-йдёт; -ешёл, -ешла́) *perf.* к пре́жнему владе́льцу.

review *n.* (*leg.*) пересмо́тр; (*mil.*) смотр, пара́д; (*survey*) обзо́р, обозре́ние; (*criticism*) реце́нзия; (*periodical*) журна́л; *v.t.* пересма́тривать *imp.*, пересмотре́ть (-рю́, -ришь) *perf.*; (*survey*) обозрева́ть *imp.*, обозре́ть (-рю́, -ри́шь) *perf.*; (of troops etc.) принима́ть *imp.*, приня́ть (приму́, -мешь; при́нял, -á, -о) *perf.* пара́д + *gen.*; (*book etc.*) рецензи́ровать *imp.*, про~ *perf.* **reviewer** *n.* рецензе́нт.

revise *v.t.* пересма́тривать *imp.*, пересмотре́ть (-рю́, -ришь) *perf.*; исправля́ть *imp.*, испра́вить *perf.*; *n.* втора́я корректу́ра. **revision** *n.* пересмо́тр, исправле́ние.

revival *n.* возрожде́ние; (to life etc.) оживле́ние. **revive** *v.t.* возрожда́ть *imp.*, возроди́ть *perf.*; оживля́ть *imp.*, оживи́ть *perf.*; *v.i.* ожива́ть *imp.*, ожи́ть (оживу́, -вёшь; о́жил, -á, -о) *perf.*

revocation *n.* отме́на. **revoke** *v.t.* отменя́ть *imp.*, отмени́ть (-ню́, -нишь) *perf.*; *v.i.* (cards) объявля́ть *imp.*, объяви́ть (-влю́, -вишь) *perf.* ренонс.

revolt *n.* бунт, мяте́ж (-á); *v.t.* вызыва́ть *imp.*, вы́звать (вы́зову, -вешь) *perf.* отвраще́ние у + *gen.*; *v.i.* бунтова́ть *imp.*, взбунтова́ться *perf.* **revolting** *adj.* отврати́тельный.

revolution *n.* (motion) враще́ние; (single turn) оборо́т; (polit. etc.) револю́ция. **revolutionary** *adj.* революцио́нный; *n.* революционе́р. **revolutionize** *v.t.* революционизи́ровать *imp.*, *perf.* **revolve** *v.t. & i.* враща́ть(ся) *imp.* **revolver** *n.* револьве́р.

revue *n.* ревю́ *neut.indecl.*

revulsion *n.* (change) внеза́пное ре́зкое измене́ние; (dislike) отвраще́ние.

reward *n.* награ́да, вознагражде́ние; *v.t.* (воз)награжда́ть *imp.*, (воз)награди́ть *perf.*

rewrite *v.t.* (recast) переде́лывать *imp.*, переде́лать *perf.*

rhapsodize v.i.: r. over, восторга́ться imp. + instr. **rhapsody** n. (mus.) рапсо́дия; pl. восхище́ние.

rhesus n. ре́зус; in comb. ре́зус-.

rhetoric n. рито́рика. **rhetorical** adj. ритори́ческий.

rheumatic adj. ревмати́ческий. **rheumatism** n. ревмати́зм. **rheumatoid** adj. ревмато́идный.

rhinestone n. иску́сственный бриллиа́нт.

rhino, rhinoceros n. носоро́г.

rhizome n. ризо́ма, корневи́ще.

rhododendron n. рододе́ндрон.

rhomb n. ромб. **rhombic** adj. ромби́ческий. **rhomboid** adj. ромбо́ид. **rhombus** n. ромб.

rhubarb n. реве́нь (-ня́) m.

rhyme n. ри́фма; pl. (verse) рифмо́ванные стихи́ m.pl.; v.t. рифмова́ть imp., с~ perf.; v.i. рифмова́ться imp.

rhythm n. ритм, ритми́чность. **rhythmic(al)** adj. ритми́ческий, -чный.

rib n. ребро́ (-а; pl. рёбра, -бер, -брам); (of umbrella) спи́ца; (knitting etc.) ру́бчик; (of leaf) жи́лка; (of ship) шпанго́ут (also collect.).

ribald adj. непристо́йный.

ribbon n. ле́нта; pl. (reins) во́жжи (-же́й) pl.; pl. (shreds) клочья́ (-ьев) m.pl.; r. development, ле́нточная застро́йка.

riboflavin n. рибофлави́н.

ribonucleic adj. рибонуклеи́новый.

rice n. рис; attrib. ри́совый.

rich adj. бога́тый; (soil) ту́чный (-чен, -чна́, -чно); (food) жи́рный (-рен, -рна́, -рно); (amusing) заба́вный. **riches** n. бога́тство. **richly** adv. (fully) вполне́.

rick[1] n. стог (loc. -е & -у́; pl. -а́), скирда́ (-а́ & -ы́; pl. скирды́, -д(о́в), -да́м).

rick[2] v.t. растя́гивать imp., растяну́ть (-ну́, -нешь) perf.

rickets n. рахи́т. **rickety** adj. рахити́чный; (shaky) расша́танный.

rickshaw n. ри́кша.

ricochet n. рикоше́т; v.i. рикошети́ровать imp. + instr.

rid v.t. освобожда́ть imp., освободи́ть (of, от + gen.); get r. of, избавля́ться imp., изба́виться perf. от + gen.

riddance n.: good r.! ска́тертью доро́га!

riddle[1] n. (enigma) зага́дка.

riddle[2] n. (sieve) гро́хот; v.t. (sift) грохоти́ть imp., про~ perf.; (with bullets etc.) изреше́чивать imp., изрешети́ть perf.

ride v.i. е́здить indet., е́хать (е́ду, е́дешь) det., по~ perf. (on horseback, верхо́м); (lie at anchor) стоя́ть (-ою́т) imp. на я́коре; v.t. е́здить indet., е́хать (е́ду, е́дешь) det., по~ perf. в, на, + prep.; n. пое́здка, езда́. **rider** n. вса́дник, -ица; (clause) дополне́ние.

ridge n. хребе́т (-бта́), гре́бень (-бня) m.; (of roof) конёк (-нька́); r.-pole, (of tent) растя́жка; r.-tile, конько́вая черепи́ца.

ridicule n. насме́шка; v.t. осме́ивать imp., осмея́ть (-ею́, -еёшь) perf. **ridiculous** adj. неле́пый, смешно́й (-шо́н, -шна́).

riding[1] n. (division of county) ра́йдинг.

riding[2] n. (horse-r.) (верхова́я) езда́; r.-habit, амазо́нка; r.-light, я́корный ого́нь (огня́) m.

Riesling n. ри́слинг (-а(у)).

rife predic. широко́ распространён (-а́), обы́чен (-чна); be r. with, изоби́ловать imp. + instr.

riff-raff n. подо́нки (-ков) pl.

rifle v.t. (search) обы́скивать imp., обыска́ть (-ыщу́, -ы́щешь) perf.; (a gun) нареза́ть imp., наре́зать (-е́жу, -е́жешь) perf.; n. винто́вка; pl. стрелки́ m.pl.; r.-range, стре́льбище.

rift n. тре́щина; (dispute) разры́в.

rig v.t. оснаща́ть imp., оснасти́ть perf.; r. out, наряжа́ть imp., наряди́ть (-яжу́, -я́дишь) perf.; r. up, стро́ить imp., по~ perf. из чего́ попа́ло; n. бурова́я устано́вка. **rigging** n. такела́ж.

right adj. (position, justified, polit.) пра́вый (прав, -а́, -о); (correct) пра́вильный; (appropriate) ну́жный (-жен, -жна́, -жно, -жны́); (suitable) подходя́щий; in one's r. mind, в здра́вом уме́; r. angle, прямо́й у́гол (угла́); r. side, (of cloth) лицева́я сторона́ (acc. -ону); v.t. исправля́ть imp., испра́вить perf.; n. пра́во (pl. -ва́); (the side) пра́вая сторона́ (*acc.* -ону́); (*R.*; *polit.*) пра́вые *sb.*; *be in the r.*, быть (*fut.* бу́ду, -дешь; был, -а́, -о; не́ был, -а́, -о) пра́вым; *by r. of*, по пра́ву + *gen.*; *by rights*, по пра́ву, по справедли́вости; *reserve the r.*, оставля́ть *imp.*, оста́вить *perf.* за собо́й пра́во; *set to rights*, приводи́ть (-ожу́, -о́дишь) *imp.*, привести́ (-еду́, -едёшь; -ёл, -ела́) *perf.* в поря́док; *r. of way*, пра́во прохо́да, проéзда; *adv.* (*straight*) пря́мо; (*exactly*) то́чно, как раз; (*to the full*) соверше́нно; (*correctly*) пра́вильно; *как* сле́дует; (*on the r.*) спра́во (*of*, от + *gen.*); (*to the r.*) напра́во.

righteous *adj.* (*person*) пра́ведный; (*action*) справедли́вый.

rightful *adj.* зако́нный.

rigid *adj.* жёсткий (-ток, -тка́, -тко), негну́щийся; (*strict*) стро́гий (-г, -га́, -го). **rigidity** *n.* жёсткость; стро́гость.

rigmarole *n.* бессмы́сленная, несвя́зная, болтовня́.

rigor mortis *n.* тру́пное окочене́ние.

rigorous *adj.* стро́гий (-г, -га́, -го), суро́вый. **rigour** *n.* стро́гость, суро́вость.

rill *n.* ручеёк (-ейка́).

rim *n.* (*of wheel*) о́бод (*pl.* обо́дья, -ьев); (*spectacles*) опра́ва. **rimless** *adj.* без опра́вы.

rind *n.* кожура́, ко́рка.

ring[1] *n.* кольцо́ (*pl.* -льца, -ле́ц, -льцам); (*circle*) круг (*loc.* -гу́, -и); (*boxing*) ринг; (*circus*) (цирковая) аре́на; *r.-dove*, вя́хирь *m.*; *r.-finger*, безымя́нный па́лец (-льца); *r.-master*, инспе́ктор (*pl.* -а́ & -ы) мане́жа; *r. road*, кольцева́я доро́га; *v.t.* (*encircle*) окружа́ть *imp.*, окружи́ть *perf.* (кольцо́м).

ring[2] *v.i.* (*sound*) звене́ть (-ню́т) *imp.*, про-~ *perf.*; звони́ть *imp.*, по-~ *perf.*; (*of shot etc.*) раздава́ться (-даётся) *imp.*, разда́ться (-а́стся, -аду́тся; -а́лся, -ала́сь) *perf.*; (*of place*) оглаша́ться *imp.*, огласи́ться *perf.* (with, + *instr.*); *v.t.* звони́ть *imp.*, по-~ *perf.* в + *acc.*; *r. off*, дава́ть (даю́, даёшь) *imp.*, дать (дам, дашь, даст, дади́м; дал, -а́,

да́ло, -и) *perf.* отбо́й; *r. up*, звони́ть *imp.*, по-~ *perf.* + *dat.*; *n.* звон, звоно́к (-нка́).

ringleader *n.* глава́рь (-ря́) *m.*, зачи́нщик.

ringlet *n.* (*of hair*) ло́кон.

ringworm *n.* стригу́щий лиша́й (-ая́).

rink *n.* като́к (-тка́).

rinse *v.t.* полоска́ть (-ощу́, -о́щешь) *imp.*, вы-~, про-~ *perf.*; *n.* полоска́ние; (*for hair*) кра́ска для воло́с.

riot *n.* бунт; *run r.*, бу́йствовать *imp.*; переступа́ть *imp.*, переступи́ть (-плю́, -пишь) *perf.* все грани́цы; (*of plants*) бу́йно разраста́ться *imp.*, разрасти́сь (-тётся; разро́сся, -сла́сь) *perf.*; *v.i.* бунтова́ть *imp.*, взбунтова́ться *perf.* **riotous** *adj.* бу́йный (бу́ен, бу́йна́, -но).

rip *v.t. & i.* рвать(ся) (рву, рвёт(ся); -а́л(ся), -ала́(сь), -а́ло/-а́ло́сь) *imp.*; поро́ть(ся) (-рю́, -рет(ся)) *imp.*; *v.t.* (*tear up*) разрыва́ть *imp.*, разорва́ть (-ву́, -вёшь; разорва́л, -а́, -о) *perf.*; *v.i.* (*rush*) мча́ться (мчи́тся) *imp.*; *n.* проре́ха, разре́з; *r.-cord*, вытяжно́й трос.

ripe *adj.* зре́лый (зрел, -а́, -о), спе́лый (спел, -а́, -о). **ripen** *v.t.* де́лать *imp.*, с-~ *perf.* зре́лым; *v.i.* созрева́ть *imp.*, созре́ть *perf.* **ripeness** *n.* зре́лость.

ripple *n.* рябь; *v.t. & i.* покрыва́ть(ся) *imp.*, покры́ть(ся) (-ро́ет(ся)) *perf.* ря́бью.

rise *v.i.* поднима́ться *imp.*, подня́ться (-ниму́сь, -ни́мешься; -ня́лся, -няла́сь) *perf.*; повыша́ться *imp.*, повы́ситься *perf.*; (*get up*) встава́ть (-таю́, -таёшь) *imp.*, встать (-а́ну, -а́нешь) *perf.*; (*rebel*) восстава́ть (-таю́, -таёшь) *imp.*, восста́ть (-а́ну, -а́нешь) *perf.*; (*sun etc.*) в(о)сходи́ть (-ит) *imp.*, взойти́ (-йдёт; взошёл, -шла́) *perf.*; (*wind*) усиливаться *imp.*, уси́литься *perf.*; *n.* подъём, возвыше́ние; (*in pay*) при-ба́вка; (*of sun etc.*) восхо́д. **riser** *n.* (*of stairs*) подступень; *he is an early r.*, он ра́но встаёт. **rising** *n.* (*revolt*) восста́ние.

risk *n.* риск; *v.t.* рискова́ть *imp.*, рискну́ть *perf.* + *instr.* **risky** *adj.* риско́ванный (-ан, -анна).

risqué *adj.* непристо́йный.

rissole *n.* котлéта.

rite *n.* обря́д. **ritual** *n.* ритуáл; *adj.* ритуáльный, обря́довый.

rival *n.* сопéрник, -ица; конкурéнт, ~ ка; *adj.* сопéрничающий; *v.t.* сопéрничать *imp.* с+*instr.*; конкурúровать *imp.* с+*instr.* **rivalry** *n.* сопéрничество.

river *n.* рекá (*acc.* рéку; *pl.* рéки, рек, рéкам); *adj.* речнóй. **riverside** *n.* прибрéжная полосá (*acc.* полосу́; *pl.* -осы, -óс, -осáм); *attrib.* прибрéжный.

rivet *n.* заклёпка; *v.t.* клепáть *imp.*; за-, клёпывать *imp.* за-, с-, клепáть *perf.*; (*attention etc.*) прикóвывать *imp.*, приковáть (-кую́, -куёшь) *perf.* (оп, к+*dat.*).

rivulet *n.* рéчка, ручеёк (-ейкá).

RNA *abbr.* рибонуклеúновая кислотá.

roach *n.* (*fish*) плотвá.

road *n.* дорóга, путь (-тú, -тём) *m.*; (*highway*) шоссé *neut.indecl.*; (*central part*; *carriageway*) мостовáя *sb.*; (*street*) у́лица; (*naut.*; *usu. pl.*) рейд; r.-block, заграждéние на дорóге; r.-hog, лихáч (-á); r.-house, придорóжный буфéт, придорóжная гостúница; r.-map, áтлас автомобúльных дорóг; r. sense, чу́вство дорóги; r. sign, дорóжный знак. **roadman** *n.* дорóжный рабóчий *sb.* **roadside** *n.* обóчина; *attrib.* придорóжный. **roadstead** *n.* рейд. **roadway** *n.* мостовáя *sb.*

roam *v.t. & i.* бродúть (-ожу́, -óдишь) *imp.* (по+*dat.*); скитáться *imp.* (по+*dat.*).

roan *adj.* чáлый.

roar *n.* (*animal's*) рёв; (*other noise*) грóхот, шум; *v.i.* ревéть (-ву́, -вёшь) *imp.*; грохотáть (-очу́, -óчешь) *imp.*, про~ *perf.*

roast *v.t. & i.* жáрить(ся) *imp.*, за-, из~ *perf.*; *adj.* жáреный; r. beef, рóстбиф *m.* в жáрком *sb.*, жáреное мя́со *sb.*

rob *v.t.* грáбить *imp.*, о~ *perf.*; красть (-аду́, -адёшь; -ал) *imp.*, у~ *perf.* у+*gen.* (of, +*acc.*); (*deprive*) лишáть *imp.*, лишúть *perf.* (of, +*gen.*). **robber** *n.* грабúтель *m.* **robbery** *n.* грабёж (-á).

robe *n.* (*also pl.*) мáнтия.

robin *n.* малúновка.

robot *n.* рóбот.

robust *adj.* здорóвый (-в, -вá), крéпкий (-пок, -пкá, -пко).

rock[1] *n.* (*geol.*) (гóрная) порóда; (*cliff etc.*) скалá (*pl.* -лы); (*large stone*) большóй кáмень (-мня; -мни, -мнéй) *m.*; on the rocks, на мелú; (*drink*) со льдом; r.-bottom, сáмый нúзкий; r.-crystal, гóрный хрустáль (-ля́) *m.*; r.-salt, кáменная соль.

rock[2] *v.t. & i.* качáть(ся) *imp.*, качну́ть(ся) *perf.*; (*sway*) колебáть(ся) (-блю́сь) *imp.*, по~ *perf.*; r. to sleep, укáчивать *imp.*, укачáть *perf.*; rocking-chair (крéсло-качáлка; rocking-horse, конь-качáлка; r. and roll, рок-н-рóлл.

rockery *n.* сад (*loc.* -у́; *pl.* -ы́) камнéй.

rocket *n.* ракéта. **rocketry** *n.* ракéтная тéхника.

rocky *adj.* скалúстый; (*unsteady*) неустóйчивый.

rococo *n.* рококó *neut.indecl.*; *adj.* в стúле рококó.

rod *n.* прут (-á; *pl.* -ья, -ьев); (*for caning*) рóзга; (*tech.*) стéржень (-жня) *m.*; (*fishing-r.*) у́дочка.

rodent *n.* грызу́н (-á).

rodeo *n.* родéо *neut.indecl.*

roe[1] *n.* (*hard*) икрá; (*soft*) молóки (-óк) *pl.*

roe[2] (*-deer*) *n.* косу́ля. **roebuck** *n.* самéц (-мцá) косу́ли.

roentgen *n.* рентгéн (*gen.pl.* -н & -нов). **roentgenography** *n.* рентгеногрáфия. **roentgenology** *n.* рентгенолóгия.

rogue *n.* плут (-á). **roguish** *adj.* плутовскóй; (*mischievous*) прокáзливый.

role *n.* роль (*pl.* -ли, -лéй).

roll[1] *n.* (*cylinder*) рулóн; (*document*) свúток (-тка); (*register*) спúсок (-ска), реéстр; (*bread r.*) бу́лочка; r.-call, переклúчка.

roll[2] *v.t. & i.* катáть(ся) *indet.*, катúть(ся) (качу́сь, кáтишься) *det.*, по~ *perf.*; (r. up) свёртывать *imp.*, сверну́ть(ся) *perf.*; *v.t.* (*road*) укáтывать *imp.*, укатáть *perf.*; (*metal*) прокáтывать *imp.*, прокатáть *perf.*; (*dough*) раскáтывать *imp.*, раскатáть *perf.*; *v.i.* (*sound*) гремéть (-мúт) *imp.*; *n.* катáние; (*of thunder*) раскáт.

roller n. ва́лик; (wave) вал (loc. -у́; pl. -ы́); pl. (for hair) бигуди́ neut.indecl.; r. bearing, ро́ликовый подши́пник; r.-skates, ро́лики m.pl., коньки́ m.pl. на ро́ликах; r. towel, полоте́нце на ро́лике.

rollicking adj. разуха́бистый.

rolling adj. (of land) холми́стый; r.-mill, прока́тный стан; r.-pin, ска́лка; r.-stock, подвижно́й соста́в.

Roman n. ри́млянин (pl. -я́не, -я́н, -я́нка; adj. ри́мский; R. alphabet, лати́нский алфави́т; R. Catholic, (n.) като́лик — ичка; (adj.) ри́мско--католи́ческий; r. type, прямо́й, све́тлый шрифт.

romance n. (tale; love affair) рома́н; (quality) рома́нтика; (mus.) рома́нс; R. languages, рома́нские языки́ m.pl.

Romanesque adj. рома́нский.

Romanian n. румы́н (gen.pl. -н), ~ ка; adj. румы́нский.

romantic adj. романти́чный, -ческий. **romanticism** n. романти́зм.

romp v.i. вози́ться (вожу́сь, во́зишься) imp.; r. home, с лёгкостью вы́играть perf.

rondo n. (mus.) ро́ндо neut.indecl.

Röntgen n.: R. rays, рентге́новские лучи́ m.pl.; (r.) see **roentgen**.

rood n. распя́тие; r.-loft, хо́ры (-р & -ров) pl. в це́ркви; r.-screen, перего-ро́дка в це́ркви.

roof n. кры́ша, кро́вля (gen.pl. -вель); r. of the mouth, нёбо; v.t. крыть (кро́ю, -о́ешь) imp., покрыва́ть imp., покры́ть (-ро́ю, -ро́ешь) perf.

rook[1] n. (chess) ладья́.

rook[2] n. (orn.) грач (-а́). **rookery** n. грачо́вник.

room n. (in house) ко́мната; pl. поме-ще́ние; (space) ме́сто; (opportunity) возмо́жность. **roomy** adj. простор-ный.

roost n. насе́ст.

root[1] n. (var. senses) ко́рень (-рня; pl. -рни, -рне́й) m.; (mus.) основно́й тон (акко́рда; (plant) корнепло́д; r. and branch, коренны́м о́бразом; r.-stock, корневи́ще; v.i. пуска́ть imp., пусти́ть (-ит) perf. ко́рни; r. to the spot, при-

гвожда́ть imp., пригвозди́ть perf. к ме́сту.

root[2] v.i. (rummage) ры́ться (ро́юсь, ро́ешься) imp.

rope n. верёвка, кана́т, трос; r.-dancer, кана́тоходец (-дца); r.-ladder, верё-вочная ле́стница; v.t. привя́зывать imp., привяза́ть (-яжу́, -я́жешь) perf.; r. in, off, о(т)гора́живать imp., о(т)горо-ди́ть (-ожу́, -о́дишь) perf. кана́том.

rosary n. (eccl.) чётки (-ток) pl.

rose n. ро́за; (nozzle) се́тка; pl. (com-plexion) румя́нец (-нца); r.-bud, буто́н ро́зы; r.-coloured, ро́зовый; r.-water, ро́зовая вода́ (acc. -ду); r.-window, розе́тка.

rosemary n. розмари́н.

rosette n. розе́тка.

rosewood n. ро́зовое де́рево.

rosin n. канифо́ль; v.t. натира́ть imp., натере́ть (-тру́, -трёшь; -тёр) perf. канифо́лью.

roster n. расписа́ние (наря́дов, де-жу́рств).

rostrum n. трибу́на, ка́федра.

rosy adj. ро́зовый; (complexion) румя́-ный.

rot n. гниль; (nonsense) вздор; v.i. гнить (-ию, -иёшь; гнил, -а́, -о) imp., с ~ perf.; v.t. гнои́ть imp., с ~ perf.

rota n. расписа́ние дежу́рств. **rotary** adj. враща́тельный, ротацио́нный. **rotate** v.t. & i. враща́ть(ся) imp. **rotation** n. враще́ние; in r., по о́череди.

rote n.: by r., наизу́сть.

rotten adj. гнило́й (гнил, -а́, -о). **rotter** n. дрянь.

rotund adj. (round) кру́глый (-л, -ла́, -ло, кру́глы́); (plump) по́лный (-лон, -лна́, по́лно). **rotunda** n. рото́нда. **rotundity** n. округлённость, полнота́.

rouble n. рубль (-ля́) m.

rouge n. румя́на (-н) pl.; v.t. & i. румя́-нить(ся) imp., на ~ perf.

rough adj. (uneven) неро́вный (-вен, -вна́, -вно); (coarse) грубый (груб, -а́, -о); (sea) бу́рный (-рен, бу́рна́, -но); (approximate) приблизи́тельный; r.-and-ready, грубый но эффекти́вный; r. copy, черновик (-а́); n. (r. ground) неро́вное по́ле; (person) хулига́н.

roughage n. грубая пища. **roughcast** n. галечная штукатурка. **roughly** adv. грубо; r. speaking, примерно.

roulette n. рулетка.

round adj. круглый (-л, -ла, -ло, круглы); (plump) полный (-лон, -лна, -полно); in r. figures, приблизительно; r.-shouldered, сутулый; n. (of object) круг (loc. -у́; pl. -и́); (circuit; also pl.) обход (pl. -ы); (ammunition) патрон, снаряд; (of applause) взрыв; adv. вокруг; (in a circle) по кругу; all r., кругом; all the year r., круглый год; prep. вокруг + gen.; кругом + gen.; по + dat.; r. the corner, (motion) за угол, (position) за углом; v.t. & i. округлять(ся) impf., округлить(ся) perf.; v.t. (pass r.) огибать impf., обогнуть perf.; r. off, (complete) завершать impf., завершить perf.; r. up, сгонять impf., согнать (сгоню, -нишь; согнал, -а, -о) perf.; r.-up, загон; (police) облава. **roundabout** n. (merry-go-round) карусель; (road junction) транспортная развязка с односторонним круговым движением машин; adj. окольный; in a r. way, окольным путём.

rouse v.t. будить (бужу, будишь) impf., раз~ perf.; (to action etc.) побуждать impf., побудить (-ужу, -удишь) perf. (to, к + dat.). **rousing** adj. возбуждающий.

rout n. (defeat) разгром; (flight) беспорядочное бегство; v.t. обращать impf., обратить (-ащу, -атишь) perf. в бегство.

route n. маршрут, путь (-ти, -тём) m.; r. march, походное движение; v.t. отправлять impf., отправить perf. по определённому маршруту.

routine n. заведённый порядок (-дка), режим; (pejor.) рутина; adj. установленный; очередной.

rove v.i. скитаться impf.; (of thoughts etc.) блуждать impf. **rover** n. скиталец (-льца).

row[1] n. (line) ряд (-á with 2, 3, 4, loc. -ý; pl. -ы́).

row[2] v.i. (in boat) грести (гребу, -бёшь; грёб, -ла) impf.; v.t. (convey) перево-

зить (-ожу, -озишь) impf., перевезти (-езу, -езёшь; -ёз, -езла) perf. на лодке.

row[3] n. (dispute) ссора; (brawl) скандал; v.i. ссориться impf., по~ perf.; скандалить impf., на~ perf.

rowan n. рябина.

rowdy adj. буйный (буен, буйна, -но); n. буян.

rowlock n. уключина.

royal adj. королевский, царский; (majestic) великолепный. **royalist** n. роялист; adj. роялистский. **royalty** n. член, члены pl., королевской семьи; (author's fee) авторский гонорар; (patentee's fee) отчисление владельцу патента.

rub v.t. & i. тереть(ся) (тру(сь), трёшь(ся)) тёр(ся)) impf.; v.t. (polish, chafe) натирать impf., натереть (-тру, -трёшь; -тёр) perf.; (r. dry) вытирать impf., вытереть (-тру, -трешь; -тер) perf.; r. in, on, втирать impf., втереть (вотру, -рёшь; втёр) perf.; r. out, стирать impf., стереть (сотру, -рёшь; стёр) perf.; r. it in, растравлять impf., растравить (-влю, -вишь) perf. рану; r. one's hands, потирать impf. руки (with joy etc.), от + gen.); r. up the wrong way, гладить impf. против шерсти.

rubber[1] n. (cured) резина; (not cured) каучук; (eraser, also r. band) резинка, ластик; attrib. резиновый; r.-stamp, (fig.) штамповать impf.

rubber[2] n. (cards) роббер.

rubbish n. мусор, хлам; (nonsense) чепуха, вздор. **rubbishy** adj. дрянной (-нен, -нна, -нно).

rubble n. бут.

rubella n. краснуха.

rubicund n. румяный.

rubric n. рубрика.

ruby n. рубин; adj. рубиновый.

ruche n. рюш.

ruck v.t. (r. up) мять (мну, мнёшь) impf., из~ (измну, -нёшь), с~ (сомну, -нёшь) perf.

rucksack n. рюкзак (-á).

rudd n. краснопёрка.

rudder *n.* руль (-ля́) *m.*

ruddy *adj.* кра́сный (-сен, -сна́, -сно); (*face*) румя́ный; (*sl.*; *damnable*) прокля́тый.

rude *adj.* гру́бый (груб, -а́, -о); (*impolite also*) неве́жливый; r. *awakening*, глубо́кое разочарова́ние; r. *health*, кре́пкое здоро́вье; r. *shock*, внеза́пный уда́р.

rudimentary *adj.* зача́точный, рудимента́рный. **rudiments** *n.* (*elements*) нача́тки (-ков) *pl.*; (*beginning*) зача́тки *m.pl.*

rue¹ *n.* (*plant*) ру́та.

rue² *v.t.* сожале́ть *imp.* o + *prep.* **rueful** *adj.* печа́льный, уны́лый.

ruff¹ *n.* (*frill*) брыжи (-жей) *pl.*; (*of feathers, hair*) кольцо́ (*pl.* -льца, -ле́ц, -льцам) (пе́рьев, ше́рсти) вокру́г ше́и.

ruff² *v.t.* (*cards*) покрыва́ть *imp.*, покры́ть (-ро́ю, -ро́ешь) *perf.* ко́зырем; *n.* покры́тие ко́зырем; ко́зырь (*pl.* -ри, -ре́й) *m.*

ruffian *n.* головоре́з, хулига́н. **ruffianly** *adj.* хулига́нский.

ruffle *v.t.* (*hair*) еро́шить *imp.*, взъ ~ *perf.*; (*water*) ряби́ть *imp.*; (*person*) раздража́ть *imp.*, раздражи́ть *perf.*

rug *n.* (*mat*) ко́врик, ковёр (-вра́); (*wrap*) плед.

Rugby (football) *n.* ре́гби *neut.indecl.*

rugged *adj.* (*uneven*) неро́вный (-вен, -вна́, -вно); (*rocky*) скали́стый; (*rough*) гру́бый (груб, -а́, -о).

ruin *n.* (*downfall*) ги́бель; (*destruction*) разоре́ние; *pl.* разва́лины *f.pl.*, руи́ны *f.pl.*; *v.t.* губи́ть (-блю́, -бишь) *imp.*, по ~ *perf.*; разори́ть *imp.*, разори́ть *perf.* **ruinous** *adj.* губи́тельный, разори́тельный; (*state*) разру́шенный (-ен).

rule *n.* пра́вило; (*carpenter's, print.*) лине́йка; as a r., как пра́вило, обы́чно; *v.t. & i.* пра́вить *imp.* (+ *instr.*); (*make lines*) линова́ть *imp.*, раз ~ *perf.*; (*give decision*) постановля́ть *imp.*, постанови́ть (-влю, -вишь) *perf.*; r. *out*, исключа́ть *imp.*, исключи́ть *perf.* **ruler** *n.* (*person*) прави́тель *m.*, ~ ница; (*object*) лине́йка. **ruling** *n.* (*of court etc.*) постановле́ние.

rum¹ *n.* ром.

rum² *adj.* стра́нный (-нен, -нна́, -нно), чудно́й (-дён, -дна́).

Rumanian *see* **Romanian**.

rumba *n.* ру́мба.

rumble *v.i.* громыха́ть *imp.*; грохота́ть (-о́чет) *imp.*; *n.* громыха́ние, грохота́ние, гро́хот.

ruminant *n.* жва́чное (живо́тное) *sb.*; *adj.* жва́чный; (*contemplative*) заду́мчивый. **ruminate** *v.i.* жева́ть (жуёт) *imp.* жва́чку; (*fig.*) размышля́ть *imp.* (over, on, o + *prep.*). **rumination** *n.* размышле́ние.

rummage *v.i.* ры́ться (ро́юсь, ро́ешься) *imp.*

rumour *n.* слух; *v.t.*: it is rumoured that, хо́дят слу́хи (*pl.*), что.

rump *n.* огу́зок (-зка); r. *steak*, ромште́кс.

rumple *v.t.* мять (мну, мнёшь) *imp.*, из ~ (изомну́, -нёшь), с ~ (сомну́, -нёшь) *perf.*; (*hair*) еро́шить *imp.*, взъ ~ *perf.*

run *v.i.* бе́гать *indet.*, бежа́ть (бегу́, бежи́шь) *det.*, по ~ *perf.*; (*roll along*) ката́ться *indet.*, кати́ться (качу́сь, ка́тишься) *det.*, по ~ *perf.*; (*work, of machines*) рабо́тать *imp.*; (*ply, of bus etc.*) ходи́ть (-ит) *indet.*, идти́ (идёт; шёл, шла) *det.*; (*compete in race*) уча́ствовать *imp.* (в бе́ге); (*seek election*) выставля́ть *imp.*, вы́ставить *perf.* свою́ кандидату́ру; (*be valid*) быть действи́тельным; (*of play etc.*) идти́ (идёт; шёл, шла) *imp.*; (*spread rapidly*) сразу распространя́ться *imp.*, распространи́ться *perf.*; (*of ink, dye*) расплыва́ться *imp.*, расплы́ться (-ывётся; -ы́лся, -ыла́сь) *perf.*; (*flow*) течь (течёт; тёк, -ла́) *imp.*; (*of document*) гласи́ть *imp.* *v.t.* (*manage, operate a machine*) управля́ть *imp.* + *instr.*; (*a business etc.*) вести́ (веду́, -дёшь; вёл, -а́) *imp.*; r. *dry, low*, иссяка́ть *imp.*, исся́кнуть (-к) *perf.*; r. *errands*, быть на посы́лках (for, y + *gen.*); r. *risks*, рискова́ть *imp.*; r. *to earth*, (*fig.*) оты́скивать (оты́щу, -щешь) *perf.*; r. *across, into*, (*meet*) встреча́ться *imp.*, встре́титься *perf.* с + *instr.*; r. *after*, (*fig.*) уха́живать *imp.* за + *instr.*; r. *away*, (*flee*) убега́ть *imp.*, убежа́ть

(-егу́, -ежи́шь) *perf.*; r. down, (*knock down*) задави́ть (-влю́, -вишь) *perf.*; (*disparage*) умаля́ть *imp.*, умали́ть *perf.*; be r. down, (*of person*) переутоми́ться *perf.* (*in past tense*) r.-down, (*decayed*) захуда́лый; r. in, (*engine*) обка́тывать *imp.*, обката́ть *perf.*; r. into see r. across; r. out, конча́ться *imp.*, ко́нчиться *perf.*; r. out of, истоща́ть *imp.*, истощи́ть *perf.* свой запа́с+gen.; r. over, (*glance over*) бе́гло просма́тривать *imp.*, просмотре́ть (-рю́, -ришь) *perf.*; (*injure*) задави́ть (-влю́, -вишь) *perf.*; r. through, (*pierce*) прока́лывать *imp.*, проколо́ть (-лю́, -лешь) *perf.*; (*money*) прома́тывать *imp.*, промота́ть *perf.*; (*glance over*) see r. over; r. to, (*money*) достига́ть *imp.*, дости́гнуть & дости́чь (-и́гну, -и́гнешь; -и́г) *perf.*+gen.; (*of money*) хвата́ть *imp.*, хвати́ть (-ит) *perf.impers.*+gen. на+acc.; the money won't r. to a car, э́тих де́нег не хва́тит на маши́ну; r. up against, ната́лкиваться *imp.*, натолкну́ться *perf.* на+acc.; n. бег; (*also distance covered*) пробе́г; (*direction*) направле́ние; (*course, motion*) ход, тече́ние; (*regular route*) маршру́т; (*mus.*) рула́да; (*bombing r.*) захо́д на цель; at a r., бего́м; r. on, большо́й спрос на+acc.; common r. of men, обыкнове́нные лю́ди (-де́й, -дям, -дьми́) *pl.*; in the long r., в конце́ концо́в.

rune *n.* ру́на.

rung *n.* ступе́нь, ступе́нька.

runner *n.* (*also tech.*) бегу́н (-á); (*messenger*) посы́льный *sb.*; (*of sledge*) по́лоз (*pl.* поло́зья, -ьев); (*cloth*) доро́жка; (*stem*) сте́лющийся побе́г; r. bean, фасо́ль; r.-up, уча́стник состяза́ния, заня́вший второ́е ме́сто. **running** *n.* бег; (*of machine*) ход, рабо́та; be in the r., име́ть *imp.* ша́нсы на вы́игрыш; make the r., задава́ть (-даю́, -даёшь) *imp.*, зада́ть (-а́м, -а́шь, -а́ст, -ади́м; за́дал, -á, -о) *perf.* темп; *adj.* бегу́щий; (*of r.*) бегово́й; (*after pl. n., in succes-*

sion) подря́д; r. account, теку́щий счёт; r.-board, подно́жка; r. commentary, (ра́дио)репорта́ж; r. title, колонти́тул; r. water, прото́чная вода́ (*acc.* -ду). **runway** *n.* (*aeron.*) взлётно--поса́дочная полоса́ (*acc.* поло́су; *pl.* -осы, -о́с, -оса́м).

rupee *n.* ру́пия.

rupture *n.* разры́в; (*hernia*) гры́жа.

rural *adj.* се́льский, дереве́нский.

ruse *n.* хи́трость, уло́вка.

rush[1] *n.* (*plant*) (*also collect.*) камы́ш (-á), тростни́к (-á); (*bot.*) си́тник.

rush[2] *v.t.* бы́стро проводи́ть (-ожу́, -о́дишь) *imp.*, провести́ (-еду́, -едёшь; -ёл, -ела́) *perf.*; торопи́ть (-плю́, -пишь) *imp.*, по~ *perf.*; *v.i.* броса́ться *imp.*, бро́ситься *perf.*; мча́ться (мчусь, мчи́шься) *imp.*; n. стреми́тельное движе́ние, поры́в; (*influx*) наплы́в; (*of blood etc.*) прили́в; (*hurry*) спе́шка; r.-hour(s), часы́ *mn.pl.* пик; r. job, авра́л.

rusk *n.* суха́рь (-ря́) *m.*

russet *adj.* краснова́то-кори́чневый.

Russia (**leather**) *n.* юфть. **Russian** *n.* ру́сский *sb.*; *adj.* ру́сский. **R. salad**, винегре́т.

rust *n.* ржа́вчина; r.-proof, нержаве́ющий; *v.i.* ржаве́ть *imp.*, за~ *perf.*

rustic *adj.* дереве́нский; (*unpolished, uncouth*) неотёсанный (-ан, -анна). n. дереве́нский, се́льский, жи́тель *m.*, ~ница. **rusticate** *v.t.* (*univ.*) вре́менно исключа́ть *imp.*, исключи́ть *perf.* из университе́та; (*arch.*) ростова́ть *imp.*; жить (живу́, -вёшь; жил, -á, -о) *imp.* в дере́вне. **rustication** *n.* (*arch.*) ростова́.

rustle *n.* ше́лест, шо́рох, шурша́ние; *v.i.* шелесте́ть (-ти́шь) *imp.*; *v.t.* & *i.* шурша́ть (-шу́, -ши́шь) *imp.* (+*instr.*); *v.t.* (*r. cattle*) красть (-аду́, -адёшь; -áл) *imp.*, у~ *perf.*

rusty *adj.* ржа́вый.

rut *n.* (*groove*) колея́.

ruthless *adj.* безжа́лостный.

rye *n.* рожь (ржи); *attrib.* ржано́й.

S

Sabbath *n.* (*Jewish*) суббо́та; (*Christian*) воскресе́нье; (*witches'*) ша́баш. **sabbatical** *adj.*: s. (*year*) годи́чный о́тпуск.

sable *n.* (*animal*; *fur*) со́боль (*pl. animal*) -ли, -ле́й & (*fur*) -ли) *m.*; (*fur*) собо́лий мех (*loc.* -е & -у́; *pl.* -а́); *attrib.* собо́лий, со́боли.

sabotage *n.* сабота́ж, диве́рсия; *v.t.* саботи́ровать *imp.*, *perf.* **saboteur** *n.* сабота́жник, диверса́нт.

sabre *n.* са́бля (*gen.pl.* -бель), ша́шка; *s.-rattling*, бряца́ние ору́жием.

sac *n.* мешо́чек (-чка).

saccharin *n.* сахари́н.

saccharine *adj.* са́харистый.

sacerdotal *adj.* свяще́ннический.

sachet *n.* поду́шечка.

sack[1] *v.t.* (*plunder*) разгра́бить *perf.*

sack[2] *n.* куль (-ля́) *m.*, мешо́к (-шка́); the s., (*dismissal*) увольне́ние; *v.t.* увольня́ть *imp.*, уво́лить *perf.* **sacking** *n.* (*hessian*) мешкови́на.

sacrament *n.* та́инство; (*Eucharist*) прича́стие. **sacred** *adj.* свяще́нный (-е́н, -е́нна), свято́й (свят, -а́, -о). **sacrifice** *n.* же́ртва; *v.t.* же́ртвовать *imp.*, по~ *perf.+instr.* **sacrificial** *adj.* же́ртвенный. **sacrilege** *n.* святота́тство. **sacrilegious** *adj.* святота́тственный. **sacristy** *n.* ри́зница. **sacrosanct** *adj.* свяще́нный (-е́н, -е́нна).

sad *adj.* печа́льный, гру́стный (-тен, -тна́, -тно). **sadden** *v.t.* печа́лить *imp.*, о~ *perf.*

saddle *n.* седло́ (*pl.* сёдла, -дел, -длам); *v.t.* седла́ть *imp.*, о~ *perf.*; (*burden*) обременя́ть *imp.*, обремени́ть *perf.* (with, +*instr.*). **saddler** *n.* седе́льник, шо́рник.

sadism *n.* сади́зм. **sadist** *n.* сади́ст. **sadistic** *adj.* сади́стский.

sadness *n.* печа́ль, грусть.

safe *n.* сейф, несгора́емый шкаф (*loc.* -у́; *pl.* -ы́); *adj.* (*uninjured*) невреди́мый; (*out of danger*) в безопа́сности; (*secure*) безопа́сный; (*reliable*) надёжный; s. and sound, цел (-а́, -о) и невреди́м. **safeguard** *n.* предохрани́тельная ме́ра; *v.t.* предохраня́ть *imp.*, предохрани́ть *perf.* **safety** *n.* безопа́сность; *s.-catch*, предохрани́тель *m.*; *s.-belt*, предохрани́тельный реме́нь (-мня́) *m.*; *s.-lamp*, рудни́чная ла́мпа; *s.-pin*, англи́йская була́вка; *s. razor*, безопа́сная бри́тва; *s.-valve*, предохрани́тельный кла́пан; (*fig.*) отду́шина.

saffron *n.* шафра́н; *adj.* шафра́нный, шафра́новый.

sag *v.i.* провиса́ть *imp.*, прови́снуть (-с) *perf.*; прогиба́ться *imp.*, прогну́ться *perf.*; *n.* прове́с, проги́б.

saga *n.* са́га.

sagacious *adj.* проница́тельный. **sagacity** *n.* проница́тельность.

sage[1] *n.* (*herb*) шалфе́й; *s.-green*, серова́то-зелёный.

sage[2] *n.* (*person*) мудре́ц (-а́); *adj.* му́дрый (мудр, -а́, -о).

Sagittarius *n.* Стреле́ц (-льца́).

sago *n.* са́го *neut.indecl.*; (*palm*) са́говая па́льма.

sail *n.* па́рус (*pl.* -а́); (*collect.*) паруса́ *m.pl.*; (*of windmill*) крыло́ (*pl.* -лья, -льев); *v.t.* (*a ship*) управля́ть *imp.+ instr.*; *v.i.* пла́вать *indet.*, плыть (плыву́, -вёшь; плыл, -а́, -о) *det.*; (*depart*) отплыва́ть *imp.*, отплы́ть (-плыву́, -ывёшь; -плы́л, -ыла́, -ы́ло) *perf.* **sailcloth** *n.* паруси́на. **sailing** *n.* (*sport*) па́русный спорт; *s.-ship*, *s.-vessel*, па́русное су́дно (*pl.* -да́, -до́в). **sailor** *n.* матро́с, моря́к (-а́).

saint *n.* свято́й *sb.* **saintly** *adj.* свято́й (свят, -а́, -о), безгре́шный.

sake n.: *for the s. of*, ра́ди + gen., для + gen.

salacious adj. непристо́йный; (*lustful*) похотли́вый.

salad n. сала́т, винегре́т; *s. days*, зелёная ю́ность; *s.-dressing*, припра́ва к сала́ту; *s.-oil*, расти́тельное, оли́вковое, ма́сло.

salamander n. салама́ндра.

salami n. саля́ми f.indecl.

salaried *adj.* получа́ющий жа́лованье. **salary** n. жа́лованье.

sale n. прода́жа; (*also amount sold*) сбыт (*no pl.*); (*at reduced price*) распрода́жа по сни́женным це́нам; *be for s.*, продава́ться (-даётся) *imp.*; *s.-room*, аукцио́нный зал. **saleable** adj. хо́дкий (-док, -дка́, -дко). **salesman** n. продаве́ц (-вца́). **saleswoman** n. продави́ца.

salient adj. (*projecting*) выдаю́щийся, выступа́ющий; (*conspicuous*) заме́тный, я́ркий; n. вы́ступ.

saline n. соляно́й.

saliva n. слюна́. **salivary** adj. слю́нный. **salivate** v.i. выделя́ть *imp.*, вы́делить *perf.* слюну́. **salivation** n. слюнотече́ние.

sallow adj. желтова́тый.

sally n. вы́лазка; (*witticism*) остро́та; v.i.: *s. forth*, отправля́ться *imp.*, отпра́виться *perf.*; *s. out*, (*mil.*) де́лать *imp.*, с~ *perf.* вы́лазку.

salmon n. лосо́сь m., сёмга, (*cul.*) лососи́на, сёмга.

salon n. сало́н. **saloon** n. (*hall*) зал; (*on ship*) сало́н; (*rly.*) сало́н-ваго́н; (*bar*) бар; *s. deck*, па́луба пе́рвого кла́сса.

salt n. соль; *s.-cellar*, соло́нка; *s. lake*, соляно́е о́зеро (*pl.* ёра); *s.-marsh*, солонча́к (-а́); *s.-mine*, соляны́е ко́пи (-пей) pl.; *s. water*, морска́я вода́ (*acc.* -ду); (*preserved in salt also*) засо́ленный (-ен); v.t. соли́ть (солю́, со́ли́шь) *imp.*, по~ *perf.*; заса́ливать *imp.*, засоли́ть (-олю́, -о́ли́шь) *perf.*; *s. away*, припря́тывать *imp.*, припря́тать (-я́чу, -я́чешь) *perf.*

saltpetre n. сели́тра.

salty adj. (*also fig.*) солёный (со́лон, -а́, -о).

salubrious adj. здоро́вый.

salutary adj. благотво́рный. **salutation** n. приве́тствие. **salute** n. приве́тствие; (*mil.*) салю́т; v.t. приве́тствовать *imp.* (*in past also perf.*); салютова́ть *imp.*, *perf.*, от ~ *perf.* + dat.

salvage n. спасе́ние; (*property*) спасённое иму́щество; (*ship*) спасённое су́дно (*pl.* -да́, -до́в); (*cargo*) спасённый груз; (*waste material*) утиль; v.t. спаса́ть *imp.*, спасти́ (-су́, -сёшь; -с, -сла́, -сло) *perf.*

salvation n. спасе́ние; *S. Army*, А́рмия спасе́ния.

salve n. мазь, бальза́м; v.t.: *s. one's conscience*, успока́ивать *imp.*, успоко́ить *perf.* со́весть.

salver n. подно́с.

salvo n. залп.

sal volatile n. ню́хательная соль.

same adj. (*monotonous*) однообра́зный; *the s.*, тот же са́мый; тако́й же, одина́ковый; *just the s.*, то́чно тако́й же; *much the s.*, почти́ тако́й же; *pron.: the s.*, одно́ и то́ же, то же са́мое; adv.: *the s.*, таки́м же о́бразом, так же; *all the s.*, всё-таки, тем не ме́нее. **sameness** n. однообра́зие.

samovar n. самова́р.

sample n. образе́ц (-зца́), про́ба; v.t. про́бовать *imp.*, по ~ *perf.* **sampler** n. образе́чик вы́шивки.

sanatorium n. санато́рий.

sanctify v.t. освяща́ть *imp.* (-яща́ю, -яти́шь) *perf.* **sanctimonious** adj. ха́нжеский. **sanction** n. са́нкция; v.t. санкциони́ровать *imp.*, *perf.* **sanctity** n. (*holiness*) свя́тость; (*sacredness*) свяще́нность. **sanctuary** n. святи́лище, алта́рь (-ря́) m.; (*refuge*) убе́жище; (*for animals etc.*) запове́дник. **sanctum** n. свята́я *sb.* святы́х; (*joc.*) рабо́чий кабине́т.

sand n. песо́к (-ска́(у́)); (*grain of s.*, *usu. pl.*) песчи́нка; (*shoal*, *sing. or pl.*) о́тмель; (*pl.*) (*beach*) пляж; (*pl.*) (*expanse of s.*) пески́ *m.pl.*; *attrib.* песо́чный, песча́ный; *s.-bar*, песча́ный бар; *s.-blast*, обдува́ть *imp.*, обду́ть (-у́ю, -у́ешь) *perf.* песо́чной струёй; *s.-dune*, дю́на; *s.-glass*, песо́чные часы́ (-со́в)

pl.; *s.-martin*, берегова́я ла́сточка; *s.-pit*, (*children's*) песо́чница.
sandal[1] *n.* санда́лия.
sandal[2], **-wood** *n.* санда́ловое де́рево.
sandbag *n.* мешо́к (-шка́) с песко́м; (*as ballast*) балла́стный мешо́к (-шка́); *v.t.* защища́ть (-ищу́, -ити́шь) *perf.* мешка́ми с песко́м.
sandbank *n.* о́тмель.
sandpaper *n.* шку́рка; *v.t.* шлифова́ть *imp.*, от ~ *perf.* шку́ркой.
sandpiper *n.* перево́зчик.
sandstone *n.* песча́ник.
sandstorm *n.* песча́ная бу́ря.
sandwich *n.* са́ндвич, бутербро́д; (*cake*) торт с просло́йкой; *s.-board*, рекла́мные щиты́ *m.pl.*; *s.-man*, челове́к-рекла́ма; *v.t.*: *s. between*, вставля́ть *imp.*, вста́вить *perf.* ме́жду + *instr.*
sandy *adj.* песча́ный, песо́чный; (*hair*) рыжева́тый.
sane *adj.* норма́льный; (*of views*) разу́мный.
sang-froid *n.* самооблада́ние.
sanguinary *adj.* крова́вый. **sanguine** *adj.* сангвини́ческий, оптимисти́ческий.
sanitary *adj.* санита́рный; гигиени́ческий; *s. towel*, гигиени́ческая поду́шка. **sanitation** *n.* санита́рия; (*disposal of sewage*) водопрово́д и канализа́ция. **sanity** *n.* норма́льная пси́хика; (*good sense*) здра́вый ум (-а́).
Santa Claus *n.* Са́нта Кла́ус; (*Russian equivalent*) дед-моро́з.
sap[1] *n.* (*juice*) сок (*loc.* -е & -у́); *v.t.* (*exhaust*) истоща́ть *imp.*, истощи́ть *perf.* (*cf.* sap[2]).
sap[2] *n.* (*mil.*) са́па; *v.t.* (*undermine*) подрыва́ть *imp.*, подорва́ть (-ву́, -вёшь; -ва́л, -вала́, -ва́ло) *perf.* (*cf.* sap[1]).
sapling *n.* молодо́е де́рево (*pl.* -вца́, -вец, -вца́м).
sapper *n.* сапёр.
sapphire *n.* сапфи́р; *adj.* (*colour*) си́ний (синь, -ня, -не).
Saracen *n.* сараци́н (*gen.pl.* -н).
sarcasm *n.* сарка́зм. **sarcastic** *adj.* сарка́сти́ческий.
sarcoma *n.* сарко́ма.
sarcophagus *n.* саркофа́г.
sardine *n.* сарди́на.

sardonic *adj.* сардони́ческий.
sari *n.* са́ри *neut.indecl.*
sartorial *adj.* портня́жный.
sash[1] *n.* (*scarf*) по́яс (*pl.* -а́), куша́к (-а́).
sash[2] *n.* (*frame*) око́нный переплёт, скользя́щая ра́ма; *s.-window*, подъёмное окно́ (*pl.* о́кна, о́кон, о́кнам).
Satan *n.* сатана́ *m.* **satanic** *adj.* сатани́нский; (*devilish*) дья́вольский.
satchel *n.* ра́нец (-нца), су́мка.
sate *v.t.* насыща́ть *imp.*, насы́тить (-ы́щу, -ы́тишь) *perf.*
sateen *n.* сати́н.
satellite *n.* спу́тник, сателли́т (*also fig.*).
satiate *v.t.* насыща́ть *imp.*, насы́тить (-ы́щу, -ы́тишь) *perf.*; *be satiated*, пресыща́ться *imp.*, пресы́титься (-ы́щусь, -ы́тишься) *perf.* **satiation** *n.* насыще́ние. **satiety** *n.* пресыще́ние, сы́тость.
satin *n.* атла́с; *adj.* атла́сный; *s.-stitch*, гладь. **satinet(te)** *n.* сатине́т. **satiny** *adj.* атла́сный, шелкови́стый.
satire *n.* сати́ра. **satirical** *adj.* сатири́ческий. **satirist** *n.* сати́рик. **satirize** *v.t.* высме́ивать *imp.*, вы́смеять (-ею, -еешь) *perf.*
satisfaction *n.* удовлетворе́ние. **satisfactory** *adj.* удовлетвори́тельный. **satisfy** *v.t.* удовлетворя́ть *imp.*, удовлетвори́ть *perf.*; (*hunger, curiosity*) утоля́ть *imp.*, утоли́ть *perf.*
saturate *v.t.* пропи́тывать *imp.*, пропита́ть *perf.*; насыща́ть *imp.*, насы́тить (-ы́щу, -ы́шешь) *perf.* **saturation** *n.* насыще́ние, насы́щенность.
Saturday *n.* суббо́та.
Saturn *n.* Сату́рн. **saturnine** *adj.* мра́чный (-чен, -чна́, -чно), угрю́мый.
satyr *n.* сати́р.
sauce *n.* со́ус; (*insolence*) на́глость; *apple s.*, я́блочное пюре́ *neut.indecl.*; *s.-boat*, со́усник. **saucer** *n.* блю́дце (*gen.pl.* -дец). **saucepan** *n.* кастрю́ля.
saucy *adj.* на́глый (нагл, -а́, -о).
sauna *n.* фи́нская ба́ня.
saunter *v.i.* прогу́ливаться *imp.*; *n.* прогу́лка.
sausage *n.* колбаса́ (*pl.* -сы), соси́ска; *s.-meat*, колба́сный фарш; *s. roll*, пирожо́к (-жка́) с колба́сным фа́ршем.

savage adj. ди́кий (дик, -á, -о); (*cruel*) жесто́кий (-о́к, -óкá, -óко); n. дика́рь (-ря́) m.; v.t. свире́по напада́ть imp., напа́сть (-аду́, -адёшь; -а́л) perf. на + acc. **savagery** n. ди́кость n.; жесто́кость n.

savanna(h) n. сава́нна.

savant n. учёный sb.

save v.t. (*rescue*) спаса́ть imp., спасти́ (-су́, -сёшь; -с, -слá, -сло) perf.; (*put aside*) откла́дывать imp., отложи́ть (-жу́, -жишь) perf.; (*spare*) бере́чь (-егу́, -ежёшь; -ёг, -еглá) imp.; v.i.: s. up, копи́ть (-плю́, -пишь), на ~ perf. де́ньги. **savings** n. сбереже́ния neut.pl.; s-bank, сберега́тельная ка́сса. **saviour** n. спаси́тель m.

savour n. вкус; v.t. смакова́ть imp.; наслажда́ться imp., наслади́ться perf. + instr.

savoury adj. (*sharp*) о́стрый (остр & остёр, остра́, о́стро́); (*salty*) солёный (со́лон, -á, -о); (*spicy*) пря́ный.

savoy n. сави́ойская капу́ста.

saw n. пила́ (pl. -лы); v.t. пили́ть (-лю́, -лишь) imp.; s. up, распи́ливать imp., распили́ть (-лю́, -лишь) perf. **sawdust** n. опи́лки (-лок) pl. **saw-edged** adj. пилообра́зный. **sawfish** n. пила́-ры́ба. **sawmill** n. лесопи́льный заво́д, лесопи́лка. **sawyer** n. пи́льщик.

saxhorn n. саксго́рн.

saxifrage n. камнело́мка.

saxophone n. саксофо́н.

say v.t. говори́ть imp., сказа́ть (-ажу́, -а́жешь) perf.; to s. nothing of, не говоря́ уже́ o + prep.; that is to s., то есть (let us) s., ска́жем; it is said (that), говоря́т (что); n. сло́во; (*opinion*) мне́ние; (*influence*) влия́ние; have one's s., вы́сказаться (-ажусь, -ажешься) perf. **saying** n. погово́рка.

scab n. (*on wound*) струп (pl. -ья, -ьев), ко́рка; (*mange*) парша́; (*strike-breaker*) штрейкбре́хер.

scabbard n. но́жны (gen. -жен) pl.

scabies n. чесо́тка.

scabious adj. скабио́за.

scabrous adj. скабрёзный.

scaffold n. эшафо́т. **scaffolding** n. леса́ (-со́в) pl., подмости (-тей) pl.

scald v.t. обва́ривать imp., обвари́ть (-рю́, -ришь) perf.; n. ожо́г.

scale [1] n. (*of fish*) чешу́йка; pl. чешуя́ (collect.); (*on boiler etc.*) на́кипь n.; v.t. чи́стить imp., o ~ perf.; соска́бливать imp., соскобли́ть (-облю́, -о́блишь) perf. чешую́ c c + gen.; v.i. шелуши́ться imp.

scale [2] n. (s.-pan) ча́ша весо́в; pl. весы́ (-со́в) pl.

scale [3] n. (*relative dimensions*) масшта́б; (*set of marks*) шкала́ (pl. -лы); (*mus.*) га́мма; (*math.*): s. of notation систе́ма счисле́ния; v.t. (*climb*) взбира́ться imp., взобра́ться (взберу́сь, -рёшься; взобра́лся, -ала́сь, -а́ло́сь) perf. (по ле́стнице) на + acc.; s. down, понижа́ть imp., пони́зить perf.; s. up, повыша́ть imp., повы́сить perf.

scalene adj. неравносторо́нний.

scallop n. (*mollusc*) гребешо́к (-шка́); pl. (*decoration*) фесто́ны m.pl.; s-shell, ра́ковина гребешка́; v.t. (*cook*) запека́ть imp., запе́чь (-еку́, -ечёшь; -ёк, -екла́) perf. в ра́ковине; (*decorate*) украша́ть imp., укра́сить perf. фесто́нами.

scalp n. ко́жа че́репа; (*as trophy*) скальп; v.t. скальпи́ровать imp., perf.

scalpel n. ска́льпель m.

scaly adj. чешу́йчатый; (*of boiler etc.*) покры́тый на́кипью.

scamp n. плути́шка m.

scamper v.i. бы́стро бе́гать imp.; (*playfully*) резви́ться imp.

scampi n. креве́тки f.pl.

scan v.t. & i. (*verse*) сканди́ровать(ся) imp.; v.t. (*intently*) внима́тельно рассма́тривать imp.; (*quickly*) бе́гло просма́тривать imp., просмотре́ть (-рю́, -ришь) perf.

scandal n. сканда́л; (*gossip*) спле́тни (-тен) pl. **scandalize** v.t. шоки́ровать imp., perf. **scandalmonger** n. спле́тник, -ица. **scandalous** adj. сканда́льный.

Scandinavian adj. скандина́вский.

scansion n. сканди́рование.

scanty adj. ску́дный (-ден, -дна́, -дно); (*insufficient*) недоста́точный.

scapegoat n. козёл (-злá) отпуще́ния.

scapula n. лопа́тка.

scar n. рубе́ц (-бца́), шрам. **scarred** adj. обезобра́женный (-ен) рубца́ми, шра́мами.

scarab n. скарабе́й.

scarce adj. дефици́тный, недоста́точный; (rare) ре́дкий (-док, -дка́, -дко); make oneself s., улизну́ть perf. **scarcely** adv. (only just) едва́; (surely not) едва́ ли. **scarcity** n. недоста́ток (-тка), дефици́т.

scare v.t. пуга́ть imp., ис~, на~ perf.; s. away, off, отпу́гивать imp., отпугну́ть perf.; n. па́ника. **scarecrow** n. пу́гало, чу́чело. **scaremonger** n. паникёр.

scarf n. шарф.

scarlet adj. (n.) а́лый (цвет); s. fever, скарлати́на; s. runner, фасо́ль многоцве́тковая.

scathing adj. е́дкий (е́док, едка́, е́дко), уничтожа́ющий.

scatter v.t. & i. рассыпа́ть(ся) imp., рассы́пать(ся) (-плю, -плет(ся)) perf.; (disperse) рассе́ивать(ся) imp., рассе́ять(ся) (-е́ю, -е́ет(ся)) perf.; v.i. (disperse, drive away) разгоня́ть imp., разогна́ть (разгоню́, -нишь; разогна́л, -а́, -о) perf.; v.i. (run) разбега́ться imp., разбежа́ться (-ежи́тся, -егу́тся) perf.; s.-brained, легкомы́сленный (-ен, -енна). **scattered** adj. разбро́санный (-ан), (sporadic) отде́льный.

scavenger n. (person) му́сорщик; (animal) живо́тное sb., пита́ющееся па́далью.

scenario n. сцена́рий. **scenarist** n. сцена́рист. **scene** n. сце́на; (part of play also) явле́ние; (place of action) ме́сто де́йствия; (scenery) декора́ция; behind the scenes, за кули́сами; make a s., устра́ивать imp., устро́ить perf. сце́ну; s.-painter, худо́жник-декора́тор; s.-shifter, рабо́чий sb. сце́ны. **scenery** n. (theat.) декора́ция; (landscape) пейза́ж. **scenic** adj. сцени́ческий.

scent n. (smell) арома́т; (perfume) духи́ (-хо́в) pl.; (trail) след (-а(у); pl. -ы́); v.t. (discern) чу́ять (чу́ю, чу́ешь) imp.; (apply perfume) души́ть (-шу́, -шишь) imp., на~ perf.; (make fragrant) наполня́ть imp., напо́лнить perf. арома́том.

sceptic n. ске́птик. **sceptical** adj. скепти́ческий. **scepticism** n. скептици́зм.

sceptre n. ски́петр.

schedule n. (timetable) расписа́ние; (inventory) о́пись; v.t. составля́ть imp., соста́вить perf. расписа́ние, о́пись, +gen.

schematic adj. схемати́ческий. **scheme** n. (plan) прое́кт; (intention) за́мысел (-сла); (intrigue) махина́ция; v.i. стро́ить imp. та́йные пла́ны. **schemer** n. интрига́н. **scheming** adj. интригу́ющий.

scherzo n. ске́рцо neut.indecl.

schism n. раско́л. **schismatic** adj. раско́льнический; n. раско́льник.

schizophrenia n. шизофрени́я. **schizophrenic** adj. шизофрени́ческий; n. шизофре́ник.

scholar n. (learned) учёный sb.; (scholarship-holder) стипендиа́т, ~ка. **scholarly** adj. учёный, нау́чный. **scholarship** n. учёность, нау́ка; (payment) стипе́ндия.

school n. шко́ла; (specialist s.) учи́лище; (univ.) факульте́т; attrib. шко́льный; v.t. (curb) обу́здывать imp., обузда́ть perf.; (accustom) приуча́ть imp., приучи́ть (-чу́, -чишь) perf. (to, к+dat., +inf.). **school-book** n. уче́бник. **schoolboy** n. шко́льник, учени́к (-а́). **schoolgirl** n. шко́льница, учени́ца. **schooling** n. обуче́ние. **school-leaver** n. выпускни́к (-а́), -и́ца. **schoolmaster** n. шко́льный учи́тель (pl. -ля́) m. **schoolmistress** n. шко́льная учи́тельница.

schooner n. шху́на.

sciatic adj. седа́лищный. **sciatica** n. и́шиас.

science n. нау́ка; (natural s.) есте́ственные нау́ки f.pl.; s. fiction, нау́чная фанта́стика. **scientific** adj. нау́чный. **scientist** n. учёный sb.; (natural s.) есте́ственник, -ица.

scintillate v.i. искри́ться imp. **scintillating** adj. блиста́тельный.

scion n. о́трыск.

scissors n. но́жницы (-ц) pl.

sclerosis n. склеро́з.

scoff[1] v.i. (mock) издева́ться imp. (at, над+instr.).

scoff[2] v.t. (eat) жрать (жру, жрёшь; жрал, -а́, -о) imp., со~ perf.

scold *v.t.* брани́ть *imp.*, вы́~ *perf.* **scolding** *n.* нагоня́й.

scollop *see* scallop.

sconce *n.* (*bracket*) бра *neut.indecl.*; (*candlestick*) подсве́чник.

scone *n.* сдобная лепёшка.

scoop *n.* черпа́к (-á), ковш (-á); *v.t.* (*s. out, up*) вычерпывать *imp.*, вычерпать *perf.*

scooter *n.* (*child's*) самока́т, ро́ллер; (*motor s.*) мотороллер.

scope *n.* преде́лы *m.pl.*, просто́р, разма́х.

scorbutic *adj.* цинго́тный.

scorch *v.t.* пали́ть *imp.*, с~ *perf.*; подпа́ливать *imp.*, подпали́ть *perf.*; *scorched earth policy*, та́ктика вы́жженной земли́; *n.* ожо́г. **scorching** *adj.* паля́щий, зно́йный.

score *n.* (*notch*) зару́бка; (*account; number of points etc.*) счёт; (*mus.*) партиту́ра; (*twenty*) два деся́тка; *pl.* (*great numbers*) деся́тки *m.pl.*, мно́жество; *v.t.* (*notch*) де́лать *imp.*, с~ *perf.* зару́бки на+*prep.*; (*points etc.*) получа́ть *imp.*, получи́ть (-чу, -чишь) *perf.*; (*mus.*) оркестрова́ть *imp.*, *perf.*; *v.i.* (*keep s.*) вести́ (веду́, -дёшь; вёл, -á) *imp.*, с~ *perf.* счёт.

scorn *n.* презре́ние; *v.t.* презира́ть *imp.*, презре́ть (-рю, -ри́шь) *perf.* **scornful** *adj.* презри́тельный.

Scorpio *n.* Скорпио́н.

scorpion *n.* скорпио́н.

Scot *n.* шотла́ндец (-дца), -дка. **Scotch** *adj.* шотла́ндский; *n.* (*whisky*) шотла́ндское ви́ски *neut.indecl.*; *the S.*, шотла́ндцы *m.pl.*

scot-free *adv.* безнака́занно.

Scots, Scottish *adj.* шотла́ндский; *see* Scotch.

scoundrel *n.* негодя́й, подле́ц (-á).

scour[1] *v.t.* (*cleanse*) отчища́ть *imp.*, отчи́стить *perf.* **scourer** *n.* металли́ческая моча́лка.

scour[2] *v.i. & i.* (*rove*) ры́скать (ры́щу, -щешь) *imp.* (по+*dat.*)

scourge *n.* бич (-á); *v.t.* бичева́ть (-чу́ю, -чу́ешь) *imp.*

scout *n.* разве́дчик; (*S.*) бойска́ут; *v.i.*: *s. about*, рыска́ть (ры́щу, -щешь) *imp.* (*for*, в по́исках+*gen.*)

scowl *v.i.* хму́риться *imp.*, на~ *perf.*; *n.* хму́рый вид, взгляд.

scrabble *v.i.*: *s. about*, ры́ться (ро́юсь, ро́ешься) *imp.*

scramble *v.i.* кара́бкаться *imp.*, вс~ *perf.*; (*struggle*) дра́ться (деру́сь, -рёшься; дра́лся, -ала́сь, -áлóсь) *imp.* (*for*, за+*acc.*); *v.t.* (*mix together*) переме́шивать *imp.*, перемеша́ть *perf.*; *scrambled eggs*, яи́чница-болту́нья.

scrap[1] *n.* (*fragment etc.*) клочо́к (-чка), обре́зок (-зка), кусо́чек (-чка); *pl.* оста́тки *m.pl.*; *pl.* (*of food*) объе́дки (-ков) *pl.*; *s.-metal*, металли́ческий лом, скрап; *v.t.* превраща́ть *imp.*, преврати́ть (-ащу́ -ати́шь) *perf.* в лом; пуска́ть *imp.*, пусти́ть (пущу́, пу́стишь) *perf.* на слом.

scrap[2] *n.* (*fight*) дра́ка; *v.i.* дра́ться (деру́сь, -рёшься; дра́лся, -ала́сь) *imp.*

scrape *v.t.* скрести́ (скребу́, -бёшь; скрёб, -ла́) *imp.*; скобли́ть (-облю́, -о́бли́шь) *imp.*; *s. off*, отскреба́ть *imp.*, отскрести́ (-ребу́ -ребёшь; -рёб, -ребла́) *imp.*; (*through, examination*) с трудом выде́рживать *imp.*, вы́держать (-жу, -жишь) *perf.*; *s. together*, наскреба́ть *imp.*, наскрести́ (-ребу́ -ребёшь; -рёб, -ребла́) *perf.*

scratch *v.t.* цара́пать *imp.*, о~ *perf.*; *v.t. & abs.* чеса́ть(ся) (чешу́(сь), -шешь(ся)) *imp.*, по~ *perf.*; *v. abs.* цара́паться *imp.*; *v.t.* (*erase, s. off, through, etc.*) вычёркивать *imp.*, вы́черкнуть *perf.*; *n.* цара́пина; *adj.* случа́йный.

scrawl *n.* кара́кули *f.pl.*; *v.t.* писа́ть (пишу́, -шешь) *imp.*, на~ *perf.* кара́кулями.

scrawny *adj.* то́щий (тощ, -á, -е), сухопа́рый.

scream *n.* крик, визг; *v.i.* крича́ть (-чу́, -чи́шь) *imp.*, кри́кнуть *perf.*; *v.t.* вы́крикивать *imp.*, вы́крикнуть *perf.*

screech *n.* визг; *v.i.* визжа́ть (-жу́, -жи́шь) *imp.*

screen *n.* ши́рма; (*cin., television, radio, etc.*) экра́н; (*sieve*) гро́хот; *s.-play*, сцена́рий; *v.t.* (*shelter*) защища́ть *imp.*, защити́ть (-ищу́ -ити́шь) *perf.*;

заслоня́ть *imp.*, заслони́ть *perf.*; (*show film etc.*) демонстри́ровать *imp.*, *perf.*; (*sieve*) просе́ивать *imp.*, просе́ять (-е́ю, -е́ешь) *perf.*; *s. off*, отгора́живать *imp.*, отгороди́ть (-ожу́, -о́дишь) *perf.* ши́рмой.

screw *n.* (*male s.; propeller*) винт (-á); (*female s.*) га́йка; (*s.-bolt*) болт (-á); *v.t.* (*s. on*) привинчивать *imp.*, привинти́ть *perf.*; (*s. up*) завинчивать *imp.*, завинти́ть *perf.*; *s. up one's eyes*, щу́риться *imp.*, со~ *perf.* **screwdriver** *n.* отвёртка.

scribble *v.t.* небре́жно, бы́стро, писа́ть (пишу́, -шешь) *imp.*, на~ *perf.*; *n.* кара́кули *f.pl.* **scribbler** *n.* писа́ка *m. & f.*

scribe *n.* писе́ц (-сца́); (*Bibl.*) кни́жник.

scrimmage *n.* сва́лка.

script *n.* по́черк, шрифт; (*of film etc.*) сцена́рий; *s.-writer*, сценари́ст. **Scripture** *n.* свяще́нное писа́ние.

scrofula *n.* золоту́ха.

scroll *n.* сви́ток (-тка); (*design*) завито́к (-тка́); *s.-work*, орна́мент в ви́де завитко́в.

scrounge *v.t.* (*steal*) тибрить *imp.*, с~ *perf.*; (*cadge*) выкля́нчивать *imp.*, вы́клянчить *perf.*; *v.i.* попроша́йничать *imp.*

scrub[1] *n.* (*brushwood*) куста́рник; (*area*) поро́сшая куста́рником ме́стность.

scrub[2] *v.t.* мыть (мо́ю, мо́ешь) *imp.*, вы́~ *perf.* щёткой; *scrubbing-brush*, жёсткая щётка; *n.* чи́стка.

scruff *n.* загри́вок (-вка); *take by the s. of the neck*, брать (беру́, -рёшь; брал, -á, -о) *imp.*, взять (возьму́, -мёшь; взял, -á, -о) *perf.* за ши́ворот.

scruffy *adj.* (*of clothes*) потрёпанный (-ан, -анна); (*of person*) неря́шливый.

scrum(mage) *n.* схва́тка вокру́г мяча́.

scruple *n.* (*also pl.*) колеба́ние, угрызе́ния *neut.pl.* со́вести; *v.i.* колеба́ться (-блюсь, -блешься) *imp.* **scrupulous** *adj.* скрупулёзный, щепети́льный.

scrutineer *n.* прове́рщик, -ица. **scrutinize** *v.t.* рассма́тривать *imp.* **scrutiny** *n.* рассмотре́ние, прове́рка.

scud *v.i.* нести́сь (несётся; нёсся, несла́сь) *imp.*, по~ *perf.*; скользи́ть *imp.*

scuffed *adj.* потёртый, поцара́панный.

scuffle *n.* сва́лка; *v.i.* дра́ться (деру́сь, -рёшься; дра́лся, -ала́сь, -а́лось) *imp.*

scull *n.* весло́; (*stern oar*) кормово́е весло́; *pl.* вёсла, -сел, -слам) *imp.* грести́ (гребу́, -бёшь; грёб, -ла́) *imp.* (па́рными вёслами); галани́ть *imp.*

scullery *n.* судомо́йня (*gen.pl.* -о́ен).

sculptor *n.* ску́льптор. **sculptural** *adj.* скульпту́рный. **sculpture** *n.* скульпту́ра.

scum *n.* пе́на, на́кипь; (*fig., people*) подо́нки (-ков) *pl.*

scupper[1] *n.* шпига́т.

scupper[2] *v.t.* (*ship*) потопля́ть *imp.*, потопи́ть (-плю́, -пишь) *perf.*

scurf *n.* пе́рхоть.

scurrility *n.* непристо́йность, гру́бость. **scurrilous** *adj.* непристо́йный, гру́бый (груб, -á, -о).

scurry *v.i.* поспе́шно, суетли́во, бе́гать *indet.*, бежа́ть (бегу́, бежи́шь) *det.*

scurvy *n.* цинга́; *adj.* по́длый (подл, -á, -о).

scuttle[1] *n.* (*coal-box*) ведёрко (*pl.* -рки, -рок, -ркам) для у́гля.

scuttle[2] *v.t.* (*ship*) затопля́ть *imp.*, затопи́ть (-плю́, -пишь) *perf.*

scuttle[3] *v.i.* (*run away*) удира́ть *imp.*, удра́ть (удеру́, -рёшь; удра́л, -á, -о) *perf.*

scythe *n.* коса́ (*acc.* ко́су; *pl.* -сы).

sea *n.* мо́ре (*pl.* -ря́); *at s.*, в (откры́том) мо́ре; *by s.*, мо́рем; *attrib.* морско́й; *s. anchor*, плаву́чий я́корь (*pl.* -ря́) *m.*; *s. anemone*, акти́ния; *s.-breeze*, ве́тер (-тра) с мо́ря; *s.-coast*, побере́жье; *s.-dog* (*person*) морско́й волк (*pl.* -и, -о́в); *s. front*, на́бережная *sb.*; *s.-gull*, ча́йка; *s.-horse*, морско́й конёк (-нька́); *s. lane*, морско́й путь (-ти́, -тём) *m.*; *s.-level*, у́ровень (-вня) *m.* мо́ря; *s.-lion*, морско́й лев (льва) *m.*; *s.-shore*, побере́жье; *s.-urchin*, морско́й ёж (-á); *s.-wall*, да́мба. **seaboard** *n.* побере́жье. **seafaring** *n.* морепла́вание. **seagoing** *adj.* да́льнего пла́вания.

seal[1] *n.* (*on document etc.*) печа́ть; *v.t.* скрепля́ть *imp.*, скрепи́ть *perf.* печа́тью; запеча́тывать *imp.*, запеча́тать *perf.*; *sealing-wax*, сургу́ч (-á).

seal[2] n. (animal) тюлень m.; (fur-s.) котик. **sealskin** n. котиковый мех (loc. -е и -ý); attrib. котиковый.

seam n. шов (шва), рубец (-бца); (stratum) пласт (-á), слой (pl. -ý); v.t. сшивать imp., сшить (сошью, -ьёшь) perf. швами.

seaman n. моряк (-á); (also rank) матрос.

seamstress n. швея.

seamy adj. со швами наружу; the s. side, (also fig.) изнанка.

seance n. спиритический сеанс.

seaplane n. гидросамолёт. **seaport** n. портовый город (pl. -á).

sear v.t. прижигать imp., прижечь (-жгу, -жжёшь, -жгут; -жёг, -жгла) perf.

search v.t. обыскивать imp., обыскать (-ыщу, -ыщешь) perf.; v.i. искать (ищу, ищешь) imp. (for, + acc.); производить (-ожу, -одишь) imp., произвести (-еду, -едёшь; -ёл, -ела) perf. обыск; n. поиски m.pl.; обыск; s.-party, поисковая группа; s.-warrant, ордер (pl. -á) на обыск. **searching** adj. (thorough) тщательный; (look) испытующий. **searchlight** n. прожектор (pl. -ы и -á).

seascape n. марина. **seasickness** n. морская болезнь. **seaside** n. берег (loc. -ý) моря; (resort) морской курорт.

season n. сезон; (period in general) период; (one of four) время neut. года; in s., то сезон; s.-ticket, сезонный билет; v.t. (mature) выдерживать imp., выдержать (-жу, -жишь) perf.; (flavour) приправлять imp., приправить perf. **seasonable** adj. по сезону; (timely) своевременный (-нен, -нна). **seasonal** adj. сезонный. **seasoning** n. приправа.

seat n. место (pl. -тá), сиденье; (chair) стул (pl. -ья, -ьев); (bench) скамейка; (buttocks) седалище; (of trousers) зад (loc. -ý, pl. -ы); (country s.) усадьба; (ticket) билет; s. belt, привязной ремень (-мня) m.; v.t. сажать imp., посадить (-ажу, -áдишь) perf.; (of room etc.) вмещать imp., вместить perf.; be seated, садиться imp., сесть (сяду, -дешь; сел) perf.

seaweed n. морская водоросль.

sebaceous adj. сальный.

sec n.: half a s.! минутку! один момент!

secateurs n.pl. секатор.

secede v.i. откалываться imp., отколоться (-люсь, -лешься) perf. **secession** n. откол.

secluded adj. укромный. **seclusion** n. укромность; (place) укромное место.

second adj. второй; be s. to, (inferior) уступать imp., уступить (-плю, -пишь) perf. + dat.; s. ballot, перебаллотировка; s.-best, второсортный; s.-class, второклассный, второсортный; s.-hand, подержанный (-ан, -анна); (of information) из вторых рук; s.-rate, второразрядный; s. sight, ясновидение; s. thoughts, взвесив всё ещё раз; have s. thoughts, передумывать imp., передумать perf. (about, + acc.); s. wind, второе дыхание; n. второй sb.; (date) второе (число) sb.; (mus.) время; angle секунда; (coll., moment) момент (in duel) секундант; pl. товар второго сорта; pl. (flour) мука грубого помола; (s. helping) вторая порция; s. in command, заместитель m. командира; s. hand (of clock etc.) секундная стрелка; v.t. (support) поддерживать imp., поддержать (-жу, -жишь) perf.; (transfer) откомандировывать imp., откомандировать perf. **secondary** adj. вторичный, второстепенный (-нен, -нна); (education) средний. **secondly** adv. во-вторых.

secrecy n. секретность. **secret** n. тайна, секрет; adj. тайный, секретный; (hidden) потайной.

secretarial adj. секретарский. **secretariat** n. секретариат. **secretary** n. секретарь (-ря) m., -рша; (minister) министр.

secrete v.t. (conceal) прятать (-ячу, -ячешь) imp., с ~ perf.; (med.) выделять imp., выделить perf. **secretion** n. укрывание; (med.) секреция, выделение.

secretive adj. скрытный.

sect n. сéкта. **sectarian** adj. сектáнтский; n. сектáнт.

section n. сéкция, отрéзок (-зка); (of book) раздéл; (of solid) сечéние, прóфиль, разрéз. **sectional** adj. секциóнный. **sector** n. сéктор (pl. -ы и -á), учáсток (-тка).

secular adj. свéтский, мирскóй; s. clergy, бéлое духовéнство. **secularization** n. секуляризáция. **secularize** v.t. секуляризовáть imp., perf.

secure adj. безопáсный, надёжный; v.t. (fasten) закреплять imp., закрепить perf.; (guarantee) обеспéчивать imp., обеспéчить perf.; (obtain) доставáть (-таю, -таёшь) imp., достáть (-áну, -áнешь) perf. **security** n. безопáсность; (guarantee) залóг; pl. цéнные бумáги f.pl.; S. Council, Совéт Безопáсности; s. risk, неблагонадёжный человéк (pl. лю́ди, -дéй, -дям, -дьми́); social s., социáльное обеспéчение.

sedan(-chair) n. портшéз.

sedate adj. степéнный (-нен, -нна). **sedation** n. успокоéние. **sedative** adj. успокáивающий; n. успокáивающее срéдство.

sedentary adj. сидя́чий.

sedge n. осóка.

sediment n. осáдок (-дка), отстóй. **sedimentary** adj. осáдочный.

sedition n. подстрекáтельство к мятежу́. **seditious** adj. подстрекáтельский, мятéжный.

seduce v.t. соблазнять imp., соблазнить perf.; совращáть imp., совратить (-ащу́, -атишь) perf. **seducer** n. соблазни́тель m. **seduction** n. обольщéние. **seductive** adj. соблазни́тельный, обольсти́тельный. **seductress** n. соблазни́тельница.

sedulous adj. прилéжный.

see[1] n. епáрхия; Holy S., пáпский престóл.

see[2] v.t. и i. ви́деть (ви́жу, ви́дишь) imp., у ~ perf.; v.t. (watch, look) смотрéть (-рю́ -ришь) imp. по ~ perf.; (find out) узнавáть (-наю́, -наёшь) imp., узнáть perf.; (understand) понимáть imp., понять (пойму́, -мёшь; пóнял, -á, -о) perf.; (meet) ви́деться (ви́жусь, ви́дишься) imp., у ~ perf.;

c + instr.; (imagine) представля́ть imp., предстáвить perf. себé; (escort) провожáть imp., проводи́ть perf.; s. about, (attend to) забóтиться imp., по ~ perf. o + prep.; s. over, осмáтривать imp., осмотрéть (-рю́, -ришь) perf.; s. through, (fig.) ви́деть (ви́жу, ви́дишь) imp. наскво́зь + acc.

seed n. сéмя (gen.pl. -мя́н) neut.; (grain) зернó; s.-bed, парни́к (-á); s.-cake, бу́лочка с тми́ном; s.-corn, посевнóе зернó; s.-pearl(s), мéлкий жéмчуг. **seedling** n. сея́нец (-нца); pl. рассáда. **seedy** adj. (shabby) потрёпанный (-ан, -анна); (ill) нездорóвый.

seeing (that) conj. ввиду́ тогó, что.

seek v.t. искáть (ищу́, -щешь) imp. + acc., gen.

seem v.i. казáться (кажу́сь, -жешься) imp., по ~ perf. (+ instr.) (often used parenthetically in impers. forms). **seeming** adj. мни́мый. **seemingly** adv. по-ви́димому, на вид.

seemly adj. прили́чный.

seep v.i. просáчиваться imp., просочи́ться perf. **seepage** n. просáчивание, течь.

seer n. прови́дец (-дца).

see-saw n. (game) кача́ние на доскé; (board) дéтские качéли (-лей) pl.; v.i. качáться imp. (на доскé).

seethe v.i. кипéть (-плю́ -пи́шь) imp., вс ~ perf.

segment n. отрéзок (-зка); (of orange etc.) дóлька; (geom.) сегмéнт.

segregate v.t. отделя́ть imp., отдели́ть (-лю́, -лишь) perf. **segregation** n. отделéние, сегрегáция.

seine n. нéвод (pl. -á).

seismic adj. сейсми́ческий. **seismograph** n. сейсмóграф. **seismology** n. сейсмолóгия.

seize v.t. хватáть imp., схвати́ть (-ачу́, -áтишь) perf.; v.i.: s. up, заедáть imp., заéсть (-éст; -éло) perf. impers. + acc.; s. upon, хвата́ться (-ачу́сь, -áтишься) imp., хвати́ться (-ачу́сь, -áтишься) perf. за + acc. **seizure** n. захвáт, заедáние; (stroke) удáр.

seldom adv. рéдко.

select adj. и́збранный; v.t. отбирáть imp., отобрáть (отберу́, -рёшь; отобрал, -á, -о) *perf.*; выбирáть *imp.*, выбрать (вы́беру, -решь) *perf.* **selection** *n.* вы́бор; (*biol.*) отбóр. **selective** *adj.* селекти́вный.

self *n.* сóбственная ли́чность; (*one's interests*) свои́ ли́чные интере́сы *m.pl.*
self- *in comb.* само-; *s.-absorbed, s.-detached* house, дом, разделённый общей эгоцентри́чный; *s.-assured,* самоуве́ренный (-ен, -енна); *s.-centred,* эгоцентри́чный; *s.-confidence,* самоуве́ренность; *s.-confident,* самоуве́ренный (-ен, -енна); *s.-conscious,* засте́нчивый; *s.-contained,* (*person*) за́мкнутый; (*flat etc.*) отде́льный; *s.-control,* самооблада́ние; *s.-defence,* самооборо́на, самозащи́та; *s.-denial,* самоотрече́ние; *s.-determination,* самоопределе́ние; *s.-effacing,* скро́мный (-мен, -мна́, -мно); *s.-esteem,* самоуваже́ние; *s.-evident,* очеви́дный; *s.-government,* самоуправле́ние; *s.-help,* самопо́мощь; *s.-importance,* самомне́ние; *s.-interest,* своекоры́стие; *s.-made,* (*man*) вы́бившийся из низо́в; *s.-portrait,* автопортре́т; *s.-possessed,* хладнокро́вный; *s.-preservation,* самосохране́ние; *s.-propelled,* самохо́дный; *s.-respect,* чу́вство со́бственного досто́инства; *s.-reliant,* наде́ющийся то́лько на себя́; *s.-righteous,* уве́ренный (-ен, -енна) в свое́й правоте́, фарисе́йский; *s.-sacrifice,* самопоже́ртвование; *s.-satisfied,* самодово́льный; *s.-service,* самообслу́живание (*attrib., in gen. after n.*); *s.-starter,* самопу́ск; *s.-styled,* самозва́ный; *s.-sufficient,* самостоя́тельный; *s.-willed,* самово́льный.

selfish *adj.* эгоисти́чный, себялюби́вый.
selfless *adj.* самоотве́рженный (-ен, -енна).
sell *v.t.* & *i.* продава́ть(ся) (-даю́, -даёт(ся)) *imp.*, прода́ть(ся) (-áм, -áшь, -áст(ся), -ади́м; -ал/-áлся, -ала́(сь), -ало/-áлось) *perf.*; *v.t.* (*deal in*) торгова́ть *imp.*+*instr.*; *s. off,* out, распродава́ть (-даю́, -даёшь) *imp.*, распрода́ть (-áм, -áшь, -áст, -ади́м; -ал, -ала́, -ало) *perf.* **seller** *n.* торго́вец (-вца). **selling** *n.* прода́жа.

selvage *n.* кро́мка.

semantic *adj.* семанти́ческий. **semantics** *n.* сема́нтика.
semaphore *n.* семафо́р.
semblance *n.* вне́шний вид.
semen *n.* се́мя *neut.*
semi- *in comb.* полу-; *s.-conscious,* полубессозна́тельный; *s.-detached house,* дом, разделённый общей стено́й; *s.-official,* полуофициа́льный; официо́зный; *s.-precious stone,* самоцве́т. **semibreve** *n.* це́лая но́та. **semicircle** *n.* полукру́г. **semicircular** *adj.* полукру́глый. **semicolon** *n.* то́чка с запято́й. **semiconductor** *n.* полупрово́дник (-á). **semifinal** *n.* полуфина́л. **semifinalist** *n.* полуфинали́ст.
seminar *n.* семина́р. **seminary** *n.* (духо́вная) семина́рия.
semiquaver *n.* шестна́дцатая но́та.
Semite *n.* семи́т, ~ка. **Semitic** *adj.* семити́ческий.
semitone *n.* полуто́н. **semivowel** *n.* полугла́сный *sb.*
semolina *n.* ма́нная крупа́.
sempstress *see* seamstress.
senate *n.* сена́т; (*univ.*) (учёный) сове́т. **senator** *n.* сена́тор. **senatorial** *adj.* сена́торский.
send *v.t.* посыла́ть *imp.*, посла́ть (пошлю́, -лёшь) *perf.*; *s. down,* (*univ.*) исключа́ть *imp.*, исключи́ть *perf.* из университе́та; *s. off,* отправля́ть *imp.*, отпра́вить *perf.*; *s. up,* (*ridicule*) высме́ивать *imp.*, вы́смеять (-ею, -еешь) *perf.*; *s.-off,* про́воды (-дов) *pl.* **sender** *n.* отправи́тель *m.*
senile *adj.* ста́рческий, дря́хлый (-л, -ла́, -ло). **senility** *n.* ста́рость, дря́хлость.
senior *adj.* (*n.*) ста́рший (*sb.*); *s. citizen,* стари́к (-á), стару́ха; *s. partner,* глава́ (*pl.* -вы) фи́рмы. **seniority** *n.* старшинство́.
senna *n.* александри́йский лист (-á).
sensation *n.* сенса́ция; (*feeling*) ощуще́ние, чу́вство. **sensational** *adj.* сенсацио́нный (-нен, -нна).
sense *n.* чу́вство, ощуще́ние; (*good s.*) здра́вый смысл; (*meaning*) смысл; *in one's senses,* в своём уме́; *v.t.* ощуща́ть *imp.*, ощути́ть (-ущу́, -ути́шь) *perf.*; чу́вствовать *imp.* **senseless** *adj.* бессмы́сленный (-ен, -енна).

sensibility *n.* чувстви́тельность.

sensible *adj.* благоразу́мный.

sensitive *adj.* чувстви́тельный; (*touchy*) оби́дчивый. **sensitivity** *n.* чувстви́тельность.

sensory *adj.* чувстви́тельный.

sensual, sensuous *adj.* чу́вственный (-ен, -енна).

sentence *n.* фра́за; (*gram.*) предложе́ние; (*leg.*) пригово́р; *v.t.* осужда́ть *imp.*, осуди́ть (-ужу́, -у́дишь) *perf.* (to, к + *dat.*); пригова́ривать *imp.*, приговори́ть *perf.* (to, к + *dat.*).

sententious *adj.* сентенцио́зный.

sentiment *n.* (*feeling*) чу́вство; (*opinion*) мне́ние. **sentimental** *adj.* сентимента́льный. **sentimentality** *n.* сентимента́льность.

sentinel, sentry *n.* часово́й *sb.*

sepal *n.* чашели́стик.

separable *adj.* отдели́мый. **separate** *adj.* отде́льный; (*independent*) самостоя́тельный; *n.* отде́льный о́ттиск; *v.t. & i.* отделя́ть(ся) *imp.*, отдели́ть(ся) (-лю́(сь), -лишь(ся)) *perf.* **separation** *n.* отделе́ние. **separatism** *n.* сепарати́зм. **separatist** *n.* сепарати́ст. **separator** *n.* сепара́тор.

sepia *n.* се́пия.

sepoy *n.* сипа́й.

sepsis *n.* се́псис.

September *n.* сентя́брь (-ря́) *m.*; *attrib.* сентя́брьский.

septet *n.* септе́т.

septic *adj.* септи́ческий; *s. tank*, септи́к. **septicaemia** *n.* се́псис, септицеми́я.

septuple *adj.* семикра́тный.

sepulchral *adj.* моги́льный, гробово́й. **sepulchre** *n.* моги́ла.

sequel *n.* (*result*) после́дствие; (*continuation*) продолже́ние. **sequence** *n.* после́довательность; (*cin.*) эпизо́д; *s. of events*, ход собы́тий.

sequester *v.t.* (*isolate*) уединя́ть *imp.*, уедини́ть *perf.*; (*confiscate*) секвестрова́ть *imp.*, *perf.* **sequestered** *adj.* уединённый. **sequestration** *n.* секве́стр.

sequin *n.* блёстка.

sequoia *n.* секво́йя.

seraph *n.* серафи́м.

Serb(ian) *adj.* се́рбский; *n.* серб, ~ ка;

Serbo-Croat(ian) *adj.* сербскохорва́тский.

serenade *n.* серена́да; *v.t.* исполня́ть *imp.*, испо́лнить *perf.* серена́ду + *dat.*

serene *adj.* (*calm*) споко́йный; (*clear*) я́сный (я́сен, ясна́, я́сно, я́сны). **serenity** *n.* споко́йствие; я́сность.

serf *n.* крепостно́й *sb.* **serfdom** *n.* крепостно́е пра́во, крепостни́чество.

serge *n.* са́ржа.

sergeant *n.* сержа́нт; *s.-major*, старшина́ (*pl.* -ны) *m.*

serial *adj.* сери́йный; (*of story etc.*) выходя́щий отде́льными вы́пусками; *n.* (*story*) рома́н в не́скольких частя́х; (*film*) сери́йный фильм; (*periodical*) периоди́ческое изда́ние. **serialize** *v.t.* издава́ть (-даю́, -даёшь) *imp.*, изда́ть (-а́м, -а́шь, -а́ст, -ади́м; изда́л, -а́, -о) *perf.* вы́пусками. **series** *n.* ряд (-а́ with 2, 3, 4, *loc.* -у́; *pl.* -ы), се́рия.

serious *adj.* серьёзный. **seriousness** *n.* серьёзность.

sermon *n.* про́поведь.

serpent *n.* змея́ (*pl.* -е́и). **serpentine** *adj.* (*coiling*) изви́листый.

serrated *adj.* зазу́бренный, зубча́тый.

serried *adj.* со́мкнутый.

serum *n.* сы́воротка.

servant *n.* слуга́ (*pl.* -ги) *m.*, служа́нка. **serve** *v.t.* служи́ть (-жу́, -жишь) *imp.*, по — *perf.* + *dat.* (as, for, + *instr.*); (*attend to*) обслу́живать *imp.*, обслужи́ть (-жу́, -жишь) *perf.*; (*food, ball*) подава́ть (-даю́, -даёшь) *imp.*, пода́ть (-а́м, -а́шь, -а́ст, -ади́м; по́дал, -а́, -о) *perf.*; (*period*) отбыва́ть *imp.*, отбы́ть (-бу́ду, -бу́дешь; о́тбыл, -а́, -о) *perf.*; (*writ etc.*) вруча́ть *imp.*, вручи́ть *perf.* (on, + *dat.*); *v.i.* (*be suitable*) годи́ться (for, на + *acc.*, для + *gen.*); (*sport*) подава́ть (-даю́, -даёшь) *imp.*, пода́ть (-а́м, -а́шь, -а́ст, -ади́м; по́дал, -а́, -о) *perf.* мяч; *it serves him right*, поде́лом ему́ (*dat.*). **service** *n.* слу́жба; (*attendance*) обслу́живание; (*set of dishes etc.*) серви́з; (*sport*) пода́ча; (*transport*) сообще́ние; *at your s.*, к ва́шим услу́гам; *v.t.* обслу́живать *imp.*, обслужи́ть (-жу́, -жишь) *perf.* **serviceable** *n.* (*useful*) поле́зный; (*durable*)

про́чный (-чен, -чна́, -чно, про́чны).
serviceman *n.* военнослужа́щий *sb.*
serviette *n.* салфе́тка. **servile** *adj.*
ра́бский; (*cringing*) раболе́пный. **servility** *n.* раболе́пие. **servo-** *in comb.*
серво-; *s.-mechanism*, сервомехани́зм;
s.-motor, сервомото́р.
sesame *n.* кунжу́т; (*open*) *s.*, сеза́м,
откро́йся.
session *n.* заседа́ние, се́ссия.
set[1] *v.t.* (*put*; *s. trap*) ста́вить *imp.*, по~
perf.; (*establish*; *s. clock*) устана́вли-
вать *imp.*, установи́ть (-влю́, -вишь)
perf.; (*table*) накрыва́ть *imp.*, накры́ть
(-ро́ю, -ро́ешь) *perf.*; (*plant*) сажа́ть
imp., посади́ть (-ажу́, -а́дишь) *perf.*;
(*bone*) вправля́ть *imp.*, впра́вить *perf.*;
(*hair*) укла́дывать *imp.*, уложи́ть
(-жу́, -жишь) *perf.*; (*jewel*) оправля́ть
imp., опра́вить *perf.*; (*print.*, *s. out*)
набира́ть *imp.*, набра́ть (наберу́,
-рёшь; набра́л, -а́, -о) *perf.*; (*bring
into state*) приводи́ть (-ожу́, -о́дишь)
imp., привести́ (-еду́, -едёшь; -ёл,
-ела́) *perf.* (in, to, в+*acc.*); (*example*)
подава́ть (-даю́, -даёшь) *imp.*, пода́ть
(-а́м, -а́шь, -а́ст, -ади́м; по́дал, -а́, -о)
perf.; (*task*) задава́ть (-даю́, -даёшь)
imp., зада́ть (-а́м, -а́шь, -а́ст, -ади́м;
за́дал, -а́, -о) *perf.*; *v.i.* (*solidify*) твер-
де́ть *imp.*, за~ *perf.*; застыва́ть *imp.*,
засты́(ну)ть (-ы́нет; -ы́л) *perf.*; (*fruit*)
завя́зываться *imp.*, завяза́ться (-я́жет-
ся) *perf.*; (*sun etc.*) заходи́ть (-ит) *imp.*,
зайти́ (зайдёт; зашёл, -шла́) *perf.*;
сади́ться *imp.*, сесть (ся́дет; сел) *perf.*;
s. eyes on, уви́деть (-и́жу, -и́дишь)
perf.; *s. free*, освобожда́ть *imp.*,
освободи́ть *perf.*; *s. one's heart on*,
стра́стно жела́ть *imp.* + *gen.*; *s. to
music*, положи́ть (-жу́, -жишь) *perf.*
на му́зыку; *s. sail*, пуска́ться *imp.*,
пусти́ться (пущу́сь, пу́стишься) *perf.*
в пла́вание; *s. about*, (*begin*) начина́ть
imp., нача́ть (начну́, -нёшь; на́чал, -а́,
-о) *perf.*; (*attack*) напада́ть *imp.*,
напа́сть (-аду́, -адёшь; -а́л) *perf.* на+
acc.; *s. back*, (*impede*) препя́тствовать
imp., вос~ *perf.* + *dat.*; *s.-back*,
неуда́ча; *s. down*, (*passenger*) выса́жи-
вать *imp.*, вы́садить *perf.*; (*in writing*)
запи́сывать *imp.*, записа́ть (-ишу́,
-и́шешь) *perf.*; (*attribute*) припи́сы-

вать *imp.*, приписа́ть (-ишу́, -и́шешь)
perf. (to, +*dat.*); *s. forth*, (*expound*)
излага́ть *imp.*, изложи́ть (-жу́, -жишь)
perf.; (*on journey*) see *s. off*; *s. in*,
наступа́ть *imp.*, наступи́ть (-ит) *perf.*;
s. off, (*on journey*) отправля́ться *imp.*,
отпра́виться *perf.*; (*enhance*) оттеня́ть
imp., оттени́ть *perf.*; *s. out*, (*state*)
излага́ть *imp.*, изложи́ть (-жу́, -жишь)
perf.; (*on journey*) see *s. off*; *s. up*,
(*business*) осно́вывать *imp.*, основа́ть
(-ну́ю, -нуёшь) *perf.*; (*person*) обеспе́-
чивать *imp.*, обеспе́чить *perf.* (with,
+ *instr.*).
set[2] *n.* набо́р, компле́кт, прибо́р; (*of
dishes etc.*) серви́з; (*of people*) круг
(*loc.* -у́; *pl.* -и́); (*radio*) приёмник;
(*television*) телеви́зор; (*tennis*) сет;
(*theat.*) декора́ция; (*cin.*) съёмочная
площа́дка.
set[3] *adj.* (*established*) устано́вленный
(-ен); (*fixed, of smile etc.*) засты́вший;
(*of intention*) обду́манный (-ан); *s.
phrase*, усто́йчивое словосочета́ние;
s. square, уго́льник.
settee *n.* дива́н.
setter *n.* (*dog*) се́ттер; (*person*) устано́в-
щик.
setting *n.* (*frame*) опра́ва; (*theat.*)
декора́ция, постано́вка; (*mus.*) му́зы-
ка на слова́; (*of sun etc.*) захо́д, зака́т.
settle *v.t.* (*decide*) реша́ть *imp.*, реши́ть
perf.; (*arrange*) ула́живать *imp.*,
ула́дить *perf.*; (*a bill etc.*) опла́чивать
imp., оплати́ть (-ачу́, -а́тишь) *perf.*;
(*colonize*) заселя́ть *imp.*, засели́ть
perf.; *v.i.* сели́ться *imp.*, по~ *perf.*;
(*subside*) оседа́ть *imp.*, осе́сть (ося́дет;
осе́л) *perf.*; *s. down*, уса́живаться *imp.*,
усе́сться (уся́дусь, -дешься; усе́лся)
perf. **settlement** *n.* поселе́ние; (*of
dispute*) разреше́ние; (*payment*) упла́-
та; (*subsidence*) оса́дка, оседа́ние;
marriage ~, бра́чный контра́кт
settler *n.* поселе́нец (-нца).
seven *adj.*, *n.* семь (-ми́, -мью́);
(*collect.*; *7 pairs*) се́меро (-ры́х);
(*cards*; *number 7*) семёрка; (*time*)
семь (часо́в); (*age*) семь лет. **seventeen**
adj., *n.* семна́дцать; (*age*) семна́дцать
лет. **seventeenth** *adj.*, *n.* семна́дцатый;
(*date*) семна́дцатое (число́). **seventh**

adj., n. седьмо́й; (*fraction*) седьма́я (часть (*pl.* -ти, -те́й)); (*date*) седьмо́е (число́). **seventieth** *adj., n.* семи-деся́тый. **seventy** *adj., n.* се́мьдесят (-мидесяти, -мьюдесятью); (*age*) се́мьдесят лет; *pl.* (*decade*) семидеся́тые го́ды (-до́в) *m.pl.*

sever *v.t.* (*cut off*) отреза́ть *imp.*, отре́-зать (-е́жу, -е́жешь) *perf.*; (*relations*) разрыва́ть *imp.*, разорва́ть (-ву́, -вёшь; -ва́л, -вала́, -ва́ло) *perf.*; (*friendship*) порыва́ть *imp.*, порва́ть (-ву́, -вёшь; порва́л, -а́, -о) *perf.*

several *pron.* (*adj.*) не́сколько (+ *gen.*).
severance *n.* разры́в; *s. pay*, выходно́е посо́бие.
severe *adj.* стро́гий (строг, -а́, -о); суро́вый; (*illness etc.*) тяжёлый (-л, -ла́). **severity** *n.* стро́гость, суро́вость.
sew *v.t.* шить (шью, шьёшь) *imp.*, с ~ (сошью́, -ьёшь) *perf.*; *s. on*, приши-ва́ть *imp.*, приши́ть (-шью́, -шьёшь) *perf.*; *s. up*, зашива́ть *imp.*, заши́ть (-шью́, -шьёшь) *perf.*
sewage *n.* сто́чные во́ды *f.pl.*, нечисто́-ты (-т) *pl.*; *s.-farm*, поля́ *neut.pl.* оро-ше́ния. **sewer** *n.* сто́чная, канализа-цио́нная, труба́ (*pl.* -бы). **sewerage** *n.* канализа́ция.
sewing *n.* шитьё; *s.-machine*, швейная маши́на.
sex *n.* (*gender*) пол; секс; *adj.* сексуа́ль-ный.
sexcentenary *n.* шестисотле́тие.
sextant *n.* секста́нт.
sextet *n.* сексте́т.
sexton *n.* понома́рь (-ря́) *m.*, моги́ль-щик.
sextuple *adj.* шестикра́тный.
sexual *adj.* полово́й, сексуа́льный. **sexuality** *n.* сексуа́льность. **sexy** *adj.* (*alluring*) соблазни́тельный; (*erotic*) эроти́ческий.
sh *interj.* ти́ше! тсс!
shabby *adj.* поно́шенный (-ен), потрё-панный (-ан, -анна); (*mean*) по́длый (подл, -á, -о).
shack *n.* лачу́га, хи́жина.
shackle *n.*: *pl.* кандалы́ (-ло́в) *pl.*; (*also fig.*) око́вы (-в) *pl.*; *v.t.* зако́вывать *imp.*, закова́ть (-кую́, -куёшь) *perf.*
shade *n.* тень (*loc.* -ни́; *pl.* -ни, -не́й),

полумра́к; (*of colour, meaning*) отте́-нок (-нка); (*lamp-s.*) абажу́р; *a s.*, чуть-чу́ть; *v.t.* затени́ть *imp.*, заслони́ть (-оню́, -о́нишь) *perf.*; (*drawing*) тушева́ть (-шу́ю, -шу́ешь) *imp.*, за ~ *perf.*; *v.i.* незаме́тно переходи́ть (-ит) *imp.* (into, в + *acc.*). **shadow** *n.* тень (*loc.* -ни́; *pl.* -ни, -не́й); *v.t.* (*follow*) та́йно следи́ть *imp.* за + *instr.* **shadowy** *adj.* тёмный (-мен, -мна́), нея́сный (-сен, -сна́, -сно). **shady** *adj.* тени́стый; (*suspicious*) подозри́тельный.
shaft *n.* (*of spear*) дре́вко (*pl.* -ки, -ков); (*arrow*) стрела́ (*pl.* -лы); (*of light*) луч (-а́); (*of cart*) огло́бля (*gen.pl.* -бель); (*axle*) вал (*loc.* -ý; *pl.* -лы́); (*mine s.*) ствол (-á) (ша́хты).
shag *n.* (*tobacco*) махо́рка; (*bird*) бакла́н. **shaggy** *adj.* лохма́тый, косма́-тый.
shah *n.* шах.
shake *v.t. & i.* трясти́(сь) (-су́(сь), -сёшь(ся); -с(ся), -сла́(сь)) *imp.*; *v.i.* (*tremble*) дрожа́ть (-жу́, -жи́шь) *imp.*; *v.t.* (*impair*) колеба́ть (-блю, -блешь) *imp.*, по ~ *perf.*; *s. hands*, пожима́ть *imp.*, пожа́ть (-жму́, -жмёшь) *perf.* ру́ку + *dat.*; *s. one's head*, пока́чать *perf.* голово́й; *s. off*, стря́хивать *imp.*, стряхну́ть *perf.*; (*fig.*) избавля́ться *imp.*, изба́виться *perf.* от + *gen.*; *s. up*, (*fig.*) встря́хивать *imp.*, встряхну́ть *perf.*
shako *n.* ки́вер (*pl.* -á).
shaky *adj.* ша́ткий (-ток, -тка́, -тко), не-про́чный (-чен, -чна́, -чно).
shale *n.* сла́нец (-нца).
shallot *n.* лук-шало́т.
shallow *adj.* ме́лкий (-лок, -лка́, -лко); (*superficial*) пове́рхностный; *n.* мел-ково́дье, мель (*loc.* -ли́).
sham *v.t. & i.* притворя́ться *imp.*, притвори́ться *perf.* + *instr.*; *n.* при-тво́рство; (*person*) притво́рщик, -ица; *adj.* притво́рный; (*fake*) подде́льный.
shaman *n.* шама́н.
shamble *v.i.* волочи́ть (-чу́, -чишь) *imp.* но́ги.
shambles *n.* бо́йня; (*muddle*) ха́ос.
shame *n.* стыд, позо́р; *v.t.* стыди́ть

imp., при~ *perf.* **shamefaced** *adj.*) стыдли́вый. **shameful** *adj.* позо́рный. **shameless** *adj.* бессты́дный.

shampoo *v.t.* мыть (мо́ю, мо́ешь) *imp.*, по~ *perf.*; *n.* шампу́нь *m.*

shamrock *n.* трили́стник.

shandy *n.* смесь (просто́го) пи́ва с лимона́дом, с имби́рным.

shank *n.* (leg) нога́ (acc. -гу; pl. -ги, -г, -га́м), го́лень; (shaft) сте́ржень (-жня) *m.*

shanty[1] *n.* (hut) хиба́рка, лачу́га; *s. town*, бидонви́ль, трущо́ба.

shanty[2] *n.* (song) матро́сская пе́сня (gen. pl. -сен).

shape *n.* фо́рма, вид, о́браз; *v.t.* придава́ть (-даю́, -даёшь) *imp.*, прида́ть (-а́м, -а́шь, -а́ст, -ади́м; при́дал, -а́, -о) *perf.* фо́рму + dat.; *v.i.* принима́ть *imp.*, приня́ть (-иму́т; при́нял, -а́, -о) *perf.* фо́рму. **shapeless** *adj.* бесфо́рменный (-ен, -енна). **shapely** *adj.* стро́йный (-о́ен, -о́йна, -о́йно).

share *n.* до́ля (pl. -ли, -лей), часть (pl. -ти, -те́й); (participation) уча́стие (pl. -ти, -те́й); (econ.) а́кция, пай (pl. пай, паёв); *v.t.* дели́ть (-лю́, -лишь) *imp.*, по~ *perf.*; разделя́ть *imp.*, раздели́ть (-лю́, -лишь) *perf.* **shareholder** *n.* акционе́р, ~ка; па́йщик, -ица.

shark *n.* аку́ла.

sharp *adj.* о́стрый (остр & остёр, остра́, о́стро); (steep) круто́й (крут, -а́, -о); (sudden, harsh) ре́зкий (-зок, -зка́, -зко); (fine) то́нкий (-нок, -нка́, -нко, то́нкий & тонки́); (mus.) дие́з; *adv.* (with time) ро́вно; (of angle) кру́то. **sharpen** *v.t.* точи́ть (-чу́, -чишь) *imp.*, на~ *perf.*; обостря́ть *imp.*, обостри́ть *perf.*

shatter *v.t.* & *i.* разбива́ть(ся) *imp.*, разби́ть(ся) (разобью́, -ьёт(ся) *perf.* вдре́безги; *v.t.* (hopes etc.) разруша́ть *imp.*, разру́шить *perf.*

shave *v.t.* & *i.* брить(ся) (бре́ю(сь), -е́ешь(ся)) *imp.*, по~ *perf.*; *v.t.* (plane) строга́ть *imp.*, вы́~ *perf.*; *n.* бритьё; *close s.*, едва́ избе́гнутая опа́сность. **shaver** *n.* электри́ческая бри́тва.

shawl *n.* шаль.

she *pron.* она́ (её, ей, ей & е́ю, о ней).

sheaf *n.* сноп (-а́); (of papers etc.) свя́зка.

shear *v.t.* стричь (-игу́, -ижёшь; -иг) *imp.*, о~ *perf.* **shearer** *n.* стрига́льщик. **shears** *n.* но́жницы (-ц) pl.

sheath *n.* (for sword etc.) но́жны (gen. -жен) pl.; (anat.) оболо́чка; (for cable etc.) обши́вка. **sheathe** *v.t.* вкла́дывать *imp.*, вложи́ть (-жу́, -жишь) *perf.* в но́жны; обшива́ть *imp.*, обши́ть (обошью́, -ьёшь) *perf.* **sheathing** *n.* обши́вка.

sheave *n.* шкив (pl. -ы́).

shed[1] *n.* сара́й.

shed[2] *v.t.* (tears, blood, light) пролива́ть *imp.*, проли́ть (-лью́, -льёшь; про́ли́л, -а́, -о) *perf.*; (skin, clothes) сбра́сывать *imp.*, сбро́сить *perf.*

sheen *n.* блеск.

sheep *n.* овца́ (pl. о́вцы, ове́ц, о́вцам); *s.-dog*, овча́рка; *s.-fold*, овча́рня (gen. pl. -рен). **sheepish** *adj.* (bashful) засте́нчивый; (abashed) сконфу́женный (-ен, -ена). **sheepskin** *n.* овчи́на.

sheer *adj.* абсолю́тный, су́щий; (textile) прозра́чный; (rock etc.) отве́сный.

sheet[1] *n.* (on bed) простыня́ (pl. про́стыни, -ы́нь, -ыня́м); (of glass, paper, etc.) лист (-а́); (wide expanse) пелена́ (gen. pl. -ён); attrib. (metal, glass, etc.) листово́й; *s. lightning*, зарни́ца.

sheet[2] *n.* (naut.) шкот (-а́); *s.-anchor*, запасно́й станово́й я́корь (pl. -ря́) *m.*; (fig.) я́корь (pl. -ря́) *m.* спасе́ния.

sheikh *n.* шейх.

sheldrake, **shelduck** *n.* пега́нка.

shelf *n.* по́лка; (of cliff etc.) усту́п; *s.-mark*, шифр.

shell *n.* (of mollusc) ра́ковина; (of tortoise) щит (-а́); (of egg, nut) скорлупа́ (pl. -пы); (of building etc.) осто́в; (explosive) снаря́д; *v.t.* очища́ть *imp.*, очи́стить *perf.*; лущи́ть *imp.*, об~ *perf.*; (bombard) обстре́ливать *imp.*, обстреля́ть *perf.*; *s. out*, (abs.) раскоше́ливаться *imp.*, раскоше́литься *perf.*

shellac *n.* шелла́к.

shellfish *n.* (mollusc) моллю́ск; (crustacean) ракообра́зное sb.

shelter *n.* прию́т, убе́жище, укры́тие; *v.t.* дава́ть (даю́, даёшь) *imp.*, дать (дам, дашь, даст, дади́м; дал, -а́, да́ло, -и) *perf.* прию́т + dat.; служи́ть

(-жу́, -жи́шь) *imp.*, по ~ *perf.* убежи́-
щем, укры́тием, + *dat.*; *v.t.* & *i.*
укрыва́ть(ся) *imp.*, укры́ть(ся) (-ро́ю-
(сь), -ро́ешь(ся)) *perf.*
shelve[1] *v.t.* (*defer*) откла́дывать *imp.*,
отложи́ть (-жу́, -жишь) *perf.* (в
до́лгий я́щик).
shelve[2] *v.i.* (*of land*) отло́го спуска́ться
imp. **shelving**[1] *adj.* отло́гий.
shelving[2] *n.* (*shelves*) стелла́ж (-а́).
shepherd *n.* пасту́х (-а́); (*fig.*) па́стырь
m.; *v.t.* проводи́ть (-ожу́, -о́дишь)
imp., провести́ (-еду́, -еде́шь; -ёл,
-ела́) *perf.* **shepherdess** *n.* пасту́шка.
sherbet *n.* шербе́т.
sheriff *n.* шери́ф.
sherry *n.* хе́рес.
shield *n.* щит (-а́); *v.t.* прикрыва́ть *imp.*,
прикры́ть (-ро́ю, -ро́ешь) *perf.*;
заслоня́ть *imp.*, заслони́ть *perf.*
shift *v.t.* & *i.* (*change position*) переме-
ща́ть(ся) *imp.*, перемести́ть(ся) *perf.*;
(*change form*) меня́ть(ся) *imp.*; (*move*; *s. responsibility etc.*) перекла́-
дывать *imp.*, переложи́ть (-жу́,
-жишь) *perf.*; *n.* перемеще́ние; переме́-
на; (*of workers*) сме́на. **shiftless** *adj.*
неуме́лый. **shifty** *adj.* ненадёжный,
нече́стный.
shilly-shally *n.* нереши́тельность; *v.i.*
колеба́ться (-блюсь, -блешься) *imp.*,
по ~ *perf.*
shimmer *v.i.* мерца́ть *imp.*; *n.* мерца́ние.
shin *n.* го́лень *f.*; *s.-bone*, большеберцо́-
вая кость (*pl.* -ти, -те́й); *s.-guard*, *-pad*,
щито́к (-тка́); *v.i.*: *s. up*, ла́зить *imp.*
по + *dat.*
shindy *n.* шум, сва́лка.
shine *v.i.* свети́ть(ся) (-и́т(ся)) *imp.*;
блесте́ть (-ещу́, -е́щешь & -ести́шь)
imp.; (*of sun etc.*) сия́ть *imp.*; *v.t.*
полирова́ть *imp.*, от ~ *perf.*; *n.* свет,
сия́ние, блеск; (*polish*) гля́нец (-нца).
shingle[1] *n.* (*for roof*) (кро́вельная)
дра́нка.
shingle[2] *n.* (*pebbles*) га́лька.
shingles *n.* опоя́сывающий лиша́й (-а́я).
shining, **shiny** *adj.* блестя́щий.
ship *n.* кора́бль (-ля́) *m.*; су́дно (*pl.* -да́,
-до́в); *v.t.* (*transport*) перевози́ть
(-ожу́, -о́зишь) *imp.*, перевезти́ (-езу́,
-езёшь; -ёз, -езла́) *perf.* (по воде́);

(*dispatch*) отправля́ть *imp.*, отпра́вить
perf. (по воде́). **shipbuilding** *n.* судо-
строи́тельство. **shipment** *n.* (*loading*)
погру́зка; (*consignment*) груз. **shipping**
n. суда́ (-до́в) *pl.* **shipshape** *adv.* в
по́лном поря́дке. **shipwreck** *n.* кора-
блекруше́ние. **shipwright** *n.* (*shipbuilder*) судострои́тель *m.*; (*carpenter*)
корабе́льный пло́тник. **shipyard** *n.*
верфь.
shire *n.* гра́фство.
shirk *v.t.* увиливать *imp.*, увильну́ть
perf. от + *gen.*
shirt *n.* руба́шка; *in s.-sleeves*, без
пиджака́.
shiver[1] *v.i.* (*tremble*) дрожа́ть (-жу́,
-жи́шь) *imp.*; *n.* дрожь.
shiver[2] *n.* (*splinter etc.*) оско́лок (-лка).
shoal[1] *adj.* (*shallow*) ме́лкий; *n.* (*bank*)
мель (*loc.* -ли́).
shoal[2] *n.* (*of fish*) ста́я, коса́к (-а́).
shock[1] *n.* (*impact etc.*) уда́р, толчо́к
(-чка́); (*med.*) шок; *attrib.* (*troops*,
brigade, *wave*) уда́рный; *s. absorber*,
амортиза́тор; *s. tactics*, та́ктика
сокруши́тельных уда́ров; *s. therapy*,
шокотерапи́я; *s.-worker*, уда́рник; *v.t.*
шоки́ровать *imp.* **shocking** *adj.* воз-
мути́тельный, ужа́сный.
shock[2] *n.* (*of sheaves*) копна́ (*pl.* -пны,
-пён, -пна́м).
shock[3] *n.* (*of hair*) копна́ воло́с.
shod *adj.* обу́тый.
shoddy *adj.* дрянно́й (-нен, -нна́, -нно).
shoe *n.* ту́фля (*gen.pl.* -фель); (*horseshoe*) подко́ва; (*tech.*) башма́к (-а́);
v.t. подко́вывать *imp.*, подкова́ть
(-кую́, -куёшь) *perf.* **shoeblack** *n.*
чи́стильщик сапо́г. **shoehorn** *n.* рожо́к
(-жка́). **shoe-lace** *n.* шнуро́к (-рка́) для
боти́нок. **shoemaker** *n.* сапо́жник.
shoe-string *n.*: *on a s.*, с небольши́ми
сре́дствами.
shoo *interj.* кш! *v.t.* прогоня́ть *imp.*,
прогна́ть (прогоню́, -нишь; прогна́л,
-а́, -о) *perf.*
shoot *v.t.* & *i.* (*discharge*) стреля́ть *imp.*
(*a gun*, из + *gen.*; *at*, в + *acc.*, по + *dat.*);
(*arrow*) пуска́ть *imp.*, пусти́ть (пущу́,
пу́стишь) *perf.*; (*kill*) застре́ливать
imp., застрели́ть (-лю́, -лишь) *perf.*;
(*execute*) расстре́ливать *imp.*, рас-

стреля́ть *perf.*; (*hunt*) охо́титься *imp.* на+*acc.*; (*football*) бить (бью, бьёшь) *imp.* (по воро́там) (*cin.*) снима́ть, снять (сниму́, -мешь; снял, -а́, -о) *perf.* (фильм); *v.i.* (*go swiftly*) проноси́ться(-ошу́сь -о́сишь-ся) *imp.*, пронести́сь(-есу́сь, -есёшься; -ёсся, -есла́сь) *perf.*; (*of plant*) пуска́ть *imp.*, пусти́ть (-щу́) *perf.* ростки́; *s. down*, (*aircraft*) сбива́ть *imp.*, сбить (собью́, -бьёшь) *perf.*; *n.* (*branch*) росто́к (-тка́), побе́г; (*hunt*) охо́та. **shooting** *n.* стрельба́; (*hunting*) охо́та; *s.-box*, охо́тничий до́мик; *s.-gallery*, тир; *s.-range*, стре́льбище.

shop *n.* (*for sales*) магази́н, ла́вка; (*for repairs, manufacture*) мастерска́я *sb.*, цех (*loc.* -е & -ý; *pl.* -и & -á) *m.*; *talk s.*, говори́ть *imp.* на узкопрофессиона́ль-ные те́мы, о дела́х; *s. assistant*, прода́вец (-вца́), -вщи́ца; *s.-floor*, (*fig.*) рабо́чие *sb.pl.*; *s.-lifter*, магази́нник; *s.-steward*, цехово́й ста́роста *m.*; *s.-window*, витри́на; *v.i.* де́лать *imp.*, с~ *perf.* поку́пки (*f.pl.*); *v.t.* (*imprison*) сажа́ть *imp.*, посади́ть (-ажу́, -а́дишь) *perf.* в тюрьму́; (*inform against*) доноси́ть (-ошу́, -о́сишь *imp.*, донести́ (-су́, -сёшь; донёс, -сла́) *perf.* на +*acc.* **shopkeeper** *n.* ла́вочник. **shopper** *n.* покупа́тель *m.*, -ница. **shopping** *n.* поку́пки *f.pl.*; *go, do one's s.*, де́лать *imp.*, с~ *perf.* поку́пки. **shopwalker** *n.* дежу́рный администра́тор магази́на.

shore[1] *n.* бе́рег (*loc.* -ý; *pl.* -á); *s. leave*, о́тпуск на бе́рег.
shore[2] *v.t.*: *s. up*, подпира́ть *imp.*, подпере́ть (подопру́, -рёшь) *perf.*
shorn *adj.* остри́женный (-ен).
short *adj.* коро́ткий (ко́роток, -тка́, ко́ротко); (*concise*) кра́ткий (-ток, -тка́, -тко); (*not tall*) ни́зкий (-зок, -зка́, -зко, ни́зки́); (*of person*) ни́зкого ро́ста; (*deficient*) недоста́точный; *be s. of*, (*have too little*) испы́тывать *imp.*, испыта́ть *perf.* недоста́ток в+*prep.*; (*not amount to*) быть (*fut.* бу́ду, -дешь; был, -á, -о; не́ был, -á, -о) ме́ньше+*gen.*; (*uncivil*) гру́бый (груб, -á, -о); (*crumbling*) рассы́п-чатый; *in s.*, одни́м сло́вом; *s.-change*, недодава́ть (-даю́, -даёшь) *imp.*,

недода́ть (-áм, -áшь, -áст, -ади́м; недо́дал, -á, -о) *perf.* сда́чу+*dat.*; *s. circuit*, коро́ткое замыка́ние; *s. circuit*, замыка́ть *imp.*, замкну́ть *perf.* на́коротко; *s. cut*, око́льный путь (-ти́, -тём) *m.*; *s. list*, оконча́тельный спи́сок (-ска); *s.-list*, включа́ть *imp.*, включи́ть *perf.* в оконча́тельный спи́сок; *s.-lived*, недолгове́чный, ми-молётный; *s. measure*, недоме́р; *at s. notice*, неме́дленно; *s.-range*, крат-косро́чный; *s. sight*, близору́кость; *s.-sighted*, близору́кий; (*fig.*) недаль-нови́дный; *s. story*, расска́з, нове́лла; *in s. supply*, дефици́тный; *s.-tempered*, вспы́льчивый; *s.-term*, краткосро́чный; *s.-wave*, коротково́лновый; *s. weight*, недове́с; *s.-winded*, страда́ю-щий оды́шкой; *n.* (*film*) короткомет-ра́жный фильм; (*drink*) спиртно́е *sb.*; (*s. circuit*) коро́ткое замыка́ние; *pl.* шо́рты (-т) *pl.*; *v.t.* замыка́ть *imp.*, замкну́ть *perf.* на́коротко. **shortage** *n.* недоста́ча (-тка); дефици́т. **short-bread** *n.* песо́чное пече́нье. **shortcoming** *n.* недоста́ток (-тка) **shorten** *v.t. & i.* укора́чивать(ся) *imp.*, укороти́ть(ся) *perf.*; сокраща́ть(ся) *imp.*, сокра-ти́ть(ся) (-ащу́, -ати́т(ся)) *perf.*; *s. sail*, убавля́ть *imp.*, уба́вить *perf.* паруса́в. **shortfall** *n.* дефици́т. **shorthand** *n.* стеногра́фия. **shorthorn** *n.* шортго́рн-ская поро́да скота́. **shortly** *adv.*: *s. after*, вско́ре (по́сле+*gen.*); *s. before*, незадо́лго (до+*gen.*).

shot[1] *n.* (*discharge of gun*) вы́стрел; (*for cannon*; *sport*) ядро́ (*pl.* я́дра, я́дер, я́драм); (*pellet*) дроби́нка; (*as pl.*, *collect.*) дробь; (*person*) стрело́к (-лка́); (*attempt*) попы́тка; (*injection*) уко́л; (*phot.*) сни́мок (-мка) (*cin.*) съёмка; *like a s.*, о́чень охо́тно, неме́дленно; *a s. in the arm*, (*fig.*) *s.-gun*, дробови́к (-á).
shot[2] *adj.* (*of material*) перели́вчатый.

shoulder *n.* плечо́ (*pl.* -чи, -н, -ча́м); (*cul.*) лопа́тка; (*of road*) обо́чина; *straight from the s.*, спле́ча; *s. to s.*, плечо́м к плечу́; *s.-blade*, лопа́тка; (*on uniform*) пого́н (*gen.pl.* -н); *v.t.* взва́ливать *imp.*, взвали́ть (-лю́, -лишь) *perf.* на пле́чи.

shout n. крик; v.i. крича́ть (-чу́, -чи́шь) imp., кри́кнуть perf.; s. down, перекри́кивать imp., перекрича́ть (-чу́, -чи́шь) perf.

shove n. толчо́к (-чка́); v.t. & i. толка́ть(ся) imp., толкну́ть perf.; s. off, (coll.) убира́ться imp., убра́ться (уберу́сь, -рёшься; убра́лся, -ала́сь, -а́ло́сь) perf.

shovel n. сово́к (-вка́), лопа́та; v.t. копа́ть imp., вы́~ perf.; (s. up) сгреба́ть imp., сгрести́ (сгребу́, -бёшь; сгрёб, -ла́) perf.

show v.t. пока́зывать imp., показа́ть (-ажу́, -а́жешь) perf.; (exhibit) выставля́ть imp., вы́ставить perf.; (film etc.) демонстри́ровать imp., про~ perf.; v.i. быть ви́дным (-ден, -дна́, -дно, ви́дны), заме́тным; s. off, (v.i.) рисова́ться imp., по~ perf.; (exhibition) выставля́ть imp., вы́ставить perf.; (theat.) спекта́кль m.; (spectacle, pageant) зре́лище; (business) де́ло (pl. -ла́); (appearance) ви́димость; s. of hands, голосова́ние подня́тием руки́; s.-case, витри́на; s.-jumping, соревнова́ние по ска́чкам; s.-room, сало́н.

showboat n. плаву́чий теа́тр. **showgirl** n. стати́стка. **showman** n. балага́нщик.

shower n. (rain) до́ждик; (hail; fig.) град; (s.-bath) душ; v.t. осыпа́ть imp., осы́пать (-плю, -плешь) perf.+instr. (on, +acc.); v.i. принима́ть imp., приня́ть (приму́, -мешь; при́нял, -а́, -о) perf. душ. **showery** adj. дождли́вый.

showy adj. я́ркий (я́рок, ярка́, я́рко); (gaudy) бро́ский (-сок, -ска́, -ско).

shrapnel n. шрапне́ль.

shred n. клочо́к (-чка́), лоскуто́к (-тка́; not a s., ни ка́пли; tear to shreds, (fig.) по́лностью опроверга́ть imp., опрове́ргнуть (-г(нул), -гла) perf.; v.t. ре́зать (ре́жу, -жешь) imp. на клочки́; рвать (рву, рвёшь; рвал, -а́, -о) imp. в клочки́.

shrew n. (woman) сварли́вая, стропти́вая, же́нщина; (animal) землеро́йка.

shrewd adj. проница́тельный.

shrewish adj. сварли́вый.

shriek n. пронзи́тельный крик, визг; v.i. визжа́ть (-жу́, -жи́шь) imp.; крича́ть (-чу́, -чи́шь) imp., кри́кнуть perf.

shrill adj. пронзи́тельный, ре́зкий (-зок, -зка́, -зко).

shrimp n. креве́тка.

shrine n. (casket) ра́ка; (tomb) гробни́ца; (sacred place) святы́ня.

shrink v.i. сади́ться imp., сесть (ся́дет; сел) perf.; (s. in size) вызыва́ть imp., вы́звать (-зовет) perf. уса́дку у+gen.; s. from, уклоня́ться imp. от+gen.; избега́ть imp.+gen.; s.-proof, безуса́дочный. **shrinkage** n. уса́дка.

shrivel v.t. & i. съёживать(ся) imp., съёжить(ся) perf.

shroud n. са́ван; pl. (naut.) ва́нты f.pl.; v.t. (fig.) оку́тывать imp., оку́тать perf. (in, +instr.).

Shrove-tide n. ма́сленица.

shrub n. куст (-а́), куста́рник. **shrubbery** n. куста́рник.

shrug v.t. & i. пожима́ть imp., пожа́ть (-жму́, -жмёшь) perf. (плеча́ми).

shudder n. содрога́ние; v.i. содрога́ться imp., содрогну́ться perf.

shuffle v.t. & i. (one's feet) ша́ркать imp. (нога́ми); (cards) тасова́ть imp., с~ perf.; (intermingle, confuse) переме́шивать imp., перемеша́ть perf.; s. off, (blame etc.) сва́ливать imp., свали́ть (-лю́, -лишь) perf. (on to, на +acc.). n. ша́рканье; тасо́вка.

shun v.t. избега́ть imp.+gen.

shunt v.i. (rly.) маневри́ровать imp., с~ perf.; v.t. (rly.) переводи́ть (-ожу́, -о́дишь) imp., перевести́ (-еду́, -едёшь; -ёл, -ела́) perf. на запа́сный путь.

shut v.t. & i. закрыва́ть(ся) imp., закры́ть(ся) (-ро́ю, -ро́ет(ся)) perf.; s. in, запира́ть imp., запере́ть (запру́, -рёшь; за́пер, -ла́, -ло) perf.; s. up, (v.i.) замолча́ть (-чу́, -чи́шь) perf.; (imper.) заткни́сь!

shutter n. ста́вень (-вня) m., ста́вня (gen.pl. -вен); (phot.) затво́р; v.t. закрыва́ть imp., закры́ть (-ро́ю, -ро́ешь) perf. ста́внями.

shuttle n. челно́к (-а́). **shuttlecock** n. вола́н.

shy[1] adj. засте́нчивый, ро́бкий (-бок, -бка́, -бко).

shy[2] v.i. (in alarm) пуга́ться imp., ис~ perf. (at, +gen.).

shy³ *v.t.* (*throw*) броса́ть *imp.*, бро́сить *perf.*; *n.* бросо́к (-ска́).

Siamese *adj.* сиа́мский; *S. twins,* сиа́мские близнецы́ *m.pl.*

Siberian *adj.* сиби́рский; *n.* сибиря́к (-а́), -я́чка.

sibilant *adj.* (*n.*) свистя́щий (звук) (*sb.*). **sic** *adv.* так!

sick *adj.* больно́й (-лен, -льна́); *be, feel, s.,* тошни́ть *imp. impers.* + *acc.*; то́шно *impers.* + *dat.*; *be s. for,* (*pine*) тоскова́ть *imp.* по + *dat.*; *be s. of,* надоеда́ть *imp.*, надое́сть (-е́м, -е́шь, -е́ст, -еди́м; -е́л) *perf.* + *nom.* (*object*) & *dat.* (*subject*); *I'm s. of her,* она́ мне надое́ла; *s.-bed,* посте́ль больно́го; *s.-benefit,* посо́бие по боле́зни; *s.-leave,* о́тпуск по боле́зни. **sicken** *v.t.* вызыва́ть *imp.*, вы́звать (-зовет) *perf.* тошноту́, (*disgust*) отвраще́ние, у + *gen.*; *v.i.* заболева́ть *imp.*, заболе́ть *perf.* **sickening** *adj.* отврати́тельный.

sickle *n.* серп (-а́).

sickly *adj.* (*ailing*) боле́зненный (-ен, -енна), хи́лый (хил, -а́, -о); (*nauseating*) тошнотво́рный. **sickness** *n.* боле́знь; (*vomiting*) тошнота́; *s. benefit,* посо́бие по боле́зни.

side *n.* сторона́ (*acc.* -ону; *pl.* -оны, -о́н, -она́м), бок (*loc.* на -у́; *pl.* -а́); *s. by s.,* бок о́ бок; ря́дом (with, c + *instr.*); *on the s.,* на стороне́, дополни́тельно; *v.i.*: *s. with,* встава́ть (-таю́, -таёшь) *imp.*, встать (-а́ну, -а́нешь) *perf.* на сто́рону + *gen.*; *s.-car,* коля́ска (мотоци́кла); *s.-effect,* (*of medicine etc.*) побо́чное де́йствие; *s.-saddle,* да́мское седло́ (*pl.* сёдла, -дел, -дла́м); *s.-slip,* боково́е скольже́ние; (*aeron.*) скольже́ние на крыло́; *s.-step,* (*fig.*) уклоня́ться *imp.*, уклони́ться (-ню́сь, -ни́шься) *perf.* от + *gen.*; *s.-stroke,* пла́вание на боку́; *s.-track,* (*distract*) отвлека́ть *imp.*, отвле́чь (-еку́, -ечёшь; -ёк, -екла́) *perf.*; (*postpone*) откла́дывать *imp.*, отложи́ть (-жу́, -жишь) *perf.* рассмотре́ние + *gen.*; *s.-view,* про́филь *m.*, вид сбо́ку. **sideboard** *n.* серва́нт, буфе́т; *pl.* ба́ки (-к) *pl.* **sidelight** *n.* боково́й фона́рь (-ря́) *m.* **sideline** *n.* (*work*) побо́чная рабо́та.

sidelong *adj.* (*glance*) косо́й.

sidereal *adj.* звёздный.

sideways *adv.* бо́ком; (*from side*) сбо́ку.

siding *n.* запа́сный путь (-ти́, -тём) *m.*

sidle *v.i.* ходи́ть (хожу́, хо́дишь) *imp.* бо́ком.

siege *n.* оса́да; *lay s. to,* осажда́ть *imp.*, осади́ть *perf.*; *raise the s. of,* снима́ть *imp.*, снять (сниму́, -мешь; снял, -а́, -о) *perf.* оса́ду с + *gen.*

sienna *n.* сие́на; *burnt s.,* жжёная сие́на.

siesta *n.* сие́ста.

sieve *n.* решето́ (*pl.* -ёта), си́то; *v.t.* проси́вать *imp.*, просе́ять (-е́ю, -е́ешь) *perf.*

sift *v.t.* проси́вать *imp.*, просе́ять (-е́ю, -е́ешь) *perf.*; (*evidence etc.*) тща́тельно рассма́тривать *imp.*, рассмотре́ть (-рю́, -ришь) *perf.* **sifter** *n.* си́то.

sigh *v.i.* вздыха́ть *imp.*, вздохну́ть *perf.*; *n.* вздох.

sight *n.* (*faculty*) зре́ние; (*view; range*) вид; (*spectacle*) зре́лище; *pl.* достопримеча́тельности *f.pl.*; (*on gun*) прице́л; *at, on, s.,* при ви́де (of, + *gen.*); *at first s.,* с пе́рвого взгля́да; *in s. of,* в виду́ + *gen.*; *long s.,* да́льнозо́ркость; *short s.,* близору́кость; *catch s. of,* уви́деть (-и́жу, -и́дишь) *perf.*; *know by s.,* знать *imp.* в лицо́; *lose s. of,* теря́ть *imp.*, по~ *perf.* из виду; (*fig.*) упуска́ть *imp.*, упусти́ть (-ущу́, -у́стишь) *perf.* из виду; *s.-reading,* чте́ние нот с листа́. **sightless** *adj.* слепо́й (слеп, -па́, -о).

sign *n.* знак; (*indication*) при́знак; (*signboard*) вы́веска; *v.t. & abs.* подпи́сывать(ся) *imp.*, подписа́ть(ся) (-ишу́(сь), -и́шешь(ся)) *perf.*; *v.i.* (*give s.*) подава́ть (-даю́, -даёшь) *imp.*, пода́ть (-а́м, -а́шь, -а́ст, -ади́м; по́дал, -а, -о) *perf.* знак.

signal¹ *adj.* выдаю́щийся, замеча́тельный.

signal² *n.* сигна́л; *pl.* (*mil.*) связь; *v.t. & i.* сигнализи́ровать *imp.*, про~ *perf.* **signal-box** *n.* сигна́льная бу́дка. **signalman** *n.* сигна́льщик.

signatory *n.* подписа́вший *sb.*; (*of treaty*) сторона́ (*acc.* -ону; *pl.* -оны, -о́н, -она́м), подписа́вшая догово́р.

signature *n.* по́дпись; (*print.*) сигнату́ра; (*mus.*) ключ (-á); *s. tune*, музыка́льная ша́пка.

signboard *n.* вы́веска.

signet *n.* печа́тка; *s.-ring*, кольцо́ (*pl.* -льца́, -ле́ц, -льца́м) с печа́ткой.

significance *n.* значе́ние. **significant** *adj.* значи́тельный. **signify** *v.t.* означа́ть *imp.*; (*express*) выража́ть *imp.*, вы́разить *perf.*; *v.i.* быть (*fut.* бу́ду, -дешь; был, -á, -о; не́ был, -á, -о) *imp.* ва́жным.

signpost *n.* указа́тельный столб (-á).

silage *n.* си́лос.

silence *n.* молча́ние, тишина́; *v.t.* заста́вить *perf.* замолча́ть. **silencer** *n.* глуши́тель *m.* **silent** *adj.* (*not speaking*) безмо́лвный; (*taciturn*) молча́ливый; (*of film*) немо́й; (*without noise*) ти́хий (тих, -á, -о), бесшу́мный; *be s.*, молча́ть (-чу́, -чи́шь) *imp.*

silhouette *n.* силуэ́т; *v.t.*: *be silhouetted*, вырисо́вываться *imp.*, вы́рисоваться *perf.* (*against*, на фо́не + *gen.*).

silica *n.* кремнезём. **silicate** *n.* силика́т. **silicon** *n.* кре́мний. **silicone** *n.* силико́н. **silicosis** *n.* силико́з.

silk *n.* шёлк (-а(у), *loc.* -е & -ý; *pl.* -á); *take s.*, станови́ться (-влю́сь, -вишься *imp.*, стать (-а́ну, -а́нешь) *perf.* короле́вским адвока́том; *attrib.* шёлковый; *s. hat*, цили́ндр. **silkworm** *n.* шелкови́чный червь (-вя́; *pl.* -ви, -ве́й) *m.* **silky** *adj.* шелкови́стый.

sill *n.* подоко́нник.

silly *adj.* глу́пый (глуп, -á, -о).

silo *n.* си́лос; *v.t.* силосова́ть *imp.*, *perf.*, за ~ *perf.*

silt *n.* ил (-а(у)); *v.i.*: *s. up*, засоря́ться *imp.*, засори́ться *perf.* и́лом.

silver *n.* серебро́; (*cutlery*) столо́вое серебро́; *adj.* (*of s.*) сере́бряный; (*silvery*) серебри́стый; (*hair*) седо́й (сед, -á, -о); *s. foil*, сере́бряная фо́льга; *s. fox*, черно-бу́рая лиса́; *s. paper*, (*tin foil*) стани́оль *m.*; *s. plate*, столо́вое серебро́; *v.t.* серебри́ть *imp.*, вы~ *perf.*, по ~ *perf.*; (*mirror*) покрыва́ть *imp.*, покры́ть (-ро́ю, -ро́ешь) *perf.* амальга́мой рту́ти. **silversmith** *n.* сере́бряных дел ма́стер (*pl.* -á). **silverware** *n.* столо́вое серебро́. **silvery** *adj.*
серебри́стый; (*hair*) седо́й (сед, -á, -о).

silviculture *n.* лесово́дство.

simian *adj.* обезья́ний.

similar *adj.* подо́бный (to, + *dat.*), схо́дный (-ден, -дна́, -дно) (to, с + *instr.*; in, по + *dat.*) *imp.* **similarity** *n.* схо́дство; (*math.*) подо́бие. **similarly** *adv.* подо́бным о́бразом.

simile *n.* сравне́ние.

simmer *v.t.* кипяти́ть *imp.* на ме́дленном огне́; *v.i.* кипе́ть (-пи́т) *imp.* на ме́дленном огне́; *s. down*, успока́иваться *imp.*, успоко́иться *perf.*

simper *v.i.* жема́нно улыба́ться *imp.*, улыбну́ться *perf.*; *n.* жема́нная улы́бка.

simple *adj.* просто́й (прост, -á, -о, про́сты́); *s.-hearted*, простоду́шный; *s.-minded*, тупова́тый. **simpleton** *n.* проста́к (-á). **simplicity** *n.* простота́. **simplify** *v.t.* упроща́ть *imp.*, упрости́ть *perf.* **simply** *adv.* про́сто.

simulate *v.t.* притворя́ться *imp.*, притвори́ться *perf.* + *instr.*; (*conditions etc.*) модели́ровать *imp.*, *perf.* **simulated** *adj.* (*pearls etc.*) иску́сственный.

simultaneous *adj.* одновреме́нный (-нен, -нна).

sin *n.* грех (-á); *v.i.* греши́ть *imp.*, со ~ *perf.*; *s. against*, наруша́ть *imp.*, нару́шить *perf.*

since *adv.* с тех пор; (*ago*) (тому́) наза́д; *prep.* с + *gen.*; *conj.* с тех пор как; (*reason*) так как.

sincere *adj.* и́скренний (-нен, -нна, -нно & -нне). **sincerely** *adv.* и́скренне; *yours s.*, и́скренне Ваш. **sincerity** *n.* и́скренность.

sine *n.* си́нус.

sinecure *n.* синеку́ра.

sine die *adv.* на неопределённый срок.

sine qua non *n.* обяза́тельное усло́вие.

sinew *n.* сухожи́лие. **sinewy** *adj.* жи́листый.

sinful *adj.* гре́шный (-шен, -шна́, -шно, гре́шны). **sinfully** *adv.* гре́шно.

sing *v.t.* & *i.* петь (пою́, поёшь) *imp.*, про ~, с ~ *perf.*

singe *v.t.* пали́ть *imp.*, о ~ *perf.*; *n.* ожо́г.

singer *n.* певе́ц (-вца́), -ви́ца.

single adj. один (одна́); (unmarried) холосто́й, незаму́жняя; (solitary) одино́кий; (bed) односпа́льный; s. combat, единобо́рство; in s. file, гусько́м; s.-handed, без посторо́нней по́мощи; s.-minded, целеустремлённый (-ён, -ённа) без одного́; s.-seater, одноме́стный автомоби́ль m.; n. (ticket) биле́т в оди́н коне́ц; pl. (tennis etc.) одино́чная игра́; v.t.: s. out, выделя́ть imp., вы́делить perf. **singlet** n. ма́йка.

singsong adj. моното́нный.

singular n. еди́нственное число́; adj. еди́нственный; (unusual) необыча́йный; (strange) стра́нный (-нен, -нна́, -нно). **singularity** n. (peculiarity) своеобра́зие.

sinister adj. (ominous) злове́щий; (evil) злой (зол, зла).

sink v.i. опуска́ться imp., опусти́ться (-ущу́сь, -у́стишься) perf.; (subside) оседа́ть imp., осе́сть (ося́дет; осе́л) perf.; (of ship) тону́ть (-нет) imp., по ~ perf.; (of sick person) умира́ть imp.; v.t. (ship) топи́ть (-плю́, -пишь) imp., по ~ perf.; (well) рыть (ро́ю, ро́ешь) imp., вы́ ~ perf.; (shaft) проходи́ть (-ожу́, -о́дишь) imp., пройти́ (пройду́, -дёшь; прошёл, -шла́) perf.; n. (also fig.) клоа́ка; (basin) ра́ковина. **sinker** n. грузи́ло.

sinner n. гре́шник, -ица.

Sino- in comb. кита́йско-. **sinologist** n. китаеве́д, сино́лог. **sinology** n. китаеве́дение, синоло́гия.

sinuous adj. изви́листый.

sinus n. (лобная) па́зуха. **sinusitis** n. синуси́т.

sip v.t. пить (пью, пьёшь; пил, -а́, -о) imp., ма́ленькими глотка́ми; n. ма́ленький глото́к (-тка́).

siphon n. сифо́н.

sir n. сэр.

sire n. (as vocative) сир; (stallion etc.) производи́тель m.; v.t. быть (fut. бу́ду, -дешь; был, -а́, -о не был, -а́, -о) imp. производи́телем + gen.

siren n. сире́на.

sirloin n. филе́ neut.indecl.

sister n. сестра́ (pl. сёстры, -тёр, -трам); s.-in-law, (husband's sister) золо́вка; (wife's sister) своя́ченица; (brother's wife) неве́стка. **sisterhood** n. (relig.) сестри́нская общи́на.

sit v.i. (be sitting) сиде́ть (сижу́, сиди́шь) imp.; (s. down) сади́ться imp., сесть (ся́ду, -дешь; сел) perf.; (parl., leg.) заседа́ть imp.; (pose) пози́ровать imp. (for, для + gen.); v.t. уса́живать imp., усади́ть (-ажу́, -а́дишь) perf.; (examination) сдава́ть (сдаю́, -аёшь) imp.; s. back, отки́дываться imp., откину́ться perf.; s. down, сади́ться imp., сесть (ся́ду, -дешь; сел) perf.; s.-down strike, италья́нская забасто́вка; s. on, (committee etc.) быть (fut. бу́ду, -дешь; был, -а́, -о; не́ был, -а́, -о) imp. чле́ном + gen.; s. up, приподнима́ться imp., приподня́ться (-ниму́сь, -ни́мешься) -ня́лся, -няла́сь) perf.; (stay out of bed) не ложи́ться imp. спать.

site n. ме́сто (pl. -та́), местоположе́ние; building s., строи́тельная площа́дка.

sitter n. пози́рующий sb.; (model) нату́рщик, -ица; s.-in, приходя́щая ня́ня. **sitting** n. (parl. etc.) заседа́ние; (for portrait) сеа́нс; (for meal) сме́на; adj. сидя́чий, сидя́щий; s.-room, гости́ная sb.

situated adj.: be s., находи́ться (-ожу́сь, -о́дишься) imp. **situation** n. местоположе́ние; (circumstances) положе́ние; (work etc.) ме́сто (pl. -та́).

six adj., n. шесть (-ти́, -тью́); (collect.; 6 pairs) ше́стеро (-ры́х); (cards; number 6) шестёрка; (time) шесть (часо́в); (age) шесть лет. **sixteen** adj., n. шестна́дцать (-ти, -тью); (age) шестна́дцать лет. **sixteenth** adj., n. шестна́дцатый; (date) шестна́дцатое (число́). **sixth** adj., n. шесто́й; (fraction) шеста́я (часть (pl. -ти, -те́й)); (date) шесто́е (число́); (mus.) се́кста. **sixtieth** adj., n. шестидеся́тый. **sixty** adj., n. шестьдеся́т (-ти́десяти, -тью́десятью); (age) шестьдеся́т лет; pl. (decade) шестидеся́тые го́ды (-до́в) m.pl.

size [1] n. (dimensions; of garment etc.) разме́р; (magnitude) величина́; (capacity) объём; (format) форма́т; v.t.: s. up, оце́нивать imp., оцени́ть (-ню́,

-нишь) perf. **sizeable** adj. поря́дочных разме́ров.

size² n. (solution) шли́хта; v.t. шлихтова́ть imp.

sizzle v.i. шипе́ть (-пи́т) imp.

skate¹ n. (fish) скат.

skate² n. (ice-s.) конёк (-нька́); (roller-s.) конёк (-нька́) на ро́ликах; v.i. ката́ться imp. на конька́х; **skating-rink**, като́к (-тка́).

skein n. мото́к (-тка́).

skeleton n. скеле́т, осто́в; s. key, отмы́чка.

sketch n. набро́сок (-ска), зарисо́вка; (theat.) скетч; s.-book, альбо́м для зарисо́вок; s.-map, кроки́ neut.indecl.; v.t. & i. де́лать imp., с ~ perf. набро́сок, -ски (+gen.); **sketchy** adj. отры́вочный; (superficial) пове́рхностный.

skew adj. косо́й; n. укло́н; on the s., ко́со; v.t. переко́шивать imp., перекоси́ть perf.; v.i. уклоня́ться imp., уклони́ться (-ню́сь, -ни́шься) perf.

skewbald adj. пе́гий.

skewer n. ве́ртел (pl. -á); v.t. наса́живать imp., насади́ть (-ажу́, -а́дишь) perf. на ве́ртел.

ski n. лы́жа; s.-jump, трампли́н; s.-run, лы́жня; v.i. ходи́ть (хожу́, хо́дишь) imp. на лы́жах.

skid n. зано́с; v.i. заноси́ть (-ошу́, -о́сишь) imp., занести́ (-сёт, -сло́) perf.impers. + acc.

skier n. лы́жник.

skiff n. я́лик, скиф.

skiing n. лы́жный спорт.

skilful adj. иску́сный, уме́лый. **skill** n. мастерство́, иску́сство, уме́ние. **skilled** adj. иску́сный; (worker) квалифици́рованный.

skim v.t. снима́ть imp., снять (сниму́, -мешь; снял, -á, -о) perf. (cream) сли́вки pl.; (skin on milk) пе́нки pl.; (scum) на́кипь, c + gen.; v.i. скользи́ть imp. (over, along, по + dat.); s. through, бе́гло просма́тривать imp., просмотре́ть (-рю́, -ришь) perf.; adj.: s. milk, снято́е молоко́.

skimp v.t. & i. скупи́ться imp. (на + acc.). **skimpy** adj. ску́дный (-ден, -дна́, -дно).

skin n. ко́жа; (hide) шку́ра; (of fruit etc.) кожура́; (on milk) пе́нка; s.-deep,

пове́рхностный; s.-diver, акваланги́ст; s.-tight, в обтя́жку; v.t. сдира́ть imp., содра́ть (сдеру́, -рёшь; содра́л, -á, -о) perf. ко́жу, шку́ру, c + gen.; снима́ть imp., снять (сниму́, -мешь; снял, -á, -о) perf. кожуру́ c + gen. **skin-flint** n. скря́га m. & f. **skinny** adj. то́щий (тощ, -á, -е).

skint adj. без гроша́ в карма́не.

skip¹ v.i. скака́ть (-ачу́, -а́чешь) imp.; (with rope) пры́гать imp. че́рез скака́лку; v.t. (omit) пропуска́ть imp., пропусти́ть (-ущу́, -у́стишь) perf.; **skipping-rope**, скака́лка.

skip² n. (container) скип.

skipper n. (naut.) шки́пер (pl. -ы & -á); (naut., other senses) капита́н.

skirmish n. схва́тка, сты́чка; v.i. сража́ться imp.

skirt n. ю́бка; v.t. обходи́ть (-ожу́, -о́дишь) imp., обойти́ (обойду́, -дёшь; обошёл, -шла́) perf. стороно́й; **skirting-board**, пли́нтус.

skit n. скетч.

skittish adj. (horse) нерови́стый; (person) игри́вый.

skittle n. ке́гля; pl. ке́гли f.pl.

skulk v.i. (hide) скрыва́ться imp.; (creep) кра́сться (краду́сь, -дёшься; кра́лся) imp.

skull n. че́реп (pl. -á); s.-cap, ермо́лка.

skunk n. скунс, воню́чка.

sky n. не́бо (pl. -беса́). **sky-blue** adj. лазу́рный. **skyjack** v.t. похища́ть imp., похи́тить (-и́щу, -и́тишь) perf. **skylark** n. жа́воронок (-нка). **skylight** n. окно́ (pl. о́кна, о́кон, о́кнам) в кры́ше. **skyline** n. горизо́нт. **skyscraper** n. небоскрёб. **skyway** n. авиатра́сса.

slab n. плита́ (pl. -ты); (of cake etc.) кусо́к (-ска́).

slack¹ n. (coal-dust) у́гольная пыль.

slack² adj. (loose) сла́бый (слаб, -á, -о); (sluggish) вя́лый; (inactive) неакти́вный; (negligent) небре́жный; (of rope) ненатя́нутый; n. (of rope) слабина́; pl. повседне́вные брю́ки (-к) pl. **slacken** v.t. ослабля́ть imp., осла́бить perf.; v.t. & i. (slow down) замедля́ть(ся) imp., заме́длить(ся) perf.; v.i. ослабева́ть imp., ослабе́ть perf. **slacker** n. безде́льник, ло́дырь m.

slag *n.* шлак.

slake *v.t.* (*thirst*) утоля́ть *imp.*, утоли́ть *perf.*; (*lime*) гаси́ть (гашу́, га́сишь) *imp.*, по ~ *perf.*

slalom *n.* сла́лом.

slam *v.t. & i.* (*door*) захло́пывать(ся) *imp.*, захло́пнуть(ся) *perf.*; *n.* (*cards*) шлем.

slander *n.* клевета́; *v.t.* клевета́ть (-ещу́, -е́щешь) *imp.*, на ~ *perf.* на + *acc.* **slanderous** *adj.* клеветни́ческий.

slang *n.* сленг, жарго́н; *v.t.* брани́ть *imp.*, вы́ ~ *perf.* **slangy** *adj.* жарго́нный, вульга́рный.

slant *v.t. & i.* наклоня́ть(ся) *imp.*, наклони́ть(ся) (-ню́, -ни́т(ся)) *perf.*; *n.* укло́н. **slanting** *adj.* пока́тый, косо́й (кос, -а́, -о).

slap *v.t.* хло́пать *imp.*, хло́пнуть *perf.* + *acc.*, *instr.*, по + *dat.*; шлёпать *imp.*, шлёпнуть *perf.*; *n.* шлепо́к (-пка́); *adv.* пря́мо. **slapdash** *adj.* поспе́шный, небре́жный. **slapstick** *n.* балага́н.

slash *v.t.* руби́ть (-блю́, -бишь) *imp.*; (*prices etc.*) ре́зко снижа́ть *imp.*, сни́зить (-и́жу, -и́зишь) *perf.*; *n.* разре́з, про́рез.

slat *n.* пла́нка, филёнка.

slate[1] *n.* сла́нец (-нца); (*for roofing*) ши́фер (*no pl.*), ши́ферная пли́тка; (*for writing*) гри́фельная доска́ (*acc.* -ску; *pl.* -ски, -со́к, -ска́м); (*s-pencil*, *graphite*) гри́фель *m.*; *v.t.* (*roof*) крыть (кро́ю, -о́ешь) *imp.*, по ~ *perf.* ши́ферными пли́тками.

slate[2] *v.t.* (*criticize*) раскритикова́ть *perf.*

slattern *n.* неря́ха. **slatternly** *adj.* неря́шливый.

slaughter *n.* (*of animals*) убо́й; (*massacre*) резня́; *v.t.* ре́зать (ре́жу, -жешь) *imp.*, за ~ *perf.*; (*people*) убива́ть *imp.*, уби́ть (убью́, -ьёшь) *perf.* **slaughter-house** *n.* бо́йня (*gen.pl.* бо́ен).

Slav *n.* славяни́н (*pl.* -я́не, -я́н) *m.*; *adj.* славя́нский.

slave *n.* раб (-а́); рабы́ня (*gen.pl.* -нь); *s.-trade*, работорго́вля; *v.i.* рабо́тать *imp.* как вол.

slaver *v.i.* пуска́ть *imp.*, пусти́ть (пущу́, пу́стишь) *perf.* слю́ни; *n.* слю́ни (-не́й) *pl.*

slavery *n.* ра́бство.

Slavic *adj.* славя́нский.

slavish *adj.* ра́бский.

Slavonic *adj.* славя́нский.

slay *v.t.* убива́ть *imp.*, уби́ть (убью́, -ьёшь) *perf.*

sleazy *adj.* (*person*) неря́шливый.

sledge *n.* са́ни (-не́й) *pl.*

sledge-hammer *n.* кува́лда.

sleek *adj.* гла́дкий (-док, -дка́, -дко).

sleep *n.* сон (сна); *go to s.*, засыпа́ть *imp.*, засну́ть *perf.*; *v.i.* спать (сплю; спал, -а́, -о) *imp.*; (*spend the night*) ночева́ть (-чу́ю, -чу́ешь) *imp.*, пере ~ *perf.*; *s.-walker*, луна́тик.

sleeper *n.* спя́щий *sb.*; (*rly.*, *beam*) шпа́ла; (*sleeping-car*) спа́льный ваго́н. **sleeping** *adj.* спя́щий, спа́льный; *s.-bag*, спа́льный мешо́к (-шка́); *s.-car(riage)*, спа́льный ваго́н; *s. partner*, пасси́вный партнёр; *s.-pill*, снотво́рная табле́тка; *s. sickness*, со́нная боле́знь. **sleepless** *adj.* бессо́нный (-нен, -нна). **sleepy** *adj.* со́нный (-нен, -нна).

sleet *n.* мо́крый снег (-а(у), *loc.* -у́).

sleeve *n.* рука́в (-а́; *pl.* -а́); (*tech.*) му́фта; (*of record*) конве́рт.

sleigh *n.* са́ни (-не́й) *pl.*; *s.-bell*, бубе́нчик.

sleight-of-hand *n.* ло́вкость рук.

slender *adj.* (*slim*) то́нкий (-нок, -нка́, -нко, то́нки); (*meagre*) ску́дный (-ден, -дна́, -дно); (*of hope etc.*) сла́бый (слаб, -а́, -о).

sleuth *n.* сы́щик.

slew *v.t. & i.* бы́стро повора́чивать(ся) *imp.*, поверну́ть(ся) *perf.*

slice *n.* ло́мтик (-мтя́) *m.*; (*share*) часть (*pl.* -ти, -те́й) *v.t.* (*s. up*) нареза́ть *imp.*, наре́зать (-е́жу, -е́жешь) *perf.*

slick *adj.* (*dextrous*) ло́вкий (-вок, -вка́, -вко, ло́вки́); (*crafty*) хи́трый (-тёр, -тра́, хи́тро́); (*sleek*) гла́дкий (-док, -дка́, -дко); *n.* нефтяна́я плёнка.

slide *v.i.* скользи́ть *imp.*; (*on ice*) ката́ться (качу́сь, ка́тишься) *imp.*, по ~ *perf.* по льду; *v.t.* (*drawer etc.*) задвига́ть *imp.*, задви́нуть *perf.* (into, в + *acc.*); *n.* (*on ice*) ледяна́я гора́ (*acc.* -ру; *pl.* -ры, -р, -ра́м), ледяна́я доро́жка; (*children's s.*) де́тская го́рка; (*chute*) жёлоб (*pl.* -á); (*microscope s.*) предме́тное стекло́ (*pl.* стёкла, -кол, -клам); (*phot.*) диапозити́в, слайд; *s.-rule*, логарифми́ческая лине́йка; *s.-valve*, золотни́к (-á). **sliding** *adj.* скользя́щий; (*door*) задвижно́й; *s. seat*, слайд.

slight[1] *adj.* (*slender*) то́нкий (-нок, -нка́, -нко, то́нки); (*inconsiderable*) незначи́тельный; (*light*) лёгкий (-сок, -гка́, -гко́, лёгки); *not the slightest*, ни мале́йшего, -шей (*gen.*); *not in the slightest*, ничу́ть.

slight[2] *v.t.* пренебрега́ть *imp.*, пренебре́чь (-егу́, -ежёшь; -ёг, -егла́) *perf.* + *instr.*; *n.* пренебреже́ние, неуваже́ние.

slightly *adv.* слегка́, немно́го.

slim *adj.* то́нкий (-нок, -нка́, -нко, то́нки); (*chance etc.*) сла́бый (слаб, -á, -о); *v.i.* худе́ть *imp.*, по ~ *perf.*

slime *n.* слизь. **slimy** *adj.* сли́зистый; (*person*) еле́йный.

sling *v.t.* (*throw*) броса́ть *imp.*, бро́сить *perf.*; швыря́ть *imp.*, швырну́ть *perf.*; (*suspend*) подве́шивать *imp.*, подве́сить *perf.*; *n.* (*for throwing*) праща́; (*bandage*) пере́вязь; (*rope*) строп.

slink *v.i.* кра́сться (-аду́сь, -адёшься; -áлся) *imp.* **slinky** *adj.* (*garment*) облега́ющий.

slip *n.* (*slipping*) скольже́ние; (*mistake*) оши́бка; (*garment*) комбина́ция; (*pillowcase*) на́волочка; (*building s.*) ста́пель (*pl.* -ля́ & -ли); (*landing s.*) э́ллинг; (*of paper etc.*) поло́ска; (*print.*) гра́нка; (*cutting*) черено́к (-нка́); (*glaze*) полива́ная глазу́рь; *s. of the pen*, опи́ска; *s. of the tongue*, обмо́лвка; *give the s.*, ускольза́ть *perf.* от + *gen.*; *v.i.* скользи́ть *imp.*, скользну́ть *perf.*; поскользну́ться *perf.*; (*from hands etc.*) выска́льзывать *imp.*, вы́скользнуть *perf.*; *v.t.* (*let go*) спуска́ть *imp.*, спусти́ть (-ущу́, -у́стишь) *perf.*; (*insert*) сова́ть (сую́, суёшь) *imp.*, су́нуть *perf.*; *s. off*, (*depart, v.i.*) ускольза́ть *imp.*, ускользну́ть *perf.*; (*clothes, v.t.*) сбра́сывать *imp.*, сбро́сить *perf.*; *s. on*, (*clothes*) наки́дывать *imp.*, наки́нуть *perf.*; *s. up*, (*make mistake*) ошиба́ться *imp.*,

ошиби́ться (-бу́сь, -бёшься; -бся) *perf.* **slipper** *n.* (*house*, дома́шняя) ту́фля (*gen. pl.* -фель); та́почка (*coll.*). **slippery** *adj.* ско́льзкий (-зок, -зка́, -зко); (*fig.*, *shifty*) увёртливый. **slip-shod** *adj.* неря́шливый, небре́жный. **slipway** *n.* (*for building*) ста́пель (*pl.* -ля́ & -ли); (*for landing*) э́ллинг.

slit *v.t.* разреза́ть *imp.*, разре́зать (-е́жу, -е́жешь) *perf.*; *n.* щель (*pl.* -ли, -ле́й), разре́з.

slither *v.i.* скользи́ть *imp.*

sliver *n.* ще́пка.

slob *n.* неря́ха *m.* & *f.*

slobber *v.i.* пуска́ть *imp.*, пусти́ть (пущу́, пу́стишь) *perf.* слю́ни; *n.* слю́ни (-не́й) *pl.*

sloe *n.* тёрн.

slog *v.t.* (*hit*) си́льно ударя́ть *imp.*, уда́рить *perf.*; (*work*) упо́рно рабо́тать *imp.*

slogan *n.* ло́зунг.

sloop *n.* шлюп.

slop *n.*: *pl.* (*water*) помо́и (-о́ев) *pl.*; (*food*) жи́дкая пи́ща; *s.-basin*, полоска́тельница; *s.-pail*, помо́йное ведро́ (*pl.* вёдра, -дер, -драм); *v.t.* & *i.* выплёскивать(ся) *imp.*, вы́плеснуть(ся) (-ещу, -ещет(ся)) *perf.*

slope *n.* накло́н, склон; *v.i.* име́ть *imp.* накло́н. **sloping** *adj.* накло́нный (-нен, -нна), пока́тый.

sloppy *adj.* (*ground*) мо́крый (мокр, -á, -о); (*food*) жи́дкий (-док, -дка́, -дко); (*work*) неря́шливый; (*sentimental*) сентимента́льный.

slot *n.* щель (*pl.* -ли, -ле́й), паз (*loc.* -ý; *pl.* -ы́); *s.-machine*, автома́т.

sloth *n.* лень; (*zool.*) лени́вец (-вца). **slothful** *adj.* лени́вый.

slouch *v.i.* (*stoop*) суту́литься *imp.*

slough *v.t.* сбра́сывать *imp.*, сбро́сить *perf.*

sloven *n.* неря́ха *m.* & *f.* **slovenly** *adj.* неря́шливый.

slow *adj.* ме́дленный (-ен(ен), -енна); (*tardy*) медли́тельный; (*stupid*) тупо́й (туп, -á, -о, ту́пы́); (*business*) вя́лый; *be slow*, (*clock*) отстава́ть (-таёт) *imp.*, отста́ть (-а́нет) *perf.*; *adv.* ме́дленно; *v.t.* & *i.* (*s. down*, *up*) замедля́ть(ся) *imp.*, замéдлить(ся) *perf.* **slowcoach** *n. n.* копýн (-á), ~ ья.

slow-worm *n.* берéтница, медянѝца.

sludge *n.* (*mud*) грязь (*loc.* -зѝ); (*sediment*) отстóй.

slug *n.* (*zool.*) слизня́к (-á); (*bullet*) пýля; (*piece of metal*) кусóк (-скá) метáлла.

sluggard *n.* лентя́й. **sluggish** *adj.* (*inert*) инéртный; (*torpid*) вя́лый.

sluice *n.* шлюз; *v.t.* заливáть *imp.*, залѝть (-лью, -льёшь; зáлѝл, -á, -о) *perf.*; *v.i.* лѝться (льётся; лѝлся, лилáсь, лилóсь) *imp.*

slum *n.* трущóба.

slumber *n.* сон (сна); *v.i.* спать (сплю, спишь; спал, -á, -о) *imp.*

slump *n.* рéзкое падéние (цен, спрóса, интерéса), *v.i.* рéзко пáдать *imp.*, (у)пáсть (-адý; -áл) *perf.*; (*of person*) тяжелó опускáться *imp.*, опустѝться (-ущýсь, -ýстишься) *perf.*

slur *v.t.* (*speak indistinctly*) невня́тно произносѝть (-ошý, -óсишь) *imp.*, произнестѝ (-есý, -есёшь; -ёс, -еслá) *perf.*; *s. over* обходѝть (-ожý, -óдишь) *imp.*, обойтѝ (обойдý, -дёшь; обошёл, -шлá) *perf.* молчáнием; *n.* (*stigma*) пятнó (*pl.* -тна, -тен, -тнам) (*mus.*) лѝга.

slush *n.* нерáха. **slushy** *adj.* сля́котный; (*fig.*) сентиментáльный.

slut *n.* нерáха. **sluttish** *adj.* неря́шливый.

sly *adj.* хѝтрый (-тёр, -трá, хѝтрó), лукáвый; *on the s.*, тайкóм.

smack[1] *n.* (*flavour*) прѝвкус; *v.i.: s. of*, пáхнуть *imp.+instr.*

smack[2] *n.* (*slap*) шлепóк (-пкá) *v.t.* шлёпать *imp.*, шлёпнуть *perf.*

smack[3] *n.* (*boat*) смэк.

small *adj.* мáленький, небольшóй, мáлый (мал, -á); (*of agent, particles*) мéлкий (-лок, -лкá, -лко); (*petty*) мéлкий; (*unimportant*) незначѝтельный; *s. capitals*, капитéль; *s. change*, мéлочь; *s. fry*, мéлкая сóшка; *s.-minded*, мéлкий (-лок, -лкá, -лко); *s.-scale*, мелкомасштáбный; *s. talk*, свéтская бесéда; *n.: s. of the back*, пояснѝца; *pl.* мéлочь.

smart[1] *v.i.* сáднить *imp. impers.*

smart[2] *adj.* (*brisk*) быстрый (быстр, -á, -о, быстры́) лóвкий (-вок, -вкá, -вко, лóвкѝ); (*sharp*) смекáлистый (*coll.*); (*in appearance*) элегáнтный.

smash *v.t. & i.* разбивáть(ся) *imp.*, разбѝть(ся разобью́, -бьёшь(ся)) *perf.*; *v.i.* (*collide*) стáлкиваться *imp.*, столкнýться *perf.* (*into, c+instr.*); *n.* (*disaster*) катастрóфа; (*collision*) столкновéние; (*blow*) тяжёлый удáр.

smattering *n.* поверхностное знáние.

smear *v.t.* смáзывать *imp.*, смáзать (-áжу, -áжешь) *perf.*; (*dirty*) пáчкать *imp.*, за~, ис~ *perf.*; (*discredit*) порóчить *imp.*, о~ *perf.*; *n.* (*slander*) клеветá; (*med.*) мазóк (-зкá).

smell *n.* (*sense*) обоня́ние; (*odour*) зáпах; *v.t.* чýвствовать *imp.* зáпах+*gen.*; ню́хать *imp.*, по~ *perf.*; *v.i.: s. of*, пáхнуть (пáх(нул), пáхла) *imp.+instr.*; *s. out*, (*also fig.*) разню́хивать *imp.*, разню́хать *perf.*; *smelling-salts*, ню́хательная соль. **smelly** *adj.* воню́чий.

smelt[1] *v.t.* (*ore*) плáвить *imp.*; (*metal*) выплáвлять *imp.*, вы́плавить *perf.*

smelt[2] *n.* (*fish*) корю́шка.

smile *v.i.* улыбáться *imp.*, улыбнýться *perf.*; *n.* улы́бка.

smirk *v.i.* ухмыля́ться *imp.*, ухмыльнýться *perf.*; *n.* ухмы́лка.

smith *n.* кузнéц (-á).

smithereens *n.: (into) to s.*, вдрéбезги.

smithy *n.* кýзница.

smock *n.* блýза.

smog *n.* тумáн с ды́мом.

smoke *n.* дым (-а(у), *loc.* -ý); (*cigarette etc.*) курéво; *s.-bomb*, дымовáя бóмба; *s.-screen*, дымовáя завéса; *v.i.* дымѝть *imp.*, на~ *perf.*; (*of lamp*) коптѝть *imp.*, на~ *perf.*; *v.t. & i.* (*cigarette etc.*) курѝть (-рю́, -ришь) *imp.*, по~ *perf.*; *v.t.* (*cure; colour*) коптѝть *imp.*, за~ *perf.*; *s. out*, вы́куривать *imp.*, вы́курить *perf.* **smokeless** *adj.* бездымный. **smoker** *n.* курѝльщик, -ица, куря́щий *sb.* **smoking** *n.: s.-compartment*, купé *neut. indecl.* для куря́щих; *s.-room*, курѝтельная *sb.* **smoky** *adj.* ды́мный; (*room*) прокýренный; (*colour*) дымчáтый.

smooth *adj.* (*surface etc.*) глáдкий (-док, -дкá, -дко); (*movement etc.*) плáвный; (*flattering*) льстѝвый; *v.t.*

приглаживать *imp.*, пригладить *perf.*; *s. over,* сглаживать *imp.*, сгладить *perf.*

smother *v.t.* (*stifle, also fig.*) душить (-шу́ -шишь) *imp.*, за~ *perf.*; (*cover*) покрывать *imp.*, покрыть (-ро́ю, -ро́ешь) *perf.*

smoulder *v.i.* тлеть *imp.*

smudge *v.t.* па́чкать *imp.*, за~, ис~ *perf.*

smug *adj.* самодово́льный.

smuggle *v.t.* провози́ть (-ожу́, -о́зишь) *imp.*, провезти́ (-езу́, -езёшь; -ёз, -езла́) *perf.* контраба́ндой; (*convey secretly*) та́йно проноси́ть (-ошу́, -о́сишь) *imp.*, пронести́ (-есу́, -есёшь; -ёс, -есла́) *perf.* **smuggler** *n.* контрабанди́ст.

smut *n.* части́ца са́жи, ко́поти; (*indecency*) непристо́йность. **smutty** *adj.* гря́зный (-зен, -зна́, -зно); непристо́йный.

snack *n.* заку́ска; *s.-bar,* заку́сочная *sb.*, буфе́т.

snaffle *n.* тре́нзель (*pl.* -ли & -ля́) *m.*; *v.t.* (*steal*) стащи́ть (-щу́, -щишь) *perf.*

snag *n.* (*branch*) сучо́к (-чка́); (*in river*) коря́га; (*fig.*) загво́здка; *v.t.* задевля́ть *imp.*, заце́пить (-плю́, -пишь) *perf.*

snail *n.* ули́тка; *at s.'s pace,* черепа́хой.

snake *n.* змея́ (*pl.* -е́и); *s.-charmer,* заклина́тель *m.*, ~ ница, змей; *s.-skin,* змеи́ная ко́жа. **snaky** *adj.* змеи́ный; (*winding*) изви́листый.

snap *v.i.* (*of dog etc.*) огрыза́ться *imp.*, огрызну́ться *perf.* (at, на + *acc.*); *v.t.* & *i.* говори́ть *imp.* серди́то, раздражённо; (*break*) обрыва́ть(ся) *imp.*, обо-рва́ть(ся) (-ву́, -вёт(ся); -ва́л(ся), -вала́(сь), -ва́ло/-вало́сь) *perf.*; *v.t.* (*make sound*) щёлкать *imp.*, щёлкнуть *perf.* + *instr.*; *s. up,* (*buy*) расхва́тывать *imp.*, расхвата́ть *perf.*; *n.* (*sound*) щёлк; (*fastener*) кно́пка, застёжка; (*cards*) де́тская ка́рточная игра́; *cold s.,* ре́зкое внеза́пное похолода́ние; *adj.* скоропали́тельный; (*parl.*) внеочередно́й. **snapdragon** *n.* льви́ный зев. **snap-fastener** *n.* кно́пка. **snapshot** *n.* момента́льный сни́мок (-мка).

snare *n.* лову́шка; *v.t.* лови́ть (-влю́, -вишь) *imp.*, пойма́ть в лову́шку.

snarl *v.i.* рыча́ть (-чи́т) *imp.*; (*person*) ворча́ть (-чу́, -чи́шь) *imp.*; *n.* рыча́ние; ворча́ние.

snatch *v.t.* хвата́ть *imp.*, (с)хвати́ть (-ачу́, -а́тишь) *perf.*; (*opportunity etc.*) ухвати́ться (-ачу́сь, -а́тишься) *perf.* за + *acc.*; *v.i.*: *s. at,* хвата́ть *imp.*, (с)хвати́ться (-ачу́сь, -а́тишься) *perf.* за + *acc.*, попыта́ться схвати́ть; (*fragment*) обры́вок (-вка); *in, by, snatches,* уры́вками.

sneak *v.i.* (*slink*) кра́сться (-аду́сь, -адёшься; -а́лся) *imp.*; (*tell tales*) я́бедничать *imp.*, на~ *perf.* (*coll.*); *v.t.* (*steal*) стащи́ть (-щу́, -щишь) *perf.*; *n.* я́бедник, -ица (*coll.*); *s.-thief,* вори́шка *m.* **sneaking** *adj.* (*hidden*) та́йный; (*of feeling etc.*) неосо́знанный.

sneer *v.i.* (*smile*) насме́шливо улыба́ться *imp.*; (*speak*) насме́шливо говори́ть *imp.*; *n.* насме́шливая улы́бка.

sneeze *v.i.* чиха́ть *imp.*, чихну́ть *perf.*; *n.* чиха́нье.

snick *n.* зару́бка.

snide *adj.* (*sneering*) насме́шливый.

sniff *v.i.* шмы́гать *imp.*, шмыгну́ть *perf.* но́сом; *v.t.* ню́хать *imp.*, по~ *perf.*

snigger *v.i.* хихи́кать *imp.*, хихикну́ть *perf.*; *n.* хихи́канье.

snip *v.t.* ре́зать (ре́жу, -жешь) *imp.* (но́жницами); *s. off,* среза́ть *imp.*, сре́зать (-е́жу, -е́жешь) *perf.*; *n.* (*purchase*) вы́годная поку́пка.

snipe *n.* (*bird*) бека́с; *v.i.* стреля́ть *imp.* из укры́тия (at, в + *acc.*). **sniper** *n.* сна́йпер.

snippet *n.* отре́зок (-зка); *pl.* (*of knowledge etc.*) обры́вки *m.pl.*

snivel *v.i.* (*run at nose*) распуска́ть *imp.*, распусти́ть (-ущу́, -у́стишь) *perf.* со́пли; (*whimper*) хны́кать (хны́чу, -чешь & хны́каю, -аешь) *imp.*

snob *n.* сноб. **snobbery** *n.* сноби́зм. **snobbish** *adj.* сноби́стский.

snook *n.*: *cock a s. at,* показа́ть (-ажу́, -а́жешь) *perf.* дли́нный нос + *dat.*

snoop *v.i.* сова́ть (сую́, суёшь) *imp.* нос в чужи́е дела́; *s. about,* шпио́нить *imp.*

snooty *adj.* чва́нный (-нен, -нна).

snooze *v.i.* вздремну́ть *perf.*; *n.* коро́ткий сон (сна).

snore *v.i.* храпе́ть (-плю́, -пи́шь) *imp.*; *n.* храп.

snorkel *n.* шно́ркель *m.*; *(diver's)* тру́бка (аквала́нга).

snort *v.i.* фы́ркать *imp.*, фы́ркнуть *perf.*; *n.* фы́рканье.

snot *n.* со́пли (-ле́й) *pl.*

snout *n.* ры́ло, мо́рда.

snow *n.* снег (-а(у), *loc.* -ý; *pl.* -á); *s.-blindness*, сне́жная слепота́; *s.-boot*, бот (*gen.pl.* -т & -тов); *s.-bound*, заснежённый (-ён, -ена́); *s.-drift*, сугро́б; *s.-plough*, снегоочисти́тель *m.*; *s.-shoes*, снегосту́пы (-пов) *pl.*; *s.-white*, белосне́жный; *v.i.*: *it is snowing, it snows*, идёт (*past* шёл) снег; *snowed up in*, занесённый (-ён, -ена́) сне́гом. **snowball** *n.* снежо́к (-жка́). **snowdrop** *n.* подсне́жник. **snowflake** *n.* снежи́нка. **snowman** *n.* сне́жная ба́ба. **snowstorm** *n.* мете́ль, вью́га. **snowy** *adj.* сне́жный; (*snow-white*) белосне́жный.

snub[1] *v.t.* относи́ться (-ошу́сь, -о́сишься) *imp.*, отнести́сь (-есу́сь, -есёшься) -ёсся, -есла́сь) *perf.* пренебрежи́тельно к + *dat.*; (*humiliate*) унижа́ть *imp.*, уни́зить *perf.*

snub[2] *adj.* вздёрнутый; *s.-nosed*, курно́сый.

snuff[1] *n.* (*tobacco*) ню́хательный таба́к (-á(у́)); *take s.*, ню́хать *imp.*, по~ *perf.* таба́к; *s.-box*, табаке́рка.

snuff[2] *n.* (*on candle*) нага́р на свече́; *v.t.* снима́ть *imp.*, снять (сниму́, -мешь; снял, -á, -о) *perf.* нага́р с + *gen.*; *s. out* (*candle*) туши́ть (-шу́, -шишь) *imp.*, по~ *perf.*; (*hopes etc.*) разруша́ть *imp.*, разру́шить *perf.*

snuffle *v.i.* (*noisily*) сопе́ть (-плю́, -пи́шь) *imp.*

snug *adj.* ую́тный, удо́бный.

snuggle *v.i.*: *s. up to*, прижима́ться *imp.*, прижа́ться (-жму́сь, -жмёшься) *perf.* к + *dat.*

so *adv.* так; (*in this way*) так, таки́м о́бразом; (*thus, at beginning of sentence*) ита́к; (*also*) та́кже, то́же, *conj.* (*therefore*) поэ́тому; *and so on*, и так да́лее; *if so*, в тако́м слу́чае; *or so*, и́ли о́коло э́того; *so-and-so*, тако́й-то; *so . . . as*, так(о́й)...как; *so as to*, с тем что́бы; *so be it*, быть по сему́; *so-called*, так называ́емый; *so far*, до сих пор; (*in*) *so far as*, насто́лько, поско́льку; *so long!* пока́! *so long as*, поско́льку; *so much*, насто́лько; *so much so*, до тако́й сте́пени; *so much the better*, тем лу́чше; *so much to self*; *so that*, что́бы; *so . . . that*, так...что; *so to say, speak*, так сказа́ть; *so what?* ну и что?

soak *v.t.* & *i.* пропи́тывать(ся) *imp.*, пропита́ть(ся) *perf.* (*in*, + *instr.*); *v.t.* мочи́ть (-чу́, -чишь) *imp.*, на~ *perf.*; (*drench*) прома́чивать *imp.*, промочи́ть (-чу́, -чишь) *perf.*; *s. up*, впи́тывать *imp.*, впита́ть *perf.*; *v.i.*: *s. through*, проса́чиваться *imp.*, просочи́ться *perf.*; *get soaked*, промока́ть *imp.*, промо́кнуть (-к) *perf.*; *n.* (*drinker*) пья́ница *m.* & *f.*

soap *n.* мы́ло (*pl.* -ла́); *attrib.* мы́льный; *v.t.* мы́лить *imp.*, на~ *perf.*; *s.-boiler*, мылова́р; *s.-box*, (*stand*) импровизи́рованная трибу́на; *s.-bubble*, мы́льный пузы́рь (-ря́) *m.*; *s.-dish*, мы́льница; *s.-flakes*, мы́льные хло́пья (-ьев) *pl.*; *s. powder*, стира́льный порошо́к (-шка́); *s.-works*, мылова́ренный заво́д. **soapy** *adj.* мы́льный.

soar *v.i.* пари́ть *imp.*; (*aeron.*) плани́ровать *imp.*, с~ *perf.*; (*building etc.*) высти́ться *imp.*; (*prices*) подска́кивать *imp.*, подскочи́ть (-и́т) *perf.*

sob *v.i.* рыда́ть *imp.*; *n.* рыда́ние.

sober *adj.* тре́звый (трезв, -á, -о); *v.t.* & *i.*: *s. up*, (*also fig.*) отрезвля́ть(ся) *imp.*, отрезви́ть(ся) *perf.*; *v.i.*: *s. up*, трезве́ть *imp.*, о~ *perf.* **sobriety** *n.* тре́звость.

sobriquet *n.* про́звище.

soccer *n.* футбо́л.

sociable *adj.* общи́тельный; (*meeting etc.*) дру́жеский. **social** *adj.* обще́ственный, социа́льный; *S. Democrat*, социа́л-демокра́т; *s. sciences*, обще́ственные нау́ки *f.pl.*; *s. security*, социа́льное обеспе́чение; *n.* вечери́нка. **socialism** *n.* социали́зм. **socialist** *n.* социали́ст; *adj.* социалисти́ческий.

socialize *v.t.* социализи́ровать *imp.*, *perf.* **society** *n.* о́бщество; (*beau monde*) свет; *attrib.* све́тский.
sociolinguistics *n.* социолингви́стика.
sociological *adj.* социологи́ческий.
sociologist *n.* социо́лог. **sociology** *n.* социоло́гия.
sock[1] *n.* носо́к (-ска́).
sock[2] *v.t.* тузи́ть *imp.*, от ~ *perf.*
socket *n.* впа́дина; (*electr.*) штéпсель (*pl.* -ля́) *m.*; (*for bulb*) патро́н; (*tech.*) гнездо́ (*pl.* -ёзда), раструб.
sod *n.* (*turf*) дёрн; (*piece of turf*) дерни́на.
soda *n.* со́да; *s.-water*, со́довая вода́ (*acc.* -ду).
sodden *adj.* промо́кший, пропи́танный (-ан) вла́гой.
sodium *n.* на́трий.
sodomite *n.* педера́ст. **sodomy** *n.* педера́стия.
sofa *n.* дива́н, софа́ (*pl.* -фы).
soft *adj.* мя́гкий (-гок, -гка́, -гко); (*sound*) ти́хий (тих, -á, -о); (*colour*) нея́ркий (-рок, -рка́, -рко); (*malleable*) ко́вкий (-вок, -вка́, -вко); (*tender*) не́жный (-жен, -жна́, -жно, не́жны́); *s.-boiled*, всмя́тку; *s. drink*, безалкого́льный напи́ток (-тка); *s. fruit*, я́года; *s. goods*, тексти́ль *m.*; *s.-headed*, придуркова́тый; *s.-hearted*, мягкосерде́чный; *s.-pedal*, преуменьша́ть *imp.*, преуме́ньшить *perf.* (значе́ние+*acc.*).
soften *v.t.* & *i.* смягча́ть(ся) *imp.*, смягчи́ть(ся) *perf.* **softness** *n.* мя́гкость. **software** *n.* програ́ммное обеспе́чение. **softwood** *n.* хво́йная древеси́на.
soggy *adj.* пропи́танный (-ан) водо́й; (*ground*) боло́тистый.
soil[1] *n.* по́чва; *s. science*, почвове́дение.
soil[2] *v.t.* па́чкать *imp.*, за~ *perf.*, ис~ *perf.*
sojourn *n.* вре́менное пребыва́ние; *v.i.* вре́менно жить (живу́, -вёшь; жил, -á, -о *imp.*
solace *n.* утеше́ние; *v.t.* утеша́ть *imp.*, уте́шить *perf.*
solar *adj.* со́лнечный.
solarium *n.* соля́рий.
solder *n.* припо́й; *v.t.* пая́ть *imp.*, спа́ивать *imp.*, спая́ть *perf.* **soldering-iron** *n.* пая́льник.

soldier *n.* солда́т (*gen.pl.* -т), вое́нный *sb.*; (*toy s.*) солда́тик; *s. of fortune*, кондотье́р. **soldierly** *adj.* во́инский.
sole[1] *n.* (*of foot, shoe*) подо́шва; (*of foot*) ступня́; (*of shoe*) подмётка; *v.t.* ста́вить *imp.*, по~ *perf.* подмётку к+*dat.*, на+*acc.*
sole[2] *n.* (*fish*) морско́й язы́к (-á).
sole[3] *adj.* еди́нственный; (*exclusive*) исключи́тельный.
solecism *n.* солеци́зм.
solemn *adj.* торже́ственный (-ен, -енна). **solemnity** *n.* торже́ственность; (*celebration*) торжество́.
solenoid *n.* соленóид.
solicit *v.t.* проси́ть (-ошу́, -о́сишь) *imp.*, по~ *perf.*+*acc.*, *gen.*, о+*prep.*; выпра́шивать *imp.*; (*prostitute*) пристава́ть (-таю́, -таёшь) *imp.*, приста́ть (-а́ну, -а́нешь) *perf.* к+*dat.* (*v. abs.*, к мужчи́нам). **solicitor** *n.* соли́ситор. **solicitous** *adj.* забо́тливый. **solicitude** *n.* забо́тливость.
solid *adj.* (*not liquid*) твёрдый (твёрд, -á, -о); (*not hollow*; *continuous*) сплошно́й; (*of time*) без переры́ва; (*firm*) про́чный (-чен, -чна́, -чно, про́чны), пло́тный (-тен, -тна́, -тно, пло́тны); (*pure*) чи́стый (чист, -á, -о, чи́сты) (*of reason etc.*) убеди́тельный; *s.-state physics*, фи́зика твёрдого те́ла; *n.* твёрдое те́ло (*pl.* -лá); *pl.* твёрдая пи́ща. **solidarity** *n.* солида́рность. **solidify** *v.t.* & *i.* де́лать(ся) *imp.*, с~ *perf.* твёрдым, *v.i.* затвердева́ть *imp.*, затверде́ть *perf.* **solidity** *n.* твёрдость; про́чность.
solidus *n.* дели́тельная черта́.
soliloquy *n.* моноло́г.
solipsism *n.* солипси́зм.
solitaire *n.* (*gem*) солите́р.
solitary *adj.* одино́кий, уединённый (-ён, -ённа); *s. confinement*, одино́чное заключе́ние. **solitude** *n.* одино́чество, уедине́ние.
solo *n.* со́ло *neut.indecl.*; (*aeron.*) самостоя́тельный полёт; *adj.* со́льный; *adv.* со́ло. **soloist** *n.* соли́ст, ~ ка.
solstice *n.* солнцестоя́ние.
soluble *adj.* раствори́мый. **solution** *n.* раство́р; (*action*) растворе́ние; (*of puzzle etc.*) реше́ние, разреше́ние.

solve *v.t.* реша́ть *imp.*, реши́ть *perf.*

solvency *n.* платёжеспосо́бность. **solvent** *adj.* растворя́ющий ; (*financially*) платёжеспосо́бный ; *n.* раствори́тель *m.*

sombre *adj.* мра́чный (-чен, -чна́, -чно).

sombrero *n.* сомбре́ро *neut.indecl.*

some *adj.*, *pron.* (*any*) како́й-нибудь ; (*a certain*) како́й-то ; (*a certain amount or number of*) не́который, *or often expressed by noun in* (*partitive*) *gen.* ; (*several*) не́сколько + *gen.* ; (*approximately*) о́коло + *gen.* ; *often expressed by inversion of noun and numeral* : (*s. people, things*) не́которые *pl.* ; *s.* day, когда́-нибудь ; *s. more*, ещё ; *s. other day*, друго́й раз ; *s. . . . others*, одни́ . . . други́е ; *to s. extent*, до изве́стной сте́пени. **somebody, someone** *n.*, *pron.* (*definite*) кто́-то ; (*indefinite*) кто́-нибудь ; (*important person*) ва́жная персо́на. **somehow** *adv.* ка́к-то ; ка́к-нибудь ; (*for some reason*) почему́-то ; *s. or other*, так и́ли ина́че.

somersault *n.* прыжо́к (-жка́) кувырко́м ; *v.i.* кувырка́ться *imp.*, кувыр(к)ну́ться *perf.*

something *n.*, *pron.* (*definite*) что́-то ; (*indefinite*) что́-нибудь ; *s. like*, (*approximately*) приблизи́тельно ; (*a thing like*) что́-то вро́де + *gen.* **sometime** *adv.* не́когда ; *adj.* бы́вший. **sometimes** *adv.* иногда́. **somewhat** *adv.* не́сколько, дово́льно. **somewhere** *adv.* (*position*) (*definite*) где́-то ; (*indefinite*) где́-нибудь ; (*motion*) куда́-то ; куда́-нибудь.

somnolent *adj.* со́нный.

son *n.* сын (*pl.* -овья́, -ове́й) ; *s.-in-law*, зять (*pl.* -я́, -ёв) *m.*

sonar *n.* гидролока́тор.

sonata *n.* сона́та.

sonde *n.* зонд.

song *n.* пе́сня (*gen.pl.* -сен) ; (*singing*) пе́ние ; *s.-bird*, певча́я пти́ца ; *s.-thrush*, певчий дрозд (-а́).

sonic *adj.* звуково́й, акусти́ческий.

sonnet *n.* соне́т.

sonny *n.* сыно́к.

sonorous *adj.* зву́чный (-чен, -чна́, -чно).

soon *adv.* ско́ро, вско́ре ; (*early*) ра́но ; *as s. as*, как то́лько ; *as s. as possible*, как мо́жно скоре́е ; *no sooner said than done*, ска́зано — сде́лано ; *sooner or later*, ра́но и́ли по́здно ; *the sooner the better*, чем ра́ньше, тем лу́чше.

soot *n.* са́жа, ко́поть.

soothe *v.t.* успока́ивать *imp.*, успоко́ить *perf.* ; (*pain*) облегча́ть *imp.*, облегчи́ть *perf.*

soothsayer *n.* предсказа́тель *m.*, -ница.

sooty *adj.* запа́чканный (-ан) са́жей, закопте́лый.

sophism *n.* софи́зм.

sophisticated *adj.* (*person*) искушённый ; (*tastes*) изощрённый (-ён, -ённа) ; (*equipment*) усоверше́нствованный.

soporific *adj.* снотво́рный ; *n.* снотво́рное *sb.*

soprano *n.* сопра́но (*voice*) *neut.* & (*person*) *f.indecl.*, дискант.

sorbet *n.* шербе́т.

sorcerer *n.* колду́н (-а́). **sorceress** *n.* колду́нья (*gen.pl.* -ний). **sorcery** *n.* колдовство́.

sordid *adj.* (*dirty*) гря́зный (-зен, -зна́, -зно) ; (*wretched*) убо́гий ; (*base*) по́длый (подл, -а́, -о).

sore *n.* боля́чка, я́зва ; *adj.* больно́й (-лен, -льна́) ; *my throat is s.*, у меня́ боли́т го́рло.

sorrel[1] *n.* (*herb*) щаве́ль (-ля́) *m.*

sorrel[2] *adj.* (*of horse*) гнедо́й ; *n.* гнеда́я ло́шадь (*pl.* -ди, -де́й, *instr.* -дьми́).

sorrow *n.* печа́ль, го́ре, скорбь. **sorrowful** *adj.* печа́льный, ско́рбный. **sorry** *adj.* жа́лкий (-лок, -лка́, -лко) ; *predic.* : *be s.*, жале́ть *imp.* (*about*, о + *prep.*) ; жаль *impers.* + *dat.* (*for*, + *gen.*) ; *s.!* извини́(те) !

sort *n.* род (*pl.* -ы́), вид, сорт (*pl.* -а́) ; *v.t.* сорти́ровать *imp.* ; разбира́ть *imp.*, разобра́ть (разберу́, -рёшь ; разобра́л, -а́, -о) *perf.* **sorter** *n.* сорти́ро́вщик, -ица.

sortie *n.* вы́лазка.

SOS *n.* (ра́дио)сигна́л бе́дствия.

sot *n.* пья́ница *m.* & *f.*

sotto voce *adv.* вполго́лоса.

soubriquet *see* **sobriquet**.

soufflé *n.* суфле́ *neut.indecl.*

soul *n.* душа́ (*acc.* -шу ; *pl.* -ши).

sound[1] *adj.* (*healthy*) здоро́вый ; (*of sleep*) кре́пкий (-пок, -пка́, -пко) ;

(*firm*) прóчный (-чен, -чнá, -чно, прóчны); *adv.* крéпко.

sound² *n.* (*noise*) звук, шум; *attrib.* звуковóй; *s.* barrier, звуковóй барьéр; *s.* effects, звуковóе сопровождéние; *s.*-proof, звуконепроницáемый; *s.*-track, звуковáя дорóжка; *s.*-wave, звуковáя волнá (*pl.* -ны, -н, вóлнам); *v.i.* звучáть (-чи́т) *imp.*, про ~ *perf.*

sound³ *v.t.* (*test depth*) измеря́ть *imp.*, изме́рить *perf.* глубину́ + *gen.*; (*med.*, *fig.*) зонди́ровать *imp.*, по ~ *perf.*; *n.* зонд.

sound⁴ *n.* (*strait*) проли́в.

soup *n.* суп (-а(у), *loc.* -е & -у́; *pl.* -ы́) *s.-*kitchen, беспла́тная столóвая *sb.*; *v.t.*: *s.* up, повыша́ть *imp.*, повы́сить *perf.* мóщность + *gen.*

sour *adj.* ки́слый (-сел, -слá, -сло); (*of milk etc.*) проки́сший; *s.* cream, смета́на; *v.i.* прокиса́ть *imp.*, проки́снуть (-с) *perf.*; *v.t.* & *i.* озлобля́ть(ся) *imp.*, озло́бить(ся) *perf.*

source *n.* истóчник; (*of river*) истóки *m.pl.*

south *n.* юг; (*naut.*) зюйд; *adj.* ю́жный; (*naut.*) зюйдовый; *adv.* к ю́гу, на юг; *s.-*east, ю́го-востóк; (*naut.*) зюйд-óст; *s.-*easterly, -eastern, ю́го-востóчный; (*naut.*) зюйд-óстовый; *s.-*west, ю́го-зáпад; (*naut.*) зюйд-вéст; *s.-*westerly, -western, ю́го-зáпадный; (*naut.*) зюйд-вéстовый; *s.* wind, зюйд. southeaster *n.* зюйд-óст. southerly *adj.* ю́жный; (*naut.*) зюйдóвый. southern *adj.* ю́жный. southerner *n.* южáнин (*pl.* -áне, -áн), южáнка (*gen. pl.* -нок); жи́тель *m.*, ~ ница юга. southernmost *adj.* сáмый ю́жный. southpaw *n.* левшá *m.* & *f.* southward(s) *adv.* к ю́гу, на юг. southwester *n.* зюйд-вéст.

souvenir *n.* сувени́р.

sou'wester *n.* (*hat*) зюйдвéстка.

sovereign *adj.* суверéнный *n.* суверéн, монáрх; (*coin*) соверéн. sovereignty *n.* суверенитéт.

soviet *n.* совéт; Supreme S., Верхóвный Совéт; S. Union, Совéтский Сою́з; *adj.* (S.) совéтский.

sow¹ *n.* свинья́ (*pl.* -ньи, -нéй, -ньям), свиномáтка.

sow² *v.t.* (*seed*) сéять (сéю, сéешь) *imp.*,

по ~ *perf.*; (*field*) засéивать *imp.*, засéять (-éю, -éешь) *perf.*; sowing-machine, сéялка. sower *n.* сéятель *m.*

soy *n.* сóевый сóус. soya *n.* сóя; *s.* bean, сóевый боб (-á).

sozzled *predic.* в дóску пьян (-á, -о).

spa *n.* вóды *f.pl.*, курóрт.

space *n.* прострáнство; (*distance*) протяжéние; (*interval*) промежу́ток (-тка); (*place*) мéсто; (*outer s.*) кóсмос; *attrib.* косм́ический; *s.-*bar, клáвиша для интервáлов; *s.* station, космúческая стáнция; *s.-*time, прострáнство-врéмя *neut.*; прострáнственно-временнóй; *v.t.* расставля́ть *imp.*, расстáвить *perf.* с промежу́тками. spacecraft *n.* космúческий корáбль (-ля́) *m.* космонáвт, астронáвт. spaceship *n.* космúческий корáбль (-ля́) *m.* spacesuit *n.* скафáндр (космонáвта). spacious *adj.* простóрный, помести́тельный.

spade¹ *n.* (*tool*) лопáта, зáступ.

spade² *n.* (*cards*) пúка.

spaghetti *n.* спагéтти *neut.indecl.*

span *n.* (*of bridge*) пролёт; (*aeron.*) размáх; (*as measure*) пядь (*pl.* пя́ди, пя́дéй); *v.t.* (*of bridge*) соединя́ть *imp.*, соедини́ть *perf.* стóроны + *gen.*, (*river*) берегá + *gen.*

spangle *n.* блёстка.

Spaniard *n.* испáнец (-нца), -нка.

spaniel *n.* спаниéль *m.*

Spanish *adj.* испáнский.

spank *v.t.* шлёпать *imp.*, шлёпнуть *perf.*; *n.* шлепóк (-пкá).

spanner *n.* гáечный ключ (-á).

spar¹ *n.* (*naut.*) рангóутное дéрево (*pl.* -éвья, -éвьев); (*aeron.*) лонжерóн.

spar² *v.i.* боксúровать *imp.*, (*fig.*) препирáться *imp.*

spare *adj.* (*in reserve*) запаснóй, запáсный; (*extra, to s.*) лúшний; (*of seat, time*) свобóдный; (*thin*) худощáвый; *s.* parts, запасны́е чáсти (-тéй) *f.pl.*; *s.* room, кóмната для гостéй (-тéй) *pl.*; *v.t.* (*grudge*) жалéть *imp.*, по ~ *perf.* + *acc.*, *gen.*; he spared no pains, он не жалéл трудóв; (*do without*) обходи́ться (-ожу́сь, -óдишься) *imp.*, обойти́сь (обойду́сь, -дёшься) *imp.*, обошёлся, -шлáсь) *perf.* без

+*gen.*; (*time*) уделя́ть *imp.*, удели́ть *perf.*; (*person, feelings, etc.*) щади́ть *imp.*, по~ *perf.*

spare-rib *n.* (свино́е) рёбрышко (*pl.* -шки, -шек, -шкам).

spark *n.* и́скра; *v.i.* искри́ть *imp.*; *sparking-plug* запа́льная свеча́ (*pl.* -чи, -че́й).

sparkle *v.i.* искри́ться *imp.*; сверка́ть *imp.*

sparrow *n.* воробе́й (-бья́); *s.-hawk*, перепеля́тник.

sparse *adj.* ре́дкий (-док, -дка́, -дко); (*population*) разбро́санный (-ан).

spasm *n.* спазм, су́дорога. **spasmodic** *adj.* спазмоди́ческий, су́дорожный.

spastic *adj.* спасти́ческий.

spate *n.* разли́в; (*fig.*) пото́к.

spatial *adj.* простра́нственный.

spatio-temporal *adj.* простра́нственно--временно́й.

spatter *v.t.* (*liquid*) бры́згать (-зжу, -зжешь) *imp.*+*instr.*; (*person etc.*) забры́згивать *imp.*, забры́згать *perf.* (*with*, +*instr.*); *n.* бры́зги (-г) *pl.*

spatula *n.* шпа́тель *m.*

spavin *n.* ко́стный шпат.

spawn *v.t.* & *abs.* мета́ть (ме́чет) *imp.* (икру́); *v.t.* (*fig.*) порожда́ть *imp.*, породи́ть *perf.*; *n.* икра́; (*mushroom s.*) грибни́ца; (*offspring*) отро́дье.

speak *v.t.* & *i.* говори́ть *imp.*, сказа́ть (-ажу́, -а́жешь) *perf.*; *v.i.* (*make speech*) выступа́ть *imp.*, вы́ступить *perf.* (с ре́чью); выска́зываться *imp.*, вы́сказаться (-ажусь, -ажешься) *perf.* (*for*, за + *acc.*; *against*, про́тив + *gen.*). **speaker** *n.* ора́тор; (*at conference etc.*) докла́дчик; (*S., parl.*) спи́кер; (*loudspeaker*) громкоговори́тель *m.* **speaking** *n.*: *not be on s. terms*, не разгова́ривать *imp.* (*with*, с + *instr.*); *s.-trumpet*, ру́пор; *s.-tube*, перегово́рная тру́бка.

spear *n.* копьё (*pl.* -пья, -пий, -пьям); *v.t.* пронза́ть *imp.*, пронзи́ть (-нжу́, -нзи́шь) *perf.* копьём. **spearhead** *n.* передово́й отря́д.

special *adj.* осо́бый, специа́льный; (*extra*) экстренный. **specialist** *n.* специали́ст. **speciality** *n.* специа́льность. **specialization** *n.* специализа́ция. **specialize** *v.t.* & *i.* специализи́ровать(ся) *imp.*, *perf.* **specially** *adv.* осо́бенно.

specie *n.* зво́нкая моне́та.

species *n.* вид.

specific *adj.* специфи́ческий; (*biol.*) видово́й; (*phys.*) уде́льный. **specification(s)** *n.* специфика́ция. **specify** *v.t.* (*mention*) специа́льно упомина́ть *imp.*, упомяну́ть (-ну́, -нешь) *perf.*+*acc.*, о + *prep.*; (*include in specifications*) специфици́ровать *imp.*, *perf.*

specimen *n.* образе́ц (-зца́), экземпля́р; *s. page*, про́бная страни́ца.

specious *adj.* благови́дный, правдоподо́бный.

speck *n.* кра́пинка, пя́тнышко (*pl.* -шки, -шек, -шкам). **speckled** *adj.* кра́пчатый.

spectacle *n.* зре́лище; *pl.* очки́ (-ко́в) *pl.*

spectacular *adj.* эффе́ктный.

spectator *n.* зри́тель *m.*, ~ница.

spectral *adj.* (*ghostlike*) при́зрачный; (*phys.*) спектра́льный. **spectre** *n.* при́зрак.

spectroscope *n.* спектроско́п. **spectroscopic** *adj.* спектроскопи́ческий.

spectrum *n.* спектр.

speculate *v.i.* (*meditate*) размышля́ть *imp.*, размы́слить *perf.* (*on*, о + *prep.*); (*in shares etc.*) спекули́ровать *imp.* **speculation** *n.* тео́рия, предположе́ние; спекуля́ция. **speculative** *adj.* гипотети́ческий; спекуляти́вный. **speculator** *n.* спекуля́нт, ~ка.

speech *n.* (*faculty*) речь; (*address*) речь (*pl.* -чи, -че́й), выступле́ние; (*language*) язы́к (-á); *s.-day*, акт; *s. therapy*, логопе́дия. **speechify** *v.i.* ора́торствовать *imp.* **speechless** *adj.* немо́й (нем, -á, -о) (*with emotion*) онеме́вший.

speed *n.* ско́рость, быстрота́; (*phot.*) светочувстви́тельность; *at full s.*, по́лным хо́дом; *s. limit*, дозво́ленная ско́рость; *v.i.* спеши́ть *imp.*, по~ *perf.*; *v.t.*: *s. up*, ускоря́ть *imp.*, ускори́ть *perf.* **speedboat** *n.* быстрохо́дный ка́тер (*pl.* -á). **speedometer** *n.* спидо́метр. **speedway** *n.* доро́жка для мотоцикле́тных го́нок. **speedwell** *n.* вероника. **speedy** *adj.* бы́стрый (быстр, -á, -о, бы́стры), ско́рый (скор, -á, -о).

speleologist *n.* спелео́лог. **speleology** *n.* спелеоло́гия.

spell[1] *n.* (*incantation*) заклина́ние.

spell [2] *v.t.* (*write*) писа́ть (пишу́, -шешь) *imp.*, на~ *perf.* по бу́квам; (*say*) произноси́ть (-ошу́, -о́сишь) *imp.*, произнести́ (-есу́, -есёшь; -ёс, -есла́) *perf.* по бу́квам; *how do you s. that word?* как пи́шется э́то сло́во?

spell [3] *n.* (*period*) промежу́ток (-тка) вре́мени.

spellbound *adj.* зачаро́ванный (-ан, -ан(н)а).

spelling *n.* правописа́ние.

spend *v.t.* (*money; effort*) тра́тить *imp.*, ис~, по~ *perf.*; (*time*) проводи́ть (-ожу́, -о́дишь) *imp.*, провести́ (-еду́, -едёшь; -ёл, -ела́) *perf.* **spendthrift** *n.* расточи́тель *m.*, ~ница *f.*; мот, ~о́вка.

sperm [1] *n.* спе́рма.

sperm [2] *n.* (*whale*) кашало́т.

spermaceti *n.* спермаце́т.

spermatic *adj.* семенно́й.

spermatozoon *n.* сперматозо́ид.

sphere *n.* (*var. senses*) сфе́ра; (*ball*) шар (-á with 2, 3, 4; *pl.* -ы́). **spherical** *adj.* сфери́ческий, шарообра́зный. **spheroid** *n.* сферо́ид.

sphincter *n.* сфи́нктер.

sphinx *n.* сфинкс.

spice *n.* спе́ция, пря́ность; *v.t.* приправля́ть *imp.*, припра́вить *perf.* спе́циями.

spick *adj.*: *s. and span,* чи́стый (чист, -á, -о, чи́сты), опря́тный; (*of person*) оде́тый с иго́лочки.

spicy *adj.* пря́ный; (*fig.*) пика́нтный.

spider *n.* пау́к (-á). **spidery** *adj.* то́нкий (-нок, -нка́, -нко, то́нки).

spike [1] *n.* (*bot.*) ко́лос (*pl.* коло́сья, -ьев).

spike [2] *n.* (*point*) остриё; (*nail*) гвоздь (-дя́; *pl.* -ди, -дей) *m.*; (*on shoes*) шип (-á); (*for papers*) нако́лка; *v.t.* снабжа́ть *imp.*, снабди́ть *perf.* шипа́ми; (*gun*) заклёпывать *imp.*, заклепа́ть *perf.*; (*drink*) добавля́ть *imp.*, доба́вить *perf.* спиртно́е в+*acc.*

spill *v.t. & i.* пролива́ть(ся) *imp.*, проли́ть(ся) (-лью́, -льёт(ся); про́ли́л/проли́лся, -á(сь), -о/про́ли́ло(сь)) *perf.*; рассыпа́ть(ся) *imp.*, рассы́пать(ся) (-плю, -плет(ся)) *perf.*; *n.* проли́тие, рассы́пка; (*fall*) паде́ние.

spin *v.t.* (*thread etc.*) прясть (пряду́, -дёшь; -ял, -яла́, -яло) *imp.*, с~ *perf.*;

(*top*) запуска́ть *imp.*, запусти́ть (-ущу́, -у́стишь) *perf.*; (*coin*) подбра́сывать *imp.*, подбро́сить *perf.*; *v.t. & i.* (*turn*) крути́ть(ся) (-учу́(сь), -у́тишь(ся)) *imp.*; кружи́ть(ся) (-ужу́(сь), -у́жишь(ся)) *imp.*; *s. out,* (*prolong*) затя́гивать *imp.*, затяну́ть (-ну́, -нешь) *perf.*; *n.* круже́ние; (*aeron.*) што́пор; (*excursion*) пое́здка. *go for a s.,* прока́тываться *imp.*, прокати́ться (-ачу́сь, -а́тишься) *perf.*

spinach *n.* шпина́т.

spinal *adj.* спинно́й; *s. column,* спинно́й хребе́т (-бта́); *s. cord,* спинно́й мозг.

spindle *n.* веретено́ (*pl.* -ёна); (*axis, pin*) ось (*pl.* о́си, осе́й) *m.*, шпи́ндель *m.* **spindly** *adj.* дли́нный (-нен, -нна́, дли́нно) и то́нкий (-нок, -нка́, -нко, то́нки).

spine *n.* (*backbone*) позвоно́чник, хребе́т (-бта́); (*bot.*) шип (-á); (*zool.*) игла́ (*pl.* -лы); (*of book*) корешо́к (-шка́). **spineless** *adj.* мягкоте́лый, бесхара́ктерный (*fig.*).

spinet *n.* спине́т.

spinnaker *n.* спи́накер.

spinner *n.* пряди́льщик, -ица; (*fishing*) блесна́.

spinney *n.* ро́щица.

spinning *n.* пряде́ние; *s.-machine,* пряди́льная маши́на; *s.-top,* волчо́к (-чка́); *s.-wheel,* пря́лка.

spinster *n.* незаму́жняя же́нщина.

spiny *adj.* колю́чий; (*fig.*) затрудни́тельный.

spiral *adj.* спира́льный, винтово́й; *n.* спира́ль.

spire *n.* шпиль *m.*

spirit *n.* дух, душа́; *pl.* (*mood*) настрое́ние; (*liquid*) спирт (*loc.* -е & -у́; *pl.* -ы́); *pl.* (*drinks*) спиртно́е *sb.*; *s.-lamp,* спирто́вка; *s.-level,* ватерпа́с; *v.t.*: *s. away,* та́йно уноси́ть (-ошу́, -о́сишь) *imp.*, унести́ (-есу́, -есёшь; унёс, -ла́) *perf.* **spirited** *adj.* энерги́чный, пы́лкий (-лок, -лка́, -лко). **spiritless** *adj.* безжи́зненный (-ен, -енна). **spiritual** *adj.* духо́вный. **spiritualism** *n.* спирити́зм. **spiritualist** *n.* спири́т. **spirituous** *adj.* спиртно́й.

spit [1] *n.* (*skewer*) ве́ртел (*pl.* -á); (*of land*) стре́лка, коса́ (*acc.* ко́су́; *pl.*

-сы); *v.t.* наса́живать *imp.*, насади́ть (-ажу́, -а́дишь) *perf.* на+ве́ртел; (*fig.*) пронза́ть *imp.*, пронзи́ть *perf.*

spit² *v.i.* плева́ть (плюю́, -юёшь) *imp.*, плю́нуть *perf.*; (*of rain*) мороси́ть *imp.*; (*of fire etc.*) шипе́ть (-пи́т) *imp.*; *v.t.*: *s. out*, выплёвывать *imp.*, вы́плюнуть *perf.*; *spitting image*, то́чная ко́пия; *n.* слюна́, плево́к (-вка́).

spite *n.* злоба́, злость; *in s. of*, несмотря́ на+*acc.* **spiteful** *adj.* зло́бный.

spittle *n.* слюна́, плево́к (-вка́).

spittoon *n.* плева́тельница.

spitz *n.* шпиц.

splash *v.t.* (*person*) забры́згивать *imp.*, забры́згать *perf.* (*with, +instr.*); (*s. liquid*) бры́згать (-зжу -зжешь) *imp. +instr.*; (*v.i.*) плеска́ть(ся) (-ещу́(сь), -е́щешь(ся)) *imp.*, плесну́ть *perf.*; (*move*) шлёпать *imp.*, шлёпнуть *perf.* (*through,* по+*dat.*); *s. money about,* сори́ть *imp.* деньга́ми; *n.* бры́зги (-г) *pl.*, плеск; *s.-down,* приводне́ние.

splatter *v.i.* плеска́ться (-е́щется) *imp.*

spleen *n.* селезёнка; (*spite*) зло́ба.

splendid *adj.* великоле́пный. **splendour** *n.* блеск, великоле́пие.

splenetic *adj.* жёлчный.

splice *v.t.* (*ropes*) сра́щивать *imp.*, срасти́ть *perf.* концы́+*gen.*; (*film, tape*) скле́ивать *imp.*, скле́ить *perf.* концы́+*gen.*; *n.* (*naut.*) сплесень (-сня) *m.*; (*film, tape*) скле́йка, ме́сто скле́йки.

splint *n.* лубо́к (-бка́), ши́на; *v.t.* накла́дывать *imp.*, наложи́ть (-жу́, -жишь) *perf.* ши́ну на+*acc.*; класть (-аду́, -адёшь; -ал) *imp.*, положи́ть (-жу́, -жишь) *perf.* в лубо́к.

splinter *n.* оско́лок (-лка), ще́пка; (*in skin*) зано́за; *s. group,* отколо́вшаяся гру́ппа; *v.t. & i.* расщепля́ть(ся) *imp.*, расщепи́ть(ся) *perf.*

split *n.* расще́лина, расщёп; (*schism*) раско́л; *pl.* шпага́т; *v.t. & i.* расщепля́ть(ся) *imp.*, расщепи́ть(ся) *perf.*; раска́лывать(ся) *imp.*, расколо́ть(ся) (-лю́, -лешь(ся)) *perf.* дели́ть(ся) (-лю́, -лит(ся)) *imp.*, раз~ *perf.* (*на ча́сти*); *v.i.: s. on,* доноси́ть (-ошу́, -о́сишь) *imp.*, донести́ (-есу́,

-есёшь; -ёс, -есла́) *perf.* на+*acc.*; *s. hairs,* спо́рить *imp.* о мелоча́х; *s. one's sides,* надрыва́ться *imp.* от хо́хота; *s.-level,* на ра́зных у́ровнях; *s. pea(s),* лущёный горо́х (-а(у)); *s. personality,* раздвое́ние ли́чности; *s. pin,* шплинт (шпли́нта); *s. second,* мгнове́ние ока.

splotch *n.* неро́вное пятно́ (*pl.* -тна, -тен, -тнам), мазо́к (-зка́).

splutter *v.i.* бры́згать (-зжу -зжешь) *imp.* слюно́й; *v.t.* (*utter*) говори́ть *imp.* невня́тно.

spoil *n.* (*pl. or collect.*) добы́ча; (*of war*) трофе́и *m.pl.*; *v.t. & i.* (*damage; decay*) по́ртить(ся) *imp.*, ис~ *perf.*; *v.t.* (*indulge*) балова́ть *imp.*, из~ *perf.*; *be spoiling for a fight,* рва́ться (рвусь, рвёшься; рва́лся, -ала́сь, -а́ло́сь) *imp.* в дра́ку.

spoke *n.* спи́ца.

spoken *adj.* (*language*) у́стный. **spokesman, -woman** *n.* представи́тель *m.*, ~ница.

sponge *n.* гу́бка; *s.-cake,* бискви́т; *s. rubber,* гу́бчатая рези́на; *v.t.* (*wash*) мыть (мо́ю, мо́ешь) *imp.*, вы́-, по~ *perf.* гу́бкой; (*obtain*) выпра́шивать *imp.*, вы́просить *perf.*; *v.i.: s. on,* жить (живу́, -вёшь; жил, -а́, -о) *imp.* на счёт +*gen.* **sponger** *n.* прижива́льщик, парази́т. **spongy** *adj.* гу́бчатый.

sponsor *n.* поручи́тель *m.*, ~ница; *v.t.* руча́ться *imp.*, поручи́ться (-чу́сь, -чишься) *perf.* за+*acc.*; (*finance*) финанси́ровать *imp.*, *perf.*·

spontaneity *n.* непосре́дственность, самопроизво́льность. **spontaneous** *adj.* непосре́дственный (-ен, -енна), самопроизво́льный.

spoof *n.* (*hoax*) мистифика́ция; (*parody*) паро́дия.

spook *n.* привиде́ние.

spool *n.* шпу́лька, кату́шка.

spoon *n.* ло́жка; *s.-bait,* блесна́(у); *v.t.* че́рпать *imp.*, черпну́ть *perf.* ло́жкой.

spoonbill *n.* коли́ца. **spoonful** *n.* по́лная ло́жка.

spoor *n.* след (-а(у); *pl.* -ы́).

sporadic *adj.* споради́ческий.

spore *n.* спо́ра.

sport *n.* спорт; *pl.* спорти́вные соревнова́ния *neut.pl.*; (*fun*) заба́ва, поте́ха, (*person*) сла́вный ма́лый *sb.*; **sports car**, спорти́вный автомоби́ль *m.*; **sports coat**, спорти́вный ку́ртка *m.*; щеголя́ть *imp.*, щегольну́ть *perf.*+ *instr.* **sportsman** *n.* спортсме́н. **sportsmanlike** *adj.* спортсме́нский.

spot *n.* (*place*) ме́сто (*pl.* -та́); (*mark*) пятно́ (*pl.* -тна, -тен, -тна́м) (*also fig.*), кра́пинка; (*pimple*) пры́щик; (*on dice etc.*) очко́ (*pl.* -ки́, -ко́в); **on the s.**, на ме́сте; (*without delay*) неме́дленно; **s. check**, вы́борочная прове́рка; *v.t.* (*mark*; *fig.*) пятна́ть *imp.*, за~ *perf.*; (*recognize*) узнава́ть (-наю́, -наёшь) *imp.*, узна́ть *perf.*; (*notice*) замеча́ть *imp.*, заме́тить *perf.*; *v.i.*: **it's spotting with rain**, накра́пывает дождь. **spotless** *adj.* чи́стый (чист, -а́, -о, чи́сты); (*fig.*) безупре́чный. **spotlight** *n.* проже́ктор (*pl.* -ы & -а́); *v.t.* освеща́ть *imp.*, освети́ть (-ещу́ -ети́шь) *perf.* проже́ктором. **spotty** *adj.* прыщева́тый.

spouse *n.* супру́г, ~а.

spout *v.i.* бить (бьёт) *imp.* струёй; хлы́нуть *perf.*; *v.t.* выпуска́ть *imp.*, вы́пустить *perf.* струю́+*gen.*; (*verses etc.*) деклами́ровать *imp.*, про~ *perf.*; *n.* (*tube*) но́сик; (*jet*) струя́ (*pl.* -у́и).

sprain *v.t.* растя́гивать *imp.*, растяну́ть (-ну́, -нешь) *perf.*; *n.* растяже́ние.

sprat *n.* ки́лька, шпро́та.

sprawl *v.i.* (*of person*) разва́ливаться *imp.*, развали́ться (-лю́сь, -лишься) *perf.*; (*of town*) раски́дываться *imp.*, раски́нуться *perf.*

spray¹ *n.* (*of flowers etc.*) ве́т(оч)ка.

spray² *n.* (*liquid*) бры́зги (-г) *pl.*; (*water*) водяна́я пыль; (*atomizer*) распыли́тель *m.*; *v.t.* опры́скивать *imp.*, опры́скать *perf.* (**with**, +*instr.*); (*cause to scatter*) распыля́ть *imp.*, распыли́ть *perf.*; **s.-gun**, краскопу́льт.

spread *v.t.* & i. (**s. out**) расстила́ть(ся) *imp.*, разостла́ть(ся) (расстелю́, -лет(ся)) *perf.*; (*unfurl, unroll*) развёртывать(ся) *imp.*, разверну́ть(ся) *perf.*; (*rumour, disease, etc.*) распространя́ть(ся) *imp.*, распространи́ть(ся) *perf.*; *v.i.* (*extend*) простира́ться *imp.*, простере́ться (-трётся) *perf.*; *v.t.* (*bread etc.*, *acc.*; *butter etc.*,

instr.) нама́зывать, ма́зать (ма́жу, -жешь) *imp.*, на~ *perf.*; *n.* распростране́ние; (*span*) разма́х; (*feast*) пир; (*paste*) па́ста; (*double page*) разворо́т.

spree *n.* (*drinking*) кутёж (-а́); **go on the s.**, кути́ть (кучу́, ку́тишь) *imp.*, кутну́ть *perf.*

sprig *n.* ве́точка.

sprightly *adj.* бо́дрый (бодр, -а́, -о), бо́дры).

spring *v.i.* (*jump*) пры́гать *imp.*, пры́гнуть *perf.*; *v.t.* (*disclose unexpectedly*) неожи́данно сообща́ть *imp.*, сообщи́ть *perf.* (**on**, +*dat.*); **s. a leak**, дава́ть (даёт) *imp.*, дать (даст, даду́т; дал, -а́, да́ло́, -и) *perf.* течь; **s. a surprise on**, де́лать *imp.*, с~ *perf.* сюрпри́з+*dat.*; **s. from**, (*originate*) исходи́ть (-ожу, -о́дишь) *imp.*, произойти́ (-ойду́, -ойдёшь; -ошёл, -ошла́) *perf.* из+*gen.*; **s. up**, (*jump up*) вска́кивать *imp.*, вскочи́ть (-чу́, -чишь) *perf.*; (*arise*) возника́ть *imp.*, возни́кнуть (-к) *perf.*; *n.* (*jump*) прыжо́к (-жка́); (*season*) весна́ (*pl.* вёсны, -сен, -снам), *attrib.* весе́нний; (*source*) исто́чник, ключ (-а́), родни́к (-а́); (*elasticity*) упру́гость; (*coil*) пружи́на; (*on vehicle*) рессо́ра; (*fig.*, *motive*) моти́в; **s. balance**, пружи́нные весы́ (-со́в) *pl.*; **s.-clean**, генера́льная убо́рка; (*v.t.*) производи́ть (-ожу́, -о́дишь) *imp.*, произвести́ (-еду́, -едёшь; -ёл, -ела́) *perf.* генера́льную убо́рку+*gen.*; **s. mattress**, пружи́нный матра́с; **s. tide**, сизиги́йный прили́в; **s. water**, ключева́я вода́ (*acc.* -ду). **springboard** *n.* трампли́н. **springbok** *n.* прыгу́н (-а́). **springy** *adj.* упру́гий.

sprinkle *v.t.* (*with liquid*) опры́скивать *imp.*, опры́скать *perf.* (**with**, +*instr.*); (*with solid*) посыпа́ть *imp.*, посы́пать (-плю, -плешь) *perf.* (**with**, +*instr.*). **sprinkler** *n.* (*for watering*) опры́скиватель *m.*; (*fire-extinguisher*) спри́нклер.

sprint *v.i.* бежа́ть (бегу́, бежи́шь) *imp.* на коро́ткую диста́нцию; *n.* спринт. **sprinter** *n.* спри́нтер.

sprit *n.* шприто́в.

sprocket n. зубе́ц (-бца́); s.-wheel, звёздочка, цепно́е колесо́ f (pl. -ёса).

sprout v.i. пуска́ть imp., пусти́ть (-ит) perf. ростки́; n. росто́к (-тка́), побе́г; pl. брюссе́льская капу́ста.

spruce[1] adj. наря́дный, элега́нтный; v.t.: s. oneself up, принаряжа́ться imp., принаряди́ться (-яжу́сь, -яди́шься) perf.

spruce[2] n. ель.

spry adj. живо́й (жив, -á, -о), бо́дрый (бодр, -á, -о, бо́дры).

spud n. (tool) моты́га; (potato) карто́шка (also collect.).

spume n. пе́на.

spur n. (rider's) шпо́ра; (fig.) сти́мул; (of mountain) отро́г; on the s. of the moment, экспро́мтом; v.t.: s. on, толка́ть imp., толкну́ть perf. (to, на + acc.).

spurge n. моло́ча́й.

spurious adj. подде́льный, подло́жный.

spurn v.t. отверга́ть imp., отве́ргнуть (-г(нул), -гла) perf.

spurt n. (jet) струя́ (pl. -у́и); (effort) рыво́к (-вка́); v.i. бить (бьёт) imp. струёй; де́лать imp., с ~ perf. рыво́к.

sputter v.t. (utter) невня́тно говори́ть imp.; v.i. шипе́ть (-пи́т) imp.

sputum n. слюна́.

spy n. шпио́н (-а); v.i. шпио́нить imp. (on, за + instr.). **spyglass** n. подзо́рная труба́ (pl. -бы). **spyhole** n. глазо́к (-зка́).

squabble n. перебра́нка; v.i. вздо́рить imp., по ~ perf.

squad n. кома́нда, гру́ппа.

squadron n. (mil.) эскадро́н; (naut.) эска́дра; (aeron.) эскадри́лья; s.-leader, майо́р авиа́ции.

squalid adj. гря́зный (-зен, -зна́, -зно), убо́гий.

squall n. шквал; v.i. визжа́ть (-жу́, -жи́шь) imp. **squally** adj. шква́листый.

squalor n. грязь (loc. -зи́), убо́гость.

squander v.t. растра́чивать imp., растра́тить perf.; (fortune) прома́тывать imp., промота́ть perf.

square n. (math.) квадра́т; (in town) пло́щадь (pl. -ди, -де́й); сквер; (on paper, material) кле́тка; (chess) по́ле; (mil.) каре́ neut.indecl.; (instrument)

науго́льник; set s., уго́льник; T-s., рейсши́на; adj. квадра́тный; (meal) пло́тный (-тен, -тна́, -тно, пло́тны); s. root, квадра́тный ко́рень (-рня) m.; s. sail, прямо́й па́рус (pl. -á); v.t. де́лать imp., с ~ perf. квадра́тным (math.) возводи́ть imp., возвести́ (-еду́, -едёшь; -ёл, -ела́) perf. в квадра́т; (bribe) подкупа́ть imp., подкупи́ть (-плю́, -пишь) perf.; s. accounts with, распла́чиваться imp., расплати́ться (-аусь, -а́тишься) perf. с + instr.

squash n. (crowd) толку́ча; (drink) (фрукто́вый) сок (-а(у), loc. -е & -у́); v.t. разда́вливать imp., раздави́ть (-влю́, -вишь) perf.; (silence) заставля́ть imp., заста́вить perf. замолча́ть; (suppress) подавля́ть imp., подави́ть (-влю́, -вишь) perf.; v.i. вти́скиваться imp., вти́снуться perf.

squat adj. корена́стый, приземи́стый; v.i. сиде́ть (сижу́, сиди́шь) imp. на ко́рточках; s. down, сади́ться imp., сесть (ся́ду, -дешь; сел) perf. на ко́рточки.

squatter n. лицо́, самово́льно поселя́ющееся в чужо́м до́ме.

squaw n. индиа́нка (в Се́верной Аме́рике).

squawk n. пронзи́тельный крик; (of bird) клёкот; v.i. пронзи́тельно крича́ть (-чу́, -чи́шь) imp., кри́кнуть perf.; (of bird) клекота́ть (-о́чет) imp.

squeak n. писк, скрип; v.i. пища́ть (-щу́, -щи́шь) imp., пи́скнуть perf.; скрипе́ть (-плю́, -пи́шь) imp., скри́пнуть perf. **squeaky** adj. пискли́вый, скрипу́чий.

squeal n. визг; v.i. визжа́ть (-жу́, -жи́шь) imp., ви́згнуть perf.

squeamish adj. брезгли́вый, привере́дливый.

squeeze n. (crush) да́вка; (pressure) сжа́тие; (hand) пожа́тие; v.t. дави́ть (давлю́, да́вишь) imp.; сжима́ть imp., сжать (сожму́, -мёшь) perf.; пожима́ть imp., пожа́ть (пожму́, -мёшь) perf.; s. in, впи́хивать(ся) imp., впи́хнуть(ся) perf.; вти́скивать(ся) imp., вти́снуть(ся) perf.; s. out, выжима́ть imp., вы́жать (вы́жму, -мешь) perf.; s.

through, проти́скивать(ся) *imp.*, проти́снуть(ся) *perf.*

squelch *n.* хлю́панье; *v.i.* хлю́пать *imp.*, хлю́пнуть(скв)ф *perf.*

squib *n.* (*firework*) пета́рда.

squid *n.* кальма́р.

squiggle *n.* (*flourish*) загогу́лина; (*scribble*) кара́кули *f.pl.*

squint *n.* косогла́зие; *adj.* косо́й (кос, -á, -о), косогла́зый; *v.i.* коси́ть *imp.*; смотре́ть (-рю́, -ришь) *imp.*, по~ *perf.* и́скоса.

squire *n.* сквайр, поме́щик.

squirm *v.i.* (*wriggle*) извива́ться *imp.*, изви́ться (изовью́сь, -вьёшься; изви́лся, извила́сь) *perf.*; (*fidget*) ёрзать *imp.*

squirrel *n.* бе́лка.

squirt *n.* струя́ (*pl.* -у́и); *v.i.* бить (бьёт) *imp.* струёй; *v.t.* пуска́ть *imp.*, пусти́ть (пущу́, пу́стишь) *perf.* струю́ (*substance*,+ *gen.*; *at*, на + *acc.*).

stab *n.* уда́р (ножо́м *etc.*); (*pain*) внеза́пная о́страя боль; *v.i.* наноси́ть (-ошу́, -о́сишь) *imp.*, нанести́ (-есу́, -есёшь; -ёс, -есла́) *perf.* уда́р (ножо́м *etc.*) (*at*, *dat.*); *v.t.* коло́ть (-лю́, -лешь) *imp.*, кольну́ть *perf.*

stability *n.* усто́йчивость, про́чность, стаби́льность, постоя́нство. **stabilization** *n.* стабилиза́ция. **stabilize** *v.t.* стабилизи́ровать *imp.*, *perf.* **stabilizer** *n.* стабилиза́тор.

stable *adj.* (*steady*) усто́йчивый; *of prices, family life etc.*) про́чный (-чен, -чна́, -чно, про́чны́); (*unwavering*) стаби́льный; (*psych.*) уравнове́шенный (-ен, -енна); *v.t.* ста́вить *imp.*, по~ *perf.* в коню́шню.

staccato *n.* (*mus.*) стакка́то *neut.indecl.*; *adv.* (*mus.*) стакка́то.

stack *n.* (*hay*) скирд(á) (-á & -ы́; *pl.* скирды́, -д(о́в), -да́м), стог (*loc.* -е & -у́; *pl.* -á); (*heap*) ку́ча, ки́па; (*building materials etc.*) штабель (-ля) *m.*; (*chimney*) (дымово́й) труба́ (*pl.* -бы); (*s.-room*) (кни́гохрани́лище; *pl.* ма́сса, мно́жество; *v.t.* скла́дывать *imp.*, сложи́ть (-жу́, -жишь) *perf.* в ку́чу; укла́дывать *imp.*, уложи́ть (-жу́, -жишь) *perf.* штабеля́ми.

stadium *n.* стадио́н.

staff *n.* (*personnel*) штат, шта́ты (-тов) *pl.*, персона́л, ка́дры (-ров) *pl.*; (*mil.*) штаб (*pl.* -ы́); (*stick*) посо́х, жезл (-á); (*mus.*) но́тные лине́йки *f.pl.*; *adj.* шта́тный; (*mil.*) штабно́й.

stag *n.* саме́ц-оле́нь (самца́-оле́ня) *m.*; *s.-beetle*, рога́ч (-á); *s.-party*, вечери́нка без же́нщин.

stage *n.* (*theat.*) сце́на, подмо́стки (-ков) *pl.*, эстра́да; (*platform*) платфо́рма; (*period*) ста́дия, фа́за, эта́п; *v.t.* (*theat.*) ста́вить *imp.*, по~ *perf.*; (*dramatize, feign*) инсцени́ровать *imp.*, *perf.*; (*organize*) организова́ть *imp.*, *perf.*; *s.-manager*, режиссёр *m.*; *s. whisper*, театра́льный шёпот.

stagger *n.* пошату́тывание, шата́ние; *v.i.* шата́ться *imp.*, шатну́ться *perf.*; кача́ться *imp.*, качну́ться *perf.*; *v.t.* (*surprise*) поража́ть *imp.*, порази́ть *perf.*; потряса́ть *imp.*, потрясти́ (-су́, -сёшь; потря́с, -ла́) *perf.*; (*hours of work etc.*) распределя́ть *imp.*, распредели́ть *perf.* **be staggered** *v.i.* поража́ться *imp.*, порази́ться *perf.* **staggering** *adj.* потряса́ющий, порази́тельный.

stagnancy, stagnation *n.* засто́й, ко́сность, ине́ртность. **stagnant** *adj.* (*water*) стоя́чий; (*fig.*) засто́йный, ко́сный, ине́ртный. **stagnate** *v.i.* застаива́ться *imp.*, застоя́ться (-ою́сь, -ои́шься) *perf.*; косне́ть *imp.*, за~ *perf.*

staid *adj.* степе́нный (-нен, -нна), тре́звый (трезв, -á, -о), соли́дный.

stain *n.* пятно́ (*pl.* -а, -тен, -тнам); (*dye*) кра́ска; *v.t.* па́чкать *imp.*, за~, ис~ *perf.*; пятна́ть *imp.*, за~ *perf.*; (*dye*) окра́шивать *imp.*, окра́сить *perf.*; *stained glass*, цветно́е стекло́. **stainless** *adj.* незапя́тнанный, безупре́чный; *s. steel*, нержаве́ющая сталь.

stair *n.* ступе́нь, ступе́нька. **staircase, stairs** *n.* ле́стница. **stair well** *n.* ле́стничная кле́тка. **flight of stairs** *n.* ле́стничный марш.

stake *n.* (*stick*) кол (-á, *loc.* -у́; *pl.* -ья, -ьев), столб (-á); (*landmark*) ве́ха; (*bet*) ста́вка, закла́д; *be at s.*, быть поста́вленным на ка́рту; *v.t.* (*mark* *out*) огора́живать *imp.*, огороди́ть (-ожу́, -о́дишь) *perf.* кольями; отмеча́ть *imp.*, отме́тить *perf.* ве́хами; (*risk*) ста́вить *imp.*, по~ *perf.* на ка́рту; рискова́ть *imp.* + *instr.*

stalactite *n.* сталакти́т.

stalagmite *n.* сталагми́т.

stale *adj.* несве́жий (несве́ж, -а́, -е) (*hard, dry*) чёрствый (чёрств, -а́, -о), сухо́й (сух, -а́, -о); (*musty, damp*) за́тхлый; (*hackneyed*) изби́тый; *become, grow s.*, черстве́ть *imp.*, за~, по~ *perf.*

stalemate *n.* пат; (*fig.*) тупи́к (-а́).

stalk *n.* сте́бель (-ля; *gen.pl.* -бле́й) *m.*; *v.t.* высле́живать *imp.*; (*stride*) ше́ствовать *imp.*

stall *n.* сто́йло; (*booth*) ларёк (-рька́) кио́ск, пала́тка; (*theat.*) кре́сло *(gen. pl.* -сел) в парте́ре; *pl.* (*theat.*) парте́р; *v.t. & i.* остана́вливать(ся) *imp.*, останови́ть(ся) (-влю́(сь), -вишь(ся)) *perf.*; *v.i.* теря́ть *imp.*, по~ *perf.* ско́рость; (*play for time*) оття́гивать *imp.*, оттяну́ть (-ну́, -нешь) *perf.* вре́мя.

stallion *n.* жеребе́ц (-бца́).

stalwart *adj.* сто́йкий (-о́ек, -о́йка́, -о́йко); *n.* сто́йкий приве́рженец (-нца), -кая -нка.

stamen *n.* тычи́нка.

stamina *n.* вынос́ливость.

stammer *v.i.* заика́ться *imp.*; *n.* заика́ние. **stammerer** *n.* заи́ка *m. & f.*

stamp *n.* печа́ть, штамп, штéмпель (*pl.* -ля́) *m.*; (*hallmark*) клеймо́ (*pl.* -ма); (*postage*) (почто́вая) ма́рка; (*feet*) то́панье; *s.-duty*, ге́рбовый сбор; *v.t.* ста́вить *imp.*, по~ *perf.* печа́ть на + *acc.*; штампова́ть *imp.*, штемпелева́ть (-лю́ю, -лю́ешь) *imp.*, за~ *perf.*; клейми́ть *imp.*, за~ *perf.*; (*trample*) то́птать (-пчу́, -пчешь) *imp.*, по~ *perf.*; *v.i.* то́пать *imp.*, то́пнуть *perf.* (нога́ми); *s. out*, подавля́ть *imp.*, подави́ть (-влю́, -вишь) *perf.*; ликвиди́ровать *imp.*, *perf.*

stampede *n.* пани́ческое бе́гство; *v.t. & i.* обраща́ть(ся) *imp.* в пани́ческое бе́гство.

stanch *v.t.* остана́вливать *imp.*, останови́ть (-влю́ -вишь) *perf.*

stanchion *n.* подпо́рка, сто́йка.

stand *n.* (*hat, coat*) ве́шалка; (*music*) пюпи́тр; (*umbrella, support*) подста́вка; (*counter*) сто́йка; (*booth*) ларёк (-рька́), кио́ск; (*taxi, bicycle*) стоя́нка; (*tribune*) ка́федра, трибу́на; (*at stadium*) трибу́на; (*position*) пози́ция, ме́сто (*pl.* -та́), положе́ние; (*resistance*) сопротивле́ние; *v.i.* стоя́ть (-ою́, -ои́шь) *imp.*; (*remain in force*) остава́ться (-аю́сь, -аёшься) *imp.*, оста́ться (-а́нусь, -а́нешься) в си́ле; *the matter stands thus*, де́ло обстои́т так; *it stands to reason*, разуме́ется; *v.t.* (*put*) ста́вить *imp.*, по~ *perf.*; (*endure*) выде́рживать *imp.*, вы́держать (-жу, -жишь) *perf.*; выноси́ть (-ошу́, -о́сишь) *imp.*, вы́нести (-су, -сешь, -с) *perf.*; терпе́ть (-плю́ -пишь) *imp.*, по~ *perf.*; (*treat to*) угоща́ть *imp.*, угости́ть *perf.* (*s.b.*, + *acc.*; *s.th.*, + *instr.*); *s. back*, отходи́ть (-ожу́, -о́дишь) *imp.*, отойти́ (-йду́, -йдёшь; отошёл, отошла́) *perf.* (*from*, от + *gen.*); (*not go forward*) держа́ться (-жу́сь, -жишься) *imp.* позади́; *s.-by*, (*store*) запа́с; (*reliable person*) надёжный челове́к (*pl.* лю́ди, -де́й, -дям, -дьми́); (*support*) опо́ра; *s. by*, (*v.i.*) (*not interfere*) не вме́шиваться *imp.*, вмеша́ться *perf.*; (*prepare*) пригота́вливаться *imp.*, пригото́виться *perf.*; (*v.t.*) (*support*) подде́рживать *imp.*, поддержа́ть (-жу́, -жишь) *perf.*; (*fulfil*) выполня́ть *imp.*, вы́полнить *perf.*; *s. for*, (*signify*) означа́ть *imp.*; (*tolerate*) *I shall not s. for it*, я не потерплю́; *s.-in*, замести́тель *m.*, ~ница; *s. in* (*for*), замеща́ть *imp.*, замести́ть *perf.*; *s.-offish*, высоко́ме́рный; *s. out*, выдава́ться (выдаётся), *imp.*, вы́даться (-астся, -адутся) *perf.*; выделя́ться *imp.*, вы́делиться *perf.*; *s. up*, встава́ть (встаю́, встаёшь) *imp.*, встать (-а́ну, -а́нешь) *perf.*; *s. up for*, (*defend*) отста́ивать *imp.*, отстоя́ть (-ою́, -ои́шь) *perf.*; защища́ть *imp.*, защити́ть (-ищу́, -ити́шь) *perf.*; *s. up to*, (*endure*) выде́рживать *imp.*, вы́держать (-жу, -жишь) perf.; (not give in to) не пасова́ть imp., с ~ perf. пе́ред + instr.

standard n. (flag) зна́мя (pl. -мёна) neut., штанда́рт (norm) станда́рт, норм.; s. of living, жи́зненный у́ровень (-вня) m.; of high s. высо́кого ка́чества; s.-bearer, знамено́сец (-сца); s. lamp, торше́р; adj. норма́льный, стандáртный, нормати́вный; (generally accepted) общепри́нятый; (exemplary) образцо́вый. **standardization** n. нормализа́ция, стандартиза́ция. **standardize** v.t. стандартизи́ровать imp., perf.; нормализова́ть imp., perf.

standing n. положе́ние, ранг, репута́ция; to be in good s. (with s.b.), быть на хоро́шем счету́ (у кого́-л.); adj. (upright) стоя́чий; (permanent) постоя́нный; s. army, постоя́нная а́рмия; s. committee, постоя́нный комите́т.

stand-pipe n. стоя́к (-а́).

standpoint n. то́чка зре́ния.

standstill n. остано́вка, засто́й, па́уза; be at a s., стоя́ть (-ою́, -ои́шь) imp. на мёртвой то́чке; bring (come) to a s. остана́вливать(ся) imp., останови́ть(ся) (-влю́(сь), -вишь(ся)) perf.

stanza n. строфа́ (pl. -фы, -ф, -фа́м), станс.

staple¹ n. (fastening) скоба́ (pl. -бы, -б, -ба́м).

staple² n. (principal product) гла́вный проду́кт, основно́й това́р; (principal element) гла́вный элеме́нт; adj. основно́й, гла́вный.

star n. звезда́ (pl. звёзды); (asterisk) звёздочка; adj. звёздный; (chief) гла́вный; (celebrated) знамени́тый; v.i. игра́ть imp., сыгра́ть perf. гла́вную роль. **starfish** n. морска́я звезда́ (pl. звёзды). **star-gazer** n. астро́лог, звездочёт.

starboard n. пра́вый борт (loc. -у́).

starch n. крахма́л; v.t. крахма́лить imp., на ~ perf. **starched** adj. крахма́льный, накрахма́ленный. **starchy** adj. крахма́листый; (prim) чо́порный.

stare n. при́стальный взгляд; v.i. при́стально смотре́ть (-рю́, -ришь)

(at, на + acc.); s. (one) in the face, (be obvious) броса́ться imp., бро́ситься perf. (+ dat.) в глаза́.

stark adj. (bare) го́лый (гол, -а́, -о); (desolate) пусты́нный (-нен, -нна); (sharp) ре́зкий (-зок, -зка́, -зко); adv. соверше́нно.

starling n. скворе́ц (-рца́).

starry adj. звёздный; s.-eyed, (coll.) мечта́тельный.

start n. нача́ло; (setting out) отправле́ние; (sport) старт; (advantage) преиму́щество; (shudder) рыво́к (-вка́); v.i. начина́ться imp., нача́ться (начнётся; на́чался́, -лась́) perf.; (engine) заводи́ться (-о́дится) imp., завести́сь (-едётся; -ёлся, -ела́сь) perf.; (set out) отправля́ться imp., отпра́виться perf.; (shudder) вздра́гивать imp., вздро́гнуть perf.; (sport) стартова́ть imp., perf.; v.t. начина́ть imp., нача́ть (-чну́, -чнёшь; на́чал, -а́, -о) perf. (gerund, inf., + inf.; by + gerund, с того́, что ...; with, + instr., с + gen.; from the beginning, с нача́ла); (set in motion) пуска́ть imp., пусти́ть (пущу́, пу́стишь) perf.; запуска́ть imp., запусти́ть (-ущу́, -у́стишь) perf. **starter** n. (tech.) пуска́тель m., ста́ртёр; (sport) ста́ртёр, **starting** adj. пусково́й. **starting-point** n. отправно́й пункт.

startle v.t. испуга́ть perf.; поража́ть imp., порази́ть perf. **startled** adj. испу́ганный (-ан), потрясённый (-ён, -ена́). **startling** adj. порази́тельный, потряса́ющий.

starvation n. го́лод, голода́ние. **starve** v.i. страда́ть imp., по ~ perf. от го́лода; (to death) умира́ть imp., умере́ть (умру́, -рёшь; у́мер, -ла́, -ло) с го́лоду; v.t. мори́ть imp., по ~, у ~ perf. го́лодом. **starving** adj. голода́ющий; (hungry) голо́дный (го́лоден, -дна́, -дно, голо́дны).

state n. (condition) состоя́ние, положе́ние; (pomp) великоле́пие, по́мпа; (nation, government) госуда́рство, штат; lie in s., поко́иться imp. в откры́том гробу́; adj. (ceremonial) торже́ственный (-ен, -енна); (apart-

ments) пара́дный; (*of State*) госуда́рственный; *v.t.* (*announce*) заявля́ть *imp.*, заяви́ть (-влю́, -вишь) *perf.*; (*expound*) излага́ть *imp.*, изложи́ть (-жу́, -жишь) *perf.*; (*maintain*) утвержда́ть *imp.* stated *adj.* (*appointed*) назна́ченный. stateless *adj.* не име́ющий гражда́нства. stately *adj.* велича́вый (-ен, -енна), велича́вый. statement *n.* (*announcement*) заявле́ние; (*exposition*) изложе́ние; (*assertion*) утвержде́ние. statesman *n.* госуда́рственный де́ятель *m.*

static *adj.* стати́чный, неподви́жный. statics *n.* ста́тика.

station *n.* (*rly.*) вокза́л, ста́нция; (*position*) ме́сто (*pl.* -та́); (*social*) обще́ственное положе́ние; (*naval etc.*) ба́за; (*meteorological, hydro-electric power, radio etc.*) ста́нция; (*post*) пост (-а́, *loc.* -у́); *v.t.* ста́вить *imp.*, по- *perf.*; помеща́ть *imp.*, помести́ть *perf.*; (*mil.*) размеща́ть *imp.*, размести́ть *perf.* station-master *n.* нача́льник вокза́ла, ста́нции.

stationary *adj.* неподви́жный; (*tech.*) стациона́рный; (*constant*) постоя́нный (-нен, -нна), усто́йчивый.

stationer *n.* продаве́ц (-вца́), -вщи́ца канцеля́рского магази́на. stationery *n.* канцеля́рские това́ры *m.pl.*; (*writing-paper*) почто́вая бума́га; *s. shop*, канцеля́рский магази́н.

statistic *n.* статисти́ческое да́нное, ци́фра. statistical *adj.* статисти́ческий. statistician *n.* стати́стик. statistics *n.* стати́стика.

statue *n.* ста́туя. statuesque *adj.* велича́вый. statuette *n.* статуэ́тка.

stature *n.* рост, стан; (*merit*) досто́инство, ка́чество.

status *n.* ста́тус; (*social*) обще́ственное положе́ние; (*state*) состоя́ние. status quo *n.* ста́тус-кво́.

statute *n.* стату́т; законода́тельный акт; *pl.* уста́в; *s.-book*, свод зако́нов. statutory *adj.* устано́вленный (-ен) зако́ном.

staunch *v.t. see* stanch; *adj.* (*loyal*) ве́рный (-рен, -рна́, -рно); (*steadfast*) сто́йкий (-о́ек, -ойка́, -о́йко), твёрдый

(твёрд, -а́, -о); про́чный (-чен, -чна́, -чно, про́чны́).

stave *n.* (*of cask*) клёпка; *v.t.* пробива́ть *imp.*, проби́ть (-бью́, -бьёшь) *perf.*; разбива́ть *imp.*, разби́ть (разобью́, -бьёшь) *perf.*; *s. off*, предотвраща́ть *imp.*, предотврати́ть (-ащу́, -ати́шь) *perf.*

stay[1] *n.* (*time spent*) пребыва́ние; (*suspension*) приостановле́ние; (*postponement*) отсро́чка; *v.i.* (*remain*) остава́ться (-аю́сь, -аёшься) *imp.*, оста́ться (-а́нусь, -а́нешься) *perf.* (*to dinner*, обе́дать); (*put up*) остана́вливаться *imp.*, останови́ться (-влю́сь, -вишься) *perf.* (at (*place*), в + *prep.*; at (*friends' etc.*), у + *gen.*); гости́ть *imp.* (with, у + *gen.*); (*live*) жить (живу́, живёшь; жил, -а́, -о) *imp.*; *s. a moment!* подожди́те мину́тку!; *s. away*, отсу́тствовать *imp.*; *s. behind*, остава́ться (-аю́сь, -аёшься) *imp.*, оста́ться (-а́нусь, -а́нешься) *perf.*; *v.t.* (*check*) заде́рживать *imp.*, задержа́ть (-жу́, -жишь) *perf.*; (*hunger, thirst*) утоля́ть *imp.*, утоли́ть *perf.*; (*suspend*) приоста́навливать *imp.*, приостанови́ть (-влю́, -вишь) *perf.*; (*postpone*) отсро́чивать *imp.*, отсро́чить *perf.*; *s. the course*, подде́рживаться *imp.*, поддержа́ться (-жу́сь, -жишься) *perf.* до конца́. stay-at-home *n.* домосе́д, ~ ка. staying-power *n.* выно́сливость.

stay[2] *n.* (*naut.*) штаг; (*support*) подде́ржка; *v.t.* (*support*) подде́рживать *imp.*, поддержа́ть (-жу́, -жишь) *perf.* stays *n.* корсе́т.

stead *n.*: *to stand s.b. in good s.*, ока́зываться *imp.*, оказа́ться (-ажу́сь, -а́жешься) *perf.* поле́зным кому́-л.

steadfast *adj.* (*firm, steady*) про́чный (-чен, -чна́, -чно, про́чны́), усто́йчивый; (*unshakeable*) сто́йкий (-о́ек, -ойка́, -о́йко), непоколеби́мый.

steady *adj.* (*firm*) про́чный (-чен, -чна́, -чно, про́чны́), усто́йчивый, твёрдый (твёрд, -а́, -о); (*continuous*) непреры́вный; (*prices*) ро́вный (-вен, -вна́, -вно); (*wind, temperature*) ро́вный (-вен, -вна́, -вно); (*speed*) постоя́нный (-нен, -нна); (*unshakeable*) непоколеби́мый; (*staid*) степе́нный (-нен, -нна); *s. hand*, твёрдая рука́ (acc. -ку; pl. -ки, -к, -ка́м); v.t. (boat) приводи́ть (-ожу́, -о́дишь) imp., привести́ (-еду́, -еде́шь; -ёл, -ела́) perf. в равнове́сие.

steak n. (before cooking) то́лстый кусо́к (-ска́) мя́са (meat), говя́дины (beef), ры́бы (fish), для жа́ренья (dish) то́лстый кусо́к (-ска́) жа́реного мя́са (meat), жа́реной ры́бы (fish) (beefsteak) бифште́кс.

steal v.t. ворова́ть imp., c~ perf.; красть (краду́, -дёшь; крал) imp., y~ perf. (also a kiss); s. a glance, укра́дкой взгля́дывать imp., взгляну́ть (-ну́, -нешь) perf. (at, на+acc.); v.i. кра́сться (краду́сь, -дёшься; кра́лся) imp.; подкра́дываться imp., подкра́сться (-аду́сь, -адёшься; -а́лся) perf. stealing n. воровство́. **stealth** n. хи́трость, уло́вка; by s., укра́дкой, тайко́м. **stealthy** adj. ворова́тый, та́йный, скры́тый.

steam n. пар (loc. -ý; pl. -ы́); at full s., на всех пара́х; get up s., разводи́ть (-ожу́, -о́дишь) imp., развести́ (-еду́, -еде́шь; -ёл, -ела́) пары́; (fig.) собира́ться imp., собра́ться (-беру́сь, -брала́сь, -брало́сь) с си́лами; let off s., (fig.) дава́ть (даю́, даёшь) imp., дать (дам, дашь, даст, дади́м; дал, -а́, да́ло, -и) perf. вы́ход свои́м чу́вствам; under one's own s., сам (-а́, -о́, -и) свои́м хо́дом; adj. парово́й, паро- in comb.; v.t. па́рить imp.; v.i. па́риться imp., по~ perf.; (vessel) ходи́ть (хо́дит) indet., идти́ (идёт); шёл, шла) det. на пара́х; s. up, (mist over) запотева́ть imp., запоте́ть perf.; потѣ́ть imp., за~, от~ perf.; s. engine, парова́я маши́на. **steamer** n. парохо́д. **steaming** adj. дымя́щийся. **steam-roller** n. парово́й като́к (-тка́). **steamship** n. парохо́д.

steed n. конь (-ня́, pl. -ни, -не́й) m.

steel n. сталь; adj. стально́й; v.t. (make resolute) ожесточа́ть imp., ожесто́чить perf.; to s. one's (own) heart, ожесточа́ться imp., ожесто́читься perf.; s. foundry, сталелите́йный заво́д; s.-making, сталепла́вильный; s.-rolling, сталепрока́тный; s. works, сталепла́вильный заво́д. **steely** adj.

стально́й; (cold) холо́дный (хо́лоден, -дна́, -дно, хо́лодны); (stern) суро́вый. **steelyard** n. безме́н.

steep[1] v.t. (immerse) погружа́ть imp., погрузи́ть perf. (in, в+acc.); (saturate) пропи́тывать imp., пропита́ть perf. (in, +instr.); be steeped in, (also fig.) погружа́ться imp., погрузи́ться perf. (in, в+acc.).

steep[2] adj. круто́й (крут, -а́, -о); (excessive) чрезме́рный; (improbable) невероя́тный. **steepness** n. крутизна́.

steeple n. шпиль m. **steeplechase** n. ска́чки f.pl. с препя́тствиями. **steeplejack** n. верхола́з.

steer[1] n. молодо́й вол (-а́), бычо́к (-чка́).

steer[2] v.t. (control, navigate) управля́ть imp., пра́вить imp. +instr.; (guide) руководи́ть imp.+instr.; v.n. пра́вить imp. рулём; рули́ть imp. (coll.); s. clear of, избега́ть imp., избежа́ть (-егу́, -ежи́шь) perf. +gen. **steering-column** n. рулева́я коло́нка. **steering-wheel** n. руль (-ля́) m., бара́нка (coll.); (naut.) штурва́л.

stellar adj. звёздный. **stellate** adj. звездообра́зный.

stem[1] n. сте́бель (-бля; pl. -бли, -бле́й) m.; (trunk) ствол (-а́); (wine-glass) но́жка; (ling.) осно́ва; (naut.) нос (loc. -ý; pl. -ы́); from s. to stern, от но́са до кормы́; v.i.: s. from, происходи́ть (-ожу́, -о́дишь) imp., произойти́ (-ойдёт; -ошёл, -ошла́) perf. от+gen.

stem[2] v.t. (dam) запру́живать imp., запруди́ть (-ужу́, -у́дишь) perf.; (stop) остана́вливать imp., останови́ть (-влю́, -вишь) perf.

stench n. злово́ние, смрад.

stencil n. трафаре́т; (tech.) шаблон; v.t. наноси́ть (-ошу́, -о́сишь) imp., нанести́ (-есу́, -есёшь; -ёс, -есла́) perf. узо́р по трафаре́ту. **stencilled** adj. трафаре́тный.

stentorian adj. громогла́сный.

step n. (pace, action) шаг (-á with 2, 3, 4, loc. -ý; pl. -и́); (gait) похо́дка; (dance) па neut.indecl.; (of stairs, ladder) ступе́нь (gen.pl. -е́ней); (measure) ме́ра; s. by s., шаг за ша́гом; in s., в но́гу; out of s., не в но́гу; *watch one's s.*, де́йствовать *imp.* осторо́жно; *take steps*, принима́ть *imp.*, приня́ть (приму́, -мешь; при́нял, -á, -о) *perf.* ме́ры; *v.i.* шага́ть *imp.*, шагну́ть *perf.*; ступа́ть *imp.*, ступи́ть (-плю́, -пишь) *perf.*; *s. aside*, сторони́ться (-ню́сь, -ни́шься) *imp.*, по~ *perf.*; *s. back*, отступа́ть *imp.*, отступи́ть (-плю́, -пишь) *perf.*; *s. down*, (*resign*) уходи́ть (-ожу́, -о́дишь) *imp.*, уйти́ (уйду́, -дёшь; ушёл, ушла́) *perf.* в отста́вку; *s. forward*, выступа́ть *imp.*, вы́ступить *perf.*; *s. in*, (*intervene*) вме́шиваться *imp.*, вмеша́ться *perf.*; *s. on*, наступа́ть *imp.*, наступи́ть (-плю́, -пишь) *perf.* на+*acc.* (*s.b.'s foot*, кому́-л. на́ ногу); *s. over*, переша́гивать *imp.*, перешагну́ть *perf.*+*acc.*, че́рез+*acc.*; *s. up*, (*increase, promote*) повыша́ть *imp.*, повы́сить *perf.*; (*strengthen*) уси́ливать *imp.*, уси́лить *perf.* **step-ladder** *n.* стремя́нка. **stepped** *adj.* ступе́нчатый. **stepping-stone** *n.* ка́мень (-мня; *pl.* -мни, -мне́й) *m.* для перехо́да че́рез ре́чку *etc.*; (*fig.*) сре́дство к достиже́нию це́ли. **steps** *n.* ле́стница.

stepbrother *n.* сво́дный брат (*pl.* -ья, -ьев). **stepdaughter** *n.* па́дчерица. **stepfather** *n.* о́тчим. **stepmother** *n.* ма́чеха. **stepsister** *n.* сво́дная сестра́ (*pl.* сёстры, сестёр, сёстрам). **stepson** *n.* па́сынок (-нка).

steppe *n.* степь (*loc.* -пи́; *pl.* -пи, -пе́й) *adj.* степно́й.

stereo *n.* (*record-player*) стереофони́ческий прои́грыватель *m.*; (*stereophony*) стереофо́ния; *adj.* (*recorded in stereo*) сте́рео. **stereophonic** *adj.* стереофони́ческий. **stereophony** *n.* стереофо́ния. **stereoscope** *n.* стереоско́п. **stereoscopic** *adj.* стереоскопи́ческий. **stereotype** *n.* стереоти́п; (*tech.*) шабло́н. **stereotyped** *adj.* (*also banal*) стереоти́пный, шабло́нный.

sterile *adj.* (*barren, germ-free*) стери́льный. **sterility** *n.* стери́льность. **sterilization** *n.* стерилиза́ция. **sterilize** *v.t.* стерилизова́ть *imp.*, *perf.* **sterilizer** *n.* стерилиза́тор.

sterling *n.* сте́рлинг; *pound s.*, фунт сте́рлингов; *adj.* сте́рлинговый; (*ir-* *reproachable*) безупре́чный; (*reliable*) надёжный.

stern[1] *n.* корма́.

stern[2] *adj.* суро́вый, стро́гий (-г, -гá, -го).

sternum *n.* груди́на.

stethoscope *n.* стетоско́п.

stevedore *n.* стивидо́р, грузчик.

stew *n.* (*cul.*) мя́со тушёное вме́сте с овоща́ми; *be in a s.*, (*coll.*) волнова́ться *imp.*; *v.t.* & *i.* туши́ть(ся) (-шу́(сь), -шишь(ся)) *imp.*, с~ *perf.*; томи́ть(ся) *imp.*; *to s. in one's own juice*, расхлёбывать *imp.* ка́шу, кото́рую сам завари́л. **stewed** *adj.* тушёный; *s. fruit*, компо́т. **stewpan**, **stewpot** *n.* кастрю́ля, соте́йник.

steward *n.* стю́ард, бортпроводни́к (-á); (*master of ceremonies*) распоряди́тель *m.* **stewardess** *n.* стюарде́сса, бортпроводни́ца.

stick[1] *n.* па́лка; (*of chalk etc.*) па́лочка; (*hockey, walking*) клю́шка; *sticks*, (*collect.*) хво́рост (-a(у)).

stick[2] *v.t.* (*spear*) зака́лывать *imp.*, заколо́ть (-лю́, -лешь) *perf.*; (*make adhere*) прикле́ивать *imp.*, прикле́ить *perf.* (*to*, к+*dat.*); прилепля́ть *imp.*, прилепи́ть (-плю́, -пишь) *perf.* (*to*, к+*dat.*); (*coll.*) (*put*) ста́вить *imp.*, по~ *perf.*; (*lay*) класть (кладу́, -дёшь; клал) *imp.*, положи́ть (-жу́, -жишь) *perf.*; *v.i.* (*adhere*) ли́пнуть (лип) *imp.* (*to*, к+*dat.*); прилипа́ть *imp.*, прили́пнуть (-нет; прили́п) *perf.* (*to*, к+*dat.*); прикле́иваться *imp.*, прикле́иться *perf.* (*to*, к+*dat.*); *s. in*, (*thrust in*) втыка́ть *imp.*, воткну́ть *perf.*; вка́лывать *imp.*, вколо́ть (-лю́, -лешь) *perf.*; *the arrow stuck into the ground*, стрела́ воткну́лась в зе́млю; (*into opening*) всо́вывать *imp.*, всу́нуть *perf.*; *s. on*, (*glue on*) накле́ивать *imp.*, накле́ить *perf.*; *s. out*, (*thrust out*) высо́вывать *imp.*, вы́сунуть *perf.* (*from*, из+*gen.*); (*project*) торча́ть (-чу́, -чи́шь) *imp.*; *s. to*, (*keep to*) приде́рживаться *imp.*, придержа́ться (-жу́сь, -жишься) *perf.*+*gen.*; (*remain at*) не отвлека́ться *imp.* от+*gen.*; *s. together*, держа́ться (-жи́мся) *imp.* вме́сте; *s. up for*, защищать *imp.*, защитить (-ищу́, -итишь) *perf.*; be, get, stuck, застревать *imp.*, застрять (-я́ну) *perf.* **sticker** n. (label) этике́тка, ярлы́к (-á). **sticking-plaster** n. ли́пкий пла́стырь m.

stickleback n. ко́люшка.

stickler n. (ярый) сторо́нник, -ица; приве́рженец (-нца), -нка (for, + gen.).

sticky adj. ли́пкий (-пок, -пка́, -пко), кле́йкий; he will come to a s. end, он пло́хо ко́нчит.

stiff adj. жёсткий (-ток, -тка́ -тко), неги́бкий (-бок, -бка́, -бко); (with cold) окочене́лый; (prim) чо́порный; (difficult) тру́дный (-ден, -дна́, -дно, тру́дны́); (breeze) си́льный (си́лён, -льна́, -льно, сильны́); be s., (ache) боле́ть (-ли́т) *imp.* **stiffen** v.t. де́лать *imp.*, с~ *perf.* жёстким; v.i. станови́ться (-влюсь, -вишься) *imp.*, стать (-а́ну, -а́нешь) *perf.* жёстким. **stiffness** n. жёсткость; (primness) чо́порность.

stifle v.t. души́ть (-шу́, -шишь) *imp.*, за~ *perf.*; (suppress) подавля́ть *imp.*, подави́ть (-влю́, -вишь) *perf.*; (sound) заглуша́ть *imp.*, заглуши́ть *perf.*; v.i. задыха́ться *imp.*, задохну́ться (-ох(ну́)лся, -ох(ну́)лась) *perf.* **stifling** adj. уду́шливый, ду́шный (-шен, -шна́, -шно).

stigma n. клеймо́ (pl. -ма) позо́ра. **stigmatize** v.t. клейми́ть *imp.*, за~ *perf.*

stile n. ступе́ньки f.pl. для перехо́да че́рез забо́р, перела́з (coll.).

stiletto n. стиле́т; s. heels, гвозди́ки m.pl., шпи́льки f.pl.

still[1] adv. (всё) ещё, до сих пор, по-пре́жнему; s. better, ещё лу́чше; (nevertheless) всё же, тем не ме́нее, одна́ко; (motionless) неподви́жно; (quietly) споко́йно; stand s., не дви́гаться (-аюсь, -аешься & дви́жусь, -жешься) *imp.*, двинуться *perf.*; time stood s. вре́мя останови́лось; sit s., сиде́ть (-жу́, сиди́шь) *imp.* сми́рно.

still[2] n. (quiet) тишина́ (pl.); (film) кадр; adj. ти́хий (тих, -á, -о), споко́йный; (immobile) неподви́жный; (not fizzy) не шипу́чий; v.t. успока́ивать *imp.*, успоко́ить *perf.*

still[3] n. перего́нный куб (pl. -ы́).

still-born adj. мертворождённый.

still life n. натюрмо́рт.

stillness n. тишина́, споко́йствие; (immobility) неподви́жность.

stilt n. ходу́ля (tech.) сто́йка, сва́я. **stilted** adj. ходу́льный.

stimulant n. возбужда́ющее сре́дство. **stimulate** v.t. возбужда́ть *imp.*, возбуди́ть *perf.*; стимули́ровать *imp.*, *perf.* **stimulating** adj. возбуди́тельный. **stimulation** n. возбужде́ние. **stimulus** n. сти́мул, возбуди́тель m., побуди́тельная причи́на.

sting n. жа́ло (also fig.); уку́с (also wound); v.t. жа́лить *imp.*, у~ *perf.*; укуси́ть (-ушу́, -у́сишь); v.i. (burn) жечь (жжёт, жгут; жёг, жгла) *imp.* **stinging** adj. (caustic) язви́тельный; s. nettle, жгу́чая крапи́ва. **sting-ray** n. скат дазиа́тис.

stinginess n. ску́пость, скаре́дность. **stingy** adj. скупо́й (скуп, -á, -о), скаре́дный.

stink n. злово́ние, вонь, смрад; v.i. воня́ть *imp.* (of, + instr.); смерде́ть (-ржу́, -рди́шь) *imp.* (of, + instr.). **stinking** adj. воню́чий, злово́нный (-нен, -нна), смра́дный.

stint n. но́рма; v.t. скупи́ться *imp.*, по~ *perf.* на + acc.

stipend n. (salary) жа́лование; (grant) стипе́ндия. **stipendiary** adj. получа́ющий жа́лование.

stipple n. рабо́та, гравирова́ние пункти́ром; v.t. & i. рисова́ть *imp.*, на~ *perf.*, гравирова́ть *imp.*, вы́~ *perf.*, пункти́ром.

stipulate v.i. ста́вить *imp.*, по~ *perf.* усло́вием (that, что); v.t. обусло́вливать *imp.*, обусло́вить *perf.* + instr.; (demand) тре́бовать *imp.* + gen. **stipulation** n. усло́вие.

stir n. шевеле́ние, движе́ние; (uproar) сумато́ха; cause a s., вызыва́ть *imp.*, вы́звать (вы́зову, -вешь) *perf.* волне́ние; v.t. (move) шевели́ть (шевелю́, -е́лишь) *imp.*, шевельну́ть *perf.* + instr.; дви́гать *imp.*, дви́нуть *perf.* + instr.; (mix) меша́ть *imp.*, по~ *perf.*, размéшивать *imp.*, размешáть *perf.*; (*excite*) волновáть *imp.*, вз~ *perf.*; *v.i.* (*move*) шевелúться (шевелю́, -éлишься) *imp.*, шевельну́ться *perf.*; двúгаться *imp.*, двúнуться *perf.*; (*be excited*) волновáться; *s. up*, возбуждáть *imp.*, возбудúть *perf.* **stirring** *adj.* волну́ющий.

stirrup *n.* стрéмя (-мени, -мян, -менáми) *neut.*

stitch *n.* стежóк (-жкá); (*knitting*) пéтля (*gen.pl.* -тель); (*med.*) шов (шва); (*pain*) кóлотье (*coll.*); *v.t.* (*embroider, make line of stitches*) строчúть (-очу́, -óчишь) *imp.*, про~ *perf.*; (*join by sewing, make, suture*) сшивáть *imp.*, сшить (сошью́, сошьёшь) *perf.*; (*med.*) наклáдывать *imp.*, наложúть (-жу́, -жишь) *perf.* швы на+*acc.*; *s. up*, зашивáть *imp.*, зашúть (-шью́, -шьёшь) *perf.* **stitching** *n.* (*sewing*) шитьё; (*stitches*) стрóчка.

stoat *n.* горностáй.

stock *n.* (*store*) запáс; (*equipment*) инвентáрь (-ря́) *m.*; (*livestock*) скот (-á); (*cul.*) бульóн; (*family*) семья́ (*pl.* -мьи, -мéй, -мьям); (*origin, clan*) род (*loc.* -ý; *pl.* -ы́); (*fin.*) áкции *f.pl.*; (*fin.*) фóнды *m.pl.*; (*punishment*) колóдки *f.pl.*; *in s.* в налúчии; *out of s.*, рáспродан; *take s. of*, обду́мывать *imp.*, обду́мать *perf.*; *adj.* стандáртный; (*banal*) избúтый; *v.t.* имéть в налúчии; *s. up*, запасáть *imp.*, запастú (-сý, -сёшь; запáс, -слá) *perf.* **stock-breeder** *n.* скотовóд. **stock-breeding** *n.* скотовóдство. **stockbroker** *n.* бúржевóй мáклер. **stock-exchange** *n.* фóндовая бúржа. **stock-in-trade** *n.* (*torgóvый*) инвентáрь (-ря́) *m.* **stockpile** *n.* запáс; *v.t.* накáпливать *imp.*, накопúть (-плю́, -пишь) *perf.* **stock-still** *adj.* неподвúжный. **stock-taking** *n.* переучёт товáра, провéрка инвентаря́. **stockyard** *n.* скотопригóнный двор (-á).

stockade *n.* частокóл.

stocking *n.* чулóк (-лкá; *gen.pl.* чулóк).

stocky *adj.* приземúстый, корена́стый.

stodgy *adj.* (*food*) тяжёлый (-л, -лá); (*boring*) ску́чный (-чен, -чна́, -чно).

stoic *n.* стóик. **stoic(al)** *adj.* стоúческий. **stoicism** *n.* стоицúзм.

stoke *v.t.* топúть (-плю́, -пишь) *imp.* **stokehold, stokehole** *n.* кочегáрка. **stoker** *n.* кочегáр, истопнúк (-á).

stole *n.* палантúн.

stolid *adj.* флегматúчный.

stomach *n.* желу́док (-дка), (*also surface of body*) живóт (-á); *adj.* желу́дочный; *v.t.* терпéть (-плю́, -пишь) *imp.*, по~ *perf.* **stomach-ache** *n.* боль в животé.

stone *n.* (*material, piece of it*) кáмень (-мня; *pl.* -мни, -мнéй) *m.*; (*fruit*) кóсточка; *adj.* кáменный; *v.t.* побивáть *imp.*, побúть (-бью́, -бьёшь) *perf.* камня́ми; (*fruit*) вынимáть *imp.*, вы́нуть *perf.* кóсточки из+*gen.*; *s. to death*, забúть (-бью́, -бьёшь) *perf.* камня́ми нáсмерть. **Stone Age** *n.* кáменный век (-а). **stone-cold** *adj.* совершéнно холóдный (хóлоден, -днá, -дно, хóлодны). **stone-deaf** *adj.* совершéнно глухóй (глух, -á, -о). **stonemason** *n.* кáменщик. **stonewall** *v.i.* устрáивать *imp.*, устрóить *perf.* обстру́кцию; мешáть *imp.*, по~ *perf.* диску́ссии. **stonily** *adv.* с кáменным выражéнием, холóдно. **stony** *adj.* кáменúстый; (*fig.*) кáменный, холóдный (хóлоден, -днá, -дно, хóлодны). **stony-broke** *predic.* I am s., у меня́ нет ни грошá.

stool *n.* табурéт, табурéтка.

stoop *n.* суту́лость; *v.t. & i.* суту́литься *imp.*, с~ *perf.*; (*bend down*) наклоня́ться *imp.*, наклонúться (-ню́(сь), -нишь(ся)) *perf.*; *s. to*, (*abase oneself*) унижáться *imp.*, унúзиться *perf.* до+*gen.*; (*condescend*) снисходúть (-ожу́, -óдишь) *imp.*, снизойтú (-ойду́, -ойдёшь; -ошёл, -ошлá) *perf.* до+*gen.* **stooped, stooping** *adj.* суту́лый.

stop *n.* останóвка; (*discontinuance*) прекращéние; (*organ*) регúстр; (*full s.*) тóчка; *request s.*, останóвка по трéбованию; *v.t.* останáвливать *imp.*, останóвить (-влю́, -вишь) *perf.*; (*discontinue*) прекращáть *imp.*, прекратúть (-ащу́, -атúшь) *perf.*; (*restrain*) удéрживать *imp.*, удержáть (-жу́, -жишь) *perf.* (*from*, от+*gen.*);

v.i. остана́вливаться *imp.*, останови́ться (-влю́сь, -ви́шься) *perf.*; (*discontinue*) прекраща́ться *imp.*, прекрати́ться (-и́тся) *perf.*; (*cease*) переставать (-таю́, -таёшь) *imp.*, переста́ть (-а́ну, -а́нешь) *perf.* (+ *inf.*); *s. up*, затыка́ть *imp.*, заткну́ть (-ну́) *perf.*; *s. at nothing*, ни перед чем не остана́вливаться *imp.*, останови́ться (-влю́сь, -ви́шься) *perf.* **stopcock** *n.* запо́рный кран. **stopgap** *n.* затычка. **stop-light** *n.* стоп-сигна́л. **stoppage** *n.* остано́вка; (*strike*) забасто́вка. **stopper** *n.* про́бка; (*tech.*) сто́пор. **stop-press** *n.* экстренное сообще́ние в газе́те. **stop-watch** *n.* секундоме́р.

storage *n.* хране́ние. **store** *n.* запа́с; (*storehouse*) склад; (*shop*) магази́н; *set s. by*, цени́ть (-ню́, -нишь) *imp.*; *what is in s. for me?* что ждёт меня впереди́? *v.t.* запаса́ть *imp.*, запасти́ (-су́, -сёшь; запа́с, -сла́) *perf.*; (*put into storage*) сдава́ть (сдаю́, сдаёшь) *imp.*, сдать (сдам, сдашь, сдаст, сдади́м; сдал, -а́, -о) *perf.* на хране́ние. **storehouse** *n.* склад, амба́р, храни́лище. **store-room** кладова́я *sb.*

storey, **story**[1] *n.* эта́ж (-а́).

stork *n.* а́ист.

storm *n.* бу́ря, гроза́ (*pl.* -зы); (*naut.*) шторм; (*mil.*) штурм, при́ступ; (*outburst*) взрыв; *v.t.* (*mil.*) штурмова́ть *imp.*; брать (беру́, берёшь) *imp.*, взять (возьму́, -мёшь; взял, -а́, -о) *perf.* при́ступом; *v.i.* бушева́ть (-шу́ю, -шу́ешь) *imp.* **storm-cloud** *n.* ту́ча. **stormy** *adj.* бу́рный (-рен, бу́рна́, -рно), бу́йный (бу́ен, бу́йна́, -но). **stormy petrel** *n.* качу́рка ма́лая.

story[1] *see* **storey**.

story[2] *n.* расска́з, по́весть; (*anecdote*) анекдо́т; (*plot*) фа́була, сюже́т; (*history*, *event*) исто́рия. **s.-teller**, расска́зчик.

stout *adj.* (*solid*) пло́тный (-тен, -тна́, -тно, пло́тны); (*portly*) доро́дный; (*strong*) кре́пкий по́ртер; **s.-hearted**, отва́жный. **stoutly** *adv.* (*stubbornly*) упо́рно; (*energetically*) энерги́чно; (*strongly*) кре́пко. **stoutness** *n.* (*strength*) про́чность; (*portliness*) доро́дство; (*courage*) отва́га; (*firmness*) сто́йкость;

stove *n.* (*with fire inside*) печь (*loc.* -чи́; *pl.* -чи, -че́й); (*cooker*) плита́ (*pl.* -ты).

stow *v.t.* укла́дывать *imp.*, уложи́ть (-жу́, -жишь) *perf.*; *s. away*, (*travel free*) е́хать (е́ду, е́дешь) *imp.*, по~ *perf.* за́йцем, без биле́та. **stowaway** *n.* за́яц (за́йца), безбиле́тный пассажи́р.

straddle *v.i.* широко́ расставля́ть *imp.*, расста́вить (-влю, -вишь) *perf.*; *v.t.* (*sit astride*) сиде́ть (сижу́, сиди́шь) *imp.* верхо́м на + *prep.*; (*stand astride*) стоя́ть (-ою́, -ои́шь) *imp.*, расста́вив но́ги над + *instr.*

straggle *v.i.* (*drop behind*) отстава́ть (-стаю́, -стаёшь) *imp.*, отста́ть (-а́ну, -а́нешь) *perf.* **straggler** *n.* отста́вший *sb.* **straggling** *adj.* (*scattered*) разбро́санный; (*untidy*) беспоря́дочный.

straight *adj.* (*unbent*) прямо́й (-м, -ма́, -мо, пря́мы); (*honest*) че́стный (-тен, -тна́, -тно); (*undiluted*) неразба́вленный; *predic.* (*properly arranged*) в поря́дке; *adv.* пря́мо; *s. away*, сра́зу. **straighten** *v.t.* & *i.* выпрямля́ть(ся) *imp.*, вы́прямить(ся) *perf.*; *v.t.* (*smooth out*) расправля́ть *imp.*, распра́вить *perf.* **straightforward** *adj.* прямо́й (-м, -ма́, -мо); (*simple*) просто́й (-т, -та́, -то); (*honest*) че́стный (-тен, -тна́, -тно). **straightness** *n.* прямизна́.

strain[1] *n.* (*pull*, *tension*) натяже́ние; (*also sprain*) растяже́ние; (*phys.*, *tech.*) напряже́ние; (*tendency*) скло́нность; (*sound*) напе́в, звук; *in the same s.*, в том же ду́хе; *v.t.* (*stretch*) натя́гивать *imp.*, натяну́ть (-ну́, -нешь) *perf.*; (*also sprain*) растя́гивать *imp.*, растяну́ть (-ну́, -нешь) *perf.*; (*phys.*, *tech.*) напряга́ть *imp.*, напря́чь (-ягу́, -яжёшь; -яг, -ягла́) *perf.*; (*filter*) проце́живать *imp.*, процеди́ть (-ежу́, -е́дишь) *perf.*; *v.i.* (*also exert oneself*) напряга́ться *imp.*, напря́чься (-ягу́сь, -яжёшься; -ягся, -ягла́сь) *perf.* **strained** *adj.* натя́нутый (*also fig.*); (*wrenched*) растя́нутый (*also sprained*). **strainer** *n.* (*tea s.*) си́течко; (*filter*) фильтр; (*sieve*) си́то.

strain[2] *n.* (*breed*) поро́да; (*hereditary trait*) насле́дственная черта́.

strait(s) *n.* (*geog.*) проли́в. **straiten** *v.t.* ограни́чивать *imp.*, ограни́чить *perf.*

straitened adj.: in s. circumstances, в стеснённых обстоятельствах. **strait-jacket** n. смирительная рубашка. **strait-laced** adj. пуританский. **straits** n. (difficulties) затруднительное положение.

strand¹ n. (hair, rope) прядь; (rope, cable) стрéнга; (thread, also fig.) нить.

strand² n. (of sea etc.) бéрег (pl. -ý; pl. -á); v.t. сажáть impr., посадить (-ажý, -áдишь) perf. на мель. **stranded** adj. (fig.) без средств.

strange adj. стрáнный (-нен, -ннá, -нно); (unfamiliar) незнакóмый; (alien) чужóй. **strangely** adv. стрáнно. **strangeness** n. стрáнность. **stranger** n. незнакóмец (-мца), -óмка; неизвéстный sb.; чужóй sb.

strangle v.t. душить (-шý, -шишь) impr., за~ perf. **stranglehold** n. мёртвая хвáтка. **strangulate** v.t. сжимáть impr., сжать (сожмý, -мёшь) perf. **strangulation** n. (strangling) удушéние; (strangulating) зажимáние.

strap n. ремéнь (-мня́) m.; v.t. (tie up) стягивать impr., стянýть (-нý, -нешь) perf. ремнём. **strapping** adj. рóслый.

stratagem n. стратагéма, хитрость. **strategic** adj. стратегический. **strategist** n. стратéг. **strategy** n. стратéгия.

stratification n. расслоéние. **stratified** adj. слóистый. **stratosphere** n. стратосфéра. **stratum** n. слой (pl. -ои), пласт (-á, loc. -ý).

straw n. солóма; (drinking) солóминка; the last s., послéдняя кáпля; adj. солóменный.

strawberry n. клубника; (wild s.) земляника collect.; adj. клубничный; земляничный.

stray v.i. сбивáться impr., сбиться (собьюсь, -ьёшься) perf.; (roam) блуждáть impr.; (digress) отклонáться impr., отклониться (-нюсь, -нишься) perf.; adj. (lost) заблудившийся; (homeless) бездóмный; n. (waif) беспризóрный sb.; (from flock) отбившееся от стáда живóтное sb.; s. bullet, шальнáя пýля.

streak n. полосá (acc. пóлосу); pl. -осы, -óс, -осáм) (of luck, тенденci (tenden-cy) жилка; (lightning) вспышка; v.t. испещрять impr., испещрить perf.; v.i. (rush) проноситься (-ошусь, -óсишься) impr., пронестись (-есусь, -есёшься; -ёсся, -еслáсь) perf. **streaked** adj. с полосáми, с прожилками (with, + gen.). **streaky** adj. полосáтый; (meat) с прослóйками жира.

stream n. (brook, tears) ручéй (-чья́); (brook, flood, tears, people etc.) потóк; (jet) струя (pl. -ýи) (current) течéние; up/down s., вверх/вниз по течéнию; with/against the s., по течéнию, прóтив течéния; v.i. течь (течёт, текýт; тёк, текла́) impr., струиться (-ится) impr.; (rush) проноситься (-ошусь, -óсишься) impr., пронестись (-есусь, -есёшься; -ёсся, -еслáсь) perf.; (blow) развевáться (-áется) impr. **streamer** n. вымпел. **stream-lined** adj. обтекáемый; (fig.) хорошó налáженный.

street n. улица; adj. уличный; s. lamp, уличный фонáрь (-ря́) m.

strength n. сила, крéпость; (numbers) численность; in full s., в пóлном состáве; on the s. of, в силу + gen. **strengthen** v.t. усиливать impr., усилить perf.; укреплять impr., укрепить perf. **strengthening** n. усилéние, укреплéние.

strenuous adj. трéбующий усилий, энергичный.

stress n. (pressure, fig.) давлéние; (tech.) напряжéние; (emphasis) ударéние; v.t. дéлать impr., с~ perf. ударéние на + acc.; подчёркивать impr., подчеркнýть perf.

stretch n. (expanse) протяжéние, прострáнство; at a s., (in succession) подря́д; v.t. & i. (widen, spread out) растягивать(ся) impr., растянýть(ся) (-ну(сь), -нешь(ся) perf.; (in length, s. out limbs) вытягивать(ся) impr., вытянуть(ся) perf.; (tauten e.g. bow) натягивать(ся) impr., натянýть(ся) (-ну(сь), -нешь(ся) perf.; (extend e.g. rope, s. forth limbs) протягивать(ся) impr., протянýть(ся) (-ну(сь), -нешь(ся) perf.; v.i.(material, land) тянýться (-нется) impr.; v.t. (exaggerate) преувеличивать impr., преувеличить perf.; s. a point, допускáть impr., допустить (-ущý, -устишь) perf. натяжку; s.

oneself, потягиваться *imp.*, потянуться (-нусь, -нешься) *perf.*; *s.* one's legs, (*coll.*) разминать (разомну, -нёшь) *perf.* ноги. **stretcher** *n.* носилки (-лок) *pl.*

strew *v.t.* разбрасывать *imp.*, разбросать *perf.*; *s.* with, посыпать *imp.*, посыпать (-плю, -плешь) *perf.* + *instr.*, усыпать *imp.*, усыпать (-плю, -плешь) *perf.* + *instr.*

stricken *adj.* поражённый (-ён, -ена), охваченный (-ен).

strict *adj.* строгий (-г, -га, -го); (*precise*) точный (-чен, -чна, -чно). **strictly** *adv.* строго, точно. **strictness** *n.* строгость, точность. **stricture(s)** *n.* (строгая) критика, осуждение.

stride *n.* (большой) шаг (-á with 2, 3, 4, *loc.* -ý; *pl.* -и) *pl.* (*fig.*) успехи *m.pl.*; to get into one's s., принимáться *imp.*, приняться (примусь, -мешься; -нялся, -нялась) *perf.* за дело; to take s.th. in one's s., преодолевать *imp.*, преодолеть *perf.* что-л. без усилий; *v.i.* шагать *imp.* (большими шагами).

stridency *n.* рéзкость. **strident** *adj.* рéзкий (-зок, -зка, -зко).

strife *n.* (*conflict*) борьба; (*discord*) раздор.

strike *n.* (*refusal to work*) забастовка, стачка; (*discovery*) открытие; (*blow*) удар; *adj.* забастовочный; *v.i.* (*be on s.*) бастовать *imp.*; (*go on s.*) забастовать *perf.*; объявлять *imp.*, объявить (-влю, -вишь) *perf.* забастовку; (*clock*) бить (бьёт) *imp.*, про~ *perf.*; *v.t.* (*hit*) ударять *imp.*, ударить *perf.*; (*mil., surprise*) поражать *imp.*, поразить *perf.*; (*discover*) открывать *imp.*, открыть (-рою, -роешь) *perf.*; (*match*) зажигать *imp.*, зажечь (-жгу, -жжёшь; -жёг, -жгла) *perf.*; (*clock*) бить (бьёт) *imp.*, про~ *perf.*; (*occur to*) приходить (-ит) *imp.*, прийти (придёт; пришёл, -шла) *perf.* в голову + *dat.*; *s.* off, вычёркивать *imp.*, вычеркнуть *perf.*; *s.* up, начинать *imp.*, начать (-чну, -чнёшь; начал, -á, -о) *perf.*; *s.* upon, нападать *imp.*, напасть (-аду, -адёшь; -ал) на + *acc.* **strike-breaker** *n.* штрейкбрехер. **striker** *n.* забастовщик, -ица. **striking** *adj.*

поразительный; *s.* distance, досягаемость.

string *n.* бечёвка, верёвка, завязка; (*mus.*) струна (*pl.* -ны); (*series*) вереница, ряд (-á with 2, 3, 4, *loc.* -ý; *pl.* -ы); (*beads*) нитка; *pl.* (*instruments*) струнные инструменты *m.pl.*; second s., запасной ресурс; pull strings, нажимать *imp.*, нажать (нажму, -мёшь) *perf.* на тайные пружины; without strings attached, без каких-либо условий; *adj.* струнный; *v.t.* (*tie up*) завязывать *imp.*, завязать (-яжу, -яжешь) *perf.*; (*thread*) низать (нижу, -жешь) *imp.*, на~ *perf.*; (*beans*) чистить *imp.*, о~ *perf.*; *s.* along, (*coll.*) (*deceive*) обманывать *imp.*, обмануть (-ну, -нешь) *perf.*; *s.* out, (*prolong*) растягивать *imp.*, растянуть (-ну, -нешь) *perf.*; strung up, (*tense*) напряжённый; *s.-bag, s.* vest, сетка. **stringed** *adj.* струнный. **stringy** *adj.* (*fibrous*) волокнистый; (*meat*) жилистый.

stringency *n.* строгость. **stringent** *adj.* строгий (-г, -га, -го).

strip[1] *n.* полоса (*acc.* полосу; *pl.* -осы, -ос, -осам), полоска, лента; *s.* cartoon, рассказ в рисунках; *s.* light, лампа дневного света.

strip[2] *v.t.* (*undress*) раздевать *imp.*, раздеть (-éну, -éнешь) *perf.*; (*deprive*) лишать *imp.*, лишить *perf.* (of, + *gen.*); (*lay bare*) обнажать *imp.*, обнажить *perf.*; *s.* off, (*tear off*) сдирать *imp.*, содрать (сдеру, -рёшь; -ал, -ала, -áло) *perf.*; *v.i.* раздеваться *imp.*, раздеться (-éнусь, -éнешься) *perf.* **strip-tease** *n.* стриптиз.

stripe *n.* полоса (*acc.* полосу; *pl.* -осы, -ос, -осам). **striped** *adj.* полосатый.

stripling *n.* подросток (-тка), юноша *m.*

strive *v.i.* (*endeavour*) стараться *imp.*, по~ *perf.*; стремиться *imp.* (for, к + *dat.*); (*struggle*) бороться (-рюсь, -решься) *imp.* (for, за + *acc.*; against, против + *gen.*).

stroke *n.* (*blow, med.*) удар; (*of oar*) взмах; (*oarsman*) загребной *sb.*; (*drawing*) штрих (-á); (*clock*) бой (*pl.* бой); (*piston*) ход (*pl.* -ы, -ов) (*swimming*) стиль *m.*; *v.t.* гла́дить *imp.*, по~ *perf.*

stroll *n.* прогу́лка; *v.i.* прогу́ливаться *imp.*, прогуля́ться *perf.*

strong *adj.* (*also able*) (*gram.*) си́льный (си́лён, -льна́, -льно, си́льны); (*also drinks*) кре́пкий (-пок, -пка́, -пко); (*healthy*) здоро́вый; (*opinion etc.*) твёрдый (-д, -да́, -до). **stronghold** *n.* кре́пость; (*fig.*) опло́т. **strong-minded, strong-willed** *adj.* реши́тельный. **strong-room** ко́мната-сейф.

strontium *n.* стро́нций.

strop *n.* реме́нь (-мня́) *m.* (для пра́вки бритв); *v.t.* пра́вить *imp.* (бри́тву).

structural *adj.* структу́рный; (*building*) конструкти́вный, строи́тельный.

structure *n.* (*composition, arrangement*) структу́ра; (*system*) строй, устро́йство; (*building*) сооруже́ние.

struggle *n.* борьба́; *v.i.* боро́ться (-рю́сь, -решься) *imp.* (*for*, за + *acc.*; *against*, про́тив + *gen.*); (*writhe, s. with* (*fig.*)) би́ться (бьюсь, бьёшься (with, над + *instr.*).

strum *v.i.* бренча́ть (-чу́, -чи́шь) *imp.* (on, на + *prep.*).

strut[1] *n.* (*vertical*) подпо́ра, сто́йка; (*horizontal*) распо́рка; (*angle brace*) подко́с.

strut[2] *v.i.* ходи́ть (хожу́, хо́дишь) *indet.*, идти́ (иду́, идёшь; шёл, шла) *det.* го́голем.

stub *n.* (*stump*) пень (пня) *m.*; (*pencil*) огры́зок (-зка); (*cigarette*) оку́рок (-рка); (*counterfoil*) корешо́к (-шка́); *v.t.*: *s. one's toe*, ударя́ться *imp.*, уда́риться *perf.* ного́й (on, на + *acc.*); *s. out*, гаси́ть (гашу́, га́сишь) *imp.*, по~ *perf.* (cigarette etc., оку́рок).

stubble *n.* стерня́, жнивьё; (*hair*) щети́на.

stubborn *adj.* упря́мый, упо́рный. **stubbornness** *n.* упря́мство, упо́рство.

stucco *n.* штукату́рка; *adj.* штукату́рный.

stuck-up *adj.* (*coll.*) наду́тый.

stud[1] *n.* (*press-button*) кно́пка; (*collar, cuff*) запо́нка; (*large-headed nail*) гвоздь (-дя́; *pl.* -ди, -дей) *m.* с большо́й шля́пкой; *v.t.* (*set with studs*)

обива́ть *imp.*, оби́ть (обью́, -ьёшь) *perf.* гвоздя́ми; (*bestrew*) усе́ивать *imp.*, усе́ять (-е́ю, -е́ешь) *perf.* (with, + *instr.*).

stud[2] *n.* (*horses*) ко́нный заво́д. **stud-horse** *n.* племенно́й жеребе́ц (-бца́).

student *n.* студе́нт, ~ка.

studied *adj.* обду́манный (-ан, -анна).

studio *n.* (*artist's, broadcasting, cinema*) сту́дия; (*artist's*) ателье́ *neut. indecl.*, мастерска́я *sb.*

studious *adj.* (*diligent*) приле́жный; (*liking study*) лю́бящий нау́ку.

study *n.* изуче́ние, иссле́дование; *pl.* заня́тия *neut.pl.*; (*essay*) о́черк; (*art*) эски́з, этю́д; (*mus.*) этю́д; (*room*) кабине́т; *v.t.* изуча́ть *imp.*, изучи́ть (-чу́, -чишь) *perf.*; учи́ться (учу́сь, у́чишься) *imp.*, об~ *perf.* + *dat.*; занима́ться *imp.*, заня́ться (займу́сь, -мёшься; заня́лся, -яла́сь) *perf.* + *instr.*; иссле́довать *imp., perf.*; (*scrutinize*) рассма́тривать *imp.*, рассмотре́ть (-рю, -ришь) *perf.*; *v.i.* учи́ться (учу́сь, у́чишься) *imp.*, об~ *perf.*

stuff *n.* (*material*) материа́л; (*substance*) вещество́; ((*woollen*) *fabric*) (шерстяна́я) мате́рия; *s. and nonsense*, вздор; *v.t.* набива́ть *imp.*, наби́ть (набью́, -ьёшь) *perf.*; (*cul.*) начиня́ть *imp.*, начини́ть *perf.*; (*cram into*) запи́хивать *imp.*, запиха́ть *perf.* (into, в + *acc.*); (*thrust, shove into*) сова́ть (сую́, суёшь) *imp.*, су́нуть *perf.* (into, в + *acc.*); *v.i.* (*overeat*) объеда́ться *imp.*, объе́сться (-е́мся, -е́шься, -е́стся, -еди́мся; -е́лся) *perf.* **stuffiness** *n.* духота́, спёртость. **stuffing** *n.* наби́вка; (*cul.*) начи́нка. **stuffy** *adj.* спёртый, ду́шный (-шен, -шна́, -шно).

stumble *v.i.* (*also fig.*) спотыка́ться *imp.*, споткну́ться *perf.* (over, о + *acc.*); *s. upon*, натыка́ться *imp.*, наткну́ться *perf.* на + *acc.* **stumbling-block** *n.* ка́мень (-мня; *pl.* -мни, -мне́й) *m.* преткнове́ния.

stump *n.* (*tree*) пень (пня) *m.*; (*pencil*) огры́зок (-зка); (*limb*) обру́бок (-бка), культя́; *v.t.* (*perplex*) ста́вить *imp.*, по~ *perf.* в тупи́к; *v.i.* (*coll.*) ковыля́ть *imp.*

stun *v.t.* (*also fig.*) оглуша́ть *imp.*, оглуши́ть *perf.*; (*also fig.*) ошеломля́ть *imp.*, ошеломи́ть *perf.* **stunning** *adj.* (*also fig.*) ошеломи́тельный; (*fig.*) сногсшиба́тельный (*coll.*).

stunt¹ *n.* трюк.

stunt² *n.* заде́рживать *imp.*, заде́ржа́ть (-жу́, -жишь) *perf.* рост + *gen.* **stunted** *adj.* ча́хлый, низкоро́слый.

stupefaction *n.* ошеломле́ние. **stupefy** *v.t.* ошеломля́ть *imp.*, ошеломи́ть *perf.* **stupendous** *adj.* изуми́тельный; (*huge*) грома́дный. **stupid** *adj.* (*foolish*) глу́пый (-п, -па́, -по), дура́цкий (*coll.*); (*dull-witted*) тупо́й (туп, -а́, -о, ту́пы). **stupidity** *n.* глу́пость, тупо́сть. **stupor** *n.* оцепене́ние; (*med.*) сту́пор.

sturdy *adj.* (*robust*) кре́пкий (-пок, -пка́, -пко), здоро́вый (-в, -ва́); (*solid, firm*) твёрдый (-д, -да́, -до).

sturgeon *n.* осётр (-а́); (*dish*) осетри́на.

stutter *n.* заика́ние; *v.i.* заика́ться *imp.* **stutterer** *n.* зайка *m.* & *f.*

sty¹ *n.* (*pigsty*) свина́рник.

sty² *n.* (*on eye*) ячме́нь (-ня́) *m.*

style *n.* стиль *m.*; (*manner*) мане́ра; (*taste*) вкус; (*fashion*) мо́да; (*sort*) род (*pl.* -ы́); *in* (*grand*) *s.*, с ши́ком; *v.t.* констру́ировать *imp.*, *perf.* по мо́де. **stylish** *adj.* мо́дный (-ден, -дна́, -дно), шика́рный. **stylist** *n.* стили́ст. **stylistic** *adj.* стилисти́ческий. **stylistics** *n.* стили́стика. **stylize** *v.t.* стилизова́ть *imp.*, *perf.*

stylus *n.* граммофо́нная иго́лка.

suave *adj.* обходи́тельный. **suavity** *n.* обходи́тельность.

subaltern *n.* (*mil.*) мла́дший офице́р. **subcommittee** *n.* подкоми́ссия, подкомите́т. **subconscious** *adj.* подсозна́тельный; *n.* подсозна́ние. **subcutaneous** *adj.* подко́жный. **subdivide** *v.t.* подразделя́ть *imp.*, подраздели́ть *perf.* **subdivision** *n.* подразделе́ние. **subdue** *v.t.* покоря́ть *imp.*, покори́ть *perf.* **subdued** *adj.* (*suppressed, dispirited*) пода́вленный; (*soft*) мя́гкий (-гок, -гка́, -гко); (*indistinct*) приглушённый. **sub-editor** *n.* помо́щник, -ица реда́ктора. **sub-heading** *n.* подзаголо́вок (-вка). **subhuman** *adj.* не дости́гший челове́ческого у́ровня.

subject *n.* (*theme*) те́ма, сюже́т; (*discipline, theme*) предме́т, (*question*) вопро́с; (*logic, philos.*) субъе́кт; (*thing on to which action is directed*) объе́кт; (*gram.*) подлежа́щее *sb.*; (*national*) по́дданный *sb.*; *adj.* (*subordinate*) подчинённый (-ён, -ена́) (*to*, + *dat.*); (*dependent*) подвла́стный (*to*, + *dat.*); *s. to*, (*susceptible to*) подве́рженный + *dat.*; (*on condition that*) при усло́вии, что..., е́сли; *s. to his agreeing*, при усло́вии, что он согласи́тся, е́сли он согласи́тся; *be s. to* (*change etc.*), подлежа́ть (-жи́т) *imp.* + *dat.*; *v.t.*: *s. to*, подчиня́ть *imp.*, подчини́ть *perf.* + *dat.*; подверга́ть *imp.*, подве́ргнуть (подве́рг, -ла) *perf.* + *dat.* **subjection** *n.* подчине́ние. **subjective** *adj.* субъекти́вный. **subjectivity** *n.* субъекти́вность. **subject-matter** *n.* (*book, lecture*) содержа́ние, те́ма; (*discussion*) предме́т.

sub judice adj. на рассмотре́нии суда́.

subjugate *v.t.* покоря́ть *imp.*, покори́ть *perf.* **subjugation** *n.* покоре́ние.

subjunctive (**mood**) *n.* сослага́тельное наклоне́ние.

sublet *v.t.* передава́ть (-даю́, -даёшь) *imp.*, переда́ть (-а́м, -а́шь, -а́ст, -ади́м; пе́редал, -а́, -о) *perf.* в субаре́нду.

sublimate *v.t.* (*chem., psych.*) сублими́ровать; (*fig.*) возвыша́ть *imp.*, возвы́сить *perf.* **sublimation** *n.* (*chem., psych.*) сублима́ция; (*fig.*) возвыше́ние. **sublime** *adj.* возвы́шенный.

subliminal *adj.* подсозна́тельный. **sub-machine-gun** *n.* пистоле́т-пулемёт, автома́т. **submarine** *adj.* подво́дный; *n.* подво́дная ло́дка. **submerge** *v.t.* погружа́ть *imp.*, погрузи́ть *perf.*; затопля́ть *imp.*, затопи́ть (-плю́, -пишь) *perf.* **submission** *n.* подчине́ние; (*for inspection*) представле́ние. **submissive** *adj.* поко́рный. **submit** *v.i.* подчиня́ться *imp.*, подчини́ться *perf.* (*to*, + *dat.*); покоря́ться *imp.*, покори́ться *perf.* (*to*, + *dat.*); *v.t.* представля́ть *imp.*, предста́вить *perf.* (*на рассмотре́ние*). **subordinate** *adj.* подчинённый *sb.*; *adj.* подчинённый

(-ён, -ена́); (*secondary*) второстепе́нный; (*gram.*) прида́точный; *v.t.* подчиня́ть *imp.*, подчини́ть *perf.* **subordination** *n.* подчине́ние. **suborn** *v.t.* подкупа́ть *imp.*, подкупи́ть (-плю́, -пишь) *perf.* **subpoena** *n.* вы́зов, пове́стка в суд; *v.t.* вызыва́ть *imp.*, вы́звать (-зову, -зовешь) *perf.* в суд. **subscribe** *v.i.* подпи́сываться *imp.*, подписа́ться (-ишу́сь, -и́шешься) *perf.* (*to*, на + *acc.*); *s. to* (*opinion*) присоединя́ться *imp.*, присоедини́ться *perf.* к + *dat.* **subscriber** *n.* (*to newspaper etc.*) подпи́счик, -ица, абоне́нт, ~ка. **subscription** *n.* (*to newspaper etc.*) подпи́ска, абонеме́нт; (*fee*) взнос. **subsection** *n.* подразде́л. **subsequent** *adj.* после́дующий. **subsequently** *adv.* впосле́дствии. **subservience** *n.* раболе́пие, раболе́пство. **subservient** *adj.* раболе́пный. **subside** *v.i.* (*water*) убыва́ть *imp.*, убы́ть (убу́ду, -дешь; у́был, -á, -о) *perf.*; (*calm down, abate*) укла́дываться *imp.*, уле́чься (уля́жется, уля́гутся; улёгся, улегла́сь) *perf.*; (*soil*) оседа́ть *imp.*, осе́сть (ося́дет; осе́л) *perf.*; (*collapse*) обва́ливаться *imp.*, обвали́ться (-ится) *perf.* **subsidence** *n.* (*abatement*) спад; (*soil*) оседа́ние. **subsidiary** *adj.* вспомога́тельный; (*secondary*) второстепе́нный. **subsidize** *v.t.* субсиди́ровать *imp.*, *perf.* **subsidy** *n.* субси́дия, дота́ция. **subsist** *v.i.* (*exist*) существова́ть *imp.*; (*live*) жить (живу́, -вёшь; жил, -á, -о) *imp.* (on, + *instr.*). **subsistence** *n.* существова́ние; (*livelihood*) пропита́ние. **subsoil** *n.* подпо́чва. **subsonic** *adj.* дозвуково́й. **substance** *n.* вещество́; (*essence*) су́щность, суть; (*content*) содержа́ние. **substantial** *adj.* (*durable*) про́чный (-чен, -чна́, -чно, про́чны); (*considerable*) значи́тельный; (*food*) пло́тный (-тен, -тна́, -тно, пло́тны); (*real*) реа́льный; (*material*) веще́ственный. **substantially** *adv.* (*basically*) в основно́м; (*considerably*) в значи́тельной сте́пени. **substantiate** *v.t.* приводи́ть (-ожу́, -о́дишь) *imp.*, привести́ (-еду́, -едёшь; -ёл, -ела́) *perf.* доста́точные основа́ния + *gen.* **substantive** *n.* (и́мя *neut.*) существи́тельное. **substitute** *n.* (*person*) замести́тель *m.*, ~ница; (*thing*) заме́на; (*tech.*) замени́тель *m.*; *v.t.* заменя́ть *imp.*, замени́ть (-ню́, -нишь) *perf.* + *instr.* (*for* + *acc.*); *S. water for milk*, заменя́ю молоко́ водо́й. **substitution** *n.* заме́на, замеще́ние. **substructure** *n.* фунда́мент. **subsume** *v.t.* относи́ть (-ошу́, -о́сишь) *imp.*, отнести́ (-су́, -сёшь; -ёс, -есла́) *perf.* к како́й-л. катего́рии. **subtenant** *n.* субаренда́тор. **subterfuge** *n.* уве́ртка, отгово́рка, уло́вка. **subterranean** *adj.* подзе́мный. **subtitle** *n.* подзаголо́вок (-вка); (*cinema*) субти́тр. **subtle** *adj.* (*fine, delicate*) то́нкий (-нок, -нка́, -нко); (*mysterious*) тайнственный (-ен, -енна); (*ingenious*) иску́сный; (*cunning*) хи́трый (-тёр, -тра́, -хи́тро). **subtlety** *n.* (*fineness, delicacy*) то́нкость; (*mystery*) тайнственность; (*ingenuity*) иску́сность; (*cunning*) хи́трость. **subtract** *v.t.* вычита́ть *imp.*, вы́честь (-чту, -чтешь; -чел, -чла) *perf.* **subtraction** *n.* вычита́ние. **suburb** *n.* при́город. **suburban** *adj.* при́городный. **subversion** *n.* (*overthrow*) сверже́ние; (*subversive activities*) подрывна́я де́ятельность. **subversive** *adj.* подрывно́й. **subvert** *v.t.* сверга́ть *imp.*, све́ргнуть (-г(нул), -гла) *perf.* **subway** *n.* тонне́ль *m.*; (*pedestrian s.*) подзе́мный перехо́д.

succeed *v.i.* удава́ться (удаётся) *imp.*, уда́ться (уда́стся, удаду́тся; уда́лся, -ла́сь) *perf.*; *the plan will s.*, план уда́стся; *he succeeded in buying the book*, ему́ удало́сь купи́ть кни́гу; (*be successful*) преуспева́ть *imp.*, преуспе́ть *perf.* (in, в + *prep.*); (*follow*) сменя́ть *imp.*, смени́ть (-ню́, -нишь) *perf.*; (*be heir*) насле́довать *imp.*, *perf.* (to, + *dat.*). **succeeding** *adj.* после́дующий. **success** *n.* успе́х, уда́ча. **successful** *adj.* успе́шный, уда́чный. **succession** *n.* прее́мственность; (*sequence*) после́довательность; (*series*) (непреры́вная) цепь (loc. -пи́; pl. -пи, -пе́й); (*to throne*) престолонасле́дие; *right of s.*, пра́во насле́дования; *in s.*, подря́д, оди́н за други́м. **successive** *adj.* (*consecutive*) после́довательный.

successor *n.* насле́дник -ица; пре́е́мник, -ица.

succinct *adj.* сжа́тый.

succour *n.* по́мощь; *v.t.* приходи́ть (-ожу́, -о́дишь) *imp.*, прийти́ (приду́, -дёшь; пришёл, -шла́) *perf.* на по́мощь + *gen.*

succulent *adj.* со́чный (-чен, -чна́, -чно).

succumb *v.i.* уступа́ть *imp.*, уступи́ть (-плю́, -пишь) *perf.* (to, + *dat.*); поддава́ться (-даю́сь, -даёшься) *imp.*, подда́ться (-а́мся, -а́шься, -а́стся, -ади́мся; -а́лся, -ала́сь) *perf.* (to, + *dat.*).

such *adj.* тако́й, подо́бный; *s. people,* таки́е лю́ди; *in s. cases,* в таки́х, в подо́бных, слу́чаях; *in such a way,* таки́м о́бразом, так; *such as, (for example)* так напри́ме́р; *(of such a kind as)* тако́й как; *s. beauty as yours,* така́я красота́ как ва́ша; *(that which)* тот (та, то, те), кото́рый; *I shall read such books as I like,* я бу́ду чита́ть те кни́ги, кото́рые мне нра́вятся; *as to,* тако́й, что́бы; *his illness was not such as to cause anxiety,* его́ боле́знь была́ не тако́й (серьёзной), что́бы вы́звать беспоко́йство; *s. and s.,* тако́й-то; *pron.* тако́в (-á, -ó, -ы́); тот (та, то, те), тако́й; *s. was his character,* тако́в был его́ хара́ктер; *s. as are of my opinion,* те, кто согла́сен со мной; *as s.,* са́мо по себе́, как таково́й, по существу́; *s. is not the case,* э́то не так.

suchlike *adj.* подо́бный, тако́й; *pron. (inanim.)* тому́ подо́бное; *(people)* таки́е лю́ди (-де́й, -дям, -дьми́) *pl.*

suck *v.t.* соса́ть (сосу́, сосёшь) *imp.*; *s. in,* вса́сывать *imp.*, всоса́ть (-су́, -сёшь) *perf.; (engulf)* заса́сывать *imp.*, засоса́ть (-су́, -сёшь) *perf.; s. out,* выса́сывать *imp.*, вы́сосать (-су, -сешь) *perf.; s. up, (coll.)* подли́зываться *imp.*, подлиза́ться (-ижу́сь, -и́жешься) *perf.* к + *dat.* **sucker** *n. (biol., rubber device)* присо́ска; *(bot.)* корнево́й о́тпрыск. **suckle** *v.t.* корми́ть (-млю́, -мишь) *imp.* + *acc.* гру́дью. **suckling** *n.* грудно́й ребёнок (-нка) *(pl.* де́ти, -те́й), сосу́н (-á).
suction *n.* соса́ние, вса́сывание.

sudden *adj.* внеза́пный, неожи́данный (-ан, -анна); *s. death,* скоропости́жная смерть. **suddenly** *adv.* внеза́пно, вдруг, неожи́данно. **suddenness** *n.* внеза́пность, неожи́данность.

suds *n.* мы́льная пе́на.

sue *v.t.* пресле́довать *imp.* суде́бным поря́дком; возбужда́ть *imp.*, возбуди́ть *perf.* де́ло про́тив + *gen.* (for, о + *prep.*); *s. s.b. for damages,* предъявля́ть *imp.*, предъяви́ть (-влю́, -вишь) *perf.* (к) кому́-л. иск о возмеще́нии уще́рба.

suede *n.* за́мша; *adj.* за́мшевый.

suet *n.* по́чечное са́ло.

suffer *v.t.* страда́ть *imp.*, по ~ *perf.*, от ~ *gen.; (experience)* испы́тывать *imp.*, испыта́ть *perf.; (loss, defeat)* терпе́ть (-плю́, -пишь) *imp.*, по ~ *perf.; (allow)* позволя́ть *imp.*, позво́лить *perf.* + *dat.;* дозволя́ть *imp.*, дозво́лить *perf.* + *dat.; (tolerate)* терпе́ть (-плю́, -пишь) *imp.; v.i.* страда́ть *imp.*, по ~ *perf.* (from, + *instr.*). **sufferance** *n. (tacit consent)* молчали́вое согла́сие; *he is here on s.,* его́ здесь те́рпят. **suffering** *n.* страда́ние.

suffice *v.i. (t.)* быть доста́точным (для + *gen.*); хвата́ть (-а́ет) *imp.*, хвати́ть (-ит) *perf. impers.* + *gen.* (+ *dat.*); *five pounds will s. me,* мне хва́тит пяти́ фу́нтов. **sufficiency** *n. (adequacy)* доста́точность; *(prosperity)* доста́ток (-тка). **sufficient** *adj.* доста́точный.

suffix *n.* су́ффикс.

suffocate *v.t.* удуша́ть *imp.*, удуши́ть (-шу́, -шишь) *perf.; v.i.* задыха́ться *imp.*, задохну́ться (-о́х(ну́л)ся, -о́х(ну́)лась) *perf.* **suffocating** *adj.* ду́шный (-шен, -шна́, -шно), удуша́ющий (-шен, -шна́, -шно), удуша́ющий. **suffocation** *n.* удуше́ние; *(difficulty in breathing)* уду́шье.

suffrage *n. (right)* избира́тельное пра́во.

suffuse *v.t. (light, tears)* залива́ть *imp.*, зали́ть (-лью́, -льёшь; за́ли́л, -á, за́ли́ло) *perf.* (with, + *instr.*); *(colour)* покрыва́ть *imp.*, покры́ть (-ро́ю, -ро́ешь) *perf.* (with, + *instr.*). **suffusion**

n. покры́тие; (*colour*) кра́ска; (*flush*) румя́нец (-нца).

sugar *n.* са́хар (-a(y)); *adj.* са́харный; *v.t.* подсла́щивать *imp.*, подсласти́ть *perf.*; **s.-basin**, са́харница; **s.-beet**, са́харная свёкла; **s.-cane**, (caxapo)paфи-на́дный тро́сти́к; **s.-refinery**, (caxapo)paфи-на́дный заво́д; **sugary** *adj.* (*sweet*) сла́дкий (-док, -дка́, -дко); (*saccharine*) caxaри́стый; (*sickly sweet*) прито́рный, слаща́вый.

suggest *v.t.* (*propose*) предлага́ть *imp.*, предложи́ть (-жу́, -жишь) *perf.*; (*advise*) сове́товать *imp.*, по~ *perf.*; (*call up*) внуша́ть *imp.*, внуши́ть *perf.*; **s. itself to**, приходи́ть (-ит) *imp.*, прийти́ (придёт; пришёл, -шла́) *perf.* кому́-л. в го́лову; *a solution suggested itself to me*, мне пришло́ в го́лову реше́ние. **suggestible** *adj.* поддаю́-щийся внуше́нию. **suggestibility** *n.* внуша́емость. **suggestion** *n.* (*proposal*) предложе́ние; (*psych.*) внуше́ние. **suggestive** *adj.* вызыва́ющий мы́сли (*of*, o + *prep.*); (*slightly indecent*) соблазни́тельный.

suicidal *adj.* самоуби́йственный; (*fig.*) губи́тельный. **suicide** *n.* самоуби́й-ство; (*person*) самоуби́йца *m. & f.*; (*fig.*) крах по со́бственной вине́; *commit s.*, соверша́ть *imp.*, соверши́ть *perf.* самоуби́йство; поко́нчить *perf.* с собо́й (*coll.*).

suit *n.* (*clothing*) костю́м; (*leg.*) иск; (*request*) про́сьба; (*cards*) масть; *follow s.*, (*cards*) ходи́ть (хожу́, хо́дишь) *imp.* в масть; (*fig.*) сле́до-вать *imp.*, по~ *perf.* приме́ру; *in one's suitable s.*, в чём мать родила́; *v.t.* (*be convenient for*) устра́ивать *imp.*, устро́ить *perf.*; (*accommodate*) при-спосо́бливать *imp.*, приспосо́бить *perf.*; (*be suitable for*, *match*) подходи́ть (-ожу́, -о́дишь) *imp.*, подойти́ (-йду́, -йдёшь; подошёл, -шла́) *perf.* (+ *dat.*); (*look attractive on*) идти́ (идёт; шёл, шла) *imp.* + *dat.*; *s. oneself*, выбира́ть *imp.*, вы́брать (-беру, -берешь) *perf.* по вку́су. **suitability** *n.* приго́дность. **suitable** *adj.* (*fitting*) подходя́щий; (*convenient*) удо́бный. **suitably** *adv.* соотве́тственно. **suitcase** *n.* чемода́н.

suite *n.* (*retinue*) сви́та; (*furniture*) гар-нитỳр; (*rooms*) апарта́менты *m.pl.*; (*mus.*) сюи́та.

suitor *n.* (*admirer*) покло́нник; (*plain-tiff*) исте́ц (истца́); (*petitioner*) проси́-тель *m.*, ~ница.

sulk *v.i.* ду́ться *imp.* **sulkiness** *n.* скве́р-ное настрое́ние. **sulky** *adj.* наду́тый, хму́рый (-р, -pá, -ро).

sullen *adj.* угрю́мый, хму́рый (-р, -pá, -ро). **sullenness** *n.* угрю́мость.

sully *v.t.* пятна́ть *imp.*, за~ *perf.*

sulphate *n.* сульфа́т. **sulphide** *n.* сульфи́д. **sulphite** *n.* сульфи́т. **sulphur** *n.* се́ра. **sulphureous** *adj.* сери́стый. **sulphuric** *adj.* се́рный; *s. acid*, се́рная кислота́.

sultan *n.* (*sovereign*) султа́н.

sultana *n.* (*raisin*) изю́мина без семя́н; *pl.* кишми́ш (-иша́) (*collect.*).

sultriness *n.* зной, духота́. **sultry** *adj.* зно́йный; ду́шный (-шен, -шна́, -шно); (*passionate*) стра́стный.

sum *n.* су́мма; (*arithmetical problem*) арифмети́ческая зада́ча; *pl.* арифме́-тика; *v.t.* (*add up*) скла́дывать *imp.*, сложи́ть (-жу́, -жишь) *perf.*; *s. up*, (*summarize*) сумми́ровать *imp.*, *perf.*; резюми́ровать *imp.*, *perf.*; (*appraise*) оце́нивать *imp.*, оцени́ть (-ню́, -нишь) *perf.* **summing-up** *n.* (*leg.*) заключи́тельная речь (*pl.* -чи, -че́й) судьи́.

summarize *v.t.* сумми́ровать *imp.*, *perf.*; резюми́ровать *imp.*, *perf.* **summary** *n.* резюме́ *neut.indecl.*, конспе́кт, сво́д-ка; *adj.* сумма́рный, ско́рый (-р, -pá, -ро).

summer *n.* ле́то (*pl.* -тá); *Indian s.*, ба́бье ле́то (*pl.* -тá); *attrib.* ле́тний; *v.i.* проводи́ть (-ожу́, -о́дишь) *imp.*, про-вести́ (-еду́, -едёшь; провёл, -á) *perf.* ле́то (*pl.* -тá). **summer-house** *n.* бесе́д-ка. **summery** *adj.* ле́тний.

summit *n.* верши́на, верх (-a(y), *loc.* -ý; *pl.* -и́ & -á); (*fig.*) зени́т, преде́л; *s. meeting*, встре́ча глав прави́тельств.

summon *v.t.* вызыва́ть *imp.*, вы́звать (-зову, -зовешь) *perf.*; (*call*) призы-ва́ть *imp.*, призва́ть (-зову́, -зовёшь; призва́л, -á, -o) *perf.*; *s. up one's courage*, собира́ться *imp.*, собра́ться

(-беру́сь, -берёшься; -бра́лся, -брала́сь, -бра́ло́сь) *perf.* с ду́хом.
summons *n.* вы́зов; (*leg.*) пове́стка в суд; *v.t.* вызыва́ть *imp.*, вы́звать (-зову, -зовешь) *perf.* в суд.

sumptuous *adj.* роско́шный.

sun *n.* со́лнце; *in the s.,* на со́лнце. **sun-bathe** *v.i.* гре́ться *imp.* на со́лнце, загора́ть *imp.* **sunbeam** *n.* со́лнечный луч (-а́). **sunburn** *n.* зага́р; (*inflammation*) со́лнечный ожо́г. **sunburnt** *adj.* загоре́лый; *become* ~, загора́ть *imp.*, загоре́ть (-рю́, -ри́шь) *perf.*

Sunday *n.* воскресе́нье; *adj.* воскре́сный.

sun-dial *n.* со́лнечные часы́ *m.pl.*

sundry *adj.* ра́зный; *all and s.,* все вме́сте и ка́ждый в отде́льности.

sunflower *n.* подсо́лнечник; *s. seeds,* сме́чки *neut.pl.* **sun-glasses** *n.* защи́тные очки́ (-ко́в) *pl.* от со́лнца.

sunken *adj.* (*hollow*) впа́лый; (*submerged*) погружённый; (*ship*) зато́пленный; (*below certain level*) ни́же (како́го-л. у́ровня).

sunlight *n.* со́лнечный свет. **sunny** *adj.* со́лнечный. **sunrise** *n.* восхо́д со́лнца. **sunset** *n.* захо́д со́лнца, зака́т. **sunshade** *n.* (*parasol*) зо́нтик; (*awning*) наве́с. **sunshine** *n.* со́лнечный свет. **sunstroke** *n.* со́лнечный уда́р. **sun-tan** *n.* зага́р. **sun-tanned** *adj.* загоре́лый.

superannuated *adj.* (*pensioner*) вы́шедший на пе́нсию; (*obsolete*) устаре́лый. **superb** *adj.* великоле́пный, превосхо́дный. **supercilious** *adj.* надме́нный (-нен, -нна), презри́тельный. **superficial** *adj.* пове́рхностный; (*outward*) вне́шний. **superficiality** *n.* пове́рхностность. **superfluity** *n.* (*surplus*) изли́шек (-шка); (*abundance*) оби́лие. **superfluous** *adj.* ли́шний, нену́жный; (*abundant*) оби́льный. **superhuman** *adj.* сверхчелове́ческий. **superimpose** *v.t.* накла́дывать *imp.*, наложи́ть (-жу́, -жишь) *perf.* **superintend** *v.t.* заве́довать *imp.*+*instr.*; (*supervise*) надзира́ть *imp.* за+*instr.* **superintendent** *n.* заве́дующий *sb.* (*of,* +*instr.*), надзира́тель *m.*, ~ница *f.* (*of,* за+*instr.*); (*police*) ста́рший полице́йский офице́р. **superior** *n.* нача́ль-

ник, -ица; ста́рший *sb.*; (*relig.*) настоя́тель *m.*, ~ница *f.*; *adj.* (*better*) лу́чший, превосхо́дящий; (*higher*) вы́сший, ста́рший; (*of better quality*) вы́сшего ка́чества; (*haughty*) высокоме́рный. **superiority** *n.* превосхо́дство. **superlative** *adj.* превосхо́дный; *n.* (*gram.*) превосхо́дная сте́пень. **super-man** *n.* сверхчелове́к. **supermarket** *n.* универса́м. **supernatural** *adj.* сверхъесте́ственный (-ен, -енна). **super-numerary** *adj.* сверхшта́тный. **superpose** *v.t.* накла́дывать *imp.*, наложи́ть (-жу́-жишь) *perf.* **superpower** *n.* одна́ из наибо́лее мо́щных вели́ких держа́в. **superscription** *n.* на́дпись. **supersede** *v.t.* заменя́ть *imp.*, замени́ть (-ню́, -нишь) *perf.* **supersonic** *adj.* сверхзвуково́й. **superstition** *n.* суеве́рие. **superstitious** *adj.* суеве́рный. **superstructure** *n.* надстро́йка. **supervene** *v.i.* сле́довать *imp.*, по~ *perf.* **supervise** *v.t.* наблюда́ть *imp.* за+*instr.*, надзира́ть *imp.* за+*instr.* **supervision** *n.* надзо́р, наблюде́ние. **supervisor** *n.* надзира́тель *m.*, ~ница *f.*; надсмо́трщик, -ица *f.*; (*of studies*) нау́чный руководи́тель *m.*

supine *adj.* (*lying on back*) лежа́щий на́взничь; (*indolent*) лени́вый.

supper *n.* у́жин; *have s.,* у́жинать *imp.*, по~ *perf.*; *the Last S.,* та́йная ве́черя.

supplant *v.t.* вытесня́ть *imp.*, вы́теснить *perf.*

supple *adj.* ги́бкий (-бок, -бка́, -бко). **suppleness** *n.* ги́бкость.

supplement *n.* (*to book*) дополне́ние; (*to periodical*) приложе́ние; *v.t.* дополня́ть *imp.*, допо́лнить *perf.* **supplementary** *adj.* дополни́тельный.

suppliant *n.* проси́тель *m.*, ~ница.

supplier *n.* поставщи́к (-а́) (*anim. & inanim.*). **supply** *n.* снабже́ние, поста́вка; (*stock*) запа́с; (*econ.*) предложе́ние; *pl.* припа́сы (-ов) *pl.*, (*provisions*) продово́льствие; *s. and demand,* спрос и предложе́ние; *s. line,* путь (-ти́, -тём) *m.* подво́за; *v.t.* снабжа́ть *imp.*, снабди́ть *perf.* (*with,* +*instr.*); поставля́ть *imp.*, поста́вить *perf.*

support *n.* подде́ржка, опо́ра; *v.t.*

поддёрживать *imp.*, поддержáть (-жý, -жишь) *perf.*; (*family*) содержáть (-жý, -жишь) *imp.* supporter *n.* сторóн-ник, -ица. supporting *adj.* (*tech.*) опóрный; *s.* actor, исполнитель *m.*, ~ница второстепéнной рóли.

suppose *v.t.* (*think*) полагáть *imp.*; (*pre-suppose*) предполагáть *imp.*, предположить (-жý, -жишь) *perf.*; (*assume*) допускáть *imp.*, допустить (-ущý, -ýстишь) *perf.* supposed *adj.* (*pre-tended*) мнимый. supposition *n.* предположéние. suppositious *adj.* предположительный.

suppress *v.t.* (*uprising, feelings*) подавлять *imp.*, подавить (-влю, -вишь) *perf.*; (*laughter, tears*) сдéрживать *imp.*, сдержáть (-жý, -жишь) *perf.*; (*forbid*) запрещáть *imp.*, запретить (-ещý, -етишь) *perf.* suppression *n.* подавлéние; (*prohibition*) запрещéние.

supremacy *n.* госпóдство, главéнство. supreme *adj.* верхóвный, высший; (*greatest*) величáйший; *S.* Soviet (*of the U.S.S.R.*), Верхóвный Совéт (СССР); *S. Court*, Верхóвный суд (-á).

surcharge *n.* приплáта, доплáта.

sure *adj.* (*convinced*) увéренный (-ен, -ена) (of, в+*prep.*; that, что); (*un-erring*) увéренный (-ен, -енна); (*certain, reliable*) вéрный (-рен, -рнá, -рно, вéрны); (*steady*) твéрдый (твёрд, -á, -о); *s. enough*, действительно, на сáмом дéле; *he is s. to come*, он обязáтельно придёт; *make s. of*, (*convince oneself*) убеждáться *imp.*, убедиться (-дишься) *perf.* в+*prep.*; (*secure*) обеспéчивать *imp.*, обеспéчить *perf.*; *make s. that*, (*check up*) проверять *imp.*, провéрить *perf.* что; *for s.*, surely *adv.* навернякá, навéрное.

surety *n.* порýка; поручитель *m.*, ~ница; *stand s. for*, ручáться *imp.*, поручиться (-чýсь, -чишься) *perf.* за + *acc.*

surf *n.* прибóй; *v.i.* занимáться *imp.*, заняться (займýсь, -мёшься; занялся, -лáсь) *perf.* сёрфингом.

surface *n.* повéрхность; (*exterior*) внéшность; *on the s.*, (*fig.*) внéшне; *under the s.*, (*fig.*) по существý; *adj.*

повéрхностный; (*exterior*) внéшний; (*ground*) назéмный; *v.i.* всплывáть *imp.*, всплыть (-ывý, -ывёшь; всплыл, -á, -о) *perf.*

surfeit *n.* (*excess*) излишество; (*surplus*) излишек (-шка); *be surfeited*, пресыщáться *imp.*, пресытиться (-ыщусь, -ытишься) *perf.* (with, + *instr.*).

surge *n.* прилив, (большáя) волнá (*pl.* -ы, вóлнáм); *v.i.* (*be agitated, choppy*) волновáться *imp.*, вз~ *perf.*; (*rise, heave*) вздымáться *imp.*; (*rush, gush*) хлынуть *perf.*; *s. forward*, ринуться *perf.* вперёд.

surgeon *n.* хирýрг; (*mil.*) воéнный врач (-á). surgery *n.* (*treatment*) хирургия; (*place*) кабинéт, приёмная *sb.*, (врачá); (*s. hours*) приёмные часы *m.pl.* (врачá). surgical *adj.* хирургический.

surly *adj.* (*morose*) угрюмый; (*rude*) грýбый (груб, -á, -о).

surmise *n.* предположéние, догáдка; *v.t.* & *i.* предполагáть *imp.*, предположить (-жý, -жишь) *perf.*; догáдываться *imp.*, догадáться *perf.*

surmount *v.t.* преодолевáть *imp.*, преодолéть *perf.*

surname *n.* фамилия.

surpass *v.t.* превосходить (-ожý, -óдишь) *imp.*, превзойти (-ойдý, -ойдёшь; -ошёл, -ошлá) *perf.* surpassing *adj.* превосхóдный.

surplus *n.* излишек (-шка), избыток (-тка) *adj.* излишний (-шен, -шня), избыточный.

surprise *n.* удивлéние, неожиданность, сюрприз; *by s.*, врасплóх; *to my s.*, к моемý удивлéнию; *s. attack*, внезáпное нападéние; *v.t.* удивлять *imp.*, удивить *perf.*; (*come upon suddenly*) застáть (-тáю, -тáешь) *imp.*, застáть (-áну, -áнешь) *perf.* врасплóх; *be surprised* (*at*), удивляться *imp.*, удивиться (*at*) *perf.* (+ *dat.*). surprising *adj.* удивительный, неожиданный (-ан, -анна).

surreal *adj.* сюрреалистический. surrealism *n.* сюрреализм. surrealist *n.* сюрреалист; *adj.* сюрреалистический.

surrender *n.* сдáча; (*renunciation*) откáз;

v.t. сдава́ть (сдаю́, сдаёшь) *imp.*,
сдать (сдам, сдашь, сласт, сдади́м;
сдал, -а́, -о) *perf.*; (*renounce*) отка́зываться *imp.*, отказа́ться (-ажу́сь,
-а́жешься) *perf.* от + *gen.*; *v.i.* сдава́ться (сдаю́сь, сдаёшься) *imp.*,
сда́ться (сда́мся, сда́шься, сда́стся,
сдади́мся; сда́лся, -ла́сь) *perf.*; *s. one-self* to, предава́ться (-даю́сь,
-даёшься) *imp.*, преда́ться (-да́мся,
-да́шься, -да́стся, -дади́мся; -да́лся,
-ла́сь) *perf.* + *dat.*

surreptitious *adj.* та́йный, сде́ланный
тайко́м. **surreptitiously** *adv.* та́йно,
тайко́м, исподтишка́ (*coll.*).

surrogate *n.* (*person*) замести́тель *m.*,
~ ница; (*thing*) замени́тель *m.*, сурро-
га́т.

surround *n.* (*frame*) обрамле́ние; (*edge,
selvage*) кро́мка; *v.t.* окружа́ть *imp.*,
окружи́ть *perf.* (with, + *instr.*); обсту-
па́ть *imp.*, обступи́ть (-пит) *perf.*; *s.
with*, (*enclose*) обноси́ть (-ошу́,
-о́сишь) *imp.*, обнести́ (-есу́, -есёшь;
-ёс, -есла́) *perf.* + *instr.* **surrounding** *adj.*
окружа́ющий, окре́стный. **surround-
ings** *n.* (*environs*) окре́стности *f.pl.*;
(*milieu*) среда́, окруже́ние; (*locality*)
ме́стность.

surveillance *n.* надзо́р, наблюде́ние.

survey *n.* обозре́ние, осмо́тр, обзо́р;
(*investigation*) обсле́дование; (*geol.*)
изыска́ние; (*topog.*) межева́ние; *v.t.*
обозрева́ть *imp.*, обозре́ть (-рю́,
-ри́шь) *perf.*; осма́тривать *imp.*,
осмотре́ть (-рю́, -ришь) *perf.*; (*investigate*) обсле́довать *imp.*, *perf.*; (*topog.*)
межева́ть (-жу́ю, -жу́ешь) *imp.* **surveyor** *n.* землеме́р.

survival *n.* (*surviving*) выжива́ние; (*relic*)
пережи́ток (-тка). **survive** *v.t.* пережи-
ва́ть *imp.*, пережи́ть (-иву́, -ивёшь;
пережи́л, -а́, -о) *perf.*; *v.i.* выжива́ть
imp., вы́жить (-иву, -ивешь) *perf.*
остава́ться (-аю́сь, -аёшься) *imp.*,
оста́ться (-а́нусь, -а́нешься) *perf.* в
живы́х. **survivor** *n.* оста́вшийся *sb.* в
живы́х.

susceptibility *n.* восприи́мчивость,
(*sensitivity*) чувстви́тельность. **susceptible** *adj.* восприи́мчивый (to, к + *dat.*)
(*sensitive*) чувстви́тельный (to, к +

dat.); (*impressionable*) впечатли́тель-
ный.

suspect *n.* подозрева́емый *sb.*; *adj.*
подозри́тельный; *v.t.* подозрева́ть
imp. (of, в + *prep.*); (*mistrust*) не
доверя́ть *imp.* + *dat.*; (*foresee*) предчу́в-
ствовать *imp.*; (*have reason to
believe*) полага́ть *imp.* (that, что).

suspend *v.t.* (*hang up*) подве́шивать
imp., подве́сить *perf.*; (*call a halt to*)
приостана́вливать *imp.*, приостано-
ви́ть (-влю́, -вишь) *perf.*; (*repeal
temporarily*) вре́менно отменя́ть *imp.*,
отмени́ть (-ню́, -нишь) *perf.*; (*dismiss
temporarily*) вре́менно отстраня́ть
imp., отстрани́ть *perf.*; *suspended sentence*, усло́вный пригово́р. **suspender**
n. (*stocking*) подвя́зка. **suspense** *n.*
(*uncertainty*) неизве́стность, неопределённость; (*anxiety*) беспоко́йство;
keep in s., держа́ть (-жу́, -жишь) *imp.*
в напряжённом ожида́нии. **suspension**
n. (*halt*) приостано́вка; (*temporary
repeal*) вре́менная отме́на; (*temporary
dismissal*) вре́менное отстране́ние;
(*hanging up*) подве́шивание; (*tech.*)
подве́с; *s.* (*stocking*) висячий мост
(мо́ста, *loc.* -ý; *pl.* -ы́).

suspicion *n.* подозре́ние; *on s.*, по
подозре́нию (of, в + *loc.*); (*trace*)
отте́нок (-нка). **suspicious** *adj.* подо-
зри́тельный.

sustain *v.t.* (*support*) подде́рживать
imp., поддержа́ть (-жу́, -жишь) *perf.*;
(*stand up to*) выде́рживать *imp.*,
вы́держать (-жу, -жишь) *perf.*; (*suffer*)
потерпе́ть (-плю́ -пишь) *perf.* **sustained** *adj.* (*uninterrupted*) непреры́в-
ный. **sustenance** *n.* пи́ща, пита́ние.

swab *n.* шва́бра; (*med.*) тампо́н; (*smear,
specimen*) мазо́к (-зка́); *v.t.* мыть
(мо́ю, мо́ешь) *imp.*, вы́~, по~ *perf.*
шва́брой; *s. the decks*, (*naut.*) дра́ить
(-а́ю, -а́ишь) *imp.*, на ~ *perf.* па́лубы.

swaddle *v.t.* пелена́ть *imp.*, за~, с~
perf. **swaddling-clothes** *n.* пелёнки
(*gen.* -нок) *pl.*

swagger *v.i.* (*walk with s.*) расха́живать
imp. с ва́жным ви́дом; (*put on airs*)
ва́жничать *imp.*

swallow[1] *n.* глото́к (-тка́); *v.t.* глота́ть
imp., глотну́ть *perf.*; проглаты́вать

imp., проглоти́ть (-очу́, -о́тишь) *perf.*; *s. up*, поглоща́ть *imp.*, поглоти́ть (-ощу́, -о́тишь) *perf.*

swallow[2] *n.* (*bird*) ла́сточка.

swamp *n.* боло́то, топь; *v.t.* залива́ть *imp.*, зали́ть (-лью́, -льёшь; за́лил, -а́, -о) *perf.*; *s. with* (*letters etc.*), засыпа́ть *imp.*, засы́пать (-плю, -плешь) *perf.* + *instr.* **swampy** *adj.* боло́тистый, то́пкий (-пок, -пка́, -пко).

swan *n.* ле́бедь (*pl.* -ди, -де́й) *m.*; *s.-song*, лебеди́ная песнь.

swank *v.i.* хва́статься *imp.*, по~ *perf.* (*about*, + *instr.*); (*coll.*) бахва́литься *imp.* (*about*, + *instr.*).

swap *n.* обме́н; *v.t.* меня́ть *imp.*, об~, по~ *perf.*; обме́нивать *imp.*, обменя́ть *perf.*; обме́ниваться *imp.*, обменя́ться *perf.* + *instr.*

sward *n.* лужа́йка, дёрн.

swarm *n.* рой (ро́я, *loc.* рою́; *pl.* рой, роёв), (*crowd*) толпа́ (*pl.* -пы); *v.i.* рои́ться (-и́тся) *imp.*; толпи́ться (-и́тся) *imp.*; кише́ть (-ши́т) *imp.* (*with*, + *instr.*).

swarthy *adj.* сму́глый (-л, -ла́, -ло).

swastika *n.* сва́стика.

swat *v.t.* прихло́пнуть *perf.*; убива́ть *imp.*, уби́ть (убью́, -ьёшь) *perf.*

swathe *n.* (*bandage*) бинт (-а́); (*puttee*) обмо́тка; *v.t.* (*bandage*) бинтова́ть *imp.*, за~ *perf.*; (*wrap up*) заку́тывать *imp.*, заку́тать *perf.*

sway *n.* колеба́ние, кача́ние; (*influence*) влия́ние; (*power*) власть; *v.t. & i.* колеба́ть(ся) (-блю(сь), -блешь(ся)) *imp.*, по~ *perf.*; кача́ть(ся) *imp.*, качну́ть(ся) *perf.*; *v.t.* (*influence*) име́ть *imp.* влия́ние на + *acc.*

swear *v.i.* (*vow*) кля́сться (кляну́сь, -нёшься, кля́лся, -ла́сь) *imp.*, по~ *perf.*; (*curse*) руга́ться *imp.*, ругну́ться *perf.*; *v.t.*: *s. in*, приводи́ть (-ожу́, -о́дишь) *imp.*, привести́ (-еду́, -едёшь, -ёл, -ела́) *perf.* к прися́ге; *s.-word*, руга́тельство, бра́нное сло́во (*pl.* -ва́).

sweat *n.* пот (*loc.* -у́; *pl.* -ы́); (*perspiration*) испа́рина; *v.i.* поте́ть *imp.*, вс~ *perf.* **sweater** *n.* сви́тер. **sweaty** *adj.* по́тный (-тен, -тна́, -тно).

swede[1] *n.* брю́ква.

Swede[2] *n.* швед, шве́дка. **Swedish** *adj.* шве́дский.

sweep *n.* вымета́ние; (*span*) разма́х; (*scope*) охва́т; (*chimney-sweep*) трубочи́ст; *v.t.* мести́ (мету́, -тёшь; мёл, -а́) *imp.*; подмета́ть *imp.*, подмести́ (-ету́, -етёшь; подмёл, -ела́) *perf.*; (*mil.*) обстре́ливать *imp.*, обстреля́ть *perf.*; (*naut.*) (*drag*) тра́лить *imp.*, про~ *perf.*; *v.i.* (*go majestically*) ходи́ть (хожу́, хо́дишь) *indet.*, идти́ (иду́, идёшь; шла, шла) *det.*, пойти́ (пойду́, -дёшь; пошёл, -шла́) *perf.* велича́во; (*move swiftly*) мча́ться (мчусь, мчи́шься) *imp.*; *s. away*, смета́ть *imp.*, смести́ (смету́, -тёшь; смёл, -а́) *perf.* **sweeping** *n.* подмета́ние; (*naut.*) тра́ление; *adj.* широ́кий (-к, -ка́, -о́ко); (*wholesale*) огу́льный. **sweepstake** *n.* тотализа́тор.

sweet *n.* (*sweetmeat*) конфе́та; (*dessert*) сла́дкое *sb.*; *adj.* сла́дкий (-док, -дка́, -дко); (*fragrant*) души́стый; (*dear*) ми́лый (мил, -а́, -о, ми́лы). **sweetbread** *n.* (*cul.*) сла́дкое мя́со. **sweeten** *v.t.* подсла́щивать *imp.*, подсласти́ть *perf.* **sweetheart** *n.* возлю́бленный, -нная *sb.* **sweetness** *n.* сла́дость. **sweet pea** *n.* души́стый горо́шек (-шка(у)) (*collect.*).

swell *v.i.* (*up*) опуха́ть *imp.*, опу́хнуть (-х) *perf.*; пу́хнуть (-х) *imp.*, вс~, о~ *perf.*; распуха́ть *imp.*, распу́хнуть (-х) *perf.*; (*a sail*) надува́ться *imp.*, -у́ется) *perf.*; (*a bud*) набуха́ть *imp.*, набу́хнуть (-нет; -х) *perf.*; (*increase*) увели́чиваться *imp.*, увели́читься *perf.*; (*sound*) нараста́ть *imp.*, нарасти́ (-тёт; наро́с, -ла́) *perf.*; *v.t.* (*a sail*) надува́ть *imp.*, наду́ть (-у́ю, -у́ешь) *perf.*; (*increase*) увели́чивать *imp.*, увели́чить *perf.*; *n.* вы́пуклость; (*naut.*) мёртвая зыбь (*pl.* -би, -бе́й). **swelling** *n.* о́пухоль; (*bud*) набуха́ние; (*increase*) увеличе́ние.

swelter *v.i.* томи́ться *imp.*, ис~ *perf.* от жары́. **sweltering** *adj.* зно́йный.

swerve *v.i.* отклоня́ться *imp.*, отклони́ться (-ню́сь, -ни́шься) *perf.*; (*sudden*) ре́зко свора́чивать *imp.*, свороти́ть (-очу́, -о́тишь) *perf.*, сверну́ть *perf.*, в сто́рону.

swift n. стриж (-á); adj. бы́стрый (быстр, -á, -о, бы́стры). **swiftness** n. быстротá.

swig n. глотóк (-ткá); v.t. потя́гивать imp. (coll.).

swill n. пóйло; v.t. (rinse) полоскáть (-ощý, -óщешь) imp., вы́~ perf.; (sluice) обливáть imp., облúть (оболью́, -льёшь; óблил, облилá, óблило) perf.

swim v.i. плáвать indet., плыть (плыву́, -вёшь; плыл, -á, -о) det.; (head) кружи́ться (кру́жится) imp.; v.t. (across) переплывáть imp., переплы́ть (-ывý, -ывёшь; переплы́л, -á, -о) perf.+ acc., че́рез+acc.; n.: in the s., в ку́рсе де́ла. **swimmer** n. пловéц (-вцá), пловчúха. **swimming** n. плáвание. **swimming-pool** n. бассéйн для плáвания. **swim-suit** n. купáльный костю́м.

swindle v.t. обмáнывать imp., обману́ть (-ну́, -нешь) perf. (coll.) надувáть imp., наду́ть (-у́ю, -у́ешь) perf.; n. обмáн; надувáтельство (coll.). **swindler** n. плут (-á), ~ óвка; мошéнник, -ица.

swine n. свинья́ (pl. -ньи, -нéй). **swineherd** n. свинопáс.

swing v.i. качáться imp., качну́ться perf.; колебáться (-блю́сь, -блешься) imp., по~ perf.; раскáчиваться imp., раскачáться perf.; v.t. качáть imp., качну́ть perf.+acc., instr.; (arms) размáхивать imp.+instr.; раскáчивать imp., раскачáть perf.; n. качáние; (stroke) мах (-a(y)); (seat) качéли (-лей) pl.; in full s., в пóлном разгáре; s. bridge, разводнóй мост (мостá, loc. -ý; pl. -ы́). **swing-door** n. дверь (loc. -ри́; pl. -ри, -рéй, instr. -рьмú & -ря́ми) открывáющаяся в любу́ю стóрону.

swingeing adj. (huge) громáдный; (forcible) сúльный (си́лён, -льнá, -льно, сúльны́).

swinish adj. свúнский (coll.). **swinishness** n. свúнство (coll.).

swipe n. удáр слéча; v.t. удáрять imp., удáрить perf. слéча.

swirl v.i. кружи́ться (-жу́сь, -у́жишься) imp., верте́ться (-рчу́сь, -ртишься)

imp.; v.t. кружи́ть (-ужу́, -у́жи́шь) imp.; n. кружéние; (whirlpool) водоворóт; (whirlwind) вихрь m.

swish v.i. (cut the air) рассекáть imp., рассéчь (-секу́, -сечёшь, -сéк, -лá) perf. вóздух со свúстом; v.t. (brandish) размáхивать imp.+instr.; v.t. & i. (rustle) шелестéть (-тúшь) imp. (+instr.); шуршáть (-шý, -ши́шь) imp. (+instr.); n. (of whip) свист; (of scythe) взмах со свúстом; (rustle) шéлест, шуршáние.

Swiss n. швейцáрец (-рца), -цáрка; adj. швейцáрский; s. roll, рулéт (с варéньем).

switch n. (electr.) выключáтель m., переключáтель m.; (rly.) стрéлка; (change) изменéние; (twig) прут (прутá; pl. -тья, -тьев); (whip) хлыст (-á); v.t. (whip) удáрять imp., удáрить perf. пру́том, хлысто́м; (electr., fig.; also s. over) переключáть imp., переключи́ть perf.; (wave) махáть (машý, мáшешь) imp., махну́ть perf.+instr.; (change direction) (of conversation etc.) направля́ть imp., напрáвить perf. (разговóр) в другу́ю стóрону; (rly.) переводи́ть (-ожу́, -óдишь) imp., перевести́ (-еду́, -едёшь, -ёл, -á) perf. (train, поезд (pl. -á)) на другóй путь; s. off, выключáть imp., вы́ключить perf.; s. on, включáть imp., включи́ть perf. **switchback** n. америкáнские гóры f. pl. **switchboard** n. коммутáтор, распределúтельный щит (-á).

swivel v.t. & i. вращáть(ся) imp.; n. вертлю́г; s. chair, вращáющийся стул (pl. -лья, -льев).

swollen adj. вздýтый. **swollen-headed** adj. чванлúвый.

swoon n. óбморок; v.i. пáдать imp., упáсть (упадý, -дёшь; упáл) perf. в óбморок.

swoop v.i.: s. down, налетáть imp., налетéть (-ечý, -ети́шь) perf. (on, на+ acc.); n. налёт; at one fell s., одни́м удáром, одни́м мáхом.

sword n. меч (-á), шпáга; s.-fish, меч-ры́ба. **swordsman** n. (искýсно) владéющий sb. холóдным орýжием; (fencer) фехтовáльщик.

sworn adj. (on oath) под прися́гой; (enemy) закля́тый; (friend) закады́чный; (brother) назва́ный.

sybaritic adj. сибари́тский.

sycamore n. я́вор.

sycophancy n. лесть. **sycophant** n. льстец (-а́). **sycophantic** adj. льсти́вый.

syllabic adj. слогово́й; (lit.) силлаби́ческий. **syllable** n. слог (pl. -и, -о́в). **syllabus** n. програ́мма.

symbiosis n. симбио́з.

symbol n. си́мвол, знак. **symbolic(al)** adj. символи́ческий. **symbolism** n. символи́зм. **symbolist** n. символи́ст. **symbolize** v.t. символизи́ровать imp.

symmetrical adj. симметри́ческий. **symmetry** n. симметри́я.

sympathetic adj. сочу́вственный (-ен, -енна); (well-disposed) благожела́тельный; (physiol.) симпати́ческий; (likeable) симпати́чный. **sympathize** v.i. сочу́вствовать imp. (with, + dat.). **sympathizer** n. (supporter) сторо́нник, -ица. **sympathy** n. сочу́вствие; (condolence) соболе́знование; (favour, liking) симпа́тия.

symphonic adj. симфони́ческий. **symphony** n. симфо́ния.

symposium n. симпо́зиум, совеща́ние.

symptom n. симпто́м, при́знак. **symptomatic** adj. симптомати́ческий.

synagogue n. синаго́га.

synchronism n. синхрони́зм. **synchronization** n. синхрониза́ция. **synchronize**
v.t. синхронизи́ровать imp., perf.; (cinema) совмеща́ть imp., совмести́ть perf. (with, с + instr.).

syncopate v.t. (mus.) синкопи́ровать. **syncopation** n. синко́па.

syndicate n. синдика́т; v.t. синдици́ровать imp., perf.

syndrome n. синдро́м.

synod n. сино́д, собо́р. **synodal** adj. синода́льный.

synonym n. сино́ним. **synonymous** adj. синоними́ческий.

synopsis n. конспе́кт. **synoptic(al)** adj. синопти́ческий.

syntactic(al) adj. синтакси́ческий. **syntax** n. си́нтаксис.

synthesis n. си́нтез. **synthesize** v.t. синтези́ровать imp., perf. **synthetic(al)** adj. синтети́ческий. **synthetics** n. синте́тика.

syphilis n. си́филис.

Syrian n. сири́ец (-и́йца), сири́йка; adj. сири́йский.

syringe n. шприц, спринцо́вка; v.t. спринцева́ть imp.

syrup n. сиро́п, па́тока. **syrupy** adj. подо́бный сиро́пу.

system n. систе́ма; (order) строй; (network) сеть (loc. се́ти; pl. -ти, -те́й); (organism) органи́зм. **systematic** adj. системати́ческий. **systematize** v.t. систематизи́ровать imp., perf. **systemic** adj. относя́щийся к всему́ органи́зму.

T

T n.: to a T, точь-в-то́чь (coll.), как раз; T-shirt, те́нниска (coll.); T-square, рейсши́на.

tab n. (loop) пете́лька; (on uniform) петли́ца; (of boot) ушко́ (pl. -ки, -ко́в); keep tabs on, следи́ть imp. за + instr.

tabby n. (cat) полоса́тая ко́шка; (gossip) зла́я спле́тница; (cloth) муа́р.

tabernacle n. (Jewish hist.) ски́ния; (receptacle) дарохрани́тельница.

table n. (furniture; food) стол (-а́); (company) о́бщество за столо́м; (list) табли́ца; (slab) доска́ (acc. -ску, pl. -ски, -со́к, -ска́м), плита́ (pl. -ты); bedside-t., ту́мбочка; t.-cloth, ска́терть; t. of contents, оглавле́ние; t.-spoon, столо́вая ло́жка; t. tennis, tableau   352   tailor

настольный теннис; *v.t.* (*for dis-cussion*) предлагать *imp.*, предложить (-жу́, -жишь) *perf.* на обсужде́ние.

tableau *n.* живая карти́на; (*dramatic situation*) драмати́ческая ситуа́ция.

tableland *n.* плоского́рье.

tablet *n.* (*medicine*) табле́тка; (*memorial t.*) мемориа́льная доска́ (*acc.* -ску́; *pl.* -ски, -со́к, -ска́м); (*name-plate*) дощечка; (*notebook*) блокно́т; (*of soap*) кусо́к (-ска́).

tabloid *n.* (*newspaper*) малоформа́тная газе́та; (*popular newspaper*) бульва́рная газета; *in t. form*, сжа́то.

taboo *n.* табу́ *neut.indecl.*, запреще́ние; *adj.* (*prohibited*) запрещённый (-ён, -ена́); (*consecrated*) свяще́нный (-е́н, -е́нна); *v.t.* налага́ть *imp.*, наложи́ть (-жу́, -жишь) *perf.* табу́ на + *acc.*

tabular *adj.* табли́чный; (*flat*) пло́ский (-сок, -ска́, -ско); (*geol.*) сло́истый, пласти́нчатый. **tabulate** *v.t.* располага́ть *imp.*, расположи́ть (-жу́, -жишь) *perf.* в ви́де табли́ц. **tabulator** *n.* (*on typewriter*) табуля́тор; (*person*) составитель *m.* табли́ц.

tacit *adj.* (*silent*; *implied*) молчали́вый; (*implied*) подразумева́емый. **taciturn** *adj.* молчали́вый, неразгово́рчивый. **taciturnity** *n.* молчали́вость, неразгово́рчивость.

tack[1] *n.* (*nail*) гво́здик, намётка; (*naut.*) галс; (*fig.*) курс; *v.t.* (*fasten*) прикрепля́ть *imp.*, прикрепи́ть *perf.* гво́здиками; (*stitch*) смётывать *imp.*, смета́ть *perf.* на живу́ю ни́тку; (*fig.*) добавля́ть *imp.*, доба́вить *perf.* ((on)to, + *dat.*); *v.i.* (*naut.*; *fig.*) лави́ровать *imp.*

tack[2] *n.* (*for riding*) сбру́я (*collect.*).

tackle *n.* (*requisites*) снасть (*collect.*), принадле́жность *f.pl.*; (*equipment*) обору́дование; (*naut.*) такела́ж; (*block and t.*) тáли (-лей) *pl.*; (*tech., t.-block*) по́лиспáст; (*sport*) блокиро́вка; *v.t.* (*try to overcome*) пыта́ться *imp.*, по ~ *perf.* преодоле́ть; (*get down to*) бра́ться (беру́сь, -рёшься *imp.*, взя́ться (возьму́сь, -мёшься; взя́лся, -ла́сь) *perf.* за + *acc.*; (*work on*) занима́ться *imp.*, заня́ться (займу́сь, -мёшься; заня́лся, -ла́сь) *perf.* + *instr.*;

(*sport*) (*intercept*) перехва́тывать *imp.*, перехвати́ть (-ачу́, -а́тишь) *perf.*; блоки́ровать *imp.*, *perf.*; (*secure ball from*) отнима́ть *imp.*, отня́ть (отниму́, -мешь; о́тнял, -а́, -о) *perf.* мяч у + *gen.*

tacky *adj.* ли́пкий (-пок, -пка́ -пко), кле́йкий.

tact *n.* такт(и́чность). **tactful** *adj.* такти́чный.

tactical *adj.* такти́ческий; (*artful*) ло́вкий (-вок, -вка́, -вко, ло́вки́). **tactician** *n.* та́ктик. **tactics** *n.* та́ктика.

tactile *adj.* осяза́тельный; (*tangible*) осяза́емый.

tactless *adj.* беста́ктный.

tadpole *n.* голова́стик.

taffeta *n.* тафта́; *attrib.* тафтяно́й.

taffrail *n.* гака́борт.

tag *n.* (*label*) ярлы́к (-á), этике́тка, би́рка; (*of lace*) наконе́чник; (*of boot*) ушко́ (*pl.* -ки, -ко́в); (*quotation*) изби́тая цита́та; *v.t.* (*label*) прикрепля́ть *imp.*, прикрепи́ть *perf.* ярлы́к на + *acc.*; *v.i.*: *t. along*, (*follow*) сле́довать *imp.*, по ~ *perf.* по пята́м (after, за + *instr.*); *may I t. along?* мо́жно с ва́ми?

tail *n.* (*of animal, aircraft, kite, pro-cession, etc.*) хвост; (*of shirt*) ни́жний коне́ц (-нца́); (*of hair; of letter*; (*mus.*) (*of note*) хво́стик; (*of coat*) фа́лда; (*of coin*) обра́тная сторона́ (*acc.* -ону) моне́ты; *heads or tails?* орёл и́ли ре́шка? *pl.* (*coat*) фрак; *t.-board*, (*of cart*) откидна́я доска́ (*acc.* -ску; *pl.* -ски, -со́к, -ска́м); (*of lorry*) откидно́й борт (*loc.* -у́; *pl.* -á); *t.-lamp, -light*, за́дний фона́рь (-ря́) *m.*; *t.-spin*, што́пор; *t. wind*, попу́тный ве́тер (-тра); *v.t.* (*fruit etc.*) острига́ть *imp.*, остри́чь (-игу́, -ижёшь, -и́г) *perf.* хво́стики + *gen.*; (*shadow*) высле́живать *imp.*; *v.i.*: *t. away, off*, постепе́нно уменьша́ться *imp.*; (*disappear*) исчеза́ть *imp.*; (*grow silent, abate*) затиха́ть *imp.* **tailcoat** *n.* фрак.

tailor *n.* портно́й *sb.*; *v.t.* шить (шью, шьёшь) *imp.*, сшить (сошью́, -ьёшь) *perf.*; *v.i.* портня́жничать *imp.* (*coll.*); *t.-made*, сши́тый, изгото́вленный на

tailpiece заказ; (*fig.*) приспособленный. **tailoring** *n.* портняжное дело.

tailpiece *n.* (*tур.*) концовка; (*appendage*) задний конец (-нца́).

taint *n.* пятно́ (*pl.* -тна, -тен, -тнам), порок; (*trace*) налёт; (*infection*) зараза; *v.t. & i.* (*spoil*) портить(ся) *imp.*, ис~ *perf.*; (*infect*) заражать(ся) *imp.*, заразить(ся) *perf.* **tainted** *adj.* испорченный (-ен).

take *v.t.* (*var. senses*) брать (беру́, -рёшь; брал, -á, -о) *imp.*, взять (возьму́, -мёшь; взял, -á, -о) *perf.*; (*also seize, capture*) захватывать *imp.*, захватить (-ачу́, -а́тишь) *perf.*; (*receive, accept*) t. breakfast; t. medicine; t. steps) принимать *imp.*, принять (приму́, -мешь; принял, -á, -о) *perf.*; (*convey, escort*) провожать *imp.*, проводить (-ожу́, -о́дишь) *perf.*; (*public transport*) t. a bath, ехать (е́ду, е́дешь) *det.*, по~ *perf.* + *instr.* на + *prep.*; (*photograph*) снимать *imp.*, снять (сниму́, снял, -á, -о) *perf.*; (*occupy*; t. time) занимать *imp.*, занять (займу́, -мёшь; занял, -á, -о) *perf.*; (*impers.*) how long does it take? сколько времени нужно? (*size in clothing*) носить (ношу́, но́сишь) *imp.*; (*exam*) сдавать (-аю́, -аёшь) *imp.*; t. courage, heart, мужа́ться *imp.*; t. cover, прятаться (-ячусь, -ячешься) *imp.*, с~ *perf.*; t. to heart, принимать *imp.*, принять (приму́, -мешь; принял, -á, -о) *perf.* близко к се́рдцу; t. a liking to, полюбить (-блю́сь, -бишься) *perf. impers.* + *dat.* (*coll.*); t. a turning, сворачивать *imp.*, свернуть *perf.* на у́лицу (*street*), доро́гу (*road*); *v.i.* (*be successful*) иметь *imp.* успех; (*of injection*) прививаться *imp.*, приви́ться (-вётся; -вился, -вилась) *perf.*; t. after, походить (-ожу́ -о́дишь) *imp.* на + *acc.*; t. away, (*remove*) убирать *imp.*, убра́ть (уберу́, -рёшь; убра́л, -á, -о) *perf.*; (*subtract*) вычитать *imp.*, вычесть (-чту, -чтешь; -чел, -чла) *perf.*; t.-*away*, магазин, где продают́ на вы́нос; t. back, брать (беру́, берёшь; брал, -á, -о) *imp.*, взять (возьму́, -мёшь; взял, -á, -о) *perf.* обратно, назад; t. down (*in writing*)

записывать *imp.*, записать (-ишу́ -и́шешь) *perf.*; t. s.b., s.th. for, to be, принимать *imp.*, принять (приму́, -мешь; принял, -á, -о) *perf.* за + *acc.*; считать *imp.*, счесть (сочту́, -тёшь; счёл, сочла) *perf.* + *instr.*, за + *instr.*; t. from, отнимать *imp.*, отнять (отниму́, -мешь; о́тнял, -á, -о) *perf.* у, от + *gen.*; t. in, (*clothing*) ушивать *imp.*, ушить (ушью́, -ьёшь) *perf.*; (*understand*) понимать *imp.*, понять (пойму́, -мёшь; по́нял, -á, -о) *perf.*; (*deceive*) обманывать *imp.*, обману́ть (-ну́, -нешь) *perf.*; t. off, (*clothing*) снимать *imp.*, снять (сниму́, -мешь; снял, -á, -о) *perf.*; (*mimic*) передразнивать *imp.*, передразнить (-ню́, -нишь) *perf.*; (*aeroplane*) взлетать *imp.*, взлететь (-ечу́, -ети́шь) *perf.*; t.-off, (*imitation*) подражание, карикату́ра; (*aeron.*) взлёт; t. on, (*undertake*) брать (беру́, -рёшь; брал, -á, -о) *imp.*, взять (возьму́, -мёшь; взял, -á, -о) *perf.* на себя́; (*at game*) сража́ться *imp.*, срази́ться *perf.* с + *instr.* (at, в + *acc.*); t. out, вынимать *imp.*, вы́нуть *perf.*; (*dog*) выводить (-ожу́, -о́дишь) *imp.*, вы́вести (-еду, -едешь; -ел) *perf.* (for a walk, на прогу́лку); (*person*) водить (вожу́, во́дишь) *indet.*, вести (веду́, -дёшь; вёл, -á) *det.*, по~ *perf.*; (*to theatre, restaurant etc.*) приглашать *imp.*, пригласить (-т, в + *acc.*); we took them out every night, мы приглашали их куда́-нибудь ка́ждый ве́чер; t. over, принимать *imp.*, принять (приму́, -мешь; принял, -á, -о) *perf.*; (*seize*) завладевать *imp.*, завладеть *perf.* + *instr.*; t. to, (*thing*) пристраститься *perf.* к + *dat.*; (*person*) привязываться *imp.*, привяза́ться (-яжу́сь, -я́жешься) *perf.* к + *dat.*; t. up, (*enter upon*) бра́ться (беру́сь, -рёшься) *imp.*, взя́ться (возьму́сь, -мёшься; взялся, -лась) *perf.* за + *acc.*; (*challenge*) принимать *imp.*, принять (приму́, -мешь; принял, -á, -о) *perf.*; (*time*) занимать *imp.*, занять (займу́, -мёшь; занял, -á, -о) *perf.*; *n.* (*fishing*) уло́в; (*hunting*) добыча; (*cin.*) дубль *m.*, кинока́др. **taking** *adj.* привлека́тельный.

takings n. сбор, барыши́ m.pl.

talc(um), t. powder n. тальк.

tale n. расска́з, ска́зка; (gossip) спле́тня (gen.pl. -тен); (coll., lie) вы́думка.

talent n. тала́нт. **talented** adj. тала́нтливый.

talisman n. талисма́н.

talk v.i. разгова́ривать imp. (to, with, c + instr.); (gossip) спле́тничать imp., на~ perf.; v.i. & t. говори́ть imp., по~ perf.; t. down to, говори́ть imp. свысока́ c + instr.; t. into, угова́ривать imp., уговори́ть perf. + inf.; t. over, (discuss) обсужда́ть imp., обсуди́ть (-ужу́, -у́дишь) perf.; t. round, (persuade) переубежда́ть imp., переубеди́ть perf.; (discuss, reaching no conclusion) говори́ть imp., по~ perf. о + prep. простра́нно, не каса́ясь существа́ де́ла; t. to, (reprimand) выгова́ривать imp + dat.; n. (conversation) разгово́р, бесе́да; (chatter, gossip) болтовня́ (coll.); (lecture) бесе́да; pl. перегово́ры (-ров) pl. **talkative** adj. болтли́вый, разгово́рчивый. **talker** n. говоря́щий sb.; (chatterer) болту́н (-á) (coll.); (orator) ора́тор. **talking-to** n. (coll.) вы́говор.

tall adj. высо́кий (-о́к, -окá, -о́ко); (in measurements) высото́й, ро́стом в + acc. **tallboy** n. высо́кий комо́д.

tallow n. са́ло. **tallowy** adj. са́льный.

tally n. (score) счёт (-a(y)); (label) би́рка, ярлы́к (-á); (duplicate) ко́пия, дублика́т; v.i. соотве́тствовать (with, + dat.); v.t. подсчи́тывать imp., подсчита́ть perf.

tally-ho interj. ату́!

talon n. ко́готь (-гтя; pl. -гти, -гтей) m.

tamarisk n. тама́риск.

tambourine n. бу́бен (-бна), тамбури́н.

tame adj. ручно́й, приручённый (-ён, -ена́); (submissive) поко́рный; (insipid) ску́чный (-чен, -чна́, -чно); v.t. прируча́ть imp., приручи́ть perf.; (also curb) укроща́ть imp., укроти́ть (-ощу́, -оти́шь) perf. **tameable** adj. укроти́мый. **tamer** n. укроти́тель m.; (trainer) дрессиро́вщик; (fig.) усмири́тель m.

tamp v.t. (road etc.) трамбова́ть imp., у~ perf.; (pack full) набива́ть imp.,

наби́ть (-бью́, -бьёшь) perf.

tamper v.i.: t. with, (meddle) вме́шиваться imp., вмеша́ться perf. в + acc.; (touch) тро́гать imp., тро́нуть perf.; (forge) подде́лывать imp., подде́лать perf.

tampon n. тампо́н.

tan n. (sun-t.) зага́р; (bark) толчёная дубо́вая кора́; adj. желтова́то-кори́чневый; v.t. (of sun) обжига́ть imp., обже́чь (обожжёт; обжёг, обожгла́) perf.; (hide) дуби́ть imp., вы́~ perf.; (beat) (coll.) дуба́сить imp., от~ perf.; v.i. загора́ть imp., загоре́ть (-рю́, -ри́шь) perf.

tandem n. (bicycle) та́ндем; (horses) упря́жка цу́гом; in t., (horses) цу́гом; (single file) гусько́м.

tang n. (taste) ре́зкий при́вкус; (smell) о́стрый за́пах; (tech.) хвостови́к; (characteristic feature) характе́рная черта́.

tangent n. (math.) каса́тельная sb.; (trigon.) та́нгенс; go off at a t., (in conversation etc.) отклоня́ться imp., отклони́ться (-ню́сь, -ни́шься) perf. от те́мы. **tangential** adj. (diverging) отклоня́ющийся.

tangerine n. мандари́н.

tangible adj. осяза́емый.

tangle v.t. & i. запу́тывать(ся) imp., запу́тать(ся) perf.; n. пу́таница.

tango n. та́нго neut.indecl.

tangy adj. о́стрый (остр & остёр, остра́, о́стро); ре́зкий (-зок, -зка́, -зко).

tank n. цисте́рна, бак; (reservoir) водоём; (mil.) танк; attrib. та́нковый; t.-engine, танк-парово́з.

tankard n. кру́жка.

tanker n. (sea) та́нкер; (road) авто-цисте́рна.

tanner n. дуби́льщик. **tannery** n. коже́венный заво́д. **tannin** n. тани́н. **tanning** n. дубле́ние.

tantalize v.t. дразни́ть (-ню́, -нишь) imp. ло́жными наде́ждами; му́чить imp., за~, из~ perf.

tantamount predic. равноси́лен (-льна, -льны) (to, + dat.).

tantrum n. вспы́шка гне́ва, при́ступ раздраже́ния.

tap[1] *n.* (*water etc.*) кран; *on* t., распи́вочно; *v.t.* (*open*) открыва́ть *imp.*, откры́ть (-ро́ю, -ро́ешь) *perf.*; (*pour out*) нали́ва́ть *imp.*, нали́ть (-лью́, -льёшь; на́ли́л, -а́, -о) *perf.*; (*med.*) выка́чивать *imp.*, вы́качать *perf.*; (*draw sap from*) подса́чивать *imp.*, подсочи́ть *perf.*; (*telephone conversation*) подслу́шивать *imp.*; t. telegraph wires, перехва́тывать *imp.*, перехвати́ть (-ачу́, -а́тишь) *perf.* телегра́фное сообще́ние; (*make use of*) испо́льзовать *imp.*, *perf.*

tap[2] *n.* (*knock*) лёгкий стук; *v.t.* стуча́ть (-чу́, -чи́шь) *imp.*, по~ *perf.* в + *acc.*, по + *dat.*; t.-dance, (*v.i.*) отбива́ть *imp.*, отби́ть (отобью́, -ьёшь) *perf.* чечётку; (*n.*) чечётка; t.-dancer, чечёточник, -ица.

tape *n.* (*cotton strip*) тесьма́; (*adhesive, magnetic, measuring, etc.*) ле́нта; (*sport*) ле́нточка; t.-measure, руле́тка; t.-recorder, магнитофо́н; t.-recording, за́пись; *v.t.* (*seal*) закле́ивать *imp.*, закле́ить *perf.*; (*record*) запи́сывать *imp.*, записа́ть (-ишу́, -и́шешь) *perf.* на ле́нту.

taper *n.* (*slender candle*) то́нкая свеча́; (*wick*) вощёный фити́ль (-ля́) *m.*; *v.t. & i.* сужива́ть(ся) *imp.*, су́зить(ся) *perf.* к концу́. **tapering** *adj.* сужива́ющийся к одному́ концу́.

tapestry *n.* гобеле́н.

tapeworm *n.* ле́нточный глист (-а́).

tapioca *n.* тапио́ка.

tapir *n.* тапи́р.

tappet *n.* толка́тель *m.*

tar *n.* дёготь (-гтя́-гтю) *m.*; (*pitch*) смола́; (*tarmac*) гудро́н; *v.t.* ма́зать (ма́жу, -жешь) *imp.*, вы́-, на ~, по ~ *perf.* дёгтем; смоли́ть *imp.*, вы́-, за ~ *perf.*; гудрони́ровать *imp.*, *perf.*

tarantella *n.* таранте́лла.

tarantula *n.* тара́нтул.

tardiness *n.* (*slowness*) медли́тельность; (*lateness*) опозда́ние. **tardy** *adj.* (*slow*) медли́тельный; (*late*) по́здний, запозда́лый.

tare[1] *n.* (*vetch*) ви́ка; *pl.* (*Bibl.*) пле́велы *m.pl.*

tare[2] *n.* (*comm.*) та́ра; (*allowance*) ски́дка на та́ру.

target *n.* мише́нь, цель.

tariff *n.* тари́ф; (*price-list*) прейскура́нт; *v.t.* тарифици́ровать *imp.*, *perf.*

tarmac *n.* (*material*) гудро́н; (*road*) гудрони́рованное шоссе́ *neut.indecl.*; (*runway*) бетони́рованная площа́дка; *v.t.* гудрони́ровать *imp.*, *perf.*

tarn *n.* го́рное озерцо́ (*pl.* -ки, -ко́в).

tarnish *v.t.* де́лать *imp.*, с~ *perf.* ту́склым; (*discredit*) поро́чить *imp.*, о~ *perf.*; *v.i.* ту́скнеть *imp.*, по~ *perf.*; *n.* (*dullness*) ту́склость; (*blemish*) пятно́ (*pl.* -тна, -тен, -тнам). **tarnished** *adj.* ту́склый (-л, -ла́, -ло).

tarpaulin *n.* брезе́нт.

tarragon *n.* эстраго́н.

tarry[1] *adj.* покры́тый дёгтем.

tarry[2] *v.i.* ме́длить *imp.*

tarsus *n.* предплюсна́ (*pl.* -сны, -сен).

tart[1] *adj.* (*taste*) ки́слый (-сел, -сла́, -сло), те́рпкий (-пок, -пка́, -пко); (*biting*) ко́лкий (-лок, -лка́, -лко). **tartness** *n.* ки́слость; ко́лкость.

tart[2] *n.* (*pie*) сла́дкий пиро́г (-а́).

tart[3] *n.* (*girl*) шлю́ха.

tartan *n.* шотла́ндка.

tartar *n.* ви́нный ка́мень (-мня) *m.* **Tartar** *n.* тата́рин (*pl.* -ры, -р), -рка; *to catch a* T., встреча́ть *imp.*, встре́тить *perf.* проти́вника не по си́лам.

task *n.* зада́ча, зада́ние; *take to* t., де́лать *imp.*, с ~ *perf.* вы́говор + *dat.*, отчи́тывать *imp.*, отчита́ть *perf.* (*coll.*); t.-force, операти́вная гру́ппа.

taskmaster *n.* эксплуата́тор.

tassel *n.* ки́сточка, кисть (*pl.* -ти, -те́й).

taste *n.* (*also fig.*) вкус; (*liking*) скло́нность (for, к + *dat.*); (*sample*) про́ба; (*small piece*) ма́ленький кусо́к (-ска́); (*sip*) ма́ленький глото́к (-тка́); t.-bud, вкусова́я лу́ковица; *v.t.* чу́вствовать *imp.*, по~ *perf.* вкус + *gen.*; (*sample*) про́бовать *imp.*, по~ *perf.*; (*fig.*) вкуша́ть *imp.*, вкуси́ть (-ушу́, -уси́шь) *perf.*; (*wine etc.*) дегусти́ровать *imp.*, *perf.*; *v.i.* име́ть *imp.* вкус, привкус (of, + *gen.*). **tasteful** *adj.* (сде́ланный) со вку́сом. **tasteless** *adj.* безвку́сный.

tasting *n.* дегуста́ция. **tasty** *adj.* вку́сный (-сен, -сна́, -сно).

tatter n. (shred) лоскут (-á); pl. лохмо́тья (-ьев) pl. **tattered** adj. обо́рванный; в лохмо́тьях.

tattle n. (chatter) болтовня́; (gossip) спле́тни (-тен) pl.; v.i. (chatter) болта́ть imp.; (gossip) спле́тничать imp., на~ perf.

tattoo[1] n. (mil.) (in evening) вече́рней зари́; (ceremonial) торже́ственная заря́; to beat the t., бить (бью, бьёшь) imp., по~ perf. зо́рю; v.i. бараба́нить imp. па́льцами.

tattoo[2] n. (design) татуиро́вка; v.t. татуи́ровать imp., perf.

taunt n. насме́шка, ко́лкость; v.t. насмеха́ться imp. над+instr. **taunting** adj. насме́шливый.

Taurus n. Теле́ц (-льца́).

taut adj. ту́го натя́нутый, туго́й (туг, -á, -о); (nerves) взви́нченный. **tauten** v.t. & i. ту́го натя́гивать(ся) imp., натяну́ть(ся) (-ну(сь), -нешь(ся)) perf. **tautness** n. натяже́ние.

tautological adj. тавтологи́ческий. **tautology** n. тавтоло́гия.

tavern n. таве́рна.

tawdriness n. мишура́. **tawdry** adj. мишу́рный; (showy) показно́й.

tawny adj. рыжева́то-кори́чневый; t. owl, нея́сыть.

tax n. нало́г; (strain) напряже́ние; direct (indirect) taxes, прямы́е (ко́свенные) нало́ги; t.-collector, сбо́рщик нало́гов; t.-dodger, неплате́льщик; t.-free, освобождённый (-ён, -ена́) от нало́га; v.t. облага́ть imp., обложи́ть (-жу́, -жишь) perf. нало́гом; (strain) напряга́ть imp., напря́чь (-ягу́, -яжёшь; напря́г, -ла́) perf.; (tire) утомля́ть imp., утоми́ть perf.; (patience) испы́тывать imp., испыта́ть perf.; (charge) обвиня́ть imp., обвини́ть perf. (with, в+prep.). **taxable** adj. подлежа́щий обложе́нию нало́гом. **taxation** n. обложе́ние нало́гом. **taxpayer** n. налогоплате́льщик.

taxi n. такси́ neut.indecl.; t.-driver, води́тель m. такси́; t. rank, стоя́нка такси́; v.i. (aeron.) рули́ть imp.

taxidermist n. наби́вщик чу́чел. **taxidermy** n. наби́вка чу́чел.

taximeter n. таксо́метр.

tea n. чай (ча́я(ю); pl. чаи́); attrib. ча́йный; t.-bag, паке́тик с сухи́м ча́ем; t.-caddy, ча́йница; t.-cloth, t.-towel, полоте́нце для посу́ды; t.-cosy, стёганый чехо́льчик (для ча́йника); t.-cup, ча́йная ча́шка; t.-leaf, ча́йный лист (-á; pl. -ья, -ьев); t.-pot, ча́йник; t.-spoon, ча́йная ло́жка; t.-strainer, ча́йное си́течко.

teach v.t. учи́ть (учу́, у́чишь) imp., на~ perf. (person, +acc.; subject, +dat., inf.); обуча́ть imp., обучи́ть (-чу́, -чишь) perf. (person, +acc.; subject, +dat., inf.); преподава́ть (-даю́, -даёшь) imp. (subject +acc.); (coll.) проу́чивать imp., проучи́ть (-чу́, -чишь) perf. **teacher** n. учи́тель (pl. -ля́ & (fig.) -ли) m., ~ница; преподава́тель m., ~ница; t.-training college, педагоги́ческий институ́т. **teaching** n. (instruction) обуче́ние; (doctrine) уче́ние.

teak n. тик; attrib. ти́ковый.

teal n. чиро́к (-рка́).

team n. (sport) кома́нда; (of people) брига́да, гру́ппа; (of horses etc.) упря́жка; t.-mate, (sport) игро́к (-á) той же кома́нды; (at work) това́рищ по рабо́те, член той же брига́ды; t.-work, брига́дная, совме́стная рабо́та; (co-operation) взаимоде́йствие, сотру́дничество; v.i. (t. up) объединя́ться imp., объедини́ться perf. в кома́нду etc.; v.t. запряга́ть imp., запря́чь (-ягу́, -яжёшь; -яг, -ягла́) perf. в упря́жку.

tear[1] n. (rent) проре́ха; (hole) дыра́ (pl. -ры); (cut) разры́в; v.t. рвать (рву, рвёшь; рвал, -á, -о) imp.; (also t. to pieces) разрыва́ть imp., разорва́ть (-ву́, -вёшь; -ва́л, -вала́, -ва́ло) perf.; v.i. рва́ться (рвётся; рва́лся, -ала́сь, -а́ло́сь) imp.; разрыва́ться imp., разорва́ться (-вётся; -ва́лся, -вала́сь, -ва́ло́сь) perf.; (rush) мча́ться (мчусь, мчи́шься) imp.; t. down, off, срыва́ть imp., сорва́ть (-ву́, -вёшь; сорва́л, -á, -о) perf.; t. away, off, отрыва́ть imp., оторва́ть (-ву́, -вёшь; оторва́л, -á, -о) perf.; t. out, вырыва́ть imp., вы́рвать (-ву, -вешь) perf.; t. up, изрыва́ть imp., изорва́ть (-ву́, -вёшь; -ва́л, -вала́, -ва́ло) *perf.*

tear² *n.* (*t.-drop*) слеза́ (*pl.* -ёзы, -ёз, -еза́м); *t.-gas,* слезоточи́вый газ (-а(у)); *perf.*

tearful *adj.* слезли́вый; (*sad*) печа́льный.

tease *v.t.* дразни́ть (-ню́, -нишь) *imp.*; (*wool*) чеса́ть (чешу́, -шешь) *imp.*; (*cloth*) ворсова́ть *imp.*, на~ *perf.*

teaser *n.* (*puzzle*) головоло́мка.

teasel, teazle *n.* (*plant*) ворся́нка; (*device*) ворси́льная ши́шка.

teat *n.* сосо́к (-ска́).

technical *adj.* техни́ческий; (*specialist*) специа́льный; (*formal*) форма́льный; *t. college,* техни́ческое учи́лище. **technicality** *n.* техни́ческая сторона́ (*acc.* -ону; *pl.* -оны, -о́н, -она́м); форма́льность. **technician** *n.* те́хник. **technique** *n.* те́хника; (*method*) ме́тод. **technology** *n.* техноло́гия, те́хника. **technological** *adj.* технологи́ческий. **technologist** *n.* техно́лог.

teddy-bear *n.* медвежо́нок (-жо́нка; *pl.* -жа́та, -жа́т).

tedious *adj.* ску́чный (-чен, -чна́, -чно), утоми́тельный. **tedium** *n.* ску́ка, утоми́тельность.

teem¹ *v.i.* (*abound in, be abundant*) кише́ть (-ши́т) *imp.* (with,+ *instr.*); (*abound in*) изоби́ловать (with imp. (with, + *instr.*).

teem² *v.i.*: *it is teeming,* дождь льёт как из ведра́.

teenage *adj.* ю́ношеский. **teenager** *n.* подро́сток (-тка). **teens** *n.* во́зраст от трина́дцати до девятна́дцати лет.

teeter *v.i.* кача́ться *imp.*, качну́ться *perf.*; пошáтываться *imp.*

teethe *v.i.*: *the child is teething,* у ребёнка прорéзываются зу́бы. **teething** *n.* прорéзывание зубо́в; *t. ring,* де́тское зубно́е кольцо́; *t. troubles,* (*fig.*) нача́льные пробле́мы.

teetotal *adj.* трéзвый (-в, -ва́, -во). **teetotalism** *n.* трéзвенность. **teetotaller** *n.* трéзвенник.

tele- *in comb.* теле-. **telecommunication(s)** *n.* да́льняя связь. **telegram** *n.* телегра́мма. **telegraph** *n.* телегра́ф; *attrib.* телегра́фный; *v.t.* телеграфи́ровать *imp.*, *perf.*; *t.-pole,* телегра́фный

столб (-а́). **telegraphese** *n.* телегра́фный стиль *m.* **telegraphic** *adj.* телегра́фный. **telegraphist** *n.* телеграфи́ст. **telegraphy** *n.* телегра́фия. **telemeter** *n.* телеме́тр. **telemetry** *n.* телеметри́я. **telepathic** *adj.* телепати́ческий. **telepathy** *n.* телепа́тия. **telephone** *n.* телефо́н; *attrib.* телефо́нный; (*message*) телефони́ровать *imp.*, *perf.* + *acc.*, о + *prep.*; (*person*) звони́ть *imp.*, по ~ *perf.* (по телефо́ну) + *dat.*; *t. box,* телефо́нная бу́дка; *t. directory,* телефо́нная кни́га; *t. exchange,* телефо́нная ста́нция; *t. number,* но́мер (*pl.* -а́) телефо́на. **telephonic** *adj.* телефо́нный. **telephonist** *n.* телефони́ст, ~ ка. **telephony** *n.* телефони́я. **telephoto lens** *n.* телеобъекти́в. **telephotography** *n.* телефотогра́фия. **teleprinter** *n.* телета́йп. **telescope** *n.* телеско́п; *v.t. & i.* телескопи́чески скла́дывать(ся) *imp.*, сложи́ть(ся) (сложу́, сло́жишь) *perf.* **telescopic** *adj.* телескопи́ческий. **televise** *v.t.* пока́зывать *imp.*, показа́ть (-ажу́ -а́жешь) *perf.* по телеви́дению; передава́ть (-даю́, -даёшь) *imp.*, переда́ть (-а́м, -а́шь, -а́ст, -ади́м; пéредал, -á, -о) *perf.* по телеви́дению. **television** *n.* телеви́дение; (*set*) телеви́зор; *attrib.* телевизио́нный. **telex** *n.* те́лекс.

tell *v.t.* (*relate*) расска́зывать *imp.*, рассказа́ть (-ажу́, -а́жешь) *perf.* (*thing told,* + *acc.*; *person told,* + *dat.*); (*utter, inform*) говори́ть *imp.*, сказа́ть (скажу́, -жешь) *perf.* (*thing uttered,* + *acc.*; *thing informed about,* о + *prep.*; *person informed,* + *dat.*); (*order*) веле́ть (-лю́, -ли́шь) *imp.*, *perf.* + *dat.*; *t. one thing from another,* отлича́ть *imp.*, отличи́ть *perf.* + *acc.* от + *gen.*; *v.i.* (*have an effect*) сказáываться *imp.*, сказа́ться (скажу́сь, -жешься) *perf.* (on, на + *prep.*); *all told,* ито́го́; *t. fortunes,* гада́ть *imp.*, по ~ *perf.*; *t. off,* (*select*) отбира́ть *imp.*, отобра́ть (отберу́, -рёшь; отобра́л, -á, -о) *perf.*; (*rebuke*) отдéлывать *imp.*, отдéлать *perf.*; *t. on, t. tales about,* ябéдничать *imp.*, на~*perf.* на + *acc.* **teller** *n.* (*of story*) расска́зчик, -ица; (*of votes*) счётчик голосо́в; (*in bank*) касси́р, ~ ша. **telling**

adj. (*effective*) эффе́ктный; (*significant*) многозначи́тельный; *t.-off*, вы́говор.

telltale *n.* доно́счик, спле́тник; *adj.* преда́тельский.

temerity *n.* (*rashness*) безрассу́дство; (*audacity*) де́рзость.

temper *n.* (*metal*) зака́л; (*character*) нрав, хара́ктер; (*mood*) настрое́ние; (*anger*) гнев; *lose one's t.*, выходи́ть (-ожу́, -о́дишь) *imp.*, вы́йти (вы́йду, -дешь; вы́шел, -шла) *perf.* из себя́; *v.t.* (*metal*) отпуска́ть *imp.*, отпусти́ть (-ущу́, -у́стишь) *perf.*; (*moderate*) смягча́ть *imp.*, смягчи́ть *perf.*

temperance *n.* (*moderation*) уме́ренность; (*sobriety*) тре́звенность.

temperament *n.* темпера́мент; (*mus.*) темпера́ция. **temperamental** *adj.* темпера́ментный.

temperate *adj.* уме́ренный (-ен, -енна).

temperature *n.* температу́ра; (*high t.*) повы́шенная температу́ра; *take s.b.'s t.*, измеря́ть *imp.*, изме́рить *perf.* температу́ру + *dat.*

tempest *n.* бу́ря. **tempestuous** *adj.* бу́рный (-рен, бу́рна́, -рно), бу́йный (бу́ен, бу́йна́, -но).

template *n.* шабло́н.

temple[1] *n.* (*relig.*) храм.

temple[2] *n.* (*anat.*) висо́к (-ска́).

tempo *n.* темп.

temporal *adj.* (*secular*) мирско́й, све́тский; (*of time*) временно́й.

temporary *adj.* вре́менный.

temporize *v.i.* приспоса́бливаться *imp.*, приспосо́биться *perf.* ко вре́мени и обстоя́тельствам; (*hesitate*) ме́длить *imp.*

tempt *v.t.* искуша́ть *imp.*, искуси́ть *perf.*; соблазня́ть *imp.*, соблазни́ть *perf.*; *t. fate*, испы́тывать *imp.*, испыта́ть *perf.* судьбу́. **temptation** *n.* искуше́ние, собла́зн. **tempter, -tress** *n.* искуси́тель *m.*, ~ница. **tempting** *adj.* зама́нчивый, соблазни́тельный.

ten *adj., n.* де́сять (-ти́, -тью́); (*collect.; 10 pairs*) де́сятеро (-ры́х); (*cards; number 10*) деся́тка; (*time*) де́сять (часо́в); (*age*) де́сять лет; (*set of 10; 10 years, decade*) деся́ток (-тка); *in tens*, деся́тками. **tenth** *adj., n.* деся́тый; (*fraction*) деся́тая (часть (*pl.*

-ти, -те́й)); (*date*) деся́тое (число́); (*mus.*) де́цима.

tenable *adj.* (*strong*) про́чный (-чен, -чна́, -чно, про́чны); (*logical*) логи́чный; (*of office*) могу́щий быть за́нятым.

tenacious *adj.* це́пкий (-пок, -пка́, -пко); (*stubborn*) упо́рный. **tenacity** *n.* це́пкость; упо́рство.

tenancy *n.* (*renting of property*) наём помеще́ния; (*period*) срок (-а(у)) аре́нды. **tenant** *n.* наима́тель *m.*, ~ница; аренда́тор.

tench *n.* линь (-ня́) *m.*

tend[1] *v.i.* (*be apt*) име́ть скло́нность (to, к + *dat.*, + *inf.*); (*move*) направля́ться *imp.*, напра́виться *perf.*

tend[2] *v.t.* (*look after*) (*person*) уха́живать *imp.* за + *instr.*; (*machine*) обслу́живать *imp.*, обслужи́ть (-жу́, -жишь) *perf.*

tendency *n.* тенде́нция, скло́нность. **tendentious** *adj.* тенденцио́зный.

tender[1] *v.t.* (*offer*) предлага́ть *imp.*, предложи́ть (-жу́, -жишь) *perf.*; (*money*) предоставля́ть *imp.*, предоста́вить *perf.*; *v.i.* (*make t. for*) подава́ть (-даю́, -даёшь) *imp.*, пода́ть (-а́м, -а́шь, -а́ст, -ади́м; по́дал, -а́, -о) *perf.* зая́вку (на торга́х); *n.* предложе́ние; *legal t.*, зако́нное платёжное сре́дство.

tender[2] *n.* (*rly.*) те́ндер; (*naut.*) посы́льное су́дно (*pl.* -да́, -до́в).

tender[3] *adj.* (*delicate, affectionate*) не́жный (-жен, -жна́, -жно, не́жны́); (*soft*) мя́гкий (-гок, -гка́, -гко); (*sensitive*) чувстви́тельный. **tenderness** *n.* не́жность; (*softness*) мя́гкость.

tendon *n.* сухожи́лие.

tendril *n.* у́сик.

tenement *n.* (*dwelling-house*) жило́й дом (-а(у); *pl.* -а́); (*flat*) кварти́ра; *t.-house*, многокварти́рный дом (-а(у); *pl.* -а́).

tenet *n.* до́гмат, при́нцип.

tennis *n.* те́ннис; *attrib.* те́ннисный; *t.-player*, тенниси́ст, ~ ка.

tenon *n.* шип (-а́).

tenor *n.* (*structure*) укла́д; (*direction*) направле́ние; (*purport*) о́бщее содержа́ние; (*mus.*) те́нор.

tense¹ *n.* вре́мя *neut.*

tense² *v.t.* напряга́ть *imp.*, напря́чь (-ягу́, -яжёшь; напря́г, -ла́) *perf.*; *adj.* (*tight*) натя́нутый; (*strained*) напряжённый (-ён, -ённа); (*excited*) возбуждённый (-ён, -ена́); (*nervous*) не́рвный (не́рвен, нервна́, не́рвно).

tenseness *n.* натя́нутость, напряжённость. **tensile** *adj.* растяжи́мый. **tension** *n.* напряже́ние (*also fig.*; *electr.*); натяже́ние.

tent *n.* пала́тка; *t.-peg*, ко́лышек (-шка) для пала́тки; *t. pole*, пала́точная сто́йка.

tentacle *n.* щу́пальце (*gen.pl.* -лец & -льцев).

tentative *adj.* (*experimental*) про́бный; (*preliminary*) предвари́тельный.

tenterhooks *n.:* *be on t.*, сиде́ть (сижу́, сиди́шь) *imp.* как на иго́лках.

tenth *see* ten.

tenuous *adj.* (*slender, subtle*) то́нкий (-нок, -нка́, -нко, то́нки́); (*flimsy*) непро́чный (-чен, -чна́, -чно); (*insignificant*) незначи́тельный; (*rarefied*) разрежённый.

tenure *n.* (*possession*) владе́ние; (*office*) пребыва́ние в до́лжности; (*period*) срок (-а(у)) (*of possession*) владе́ния, (*of office*) пребыва́ния в до́лжности.

tepid *adj.* теплова́тый.

tercentenary, **-ennial** *n.* трёхсотле́тие; *adj.* трёхсотле́тний.

term *n.* (*period*) срок (-а(у)); (*univ.*) семе́стр; (*school*) че́тверть (*pl.* -ти, -те́й); (*math.*) член; (*leg.*) се́ссия; (*technical word, expression*) те́рмин; (*expression*) выраже́ние; (*med.*) норма́льный пери́од бере́менности; *pl.* (*conditions*) усло́вия *neut.pl.* (*of payment*, опла́ты)*.*; (*relations*) отноше́ния *neut.pl.*; *on good terms*, в хоро́ших отноше́ниях; (*language*) язы́к (-а́), выраже́ния *neut.pl.*; *come to terms with*, (*resign oneself to*) покоря́ться *imp.*, покори́ться *perf.* к + *dat.*; (*come to an agreement with*) приходи́ть (-ожу́, -о́дишь) *imp.*, прийти́ (приду́, -дёшь; пришёл, -шла́) *perf.* к соглаше́нию с + *instr.*; *v.t.* называ́ть *imp.*, назва́ть (назову́, -вёшь; назва́л, -а́,

-о) *perf.*; *I do not t. impatience a shortcoming*, я не называ́ю нетерпе́ние недоста́тком.

termagant *n.* сварли́вая же́нщина, меге́ра (*coll.*).

terminable *adj.* ограни́ченный сро́ком, сро́чный (-чен, -чна, -чно).

terminal *adj.* коне́чный, заключи́тельный; (*univ.*) семестро́вый; (*school*) четвертно́й; (*leg.*) сессио́нный; *n.* (*electr.*) зажи́м; (*computer*) термина́л; (*terminus*) (*rly.*) коне́чная ста́нция, (*bus etc.*) коне́чная остано́вка; (*aeron.*) (*airport buildings*) зда́ния *neut.pl.* аэропо́рта; *air-t.*, аэровокза́л.

terminate *v.t.* & *i.* конча́ть(ся) *imp.*, ко́нчить(ся) *perf.* (*in*, + *instr.*). **termination** *n.* коне́ц (-нца́), оконча́ние.

terminology *n.* терминоло́гия. **terminological** *adj.* терминологи́ческий.

terminus *n.* (*rly.*) коне́чная ста́нция, (*bus etc.*) коне́чная остано́вка.

termite *n.* терми́т.

tern *n.* кра́чка.

terra *n.:* *t. firma*, су́ша; *t. incognita*, неизве́стная страна́.

terrace *n.* терра́са; (*row of houses*) ряд (-á *with* 2, 3, 4, *loc.* -у; *pl.* -ы́) домо́в; *v.t.* терраси́ровать *imp.*, *perf.*

terracotta *n.* террако́та; *adj.* терракотовый.

terrain *n.* ме́стность.

terrapin *n.* (*turtle*) во́дная черепа́ха.

terrestrial *adj.* земно́й; (*ground*) назе́мный.

terrible *adj.* (*frightening, dreadful, very bad*) ужа́сный; (*excessive*) стра́шный (-шен, -шна́, -шно, стра́шны́) (*coll.*). **terribly** *adv.* ужа́сно, стра́шно.

terrier *n.* терье́р.

terrific *adj.* ужаса́ющий; (*coll.*) (*huge*) огро́мный; (*splendid*) великоле́пный. **terrify** *v.t.* ужаса́ть *imp.*, ужасну́ть *perf.*

territorial *adj.* территориа́льный. **territory** *n.* террито́рия, (*fig.*) о́бласть, сфе́ра.

terror *n.* у́жас, страх; (*person, thing causing*) терро́р. **terrorism** *n.* террори́зм. **terrorist** *n.* террори́ст, ~ ка. **terrorize** *v.t.* терроризи́ровать *imp.*, *perf.*

terse adj. сжа́тый, кра́ткий (-ток, -тка́, -тко). **terseness** n. сжа́тость, кра́ткость.

tertiary adj. трети́чный; (education) вы́сший.

tessellated adj. моза́ичный.

test n. испыта́ние, про́ба; (exam) экза́мен; контро́льная sb. (coll.); (standard) крите́рий; (analysis) ана́лиз; (chem., reagent) реакти́в; t. ban, запреще́ние испыта́ний я́дерного ору́жия; t. case, де́ло (pl. -ла́) име́ющее принципиа́льное значе́ние для разреше́ния аналоги́чных дел; t. flight, испыта́тельный полёт; t. paper, (exam) экзаменацио́нный биле́т; t. pilot, лётчик-испыта́тель m.; t.-tube, проби́рка; v.t. (try out) испы́тывать imp., испыта́ть perf.; (check up on) проверя́ть imp., прове́рить perf.; (give exam to) экзаменова́ть imp., про ~ perf.; (chem.) подверга́ть imp., подве́ргнуть (-г) perf. де́йствию реакти́ва.

testament n. завеща́ние; Old, New T., Ве́тхий, Но́вый заве́т. **testamentary** adj. завеща́тельный. **testator** n. завеща́тель m., ~ ница.

testicle n. яи́чко (pl. -чки, -чек).

testify v.i. свиде́тельствовать imp. (to, в по́льзу + gen.; against, про́тив + gen.); v.t. (declare) заявля́ть imp., заяви́ть (-влю́, -вишь) perf.; (be evidence of) свиде́тельствовать о + prep.

testimonial n. рекоменда́ция, характери́стика. **testimony** n. показа́ние, -ния pl., свиде́тельство; (declaration) заявле́ние.

testy adj. раздражи́тельный.

tetanus n. столбня́к (-á).

tetchy adj. раздражи́тельный.

tête-à-tête n., adv. тет-а-те́т.

tether n. при́вязь; be at, come to the end of one's t., дойти́ (дойду́, -дёшь; дошёл, -шла́) perf. до то́чки; v.t. привя́зывать imp., привяза́ть (-яжу́, -я́жешь) perf.

tetra- in comb. четырёх-, тетра-. **tetrahedron** n. четырёхгра́нник. **tetralogy** n. тетрало́гия.

Teutonic adj. тевто́нский.

text n. текст; (theme) те́ма. **textbook** n. уче́бник.

textile adj. тексти́льный; n. ткань; pl. тексти́ль m. (collect.).

textual adj. текстово́й.

texture n. факту́ра; (consistency) консисте́нция; (quality) ка́чество; (structure) строе́ние.

thalidomide n. талидоми́д.

than conj. (comparison) чем; other t., (except) кро́ме + gen.; none other t., не кто ино́й, как; nothing else t., не что ино́е, как.

thank v.t. благодари́ть imp., по ~ perf. (for, за + acc.); t. God, сла́ва Бо́гу; t. you, спаси́бо, благодарю́ вас; n.pl. благода́рность; thanks to (good result) благодаря́ + dat.; (bad result) из-за + gen. **thankful** adj. благода́рный. **thankless** adj. неблагода́рный. **thank-offering** n. благода́рственная же́ртва. **thanksgiving** n. (service of) благода́рственный моле́бен (-бна); благодаре́ние.

that dem.adj., dem.pron. тот (та, то; pl. те); э́тот (э́та, э́то; pl. э́ти); t. which, тот (та, то; те) кото́рый; rel.pron. кото́рый; conj. что; (purpose) что́бы; adv. так, до тако́й сте́пени.

thatch n. (straw) соло́менная, (reed) тростнико́вая кры́ша; v.t. крыть (кро́ю, кро́ешь) imp., по ~ perf. соло́мой (straw), тростнико́м (reed).

thaw v.t. раста́пливать imp., растопи́ть (-плю́, -пишь) perf.; v.i. та́ять (та́ет) imp., рас ~ perf.; (fig.) смягча́ться imp., смягчи́ться perf.; n. о́ттепель f.; (fig.) смягче́ние.

the adj. definite article not translated; adv. тем; the ... the, чем ... тем; t. more t. better, чем бо́льше тем лу́чше.

theatre n. теа́тр; (lecture etc.) аудито́рия; (operating) операцио́нная sb.; t.-goer, театра́л. **theatrical** adj. театра́льный.

theft n. воровство́, кра́жа.

their, theirs poss.pron. их; свой (-оя́, -оё; -ои́).

theism n. теи́зм. **theist** n. теи́ст. **theistic(al)** adj. теисти́ческий.

theme *n.* тéма, предмéт. **thematic** *adj.* темати́ческий.

themselves *pron.* (*emph.*) (они́) са́ми (-и́х, -и́м, -и́ми); (*refl.*) себя́ (себé, собо́й); -ся (*suffixed to v.t.*).

then *adv.* (*at that time*) тогда́, в то врéмя; (*after that*) пото́м, зате́м; *now and t.*, врéмя от врéмени; *conj.* в тако́м слу́чае, тогда́; *n.* то врéмя *neut.*; *adj.* тогда́шний.

thence *adv.* отту́да; (*from that*) из э́того. **thenceforth, -forward** *adv.* с того́/э́того врéмени.

theodolite *n.* теодоли́т.

theologian *n.* тео́лог. **theological** *adj.* теологи́ческий. **theology** *n.* теоло́гия.

theorem *n.* теорéма. **theoretical** *adj.* теорети́ческий. **theorist** *n.* теорéтик.

theorize *v.i.* теоретизи́ровать *imp.*

theory *n.* тео́рия.

theosophy *n.* теосо́фия.

therapeutic(al) *adj.* терапевти́ческий. **therapeutics** *n.* терапéвтика. **therapy** *n.* терапи́я.

there *adv.* (*place*) там; (*direction*) туда́; *interj.* вот! ну! *t. is, are,* есть, имéется (-éются); *t. you are,* (*on giving s.th.*) пожа́луйста. **thereabouts** *adv.* (*near*) поблизости; (*approximately*) приблизи́тельно. **thereafter** *adv.* по́сле э́того. **thereby** *adv.* таки́м о́бразом. **therefore** *adv.* поэ́тому, слéдовательно. **therein** *adv.* в э́том; (*in that respect*) в э́том отношéнии. **thereupon** *adv.* зате́м.

thermal *adj.* теплово́й, терми́ческий; *t. capacity,* теплоёмкость; *t. springs,* горя́чие исто́чники *m.pl.*; *t. unit,* едини́ца теплоты́.

thermo- *in comb.* термо-, тепло-. **thermocouple** *n.* термопа́ра. **thermodynamics** *n.* термодина́мика. **thermoelectric(al)** *adj.* термоэлектри́ческий. **thermometer** *n.* термо́метр, гра́дусник. **thermonuclear** *adj.* термоя́дерный. **thermos** *n.* тéрмос. **thermostat** *n.* термоста́т.

thesis *n.* (*proposition*) тéзис; (*dissertation*) диссертáция.

they *pron.* они́ (их, им, и́ми, о них).

thick *adj.* то́лстый (-т, -та́, -то, то́лсты́); (*in measurements*) толщино́й в + *acc.*; (*line*) жи́рный (-рен, -рна́,

-рно); (*dense*) пло́тный (-тен, -тна́, -тно, пло́тны́); густо́й (-т, -та́, -то, гу́сты́); (*turbid*) му́тный (-тен, -тна́, -тно, му́тны́); (*stupid*) тупо́й (туп, -а́, -о, ту́пы)́; *t.-headed,* тупоголо́вый (*coll.*); *t.-skinned,* толстоко́жий; в гу́ща; (*of fight*) разга́р; *through t. and thin,* не колéблясь; несмотря́ ни на каки́е препя́тствия. **thicken** *v.t.* утолща́ть(ся) *imp.*, утолсти́ть(ся) *perf.*; (*make, become denser*) сгуща́ть(ся) *imp.*, сгусти́ть(ся) *perf.*; *v.i.* (*become more intricate*) усложня́ться *imp.*, усложни́ться *perf.* **thicket** *n.* ча́ща. **thickness** *n.* (*also dimension*) толщина́; (*density*) пло́тность, густота́; (*layer*) слой (*pl.* слои́). **thickset** *adj.* корена́стый.

thief *n.* вор (*pl.* -ы, -о́в), ~о́вка. **thieve** *v.i.* ворова́ть *imp.*; *v.t.* красть (-аду́, -адёшь; -ал) *imp.*, у ~ *perf.* **thievery** *n.* ворово́во. **thievish** *adj.* ворова́тый.

thigh *n.* бедро́ (*pl.* бёдра, -дер, -драм). *t.-bone,* бе́дренная кость (*pl.* -ти, -тéй).

thimble *n.* напёрсток (-тка).

thin *adj.* (*slender; not thick*) то́нкий (-нок, -нка́, -нко, то́нки́); (*lean*) худо́й (худ, -а́, -о, ху́ды́); (*too liquid*) жи́дкий (-док, -дка́, -дко); (*sparse*) рéдкий (-док, -дка́, -дко); (*weak*) сла́бый (-б, -ба́, -бо); *v.t. & i.* дéлать(ся) *imp.*, с ~ *perf.* то́нким, жи́дким; *v.i.*: *t. down,* худéть *imp.*, по ~ *perf.*; *t. out,* редéть *imp.*, по ~ *perf.*; *v.t.*: *t. out,* прорéживать *imp.*, проредить *perf.*

thing *n.* вещь (*pl.* -щи, -щéй); (*object*) предмéт; (*matter*) дéло (*pl.* -ла́); *poor t.*, (*person*) бедня́жка *m. & f.* (*coll.*); *pl. (belongings*) пожи́тки (-ков) *pl.* (*coll.*); (*clothes*) оде́жда; (*implements*) у́тварь (*collect.*); (*affairs*) дела́ *neut.pl.*

thingamy *n.* (*person*) как бишь его́? (*thing*) шту́ка.

think *v.t. & i.* ду́мать *imp.*, по ~ *perf.* (*about, of,* o + *prep.*, над + *instr.*); (*consider*) счита́ть *imp.*, счесть (сочту́, -тёшь; счёл, сочла́) *perf.* (*to be,* + *instr.*, за + *acc.*; *that,* что); *v.i.* (*think, reason*) мы́слить *imp.*; (*intend*) намерева́ться *imp.* (*of doing,* + *inf.*); *t. out,* проду́мывать *imp.*, проду́мать perf.; *t. over*, обду́мывать *imp.*, обду́мать *perf.*; *t. up, of*, приду́мывать *imp.*, приду́мать *perf.* **thinker** *n.* мысли́тель *m.* **thinking** *adj.* мы́слящий; *n.* (*reflection*) размышле́ние; *to my way of t.*, по моему́ мне́нию.

thinly *adv.* то́нко. **thinness** *n.* то́нкость; (*leanness*) худоба́. **thin-skinned** *adj.* (*fig.*) оби́дчивый.

third *adj., n.* тре́тий (-тья, -тье); (*fraction*) треть (*pl.* -ти, -те́й); (*date*) тре́тье (число́); (*mus.*) те́рция; *t. party*, тре́тья сторона́ (*acc.* -ону; *pl.* -оны, -о́н, -она́м); *t.-rate*, третьестепе́нный; *T. World*, стра́ны *f.pl.* тре́тьего ми́ра.

thirst *n.* жа́жда (for, +*gen.* (*fig.*)); *v.i.* (*fig.*) жа́ждать (-ду, -дешь) *imp.* (for, +*gen.*). **thirsty** *adj.*: *be t.*, хоте́ть (хочу́, -чешь) *imp.* пить.

thirteen *adj., n.* трина́дцать (-ти, -тью); (*age*) трина́дцать лет. **thirteenth** *adj., n.* трина́дцатый; (*date*) трина́дцатое (число́).

thirtieth *adj., n.* тридца́тый; (*date*) тридца́тое (число́). **thirty** *adj., n.* три́дцать (-ти, -тью); (*age*) три́дцать лет; *pl.* (*decade*) тридца́тые го́ды (-до́в) *m.pl.*

this *dem.adj., dem.pron.* э́тот (э́та, э́то; *pl.* э́ти); *t. way*, сюда́; *like t.*, вот так.

thistle *n.* чертополо́х.

thither *adv.* туда́.

thong *n.* реме́нь (-мня́) *m.*

thorax *n.* грудна́я кле́тка.

thorn *n.* шип (-а́), колю́чка (*coll.*). **thorny** *adj.* колю́чий; (*fig.*) терни́стый; (*ticklish*) щекотли́вый.

thorough *adj.* основа́тельный, тща́тельный; (*complete*) по́лный (-лон, -лна́, по́лно), соверше́нный (-нен, -нна). **thoroughbred** *adj.* чистокро́вный, поро́дистый. **thoroughfare** *n.* прое́зд, (*walking*) прохо́д. **thoroughgoing** *adj.* радика́льный. **thoroughly** *adv.* (*completely*) вполне́, соверше́нно. **thoroughness** *n.* основа́тельность, тща́тельность.

though *conj.* хотя́; несмотря́ на то, что; *as t.*, как бу́дто; *adv.* одна́ко, всё-таки.

thought *n.* мысль; (*heed*) внима́ние; (*meditation*) размышле́ние; (*intention*)

наме́рение; *pl.* (*opinion*) мне́ние. **thoughtful** *adj.* заду́мчивый; (*considerate*) внима́тельный, забо́тливый. **thoughtless** *adj.* необду́манный (-ан, -анна); (*inconsiderate*) невнима́тельный. **thought-reader** *n.* тот, кто уме́ет чита́ть чужи́е мы́сли.

thousand *adj., n.* ты́сяча (*instr.* -чей & -чью). **thousandth** *adj., n.* ты́сячный; (*fraction*) ты́сячная (часть (*pl.* -ти, -те́й)).

thraldom, thrall *n.* (*state*) ра́бство; *in t.*, обращённый (-ён, -ена́) в ра́бство.

thrash *v.t.* бить (бью, бьёшь) *imp.*, по ~ *perf.*; *t. out*, (*discuss*) тща́тельно обсужда́ть *imp.*, обсуди́ть (-ужу́ -у́дишь) *perf.*; *v.i.*: *t. about*, мета́ться (мечу́сь, -чешься) *imp.* **thrashing** *n.* (*beating*) взбу́чка (*coll.*).

thread *n.* ни́тка, нить (*also fig.*); (*of screw etc.*) наре́зка, резьба́; *v.t.* (*needle*) продева́ть *imp.*, проде́ть (-е́ну, -е́нешь) *perf.* ни́тку в+*acc.*; (*beads etc.*) нани́зывать *imp.*, наниза́ть (-ижу́, -и́жешь) *perf.*; *t. one's way*, пробира́ться *imp.*, пробра́ться (-беру́сь, -берёшься; -бра́лся, -брала́сь, -бра́ло́сь) *perf.* (through, че́рез+*acc.*). **threadbare** *adj.* (*clothes etc.*) потёртый, изно́шенный; (*hackneyed*) изби́тый.

threat *n.* угро́за. **threaten** *v.t.* угрожа́ть *imp.*, грози́ть *imp.*, при ~ *perf.* (*person*, +*dat.*; with, +*instr.*; to do, +*inf.*).

three *adj., n.* три (трёх, -ём, -емя́, -ёх); (*collect.; 3 pairs*) тро́е (-ои́х); (*cards, number 3*) тро́йка; (*time*) три (часа́); (*age*) три го́да; *t. times*, три́жды; *t. times four*, три́жды четы́ре; *t.-cornered*, треуго́льный; *t.-dimensional*, трёхме́рный; *t.-ply*, (*wood*) трёхсло́йный; (*rope*) тройно́й; *t.-quarters*, три че́тверти; **threefold** *adj.* тройно́й; *adv.* втро́йне. **threesome** *n.* тро́йка.

thresh *v.t.* молоти́ть (-очу́, -о́тишь) *imp.* **threshing** *n.* молотьба́; *t.-floor*, ток (*loc.* -у́; *pl.* -а́) *m.*; *t.-machine*, молоти́лка.

threshold *n.* поро́г.

thrice *adv.* три́жды.

thrift *n.* бережли́вость; (*plant*) арме́-

рия. **thriftless** *adj.* расточи́тельный. **thrifty** *adj.* бережли́вый.

thrill *n.* (*trepidation, excitement*) тре́пет, волне́ние; (*s.th. thrilling*) что-л. захва́тывающее; *vt. & i.* си́льно волнова́ть(ся) *imp.*, вз ~ *perf.* **thriller** *n.* приключе́нческий, детекти́вный, (*novel*) рома́н, (*film*) фильм. **thrilling** *adj.* волну́ющий, захва́тывающий.

thrive *v.i.* процвета́ть *imp.*; (*grow*) разраста́ться *imp.*, разрасти́сь (-тётся); разрося́-сла́сь) *perf.*

throat *n.* го́рло. **throaty** *adj.* горта́нный; (*hoarse*) хри́плый (-л, -ла́, -ло).

throb *v.i.* (*heart*) си́льно би́ться (бётся) *imp.*; пульси́ровать *imp.*; *his head throbbed,* кровь стуча́ла у него́ в виска́х; *n.* бие́ние; пульса́ция.

throe *n.* о́страя боль; *pl.* му́ки *f.pl.*; (*of birth*) родовы́е му́ки *f.pl.*; (*of death*) аго́ния.

thrombosis *n.* тромбо́з.

throne *n.* трон, престо́л; *come to the t.,* вступа́ть *imp.*, вступи́ть (-плю́, -пишь) *perf.* на престо́л.

throng *n.* толпа́ (*pl.* -пы); *v.i.* толпи́ться *imp.*; *v.t.* заполня́ть *imp.*, запо́лнить *perf.* (толпо́й).

throttle *n.* (*gullet*) гло́тка; (*tech.*) дро́ссель *m.*; *v.t.* (*strangle*) души́ть (-шу́, -шишь) *imp.*, за ~ *perf.*; (*tech.*) дроссели́ровать *imp., perf.*; *t. down,* сбавля́ть *imp.*, сба́вить *perf.* ско́рость + *gen.*

through *prep.* (*across, via, t. opening*) че́рез + *acc.*; (*esp. t. thick of*) сквозь + *acc.*; (*air, streets etc.*) по + *dat.*; (*agency*) посре́дством + *gen.*; (*reason*) из-за + *gen.*; *adv.* наскво́зь; (*from beginning to end*) с нача́ла до конца́; *be t. with,* (*s.th.*) ока́нчивать *imp.*, око́нчить *perf.*; (*s.b.*) порва́ть (-ву́, -вёшь; порва́л, -а́, -о) *perf.* с + *instr.*; *put t.,* (*on telephone*) соединя́ть *imp.*, соедини́ть *perf.*; *t. and t.,* до конца́, соверше́нно; *adj.* сквозно́й. **throughout** *adv.* повсю́ду, во всех отноше́ниях; *prep.* по всему́ (всей, всему́); *dat.* всем) + *dat.*; (*from beginning to end*) с нача́ла до конца́ + *gen.*

throw *n.* бросо́к (-ска́), броса́ние; *v.t.*

броса́ть *imp.*, бро́сить *perf.*; кида́ть *imp.*, ки́нуть *perf.*; (*rider*) сбра́сывать *imp.*, сбро́сить *perf.*; (*pottery*) формова́ть *imp.*, с ~ *perf.*; (*party*) устра́ивать *imp.*, устро́ить *perf.*; *t. oneself at,* набра́сываться *imp.*, набро́ситься *perf.* на + *acc.*; *t. oneself into,* броса́ться *imp.*, бро́ситься *perf.* в + *acc.*; *t. about,* разбра́сывать *imp.*, разброса́ть *perf.*; *t. money about,* сори́ть *imp.* деньга́ми; *t. aside, away,* отбра́сывать *imp.*, отбро́сить *perf.*; *t. away, out,* выбра́сывать *imp.*, вы́бросить *perf.*; *t. back,* отбра́сывать *imp.*, отбро́сить *perf.* наза́д; *t.-back,* регре́сс, возвра́т к про́шлому, атави́зм; *t. down,* сбра́сывать *imp.*, сбро́сить *perf.*; *t. in,* (*add*) добавля́ть *imp.*, доба́вить *perf.*; (*sport*) вбра́сывать *imp.*, вбро́сить *perf.*; *t.-in,* вбра́сывание мяча́; *t. off,* сбра́сывать *imp.*, сбро́сить *perf.*; *t. open,* распа́хивать *imp.*, распахну́ть *perf.*; *t. out,* (*see also t. away*) (*expel*) выгоня́ть *imp.*, вы́гнать (вы́гоню, -нишь) *perf.*; (*reject*) отверга́ть *imp.*, отве́ргнуть (-г(нул), -гла) *perf.*; *t. over, t. up,* (*abandon, renounce*) броса́ть *imp.*, бро́сить *perf.*

thrush[1] *n.* (*orn.*) дрозд (-а́).

thrush[2] *n.* (*disease*) моло́чница.

thrust *n.* (*shove*) толчо́к (-чка́); (*lunge*) вы́пад; (*blow, stroke, mil.*) уда́р; (*tech., of rocket*) тя́га; *v.t.* (*shove*) толка́ть *imp.*, толкну́ть *perf.*; (*t. into, out of*) give quickly, carelessly*) сова́ть (сую́, суёшь) *imp.*, су́нуть *perf.*; *t. one's way,* пробива́ть *imp.*, проби́ть (-бью́, -бьёшь) *perf.* себе́ доро́гу; *t. aside,* отта́лкивать *imp.*, оттолкну́ть *perf.*; *t. out,* высо́вывать *imp.*, вы́сунуть *perf.*

thud *n.* глухо́й звук, стук; *v.i.* (*fall with t.*) па́дать *imp.*, (у)па́сть (у)паду́, -дёшь; (у)па́л) *perf.* с глухи́м сту́ком; шлёпаться *imp.*, шлёпнуться *perf.* (*coll.*).

thug *n.* головоре́з (*coll.*).

thumb *n.* большо́й па́лец (-льца); *thumbs down,* знак отрица́ния; *thumbs up!* недурно́! *under the t. of,* под башмако́м у + *gen.*; *v.t.: t. through,* перели́стывать *imp.*, перелиста́ть *perf.*; *t.* a lift, голосова́ть *imp.*, про~ *perf.* (*coll.*). **thumbscrew** *n.* тиски́ (-ко́в) *pl.* для больши́х па́льцев.

thump *n.* (*heavy blow*) тяжёлый уда́р; (*thud*) глухо́й звук, стук; *v.t.* наноси́ть (-ошу́, -о́сишь) *imp.*, нанести́ (-есу́, -есёшь; -ёс, -есла́) *perf.* уда́р+*dat.*; колоти́ть (-очу́, -о́тишь) *imp.*, по~ *perf.* в+*acc.*, по+*dat.*; *v.i.* (*strike with t.*) би́ться (бьюсь, бьёшься) *imp.* с глухи́м шу́мом.

thunder *n.* гром (*pl.* -ы, -о́в); (*fig.*) гро́хот; *t.-cloud*, грозова́я ту́ча; *v.i.* греме́ть (-млю, -ми́шь) *imp.*; грохота́ть (-очу́, -о́чешь) *imp.*; (*fulminate* (*fig.*)) мета́ть (мечу́, -чешь) *imp.*; *it thunders*, гром греми́т. **thunderbolt** *n.* уда́р мо́лнии; (*fig.*) гром среди́ я́сного не́ба. **thunderclap** *n.* уда́р гро́ма. **thunderous** *adj.* громово́й. **thunderstorm** *n.* гроза́ (*pl.* -зы). **thunderstruck** *adj.* (*fig.*) как гро́мом поражённый (-ён, -ена́). **thundery** *adj.* грозово́й.

Thursday *n.* четве́рг (-а́).

thus *adv.* (*in this way*) так, таки́м о́бразом; (*accordingly*) ита́к; *t. far*, до сих пор.

thwack *n.* си́льный уда́р; *v.t.* бить (бью, бьёшь) *imp.*, по~ *perf.*

thwart *v.t.* меша́ть *imp.*, по~ *perf.*+ *dat.*; (*plans*) расстра́ивать *imp.*, расстро́ить *perf.*; *n.* (*bench*) ба́нка.

thyme *n.* тимья́н.

thyroid *n.* (*t. gland*) щитови́дная железа́.

tiara *n.* тиа́ра.

tibia *n.* больша́я берцо́вая кость (*pl.* -ти, -те́й).

tic *n.* тик.

tick[1] *n.* (*noise*), ти́канье; (*moment*) моме́нт, мину́точка; (*mark*) пти́чка; *v.i.* ти́кать *imp.*, ти́кнуть *perf.*; *v.t.* отмеча́ть *imp.*, отме́тить *perf.* пти́чкой; *t. off*, (*scold*) отде́лывать *imp.*, отде́лать *perf.* (*coll.*).

tick[2] *n.* (*mite*) клещ (-а́).

tick[3] *n.* (*of mattress*) чехо́л (-хла́); (*of pillow*) на́воло(ч)ка; (*ticking*) тик.

tick[4] *n.* (*coll.*) креди́т; *on t.*, в креди́т.

ticket *n.* биле́т; (*label*) ярлы́к (-а́); (*season t.*) ка́рточка; (*cloakroom t.*)

номеро́к (-рка́); (*receipt*) квита́нция; *t.-collector*, контролёр; *t.-office*, (биле́тная ка́сса; *t.-punch*, компо́стер; *v.t.* прикрепля́ть *imp.*, прикрепи́ть *perf.* ярлы́к к+*dat.*

tickle *n.* щеко́тка; *v.t.* щекота́ть (-очу́, -о́чешь) *imp.*, по~ *perf.*; (*amuse*) весели́ть *imp.*, по~, раз~ *perf.*; *v.i.* щекота́ть (-о́чет) *imp.*, по~ *perf. impers.*; *my throat tickles*, у меня́ щеко́чет в го́рле. **ticklish** *adj.* щекотли́вый (*also fig.*); *to be t.*, боя́ться (бою́сь, бои́шься) *imp.* щеко́тки.

tidal *adj.* прили́во-отли́вный; *t. wave*, прили́вная волна́ (*pl.* -ны, -н, волна́м).

tiddlywinks *n.* (игра́ в) блю́шки (-шек) *pl.*

tide *n.* прили́в и отли́в; *high t.*, прили́в; *low t.*, отли́в; (*current, tendency*) тече́ние; *the t. turns*, (*fig.*) собы́тия принима́ют друго́й оборо́т; *t.-mark*, отме́тка у́ровня по́лной воды́; *v.t.*: *t. over*, помога́ть *imp.*, помо́чь (-огу́, -о́жешь; -о́г, -огла́) *perf.*+*dat.* of *person* справля́ться (*difficulty*, c+ *instr.*); *will this money t. you over?* вы протя́нете с э́тими деньга́ми?

tidiness *n.* опря́тность, аккура́тность.

tidy *adj.* опря́тный, аккура́тный; (*considerable*) поря́дочный; *v.t.* убира́ть *imp.*, убра́ть (уберу́, -рёшь; убра́л, -а́, -о) *perf.*; приводи́ть (-ожу́, -о́дишь) *imp.*, привести́ (-еду́, -едёшь; -ёл, -ела́) *perf.* в поря́док.

tie *n.* (*garment*) га́лстук; (*string, lace*) завя́зка; (*link, bond, tech.*) связь; (*equal points etc.*) ра́вный счёт; *end in a t.*, зака́нчиваться *imp.*, зако́нчиться *perf.* вничью́; (*match*) матч; (*mus.*) ли́га; (*burden*) обу́за; *pl.* (*bonds*) у́зы (уз) *pl.*; *t.-pin*, була́вка для га́лстука; *v.t.* свя́зывать *imp.*, связа́ть (свяжу́, -жешь) *perf.* (*also fig.*); (*t. up*) завя́зывать *imp.*, завяза́ть (-яжу́, -я́жешь) *perf.*; (*restrict*) ограни́чивать *imp.*, ограни́чить *perf.*; *t. down*, (*fasten*) привя́зывать *imp.*, привяза́ть (-яжу́, -я́жешь) *perf.*; *t. up*, (*tether*) привя́зывать *imp.*, привяза́ть (-яжу́, -я́жешь) *perf.*; (*parcel*) перевя́зывать *imp.*, перевяза́ть (-яжу́, -я́жешь) *perf.*; *v.i.* (*be tied*) завя́зываться *imp.*, завяза́ться (-я́жется) *perf.*; (*sport*) равня́ть *imp.*, с~

perf. счёт; сыгра́ть *perf.* вничью́; *t. in, up, with,* совпада́ть *imp.,* совпа́сть (-адёт, -а́л) *perf.* c + *instr.*

tier *n.* ряд (-а́ *with* 2, 3, 4, *loc.* -у́; *pl.* -ы́), я́рус.

tiff *n.* размо́лвка; *v.i.* ссо́риться *imp.,* по~ *perf.* (with, c + *instr.*).

tiger *n.* тигр. **tigress** *n.* тигри́ца.

tight *adj.* (*compact*) пло́тный (-тен, -тна́, -тно, пло́тны́); (*cramped*) те́сный (-сен, -сна́, -сно), у́зкий (-зок, -зка́, -зко); (*impenetrable*) непроница́емый; (*strict*) стро́гий (-г, -га́, -го); (*tense, taut*) туго́й (туг, -а́, -о), натя́нутый; *t.-fisted,* скупо́й (-п, -па́, -по); *t. corner,* (*fig.*) тру́дное положе́ние. **tighten** *v.t. & i.* натя́гивать(ся) *imp.,* натяну́ть(ся) *perf.*; (*clench, contract*) сжима́ть(ся) *imp.,* сжа́ть(ся) (сожму́(сь), -мёшь(ся)) *perf.*; *t. one's belt,* потуже затя́гивать *imp.,* затяну́ть *perf.* по́яс (*also fig.*); *t. up,* (*discipline etc.*) подтя́гивать *imp.,* подтяну́ть *perf.* (*coll.*) **tightly** *adv.* (*strongly*) про́чно; (*closely, cramped*) те́сно. **tightness** *n.* теснота́; напряжённость. **tightrope** *n.* ту́го натя́нутый кана́т. **tights** *n.* колго́тки (-ток) *pl.*

tilde *n.* ти́льда.

tile *n.* (*roof*) черепи́ца (*also collect.*); (*decorative*) ка́фель *m.* (*also collect.*); *v.t.* крыть (кро́ю, кро́ешь) *imp.,* по~ *perf.* черепи́цей, ка́фелем. **tiled** *adj.* (*roof*) черепи́чный; (*floor*) ка́фельный.

till[1] *prep.* до + *gen.*; *not t.,* то́лько (Friday, в пя́тницу; the next day, на сле́дующий день); *conj.* пока́ не; *not t.,* то́лько когда́.

till[2] *n.* ка́сса.

till[3] *v.t.* возде́лывать *imp.,* возде́лать *perf.* **tillage** *n.* обрабо́тка земли́.

tiller[1] *n.* земледе́лец (-льца).

tiller[2] *n.* (*naut.*) ру́мпель *m.*

tilt *n.* накло́н; (*naut., aeron.*) крен; on the *t.,* в накло́нном положе́нии; at full *t.,* и́зо всех сил; по́лным хо́дом; *v.t. & i.* наклоня́ть(ся) *imp.,* наклони́ть(ся) (-ню́(сь), -нишь(ся)) *perf.*; (*heel (over)*) крени́ть(ся) *imp.,* на~ *perf.*

timber *n.* лесоматериа́л, лес (-а(у)) (*collect.*); (*beam*) ба́лка (*pl.* -ки); (*naut.*) ти́мберс. **timbered** *adj.* обши́тый де́ревом; деревя́нный. **timbering** *n.* (*work*) пло́тничная рабо́та.

timbre *n.* тембр.

time *n.* вре́мя *neut.*; (*occasion*) раз (*pl.* -зы, -з); (*term*) срок (-а(у)); (*period*) пери́од, эпо́ха; (*mus.*) темп, такт; (*sport*) тайм; *pl.* (*period*) времена́ *pl.*; (*in comparison*) раз; *five times as big,* в пять раз бо́льше; (*multiplication*) *four times four,* четы́режды четы́ре; *five times four,* пя́тью четы́ре; *t. and t. again, t. after t.,* не раз, ты́сячу раз; *at a t.,* ра́зом, одновре́менно; *at the t.,* в э́то вре́мя; *at times,* по времена́м; *at the same t.,* в то же вре́мя; *before my t.,* до меня́; *for a long t.,* до́лго; (*up to now*) давно́; *for the t. being,* пока́; *from t. to t.,* вре́мя от вре́мени; *in t.,* (*early enough*) во́-время; (*with t.*) со вре́менем; *in good t.,* своевре́менно; *in t. with,* в такт + *dat.*; *in no t.,* момента́льно; *on t.,* во́-время; *one at a t.,* по одному́; *I do not have t. for him,* (*fig.*) я не хочу́ тра́тить вре́мя на него́; *have t. to,* (*manage*) успева́ть *imp.,* успе́ть *perf.* + *inf.*; *have a good t.,* хорошо́ проводи́ть (-ожу́, -о́дишь) *imp.,* провести́ (-еду́, -едёшь; -ёл, -ела́) *perf.* вре́мя; *it is t.,* пора́ (to, + *inf.*); *what is the t.?* кото́рый час? *kill t.,* убива́ть *imp.,* уби́ть (убью́, -ьёшь) *perf.* вре́мя; *work full (part) t.,* рабо́тать *imp.* по́лный (непо́лный) рабо́чий день; *t.-bomb,* бо́мба заме́дленного де́йствия; *t.-consuming,* отнима́ющий мно́го вре́мени; *t.-honoured,* освящённый века́ми; *t.-lag,* отстава́ние во вре́мени; (*tech.*) запа́здывание; *t.-limit,* преде́льный срок (-а(у)); *t. off,* о́тпуск; *t.-signal,* сигна́л вре́мени; *t.-signature,* та́ктовый разме́р; *v.t.* (*choose*) выбира́ть *imp.,* вы́брать (-беру, -берешь) *perf.* вре́мя + *gen.*; (*arrange t.*) назнача́ть *imp.,* назна́чить *perf.* вре́мя + *gen.*; (*ascertain t.*) засека́ть *imp.,* засе́чь (-еку́, -ечёшь,

засе́к, -ла́, -ло) *perf.* вре́мя; хроно-
метри́ровать *imp.*, *perf.* **timekeeper** *n.*
(*person*) та́бельщик; (*sport*) хроно-
метри́ст. **timeless** *adj.* ве́чный. **timely**
adj. своевре́менный. **timepiece** *n.*
часы́ (-со́в) *pl.*; хроно́метр. **timetable**
n. расписа́ние; (*of work*) гра́фик.
timid *adj.* ро́бкий (-бок, -бка́, -бко),
засте́нчивый. **timidity** *n.* ро́бость,
засте́нчивость. **timorous** *adj.* боязли́-
вый.
tin *n.* (*metal*) о́лово; t. plate, бе́лая
жесть; *attrib.* оловя́нный, жестяно́й;
(*container*) (консе́рвная) ба́нка, жес-
тя́нка; (*cake-t.*) фо́рма; (*baking t.*)
про́тивень (-вня) *m.*; t. foil, оловя́н-
ная фо́льга; t.-opener, консе́рвный
нож (-а́); *v.t.* (*coat with t.*) луди́ть
(лужу́, лу́ди́шь) *imp.*, вы~, по~ *perf.*;
(*pack in t.*) консерви́ровать *imp.*,
perf.; tinned food, консе́рвы (-вов) *pl.*
tinny *adj.* (*thin*) то́нкий (-нок, -нка́,
-нко, то́нки́); (*piano etc.*) издаю́щий
металли́ческий звук; (*sound*) металли́ческий. **tinsmith** *n.* жестя́нщик.
tincture *n.* (*colour, fig.*) отте́нок (-нка);
(*taste, fig.*) при́вкус; (*fig.*) налёт; t.
(*colour; fig.*) слегка́ окра́шивать *imp.*,
окра́сить *perf.*; (*flavour*) придава́ть
(-даю́, -даёшь) *imp.*, прида́ть (-а́м,
-а́шь, -а́ст, -ади́м; при́дал, -а́, -о)
perf. вкус + *dat.*
tinder *n.* (*colour, fig.*) трут; t.-box, тру́тница.
tinge *n.* (*colour; fig.*) отте́нок (-нка);
(*taste; fig.*) при́вкус; (*fig.*) налёт; *v.t.*
(*also fig.*) слегка́ окра́шивать *imp.*,
окра́сить *perf.*
tingle *n.* пока́лывание, (*from cold*)
пощи́пывание, *v.i.* (*sting*) коло́ть
(ко́лет) *imp. impers.*; my fingers t., у
меня́ ко́лет па́льцы; his nose tingled
with the cold, моро́з пощи́пывал ему́
нос; (*burn*) горе́ть (гори́т) *imp.*;
(*jingle*) звене́ть (-ни́т) *imp.* в уша́х
(*person*, y + *gen.*).
tinker *n.* ме́дник, луди́льщик; *v.i.*
(*work as a t.*) рабо́тать *imp.* луди́ль-
щиком; t. with, вози́ться (вожу́сь,
во́зишься) *imp.* c + *instr.*
tinkle *n.* звон, звя́канье; *v.i.(t.)* звене́ть
(-ню́, -ни́шь) *imp.* (+ *instr.*); звя́кать
imp., звя́кнуть *perf.* + *instr.*; (*on*

instrument) бренча́ть (-чу́, -чи́шь)
imp. (*on*, на + *prep.*).
tinsel *n.* мишура́ (*also fig.*); *attrib.*
мишу́рный.
tint *n.* отте́нок (-нка); (*faint t.*) бле́д-
ный тон (*pl.* -а́); *v.t.* слегка́ окра́ши-
вать *imp.*, окра́сить *perf.* **tinted** *adj.*
окра́шенный; t. glasses, тёмные очки́
(-ко́в) *pl.*
tiny *adj.* о́чень ма́ленький; кро́шечный
(*coll.*).
tip[1] *n.* (*end*) ко́нчик; (*of stick, spear etc.*)
наконе́чник; *v.t.* приставля́ть *imp.*,
приста́вить *perf.* наконе́чник к + *dat.*;
be on the t. of s.b.'s tongue, верте́ться
(ве́ртится) *imp.* на языке́ y + *gen.*
tip[2] *n.* (*money*) чаевы́е (-ы́х) *pl.*; (*advice*)
сове́т, намёк; (*private information*)
све́дения *neut.pl.*, полу́ченные час́т-
ным о́бразом; (*dump*) сва́лка; (*slight
push*) лёгкий толчо́к (-чка́); *v.t.* & *i.*
наклоня́ть(ся) *imp.*, наклони́ть(ся)
(-ню́(сь), -ни́шь(ся)) *perf.*; *v.t.* (*hit
lightly*) слегка́ ударя́ть *imp.*, уда́рить
perf.; (*give*) дава́ть (даю́, даёшь)
imp., дать (дам, дашь, даст, дади́м;
дал, -а́, да́ло́, -и) *perf.* (*person*, + *dat.*;
money, де́ньги на чай, *information*,
ча́стную информа́цию); t. out,
выва́ливать *imp.*, вы́валить *perf.*; t.
over, up, (*v.t.* & *i.*) опроки́ды-
вать(ся) *imp.*, опроки́нуть(ся) *perf.*;
t. up, back, (*seat*) отки́дывать *imp.*,
отки́нуть *perf.*; t. the scales, (*fig.*)
реша́ть *imp.*, реши́ть *perf.* исхо́д
де́ла; t.-up lorry, самосва́л.
tipple *n.* (алкого́льный) напи́ток (-тка);
v.i. выпива́ть *imp.*; *v.t.* & *i.* попива́ть
imp. (*coll.*). **tippler** *n.* пья́ница *m.* & *f.*
tipster *n.* жучо́к (-чка́).
tipsy *adj.* подвы́пивший.
tiptoe *n.*: on t., на цы́почках.
tip-top *adj.* первокла́ссный, превосхо́д-
ный.
tirade *n.* тира́да.
tire[1] (*metal*) колёсный банда́ж (-а́).
tire[2] *see* tyre.
tire[3] *v.t.* (*weary*) утомля́ть *imp.*,
утоми́ть *perf.*; (*bore*) надоеда́ть *imp.*,
надое́сть (-е́м, -е́шь, -е́ст, -еди́м; -е́л)
perf. + *dat.*; *v.i.* утомля́ться *imp.*,
утоми́ться *perf.*; устава́ть (устаю́,

-аёшь) *imp.*, уста́ть (-а́ну, -а́нешь) *perf.* тиза́ль adj. уста́лый, утомлённый; be t. of: I am t. of him, он мне надое́л; I am t. of playing, мне надое́ло игра́ть; t. out, изму́ченный. **tiredness** *n.* уста́лость. **tireless** adj. неутоми́мый. **tiresome** adj. утоми́тельный, надое́дливый. **tiring** adj. утоми́тельный.

tiro *n.* новичо́к (-чка́).

tissue *n.* ткань; (*handkerchief*) бума́жная салфе́тка; t.-paper, папиро́сная бума́га.

tit¹ *n.* (*bird*) сини́ца.

tit² *n.*: t. for tat, зуб за́ зуб.

titanic adj. (*huge*) титани́ческий.

titbit *n.* ла́комый кусо́к (-ска́); (*news*) пика́нтная но́вость.

tithe *n.* деся́тая часть (*pl.* -ти, -те́й); (*hist.*) десяти́на.

titillate *v.t.* щекота́ть (-очу́, -о́чешь) *imp.*, по~ *perf.*; прия́тно возбужда́ть *imp.*, возбуди́ть *perf.*

titivate *v.t. & i.* (*coll.*) прихора́шивать(ся) *imp.* (*coll.*).

title *n.* (*of book etc.*) назва́ние; (*heading*) загла́вие; (*rank*) ти́тул, зва́ние; (*cin.*) титр; (*sport*) зва́ние чемпио́на, t.-deed, докуме́нт, даю́щий пра́во со́бственности; t.-holder, чемпио́н; t.-page, ти́тульный лист (*pl.* -ы́); t.-role, загла́вная роль (*pl.* -ли, -ле́й). **titled** adj. титуло́ванный.

titter *n.* хихи́канье; *v.i.* хихи́кать *imp.*, хихи́кнуть *perf.*

tittle *n.* чу́точка, ка́пелька; t.-tattle, болтовня́ (*coll.*).

titular adj. номина́льный; титуло́ванный.

to *prep.* (*town, a country, theatre, school, etc.*) в + *acc.*; (*the sea, the moon, the ground, post-office, meeting, concert, north, etc.*) на + *acc.*; (*the doctor; towards, up* t.; t. *one's surprise etc.*) к + *dat.*; (*with accompaniment of*) под + *acc.*; (*in toast*) за + *acc.*; (*time*): ten minutes t. three, без десяти́ три; (*compared with*) в сравне́нии с + *instr.*; it is ten t. one that, де́вять из десяти́ за то, что; t. the left (right), нале́во (напра́во); (*in order to*) что́бы + *inf.*; adv.: shut the door t., закро́йте дверь; come

t., приходи́ть (-ожу́, -о́дишь) *imp.*, прийти́ (-йду́, -йдёшь; пришёл, -шла́) *perf.* в созна́ние; bring t. приводи́ть (-ожу́, -о́дишь) *imp.*, привести́ (-еду́, -едёшь; ёл, -ела́) *perf.* в созна́ние; t. and fro, взад и вперёд.

toad *n.* жа́ба. **toadstool** *n.* пога́нка.

toady *n.* подхали́м; *v.t.* льстить *imp.*, по~ *perf.* + *dat.*; пресмыка́ться, ни́зкопокло́нничать *imp.* (то, пе́ред + *instr.*).

toast *n.* (*bread*) поджа́ренный хлеб; (*drink*) тост; t.-master, тамада́ *m.*; t.-rack, подста́вка для поджа́ренного хле́ба; *v.t.* (*bread*) поджа́ривать *imp.*, поджа́рить *perf.*; (*drink*) пить (пью, пьёшь; пил, -а́, -о) *imp.*, вы~ *perf.* за здоро́вье + *gen.* **toaster** *n.* то́стер.

tobacco *n.* таба́к; *attrib.* таба́чный; t.-pouch, кисе́т. **tobacconist** *n.* торго́вец (-вца) таба́чными изде́лиями; t.'s shop, таба́чный магази́н.

toboggan *n.* табо́гган, са́ни (-не́й) *pl.*; *v.i.* ката́ться *imp.* на саня́х.

today adv. сего́дня; (*nowadays*) в на́ши дни; *n.* сего́дняшний день (дня) *m.*; today's newspaper, сего́дняшняя газе́та; the writers of t., совреме́нные писа́тели *m.pl.*

toddle *v.i.* ковыля́ть *imp.* (*coll.*); (*learn to walk*) учи́ться (учу́сь, у́чишься) *imp.* ходи́ть; (*stroll*) прогу́ливаться *imp.* **toddler** *n.* ребёнок (-нка; *pl.* де́ти, -те́й), начина́ющий ходи́ть; малы́ш (-а́) (*coll.*).

toddy *n.* горя́чий пунш.

to-do *n.* сумато́ха, суета́.

toe *n.* па́лец (-льца) ноги́; (*of sock etc.*) носо́к (-ска́); t.-cap, носо́к (-ска́); from top to t., с головы́ до пят; *v.t.* (*touch with t.*) каса́ться *imp.*, косну́ться *perf.* носко́м + *gen.*; t. the line, (*fig.*) подчиня́ться *imp.*, подчини́ться *perf.* тре́бованиям.

toffee *n.* (*substance*) ири́с; (*a t.*) ири́ска (*coll.*).

toga *n.* то́га.

together adv. вме́сте, сообща́; (*simultaneously*) одновре́менно; t. with, вме́сте с + *instr.*; all t., все вме́сте; get t., собира́ть(ся) *imp.*, собра́ть(ся) (-беру́, -берёшь; -бра́л(ся), -брала́(сь),

-брáло, -брáлóсь) perf.; join t. объединя́ть(ся) imp., объедини́ть(ся) perf. (with, c + instr.).

toggle n. (button) продолговáтая (деревя́нная) пу́говица.

toil n. тяжёлый труд; v.i. труди́ться (-ужу́сь, -у́дишься) imp.; (drag oneself along) тащи́ться (тащу́сь, -щишься) imp. **toiler** n. тру́женик, -ица.

toilet n. туалéт; t.-paper, туалéтная бумáга; t. water, туалéтная водá (acc. вóду).

toilsome adj. утоми́тельный.

token n. (sign) знак; (keepsake) подáрок (-рка) на пáмять; (coupon, counter) талóн, жетóн; as a t. of, в знак + gen.; attrib. символи́ческий; t. resistance, ви́димость сопротивлéния; by the same t., (similarly) к тому́ же; (moreover) крóме тогó.

tolerable adj. (bearable) терпи́мый; (satisfactory) удовлетвори́тельный, снóсный (coll.). **tolerance** n. терпи́мость; (tech.) дóпуск; (med.) толерáнтность. **tolerant** adj. терпи́мый; (med.) толерáнтный. **tolerate** v.t. терпéть (-плю́, -пишь) imp., по ~ perf.; (allow) допускáть imp., допусти́ть (-ущу́, -у́стишь) perf.; (med.) быть толерáнтным. **toleration** n. терпи́мость.

toll[1] n. (duty) пóшлина; take its t., наноси́ть (-ошу́) imp., нанести́ (-сёт; нанёс, -еслá) perf. тяжёлый урóн; t.-bridge, платны́й мост (мостá, loc. -ý; pl. -ы́); t.-gate, застáва, где взимáется сбор.

toll[2] v.t. (мéдленно и мéрно) ударя́ть imp., удáрить perf. в кóлокол; v.i. звони́ть imp., по ~ perf. (мéдленно и мéрно).

tom(-cat) n. кот (-á).

tomahawk n. томагáвк; v.t. бить (бью, бьёшь) imp., по ~ perf. томагáвком.

tomato n. помидóр; attrib. томáтный.

tomb n. моги́ла. **tombstone** n. моги́льная плитá (pl. -ты).

tomboy n. сорванéц (-нцá).

tome n. большáя (тяжёлая) кни́га.

tomfoolery n. дурáчества neut.pl.

tommy-gun n. автомáт.

tomorrow adv. зáвтра; n. зáвтрашний

день (дня) m.; t. morning, зáвтра у́тром; the day after t., послезáвтра; see you t., (coll.) до зáвтра.

tom-tit n. сини́ца.

tom-tom n. тамтáм.

ton n. (a lot) мáсса.

tonal adj. тонáльный. **tonality** n. тонáльность. **tone** n. тон (pl. -ы (mus. & fig.), -á (colour)); (atmosphere, mood) атмосфéра, настроéние; (med.) тóнус; t.-arm, звукоснимáтель m.; t. control, регуля́ция тéмбра; t.-deaf, с слáбым музыкáльным слýхом; v.t. придавáть (-даю́, -даёшь) imp., придáть (-áм, -áшь, -áст, -адим; при́дал, -á, -о) perf. желáтельный тон + dat.; v.i. (harmonize) гармони́ровать imp. (with, c + instr.); t. down, смягчáть(ся) imp., смягчи́ть(ся) perf.; t. up, уси́ливать imp., уси́лить perf.; (med.) тонизи́ровать imp., perf.

tongue n. (var. senses) язы́к (-á); (of shoe) язычóк (-чкá); t.-in-cheek, с насмéшкой, иронически; t.-tied, косноязы́чный; t.-twister, скороговóрка; give t., (of dog) поддавáть (-аю́, -аёшь) imp., поддáть (-áм, -áшь, -áст, -ади́м; пóддал, -á, -о) perf. гóлос; (of person) грóмко говори́ть imp.; hold one's t., держáть (-жý, -жишь) imp. язы́к за зубáми; lose one's t., проглáтывать imp., проглоти́ть (-очý, -óтишь) perf. язы́к; put out one's t., покáзывать imp., показáть (-ажý, -áжешь) perf. язы́к.

tongs n. щипцы́ (-цóв) pl.

tonic n. (med.) тонизи́рующее срéдство; (mus.) тóника; adj. (med.) тонизи́рующий; (mus.) тони́ческий.

tonight adv. сегóдня вéчером; n. сегóдняшний вéчер.

tonnage n. тоннáж, грузовмести́мость; (charge) корáбельный сбор.

tonsil n. миндáлина. **tonsillitis** n. ангина.

tonsure n. тонзýра; v.t. выбривáть imp., вы́брить (-рею, -реешь) perf. тонзýру + dat.

too adv. сли́шком; (also) тáкже, тóже; (very) óчень; (indeed) действи́тельно; (moreover) к тому́ же; none t., не сли́шком.

tool n. инструме́нт; (*machine-t.*) стано́к (-нка́); (*implement*; *fig.*) ору́дие; *t.-box*, я́щик с инструме́нтами.

toot n. гудо́к (-дка́); v.i. гуде́ть (-ди́т) *imp.*; (*give a hoot*) дава́ть (даю́, даёшь) *imp.*, дать (дам, дашь, даст, дади́м) *imp.*; дал, -а́, да́ло, -и) *perf.* гудо́к; v.t. (*blow*) труби́ть *imp.* в + *acc.*

tooth n. зуб (*pl.* -ы, -о́в); (*tech.*) зубе́ц (-бца́); *attrib.* зубно́й; *t.-brush*, зубна́я щётка; *t.-comb*, ча́стый гребень (-бня) *m.*; *false teeth*, вставны́е зу́бы (-бо́в) *pl.*; *first t.*, моло́чный зуб (*pl.* -ы, -о́в); *loose t.* шата́ющийся зуб (*pl.* -ы, -о́в); *second t.*, постоя́нный зуб (*pl.* -ы, -о́в); *t. and nail*, (*fiercely*) не на жизнь, а на́ смерть; (*energetically*) энерги́чно; *in the teeth of*, (*in defiance of*) напереко́р + *dat.*; (*directly against*) пря́мо про́тив + *gen.*; *have one's teeth attended to*, лечи́ть (-чу́, -чишь) зу́бы (-бо́в) *pl.*; *he has cut a t.*, у него́ проре́зался зуб. **toothache** n. зубна́я боль. **toothed** adj. зубча́тый. **toothless** adj. беззу́бый. **toothpaste** n. зубна́я па́ста. **toothpick** n. зубочи́стка. **toothsome** adj. вку́сный (-сен, -сна́, -сно). **toothy** adj. зуба́стый (*coll.*).

top[1] n. (*toy*) волчо́к (-чка́).

top[2] n. (*of object*; *gen.*) верх (-а(у), *loc.* -у́; *pl.* -и́); (*of hill etc.*) верши́на; (*of tree*) верху́шка; (*of head*) маку́шка; (*of milk*) сли́вки (-вок) *pl.*; (*lid*) кры́шка; (*upper part*) ве́рхняя часть (*pl.* -ти, -те́й); *t.* сору, оригина́л; *t. drawer*, (*fig.*) вы́сшее о́бщество; *t. hat*, цили́ндр; *t.-heavy*, переве́шивающий в свое́й ве́рхней ча́сти; (*at*) *t. level*, на вы́сшем у́ровне; (*of high rank*) высокопоста́вленный; *t. secret*, соверше́нно секре́тный; *on t. of*, (*position*) на + *prep.*, сверх + *gen.*; (*on to*) на + *acc.*; *on t. of everything*, сверх всего́; *from t. to bottom*, све́рху до́низу; *at the t. of one's voice*, во весь го́лос; *at t. speed*, на весь опо́р; adj. ве́рхний, вы́сший, са́мый высо́кий; (*foremost*) пе́рвый; v.t. (*cover*) покрыва́ть *imp.*, покры́ть (-ро́ю, -ро́ешь) *perf.*; (*reach t. of*) подни-ма́ться (-нимусь,

tool n. инструме́нт
-ни́мешься; -ня́лся, -няла́сь) *perf.* на верши́ну + *gen.*; (*excel*) превосходи́ть (-ожу́, -о́дишь) *imp.*, превзойти́ (-ойду́, -ойдёшь; -ошёл, -ошла́) *perf.*; (*cut t. off*) обреза́ть *imp.*, обре́зать (-е́жу, -е́жешь) *perf.* верху́шку + *gen.*; *t. off*, заверша́ть *imp.*, заверши́ть *perf.*; *t. up*, (*with liquid*) долива́ть *imp.*, доли́ть (-лью́, -льёшь; до́лил, -а́, -о) *perf.*; (*with grain etc.*) досыпа́ть *imp.*, досы́пать (-плю -плешь) *perf.*

topaz n. топа́з.

topcoat n. пальто́ *neut. indecl.*

topiary n. иску́сство фигу́рной стри́жки кусто́в.

topic n. те́ма, предме́т. **topical** adj. актуа́льный; *t. question*, злободне́вный вопро́с. **topicality** n. актуа́льность.

topknot n. (*tuft*, *crest*) хохо́л (-хла́); (*knot*) пучо́к (-чка́) лент (*of ribbons*), воло́с (*of hair*).

topmost adj. са́мый ве́рхний; са́мый ва́жный.

topographer n. топо́граф. **topographic(al)** adj. топографи́ческий. **topography** n. топогра́фия.

topology n. тополо́гия. **toponymy** n. топони́мика.

topple v.t. & i. опроки́дывать(ся) *imp.*, опроки́нуть(ся) *perf.*; v.i. вали́ться (-лю́сь, -лишься) *imp.*, по~, с~ *perf.*

topsail n. ма́рсель *m.*

topsoil n. ве́рхний слой по́чвы.

topsy-turvy adj. повёрнутый вверх дном; (*disorderly*) беспоря́дочный; adv. вверх дном, ши́ворот-навы́ворот.

torch n. фа́кел; (*electric t.*) электри́ческий фона́рик; (*fig.*) све́точ; *t.-bearer*, факельщик, -ица. **torchlight** n. свет фа́кела, фона́рика.

toreador n. тореадо́р.

torment n. муче́ние, му́ка; v.t. му́чить *imp.*, за~, из~ *perf.* **tormentor** n. мучи́тель *m.*

tornado n. торна́до; (*fig.*) урага́н.

torpedo n. торпе́да; *t.-boat*, торпе́дный ка́тер (-а́); v.t. торпеди́ровать *imp.*, *perf.*; (*fig.*) прова́ливать *imp.*, провали́ть (-лю́, -лишь) *perf.*

torpid adj. (*numb*) онеме́лый; (*sluggish*)

вялый; (*zool.*) находящийся в спячке.
torpor *n.* онемелость; апатия.

torque *n.* (*phys.*, *mech.*) вращающий момент.

torrent *n.* стремительный поток; (*fig.*) поток; *pl.* ливень (-вня) *m.* **torrential** *adj.* текущий быстрым потоком; (*of rain*) проливной; (*fig.*) обильный.

torrid *adj.* знойный.

torsion *n.* скрученность; (*tech.*) кручение.

torso *n.* туловище; (*of statue*) торс.

tort *n.* гражданское правонарушение.

tortoise *n.* черепаха. **tortoise-shell** *n.* панцирь *m.* черепахи; (*material*) черепаха; *attrib.* черепаховый; (*cat*) пёстрый.

tortuous *adj.* извилистый; (*evasive*) уклончивый.

torture *n.* пытка; *v.t.* пытать *imp.*; (*torment*) мучить *imp.*, за~, из~ *perf.*; (*distort*) искажать *imp.*, исказить *perf.* **torturer** *n.* мучитель *m.*, палач (-а).

toss *n.* бросок (-ска), бросание; t. of coin, подбрасывание монеты, жеребьёвка (*fig.*); win (lose) the t., (не) выпадать *imp.*, выпасть (-адет; -ал) *perf.* жребий impers. (I won the t., мне выпал жребий); *v.t.* бросать *imp.*, бросить *perf.*; (*coin*) подбрасывать *imp.*, подбросить *perf.*; (*rider*) сбрасывать *imp.*, сбросить *perf.*; (*of bull etc.*) поднимать *imp.*, поднять (-ниму, -нимешь; поднял, -а, -о) *perf.* на рога; (*head*) вскидывать *imp.*, вскинуть *perf.*; (*salad*) перемешивать *imp.*, перемешать *perf.*; t. a pancake, переворачивать *imp.*, перевернуть *perf.* блин, подбросив его; *v.i.* (*of ship*) качаться *imp.*, качнуться *perf.*; (*in bed*) метаться (мечусь, -чешься) *imp.*; t. aside, away, отбрасывать *imp.*, отбросить *perf.*; t. off, (*work*) делать *imp.*, с~ *perf.* наспех; (*drink*) пить (пью, пьёшь) *imp.*, вы~ *perf.* залпом; t. up, бросать *imp.*, бросить *perf.* жребий. **toss-up** *n.* жеребьёвка; (*doubtful matter*) it is a t., это ещё вопрос.

tot[1] *n.* (*coll.*) (*child*) малыш (-а) (*coll.*);

(*glass*) маленькая рюмка; (*dram*) маленький глоток (-тка).

tot[2]: t. up, (*coll.*) (*v.t.*) складывать *imp.*, сложить (-жу, -жишь) *perf.*; (*v.i.*) равняться *imp.* (to, + *dat.*).

total *n.* итог, сумма; *adj.* общий, (*complete*) полный (-лон, -лна, -лно); in t., в целом, вместе; t. recall, фотографическая память; t. war, тотальная война; sum t., общая сумма; *v.t.* подсчитывать *imp.*, подсчитать *perf.*; (*v.i.*) равняться *imp.* + *dat.* **totalitarian** *adj.* тоталитарный. **totality** *n.* вся сумма целиком; the t. of, весь (вся, всё; все); in t., в целом вместе. **totalizator** *n.* тотализатор. **totalize** *v.t.* соединять *imp.*, соединить *perf.* воедино. **totally** *adv.* совершенно.

totem *n.* тотем; t.-pole, тотемный столб (-а).

totter *v.i.* (*walk unsteadily*) ходить (хожу, ходишь) indet., идти (иду, идёшь; шёл, шла) det., пойти (пойду, -дёшь; пошёл, -шла) *perf.* неверными шагами; (*reel*) шататься *imp.*; (*toddle*) ковылять *imp.*; (*perish*) гибнуть (-ну) *imp.*, по~ *perf.*

toucan *n.* тукан.

touch *n.* прикосновение; (*sense*) осязание; (*stroke of brush etc.*) штрих (-а); (*mus. or art style*) туше; (*of piano etc.*) удар; (*shade*) оттенок (-нка); (*taste*) привкус; (*small amount*) чуточка; (*of illness*) лёгкий приступ; (*of sport*) площадь (*pl.* -ди, -дей) за боковыми линиями; (*personal t.*) личный подход; get in t. with, связываться *imp.*, связаться (-яжусь, -яжешься) *perf.* с + *instr.*; keep in (lose) t. with, поддерживать *imp.*, поддержать (-жу, -жишь) *perf.* терять *imp.*, по~ *perf.* связь, контакт с + *instr.*; put the finishing touches to, отделывать *imp.*, отделать *perf.*; t.-line, боковая линия; t. typing, слепой метод машинописи; common t., чувство локтя; to the t., на ощупь; *v.t.* (*lightly*) прикасаться *imp.*, прикоснуться *perf.* к + *dat.*; касаться *imp.*, коснуться *perf.* + *gen.*; (*also disturb*; *affect*) трогать *imp.*, тронуть *perf.*; (*momentarily reach*) подска́кивать *imp.*, подскочи́ть (-чи́т) *perf.* до +*gen.* (*coll.*); (*be comparable with*) идти́ (иду́, идёшь; шёл, шла) *imp.* в сравне́нии с+*instr.*; *v.i.* (*be contiguous; come into contact*) соприкаса́ться *imp.*, соприкосну́ться *perf.*; *t. down*, приземля́ться *imp.*, приземли́ться *perf.*; *t.-down*, поса́дка; *t. off*, (*provoke*) вызыва́ть *imp.*, вы́звать (вы́зову, -вешь) *perf.*; *t.* (*up*)*on*, (*fig.*) каса́ться *imp.*, косну́ться *perf.*+*gen.*; *t. up*, поправля́ть *imp.*, попра́вить *perf.*; *t.-and-go*, риско́ванное де́ло; *t. wood!* не сгла́зить бы! **touched** *adj.* тро́нутый. **touchiness** *n.* оби́дчивость. **touching** *adj.* тро́гательный. **touchstone** *n.* проби́рный ка́мень (-мня; *pl.* -мни, -мне́й) *m.* **touchy** *adj.* оби́дчивый.

tough *adj.* жёсткий (-ток, -тка́, -тко); (*durable*) про́чный (-чен, -чна́, -чно, про́чны); (*strong*) кре́пкий (-пок, -пка́, -пко); (*difficult*) тру́дный (-ден, -дна́, -дно, тру́дны); (*hardy*) выно́сливый; *n.* хулига́н, банди́т. **toughen** *v.t. & i.* де́лать(ся) *imp.*, с~ *perf.* жёстким. **toughness** *n.* жёсткость; (*durability*) про́чность.

toupee *n.* небольшо́й пари́к (-á).

tour *n.* (*journey*) путеше́ствие, пое́здка; (*excursion*) экску́рсия; (*of artistes*) турне́ *neut.indecl.*; (*of duty*) объе́зд; *t. de force*, проявле́ние си́лы (*strength*), ло́вкости (*skill*); *v.i.* (*t.*) соверша́ть *imp.*, соверши́ть *perf.* путеше́ствие, турне́, объе́зд (по+*dat.*). **tourism** *n.* тури́зм. **tourist** *n.* тури́ст, ~ка; путеше́ственник, -ица; *t. class*, второ́й класс.

tournament *n.* турни́р. **tourney** *v.i.* уча́ствовать *imp.* в турни́ре.

tourniquet *n.* турникет.

tousle *v.t.* взъеро́шивать *imp.*, взъеро́шить *perf.* (*coll.*).

tout *n.* навя́зчивый торго́вец (-вца); (*of horses*) челове́к (*pl.* лю́ди, -де́й, -дям, -дьми) добыва́ющий и продаю́щий све́дения о лошадя́х пе́ред ска́чками; *v.t.* навя́зывать *imp.*, навяза́ть (-яжу́, -я́жешь) *perf.* (*thing*, +*acc.*; *person*, +*dat.*).

tow[1] *v.t.* букси́ровать *imp.*; *n.* букси-

ро́вка; *on t.*, на букси́ре; *t.-boat*, букси́рное су́дно (*pl.* -дá, -до́в); *t.-path*, бечевни́к (-á); *t.-rope*, букси́р, бечевá *no pl.*

tow[2] *n.* (*text.*) па́кля.

towards *prep.* (*in direction of*) (по направле́нию) к+*dat.*; (*fig.*) к+*dat.*; (*for*) для+*gen.*

towel *n.* полоте́нце; *t. rail*, ве́шалка для полоте́нец. **towelling** *n.* махро́вая ткань.

tower *n.* ба́шня; (*tech.*) вы́шка; (*fig.*): *t. of strength*, надёжная опо́ра; *v.i.* вы́ситься *imp.*, возвыша́ться *imp.* (*above*, над+*instr.*). **towering** *adj.* (*high*) высо́кий (-о́к, -ока́, -о́ко); (*rising up*) возвыша́ющийся; (*furious*) нейсто́вый.

town *n.* го́род (*pl.* -á); *attrib.* городско́й; *t. clerk*, секрета́рь *m.* городско́й корпора́ции; *t. council*, городско́й сове́т; *t. councillor*, член городско́го сове́та; *t. crier*, глаша́тай; *t. hall*, ра́туша; *t. planning*, градострои́тельство. **townsman, -swoman** *n.* горожа́нин (*pl.* -áне, -áн), -áнка.

toxic *adj.* ядови́тый, токси́ческий.

toxin *n.* яд (-а(у)); (*med.*) токси́н.

toy *n.* игру́шка; *t. dog*, ма́ленькая ко́мнатная соба́чка; *t. soldier*, оловя́нный солда́тик; *v.i.*: *t. with*, (*s.th. in hands*) верте́ть (верчу́, -ртишь) *imp.* в рука́х; (*trifle with*) игра́ть *imp.* (с)+*instr.*

trace[1] *n.* (*track, mark*) след (*pl.* -ы́); (*small amount*) небольшо́е коли́чество; *t. element*, микроэлеме́нт; *v.t.* (*track down*), (*trace through*) просле́живать *imp.*, проследи́ть *perf.*; (*make copy*) кальки́ровать *imp.*, с~ *perf.*; *t. back*, (*v.i.*) восходи́ть (-ожу́, -о́дишь) *imp.* (*to*, к+*dat.*); *t. out*, (*plan*) набра́сывать *imp.*, наброса́ть *perf.*; (*map, diagram*) черти́ть (черчу́, -ртишь) *imp.*, на~ *perf.* (*design*) узо́р. **tracing** *n.* (*copy*) чертёж (-á) на ка́льке; *t. paper*, ка́лька.

trace[2] *n.* (*of harness*) постро́мка.

trachea *n.* трахе́я.

track *n.* (*path*) доро́жка, тропи́нка; (*mark*) след (*pl.* -ы́); (*rly.*) путь (-ти́,

-тём) *m.*, колея́; (*sport*) трек, доро́жка; (*on tape*) (звукова́я) доро́жка; (*on record*) за́пись; t. events, соревнова́ния *neut.pl.* по бегу́; t. suit, трениро́вочный костю́м; off the t., на ло́жном пути́; (*fig.*) отклони́вшийся от те́мы; off the beaten t., в глуши́; be on the t. of, пресле́довать *imp.*; go off the t., (*fig.*) отклони́ться *imp.*, отклони́ться (-ню́сь, -ни́шься) *perf.* от те́мы; keep t. of, следи́ть *imp.* за + *instr.*; lose t. of, теря́ть *imp.*, по~ *perf.* след + *gen.*; *v.t.* просле́живать *imp.*, проследи́ть *perf.*; t. down, высле́живать *imp.*, вы́следить *perf.*

tract¹ *n.* (*expanse*) простра́нство; (*anat.*) тракт.

tract² *n.* (*treatise*) тракта́т; (*pamphlet*) брошю́ра.

tractability *n.* (*of person*) сгово́рчивость; (*of material*) ко́вкость. tractable *adj.* (*person*) сгово́рчивый; (*material*) ко́вкий (-вок, -вка́, -вко). traction *n.* тя́га; (*therapy*) тра́кция; t.-engine, тра́ктор-тяга́ч (-á). tractor *n.* тра́ктор; t.-driver, тракторист.

trade *n.* торго́вля; (*occupation*) профе́ссия, ремесло́ (*pl.* -ёсла, -ёсел, -ёслам); (*collect.*) торго́вцы *m.pl.*; t. mark, фабри́чная ма́рка; (*fig.*) отличи́тельный знак; t. name, (*of firm*) назва́ние фи́рмы; t. secret, секре́т фи́рмы; t. union, профсою́з; t.-unionist, член профсою́за; t. wind, пасса́т; *v.i.* торгова́ть *imp.* (in, + *instr.*); *v.t.* (*swap like things*) обме́ниваться *imp.*, обменя́ться *perf.* + *instr.*; (t. for s.th. different) обме́нивать *imp.*, обменя́ть *perf.* (for, на + *acc.*); t. in, сдава́ть (сдаю́, сдаёшь) *imp.*, сдать (сдам, сдашь, сдаст, сдади́м; сдал, -á, -о) *perf.* в счёт поку́пки но́вого; t. on, (*exploit*) испо́льзовать *imp.*, *perf.* trader, tradesman *n.* торго́вец (-вца). trading *n.* торго́вля, комме́рция; *attrib.* торго́вый; t. station, факто́рия. tradition *n.* тради́ция; (*legend*) преда́ние. traditional *adj.* традицио́нный (-нен, -нна). traditionalism *n.* приве́рженность к тради́циям. traditionally *adv.* по тради́ции.

traduce *v.t.* клевета́ть (-ещу́, -ещешь)

imp., на~ *perf.* на + *acc.* traducer *n.* клеветни́к (-á), -и́ца.

traffic *n.* движе́ние; (*trade*) торго́вля; (*transportation*) тра́нспорт; t. island, острово́к (-вка́) безопа́сности; t. jam, про́бка; t. lights, светофо́р; *v.i.* торгова́ть *imp.* (in, + *instr.*). trafficator *n.* указа́тель *m.* поворо́та. trafficker *n.* торго́вец (-вца) (in, + *instr.*).

tragedian *n.* тра́гик. tragedy *n.* траге́дия. tragic *adj.* траги́ческий. tragicomedy *n.* трагикоме́дия.

trail *n.* (*trace*, *track*) след (*pl.* -ы́); (*path*) тропи́нка; (*course*: *road*) путь (-ти́, -тём) *m.*; *v.t.* (*track*) высле́живать *imp.*, вы́следить *perf.*; *v.t.* & *i.* (*drag*) таска́ть(ся) *indet.*, тащи́ть(ся) (-щу́(сь), -щишь(ся)) *det.*; волочи́ть(ся) (-чу́(сь), -чишь(ся)) *imp.* trailer *n.* (*on vehicle*) прице́п; (*plant*) сте́лющееся расте́ние; (*cin.*) (кино)ро́лик.

train *n.* по́езд (*pl.* -á); (*of dress*) шлейф; (*retinue*) сви́та; (*mil.*) обо́з; (*convoy*) карава́н; (*series*) цепь (*loc.* -пи́; *pl.* -пи, -пе́й) *v.t.* (*instruct*) обуча́ть *imp.*, обучи́ть (-чу́, -чишь) *perf.* (in, + *dat.*); (*prepare*) гото́вить *imp.* (for, к + *dat.*); (*sport*) тренирова́ть *imp.*, на~ *perf.*; (*animals*) дрессирова́ть *imp.*, вы́~ *perf.*; (*break in*) объезжа́ть *imp.*, объе́здить *perf.*; (*aim*, *point*) направля́ть *imp.*, напра́вить *perf.*; (*plant*) направля́ть *imp.*, напра́вить *perf.* рост + *gen.*; *v.i.* (*prepare*) приготовля́ться *imp.*, пригото́виться *perf.* (for, к + *dat.*); (*sport*) тренирова́ться *imp.*, на~ *perf.* trainee *n.* стажёр, практика́нт. trainer *n.* инстру́ктор; (*sport*) тре́нер; (*of animals*) дресси́ровщик. training *n.* обуче́ние; (*sport*) трениро́вка; (*of animals*) дрессиро́вка; t.-college, (*teachers'*) педагоги́ческий институ́т; t.-school, специа́льное учи́лище.

traipse *v.i.* таска́ться *indet.*, тащи́ться (-щу́сь, -щишься) *det.*

trait *n.* (характе́рная) черта́; штрих (-á).

traitor *n.* преда́тель *m.*, изме́нник. traitorous *adj.* преда́тельский. traitress *n.* преда́тельница, изме́нница.

trajectory *n.* траекто́рия.

tram *n.* трамва́й; *t.-driver,* вагоново́-
жа́тый *sb.; t.-line,* трамва́йная ли́ния.

trammel *n.* (*net*) не́вод (*pl.* -а́); *t.*
(*fig.*) поме́ха, препя́тствие; *v.t.* (*fig.*)
препя́тствовать *imp.,* вос~ *perf.*
+ *dat.*

tramp *n.* (*vagrant*) бродя́га *m.;* (*tread*)
то́пот; (*journey on foot*) путеше́ствие
пешко́м; *v.i.* (*of vagrant*) бродя́жни-
чать *imp.;* (*go with heavy tread*)
то́пать *imp.;* (*go on foot*) ходи́ть
(хожу́, хо́дишь) *indet.,* идти́ (иду́,
идёшь; шёл, шла) *det.,* пойти́
(пойду́, -дёшь; пошёл, -шла́) *perf.*
пешко́м. trample *v.t.* топта́ть (топчу́,
-чешь) *imp.,* по~, ис~ *perf.; t.* down,
выта́птывать *imp.,* вы́топтать (-пчу,
-пчешь) *perf.; t. on,* (*fig.*) попира́ть
imp., попра́ть (-ру́, -рёшь) *perf.*

trampoline *n.* батут́, бату́д.

trance *n.* транс; (*rapture*) состоя́ние
экста́за.

tranquil *adj.* споко́йный. tranquillity *n.*
споко́йствие. tranquillize *v.t.* успока́и-
вать *imp.,* успоко́ить *perf.* tranquillizer
n. транквилиза́тор.

transact *v.t.* (*business*) вести́ (веду́,
-дёшь; вёл, -а́) *imp.;* (*a deal*) заклю-
ча́ть *imp.,* заключи́ть *perf.* transaction
n. де́ло (*pl.* -ла́), сде́лка; *pl.* (*publica-
tions*) труды́ *m.pl.;* (*minutes*) прото-
ко́лы *m.pl.*

transatlantic *adj.* трансатланти́ческий.

transceiver *n.* приёмо-переда́тчик.

transcend *v.t.* преступа́ть *imp.,* престу-
пи́ть (-плю́, -пишь) *perf.* преде́лы
+ *gen.;* (*excel*) превосходи́ть (-ожу́,
-о́дишь) *imp.,* превзойти́ (-ойду́, -ой-
дёшь; -ошёл, -ошла́) *perf.* transcen-
dency *n.* превосхо́дство. transcendent
adj. превосхо́дный. transcendental *adj.*
(*philos.*) трансцендента́льный.

transcontinental *adj.* трансконтинента́-
льный.

transcribe *v.t.* (*copy out*) перепи́сывать
imp., переписа́ть (-ишу́, -и́шешь)
perf.; (*shorthand*) расшифро́вывать
imp., расшифрова́ть *perf.;* (*mus.*)
аранжи́ровать *imp.,* *perf.* (*phon.*) тран-
скри́бировать *imp.,* *perf.* transcript *n.*
ко́пия; (*shorthand*) расшифро́вка.
transcription *n.* (*copying out*) пере-

пи́сывание; (*copy*) ко́пия; (*mus.*)
аранжиро́вка; (*phon.*) транскри́пция.

transducer *n.* преобразова́тель *m.,*
да́тчик.

transept *n.* трансе́пт.

transfer *n.* (*of objects*) перено́с, пере-
меще́ние; (*of money; of people*) пере-
во́д; (*leg.*) переда́ча; (*design*) перевод-
на́я карти́нка; *v.t.* (*objects*) переноси́ть
(-ошу́, -о́сишь) *imp.,* перенести́
(-есу́, -есёшь; -ёс, -есла́) *perf.;*
перемеща́ть *imp.,* перемести́ть *perf.;*
(*money; people; design*) переводи́ть
(-ожу́, -о́дишь) *imp.,* перевести́
(-еду́, -едёшь; -ёл, -ела́) *perf.;* (*leg.*)
передава́ть (-даю́, -даёшь) *imp.,*
переда́ть (-а́м, -а́шь, -а́ст, -ади́м;
пе́редал, -а́, -о) *perf.; v.i.* (*to different
job*) переходи́ть (-ожу́, -о́дишь) *imp.,*
перейти́ (-ейду́, -ейдёшь; -ешёл,
-ешла́) *perf.;* (*change trains etc.*) пере-
са́живаться *imp.,* пересе́сть (-ся́ду
-ся́дешь; -се́л) *perf.* transferable *adj.*
допуска́ющий переда́чу; (*replaceable*) заменя́емый, замени́мый. trans-
ference *n.* переда́ча.

transfiguration *n.* преобразова́ние;
(*spiritual*) преображе́ние. transfigure
v.t. преобразо́вывать *imp.,* преобра-
зова́ть *perf.;* (*in spirit*) преобража́ть
imp., преобрази́ть *perf.*

transfix *v.t.* (*pierce*) пронза́ть *imp.,*
пронзи́ть *perf.;* (*fig.*) пригвожда́ть
imp., пригвозди́ть *perf.* к ме́сту.

transform *v.t. & i.* (*also electr.*) пре-
образо́вывать(ся) *imp.,* преобразо-
ва́ть(ся) *perf.; t. into, v.t.(i.)* превра-
ща́ть(ся) *imp.,* преврати́ть(ся)
(-ащу́(сь), -ати́шь(ся)) *perf.* в + *acc.*
transformation *n.* преобразова́ние;
превраще́ние. transformer *n.* (*electr.*)
трансформа́тор.

transfuse *v.t.* (*med.*) перелива́ть *imp.,*
перели́ть (-лью́, -льёшь; -ли́л, -лила́)
perf.; (*steep*) пропи́тывать *imp.,* про-
пита́ть *perf.* (in, + *instr.*); (*convey*) пере-
дава́ть (-даю́, -даёшь) *imp.,* переда́ть
(-а́м, -а́шь, -а́ст, -ади́м; пе́редал, -а́,
-о) *perf.* transfusion *n.* перелива́ние
(кро́ви).

transgress *v.t.* переступа́ть *imp.,* пере-
ступи́ть (-плю́, -пишь) *perf.;* нару-

шáть *imp.*, нарýшить *perf.* **transgression** *n.* простýпок (-пка), нарушéние; (*sin*) грех (-á). **transgressor** *n.* правонарушитель *m.*; (*sinner*) грéшник, -ица.

transience *n.* быстротéчность, мимолётность. **transient** *adj.* преходящий; (*fleeting*) мимолётный.

transistor *n.* транзистор; *t. radio*, транзисторный приёмник. **transistorized** *adj.* на транзисторах.

transit *n.* транзит, прохождéние; (*astron.*) прохождéние планéты; *in t.*, в пути; *t. camp*, лáгерь (*pl.* -ря, -рéй) *m.* перемещённых лиц; *t. visa*, транзитная виза. **transition** *n.* перехóд. **transitional** *adj.* перехóдный; (*interim*) промежýточный. **transitive** *adj.* перехóдный. **transitory** *adj.* мимолётный; (*temporary*) врéменный.

translate *v.t.* переводить (-ожý, -óдишь) *imp.*, перевести (-едý, -едёшь; -ёл, -елá) *perf.*; (*explain*) объяснять *imp.*, объяснить *perf.* **translation** *n.* перевóд. **translator** *n.* перевóдчик, -ица.

transliterate *v.t.* транслитерировать *imp.*, *perf.* **transliteration** *n.* транслитерáция.

translucency *n.* полупрозрáчность. **translucent** *adj.* просвéчивающий, полупрозрáчный.

transmigration *n.* переселéние.

transmission *n.* передáча; (*tech.*) трансмиссия; *attrib.* передáточный. **transmit** *v.t.* передавáть (-даю, -даёшь) *imp.*, передáть (-áм, -áшь, -áст, -адим; пéредал, -á, -о) *perf.* **transmitter** *n.* (*radio*)передáтчик.

transmutation *n.* превращéние. **transmute** *v.t.* превращáть *imp.*, превратить (-ащý, -атишь) *perf.*

transom *n.* переплёт.

transparency *n.* прозрáчность; (*picture*) транспарáнт; (*phot.*) диапозитив. **transparent** *adj.* прозрáчный; (*obvious*) очевидный; (*frank*) откровéнный (-нен, -нна).

transpire *v.t. & i.* испарять(ся) *imp.*, испарить(ся) *perf.*; *v.i.* (*fig.*) обнарýживаться *imp.*, обнарýжиться *perf.*; (*occur*) случáться *imp.*, случиться *perf.*

transplant *v.t.* пересáживать *imp.*, пересадить (-ажý, -áдишь) *perf.*; (*surg.*) дéлать (*impf.*) *c* ~ *perf.* пересáдку + *gen.*; *n.* (*surg.*) пересáдка.

transport *n.* (*var. senses*) трáнспорт; (*conveyance*) перевóзка; (*of rage etc.*) порыв; *attrib.* трáнспортный; *v.t.* перевозить (-ожý, -óзишь) *imp.*, перевезти (-езý, -езёшь; -ёз, -езлá) *perf.*; (*exile*) ссылáть *imp.*, сослáть (сошлю, -лёшь) *perf.* **transportation** *n.* трáнспорт, перевóзка; (*exile*) ссылка.

transpose *v.t.* перемещáть *imp.*, переместить (-ещý, -естишь) *perf.*; (*words*) переставлять *imp.*, переставить *perf.*; (*mus.*) транспонировать *imp.*, *perf.* **transposition** *n.* перемещéние, перестанóвка; (*mus.*) транспонирóвка.

trans-ship *v.t.* перегружáть *imp.*, перегрузить (-ужý, -узишь) *perf.*

transverse *adj.* поперéчный.

transvestism *n.* трансвестизм. **transvestite** *n.* трансвестит.

trap *n.* ловýшка (*also fig.*), западня, капкáн; (*tech.*) сифóн; (*cart*) рессóрная двукóлка; *v.t.* (*catch*) ловить (-влю, -вишь) *imp.*, поймáть *perf.* (в ловýшку); (*fig.*) заманивать *imp.*, заманить (-ню, -нишь) *perf.* в ловýшку. **trapdoor** *n.* люк.

trapeze *n.* трапéция. **trapezium** *n.* трапéция.

trapper *n.* охóтник, стáвящий капкáны.

trappings *n.* сбрýя (*collect.*); (*exterior attributes*) внéшние атрибýты *m.pl.*; (*adornments*) украшéния *neut.pl.*

trash *n.* дрянь (*coll.*). **trashy** *adj.* дрянной (-нен, -нна, -нно).

trauma *n.* трáвма. **traumatic** *adj.* травматический.

travel *n.* путешéствие; (*tech.*) передвижéние; *t. bureau*, бюрó *neut.indecl.* путешéствий; *t.-sick*: *be t.-sick*, укáчивать *imp.*, укачáть *perf. impers.* + *acc.*; *I am t.-sick in cars*, меня в машине укáчивает; *v.i.* путешéствовать *imp.*; (*tech.*) передвигáться *imp.*, передвинуться *perf.*; *v.t.* объезжáть *imp.*, объéхать (-éду, -éдешь) *perf.* **traveller** *n.* путешéственник, -ица.

(*salesman*) коммивояжёр; *t.'s cheque.*
дорожный чек. **travelling** *n.* путешéствие; *attrib.* дорóжный; (*itinerant*)
передвижнóй. **travelogue** *n.* (*film*)
фильм о путешéствиях; (*lecture*)
лéкция о путешéствиях с диапозити́-
вами.

traverse *v.t.* пересекáть *imp.*, пересéчь
(-екý, -ечёшь; -ёк, -еклá) *perf.*; (*discuss*) подрóбно обсуждáть *imp.*,
обсуди́ть (-ужý, -ýдишь) *perf.*

travesty *n.* парóдия; *v.t.* пароди́ровать
imp., *perf.*

trawl *n.* трал; *v.t.* трáлить *imp.*; *v.i.*
лови́ть (-влю́, -вишь) *imp.* ры́бу
трáловой сéтью. **trawler** *n.* трáулер.
trawling *n.* трáление.

tray *n.* поднóс; *in-*(*out-*)*t.*, корзи́нка для
входя́щих (исходя́щих) бумáг.

treacherous *adj.* предáтельский; (*unreliable*) ненадёжный. **treachery** *n.*
предáтельство.

treacle *n.* пáтока. **treacly** *adj.* пáточный.

tread *n.* пóступь, похóдка; (*stair*)
ступéнька; (*of tyre*) протéктор; *v.i.*
ступáть *imp.*, ступи́ть (-плю́, -пишь)
perf.; шагáть *imp.*, шагнýть *perf.*; *v.t.*
топтáть (-пчý, -пчешь) *imp.*; дави́ть
(-влю́, -вишь) *imp.* **treadle** *n.* (*of
bicycle*) педáль; (*of sewing-machine*)
поднóжка.

treason *n.* измéна; *high t.*, госудáрственная измéна. **treasonable** *adj.*
измéннический.

treasure *n.* сокрóвище, клад; *t. trove*,
нáйденный клад; *v.t.* (*preserve*)
храни́ть *imp.*; (*value*) дорожи́ть *imp.*+
instr.; высокó цени́ть (-ню́, -нишь)
imp. **treasurer** *n.* казначéй. **treasury**
n. (*also fig.*) сокрóвищница; (*T.*) казнá
no pl.; *the T.*, госудáрственное казнá-
чéйство.

treat *n.* (*pleasure*) удовóльствие;
(*entertainment*) угощéние; *v.t.* (*have
as guest*) угощáть *imp.*, угости́ть *perf.*
(*to*, + *instr.*); (*med.*) лечи́ть (-чý,
-чишь) *imp.* (*for*, от + *gen.*; *with*,
+ *instr.*); (*behave towards*) обращáться
imp. с + *instr.*; (*process*) обрабáтывать
imp., обрабóтать *perf.* (*with*, + *instr.*);
(*discuss*) трактовáть *imp.* о + *prep.*; (*regard*) относи́ться (-ошýсь, -óсишься)

imp., отнести́сь (-есýсь, -есёшься;
-ёсся, -еслáсь) *perf.* к + *dat.* (*as*, как к +
dat.). **treatise** *n.* трактáт. **treatment** *n.*
(*behaviour*) обращéние; (*med.*) лечé-
ние; (*processing*) обрабóтка; (*discussion*) трактóвка. **treaty** *n.* договóр.

treble *adj.* тройнóй; (*trebled*) утрóен-
ный (-ен); (*mus.*) дискáнтовый; *adv.*
втрóе, втройнé; *n.* тройнóе коли́-
чество; (*mus.*) дискáнт; *v.t.* & *i.*
утрáивать(ся) *imp.*, утрóить(ся) *perf.*

tree *n.* дéрево (*pl.* дерéвья, -ьев).
treeless *adj.* безлéсный.

trefoil *n.* трили́стник.

trek *n.* (*migration*) переселéние; (*journey*) путешéствие; *v.i.* (*migrate*) пере-
селя́ться *imp.*, пересели́ться *perf.*;
(*journey*) путешéствовать *imp.*

trellis *n.* шпалéра; (*for creepers*)
решётка.

tremble *v.i.* трепетáть (-ещý, -éщешь)
imp. (*at*, при + *prep.*); дрожáть (-жý,
-жи́шь) *imp.* (*with*, от + *gen.*); трясти́сь
(-сýсь, -сёшься, -сся, -слáсь) *imp.*
(*with*, от + *gen.*). **trembling** *n.* трéпет,
дрожь; *in fear and t.*, трепещá.

tremendous *adj.* (*enormous*) огрóмный;
(*excellent, remarkable*) потрясáющий.

tremor *n.* дрожь, трéпет; (*earthquake*)
толчóк (-чкá). **tremulous** *adj.* дро-
жáщий; (*uneven*) нерóвный (-вен,
-внá, -вно); (*shy*) рóбкий (-бок, -бкá,
-бко).

trench *n.* канáва, ров (рва, *loc.* во рву́);
(*mil.*) окóп; *t. coat*, тёплая полуши́-
нéль; *v.t.* рыть (рóю, рóешь) *imp.*,
вы ~ *perf.* канáвы, рвы, окóпы в +
prep.; (*dig over*) перекáпывать *imp.*,
перекопáть *perf.*

trenchant *adj.* óстрый (остр & остёр,
острá, óстро), рéзкий (-зок, -зкá,
-зко). **trenchancy** *n.* острота́, рéзкость.

trend *n.* направлéние, тендéнция.
trendy *adj.* мóдный (-ден, -днá, -дно).

trepidation *n.* (*trembling*) трéпет; (*alarm*)
тревóга.

trespass *n.* (*on property*) нарушéние
грани́ц; (*misdemeanour*) просту́пок
(-пка); *v.i.* нарушáть *imp.*, нарýшить
perf. прáво владéния; *t. on*, (*property*)

нарушать *imp.*, нарушить *perf.* границу + *gen.*; (*selfishly exploit*) злоупотреблять *imp.*, злоупотребить *perf.* + *instr.* trespasser *n.* нарушитель *m.*, ~ ница границ.

tress *n.* локон, коса (*acc.* косу; *pl.* -сы).

trestle *n.* козлы (-зел, -злам) *pl.*

trial *n.* (*test*) испытание (*also ordeal*), проба; (*leg.*) процесс, суд (-а́); (*sport*) попытка; *on t.* (*probation*) на испытании; (*of objects*) взятый на пробу; (*leg.*) под судом; *t. period*, испытательный срок (-а(y)); *t. run*, пробный пробег (*of ship*) пробное плавание; (*of plane*) испытательный полёт; *t. and error*, метод подбора.

triangle *n.* треугольник. triangular *adj.* треугольный; (*three-edged*) трёхгранный.

tribal *adj.* племенной, родовой. tribe *n.* племя *neut.*, род (-а(y), *loc.* -ý; *pl.* -ы). tribesman *n.* член племени, рода.

tribulation *n.* горе, несчастье.

tribunal *n.* трибунал; (*court*, *fig.*) суд (-á).

tribune[1] *n.* (*leader*) трибун.

tribune[2] *n.* (*platform*) трибуна; (*throne*) кафедра.

tributary *n.* (*geog.*) приток; (*hist.*) данник. tribute *n.* дань (*also fig.*); *pay t.*, (*fig.*) отдавать (-даю, -даёшь) *imp.*, отдать (-ám, -áшь, -áст, -адим; отдал, -á, -о) *perf.* дань (уважения) (to, + *dat.*).

trice *n.*: *in a t.*, мгновенно.

trick *n.* (*ruse*) хитрость; (*deception*) обман; (*conjuring*) фокус; (*feat*, *stunt*) трюк; (*joke*) шутка; (*of trade etc.*) приём; (*habit*) привычка; (*cards*) взятка; *play a t. on*, играть *imp.*, сыграть *perf.* шутку с + *instr.* с; *t.* обманывать *imp.*, обмануть (-ну, -нешь) *perf.* trickery *n.* обман, надувательство (*coll.*).

trickle *v.i.* капать *imp.*; сочиться *imp.*; *n.* струйка.

trickster *n.* обманщик, -ица. tricky *adj.* (*complicated*) сложный (-жен, -жна, -жно); (*crafty*) хитрый (-тёр, -трá, -хитро́).

tricot *n.* трико́ *neut.indecl.*

tricycle *n.* трёхколёсный велосипед.

trident *n.* трезубец (-бца).

triennial *adj.* трёхлетний.

trifle *n.* пустяк (-á), мелочь (*pl.* -чи, -чей); (*dish*) вид сладкого блюда; *a t.*, (*adv.*) немного + *gen.*; *v.i.* шутить (шучу, шутишь) *imp.*, по ~ *perf.* (with, с + *instr.*); относиться (-ошусь, -осишься) *imp.*, отнестись (-есусь, -есёшься; -ёсся, -еслась) *perf.* несерьёзно (with, к + *dat.*). trifling *adj.* пустяковый.

trigger *n.* (*of gun*) курок (-рка́), спусковой крючок (-чка́); (*releasing catch*) защёлка; *v.t.*: *t. off*, вызывать *imp.*, вызвать (вызову, -вешь) *perf.*

trigonometry *n.* тригонометрия.

trilby (*hat*) *n.* мягкая фетровая шляпа.

trill *n.* трель; *v.i.* выводить (-ожу, -о́дишь) *imp.*, вывести (-еду, -едешь; -ел) *perf.* трель.

trilogy *n.* трилогия.

trim *n.* порядок (-дка), готовность; *in fighting t.*, в боевой готовности; *in good t.*, (*sport*) в хорошей форме; (*haircut*) подстрижка; (*clipping*, *pruning*) подрезка; *adj.* (*neat*) аккуратный, опрятный; (*smart*) нарядный; *v.t.* (*cut*, *clip*, *cut off*) подрезать *imp.*, подрезать (-éжу, -éжешь) *perf.*; (*hair*) подстригать *imp.*, подстричь (-игу, -ижёшь; -йг) *perf.*; (*square*) обтёсывать *imp.*, обтесать (-ешу, -éшешь) *perf.*; (*a dress etc.*) отделывать *imp.*, отделать *perf.*; (*a dish*) украшать *imp.*, украсить *perf.* trimming *n.* (*on dress*) отделка; (*to food*) гарнир, приправа.

trimaran *n.* тримаран.

Trinity *n.* троица; *T. Sunday*, троицын день (дня) *m.*

trinket *n.* безделушка, брелок.

trio *n.* трио *neut.indecl.*; (*of people*) тройка.

trip *n.* поездка, путешествие, экскурсия; (*business trip*) командировка; (*stumbling*) спотыкание; (*sport*) подножка; (*light step*) лёгкая походка; (*mistake*) ошибка; (*tech.*) расцепляющее устройство; *v.i.* (*run lightly*) бегать *indet.*, бежать (бегу, бежишь) *det.*, по ~ *perf.* вприпрыжку; (*stumble*) спотыкаться *imp.*, споткнуться *perf.*

(over, o + acc.); (make a mistake) ошиба́ться imp., ошиби́ться (-бу́сь, -бёшься; -бся) perf.; v.t. подставля́ть imp., подста́вить perf. но́жку + dat. (also fig.); (confuse) запу́тывать imp., запу́тать perf.

tripartite adj. трёхсторо́нний.

tripe n. (dish) рубе́ц (-бца́).

triple adj. тройно́й; (tripled) утро́енный (-ен); v.t. & i. утра́ивать(ся) imp., утро́ить(ся) perf. (mus.) трио́ль; (one of triplets) близне́ц (-а́) (из тро́йни); pl. тро́йня. **triplicate** n.: in t., в трёх экземпля́рах.

tripod n. трено́жник.

triptych n. три́птих.

trite adj. бана́льный, изби́тый.

triumph n. триу́мф (also event), торже́ство, побе́да; v.i. торжествова́ть imp., вос~ perf. (over, над + instr.). **triumphal** adj. триумфа́льный. **triumphant** adj. (exultant) торжеству́ющий, лику́ющий; (victorious) победоно́сный.

trivia n. ме́лочи (-че́й) pl. **trivial** adj. незначи́тельный. **triviality** n. тривиа́льность, бана́льность. **trivialize** v.t. упроща́ть imp., упрости́ть perf.

troglodyte n. троглоди́т.

troika n. тро́йка.

Trojan adj. троя́нский; n.: work like a T., рабо́тать imp. энерги́чно, усе́рдно.

troll n. (myth.) тролль m.

trolley n. теле́жка, вагоне́тка; (table on wheels) сто́лик на колёсиках. **trolleybus** n. тролле́йбус.

trollop n. неря́ха; проститу́тка.

trombone n. тромбо́н.

troop n. гру́ппа, отря́д; pl. (mil.) войска́ neut.pl., солда́ты m.pl.; t.-ship, войсково́й тра́нспорт; v.i. (move in a crowd) дви́гаться (-ается & дви́жется) imp. толпо́й. **trooper** n. кавалери́ст. **trooping the colour(s)** n. торже́ственный вы́нос зна́мени (зна́мен).

trophy n. трофе́й; (prize) приз (pl. -ы́).

tropic n. тро́пик; T. of Cancer, тро́пик Ра́ка; T. of Capricorn, тро́пик Козеро́га. **tropical** adj. тропи́ческий.

trot n. рысь (loc. -си́); v.i. рыси́ть imp.; (rider) е́здить indet., е́хать (е́ду, е́дешь) det., по ~ perf. ры́сью; (horse)

ходи́ть (-ди́т) indet., идти́ (идёт; шёл, шла) det., пойти́ (пойду́, -дёшь; пошёл, -шла́) perf. ры́сью; t. out, (present for inspection) представля́ть imp., предста́вить perf. на рассмотре́ние; (show off) щеголя́ть imp., щегольну́ть perf. + instr. **trotter** n. (horse) рыса́к (-а́); pl. (dish) но́жки f.pl.

troubadour n. трубаду́р.

trouble n. (worry) беспоко́йство, трево́га; (misfortune) беда́ (pl. -ды), го́ре; (unpleasantness) неприя́тности f.pl.; (effort, pains) хло́поты (-от) pl., труд; (care) забо́та; (disrepair) пробле́ма, неиспра́вность f.pl. (with, c + instr.), неиспра́вность (with, в + prep.); (illness) боле́знь; heart t., боле́знь се́рдце; t.-maker, наруши́тель m., ~ ница споко́йствия; t.-shooter, авари́йный монтёр; ask for t., напра́шиваться imp., напроси́ться (-ошу́сь, -о́сишься) perf. на неприя́тности; be in t., име́ть imp. неприя́тности; cause t. to, доставля́ть imp., доста́вить perf. хло́поты + dat.; get into t., попа́сть (-аду́, -адёшь; -а́л) perf. в беду́; make t. for, причиня́ть imp., причини́ть perf. неприя́тности + dat.; take t., стара́ться imp., по ~ perf.; take the t., труди́ться (-ужу́сь, -у́дишься) imp., по ~ perf. (to, + inf.); the t. is (that) беда́ в том, что; v.t. (make anxious, disturb, give pain) беспоко́ить imp.; may I t. you for, мо́жно попроси́ть у вас + acc.; may I t. you to, мо́жно попроси́ть вас + inf.; v.i. (worry) беспоко́иться imp.; (take the t.) труди́ться (тружу́сь, тру́дишься) imp. **troubled** adj. беспоко́йный. **troublesome** adj. (restless, fidgety) беспоко́йный; (capricious) капри́зный; (difficult) тру́дный (-ден, -дна́, -дно, тру́дны).

trough n. (for food) корму́шка, коры́то; (gutter) жёлоб (pl. -а́); (of wave) подо́шва; (meteorol.) ложби́на ни́зкого давле́ния.

trounce v.t. (beat) бить (бью, бьёшь) imp., по ~ perf.; (punish) суро́во нака́зывать imp., наказа́ть (-ажу́,

-а́жешь) *perf.*; (*scold*) суро́во брани́ть *imp.*, вы ~ *perf.* (*coll.*).

troupe *n.* тру́ппа.

trouser-leg *n.* штани́на (*coll.*). **trousers** *n.* брю́ки (-к) *pl.*, штаны́ (-но́в) *pl.* **trouser-suit** *n.* брю́чный костю́м.

trousseau *n.* прида́ное *sb.*

trout *n.* форе́ль.

trowel *n.* (*for plastering etc.*) лопа́тка; (*garden t.*) садо́вый сово́к (-вка́).

truancy *n.* прогу́л. **truant** *n.* прогу́льщик, -ица; *play t.*, прогу́ливать *imp.*, прогуля́ть *perf.*; *adj.* пра́здный.

truce *n.* переми́рие; (*respite*) передышка.

truck[1] *n.*: have no t. with, избега́ть *imp.*, избежа́ть (-eгу́, -eжи́шь) *perf.* + *gen.*

truck[2] *n.* (*lorry*) грузови́к (-а́); (*rly.*) ваго́н-платфо́рма.

truckle *v.i.* раболе́пствовать *imp.* (to, пе́ред + *instr.*).

truculence *n.* свире́пость. **truculent** *adj.* свире́пый.

trudge *n.* утоми́тельная прогу́лка; *v.i.* уста́ло тащи́ться (-щу́сь, -щишься) *imp.*

true *adj.* (*faithful, correct*) ве́рный (-рен, -рна́, -рно, ве́рны́); (*correct*) пра́вильный; (*genuine*) по́длинный (-нен, -нна); (*exact*) то́чный (-чен, -чна́, -чно); *t. to life*, реалисти́ческий; *come t.*, сбыва́ться *imp.*, сбы́ться (сбу́дется; сбы́лся, -ла́сь) *perf.*

truffle *n.* трю́фель (*pl.* -ли, -ле́й) *m.*

truism *n.* трюи́зм. **truly** *adv.* (*sincerely*) и́скренне; (*faithfully*) ве́рно; (*really, indeed*) действи́тельно, пои́стине; (*accurately*) то́чно; *yours t.*, пре́данный Вам.

trump *n.* ко́зырь (*pl.* -ри, -ре́й) *m.* (*also fig.*); *v.i.* козыря́ть *imp.*, козырну́ть *perf.* (*coll.*); *v.t.* бить (бью, бьёшь) *imp.*, по ~ *perf.* ко́зырем; *t. up*, выду́мывать *imp.*, вы́думать *perf.*; фабрикова́ть *imp.*, с ~ *perf.*

trumpery *n.* мишура́; (*rubbish*) дрянь (*coll.*).

trumpet *n.* труба́ (*pl.* -бы́); *v.i.* труби́ть *imp.* (on, в + *acc.*); (*elephant*) реве́ть (-ву́, -вёшь) *imp.*; *v.t.* (*proclaim*) возвеща́ть *imp.*, возвести́ть *perf.* **trumpeter** *n.* труба́ч (-а́).

truncate *v.t.* усека́ть *imp.*, усе́чь (-еку́, -ечёшь; усёк, -ла́) *perf.*; (*cut top off*) среза́ть *imp.*, сре́зать (-е́жу, -е́жешь) *perf.* верху́шку + *gen.*; (*abbreviate*) сокраща́ть *imp.*, сократи́ть (-ащу́, -ати́шь) *perf.*

truncheon *n.* (*police*) дуби́нка; (*staff, baton*) жезл (-а́).

trundle *v.t.* & *i.* ката́ть(ся) *indet.*, кати́ть(ся) (качу́(сь), ка́тишь(ся)) *det.*, по ~ *perf.*

trunk *n.* (*stem*) ствол (-а́); (*anat.*) ту́ловище; (*elephant's*) хо́бот; (*box*) сунду́к (-а́); *pl.* (*swimming*) пла́вки (-вок) *pl.*; (*boxing etc.*) трусы́ (-со́в) *pl.*; *t.-call*, вы́зов по междугоро́дному телефо́ну; *t.-line*, магистра́льная ли́ния; *t.-road*, магистра́льная доро́га.

truss *n.* (*girder*) ба́лка, фе́рма; (*med.*) грыжево́й банда́ж (-а́); (*sheaf, bunch*) свя́зка; *v.t.* (*tie up*, *bird*) свя́зывать *imp.*, связа́ть (-яжу́, -я́жешь) *perf.*; (*reinforce*) укрепля́ть *imp.*, укрепи́ть *perf.*

trust *n.* дове́рие, ве́ра; (*body of trustees*) опе́ка; (*property held in t.*) довери́тельная со́бственность; (*econ.*) трест; (*credit*) креди́т; (*responsibility*) отве́тственность; *breach of t.*, злоупотребле́ние дове́рием; *on t.*, (*credit*) в креди́т; *take on t.*, принима́ть *imp.*, приня́ть (приму́, -мешь; при́нял, -а́, -о) *perf.* на ве́ру; *v.t.* доверя́ть *imp.*, дове́рить *perf.* + *dat.* (with, + *acc.*; to, + *inf.*); ве́рить *imp.* по ~ *perf.* + *dat.*, в + *acc.*; (*entrust*) поруча́ть *imp.*, поручи́ть (-чу́, -чишь) *perf.* (to, + *dat.*); (*a secret etc.*) вверя́ть *imp.*, вве́рить *perf.* (to, + *dat.*); *v.i.* (*hope*) наде́яться *imp.*, по ~ *perf.* **trustee** *n.* попечи́тель *m.*, ~ ница, опеку́н, ~ ша. **trustful, trusting** *adj.* дове́рчивый. **trustiness** *n.* ве́рность; (*reliability*) надёжность. **trustworthy, trusty** *adj.* надёжный, ве́рный (-рен, -рна́, -рно, ве́рны́).

truth *n.* и́стина, пра́вда; *tell the t.*, говори́ть *imp.*, сказа́ть (скажу́, -жешь) *perf.* пра́вду; *to tell you the t.*, по пра́вде говоря́. **truthful** *adj.* правди́вый.

try n. (attempt) попы́тка; (test, trial) испыта́ние, про́ба; v.t. (taste; examine effectiveness of) про́бовать imp., по~ perf.; (test) испыта́ывать imp., испыта́ть perf.; (leg.) суди́ть (сужу́, су́дишь) imp. (for, за + acc.); v.i. (endeavour) стара́ться imp., по~ perf.; (make an attempt) пыта́ться imp., по~ perf.; t. on, (clothes) примеря́ть imp., приме́рить perf. **trying** adj. тяжёлый (-л, -ла́); (tiresome) докучли́вый (coll.).

tsar n. царь (-ря́) m. **tsarina** n. цари́ца.

tub n. ка́дка, лоха́нь.

tuba n. ту́ба.

tubby adj. то́лстенький.

tube n. тру́бка, труба́ (pl. -бы); (toothpaste etc.) тю́бик; (underground) метро́ neut.indecl.; cathode-ray t., электроннолучева́я тру́бка; inner t., ка́мера.

tuber n. клу́бень (-бня) m. **tubercular** adj. туберкулёзный. **tuberculosis** n. туберкулёз. **tuberose** n. тубероза.

tubing n. тру́бы m.pl.; (pipe-line) трубопрово́д. **tubular** adj. тру́бчатый.

tuck n. (in garment) скла́дка; v.t. (make tucks in) де́лать imp., с~ perf. скла́дки на + loc.; (thrust into, t. away) засо́вывать imp., засу́нуть perf.; (hide away) пря́тать (-я́чу, -я́чешь) imp., с~ perf.; t. in (shirt etc.) завля́ть imp., запра́вить perf.; t. in, up, (blanket, skirt) подтыка́ть imp., подоткну́ть perf.; t. up (sleeves) засу́чивать imp., засучи́ть (-чу́, -чишь) perf.; (in bed) укрыва́ть imp., укры́ть (-ро́ю, -ро́ешь) perf.; (hair etc. out of the way) подбира́ть imp., подобра́ть (подберу́, -рёшь; подобра́л, -а́, -о) perf.

Tuesday n. вто́рник.

tuft n. пучо́к (-чка́). **tufted** adj. с хохолко́м.

tug v.t. (sharply) дёргать imp., дёрнуть perf.; (pull) тяну́ть (-ну́, -нешь) imp., по~ perf.; (tow) букси́ровать imp.; n. рыво́к (-вка́); (tugboat) букси́рное су́дно (pl. -да́, -до́в); t. of war, перетя́гивание на кана́те.

tuition n. обуче́ние (in, + dat.).

tulip n. тюльпа́н.

tulle n. тюль m.

tumble v.i. (fall) па́дать imp., (у)па́сть (у)паду́, -дёшь; (у)па́л) perf.; (go head over heels) кувырка́ться imp., кувыркну́ться perf.; (rush headlong) броса́ться imp., бро́ситься perf.; v.t. (disarrange) приводи́ть (-ожу́, -о́дишь) imp., привести́ (-еду́, -едёшь; -ёл, -ела́) perf. в беспоря́док; n. паде́ние; кувырка́нье. **tumbledown** adj. полуразру́шенный (-ен), развали́вшийся. **tumbler** n. (acrobat) акроба́т; (glass) стака́н; (pigeon) ту́рман.

tumour n. о́пухоль.

tumult n. (uproar) сумато́ха, шум (-a(y)); (agitation) волне́ние. **tumultuous** adj. шу́мный (-мен, -мна́, -мно).

tumulus n. курга́н, моги́льный холм (-á).

tun n. больша́я бо́чка.

tuna n. туне́ц (-нца́).

tundra n. ту́ндра.

tune n. мело́дия, моти́в; in t., в тон, (of instrument) настро́енный (-ен); out of t., не в тон, фальши́вый; (of instrument) расстро́енный (-ен); be in t. with, (fig.) гармони́ровать imp. c + instr.; be out of t. with, (fig.) (thing) идти́ (иду́, идёшь; шёл, шла) imp. вразре́з c + instr.; (person) быть не в ладу́ c + instr.; call the t., распоряжа́ться imp.; change one's t., (пере)меня́ть imp., перемени́ть (-ню́, -нишь) perf. тон; v.t. (instrument; radio) настра́ивать imp., настро́ить perf. (engine etc.) регули́ровать imp., от~ perf.; (fig.) приспоса́бливать imp., приспосо́бить perf.; t. in, настра́ивать imp., настро́ить (radio) ра́дио (to, на + acc.); v.i.: t. up, настра́ивать imp., настро́ить perf. инструме́нт(ы). **tuneful** adj. мелоди́чный, гармони́чный. **tuneless** adj. немелоди́чный. **tuner** n. настро́йщик.

tungsten n. вольфра́м.

tunic n. (of uniform) ки́тель (pl. -ля & -ли) m.

tuning n. настро́йка; (of engine) регулиро́вка; t.-fork, камерто́н.

tunnel n. тунне́ль m.; v.i. прокла́дывать imp., проложи́ть (-жу́, -жишь) perf. тунне́ль m.

tunny n. туне́ц (-нца́).

turban *n.* тюрбáн, чалмá.

turbid *adj.* мýтный (-тен, -тнá, -тно); (*fig.*) тумáнный (-нен, -нна).

turbine *n.* турбина. **turbo-jet** *adj.* (*n.*) турбореактивный (самолёт). **turbo-prop** *adj.* (*n.*) турбовинтовóй (самолёт).

turbot *n.* тюрбó *neut.indecl.*

turbulence *n.* бýйность, бýрность; (*tech.*) турбулéнтность, **turbulent** *adj.* бýйный (бýен, бýйнá, -но), бýрный (-рен, бýрнá, -но); (*tech.*) турбулéнтный.

tureen *n.* сýпник, сýпница.

turf *n.* дёрн; *the t.*, (*track*) беговáя дорóжка; (*races*) скáчки *f.pl.*; *v.t.* дерновáть *imp.*

turgid *adj.* (*swollen*) опýхший; (*pompous*) напыщенный (-ен, -енна).

Turk *n.* тýрок (-рка), турчáнка.

turkey *n.* индю́к (-á), -ю́шка; (*dish*) индéйка.

Turkic *adj.* тю́ркский. **Turkish** *adj.* турéцкий; *T. bath*, турéцкие бáни *f.pl.*; *T. delight*, рахáт-лукýм. **Turkoman, Turkmen** *n.* туркмéн, ~ка *adj.* туркмéнский.

turmoil *n.* (*disorder*) беспорáдок (-дка); (*uproar*) суматóха, шум (-а(у)).

turn *n.* (*change of direction*) поворóт; (*revolution*) оборóт; (*service*) услýга; (*change*) изменéние; (*one's t. to do s.th.*) óчередь; (*character*) склад харáктера; (*circus, variety*) нóмер (*pl.* -á); *t. of phrase*, оборóт рéчи; *at every t.*, на кáждом шагý; *by, in turn(s)*, по óчереди; *to a t.*, как раз в мéру; *take a bad t.*, принимáть *imp.*, принять (приму́, -мешь; принял, -á, -о) рот дурнóй оборóт; *take a t. for the worse*, изменя́ться *imp.*, измениться (-ню́сь, -нишься) *perf.* к худшему; *v.t.* (*handle, key, car around etc.*) повора́чивать *imp.*, повернуть *perf.*; (*revolve, rotate*) враща́ть *imp.*; (*spin, twirl*) вертéть (-рчу́, -ртишь) *imp.* + *acc.*, *instr.*; (*page; on its face*) перевёртывать *imp.*, переверну́ть *perf.*; (*direct*) направля́ть *imp.*, напра́вить *perf.*; (*cause to become*) дéлать *imp.*, с~ *perf.* + *instr.*; (*on lathe*) точи́ть (-чу́, -чишь) *imp.*; *t. s.b.'s head*, кружи́ть

(кружу́, кру́жи́шь) *imp.*, вс~ *perf.* гóлову + *dat.*; *t. one's stomach*: *that turns my stomach*, меня́ от э́того тошни́т; *v.i.* (*change direction*) повора́чивать *imp.*, поверну́ть *perf.*; завёртывать *imp.*, заверну́ть *perf.*; (*rotate*) враща́ться *imp.*; (*t. round*) повора́чиваться *imp.*, поверну́ться *perf.*; (*become*) станови́ться (-влю́сь, -вишься *imp.*, стать (стáну, -нешь) *perf.* + *instr.*; *t. against*, ополча́ться *imp.*, ополчи́ться *perf.* на + *acc.*, про́тив + *gen.*; *t. around, see t. round*; *t. away*, (*v.t. & i.*) отвора́чивать(ся) *imp.*, отверну́ть(ся) *perf.*; *t. back*, (*v.i.*) повора́чивать *imp.*, поверну́ть назáд; (*v.t.*) (*bend back*) отгибáть *imp.*, отогну́ть *perf.*; *t. down*, (*refuse*) отклоня́ть *imp.*, отклони́ть (-ню́, -нишь) *perf.*; (*collar*) отгибáть *imp.*, отогну́ть *perf.*; (*make quieter*) дéлать *imp.*, с~ *perf.* ти́ше; *t. grey*, (*v.i.*) седéть *imp.*, по~ *perf.*; *t. in*, (*v.t.*) (*hand back*) возвраща́ть *imp.*, верну́ть *perf.*; (*so as to face inwards*) повора́чивать *imp.*, поверну́ть *perf.* вовну́трь; *t. inside out*, вывора́чивать *imp.*, вы́вернуть *perf.* наизна́нку; *t. into*, (*change into*) (*v.t. & i.*) превраща́ть(ся) *imp.*, преврати́ть(ся) (-ащу́(сь), -ати́шь(ся) *perf.* в + *acc.*; (*street*) свора́чивать *imp.*, сверну́ть *perf.* на + *acc.*; *t. off*, (*light, radio, etc.*) выключа́ть *imp.*, выключить *perf.*; (*tap*) закрывáть *imp.*, закры́ть (-рóю, -рóешь) *perf.*; (*branch off*) свора́чивать *imp.*, сверну́ть *perf.*; *t. on*, (*light, radio, etc.*) включа́ть *imp.*, включи́ть *perf.*; (*tap*) открывáть *imp.*, откры́ть (-рóю, -рóешь) *perf.*; (*attack*) напада́ть *imp.*, напáсть (-аду́, -адёшь; -ал) *perf.*; *t. out*, (*light etc.*) *see t. off*; (*prove to be*) оказывáться *imp.*, оказáться (-ажу́сь, -áжешься) *perf.* (*to be*, + *instr.*); (*drive out*) выгоня́ть *imp.*, вы́гнать (вы́гоню, -нишь) *perf.*; (*pockets*) вывёртывать *imp.*, вы́вернуть *perf.*; (*be present*) приходи́ть (-ожу́, -óдишь) *imp.*, прийти́ (приду́, -дёшь; пришёл, -шлá) *perf.*; (*product*) выпускáть *imp.*, вы́пустить *perf.*; *t. over*, (*egg, page, on its face, roll over*) (*v.t. & i.*) перевёртывать(ся) *imp.*, перевернуть(ся) *perf.*; (*hand over*) передавать (-даю, -даёшь) *imp.*, передать (-ам, -ашь, -аст, -адим; передал, -а, -о) *perf.*; (*think about*) обдумывать *imp.*, обдумать *perf.*; (*overturn*) (*v.t. & i.*) опрокидывать(ся) *imp.*, опрокинуть(ся) *perf.*; (*switch over*) переключать *imp.*, переключить *perf.* (to, на + *acc.*); *t. pale*, бледнеть *imp.*, по ~ *perf.*; *t. red*, краснеть *imp.*, по ~ *perf.*; *t. round*, (*v.i.*) (*rotate*) *t. one's back*; *t. to face s.th.*) повёртываться *imp.*, повернуться *perf.*; (*t. to face*) оборачиваться *imp.*, обернуться *perf.*; (*v.t.*) повёртывать *imp.*, повернуть *perf.*; (*t. sour*, скисать *imp.*, скиснуть (скис) *perf.*; *t. to*, обращаться *imp.*, обратиться (-ащусь, -атишься) *perf.* к + *dat.* (for, за + *instr.*); *t. up*, (*appear*) появляться *imp.*, появиться (-влюсь, -вишься) *perf.*; (*be found*) находиться (-ожусь, -одишься) *imp.*, найтись (-йдусь, -йдёшься) *imp.*, нашёлся; нашлась, -шлась) *perf.*; (*shorten garment*) подшивать *imp.*, подшить (-шью, -шьёшь) *perf.*; (*crop up*) подвёртываться *imp.*, подвернуться *perf.*; (*bend up*; *stick up*) (*v.t. & i.*) загибать(ся) *imp.*, загнуть(ся) *perf.*; (*make louder*) делать *imp.*, с ~ *perf.* громче; *t. up one's nose*, воротить (-очу, -отишь) *imp.* нос (gl, от + *gen.*) (*coll.*); *t. upside down*, перевора́чивать *imp.*, переверну́ть *perf.* вверх дном. **turn-out** *n.* (*people*) количество приходящих; (*goods*) выпуск. **turn-up** *n.* (*on trousers etc.*) отворот, обшлаг (-á; *pl.* -á).

turncoat *n.* ренегат, перебежчик.

turner *n.* токарь (*pl.* -ри & -ря) *m.*

turning *n.* (*road*) поворот; *t.-point*, поворотный пункт.

turnip *n.* репа.

turnover *n.* (*turning over*) опрокидывание; (*econ.*) оборот; (*fluctuation of manpower*) текущесть рабочей силы; (*pie*) полукруглый пирог (-á) с начинкой.

turnpike *n.* (*toll-gate*) застава (где взимается подорожный сбор).

turnstile *n.* турникет.

turntable *n.* (*rly.*) поворотный круг

(*loc.* -е & -ý; *pl.* -и); (*gramophone*) диск.

turpentine *n.* скипидар.

turpitude *n.* низость, порочность.

turquoise *n.* (*material, stone*) бирюза; *adj.* бирюзовый.

turret *n.* башенка; (*gun t.*) орудийная башня.

turtle *n.* черепаха.

turtle-dove *n.* горлица.

tusk *n.* бивень (-вня) *m.*, клык (-á).

tussle *n.* драка; *v.i.* драться (дерусь, -рёшься *perf.*; дрался, -лась, дралось) *imp.* (for, за + *acc.*).

tut *interj.* ах ты!

tutelage *n.* (*guardianship*) опекунство; (*instruction*) обучение. **tutelar(y)** *adj.* опекунский. **tutor** *n.* (*private teacher*) частный домашний учитель (*pl.* -ля) *m.*, ~ ница; (*coach*) репетитор; (*univ.*) руководитель *m.* ~ ница; (*primer*) учебник; (*mus. primer*) школа игры; *v.t.* (*instruct*) обучать *imp.*, обучить (-чу, -чишь) *perf.* (in, + *dat.*); (*give lessons to*) давать (даю, даёшь) *imp.*, дать (дам, дашь, даст, дадим; дал, -á, дало, -и) *perf.* уроки + *dat.*; (*guide*) руководить *imp.* + *instr.* **tutorial** *n.* консультация, встреча с руководителем.

tutu *n.* (*ballet*) пачка.

twaddle *n.* пустая болтовня, чепуха.

twang *n.* (*string*) резкий звук (натянутой струны); (*voice*) гнусавость; *v.i.* (*string*) звучать (-чу, -чишь) *imp.*, про ~ *perf.*; (*voice*) гнусавить; *v.t.* (*pluck*) перебирать *imp.*

tweak *n.* (*pinch*) щипок (-пка); *v.t.* щипать (-плю, -плешь) *imp.*, (у)щипнуть *perf.*

tweed *n.* твид.

tweet *n.* щебет; *v.i.* щебетать (-ечу, -ечешь) *imp.*

tweezers *n.* пинцет.

twelfth *adj.*, *n.* двенадцатый; (*date*) двенадцатое (число); *T.-night*, канун крещения. **twelve** *adj.*, *n.* двенадцать (-ти, -тью); (*time*) двенадцать (часов); (*age*) двенадцать лет.

twentieth *adj.*, *n.* двадцатый; (*date*) двадцатое (число). **twenty** *adj.*, *n.* двадцать (-ти, -тью); (*age*) двадцать лет; *pl.* (*decade*) двадцатые годы (-дов) *m.pl.*

twice adv. (2 times, on 2 occasions) два́жды; t. as, вдво́е, в два ра́за + comp.

twiddle v.t. (turn, twirl) верте́ть (-рчу́, -ртишь) imp., + acc., instr.; (toy with) игра́ть imp. + instr.; t. one's thumbs, (fig.) безде́льничать imp.

twig n. ве́точка, прут (пру́та́; pl. -тья, -тьев).

twilight n. су́мерки (-рек) pl.; (decline) упа́док (-дка). **twilit** adj. су́меречный.

twill n. твил, са́ржа.

twin n. близне́ц (-а́); pl. (Gemini) Близнецы́ m.pl.; t. beds, па́ра односпа́льных крова́тей; t. brother, брат (pl. -тья, -ьев) -близне́ц (-а́). t.-engined, двухмото́рный. t. town, го́род (pl. -а́) -побрати́м; v.t. (unite) соединя́ть imp., соедини́ть perf.

twine n. бечёвка, шпага́т; v.t. (twist, weave) вить (вью, вьёшь; вил, -а́, -о) imp., с ~ perf.; t. & i. (t. round) обвива́ть(ся) imp., обви́ть(ся) (обовью́(сь), -вьёшь(ся); обви́л(ся), -ла́(сь), -ло(сь)) perf.

twinge n. при́ступ (бо́ли), о́страя боль; (of conscience) угрызе́ние.

twinkle n. мерца́ние, огонёк (-нька́); v.i. мерца́ть imp., сверка́ть imp. **twinkling** n. мерца́ние; in the t. of an eye, в мгнове́ние о́ка.

twirl n. враще́ние, круче́ние; (flourish) ро́счерк; v.t. & i. (twist, turn) верте́ть(ся) (-рчу́(сь), -ртишь(ся)) imp.; (whirl, spin) кружи́ть(ся) (-жу́(сь), кружи́шь(ся) imp.

twist n. (bend) изги́б, поворо́т; (twisting) круче́ние; (distortion) искаже́ние; (sprain) вы́вих; (dance) твист; (characteristic) характе́рная осо́бенность; (in story) поворо́т фа́булы; v.t. скру́чивать imp., крути́ть (-учу́, -у́тишь) imp., с ~ perf.; (wind together) вить (вью, вьёшь; вил, -а́, -о) imp., с ~ perf.; (distort) искажа́ть imp., искази́ть perf.; (sprain) вывихивать imp., вы́вихнуть perf.; v.i. (bend, curve) изгиба́ться imp., изогну́ться perf.; (climb, meander, twine) ви́ться (вьётся) imp. **twisted** adj. (bent, distorted) искривлённый (-ён, -ена́) (also fig.). **twister** n. обма́нщик, -ица.

twit v.t. упрека́ть imp., упрекну́ть perf. (with, в + prep.).

twitch n. (twitching, jerk) подёргивание; (spasm) су́дорога; v.t. & i. дёргать(ся) imp., дёрнуть(ся) perf. (at, за + acc.).

twitter n. щебет; v.i. щебета́ть (-ечу́, -е́чешь) imp., чири́кать imp.

two adj. n. два, две (f.) (двух, -ум, -умя́, -ух); (collect.; 2 pairs) дво́е (-ои́х); (cards, number 2) дво́йка; (time) два (часа́); (age) два го́да; t. times, два́жды; t. times four, два́жды четы́ре; in t., (in half) надво́е, попола́м; t.-edged, обоюдоо́стрый (also fig.); (ambiguous) двусмы́сленный (-ен, -енна); t.-ply, (wood) двухсло́йный; (rope) двойно́й; t.-seater, двухмéстный (автомоби́ль); t.-stroke, двухта́ктный; t.-way, двусторо́нний.

twofold adj. двойно́й; adv. вдвойне́.

twosome n. па́ра, дво́йка.

tycoon n. магна́т.

tympanum n. (anat.) бараба́нная перепо́нка.

type n. (var. senses) тип; (model) типи́чный образе́ц (-зца́); (sort, kind) род (pl. -ы́); (letter) ли́тера; (collect.) шрифт (pl. -ы́); true to t., типи́чный; v.t. писа́ть (пишу́, -шешь) imp., на ~ perf. на маши́нке. **typescript** n. машинопись. **typewriter** n. пи́шущая маши́нка. **typewritten** adj. машинопи́сный.

typhoid fever n. брюшно́й тиф.

typhoon n. тайфу́н.

typhus n. сыпно́й тиф.

typical adj. типи́чный. **typify** v.t. служи́ть (-жу́, -жишь) imp., по ~ perf. типи́чным приме́ром + gen.; (personify) олицетворя́ть imp., олицетвори́ть perf.

typist n. машини́стка.

typographical adj. типогра́фский, книгопеча́тный. **typography** n. книгопеча́тание; (style) оформле́ние.

tyrannical adj. тирани́ческий, деспоти́чный. **tyrannize** v.i. (t.) тира́нствовать imp. (над + instr.). **tyrant** n. тира́н, де́спот.

tyre n. ши́на; t.-gauge, маноме́тр для шин.

U

U-boat *n.* неме́цкая подво́дная ло́дка; *U-tube*, U-обра́зная тру́бка; *U-turn*, разворо́т.

ubiquitous *adj.* вездесу́щий; (*universal*) повсеме́стный. **ubiquity** *n.* вездесу́щность; повсеме́стность.

udder *n.* вы́мя *neut.*

U.F.O. *abbr.* НЛО (неопо́знанный лета́ющий объе́кт); (*flying saucer*) лета́ющая таре́лка.

ugh *interj.* тьфу!

ugliness *n.* уро́дство. **ugly** *adj.* некраси́вый, уро́дливый, безобра́зный; (*unpleasant*) неприя́тный; (*repulsive*) проти́вный; *u.* duckling, (*fig.*) га́дкий утёнок (-нка; *pl.* утя́та, -т).

Ukrainian *n.* украи́нец (-нца), -нка; *adj.* украи́нский.

ukulele *n.* гава́йская гита́ра.

ulcer *n.* я́зва. **ulcerate** *v.t.* & *i.* изъязвля́ть(ся) *impf.*, изъязви́ть(ся) *perf.* **ulcered**, **ulcerous** *adj.* изъязвлённый.

ulna *n.* локтева́я кость (*pl.* -ти, -те́й)

ulterior *adj.* скры́тый.

ultimate *adj.* (*final*) после́дний, оконча́тельный; (*fundamental*) основно́й. **ultimately** *adv.* в коне́чном счёте, в конце́ концо́в. **ultimatum** *n.* ультима́тум.

ultra- *in comb.* ультра-, сверх-.

ultramarine *n.* ультрамари́н; *adj.* ультрамари́новый. **ultra-violet** *adj.* ультрафиоле́товый.

umber *n.* у́мбра; *adj.* тёмно-кори́чевый.

umbilical *adj.* пупо́чный; *u.* cord пупови́на.

umbra *n.* по́лная тень (*loc.* -ни́; *pl.* -ни, -не́й) **umbrage** *n.* оби́да; *take u.*, обижа́ться *impf.*, оби́деться (оби́жусь, -и́дишься) *perf.* (at, на + *acc.*).

umbrella *n.* зо́нтик, зонт (-а́); *u.* stand, подста́вка для зонто́в.

umpire *n.* судья́ (*pl.* -дьи, -де́й, -дьям) *m.*; *v.t.* & *i.* суди́ть (сужу́, су́дишь) *impf.*

unabashed *adj.* нерастеря́вшийся; без вся́кого смуще́ния. **unabated** *adj.* неосла́бленный, неосла́бный. **unable**

adj.: *be u. to*, не мочь (могу́, мо́жешь; мог, -ла́) *impf.*, с ~ *perf.*; быть не в состоя́нии; (*not know how to*) не уме́ть *impf.*, с ~ *perf.* **unabridged** *adj.* несокращённый, без сокраще́ний. **unaccompanied** *adj.* несопровожда́емый; (*mus.*) без аккомпанеме́нта. **unaccountable** *adj.* (*inexplicable*) необъясни́мый. **unaccustomed** *adj.* (*not accustomed*) непривы́кший (to, к + *dat.*); (*unusual*) непривы́чный. **unadulterated** *adj.* настоя́щий, нефальсифици́рованный; чисте́йший. **unaffected** *adj.* и́скренний (-нен, -нна, -нне & -нно); (*not affected*) незатро́нутый. **unaided** *adj.* без по́мощи, самостоя́тельный. **unalloyed** *adj.* беспри́месный, чи́стый (чист, -а́, -о, чи́сты) **unalterable** *adj.* неизменя́емый, неизме́нный (-нен, -нна). **unambiguous** *adj.* недвусмы́сленный (-ен, -енна) **unanimity** *n.* единоду́шие. **unanimous** *adj.* единоду́шный. **unanswerable** *adj.* (*irrefutable*) неопроверж́имый. **unapproachable** *adj.* непристу́пный; (*unmatched*) несравни́мый. **unarmed** *adj.* безору́жный, невооружённый. **unashamed** *adj.* бессо́вестный, на́глый (нагл, -а́, -о). **unasked** *adj.* доброво́льный, непро́шеный (*coll.*). **unassailable** *adj.* непристу́пный; (*irrefutable*) неопроверж́имый. **unassuming** *adj.* скро́мный (-мен, -мна́, -мно), непритяза́тельный. **unattainable** *adj.* недосяга́емый. **unattended** *adj.* (*unaccompanied*) несопровожда́емый. **unattractive** *adj.* непривлека́тельный. **unauthorized** *adj.* неразрешённый; (*person*) неправомо́чный. **unavailable** *adj.* не име́ющийся в нали́чии, недосту́пный; *be u.*, в нали́чии нет + *gen.* **unavailing** *adj.* беспол́езный, тще́тный. **unavoidable** *adj.* неизбе́жный, немину́емый. **unaware** *predic.*: *be u. of*, не сознава́ть (-аю́, -аёшь) *impf.* + *acc.*; не знать *impf.* о + *prep.* **unawares** *adv.* враспло́х, неожи́данно; (*unintentionally*) неча́янно. **unbalance** *v.t.* (*psych.*) лиша́ть *impf.*, лиши́ть *perf.* душе́вного равнове́сия. **unbalanced** *adj.* (*psych.*) неуравнове́шенный (-ен, -енна). **unbearable** *adj.* невыноси́мый. **unbeatable** *adj.* (*unsurpassable*) не могу́щий быть превзойдённым; (*invincible*) непобеди́мый. **unbeaten** *adj.* (*unsurpassed*) непревзойдённый (-ён, -ённа). **unbecoming** *adj.* (*inappropriate*) неподходя́щий; (*unseemly*) неприли́чный; *be u.*, быть не к лицу́ (to, +*dat.*). **unbelief** *n.* неве́рие. **unbelievable** *adj.* невероя́тный. **unbeliever** *n.* неве́рующий *sb.* **unbend** *v.t. & i.* (*straighten*) выпрямля́ть(ся) *imp.*, вы́прямить(ся) *perf.*; разгиба́ть(ся) *imp.*, разогну́ть(ся) *perf.*; *v.i.* (*become affable*) станови́ться (-влю́сь, -вишься) *imp.*, стать (-а́ну, -а́нешь) *perf.* приве́тливым. **unbending** *adj.* непреклóнный (-нен, -нна). **unbias(s)ed** *adj.* беспристра́стный. **unblemished** *adj.* незапя́тнанный. **unblushing** *adj.* бессты́дный. **unbolt** *v.t.* отпира́ть *imp.*, отпере́ть (отопру́, -рёшь; о́тпер, -ла́, -ло) *perf.* **unborn** *adj.* ещё не рождённый (-ён, -ена́). **unbosom** *v.t.*: *u. oneself*, открыва́ть *imp.*, откры́ть (-ро́ю, -ро́ешь) *perf.* ду́шу. **unbound** *adj.* (*free*) свобо́дный; (*book*) непереплетённый. **unbounded** *adj.* (*not limited*) неограни́ченный (-ен, -енна); (*joy*) безме́рный; (*infinite*) безграни́чный. **unbreakable** *adj.* небью́щийся. **unbridled** *adj.* разну́зданный (-ан, -анна). **unbroken** *adj.* (*intact*) неразби́тый, це́лый; (*continuous*) непреры́вный; (*unsurpassed*) непоби́тый; (*horse*) необъе́зженный. **unbuckle** *v.t.* расстёгивать *imp.*, расстегну́ть *perf.* **unburden** *v.t.*: *u. oneself*, отводи́ть (-ожу́, -о́дишь) *imp.*, отвести́ (-еду́, -едёшь; -ёл, -ела́) *perf.* ду́шу. **unbutton** *v.t.* расстёгивать *imp.*, расстегну́ть *perf.* **uncalled-for** *adj.* неуме́стный. **uncanny** *adj.* жу́ткий (-ток, -тка́, -тко), сверхъесте́ственный (-ен, -енна). **uncared-for** *adj.* забро́шенный. **unceasing** *adj.* непреры́вный, безостано́вочный. **unceremonious** *adj.* бесцеремо́нный (-нен, -нна). **uncertain** *adj.* (*not certainly known*) то́чно неизве́стный,

нея́сный (-сен, -сна́, -сно); (*indecisive, hesitating*) неуве́ренный (-ен, -енна); (*lacking belief, confidence*) неуве́ренный (-ен, -ена); (*indeterminate*) неопределённый (-нен, -нна); (*changeable*) изме́нчивый; *be u.*, (*not know for certain*) то́чно не знать *imp.*; *in no u. terms*, в недвусмы́сленных выраже́ниях. **uncertainty** *n.* неизве́стность; неуве́ренность; неопределённость; изме́нчивость. **unchain** *v.t.* спуска́ть *imp.* спусти́ть (-ущу́, -у́стишь) *perf.* с це́пи. **unchallenged** *adj.* не вызыва́ющий возраже́ний. **unchangeable** *adj.* неизмени́мый, неменя́емый. **unchanged** *adj.* неизмени́вшийся. **unchanging** *adj.* неменя́ющийся. **uncharacteristic** *adj.* нетипи́чный, нехара́ктерный. **uncharitable** *adj.* немилосе́рдный, жесто́кий (-о́к, -о́ка́, -о́ко). **uncharted** *adj.* (*fig.*) неиссле́дованный. **unchecked** *adj.* (*unrestrained*) необу́зданный (-ан, -анна). **uncivil** *adj.* неве́жливый. **uncivilized** *adj.* нецивилизо́ванный. **unclaimed** *adj.* невостре́бованный. **unclassified** *adj.* неклассифици́рованный; (*secret*) несекре́тный.

uncle *n.* дя́дя (*pl.* -ди, -дей & -дья́, -дьёв) *m.*

unclean *adj.* (*not clean*; *Bibl. of food*) нечи́стый (-т, -та́, -то). **unclear** *adj.* нея́сный (-сен, -сна́, -сно), непоня́тный. **uncoil** *v.t. & i.* разма́тывать(ся) *imp.*, размота́ть(ся) *perf.* **uncomfortable** *adj.* неудо́бный; (*awkward*) нело́вкий (-вок, -вка́, -вко). **uncommon** *adj.* (*unusual, remarkable*) необыкнове́нный (-нен, -нна), замеча́тельный; (*rare*) ре́дкий (-док, -дка́, -дко). **uncommunicative** *adj.* необщи́тельный, молчали́вый. **uncomplaining** *adj.* безро́потный. **uncompleted** *adj.* неоко́нченный, незако́нченный. **uncomplimentary** *adj.* нелестный. **uncompromising** *adj.* не иду́щий на компроми́ссы; (*inflexible*) непрекло́нный (-нен, -нна). **unconcealed** *adj.* нескрыва́емый. **unconcern** *n.* (*freedom from anxiety*) безза́ботность; (*indifference*) равноду́шие. **unconcerned** *adj.* безза́ботный; равноду́шный. **unconditional**

adj. безогово́рочный, безусло́вный. **unconfirmed** *adj.* неподтверждённый. **unconnected** *adj.*: *u. with,* не свя́занный (-ан) с + *instr.* **unconquerable** *adj.* непобеди́мый. **unconscionable** *adj.* бессо́вестный; (*excessive*) неуме́ренный (-ен, -енна). **unconscious** *adj. (also unintentional)* бессозна́тельный; (*predic.*) без созна́ния; (*unintentional*) нево́льный; *be u. of,* не сознава́ть (-аю́, -аёшь) *imp.* + *gen.*; *n.* подсозна́тельное *sb.* **unconsciousness** *n.* бессозна́тельное состоя́ние; бессозна́тельность. **unconstitutional** *adj.* неконституцио́нный (-нен, -нна). **unconstrained** *adj.* непринуждённый (-ён, -ённа). **uncontrollable** *adj.* неудержи́мый, неукроти́мый. **uncontrolled** *adj.* (*unbridled*) необу́зданный (-ан, -анна). **unconventional** *adj.* чу́ждый (-д, -да́, -до) усло́вности; необы́чный. **unconvincing** *adj.* неубеди́тельный. **uncooked** *adj.* сыро́й (-р, -ра́, -ро). **unco-operative** *adj.* неотзы́вчивый, безуча́стный. **uncork** *v.t.* отку́поривать *imp.*, отку́порить *perf.* **uncouple** *v.t.* расцепля́ть *imp.*, расцепи́ть (-плю́, -пишь) *perf.* **uncouth** *adj.* гру́бый (-б, -ба́, -бо). **uncover** *v.t.* (*remove cover from*) снима́ть *imp.*, снять (сниму́, -мешь; снял, -á, -о) *perf.* кры́шку с + *gen.*; (*reveal*) открыва́ть *imp.*, откры́ть (-ро́ю, -ро́ешь) *perf.*; (*disclose*) обнару́живать *imp.*, обнару́жить *perf.* **uncovered** *adj.* незакры́тый, откры́тый. **uncritical** *adj.* некрити́чный. **unction** *n.* (*ceremony*) пома́зание; (*process*) втира́ние ма́зи; (*ointment*) мазь; (*balm*) еле́й; (*piety*) на́божность; (*affectedness*) еле́йность; *extreme u.,* соборова́ние. **unctuous** *adj.* еле́йный. **uncultivated** *adj.* (*land*) невозде́ланный; (*talent*) неразви́тый (-развит, -á, -о) (*uncultured*) некульту́рный. **uncultured** *adj.* некульту́рный. **uncurl** *v.t. & i.* развива́ть(ся) *imp.*, разви́ть(ся) (разовью́, -ёт(ся); разви́л(ся), -лá(сь), разви́ло́(сь)) *perf.* **uncut** *adj.* (*unabridged*) несокращённый, без сокраще́ний.

undamaged *adj.* неповреждённый, неиспо́рченный. **undaunted** *adj.* бесстра́шный. **undeceive** *v.t.* выводи́ть (-ожу́, -о́дишь) *imp.*, вы́вести (-еду, -едешь; -ел) *perf.* из заблужде́ния. **undecided** *adj.* (*not settled*) нерешённый; (*irresolute*) нереши́тельный. **undemanding** *adj.* нетре́бовательный. **undemocratic** *adj.* недемократи́ческий, антидемократи́ческий. **undemonstrative** *adj.* сде́ржанный (-ан, -анна). **undeniable** *adj.*, неоспори́мый, несомне́нный (-нен, -нна).

under *prep.* (*position*) под + *instr.*; (*direction*) под + *acc.*; (*fig.*) под + *instr.*; (*less than*) ме́ньше + *gen.*, ни́же + *gen.*; (*according to*) по + *dat.*; (*in view of, in the reign, time, of*) при + *prep.*; *u. age,* несовершенноле́тний; *u. repair,* в ремо́нте; *u. way,* на ходу́; *from u.,* из-под + *gen.*; *adv.* (*position*) внизу́, ни́же; (*direction*) вниз; (*less*) ме́ньше; *adj.* ни́жний; (*subordinate*) ни́зший; *u.-secretary,* замести́тель *m.* мини́стра; *u.-side,* ни́жняя пове́рхность.

undercarriage *n.* шасси́ *neut. indecl.* **underclothes, underclothing** *n.* ни́жнее бельё. **undercoat** *n.* (*of paint*) грунто́вка. **undercover** *adj.* та́йный, секре́тный. **undercurrent** *n.* подво́дное тече́ние; (*fig.*) скры́тая тенде́нция. **undercut** *v.t.* (*cut away*) подреза́ть *imp.*, подре́зать (-е́жу, -е́жешь) *perf.*; (*price*) назнача́ть *imp.*, назна́чить *perf.* бо́лее ни́зкую це́ну чем + *nom.* **underdeveloped** *adj.* недора́звитый, слабора́звитый; (*photog.*) недопроя́вленный. **underdog** *n.* неуда́чник. **underdone** *adj.* недожа́ренный (-ен). **underemployment** *n.* непо́лная за́нятость. **underestimate** *v.t.* недооце́нивать *imp.*, недооцени́ть (-ню́, -нишь) *perf.*; *n.* недооце́нка. **underexpose** *v.t.* недоде́рживать *imp.*, недодержа́ть (-жу́, -жишь) *perf.* **underfed** *adj.* недоко́рмленный. **underfelt** *n.* грунт ковра́. **underfloor** *adj.* находя́щийся под по́лом. **underfoot** *adv.* под нога́ми. **undergarment** *n.* предме́т ни́жнего белья́.

undergo *v.t.* подверга́ться *imp.*, подве́ргнуться (-гся) *perf.* + *dat.*; (*endure*) переноси́ть (-ошу́, -о́сишь) *imp.*, перенести́ (-есу́, -есёшь; -ёс, -есла́) perf. **undergraduate** n. студе́нт, ~ка. **underground** n. (rly.) метро́ neut. indecl.; (fig.) подпо́лье; adj. подзе́мный; (fig.) подпо́льный; adv. под землёй; (fig.) подпо́льно; go u., уходи́ть (-ожу́, -о́дишь) imp., уйти́ (уйду́, -дёшь; ушёл, ушла́) perf. в подпо́лье. **undergrowth** n. подле́сок (-ска). **underhand** adj. закули́сный, та́йный. **underlie** v.t. (fig.) лежа́ть (-жи́т) imp. в осно́ве + gen. **underline** v.t. подчёркивать imp., подчеркну́ть perf. **underling** n. подчинённый sb.

undermanned adj. испы́тывающий недоста́ток в рабо́чей си́ле. **undermentioned** adj. нижеупомя́нутый. **undermine** v.t. де́лать imp., с~ perf. подко́п под + instr.; (wash away) подмыва́ть imp., подмы́ть (-мо́ю, -мо́ешь) perf.; (authority) подрыва́ть imp., подорва́ть (-ву́, -вёшь; подорва́л, -а́, -о) perf.; (health) разруша́ть imp., разру́шить perf. **underneath** adv. (position) внизу́; (direction) вниз; prep. (position) под + instr.; (direction) под + acc.; n. ни́жняя часть (pl. -ти, -те́й); adj. ни́жний. **undernourished** adj. недоко́рмленный; be u., недоеда́ть imp. **undernourishment** n. недоеда́ние.

underpaid adj. низкоопла́чиваемый. **underpants** n. кальсо́ны (-н) pl., трусы́ (-со́в) pl. **underpass** n. прое́зд под полотно́м доро́ги, тонне́ль m. **underpin** v.t. подводи́ть (-ожу́, -о́дишь) imp., подвести́ (-еду́, -едёшь; -ёл, -ела́) perf. фунда́мент под + acc. **underpopulated** adj. малонаселённый (-ён, -ённа). **underprivileged** adj. по́льзующийся ме́ньшими права́ми; (poor) бе́дный (-ден, -дна́, -дно, бе́дны́). **underrate** v.t. недооце́нивать imp., недооцени́ть perf.

undersell v.t. продава́ть (-даю́, -даёшь) imp., прода́ть (-а́м, -а́шь, -а́ст, -ади́м; про́дал, -а́, -о) perf. деше́вле + gen. **undersigned** adj. (n.) нижеподписа́вшийся (sb.). **undersized** adj. маломе́рный, нестанда́ртный; (dwarfish) ка́рликовый. **underskirt** n. ни́жняя ю́бка.

understaffed adj. неукомплекто́ванный.

understand v.t. понима́ть imp., поня́ть (пойму́, -мёшь; по́нял, -а́, -о) perf.; (have heard say) слы́шать imp. **understandable** adj. поня́тный. **understanding** n. понима́ние; (intellect) ра́зум; (mutual u.) взаимопонима́ние; (agreement) соглаше́ние; (harmony) согла́сие; adj. (sympathetic) чу́ткий (-ток, -тка́, -тко), отзы́вчивый. **understate** v.t. преуменьша́ть imp., преуме́ньшить perf. **understatement** n. преуменьше́ние. **understudy** n. дублёр; v.t. дубли́ровать imp. роль + gen.

undertake v.t. (engage in, enter upon) предпринима́ть imp., предприня́ть (-иму́, -и́мешь; предпри́нял, -а́, -о) perf.; (responsibility) брать (беру́, берёшь) imp., взять (возьму́, -мёшь; взял, -а́, -о) perf. на себя́; (+ inf.) обя́зываться imp., обяза́ться (-яжу́сь, -я́жешься) perf.; (guarantee) руча́ться imp., поручи́ться (-чу́сь, -чишься) perf. (that, что). **undertaker** n. гробовщи́к (-а́). **undertaking** n. предприя́тие; (obligation) обяза́тельство. **undertone** n. (half-tint) полуто́н (pl. -ы & -а́); (nuance) отте́нок (-нка); speak in undertones, говори́ть imp. вполго́лоса. **undertow** n. глуби́нное тече́ние, противополо́жное пове́рхностному; подво́дное тече́ние. **underwater** adj. подво́дный. **underwear** n. ни́жнее бельё. **underworld** n. (myth.) преиспо́дняя sb.; (criminals) престу́пный мир (pl. -ы́). **underwrite** v.t. (sign) подпи́сывать imp., подписа́ть (подпишу́, -и́шешь) perf.; (accept liability for) принима́ть imp., приня́ть (приму́, -мешь; при́нял, -а́, -о) perf. на страх; (guarantee) гаранти́ровать imp., perf. **underwriter** n. подпи́счик; страхо́вщик; (company) страхова́я компа́ния.

undeserved adj. незаслу́женный (-ен, -енна). **undeserving** adj. незаслу́живающий; u. of, не заслу́живающий + gen. **undesirable** adj. нежела́тельный; n. нежела́тельное лицо́ (pl. -ца). **undeveloped** adj. нера́звитый.

(*land*) незастро́енный. **undignified** *adj.* недосто́йный (-о́ин, -о́йна). **undiluted** *adj.* неразба́вленный. **undisciplined** *adj.* недисциплини́рованный (-ан, -анна). **undiscovered** *adj.* неоткры́тый; (*unknown*) неизве́стный. **undiscriminating** *adj.* непроница́тельный, неразбо́рчивый. **undisguised** *adj.* откры́тый, я́вный. **undismayed** *adj.* необескура́женный. **undisputed** *adj.* бесспо́рный. **undistinguished** *adj.* невыдаю́щийся. **undisturbed** *adj.* (*untouched*) нетро́нутый; (*peaceful*) споко́йный; (*in order*) в поря́дке. **undivided** *adj.* (*unanimous*) единоду́шный; *give* u. *attention*, посвяща́ть *imp.*, посвяти́ть (-ящу́, -яти́шь) *perf.* все си́лы (to, +*dat.*). **undo** *v.t.* (*open*) открыва́ть *imp.*, откры́ть (-ро́ю, -ро́ешь) *perf.*; (*untie*) развя́зывать *imp.*, развяза́ть (-яжу́, -я́жешь) *perf.*; (*unbutton, unhook, unbuckle*) расстёгивать *imp.*, расстегну́ть *perf.*; (*destroy, cancel*) уничтожа́ть *imp.*, уничто́жить *perf.* (*be the undoing of*) губи́ть (гублю́, -бишь) *imp.*, по- *perf.* **undoing** *n.* (*ruin, downfall*) ги́бель; (*destruction*) уничтоже́ние. **undoubted** *adj.* несомне́нный (-нен, -нна). **undoubtedly** *adv.* несомне́нно. **undress** *v.t. & i.* раздева́ть(ся) *imp.*, разде́ть(ся) (-е́ну(сь), -е́нешь(ся)) *perf.* **undrinkable** *adj.* него́дный (-ден, -дна́, -дно) для питья́. **undue** *adj.* чрезме́рный. **unduly** *adv.* чрезме́рно.

undulate *v.i.* быть волни́стым, холми́стым. **undulating** *adj.* волни́стый. **undulation** *n.* волни́стость; (*motion*) волнообра́зное движе́ние; (*of surface*) неро́вность пове́рхности.

undying *adj.* (*eternal*) ве́чный.

unearned *adj.* незарабо́танный; (*undeserved*) незаслу́женный (-ен, -енна); u. *income*, трудово́й дохо́д. **unearth** *v.t.* (*dig up*) выка́пывать *imp.*, вы́копать *perf.* из земли́; (*fox etc.*) выгоня́ть *imp.*, вы́гнать (вы́гоню, -нишь) *perf.* из норы́; (*fig.*) раска́пывать *imp.*, раскопа́ть *perf.* **unearthly** *adj.* неземно́й, сверхъесте́ственный (-ен, -енна); (*inconvenient*) кра́йне неудо́бный. **uneasiness** *n.* (*anxiety*)

беспоко́йство, трево́га; (*awkwardness*) нело́вкость. **uneasy** *adj.* беспоко́йный, трево́жный; нело́вкий (-вок, -нел́вка́, -вко). **uneatable** *adj.* несъедо́бный. **uneconomic** *adj.* нерента́бельный, неэкономи́чный. **uneconomical** *adj.* (*car etc.*) неэкономи́чный; (*person*) неэконо́мный. **uneducated** *adj.* необразо́ванный (-ан, -анна). **unemployed** *adj.* безрабо́тный; (*unoccupied*) незаня́тый (-т, -та́, -то); (*unused*) неиспо́льзованный. **unemployment** *n.* безрабо́тица; u. *benefit*, посо́бие по безрабо́тице. **unending** *adj.* бесконе́чный, несконча́емый. **unenlightened** *adj.* непросвещённый (-ён, -ённа); (*uninformed*) неосведомлённый. **unenterprising** *adj.* непредприи́мчивый, безынициати́вный. **unenviable** *adj.* незави́дный. **unequal** *adj.* нера́вный; (*of u. value*) неравноце́нный (-нен, -нна); (*unjust*) несправедли́вый; (*inadequate*) неадеква́тный; u. *to*, неподходя́щий для+*gen.* **unequalled** *adj.* бесподо́бный, невзойдённый (-ён, -ённа). **unequivocal** *adj.* недвусмы́сленный (-ен, -енна). **unerring** *adj.* безоши́бочный.

UNESCO *abbr.* ЮНЕ́СКО.

uneven *adj.* неро́вный (-вен, -вна́, -вно). **uneventful** *adj.* не бога́тый собы́тиями, ти́хий (тих, -а́, -о). **unexceptionable** *adj.* безукори́зненный (-ен, -енна). **unexceptional** *adj.* обы́чный. **unexpected** *adj.* неожи́данный (-ан, -анна); (*sudden*) внеза́пный. **unexplainable** *adj.* необъясни́мый. **unexplored** *adj.* неиссле́дованный. **unexpurgated** *adj.* без купю́р, неподве́ргшийся цензу́ре.

unfailing *adj.* неизме́нный (-нен, -нна); (*faithful*) ве́рный (-рен, -рна́, -рно, ве́рны); (*reliable*) надёжный; (*inexhaustible*) неисчерпа́емый. **unfair** *adj.* несправедли́вый; (*dishonest*) нече́стный (-тен, -тна́, -тно). **unfaithful** *adj.* неве́рный (-рен, -рна́, -рно, неве́рны); (*treacherous*) вероло́мный. **unfamiliar** *adj.* незнако́мый; (*unknown*) неве́домый. **unfashionable** *adj.* немо́дный (-ден, -дна́, -дно). **unfasten** *v.t.* (*detach untie*) открепля́ть *imp.*, открепи́ть perf.; (detach, unbutton) отстёгивать imp., отстегну́ть perf.; (undo, unbutton, unhook) расстёгивать imp., расстегну́ть perf. **unfathomable** adj. (immeasurable) неизмери́мый, бездо́нный; (incomprehensible) непостижи́мый. **unfavourable** adj. неблагоприя́тный; (not approving) неблагоскло́нный (-нен, -нна). **unfeeling** adj. бесчу́вственный (-ен, -енна). **unfeigned** adj. и́стинный (-нен, -нна), неподде́льный. **unfinished** adj. незако́нченный; (crude) необрабо́танный (-ан, -анна). **unfit** adj. него́дный (-ден, -дна́, -дно), непригодный, неподходя́щий; (unhealthy) нездоро́вый. **unfix** v.t. открепля́ть imp., открепи́ть perf. **unflagging** adj. неослабева́ющий. **unfledged** adj. неоперивший ся (also fig.). **unfold** v.t. & i. развёртывать(ся) imp., разверну́ть(ся) perf.; (open up) раскрыва́ть(ся) imp., раскры́ть(ся) (-ро́ю(сь), -ро́ешь(ся)) perf. **unforeseen** adj. непредви́денный. **unforgettable** adj. незабыва́емый. **unforgivable** adj. непрости́тельный. **unforgiving** adj. непроща́ющий. **unfortunate** adj. несча́стли́вый, несча́стный; (regrettable) неуда́чный; n. несча́стли́вец (-вца), неуда́чник, -ица. **unfortunately** adv. к несча́стью, к сожале́нию. **unfounded** adj. необосно́ванный (-ан, -анна). **unfreeze** v.t. & i. размора́живать(ся) imp., разморо́зить(ся) perf. **unfriendly** adj. недружелю́бный, приве́тливый. **unfrock** v.t. лиша́ть imp., лиши́ть perf. духо́вного са́на. **unfruitful** adj. беспло́дный. **unfulfilled** adj. (promise etc.) невы́полненный; (hopes etc.) неосуществлённый. **unfurl** v.t. & i. развёртывать(ся) imp., разверну́ть(ся) perf. **unfurnished** adj. немеблиро́ванный.

ungainly adj. неskла́дный, неуклю́жий. **ungentlemanly** adj. неблагоро́дный, неве́жливый. **ungodliness** n. безбо́жие. **ungodly** adj. (also outrageous) безбо́жный. **ungovernable** adj. необу́зданный (-ан, -анна), неукроти́мый. **ungracious** adj. нелюбе́зный. **ungrammatical** adj. граммати́чески непра́вильный. **ungrateful** adj. небла-

года́рный. **unguarded** adj. (incautious) неосторо́жный.
unguent n. мазь.
unhappiness n. несча́стье. **unhappy** adj. несча́стли́вый, несча́стный. **unharmed** adj. невреди́мый. **unhealthy** adj. (in var. senses) нездоро́вый, боле́зненный (-ен, -енна); (harmful) вре́дный (-ден, -дна́, -дно). **unheard-of** adj. неслы́ханный (-ан, -анна). **unheeded** adj. незаме́ченный. **unheeding** adj. невнима́тельный. **unhelpful** adj. бесполе́зный. **unhesitating** adj. реши́тельный. **unhesitatingly** adv. без колеба́ния. **unhinge** v.t. снима́ть imp., снять (сниму́, -мешь; снял, -а́, -о) perf. с пе́тли; (fig.) расстра́ивать imp., расстро́ить perf. **unholy** adj. (impious) нечести́вый; (awful) ужа́сный. **unhook** v.t. снима́ть imp., снять (сниму́, -мешь; снял, -а́, -о) perf. с крючка́; (undo hooks) расстёгивать imp., расстегну́ть perf.; (uncouple) расцепля́ть imp., расцепи́ть (-плю́, -пишь) perf. **unhoped-for** adj. неожи́данный (-ан, -анна). **unhorse** v.t. сбра́сывать imp., сбро́сить perf. с ло́шади. **unhurt** adj. невреди́мый.
unicorn n. единоро́г.
unification n. объедине́ние, унифика́ция (also standardization).
uniform n. фо́рма, фо́рменная оде́жда; adj. единообра́зный; (homogeneous) одноро́дный; (of u.) фо́рменный. **uniformity** n. единообра́зие; одноро́дность. **unify** v.t. объединя́ть imp., объедини́ть perf.; унифици́ровать imp., perf. (also standardize).
unilateral adj. односторо́нний.
unimaginable adj. невообрази́мый. **unimaginative** adj. лишённый (-ён, -ена́) воображе́ния, проза́ичный. **unimpeachable** adj. безупре́чный. **unimportant** adj. нева́жный. **uninformed** adj. (ignorant) несве́дущий (about, в + prep.); (ill-informed) неосведомлённый. **uninhabitable** adj. непригодный для жилья́. **uninhabited** adj. необита́емый. **uninitiated** adj. непосвящённый. **uninspired** adj. бана́льный. **unintelligible** adj. неразбо́рчивый. **un-**

intentional *adj.* неумы́шленный (-ен, -енна). **unintentionally** *adv.* неумы́шленно. **uninterested** *adj.* незаинтересо́ванный. **uninteresting** *adj.* неинтере́сный. **uninterrupted** *adj.* непреры́вный. **uninviting** *adj.* непривлека́тельный.

union *n.* (*alliance*) сою́з; (*joining together, alliance*) объедине́ние; (*combination*) соедине́ние; (*marriage*) бра́чный сою́з; (*harmony*) согла́сие; (*trade u.*) профсою́з; (*polit.*) унио́нист. **unionist** *n.* член профсою́за; (*polit.*) унио́нист.

unique *adj.* еди́нственный (в своём ро́де), уника́льный.

unison *n.* (*mus.*) унисо́н; (*fig.*) согла́сие; *in u.*, (*mus.*) в унисо́н; (*fig.*) в согла́сии.

unit *n.* едини́ца; (*mil.*) часть (*pl.* -ти -те́й).

unite *v.t.* & *i.* соединя́ть(ся) *imp.*, соедини́ть(ся) *perf.*; объединя́ть(ся) *imp.*, объедини́ть(ся) *perf.* **united** *adj.* соединённый, объединённый; *U. Nations*, Организа́ция Объединённых На́ций; *U. States*, Соединённые Шта́ты *m.pl.* Аме́рики. **unity** *n.* еди́нство; (*cohesion*) спло́ченность; (*math.*) едини́ца.

universal *adj.* (*general*) всео́бщий; (*world-wide*) всеми́рный; (*many-sided*) универса́льный. **universe** *n.* вселе́нная *sb.*; (*world*) мир; (*cosmos*) ко́смос. **university** *n.* университе́т; *attrib.* университе́тский.

unjust *adj.* несправедли́вый. **unjustifiable** *adj.* не име́ющий оправда́ния. **unjustified** *adj.* неопра́вданный.

unkempt *adj.* нечёсаный (-ан); (*untidy*) неопря́тный. **unkind** *adj.* недо́брый, злой (зол, зла, зло). **unknown** *adj.* неизве́стный.

unlace *v.t.* расшнуро́вывать *imp.*, расшнурова́ть *perf.* **unlawful** *adj.* незако́нный (-нен, -нна). **unlearn** *v.t.* разу́чиваться *imp.*, разучи́ться (-чу́сь, -чишься) *perf.* (*how to*, +*inf.*); *v.t.* забыва́ть *imp.*, забы́ть (забу́ду, -дешь) *perf.* **unleash** *v.t.* (*dog*) спуска́ть *imp.*, спусти́ть (-ущу́, -у́стишь) *perf.* с при́вязи; (*also fig.*) развя́зывать *imp.*, развяза́ть (-яжу́, -я́жешь) *perf.*

unleavened *adj.* бездро́жжево́й, пре́сный (-сен, -сна́, -сно).

unless *conj.* е́сли…не.

unlike *adj.* непохо́жий (на+*acc.*); (*in contradistinction to*) в отли́чие от+ *gen.* **unlikely** *adj.* малове́роятный, неправдоподо́бный; *it is u. that*, вряд ли, едва́ ли. **unlimited** *adj.* (*unrestricted*) неограни́ченный (-ен, -енна); (*boundless*) безграни́чный. **unlined** *adj.* (*clothing*) без подкла́дки. **unload** *v.t.* (*remove load from*) разгружа́ть *imp.*, разгрузи́ть (-ужу́, -у́зишь) *perf.*; (*remove load from, remove from*) выгружа́ть *imp.*, вы́грузить *perf.*; (*gun*) разряжа́ть *imp.*, разряди́ть *perf.* **unlock** *v.t.* отпира́ть *imp.*, отпере́ть (отопру́, -рёшь; о́тпер, -ла́, -ло) *perf.*; открыва́ть *imp.*, откры́ть (-ро́ю, -ро́ешь) *perf.* **unlucky** *adj.* несчастли́вый; (*unsuccessful, unfortunate*) неуда́чный.

unmake *v.t.* (*destroy*) уничтожа́ть *imp.*, уничто́жить *perf.*; (*annul*) аннули́ровать *imp.*, *perf.*; (*depose*) понижа́ть *imp.*, пони́зить *perf.* **unman** *v.t.* (*discourage*) лиша́ть *imp.*, лиши́ть *perf.* му́жества. **unmanageable** *adj.* тру́дно поддаю́щийся контро́лю; (*of child*) тру́дный (-ден, -дна́, -дно, тру́дны). **unmanly** *adj.* недосто́йный (-о́ин, -о́йна) мужчи́ны. **unmannerly** *adj.* невоспи́танный (-ан, -анна). **unmarketable** *adj.* него́дный (-ден, -дна́, -дно) для прода́жи. **unmarried** *adj.* холосто́й (хо́лост, -а́, -о); (*of man*) нежена́тый; (*of woman*) незаму́жняя. **unmask** *v.t.* (*fig.*) разоблача́ть *imp.*, разоблачи́ть *perf.* **unmentionable** *adj.* незатра́гиваемый, необсужда́емый. **unmerciful** *adj.* безжа́лостный. **unmerited** *adj.* незаслу́женный (-ен, -енна). **unmethodical** *adj.* несистема́тический, неметоди́чный. **unmindful** *adj.* невнима́тельный (of, к+*dat.*). **unmistakable** *adj.* несомне́нный (-нен, -нна), я́сный (я́сен, ясна́, я́сно, я́сны́). **unmitigated** *adj.* несмягчённый; (*absolute*) абсолю́тный; (*thorough*) отъя́вленный. **unmoved** *adj.* (*indifferent*) равноду́шный; (*adamant*) непрекло́нный (-нен, -нна).

unnatural *adj.* неесте́ственный (-ен.

-енна), противоесте́ственный (-ен, -енна). **unnecessary** adj. нену́жный, изли́шний (-шен, -шня). **unnerve** v.t. лиша́ть imp., лиши́ть perf. реши́мости, му́жества. **unnoticed** adj. незаме́ченный.

unobjectionable adj. прие́млемый. **un-observant** adj. невнима́тельный, ненаблюда́тельный. **unobserved** adj. незаме́ченный. **unobtainable** adj. тако́й, кото́рого нельзя́ доста́ть; недосту́пный. **unobtrusive** adj. ненавя́зчивый. **unoccupied** adj. неза́нятый (-т, -та́, -то), свобо́дный; (uninhabited) необита́емый. **unofficial** adj. неофициа́льный. **unopposed** adj. не встре́тивший сопротивле́ния. **unorthodox** adj. неортодокса́льный.

unpack v.t. распако́вывать imp., распакова́ть perf. **unpaid** adj. (not receiving pay) не получа́ющий пла́ты; (work) беспла́тный. **unpalatable** adj. невку́сный; (unpleasant) неприя́тный. **unpardonable** adj. непрости́тельный. **unpin** v.t. отка́лывать imp., отколо́ть (-лю́, -лешь) perf. **unpleasant** adj. неприя́тный. **unpleasantness** n. непривлека́тельность; (also occurrence) неприя́тность; (quarrel) ссо́ра. **un-popular** adj. непопуля́рный. **un-precedented** adj. беспрецеде́нтный, бесприме́рный. **unpredictable** adj. не могу́щий быть предска́зчастный. **un-prejudiced** adj. беспристра́стный. **un-premeditated** adj. непреднаме́ренный (-ен, -енна). **unprepared** adj. неподгото́вленный, негото́вый. **unpossessing** adj. непривлека́тельный. **un-pretentious** adj. просто́й (прост, -а́, -о, про́сты́) без прете́нзий. **unprincipled** adj. беспринци́пный; (immoral) безнра́вственный (-ен(ен), -енна). **unprintable** adj. нецензу́рный. **un-productive** adj. непродукти́вный. **un-profitable** adj. невы́годный. **unpromising** adj. не обеща́ющий ничего́ хоро́шего. **unpronounceable** adj. непроизноси́мый. **unpropitious** adj. неблагоприя́тный. **unprotected** adj. (defenceless) беззащи́тный; (area) откры́тый. **unproven** adj. недока́занный. **unprovoked** adj. ниче́м не вы́званный.

unprovoked adj. непровоци́рованный. **unpublished** adj. неопубликова́нный, неи́зданный. **un-punctual** adj. непунктуа́льный. **un-punished** adj. безнака́занный (-ан, -анна).

unqualified adj. неквалифици́рованный (-ан, -анна); (unconditional) безогово́рочный. **unquenchable** adj. неутоли́мый; (fig.) неугаси́мый. **unquestionable** adj. несомне́нный (-нен, -нна), неоспори́мый. **unquestionably** adv. несомне́нно. **unquestioned** adj. не вызыва́ющий сомне́ния.

unravel v.t. & i. распу́тывать(ся) imp., распу́тать(ся) perf.; v.t. (solve) разга́дывать imp., разгада́ть perf. **unread** adj. (book etc.) непрочи́танный. **un-readable** adj. (illegible) неразбо́рчивый; (boring) ску́чный (-чен, -чна́, -чно). **unready** adj. негото́вый; (slow-witted) несообрази́тельный. **unreal** adj. ненасто́ящий. **unrealistic** adj. нереа́льный. **unreasonable** adj. (unwise) неблагоразу́мный; (excessive) непоме́рный; (expensive) непоме́рно дорого́й (до́рог, -а́, -о); (of price) непоме́рно высо́кий (-о́к, -ока́, -о́ко); (unfounded; of demand) необосно́ванный (-ан, -анна). **unreasoned** adj. непроду́манный. **unreasoning** adj. не-мы́слящий. **unreceptive** adj. невосприи́мчивый. **unrecognizable** adj. неузнава́емый. **unrecognized** adj. не-при́знанный. **unrefined** adj. неочи́щенный; (manners etc.) гру́бый (груб, -а́, -о). **unrelenting** adj. (ruthless) безжа́лостный; (unremitting) неосла́бный; (not abating) неуменьша́ющийся. **unreliable** adj. ненадёжный. **unremitting** adj. неосла́бный; (incessant) беспреста́нный (-нен, -нна). **unremunerative** adj. невы́годный. **un-repeatable** adj. (unique) неповтори́мый; (indecent) неприли́чный. **un-repentant** adj. нераска́явшийся. **un-representative** adj. нехара́ктерный. **unrequited** adj.: u. love, любо́вь без взаи́мности. **unreserved** adj. (full) по́лный (-лон, -лна́, по́лно́); (open) открове́нный (-нен, -нна); (unconditional) безогово́рочный; u. seats, незаброни́рованные места́ neut.pl.

unresisting adj. несопротивля́ющийся. **unrest** n. беспоко́йство; (polit.) беспоря́дки m.pl.; волне́ния neut.pl. **unrestrained** adj. несде́ржанный (-ан, -анна). **unrestricted** adj. неограни́ченный (-ен, -енна). **unripe** adj. незре́лый, неспе́лый. **unrivalled** adj. бесподо́бный. **unroll** v.t. & i. развёртывать imp., разверну́ть(ся) perf. **unruffled** adj. (smooth) гла́дкий (-док, -дка́, -дко); (calm) споко́йный. **unruly** adj. (wild) бу́йный (буен, буйна́, -но), (disobedient) непослу́шный.

unsafe adj. опа́сный; (insecure) ненадёжный. **unsaid** adj.: leave u., молча́ть (-чу́, -чи́шь) imp. о+prep. **unsaleable** adj. нехо́дкий. **unsalted** adj. несолёный (несо́лон, -а́, -о). **unsatisfactory** adj. неудовлетвори́тельный. **unsatisfied** adj. неудовлетворённый (-ён, -ена́ & -ённа). **unsatisfying** adj. неудовлетворя́ющий; (food) несы́тный (-тен, -тна́, -тно). **unsavoury** adj. невку́сный; (distasteful) проти́вный. **unscathed** adj. невреди́мый; (fig.) жив и невреди́м. **unscheduled** adj. внеочередно́й. **unscientific** adj. ненау́чный. **unscrew** v.t. & i. отви́нчивать(ся) imp., отвинти́ть(ся) perf. **unscrupulous** adj. неразбо́рчивый в сре́дствах, беспринци́пный, бессо́вестный. **unseasonable** adj. не по сезо́ну; (inopportune) несвоевре́менный (-нен, -нна). **unseasoned** adj. (food) неприпра́вленный; (wood) невы́держанный; (unaccustomed) непривы́кший. **unseat** v.t. (of horse) сбра́сывать imp., сбро́сить perf. с седла́; (parl.) лиша́ть imp., лиши́ть perf. парла́ментского манда́та. **unseemly** adj. неподоба́ющий, непристо́йный. **unseen** adj. неви́данный; u. translation, перево́д с листа́. **unselfish** adj. бескоры́стный, неэгоисти́чный. **unserviceable** adj. неприго́дный. **unsettle** v.t. наруша́ть imp., нару́шить perf. распоря́док+gen., выбива́ть (-ва́ю) imp., вы́бить (-бью, -бьешь) perf. из колеи́; (upset) расстра́ивать imp., расстро́ить perf. **unsettled** adj.: the weather is u., пого́да не установи́лась. **unshakeable** adj. непоколеби́мый. **unshaven** adj. не-

бри́тый. **unsheathe** v.t. вынима́ть imp., вы́нуть perf. из но́жен. **unship** v.t. (cargo) выгружа́ть imp., вы́грузить perf.; (passenger) выса́живать imp., вы́садить perf. на бе́рег. **unsightly** adj. непригля́дный, уро́дливый. **unskilful** adj. неуме́лый. **unskilled** adj. неквалифици́рованный (-ан, -анна). **unsociable** adj. необщи́тельный. **unsold** adj. непро́данный. **unsolicited** adj. непро́шеный. **unsolved** adj. нерешённый. **unsophisticated** adj. просто́й (прост, -а́, -о, про́сты), безыску́сственный (-ен, -енна). **unsound** adj. (unhealthy, unwholesome) нездоро́вый; (rotten, also fig.) гнило́й (гнил, -а́, -о); (unreliable) ненадёжный; (unfounded) необосно́ванный (-ан, -анна); (faulty) дефе́ктный; of u. mind, душевнобольно́й. **unsparing** adj. (lavish) ще́дрый (щедр, -а́, -о); (merciless) беспоща́дный. **unspeakable** adj. (inexpressible) невырази́мый; (very bad) отврати́тельный. **unspecified** adj. то́чно не устано́вленный (-ен), неопределённый (-нен, -нна). **unspoilt** adj. неиспо́рченный. **unspoken** adj. невы́сказанный. **unsporting**, **unsportsmanlike** adj. неспорти́вный, недосто́йный (-о́ин, -о́йна) спортсме́на. **unstable** adj. неусто́йчивый; (emotionally) неуравнове́шенный (-ен, -енна). **unsteady** adj. неусто́йчивый. **unsuccessful** adj. неуда́чный, безуспе́шный. **unsuitable** adj. неподходя́щий, неподоба́ющий; (incompatible) несовмести́мый. **unsuited** adj. (incompatible) несовмести́мый. **unsullied** adj. незапя́тнанный. **unsupported** adj. неподдёржанный. **unsure** adj. (not convinced) неуве́ренный (-ен, -ена) of oneself; (hesitating) неуве́ренный (-ен, -енна) в себе́. **unsurpassed** adj. непревзойдённый (-ён, -ённа). **unsuspected** adj. не вызыва́ющий подозре́ний; (unforeseen) непредви́денный. **unsuspecting** adj. неподозрева́ющий. **unsweetened** adj. неподслащённый. **unswerving** adj. непоколеби́мый. **unsymmetrical** adj. несимметри́ческий. **unsympathetic** adj. несочу́вствующий; (unattractive) несимпати́чный. **unsystematic** adj. несистемати́чный.

untainted   392   up

untainted adj. неиспо́рченный. **untalented** adj. нетала́нтливый. **untameable** adj. не поддаю́щийся прируче́нию; (*indomitable*) неукроти́мый. **untapped** adj.: *u. resources*, неиспо́льзованные ресу́рсы *m.pl.* **untarnished** adj. непотускне́вший; (*fig.*) незапя́тнанный. **untenable** adj. несостоя́тельный. **unthinkable** adj. (*inconceivable*) невообрази́мый; (*unlikely*) невероя́тный; (*out of the question*) исключённый (-ён, -ена́). **unthinking** adj. легкомы́сленный (-ен, -енна). **unthread** v.t. вынима́ть *imp.*, вы́нуть *perf.* ни́тку из+*gen.* **untidiness** n. неопря́тность; (*disorder*) беспоря́док (-дка). **untidy** adj. неопря́тный; (*in disorder*) в беспоря́дке. **untie** v.t. развя́зывать *imp.*, развяза́ть (-яжу́, -я́жешь) *perf.*; (*set free*) освобожда́ть *imp.*, освободи́ть *perf.*

until prep. до+*gen.*; *not u.*, не ра́ньше+*gen.*; *u. then*, до тех пор; *conj.* пока́, пока́...не; *not u.*, то́лько когда́.

untimely adj. (*premature*) безвре́менный; (*inopportune*) несвоевре́менный (-нен, -нна) (*inappropriate*) неуме́стный. **untiring** adj. неутоми́мый. **untold** adj. (*innumerable*) бессчётный, несме́тный; (*inexpressible*) невырази́мый. **untouched** adj. (*also pure*) нетро́нутый; (*indifferent*) равноду́шный. **untoward** adj. (*unfavourable*) неблагоприя́тный; (*refractory*) непоко́рный. **untrained** adj. необу́ченный. **untranslatable** adj. непереводи́мый. **untried** adj. неиспы́танный. **untroubled** adj. споко́йный. **untrue** adj. (*incorrect, disloyal*) неве́рный (-рен, -рна́, -рно, неве́рны); (*incorrect*) непра́вильный; (*false*) ло́жный. **untrustworthy** adj. ненадёжный. **untruth** n. непра́вда, ложь. **untruthful** adj. лжи́вый.

unusable adj. непри́годный. **unused** adj. (*not › employed*) неиспо́льзованный; (*not accustomed*) непривы́кший (to, к+*dat.*). **unusual** adj. необыкнове́нный (-нен, -нна), необы́чный. **unusually** adv. необыкнове́нно. **unutterable** adj. невырази́мый.

unvarnished adj. (*fig.*) неприкра́шенный. **unvarying** adj. неизменя́ющийся.

unveil v.t. снима́ть *imp.*, снять (сниму́, -мешь; снял, -а́, -о) *perf.* покрыва́ло с+*gen.*; (*statue*) торже́ственно открыва́ть *imp.*, откры́ть (-ро́ю, -ро́ешь) *perf.*; (*disclose*) открыва́ть *imp.*, откры́ть (-ро́ю, -ро́ешь) *perf.* **unversed** adj. несве́дущий (in, в+*prep.*); (*inexperienced*) нео́пытный (in, в+*prep.*).

unwanted adj. нежела́нный. **unwarranted** adj. (*unjustified*) неопра́вданный. **unwary** adj. неосторо́жный. **unwavering** adj. непоколеби́мый. **unwelcome** adj. нежела́нный, нежела́тельный; (*unpleasant*) неприя́тный. **unwell** adj. нездоро́вый. **unwholesome** adj. нездоро́вый, вре́дный (-ден, -дна́, -дно). **unwieldy** adj. громо́здкий, неуклю́жий. **unwilling** adj. нерасполо́женный. **unwillingly** adv. неохо́тно, про́тив жела́ния. **unwillingness** n. нерасположе́ние, неохо́та. **unwind** v.t. & i. разма́тывать(ся) *imp.*, размота́ть(ся) *perf.*; (*rest*) отдыха́ть *imp.*, отдохну́ть *perf.* **unwise** adj. не(благо)разу́мный. **unwitting** adj. нево́льный, неча́янный. **unwittingly** adv. нево́льно, неча́янно. **unwonted** adj. непривы́чный. **unworkable** adj. непримен	и́мый. **unworldly** adj. не от ми́ра сего́; (*spiritual*) духо́вный. **unworthy** adj. недосто́йный (-о́ин, -о́йна). **unwrap** v.t. развёртывать *imp.*, развернуть *perf.* **unwritten** adj.: *u. law*, непи́саный зако́н.

unyielding adj. упо́рный, неподатли́вый.

unzip v.t. расстёгивать *imp.*, расстегну́ть (-ну́, -нёшь) *perf.* (мо́лнию с+*gen.*).

up adv. (*motion*) наве́рх, вверх; (*position*) наверху́, вверху́; *up and down*, вверх и вниз; (*back and forth*) взад и вперёд; *up to* (*towards*) к+*dat.*; *up to now*, до сих пор; *be up against*, име́ть *imp.* де́ло с+*instr.*; *it is up to you+inf.*, э́то вам+*inf.*, вы должны́+*inf.*; *not up to much*, нева́жный; *what's up?* что случи́лось? в чём де́ло? *your time is up*, ва́ше вре́мя истекло́; *up and about*, на нога́х; *he isn't up yet*, он ещё не встал; *he isn't up to this job*, он не годи́тся для э́той рабо́ты; *prep.* вверх по + *dat.*; (*along*) (вдоль) по + *dat.*; *up wind*, про́тив ве́тра; *v.t. & i.* поднима́ть(ся) *imp.*, подня́ть(ся) (-ниму́(сь), -ни́мешь(ся)); по́днял/подня́лся, -ла́(сь), -ло/-ло́сь) *perf.*; (*leap up*) вска́кивать *imp.*, вскочи́ть (-чу́, -чишь) *perf.*; *adj.*: *up-to-date*, совреме́нный (-нен, -нна); (*fashionable*) мо́дный (-ден, -дна, -дно); *up-and-coming*, напо́ристый, многообеща́ющий; *n.*: *ups and downs*, (*fig.*) превра́тности *f.pl.* судьбы́.

upbraid *v.t.* брани́ть *imp.*, вы~ *perf.* (*for*, за + *acc.*).

upbringing *n.* воспита́ние.

update *v.t.* модернизи́ровать *imp.*, *perf.*; (*book*) дополня́ть *imp.*, допо́лнить *perf.*

upgrade *v.t.* повыша́ть *imp.*, повы́сить *perf.* (*по службе*).

upheaval *n.* сдвиг; (*revolution*) переворо́т; (*geol.*) смеще́ние пласто́в.

uphill *adj.* иду́щий в го́ру; (*fig.*) тяжёлый (-л, -ла́); *adv.* в го́ру.

uphold *v.t.* подде́рживать *imp.*, поддержа́ть (-жу́, -жишь) *perf.*; *u. a view*, приде́рживаться *imp.* взгля́да. **upholder** *n.* сторо́нник.

upholster *v.t.* обива́ть *imp.*, оби́ть (обобью́, -ьёшь) *perf.* (*with*, *in*, + *instr.*). **upholsterer** *n.* обо́йщик. **upholstery** *n.* оби́вка.

upkeep *n.* (*maintenance, support*) содержа́ние; (*repair(s)*) ремо́нт; (*cost of u.*) сто́имость содержа́ния.

upland *n.* гори́стая часть (*pl.* -ти, -те́й) страны́, наго́рная страна́ (*pl.* -ны); *adj.* наго́рный; (*inland*) лежа́щий внутри́ страны́.

uplift *v.t.* поднима́ть *imp.*, подня́ть (-ниму́, -ни́мешь; по́днял, -а́, -о) *perf.*; *n.* подъём.

upon *prep.* (*position*) на + *prep.*, (*motion*) на + *acc.*; *see* **on.**

upper *adj.* ве́рхний; (*socially, in rank*) вы́сший; *gain the u. hand*, одержа́ть *imp.*, одержа́ть (-жу́, -жишь) *perf.* верх (*over*, над + *instr.*); *u. crust*, верху́шка о́бщества; *the U. House*, ве́рхняя пала́та; *n.* передо́к (-дка́).

uppermost *adj.* са́мый ве́рхний, вы́сший; *be u. in person's mind*, бо́льше

всего́ занима́ть *imp.*, заня́ть (займу́, -мёшь; за́нял, -а́, -о) *perf.* мы́сли кого́-л.

uppish *adj.* спеси́вый, высокоме́рный.

upright *n.* подпо́рка, сто́йка; *adj.* вертика́льный; (*straight*) прямо́й (-м, -ма́, -мо, пря́мы); (*honest*) че́стный (-тен, -тна́, -тно); *u. piano*, пиани́но *neut.indecl.*; *adv.* вертика́льно, пря́мо, сто́йма.

uprising *n.* восста́ние.

uproar *n.* шум (-а(у)), гам. **uproarious** *adj.* шу́мный (-мен, -мна́, -мно); бу́йный (бу́ен, буйна́, -но).

uproot *v.t.* вырыва́ть *imp.*, вы́рвать (-ву, -вешь) *perf.* с ко́рнем; (*eradicate*) искореня́ть *imp.*, искорени́ть *perf.*

upset *n.* (*disorder, confusion, discomposure*) расстро́йство; *v.t.* (*disorder, discompose, spoil (plans etc.)*) расстра́ивать *imp.*, расстро́ить *perf.*; *v.t. & i.* (*overturn*) опроки́дывать(ся) *imp.*, опроки́нуть(ся) *perf.*; *adj.* (*miserable*) расстро́енный (-ен); *u. stomach*, расстро́йство желу́дка.

upshot *n.* развя́зка, результа́т.

upside-down *adj.* переверну́тый вверх дном; *adv.* вверх дном; (*in disorder*) в беспоря́дке.

upstairs *adv.* (*position*) наверху́; (*motion*) наве́рх; *n.* ве́рхний эта́ж (-а́); *adj.* находя́щийся в ве́рхнем этаже́.

upstart *n.* вы́скочка *m. & f.*

upstream *adv.* про́тив тече́ния; (*situation*) вверх по тече́нию.

upsurge *n.* подъём, волна́ (*pl.* -ны, -н, во́лна́м).

uptake *n.*: *be quick on the u.*, бы́стро сообража́ть *imp.*, сообрази́ть *perf.*

upturned *adj.* (*face etc.*) по́днятый (по́днят, -а́, -о) кве́рху; (*inverted*) переве́рнутый.

upward *adj.* напра́вленный (-ен) вверх, дви́жущийся вверх. **upwards** *adv.* вверх; *u. of*, свы́ше + *gen.*

uranium *n.* ура́н; *attrib.* ура́новый.

urban *adj.* городско́й.

urbane *adj.* ве́жливый, с изы́сканными мане́рами. **urbanity** *n.* ве́жливость.

urchin *n.* мальчи́шка *m.*

urge *n.* (*incitement*) побужде́ние, толчо́к (-чка́); (*desire*) жела́ние; *v.t.* (*impel, u. on*) подгоня́ть *imp.*, подогна́ть (подгоню́, -нишь) подогна́л, -á, -о) *perf.*; (*induce, prompt*) побужда́ть *imp.*, побуди́ть *perf.*; (*advocate*) настоя́тельно убежда́ть *imp.*; (*give as reason*) обраща́ть *imp.*, обрати́ть (-ащу́, -ати́шь) *perf.* внима́ние на + *acc.* **urgency** *n.* (*also insistence*) настоя́тельность; (*immediate importance*) безотлага́тельность; *a matter of great u.*, сро́чное де́ло (*pl.* -ла́). **urgent** *adj.* сро́чный (-чен, -чна́, -чно); (*also insistent*) настоя́тельный; (*absolutely essential*) кра́йне необходи́мый. **urgently** *adv.* сро́чно.

uric *adj.* мочево́й. **urinal** *n.* писсуа́р. **urinate** *v.i.* мочи́ться (-чу́сь, -чишься) *imp.*, по ~ *perf.* **urination** *n.* мочеиспуска́ние. **urine** *n.* моча́.

urn *n.* у́рна.

usable *adj.* го́дный (-ден, -дна́, -дно) к употребле́нию. **usage** *n.* употребле́ние; (*custom*) обыча́й; (*treatment*) обраще́ние. **use** *n.* (*also benefit*) по́льза; (*application*) употребле́ние, примене́ние, испо́льзование; *it is of no u.*, бесполе́зно; *make u. of*, испо́льзовать *imp.*, *perf.*; по́льзоваться *imp.* + *instr.*; *v.t.* употребля́ть *imp.*, по́льзоваться *imp.* + *instr.*; применя́ть *imp.*, примени́ть (-ню́, -нишь) *perf.*; (*treat*) обраща́ться *imp.* c + *instr.*; *I used to see him often*, я ча́сто его́ встреча́л (*imp. p.t.*); *be, get, used to*, привыка́ть *imp.*, привы́кнуть (-к) *perf.* (*to*, к + *dat.*); *u. up*, расхо́довать *imp.*, из ~ *perf.* **used** *adj.* (*second-hand*) поде́ржанный, ста́рый (стар, -á, ста́ро). **useful** *adj.* поле́зный; *come in u., prove u.*, пригоди́ться *perf.* (*to*, + *dat.*). **useless** *adj.* бесполе́зный, никуда́ не го́дный (-ден, -дна́, -дно). **user** *n.* потреби́тель *m.*

usher *n.* (*door-keeper*) швейца́р; (*theat.*) билетёр; *v.t.* (*lead in*) вводи́ть (введу́, -о́дишь) *imp.*, ввести́ (-еду́, -едёшь; -ёл, -ела́) *perf.*; (*proclaim, u. in*)

возвеща́ть *imp.*, возвести́ть *perf.* **usherette** *n.* билетёрша.

usual *adj.* обыкнове́нный (-нен, -нна), обы́чный; *as u.*, как обы́чно. **usually** *adv.* обыкнове́нно, обы́чно.

usurer *n.* ростовщи́к (-á). **usurious** *adj.* ростовщи́ческий.

usurp *v.t.* узурпи́ровать *imp.*, *perf.*; незако́нно захва́тывать *imp.*, захвати́ть (-ачу́, -а́тишь) *perf.* **usurper** *n.* узурпа́тор, захва́тчик.

usury *n.* ростовщи́чество.

utensil *n.* инструме́нт, ору́дие; *pl.* у́тварь; принадле́жности *f.pl.*; (*kitchen utensils*) посу́да.

uterine *adj.* ма́точный; (*of one mother*) единоутро́бный. **uterus** *n.* ма́тка.

utilitarian *adj.* утилита́рный; *n.* утилитари́ст. **utilitarianism** *n.* утилитари́зм. **utility** *n.* поле́зность; (*profitableness*) вы́годность; *adj.* утилита́рный; (*practical*) практи́чный. **utilize** *v.t.* испо́льзоваться *imp.*, *perf.*; утилизи́ровать *imp.*, *perf.*

utmost *adj.* (*extreme*) кра́йний, преде́льный; (*furthest*) са́мый отдалённый (-ён, -ённа); *this is of the u. importance to me*, э́то для меня́ кра́йне ва́жно; *n.*: *do one's u.*, де́лать *imp.*, с ~ *perf.* всё возмо́жное.

Utopia *n.* уто́пия. **utopian** *adj.* утопи́ческий; *n.* утопи́ст.

utter *attrib.* по́лный, соверше́нный, абсолю́тный; (*out-and-out*) отъя́вленный (*coll.*); *v.t.* произноси́ть (-ошу́, -о́сишь) *imp.*, произнести́ (-есу́, -есёшь; -ёс, -есла́) *perf.*; (*let out*) издава́ть (-даю́, -даёшь) *imp.*, изда́ть (-а́м, -а́шь, -а́ст, -ади́м; и́здал, -á, -о) *perf.* **utterance** *n.* (*uttering*) произнесе́ние; (*pronouncement*) выска́зывание; (*diction*) ди́кция; (*pronunciation*) произноше́ние; *gift of u.*, дар сло́ва; *give u. to*, выража́ть *imp.*, вы́разить *perf.* слова́ми. **utterly** *adv.* кра́йне, соверше́нно.

uvula *n.* язычо́к (-чка́).

Uzbek *n.* узбе́к, -е́чка; *adj.* узбе́кский.

V

V-neck n. V-образный вырез; *V sign*, (*victory*) знак победы.

vacancy n. (*for job*) вакансия, свободное место (*pl.* -та́); (*at hotel*) свободный номер (*pl.* -а́); (*emptiness*) пустота; (*apathy*) безучастность; (*absent-mindedness*) рассеянность.

vacant adj. (*post*) вакантный; (*post; not engaged, free*) свободный; (*empty*) пустой (пуст, -а́, -о, пусты́); (*look*) рассеянный (-ян, -янна); ,,*v. possession*", ,,помещение готово для въезда". **vacantly** adv. рассеянно. **vacate** v.t. освобождать *impf.*, освободить *perf.*; покидать *impf.*, покинуть *perf.* **vacation** n. (*school, univ.*) каникулы (-л) *pl.*; (*leave*) отпуск; (*vacating*) оставление, освобождение.

vaccinate v.t. прививать *impf.*, привить (-вью, -вьёшь; привил, -а́, -о) *perf.* + *dat.* (*against, + acc.*). **vaccination** n. прививка (*against*, от, против + *gen.*). **vaccine** n. вакцина.

vacillate v.i. колебаться (-блюсь, -блешься) *impf.* **vacillation** n. колебание; (*inconstancy*) непостоянство.

vacuity n. пустота. **vacuous** adj. пустой (пуст, -а́, -о, пусты́); (*foolish*) бессмысленный (-ен, -енна). **vacuum** n. вакуум; (*fig.*) пустота; (*v. brake*, вакуумный тормоз); *v.-clean*, чистить *impf.*, вы~, по~ *perf.* пылесосом; *v. cleaner*, пылесос; *v. flask*, термос; *vacuum-gauge*, вакуумметр; *v. pump* вакуум-насос.

vade-mecum n. путеводитель m.

vagabond n. бродяга m.; attrib. бродячий. **vagabondage** n. бродяжничество. **vagabondize** v.i. скитаться *impf.*, бродяжничать *impf.*

vagary n. каприз, причуда.

vagina n. влагалище. **vaginal** adj. влагалищный.

vagrancy n. бродяжничество. **vagrant** adj. бродячий; n. бродяга m.

vague adj. (*indeterminate, uncertain*) неопределённый (-нен, -нна); (*unclear*) неясный (-сен, -сна́, -сно); (*dim*) смутный (-тен, -тна́, -тно); (*absent-minded*) рассеянный (-ян, -янна). **vagueness** n. неопределённость, неясность; (*absent-mindedness*) рассеянность.

vain adj. (*futile*) тщетный, напрасный; (*empty*) пустой (пуст, -а́, -о, пусты́); (*conceited*) самолюбивый, тщеславный; *in v.*, напрасно, тщетно, зря. **vainglorious** adj. тщеславный, хвастливый. **vainglory** n. тщеславие, хвастливость.

valance n. подзор, оборка, занавеска.

vale n. дол, долина.

valediction n. прощание. **valedictory** adj. прощальный.

valency n. валентность.

valentine n. (*sweetheart*) возлюбленный, -нная (выбирается 14-ого февраля); (*card*) поздравительная карточка с днём святого Валентина.

valerian n. валериана; (*med.*) валериановые капли (-пель) *pl.*

valet n. камердинер, слуга (*pl.* -ги) m.

valetudinarian adj. болезненный (-ен, -енна); (*hypochondriac*) мнительный.

valiant adj. храбрый (храбр, -а, -о), доблестный.

valid adj. действительный, имеющий силу; (*weighty*) веский. **validate** v.t. (*ratify*) утверждать *impf.*, утвердить *perf.*; (*declare valid*) объявлять *impf.*, объявить (-влю, -вишь) *perf.* действительным. **validity** n. действительность; (*weightiness*) вескость.

valise n. саквояж, чемодан.

valley n. долина.

valorize v.t. устанавливать *impf.*, установить (-влю, -вишь) *perf.* цены + *gen.* (by government action, путём государственных мероприятий).

valorous adj. доблестный. **valour** n. доблесть.

valuable adj. ценный (-нен, -нна); (*costly*) дорогой (дорог, -а́, -о); *pl.* ценные вещи (-щей) *pl.*, драгоценности f.*pl.* **valuation** n. оценка. **value** n. ценность; (*cost, worth*) цена (*pl.* -ны); (*worth; econ.*) стоимость; (*significance*) значение; (*math.*) величина́; (*mus.*) дли́тельность; *pl.* це́нности *f.pl.*; v.-added tax, нало́г на доба́вленную сто́имость; v.-judgement, субъекти́вная оце́нка; *v.t.* (*estimate*) оце́нивать *imp.*, оцени́ть (-ню́, -нишь) *perf.*; (*hold dear*) цени́ть (-ню́, -нишь) *imp.*, дорожи́ть *imp.+instr.*

valueless *adj.* беспо́лезный, ничего́ не сто́ящий. **valuer** *n.* оце́нщик.

valve *n.* (*tech.*, *med.*, *mus.*) кла́пан; (*tech.*) ве́нтиль *m.*; (*bot.*) ство́рка; (*radio*) электро́нная ла́мпа.

vamp[1] *n.* (*of shoe*) передо́к (-дка́); (*patched-up article*) что-л. почи́ненное на ско́рую ру́ку; (*mus.*) импровизи́рованный аккомпанеме́нт; *v.t.* (*repair*) чини́ть (-ню́, -нишь) *imp.*, по~ *perf.*; (*mus.*) импровизи́ровать *imp.*, сымпровизи́ровать *perf.* аккомпанеме́нт к+*dat.*

vamp[2] *n.* (*flirt*) соблазни́тельница.

vampire *n.* (*also fig.*; *also v. bat*) вампи́р.

van[1] *n.* (*road vehicle*, *caravan*) фурго́н; (*rly.*) бага́жный (*luggage*), това́рный (*goods*), служе́бный (*guard's*), ваго́н.

van[2] *n.* (*vanguard*) аванга́рд.

vanadium *n.* вана́дий.

vandal *n.* ванда́л, хулига́н. **vandalism** *n.* вандали́зм, ва́рварство. **vandalize** *v.t.* разруша́ть *imp.*, разру́шить *perf.*

vane *n.* (*weathercock*) флю́гер (*pl.* -á); (*of windmill*) крыло́ (*pl.* -лья, -льев); (*of propeller*) ло́пасть (*pl.* -ти, -те́й); (*of turbine*) лопа́тка.

vanguard *n.* аванга́рд.

vanilla *n.* вани́ль; *attrib.* вани́льный.

vanish *v.i.* исчеза́ть *imp.*, исче́знуть (-ёз) *perf.*; пропада́ть *imp.*, пропа́сть (-аду́, -адёшь; -а́л) *perf.*; vanishing-point, то́чка схо́да.

vanity *n.* (*futility*) тщета́, суета́; (*vainglory*) тщесла́вие; v. bag, су́мочка, несессе́р.

vanquish *v.t.* (*enemy*) побежда́ть *imp.*, победи́ть (-еди́шь, -еди́т) *perf.*; (*fig.*) преодолева́ть *imp.*, преодоле́ть *perf.*

vantage *n.* преиму́щество; v.-point, вы́годная пози́ция; (*for observation*) пункт наблюде́ния.

vapid *adj.* безвку́сный; (*also fig.*) пре́сный (-сен, -сна́, -сно); (*fig.*) ску́чный (-чен, -чна́, -чно).

vaporize *v.t.* & *i.* испаря́ть(ся) *imp.*, испари́ть(ся) *perf.* **vaporizer** *n.* испари́тель *m.* **vaporous** *adj.* парообра́зный; (*vague*) тума́нный (-нен, -нна).

vapour *n.* (*steam etc.*) пар (*loc.* -у́; *pl.* -ы́); (*mist*, *haze*) тума́н.

variable *adj.* изме́нчивый, непостоя́нный (-нен, -нна); (*weather*) неусто́йчивый, (*also math.*) переме́нный; *n.* (*math.*) переме́нная (величина́). **variance** *n.* (*disagreement*) разногла́сие; (*change*) измене́ние; (*disparity*) несоотве́тствие; be at v. with, расходи́ться (-ожу́сь, -о́дишься) *imp.*, разойти́сь (-йду́сь, -йдёшься; -ошёлся, -ошла́сь) *perf.* во мне́ниях с+*instr.* **variant** *n.* вариа́нт; *adj.* ра́зный. **variation** *n.* (*varying*) измене́ние, переме́на; (*variant*) вариа́нт; (*variety*) разнови́дность; (*mus.*, *math.*) вариа́ция.

varicose *adj.*: v. veins, расшире́ние вен.

variegate *v.t.* де́лать *imp.*, с~ *perf.* пёстрым; (*diversify*) разнообра́зить *imp.* **variegated** *adj.* разноцве́тный, пёстрый (-р, -ра́, пёстро́); (*diverse*) разнообра́зный. **variety** *n.* разнообра́зие; (*sort*) разнови́дность; (*multitude*) мно́жество; v. show, варьете́ neut.indecl., эстра́дный конце́рт. **various** *adj.* (*of several kinds*) разли́чный; (*different*, *several*) ра́зный; (*diverse*) разнообра́зный.

varnish *n.* лак; (*fig.*) лоск; *v.t.* лакирова́ть *imp.*, от~ *perf.* (*also fig.*). **varnishing** *n.* лакиро́вка.

vary *v.t.* разнообра́зить *imp.*, меня́ть *imp.*; *v.i.* (*change*) меня́ться *imp.*, изменя́ться *imp.*, измени́ться (-ню́сь, -нишься) *perf.*; (*differ*) ра́зниться *imp.*; (*disagree*) не соглаша́ться *imp.*

vase *n.* ва́за.

vaseline *n.* вазели́н.

vassal *n.* васса́л.

vast *adj.* грома́дный, обши́рный. **vastly** *adv.* значи́тельно. **vastness** *n.* грома́дность, обши́рность.

vat *n.* чан (*pl.* -ы́), бак.

Vatican *n.* Ватика́н.

vaudeville *n.* водеви́ль *m.*; (*variety*) варьете́ neut.indecl.

vault[1] *n.* (*leap*) прыжо́к (-жка́); *v.t.*

перепры́гивать *imp.*, перепры́гнуть *perf.*; *v.i.* пры́гать *imp.*, пры́гнуть *perf.* **vaulting-horse** *n.* гимнасти́ческий конь -ня́; *pl.* -ни, -не́й) *m.*

vault[2] *n.* (*arch, covering*) свод; (*cellar*) по́греб, подва́л; (*burial v.*) склеп; *v.t.* возводи́ть *imp.* (-ожу́, -оди́шь) *imp.*, возвести́ (-еду́, -едёшь; -ёл, -ела́) *perf.* свод над + *instr.* **vaulted** *adj.* сво́дчатый.

vaunt *n.* хвастовство́; *v.i.*(*t.*) хва́статься *imp.*, по ~ *perf.* (+ *instr.*).

veal *n.* теля́тина; *attrib.* теля́чий.

vector *n.* (*math.*) ве́ктор; (*carrier of disease*) перено́счик инфе́кции.

veer *v.i.* (*change direction*) изменя́ть *imp.*, измени́ть (-ню́, -нишь) *perf.* направле́ние; (*turn*) повора́чивать *imp.*, повороти́ть (-очу́, -о́тишь) *perf.*; *v. away from*, отша́тываться *imp.*, отшатну́ться *perf.* от + *gen.*

vegetable *n.* о́вощ; *adj.* расти́тельный; (*of vegetables*) овощно́й. **vegetarian** *n.* вегетариа́нец, -нка; *attrib.* вегетариа́нский. **vegetarianism** *n.* вегетариа́нство. **vegetate** *v.i.* расти́ (-ту́, -тёшь; рос, -ла́) *imp.*; (*fig.*) прозяба́ть *imp.* **vegetation** *n.* расти́тельность; (*fig.*) прозяба́ние. **vegetative** *adj.* расти́тельный; (*biol.*) вегетати́вный; (*fig.*) прозяба́ющий.

vehemence *n.* (*force*) си́ла; (*passion*) стра́стность. **vehement** *adj.* (*forceful*) си́льный (си́лён, -льна́, -льно, си́льны́); (*passionate*) стра́стный (-тен, -тна́, -тно).

vehicle *n.* сре́дство передвиже́ния/ перево́зки; (*motor v.*) автомоби́ль *m.*; (*medium*) сре́дство; (*chem.*) носи́тель *m.* **vehicular** *adj.* (*conveying*) перево́зочный; (*of motor transport*) автомоби́льный; *v. transport*, автогрузево́й тра́нспорт.

veil *n.* вуа́ль, покрыва́ло; (*fig.*) заве́са, покро́в; (*pretext*) предло́г; *v.t.* покрыва́ть *imp.*, покры́ть (-ро́ю, -ро́ешь) *perf.* вуа́лью, покрыва́лом; (*fig.*) скрыва́ть *imp.*, скрыть (-ро́ю, -ро́ешь) *perf.*

vein *n.* ве́на; (*of leaf; streak*) жи́лка; *in the same v.*, в том же ду́хе. **veined** *adj.* испещрённый (-ён, -ена́) жи́лками.

veld *n.* вельд.

vellum *n.* (*parchment*) то́нкий перга́мент; (*paper*) веле́невая бума́га.

velocity *n.* ско́рость.

velour(s) *n.* велю́р; (*attrib.*) велю́ровый.

velvet *n.* ба́рхат; *adj.* ба́рхатный. **velveteen** *n.* вельве́т. **velvety** *adj.* барха́тистый.

venal *adj.* прода́жный, подку́пный. **venality** *n.* прода́жность.

vend *v.t.* продава́ть (-даю́, -даёшь) *imp.*, прода́ть (-а́м, -а́шь, -а́ст, -ади́м; про́дал, -а́, -о) *perf.* **vending-machine** *n.* торго́вый автома́т. **vendor** *n.* продаве́ц (-вца́), -вщи́ца.

vendetta *n.* венде́тта, кро́вная месть.

veneer *n.* фанеро́вка; (*fig.*) лоск; *v.t.* фанерова́ть *imp.*

venerable *adj.* почте́нный (-нен, -нна); (*V.*) преподо́бный. **venerate** *v.t.* благогове́ть *imp.* пе́ред + *instr.* **veneration** *n.* благогове́ние, почита́ние. **venerator** *n.* почита́тель *m.*

venereal *adj.* венери́ческий.

venetian blind *n.* жалюзи́ *neut.indecl.*

vengeance *n.* месть, мще́ние; *take v.*, мстить *imp.*, ото ~ *perf.* (*on, + dat.*; *for,* за + *acc.*); *with a v.*, в по́лном смы́сле сло́ва; (*with might and main*) вовсю́. **vengeful** *adj.* мсти́тельный.

venial *adj.* прости́тельный.

venison *n.* оле́нина.

venom *n.* яд (-а(у)). **venomous** *adj.* ядови́тый.

vent[1] *n.* (*opening*) вы́ход (*also fig.*), отве́рстие; (*air-hole*) отду́шина; (*anus*) за́дний прохо́д; (*feelings*) дава́ть (даю́, даёшь) *imp.*, дать (дам, дашь, даст, дади́м; дал, -а, да́ло, -и) *perf.* вы́ход + *dat.*; (*opinion*) выска́зывать *imp.*, вы́сказать (-ажу, -ажешь) *perf.*

vent[2] (*slit*) разре́з.

ventilate *v.t.* прове́тривать *imp.*, прове́трить *perf.*; (*fig.*) обсужда́ть *imp.*, обсуди́ть (-ужу́, -у́дишь) *perf.* **ventilation** *n.* вентиля́ция, прове́тривание. **ventilator** *n.* вентиля́тор.

ventral *adj.* брюшно́й.

ventricle *n.* желу́дочек (-чка).

ventriloquism, -quy *n.* чревовеща́ние. **ventriloquist** *n.* чревовеща́тель *m.* **ventriloquize** *v.i.* чревовеща́ть *imp.*

venture *n.* риско́ванное предприя́тие; (*speculation*) спекуля́ция; *at a v.*, науда́чу; *v.i.* (*hazard, dare*) отва́живаться *imp.*, отва́житься *perf.*; *v.t* (*risk*) рискова́ть *imp.*+*instr.*, рискну́ть *imp.*, по~ *perf.* на ка́рту; *v. an opinion, guess*, осме́ливаться *imp.*, осме́литься *perf.* вы́сказать мне́ние, дога́дку.

venturesome *adj.* (*person*) сме́лый (смел, -а́, -о); (*enterprise*) риско́ванный (-ан, -анна).

venue *n.* ме́сто (*pl.* -та́) сбо́ра.

veracious *adj.* правди́вый. **veracity** *n.* правди́вость.

veranda(h) *n.* вера́нда.

verb *n.* глаго́л. **verbal** *adj.* (*oral*) у́стный; (*relating to words*) слове́сный; (*gram.*) отглаго́льный. **verbalize** *v.t.* выража́ть *imp.*, вы́разить *perf.* слова́ми; *v.i.* быть многосло́вным. **verbatim** *adj.* досло́вный; *adv.* досло́вно. **verbiage** *n.* многосло́вие. **verbose** *adj.* многосло́вный. **verbosity** *n.* многосло́вия.

verdant *adj.* зелёный (зе́лен, -а́, -о).

verdict *n.* верди́кт, реше́ние; (*opinion*) мне́ние.

verdigris *n.* я́рь-медя́нка.

verdure *n.* зе́лень.

verge[1] *n.* (*also fig.*) край (*loc.* -а́е & -аю́; *pl.* -а́й); (*of road*) обо́чина; (*fig.*) грань; (*eccl.*) жезл; *on the v. of*, на гра́ни; *he was on the v. of telling all*, он чуть не рассказа́л всё.

verge[2] *v.i.* клони́ться (-ню́сь, -нишься) *imp.* (*towards*, к+*dat.*); *v. on*, грани́чить *imp.* c+*instr.*

verger *n.* церко́вный служи́тель *m.*; (*bearer of staff*) жезлоно́сец (-сца).

verification *n.* прове́рка; (*confirmation*) подтвержде́ние. **verify** *v.t.* проверя́ть *imp.*, прове́рить *perf.*; (*confirm*) подтвержда́ть *imp.*, подтверди́ть *perf.* **verisimilitude** *n.* правдоподо́бие. **veritable** *adj.* настоя́щий. **verity** *n.* и́стина.

vermicelli *n.* вермише́ль.

vermilion *adj.* я́рко-кра́сный (-сен, -сна́, -сно); *n.* кинова́рь.

vermin *n.* вреди́тели *m.pl.* парази́ты *m.pl.*; (*fig.*) подо́нки (-ков) *pl.* **verminous** *adj.* киша́щий парази́тами; (*fig.*) отврати́тельный.

vermouth *n.* ве́рмут.

vernacular *adj.* (*native, of language*) родно́й; (*local, of dialect*) ме́стный; (*national, folk*) наро́дный; (*colloquial*) разгово́рный; *n.* родно́й язы́к (-а́); ме́стный диале́кт; (*homely language*) разгово́рный язы́к (-а́).

vernal *adj.* весе́нний.

vernier *n.* но́ниус, верньёр.

verruca *n.* борода́вка.

versatile *adj.* многосторо́нний; (*flexible, of mind*) ги́бкий (-бок, -бка́, -бко). **versatility** *n.* многосторо́нность, ги́бкость.

verse *n.* (*also Bibl.*) стих (-а́); (*stanza*) строфа́ (*pl.* -фы); (*poetry*) стихи́ *m.pl.*, поэ́зия. **versed** *adj.* о́пытный, све́дущий (*in*, в+*prep.*). **versicle** *n.* во́зглас. **versify** *v.i.* писа́ть (пишу́, -шешь) *imp.*, на~ *perf.* стихи́; *v.t.* перелага́ть *imp.*, переложи́ть (-жу́, -жишь) *perf.* в стихи́.

version *n.* (*variant*) вариа́нт; (*interpretation*) ве́рсия; (*text*) текст.

versus *prep.* про́тив+*gen.*

vertebra *n.* позвоно́к (-нка́); *pl.* позвоно́чник. **vertebral** *adj.* позвоно́чный. **vertebrate** *n.* позвоно́чное живо́тное *sb.*

vertex *n.* верши́на; (*anat.*) маку́шка. **vertical** *adj.* вертика́льный; *n.* вертика́ль.

vertiginous *adj.* (*dizzy*) головокружи́тельный; (*rotating*) крутя́щийся. **vertigo** *n.* головокруже́ние.

verve *n.* подъём, энтузиа́зм.

very *adj.* (*that v. same*) тот са́мый; (*this v. same*) э́тот са́мый; *at that v. moment*, в тот са́мый моме́нт; (*precisely*) как раз; *you are the v. person I was looking for*, как раз вас я иска́л; *the v.*, (*even the*) да́же, вплоть; *the v. thought frightens me*, одна́, да́же, мысль об э́том меня́ пуга́ет; (*the extreme*) са́мый; *at the v. end*, в са́мом конце́; *adv.* о́чень; *v. much*, о́чень; *v. much*+

comp., гораздо + *comp.*; *v.* + *superl.*, *superl.*; *v. first*, самый первый; *v. well*, (*agreement*) хорошо, ладно; *not v.*, не очень, довольно + *neg.*

vesicle *n.* пузырёк (-рька).

vespers *n.* вечерня.

vessel *n.* сосуд; (*ship*) корабль (-бля) *m.*, судно (*pl.* суда, -дов).

vest[1] *n.* майка; (*waistcoat*) жилет.

vest[2] *v.t.* (*with power*) облекать *imp.*, облечь (-еку, -ечёшь; -ёк, -екла) *perf.* (*with*, + *instr.*); (*rights*) наделять *imp.*, наделить *perf.* + *instr.* (*in*, + *acc.*).

vested *adj.*: *v. interest*, личная заинтересованность; *v. interests*, (*property rights*) имущественные права *neut. pl.*; (*entrepreneurs*) крупные предприниматели *m.pl.*; *v. rights*, безусловные права *neut.pl.*

vestal (*virgin*) *n.* весталка.

vestibule *n.* вестибюль *m.*, передняя *sb.*

vestige *n.* (*trace*) след (*pl.* -ы); (*sign*) признак.

vestments *n.* одеяние, одежда; (*eccl.*) облачение. **vestry** *n.* ризница. **vesture** *n.* одеяние.

vet *n.* ветеринар; *v.t.* (*fig.*) проверять *imp.*, проверить *perf.*

vetch *n.* вика *collect.*

veteran *n.* ветеран; *adj.* старый (стар, -á, старо).

veterinary *adj.* ветеринарный; *n.* ветеринар.

veto *n.* вето *neut.indecl.*, запрещение; *v.t.* налагать *imp.*, наложить (-жу, -жишь) *perf.* вето на + *acc.*; запрещать *imp.*, запретить (-ещу, -етишь) *perf.*

vex *v.t.* досаждать *imp.*, досадить *perf.* + *dat.* **vexation** *n.* досада. **vexed** *adj.* (*annoyed*) раздосадованный (-ан); (*question*) спорный *adj.* **vexatious**, **vexing** *adj.* досадный.

via *prep.* через + *acc.*

viable *adj.* жизнеспособный; (*practicable*) осуществимый.

viaduct *n.* виадук.

vial *n.* пузырёк (-рька).

vibrant *adj.* (*vibrating*) вибрирующий; (*resonating*) резонирующий; (*trembling*) дрожащий (*with*, от + *gen.*).

vibraphone *n.* вибрафон. **vibrate** *v.i.*

vibrate *imp.*, дрожать (-жу, -жишь) *imp.*; (*to sound*) звучать (-чу, -чишь) *imp.*, про ~ *perf.*; *v.t.* (*make v.*) вызывать *imp.*, вызвать (вызову, -вешь) *perf.* **vibration** *n.* вибрация, дрожание. **vibrato** *n.* вибрато *neut.indecl.*

vicar *n.* приходский священник. **vicarage** *n.* дом (*pl.* -á) священника.

vicarious *adj.* (*deputizing for another*) замещающий другого; (*indirect*) косвенный.

vice[1] *n.* (*evil*) порок, зло; (*shortcoming*) недостаток (-тка).

vice[2] *n.* (*tech.*) тиски (-ков) *pl.*

vice- *in comb.* вице-, заместитель *m.*; *v.-admiral*, вице-адмирал; *v.-chairman*, заместитель *m.* председателя; *v.-chancellor*, (*univ.*) проректор; *v.-consul*, вице-консул; *v.-president*, вице-президент. **viceroy** *n.* вице-король (-ля) *m.*

vice versa *adv.* наоборот.

vicinity *n.* окрестности *f.pl.*, соседство, близость; *in the v.*, поблизости (*of*, от + *gen.*).

vicious *adj.* порочный; (*spiteful*) злобный; (*cruel, brutal*) жестокий (-ок, -ока, -око); *v. circle*, порочный круг (*loc.* -e & -ý; *pl.* -и). **viciousness** *n.* порочность; злобность.

vicissitude *n.* превратность.

victim *n.* жертва. **victimization** *n.* преследование. **victimize** *v.t.* (*harass*) мучить *imp.*, за ~, из ~ *perf.*; (*persecute*) преследовать *imp.*

victor *n.* победитель *m.*

Victorian *adj.* викторианский; (*fig.*) старомодный.

victorious *adj.* (*army*) победоносный; (*procession etc.*) победный. **victory** *n.* победа.

victual *v.t.* снабжать *imp.*, снабдить *perf.* провизией. **victualler** *n.* поставщик продовольствия. **victuals** *n.* пища, провизия *collect.*

vide imper. смотри.

video *adj.* телевизионный. **videotape** *n.* магнитная лента для записи изображения и звука.

vie *v.i.* соперничать *imp.* (*with*, c + *instr.*; *for*, в + *prep.*).

view *n.* (*prospect, picture*) вид; (*opinion*) взгляд, мнéние; (*viewing*) просмóтр; (*inspection*) осмóтр; *in v. of*, ввидý + *gen.*; *on v.*, выставленный (-ен) для обозрéния; *with a v. to*, с цéлью + *gen.*, + *inf.*; *v.t.* (*pictures etc.*) рассмáтривать *imp.*, осмотрéть (-рю, -ришь) *perf.*; (*mentally*) смотрéть (-рю, -ришь) *imp.* на + *acc.*; *v.i.* смотрéть (-рю, -ришь) *imp.*, по ~ *perf.* телевúзор. **viewer** *n.* зрúтель *m.*, ~ница; (*for slides*) проéктор. **viewfinder** *n.* видоискáтель *m.* **viewpoint** *n.* тóчка зрéния.

vigil *n.* бóдрствование; *keep v.*, бóдрствовать *imp.*, дежýрить *imp.* **vigilance** *n.* бдúтельность. **vigilant** *adj.* бдúтельный. **vigilante** *n.* дружúнник.

vignette *n.* виньéтка.

vigorous *adj.* сúльный (сúлён, -льнá, -льно, сúльны), энергúчный. **vigour** *n.* сúла, энéргия.

vile *adj.* (*base*) пóдлый (подл, -á, -о); нúзкий (-зок, -зкá, -зко); (*disgusting*) отвратúтельный. **vileness** *n.* пóдлость; отвратúтельность. **vilify** *v.t.* чернúть *imp.*, о ~ *perf.*

villa *n.* вúлла.

village *n.* дерéвня, селó; *attrib.* дерéвенский, сéльский. **villager** *n.* дерéвенский, сéльский, жúтель *m.*

villain *n.* злодéй. **villainous** *adj.* злодéйский; (*foul*) мéрзкий (-зок, -зкá, -зко). **villainy** *n.* злодéйство.

villein *n.* крепостнóй *sb.*

vim *n.* энéргия.

vinaigrette *n.* (*dressing*) припрáва из ýксуса и олúвкового мáсла.

vindicate *v.t.* (*justify*) опрáвдывать *imp.*, оправдáть *perf.*; (*stand up for*) отстáивать *imp.*, отстоять (-оύ, -оúшь) *perf.* **vindication** *n.* (*justification*) оправдáние; (*defence*) защúта.

vindictive *adj.* мстúтельный.

vine *n.* виногрáдная лозá (*pl.* -зы).

vinegar *n.* ýксус; *attrib.* ýксусный. **vinegary** *adj.* кúслый (-сел, -слá, -сло).

vineyard *n.* виногрáдник.

vintage *n.* сбор, урожáй, виногрáда; (*wine*) винó из сбóра определённого

гóда; *attrib.* (*wine*) мáрочный; (*car*) стáрый (стар, -á, стáро).

viola[1] *n.* (*mus.*) альт.

viola[2] *n.* (*bot.*) фиáлка.

violate *v.t.* (*treaty, privacy*) нарушáть *imp.*, нарýшить *perf.*; (*grave*) осквернять *imp.*, осквернúть *perf.*; (*rape*) насúловать *imp.*, из~ *perf.* **violation** *n.* нарушéние; осквернéние; насúлие. **violator** *n.* нарушúтель *m.*

violence *n.* (*physical coercion, force*) насúлие; (*strength, force*) сúла. **violent** *adj.* (*person*) свирéпый, жестóкий (-ók, -óкá, -óко); (*storm etc.*) сúльный (сúлён, -льнá, -льно, сúльны); (*quarrel*) бýрный (бýрен, бýрнá, -но), свирéпый; (*pain*) сúльный (сúлён, -льнá, -льно, сúльны); (*epoch*) бýрный (бýрен, бýрнá, -но), жестóкий (-ók, -óкá, -óко); (*death*) насúльственный. **violently** *adv.* сúльно, óчень.

violet *n.* (*bot.*) фиáлка; (*colour*) фиолéтовый цвет; *adj.* фиолéтовый.

violin *n.* скрúпка. **violinist** *n.* скрипáч (-á), ~ка.

V.I.P. *abbr.* óчень вáжное лицó (*pl.* -ца).

viper *n.* гадю́ка; (*fig.*) змея (*pl.* -éи). **viperous** *adj.* ядовúтый.

virago *n.* мегéра.

viral *adj.* вúрусный.

virgin *n.* дéвственник, -ица; *V. Mary*, дéва Марúя; *adj.* (*also fig.*) дéвственный (-ен, -енна); *v. lands, soil*, целинá. **virginal** *adj.* дéвственный (-ен, -енна); (*innocent*) невúнный (-нен, -нна; *virginals*) спинéт без нóжек. **virginity** *n.* дéвственность. **Virgo** *n.* Дéва.

virile *adj.* (*mature*) возмужáлый; (*manly*) мýжественный (-ен, -енна). **virility** *n.* возмужáлость; мýжество.

virtual *adj.* фактúческий. **virtually** *adv.* фактúчески. **virtue** *n.* (*excellence*) добродéтель; (*merit*) достóинство; *by v. of*, посрéдством + *gen.*, благодарá + *dat.* **virtuosity** *n.* виртуóзность. **virtuoso** *n.* виртуóз. **virtuous** *adj.* добродéтельный; (*chaste*) целомýдренный (-ен, -енна).

virulence *n.* (*toxicity*) ядовúтость; (*power*) сúла; (*med.*) вирулéнтность; (*fig.*) злóба. **virulent** *adj.* (*poisonous*) ядови́тый; (*of disease*) опа́сный; (*fig.*) зло́бный.

virus *n.* ви́рус.

visa *n.* ви́за; *v.t.* визи́ровать *imp., perf.,* за ~ *perf.*

visage *n.* лицо́ (*pl.* -ца); (*aspect*) вид.

vis-à-vis *adv.* визави́, напро́тив; *n.* визави́ *neut.indecl.; prep.* (*with regard to*) в отноше́нии + *gen.;* (*opposite*) напро́тив + *gen.*

viscera *n.* вну́тренности *f.pl.*

viscose *n.* виско́за.

viscosity *n.* вя́зкость.

viscount *n.* вико́нт. **viscountess** *n.* виконте́сса.

viscous *adj.* вя́зкий (-зок, -зка́, -зко).

visibility *n.* ви́димость. **visible** *adj.* ви́димый. **visibly** *adv.* я́вно, заме́тно.

vision *n.* (*sense*) зре́ние; (*apparition*) виде́ние; (*insight*) проница́тельность; (*foresight*) предви́дение; (*on television screen*) изображе́ние. **visionary** *adj.* (*spectral; illusory*) при́зрачный; (*imaginary, fantastic*) вообража́емый, фантасти́ческий; (*impracticable*) неосуществи́мый; (*given to having visions*) скло́нный к галлюцина́циям; *n.* (*dreamer*) мечта́тель *m.,* ~ ница, фантазёр (*one who has visions*) визионе́р.

visit *n.* посеще́ние, визи́т; (*trip*) пое́здка; *v.t.* навеща́ть *imp.,* навести́ть *perf.;* посеща́ть *imp.,* посети́ть (-ещу́, -ети́шь) *perf.;* (*call on*) заходи́ть (-ожу́, -о́дишь) *imp.,* зайти́ (-йду́, -йдёшь; зашёл, -шла́) *perf.* к + *dat.;* ходи́ть (хожу́, хо́дишь) *indet.,* идти́ (иду́, идёшь; шёл, шла) *det.,* пойти́ (пойду́, -дёшь; пошёл, -шла́) *perf.* в го́сти к + *dat.; be visiting,* быть в гостя́х у + *gen.* **visitation** *n.* (*official visit*) официа́льное посеще́ние; (*eccl.*) бо́жье наказа́ние. **visiting-card** *n.* визи́тная ка́рточка. **visitor** *n.* гость (*pl.* -ти, -те́й) *m.,* посети́тель *m.*

visor *n.* (*of cap*) козырёк (-рька́); (*in car*) солнцезащи́тный щито́к (-тка́); (*of helmet*) забра́ло.

vista *n.* перспекти́ва, вид.

visual *adj.* (*of vision*) зри́тельный; (*graphic*) нагля́дный; *v. aids,* нагля́дные посо́бия *neut.pl.* **visualize** *v.t.*

представля́ть *imp.,* предста́вить *perf.* себе́.

vital *adj.* (*also fig.*) жи́зненный (-ен, -енна); (*essential*) суще́ственный (-ен, -енна); (*lively*) живо́й (жив, -á, -о); *v. statistics,* стати́стика есте́ственного движе́ния населе́ния. **vitality** *n.* жизнеспосо́бность; (*liveliness*) жи́вость. **vitalize** *v.t.* оживля́ть *imp.,* оживи́ть *perf.* **vitals** *n.* жи́зненно ва́жные о́рганы *m.pl.*

vitamin *n.* витами́н.

vitiate *v.t.* по́ртить *imp.,* ис~ *perf.;* (*invalidate*) де́лать *imp.,* с~ *perf.* недействи́тельным; лиша́ть *imp.,* лиши́ть *perf.* си́лы. **vitiation** *n.* по́рча; (*leg.*) лише́ние си́лы; призна́ние недействи́тельным.

viticulture *n.* виногра́дарство.

vitreous *adj.* стекови́дный; (*of glass*) стекля́нный. **vitrify** *v.t. & i.* превраща́ть(ся) *imp.,* преврати́ть(ся) (-ащу́(сь), -ати́шь(ся)) *perf.* в стекло́, в стекови́дное вещество́.

vitriol *n.* купоро́с; (*fig.*) язви́тельность. **vitriolic** *adj.* купоро́сный; (*fig.*) язви́тельный.

vituperate *v.t.* брани́ть *imp.,* вы́~ *perf.* **vituperation** *n.* брань.

vivacious *adj.* живо́й (жив, -á, -о) оживлённый (-ён, -ена́). **vivacity** *n.* жи́вость, оживлённость.

viva voce *adj.* у́стный; *n.* у́стный экза́мен.

vivid *adj.* (*bright*) я́ркий (я́рок, ярка́, я́рко); (*lively*) живо́й (жив, -á, -о); (*imagination*) пы́лкий (пы́лок, -лка́, -лко). **vividness** *n.* я́ркость; жи́вость; пы́лкость.

vivify *v.t.* оживля́ть *imp.,* оживи́ть *perf.*

vivisection *n.* вивисе́кция.

vixen *n.* лиси́ца-са́мка; (*fig.*) мегéра.

viz. *adv.* то есть, а и́менно.

vizier *n.* визи́рь *m.*

vocabulary *n.* слова́рь (-ря́) *m.;* (*range of language*) запа́с слов; (*of a language*) слова́рный соста́в.

vocal *adj.* голосово́й; (*mus.*) вока́льный; (*noisy*) шу́мный (шу́мен, -мна́, -мно); *v. cord,* голосова́я свя́зка. **vocalic** *adj.* гла́сный. **vocalist** *n.* певе́ц (-вца́), -ви́ца.

vocation *n.* призва́ние; (*profession*) профе́ссия. **vocational** *adj.* профессиона́льный. **vocative** *adj.* (*n.*) зва́тельный (паде́ж -á).

vociferate *v.t.* крича́ть (-чу́, -чи́шь) *imp.*, кри́кнуть *perf.* **vociferous** *adj.* (*clamorous*) крикли́вый; (*noisy*) шу́мный (шу́мен, -мна́, -мно).

vodka *n.* во́дка.

vogue *n.* мо́да; (*popularity*) популя́рность; *in v.*, в мо́де.

voice *n.* го́лос; (*gram.*) зало́г *v.t.* (*express*) выража́ть *imp.*, вы́разить *perf.* **voiced** *adj.* (*phon.*) зво́нкий (-нок, -нка́, -нко). **voiceless** *adj.* (*phon.*) глухо́й (глух, -á, -о).

void *n.* пустота́; *adj.* пусто́й (пуст, -á, -о, пусты́); (*invalid*) недействи́тельный; *v. of*, лишённый (-ён, -ена́) + *gen.*; *v.t.* (*render invalid*) де́лать *imp.*, с~ *perf.* недействи́тельным; (*excrete*) опорожня́ть *imp.*, опорожни́ть *perf.*

volatile *adj.* (*chem.*) лету́чий; (*inconstant*) непостоя́нный (-нен, -нна); (*elusive*) неулови́мый. **volatility** *n.* лету́честь; непостоя́нство. **volatilize** *v.t. & i.* (*chem.*) улету́чивать(ся) *imp.*, улету́чить(ся) *perf.*; (*also fig.*) испаря́ть(ся) *imp.*, испари́ть(ся) *perf.*

vol-au-vent *n.* слоёный пирожо́к (-жка́).

volcanic *adj.* вулкани́ческий (*also fig.*). **volcano** *n.* вулка́н.

vole *n.* (*zool.*) полёвка.

volition *n.* во́ля; *by one's own v.*, по свое́й во́ле.

volley *n.* (*missiles*) залп; (*fig.*; *of arrows etc.*) град; (*sport*) уда́р с лёта; *v.t.* (*sport*) ударя́ть *imp.*, уда́рить *perf.* с лёта. **volley-ball** *n.* волейбо́л.

volt *n.* вольт. **voltage** *n.* вольта́ж, напряже́ние. **voltaic** *adj.* гальвани́ческий. **voltmeter** *n.* вольтме́тр.

volte-face *n.* (*fig.*) ре́зкая переме́на.

volubility *n.* говорли́вость. **voluble** *adj.* говорли́вый.

volume *n.* (*book*) том (*pl.* -á); (*capacity*, *bulk*; *also fig.*) объём; (*loudness*) гро́мкость; (*mus.*; *strength*) си́ла. **voluminous** *adj.* (*bulky*) объёмистый, обши́рный; (*of writer*) плодови́тый; (*of many volumes*) многото́мный.

voluntary *adj.* доброво́льный; (*deliberate*) умы́шленный (-ен, -енна); *n.* (*mus.*) со́ло *neut.indecl.* на орга́не. **volunteer** *n.* доброво́лец (-льца); *v.t.* предлага́ть *imp.*, предложи́ть (-жу́, -жишь) *perf.*; *v.i.* (*offer*) вызыва́ться *imp.*, вы́зваться (вы́зовусь, -вешься) *perf.* (*inf.* + *inf.*; *for*, в + *acc.*); (*mil.*) идти́ (иду́, идёшь; шёл, шла) *imp.*, пойти́ (пойду́, -дёшь; пошёл, -шла́) *perf.* доброво́льцем.

voluptuary *n.* сластолю́бец (-бца). **voluptuous** *adj.* сластолюби́вый, чу́вственный (-ен, -енна). **voluptuousness** *n.* сластолю́бие.

volute *n.* (*archit.*) волю́та.

vomit *n.* рво́та; *v.t.* рвать (рвёт) *imp.*, вы́рвать (-вет) *perf. impers.* + *instr.*; *he was vomiting blood*, его рва́ло кро́вью; (*fig.*) изверга́ть *imp.*, изве́ргнуть *perf.*

voracious *adj.* прожо́рливый; (*fig.*) ненасы́тный. **voracity** *n.* прожо́рливость; ненасы́тность.

vortex *n.* (*whirlpool*; *also fig.*) водоворо́т; (*whirlwind*; *also fig.*) вихрь *m.*

votary *n.* почита́тель *m.*, ~ница; сторо́нник, -ица.

vote *n.* (*poll*) голосова́ние; (*individual v.*) го́лос (*pl.* -á); *the v.*, (*suffrage*) пра́во го́лоса; (*resolution*) во́тум *no pl.*; *v. of no confidence*, во́тум недове́рия (*in*, + *dat.*); *v. of thanks*, выраже́ние благода́рности; *v.i.* голосова́ть *imp.*, про~ *perf.* (*for*, за + *acc.*; *against*, про́тив + *gen.*); *v.t.* (*grant by v.*) ассигнова́ть *imp.*, *perf.*; (*deem*) признава́ть *imp.*, призна́ть *perf.*; *the film was voted a failure*, фильм был при́знан неуда́чным; *v. in*, избира́ть *imp.*, избра́ть (изберу́, -рёшь; избра́л, -á, -о) *perf.* голосова́нием. **voter** *n.* избира́тель *m.* **voting-paper** *n.* избира́тельный бюллете́нь *m.*

votive *adj.* испо́лненный по обе́ту; *v. offering*, приноше́ние по обе́ту.

vouch *v.i.*; *v. for*, руча́ться *imp.*, поручи́ться *perf.* за + *acc.* **voucher** *n.* (*receipt*) распи́ска; (*coupon*) тало́н. **vouchsafe** *v.t.* удоста́ивать *imp.*, удосто́ить + *instr.* (*person to whom granted*, + *acc.*).

vow *n.* кля́тва, обе́т; *v.t.* кля́сться

(кляну́сь, -нёшься; кля́лся, -ла́сь) *imp.*, по ~ *perf.* в + *prep.*

vowel *n.* гла́сный *sb.*

voyage *n.* путеше́ствие; *v.i.* путеше́ствовать *imp.*

vulcanization *n.* вулканиза́ция.

vulgar *adj.* вульга́рный, гру́бый (груб, -а́, -о), по́шлый (пошл, -а́, -о); (*of the common people*) простонаро́дный.

vulgarism *n.* вульга́рное выраже́ние.

vulgarity *n.* вульга́рность, по́шлость.

vulgarization *n.* вульгариза́ция. **vulgarize** *v.t.* вульгаризи́ровать *imp.*, *perf.*

vulnerable *adj.* уязви́мый.

vulture *n.* гриф; (*fig.*) хи́щник.

vulva *n.* ву́льва.

W

wad *n.* кусо́к (-ска́) ва́ты; (*in gun*) пыж (-а́) *w. of money*, па́чка бума́жных де́нег; *v.t.* (*stuff with wadding*) набива́ть *imp.*, наби́ть (набью́, -бьёшь) *perf.* ва́той. **wadding** ва́та; (*padding, packing*) набивка.

waddle *v.i.* ходи́ть (хожу́, хо́дишь) *indet.*, идти́ (иду́, идёшь; шёл, шла) *det.*, пойти́ (пойду́, -дёшь; пошёл, -шла́) *perf.* вперева́лку (*coll.*).

wade *v.t.* & *i.* (*river*) переходи́ть (-ожу́, -о́дишь) *imp.*, перейти́ (-йду́, -йдёшь; перешёл, -шла́) *perf.* вброд; *v.i.*: *w. through*, (*mud etc.*) пробира́ться *imp.*, пробра́ться (проберу́сь, -рёшься; пробра́лся, -ала́сь, -а́лось) *perf.* по + *dat.*; (*s.th. boring etc.*) одолева́ть *imp.*, одоле́ть *perf.* **wader** *n.* (*bird*) боло́тная пти́ца; (*boot*) боло́тный сапо́г (-а́; *gen.pl.* -г).

wafer *n.* ва́фля (*gen.pl.* -фель); (*eccl.*; *paper seal*) обла́тка.

waffle[1] *n.* (*dish*) ва́фля (*gen.pl.* -фель).

waffle[2] *n.* (*blather*) трёп; *v.i.* трепа́ться (-плю́сь, -пле́шься) *imp.*

waft *v.t.* & *i.* нести́(сь) (несу́(сь), -сёшь(ся); нёс(ся), несла́(сь)) *imp.*, по ~ *perf.*

wag[1] *n.* (*wave*) взмах; (*of tail*) виля́ние; *v.t.* (*tail*) виля́ть *imp.*, вильну́ть *perf.* + *instr.*; (*finger*) грози́ть *imp.*, по ~ *perf.* + *instr.*; *v.i.* кача́ться *imp.*, качну́ться *perf.*

wag[2] *n.* (*joker*) шутни́к (-а́).

wage[1] *n.* за́работная пла́та; *w.-earner*, рабо́чий *sb.*; (*bread-winner*) корми́лец (-льца); *w.-freeze*, замора́живание за́работной пла́ты; *living w.*, прожи́точный ми́нимум. **wages** *n.* *see* **wage**[1].

wage[2] *v.t.*: *w. war*, вести́ (веду́, -дёшь; вёл, -а́) *imp.*, про ~ *perf.* войну́.

wager *n.* пари́ *neut.indecl.*; (*stake*) ста́вка; *v.i.(t.)* держа́ть (-жу́, -жишь) *imp.* пари́ (на + *acc.*) (that, что).

waggish *n.* шаловли́вый.

wag(g)on *n.* (*carriage*) пово́зка; (*cart*) теле́га; (*rly.*) ваго́н-платфо́рма; (*van*) фурго́н; (*trolley*) вагоне́тка. **wag(g)oner** *n.* во́зчик.

wagtail *n.* трясогу́зка.

waif *n.* беспризо́рник.

wail *n.* вопль *m.*; *v.i.* вопи́ть *imp.* (*coll.*), выть (во́ю, во́ешь) *imp.* (*coll.*).

wainscot *n.* пане́ль; *v.t.* обшива́ть *imp.*, обши́ть (обошью́, -ьёшь) *perf.* пане́лью.

waist *n.* та́лия; (*level of w.*) по́яс (*pl.* -а́); *w.-deep*, (*adv.*) по по́яс. **waistband** *n.* по́яс (*pl.* -а́). **waistcoat** *n.* жиле́т. **waistline** *n.* та́лия.

wait *n.* ожида́ние; *lie in w.*, быть в заса́де; *lie in w.* (*for*), поджида́ть *imp.*; *lie in w. also w. for*) ждать (жду, ждёшь; ждал, -а́, -о) *imp.* (+ *gen.*); *v.i.* (*be a waiter, waitress*) быть официа́нтом, -ткой; *v.i. w. on*, обслу́живать *imp.*, обслужи́ть (-жу́, -жишь) *perf.*

waiter n. официа́нт. **waiting** n. ожида́ние; w.-list, спи́сок (-ска) кандида́тов; w.-room, приёмная sb.; (rly.) зал ожида́ния. **waitress** n. официа́нтка.

waive v.t. отка́зываться imp., отказа́ться (-ажу́сь, -а́жешься) perf. от + gen.

wake¹ n. (at funeral) поми́нки (-нок) pl.

wake² n. (naut.) кильва́тер; in the w. of, в кильва́тере + dat., по пята́м за + instr.

wake³ v.t. (also w. up) буди́ть (бужу́, бу́дишь) imp., раз~ perf.; v.i. (also w. up) просыпа́ться imp., просну́ться perf.; v.t. & i. (also fig.) пробужда́ть(ся) imp., пробуди́ть (-ужу́(сь), -у́дишь(ся)) perf. **wakeful** adj. (sleepless) бессо́нный; (vigilant) бди́тельный. **wakefulness** n. бди́тельность. **waken** see **wake³**.

walk n. (walking) ходьба́; (gait) похо́дка; (stroll) прогу́лка пешко́м; (path, avenue) тропа́ (-пы, -пу́, тро́пам), алле́я; w.-out, (strike) забасто́вка; (exit) демонстрати́вный ухо́д; w.-over, лёгкая побе́да; ten minutes' w. from here, де́сять мину́т ходьбы́ отсю́да; go for a w., идти́ (иду́, идёшь; шёл, шла) imp., пойти́ (пойду́, -дёшь; пошёл, -шла́) perf. гуля́ть; from all walks of life, всех слоёв о́бщества; v.i. ходи́ть (хожу́, хо́дишь) indet., идти́ (иду́, идёшь; шёл, шла) det., пойти́ (пойду́, -дёшь; пошёл, -шла́) perf.; гуля́ть imp., по~ perf.; w. away, off, уходи́ть (ухожу́, -о́дишь) imp., уйти́ (уйду́, -дёшь; ушёл, ушла́) perf.; w. in, входи́ть (вхожу́, -о́дишь) imp., войти́ (войду́, -дёшь; вошёл, -шла́) perf.; w. out, выходи́ть (-ожу́, -о́дишь) imp., вы́йти (-йду, -йдешь; вы́шел, -шла) perf.; v.t. (traverse) обходи́ть (-ожу́, -о́дишь) imp., обойти́ (-йду́, -йдёшь; обошёл, -шла́) perf.; (take for w.) выводи́ть (-ожу́, -о́дишь) imp., вы́вести (-еду, -едешь; -ел) perf. гуля́ть. **walker** n. ходо́к (-á). **walkie-talkie** n. (перено́сная) ра́ция. **walking** n. ходьба́; v. stick, трость (pl. -ти, -те́й); adj. гуля́ющий; (med.); encyclopaedia) хо-

дя́чий; w.-on part, роль (pl. -ли, -ле́й) без слов.

wall n. стена́ (acc. -ну; pl. -ны, -н, -на́м); (of object) сте́нка; attrib. стенно́й; v.t. обноси́ть (-ошу́, -о́сишь) imp., обнести́ (-есу́, -есёшь; -ёс, -есла́) perf. стено́й. **w. up**, (door, window) заде́лывать imp., заде́лать; (brick up) замуро́вывать imp., замурова́ть perf.

wallet n. бума́жник.

wallflower n. желтофио́ль.

wallop n. си́льный уда́р; v.t. си́льно ударя́ть imp., уда́рить perf.; бить (бью, бьёшь) imp., по~ perf.

wallow v.i. валя́ться imp., бара́хтаться; w. in, (give oneself up to) предава́ться (-даю́сь, -даёшься) imp., преда́ться (-а́мся, -а́шься, -а́стся, -ади́мся; преда́лся, -ла́сь) perf. + dat.

wallpaper n. обо́и (обо́ев) pl.

walnut n. гре́цкий оре́х; (wood, tree) оре́ховое де́рево (pl. (tree) -е́вья, -е́вьев), оре́х.

walrus n. морж (-á).

waltz n. вальс; v.i. вальси́ровать imp.

wan adj. (pale) бле́дный (-ден, -дна́, -дно, бле́дны); (faint) ту́склый (-л, -ла́, -ло).

wand n. (of conductor, magician) па́лочка; (of official) жезл (-á).

wander v.i. броди́ть (брожу́, -о́дишь) imp.; (also of thoughts etc.) блужда́ть imp.; w. from the point, отклоня́ться imp., отклони́ться (-ню́сь, -ни́шься) perf. от те́мы. **wanderer** n. стра́нник, скита́лец (-льца). **wandering** adj. бродя́чий; блужда́ющий; (winding) изви́листый.

wane n. убыва́ние; v.i. убыва́ть imp., убы́ть (убу́дет; у́был, -á, -о) perf.; (diminish) уменьша́ться imp., уме́ньши́ться perf.; (weaken) ослабева́ть imp., ослабе́ть perf.

wangle v.t. ухитря́ться imp., ухитри́ться perf. получи́ть.

want n. (lack) недоста́ток (-тка); (need) нужда́; (requirement) потре́бность; (desire) жела́ние; v.t. хоте́ть (хочу́, -чешь, хоти́м) imp., за~ perf. + gen., acc.; (need) нужда́ться imp. в + prep.; I want you to come at six, я хочу́, чтобы ты пришёл в шесть. **wanting**

adj. (*absent*) отсу́тствующий; *be w.*, недостава́ть (-таёт) *imp.* (*impers.* + *gen.*); *experience is w.*, недостаёт о́пыта.

wanton *adj.* (*licentious*) распу́тный; (*senseless*) бессмы́сленный (-ен, -енна); (*luxuriant*) бу́йный (бу́ен, буйна́, -но).

war *n.* война́ (*pl.* -ны); (*attrib.*) вое́нный (*in w. crime, w. correspondent, w. debts, w. loan etc.*); *at w.*, в состоя́нии войны́; *w.-cry,* боево́й клич; *w.-dance,* войнственный та́нец (-нца); *w.-game,* вое́нная игра́; *w.-horse,* боево́й конь (-ня́; *pl.* -ни, -не́й) *m.*; *w. memorial,* па́мятник па́вшим в войне́; *w.-paint,* раскра́ска те́ла пе́ред похо́дом; *w.-path,* (*fig.*): *be on the w.-path,* быть в войнственном настрое́нии; *v.i.* воева́ть (вою́ю, -юёшь) *imp.*

warble *n.* трель; *v.i.* издава́ть (-даю́, -даёшь) *imp.*, изда́ть (-а́м, -а́шь, -а́ст, -ади́м; изда́л, -а́, -о) *perf.* тре́ли.

ward[1] *n.* (*hospital*) пала́та *n.*; (*child etc.*) подопе́чный *sb.*; (*district*) администрати́вный райо́н го́рода.

ward[2] *v.t.*: *w. off,* отража́ть *imp.*, отрази́ть *perf.*

warden *n.* (*prison*) нача́льник *m.*; (*college*) ре́ктор.

warder *n.* тюре́мщик.

wardrobe *n.* гардеро́б.

warehouse *n.* склад, пакга́уз. **wares** *n.* изде́лия *neut.pl.*, това́ры *m.pl.*

warfare *n.* война́.

warhead *n.* боева́я голо́вка.

warily *adv.* осторо́жно. **wariness** *n.* осторо́жность.

warlike *adj.* войнственный (-ен, -енна).

warm *adj.* тёплый; *adj.* (*also fig.*) тёплый (тёпел, -пла́, -пло́, -плы); *v.t.* гре́ть(ся) *imp.*, согре́ть(ся) *perf.*; *w. up,* (*food etc.*) подогрева́ть(ся) *imp.*, подогре́ть(ся) *perf.*; (*liven up*) оживля́ть(ся) *imp.*, оживи́ть(ся) *perf.*; (*sport*) размина́ться *imp.*, размя́ться (разомну́сь, -нёшься) *perf.*; (*mus.*) разыгрыва́ться *imp.*, разыгра́ться *perf.* **warmth** *n.* тепло́; (*cordiality*) серде́чность.

warmonger *n.* поджига́тель *m.* войны́.

warn *v.t.* предупрежда́ть *imp.*, преду-

преди́ть *perf.* (*about,* о + *prep.*). **warning** *n.* предупрежде́ние.

warp *n.* (*of cloth*) осно́ва; (*of wood*) коробле́ние; *v.t. & i.* (*wood*) коро́бить(ся) *imp.*, по~, с~ *perf.*; *v.t.* (*pervert, distort*) извраща́ть *imp.*, изврати́ть (-ащу́, -ати́шь) *perf.*

warrant *n.* (*for arrest etc.*) о́рдер (*pl.* -а́); (*justification*) оправда́ние; (*proof*) доказа́тельство; *v.t.* (*justify*) опра́вдывать *imp.*, оправда́ть *perf.*; (*guarantee*) гаранти́ровать *imp.*, *perf.*; руча́ться *imp.*, поручи́ться (-чу́сь, -чишься) *perf.* за + *acc.* **warrantable** *adj.* допусти́мый. **warranty** *n.* (*basis*) основа́ние; (*guarantee*) гара́нтия.

warren *n.* уча́сток (-тка), где во́дятся кро́лики.

warring *adj.* противоречи́вый, непримири́мый.

warrior *n.* во́ин, бое́ц (бойца́).

warship *n.* вое́нный кора́бль (-ля́) *m.*

wart *n.* борода́вка; *w.-hog,* борода́вочник. **warty** *adj.* борода́вчатый.

wartime *n.*: *in w.,* во вре́мя войны́.

wary *adj.* осторо́жный.

wash *n.* мытьё; (*thin layer*) то́нкий слой (*pl.* -ои́); (*lotion*) примо́чка; (*surf*) прибо́й; (*backwash*) попу́тная струя́ (*pl.* -у́и); *at the w.,* в сти́рке; *have a w.,* мы́ться (мо́юсь, мо́ешься) *imp.*, по ~ *perf.*; *w.-basin,* умыва́льник; *w.-house,* пра́чечная *n.*; *w.-out,* (*fiasco*) прова́л; *w.-room,* умыва́льная *sb.*; *w.-tub,* лоха́нь для сти́рки; *v.t. & i.* мы́ть(ся) (мо́ю(сь), мо́ешь(ся) *imp.*, вы́~, по~ *perf.*; *v.t.* (*clothes*) стира́ть *imp.*, вы́~ *perf.*; (*of sea*) омыва́ть *imp.*; *v.i.* (*clothes*) стира́ться *imp.*; *w. ashore: the body was washed ashore,* труп прибило́ к бе́регу (*impers.*); *w. away, off, out,* смыва́ть(ся) *imp.*, смыть(ся) (смо́ю, -о́ешь. -о́ет(ся) *perf.*; (*carry away*) сноси́ть (-ошу́, -о́сишь) *imp.*, снести́ (-есу́, -есёшь; -ёс, -есла́) *perf.*; *w. out,* (*rinse*) спола́скивать *imp.*, сполосну́ть *perf.*; *w. up,* (*dishes*) мыть (мо́ю, мо́ешь) *imp.*, вы́~, по ~ *perf.* (посу́ду); *w. one's hands* (*of it*), умыва́ть *imp.*, умы́ть (умо́ю, -о́ешь *perf.* ру́ки. **washed-out** *adj.* (*exhausted*) утомлённый. **washer** *n.* (*tech.*) ша́йба.

washerwoman *n.* пра́чка. **washing** *n.* (*of clothes*) сти́рка; (*clothes*) белье́; *w.-machine*, стира́льная маши́на; *w.-powder*, стира́льный порошо́к (-шка́); *w.-up*, (*action*) мытье́ посу́ды; (*dishes*) гря́зная посу́да.

wasp *n.* (*pl.* о́сы) оса́; *w.'s nest*, оси́ное гнездо́ (*pl.* -ёзда). **waspish** *adj.* (*irritable*) раздражи́тельный; (*caustic*) язви́тельный.

wastage *n.* уте́чка. **waste** *n.* (*desert*) пусты́ня; (*wastage*) уте́чка; (*refuse*) отбро́сы *m.pl.*; (*of time, money etc.*) (бесполе́зная) тра́та; *go to w.*, пропада́ть *imp.*, пропа́сть (-аду́, -адёшь; -а́л) *perf.* да́ром; *w.-pipe*, сто́чная труба́ (*pl.* -бы); *adj.* (*desert*) пусты́нный (-нен, -нна); (*superfluous*) нену́жный; (*uncultivated*) невозде́ланный; *w. land*, пусты́рь (-ря́) *m.*; *lay w.*, опустоша́ть *imp.*, опустоши́ть *perf.*; *w. paper*, нену́жная бума́га *f.pl.*; (*for recycling*) макулату́ра; *w. products*, отхо́ды (-дов) *pl.*; *w.-paper basket*, корзи́на для (нену́жных) бума́г; *v.t.* тра́тить *imp.*, по ~ *perf.*; (*time*) теря́ть *imp.*, по ~ *perf.*; *v.t.* & *i.* (*weaken*) истоща́ть(ся) *imp.*, истощи́ть(ся) *perf.*; *v.i.*; *w. away*, ча́хнуть (-х) *imp.*, за ~ *perf.* **wasteful** *adj.* расточи́тельный. **wastrel** *n.* (*idler*) безде́льник.

watch *n.* (*timepiece*) часы́ (-со́в) *pl.*; (*duty*) дежу́рство; (*naut.*) ва́хта; *keep w. over*, наблюда́ть *imp.* за + *instr.*; *w.-chain*, цепо́чка для часо́в; *w.-dog*, стороже́вой пёс (пса); *w.-maker*, часовщи́к (-а́); *w.-spring*, часова́я пружи́на; *w.-tower*, стороже́вая ба́шня (*gen.pl.* -шен); *v.t.* наблюда́ть *imp.*; следи́ть *imp.* за + *instr.*; (*guard, w. over*) охраня́ть *imp.*, охрани́ть *perf.*; (*look after*) смотре́ть (-рю́, -ришь) *imp.*, по ~ *perf.* за + *instr.*; *w. television, a film*, смотре́ть (-рю́, -ришь) *imp.*, по ~ *perf.* телеви́зор, фильм; *w. out!* осторо́жно! **watchful** *adj.* бди́тельный. **watchman** *n.* (*ночно́й*) сто́рож (*pl.* -а́, -е́й). **watchword** *n.* ло́зунг.

water *n.* вода́ (*acc.* -ду; *pl.* -ды, -д, во́да́м); *attrib.* водяно́й, во́дный; *w.-*

bath, водяна́я ба́ня; *w.-bird*, водяна́я пти́ца; *w.-bottle*, графи́н для воды́; *w. bus*, речно́й трамва́й; *w.-butt*, бо́чка для дождево́й воды́; *W.-carrier*, Водоле́й; *w.-closet*, убо́рная *sb.*; *w.-colour*, акваре́ль; *w.-heater*, кипяти́льник; *w.-hole*, (*in desert*) ключ (-а́); *w.-jump*, во́дное препя́тствие; *w.-level*, у́ровень (-ня) *m.* воды́; *w.-lily*, водяна́я ли́лия; *w.-line*, ватерли́ния; *w.-main*, водопрово́дная магистра́ль; *w.-melon*, арбу́з; *w. mill*, водяна́я ме́льница; *w.-pipe*, водопрово́дная труба́ (*pl.* -бы); *w. polo*, во́дное по́ло *neut.indecl.*; *w.-power*, гидроэне́ргия; *w.-rat*, водяна́я кры́са; *w.-ski*, (*n.*) во́дная лы́жа; *w.-supply*, водоснабже́ние; *w.-tower*, водонапо́рная ба́шня (*gen.pl.* -шен); *w.-way*, во́дный путь (-ти́, -тём) *m.*; *w.-weed*, водоро́сль; *w.-wheel*, водяно́е колесо́ (-ёса); *v.t.* (*flowers etc.*) полива́ть *imp.*, поли́ть (-лью́, -льёшь; по́ли́л, -а́, -о) *perf.*; (*animals*) пои́ть (пою́, по́ишь) *imp.*, на ~ *perf.*; (*irrigate*) ороша́ть *imp.*, ороси́ть *perf.*; *v.i.* (*eyes*) слези́ться *imp.*; (*mouth*) *my mouth waters*, у меня́ слю́нки теку́т; *w. down*, разбавля́ть *imp.*, разба́вить *perf.* **watercourse** *n.* (*brook*) руче́й (-чья́); (*bed*) ру́сло (*gen.pl.* -л); (*channel*) кана́л. **watercress** *n.* кресс водяно́й. **waterfall** *n.* водопа́д. **waterfront** *n.* часть (*pl.* -ти, -те́й) го́рода примыка́ющая к бе́регу. **watering-can** *n.* ле́йка. **waterlogged** *adj.* заболо́ченный (-ен); (*impregnated*) пропи́танный (-ан) водо́й. **watermark** *n.* (*in paper*) водяно́й знак. **waterproof** *adj.* непромока́емый; *n.* непромока́емый плащ (-а́). **watershed** *n.* водоразде́л. **waterside** *n.* бе́рег (*loc.* -ý; *pl.* -а́). **watertight** *adj.* водонепроница́емый; (*hermetic*) гермети́ческий. **waterworks** *n.* водопрово́дные сооруже́ния *neut.pl.* **watery** *adj.* водяни́стый; (*pale*) бле́дный (-ден, -дна́, -дно, бле́дны́).

watt *n.* ватт.

wattle *n.* (*fencing*) плете́нь (-тня́) *m.*; *attrib.* плетёный.

wave *v.t.* (*hand etc.*) маха́ть (машу́, -шешь) *imp.*, махну́ть *perf.* + *instr.*

(*hair*) завива́ть *imp.*, зави́ть (-вью́, -вьёшь; зави́л, -á, -о) *perf.*; *v.i.* (*flutter*) развева́ться *imp.*; (*rock, swing*) кача́ться *imp.*, качну́ться *perf.*; w. aside; (*spurn*) отверга́ть *imp.*, отве́ргнуть (-г) *perf.*; w. down, дава́ть (даю́, даёшь) *imp.*, дать (дам, дашь, даст, дади́м; дал, -á, да́ло, -ли) *perf.* знак остано́вки + *dat.*; *n.* (*in var. senses*) волна́ (*pl.* -ны, -н, во́лна́м); (*of hand*) взмах; *v.i.* (*in hair*) зави́вка.
wavelength *n.* длина́ волны́. **waver** *v.i.* (*also fig.*) колеба́ться (-блюсь, -блешся) *imp.*; (*flicker, flutter*) колыха́ться (-ы́шется) *imp.*; колыхну́ться *perf.* **wavy** *adj.* волни́стый.

wax *n.* воск; (*in ear*) се́ра; *attrib.* восково́й; *v.t.* воща́ть *imp.*, на~ *perf.* **waxen, waxy** *adj.* восково́й; (*like wax*) похо́жий на воск. **waxwork** *n.* восковáя фигу́ра; *pl.* галере́я восковы́х фигу́р.

way *n.* (*road, path, route*; *fig.*) доро́га, путь (-ти́, -тём) *m.*; (*manner*) о́браз; (*method*) спо́соб; (*condition*) состоя́ние; (*respect*) отноше́ние; (*habit*) привы́чка; *by the w.*, (*fig.*) кста́ти, ме́жду про́чим; *on the w.*, по доро́ге, по пути́; *this w.* (*direction*) сюда́; (*in this w.*) таки́м о́бразом; *the other w. round*, наоборо́т; *under w.*, на ходу́; *be in the w.*, меша́ть *imp.*; *get out of the w.*, уходи́ть (-ожу́, -о́дишь) *imp.*, уйти́ (уйду́, -дёшь; ушёл, ушла́) *perf.* с доро́ги; *give w.*, (*yield*) поддава́ться (-даю́сь, -даёшься) *imp.*, подда́ться (-áмся, -áшься, -áстся, -ади́мся; -дался, -лáсь) *perf.* (*to,* + *dat.*); (*collapse*) обру́шиваться *imp.*, обру́шиться *perf.*; *go out of one's w. to*, стара́ться *imp.*, по~ *perf.* из всех сил + *inf.*; *have it one's own w.*, де́йствовать *imp.* по-сво́ему; *make w.*, уступа́ть *imp.*, уступи́ть (-плю́, -пишь) *perf.* доро́гу (*for,* + *dat.*).
wayfarer *n.* пу́тник. **waylay** *v.t.* (*lie in wait for*) подстерега́ть *imp.*, подстере́чь (-егу́, -ежёшь) подстерёг, -лá) *perf.*; (*stop*) перехва́тывать *imp.*, перехвати́ть (-ачу́, -áтишь) *perf.* по пути́. **wayside** *n.* обо́чина; *adj.* придоро́жный.

wayward *adj.* своенра́вный, капри́зный. **waywardness** *n.* своенра́вие, капри́зность.

we *pron.* мы (нас, нам, на́ми, нас).
weak *adj.* (*in var. senses*) слáбый (слаб, -á, -о); (*indecisive*) нереши́тельный; (*unconvincing*) неубеди́тельный. **weaken** *v.t.* ослабля́ть *imp.*, осла́бить *perf.*; *v.i.* слабе́ть *imp.*, о~ *perf.* **weakling** *n.* слáбый челове́к (*pl.* лю́ди, -де́й, -дям, -дьми́). **weakness** *n.* слáбость; *have a w. for*, име́ть *imp.* слáбость к + *dat.*

weal *n.* (*mark*) рубе́ц (-бцá).

wealth *n.* богáтство; (*abundance*) изоби́лие. **wealthy** *adj.* богáтый, состоя́тельный.

wean *v.t.* отнима́ть *imp.*, отня́ть (отниму́, -мешь) *perf.* от груди́; (*fig.*) отучáть *imp.*, отучи́ть (-чу́, -чишь) *perf.* (*of, from,* от + *gen.*).

weapon *n.* ору́жие. **weaponless** *adj.* безору́жный. **weaponry** *n.* вооруже́ние, ору́жие.

wear *n.* (*wearing*) но́ска; (*clothing*) оде́жда; (*w. and tear*) изнáшивание; *v.t.* носи́ть (ношу́, но́сишь) *imp.*, быть в + *prep.*; *v.i.* носи́ться (но́сится) *imp.*; w. off, (*cease to have effect*) перестава́ть (-таю́, -таёшь) *imp.*, переста́ть (-áну, -áнешь) *perf.* де́йствовать; w. out, (*clothes*) изнáшивать(ся) *imp.*, износи́ть(ся) (-ошу́(сь), -о́сишь(ся)) *perf.*; (*exhaust, become exhausted*) истощáть(ся) *imp.*, истощи́ть(ся) *perf.*

weariness *n.* (*tiredness*) устáлость, утомле́ние; (*tedium*) утоми́тельность. **wearing, wearisome** *adj.* утоми́тельный. **weary** *adj.* устáлый, утомлённый (-ён, -енá); *v.t. & i.* утомля́ть(ся) *imp.*, утоми́ть(ся) *perf.*

weasel *n.* лáска (*gen.pl.* -сок).

weather *n.* погóда; w.-beaten, повреждённый (-ён, -енá) бу́рями; (*of face*) обве́тренный (-ен, -ена́); (*of person*) закалённый (-ён, -енá); w.-chart, синопти́ческая кáрта; w. forecast, прогнóз погóды; w.-station, метеорологи́ческая стáнция; *v.t.* (*storm etc.*) выде́рживать *imp.*, вы́держать (-жу, -жишь) *perf.*; (*expose to atmosphere*) подвергать *imp.*, подвергнуть (-г) *perf.* атмосферным влияниям. **weather-cock, weathervane** *n.* флюгер (*pl.* -á). **weatherman** *n.* метеоролог.

weave[1] *v.t. & i.* (*fabric*) ткать (тку, ткёшь; ткал, -á, -о) *imp.*, co ~ *perf.*; *v.t.* (*fig.*; *also* wreath *etc.*) плести (плету, -тёшь; плёл, -á) *imp.*, c ~ *perf.*; *n.* узор ткáни. **weaver** *n.* ткач, -á; -иха. **weaving** *n.* (*the art of w.*) ткáчество (*the w.*) тканьё.

weave[2] *v.i.* (*sway*) покáчиваться *imp.*

web *n.* (*cobweb, gossamer*; *fig.*) паутина; (*membrane*) перепонка; (*tissue*) ткань; (*fig.*) сплетение. **webbed** *adj.* перепончатый. **webbing** *n.* ткáная лента, тесьмá.

wed *v.t.* (*of man*) жениться (-нюсь, -нишься) *imp.*, *perf.* на+*prep.*; (*of woman*) выходить (-ожу, -одишь) *imp.*, выйти (выйду, -дешь; вышла) *perf.* зáмуж за+*acc.*; (*unite*) сочетáть *imp.*, *perf.*; *v.i.* жениться (-нюсь, -нишься) *perf.* (*coll.*) вступáть *imp.*, вступить (-плю, -пишь) *perf.* в брак. **wedded** *adj.* супружеский; w. to, (*fig.*) преданный (-ан) +*dat.* **wedding** *n.* свáдьба, бракосочетáние; w.-cake, свáдебный торт; w.-day, день (дня) *m.* свáдьбы; w.-dress, подвенечное плáтье (*gen.pl.* -в); w.-ring, обручáльное кольцо (*pl.* -льца, -лéц, -льцам).

wedge *n.* клин (*pl.* -ья, -ьев); *v.t.* (*w. open*) заклинивать *imp.*, заклинить *perf.*; *v.t. & i.*: w. in(to), вклинивать(ся) *imp.*, вклинить(ся) *perf.* (в+*acc.*).

wedlock *n.* брак, супружество; *born out of w.*, рождённый (-ён, -енá) вне брáка, внебрáчный.

Wednesday *n.* средá (*acc.* -ду; *pl.* -ды, -д, -дáм).

weed *n.* сорняк (-á); w.-killer, гербицид; *v.t.* полоть (полю, -лешь) *imp.*, вы ~ *perf.* w. out, удалять *imp.*, удалить *perf.* **weedy** *adj.* заросший сорнякáми; (*person*) тощий (тощ, -á, -е).

week *n.* неделя; w.-end, суббóта и воскресéнье, уикэнд. **weekday** *n.* будний день (дня) *m.* **weekly** *adj.* еженедельный; (*wage*) недельный;

adv. раз в неделю; еженедельно; *n.* еженедельник.

weep *v.i.* плáкать (плáчу, -чешь) *imp.*; w. over, оплáкивать *imp.*, оплáкать (оплáчу, -чешь) *perf.* **weeping** *n.* плач; *adj.*: w. willow, плакучая ива. **weepy** *adj.* слезливый.

weevil *n.* долгоносик.

weft *n.* уток (уткá).

weigh *v.t.* (*also fig.*) взвешивать *imp.*, взвесить *perf.*; (*consider*) обдумывать *imp.*, обдумать *perf.*; *v.t. & i.* (*so much*) весить *imp.*; w. down, отягощáть *imp.*, отяготить (-ощу, -отишь) *perf.*; w. on, тяготить (-ощу, -отишь) *imp.*; w. out, отвешивать *imp.*, отвесить *perf.*; w. up, (*appraise*) оценивать *imp.*, оценить (-ню, -нишь) *perf.* **weight** *n.* (*also authority*) вес (*pl.* -á); (*load, also fig.*) тяжесть; (*sport*) гиря, штáнга; (*influence*) влияние; *lose w.*, худеть *imp.*, по ~ *perf.*; *put on w.*, толстеть *imp.*, по ~ *perf.*; прибавлять *imp.*, прибáвить *perf.* в весе; *w.-lifter*, гиревик (-á), штангист; *w.-lifting*, поднятие тяжестей; *v.t.* (*make heavier*) утяжелять *imp.*, утяжелить *perf.* **weightless** *adj.* невесомый. **weightlessness** *n.* невесомость. **weighty** *adj.* (*also fig.*) веский; (*heavy*) тяжёлый (-л, -лá); (*important*) вáжный (-жен, -жнá, -жно, -жны).

weir *n.* плотина, запруда.

weird *adj.* (*strange*) стрáнный (-нен, -ннá, -нно).

welcome *n.* (*greeting*) приветствие; (*reception*) приём; *adj.* желáнный (-ан); (*pleasant*) приятный; *you are w.*, (*don't mention it*) не стóит благодáрности, пожáлуйста; *you are w. to use my bicycle*, мой велосипед к вáшим услугам; *you are w. to stay the night*, вы мóжете переночевáть у меня/нас; *v.t.* приветствовать *imp.* (& *perf.* in past tense); *interj.* добро пожáловать!

weld *n.* сварнóй шов (шва); *v.t. & i.* свáривать(ся) *imp.*, сварить(ся) *perf.*; (*fig.*) сплачивать *imp.*, сплотить *perf.* **welder** *n.* свáрщик. **welding** *n.* свáрка.

welfare *n.* благосостояние, благополучие; *W.* State, госудáрство всеобщего благосостояния; w. work, рабóта по социáльному обеспечéнию.

well[1] *n.* колóдец (-дца); (*for stairs*) лéстничная клéтка.

well[2] *v.i.*: w. forth, up, бить (бьёт) *imp.* ключóм; хлы́нуть *perf.*

well[3] *adj.* (*healthy*) здорóвый; feel w., чýвствовать *imp.*, по ~ *perf.* себя́ хорошó, здорóво; get w., поправля́ться *imp.*, попра́виться *perf.*; look w., хорошó вы́глядеть (-жу, -дишь) *imp.*; all is w., всё в поря́дке; *interj.* ну(!); *adv.* хорошó; (*very much*) óчень; as w., тóже; as w. as, (*in addition to*) крóме + *gen.*; it may w. be true, вполнé возмóжно, что э́то так; very w.! хорошó! w. done! молодéц! w.-advised, благоразýмный; w.-balanced, уравновéшенный (-ен, -енна); w.-behaved, благонра́вный; w.-being, благополýчие; w.-bred, благовоспи́танный (-ан, -анна); w.-built, крéпкий (-пок, -пка́, -пко); w.-defined, чёткий (-ток, -тка́, -тко); w.-disposed, благоскло́нный (-нен, -нна), благожела́тельный; w. done, (*cooked*) (хорошó) прожа́ренный (-ен); w.-fed, откóрмленный (-ен); w.-groomed, (*person*) хóленый; w.-grounded, обоснóванный (-ан, -анна) (*versed*) свéдущий (in, в + *prep.*); w.-informed, (хорошó) осведомлённый (-ён, -ена́) (about, в + *prep.*); w.-known, извéстный; w.-mannered, воспи́танный (-ан); w.-meaning, имéющий хорóшие намéрения; w. paid, хорошó опла́чиваемый; w. preserved, хорошó сохрани́вшийся; w.-proportioned, пропорциона́льный; w.-read, начи́танный (-ан, -анна); w.-spoken, умéющий изы́сканно говори́ть; w. timed, своеврéменный (-нен, -нна); w.-wisher, доброжела́тель *m.*; w.-worn, (*fig.*) избитый. **wellnigh** *adv.* почти́.

wellington (boot) *n.* рези́новый сапóг (-á; *gen.pl.* -г).

Welsh[1] *adj.* валли́йский, уэ́льский. **Welshman** *n.* валли́ец. **Welshwoman** *n.* валли́йка.

welsh[2] *v.t.*: w. on, (*swindle*) надува́ть *imp.*, наду́ть (-у́ю, -у́ешь) *perf.* (*coll.*); (*fail to keep*) не сдéрживать *imp.*,

сдержа́ть (-жу́, -жишь) *perf.* + *gen.*

welt *n.* (*of shoe*) рант (*loc.* -ý); (*weal*) рубéц (-бца́).

welter *n.* (*confusion*) сумбýр, пýтаница; *v.i.* валя́ться.

wench *n.* дéвка.

wend *v.t.*: w. one's way, держа́ть (-жу́, -жишь) *imp.* путь.

wer(e)wolf *n.* оборотень (-тня) *m.*

west *n.* зáпад; (*naut.*) вест; *adj.* зáпадный; *adv.* на зáпад, к зáпаду. **westerly** *adj.* зáпадный; *n.* зáпадный вéтер (-тра). **western** *adj.* зáпадный; *n.* (*film*) вéстерн. **westernize** *v.t.* европеизи́ровать *imp.*, *perf.* **westward(s)** *adv.* на зáпад, к зáпаду.

wet *adj.* мóкрый (-р, -рá, -ро); (*paint*) непросóхший; (*rainy*) дождли́вый; w.-nurse, корми́лица; "w. paint" „осторóжно окра́шено"; w. through, промóкший до ни́тки; w. suit, водонепроница́емый костю́м; *n.* (*dampness*) влáжность; (*rain*) дождь (-дя́) *m.*; *v.t.* мочи́ть (-чу́, -чишь) *imp.*, на ~ *perf.* **wetness** *n.* влáжность.

whack *n.* (*blow*) си́льный удáр; *v.t.* колоти́ть (-очу́, -óтишь) *imp.*, по ~ *perf.*

whale *n.* кит (-á).

wharf *n.* при́стань (*pl.* -ни, -нéй).

what *pron.* (*interrog.*, *interj.*) что (чегó, чемý, чем, чём); (*how much*) скóлько; (*rel.*) (то,) что (чегó, чемý, чем, чём); what (...) for, зачéм; w. if, а что éсли; w. is your name? как вас зовýт? *adj.* (*interrog.*, *interj.*) какóй; w. kind of, какóй. **whatever** *pron.* что бы ни + *past* (w. you think, что бы вы ни дýмали); всё, что (take w. you want, возьми́те всё, что хоти́те); *adj.* какóй бы ни + *past* (w. books he read(s), каки́е бы кни́ги он ни прочита́л); (*at all*): there is no chance w., нет никакóй возмóжности; is there any chance w.? есть ли хоть какáя-нибудь возмóжность?

wheat *n.* пшени́ца. **wheaten** *adj.* пшени́чный.

wheedle *v.t.* (*coax into doing*) угова́ривать *imp.*, уговори́ть *perf.* с помощью лéсти; w. out of, выма́нивать *imp.*, вы́манить *perf.* у + *gen.* **wheedling** *adj.* вкра́дчивый, льсти́вый.

wheel n. колесо́ (pl. -ёса); (steering-w., helm) руль (-ля́) m., штурва́л; (potter's) гонча́рный круг; v.t. (push) ката́ть indet., кати́ть (качу́, ка́тишь) det., по~ perf.; v.t. & i. (turn) пове́ртывать(ся) imp., поверну́ть(ся) perf.; v.i. (circle) кружи́ться (-ужу́сь, -у́жишься) imp. **wheelbarrow** n. та́чка. **wheelchair** n. инвали́дное кре́сло (gen.pl. -сел) (на колёсах). **wheelwright** n. коле́сник.

wheeze n. сопе́ние, хрип; v.i. сопе́ть (-плю́, -пи́шь) imp., хрипе́ть (-плю́, -пи́шь) imp. **wheezy** adj. хри́плый (-л, -ла́, -ло).

whelk n. (mollusc) брюхоно́гий моллю́ск.

when adv. когда́; conj. когда́, в то вре́мя как; (whereas) тогда́ как; (although) хотя́. **whence** adv. отку́да. **whenever** adv. когда́ же; conj. (every time) вся́кий раз когда́; (at any time) в любо́е вре́мя, когда́; (no matter when) когда́ бы ни+past; we shall have dinner w. you arrive, во ско́лько бы вы ни прие́хали, мы пообе́даем. **where** adv., conj. (place) где; (whither) куда́; from w., отку́да. **whereabouts** adv. где; n. местонахожде́ние. **whereas** conj. тогда́ как; хотя́; (official) поско́льку. **whereby** adv., conj. посре́дством чего́. **wherein** adv., conj. в чём. **wherever** adv., conj. (place) где бы ни+past; (whither) куда́ бы ни+past; w. he goes, куда́ бы он ни шёл; **wherewithal** n. сре́дства neut. pl.

whet v.t. точи́ть (-чу́, -чишь) imp., на~ perf.; (stimulate) возбужда́ть imp., возбуди́ть perf. **whetstone** n. точи́льный ка́мень (-мня; pl. -мни, -мне́й) m.

whether conj. ли; I don't know w. he will come, я не зна́ю, придёт ли он; w. he comes or not, придёт (ли) он и́ли нет.

whey n. сы́воротка.

which adj. (interrog., rel.) како́й; pron. (interrog.) како́й? (person) кто; (rel.) кото́рый; (rel. to whole statement) что; w. is w.? (persons) кто из них кто? (things) что-что? **whichever** adj., pron. како́й бы ни+past (w. book you choose, каку́ю бы кни́гу ты ни

вы́брал); любо́й (take w. book you want, возьми́те любу́ю кни́гу).

whiff n. (wind) дунове́ние; (smoke) дымо́к (-мка́); (odour) за́пах.

while n. вре́мя neut.; промежу́ток (-тка) вре́мени; a little w., недо́лго; a long w., до́лго; for a long w., (up to now) давно́; for a w., на вре́мя; in a little w., ско́ро; once in a w., вре́мя от вре́мени; it is worth w., сто́ит э́то сде́лать; v.t.: w. away, проводи́ть (-ожу́, -о́дишь) imp., провести́ (-еду́, -едёшь; -ёл, -ела́) perf.; conj. пока́; в то вре́мя как; (although) хотя́, несмотря́ на то, что; (contrast) a; we went to the cinema w. they went to the theatre, мы ходи́ли в кино́, а они́ в теа́тр. **whilst** see while.

whim n. при́хоть, причу́да, капри́з. **whimper** n. хны́канье; v.i. хны́кать (хны́чу, -чешь & хны́каю, -аешь) imp. **whimsical** adj. капри́зный; (odd) причу́дливый. **whimsy** n. капри́з, при́хоть, причу́да.

whine n. (wail) вой; (whimper) хны́канье; v.i. скули́ть imp.; (wail) выть (во́ю, во́ешь); (whimper) хны́кать imp.

whinny n. ти́хое ржа́ние; v.i. ти́хо ржать (ржу, ржёшь) imp.

whip n. кнут (-а́), хлыст (-а́); w. hand, контро́ль (-ля) m.; v.t. (lash) хлеста́ть (-ещу́, -е́щешь) imp., хлестну́ть perf.; (urge on) подгоня́ть imp., подогна́ть (подгоню́, -нишь; подогна́л, -а́, -о) perf.; (cream) сбива́ть imp., сбить (собью́, -ьёшь) perf.; w. off, ски́дывать imp., ски́нуть perf.; w. out, выхва́тывать imp., вы́хватить perf.; w. round, бы́стро пове́ртываться imp., поверну́ться perf.; w.-round, сбор де́нег; w. up, (stir up) разжига́ть imp., разже́чь (разожгу́, -ожжёшь; разжёг, разожгла́) perf. **whipper-snapper** n. ничто́жество. **whipping** n. по́бои (-оев) pl.

whirl n. круже́ние; (of dust etc.) вихрь (-ря) m.; (turmoil) сумато́ха, смяте́ние; v.t. & i. кружи́ть(ся) (кружу́(сь), кру́жишь(ся)) imp., за~ perf. **whirlpool** n. водоворо́т. **whirlwind** n. вихрь (-ря) m.

whirr n. жужжа́ние; v.i. жужжа́ть (жужжу́, -жжи́шь) imp.

whisk n. (of twigs etc.) ве́ничек (-чка); (utensil) мутовка; (movement) пома́хивание; v.t. (cream etc.) сбива́ть imp., сбить (собью, -ьёшь) perf.; (wag, wave) маха́ть (машу́, -шешь) imp., махну́ть perf. + instr.; w. away, off, (brush off) смахивать imp., смахну́ть perf.; (take away) быстро уноси́ть (-ошу́, -о́сишь) imp., унести́ (-есу́, -есёшь; -ёс, -есла́) perf.; v.i. (scamper away) юркну́ть perf.

whisker n. (human) во́лос (pl. -осы, -о́с, -оса́м) на лице́; (animal) ус (pl. -ы́); pl. (human) бакенба́рды f.pl.

whisky n. ви́ски neut.indecl.

whisper n. шёпот; (rustle) ше́лест; v.t. & i. шепта́ть (шепчу́, -чешь) imp., шепну́ть perf.; (rustle) шелесте́ть (-ти́шь) imp.

whist n. вист.

whistle n. (sound) свист; (instrument) свисто́к (-тка́); v.i. свисте́ть (-ищу́, -исти́шь) imp., сви́стнуть perf. (also to dog etc.); v.t. насви́стывать imp.

whistler n. свисту́н (-а́) (coll.).

whit n.: no w., not a w., ничу́ть, ниско́лько.

white adj. бе́лый (бел, -а́, бе́ло); (hair) седо́й (сед, -а́, -о); (pale) бле́дный (-ден, -дна́, -дно, бле́дны); (transparent) прозра́чный; (with milk) с молоко́м; paint w., кра́сить imp., по~ perf. в бе́лый цвет; w.-collar, конто́рский; w.-collar worker, служа́щий sb.; w.-hot, раскалённый добела́; W. House, Бе́лый дом; w. lie, неви́нная ложь (лжи, instr. ло́жью); W. Russian, (n.) белору́с, ~ка; (adj.) белору́сский; (colour) бе́лый цвет; (egg, eye) бело́к (-лка́); (w. man) бе́лый sb. whitebait n. малёк (-лька́). snето́к (-тка́). **whiten** v.t. бели́ть (белю́, бе́лишь) imp., на~, по~, вы~ perf.; (blanch, bleach) отбе́ливать imp., отбели́ть perf.; v.i. беле́ть imp., по~ perf. **whiteness** n. белизна́. **whitewash** n. раство́р для побе́лки; v.t. бели́ть (белю́, бе́лишь) imp., по~ perf.; (fig.) обеля́ть imp., обели́ть perf.

whither adv., conj. куда́.

whiting n. (fish) мерла́нг.

Whitsun n. тро́ица.

whittle v.t. строга́ть imp., вы́~ perf., ножо́м; w. down, (decrease) уменьша́ть imp., уме́ньшить perf.

whiz(z) n. свист; v.i. свисте́ть (-ищу́, -исти́шь) imp.

who pron. (interrog.) кто (кого́, кому́, кем, ком); (rel.) кото́рый.

whoa interj. тпру!

whoever pron. кто бы ни + past; (he who) тот, кто.

whole adj. (entire) весь (вся, всё; все); це́лый; (intact, of number) це́лый; w.-heartedly, от всего́ се́рдца; w. meal, непросе́янная мука́; n. (thing complete) це́лое sb.; (all there is) (вся, всё; все) sb.; (sum) су́мма; as a w., в це́лом; on the w., в о́бщем. **wholesale** adj. опто́вый; (fig.) ма́ссовый; n. опто́вая торго́вля; adv. о́птом. **wholesaler** n. опто́вый торго́вец (-вца). **wholesome** adj. здоро́вый, благотво́рный. **wholly** adv. по́лностью, целико́м.

whom pron. (interrog.) кого́ etc. (see who); (rel.) кото́рого etc.

whoop n. крик, ги́канье (coll.); v.i. крича́ть (-чу́, -чи́шь) imp., кри́кнуть perf.; ги́кать imp., ги́кнуть perf. (coll.); whooping cough, коклю́ш.

whore n. проститу́тка.

whorl n. (bot.) муто́вка; (on shell) зави́ток (-тка́); (of spiral) вито́к (-тка́).

whose pron. (interrog., rel.) чей (чья, чьё; чьи) (?); (rel.) кото́рого.

why adv. почему́; n. причи́на; interj. (surprise) да ведь!; (impatience) ну!

wick n. (of lamp etc.) фити́ль (-ля́) m.

wicked adj. злой (зол, зла); (immoral) безнра́вственный (-нен, -нна). **wickedness** n. зло́бность.

wicker n. пру́тья m.pl. для плете́ния; attrib. плетёный.

wicket n. кали́тка; (cricket) воро́тца.

wide adj. широ́кий (-к, -ка́, широ́ко); (extensive) обши́рный; (in measurements) в + acc. ширино́й; w. awake, бо́дрствующий; (wary) бди́тельный; w. open, широко́ откры́тый; (defenceless) незащищённый; adv. (off target) ми́мо це́ли. **widely** *adv.* широко́. **widen** *v.t.* & *i.* расширя́ть(ся) *imp.*, расши́рить(ся) *perf.* **widespread** *adj.* широко́ распространённый (-ён, -ена́).

wi(d)geon *n.* ди́кая у́тка.

widow *n.* вдова́ (*pl.* -вы). **widowed** *adj.* овдове́вший. **widower** *n.* вдове́ц (-вца́). **widowhood** *n.* вдовство́.

width *n.* ширина́; (*fig.*) широта́; (*of cloth*) полотни́ще.

wield *v.t.* держа́ть (-жу́, -жишь) *imp.* в рука́х; владе́ть + *instr.*

wife *n.* жена́ (*pl.* жёны).

wig *n.* пари́к (-а́).

wiggle *v.t.* & *i.* (*move*) шевели́ть(ся) *imp.*, по ~, шевельну́ть(ся) *perf.*

wigwam *n.* вигва́м.

wild *adj.* ди́кий (дик, -а́, -о); (*flower*) полево́й; (*uncultivated*) невозде́ланный; (*tempestuous*) бу́йный (бу́ен, бу́йна, -но); (*furious*) нето́вый; (*ill-considered*) необду́манный (-ан, -анна); *be w. about*, быть без ума́ от + *gen.*; *w.-goose chase*, сумасбро́дная зате́я; *n.*: *pl.* пусты́ня, де́бри (-рей) *pl.* **wildcat** *adj.* (*reckless*) риско́ванный; (*unofficial*) неофициа́льный. **wilderness** *n.* ди́кая ме́стность; (*desert*) пусты́ня. **wildfire** *n.*: *spread like w.*, распространя́ться *imp.*, распространи́ться *perf.* со сверхъесте́ственной быстрото́й. **wildlife** *n.* жива́я приро́да. **wildness** *n.* ди́кость.

wile *n.* хи́трость, уло́вка.

wilful *adj.* (*obstinate*) упря́мый; (*deliberate*) преднаме́ренный (-ен, -енна), умы́шленный (-ен, -енна). **wilfulness** *n.* упря́мство; преднаме́ренность.

will *n.* во́ля; (*w.-power*) си́ла во́ли; (*desire*) во́ля, жела́ние; (*at death*) завеща́ние; *against one's w.*, про́тив во́ли; *at w.*, по жела́нию; *of one's own free w.*, доброво́льно; *with a w.*, с энтузиа́змом; *good w.*, до́брая во́ля; *make one's w.*, писа́ть (пишу́, -шешь) *imp.*, на ~ *perf.* завеща́ние; *v.t.* (*want, desire*) хоте́ть (хочу́, -чешь, хоти́м) *imp.*, за ~ *perf.* + *gen.*; *желáть imp.*, по ~ *perf.* + *gen.*; (*order*) веле́ть (-лю́, -ли́шь) *imp., perf.*; (*compel by one's w.*) заставля́ть *imp.*, заста́вить *perf.*; (*bequeath*) завеща́ть *imp., perf.*

willing *adj.* гото́вый, согла́сный; (*assiduous*) стара́тельный. **willingly** *adv.* охо́тно. **willingness** *n.* гото́вность.

will-o'-the-wisp *n.* блужда́ющий огонёк (-нька́).

willow *n.* и́ва.

willy-nilly *adv.* во́лей-нево́лей.

wilt *v.i.* вя́нуть (вял) *imp.*, за ~ *perf.*; поника́ть *imp.*, пони́кнуть (-к) *perf.*; (*weaken*) слабе́ть *imp.*, о ~ *perf.*

wily *adj.* хи́трый (-тёр, -тра́, хи́тро), кова́рный.

win *n.* вы́игрыш, побе́да; *v.t.* & *i.* выи́грывать *imp.*, вы́играть *perf.*; *v.t.* (*obtain*) добива́ться *imp.*, доби́ться (-бью́сь, -бьёшься) *perf.* + *gen.*; *w. over*, (*convince*) убежда́ть *imp.*, убеди́ть (-ди́шь) *perf.*; (*gain favour of*) располага́ть *imp.*, расположи́ть (-жу́, -жишь) *perf.* к себе́; *w. through*, (*overcome*) преодолева́ть *imp.*, преодоле́ть *perf.*

wince *n.* содрога́ние, вздра́гивание; *v.i.* вздра́гивать *imp.*, вздро́гнуть *perf.*

winch *n.* (*windlass*) лебёдка.

wind¹ *n.* (*air*) ве́тер (-тра); (*breath*) дыха́ние; (*flatulence*) ве́тры *m.pl.*; *w. instrument*, духово́й инструме́нт; *w.-swept*, откры́тый ветра́м; *get w. of*, проню́хивать *imp.*, проню́хать *perf.*; *v.t.* (*make gasp*) заставля́ть *imp.*, заста́вить *perf.* задохну́ться.

wind² *v.i.* (*meander*) ви́ться (вьюсь, вьёшься; ви́лся, -ла́сь) *imp.*; извива́ться *imp.*; *v.t.* & *i.* (*coil*) нама́тывать(ся) *imp.*, намота́ть(ся) *perf.*; *v.t.* (*watch*) заводи́ть (-ожу́, -о́дишь) *imp.*, завести́ (-еду́, -едёшь; -ёл, -ела́) *perf.*; (*wrap*) уку́тывать *imp.*, уку́тать *perf.*; *w. down*, разма́тывать(ся) *imp.*, размота́ть(ся) *perf.*; *w. up*, (*v.t.*) (*reel*) сма́тывать *imp.*, смота́ть *perf.*; (*watch*) *see* **wind²**; (*v.t.* & *i.*) (*end*) конча́ть(ся) *imp.*, ко́нчить(ся) *perf.* **winding** *adj.* (*twisted*) вито́й, спира́льный; (*meandering*) изви́листый.

windfall *n.* (*lit.*) плод (-а́), сби́тый ве́тром; (*fig.*) неожи́данное сча́стье.

windlass *n.* лебёдка.

windmill *n.* ветряна́я ме́льница.

window n. окно́ (pl. о́кна, о́кон, о́кнам); (of shop) витри́на; w.-box, нару́жный я́щик для расте́ний; w.-dressing, украше́ние витри́н; w.-frame, око́нная ра́ма; w.-ledge, подоко́нник; w.-pane, око́нное стекло́ (pl. стёкла, -кол, -клам); w.-shopping, рассма́тривание витри́н; w.-sill, подоко́нник.

windpipe n. дыха́тельное го́рло, трахе́я.

windscreen n. пере́днее/ветрово́е стекло́ (pl. стёкла, -кол, -клам); w. wiper, стеклоочисти́тель m., дво́рник (coll.).

windward n. наве́тренная сторона́ (acc. -ону); adj. наве́тренный. **windy** adj. (verbose) многосло́вный.

wine n. вино́ (pl. -на); w.-cellar, ви́нный по́греб (pl. -а́); w.-coloured, тёмно-кра́сный; w.-grower, виногра́дарь m.; w.-growing, виногра́дарство; w.-list, ка́рта вин; w.-merchant, торго́вец (-вца) вино́м; w.-tasting, дегуста́ция вин; v.t. (take wine) пить (пью, пьёшь; пил, -а́, -о) imp., вы́~ perf. вино́; v.t. угоща́ть imp., угости́ть perf. вино́м. **winebottle** n. ви́нная буты́лка. **wineglass** n. рю́мка. **winery** n. ви́нный заво́д. **winy** adj. ви́нный.

wing n. (also polit.) крыло́ (pl. -лья, -льев); (archit.) фли́гель (pl. -ля́, -ле́й) m.; (sport) фланг; pl. (theat.) кули́сы (pl.); w.-nut, крыла́тая га́йка; w.-span, разма́х кры́льев; v.i. лета́ть indet., лете́ть (лечу́, лети́шь) det., по~ perf.; v.t. (provide with wings) снабжа́ть imp., снабди́ть perf. кры́льями; (quicken) ускоря́ть imp., уско́рить perf.; (inspire) окрыля́ть imp., окрыли́ть perf. **winged** adj. крыла́тый.

wink n. (blink) морга́ние; (as sign) подми́гивание; in a w., момента́льно; v.i. морга́ть imp., моргну́ть perf.; мига́ть imp., мигну́ть perf. (at, + dat.); подми́гивать imp., подми́гнуть perf. (at, + dat.); (fig.) смотре́ть (-рю́, -ришь) imp., по~ perf. сквозь па́льцы на + acc.

winkle n. берегова́я ули́тка; v.t.: w. out, выко́вы́ривать imp., вы́ковырять perf.

winner n. победи́тель m., ~ница. **winning** adj. вы́игрывающий, побежда́ю-

щий; (of shot etc.) реша́ющий; (charming) обая́тельный; n.: pl. вы́игрыш; w.-post, фи́нишный столб (-а́).

winnow v.t. (grain) ве́ять (ве́ю, ве́ешь) imp.; (sift) просе́ивать imp., просе́ять (-е́ю, -е́ешь) perf.

winsome adj. привлека́тельный, обая́тельный.

winter n. зима́; attrib. зи́мний; v.i. проводи́ть (-ожу́, -о́дишь) imp., провести́ (-еду́, -едёшь; -ёл, -ела́) perf. зи́му; зимова́ть imp., пере~ perf. **wintry** adj. зи́мний; (cold) холо́дный (хо́лоден, -дна́, -дно, холодны́).

wipe v.t. (also w. out inside of) вытира́ть imp., вы́тереть (вы́тру, -решь; вы́тер, -ла) perf.; w. away, off, стира́ть imp., стере́ть (сотру́, -рёшь; стёр, -ла) perf.; w. out, (exterminate) уничтожа́ть imp., уничто́жить perf.; (disgrace etc.) смыва́ть imp., смыть (смо́ю, -о́ешь) perf.

wire n. про́волока; (carrying current) про́вод (pl. -а́); (telegram) телегра́мма; attrib. про́волочный; w. netting, про́волочная сеть; v.t. (electr.) де́лать imp., с~ perf. электри́ческую прово́дку в + acc.; (telegraph) телеграфи́ровать imp., impf.; **wireless** n. ра́дио neut.indecl.; w. set, радиоприёмник. **wiring** n. электропрово́дка. **wiry** adj. жи́листый.

wisdom n. му́дрость; w. tooth, зуб (pl. -ы, -о́в) му́дрости. **wise** adj. му́дрый (-р, -ра́, -ро); (prudent) благоразу́мный.

wish n. жела́ние; with best wishes, всего́ хоро́шего, с наилу́чшими пожела́ниями; v.t. хоте́ть (-чешь, -чешь, хоти́м) imp., за~ perf. (I w. I could see him, мне хоте́лось бы его́ ви́деть; I w. to go, я хочу́ пойти́; I w. you to come early, я хочу́, что́бы вы ра́но пришли́; I w. the day were over, хорошо́ бы день уже́ ко́нчился); жела́ть imp. + gen. (I w. you luck, жела́ю вам уда́чи); (congratulate on) поздравля́ть imp., поздра́вить perf. (I w. you a happy birthday, поздравля́ю тебя́ с днём рожде́ния); v.i.: w. for, жела́ть imp. + gen.; хоте́ть (хочу́,

-чешь, хотим) imp., за ~ perf.+gen.;
acc. **wishbone** n. ду́жка. **wishful** adj.
жела́ющий; w. thinking, приня́тие
жела́емого за действи́тельное.

wishy-washy adj. (too liquid) жи́дкий
(-док, -дка́, -дко); (fig.) сла́бый (-б,
-ба́, -бо), бессве́тный.

wisp n. (of straw) пучо́к (-чка́); (hair)
клочо́к (-чка́); (smoke) стру́йка.

wistaria n. глици́ния.

wistful adj. (pensive) заду́мчивый;
(melancholy) тоскли́вый.

wit[1] n. (mind) ум (-а́); (wittiness) остро-
у́мие; (person) остря́к (-а́); be at one's
w.'s end, не знать imp. что де́лать.

wit[2] v.i.: to w., то есть, а и́менно.

witch n. ве́дьма, колду́нья (gen.pl.
-ний); (person) остря́к+acc.; w.-hunt,
охо́та на ве́дьм. **witchcraft** n. кол-
до́вство.

with prep. (in company of, together w.)
(вме́сте) с+instr.; (as a result of)+
gen.; (at house of, in keeping of) y+
gen.; (by means of)+instr.; (in spite
of) несмотря́ на+acc.; (including)
включа́я+acc.; w. each/one another,
друг с дру́гом.

withdraw v.t. (retract) брать (беру́,
-рёшь; брал, -а́, -о) imp., взять
(возьму́, -мёшь; взял, -а́, -о) perf.
наза́д; (curtain, hand) отдёргивать
imp., отдёрнуть perf.; (cancel) сни-
ма́ть imp., снять (сниму́, -мешь;
снял, -а́, -о) perf.; (mil.) отводи́ть
(-ожу́, -о́дишь) imp., отвести́ (-еду́,
-едёшь; -ёл, -ела́) perf.; (money from
circulation) изыма́ть imp., изъя́ть
(изыму́, -ы́мешь) из обраще́ния;
(diplomatic representative) отзыва́ть
imp., отозва́ть (отзову́, -вёшь; отоз-
ва́л, -а́, -о) perf.; (from bank) брать
(беру́, -рёшь; брал, -а́, -о) imp., взять
(возьму́, -мёшь; взял, -а́, -о)
perf.; v.i. удаля́ться imp., удали́ться
perf.; (mil.) отходи́ть (-ожу́, -о́дишь)
imp., отойти́ (-йду́, -йдёшь; отошёл,
-шла́) perf. **withdrawal** n. (retraction)
взя́тие наза́д; (cancellation) сня́тие;
(mil.) отхо́д; (money from circulation)
изъя́тие; (departure) ухо́д. **withdrawn**
adj. за́мкнутый.

wither v.i. вя́нуть (вял) imp., за ~ perf.;

высыха́ть imp., вы́сохнуть (-x) perf.;
v.t. иссуша́ть imp., иссуши́ть (-шу́,
-шишь) perf. **withering** adj. (fig.)
испепеля́ющий.

withers n. хо́лка.

withhold v.t. (refuse to grant) не дава́ть
(даю́, даёшь) imp., дать (дам, дашь,
даст, дади́м; дал, -а́, да́ло́, -и) perf.+
gen.; (hide) скрыва́ть imp., скрыть
(скро́ю, -о́ешь) perf.; (restrain) уде́р-
живать imp., удержа́ть (-жу́, -жишь)
perf.

within prep. (inside) внутри́+gen., в+
prep.; (w. the limits of) в преде́лах+
gen.; (time) в тече́ние+gen.; adv.
внутри́; (at home) до́ма.

without prep. без+gen.; (outside) вне+
gen., за+instr.; w. saying good-bye,
не проща́ясь; do w., обходи́ться
(-ожу́сь, -о́дишься) imp., обойти́сь
(-йду́сь, -йдёшься; обошёлся, -шла́сь)
perf. без+gen.

withstand v.t. противостоя́ть (-ою́
-ои́шь) imp.+dat.; вы́держивать imp.,
вы́держать (-жу, -жишь) perf.

witless adj. глу́пый (-п, -па́, -по).

witness n. (person) свиде́тель m.; (eye-
witness) очеви́дец (-дца); (to signature
etc.) завери́тель m.; (evidence) свиде́-
тельство; bear w. to, свиде́тель-
ствовать imp., за ~ perf.+acc.; w.-box, ме́сто
(pl. -та́) для свиде́телей; v.t. быть
свиде́телем+gen.; (document etc.) за-
веря́ть imp., заве́рить perf.

witticism n. остро́та. **wittiness** n.
остроу́мие. **witty** adj. остроу́мный.

wizard n. волше́бник, колду́н (-а́).
wizardry n. волшебство́.

wizened adj. (wrinkled) морщи́нистый.

wobble v.t. & i. шата́ть(ся) imp.,
шатну́ть(ся) perf.; кача́ть(ся) imp.,
качну́ть(ся) perf.; v.i. (voice) дрожа́ть
(-жу́, -жи́шь) imp. **wobbly** adj. ша́ткий.

woe n. го́ре; w. is me! го́ре мне! **woe-
begone** adj. удручённый, мра́чный
(-чен, -чна́, -чно). **woeful** adj. ско́рб-
ный, го́рестный.

wolf n. волк (pl. -и, -о́в); w.-cub,
волчо́нок (-нка; pl. волча́та, -т); v.t.
пожира́ть imp., пожра́ть (-ру́, -рёшь;
пожра́л, -а́, -о) perf. (coll.). **wolfhound**
n. волкода́в.

woman n. же́нщина. **womanhood** n. (maturity) же́нская зре́лость. **womanish** adj. женоподо́бный. **womanly** adj. же́нственный (-ен, -енна).

womb n. ма́тка; (fig.) чре́во.

womenfolk n. же́нщины f.pl.; (of one's family) же́нская полови́на семьи́.

wonder n. чу́до (pl. -деса́, -де́с); (amazement) изумле́ние; (it's) no w., неудиви́тельно; v.t. интересова́ться imp. (I w. who will come, интере́сно, кто придёт); v.i.: I shouldn't w. if, неудиви́тельно бу́дет, е́сли; I w. if you could help me, не могли́ бы вы мне помо́чь? w. at, удивля́ться imp., удиви́ться perf.+dat. **wonderful, wondrous** adj. замеча́тельный, удиви́тельный, чуде́сный.

wont n.; as is his w., по своему́ обыкнове́нию; predic.: be w. to, име́ть привы́чку+inf. **wonted** adj. привы́чный.

woo v.t. уха́живать imp. за+instr.; (fig.) добива́ться+gen.

wood n. (forest) лес (a(y), loc. -ý; pl. -á); (material) де́рево; (firewood) дрова́ (-в, -ва́м) pl.; **w.-louse**, мокри́ца; **w.-pigeon**, лесно́й го́лубь (pl. -би, -бе́й) m.; **w.-pulp**, древе́сная ма́сса; **w.-shed**, сара́й для дров; **w.-wind**, деревя́нные духовы́е инструме́нты m.pl.; **w.-wool**, то́нкая, упако́вочная стру́жка. **woodbine** n. жи́молость. **woodcock** n. ва́льдшнеп. **woodcut** n. гравю́ра на де́реве. **wooded** adj. леси́стый. **wooden** adj. (also fig.) деревя́нный. **woodland** n. леси́стая ме́стность; attrib. лесно́й. **woodman** n. лесни́к (-á). **woodpecker** n. дя́тел (-тла). **woodwork** n. столя́рная рабо́та; (wooden articles) деревя́нные изде́лия neut.pl.; (wooden parts of s.th.) деревя́нные ча́сти (-те́й) pl. (строе́ния). **woodworm** n. (жук-)древото́чец (-чца). **woody** adj. (plant etc.) древя́нистый; (wooded) леси́стый.

wool n. шерсть (pl. -ти, -те́й). **woollen** adj. шерстяно́й. **woolly** adj. (covered with w.) покры́тый ше́рстью; (fleecy) шерсти́стый; (indistinct) нея́сный; w. mind, thinking пу́таница в голове́; n. (coll.) сви́тер.

word n. (unit of language; utterance; promise) сло́во (pl. -ва́); (remark) замеча́ние; (news) изве́стие; have a w. with, поговори́ть perf. c+instr.; by w. of mouth, на слова́х, у́стно; in a w., одни́м сло́вом; in other words, други́ми слова́ми; w. for w., сло́во в сло́во; v.t. выража́ть imp., вы́разить perf.; формули́ровать imp., с~ perf. **wordiness** n. многосло́вие. **wording** n. формулиро́вка, реда́кция. **wordy** adj. многосло́вный.

work n. рабо́та; (labour; toil; scholarly w.) труд (-á); (occupation) заня́тие; (studies) заня́тия neut.pl.; (of art) произведе́ние; (book) сочине́ние; pl. (factory) заво́д; (mechanism) механи́зм; at w., (doing w.) за рабо́той; (at place of w.) на рабо́те; out of w., безрабо́тный; **w.-bench**, верста́к (-á); **w.-force**, рабо́чая си́ла; **w.-load**, нагру́зка; **w.-room**, рабо́чая ко́мната; **w.-shy**, лени́вый; v.i. (also function) рабо́тать imp. (at, on, над+instr.); (study) занима́ться imp., заня́ться (займу́сь, -мёшься; заня́лся, -ла́сь, -ло́сь) perf.; (also toil, labour) труди́ться (-ужу́сь, -у́дишься) imp.; (function) де́йствовать imp.; w. to rule, рабо́тать imp., выполня́я сли́шком пунктуа́льно все пра́вила, с це́лью уме́ньшить производи́тельность; v.t. (operate) управля́ть imp.+instr.; обраща́ться imp.+instr.; (wonders) твори́ть imp., со~ perf.; (soil) обраба́тывать imp., обрабо́тать perf.; (mine) разраба́тывать imp., разрабо́тать perf.; (compel to w.) заставля́ть imp., заста́вить perf. рабо́тать; **w. in**, вставля́ть imp., вста́вить perf.; **w. out**, (solve) реша́ть imp., реши́ть perf.; (plans etc.) разраба́тывать imp., разрабо́тать perf.; (exhaust) истоща́ть imp., истощи́ть perf.; everything worked out well, всё ко́нчилось хорошо́; w. out at, (amount to) составля́ть imp., соста́вить perf.; **w. up**, (perfect) обраба́тывать imp., обрабо́тать perf.; (excite) возбужда́ть imp., возбуди́ть perf.; (appetite) нагу́ливать imp., нагуля́ть perf. **workable** adj. осуществи́мый, реа́льный.

workaday *adj.* бу́дничный. **worker** *n.* рабо́чий *sb.*; рабо́тник, -ица. **working** *adj.*: *w.* class, рабо́чий класс; *w.* conditions, усло́вия *neut.pl.* труда́; *w.* day, рабо́чий день (дня) *m.*; *w.* hours, рабо́чее вре́мя *neut.*; *w.* party, коми́ссия *sb.*, рабо́тник. **workmanlike** *adj.* иску́сный. **workmanship** *n.* иску́сство, мастерство́. **workshop** *n.* мастерска́я *sb.*

world *n.* мир (*pl.* -ы́), свет; *attrib.* мирово́й; *w.-famous*, всеми́рно изве́стный; *w.-view*, мировоззре́ние; *w.* war, мирова́я война́ (*pl.* -ны); *w.-weary*, уста́вший от жи́зни; *w.-wide*, распространённый (-ён, -ена́) по всему́ све́ту; всеми́рный. **worldly** *adj.* (*earthly*) земно́й; (*temporal*) мирско́й; (*experienced*) о́пытный.

worm *n.* червь (-вя́; *pl.* -ви, -ве́й) *m.*; (*also tech.*) червя́к (-а́); (*intestinal*) глист (-а́); *v.t.*: *w.* oneself into, вкра́дываться *imp.*, вкра́сться (-аду́сь, -адёшься; -а́лся) *perf.* в + *acc.*; *w.* out, выве́дывать *imp.*, вы́ведать *perf.* (of, y + *gen.*); *w.* one's way, проби́раться *imp.*, пробра́ться (-беру́сь, -берёшься; -бра́лся, -брала́сь, -брало́сь) *perf.* **worm-eaten** *adj.* исто́ченный (-ен) червя́ми. **wormwood** *n.* полы́нь.

worry *n.* (*anxiety*) беспоко́йство, трево́га; (*care*) забо́та; *v.t.* беспоко́ить *imp.*, о ~ *perf.*; трево́жить *imp.*, вс ~ *perf.*; (*of dog*) терза́ть *imp.*; *v.i.* беспоко́иться *imp.*, о ~ *perf.* (about, о + *prep.*); му́читься *imp.*, за ~, из ~ *perf.* (about, из-за + *gen.*).

worse *adj.* ху́дший; *adv.* ху́же; *n.*: from bad to *w.*, всё ху́же и ху́же; *adv.* & *i.* ухудша́ться *imp.*, уху́дшиться *perf.* **worsen** *v.t.* & *i.* ухудша́ть *imp.*, уху́дшить *perf.*

worship *n.* поклоне́ние (of, + *dat.*); (*relig.*) богослуже́ние; *v.t.* поклоня́ться *imp.* + *dat.*; (*adore*) обожа́ть *imp.* **worshipper** *n.* покло́нник, -ица.

worst *adj.* наиху́дший, са́мый плохо́й; *adv.* ху́же всего́; *n.* са́мое плохо́е; *v.t.* побежда́ть *imp.*, победи́ть (-и́шь) *perf.*

worsted *n.* шерстяна́я/камво́льная пря́жа.

worth *n.* (*value*) цена́ (*acc.* -ну; *pl.* -ны); (*fig.*) це́нность; (*merit*) досто́инство; give me a pound's *w.* of petrol, да́йте мне бензи́на на фунт; *adj.*: be *w.*, (*of value equivalent to*) сто́ить *imp.* (what is it *w.*? ско́лько э́то сто́ит?); (*deserve*) сто́ить *imp.* + *gen.* (is this film *w.* seeing? сто́ит посмотре́ть э́тот фильм?); (*of merit*) сто́ить *imp.*, изо всех сил. **worthless** *adj.* ничего́ не сто́ящий; (*useless*) бесполе́зный. **worthwhile** *adj.* сто́ящий. **worthy** *adj.* досто́йный (-о́ин, -о́йна).

would-be *adj.*: *w.* actor, челове́к (*pl.* лю́ди, -де́й, -дям, -дьми́) мечта́ющий стать актёром.

wound *n.* ра́на, ране́ние; (*fig.*) оби́да; *v.t.* ра́нить *imp.* & *perf.*; обижа́ть *imp.*, оби́деть (-и́жу, -и́дишь) *perf.* **wounded** *adj.* ра́неный.

wraith *n.* виде́ние.

wrangle *n.* перека́ние, спор; *v.i.* перека́ться *imp.*; спо́рить *imp.*, по ~ *perf.*

wrap *n.* (*shawl*) шаль; (*stole*) палантин; *v.t.* (*also w.* up) завёртывать *imp.*, заверну́ть *perf.*; *w.* up (*fig.* & *i.*) (in wraps) заку́тывать(ся) *imp.*, заку́тать(ся) *perf.*; (*v.t.*) (*conclude*) заверша́ть *imp.*, заверши́ть *perf.*; wrapped up in, (*fig.*) поглощённый (-ён, -ена́) + *instr.* **wrapper** *n.* обёртка. **wrapping** *n.* обёртка; *w.* paper, обёрточная бума́га.

wrath *n.* гнев, я́рость. **wrathful** *adj.* гне́вный (-вен, -вна́, -вно).

wreak *v.t.*: *w.* havoc, производи́ть (-ожу́, -о́дишь) *imp.*, произвести́ (-еду́, -едёшь; -ёл, -ела́) *perf.* ужа́сные разруше́ния; *w.* vengeance, мстить *imp.*, ото ~ *perf.* (on, + *dat.*).

wreath *n.* вено́к (-нка́) (of smoke) кольцо́ (*pl.* -льца, -ле́ц, -льцам). **wreathe** *v.t.* (*form into wreath*) сплета́ть *imp.*, сплести́ (-ету́, -етёшь; -ёл, -ела́) *perf.*; (*encircle*) обвива́ть *imp.*, обви́ть (обовью́, -ьёшь; обви́л, -ла́, -ло) *perf.* (with, + *instr.*); *v.i.* (*wind round*) обвива́ться *imp.*, обви́ться (обовью́сь, -ьёшься; обви́лся, -ла́сь) *perf.*; (*of smoke*) клуби́ться *imp.*

wreck *n.* (*destruction*) круше́ние, ава́-

рия; (*wrecked ship*) о́стов разби́того су́дна; (*vehicle, person, building etc.*) разва́лина; *v.t.* (*cause destruction of*) вызыва́ть *imp.*, вы́звать (вы́зову, -вешь) круше́ние + *gen.*; (*ship*) топи́ть (топлю́, -пишь) *imp.*, по~ *perf.*; (*destroy, also dopes etc.*) разруша́ть *imp.*, разру́шить *perf.*; *be wrecked*, терпе́ть (-плю́, -пишь) *imp.*, по~ *perf.* круше́ние; (*of plans etc.*) ру́хнуть *perf.* **wreckage** *n.* обло́мки *m.pl.* круше́ния.

wren *n.* крапи́вник.

wrench *n.* (*jerk*) дёрганье; (*sprain*) растяже́ние; (*tech.*) га́ечный ключ (-á); (*fig.*) боль; *v.t.* (*snatch, pull out*) вырыва́ть *imp.*, вы́рвать (-ву, -вешь) *perf.* (*from*, у + *gen.*); (*sprain*) растя́гивать *imp.*, растяну́ть (-ну́, -нешь) *perf.*; *w. open*, взла́мывать *imp.*, взлома́ть *perf.*

wrest *v.t.* (*wrench*) вырыва́ть *imp.*, вы́рвать (-ву, -вешь) *perf.* (*from*, у + *gen.*); (*agreement etc.*) исторга́ть *imp.*, исто́ргнуть (-г) *perf.* (*from*, у + *gen.*); (*distort*) искажа́ть *imp.*, искази́ть *perf.*

wrestle *v.i.* боро́ться (-рю́сь, -решься) *imp.* **wrestler** *n.* боре́ц (-рца́). **wrestling** *n.* борьба́.

wretch *n.* несча́стный *sb.*; (*scoundrel*) негодя́й. **wretched** *adj.* жа́лкий (-лок, -лка́, -лко); (*unpleasant*) скве́рный (-рен, -рна́, -рно).

wriggle *v.i.* извива́ться *imp.*, изви́ться (изовью́сь, -вьёшься *imp.*; извился́, -ла́сь) *perf.*; (*fidget*) ёрзать *imp.*; *v.t.* виля́ть *imp.*, вильну́ть *perf.* + *instr.*; *w. out of*, уви́ливать *imp.*, увильну́ть от + *gen.*

wring *v.t.* (*also w. out*) выжима́ть *imp.*, вы́жать (вы́жму, -мешь) *perf.*; (*extort*) исторга́ть *imp.*, исто́ргнуть (-г) *perf.* (*from*, у + *gen.*); (*hand*) кре́пко пожима́ть *imp.*, пожа́ть (пожму́, -мёшь) *perf.* (*of*, + *dat.*); (*neck*) свёртывать *imp.*, сверну́ть *perf.* (*of*, + *dat.*); *w. one's hands*, лома́ть *imp.* с~ *perf.* ру́ки. **wringer** *n.* маши́на для отжима́ния белья́.

wrinkle *n.* морщи́на; (*tip*) поле́зный сове́т; *v.t. & i.* мо́рщить(ся) *imp.*, с~ *perf.*

wrist *n.* запя́стье; *w.-watch*, нару́чные часы́ (-со́в) *pl.*

writ *n.* пове́стка, предписа́ние.

write *v.t. & i.* (*also fig.*) писа́ть (пишу́, -шешь) *imp.*, на~ *perf.*; *w. down*, запи́сывать *imp.*, записа́ть (запишу́, -шешь) *perf.*; *w. off*, (*cancel*) аннули́ровать *imp.*, *perf.*; (*dispatch letter*) отсыла́ть *imp.*, отосла́ть (отошлю́, -шлёшь) *perf.*; *the car was a w.-off*, маши́на была́ соверше́нно испо́рчена; *w. out*, выпи́сывать *imp.*, вы́писать (-ишу, -ишешь) *perf.* (*in full*, по́лностью); *w. up*, (*account of*) подро́бно опи́сывать *imp.*, описа́ть (-ишу́, -и́шешь) *perf.*; (*notes*) перепи́сывать *imp.*, переписа́ть (-ишу́, -и́шешь) *perf.*; *w.-up*, (*report*) отчёт. **writer** *n.* писа́тель *m.*, ~ница.

writhe *v.i.* (*from pain*) ко́рчиться *imp.*, с~ *perf.*; (*fig.*) му́читься *imp.*, за~ *perf.*, из~ *perf.*

writing *n.* (*handwriting*) по́черк; (*work*) произведе́ние; *in w.*, в пи́сьменной фо́рме; *the w. on the wall*, злове́щее предзнаменова́ние; *w.-case*, несессе́р для пи́сьменных принадле́жностей; *w.-desk*, конто́рка, пи́сьменный стол (-á); *w.-paper*, почто́вая бума́га.

wrong *adj.* (*incorrect*) непра́вильный, неве́рный (-рен, -рна́, -рно, неве́рны), оши́бочный; *not the right* (*I have bought the wrong book*, я купи́л не ту кни́гу; *you've got the wrong number*, (*telephone*) вы не туда́ попа́ли); (*mistaken*) непра́вый (-в, -ва́, -во) (*you are w.*, ты непра́в); (*unjust*) несправедли́вый; (*sinful*) дурно́й (ду́рён, -рна́, -рно, ду́рны́); (*defective*) неиспра́вный; (*side of cloth*) ле́вый; *w. side out*, наизна́нку; *w. way round*, наоборо́т; *in the w.*, непра́в; *be in the w.*, быть непра́вым; *do w.*, греши́ть *imp.*, со~ *perf.*; *adv.* непра́вильно, неве́рно; *go w.*, не получа́ться *imp.*, получи́ться (-ится) *perf.*; (*harm*) вреди́ть *imp.*, по~ *perf.* + *dat.*; обижа́ть *imp.*, оби́деть *perf.*; (*be unjust to*) быть несправедли́вым к + *dat.* **wrongdoer** *n.* престу́пник, гре́шник, -ица. **wrongful** *adj.* неспра-

ведли́вый, непра́вильный. **wrongly**
adv. непра́вильно, неве́рно.
wrought *adj.*: w. *iron,* сва́рочное
желе́зо.

wry *adj.* криво́й (-в, -ва́, -во), пере-
ко́шенный; w. *face,* грима́са.

X

xenophobia *n.* ксенофо́бия.
Xerox *v.t.* размножа́ть *imp.,* раз-
мно́жить *perf.* на ксе́роксе. **Xerox
copy** *n.* ксероко́пия.
X-ray *n.* (*picture*) рентге́н(овский сни́-
мок (-мка)); *pl.* (*radiation*) рентге́но-
вы лучи́ *m.pl.*; *v.t.* (*photograph*)
де́лать *imp.,* с~ *perf.* рентге́н + *gen.*;
(*examine*) иссле́довать *imp., perf.*
рентге́новыми луча́ми.
xylophone *n.* ксилофо́н.

Y

yacht *n.* я́хта; y.-*club,* яхт-клу́б. **yacht-
ing** *n.* па́русный спорт. **yachtsman** *n.*
яхтсме́н.
yak *n.* як.
Yale lock *n.* америка́нский замо́к
(-мка́).
yam *n.* ям.
yank *n.* рыво́к (-вка́); *v.t.* рвану́ть *perf.*
yap *n.* тя́вканье; *v.i.* тя́вкать *imp.,*
тя́вкнуть *perf.*
yard[1] *n.* (*piece of ground*) двор (-а́).
yard[2] *n.* (*measure*) ярд; (*naut.*) рей.
yardstick *n.* (*fig.*) мери́ло.
yarn *n.* пря́жа; (*story*) расска́з.
yarrow *n.* тысячели́стник.
yashmak *n.* чадра́.
yawl *n.* ял.
yawn *n.* зево́к (-вка́); *v.i.* (*person*) зева́ть
imp., зевну́ть *perf.*; (*chasm etc.*) зия́ть
imp.
year *n.* год (*loc.* -у́; *pl.* -ы & -а́, -о́в &
лет, -а́м); *from* y. *to* y., год о́т году;
y. *in,* y. *out,* из го́да в год; y.-*book,*
ежего́дник. **yearly** *adj.* ежего́дный,

годово́й; *adv.* ежего́дно, раз в год.
yearn *v.i.* тоскова́ть *imp.,* (for, по +
dat., prep.). **yearning** *n.* тоска́ (for, по +
dat., prep.).
yeast *n.* дро́жжи (-же́й) *pl.*
yell *n.* крик; *v.i.* крича́ть (-чу́, -чи́шь)
imp., кри́кнуть *perf.*; *v.t.* выкри́кивать
imp., вы́крикнуть *perf.*
yellow *adj.* жёлтый (-т, -та́, жёлто);
(*cowardly*) трусли́вый; *n.* жёлтый
цвет; *v.i.* желте́ть *imp.,* по~ *perf.*
yellowhammer *n.* овся́нка. **yellowish**
adj. желтова́тый.
yelp *n.* визг; *v.i.* визжа́ть (-жу́, -жи́шь)
imp., ви́згнуть *perf.*
yen *n.* (*money*) ие́на.
yes *adv.* да; *n.* утвержде́ние, согла́сие;
(*in vote*) го́лос (*pl.* -а́) „за“; y.-*man,*
подпева́ла *m. & f.* (*coll.*).
yesterday *adv.* вчера́; *n.* вчера́шний
день (дня) *m.*; y. *morning,* вчера́
у́тром; *the day before* y., позавчера́;
yesterday's newspaper, вчера́шняя га-
зе́та.

yet adv. (still) ещё; (so far) до сих пор; (with compar.) да́же, ещё; (in questions) уже́; (nevertheless) тем не ме́нее; as y., пока́, до сих пор; not y., ещё не; conj. одна́ко, но.

yew n. тис.

Yiddish n. и́диш.

yield n. (harvest) урожа́й; (econ.) дохо́д; v.t. (fruit, revenue, etc.) приноси́ть (-ошу́, -о́сишь) imp., принести́ (-есу́, -есёшь; -ёс, -есла́) perf.; (give up) сдава́ть (сдаю́, сдаёшь) imp., сдать (-ам, -ашь, -аст, -ади́м; сдал, -а́, -о) perf.; v.i. (give in) (to enemy etc.) уступа́ть imp., уступи́ть (-плю́, -пишь) perf. (to, +dat.); (to temptation etc.), поддава́ться (-даю́сь, -даёшься) imp., подда́ться (-а́мся, -а́шься, -а́стся, -ади́мся; -а́лся, -ала́сь) perf. (to, +dat.).

yodel n. йодль m.; v.i. петь (пою́, поёшь) imp., про ~, с ~ perf. йо́длем.

yoga n. йо́га. **yogi** n. йог.

yoghurt n. простоква́ша.

yoke n. (also fig.) ярмо́ (pl. -ма); (fig.) и́го; (for buckets) коромы́сло (gen.pl. -сел); (of dress) коке́тка; y. of oxen, па́ра запряжённых воло́в; v.t. впряга́ть imp., впрячь (-ягу́, -яжёшь; -яг, -ягла́) perf. в ярмо́.

yokel n. дереве́нщина m. & f.

yolk n. желто́к (-тка́).

yonder adv. вон там; adj. вон тот (та, то; pl. те).

yore n.: (in days) of y., во вре́мя о́но.

you pron. (familiar sing.) ты (тебя́, тебе́, тобо́й, тебе́); (familiar pl., polite sing. & pl.) вы (вас, вам, ва́ми, вас); (one) not usu. translated; verb translated in 2nd pers. sing. or by impers. construction: y. never know, никогда́ не зна́ешь.

young adj. молодо́й (мо́лод, -а́, -о); ю́ный (юн, -а́, -о); (new) но́вый (нов, -а́, -о); (inexperienced) нео́пытный; the y., молодёжь; n. (collect.) молодня́к (-а́), детёныши m.pl. **youngish** adj. моложа́вый. **youngster** n. ма́льчик, ю́ноша m.

your(s) poss. pron. (familiar sing.; also in letter) твой (-оя́, -оё; -ои́); (familiar pl., polite sing. & pl.; also in letter) ваш; свой (-оя́, -оё; -ои́). **yourself** pron. (emph.) (familiar sing.) (ты) сам (-ого́, -ому́, -и́м, -о́м) (m.), сама́ (-мо́й, асс. -му́) (f.); (familiar pl., polite sing. & pl.) (вы) са́ми (-и́х, -и́м, -и́ми); (refl.) себя́ (себе́, собо́й) -ся (suffixed to v.t.); by y., (independently) самостоя́тельно, сам (-а́; -и); (alone) оди́н (одна́; одни́).

youth n. (age) мо́лодость, ю́ность; (young man) ю́ноша m.; (collect., as pl.) молодёжь; attrib. молодёжный; y. club, молодёжный клуб; y. hostel, молодёжная турба́за. **youthful** adj. ю́ношеский.

yo-yo n. йо-йо́.

Yugoslav(ian) adj. югосла́вский; n. югосла́в, ~ ка.

Z

zany adj. смешно́й (-шо́н, -шна́).

zeal n. рве́ние, усе́рдие. **zealot** n. фана́тик. **zealous** adj. ре́вностный, усе́рдный.

zebra n. зе́бра.

zenith n. зени́т.

zephyr n. зефи́р.

zero n. нуль (-ля́) m., ноль (-ля́) m.;

attrib. нулево́й; z. hour, час „Ч".

zest n. (piquancy) пика́нтность; (ardour) жар, энтузиа́зм; z. for life, жизнелю́бие.

zigzag n. зигза́г; adj. зигзагообра́зный; v.i. де́лать imp., с~ perf зигза́ги.

zinc n. цинк; attrib. ци́нковый.

Zionism *n.* сиони́зм. **Zionist** *n.* сиони́ст.
zip *n.* (*z. fastener*) (застёжка-)мо́лния;
v.t. & i.: *z. up*, застёгивать(ся) *imp.*,
застегну́ть *perf.* на мо́лнию.
zither *n.* ци́тра.
zodiac *n.* зодиа́к; *sign of the z.*, знак
зодиа́ка. **zodiacal** *adj.* зодиака́льный.
zonal *adj.* зона́льный. **zone** *n.* зо́на;
(*geog.*) по́яс (*pl.* -а́).

zoo *n.* зоопа́рк. **zoological** *adj.* зооло-
ги́ческий; *z. garden(s)*, зоопа́рк,
зоологи́ческий сад (*loc.* -у́; *pl.* -ы́).
zoologist *n.* зоо́лог. **zoology** *n.* зооло́-
гия.
zoom *v.i.* (*aeron.*) де́лать *imp.*, с ~ *perf.*
го́рку; *n.* го́рка; *z. lens*, объекти́в с
переме́нным фо́кусным расстоя́нием.
Zulu *adj.* зулу́сский; *n.* зулу́с, ~ ка.